Footprint
Mexico & Central America

Peter Hutchison
16th edition

"A border is always a temptation"

Larry McMurtry

❶ **Baja California**
Grey whales bask with their young near the beautifully barren landscapes of the Viscaíno desert

❷ **The Copper Canyon**
A rail journey to remember and one dizzily deep canyon

❸ **Zacatecas**
Rich colonial architecture built on the wealth of the silver mines

❹ **Lago de Pátzcuaro**
Cobbled streets, craft villages and Mexico's most famous Day of the Dead

❺ **Mexico City**
A mad and chaotic metropolis

❻ **Teotihuacán**
The third largest pyramid in the world

❼ **Oaxaca**
Colonial charm, vibrant culture and ruins

❽ **Pacific coast**
From mega resorts to quiet beaches

❾ **San Cristóbal de las Casas**
Capital of Mexico's indigenous culture; Zapatista heartland

❿ **Palenque**
Eerily atmospheric Maya ruins with rainforest backdrop shrouded in cloud

⓫ **Chichén Itzá**
Laid-back ruins at the water sorcerer's well

Mexico & Central America Highlights

See colour maps at back of book

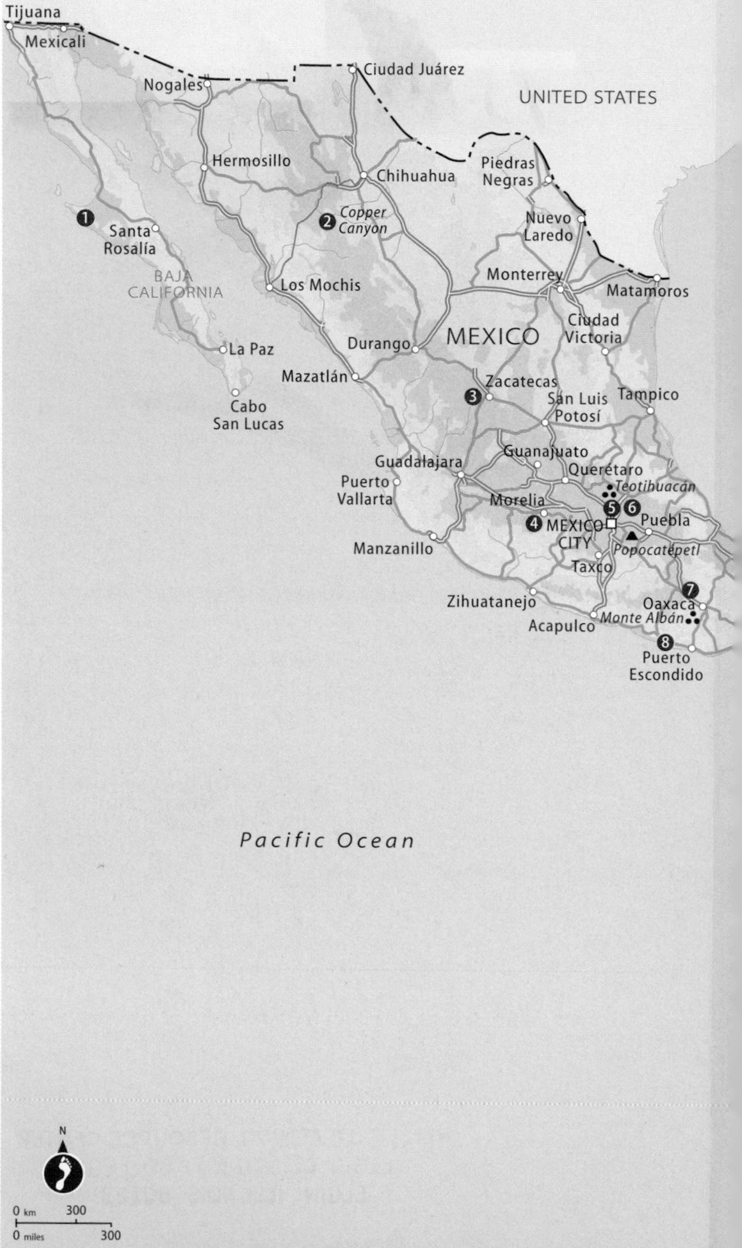

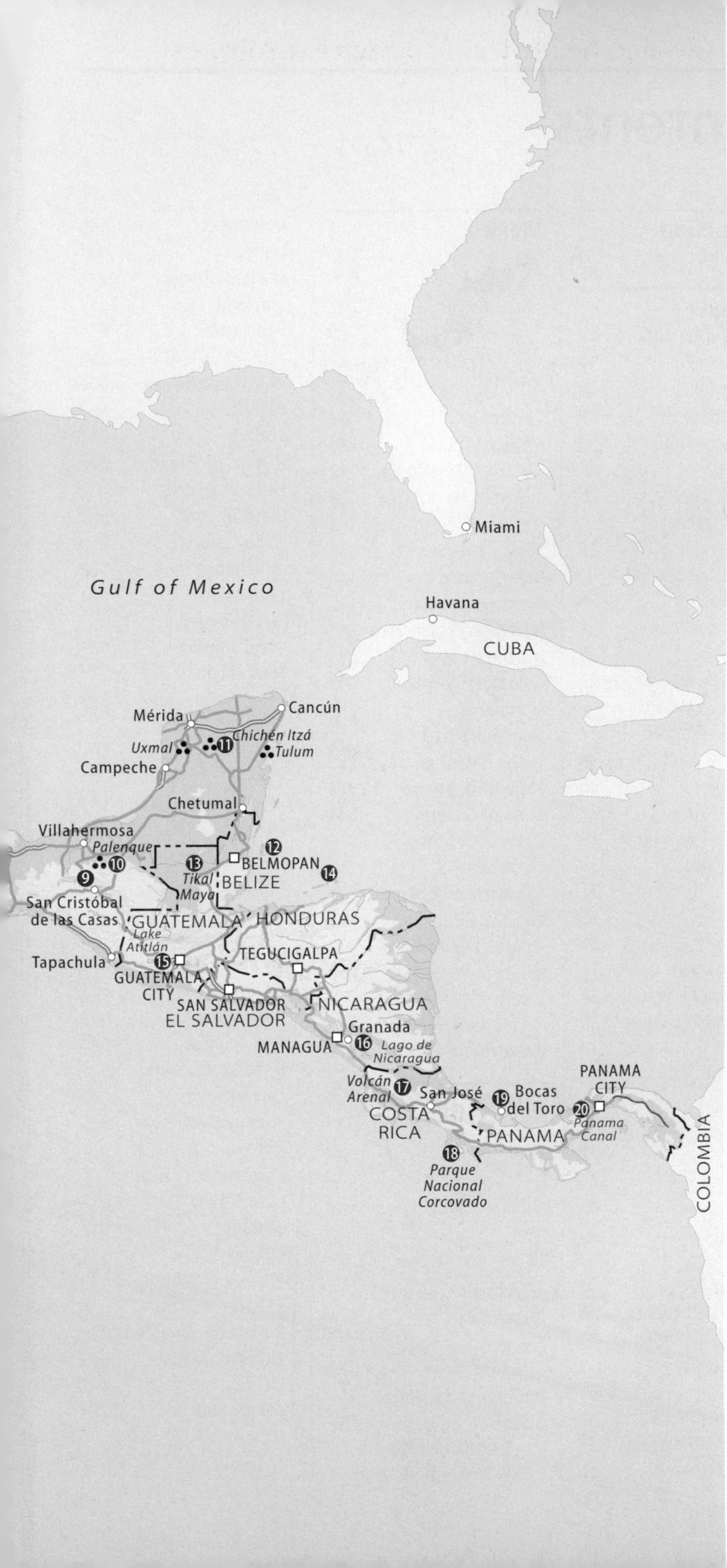

⓬ Blue holes and offshore cayes
A marine wonderland with world-class diving

⓭ Tikal
Maya skyscrapers pushing up through the rainforest canopy

⓮ Bay Islands
Dreamy Caribbean islands with fine coral and excellent, cheap diving

⓯ Antigua, Lake Atitlán and Chichicastenango
A hat-trick of colonial charm, sheer beauty and bartered bargains at Chichi's top-notch market

⓰ Isla de Ometepe and Granada
Volcanic peaks rise from Lake Nicaragua, close to the country's most appealing colonial town

⓱ Volcán Arenal
Central America's most active volcano

⓲ Parque Nacional Corcovado
One of Central America's best-protected rainforest reserves

⓳ Bocas del Toro
Central America's emerging backpacker beach stop

⓴ Panama Canal
The ultimate ocean-linking shortcut

Contents

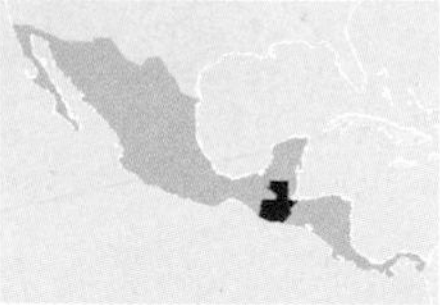

Belize

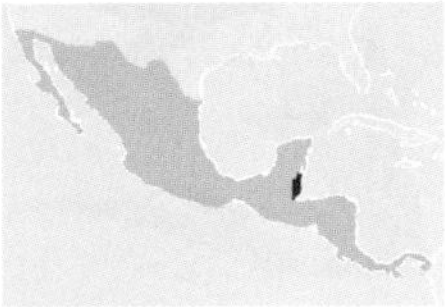

El Salvador

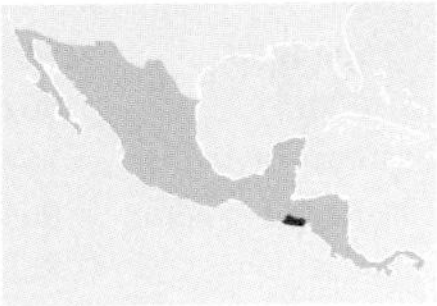

Honduras

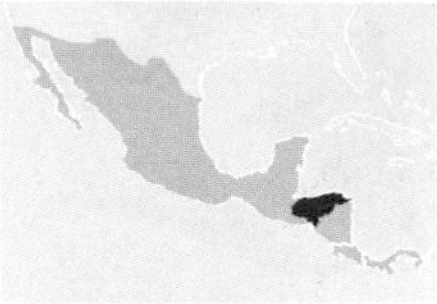

Nicaragua

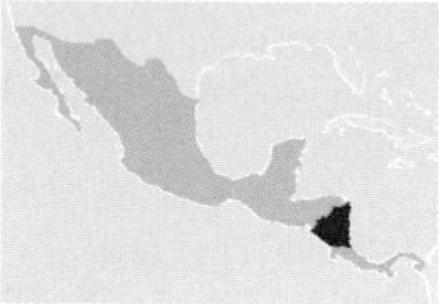

Costa Rica

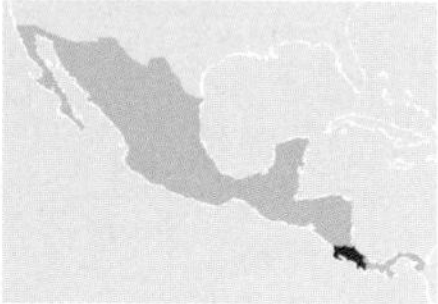

Panama

Background

Footnotes

Inside front cover

Inside back cover

Chichicastenango
Famous for being Central America's best market town, Chichicastenango is a curious blend of mysticism and commercialism.

A foot in the door

Images of Central America and Mexico flow as freely as tequila in a Mexican cantina: colourful indigenous markets, chaotic mega-cities, serene countryside, stunning beaches, pristine national parks and marine reserves filled with wildlife. Volcanoes and earthquakes have shaped and moulded these mountainous lands for millennia. Impressive tropical storms illuminate the night sky, while the wreckage left by hurricanes is a reminder of the power of nature and the fragility of life.

Human impact on this land is no less impressive. Ruined remnants of ancient civilizations litter the region. Spectacular architecture, ancient and modern, is profuse. Massive pyramids dominate the barren plain north of Mexico City, while Maya monuments tower above the rainforest canopy to the south. The conquistadors barely crossed a river without founding a town and the local peculiarities and indigenous influences that characterize each colonial church usually make a pilgrimage worthwhile. Architecture has undergone constant evolution, marking the region's progress through despots and dictators, civil war and revolution. From the Maya to these modern digital days, each ruling power has commemorated its success either by building on the past or by trying to destroy its legacy. For the traveller, the journey is a collection of snapshots through history.

Today, modern life develops at great speed in the region's cities but, hidden in rural pockets, culture remains stubbornly unchanged. People live as their forebears have for centuries – with perhaps the addition of a fuzzy black-and-white TV emitting a dependable hiss. Signs of wealth range from absent to obscene but two traits are shared by all: friendliness and an almost obsessive desire for a damn good fiesta. Whatever the celebration, every Central American and Mexican worth their tortilla will mark the occasion in style.

Mexico

Encapsulating Mexico is difficult, but imagine countries within countries. Gloriously manic Mexico City is a world away from the serenity of the quieter spots. Little remains of the pre-conquest island city of Tenochtitlán, but the vast ruins of Teotihuacán stand as monument to the value of these prized central highlands. Today's capital is equally impressive. Struggling to move for congestion and gasping for air in the pollution, the Federal District remains one of the world's great cities: a living, working, just-breathing metropolis.

To the north, colonial cities founded on the wealth of silver mines rest assuredly on architectural laurels, while beyond, the endless deserts are punctuated by hot spots such as the Baja California Peninsula and the spectacular train journey through the Copper Canyon. The Pacific coast, stretching southeast from Puerto Vallarta, entices the traveller with glorious, surf-pummelled beaches, and the Yucután Peninsula, jutting out into the Caribbean, is home to both mega-resorts and quiet palm-backed strands, spiced up with unmissable Maya ruins.

Battered by the vicious winds of Hurricane Wilma, the Yucatán bore the brunt of a region that was hit three times in the hurricane season of 2005. The rebuild was impressive and quick. Change is slower in the southern state of Chiapas, where campaigners champion the rights of

Taxco

The striking pink stone of gold-filled Santa Prisca stands out against the houses of one of Mexico's prettiest silver towns.

Mexico's 24 million indigenous peoples. Others question the merits of NAFTA membership, or the evolving political landscape as Mexico's electorate continues to move away from seven decades of PRI rule. Mexico has always been a cauldron for change. Viva variety, viva confusion, viva Mexico!

Guatemala

Surely nobody could fail to be impressed by Guatemala. The expansive ruins of Tikal symbolize this rich and complex country, with majestic temples looking out across the endless rainforest canopy. To the south, the Maya, who once ruled these massive cities of stone, live on in hundreds of towns and villages, nestled among the intensely farmed foothills of scenic mountains and volcanoes. Each Guatemalan community has its own textile and its own fiesta; colourful markets welcome visitors, while packed buses ignore your pleas for a ride. Serenity and calm await. Not in the chaos of Guatemala City but in the colonial charm of Antigua, the former capital, and in the hypnotic beauty of Lake Atitlán. To the east, the lowland sierras offer trekking and hiking, with the Caribbean coast promising laid-back beach life and Garífuna culture. And, to the west, a fledgling ecotourism interest supports nesting turtles on Guatemala's forgotten Pacific shores.

Volcán Poás
The steaming vents of Costa Rica's sleeping giant.

1

2

4

5

7

8

10

11

1 *The Mexican Pipeline, near Puerto Escondido, produces the fastest-breaking waves anywhere in the world.*
▸▸ See page 368.

2 *Semana Santa at Zunil, near Quetzaltenango, is a very colourful event.*
▸▸ See page 591.

3 *Glyphs on the stelae at Copán in Honduras reveal some of the mysteries of the Maya.*
▸▸ See page 805.

4 *On beautiful Roatán, even the iguana run around proposing with flowers.*
▸▸ See page 858.

5 *Chubby ceramics from a roadside stall; in Nicaragua you'll also find good-quality cotton hammocks, leather goods, colourful woven rugs and wicker furniture.*
▸▸ See page 898.

6 *The white-sand beaches of Cabo San Lucas attract tourists to the southernmost tip of Mexico's wild Baja California Peninsula.* *▸▸ See page 183.*

7 *El Salvador's Izalco Volcano used to be known as the Lighthouse of the Pacific.*
▸▸ See page 747.

8 *There are canyons, coves, overhangs, ledges, walls and endless possibilities for underwater photography off the coast of Belize.* *▸▸ See page 661.*

9 *The global financial centre of Panama City is a curious blend of old Spain, US-style mall developments and the bazaar atmosphere of the East.* *▸▸ See page 1123.*

10 *Many of the Sandinista murals and images of the Revolution have been removed, but Nicaragua still paints its political colours on the wall.* *▸▸ See page 925.*

11 *Maya skyscrapers push up through the rainforerst canopy at Tikal.*
▸▸ See page 635.

12 *Processing molasses; some methods of production have remained unchanged for centuries in El Salvador.* *▸▸ See page 1239.*

Belize

Compact and accessible, but just a bit more expensive than its immediate neighbours, tiny Belize often gets overlooked. Yet this Caribbean country is home to the Mesoamerican Barrier Reef – the longest in the western hemisphere – and offers some of the best diving in the world, along with a boatload of other watersports worth getting wet for. Over 35% of the country is protected in national parks and reserves, including the world's only jaguar sanctuary at Cockscomb Basin. To the east, an intricate system of caves provide a glimpse into the Maya underworld. And in the pine-clad hills to the south, Caracol, the largest of Belize's ruins, remains mostly unexplored, comfortable in the little-known fact that it once ruled over nearby Tikal.

El Salvador

El Salvador gets short shrift due to the popularity of its neighbours, but the volcanic highlands and contrasting coastal plains are stunningly beautiful. The country was rocked in 2001 by a massive double earthquake and again in 2005 by the eruption of Santa Ana volcano. It has only recently started to welcome travellers, but is an ultimately enjoyable experience thanks to its genuinely friendly people. San Salvador, the capital, is close to volcanoes, lakes and national parks; northern towns have moved out from the shadows of civil war and are enjoying a cultural revival; to the south, long sandy beaches have been prized by surfers for decades; to the west are coffee plantations and the beautiful Ruta de las Flores. And if you're seeking a challenge, try the national park called 'El Imposible'.

Goff's Caye , one of Belize's idyllic offshore islands.

Capuchin monkeys in Costa Rica's Manuel Antonio National Park – curious, chatty and chastising.

Honduras

One of Central America's dark horses, Honduras has been pushing for a place in the limelight for years. The Bay Islands, off the Caribbean coast, are still the cheapest place to learn to scuba dive and, onshore, the adventure continues with whitewater rafting, hiking and birdwatching. Along the Atlantic, you can relax in the coastal communities of Omoa, Tela, La Ceiba and Trujillo and visit the isolated rainforest of La Mosquitia – Central America's 'Little Amazon'. Close to the border with Guatemala, the stunning Copán ruins mark the southernmost reach of the Maya Empire. Beyond this well-trodden route, in the western hills, villages are quieter and the hillside paths less travelled, with colonial treasures and indigenous communities to discover.

Nicaragua

Although memories of the 1979 Sandinista Revolution still evoke images of work crews, *comandantes* and communist sympathies, the Nicaragua of today is a very different and rapidly changing place. The country is embracing a deluge of tourist dollars that is set to increase as word gets around – Nicaragua is cool. There is a freshness about a country where the smiles are still warm and the eyes undimmed by the attitudes of thoughtless travellers. The memorable sites of the Island of Ometepe, Volcán Masaya, the Corn Islands, the Río San Juan and Pacific beaches are matched by some of Central America's oldest towns, including conservative Granada and liberal León. It's the contrasts that make Nicaragua so appealing.

The San Blas Islands are home to the Kuna people, Panama's largest indigenous group.

Costa Rica

Peaceful, calm and 100% democratic... ah, that'll be Costa Rica. The place is packed with national parks, private reserves and national monuments. What makes the difference in tiny Costa Rica is the sheer variety of wildlife on offer: quetzales here, nesting turtles there, big cats at all points of the compass. World-class whitewater rafting from Turrialba; surfing on both coasts; the eruptions of Arenal volcano and the steaming mudpools of Rincón de la Vieja nearby; walking and hiking in the cloud forests of Monteverde or the rainforest of the Osa Peninsula; other countries may offer these things, but they don't pack them into a such a compact, attractive bundle as Costa Rica. And they don't do it in quite the same laid-back way as the Ticos, who espouse *la pura vida*.

Panama

Panama is the crossroads of the world. The Panama Canal may not be natural but it is a spectacular engineering marvel and pure Panamanian since the country successfully took control of the world's greatest shortcut at the end of 1999. Beyond modern Panama City, national and international visitors are opening their eyes to new discoveries on the Azuero Peninsula and in the Chiriquí Highlands, while Bocas del Toro on the Atlantic is developing into a hip coastal destination, with beaches, surfing, glassy waters and islands full of tiny multicoloured frogs. The autonomous San Blas Islands provide a precious haven of calm and tranquillity and, for the true adventurer, the wilderness of the Darién still offers one of the great challenges this side of space travel.

Essentials

Footprint features

Planning your trip

'Where to go?' is perhaps the most frequently asked question about Mexico and Central America. The sheer variety of options means that for once the cliché is true – there is something for everyone. The sheer variety of landscapes, cultures and opportunities excites, entices and, to start with, just bewilders.

The scope for adventurous holidays is vast, whether it be branching out from a mega-resort like Puerto Vallarta or Cancún, climbing a volcano, scuba diving and snorkelling, whitewater rafting or seeking out the elusive quetzal bird from the forests of Guatemala right down to Panama. Equally enticing is the cultural variety; the pyramids and sculptures of the Aztecs, Maya and other cultures; the Spanish colonial heritage, from the grandest cathedral to the smallest village church; the flora and fauna; indigenous markets; the modern and dynamic museums and art of the region; learning the language or local cooking techniques; or the mere prospect of lazing at some palm-shaded hideaway fringed with golden sands. One especially rewarding aspect of travel in Central America is the relatively compact size of many of the countries making it easy to move from one place to the next.

Detailed planning information is given for each country: Belize, page 654; Costa Rica, page 974; El Salvador, page 722; Guatemala, page 510; Honduras, page 782; Mexico, page 62; Nicaragua, page 892; Panama, page 1112.

Where to go

Choosing which country or countries to visit can be a strangely paralyzing experience. Each is worth visiting on its own merits and deserves time – your dilemma is deciding whether to skim the surface of a few countries or get to grips with a couple of spots.

Three weeks

Not long enough to cover the region, but you don't have to 'do' the whole isthmus in one trip. Breaking down the options, three weeks could comfortably be spent exploring Guatemala, with a fortnight taking in the essentials of **Antigua, Tikal** and **Lake Atitlán**. Spend an extra week in the **Cayo district** of **Belize**, the **Caribbean** coast of Guatemala crossing into **Honduras** for a bit of diving in the **Bay Islands** or heading north to the indigenous homelands of **Chiapas**, Mexico. Any version of the **Ruta Maya**, taking in the main Maya sites of Guatemala, Belize and southern Mexico is possible in three weeks but doesn't really allow time for deviation. Another three-week trip could focus on **Costa Rica**, with a great variety of national parks on offer. The particular recommendation will depend on the time of year, but the most popular include **Manuel Antonio National Park, Monteverde Cloud Forest Reserve** and **Tortuguero National Park** to the east, and **Corcovado National Park** to the south. The explosive **Volcán Arenal** never disappoints unless it is shrouded in cloud. For the active there is whitewater rafting, surfing, horse riding and trekking. You could just about manage an overland trip from **Guatemala** through to **Costa Rica** in three weeks. If you're feeling particularly manic, you could even manage a mad dash down the **Pan-American Highway** from **Mexico City** all the way to **Panama City**.

Six to eight weeks

Six to eight weeks is long enough to travel across a few countries without feeling you've rushed too much. Arriving in **Mexico City**, and after a few days' exploring the sights and sounds, the **architecture** ancient and modern, and dodging the traffic, you can head south to the beaches of **Oaxaca**, before making your way east to **Chiapas** and the Maya ruins of **Palenque**. From here continue south to Guatemala or west out to the **Yucután Peninsula** for the beautiful beaches and more **Maya** ruins. Dropping south, **Belize** is worth some time. **Diving**, though more expensive than Honduras, is some of the best in the world and includes the **Blue Hole**. Head west for **Guatemala** and the eerie cave and river trips of the **Cayo District** or, to the south, the serenity around **Plancencia**, the jaguar sanctuary at **Cockscomb Basin** and the Maya villages close to **Punta Gorda**.

Six weeks is long enough to include a short Spanish language course in **Antigua**, **Quetzaltenango** or even **Todos Santos** – world famous for its annual festival in November. After Guatemala, **Honduras** draws many to the affordable diving of the **Bay Islands** which need at least a week. Other attractions include whitewater rafting on the **Río Cangrejo** close to **La Ceiba**. Inland, treks and hikes in the quiet hills around **Gracias** go through beautiful scenery and small indigenous communities, the very heart of Honduras. An alternative six-week trip might arrive in **Guatemala City** and head south overland flying out of **San José**, Costa Rica. While experiencing Guatemala and Costa Rica, you can travel at leisure through **Honduras**, dip into the lakes and volcanic beauty of **El Salvador** and visit **Nicaragua** where revolutionary history merges with colonial legacy to create one of Central America's most endearing nations. Honduras and Nicaragua are, for many travellers, the most challenging destinations, but for many the most memorable.

Three months

Entering the realms of comfortably travelling from top to bottom, three months is plenty to enter into the classic trip – to follow the **Pan-American Highway** from the Río Grande to the Darién Gap. Equally you could start at Panama and head north. You can cross the US-Mexico border at several points. From **Laredo**, the route heads south through **Monterrey** and the port of **Tampico** before veering inland through the silver-mining centre of **Pachuca** and on to **Mexico City**. From **Ciudad Juárez** on the border, it's a short trip to **Chihuahua**, the vast **Copper Canyon** and the glorious railroad down to the Pacific Ocean. The famous train journey is one of several options for leaving **Chihuahua** on a route heading south that takes in the old silver towns of **Zacatecas** and **San Luis Potosí**, in the **Colonial Heartland**. On the west coast **Tijuana** offers the simplest route to the rugged desert beauty of the **Baja California Peninsula**, popular for beaches and whale watching. This is also an alternative (and longer) route to the Copper Canyon via **Los Mochis**. After the Pacific **Costa Alegre**, head inland for **Guadalajara** and then **Mexico City**. Make your way southeast from the Mexican Central Highlands to **Guatemala** and continue the route south, or take in **Belize** after travelling through the **Yucután Peninsula**.

A gentle meander through **Honduras, El Salvador** and **Nicaragua** can involve a switch of coastlines in **Costa Rica**, to the Caribbean coast and enjoy the idyllic alternative of the southern beaches and the dive sites of **Bocas del Toro**. Or continue south to Costa Rica's **Osa Peninsula** before taking the Pan-American Highway across the final border to **David** and on to **Panama City**. From David, you can blend adventure and beauty with a visit to the **Chiriquí Highlands**. A voyage through the **Panama Canal** would be the ideal way to end a trip of trans-continental travel before heading further south or returning home. The great adventure challenge of the region is still travelling through the **Darién Gap**.

Over three months

Longer than three months is worth sketching out into some form of plan. In addition to suggestions mentioned above, you might want to consider stopping for **language courses, diving instruction**, or a whole range of **cultural** and **activity** courses available throughout the region. You can stay in one place or choose to stagger your studies over several countries. **Work,** both voluntary and paid, can also be found if you want to stop moving for a while.

The first pages of each country chapter give a more detailed look at the highlights and pertinent information for each country. The suggestions are, of course, not definitive. Travellers can move freely through the region, with a guarantee of finding lodging, food and services in all but the most basic places.

When to go

Climate

The best time to go is between October and April, although there are slight regional variations. The rainy season works its way up from the south beginning in May and running through until August, September and even October. This is also hurricane season along the Caribbean. Despite the high profile storm of Hurricane Wilma and a few lesser-known local hurricanes and tropical storms, landfall is relatively rare. If one does arrive while you're in the area you can get details at www.nhc.noaa.gov. But don't be put off by the term 'rainy season' – in most places and in most years, heavy rain falls for an hour or two a day.

Fiestas

In terms of events, regional celebrations are around Easter (*Semana Santa*), the Day of the Dead (2 November) and Christmas. Beyond that each country celebrates wildly on its Independence day, 15 September for all nations apart from Belize (21 September), Mexico (16 September) and Panama (3 November). Other fiestas are held throughout the year. As well as national and regional holidays, August is vacation time for Mexicans and Central Americans and accommodation is scarce especially in the smaller resorts.

Tour operators

In the UK

Condor Journeys and Adventures, 2 Ferry Bank, Colintraive, Argyll, PA22 3AR, T01700-841-318, www.condorjourneys-adventures.com, also offices in France

Explore, 1 Frederick St, Aldershot, Hants, GU11 1LQ, T01252-760-100, www.explore.co.uk.

Galapagos Classic Cruises, 6 Keyes Rd, London, NW2 3XA, T020-8933-0613, www.galapagoscruises.co.uk.

Journey Latin America, 12-13 Heathfield Terrace, London, W4 4JE, T020-87478315; 12 St Ann's Sq, Manchester, M2 7HW, T0161-832-1441, www.journeylatinamerica.co.uk.

Last Frontiers, Fleet Marston Farm, Aylesbury, Buckinghamshire, HP18 OQT, T01296-653000, www.lastfrontiers.com.

Select Latin America, 79 Maltings Place, 169 Tower Bridge Rd, London, SE1 3LJ, T020-7407-1478, www.selectlatinamerica.com.
South American Experience, 47 Causton St, London, SW1P 4AT, T020-7976-5511, www.southamericanexperience.co.uk.
Trips Worldwide, 14 Frederick Place, Clifton, Bristol, BS8 1AS, T0117-311-4404, www.tripsworldwide.co.uk.
Tucan Travel, 316 Uxbridge Rd, London, W3 9RE, T020-8896-1600, www.tucantravel.com.
Veloso Tours, 34 Warple Way, London, W3 0RG, T020-8762-0616, www.veloso.com.

In North America
Exito Travel, 108 Rutgers St, Fort Collins, CO 80525, T970-482-3019, www.exito-travel.com.
GAP Adventures, 19 Charlotte St, Toronto, Ontario, M5V 2H5, T1-800-708- 7761, www.gapadventures.com.

Mila Tours, 100 S Greenleaf Av, Gurnee, Il 60031, T1-800-367-7378, www.milatours.com.
S and Stours, 3366 E Trevino Dr, Sierra Vista, AZ 85650, T800-499-5685, www.ss-tours.com.

In Latin America
CAT Mexico, Calzada las Aguilas 1075, Col San Clemente las Aguilas, México DF, www.cat-travel.com.

International
The following have operations in the US, Canada, Europe , Australia and New Zealand.
Dragoman, T01728-861133, www.dragoman.co.uk.
Exodus Travels, T020-8675-5550, www.exodus.co.uk.
LADATCO tours, 2200 S Dixie Highway, Suite 704, Coconut Grove, FL 33133, T1-800-327-6162, www.ladatco.com.

Finding out more

All countries in the region have a tourist board but not all have an international presence. The internet makes it possible to get the latest information on developments in a country. **South American Explorers** ⓘ *Head Office in the USA at 126 Indian Creek Rd, Ithaca, NY 14850, USA T607-277-0488, www.samexplo.org.* Despite the name, the whole of Latin America is covered and members receive help with travel planning as well as informed access on books and maps covering the region. Many countries in the region have tourist boards in North America. Some also have a presence in Europe and other parts of the world.

Useful websites → *A list of useful websites for each country is given at the start of each chapter.*

www.centralamerica.com Covers mainly Costa Rica but also touches on Guatemala, Belize, Nicaragua and Panama.
www.latinnews.com Up-to-date site with political comment.
www.odci.gov/cia/publications/factbook/index.html For information on all sorts, from birth rates to natural resources.
www.planeta.com A phenomenal resource which is staggering for its detail on everything from ecotourism and language schools to cybercafés.
www.revuemag.com Growing regional guide, focusing on Guatemala with coverage of El Salvador, Honduras and Belize.
www.visitcentromerica.com Central American nations have pooled marketing resources on this website.
Google has country search engines for Mexico (.com.mx), El Salvador (.com.sv), Honduras (.com.hn), Nicaragua (.com.ni), Costa Rica (.com.cr) and Panama (.com.pa).

Language → *See Footnotes, page 1272, for a list of useful words and phrases.*

Spanish is spoken throughout Mexico and Central America and, while you will be able to get by without knowledge of Spanish, you will become very frustrated and feel helpless in many situations. English, or any other language, is absolutely useless off the beaten track (except in Belize). A pocket dictionary and phrase book together with some initial study or a beginner's Spanish course before you leave are strongly recommended. If you have the time, booking a week or two of classes at the beginning of your travels is a good idea, and best if you can immerse yourself completely.

Some areas have developed a reputation for language classes, for instance Cuernavaca in Mexico, Antigua and Quetzaltenango in Guatemala and San José in Costa Rica. Many other locations also provide tuition. The merits of a well-known centre normally include a wide-range of cultural activities and supporting options for homestay. For details, see Language schools in the Directory sections of individual towns. Not all the locals speak Spanish, of course; you will find that some indigenous people in the more remote areas – the highlands of Guatemala for example – speak only their indigenous languages, although there will usually be at least one person in a village who can speak Spanish.

Arranging language tuition internationally is increasingly popular. One of the most comprehensive options is provided by **AmeriSpan** ⓘ *PO Box 58129, 117 South 17th St, Philadelphia, PA 19102, T+1-215-751-1100, www.amerispan.com*, also with offices in Antigua, Guatemala, offers Spanish immersion programmes, educational tours, volunteer and internship positions throughout Latin America. Spanish language courses from one week in duration in Mexico and Central America, with pre-trip classes in the UK, are available from **Cactus Language** ⓘ *4 Clarence House, 30-31 North St, Brighton, East Sussex, BN1 1EB, T0845-130-4775, www.cactuslanguage.com*, has additional options for volunteer work, diving and staying with host families. **Spanish Abroad** ⓘ *5112 N 40th St, Suite 103, Phoenix, AZ 85018, USA, T1-888-722-7623 (USA and Canada), T+1-602 778 6791 (worldwide), www.spanishabroad.com*, run intensive Spanish immersion programmes throughout Latin America for those wishing to study abroad. **Institute for Spanish Language Studies** ⓘ *in the US on T1-800-765-0025, www.isls.com*, has schools in Mexico, Costa Rica and Panama, offering innovative and flexible programmes.

Disabled travellers

As in most Latin American countries, facilities for disabled travellers are severely lacking. Most airports and hotels and restaurants in major resorts have wheelchair ramps and adapted toilets. While some cities such as San José in Costa Rica are all ramped, in general pavements are often in such a poor state of repair that walking is precarious.

Some travel companies are beginning to specialize in exciting holidays, tailor-made for individuals depending on their level of disability. The Global Access-Disabled Travel Network Site, www.globalaccessnews.com, provides travel information for disabled adventurers and includes a number of reviews and tips from members of the public. You might also want to read *Nothing Ventured* edited by Alison Walsh (Harper Collins), which gives personal accounts of worldwide journeys by disabled travellers, plus advice and listings.

Gay and lesbian travellers

Most of Latin America is not particularly liberal in its attitudes to gays and lesbians. Even in the cities people are fairly conservative, and more so in provincial towns and rural areas. Having said that, things are changing and you'll find there is a gay scene with bars and clubs at least in most of the bigger cities and resorts.

Student and teacher travellers

If you are in full-time education you will be entitled to an **International Student Identity Card** (ISIC), which is distributed by student travel offices and travel agencies in over 100 countries. ISIC gives you special prices on all forms of transport (air, sea, rail, etc), and a variety of other concessions and services, contact **International Student Travel Confederation** (ISTC) ⓘ *Herengracht 479, 1017 BS Amsterdam, The Netherlands, T+31-20-421 2800, www.isic.org*. Student cards must carry a photograph if they are to be of any use for discounts in Latin America. The ISIC website provides a list of card issuing offices around the world. Teachers may want to take an **International Teacher Identity Card** (ITIC) distributed by ISTC above as discounts are often extended to teachers.

Travelling with children

Travel with children can bring you into closer contact with Latin American families and generally presents no special problems – in fact the path is often smoother for family groups. Officials tend to be more amenable where children are concerned and they are pleased if your child knows a little Spanish. Moreover, even thieves and pickpockets seem to have some of the traditional respect for families, and may leave you alone because of it! Always carry a copy of your child's birth certificate and passport photos. For an overview of travelling with children, visit www.babygoes2.com.

Overland travel in Latin America can involve a lot of time spent waiting for public transport, so make sure you pack enough toys, books and so forth. Food can be a problem if the children are not adaptable. It is easier to take biscuits, drinks, bread, etc with you on longer trips than to rely on meal stops where the food may not be to taste. A small immersion heater and jug for making hot drinks is invaluable, but remember that electric current varies. Try and get a dual-voltage one (110v and 220v). All airlines charge a reduced price for children under 12 and less for children under two. Double check the child's baggage allowance – some are as low as 7 kg. On long-distance buses children generally pay half or reduced fares. For shorter trips it is cheaper, if less comfortable, to seat small children on your knee. Often there are spare seats which children can occupy after tickets have been collected. In city and local excursion buses, small children do not generally pay a fare, but are not entitled to a seat when paying customers are standing. On sightseeing tours you should *always* bargain for a family rate; often children can go free. Note that a child travelling free on a long excursion is not always covered by the operator's travel insurance.

In **hotels** try to negotiate family rates. If charges are per person, always insist that two children will occupy one bed only, therefore counting as one tariff. If rates are per bed, the same applies. It is quite common for children under 10 or 12 to be allowed to stay for no extra charge as long as they are sharing your room.

Women travellers

Some women experience problems, whether accompanied or not; others encounter no difficulties at all. You should be aware that unaccompanied Western women will be subject to close scrutiny and exceptional curiosity. Don't be unduly scared – or flattered. Simply be prepared and try not to over-react. When you set out, err on the side of caution until your instincts have adjusted to the new culture. Women travelling alone could consider taking a wedding ring (a fake one if necessary) to prevent being hassled. To help minimize unwanted attention, do not wear suggestive clothing. Do not feel bad about showing offence. When accepting an invitation, make sure that someone else knows the address and the time you left. Ask if you can bring a friend (even if you do not intend to do so). A good rule is always to act with confidence, as though you know where you are going, even if you do not. Someone who looks lost is more likely to attract unwanted attention. Do not disclose to strangers where you are staying.

Working in Mexico and Central America

Two main areas provide opportunities for unskilled volunteers: childcare – often at orphanages or schools – and nature projects. Be warned, spontaneous volunteering is becoming more difficult. Organizations that use volunteers have progressed and plan their personnel needs so you may be required to make contact before you visit. Many organizations now charge volunteers for board and lodging and projects are often for a minimum of four weeks.

Guatemala and Costa Rica have fairly well-developed and organized volunteer programmes. Instinct suggests that strong hands, a generous spirit and genuine charity will also be much appreciated in El Salvador for several years to come as the clear up after the earthquakes of 2002 continues.

Many developed countries have nationally organized volunteer programmes. The **US Peace Corps** ⓘ *Paul D Coverdell Peace Corps Headquarters, 1111 20th St NW, Washington, DC 20526, T1-800-424-8580, www.peacecorps.gov*, is the most prominent in the region, working with countries on development projects with two-year assignments for US citizens in countries throughout the region.

Variations on the volunteering programme are to enrol on increasingly popular GAP year programmes. These normally incorporate a period of volunteer work with a few months of free time at the end of the programme for travel. **Experiment in International Living** ⓘ *T+44-1684-562577, www.eiluk.org*, is the UK element of a US international homestay programme that arranges stays with families in Mexico and Central America with social projects based on the ethos that if you want to live together you need to work together. It's an excellent way to meet people and learn the language.

Before you travel

Getting in

All international travel requires that you have at least six months remaining on a valid passport. Beyond a passport, very little is required of international travellers to Central America and Mexico. However, there are a few little tricks that can make your life a lot easier. Latin Americans, especially officials, are very document-minded. You should always carry some form of identification, ideally your passport or even better a laminated copy of it, in a safe place about your person. If staying in a country for several weeks, it is worthwhile registering at your embassy or consulate. Then, if your passport is stolen, the process of replacing it is faster and easier. It can also be handy to keep some additional passport-sized photographs together with photocopies of essential documents – including your flight ticket – separately from the originals.

Visas, immigration, insurance and documents: see each individual country for specific details.

It is your responsibility to ensure that your passport is stamped in and out when you cross borders. The absence of entry and exit stamps can cause serious difficulties; seek out the proper immigration offices if the stamping process is not carried out as you cross. Also, do not lose your entry card; replacing it can cause you a lot of trouble and possibly expense. If planning to study in Latin America for a long period, make every effort to get a student visa in advance.

Insurance is strongly recommended and policies are very reasonable. If you have financial restraints the most important aspect of any insurance policy is medical care and repatriation. Ideally you want to make sure you are covered for personal items too. Make sure you read the small print *before* heading off so you are aware of what is covered and what is not, what is required to submit a claim and what to do in the event of an emergency. Don't take anything you can't afford to replace.

If driving, or considering renting, an international driving licence is very useful, although not always essential. Membership of British, European and US motoring organizations can also be useful for discounts such as hotel charges, car rentals, maps and towing charges. Business people should carry a good supply of visiting cards, which are essential for good business relations in Latin America. Identity, membership or business cards in Spanish (or a translation) and an official letter of introduction (also in Spanish) are useful too.

For US nationals, the implications of the **Western Hemisphere Travel Initiative**, which comes into force on 1 January 2008 should be considered if entering Mexico and Panama. You will need a passport to reenter the US once you have left and visited these countries.

Customs, duty free and export restrictions

Duty free allowances and export restrictions for each country are listed in the beginning sections of each chapter. It goes without saying that drugs, firearms and banned products should not be traded or taken across international boundaries.

Vaccination and immunization

Vaccinations and immunizations are an important part of the pre-trip planning, with some being required several months before you arrive in a country (see Health, page 53).

What to take

Take as little as possible. Clothes that are quick and easy to wash and dry are a good idea. Loose-fitting clothes are more comfortable in hot climates and can be layered if it gets cooler. Sarongs are versatile: they can be used as a towel, a beach mat, a skirt, a sheet, or a scarf, to name but a few. But don't pack too many clothes; you can easily, and cheaply, buy things en route. Four musts are good walking shoes, a sun hat, sunglasses and flip-flops.

Don't load yourself down with toiletries either. They're heavy and can usually be found cheaply and easily everywhere. Items like contact lens solutions and tampons may be harder to find, but stock up in major cities as you go along and there shouldn't be a problem. Throughout Central America, but not Mexico, lens solution is hard to find. One thing you don't want to get stuck without is toilet paper, so keep a stash close by, and dental floss, which can be useful for backpack repairs as well.

Probably the most useful single item is a Swiss Army knife (with corkscrew), followed by a money belt, a headtorch/flashlight (not everywhere has 24-hour electricity), the smallest alarm clock you can find and a basic medical kit. Also, don't forget to pack photocopies of essential documents like passport, visas and traveller's cheque receipts just in case you lose the originals. For security a small padlock is useful for locking up your bag, and on the doors of some the more basic hotels. Finally, a climbing karabiner can be handy for clipping your bag on to something and foiling the grab thief.

Photographers using print will want to take all the film that they will require for the trip, ideally in a bag that is both water and dust proof – if not available triple wrap them in plastic bags. Obtaining film in the region is getting easier, but you may not be able to get the precise film you want when you want it. Digital photographers will want to find a way of clearing the camera memory either by burning to CD, downloading to a website or some other method.

Money

While most – but not all – countries in Central America and Mexico have their own currencies, the most useful foreign currency in the region is the US dollar. Both Panama and El Salvador actually use the currency as if it were their own. Consequently that proportion of your money you take in cash and traveller's cheques should be in US dollars. Banks and *casa de cambios* are increasingly able to change euros but the dollar is still the most readily accepted and changed.

How much?

As a rough calculation budget travellers can get by on US$25-US$30 a day, but that means that you won't be able to afford to take many excursions. A more realistic and sustainable budget is US$30-US$45. Plenty of travellers manage on smaller budgets but it's probably better to spend a little longer at home saving up, and then have a good time while you're away, rather than find yourself adding up the small change on a Saturday night to see if you can afford a weekly beer. The three main ways of keeping in funds while travelling are with US dollars cash, US dollars traveller's cheques (TCs), or plastic (credit cards). It is recommended that you take all three.

Cash

The chief benefit of taking US dollars is that they are accepted almost everywhere. They are used as national currency in El Salvador and Panama, and rates and commissions are more competitive than for other currencies.

Exchange rates (June 2006)

Country	Unit of currency	US$	Euro	Sterling
Belize	Belize dollar	2.00	2.40	3.51
Costa Rica	Colón	491	620	906
El Salvador*	Colón	8.75	10.53	15.39
Guatemala	Quetzal	7.28	9.18	13.41
Honduras	Lempira	18.11	22.83	33.36
Mexico	Peso	11.37	14.34	20.95
Nicaragua	Córdoba	16.47	20.77	30.34
Panama*	Balboa	1.00	1.21	1.78

* US notes and coins are legal tender.

In many countries, US dollar notes are only accepted if they are in excellent condition – no small tears, rips, nicks, holes or scribbles. When ordering money at home bear this in mind. Take a selection of bills including several low-value US dollar bills (US$5 or US$10) which can be carried for changing into local currency if arriving in a country when banks or *casas de cambio* are closed, and for use in out of the way places when you may run out of local currency. They are also very useful for shopping: shopkeepers and *casas de cambio* tend to give better exchange rates than hotels or banks (but see below).

In Mexico, casas de cambio may be open longer hours than banks, but they do not offer better exchange rates.

If your budget is tight it is essential to avoid situations where you are forced to change money regardless of the rate; watch weekends and public holidays carefully and never run out of local currency. Take plenty of local currency, in small denominations, when making trips away from the major towns and resorts.

Traveller's cheques

Traveller's cheques provide reasonably accessible cash with peace of mind against theft. Denominations of US$50 and US$100 are preferable, with a few of US$20 to increase your options. Some banks will change the cheques for US dollars cash if you need to top up your supply. **American Express**, **Visa** or **Thomas Cook** US dollar traveller's cheques are recommended, but less commission is often charged on **Citibank** or **Bank of America** traveller's cheques if they are cashed at Latin American branches of those banks. American Express now has a plastic **Traveller's Cheque Card,** used in a similar way to paper traveller's cheques. While this should work in theory, experience shows that new financial ideas are not quickly adopted in Central America and you may have trouble using it.

Several banks charge a high fixed commission for changing traveller's cheques because they don't really want the bother. *Casas de cambio* are usually a much better bet for this service. Some establishments may ask to see a passport and the customer's record of purchase before accepting. Keep the original purchase slip in a separate place to the traveller's cheques and make a photocopy for security. The better hotels will normally change traveller's cheques for their guests (often at a poor rate).

Credit cards

Credit cards are ideal for travelling providing ready access to funds without carrying large amounts of cash on your person. In an ideal world taking a couple of cards (one Visa and one MasterCard) will make sure you are covered in most options. It is straightforward to obtain a cash advance against a credit card and even easier to withdraw cash from ATMs. There are two acceptance systems, **Plus** and **Cirrus**. You may have to experiment to see what combination of options your require. Fortunately, most ATMs give you a 'language' option after you enter your card. The rates of exchange on ATM withdrawals are the best available for currency exchange but your bank or credit card company imposes a handling charge. With a credit card, obtain a credit limit sufficient for your needs, or pay money to put the account in credit. If travelling for a long time, consider a direct debit to clear your account regularly. If you lose a card, immediately contact the 24-hour helpline of the issuer in your home country (find out the numbers to call before travelling and keep them in a safe place). Most card issuers provide a telephone number where you can call collect from anywhere in the world in case of card loss or theft; be sure to request it before travelling.

Remove your credit card from the machine immediately after the transaction to avoid it being retained – getting it back can be difficult.

For purchases, credit cards of the **Visa** and **MasterCard** groups, **American Express** (Amex), **Carte Blanche** and **Diners Club** can be used. Make sure you know the correct procedure if they are lost or stolen. Credit card transactions are normally at an officially recognized rate of exchange; they are often subject to sales tax. In addition, many establishments in Latin America charge a fee of about 5% on credit card transactions; although forbidden by credit card company rules there is not a lot you can do about this, except get the charge itemized on the receipt and complain to the card company. For credit card security, insist that imprints are made in your presence. Any imprints incorrectly completed should be torn into tiny pieces. Also destroy the carbon papers after the form is completed (signatures can be copied from them).

Changing money

Whenever possible change your money at a bank or a *casa de cambio*. Black markets have largely disappeared; avoid them if you can as you are unlikely to get a significantly better rate and you place yourself a greater risk of being ripped off. If you need to change money on the street, do not do so alone. If you are unsure about rates of exchange when you enter a country, check at the border with more than one changer, or ask locals or any traveller who may be leaving that country. Whenever you leave a country, sell any local currency before leaving – the further you get away from a country, the less the value of a country's money; in some cases you may not be able to change it at all.

Getting there

All countries in Latin America officially require travellers entering their territory to have an onward or return ticket. This regulation is rarely enforced, but it can create problems. In lieu of an onward ticket out of the country you are entering, any ticket out of another Latin American country may suffice, or proof that you have sufficient funds to buy a ticket (a credit card will do). International air tickets are very expensive if purchased in Latin America.

Air

Certain Central American countries impose local tax on flights originating there. Among these are Guatemala, Costa Rica, Panama and Mexico. Details of all the main airlines flying to each country are given in the relevant Essentials sections.

Fares from Europe and North America to Latin American destinations vary. Peak periods, and higher prices, correspond to holiday season in the northern hemisphere. The very busy seasons are as follows: 7 December to 15 January, and July to

Airline and internet travel resources

Most international and several domestic airlines have websites which are useful for gaining information about flights. As yet you are unlikely to get the best price online, so use the websites in an advisory capacity only.

AeroMéxico www.aeromexico.com
Air France www.airfrance.com
Alaska Airlines www.alaskaairlines.com
Alitalia www.alitalia.it
American Airlines www.aa.com
Avianca www.avianca.com
British Airways www.ba.com
Condor www.condor.de
Continental www.continental.com
Copa www.copaair.com
Cubana www.cubana.cu
Delta www.delta.com
Grupo Taca www.grupotaca.com
Iberia www.iberia.com
Japan Airlines www.jal.com
KLM www.klm.com
Lacsa www.grupotaca.com
LanChile www.lanchile.com
Lufthansa www.lufthansa.com
Martinair www.martinair.com
Mexicana www.mexicana.com
Northwest www.nwa.com
Qantas www.qantas.com.au
Taca www.grupotaca.com
United www.ual.com
Varig www.varig.com.br

Mexican low-cost airlines
ABC Interjet www.interjet.com.mx
Avolar www.avolar.com.mx
Click Mexicana www.clickmexicana.com
Volaris www.volaris.com.mx

For a full list of airline websites visit www.evasions.com/airlines1.htm

Web resources
www.expedia.com
www.travelocity.com
www.orbitz.com
www.opodo.com
www.priceline.com
www.lastminute.com

mid-September. If you intend travelling during those times, book as far ahead as possible. Check with an agency for the best deal for when you wish to travel. There is a wide range of offers to choose from in a highly competitive environment. Check the lists of discount flight agents for UK and Ireland, North America, and Australia and New Zealand. Also check the list of airline websites here and the list of tour operators in the UK and North America, on page 23. Many airlines share passengers across journeys so you many fly the transatlantic leg with one airline before changing to a different airline for the final leg

Most airlines offer discounted (cheaper than official) fares of one sort or another on scheduled flights. These are not offered by the airlines direct to the public, but through agencies who specialize in this type of fare. An indication of cost is difficult to give due to the large number of variables. The main factors are frequency of flights and popularity of destination at a particular time of year and there is a great price fluctuation. As a rough guide a three-month London-Mexico return in August is approximately US$950. In November the same flight falls to US$675. A three-month London-Costa Rica return is US$1125 in August, but US$675 in November. Flying into one place and out of another can be very useful. Flying into Mexico City and out of Costa Rica in August is around US$1000, while in November look to pay around US$765. While these are prices from London, the European prices are usually similar or cheaper as flights often involve European airlines such as **Martinair** or **Iberia**.

From the US flight costs are highly variable. Travellers from Australia and New Zealand will struggle to see change out of AUS$2500 coming in through Los Angeles.

Discount flight agents in Europe

In the UK
Journey Latin America, 12-13 Heathfield Terr, London, W4 4JE, T020 8747 8315; 12 St Ann's Square, Manchester, M27HW, T0161 8321441, www.journeylatinamerica.co.uk.
South American Experience, 47 Causton St, London, SW1P 4AT, T020 7976 5511, www.south american experience.co.uk.
STA Travel, 6 Wrights Lane, London, W8 6TA, T0870-1630026, www.statravel.co.uk, with branches throughout the world. Specialists in low-cost student/youth flights and tours, also good for student Ids.
Trailfinders, 194 Kensington High St, London, W8 7RG, T0845-0585858, www.trailfinders.com.

In France
Images du Monde, 14 rue Lahire, 75013 Paris, T1-4424-8788, www.imagenes-tropicales.com.

In Holland
Thika Travel, Kerkplein 6, 3628 ZN, Kockengen, T0346-242526, www.thika.nl.

In Germany
Die Reisegalerie, Grüneburgweg 84, 60323 Frankfurt, T069-9720-6000, www.reisegalerie.com.

Other fares fall into three groups, and are all on scheduled services: **Excursion** (return) fares: these have restricted validity either 7-90 days, or 7-180 days (Mexico), depending on the airline; 7-90 days (Central America). These are fixed-date tickets where the dates of travel cannot be changed after issue without incurring a penalty. **Yearly fares**: these may be bought on a one-way or return basis, and usually the returns can be issued with the return date left open. You must, however, fix the route. **Student** (or Under-26) fares: one way and returns available, or 'open jaws' (see below). There is also a wider range of cheap one-way student fares originating in Latin America than can be bought outside the continent. There is less availability in the busy seasons. There is a wider range of student fares to Mexico than elsewhere. Some airlines are flexible on the age limit, others strict.

Open jaw fares

For people intending to travel a linear route and return from a different point from that which they entered, there are 'open jaw' fares, which are available on student, yearly, or excursion fares. All airlines can provide open jaw fares simply calculated on the extra distance travelled.

Flights from Europe

Airfares from Europe to Mexico City between February and June can be very low (see above), commensurate with some transatlantic fares (the same does not apply to holiday destinations like Cancún or Acapulco). Most European airlines have a regular weekly service to the capital throughout the year so it is worth considering Mexico City as an entry/exit point for a Mexican trip for the widest range of options and prices. If you do not stop over in Mexico City, low-cost add-ons are available to Mexican domestic destinations through link with the main airlines.

With the promotion of Cancún as a gateway from Europe, there has been an increase in the number of scheduled flights to Mexico (for example **Iberia** flies daily from Madrid and Barcelona to Cancún via Miami; **Air France/American Airlines** daily Paris to Cancún; **Condor Flugdienst** from Frankfurt once a week to Cancún, **British Airways** operates a daily flight London Gatwick to Cancún via Dallas Fort Worth). If starting in the US and crossing Mexico's northern border,

Discount flight agents in the rest of the world

North America
Air Brokers International, 685 Market St, Suite 400, San Francisco, CA94102, T01-800-883-3273, www.airbrokers.com.
Discount Airfares Worldwide On-Line, www.etn.nl/discount.htm Discount agent links.
Exito Latin American Travel Specialists, 108 Rutgers St, Fort Collins, CO 80525, T1-800-655-4053; worldwide T970-482-3019, www.exito-travel.com.
STA Travel, T1-800-781-4040, www.statravel.com Branches throughout the US and Canada.
Travel CUTS, 187 College St, Toronto, ON, M5T 1P7, T1-866-246-9762, www.travelcuts.com Student discount fares.

Australia and New Zealand
Flight Centres, 82 Elizabeth St, Sydney, T133-133, www.flightcentre.com.au; 205 Queen St, Auckland, T0800-243544, www.flightcentre.co.nz. With branches in other towns and cities.
STA Travel, 260 Hoddle St, Abbotsford VIC 3067, toll free on T1300-733035, www.statravel.com.au. In NZ: Level 8, 229 Queen St, Auckland, www.statravel.co.nz, T0508-782-872. Also in major towns and university campuses.
Travel.com.au, 76-80 Clarence St, Sydney, T1300-130483, www.travel.com.au.
Trailfinders, 8 Spring St, Sydney, NSW 2000, www.trailfinders.com.au, T1300-780212.

flights can be surprisingly cheap if you get a special offer linking with one of the US international carriers.

Moving beyond Mexico there are few direct flights and asking a local discount supplier for the cheap options is the best way of finding out about flights. Seasonal charter flights can work out to be very affordable. **Martinair**, a subsidiary of **KLM**, flies Costa Rica-Netherlands, for around US$500 return. There are several cheap French charters to Mexico and Guatemala. There are a number of 'packages' that include flights from Mexico to Cuba which can be bought locally in Mexico, Guatemala, Costa Rica or in advance. Travellers starting their journey in continental Europe should make local enquiries about charters and agencies offering the best deals.

Flights from the US and Canada

Flying to Mexico from the US and Canada offers a very wide range of options. The main US carriers – **American Airlines, Continental** and **United** – offer flights to many cities in Mexico in addition to daily flights to Mexico City, Guadalajara, Cancún, Monterrey and Puerto Vallarta. Direct international flights also serve many other cities in the country; the main through points are Miami, Dallas/Fort Worth, Los Angeles and San Francisco. From Canada the options are less varied, but regular flights serve the main cities with direct flights from Montreal and Toronto. Keep an eye out for special offers. Flights to Central America from the US and Canada offer fewer options. All capital cities receive a regular service, with connections to regional cities and large towns.

If buying airline tickets routed through the USA, check that US taxes are included in the price.

Flights from Central and Latin America

Links throughout the isthmus are provided by **Grupo Taco,** a regional association linking Central America's national carriers. Main connections within the region and to other countries in Latin America and the Caribbean are provided through Mexico, San Salvador and Panama City. Regional services are beginning to drop and are worth considering.

Flights from Australia and New Zealand

Flights to Central America and Mexico from Australia and New Zealand are with **United Airlines** and generally connect through Los Angeles, where the range of flights available to US travellers can be used for connections.

General hints

Given complete free choice many people do not know where they will end up after several months travelling and would like to leave arranging the return leg of a ticket open in terms of date and departing airport or better still purchase a return leg when the time is right. In reality this is not a good idea. Two one-way tickets are always more expensive than a return and purchasing a ticket to return to the US or Europe is almost always more expensive than it would be from home. If you have a return ticket you can normally change the return leg date of travel and often the airport (normally at a charge) at local travel agents.

When departing by air, don't forget that you will have to pay airport departure tax if it isn't already included in your ticket.

If you buy discounted air tickets always check the reservation with the airline concerned to make sure the flight still exists. Also remember that airlines' schedules change in March and October each year, so if you're going to be away a long time it's best to leave return flight coupons open. If you know that you will be returning at the very busy seasons you should make a reservation. In addition, it is vital to check in advance whether you are entitled to any refund or re-issued ticket if you lose, or have stolen, a discounted air ticket.

Weight allowances if going direct from Europe are generally 22 kg for economy and business class or 30 kg for first class. If you have special baggage requirements, check with an agency about anomalies which exist on different weight allowances one way, for example. Certain carriers (for example **Iberia, Air France**) offer a two-piece allowance out of the UK only, each piece up to 32 kg. Many people travel to Mexico and Central America via the US, and all carriers via the USA offer this allowance in both directions. Weight limits for internal flights are often lower, so it's best to enquire beforehand.

Boat

Sailing your own vessel

Following the coastal route doesn't have to be done from the land side, as thousands of sailors who follow the good-weather sailing around the coast of Mexico and Central America can confirm. Between California, the Panama Canal and Florida dozens of marinas await the sailor looking to explore the region from the sea. A guide to the marinas and sailing ports of the region is *Cruising Ports: Florida to California via Panama*, by Capt John Rain, published by Point Loma Publishing in San Diego. Captain Rain is an experienced navigator of Mexican and Central American waters with over 60 Panama transits under his cap (his website is home.san.rr.com/caprains).

Travelling by boat to the region is not cheap and is really only worth considering if you are shipping a vehicle from Europe or the US. Enquiries regarding passages should be made through agencies in your own country. In the UK, **Strand Voyages** have information on occasional one-way services to the Gulf of Mexico from Europe. Details on shipping cars are given in the relevant country sections.

In the UK

The Cruise People, 88 York St, London, W1H 1DP, T020-7723-2450, www.cruisepeople.co.uk; 1252 Lawrence Av East, Toronto, Canada, M3A 1C3, T416-444-2410.

Strand Voyages, 1 Adam St, London, WC2N 6AB, T020-7766-8220, www.strandtravel.co.uk.

In the rest of Europe

SGV Reisenzentrum Weggis, Seestrasse 7, 6353 Weggis, Switzerland, T+41-390-1133, www.frachtschiffreisen.ch.

In the USA

Freighter World Cruises, 180 South Lake Av, Pasadena, CA 91101-2655, T1-800-531-7774, www.freighterworld.com.

Travltips Cruise and Freighter Travel Association, PO Box 580188, Flushing, New York 11358, T1-800-872-8584, www.travltips.com.

Road

Travel from the USA

There are a multitude of entry points from the US that can be used the main ones being Tijuana, Nogales, Ciudad Juaréz, Piedras Negras, Nuevo Laredo and Matamoros. These and others are covered in detail within the Mexico chapter. Crossing the border is simple and hassle free for foot passengers and reasonably straightforward for people travelling with their own vehicle. All border towns have a bus terminal that offers long-distance bus services.

An alternative is to consider catching a long-distance bus from inside the US. **Greyhound** and several other companies offer the service from border towns and towns further north such as Arizona, Los Angeles and even as far as Chicago.

If you are thinking of travelling via the USA, or of visiting the USA after Latin America, you are strongly advised to get your visa and find out about any other requirements from a US Consulate in your own country before travelling. Although visa requirements for air travellers with round-trip tickets to the USA have been relaxed, it is advisable to have a visa to allow entry by land, or on airlines from South and Central America which are not 'participating carriers' on the Visa Waiver scheme.

Travellers are not permitted to bring any meats, fruits, vegetables, plants, animals, and plant and animal products into the country. Travellers who fail to declare items can be fined up to US$100 on the spot, and their exit from the airport will be delayed. Call 301-436-5908 for a copy of the helpful pamphlet, 'Travelers Tips'.

Touching down

Airport information As a general rule, try to avoid arriving at night and if you can't, have a hotel booked and take a taxi straight there. It may not be the cheapest way out of the airport, but it is the simplest and safest. Each country in the region charges an airport departure tax – information is given in each chapter for the relevant country.

Local customs and laws

Clothing

Most Latin Americans, if they can afford it, devote great care to their clothes and appearance; it is appreciated if visitors do likewise. How you dress is mostly how people will judge you.

Courtesy

Remember that politeness – even a little ceremoniousness – is much appreciated. Men should always remove any headgear and say '*con permiso*' when entering offices. Shaking hands is much more common in Latin America than in Europe or North America; always say *Buenos días* before midday, *Buenas tardes* in the

How big is your footprint?

Where possible choose a destination, tour operator or hotel with a proven ethical and environmental commitment – if in doubt ask; spend money on locally produced (rather than imported) goods and services and use common sense when bargaining – your few dollars saved may be a week's salary to others.

Use water and electricity carefully – travellers may receive preferential supply while the needs of local communities are overlooked.

Consider staying in local accommo dation rather than foreign-owned hotels – the economic benefits for host communities are far greater – and there are greater opportunities to learn about local culture.

Protect wildlife and other natural resources – don't buy souvenirs or goods unless they are made from materials that are clearly sustainably produced and are not protected under CITES legislation (CITES controls trade in endangered species).

Learn about local etiquette and culture – consider local norms and behaviour and dress appropriately for local cultures and situations.

Always ask before taking photographs or videos of people.

Make a voluntary contribution to counter the pollution caused by international air travel. **Climate Concern** calculates the amount of carbon dioxide you generate, and then offsets it by funding projects that reduce it; visit www.co2.org. Alternatively, you can offset CO2 emissions from air travel through **Climate Care**'s CO2 reduction projects, www.climatecare.org.

afternoon or *Buenas noches* later in the evening, and it's normal to wait for a reply before proceeding further. In shops and markets, saying *No, gracias* with a smile is always better than an arrogant dismissal. Try not to be impatient and avoid criticizing situations in public; the officials may know more English than you think and gestures and facial expressions are certainly open to interpretation. Be judicious about discussing politics with strangers (especially in Guatemala, Honduras, Nicaragua and El Salvador). In certain situations, however, politeness can be a liability: for example when queuing, as, with the exception of Mexicans, most Latin Americans are disorderly queuers.

Punctuality is more of a concept than a reality in Latin countries. The *mañana* culture reigns supreme and any arrangement to meet at, say 1900, will normally rendezvous about 2100. However, the one time you are late to catch a bus, boat or plane, it will leave on time – the rule is hurry up and wait.

Prohibitions

Users of drugs, even of soft ones, without medical prescription should be particularly careful, as some countries impose heavy penalties – up to 10 years' imprisonment – for even the simple possession of such substances. The planting of drugs on travellers, by traffickers or the police, is not unknown. If offered drugs on the street, make no response at all and keep walking. Note that people who roll their own cigarettes are often suspected of carrying drugs and are subjected to close searches.

If you are taking illegal drugs – even ones that are widely and publically used – be aware that authorities do set traps from time to time. Should you get into trouble, your embassy is unlikely to be very sympathetic.

Responsible tourism

The travel industry is growing rapidly and increasingly the impact is becoming apparent. These impacts can seem remote and unrelated to an individual trip or holiday. But air travel is clearly implicated in global warming and damage to the ozone layer and resort location and construction can destroy natural habitats and restrict traditional rights and activities. With this in mind, individual choice and awareness can make a difference in many instances (see box); collectively, travellers can have a significant effect in shaping a more responsible and sustainable industry.

In an attempt to promote awareness of and credibility for responsible tourism, organizations such as **Green Globe 21** ① *Suite 8, Southern Cross House, 9 McKay Street, Turner, ACT, 2612, Australia, T+61-2-6257-9102, www.greenglobe21.com*, offer advice on selecting destinations and sites that aim to achieve certain commitments to conservation and sustainable development. Generally these are larger mainstream destinations and resorts but they are still a useful guide and increasingly aim to provide information on smaller operations.

Of course travel can have beneficial impacts and this is something to which every traveller can contribute – many national parks are part funded by receipts from visitors. Similarly, travellers can support small-scale enterprises by staying in locally run hotels and hostels, eating in local restaurants and by buying local goods, supplies and crafts.

There has been a phenomenal growth in tourism that promotes and supports the conservation of natural environments and is also fair and equitable to local communities. This 'eco-tourism' segment provides a vast and growing range of destinations and activities in Central America. For example, in **Mexico**, cultural heritage and ecotourism is being promoted by **Bioplanet@** ① *T+52-55-5661-6156, www.bioplaneta.com*, and in **Belize** through the **Belize Ecotourism** Association ① *T+501-722-2119, www.bzecotourism.org*, and **PACT** (the Protected Areas Conservation Trust) ① *T+501 822-3637, www.pactbelize.org*.

Ecotourism organizations

Conservation International, T1-202-429-5660, www.ecotour.org.
The International Ecotourism Society, T1-202-347-9203, www.ecotourism.org.
Planeta, www.planeta.com.
Tourism Concern, T020-7133-3330, www.tourismconcern.org.uk, have begun to develop and/or promote eco-tourism projects and destinations; an excellent source of information.
Earthwatch, North America on T1-800-776-0188, in Europe on T+44-(0)1865-318838, www.earthwatch.org. Offers to participate in various projects throughout the region.
Discovery International T+44-(0)1285-643333, www.discoveryinitiatives.com. Offers a changing selection of opportunities to participate directly in scientific research and development projects throughout the region.

Safety

Generally speaking, most places in Latin America are no more dangerous than any major city in Europe or North America and the people, if anything, are friendlier and more open. In provincial towns, main places of interest, on daytime buses and in ordinary restaurants the visitor should be quite safe. Nevertheless, in large cities (particularly in crowded places such as markets and bus stations) crime exists, mostly of the opportunistic kind. If you are aware of the dangers, act confidently and use your common sense you will lessen many of the risks. The following tips, all endorsed by travellers, are meant to forewarn, not alarm.

Keep all documents secure; hide your main cash supply in different places or under your clothes. Extra pockets sewn inside shirts and trousers, pockets closed with a zip or safety pin, moneybelts, neck or leg pouches, and elasticated support bandages for keeping money and cheques above the elbow or below the knee have been repeatedly recommended. Pouches worn outside the clothes are not safe. Keep cameras in bags (preferably with a chain or wire in the strap to defeat the slasher) and don't wear fancy wrist-watches or jewellery. Carry your small day pack in front of you.

Safety on public transport

When you have all your luggage with you at a bus or railway station, be especially careful: don't get into arguments with any locals if you can help it and clip, tie or lock all the items together with a chain or cable if you are waiting for some time, or simply sit on top of your backpack. Take a taxi between airport/bus station/railway station and hotel, if you can afford it. Keep your bags with you in the taxi and pay only when you and your luggage are safely out of the vehicle (but keep an eye on it!). Avoid night buses unless essential or until you are comfortable travelling in the area; avoid arriving at night whenever possible; and watch your belongings whether they are stowed inside or outside the cabin (rooftop luggage racks create extra problems, which are sometimes unavoidable – many bus drivers cover rooftop luggage with plastic sheeting, but a waterproof bag or outer sack can be invaluable for protecting your luggage and for stopping someone rummaging through the top of your bag). Major bus lines often issue a luggage ticket when bags are stored in the hold; this is generally a safe system. When getting on a bus, keep your ticket handy as you will probably have to show it at some point. Finally, be wary of accepting food, drink, sweets or cigarettes from unknown fellow travellers on buses or trains; although extremely rare, they may be drugged, and you could wake up hours later without your belongings. In this connection, never accept a bar drink from an opened bottle (unless you can see that the bottle is in general use); always have it uncapped in front of you.

For specific local problems, see under the individual countries.

Scams

A number of distraction techniques such as mustard smearers and paint or shampoo sprayers and strangers' remarks like 'what's that on your shoulder?' or 'have you seen that dirt on your shoe?' are designed to distract you for a few critical moments in which time your bag may be grabbed. Furthermore, supposedly friendly assistance asking if you have dropped money or other items in the street work on the same premise. If someone follows you when you're in the street, let him catch up with you and 'give him the eye'. While you should take local advice about being out at night, do not assume that daytime is any safer. If walking after dark on quiet streets, walk in the road, not on the pavement.

Be wary of 'plain-clothes policemen'; insist on seeing identification and on going to the police station by main roads. Do not hand over your identification (or money – which he should not need to see anyway) until you are at the station. On no account take them directly back to your lodgings. Be even more suspicious if he seeks confirmation of his status from a passer-by. If someone implies they are asking for a bribe, insist on a receipt. If attacked, remember your assailants may well be armed, and try not to resist.

It is best, if you can trust your hotel, to leave any valuables you don't need in a safe-deposit. Always keep an inventory of what you have deposited. If you don't trust the hotel, lock everything in your pack and secure that in your room. If you do lose valuables, you will need to report the incident to the police for insurance purposes.

Rape

This is extremely rare, but if you are the victim of a sexual assault, you are advised in the first instance to contact a doctor (this can be your home doctor if you prefer). You will need tests to determine whether you have contracted any sexually transmitted diseases; you may also need advice on post-coital contraception. You should also contact your embassy, where consular staff are very willing to help in cases of assault.

Police

Probably the best advice with regards the police in Mexico and Central America is to have as little to do with them as possible. An exception to this rule are the Tourist Police, who operate in some of the big cities and resorts, and provide assistance. In general, law enforcement in Latin America is achieved by periodic campaigns, not systematically.

You may well be asked for identification at any time and should have some form of identification with you at all times. If you cannot produce it, you may be jailed. If a visitor is jailed his or her friends should provide food every day. This is especially important for people on a special diet, such as diabetics. If you are jailed, you should contact your embassy or consulate and take advice. In the event of a vehicle accident in which anyone is injured, all drivers involved are automatically detained until blame has been established, and this does not usually take less than two weeks.

The giving and receiving of bribes is not recommended. However, the following advice may prove useful for people travelling in Mexico and Central America. Never offer a bribe unless you are fully conversant with the customs of the country. Wait until the official makes the suggestion, or offer money in some form which is apparently not bribery, for example 'In our country we have a system of on-the-spot fines (*multas de inmediato*). Is there a similar system here?' Do not assume that officials who accept a bribe are prepared to do anything else that is illegal. You bribe them to persuade them to do their job, or to persuade them not to do it, or to do it more quickly, or more slowly. You do not bribe them to do something which is against the law. The mere suggestion would make them very upset. If an official suggests that a bribe must be paid before you can proceed on your way, be patient (assuming you have the time) and he may relent. Bear in mind that by bribing you are participating in a system that may cause you immense frustration.

Getting around

By far the most popular style of transport for the 'independent' traveller is public transport, in particular bus travel. An excellent network of buses criss-cross Mexico and Central America varying in quality from luxurious inter-city cruisers with a/c, videos and fully reclining seats, to beaten-up US-style school buses or 'chicken buses'.

Travelling under your own steam is also very popular. Driving your own vehicle – car, camper van, motorbike and bicycle – offers wonderful freedom and may not be as expensive or as bureaucratic as you think. From the letters we receive, the ever-greater co-operation between the nations of Central America is producing dramatic benefits at border crossings for those who decide to go it alone. With the comprehensive road network it's easy to miss out on other sensible choices. Don't shun the opportunity to take a short flight. While you'll need to enquire about precise costs, the view from above provides a different perspective and the difference in cost may not be as great as you think. Getting around in Central America is rarely a problem whether travelling by bus, car, bike, in fact almost any mode of transport.

There is just one caveat that stands good across all situations: be patient when asking directions. Often Latin Americans will give you the wrong answer rather than admit they do not know. Distances are notoriously inaccurate so ask a few people.

Air

With the exception of El Salvador, all countries have a domestic flight service. Prices vary but it is definitely worth considering an aerial 'hop' if it covers a lot of difficult terrain and you get the bonus of a good view. If you know the outline of your itinerary, it may be worth booking internal flights before you arrive in the country. They are often cheaper.

Air passes

An option worth exploring is the airpass, usually offered by an airline or group of airlines. The standard scheme works on system of vouchers. A voucher covers a set distance between any two destinations. You simply buy as many vouchers as you want. **Mexicana** operates one such scheme and there is **All-America Airpass**, with 27 participating airlines from the US, Mexico, the Caribbean, Central and South America. These passes must be purchased in conjuction with an international air ticket.

Low-frills airlines have arrived in the region, with four operating in Mexico. Keep an eye on websites for special offers. See page 32.

Boat

Keeping all options open, water transport has to be a consideration – although not a very realistic one in terms of reaching a set destination. Beyond the value of sightseeing particularly in small, quiet tropical rivers, genuine water transportation is on the decline. You'll find a few regular ferry schedules that avoid circuitous land routes. The main journeys are from the tip of Baja California to the Mexican mainland; between the Cayes of Belize and skipping down the coastline; from the Bay Islands of Honduras to the mainland; across Lake Nicaragua; and in Costa Rica, where there are connections between the mainland and the Osa and Nicoya peninsulas on the Pacific Coast. If heading from Panama to South America you can work your way along the Caribbean coastline to Colombia using a number of small sporadically available vessels.

Beyond this functional travel one journey stands out. Travelling the Panama Canal (as opposed to just seeing it!) and crewing a private yacht. Both of these requiring flexible schedules and good timing, but you might get lucky. Conditions of 'employment' vary greatly – you may get paid, you may get board and lodgings, you may even have to pay. See the Panama chapter for further information.

Road

Bus

There is an extensive road system with frequent bus services throughout Mexico and Central America. Some of these services are excellent. In mountainous country, however, do not expect buses to get to their destination, after long journeys, anywhere near on time. Avoid turning up for a bus at the last minute; if it is full it may depart early. In general travellers tend to sit near the front – going round bends and over bumps has less impact on your body and sense near the front axle, making the journey more comfortable and reducing the likelihood of motion sickness. Tall travellers are advised to take aisle, not window, seats on long journeys as this allows more leg room. When the journey takes more than three or four hours, meal stops at country inns or bars, good and bad, are the rule. Often no announcement is made on the duration of the stop; ask the driver and follow him, if he eats, eat. See what the locals are eating – and buy likewise, or make sure you're stocked up on food and drink at the start. For drinks, stick to bottled water, soft drinks or coffee (black). The food sold by vendors at bus stops may be all right; watch if locals are buying, though unpeeled fruit is, of course, reliable. See above for security in buses. Make sure you have a sweater or blanket to hand for long bus journeys, especially at night; even if it's warm outside, the air-conditioning is often fierce.

International buses link the capital cities providing an effective way of quickly covering a lot of ground. There are several companies but the main operator is **Ticabus** with headquarters in Costa Rica, www.ticabus.com. However, bear in mind that Panama-Guatemala with **Ticabus** takes about four days and costs around US$70, plus accommodation in Managua and San Salvador. You may want to consider flying if you need to get through more than one country quickly.

Car

What kind of motoring you do will depend on what kind of car you set out with. Four-wheel-drive is not necessary, although it does give you greater flexibility in mountain and jungle territory. Wherever you travel you should expect from time to time to find roads that are badly maintained, damaged or closed during the wet season, and delays because of floods, landslides and huge potholes.

Be prepared for all manner of mechanical challenges. The electronic ignition and fuel metering systems on modern emission-controlled cars are allergic to humidity, heat and dust, and cannot be repaired by mechanics outside the main centres. Standard European and Japanese cars run on fuel with a higher octane rating than is commonly available in North, Central or South America. Note that in some areas gas stations are few and far between. Fill up when you see one: the next one may be out of fuel.

Documents Land entry procedures for all countries are simple though time-consuming, as the car has to be checked by customs, police and agriculture officials (see Mexico, Getting around by car). All you need is the registration document in the name of the driver, or, in the case of a car registered in someone else's name, a notarized letter of authorization. Note that Costa Rica does not recognize the International Driving Licence, which is otherwise useful. In Guatemala, Honduras and Costa Rica, the car's entry is stamped into the passport so you may not leave the country even temporarily without it. A written undertaking that the vehicle will be re-exported after temporary importation is useful and may be requested in Nicaragua, Costa Rica and Panama.

Most countries give a limited period of stay, but allow an extension if requested in advance. Of course, do be very careful to keep **all** the papers you are given when you enter, to produce when you leave. An army of 'helpers' loiters at each border crossing, waiting to guide motorists to each official in the correct order, for a tip. They can be very useful, but don't give them your papers. Bringing a car in by sea or air is much more complicated and expensive; generally you will have to hire an agent to clear it through.

Insurance for the vehicle against accident, damage or theft is best arranged in the country of origin. In Latin American countries it is very expensive to insure against accident and theft, especially as you should take into account the value of the car increased by duties calculated in real (that is non-devaluing) terms. If the car is stolen or written off, you will be required to pay very high duty on its value. A few countries (for example Costa Rica) insist on compulsory third-party insurance, to be bought at the border; in other countries it's technically required, but not checked up on (again, see Mexico, Getting around by car, for details on **Sanborn's** and other insurers, who will insure vehicles for driving in Mexico and Central America). Get the legally required minimum cover – not expensive – as soon as you can, because if you should be involved in an accident and are uninsured, your car could be confiscated. If anyone is hurt, do not pick them up (you become liable). Seek assistance from the nearest police station or hospital if you are able to do so. You may find yourself facing a hostile crowd, even if you are not to blame. Expect frequent road checks by police, military (especially Honduras, where there is a check point on entering and leaving every town), agricultural and forestry produce inspectors, and any other curious official who wants to know what a foreigner is doing driving around in his domain. Smiling simple-minded patience is the best tactic to avoid harassment.

For a good, first-hand overview of the challenges of travelling overland in your own vehicle, get hold of a copy of *Panama or Bust*, by Jim Jaillet, www.panamaorbust.com, which covers the challenges of preparing for and completing a year-long trip from the US to Panama and back.

Security Spare no ingenuity in making your car secure. Try never to leave the car unattended except in a locked garage or guarded parking space. Remove all belongings and leave the empty glove compartment open when the car is unattended. Also lock the clutch or accelerator to the steering wheel with a heavy, obvious chain or lock. Street children will generally protect your car fiercely in exchange for a tip. Be sure to note down key numbers and carry spares of the most important ones, but don't keep all spares inside the vehicle.

Shipping a vehicle to and beyond Central America Two shipping lines recommended for shipping cars to Central America from around the world are **Wallenius Wilhelmsen** ⓘ *head office in Norway at Box 33, N-1324 Lysaker, T+47-6758-4100, for other offices visit www.2wglobal.com*; and in the US **American Cargo Service Inc** ⓘ *2305 Northwest 107 Av, Box 122, Miami, FL 331720, T305-592-8065*. You'll find good online recommendations at www.horizonsunlimited.com.

Shipping from Panama to mainland South America is expensive; shop around to find the cheapest way. The shipping lines and agents, and the prices for the services from Panama and elsewhere change frequently. Current details and recommendations will be found in the Panama chapter under Shipping a vehicle, page 1118.

Car hire

While not everyone has the time or inclination to travel with their own car, the freedom that goes with renting for a few days is well worth considering, especially if you can get a group of three or four together to share the cost. The main international car hire companies operate in all countries, but tend to be expensive. Hotels and tourist agencies will tell you where to find cheaper rates, but you will need to check that you have such basics as a spare wheel, toolkit and functioning lights, etc. If you plan to do a lot of driving and will have time at the end to dispose of it, investigate the possibility of buying a second-hand car locally; since hiring is so expensive it may well work out cheaper and will probably do you just as well. For visiting Mexico and beyond, investigate the cost of buying a car in the USA and selling it there at the end of a trip (do not try to sell a car illegally in Mexico or Central America).

Car hire insurance Check exactly what the hirer's insurance policy covers. In many cases it will only protect you against minor bumps and scrapes, not major accidents, or 'natural' damage (for example flooding). Ask if extra cover is available. Also find out, if using a credit card, whether the card automatically includes insurance. Beware of being billed for scratches which were on the vehicle before you hired it. When you return the vehicle make sure you check it with someone at the office and get signed evidence that it is returned in good condition and that you will not be charged.

Cycling

Unless you are planning a journey almost exclusively on paved roads – when a high-quality touring bike would probably suffice – a mountain bike is recommended. The good-quality ones are incredibly tough and rugged. Although touring bike and to a lesser extent mountain bike spares are available in the larger Latin American cities, you'll find that locally manufactured goods are often shoddy and rarely last. In some countries, such as Mexico, imported components can be found but they tend to be very expensive. Buy everything you can before you leave home.

Recommended reading: *Richard's New Bicycle Book* (Pan, £12.99) makes useful reading for even the most mechanically minded. Also recommended is *Latin America by Bike – A Complete Touring Guide,* Walter Sienko (The Mountaineers, 1993).

The **Expedition Advisory Centre** ⓘ *at the Royal Geographical Society, 1 Kensington Gore, London, SW7 2AR, T+44-(0)20-7591-3030, www.rgs.org*, has published a booklet on planning a long-distance bike trip titled *Bicycle Expeditions,* by Paul Vickers. Published in March 1990, it is available as a PDF from the website or £5 for a photocopy. In the UK the **Cyclists' Touring Club** ⓘ *CTC, Parklands, Railton Rd, Guildford, Surrey, GU2 9JX, T0870-873-0060, www.ctc.org.uk*, has information on touring, technical information and discusses the relative merits of different types of bikes.

From Guatemala to Panama, border officials ask for a document of ownership and a frame number for your bicycle.

For a first-hand account of travelling through the entire region by bike, look at *The Road That Has No End*, by Tim Travis (www.downtheroad.org). Tim and Cindie are on a round the world trip, but this book covers the stretch from Mexico to Panama.

Hitchhiking

Hitchhiking in Latin America is reasonably safe and straightforward for males and couples, provided you speak some Spanish. It is a most enjoyable mode of transport – a good way to meet the local people, to improve one's languages and to learn about the country. If trying to hitchhike away from main roads and in sparsely populated areas, however, allow plenty of time, and ask first about the volume of traffic on the road. On long journeys, set out at crack of dawn, which is when trucks usually leave. They tend to go longer distances than cars. However, it should be said that hitchhiking involves inherent risks and should be approached sensibly and with caution.

Motorbikes

People are generally very friendly to motorcyclists and you can make many friends by returning friendship to those who show an interest in you. Buying a bike in the States and driving down works out cheaper than buying one in Europe. In making your choice go for a comfortable bike. The motorcycle should be off-road capable without necessarily being an off-road bike. A passport, International Driving Licence, and bike registration document are required.

Security This is not a problem in most countries. Try not to leave a fully laden bike on its own. A D-lock or chain will keep the bike secure. An alarm gives you peace of mind if you leave the bike outside a hotel at night. Look for hotels that have a courtyard or more secure parking and never leave luggage on the bike overnight or whilst unattended. Also take a cover for the bike.

Shipping Bikes may be sent from Panama to Colombia by cargo flight. You must drain the fuel and oil and remove the battery, but it is easier to disconnect and seal the overflow tube. Tape cardboard over fragile bits and insist on loading the bike yourself. The Darién Gap is impossible unless you carry the bike. For details on shipping to and from Panama see page 1118.

Border crossings All borders in Central America seem to work out at about US$20 per vehicle. The exceptions to this are Mexico (see Getting around by car in Mexico) and Panama (approximately US$4.50). All borders are free on exit, or should be on most occasions. Crossing borders on a Sunday or a holiday normally incurs double the standard charges in Central American countries. It is sometimes very difficult to find out exactly what is being paid for. If in doubt ask to see the boss and/or the rule book.

If you like the idea of a motorbike trip, but can't see yourself putting together the full expediction, **ACS Motorcycle Tours** ⓘ *T+507-236-7232, www.acs-panama.com*, in Panama have put together some good itineraries covering the region.

Train

Trains are like nature – they are treasured when threatened with extinction. Now that the privatization and subsequent closure of train lines in Mexico and Central America is almost complete there is a renaissance of interest in the classic journeys including the **Copper Canyon** in northern Mexico, the **Tequila Express** running from Guadalajara to Tequila, a fledgling tourist service in **Costa Rica** offering a couple of short runs and the **Trans-Isthmus** railroad in Panama. With the exception of the Copper Canyon, none of these are genuine train journeys. Trains do run in a few countries – Mexico, El Salvador and Honduras – but they are slower than buses and there is no such thing as a scheduled service. Train travel is no longer a viable means of transport for the region.

Maps

Maps from the **Institutos Geográficos Militares** in respective capitals are often the only good maps available in Latin America. It is therefore wise to get as many as possible in your home country before leaving, especially if travelling overland. An excellent series of maps covering the whole region and each country is published by **International Travel Maps** (ITM) ⓘ *530 West Broadway, Vancouver BC, V5Z 1E9, Canada, T604-879-3621, www.itmb.com*, most with historical notes by the late Kevin Healey.

An excellent source of maps is **Stanfords** ⓘ *12-14 Long Acre, Covent Garden, London, WC2E 9LP, T+44-(0)20-7836-1321, www.stanfords.co.uk, also in Bristol and Manchester*. Internet ordering and international delivery service available.

Sleeping

Hotels

At the top end of the market, mid- and upper-range hotel chains can be found throughout the region. A cheap but not bad hotel might be US$15 a night upwards in Mexico, less in some but not all of the Central American countries. In many of the popular destinations, there is often an established preferred choice budget option. The quality of these fluctuates. The good ones stay on top of the game, the mediocre ones fade and bloom with the fashions. For those on a really tight budget, it is a good idea to ask for a boarding house – *casa de huéspedes, hospedaje, pensión, casa familial* or *residencial*, according to the country; they are normally to be found in abundance near bus and railway stations and markets. The very cheapest hotels often do not have 24-hour water supplies so ask when the water is available. There are often great seasonal variations in hotel prices in resorts. In Mexico, couples should ask for a room with *cama matrimonial* (double bed), which is normally cheaper than a room with two beds. Note that in the text the term 'with bath' usually means 'with shower and toilet', not 'with bath tub'.

See box, page 46, and inside front cover for hotel grade and price guide.

Motels, particularly in northern Mexico, are extremely popular and tend to provide accessible, economic accommodation close to the main roads. Further south, the term 'motel' picks up an altogether seedier interpretation.

Making reservations is a good idea, particularly at times you know are going to be busy or if you are travelling a long distance and won't have the energy to look around for a room. At the lower end of the market, having reservations honoured can be difficult. Ask the hotel if there is anything you can do to secure the room. If arriving late, make sure the hotel knows what time you plan to arrive.

Hotel prices and facilities

LL (over US$150) to **A** (US$46-65) Hotels in these categories can be found in most of the large cities but especially where there is a strong concentration of tourists or business travellers. They should offer pool, sauna, gym, jacuzzi, all business facilities (including email), several restaurants and bars. A safe box is usually provided in each room. Credit cards are usuallly accepted and dollars cash changed typically at poor rates.

B (US$31-45) Hotels in this category should provide more than the standard facilities and a fair degree of comfort. Many include a good breakfast and offer extras such as a colour TV, minibar, air conditioning and a swimming pool. They may also provide tourist information and their own transport for airport pick-ups. Service is generally good and most accept credit cards although a lower rate is often offered for cash.

C (US$21-30) and **D** (US$12-20) Hotels in these categories range from very comfortable to functional and there are some real bargains to be had. You should expect your own bathroom, constant hot water, a towel, soap and toilet paper. There is sometimes a restaurant and a communal sitting area. In tropical regions rooms are usually equipped with air conditioning although this may be rather old. Hotels used to catering for foreign tourists and backpackers often have luggage storage, money exchange and kitchen facilities.

E (US$7-11) and **F** (under US$6) Hotels in these categories are often extremely simple with bed-side or ceiling fans, shared bathrooms and little in the way of furniture. Standards of clean-liness may not be high and rooms may also be rented to couples by the hour.

Youth hostels

The **International Youth Hostel Association** ⓘ *www.hihostels.com*, has a growing presence in the region with several places in Mexico and Costa Rica. With other affiliated hostals joining it is worth considering getting membership if you are staying in Mexico for a while. While there is no shortage of cheap accommodation in the region, youth hostals do still offer a fairly reliable standard of cleanliness. Members with an identity card normally get a small discount.

Camping

Organized campsites are referred to in the text immediately below hotel lists, under each town. If there is no organized site in town, a football pitch or gravel pit might serve. Obey the following rules for 'wild' camping: (1) arrive in daylight and pitch your tent as it gets dark; (2) ask permission to camp from a person in authority; (3) never ask a group of people – especially young people; (4) avoid camping on a beach (because of sandflies and thieves). If you can't get information, camp in a spot where you can't be seen from the nearest inhabited place and make sure no one saw you go there.

If taking a cooker, the most frequent recommendation is a multifuel stove (for example MSR International Coleman Peak 1, which will burn unleaded petrol or, if that is not available, kerosene, *benzina blanca*, etc. Alcohol-burning stoves are simple, reliable, but slow and you have to carry a lot of fuel: for a methylated spirit-burning stove buy *alcohol desnaturalizado, alcohol metílico, alcohol puro (de caña)* or *alcohol para quemar* (avoid this in Honduras as it does not burn). Ask for 95%, but 70% will suffice. In Mexico fuel is sold in supermarkets; in all countries it can be found in pharmacies. Gas cylinders and bottles are usually exchangeable, but if not can be recharged; specify whether you use butane or propane. Gas canisters are not always available. Camping supplies are usually only available in the larger cities, so stock up on them when possible.

Hammocks

A hammock can be an invaluable piece of equipment, especially if travelling on the cheap. It will be of more use than a tent because many places have hammock-hooks, or you can sling a hammock between trees, etc. A good tip is to carry a length of rope and some plastic sheeting. The rope gives a good choice of tree distances and the excess provides a hanging frame for the plastic sheeting to keep the rain off. Metal S-hooks or a couple of climbing karabiners can also be very useful. Don't forget a mosquito net if travelling in insect-infected areas.

Toilets

Almost without exception, used toilet paper should be placed in the receptacle provided not flushed down the pan. This applies even in quite expensive hotels. Failing to observe this custom blocks the pan or drain.

Eating

→ *See inside front covers for price codes.*

There is a section on each nation's food at the start of each chapter. We don't attempt to include everywhere listed, but a cross section of the type of places available, and hopefully managing to include the best of what is on offer. Naturally the dining experience varies greatly. An excellent general rule when looking for somewhere to eat is to ask locally.

The golden rule is boil it, cook it, peel it, or forget it – but if you did that every day, every meal, you'd never eat anywhere...

Most restaurants serve a daily special meal, usually at lunchtime called a *comida corrida* or *comida corriente*, which works out much cheaper and is usually filling and nutritious. Vegetarians should be able to list all the foods they cannot eat; saying '*Soy vegetariano/a*' (I'm a vegetarian) or '*No como carne*' (I don't eat meat) is often not enough. Universally the cheapest place to eat is the local market.

Shopping

Souvenirs

The range of gifts available is daunting, from the fine silver of Mexico's Colonial Heartlands, the tacky T-shirts of the more popular spots and the textiles and clothing of Guatemala to the leather goods from Nicaragua and the finely crafted *molas* of Panama. The best place to buy souvenirs without doubt is Guatemala, in particularly the market at Chichicastenango. If buying more expensive items, research before you leave home so you know if you're gettting a good deal.

Shipping items home is a good option.

Best buys and regional items are highlighted in each chapter. Generally, choice is better in the capital, but the price is steeper . Always make sure you know the price before purchasing an item. Bargaining seems to be the general rule in most countries' street markets.

Photography

If photography is important to you, plan for your trip before arriving in the region. Your plans will depend on whether you're taking print or digital pictures. When shopping for film for the rainforest bear in mind that 400 ASA is impossibly slow. Film prices are similar to Europe, and more expensive than the US. While print film is readily available (check the expiry date), slide film is difficult to find. Some travellers advise against mailing exposed films home; either take them with you, or have them developed, but not printed, once you have checked the laboratory's quality.

Developing film in Latin America is often, but not always, a problem. If you want to develop the film, try and get a local recommendation. Ask the store if you can see an example of their laboratory's work and if they hand-develop. Exposed film can be protected in humid areas by putting it in a balloon and tying a knot. Similarly, keeping your camera with a sachet of silica gel crystals or in a plastic bag may reduce the effects of humidity.

For digital photography (and video) you will need to work out how you are going to clear the memory of your camera once it is full. Options include burning to CD, downloading to website or buying more memory sticks. Whatever you do, make sure you have all the relevant cables and have tested them fully on other people's machines before travelling.

Festivals and events

If the time and mood is right, there is little to beat a Latin festival. Fine costumes, loud music, the sounds of firecrackers tipped off with the gentle wafting of specially prepared foods all (normally) with a drink or two. Whether you seek out the carnival or happen to stumble across a celebration, the events – big or small – are likely to be memorable.

If you want to hit the carnivals there are a few broad dates generally significant throughout the region. Carnival is normally the week before the start of Lent. It's more important in Mexico but you'll probably find regional celebrations in most places. *Semana Santa* (Easter Week) is an understandably more spiritual affair. On 2 November is *Día de los Muertos* (Day of the Dead), again most popular in Mexico but significant throughout the region when families visit cemetaries to honour the dead. Christmas and New Year result in celebrations of some kind, but not always public.

Public holidays throughout the region lead to a complete shut-down in services. No banks, government offices, usually no shops and often far fewer restaurants and bars. It is worth keeping an eye on the calendar to avoid changing money or trying to make travel arrangements on public holidays.

Mexico

A week before Lent Carnival/Mardi Gras Traditionally throughout Latin America, this week is a time for celebration before the hardships of Lent; in Mexico it is particularly popular in La Paz (Baja California Sur) and the port of Veracruz.

15 Sep Cry for Independence, celebrations that are particularly impressive in Mexico City.

16 Sep Independence Day, with regional festivities and parades.

2 Nov Day of the Dead, in which the souls of the deceased return to earth and family and friends turn out in costume and festival to meet them – particularly colourful around Lake Pátzuaro.

12 Dec Pilgrimage of thousands to the Basílica de Guadalupe, in northeast Mexico City, to the most venerated shrine in Mexico. Well worth a visit.

Guatemala

Mar/Apr Semana Santa, particularly colourful in Antigua with floats carrying Christ over wonderfully coloured and carefully placed carpets of flowers; also spectacular is Santigo Atitlán.

Nov Todos Santos Cuchumatán, All Saints' Day in the small town of Todos Santos, a colourful and drunken horse race with lots of dancing and antics.

Belize

10 Sep St George's Cay Day, with celebrations in Belize City which start with river races in San Ignacio.
19 Nov Settlement Day, celebrating the liberation (or arrival) of the Garífuna from distant shores. Also celebrated in Guatemala and Honduras.

El Salvador

29 Nov Nuestra Señora de la Paz. Big celebrations in San Miguel.

Honduras

15 May San Isidro, La Ceiba's patron saint, followed by a fortnight of celebrations. The highlight is a huge carnival on the third Sat in May.
1-4 Feb Supaya, southeast of Tegucigalpa, the most important shrine in Honduras with a tiny wooden image of the Virgen de Supaya.

Nicaragua

Keep an eye out for patron saints of villages and towns.

Costa Rica

Late Jan/early Feb Fiesta de los Diablitos in the small towns of Boruca and Rey Curre, south Costa Rica, symbolic of the fight between cultures, religion and colonization.
2 Aug Virgin of Los Angeles, celebrated with pilgrimages to the basilica in Cártago.
15 Sep Independence Day with celebrations and parades in the capital San José and throughout the country.
12 Oct Día de la Raza (Columbus Day) celebrated with particular gusto in the Caribbean city of Puerto Limón.

Panama

3 Nov Independence Day.

Sport and activities

Special interest travel in the region is widespread. Whether seeking cookery courses or specializing in sun-bathing you can find somewhere to do your thing. Adventure sports tourism tends to develop in correlation with general tourist services. Carrying out a dangerous sport in a location where supporting infrastructure is limited probably indicates that the risks are not worth it. You should always make sure you have the necessary equipment for the activity you are doing. If you have any worries about safety you have a responsibility to yourself and to others who will follow you to speak out and voice your concerns until you are reassured.

Archaeology

For both the generalist and the specialist the region is dotted with ruins from Central Mexico down to northern Honduras. The main Maya sites in **Mexico** are Palenque, Yaxchilán, Bonampak, Uxmal, Chichén Itzá and Tulum. Close to Mexico City is the truly monumental site of Teotihuacán. Towards the Gulf of Mexico the site of El Tajín near Papantla is impressive and relatively quiet due to being off the more popular travel routes. South near Oaxaca is the site of Monte Albán, the former capital of the Zapotec culture.

In **Guatemala** Tikal is one of the region's must-see attractions, and a visit to Quiriguá is worthwhile. In **Belize,** Lamanai and Cahal Pech are the easiest sites to visit, with trips to Caracol near San Ignacio and Lubaantun in the far south more demanding. Copán in **Honduras** is particularly noted for the large number of detailed stelae. In **El Salvador** the sites of Joya de Cerén and San Andrés have a low-key charm.

South of Honduras, archaeological sites are significantly fewer and generally require either specialist knowledge or interest with the highlight possibly being the largely unresearched site of Guayabo in **Costa Rica**.

Bullfighting

A strong part of Mexican life if you're interested, the bullfight is rich with tradition and ceremony. In Mexico City bullfights take place on Sundays from November/December to March/April. Another lively event in quieter spots are rodeos or *charreadas*, found both in Mexico and less commonly further south.

Canopy tours

Canopy tours are developing like a rash from Costa Rica outwards to Panama, Nicaragua and beyond. The more sedate options follow aerial walkways retaining a degree of quiet and decorum that make birdwatching a possibility. The more popular type is zipping down high-tension cables strung between forest giants.

Canyoning and caving

Options for caving and canyoning are developing in Mexico and Guatemala but the best caving in the region and the western hemisphere is found in Belize which has some of the longest cave systems in the world.

Courses and learning

Language courses are a natural choice. But if looking to learn some new skills try Mexican cooking in one of many culinary schools popping up in Oaxaca. The colourful textiles of Guatemala can be slightly demystified with classes in weaving – easiest to arrange through language schools in the highlands.

Diving and snorkelling → *Refer to* Footprint Diving the World.

Opportunities for diving and snorkelling can be found throughout the region. Overall the best diving for safety and opportunity is probably in **Belize**, especially in the offshore cayes, but prices tend to be more expensive than elsewhere. The cheapest place to learn to dive is off the Bay Island of Utila, **Honduras** – just US$200, less in low season. If arriving in Cancún, learning to dive in the area is surprisingly affordable meaning you can dive off Isla Mujeres on your way south. Good diving in **Costa Rica** is limited to the area around Puerto Viejo and Manzanillo on the Caribbean south coast, with the same good conditions continuing south to Bocas del Toro in **Panama**. Two diving hotspots in the region are the Blue Hole in **Belize** and the Cocos Islands off **Costa Rica.** The Blue Hole costs around US$180 for a day trip but you'll need around US$3600 for the 10-day trip to the Cocos Islands.

Fishing

Sea and freshwater fishing are world class with marlin and sailfish in the deep waters off Costa Rica and Mexico, bonefish a little closer to shore on the flats in Belize, while the freshwater dreams of snook and tarpon lurk in tropical streams along the Caribbean. Costs, however, are generally prohibitive, running to several hundred dollars for the day.

Hiking and trekking → *For recommended maps, see page 45.*

A network of paths and tracks covers much of Central America. In Guatemala, which has a large indigenous population, you can walk just about anywhere, but in other countries, particularly Costa Rica, you can be limited to the many excellent national parks with hiking trails. Most Central American countries have an **Instituto Geográfico Militar** which sells topographical maps, scale 1:100,000 or 1:50,000. The physical features shown on these are usually accurate; the trails and place names less so. National parks offices also sell maps.

Trekking should not be approached casually. Even if you only plan to be out a couple of hours you should have comfortable, safe footwear (which can cope with the wet) and a daypack to carry your sweater and waterproof. At high altitudes the

Protect the reef!

Belize, Mexico, Honduras and Panama offer some of the finest marine environments in the Caribbean Basin, but the major challenge is to keep it that way. It's important that if you dive or snorkel you take responsibility for your own actions, and that your trip contributes to the preservation, rather than the destruction of the reef.

Here are a few ways to help:

1. Don't touch the reef! Even a gentle brush can remove the protective covering of mucus from a coral colony and cause the death of an animal community that has taken hundreds of years to develop.
2. Don't remove anything from the reef, however pretty.
3. Be aware of your fins and where they go! It's easy to lose track of that deadly (for the coral) 50 cm on the end of your foot.
4. If you want to snorkel but haven't tried it before, practise your technique before you get close to a coral reef. A shallow bottom of a sandy beach, or a swimming pool is perfect.
5. When diving, stop your initial descent before you whack straight into the reef below.
6. Lend a hand! Collect any plastic or rubbish you find on the reef or the cayes and make sure it's correctly disposed of. Lost fishing nets can be huge problem for marine life, killing fish, turtles, even dolphins for years afterwards.
7. Support an organization working to project coral reefs, locally or worldwide. There are many excellent small-scale grassroots organizations which deserve your support.

For more information visit www.reefbase.org.

difference in temperature between sun and shade is remarkable. The longer trips mentioned in this book require basic backpacking equipment. Essential items are: a good backpack, sleeping bag, foam mat, stove, tent or tarpaulin, dried food (not tins), water bottle, compass, trowel for burying excreta.

Hikers have little to fear from the animal kingdom apart from insects, and robbery and assault are very rare. You are much more of a threat to the environment than vice versa. Leave no evidence of your passing; don't litter and don't give gratuitous presents of sweets or money to rural villagers. Respect their system of reciprocity; if they give you hospitality or food, then is the time to reciprocate with presents.

Horse riding

As much a mode of transport as a pleasure in itself, wherever there is open space and nature you'll probably find horse riding.

Mountain biking and cycling

It's a widely held belief that anyone can go mountain biking and to some extent that is true. However, if you're looking for a genuinely challenging ride it is worth seeking out a specialist regional guide.

Mountaineering and climbing

If you have a serious interest in rock climbing the only place to head for is the massive limestone cliffs and big-wall appeal of Potrero Chico near Hidalgo, just outside Monterrey in northern **Mexico**. There are also opportunities in Humira outside Creel. This sport requires specialist knowledge and thorough safety systems.

The main climbing in the region is found in the highlands of **Mexico** with several peaks over 5000 m (see page 78). In all countries further south there are several volcanic peaks, active and dormant, that give excellent views and a challenging climb all the way through the isthmus down to **Panama**. In **Guatemala** the active volcanic peak of Pacaya is a popular and safe excursion, while the Cuchumatanes Mountains in the mid-west of the country have the country's highest non-volcanic peaks. In **Belize** the highest climb is at Victoria Peak, best reached from the Cockscombe Basin Jaguar Sanctuary. Moving further south, climbing tends towards trekking. The peaks in **Honduras** include the hills around Gracias including Celaque (the highest, at 2849m) Puca and Opulaca. Close to La Ceiba is the rarely climbed Pico de Bonito. In **Nicaragua** Volcán Concepción and Madera on Isla de Omotepe are highlights of any trip through the region. In **Costa Rica** the highest peak is Cerro Chirripó and in **Panama** Volcán Barú is a 'drive' from the nearby town of Boquete.

Surfing → *Refer to* Footprint Surfing the World.

It's an endless summer of surfing all the way down the Pacific coast. From the north to the south there are popular breaks. From Baja California and Cabo San Lucas down to the Mexican Pipeline at Puerto Escondido there are popular breaks along the Mexican Pacific coast. In **El Salvador** there are good breaks close to La Libertad, with several all down the Pacific coast of **Nicaragua**. **Costa Rica** has well-documented breaks down the coast with the main centres at Tamarindo, Malpaís, Jacó and Dominical. Particular breaks are mentioned in the text. If looking to learn your best chance is probably in **Mexico** and **Costa Rica**.

Whitewater rafting

Being a potentially dangerous sport, whitewater rafting is not as widespread as it could be, but there are many world-class opportunities in the region. In **Mexico** try the Rivers Antigua/Pescados and Filo-Bobos near Veracruz. In **Guatemala** there are operators using the Cahabón, Motagua and Esclavos. In **Honduras** try the Cangrejal near La Ceiba in North Honduras, in **Costa Rica** the Reventazón and Pacuare are popular rivers, as is the River Chiriquí in Boquete, **Panama**.

Wildlife and birdwatching

→ *See page 1265 for an introduction to the region's wildlife.*

Central America and Mexico is home to spectacular wildlife-watching opportunities. Whale watching off the coast of Baja California is popular between mid-December and mid-March, and you have the chance to dive with whale sharks between March and May in southern Belize and the Bay Islands off Honduras. Another popular animal to see is the manatee, most likely to be in the coastal lagoons of Belize and Honduras.

On land it is the mammals, particularly monkeys and the elusive cat family, that quicken the heartbeat, whilst in the air, or at least close to the ground the sheer number of bird species mean ornithologists get positively over-excited by the opportunities found throughout the region. From Mexico to Panama there are countless sites. Wetland lagoons and rainforest sites provide some of the most colourful birdlife. For the novice the resplendent quetzal, with its beautifully flamboyant tail feather, is an essential sighting to start any twitchers career.

Health

Before you go

Ideally, you should visit your GP/practice nurse or travel clinic at least six weeks before your departure for general advice on travel risks, malaria and recommended vaccinations. Your local pharmacist can also be a good source of readily accessible advice. Make sure you have travel insurance, get a dental check (especially if you are going to be away for more than a month), know your own blood group and, if you suffer a long-term condition such as diabetes or epilepsy, make sure someone knows or that you have a Medic Alert bracelet/necklace with this information on it.

Recommended vaccinations

Vaccinations for **tetanus, hepatitis A** and **typhoid** are commonly recommended for all countries covered in this book. In addition, **yellow fever** vaccination is recommended for some areas of Panama; in most of the countries a yellow fever certificate is required if entering from an infected area (this doesn't usually apply to babies). In all eight countries vaccinations may also be advised advised against **tuberculosis, hepatitis B, rabies** and **diptheria** and, in the case of Guatemala, **cholera.** The final decision, however, should be based on a consultation with your GP or travel clinic. In all cases you should confirm your primary courses and boosters are up to date.

Malaria

Malaria precautions (see below) are essential for some parts of Mexico and Central America, particularly some rural areas. Once again, check with your GP or travel clinic well in advance of departure.

A-Z of health risks

Altitude sickness

Acute mountain sickness can strike from about 3000 m upwards and in general is more likely to affect those who ascend rapidly (for example by plane) and those who over-exert themselves. Acute mountain sickness takes a few hours or days to come on and presents with heachache, lassitude, dizziness, loss of appetite, nausea and vomiting. Insomnia is common and often associated with a suffocating feeling when lying down in bed. You may notice that your breathing tends to wax and wane at night and your face is puffy in the mornings – this is all part of the syndrome. If the symptoms are mild, the treatment is rest and painkillers (preferably not aspirin-based) for the headaches. Should the symptoms be severe and prolonged it is best to descend to a lower altitude immediately and reascend, if necessary, slowly and in stages. The symptoms disappear very quickly – even after a few hundred metres of descent.

The best way of preventing acute mountain sickness is a relatively slow ascent. When trekking to high altitude, some time spent walking at medium altitude, getting fit and acclimatising is beneficial. When flying to places over 3000 m a few hours' rest and the avoidance of alcohol, cigarettes and heavy food will go a long way towards preventing acute mountain sickness.

Bites and stings

This is a very rare event indeed for travellers, but if you are unlucky (or careless) enough to be bitten by a venomous snake, spider, scorpion or sea creature, try to identify the culprit, without putting yourself in further danger (do not try to catch a live snake).

Snake bites in particular are very frightening, but in fact rarely poisonous – even venomous snakes bite without injecting venom. Victims should be taken to a hospital or a doctor without delay. It is not advised for travellers to carry snake bite antivenom as it can do more harm than good in inexperienced hands. Reassure and comfort the victim frequently. Immobilize the limb with a bandage or a splint and get the patient to lie still. Do not slash the bite area and try to suck out the poison. This also does more harm than good. You should apply a tourniquet in these circumstances, but only if you know how to. Do not attempt this if you are not experienced.

Certain tropical fish inject venom into bathers' feet when trodden on, which can be exceptionally painful. Wear plastic shoes if such creatures are reported. The pain can be relieved by immersing the foot in hot water (as hot as you can bear) for as long as the pain persists.

Dengue fever

This is a viral disease spread by mosquitoes that tend to bite during the day. The symptoms are fever and often intense joint pains, also some people develop a rash. Symptoms last about a week but it can take a few weeks to recover fully. Dengue can be difficult to distinguish from malaria as both diseases tend to occur in the same countries. There are no effective vaccines or antiviral drugs though, fortunately, travellers rarely develop the more severe forms of the disease (these can prove fatal). Rest, plenty of fluids and **paracetamol** (not aspirin) is the recommended treatment.

Diarrhoea and intestinal upset

Diarrhoea can refer either to loose stools or an increased frequency of bowel movement, both of which can be a nuisance. Symptoms should be relatively short-lived but if they persist beyond two weeks specialist medical attention should be sought. Also seek medical help if there is blood in the stools and/or fever.

Adults can use an antidiarrhoeal medication such as loperamide to control the symptoms but only for up to 24 hours. In addition keep well hydrated by drinking plenty of fluids and eat bland foods. Oral rehydration sachets taken after each loose stool are a useful way to keep well hydrated. These should always be used when treating children and the elderly.

Bacterial traveller's diarrhoea is the most common form. **Ciproxin (Ciprofloxacin)** is a useful antibiotic and can be obtained by private prescription in the UK. You need to take one 500 mg tablet when the diarrhoea starts. If there are so signs of improvement after 24 hours the diarrhoea is likely to be viral and not bacterial. If it is due to other organisms such as those causing giardia or amoebic dysentery, different antibiotics will be required.

The standard advice to prevent problems is to be careful with water and ice for drinking. Ask yourself where the water came from. If you have any doubts then boil it or filter and treat it. There are many filter/treatment devices now available on the market. Food can also transmit disease. Be wary of salads (what were they washed in, who handled them), re-heated foods or food that has been left out in the sun having been cooked earlier in the day. There is a simple adage that says wash it, peel it, boil it or forget it. Be wary of unpasteurised dairy products as these can transmit a range of diseases.

Hepatitis

Hepatitis means inflammation of the liver. Viral causes of the disease can be acquired anywhere in the world. The most obvious symptom is a yellowing of your skin or the whites of your eyes. However, prior to this all that you may notice is itching and tiredness. Pre-travel hepatitis A vaccine is the best bet. Hepatitis B (for which there is a vaccine) is spread through blood and unprotected sexual intercourse, both of which can be avoided.

Japanese encephalitis B

This is a viral disease of the brain spread by mosquitoes in parts of Asia. It is very rare in travellers but those visiting rural areas during the wet season may be advised to have the vaccine.

Malaria

Malaria can cause death within 24 hours and can start as something just resembling an attack of flu. You may feel tired, lethargic, headachy, feverish; or more seriously, develop fits, followed by coma and then death. Have a low index of suspicion because it is very easy to write off vague symptoms, which may actually be malaria. If you have a temperature, visit a doctor as soon as you can and ask for a malaria test. On your return home, if you suffer any of these symptoms, have a test as soon as possible. Even if a previous test proved negative, this could save your life.

Treatment is with drugs and may be oral or into a vein depending on the seriousness of the infection. Remember ABCD: Awareness (of whether the disease is present in the area you are travelling in), Bite avoidance, Chemoprohylaxis, Diagnosis.

To prevent mosquito bites wear clothes that cover arms and legs, use effective insect repellents in areas with known risks of insect-spread disease and use a mosquito net treated with an insecticide. Repellents containing 30-50% DEET (Di-ethyltoluamide) are recommended when visiting malaria endemic areas; lemon eucalyptus (Mosiguard) is a reasonable alternative. The key advice is to guard against contracting malaria by taking the correct anti-malarials and finishing the recommended course. If you are popular target for insect bites or develop lumps quite soon after being bitten use antihistamine tablets and apply a cream such as hydrocortisone.

Remember that it is risky to buy medicine, and in particular anti-malarials, in some developing countries. These may be sub-standard or part of a trade in counterfeit drugs.

Rabies

Rabies is endemic throughout certain parts of the world so be aware of the dangers of the bite from any animal. Rabies vaccination before travel can be considered but if bitten always seek urgent medical attention – whether or not you have been previously vaccinated – after first cleaning the wound and treating with an iodine base disinfectant or alcohol.

Sun

Take good heed of advice regarding protecting yourself against the sun. Overexposure can lead to sunburn and, in the longer term, skin cancers and premature skin aging. The best advice is simply to avoid exposure to the sun by covering exposed skin, wearing a hat and staying out of the sun if possible, particularly between late morning and early afternoon. Apply a high factor sunscreen (greater than SPF15) and also make sure it screens against UVB. A further danger in tropical climates is heat exhaustion or more seriously heatstroke. This can be avoided by good hydration, which means drinking water past the point of simply quenching thirst. Also when first exposed to tropical heat take time to acclimatise by avoiding strenuous activity in the middle of the day. If you cannot avoid heavy exercise it is also a good idea to increase salt intake.

Underwater health

If you plan to dive make sure that you are fit do so. The British Sub-Aqua Club (BSAC), Telford's Quay, South Pier Road, Ellesmere Port, Cheshire CH65 4FL, UK, T01513-506200, F01513-506215, www.bsac.com, can put you in touch with doctors who will carry out medical examinations. Check that any dive company you use are reputable and have appropriate certification from BSAC or Professional Association of Diving Instructors (PADI), Unit 7, St Philips Central, Albert Rd, St Philips, Bristol, BS2 0TD, T0117-3007234, www.padi.com.

Water

There are a number of ways of purifying water. Dirty water should first be strained through a filter bag and then boiled or treated. Bring water to a rolling boil for several minutes. There are sterilising methods that can be used and products generally contain chlorine (eg *Puritabs*) or iodine (eg *Pota Aqua*) compounds. There are a number of water sterilisers now on the market available in personal and expedition size. Make sure you take the spare parts or spare chemicals with you and do not believe everything the manufacturers say.

Other diseases and risks

There are a range of other insect borne diseases that are quite rare in travellers, but worth finding out about if going to particular destinations. Examples are sleeping sickness, river blindness and leishmaniasis. Fresh water can also be a source of diseases such as bilharzia and leptospirosis and it is worth investigating if these are a danger before bathing in lakes and streams. Also take heed of advice regarding protecting yourself against the sun (see above) and remember that unprotected sex always carries a risk and extra care is required when visiting some parts of the world.

Further information

Websites

Foreign and Commonwealth Office (FCO) (UK), www.fco.gov.uk

The National Travel Health Network and Centre (NaTHNaC) www.nathnac.org/

World Health Organisation, www.who.int

Fit for Travel (UK), www.fitfortravel.scot.nhs.uk This site from Scotland provides a quick A-Z of vaccine and travel health advice requirements for each country.

Books

Dawood R, editor. *Travellers' health*. 3rd Ed. Oxford: Oxford University Press, 2002.

Expedition Medicine (The Royal Geographic Society) Editors David Warrell and Sarah Anderson ISBN 1 86197 040-4.

Keeping in touch

Internet

Email is becoming more common and public access to the Internet is becoming endemic with cybercafés opening in both large and small towns. We list cybercafés in the text, but obviously these change as new ones open and old ones close. If you can't find the cybercafes listed, just ask someone locally. One website giving information on cybercafés is **www.world66.com** but it is very difficult keep pace with the changing situation.

The symbol @ is called arroba in Spanish.

Telephone → *See inside back cover for telephone dialling codes.*

Many of the telecommunications networks have been privatized and prices have fallen considerably and in some areas have even improved. Consequently keeping in touch by phone is no longer prohibitive. Alternatively international telecom chargecards are useful and available from most countries; obtain details before leaving home. For the US **AT&T**'s 'USA Direct', **Sprint** and **MCI** are all available for calls to the USA. It is much cheaper than operator-assisted calls. Communicating by fax is a convenient way of sending messages home. Many places with public fax machines (post offices, telephone companies or shops) will receive as well as send messages. Internet calls through the Hotmail system may be possible if an Internet café is set up for calls.

Using a **mobile telephone** in most of Mexico and Central America is very expensive. In addition to the hassle of having to recharge your telephone, research carefully whether it is worth you while. Mobile phone calls will be cheaper if you buy a SIM card for the local network; in-country calls are likely to be considerably cheaper than using your home based account. However, bear in mind that the initial cost of the SIM card may make this a more expensive option. And your personal mobile number will not work.

Post

Postal services vary in efficiency from country to country and prices are quite high; pilfering is frequent. All mail, especially packages, should be registered. Check before leaving home if your embassy will hold mail and if so for how long, in preference to the Poste Restante/General Delivery (*Lista de Correos*) department of a country's Post Office. Cardholders can use American Express agencies. If you're expecting mail and there seems to be no mail at the Lista under the initial letter of your surname, ask them to look under the initial of your forename or your middle name. If your name begins with 'W', look for letters under 'V' as well, or ask. For the smallest risk of misunderstanding, use title, initial and surname only.

Media

World Band Radio Latin America has more local and community radio stations than practically anywhere else in the world; a shortwave (world band) radio offers a practical means to brush up on the language, sample popular culture and absorb some of the richly varied regional music. International broadcasters also transmit across Central America in both English and Spanish, these include the **BBC World Service**, www.bbc.co.uk/worldservice/index.shtml for schedules and frequencies, the **Voice of America**, www.voa.gov, and Boston (Mass)-based **Monitor Radio International** , operated by Christian Science Monitor, www.csmonitor.com. **Putumayo World Music**, www.putumayo.com specialise in the exotic sounds of Mexican music.

Details of the national newspapers, television and radio are given at the beginning of each chapter.

Essentials

Telephone

[illegible]

Post

[illegible]

Media

World Band Radio [illegible]

Mexico

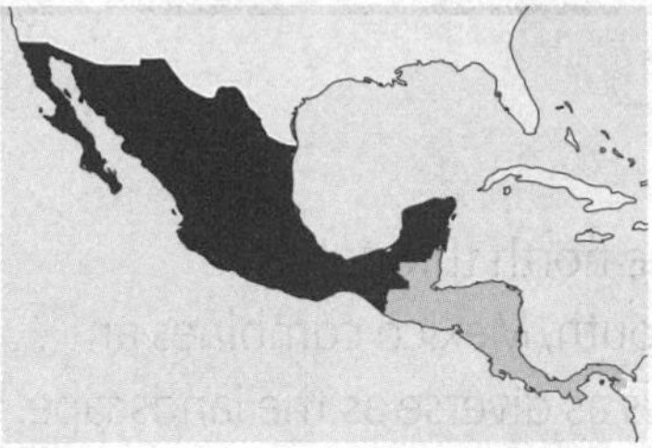

Footprint features

Introduction

Embracing scorched desert in the north through to body-hugging humidity in the south, Mexico combines an invigorating cocktail of influences as diverse as the landscape. As an emerging global market, Mexico's economy ebbs and flows to the tide of world trade, yet in rural communities market stallholders barter produce as they have for millennia. City wealth contrasts with rural poverty, and globalisation creeps in through fast-food outlets and shopping malls as centuries-old cultures cling to ancient traditions.

Underlying everything in Mexico is the improvisation of history. The growth of regional powers – the Olmecs, Teotihuacán, Toltecs and Mixtecs – were precursors for the Maya in the south and the terrifying Aztecs in the Central Highlands. Later, the Spanish conquest exploited regional rivalries before eventually replacing the Aztec capital, Tenochtitlán, with the first foundations of today's Mexico City.

For the visitor it's the chaotic confusion and juxtapositions that are so invigorating: the stark barren beauty of the Vizcaíno Desert in Baja California contrasts with the natural wonder of breeding grey whales lolling in the waters of Scammon's Lagoon; along the south Pacific coastline, isolated international resorts sit unnervingly close to deserted beaches; in the colonial cities winding cobbled lanes echoing with the memories of Mexico's silver mining history are lit with the electronic flash of neon light; in Chiapas, Zapatista rebels use mobile phones to galvanise support for Mexico's indigenous population. And all over the country hundreds of vibrant festivals celebrate Mexico's rich cultural heritage.

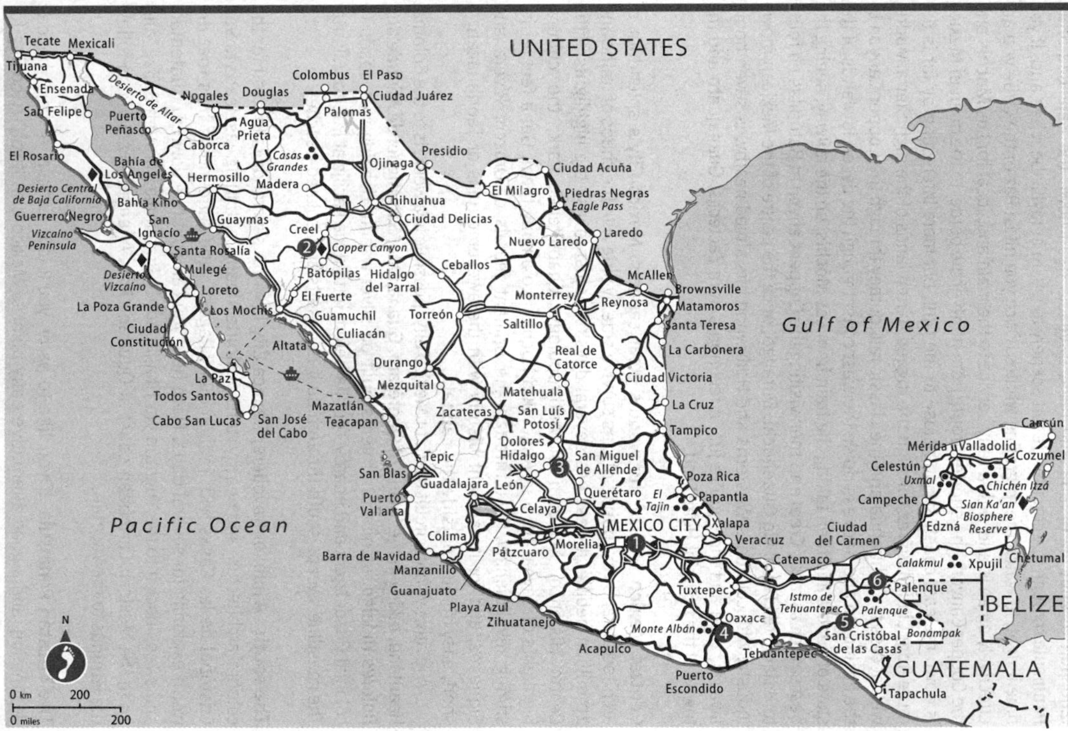

★ Don't miss...

1. **Mexico City** A nightmarishly busy metropolis, founded by the Aztecs and pulsating with colour, page 84.
2. **Barranca del Cobre (Copper Canyon)** Los Mochis to Chihuahua: one of the world's great train journeys, with peaceful hiking near Creel, page 221.
3. **Colonial Heartland** Elegant cities built on the wealth of the silver buried deep in the mountains of Central Mexico, page 245.
4. **Oaxaca** A colonial treasure of cobbled streets, with the ruins of Monte Albán nearby, page 357.
5. **San Cristóbal de las Casas** Chiapas highlands, a popular base for visiting travellers, page 400.
6. **Palenque** Hidden in the rainforest of Mexico's deep south, page 408.

Planning your trip

Mexico's size makes it impossible for anyone to see it all in one go. Fortunately, with so many attractions, and with relatively good transport links, it is not difficult to select a good variety of options. The Pacific, Gulf of Mexico and Caribbean Sea provide thousands of miles of beaches on either side of the country. The bulk of the interior is made up of mountains and plateaux, in the north predominantly arid, but, in the south, more densely forested and wet. For those flying in, there are two main ports of entry to Mexico, the capital and Cancún. To the north there is one long and wonderfully permeable border across which most driving traffic arrives.

Where to go

Northern Mexico If you're making the full sweep from the US border, the busiest land port of entry is Tijuana and most travellers head down the **Baja California Peninsula** through spectacular desert scenery to lay up at idyllic beaches and, if you time it right, to watch the migrating whales. Once you hit La Paz or the Cape you are effectively on an island with a ferry service to the mainland, ideal for **Los Mochis** and the Copper Canyon. The shortest route from north of the border to the heart of Mexico is down the east coast, staying close to the **Gulf**, but more interesting by far is the route from **Ciudad Juárez** through the rugged barren lands of the high Sierra Madre, with access to Chihuahua and the classic rail journey through the **Copper Canyon to the Pacific**. An alternative is down the west coast through the desert lowlands of the state of Sonora and then taking the train from **Los Mochis**, up the railway, seeing the best stretch as far as **Creel** and then visiting the **Copper Canyon** at Batópilas en route to Hidalgo del Parral via Guachochi. Durango, once the centre of the Mexican movie industry with countless Westerns and Hollywood hits filmed nearby, is seven hours away by road and then you're just a few hours from **Zactecas, Guanajuato** and the towns of the **Colonial Heartland.**

Central Mexico One of the world's great capitals, **Mexico City's** splendour of architecture and vast public plazas survive side by side with the chaos of traffic and 20 million people. It deserves several days' stay just to visit the highlights – the Centro Histórico, Museum of Anthropology, Chapultepec Park, the cultural highlights of Coyoacán, San Angel and Xochimilco among them. Get a feel for its stirring revolutionary past through the brilliant murals of Orozco, Rivera and Siqueiros, and for its ancient history with the awesome ruins of Teotihuacán, a short, easy trip just outside the capital.

A relatively short circuit north of Mexico City, possible in a week, is to the Colonial Heartland, taking in the towns of **Querétaro, Guanajuato, San Miguel de Allende** and **Dolores Hidalgo,** architectural gems built on silver wealth. Heading west leads to colonial **Guadalajara** and nearby **Tequila** before hitting the Pacific at Puerto Vallarta. The coastline sweeps south through built-up resorts and isolated beaches.

The south A hub for travellers, **Oaxaca City** is worth several days in itself for the colonial architecture and nearby ruins of **Monte Albán.** Continuing east leads to **San Cristóbal de las Casas** with indigenous villages in the surrounding hills that are worth exploring for several days. From here you can continue down to Guatemala and sweep back into the Yucatán via Tikal in north Guatemala, through Belize, and on to the **Mexican Caribbean** coast at Quintana Roo. Alternatively, you can follow the isthmus to the Yucatán.

The Yucatán Peninsula If you like to party, you'll love **Cancún,** a major holiday destination, and a good alternative entry point to Mexico City. If you're looking for something a little quieter, a short journey will take you to beaches nearby where you can snorkel and dive, relaxing in the warm, soothing waters. Cancún is the perfect starting point for the Ruta Maya – an eliptical route that takes in the major Maya ruins in Mexico, Belize, Guatemala and Honduras. South of Cancún, towards Belize is **Tulum**, while heading inland to **Mérida** it's a short trip to **Uxmal** and **Chichén Itzá**. Heading southwest towards Guatemala the fine ruins of **Palenque** are close to the waterfalls of Misol-Há and Agua Azul and the ruins of **Yachilán** and **Bonampak**.

Suggested itinerary The ultimate trip has to start by crossing from San Diego to **Tijuana**, down the **Baja California Peninsula** and over to **Los Mochis** for the **Copper Canyon**. From there, drop into a couple of the colonial towns – **Zacatecas** and **Guanajuato** stand out – and then to **Mexico City**. After a few days in the capital, head down to **Oaxaca City** and and then the **Oaxaca coast**, on to **San Cristóbal de las Casas** and nearby **Palenque**. That will take about four to six weeks, once you've added on the inevitable side trips. From Palenque you have three options. Head up to the **Yucatán Peninsula**, its beaches and the Maya ruins of **Chichén Itzá**, **Uxmal**, **Tulum** and the many lesser known sites, and then down to Belize through **Chetumal** – about three weeks. Cross from Palenque through the **La Palma-El Naranjo** crossing, or **Frontera-Echeverría**, for good, direct access to Santa Elena and Tikal. If heading for the Guatemalan highlands, cross at Ciudad Tecún Umán or Talismán from southern Mexico, the quickest option.

When to go

The best time to go is between October and April when there is virtually no rain. The rainy season works its way up from the south beginning in May and running until August, September and even October. This is also hurricane season in the Caribbean and on rare occasions the Yucatán and Gulf states get hit. But don't be put off by the term 'rainy season' – most years, the rains only really affect travellers for an hour or two a day. In the northern states of Baja California, Sonora, Chihuahua and Coahuila, it can remain very hot and dry.

August is holiday time for Mexicans and this can make accommodation scarce in the smaller resorts and in popular places close to Mexico City. Semana Santa (Easter week) and the Christmas holidays can also affect room availability. Day of the Dead celebrations (at the beginning of November and particularly around Pátzcuaro) and other important local fiestas also make it advisable to pre-book.

Finding out more

In Mexico, tourists can call T01-800-446-3942 to clarify problems. See under Mexico City for full details of Mexican tourist agencies.

Mexican tourist offices

In **Europe**, multilingual telephone coverage on T00 800 1111-2266.
In North American for **Canada** and **US** call T1-800-446-3942.

Useful websites

Mexico's web presence is phenomenal, some of the reliable, informative and useful websites that have been round for a while include:

www.visitmexico.com Mexico Tourist Board site, a comprehensive multilingual site with information on the entire country.
www.sectur.gob.mx Tourism Secretariat's site, with less glossy links but equally comprehensive information.
www.mexicanwave.com and **www.mexperience.com** Well-constructed site updated daily, with current affairs, feature articles and advice on travel in Mexico. Look out for the forum where comments from fellow travellers are exchanged.
www.mexconnect.com Also worth a look.

Language

The official language of Mexico is Spanish. Outside of the main tourist centres, travelling without some knowledge of Spanish is a major hindrance. Adding to the challenges of communication, there are also some 50 indigenous languages spoken in Mexico, the most common of which are Nahuatl, Maya, Zapotec and Mixtec.

Before you travel

Visas and immigration

US citizens need only show an original birth certificate and photo ID to enter Mexico. A passport is required for citizens of Western European countries, Canada, Australia, New Zealand, Hungary, Iceland, Japan, Singapore, South Korea, Argentina, Bermuda, Chile, Costa Rica, Uruguay, Venezuela and Israel.

Once proof of nationality has been verified you receive a Mexican Tourst Card (FM-T) at the point of entry or in advance at a consulate or embassy. The tourist card is issued for up to 180 days and should be returned to immigration officials when departing the country. Citizens of other countries need to obtain a visa before travelling – check in advance.

Although technically you are only supposed to stay 180 days a year on a tourist card, one correspondent lived in Mexico for five years on a tourist card, making short visits to the US three to four times a year, with no problems. Tourist cards are not required for cities close to the US border.

Renewal of entry cards or visas must be done at **Servicios Migratorios** ⓘ *862 Ejército Nacional, Mexico City, Mon-Fri 0900-1300*. Only 60 days are given, and you can expect to wait up to 10 days for a replacement tourist card. To get there, take metro to Polanco then a taxi. There are immigration offices at international airports and in cities such as Guadalajara, Oaxaca or Acapulco, which can renew tourist cards. To renew a tourist card by leaving the country, you must stay outside Mexico for at least 72 hours. Take traveller's cheques or credit card as proof of finance.

At the border crossings with Belize and Guatemala, you may be refused entry into Mexico if you have less than US$200 (or US$350 for each month of intended stay, up to a maximum of 180 days). Likewise, if you are carrying more than US$10,000 in cash or traveller's cheques, you must declare it.

If a person **under 18** is travelling alone or with one parent, both parents' consent is required, certified by a notary or authorized by a consulate. A divorced parent must be able to show custody of a child. (These requirements are not always checked by immigration authorities and do not apply to all nationalities.) Exact details are available from any Mexican Consulate.

Mexican embassies and consulates

Australia, 14 Perth Av, Yarralumia, 2600 ACT, Canberra, T6273-3963, www.embassyofmexicoinaustralia.org.
Belize, 18 North Park St, Belize City, T223-0193.
Canada, 45 O´Connor St, Suite 1000, K1P 1A4, Ottawa, Ont, T613-233-8988, www.embamexcan.com.
Denmark, Strandvejen 64E, Hellerup, DK 2900, Copenhagen, T3961-0500, www.mexican-embassy.dk.
France, 9 rue de Longchamp, 75116 Paris, T5370 2770.
Germany, Klingelhöferstrasse 3, 10785 Berlin, T30-269-3230, www.embamex.de.
Holland, Burgemeester Patijnlaan 1930, 2585 CB La Haya, T360-2900, www.embamex-nl.com.
Israel, Trade Tower 25, Hamered St, 5th floor, Tel Aviv 68125, T516-3938.
New Zealand, 111-115 Customhouse Quay, 8th floor, Wellington, T472-5555, www.mexico.org.nz.
Switzerland, Bernastrasse 57, 3005, Berne, T351-1875.

UK, 42 Hertford St, Mayfair, London, W1Y 7JR, T7499-8586, www.embamex.co.uk.
USA, 1911 Pennsylvania Av, NW, 20006 Washington DC, T728-1600.

You'll find contact details for other embassies at www.sre.gob.mx.

Customs

The list of permitted items is extensive and generally allows for items that could reasonably be considered for personal use. Large quantities of any item may attract suspicion. Adults entering Mexico are allowed to bring in up to 3 litres of wine, beer or spirits; 20 packs of cigarettes, or 25 cigars, or 200 g of tobacco and medicines for personal use. Goods imported into Mexico with a value of more than US$1000 (with the exception of computer equipment, where the limit is US$4000) have to be handled by an officially appointed agent. Latest updates are available at www.aduanas.sat.gob.mx (Spanish only).

Vaccinations

A vaccination certificate is generally required for travellers arriving from countries where yellow fever is present. See also Health, page 82.

What to take

In the Highlands it can be cold at night especially in winter, and most hotels do not have heating. Cheaper hotels often provide only one blanket and, while they will certainly provide a second if available, a light sleeping bag that packs up small can be useful. This applies in popular tourist centres such as San Cristóbal de las Casas and Pátzcuaro. ▸▸ *See also Essentials, page 29.*

Money

Currency → *US$1=$11.39 Mexican pesos (June 2006).*

The monetary unit is the Mexican peso, represented by '$' – the dollar sign – providing great potential for confusion, especially in popular tourist places where prices are higher and often quoted in US$.

Exchange

Cash Dollars are easily changed in all cities and towns at banks and *casas de cambio* and in the more popular places can sometimes be used if you're running short of pesos. Take a mix of large and small denominations – you don't want to get stuck trying to change a US$100 bill in a dusty village in the middle of nowhere. Along the with the United States the most-used currency is the US dollar. While it is possible to change the euro, sterling and other currencies, not all banks or *casas de cambio* will take them.

Traveller's cheques Cheques from any well-known bank can be cashed in most towns if drawn in US dollars; traveller's cheques from other currencies (including Euros) are harder to cash, and certainly not worth trying to change outside the largest of cities. If you are stuck, large branches of BITAL have been known to change other currencies. *Casas de cambio* are generally quicker than banks for exchange transactions and stay open later; fees are not charged but their rates may not be as good. You may be asked to show your passport, another form of ID or even proof of purchase (but keep it separate from your traveller's cheques). Denominations of US$50 and US$100 are preferable, though you will need a few of US$20. American Express and Visa US dollar traveller's cheques are recommended as the easiest to change.

Transfer If you need to make a transfer ask your bank if they can transfer direct to a Mexican bank without using an intermediary, which usually results in greater delays. Beware of short-changing at all times. **Western Union,** www.westernunion.com, have outlets throughout Mexico but the service is more expensive than a traditional bank wire.

Credit cards ATMs are now found even in small towns allowing you to travel without carrying large amounts of cash or TCs. **MasterCard, Visa** and **American Express** are widely accepted in Mexico either when paying for goods, withdrawing cash from ATMs (*cajero automático*) or obtaining cash over the counter from banks. Many banks are affiliated to MasterCard and/or Visa so travel with both if possible. Credit cards are useful in hotels, restaurants, shops and when hiring equipment to put down a deposit. There is often a 6% tax on the use of credit cards.

Lost or stolen cards: MasterCard: T001-800-307-7309. Visa: T001-800-847-2911.

Cost of living

A basic room is likely to set you back about US$15 on average, with occassionally cheaper prices available. Comfortable rooms will start at around US$20. Some hotels offer no single rooms, or they may charge 80% of the price of a double. If you are travelling alone this should be built into your budget. Meals start from US$10 a day for those on tight budgets. Activities will tend to be in the region of US$30 and upwards a day, depending on the activity.

Travel eats up more of your budget. Travel in Mexico is considerably more expensive (and more comfortable) than in the rest of Central America, partly because of the vast distances covered. » *See Getting around, page 69.*

Budget travellers should note that there is a definite tourist economy in resort areas, with high prices and, on occasion, unhelpful service. This can be avoided by seeking out those places used by locals; an understanding of Spanish is useful.

Student cards Although an international student (ISIC) card offers student discounts, only national Mexican student cards permit free entry to archaeological sites, museums, etc (see SETEJ, page 85).

Getting there

Air

Airports There are several international airports, the two busiest are **Mexico City** and **Cancún**. Services from the US and Canada arrive at almost 30 Mexican cities. Air passes are often bought in conjunction with international flights so ask when booking if planning internal flights, see page 31. For those arriving at Mexico City who are going straight on to Cuernavaca, Puebla, Toluca or Pachuca, there are bus services at frequent intervals departing from outside Sala D of the airport.

Student/youth and discount fares Some airlines are flexible on the age limit, others strict. One way and returns available, or 'Open Jaws' (flying into one point and returning from another). Do not assume student tickets are the cheapest, though they are often very flexible.

From Europe To Mexico City: There are several airlines that have regular direct flights. From Amsterdam with **KLM**; from Frankfurt with **Lufthansa** and **AeroMéxico** (LTU and **Condor** charter flights to Mexico City or Cancún); from London and Manchester with **British Airways**; from Barcelona with **Iberia**; from Madrid with

Iberia and **AeroMéxico**; from Paris with **Air France** and **AeroMéxico.** Most connecting flights in Europe are through Madrid or Gatwick. Fares vary from airline to airline and according to time of year. Check with an agency for the best deal for when you wish to travel. **To Cancún**: From Amsterdam with **Martinair**, Dusseldorf with **LTU**, Frankfurt with **LTU** and **Condor**, Munich with **LTU** and **Condor**; Madrid with **AeroMéxico** and **Avianca**, Milan with **Lauda Air** and Paris with **American Airlines.**

From USA **To Mexico City**: A large number of airlines fly this route, including **American Airlines, AeroMéxico, Delta, Continental, United, Northwest, Taesa** and **Americawest**. Flights are available from most major cities, with the cheapest generally going through Miami, Dallas, Houston and sometimes Los Angeles. **To Cancún**: From Albany, Atlanta, Baltimore, Buffalo (New York), Charlotte (NC), Chicago, Dallas/Fort Worth, Detroit, Houston, Indianapolis, Las Vegas, Los Angeles, Memphis, Miami, New Orleans, New York, Philadelphia, Phoenix, Pittsburgh, St Louis, San Francisco, Seattle/Tacoma and Washington DC.

If you foresee returning home at a busy time (eg between Christmas and the beginning of January, or August), a booking is advisable on open-return tickets.

From Canada **To Mexico City**: From Montreal and Sault Ste Marie with **Mexicana**; from Toronto with **Mexicana** and **United**; and from Vancouver with **Japan Airlines. To Cancún**: From Montreal and Vancouver with **Mexicana.**

From Australia and New Zealand From Sydney with **United** and from Auckland with **Air New Zealand**, all flying through Los Angeles.

From Latin America and the Caribbean Flights from Latin America have increased in recent years. Central America is covered by the **TACA** network, connecting the capitals of each country to Mexico City and some of the smaller regional cities. In South America, connections are to capitals and major cities. If planning a trip to Cuba there are flights from Cancún, Mérida and Mexico City with **Mexicana, Cubana** and **Aerocaribe.**

Road

From US There are many crossings along the border with the US, the main ones are at Tijuana, Mexicali, Nogales, Ciudad Juárez, Piedras Negras, Nuevo Laredo and Matamoros.

From Guatemala The main border town is Tapachula, with a crossing over the Talismán Bridge or at Ciudad Hidalgo. A more interesting route is via Ciudad Cuauhtémoc or heading northwest from Santa Elena/Flores towards Tenosique. There are also options for road and river travel.

From Belize The border crossing at Santa Elena is near Chetumal, where public transport can be arranged. A second very quiet crossing is at Blue Creek – good for a challenge but little else.

Touching down

Airport information and exit tax

When arriving in Mexico by air, make sure you fill in the immigration document before joining the queue to have your passport checked. Also at Mexico City airport you may be subject to a brief interview by the Federal District Health Service, in relation to the control of cholera, yellow fever and other diseases.

Touching down

Business hours All banks open Mon-Fri 0900-1330 (some stay open later), Sat 0900-1230. Business offices usually open at 0900 or 1000 and close at 1300 or 1400. They reopen at 1400 or 1500 and stay open until 1900 or later. Business hours in other parts of the country vary considerably according to the climate and local custom.
Telephone Country code T+52; operator T020; international operator T090; directory enquiries T040.
Official time 6 hrs behind GMT, US Central Standard Time; Daylight Saving Time, from first Sunday in April to last Sunday in October, 5 hrs behindGMT. Sonora, Sinaloa, Nayarit and Baja California Sur are seven hours behind GMT; Baja California Norte (above 28th Parallel) is eight hours behind GMT (but seven hours behind GMT between 1 April and end October).
Weights and measures The metric system is used everywhere.

Airport departure tax is US$40 on international flights (dollars or pesos accepted); always check when purchasing if departure tax is included in ticket price. A sales tax of 15% is payable on domestic plane tickets bought in Mexico.

Local customs and laws

Clothing Casual clothing is adequate for most occasions although men may need a jacket and tie in some restaurants. Topless bathing is increasingly acceptable in parts of Baja California, but take guidance from others.
Complaints If you have any complaints about faulty goods or services contact **Profeco** or Procuraduría Federal del Consumidor ⓘ *T01-800-468-8722, www.profeco.gob.mx*, or visit the nearest city branch.
Identification ID is increasingly required when visiting offices or tourist sites within government buildings. It's handy to have some form of identification (*identificación* or *credencial*; photocopied passport will usually do), to register one's name, and leave the ID with the security guard in exchange for a pass when entering a building.
Photography There is a charge of US$3-5 for the use of video cameras at historical sites. If you want to use professional camera equipment, including a tripod, the fee is usually much higher.
Tipping Normally 10-15%; the equivalent of US$0.25 per bag for porters, the equivalent of US$0.20 for bell boys, and nothing for a taxi driver unless some kind of exceptional service.

Safety

Mexico is generally a safe country to visit, although precautions over personal safety should be taken, especially in Mexico City. Never carry valuables visibly or in easily picked pockets. Leave passports, tickets and important documents in a hotel safety deposit, not in your room. Cars are a prime target for theft; never leave possessions visible inside the car and at night park in hotel car parks. Avoid travelling at night; if at all possible make journeys in daylight. Couples and, even more, women on their own, should avoid lonely beaches. Those on the west coast are gaining a reputation as drug-landing points. The police service has an equivalent to the **Green Angels** (**Angeles Verdes**, see page 72), the **Silver Angels**, who help victims of crime to file a report. US citizens should present this report to the nearest embassy or consulate. Otherwise, it is best to avoid the police if at all possible; they are rarely helpful and tend to make complicated situations even worse. Should you come into contact with them, try to stay as calm and polite as possible. Never offer a bribe unless you are fully conversant with the customs of the country (see Warnings page 72). Speaking Spanish is a great asset for avoiding rip-offs targeting gringos, especially short changing and overcharging (both rife), and for making the most of cheap *comedores* and market shopping.

Getting around

It may sound obvious but Mexico is larger than many people realize. Travelling Tijuana to Cancún non-stop by bus and assuming good links would take at least three days and cost in the region of US$200. Be realistic about the distances you hope to travel. And, if time is short, consider taking an internal flight – a short flight might seem expensive but add the cost of bus travel, food en route and recovery time it's worth keeping an open mind especially as internal flights on popular routes can be surprisingly cheap.

Air

Most medium-sized towns are served with internal flights. If you're looking to cover a great distance in a short time it is worth exploring the option of an airpass. **Mexicana** and **AeroCalifornia** provide Airpasses, covering much of the country; the pass is eligible only to those arriving on transatlantic flights, valid three to 90 days and must be purchased before arrival in Mexico. Fares range from US$50-400 per coupon; extra coupons may be bought and reservations may be changed. Several other airlines fly internal routes (a few with international flights as well), including **Aero California, Aeromar, Aerolitoral, Taesa, Saro, Aviacsa** and **Aerocaribe.**

Low-cost flights have arrived in Mexico with **Avolar** (www.avolar.com.mx), **ABC Interjet** (www.interjet.com.mx), **Volaris** (www.volaris.com.mx) and **Mexicana Airline's Click Mexicana** (www.clickmexicana.com) providing services to different parts of Mexico. Toluca's Adolfo López Mateos International Airport, about 40 miles west of Mexico City, is the central hub for the low-cost airlines. General costs are comparable with the older airlines. You get the bargain if you can book ahead, travel at inconventient times or if there is a special offer.

Bus

The Mexican bus system is good, but at times both complicated and confusing. The system favours the frequent, resident traveller. When the visitor tries to use the system you can be confronted with a daunting range of options, sometimes leaving from different terminals. The bottom line is that there is normally a bus going from where you are to where you want to go. The problem is trying to locate where that bus leaves from. In some cities there is a central bus terminal (in Mexico City there are four – one at each point of the compass broadly serving their respective areas), in others there are a couple – one for first-class buses, one for second. A third variation is division by companies.

> *Buses are often called camiones, hence Central Camionero for bus station.*

Bus travel can use up a lot of your budget because the distances covered are great. As a very rough calculation bus travel works out at around US$3.80 per hour, with tickets falling between US$3.20 to US$4.60 an hour.

Bus services have been upgraded in recent years and are generally organized, clean and prompt. Services range from luxury, to first and second class. However, travellers should not be beguiled into thinking that it is necessary to purchase an expensive ticket in order to travel comfortably. The service varies greatly between routes. A journey between two cities will almost certainly have a luxury service; a short trip between villages may be on a battered old bus.

The superior classes, called **Primera Plus** and **Ejecutiva,** offer varying degrees of comfort and some extra services. A number of bus companies offer this option providing reclining seats, toilets, drinks, videos, etc. ETN has exceptional buses with very comfortable, extra-wide seats but prices are about 35-40% above regular first class. The superior classes are probably best for journeys over six hours. First-class buses are also comfortable and have reclining seats, toilets and videos.

For many long-distance routes, the second-class buses have disappeared. Second-class buses usually operate from a different terminal to first-class buses and are often antiques (interesting, but frustrating when they break down). They call at towns and villages and go up side roads the first-class buses never touch.

In general, it is a good idea to take food and drink with you on a long bus ride, as stops may depend on the driver. When a bus stops for refreshment, remember who your driver is and follow him; also memorize your bus number so you don't miss it when it leaves. On daytime journeys consider whether you want to see the scenery or a video. If going on an overnight bus, book seats at the front as toilets can get smelly by morning. Also make sure you have a jacket, jumper or blanket to hand as the air conditioning can be very cold at night. You must book in advance for buses travelling in the Yucatán Peninsula, especially around Christmas; it is also advisable to book if going elsewhere. Bus seats are particularly hard to get during school holidays, August and the 15 days up to New Year when many public servants take holidays in all resorts; transport from Mexico City is booked up in advance and hotels are filled too. On intercity services luggage is checked into the hold of the bus with a receipt provided, offering a degree of security. But however well organized a company, always check your luggage is on your bus if you are putting it in the hold.

Inside the bus, lock or clip your luggage to the rack with a cycle lock and chain. Luggage racks on both classes of long-distance bus are spacious and will take a rucksack with a little persuasion (either of the rucksack itself, or the bus driver).

Fares First-class fares are usually 10% dearer than second-class ones and the superior classes are even more. On a long journey you can save the price of a hotel room by travelling overnight, but in many areas this is dangerous and not recommended. Look out for special offers, including discounts at some hotel chains.

Useful bus links

ADO GL www.adogl.com.mx, T01-800-702-8000. The Yucatán, southeast, Gulf and northeast Mexico.
Cristóbal Colón, T01-800-702-8000. South of Mexico City.
ETN www.etn.com.mx, T01-800-360-4200.
Estrella de Oro www.estrelladeoro.com.mx, T01-800-9000-105. Mainly southwest of Mexico City.
Grupo Estrella www.estrellablanca.com.mx, T01-800-507-5500. Most of Mexico through several companies.
Omnibus www.odm.com.mx,T01-800-849-0208. North of Mexico City.
Primera Plus www.primeraplus.com.mx. Mid-central to southern Mexico.
UNO www.uno.com.mx, T01-800-702-8000. North of Mexico City.

Some bus tickets can be purchased at **www.ticketbus.com.mx**, information on T01-800-702-8000. If travelling from north of the border, you might want to hook up with Green Tortoise, www.greentortoise.com who have a range of trips throughout Mexico.

Car

Permits Vehicles may be brought into Mexico on a Tourist Permit for 180 days each year. The necessary documents are: passport, birth certificate or naturalization papers; tourist card; vehicle registration (if you do not own the car, a notarized letter from the vehicle's owner, be it the bank, company, is necessary); a valid driver's licence. National or international driving licences are accepted. The original and two photocopies are required for each. It takes 10 days to extend a permit, so ask for more time than you expect to need. Don't overstay; driving without an extension gets a US$50 fine for the first five days and then rises abruptly to half the value of the car! US$16.50 is charged for the permit, payable only by credit card (Visa, MasterCard, American Express or Diners Club), not a debit card, in the name of the car owner, as recorded on the vehicle registration. The **American Automobile Association** (AAA) issues Tourist Permits for 'credit card' entry, free to members, US$18 to non-members; in California this service is available only to members. If you do not have a credit card, you have to buy a refundable bond in cash to the value of the vehicle according to its age (a set scale exists), which is repaid on leaving Mexico. The bond is divided into two parts, the bond itself and administration; the latter, accounting for about 43% of the total cost, is retained by the authorities; the bond is refunded. The bond is issued by Afianziadora Mexicana at US/Mexican border crossings, or by **Sanborn's** (see page 71). It may be waived if you are only going to the State of Sonora.

English versions of leaflets giving the rules on temporary importation of vehicles state that you must leave at the same crossing by which you entered. The Spanish versions do not say this and in practice it is not so. The temporary importation permit is multiple entry for 180 days; within that period you can enter and leave by whatever crossing, and as often as you like. Remember, though, that you must have a new tourist card or visa for each new entry. The Sanborn's website (www.sanbornsinsurance.com), is an excellent source of information.

On entry, go to Migración for your tourist card, on which you must state your means of transport. This is the only record of how you entered the country. At the **Banjército** desk sign an *Importación Temporal de Vehículos/Promesa de retornar vehículo*, which bears all vehicle and credit card details so that, if you sell your car illegally, your credit card account can be debited for the import duty. Next you purchase the *Solicilud de importación temporal*, which costs US$12; it bears a hologram that matches the dated sticker, which must be displayed on the windscreen or, on a motorcycle, on some safe surface. Then go to *Copias* to photocopy all necessary documents and papers issued. The sticker and other entry documents must be surrendered on departure. They can only be surrendered at a Mexican border crossing, with date stickers cancelled by **Banjército** at Immigration. If you neglect to do this, and re-enter Mexico with an expired uncancelled sticker on you car, you will be fined heavily for each 15-day period that has elapsed since the date of expiry. If you intend to return to Mexico within the 180-day period, having surrendered your sticker and documents, keep safe the *Importación Temporal de Vehículos* form, stamped *Cancelado*, as a receipt. If entry papers are lost there can be much delay and expense (including enforcement of the bond) in order to leave the country. **Banjército** (**Banco del Ejército**) offices at borders are open daily, some for 24 hours. Each vehicle must have a different licensed driver (that is, you cannot tow another vehicle into Mexico unless it has a separate driver).

On arrival, you have to find the place where car permits are issued; this may not be at the border.

Insurance In Mexico foreign insurance will not be honoured; you must ensure that the company you insure with will settle accident claims outside Mexico. According to latest official documents, insurance for foreign cars entering Mexico is not mandatory, but it is highly recommended to be insured. Arranging insurance when crossing from the USA is very easy as there are many offices at US border crossings. Policy prices vary enormously between companies, according to age and type of vehicle, etc. **Sanborn's Mexican Insurance Service**, with offices in every US border town, and many more, will provide comprehensive insurance, including full-year cover, within Mexico and other parts of Latin America, and provides free 'Travelogs' for Mexico and Central America with useful tips. Sanborn's Insurance head office is at 2009 S 10th Street, McAllen, TX 78505-0310, T956-686-0711, toll free 800-222-0158, www.sanbornsinsurance.com. **Tepeyac**, with offices in most Mexican cities, and towns and at border crossings (including Tapachula), and in US (eg in San Diego, **Mexican American Insurance Agency**, 1506 India Street, corner of 6th and A streets, downtown, T233-7767).

Entering Mexico from Guatemala presents few local insurance problems now that **Tepeyac** (see above), has an office in Tapachula, and **Seguros La Provincial**, Avenida General Utrillo 10A, upstairs, San Cristóbal de las Casas, have an office in Cuauhtémoc, Avenida Cuauhtémoc 1217 ground floor, Sr García Figueroa, T5-604-0500. Otherwise, try **Segumex** in Tuxtla Gutiérrez. In Mexico City, try **Grupo Nacional Provincial**, Río de la Plata 48, T528-67732, who have offices in many towns.

Petrol/disesel All *gasolina* is now unleaded. All petrol stations in Mexico are franchised by Petróleos Mexicanos (PEMEX) and fuel costs the same throughout the country except near the US border, where it may be a bit cheaper. Roughly US$0.65 a litre. Unleaded petrol is classified either as *Magna*, from the green pumps, or the more expensive *Premium*, from the red ones. Diesel is also available. Petrol stations are not self-service. Make sure the pump is set at zero before your tank is filled and that your filler cap is put back on before you drive off. Specify how much you want either in litres or in money; it is normal to give the attendant a small tip.

Assistance The free assistance service of the Mexican Tourist Department's green jeeps (**Angeles Verdes**) patrol many of Mexico's main roads. Call toll free number on 01-800-903-9200; every state also has an Angeles Verdes hotline. The drivers speak English, are trained to give first aid, make minor auto repairs and deal with flat tyres. They carry gasoline and have radio connection. All help is completely free, and you pay cost price for the gasoline. Although the idea is great, few Mexicans rely on the service in outlying areas and your best bet is to keep your vehicle in good condition and carry out the usual regular checks.

Road tolls A toll is called a *cuota*, as opposed to a non-toll road, which is a *vía libre*. There are many toll charges and the cost works out at around one peso per kilometre. Check your route at http://portal.sct.gob.mx. Some new freeways bypassing city centres charge US$4-12, or more. Because of the high cost of toll roads, they are often quite empty, which means that good progress can be made. Some tolls can be avoided if you seek local or motoring club advice on detours around toll gates (follow trucks). This may involve unpaved roads, which should not be attempted in the wet. However, the *carreteras libres* are normally perfectly acceptable and more interesting as they often travel through small towns and sometimes beautiful countryside.

In case of accident Do not abandon your vehicle. Call your insurance company immediately to inform it of the accident. Do not leave Mexico without first filing a claim in Mexico. Do not sign any contract or agreement without a representative of the insurance company being present. Always carry with you, in the insured vehicle, your policy identification card and the names of the company's adjusters (these are the recommendations of Asemex). If, in an accident, bodily injury has occurred or the drivers involved cannot agree who is at fault, the vehicles may be impounded. Drivers will be required to stay in the vicinity in cases of serious accidents, the insured being confined to a hotel (or hospital) until the claim is settled (according to **Sanborn's**). A helpline for road accidents is available by phoning T02 and asking the operator to connect you to Mexico City T5684-9715 or 5684-9761.

Warnings On all roads, when two vehicles converge from opposite directions, or when a vehicle is behind a slow cart, bicycle, etc, the driver who first flashes his lights has the right of way. This also applies when a bus or truck wishes to turn left across the opposing traffic: if the driver flashes his lights he is claiming right of way and the oncoming traffic must give way. At *Alto* (Halt) signs, all traffic must come to a complete stop. Do not drive at night. Night-time robberies on vehicles are on the increase especially in Guerrero and Oaxaca states. 'Sleeping policemen' or road bumps can be hazardous in towns and villages as often there are no warning signs; they are sometimes marked *zona de topes*, or incorrectly marked as *vibradores*. In most instances, their distinguishing paint has worn away.

Roadworks are usually well marked. If your vehicle breaks down on the highway and you do not have a warning triangle or a piece of red cloth to act as a warning, cut branches from the roadside and lay them in the road some distance in front of and behind your vehicle.

If you are stopped by police in town for an offence you have not committed and you know you are in the right, do not pay the 'fine' on the spot. Take the policeman's identity number, show him that you have his number and tell him that you will see his chief (*jefe*) at the tourist police headquarters instead. It is also advisable to go to the precinct station anyway whenever a fine is involved, to make sure it is genuine. If stopped in a remote area, it is not advisable to get into a dispute with a policeman; drugs may be planted in your vehicle or problems may occur.

Further information A useful source of information and advice (whose help we acknowledge here) is the **Recreation Vehicle Owner's Association of British Columbia** ⓘ *RVOABC, PO Box 3003, Langley, BC, V3A 4R3, T604-856-4803, www.rvoa.bc.ca (Membership US$35 a year, members receive RV Times publication*; Mexican insurance can be arranged for members). RV tours including Mexico are available from **RV Adventuretours** ⓘ *305 West Nolana Loop 2, McAllen, TX78505, US*. *RVing in Mexico, Central America and Panamá*, by John and Liz Plaxton (Travel 'N Write, Canada, 1996), has been recommended as full of useful information, although it can be difficult to get hold of.

Car hire Car rental is very expensive in Mexico, from US$35-45 a day for a basic model with 15% sales tax added to rental costs. Rates will vary from city to city. Make sure you have unlimited mileage. Age limit is normally at least 25 and you'll need to place a deposit, normally against a credit card, for damage. It can be cheaper to arrange hire in the US or Europe. Proceed with caution. At some tourist resorts, however, such as Cancún, you can pick up a VW Beetle convertible for US$25 per day. Renting a vehicle is nearly impossible without a credit card. It is twice as expensive to leave a car at a different point from the starting point than it is to make a round trip.

Cycling

Mexico offers plenty of enjoyable places for cycling. The main problems facing cyclists are the heavy traffic that will be encountered on main roads, the poor condition of these roads and the lack of specialized spare parts, particularly for mountain bikes. It is possible to find most bike spares in the big cities, but outside these places it is only possible to find the basics: spokes, tyres, tubes, etc. Traffic is particularly bad around Mexico City. The easiest region for cycling is the Gulf of Mexico coast; however, many of the roads are dead flat, straight and generally boring. The mountains may appear intimidating, but gradients are not difficult as clapped-out buses and trucks have to be able to climb them. Consequently, much of the best riding is in the sierra. If cycling in Baja, avoid riding in mid-summer; even during October temperatures can reach 45°C+ and water is very scarce all the time. The toll roads are generally preferable to the ordinary highways for cyclists; there is less traffic, more lanes and a wide paved shoulder. Some toll roads have 'no cyclists' signs but usually the police pay no attention. If you walk your bicycle on the pavement through the toll station you don't have to pay. If using the toll roads, take lots of water as there are few facilities. Cycling on some main roads can be very dangerous; it is useful to fit a rear-view mirror.

Motorcycle

Motorcycling is good in Mexico as most main roads are in fairly good condition and hotels are usually willing to allow the bike to be parked in a courtyard or patio. In the major tourist centres, such as Acapulco, Puerto Vallarta or Cancún, motorbike parts can be found as there are Honda dealers for bike and jet-ski rentals.

Hitchhiking

Hitchhiking is usually possible for single hikers, but apparently less easy for couples. It is generally quick, but not universally safe (seek local advice). Do not, for example, try to hitch in parts of Guerrero and Oaxaca states where even driving alone is not recommended. Yet in Baja California in some ways it is the best way to travel. In more out-of-the-way parts, short rides from village to village are usually the rule, so progress can be slow. Getting out of big cities is best done by taking a local bus out of town in the direction of the road you intend to take. Ask for the bus to take the *Salida* (Exit) to the next city on that road. It is very easy to hitch short distances, such as the last few km to an archaeological site off the main road; offer to pay something, like US$0.50.

Taxis

To avoid overcharging, the government has taken control of taxi services from airports to cities. Only those with government licences are allowed to carry passengers from the airport and you can usually buy a ticket from a booth at the terminal. No further tipping is then required, except when the driver handles heavy luggage or provides some extra service for you. The same system has been applied at bus stations but it is possible to pay the driver direct. Avoid flagging down taxis in the street at night in Mexico City. It is safer to phone for a *sitio* taxi from your hotel.

Train

Apart from the **Chihuahua-al-Pacífico**, between Los Mochis, Creel and Chihuahua, considered one of the world's greatest rail routes (see page 219), and the **Tequila Express**, a rather cutesy way of moving people from Guadalajara to Tequila so they can drink and not drive, there are no official passenger services running. However, some freight trains do have passenger wagons and if you have a great deal of time and patience and are train mad then you probably can travel through Mexico on trains. Services are said to be ridiculously cheap and stupidly slow – walking may be quicker. Reaching your destination is also likely to be more through luck and persistence than planning.

Maps

Internationally, **ITM** (see page 45), www.itmb.com, provide several maps including one covering all Mexico, Mexico City, Baja California, Mexico North West, Mexico South East, Yucatán Peninsula and a growing selection of regional road maps. The Mexican Government Tourist Highway Map is free at tourist offices (when in stock). If driving from the US you get a free map if you buy your insurance at **Sanborn's** in the border cities.

Guía Roji publish a wide range of regional maps, city plans and gazettes, available at most bookshops and news stands. The **Dirección General de Oceanografía**, Calle Medellín 10, near Insurgentes metro station, sells excellent maps of the entire coastline of Mexico. Buy good detailed maps of states of Mexico and the country itself from **Dirección General de Geografía y Meteorología**, Avenida Observatorio 192, México 18 DF, T5515-1527 (go to Observatorio metro station and up Calle Sur 114, then turn right a short distance down Avenida Observatorio). Maps are also available from **Instituto Nacional de Estadística, Geografía e Informática** (**INEGI**), which has branches in Mexico City (see page 84) and in state capitals (US$3 per sheet). Pemex road atlas, *Atlas de Carreteras y Ciudades Turísticas*, US$5 in bookshops (for example **Sanborn's**), which has 20 pages of city maps, almost every road one may need, contour lines, points of interest, service stations, etc (it is rarely on sale in Pemex stations), is recommended.

Sleeping

Hotels and hospedajes

Hotel prices in the lower and middle categories are still very reasonable by US and European standards. Prices of top and luxury hotels have risen more steeply as tourism has increased. English is spoken at the best hotels and is increasingly common throughout Mexico. There is a hotel tax, ranging between 1% and 4%, according to the state, although it is generally levied only when a formal bill is issued.

Beware of 'helpfuls' who try to find you a hotel, as prices quoted at the hotel desk rise to give them a commission.

Always check the room before paying in advance. Also ask if there is 24-hour running water. Check-out time from hotels is commonly 1100 but bag storage is commonplace. Rooms are normally charged at a flat rate, or if there are single rooms they are around 80% the price of a double, so sharing works out cheaper. A room with a double bed is are usually cheaper than one with two singles and a room with three or more sharing is often very economical even in the mid-price range.

During peak season (November to April) it may be hard to find a room. The week after Easter is normally a holiday, so prices remain high, but resorts are not as crowded as the previous week. Discounts on hotel prices can often be arranged in the low season (May to October), but this is more difficult in the Yucatán and Baja California.

Casas de huéspedes are usually the cheapest places to stay, although they are often dirty with poor plumbing. Motels and auto-hotels, especially in central and south Mexico, are not usually places where guests stay the whole night (you can recognize them by curtains over the garage and red and green lights above the door to show if the room is free). If driving, and wishing to avoid a night on the road, they can be quite acceptable (clean, some have hot water, and in the Yucatán they have a/c), and they tend to be cheaper than other, 'more respectable' establishments.

Youth hostels

Fourteen *albergues* exist in Mexico, mostly in small towns; they are usually good value and clean. While the hostels take YHA members and non-members, members pay a slightly reduced rate and, after about four nights, it normally works out to be cost effective to become a member. Services vary from place to place, but you may have to pay a key deposit. Hostels often have lockers for valuables. For information contact **Hostelling Mexico** ⓘ *Guatemala 4, Col Centro, Mexico City, T5211-1113, www.hostels.com*

Many towns have a **Villa Deportiva Juvenil**. While these are essentially the Mexican equivalent of a youth hostel their main market is for groups of student Mexicans who may, for example, be taking part in a regional event. It's worth looking out for the option as they are normally very cheap. But while some cater very well for the international traveller, others are barely interested. Details within text.

Camping

Most sites are called Trailer Parks, but tents are usually allowed. **Playas Públicas**, with a blue and white sign of a palm tree, are beaches where camping is allowed. They are usually cheap, sometimes free and some have shelters and basic amenities. You can often camp in or near national parks, although you must speak first with the guards, and usually pay a small fee. Paraffin oil (kerosene) for stoves is called *petróleo para lámparas* in Mexico. It is available from an *expendio*, or *despacho de petróleo*, or from a *tlapalería*, but not from gas/petrol stations. Methylated spirits is called *alcohol desnaturalizado* or *alcohol del 96* and is available from chemists. Calor gas is widely available, as it is throughout Central America. *Gasolina blanca* (white gas) may be bought in *ferreterías* (ironmongers) or paint shops; prices vary widely, also ask for Coleman fuel. Alcohol for heating the burner can be obtained from supermarkets.

Eating

Food

Food for most Mexicans represents an integral part of their national identity, a fact immediately seen in their desire to offer visitors an excess of the most typical dishes and specialities. Much has been written since the 1960s about the evolution of Mexican food and experts suggest that there are three important stages: first, the combination of the indigenous and the Spanish; later, the influence of other European cuisines, notably the French in the 19th century; and finally the adoption of exotic oriental dishes and fast-food from the US in the 20th century.

Because of the use of chilli as the principal seasoning in Mexican cooking, it is usually perceived as spicy or hot. However, there is another element that is even more characteristic and which visitors become aware of as they get to know the wide range of Mexican dishes. Maize, or corn, has been a staple crop from oldest times not only in Mexico but in the continent as a whole. Maize is consumed in *antojitos* (snacks), some of the most common of which are *quesadillas, sopes, tostadas, tlacoyos* and *gorditas*, which consist of various shapes and sizes of *tortillas*, with a variety of fillings and usually garnished with a hot sauce.

Certain dishes such as *mole* (chicken or turkey prepared in an elaborate chilli-based sauce, see box page 371) or *pozole* (a pot-au-feu with a base of maize kernels and stock) are close to their indigenous traditions. Others, however, are of more recent creation, for example the following breakfast dishes, all with eggs: *huevos rancheros* (fried, with spicy sauce on a bed of *tortillas*), *machaca norteña* (scrambled with dried minced beef), *huevos motuleños* (fried with sauce of tomatoes, peas, cheese and fried banana) and *huevos a la mexicana* (scrambled with chilli and tomatoes).

Usual meals are breakfast, a heavy lunch between 1400 and 1500 and a light supper between 1800 and 2000. Meals in modest establishments cost US$2-3 for breakfast, US$2.50-3.50 for set lunch (US$4-6 for a special *comida corrida*) and US$5-10 for dinner (generally no set menu). A la carte meals at modest establishments cost about US$8; a very good meal can be had for US$13 at a middle-level establishment. Much higher prices are charged by the classiest restaurants in Mexico City and some resorts. Some restaurants give foreigners the menu without the *comida corrida* (set meals), so forcing them to order à la carte which is often double the price.

The best value is undoubtedly in small, family-run places.

Street stalls are by far the cheapest – although not always the safest – option and often the best chance of trying truly local food. If self-catering, markets are cheaper than supermarkets. In resort areas hotels often include breakfast and dinner.

Drink

The **beer** is good: brands include **Dos Equis-XX, Montejo, Bohemia, Sol, Superior** and **Tecate. Negra Modelo** is a dark beer; it has the same alcohol content as the other beers. Some beer is drunk with lime juice and a salt-rimmed glass, or *michelada* with chilli sauce (both available in Oaxaca). Local **wine** is cheap and improving in quality; try **Domecq, Casa Madero** or **Santo Tomás**; the white sold in *ostionerías*, oyster restaurants, is usually good. **Cetto Reisling Fumé** has been recommended. Some of the best wines produced in Mexico are those from Monte Xanic, produced near Ensenda, Baja California, but thry are very expensive. The native drinks are **pulque**, the fermented juice of the agave plant (those unaccustomed to it should not over-indulge), **tequila**, made in Jalisco, and **mezcal** from Oaxaca; also distilled from agave plants. Mezcal usually has a *gusano de maguey* (worm) in the bottle, considered to be a particular delicacy. Tequila and mezcal rarely have an alcoholic content above 40-43%; tequila Herradura is particularly recommended. Also available is the Spanish aniseed spirit,

There are few outdoor drinking places in Mexico except in tourist spots.

anís, which is made locally. Imported whiskies and brandies are expensive. Rum is cheap and good. *Puro de caña* (called *chingre* in Chinanteca and *posh* in Chamula) is distilled from sugar cane; it is stronger than *mezcal* but with less taste; it is found in Oaxaca and Chiapas.

There are always plenty of non-alcoholic soft drinks (*refrescos*) and mineral water. *Agua fresca* – fresh fruit juices mixed with water or mineral water – and milk shakes (*licuados*) are good and usually safe. If you don't like to drink out of a glass ask for a straw, *popote*. Herbal teas, for example chamomile and mint (*manzanilla* and *hierba buena*), are readily available.

Festivals and events

If any of these holidays falls on a Thursday or a Tuesday, they are usually an excuse for a *puente*, a 'bridge' or long weekend (which can have implications for travel, hotel accommodation and services).

National holidays
I Jan New Year.
5 Feb Constitution Day
21 Mar Birthday of Benito Juárez
Maundy Thu, Good Fri and Easter Sat
1 May Labour Day
5 May Battle of Puebla
1 Sep El Informe (Presidential Message)
16 Sep Independence Day
12 Oct Día de la Raza (Discovery of America)
20 Nov Día de la Revolución (Revolution Day)
25 Dec Christmas Day

Religious fiestas
The Mexican calendar of religious fiestas lists over 5000 each year. The most widely celebrated are:
6 Jan Santos Reyes (Three Kings)
10 May Día de las Madres (Mothers' Day)
1-2 Nov Día de los Muertos (All Souls' Day)
12 Dec La Virgen de Guadalupe

Shopping

Ceramics

Ceramics are generally crafted out of baked clay or plaster and are polished, glazed or polychrome. In some parts such as Michoacán men paint the pieces but in the main pot-making is done by women. Some of the best pots have a brilliant glaze such as the Patambán pottery found in Michoacán. The green finish comes from the oxidization of copper while its fragility comes from 'eggshell' thin clay working.

Crafts

The colourful markets and craft shops are one of the highlights of any visit to Mexico. *Artesanía* in Mexico is an amalgam of ancient and modern design. The strongest influence are the traditional popular art forms of indigenous communities the length and breadth of the country, which pour into colonial towns such as Oaxaca, San Cristóbal, Pátzcuaro and Uruapan. These are convenient market centres for seeing the superb range of products from functional pots to scary masks hanging over delicately embroidered robes and gleaming lacquered chests.

A useful online resource promoting fair trade and sustainable production can be found at www.bioplaneta.com.

Masks

Textile art is heavily influenced by religious ritual, particularly dances to master natural forces, but as well as being impressively robed, priests, witches and shamans are often masked in the guise of animals such as eagles, jaguars, goats, monkeys, and coyotes, particularly in the states of Guerrero (for example in Chilapa), Sinaloa, Sonora and Nayarit.

Silver and gold

For silver and gold work, known as *orfebrería*, look under Taxco and the markets in Mexico City. Jade jewellery is made in Michoacán while semi-precious stones such as onyx, obsidian, amethyst and turquoise are found in Oaxaca, Puebla, Guerrero, Zacatecas and Querétaro.

Textiles

Weaving and textile design go back a long way in Mexico and the variety on offer is huge. Textiles can be spun in cotton or wool on the traditional *telar de cintura*, a 'waist loom', or *telar de pie*, a pedal-operated loom introduced by the Spanish. Many woven items are on sale in the markets, from sarapes and *morrales* (shoulder bags) to wall-hangings, rugs and bedspreads. Synthetic fibres are often used too, so make sure you know what you're getting before you buy.

Sport and activities

Mexico's coastline of reefs and swells, expanse of mountain ranges cut by long rivers and protected areas make it extremely well suited to many types of outdoor adventure. AMTAVE are making steady progress in promoting and protecting ecotourism alongside adventure-related pursuits. The need for standards – safety and otherwise – is important in some activities and AMTAVE is doing plenty to develop awareness in this field. **Associación Mexicana de Turismo de Aventura y Ecoturismo** ⓘ *Félix Cuevas 224-b, Col del Valle, CP 03100, México DF, T/F5575-7887, www.amtave.org*.

Aerial sports

See under Specialists in adventure and ecotourism, page 123. **Guanajuato, Valle de Bravo** (for hang-gliding) and the state of **Hidalgo** are most often the backdrop.

Canyoning

Rappel, or abseiling, is often the only way to reach some sites so canyoning is frequently a part of any trip. Two of the best locations for this new sport are the **Cañadas de Cotlamani,** near Jalcomulco in Veracruz and, in the **Cumbres de Monterrey National Park,** the Recorrido de Matacanes circuit (based on the Cascada Lagunillas) and a circuit spilling out from the Cascada El Chipitín, known locally as Recorrido Hidrofobia.

Caving

Caving, or speleology, in Mexico is more than just going down into deep dark holes. Sometimes it is a sport more closely related to canyoning as there are some excellent underground river scrambles. The best of these is probably the 8-km-long **Chontalcuatlán,** a part of the Cacahuamilpa cave system near Taxco. There is an underground lagoon here in **Zacatecolotla** cave. There are also well-publicized options for caving in **Cuetzalan,** near Puebla. Beside the **Matacanes** river circuit in Nuevo León, near Monterrey (see Canyoning) there are some large caves, the **Grutas de La Tierrosa, La Cebolla** and **Pterodáctilo.**

For purist potholers there are many vertical caves or *sótanos* (cellars) such as **El Jabalí, El Nogal** and **Tilaco** in the Sierra Gorda de Querétaro and **La Purificación** near Ciudad Victoria. The biggest cave systems are in Chiapas especially around Tuxtla

Gutiérrez. One of the best elsewhere is the **Sótano de las Golondrinas** on the Santa María river, San Luis Potosí (see rafting), although perhaps the most challenging is **Pozo Verde**, 1070 m deep, near Ocotempa, Puebla.

And finally you have the option of diving in water-filled caves known as *cenotes*, a common and popular sport in the Yucatán, particularly around Tulum.

Climbing

The big glaciated volcanoes are within relatively easy reach of Mexico City. Although there are few technical routes, crampons, ice-axe and occasionally rope are required for safe ascents. The season is October to May. Now that **Popocatépetl** (5452 m) and **Colima Volcano** (3842 m) are sporadically erupting (although it may still be possible to climb **El Nevado** 4339 m, behind Colima Volcano), the two remaining high-altitude challenges are **Pico de Orizaba** (Citlatépetl, 5760 m, Mexico's highest volcano) and **Iztaccíhuatl** (5286 m, the best technical climbing with great views over 'Popo'). Two good acclimatization climbs are **Cofre de Perote** (Nouhcampatépetl, 4282 m) and **Nevado de Toluca** (Xinantécatl, 4583 m). Further afield, near Tapachula in Chiapas, **Volcán Tacaná** (4150 m) is a worthwhile but little-climbed mountain.

Rock climbing is an increasingly popular sport for Mexicans and there is good to great climbing in most parts of the country. Specialist opportunities can be found near **Pueblo Viejo** and also in the area surrounding **Creel**, in Chihuahua. Also in the north, near Hidalgo (40 km from Monterrey), is the the massive limestone cliff of **Potrero Chico**, a magnet for big-wall climbers.

Diving

This is practised off most of Mexico's coastline but two regions, **Quintana Roo** and **Baja California** at opposite ends of the country, are particularly noteworthy. The first offers warm-water reefs close to the shore and visibility of over 30 m. Southern Baja has adventurous diving in deep waters. **Cozumel**, in Quintana Roo, has some of the best diving in the world, but the extent of the damage caused by Hurricane Wilma in October 2005 is still being explore. There are marine parks at Chankanaab and at Palancar Reef with numerous caves and gullies and a horseshoe-shaped diving arena. Also excellent on the west side of the island are Santa Rosa and sites off San Francisco beach. To the southwest are good sites off Laguna Colombia, while off Punta Sur there is excellent deep diving. There is concern, however, over the damage to the reef inflicted by the new cruise ship pier, and more of these piers are planned. At Isla Mujeres, also in Quintana Roo, the most dived sites include Los Manchones, La Bandera, a shallow dive south of the island, and El Frío, a deep wreck an hour and a half to the north.

Diving in the water-filled *cenotes* of the Yucatán, particularly around Tulum, is also popular.

Rafting

The variety in Mexico's rafting rivers opens the activity up to all types of traveller. The attraction is not just the run but the trek or rappel to the start and the moments between rapids, drifting in deep canyons beneath hanging tropical forests, some of which contain lesser-known and quite inaccessible ruins. For sheer thrills many of the best are in the centre of the country.

The season for whitewater rafting is generally July to September, when rivers are fuller, in Central Mexico, but in Chiapas, January and February are preferred because the climate is cooler.

The most popular river is the **Río Antigua/Pescados** in Veracruz. The upper stretch, the Antigua, has some good learning rapids (Grade II) running into Grade III, but, if you have more than one day, the Pescados (the lower Antigua), nearer to Jalcomulco, can give a bigger adrenalin rush with some Grade IV whitewater. The biggest rush in the country, however, is on the **Barranca Grande** and at **Cañón Azul** where there is excellent quality Grade V water. To complete the pre-eminence of **Veracruz** as a rafting destination is the **Filo-Bobos**. The Alto Filo (Grades IV and V) and the 25-km-long Tlapacoyan to Palmilla stretch, halfway along which the Bobos enters the Filo, are the areas of most interest to rafter-archaeologists.

Rafting in **Chiapas** covers the spectrum from sedate floats on rivers such as the Lacan-Há through the Lacandón jungle to Grade IV/V rapids on the Río Jataté, which gathers force where the Lacan Tum enters it and gradually diminishes in strength as it nears the Río Usumacinta.

Sea kayaking

The simplest kayaks are more like rafts and have no open compartments that you need to worry about flooding. Agencies will assess your experience when renting out more advanced equipment and for longer periods. The warm waters of the **Sea of Cortés**, off Baja California Sur, are kayak heaven. **Isla Espíritu Santo** and **Isla Partida** are easily accessible from La Paz and whether in or out of your kayak you can experience a wild party of stingrays, sea-lions, dolphins, porpoises and occasionally grey whales and hammerheads. Another good spot for kayaking is in the **Bahía de Sayulita** just north of Puerto Vallarta and around the nearby **Islas Marietas**.

Sport fishing

There are resort-based sports fishing fleets along much of Mexico's Pacific coast, from **Acapulco** to **Bahía Kino**, where there is a tournament at the end of June/ beginning of July. There is also a big tournament in **Manzanillo** in February.

Surfing

Some of the world's most exhilarating surfing can be experienced along Mexico's Pacific coast. The highlights are the huge Hawaiian-size surf that pounds the **Baja California** shoreline and the renowned *Mexican Pipeline* at **Puerto Escondido**. There are numerous possibilities, ranging from developed beaches to remote bays accessible only by 4WD vehicles. Many are to be found at the estuaries of rivers where sandbars are deposited and points are formed. It is impossible to name all the good beaches; the following is a selection starting in the north.

Isla de Todos Santos in front of Ensenada has big swells. It is much frequented by US surfers and is best in winter. A wetsuit is usually necessary when surfing in Baja. **Mazatlán** is the point on the mainland where currents escape the shielding effects of the peninsula and surfing is possible. As the geographical centre point on Mexico's surfing coast it has been chosen as home to the **Surfing Association** ① *PO Box 310*. In front of the town Isla de la Piedra is good along with Playa Cerritos just north of the town and also **El Caimanero** and near **Teacapan**, 100 km to the south. **San Blas** is an excellent learning centre. The waves are normally not too big and there are few rocks or dangerous currents. Surfing is best in the spring and summer, particularly between July and October.

Trekking

The **Copper Canyon** is a vast wilderness for trekking. Creel is the obvious base but an excellent trek is from Batópilas to Urique – three days in the heat of the *barranca*, through Tarahumara lands – there's no better way to experience the abyss after you have spent a day or two wondering, from a mirador on its rim, what it is like down there. Be careful about where you camp. Ask landowners' permission and don't slow down too much should you stumble across a marijuana plantation.

Bahía de Matanchén, near San Blas is said to have the longest surf break in the world.

The best trekking within easy reach of a major city is from Monterrey, particularly in the **Cumbres de Monterrey National Park**. There are several organizations in Mexico City that arrange weekend mountain hiking excursions.

One of the attractions of more remote trekking – in the states of **Oaxaca** and **Nayarit**, for example – is to visit indigenous communities such as Cora and Huichol villages. However, one should be sensitive to local reaction to tourist intrusion. Baja California's petroglyph cave sites can often only be visited on foot, which adds to the mystical experience, but here too remember that most sites are sacred and you should be accomanied by a guide. Seek advice before trekking in **Chiapas** and **Guerrero**, both hideouts for rebel groups, with the hefty military presence that goes with them.

National parks

Mexico has an immense range of habitats and wildlife; the far south is in the Neotropical kingdom, with a wealth of tropical forest species, while the far north is very much part of the Neoarctic kingdom, with typically North American species, and huge expanses of desert with unique ecosystems. The greater part of the country is a transition zone between the two, with many strange juxtapositions of species that provide invaluable information to scientists, as well as many endemic species. Mexico's national parks were set up a long time ago primarily to provide green recreation areas for city dwellers; they are generally small and have often been planted with imported species such as eucalyptus, and are thus of no biological value. However, the country does also have a good number of biosphere reserves, which are both of great biological value and suitable for tourism.

Starting in the far south, in Chiapas, **El Triunfo Biosphere Reserve** protects Mexico's only cloud forest, on the mountains (up to 2750 m) above the Pacific coast; the main hiking route runs from Jaltenango (reached by bus from Tuxtla) to Mapastepec on the coastal highway. Groups need to book in advance through the **Instituto de Historia Natural** ⓘ *Calzada de Hombres de la Revolución, by the botanical garden and Regional Museum (Apdo 391, Tuxtla 29000; T961-612-3663)*.

Also in Chiapas is the immense **Selva Lacandona**, supposedly protected by the Azules Biosphere Reserve but in reality still being eaten away by colonization and logging. New plant species are still being discovered in this rainforest, best visited either from the Bonampak and Yaxchilán ruins, or by the road/boat route via Pico de Oro and Flor de Café to Montebello.

In the Yucatán the **Sian Ka'an Biosphere Reserve**, south of Cancún, is a mixture of forest, savanna and mangrove swamp, best visited on a day-trip run by **Amigos de Sian Ka'an** ⓘ *Calle Fuego 2 SM, Cancún, T(998)-892-2958, www.amigosdesiankaan.org*. Also useful is the **Sian Ka'an Information Centre** ⓘ *Av Tulum between Satelite and Geminis, Tulum, T/F(984) 871-2363, siankaan_tours@hotmail.com*. It is also well worth visiting the **Río Lagartos** and **Río Celestún** reserves on the north and west coasts of Yucatán, well known for their flamingos. The **Calakmul Biosphere Reserve** is important mainly for its Mayan ruins, seeming to the layman more like scrub than forest.

Across the country's centre is the **Transversal Volcanic Belt**, one of the main barriers to Nearctic and Neotropic species; it's easiest to head for the **Parque Nacional Izta-Popo** (from Amecameca), the **Parque Nacional Zoquiapan** (on the main road to Puebla) or the **Parque Nacional El Tepozteco** (on the main road to Cuernavaca), and naturally the volcanoes themselves are well worth climbing.

Only small areas of the northern deserts and sierras are formally protected. The most accessible areas are in Durango state, including **La Michilía Biosphere Reserve**, with pine, oak and red-trunked *Arbutus* and *Arctostaphylus* trees typical of the Sierra Madre Occidental. A daily bus runs to San Juan de Michis, and you should get off at a T-junction 2 km before the village and walk west, first getting permission from the Jefe de Unidad Administrativo, **Instituto de Ecología** ⓘ *Apdo 632, 34000 Durango, T(618) 812 1483*; their offices are at Km 5 on the Mazatlán highway. The **Mapimí Biosphere Reserve** covers an area of desert *matorral* (scrub) that receives just 200 mm of rain a year; it lies to the east of Ceballos, on the Gómez Palacio-Ciudad Jiménez highway. In addition to the many species of bush and cactus, this is home to giant turtles, now in enclosures at the Laboratory of the Desert.

There is a great variety of protected areas in Baja California, all of considerable biological value: the highest point (3000 m) is the **Sierra de San Pedro Mártir**, in the north, which receives plenty of precipitation and has largely Californian fauna and flora. A dirt road starts at the Puente San Telmo, on the main road down the west coast, and leads almost 100 km to an astronomical observatory. Desert environments are, of course, unavoidable here, with 80 endemic cacti: the **Gran Desierto del Altar** is a dry lunar landscape, best seen from the main road along the US border, while the **El Vizcaíno Biosphere Reserve** protects a huge area of central Baja, characterized by agaves and drought-resistant scrub. However, the main reason for stopping here is to see the migration of the grey whale to its breeding grounds. In the far south, the **Sierra de la Laguna** boasts a unique type of cloud forest, with several endemic species; to get here you have to cross about 20 km of desert from just south of Todos Santos to La Burrera, and then follow a trail for 11 km to a rangers' *campamento* at about 1750 m.

Information on national parks and biosphere reserves can be obtained from the **Instituto Nacional de Ecología** ⓘ *Periférico 5000, Col Insurgentes Cuicuilco, CP 04530, Delegación Coyoacán, México DF, www.ine.gob.mx*, a decentralized body of the Secretaría de Medio Ambiente y Recursos Naturales.

Non-governmental conservation organizations include **Naturalia** ⓘ *Apdo Postal 21541, 04021 México DF, T(55) 5674-6678, www.naturalia.org.mx*, and **Pronatura, Asociación Mexicano por la Conservación de la Naturaleza,** *Aspérgulas 22, Col San Clemente, CP 01740, México, DF T/F(55) 5635-5054, www.pronatura.org.mx.*

Health

Social Security hospitals are restricted to members, but will take visitors in emergencies; they are more up to date than the Centros de Salud and Hospitales Civiles found in most centres, which are very cheap and open to everyone. It's advisable to vaccinate against hepatitis, typhoid, paratyphoid and poliomyelitis if visiting the low-lying tropical zones, where there is also some risk of malaria. Dengue fever is spreading in Mexico so seek advice and protect yourself against being bitten. Note also that cholera is on the rise. Hepatitis is also a problem in Mexico and, if you have not been vaccinated in advance, gamma globulin is available at better pharamacies/chemists.

Keeping in touch

Communications

Internet A list of useful websites is given on page 23. Every major town now has at least one internet café, with more springing up daily. If money is tight and you have time, look around; prices vary from place to place but are normally US$1-2 an hour.

Post Rates are raised in line with the peso's devaluation against the dollar. International service has improved and bright red mailboxes, found in many parts of the city, are reliable for letters. Parcel counters often close earlier than other sections of the post office in Mexico. Not all these services are obtainable outside Mexico City; delivery times in/from the interior may well be longer than those from Mexico City.

Poste Restante (*lista de correos* in Mexico) functions quite reliably, but you may have to ask under each of your names; mail is sent back after 10 days (for an extension write to the Jefe de la Administración of the post office holding your mail, any other post office will help you do this). Addressthe envolope: *'Favor de retener hasta llegada'*.

Prices North America, Central America and the **Caribbean**: under 20 g, 10.50 pesos; 20-50 g, 17.50 pesos; 500 g-1 kg, 108.50 pesos. **South America** and Europe: under 20 g, 13 pesos; 20-50 g, pesos 20.50; 500 g-1 kg, 275 pesos. **Asia, Africa** and **Oceania**: under 20 g, 14.50 pesos; 20-50 g, 24.50 pesos; 500 g-1 kg, 357.50 pesos.

Telephone

Calls made to Mexican numbers are either local, regional or international. Most destinations have a seven-digit number (except Mexico DF, Guadalajara and Monterrey which have eight-digit numbers). Most regions have a three-digit code (except Mexico DF, Guadalajara and Monterrey which have two-digit codes). The format of a number, depending on the type of call, should be as follows: **local** – use 7- or 8-digit numbers; **regional** – long-distance access (01) + regional code (three- or two-digit code) + seven- or eight-digit number; **international** – international access + country code (52) + regional code + seven- or eight-digit number.

Mexico City (code 55), Guadalajara (code 33), Monterrey (code 81).

Most public phones take phone cards only (**Ladatel**) costing 30 or 50 pesos from shops and news kiosks everywhere. **AT&Ts US Direct** service is available; for information in Mexico dial 412-553-7458, ext 359. From **LADA** phones (see below), dial **01, similar for AT&T credit cards. To use calling cards to Canada T95-800-010-1990. Commercially run *casetas*, or booths (for example **Computel**), where you pay after phoning, are up to twice as expensive as private phones, and charges vary from place to place. **Computel** have offices countrywide with long opening hours. It is better to call collect from private phones, but better still to use the LADA system. Reverse-charge (collect) calls on **LADA** can be made from any blue public phone, say you want to *llamar por cobrar*; silver phones are for local and direct long-distance calls, some take coins. Others take foreign credit cards (Visa, MasterCard, not Amex; not all phones that say they take cards accept them, others that say they don't do).

Pre-paid phone cards (eg **Ladatel**, above) are available, but expensive for international calls. Of other pre-paid cards, the best value are those issued by **Ekofon**, available at various airport and other outlets, and through a pre-chargeable account service, which may be opened by Internet; go to www.amistadbm.org.mx and then to the Ekofon link. Accounts may opened with as little as US$5, and are rechargeable. Calls, which can be made from any telephone in the country, cost 3 pesos per minute to the US, 5 pesos per minute to Europe, 2.75 pesos per minute to Asia. The same account can be used for calls made from the US and Canada, at even cheaper rates. Recommended.

Media

Newspapers and magazines The influential dailies are: *Excelsior*, *Novedades*, *El Día*, *Uno Más Uno*, *El Universal*, *El Heraldo*, *La Jornada* (www.jornada.unam.mx, more to the left), *La Prensa* (a popular tabloid, with the largest circulation), *El Nacional* (mouthpiece of the government). In **Guadalajara**, *El Occidental*, *El Informador* (www.informador.com.mx) and *Siglo 21*. There are influential weekly magazines *Proceso*, *Siempre*, *Epoca* and *Quehacer Político*. The political satirical weekly is *Los Agachados*.
The New York edition of the *Financial Times* and other British and European papers are available at Mexico City Airport and from the **Casa del Libro**, Calle Florencia 37 (Zona Rosa), Hamburgo 141 (Zona Rosa) and Calle Homero (Polanco), all in Mexico City. *The Miami Herald* is stocked by most newspaper stalls.

La Jornada's Thursday supplement, Tiempo Libre, lists the week's cultural activities.

Mexico City

→ *Phone code: 55. Colour map 3, B4. Altitude: 2240 m.*

Although very little remains of the ancient Aztec capital, the island city of Tenochtitlán that ruled the Central Highlands for a couple of hundred years, the city that has replaced it is equally impressive. Founded by the Spaniards in 1521, Mexico City is colourful, bawdy, vibrant, gaudy, cultured, noisy, sometimes dangerous, always fascinating and increasingly hip – a celebration of chaotic humanity, good and bad.

One of the largest cities in the world, the Ciudad de México, Distrito Federal or DF as it is often called, needs some time to do it justice, especially the Centro Histórico. Monumental architecture, magnificent church interiors, museums and vibrant pulsating murals full of the optimism of the post-Revolution period, invite you to drift around savouring the delights (and pollution) of this vast metropolis. There is music, dance and theatre in parks and plazas round every corner, while beyond the city centre you can explore San Angel, Coyoacán, Xochimilco and the Villa de Guadalupe.

» *For Sleeping, Eating and other listings, see pages 111-131.*

Ins and outs

Getting there

The airport is 13 km east of the city centre, 88 pesos (US$8.50) fixed fare to the centre. For details of international scheduled flights see Essentials, page 67, and for airport information see page 123. Domestic flights go to all major towns in Mexico. There are four long-distance bus terminals: North, South, East and West, divided, more or less, according to the regions they serve. The railway station is fairly central but there are currently no scheduled services. » *See also Transport, page 123.*

Getting around

If visiting for the first time, get yourself a hotel close to the Centro Histórico or Zócalo. In the heart of everything, you can walk to many of the major sights or just sit and watch the world go by. The metro is straightforward, cheap and the most convenient form of public transport, see page 123. It is also less polluted than the alternatives, such as buses and taxis, which are frequently stuck in the congested traffic. The Centro Histórico is best managed on foot and most other sights are within easy walking distance of a metro station. If driving, enjoy the challenge!

Maps Specialized maps can be bought from the **Instituto Nacional de Estadística Geografía e Informática (INEGI)** ⓘ *Metro Insurgentes, Mon-Fri 0800-2000, Sat 0800-1600*. You'll find it in the arcade below the traffic roundabout at Insurgentes; all maps are available, including topographical maps for trekking. **La Rosa de los Vientos** ⓘ *Higuera, Coyoacán*, in the south of the city, sells maps of all parts of the country.

Best time to visit

Spring is the hottest time of year but because of the high altitude, the climate is usually mild save for a few days in mid-winter, when it can get quite cold. Even in summer the temperature at night is rarely above 13°C and in winter there can be sharp frosts. The normal annual rainfall is 660 mm and most of it falls between May and October, usually in the late afternoon.

Orientation

You will find, as you explore the city, that you use two thoroughfares more than any others. The most famous is **Paseo de la Reforma**, with a tree-shaded, wide centre section and two side lanes. From the west it skirts the north edge of the Bosque de Chapultepec and then runs diagonally northeast past the Centro Histórico and on towards the Basílica de Guadalupe, still fairly wide but without side lanes. The other thoroughfare is **Avenida Insurgentes**, a diagonal north-south artery about 35 km long. Reforma and Insurgentes bisect at a *glorieta* (roundabout) with a statue of Cuauhtémoc, the last of the Aztec emperors.

Other important thoroughfares are the **Eje Central** (**Lázaro Cárdenas**), which runs south to north from the Circuito Interior (near the Olympic swimming pool) via Bellas Artes and the Torre Latino Americana, through Tlatelolco, past the Terminal del Norte (North Bus Terminal) and beyond; the **Calzada de Tlalpan**, which runs north-south from near the city centre, past the Terminal del Sur (South Bus Terminal) and leads out of the city towards Cuernavaca; the **Circuito Interior**, which encircles most of the city at an average distance of about 5 km from the centre; the **Periférico** which does the same thing further out (some sections now are two-storey); and the **Viaducto Miguel Alemán** crossing from the east, near the airport, and joining the Periférico in the west.

City Maps An excellent free pocket map is available (until they run out) from tourist information booths – there's one on the northwest corner of the Zócalo. The best maps of the city are from *Guía Roji* (an excellent A to Z, US$14). Metro stations have useful large-scale wall maps of the immediate area.

Tourist information

Dotted around town are sporadically manned **tourist information booths**, operated by the Mexico City Government, which have handy maps and can provide information.

Tourist assistance ⓘ *T5250-0123*, provides information on the phone. They have a **main office** ⓘ *Nuevo León 56, 9th floor, 06100, T5553-1260, www.mexicocity.gob.mx*, and the website is very wide ranging. The **Secretaría de Turismo** ⓘ *Masaryk 172, 5th floor, between Hegel and Emerson*, is in the Colonia Polanco (bus No 32).

Most museums and galleries are closed on Mondays.

Refer complaints to the tourist information centres or Tourist Police, in blue uniforms. For problems such as theft, fraud, abuse of power by officials, call **Protectur** ⓘ *T5516-0490*.

Students

SETEJ (Mexican Students' Union) ⓘ *Hamburgo 305, Col Juárez, Metro Sevilla, T5211-0743, www.setej.org, Mon-Fri 0900-1800, Sat 0900-1400*, issues student cards and deals with ISIS insurance. To obtain a national student card you need two photos, passport, confirmation of student status and US$13.

Most museums are free to students and teachers with ID.

Safety and pollution

As with any large city there are grounds for caution at times. Take care in the centre at quiet times, and in Chapultepec, where Sunday is the safest day. At night you are advised to phone for a taxi.

The city lies in the Valley of Mexico, a huge basin roughly 110 km long by 30 km wide. Rimming this valley is a sentinel-like chain of peaks of the Sierra Nevada mountains. About one in five of Mexico's population share the enclosed area with half the country's manufacturing employment breathing in much of the nation's industrial smog (the worst months being December to February). Common ailments that creep up over hours or days are a burning sensation in the eyes (contact lens wearers take note) and nose, and a sore throat. Local authorities advise citizens not to smoke and not to take outdoor exercise. Newspapers provide information showing air quality, with warnings and advice.

History

The vast metropolis of Mexico City has a history stretching back some 15,000 years when the first indigenous groups arrived in the fertile valley, eventually settling around 4000 BC with the domestication of corn. External influences always pushed and it was maize cultivation by the Olmec civilization on the Pacific coast that supported the settlement of Teotihuacán, 49 km north of Mexico City. The city grew to house some 250,000 before rapidly declining in the 7th century.

Dominant cultures failed to appear until the 14th century when the warring Aztecs founded a city where an eagle was seen devouring a snake. The city of Tenochtitlán began its growth on an island located at the modern-day Plaza Santo Domingo. The city grew, fed by produce grown on floating islands, *chinampas,* and fuelled by an unquenchable bloodthirst that demanded ritual sacrifice to the gods.

The city state was suffering with 200,000 inhabitants – and a population of some 1.5 million in the wider Valley of Mexico – when Moctezuma's messengers informed him of the arrival of vessels off the Yucatán. Cortés' arrival in 1519 coincided with the predicted return of Quetzalcoatl, the Plumed Serpent, from the east. The 33-year-old conqueror exploited friction between Mexico's regional groups and within seven months had walked Tenochtitlán. Moctezuma was taken hostage and murdered and within two years the Aztec empire had been destroyed.

Development of Mexico and the capital in the 16th and 17th century was fuelled by silver mining to the north and the development of agriculture. New Spain flourished through trade with Europe and the Orient, while Spain suffered its steady decline. By Independence in 1821 the city's population was around 160,000.

Mexico City boomed under the industrialization of the 20th century, and the promise of employment through the 1930s depression pushed the population to over 1.5 million by the 1940s. Sheer numbers created pressure on services and shanty towns sprung up around the city. The momentum was set and the die cast of a city infrastructure that struggles to cope with a population that numbers some 20 million – and counting.

Sights

Starting at the Zócalo (main square) and the streets around it, moving westwards, to the Palacio de Bellas Artes, through the Alameda Central, down Reforma and skirting the Zona Rosa, the following route will eventually lead to Chapultepec Park, and the fashionable area of Polanco, to the north of the park.

Centro Histórico

The tourist information booth on the northwest corner of Zócalo has free city maps.

Much of the Historic Centre has been refurbished in recent years and **Calle Tacuba** is especially fine. This central area forms a rough rectangle bordered by Alhóndiga/Santísma to the east of the Zócalo, Guerrero to the west of the Alameda, República de Honduras (by Plaza Garibaldi) to the north, and Arcos de Belén/Izazaga to the south. The *Guía Peatonal* of Sacbé (US$1.15) is recommended, giving eight suggested walking routes, all starting from metro stations. One good way of familiarizing yourself quickly with the Centro Histórico is to take a ride on a form of rickshaw (*bici-taxi*) from the Zócalo, US$2 for 30 minutes.

Zócalo

The great main square, or Plaza Mayor, centre of the oldest part, is always alive with people and often vivid with official ceremonies and celebrations, or with political demonstrations and marches. The huge flag in the centre of the square is raised at 0600 (0500 in winter), and taken down, with great pomp and ceremony, at 1800 (1700 in winter) on most days. On the north side, on the site of the Great Teocalli or temple of the Aztecs, is the cathedral.

Mexico City orientation

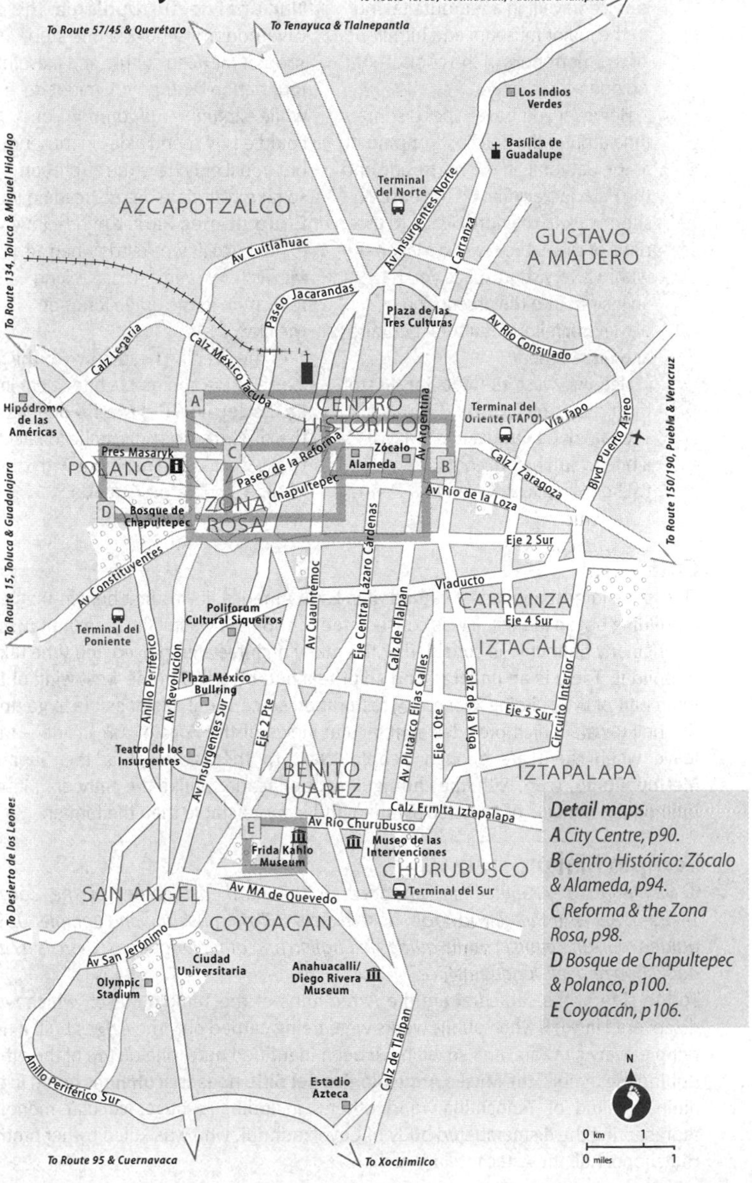

24 hours in Mexico City

If you only have one day to explore Mexico City you cannot do the place justice, you'll be exhausted by the altitude and dazed by the number of people. The **Turibus City Tour** (US$13, T5598-2417, www.turibus.com.mx) provides a hop-on, hop-off service travelling a set route taking in the major museum and highlights of the metropolis in the comfort of an open-top bus.

However you travel, spend some time around the Zócalo, dropping in at the Catedral on the north side and the Palacio Nacional on the east. A short walk to the north leads to the ruins of the Aztec Templo Mayor – within a very short space you have an insight into the driving forces of Mexico; religion, cultural heritage and government.

Heading west from the Zócalo stop by at the **Café Tacuba** (Calle Tacuba) or **La Opera** (5 de Mayo) for a bite to eat, before continuing west to the leafy plaza of Alameda Central. If you've a head for heights take the lift to the 44th floor of the **Torre Latinoamericana** for a great view of the city, smog permitting.

Jump on the metro (or back on the Turibus) and head down to Chapultepec and the **Museo Nacional de Antropología**. This cavernous museum is a one-stop shop of Mexican culture and a useful foundation for trips you might do while exploring the country. You could easily spend a day in museum, but you'll only have the afternoon so take your time before heading into **Chapultepec Park**, a mind-blowing experience at weekends when all Mexico City seems to be seeking relaxation in the green lungs of the city.

In the evening head down to the **Zona Rosa** and grab a bite to eat in **La Bodeguita del Medio** or one of the city's trendy spots, or head back to the Zócalo and hang out with the locals at the **Salón Corona**.

Cathedral

This is the largest and oldest cathedral in Latin America. It was first built in 1525 and rebuilding began in 1573; it was consecrated in 1667 but wasn't finished until 1813. It is singularly harmonious considering the many architects employed and time taken to build it. There is an underground crypt reached by stairs in the west wing of the main part of the building (closed for restoration since 1993). It's possible to go up to the bell-towers which provides spectacular views of the Zócalo. Ask inside – trips leave when there are enough people. Next to the cathedral is the **Sagrario Metropolitano**, 1769, with fine churrigueresque façade. Unlike the cathedral, it was built on the remains of an Aztec pyramid and is more stable than the former.

Templo Mayor

ⓘ *Seminario 4 y Guatemala, entrance in the northeast corner of the Zócalo, T5542-4784, Tue-Sun 0900-1700, last tickets 1630, museum and temple US$4; guided tours in Spanish, audio guides in English and other languages; there is a café, bookshop and left-luggage office.*

To the side of the cathedral are the Aztec ruins of the Templo Mayor, which were discovered in 1978 when public works were being carried out. The Aztecs built a new temple every 52 years, and seven have been identified here, one on top of the other. Behind the temple, the **Museo Arqueológico del Sitio** houses sculptures found in the main pyramid of Tenochtitlán and others, including a huge, circular monolith representing the dismembered body of Coyolxauhqui, who was killed by her brother Huitzilopochtli, the Aztec tutelary god.

Palacio Nacional

ⓘ *Tue-Sun 1000-1700, free, photo ID requested.*

The National Palace takes up all the eastern side of the Zócalo. Built on the site of the Palace of Moctezuma and rebuilt in 1692 in colonial baroque, it has a façade of the red volcanic stone called *tezontle*; the top floor was added by President Calles in the 1920s. Today it houses various government departments. Over the central door hangs the Liberty Bell, rung every year at 2300 on 15 September by the President, who commemorates independence from Spain and gives **El Grito**: *'¡Viva México!'*

The staircase leading to the first floor of the inner courtyard and two of the walls of the first floor are decorated with superb frescoes by Diego Rivera. The right-hand panel on the staircase (1929) depicts prehispanic Mexico; the large central panel (275 sq m, started 1929, finished 1935) shows the history of Mexico from 1521 to 1930 and the panel on the left is known as *El mundo de hoy y de mañana* (The World Today and Tomorrow, 1934). The first fresco (4.92 x 9.71 m) on the first floor is known variously as *La Gran Tenochtitlán* and *El mercado de Tlatelolco* (1945), and shows the market of Tlatelolco against a background of the ancient city of Tenochtitlán. There follow representations of various indigenous cultures – Purépecha, Mixteca-Zapoteca, Totonaca and Huasteca (the last showing the cultivation and worship of maize), culminating in the final fresco, which shows in narrative form the arrival of Hernán Cortés in Veracruz. These murals were done between 1942 and 1951. There are knowledgeable guides who speak English. They also sell postcards of the murals, but much better reproductions of the same works are available in most museums in the city.

On the first and second floors of the Palacio Nacional, on the left as one enters the great courtyard, an area formerly occupied by government offices has been transformed into elegant galleries open to the public and housing temporary exhibitions. Across from the main entrance and beyond the courtyard is a pleasant open-air area that the public can also visit. The **Museo de las Culturas** ⓘ *Moneda 13, behind the Palacio Nacional*, holds exhibitions from countries worldwide.

Around the Zócalo

The **Suprema Corte de Justicia de la Nación** ⓘ *opposite the Palacio Nacional, on the southeast corner of the Zócalo, closes at 1400*, has frescoes by Orozco (*National Riches* and *Proletarian Struggle*). The ornate building in the southwest corner of the Zócalo, the **Antiguo Ayuntamiento** (Old City Hall), is now used for ceremonial purposes and is where visiting dignitaries are granted the Keys of the City.

On the west side of the Zócalo are the **Portales de los Mercaderes** (Arcades of the Merchants), which have been very busy since they were built in 1524. North of them, opposite the cathedral, is the **Monte de Piedad** (National Pawnshop), established in the 18th century and housed in a 16th-century building. Prices are government controlled and bargains can often be found. Auctions are held each Friday at 1000 (first, second and third Friday for jewellery and watches, fourth for everything else). US dollars are accepted.

North of the Zócalo

On Calle Justo Sierra, north of cathedral between Guatemala and San Ildefonso, is the **Mexican Geographical Society**, in whose courtyard is a bust of Humboldt and a statue of Benito Juárez, plus a display of documents and maps (ask at the door to be shown in); opposite are the **Anfiteatro Simón Bolívar**, with murals of his life in the lobby and an attractive theatre, entered through the former **Colegio de San Ildefonso**, which was built in splendid baroque style in 1749 as a Jesuit school and later became the Escuela Nacional Preparatoria. There are important frescoes by Orozco (including *Revolutionary Trinity* and *The Trench*) and, in the Anfiteatro Bolívar, by Diego Rivera (*Creation*) and Fernando Leal, all in excellent condition. There is another Leal mural,

Lord of Chalma, in the stairwell separating the two floors of Orozco works, as well as Jean Charlot's *Massacre in the Templo Mayor*. In a stairwell of the Colegio Chico there are experimental murals by Siqueiros. The whole interior has been magnificently restored. There are occasional important temporary exhibitions. More Orozco frescoes can be seen at the **Biblioteca Iberoamericana** on Cuba between República de Brasil and Argentina (for more information on the muralists and their work, see pages 96 and 102). Just along the road is the **Museo de la Caricatura** ⓘ *Donceles 97,*

Mexico City centre

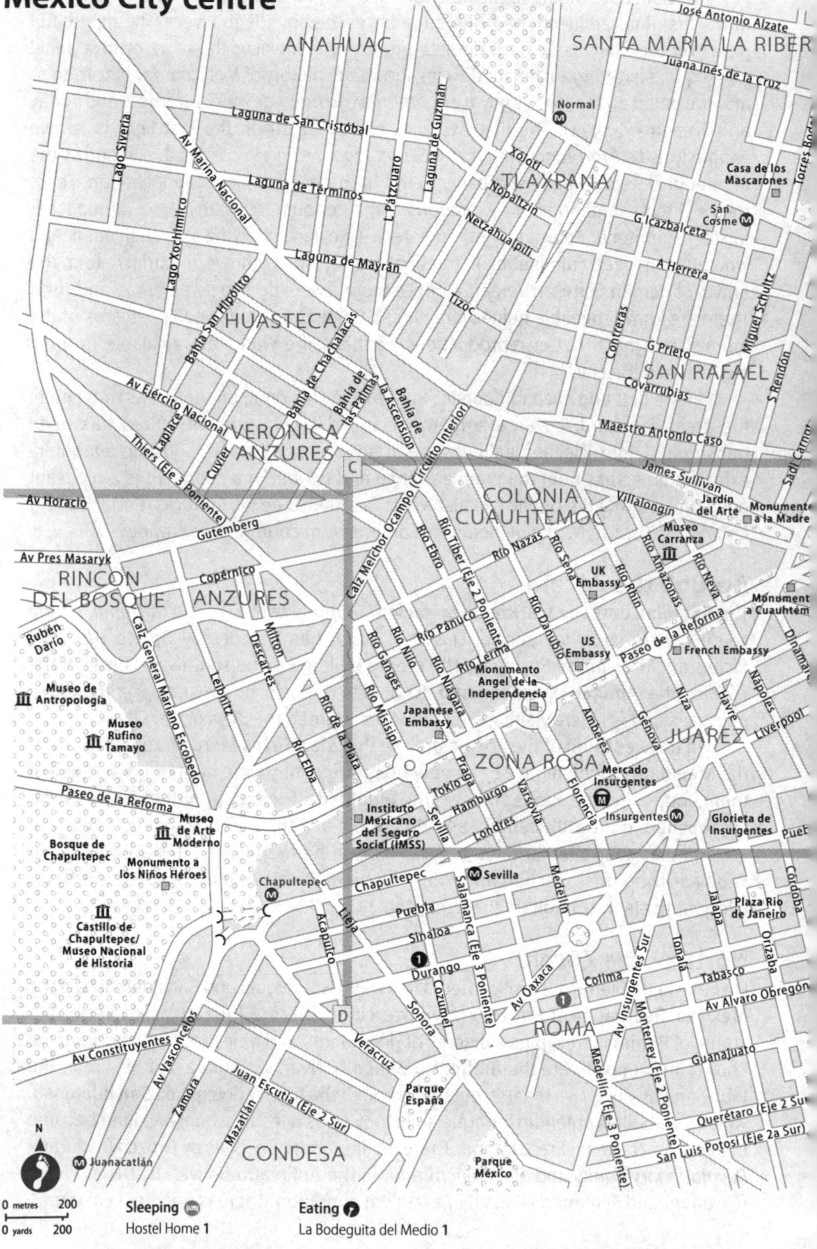

Tue-Sun 1000-1800, US$1.50. Housed in the former Colegio de Cristo, this collection includes works by contemporary cartoonists as well as the influential artist José Guadalupe Posada, famous for his skeletal images.

The **Secretaría de Educación Pública** ⓘ *Argentina 28, 3 blocks from the Zócalo, daily 1000-1730, free,* was built in 1922. For lovers of Mexican murals there are over 200 to view by a number of different painters, including some of Diego Rivera's

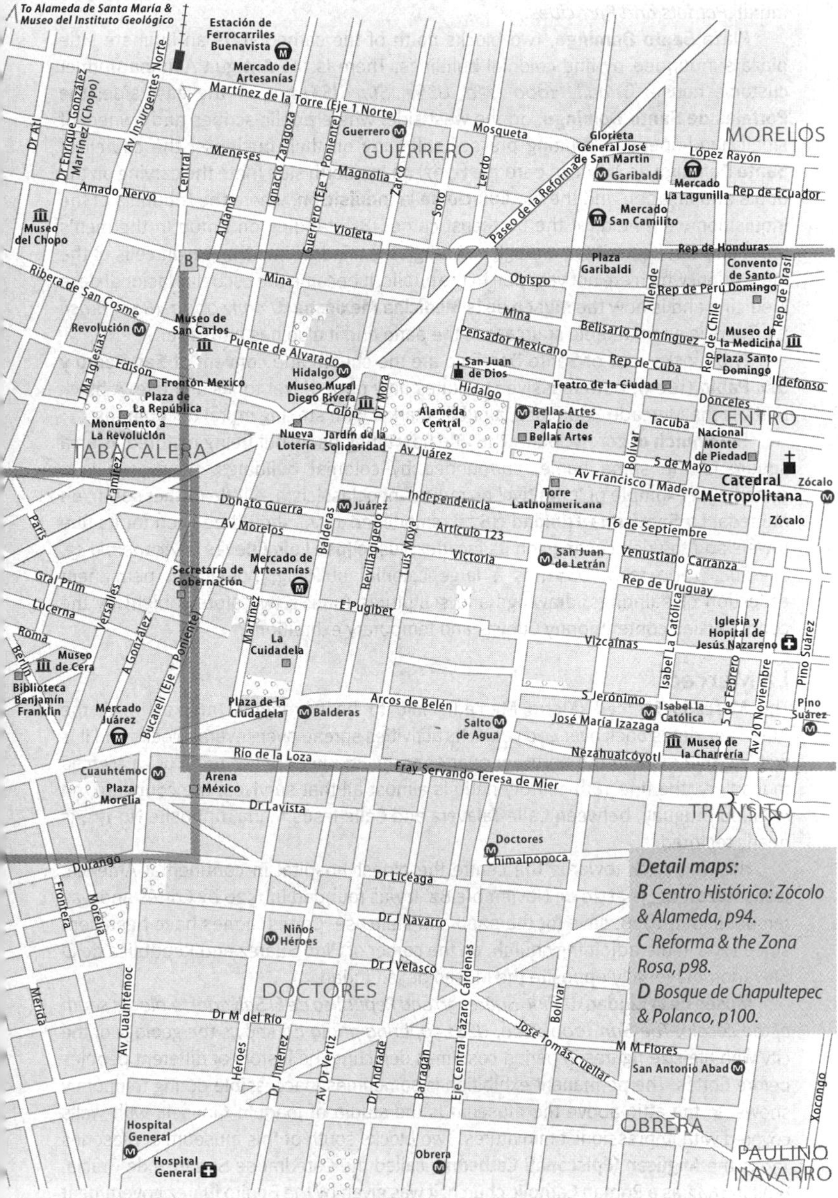

masterpieces. Painted between 1923 and 1928, they illustrate the lives and sufferings of the common people, as well as satirizing the rich. Look out for *Día de Muertos* (Day of the Dead) on the ground floor (far left in second courtyard) and, on the first floor, *El pan nuestro* (Our Daily Bread) showing the poor at supper, *El banquete de Wall Street* (The Wall Street Banquet) and the splendidly restored *La cena del capitalista* (The Capitalist's Supper). A long passageway connecting the Secretaría with the older Antigua Aduana de Santo Domingo (see below) displays the dynamic Siqueiros mural, *Patriots and Parricides*.

Plaza Santo Domingo, two blocks north of the cathedral, is an intimate little plaza surrounded by fine colonial buildings. There is the **Antigua Aduana** (former customs house) ⓘ *daily 1000-1730, US$2, Sun US$1.30*, on the east side; the **Portales de Santo Domingo**, on the west side, where public scribes and owners of small hand-operated printing presses still carry on their business; the church of **Santo Domingo**, in Mexican baroque (1737) on the north side (note the carving on the doors and façade); and the old **Edificio de la Inquisición**, where the tribunals of the Inquisition were held, at the northeast corner. By standing on tiptoe in the men's room one can see – if tall enough – through the window into the prison cells of the Inquisition, which are not yet open to the public. It became the Escuela Nacional de la Medicina and is now the **Museo de la Medicina Mexicana** ⓘ *daily 0900-1800, Brasil 33*. There is a remarkable staircase in the patio and it also has a theatre.

Two blocks east of Santo Domingo are the church and convent of **San Pedro y San Pablo** (1603), both massive structures now turned over to secular use. A block north is the Mercado Rodríguez, a public market with striking mural decorations.

The **Church of Loreto**, built 1816 and now tilting badly but being restored, is on a square of the same name, surrounded by colonial buildings. Its façade is a remarkable example of 'primitive' or 'radical' neoclassicism. A little further south, on Moneda, **La Santísima Trinidad** (1677, remodelled 1755) should be seen for its fine towers and the rich carvings on its façade. **Museo José Luis Cuevas** ⓘ *Academia 13, Tue-Sun, 1000-1730, US$1*, is a large colonial building, housing a permanent collection of paintings, drawings and sculptures (one is two storeys high) by the controversial, contemporary Cuevas and temporary exhibitions.

La Merced

The **Mercado Merced** (Metro Merced), said to be the largest market in all the Americas, dates back over 400 years. Its activities spread over several blocks and it is well worth a visit. In the northern quarter of this market are the ruins of La Merced monastery; the fine 18th-century patio is almost all that survives; the courtyard, on Avenida Uruguay, between Calle Talavera and Calle Jesús María, opposite No 171, is nearly restored.

Heading back towards the centre the oldest hospital in continental America, **Jesús Nazareno**, is at 20 de Noviembre 82. It was founded in 1526 by Cortés and was remodelled in 1928, save for the patio and staircase. Cortés' bones have been kept since 1794 in the adjoining church, on the corner of Pino Suárez and República de El Salvador, diagonally opposite the Museo de la Ciudad.

Museo de la Ciudad ⓘ *Pino Suárez 30 and República de El Salvador, 2 blocks south of the Zócalo, Tue-Sun 1000-1800, US$1.50, bring photo ID*, shows the geology of the city with life-size figures in period costumes depicting the history of different peoples before Cortés. The permanent exhibition is sometimes inaccessible during temporary shows. In the attic above the museum is the studio of Joaquín Clausell, with walls covered with Impressionist miniatures. Two blocks south of this museum at Mesones 139 is the **Anglican (Episcopal) Cathedral**, called the Catedral de San José de Gracia. Built in 1642 as a Roman Catholic church, it was given by the Benito Juárez government to the Episcopal Mission in Mexico. Juárez himself often attended services here.

Further south, **Museo de la Charrería** ⓘ *Isabel la Católica and José María Izazaga,* close to Metro Isabel la Católica, free, is small, with interesting artefacts and a history of the *charro* (Mexican cowboy).

Zócalo to La Alameda

On Avenida Madero, which leads from the Zócalo west to the Alameda, is the late 16th-century **La Profesa** church with a fine high altar and a leaning tower. The 18th-century **Palacio de Iturbide** ⓘ *Av Madero 17, Tue-Sun 1000-1700, free*, once the home of Emperor Agustín (1821-1823), has been restored and has a clear plastic roof. Wander around, it is now the head office of a bank.

Also on Avenida Madero, near the Alameda, is the 16th-century **Casa de los Azulejos** (House of Tiles). It is brilliantly faced with blue and white 18th-century Puebla tiles. Occupied by the Zapatista army during the Revolution, it is now home to **Sanborn's** restaurant. The staircase walls are covered with an Orozco fresco *Omniscience* (1925). Opposite is the **Church of San Francisco**, founded in 1525 by the 'Apostles of Mexico', the first 12 Franciscans to reach the country. It was by far the most important church in colonial days, attended by the Viceroys themselves. Cortés' body rested here for some time, as did the body of 'Emperor' Iturbide.

The **Museo Nacional de Arte** ⓘ *Tacuba 8, Tue-Sun 1030-1730, US$3*, is opposite the Palacio de Minería, near the main Post Office. It was built in 1904 and designed by the Italian architect Silvio Contri as the Palacio de Comunicaciones. The building has magnificent staircases made by the Florentine firm Pignone. It houses a large collection of Mexican paintings, drawings, sculptures and ceramics dating from the 16th century to 1950. It has the largest number of paintings (more than 100) by José María Velasco in Mexico City, as well as works by Miguel Cabrera, Gerardo Murillo, Rivera, Orozco, Siqueiros, Tamayo and Anguiano. The museum building has been completely restored and facilities modernized.

On the corner of Tacuba and the Eje Central (Lázaro Cárdenas) is the magnificent **Correo Central** (Post Office) ⓘ *Mon-Fri 0900-1800, Sat 1000-1400, free*, commissioned in 1902 and completed in 1907.

Palacio de Bellas Artes

ⓘ *Tue-Sun 1000-1800, US$3, performances by the Ballet Folklórico de México, Sun 0930 and 2030, Wed 2030; tickets from US$25, T5521-9251, www.balletamalia.com, for details.*

A large, showy building, interesting for Art Deco lovers (see the fabulous stained-glass skylight in the roof), it houses a museum, theatre, a *cafetería* at mezzanine level (light, serving average continental food at moderate prices) and an excellent bookshop on the arts. The museum has old and contemporary paintings, prints, sculptures and handicrafts. There are spirited Riveras in the room of oils and watercolours. Other frescoes are by Orozco, Tamayo and Siqueiros. There are also prestigious temporary fine art exhibitions (no extra charge). On the top floor is a museum of architecture, which holds temporary exhibitions and shows the building's history. The most remarkable thing about the theatre is its glass curtain designed by Tiffany. It is solemnly raised and lowered before each performance of the Ballet Folklórico de México. Operas are also performed here and there are frequent orchestral concerts. The Palacio was refurbished, inside and out, in 1994 to celebrate its diamond jubilee; the garden in front of the marble apron has been laid out as originally designed. But the Palacio is listing badly and has sunk 4 m since it was built.

> *The fresco by Rivera is a copy of the one rubbed out in disapproval at Radio City, New York.*

La Alameda

Across the road is the **Torre Latinoamericana** ⓘ *daily 0930-2230, US$4.50 to go up*, which has a viewing platform with telescopes on the 44th floor. This great glass tower dominates the gardens of the **Alameda Central**, once the Aztec market and later the place of execution for the Spanish Inquisition. Beneath the broken shade of eucalyptus, cypress and ragged palms, wide paths link fountains and heroic statues. The Alameda became a popular area for all social classes to stroll casually in the 19th century. It is now much more a common thoroughfare, with many temporary stalls at certain festive times of year. The park is illuminated at night.

Along the south side of the Alameda runs Avenida Juárez, a broad street with a mixture of old and new buildings. Opposite the Palacio de Bellas Artes is a building known as **La Nacional**, which was Mexico City's first skyscraper in the 1930s. Look carefully at its perpendicularity, a result of the 1985 earthquake.

Also on the south side of the Alameda is the **Hemiciclo a Juárez** statue (now on the 20 peso note), designed by Guillermo de Heredia in white marble and inaugurated in 1910 to mark the centenary of Independence. Opposite, the colonial

Centro Histórico: Zócalo & Alameda

Sleeping
Avenida **2** *C3*
Buenos Aires **3** *B4*
Canadá **4** *B4*
Capitol **5** *C3*
Carlton **6** *B1*
Casas de los Amigos **1** *B1*
Catedral **7** *B5*
Congreso **10** *B4*
Cortés **11** *B2*
Cuba **12** *B4*
Danky **13** *C1*
El Roble **14** *C5*
Fleming **16** *C2*
Fornos **17** *D2*
Frimont **18** *B1*
Gillow **20** *B4*
Habana **19** *B4*
Hostal Catedral **8** *B4*
Hostal Moneda **31** *B5*
Isabel la Católica **21** *C4*
Jena **22** *B1*
Juárez **23** *B4*
Lafayette **24** *C4*
La Marina **25** *A4*
Majestic **26** *C4*
Marlowe **27** *C3*

N
0 metres 100
0 yards 100

church of Corpus Christi is used to display and sell folk arts and crafts. Further west a sunken section of the pavement shelters the **Plaza de las Esculturas** (1998), with 19th-century sculptures. A stroll down Calle Dolores, a busy and fascinating street, leads to the market of San Juan. Three blocks west, on Plaza Ciudadela, is the lively **Mercado de la Ciudadela**, which sells crafts from all over Mexico.

Diego Rivera's huge (15 m by 4.8 m) and fascinating mural, the *Sueño de una Tarde Dominical en la Alameda Central*, was removed from the earthquake-damaged **Hotel del Prado** on Avenida Juárez in 1985 and now occupies its own purpose-built museum, the **Museo Mural Diego Rivera** ⓘ *north side of the Jardín de la Solidaridad at the west end of the Alameda Central, Tue-Sun 1000-1800, US$1.50*. One of Rivera's finest works, it presents a pageant of Mexican history from the Conquest up to the 1940s with vivid portraits of national

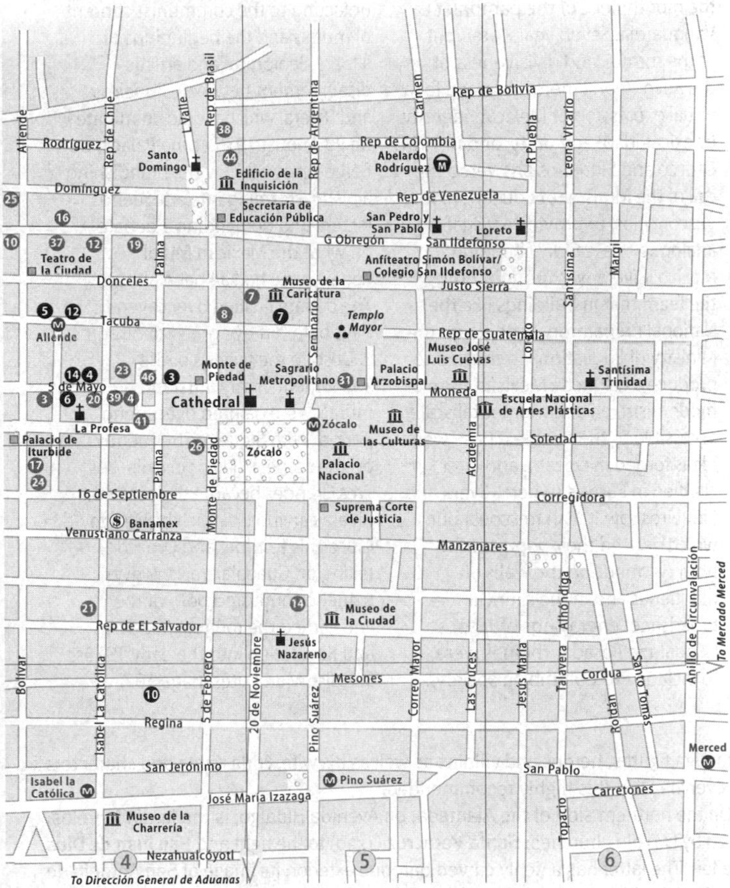

Meave **28** *C3*
Mina **29** *A1*
Monaco **30** *A1*
Oxford **34** *B1*
República **37** *B4*
Río de Janeiro **38** *A4*
Rioja **39** *B4*
Royalty **40** *B1*
San Antonio **41** *B4*
San Francisco **42** *C2*
Sheraton Centro Histórico **43** *B2*
Texas **9** *B1*
Tuxpan **44** *A4*
Zamora **46** *B4*

Eating

Bamerette **1** *B2*
Bar la Opera **2** B3
Café El Popular **3** *B4*
Café La Blanca **4** *B4*
Café Tacuba **5** *B4*
Dulcería de Celaya **6** *B4*
La Casa de las Sirenas **7** *B5*
Los Girasoles **8** *B3*
Mr Lee **9** *C3*
Nadja **10** *D4*
Sanborn's **11** *B3*
Super Soya **12** *B4*
Sushi Roll **13** *B3*
Torta Brava **14** *B4*
Trevi **15** *B2*

Bars & clubs

La Perla **16** *A4*
Salón Corona **17** *C4*

Los Tres Grandes

The story of muralism in Mexico has largely been that of 'Los Tres Grandes', Diego Rivera, José Clemente Orozco and David Alfaro Siqueiros, although there were many other artists involved from the start. In 1914 Orozco and Siqueiros were to be found in the Carranza stronghold of Orizaba fomenting social and artistic revolution through the mouthpiece of the pamphlet La Vanguardia. Seven years later, out of the turmoil and divisiveness of the Revolution emerged a need for a visual expression of Mexican identity (mexicanidad) and unity, and in 1921 Orozco and Siqueiros answered the call of the Minister of Education, José Vasconcelos, to provide a visual analogue to a rapidly changing Mexico. Rivera was brought onto the team that in buildings like the National Preparatory School and the Ministry of Education, attempted to produce a distinctly Mexican form of modernism, on a monumental scale, accessible to the people. These were ideas forged in Orizaba and later clarified in Europe (where Rivera and Siqueiros saw Italian frescoes) but which derived their popular form from paintings on the walls of pulquerías and in the satirical broadsheet engravings of José Guadalupe Posada. Themes were to include Pre-Columbian society, modern agriculture and medicine and a didactic Mexican history pointing to a mechanized future for the benefit of all. Siqueiros in particular was keen to transform the working practice of artists who would henceforth work as members of co-operatives.

The 'movement' fell apart almost from its inception. There were riots objecting to the communist content of murals and the beginnings of a long ideological and artistic disagreement between Siqueiros and Rivera, which would culminate on 28 August 1935 at the Palacio de Bellas Artes with Rivera, brandishing a pistol, storming into a Siqueiros lecture and demanding a debate on what the Mexican Mural Renaissance had all been about! The debate ensued over several days before they agreed to disagree.

Despite the failings of the 'movement' many outstanding murals were painted over a long period. With Siqueiros frequently off the scene, in jail or in exile, Los Tres Grandes became the big two; Rivera carving up much of Mexico City as his territory and Orozco taking on Guadalajara. However, Siqueiros outlasted both of them and carried the torch of Muralism and Revolution into the early 1970s. See also Mural sites, page 102.

and foreign figures, heroes and villains as well as his wife, Frida Kahlo and characters from everyday life. It is highly recommended.

On the northern side of the Alameda, on Avenida Hidalgo, is the Jardín Morelos, flanked by two old churches: **Santa Veracruz** (1730) to the right and **San Juan de Dios** to the left. The latter has a richly carved baroque exterior; its image of San Antonio de Padua is visited by those who are broken-hearted from love. Next door, the **Museo Franz Mayer** ⓘ *T5518-2265, Tue-Sun 1000-1700, US$2*, in the former Hospital de San Juan de Dios, was built in the 17th century. Recently rebuilt and exquisitely restored, it houses a library and an important decorative arts collection of ceramics, glass, silver, timepieces, furniture and textiles, as well as Mexican and European paintings from the 16th-20th centuries. Its cloister is an oasis of peace in the heart of the city.

North of La Alameda

Plaza Garibaldi

About four blocks north of the post office off Eje Central Lázaro Cárdenas is Plaza Garibaldi, an absolute must one evening, ideally on a Friday or Saturday (it tends to be quiet on Mondays) when up to 200 *mariachis* in their traditional costume of huge sombrero, tight silver-embroidered trousers, pistol and *sarape*, will play your favourite Mexican serenade for between US$5 (for a bad one) and US$10 (for a good one). If you arrive by taxi you will be besieged. The whole square throbs with life and the packed bars are cheerful. The **Lagunilla** market is held about four blocks northeast of the plaza, a hive of activity particularly on Sundays.

On one side of Plaza Garibaldi is a gigantic and very entertaining eating hall where different stalls sell different courses.

Plaza de las Tres Culturas

Further north still, Lázaro Cárdenas leads to Santa María la Redonda, at the end of which is **Plaza Santiago de Tlatelolco** (metro line 3 to Tlatelolco), the city's oldest plaza after the Zócalo. The main market of the Aztecs was here, and on it, in 1524, the Franciscans built a huge church and convent. It is now known as the Plaza de las Tres Culturas since it shows elements of Aztec, colonial and modern architecture. The Aztec ruins have been restored and the magnificent Franciscan church of Santiago Tlatelolco, completed 1609, is now the focus of the massive, multi-storey Nonoalco-Tlatelolco housing scheme (heavily damaged in the 1985 earthquake), a garden city within a city, with pedestrian and wheeled traffic entirely separate. In October 1968, the Plaza de las Tres Culturas was the scene of serious distubances between the authorities and students, in which a large number of students were killed.

You could combine this with a visit to the Basílica de Guada lupe, see page 110, a bit further north.

West of La Alameda

West of the Paseo de la Reforma is the **Monumento a la Revolución**, a great copper dome, soaring above supporting columns set on the largest triumphal arches in the world. Beneath the monument, the **Museo Nacional de la Revolución** ⓘ *Tue-Sun 1000-1700, US$1.50*, which deals with the period 1867-1917, is very interesting and has lots of exhibits, original photographs and videos.

The **Museo de San Carlos** ⓘ *Puente de Alvarado 50 (Metro Revolución), Wed-Mon 1000-1800, US$2*, reached by crossing Reforma near Metro Hidalgo, is in a 19th-century palace, with fine Mexican colonial painting and a first-class collection of European paintings. It was the home of Señora Calderón de la Barca who wrote *Life in Mexico* while living there.

Santa María la Ribera and San Cosme

These are two wards north of Metro San Cosme, which became fashionable residential areas in the late 19th century, and many elegant, if neglected façades are to be seen. On the corner of Ribera de San Cosme and Naranjo next to San Cosme metro note the **Casa de los Mascarones.** Built in 1766, this was the country house of the Conde del Valle de Orizaba, later the Escuela Nacional de Música. Recently restored, it now houses a university computer centre. The **Museo Universitario del Chopo** ⓘ *Enrique González Martínez 10, between Metro San Cosme and Av Insurgentes Norte, Wed-Sun 1000-1400, 1600-1900*, holds contemporary international photography and art exhibitions in a church-like building designed by Eiffel. In the pleasant **Alameda de Santa María**, between Pino and Torres Bodet, stands an extraordinary Moorish pavilion designed by Mexicans for the Paris Exhibition in 1889. On its return to Mexico, the *kiosko* was placed in the Alameda Central before being transferred to its present site in 1910. On the west side of this square, on Torres Bodet, is the **Museo del Instituto Geológico** ⓘ *Tue-Sun 1000-1700, free.* Apart from its collection of fossils and minerals (and magnificent early 20th-century showcases), the building itself (1904) is worth a visit for its swirling wrought-iron staircases and unusual stained-glass windows of mining scenes by Zettler (Munich and Mexico).

Paseo de la Reforma and Zona Rosa

The wide and handsome Paseo de la Reforma continues southwest from the Alameda to the Bosque de Chapultepec. It is lined with shops, offices, hotels and some striking modern buildings: the Hotel Crowne Plaza, the Mexican Stock Exchange (*Bolsa de Valores*) and the Hotel María Cristina, as well as a red-and-black cuboid office structure on the left. Along it are monuments to Columbus, Cuauhtémoc and, at the intersection with Tiber/Florencia, a 45-m marble column supporting the golden form of a female angel representing Independence. Known as 'El Angel', the statue, which used to be on an even higher column, fell to the ground in the 1957 earthquake. This is a favourite spot for political demonstrations, as well as sporting and national celebrations. One block north of Reforma, the **Museo Carranza** ⓘ *Lerma y Amazonas*, is a museum with items linked to the life of the famous revolutionary and constitutionalist, and to the Revolution itself. It is worth a visit.

Reforma & Zona Rosa

Sleeping
Casa González **1**
Imperial **2**
Mansión Havre **3**
María Cristina **4**
NH México **5**
Parador Washington **6**
Prim **7**
Suites Amberes **8**
Suites Havre **9**
Uxmal **10**
Viena **11**

Zona Rosa

The famous Zona Rosa (Pink Zone) lies to the south of Reforma, contained approximately by Reforma, Sevilla, Avenida Chapultepec and Insurgentes Sur. This was formerly the setting for Mexico City's most fashionable stores, restaurants and nightclubs. It suffered considerable damage in the 1985 earthquake and subsequently lost ground to Polanco (see below). In recent times it has seen a revival and is once again a very pleasant area in which to stroll, shop (or window-shop) and dine, in the many open-air or half-covered restaurants.

Bosque de Chapultepec and Polanco

The park, with its thousands of *ahuehuete* trees (so sacred to the Aztecs), is beautiful and is now being kept litter free and well policed (park closes at 1700). The best day to visit is Sunday when it is all much more colourful (and more crowded). The park is divided into three sections. The first, the easternmost, was a wood inhabited by the Toltecs and Aztecs. Most of the interesting sites are in this section (see below).

The second section, west of Bulevar Manuel Avila Camacho, was added in 1964. It has a large **amusement park** ⓘ *Wed and Fri-Sun 1030-2000, US$1; Montaña Rusa Sat and Sun only, US$0.40*, with a wonderful section for children and another for adults and the *Montaña Rusa*, one of the world's largest roller coasters. There are bridle paths and polo grounds. Diego Rivera's famous fountain, the **Fuente de Tlaloc**, is near the children's amusement park. Close by are the Fuentes de las Serpientes (Snake Fountains). Both the Lago Menor and Lago Mayor are popular for boating; on the shore of each is a restaurant.

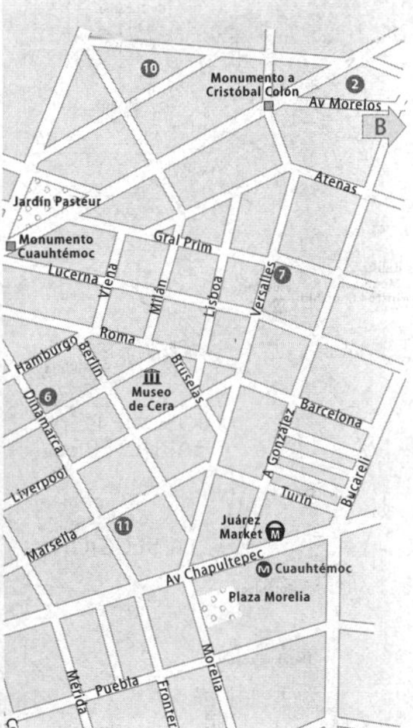

The third section, which was added in 1974, stretches a long way beyond the Panteón Civil de Dolores (cemetery) and has little to interest the tourist.

The first section contains a maze of pathways, the **Plaza del Quijote** and **Monumento a los Niños Héroes**, a large lake and a smaller one (with an outdoor theatre used for performances of *Swan Lake* and similar). There are shaded areas, and stalls selling snacks of all kinds, especially at weekends. There is also a **zoo** ⓘ *Tue-Sun, shuts 1630, free*, with giant pandas and other animals from around the world; it is well laid out, the cages are spacious and most animals seem content. The official residence of the President, **Los Pinos**, is also situated in the first section.

At the top of a hill, and visible from afar (a long climb on foot; train to the top US$0.20 return journey) is the imposing **Castillo de Chapultepec** ⓘ *Tue-Sun 0900-1700, US$2.50 (long queues on Sun)*. Free classical music concerts are given on Sunday at 1200 by the Bellas Artes Chamber Orchestra; arrive early for a seat, with a view over the Valley of Mexico from its beautiful balconies – a total refurbishment was completed in 2000. The castle now houses the **Museo Nacional de Historia** but its rooms were once used by the Emperor Maximilian and the Empress Carlota during their brief reign. There is an impressive mural by Siqueiros, *From the Dictatorship of Porfirio Díaz to the Revolution* (in Sala XIII, near the entrance), and a mural by O'Gorman on the theme of Independence, as well as several by Camarena.

Halfway down the hill is the **Galería de Historia**, which has dioramas, with tape-recorded explanations of Mexican history, and photographs of the 1910 Revolution. Just below the castle are the remains of the famous **Arbol de Moctezuma**, known locally as *El Sargento*. This immense tree, which has a circumference of 14 m, was about 60 m high before it was cut down to 10 m.

Also in the first section of the Bosque de Chapultepec, and on the same side of Reforma as Chapultepec Castle, is the **Museo de Arte Moderno** ⓘ *Tue-Sun 1000-1700, US$1.50, free with ISIC card.* There is a good bookshop, gift shop and an open-air cafeteria behind the first building. A free galleries map and monthly calendar of exhibitions is available here and at other museums and galleries. The museum has a permanent collection of modern Mexican art and regularly stages temporary national and international exhibitions. It consists of two circular buildings pleasantly

Bosque de Chapultepec & Polanco

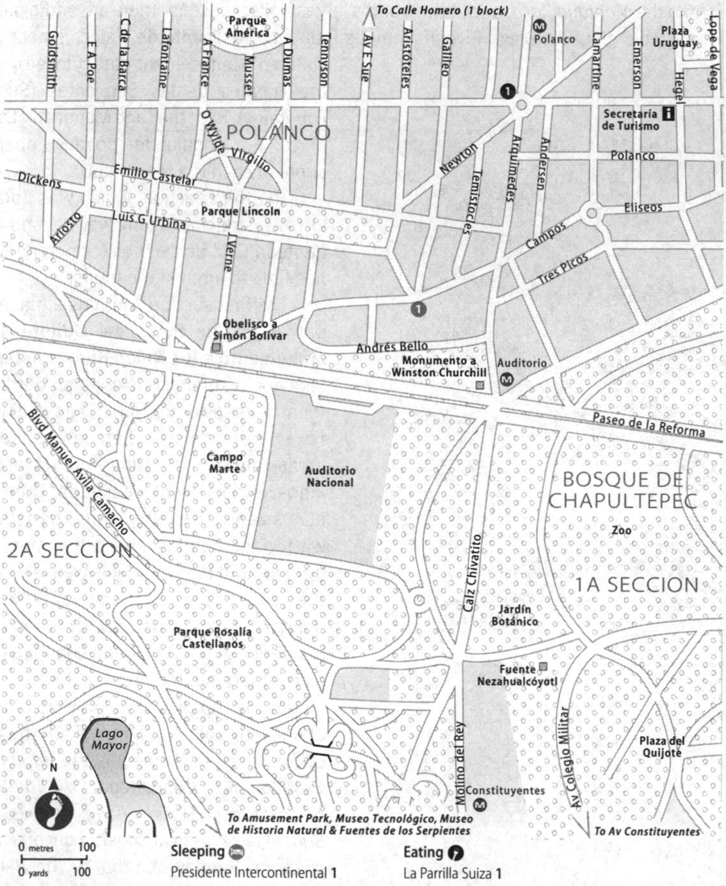

set among trees with sculptures in the grounds. The temporary exhibitions are usually held in the smaller of the two buildings; entrance through the larger one. The delightfully light architecture of the larger building is balanced by a heavy, marble staircase, with a curious acoustic effect on the central landing under a translucent dome, which must have been unplanned.

The **Museo Rufino Tamayo** ⓘ *on the other side of Reforma, cross near the Museo de Arte Moderno, on the way to the Anthropological Museum, Tue-Sun 1000-1800, US$1.70, free to students with ISIC card*, has a fine collection of works by Rufino Tamayo and shows contemporary Mexican and other painters. The interior space of the museum is unusual in that it is difficult to know which floor you are on. There is a very pleasant restaurant.

Museo Nacional de Antropología

ⓘ *Tue-Sun, US$4 from 0900-1700, US$13.50 from 1700-1900, free on Sundays, www.mna.inah.gob.mx. Written explanations in Spanish and English, audio guide available in English, US$4, which describes 130 of the exhibits. Guided tours in English or Spanish free with a minimum of 5 people. If you want to see everything, you need at least 2 days. Permission to photograph (no tripod or flash allowed) US$1,*

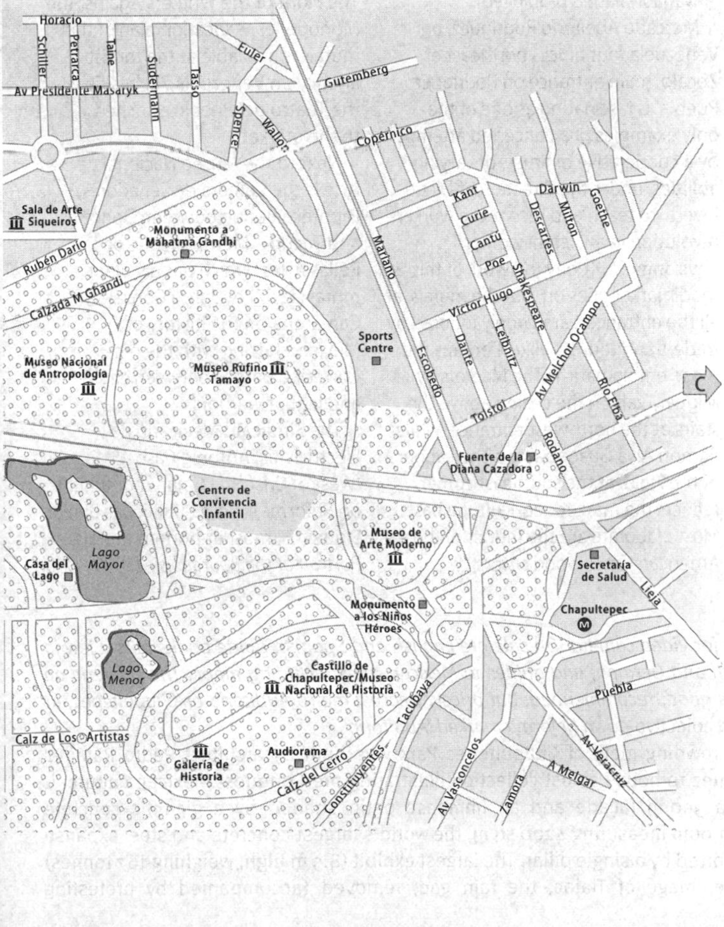

Mural sites

Apart from the main centres of mural painting already listed geographically in the text (Palacio Nacional, Suprema Corte de Justicia, Palacio de Bellas Artes, Museo Mural Diego Rivera, Escuela Nacional Preparatoria-San Ildefonso, Secretaría de Educación, Castillo de Chapultepec and below Polyforum Cultural Siqueiros), there are other sites well worth visiting that all lie within walking distance or short metro ride from the centre. Some of these are functioning workplaces, so tact should be shown when visiting: ask permission before heading off into labyrinthine buildings and always check about photo restrictions (invariably flash is prohibited).

Mercado Abelardo Rodríguez, on Venezuela four blocks northeast of Zócalo, main entrance on Rodríguez Puebla, is fascinating as one of the only examples of a concerted attempt by a cooperative of artists of varying abilities, under the direction of Diego Rivera, to teach and record the workers' revolution in an actual workers' environment. Today the work of this food market goes on, but the murals, at all the entrances, are largely ignored by traders and tourists alike. Perhaps the most emblematic is The Markets by Miguel Tzab on the ceiling above the stairs at the northwest entrance, while Ramón Alva Guadarrama's The Labours of the Field, at the southeast corner, reflects the market's agricultural base. Most elaborate are the murals of the American Greenwood sisters, Marion and Grace, showing *Industrialization of the Countryside and The Mine*, on the stairs either side of the main entrance. Opposite, upstairs, is a relief mural by Isamu Noguchi. For permission to take photos go to the market office behind the restaurant at the southwest entrance.

In the theatre foyer is Antonio Pujol's Problems of the Worker, much praised at the time of its completion in 1936. In the cloisters of the confusingly named Patio Diego Rivera, behind the ticket office, is Pablo O'Higgins's tirade against international fascism, The Fight of the Workers Against the Monopolies. A location plan of the murals is available at the tourist agency on Venezuela 72, beside the Teatro del Pueblo attached to the market.

Next to the Museo Nacional de Arte is the Cámara de Senadores, Hipoteca Beride between Donceles and Tacuba, Metro Allende or Bellas Artes, which has a violent mural (1957) by Jorge González Camarena on the history of Mexico, starting with the pre-Cortesian battles between eagle and jaguar warriors.

The Sindicato Mexicano de Electricistas, Antonio Caso 45 (west of Cristóbal Colón monument on Reforma), T5535-0386, has one of Siqueiros' most important murals, *Portrait of the Bourgeoisie* (1939-1940),

US$5 for video camera. On sale are English and Spanish guide books plus a few in French and German, and guides to Mexican ruins including maps. The cafeteria on site is good, recommended, but pricey. Nearest metro Auditorio or Chapultepec, or take a colectivo *down Reforma marked 'Auditorio'.*

The crowning glory of Chapultepec Park was built by architect Pedro Ramírez Vásquez to house a vast collection illustrating pre-Conquest Mexican culture. It has a 350-m façade and an immense patio shaded by a gigantic concrete mushroom measuring 4200 sq m, the world's largest concrete and steel expanse supported by a single pillar. The largest exhibit (8.5 m high, weighing 167 tonnes) is the image of Tlaloc, the rain god, removed (accompanied by protesting located up the second floor stairwell to the left of the entrance. It depicts the revolutionary struggle against international fascism and is considered a seminal work for its use of cinematic montage techniques and viewing points. Before taking photos ask permission in the secretaría office on the right at the end of the corridor on the second floor.

A 15-minute walk away at Altamirano 118, Colonia San Rafael, T5535-2246, is the Teatro Jorge Negrete, in the foyer of which is a later Siqueiros mural, *Theatrical Art in the Social Life of Mexico* (1957), precursor in its expression of movement to his mural in Chapultepec Castle. Ask permission to see it in the office at No 128. No photos (nearest Metro San Cosme).

At the Hospital de La Raza in what was once an outer entrance hall (but is now at the centre of the building) is Rivera's *History of Medicine* (1953), and to the left of the main entrance, in a naturally lit theatre foyer (usually locked but you can see it through the large frontal windows if there is nobody about with keys), is Siqueiros' *For the Complete Safety of All Mexicans at Work* (1952-1954). Ask a security guard or at main reception for directions to the murals. Take Metro La Raza and from the station head south along the right side of Insurgentes Norte, cross the railway, go straight ahead and then cross the freeway by the footbridge to the hospital. For permission to take photos here and at other medical centres you must ask at the Sede IMSS, Hidalgo 230, Metro Bellas Artes.

Another hospital with a relevant themed mural is the Centro Médico Nacional, Avenida Cuauhtémoc, where Siqueiros' *Apology for the Future Victory of Medicine over Cancer* (1958) has been restored following damage in the 1985 earthquake. Since 1996 it has been on display in the waiting area of the oncology building beyond the main entrance building on the right. At the entrance, as you come up the stairs from the metro station Centro Médico, is a mural by Chávez Morado commemorating the rebuilding of the hospital in which many died during the earthquake.

Before or after visiting the mural sites we recommend reading one or more of the following: *The Murals of Diego Rivera*, by Desmond Rochfort, London, 1987; *Mexican Muralists*, same author, New York, 1984. *Dreaming with his Eyes Open*, by Patrick Marnham, New York and London, 1998, is an immensely readable though not entirely scholastic biography of Diego Rivera, which deals with Orozco, Siqueiros and the other muralists as well as Rivera. See also box, page 96.

cloudbursts) from near the town of Texcoco to the museum. Upstairs is a display of folk costumes, which may be closed on Sundays. Added attractions include *voladores* and musicians.

Inside, the museum is very well organized; each major culture that contributed to the evolution of Mesoamerican civilization is well represented in its own room or *sala*: pre-Classic, Teotihuacán, Toltec, Aztec, Oaxaca, Gulf Coast, Maya, Northwestern and Western Mexico. Two areas are often missed by visitors: the Torres Bodet Auditorium, where visiting archaeologists, art historians, anthropologists etc give seminars, often in English and usually free; and the Temporary Exhibitions Hall, which is also worth checking out.

Polanco

ⓘ *To get to Polanco, take a* colectivo *marked 'Horacio' from Metro Chapultepec or Metro Polanco. To get to Lomas de Chapultepec, take a bus marked 'Km 15' or 'Cuajimalpa' from Antropología or the bus station by Metro Chapultepec. To get to Las Palmas, take a* colectivo *or bus marked 'Las Palmas' from Antropología or from the bus station by Metro Chapultepec. To get to Santa Fe, take a* colectivo *marked 'Centro Comercial Santa Fe' from Antropología or a bus from Metro Chapultepec.*

To the right of this section of Reforma, and behind the Museo de Antropología, lies the luxury residential area known as Polanco, which has many interesting art galleries and shops. It does not suffer from the tourists that crowd the Zona Rosa and other so-called chic areas. Many of the old houses have carved stone façades, tiled roofs and gardens, especially on **Calle Horacio**, a pretty street lined with trees and parks. Polanco also contains some of the most modern (and conspicuous) hotels in the city, such as the **Nikko, Presidente** and **Camino Real**, which are at least worth a walk-in visit. Also here are exclusive private residences, commercial art galleries, fashion stores, expensive restaurants and other establishments that are collectively a monument to the consumer society; one glaring example of this is the huge **Palacio de Hierro** department store and offices along **Mazaryk**. There are also a couple of fairly unremarkable modern churches and, in fact, little of cultural value, with the exception of the **Sala de Arte Siqueiros** ⓘ *Tres Picos 29*. Traffic is frequently very congested; avoid taking a taxi if possible; Metro Polanco on Horacio is centrally situated.

Beyond the Auditorio Nacional, Reforma continues southwest towards the area known as **Lomas de Chapultepec** (or simply *Las Lomas*), which gradually rises through broad tree-lined avenues to an altitude that leaves most of the pollution behind. It is mostly residential, including many embassies or ambassadorial residences.

To the north, taking a right at the Fuente de Petróleos up Bulevar Manuel Avila Camacho, you come to the modern office and commercial area of **Las Palmas**, while straight ahead, some 8 km further, beyond Lomas de Chapultepec and on the way out towards Toluca, lies the district of **Santa Fe**, perched on some of the highest ground and therefore in one of the least polluted areas in the city, with some extraordinary, futuristic architecture.

South of the city centre

When you have exhausted the centre of Mexico City, or perhaps when it has exhausted you, the surrounding areas have much to offer in the way of museums, colonial architecture, markets, shops, restaurants and parks. At Xochimilco you can float in a colourful *trajinera* and enjoy a picnic on the banks of the *chinampas*, or floating gardens. The enormous Ciudad Universitaria should not be missed, nor should the botanical gardens. Visit the Saturday bazaar in San Angel, try a glass of pulque or take in a theatrical performance at Coyoacán.

Insurgentes Sur

Heading out of the city centre along Insurgentes towards the delightful suburbs, or *colonias*, of San Angel and Coyoacán, there are several sites that should not be missed. A little to the west of where Insurgentes crosses Chapultepec, and on Avenida Chapultepec itself between Calle Praga and Calle Varsovia, are the remains of the old **aqueduct** built in 1779. South of the Viaducto and next door to the towering World Trade Center, the **Polyforum Cultural Siqueiros** ⓘ *Insurgentes Sur, US$0.40, daily 1000-1900, closed for lunch*, includes a handicraft shop and an art museum, with huge frescoes by Siqueiros, one of the largest in the world, inside the ovoid dome.

A little further south is the **Plaza México**, the largest bullring in the world, with capacity for some 55,000 spectators. It is situated in the **Ciudad de los Deportes**, ⓘ *just* *off Insurgentes Sur, T5563-1659, US$1-18 in the cheaper* sol (sun) *half of the Plaza; seats in the* sombra *(shade) are more expensive, up to US$35 in the barreras.* It's best to buy tickets, especially for important fights, early on Saturday morning from the *taquillas* at the Plaza. The 'México' is one of the world's three most important bullfighting venues and, as virtually every great matador comes to fight in Mexico in the winter months, the chances of seeing an important event are high. The closest metro station is San Antonio or take a *colectivo* to junction of Insurgentes Sur with Eje 5.

Further south still on Avenida Insurgentes Sur at the corner of Mercaderes is a remarkable building by Alejandro Prieto: the **Teatro de Los Insurgentes**, a theatre and opera house seating 1300 people. The main frontage consists of a high curved wall covered with mosaic decoration, the work of Diego Rivera.

San Angel

ⓘ *Reach San Angel by bus from Chapultepec Park or by metro Line 3 to Miguel Angel de Quevedo.*

Thirteen kilometres southwest of the centre, Villa Obregón, popularly known as San Angel, has narrow, cobblestone streets, many old homes, huge trees and the charm of an era now largely past. Most of the distinguished architecture is from the 19th century. See the triple domes of its **Iglesia del Carmen**, covered with coloured tiles, and of the former Convento del Carmen, now the **Museo Colonial del Carmen** ⓘ *daily 1000-1700*, which houses 17th- and 18th-century furniture and paintings. In the crypt, several mummified bodies are displayed in glass-topped cases. The **Centro Cultural San Angel** ⓘ *Revolución opposite Museo del Carmen*, stages exhibitions, concerts, lectures, etc. See also the beautifully furnished and preserved 18-century **Casa del Risco** ⓘ *Callejón de la Amargura, near the Bazar del Sábado, Tue-Sun 1000-1700, free; library Mon-Fri 0900-2000, Sat 1000-1400, photographic ID required for entry.* The house contains a collection of Mexican and European paintings from the 15th to the 20th centuries as well as a library devoted to international law and the Mexican Revolution. Also worth a visit is the church of **San Jacinto**, once belonging to a Dominican convent (1566). The **Museo de Arte Carrillo Gil** ⓘ *Av Revolución 1608, US$3.35*, has good changing exhibits and a permanent collection including paintings by Orozco and Siqueiros as well as several of Diego Rivera's Cubist works. There is a good bookshop and *cafetería*.

The **Museo Estudio Diego Rivera** ⓘ *Av Altavista y Calle Diego Rivera, Tue-Sun 1000-1800, US$1*, is where Diego and his wife, Frida Kahlo lived and worked. It contains several works by Rivera, as well as belongings and memorabilia. The building was designed by Juan O'Gorman. Opposite is the **Antigua Hacienda de Goicochea** – now the **San Angel Inn**. Many tourists come to San Angel on a Saturday to visit the **Bazar del Sábado** ⓘ *0900-1400*, a splendid folk art and curiosity market. Between San Angel and Coyoacán is the monument to Alvaro Obregón on the spot where the former president was assassinated in 1928 (by the junction of Avenida Insurgentes Sur and Arenal).

Coyoacán

ⓘ *From the city centre, it is easiest to take the metro to Viveros, Miguel Angel de Quevedo or General Anaya. The* colectivo *from Metro General Anaya to the centre of Coyoacán is marked 'Santo Domingo', get off at Abasolo or at the Jardín Centenario.*

▸▸ *For Sleeping, Eating, Bars, Entertainment and Shopping in Coyoacán, see pages 117, 114, 119 and 120.*

The oldest part of Mexico City, Coyoacán is the place from which Cortés launched his attack on the Aztec city of Tenochtitlán. It is also one of the most beautiful and best-preserved parts of the city, with hundreds of fine buildings from the 16th to 19th centuries, elegant tree-lined avenues and carefully tended parks and, in the Jardín Centenario and the Plaza Hidalgo, two very attractive squares. It's best explored on foot, which will take most of a day, although it's often combined with a visit to San Angel.

Coyoacán is culturally one of the liveliest parts of Mexico City and with its attractive cafés and good shops it is much frequented by the inhabitants of the capital, particularly at weekends. From San Angel, you can get to Coyoacán via a delightful walk through Chimalistac, across Avenida Universidad and down Avenida Francisco Sosa; or you can take a bus or *pesero* marked 'Taxqueña' as far as Calle Caballocalco.

If coming from Metro Viveros (a large park in which trees are grown for other city parks) or Miguel Angel de Quevedo it is worth making a slight detour in order to walk the length of **Francisco Sosa**, said to be the first urban street laid in Spanish America. At the beginning of this elegant avenue is the 18th-century church of **San Antonio Panzacola** by the side of Río Churubusco. Nearby, on Universidad, is the remarkable, beautiful (and modern) chapel of **Nuestra Señora de la Soledad**, built in the grounds of the 19th-century ex-hacienda El Altillo. A little way down is the **Museo Nacional de la Acuarela** ⓘ *Salvador Novo*, the National Watercolour Museum. The terracotta-fronted residence at **Francisco Sosa 383** ⓘ *Tue-Sun, free; courtyard and garden Mon-Fri 0900-1600*, is said to have been built by Alvarado. Many fine houses follow, mostly built in the 19th century. **Santa Catarina**, in the square of the same name, is a fine 18th-century church; on Sunday, at about one o'clock, people assemble under the trees to tell stories (all are welcome to attend or participate). In the same square, the **Casa de la Cultura Jesús Reyes Heroles** should not be missed, with its delightful leafy gardens. Just before arriving at the **Jardín Centenario**, with its 16th-century arches, is the 18th-century **Casa de Diego Ordaz**.

If time in Coyoacán is limited, take in La Casa de Trotsky, Museo Frida Kahlo, Museo de las Culturas Populares and the church of San Juan Bautista.

The centre of Coyoacán, with its two adjacent plazas, is dominated by the 16th-century church of **San Juan Bautista**, with later additions and a magnificent interior. Jardín Centenario was once the atrium of this 16th-century Franciscan monastery. On the north side of Plaza Hidalgo, the **Casa de Cortés** was in fact built 244 years after the Conquest, on the site of Cortés' house.

Coyoacán

Frida Kahlo

The life of Frida Kahlo was not a very happy one; she questioned her European and Mexican roots, very much like the artists of an earlier era who were infuenced by styles and subjects originating in the Old World, which they attempted to express in New World terms. Frida suffered greatly because her treatment after an accident when she was young went terribly wrong, added to which she and her spouse, Diego Rivera, were not the most compatible of couples. Her anguish is expressed in many of her paintings on display at the Museo Frida Kahlo, in Coyoacán.

Frida's life was the subject of the big budget film *Frida*, filmed on location in San Luis Potosí with Salma Hayek in the title role and Alfredo Molina as Diego Rivera.

The **Museo Nacional de Culturas Populares** ⓘ *Av Hidalgo, Tue-Sun 1000-1600, free*, just off Plaza Hidalgo, houses permanent and temporary exhibitions on popular Mexican culture.

At weekends there are many open-air events especially on Plaza Hidalgo and in the *artesanía* market, off Plaza Hidalgo, which is well worth a visit.

The beautiful 18th-century church of **La Conchita** ⓘ *Fri evenings and Sun mornings*, in a pretty square of the same name is reached by walking down Higuera from Plaza Hidalgo; the interior, especially the altarpiece, is magnificent. On the corner of Higuera and Vallarta is what is reputed to be the **Casa de La Malinche**, Cortés' mistress and interpreter.

Admirers of Frida Kahlo will want to visit the **Museo Frida Kahlo**, or **Casa Azul** ⓘ *Allende and Londres 247, Tue-Sun 1000-1800, US$3, no photos*. Two rooms are preserved as lived in by Frida Kahlo and her husband Diego Rivera, and the rest contain drawings and paintings by both. Frida was very interested in folk art, an interest that is illustrated by the small collection of regional costumes on display. In the **Jardín Cultural Frida Kahlo**, near Plaza de La Conchita, there is a striking bronze statue of Frida by the contemporary Mexican sculptor Gabriel Ponzanelli.

La Casa de Trotsky ⓘ *Río Churubusco 410, between Gómez Farías and Morelos, Tue-Sun 1000-1700, US$2, half-price with ISIC card*, is where the Russian revolutionary lived before he was murdered in the study in 1940. The house is dark and sombre, and there is a tomb in the garden where his ashes were laid.

To reach the centre of Coyoacán from Metro General Anaya, there is a pleasant walk along Héroes del 47 (one block along on the left is the 16th-century church of **San Lucas**), across División del Norte and down Hidalgo (one block along on the left, and two blocks down San Lucas is the 18th-century church of **San Mateo**).

Ciudad Universitaria

ⓘ *Take a bus marked 'CU', along Eje Lázaro Cárdenas; also bus 17, marked 'Tlalpan', which runs the length of Insurgentes (about 1 hr); alternatively, take metro Line 3 to Copilco station (20 mins' walk to University) or to Universidad station (30 mins' walk). At University City free buses ferry passengers to the different areas of the campus.*

The world-famous University City, 18 km from the centre via Insurgentes Sur on the road towards the Cuernavaca highway, was founded in 1551. Perhaps the most notable building is the 10-storey **Biblioteca** (library), by Juan O'Gorman, its outside walls iridescent with mosaics telling the story of scientific knowledge, from Aztec astronomy to molecular theory.

Across the highway is the **Estadio Olímpico**, with seats for 80,000 and a sculpture-painting by Diego Rivera telling the story of Mexican sport. In shape, colour and situation a world's wonder, but now closed and run down. Beyond the Olympic Stadium is the **Jardín Botánico Exterior** ⓘ *daily 0700-1630, 30-min walk, ask directions*, which shows all the cactus species in Mexico. Beyond the Ciudad Universitaria, but still a part of the university, is a complex which includes the **Museo Universitario Contemporáneo de Arte** and the extraordinary **Espacio Escultórico**, a large circular area of volcanic rock within a circle of cement monoliths; on the opposite side of the road is another large area with many huge sculptures; stick to the path as it is possible to get lost in the vegetation.

Anahuacalli

ⓘ *Off División del Norte, Museo 150, T5617-4310, Tue-Sun 1000-1400, 1500-1800, closed Holy Week, US$1.70. The museum is reached by Combi 29 from the Taxqueña metro station to Estadio Azteca, or take the bus marked División del Norte from outside Metro Salto del Agua.*

Further east is the **Diego Rivera Museum**, also called Anahuacalli. There is a fine collection of pre-Columbian sculpture and pottery, effectively displayed in a pseudo-Mayan tomb purpose built by Diego Rivera. There is a big display here for the Day of the Dead at the beginning of November.

Xochimilco

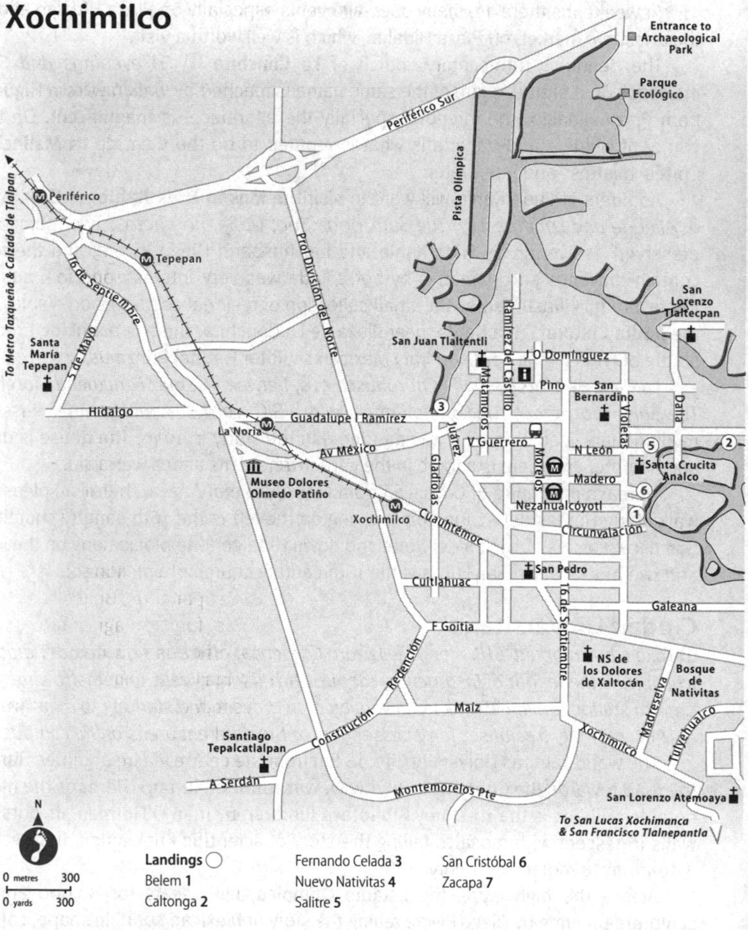

Churubusco

ⓘ *Reached from the Zócalo by Coyoacán or Tlalpan buses; or from Metro General Anaya.*
Situated 10 km southeast in the area of Churubusco is the picturesque and partly ruined convent (1762) that is now the **Museo Nacional de las Intervenciones** ⓘ *General Anaya y 20 de Agosto, Tue-Sun 0900-1800, US$3.35*. The museum's 17 rooms are filled with mementoes, documents, proclamations and pictures recounting foreign invasions, incursions and occupations since Independence. It also holds temporary exhibitions. The site of the museum was chosen because it was the scene of a battle when the US Army marched into Mexico City in 1847. This was where the San Patricios, the famous Saint Patrick's Brigade who fought as volunteers on the Mexican side, were captured by the US Army. Next door is the 16th-century **church of San Diego**, with 17th- and 18th-century additions. Near the church, on the other side of Calzada General Anaya, is the delightful **Parque de Churubusco**. One block from Tlalpan along Héroes del 47, to the left, is the 18th-century **church of San Mateo.**

Tlalpan

A further 6.5 km, or direct from San Angel (see page 105), is this suburb with colonial houses, gardens and, near the Plaza de la Constitución, the early 16th-century **church of San Agustín** with a fine altar and paintings by Cabrera. It can be reached by bus or trolley bus from the Taxqueña metro station. The suburb of **Peña Pobre** is 2.5 km west, near which, to the northeast, is the **Pyramid of Cuicuilco** ⓘ *Insurgentes Sur Km 16 y Periférico, Tue-Sun 0800-1800*, believed to be the oldest in Mexico. It dates from the fifth or sixth century BC and is over 100 m in diameter but only 25 m high. There is an archaeological museum on site.

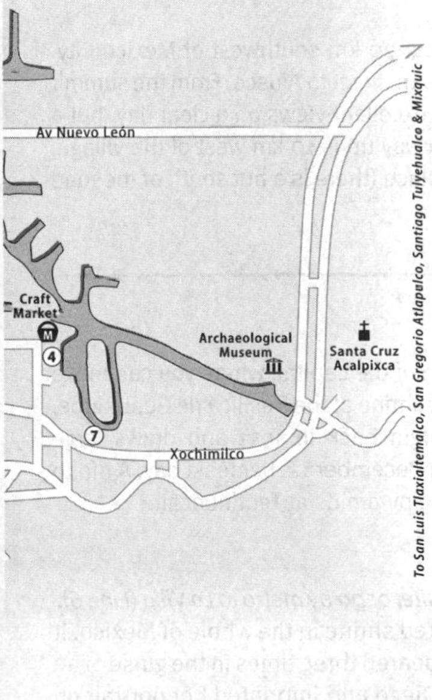

Xochimilco → *Colour map 3, B5.*

ⓘ *Easiest access is by bus,* colectivo *or metro to Metro Taxqueña, then* tren ligero *(about 20 mins). Get off at the last stop.*
Some 20 km to the southeast of the city centre, Xochimilco has many attractions, not least the fact that it lies in an unpolluted area. Meaning 'the place where flowers grow', Xochimilco was an advanced settlement long before the arrival of the Spaniards. Built on a lake, it developed a form of agriculture using *chinampas* (**floating gardens**); the area is still a major supplier of fruit and vegetables to Mexico City. The Spaniards recognized the importance of the region and the need to convert the indigenous population; evidence of this is the considerable number of 16th- and 17th-century religious buildings in Xochimilco itself and in the other 13 *pueblos* that make up the present-day *delegación*, or municipality.

Xochimilco is famous for its canals and colourful punt-like boats, *trajineras*, which bear girls' names. There are seven landing-stages, or *embarcaderos*, the largest of which are **Fernando Celada** and **Nuevo Nativitas** (the latter is a large craft market where most coachloads of tourists are set down). All are busy at weekends, especially Sunday afternoon. Official tariffs operate, although prices are sometimes negotiable; a boat taking six passengers costs US$5.75 per hour (a trip of at least 1½ hours is desirable); floating *mariachi* bands will charge US$3.50 per song, *marimba* groups US$1.50. There are reasonably priced tourist menus (lunch US$2) from passing boats or, even better, stock up with a picnic and beers before setting off.

The indisputable architectural jewel of Xochimilco is the church of **San Bernardino de Siena** (begun in 1535, completed 1595; magnificent Renaissance-style altarpiece, 1580-90) and its convent (circa 1585). The oldest Spanish-built religious edifice is the tiny **Capilla de San Pedro** (1530). Also worthy of mention are **Nuestra Señora de los Dolores de Xaltocán** (17th-century façade, 18th-century retable), **Santa Crucita Analco** and **San Juan Tlaltentli**. All are within walking distance of the centre of Xochimilco. For those interested in church architecture, the villages to the west, south and east of Xochimilco are worth visiting, all reachable by *colectivo* or bus from the centre of Xochimilco. In nearby **Míxquic**, famous for its **Día de los Muertos** (Day of the Dead) celebrations, the church of **San Andrés** (second quarter of 16th century; façade 1620; many alterations) was built on the site of an earlier temple using some of the original blocks, with traces of prehispanic designs.

Museo Dolores Olmedo Patiño ⓘ *Av México 5843 and Antiguo Camino a Xochimilco, 1 block southwest from La Noria tren ligero station, Tue-Sun 1000-1800, US$3, students US$1.50, T5555-1016, www.mdop.org.mx*, is highly recommended. It is set in 3 ha of beautiful garden and grassland on the site of an old estate, probably dating from the 16th century. Rare Mexican hairless dogs and peacocks parade through the grounds. The museum houses 137 works by Diego Rivera, 25 by Frida Kahlo, and an important collection of drawings by Angelina Beloff. There are also preispanic artefacts, 19th-century antiques and Mexican folk art. There is also a very pleasant open and covered café and a **tourist office** ⓘ *Pino 36, daily 0800-2100.*

Ajusco

Another excursion can be made to Ajusco, about 20 km southwest of Mexico City. Catch a bus from Estadio Azteca on Calzada Tlalpan direct to Ajusco. From the summit of the extinct **Volcán Ajusco** (3929 m) there are excellent views on a clear day, but a stroll through the foothills is also pleasant. The way up is 10 km west of the village, 400 m west of where the road branches to Xalatlaco (there is a hut south of the road where the path goes to the mountain).

North of the city centre

Another escape from the city centre heads north of the capital, where you can make your own pilgrimage to Mexico's most important shrine at the Basílica de Guadalupe. The site celebrates two apparitions of the Virgin back in 1531 and draws large numbers throughout the year, and especially on December 12, her feast day. A trip to the Basílica is easily combined with a visit to the pyramids at Teotihuacán.

Basílica de Guadalupe

ⓘ *US$3, buses marked 'La Villa' go close to the site, or go by metro to La Villa (Line 6).* The Basílica de Guadalupe is the most venerated shrine in the whole of Mexico. It was here, in December 1531, that the Virgin appeared three times in the guise of an indigenous princess to local *campesino* Juan Diego and imprinted her portrait on his cloak. The cloak is preserved, set in gold, but was moved into the new basilica next door as a massive crack had appeared down the side of the old building. The huge, modern basilica, completed in 1976, was designed by architect Pedro Ramírez Vázquez (who was also responsible for the Museo Nacional de Antropología). It's an impressive building and holds over 20,000 people (very crowded on Sunday) and an estimated 20 million pilgrims visit the shrine every year. The original basilica has been converted into a **museum**. It still houses the original magnificent altar, but otherwise mostly representations of the image on the cloak, plus interesting painted tin plates offering votive thanks for cures, etc from about 1860. A chapel stands over the well that gushed at the spot where the Virgin appeared. Indigenous dance groups provide entertainment in front of the basilica. There are, in fact, about seven churches in the immediate neighbourhood, including one on the hill above, the **Iglesia del Cerrito** (which has excellent views over the city); most of them are at crazy angles to each other and to the ground, because of subsidence. The **Templo de los Capuchinos** has been the subject of a remarkable feat of engineering in which one end has been raised 3.4 m so that the building is now horizontal.

Hundreds of thousands of people come from all over Mexico to celebrate the feast of La Virgen de Guadalupe, on 12 December.

Northern suburbs

The **pyramid of Tenayuca** ⓘ *daily 1000-1645, US$1.50*, 10 km to the northwest of the city centre, is about 15 m high and the best preserved in Mexico. The Aztecs rebuilt this temple every 52 years; this one was last reconstructed about 1507 and is well worth seeing, for it is surrounded with serpents in masonry. To get there, take the metro to the Terminal de Autobuses del Norte, La Raza, and catch the bus from there. By bus from Tlatelolco, ask the driver and passengers to advise you on arrival as the site is not easily visible. Not far from Tenayuca is the old town of **Tlalnepantla** where you can see the ancient convent (ask for the Catedral) on the Plaza Gustavo Paz, and the church (1583), which contains the first image, a Christ of Mercy, brought to the New World. The smaller pyramid of **Santa Cecilia Acatitlán** ⓘ *US$1.50*, which is interesting for its restored sanctuary, is 2.5 km to the north. It is difficult to find; head for the church tower visible from the footbridge over the highway.

These sites are only worth visiting if you are seriosly interested; it's a fair trek to reach them.

It **Naucalpan**, northwest of the city just outside the city boundary on Bulevar Toluca, pre-Classic Olmec-influenced figurines can be seen in the **Museo de la Cultura de Tlatilco** ⓘ *Tue-Sun*, opposite the **Hotel Naucalpan** on Vía Gustavo Paz. This is said to be the oldest settlement in the Cuenca de México; now a rather grim suburb.

Sleeping

Prices of the more expensive hotels do not normally include 15% tax; service is sometimes included. Always check in advance. Discounts are often available; breakfast is rarely included in the room price. There are hotel reservation services at the airpoRt and bus stations.

Centro Histórico

Zócalo *p87, map p94*

LL Gran Hotel de México, 16 de Septiembre 82, T/F5510-4040 to 47. Has an incredible foyer, 30s style, 4th-floor restaurant and balcony good for Zócalo-watching, especially on Sun morning (breakfast buffet US$10).

AL Majestic (Best Western), Madero 73 on Zócalo, T5521-8609. Interesting rooms, lots of tiles, carved wooden beams, large beds, quiet rooms overlook courtyard, magnificent breakfast in 7th-floor restaurant with excellent views of centre.

A Catedral, Donceles 95, behind cathedral, T5518-5232, www.hotelcatedral.com. Clean, spacious, good service. Recommended.

A Gillow, 5 de Mayo and Isabel la Católica 17, T5518-1440, www.hotelgillow.com. Central, large, clean, best rooms on 6th floor, many services, attractive, hospitable, good value, mediocre restaurant.
C Canadá, Av 5 de Mayo 47, T5518-2106. Smart place with bath, hot water, TV, a little overpriced but friendly and helpful.
C-D San Antonio, 2nd Callejón, 5 de Mayo 29, T5512-1625. Clean, pleasant, popular, friendly, TV in room. Recommended but get a receipt if staying for several days and paying in advance.
C-E Hostal Moneda, Moneda 8, 1 block east of the cathedral, T5522-5821, www.hostalmoneda.com.mx. Clean, friendly, safe and very good location. Happening meeting place, rooftop terrace used for serving great inclusive breakfasts with a beautiful view of the cathedral and other surrounding buildings. Free internet with a couple of machines, a wide range of ready to go tours and free city centre walking tour. Recommended.
D El Roble, Uruguay y Pino Suárez, 2 blocks south of the Zócalo. Bath, TV, restaurant closes early. Recommended.
D Hostel Catedral, Guatemala 4, T5518-1726, www.hostelcatedral.com. Hostel just behind the cathedral, 209 beds (private rooms and dorms), restaurant, kitchen, laundry, internet centre, secure storage, travel agency has booking service, great roof terrace and happy to accommodate late arrivals.
D Juárez, up a quiet alley off 5 de Mayo 17, 1-min walk from Zócalo, T5512-6929. Ask for room with window, safe, clean, with marble bathrooms (!), phone, radio, TV. Will hold bags, try to book in advance as often full. Great location near the Zócalo. Good budget choice. Highly recommended.
D Washington, Av 5 de Mayo 54, T5512-3502. Clean, small rooms, cable TV. A regular cheap hotel in the centre of town. Credit cards accepted. Euros changed.
D-E Rioja, Av 5 de Mayo 45, next door to Canadá, T5521-8333. Shared or private baths, reliable hot water, clean, popular, luggage store, well placed and recently remodelled. Normally recommended, but we have received a report of theft from rooms in the hotel – watch your gear just to be safe.
D-E Zamora, 5 de Mayo 50, T5512-1832. Generally ok, although the bathrooms a bit tired. Some big rooms which work out very cheap when more than 2 people.

North of the Zócalo *p89, map p94*
E Tuxpan, Colombia 11, near Brasil, T5526-1118. In the heart of a street market so a lively spot, but modern, clean, TV, hot showers and each room has a mirror on the ceiling!
E-F Río de Janeiro, Brasil 45l, near Colombia close to Plaza Santa Domingo, T5526-2905. Grubby, extremely basic. Probably cheapest in town. OK if money is really tight.

Zócalo to La Alameda *p93, map p94*
The best of the cheaper hotels are between the Zócalo and the Alameda.
C Buenos Aires, Av 5 de Mayo, T5518-2104. Safe, friendly, TV, stores luggage, hot water.
C Capitol, Uruguay 12, T5518-1750. Attractive lobby, recently remodelled, TV, bath, clean, friendly, don't miss the restaurant in the same building: **El Malecón**.
C Congreso, Allende 18, T5510-4446. With bath, hot water, good, central, clean, quiet, TV, garage.
C Habana, República de Cuba 77 (near Metro Allende), T5518-1589. Spacious rooms, huge beds, renovated, very clean, phone, TV, friendly and helpful staff. Can be noisy, but good location, good choice if you're looking to avoid the crowds. Highly recommended.
D Avenida, Lázaro Cárdenas 38 (Metro San Juan de Letrán), T5518-1007. With bath, central, friendly, will store luggage, good value, cheapest hotel that can be booked at airport. Recommended.
D Lafayette, Motolinia 40 and 16 de Septiembre, T5521-9640. With bath and TV, good, clean, quiet (pedestrian precinct), but check rooms, there's a variety of sizes.
D La Marina, Allende 30 y Blv Domínguez, T5518-2445. Clean, comfortable, safe, friendly, TV, hot water, will store luggage. Recommended.

***Phone code** Mexico City 55. For further telephone information see pages 56 and 82.*

D República, Cuba 57, T5512-9517. Wonderful old building, rooms a bit tired, but charming in a run-down way. With bath, hot water, rooms upstairs quieter. Recommended.
D-E Cuba, Cuba 69, T5518-1380. With bath, TV, good beds but some of the sheets too small.
D-E Isabel la Católica, Isabel la Católica 63, T5518-1213. Pleasant, popular, clean, helpful, safe (taxi drivers must register at desk before taking passengers), roof terrace, large shabby rooms with bath and hot water (some without windows), central, a bit noisy, quite good restaurant, luggage held, rooms on top floor with shared bathroom are cheaper. Recommended.

La Alameda *p93, map p94*
LL Sheraton Centro Histórico, Juárez 70, T5130-5300, www.sheratonmexico.com. Great site, overlooking the Alameda Central. Built on the site of the former **Hotel del Prado**, which collapsed in the 1985 earthquake; interesting collage of Diego Rivera murals.
L Cortés (Best Western), Av Hidalgo 85, T5518-2181, www.bestwestern.com. This is the only baroque-style hotel in Mexico City, a former pilgrims' guesthouse, with a pleasant patio, TV, good bathroom, no a/c or pool, quiet, good but touristy floor show, good food.
A San Francisco, Luis Moya 11, T5521-8960, just off Alameda. Great views, friendly, excellent value, takes credit cards, good set meals.
B Fleming, Revillagigedo 35, T5510-4530, www.hotelfleming.com.mx. Good value, central.
C Marlowe, Independencia 17, T5521-9540. Clean, modern, finished to a high standard, safe parking, lift, restaurant good but service is slow (tourist office at airport refers many travellers here – if this one is too expensive, the cheaper Concordia, see below, is round the corner).
D Danky, Donato Guerra 10, T5546-9960/61. With bath, central, hot water, phone, clean, easy parking. Recommended.
D-E Fornos, Revillagigedo 92, near Metro Balderas, 10 mins' walk to Alameda. Extremely clean, bathroom, TV, radio, restaurant, large indoor car park, friendly staff, Dutch-speaking Spanish owner, very good value. Highly recommended.
E Meave, Meave 6, esq Lázaro Cárdenas, T5521-6712. Bath, TV, clean, quiet, very friendly, ground-floor rooms rented by hour, but very discreet. Recommended.

North of La Alameda *p97, map p90*

D Nueva Estación, Zaragoza opposite Buenavista train station. With bath, clean, quiet, friendly, colour TV.
D Yale, Mosqueta 200, 5 mins' walk from Buenavista train station. Showers, toilet, large room with TV and phone, very good value. Recommended.

West of La Alameda *p97, map p90*

A fairly run-down part of town, but close to the working heart of the city.
A Jena, Jesús Terán 12, T5566-0277. New, central. Recommended (but not the travel agency on the premises).
B Mayaland, Maestro Antonio Caso 23, T5566-6066. Very clean rooms, with bath, good value, good restaurant. Recommended.
B Palace, Ignacio Ramírez 7, T5566-2400. Very friendly, good restaurant.
C Oxford, Ignacio Mariscal 67, T5566-0500. Very clean, radio and satellite TV, helpful, but short stay.
C Texas, Ignacio Mariscal 129, T5564-4626. With bath, clean, hot water, small rooms, good breakfasts.
D Detroit, Zaragoza 55, T5591-1088. Hot shower, central, clean, has parking.
D Mina, José T Salgado 18, esq Mina, T5703-1682. Modern, clean, TV, large beds.
D Monaco Guerrero 12, T5566-8333. Comfortable, TV, modern, good service.
D Royalty, Jesús Terán 21, opposite **Hotel Jena**. With bath, TV, clean, very quiet, near Metro Hidalgo.
D-E Frimont, Jesús Terán 35, T5705-4169. Clean and central, with good views from rooms up on the 5th floor. Good, cheap restaurant.
D-F Casa de los Amigos, Ignacio Mariscal 132, T5705-0521, near Metro Revolución, www.casadelosamigos.org. Dormitory, slightly more in a double room, pay 2 nights in advance, use of kitchen, maximum 15-day stay, separation of sexes, run by

Quakers for Quakers, or development-work-related travellers; other travellers taken only if space is available, good information on volunteer work, travel and language schools, breakfast and laundry facilities on roof, safe-keeping for luggage, English library; advance booking advisable. Recommended.

E Carlton, Ignacio Mariscal 32-bis, T5566-2911. Getting rough around the edges, small rooms but some with fine views, rooms at front noisy, good restaurant. Recommended.

E El Paraíso, Ignacio Mariscal 99, T5566-8077. Hot water, clean, private bath, TV, phone, recently renovated. Friendly.

Paseo de la Reforma and Zona Rosa *p98, map p98*

LL Imperial, Reforma 64, T5705-4911. Very good, restaurant, café, bar, 24-hr service, all business facilities.

LL NH México, Liverpool 155, T5228-9928. Www.nh-hotels.com. Good hotel, aimed at the North American business traveller. Recommended.

LL Royal Zona Rosa, Amberes 78, T5228-9918, www.hotelesroyal.com.mx. A good Spanish hotel with fine suites ideal for both businesspeople and holiday-makers.

AL María Cristina, Lerma 31, T5566-9688. Attractive colonial style, comfortable, helpful, safe parking. Recommended.

A Prim, Versalles 46, T5592-4600, www.hotelprim.com.mx. Clean, good in all respects.

A Viena, Marsella 28 (close to Juárez market and Metro Cuauhtémoc), T5566-0700. Quiet, Swiss decor, garage, dining room. Recommended.

C Casa González, Lerma y Sena 69 (near British Embassy), T5514-3302. Full board available, shower, clean, quiet and friendly, English spoken by Sr González, no credit cards. Recommended.

C Parador Washington, Dinamarca 42 y Londres. With bath, clean, safe area, café next door.

C Uxmal, Madrid 13, quite close to Zona Rosa. Clean rooms, same owner as more expensive **Madrid** next door (**AL**). With access to their better facilities. Recommended.

D-E Mansión Havre, Havre 40, T5533-1271, mansionhavre@hotmail.com. Good hostel with dorm rooms, kitchen and small balcony.

Apartments

Suites Amberes, Amberes 64, Zona Rosa, T5533-1306. Kitchenette, good value.

Suites Havre, Havre 74, T5533-5670,near Zona Rosa. 56 suites with kitchen, phone and service. Recommended for longer stays.

Bosque de Chapultepec and Polanco *p99, map p100*

LL Presidente Intercontinental, Campos Elíseos 218, overlooking Chapultepec Park, T5327-7700, www.interconti.com. Ideal hotel for business and pleasure.

Insurgentes Sur *p104, map p87*

E Hostel Home, Tabasco 303, Col Roma, T5511-1683, www.hostelhome.com.mx. Great little hostel with the cleanliness and services you expect (kitchen, friendly staff, dormitory accommodation) in a quiet part of town without the numbers at hostels in the Centro Histórico.

Apartments

A Hotel Suites del Parque, Dakota 155, Col Nápoles, T5536-1450, hotelsuitesdelparque@prodigy.net.mx Extremely spacious suites, usual amenities, price good for up to 4 people, very convenient for the World Trade Center (across the street), good restaurant. Any length of stay.

South of the city centre *p105, map p106*

AL Suites Coyoacán, Av Coyoacán 1909, Col del Valle T5534-8353, suitescoyoacan@mexis.com. One of the few hotels in the area with a restaurant, catering facilities and gym.

Apartments

Suites Quinta Palo Verde, Cerro del Otate 20, Col Romero de Terreros, México 21 DF, T5554-3575. Pleasant, diplomatic residence turned guesthouse, near the University; run by a veterinary surgeon, Miguel Angel, very friendly, speaks English and German, but the dogs are sometimes noisy.

North of the city centre *p110, map p87*

B Brasilia, near Terminal del Norte bus station, on Av Cien Metros 48-25, T5587-8577. Excellent modern hotel, king-size bed, TV. 24-hr traffic jam in front.
C La Villa de los Quijotes, Moctezuma 20, near Basílica de Guadalupe (Metro La Villa), T5577-1088. Modern, quiet, clean, expensive restaurant.

Elsewhere *map p87*

AL JR Plaza, Blv Puerto Aéreo 390, T5785-5200, www.hoteljrplaza.com. Free airport transport, expensive restaurant, quiet, good rooms with solid furniture, close to metro.

Youth hostels and campsites

Asociación Mexicana de Albergues de la Juventud, Madero 6, Oficina 314, México 1, DF. Write for information.
Comisión Nacional del Deporte (Condep), runs the **Villas Deportivas Juveniles** (see below); information office at Glorieta del Metro Insurgentes, Local C-11, T5525-2916. Condep will make reservations for groups of 10 or more; to qualify you must be between 8 and 65 and have a *Tarjeta Plan Verde* membership card, US$6, valid for 2 years, obtainable within 24 hrs from office at Tlalpan 583, esq Soria, Metro Xola, or a IYHF card.

See also **SETEJ**, page 85, for information on hotels and other establishments offering lodging for students.

For the nearest camping, see **Tepozotlán**, page 137, and the road to **Toluca**, page 142.

Eating

All the best hotels have good restaurants. The number and variety of eating places is vast; this is only a small selection.

Centro Histórico

Zócalo *p87, map p94*

₸₸₸ Centro Catalán, Bolívar 31, open 1100-1700 only. Excellent paella and other Spanish cuisine (2nd floor).
₸₸₸ El Café, 5 de Mayo 23, close to the Zócalo. Very good restaurant.
₸₸₸ La Casa de las Sirenas, Tacuba y Seminario, behind the cathedral. Mexican menu, fantastic selection of tequilas. Excellent food and service. Recommended.
₸₸₸ Mesón del Castellano, Bolívar y Uruguay, T5518-6080. Good atmosphere, plentiful and not too dear, excellent steaks. Daytime only. Recommended.
₸₸ Centro Castellano, Uruguay. Excellent, cheap, try the steaks.
₸₸ Los Girasoles, corner of Tacuba and Gante. Mexican cuisine, adds a cover charge of US$1.20, which is not mentioned in the menu. Reasonable food.
₸ Maple, Uruguay 109, next to **Hotel Roble**. Recommended for its *comida*.
₸ Mariscos, República de Uruguay, opposite No 28. Bustling lunch stop, good seafood meals and fish soup.
₸ Nadja, Mesones 65, near Pino Suárez. Typical food, set menu for US$1.30, large portions, friendly. Recommended.
₸ Pancho Uruguay 84. Recommended for its breakfasts, cheap meals and service.
₸ Restaurante Vegetariano, Filomeno Mata 13, open until 2000, Sun 0900-1900. Good and cheap *menú del día*.
₸ Shakey's, Monte de Piedad (at the Zócalo). Self-service, large helpings of pizza and chicken.
₸ Zenón, corner of Madero 65 and Palma. Trendy decor, average Mexican food, cheap *comida corrida*.

Cafés and bakeries

El 20 de Bolívar, Bolívar 20. Excellent service and highly recommended for breakfasts.
Pastelería Madrid, 5 de Febrero 25, 1 block from **Hotel Isabel la Católica**. Good pastries and breakfasts.
Rex, 5 de Febrero 40, near Zócalo. Good *café con leche* and cheap *comidas*.

North of the Zócalo *p89, map p94*

₸₸₸ Hostería Santo Domingo, 70 and 72 Belisario Domínguez, 2 blocks west of Plaza Santo Domingo, T5510-1612. Oldest restaurant in town with former diners creating a who's who of Mexican history. Good food and service and excellent live music.

ꝑ **Comida Económica Verónica**, República de Cuba, 2 doors from **Hotel Habana** (No 77). For tasty breakfasts and set *comida corrida*, very hot *chilaquiles*, good value and delightful staff. Recommended. Closed Sun.

Zócalo to La Alameda *p93, map p94*

ꝑꝑꝑ **Bar La Opera**, 5 de Mayo near Bellas Artes, T5512-8959. Mon-Sat 1300-0000, Sun 1300-1800. One of the city's most elegant watering holes, open since 1870. Relaxing atmosphere, Mexican appetizers and entrées, and an expensive drinks list. And the bullet hole in the ceiling was left by Mexican revolutionary hero Pancho Villa, allegedly.

ꝑꝑꝑ **Café Tacuba**, Tacuba 28. A very old restaurant with stunning tile decor, not touristy and specializing in Mexican food. Very good *enchiladas*, excellent meat dishes, *tamales* and fruit desserts although portions are a little small and service a bit slow, live music and mariachis, very popular with local business people. It's also where renowned Mexican politician, Danilo Fabio Altamirano, was assassinated in 1936. Expensive but recommended.

ꝑꝑꝑ **Sanborn's Casa de los Azulejos**, Av Madero 17. Known as the foreigners' home-from-home, **Sanborn's** has 36 locations in Mexico, with soda fountain, drugstore, restaurant, English, German and Spanish-language magazines, handicrafts, chocolates, etc. This, the most famous branch, is in the 16th-century the 'house of tiles'. Service can be poor, but there are many delicious local dishes in beautiful high-ceilinged room, with Orozco mural on staircase. About US$10-15 per person without wine (also has handicraft shops).

ꝑꝑ **El Patio del Gaucho**, Uruguay. Moderate prices, attentive, good *asado*. Recommended.

ꝑꝑ **Sushi Roll**, 5 de Mayo and Filomeno Mata, about 5 blocks west of the Zócalo. Large selection of sushi rolls, very good.

ꝑꝑ-ꝑ **Café El Popular**, 5 de Mayo 52, on corner of alley to **Hotel Juárez**. Cheap, rushed, open 24 hrs, good meeting place.

ꝑ **Gili's Pollo**, 5 de Mayo, opposite **Hotel Rioja**. Excellent chicken, eat in or takeaway, cheap, filling and friendly

ꝑ **París**, 5 de Mayo 10. Good breakfast and dinner.

ꝑ **Super Soya**, Tacuba, Metro Allende. Good juices and fruit salads, health food shop.

ꝑ **Torta Brava**, 5 de Mayo, near Zócalo. Good *comida*, friendly.

Cafés, bakeries and sweet shops

Café La Blanca, 5 de Mayo 40. Popular and busy atmosphere, good expresso coffee, open for Sun breakfast and early on weekdays. Recommended.

Dulcería de Celaya, 5 de Mayo 39. Famous traditional (and expensive), hand-made candy store in lovely old premises.

Panadería La Vasconia, Tacuba 73. Good bread, also sells cheap chicken and fries.

La Alameda *p93, map p94*

ꝑꝑ **Trevi**, Dr Mora y Colón (west end of Alameda). Italian/US/Mexican, reasonable prices.

ꝑ **Dinastía Lee**, Independencia y Dolores. Reasonable Chinese food, 0800-2400.

ꝑ **Mr Lee**, Independencia 19-B. Chinese, seafood, good food, value and service.

Cafés

Bamerette, Av Juárez 52 (**Hotel Bamer**). Excellent breakfast, and a fine spot to watch the world go by.

West of La Alameda *p97, map p90*

ꝑꝑ **La Habana**, Bucareli y Morelos. Not cheap but good food and famed for its excellent coffee and *banderilla* pastries. A great place for breakfast.

ꝑ **El Sol**, Gómez Farías 67, Col San Rafael. Frequented by journalists, superb Mexican cuisine and *comida corrida*.

Paseo de la Reforma and Zona Rosa *p98, map p98*

ꝑꝑꝑ **Cardenal**, Palma 23. Food, service and music (from 1530) is outstanding, 1930s ambience.

ꝑꝑꝑ **Carousel Internacional**, Hamburgo and Niza, Zona Rosa. Very popular drinking-hole for smartly dressed Mexicans, resident *mariachi*, food not gourmet but fun atmosphere.

ꝑꝑꝑ **Chalet Suizo**, Niza 37. Very popular with tourists, specializes in Swiss and German food.

ꝑꝑꝑ **Karl**, on Amberes near junction Londres. Excellent vegetarian buffet lunch and dinner.

TTT La Costa Azul, López 127 y Delicias. Central, good, stark lighting, reasonable prices.

TTT Le Gourmet, Dakota 155. French cuisine and said to be the most expensive restaurant in Mexico, and also said to be worth it!

TTT Milomita, Mesones 87, Centro, 0800-2000. Specializes in American cuts of meat.

TTT Sir Winston Churchill, Avila Camacho 67. Serves British food, smart and popular.

TT Keops, Hamburgo 146, near Amberes in Zona Rosa, T5525-6706. Reasonable food, good, live music.

TT La Puerta del Angel, Varsovia y Londres. Local food and specializing in American cuts, very good.

T El Huequito, Bolívar 58. Casual, friendly, cheap meals for US$2.

T Yug, Varsovia 3. Vegetarian, 4-course set lunch US$3.50. Health food shop.

Cafés

Duca d'Este, Av Florencia y Hamburgo. Good coffee and pastries.

El Núcleo, Lerma y Marne. Excellent fruit salads, breakfasts and lunches, closes 1800 and all day Sun.

Bosque de Chapultepec and Polanco *p99, map p100*

TTT Cambalache, Arquimedes north of Presidente Masaryk. Argentine steakhouse, good steaks, wide selection of wines, cosy atmosphere.

TTT Charlotte´s, Lope de Vega 341, north of Horacio. Serves finest English and international cuisine, also stunningly inventive dishes.

TTT El Buen Comer Marcelín, Edgar Allan Poe 50, T5203-5337. Mainly French, very good.

TTT Fisher's, Taine 311, Polanco. Superb seafood, not expensive considering the quality and presentation. No reservations accepted.

TTT La Parrilla Suiza, Arquimedes y Presidente Masaryk. For grilled meats, *alambres*, *sopa de tortilla* and other meat-and-cheese dishes, very popular, especially 1400-1600, service fair.

TT Chilango's, Molière between Ejército Nacional and Homero. Good value and service, MTV videos. Recommended.

TT Embers, Séneca y Ejército Nacional. 43 types of excellent hamburger, good French fries. Recommended.

T El Jarocho, Homero between Emerson and Hegel. Informal, eat-at-counter place.

South of the city centre

Insurgentes Sur *p104, map p87*

TT La Bodeguita del Medio, Cozumel 37, Condesa, T5553-0246. Cuban bar covered in graffiti, very good *mojitos*.

TT La Cava, Insurgentes Sur 2465. Excellent food and steaks, lavishly decorated as an old French tavern.

Cafés

Enanos de Tapanco y Café, Orizaba 161, between Querétaro and San Luis Potosí. Great coffee, warm friendly atmosphere.

Gaby's, Liverpool y Nápoles. Excellent Italian-style coffee, decor of old coffee machines.

Il Mangiare, opposite Poliforum Cultural Siqueiros (see page 104). Very good sandwiches.

Roxy, Montes de Oca y Mazatlán, Col Condesa. Good ice cream.

San Angel *p105, map p87*

TTT San Angel Inn, Diego Rivera 50, T5616-2222, www.sanangelinn.com Mon-Sat 1230-0030, Sun 1300-2130. Top-quality dining in the former Carmelite monastery. If you can't afford a meal, it's worth going for a drink.

Coyoacán *p105, map p106*

There are several pleasant *cafeterías* in the Jardín Centenario, some of which serve light snacks and *antojitos*.

TTT Caballocalco, Plaza Hidalgo. Expensive, but very good, especially for breakfast.

TTT El Jolgorio, tucked away down Higuera, opposite the post office. Excellent lunch menu, reasonable set-meal prices, good salads and vegetarian dishes.

TTT Mesón Antiguo Santa Catarina, delightfully situated restaurant in the square of the same name. Good Mexican cuisine at reasonable prices, splendid atmosphere, especially for breakfast or supper.

TTT Pacífico, Av Pacífico, in restored 19th-century residence. Specialities include prehispanic dishes, good value.

ΨΨΨ-ΨΨ **Hacienda de Cortés**, Fernández Leal 74, behind Plaza de la Conchita, T5659-3741, www.haciendadecortes.com.mx. Exceptionally pleasant surroundings, large shaded outdoor dining area, excellent breakfast, good value *comida corrida* US$5, try the *sábana de res con chilaquiles verdes*. Come at the weekend (book in advance) and see the heart of Mexican family life.

ΨΨ **Vegetariano**, Carranza y Caballocalco. Offers an excellent buffet lunch.

ΨΨ-Ψ **El Morral**, Allende 2. Set lunch, good Mexican food, handmade tortillas, price doubles at weekends, no credit cards, quieter upstairs, palatial lavatories. Highly recommended.

ΨΨ-Ψ **La Guadalupana**, Higuera and Caballocalco, a few steps behind the church of San Juan Bautista in the centre of Coyoacán, T5554-6253. Mon-Sat 0900-2300. One of the best-known *cantinas* in Mexico, dating from 1932, fantastic food and a great atmosphere and no apologies for the passionate interest in bull fighting.

Ψ **Fabio's**, overlooking Plaza Hidalgo and the Delegación. Good *comida corrida*, credit cards accepted.

Ψ **Mercado**, between Malintzin and Xicoténcatl, opposite Jardín del Carmen. Exquisite *quesadillas* at Local 31, outside try the seafood at **El Jardín del Pulpo** if you can get a seat. Fruit and vegetable sellers are ready to explain the names and uses of their goods; frequent musical entertainment particularly lunchtime and weekends.

Ψ **Rams**, Hidalgo, almost opposite Museo Nacional de las Culturas Populares. Excellent fish, very-good value *comida corrida*.

Cafés, bakeries and ice creams

Como a La Antigua, Allende 14, just past the Foro Cultural Hugo Argüelles. Very fine home-made pastries.

Xochimilco *p109, map p108*

Ψ **Beto's**, opposite Fernando Celada. Good, clean and cheap restaurant, US$2 for lunch.

Ψ **Restaurante del Botas**, Pino, to the left of the cathedral. First-rate cheap lunch (US$2).

Bars and clubs

Nightlife in Mexico City is as lively and varied as everything else the city has to offer. From gentle supper clubs with floorshows to loud, brash nightclubs, and from piano bars to *antros* (or disco-bars) and bars that offer traditional Mexican music – all tastes are catered for. The most popular districts are Condesa, Roma, Zona Rosa, Polanco, San Angel and Coyoacán. You can go for a drink at any time, clubbing starts late with most just getting going by midnight. Prices of drinks and admission vary enormously depending on the area. Remember that, because of the high altitude, 1 alcoholic drink in Mexico City can have the effect of 2 at lower altitudes. Many bars and nightclubs are closed on Sun.

Centro Histórico *p86, map p94*

Bar Mata, Filomeno Mata 11, Alameda Central, T5518-0237, Thu-Sat. On the 4th and 5th floors of a colonial building near Palacio de Bellas Artes. Atmosphere conducive to dancing and mingling, especially in the rooftop (5th-floor) bar, with great views of the city at night.

La Perla, República de Cuba 44. Seedy but popular little club in the centre, Thu-Sat 2000-0400, US$4.

Salón Corona, Bolívar, betwen Madero and 16 de Septiembre. Big, basic bar full of locals (and watching visitors). Good atmosphere. Closes around midnight.

North of La Alameda *p97, map p94*

Salón México, 25 Callejón de San Juan, Col Guerrero, T5518-0931. Spectacular dance hall built in a converted factory.

Paseo de la Reforma and Zona Rosa *p98, map p98*

Casa Rasta, Insurgentes 149, T5705-0086, Thu-Sat from 2200. US$20 for men, US$5 for women, but with free bar. For reggae lovers.

El Colmillo, Versailles 52, T5553-0262, Wed-Sat from 2200. Attracting a young, chic crowd, techno music downstairs and an exclusive jazz bar upstairs.
El Taller, Florencia and Reforma, Tue-Sun, 2200. Underground gay bar, one of the first in Mexico City.
Yuppie's Sports Café, Génova 34, Zona Rosa, T5208-2267, daily 1300-0100. Good Tex-Mex and American-style fare in a pub with every corner adorned with sports memorabilia, TVs broadcast games from Mexico and around the world.

Bosque de Chapultepec and Polanco *p99, map p100*
Barfly, Plaza Mazarik Mall, T5282-2906, Tue-Sat from 2000. Cosy bar with small dance floor and Cuban dance bands from 2300.
Mezzanote, Masaryk 407, T5282-0130, daily from 1400. Art nouveau decor, ideal for drinking, dining or dancing, especially later in the night. Franchise from the original in Miami, frequented by thirty-somethings.

Insurgentes Sur *p104, map p87*
La Bodeguita del Medio, Cozumel 37, T5553-0246. Extremely popular Cuban bar-cum-restaurant where drinks like *mojitos* became famous, and graffiti an art form.

Mamá Rumba, Querétaro 230 and Medellín, Col Roma, T5564-6920. One of the first places in Mexico City with Cuban rhythms, famous for its *rumba*, now with a couple of floors. Live music Thu-Sat from 2300. Also a new branch opened in San Angel (T5550-8099) with live music Wed-Sat from 2100. Get there early, it gets packed. US$6.
Meneo, Nueva York 315, T5523-9448, Thu-Sat. Modern dance hall for live salsa and merengue, with 2 dance floors.
Metal Night Club, Insurgentes Sur 226, Roma, T5511-4460, Fri-Sat from 2000. Gay bar with house, pop and progressive music.
Rexo, Saltillo 1 and Nuevo León, Condesa, T5553-5337, daily from 1330. Restaurant-bar with Mediterranean food, one of the most fancied places in the area.

Coyoacán *p105, map p106*
El Hijo del Cuervo, Jardín Centenario 17, Coyoacán, T5658-5306, daily 1300-0000. Small cover (up to US$7) depending on show. Attracting students and hip intellectuals of all ages for an interesting mix of rock and *nueva canción*, and the occasional theatre show.
La Guadalupana, Higuera and Caballocalco, see Eating, page 118.

Entertainment

For all cultural events, consult *Tiempo Libre*, every Thu from newsstands, US$1, or monthly programmes from Bellas Artes bookshop.

Cinema

A number show non-Hollywood films in original language (Spanish subtitles); check *Tiempo Libre* magazine for details. Most cinemas, except **Cineteca Nacional**, offer reduced prices on Wed.
Cine Diana, Av Reforma, at the end where Parque Chapultepec starts.
Cine Electra, Río Guadalquivir (near El Angel).
Cine Latino, Av Reforma between the statue of Cuauhtémoc and El Angel.
Cine Palacio Chino, in the Chinese *barrio* *south of Av Juárez (also interesting for restaurants).*
Cine Versalles, Versalles (side street off Av Reforma, near statue of Cuauhtémoc).
Cinematógrafo del Chopo, Dr Atl, non-commercial films daily 1700 and 1930.
Cineteca Nacional, Metro Coyoacán (excellent bookshop on the cinema and related topics, library).
Ciudad Universitaria, the Centro Cultural has a good cinema.

Theatre

Centro Histórico *p86, map p94*
Palacio de Bellas Artes (for Ballet Folklórico, opera and classical concerts, see page 93).
Teatro la Blanquita, Av Lázaro Cárdenas

Sur near Plaza Garibaldi. Variety show nightly with singers, dancers, comedians, magicians and ventriloquists, very popular with locals. **Teatro de la Ciudad**, Donceles 36, T5510-2197, has the Ballet Folklórico Nacional Aztlán, US$3-US$15 for tickets, very good shows Sun morning and Wed.

Bosque de Chapultepec and Polanco *p99, map p100.*
Auditorio Nacional, Paseo de la Reforma, Chapultepec. Major concerts and spectaculars (eg presidential inauguration) are often staged here. There are a couple of theatres behind the Auditorio (check at tourist office for details of programmes).

Insurgentes Sur *p104, map p87.*
Teatro de los Insurgentes, south of the centre.

Coyoacán *p105, map p106.*
Coyoacán has several small and medium-sized theatres, for example the **Teatro Coyoacán** and **Teatro Usigli**, Eleuterio Méndez, 5 blocks from Metro General Anaya; the **Foro Cultural de Coyoacán**, Allende (most events free of charge); the **Museo Nacional de Culturas Populares**, Hidalgo; the **Foro Cultural Ana María Hernández**, Pacífico 181, the **Teatro Santa Catarina**, Plaza Santa Catarina, the **Teatro Rafael Solana**, Miguel Angel de Quevedo (nearly opposite Caballocalco, the **Casa del Teatro**, Vallarta 31; and **Foro de la Conchita**, Vallarta 33.

Also note **El Hábito**, Madrid, and **El Hijo del Cuervo**, Jardín Centenario, for avant-garde drama and cabaret; **Los Talleres de Coyoacán**, Francisco Sosa, for dance and ballet; **CADAC**, Centenario, for traditional and experimental drama.

On the edge of the Delegación Coyoacán, at the southeast corner of Churubusco and Tlalpan (Metro General Anaya) is the **Central Nacional de las Artes**, a huge complex of futuristic buildings dedicated to the training and display of the performing and visual arts. It has a good bookshop, library and *cafeterías*.

Ciudad Universitaria *map p87*
Teatro Universitario at the UNAM's Centro Cultural (see p107).

Festivals and events

15 Sep, **Independence** celebration; largest in the capital when the President gives the *Grito*: 'Viva México' from the Palacio Nacional on the Zócalo at 2300, and rings the Liberty Bell (now, sadly, electronic!). This is followed by fireworks. Just as much fun, and probably safer, is the *Grito* that takes place at the same time in the Plaza in Coyoacán.
16 Sep, military and traditional regional **Independence parades** in the Zócalo and surrounding streets, 0900-1400, great atmosphere.
12 Dec, **Guadalupana** at the Basílica de Guadalupe, definitely worth a visit if you're in town (see page 110).

Shopping

Art and handicrafts

Fonart, Fondo Nacional para el Fomento de las Artesanías, a state organization founded in 1974 in order to rescue, promote and diffuse the traditional crafts of Mexico. Main showroom at Av Patriotismo 594 (Metro Mixcoac), T5598-1666, and a branch at Av Juárez 89 (Metro Hidalgo). Competitive prices, superb quality.
Mercado de Artesanías Finas Indios Verdes, Galería Reforma Norte SA, González Bocanegra 44 (corner of Reforma Norte, near statue of Cuitláhuac, Tlatelolco). Good prices and quality but no bargaining.
Uriarte, Emilio Castelar 95-E, Polanco,

T5282-2699, and Pabellón Altavista, Calzada Desierto de los Leones 52 D-6, San Angel, T5616-3119, www.talavera.com. For Talavera pottery from Puebla.

There are many gift shops in **Coyoacán**: **Mayolih**, Aldama with Berlín, 2 blocks from Museo Frida Kahlo; and **La Casita** on Higuera.

Books, posters and music

American Bookstore, Madero 25, also on Revolución (5-min bus ride south from Metro Barranca del Muerte) large stocks of Penguins and Pelicans, low mark-up.

Casa Libros, Monte Athos 355, Lomas, large stock of second-hand English books, the shop is staffed by volunteers, gifts of books welcome, all proceeds to the American Benevolent Society.

El Parnaso, Jardín Centenario, Coyoacán, is one of the most famous bookshops in Mexico City (its coffee is equally well known).

Fondo de Cultura Económico, Miguel Angel de Quevedo. Inexpensive editions in Spanish.

Gandhi has several shops with a large selection and keen prices. Large branches on MA de Quevedo, another opposite Palacio de Bellas Artes. Also has good range of music excellent prices.

John Gibbs Publications, T/F 5658-5376, www.johngibbs.com. Supplies fine art posters, including images by Diego Rivera and Frida Kahlo, to the city's principal museums and bookshops.

La Torre de Papel, Filomeno Mata 6-A, in Club de Periodistas, sells newspapers from all over Mexico and US.

Librería del Sótano, several branches: Av Juárez, Antonio Caso, MA de Quevedo). Inexpensive editions in Spanish.

Libros y Arte is a good chain of literary and art bookshops with branches in the Palacio de Bellas Artes, the airport (area D), the Centro Nacional de Las Artes, the Cineteca Nacional, Coyoacán (Av Hidalgo), Museo del Carmen (San Angel) and the Museo Nacional de las Culturas (Moneda 13, Centro).

Librería Madero, Madero 12, Centro. Good, stocks antiquarian books.

Sanborn's chain has the largest selection of English-language magazines in the country and stocks some best-selling paperbacks in English.

Second-hand book market, Independencia just past junction with Eje Lázaro Cárdenas. Has some English books; also Puente de Alvarado, 100 m from Metro Hidalgo, and Dr Bernard 42, Metro Niños Héroes. Second-hand Spanish and antiquarian booksellers on Donceles between Palma and República de Brasil, about 1½ blocks from Zócalo.

UNAM bookshop, Ciudad Universitaria. Has a comprehensive range of books in Spanish.

Clothing and accessories

Mexican jewellery and handmade silver can be bought everywhere. Among the good silver shops are **Sanborn's**, **Calpini**, **Prieto**, and **Vendome**.

Joyería Sobre Diseño, Local 159, at the Ciudadela market. Helpful and will produce personalized jewellery cheaply. There are also good buys in perfumes, quality leather and suede articles.

Many small tailors are found in and around República de Brasil; suits made to measure in a week or less at a fraction of European prices. Also many off-the-peg tailors, eg **Beleshini**, Juárez 12, opposite the Palacio de Bellas Artes.

At Metro Pino Suárez are several shops selling *charro* clothing and equipment (leggings, boots, spurs, bags, saddles, etc), eg **Casa Iturriaga**. Recommended.

Cycle shops

Benolto, near Metro Polanco, stocks almost all cycle spares.

Escuela Médico Militar, near Metro Pino Suárez, has a very good shop, stocking all the best-known international makes for spare parts.

Hambling González Muller, Ezequiel Ordóñez 46-1, Col Copilco el Alto, Coyoacán, T/F5658-5591. The best cycle repair in Mexico City. Builds wheels and frames for Mexican racers, reasonable prices, highly recommended.

Tecno-Bici, Av Manuel Acuña 27 (Metro Camarones, line 7), stocks almost all cycle spares, parts. Highly recommended.

Markets

Bazar del Sábado, San Angel (page 105). Although expensive, many items are exclusive to it; good leather belts, crafts and silver; Sat only from about 1100.

Buena Vista craft market, Aldama 187 y Degollado (Metro Guerrero. Excellent quality. Mon-Sat 0900-1800, Sun 0900-1400.
La Ciudadela, Mercado Central de Artesanías, beside Balderas 95 between Ayuntamiento y Plaza Morelos. Mon-Sat 1100-1800, Sun 1100-1400. Government-sponsored, fixed prices, good selection, reasonable and uncrowded, is cheaper than San Juan, but not for leather; craftworkers from all Mexico have set up workshops here (best for papier mâché, lacquer, pottery and Guatemalan goods), but prices are still cheaper in places of origin.
Mercado Insurgentes, Londres, Zona Rosa. Good for silver, but other things expensive, stallholders pester visitors, only place where they do so.
Mercado Jamaica, Metro Jamaica, line 4. Has a huge variety of fruits and vegetables, also flowers, pottery, canaries, parrots, geese, and ducks, indoor and outdoor halls.
Mercado La Lagunilla, near Glorieta Cuitláhuac (take *colectivo* from Metro Hidalgo). A flea market covering several blocks where antique and collectable bargains are sometimes to be found, also a lot of rubbish. Open daily, but Sun best day. Good atmosphere, watch your bag.
Mercado Merced (page 92), Metro Merced. Vast general market.
Mercado San Juan, Ayuntamiento and Arandas, near Metro Salto del Agua. Good prices for handicrafts, especially leather goods and silver (also cheap fruit and health food). Mon-Sat 0900-1900, Sun 0900-1600 (don't go before 1000).
Mercado Sonora, secret potions and remedies, animals and birds as well as *artesanías*.
Tianguis del Chopo, Aldama, No 211, between Sol and Luna. Sat 1000-1600. Clothes, records, etc, frequented by hippies, punks, rockers and police.

Photography

Foto Regis, Balderas 32, 4th floor, T5521-5010, www.fotoregis.com Good service on a range of makes including Canon, Minolta, Pentax, Hasselblad, Konica and Leica. Reasonably priced as well. Mon-Fri 0900-1800, Sat 0900-1400. Also provides good-quality, reliable development at shop on Juárez 80, T5521-0346.

▲ Activities and tours

Hiking

At weekend with Alpino and Everest clubs.
Club Alpino Mexicano, Coahuila 40 esq Córdoba, Roma, T5574-9683 , T/F5574-9683, www.clubalpinomexicano.com.mx, small shop (if club door is closed ask here for access). Helpful, also arranges (free) mountain hiking at weekends, runs ice climbing courses.
Club de Exploraciones de México, Juan A Mateos 146, Col Obrero (Metro Chabacano), DF 06800, T5740-8032, www.cemac.org.mx, Wed and Fri 1930-2200, organizes several walks in and around the city on Sat and Sun, cheap equipment hire.

Supplies and repairs

Deportes Rubens, Venustiano Carranza 17, T5518-5636. Supplies equipment.
Servicio Coleman, Marqués Sterling 23. Stove repairs.
Vertimania, Federico T de la Chica 12, Plaza Versailles, Local 11-B, Col Satélite, T/F5393-5287. Supplies equipment.

Spectator sports

Football

Estadio Azteca, south of the City. Sun 1200. To get to the Aztec Stadium take metro to Taxqueña terminus, then tram en route to Xochimilco to Estadio station; about 75 mins from Zócalo.

Horse races

Hipódromo de las Américas, west of Blv Avila Camacho, off Av Conscriptos, www.hipodromo.com.mx. Beautiful track with infield lagoons and flamingoes, and plenty of atmosphere. Incorporates exhibition and convention centre.

Tour operators

Shop around as prices vary considerably, although deals regularly available in Europe or the USA are rare or impossible to find. If possible, use a travel agent that has been recommended to you, as not all are efficient or reliable.

American Express, Reforma 234 y Havre, T5533-0380. Mon-Fri 0900-1800, Sat 0900-1300. Service slow but helpful.

Corresponsales de Hoteles, Blv Centro 224-4, T5360-3356, www.corresponsales.com.mx. For hotel reservations (upmarket).

Grey Line Tours, Londres 166, T5208-1163. Reasonably priced tours, car hire, produces *This is Mexico* book (free).

Hivisa Viajes, Río Támesis 5, Col Cuauhtémoc, T5703-0911, www.hivisaviajes.com.mx. One of the most reliable. Good for flights to Europe, Central and South America, and for changing flight dates, English spoken, ask for Icarus Monk.

Mundo Joven Travel Shop, Guatemala 4, Col Centro, T5518-1755, www.mundojoven.com. Issues ISIC card, agents for International Youth Hostel Federation.

Protures Viajes, Av Baja California 46, Col Roma Sur, T5264-4497. Recommended agency for flights to Central and South America and Cuba.

Viajes Tirol, José Ma Rico 212, Depto 503, T5534-5582, English and German spoken, recommended.

Specialists in adventure and ecotourism

Al Aire Libre, Centro Comercial Interlomas, Local 2122, Lomas Anáhuac Huixquilucan, T5291-9217. Rafting (Ríos Pescados-Antigua, Santa María, Amacuzac), climbing, caving (Chontalcuatlán, Zacatecoltla, La Joya), ballooning, parapenting.

Asociación Mexicana de Turismo de Aventura y Ecoturismo (AMTAVE), Río y Montaña, Prado Norte 450-T, Lomas de Chapultepec, T/F5520-2041, www.amtave.org. Regulates and promotes many of the agencies listed. Not all areas of adventure sport come under their umbrella, for instance specialist diving agencies remain unattached to any Mexico based organization, as diving is a mainly regional activity. But a very good wide ranging list of members.

Transport

Air

Airport information

The airport terminal is divided into sections, each designated by a letter. A row of shops and offices outside each section contains various services.

Section A National Arrivals; post office, city of Mexico tourist office, exit to taxis and metro, INAH shop, telecommunications office.

Section A-B AeroMéxico; Bancomer ATM.

Section B Banamex.

Sections B-C Entrance to Continental Plaza hotel, *casa de cambio*.

Section C Mexicana; map shop.

Sections C and D Ladatel phones just after C (Ladatel cards are sold at many outlets in the airport). **Exposición Diego Rivera** exhibition hall. Other national airline offices; bookshop.

Section D National and International Departures; *cambio* opposite; more national airline desks; long-distance phones; a bar and restaurant.

From Section D you have to leave the building to get to:

Section E International Arrivals; car hire offices; exchange (Banamex); 24-hr luggage lockers (US$5 per day).

Sections E-F Upstairs are shops, fast-food restaurants (mostly US-style), exchange and phones.

Section F International check-in; banks.

Money exchange

Pesos may be bought at any of the bank branches liberally spread throughout the airport. Most foreign currencies or TCs are accepted, also most credit cards.

Telephones

Many phones at the airport, you'll have to keep looking until you find one that works. Look for the Lada *multitarjeta* phones. There is a phone office at the far end of Section F, which accepts Amex and, in theory, Visa, MasterCard and other cards. It is very expensive though.

Hotel bookings

There are airport information kiosks at Salas A, D, E and F. There is a hotel desk before passing through customs. The tourist office at A has phones for calling hotels, no charge, helpful, but Spanish only. The travel agency at east exit will book hotels or reconfirm flights, charges 5 pesos.

Transport from the airport

Taxis Fixed-price taxis by zone, buy tickets from booths at exits by Sections A, E and F; you can buy tickets before passing customs but they are cheaper outside the duty-free area; rates vary, US$10 to the **Centre/Zócalo**, according to distance (per vehicle, not per person), drivers may not know or may be unwilling to go to cheaper hotels. For losses or complaints about airport taxis, T5571-3600 Ext 2299; for reservations T5571-9344, daily 0800-0200. The fixed-price taxi system is efficient and safe. A cheaper alternative (about 50%) if you don't have too much luggage is to cross the Blv Puerto Aéreo by the Metro Terminal Aérea and flag down an ordinary taxi outside the Ramada hotel.

Buses There are regular buses from the city centre to the airport (eg No 20, along north side of Alameda), but the drawback is that you have to take one to Calzada Ignacio Zaragoza and transfer to trolley bus at the Blv Puerto Aéreo (ie at Metro Terminal Aérea). Buses to airport may be caught every 45 mins until 0100 from outside **Hotel de Carlo**, Plaza de la República 35. It takes 1 hr from downtown (and, in the rush hour, most of the day, it is jam-packed), but you can take baggage if you can squeeze it in.

See map, page 87, for location of terminals. For details of bus services, see destinations in text.

Metro To get to the airport cheaply, take the metro to Terminal Aérea and walk, or take metro to Blv Puerto Aéreo and then a *pesero* marked 'Oceanía', which will leave you at the Terminal metro station.

Airline offices

See page 32 for web addresses. Many airline offices are on Paseo de la Reforma or Hamburgo.

Aero California, Reforma 332, T5207-1392. **Air Canada**, Reforma 398-14T5207-6611. **AeroMéxico**, Reforma 445, T5133-4198. **Air France**, Edgar Allan Poe 90, T5627-6000. **Alitalia**, Río Tiber 103, 6th floor, T5533-1240. **American Airlines**, Reforma 300, T5209-1400. **Avensa**, Reforma 325, T5208-4998. **Avianca**, Reforma 195, T5566-8580. **British Airways**, Jaime Balmes 8, Los Morales, T5387-0300. **Canadian Airlines**, Reforma 390, T5207-6611. **Continental**, Andrés Bello 45, T5280-1567. **Delta**, Horacio 1855 1st floor, Polanco, T5279-0820. **El Al**, Paseo de las Palmas, T5735-1105. **Iberia**, Av Ejército Nacional 436, 9th floor, T1101-1515. **Japan Airlines**, Reforma 295, T5533-6580. **KLM**, Paseo de las Palmas 735, T5202-4444. **Lufthansa**, Paseo de las Palmas 239, T5230-0000. **Mexicana**, Xola 535, Col del Valle, T5448-3000. **Northwest Airlines**, Reforma y Amberes 312, T5511-3579, Reforma 300, T5525-7090. **SAS**, Hamburgo 61, T5533-0098. **Swissair**, Hamburgo 66, T5533-6363. **Taca**, Morelos 108, Col Juárez, T5546-8807. **United Airlines**, Hamburgo 213, loc 23-24, T5250-1657.

Bus

Local

Buses have been coordinated into 1 system: odd numbers run north–south, evens east–west. Fares on large buses, which display routes on the windscreen, are US$0.20, exact fare only. There are 60 direct routes and 48 feeder (SARO) routes. Thieves and pickpockets haunt the buses plying along Reforma and Juárez. A useful route for tourists (and well known to thieves, so don't take anything you don't require immediately) is No 76, which runs from Uruguay (about the level of the Juárez Monument at Parque Alameda) along Paseo de la Reforma, beside Chapultepec Park. A *Peribus* service goes round the entire Anillo Periférico. Trolley buses charge US$0.15.

Long distance

At all bus stations there are many counters for the bus companies, not all are manned and it is essential to ask which is selling tickets for the destination you want (don't take notice boards at face value). On the whole, the bus stations are clean and well organized. Book ahead where possible.

Terminal del Norte, Av Cien Metros 4907, for destinations in north Mexico, including US borders. There is a *casa de cambio*, 24-hr cafés, left luggage, pharmacy, bakery and phone offices for long-distance calls (often closed and poorly informed, very high charges). The bus station is at Metro Autobuses del Norte, Line 5. City buses marked Cien Metros or Central del Norte go directly there.

Terminal del Sur, at corner of Tlalpan 2205, across from Metro Taxqueña, Line 2, serves Cuernavaca, Acapulco, Oaxaca and Zihuatanejo areas. Direct buses to centre (Donceles) from Terminal del Sur, and an express bus connects the Sur and Norte terminals. It can be difficult to get tickets to the south, book as far in advance as possible; the terminal can be chaotic.

Terminal Poniente is situated opposite the Metro Observatorio, Line 1 of the metro, to serve the west of Mexico. You can go to the centre by bus from the *urbano* outside the bus station, Terminal Poniente (US$0.10).

Terminal Oriente, known as **TAPO**, Calzada Ignacio Zaragoza, Metro San Lázaro, Line 1 for buses to Veracruz, Yucatán and southeast, including Oaxaca and Puebla (2 hrs). It has a tourist information office open from 0900; luggage lockers, US$2.65 per day, key is left with guard; post office, *farmacia* changes TCs. To **Guatemala**, from TAPO, take a bus to Tapachula, Comitán or Cd Cuauhtémoc, pesos only accepted.

Mexico City Airport There are also buses departing from the airport (outside Sala D), to Puebla, Toluca, Cuernavaca and Querétaro, very convenient.

Booking

Advance booking is recommended for all trips, and very early reservation if going to fiestas during Holy Week etc. At Christmas, many Central American students return home via Tapachula, and buses from Mexico City are booked solid for 2 weeks before, except for those lines that do not make reservations. You must go and queue at the bus stations, which can involve a long wait, sometimes 2-2½ hrs. Even if you are travelling, you may sometimes be required to buy a *boleto de andén* (platform ticket) at many bus stations. Note that many bus companies require luggage to be checked in 30 mins in advance of departure.

Transport from terminals

All bus terminals operate taxis with voucher system and there are long queues (check change carefully at the taxi office). It is much easier to pay the driver, although beware of extra charges. In the confusion at the terminals some drivers move each other's cabs to get out of the line faster and may take your voucher and disappear. The terminals are connected by metro, but this is not a good option at rush hour, or if carrying too much luggage.

Bus companies

Going north Transportes del Norte, at Av Insurgentes Centro 137, near Reforma, T5587-5511/5400; depart from Terminal del Norte. **Omnibus de México**, Insurgentes Norte 42, at Héroes Ferrocarrileros, T5567-6756/5858. **Greyhound**, Reforma 27, T5535-2618/4200, closed 1400-1500 and all day Sun; information at Terminal del Norte from **Transportes del Norte (Chihuahuenses)** or **Tres Estrellas** bus counters.

Going to central states Autobuses **Anáhuac**, Bernal Díaz 6, T5591-0533; Terminal del Norte departures.

Going northwest ETN, Terminal del Norte, T5567-3773, or Terminal Poniente, T5273-0251. **Tres Estrellas de Oro**, Calzada Vallejo 1268 Norte, Col Santa Rosa, T5391-1139/3021, Terminal del Norte.

Going northeast ADO, Av Cien Metros 4907, T5567-8455/5322. Beware of **ADO** selling tickets for buses and then not running the service. Although the ticket will be valid for a later bus, there are then problems with overbooking (your seat number won't be valid).

Going south (including Guatemala) Cristóbal Colón, Blv Ignacio Zaragoza 200,

T5542-7263 to 66; from Terminal de Oriente; **ADO**, Buenavista 9 (T5592-3600 or 5542-7192 at terminal). **Estrella de Oro**, Calzada de Tlalpan 2205 (T5549-8520 to 29).

Car

If you have a car in the city, find a cheap hotel to park and explore the city by bus, metro or on foot. If you are planning to hire a car, it is generally cheaper to organize it from the USA or Europe. When driving in the capital you must check which *día sin auto hoy no circula* applies to your vehicle's number plate; if your car is being driven when its number is prohibited, you could be fined US$80. This should not apply to foreign-licensed cars. The regulation covers the State of México as well as the Distrito Federal. The ban applies to the last digit of your number plate: **Mon** 5, 6; **Tue** 7, 8; **Wed** 3, 4; **Thu** 1, 2; **Fri** 9, 0. Occasionally, when contamination levels are even worse than usual, the programme runs at weekends too: **Sat**, all even numbers and 0; **Sun**, all odd numbers. Normally, you can drive freely in 'greater' Mexico City on Sat, Sun and between 2200 and 0500 all week.

Car hire

Auto Rent, Reforma Norte 604; quick service at Av Chapultepec 168, T5533-5335 (5762-9892 airport). **Avis**, Medellín 14. **Budget Rent Auto**, Reforma 60. **Hertz**, Revillagigedo 2. **VW**, Av Chapultepec 284-6. **National Car Rental**, Insurgentes Sur 1883. **Odin**, Balderas 24-A; and many local firms, which tend to be cheaper. **Pamara**, Hamburgo 135, T5525-5572, 200 km free mileage.

Metro

Beware of pickpocketing on the metro. Pino Suárez, Hidalgo and Autobuses del Norte are particularly infamous for thieves.

An efficient, modern system and the best method of getting around the city, especially when the pollution is bad. Trains are fast, frequent, clean and quiet although overcrowded at certain times. Between 1800 and 2100 men are separated from women and children at Pino Suárez and certain other central stations. 2 pieces of medium-sized luggage are permitted.

Tickets and times

Tickets cost 2 pesos, buy several to avoid queuing, check train direction before entering turnstile or you may have to pay again.

Lines 1, 2, 3 and A run Mon-Fri 0500-0030, Sat 0600-0130 and Sun and holidays 0700-0030; the other lines open 1 hr later on weekdays (same hours on weekends and holidays).

Metro information

There is a metro information service at Insurgentes station on the Pink Line 1, which dispenses maps, and most interchange stations have information kiosks. The *Atlas de Carreteras*, US$1.65, has a map of Mexico City, its centre and the metro lines marked. *Pronto's* map of the metropolitan area displays the metro clearly. Good metro and bus maps at the Anthropology Museum, US$1.25. *Guía práctica del Metro*, US$9, explains all the station symbols; also *Guía cultural del Metro*, US$3, both for sale at Zócalo station. All the stations have a symbol, eg the grasshopper signifying Chapultepec and there is a detailed local street map of the immediate vicinity – *planos de barrio* – at every station. There are 9 lines in service.

Line 1 (pink) from **Observatorio** (by Chapultepec Park) to **Pantitlán** in the eastern suburbs. It goes under Av Chapultepec and not far from the lower half of Paseo de la Reforma, the Mercado Merced, and 3 km from the airport.

Line 2 (blue) from **Cuatro Caminos** in the northwest to the Zócalo and then south above ground to **Taxqueña**.

Line 3 (olive) from Indios Verdes south to the University City (free bus service to Insurgentes).

Line 4 (turquoise) from **Santa Anita** on the southeast side to **Martín Carrera** in the northeast.

Line 5 (yellow) from **Pantitlán**, via Terminal Aérea (which is within walking distance of gate A of the airport, but some distance from the international gates – opens 0600), up to **Politécnico** (if using La Raza to connect with Line 3, note that there is a long walk between Lines 5 and 3, through the Tunnel of Knowledge).

Line 6 (red) from **El Rosario** in the northwest to **Martín Carrera** in the northeast.

Line 7 (orange) from **El Rosario** in the northwest to **Barranca del Muerto** in the southwest.
Line 8 (green) from **Garibaldi** (north of Bellas Artes, Line 2), through Chabacano (Line 9) and Santa Anita (Line 4), to **Constitución de 1917** in the southeast.
Line 9 (brown) parallel to Line 1 to the south, running from **Tacubaya** in the west (where there are interesting paintings in the station) to **Pantitlán** in the east.
In addition to the numbered lines:

Line A (*metro férreo*) southeast from Pantitlán as far as La Paz (10 stations in all).
Line B, from Buenavista to Cd Azteca in Ecatepec, north of the city.
Tren ligero From Taxqueña to Xochimilco, a very convenient route.

Art in the metro

At the **Zócalo** metro station there is an interesting permanent exhibit about the city. At **Pino Suárez**, the station has been built around a small, restored Aztec temple.

Mexico City metro

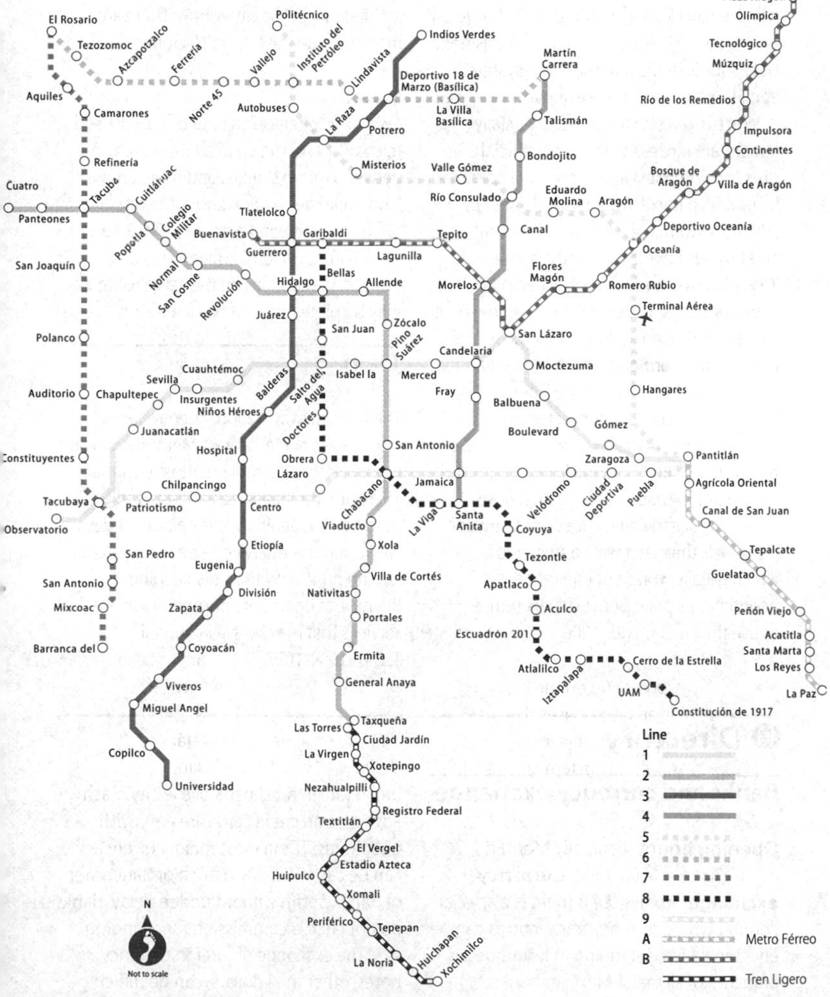

Art in the metro: **Line 1**, Pino Suárez and Tacubaya; **Line 2**, Bellas Artes and Panteones; **Line 3**, La Raza, scientific display in the Tunnel of Knowledge, and south of Coyoacán; **Line 4**, Santa Anita; **Line 5**, Terminal Aérea; **Line 6**, all stations, **Line 7**, Barranca del Muerto; **Line 9**, Mixuca.

Taxi

Turismo taxis Operate from 1st-class hotels, the Museo Nacional de Antropología etc and are the most expensive.
Sitio taxis (fixed ranks) Operate from bus terminals, railway station and other locations; no meters. About double the normal price but safer. You pay in advance at a booth (check your change); they charge on a zone basis, US$4.60 for up to 4 km, rising to US$22 for up to 22 km (the same system applies at the airport – see above).

Warning Lone travellers, especially female, are advised to take only official *Sitio* taxis (not VW ones) from hotels or ordered by phone, particularly at night. Tourist police advise that you make a note of registration and taxi numbers before getting in.
Taxis on unfixed routes (green or white with a broad red horizontal band; yellow ones should be avoided as they are supposed to have been phased out). These can be flagged down anywhere; tariffs US$0.35 plus 5 cents for each 250 m or 45 seconds; between 2200 and 0600 they charge 20% extra. They have meters (check they are working properly and set at zero); if you do not bargain before getting in, or if the driver does not know the route well, the meter will be switched on, which usually works out cheaper than negotiating a price. Some drivers refuse to use their meter after 1800.

Drivers often do not know where the street you want is; try to give the name of the intersection between 2 streets rather than a number, because the city's numbering can be erratic.

Tips and complaints

A tip is not normally expected, except when special help has been given.

For information, or complaints, T5605-5520; if complaining, make sure you take the taxi's ID number.

Bicitaxi

Another type of taxi travel, the tricycle, is now being encouraged to counter exhaust pollution, and is a good way to see the architecture of the city centre. There are many outside the Palacio Nacional.

Colectivos

Colectivos (often called *peseros* – they used to cost 1 peso) run on fixed routes, often between metro stations and other known landmarks; destination and route displayed on the windscreen. Fares are US$0.20 up to 5 km, US$0.25 up to 10 km and US$0.35 beyond. If a bus runs on the same route, it may be preferable as it has fixed stops.

Train

The main railway station, Buenavista, on Insurgentes Norte, nearest Metro Revolución, is now almost a complete ghost terminal. There are just 2 passenger services still running, to Querétaro and Apizalco 3 days a week, and these services – each very slow – are run principally to justify keeping Buenavista open. For information on any services that may be available, call T5547-1084/1097.

Directory

Banks and currency exchange

Opening hours Generally Mon-Fri 0930-1700, Sat 0900-1300. **Currency exchange** Always see if there is a special counter where currency transactions can be effected to avoid standing in long queues. Branches of all major Mexican banks proliferate in most parts of the city. Cash advances on credit cards are easy with good rates. TCs in most major currencies can be cashed at any branch of **Bancomer** or **Banca Serfín** without undue delay. Banks do not charge commission for changing TCs. The exchange of foreign currency notes, other than dollars, can be difficult apart from at the airport and main bank branches in the city centre. There are 2 *casas de cambio* at the airport that specialize in 'obscure' currencies. Before buying or selling currency, check the day's exchange rate from a newspaper and then shop around. There is often a great disparity between different banks and *casas de cambio*, particularly in times of volatile currency markets. Hotels usually offer very poor rates.

Banks Banco de Comercio (Bancomer, Visa agent), head office at Av Universidad 1200, also Venustiano Carranza y Bolívar, good quick *cambio*, same rate for cash and TCs. **Banco Nacional de México (Banamex)**, Palmas, **Banamex**'s offices nearby, at Av Isabel la Católica 44, are in a converted baroque palace, ask the porter for a quick look into the magnificent patio. Another worthwhile building is the bank's branch in the Casa Iturbide, Madero 17 and Gante, where Agustín de Iturbide lived as emperor. **Banco Internacional** recommended, they deal with MasterCard (Carnet) and Visa (usually quicker than Bancomer or Banamex for cash advances against credit card). **Banca Serfín**, corner of 16 de Septiembre y Bolívar, or Madero 32, near Bolívar. **Citibank**, Paseo de la Reforma 390, for Citicorp TCs, they also give cash advances against credit cards with no commission. **American Express** emergency number, T5326-2626, platinum, T5326-2929; also office at Reforma 234 esq Havre, T5533-0380, will change cheques on Sat 0930-1330, also Mon-Fri until 1800 (there are 5 other Amex offices in Mexico City, including Campos Elíseos 204, Local 5, Polanco; Centro Comercial Perisur). For more details on Visa and MasterCard, see Credit cards, page 65.

Casas de cambio There are many *casas de cambio*, especially on Reforma, Madero and throughout the city centre. Their hours may be more convenient, but their rates can be poor. **Central de Cambios** (Suiza), Madero 58, west of Zócalo, and **Casa de Cambio Plus**, Av Juárez, have been recommended for rates. The **Perisur** shopping centre, Insurgentes and Periférico Sur, has a *casa de cambio*, T5606-3698, which is usually open until 1900, with a better exchange rate in the morning. See also Airport, above.

Cultural centres

Amistad Británico-Mexicana, T5286-0017, www.amistadbm.org.mx Benjamin Franklin Library, Londres 116 (has New York Times 2 days after publication). **Anglo-Mexican Cultural Institute**, Maestro Antonio Caso 127, T5566-6144. **British Council**, Lope de Vega 316, Polanco, T5263-1900, www.britishcouncil.org.mx. **Goethe-Institut**, Tonalá 43 (Metro Insurgentes), T5207-0487, www.goethe.de/mexiko. **Instituto Francés de América Latina**, Lafontaine 32, free films every Thu at 2030, T9171-9840, www.paginasculturales.org.mx. **Instituto Italiano**, Francisco Sosa 77, Coyoacán, T5554-0044, www.iic.org.mx, has 3-week intensive yet painless courses in Spanish, 3 hrs a day.

Embassies and consulates

Most take 24 hrs for visas; check to make sure you have a visa and not just a receipt stamp. Check www.sre.gob.mx/acreditadas for details.

Australia, Rubén Darío 55, Col Polanco, T1101-2200, www.mexico.embassy.gov.au. **Belize**, Bernardo de Gálvez 215, Lomas Virreyes, T5520-1346, Mon-Fri 0900-1330. **Canada**, Schiller 529 (corner Tres Picos), near Anthropology Museum, T5724-7900, www.canada.org.mx **Costa Rica**, Río Po 113, Col Cuauhtémoc, T5525-7765. **Denmark**, Tres Picos 43, Col Polanco, T5255-3405, Mon-Thu 0830-1600, Fri 0830-1300, Metro Auditorio. **El Salvador**, Temístocles 88, T5281-5725, Metro Auditorio. **France**, Lafontaine 32,T9171-9840. **Germany**, Byron 737, Col Polanco, T5283-2200, Mon-Thu, 0730-1530, Fri 0730-1500. **Guatemala**, Explanada 1025, Lomas de Chapultepec, T5540-7520, Mon-Fri 0900-1300 . **Honduras**, Alfonso Reyes 220, T5211-5250. **Ireland**, Cda Blv Manuel Avila Camacho 76, 3rd floor, T5520-5803, Mon-Fri 0900-1700. **Israel**, Sierra Madre 215 (Metro Auditorio), T5201-1500, www.mfa.gov.il, Mon-Thu 0900-1600, Fri 0900-1400. **Italy**, Paseo de las Palmas 1994, Col Lomas de Chapultepec, T5596-3655. **Japan**, Paseo de la Reforma 395, Col Cuauhtémoc, T5211-0028. **Netherlands**, Vasco de

Quiroga No. 3000, piso 7, Edificio Calakmul (Santa Fe), T5258-9921, www.paisesbajos.com.mx. **New Zealand**, Jaime Balmer 8, 4th floor, Edificio Corporativo, Polanco, T5283-9460. **Nicaragua**, Prado Norte 470, T5540-5625, **Panama**, Sócrates 339, T5280-7857. **Sweden**, Paseo de las Palmas 1375, T9178-5010, www.suecia.com.mx. **Switzerland**, Paseo de las Palmas 405, 11th floor, Edificio Torre Optima, Col Lomas de Chapultepec, T5520-3003, Mon-Thu 0900-1200, Fri 0900-1100. **UK**, Río Lerma 71, T5242-8500, www.embajadabritanica.com.mx, Mon-Thu 0800-1600, Fri 0800-1330. **USA**, Paseo de la Reforma 305, Col Cuauhtémoc, T5080-2000, www.usembassy-mexico.gov, Mon-Fri 0830-1730. If requiring a visa for the USA, it is best to get it in your home country.

Immigration

Servicios Migratorios, of the Secretaría de Gobernación, Ejército Nacional 862, between Platón and Séneca. Not easy to get to; best to take metro to Polanco, then taxi. Mon-Fri 0900-1330. Get there early, usually long queues, little English spoken. Here you can extend tourist cards for stays over 90 days or replace lost cards; new cards can take just a couple of hours, but charges are as high as US$40; you may be given 10 days to leave the country.

This is also where you have to come to exchange a tourist card for a student visa and for any other immigration matter concerning foreigners. It is essential to be armed with a lot of patience, and to attend with a Spanish speaker if you don't speak the language. The normal procedure is to fill out a form indicating which service you need; you are then given a receipt with a number. See page 64 for more information on visas.

Internet

Rates US$2-3 per hr. Currently one of the handiest non-hotel options is **Lafoel Internet Service**, Donceles 80 y Brasil, 1st floor, T5512-3584, a couple of blocks north of the Zócalo. Opens at 0800. Many others throughout the city to choose from – ask in your hotel for the closest.

Language schools

The UNAM (see page 107) has excellent classes of Spanish language and Mexican culture: **Centro de Enseñanza para Extranjeros**, US$200 for 6 weeks, 5 different levels, free additional courses in culture, free use of medical service, swimming pool, library, a student card from here allows free entry to all national monuments and museums and half price on many bus lines (eg **ADO** during summer vacations). See also Learning Spanish, page 25, and Cultural centres above.

Laundry

Laundrette, Río Danubio, between Lerma and Pánuco and at Chapultepec and Toledo, near Metro Sevilla, expensive. **Lavandería** at Chapultepec y Toledo. **Lavandería Automática Edison**, Edison 91 (Metro Revolución), between José María Iglesias y Ponciano Arriaga, Col Tabacalera (centre). Mon-Fri 0900-1900, Sat 0900-1800. Has automatic machines, US$1.50 per 3 kg, US$1.50 drying. **Lavandería** at Parque España 14 and Antonio Caso 82, near British Council, US$4 for 3 kg, quick service.

Medical services

Doctors

Dr César Calva Pellicer (who speaks English, French and German), Copenhague 24, 3rd floor, T5514-2529. **Dr Smythe**, Campos Elíseos 81, T5545-7861, recommended by US and Canadian Embassies.

Hospitals and clinics

Most embassies have a list of recommended doctors and dentists who speak languages other than Spanish. **American British Cowdray Hospital** (also known as **El Hospital Inglés**, or ABC), on Observatorio past Calle Sur 136, T5277-5000 (emergency T5515-8359); very helpful. **Hospital de Jesús Nazareno**, 20 de Noviembre 82, Spanish-speaking, friendly, drugs prescribed cheaply. It is a historical monument (see page 92).

Vaccination centres

Vaccination centre Benjamín Hill 14, near Metro Juanacatlán (Line 1). Mon-Fri 0830-1430, 1530-2030, avoid last 30 mins,

Sat 0830-1430; typhoid (free throughout Mexico), cholera and yellow fever (US$2), Tue and Fri only; will give a prescription for gamma globulin. For hepatitis shots you have to buy gamma globulin in a pharmacy (make sure it's been refrigerated) and then an injection there or at a doctor's surgery or the ABC Hospital (see above).

Pharmacies

Farmacia Homeopática, Mesones 111-B. **Farmacia Nosarco**, corner of 5 de Febrero and República de El Salvador, stocks wide range of drugs for stomach bugs and tropical diseases, may give 21% discount. **Sanborn's** chain and **El Fénix** discount pharmacies are the largest chains with the most complete selection. Many supermarkets have good pharmacies.

Post office

Correo Central Tacuba y Lázaro Cárdenas, opposite Palacio de Bellas Artes, open for **letters** Mon-Fri 0800-2400, Sat 0800-2000, Sun 0900-1600. For **parcels** Mon-Fri 0800-1800, Sat 0800-1600. Parcels up to 2 kg (5 kg for books) may be sent. It is an interesting historic building with a stunning interior, worth a visit. Philatelic sales at windows 9 to 12. Mail kept for 10 days at Poste Restante, window 3, recommended, but closed Sat and Sun (see page 83). If they can't find your mail under the initial of your surname, ask under the initials of any other names you may happen to have.

EMS Mexpost, accelerated national and international postage, is available at the Central Post Office, the airport, Zona Rosa, Coyoacán and 13 other post offices in the city; payable by weight.

Other post offices (Mon-Fri 0800-1900, Sat 0800-1300), which travellers may find useful: **Centre**, Nezahualcóyotl 184 and Academia 4; **P Arriaga** and Ignacio Mariscal, 2 blocks north of Monumento a la Revolución; **Zona Rosa**, Londres 208; **Tlatelolco**, Flores Magón 90; **San Rafael**, Schultz 102; **Lomas de Chapultepec**, Prado Norte 525; **Buenavista**, Aldama 216; **San Angel**, Dr Gálvez 16; **Coyoacán**, Higuera 23; **Iztapalapa**, Calzada Ermita Iztapalapa 1033; **Xochimilco**, Prolongación Pino 10; also at the **airport** and bus terminals. In all there are 155 branches in the federal capital, so there is no need to go to the Correo Central.

Telephone

Finding a public phone that works can be a problem. Most now take phone cards (Ladatel, provided by Telmex), costing 30 and 50 pesos, from shops and news kiosks everywhere. Calls abroad can be made from phone booths with credit cards (via **LADA** system), but this is very expensive. See page 83 for details of the **LADA** phone system. International calls can easily be made from the phone offices in bus terminals. There are several places, including some shops, all officially listed, with long-distance phones. One of the best options for international calls is an **Ekofon** card or account (see page 83).

Telephone numbers Most numbers are 7 digit with 3 exceptions. When calling long distance dial 01+ regional code (3 digits) + 7- digit number.

North of Mexico City

Right in the centre of the country, Mexico City is well suited for exploring the colonial towns, villages, national parks, prehispanic sites, volcanoes, caves and hot springs that are within easy reach for a day or weekend trip. Everyone heads north to see Mexico's most visited pyramids at the vast and awe-inspiring site of Teotihuacán, 'the place of the gods'. Less crowded are the towering Atlantes at Tula, the Toltec capital, and the pretty villages in the hills near Pachuca where you can eat the Cornish pasties that are a legacy of the English who once mined gold in the region. » *For Sleeping, Eating and other listings, see pages 136-138.*

Acolman

Acolman, 35 km northeast of Mexico City, is easily visited after the Basílica de Guadalupe (see page 110) and on the way to Teotihuacán. It has the formidable fortress-like convent and church of San Agustín. This dates from 1539-1560, with much delicate detail on the façade and some interesting murals inside. Note the fine portal and the carved stone cross at the entrance to the atrium. An interesting architectural feature is the open chapel just above and to the right of the main entrance. While Mass was being celebrated inside the monastery for the benefit of the Spaniards, the spiritual needs of the indigenous worshippers were catered for by the friar who celebrated the Mass in this tiny balcony chapel. Acolman can be reached by bus from Metro Indios Verdes, or from the Zócalo.

Teotihuacán » *pp136-138. Colour map 3, B4.*

ⓘ *Daily 0800-1700. US$3.50 (extra charge for videos, tripods not permitted). Son et lumière display, US$4 per person (good lumière, not so good son); lasts 45 mins, 1900 in Spanish, 2015 in English (Oct-Jun only); take blanket or rent one.*

Arrive early before the vast numbers of ambulantes *(wandering vendors) and the tour groups at 1100. Reckon on two or three hours, longer if you're really keen. There is a perimeter road with a number of car parking places.*

The simplest way to visit Teotihuacán is on an organized tour although you can catch an ordinary buses from Terminal del Norte and Indios Verdes. » *For Transport details, see page 137.*

This site, 49 km north of Mexico City, has some of the most remarkable relics of an ancient civilization in the world. Thought to date from around 300 BC-AD 600, the builders of Teotihuacán, or 'place of the gods', remain a mystery. Where they came from and why the civilization disappeared is pure conjecture. It seems that the city may have housed 250,000 people who were peace-loving but whose influence spread as far as Guatemala. However, the 'peace-loving' theory is constantly being challenged. There are definite indications that human sacrifice was being practised at Teotihuacán long before the arrival of the Aztecs to the Valley of Mexico. Recent research indicates that an individual from Teotihuacán arrived at Copán in Honduras and usurped the power of the rightful ruler, thus continuing to spread the influence of Teotihuacán throughout the Maya region. Teotihuacán was not just a ceremonial centre; vast areas of enclaves have been excavated showing that, apart from those zones designated as sacred, there were also areas occupied by artisans, labourers, merchants and representatives of those crafts and professions that contribute to a functioning city. One zone housed merchants from the Maya area, another was occupied by representatives from Monte Albán in Oaxaca. Some time in the seventh century, Teotihuacán was ravaged by fire and may also have been looted, causing an exodus of its inhabitants. So completely was it abandoned that it was left to the Aztecs to give names to its most important features. There are many questions still to be answered about Teotihuacán culture and new dicoveries are being made all the time.

Sights

There are three main areas: the **Ciudadela**, the **Pyramid of the Sun** and the **Pyramid of the Moon**. The whole is connected by the Avenue of the Dead, which runs almost due north for nearly 4 km. To the west lie the sites of Tetitla, Atetelco, Zacuala and Yayahuala (see below). To the northeast lies Tepantitla, with fine frescoes. The old

Teotihuacán

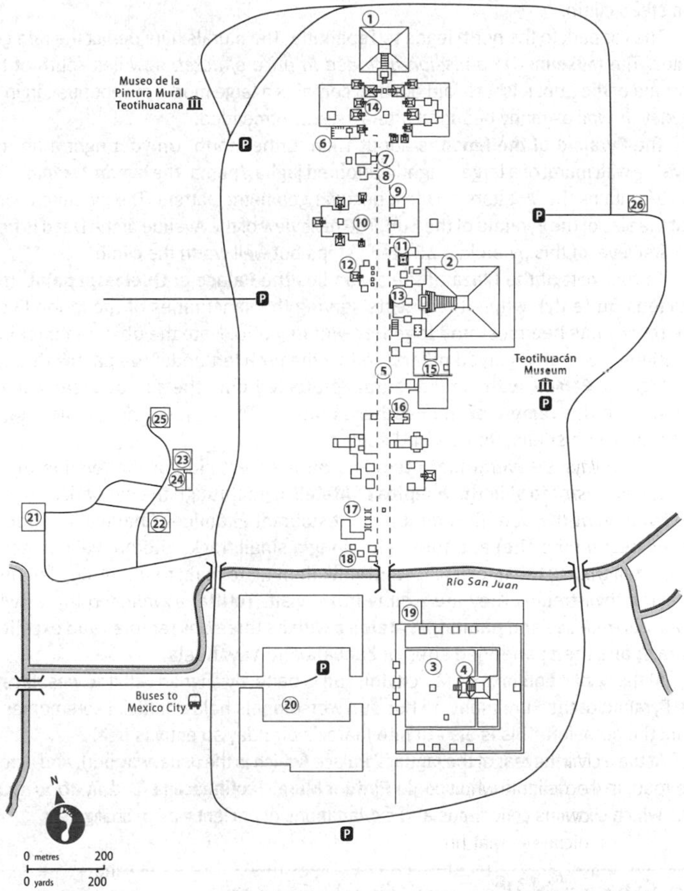

Pyramid of the Moon **1**
Pyramid of the Sun **2**
Ciudadela **3**
Temple of Quetzalcoatl **4**
Avenue of the Dead **5**
Palaces of Quetzalpapalotl,
Jaguars & Feathered Shells **6**
Temple of Agriculture **7**
Mural of the Mythological Animals **8**
Jaguar Temple & Mural **9**
Plaza of the Columns **10**
Palace of the Sun **11**
Patio of the Four Little Temples **12**
Plaza of the Sun **13**
Plaza of the Moon **14**
House of the Priest **15**
Viking Group **16**
Avenue of the Dead complex with
'Superimposed Buildings' group **17**
Northwest Cluster **18**
Plaza Two **19**
Great Compound **20**
Palace of Atetelco **21**
Palace of Tetitla **22**
Palace of Zacuala **23**
Patio of Zacuala **24**
Palace of Yayahuala **25**
Palace of Tepantitla **26**

city is traceable over an area of 3.5 by 6.5 km. Capable of holding 60,000 people, the citadel's main feature is the **Temple of Quetzalcoatl** (the Plumed Serpent, Lord of Air and Wind). Go to the east side of the 1-km square. Behind the largest of the temples (take the right-hand path) lies an earlier pyramid, which has been partially restored. Lining the staircase are huge carved heads of the feathered serpents.

Follow the Avenue of the Dead to the **Plaza of the Sun**. You will pass small grassy mounds, which are unexcavated temples. The Plaza contains many buildings, probably for the priests, but is dominated by the massive **Pyramid of the Sun** (64 m high, 213 sq m at the base) and covering almost the same space as the Great Pyramid of Cheops in Egypt. The sides are terraced, and wide stairs lead to the summit. The original 4-m covering of stone and stucco was removed by mistake in 1910. The view from the top gives a good impression of the whole site. But beware, it is a steep climb.

The car park to the north leads to Tepantitla. The murals here depict the rain god Tlaloc. The **museum** ⓘ *admission included in price of ticket*, now lies south of the Pyramid of the Sun. It is well laid out and contains a large model of Teotihuacán in its heyday as well as many beautiful artefacts; recommended.

The **Pyramid of the Moon** is about 1 km further north. On your right a tin roof covers a wall mural of a large, brightly coloured jaguar/puma (the **Jaguar Temple**). The plaza contains the 'A' altars – 11 in a peculiar geometric pattern. The pyramid is only half the size of the Pyramid of the Sun. The best view of the Avenue of the Dead is from the first level of this pyramid – 48 steep steps but well worth the climb.

To the west of the Plaza of the Moon lies the **Palace of Quetzalpapalotl** (the Precious Butterfly), where the priests serving the sanctuaries of the Moon lived. The palace has been restored together with its patio. Note the obsidian inlet into the highly decorated carved pillars. Follow the path left under the palace through the **Jaguars' Palace**, with catlike murals protected from the sun by green canvas curtains, to the **Temple of the Feathered Shells**. The base of the simple altar is decorated with shells, flowers and eagles.

You will pass several more temples on the west side of the Avenue of the Dead. If you want to visit the **temples of Atetelco**, go through the car park opposite the Pyramid of the Sun, turn right past **Restaurant Pirámides Charlies** (reputed to be the best on the site) and turn right along a small track. Alternatively, to get to them from the museum, exit west and walk right up to main road, turning left after crossing the stream. They are well worth a visit: **Tetitla**, a walled complex with beautiful frescoes and paintings; **Atetelco** with its three tiny temples and excellent murals; and the abandoned sites of **Zacuala** and **Yayahuala**.

At the spring equinox, 21 March, the sun is perfectly aligned with the west face of the Pyramid of the Sun; many ad hoc sun worshippers hold unofficial ceremonies to mark the occasion. This is also Benito Juárez's birthday so entry is free.

At the exit to the rear of the Jaguars' Palace (which is the usual way out), and across the road, is the delightful **Museo de Pintura Mural Teotihuacana** ⓘ *daily 1000-1700, free*, which contains collections and explanations of ancient wall painting.

Pachuca

» *pp136-138. Colour map 3, B4.*

→ *Phone code: 771. Altitude: 2445 m.*

Capital of Hidalgo state (www.hidalgo.gob.mx), Pachuca, 94 km northeast of Mexico City, is also one of the oldest silver mining centres in Mexico. The Aztecs, the Spaniards and more recently the English all mined here leaving the hills honeycombed with old workings and terraced with tailings. The English left a small culinary legacy with a Mexicanized version of a Cornish pasty, available in some of the town's cafés.

The town centre is partly pedestrianized and, although the centre is largely modern, there are a number of colonial buildings among its narrow, steep and crooked streets. These include the treasury for the royal tribute, **Las Cajas Reales** (1670), Venustiano Carranza 106, now used as offices; **Las Casas Coloradas** (1785), on Plaza Pedro María Anaya, now the Tribunal Superior de Justicia; and a former **Convento de San Francisco** (1596) on Arista and Hidalgo next to Parque Hidalgo. An outstanding **photographic museum** ⓘ *T714-3653, Tue-Sun 1000-1800, free,* is in the large cloister on the far side of the convent. **Casa de las Artesanías** for Hidalgo state is at the junction of Avenida Revolución and Avenida Juárez. In the Plaza Independencia is a huge clock with four Carrara marble figures.

The **Museo de la Minería** ⓘ *Mina 110, Tue-Sun 1000-1400, 1500-1800, free,* has an excellent display of the history of mining in Pachuca. An industrial heritage programme is under way to restore some of the old mining settlements; up-to-date information is available in the museum. The **Museo Regional de Hidalgo** ⓘ *Centro Cultural Hidalgo, Tue-Sun 0900-1800, may close early on Sun afternoon,* displays chronological exhibits of the state's history. In the complex there is a souvenir shop with reproductions of ceramic and metal anthropological items and recordings of indigenous music, a library and exhibition hall.

The modern buildings include a **theatre**, the **Palacio de Gobierno** (which has a mural depicting ex-President Echeverría's dream of becoming Secretary-General of the UN), and the **Banco de Hidalgo**. There is a **tourist office** ⓘ *Av Revolución 1300, T718-3937.*

Around Pachuca

Real del Monte, a very interesting and attractive small town, is one of a number of mining centres in the area, most of which are no longer operative. Cornish miners came here from England in large numbers in the second quarter of the 19th century. Traces of their presence can still be seen in blue-eyed inhabitants, surnames and, of course, the pasties or *pastes*. Most of the buildings have sloping roofs or *techos de dos aguas* and are carefully preserved. The **Panteón Inglés** (English cemetery) is on a wooded hill opposite the town; the caretaker will recite stories about families buried there. No lodging is available at present; take a *colectivo* from Pachuca, 10 minutes' drive.

North of Pachuca via Atotonilco el Grande, there is a chapel and convent halfway down a beautiful canyon, the impressive **Barranca de Metztitlán**, which has a wealth of different varieties of cacti, including the 'hairy old man' cactus, and a huge 17th-century monastery. The death of Ome Tochtli (Two Rabbit) at the hands of Tezcatlipoca (Smoking Mirror) occurred at Metztitlán. Further north on a difficult road is Molango, where there is a restored convent, Nuestra Señora de Loreto. **San Miguel Regla,** 34 km northeast of Pachuca, is a mid-18th-century hacienda built by the Conde de Regla, and now run as a resort. A road continues towards **Tulancingo** on the Pachuca-Poza Rica road, Route 130, with a handful of hotels. **Epazoyucan**, 17 km east of Pachuca, and a further 4 km off Route 130 to the right, is a village with the interesting convent of San Andrés. After Tulancingo, Route 119 branches off to the right to **Zacatlán**, famous for its apple orchards, plums, pears and cider. Its alpine surroundings include an impressive national park, the **Valle de las Piedras Encimadas** (stacked rocks), where camping is possible. Some 16 km south of Zacatlán and about 1½ hours from Puebla (see page 156) is **Chignahuapan**, a leading producer of *sarapes*, surrounded by several curative spas.

Tepotzotlán » pp136-138. Colour map 3, B4.

→ *Phone code: 55.*

In the town of Tepotzotlán, about 43 km northwest of Mexico City, just off the road to Querétaro, is the splendid Jesuit church of **San Francisco Javier** in churrigueresque style and with fine colonial paintings in the convent corridors. The old Jesuit monastery has been converted into the **Museo Nacional del Virreinato** ⓘ *Tue-Sun 1000-1700, US$4.35*, a comprehensive and well-displayed collection covering all aspects of life under Spanish rule. It is also a tourist centre with restaurants. There is a big market on Wednesday and Sunday when the town gets very congested; there is a good selection of handicrafts and jewellery, as well as meat, cheese and other foods.

Don't confuse Tepotzotlán with Tepoztlán, which is south of Mexico City, Cuernavaca.

In the third week of December, **pastorelas**, plays based on the temptation and salvation of Mexican pilgrims voyaging to Bethlehem, are held. Tickets are about US$10. Contact **Viajes Roca** ⓘ *Neva 30, Col Cuauhtémoc, Mexico City*, for tickets.

Tula

» *pp136-138. Colour map 3, B4.*

→ *Phone code: 773.*

ⓘ *Tue-Sun 0930-1630 (museum Wed-Sun). Site and museum, US$3 weekdays, reduction with ISIC card. The small restaurant is not always open. Multilingual guidebooks at entrance, fizzy drinks on sale.*

A half-day excursion from Mexico City can be made to Tula, 65 km north of Mexico City, thought to be the most important Toltec site in Mexico. In all, two ball courts, pyramids, a frieze in colour, and remarkable sculptures over 6 m high have been uncovered. There are four huge warriors in black basalt on a pyramid, these are the great Atlantes anthropomorphic pillars. One is a reproduction; the original is on display at the Museo de Antropología in Mexico City. The platform on which the four warriors stand is encircled by a low relief frieze depicting jaguars and coyotes, and Tlaloc masks adorn the walls. Note the butterfly emblem on the chests of the warriors and the *atlatl* (spear-thrower) held by their sides. The butterfly, so important an element in Toltec iconography, was once more to become associated with the warrior class during the Aztec period, when dead warriors became butterflies who escorted the sun to midday. The museum is well worth visiting and there is a massive fortress-style church, dating from 1553, near the market.

The town of Tula itself is pleasant, clean and friendly. If driving from Mexico City, take the turn for Actopan before entering Tula, then look for the Parque Nacional sign (and the great statues) on your left.

Sleeping

Teotihuacán *p132*

AL Villas Arqueológicas, San Juan Teotihuacán, T594-956-0909. Close to the pyramids, with a pool.

Pachuca *p136*

B Emily, Plaza Independencia, T715-0828, www.hotelemily.com.mx. Tidy hotel with TV and phone, good restaurant. Parking.

C De los Baños, Matamoros 205, T713-0700. Rooms not up to standard of entrance, good, friendly and helpful. Recommended.

C San Antonio, 6 km from Pachuca on road to Mexico City (ask for directions), T711-0599. Spacious rooms, good value, clean, quiet, restaurant.

D Juárez, Barreda 107, just before Real del Monte. Superb wooded surroundings. With bath, some rooms without windows.

D-F Grenfell, Plaza Independencia 116, T715-0277. With bath, clean, friendly, pleasant, good value. Some cheaper rooms but undergoing renovation so prices may rise. Bus from bus station passes the door.

Phone codes *Pachuca 771; Tepotzotlán 55; Tula 773.*

Around Pachuca *p135*
A Mi Ranchito, Xicotepec de Juárez, T771-764-0212. One of the best small hotels in Mexico.
B Hacienda San Miguel Regla, San Miguel Regla, T771-792-0102. A fine atmosphere, excellent service, pool, lush gardens, tennis, horse riding and log fires. Highly recommended.
D Posada Don Ramón, Zacatlán. Best hotel in town, with pleasant furnished rooms in a colonial-style building.

Tepotzotlán *p135*
AL Tepotzotlán, Industrias, about 3 blocks from centre. TV, restaurant, swimming pool, good views, secure parking. Recommended.
A Posada San José, Plaza Virreinal No 13, T55-5876-0835. Nice rooms, but not great value.

Camping
Pepe's (Eva Sámano de López, Mateos 62, T5876-0515/0616, in Mexico City, or contact **Mallorca Travel Service**, Paseo de la Reforma 105, T5705-2424). The nearest trailer park to the capital, it costs about US$12 a night, 55 pads with full hook-ups, very friendly, clean, hot showers, Canadian run. Recommended (owner has a hotel in Mexico City if you want to leave your trailer here and stay in the capital).

Tula *p136*
B Sharon, Blv Tula-Iturbe 1, T732-0976, hotel_sharon@hotmail.com. Large clean rooms, secure car parking, restaurant, lift. A business hotel, so a little sterile, but recommended nonetheless.
C Catedral, Zaragoza No 106, T732-0813. Clean, pleasant, TV.

Eating

Teotihuacán *p132*
¥ Los Pinos, Guadalupe Victoria, in the village of San Juan Teotihuacán, is one of a few decent eating options, and the village makes an interesting detour.

Pachuca *p136*
¥¥ Casino Español, Blv Everardo Márquez 202. Old-time favourite serving Mexican, Spanish and international dishes, open all day.
¥ El Buen Gusto, Arista y Viaducto Nuevo Hidalgo. Clean, good-value *comida corrida*.

Tepotzotlán *p135*
¥¥ Hostería del Monasterio. Very good Mexican food and a band on Sun; try their *café de olla* (sweet coffee with cinnamon).
¥ Restaurant Artesanías, opposite church. Cheap. Recommended.

Tula *p136*
¥ Nevería, on main square. Good soup.
¥ Restaurant la Cabaña, on main square. Local dishes.

Activities and tours

Teotihuacán *p132*
Tour operators
Mexbus, T5514-2233 or T01800-523-9412, www.mexbus.net, provides day trips, including a stop at the Basílica de Guadalupe, pick-up and return from central hotels, English-speaking guide and lunch for US$27.

Transport

Teotihuacán *p132*
The site is more generally known as 'Pirámides' than as 'Teotihuacán'.
Bus Ordinary buses leave from Terminal del Norte, Gate 8, platform 6 (Metro Autobuses del Norte), Mexico City; at least 45 mins, US$2 1 way (**Pirámides** buses are white with a yellow stripe). You can also take the metro to Indios Verdes (last stop on line 3), then a public bus (US$2.50) to the pyramids. Bus returns from Door 1 (some others from 2 and 3) at Teotihuacán site, supposedly every 30 mins. Some return buses to the capital terminate in the outskirts in rush hour without warning. You can ride back to town with one of the tourist buses for about US$3.

Pachuca *p136*
Bus There are frequent departures from Terminal del Norte. In Pachuca the bus terminal is outside town; take any bus marked 'Central'. A 4-lane highway now runs from Mexico City to Pachuca via Venta de Carpio, Km 27, from which a road runs east to Acolman, 12 km, and Teotihuacán, another 10 km.

Tepotzotlán *p135*
Bus From near Metro El Rosario, US$1.50, 1-hr ride. Many Querétaro or Guanajuato buses from Terminal del Norte pass the turn-off at 'Caseta Tepotzotlán' from where you can take a local bus or walk (30 mins) to the town.

Tula *p136*
Bus Regular 1st-class bus from Terminal del Norte, Av de los Cien Metros, which goes to Tula bus terminal in 1½ hrs; US$4, every 40 mins, 0600-2100; Tula bus terminal is 3 km from the site, take a 'Chapantago' bus (every 20 mins) to the entrance, 5 mins (ask where to get off), or a taxi, or walk, turning right out of the bus station. At the main road, cut diagonally left across road and take first right, which will take you to a bridge over an evil-smelling river. Carry on to the main highway, then turn left. Tula-Pachuca US$3.30; safe to leave belongings at bus station. **Grey Line, Londres 166, T5208-1163,** excursions from Mexico City have been recommended. There are also services to Queretaro (2¼ hrs), Guanajuato and León.

West of Mexico City

Heading west takes you through the mountains that form the western fringe of the Central Valley and which, on clear days (quite rare), provide spectacular views of the city. Time it right and go on a Friday, travelling through cool pine forests, for Toluca's massive street market. You can hike on the slopes of Nevado de Toluca, explore the forests of Ixtapan de la Sal or visit the lesser-known ruins of Malinalco. ▸▸ *For Sleeping, Eating and other listings see pages 141-143.*

Toluca ▸▸ *pp141-143. Colour map 3, B3.*

→ *Phone code: 722. Altitude: 2639 m.*

From Mexico City head towards **Parque Nacional Miguel Hidalgo**, or **La Marquesa,** with lakes suitable for watersports and other activities such as hiking and camping in nearby hills. Turning south off Route 15 leads to Chalma and Santiago Tianguistenco with incredible panoramic views of the city and the Valley of Mexico, smog permitting. Entering the Basin of Toluca, the proud form of the ice-capped Toluca volcano (see page 139) dominates the landscape.

At 2680 m, Toluca – 64 km west of Mexico City by dual carriageway – is the highest city in Mexico and capital of the state of the same name. Well known for confectionery and the local *chorizo* sausage, Toluca's real fame is down to the huge Friday market, close to the bus station on Paseo Tollocán and Idisro Fabela. Spreading out across several blocks, modern manufactured goods are sold alongside more traditional goods of woven baskets, *sarapes*, *rebozos*, pottery and embroidered goods. The city is easily visited as a day trip starting out early from Mexico City (very regular buses from Terminal Poniente, one hour), or stopping en route heading west. The **tourist office** ⓘ *Lerdo de Tejada Pte 101, Edificio Plaza Toluca, 1st floor, T215-0131,* has a free *Atlas Turístico* of the state of México, including street maps of all towns of interest.

Sights

The centre of the city is the **Plaza de los Mártires**, a very open space. On its south side is the **cathedral**, begun in 1870, but not completed until 1978. Incorporated in its interior is the baroque façade of the 18th-century church of the Tercera Orden. Also on the south side is the **Church of Veracruz**, housing a Black Christ and with a very attractive interior. On three sides of the block containing these two churches are **Los Portales** (Calle Bravo, Calle Hidalgo and Calle Constitución), arcaded shops and restaurants. Northeast of Plaza de los Mártires is a park, Plaza Angel María Garibay, with trees and fountains, on which is the **Museo de Bellas Artes** ⓘ *Tue-Sun 1000-1800, US$0.25, concessions half price, booklet US$1.35*, formerly the Convento del Carmen, with seven halls of paintings from 18th-century colonial baroque to the 20th century, and temporary exhibitions. A tunnel is said to run from the ex-Convento to all the central churches. Next door is the **Templo del Carmen**, a neoclassical church with a gold and white interior, and next to that is Plaza España. At the eastern end of Plaza Garibay is the **Cosmovitral** and **Jardín Botánico** ⓘ *Tue-Sun 0900-1700, US$0.60*. From 1933 to 1975 the building was the 16 de Septiembre market; it was reopened in 1980 as a formal garden in honour of the Japanese Eizi Matuda, who set up the herbarium of the Estado de Mexico, with fountains and exhibitions, all bathed in the blues, oranges and reds of the vast stained-glass work of Leopoldo Flores Valdez. One block west of Plaza Garibay is the **Palacio de Gobierno**. Four blocks west of Los Portales is the **Alameda**, a large park with a statue of Cuauhtémoc and many tall trees; on Sunday morning it is popular with families strolling among the many stalls. The entrance is at the junction of Hidalgo and Ocampo. At Ocampo and Morelos is the **Templo de la Merced**. The **Casa de las Artesanías (Casart)** ⓘ *Paseo Tollocán 700*, has an excellent display of local products for sale.

Look out for an orange liqueur known as moscos, a local speciality.

Around Toluca

» *pp141-143.*

From Toluca take a bus north to the pyramids and Aztec seminary of **Calixtlahuaca** ⓘ *US$4.35*, 2 km off the road to Ixtlahuacan. The pyramids are to Quetzalcoatl (circular) and to Tlaloc. They are just behind the village, 10 minutes' walk from the final bus stop. Forty-five minutes north of Toluca by car, near the town of **Temoaya**, is the **Centro Ceremonial Otomí**, a modern site for cultural events in a beautiful setting.

A road branches off the Toluca to Valle de Bravo road at Km 75 to the Toluca volcano, **Nevado de Toluca**, or Xinantécatl. At 4583 m this is the fourth highest mountain in Mexico. The road climbs to the deep blue lakes of the Sun and the Moon in its two craters, at about 4270 m, from which there is a wide and awe-inspiring view. It is 27 km from the turning off the main road to the heart of the craters. During winter it is possible to ski on the slopes; 2 km from the entrance is an *albergue* with food and

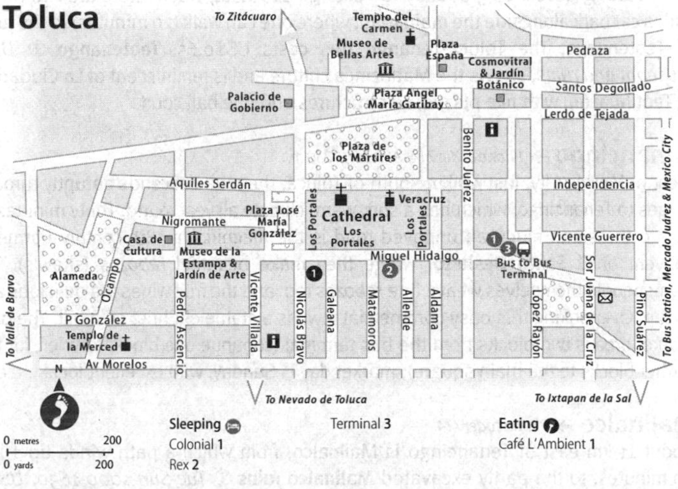

cooking facilities. From here it is 10 km to the entrance to the crater, where there is a smaller *albergue* (cooking facilities, food sold at weekends only, no bathroom or water, dirty), and then a further 6 km to the lakes. A shortcut from the small *albergue* takes 20 minutes to the crater; it is not possible to drive. At the third refuge, 21 km from the turn-off is an attendant. Trips to the volcano are very popular at weekends. You can stay overnight at any of the refuges (F), although they are sometimes closed during the week; there is a restaurant, but the trip can be done in one day from Toluca. If walking remember the entrance to the crater, as you face it, is on the far left side of the volcano.

To reach the Toluca volcano take the first bus to Sultepec from Toluca at about 0700 (every two hours thereafter). Leave the bus where the road to the radio station branches off, just after Raíces village (US$1); from there it is about 20 km to the crater, hitching is fairly easy, especially at weekends. Aim to get to the crater by midday, otherwise clouds will cover everything. Visitors must leave by 1700.

South of Toluca

Along Route 55 south of Toluca, or reached from it, are a number of interesting art- and craft-producing villages, all with fine old churches. The first village is **Metepec**, the pottery-making centre of the valley, 1.5 km off the road to Tenango. The clay figurines made here, painted bright fuchsia, purple, green and gold, are unique. This is the source of the *árboles de la vida*, the gaudily painted pottery 'trees of life and death' sold all over Mexico. Craft workshops are very spread out; market day is Monday.

If you're feeling brave, try atepocates: embryo frogs with tomato and chillies, boiled in maize leaves.

A detour east off Route 55 or south from Route 15, the Toluca-Mexico City highway, goes to the town of **Santiago Tianguistenco**, where there are good pottery bowls, baskets and *sarapes*. Try blue corn *gordas* or *tlacoyos* which are stuffed with a bean paste. Market day is Wednesday and the town is crowded at weekends.

San Mateo Atenco (altitude 2570 m) is situated south of the Toluca-Lerma 'corridor'. Settled in ancient times, it has featured in several important historical moments by virtue of occupying a bridge-head between lagoons: Axayácatl, Hernán Cortés and Hidalgo all passed this way. There is a Franciscan church and monastery, the earliest parts of which date from 1550. The town is famous for its shoes, and leather goods of all descriptions and you can pick up some excellent bargains. On 25 October St Crispin, the patron saint of shoemakers, is honoured in the open chapel of the church in the presence of the local bishop. Market is on Friday and Saturday.

Route 55 descends gradually to **Tenango de Arista**, where there are two hotels with a car park alongside the main road, where one can walk (20 minutes) to the ruins of Teotenango. The Toluca-Tenango bus costs US$0.65. **Teotenango** ⓘ *US$1 museum and ruins*, shows the Matlazinca culture and is reminiscent of La Ciudadela at Teotihuacán, with five plazas, 10 structures and one ball court.

Tenancingo → *Phone code: 714. Altitude: 1830 m.*

West of Mexico City, just 48 km south of Toluca, the road descends abruptly through gorges to Tenancingo, which has a soft, warm climate all year round. Thirty minutes by bus to the south along an unpaved road is the magnificent 18th-century Carmelite convent of **El Santo Desierto**, where they make beautiful *rebozos* (shawls). The townspeople themselves weave fine *rebozos* too, and the fruit wines are delicious and cheap. Overlooking this busy commercial town is a statue of Christ on a hill. The daily market area is two blocks from the bus terminal (continue one block, turn left for two further blocks to the main square); market day is Sunday, with excellent local cheese.

Malinalco → *Phone code: 714.*

About 11 km east of Tenancingo is Malinalco, from which a path winds up 1 km, 20 minutes, to the partly excavated **Malinalco ruins** ⓘ *Tue-Sun 1000-1630, US$2,* dating from 1188, and one of the most remarkable prehispanic ruins in Mexico. A fantastic rock-cut temple in the side of a mountain, 430 steps up, conceals in its interior eagle and jaguar effigies. Apparently, you can feel movement in the rock if you lie on it or lean against it. The site, which shows Matlatzinca culture with Aztec additions, is very small, but in a commanding position overlooking the valley.

The site is visible from the town as a ledge on the hillside; the walk up passes a tiny, blue colonial chapel. For an even better view of the ruins carry straight on where the path leading to the ruins branches off to the right. This old road is cobbled in places and rises up the mountainside pretty steeply, arriving (after about 1½ hours' walk) at a small shrine with two crosses. It is possible to camp here but there is no water. Breathtaking views can be seen from here off both sides of the ridge. The trail then carries on gently down the other side, past avocado trees, for 20 minutes, to the paved road to Tenancingo, almost opposite a new brick house with arches. It is possible to catch a bus back over the mountains to Malinalco. It would also be much easier, a downhill walk mostly, to do this whole hike in reverse; catch the bus out, ask for the old road, and walk back.

You also should not fail to visit the Augustinian **Templo y Ex-convento del Divino Salvador** (1552), in the centre of town, the nave of which has a patterned ceiling, while the two-storey cloisters are painted with elaborate, early frescoes. Just below the main square in front of the convent is the market (market day Wednesday). There is a **fiesta** in Malinalco on 6 August.

You can also get to Malinalco from Toluca, or Mexico City, by taking a second-class bus to **Chalma**. This is a popular pilgrimage spot. From the bus stop, walk uphill, past the market stalls, to the crossroads where blue *colectivos* leave for Malinalco until 2000 (10 km, 20 minutes, US$1), or take a taxi.

Ixtapan de la Sal → *Phone code: 721. Colour map 3, B3.*

On Route 55, 23 km from Tenancingo, is Ixtapan de la Sal, a pleasant leisure resort with medicinal hot springs surrounded by forest. In the centre of this quiet whitewashed town is the **municipal spa** ⓘ *daily 0700-1800, not always open, US$1.60*. At the edge of town is the privately run **Parque Los Trece Lagos** ⓘ *US$1.55, US$0.90 for two slides, US$2.20 for slides all day, free midweek 1200-1400 (slide prohibited to those over 40)*, which has a train running around it and numerous picnic spots. Private baths charge US$6 for admission only, everything else is extra. For the hedonist there are private 'Roman' baths; for the stiff-limbed, a medicinal hot-water pool; for the vain, mud baths. Ther's also an Olympic swimming pool, rowing boats and, for the adventurous, a 150-m **water slide**. Market day is Sunday and there is a **fiesta** on the second Friday in Lent.

Tonatico, 5 km past Ixtapan de la Sal, is a much cheaper village with a pleasant municipal *balneario* filled with medicinal hot water supposed to help blood circulation, rheumatism and other illnesses. There is also a waterslide, open at weekends only, and a cheap hotel (see Sleeping, page 142).

Valle de Bravo → *Phone code: 726. Colour map 3, B3.*

The mountain resort of Valle de Bravo, located on a branch road of Route 134, is a charming old town on the edge of an attractive artificial lake and close to an important Monarch butterfly wintering area. Cool weekend bolt-hole for rich *capitalinos*. Valle de Bravo's **fiesta** is 26 February to 14 March. From Valle del Bravo it's an easy excursion to **Colorines** with six series of rock paintings dating from AD 800.

Sleeping

Toluca *p138, map p139*

AL Del Rey Inn, Km 63 Mexico City-Toluca Highway, T212-2122. Motel with resort facilities.

C Colonial, Hidalgo Ote 103, T214-7066. Pleasant courtyard with stained glass, with bath, clean, TV, cheap food (good

restaurant). Recommended (bus from Terminal de Autobuses to Centro passes in front).
C **La Mansión**, Hidalgo Pte 408, T215-6578. With hot water, clean, garage, TV.
D **Rex**, Matamoros Sur 101, T215-9300. With bath, hot water, no restaurant.
D **Terminal**, adjoining bus terminal, T215-7960 (prices vary according to floor). Restaurant next door.
E **Maya**, Hidalgo Pte 413, no check-in before 2000. Shared bath, hot water, clean, small rooms without door locks, towels extra.

Camping
Campo Escuela Nacional de Tantoco, Km 29.5 on Mexico City-Toluca road, T5512-2279. Cabins and campsite.

Tenancingo *p140*
D **Lazo**, Guadalupe Victoria 100 (1½ blocks straight on from market, away from bus terminal), T142-0083. Clean rooms in annex with shower, leafy courtyard, **El Arbol de la Vida** restaurant.
E **Don Ale**, corner of Insurgentes y Netzahualcóyotl, T142-0516. Good value, with clean rooms, nice balcony and garden and no bugs. Loud TV may annoy some.

Malinalco *p140*
E **Santa Mónica**, Hidalgo 109, T147-0031. With bath, pretty courtyard, good value.

Camping
El Paraíso, opposite the small blue chapel, camping and trailer park, not well named; no facilities other than a dirty toilet.

Ixtapan de la Sal *p141*
LL **Ixtapan**, Blv Arturo San Román, T143-2440, www.spamexico.com. Including food and entertainment.
AL **Vista Hermosa**, T143-0092. Next door to Ixtapan, full board only, good, friendly.
D **Casa de Huéspedes Margarita**, Juárez. Clean. Recommended.
D **Casa Guille**, José María Morelos 12, T143-0220. With bath, clean.
D **Hotel**, Tonatico, 5 km from Ixtapan, at the entrance to the *balneario*, T141-0691. With bathroom.

E **Casa Yuyi**. With bath, clean, good.

Valle de Bravo *p141*
There are a few cheap *posadas familiares* around the plaza.
A-B **Los Arcos**, Bocanegra 310, T262-0042. Some rooms with excellent view, swimming pool, restaurant (weekends only), not very helpful staff (more expensive at weekends).
D **Blanquita's**, opposite church off main plaza. Basic, fairly clean, OK.

Camping
Trailer park Av del Carmen 26, T262-1972. Familia Otero, English spoken, 5 hook-ups, 7 dry camping, 3 rentals, small private grounds. Recommended.

Eating

Toluca *p138, map p139*
₸₸ **Ostionería Escamilla**, Rayón Norte 404. Good fish.
₸ **Café L'Ambient**, Hidalgo 231 Pte. Snacks, meals, quite simple.
₸ **Fonda Rosita**, Los Portales central avenue going through to Plaza de los Mártires. Pleasant, Mexican. Also open Sun morning.
₸ **Impala**, Los Portales. For *comida corrida*, coffee. Open daily; Sun from 0930 for good set breakfasts.
₸ **Panadería Libertad**, Hidalgo, next door to Café L'Ambient. Good pizza takeaway.

South of Toluca *p140*
₸ **Mesón del Cid**, Santiago Tianguistenco. Serves good regional food, try *sopa de hongos* (mushroom soup).

Malinalco *p140*
₸₸ **La Salamandra**, on road to ruins. Trout farm and fishery with a restaurant; superb, bring own beverages, bread, salad. Good value.

Valle de Bravo *p141*
Restaurants on pier are expensive.
₸₸ **Los Pericos**, Embarcadero Municipal, T262-0558. International menu, specializes in fish dishes, daily 0900-2000.

Phone codes Toluca 722; Tenancingo 714; Malialco 714; Ixtapan de la Sal 721; Valle de Bravo 726.

🍴 **Alma Edith**, Zócalo. One of the few places to be open for breakfast by 0900. Very good, but slow service, good *comida corrida*.
🍴 **El Monarca**, Juárez 203. Excellent *comida corrida*.
🍴 **Mercado**. Good, cheap food. The *cecina* (salted beef) in this part of the country is magnificent and highly recommended.

Transport

Toluca *p138*
Bus
Local The bus station is some distance from the centre; information is difficult to gather inside and all is confusion outside – look for a bus marked 'Centro', US$0.15; from centre to terminal buses go from, among other places, Ignacio Rayón Norte and Hidalgo Ote; look for 'Terminal' on window (yellow or orange bus).

Long distance To **Mexico City** (Terminal Poniente, close to Metro Observatorio), US$3.50, 1 hr. Bus to **Pátzcuaro**, 6 hrs, US$23, several daily; to **Taxco**, 4 buses a day, 3 hrs, US$8 with Frontera, a spectacular journey. To **Morelia**, several buses daily with Herradura de Plata, 4 hrs, US$11. Many buses to **Tenango de Arista** (30 mins, US$1), **Tenancingo**; also regular buses to **Calixtlahuaca** 1 hr, US$3.50 from platform 7.

Ixtapan de la Sal *p141*
Bus To **Mexico City** every 30 mins from Terminal Oriente, 3 hrs, US$7; to **Toluca** every 30 mins, 2 hrs, US$5.80. Also to **Taxco**, **Coatepec**, **Cuernavaca**.

Car About 2 hrs from Mexico City: turn off Route 15, the Toluca highway, at La Marquesa, go through Santiago Tianguis tenco and join Route 55 at Tenango. The road goes on to the **Grutas de Cacahuamilpa** (see page 147), from where you can continue either to Cuernavaca or Taxco.

Valle de Bravo *p141*
Bus There are 2 direct buses a day from **Zitácuaro**, 1½ hrs, US$4; hourly buses to **Toluca** and **Mexico City**; 1st-class bus to Toluca, US$4.80.

South of Mexico City

Heading south has been a popular route for centuries. Visit Cuernavaca and follow in the footsteps of Aztec nobility, Cortés and modern Mexicans who have used the gentle climate of the 'city of eternal spring' as a bolt-hole to relax and get away from the metropolis. As a centre of learning it is one of the most popular spots for Spanish language schools in Mexico. Further south lies the colonial mining centre of Taxco with red-tiled roofs and pretty up-and-down cobbled streets; the magnificent Santa Prisca church is one of the most elaborate in all Mexico. The shops and market stalls are an attraction too, and you can seek out bargains in beautifully crafted silver. » *For Sleeping, Eating and other listings see pages 149-154.*

Cuernavaca

» *pp149-154. Colour map 3, B4.*

→ *Phone code: 777. Altitude: 1542 m.*

Cuernavaca lies just outside the Valley of Mexico. It is more than 700 m lower than Mexico City and the mild climate has made the town a popular escape from the heat of the city. With the Nahuatl name of Cuauhnáhuac, meaning 'adjacent to the tree', the area was popular with the Aztec nobility, and Hernán Cortés built a palace here, a tradition which continues today with the modern walled homes of rich *capitalinos*. The town is a buzzy centre of arts and intellectuals, with visitors from foreign lands joining the quest for knowledge at the town's many language schools.

This area gets the weekend crowd from Mexico City.

Ins and outs

Getting there Buses leave the capital from the Terminal del Sur to one of Cuernavaca's four bus stations, each serving a different bus company (for details see Transport, page 152). To drive the 89 km to Cuernavaca, follow Insurgentes Sur all the way south beyond Ciudad Universitaria and then take either the fast *cuota* (toll), or the picturesque *libre*. Beyond Cuernavaca, Route 95 and 95D continue south towards Taxco and Acapulco, or you can head east to Tepoztlán, Cuautla and on to the state of Puebla. There is a small airport at Cuernavaca with some domestic flights (see Transport page, 152).

Getting around Most of the sights in Cuernavaca are near the centre of town, within easy walking distance of each other. Local buses can be confusing as they take long, roundabout routes through the *colonias*. Buses marked 'Centro' or 'Buena Vista' all go to the cathedral. Taxis are plentiful and easy to flag down; agree on the price before travelling.

Tourist information There is a state **tourist office** ⓘ *Av Morelos Sur 187, T/F314-3872*, and a **tourist kiosk** i *Vicente Guerrero outside Posada San Angelo*. For cultural activities, go for information to the university building behind the cathedral on Morelos Sur.

Sights

The centre of the city has two adjacent squares, the larger **Zócalo** and the smaller **Alameda**. At the western end of the Zócalo is the Palacio de Gobierno; north of the Zócalo, east of the Alameda is the Centro Las Plazas shopping mall. Heading north from the Alameda, Calle Vicente Guerrero is lined with shops in arcades. Calle Degollado leads down to the main market in a labyrinth of shops and alleys.

The **Palacio Cortés** built in 1531 for his second wife stands at the eastern end of the tree-shaded Zócalo; on the rear balcony is a Diego Rivera mural depicting the Conquest of Mexico. It was the seat of the State Legislature until 1967, when the new legislative building opposite was completed; it has now become the **Museo Regional de Historia Cuauhnáhuac** ⓘ *Tue-Sun 1000-1700, US$1.60*, showing everything from mammoth remains to contemporary indigenous culture. Explanations are not very logical and most are in Spanish.

West of the centre, Calle Hidalgo leads to one of the main areas of historical interest in the city. The **cathedral** ⓘ *entrance on Hidalgo, near Morelos,* was finished in 1552. Some 17th-century murals were discovered during restoration depicting the martyrdom of the Mexican saint San Felipe de Jesús on his journey to Japan. The scenes show monks in open boats, and mass crucifixions. The interior is bathed in different colours from the modern stained-glass windows. At the west end is a stone font full of water; the east end, painted gold, contains the modern altar. In the entrance to the chapel of the Reserva de la Eucarista is a black and white fresco of the crucifixion. There are also two-storey cloisters with painted friezes and a fragment of massed ranks of monks and nuns. By the cathedral entrance stands the charming small church of the **Tercera Orden** (1529), whose quaint façade carved by local indigenous craftsmen contains a small figure suspected to be one of the only two known statues of Cortés in Mexico. (The other is a mounted statue near the entrance of the **Casino de la Selva** hotel.) The gates to the cathedral and the Tercera Orden are closed each day at 1400. Next to the cathedral, in the Casa de la Torre is the **Museo Robert Brady** ⓘ *Calle Nezahualcoyotl 4, Tue-Sun 1000-1800, US$2, café and shop*, housing a collection of paintings by, among others, Diego Rivera, Frida Kahlo, Paul Klee and Francisco Toledo. It also has colonial furniture, textiles, prehispanic objects and African art and ceramics and is well worth a visit.

The Sun morning Mass at 1100 is accompanied by a special mariachi band. Mariachis also perform on Sun and Wed evenings in the cathedral.

Descriptions are in English and Spanish. The 18th-century **Jardín Borda** ⓘ *Calle Morelos, Tue-Sun 1000-1730, US$10*, was a favourite resort of Maximilian and Carlota. It has been restored and is in fine condition. It holds open-air concerts and there are exhibition rooms, café, good bookshop and museum. Boats can be rented on the small lake, US$1-2 depending on duration. Next to the Jardín Borda is the neoclassical church of Nuestra Señora de Guadalupe. Two kilometres on the right up Morelos (*pesero*), side by side are the churches of **San José Tlaltenango** (1521-1523) and the early 19th-century **Nuestra Señora de la Natividad**; there's a bazaar on Sunday, seeling second-hand English books.

Casa de Maximiliano, the weekend retreat of the ill-fated imperial couple Emperor Maximilian and Empress Charlotte, in the pleasant district of Acapatzingo, is now the **Herbolario y Jardín Botánico** ⓘ *Matamoros 200, Col Acapatzingo, daily 0900-1700, free*, with a peaceful and interesting museum. To get there take a bus from the centre to Acapatzingo and ask the driver for the Museo del Herbolario, or take a taxi (US$1.75).

The house of David Alfaro Siqueiros, the painter, is now a museum, **Taller Siqueiros** ⓘ *Calle Venus 7, daily 1000-1630, US$1.50*, a long way east of the centre. It

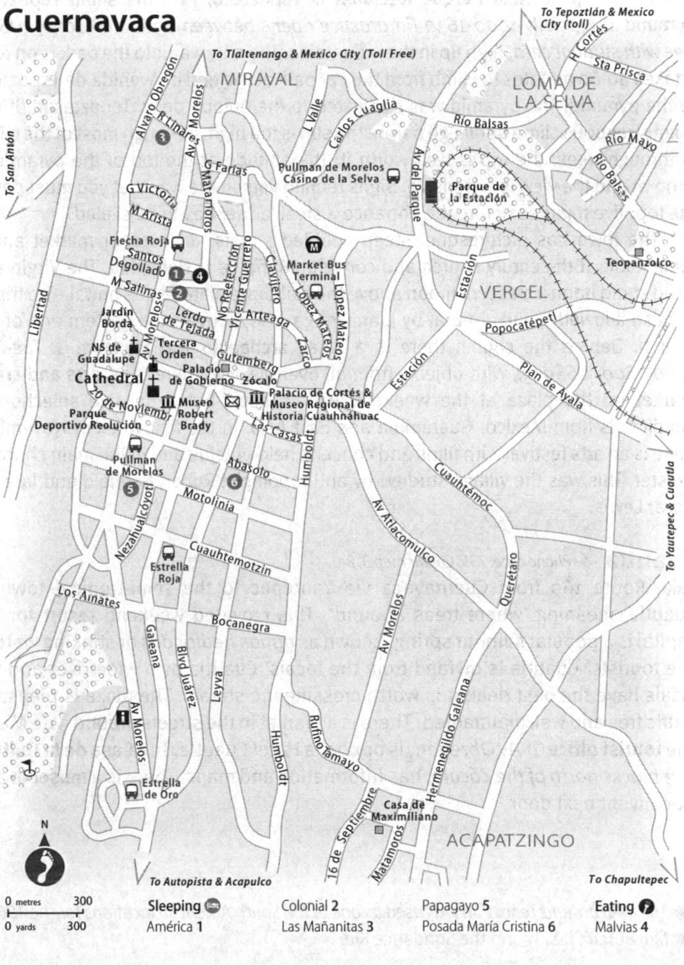

 contains lithographs and personal photographs. The very unusual **Teopanzolco** pyramid is to be found just east of the railway station. At the pyramid's summit, remains of the temple can be seen. Also in the complex are various structures including a circular building, probably dedicated to Quetzalcoatl.

Around Cuernavaca » pp149-154.

Chapultepec Park, southeast of the city centre, has boating facilities, a small zoo, water gardens, with a small admission charge. Also east of the centre is a zoo and recreation centre at **Jungla Mágica**, built around a series of natural springs. The potters' village of **San Antón** is perched above a waterfall a little west of the city, where divers perform on Sundays for small donations. In the vicinity of Cuernavaca are many **spas**, such as Xochitepec, Atotonilco, Oaxtepec, Temixco, Las Huertas and Los Manantiales at Xicatlocatla.

Tepoztlán → *Phone code: 739. Colour map 3, B4.*

Tepoztlán, meaning 'where copper abounds', is 24 km northeast of Cuernavaca at the foot of the spectacular **Parque Nacional El Tepozteco**, with the small **Tepozteco pyramid** ⓘ *officially 1000-1630 (in practice opens between 0900 and 1030), US$3, free with student card*, high up in the mountains. The only way into the park is on foot. It takes 40-60 minutes to climb from the car park at the end of Avenida de Tepozteco to the pyramid. The pyramid was dedicated to the pulque deity, Tepoztecatl. It is a 2-km strenuous climb uphill; go before the sun is too high, although most of the climb is through trees; the trip is well worth it; the altitude at the top of the pyramid is 2100 m and the view is expansive. Signs remind you on the way that you must pay at the top; five minutes before the entrance a steel ladder has to be scaled.

The town has picturesque, steep cobbled streets, an outdoor market and a remarkable 16th-century church and convent, **María de la Natividad**. The Virgin and Child stand upon a crescent moon above the elaborate plateresque portal – no tripod or flash allowed – and a mural by Juan Ortega (1887) covers the eastern end of the church. Behind the church there is a small **archaeological museum** ⓘ *Tue-Sun 1000-1800, US$0.75*, with objects from all over Mexico. There is an **arts and crafts market** on the plaza at the weekend with a good but expensive selection of handicrafts from Mexico, Guatemala and East Asia. In the first week of November, there is an arts festival with films and concerts held outside and in the main church's cloister. This was the village studied by anthropologist Robert Redfield and later by Oscar Lewis.

Cuautla → *Phone code: 735. Colour map 3, B4.*

Take Route 160 from Cuernavaca via Yautepec to the semi-tropical town of Cuautla, meaning 'where trees abound'. This crowded weekend resort for the capital is a popular sulphur spring, known as *aguas hediondas* or stinking waters. The tourists' Cuautla is divided from the locals' Cuautla by a wide river and the locals have the best deal; it is worth crossing the stream. The plaza is pleasant, traffic free and well maintained. There is a market in the streets around 5 de Mayo. The **tourist office** ⓘ *Av Obregón*, is opposite Hotel Cuautla. The **Casa de la Cultura** ⓘ *3 blocks north of the Zócalo*, has information and maps. There is a **museum** and ex-convent next door.

The area around Tepoztlán was used as one of the South American locations for the 1969 film Butch Cassidy and the Sundance Kid.

South of Cuernavaca » pp149-154.

Alpuyeca, Km 100, has a church with indigenous murals. A road to the left runs to **Lago Tequesquitengo** (Paraíso Ski Club) and the lagoon and sulphur baths of **Tehuixtla**. East of the lake is **Jojutla** and a nearby old Franciscan convent of **Tlaquiltenango** (1540) (frequent bus service from Cuernavaca, US$1.75, **Pullman de Morelos**). Use the route through Jojutla if coming from the coast heading for Cuautla, to avoid Cuernavaca. Enquire locally for road conditions off the major highways.

Xochicalco → *Colour map 3, B4.*

ⓘ *Daily 1000-1700, US$2, free with ISIC card, tickets must be bought at the museum.*

At 15 km on the westerly road from Alpuyeca is the right-hand turn to the Xochicalco ruins, 36 km southwest of Cuernavaca, topped by a pyramid on the peak of a rocky hill, dedicated to the Plumed Serpent whose coils enfold the whole building and enclose fine carvings which represent priests.

Xochicalco was at its height between AD 650 and 900. It is one of the oldest known fortresses in Middle America and a religious centre as well as an important trading point. The name means 'Place of the flower house' although now the hilltops are barren. The sides of the Pyramid of the Plumed Serpent are faced with andesite slabs, fitted invisibly without mortar. After the building was finished, reliefs 3 to 4 inches deep were carved into the stone as a frieze. There are interesting **underground tunnels** ⓘ *daily 1100-1400*; one has a shaft to the sky and the centre of the cave. There are also ball courts, the remains of 20 large circular altars and of a palace and dwellings. Xochicalco is well worth the 4-km walk from the bus stop; take a torch for the underground part. There is a **museum** about 500 m from ruins, incorporating many ecological principles and housing magnificent items from the ruins; descriptions in Spanish only.

Xochicalco was the meeting place of northern and southern cultures and, it is believed, both calendar systems were correlated here.

Cacahuamilpa

ⓘ *Daily 1000-1700, US$2.50, children US$1.50, including 2¼-hr tour, every hr on the hr up to 1600 (crowded after 1100 and at weekends), take a torch.*

From Alpuyeca, a road runs west for 50 km to the Cacahuamilpa caverns known locally as 'Las Grutas'. These are some of the largest caves in North America and are well worth a visit.

Taxco » pp149-154. *Colour map 3, C4.*

→ *Phone code: 762.*

The first silver shipped to Spain came from the mines of Taxco. José de la Borda made and spent three fortunes here in the 18th century; he founded the present town and built the magnificent twin-towered, rose-coloured parish church of Santa Prisca, which soars above everything but the mountains. The picturesque town is now a national monument and all modern building is forbidden.

Ins and outs

Getting there Shortly after Amacuzac (Km 121) a branch *autopista* scales mountainsides with breathtaking views taking you right to the outskirts of Taxco, a colonial town with steep, twisting, cobbled streets and many picturesque buildings, now wholly dedicated to tourism. Taxco is a fairly small town and, although hilly and cobbled, it is best experienced on foot. Buses to Taxco leave from Mexico City's Terminal del Sur. You should book onward or return bus tickets to Mexico City on arrival. Some buses en route to Mexico City drop passengers on the main highway, some way from the centre. Taxco is connected to Mexico City and Acapulco via Route 95 and the fast *supercarretera* Route 95D. Combis or taxis will take you up the hill from the bus terminal. For international flights, Mexico City or Acapulco airports are the closest. Some domestic routes are served by Cuernavaca airport (see Transport, page 152).

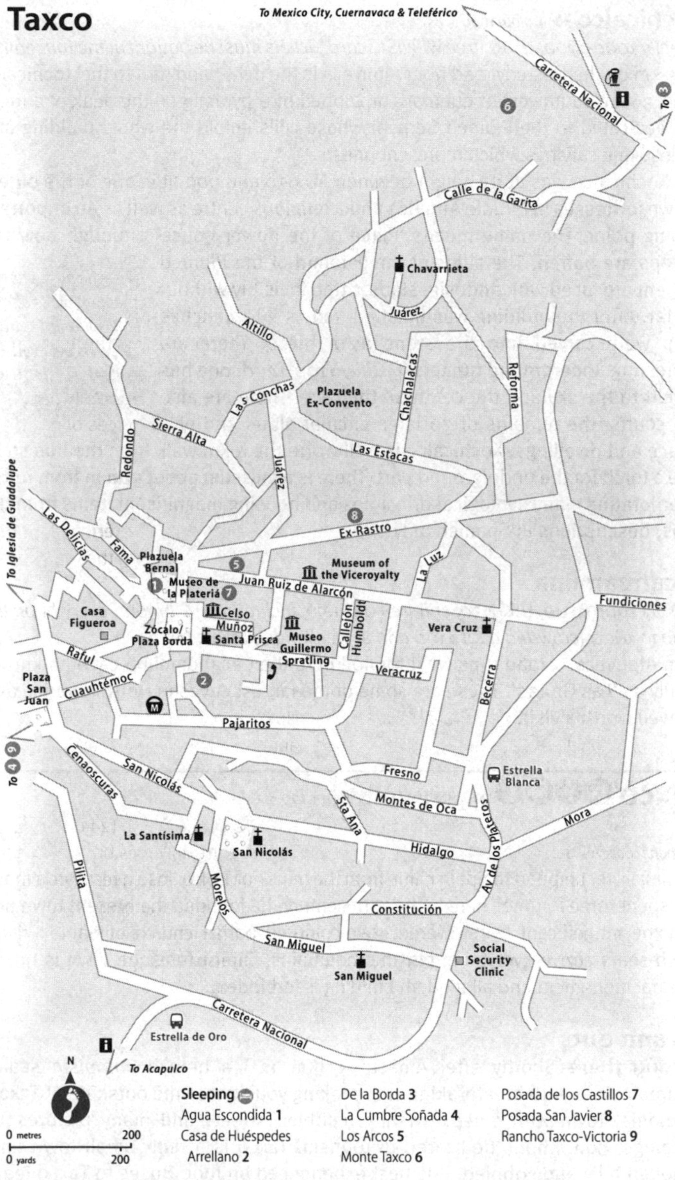

Tourist information Tourist office ⓘ *Av de los Plateros 1, T622-2274, daily 0900-1400, 1600-2000.* You can take a city tour from the tourist office ⓘ*US$35 for up to 5 people.*

Sights

Dominating the central **Plaza Borda** the rose-coloured churrigueresque **Iglesia de Santa Prisca** with its tiled octagonal dome is magnificent. The gilded interior is dazzling too and there is a fine carved pulpit and paintings by 18th-century artist, Miguel Cabrera. The **Museo de Arte Virreinal** ⓘ *J Ruiz de Alarcón 12, Tue-Sat 1000-1700, Sun 0900-1500, US$1, concessions US$0.50*, formerly **Casa Humboldt,** where Baron von Humboldt once stayed, has been renovated and exhibits include beautiful religious art from Santa Prisca and elsewhere. **Casa Figueroa**, the 'House of Tears', so called because the colonial judge who owned it forced indigenous labourers to work on it to pay their fines, is now a private house. **Museo Guillermo Spratling** ⓘ *Tue-Sun 1000-1700, US$1.80*, behind Santa Prisca, houses prehispanic artefacts bought by William Spratling, a North American architect who came to Taxco in the 1920s. His designs in silver helped bring the city to world recognition and revived a dwindling industry. On his death bed Spratling donated his collection to the state. The **Museo de la Platería** ⓘ *Plaza Borda 1, US$0.80*, is devoted to modern silverworking and at the **Platería La Mina** ⓘ *Av de los Plateros*, you can see mining techniques. The main central area of Taxco is full of shops and shopping tourists; the district between the four-storey Mercado and the Carretera Nacional is quieter and free of tourists. Also quieter are those parts up from the main street where the taxis can't go.There is a silver market just below Santa Prisca. And at weekends next to the bus station, prices of silver are around 50% lower than in the shops in town.

Make sure the silver you buy is authentic and has the '925' stamp; alpaca, or nickel silver, contains no silver at all.

There is much festivity in **Semana Santa** (Holy Week). At this time the price of accommodation rises steeply; book a room in advance.

On the outskirts of town there are superb views from the **Teleférico to Monte Taxco** ⓘ *US$1.50 return*. The cable car is reached by microbus along the main street from Santa Prisca.

Sleeping

Cuernavaca *p143, map p145*

LL Las Mañanitas, Ricardo Linares 107, T314-1466, www.lasmananitas.com.mx. One of the best hotels in Mexico, built in Mexican colonial style, many birds in lovely gardens, excellent food, reservation necessary.

L Hostería Las Quintas, Av Díaz Ordáz 9, Col Cantarranas, T318-3949. Built in traditional Mexican style, the owner has a splendid collection of bonsai trees, restaurant, 2 pools, spa, outdoor jacuzzi, magnificent setting, fine reputation.

AL Hacienda de Cortés, Plaza Kennedy 90, T315-8844. 16th-century sugar hacienda. Magnificent colonial architecture, garden, suites, pool, excellent restaurant, access by car.

A Posada Cuernavaca, Paseo del Conquistador, T313-0800. Motel with restaurant, grounds.

A Posada María Cristina, Francisco Leyva 200, near Zócalo, T318-5767. Restaurant, pool, garden, secure parking, extensively refurbished.

A Posada Quinta Las Flores, Tlaquepaque 210, Col Las Palmas, T314-1244, 30 mins' walk from centre. Includes breakfast, no TV, helpful, pool, gardens, restaurant (set evening meal), small parking space, very pleasant. Highly recommended.

A Suites Paraíso, Av Domingo Díaz 1100, T313-2444. Family accommodation.

B Hostería del Sol, Hidalgo, close to the Palacio de Cortés, T318-3241. Loaded with charm and authentically Mexican, lots of tiles, courtyards, flowers. Recommended.

B Papagayo, Motolinia 13, T314-1711, 5 blocks from Zócalo, 1 block from Estrella

Roja bus station. 25-m pool, gardens, convenient, good value, suitable for families, parking.

C **Las Hortensias**, Hidalgo 22, T318-5265. Pretty courtyard, central, long-distance phone service, takes Visa.

C **Royal**, Matamoros 11, T318-6480. Motel with hot water 0700-2300, central, clean. Recommended.

C-D **Cuernaback**, Humboldt 46, T310-1050, www.cuernabackhostel.com. Dorms and private rooms, pleasant garden and swimming pool. Linked with **Hostal Moneda** in Mexico City.

D **Colonial**, Aragón y León 104, T318-6414. Friendly, pleasant courtyard, clean airy rooms.

E **América**, Aragón y León between Morelos and Matamoros 111. Safe, good value but noisy, clean, basic; some rent rooms by the hr. One of several cheaper hotels in this street.

Apartments

Suites OK Motel, Zapata 71, T313-1270. Special student and long-term rates, apartments, swimming pool, with Restaurant Las Margaritas.

Tepoztlán *p146*

L-AL **Posada del Tepozteco**, T395-0010. A very good inn, quiet, old fashioned, with swimming pool, excellent atmosphere and view. Highly recommended.

AL **Hotel Restaurant Anatlán de Quetzalcoatl**, T395-1880. Pool, children's park, gardens.

AL-A **Posada Ali**, Nezahualcóyotl 2 C, off Av del Tepozteco, T395-1971. 4 rooms, 2 family suites, breakfast, pool, fine view.

A **Casa Iccemanyan**, Familia Berlanga, Calle del Olvido 26, T395-0096. With 3 meals (**B** without meals), monthly rates available, 4 *cabañas*, swimming pool, clothes-washing facilities, use of kitchen, laundry, restaurant, English, French and German spoken, beautiful garden.

Cuautla *p146*

C **Jardín de Cuautla**, 2 de Mayo 94, opposite Colón bus station, T352-0088. Modern, clean, but bad traffic noise, pool.

C-D **España**, 2 de Mayo 22, 3 blocks from bus station, T352-2186. Very good, clean. Recommended.

D **Hotel Colón**, on the main square. Good, clean.

E **Casa de Huéspedes Aragón**, Guerrero 72. Hot water, friendly, basic, clean, good value. Recommended.

South of Cuernavaca *p147*

There are several lakeside hotels at Tequesquitengo.

AL **Hacienda Vista Hermosa**, Tequesquitengo, T5662-4918. Hernán Cortés' original *ingenio* (sugar mill), now a popular resort, with swimming, boating, waterskiing and fishing on the lake.

Taxco *p147, map p148*

LL **Monte Taxco**, on right entering Taxco, T622-1300, www.montetaxco.com.mx. Spectacular hilltop setting, pool, horse riding, golf course. Some mosquitoes.

AL **De la Borda**, on left as you enter Taxco, T622-0225. Large, all facilities, great views, most expensive and best.

AL **La Cumbre Soñada**, 1.5 km or so towards Acapulco on a mountain top. Colonial, exquisite.

AL **Rancho Taxco-Victoria**, Soto la Marina 15, walk to centre. Fantastic view, good restaurant. Recommended.

B **Posada Don Carlos**, Consuelo 8, T622-0075. Converted old mansion, restaurant, good view.

B-C **Agua Escondida**, Guillermo Spratling 4, www.aguaescondida.com, on Plaza Borda, T622-1166. Comfortable rooms, with bath, rooftop bar with great view over Santa Prisca, parking, pool. Recommended.

C **Posada San Javier**, down a small street opposite Municipalidad, T622-3177. Clean, lovely garden, pool (sometimes dirty), excellent value.

C **Posada Santa Anita**, Av de los Plateros 106, T622-0752. With hot shower and toilet, cheaper without, very clean, basic, overpriced, noisy at night, friendly, secure parking; the cheapest hotels are in this area.

C-D **Los Arcos**, Juan Ruiz de Alarcón 2, T622-1841. Reconstructed 17th-century

Phone codes *Cuernavaca 777; Tepoztlán 739; Cuautla 735; Taxco 762.*

ex-convent, rooftop garden, breakfast available, best rooms for views are 18 and 19, rooms overlooking street are noisy.
C-D **Posada de los Castillos**, Alarcón 7, T622-1396, off main square. Mexican style, friendly, excellent value. Book ahead where possible.
D **Casa Grande**, Plazuela San Juan 7, T622-0969. Pleasant, well furnished but a bit ramshackle, rooms at the top are better, takes credit cards, good value.
D-F **Casa de Huéspedes Arrellano**, Pajaritos 23, below Santa Prisca and Plaza Borda. Terrace, quiet at night, with bath, basic, old beds, hot water.
E **El Jumil**, Reforma 6, near Tourist Office North. Without bath, hot water, basic, friendly, but noisy.
F **Central**, round the left-hand corner of Casa de Huéspedes Arrellano. Shared bath, quite clean, some rooms without windows.

Eating

Cuernavaca *p143, map p145*
Fruit juices are sold from stalls beneath the bandstand on the Zócalo.
TTT **Las Mañanitas**, see Sleeping above. Beautiful and very well known, but expensive, only Amex accepted.
TTT-TT **Marco Polo**, opposite cathedral. Good, Italian, good pizzas, popular meeting place. Recommended.
TT **La India Bonita**, Morrow 20. Excellent Mexican food.
TT **Los Vikingos**, near the Glorieta Niña in Col Las Palmas. Restaurant and a good *pastelería*.
TT **Vivaldi**, Pericón 102. Restaurant and *pastelería*. Reasonable, popular with locals.
T **California**, Morelos, just down from the Comercial Mexicana supermarket. Excellent buffet lunches at this branch of the chain.
T **La Pasadita**, Morelos esq Abasolo. Amazingly wide choice at very good prices, quieter upstairs.
T **Malvias**, Matamoros, next to Motel Royal. Friendly, good-value *comida corrida*.
T **Pollo y Más**, Galeana. Decent, cheap *comida corrida*.

Tepoztlán *p146*
TTT-TT **El Ciruelo**, Zaragoza 17. Quiet, nice decor, popular with wealthy Mexicans.
TT **La Costa de San Juan**, by plaza on opposite side of street. Meat and seafood.
TT **Los Colorines**, Av del Tepozteco 13-B. Good Mexican vegetarian.
TT **Tapatía**, Av Revolución 1910 (just across street from church wall). Good food and pleasant view from 1st floor, takes credit cards.
TT-T **Axitla**, at beginning of path up to Tepozteco. Open Fri, Sat, Sun and holidays. Mexican and international menus.

Taxco *p147, map p148*
TTT-TT **La Ventana**, in La Hacienda del Solar, T622-0587. Wonderful view of the city, Italian and Mexican menu, main course about US$9. Recommended.
TT **La Hacienda**, Plaza Borda 4 (entrance is off the square). Excellent Mexican food and wine at reasonable prices, chic decor and a nice atmosphere.
TT **Pizzería Mario**, Plaza Borda. Beautiful view over city, excellent pizzas, the 1st pizzeria in town, opened 30 years ago, pleasant service. Highly recommended.
TT **Pozolería Betty**, Mora 20 (below bus station). Good food includes the local beetle (*jumil*) sauce.
TT-T **Concha Nuestra**, Plazuela San Juan (above Hotel Casa Grande). Mediocre food and poor service, live Latin American music excellent, cheap for breakfasts, other meals pricey.
TT-T **La Pagaduría del Rey**, Cerro de Bermeja, T622-0075. Panoramic view over city, international menu, excellent food but overpriced wine, closes 2130, closed Mon.
TT-T **Santa Fe**, Hidalgo 2, opposite Hotel Santa Prisca, T622-1170. Excellent *comida corrida* (US$6) but disappointing *enchiladas*. Used by locals.
T **La Hamburguesa**, off Plaza San Juan. Excellent *comida corrida*, US$1.80, home-cooked food, despite name.
T **Mercado** Cheap *comida corrida* in market and good cheap restaurants on San Nicolás.

Cafés and ice cream parlours
Freddie's, J Ruiz de Alarcón 8, next to Museo de Arte Virreinal. Excellent coffee and cakes.
Nevería. Exquisite *quesadillas* in the ice cream parlour on top of the silver shop **Perlita**.

Shopping

Cuernavaca *p143, map p145*

Bookshops Particularly good on art and history in the **Palacio de Cortés**, to the left of the main entrance; also at **Jardín Borda** in Morelos. Another good bookshop, **Gandhi Colorines**, Av Teopanzoclo 401, not far from the archaeological site of the same name. Second-hand English books at **Guild House**, Tuxtla Gutiérrez, Col Chipitlán, T312-5197.

Handicrafts Market behind Palacio de Cortés, moderately priced and interesting silver, textiles and souvenirs.

Activities and tours

Cuernavaca *p143, map p145*

Travel agents

Marín, Centro Las Plazas, Local 13, Amex agent, changes Amex TCs but poorer rate than *casas de cambio*, charges US$1 to reconfirm flights. Also in Centro Las Plazas, Pegaso, French, Italian, German, English spoken (the sign says), charges US$2 to reconfirm.

Viajes Adelina, Pasaje Bella Vista, on Zócalo.

Transport

Cuernavaca *p143, map p145*

Air

Flights from **Acapulco**, **Culiacán**, **Guadalajara**, **Hermosilla**, **León**, **Monterrey**, **Tijuana** and **Veracruz** with Aerolíneas Internacionales.

Bus

Each bus company has its own terminal: **Estrella de Oro**, Morelos Sur 900, Col Las Palmas, T312-3055. Local buses from the bus station up Morelos, marked Centro, or Buena Vista, all go to the cathedral. From the centre take bus on Galeana marked Palmas. **Pullman de Morelos**, Abasolo 106 y Netzahualcóyotl in the centre, T318-0907, for **Mexico City** and some local departures to **Alpuyeca**, **Tehuixtla**, **Zacatepec**, **Jojutla** and **Grutas de Cacahuamilpa**. There's a second Pullman terimnal at **Casino de la Selva**, Plan de Ayala 102, opposite Parque de la Estación, T318-9205, for **Ejecutivo Dorado** buses to **Mexico City** and 10 daily buses to Mexico airport. **Flecha Roja** on Morelos Norte 503 y Arista, T312-5797. **Estrella Roja**, Galeana y Cuauhtemotzín, south of the centre.

Many minibuses and 2nd-class buses leave from a terminal by the market: to **Mexico City** 1½ hrs, fares US$4.30 ordinary to US$5.50 **Ejecutivo Dorado** is said to be the most comfortable and fastest, from Terminal del Sur, Mexico City every 30 mins. To **Acapulco**, 4 hrs, **Estrella de Oro**, US$23 (US$27 *plus*). For advance tickets for Acapulco or other points on the Pacific Coast, be at **Estrella de Oro** office between 1645 and 1700, 2-3 days before you want to travel, this is when seats are released in Mexico City and full fare from Mexico City to the coast must be paid.To **Zihuatanejo**, Estrella de Oro, 1 a day, US$31. To **Taxco**, **Flecha Roja**, 2nd-class buses, hourly on the ½ hr (not recommended), or **Estrella de Oro**, 1st class, US$5.80. To **Puebla**, **Estrella de Oro**, *gran turismo* service, US$7, 1st class hourly, US$5.50, 2 stops. To **Cuautla** either **Estrella Roja** every 20 mins, US$2.50, or 2nd class or minibus from market terminal, via Yautepec every hr, 1 hr, interesting trip; go there for long-distance buses going south (Puebla buses do not stop at Cuautla).

Tepoztlán *p146*

Bus Local **Autobus Verde**, from Cuernavaca market terminal, takes 1 hr to **Mexico City**, US$1 (bus returns to Cuernavaca from the top of the Zócalo); bus to Mexico City, US$4.50 1st class, US$4.80 **Primera Plus**, hourly. There are buses from Tepoztlán to Yautepec (Marigold Hill).

Xochicalco *p147*

Bus Take a **Pullman de Morelos** bus from Cuernavaca en route to El Rodeo (every 30 mins), Coatlán or Las Grutas; get off at turn-off, 4 km from the site, then take a *colectivo* taxi, US$0.35-US$1.20 per person, or walk up the hill. From Taxco, take bus to Alpuyeca (US$1.60, 1 hr 40 mins) and pick up bus from Cuernavaca to turn-off, or taxi from junction at Alpuyeca directly to ruins (12 km, US$2.50).

Cacahuamilpa *p147*

Bus There are direct **Pullman de Morelos** buses from **Cuernavaca** at 1030 and 1200, returning 1700 and 1830, 1 hr, US$2; also Flecha Roja; usually overcrowded at weekends, enquire about schedules for local buses or buses from **Taxco** to **Toluca**, which stop there (from Taxco, 30 km, 40 mins).

Taxco *p147, map p148*

Bus Local: Little 24-seater combis take you up the hill from the bus terminal on main road, US$0.35, same fare anywhere in town.

Long distance: Taxco is reached from **Mexico City** from the Terminal del Sur, Estrella de Oro, 2½ hrs, luxury US$15, *plus* US$12, non-stop, with video, 3 a day, 1st class US$11, quick, no overcrowding; also Estrella Blanca, on the hr US$11, up to 5 hrs. Buses to **Cuernavaca**; 4 1st-class buses, 5 2nd-class, 1½ hrs, US$4. Spectacular journey to **Toluca**, missing out Mexico City, 2nd-class buses only, 3 hrs, US$8, change at Toluca for Morelia. To **Acapulco**, Estrella de Oro, or Estrella Blanca, 5 hrs, US$15.

Directory

Cuernavaca *p143, map p145*

Banks Cambio Gesta, Morrow 9, T318-3750, daily 0900-1800. Divisas de Cuernavaca, Morrow 12; many banks in the vicinity of the Zócalo. **Internet** Axon Cyber Café, Av Cuauhtémoc 129-B. California Cybercafé, Lerdo de Tejada 10b, Mon-Sat 0800-2000, Sun 0900-1400. **Language schools** Spanish courses start from about US$250-300 per week for 5-6 hrs a day. Some schools also have a registration fee of as much as US$100. Staying with a local family will be arranged by a school and costs US$25-40 a day including meals; check with individual schools, as this difference in price may apply even if you stay with the same family. The peak time for tuition is summer: at other times it may be possible to arrive and negotiate a reduction of up to 25%. Cemanahuac, San Juan 4, Col Las Palmas, CP 62051, T318-6407, www.cemanahuac.com. Claims high academic standards, field study, also weaving classes. **Center for Bilingual Multicultural Studies**, Apdo Postal 1520, T317-1087, www.bilingual-center.com. **Centro de Artes y Lenguas**, Nueva Tabachín 22-A, T317-3126, scale@infosel.net.mx. 5 hrs a day, registration US$100, 1 week minimum, classes US$160, US$300 a week accommodation with families including meals. **Centro de Lengua, Arte e Historia para Extranjeros**, Universidad Autónoma del Estado de Morelos, Río Pánuco 20, Col Lomas del Mirador, T316-1626 (accommodation with families can be arranged). **Cetlalic**, Madero 721, Col Miraval, CP 62270, T313-5450, www.cetlalic.org.mx. Themed courses, plus Mexican and Central American history and culture. Non-profit making. Various levels. Small groups (maximum 5 people). Stay with families. Recommended. **Cuauhnáhuac**, Morelos Sur 123, Col Chipitlán, CP 62070, T312-3673, www.cuauhnahuac.edu.mx. A cooperative language centre offering standard and intensive Spanish options, and private classes, registration US$70, US$300 per week or US$800 per month high season, US$230 per week, US$690 per month low season, family stays US$22 per day shared room with meals or US$35 single room with meals, efficient, helpful. **Cuernavaca Language School**, T311-8956, www.cls.com.mx, or PO Box 4133, Windham, New Hampshire, USA, T603-4379714. **Encuentros**, Morelos 36, Col Acapantzingo, CP 62440, T/F312-5088, www.learnspanishinmexico.com. A fun, functional approach to acquiring Spanish including twice-weekly visits to places in Cuernavaca. Registration US$100, tuition US$210. **Experiencia,** Apdo Postal 5-96, Leyva 200, Col Miguel Hidalgo, CP 62050, T312-6579, www.experienciaspanish.com. One-to-one, class and hourly sessions. Free *intercambios* (Spanish-English practice sessions) Tue and Wed afternoon, open 5 days a week. **Fenix Language Institute**, Nueva Francia 8, Col Recursos, T/F313-3285, www.fenixmex.com. **Idel**, Apdo 1271-1, Calz de los Actores 112, Col Atzingo, T/F313-0157, del-site.tripod.com/idel.html, 5 levels of course. **Ideal Latinoamerica**, Privada Narciso Mendoza 107, Col La Pradera, CP 62170, T311-7551, www.ideal-school.com. A variety of courses, including a professional vocabulary program; family homestay is an option. **IMEC**, Piñanonas 26, Col Jacarandas, CP 62420, www.imeccuernavaca.com.mx. A variety of pachages are offered and homestay can be arranged. **Instituto Chac-Mool**, Privada de la Pradera 108, Col Pradera, T317-1163, www.chac-mool.com. Family homestay arranged. **KUKULCAN**, Manuel Mazarí 208, Col Miraval, CP62270, T312-5279, www.kukulcan.com.mx. A variety of Spanish courses, including one for health care professionals, and free cultural activities such as salsa, folk dancing and cooking. **Spanish Language Institute** (SLI), Pradera 208, Col La Pradera, CP 62170, T311-0063, www.asli.com.mx. Open 5 days a week, minimum 6 hrs per day, classes start every Mon. **Universal**, JH Preciado 171, Col San Antón, CP 62020, T312-4902, www.universal-spanish.com, 3 levels of language course, tutorials and mini courses on culture.

Laundry On Galeana, 1½ blocks from the Zócalo. **Post office** On Hidalgo, just off the Alameda. **Telephone** Telmex on Hidalgo, just off the Alameda, LADA phones are outside, almost opposite junction of Nezahualcoyotl. There is a telephone office at **Parrots** restaurant and bar on the Alameda, next to the Museo Regional.

Tepoztlán *p146*

Language schools Tepoztlán is a definite alternative to Cuernavaca. Try **Spanish Communications Institute**, Cuauhtemotzín, T315-1709, USA T956-994-9977.

Taxco *p147, map p148*

Banks Good rates at **Cambio de Divisar Argentu** on Plazuela San Juan 5. **Bancomer**, between Plazuela San Juan and Plaza Principal, is OK. **Internet** Azul Cybercafé, Hidalgo, near Plaza San Juan, Mon-Sat 0900-2200. **Laundry** Lavandería La Cascada, Delicias 4. **Post office** On Carretera Nacional about 100 m east of **Estrella de Oro** bus terminal.

East of Mexico City

Snow-capped Popocatépetl, the smoking-mountain warrior, and his princess Iztaccíhuatl rise majestically to the east of the capital en route to Puebla, City of the Angels, or tucked-away Tlaxcala, delightful capital of Mexico's smallest state. Nearby are the dramatic murals of Cacaxtla and Cholula's artificial 'mountain', in fact the largest pyramid in all Mesoamerica. *» For Sleeping, Eating and other listings see pages 163-167.*

Amecameca → *Phone code: 587. Colour map 3, B4. Altitude: 2315 m.*

At Km 29 on Route 190 is **Ixtapaluca**, where a road heading south leads to the small town of Amecameca, once the starting point for exploring Popocatépetl (5452 m), smoking mountain, and Iztaccíhuatl (5286 m), the white woman. On the way to Amecameca, see the restored 16th-century convent and church at **Chalco**, and the fine church, convent and open-air chapel of the same period at **Tlalmanalco**.

The Zócalo at Amecameca, 60 km from Mexico City, is pleasant with good taco stands. A road reaches the sanctuary of El Sacromonte, 90 m above the town, with magnificent views, a small and very beautiful church built round a cave once inhabited by Fray Martín de Valencia, a conquistador who came to Mexico in 1524. It is, after the shrine of Guadalupe, the most sacred place in Mexico and has a much-venerated full-sized image of Santo Entierro weighing only 1.5 kg. From the Zócalo, take the exit under the arch and head for the first white station of the cross; the stations lead to the top. Market day is Saturday, and there is an excellent non-touristy market on Sunday. The **tourist office** ⓘ *near the plaza, daily 0900-1500*, can provide information and guides for Iztaccíhuatl. To get to Amecameca from Mexico City, take the metro to Pantitlán, then a bus or *pesero* to Ixtapaluca. Behind the Mercado Municipal take another *pesero* on the 'Avila Camacho' route and get off at La Vereda.

Check locally whether the Amecameca-Cholula road through the volcanoes is still closed. The saddle, which is reached by car via a paved road up to the Paso de Cortés (25 km from Amecameca), gives particularly fine views.

Popocatépetl

In December 2000, Popocatépetl, known familiarly as Don Goyo, had its largest eruption for 500 years. The crater lid, which was in part blown sky-high, had increased, according to experts, to 14 million cubic metres; not only did smoke and ash rise to a height of more than 10 km, but the volcano also threw out incandescent rocks for a radius of up to 2 km. There was another similar eruption less than a month later.

Popo has been closed to climbers since 1994; access is restricted in a radius of 12 km from the crater.

For the foreseeable future it will not be possible to climb, or get close to, Popocatépetl; furthermore, outsiders should exercise discretion about visiting villages in the danger area out of respect for the inhabitants. Ask locally for up-to-date information and advice.

Iztaccíhuatl

From Paso de Cortés a road goes left, north along another dirt road, which leads past a TV station for 8 km to the parking nearest to the summit of Iztaccíhuatl at La Joya. Near the antennae is a *refugio* called Atzomani, which is the safest place to park, and there is a *buzón* (box) for notifying potential rescue groups of your intended route. From there you find various routes to the summit (12 to 15 hours return) and three to four refuges in which to stay overnight (no furniture, bare floors, dirty). Iztaccíhuatl has been described as 'an exhilarating rollercoaster of successive summits'. To climb Iztaccíhuatl take a taxi to La Joya; from there, follow the tracks up the grassy hill on the right; it's four to six hours to the first huts. The first two huts are at 4750 m (space for

30 people), the third at 4850 m (10-15 people), and the last hut is at 5010 m (in poor condition, 10-12 people); the Luis Menéndez hut is the most salubrious. From the last hut it is 2½ to three hours to the top; set off at 0400, over two glaciers. Some rock climbing is required, so crampons and ice-picks are necessary and can be hired in Amecameca.

The best time to climb the volcano is late Oct to early Mar when skies are clear; from May to Oct the weather is good before noon only.

A more technical route starts at the *buzón* and at first descends left into the valley. Walk three to four hours from La Joya to the Ayoloco glacier before which is a refugio for eight to 10 people at 4800 m. From here it is three to four hours to the summit. Guides are available in Amecameca. They charge about US$110 and are worth it, as walking on glaciers without knowing the conditions is hazardous.

It's also possible to climb Iztaccíhuatl from Puebla. Take a second-class bus to Cholula from Puebla, then a combi from the centre to **San Nicolás de los Ranchos**. From here bargain with one of the few local taxis for a ride to **La Joya** (US$20).

The route to Puebla

Heading east from Mexico City you could make a small detour to **Chapingo**, where there are some fine Rivera frescoes in the **college chapel** ⓘ *Mon-Fri 0900-1800*. You can get there by *colectivo* from General Anaya y San Ciprián or by bus from TAPO (**Autotransportes Mexico-Texcoco**, US$0.70).

Near Chapingo a road runs to **Huexotla**, which has an Aztec wall, ruined fortifications and pyramid, and the 16th-century Franciscan convent of San Luis Obispo. Another road from the town of Texcoco runs through the public park of **Molino de las Flores**. From the old hacienda buildings, now in ruins, a road (right) runs up the hill of Tetzcotzingo, near the top of which are the **Baños de Nezahualcóyotl**, the poet-prince. **San Miguel de Chiconcuac**, on the road to San Andrés and left at its church, 4 km away, is famous for its rugs, sweaters and *sarapes*. Tuesday is market day and there is a rousing **fiesta** in honour of their patron saint on 29 September.

Beyond Ixtapaluca, southeast of Los Reyes on Route 190, the road climbs through pine forests to reach 3196 m, about 63 km from Mexico City, and then descends in a series of sharp bends to the town of **San Martín Texmelucan**, Km 91. The old Franciscan convent here has a beautifully decorated interior, and a former hacienda displays weaving and old machinery. The Zócalo too is beautiful, with benches covered in ceramic tiles and a central gazebo. Market day is Tuesday.

Puebla

» *pp163-167. Colour map 3, B4.*

→ *Phone code: 222. Population: 1,346,176. Altitude: 2060 m.*

'City of the Angels', Puebla de los Angeles is one of Mexico's oldest and most famous cities and the capital of Puebla state. It was founded in 1531 by Fray Julián Garcés who saw angels in a dream indicating where the city should be built, hence its name. It is also one explanation of why Puebla wasn't built over prehispanic ruins like many other colonial cities. Talavera tiles are an outstanding feature of Puebla's architecture and their extensive use on colonial buildings distinguishes Puebla from other colonial cities. Puebla is a charming, pleasant and friendly city, always popular with travellers.

Ins and outs

Getting there **Aeropuerto Hermanos Serdán** (PBC) has mostly domestic flights. The CAPU bus station is to the north of the city. Taxis from the terminal to the city centre

Puebla is said to have had 365 churches, one for each day of the year.

leave from outside the departure terminal. From the centre to the terminal, take any form of public transport marked 'CAPU'. Puebla is on the main Highway 150 from Mexico City to the Gulf Coast, the same *supercarretera* that branches south, beyond Puebla, to Oaxaca. An important commercial centre, Puebla is also the hub of other lesser routes to towns and villages in the surrounding area.

Getting around Although Puebla is a big city, most of the major sites are around the centre, within easy walking distance of each other. City buses, *colectivos* or taxis will take you to any of the more distant sites.

Information The **tourist office** ⓘ *5 Ote 3, Av Juárez, T246-2044, www.turismopuebla.com.mx, Mon-Fri,* is behind the cathedral, next to the post office.

Sights

The centre, although still beautifully colonial, is cursed with traffic jams and pollution, except in those shopping streets reserved for pedestrians. Puebla is said to have had 365 churches dating from the early colonial period, one for each day of the year. The din from the church bells was so loud that the residents requested that it be toned down a little since they were driven to distraction on Sundays and feast days.

The **Congreso del Estado** ⓘ *Calle 5 Poniente 128*, formerly the Consejo de Justicia, near the post office, is a converted 19th-century Moorish-style town house. The tiled entrance and courtyard are very attractive and it had a theatre inside, shown to visitors on request. It is now the seat of the state government. The **Patio de los Azulejos** ⓘ *3 Sur between 9 and 11 Poniente 110*, should also be visited; it has fabulous tiled façades on the former almshouses for old retired priests of the order of San Felipe Neri. The colours and designs are beautiful. The tiny entrance on 16 de Septiembre is hard to find; ring the bell on the top right and you may get a guided tour. Also worth visiting is the **Biblioteca Palafoxiana** ⓘ *Casa de la Cultura, opposite the cathedral, 5 Oriente 5, open 1000*, or the library of Bishop Palafox; it has 46,000 antique volumes. It is in a colonial building with a large courtyard, which also houses paintings and art exhibitions. Next door at 5 Oriente 9 is another attractive building, the **Tribunal Superior de Justicia**, built in 1762; you may go in the courtyard.

The **Plaza y Mercado El Parián** is between Avenida 2 y 4 Oriente and Avenida 6 y 8 Norte. On Calle 8 Norte between Avenida 6 Oriente and Avenida 4 Oriente there are many small shops selling paintings. The area is also notable for onyx souvenir shops. Onyx figures and chess sets are attractive and cheaper than elsewhere, but the *poblanos* are hard bargainers. In the adjoining Barrio del Artista the artists' studios are near to **Hotel Latino**. Live music and refreshments at small **Café del Artista** ⓘ *Calle 8 Norte y Avenida 6 Oriente.*

The **Teatro Principal** (1550) ⓘ *Av 8 Ote y Calle 6 Norte*, is possibly the oldest in the Americas although it was badly damaged by fire in 1902 and had to be

Puebla

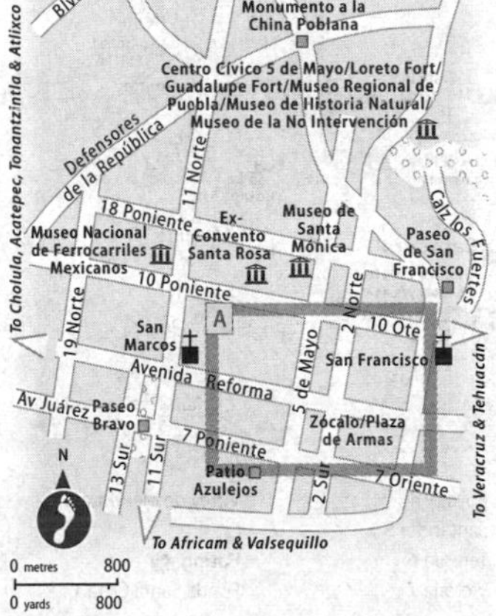

rebuilt. The Jesuit church of **La Compañía** ⓘ *Av Don Juan de Palafox y Mendoza y 4 Sur*, has a plaque in the sacristy showing where China Poblana is said to be buried. Also worth visiting is the house of Aquiles Serdán, a liberal activist who opposed the dictatorship of Porfirio Díaz. A conflict which took place in this house – in which he and about 17 others were killed – is said to have sparked the 1910 Revolution. It is now full of memorabilia and houses the **Museo de la Revolución Mexicana** ⓘ *6 Oriente 206, daily 1000-1630, US$1*. The tiled façade of the **Casa de los Muñecos**, on the corner of the main square, is famous for its caricatures in tiles of the enemies of the 18th-century builder. Inside, in the **Museo Universitario** ⓘ *2 Norte 1, US$1*, some rooms contain old physics instruments, seismographs, cameras and telescopes, another has stuffed animals, but most rooms contain religious paintings from the 17th and 18th centuries. Avenida Reforma has many fine buildings, for example No 141, **Hotel Alameda**, which is tiled inside and out. The **Palacio Municipal** is on the north side of the Zócalo. To the right of the entrance is the **Biblioteca del Palacio** (opened 1996) with some tourist information and books on the city. To the left is the **Teatro de la Ciudad**, opened 1995, where music and drama are performed. There is also an art gallery in the building.

The **Casa del Dean** ⓘ *16 de Septiembre y 7 Poniente, US$2.20 plus tip for the guide if wanted*, was built in 1580. The walls of the two remaining rooms are covered with 400-year-old murals in vegetable and mineral dyes, which were discovered in 1953 under layers of wallpaper and paint. In 1984, the house, previously used as a cinema, was taken over by the government and opened to the public. The murals were inspired by the poems of the Italian poet and humanist, Petrarch, and are believed to have been painted by indigenous craftsmen under the direction of the Dean, Don Tomás de la Plaza, whose house it was. The murals contain a mixture of classical Greek, pagan (indigenous) and Christian themes. About 40% have been restored.

Churches

On the central arcaded plaza is the fine **Cathedral**, notable for its marble floors, onyx and marble statuary and gold-leaf decoration. There are statues flanking the

Puebla centre

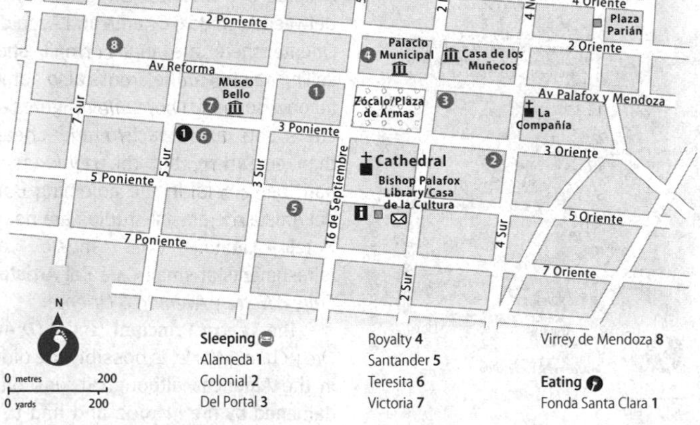

altar, which are said to be of an English king and a Scottish queen. The bell tower gives a grand view of the city and snow-capped volcanoes, although recently visitors have not been allowed access.

One of the most stunning sights in Puebla is the **Capilla del Rosario** of the church of **Santo Domingo** ⓘ *5 de Mayo 407* (1596-1659). The baroque here displays a beauty of style and prodigality of form that served as example and inspiration for all later baroque in Mexico. Inside, the chapel is a riot of detailed gold leaf. The altar of the main church is also decorated with gold leaf with four levels from floor to ceiling of life-size statues of religious figures. There is a strong indigenous flavour to Puebla's baroque; this can be seen in the churches of Tonantzintla and Acatepec (see page 160); it is not so evident, but it is still there, in the opulent decorative work in the cathedral. Beyond the church, up towards the Fuerte Loreto (see below), there is a spectacular view of the volcanoes.

Other places well worth visiting are the churches of **San Cristóbal** (1687) ⓘ *4 Norte y 6 Ote*, with modern churrigueresque towers and Tonantzintla-like plasterwork inside, as well as the 18th-century **San José** ⓘ *2 Norte y 18 Ote*, with attractive tiled façade and decorated walls around the main doors and beautiful altarpieces inside. One of the most famous and oldest local churches is **San Francisco** ⓘ *14 Ote 1009*, with a glorious tiled façade and a mummified saint in its side chapel; see also the pearl divers' chapel, given by the poor divers of Veracruz. The **Capilla de Dolores** ⓘ *the other side of Blv 5 de Mayo from San Francisco*, is small but elaborately decorated. **Santa Catalina** ⓘ *3 Norte with 2 Pte* has beautiful altarpieces; **Nuestra Señora de la Luz** ⓘ *14 Norte and 2 Ote*, has a good tiled façade and so has **San Marcos** ⓘ *Av Reforma and 9 Norte*. The Maronite church of **Belén** ⓘ *7 Norte and 4 Pte*, has a lovely old tiled façade and a beautifully tiled interior. The church **La Puerta del Cielo** ⓘ *at the top of the Cerro de San Juan in Col La Paz*, has over 80 figures of angels inside.

Museums

The **Museo de Artesanías del Estado** ⓘ *3 Norte 1203, Tue-Sun 1000-1630*, in the **ex-Convento de Santa Rosa**, is well worth a visit. It has a good display of the many crafts produced in the State of Puebla, although the highlight is a priceless collection of 16th-century Talavera tiles on the walls and ceilings of its extraordinary vaulted kitchen, well worth a visit. It was here that the nuns are said to have invented the famous *mole poblano*.

The fragile-looking and extravagantly ornamented **Casa del Alfeñique** (Sugar Candy House) ⓘ *Av 4 Ote 418, US$0.40*, a few blocks from the cathedral, now the Museo Regional del Estado, is worth seeing.

Museo Bello ⓘ *Av 3 Pte 302, Tue-Sun US$1.10, free Tue, guided tours*, is the house of the collector and connoisseur Bello who died in 1938. It has good displays of Chinese porcelain and Talavera pottery and is beautifully furnished. **Museo de Santa Mónica** ⓘ *18 Pte 103, Tue-Sun 1000-1800*, is housed in a former convent where generations of nuns hid, after the reform laws of 1857 made the convent illegal. This is where the nuns invented the local speciality and national dish, *chiles en nogada*. **Museo Amparo** ⓘ *2 Sur 708, esquina 9 Ote, Wed-Sun 1000-1800, free guided tour 1200 Sun, US$2, students half price* has an excellent anthropological exhibition with one of the best prehispanic collections in Mexico and audiovisual explanations in Spanish, English, French and Japanese (take your own headphones, or hire them). Colonial art and furniture are on show upstairs. Recommended.

In the suburbs of Puebla. the **Cinco de Mayo Civic Centre**, with a stark statue of Benito Juárez, is, among other things, a regional centre of arts, crafts and folklore. It is near the **Museo Regional de Puebla** ⓘ *daily 1000-1700*, which has magnificent collections but little information. Also nearby is the **Museo de Historia Natural**, auditorium, planetarium, fairgrounds and an open-air theatre. In the same area, the forts of Guadalupe and Loreto were the scene of the **Battle of Puebla**, in which 2000

 Mexican troops defeated Maximilian's 6000 European troops on 5 May 1862 (although the French returned victorious 10 days later). This is why 5 May is a holiday in Mexico. Inside the **Fuerte Loreto**, which has views of the city (and of its pollution), is a small museum, **Museo de la No Intervención** ⓘ *Tue-Sun 1000-1700, US$1.30*, depicting the battle of 1862.

Around Puebla

» pp163-167.

The small somnolent town of **Cholula**, with the Universidad de las Américas, was once as influential as Teotihuacán. When Cortés arrived, it was a holy centre with 100,000 inhabitants and 400 shrines, or *teocallis*, grouped round the great pyramid of Quetzalcoatl. When razing the shrines, Cortés vowed to build a chapel for each one destroyed; in fact there are 'only' about 70 churches in Cholula.

The excavated **pyramid**, a man-made mountain, has 8 km of tunnels and some recently discovered frescoes inside; 1 km of tunnel is open to the public, giving an idea of the layers that were superimposed to create the pyramid. Near the tunnel entrance is a **museum** ⓘ *daily 1000-1700, US$2 weekdays, guides charge US$6.50, (recommended as there are no signs inside; some guides speak English)*, has a copy of the frescoes (the originals are not open to the public). To get there from the Zócalo follow Avenida Morelos and cross the railway. The 16th-century chapel of **Los Remedios** on top of the pyramid gives a fine view. The Franciscan fortress church of **San Gabriel** (1552) ⓘ *Mon-Sat 0600-1200, 1600-1900, Sun 0600-1900*, is in the plaza. Next to it is the **Capilla Real** ⓘ *Mon-Sat 1000-1200, 1530-1800, Sun 0900-1800*, which has 49 domes.

In the neighbouring village of **Tonantzintla** the 16th-century church of **Santa María de Tonantzintla** ⓘ *daily 1000-1800*, or 'the place of our venerable mother', is one of the most beautiful churches in Mexico. It can be reached by paved road from **San Francisco Acatepec** ⓘ *daily 0900-1800 (supposedly, but not always so), the key is held by José Ascac, ask for his shop*, another village with an equally beautiful but less ornate 16th-century church, whose interior has been restored following a fire, but whose wonderful tiled façade is still intact. These two tiny churches are exquisite and should not be missed; they are resplendent with Poblano tiles and their interiors, especially that of Tonantzintla, are a riot of indigenous stuccowork and carving. Best light for photography is after 1500; photography *inside* the churches is frowned upon.

You can visit Tonantzintla and Acatepec from Cholula with a *pesero* (from main square) or combi (US$0.55 from junction of Avenida 5 and Miguel Alemán) to Acatepec or to Tonantzintla (marked Chilipo or Chipanco; ask which combi goes to the church you want). You can walk the 1 km to the other church, and then take a bus or combi back to Cholula or Puebla. The Acatepec bus from CAPU in Puebla (US$0.45, 30 minutes) stops outside the church. The villages are off Highway 190 en route from Puebla to Izúcar de Matamoros.

Huejotzingo, Km 106, has the second oldest church and monastery in Mexico. It was built in 1529 and is now a museum. Market is held on Saturday and Tuesday. There is a dramatic carnival on Shrove Tuesday, portraying the story of Agustín Lorenzo, a famous local bandit.

Tlaxcala

» pp163-167. Colour map 3, B4.

➔ *Phone code: 246. Altitude: 2240 m.*

North of Puebla the quaint old town of Tlaxcala, capital of Mexico's smallest state, has a very pleasant centre of simple buildings washed in ochre, pink and yellow, and vast not-so-quaint suburbs. It is the capital of the state of the same name whose wealthy ranchers breed fighting bulls, but whose landless peasants are still poor. The annual **fair** is held 29 October-15 November each year.

The **tourist office** ⓘ *Av Juárez y Landizábal, T465-0960*, has many maps and leaflets and is very helpful.

Dating from 1521, the **Church of San Francisco** is the oldest in Mexico, from whose pulpit the first Christian sermon was preached in New Spain (Mexico). Of course, the sermon would have been for the benefit of the Spanish residents; the local indigenous people would have congregated outside at the open chapel. Almost next door is the **Museo del Estado de Tlaxcala** ⓘ *daily 0900-1700, US$1*, with two floors of interesting historical and artistic exhibits. In the Palacio de Gobierno on the main square are the extremely colourful murals depicting the indigenous story of Tlaxcala, the history of Mexico and of humankind. **The Museo de Artes y Tradiciones Populares** ⓘ *Tue-Sun, US$0.60*, is a 'living museum' where local Otomí people demonstrate traditional arts and customs including the sweat bath, cooking, embroidery, weaving and pulque-making. It is highly recommended.

Around Tlaxcala

The churrigueresque **Basílica de Ocotlán** (1541), on a hill in the outskirts of Tlaxcala (a stiff 20-minute climb from Juárez via Guribi and Alcocer), commands a view of valley and volcano. It was described by Sacheverell Sitwell as "the most delicious building in the world". Its façade of lozenge-shaped vermilion bricks, framing the white stucco portal and surmounted by two white towers with fretted cornices and salomonic pillars, is beautiful. The sumptuous golden interior, comparable with those of Taxco and Tepotzotlán, was worked on for 25 years by the indigenous artist Francisco Miguel.

The ruined pyramid of **Xicoténcatl** at San Esteban de Tizatlán, 5 km from Tlaxcala, has two sacrificial altars with original colour frescoes preserved under glass. The pictures tell the story of the wars with Aztecs and Chichimecs. Amid the archaeological digs at Tizatlán are a splendid 19th-century church and the 16th-century chapel of San Esteban. To get there, take a *colectivo* to Tizatlán from 1 de Mayo y 20 de Noviembre, Tlaxcala; at the main square, alight when you see a yellow church dome on the left.

Cacaxtla → *Colour map 3, B4.*

ⓘ *Tue-Sun 1000-1630, US$2, which also includes access to the nearby ruins of Xochitecatl. From Puebla take a Flecha Azul bus marked 'Nativitas' from Calle 10 Pte y Calle 11 Norte to just beyond Nativitas where a sign on the right points to San Miguel del Milagro and Cacaxtla (US$1). Walk up the hill (or colectivo US$0.20) to a large sign with its back to you, turn left here for the ruins.*

A remarkable series of pre-Columbian frescoes are to be seen at the ruins of Cacaxtla near San Miguel del Milagro, between Texmelucan and Tlaxcala. The colours are still sharp and some of the figures are larger than life size. To protect the paintings from the sun and rain, a huge roof has been constructed. An easily accessible visitors' centre has been opened but there is disappointingly little published information on the site. In theory there is a 'per picture' charge for photography, but this is not assiduously collected although flash and tripod are strictly prohibited.

Cuetzalan and around → *Phone code: 233. Colour map 3, B5.*

An interesting day trip from Puebla is to Cuetzalan market (via Tetela-Huahuaxtla), which is held on Sunday in the Zócalo (three hours' walk up). In the first week of October each year dancers from local villages gather and *voladores* 'fly' from the top of their pole. The Nahua sell cradles (*huacales*) for children, machetes and embroidered garments. Women decorate their hair with skeins of wool. The *Día de los*

> *It can be very foggy at Cuetzalan, even when it is fine in Puebla.*

 Muertos (2 November) is interesting here. Big clay dogs are made locally: unusual stoves that hold large flat clay plates on which *tortillas* are baked and stews are cooked in pots; these are also available in nearby Huitzilán. You can also go via Zaragoza, Zacapoaxtla and Apulco, where you can walk along a path, left of the road, to the fine 35-m waterfall of **La Gloria. Tourist information** is available at Calle Hidalgo y Bravo, helpful, good map.

From Cuetzalan it is a one-and-a-half-hour walk to the well-preserved, niched pyramids of **Yohualichan** ⓘ *Wed-Sun, US$2*, from the Totonac culture. There are five excavated pyramids, two of them equivalent to that at El Tajín (see page 327), and three still uncovered. There has been earthquake damage, though. Take a bus from Calle Miguel Alvarado Avila y Calle Abosolo, more frequent in morning and market days, to San Antonio and get off at the sign Pirámides Yohualichan (30 minutes, bad road), then walk 2 km to the site. In the Cuetzalan area are 32 km of caverns with lakes, rivers and wonderful waterfalls. These include Tzicuilan (follow Calle Emiliano Zapata, east of town) and Atepolihuit (follow Carretera Antigua up to the Campo Deportivo, west of town). Children offer to guide visitors to the ruins and caves.

South of Puebla » pp163-167.

From Puebla, Route 150 continues to **Amozoc,** where tooled leather goods and silver decorations on steel are made, both mostly as outfits for the *charros*, or Mexican cattlemen. Beyond Amozoc lies **Tepeaca** with its late 16th-century monastery, well worth a visit; its weekly market is very extensive. On the main square is **Casa de Cortés** ⓘ *daily 1000-1700*, where Hernán Cortés signed the second of five *Cartas de Relación* in 1520. An old Spanish tower (1580) stands between Tepeaca's main square and the parish church. Beyond Tepeaca, 57 km from Puebla, lies **Tecamachalco**, where the vast 16th-century Franciscan monastery church has beautiful murals on the choir vault, in late medieval Flemish style, by a local indigenous artist.

Tehuacán → *Phone code: 238. Colour map 3, C5. Altitude: 1676 m.*

This charming town, southeast of Puebla, has a pleasant, sometimes cool, climate. Water from the mineral springs is bottled and sent all over the country by **Garci Crespo, San Lorenzo** and **Peñafiel.** From the small dam at Malpaso on the Río Grande, an annual race is held for craft without motors as far as the village of Quiotepec. The central plaza is pleasant and shaded. The **Museo de Minerología Romero** ⓘ *Av Reforma, 7 Norte 356, daily 0900-1200, 1600-1800, morning only on Sat, free*, is in the ex-Convento del Carmen. It has one room with a good collection of minerals from all over the world. The Ayuntamiento on the Zócalo is decorated inside and out with murals and tiles. A short bus ride beyond Peñafiel Spa is the spa of **San Lorenzo** ⓘ *US$2*, with spring-fed pools surrounded by trees.

Huautla de Jiménez

From Teotitlán it is possible to drive into the hills to the indigenous town of Huautla de Jiménez, where the local Mazatec population consume the hallucinogenic 'magic' mushrooms made famous by Dr Timothy Leary. Huautla has all four seasons of the year in each day: springlike mornings, wet, foggy afternoons, fresh, autumn evenings and freezing nights. Hiking in the mountains here is worthwhile. There are many police and military; drivers may be waved down by people in the road up to Huautla; do not stop for them, they may be robbers.

Sleeping

Amecameca *p155*

E San Carlos, Constitución 10, T978-0746. The only hotel, simple basic rooms.

Camping

Permitted at the railway station, ask the man in the office (leaving town, it's after the road to Tlamacas, on the right, 1-2 km away).

Puebla *p156, maps p157 and 158*

LL-AL Puebla Marriott Real, Hermanos Serdán 807, near 1st Puebla interchange on Mexico City-Puebla motorway. T223-8300, www.pueblamarriott.gruporeal.com. The best hotel in town but far from the centre.

L-AL Camino Real, 7 Pte 105, T229-0909, www.caminoreal.com/puebla. In ex-Convento de la Concepción, built 1593 and beautifully restored, all rooms are different, quiet, bar, restaurant, room service, boutiques, dry cleaning.

A Del Portal, Portal Morelos 205, T246-0211. Very good, but ask for a room away from Zócalo side (noisy); restored colonial, plain rooms, TV, phone, parking across the street.

A-C Aristos, Av Reforma, esq 7 Sur, T232-0565. Good facilities in rooms and bathrooms, gym with sauna, pool, attractive public areas, restaurant, piano bar, cheaper rates at weekends.

B-C Palace, 2 Ote 13, T242-4030. Price depends on number and size of beds, attractive, modern lobby, *cafetería*, satellite TV, phones, 60 rooms.

B-C Royalty, Portal Hidalgo 8, T242-4740. Pleasant, central, quiet, restaurant good but expensive and service slow, tables outside under the portales where a marimba band sometimes plays.

C Colonial, 4 Sur 105, T246-4199. Across pedestrian street from La Compañía church, old-fashioned and charming, very friendly, colonial style, restaurant, accepts Amex, ask for back room, with bath, TV and phone.

C Gilfer, 2 Ote 11, T246-0611. Attractive, modern building, large rooms, reasonable restaurant, excellent service.

C Granada, Blv de la Pedrera 2303, T232-0966. Very close to bus terminal, bus to centre leaves from front door, quiet, comfortable, restaurant, room service, TV in rooms. Also close to the bus terminal.

C Imperial, 4 Ote 212, T242-4980. Good-sized plain rooms with TV and phones, shower, clean, some rooms noisy, laundry, restaurant, gym, parking, 30% discount for *Footprint* owners, good value.

D Alameda, Reforma 141, close to the Zócalo, T242-0882. Most rooms windowless, parking, TV, phone, bath, very clean, friendly, good value.

D Ritz, 2 Norte 207 y 4 Ote, 2 blocks from Zócalo, T232-4457. Reasonable, drab front but good rooms with balcony.

D Virrey de Mendoza, Reforma 538, T242-3903. Old colonial house, plain, fairly basic rooms, high ceilings, TV, bath, beautiful wooden staircase.

D-E Santander, 5 Pte 111, near cathedral, T246-3175. Colonial façade, hot showers, clean, simple, big bright rooms towards street, TV, enclosed parking. Recommended.

D-E Teresita, 3 Pte 309, T232-7072. Small modern rooms, with bath (although the 'comedy showers' manage to get everything soaked!), hot water, friendly.

E Casa de Huéspedes Los Angeles, Calle 4 Norte 9. Basic, communal bathrooms, irregular hot water, *comedor*, central.

E Victoria, near Zócalo, 3 Pte 306, T232-8992. Clean, quiet, hot showers. Friendly and recommended.

Around Puebla *p160*

B Villas Arqueológicas, 2 Pte 501, Cholula, T247-1966. Behind pyramid, affiliated to Club Med. Heated pool, pleasant garden, tennis, French restaurant, rooms have heating, TV, phone, English and French spoken.

C Cali Quetzalcoatl, on Zócalo, Portal Guerrero 11, Cholula, T247-4199. Clean, good restaurant.

E Hostal Cholollan, 2Calle Norte 2003, Barrio de Jesús, Cholula, T247-7038. Dormitory accommodation, in a lively place with great

***Phone codes** Amecameca 587; Puebla and around 222; Tlaxcala 246; Cuetzalan and around 233; Tehuacán 238.*

views of Popo and Izta from the terrace. Free use of kitchen, and great meeting spot.

E Las Américas, 14 Ote 6, San Andrés, Cholula, T247-0991. Near pyramid, actually a motel, modern with rooms off galleries round paved courtyard (car park), small restaurant, clean, good value.

E Trailer Park Las Américas, 30 Ote 602, Cholula. Hot showers, secure, as are the furnished apartments.

Tlaxcala *p160*

A Posada San Francisco (Club Med), Plaza de la Constitución 17, T462-6022. Lavishly decorated in colonial style, 2 restaurants, good food, secure parking, swimming pool, tennis courts. Highly recommended.

B Alifer, Morelos 11, uphill from plaza, T462-5678. Central, quite comfortable but fairly characterless. Safe parking.

Cuetzalan and around *p161*

C Hotel Taselotzin, by La Gloria waterfall, near Cuetzalan. A set of *cabañas*, very clean, great views, 2 beds per cabin, and bathroom (**E** per person per night). Recommended.

E-F Hotel Rivello, G Victoria 3, T331-0139, 1 block from Zócalo. With bath (cheaper without), basic, friendly, clean.

Tehuacán *p162*

A México, Reforma Norte and Independencia Pte, 1 block from Zócalo, T382-2419. With garage, TV, restaurant, renovated colonial building, pool, quiet.

C Inter, above restaurant of same name, close to bus station (ask there), T383-3620. Hot shower, clean, modern.

D Iberia, Independencia Ote 217, T383-1500. With bath, clean, airy, pleasant restaurant, noisy weekends, public parking nearby at reduced fee with voucher from hotel. Recommended.

E Madrid, 3 Sur 105, T382-0272, opposite Municipal Library. Comfortable, pleasant courtyard, cheaper without bath. Recommended.

Eating

Amecameca *p155*

There are several eating places and a good food market. A good-quality pulque is available at the *pulquería* on the main plaza.

Puebla *p156, maps p157 and p158*

Local specialities include *chiles en nogada* (poblano chillies stuffed with minced meat and almonds and topped with a sweet cream sauce made with ground nuts, then topped with pomegranate seeds; the green, white and red colours are supposed to represent the Mexican flag); and *mole poblano* (chicken or turkey with sauce of chillies, spices, nuts and chocolate).

TT La Poblanita, 10 Norte 1404-B, and **TT Fonda Santa Clara**, 3 Pte 307. 2nd larger location with parking a couple of blocks west on 3 Pte. Both very good for local specialities, very popular, often crowded. Excellent *mole*, *mixiote* (lamb with chilli, wrapped in paper with spicy sauce), *chiles en nogada* (best in Jul-Sep), delicious.

TT Hotel Royalty, Portal Hidalgo 8. Nice restaurant with traditional dishes including *platillos poblanos*, tables under the portales, sometimes with *marimba* band.

TT La Gardenia, Palafox 416. Local dishes, a bit cramped but very good quality, selection and value. Recommended.

TT Librería Cafetería Teorema, Reforma 540, esq 7 Norte. Café, books and art, live music at night, good coffee and snacks, pastries, *platillos mexicanos*. Recommended.

TT Mesón Sacristía de la Compañía, 6 Sur 304, T242-3554. In the old sacristy, marvellous patio, lots of plants, very cosy.

TT Restaurant Van Gogh, 3 Pte 145-A. Opens 0830 for good breakfast and cheap *menú del día*.

TT Woolworth's, corner of 2 Pte and 5 de Playo, 1½ blocks from northwest corner of Plaza Mayor. Daily 0800-2200. Good range of cheap, reasonable meals and some expensive dishes.

TT-T El Vegetariano, 3 Pte 525 (near **Hotel San Agustín**). Good, opens 0730 for breakfast. Recommended.

T Al Kalifa, 2 Sur between 15 y 17 Ote. Cheap tacos, very good *taco árabe*. Recommended.

T La Princesa, Portal Juárez 101. Good variety and good prices, several other similar places nearby to choose from on Zócalo.

T Mercado El Alto, in the San Francisco quarter. Beautiful market covered with *azulejos*, with good local cuisine. Breakfast and lunch, 8 different menus.

Cafés, sweet shops and ice cream parlours

Nieves – drinks made of alcohol, fruit and milk – are worth trying. **Calle 6 Ote** specializes in shops selling traditional handmade *dulces* (sweets), *camotes* (candied sweet potatoes) and *rompope* (egg nog).
Café Britannia, Reforma 528. Cheap and good coffee. Recommended.
Cafetería Tres Gallos, 4 Pte 110. Good coffee and pastries.
Super-Soya, 5 de Mayo. Good for fruit salads and juices. Several other good places for *comidas corridas* on 5 de Mayo.
Tepoznieves, 3 Pte 150 esq 3 Sur. Rustic Mexican decor, serves all varieties of tropical fruit ice cream and sherbet.

Around Puebla *p160*

There are many good restaurants and food stops in Cholula due to the large number of North Americans in town. Try the *licuados* at market stalls (fruit and milk and 1 or 2 raw eggs if you wish); *mixiote* is a delicious local dish of spicy lamb or goat barbecued in a bag.
ΨΨ **Restaurant Choloyán**, Av Morelos. Good, clean, friendly. Also sells handicrafts.

Tlaxcala *p160*

ΨΨ **Fonda del Convento**, San Francisco 1. Serves excellent 4-course traditional meals.
ΨΨ **Los Portales**, main square. Popular, with regional dishes.
Ψ **Oscar's**, Av Juárez, by corner of Zitlalpopocatl. Excellent sandwiches and juices.

Cuetzalan and around *p161*

Ψ **Posada Quetzal**, Zaragoza, Cuetzalan. Good, cheap restaurant.
Ψ **Yoloxochitl**, 2 de Abril, Cuetzalan. Good for breakfasts, huge juices.

Cafés

Café-Bazar Galería, in centre, Cuetzalan. Good sandwiches and tea, nice garden, English magazines. Recommended.

Tehuacán *p162*

There are many reasonably priced eating places on the Zócalo.
ΨΨ **Restaurant Santander**. Good but pricey.
Ψ **Pizzería Richards**, Reforma Norte 250. Good pizzas, good fresh salads.

Cafés bars and juice stalls

Cafetería California, Independencia Ote 108. Excellent juices and *licuados*.
La Pasita, 5 Ote between 2 y 4 Sur, in front of Plaza de los Sapos. The oldest bar in Puebla, sells a drink by the same name, a local speciality. Recommended.

Festivals and events

Puebla *p156, map p157*

Mid-Apr Feria for 2 weeks.
Sep-Nov The Fiesta Palafoxiana runs from the last Fri in Sep until mid-Nov for 9 weekends of dancing, music, theatre, exhibitions, etc; some free performances.

Shopping

Puebla *p156, map p157*

5 de Mayo is a pedestrian street closed to traffic from the Zócalo to Av 10. The entire block containing the Capilla del Rosario/ Templo de Santo Domingo in the southeast corner has been made into a shopping mall (opened 1994), called the **Centro Comercial La Victoria** after the old La Victoria market. The old market building still exists.

Bookshops **Librería Británica**, Calle 25 Pte 1705-B, T240-8549.

Crafts The famous Puebla Talavera tiles may be purchased from factories outside Puebla, or from the famous **Taller Uriarte**, Av 4 Pte 911 (spectacular building, tours at 1100, 1200 and 1300). Recommended.

Other government-sponsored shops include **Tienda Convento Santa Rosa**, 3 Norte 1203, T240-8904; **Talavera de la Reyna**, Camino a la Carcaña 2413, Recta a Cholula. Recommended (also in Hotel Mesón del Angel); **Centro de Talavera**, Calle 6 Ote 11; **D Aguilar**, 40 Pte 106, opposite Convento de Santa Mónica; and **Casa Rugerio**, 18 Pte 111. **Margarita Guevara**, 20 Pte 30.

Transport

Amecameca *p155*

Bus From Mexico City with Cristóbal Colón. Los Volcanes 2nd-class bus 1-1½ hrs, US$2.80, from the Terminal del Oriente.

Air

Aeropuerto Hermanos Serdán (PBC) has flights to **Guadalajara**, **León**, **Mexico City**, **Monterrey** and **Tijuana**. For website addresses, see page 32.

Airline offices Aero California, Blv Atlixco 2703, Locales B y C, Col Nueva Antequera, T230-4855. **AeroMéxico**, Av Juárez 1514, Col La Paz, T232-0013. **Aeromar**, T232-9633. **Mexicana**, Av Juárez 2312, between Calle 23 Sur and 25 Sur, T248-5600. **Lufthansa** and **LanChile**, at Av Juárez 2916, Col La Paz, T248-4400.

Bus

The huge CAPU bus terminal is north of city. From the centre take any form of transport marked 'CAPU', many *colectivos* and buses (route 12) on Av 9 Norte, US$3.50 per person flat rate; or bus 37 or 21 at Av Camacho. To the centre from the terminal take combi No 14, US$0.30, which stops at 11 Norte and Reforma at Paseo de Bravo (make sure it's a No 14 'directo', as there is a No 14 that goes to the suburbs). The departure terminal has banking services (with ATM), and a good practical mix of shops including gift shops, phone booths, food shops and luggage storage. The arrivals terminal has some shops including small grocery, free toilets, long-distance pay phones and taxi ticket booth (but you have to take ramp to the departure terminal to get the taxi).

Buses services from Puebla run to most parts of Mexico. To **Mexico City**, ADO *GL* to TAPO (eastern) terminal every 20 mins from 0640 to 2010, 2 hrs, US$9; to Terminal del Sur every hr from 0635 to 2135, US$6.50; to Terminal del Norte every 20-40 mins from 0520-2150, US$6.50, **Estrella Roja** to Mexico City airport every hour from 0300 to 2000, 2 hrs, US$9. To Mexico City 2nd class every 10 mins, US$5, *plus* service US$5.50; **AU**, every 12 mins from 0510 to 2300. To **Acapulco**, **Estrella Blanca**, *plus* service, 2200, US$33, 1st class, 1030, 1230, 2130, 2230, 2300, US$28. To **Chetumal**, ADO, 1145, US$58. To **Mérida**, ADO, 2105, US$59. To **Oaxaca**, all take new *autopista*, 4½ hrs; **ADO** at 0800 and 1900, US$24; *UNO* at 1800, US$21. To **Reynosa**, **ADO** at 1155, US$44. To **San Cristóbal de las Casas**, **Cristóbal Colón**, *plus* service, 1715, 1845, 2215, US$50. To **Tapachula**, **UNO**, 1830, 16 hrs, US$71; **Cristóbal Colón**, *plus* service, 2115, US$46. To **Tehuacán** direct ADO every 30-45 mins 0600-2100, US$5.50. To **Tuxtla Gutiérrez**, ADO, 2010, US$42; UNO, 2215, 14 hrs, US$65; To **Villahermosa**, ADO *GL plus* service via *autopista*, 1115, 1535 and 2200, US$46, 1st class, 1900, 2145, US$32; UNO at 2100, 8 hrs, US$53. To **Xalapa**, **ADO** *GL plus* service at 0805 and 1700, US$9, 1st class, 8 a day, 4 hrs, US$7.50; **AU**, 2nd class.

Bus companies Autobuses de Oriente (ADO), T01800-7028000. Mercedes Benz buses, 1st class and *'GL' plus* service. **Oro**, T249-7775, *gran turismo* or 1st-class service. **UNO**, T230-4014, luxury service. **Estrella Roja**, T249-7099, 2nd class, 1st class and *plus* service. **Cristóbal Colón**, T249-7144 ext 2860, *plus* service. **Estrella Blanca**, T249-7561, 1st class, *plus* and *élite* services. **Autobuses Unidos** (AU), T249-7366, all 2nd class without toilets.

Bicycle

Bike shops Several shops in 7 Norte, north of 4 Pte, have international spare parts.

Taxi

Radio Omega, T240-6299, radio taxi service, with new Chevrolet cars, 24-hr service, will deliver packages or pick up food or medicine and deliver it to your hotel.

Train

The train station is a long way from the centre, so before going there check at the tourist office to see if any passenger services are running.

Around Puebla *p160*

Bus Frequent 2nd-class **Estrella Roja** buses from Puebla to **Cholula** from 6 Pte y 13 Norte, 9 km on a new road, 20 mins, also 1st- and 2nd-class **Estrella Roja** buses from CAPU bus terminal hourly (be ready to get out, only a quick stop in Cholula); from Cholula take a 'Pueblo Centro' bus to the city centre, or a 'Puebla-CAPU' bus for the terminal; *colectivos* to Cholula. From **Mexico City**, leave for Cholula from Terminal del Oriente with **Estrella Roja**, every 30 mins, 2½ -3 hrs, US$4.20, 2nd class every 20 mins, a very scenic route through steep wooded hills. Good views of volcanoes.

Tlaxcala *p160*
Bus Tlaxcala's bus station is about a 10-min walk from the centre. Frequent **Flecha Azul** buses from **Puebla**, central bus station (platform 81/82) between 0600 and 2130, 45 mins, US$1.50. To **Cacaxtla** US$0.55.

Cuetzalan *p161*
Bus Direct buses from **Puebla** (Tezuitecos line only), 5 a day from 0500 to 1530, US$8.50; quite a few return buses, but if none direct, go to Zaragoza and change buses there. There are many buses to Zacapoaxtla with frequent connections for Cuetzalan.

Tehuacán *p162*
Bus ADO bus station on Av Independencia (Pte). Direct to **Mexico City**, 5 hrs, US$13; to **Puebla**, 2½ hrs, US$5.50; to **Oaxaca** 5½ hrs, US$16, **Autobuses Unidos** at 1430, coming from Mexico City, may be full), **Veracruz**, US$11, and the Gulf: **Autobuses Unidos**, 2nd class on Calle 2 Ote with several buses daily to Mexico City and Oaxaca. Local bus to **Huajuapan**, 3 hrs, US$7; from there, frequent buses to Oaxaca.

Huautla de Jiménez *p162*
Bus Several daily buses to/from **Mexico City** and **Oaxaca** (US$6.50); children meet buses offering lodging in their homes.

❶ Directory

Puebla *p156, map p157*
Banks Bancomer, 3 Pte 116, changes TCs 0930-1300, good rates. On the Zócalo are **Banco Santander Mexicano**; **Banco Inverlat** at Portal Benito Juárez 109, changes money 0900-1400; and a *casa de cambio* at Portal Hidalgo 6 next to Hotel Royalty. On Av Reforma are: **Banamex**, No 135; **Bancomer**, No 113; **HSBC**, across the street. Most banks have ATMs. **Internet** Escuela Sandoval, on 5 Ote, you can email for US$2 per hr. **Soluciones Alternativas**, Calle 4 Norte 7, 101, 1st flr, no sign, email service US$2 per hr. At the **BUAP University**, Av San Claudio esq 22 Sur, T244-4404, Mon-Fri 0700-2100, Sat and Sun 0800-1800, 48 PCs, but slow, US$2.50 per hr. **Laundry** Commercial centre on Av 21 Pte and Calle 5 Sur, US$4 wash and dry, 3 hrs. Another on 9 Norte, between 2 and 4 Pte, US$2.80, good service wash. **Medical services** Dentist: Dr A Bustos, 2 Pte 105-8, T232-4412, excellent service, recommended. **Doctors** Dr Miguel Benítez Cortázar, 11 Pte 1314, T242-0556, US$15 per consultation; Dr Cuauhtémoc Romero López, same address and phone. Hospitals: **Beneficiencia Española**, 19 Norte 1001, T232-0500. **Betania**, 11 Ote 1826, T235-8655. **UPAEP**, 5 Pte 715, T246-6099. The cheapest is **Universitario de Puebla**, 25 Pte y 13 Sur, T243-1377, where an outpatient consultation is US$5. **Post office** 5 Ote between 16 de Septiembre and 2 Sur, Mon-Fri 0800-2000.

Around Puebla *p160*
Banks There is a *casa de cambio* on the corner of the main plaza in Cholula.

Tlaxcala *p160*
Internet Café Internet, Independencia 21, south of Av Guerrero. **Laundry** Servi-Klim, Av Juárez, 1½ blocks from plaza, dry cleaners, will launder but at dry-cleaning prices. **Lavandería Acuario**, Alonsa Escalona 17, between Juárez and Lira y Ortega, 3 kg US$3, self-service 4 kg US$1, daily 0830-2000.

South of Puebla *p162*
Language school Escuela de Español en Tecamachalco, Calle 29 Sur 303, Barrio de San Sebastián, Tecamachalco, CP 75480, Apdo Postal 13, T422-1121, run by Patricia Martínez, very good; possible to live with families.

Baja California

Baja California (Lower California) is that long, narrow appendage that dangles southwards from the US border between the Pacific Ocean and the Gulf of California for 1300 km. Rugged and almost uninhabited mountains split its tapering length, which has an average width of only 80 km. The tourist hotspots are found at the far north and south. Bordering the US is the brassy and gaudy Tijuana and nearby northern beaches, and in the far south the up-market resorts of Cabo San Lucas and San José del Cabo of the southern Cape zone and La Paz with its colourful carnival. In between is the wilderness that attracts vsitors to watch the whales and dolphins at Guerrero Negro or nearby San Ignacio, comb the beaches, explore the national parks, discover the ancient cave paintings, and enjoy the awe-inspiring and ever-changing desert landscapes. For them, the peninsula, with its hundreds of kilometres of virgin coastline, is a magical place of blue skies, fresh air, solitude and refuge from the rat race north of the border. ▸▸ *For Sleeping, Eating and other listings, see pages 183-196.*

History

Cortés attempted to settle at La Paz in 1534 after one of his expeditions had brought the first Europeans to set foot in Baja, but the land's sterile beauty disguised a chronic lack of food and water; this, and sporadic hostility from local tribes, forced the abandonment of most early attempts at settlement. Jesuit missionary fathers arrived at Loreto in 1697 and founded the first of their 20 missions. The Franciscans and then Dominicans took over when the Jesuits were expelled in 1767. The fathers were devoted and untiring in their efforts to convert the peninsula's ethnic groups, but diseases introduced unknowingly by them and by ships calling along the coasts soon decimated the local population; some indigenous people remain today, but without tribal organization. Scattered about the sierras are the remains of these missions, some beautifully restored, others no more than eroded adobe foundations.

Essentials

Food and accommodation tend to be more expensive than they are in the rest of Mexico, but cheaper than in the US. Tijuana, Ensenada and La Paz all have a good range of duty-free shopping. Make a note of departure times of buses in Tijuana or Ensenada when travelling south: between Ensenada and Santa Rosalía it can be difficult to obtain bus information. Don't ask for menus in English if you can help it; prices are often cheaper in the Spanish version. Check change as overcharging is not uncommon. Note that hotels have widely divergent winter and summer rates; between June and November tariffs are normally lower than those given in the text below (especially in expensive places). The US dollar is preferred in most places north of La Paz.

If you're planning the Big Trip from Mexico to Panama you have to start or end at the Mexican border with the US. It's long, stretching from Tijuana on the Pacific Coast east to the outlet of the Río Grande near Matamoros in the Gulf of Mexico.

Stretching 1704 km from Tijuana to Cabo San Lucas, Highway 1 is generally in good repair, although slightly narrow and lacking hard shoulders. Roads in Baja California Norte are more potholed than those in Baja California Sur. Service stations are placed at adequate intervals along the route, but motorists should fill their tanks at every opportunity and carry spare fuel, particularly if venturing off the main roads. Stations in small towns may not have fuel, or may sell from barrels at inflated prices. The same conditions apply for Highway 5 (Mexicali-San Felipe), Highway 3 (Tecate-Ensenada-San Felipe) and Highway 2 (Tijuana 196, Mexicali-San Luis-Sonoyta). Hitchhiking is not difficult although you may have long waits, and there is very little public transport off the main highway.

Border essentials Mexico-USA

Crossing into Mexico
There is no immigration check on the Mexican side of the border. The buffer zone for about 120 km south of the border allows US citizens to travel without a tourist card. Some have reported travelling in Baja California Sur without a tourist card. If you are bringing in a vehicle you should try to get a tourist card/ vehicle permit in Tijuana (see page 170); if you are travelling beyond Baja California, with or without a vehicle, getting a tourist card in Tijuana will save a lot of trouble later. Immigration authorities are also encountered at Mexicali, Ensenada, Quitovac (28 km south of Sonoyta, Sonora on Highway 2), and when boarding the ferries to cross the Gulf of California, see box, page 194. As a car needs an import permit, make sure you get to the ferry with lots of time to spare and preferably with a reservation.

Crossing into Mexico

» pp 183-196. Colour map 1, A1.

Calexico/Mexicali

The border is open 24 hours a day. Day visitors may prefer to park on the California side, since the extremely congested Avenida Cristóbal Colón in Mexicali, which parallels the frontier fence, is the access route to the US port of entry. Southbound flow is generally better than northbound; entering Mexico, follow the diagonal Calzada López Mateos, which leads to the tourist office and train and bus stations. Pedestrians travelling from Mexicali to Calexico should take the underpass beneath Calzada López Mateos, which passes through the Mexican immigration office before continuing to the US side.

Highway 2 runs east from Mexicali through San Luis Río Colorado, Sonoyta and Caborca to join the Pacific Highway at Santa Ana; see page 198.

Mexicali → *Phone code: 686. Colour map 1, A1.*

Capital of Baja California, Mexicali is not as geared to tourism as Tijuana and thus retains its busy, business-like border-town flavour. The University of Baja California's **Museo Regional** ⓘ *Av Reforma y Calle L, Tue-Fri 0900-1800, weekend 1000-1500, free,* has interesting exhibits illustrating Baja's archaeology, ethnography and missions.

Calexico, the much smaller city on the California side of the border, is so thoroughly Mexicanized that it can be difficult to find a newspaper from San Diego or Los Angeles. Mexican shoppers flock here for clothing bargains.

West of Mexicali

The road from Mexicali to Tijuana is fast and well surfaced, running across barren desert flats, below sea level and with organ-pipe cacti in abundance, until reaching the eastern escarpment of the peninsula's spine; it winds its way up the Cantú Grade to La Rumorosa, giving expansive, dramatic vistas of desert and mountain.

Tecate → *Phone code: 665. Colour map 1, A1.*

The border crossing is open from 0600-2400. Immigration facilities are three blocks north, uphill, from the west side of the parque. **Mexican immigration offices** ⓘ *Lázaro Cárdenas and Callejón Madero, T654-0280*, are on the left, US on the right. The friendly Mexican immigration and customs officers will only process vehicle papers between 0800 and 1600; at other hours, continue to Mexicali or Sonoyta. All documents are obtainable at the border. Tourist cards may also be obtained at the bus terminal. Services to the interior resemble those from Tijuana (**Tres Estrellas de**

Oro to Mexico City, US$93.50). The **Baja California Secretary of Tourism** ⓘ *opposite the park at Libertad 1305, T6540-1095*, provides a useful map of the town and other information. English spoken.

Visitors will find that placid Tecate is more like a Mexican city of the interior than a gaudy border town, perhaps because there is no town centre on the US side.

San Diego/Tijuana

The big trip through Mexico and Central America starts at Tijuana, well San Diego in reality. It is worth considering staying in San Diego for a couple of nights, and popping over the border to orientate yourself, check out bus times and so forth without weighty baggage. You can cross the border and return without completing formalities if you stay within a few miles of Tijuana.

Arriving in San Diego International Airport, bus No 992 stops outside all terminals and gets you from the airport to the downtown Gaslamp district and the Greyhound station ⓘ *120 Broadway, T1-800-229-9424, www.greyhound.com*, with many services to Los Angeles. The trolley bus service that covers most of the city goes right to the border at San Ysidro.

A tourist office at the border gives out maps of the border area explaining money changing, buses, etc.

Due to the sheer volume of people crossing the border, it is very easy to enter Mexico without completing formalities for foot and vehicle passengers. If travelling on into Mexico, don't follow the crowds who cross without visiting immigration. When you actually leave the US try to complete US exit formalities (hand your US entry card to the US immigration office where people are entering Mexico) and get a Mexico entry stamp at the border as it will avoid serious problems later on.

If entering without a vehicle, you can get a tourist card from the office just over the pedestrian bridge – the office faces the traffic and you will have to look around. After completing immigration procedures walk over another pedestrian bridge before you get to Tijuana proper where you're greeted by money changers. From there, it's a short walk to the downtown bus terminal. The main terminal is 5 km southeast of town.

For drivers, US freeways funnelling 12 lanes of traffic into three on the Mexican side means great congestion, particularly at weekends. As for pedestrians there is no passport check at the border for vehicles, so try to deal with US exit formalities and get an entry stamp at the border as it will avoid serious problems later on. Be sure to get an entry stamp on your tourist card as well as your passport. The immigration office is difficult to find; try the right-hand lane marked 'Customs'. When entering with a vehicle or motorcycle you should be able to obtain your tourist card/vehicle permit at this office, then you are supposed to get a stamp from a vehicle registry office about 100 m south. The officials will ask for copies of your documents, including the vehicle permit. If looking for insurance try **Baja Bound Insurance Services** ⓘ *920 E St 301, San Diego, T888-552-2252, www.bajabound.com*, who can also provide good, up to date information on travelling requirements.

If entering by bicycle, go to 'secondary', the immigration area to the right, where an official will process your tourist card to travel beyond Ensenada. Cyclists are not allowed on Highway 1-D (the toll road), so head for Highway 1 (*libre*) to Ensenada. Going into the US, be prepared for tough immigration procedures.

A quieter recommended alternative is the **Otay Mesa crossing** ⓘ *8 km east of Tijuana, 0600-2200*, reached from the US side by SR-117. Car insurance and vehicle permit facilities are no longer available here. From the Mexican side it is harder to find; continue on the bypass from Highway 1-D to near the airport and the 'Garita de Otay' sign.

Tijuana pp 183-196. Colour map 1, A1.

→ *Phone code: 664.*

Sitting on the south side of the River Tijuana, 35 million people annually cross the border to Tijuana, fuelling the city's claim to be 'the world's most-visited city'; this is the frontline at which the US and Mexico face up to each other in pleasure and politics. Often criticized as 'not being the real Mexico', it is nevertheless an historic and impassioned place. It came to prominence with Prohibition in the US in the 1920s when Hollywood stars and thirsty Americans flocked to the sleazy bars and enterprising nightlife of Tijuana and Mexicali, both at this time little more than large villages.

Although countless bars still vie for the visitor's dollar, it is the duty-free bargains, horse racing, cheap medicines and inexpensive English-speaking dentists which attract many visitors. Modern Tijuana is Mexico's fourth-largest city and one of the most prosperous. However, a walk along the barrio beside the border (don't go alone) to see the breached fence will demonstrate the difference between the first and third worlds.

Ins and outs

Getting there It is cheaper to fly south from Aeropuerto Rodríguez (TIJ), 17 km (20 minutes) from San Diego, CA, than it is from any US airports. For further details, see Transport, page 192. The bus station is 5 km southeast of the centre at the end of Vía Oriente (at La Mesa); take any local bus marked 'Central Camionera' or 'Buena Vista'. Local buses marked 'La Línea/Centro' go from the bus station to the border.

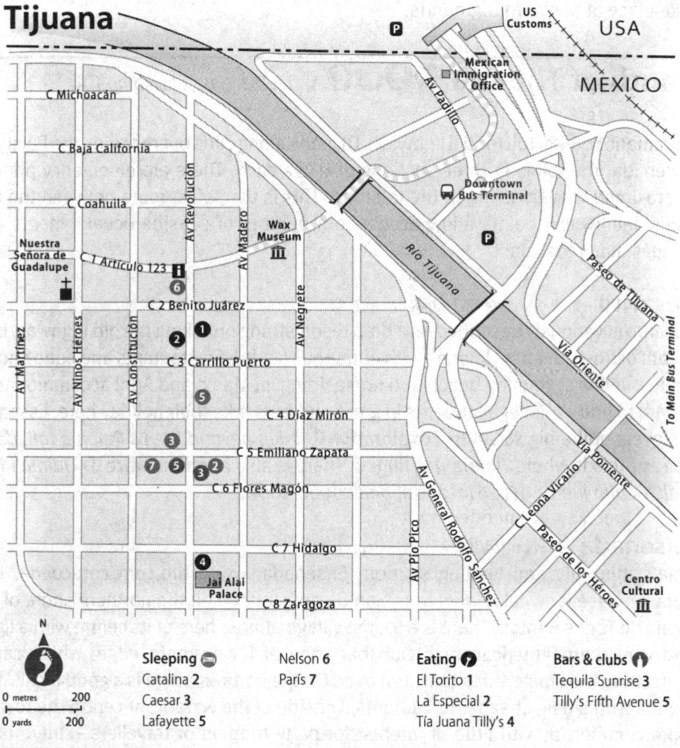

Getting around In the centre a selection of long distance buses leave from Calle 2 near Revolución. When taking a taxi in Mexico (unless it is a fixed-price airport service), it is often a good idea to agree on a price before travelling (some bargaining may be acceptable).

Tourist information The main **tourist office** ⓘ *Plaza Patria, Blv Agua Caliente, T688-0555, Mon-Fri 1000-1900*, is not as convenient as the one at the top of Avenida Revolución and Calle 1 ⓘ *T688-1685, Mon-Fri 0900-1400, 1600-1900; Sat 0900-1300*, which has helpful, English-speaking staff.

Sights

The main drag, **Avenida Revolución**, runs directly south from the tourist kiosk on the edge of the red-light district, with many bars and restaurants and souvenir shops (generally open 1000-2100). The **Centro Cultural** ⓘ *Paseo de los Héroes y Av Independencia*, contains the excellent **Museo de las Identidades Mexicanas**, which lets visitors know in no uncertain terms that they are in Mexico. There are also handicraft shops, restaurant, concert hall, and the ultra-modern spherical **Omnimax Cinema** ⓘ *T684-1111, English performance 1400 daily, Spanish version 1900*, where three films are shown on a 180° screen; it is best to sit at the back/top so you don't have to lean too far back. There is a small **Wax Museum** ⓘ Calle *1 y Madero, daily 1000-1800, US$1.80*, with historical figures and movie stars. The **Catedral of Nuestra Señora de Guadalupe** is at Calle 2. Tijuana has two bullrings: the **Plaza de Toros Monumental** ⓘ *Playas de Tijuana*, is the only one in the world built on the sea shore; **El Toreo** ⓘ *Blv Agua Caliente, T680-1808, May-Sep Sun 1600, tickets from US$4.50 in the sun (sol) to US$16 in the shade (sombra)*, is 3 km east of downtown. *Corridas* alternate between the two. *Charreadas* (rodeos) ⓘ *every Sun from May-Sep, free*, take place at one of four grounds.

South of Tijuana » *pp 183-196. Colour map 1, A1.*

A dramatic 106-km toll road (Highway 1-D) leads along cliffs overhanging the Pacific to Ensenada; the toll is in three sections of US$2 each. There are emergency phones approximately every 2 km on the toll road. This is the safest route between the two cities and 16 exit points allow access to a number of seaside developments and villages along the coast.

Rosarito → *Phone code: 661. Colour map 1, A1.*

Rosarito is variously described as a drab resort strung out along the old highway, or 'a breath of fresh air after Tijuana', with numerous seafood restaurants and curio shops. There is a fine swimming beach and horse riding. In March and April accommodation is hard to find as college students in great numbers take their holiday here. Essential for lovers of the big screen is **Foxploration** ⓘ *2 km beyond the La Paloma toll, daily, US$21* . This is where *Titanic* was filmed. There is also a **tourist office** ⓘ *Quinta Plaza Mall, Benito Juárez 96, T612-0200, daily 0900-1600*.

Ensenada → *Phone code: 646. Colour map 1, A1.*

Baja's third city and leading seaport, Ensenada, www.sdro.com/cotucoeda, is a popular place for weekenders from San Diego, situated on the northern shore of the Bahía de Todos Santos. There is a tourist village atmosphere at its centre with a lively and very North American nightclub/bar zone at its northern edge, which caters perfectly to the cruise ships that stop over. On the harbour fringe is a good locals' fish market with small, cheaper restaurants. Outside of the waterfront centre the town is more commercial with little of interest for party trippers or travellers – there is no beach in the centre. Sport and commercial fishing, and agriculture (with canning, wineries and olive growing) are the chief activities. The port itself is rather unattractive and the beach is dirty. Out of town, go and see **La Bufadora** blowhole. The **tourist office** ⓘ *Blv Costero y Azueta, daily 1000-1900*, is on the main seafront boulevard.

Tourist activity concentrates along **Avenida López Mateos** and, especially, along its northern section, where most of the hotels, restaurants and shops are located. The twin white towers of **Nuestra Señora de Guadalupe** ⓘ *Calle 6*, are a prominent landmark; on the seafront is the new **Plaza Cívica**, a landscaped court containing large busts of Juárez, Hidalgo and Carranza. The **Museo Histórico Regional** ⓘ *Gastelum, near Calle 1, closed Mon*, has an ethnographic collection on Mesoamerican people. A splendid view over the city and bay can be had from the road circling the Chapultepec Hills on the western edge of the business district. Steep but paved access is via the west extension of Calle 2, two blocks from the bus station. The **Bodegas de Santo Tomás** ⓘ *Av Miramar 666, between Calle 6 y 7, T178-2509, daily tours at 1100, 1300, 1500, US$2*, is Mexico's premier winery. *Charreadas* (rodeos) are held on summer weekends at the **charro ground** ⓘ *Blancarte y Calle 2*. There's a weekend **street market** ⓘ *Av Riveroll y Calle 7, 0700-1700*, and the fish market at the bottom of Avenida Macheros specializes in *tacos de pescado* (fish finger wrapped in tortilla!).

Highway 1 south from Ensenada passes turn-offs to several beach resorts. Just before the agricultural town of **Maneadero**, a paved highway runs 23 km west on to the Punta Banda pensinsula, where you can see **La Bufadora** blowhole, one of the most powerful on the Pacific, apparently best seen on a rising tide. Air sucked from a sea-level cave is expelled as high as 16 m through a cleft in the cliffs.

Southeast to San Felipe

» pp 183-196. Colour map 1, A1.

Highway 3 heading east to San Felipe leaves Ensenada at the Benito Juárez *glorieta* monument on the Calzada Cortés.

At Km 39, a paved road leads off 3 km to **Ojos Negros**, continuing east (graded, dry weather) into scrub-covered foothills. It soon climbs into the *ponderosa* pine forests of the Sierra de Juárez. The road enters the **Parque Nacional Constitución de 1857**, 37 km from Ojos Negros. The jewel of the park is the small **Laguna Hanson**, a sparkling shallow lake surrounded by Jeffery pines; camping here is delightful, but note that the lake is reduced to a boggy marsh in dry seasons and that the area receives snow in midwinter.

Highway 3 descends along the edge of a green valley to the rapidly developing town of Valle de Trinidad. A reasonable dirt road runs south into the **Parque Nacional Sierra San Pedro Mártir.**

After leaving the valley, Highway 3 follows a canyon covered in dense stands of barrel cacti to the **San Matías Pass** between the Sierras Juárez and San Pedro Mártir, which leads on to the desolate **Valle de San Felipe**. The highway turns east and emerges on to open desert hemmed in by arid mountains; 201 km from Ensenada it joins Highway 5 at the La Trinidad T-junction, 142 km south of Mexicali and 51 km north of San Felipe.

Mexicali to San Felipe

Highway 5 heads south from Mexicali for 193 km to San Felipe, passing at about Km 34 the Cerro Prieto geothermal field. After passing the Río Hardy and the Laguna Salada (Km 72), a vast, dry alkali flat sometimes turned into a muddy morass by rare falls of rain, the road runs straight across sandy desert until entering San Felipe around a tall, white, double-arched monument. Floods can cut the road across the Laguna Salada; when it is closed, motorists have to use Highway 3 from Ensenada (see above) to get to San Felipe.

San Felipe → *Phone code: 686. Colour map 1, A2.*

San Felipe is a pleasant, tranquil fishing and shrimping port on the Gulf of California although at weekends it can become overcrowded and noisy. Long a destination for devoted sportfishermen and a weekend retreat for North Americans, San Felipe is now experiencing a second discovery, with new trailer parks and the paving of many of the town's sandy streets. The **tourist office** ⓘ *Mar de Cortés y Manzanillo, opposite Motel El Capitán, T577-1600, Tue-Sun 0900-1400 and 1600-1800, www.sanfelipe.com.mx*, is helpful. Navy Day is celebrated on 1 June with a carnival, street dancing and boat races.

South from Ensenada » *pp 183-196. Colour map 1, A1.*

Santo Tomás → *Colour map 1, A1.*

Chaparal-clad slopes begin to close in on the highway as it winds its way south, passing through the small town of **Santo Tomás**. Nearby are the ruins of the Dominican Mission of 1791 (local Santo Tomás wine is cheaper out of town). A little north of San Vicente a road heads west to **Eréndira**, a beach resort made popular and accessible by **Coyote Cal's** (see Sleeping, page 185). **San Vicente** comes next, with two Pemex stations, cafés, tyre repairs and several stores. **Colonet**, further south, is a supply centre for surrounding ranches with several services. A dry-weather dirt road runs 12 km west to **San Antonio del Mar** where there are many camping spots amid high dunes fronting a beautiful beach renowned for surf fishing and clam-digging.

A reasonable, graded road branches east, 7 km south of Colonet, to San Telmo and climbs into the mountains. At 50 km it reaches the **Meling Ranch** (also called San José), which offers resort accommodation for about 12 guests. About 15 km beyond, the road enters the **Parque Nacional Sierra San Pedro Mártir** and climbs through forests (4WD recommended) to three astronomical observatories perched on the dramatic eastern escarpment of the central range. The view is one of the most extensive in North America: east to the Gulf, west to the Pacific, and southeast to the overwhelming granite mass of the **Picacho del Diablo** (3096 m), Baja's highest peak. Turning west off the main road goes to **Campo 4 Casas** ⓘ *small entrance fee*, a good beach resort with services and good surfing.

El Rosario → *Colour map 1, B1.*

After leaving the San Quintín valley the scenery starts to get spectacular, bypassing Santa María (fuel), the Transpeninsular Highway (officially the Carretera Transpeninsular Benito Juárez) runs along the Pacific before darting inland at Rancho El Consuelo. It climbs over a barren spur from which there are fine views, then drops in a succession of tight curves into El Rosario, 58 km from San Quintín. This small, agricultural community has a Pemex station, small supermarket, a basic museum, and meals, including Espinosa's famous lobster burritos (expensive and not particularly good) and omelettes.

Central desert of Baja California » *pp 183-196.*

Highway 1 makes a sharp 90° turn at El Rosario and begins to climb continuously into the central plateau; gusty winds increase and astonishingly beautiful desertscapes gradually become populated with many varieties of cacti. Prominent are the stately cardones; most intriguing are the strange, twisted cirios growing to heights of 6-10 m. They are unique to this portion of Baja California and extend as far south as the Vizcaíno Desert, and to a small area of Sonora state on the mainland. At Km 62, a 5-km track branches south to the adobe remains of **Misión San Fernando Velicatá**, the only Franciscan mission in Baja, founded by Padre Serra in 1769. About 26 km north of Cataviña a strange region of huge boulders begins, some as big as houses; interspersed by cacti and crouching elephant trees, this area is one of the most picturesque on the peninsula.

Cataviña → *Colour map 1, A2.*

Cataviña only has a small grocery store/**Café La Enramada** and the only Pemex station on the 227-km stretch from El Rosario to the Bahía de Los Angeles junction (there are in fact two fuel stations, but do not rely on either having supplies). Just 2 km north of Cataviña there are easily accessible cave paintings near Km 170 on the Transpeninsular Highway.

Highway 1 continues southeast through an arid world of boulder-strewn mountains and dry salt lakes. The new graded road to Bahía San Luis Gonzaga (see under South of San Felipe, above) branches off to the east.

Bahía de los Angeles → *Colour map 1, B2.*

The side road runs 68 km through cirios and datilillo cactus-landscapes and crosses the Sierra de la Asamblea to Bahía de los Angeles (no public transport but hitchhiking possible), a popular fishing town, which, despite a lack of vegetation, is one of Baja's best-known beauty spots. The bay, sheltered by the forbidding slopes of **Isla Angel de la Guarda** (Baja's largest island), is a haven for boating, although winds can be tricky for kayaks and small craft. There is good clamming and oysters. There are facilities in town and also a modest but interesting **museum**, which is good for information on the many mines and on mining techniques used in the region around the turn of the 20th century.

There are thousands of dolphins in the bay between June and December. Some stay all year. There are large colonies of seals and many exotic seabirds. Fishing is excellent. **La Gringa**, a beautiful beach 13 km north of town, charges a small fee for its many camping sites, pit toilets and rubbish bins. The series of tiny beaches at the foot of **Cabañas Díaz** are good for swimming, but watch out for stingrays when wading.

Baja California Sur » *pp 183-196.*

State border → *Colour map 1, B2.*

Back on the main route, Highway 1 now runs due south. Before you enter Baja California Sur you pass Rosarito (one store and one restaurant) and go through **Villa Jesús María** (gas station, store, cafés) to the 28th parallel, which marks the state border (with a soaring stylized eagle monument) between Baja California and Baja California Sur.

Advance clocks one hour to Mountain time when entering Baja California Sur, but note that Northern Baja observes Pacific Daylight Saving Time from first Sunday in April to last Sunday in October; time in both states and California is thus identical during the summer.

Guerrero Negro → *Phone code: 615. Colour map 1, B2.*

Three kilometres beyond the state line and 4 km west of the highway, Guerrero Negro is the halfway point between the US border and La Paz. There are gas stations, bank (**Banamex**, does not change traveller's cheques), hospital, cafés, stores, an airport, and the headquarters of **Exportadora de Sal**, the world's largest salt-producing firm and a cause for much concern among environmentalists.

In July and August you can hear the whales breathe as you stand on shore.

At the far western end of town is the skeleton of a grey whale, a fitting memorial to a town that is recognized for whale watching. Many hotels and agencies in town thrive or die on the backs of the tourists who migrate to the region from mid-December to mid-March. The alternative base for whale-watching tours is San Ignacio 142 km to the east. See box, page 178.

Desierto Vizcaíno → *Colour map 1, B2.*

After Guerrero Negro the highway enters the grim Vizcaíno Desert. A gravel road branches off due east for 42 km to El Arco and other abandoned mining areas. The road then crosses the peninsula to **San Francisquito** on its beautiful bay overlooking the Gulf of California (77 km). A new gravel road from Bahía de Los Angeles (135 km) gives easier road access than from El Arco and opens up untouched stretches of the Gulf coast.

Vizcaíno Peninsula → *Colour map 1, B2.*

Vizcaíno Peninsula, which thrusts into the Pacific south of Guerrero Negro, is one of the most remote parts of Baja. Although part of the Vizcaíno Desert, the scenery of the peninsula is varied and interesting; isolated fish camps dot the silent coast of beautiful coves and untrodden beaches. A dry-weather road cuts west through the peninsula to Bahía Tortugas and the rugged headland of Punta Eugenia. It leaves Highway 1, 70 km beyond Guerrero Negro at the Vizcaíno Junction (also called Fundolegal). The new road is paved for 8 km to Ejido Díaz Ordaz. It passes **Rancho San José** (116 km) and the easily missed turn-off to Malarrimo Beach (where beachcombing is unparalleled). After another bumpy 50 km is **Bahía Tortugas**, a surprisingly large place considering its remoteness. Two roads leave the Vizcaíno-Bahía Tortuga road for Bahía Asunción, which has the peninsula's only other gas station. From here there is a coast road south to **Punta Prieta, La Bocana** and **Punta Abreojos** (93 km). A lonely road runs for 85 km back to Highway 1, skirting the Sierra Santa Clara before crossing the salt marshes north of Laguna San Ignacio and reaching the main road 26 km before San Ignacio.

It should be stressed that the minor Bajan roads require high-clearance, preferably 4WD, vehicles carrying adequate equipment and supplies, water and fuel.

San Ignacio → *Phone code: 615. Colour map 1, B2.*

The highway continues southeast and, 20 km from the Vizcaíno Junction, reaches the first of 23 microwave relay towers that follow Highway 1 almost to the cape. They are closed to the public but make excellent landmarks and, in some cases, offer excellent views. The turn-off right for the oasis town of San Ignacio, marked by a grey whale skeleton, is at **San Lino**, 143 km from Guerrero Negro. A road of about 3 km (US$2 in a taxi) leads to a small, attractive town with pastel-coloured commercial buildings and a good old mission church; there is a service station with mechanical assistance. Whale-watching tours can be arranged from here and it's a far more enjoyable place to spend time than Guerrero Negro.

The best season for whale- watching is January-March, US$25 per hour for up to six people.

Several tours can be arranged around town, including whale watching and nearby cave paintings. Whale-watching trips are US$40 per person for 2½ hours, with transport costs of US$130 per person shared between the number of people travelling. Try **Ecoturismo Kuyima** ⓘ *on the main plaza, T/F154-0070, www.kuyima.com*, who can organize the trip and other excursions. ⏩ *See page 191 for details of excursions.*

Around San Ignacio → *Colour map 1, B2.*

A 70-km road from San Ignacio leads to Laguna San Ignacio, one of the best whale-viewing sites; mothers and calves often swim up to nuzzle boats and allow their noses to be stroked. The **Cooperativa Laguna de San Ignacio** ⓘ *Juárez 23, off the Zócalo in San Ignacio*, takes fishermen to the lagoon every day and can sometimes accommodate visitors.

There are many **cave painting sites** around San Ignacio; colourful human and animal designs left by Baja's original inhabitants still defy reliable dating or full understanding. To reach most requires a mule trek over tortuous trails; Oscar Fischer, at **Motel La Posada**, arranges excursions into the sierras (about US$10 per person to Santa Teresa cave). The cave at the **Cuesta del Palmarito**, 5 km east of **Rancho Santa Marta** (50 km northwest of San Ignacio), is filled with designs of humans with uplifted arms, in brown and black; a jeep and guide (if one can be found) are required. A better road leads east from the first microwave station past Vizcaíno Junction up to **San Francisco de la Sierra**, where there are other paintings and petroglyphs.

Santa Rosalía

» *pp 183-196. Colour map 1, B3.*

→ *Phone code: 615.*

Seventy-two kilometres from San Ignacio is Santa Rosalía, squeezed into a narrow bottleneck valley running off the harbour. It was built by the French **El Boleo Copper Company** in the 1880s, laid out in neat rows of wood-frame houses, many with broad verandas, and there is something intangible about Santa Rosalía that doesn't quite make it French but neither is it Mexican in appearance.

Santa Rosalía's streets are narrow and congested; larger vehicles should park along the highway or in the ferry dock parking lot.

Up the hill near the **Hotel Francés**, the dusty old street of shaded verandas is split down the middle by half-a-dozen rusting old engines. Subject to the fierce elements, their display is both nostalgic and pointless, but still good to see. There is a small museum off Calle Francisco next to the **Impecsa** warehouse, with historic exhibits of mining. The church of **Santa Bárbara** ⓘ*Obregón y Calle 3*, a block north of the main plaza, was built of prefabricated galvanized iron for the 1889 Paris World's Fair from a design by Eiffel. It was then shipped around the Horn to Baja. Also visit the *panadería* **El Boleo**, which has been baking and selling fresh bread for over 100 years.

The Pemex station is conveniently located on the highway, unlike the one at Mulegé (see below), so larger RVs and rigs should fill up here. There is a 24-hour store a couple of hundred yards south.

Mulegé

» *pp 183-196. Colour map 1, B3.*

→ *Phone code: 615.*

Sixty-one kilometres south of Santa Rosalía, is another oasis community, a tranquil retreat outside of spring break, which is an increasingly popular hideaway for US and Canadian retirees. There are lovely beaches, good diving, snorkelling and boating in Bahía Concepción. The old Federal territorial prison (**La Cananea**) has been converted into a museum. It became known as the 'prison without doors' because the inmates were allowed out during the day to work in the town. A pleasant walk leads for 3 km out of town to the stony beach complete with lighthouse with good views. The tidal lagoons are popular for collecting clams.

Just upstream from the highway bridge on the south side of the river is the **Misión de Santa Rosalía de Mulegé**, founded by the Jesuits in 1705. Above the mission there is a good lookout point over the town and its sea of palm trees. Looking the other way there is a fine view at sunset over the inland mesas. Locals swim at an excellent spot about 500 m inland from the bridge and to the right of the track to the Mission. There are tours to cave painting sites, US$30 per person including drinks; a guide is necessary; recommended is Salvador Castro, ask for him at the taxi rank in the plaza. The Pemex station is in Calle General Martínez, one block

There are no banks in Mulegé, but you can change dollars – make sure you come with cash.

Whales

Whale watching

Whale watching is the main attraction on **Laguna Ojo de Liebre**, usually known as **Scammon's Lagoon** after the whaling captain who entered in 1857. California grey whales mate and give birth between end-December and February, in several warm-water lagoons on central Baja's Pacific coast. Most leave by the beginning of April, but some stay as late as May or June. They can be seen cavorting and sounding from the old salt wharf 10 km northwest of Guerrero Negro on the Estero San José, or from a designated 'whale-watching area' with observation tower on the shore of Scammon's Lagoon, 37 km south of town. The access road branches off Highway 1, 8 km east of the junction (if going by public transport, leave bus at the turn-off and hitch). There is a small fee for camping at the watching area, which pays to keep it clean. The shores of Scammon's Lagoon are part of the **Parque Natural de la Ballena Gris**. *Pangas* are available for hire (US$10 per person), but a more straightforward way of seeing the whales is on one of the daily tours from Guerrero Negro including a 1½-hour boat trip, sandwiches and transport to the lagoon, US$40-45 per person, with departures at 0800 and 1100, between mid-December and mid-March, when as many as 50 whales are in the lagoon. One reader saw a dozen on a trip in mid-January. There are also some trips from San Ignacio.

Whale conservation

Mexico was the first country in the world to set aside habitat for whales. In 1971, Scammon's Lagoon was designated a grey whale refuge. A few years later, two more grey whale lagoons were protected – Guerrero Negro and San Ignacio. Whale watching and some fishing is still permitted in the lagoons under special regulations but other industrial activities are prohibited.

In 1988, a new biosphere reserve and world heritage site was created, which included all of Laguna Ojo de Liebre, Laguna Guerrero Negro and Laguna San Ignacio as well as the desert areas all around – a total area of more than 2.5 million hectares. Called the **Vizcaíno Desert Biosphere Reserve**, it is the largest nature reserve in Latin America. It is definitely worth visiting. Besides whales and dolphins, it is possible to see California sea lions, black and green turtles, osprey, brown pelicans, Caspian terns, great blue herons, great egrets and peregrine falcons.

With such habitat protection, the return of grey whale numbers, and the sightings of more and more hump-back, blue, fin and Bryde's whales in the Gulf of California, Mexico's whales seemed to be in good shape.

In 1995, however, the Mexican government in partnership with Mitsubishi, the Japanese conglomerate, announced plans to build the largest salt mine in the world inside the reserve, greatly expanding existing salt factories. The US$120 million development, which would create 208 permanent jobs in a relatively underdeveloped area. Direct impact from the construction and operation of the facility on the shore of Laguna San Ignacio would impact the temperature and salinity of the critical grey whale habitat. Intervention and pressure from Mexican and international conservation bodies has led to expansion plans being shelved.

before plaza in the centre; not convenient for large vehicles, which also have a one-way system to contend with. But there is another Pemex station 4½ km south of the bridge, on the road out of town towards Loreto, with restaurant and mini-market. There is good free tourist information in the town centre.

South of Mulegé

Beyond Mulegé the highway runs along the shores of Bahía Concepción for 50 km. This stretch is the most heavily used camping and boating area on the peninsula; the water is beautiful, swimming safe, camping excellent and there is varied marine life. **Playa Santispac**, in the cove called **Bahía Coyote**, 23 km south of Mulegé (about a 30-minute ride) is recommended. There are many small restaurants (for example **Ana's**, which sells water and bakes bread, food good value, and **Ray's**, good food, a bit pricey) and palapas (shelters) for hire (day or overnight, US$2.50). You can get to Santispac from Mulegé on the La Paz bus (taxi, US$12); it is also quite easy to hitch. Just south of here, in the next cove, at **Playa Concepción**, tents, palapas and kayaks can be hired at **Ecomundo**, see page 186.

Further south from El Coyote is **Playa Buenaventura**, which has rooms at **A George's Olé**, palapas and three *cabañas* for rent (US$20), and an expensive restaurant. From the entrance to the beach at Requesón, veer to the left for **Playa La Perla**, which is secluded.

A new graded dirt road branches off Highway 1 to climb over the towering **Sierra Giganta**, whose desert vistas of flat-topped mesas and cardón cacti are straight out of the Wild West. The road begins to deteriorate after the junction (20 km) to San José de Comondú and limps another 37 km into San Isidro after a spectacular drop into the **La Purísima** valley. The paved road leads on southwards to **La Poza Grande** (52 km) and **Ciudad Insurgentes** (85 km).

Loreto

▸▸ *pp 183-196. Colour map 1, C3.*

→ *Phone code: 613.*

Some 1125 km from Tijuana, Loreto is one of the most historic places in Baja. Here Spanish settlement of the peninsula began with Father Juan María Salvatierra's founding of the **Misión de Nuestra Señora de Loreto** ⓘ *Zócalo, Tue-Sun 0900-1300, 1345-1800, US$1.80*, on 25 October 1697. It was the first capital of the Californias. Nestled between the slopes of the Sierra Giganta and the offshore Isla del Carmen, Loreto has experienced a tourist revival; fishing here is some of the best in Baja California. The mission is the largest structure in town and perhaps the best restored of all the Baja California mission buildings. It has a gilded altar. The **museum** is also worth a visit.

Route south of Loreto

Just south of Loreto a rough road runs 37 km through impressive canyon scenery to the village of **San Javier**, tucked in the bottom of a steep-walled valley; the settlement of some 120 people has only one store but the **Misión de San Javier** is one of the best preserved in North America; it was founded by the Jesuits in 1699 and took 59 years to complete. The thick volcanic walls, Moorish ornamentation and bell tower are most impressive in so rugged and remote a location. Taxis from Loreto can be arranged at roughly US$65 for the day, but hitching is quite possible. The trip is worth the effort.

The highway south of Loreto passes a picturesque stretch of coast. There are three lovely public beaches between Loreto and Puerto Escondido (none has drinking water): **Notrí, Juncalito** and **Ligüí** are palm-lined coves, which are a far cry from the bustle of the new resort developments nearby. Beyond Ligüí (36 km south of Loreto)

Highway 1 ascends the eastern escarpment of the Sierra Giganta (one of the most fascinating legs of Highway 1) before leaving the Gulf to strike out southwest across the peninsula again to Ciudad Constitución.

Ciudad Constitución and around → *Phone code: 613. Colour map 1, C3.*

The highway passes by Ciudad Insurgentes, a busy agricultural town with two service stations, banks, auto repairs, shops and cafés (no hotels/motels), then runs dead straight for 26 km to Ciudad Constitución, which is the marketing centre for the Magdalena Plain agricultural development and has the largest population between Ensenada and La Paz (50,000). It has department stores, restaurants, banks, service stations, car repairs, hospital and airport.

> *'Mag Bay' is considered the finest natural harbour between San Francisco and Acapulco.*

Whales can be seen at **Puerto López Mateos** further north (access from Ciudad Insurgentes or Ciudad Constitución); there's no hotel, but ask for house of María del Rosario González who rents rooms, or take a tent and camp at the small harbour near the fish plant.

La Paz » pp 183-196. *Colour map 1, C3.*

→ *Phone code: 612.*

Capital of Baja California Sur, La Paz is a relaxed modern city, nestled at the southern end of **Bahía La Paz** (where Europeans first set foot in Baja in 1533). Sunsets can be spectacular. Prices have risen as more tourists arrive to enjoy its winter climate, but free port status ensures that there are plenty of bargains (although some goods, like certain makes of camera, are cheaper to buy in the US). Oyster beds attracted many settlers in the 17th century, but few survived long. The **Jesuit mission**, founded in 1720, was abandoned 29 years later. La Paz became the territorial capital in 1830 after Loreto was wiped out by a hurricane. Although

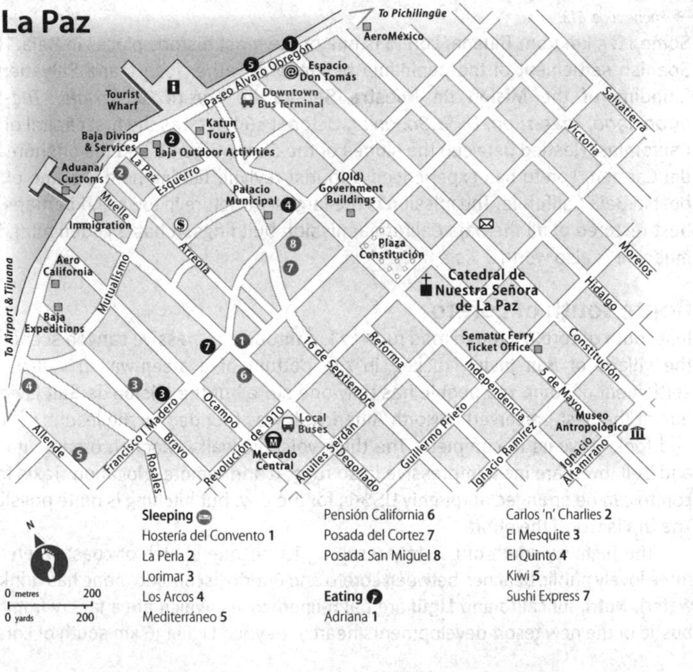

bursting with new construction, there are still many touches of colonial grace, arched doorways and flower-filled patios. The early afternoon siesta is still observed by many businesses, especially during summer.

If you're looking for a challenging way to move on, hang around a while and visit one of the marinas at the northern end of town to see if you can get a crewing job with a boat heading down the coast.

The **tourist office** ⓘ *Tourist Wharf at the bottom of 16 de Septiembre, Mon-Fri 0800-1500, Sat 0900-1300, 1400-1500, open till 1900 in high season*, will make hotel reservations, English spoken; they have some literature and town maps and there's a noticeboard for rides offered, crew wanted, etc.

Sights

The street grid is rectangular; westerly streets run into the Paseo Alvaro Obregón, the waterfront **Malecón**, where the commercial and tourist wharves back on to a tangle of streets; here are the banks, **Palacio Municipal**, **Chinatown** and many of the cheaper *pensiones*. The local landmark is **Carlos 'n' Charlies** restaurant from where you can find most things within a couple of blocks. The more expensive hotels are further southwest. The heart of La Paz is the **Plaza Constitución**, a little east of the main tourist area, facing which are the government buildings and the graceful **Catedral de Nuestra Señora de la Paz**, built in 1861-1865 on or near the site of the original mission. The **Museo Antropológico de Baja California Sur** ⓘ *Ignacio Altamirano y 5 de Mayo, Mon-Fri 0800-1800, Sat 0900-1400, free*, is well worth a visit, with a small but admirable display of Peninsular anthropology, history and pre-history, folklore and geology. The bookshop has a wide selection on Mexico and Baja. The **Museum of the Whale** ⓘ *Navarro and Ignacio Altamirano*, and a carved mural depicting the history of Mexico, can be seen at the **Palacio de Gobierno** on Isabel La Católica, corner of Bravo.

Beaches

There are many beaches around La Paz, the most popular are on the **Pichilingüe Peninsula**. Most have restaurants (good seafood restaurant under a *palapa* at Pichilingüe). Going north from La Paz to the ferry terminal on Highway 11 you will pass **Palmira**, **Coromuel** (popular with *paceños*), **El Caimancito** ⓘ *admission fee*, and **Tesoro**. Wind-surfing and catamaran trips can be arranged. Buses to Pichilingüe run from 1000-1400 and 1600-1730, US$1.30 from station at Paseo Alvaro Obregón and Independencia; 100 m north of ferry terminal is a *playa pública*. **Balandra** ⓘ *rubbish bins, palapas, US$2*, and **Tecolote** ⓘ *camping free under palapas*, are reached by the road beyond the ferry terminal (paved for some distance beyond this point; some buses on this route run beyond the ferry terminal at weekends). The road ends at a gravel pit at Playa Cachimba (good surf fishing), 13 km northeast of Pichilingüe; the north-facing beaches are attractive but can be windy, and there are some sandflies. El Coyote (no water or facilities), on the east coast, is reached by a road/track from La Paz running inland along the middle of the peninsula. Southwest of La Paz on the bay are the tranquil, no-surf beaches of Comitán and El Mogote. In October (at least) and after rain, beware of stinging jellyfish in the water.

Around La Paz

There are boat tours from the Tourist Wharf on the Malecón around the bay and to nearby islands like **Espirítu Santo**. Travel agencies offer a daily boat tour to **Los Lobos Islands** ranging from US$40-80; the tour should include lunch and snorkelling, six hours, you can see pelicans, sea-lions and dolphins, with luck whales, too. About 17 km west of La Paz a paved road branches northwest off Highway 1 around the bay leading to the mining village of **San Juan de la Costa**, allowing a closer look at the rugged coastal section of the Sierra de la Giganta. After San Juan (45 km), the road is passable for medium-size vehicles to **Punta Coyote** (90 km), closely following the narrow space between mountains and coast with wonderful untouched camping spots. From Coyote to **San Evaristo** (27 km) the track is poor and a rugged vehicle is recommended. San Evaristo is a sleepy fishing village on a delightful cove sheltered on the east by Isla San José. This is a rewarding excursion for those with smaller, high-clearance vehicles (vans and pick-ups) for the steep final 20-mile stretch.

State Highway 286 leads southeast out of La Paz 45 km to **San Juan de Los Planes**. A fair road continues another 15 km to the beautiful **Ensenada de los Muertos**, where there is good fishing, swimming and 'wild' camping. A further 11 km is the headland of **Punta Arena de la Ventana**, with a magnificent view of the sterile slopes of Isla Cerralvo. Six kilometres before Los Planes, a graded road leads to the **Bahía de la Ventana** and the small fishing villages of La Ventana and El Sargento, which have lovely beaches facing **Isla Cerralvo**.

South of La Paz » *pp 183-196. Colour map 2, C1.*

South of La Paz, the central mountain spine rises again into the wooded heights of the **Sierra de la Laguna** and bulges out into the 'Cape Region', Baja's most touristically developed area.

Eight kilometres beyond **El Triunfo** is the lovely mountain town and farming centre of **San Antonio** (gasoline, groceries, meals), which was founded in 1756 and served briefly as Baja's capital (1828-1830) when Loreto was destroyed. Eight kilometres south of San Antonio was the site of **Santa Ana**, where silver was first discovered in 1748. It was from this vanished village that the Viceroy and Padre Junípero Serra planned the expedition to establish the chain of Franciscan missions in Alta California.

Highway 1 climbs sharply from the canyon and winds past a number of ancient mines, through the peaceful orchard-farming town of **San Bartolo** (groceries and meals) and down to the coastal flats around **Los Barriles**. A number of resort hotels are situated near here along the beautiful **Bahía de Palmas** and at nearby **Buena Vista**; none is in the 'budget' class but all are popular.

The highway turns inland after Los Barriles (106 km from La Paz). An 'East Cape Loop' turns east off the highway through **La Rivera**. A new spur leads towards **Cabo Pulmo**, paralleling the coast to San José del Cabo. Off Cabo Pulmo, a beautiful headland, is the Northern Pacific's only living coral reef; fishing, diving and snorkelling are excellent.

Santiago is a pleasant, historic little town 3 km off Highway 1 (bus stop at junction, two hours from La Paz, US$3.50 in a taxi from the highway). A Pemex station, café and stores grouped around the town plaza. The Jesuits built their tenth mission in Santiago in 1723 after transferring it from Los Barriles. The town was one of the sites of the uprising of the Pericué people in 1734. There are hot springs (warm), behind a mini dam, in a pleasant setting, 12 km away along a dirt road at the foot of the mountains. Head towards the village of **Aguascalientes** (8 km) and the hot springs are 4 km beyond this. You can walk on from the spring to a waterfall.

Some 3.5 km south of the Santiago turn-off, Highway 1 crosses the **Tropic of Cancer**, marked by a large concrete sphere, and runs south down the fertile valley between the lofty **Sierra de la Laguna** (west) and the **Sierra Santa Clara** (east), to Los Cabos International Airport. San José del Cabo is 14 km further south.

San José del Cabo → *Phone code: 624. Colour map 2, C1.*

The largest town south of La Paz and founded in 1730, San José del Cabo is now a modern town divided into two districts: the very Americanized resort sectors and new **Fonatur** development on the beach, and the downtown zone to the north, with the government offices and many businesses grouped near the tranquil **Parque Mijares**.

The attractive church on the **Plaza Mijares** was built in 1940 on the final site of the mission of 1730; a tile mosaic over the entrance depicts the murder of Padre Tamaral by rebellious locals in 1734.

Cabo San Lucas → *Phone code: 624. Colour map 2, C1.*

The resort town of Cabo San Lucas has grown rapidly in recent years from the sleepy fishing village of 1500 inhabitants it was in 1970. It is now an expensive international resort with a permanent population of 8500. The place is full of North Americans who come for the world-famous fishing or to find a retirement paradise.

Everything is quoted in US dollars and food is more American than Mexican.

Ringed by pounding surf, columns of fluted rock enclose **Lover's Beach** (be careful if walking along the beach, as huge waves sweep away several visitors each year), a romantic sandy cove with views out to the seal colonies on offshore islets. At the very tip of the Cabo is the distinctive natural arch, **El Arco**; boats can be hired to see it close up, but care is required because of the strong currents. At the harbour entrance is a pinnacle of rock, **Pelican Rock**, which is home to vast shoals of tropical fish; it is an ideal place for snorkelling and scuba diving, and glass-bottomed boats can be rented at the harbour-side.

Todos Santos → *Phone code: 612. Colour map 2, C1.*

Highway 9 was not paved until 1985 and the superb beaches of the west coast have yet to suffer the development of the east. The road runs due south through a cactus-covered plain from just after **San Pedro** to Todos Santos. This quiet farming town just north of the Tropic of Cancer is slowly becoming a tourist and expat centre.

West coast beaches

Two kilometres from Todos Santos is a stretch of the Pacific coast with some of the most beautiful beaches of the entire Baja California Peninsula. Nearest to the town is **Playa Punta Lobos** where the local fishermen shore up (the *pangas* come in early afternoon); it is a popular picnic spot, but with too much rubbish and too many unfriendly dogs for wild camping. Next comes **Playa Las Palmas**, good for swimming. Cleaner for camping is the sandy cove at **Playa San Pedrito** (4 km southeast). Backed by groves of Washingtonia fan palms and coconut palms, this is one of the loveliest wild camping spots anywhere; it is also good for surfing. Opposite the access road junction is the **Campo Experimental Forestal**, a botanical garden with a well-labelled array of desert plants from all regions of Baja. Here too is the **Trailer Park San Pedrito** (see Sleeping, below), an open area on the beach and one of the most beautifully sited RV parks in Baja California.

Parque Nacional Sierra de la Laguna

In the rugged interior east of Todos Santos is the Parque Nacional Sierra de la Laguna. Its crowning peak is the **Picacho La Laguna** (2163 m), which is beginning to attract a trickle of hikers to its 'lost world' of pine and oak trees, doves and woodpeckers, grassy meadows and luxuriant flowers; there is nothing else like it in Baja. The trail is steep but straightforward; the panoramic view takes in La Paz and both the Gulf and Pacific coasts. It gets cold at night. The park can be reached from Todos Santos; three-day guided pack trips are also offered by the **Todos Santos Inn**. Alternatively, take a taxi from Todos Santos to **La Burrera**, from where it is eight hours' walk along the littered path to La Laguna.

Sleeping

Crossing into Mexico: Mexicali *p169*

A **Azteca de Oro**, Industria 600, T557-1433. Motel opposite train station and only a few blocks from bus terminal. A/c, TV, a bit scruffy but convenient.

A Del Norte, Melgar y Av Madero, T552-8102. Some a/c and TV, across from border crossing, pleasant but a little noisy, has free parking for guests, offers discount coupons for breakfast and dinner.
B-C Hotel De Anza, motel on the Calexico side. Excellent value for money.
D Rivera, near the railway station. A/c, best of the cheaper hotels.

Crossing into Mexico: Tecate *p169*

D Frontera, Callejón Madero 131, T654-1342. Basic but clean and friendly (Antonio Moller Ponce, who resides here, is knowledgeable on the area's history and ethno-history).
E Juárez, Juárez 230. Rooms with or without bath, hot water.

Crossing into Mexico: Tijuana *p170, map p171*

LL Grand Hotel Tijuana, Blv Agua Caliente 4500, T01-800-026-6007 (toll free in Mexico), www.grandhoteltij.com.mx. Heated pool, suites, etc. First rate.
B Caesar, Calle 5 y Av Revolución, T685-1606. A/c, restaurant, decorated with bullfight posters, unique character. Good.
B Nelson, Av Revolución 721, T685-4302. Central, simple clean rooms, coffee shop.
C Catalina, Calle 5 and Madero, T685-9748. Clean and good for Tijuana.
C Lafayette, Av Revolución 325, between Calle 3 and 4, T685-3940. Clean and safe rooms, and right in the centre of things.
C París, Calle 5, No 8181, T685-3023. Adequate, value-for-money budget hotel.
D San Diego Downtown Hostel, 521 Market St, T(619) 525-1531, www.sandiegohostels.org. With clean, tidy dorm rooms, breakfast included. It's a good spot and close to the Greyhound station.

Ensenada *p172*

Some of the larger hotels have different rates for summer and winter; check first! All hotels are filled in Ensenada at weekends, get in early.
LL Las Rosas Hotel and Spa, Highway 1 at Km 105.5, 7 km west of town, T/F174-4310, www.lasrosas.com. Suites, spectacular ocean views, pool, sauna, restaurant.
LL-A Bahía, Blv Costero and Av Alvarado, T178-2101, www.hotelbahia.com.mx/ing/. Balconies, suites, fridges, quiet, clean, parking, a/c, good value, popular.
LL-A Quintas Papagayo, 1.5 km north on Highway 1, T174-4155, www.hussongs.com.mx. Landscaped beach resort complex with all facilities, **Hussong's Pelícano** restaurant attached.
AL-A Ensenada Travelodge, Av Blancarte 130, T178-1601. Motel with a/c, heated pool, whirlpool, family rates available, restaurant.
C Perla del Pacífico, Av Miramar 229. Quite clean, hot water, parking.
D América, López Mateos, T176-1333. Basic, hard beds, kitchenettes, good.
D Hostal Sauzal, El Sauzal de Rodríguez, 9.5 km before Ensenada, 2½ blocks from the highway up Av L (get off the bus at the traffic light in El Sauzal and walk) T(646)174-6381, http://hostelsauzal.tripod.com. Price per person. Has 4-bed dorms, hot water, storage lockers, use of kitchen and a library of books and maps on Baja – a good place to stop, chill, and pick up info before rushing south. María is very friendly and welcoming and will give you the complete low down on the latest developments throughout Baja.
D Río, Av Miramar 231 and Calle 2, opposite Perla. Basic, but cheapest in town.
D Ritz, Av Ruiz y Calle 4, No 379, T174-0501. Central, a/c, TV, phone, coffee shop, parking.

Southeast to San Felipe *p173*

E Mike's Sky Rancho, Parque Nacional Sierra San Pedro Mártir, T(664) 681-5514 (Tijuana). A working ranch that offers motel-style accommodation, pool, camping and guided trips into the surrounding mountains. Good meals.

San Felipe *p174*

AL Castel, Av Misión de Loreto 148, T577- 1282. A/c, 2 pools, tennis, etc. Best in town.

Phone codes *Mexicali 686; Tijuana 664; Rosarito 661; Ensenada 646; San Felipe 686; Santo Tomás 646; El Rosario 616; Guerrero Negro 615; San Ignacio 615; Santa Rosalía 615; Mulegé 615; Loreto 613; Ciudad Constitución 613; La Paz 612; San José del Cabo 624; Cabo San Lucas 624; Todos Santos 612.*

B Cortez, on Av Mar de Cortés, T577-1055, cortezho@telnor.net. Beachside esplanade. Motel with a/c, pool, *palapas* on beach, launching ramp, disco, restaurant.
B La Trucha Vagabunda, Mar Báltico, near Motel Cortés, T577-1333. Also a few RV spaces and **Restaurant Alfredo** (Italian), seafood, international cuisine.
C El Pescador, T577-1044, Mar de Cortés and Calzada Chetumal. A/c, modest but comfortable motel.

Camping

Many trailer parks and campgrounds in town and on coast to north and south.
El Faro Beach and RV Park, on the bay 18 km south at Km 14.
La Jolla, Playa de Laura. US$12.
Mar del Sol, Av Misión de Loreto, T577-1088. US$18.
Playa Bonita, Golfo de California 784, T577-1215, playabonita@aol.com. US$15-25.
Ruben's, Golfo de California 703, T577-1442. Nice beach. US$12.

South from Ensenada *p174*

L-AL Meling Ranch (also called San José), www.melingguestranch.com. Resort accommodation for about 12 guests.
B-D Coyote Cal's, Eréndira,T154-4080, www.coyotecals.com. Dorms and rooms. Good range of activities including beaches, surfing, whale watching and hiking.
D Campo 4 Casas, Punta San Telmo, T165-0010. International hostel. Good beach resort with services and good surfing. Small entrance fee.
D El Palomar Motel, Santo Tomás, T/F(646) 178-8002. Adequate but overpriced rooms, restaurant, bar, general store and gas station, RV park with full hook-ups, campsite with swimming pool, clean, refurbished, US$10).
E Motel El Cammo, Highway 1, south of San Vicente. Without bath, friendly, OK restaurant.

El Rosario *p174*

D Sinai. Comfortable, very clean, small RV park, friendly owner makes good meals, but beware of overcharging.

Bahía de los Angeles *p175*

C-F Camp Gecko, T151-9454, www.campgecko.com. Good, quiet spot, *cabañas* and camping under *palapas*.

Camping

Guillermo's Trailer Park, T650-3209. Flush toilets, showers, restaurant, gift shop, boat ramp and rentals. It has a restaurant on main street, above the gift shop, well-prepared Mexican food, attractive, reservations advised at weekends. US$8-12.
Sal y Mauro, campsite. First gravel road on left before entering town, friendly.

State border *p175*

AL Hotel La Pinta, Guerrero Negro, T157-1304, www.lapintahotels.com. A/c, pool, dining room, bar, trailer park attached, 60 spaces, full hook-ups, laundry and gasoline at hotel.

Guerrero Negro *p175*

B Malarrimo, east end of town, T157-0100, www.malarrimo.com. Mix of family rooms, *cabañas* and rooms. Tour operator arranging whale-watching tours, good surf 'n' turf restaurant. Very clean, TV, fan, quiet. Good deal overall.
C San José, opposite bus terminal, T157-1420. Clean, will help to organize whale-watching tours.
C-D El Morro, on road into town from highway, T157-0414. Modest, clean.
E Las Dunas, few doors from **El Morro**. Friendly, modest, clean. Recommended.

San Ignacio *p176*

AL La Pinta, on road leading into town, T154-0300, www.lapintahotels.com. A/c, pool, all facilities, built in mission style. Attractive but overpriced.
C Motel La Posada, on rise 2 blocks from Zócalo, just ask in town, T154-343. Well maintained, fans, shower, best value in town, worth bargaining.
D Chalita, south side of the plaza, T154-0082. Cheap and cheerful.

Santa Rosalía *p177*

B Francés, Calle Jean Michel Cousteau up the hill, T152-2052. This 2-storey French colonial building is a living piece of history – you can visit, but there is a charge. A/c, restaurant, bar, pool excellent views overlooking the Gulf. Charming.
B-C Real, Av Manuel Montoya near Calle 1, T152-0068. Similar to **Olvera**. Recommended.

C **Olvera**, on plaza at entrance to town, 2nd floor, T152-0057. A/c, showers, clean, could do with a lick of paint. Good value.
E **Blanco y Negro**, Calle 3 and Serabia, T152-0080. Basic but clean.

Camping

It's possible to camp on the beach under *palapas*; access via an unmarked road 500 m south of El Morro, free, no facilities, a beautiful spot.
Las Palmas, 3 km south of town. Trailer park, 30 spaces, showers, laundry, good value.
San Lucas RV Park, on beach, San Lucas, no hook-ups, flush toilets, boat ramp, ice, restaurant, US$6 per vehicle, 75 spaces. Recommended.

Mulegé *p177*

Prices change dramatically between high and low season.
A **Serenidad**, 4 km south of town near the river mouth on beachside road, T153-0530, www.hotelserenidad.com. Good views over the Gulf and a relaxing away-from-it-all ambience. RV hook-ups too.
B-C **Las Casitas**, Callejón de los Estudiantes y Av Madero 50, T152-3023. Central, a/c, showers, restaurant and bar, shady garden patio, fishing trips arranged, pleasant older hotel, well run.
C **Vieja Hacienda**, Madero 3, T153-0021. Lovely courtyard, pool, rooms refurbished, bar, trips to cave paintings offered. Recommended.
D **Manuelita's**, with a beautiful patio, basic with private shower.
D **Suites Rosita**, Av Madero near main plaza. A/c, kitchenettes, clean and pleasant, hot water, a bit run-down but good value.
E-F **Nachita**, **Canett** and **Sorpresa**. *Casas de huéspedes* on the road into town. All basic but reasonably clean.

Camping

The Orchard (Huerta Saucedo) RV Park, on river south of town, partly shaded, off Highway 1, T153-0300. Pool, free coffee, book exchange, boat ramp, fishing, discount with AAA/AA membership. Recommended.
Villa María Isabel RV Park, on river and highway east of Orchard, T153-0246. Pool, recreation area, disposal station, American-style bakery.

South of Mulegé *p179*

E **Ecomundo** T153-0409, Apdo Area 60, ecomundo@aol.com (office in Mulegé at Las Casitas hotel). Tents, *palapas* and kayaks can be hired, and there is also a bookshop, gallery, bar and restaurant. Idyllic place to hang out, run by an American couple.

Loreto *p179*

AL **La Pinta**, on Sea of Cortés, 2 km north of Zócalo, T135-0025, www.lapintahotels.com. A/c, showers, pool, tennis, restaurant, bar, considered by many the best of the original 'Presidente' *paradores*, 30 rooms, fishing boat hire. Recommended.
C **Salvatierra**, Salvatierra, on south approach to town, T135-0021. Motel with a/c, hot showers but poor water pressure, limited cable TV, clean, good value.
D **Posada San Martín**, Juárez and Calle Davis 4, 2 blocks from the beach, T135-0792. Clean motel with small patio and very friendly owner. Laundry service. Recommended.

Camping

Ejido Loreto RV Park, on beach 1 km south of town. Full hook-ups, toilets, showers, free coffee, laundry, fishing and boat trips. Butter clams are plentiful in the sand.

Route south of Loreto *p179*

Tripui Trailer Park, 25 km south of Loreto, PO Box 100, Loreto, T133-0818. Claimed to be the best in Mexico. Landscaped grounds, paved roads, coin laundry, groceries, restaurant and pool, lit tennis court, playground; 31 spaces, US$15.

Ciudad Constitución and around *p180*

C **Casino**, Guadalupe Victoria, a block east of the Maribel, Cd Constitución, T132-1415. Quiet, 36 clean rooms, restaurant, bar.
C **Maribel**, Guadalupe Victoria and Highway 1, T132-0155, 2 blocks south of San Carlos road junction, Cd Constitución. A/c, TV, restaurant, bar, suites available, clean, fine for overnight stop.
D-E **El Arbolito**, Hidalgo, Cd Constitución. Basic, clean, central.
E **Motel Las Brisas**, Bahía Magdalena, 1 block behind bus station. Clean, friendly, quiet.
E **Reforma**, Obregón, 2 blocks from the plaza, Cd Constitución. Basic, with bath. Friendly.

Camping

Campestre La Pila, 2.5 km south of Cd Constitución on unpaved road off Highway 1, T132-0562. Farmland setting, full hook-ups, toilets, showers, pool, laundry, groceries, tennis courts, ice, restaurant, bar, no hot water, US$12.

RV Park Manfred, on left of main road going north into Cd Constitución, T132-1103. Very clean, friendly and helpful, Austrian owner (serves Austrian food). US$13-18.

La Paz *p180*

L-AL Los Arcos, Paseo Alvaro Obregón 498 at Allende, T122-2744, www.losarcos.com A/c, pool, restaurant, across the Malecón from the beach, walking distance of centre, fishing trips. Excellent value.

AL Mediterráneo, Allende 36, T/F125-1195, www.hotelmed.com Beautiful Greek-style hotel with classic standards as you would expect. Great service, outstanding **La Pazta** restaurant with Greek and Italian dishes. Internet access.

A La Perla, Obregón 1570, on the water front, T122-0777, perla@lapaz.cromwell.com.mx. Clean, a/c, friendly, expensive restaurant, swimming pool, locked garage.

C Lorimar, Bravo 110, T125-3822. Hot showers, clean, very helpful, run by a Mexican/American couple, popular, good place to meet fellow travellers, good-value restaurant, can organize trip to Tecolote beach. Best value for money in town by a long shot. Recommended.

D Posada del Cortez, Av 16 de Septiembre, T122-8240. Pretty basic uninspiring rooms, but good for the price and safe.

D Posada San Miguel, Belisario Domínguez Norte 45, T122-1802, near plaza. Colonial-style, bathroom, limited hot water, quiet. Looks better on the outside than it is inside. Often full and recommended but a little overpriced.

E Hostería del Convento, Madero 85, T122-3508. Friendly enough but pretty basic, fans, clean, shower, tepid water between 0700-0900. Cheapest in town.

E Pensión California, Degollado 209, near Madero, T122-2896. Basic, fan, shower, garden patio, noisy, friendly, weekly deals, not too clean. Good budget choice.

Camping

Aquamarina RV Park, 3500 m southwest, 400 m off Highway 1 at Calle Nayarit, on bay, T122-3765. Nicely landscaped, all facilities, marina, boat ramp, fishing, scuba trips. US$15.

El Cardón Trailer Park, 4 km southwest on Highway 1, T122-0078. Partly shaded area away from beach, full facilities.

La Paz Trailer Park, 1500 m south of town off Highway 1, access via Calle Colima, T125-0602. Deluxe, nearest RV park to La Paz, very comfortable.

South of La Paz *p182*

C Palomar, by the hot springs, 12 km from Santiago. A/c, hot showers, restaurant, bar, on main street, modest, good meals. Camping in hotel grounds, with cold shower and toilets available.

E La Rivera RV Park, La Rivera, in palm grove next to beach. Excellent swimming, hot showers, laundry, friendly. Recommended.

San José del Cabo *p182*

Several top-quality hotels along the beach front, about 1 km south of town, of varying excellence and seclusion. All are booked as part of resort holidays; some won't even allow passing trade to enter.

LL One & Only Palmilla, 8 km west at Punta Palmilla T146-7000. One of the top resorts in Baja with outstanding surf nearby. Some a/c, showers, pool, beach, tennis, restaurant, bar, skin diving, fishing cruisers and skiffs for hire (daily happy hour allows mere mortals to partake of margarita and appetizers and see how royalty and film stars live!).

LL-AL El Encanto Inn, Calle Morales and Alvaro Obregón, T142-0388, www.elencantoinn.com. Easy Mediterranean feel to the place with stylish decor. Good choice.

A Posada Terranova, Degollado between Doblado and Zaragoza, T142-0534, www.hterranova.com.mx. Pleasant rooms in a quietly professional atmosphere. Fine mid-price restaurant with patio dining.

B Señor Mañana, Alvaro Obregón 1, just off the main square, T/F142-0462, www.srmanana.net. Several options of rooms ranging from basic to quite comfortable. None of the rooms are fantastic, but the small pool, use of kitchen and hammock area make it a good choice for the cheaper rooms

B-C Ceci, Zaragoza 22, 1 block west of plaza, T142-0041. Central, with fans, hot showers (occasionally), cable TV, basic but clean, good value.
C-D Collí, close to the centre, T142-0725. Fans, hot showers, 12 clean and adequate rooms in a family-run hotel.
D Brisa del Mar, on Highway 1, 3 km southwest of town. Motel with 10 rooms, restaurant, bar, pool, modest but comfortable, behind trailer park on outstanding beach.
D Nuevo San José, Alvaro Obregón. Clean, quiet, cool, comfortable, ceiling fans. Good value.

Camping
Unofficial camping is possible on those few beaches not fronted by resort hotels.
Brisa del Mar Trailer Park, 100 RV sites in fenced area by great beach. Full hook-ups, flush toilets, showers, pool, laundry, restaurant, bar, fishing trips arranged, popular, good location. Recommended. US$18-25.

Cabo San Lucas *p183*
Cheap accommodation doesn't exist in Cabo.
LL-L Finisterra, perched on promontory near Land's End, T143-3333, www.finisterra.com. A/c, TV, shower, pool, steps to beach, poolside bar with unsurpassed view, restaurant, entertainment, sport-fishing cruisers.
AL-A Marina, Blv Marina y Guerrero, T143-3332. Central, a/c, restaurant, bar, can be noisy, pricey.
A Mar de Cortés, on Cárdenas and Guerrero in town centre, T143-0032, www.mardecortez.com. A/c, showers, helpful, pool, outdoor bar/restaurant, good value.
B Dos Mares, Calle Emiliano Zapata, T143-0330. A/c, TV, clean, small pool, parking space. Don't get drunk and fall down the stairs – survival unlikely. Recommended.
C San Antonio, Av Morelos between Obregón and Carranza, 3 blocks back from the main street, T143-7353. Cheapest option in town really, and much better than the rest.
D El Dorado, Morelos, 4 blocks from bus terminal. Clean, fan, hot water, private bath.

Camping
El Faro Viejo Trailer Park, 1.5 km northwest at Matamoros y Morales, T143-4211. Shade, laundry, ice, restaurant, bar, clean, out of town but good. US$15.

Todos Santos *p183*
LL-L Todos Santos Inn, Calle Legaspi 33, 2 blocks north of Plaza T/F145-0040, www.todossantosinn.com. Refurbished 19th-century house, some en suite rooms, very tranquil. Worth splashing out.
B Hotel California, formerly the **Misión de Todos Santos Inn**, Juárez and Morelos, T145-0525, hotelcaliforniareservations@hotmail.com. Historic brick building near town centre, a block north of Highway 9. Fans, showers, pool, a/c, dining room.
C Miramar, south end of village, T145-0341. New, with bath, hot water, fan, pool, clean, safe, parking. Recommended.
C Motel Guluarte. Calle Morelos, T145-0006. Fan, fridge, shower, pool, good value.
C Way of Nature, bed and breakfast, along dirt road signposted at southern end of Juárez, 2 blocks south of **Hotel California**. Large circular *palapa* with rooms. Very quiet. Tent camping too.

Camping
El Molino Trailer Park, off highway at south end of town, 30 mins from beach, T124-0140. Full hook-ups, flush toilets, showers, laundry, American owner, very helpful, US$8 for 4. No camping here but apparently OK to use the beach (clean, but look out for dogs).
Trailer Park San Pedrito, several kilometres south of Todos Santos, T125-0170. This is a great location on the beach. Full hook-ups, flush toilets, showers, pool, laundry, restaurant, bar, US$13 for RVs.

Eating

Crossing into Mexico: Tecate *p169*
₸ El Passetto, Libertad 200 near Parque Hidalgo. Excellent Mexican and Italian specialities.

Crossing into Mexico:Tijuana *p170, map p171*
₸₸₸-₸₸ Tía Juana Tilly's, Av Revolucion at Calle 7, T685-6024. Excellent food, popular local open-air spot, reasonably priced.

Ψ El Torito, Av Revolución between Calle 2 and 3. Mexican-diner style, with rock music in the evenings.
ΨΨ-Ψ La Especial, Av Revolución 718, T685-6654. Surprisingly authentic Mexican food by Tijuana standards.

Ensenada *p172*
Plenty of places to choose from down the Blv Costero promenade, or the upper section of Av Lopéz Mateos.
ΨΨΨ El Rey Sol, López Mateos 1000 y Blancarte. French/Mexican, elegant, reasonable prices for the style.
ΨΨΨ Mandarín, López Mateos 2127, between Soto and Balboa (Chinese). Elegant surroundings, good food, expensive, considered to be the best *chifa* in Ensenada.
ΨΨ Cantina Hussong's, Av Ruiz 113. An institution in both the Californias, more of a bar than a restaurant, 1000-0100.
ΨΨ Cha-Cha Burgers, Blv Costero 609. American-style burgers, fish, chicken, fast food 1000-2200.
ΨΨ El Pollo, Macheros y Calle 2. Grilled chicken 'Sinaloa style', fast food 1000-2200 every day of year.
ΨΨ Las Brasas, López Mateos 486, between Ruiz and Gastelum. Barbecue chicken and fish, Mexican specialities, attractive mid-priced patio dining, 1100-2200, closed Tue.
ΨΨ-Ψ Mesón de Don Fernando, López Mateos. Good breakfasts, tacos and seafood, good value.
Ψ Lonchería La Terminal, opposite bus station. Cheap and filling *comida*, good but basic.

San Felipe *p174*
ΨΨ George's, 336 Av Mar de Cortés. Steaks, seafood, live music, pleasant, friendly, popular with US residents. Recommended.
ΨΨ Green House, Av Mar de Cortés 132 y Calzada Chetumal. Good food, beef or chicken *fajitas* a speciality, friendly service, cheap breakfasts, 'fish fillet for a fiver'. Daily 0730-0300.
ΨΨ-Ψ Las Misiones in Mar del Sol RV park. Small menu, moderately priced, seafood crêpes a speciality, popular with families, good service.
Ψ Clam Man's Restaurant, Calzada Chetumal, 2 blocks west of Pemex station. Used to belong to the late, famous Pascual 'The Clam Man'. Oddly decorated, but excellent clams, steamed, fried, barbecued, at budget prices.

Bahía de los Angeles *p175*
ΨΨ-Ψ Restaurant Las Hamacas, on north edge of town. Budget café with bay view, slow service, popular for breakfast.

Guerrero Negro *p175*
ΨΨ Malarrimo Restaurant-Bar, east end of town, T157-0100, www.malarrimo.com. In hotel of the same name. Good fish and steak menu, moderate prices, music, open for breakfast.
ΨΨ Mario's Restaurant-Bar, next to El Morro. Modest surroundings and fare, disco.
Ψ Taco stall, a few blocks towards town from El Morro. Excellent.

San Ignacio *p176*
ΨΨ-Ψ Lonchería Chalita, on Zócalo. Excellent value.
Ψ Rice'n'Beans, on the plaza. Good and cheap.

Santa Rosalía *p177*
ΨΨ Balneario Selene, on highway opposite Pemex, T152-0685. Seafood.

Bakeries
Panadería El Boleo, Av Constitución. A Santa Rosalía institution, they were selling bread when the West was Wild.

Mulegé *p177*
A few bars in town will offer you the full range of tequilas.
ΨΨΨ-ΨΨ Patio El Candil, Zaragoza. Simple outdoor dining with good breakfasts.
ΨΨ El Mezquite, Zaragoza. Good burgers, live music.
ΨΨ Equipales, Zaragoza, upstairs. Recommended for good local cooking and for breakfasts.
ΨΨ-Ψ Donna Moe's Pizza, Zaragoza, on corner of Plaza Corona. Pleasant rooftop breakfast patio and bar.
ΨΨ Jungle Jim, signed turn-off from highway, 2 km south. Rustic, Mexican, friendly.

Loreto *p179*
ΨΨΨ-ΨΨ La Palapa, Av Hidalgo, ½ block from seafront. Excellent seafood.
ΨΨ César's, Zapata y Juárez. Good food and service, candlelit, moderate prices.

YY-Y **Café Olé**, Madero 14. Mexican and fast food, *palapa* style, open-air breakfasts, budget rates.

Ciudad Constitución *p180*

YY **Nuevo Dragón de Oro**, Av Olachea with Esgrima, 5 blocks north of plaza. Chinese.

Bakeries

Panadería Superpan, north of market hall. Excellent pastries.

La Paz *p180*

YYY-YY **Carlos 'n' Charlies**, right on the seafront. A popular Mexican staple, good to know where it is, but probably not the best food.

YYY-YY **Kiwi**, on the sea front. Open 0800-2400. A mix of Mex and international dishes. Good prices through the day.

YY **Adriana**, on beachfront. Open air, excellent service and stylish.

YY **Sushi Express**, Madero and Degollado, good, sushi eat in or takeaway.

YY-Y **El Quinto**, Independencia y Belisario Domínguez. Very good vegetarian with lots of wholesome foodstuffs.

Y **El Mesquite**, Madero between Ocampo and Bravo. A wicked little streetside burger bar. Cheap, tasty and filling. Evenings only.

Y **Mercado**. Good *lonchería* and juice bars in the market.

Y **Taquerías**. Superb seafood tacos at stands outside Pensión California and Posada San Miguel.

San José del Cabo *p182*

The town is full of tasty options, many of them courting the dollars of visiting vacationers over travellers on a budget. For more realistic budget options you have to head west of the centre.

YYY **Casa Natalia**, Blv Mijares, in the hotel of the same name. A stylish setting with a chic approach to romance.

YY **Baan Thai**, Morelos and Comonfort, opposite Encanto Inn, T142-3344. Wonderful atmosphere, quiet patio at the back.

YY **Damiana**, at the top of Blv Mijares. Mexican and international dishes under the most spectacular bougainvillea tree. Very romantic.

Cabo San Lucas *p183*

Many expensive but good eateries, particular on the promenade in front of the marina.

YYY-YY **The Giggling Marlin**, Marina Blv. A landmark used for directions, and a fine place to experience what makes Cabo San Lucas tick. The food is good, the prices reasonable and the self-deprecating humour on the walls refreshing.

YY **Flor de Guadalajara**, Lázaro Cárdenas, on the way out of town a few blocks beyond 'Skid Row'. Good local dishes.

YY **Rays Tequila – The Corner Café**, Los Cabos. Does what is says on the tin – a fine chap called Ray serving fine tequila.

YY-Y **Paty's Garden**, Niños Héroes between Zaragoza and Ocampo, T143-0689. An authentic atmosphere, complete with pool table, and tasty as well. A good budget choice.

Todos Santos *p183*

YYY **Café Santa Fe**, on main plaza. Gourmet Italian food, pricey but very highly rated restaurant.

YYY-YY **Tequila Sunrise**, opposite the Hotel California. A colourful spot serving drinks and snacks to those venturing up from Cabo San Lucas.

Entertainment

Crossing into Mexico:Tijuana *p170, map p171*

Bars and clubs

Flamingos, south on old road to Ensenada, and **Chantecler** are also both recommended nightclubs.

Tequila Sunrise, Av Revolución, between Calle 5 and 6. Balcony bar with great opportunity to get your bearings without being hassled on the street.

Tilly's Fifth Avenue, Revolución and Calle 5, T685-9015. Good lively bar.

Festivals and events

La Paz *p180*

Feb/Mar Pre-Lenten Mardi Gras (carnival), inaugurated in 1989, is one of Mexico's finest. The Malecón is converted into a swirling mass of dancing, games, restaurants and stalls, and the street parade is happy and colourful.

Shopping

Crossing into Mexico: Tijuana *p170, map p171*
Plaza Río Tijuana Shopping Centre, Paseo de Los Héroes; opposite are the **Plaza Fiesta** and **Plaza del Zapato** malls, the latter specializing in footwear. Nearby is the colourful public **market**. Downtown shopping area is **Av Revolución** and **Av Constitución**. Bargaining is expected at smaller shops, and everyone except bus drivers are happy to accept US currency.

La Paz *p180*
A duty-free port. Tourist shops are concentrated along the Malecón between the Tourist and Commercial wharves.

Crafts
Bazar del Sol, Obregón 1665, for quality ceramics and good Aztec art reproductions.
Casa de las Artesanías de BCS, Paseo Alvaro Obregón at Mijares, just north of **Hotel Los Arcos**. Souvenirs from all over Mexico.
Centro de Arte Regional, Chiapas y Encinas, 5 blocks east of Isabel la Católica. Pottery workshop, reasonable prices.
Fortunato Silva, Highway 1 (Abasolo) y Jalisco at south end of town. Good quality woollen and hand-woven cotton garments and articles.
Solco's, Obregón y 16 de Septiembre. Large selection of Taxco silver, leather, onyx chess sets.

General supplies
CCC Supermarket, opposite Palacio de Gobierno, is good for supplies.
Ferretería,hardware store across from the main city bus terminal, sells white gas stove fuel (*gasolina blanca*).
Mercado Central, Revolución y Degollado, and another at Bravo y Prieto, has a wide range of goods (clothes, sandals, guitars, etc), plus fruit and vegetables.
La Perla de la Paz department store, Arreola y 21 de Agosto. General camping supplies.

Todos Santos *p183*
Bookshop El Tecolote Libros is an excellent bookshop selling good maps, books, book swap (no romance though!) and very useful general information on the area.

Activities and tours

Crossing into Mexico: Tijuana *p170, map p171*
Tour operators
Honold's Travel, Av Revolución 828, T688-1111. Provides all standard services and plane ticketing services.

Mulegé *p177*
Diving
Diving is off Punta Concepción or Isla Santa Inés. The best snorkelling from the shore is just past the point, opposite way up from beach by lighthouse.
Cortez Explorers, Calle Moctezuma 75A, T/F153-0500, www.cortez-explorer.com. Mon-Sat 1000-1300, 1600-1900. Friendly, English spoken, US$60 for 2-tank boat dive excluding equipment. US$35 snorkelling from boat with minimum of 3 people.

Tour operators
There is a small sports fishing fleet operating out of the harbour here. Also hires out quadbikes (must be 16 or over), mountain bikes, horse riding and fishing tours.

Day trips to nearby cave paintings at La Trinidad can be arranged from Mulegé. US$40 per person, slightly less with groups. T/F153-0232 or book through **Hotel Las Casitas**.

Loreto *p179*
Diving and fishing
Scuba and snorkelling information and equipment booth on municipal beach near the fishing pier; the beach itself stretches for 8 km, but is dusty and rocky. Beware of stingrays on the beach.
Arturos Sports Fishing Fleet, T135-0409, www.arturosport.com. Full sports fishing, scuba and snorkelling.

La Paz *p180*
Diving
Baja Diving and Service, Obregón 1680, T122-1826, www.bajadivingservice.com. Hires diving equipment and takes diving trips. Resort and diving packages available.

Tour operators
You can hire a bike and head out on your own, or take a tour – all day tour around

mountains visiting local ranches (US$55) – it's worth the effort.

Baja Outdoor Activities, right on the seafront, T125-5636, www.kayakinbaja.com. Run by Ben and Alejandra Gillam. Simple ½-day tours or full trips out to Espíritu Santo Island in the Gulf, also whale watching. Prices start at US$35. Excellent.

Katun Tours, 16 de Septiembre 15, across the street from **Carlos 'n' Charlies**.

Baja Outdoor Activities, T348-5609, www.katun-tours.com.

Cabo San Lucas *p183*

There's absolutely no shortage of sporting activities, including **scuba diving** (US$60 for a 2-tank dive), **snorkelling** (US$35), **horse riding** (US$57 for 2 hrs), **parasailing** (US$35) and so on. The latest craze is **personal submarines** (US$85 for 30 mins)! There are plenty of operators.

Todos Santos *p183*

Surfing

Todos Santos surf shop, Rangel and Zaragoza. Board hire at US$10.50 per day, US$5.25 for body board. They have kiosk at Playa Los Cerritos beyond El Pescadero. They also hire out tents (US$5.50 per day) and mountain bikes (US$10) at the main shop.

Transport

Crossing into Mexico: Mexicali *p169*

Air

Airport (MXL) 25 km east, Blv Aviación. Flights to **Chihuahua**, **Cd Obregón**, **Guadalajara**, **Hermosillo**, **Mexico City**, **Monterrey** and **Torreón**.

Airline offices AeroMéxico, T91-800-90999. Mexicana, T553-5402.

Bus

All buses leave from the central bus station (Camionera Central) on Av Independencia. 'Central Camionera' bus to Civic Centre and bus station. To **Ensenada**, 4 a day, 4 hrs, US$16. To **Guadalajara**, 1 service, 34 hrs, US$100. To **Hermosillo**, regular service, 10 hrs, US$29. To **La Paz**, daily 1630, 24 hrs, US$82. To **Mazatlán**, every 30 mins, 24 hrs, US$68. To **Mexico City**, 1 a day, 40 hrs, US$120. To **San Felipe**, 4 a day, 3 hrs, US$12. To **Tijuana** every 30 mins, 3 hrs, US$12.

To USA Golden State buses to **Los Angeles** (US$44) tickets available at trailer/kiosk across from **Hotel del Norte**, also with services within Mexico. **Greyhound** from **Los Angeles** to **Calexico** (901 Imperial Av), US$35, 6 hrs. **San Diego** to **Calexico** via **El Centro**, US$24, 3 hrs. The 1300 bus from **San Diego** may connect with the **Pullman** bus to **Mazatlán**, US$40, 21 hrs. Local buses are cheap, about US$0.55.

Crossing into Mexico: Tijuana *p170, map p171*

Air

Aeropuerto Rodríguez (TIJ), T683-2102. To **Mexico City**, with good connections to regional airports. Also international flights to **Las Vegas**, **Los Angeles** in the US and **Panama City**. Taxi between airport and centre is quoted at US$15.

Airline offices Aero California, T684-9268. AeroMéxico, T685-4401. Mexicana, T634-6545.

Bus

Local General information at bus station, T621-2606. It is possible to get buses to most destinations from **Tijuana's Downtown station**, Calle 2 near Av Revolución, with the office close to the pedestrian bridge. Local buses go to the border from the bus station, every 30 mins up to 2300, marked **'La Línea/Centro'**, US$0.50.

Long distance There are local buses to the Central Camionera, the main bus station 5 km southeast of the centre at the end of Vía Oriente, from Constitución and Calle 3, about US$0.50, taxis ask US$10. Good facilities including *casa de cambio*, ATM, pharmacy and a couple of fast-food outlets. Services provided by **Estrella Blanca**, T621-2955, **TAP**, T621-3903, and **Transportes del Pacífico**, T621-2606, for services throughout Mexico. For Baja California the main option is ABC,T621-2424.

All services hourly unless stated. To **Culiacán**, 22 hrs, US$76. To **Guadalajara**, 34 hrs, US$90. To **Hermosillo**, 11 hrs, US$35. To **Los Mochis**, 19 hrs, US$65. To **Mazatlán**, 26 hrs, US$81. To **Mexicali**, 2 hrs, US$16. To **Mexico City**, 38 hrs, US$122-150. To **Sonoyta**, 2½ hrs, US$33.

Heading down the peninsula from north to south, with ABC departures every 30 mins, the options are: **Ensenada**, 1½ hrs, US$8; **El Rosario**, 6½ hrs, US$23; **Guerrero Negro**, 12 hrs, US$43; **Santa Rosalía**, 17 hrs, US$56; **Mulegé** 18 hrs, US$62; **La Paz**, 24 hrs, US$90.

To USA From Tijuana bus terminal Greyhound has buses every 2 hrs, US$12, 1 hr 10 mins, to **San Diego** via the Otay Mesa crossing, except after 2200, when it uses the Tijuana crossing; coming from **San Diego** stay on the bus to the main Tijuana terminal, entry stamp given at border (ask driver to get it for you), or at bus station. Long queues for immigration at lunchtime. Walk across La Línea (border) and catch a Golden State bus to downtown **Los Angeles**, US$13 (buy ticket inside McDonald's restaurant), 12 a day, or take trolley to downtown **San Diego** and get a Greyhound, US$20, or Amtrak train, US$25, to **Los Angeles**. Golden State is the cheapest and fastest; its terminal is about 1 km from Greyhound terminal in downtown LA, but stops first at **Santa Ana** and else where if requested.

Ensenada *p172*

Bus To **Tijuana**, US$7, 1½ hrs. ABC have a service heading south through the peninsula. Transportes ABC and TNS buses to **San Felipe**, direct, over the mountains, at 0800 and 1800, 3½ hrs, US$13.

Hitchhiking Hitching is a great way to get around the Baja and used by many budget travellers. There seems to be a slightly different approach on the peninsula to the 'mainland'. Hitching out of Tijuana would range between pointless and dangerous; Ensenada would be a good starting point if heading south.

San Felipe *p174*

Bus Bus station is on Mar Báltico near corner of Calzada Chetumal, in town centre. Transportes ABC and TNS buses to **Ensenada**, direct, over the mountains, at 0800 and 1800, 3½ hrs, US$13. Bus to **Mexicali**, 4 a day from 0730, 2 hrs, US$12.

Guerrero Negro *p175*

Air Airport (GUB), 3 km from town, very handy if you want to go to **Hermosillo**. There are regular flights to **Isla Cedros** and **Bahía Tortugas**; information from airfield downtown.

Bus To **La Paz**, 0030, 0600, 2030, 2100, 11 hrs, US$40. To **Mexicali**, 2400, 14 hrs, US$60. To **Mulegé**, 4½ hrs, US$21. To **Santa Rosalía**, 0530, 3 hrs, US$24. To **Tijuana**, 0630, 0830, 2030 and 2200, 11 hrs, US$43.

Santa Rosalía *p177*

Bus **ABC/Autobus Aguila** station, T152-0150, 400 m south of ferry terminal; stop for most Tijuana-La Paz buses, several per day. To **La Paz**, 1100, US$33. To **Tijuana**, US$56.

Mulegé *p177*

Bicycle Bike repairs near Doney's Tacos, 1 block before Casa de la Cultura, on left.

Bus Buses to the south do not leave at scheduled times, ask in town as everyone knows when they come through. Allow plenty of time to complete your journey. Bus stop is on highway, north of bridge, at entrance to town. There is an airstrip for private planes beside the currently closed Hotel Vista Hermosa.

Loreto *p179*

Air Airport 7 km south of town. Flights to **Cd Obregón**, **Guadalajara**, **Hermosillo**, **La Paz** and internationally to **Los Angeles**. Other destinations in high season.

Bus Station at Salvatierra opposite intersection of Zapata. To **La Paz** 6 a day, from 0700, US$10.75. To **Tijuana** throughout the day, US$70, 19 hrs. To **Mulegé** with Aguila 2½ hrs, US$8.

La Paz *p180*

Air

General Manuel Márquez de León International Airport (LAP), 11 km southwest on paved road off Highway 1. Taxi fare US$20, *colectivo* US$14. Flights within Mexico to **Chihuahua**, **Cd Obregón**, **Culiacán**, **Guadalajara**, **Hermosillo**, **Loreto**, **Los Mochis**, **Mazatlán**, **Mexico City**, **Monterrey**, **Tijuana**. US destinations include **Los Angeles** and **Phoenix**. More charter flights in high season.

Airline offices Aero California, Alvaro Obregón, T122-0093. AeroMéxico, T122-0091.

Ferry schedule from Baja California

	La Paz-Topolobampo	Topolobampo-La Paz	La Paz-Mazatlán	Mazatlán-La Paz
Frequency	Daily	Daily	Tue, Thu, Sat	Mon, Wed, Fri
Time	1500	2300	1600	1500
Salón price	US$59	US$59	N/A	N/A
Turista price	N/A	N/A	US$69	US$69
Cabina price	N/A	N/A	US$69	US$69

Salón: General seating
Turista: Cabin with bunkbeds and washbasins
Cabina: Cabin with bunkbeds and bathrooms
Especial: Cabin with living room, bedroom, bathroom and closet

Baja Ferries (www.bajaferries.com.mx)
La Paz: T125-7443
Mazatlán: T985-0470
Los Mochis: T817-3725

Bicycle
Viajes Palmira, Av Obregón, opposite **Hotel los Arcos**, T122-4030. Rents cycles and mopeds.

Bus
Local Buses about US$0.50, depot at Revolución de 1910 y Degollado by the Mercado Central. The Central Camionera (main bus station) is at Jalisco y Héroes de la Independencia, about 16 blocks from centre (taxi US$2). You can get most buses you need from the promenade Aguila terminal on Obregón between Independencia and 5 de Mayo, 1 block up from **Carlos 'n' Charlies**.

Long distance: Buses heading for the Cape go clockwise or counter clockwise. Head counter clockwise if going for **Todo Santos** or **Cabo San Lucas**. Services at 0730, 1030, 1130, 1530 and 1930, 2½ hrs, US$11. Head counter clockwise if going to **San José del Cabo**. Services at 0800, 1000, 1200, 1430, 1630 and 1830, 3 hrs, US$11. Information T122-7094 ext 111.

For most long-distance journeys you will have to go to the main terminal. To **Guerrero Negro**, 6 per day, US$40. To **Loreto**, 3 per day, US$20. To **Tijuana**, 1300 and 2000, 22 hrs, US$89. Try to book at least 2 weeks ahead (6 weeks at Christmas, Easter and in Jul and Aug).

Car
Budget, **Avis**, **Hertz**, **Auto Renta Sol** and **Auto Servitur** booths at airport.

Ferry
For schedule to **Mazatlán** and **Topolobampo**, see above. Modern ferry terminal at Pichilingüe, 21 km north on paved highway.

Tickets for the same day are sold at the terminal. Advance tickets may be bought at **Baja Ferries** at I La Católica y Navarro, toll free on 01-800-122-1414, www.bajaferries.com.mx, and some local travel agents. They also have offices in Los Mochis and several other towns in the area.

In general book in advance whenever possible, especially if travelling by vehicle and your journey time is critical. **Tourist cards** must be valid, allow 2 hrs as there are long queues when buying tickets and boarding. In the past, many motorists have had difficulty getting reservations or having them honoured. Vehicles must have **car permits**, obtainable at ferry terminal or at Registro Federal de Vehículos in Tijuana; automobile clubs will provide information. Service and conditions on the ferry are improving. Bus to Pichilingüe from seafront terminal in La Paz. Reasonable facilities at terminal but crowded; large parking lots, officials may permit RVs to stay overnight while awaiting ferry departures. On all ferry crossings, **delays** can occur from Sep if there is bad weather. Keep a flexible schedule if travelling to the mainland.

San José del Cabo *p182*
Air To Los Cabos International Airport (SJD), 14 km, take a local bus, US$3, which drops at the entrance road to the airport, leaving a 2-km walk, otherwise take a taxi. Airport to San José del Cabo in *colectivo*, US$7. Good regional connections and international to the US.

Airline offices Aero California, T167-200-21. Mexicana, T143-5353.

Bus Bus station on Valerio González Canseco, about 600 m south of the main road into town. To **Cabo San Lucas** with Tres Estrellas, daily from 0700, US$1.25, 30 mins. To **La Paz** daily from 0630, US$9, 3 hrs.

Cabo San Lucas *p183*
Bus Bus station at 16 de Septiembre y Zaragoza, central, few facilities. Regular service to **San José del Cabo**, 30-45 mins depending on traffic, US$2. To **La Paz**, 6 a day from 0630, US$8.

Ferry There are no ferries from Cabo San Lucas to Puerto Vallarta.

Directory

Crossing into Mexico: Mexicali *p169*
Banks all major banks: currency exchange from 0900-1330 only. *Casas de cambio* in Calexico give a slightly better rate. There are several on López Mateos.
Immigration Mexican Consulate in Calexico, T357-3863.

Crossing into Mexico: Tijuana *p170, map p171*
Banks Many banks, all dealing in foreign exchange. For Visa TCs, go to Bancomer. Better rate than *casas de cambio* but less convenient. Countless *casas de cambio* throughout Tijuana open day and night. Most *cambios* charge a commission (up to 5%), even for cash dollars; ask before changing. **Embassies and consulates** Canada, Germán Gedovius 10411-101, T684-0461, tijuana@canada.org.mx. France, Av Revolución 1651, T685-7177. Germany, Av Sánchez Taboada 9210, T680-1830. Spain, Av de los Olivos 305, T686-5780. UK, Blv Salinas 1500, Fraccionamiento Aviación, T686-5320, www.britishconsulate tijuana.com. US, Tapachula 96, between Agua Caliente racetrack and the Country Club, Mon-Fri 0800-1630, T681-7400.
Emergencies Fire: T135. Police: T134.
Immigration Mexican Consulate-General, San Diego, CA, 1549 India St, T619-231-8414, portal.sre.gob.mx/sandiego, Mon-Fri 0900-1400, for visas and tourist information. **Internet** Revolución just beyond Calle 3. **Medical services** Red Cross: 132; valid for Tijuana, Rosarito, Ensenada, Tecate, Mexicali and San Luis Río Colorado. **Telephone** Computel, Calle 7 y Av Negrete, metered phones, fax, computer facilities.

Ensenada *p172*
Immigration Beside the shipyard, for tourist entry permits. **Internet** **Equinoxio**, Blv Lázaro Cárdenas 267 in front of Plaza Marina, T179-4646, US$2 per hr, with a mighty fine cappuccino served on the side.
Language schools Baja California Language College, east of the town towards San Quintín, PO Box 7556, San Diego, CA 92167, USA 1-877-444-2252, www.bajacal.com. Spanish immersion for business executives, teachers, travellers and students.

Santa Rosalía *p177*
Banks Banamex and Bancomer, both with ATMs. **Internet** Centcom, Obregón and Calle 9, with another place just behind the main junction entrance to the town.
Laundry Opposite Hotel Central, wash and dry US$2.50 per load. **Post office** Only from here and La Paz can parcels be sent abroad; customs check necessary first, at boat dock.

Mulegé *p177*
Banks There are none in town and very few places take TCs. You can change dollars at most stores. **Laundry** Claudia, Zaragoza and Moctezuma, next to Hotel Terrazas, self-service and with good information boards. **Post office** and **police** in old city hall, 1 block up from Pemex. **Telephone**

Mini-supermarket Padilla, Zaragoza, 1 block from Pemex station (also fax); also from video store, nearby.

Loreto *p179*
Bank Bancomer on southwest corner of plaza. **Internet** Gigante, estate agent above shoe shop, on Salvatierra.

La Paz *p180*
Banks Plenty of banks and ATMs down 16 de Septiembre: Banamex, Arreola y Esquerro. 2 *casas de cambio* on 5 de Mayo off Obregón, 0800-2000, better rates than banks.
Immigration 2nd floor of large building on Paseo Alvaro Obregón, opposite the pier, very helpful, able to extend visa here.
Internet Espacio Don Tomás, Obregón between 5 de Mayo and Constitución. In an art gallery with fine snacks and coffee.
Laundry Laundromat Yoli, 5 de Mayo y Rubio. Also at Marina de La Paz.

San José del Cabo *p182*
Banks Several *casas de cambio* around town. There is a branch of Bancomer on Zaragoza and a branch of BanCrecer with an ATM, just off the junction of the Transpeninsular Highway and Doblado.
Internet Several places in town, many asking ridiculous prices. Try Espacio Café Internet (discounts for students) on the 2nd floor opposite the hospital on Doblado.
Laundry Lavamática San José, on Valerio Gonzaléz. **Post office** A few blocks from the town centre down Blv Mijares.

Cabo San Lucas *p183*
Banks Plenty of branches with ATMs in town. **Internet** Kill 2 birds with one stone, log on while doing your washing at the **Laundromat** on Leona Vicario and 20 de Noviembre, 30 mins US$2.40, 1 load wash and dry US$2.40. Cafés on the main drag are pricey. **Post office** Morelos y Niños Héroes.

Todos Santos *p183*
Banks BanCrecer, with ATM but doesn't change TCs, *casa de cambio* on Colegio Militar with Hidalgo does.
Laundry Lavandería Misión. US$3.50 wash and dry.

Northwest coast

The Northwest coast of Mexico includes the scenic Sierra de Pintos, the copper-mining centre at Cananea, the longest sand dunes in North America at Algodones, and the desert conditions of the Desierto de Altar and the beaches and watersports of Puerto Peñasco. At the Pinacate Natural Park the moonscape of volcanic craters and lava fields is very impressive and so is the wildlife. With a little more time, you can explore the Kino Missions and enjoy sportfishing at Kino Nuevo, participate in fishing tournaments at La Choya and San Carlos or take a boat excursion from Rocky Point. There are many opportunities to take boat trips to the islands just off the coast and you can take an overnight ferry to Baja California.

Heading south, detour to the beautiful colonial town of Alamos, home of the original Mexican jumping bean. Relax in the streets of Los Mochis and enjoy the music of the roaming mariachis before boarding the famous Copper Canyon train for the journey of a lifetime. The popularity of Mazatlán as a holiday resort is well established; from here, you can travel northeast to Durango and the Colonial Heartland, or southeast to Tepic and Guadalajara, pleasant resting places if you are travelling on to Mexico City.

Like the west coast of all continents between latitudes 20° and 30°, the whole area is desert, but fruitful wherever irrigated by water flowing from the mountains. Summers are very hot, sometimes rainy, winters mild and very dry. »» *For Sleeping, Eating and other listings, see pages 205-213.*

Crossing into Mexico: Nogales(US)/ Nogales → *Colour map 1, A3.*

The Nogales crossing is open 24 hours. There's no checkpoint on the Mexican side although there is a customs area that is sometimes staffed and sometimes not. If it is staffed, you push a button and if you get a green light you can pass without being inspected; no such luck if you get a red light. After you cross the border, if you keep walking straight ahead about 50 m you'll get to the immigration office (on your right) where you can pick up your tourist card (FM-T).

It is important to get tourist cards validated before leaving the area. Customs agents at the bus station will turn a blind eye if you get on a bus without a tourist card, but if the bus is stopped for routine checks (frequent) you may get sent back to the border.

To avoid the congestion of the downtown route, motorists are generally advised to use the truck crossing (0600-2000, currency exchange available), which is reached by the Mariposa Avenida exit from Interstate 19, 4 km north of downtown Nogales, Arizona. Returning from Mexico to the US, follow the sign to the 'Periférico', which avoids the downtown area.

Motor vehicle documents can be obtained at the Mexican Customs Post 21 km south of Nogales, on Highway 15 to Santa Ana, along with US insurance (which may also be obtained at the border). There is a **tourist office** and a *casa de cambio* here. You need to have title to the car with you (ie you can't drive someone else's car into Mexico). You also need two photocopies of vehicle registration, driver's licence, insurance papers, credit card and visitor's permit (approved); a photocopy machine is available. In the same building as the immigration office on the border is a **Seguros Tepeyac** ⓘ *www.mapfretepeyac.com.mx*, outlet where you can buy car insurance. If you only want liability insurance, not collision waiver, they charge US$2.24 per day. To insure a car worth US$7000 with both liability and collision insurance costs US$5.63 daily. There are also a few other insurance agencies.

Nogales → *Phone code: 631. Colour map 1, A3.*

Nogales lies astride a mountain pass at 1120 m across from Nogales, Arizona, and is the largest town in the Pimería Alta, the area of southern Arizona and northern Sonora occupied by the Pima people at the arrival of the Spaniards. The **Pimería Alta Historical Society** ⓘ *Mon-Fri 0900-1700, Sat 1000-1600, Sun 1300- 1600, free*, a block from the border in Nogales, Arizona, has excellent exhibits on the history of the region, a valuable library and archives, and also organizes tours to the Sonoran missions. The staff are a good source of information on the Mexican side. The **tourist office** is just past the immigration office. The staff are friendly, helpful and have brochures.

Northwest border

San Luis Río Colorado → *Phone code: 653. Colour map 1, A2.*

Route 2 from Tijuana runs close to the border, going through Mexicali (see page 169), San Luis Río Colorado, Sonoyta and Caborca to Santa Ana, where it joins the West Coast Highway (Route 15) to Mexico City. East of Mexicali the fast four-lane highway crosses the fertile Mexicali Valley to a toll bridge over the diminished Colorado River, and continues to San Luis Río Colorado, a cheerfully tourist-oriented border town in the 'free zone' and serving cotton country. There are summer bullfights and small nightlife districts like those of the Old West, including a so-called *Zona de Tolerancia*.

Algodones → *Colour map 1, A2.*

North of San Luis (35 km) is Baja California's last international border-crossing point, the farming town of Algodones. The border is open 0600-2000, but motor vehicle documents are processed weekdays only, 0800-1500. The road north from San Luis skirts the Algodones dunes, the longest in North America. Algodones has one hotel, Mexican car insurance is readily available, and there are several *casas de cambio*.

At **Andrade**, on the California side, the Quechan people from the nearby Fort Yuma Reservation operate an RV park and campground (see Sleeping, page 205).

Desierto de Altar

After leaving San Luis Río Colorado, Route 2 crosses the sandy wastes of the Desierto de Altar – Mexico's own mini-Sahara. The road is very narrow in places, watch out for overloaded Mexican trucks. For 150 km there are no facilities (petrol at Los Vidrios), only three houses and an enveloping landscape of sand dunes, cinder cones and a dark lava flow from the Cerro del Pinacate. All the area around the central range is protected by the **Parque Natural Pinacate**. A gravel road 10 km east of **Los Vidrios** gives access to the northern sector of the park, which contains much wildlife, for example puma, deer, antelope, wild boar, Gila monster, wild sheep, quail and red-tailed eagle.

Lukeville/ Sonoyta → *Colour map 1, A2.*

After a hot and monotonous 200 km from San Luis, Route 2 reaches the sun-bleached bordertown of Sonoyta, a short distance from Lukeville, Arizona. Sonoyta has little of interest itself, but there are several American-style hotels. Arizona's picturesque Organ Pipe Cactus National Monument is just across the border from Sonoyta.

The border crossing between Lukeville and Sonoyta is open from 0800 to 2400. Camping is possible at developed sites near the visitor centre at Organ Pipe National Monument for US$8 (US$3 visitor permit is valid for 15 days).

Highway 8 goes southwest from Sonoyta through 100 km of sand dunes; a sign, 'Dunas – 10 km', at Km 80, points along a sandy road that leads to dramatic, desolate inland dunes through mountain-rimmed black lava fields; 4WD is recommended.

Puerto Peñasco → *Phone code: 638. Colour map 1, A2.*

One of the most important shrimping ports on the Gulf; the huge shrimp are too expensive for the US market and are mostly exported to Japan. It is very popular with Arizona and California RV drivers for fishing, surfing and the beach. On the north side of the bay, 12 km, is **La Choya**, largely a gringo place, sandy streets, full of trailers and beach cottages, and several fine beaches.

Caborca → *Phone code: 637. Colour map 1, A3. Altitude: 286 m.*

Route 2 runs from Sonoyta to Caborca (150 km), passing through a number of small towns (San Emeterio, San Luisito) and a more mountainous but still arid land. There is a Customs and Immigration station near Quitovac (28 km south of Sonoyta). The paved State Highway 37 continues southeast, roughly following the rail line to Caborca (180 km) – an alternative to the inland Highway 2 route.

Keep an eye out for semi-wild longhorn cattle along the road to El Sásabe.

Caborca lies on the Mexicali-Benjamín Hill railway in the midst of a gently sloping plain. Caborca's restored church of **Nuestra Señora de la Concepción** was one of the 25 missions founded by the legendary missionary and explorer Padre Kino in Sonora and Arizona between 1687 and 1711. Caborca is the best base for exploring the **Kino Missions**.

Altar to the Arizona border → *Colour map 1, A3.*

Highway 2 continues east through Altar (café, gas station) to join Highway 15 at **Santa Ana** , a small town of little note. The **Fiesta de Santa Ana** is held 17-26 July, with horse racing, fireworks, etc.

The border at **El Sásabe** is open from 0800 to 2000, but there is no public transport on either side, nor is there any Mexican automobile insurance agency. For information as to road conditions, phone US Customs (T602-823-4231); although they appear not to encourage traffic over this route.

The Desierto de Altar was used to train US astronauts during the Moon Missions.

South of Nogales

Nogales to Mazatlán: the Pacific Highway

The road along the Pacific coast gives access to several resorts (Guaymas, Mazatlán and Puerto Vallarta), to ferry terminals for Baja California, and to the Los Mochis end of the Chihuahua al Pacífico railway passing beside the Copper Canyon. From Nogales to Guaymas on the Gulf of California, the road runs along the western slopes of the Sierra Madre, with summits rising to 3000 m. From Guaymas on to Mazatlán it threads along the lowland, with the Sierra Madre Occidental's bold and commanding escarpment to the east.

The Pacific Highway down the coast to Acapulco and Salina Cruz is completely paved but has military searches in the State of Guerrero (for narcotics and arms). There are many motels along the whole route, so that each town of any importance has one or more nearby.

Magdalena Valley

South of the border at Nogales, Route 15 passes through the Magdalena Valley. The Cocóspera mines are near Imuris and there are famous gold and silver mines near Magdalena, which has a great indigenous fiesta in the first week of October.

From Imuris, Route 2 heads east (to Naco and Agua Prieta) through the scenic Sierra de Pintos to the historic and still important copper mining centre of Cananea. This was the site of a 1906 miners' strike against the American-owned **Cananea Consolidated Copper Company**, one of the critical events in the last years of the Porfirio Díaz dictatorship. Hundreds of Arizona Rangers crossed the border to join the Sonora militia in putting down the strike, which is commemorated at the **Museo de La Lucha Obrera** ⓘ *Av Juárez*, the former city jail. Back on Route 15, 120 km from Nogales, is Santa Ana, where the road enters from Tijuana and Mexicali.

Hermosillo → *Phone code: 662. Colour map 1, B3. Altitude: 237 m.*

Capital of Sonora state, Hermosillo is a modern city, resort town and centre of a rich orchard area with a rich strip of cotton fields, vegetables, melons, oranges and grapes just to the east. There's a **tourist office** ⓘ *Paseo del Canal y Comonfort Edificio Sonora, 3rd floor, T/F217-0176, www.sonoraturismo.gob.mx.*

Reminders of an illustrious colonial past can be found around the central Plaza Zaragoza (invaded by noisy birds at sunset). The imposing neoclassical **Catedral de La Asunción** (1779), has a baroque dome and three naves, and the **Palacio de Gobierno** has intricately carved pillars and pediment, historical murals and grandiose statues amid landscaped gardens.

Not far north of downtown (Rosales y Transversal) is **University City**, with its modern buildings of Mexican architecture blended tastefully with Moorish and Mission influences. There is an active fine arts and cultural life, with many events throughout the year open to visitors (check at the tourist office for details). Two kilometres south of Plaza Zaragoza, near the Periférico Sur, is the wonderful **Centro Ecológico de Sonora**, a botanical garden and zoo displaying Sonoran and other desert flora and fauna in well-cared-for surroundings.

Bahía Kino → *Phone code: 662. Colour map 1, B3.*

A paved 118-km road runs west past the airport to Bahía Kino, divided into the old, somnolent and somewhat down-at-heel fishing village, and the new **Kino Nuevo**, a 'winter gringoland' of condos, trailer parks and a couple of expensive hotels. Although the public beaches are good, most North American visitors come for the sportfishing. The Seri people, who used to live across El Canal del Infiernillo (Little Hell Strait) on the mountainous **Isla Tiburón** (Shark Island), have been displaced by the Navy to the mainland. They come into Kino on Saturday and Sunday to sell their ironwood animal sculptures and traditional basketware. They can usually be found at the **Posada del Mar Hotel**. For the visitor interested in exploring nature reserves, Isla Tiburón is of especial interest. Protected in the nearly 400 sq m preserve, the population of both the big horn sheep and mule deer has grown enormously. On the south end of the island, water depths of 50 m or more are common. It is an excellent area not only for scuba diving but also for fishing, and **Dog Bay** provides shelter and ideal anchorage for spending the night. **Isla Patos** (Duck Island), 30 minutes north of Isla Tiburón, offers the opportunity to explore the submerged Spanish vessels that once sailed the Sea of Cortés. Other islands worth visiting are **Alcatraz** (also known as **Pelican Island**), **Turner**, and **San Esteban**. In Kino Nuevo, there is the fine **Museo Regional de Arte Seri** on Mar de Cortés, the main boulevard.

Guaymas and Bahía San Carlos → *Phone code: 622. Colour map 1, B3.*

Guaymas is set on a lovely bay backed by desert mountains. It has excellent deep-sea fishing and seafood for the gourmet. **Miramar beach**, on **Bocachibampo Bay** with its blue sea sprinkled with green islets, is the resort section. The climate is ideal in winter but unpleasant in summer. The 18th-century church of **San Fernando** is worth a visit; so, too, outside the town, is the 17th-century church of **San José de Guaymas**. The port area also boasts some worthy buildings, among which are the **Templo del Sagrado Corazón de Jesús**, the **Banco de Sonora**, the **Palacio Municipal** (constructed in 1899), the **Ortiz Barracks** and the **Antigua Carcel Municipal** (old Municipal Prison) constructed in 1900. Guaymas acquired the title 'heroic' in 1935, in memory of the valiant defence by its inhabitants during the French Invasion of 1854.

! The Alamos Music Festival is an annual event held for seven days at the end of January, www.alamosmexico.com.

Fifteen kilometres north of Guaymas (or 12 km from Highway 15) is Bahía San Carlos, very Americanized and touristy, where *Catch-22* was filmed. Above the bay a twin-peaked hill, the **Tetas de Cabra**, is a significant landmark. There is good fishing with an international tournament in July. There's a **tourist office** ⓘ *Av Serdán, www.visitguaymas.com.*

South of Guaymas

From **Ciudad Obregón**, a good place for buying leather goods, such as western boots and saddles, to **Navojoa** is a four-lane highway in poor condition (toll at Navojoa, US$7). West of Navojoa, on **Huatabampo Bay**, are the survivors of the Mayo people; their festivals are in May. Hourly buses to Alamos.

Alamos → *Phone code: 647. Colour map 2, B1.*

Fifty-two kilometres into the hills is the delightful old colonial town of Alamos, now declared a national monument. It is set in a once famous mining area fascinating for rock enthusiasts. Although the area was explored by the Spanish in the 1530s, development did not begin for another 100 years when the Jesuits built a mission nearby. With a rich history in silver mining, trips to old mine sites can easily be arranged. The area is also rich in birdlife, with many species arriving to overwinter.

Another, altogether more lighthearted reason for visiting in June in particular, is to see the famous jumping beans: a symbiotic relationship between a plant and a moth larvae. The two develop simultaneously giving the impression that the seed pod or bean is actually jumping.

Los Mochis → *Phone code: 668. Colour map 2, B1.*

In spite of being 25 km from the sea, Los Mochis is a fishing resort with a sizeable US colony. The name is derived either from a local word meaning 'hill like a turtle', or possibly, from *mocho*, meaning one-armed, perhaps after a cowboy thus mutilated. The city, in a sugar cane area, was founded in 1904 around a sugar mill built by the American, Benjamin Johnson, and his wife was responsible for building the Sagrado Corazón church. The family lost everything in the Revolution. This is the starting point for the uphill railway journey passing the Copper Canyon. Try doing anything else in town, and you'll probably be looked at rather strangely. There are plenty of nightspots and bars visited by roaming mariachis, who play excellent music.

Los Mochis is the departure point for the Chihuahua al Pacífico Copper Canyon train journey.

Tourist information for Los Mochis and the state of Sinaloa in the municipal building, Marcial Ordoñes and Allende.

Topolobampo → *Phone code: 668. Colour map 2, B1.*

A side road, running southwest from Los Mochis, crosses the salt flats to Topolobampo (20 km, 30 minutes). The town is built on several hills facing the beautiful bay-and-lagoon-indented coast. In the bay, which has many outlets, there are a number of islands; sunsets here are lovely. You can get a ferry from here to La Paz.

Towards Chihuahua by train

The famous Chihuahua al Pacífico train journey shows the spectacular scenery of the Sierra Madre and the Barranca del Urique/Cobre (Urique/Copper Canyon). The **Servicio Estrella** train should leave daily at 0600 (but often at 0700), US$65 to Creel

Los Mochis

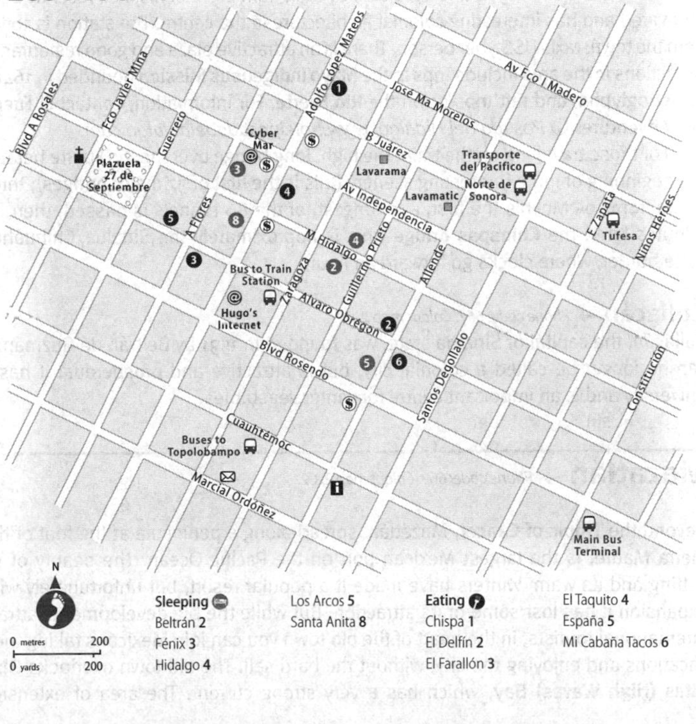

Sleeping
Beltrán 2
Fénix 3
Hidalgo 4
Los Arcos 5
Santa Anita 8

Eating
Chispa 1
El Delfín 2
El Farallón 3
El Taquito 4
España 5
Mi Cabaña Tacos 6

(about 10 hours), US$120 to Chihuahua (about 16.5 hours, but expect delays). For train information and prices, check www.chepe.com.mx. Bring your own food, drinking water and toilet paper for the journey.

Tickets must be bought in advance either on morning of departure or, in high season (July to August, New Year, Holy Week), a day or more before. **Estrella** class tickets can be bought from tour operators in Los Mochis, with an 8% surcharge, but they will try to persuade you to book into preferred (expensive) hotels. It may be worth buying tickets from them to avoid long queues at the station. If you are only going as far as Creel buy return tickets as it is impossible to reserve seats from Creel back to Los Mochis. Local buses leave from Los Mochis on Obregón and Zaragoza (US$0.40) for the train station, departing 0515, in time for the queues.

For Creel, the Copper Canyon and more train information, see page 219.

On the **Primera Especial** the windows do not open, so, to take photos, stand between the carriages if you can. Motorists taking the train to Creel have been advised to park in front of the station as there are lights and people at all times. Alternatively, ask for Sr Carlos at the station ticket office, who will guard the car at his home for a modest fee. There is more expensive parking downtown.

Sit on the right for the best views, except when approaching Temoris when it's all jump to the left, then return to the right until the first tunnel after Temoris when the views are good on both sides.

The ordinary second-class train, **Tarahumara**, aims to leave at 0700, with prices roughly half that of the first class, but it is not possible to reserve seats. Second-class trains make many stops but are reasonably comfortable and it is possible to open the windows. On either train, sit on the right for the best views, except when approaching Temoris when it's all jump to the left, then return to the right until the first tunnel after Temoris when the views are good on both sides.

El Fuerte → *Phone code: 698. Colour map 2, B1.*

This town, founded in 1564 and 1½ hours by train from Los Mochis, has recently been renovated and has interesting colonial architecture in the centre. The station is 10 km from the town; taxis US$4 per person. There is an attractive plaza and good restaurants. Attractions in the area include trips to the **Mayo Indigenous Mission** (founded in 1648), to **petroglyphs**, and raft trips down the **Río Fuerte**. For information, contact **El Fuerte Eco-Adventures** ⓘ *Posada del Hidalgo, www.hotelposadadelhidalgo.com.*

For those travelling on the train, the high, long bridge over the Río Fuerte heralds the beginning of more interesting scenery (this is the first of 37 major bridges); three hours from Los Mochis the first, and longest, of the 86 tunnels is passed, then, 10 minutes later, the **Chinapas bridge** (this is approximately the Sinaloa/Chihuahua state border, where clocks go forward an hour).

Culiacán → *Phone code: 667. Colour map 2, C2.*

Culiacán, the capital of Sinaloa state, was founded in 1531 by Beltrán de Guzmán. It can no longer be called a colonial city, but is attractive and prosperous; it has a university and is an important centre for winter vegetables.

Mazatlán → *Phone code: 669. Colour map 2, C2.*

Beyond the **Tropic of Cancer**, Mazatlán, spread along a peninsula at the foot of the Sierra Madre, is the largest Mexican port on the Pacific Ocean. The beauty of its setting and its warm winters have made it a popular resort, but unfortunately with expansion it has lost some of its attraction. But while the big developments attract international tourists, in the heart of the old town you can join Mexicans taking their vacations and enjoying the city, without the hard sell. The old town overlooks **Olas Altas (High Waves) Bay**, which has a very strong current. The area of extensive development, called the **Zona Dorada**, stretches for several kilometres to the north of the Old Town. Entering Mazatlán by sea from Baja shows the city at its most impressive – two pyramid-shaped hills, one topped by a lighthouse, the other the 'rock' of **Isla Piedra**, guards the harbour entrance.

Ins and outs

Getting there First-class buses go to and from most major cities west and north of the capital, while second-class buses will take you to smaller towns such as San Blas. The main bus station is north of the old town centre, with local buses and taxis providing links to the old town. A ferry service operates between Mazatlán and La Paz, in Baja California (see page 194 for ferry schedules). For drivers, Route 15, the coastal road, heads north to the US border, and south to Tepic then inland to Guadalajara; Route 40 is the picturesque but hair-raising road to Durango. The local airport has flights to Mexico City and destinations in northern and western Mexico and in the US. Planes are met by the usual fleet of fixed-fare taxis and microbuses.

Getting around Most local buses leave from the market. There is an express service (green and white buses), which runs from the centre along the seafront to the Zona Dorada and beyond. Taxis are readily available and pulmonias, taxis that look like golf carts, will ferry you between the bus station and your hotel.

Mazatlán

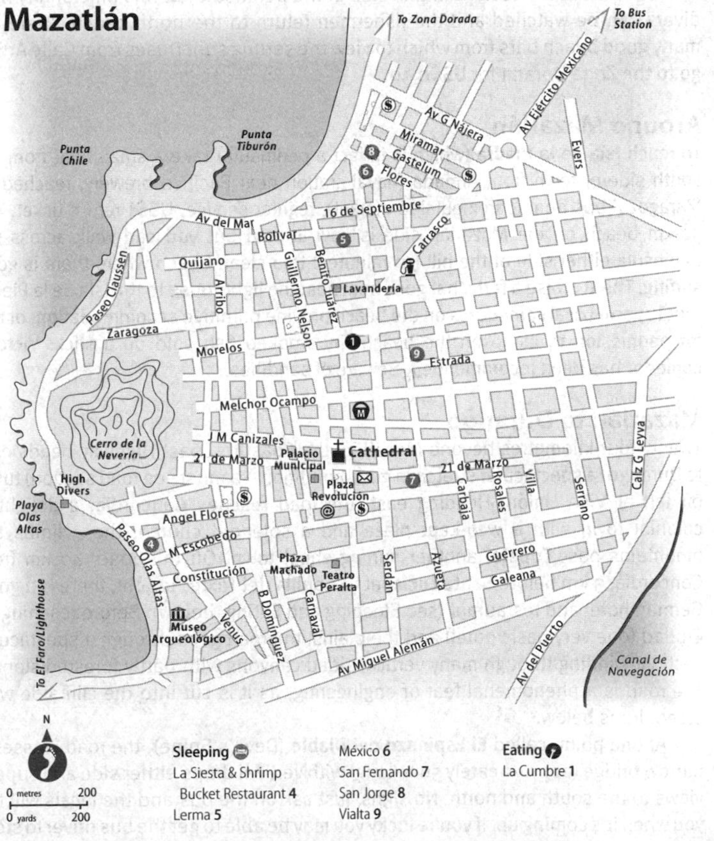

Sleeping
La Siesta & Shrimp Bucket Restaurant **4**
Lerma **5**
México **6**
San Fernando **7**
San Jorge **8**
Vialta **9**

Eating
La Cumbre **1**

 Tourist information The **tourist office** ⓘ *Edif Banrual 4th floor, Av Camarón Sábalo and Tiburón, www.sinaloa-travel.com*, is at the northern end of Zona Dorada. However, information can easily be obtained at any travel agency or hotel information desk.

Sights

The old part of town is located around Plaza Machado, which is on Calle Carnaval. This is far and away the most interesting part of the city. Half a block from the plaza is the **Teatro Peralta**, the 17th-century opera house, which has been restored and reopened to the public. The **Aquarium** ⓘ *Av de los Deportes III, just off the beach, behind Hotel Las Arenas, 0900, US$3, children US$1.50*, is interesting, and includes sharks and blindfish. The **Museo Arqueológico de Mazatlán** ⓘ *Sixto Osuna 115, ½ block from Hotel Freeman, US$1*, is small, covering the state of Sinaloa. Recommended.

The lighthouse on El Faro peninsula is 157 m above sea level.

Tourism is now concentrated in the **Zona Dorada**, which includes the beaches of **Gaviotas, Los Sábalos, Escondida, Delfín, Cerritos, Cangrejo** and **Brujas** (north of Playa Brujas is a rocky area, which is good for snorkelling); the area is built up and accommodation is expensive. The **Old Town** around **Olas Altas** bay has a distinctly more relaxing feel with a promenade lined by hotels; a long beach at its foot, curves northwards around the bay, first as Paseo Claussen, then Avenida del Mar, which leads to Avenida Camarón Sábalo in the Zona Dorada (take bus from Juárez – best from in front of market – marked Sábalo Centro US$0.30). The sunsets are superb seen from this side of the peninsula; at this time of day high divers can be watched and the fishermen return to the north beach. There are many good beach bars from which to view the setting sun. Buses from Calle Arriba go to the Zona Dorada for US$0.50.

Around Mazatlán

To reach **Isla de la Piedra** (which is in fact a peninsula) take a small boat from the south side of town from Armada (naval station near Pacífico brewery, reached by 'Zaragoza' bus from Juárez outside market), regular service, US$1 return ticket. The 30-km beach on the Mazatlán side is now littered but you can walk across the peninsula either side of the hill (10 minutes) to a clean beach where there is good surfing. There is also a ferry that goes from near the lighthouse to the Isla de la Piedra (until 1700). Local *comedores* on the beach provide primitive accommodation, or ask for permission to camp on the beach. Try smoked fish sold on a stick; **Victor's comedor** has been recommended. Beware of sandflies.

Mazatlán to Durango

Twenty-four kilometres beyond Mazatlán, the Coast-to-Coast Highway heads east to Durango (a spectacular stretch in good condition – a must see road section) turns off left at Villa Unión. Heading east, the road reaches **Concordia**, a delightful colonial town with a well-kept plaza and a splendid church, then climbs the mountains past **Copala**, another mining ghost town. On this road, 40 km from Concordia, 3 km before **Santa Lucía**, at La Capilla del Taxte, 1240m, there is a good German hotel and restaurant (see Sleeping and Eating, below). Before reaching La Ciudad (one very basic hotel) and the plains, the road goes through a spectacular section, winding through many vertical-sided canyons with partly forested slopes. The road is a phenomenal feat of engineering, as it is cut into the cliff side with steep drops below.

At one point, called **El Espinazo del Diablo** (Devil's Spine), the road crosses a narrow bridge (approximately 50 m long) with vertical drops either side and superb views to the south and north. No signs, just ask on the bus and the locals will tell you when it's coming up. If you're lucky you may be able to get the bus driver to stop.

Music in Mazatlán

Firmly rooted and extremely popular in the State of Sinaloa is a type of orchestra known as the **Banda Sinaloense** or **Tamborera**, which plays *Chaparral* at almost any time of day or night in restaurants, dance halls, bars, at family parties or on the street. It usually has from 14 to 16 musicians: four saxophones, four trumpets, clarinets, tuba, three or four men on drums and other percussion instruments, including maracas and *guiro*, and loud, strong voices. It is unabashed, brutal music, loud and lively. One such *banda* plays every afternoon at the **Chaparral** bar, opposite the Conasupo market near the bus station.

After reaching the high plateau, the road passes through heavily logged pine forests to Durango (see page 225). Cyclists will find this road hard work in this direction, as there are many bends and steep hills. Trucks are frequent but they travel at very reduced speeds.

South of Mazatlán

Route 15 continues south from Villa Unión. At **Rosario**, 68 km south of Mazatlán, an old mining town riddled with underground workings. There is an attractive and generally clean beach at **Playas El Caimanero**, about 45 km southwest of Rosario. Try the fish. Be careful of hiking around the Baluarte River valley as there are *caimanes* (alligators), hence the name of the beach. There is a good seafood restaurant on the left at the entrance to Escuinapa coming from Mazatlán.

Teacapan → *Phone code: 695.*

In **Escuinapa** a good road turns off 30 km to the coast at Teacapan. There is a bus that connects the two towns. The fishing is excellent and you can buy fresh fish directly from the fishermen on Teacapan beach. There are fine beaches such as **Las Cabras**, **La Tambora** and **Los Angeles**. Dolphins can be seen at certain times of year. Buses from Escuinapa; tours from Mazatlán US$45.

South of Escuinapa the road passes several quaint little towns: **Acaponeta** (turn-off for El Novillero beach, large waves and many sandflies), **Rosamorada**, **Tuxpan** and **Santiago Ixcuintla** (several hotels), all with colonial religious buildings and archaeological museums. Nearby is the tiny island of **Mexcaltitán** and, further south, the beaches at San Blas (see page 303). After Tepic, Route 15 heads inland to Guadalajara (see page 290).

Sleeping

Nogales *p197*

B **Miami**, Campillo and Ingenieros, T312-5450. Friendly, good restaurant. Recommended.

B **Olivia**, Obregón 125, T312-2200. A/c, TV, reasonable.

There is a wide selection of cheaper hotels on Juárez, a 1-block extension of Av López Mateos between Campillo and the border, 2 blocks from the Mexican port of entry.

Algodones *p197*

E **Motel Olímpico**. Algodones' only hotel, rather misnamed.

Camping

RV park and campground, run by the Quechan people from the nearby Fort Yuma Reservation, US$12 per site with electricity, US$8 without; including hot showers and access to laundry room.

Puerto Peñasco *p198*

AL **Viña del Mar**, Calle 1 de Junio y Blv Malecón Kino, T383-3600, www.vinadelmarhotel.com. Modern resort, cliffside jacuzzi, video-disco, etc, attractive rooms, good value.
D **Motel Mar y Sol**, Km 94 on road to Sonoyta, T383-3190. Pleasant gardens, restaurant, a/c, friendly.
E **Motel Davis**, Emiliano Zapata 100, T383-4314. Pleasant.

Camping

Playa Bonita RV Park, on lovely Playa Bonita, T383-2596, 300 spaces, restaurant, shop, laundry. US$17-25.
Playa de Oro Trailer Resort, Matamoros 36, T383-2668, 2 km east. Laundry, boat ramp, 200 sites, US$19-25.

Caborca *p198*

D **Hotel Yaqui**, T411-3377. All clean with a/c, TV, service station and general facilities.

Altar to the Arizona border *p198*

B **Motel San Francisco**, T641-324-1380. A/c, shower, baths, restaurant.

Camping

Canadian-Mexican trailer park, south of town, on the right going south, space for 9-10 trailers, rustic, useful overnight stop.

Magdalena Valley *p199*

B-C **Hotel El Cuervo**, near plaza, cheaper without TV.

Hermosillo *p199*

AL **Señorial**, Blv Kino y Guillermo Carpena, T215-5155. At the top end with a/c, pool, parking, restaurant, bar.
C **Monte Carlo**, Juárez y Sonora, T212-3354. With a/c, old, clean, very popular, as is adjoining restaurant.
C **San Alberto**, Serdán y Rosales, T213-1840. With breakfast, a/c, cable TV, pool, good value.
D **Washington**, Dr Noriega Pte 68, T213-1183. With a/c, clean, basic rooms off narrow courts, with bath, best budget hotel, parking for motorbikes.
E **Casa de los Amigos**, contact the **Asociación Sonorense de los Amigos**, Felipe Salido 32, Col Centro, T/F217-0142. Dormitories, living room, library, garden, laundry and kitchen. Cheap hotels and *casas de huéspedes* can be found around Plaza Zaragoza and along Sonora near Matamoros (red-light activity, choose carefully).

Bahía Kino *p199*

A **The Anchor House**, T242-0141. Beautiful bed and breakfast house on the beach, American-run.
C **Hotel Saro**, Mar de Cortés, between Nueva York and Vancouver, T242-007. 5 rooms, on beach.

Camping

It's possible to camp on the beaches with or without a tent.
Kino Bay RV Park, Av Mar de Cortés, T242-0216, www.kinobayrv.com, US$20.

Guaymas and Bahía San Carlos *p200*

A **Fiesta San Carlos**, Bahía San Carlos, T226-1318, hotelfiesta10@hotmail.com. Clean, good food, pool.
B **Santa Rita**, Serdán and Calle 9, Guaymas, T224-1919. With bath, a/c, clean, good.
C **Dorada Rental Units**, Bahía San Carlos, T226-0307, PO Box 48. After 10 km from the highway a road branches here. On beach, pleasant.
C **Ferrer Apartments**, Bahía San Carlos. Cooking facilities, hot water, pleasant patio, good value.
D **Motel Cominse**, Calle 14, Guaymas. Clean and simple motel, but a good choice.
F **Casa de Huéspedes Martha**, Calle 13, Guaymas. With bath, fan, hot water, a little run-down.

Camping

At Km 13 the road forks: left 1 km to 2 secluded bays with limited trailer camping, and right to the **Marina Real** on Sonora Bay, and beyond a beach with open camping.

Phone codes *Nogales 631; San Luis Río Colorado 653; Puerto Peñasco 683; Caborca 637; Altar 637; Hermosillo 662; Bahía Kino 662; Guaymas 622; Bahía San Carlos 622; Alamos 647; Los Mochis 668; Topolobampo 668; El Fuerte 698; Culiacán 667; Mazatlán 669; Teacapan 695.*

South of Guaymas *p200*
A Costa de Oro, M Alemán 210, Cd Obregón, T414-1765. Well-kept and pleasant.
AL Great Western San Jorge, M Alemán 929 Norte, Cd Obregón, T414-9514. With a/c, TV, restaurant, bar, pool, safe parking, clean, friendly, with colonial Spanish decor.

Camping
Trailer park, in the north of Navojoa on Route 15. Run-down, shaded, US$10 for full hook-up, US$5 for car or small jeep, dollars preferred to pesos.

Alamos *p200*
B Los Portales Hotel, Juaréz 6, T428-0111. With beautiful frescoes, on plaza.
D Somar, on the road into Alamos, T428-0195, Madero 110, standard Mexican hotel rooms.

Camping
El Caracol Trailer Park. Rustic, good pool, not always open (US$15).

Los Mochis *p201, map p201*
AL-A Santa Anita, Leyva and Hidalgo, T818-7046, www.santaanitahotel.com. Comfortable, clean dining-room (good), noisy a/c, stores luggage.
A-B El Dorado, Gabriel Leyva 525 Norte, 20 mins from centre, T815-1111, www.eldoradomochis.com.mx. A/c, pool, friendly, very good.
B Beltrán, Hidalgo 281 Pte, T812-0688. Noisy a/c, TV, has all travel timetables and will make reservations. Recommended.
B Fénix, A Flores 365 Sur, T812-2623, hotelfenix@email.com. Safe, clean, wake-up call, very good, credit cards accepted.
C Hidalgo, opposite Beltrán at 260 Pte, T/F818-3453. Cheap *cafetería*, friendly, occasionally no hot water.
D-E Los Arcos, Allende 524, between Castro and Obregón, T812-3253. Without bath, clean but dingy, fills up quickly, some rooms noisy, more expensive with a/c, but a good deal and the best budget choice.

Camping
RV Park Copper Canyon, Ruta 15, on the right side of the road when entering town. Good place to leave vehicles when visiting the Copper Canyon.

Topolobampo *p201*
For other accommodation go to Los Mochis.
B Yacht Hotel, 3-4 km south of town. Modern, a/c, clean and good food, quiet, good views, but seems to close for the winter.
E Estilo Europeo Poama, at the ferry terminal, 10 mins' walk from Los Mochis bus.

El Fuerte *p202*
AL Posada del Hidalgo (details from Hotel Santa Anita, T818-7046, www.mexicoscoppercanyon.com, in Los Mochis), a historical mansion. They have a booklet providing an 1½-hr walk with the colonial highlights of the town.
D Hotel San Francisco, T893-0055. Good value.

Camping
Trailer park (no name but linked with the Hotel Santa Anita in Los Mochis, see above).

Culiacán *p202*
AL Los 3 Ríos, 1 km north of town on highway 15, at Km 1423, T750-5280. Trailer park, US$10, pool, resort-style, good restaurant.
A Los Caminos, Blv Colegio Militar y Blv Leyva Solano, T715-3300. With a/c, phone, satellite TV, restaurant, pool, nightclub, safe parking, clean rooms.
C San Francisco, Hidalgo 227, T713-5903. With bath, clean, friendly, free parking.

Mazatlán *p202, map p203*
The expensive hotels are in the area known as the Zona Dorada. Along the northern beach on Av Camarón Sábalo or just off it there are many full service resorts. Budget hotels are around the Old Town where there are generally better deals. Ask taxi drivers for the cheaper places.
LL-AL Océano Palace, Av Camarón Sábalo, T913-0666, north end of Zona Dorada. All-inclusive resort.
AL-A Aquamarina, Av del Mar 110, T981-7080, across the road from the beach (front rooms are likely to be noisy).
A Las Palmas, Camarón Sábalo 305, Zona Dorada, PO Box 135, T916-5664. Good value. Recommended.
A Las Arenas, Av del Mar, across the road from the beach, T982-0000, www.sandsarenas.com. Front rooms are likely to be

noisy. With swimming pool, a/c, TV, fridge, garden, good restaurant, on beach.
A La Siesta, No 11 Sur, Old Town, T981-2640. With a/c, clean, friendly, safe, very good, nice patio, restaurant (**Shrimp Bucket**).
B San Jorge, Aguiles Serdán 2710, T981-3695. Quiet spot, tidy rooms close to the beach.
D-E Vialta, Azueta 2006, 3 blocks from market, T981-6027. With bath and fan, nice central patio, friendly, helpful, comfortable.
E Lerma, Simón Bolívar 622 and Aquiles Serdán, near beach, T981-2436. With fan and hot showers, friendly, spotless, simple, but quiet and cool. Shared balconies. Secure parking. A good choice.
E México, México 201 and Aquiles Serdán, T981-3806. Good tidy rooms, basic, but the popular budget option.
E San Fernando, 21 de Marzo 926, T981-7990. With bath, hot water eventually, very basic, very friendly. Recommended.

Camping

North of the city there are undeveloped beaches with free overnight camping; it is safer to camp in a group (take bus to Sábalos and get out where it turns round). There are at least 10 trailer parks on Playa del Norte/ Zona Dorada and on towards the north.
RV Park Villas al Mar, quiet place directly on the beach at the Camarón Sábalo. Good shade amongst the palms and bamboo.

Mazatlán to Durango *p197*

D Villa Blanca, La Capilla del Taxte, 3 km from Santa Lucía, T(244) 442-1628. A good German hotel and restaurant.

South of Mazatlán *p205*

B Motel Virginia, Carretera Internacional Km 1107, south of Rosario and several kilometres north of Escuinapa, T(694) 953-2755. Good clean, *palapa* restaurant next door, possible trailer parking.

Teacapan *p205*

A Rancho Los Angeles, Teacapan Ecológico (Las Palmas 1-B, Col Los Pinos, Mazatlán, T/F695-953-1344). Former home of a drug baron (deceased), 16 km north from Teacapan towards Escuinapa, on beach. Good value, luxurious swimming pool. Recommended.

D Hotel Denisse, on square, T/F(695) 954-5266, José Morales and Carol Snobel. Clean, next to phone office, noisy, local trips arranged.

Camping

Oregon. US$8, no signs, on beach in town, run-down but one of better places to stay, new Mexican hotel next door.

Eating

Nogales *p199*

ΨΨΨ-ΨΨ El Greco, upstairs at Obregón and Pierson. Attractive, fairly priced international menu. Occasionally has live mariachi music.
ΨΨΨ-ΨΨ Elvira's Restaurant, Obregón 1. Very colourful, relaxed and informal atmosphere.
ΨΨ Café Olga, Juárez 37 next to bus station. Open all hours.

Puerto Peñasco *p198*

ΨΨ Costa Brava Restaurant, Kino y 1 de Junio. Best in town, modest prices, exotic menu, pleasant.
ΨΨ La Gaviota, coffee shop at **Hotel Viña del Mar**. Good breakfasts and views.
Fresh fish is available from the open-air fish market on the Malecón (old town).
Ψ Café La Cita, 1 de Junio near the petrol station. Authentic Mexican, budget.

Hermosillo *p199*

ΨΨΨ Jardín Xochimilco, Obregón 51, T250-4052, Villa de Seris. Very good beef, not cheap.
ΨΨΨ San César, Plutarco Elías Calles 71 Pte. Excellent chop sueys, seafood and expensive gringo food.
ΨΨΨ-ΨΨ Mariscos Los Arcos de Hermosillo, Michel y Ocampo (4 blocks south of Plaza), T213-2220. Fresh seafood, attractive and expensive.

Bahía Kino *p199*

ΨΨ El Pargo Rojo. For really good seafood. Recommended.
ΨΨ La Palapa, Old Kino. Reasonably priced meals are available.
ΨΨ Marlín, next to **Islandia Marina Trailer Park**. Fresh seafood and snacks.

Guaymas and Bahía San Carlos *p200*

Generally, restaurants are overpriced.
ΨΨ Todos Comen, Serdán, Guaymas. Good food at reasonable prices.

ŸŸ **Piccolo**, Bahía San Carlos, good pasta, salads, good value.

Los Mochis *p201, map p201*
Many *birrierías* serving *birria*, a local beef dish.
ŸŸŸ **España**, Obregón. Very good, with style and grace.
ŸŸ **El Farallón**, Flores and Obregón. Good seafood and service, reasonably priced.
ŸŸ-Ÿ **El Delfín**, Allende Sur near Obregón. Restaurant and bar, nice atmosphere if a little rough and ready. Get thrown out... through the swing doors.
ŸŸ-Ÿ **El Taquito**, Leyva, 1 block from Santa Anita. Open 24 hrs.
Ÿ **Chispa**, Leyva Sur 117, near Morelos. Art deco design, clean, good.
Ÿ **Mi Cabaña Tacos**, corner of Obregón y Allende. Popular with locals, friendly. Recommended.

Mazatlán *p202, map p203*
Many cheap street places selling fruit shakes and simple Mexican dishes at the beach end of Av Manuel G Nájera.
ŸŸ **Shrimp Bucket**, Olas Altas 11 and Av del Mar. Rightly famous for seafood, good environment, popular, good.
ŸŸ-Ÿ **La Cumbre**, Benito Juárez and Hidalgo. Few seats, very busy, not many tourists, 1100-1500. Recommended.
Ÿ **Mercado**. The best deal is at the market where you can get an excellent fish lunch for US$1.50.

Entertainment

Mazatlán *p202, map 203*
Bars and clubs
Joe's Oyster Bar. Very good disco behind Hotel Los Sábalos, open-air, US$10 cover charge and open bar. Good music and busy in the tourist season.
Edgar's Bar, Aquiles Serdán. 1 of Mazatlán's oldest drinking joints.

Activities and tours

Los Mochis *p201, map p201*
Tour operators
Aracely, Obregón 471 Pte, T812-5090. Amex agents, and full services with reservations for first-class train.
Viajes Flamingo, www.mexicoscoppercanyon.com/flamingo/ in the lobby of Hotel Santa Anita, Leyva and Hidalgo, T812-1613. Bookings for the trains attract a commission of 8%.

Mazatlán *p202, map 203*
Always check with the locals whether **swimming** is safe, since there are strong rip currents in the Pacific, which run out to sea and are extremely dangerous. **Fishing** is the main sport (sailfish, tarpon, marlin, etc). Mazatlán's famous fishing tournament follows Acapulco's and precedes the one at Guaymas. **Birdwatching** is popular too: in the mangrove swamps are egrets, flamingos, pelicans, cranes, herons and duck. Nearby at Camarones there is **parasailing**, drawn by motorboats. The northern beach tourist strip offers boat trips to nearby deserted islands, snorkel hire and paragliding. **Bungee jumping** is done at junction Camarón Sábalo y Rafael Buelna opposite McDonald's.

There are **bullfights** at Mazatlán, good view from general seats in the shade (*sombra*), although you can pay much more to get seats in the first 7 rows – Sun at 1600, very touristy.

Tour operators
Explora Tours, Centro Comercial Lomas, Av Camarón Sábalo 204-L-10, T913-9020. Very helpful. Recommended.
Zafari Tours, Paseo Claussen 25. Ferry bookings, helpful. **Hudson Tours**, T913-1764. For mountain biking.

Transport

Nogales *p199*
Bus
Nogales' bus terminal is 8 km south of the city centre, along the highway to Magdalena and Hermosillo; parking US$1 per hr. Taxis at the border ask US$5 to take you to the bus station, but on the return journey the booth selling taxi vouchers charges less than US$4. A local bus, 1 peso, leaves 1 block from the border. Bus 46 from Juárez goes to the terminal (US$0.25). The bus station has a booth to change money. It also has a **Computel** outlet with long-distance phone service.

There are 3 bus lines that go into Mexico using the terminal: **Norte de Sonora**, **Transportes del Pacífico** and **Elite**. They all seem to have high-quality buses; **Transportes del Pacífico** also runs 2nd-class buses to most of their destinations.
To **Chihuahua**, with **Elite** 0800, 1915, $42. To **Cd Obregón**, 7 throughout the day, US$27. To **Culiacán**, several mid-afternoon departures. To **Durango**, 1530, US$72. To **Guadalajara**, every couple of hrs, US$110. To **Guaymas**, regular hourly service, US$20. To **Hermosillo**, hourly, US$13. To **Los Mochis**, hourly, US$32. To **Mazatlán**, hourly, US$74. To **Mexicali**, with **Norte de Sonora** US$24.10, hourly, with various route options, US$140. To **Puerto Peñasco (Rocky Point)**, 1 bus at 1530. **Tepic**, hourly service, US$90. To **Zacatecas**, direct, US$87.

To USA Autobuses Crucero to **Los Angeles**, US$52.00. **Phoenix**, US$19.00. **Tucson**, US$7.00. There are also links to the **Greyhound** network in the US.

To get to the US border, turn left as you leave the building and walk to the 1st traffic light and cross the street you can pick up the buses to the border, referred to by the locals as *La Línea*. The buses run-down the same street you'd be walking on. Nearby is another private bus terminal for the **Tufesa** line, which run buses down the coast as far as **Culiacán** (US$33). They have several departures daily and have nice, modern buses.

On the Arizona side, 1 block from the port of entry, **Citizen Auto Stage Company**, T287-5628, runs 10 buses daily between **Tucson** and Nogales (US$6.50); stops at Tucson airport en route. Stopovers (no additional charge) are possible to visit **Tumacacori Mission**, north of Nogales. US **Greyhound** is about ¼ block from the border.

If you're entering the US from Mexico, you'll see a ramp and stairs on your left on the street after you've crossed the border. The **Greyhound** station is at the top of the stairs, where you can catch buses to Tucson (US$7) and points beyond. Buses leave for **Tucson** almost hourly 0630-2000. There are smaller vans that leave at 0800, 1200, and 1600. Buses leave for **Phoenix**, AZ (Arizona's largest city, about 2 hrs north of Tucson) at 0700, 1400 and 1930, US$19.00. They also have buses for **Hermosillo** (US$10) and **Cd Obregón** (US$20) that don't require a transfer in Nogales, at 0715, 1215, 0230, 0545, and 0945, which stop across the border on the Mexican side to pick up passengers. The **Greyhound** bus station is a small, 1-room building with toilets, lockers, pay phones and a few fast-food outlets.

Car

Road tolls If driving from Nogales to Mazatlán by the 4-lane, divided toll road (Route 15), there are 12 toll gates. The first is 88 km south of Nogales. No motorcycles, bikes (but see page 73), pedestrians or animals are allowed on the highway, which is fenced and patrolled. The toll stations are well lit, have good public conveniences, fuel and food. The total distance from Nogales to Mazatlán is 1118 km. It is not possible to list every toll location and every deviation to avoid it. Most deviations are dirt roads and should not be taken in the rainy season. On toll routes and their avoidance, seek advice from US motoring associations and clubs (see page 73) as costs and conditions change rapidly.

Hermosillo *p199*

Air The Gen **Pesquira/García airport (HMO)** is 12 km from town. Daily flights to **Mexico City** with **Aero California**, **AeroMéxico** and **Mexicana**. Good domestic connections. International flights to **Los Angeles**, **Tucson** and **Phoenix**.

Bus Bus station on Blv Transversal 400, north of the university. To **Agua Prieta**, 6 a day, 7 hrs, US$18. To **Guaymas**, hourly round the clock, 2½ hrs, US$8. To **Kino**, 4 a day, 2 hrs, US$4. To **Los Mochis**, 7½ hrs through scrubland and wheat fields, US$29. To **Mazatlán**, 10-12 hrs, US$42. To **Nogales**, hourly 0230-1830, 4 hrs, US$14. To **Tijuana**, 11 hrs, US$47.

Guaymas and Bahía San Carlos *p200*

Air The Gen **José M Yáñez airport (GYM)** is 5 km from Guaymas on the way to San Carlos. **AeroMéxico** (T226-0123) has flights to **La Paz**, **Mexico City** and **Phoenix**.

Bus 1st-class bus to **Hermosillo**, 2½ hrs, US$8. To **Mazatlán**, frequent, 12 hrs, US$42; **Tijuana**: 18 hrs, US$62. To **Culiacán**, 9 hrs,

US$22. Buses from Empalme to **Los Mochis**/Sufragio with **Autotransportes Tufesa**, 5½ hrs, US$13.

Alamos *p200*

Bus **Navojoa**-Alamos every hr on the ½ hr from 0630-1830, 1 hr, US$2, good road. Bus station for Alamos is about 8 blocks from main bus station in Navojoa, but you must ask directions because it is a confusing route.

Los Mochis *p201*

Air

Aeropuerto Federal (LMM) is 6½ km from town. Flights to **Mexico City** and major towns in Northern Mexico. International flights to **Los Angeles**, **Phoenix** and **Tucson** with **AeroMéxico** and **Aero California**.

Airline offices Aero California, T818-1616.

Bus

Local Buses to the train station leave from the corner of Obregón and Zaragoza, first leaves at 0515 in time to get tickets for the train, US$0.40. Local buses to destinations around Sinaloa, eg Topolobampo, Guasave, San Blas (Sufragio) and Culiacán leave from Cuauhtémoc, near the post office.

Long distance There is a bus station in town on the corner of Castro and Constitución, to the south of town, about 10 mins' walk. **Estrella Blanca** group of bus companies (**Futura** and **Elite**) with long-distance services leave from here as well as international services coming down from the US. The terminals of **Norte de Sonora**, T812-1757, **Transporte del Pacífico**, T812-0341, and **Tufesa**, T818-2222, for services along the western coast leave from several terminals clustered together near Degollado and Juárez, to the east of town. Check locally for the best option for your destination if it is slightly unusual.

To **Cd Obregón**, US$29. To **Guadalajara**, hourly, 13 hrs, US$43. To **Guaymas**, 6 hrs, US$15. To **Mazatlán**, hourly, 6 hrs, US$19. To **Mexico City**, every couple of hrs, 24 hrs, US$80. To **Monterrey**, 0900 and 2000, 24 hrs, US$90. To **Nogales**, 1930 and 2030, 12 hrs, US$26. To **Tepic**, hourly, 10 hrs, US$38. **Tijuana**, hourly, 20 hrs, US$65.

Train

For **Creel** and **Chihuahua**, see page 232. If coming from Chihuahua and you don't want to stay in Los Mochis (assuming the train is not over-delayed), you can take a night bus to Mazatlán at 2200, arriving 0630. Los Mochis station has toilets and local phones; ticket office is open 1 hr before train leaves. The station is 8 km from town; do not walk there or back in the dark. There is a bus service from 0500, US$0.15 from corner of hotels **Hidalgo** and **Beltrán**, otherwise take the 0500 bus from **Hotel Santa Anita**, US$3.50 (for house guests only), or taxi. Taxis in the centre go from Hidalgo y Leyva; fare to station US$5 per car, bargaining not possible, make sure price quoted is not per person, rip-offs are common. Bus to town from corner of 1st junction from station from 0530.

Topolobampo *p201*

Ferry To **La Paz**, Baja California Sur. For schedule, fares and information, see page 194. Enquiries in Los Mochis on T817-3752 or on day of travel at Muelle Topolobampo office, opens 3 hrs prior to departure (be there at least 2 hrs before sailing), T862-0141.

Culiacán *p202*

Air The **Aeropuerto Federal de Bachigualato (CUL)** is 10 km from centre. **Aero California**, T716-0250; **AeroMéxico**, T715-3772; have flights to **Mexico City**, **Acapulco**, and major cities in Northern Mexico. International flights to **Los Angeles** and **Tucson**.

Bus Buses to all places along the west coast, including **Guaymas**, 9 hrs, US$32. **Tepic**, 8½ hrs, US$28.

Car North of the city, the north and southbound carriageways are on different levels with no divide (very dangerous). A toll section of freeway heads nearer to the coast, past Navolata, bypasses Culiacán and rejoins Highway 15 a few km south of that city.

Mazatlán *p202, map p203*

Air

Aeropuerto General Rafael Buelna (MZT), 3 km from centre. Domestic flights to **Guadalajara**, **Mexico City**, and major cities in Northern Mexico. International connections to **San José** (Costa Rica), **Calgary** (Canada), **Denver**, **Houston**, **Los Angeles**, **Phoenix**, **Portland**, **Salt Lake City**, **San Francisco**, **Seattle** and **Spokane** (Washington).

Airline offices Aero California, T913-2042. AeroMéxico, T984-1111. Mexicana, T913-0770.

Bicycle
Beware, the Mazatlán-Tepic-Guadalajara road has been described as 'the most dangerous in the world for cyclists'.

Bus
Local Green and white express buses on the 'Sábalo Centro' route run from Playa Cerritos to the city centre along the seafront road, US$0.35.

Long distance A big central terminal, making travel a bit easier, is just off the Carretera Internacional and Ferrusquilla s/n, about 3 km north of the Old Town, 4 km south of the Zona Dorado. Take 'Insurgentes' bus from terminal to Av Ejército Mexicano for the centre, via market at Aquiles Serdán.

Bus companies Transporte Norte de Sonora, T981-2335, **Transportes del Pacífico**, T981-5156, **Estrella Blanca**, T982-1949.

To **Chihuahua**, 1400 and 1800, 16 hrs, US$55. To **Durango**, hourly 0600-1900, 7 hrs, US$27. To **Guadalajara**, 8 hrs, US$28. To **Guaymas**, hourly, 11 hrs, US$36. To **Los Mochis**, 6 hrs, US$19. To **Mexicali**, 24 hrs, US$72. To **Mexico City**, 17 hrs, US$65. **Navojoa**, every 1½ hrs, 18 hrs, US$59. To **Nogales**, every 1½ hrs, 18 hrs, US$58. To **Puerto Vallarta**, 1600, 8 hrs, US$32. To **Tepic**, 5 hrs, US$15. To**Tijuana**, hourly, 26 hrs, US$82. To **Rosario**, US$1.65, you can then (with difficulty) catch bus to **Caimanero** beach. Terminal Alamos, Av Guerrero Ote 402, 2 blocks from market, buses to **Alamos** every hr on the ½-hr.

Car
Budget, Camarón Sábalo 402, T913-2000. National, Camarón Sábalo 7000, T913-6000, US$280 per week. AGA, Camarón Sábalo 316, T914-4405.

Ferry
La Paz (Baja California Sur), see schedule, page 194, for other information see under La Paz, Baja California section. Allow plenty of time for booking and customs procedure. Tickets from **Hotel Aguamarina**, Av del Mar 110, with 10% commission, also from travel agents. Ferry terminal is at the southern end of Av del Puerto, quite a way from the centre (take bus marked 'Playa Sur', which also goes from the street corner opposite ferry terminal to Av Ejército Méxicano near bus station).

Ticket office for La Paz ferry 0830-1300 only, on day of departure, arrive before 0800, unclaimed reservations on sale at 1100. Don't expect vehicle space for same-day departure.

Taxi
Taxis charge an average US$3.50-US$5 between Zona Dorada and city centre. From Bahía del Puerto Viejo to centre, taxi US$1, bus US$0.20.

Directory

Nogales *p199*
Banks Casa de Cambio Money Exchange, Campillo y López Mateos. **Casa de Cambio 'El Amigo'**, Campillo y López Mateos, local 14. **Compra-venta de Dólares Serfín**, Av López Mateos y Calle Pierson 81, 1st floor. **Medical services** Hospital: According to the tourist office, the best private hospital in Nogales is the **Hospital del Socorro**, Dirección Granja, T314-6060. Any taxi driver will know how to get there. **Pharmacy: Farmacia Benavides**, behind the immigration office. They give injections. There are several other pharmacies nearby.

Puerto Peñasco *p198*
Banks There are 2 banks. **Laundry** Laundromat Liz, Altamirano y Simón Morua.

Bahía Kino *p199*
Banks There is no bank in the area. The nearest is **Bancomer** in Miguel Alemán, between Kino and Hermosillo, 48 km away.

Guaymas and Bahía San Carlos *p200*
Bank, phone and fax After 10 km, near the Pemex station. **Post office and police station** 7 km from the Highway, behind the shops.

Los Mochis *p201, map p201*

Banks Many banks on Leyva, with ATMs, and a *casa de cambio* open a little later. **Internet** Hugo's Internet Café, Leyva 537, with printers and scanners, also same price at Cyber Más, Independencia 421. **Laundry** Lavamatic, Allende 218, self-service if you want; Lavarama at Juárez 225. **Medical services** Hospital Fátima, Loaizo 606 Pte, T815-5703, private, English spoken. **Post office** Ordóñez Pte, between Prieto y Zaragoza Sur, south of centre, Mon-Fri 0900-1400,1600-1800.

Mazatlán *p202, map p203*

Banks Many banks in the centre, near the plaza. Banamex, Juárez and Angel Flores, also Av Camarón Sábalo 434. Open 0900-1330, 1530-1730. *Casas de cambio* on Camarón Sábalo 109, 1009 and at junction with RT Loaiza; also at R T Loaiza 309. American Express, Camarón Sábalo, T913-0600, Mon-Fri 0900-1700, Sat 0900-1400. **Embassies and consulates** Canada, Hotel Playa Mazatlán, Av Playa Gaviotas 202, Local 9, Zona Dorado, T913-7320. France, B Dominguez 1008, T985-1228. Netherlands, Av Sábalo Cerritos, T913-5155. Germany, Jacarandas 10, T981-2077. Italy, Av Olas Altas 66-105, T981-4855. Norway, F Alcalde 4, T981-3237. US, RT Loaiza, opposite Hotel Playa Mazatlán, T/F916-5889, Mon-Fri 0930-1300, T913-4455 ext 285. **Emergency** General emergency T06; Red Cross T981-3690; Ambulance T985-1451; Police T982-1867. **Hospitals** Hospital General, Av Ferrocarril, T984-0262. Cruz Roja Mexicana, Alvaro Obregón 73, T981-3690. There is a free Red Cross treatment station on Camarón Sábalo, opposite the Beach Man. **Internet and telephone** Mail Boxes Etc, Camarón Sábalo 310, T916-4009, mail boxes, courier service; across the street at Centro Comercial Lomas. In the Old Town, a couple of internet cafés on the south side of the main plaza, US$1.50/hr. Also cheap international calls (US$1.80 per hr) and international calls and faxes, Mon-Fri 0600-2200, Sat-Sun 0900-1700. **Laundry** Lavandería, on Zúñiga and Juárez, near Hotel Lerma. **Post office** Juárez y 21 de Marzo, opposite Palacio Municipal, T981-2121. DHL is a couple of doors from Mail Boxes Etc (see above), Mon-Fri 0900-1330, Sat 1500-1800, 0830-1330. **Telephones** Camarón Sábalo, 1 block from American Express; also 21 de Marzo y Juárez. Computel phone and fax service, Aquiles Serdán 1512, T985-0109. Phone rental, Accetel, Camarón Sábalo 310-4, T916-5056. There are public phones taking international credit cards all along Camarón Sábalo and RT Loaiza in the Zona Dorada for long-distance calls.

Northern Highlands

The imposing Sierra Madre highlands of northern Mexico are rarely a destination in their own right. But these vast landscapes, at times barren and monotonous, hold some of Mexico's most spectacular surprises. The most important archaeological site in Northern Mexico is just a couple of hours' drive south of the border at Casas Grandes or Paquimé, a maze of multi-storeyed adobe buildings, once a thriving community with over 3000 inhabitants. Don't expect to see too many dainty little dogs in Chihuahua; this, Mexico's biggest state, is the rugged land of Pancho Villa and there are museums and memorabilia dedicated to the Bandido-turned-Hero of the Revolution – even the bullet-ridden Dodge car he was finally gunned down in. It's dramatic stuff; and so is the Chihuahua-al-Pacífico, billed as 'the world's most scenic railroad', which wends its way across bridges, through tunnels and over the Sierra Madre down to the Pacific coast at Los Mochis. It's a journey of a lifetime. Hikers will want to stop off at Creel or Divisadero to absorb the views, discover the awe-inspiring landscapes, strange rock formations and wildlife, visit Mexico's tallest waterfall and penetrate the vertiginous depths of the Barranca del Cobre, the Copper Canyon, bigger than Colorado's Grand Canyon. This is the craggy land of the Tarahumara people, and some 60,000 live in the Sierra where you can buy their hand-carved and woven crafts in any of the towns or villages. And if you're still looking for action, why not try some of the Wild-West kind and walk the streets of real Western film sets in the state of Durango. ▸▸ *For Sleeping, Eating and other listings, see pages 226-234.*

Crossing into Mexico: El Paso/Ciudad Juárez

From El Paso you can get on a bus outside Gate 9 of the **Greyhound** terminal and pay the driver (US$5); as you cross the border he should stop and wait for your documents to be processed. On entry you are automatically given 30 days to stay in Mexico, unless you ask for longer. Trolley buses cross the border for short trips. Alternatively, you can walk across (US$0.35 toll per person). Walking from Mexico to the US costs US$0.55 (toll for cars leaving Mexico US$2.05). Border formalities are minimal. If you cross into the US as a non-US citizen and with a view to leaving the US by plane, you must ask for an immigration card for when you do leave. Remember, also, to make sure you have your US visa if you require one.

El Paso is on Mountain Standard Time, which is one hour behind Central Standard Time and General Mexican Time.

There is a new border crossing at **Santa Teresa**, New Mexico, west of El Paso. It is good for trucks and southbound travellers avoiding the congestion of Ciudad Juárez.

Ciudad Juárez → *Phone code: 656. Colour map 2, A2. Altitude: 1150 m.*

Crossing the border from El Paso, Texas you'll reach Ciudad Juárez. Ciudad Juárez and El Paso have over 1.2 million people each; the cross-border industry has made Ciudad Juárez the largest *maquiladora* or workshop city in the world. Twin plant assembly and manufacturing operations now supersede tourism and agriculture in the city.

The Spanish conquistador Cabeza de Vaca discovered the Paso del Norte (Northern Pass) on the Camino Real. The name was retained until 1888 when Porfirio Díaz renamed the city after Benito Juárez. Today four bridges link the two cities.

The **tourist office** ⓘ *Malecón y Francisco Villa, T615-2301*, is on the ground floor of the Presidencia Municipal (City Hall), on the left as you cross the Sante Fe bridge.

In Ciudad Juárez, the **Nuestra Señora de Guadalupe de El Paso del Norte** mission was the first established in the region; the building was completed in 1668. The mission, and the nearby **cathedral**, are two blocks west of Avenida Juárez on 16 de Septiembre. At the junction of Avenida Juárez and 16 de Septiembre is the Aduana, the former customs building, now the **Museo Histórico**. In Parque Chamizal, just across the Córdova bridge, are the **Museo de Arte Prehispánico,** with exhibits from each Mexican state, the Botanic Gardens and a memorial to Benito Juárez. Continuing south down Avenida Lincoln, you come to the Pronaf area with the **Museo de Arte e Historia.**

Ciudad Juárez/El Paso

The **University Cultural Centre** and the **Fonart artisan centre**, which acts as a Mexican 'shop window', are well worth a look for the uninitiated tourist. The **Plaza Monumental de Toros** ⓘ *López Mateos y Triunfo de la República*, holds bullfights between April and August, and *charreadas* (rodeos) are held at the **Lienzo Charro** ⓘ *Av del Charro*. The main street is **Avenida Juárez**, on or near which are most of the souvenir shops, hotels, cheap and expensive restaurants, clubs and bars.

To the east of **El Paso**, over the border, the **Ysleta Mission** is the oldest in Texas (1680), built by Franciscan monks and local Tigua tribesmen, who have a 'reservation' (more like a suburb) nearby; the **Socorro Mission** (1681) and **San Elizario Presidio** (1789, rebuilt 1877-1887) are in the same direction. There are a number of museums, including the **Americana Museum** in the **Civic Centre** (which also houses a performing arts centre, convention centre and tourist office), the **Museum of Art** ⓘ *1211 Montana*, and the **Fort Bliss Air Defence Museum** of the nearby Air Base. Conducted tours of El Paso (US$10 – same price for Ciudad Juárez) usually take in Fort Bliss, the University, the Scenic Drive and the Tigua Reservation. **El Paso Tourist Office** ⓘ *Civic Centre Plaza, T534-0686; also at the airport.*

Crossing into Mexico: Presidio/Ojinaga → *Phone code: 626.*

Chihuahua may also be reached from the border at Ojinaga, east of El Paso/Ciudad Juárez. This route is recommended not only for the ease of crossing, but also for the spectacular scenery either side of the border.

Crossing the border Follow signs to Ojinaga; pass US immigration on left (if you need to, surrender US visa waiver form here). On the Mexican side, a guard will check your passport. Those with vehicles then park before doing paperwork. Boys selling chewing gum will look after your car/bike, but you can see it through the office windows. There are separate desks for personal and vehicle papers. Photocopying can be done for US$1. Get insurance before Presidio, no one sells it there, but you could ask **Stella McKeel Agency** ⓘ *T915-229-3221/5*. Full details of entry requirement for drivers is given in Essentials, page 70. The border is open 24 hours.

Leaving Mexico, note that the bus station is 2 km from the border. Make sure all your papers are stamped correctly.

Forty-two kilometres from Ojinaga on Route 16 towards Chihuahua is **El Peguis**, overlooking an extraordinary canyon. There is also a *garita*, where vehicle papers are checked.

Crossing into Mexico: Columbus/Palomas

Route 2 runs west from Ciudad Juárez, roughly parallel with the Mexico-US border. Between Juárez and Janos, at the northern end of lateral Mexico 24, is the dusty border town of Palomas, Chihuahua, opposite Columbus, New Mexico. The modern border facilities are open 24 hours. Palomas itself has few attractions apart from limited duty-free shopping for liquor and pharmaceuticals, but Columbus was the site of Pancho Villa's 1916 incursion into New Mexico, which led to reprisals by the forces of American General John J Pershing. The **Columbus Historical Museum** ⓘ *daily 1000-1600*, on the southeast corner of the highway intersection, contains many old photos of Pancho Villa, a copy of his death mask, and one of his *sombreros*; it also has exhibits on Villa's sacking and burning of Columbus. There is a small shelf of books on the history of the town that you can browse through. The father of the museum's curator played a part in the battle.

It's nearly 5 km from Columbus to the border, south on Highway 11. Palomas is just across the border, and you park for free in a paved lot just before the border and walk across. The Mexican immigration office is just on the right as you cross the border. If you're driving, there's also a customs checkpoint at the border crossing. The customs' administrative building is about 60 m south of the immigration office.

Janos and around → *Phone code: 636. Colour map 2, A2.*

At the intersection of border Route 2 and Chihuahua Route 10 to Nuevo Casas Grandes is Janos. Nearby are the northernmost Mennonite colonies in Mexico; numerous vendors sell Mennonite cheese, which also has a market in upscale restaurants across the border in New Mexico. The German-speaking Mennonites are very conspicuous, the men in starched overalls and the women in long dresses and leggings, their heads covered with scarves.

Crossing into Mexico: Douglas/Agua Prieta

→ *Phone code: 633. Colour map 2, A1.*

Northwest of Janos, via border Route 2, are the border crossings of Agua Prieta (opposite Douglas, Arizona) and **Naco** (adjacent to its Arizona namesake and a short distance south of the historic, picturesque copper mining town of Bisbee). Agua Prieta is growing rapidly with the proliferation of *maquiladoras* on both sides of the border.

Crossing into Agua Prieta on foot, walk on the right-hand side of the road to enter Mexico. There are no obligatory checkpoints if you just want to see Agua Prieta. Otherwise, the immigration office for your FM-T (tourist card) is on the right just as you cross the border, and customs is just past it. You also pick up papers for your car here if you're driving, and get auto insurance. If you keep walking straight ahead you'll cross a street, which has buses running to the Agua Prieta bus station. Take buses running east, which have '13-20', 'Ejidal' or 'P Nuevo' on their front windows. Taxis charge US$3 from the border to the bus station, a five- or ten-minute ride.

Winter Arizona time is the same as Agua Prieta time but during summer Agua Prieta is one hour ahead.

On the Douglas side, the **Chamber of Commerce** ⓘ *T364-2477, at 1125 Pan American*, has good information on Mexico as well as Arizona, with a wealth of maps (including Agua Prieta) and brochures.

Agua Prieta is 162 km from Janos via Route 2, which crosses the scenic Sierra San Luis, covered by dense oak-juniper woodland, to the continental divide (elevation 1820 m) at **Puerto San Luis**, the border between the states of Sonora and Chihuahua. There are outstanding views of the sprawling rangelands to the west. Southbound motorists from the US must present their papers to Mexican customs at **La Joya**, a lonely outpost 70 km northwest of Janos.

South of Ciudad Juárez

The road between Ciudad Juárez and Chihuahua is wide, mostly flat, easy to drive, and not as interesting as the Gulf and Pacific routes. From Ciudad Juárez for some 50 km along the Río Bravo there is an oasis that grows cotton of an exceptionally high grade. The next 160 km of the road to Chihuahua are through desert.

Casas Grandes (Paquimé) → *Phone code: 636. Colour map 2, A2.*

ⓘ *Daily, 1000-1700, US$3.50.*

The archaeological site of Casas Grandes (Paquimé) can be reached from Chihuahua, Ciudad Juárez or Agua Prieta, roughly 60 km south of Janos on Route 2. **Nuevo Casas Grandes** is a town built around the railway; it is very dusty when dry, the wind blowing clouds of dust down the streets, and when wet the main street becomes a river. There is not much to do, but there are cinemas that show US and Mexican films.

Casas Grandes/Paquimé was probably a trading centre, reaching its peak between 1210 and 1261. The city was destroyed by fire in 1340. Its commercial influence is said to have reached as far as Colorado in the north and into southern Mexico. At its height, it had multi-storeyed buildings; the niches that held the beams for the upper floors are still visible in some structures. A water system, also visible, carried hot water from thermal springs to the north, and acted as drainage. Most of the buildings are of a type of adobe, but some are faced with stone. You can see a ball court and various plazas among the buildings. The site is well tended. To get there take a yellow bus from outside the furniture shop at 16 de Septiembre y Constitución Poniente, US$0.20, 15 minutes. From the square in Casas Grandes village either take Calle Constitución south out of the square past the school, walk to the end of the road, cross a gully, then straight on for a bit, turn right and you will see the site, or take Avenida Juárez west out of the square and turn left at the sign to Paquimé, 1 km.

Paquimé ceramics, copying the original patterns, either black on black, or beige with intricate red and grey designs, are made in the village of **Mata Ortiz**, 21 km southwest of Nuevo Casas Grandes.

Madera and around → *Phone code: 157. Colour map 2, A2. Altitude: 2100 m.*

Madera is in the Sierra Madre, northwest of Chihuahua, surrounded by rugged mountain scenery. It is high enough to receive snow in winter (rainy season September-March, best time to visit May-August). The region around Madera has ample scope for tourism: archaeological sites, birdwatching, fine landscapes and good infrastructure.

Madera is on an important waterfowl migratory route, with white-fronted, blue and snow geese, mallard, pintail, teal, widgeon and redhead duck, and sandhill crane passing through. This does mean that it has become a popular centre for shooting (season mid-November to February), but birdwatching expeditions can be arranged at **Motel Real del Bosque.**

Taking Calle 3 in a northerly direction out of town you come to a signed turning right to Las Varas, which leads to Casas Grandes (there is another, unsigned turning to Las Varas further on). Straight on is **El Salto**, a 35-m waterfall, best seen after the spring thaw (March-April). The fall is along a track to the left; to see it you have to walk around the rim of a little canyon. It is possible to hike down to the river below (about one hour). Ask at the house on the track to the fall if you want to camp (no facilities).

Four kilometres from the turn-off to El Salto is the entrance to **Cuarenta Casas** (40 houses) ⓘ *1½ hrs from Madera, daily 0900-1600 (except 16 Sep), free.* Cuarenta Casas is a series of cave dwellings, inhabited originally by indigenous people of the Paquimé culture. Some of the houses have the palet-shaped windows/doorways also seen at Casas Grandes (called here La Cueva de las Ventanas); some are two storeys high. There is a good view of the cave houses from the visitors' hut at the entrance. A trail descends to the river before climbing steeply to the cave, a hike that takes 45 minutes to one hour one way. Camping is possible only when personnel are staying the night; there are no facilities other than water. (Tour from **Motel Real del Bosque,** Carretera Chihuahua-Madera, T572-0066, takes six hours, US$65, minimum four people; alternatively, hitchhiking is possible.)

South of Madera is the **Misión Tres Ojitos**, where the Spanish priest, Padre Espronceda, makes ham. Take the road to La Junta from Madera and at the signpost, turn off right. On the dirt road, take the left fork through the village. Go past the church and on the right the Mission is signed (10 km from Madera).

In Madera there is a sign indicating **Zona Arqueológica Huapoca**, going west on Independencia. At Km 13 on this good dirt road is Lago Campo 3, shallow and marshy, with wildlife. Eighteen kilometres from town you reach an altitude of 2500 m, with stunning views of the Sierra Madre. Plenty of birdlife can be seen from the road. At Km 41 is the entrance to the **Zona Arqueológica Anasazi**, which contains the Nido del Aguila (Eagle's Nest) cave dwellings and the Cueva del Serpiente (Serpent's Cave). The 2-km road to the site is terrible and about 300 m are impassable (you have to find somewhere to leave your car before the so-called 'car park'). There is no path to the Nido del Aguila, and a guide is recommended.

Chihuahua

→ *Phone code: 614. Colour map 2, B2. Altitude: 1420 m.*

The capital of Chihuahua state and centre of a mining and cattle area, Chihuahua City, 375 km from the border, is mostly a modern and rather run-down industrial city, but has strong historical connections, especially with the Mexican Revolution. Pancho Villa operated in the surrounding country, and once captured the city by disguising his men as peasants going to market. There are also associations with the last days of Independence hero Padre Hidalgo. Summer temperatures often reach 40°C but be prepared for ice at night as late as November. Rain falls from July to September.

The **tourist office** ⓘ *Libertad 1300, Edificio Agustín Melgar, 1st floor, T/F429-3421, www.chihuahua.gob.mx, Mon-Fri 0900-1900, Sat-Sun 0900-1400*, has general information, but not that up to date. The cinema on Universidad near the post office shows films from the US.

Sights

The old tower of the Capilla Real where Hidalgo awaited his execution is now in the **Palacio Federal** ⓘ *Libertad y Guerrero*. The dungeon (*calabozo*) is quite

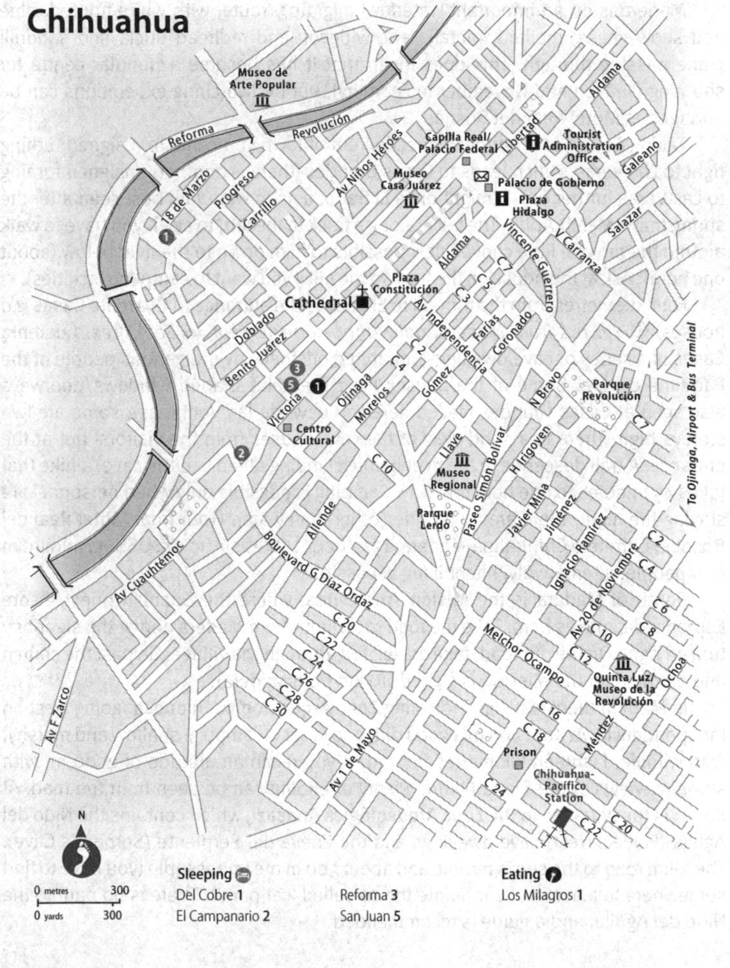

unremarkable and the Palacio itself is very neglected. The **Palacio de Gobierno**, on the other hand, is in fine condition, with a dramatic set of murals by Aaron Piña Morales depicting Chihuahua's history. There are a number of old mansions and the **Paseo Bolívar** area is pleasant. **Calle Libertad** is for pedestrians only from Plaza Constitución to the Palacio de Gobierno and Palacio Federal. Calle 4 and streets that cross it northwest of Juárez are bustling with market stalls and restaurants. Worth looking at is the **cathedral** ⓘ *Plaza Constitución*, which was built between 1717 and 1789; its Baroque façade dates from 1738, the interior is mostly unadorned, with square columns, glass chandeliers and a carved altarpiece. In the southeast of the town near Calle Zarco are ancient **aqueducts**. Walk north along Ocampo and over the river for fine views of the city at sunset.

The **Quinta Luz** (1914), where Pancho Villa lived, is now the **Museo de la Revolución** ⓘ Calle *10 No 3014, daily 0900-1300, 1500-1900, US$1*, is well worth a visit, with many old photographs, the car in which Villa was assassinated (looking like a Swiss cheese from all the bullet holes), his death mask and postcards of the assassinated leader. The **Museo Regional** ⓘ *Bolívar 401, Tue-Sun 0900-1300, 1600-1900, US$2.70*, in the former mansion Quinta Gameros, has interesting exhibits and extremely fine art nouveau rooms: the dining room, the child's room that features Little Red Riding Hood scenes; the bathroom, with frogs playing among reeds, etc, an exhibition of Paquimé ceramics, as well as temporary exhibitions. The **Museo de Arte e Industria Populares** ⓘ *Av Reforma 5, Tue-Sat 0900-1300, 1600-1900, free*, has displays Tarahumara art and lifestyle as well as shops. The **Museo Casa Juárez** ⓘ *Juárez y Calle 5, Mon-Fri 0900-1500, 1600-1800*, was once the house and office of Benito Juárez himself.

Towards the Basaseachi Falls → *Colour map 2, B2.*

Route 16 leads west through **Ciudad Cuauhtémoc**, which has the **Museo y Centro Cultural Menonita** ⓘ *Km 10 on the road to Alvaro Obregón, T428-7508*, and **La Junta** to the Basaseachi Falls, which, at 311 m. This is the highest single-jump waterfall in North America and is worth the effort of getting there. The top of the falls is 3 km from town (2 km by good dirt road, 1 km by signed trail). A paved road leads to a car park (with taco stalls) and mirador 1.5 km above the falls. From here a path leads to the top of the falls and continues steeply to the pool at the bottom (best to swim in the morning when the sun still strikes the pool). Hitching is difficult here; better to take a tour (US$16). The falls can also be reached from Creel (see below) via San Juanito along a very rough road.

Chihuahua to Los Mochis: the Copper Canyon

The **Chihuahua al Pacífico** train journey to Los Mochis is spectacular and exciting especially on the descent through the **Barranca del Cobre**, the Copper Canyon, to the coast beyond Creel: it's lauded as one of the great train journeys in the world and with good reason. As a result it's popular and at busy times you will need to book seats in advance. Sit on the left-hand side of the carriage going down to Los Mochis; right-hand side coming up from Los Mochis.

For train enquiries, contact the information and reservations office on T01-800-122-4373, www.chepe.com.mx. *Primera* (first class) tickets can be pre-booked at travel agents in Chihuahua, Los Mochis (see page 201) and some stations along the way. The schedule is an approximation of intent, but check details as they are subject to change. On average trains are about one hour late by the time they arrive in Los Mochis. Bring your own drinking water and toilet paper. Do not take large amounts of cash or jewellery, there can be security problems on the railway.

A second-class train (*mixto* or *clase económica*) also runs but travelling on it is much more difficult. You can only buy tickets in person; they are sold once the first

Chihuahua al Pacífico Primera Express

From Chihuahua to Los Mochis				
Time	Price	Destination	Price	Time
0600		Chihuahua	US$96	1925
0815	US$20	Cuauhtémoc	US$77	1703
1115	US$44	Creel	US$53	1404
1234 (20-min)	US$52	Divisadero	US$44	1225 (20 min)
1302	US$53	Posada	US$43	1219
1318 (7-min)	US$54	San Rafael	US$42	1200 (5-min)
1417	US$59	Bahuichivo	US$37	1107
1515	US$65	Temoris	US$31	1006
1756	US$84	El Fuerte	US$18	0726
1930	US$96	Los Mochis		0600
			From Los Mochis to Chihuahua	

Económica class tickets are roughly half price, see text for details.

train has left or passed through; the train leaves in theory about one hour after the first-class train and the timetable is quintessentially latino – the train may be along, it may be along tomorrow. Prices are roughly half that of the first-class train.

The most interesting part of the journey is between Creel and Los Mochis. If wishing to see the best scenery, there is little point in taking the train Chihuahua-Creel-Chihuahua (on this stretch, the cheaper train is just as good as the *Primera Especial*). If planning to spend a few days in Creel, there are frequent buses Chihuahua-Creel. Delays are possible in the rainy season.

West of Chihuahua are high, windy and sparsely populated plains. From Chihuahua, the railway and road (Route 16, *cuota* and *libre* after Km 45; the latter is good) cross the Sierra of the **Tarahumara** people, who call themselves the **Raramuri** ('those who run fast'). They were originally cave-dwellers and nomads, but now work as day-labourers in the logging stations and have settled around the mission churches built by the Spanish in the 17th century.

Creel and around → *Phone code: 635. Colour map 2, B2. Altitude: 2356 m.*

Creel is the commercial centre of the Tarahumara region and is named after Enrique Creel (1854-1931), economist and entrepreneur, governor of Chihuahua state in 1907, who initiated the building of the railway and planned to improve the Tarahumara's lives by establishing a colony here.

Creel is an excellent centre for trekking and horse riding. It is also a good centre for reaching several deep canyons, including that of the Río Urique, known as the Barranca del Urique, or del Cobre (the Urique, or Copper Canyon – see below).

Cusárare → *Colour map 2, B2.*

Twenty kilometres south of Laguna Arareco, is Cusárare (place of the eagles), with a **Jesuit church** ⓘ *US$1*, dating back to 1767 and painted by indigenous craftsmen. To get to the 30-m waterfall, continue 100 m after the junction to Cusárare where there is a hotel sign on the right; turn right, pass the hotel and then the bridge, at the junction turn right; it's about 45 minutes' walk and is not well-signposted. There is very good hiking around Cusárare, but a guide may be necessary (Sr Reyes Ramírez and his son have been

The falls are at their best July-September.

recommended for tours to the canyon). Allow four days to see the canyon properly, as hiking is tough. The canyon is hot by day and cold by night. The American guide Cristóbal, at **Margarita's**, has also been recommended.

Guachochi → *Phone code: 649. Colour map 2, B2.*

Guachochi, 156 km south of Creel, has a Wild West appearance. There is a bank. From Guachochi you can walk four hours to the impressive **Barranca de Sinforosa**. The canyon is not visible until you reach the edge. From a point several hundred metres above the Río Verde you can see an unforgettable extended system of immense canyons, grander (according to some) than the view you can see from El Divisadero or on crossing the Barranca del Cobre. There's a path down to the river.

Barranca del Urique/Copper Canyon → *Colour map 2, B2.*

The road south out of Cusárare leads eventually to Batópilas, passing a turn-off to El Tejabán above the Barranca del Urique/Cobre (this is claimed to be the 'real' Copper Canyon); **Basíhuare** ('Sash') village, surrounded by pink and white rock formations (40 km from Creel); and the **Puente del Río Urique**, spanning the Urique Canyon. The climate is ideal for camping. At the junction Creel-Guachochi-Bufa, near Samachique, is a small restaurant/hotel, **La Casita** (F), which is very primitive and romantic. The road is paved as far as the junction but is bumpy from then on. Just after the junction, 3 km down into the valley is **Samachique**, where the *rari-pame* race, kicking a wooden ball for 241 km without rest, often takes two or three days and nights in September. Stranded travellers can find a room and food at the bus stop (no more than a shack) in Samachique, which is 1 km off the main route to Batópilas (1330 bus from Guachochi arrives at 1500 after the Creel bus has gone through). If wishing to hitch to Batópilas (2½-hour drive) take the right fork as you walk back out of Samachique; it rejoins the route at a junction where you can wait for traffic both coming through and by-passing the village. **Quírare,** 65 km from Creel, offers views of the beautiful Batópilas Canyon. After Quírare there is an awesome 14-km descent to **La Bufa,** in the Batópilas canyon, and on to Batópilas, possibly the most scenic road in northern Mexico.

Creel

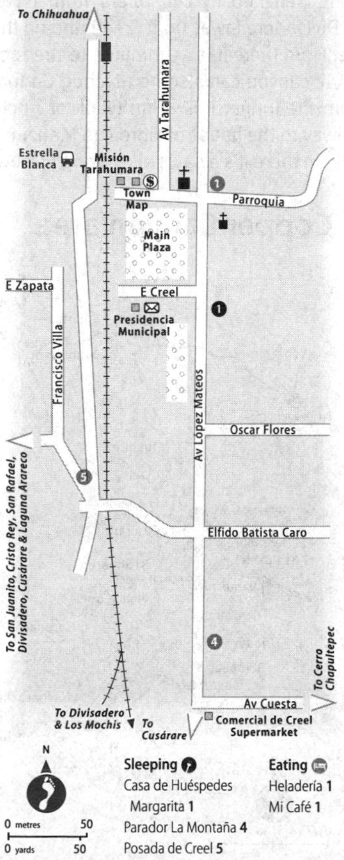

Batópilas and around

Batópilas, 120 km from Creel, is a delightful little palm-fringed town of 1100 inhabitants hemmed in by the swirling river and the cactus-studded canyon walls. It is an excellent centre for walking and within easy reach of the Urique Canyon (see box, page 223). The **Mina de Guadalupe** was discovered in 1780 by

Pedro de la Cruz. Batópilas became a thriving silver-mining centre, with mines owned by the Shepard family. Their mansion (near the bridge), abandoned during Pancho Villa's campaign, must be one of the most elaborate adobe houses anywhere, but it is now overgrown and dilapidated.

The **Porfirio Díaz Mine** above the bridge into town can be explored to about 3 km into the mountain (take torch); as you get into the mine there is the sickly, sweet smell of bat droppings, after about 1 km the air is thick with disturbed bats. There is a Jesuit mission at **Satevo**, a 7-km walk from Batópilas along the river.

Towards Divisadero → *Colour map 2, B2.*

Beyond Creel, the Chihuahua al Pacífico train passes its highest point, **Los Ojitos** and, soon after, the **Lazo loop**, in which the track does a 360° turn. At Divisadero there is an all-too-brief 20-minute stop to view the canyon and buy souvenirs from the Tarahumara women. Five minutes further on, the train comes to **Hotel Posada Barrancas**. See page 220 for schedule.

For those who aren't travelling on the train the Barranca de Urique/Cobre (Urique/Copper Canyon) is quite a long way from Creel. Apart from the access from Batópilas (see box, page 223), or from Bahuichivo (see below), the simplest way to see the canyon is to take a bus or hitch to Divisadero or **Posada Barrancas** on the rough road, paved halfway from Creel, or else take the train.

The **Balancing Rock** is at the edge of the canyon; it wobbles in a stomach-churning way as you stand on it. Reached by *camioneta* from **Hotel Divisadero Barrancas**, or walk 1-2 km from Divisadero (away from Creel) and on the left you will see the wooden entrance gate. From there it is 45 minutes to the rock with stops at the canyon viewing points. The canyon can also be reached on foot from Divisadero or **Posada Barrancas**; from the former it is 6 km (walk or hitch) along the dirt road that runs beside the railway to the house of Florencio Manzinas (at the first group of houses you come to). From there it's a day's hike along narrow, slippery, often steep and sometimes overgrown trails into the canyon, descending from cool pine forest into gradually more subtropical vegetation as you approach the river and the canyon floor. Take plenty of water for the hike as, after descending the first section following a stream, you have to go over another hill before getting down to the river, which means several hours without access to water.

Divisadero to Bahuichivo → *Colour map 2, B2.*

Twenty-five minutes beyond the **Hotel Posada Barrancas** the **Chihuahua al Pacífico** reaches **San Rafael**, where there is a 10-minute stop, and then passes the **La Laja** bridge and tunnel. It is a further 20 minutes to **Cuiteco**. Next on the line comes Bahuichivo; if you don't want to go all the way to Los Mochis you can return from here . From Bahuichivo to Los Mochis is five hours on the train.

Copper Canyon area

Batópilas to Urique

A three-day hike goes from the Batópilas Canyon to Urique (once known as the Camino Real), from where you can get a ride to Bahuichivo for a train to Creel or Los Mochis (colour map2, B2).

Routes Batópilas-Cerro Colorado-Piedra Redonda-Cerro El Manzano-La Estación-Los Alisos-Urique. You climb from 500 m, reaching 2200 m before descending to Urique at 600 m. It can be very hot in the canyons; drink at least four litres of water a day (you can fill up at settlements along the way) and take plenty of sunblock. There are many junctions of paths and so if you are without a guide it is vital to check that you are on the correct route as often as possible (try not to wander into marijuana plantations). One recommendation if you are using the 'Batópilas' survey map (1:50,000 sheet G13A41, covering the entire route, available from the Misión Tarahumara in Creel US$5) is that you take the ridge path (not marked on the 1979 edition) after Cerro El Manzano to La Estación, both for the views and directness.

Horse riding A recommended guide (not cheap) is Librado Balderrama Contreras who will guide you to Urique or to surrounding attractions such as Mesa Quimoba, Mesa de San José and Monerachi. There are several places in town where you can hire mules (with a handler) for carrying gear.

Urique → *Phone code: 635. Colour map 2, B2.*

From Bahuichivo, bus and pick-ups make the five-hour journey to Urique, in the heart of the Barranca de Urique. At the lip of the canyon is a mirador offering fine views. The road into the canyon is spectacular, only rivalled by the road to Batópilas.

Témoris → *Phone code: 635.*

Near Témoris, the train track enters a tunnel in which the railway turns through 180°. Témoris, an attractive town 11 km above the train station, in the mining and cattle country of the lower western Sierra Madre, is a good base for visiting working ranches, Tarahumara villages, waterfalls and swimming holes, on foot, horse or mountain bike. *Colectivos* make the trip or you may be able to hitch with local merchants. There are three hotels in the area and several cheap restaurants.

South from Chihuahua

Ciudad Delicias to Zacatecas → *Phone code: 639. Colour map 2, B3-C4.*

At Ciudad Delicias, the first major town southeast of Chihuahua on Route 45, Ciudad Delicias, there is a **Museo de Paleontología** ⓘ *Av Río Chuvíscar Norte y Círculo de la Plaza de la República, T472-8513, Mon-Sat 0900-2000*, with fossils from the Zona de Silencio (see below) and from the inland sea that covered the area 80 million years ago.

Further south is **Ciudad Camargo** (phone code: 648), famous for its eight days of **Fiesta de Santa Rosalía** beginning on 4 September, when there are cockfights, horse racing and dancing.

From **Ciudad Jiménez** (1263 km from Mexico City) there are two routes south to Fresnillo and Zacatecas: the Central Highway through Durango, or a more direct route via Torreón (237 km from Ciudad Jiménez), passing Escalón, **Ceballos, Yermo** and **Bermejillo**, on Route 49.

Between Escalón and Ceballos is the **Zona del Silencio** (the Silent Zone), a highly magnetic area where, it is claimed, electrical appliances fall silent, aircraft radar goes haywire, and so on. It inspires much interest and research.

Between Gómez Palacio and Zacatecas are **Cuéncame**, **Río Grande** and **Fresnillo**. This last town is the birthplace of the artist Francisco Goitia and musician Manuel M Ponce.

Hidalgo del Parral → *Phone code: 627. Colour map 2, B3.*

Connecting to the north through Ciudad Jiménez (77 km) Hidalgo del Parral, or often just Parral, is an old mining town with narrow streets. In 1629, Juan Rangel de Viezma discovered La Negrita, the first mine in the area. Now known as La Prieta, it overlooks the city from the top of Cerro la Prieta. Rangel founded the town in 1631 under the name of San Juan del Parral. The mine owners were generous benefactors to the city, leaving many beautiful buildings that still stand. On 8 September 1944, severe damage was caused by a flood. The decrease in population, either through drowning or flight, led to a recession. Hidalgo del Parral is a pleasant, safe, affluent city with acompact centre with a string of shaded plazas, many bridges over the sinuous, and often dry, Río del Parral, and several churches.

The city's history is split between its mining heritage and the fact that Pancho Villa was assassinated here.

Sights

On the Plaza Principal is the **Parroquia de San José**, with a beautiful interior. Plaza Baca has a statue to *El Buscador de Ilusiones* (the Dream Seeker), a naked man panning for gold. The **cathedral** is on this square and, on the opposite side, is the **Templo San Juan de Dios** with an exuberant altarpiece, painted gold. Across the road from the cathedral is the former **Hotel Hidalgo** (not in use), built in 1905 by mine owner Pedro Alvarado and given to Pancho Villa in the 1920s. Next door is **Casa Stallforth** (1908), the shop and house of a German family who supplied everything imaginable to the city. It is still a shop, with the original interior. Continuing on Mercaderes, before the bridge, is **Casa Griensen**, now the Colegio Angloamericano Isaac Newton. Griensen, another German, married Alvarado's sister. Behind this house is **Casa Alvarado**, still a private residence, only for viewing from the outside. Crossing the bridge at the end of Mercaderes, you come to the site of Villa's death, on the corner of Plaza Juárez.

Around Hidalgo del Parral

Twenty-six kilometres east of Parral on the Jiménez road, a well-signed road leads 5 km south to **Valle de Allende**. Originally called Valle de San Bartolomé, it was the site of the first **Franciscan mission** in Chihuahua, founded in the late 16th century by Fray Agustín Rodríguez. The original monastery building still stands on the main square, but it is unused (it has been used as a *refrigeradora* to store apples).

Hidalgo del Parral to Durango

Route 45 is in good condition all the way to Durango. At **Villa de Nieve,** 3 km down a winding road, well signed, is Pancho Villa's hacienda, with an excellent **museum** ⓘ *give a donation to the man who opens the door*. Villa was given the hacienda in exchange for promising to lay down his arms and retire to private life (28 July 1920).

Cinema enthusiasts can visit the Western sets of **Villa del Oeste** (9 km from Durango) and **Chupaderos** (14 km), both decaying (especially the latter) but smelling authentically of horse. San Juan del Río buses go there or take a taxi, US$14; 4 km east off the road, at San Juan del Río, is a Pemex station. Halfway down

The assassination of Pancho Villa

The infamous assassination of Pancho Villa took place in the centre of Hidalgo del Parral on 20 July 1923. Villa owned a house on Calle Zaragoza (now a shop called Almacenes Real de Villa, painted bright pink) and was making his way from there to the Hotel Hidalgo, which he also owned, when he was ambushed on Avenida Juárez. The house chosen by the assassins is now the Museo Pancho Villa (Monday-Friday 0900-2000, Saturday 0900-1300.) Twelve of the 100 bullets fired hit Villa, who was taken immediately to the Hotel Hidalgo. The death mask taken there can be seen in the museum and also in the museum in Chihuahua. His funeral took place the next day and he was buried in the Panteón Municipal; his tomb is still there even though the body has been transferred to Mexico City.

the side road to San Juan is a signed road to **Coyotada**, off which is a 4-km road to **Pancho Villa's birthplace and museum** ⓘ *free, donation welcome*, which is modest, a few artefacts and photos.

Santiago Papasquiaro is three hours north of Durango on Route 23. On the way, in Canatlán, are Mennonite colonies. There are a number of hot springs in the area; **Hervideros** is the most popular, take the bus to Herreras, then it's a 30-minute walk. **Tepehuanes**, one hour further on, is a small pleasant town with a couple of hotels. Walk to Purísima and then to a small, spectacular canyon. A dirt road continues to **Guanacevi**, a mining town in the Sierra.

Seven kilometres north of the Durango road, 12 km before Sombrerete, is the **Sierra de los Organos** (Valley of the Giants), now a national park, where John Wayne made several of his westerns. It is named after the basalt columns, which are supposed to resemble organ pipes.

Durango → *Phone code 618. Colour map 2, C3. Altitude: 1924 m.*

Victoria de Durango, capital of Durango state was founded in 1563. It is a modernizing city but with many beautiful old buildings (see the 18th-century **Casa de los Condes de Suchill**, now Bancomer, on 5 de Febrero, and the French-style

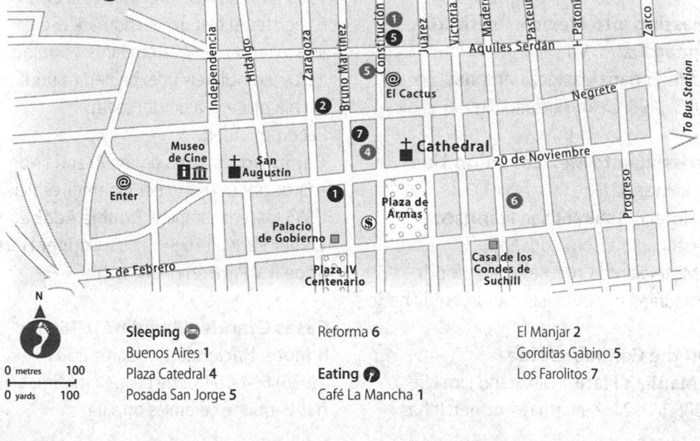

 Teatro Ricardo Castro), with wonderfully calming murals in the auditorium, a cathedral (1695) and a famous iron-water spring.

The town is all pretty much within a couple of blocks of the main plaza. The main street is Avenida 20 de Noviembre, a wide dominating thoroughfare that reflects the 'Wild West' image of the state of Durango, so often a backdrop to not only Hollywood movies but also the Mexican film industry at its height. Lest you think the city rests on the laurels that made such classics as *The Wild Bunch* by Sam Peckinpah (1968), more recent classics include The *Mask of Zorro I* (1998).

There is a small **Museo de Cine** ⓘ *Florida 1106, Barrio El Calvario, Tue-Sun 1000-1800, US$0.50*, with a good collection of Mexican film posters plus old cameras. The **tourist office** is above the Museo de Cine.

Sleeping

Ciudad Juárez *p214, map p214*
L **Holiday Inn Express**, Paseo Triunfo de la República 8745, T629-6000, www.ichotelsgroup.com/h/d/ex/1/en/hd/juaex. Reliable Holiday Inn quality.
B **Plaza Continental**, Lerdo Sur 112, downtown, T615-0084. Clean, TV, noisy, friendly, restaurant good.
D **Hotel D'Manely**, Blv Oscar Flores 4431, T610-7330, close to bus station. Go out of the west (taxi) entrance, walk straight across the parking lot to the street, cross the street, and walk left 2 blocks. Heating, private bath.
E **Juárez**, Lerdo Norte 143, close to Stanton St bridge, T615-0358. Comfortable, hot water, good value.

On the El Paso side
B **International Hotel**, Oregon. A/c, TV, clean. Recommended.
D **Gardner**, 311 East Franklin Av, T532-3661. Hot water, shared bath, TV and phone in room, rooms with bath available, also serves as youth hostel.

Crossing into Mexico: Presidio/ Ojinaga *p215*
C **Armendariz**, Zaragoza 713, near Zócalo, T453-1198. Clean, safe parking.

Crossing into Mexico: Columbus/ Palomas *p215*
D **Hotel Restaurant San Francisco**. Reasonable accommodation.
E **Motel Santa Cruz**. Behind seafood restaurant, opposite gas station. Fairly basic.

On the Columbus side
A **Martha's Place**, Main Stand Lima St, T505-531-2467, marthas@vtc.net. It has a very attractive lobby and a pleasant breakfast area.
C **Suncrest Inn**, Highway 11, just north of Highway 9. TV and phones in rooms.
Camping **Pancho Villa State Park**, opposite the Columbus Historical Museum, Excellent, well-maintained sites, additional charge for electrical hook-up.

Crossing into Mexico: Douglas/Agua Prieta *p216*
A **Motel La Hacienda**, Calle Primera and Av 6, T338-0621, a few blocks from the border. Best in town.
B **Motel Arizona**, Av 6 between Calle 17 and 18, T338-2522. With heating, pleasant.
D **Motel Colonial**, Naco. The only formal accommodation, often full, but the manager may tolerate a night's auto camping within the motel compound.

On the Douglas side
AL-A **Gadsden Hotel**, 1046 G Av, T364-4481, www.hotelgadsden.com. A registered historical landmark used as a location for Western films. Fabulous lobby, completely unexpected to find such a place in a border town. Recommended.
Camping RV parks on the Arizona side charge about US$10 per night for vehicle, US$5 for tent camping: **Double Adobe Trailer Park** off Highway 80, **Copper Horse Shoe R V Park** on Highway 666.

Casas Grandes/Paquimé *p216*
B **Motel Hacienda**, Av Juárez 2603, T(636) 694-1048. The best. Sometimes has Paquimé ceramics on sale.

C Paquimé, Av Benito Juárez, T(636)694-1320. With fan and a/c, clean, large, pleasant. Recommended.

Madera and around *p217*

C María, Calle 5 y 5 de Mayo. Cheaper rooms available, heating, clean, limited parking, restaurant open 24 hrs. Good.

F Motel Maras, Calle 5, 1 block south of Mirmay. Hot water, noisy, clean but dusty rooms.

Chihuahua *p218, map p218*

The cheaper hotels are on Juárez and its cross-streets; the cheapest are behind the cathedral.

B El Campanario, Blv Díaz Ordaz 1405, southwest of cathedral, T415-4545. Good rooms, clean, TV. Recommended.

C Del Cobre, Calle 10A y Progreso 905, T415-1730. With bathroom, hot water, TV, very comfortable, **Bejarano** restaurant good, reasonable laundry.

D-E Reforma, Victoria 809, T410-6848. Colonial-style, friendly, clean, fan, hot water, restaurant, TV in reception, safe, parking next door for cars and motorbikes. Recommended.

E San Juan, Victoria 823, T410-0035. In old colonial house, but rooms (repairs needed, a bit sombre) are in another part, reasonable food, water sometimes scarce, friendly.

Creel and around *p220, map p221*

You'll need to make reservations in advance.

AL The Lodge at Creel, used to be **Pensión Creel**, Av López Mateos 61, about 1 km from the plaza and railway station, T456-0071, www.thelodgeatcreel.com. Price includes breakfast and dinner.

B Parador La Montaña, Av López Mateos 44, T456-0075 (full board available). Will exchange foreign currency at reasonable rates, TV, clean, quiet, restaurant, bar, organizes excursions, safe parking. Live music.

B-D Casa de Huéspedes Margarita, López Mateos 11, T456-0045. Cheapest in dormitory (packed in high season with mattresses on floor). More expensive in double with bath, breakfast and dinner included, good communal meals, very popular meeting place (book in advance in high season), Margarita's reps meet arriving train passengers, quite pushy, organizes tours (see below), horses can be hired. Highly recommended. (If full, Margarita's sister will put you up, **E**, with dinner and breakfast, enjoyable.)

C Korachi, Francisco Villa 116, T456-0207. Right beside the station, and a good budget choice.

C-E Cabañas Berti's, Av López Mateos 31, T456-0086. Heating, soap and towels, parking, 1 kitchenette, excursions. Friendly owner Sr Sergio Arnoldo Rascón plays guitar in local clubs.

C-E Posada de Creel, T/F456-0142, Apdo Postal 7. Remodelled building, gas fires in rooms, very clean. Cheaper without bath in dormitory. Hot water, helpful, English-speaking managers. Recommended.

Guachochi *p221*

B Melina, Belisario Domínguez 14, T30255. Clean, hot water, bar.

D Chaparro, Francisco Villa 1, T543-0004. Overpriced but good restaurant, bath, TV, hot water.

Copper Canyon *p221*

F La Casita, at the junction Creel-Guachochi-Bufa, near Samachique. A small restaurant/ hotel, very primitive and romantic.

Batópilas and around *p221*

B-C Juanita, on central plaza, T456-9043. Very clean. Recommended.

E Chulavista, on way into town, T456-9093, owned by Don Mario, near bridge at entrance to village. Clean, hot water, tiny rooms.

Towards Divisadero *p222*

A Posada Barrancas Mirador, mirador.mexicoscoppercanyon.com. Views from every room, full board, free lemonade on arrival and free margarita later. Tours arranged, including hike or horse riding trip to a Tarahumara village. Recommended.

C Casa de Huéspedes Díaz, Posada Barrancas. Rooms with 2 double beds, hot water on request, prepares meals.

Phone codes *Ciudad Juárez 656; Ojinaga 626; Janos 636; Agua Prieta 633; Casas Grandes 636; Madera 157; Chihuahua 614; Creel 635; Guachochi 649; Urique 635; Témoris 635; Ciudad Delicias 639; Hidalgo del Parral 627; Durango 618.*

D **Rancho de Lancho**, Posada Barrancas, with a couple of basic rooms, dirty bathrooms, but very helpful with walks and breakfast available.

D-F **Trail Head Inn**, T578-3007. Run by Rogelio Domínguez who often meets the train saving the 2 km walk from town. Basic, dormitory accomodation. Great location for canyon hikes to the river and great views.

F **Room**, Posada Barrancas. Walk 1.5 km down the road, past the 'camping' sign to a hamlet of 3 houses. 1st house on left has a rustic room with earth floor and lantern with a double and a single bed.

Divisadero to Bahuichivo *p222*

B **Hotel Cuiteco**, Cuiteco, delightful, with a patio that has an unimpeded view of the mountains, quiet, oil lamps, gas stove in courtyard.

Témoris *p223*

D-F **Campamento Adame**, a good choice for backpackers, has *cabañas*, dormitories and tent sites with shower and cooking facilities.

Ciudad Delicias to Zacatecas *p223*

A **Hotel Santa Fe**, south edge of Ciudad Camargo on highway, T462-4022. Very quiet, secure parking, good breakfast, some English spoken. Recommended.

A **Motel La Fortuna**, Panamericana Km 724, Fresnillo, T(493) 932-5664, www.motellafortuna.com, comfortable, hot water.

A-D **Posada de Sol**, Blv Revolución 3501, Torreón, T720-2991. Modern motel, secure parking, small restaurant, bar, hot showers, rooms range from basic, windowless, clean *cabañas* to large, US-style rooms with TV, good value.

B **Hacienda del Norte**, Av Agricultura Norte 5, T472-0200. Good all-round comforts.

B **Motel La Siesta**, Av Madero 320 Norte, Gómez Palacio, Torreón, T714-0291. Clean, hot water, safe parking. Good.

B-C **Baeza**, Calle 2 Norte 309, T472-1000. Also a good choice.

C-D **Maya**, Ensaye 9, Fresnillo, T(493)932-0351, good travelling option.

C-D **La Posta**, Gral Ceniceros 68 Norte, Cuéncame, T(671)763-0029, hot water, with parking.

D **Victoria**, Comonfort y Jiménez, Cd Camargo, T462-0801. Clean and cheap motel.

Hidalgo del Parral *p224*

B **Acosta**, Agustín Barbachano 3, T522-0221, off Plaza Principal. Quiet, car or motorbike parking, rooftop terrace with fine view, laundry facilities, very clean, central, friendly, helpful, hot water, excellent value. Recommended.

B **Adriana**, Colegio 2, between Plaza Principal and Plaza Baca, T522-2570. A/c, restaurant, bar, parking.

C **San José**, Santiago Méndez 5, near Plaza Principal, T522-2453. With bath, safe parking, clean, central.

D **Chihuahua**, Jesús García and Colón 1, T522-1513. Clean, simple.

E **Casa Peréz**, Calle Oscar Flores 257, T456-0047. Good, clean rooms with hot water, and friendly service.

E **Margarita**, near bus station. A bit noisy, but excellent value, well-run with friendly staff and a café next door. 24-hour parking available in supermarket next door. Recommended.

Hidalgo del Parral to Durango *p224*

D **Hotel División del Norte**, Madero 35, Santiago Papasquiaro, T(674)- 862-0013. In a former convent; the owner's husband was in Pancho Villa's División del Norte.

Durango *p225, map p225*

L-AL **Posada San Jorge**, Constitución 102 Sur, T811-3526, www.hotelposadasanjorge.com.mx. Old colonial building, patio, large rooms, friendly, parking. Recommended.

C **Plaza Catedral**, Constitución 216 Sur, T813-2480. Great old building with private bathrooms and parking at the back. Good value.

C **Reforma**, 5 de Febrero y Madero, T813-1622. Authentic 1960s lobby, clean, comfortable rooms, free indoor parking, good restaurant. A little overpriced.

E **Oasis**, Zarco between 20 de Noviembre y 5 de Febrero. With bath, hot water, rooms on the top floor have a good view.

E-F **Buenos Aires**, Constitución 126 Norte, T812-3128. Clean, tidy and very safe. A good budget choice.

Eating

Ciudad Juárez *p214, map p214*

¥¥ **El Saucito**, Lerdo Sur 263. Popular, good breakfasts.

¥¥ **Florida**, Juárez 301, 2 blocks from **Hotel Impala**. Clean, good food and service.

¥ **El Gordo No 2**, Francisco Madero, ½ block from 16 de Septiembre. Good for tacos and burritos.

Crossing into Mexico: Douglas/Agua Prieta *p216*

¥¥ **El Pollo Loco**, Agua Prieta, near the plaza, for roasted chicken.

¥¥ **Mariscos y Carnes 'La Palapa'**, Calle 6 between Av 11 and 12. Seafood and meat.

Janos and around *p216*

¥¥-¥ **Restaurant Durango**, de facto bus station at the intersection. Good inexpensive food.

Casas Grandes/Paquimé *p216*

¥ **Café de la Esquina**, 5 de Mayo y Obregón, near bus offices, Nuevo Casas Grandes. Cheap, clean, friendly, popular.

Chihuahua *p218, map p218*

The smartest and best are in the Zona Dorada, northeast of the centre on Juárez, near Colón.

¥¥ **Los Milagros**, Victoria 812. Young people's meeting place, good atmosphere.

¥¥ **Quijote's**, Victoria 807. Good food and value, buffet meals till 1700, dinner also, friendly.

¥ **La Galatea**, Juárez y Calle 2. Restaurant within department store, recommended for breakfast, cheap.

Mercado. The market is between Calle 2 and 6, southeast of Av Niños Héroes, small but good for fruit and vegetables.

Creel and around *p220, map p221*

Water shortages are common.

¥¥-¥ **Verónica**, López Mateos. Good *comida corrida*.

¥¥ **Bar Plaza Mexicana**, on Elfido Batista Caro, owned by **Margarita's** (see Sleeping). Recommended.

¥ **Mi Café**, next door to **Bar Plaza Mexicana**. Good food, cheap, try the apple *empanadas*, friendly.

Bakeries and ice cream parlours

Heladería, López Mateos between Parroquía and Oscar Flores. Good ice cream shop.

Batópilas and around *p221*

¥¥ **Carolina**, between bridge and centre. Friendly owner.

¥ **El Puente Colgante**. New, pleasant and friendly, garden, cold beer, a b it pricey.

¥ Meals at the private house of Sra Enedina Caraveo de Hernández, Plaza Constitución, are good and cheap, large portions.

Hidalgo del Parral *p224*

¥¥ **La Parroquia** in **Hotel San José**. Good-value meals, including breakfast.

¥¥ **Morelos**, Plazuela Morelos 22, off Plaza Principal. Clean, rather expensive, 0700-2300, Fri and Sat open 24 hrs.

¥¥-¥ **Café Corales**, Flores Magón opposite Buses Ballezano. Good beef sandwiches.

Cafés and bakeries

El Parralense, off Independencia on Calle Los Ojitos. Wide choice of bread and cakes.

Durango *p225, map p225*

¥¥ **Café La Mancha**, 20 de Noviembre 807 Pte. Relaxed, tables outside at back, cheap lunches.

¥¥ **El Manjar**, Negrete and Zaragoza, vegetarian Mexican dishes – open for breakfast.

¥¥-¥ **Gorditas Gabino**, Constitución 112 Norte. Mexican food in a US-diner style. Cheap, good and central.

¥¥-¥ **Samadhi**, a couple of blocks from the cathedral on Negrete 403 Pte. Good-value vegetarian food, delicious soups, popular with locals.

¥ **Gardy**, F de Urdiñola 239, Nueva Viscaya, T818-7162. Vegetarian.

¥ **Los Farolitos**, Martínez and 20 de Noviembre. Exquisite tacos and *burritos*.

For an explanation of sleeping and eating price codes used in this guide, see inside the front cover. Other relevant information is found in Essentials, see pages 45-47.

Festivals and events

Ciudad Juárez *p214, map p214*
2-5 May Festival de la Raza; music, dance, cultural events.
5 May Celebrations on Av Juárez (Battle of Puebla).
15 Sep Independence Day.
Jun-Jul Feria Juárez, Parque Chamizal.
1-4 Jun Festival Ojinaga.

Creel and around *p220, map p221*
12 Dec Tarahumara festival.

Shopping

Chihuahua *p218, map p218*
Artesanías Tarahumaras, Calle 5 y Doblado 312, T413-0627. Crafts, baskets, wood carvings, jewellery.

Activities and tours

Creel and around *p220, map p221*
Rock climbing
Expediciones Umarike, www.umarike.com.mx (see Bicycle hire below), US$50 per ½ day, at Humira (road to Batópilas), Chapultepec rock (in town) abseil at Basaseachi, bouldering. Generally top rope climbing because of loose volcanic rock. Rents out tents (US$6.50 per night), sleeping bags, stoves.

Chihuahua *p218, map p218*
Tour operators
Guillermo Bechman, T413-0253. Arranges stays at cabins above Bahuichivo, near Copper Canyon.
Viajes Flamingo, Santa Anita Hotel, T412-1613. Will book train tickets in advance, no commission charged, English spoken.
Turismo Al Mar, T416-5950. Accommodation and rail packages to Copper Canyon, 5 nights and some meals, US$500 for 2 people.

Creel and around *p220, map p221*
Horse riding
Horses can be rented at several locations, eg **Rarajipa 18** (near **Expediciones Umarike**), to visit the Cristo Rey statue above town or to waterfalls.

Tour operators
Many people hang around the square offering tours in a variety of vehicles, or other means of transport. **Roberto Venegas**, T456-0049, who has a van, is recommended.

Batópilas and around *p221*
Tour operators
Several people in Creel offer trips to Batópilas. A recommended guide is **Pedro Estrada Pérez** (limited English but patient), T456-0079. An overnight trip for 4 (minimum) costs US$60 per person, plus lodging and meals, including trip to Jesuit Mission at Satevo (see below). Many hotels arrange tours including **Hotel Los Pinos**, Av López Mateos. Some examples: to Cusárare (US$12-15), mission and falls, and Basíhuare; Recohauta hot springs (US$8 plus US$1.50 entrance); San Ignacio, Valle de los Hongos and Laguna Arareco; to Basaseachi (US$58 includes lunch, minimum 4, from Parador La Montaña); Divisadero (US$20, minimum 5, from Margarita's). These tours are pricey, but good fun and may involve more walking or climbing than advertised.

Durango *p225, map p225*
Tour operators
Excursiones Pantera , T825-8676, www.aventurapantera.com.mx. Good selection of adventure tours in the area.

Transport

Ciudad Juárez *p214*
Air
Abraham González (CJS) airport is 19 km south of the city (T619-0734). Flights to **Mexico City**, **Chihuahua**, **Cd Obregón**, **Culiacán**, **Durango**, **Guadalajara**, **Hermosillo**, **Ixtapa**, **León**, **Los Cabos**, **Mazatlán**, **Monterrey**, **Torreón**, **Tijuana** and **Zacatecas**.

El Paso's airport (ELP) is near Fort Bliss and Biggs Field military airbase with flights by **American**, **Delta**, **America West Airlines** and **Southwest Airlines** to all parts of the US. There are also flights to El Paso from **Chihuahua** and **Guadalajara**. *Colectivo* from Cd Juárez airport to El Paso or El Paso airport, US$15.50.

Airline offices Aero California, T618-3399. AeroMéxico, T613-8719.

Bus
Terminal is at Blv Oscar Flores 4010, T613-2083, south of the centre. There is a taxi information booth, which can give you estimated fares before you approach a driver. From the terminal to centre or Santa Fe bridge, taxi fare is about US$8. If you walk from the terminal to the highway, take any bus going to the right marked 'Centro' for US$0.30. Shuttle bus to **El Paso Greyhound Terminal**, US$5, hourly. From the Greyhound Terminal, corner of San Antonio and Santa Fe streets, you can get buses to **Laredo**, **Tucson**, etc, and other connections in the US. They have buses every hr on the ½ hr to Cd Juárez, 0630-2130, US$5. You can buy your ticket on the bus. It stops at the Mexican side of the border for immigration where you can pick up your FM-T (tourist card) there.

The Cd Juárez bus station has good sevices including long-distance telephones, money-changing facilities and left-luggage. On the west side of the building is a taxi booth (US$4.80 to the city centre). Exit the west side (the same door you use to get taxis) and cross the parking lot to take any northbound bus to the city centre. Ticket counters are on the north side of the terminal.

To **Chihuahua**, every ½ hr, 0700-0200, 4½ hrs, US$20, with **Chihuahenses Plus** hourly, 0400-2400; with **Turistar Ejecutivo**, 3 daily, US$28. **Durango**: every couple of hrs, US$62-51. To **Guadalajara**, 1000, 1300 and 2200, US$81. To **León**, 5 a day, US$75.To **Matamoros**, 1630 and 2145, US$72. To **Mexico City**, 25 hrs, US$100. To **Monterrey**, 1330, 1630 and 2145, US$62. To **San Luis Potosí**, US$72. To **Zacatecas**, hourly 0800-2400, US$62.

You can also buy tickets with **Omnibus de México**, www.odm.com.mx, for points in the US: to **Alburquerque, NM**, 1000, 1700, 2000, US$25. To **Denver, Colorado**, 1000, 1900, US$45. To **Los Angeles, CA**, 1030, 1600, 1845, US$50. **Greyhound**, El Paso, T532-2365. **Turismos Rápidos**, 828 South El Paso, off Santa Fe Bridge, to many US destinations.

Car
Sanborn's, for insurance and information, 440 Raynolds, El Paso, T1-800-222-0158, www.sanbornsinsurance.com, Mon-Fri 0830-1700.

Taxi
Charged by zone, from US$2.75 to US$7.25. You can also negotiate with the driver for hourly rates. The going rate about US$20 per hr. Some are allowed to cross the border and take you to downtown El Paso; US$30.

Crossing into Mexico: Presidio/ Ojinaga *p215*

Bus
The bus station in Agua Prieta is one small room with an adequate restaurant called Don Camione, and a phone service.

To **Chihuahua**, every couple of hrs from 0600, US$32. To **Cd Juárez**, 0900, 0930 and 2230. To **Durango**, 1930, US$65. To **Hermosillo**, every couple of hrs from 0600-1400, US$18. To **Mexico City**, 1700. To **Nogales**, every couple of hrs from 0830-1600, US$15. To **Phoenix**: every 3 hrs from 0515-1630, US$42. To **Tijuana**, Norte de Sonora, 2030. To **Zacatecas**, Cabellero Azteca (all 2nd class), 2130, US$56.

Douglas has a small bus terminal, 538 14th St, between Av F and Av G, T364-2233, operated by **Greyhound** and **Autobuses** Crucero. **Tucson**, US$19. **Phoenix**, US$30. **Los Angeles**: US$65. The schedules for all the buses are the same: 0545, 1145, 1515, and 1715. The terminal closes at 1600 so you'd have to wait outside for the 1715 bus.

Taxi
Armando Chávez, T335-2162. Recommended. If you are crossing the border, when you come to the first cross street, take a left and the office is just around the corner on the north side of the street.

Casas Grandes/Paquimé *p216*

Bus All offices are on Alvaro Obregón. To **Cd Juárez**, several daily, 4 hrs, US$15. To **Chihuahua**, 5 hrs, US$18. To **Mexico City**: once a day via El Sueco, once via Cuauhtémoc. 3 a day to **Agua Prieta**. Also one service a day to **Cuauhtémoc**, **Hermosillo**, **Madera**, **Monterrey**, **Nogales** and **Tijuana**.

Madera and around *p217*

Bus Estrella Blanca, T572-0431, to/from **Chihuahua** every hr, takes 5 hrs, bus stop on Calle 5.

Chihuahua *p218, map p218*

Air

Airport Gen Fierro Villalobos (CUU) on Blv Juan Pablo II, 18 km from centre on road to Ojinaga. Airport buses collect passengers from hotels, fare US$1.10. Also minibuses. Taxi US$16 (no other transport at night). Flights to **Cd Juárez**, **Cd Obregón**, **Culiacán**, **Guadalajara**, **Hermosillo**, **La Paz**, **Loreto**, **Los Cabos**, **Los Mochis**, **Manzanillo**, **Mazatlán**, **Mexico City**, **Monterrey**, **Tijuana** and **Torreón**. AeroMéxico to **Los Angeles** daily, and Aerolitoral to **Dallas** and **El Paso** in the US.

Airline offices AeroMéxico, T415-6303.

Bicycle

Bicycle spares Independencia 807, 0900-2000.

Bus

Local Town buses cost US$0.20.

Long distance Bus terminal on Blv Juan Pablo II, 8 km from centre on way to airport, southeast of town, T420-2286, 20 mins by bus to centre (US$0.30), or taxi US$4 (fixed price). Buses from centre at Niños Héroes between Ocampo and Calle 10. There is an exchange office (beware short-changing), cafetería and left luggage.

To **Aguascalientes**, US$48. To **Creel**, every couple of hrs from 0600, 4-5 hrs, US$16, paved all the way. To **Durango**, US$45. To **Guadalajara**, several, US$57, including Estrella Blanca, which also goes to **Acapulco**, US$88, and **Puerto Vallarta**, US$81. 2nd class bus, to **Hidalgo del Parral**, 2½ hrs, US$11. To **Nuevo Casas Grandes**, see above (note that Chihuahua-Madera buses go either via El Sueco, or via the Sierra). To **Nuevo Laredo**, at 2030, US$48; also to **Monterrey**, US$44, to **Mazatlán**, 2 companies, US$53, 19 hrs, heart-stopping view; to **Mexico City** (and intermediate destinations), frequent services with several companies, 20 hrs, US$79. To **Querétaro**, US$62. To **San Luis Potosí**, US$48. To **Saltillo**, US$35. To **Torreón**, US$22. To **Zacatecas**, 12 hrs, US$48.

Taxi

Taxis work on a zone system. Agree price before boarding.

Train

The station for the 631-km **Chihuahua al Pacífico** railway is 1 block behind the prison (take bus marked Rosario, or walk); in the early morning you may have to take a taxi. Information and tickets by post: **Departamento Regional de Pasajeros**, Apdo Postal 46, Chihuahua, CHIH, México, T415-7756. To **Los Mochis** daily at 0700, arrives 1950, returns 0600 arrives 2050, also Mon, Wed, Fri at 0800, arrives 2225, returns Tue, Thu, Sat 0700, arrives 2325 (see page 219 for details). There is another station (currently freight only) 3 km along Av Niños Héroes, left at Av Colón, which becomes Av Tecnológico, past the river and right along Av División del Norte, T413-0714.

Creel and around *p220, map p221*

Bicycle

Bike hire Expediciones Umarike, Av Ferrocarril s/n, north of tracks west of Plaza, PO Box 61, T/F456-0632, www.umarike.com.mx. Run by Arturo Gutiérrez and his Welsh wife Audrey, very friendly, open every day, cosy offices with books and real coffee. US$6.50 for ½ day, US$10.50 whole day, provide map, good bikes, must deposit ID; longer guided tours available on bike or in 4WD, eg to **Tararecua Canyon**.

Bikes from several other places roughly US$13 for the day; look around if you need better bikes.

Bus

Buses to surrounding villages all leave from outside **Hotel Korachi**, across railway track from square. To **Chihuahua**, every couple of hrs from 0600, US$16, 4-5 hrs. To **Cd Juárez**, 0800. To **Cusárare** (see below): at 0700, US$2.50, or lift in Margarita's transport US$6, or hitchhike. To **Guachochi**, 1200, 1730, US$4.50. To **León**, 1600, 15 hrs, US$60. To **San Rafael** via **Divisadero**, at 1030, 1500 and 1830, US$3 to Divisadero.

Train

For schedule see page 219. Station office Mon 0800-1000, 1100-1600, Tue-Fri 1000-1600, Sat 1000-1300. From Creel to Los Mochis takes about 8 hrs on the train.

Guachochi *p221*
Bus To **Creel** twice daily 0730 and 1330, US$4 (check at **Hotel Korachi** for schedule from Creel); also reached from Hidalgo del Parral, bus leaves for **Parral** at 0800 and 1200, now paved, but not spectacular.

Batópilas and around *p221*
Bus Buses from **Creel**, Tue, Thu and Sat at 0700, 5-6 hrs (paved as far as Samachique turn-off) depending on weather, US$16, buy ticket the day before, very crowded. Tickets are sold from **Restaurant La Herradura** in the main street. Return to **Creel**, Mon, Wed, and Fri; it leaves Batópilas at 0500 (have a torch handy as it is very dark). Also a 10-seater van on Mon, Wed and Fri, leaving at 0930, US$17, returns following day at 0500. Supply lorry leaves for **Chihuahua** Tue, Thu, Sat at 0600, takes passengers.

Towards Divisadero *p222*
Bus Regular daily buses from Divisadero to **Creel** (US$2.30) connecting to Chihuahua.

Ciudad Delicias to Zacatecas *p223*
Air Torreón airport (14.5 km from the centre). To **Chihuahua**, **Cd Juárez**, **Culiacán**, **Durango**, **Guadalajara**, **Hermosillo**, **Ixtapa**, **Mazatlán**, **Mexico City**, **Monterrey**, **Piedras Negras** and **Tijuana**. International flights to **Houston** and **Los Angeles** in the US, **Panama City** and **Sao Paulo**, Brazil.

Bus To/from **Chihuahua** hourly, US$4; **Omnibus de México**, Av 6 y Calle 2 Norte, T472-1020; **Estrella Blanca**, Av 6 Norte 300, T472-1509; **Rápidos Delicias**, Av 5 Norte 301, T472-1030.

From Torreón to **Chihuahua**, 6 hrs, US$24; to **Cd Juárez**:, US$42; to **Durango**, about 6 a day, 4½ hrs; to **Tepic**, US$42.

Gómez Palacio has its own bus station, without a shuttle to the centre. City buses outside have frequent services to all 3 city centres, US$0.33.

Hidalgo del Parral *p224*
Bus The bus station is 20 mins' walk out of town on Av Independencia, east of centre, taxi about US$2. Few bus lines start here so it is difficult to reserve seats. To **Durango**, 6 hrs, US$24. To **Zacatecas**, 9 hrs, US$42. To **Chihuahua**, frequent departures, 2½ hrs, US$11. Also to **Guachochi**. Buses Ballezano to Guachochi leave from office on Carlos Fuero y Flores Magón at 0800, 1230, 1545, US$4.

Durango *p225, map p225*
Air Guadalupe Victoria Airport (DGO), 12 km from centre (taxi US$8.50). To **Chihuahua**, **Guadalajara**, **Mazatlán**, **Mexico City**, **Monterrey**, **Tijuana** and **Torreón**. There are international flights to **Chicago**, **El Paso** and **Los Angeles**.

Airline offices Mexicana, T813-3030, Aero California, T817-7177. AeroMéxico, next to cathedral, T817-8828.

Bus Bus station out of town: minibus No 2 to centre, every 5 mins from 0600 to 2130, US$0.25. Services with **Omnibus de México** and **Estrella Blanca**. Across the Sierra Madre Occidental to **Mazatlán** there are several buses daily, 7 hrs, US$26. The views are fantastic and recommended if you cannot do the Chihuahua-Los Mochis train journey; sit on left side.

To **Chihuahua**, several daily, 8 hrs, US$36. To **Hidalgo del Parral**, 7 hrs, US$24. To **Guadalajara**, 2000 and 2200, 8 hrs, US$40. To **Mexico City**, every couple of hours, 12 hrs, US$58. To **Zacatecas**, 4½ hrs, US$18.

Directory

Ciudad Juárez *p214, map p214*
Banks Most *cambios* are on Av Juárez and Av de las Américas; there is also a *cambio* at the bus terminal. Rates vary little. The best and most convenient exchange houses are in El Paso: **Valuta Corp**, 301 Paisano Drive, buys and sells all foreign currencies but at poor rates, wires money transfers, open 24 hrs including holidays. **Melek Corp**, 306 Paisano Drive, offers most of the same services as Valuta but only dollars and pesos, not open 24 hrs. If coming from US Immigration, when you reach Paisano Drive/Highway 62, turn east for these places. (In El Paso, banks are closed on Sat.) **Embassies and consulates** Mexico, 910, E San Antonio, El Paso, T533-4082. **US**, López Mateos 924, Cd Juárez, T613-4048. **UK**, Fresno 185, Campestre Juárez, T617-5791. **Post office** Corner of Lerdo Sur and Ignacio de la Peña.

Crossing into Mexico: Presidio/ Ojinaga *p215*
Banks Bancomer on Zócalo, changes TCs, no commission; opposite is **Casa de Cambio Allende**, cash only, poorer rates.

Crossing into Mexico: Douglas/ Agua Prieta *p216*
Medical services Cruz Roja, corner of Calle 17 and Av 6. From there they can take you to other hospitals. **Pharmacies:** open 24 hrs, 1 on the corner of Calle 3 and Av 8, and another on the corner of Av 5 and 7.

Casas Grandes/Paquimé *p216*
Banks Several on 5 de Mayo and Constitución Ote; **Casa de Cambio California** next to hotel of that name, in Nuevo Casas Grandes. **Telephone** Long-distance calls from **Rivera** bus office, on Alvaro Obregón, in Nuevo Casas Grandes.

Madera and around *p217*
Banks Banamex, Bancomer and Banrural with ATMs and will change dollars (and TCs).

Chihuahua *p218, map p218*
Banks **Bancomer** on Plaza Constitución offers better rates than **Multibanco Comermex** on same square. **Casa de Cambio Rachasa**, Independencia y Guadalupe Victoria, on Plaza, poorer rates, no commission on cash, 2 on TCs, Mon-Sat 0900-2100 (also at Aldama 711). Exchange is available in the bus terminal, but rates are slightly better downtown.
Internet **Cyber Café Canaco**, Chamber of Commerce, Av Cuauhtémoc 1800, 2nd floor. **Laundry** Ocampo 1412. Julián Carrillo 402. **Telephone** Libertad, in the Palacio Federal. Also in Central Camionera. Credit card phone outside **AeroMéxico** office on Guadalupe Victoria, ½ block from Plaza Constitución (towards Carranza). Main phone office on Av Universidad.

Creel and around *p220, map p221*
Banks **Banca Serfín**, on the square, very friendly, 0900-1300, changes dollars cash with no commission, but commission charged on TCs (US$1 per cheque), TCs must be authorized by manager, Visa and MasterCard advances, no commission.
Laundry Pink house opposite side of tracks from square, US$3 per load, 2 hrs, good, Mon-Sat 0900-2000, restricted hrs on Sun.
Post office On main square in Presidencia Municipal, no sign. **Telephone** Long-distance phone office in **Hotel Nuevo**.

Batópilas and around *p221*
Banks **Tienda Grande** (Casa Morales), the store on the plaza, can change TCs at a poor rate.

Hidalgo del Parral *p224*
Banks **Banco Unión**, in Hotel Adriana complex, exchange until 1200, poor rates, similarly at **Banamex** opposite. Good rates at **Bancomer**, Plaza Principal until 1200. Opposite is **Cambios de Oro**, no commission, good rates, Mon-Fri 0900-1900, Sat until 1400. Also at **Gasolinera Palmilla** on road to Santa Bárbara, 3 km out of town. **Post office** Calle del Rayo, just over bridge from centre, 0800-1500.

Durango *p225, map p225*
Banks **Bancomer**, and many others with ATMs neatly on the west side of the plaza by cathedral. **Internet** **El Cactus**, Constitución, 1 block past the cathedral heading north, open 1000-2200. Many others in town. **Post office** Av 20 de Noviembre 500 B Ote.

Northeast Mexico

Some of the most crucial battles of the 1846-1848 War between Mexico and the United States were fought in the northeast of Mexico. Brownsville and Matamoros experienced the first outbreak of hostilities and it was here that many US troops deserted and joined the Mexican forces, giving rise to the St Patrick's Battalion. Museums in the towns and cities along the way tell this and other stories of the region. On a more contemporary note, the galleries of Monterrey are at the cutting edge of modern Mexican art. Outside the city you can explore Mexico's largest national park, venture into vast caves with stalactites and stalagmites, try rock climbing on mountains that tower above chasms, or set out on a two-day adventure circuit involving river canyoning, abseiling or swimming through tunnels. Further south you can enjoy tropical bird sanctuaries, jungle and even cloud forest and visit archaeological sites of the enigmatic Huastec civilization. You could even take in some deep-sea fishing before finally reaching Tampico and the Gulf coast or heading inland to the Colonial Highlands.

The Gulf Route from Laredo, along the Pan-American Highway, takes in the major industrial centre of Monterrey and the port of Tampico. The route passes through the coastal state of Tamaulipas before entering the regions of the Huastec and Otomí people. Then there is a choice of either continuing south or heading west to the Central Highlands via the old silver-mining centre of Pachuca. » *For Sleeping, Eating and other listings, see see pages 241-244.*

Crossing into Mexico

The first route to be opened to Mexico was the Gulf Route. Traffic from the central and eastern parts of the US can enter northeast Mexico through five gateways along the Río Bravo; at Matamoros, opposite Brownsville; at Reynosa opposite McAllen; east to west: at Ciudad Miguel Alemán, opposite Roma; at Nuevo Laredo, opposite Laredo; and at Piedras Negras, opposite Eagle Pass. The roads from these places all converge upon Monterrey (a new toll road from Nuevo Laredo is the quickest route, US$12).

By car, the best way is over the Colombia Bridge, north of Laredo: on Interstate 35, take the exit to Milo (the first exit north of the Tourist Bureau, then take Farm Road 1472 west). This crossing has little traffic and friendly staff, but it does involve a 40-km detour (it is well-signposted on the Mexican side). There is a toll on the international bridge. Once in Mexico, you can continue to Monterrey either on Route 85 via Nuevo Laredo, or by following the railway line via Ciudad Anáhuac and Lampazos.

Laredo/Nuevo Laredo → *Phone code: 867. Colour map 2, B6.*

This is the most important town of the eastern border crossings. Nuevo Laredo is a bit of a tourist trap but it is fun to stroll through the souvenir shops.

After 130 km of grey-green desert, the road from Nuevo Laredo climbs the Mamulique Pass, which it crosses at 700 m, before descending to Monterrey. From Laredo to Monterrey there is a toll road (*cuota*) and a non-toll road (*vía libre*). The latter goes through **Sabinas Hidalgo.** There is a toll bypass around Monterrey.

McAllen/Reynosa → *Phone code: 899.*

Opposite McAllen on the border, Reynosa has a population of just over 400,000 but there's not much to see.

Brownsville/Matamoros → *Phone code: 868. Colour map 2, B6.*

Matamoros is a town with a bright and unforbidding museum, designed to let prospective tourists know what they can expect in Mexico. Visas can be obtained in Brownsville on the US side of the border from the Mexican Consulate at 940 East Washington. Crossing the border by car here is quick and easy; permission is usually granted for six months (multiple entry) for passengers and vehicle, paperwork takes only about 10 minutes if everything is in order.

Eagle Pass/Piedras Negras → *Phone code: 878. Colour map 2, B5.*

Piedras Negras, is across the Río Bravo from Eagle Pass, Texas. Beyond Hermanas (137 km), the highway climbs gradually up to the plateau country. There is the **Centro Artesanal Piedras Negras** ⓘ *Edif la Estrella, Puerta México, T782-1087*, craft shop.

Saltillo → *Phone code: 884. Colour map 2, B5. Altitude: 1600 m.*

The capital of Coahuila state is a cool, dry popular resort noted for the excellence of its *sarapes* (poncho). Its 18th-century **cathedral**, a mixture of romanesque, churrigueresque, baroque and plateresque styles, is the best in northern Mexico. College students from the US attend the popular **Summer School** ⓘ *T414-9541*. There's a **tourist office** ⓘ *Blv Venustiano Carranza 3206, T/F439-2745*.

The **Museo de las Aves (Bird Museum)** ⓘ *Hidalgo y Bolívar 151 (a few blocks north of sarape factory), T140167, Tue-Sat 1000-1800, Sun 1100-1800, small admission charge, guides available*, contains hundreds of stuffed birds. Also check out the **Museo del Desierto** ⓘ *Prolongación Pérez Treviño 3745, www.museodeldesierto.org, daily 1000-1700, US$5.75*, to learn all you need to know about the Mexican desert. The house of the artist **Juan Antonio Villarreal Ríos** ⓘ *Blv Nazario Ortiz Garza, Casa 1, Manzana 1, Col Saltillo 400, T415-2707, free*, has an exhibition in every room of Dali-esque work; visitors are welcome, phone first. There are good views from **El Cerro del Pueblo** overlooking the city. An 87-km road runs east to Monterrey (both toll and non-toll).

Matehuala → *Phone code: 488.*

From Saltillo, two roads run south: one heads southwest to Zacatecas (see page 257) and the other south to Matehuala and San Luis Potosí (see page 259). Along the Saltillo-Matehuala section the scenery is worthwhile, as the road winds its way through wooded valleys. The final section passes through undulating scrub country to Matehuala, an important road junction with a fiesta from 6-20 January. It's also a good jumping-off point to visit the important mining town of Real de Catorce (see page 261). From Matehuala you go via the Colonial Heartland route to Mexico City.

Monterrey → *Phone code: 81. Colour map 2, B5. Altitude: 538 m.*

Capital of Nuevo León state and third largest city in Mexico, Monterrey, 253 km south of the border, is dominated by the **Cerro de la Silla** (saddle) from the east and the **Cerro de las Mitras** in the west. It is an important cultural centre in Mexico and there are many fine museums to visit. Its streets are congested, its layout seems unplanned and its architecture uninspiring except in the centre, which has undergone renewal and remodelling in recent years.

Ins and outs

Getting there **Aeropuerto Internacional General Mariano Escobedo** (MTY), 24 km from city centre, has flights to most cities in Mexico and to many in the US, Canada, Caribbean and Latin America. A taxi from the airport to the city centre costs US$10. The vast, long-distance bus terminal is north of the city centre on Avenida Colón (Metro Cuauhtémoc). Several major routes converge at Monterrey, connecting the industrial city to the rest of Mexico and to Nuevo Laredo, Reynosa and Matamoros on the US border.

Getting around The Monterrey metro system has two intersecting lines, which run north-south and east-west of the city. Buses run to all areas within the city; ask at the tourist office for a map.

Tourist information The **State Tourist Office** ⓘ *3rd floor, Edif Elizondo Páez, 5 de Mayo 525, T8344-4343*, provides large city maps free of charge. Another **tourist office** ⓘ *Padre Mier y Dr Coss on the east side of the Macro Plaza, Tue-Sun 1000-1700*, sometimes closes at lunchtime, but is easier to find.

Best time to visit Monterrey climate is fairly unattractive: it's too cold in winter, too hot in summer (though evenings are cool), dusty at most times and a there's shortage of water.

Sights

The centre lies just north of the Río Santa Catarina. Plaza Zaragoza, Plaza 5 de Mayo, the Explanada de los Héroes and Parque Hundido link with the Gran Plaza to the south to form the **Macro Plaza**, claimed to be the biggest civic square in the world. Its centrepiece is the **Faro de Comercio** (Commerce Beacon). To the east of the Faro is the 18th-century **cathedral**, badly damaged in the war against the US in 1846-1847, when it was used by Mexican troops as a powder magazine. Running along the west side of the northern part of the Plaza are the **Torre Latina**, **High Court** and **State Congress**; opposite, on the east side are the **Biblioteca** and the **Teatro de La Ciudad**, all modern buildings. The Macro Plaza is bordered at its southern end by the **Palacio Municipal**, and at its northern limit is the **Palacio de Gobierno**.

Museums

Calle Morelos is a pedestrian-only shopping centre. Its famous **Instituto Tecnológico**, ⓘ *Av Garza Sada 2501*, has valuable collections of books on 16th-century Mexican history. The **Museo de la Historia Mexicana** (Mexican History Museum) ⓘ *Dr Coss 445 Sur, off the north end of the Plaza, T8342-4820, 1100-1900, closed Mon, free Tue*, is an excellent interactive museum, good for children.

The **Museo de Monterrey** ⓘ *Av Alfonso Reyes 2202 Norte (500 m north of Metro Central), T8328-6060, Tue-Sun 1100-2000, Wed 1000-2000*, is in the grounds of the **Cuauhtémoc Brewery** ⓘ *visits to the brewery Mon-Fri 0930-1530, Sat 0930-1300*.

Monterrey centre

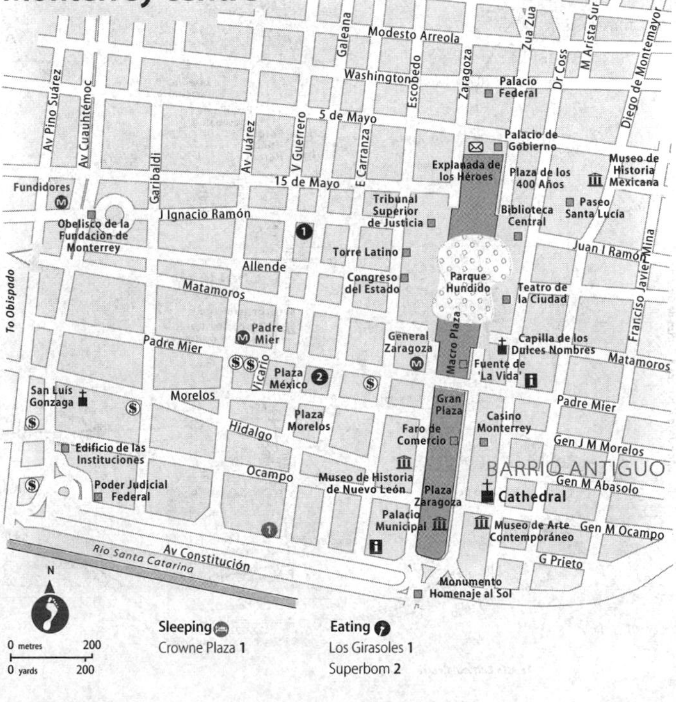

The **Museo de Arte Contemporáneo (MARCO)** ⓘ *Zua Zua y PR Jardon, T8342-4820, Wed and Sun 1100-2100, Tue, Thu-Sat 1100-1900, US$2, free Wed*, is one of the best modern art galleries in Mexico; it holds temporary shows and has a good bookshop. Two other art galleries with temporary shows are the **Pinacoteca de Nuevo León** ⓘ *Parque Niños Héroes, T8331-5462, Tue-Sun 1000-1800*, and **Centro Cultural de Arte** ⓘ *Belisario Domínguez 2140 Pte, Col Obispado, T8347-1128, Mon-Fri 0900-1300, 1500-1800*.

The **Centro Cultural Alfa** ⓘ *Garza García suburb, T8356-5696, Tue-Fri 1500-2100, Sat 1400-2100, Sun 1200-2100, closed Mon*, has a fine planetarium, an astronomy and a physics section. In a separate building is a Rufino Tamayo stained-glass window. The centre is reached by special bus from the west end of the Alameda, hourly on the hour 1500-2000.

Around Monterrey

In the hills around Monterry is the bathing resort of **Topo Chico**, 6.5 km to the northwest; water from its hot springs is bottled and sold throughout Mexico. Reached by a road heading south (extension of Avenida Gómez Morín), is **Chipinque**, an ecological park in the Sierra Madre, with magnificent views of the Monterrey area. It is popular for hiking, mountain biking and climbing, with peaks reaching 2200 m.

West of Monterrey, off the Saltillo road, are the **Grutas de García** ⓘ *about 10 km from Villa García, which is 40 km from Monterrey*. The entrance to the caves is 800 m

Monterrey

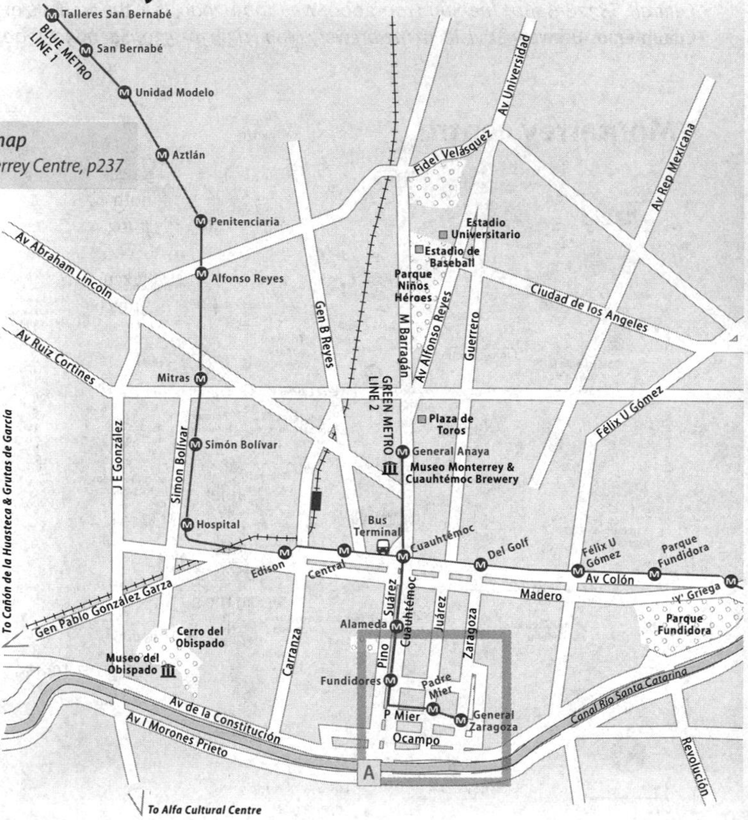

up, by cable car, and inside are beautiful stalagmites and stalactites. A tour of the caves takes 1½ hours, and it is compulsory to go in a group with a guide. You can take a bus to Villa García, but it is a dusty walk to the caves. On Sunday, **Transportes Saltillo-Monterrey** run a bus to the caves at 0900, 1000 and 1100. Otherwise, take an agency tour, for example **Osetur**; book at **Hotel Ancira.**

Hidalgo is a small town 38 km northwest of Monterrey on the Monclova road (Route 53). Dominating the area are the massive limestone cliffs of **Potrero Chico** (4 km west of town, take road leading on from Calle Francisco Villa). The cliffs are a magnet for big-wall climbers, particularly during the US winter, and have some of the hardest pitches in the world (up to 5.12d), including the 650-m-long **Sendero Luminoso** route on the central pillar of **El Toro.** A sheet guide by Jeff Jackson describing 80 of the best climbs and places to camp is available at the store on the left before you reach the *balneario.* Accommodation (**F**) at the rancho. **Autobuses Mina** leave at hourly intervals from Monterrey bus station to Hidalgo (bus station on plaza).

Monterrey to the Colonial Heartland

Heading south from Monterrey, the road threads through the narrow and lovely **Huajuco Canyon**; from the village of Santiago, a road runs to within 2 km of the **Cola de Caballo**, or Horsetail Falls, in the **Parque Nacional Cumbres de Monterrey** ⓘ *US$2.40; cost of guide US$5*, the largest in Mexico. There is a first-class hotel on the way, and you can take a *colectivo*, US$1.65, from the bus stop to the falls, and hire a horse, US$1.65, to take you to the top of the falls. Deeper into the park are other waterfalls: the 75-m **Cascada El Chipitín** and **Cascada Lagunillas**. There is a two-day circuit, *Recorrido de Matacanes*, starting at Las Adjuntas, taking in both these falls and involving river canyoning, abseiling and swimming through tunnels. Ask at **Asociación de Excursionismo y Montañismo** in Monterrey (see page 242).

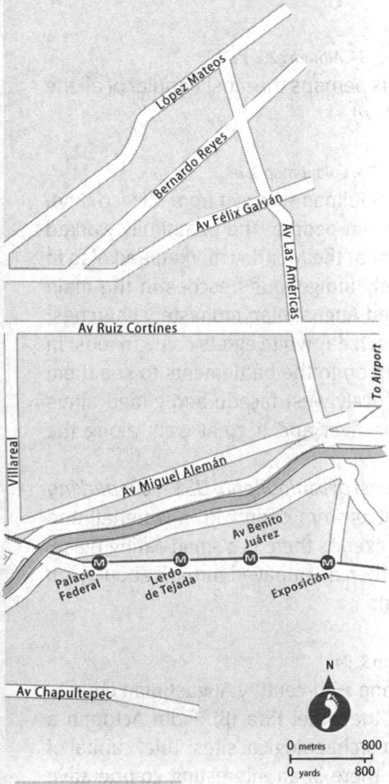

Ciudad Victoria → *Phone code: 834.*

Colour map 2, C6. Altitude: 336 m.

Capital of Tamaulipas state, Ciudad Victoria is a quiet, clean, unhurried city with a shaded plaza. The Parque Siglo 21 is the same end of town as the bus station. The centrepiece is a planetarium, which looks like a huge red ball that landed on the banks of the Río San Marcos. The **Museo de Antropología e Historia** ⓘ *on the plaza*, has a good section on the Huastec culture. There's a **tourist office** ⓘ Calle *8 Anaya y Olivia Ramírez 1287, T/F316-1074.*

The north-south streets (parallel to the Sierra) have names and numbers, the east-west streets have only names.

Ciudad Mante and around → *Phone code: 831. Colour map 2, C6.*

After crossing the Tropic of Cancer the road enters the solid green jungle of the tropical lowlands. Ciudad Mante (Route 85), 137 km south of Ciudad Victoria, is almost exactly the mid-way point between Matamoros and Mexico City and makes a convenient stopover place despite being a grubby city. It has a **Museo de Antropología e Historia**, with objects from the Huastec culture.

Forty-five kilometres north of Ciudad Mante is the village of **Gómez Farías**, an important centre for ornithological research: the highlands above the village represent the northernmost extent of several tropical vegetation formations. Many tropical bird species reach the northern limit of their range. Gómez Farías is reached by turning west off the main highway, 14 km over a paved road to the town plaza. From there, an easy 2-km walk provides excellent views of bird habitats.

South of Ciudad Mante, at Km 548 from Mexico City, is **Antiguo Morelos** where a road turns off west to San Luis Potosí (see page 259) 314 km, and Guadalajara (see page 290).

Tampico → *Phone code: 833. Colour map 2, C6.*

The port of Tampico, on the Gulf of Mexico, is definitely not a tourist attraction, although fishing (both sea and river) is excellent. It is reached by a fine road from Ciudad Mante, in a rich sugar-growing area. Tampico was founded in 1522 by Gonzalo de Sandoval but was sacked by pirates in the 17th century and refounded in 1823.

Ciudad Valles → *Phone code: 481. Colour map 2, C6.*

Ciudad Valles, on a winding river, is a popular stopover with many hotels. **Museo Regional Huasteco** ⓘ *Rotarios y Artes (or Peñaloza), Mon-Fri 1000-1200, 1400-1800*, is the centre of archaeological and ethnographic research for the so-called Huasteca region.

Tamazunchale → *Phone code: 483. Colour map 3, B4. Altitude: 206 m.*

With riotous tropical vegetation, Tamazunchale is perhaps the most popular of all the overnight stops on this route (see Sleeping, below).

Ixmiquilpan and around → *Phone code: 759. Colour map 3, B4.*

An area of 23,300 sq km north and south of Ixmiquilpan (Km 169 from Mexico City), just off the highway, is inhabited by 65,000 Otomí people. The beautifully worked Otomí belts and bags may sometimes be bought at the Monday market, and also in the *artesanía* shop in the main street. See early indigenous frescoes in the main church, one of several 16th-century battlemented Augustinian monastery-churches; the monastery is open to the public. At sunset each day white egrets come to roost in the trees outside the church; it's worth going up on to the battlements to see them swoop down. The church of **El Carmen** has a lovely west façade and gilded altars inside. There is a 16th-century **bridge** over the river and a great walk along the *ahuehuete* tree-lined banks.

The **Barranca de Tolantongo** ⓘ *37 km northeast of Ixmiquilpan, US$2, car parking US$2 at entrance to recreational area*, is about 1500 m deep with a waterfall and thermal spring; camping is permitted and at weekends there is a small eating place. To get there take the road towards **El Cardonal**, then an unpaved turn-off about 3 km before El Cardonal (there is a bus from Pachuca).

Actopan to Tula → *Phone code: 772. Colour map 3, B4.*

Actopan (Km 119 from the capital) has another fine 16th-century Augustinian church, convent, and an impressive open chapel and the **Hotel Rira** (B). From Actopan a 56-km branch road runs to one of Mexico's great archaeological sites: Tula, capital of the Toltecs (see page 136).On the way to Tula there is an interesting co-operative village, **Cruz Azul**, where there are free Sunday-morning concerts at 1000 in front of main market. At **Colonia** (Km 85), a road runs left for 8 km to Pachuca (see page 138).

Sleeping

Laredo/ Nuevo Laredo *p235*
B **Reforma**, Av Guerrero 822, T712-6250. Good, clean rooms.
C **Alameda**, Gonzalez 2715, on plaza, T712-5050. Good spot, and bright rooms.
E **Calderón**. With bath, hot water, fan, run-down, friendly.

Camping
The better of the 2 trailer parks is on the east side of Interstate 35, Main St, exit, 10 mins from border.

McAllen/Reynosa *p235*
E **Arcade**, corner of Cedar and North 12th St, 2 blocks from **Greyhound** terminal, south from **Valley Transit** bus terminal.

Brownsville/Matamoros *p235*
A **Ritz**, Matamoros 612 y Siete, T812-1190. Good all-round services, including a gym.

Saltillo *p236*
There are several hotels a short distance from the plaza at the intersection of Allende and Aldama, the main streets. Saltillo is a conference centre with many hotels in the luxury range.
A **Rancho El Morillo**, Prolongación Obregón Sur y Echeverría, T417-4376, www.elmorillo.com. A converted hacienda, excellent value, meals available.
C **Jardín**, Padre Flores 211, T412-5916. Basic, cold water, safe motorcycle parking.
D **Brico**, Ramos Arizpe Pte 552, T412-5146. Cheap, noisy, clean, tepid water.

Camping
Trailer park, turn right on road into town from Monterrey between **Hotel del Norte** and **Kentucky Fried Chicken**. Hook-ups, toilets, basic.

Matehuala *p236*
A **Trailerpark Las Palmas**, north of town (Km 617), T882-0001. Clean, English spoken and paperbacks sold, bowling alley and miniature golf.
C **El Dorado**, nearby, T882-0174. Cheaper. Recommended.
E **Alamo**, Guerrero 116, T882-0017. Hot showers, clean and very pleasant rooms, safe motorcycle parking, friendly. Recommended.

Monterrey *p236, map p237*
It can be difficult to get accommodation. There are many hotels between Colón and Reforma, but nothing below US$15. Most of the cheap hotels are in the area around the bus station (metros Central and Cuauhtémoc).
L **Crowne Plaza**, Av Constitución 300 Ote, near Plaza Zaragoza, T8319-6000, www.hotelesmilenium.com. The best.
B **Yamallel**, Zaragoza 912, Norte Madero, T8375-3500, www.hotelyamallel.com.mx. Good.
C **Motel/Trailerpark Nueva Castilla**, on Highway 85 before Saltillo bypass. Motel with spaces for RVs, pool, hot showers, clean but drab.
D **La Silla**, Juan Méndez, opposite Monterrey La Silla (**B**), its sister hotel. Clean, friendly. Recommended.

Ciudad Victoria *p239*
There are several cheaper hotels by the bus station and in the centre.
AL **Best Western Santorín**, Cristóbal Colón Norte 349, T318 1515. A/c, TV, parking, restaurant.
C **Los Monteros**, Plaza Hidalgo, T312-0300. Downtown motel. OK for the price.

Camping
Victoria RV Trailer Park, Libramiento 101-85 (follow signs), T/F312-4824. Good service, electricity, hot showers. US$15.

Ciudad Mante and around *p240*
A **Mante**, Guerrero 500 Norte, T232-0990. Probably the best hotel, in shaded grounds at north edge of business sector.
C **Monterrey**, Av Juárez 503 Ote, T232-2712, in old sector. With bath, hot water, a/c, cable TV, helpful manager speaks English, safe parking, restaurant not so good. Recommended.

Tampico *p240*
B **Nuevo León**, 2½ blocks north of Plaza de la Libertad, Aduana N 107, T124-370. With a/c, shower, clean.
E **Hawaii**, Héroes del Cañonero 609, 2 blocks east of Plaza Libertad, T234-1887. Dark rooms, clean. There are others on this street.

Camping
RVs can stay in the parking lot of the airport, US$15 per vehicle, noisy from traffic.

Ciudad Valles *p240*
B **San Fernando**, T382-0184, on main highway. Clean, large rooms, a/c, TV, parking.
D **Condesa**, Av Juárez 109, T382-0015. Clean, basic, fan, friendly, OK.

Camping
El Bañito, 11 km south of town. With warm sulphur pools.

Ixmiquilpan *p240*
C **Hotel Diana**, Av Insurgentes Pte 5, T723-0758. Rear buildings slightly dearer rooms, safe parking. Recommended.
E **Hotel/Restaurant Los Portales**, 1 block from main square. Clean, safe parking.

Eating

Saltillo *p236*
ƚƚ **El Campanario Saloon and Grill**, Ocampo, 1200-2400. Recommended.
ƚ **Arcasa**, Victoria. Good local food.
ƚ **Victoria**, Padre Flores 221, by Hotel Hidalgo. Has reasonable *comida*.

Monterrey *p236, map p237*
ƚƚ-ƚ **Los Girasoles**, Juan Ignacio Ramón 200 Ote (esq Guerrero, 1 block from Juárez). Good-value vegetarian.
ƚ **Superbom**, Padre Mier. Good menu.

Ciudad Victoria *p239*
ƚƚ **Chavos**, Calle 12, Hidalgo y Juárez. All-you-can-eat buffet.
ƚƚ **Daddy's** on the plaza. A sort of Denny's, with a Mexican touch for the homesick North American.
ƚ **Café Cantón**, ½ a block from the plaza on Calle 9. Congregation place for locals.

Tampico *p240*
ƚ **Centro Gastronómico Mercado de Comida** east of the market, for many cheap restaurants.
ƚ **Emir**, Olmos between Díaz Mirón and Madero. Good for breakfast.

Festivals and events

Saltillo *p236*
Aug Local feria during the 1st half of the month; cheap accommodation impossible to find at this time.
30 May and **30 Aug** Indigenous dances and picturesque ceremonies
Oct Bullfights during fiestas.
Dec *Pastorelas*, telling the story of the Nativity, are performed in the neighbourhood in Christmas week.

Activities and tours

Monterrey *p236, map p237*
Adventure sports
Asociación de Excursionismo y Montañismo, Washington Pte 2222-B, Col María Luisa, T8327-1929 (ask for Sr Angel Medina).

Spectator sports
Baseball **Estadio de Baseball Monterrey**, Parque Niños Héroes, T8351-8022.
Bullfighting **Plaza de Toros**, M Barragán y Alfonso Reyes, north of bus station, T8374-0505.
Football **Estadio Tecnológico**, off Av Garza Sada, southeast of centre, T8375-8200; **Estadio Universitario**, Parque Niños Héroes, north of centre, T8376-2238.

Tampico *p240*
Fishing
Apr-Aug is the Deep-Sea Fishing competition season, with several major competitions.

Phone codes *Nuevo Laredo 867; Reynosa 899; Matamoros 868; Piedras Negras 878; Saltillo 884; Matehuala 488; Monterrey 81; Ciudad Victoria 834; Ciudad Mante 831; Tampico 833; Ciudad Valles 481; Tamazunchale 483; Ixmiquilpan 759; Actopan 772.*

Transport

Laredo/Nuevo Laredo *p235*

Bus

The Nuevo Laredo bus station is not near the border; take a bus to the border, then walk across. You cannot get a bus from the Laredo Greyhound terminal to the Nuevo Laredo terminal unless you have an onward ticket. Connecting tickets from Houston via Laredo to Monterrey are available, 14 hrs. Some buses to Laredo connect with Greyhound buses in the US.

To **Guadalajara**, 9 a day, 18 hrs, US$72. To **Mexico City** with Estrella Blanca/ Transportes del Norte, 9 buses a day, 16 hrs, US$68-92. To **Monterrey**, hourly departures, 4 hrs, US$12. To **San Luis Potosí**, US$52. To **Tampico** and **Morelia** 17 hrs, US$56.

Car

Car insurance Johnson's Mexico Insurance, Tepeyac Agent, Lafayette and Santa Ursula (59 and Interstate 35), US$2.60 per day, open 24 hrs, recommended. Sanborn's, 2212 Santa Ursula (Exit 16 on Interstate 35), T723-3657, www.sanbornsinsurance.com Expensive, open 24 hrs.

Brownsville/Matamoros *p235*

Bus Several lines run 1st-class buses to **Mexico City**, 14 hrs. Transportes del Norte to **Cd Victoria** regular departures, US$15.50, 4 hrs.

Saltillo *p236*

Air

The airport (SLW) is 16 km from town. Flights to **Mexico City** daily with Mexicana. Aerolitoral flies to **Guadalajara** and **Monterrey**.

Bus

The terminal is on Blv Echeverría, 3 km south of centre (yellow bus marked 'Periférico' from Allende y Lerdo de Tejada in centre); minibuses to Pérez Treviño y Allende (for centre) will take luggage. Bus to **Cd Acuña**, 2nd class, 8 hrs, US$23. To **Hidalgo de Parral**, 9 hrs, US$32. To **Mexico City**, 1st class, 11 hrs, US$48. To **San Luis Potosí**, US$20. To **Monterrey** and **Nuevo Laredo** with Transportes del Norte. For **Torreón** 3 hrs, US$16, all buses originate in Monterrey and tickets are only sold when bus arrives; be prepared to stand.

Matehuala *p236*

Bus **Mexico City**: 8 hrs, US$31. **Monterrey**: 4 hrs, US$18. **Real de Catorce**: US$3. **San Luis Potosí**: with Estrella Blanca, 2½ hrs, US$8.50.

Monterrey *p236, map p237*

Air

Gen Mariano Escobedo airport (MTY), 24 km from centre. Daily flights from **Mexico City** take 1 hr 20 mins. Good links to many other Mexican cities and numerous flights to the **US** and **Canada** and to **Havana**, Cuba.

Airline offices AeroCalifornia, T8345-9700. AeroMéxico, T8343-5560. American Airlines, T8340-3031. Aviacsa, T8153-4304. Mexicana, T800-715-0220.

Bus

Terminal on Av Colón, between Calzada B Reyes and Av Pino Suárez (Metro Cuauhtémoc), T318-3737. To **Santiago**, for Cola de Caballo falls, US$2.20. To **Mexico City**, 12 hrs. A more scenic trip is from Mexico City (northern bus terminal) to **Cd Valles**, 10 hrs, from where there are many connecting buses to Monterrey. To **Chihuahua**, with Transportes del Norte, 8 a day, 12 hrs, US$46. To **Guadalajara**, US$42. To **Matamoros**, with Transportes del Norte, 4 hrs, US$18. To **Nuevo Laredo**, departures every hr, 4 hrs, US$14. Frequent buses to **Saltillo**, but long queues for tickets. To **San Luis Potosí**, US$26. To **Tampico**, 7-8 hrs, US$26. To **Torreón**, US$20.

Car

If driving to **Saltillo**, there is nothing to indicate you are on the toll-road until it is too late. The toll is US$7. Look for the old road.

Car rental Monterrey, Serafín Peña 740-A Sur, T344-6510. **National**, Escobedo Sur 1011 Local 8, T344-6363.

Metro

There are 2 metro lines. The **blue line**, the longer one, runs south from the suburb of San Bernabé and then makes a right-angle turn traversing the city eastwards passing by the bus and train stations. It connects with the **green line** (at Cuauhtémoc near the bus station), which runs south into the centre. Tickets bought from machines (2 pesos a ticket, less for more than one).

Ciudad Victoria *p239*
Bus The terminal is on the outskirts near the ring road northeast of the town centre. Omnibuses Blancos to **Cd Valles**, US$12. To **Mexico City**, 10 hrs, US$43-63.

Tampico *p240*
Air
The Francisco Javier Mina Airport (TAM), T238-0571, is 8 km from the centre. Mexicana has daily flights to **Mexico City** and Aerolitoral flies to **San Antonio** (Texas). There are good links with towns in Northern Mexico and on the Gulf coast, and Aero California flies to **Los Angeles** via **Mexico City**, **Tepic** and **Tijuana**. Continental Express flies to **Dallas** and **Houston**.

Airline offices Aero California, T213-8400. AeroMéxico, T217-0939. Mexicana, T213-9600.

Bus
The bus station is several km from the centre on Av Ejército Mexicano on the far side of Laguna del Carpintero. *Colectivos* to bus station leave from Olmos between market and plaza. To **Cd Valles**, US$9. To **Mexico City**, 8 hrs, US$27. To **Monterrey**, 7-8 hrs, US$29. To **San Luis Potosí**, 7 hrs, US$24.

Ciudad Valles *p240*
Bus Omnibus Ote to **San Luis Potosí**, US$11, 4 hrs; **Mexico City**, US$26, 10 hrs.

Directory

Laredo/Nuevo Laredo *p235*
Banks UNB Convent and Matamoros charges 1% commission on TCs, Mon-Fri 0830-1600. IBC, no commission under US$500. **Embassies and consulates** Mexican Consulate, Farragut and Maine, 4th light on the right after leaving Interstate 35, Mon-Fri 0800-1400, helpful.

Saltillo *p236*
Banks Bancomer, Allende y Victoria. Banamex, Allende y Ocampo.
Telephones Long-distance calls from Café Victoria, Padre Flores 221, near market.
Post office Victoria 223.

Monterrey *p236, map p237*
Banks Plenty of ATMs in town. **Embassies and consulates** British (Honorary), T8333-7598. Canadian, T8344-3200. Mon-Fri 0900-1330 and 1430-1730. French, T8336-4498. German, T8338-5223. Guatemalan, T8372-8648. Israeli, T8336-1325. Netherlands, T8342-5055. Swedish, T8346-3090. Swiss, T8338-3675. US, T8345-2120. **Medical services** Hospital General de IMSS, Pino Suárez y J I Ramón, T8345-5355. Angeles Verdes, T8340-2113. Red Cross, T8375-1212. **Post office** Palacio Federal, Av 5 de Mayo y Zaragoza (behind Government Palace), T342-4003.

Tampico *p240*
Post office Madero 309 Ote, T212-1927.
Embassies and consulates Germany, 2 de Enero, 102 Sur-A, T212-9784. Also deals with British affairs. **Medical services** Red Cross, T212-1313.

Colonial Heartland

For centuries, the mines of Central Mexico churned out much of the world's silver and a fair amount of gold and precious stones too. Spanish-style architecture, built with the fortunes amassed from silver and gold, is at its most opulent and impressive in the magnificent towns and cities of the colonial highlands. While the mines of Zacatecas, San Luis Potosí and Guanajuato supplied the precious metal to the Spanish crown, the states of Aguascalientes and Querétaro were important supply centres and stopovers on the silver route to the capital and the port of Veracruz. Mining is still important in this area and many of these old cities are today important modern industrial centres, mostly with sprawling suburbs; but they mostly manage to retain at their core the magnificence of their colonial past. The 'ghost towns' of Pozas and Real de Catorce, once thriving mining centres, have not fared so well, but it is fascinating to wander through their semi-deserted streets. The years of heavy-handed Spanish rule and obvious inequalities led to discontent and in the early 19th century this region was the Cradle of Independence; nearly every town or village played a part in the break with Spain and many museums and monuments tell the story. Colonial rule relied heavily on the work of the missionaries and a tour of the 18th-century Missions of Querétaro, well off the beaten track, with a stop-off at the thermal baths and opal mines of Tequisquiapan, is well worth the hair-raising journey of 700 curves. *» For Sleeping, Eating and other listings, see pages 262-275.*

Querétaro *» pp262-275. Colour map 3, B3.*

→ Phone code: 442. Altitude: 1865 m.

An important industrial centre and state capital, Querétaro was founded in 1531 and the name means 'Place of Rocks' in Tarascan. As gateway to the Colonial Heartland, the sprawling city hides a treasured city centre of pedestrian walkways and colonial architecture. Sights are somewhat limited, but the ambience makes a visit worthwhile and provides time to contemplate the historical significance of the city. Hidalgo's rising in 1810 was plotted here, and it was here that Emperor Maximilian surrendered after defeat, was tried and shot on 19 June 1867, on the Cerro de las Campanas (the Hill of Bells), outside the city. It's also a good base to plan trips to the Peñón de Bernal and the rarely visited Missions of Querétaro in the Sierra Gorda to the east.

Ins and outs

Getting there The Central Camionera (bus station) is 5 km southeast of the centre on the Mexico City-León highway. There are regular services to Mexico City's Terminal del Norte and the airport (Sala D). Querétaro is at the crossroads of Route 57 (San Luis Potosí-Mexico City) and Route 45 to Celaya, León and Aguascalientes.

Getting around Querétaro centre is reasonably compact; walking tours are very popular. City buses Nos 8 and 19 link the town centre and bus station; make sure they say 'Central Camionera' or 'Terminal de Autobuses'. There is a **tourist office** ⓘ *Pasteur Norte 4, on Plaza Independencia at the junction with Libertad, T212-1412.*

Sights

In 1810, Doña Josefa Ortiz de Domínguez, wife of the mayor and prominent member of a group plotting for Independence, got word to Father Hidalgo that their plans for revolt had been discovered. Hidalgo immediately gave the cry (*El Grito*) for Independence. Today, every 15 September at 2300, El Grito is given from the balcony of the **Palacio Municipal** ⓘ *T238-5000, Mon-Fri 0800-2000, Sun 0800-1800*, which was once home of Doña Josefa La Corregidora and can be visited. (El Grito is echoed on every civic balcony thoughout Mexico).

The **Santa Rosa de Viterbo** church and monastery was remodelled by Francisco Tresguerras. He also reconstructed the **Templo de Santa Clara**, one of the loveliest churches in Mexico, with fine gilded carvings. The 16th-century church and monastery of **Santa Cruz** served as the headquarters of Maximilian and his forces and later as the Emperor's prison before he faced the firing squad in 1867. There is a good view from the bell tower. The church of **San Felipe**, recently restored, is now the cathedral. The splendid **Palacio Federal**, once an Augustinian convent with exceptionally fine cloisters, has been restored and houses an art gallery containing some beautiful works. The **Teatro de la República**, by Jardín Zenea, is where Maximilian and his generals were tried, and where the Constitution of 1917 (still in force) was drafted.

A little out of town to the west on Avenida Zaragoza **Los Arcos** form an impressive **aqueduct**, built in 1726, and the enduring symbol of Querétaro.

The important and elegant **Museo Regional** ⓘ *Tue-Sun 1000-1900, US$3*, is on the main plaza, known as Plaza de Armas or as Jardín Obregón. It contains much material on the Independence movement and the 1864 to 1867 period leading to the imprisonment and death of Maximilian.

Around Querétaro » pp262-275.

Missions of Querétaro

The road to the Missions of Querétaro goes through the small market town of **Ezequiel Montes**, reached either by a road turning northeast from the main

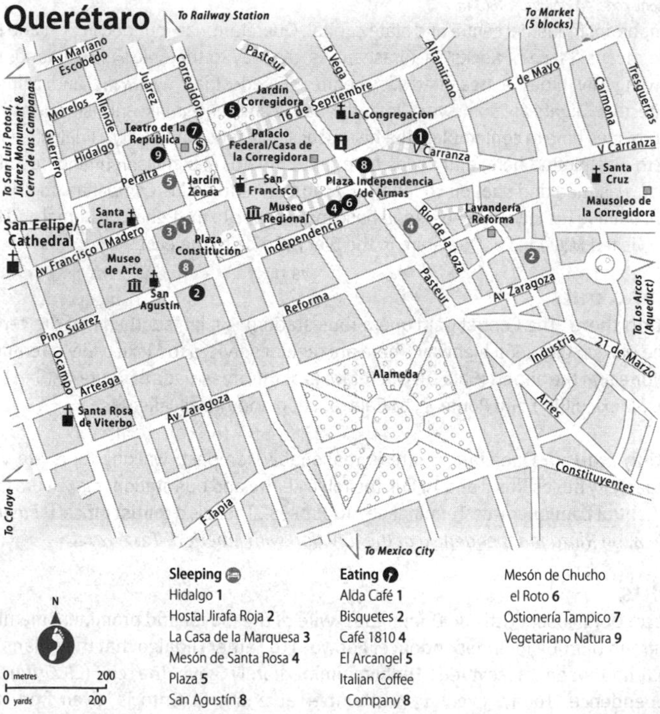

Missions of Querétaro

A little-known feature of Querétaro is the existence of five 18th-century missions in the far northeast of the state. The missions were founded by Fray Junípero de la Serra, who later went on to establish missions in California. He is also said to have planted a miraculous tree in the convent of Santa Cruz in the city of Querétaro by thrusting his staff into the ground. The tree is apparently the only one of its kind in the world to have cruciform thorns.

All five missions – Jalpan, Concá, Landa de Matamoros, Tilaco and Tancoyol – most easily visited from Jalpan, have been restored, and two of them have hotels nearby. The journey itself requires something of a head for heights – while it is a dramatic and scenic journey climbing the massif of the Sierra Gorda, there are said to be 700 curves en route. There is a slightly shorter way, but that has over 1000. If travelling by bus, allow at least three days to enjoy the tour of the missions.

highway, 21 km east of Querétaro, or by Route 120 from San Juan del Río (see below). Two places of interest off the first-mentioned road are the towns of **Colón**, 14 km off the road with 17th-century Templo de Nuestra Señora de los Dolores de Soriana, and **Bernal**, 75 km from Querétaro, a centre for clothing, blankets, wall hangings and carpets. Near Bernal is the remarkable **Peñón de Bernal**, a massive rocky outcrop 350 m high. On the night before and the day of the spring equinox (21 March) there is a **festival** held here. Local indigenous people believe the mountain is an energy point, because of its distinctive shape, and come to get energy from the first sun of the year. Of its kind, it is considered the third largest after the Rock of Gibraltar and the Sugarloaf Mountain in Rio de Janeiro.

Jalpan, the first of the missions in the region, becomes visible way below in a broad, lush valley. It is the largest of the missions, which are located in the high valleys spreading out from the town. Jalpan was the first to be founded in 1774 and has cloisters in addition to the main church. The town itself is picturesque without being spoilt. It makes a good base for day trips to the other missions. There are also pleasant walks along tree-lined riverbanks.

The missions in the area (see box, page 247) are distinguished by the profusion of baroque carving, their superb location and the care with which they have been conserved. They make a good trip of a few days by bus or car: **Landa de Matamoros**, 18 km east of Jalpan; **Tilaco**, 25 km beyond Landa to the east; and **Tancoyol**, 37 km to the north of Landa. The roads are good apart from the last 15 km into Tilaco.

San Juan del Río → *Phone code: 427. Colour map 3, B3.*

Forty-eight kilometres from Querétaro is San Juan del Río, near where some of the best fighting bulls are raised; the town is a centre for handicrafts, and also for polishing gemstones: opals and amethysts.

Tequisquiapan → *Phone code: 414. Colour map 3, B3.*

A branch road runs northeast from San Juan to the picturesque town of Tequisquiapan, with thermal baths, a fine climate, watersports, weekend residences and expensive, good hotels. The town is deserted from Monday to Thursday and big reductions in hotel prices can be found. There is a geyser, at **Tecozautla**, one hour 15 minutes from Tequisquiapan.

Cadereyta → *Phone code: 441. Colour map 3, B3.*

North of Tequisquiapan is Cadereyta (Km 75), colonial in style, with two noteworthy churches in the main square, one dedicated to St Peter, the other to St Paul. The latter houses an important collection of colonial religious art.

San Joaquín → *Phone code: 441. Colour map 3, B3.*

East of Route 120, the ruins at San Joaquín (Km 138), Ranas and Toluquilla, have been only partially excavated. You must register upon arriving and a donation is requested. The sites have been attributed to the Toltecs and the Chichimecs. **Ranas** ⓘ *US$1*, is a 30-minute walk from the village and has stupendous views from a series of terraced platforms and pyramids; **Toluquilla** lies 10 km from the village (poorly marked road). Although there were only, at most, 200 inhabitants, there are six ball courts. Tarantulas abound! Fifteen minutes' walk from San Joaquín is a beautiful cave (**Las Grutas**). San Joaquín is famous for the annual Huapango dance festival on 15 April.

The roads to both ruins are steep and the ruins are often swathed in mist.

The bends really start after Vizarrón. Much of the journey from here on is through rather arid and dramatic terrain with gorges and panoramic views. The high point is called **La Puerta del Cielo** (Door to the Sky), which is apt as you can actually look down on the clouds. As the road begins to descend, so the vegetation becomes more tropical and the weather gets much warmer. If driving there are plenty of petrol stations, but keep topping up just to be safe.

Jalpan → *Phone code: 441. Colour map 3, B4. Altitude: 700 m.*

Jalpan, the first of the missions in the region, becomes visible way below in a broad, lush valley. It is the largest of the missions, which are located in the high valleys spreading out from the town. Jalpan was the first to be founded in 1774 and has cloisters in addition to the main church. The town itself is picturesque without being spoilt. It makes a good base for day trips to the other missions. There are also pleasant walks along tree-lined riverbanks. The town **museum** ⓘ *daily 1000-1500, US$0.50 is worth a visit.*

The missions in the area (see box, page 247) are distinguished by the profusion of baroque carving, their superb location and the care with which they have been conserved. They make a good trip of a few days by bus or car: **Landa de Matamoros,** 18 km east of Jalpan; **Tilaco,** 25 km beyond Landa to the east; and **Tancoyol,** 37 km to the north of Landa. The roads are good apart from the last 15 km into Tilaco.

Concá → *Altitude: 500 m.*

Thirty-eight kilometres northwest of Jalpan is Concá. At the bridge of Concá a hot-water river flows into one with cold water. The church is built on a ridge, creating a dramatic skyline when viewed from below. The village is very small with two restaurants. *Acamaya* (freshwater crayfish) are a local speciality. There's an hourly bus to Concá from Jalpan, US$1.30.

Xilitla → *Phone code: 489. Colour map 3, B4.*

About 87 km west of Jalpan is the charming village of Xilitla which would normally be overlooked but for the lush tropical valley and comfortable climate. The late Edward James, born 1907, millionaire heir to the Phelps Dodge copper fortune and with connections to the British royal family, fell in love with the place and built Las Pozas, a house and gardens of architectural eccentricity that are matched only by their setting. Las Pozas is 30 minutes' walk from Xilitla and is fascinating with extravagant concrete structures intertwined with exuberant vegetation, waterfalls, birds and butterflies.

Celaya

→ *Phone code: 461. Colour map 3, B3. Altitude: 1800 m.*

Celaya is famous for its confectionery, especially a caramel spread called *cajeta* or *dulce de leche*, and its churches, built by Mexico's great architect Francisco Eduardo Tresguerras (1759-1833), a native of the town. His best is considered to be **El Carmen**, with an elegant tower and dome. He also built a fine bridge over the Río de la Laja. Founded on 1 January 1571, the city's prosperity came from the fertile soils of the region, which helped the growing town to develop as an important trade and supply centre for mining communities in the region. The **tourist office** ⓘ *Casa del Diezmo, Juárez 204, T/F613-4313*, is helpful.

Not surprisingly the appeal of the town lies in the architecture of Tresguerras. **Templo del Carmen** was built by Tresguerras in 1802-1807; the interior and exterior are neoclassical with a simple elegance, and you can see Tresguerras' own paintings inside. **Convento de San Francisco** is one of the largest in the country, with a 17th-century baroque interior; the façade of the cloisters was rebuilt by Tresguerras. **Templo de San Francisco** was rebuilt in 1683 after the original chapel was demolished. The façade is neoclassical and was rebuilt, together with the altars, by Tresguerras in 1810-1820. **Claustro Agustino** dates from the beginning of the 17th century and was the municipal prison until 1961, but now doubles as the Casa de la Cultura. **Templo de San Agustín** was built in 1609 in the plateresque style. **Templo de la Tercera Orden** is another of Tresguerras' neoclassical works, built in 1820 with marvellous altars. The **Columna de la Independencia** was designed by Tresguerras and was the first monument in the country to celebrate Mexico's freedom in 1828. **Torre Hidráulica**, also known as the **bola de agua** (ball of water), has been adopted as the symbol of the city; it was inaugurated on the centenary of Mexico's Independence from Spain and holds one million litres of water. **Casa del Diezmo**, built at the end of the 17th century, now houses the tourist office. The **Presidencia Municipal** has impressive murals up the stairways in the entrance off the main square, a metamorphosis of people and events in Mexico's history, created in 1980 by local artist Octavio Ocampo González. The **Mausoleo de Tresguerras** is a baroque chapel where the famous architect is buried.

Irapuato

» *pp262-275. Colour map 3, B3.*

→ *Phone code: 462.*

Irapuato is **World Strawberry Capital** and is justly noted for the delicious fruit. In the town centre, around **Plaza de los Fundadores** and the **Jardín Hidalgo**, there is a cluster of historic buildings. The **Templo del Hospital**, built around 1550, rebuilt 1617, façade completed 1733, is said to have the country's largest chandelier. Outside, the **Cruz Monolítica** commemorates the visit of San Sebastian of Aparicio. The façade of the **Templo de San Francisco**, also known as El Convento (1799), is a mixture of baroque and neoclassical. The huge **Parroquia** (parish church) was rebuilt in the mid-18th century. The **Presidencia Municipal**, 19th century, incorporates a former 18th-century school, the **Colegio de Enseñanza para Niños**. The fountain, **Fuente de los Delfines**, was given to the town by Emperor Maximilian. There's a **tourist office** ⓘ *Escuela Médico Militar 60, Col Jardines, T624-7174, www.irapuato.gob.mx*.

Unfortunately, the centre of town has been invaded by unsightly and incongruous modern buildings, but just to the edge is the 16th-century church of **San José**, with fine examples of American indigenous art, and the **Templo of Nuestra Señora de Guadalupe** (1890), with a striking late neoclassical gold-leaf-decorated interior.

San Miguel de Allende

▸▸ *pp262-275. Colour map 3, B3.*

➔ *Phone code: 415. Altitude: 1850 m.*

This charming old town on a steep hillside facing the broad sweep of the Río Laja and the distant blue of the Guanajuato mountains is 50 km north of Querétaro by paved road and has pretty much been taken over by North Americans seeking the combination of language schools and relaxed living with an arty edge that this pleasant colonial town has. It was founded as San Miguel in 1542, with Allende added in honour of the Independence patriot who was born there. Its twisting cobbled streets rise in terraces to the mineral spring of El Chorro, from where the blue and yellow tiled cupolas of some 20 churches can be seen. It has been declared a national monument.

Ins and outs

Getting there The long-distance bus station is west of the town centre along Calle Canal. The town centre can be reached by taxi or bus. The nearest airport is at Silao, close to León, also called Aeropuerto del Bajío.

Getting around Most places of interest can be reached on foot. **Walking tours** of old houses and gardens leave from the **Jardín** ⓘ *Insurgentes 25, between Reloj and Hidalgo, T152-0293, Sun 1200, 4 hrs, US$10.* The **tourist office** ⓘ *Plaza Prinicpal, next to the church, T152-6565,* is good for finding hotels, English spoken, city map.

Sights

Social life revolves around the market and the Jardín, or Plaza Principal, an open-air living room for San Migueleans. Around it are the colonial **Palacio Municipal**, several hotels and **La Parroquia** (parish church), adorned in the late 19th century by Zeferino Gutiérrez, an indigenous stonemason who provided the austere Franciscan front with a beautiful façade and a Gothic tower. See also the mural in the chapel. The church of **San Felipe Neri**, with its fine baroque façade, is at the southwest end of the market. Notable among the baroque façades and doors rich in churrigueresque details are the **Casa del Mayorazgo de Canal** and the **San Francisco** church, which was designed by Tresguerras. The convent of **La Concepción**, built in 1734, now houses an art school, the **Centro Cultural Ignacio Ramírez Nigromonte,** locally known as Escuela de Bellas Artes

San Miguel de Allende

Sleeping
Casa de Huéspedes 1
Casa de Sierra Nevada 11
Casa Luna B&B 2
Hostal Alcatraz 4
La Mansión del Bosque 5
Parador San Sebastián 7
Posada Carmina 8
Posada de las Monjas 9
Posada 'El Mayorazgo' 3
Rincón del Cielo 12
Sautto 13
Vista Hermosa Taboada 14

Eating
Café etc 1
Casa Mexas 2
El Buen Café 3
El Infierno 4
El Jardín 5
El Tomate 6
La Piñata 7
Mama Mía 8
Mesón de San José 9
Tío Lucas 10

(good *cafetería* in its courtyard). The summer residence of the Condes de Canal, on San Antonio, contains the art school and a language school, the **Instituto Allende**, started by Stirling Dickinson (which has an English-language library and runs Spanish courses). A magnificent view of the city can be gained from the mirador on the Querétaro road.

Around San Miguel de Allende

A good all-day hike can be made to the **Palo Huérfano** mountain on the south side of town. Take the road to just before the radio pylon then take the trails to the summit, where there are oaks and pines. **El Charco del Ingenio** ⓘ *T154-4715, daily, US$2.75*, are botanical gardens that cover an area of 64 ha, with lovely views, a deep canyon, an artificial lake and cacti garden of many species. There are great views and hikes around the canyon and lakes, and it's a good spot for watching the sunset – but don't wander too far, it closes at dusk. To get there, take a bus to El Gigante shopping centre, turn left and continue for 15 minutes, or go up Calle Homobono, a more interesting and attractive route.

Dolores Hidalgo

» *pp262-275. Colour map 3, B3.*

➔ *Phone code: 418.*

The home of Father Hidalgo, 54 km from Guanajuato, is a most attractive, tranquil small town. The main square, or Jardín, is lovely, dominated by a statue of Hidalgo. On one side is the church of **Nuestra Señora de los Dolores** (1712-1778) in which Hidalgo gave *El Grito de la Independencia* (the Cry for Independence from Spain); the façade is impressive, and the churrigueresque side altar pieces, one of gold leaf, one of wood, are more ornate than the main altar – not always open. On the main square there are many restaurants, cafés and banks. The **tourist office** ⓘ *main square, T/F182-1164*, can direct you to places making traditional Talavera tiles and ceramics, available at very good prices. Dolores Hidalgo can be a good, quiet base for visiting livelier Guanajuato and more expensive San Miguel de Allende.

The **Iglesia de La Asunción** ⓘ *Puebla y Sonora*, has a large tower at one end, a dome at the other, with extensive murals and a tiled floor inside. Two blocks away, at Puebla and Jalisco, is **Plaza de los Compositores Dolorenses** with a bandstand. Between these two sites on Puebla is the post and telegraph office. Visit Hidalgo's house, the **Museo Casa Hidalgo** ⓘ *Morelos and Hidalgo, Tue-Sat 1000-1800, Sun 1000-1700, US$4.35*, a beautiful building with a courtyard and wells, memorabilia

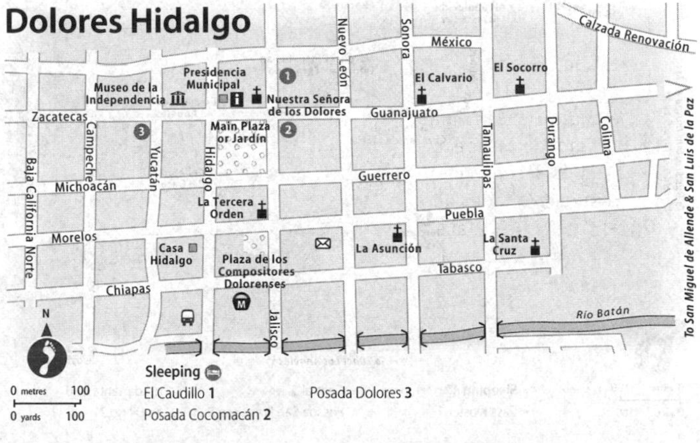

and one room almost a shrine to the Father of Independence. The **Museo de la Independencia** ⓘ *Zacatecas, US$0.70*, was formerly a jail, but now has displays of striking paintings of the path to Independence.

Around Dolores Hidalgo

About 5 km southeast of town on a dirt track are the ruins of the **Hacienda de la Erre** ⓘ *free entrance to the untended ruins and grounds*, Padre Hidalgo's first stop on the Independence route after leaving Dolores. The standing walls are only 3-4 m high; there are about four rooms with ceilings, the patio is overgrown, but the chapel has been rebuilt. Outside is the huge mezquite tree under which Hidalgo is supposed to have said Mass for his insurgent troops. The walk to the ruins (1½-2 hours) starts from the plaza. Take Calle Guerrero to the east, then Tamaulipas to the main road. Turn left for 1 km to a gravel road on the left on a long curve. Follow this to the hacienda in a fertile area with plenty of trees.

Guanajuato

» pp262-275. Colour map 3, B3.

→ *Phone code: 461. Altitude: 2010 m.*

The beautiful university city in the central state of Guanajuato, declared a UNESCO World Heritage Site, has been important for its silver since 1548. Its name derives from the Tarascan Quanax-Huato, 'place of frogs'. It stands in a narrow gorge amid wild and striking scenery; the Guanajuato River which cuts through the city has been covered over and several underground streets wind their way underneath the city like a human rabbit warren – an unusual and confusing system, especially if you try driving in the city, which only gets better when you start to take the situation humourously.

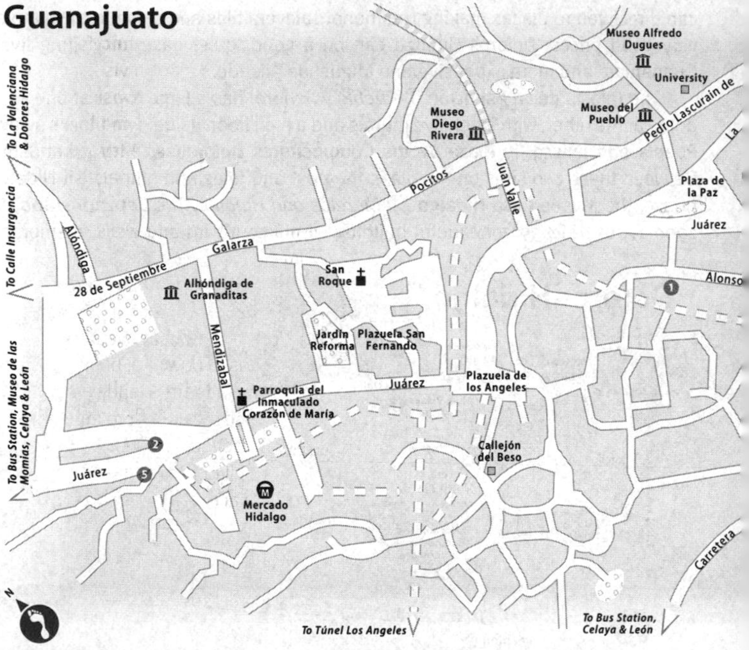

Sleeping
Casa Kloster 1
Central 2
Posada San Francisco 5
Posada Santa Fe 6
San Diego 7

Ins and outs

Getting there The international Aeropuerto del Bajío (BJX), 40 km west of Guanajuato near the town of Silao, has flights within Mexico and to the USA. The long-distance bus terminal is on the outskirts, southwest of town (see page 272); taxis or buses ('Centro') will ferry you into town.

Getting around Many of the interesting places are along and around Juárez and can be visited on foot in a day or two. Some streets, like Padre Belaunzarán, are not entirely enclosed; others, such as Hidalgo, are, so they fill with traffic fumes. The Túnel Los Angeles leads from the old subterranean streets to the modern roadway that connects with the Carretera Panorámica and the monument to Pípila (see below). Taking traffic underground has not relieved the congestion of the surface streets, which are steep, twisted and narrow. Parking for hotels is often a fair distance away.

Tourist information The **tourist office** ⓘ *Plaza de la Paz 14, beside the Basílica, T732-7622, www.guanajuato.gob.mx*, sells maps and has information about the area.

Sights

The best of many colonial churches are the Jesuit **La Compañía** (1765), by the University, note the brick ceiling; **San Diego** (1663) on the Jardín de la Unión; the **Parroquia del Inmaculado Corazón de María**, on Juárez, opposite Mercado Hidalgo, which has interesting statues on the altar; and the cathedral, or **Basílica de Nuestra Señora de Guanajuato** (1693), on Plaza de la Paz, which has a beautiful yellow interior and an ornately painted vaulted ceiling. **San Roque** (1726), on Plazuela de San Roque, a small park between Juárez and Pocitos, also has a pretty vaulted ceiling, reached by a walkway that goes from the northeast side of the Jardín Reforma. The **Templo de San Francisco** (1671), on Sopeña, is also worth visiting.

The Festival Cervantino, said to be Latin America's biggest arts festival, takes place in October each year.

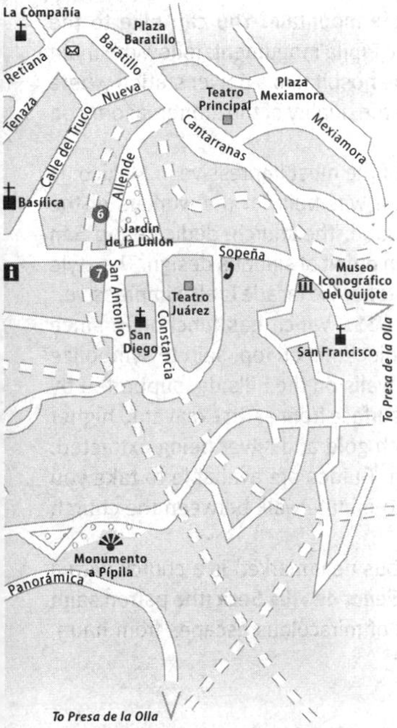

Probably the most famous of Guanajuato's alleys and lanes is the **Callejón del Beso** (Alley of the Kiss), which is so narrow that, according to legend, two lovers kept apart by their families were able to exchange kisses from opposite balconies.

Guanajuato has a series of fine museums too. One most interesting building is the massive **Alhóndiga de Granaditas** ⓘ *US$2.80*, built as a granary, turned into a fortress, and now a museum with artefacts from the pre-Columbian and colonial periods. When Father Hidalgo took the city in 1810, the Alhóndiga was the last place to surrender, and there was a wanton slaughter of Spanish soldiers and royalist prisoners. Later when Hidalgo was himself caught and executed, along with three other leaders, in Chihuahua, their severed heads were fixed, in revenge, at the four corners of the Alhóndiga.

An unusual sight shown to visitors is of mummified bodies in the small **Museo de las Momias** ① *daily 0900-1800, US$2.60, long queues on Sun,* in the Panteón Municipal, above the city off Tepetapa; buses go there ('Momias', signposted Panteón Municipal, 10 minutes, along Avenida Juárez), but you can walk. The **Museo Iconográfico del Quijote** ① *Manuel Doblado 1, Tue-Sat 1000-1830, Sun 1000-1430, US$2, free Sun*, is highly recommended for its paintings, drawings and sculptures of the Don. The painter **Diego Rivera** was born at Pocitos 47, now a **museum** ① *Tue-Sat 1000-1900, Sun 1000-1500, US$1.40*, with a permanent collection of his work on various floors, showing his changing styles; on the ground floor are his bed and other household objects. Also on Pocitos, at No 7, just across from the university, is the **Museo del Pueblo** ① *Tue-Sat 1000-1900, Sun 1000-1500, US$1.40*, in a beautiful 17th-century mansion; it has one room of work by the muralist **José Chávez Morado**, a room of selected items of all Mexican art forms and temporary exhibitions. The **University** was founded in 1732; its façade of coloured stone, above a broad staircase, glows richly at sunset.

Around Guanajuato » *For tours of the surrounding area, see page 271.*

Crowning the high hill of Hormiguera is the **Monumento a Pípila**, the man who fired the door of the Alhóndiga so that the patriots could take it. There is a fine view from the top. Look for the 'Al Pípila' sign. A number of cobbled stairways through picturesque terraces, such as Callejón del Calvario, leading off Sopeña, go up to the monument. It's a steep but short climb (about 15 minutes) rewarded with fine panoramic views of the city. Otherwise take a local bus from **Hotel Central**, on Juárez. The Carretera Panorámica, which encircles the city, passes the Pípila monument. At its eastern end the Panorámica goes by the **Presa de la Olla**, a favourite picnic spot with good cheap food available from roadside stalls. From the dam, Paseo de la Olla runs to the city centre, passing mansions of the wealthy silver barons and the **Palacio de Gobierno** (note the use of local stone).

Over the city looms the shoulder of **La Bufa** mountain. You can hike to the summit up a trail, which takes one hour: from the Pípila monument, follow the main road for about 1 km to the hospital. Walk past the hospital to a power station where the main trail starts; if you pass the quarry, note the quality of the stonemasonry on the mason's shelter.

The splendid church of **La Valenciana**, one of the most impressive in Mexico, is 5 km out of town on the Dolores Hidalgo road; it was built for the workers of the Valenciana silver mine, once the richest in the world. The church, dedicated to San Cayetano, has three huge gilt altars and a wooden pulpit of sinuous design. The style is churrigueresque, done in grey-green and pink stone; the façade is also impressive.

The **Valenciana mine** ① *daily 0900-1700, US$1*, which has functioned since 1548, is surrounded by a wall with triangular projections on top, said to symbolize the crown of the King of Spain. The huge stone walls on the hillside, supported by enormous buttresses, created an artificial level surface from earth excavated higher up the slope. The mine is still working with both gold and silver being extracted. With care you can walk freely in the whole area. Guides are available to take you round on an interesting 30-minute tour. It is a 10-minute walk between the church and the mine pit-head.

At the old site of **La Cata** silver mine (local bus near market) is a church with a magnificent baroque façade and the shrine of **El Señor de Villa Seca** (the patron saint of adulterers) with *retablos* and crude drawings of miraculous escapes from harm, mostly due to poor shooting by husbands.

León » pp262-275. Colour map 3, B2.

➔ *Phone code: 477. Altitude: 1885 m.*

In the fertile plain of the Río Gómez, León is now said to be Mexico's fifth city. Nuño de Guzmán reached the area on 2 December 1530 and subsequently local farms and estates were granted to the Spaniards. Eventually Don Martín Enríquez de Almanza decreed on 12 December 1575 that a city, called León, would be founded if 100 volunteers could be persuaded to live there for 10 years, or a town if only 50 could be found. On 20 January 1576 a town was founded by Dr Juan Bautista de Orozco, and it wasn't until 1830 that León became a city. The business centre is the delightful **Plaza de la Constitución.**

The **tourist office** ⓘ *Edificio Cielo 501, López Mateos Poniente and M Alemán, www.leon-mexico.com*, provides helpful but limited information; a good city map is available free at the Palacio Municipal.

Sights

There are many shaded plazas and gardens in León. The Palacio Municipal, by the Plaza de la Constitución, is said to have been built as a result of a winning lottery ticket bought by a local doctor! The small **cathedral** was started by Jesuits in 1744, but they were expelled from Mexico in 1767 by Carlos III. It was eventually finished in 1837 and consecrated in 1866. The catacombs are well worth seeing at the **Templo Expiatorio** ⓘ *Thu-Sun 1000-1200*, which has been under construction for most of the last century. The **Teatro Doblado** ⓘ *Av Hermanos Aldama*, stages events. There is also a **Casa de Cultura** which houses exhibitions and is buzzing at night. Also worth seeing is the **Casa de Las**

León is the main shoe centre of the country and is noted for its leather work, fine silver-trimmed saddles and rebozos (shawls).

Monas ⓘ *5 de Mayo 127-29*, where Pancho Villa issued the Agrarian Reform Law on 24 May 1915, and the beautiful **Santuario de Guadalupe**.

The **Museo de León** ⓘ *Hermanos Aldama, Tue-Sat 1000-1400 and 1630-1930, Sun 1000-1400*, has art exhibitions. On Justo Sierra, the **Museum of Anthropology and History** is housed in a beautiful building.

Aguascalientes

▸▸ *pp262-275. Colour map 3, B2.*

→ *Phone code: 449. Altitude: 1987 m.*

Founded in 1575, capital of its state, the name (hot waters) comes from its hot mineral springs. An oddity is that the city is built over a network of tunnels dug out by a forgotten people. It has pretty parks, a pleasant climate and delicious fruits. Local specialities include drawn-linen threadwork, pottery and leather goods.

The **Federal Tourist Office** ⓘ *T915-1155, www.aguascalientes.gob.mx, daily 0800-2000*, is in the Palacio de Gobierno on Plaza Patria, and a good town plan is available from the entrance booth of the Palacio Municipal.

Sights

Palacio de Gobierno, started in 1665, once the castle home of the Marqués de Guadalupe, has a splendid courtyard, with decorated arches on two levels. The grand staircase in the centre, built in the 1940s, blends in magnificently. There are also colourful murals by the Chilean artist Osvaldo Barra. Among the churches, **San Antonio**, on Zaragoza, should not be missed, neither should the Carmelite **Templo de San Marcos**, with a baroque façade, built 1655-1765 on the site of a chapel that had existed since the mid-16th century, in the *barrio* of San Marcos west of the centre.

Teatro Morelos ⓘ *next to the cathedral, T915-0097*, is where the revolutionary factions led by Pancho Villa, Emiliano Zapata and Venustiano Carranza attempted to find some common ground on which they could all work together. The attempt ended in failure. The **university** is 30 minutes from the city centre. Its administrative offices are in the ex-Convento de San Diego, by the attractive Jardín del Estudiante, and the Parían shopping centre.

Museums

Museo de Aguascalientes ⓘ *Zaragoza 507, Tue-Sun 1100-1800*, by the church of San Antonio, has a collection of contemporary art, including fine paintings by Saturnino Herrán, and works by Orozco, Angel, Montenegro and others. The **Museo José Guadalupe Posada** ⓘ *Tue-Sun 1100-1800, US$.60*, is in a gallery by the Templo del Cristo Negro, close to the pleasant Jardín del Encino or Jardín Francisco, on Díaz de León. The museum has a remarkable collection of prints by the artist Posada, best known for his engravings of *calaveras*, macabre skeletal figures illustrating and satirizing the events leading up to the Revolution. There are cultural events in the courtyard on Saturday and Sunday.

The **Casa de la Cultura**, on Venustiano Carranza and Galeana Norte, is a fine colonial building. It holds a display of *artesanía* during the April **feria**.

Around Aguascalientes

Hacienda de San Blas, 34 km away, contains the **Museo de la Insurgencia**, with murals by Alfredo Zermeño.

Forty-two kilometres southwest en route to Guadalajara is the colonial town of **San Juan de los Lagos**, a major pilgrimage centre and crowded during Mexican holidays. There is also a fine view on entering this town: as the road descends you see the twin-towered church with its red, blue and yellow tiled dome. San Juan is famous for glazed fruits. There are many hotels in the town.

Zacatecas » pp262-275. Colour map 3, B2.

→ *Phone code: 493. Altitude: 2495 m.*

Founded in 1548, and capital of Zacatecas State, this picturesque up-and-down mining city is built in a ravine with pink stone houses scattered over the hills. The largest silver mine in the world, processing 10,000 tonnes of ore a day or 220 tonnes of silver, is at **Real de Angeles**. Silver has bestowed an architectural grandeur on Zacatecas to match that of Guanajuato. Many travellers believe it to be the most pleasant town in this part of Mexico. You could easily spend days soaking up the atmosphere. There's also a lively nightlife with bars and discos » *For Sleeping, Eating and other listings, see pages 262-275.*

Ins and outs

Getting there The international **Aeropuerto La Calera** (ZCL) is 27 km north of the city, with flights to domestic locations and several cities in the USA. The bus terminal is 4 km south of town. Bus No 8 from outside the terminal leaves for the town centre every 10-15 minutes.

Getting around Bulevar López Mateos, a busy highway, runs close to the centre of town from the bus station (about 4 km south of town) and down the ravine. Driving can be a nightmare with many one-way systems. The **tourist office** ⓘ *Av Hidalgo 403, 2nd floor, T924-0552, www.turismozacatecas.gob.mx*, is friendly and helpful; they provide free maps and good hotel and language class.

Sights

The **Cathedral** (1730-1752) is the centrepiece of town with a fine churrigueresque façade; to the west is the **San Agustín** church, with interior carvings, and the Jesuit church of **Santo Domingo** (frescoes in the sacristy by Francisco Antonio Vallejo (ask the sacristan to turn the lights on)). Also worth seeing are the **Casa Moneda** (better known as the **Tesorería**), founded 1810, and the **Teatro Calderón**, opposite the cathedral. The **Mina del Edén** ⓘ *Av Torreón y Quebradilla, daily 1000-1800, US$2.50*, at the western side of town, is an old mine with a short section of mine railway in operation; the tour in fast Spanish lasts about one hour. In the mine there is also a **disco** ⓘ *Thu, Fri and Sat, 2200-0230, varied music.* You can leave the mine the way you went in or work your way through to the end and **El Teleférico**, which carries you over the city, with spectacular views, to Cerro de la Bufa and the **Capilla de Los Remedios** (1728).

Museums

Close to the centre of town is **Museo Pedro Coronel** ⓘ *Plaza Santo Domingo, Thu-Tue 1000-1630US$2.50*, which houses an excellent collection of European and modern art (including Goya, Hogarth, Miró and Tàpies), as well as folk art from Mexico and around the world (take a guide to make the most of the collections). A couple of blocks to the south, east of San Agustín, is the **Museo Zacatecano** ⓘ *Wed-Mon 1000-1630, US$1.50*, which contains religious paintings, Huichol handicrafts and some colonial items.

To the north of town the **Museo Rafael Coronel** ⓘ *Wed-Mon, US$2.50*, housed in the ex-Convento de San Francisco, has a vast collection of masks and puppets, primarily Mexican, and an attractive garden perfect for a small picnic.

Heading south near the fine, old **Acueducto El Cubo** is the **Museo Francisco Goitia** ⓘ *Tue-Sun 1000-1700, US$2.50*, housed in what was once the governor's mansion, by the Parque General Enrique Estrada, Colonia Sierra de Alicia. The museum has modern paintings by Zacatecans, but its main attractions are the paintings of small-town poverty in Mexico by Francisco Goitia. Behind the museum is the spectacular and modern **Parroquia de Fátima**; built in 1975, it pays tribute to the heritage of the city.

Up on the hill, best visited after going through Mina El Edén and El Teleférico, is **Museo de la Toma de Zacatecas** ⓘ *daily 1000-1700, US$1.50*, on the Cerro de la Bufa, commemorates Pancho Villa's victory over Huerta's forces in 1914. The hill, northeast of the city centre, is recommended for views over the city. It is a pleasant walk, although crowded on Sundays. There is also a statue of Villa, an observatory and the **Mausoleo de Los Hombres Ilustres.** It's a 10- or 15-minute walk down the hill, with a small café on the first road you meet with good views over the city.

Around Zacatecas

Beyond Zacatecas to the east lies the **Convento de Guadalupe**, a national monument, with a fine church and convent, which now houses a **Museum of Colonial Religious Art** ⓘ *daily 1000-1700, US$1.50*. The galleries of the convent are full of paintings covering the life of St Francis and huge frescoes. The labyrinthine convent is well worth a visit, with the Virgin as a child set in gold held in the church. To get there, take bus No 13 from López Mateos y Salazar, near the terminal, US$0.15, 20 minutes.

Visit the **Chicomostoc** ruins, also known as **La Quemada** ⓘ *US$3.50*, 56 km south. To get there, take the 0800 or 1100 **Línea Verde** bus from the main terminal to

Adjuntas (about 45 minutes, US$0.60), on the Villanueva road. Walk 30 minutes through beautiful, silent, nopal-cactus scenery to the ruins, which offer an impressive view. There is the Palace of the Eleven Columns, a Pyramid of the Sun and other remains on a rocky outcrop, in various stages of restoration. In themselves the ruins are not spectacular, but together with the setting they are worth the trip. For the return from the junction at Adjuntas, wait for a bus or hitch back to Zacatecas.

Jerez is an old colonial town about 65 km from Zacatecas, where the wide-brimmed *sombrero charro* is worn. There are two interesting churches in the town: **La Soledad**, begun 1805, completed later that century, which has a baroque façade, but most elaborate are the three gateways – composites of all manner of over-the-top classical styles; **La Inmaculada**, also with a baroque façade, has a neo-Romanesque interior.

San Luis Potosí

» *pp262-275. Colour map 3, B3.*

→ *Phone code: 444. Altitude: 1880 m.*

Lying 423 km from Mexico City, glazed, many-coloured tiles are a feature of the city; one of its shopping streets, the main plaza, and the domes of many of its churches are covered with them. It became an important centre after the discovery of the famous San Pedro silver mine in the 16th century, and a city in 1658. There is a festival in the second half of August.

San Patricio Caffe **11**
Viva Pizza **12**

The **tourist office** ⓘ *Obregón 520, T812-9906, www.visitasanluispotosi.com*, is half a block west of Plaza de los Fundadores. It's in a beautiful colonial house with lovely gardens. They are helpful with good brochures and maps.

The **Cathedral** is on **Plaza Hidalgo**; fronting the east side. It has a beautiful exterior of pink cantera (a type of local stone), with ornately carved bell towers. The interior is also very beautiful. There are rows of stone columns running down the length of each side of the church's interior, each column being about 2 m in diameter. Also on the east side of the plaza, just the north of the cathedral, is the **Palacio Municipal**. In the interior, over the double branching staircase, you can admire the glasswork representing the city's coat of arms. In the upper floor, the Cabildo Hall has a ceiling painted by Italian artist Erulo Eroli, featuring mythological Christian themes. Do not miss the church of **San Francisco**, which fronts the plaza of the

Parking is very difficult. There is a car park near the police station on Eje Vial, US$1 for 1st hr, US$0.65 for each subsequent hr.

same name. This church is one of the baroque jewels of the city. The construction dates back to 1686. In that year, the work of the beautiful pink limestone façade was begun. But it wasn't until the next century that some of its most important features were added, such as the baroque tower and the main altar. The interior is embellished with wonderful paintings, among which the works by Miguel Cabrera and Antonio Torres are the most outstanding. Worthy of admiration is the sacristy, the most magnificent in San Luis Potosí. The **Templo del Carmen**, in **Plaza del Carmen**, has a grand tiled dome, an intricate façade, and a fine pulpit and altar inside. The room to the left of the main altar has another exquisite, very striking altar covered in gold leaf. The **Teatro de la Paz** is next door. The baroque **Capilla de Aranzazú**, behind San Francisco, inside the regional museum (see below), must not be missed; the carved stone framework of the chapel window is one of the most beautiful pieces of baroque art in the city.

Then there is the **Capilla de Loreto** with a baroque façade; the **Templo de San Miguelito**, in the oldest part of the city; **San Agustín**, with its ornate baroque tower; and the startling modern **Iglesia de la Santa Cruz**, in the Industria Aviación district, designed by Enrique de la Mora. The **Palacio de Gobierno**, begun 1789, contains oil paintings of past governors. There is also the colonial treasury, **Antigua Caja Real** ⓘ *some rooms may be visited Mon-Fri 0930-1330*, which was built in 1767. Of great artistic merit are the doors and windows of the chapel, carved in stone in the purist baroque style. Of special interest is the stairway leading to the first floor. It has very low steps, so that the mules, laden with precious metals, could climb easily.

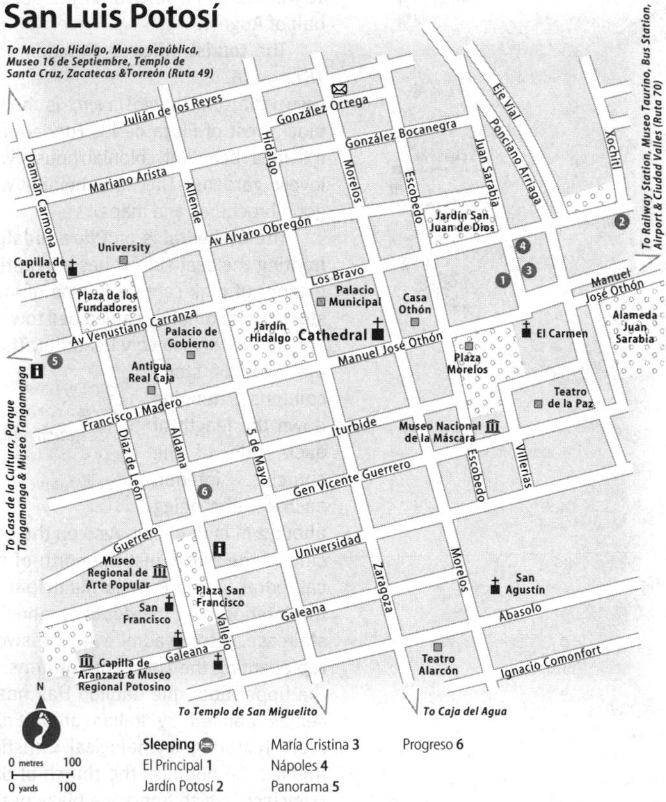

Other points of interest are the pedestrian precinct surrounding **Jardín Hidalgo** and the **Caja del Agua** fountain (1835) in Avenida Juárez. **Plaza de San Francisco** is very pleasant. The modern railway station has frescoes by Fernando Leal. The **Teatro Alarcón**, on Calle Abasolo, between Zaragoza and Morelos, is by Tresguerras (see under Celaya, page 249). It is now being used as offices for a miners' union. The **university** was founded in 1804.

Museums

The **Museo Regional de Arte Popular** ⓘ *Tue-Sat 1000-1345, 1600-1745, Sun 1000-1400, Mon 1000-1500,* next to San Francisco church, is housed in what used to be a private residence. Handicrafts from various parts of the state can be seen, including ceramics, woodwork, *rebozos*, textiles etc. There are also items for sale. Nearby is the **Museo Regional Potosino** ⓘ *Tue-Fri 1000-1300, 1500-1800, Sat 1000-1200, Sun 1000-1300*, located in the building that originally was a Franciscan convent. The ground floor has an exhibition of prehispanic artefacts, mainly from the Huastec culture. The **Museo Nacional de la Máscara** ⓘ *daily 1000-1400, 1600-1800, US$0.50 plus US$0.50 for use of camera*, in what used to be the Palacio Federal, has an excellent collection of masks. The most impressive are the masks used in colonial and prehispanic times in pagan religious ceremonies. In Parque Tangamanga is the **Museo Tangamanga** ⓘ *daily 0600-1800*, in an old hacienda, and also a planetarium, observatory and open-air theatre. In Plaza España, next to Plaza de Toros, is a **Museo Taurino** (bullfighting museum) ⓘ *Tue-Sat 1100-1330, 1730-1930*, east of Alameda on Universidad y Triana.

Around San Luis Potosí

South of San Luis Potosí, east of the junction with Route 110, is **San Luis de la Paz**. Nearby is one of Mexico's mining ghost-towns, **Pozos** (altitude: 2305 m), once one of the most important mining centres of Mexico. It's very silent and a complete contrast to Real de Catorce (see below). Pozos was founded in 1576 when silver was discovered. In the 19th century the population reached 80,000 but following the Revolution most of the foreign (French and Spanish) owners left and the workforce migrated to Mexico City. Today the population is around 2000, but the town is very quiet and the whole area was decreed a historical monument in 1982. Pozos can be reached by bus from San Miguel de Allende (change at San Luis de la Paz) or San José Iturbide.

Real de Catorce

» *pp262-275. Colour map 3, A3.*

→ *Phone code 488. Altitude: 2765 m.*

Real de Catorce 56 km west of Matehuala, is one of Mexico's most interesting old mining towns. This remarkable city, founded in 1772, clustering around the sides of a valley, used to be so quiet that you could hear the river in the canyon, 1000 m below. It is becoming increasingly popular as a tourist destination and new hotels are being built.

The first church was the **Virgen del Guadalupe** (1779), a little way out of town. Beautiful ceiling paintings remain, as well as the black coffin used for the Mass of the Cuerpo Presente. Many of the images from this church were moved to the **Church of San Francisco** (1817), which is believed to be miraculous. The floor of the church is made of wooden panels, which can be lifted to see the catacombs below. In a room to one side of the main altar are *retablos*, touchingly simple paintings on tin, as votive offerings to the saint for his intercession. Next to the church is a small but worthwhile **museum** showing mining equipment, etc.

Sleeping

Querétaro *p245, map p246*

LL-L La Casa de la Marquesa, Madero 41, T212-0092, www.lacasadellamarquesa.com. 3 categories of rooms, the cheapest a steal at US$135. Opulence and comfort as it should be. Mid-priced rooms equally luxurious.

L-AL Mesón de Santa Rosa, Pasteur Sur 17, Centro, T224-2623, www.mesonsanta rosa.com. Small, 300-year-old inn, crammed with colonial detail but tastefully modernized, good restaurant with international and Mexican cuisine.

B Hidalgo, Madero 11 Pte, near Zócalo, T212-0081, www.hotelhidalgo.com.mx. With bath, quiet, friendly, excellent value for 2 or more, restaurant.

C Plaza, Juárez Norte 23, T212-1138. With bath, TV and phone, good location, airy, lovely inner patio, modernized, safe, clean, comfortable. Recommended.

C San Agustín, Pino Suárez 12, T212-3919. Small, dark rooms, handy restaurant next door.

D El Cid, Prolongación Corregidora Sur 10, T214-1165. More of a motel, clean, good value.

E Posada Familiar, Independencia 22, T212-0584. Basic but OK, courtyard.

E Hostel Jirafa Roja, Calle 20 de Noviembre 72, T212-4825. Promising new hostel, reasonably close to the centre of town. Kitchen facilities available. Reception desk not always manned, call in advance to say what time you're going to arrive. Good local information.

Jalpan *p247*

A Hotel Inn Misión Jalpan, main square next to the mission, T296-0255, www. hotelesmision.com.mx. Best place in town, good-sized rooms, tastefully decorated, good restaurant and swimming pool.

C Posada Fray Junípero, Ezequiel Montes 124, opposite church, T412-1241. With bath and TV, clean, friendly, credit cards, colonial style, pool, restaurant, good value but noisy because of bus station.

D El Económico, on main road just downhill of first Pemex in town, T441-2960. Clean, basic with laundry. Helpful staff.

D El Aguaje del Morro, down walkway on north side of the main plaza, just before the bridge, T296-0245. Very friendly staff, can be noisy. Also provides excellent, cheap local food.

E Posada Aurora, Calle Hidalgo. With bath, hot water, fan, clean, friendly. Recommended.

San Juan del Río *p247*

AL Hotel Mansión Galindo, just outside town, T272-0050. Beautiful restored hacienda; apparently given by Cortés to his mistress, La Malinche.

C Layseca, Av Juárez 9 Ote, T272-0110. Colonial building, large rooms, nice furniture, excellent, car parking, no restaurant.

Tequisquiapan *p247*

L-AL El Relox, Morelos 8, T273-0006, www.relox.com.mx. Attractive with spa pool, open to non-residents.

A Posada Los Arcos, Moctezuma 12, T273-0566. Pleasant spot, well maintained. Private bath, fan and TV.

B Posada Tequisquiapan, Moctezuma 6, T273-0010. Large rooms, some with balconies looking out onto gardens. Private bath and TV.

San Joaquín *p248*

D Mesón de Joaquín, T272-5315, next to bus park. Good-value rooms for 4 and a campground with shelters and barbecue stands on the outskirts above the town.

Concá *p248*

AL Hotel Misión Hacienda Conca, Carretera Jalpan-Río Verde, km 57, T01-800-029-4240, www.hotelesmision.com. A spot of all-inclusive luxury in the middle of nowhere.

Xilitla *p248*

AL-B El Castillo, T365-0038. Includes breakfast, pool, fine views, run by Avery and Leonore Danzinger.

Phone codes *Querétaro 442; Jalpan 441; San Juan del Río 427; Tequisquiapan 414; Cadereyta 441; San Joaquín 441; Xilitla 489; Celaya 461; Irapuato 462; San Miguel de Allende 415; Dolores Hidalgo 418; Guanajuato 461; León 477; Aguascalientes 449; Zacatecas 493; San Luis Potosí 444; Pozos 478; Real de Catorce 488.*

C **El Lobo**, in El Lobo, between the northern missions and Xilitla, T441-234-9103. Simple but OK hotel in case you need or want to stop.

Celaya *p249*
Many of the better hotels are outside the centre.
B **Plaza Bajío Inn**, Libertad 133, T613-8600. 80 rooms, central, restaurant, parking, medical service, laundry.
C **Isabel**, Hidalgo 207, T612-2096. Restaurant, bar, laundry, parking.
E **Guadalupe**, Portal Guadalupe 108, T612-1839. Very old hotel with historical connections, central, cheaper rooms without bath.

Irapuato *p249*
B-C **Hotel Real de Minas**, Portal Carrillo Puerto 1, T627-7330. Overpriced, with equally overpriced restaurant, on Portal Carrillo Puerto, quiet rooms on church side.
C **Kennedy**, Kennedy 830, T627-4110. Simple rooms with TV.

San Miguel de Allende *p250, map p250*
Many weekend visitors, so book ahead. A good source of information on cheap accommodation is the English-language paper published weekly by the Anglo-Mexican Library on Insurgentes.
LL **Casa de Sierra Nevada** , Hospicio 35, T01-800-509-0745, www.casadesierranevada.com. Best hotel in town combining colonial grace and top service.
LL-L **Casa Luna B&B**, Pila Seca 11, T/F152-1117, www.casaluna.com. American run, excellent breakfast included, beautiful themed rooms, no smoking inside. Also operates Casa Luna Quebrada.
L-B **La Mansión del Bosque**, Aldama 65, T152-0277, www.infosma.com/mansion. Possibly the most relaxing and friendly guest house in San Miguel. The rooms are normally fully booked and the service is warming and as if family.
LL-L **Rincón del Cielo**, Correo 10, next to main plaza, T152-1647. Rooms are large and have 2 storeys, the bedroom is upstairs with fireplace and huge bathroom with tub, living room has wet bar, attractive and good value.
LL-AL **Posada Carmina**, Cuna de Allende 7, T152-0458, www.posadacarmina.com. Colonial building, courtyard for meals. Recommended.
A **La Siesta**, Salidad a Celaya 82, near Jardín, T152-0207, www.hotellasiesta.com. Pool, fireplaces in rooms (US$34 with breakfast).
A **Posada de las Monjas**, Canal 37, T152-0171, www.posadalasmonjas.com. With shower, excellent set meals in restaurant, bar, clean and attractive, very good value, a converted convent.
B **Vista Hermosa Taboada**, Allende 11, T152-0078. Popular, nice old colonial building.
B **Sautto**, Dr Macías 59, T152-0052. Rooms with fridge, fireplace and bath, new rooms best, rustic, garden, hot water, parking. Recommended.
C **Hotel Posada 'El Mayorazgo'**, Hidalgo 8, T152-1309. If you stay 6 days, the 7th is free. Also rent by the month and has 1-bed apartments.
C **Parador San Sebastian**, Mesones 7, near market, T152-7084. With bath, charming, large rooms with fireplace, clean, car park, noisy at front (most rooms are at the back), and beautiful courtyard. Recommended.
D **Casa de Huéspedes**, Mesones 27, T152-1378. Looks grubby on the outside but it's clean with hot water, popular, roof garden, nice location, good value.
E **Hostal Alcatraz**, Relox 54, T152-8543, alcatrazhostel@yahoo.com. Clean and tidy dormitory accommodation, hot water and kitchen available. Very friendly and helpful. Recommended.
F **La Villa de Pancho**, Quebrada 12 (1 block west of Hotel Sautto), T152-1247. Tidy little rooms up a cranky set of stairs, but good value and very friendly.

Camping
KAO campgrounds further out than Siesta on road to Guanajuato. Quiet, grassy site, all facilities, pleasant, Dutch owner.
Siesta, on road to Guanajuato, with trailer park, gardens.

Dolores Hidalgo *p251, map p251*
B **El Caudillo**, Querétaro 8, just off plaza, opposite the church of Nuestra Señora de los Dolores, T182-0198. Clean, good value.
B **Posada Cocomacán**, T182-6087, on the Járdin. Pleasant colonial house where Juárez stayed, comfortable, good value, good food, parking. Recommended.

D **Posada Dolores**, Yucatán 8, T182-0642. With bath, clean, OK, small rooms.

Guanajuato *p252, map p252*
Hotel rooms can be hard to find after 1400. For holidays and weekends it is advisable to book ahead.
L-AL **Parador San Javier**, Plaza Aldama 92, http://hotelmex.com/paradorsanjavier, T732-0696. Very extensive grounds, some rooms have fireplaces.
L-AL **Posada Santa Fe**, Jardín de la Unión 12, T732-0084, www.posadasantafe.com/hpsf.htm. Plain regular rooms but the suites are very attractive with colonial-style furniture. Good restaurant on open terrace with excellent service. Tables on the plaza for dining. Recommended.
AL **San Diego**, Jardín de la Unión 1, T732-1321, www.hotelerasandiego.com. Good bar and restaurant but slow, colonial style, very pleasant.
AL **Suites Casa de las Manrique**, Juárez 116 (between the Mercado and the Callejón del Beso), T732-7678. Large, attractive suites, colonial decor, very good value for price.
A **El Insurgente Allende**, Juárez 226, T732-3192. Pleasant, clean, avoid rooms on 4th floor where there is a disco, good breakfasts.
B **Alhóndiga**, Insurgentes 49, T732-0525. Good, clean, quiet, TV in rooms, parking, restaurant **La Estancia**.
B **La Fragua**, Juárez, T732-2715, at the western end. Very clean, good staff, 5 mins' walk from the centre of town.
B **Mineral de Rayas**, Alhóndiga 7, T732-1967. With bath, clean linen, pool, garage, restaurant, bar and **Danny's Bar**. Recommended.
B **Socavón**, Alhóndiga 41A, T732-6666. Pretty restaurant/bar. Colonial decor, attractive interior courtyard, nice rooms for price, with TV and phones.
C **Central**, Juárez 111, T732-0080, near Cine Reforma. Friendly, good restaurant but noisy for rooms beside it.
C **Dos Ríos**, Alhóndiga 29, T732-0749. TV in rooms, good value, rooms on street noisy.
C **Posada San Francisco**, Juárez 178, corner of Gavira, on Zócalo, T732-2084. Good value but outside rooms noisy, lovely inner patio.
D **Mineral de Rayas**, Alhóndiga 7, T732-1967. With bath, clean linen, pool, garage, restaurant, bar and **Danny's Bar**. Recommended.
D **Posada La Condesa/Los Arcos**, Plaza de La Paz 60 (west end of plaza), T732-1462. Small, basic rooms, clean, hot water, drinking water available.
D-E **Casa Kloster**, Alonso 32, T732-0088. Book ahead, good location, very friendly, dormitory rooms for 4, a few with private bath, some without windows, clean, very good value. Often recommended, but not right for all. Have a look and see.
F **Marilú Ordaz**, Barranca 34, T732-4705. Accommodation in private home. Price per person. Friendly, 5 mins' walk from market.

Camping
L-A **Villa de Plata**, T732-1173, www.hotelvillaplata.com. Trailer Park 1 km north of Mineral de Rayas, there is a sign on the Carretera Panorámica. Hot showers and funky decor.

Around Guanajuato *p254*
D **Hotel El Crag**, Santa Rosa. A storybook setting in the forest.

León *p255, map p255*
AL **La Nueva Estancia**, López Mateos 1317 Pte, T637-0000, www.nehotel.com.mx/inicio.html. Restaurant recommended.
AL **Real de Minas**, López Mateos 2211, T710-4090, www.realdeminas poliforum.com.mx. Recommended.
A **Howard Johnson Condesa**, on Plaza, Portal Bravo 14, T713-1120, www.hjleon.com. 3 star. Restaurant recommended.
B-C **Rex**, 5 de Febrero 104, near Plaza, T714-2415, www.hotelrealrex.com/. Modern. Recommended.
C **Fundadores**, Ortiz de Domínguez 218, T716-1727. Better than similarly priced hotels in centre.
C **Monte Carlo**, Justo Sierra 432, T713-1597. Clean, friendly, central.
D **Posada de Fátima**, Belisario Domínguez 205. Clean, central.
D **Tepeyac**, Obregón 727, T716-8365. 1 star, OK, rooms a bit dark.

Aguascalientes *p256*
LL **Gran Hotel Hacienda de la Noria**, Av Héroe de Nacozari Sur 1315, Col La Salud, T918-4343, www.granhotellanoria.com.mx. Very comfortable, jacuzzi in all rooms.

Mexican, Japanese and international cuisine, gardens, swimming pool.
AL Hotel de Andrea Alameda, Alameda esq Av Tecnológico, T970-3800. Old hacienda, large rooms, good restaurant.
B Imperial, Moctezuma y 5 de Mayo 106, on plaza, T915-1650. Large, sparse rooms.
D Señorial, Colón 104, T915-1630. Rooms with phone, helpful lady speaks English.
D-E Don Jesús, Juárez 429, T915-5598. Hot water 3 hrs morning and evening, good value.
E Brasil, Guadalupe 110, T915-1106. With bath, quiet. One of several cheap hotels around Juárez market.
E Reforma, Nieta y Galeana, 1 block west of main plaza. Colonial style, large courtyard, rooms a bit dark, friendly, clean.
F Casa Belén, López Mateos y Galeana, T915-8593. Central, hot water, clean, friendly.

Around Aguascalientes *p256*

B Posada Santa Cecilia, Constitución/San Francisco 4, Jerez, T(494) 945-2412. Old style, pleasant atmosphere.
C Hotel Casa Blanca, Anguiano 107 on the plaza, Encarnación de Díaz, T(475) 953-2007. Hot water, secure parking nearby, reasonable restaurant) is halfway to Lagos de Moreno.

Zacatecas *p257, map p258*

L Mesón de Jobito, Jardín Juárez 143, in the heart of Centro Histórico, T924-1722, www.mesondejobito.com. Small, select and very stylish hotel, attractive restaurant with international and Mexican cuisine.
L Quinta Real, Av González Ortega, T922-9104. Beautiful, built around old bullring (said to be the 2nd oldest in Latin America), aqueduct goes past the front door. Excellent.
B Condesa, opposite **Posada de los Condes**, Av Juárez 102, T922-1160. OK, quiet with good views of Cerro de la Bufa, cheap restaurant.
C Colón, Av López Velarde 508, Barrio La Paz, near old bus station, T922-8925. Clean, with showers.
C Hostal Villa Colonial, 1 de Mayo y Callejón Mono Prieto, just south of the cathedral, right in the historic centre, T/F922-1980. Shared bath in a mix of dormitories and private rooms. Great views from the rooftop patio. Can provide information on sites and transport. Use of kitchen, internet access. Good deal, recommended. Also run **Hostal Plata** to meet demand.
C Posada de los Condes, Juárez 107, T922-1093. A bit noisy, rooms darkish except those at front with balconies.
C-D Gami, Av López Mateos 309, to the southeast of town, near old bus station, T922-8005. Rooms with TV, OK.
D Zamora, Plaza de Zamora 303, T922-1200. With bath, central, very basic.
E Youth hostel Parque del Encantado 103, CP 98000, on bus route to centre from bus station, T922-1151. No singles.

Camping

Trailer park, at Morelos junction, about 20 mins northwest of the city, where Route 54 Saltillo-Guadalajara crosses Route 49. Hook-ups, basic, behind Pemex.

San Luis Potosí *p259, map p260*

There are many hotels between the railway station and the cathedral.
AL Panorama, Av Venustiano Carranza 315, T812-1777, www.hotelpanorama.com.mx. Price includes breakfast and a 20% discount on other meals. Large, attractive rooms. Very good views of the city from the upper floors.
A Mansión Los Arcos, Highway 57, km 191, a few kilometres south of San Luis Potosí, signposted, T824-0530. Motel with restaurant and safe parking.
A María Cristina, Juan Sarabia 110, Altos, T128-8550, www.mariacristina.com.mx. Modern, clean, small rooms with phone and TV, with restaurant, good value.
A Nápoles, Juan Sarabia 120, T812-8418. Good restaurant, TV, phones, ceiling fans. Recommended.
B Hotel Guadalajara, Jiménez 253, near train station, T812-4404. Small rooms with TV and phone; has enclosed parking.
C El Principal, Juan Sarabia 145 opposite **María Cristina**, T812-0784. With bath. OK, loud TV in hall.
C Progreso, Aldama 415, less than a block from Plaza San Francisco, T812-0366. Attractive colonial façade. Rooms are large but rather dark and a little run-down. Not bad for the price.
D Universidad, Universidad 1435, between train and bus station, T816-0707. Clean, friendly, hot showers.

D-E Jardín Potosí, Los Bravo 530, T812-3152. Good, hot water, restaurant. Recommended.

Pozos *p261*

L Casa Montana, T293-0032, www.casamontanahotel.com. Extreme comfort blended with great style. A wonderful place to stay in the heart of the colonial centre, but away from the crowds.

Real de Catorce *p261*

Accommodation is easy to find: boys greet new arrivals and will guide motorists through the peculiar one-way system (otherwise possible police fine).

A El Corral del Conde, Morelos, close to Mesón de la Abundancia, T887-5048. 6 rooms, fine furniture, clean, big bathrooms.

B Quinta Puesta del Sol, Calle del Cementerio 16, T887-5050. With bath, TV, beautiful views, poor restaurant.

A Hotel El Real, Morelos 20. Clean, nice atmosphere, friendly owner, good restaurant. Recommended.

E Providencia, on main street. Hot water, clean, restaurant. Several other hotels, and various restaurants.

Eating

Querétaro *p245, map246*

TTT Mesón de Chucho el Roto, Plaza Independencia. Very popular at night with drinks, music, good food and service. Surprisingly affordable and good value.

TTT Mesón Santa Rosa, Pasteur 17, in courtyard of hotel of same name. Good but expensive, restored colonial building.

TT Alda Café, Río de la Loza 4, T224-4077. Modern, breezy and stylish Italian café/restaurant. Chic and popular.

TT Bisquetes, in arcade of old **Gran Hotel** on Zócalo. Good value. Try local Hidalgo Pinot Noir wine.

TT Café 1810, Plaza Independencia. Enjoyable plaza-side restaurant perfect for watching the world go by.

TT El Arcangel, Plaza Jardín Guerrero. Stylish spot with a good *menú del día*.

TT Lonergan's, Plaza de Armas. Pleasant café with small art gallery, magazines in English, French and German.

TT Ostionería Tampico, Corregidora Norte 3. Specialists in fish, and with good reason.

T La Mariposa, A Peralta 7. Excellent coffee, *tortas* and fruit shakes.

T Leo's, at La Cruz market. Excellent tacos and *quesadillas*, popular.

T The Italian Coffee Company, on the plaza. Pure Italian heaven in a cup.

T Vegetariano Natura, Av Juárez 47. Good, cheap vegetarian food, with health food supplements available for sale.

Tequisquiapan *p247*

TTT K'puchinos, north side of main square. Excellent Mexican dishes in a stylish restaurant. The place to sit and watch the world go by.

TT Maridelphi, on south side of main square. Popular local choice.

Jalpan *p247*

T Las Cazuelas, to right of church. Delicious tacos, very clean.

T Las Jacarandas, next to bus station. Good *comida corrida*, reasonably priced, clean. Shrimp cocktails at stalls on plaza.

Xilitla *p248*

T Restaurant Los Cayos. Good view. Try *enchiladas huastecas* and local coffee.

Celaya *p249*

TTT El Mezquital, Blv López Mateos 1113 Ote. Meat and traditional barbeque.

TT La Mansión del Marisco, Blv López Mateos 1000, esq Juárez. Fish and seafood, live music at weekends.

San Miguel de Allende *p250, map p250*

TTT-TT Mesón de San José, Mesones 38, T152-3848. Mexican and international cuisine including vegetarian dishes, excellent breakfasts, in a pleasant patio. German/Mexican owners, 0800-2200, live music Sun, gift shop. Well hidden so quite quiet at times.

TT Café etc, Calle Reloj 37, Mon-Sat 0800-2100, Sun 1000-1800. Great café atmosphere in a gallery, with internet and excellent music – some 2000 CDs from classical to the very latest sounds – most of which is available to buy.

TT Casa Mexas, Canal 15. Good American food, clean, popular with gringos.

TT El Buen Café, Jesús 23, T152-5807. Good quiche, pies, cakes and juices.

🍴🍴 **El Infierno**, Mesones, just below Plaza Allende. Excellent *sopa azteca*, good value.
🍴🍴 **El Jardín**, San Francisco, close to plaza. Friendly service, good food, also vegetarian, violinist plays upstairs at weekends for price of a drink.
🍴🍴 **El Tomate**, on Mesones. Vegetarian restaurant, attractive, spotless, excellent food, generous helpings, not cheap.
🍴🍴 **Mama Mía**, Umarán, west of main square. Main meals good but not cheap, free live folk music or films in the afternoon, excellent cheap breakfasts.
🍴🍴 **Restaurant La Fonda**, Hidalgo 28 between Insurgentes and Mesones. Excellent Mexican food and very friendly staff. Impromptu music and readings.
🍴🍴 **Rincón Español**, opposite post office. Good *comida corrida*, flamenco at weekends. Recommended.
🍴🍴 **San Agustín**, on San Francisco. Good food with *fajitas*, excellent *churros* and Mexican hot chocolate, lively music and quirky decor.
🍴🍴 **Tío Lucas**, Mesones 103, T152-4996, opposite Teatro Angela Peralta. Very good. Recommended.
🍴 **La Piñata**, Umarán. One of the few cheap, family-run Mexican restaurants left in town. No airs and graces, but great food.
🍴 **Chicken restaurant**, corner of Juárez and Mesones. Roast chicken in windows, good.

Dolores Hidalgo *p251, map p251*
Cafés and ice cream parlours
Fruti-Yoghurt, Hidalgo y Guerrero, just off Jardín. Delicious yoghurt, wholefood cakes and biscuits.
Helado Torres, southwest corner of Jardín. Excellent ice cream.

Guanajuato *p252, map p252*
Tourists are often given the à la carte menu; ask for the *menú del día* or *comida corrida*. You can eat well and cheaply in the market (eg sandwiches and fresh fruit juices) and in the *locales* behind Mercado Hidalgo.
🍴🍴🍴 **La Lonja**, on the corner of the Jardín de la Unión, opposite Hotel San Diego. Pleasant and lively bar, beers come with complimentary dish of tacos with salsa.
🍴🍴 **El Mexicano**, Juárez 214. Good *comida corrida* with dessert and drink, a little overpriced.
🍴🍴-🍴 **Café Truco 7**, Callejón Truco, off Plaza de la Paz. *Menú del día* US$3, relaxed family atmosphere. Theatre in back room Fri and Sat afternoon. Recommended.
🍴🍴-🍴 **El Retiro**, Sopeña 12, near Jardín de la Unión. Reasonable food, *comida corrida* very good value.
🍴🍴-🍴 **La Mancha**, Galarza 7. Reasonable price. Recommended for *comida corrida*.
🍴🍴-🍴 **Pizza Piazza**, Plaza San Fernando and several other locations. Cheap and good.
🍴 **Café Las Musas**, Plaza Baratillo. Good-value breakfast.
🍴 **Vegetariano**, Callejón Calixto 20. Inexpensive, sells wholewheat bread.

Cafés, bakeries and ice cream parlours
El Unicornio Azul, Plaza Baratillo. Good healthfood shop, *pan integral*, also sells cosmetic products.

Around Guanajuato *p254*
🍴🍴 **Rancho de Enmiedo**, Santa Rosa. Good dried meat specialities and beautiful scenery.

León *p255, map p255*
🍴🍴🍴 **Panteón Taurino**, Calzado de Los Héroes 408, T713-4969. Expensive but worth visiting for the incredible decor.
🍴🍴 **Cadillac**, ½ block from cathedral on Hidalgo. Good *comida corrida*.
🍴🍴 **La Pagoda de Ling Choy**, López Mateos 1501 Ote, T714-9026. Chinese.
🍴🍴 **Lupillos**, López Mateos 2003 Ote, opposite stadium, T771-1868. Pasta and pizza.
🍴 **GFU**, López Mateos, near IMSS building. Vegetarian snacks.

Aguascalientes *p256*
Try the area around 5 de Mayo for *pollo rostizado*.
🍴🍴 **Freeday**, near Benito Juárez statue. Video bar and restaurant, lively at weekends.
🍴🍴-🍴 **Mitla**, Madero 220. Good breakfast, moderate prices.
🍴 **Café Parroquia**, Hidalgo, 1 block west of Madero. Good, cheap.
🍴 **Jacalito**, López Mateos, also near Plaza Crystal. Cheap *tortas*, clean.
🍴 **Jugos Acapulcos**, Allende 106. Good *comida corrida*.
🍴 **Lonchería Gorditas Victoria**. Popular with locals especially for tacos.

Zacatecas *p257, map p258*
¥¥ **Divino Brazil**, Hidalgo 802, T922-9710. Good Brazilian food with live music in the evenings, open until 0230.
¥¥ **El Jacalito**, Juárez 109. Excellent *comida corrida* and breakfast. Daily 0800-2230.
¥¥ **El Paraíso**, Av Hidalgo y P Goitia, corner of market. Bar/restaurant, nice atmosphere, closed Sun.
¥¥ **La Cuija**, in old Centro Comercial on Av Tacuba. Good food, music, atmosphere.
¥¥ **Viva Pizza**, Callejón de Veyna, up a small alley almost opposite the cathedral. Good pizza.
¥¥-¥ **La Cantera Musical**, Av Tacuba. Good atmosphere, poor a/c, good Mexican food but drinks limited after 2000.
¥¥-¥ **Nueva Galicia**, Plazuela Goitia 102. Wide range of Mexican food, also offers delicious sushi. Recommended.
¥ **El Tragadero**, Juárez 232. Pretty basic café-set up but good local Zacatecan dishes, veggie dishes, very friendly, cheap and excellent value. 0900-2100, 365 days a year, with special dishes on Christmas Day.
¥ **La Unica Cabaña**, Jardín de la Indepen dencia. Cheap, excellent set meals.
¥ **Recovedi**, facing Plaza Alameda. All-you-can eat buffets, good veggie options, good wholesome food. Cheap.

Cafés
Acrópolis, opposite cathedral. 50-year-old café and diner, good breakfast, slow service.
Café Zaz, Av Hidalgo 201. Reasonably priced in a smart café setting.
Healthfood store, Rayón 413. Serves excellent food at reasonable prices.
San Patricio Caffe, Av Hidalgo. Wonderful (and pricey) coffees, where the smart, young and rich Zacatecanos hang out.

San Luis Potosí *p259, map p260*
Many reasonably priced eating places at western end of Alameda Juan Sarabia.
¥¥ **Los Molinos**, in Hostal del Quijote. Excellent, well-served food.
¥¥-¥ **Café Pacífico**, corner of Los Bravo and Constitución, a couple of blocks from the train station. 24 hrs. Good hot chocolate. Nice atmosphere.
¥¥-¥ **La Parroquia**, corner of Díaz de León and Carranza, on the Plaza de los Fundadores. In old building but modern inside. Attractive wood panelling. Good food and *comida corrida*.
¥¥-¥ **La Posada del Virrey**, north side of Jardín Hidalgo. The restaurant is in a beautiful covered courtyard of an old colonial building. They also have a dining room facing the plaza.

Real de Catorce *p261*
¥¥¥-¥¥ **El Eucalyptus**, on way to Zócalo. Italian-Swiss run. Excellent home-made pasta, vegetarian food, cakes. Pricey but recommended.

Entertainment

Querétaro *p245, map246*
Music
Mariachis play in the Jardín Corregidora, 16 de Septiembre y Corregidora, in the evenings. The town band plays in the Jardín Obregón on Sun evening, lovely atmosphere.

Theatre
Corral de Comedias, Carranza 39, T212-0765. An original theatre company, colonial surroundings and suppers.

San Miguel de Allende *p250, map p250*
Cinema
Villa Jacaranda, hotel video bar. English-language films, US$5 including alcoholic drink and popcorn.

Theatre
Teatro Angela Peralta, Mesones 82, has theatre, musical events and dance. There's a coffee house in the front entrance hall.

Guanajuato *p252, map p252*
Bars and clubs
2 nightclubs have been recommended: **Disco El Grill**, Calle Alonso (100 m from Casa Kloster) and **Disco Los Comerciales**, Juan Valle.

Music
A band plays in Jardín de la Unión 3 times a week.

Theatre
Theatre sketches from classical authors out of doors in lovely old plazas from Apr-Aug.

Teatro Juárez, on Sopeña, a magnificent French-type Second Empire building (US$0.50 to view, US$0.35 to take photos), shows art films and has symphony concerts. **Teatro Principal**, Cantarranas, by Plaza Mexiamora.

León *p255, map p255*
Bars and clubs
Good bars include **JJ Sport**, Rocío 115-A, Jardines del Moral; **Pepe's Pub**, Madero 120, Zona Centro; **Fut-bol Bar**, Hidalgo 923-B, T717-8020. Clubs include **Domus**, López Mateos 2611 Ote, T711-6614; **Ossy's**, Av Paseo de los Insurgentes, on exit road to Lagos de Moreno, T717-6880; **La Iguana**, Centro Comercial Insurgentes, Local 4 y 5B, T718-1416; **Piano Bar Maya**, Prolongación Calzada 112, T716-9734.

Festivals and events

Querétaro *p245, map246*
Dec Feria Agrícola (agricultural rair) from 2nd week of Dec until Christmas with bullfights and cock fights.
Dec 31 New Year's Eve there is a special market and performances in the main street.

Celaya *p249*
10-20 Jan Fiesta of the appearance of the **Virgen de Guadalupe** in the Tierrasnegras barrio, one of the oldest districts of Celaya. There is theatre, dancing, fireworks and eating a typical local *antojito*: *gorditas de Tierrasnegras*.
Mar/Apr Easter is marked by visiting several *balnearios* in the area and there are processions through the streets, much eating of local delicacies, and on Easter Sun, a **Judas** image is burned in many places in the city.
16 Jul The Virgen del Carmen.

San Miguel de Allende *p250, map p250*
Feb Pre-Lenten carnival.
Mar/Apr Easter Week.
Jun Corpus Christi.
End-Jul to mid-Aug Classical Chamber Music Festival; information from Bellas Artes.
15-16 Sep Independence Day.
28 Sep-1 Oct Fiesta de San Miguel, with *conchero* dancers from many places.
2 Nov Day of the Dead.
16-24 Dec Christmas Posadas, celebrated in the traditional colonial manner. There is a **Christmas season musical celebration**, which attracts musicians of an inter-national level.

Dolores Hidalgo *p251, map p251*
15-16 Sep Independence celebrations.

Guanajuato *p252, map p252*
Mar/Apr Viernes de las Flores (Friday of Flowers) is held on the Fri before Good Fri, starting with the **Dance of the Flowers** on Thu night at about 2200 right through the night, adjourning to Jardín de la Unión to exchange flowers. Very colourful and busy.
End Oct Festival Cervantino de Guanajuato, T732-0959, www.festivalcervantino.gob.mx, is an important cultural event in the Spanish-speaking world, encompassing theatre, song and dance over the last 2 weeks of Oct. There is a mixture of free, open-air events, and paying events. Well-known artists from around the world perform. The festival, in honour of Cervantes, is highly recommended and crowded; book accommodation in advance.
Dec During the **Christmas** period students dress up in traditional *estudiantina* costumes and wander the streets singing carols and playing music. Groups leave from in front of the theatre at 2030.

León *p255, map p255*
19-24 Jan Fiesta de San Sebastián, very crowded and good fun.

Aguascalientes *p256*
Mid-Apr Start of a 3-week wine festival, **Feria de San Marcos** (the area is famous for viticulture and the local wine is named after San Marcos). There are processions, cockfights (in Mexico's largest *palenque*, seating 4000), bullfights, agricultural shows, etc. Plaza de Armas is lavishly decorated for the occasion. The *feria*, covered by national TV networks, is said to be the biggest in Mexico. Book accommodation in advance.

Zacatecas *p257, map p258*
Sep The **fiestas** spread over most of the month. There are bullfights on Sun, but given the growth in popularity of the town you could stumble across an impromtu celebration at any time of year.

Real de Catorce *p261*
Mar/Apr On Good Fri, thousands of visitors gather to watch a lively **Passion play**, with realistic Roman soldiers and very colourful Jews and apostles.
3-4 Oct Pilgrimage for **San Francisco**, on foot from Matehuala. Take the local bus from Matehuala to La Paz and join the groups of pilgrims who set out from early evening onwards.

Shopping

Querétaro *p245, map246*
Gems and jewels There are local opals, amethysts and topazes for sale; mineral specimens are shaped into spheres and then polished until they look like jewels. Prices are cheaper than San Juan del Río, but more expensive than Taxco. Recommended is **Joyería Villalón**, Andador Libertad 24a, for fine opals at good prices. **La Cruz market**, 10 mins' walk from the centre, is very well stocked, busy and clean. Open daily, with a street market on Sun.

San Juan del Río *p247*
Gems and jewels **La Guadalupana**, 16 de Septiembre 5. A friendly shop. Recommended.

San Miguel de Allende *p250, map p250*
Bookshop **El Tecolote**, Calle Jesús, good selection of French and English books.

Handicrafts Pottery, cotton cloth and brasswork are the main local crafts. The **Mercado de Artesanías** tends to sell tacky souvenirs rather than real handicrafts; prices are high and the selection poor. **La Casa del Vidrio**, Correo 11, offers an excellent selection of brown-glass items at fair prices (sale prices in the summer, 40% off).

Dolores Hidalgo *p251, map p251*
Crafts **Artesanías Castillo**, Ribera del Río, between Hidalgo and Jalisco. Beautiful ceramics at low prices. Visits to the factory can be arranged.

Markets **Tabasco**, south side, between Jalisco and Hidalgo. There's another market, near Posada Dolores, on **Yucatán**.

Guanajuato *p252, map p252*
Crafts **Fonart**, opposite La Valenciana church (see above) has an excellent selection of handicrafts; high prices but superb quality. Local pottery is for sale in the **Mercado Hidalgo** (1910), in the centre of town, and there is a **Casa de Artesanías** behind the Teatro Juárez (see Entertainment above).

León *p255, map p255*
Leatherwork Shops along **Belisario Domínguez** and **Plaza Piel**, Hilario Medina y López Mateos.

Shopping centres **La Gran Plaza**, Blv López Mateos 1902 Pte; **Plaza Mayor**, Av de las Torres, corner of Prolongación Morelos; **Plaza León**, Blv López Mateos 1102 Ote.

Aguascalientes *p256*
Bootmakers **Zapatería Cervantes**, Guerrero 101 Sur y Nieto, T915-1943. One of many shops selling boots made to order.

Market The main market is at 5 de Mayo y Unión, large and clean, with toilet on upper floor.

Zacatecas *p257, map p258*
Market Between Hidalgo and Tacuba the elegant 19th-century market building has been converted into a pleasant shopping centre (popular café on balcony, reasonable). The market is now dispersed in various locations a few blocks to the southwest. Zacatecas is famous for its *sarapes* and has two delicacies: the local cheese, and *queso de tuna*, a candy made from the fruit of the nopal cactus (do not eat too much, as it has powerful laxative properties).

San Luis Potosí *p259, map p260*
Markets Head north on Hidalgo and you come to **Mercado Hidalgo**, then **Mercado República** and **Mercado 16 de Septiembre**. Locally made *rebozos* (the best are from Santa María del Río) are sold in the markets. **Chalita**, a 3-storey hypermarket, is on Jardín San Juan de Dios between Av Alvaro Obregón and Los Bravo.

Food **Casa de Nutrición**, 5 de Mayo 325, is a healthfood store.

Activities and tours

San Miguel de Allende *p250, map p250*
Tour operators **Viajes Vertiz**, Hidalgo 1A, T152-1856, vvertiz@unisono.net.mx. Good travel agent, American Express agent.
PMC, Hidalgo 18, T152-0121, www.pmexc.com. A wide range of tours and trips from walking tours of the town, workshops and language classes, through to adventure and nature tours and visits to nearby archaelogical sites.

Guanajuato *p252, map p252*
Tour operators Tours of the city and outskirts and south of the state are possible; if you want an English-speaking guide, prices multiply. **Transportes Turísticos de Guanajuato**, underneath the Basílica on Plaza de la Paz, T732-2838, offers tours to sites outside the city.

León *p255, map p255*
Tour operators **Viajes Sindy de León**, 20 de Enero 319, T713-1224. **Jovi de León**, Madero 319 Centro, T714-5094.

Zacatecas *p257, map p258*
Tour operators **Cantera Tours**, Centro Comercial El Mercado, Av López Velarde 602-6, Local A-21, T922-9065.**Operadora Zacatecas**, T924-0050, offers several interesting tours. **Viajes Masoco**, Enlace 115, Col Sierra de Alca, T922-5559, tours to Chicomostoc and Jerez, US$15.50.

Transport

Querétaro *p245, map246*
Air
Flights to **Guadalajara**, **Mexico City**, **Monterrey** and **San Luis Potosí**.
Airline offices Aeromar, T220-6936.

Bus
The bus station is 5 km southeast of the centre, near Estadio Corregidora. Terminal A, modules 1 and 2, 1st class and *plus*; Terminal B, modules 3, 4 and 5, 2nd class. No buses run directly to the centre; the closest you'll get is the south end of Corregidora. There are fixed-price taxis and buses. The bus station has luggage storage, restaurants (with a bar upstairs), travel agency,

newsagents, telephones and toilets.

There are good connections with most towns on the US border if you are heading north. Likewise, if heading south, Querétero is a target to aim for, with good connections. To **Acapulco**, 2200 and 0040, US$42. To **Aguascalientes**, 1315 and 0215, US$19. To **Chihuahua**, 1930 and 2030, US$62. To **Cd Juárez**, 16 a day, US$114. To **Durango**, 1120 and 2100, US$36. To **Guadalajara**, frequent services, 5 hrs, US$27. To **Guanajuato**, 6 a day between 0800 and 1700, 3 hrs, US$9. To **León**, every couple of hours, US$11. To **Mazatlán**, 1000, 1210 and 1830, US$58. To **Mexico City**, an endless stream of buses of all classes, 3 hrs, US$11-14. To **Monterrey**, 15 per day, US$33. To **Morelia**, 16 per day, US$9. To **Nogales**, US$135. To **Piedras Negras**, 1540, 1900 and 1955, US$75. To **San Juan del Río**, every 15 mins, 1 hr. To **San Luis Potosí**, regular throughout the day, 3 hrs, US$12. To **San Miguel de Allende**, hourly, 1 hr, US$5. To **Tijuana**, 1000, 1210 and 1830, US$130. To **Tula**, 2¼ hrs, US$7.50. To **Zacatecas**, almost hourly, US$24.

Car
There is a 4-lane motorway from Irapuato past Querétaro to Mexico City. The Mexico City motorway passes close to Tula and Tepozotlán.

Tequisquiapan *p247*
Bus **San Juan del Río**-Tequisquiapan, regular services, 20 mins, US$1.

San Joaquín *p248*
Bus San Joaquín can be reached in 3 hrs by car or bus on a windy road going through desert and then misty pine forests. Flecha Amarilla runs 6 buses a day, earliest from Querétaro 0620, last 1620, US$4; Flecha Azul also runs buses San Joaquín-**San Juan del Río**.

Jalpan *p247*
Bus To **Mexico City**, 3 direct, 6 hrs, US$18, beautiful trip. To **Landa de Matamoros**, hourly, US$0.80, 20 mins. To **Tilaco** and **Tancoyol**, 40-min bus journey to **La Lagunita**, hourly, then combis (on market day, Sat) or hitchhike. To **Querétaro**, every hr, 5 hrs, US$5. To **Cd Valles**, frequent, via Landa de Matamoros and Xilitla.

Xilitla *p248*

Bus From **Jalpan** every hr, US$2.30, 2½ hrs.

Celaya *p249*

Bus 6 buses a day to **Mexico City** airport with Primera Plus. 24-hr pharmacy at the bus station.

San Miguel de Allende *p250, map p250*

Bus The bus station is on the outskirts, regular bus to the centre US$0.25, returns from the market or outside **Posada San Francisco** on the Jardín. A taxi costs about US$1 to the centre. Buses to the centre leave from in front of the terminal.

To **Aguascalientes**, 1235 and 1435, 2 hrs, US$11. To **Celaya**, every 15 mins, 1 hr, US$2.60. If there are no buses leaving for Guadalajara from San Miguel at the time you want to go, it's best to go to Celaya and catch a bus from there. To **Guadalajara**, 0730, 0930 and 1730, 4 hrs, US$28. To **Guanajuato**, 0745, 0945, 1245 and 1700, US$5. To **León**, 0730, 0930 and 1730, US$10. To **Mexico City** (northern terminal), 0940 and 1600, US$19, cheaper services every 40 mins from 0520 to 2000, US$15. To Querétaro, every 40 mins 0520-2000, US$3.50. To **San Luis Potosí**, 7 per day, US$9.

International connections Daily buses to **Laredo**, Texas, US$44, **San Antonio** and on to **Dallas**, US$67, at 1800. Also daily buses to **Houston** at 1800. And every Wed at 1800 to **Chicago**, US$116.

Dolores Hidalgo *p251, map p251*

Bus Station is at Hidalgo y Chiapas, 5 mins from main square; with restaurant, toilets, left-luggage and telephones. Frequent buses to **Guanajuato**, US$2.50; **Querétaro**, US$3.80; **León**, US$3.65; **Mexico City**, US$10.50; **San Luis Potosí**, US$5; **San Luis de la Paz**, US$2; and **San Miguel de Allende**, US$2.50. To **Aguascalientes**, US$6.50, 2nd class, via San Felipe.

Guanajuato *p252, map p252*

Bus

Local Set fare for city buses US$0.25.

Long distance A new bus terminal has opened on the road to Silao, near toll gate, 20 mins from centre by bus, US$0.30. Taxi to centre, US$2. Buses leave for the centre from right outside the front of the terminal. Look for 'Centro' on the front window of the bus, or the sign above the front window. To get to the bus station from the centre, you pick up buses on Av Juárez in front of the **Hotel Central**, about a block west of the Mercado Hidalgo. The bus stop has a sign saying 'C Camionera'. The bus terminal has a place for storing luggage.

To **Cuidad Juárez**, transferring in León 1015, US$105. To **Guadalajara**, 19 buses a day between 0900 and 2330, US$22. To **Irapuato**, 5 between 0530 and 1830, US$4. To **León**, 0830, 1230 and 1730, 45 mins, US$4.50. To **Mexico City**, regular service, 4½ hrs, US$26. To **Monterrey**, 7 all running in the afternoon, US$42. To **Morelia**, 0700, 0820, 1210 and 1620, US$11. To **Nuevo Laredo**, 1930, US$67. To **Querétaro**, 6 between 0710 and 1820, US$11. To **San Luis Potosí**, 5 through the day, US$13. To **San Miguel de Allende**, regular service from 0700 until 1915, 1½ hrs, US$5. To **Tijuana**, 1800, US$125.

To many destinations it is better to go to León and pick up the more frequent services from there (buses every 10 mins Guanajuato-**León**, US$1.30).

Around Guanajuato *p254*

Bus For **La Valenciana** mine, a local 'Valenciana' bus starts in front of **Hotel Mineral de Rayas**, Alhóndiga 7, leaving every 30 mins during the day, US$0.10, 10 mins' ride.

For **Cerro del Cubilete**, take local buses from Guanajuato, 1½ hrs, US$1.15, 0700, 0900, 1100, 1400, 1600 (also from **Silao**, US$0.75). Last bus up leaves at 1600 from Silao and Guanajuato.

León *p255, map p255*

Air

International airport, Del Bajío (BJX), 18 km from León, 6 km from Silao. Good domestic connections, international flights to several US cities, also to Guatemala and South American cities.

Airline offices Mexicana, Blv López Mateos 401 Ote, T714-9500. **AeroMéxico**, Madero 410, T716-6226. **Continental**, Blv López Mateos 2307 Pte, T713-5199.

Bus
The terminal has a post office, long-distance phones, restaurant and shops. To **Chihuahua**, US$52. Many buses run to **Cd Juárez**, US$50. To **Durango**, US$16.50. To **Guadalajara**, every 30 mins, first at 0600, 4 hrs, US$16. To **Guanajuato**, all the time, 40 mins, US$3. To **Mexico City**, more buses than you can count, 5 hrs, US$23. To **Monterrey**, US$25. To **Poza Rica**, US$21. To **Querétaro**, hourly, 2 hrs, US$8. To **Zacatecas**, 4½ hrs, US$16.

Taxi
Taxis are expensive from the airport to León; take one to Silao, US$10, and then take a bus to León or Guanajuato, or walk 1½ km to the main road and take a bus from there.

Aguascalientes *p256*
Air
The airport (AGU) is 21 km from the town centre. Good domestic flights and flights to **Los Angeles** with AeroMéxico.

Airline offices Aero California, Juan de Montoro 203, T915-2400. AeroMéxico, Madero 474, T916-1362.

Bus
Bus station about 1 km south of centre on Av Circunvalación Sur with post office and pharmacy, take city bus from Galeana near López Mateos. To **Cd Juárez**, US$68. To **Chihuahua**, US$88. To **Guadalajara**, several through the day, 6 hrs, US$18. To **Guanajuato**, 5 daily, 3½ hrs, US$5. To **León**, 21 a day, 2 hrs, US$9. To **Mexico City**, 9 a day, 7 hrs, US$30. To **Monterrey**, US$48. To **Morelia**, Primera Plus, 4 a day, US$17. To **Nuevo Laredo**, US$72. To **Puerto Vallarta**, at 2230, US$46. To **Querétaro**, 8 a day, 6 hrs, US$21. To **San Luis Potosí**, Futura, 16 a day 0600-2300, US$9. To **Tijuana**, 1530 and 2100, US$145. To **Zacatecas**, every 30 mins, 2½ hrs, US$6.

Zacatecas *p257, map p258*
Air
Aeropuerto La Calera (ZCL), 27 km north of city, flights daily to **Mexico City**, **Tijuana**, **Guadalajara**, **Cd Juárez**, **Morelia**, **Aguascalientes** and direct flights to several US cities.

Airline offices Mexicana, T922-3248.

Bus
New terminal 4 km south of town; taxi US$1.20; red No 8 buses from Plaza Independencia (US$0.15) or white *camionetas* from Av González Ortega (old bus station on Blv López Mateos only serves local destinations). Apart from buses to Mexico City, Chihuahua and a few other major towns, most routes do not have bookable seats. Frequent buses passing through Jerez back to Zacatecas with Rojo de Los Altos, US$2.20.

To **Aguascalientes**, every 30 mins, 2½ hrs, US$5. To **Chihuahua**, via Torreón, 12 hrs, US$45. To **Durango**, 5 hrs, many throughout the day, US$8 (if continuing to Mazatlán, stay the night in Durango in order not to miss the views on the way to the coast). To **Guadalajara**, hourly, 4 hrs, US$18. To **Hidalgo del Parral**, 10 hrs, US$39. To **León**, 3½ hrs, US$11. To **Mexico City**, almost hourly, 8 hrs, US$38. To **San Luis Potosí**, 7 daily, 2½ hrs, US$8.

Train
Zacatecas is on the Mexico City-Querétaro-Chihuahua line. No scheduled trains running but if a cargo train is passing through, there may be a passenger wagon.

San Luis Potosí *p259, map p260*
Air
The airport (SLP) is 6 km from the centre. Many daily to **Mexico City**, also flights to **Aguascalientes**, **Guadalajara**, **Monterrey**, **Tampico** Flights to **Chicago**, **San Antonio** (Texas).

Airline offices Aeromar, Av Carranza 1160-2; T911-4671. Mexicana, T917-8836. Aero California, T911-8050. Mexicana de Aviación, T917-8920.

Bus
Bus station on outskirts of town 1½ km from centre. Left-luggage, telephone office and a few shops at the terminal. Also taxi ticket booth, US$2 to centre. For local buses to the centre, walk out the front door of the terminal and turn right. Walk down the street to the first traffic light. Then take buses heading south on the cross street (ie to your right as you're facing it) marked 'de Mayo' or 'Los Gómez'.

To **Aguascalientes**, hourly, 2½ hrs, US$18. To **Chihuahua**, 9 buses per day, US$68. To

Cd Juárez, 9 buses per day, US$92. To **Durango**, 1405, 2045 and 2330, US$29. To **Guadalajara**, hourly service, 5 hrs, US$20. To **Guanajuato**, regular service, 4 hrs, US$11. To **Nuevo Laredo**, 10 hrs, US$45. To **Matehuala**, 13 buses per day, 1½ hrs, US$11. To **Mexico City**, very regular service, 5 hrs, US$25. To **Monterrey**, 14 daily, 6 hrs, US$25. To **Morelia**, regular service, US$19. To **Querétaro**, hourly from 0900, 2½ hrs, US$13. To **San Miguel de Allende**, 6 a day, 3 hrs. To **Tijuana**, 1530 and 1830, US$140. To **Zacatecas**, 7 buses daily, 2½ hrs, US$8.

Autobuses Americanos; 2 buses daily, stopping at **Laredo**, **San Antonio**, **Dallas**, and **Houston**, in Texas, and **Chicago.**

Real de Catorce *p261*

Bus Many buses a day to **Matehuala**, from the corner of Guerrero and Mendiz, US$2 one way. A taxi can be hired for US$25, economic for 4 people; local buses from office 1 block north of the Zócalo.

Directory

Querétaro *p245, map p246*

Banks There is a Banamex ATM on the Jardín Obregón at Juárez and 16 de Septiembre that accepts Visa and MasterCard. Banco Inverlat ATM (that should accept Amex cards) at Corregidora Norte 60. Casa de Cambio at Corregidora Norte 134. **Internet** Café Internet Asodi, Francisco Márquez 219, Col Las Campanas. Café Internet Cibers Pace, Av Universidad 297, Col Las Brujas. Café Internet Welo, Ezequiel Montes 67 Sur (close to corner of Constituyentes), T212-7272. Wave Internet, Carraza, open daily 0900-2200 or thereabouts, US$1 per hr. Simple set-up but good machines. **Language schools** Centro Intercultural de Querétaro, Reforma 41, Centro, T/F212-2831. FEPE (Franco Español para Extranjeros), Luis Pasteur Norte 29, Col Centro, office in Mexico City on T5666-0875. Classes have a maximum of 5 students, 25 hrs per week, also 1-to-1 tuition, 'Spanish for travellers' course and homestays available. **Post office** Arteaga Pte 5.

San Miguel de Allende *p250, map p250*

Banks Casa de Cambio Deal on Correo, opposite post office, and on Juárez. **Embassies and consulates** US Consular Agent, Plaza Golondrinas arcade, Hernández Macías, interior 111, T152-2357, Mon-Fri 0900-1300. **Immigration** 2nd floor Plaza Real del Conde, T152-2542, daily 0900-1300. For tourist card extensions, etc, take 2 copies of passport, tourist card and credit card or TCs. **Internet** Café etc, Calle Reloj 37, Mon-Sat 0800-2100, Sun 1000-1800. Good machines and so much more than an internet café with excellent music and coffee. La Conexión, Aldama 1, T/F152-1599. Border Crossings, Correo 19, phone, fax, and email service. Estación Internet, Recreo 11. **Language schools** Many of the schools demand payment in US dollars (technically illegal) and you may prefer to arrange private tuition for US$3-4 per hr. Academia Hispanoamericana, Mesones 4, T152-0349, www.ahaspeakspanish.com, recommended for language lessons and sessions on Mexican history, folklore, literature, singing and dancing; very helpful; accommodation with families. Warren Hardy Spanish, San Rafael 6, T152-4728, www.warrenhardy.com, intensive courses for beginners or intermediate level, run by Warren Hardy, the inventor of the Card Game method. Habla Hispana Spanish School, Calzada de la Luz 25, Aptdo 689, T152-1535, www.mexicospanish.com, has also received good reports. Mexican Cooking Classes, ask at El Buen café, Jesús 23, different menu every week. **Laundry** On Pasaje de Allende, same-day service; unnamed laundry at Correo 42, good. **Libraries** English-language library Biblioteca Pública on Insurgentes has an excellent selection on Mexico; very extensive bilingual library, with computer centre and English-speaking staff. Distribute the weekly *Atención San Miguel*, which has listings of Spanish classes, tutors and local events. **Telephone** There is a long-distance phone service at Diez de Sollano 4, just off the plaza.

Guanajuato *p252, map p252*

Banks Bancomer, Banca Serfín, Banamex, daily 0900-1100. **Internet** Alonso 70B, Mon-Sat 0900-1800. **Language schools** Academia Falcón, Paseo de la Presa 80, Guanajuato, 36000, T731-1084,

www.academiafalcon.com. Good-quality instruction, regular recommendations. Universidad de Guanajuato, T732-0006, montesa@quijote.ugto.mx. The university has many US exchange students.
Laundry Lavandería Internacional, Alhóndiga 35A, self or service wash. La Burbuja Express, Plazuela Baratillo. Lavandería Automática Internacional, Manuel Doblado 28. **Post office** Corner of Subida San José, by La Compañía church.
Telephone International phone calls from phone booths with coins, or collect. Long-distance offices in Miscelánea Unión shop, by Teatro Principal and on Pocitos, opposite Alhóndiga de Granaditas.

León *p255, map p255*
Banks Bancomer, Belisario Domínguez 322, and HSBC on the plaza. **Post office** Obregón y 5 de Mayo, Mon-Fri 0800-1900.

Aguascalientes *p256*
Banks On Plaza Inverlat, ATM takes Amex. Banamex, ATM. **Cultural centres** El Centro Cultural Los Arquitos, Narcozari y Alameda, T917-0023, formerly a 19th-century bathhouse, restored 1993, museum, bookshop, café. **Internet** Sistemas Alt 64, Vásquez del Mercado 206, T915-7613, Mon-Sat 1000-1400, 1600-2100. Acnet, Edificio Torreplaza Bosques 2nd flr, Av Aguascalientes near university, bus from Rivero Gutiérrez. **Post office** Hospitalidad, near El Porián shopping centre. **Red Cross** T915-2055.

Zacatecas *p257, map p258*
Banks Banamex, Av Hidalgo. Bancomer, Av Hidalgo, has a Visa cash dispenser and gives cash (pesos) on Visa cards. Several other banks with ATMs on Av Hidalgo.
Cultural centres Alianza Francesa, Callejón del Santero 111, T924-0348, French film every Tue at 1900 (free). **Internet** Café@rroba, Félix U Gómez 520 B ,daily 0900-2200. Cybertech, Hidalgo 771, T922-0870, Mon-Sat 0930-2130. **Language school** Fénix Language Institute, T922-1643, www.fenixlanguage institute.com. **Laundry** At the north end of town are Lavandería El Indio Triste, Juan de Tolosa 828 and Lavasolo, similar prices.
Medical services Santa Elena Clinic, Av Guerrero, many specialists, consultation, US$15. **Post office** Allende between Independencia and Hidalgo, towards the south of town. **Telephone** Telégrafos, Av Hidalgo y Juárez.

San Luis Potosí *p259, map p260*
Internet Café Cibernético, Av Carranza 416. **Medical services** Red Cross, Av Juárez and Diez Gutíerrez, T915-3332. Hospital Central (public), Av Carranza 2395, T913-0343. Sociedad de Beneficios Española (private), Av V Carranza 1090, T913-4048. Hospital de Nuestra Señora de la Salud (private), Madre Perla 435, Frac Industrias (4 blocks behind Holiday Inn Hostal del Quixote), T924-5424. Clínica Díaz Infante (private), Arista 730, T912-3737. **Post office** Morelos y González Ortega.

Michoacán

West of Mexico City the state of Michoacán, home to the Purépecha (or Tarascan) people, is a country of deep woods, fine rivers and great lakes, with abundant fruit, fish and game. Visitors are drawn by the Tarascan customs, folklore, way of life, craft skills (pottery, wood work and lacquer), music and especially dance. Try to catch one of the festivals. The Day of the Dead, an important date in the Mexican calendar of festivals, is prominent in Michoacán, particularly around Pátzcuaro, where on 1 November every village around the lake honours its dead; it is a festive occasion, but also profoundly spiritual. People flock to El Campanario Ecological Reserve each year to see millions of Monarch butterflies take to the wing, one of the most impressive sights in all of Mexico.

There are many small prehispanic sites to be explored en route, and the open chapel at Cuitzeo is well worth a stop. As elsewhere in Mexico, the colonial architecture will impress and the natural beauty of Volcán Paricutín will bemuse. A few days relaxing on the almost deserted beaches of Playa Azul will prepare you for the next stage of your journey. ▸▸ *For Sleeping, Eating and other listings, see pages 283-289.*

Morelia ▸▸ *pp283-289. Colour map 3, B3.*

→ *Phone code: 443. Altitude: 1950 m.*

Founded in 1541, Morelia, capital of Michoacán State, is a rose-tinted city with grand, attractive colonial buildings, delightful courtyards and shady plazas.

Ins and outs

Getting there The airport is about 27 km north of Morelia. Blue and white Aeropuerto buses will take you to the centre. The new bus terminal is a long way from town. It is best to get a taxi for the 15- to 20-minute drive; or take a local bus. Morelia is connected by Route 43 to Salamanca, Route 14 to Uruapan and Route 15 to Zamora and Mexico City.

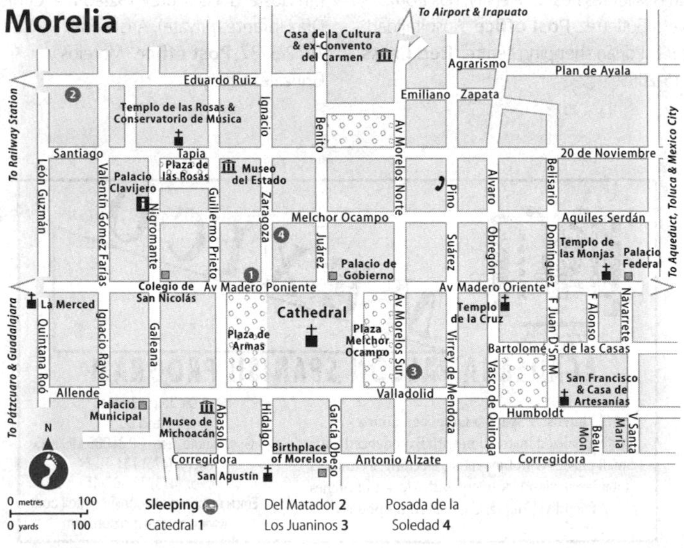

Tourist information The **tourist office** ⓘ *Nigromante 79, T312-8081, www.turismomichoacan.gob.mx, Mon-Fri 0800-2000, Sat and Sun 0900-1900*, is inside Palacio Clavijero (south end), and has local hotel information and map; English spoken. Good city maps are available from **Casa de Cambio Troca Mex** ⓘ *Melchor Ocampo y Zaragoza and on Guillermo Preito.*

Sights

The **cathedral** (1640) is set between the two main plazas, with graceful towers and a fine façade, in what is called 'sober baroque' style. The **Santuario de la Virgen de Guadalupe**, east of the aqueduct, has an ornate interior of terracotta garlands and buds, painted in pastels. There are four huge oil paintings of the missionaries 'Christianizing the Indians'. Other important churches are the modernized **Templo de la Cruz** and the 18th-century **Templo de las Rosas** in the delightful plaza of the same name (its ex-Convento now houses the Conservatorio de Música). The oldest of Morelia's churches is the **Templo de San Francisco** of the Spanish Renaissance period, although it lacks many of the decorative features of that style. The **Templo de las Monjas** has an extravagant baroque façade, constructed in 1727. The **Templo de San Agustín** (16th century) has a more Gothic influence but is also imposing.

There are some good language schools in Morelia (see Directory page 288).

Even more interesting than the colonial churches are the many fine colonial secular buildings still standing. The Independence hero José María Morelos, the reformer Melchor Ocampo and the two unfortunate Emperors of Mexico (Agustín de Iturbide and the Archduke Maximilian of Austria) are commemorated by plaques on their houses. **Morelos' birthplace**, at Corregidora 113, is open to visitors, admission free. The **Colegio de San Nicolás** (1540) is the oldest surviving institution of higher education in Latin America. (It has a summer school for foreign students.) Opposite is the **Centro Cultural Universitario**, with many free events. The fine former Jesuit college, now called the **Palacio Clavijero**, corner of Madero and Nigromante, contains government offices and an extensive market selling *artesanía* and sweets in the arcades, with a helpful **tourist office** on the ground floor. At the east edge of the downtown area, on the road to Mexico City, are the 224 arches of a ruined **aqueduct**, built in 1788 (walk 11 blocks east from cathedral along Avenida Madero). Both **Banamex** and **Bancomer** have their offices in magnificent old houses on Madero Poniente, near the plaza; the patio of the former is especially fine. Also notable are the **Law School**, in the former monastery of **San Diego**, next to the **Santuario de la Virgen de Guadalupe**, past the aqueduct; the **Palacio de Gobierno** (1732-1770), facing the cathedral; the **Palacio Municipal**; and the **Palacio Federal**, built in the 18th century, and formerly a convent. Visit also the churches of **La Merced**, with its lovely tower and strange, bulging *estípites* (inverted pyramidal supports), **Las Capuchinas**, Ortega y Montaño, southeast of the centre, which has some churrigueresque *retablos*, and **Santa María**, on a hilltop south of the city.

Next to the Plaza de Morelos is the **Calzada Fray Antonio de San Miguel**, a shady pedestrianized walkway with restored mansions leading three blocks to the **Fuente Tarasca**, a fountain with three bare-breasted women holding up a giant basket of fruit.

Thursday and Sunday are **market days**: specialities are pottery, lacquerwork, woodcarving, jewellery, blankets and leather sandals; in this connection see the **Casa de Artesanías de Michoacán**, in the ex-Convento de San Francisco, next to the church of the same name; it is full of fine regional products for sale but they are not cheap. The small shops upstairs, some of which have local artisans at work, have better quality crafts than the shops downstairs. The masks are particularly fine.

Museums

The **Museo de Michoacán** ⓘ *Calle Allende 305, Mon-Sat 0900-1900, Sun 0900-1400, US$4.505*, has a collection of objects relating to the history of Michoacán from prehispanic times to the present day. The **Casa de la Cultura** ⓘ *Av Morelos Norte, daily, free*, housed in the ex-Convento del Carmen, has a good collection of masks from various regions, and also of crucifixes. The centre hosts arts workshops (nominal fee), daily music and dance performances, exhibitions, etc. The **Museo del Estado** ⓘ *southeast corner of Jardín de las Rosas, Mon-Sat 0900-1400, 1600-2000, Sun 0900-1400, 1600-1900, free*, in the house of Empreror Iturbide's wife (Casa de la Emperatriz), is well worth a visit. Most of the ground floor is dedicated to Tarascan history and culture, with lots of information about Michoacán and, at the front, an old pharmacy with all its bottles, cabinets, scales, etc intact. The **Museo Casa de Morelos** ⓘ *Morelos Sur, daily 0900-1900, US$1.20*, about three blocks south of the cathedral, has exhibits on the Independence movement and its hero, José María Morelos. **Museo de Arte Contemporáneo Alfredo Zalce** ⓘ *Av Acueducto, Tue-Sun, closes for siesta, reopens 1600*, in a 19th-century French-style building, has temporary exhibitions. For a guided tour of the city, contact David, front desk, Villa Montaña Hotel, where there are many other tours on offer, including one to the Monarch Butterfly Reserve (see page 279).

Around Morelia

» pp283-289.

The road east of Morelia soon climbs through 50 km of splendid mountain scenery of forests, waterfalls and gorges, to the highest point (Km 253), Puerto Gartan, and **Mil Cumbres** (2886 m), with a magnificent view over mountain and valley, and then descends into a tropical valley. A new, four-lane highway avoids the Mil Cumbres pass.

Zitácuaro is a small town with a pleasant plaza and a good covered market. The **tourist office** ⓘ *T153-0675, www.zitacuaro.com.mx*, is at Km 4 on the Zitácuaro-Toluca road. North of here, a turning off the main road at **Angangueo** brings you to a unique site, the wintering grounds of the Monarch butterfly in **Reserva Ecológica El Campanario** ⓘ *daily 0900-1700, US$2, plus a tip for your guide, Spanish only, see box, page 279*, above the village of **El Rosario**. Try to form a small group to go round the reserve. There is a visitors' centre and food kiosks near the entrance.

Just north of Morelia there is a good road to two lakeside villages in the neighbouring state of Guanajuato. At **Cuitzeo**, the first one, there is a fine Augustinian church and convent (begun in 1550), with a cloister, a huge open chapel, and good choir stalls in the sacristy. The church houses a collection of Mexican graphic art, spanning four centuries, in a gallery in the basement. **Laguna de Cuitzeo**, beside which it stands, is the second largest lake in Mexico; the road crosses it on a causeway. From here one can go through the attractive mountain scenery around **Valle de Santiago**. The second village, 33 km to the north, **Yuriria**, has a large-scale indigenous version of the splendid church and convent at Actopan. It is on Laguna de Yuriria, which looks like a grassy swamp.

Quiroga heart of Tarascan (Purépecha) country, is named after Bishop Vasco de Quiroga, who was responsible for most of the Spanish building in the area and for teaching the Purépecha people the various crafts they still practise: work in wool, leather, copper, ceramics and cane. There are many indigenous people here and few tourists. There is a fair and craft exhibitions in December.

Tzintzuntzan (pronounced rapidly *sin-sun-san*) was the pre-Conquest Tarascan capital; the **ruins** ⓘ *daily 0900-1700, US$2*, are just behind the village; a Purépecha ceremonial centre, with five pyramids, is across the road and up the hill (10 minutes' walk) from the monastery. The **monastery**, on Magdalena, was built in 1533 but closed over 250 years ago. It has been restored, but its frescoes have deteriorated badly. The church bells date from the 16th century; a guard will show you round. In the grounds are some very old olive trees which are still bearing fruit, said to have been planted by Vasco de Quiroga. Fortuitously they were missed in a Spanish edict to

Monarch butterflies

The wintering ground of the Monarch butterfly in Reserva Ecológica El Campanario is one of the natural wonders of the world. Every year millions of bright orange-coloured butterflies gather to enjoy the warm climate having migrated from southeast Canada and northeast USA. Huge clusters of butterflies hang from branches, which bow under their weight, eventually rising in a swirling mass of red clouds when warm air blows through the reserve. Most impressive is the sound of their wings, like a strong breeze blowing through the trees. The butterflies arrive between December and March, with the best time of year to visit being January and February. They leave in March, after which there is nothing to see until the following November/December. The reserve is at a high altitude and you need to walk a few kilometres (30 minutes) to see the butterflies. Bring warm clothes. It is very cold at night. It gets very busy at week-ends, when all the accommodation will be full; your best bet is to arrive at the sanctuary when it opens at 0900 to avoid the rush of tourists, US$2.

The reserve can easily be visited from the villages of **Angangueo** or **Zitácuaro**, both of which cater for the influx of butterfly-watchers. Alternatively, you can arrange transport from Mexico City. (See Zitácuaro and Angangueo, page 284, for hotel options.) Half-hourly local bus (marked Angangueo) from Zitácuaro (Avenida Santos Degollado Oriente, or from bus station on outskirts of town) to Ocampo, one hour, US$1.20, and from Ocampo another local bus via El Rosario (one every hour, 75 minutes, US$2.80, 12 km on a mountainous dirt road) to the parking lot below the reserve from where it is a 15-minute walk to the reserve. A truck from Ocampo to the butterfly refuge costs US$17; this can be shared, especially at week-ends. All hotels will arrange transport to the reserve, about US$20 per vehicle, one hour. Four direct buses a day to Mexico City (west), US$11.

destroy all Mexican olive trees when it was thought that Mexican olive oil would compete with Spain's. A most interesting **Passion play** is given at Tzintzuntzan and fiestas, such as **El Señor del Rescate** on 1 February, are very colourful. Beautiful, hand-painted pottery, displayed everywhere, is very cheap but also brittle. (It is also available in other markets in Mexico.) Other handicrafts on sale include woodcarving, leather and basket-woven Christmas tree ornaments; good bargaining opportunities.

Pátzcuaro and around

» *pp283-289. Colour map 3, B2.*

→ *Phone code: 434. Altitude: 2110 m.*

Twenty-three kilometres south of Quiroga, Pátzcuaro is one of the most picturesque towns in Mexico, with narrow cobbled streets and deep overhanging eaves. The houses are painted white and brown. It is built near Lago de Pátzcuaro, about 50 km in circumference, with Tarascan villages on its shores and many islands. At these villages, the Day of the Dead commemorations are worth visiting.

Ins and outs

Getting there The nearest airports are at Morelia to the east and Uruapan to the west. The bus station is on the outskirts of town. A local bus, *colectivo* or taxi will take you to the centre. Pátzcuaro is connected by Route 14 to Morelia and Uruapan.

Getting around It is a steep 3-km walk uphill from the lake shore to the plaza; *colectivos* run every few minutes to Plaza Chica.

Tourist information The **tourist office** ⓘ *on the north side of Plaza Grande next to Banca Serfín, Mon-Fri 0900-1500, variable in afternoon, usually 1700-1900, Sat and Sun 0900-1500*, is friendly and provides good information.

Sights

There are several interesting buildings: the unfinished **La Colegiata** (1603), known locally as La Basílica, with its much-venerated Virgin fashioned by an indigenous craftsman from a paste made with cornstalk pith and said to have been found floating in a canoe. Behind the Basílica there are remains of the pre-Columbian town and of a pyramid in the precincts of the Museo de Artes Populares; the restored Jesuit church of **La Compañía** (and, almost opposite, the early 17th-century church of the **Sagrario**) at the top of Calle Portugal. Behind this street are two more ecclesiastical buildings: the **Colegio Teresiano** and the restored **Templo del Santuario**; on Calle Lerín is the old monastery, with a series of small patios. There are murals by Juan O'Gorman in the **Library**, formerly San Agustín. On Calle Allende is the residence of the first governor. On Calle Terán is the church of **San Francisco**; nearby is **San Juan de Dios**, on the corner of Calle Romero. Visit also the **Plaza Vasco de Quiroga**. The chapel of **El Calvario** is 15 minutes' walk outside the town, on the summit of Cerro del Calvario, a hill giving wide views. The views are also good from the old chapel of the **Humilladero**, above the cemetery on the old road to Morelia. This chapel is said to have been built on the spot where the last Tarascan emperor knelt in submission to the Spanish conquistador, Cristóbal de Olid.

The very well-arranged **Museo de Artes Populares** ⓘ *Tue-Sat 0900-1900, Sun 0900-1430, English speaking, friendly guide, US$2*, is in the former Colegio de San Nicolás (1540) and is excellent for seeing regional ceramics, weaving, woodcarving and basketware. Ask there for the **Casa de los Once Patios**, which contains boutiques selling handicrafts; you can see weavers and painters of lacquerwork in action.

The best-known lake island is **Janitzio**, which has been spoilt by the souvenir shops and the tourists (visit during the week if possible). It is 45 minutes by motorboat; boats leave when full from 0800 onwards, US$2.50 return from Muelle General; cheaper from Muelle San Pedrito, 500 m further on, tickets from office at dock, last boat back (return by any boat) at 2000. It is a 45-minute walk from the centre of Pátzcuaro or take a bus marked 'Lago' from Plaza Bocanegra. There is an unfortunate **Monumento a Morelos** ⓘ *US$0.60*, crowning a hill on the island, with a mural glorifying Independence inside. It nevertheless affords magnificent views although there are often queues to climb the spiralling stairs inside to the top. A circular path goes around the island where there are lots of good restaurants; those on the waterfront charge more than those on the hill, same quality.

For information on the Day of the Dead, see Festivals and events, page 287.

Another lake island to visit, less touristy than Janitzio, is **Yunuen**, boat from Muelle General, US$2.70. The island is clean and quiet. There are few *lanchas* during the week, so be sure to arrange a return trip unless you want to spend the night. Bring provisions. On a lakeside estate (formerly the country house of General Lázaro Cárdenas) is the **Educational Centre for Community Development in Latin America** ⓘ *T342-8153, www.crefal.edu.mx*, better known as CREFAL (free films every Wednesday at 1930).

For a truly spectacular view of the lake, the islands and the surrounding countryside, walk to **Cerro del Estribo**; an ideal site for a quiet picnic. It is a one-and-a-half-hour walk to the top from the centre of Pátzcuaro. The areas round Pátzcuaro are also recommended for birdwatching.

From Pátzcuaro, you can also visit **Tzintzuntzan** and **Quiroga** (see page 278) by regular bus service. Thirty minutes by local bus from Plaza Chica is **Ihuatzio** ⓘ *US$1.10, leaflets in Spanish or English, US$0.40*, on a peninsula 12 km north of Pátzcuaro town, 8 km from Tzintzuntzan. This was the second most important Tarascan city; two pyramids are well preserved and afford good views of the lake. The pyramids are signposted, 1 km from the village, but the road is very bad. To get to Tzintzuntzan from Ihuatzio, take bus or hitch back to main road and wait for Pátzcuaro-Quiroga bus.

Uruapan and around

» *pp283-289. Colour map 3, B2.*

→ *Phone code: 452. Altitude: 1610 m.*

From Pátzcuaro, the road continues southwest to Uruapan, the 'place where flowers are plentiful'. The most attractive of its three plazas is the **Zócalo**, which has the **Jardín de los Mártires** at its west end. Opposite the Jardín is part of the former **Collegiate church of San Francisco** (17th century with later additions such as an interesting 1960s modern art interior), which houses the attractive **Casa de la Cultura** (small museum upstairs, free, with excellent display of the history of Uruapan). Local crafts can be bought in the *portales* or at the market. At the east end of the Zócalo is the restored hospital, built by Fray Juan de San Miguel in the 16th century; now a ceramics museum, the **Museo La Huatápera**. Adjoining it is a 16th-century chapel now converted into a craft shop. Behind the chapel and museum is the **Mercado de Antojitos** and, beyond it, the clothes and goods market permanently occupying several streets. The **food market** has now moved out of the centre to two sites, one at Obregón and Francisco Villa with cheap eateries upstairs, and the other on Calzada Benito Juárez at the end of the goods market that extends up Constitución from the centre.

On M Treviño, between A Isaac and Amado Nervo, there is a house just 1.5 m wide and several storeys high – possibly Mexico's narrowest building.

The **tourist office** ⓘ *Ayala, T524-7199, Mon-Sat 0900-1400 and 1600-2000, Sun 1000-1400*, is between Independencia and Pino Suárez.

The town suffers badly from traffic fumes although it is set beside streams, orchards and waterfalls in the **Parque Nacional Eduardo Ruiz** ⓘ *US$0.35*, which is cool at night, and well worth a visit. To get there, walk or catch a bus one block south of the Zócalo marked 'El Parque'. At the entrance to the Parque, on the corner of Independencia and Culver City, 1 km from the town centre, is a **Mercado de Artesanías** selling wooden boxes and bracelets. Local foods are sold in the park.

It is 10 km through coffee groves and orchards along Río Cupatitzio (meaning Singing River) to the **Tzararacua Falls** ⓘ *US$0.25*. There are restaurants at the bus stop where you can hire a horse to the falls ; it is not advisable to walk to the falls alone. A bus (marked 'Tzararacua', or 'Zupomita'; but ask if it goes all the way) will take you from the Zócalo at Uruapan to Tzararacua, US$1 (15-25 minutes), weekends and public holidays only.

Volcán Paricutín → *Colour map 3, B2.*

The volcano of Paricutín can be visited from Uruapan. It started erupting on 20 February 1943, became fiery and violent and rose to a height of 1300 m above the 2200-m-high region, and then died down after several years into a quiet grey mountain (460 m) surrounded by a sea of cold lava. The church tower of **San Juan**, a buried village, thrusting up through cold lava is a fantastic sight (the lava flow stopped at the foot of the altar). If you are not taking an organized tour (with horses and guides included), Paricutín is best reached by taking a 'Los Reyes' bus on a paved road to **Angahuan**, 34 km from Uruapan, US$0.85, one hour, nine a day each way (from 0500 to 2000) with **Galeana**, then hire a horse or mule or walk (one hour).

A full day's excursion with mules to the area costs about US$8-12 per mule, with US$3-4 tip for the guide (six to seven hours); shorter journeys cost less. To go on foot with a guide costs US$10. It is 3 km from Angahuan to the San Juan ruins, an easy walk: as you enter the village square from Uruapan (the church is south of that street) follow the road and after the square take the second street to you left (it is the only road that goes at an angle of 45°) and follow this cobbled street with telegraph poles on the left-hand side for 750 m to a stone pillared gateway. At the gate turn right down a dirt path that leads to a parking area and a viewpoint of the site (overnight parking possible). Just before you enter the parking lot a wide, dirt path with many horse tracks and footprints leads to your right and down through the forest and directly to the lava field and the church. Alternatively, start at the new hostel from where you can also see the church. Guide on foot to church US$5 per group.

To the crater of the volcano is 10 km, a long, tough walk (also a long day on horseback for the unaccustomed, especially if you get a wooden saddle). Walk westwards round the lava field, through an avocado plantation. Wear good walking shoes with thick soles as the lava is very rough and as sharp as glass in places (some people find they cannot make the last stretch over the tennis-ball size rocks); bear in mind the altitude too, as the return is uphill. It takes seven to nine hours to the volcano and back. The cone itself is rather small and to reach it there is a stiff 30-minute climb from the base. A path goes around the tip of the crater, where activity has ceased. If going in one day, leave Uruapan by 0800 so that you don't have to rush. Go even earlier in the rainy season as clouds usually build up by midday. Take a sweater for the evening and for the summit where it can be windy and cold after a hot climb. The last bus back to Uruapan leaves at 1900; but it's best not to rely on it. Much better is to stay the night in **Angahuan**, where there is an *albergue* (see Sleeping, page 283). It is possible to drive to the *albergue* where they try to charge US$1.60 for the free car park. Camping is possible near the hostel. In the village are shops selling food and drink and there is a good local restaurant in the street behind the church. Two reasonable restaurants are on the road to the *albergue*. There is a water tap near the church; follow the signs. Just outside the village, on the dirt track to the main road, is the cemetery.

Zamora and Paracho

→ Phone codes: 351 and 423. Colour map 3, B2.

Zamora (58 km east of Jiquilpan) is an agricultural centre founded in 1540. In the centre is the **Catedral Inconclusa**, a large, interesting Gothic-style church, started in 1898, but work was suspended during the Revolution. There are several other fine churches, and a market on Corregidora. Much of the area around the plaza is pedestrianized. Nearby is tiny Laguna de Camécuaro, with boats for hire, restaurants and wandering musicians; popular at holiday times. There is a **tourist office** ⓘ *Morelo Sur 76, T512-4015*.

South east of Zamora is **Charapán** where a branch road runs 32 km south through pine woods to Paracho, a quaint, very traditional village of small wooden houses; in every other one craftworkers make guitars, violins and mandolins, worth from US$15 to US$1500. A recommended workshop is that of **Ramiro Castillo** ⓘ *Av Independencia 259, Galeana 38*, good value, friendly. Bargaining is possible in all workshops.

Pacific coast

» *pp283-289. Colour map 3, B2.*

The Pacific coast of Michoacán is only just coming under development. From Uruapan, Route 37 goes to Playa Azul, 350 km northwest of Acapulco (bus US$12, 10½ hours minimum) and 122 km from Zihuatanejo (see page 349). **Playa Azul** is a coconut-and-hammock resort (reported dirty and dilapidated) frequented much more by Mexicans than foreigners, with a few large hotels. The town of **La Mira**, on the main road, is larger than Playa Azul. Forty kilometres of excellent deserted beaches stretch to the north of Playa Azul. At night there is beautiful phosphorescence at the water's edge.

Northwest up the coast, 76 km from Playa Azul, is **Caleta de Campos**. Buses run along the coast road to La Mira, then a short distance to Caleta de Campos. In this poor village perched above a beautiful bay, there is little to eat other than seafood. At the beach here, five minutes from the village, there are bars and restaurants, popular with surfers. Be careful as there are strong currents. The main **fiesta** runs from 10-13 December; at 0200 on 13 December **El Torito**, a bull mask and sculpture loaded with fireworks, makes its spectacular appearance (watch out for elaborate, if dangerous, fireworks at fiesta time).

> *Avoid night-time driving in this area as hold-ups have been reported.*

Eighty-six kilometres further up the coast, to the northwest, is **Maruata**, unspoilt and beautiful. This is a turtle conservation area. There are floods in the rainy season and the river has washed away some of the beach. There are *cabañas* for rent and *palapas* under which you can camp. For southbound traffic seeking Maruata, road signs are inadequate.

Lázaro Cárdenas is the connecting point for buses from Uruapan, Manzanillo and Zihuatanejo. There is a **tourist office** ⓘ *in the Hotel Casablanca building, Nicolás Bravo 475, T532-1547*.

Sleeping

Morelia *p276, map p276*

Some of the cheaper hotels may have water only in the morning; check.

LL Los Juaninos, Morelos Sur 39, T312-0036, www.hoteljuaninos.com.mx. At one time the Episcopal Palace (1685), beautifully restored in 1998, rooftop restaurant overlooking the Zócalo. Luxurious.

LL Villa Montaña, Patzimba 201, T314-0231, www.villamontana.com.mx. On Santa María hill, south of the city, with glorious views. Each room is a house on its own, run by French aristocrats; very expensive but worth it, superb restaurant.

L-AL Posada de la Soledad, Zaragoza 90 and Ocampo, T312-1888, www.hsoledad.com. Off Plaza de Armas and quiet. Fine courtyards, converted chapel as dining room, TV and fireplaces in rooms, parking opposite, good value. Recommended.

AL-A Catedral, Zaragoza 37, T313-0783, hotel_catedral@infosel.net.mx. Close to plaza. Spacious, nice bar, restaurant closes quite early. Recommended.

A Concordia, Gómez Farías 328, T312-3052, round corner from bus station. TV and phone in rooms.

C Villa Centurión, on road to Morelos, T313-2272. Good antiques, pool, TV.

C Del Matador, E Ruiz 531, opposite bus station, T/F312-4649. Simple, with bath.

C Don Vasco, Vasco de Quiroga 232, T/F312-1484. With shower and hot water, clean, safe, some rooms dingy. Recommended.

C Las Palmas, on road to Guadalajara, also trailer park. 2 good trailer parks on Route 126 between Morelia and the capital.

C Mintzicuri, Vasco de Quiroga 227 (opposite Don Vasco), T312-0664. Clean, small rooms, hot shower, TV, parking, helpful tourist office.

D Colonial, Morelos Norte, corner with 20 de Noviembre 15, T312-1897. Pleasant, lots of hot water, good value.

D Posada del Cortijo, E Ruiz 673, T312-9642. Good value, but small rooms, overlooks the Casa de la Cultura, hot water.

D Posada Lourdes, Madero Pte 340, T312-5603. Basic, clean, quiet, hot water.

E Señorial, Santiago Tapiá 543, 1 block south from bus terminal. Basic, with bath.

E Youth hostel, corner of Oaxaca and Chiapas 180, 1 km southwest of bus station (walk west to Cuautla, then south along Cuautla to Oaxaca), T313-3177. Price per person. Known by its initials IMJUDE, although some people refer to it as CREA, its former initials.

Around Morelia *p278*

L-AL Villa Monarca Inn, Zitácuaro, on the road to Morelia, T715-153-5346, www.villamonarca.com. Has a pool.

AL Rancho San Cayetano, Zitácuaro, 3 km out on Huetamo road, T153-1926, hotel@ranchosancayetano.com. Chalets, friendly, clean. Highly recommended.

A Lorenz, Av Hidalgo Ote 14, Zitácuaro, 9 blocks from bus station, T715-253-0991. Quiet, clean, TV, friendly.

C Albergue Don Bruno, Morelia 92, Angangueo, T156-0026. Good but a little overpriced, nice setting, restaurant.

C La Margarita, Morelia, Angangueo, very clean, highly recommended, owner does tours to butterfly sanctuary.

C México, Revolución Sur 22, Zitácuaro, T(715)153-2811. Clean, large rooms with cable TV, parking, restaurant.

C Quiroga, Vasco de Quiroga Pte 340, Quiroga, T354-0035. Modern with parking.

C Tarasco, Vasco de Quiroga Ote 9, Quiroga, T354-0100, eduardo_carreon_valadez@yahoo.com.mx. Colonial style, with a courtyard, clean, hot water, pleasant but front rooms noisy. Parking.

D América, Revolución Sur 8, Zitácuaro, 1st block, T(715)-153-1116. TV, pleasant, clean.

D Mary, Revolución Sur 4, Zitácuaro, T(715) 153-0847. Hot shower, TV, clean.

D Posada Michoacán, 5 de Mayo, main square, Zitácuaro, T(715) 153-0008. TV, clean, friendly, luggage store.

D-E Paso de la Monarca, Nacional 20, Angangueo, T158-0187. Large comfortable rooms, hot water, friendly, meals. Highly recommended.

E Carolina, Zitácuaro, 1 block north of the plaza between Revolución. Big rooms, friendly and hot water until 2100, cheap option.

E Hotel Imperial, Queréndaro, near church. Pleasant rooms and courtyard, hot water, good value.

Camping

Trailer park 3 km north of Quiroga. Old summer residence of a former Mexican president, good view over Lake Pátzcuaro.

Pátzcuaro and around *p279, map p280*

Rooms in some hotels are reserved 4 weeks prior to Día de los Muertos; other hotels do not take reservations, so it's pot luck at this time.

L Posada La Basílica, Arciga 4, T342-1108. 12 rooms, nice restaurant with good views, central.

L Mansión Iturbe, Portal Morelos 59, T342-3628, www.mexonline.com/iturbe.htm. 14 rooms, English, French and

Phone codes *Morelia 443; Zitácuaro 715; Quiroga 454; Pátzcuaro 434; Uruapan 452; Zamora 351; Paracho 423; Lázaro Cárdenas 753.*

German spoken, beautiful restored 1790s mansion on main plaza, *El Gaucho Viejo* restaurant, Argentine *churrasco*. Open Wed-Sun 1800-2400; folk music. Recommended.

L-AL Fiesta Plaza, Plaza Bocanegra 24, T342-2516. Beautiful interior patio, good.

L-AL Posada de don Vasco, Av Lázaro Cárdenas 450, towards the lake, T342-0227. Attractive, colonial-style hotel (halfway between lake and town), breakfast good, other meals poor, presents the *Baile de los Viejitos* (Dance of the Old Men) on Wed and Sat at 2100 at no charge, non-residents welcome but drinks very expensive.

AL Misión San Manuel, Portal Aldama 12 on main plaza, T342-1050. Restaurant. Highly recommended.

A Gran Hotel, Portal Regules 6, on Plaza Bocanegra, T342-0443, www.granhotel patzcuaro.com.mx. Small rooms, clean, friendly, pleasant, good food.

A Los Escudos, Portal Hidalgo 73, T342-1290. 17th-century building, ask for room with fireplace, good food. *Baile de los Viejitos* (Dance of the Old Men) every Sat at 2000. Recommended.

A Mesón del Gallo, Dr Coss 20, T342-1474, hmeson@yahoo.com. 25 rooms, good value, flower garden, tasteful furnishings.

A-B Villa Pátzcuaro, Av Lázaro Cárdenas 506, T342-0767, 1 km from centre. Very quiet, pleasant, hot water, gardens, lots of birds, tennis, also camping and caravan site.

B Hostería de San Felipe, Av Lázaro Cárdenas 321, T/F342-1298, www.mexon line.com/hosteria-sanfelipe.htm. Friendly, clean, fireplaces in rooms, good restaurant (closes 2030). Highly recommended.

B Mesón del Cortijo, Obregón, just off Américas, towards the lake, T342-1295. Often fully booked at weekends. Recommended.

B Posada de la Salud, Benigno Serrato 9, T342-0058. Clean, quiet, pleasant, nice garden, excellent value, no hot water during middle of day, some rooms with individual fireplaces. Recommended.

D Valmen, Padre Lloreda 34-A, T342-1161. Good, friendly.

D-E Posada de la Rosa, Portal Juárez 29 (Plaza Chica), T342-0811. With bath, cheaper without, colonial style, clean, doors to rooms not very secure, parking.

D-E Posada San Agustín, Portal Juárez 27 (Plaza Chica), T342-0442. Very good value, clean, hot water.

Camping

See also Villa Pátzcuaro, above.

Trailer Park El Pozo, on lakeside, opposite Chalamu, Km 20, Carretara 15, T342-0937. Hot showers am, large, delightful, well equipped, owner speaks English, also camping.

Uruapan and around *p281*

L Mansión del Cupatitzio, motel on the road to Guadalajara, T523-2100, www.mansiondel cupatitzio.com. Outstanding.

AL El Tarasco, Independencia 2, T524-1500. Pool, lovely, good restaurant.

A Concordia, Portal Carrillo 8, on main plaza, T/F523-0400, www.hotelconcordia.com.mx. Comfortable rooms and a nice restaurant.

A Pie de la Sierra, Km 4 Carretera a Charapán, on north outskirts, T524-2510. Good motel with moderately priced restaurant.

B Nuevo Hotel Alameda, Av 5 de Febrero, T523-4100. With bath, clean, TV, good value.

B-C Villa de Flores, Emilio Carranza 15, west of centre, T524-2800. Quiet, pleasantly furnished, lovely flowers. Recommended.

C Del Parque, Av Independencia 124. With bath, very nice, by entrance to national park, clean, quiet, enclosed parking. Recommended.

C-D Mi Solar, Juan Delgado 10, T522-0912, www.hotelmisolaruruapan.com. Good value, hot water, clean. Recommended.

E Betty's, near bus station. Price per person. With bath.

E Moderno, main plaza. Lovely building, with bath, water spasmodic, friendly, very basic.

Volcán Paricutín *p282*

B-E Cabañas, Angahuan. Sleep 6, with a log fire, or cheaper per person in dormitory with bunk beds (dormitories closed in low season). Both have hot showers; meals available, restaurant closes 1900 in low season, basic facilities, but clean and peaceful, warm and recommended but service poorer when few people are staying.

D Albergue Centro Turístico de Angahuan, T(452) 523-3934 (Uruapan). The *albergue* is signposted from the bus stop, and is about 30-min walk from there.

Zamora and Paracho *p283*
L-B **Fénix**, Madero Sur 401, Zamora, T512-0266, www.hotelfenix.com. Clean, big swimming pool, poor ventilation, pleasant balconies.
C-D **Posada Fénix**, Morelos y Corregidora Ote 54, T515-1265, 1 block from Zócalo, Zamora. Rooms of varying quality, nice owner (also owns **Fénix**, see above), good laundry service.
E **San Sebastián**, Piedad de Cabadas. Central, hot water, old but nice, parking across the street.

Pacific coast *p283*
AL **De la Curva**, Nicolás Bravo 235, Lázaro Cárdenas, T537-3658, www.hoteldelacurva.com. Good services across the board.
A **Playa Azul**, Venustiano Carranza s/n, Playa Azul, T536-0089. Has a trailer park with 20 spaces, full hook-up, bathrooms, cold shower, 2 pools, bar and restaurant, US$13 for car and 2 people.
C **Los Arcos**, Caleta de Campos, T531-5038. With bath, good views from most rooms.
C **Delfín**, Venustiano Carranza s/n, Playa Azul, T536-0007. No a/c, but clean, pleasant and there's a swimming pool.
D **Del Pacífico**, Blv Francisco Villa, Playa Azul, opposite beach, T536-0106. Bath, fan, clean, hammocks on roof, friendly. A bit run-down but recommended.
D-E **Hotel Yuritzi**, Caleta de Campos, T531-5010, www.hotelyuritzi.com. With bath, a/c, TV, cheaper without, clean, no hot water, good views from front, changes TCs at reasonable rates.
E **Cabañas**, Caleta de Campos. With hammock space at US$1 per person, northwest of village, where Río Nexpa reaches the coast.
E **Costa Azul**, 5 de Mayo 276, Lázaro Cárdenas, T532-0780. With bath.
F **Cabañas**, Maruata. There are *cabañas* for rent and *palapas* under which you can camp.

Eating

Morelia *p276, map p276*
TTT-TT **La Flor de las Mercedes**, León Guzmán. Colonial-style house, beautiful decor, moderate prices.
TT **Boca del Río**, Gómez Farías185. Good fish.
TT **La Bodega de la Iguana**, Av Camelinsa 3636, T314-4204. Very good traditional cuisine. Highly recommended.
TT **Quinta Sol**, Aquiles Serdán 729, 5 blocks east of Morelos. Also vegetarian, good *comida corrida*, served from 1400; both close daily at 1700 and both closed Sun.
TT **Viandas de San José**, Alvaro Obregón 263 and Zapata. Good cheap *comida corrida*, excellent service. Recommended.
TT **Woolworth's**, Virrey de Mendoza and Madero. Pretty old building with stone-vaulted ceilings.
T **Los Pioneros**, Aquiles Serdán y Morelos Norte. Cheap, good local food.

Cafés, bakeries and sweet shops
Café Colón, Aquiles Serdán 265. Good coffee.
Café de Conservatorio, on Plaza de las Rosas (opposite music academy). Not cheap but nice atmosphere and tasty cakes.
Casa de la Cultura. Has a good café with delicious home-made cakes.
Mercado de Dulces, Gómez Farías at the western end of the Palacio Clavijero. Famous for *ates* (fruit jellies), candies and *rompope* (an alcoholic drink similar to advocaat).

Around Morelia *p278*
TT **Los Arcos**, Angangueo. One of several cafés and restaurants near the plaza, wholesome food, but not gourmet.

Pátzcuaro and around *p279, map p280*
Local speciality is *pescado blanco* (white fish), and several lakeside restaurants serve fish dishes but, due to over-fishing and pollution, it is advisable to avoid locally caught fish.

Breakfast available from small stands in the market, usually 0600-0700 (milk shakes, rice pudding, etc). *Comida corrida* at restaurants around Plaza Grande and Plaza Chica is usually the same each day. Many places close before 2000.
TT **El Gaucho Viejo**, Mansión Iturbide (see Sleeping, above). Argentine *churrasco*, Wed-Sun 1800-2400, folk music.
TT **Gran Hotel**. Filling *comida corrida*, excellent *café con leche*.
TT **Los Escudos**, Plaza Quiroga. Open until 2200, popular with tourists, try *sopa tarasca* (a soup made with toasted *tortillas*, cream and cheese), which is good value, and coffee.

¥¥ T'irekua, Plaza Vasco de Quiroga 29. Beautiful patio, peaceful, good breakfast.
¥¥-¥ El Patio, Plaza Vasco de Quiroga 19, T342-0484. Fruit and yoghurt for breakfast, also serves good meals, good service too. Daily 0800-2200. Recommended.
¥ Cafetería El Buho, Tejerías 8. Meals, drinks, slow but very good food, good value, stylish, friendly. Recommended.
¥ Camino Real, next to Pemex, 100 m from El Pozo Trailer Park. Very good *comida corrida*, quick service.
¥ La Casona, Plaza Quiroga. Reasonable prices (cheapest breakfast in town).
¥ Mercado. Good chicken with vegetables and *enchiladas* over the market (budget restaurants here are usually open in the evening).

Cafés and ice cream parlours
Paletería, Codallos 24. Excellent ice cream parlour which also sells frozen yoghurt.

Uruapan and around *p281*
The local speciality is *cecina*, dried meat.
¥¥ Café El Sol y La Luna, Independencia between Zócalo and Parque. Arty/student bar, sometimes live music at weekends.
¥¥ Calypso, Alvaro Obregón 2A. Excellent cakes and hamburgers, ask for local drink speciality: *agua fresca de rompope*.
¥ La Pérgola, on plaza. Good breakfasts and coffee. Recommended.
¥ Mercado de Antojitos. Cheap meals from *comedores*. Locals eat at open-air food stalls under 1 roof at back of church, very picturesque.

Zamora and Paracho *p283*
¥¥ Carnes Toluca, Madero Sur and Leonardo, Zamora, and **Antigua Carnes Toluca** over the road. Not much more than meat, but plenty of it.
¥ Café D'Gribet, on main street, cheap and good snacks. Try local pancakes.
¥ El Patio, La Piedad de Cabadas, near church. Very good, dish of the day good value.

Entertainment

Morelia *p276, map p276*
Peña Bola Suriana, Allende 355. Live traditional guitar music, open courtyard, small cover charge.
Teatro Municipal. Free weekly concerts.

Festivals and events

Pátzcuaro and around *p279, map p280*
1 Jan Los Viejitos (Old Men), in Janitzio.
2 Feb Los Sembradores (The Sowers).
4 Feb Los Apaches (at the churches).
Feb Carnaval in the Lake Pátzcuaro region; the **Danza de los Moros** (The Moors) is performed.
12 Oct Día de la Raza, when Columbus reached America, there is also a procession with the Virgin and lots of fireworks.
1-2 Nov Día de los Muertos (All Souls' Day), ceremony at midnight, at almost every village around the lake; if you are in the region at this time it is well worth experiencing. The ceremony is most touristy on Janitzio island and at Tzintzuntzan, but at villages such as Ihuatzio, Jarácuaro and Urandén it is more intimate. The tourist office has leaflets listing all the festivities.
6-9 Dec Virgen de la Salud, when authentic Tarascan dances are performed in front of the Basílica.
12 Dec There is an interesting fiesta on for the Virgen de Guadalupe.

Uruapan and around *p281*
1st week of Apr The Zócalo is filled with pottery, brought from all the surrounding indigenous villages.
Jun Las Canacuas (Crown Dance), on Corpus Christi.
16 Sep In nearby village of **San Juan**, to celebrate the saving of an image of Christ from the San Juan church at the time of the Paricutín eruption.
15 Sep Feria in Uruapan (2 weeks either side).

Activities and tours

Pátzcuaro and around *p279, map p280*
Fishing
Winter is the best time for fishing in the somewhat fish-depleted lake, where locals traditionally threw nets shaped like dragonflies, now a rather rare event.

Transport

Morelia *p276, map p276*
Air
Mexican destinations include **Cuernavaca**, **León**, **Mexico City**, **Tijuana**, **Uruapan**,

Veracruz and Zacatecas. There are international flights to Chicago, LA, San Francisco and San José (CA).

Airline offices Aeromar, T312-8545.

Bus

The new terminal is out of town, a 15- or 20-min taxi ride. To **Aguascalientes**, 0230, 0805, 1205, 1605 and 1705, 7 hrs, US$23. To **Celaya**, 18 per day, US$9. To **Colima**, 0740, 1200, US$20. To **Guadalajara**, at least hourly, 3-5 hrs, quicker on the *autopista*, US$23-16. To **Guanajuato**, 8 daily from 0650 to 1525, 3½ hrs, US$9. To **León**, regular throughout the day, 4 hrs, US$12. To **Manzanillo**, 2230, US$33. To **Mexico City**, very regular services, some to the North terminal, some to the West terminal, 4 hrs, US$21. To **Monterrey**, 1700, US$72. To **Nogales**, 2000, US$110. To **Nuevo Laredo**, 1700, US$92. To **Pátzcuaro**, very regular service, 1 hr, US$4. To **Querétaro**, very regular, US$7-8.60. To **San Luis Potosí**, hourly, US$13. To **Uruapan**, very regular departures, 2 hrs, US$8.

Around Morelia *p278*

Bus From Zitácuaro to **Guadalajara**, 11 hrs, US$14.80. To **Mexico City**, 1½ hrs, US$9. To **Morelia**, hourly, 3½ hrs, US$5. Fixed price taxi to and from town, US$1.50; minibuses US$0.40. **Quiroga** from **Pátzcuaro** station every 15 mins. Bus Quiroga-**Mexico City**, US$17. Bus to Tzintzuntzan from Pátzcuaro bus station every 15 mins, US$0.50, same bus as for Quiroga. If taking the route Uruapan-Pátzcuaro-Morelia, Tzintzuntzan and Quiroga come after Pátzcuaro.

Pátzcuaro and around *p279, map p280*

Bus New bus station (called Central) out of town, with left-luggage office, *colectivo* from centre US$0.30, taxi US$1.70. Bus US$0.20 from Plaza Bocanegra. You can pick up buses from large roundabout 1 km north of centre. Taxi US$1.45.

To **Guadalajara**, late morning service, 6 hrs, US$15. To **Lázaro Cárdenas**, hourly from 0600, 8 hrs, long but spectacular ride through mountains and lakes (police checks likely), US$16. To **Mexico City**, regular service through the day, 6 hrs, US$18. To **Morelia**, every 30 mins, 1 hr, US$3. To **Toluca**, from 0915, 5 hrs, 1st class US$17.50. Local buses from corner of market in town to lakeside (*colectivo* to lakeside US$0.25). To **Uruapan**, 1 hr, US$2.50.

Uruapan and around *p281*

Air

Daily to **Mexico City**. Also flights to **Culiacán**, **Guadalajara** and **Tijuana**.

Airline offices Aeromar, T523-5050.

Bus

Bus station on the northeast edge of town, necessary to get a city bus into town (US$0.25), finishing at about 2100, or a taxi to the plaza, US$3. Left-luggage. To **Colima**, 6 hrs, US$14. To **Guadalajara**, roughly hourly, 4½ hrs, US$18. To **Lázaro Cárdenas**, every 30 mins, 6 hrs, US$15. To **Mexico City**, more than 1 per hr, 6 hrs, US$28. To **Morelia**, every 20 mins, 2½ hrs, US$7. To **Pátzcuaro**, frequent, 1 hr, US$3.

Zamora and Paracho *p283*

Bus Bus station at north edge of Zamora, local bus to centre US$0.25, taxi US$3.50, from centre to bus station from 5 de Mayo in front of Catedral Inconclusa. Bus to **Mexico City** and to **Guadalajara**, US$16. To **Morelia**, US$15. To **Pátzcuaro**, 2½ hrs. To **Tamazula**, for Cd Guzmán, 3½-4 hrs, US$9.

From Paracho there are buses to **Uruapan** US$0.80, 45 mins. Also to **Morelia** via Pátzcuaro.

Pacific coast *p283*

Bus Buses ply up and down the coast road, stopping at the road junction 4 km from Plaza Azul. *Colectivos* take you between town and junction. If driving north it is 5 hrs to **Tecomán** (where the road from Colima comes down to the coast).
From Lázaro Cárdenas **Galeana** to **Manzanillo** 7¾ hrs, US$15; to **Uruapan**, 6½ hrs, US$16; to **Guadalajara**, US$31 with La Línea; to **Mexico City** US$43, luxury.

Directory

Morelia *p276, map p276*

Banks Bancomer, Av Madero Oriente, Visa ATM. There is an ATM just east of the Hotel Casino that accepts Visa and MasterCard. There is a **Banco Inverlat** ATM next to the bus station that accepts American Express cards. **Internet** Chatroom Cybercafé, Nigromante 132A, Mon-Sat 0900-2200, Sun 1200-2100, spacious, tranquil. Shareweb Cybercafé, Av Madero Ote 573-C, Mon-Sat 0900-2200, Sun 1400-2200. **Language schools** Centro Mexicano de Idiomas, Calzada Fray Antonio de San Miguel 173, T312-4596. Intensive weekly classes; other courses available include handicrafts. Accommodation with families. **Baden-Powell Institute**, Antonio Alzate 565, T312-4070. Courses for all levels, plus cultural, social science and extracurricular courses. Highly recommended. (See also Learning Spanish in Essentials, page 25). **Laundry** Lavandería Chapultepec, Ceballos 881. Lavandería on Santiago Tapiá towards bus station. **Medical services** Dentist: Dr Leopoldo Arroyo Contreras, Abraham González 35, T312-0751, near the cathedral. Recommended. **Post office** In Palacio Federal. Long-distance phone and fax, Gómez Farías 113, near the sweet market.

Pátzcuaro and around *p279, map p280*
Banks Several ATMs in the centre. Banamex, Portal Juárez 32. Promex, Portal Regules 9. Serfín, Portal Allende 54. Bancomer, Zaragoza 23; *casa de cambio* at Benito Mendoza 7. **Internet** México en Línea, Fed Tena 30-L9, T342-4566. **Laundry** Lavandería San Francisco, Terán 16, Mon-Sat 0900-2000. **Medical services** Dentist: Dr Antonio Molina, T342-3032. Doctor: Dr Jorge Asencio Medina, T342-4038. Dr Guadalupe Murillo, T342-1209. Pharmacy: Gems, Benito Mendoza 21, T342-0332, daily 0900-2100. **Post office** Obregón, 1 block from Plaza Chica, Mon-Fri 0800-1600, Sat 0900-1300.

Uruapan and around *p281*
Banks Banamex, Cupatitzio y Morelos, visa agent. Bancomer, Carranza y 20 de Noviembre. Serfín, Cupatitzio. **Internet** Logicentro Cyber Café, Av Juárez 57, T524-9494, Mon-Sat 0900-1400, 1600-2100. Computer shop, basement of Hotel Plaza. **Laundry** Carranza 47, Mon-Sat 0900-1400, 1600-2000. Mujer Santayo Lavandería, Michoacán 14, T523-0876. **Medical services** Red Cross, T524-0300. **Post office** Reforma 13. **Telephone** Computel, Ocampo, on plaza, daily 0700-2200.

Zamora *p283*
Internet In small mall on Morelos, between Colón and Ocampo.

Guadalajara to the Pacific coast

If it's the Mexican stereotype you're after, make your way to the state of Jalisco. This is where you'll find the town of Tequila, the lasso-swinging charros, the swirling Jarabe Tapatío (Mexican hat dance) and the romantic mariachis, those roving musicians dressed in fine, tight-trousered gala suits and massive sombreros of the early 19th-century rural gentry. All these originated in Jalisco, but there are other attractions worth making a song and dance about.

Guadalajara, the state capital, is today a huge, modern metropolis. But the 'pearl of the west' has a magnificent and elegant Spanish core with shady plazas, impressive colonial architecture, some fine museums and the vast Mercado Libertad. A short visit to the famous craft centre suburbs of Tlaquepaque orTonalá is relaxing and rewarding, take a boat ride on Mexico's largest lake,Lago de Chapala, go and see the volcanically activeNevado de Colima, cool off in the pine forests around the delightful old town of Tapalpa, or visit a distillery in Mexico's most famous small town, Tequila.

Jalisco is also gateway to the Pacific coast and the mega resort of Puerto Vallarta on the vast Bahía de Banderas. But there are other beautiful and secluded beaches both north and south of Vallarta. Up the coast, in the neighbouring state of Nayarit, sleepy San Blasis popular with surfers and birdwatchers. Away from the resorts, remote in the Sierra Madre Occidental, live the Cora and Huichol people, renowned for their stunningly beautiful chaquira beadwork and colourful nierika yarn paintings, as well as for the ancestral ritual that takes them hundreds of miles every year on a pilgrimage to the sacred peyote grounds near Real de Catorce to collect the hallucinogenic cactus. » *For Sleeping, Eating and other listings, see page 306-324.*

Guadalajara » *pp306-324. Colour map 3, B2.*

→ *Phone code: 33. Population: 5,000,000. Altitude: 1650 m.*

Guadalajara, Mexico's second city, was founded on 14 February 1542. In the Centro Histórico, graceful colonial arcades, or portales, flank scores of old plazas and shaded parks. Efforts are being made to preserve the colonial atmosphere and restore noteworthy buildings. At weekends and on public holidays, the town fills with Guadalajarans meandering through the town.

Ins and outs

Getting there Frequent flights to Mexico City and many other domestic and international destinations from Aeropuerto Internacional Miguel Hidalgo (GDL) 20 km south of the city. Fixed-rate taxis will take you into the city; tickets available in airport. Two local bus routes also service the airport. » *See Transport, page 317.*

An important commercial centre, Guadalajara is the hub of several major land routes. The appropriately vast **bus terminal** is 10 km southeast of the centre; allow at least 30 minutes to get there on one of the luxury bus services (**Línea Azul** and **Línea Cardenal**). The terminal is a nightmare if you try to understand it; fortunately that's not

Sleeping
Aranzazú 2 *C2*
Azteca 3 *B3*
Francés 5 *B2*
Hostal Guadalajara 7 *B3*
Janeiro 10 *B3*
León 11 *C2*
Plaza Génova 15 *B2*
Posada San Pablo 16 *C1*
Posada Tapatía 17 *B1*
Rotonda 18 *A2*

Eating
Café D'Osio 1 *C1*
Café Madoka 2 *B1*
Carnes Asadas Rigo's 3 *C3*
El Mexicano 4 *B3*
La Playita 5 *B2*
La Rinconada 6 *B3*

Bars & clubs
Femina La Latina 8 *B2*
La Jaula 9 *B2*
La Mansión 10 *B2*
La Maskara 11 *B2*
La Maestranza 12 *B2*

too important. Simply put, there are seven modules at the terminal, each serving different bus companies rather than towns or regions within Mexico.

The **old bus station**, a few blocks south of the city centre, serves towns within 100 km of Guadalajara, mainly with second-class buses and *colectivos* which run to the towns on Lake Chapala. There is a train station at the south end of Calzada de la Independencia operating the **Tequila Express**.

Getting around The most pleasant way of seeing the city is by horse-drawn carriage; these are to be found outside the Museo Regional at the corner of Liceo and Hidalgo and a few other places. More conventional buses and *colectivos* run to most areas of the city, although regular services can be frustratingly bad. Trolley buses and the new luxury buses with guaranteed seats on a few fixed routes are a much better option. The city also has two 'metro', or rather *tren ligero* lines, one running north-south and the other west-east. Taxis tend not to use meters so agree on a price before setting off.

Best time to visit The climate is mild, and clear all through the year, although in summer it can be thundery at night. Pollution from vehicles can be bad downtown and the winter is the worst time for smog. However, afternoons are usually clear and sunny and during the rainy summer season smog is less of a problem.

Tourist offices State and Federal tourist office (**Sectur**) ⓘ *Morelos 102, Plaza Tapatía, T3668-1602, Mon-Fri 0800-2000, Sat and Sun 1000-1600,* has information in German and English, including a good walking tour map of the historic centre, helpful. There are also tourist booths in front of the cathedral and at the eastern end of Plaza Tapatía. *Siglo 21* newspaper has a good entertainments section, *Tentaciones*, on Friday, and music, film and art listings every day.

Safety Guadalajara is generally a safe city. Normal precautions are required against pickpockets, but little more.

The cathedral and Plaza de Armas

The heart of the city is the Plaza de Armas. On its north side is the **cathedral**, begun in 1561, finished in 1618, in a medley of styles; its two spires are covered in blue and yellow tiles. There is a reputed Murillo Virgin inside (painted 1650), and the famous *Virgen del Carmen*, painted by Miguel Cabrera, a Zapotec artist from Oaxaca. In the dome are frescoes of the four gospel writers and in the Capilla del Santísimo are more frescoes and paintings of the Last Supper. From inside you can see the evening sun's rays streaming through the dome's stained glass. The cathedral's west façade is on Plaza de los Laureles, on the north side of which is the **Palacio Municipal** (1952), which contains murals by Gabriel Flores depicting the city's founding.

Also on Plaza de Armas is the **Palacio de Gobierno** (1643) where, in 1810, Hidalgo issued his first proclamation abolishing slavery. **José Clemente Orozco**'s great murals can be seen on the central staircase; they depict social struggle, dominated by Hidalgo, with the church on the left, fascism on the right and the suffering peasants in the middle. More of Orozco's work can be seen in the **Congreso** ⓘ *free*, an integral part of the Palacio de Gobierno (and also at the university Rectoría, the Instituto Cultural Cabañas, and the Casa José Clemente Orozco, see below, as well as at the university's main library, Glorieta Normal, north of the centre).

East of the cathedral

East from the cathedral is the **Plaza de la Liberación**, with a statue of Hidalgo, where the national flag is raised and lowered daily (with much ceremony). On the north side, the **Museo Regional de Guadalajara** ⓘ *Liceo 60, between Hidalgo and Independencia, Tue-Sat 0900-1730, Sun 0900-1700 US$2, free on Sun, Tue and* holidays, free for children and senior citizens, is in an old seminary (1710), with a good prehistoric section (including the complete skeleton of a mammoth found in Jalisco). This museum has an interesting display of shaft tombs, an excellent display of Colima, Nayarit and Jalisco terracotta figures (but less extensive than the Museo de Arqueología, see below), and one of the finest displays of 17th- to 18th-century colonial art in Mexico. There are also musical instruments, indigenous art and one room devoted to the history of Jalisco from the Conquistadores to Iturbide; highly recommended.

The **Palacio Legislativo** ⓘ *Plaza de la Liberacón, open to the public 0900-1800*, a neoclassical building, remodelled in 1982, has a list of the names of all the Constituyentes, from Hidalgo to Otero (1824-1857 and 1917). At the eastern end of this plaza is the enormous and fantastically decorated **Teatro Degollado** ⓘ *daily 1000-1400* (1866, see Entertainment, page 314), which is well worth seeing even if you do not go to a performance.

A pedestrian mall, **Plaza Tapatía**, has been installed between the Teatro Degollado and the Hospicio Cabañas, crossing the Calzada de la Independencia, covering 16 blocks. It has plants, fountains, statuary and a tourist office. The massive **Hospicio Cabañas** near the Mercado Libertad, to the east is now known as **Instituto Cultural Cabañas** ⓘ *Tue-Sat 1000-1600, Sun 1000-1500*. The ex-orphanage is a beautiful building with 22 patios, which is floodlit at night. The contents of the former Museo Orozco in Mexico City have been transferred here. See also Orozco's famous *Man of Fire* painted in the dome. The Cabañas also has exhibitions of Mexican and international art and other events, listed under Entertainment below.

Facing the Cabañas, on Morelos, is a sculpture in bronze by Rafael Zamarripa of Jalisco's symbol: two lions supporting a tree. Immediately in front of the Instituto Cultural Cabañas are four bronze seats/sculptures by local artist Alejandro Colunga, which could be regarded as amusing or macabre, depending on your sense of humour. They include skeletons, an empty man's suit topped by a skull, a large pair of ears, etc. Just south of the Cabañas is the vast **Mercado Libertad**, known locally as San Juan de Dios, see Shopping, page 315, and opposite, on Obregón and Leonardo Vicario, is the **Plaza de los Mariachis**.

Museo de la Ciudad ⓘ *Calle Independencia 684, Tue-Sun 1000-1730, Sat 1000-1400, US$0.50*, in a pretty colonial building with two columned patios, has information on the city from its founding to the present day, including maps and population statistics.

West of the cathedral

West of the cathedral, along Avenida Juárez, is the *Rectoría* of the **University of Guadalajara** ⓘ *Av Juárez y Tolsá (Enrique Díaz de León)*. Inside, in the *Paraninfo* (main hall), is another Orozco mural portraying 'man asleep, man meditating, and man creating'; lie on your back or look in a mirror. The building also houses the **Museo de Arte** ⓘ *Tue-Fri 1000-1800, Sat-Sun 1000-1600, good café*.

Not far from the university is the strange-looking **Templo Expiatorio** ⓘ *Av Enrique Díaz de León y Madero*, with fine stained glass and intricate ceiling, Gothic style but still unfinished after a century.

Further west along Avenida Vallarta, the **Casa Taller José Clemente Orozco** ⓘ *Aurelio Aceves 29, Tue-Sat 1000-1600, Sun 1000-1500*, on a pedestrian street half a block from Los Arcos, was built in the 1940s and donated to the state of Jalisco by the family after the artist's death in 1951.

South of the cathedral

Not far from the centre a couple of churches are worth visiting. **San Francisco Neri** (1550), off Avenida 16 de Septiembre, has a three-tiered altar with columns, a feature repeated on the façade. To the north is the **Jardín San Francisco**, a pleasantly shaded plaza, and the starting point for horse-drawn carriages. To the west is the old church of **Nuestra Señora de Aranzazú**, with three fantastic churrigueresque altarpieces; equally impressive are the coloured ceilings and the finely carved dado, the only light coming from high-up windows and from the open east door.

The **Museo de Arqueología de Occidente de México** ⓘ *Av 16 de Septiember 889, Zona Agua Azul, Tue-Sun 1000-1330, 1700-1900, Sat 1200-1400, 1600-1900, US$0.50*, has a comprehensive collection of objects from Jalisco, Colima and Nayarit, including pottery, ornaments, weapons, figures and illustrations of tombs. A small booklet in English is available. Nearby, is **Parque Agua Azul** ⓘ *Calzada Independencia Sur, Tue-Sun 0800-1900, US$0.20*, a park with a good aviary, trees, flowers and fountains. It also contains an outdoor concert bowl, the **Teatro Experimental** and the **Casa de las Artesanías de Jalisco** (see Crafts, page 316). It's about 15 blocks south of the centre at the intersection of Constituyentes and González Gallo; to get there take bus 52 or 54 up Avenida 16 de Septiembre or No 60 or 62 up Calzada Independencia back to centre.

North of the cathedral

North of the cathedral, is the **Museo de Periodismo y Artes Gráficas** ⓘ *Av Alcalde 225, Tue-Sat 1000-1800, Sun 1100-1500, US$1, students with ID half price, over 60s free*. The building is known as the Casa de los Perros because of two large dog statues on the roof. The first printing shop in Guadalajara was here and the first *periódico insurgente* (insurgent newspaper) in the Americas, *El Despertador Americano*, was published here in 1810. The museum contains old printing presses, newspapers, etc. When Avenida Alcalde was widened in 1950, the building's façade was moved back 9 m. **Casa Museo López Portillo** ⓘ Calle *Liceo 177, Tue-Sat 1000-1700, Sun 1000-1500*, formerly the family home of the ex-President, was restored in 1982 when he was in office. It is a colonial house with a large tiled courtyard, and surrounding rooms furnished with 18th- and 19th-century Italian and French furniture. It is also used as a cultural centre with classes in music, dance, literature, chess, indigenous culture and languages.

Churches worth seeing north of the cathedral include **Santa Mónica** ⓘ *Santa Mónica y Reforma* (1718), which is small, but very elaborate with impressive arches full of gold under a clear atrium and a richly carved façade. Nearby, is the church of **San José** ⓘ *Alcalde y Reforma*, a 19th-century church with a fine gilded rococo pulpit, has eight pillars in a semicircle around the altar, painted deep red and ochre behind, giving an unusual effect, the overall light blue gives an airy feel; in the plaza outside is a statue of Núñez, defender of the Reforma who was killed in 1858. The **Santuario de Guadalupe** ⓘ *Av Alcalde and Juan Alvarez*, is lovely inside; outside, in the Jardín del Santuario, are massive celebrations on 12 December, the day of the Virgin of Guadalupe, with fireworks, musicians, vendors and games. Five minute's walk away, **San Miguel de Belén** ⓘ *Hospital 290*, is enclosed in the Hospital Civil Viejo and contains three fine late 18th-century *retablos*; behind the hospital is the **Panteón de Belén** ⓘ *entrance at Calle Belén 684 at the corner of Eulogio Parra, open until 1500*, a beautiful old cemetery closed to new burials for many years.

Parque Alcalde ⓘ *Jesús García y Av de los Maestros, small entry fee*, is a pleasant enough park with a lake, rowing boats and a children's playground.

On the way out of the city going north along Calzada Independencia, near the Barranca de Oblatos, a huge canyon, there is a large and well-kept **Jardín Zoológico** ⓘ *US$0.50, bus 600, 60 and 62 heading north on Independencía*, with plenty of Central American animals and aviaries in a delightful atmosphere. **Selva Mágica** amusement park is inside the zoo; it has a dolphin and seal show three or four times a day. There is also a **Planetarium** nearby.

Zapopan

In a northwest suburb of Guadalajara is the **Basílica de Zapopan**, completed 1690, with a miraculous image of Nuestra Señora, known as *La Generala* on the main altar, given to the local people in 1542. There is a huge **Fiesta de la Virgen de Zapopan** on 12 October. Next door is the **Museo de Arte Huichol Wixárica** ⓘ *Mon-Sat 0930-133, 1500-1800, Sun 1000-1500*. At one end of the pedestrian street, **Paseo Teopitzintli**, leading to the plaza and basilica, is the colonial-style **Arco de Ingreso**. The **tourist office** ⓘ *Guerrero, T3110-0754, Mon-Fri 0900-2100, Sat 0900-1300*, is in the Casa de la Cultura, two blocks behind the Basílica. To get to Zapopan, take bus No 275 on Avenida Alcalde, or take line 1 of the *tren ligero* to the Avila Camacho stop and pick up bus No 175 to Zapopan (there are several different 175s, so check with driver that the bus goes all the way to Zapopan).

A visit to Tequila is an easy day trip from Guadalajara – see page 321.

Tlaquepaque

About 7 km southeast of the city centre is the attractive suburb of Tlaquepaque, which is well worth a visit. Calle Independencia runs from Bulevar Tlaquepaque (the main avenue into Guadalajara) to the main plaza where you can see the restored **Parroquia de San Pedro Tlaquepaque** and the **Basílica La Teranensis**. Further on is the **Parián**, a very large, square building occupying most of another plaza, with bars (pretty woodwork and tiling) and kitchens around the perimeter. The rest is an open courtyard. By day Tlaquepaque is a fusion of craft ideas ranging from red-hot and pricey minimalist style through to stack-it-high and sell-it-cheap tack (see Shopping, page 315); at night the boulevards and main square fill with diners and *mariachis*, who play Friday, Saturday, Sunday, 1530 and 2130; also roving *mariachis* play for a fee. If you're looking to stay in the area for a couple of days there is good accommodation, see Sleeing, page 306. The **Museo Regional de la Cerámica** ⓘ *Independencia 237, T3635-5404, Tue-Sat 1000-1800, Sun 1000-1500*, in a beautiful colonial building displays examples of Jalisco's ceramics and other handicrafts. There are also items for sale.

Tlaquepaque and Tonalá can be easily combined as one trip from Central Guadalajara

Around Guadalajara » pp306-324.

Tonalá → *Phone code: 33. Colour map 3, B2.*

Fifteen kilometres southwest of Guadalajara on the road to Mexico City is Tonalá, noted for its Sunday and Thursday **markets**, where you can pick up bargains in pottery, glass and ceramics. The market is held on the central avenue, where all the buses from Guadalajara stop. Calle Benito Juárez intersects this avenue and is a main shopping street. It runs to the main plaza (where it intersects with Calle Madero, the other main shopping street in the centre) and on another block to the **Parroquía de Santiago de Tonalá**, a very beautiful church built in the mid-17th century. On the plaza is the cream-coloured **Iglesia del Sagrado Corazón**. The walls are lined with crucifixion paintings. Also on the plaza are the **Presidencia Municipal**, a pastel blue-green colonial-style building, and the municipal market (food and crafts).

Chapala → *Phone code: 376. Colour map 3, B2.*

Chapala town, 64 km to the southeast of Guadalajara on the northern shore of **Laguna de Chapala** (113 km long, 24-32 km wide), has thermal springs, several good and pricey hotels, three golf courses, and is a popular resort particularly with retired North Americans and Mexican day-trippers.

Laguna de Chapala is set in beautiful scenery. There are boats of all kinds for hire, some go to the **Isla de los Alacranes** (restaurant), and there is water-fowl shooting in autumn and winter. Most fish in the lake have been killed by pollution, but the 5-cm 'XYZ' fish, called *charales*, are a delicacy similar to whitebait. There is a market on the east side of the Zócalo with stalls selling handicrafts, some places to eat, and dirty public conveniences (1 peso); entrance on street behind the market. There is a regional **tourist office** ⓘ *Aquiles Serdán 26, T765-3141.* A free English-language newspaper, *El Ojo del Lago*, is available at hotels and online at www.chapala.com.

Ajijic to Jocotepec → *Phone code: 376. Colour map 3, B2.*

Seven kilometres to the west of Chapala, **Ajicjic** a smaller, once indigenous village, has an arty-crafty American colony with many retired North Americans. The village is pleasant, with cobbled streets, a pretty little plaza and many single-storey villas. One block east of the plaza at the end of Calle Parroquia is the very pretty church of San Andrés, started in 1749. On Colón, in the two blocks north of the plaza, are several restaurants, boutiques and galleries. Going south from the plaza, Colón becomes Morelos, crossing Calle Constitución and continuing some five blocks to the lake with lots of restaurants, galleries and shops. The lake shore has receded about 200 m from the original shoreline and is a bit smelly. The Way of the Cross and a Passion Play are performed at Easter in a chapel high above the town. **House and garden tours** ⓘ *Thu 1030, 2½ hrs, US$10, T766-1881 for reservation*, in aid of Lakeside School for the Deaf.

Beyond Ajijic to the west lies the small town of **San Juan Cosalá**, less prosperous than Ajijic but pleasant, with cobblestone streets and fewer gringos. There are thermal springs (varied temperatures, crowded and noisy at weekends, five pools of different sizes). Fish restaurants are squeezed between the carretera and the lake at **Barrenada**, 1 km east of town.

Forty kilometres due south of Lake Chapala is the colonial town of **Mazamitla** (2200 m), a pleasant place on the side of a range of mountains, but cold at night. It has a charming Zócalo.

Tapalpa → *Phone code: 343. Colour map 3, B2.*

About 130 km south of Guadalajara off Route 54 to Sayula and Ciudad Guzmán is Tapalpa, a very pretty village indeed and a popular place for weekend homes for rich Tapatíos. It is a three-and-a-half-hour drive from Guadalajara. The bus makes several detours into the hills to stop at small places such as **Zacoalco** (Sunday market) and **Amacueca**. The road up to Tapalpa is winding and climbs sharply and the air becomes noticeably cooler. The town itself, with only 11,000 inhabitants, shows ample signs of the influx of prosperity. There are two churches (one with a curious atrium) and an imposing flight of stone steps between them, laid out with fountains and ornamental lamps. Tapalpa is in cattle country; the rodeo is a popular sport at weekends. The main street is lined with stalls, selling *sarapes* and other tourist goods on Sunday and fresh food the other days of the week. The local speciality is *ponche*, an improbable blend of tamarind and mezcal, which is sold in gallon jars and recommended only for the curious or foolhardy.

Colima and around » *pp306-324. Colour map 3, B2.*

→ *Phone code: 312. Altitude: 494 m.*

The capital of Colima State is a most charming and hospitable town. In January of 2003 a large earthquake damaged many buildings and killed at least 25 people, but the town is recovering quickly and is rebuilding and repairing its churches and historical buildings. The main square is the focal point of the town, with a 19th-century Moorish-style arcade and a strange rebuilt Gothic ruin on the road beyond the **cathedral** (late 19th century). Also on the east side of the main square is the **Palacio de Gobierno**, which contains interesting murals of the history of Mexico. Behind them is the **Jardín Torres Quintero**, another pretty plaza but smaller.

The volcanoes of Colima

Protected by Parque Nacional Volcán Nevado de Colima, the **Volcano of Colima** (3860 m) and **El Nevado de Colima** (4330 m) are to the north of the city of Colima. The former, which erupted with great loss of life in 1941, used to be one of the most exciting climbs in Mexico. However, in recent years, activity has increased dramatically and a curfew radius of 11 km has been put in place, with nearby villages poised for immediate evacuation. In the first half of 2002 reports from the University of Colima said there were slow emissions of lava on the western and southeastern flanks of the volcano. The emissions are part of a period of greater activity that peaked in 1999 with explosions that sent columns of dust 8 km into the sky. Colima volcano has been erupting periodically for 500 years with over 30 major eruptions dating as far back as 1585. This latest period of activity puts the volcano off limits for the time being – you can check on the current situation on the web at www.ucol.mx/volcan

A huge **earthquake** measuring 7.8 on the Richter scale hit Colima State in January 2003. At least 25 people died in the 10-second-long quake that caused greatest damage in the city of Colima where almost half the fatalities occurred. The epicentre was some 10 km off the Pacific coast, but tremors were felt in nearby Guadalajara and as far away as Mexico City. It was estimated that some 10,000 homes were damaged in the earthquake and around 800 were completely destroyed.

The **Museo Regional de Historia** ⓘ *on the Zócalo, Tue-Sat 0900-1800, Sun 1700-2000*, has a comprehensive collection of prehispanic ceramics; look out for the figurines of dogs, which were clearly being fattened for the supper table. The ceramicists attained a high level of perfection in portraying realistically the facial expressions of people engaged in their daily tasks.

Andador Constitución is a pedestrian street, with people selling paintings, several small, attractive restaurants and a state-run artisan's shop at the north end on the corner of Zaragoza. Crossing Zaragoza, Constitución is open to traffic and one block north on the corner with Vicente Guerrero is the church of **San Felipe de Jesús** (early 18th-century plateresque façade) where Miguel Hidalgo was at one time parish priest. There is a public swimming pool in the **Parque Regional Metropolitano** on Calle Degollado about five to six blocks from the southwest corner of the main plaza. **Teatro Hidalgo** on the corner of Degollado and Morelos, has a pink colonial façade and large carved wooden doors (only open during functions). Parque Núñez, five blocks east of the plaza is also attractive and twice the size of the plaza. There's also a **tourist office** ⓘ *Hidalgo 96, corner of 27 de Septiembre, T312-4360, www.visitacolima.com.mx, Mon-Fri.*

The **Museo de las Culturas de Occidente María Ahumada** ⓘ *Calzada Pedro Galván, Tue-Sun 0900-1900*, in the Casa de Cultura complex, deserves a visit if only for its ample collection of prehispanic figurines. The region specialized in the production of pottery figures concerned with earthly problems and not cosmological events, as in other areas. The **Museo Universitario de Artes Populares 'Ma Teresa Pomar'** ⓘ *Calle 27 de Septiembre y Manuel Gallardo, Tue-Sun 1000-1300, 1700-2000*, exhibits folklore and handicrafts and has items for sale.

Around Colima

El Chanal ⓘ *Tue-Sun 0100-1700*, is an archaeological site, about 15 km to the north of Colima, which has a small pyramid with 36 sculptured figures, discovered in 1944. Another site, closer by, is **La Campana** ⓘ *just off Av Tecnológico, Tue-Sun 1000-1700, US$1.30*. These largely unexcavated, extant remains include a ball court and a few temples and platforms aligned with Colima Volcano 30 km to the north. **El Hervidero**, 22 km southeast of Colima, is a spa in a natural lake of hot springs that reach 25°C.

Comala, a pretty colonial town with whitewashed adobe buildings near Colima, is worth a few hours' visit (bus US$0.25, 20 minutes, every half an hour, from Suburbana bus station). The climate in Comala is somewhat cooler and more comfortable than Colima, and there are excellent views of the volcanoes of Colima, especially the active Volcán de Fuego. The surrounding vegetation is lush with coffee plantations.

Manzanillo and the Pacific coast

›› *pp306-324. Colour map 3, B1.*

→ *Phone code: 314.*

A beautiful, three-hour hilly route runs from Colima to Manzanillo, which has become an important port on the Pacific. A fast toll road has been opened between Guadalajara and Manzanillo. Activities for tourists at Manzanillo, which is not a touristy town, include deep-sea fishing (US$250 to hire a boat for a day, with beer, *refrescos* and *ceviche*), bathing, and walking in the hills. There is a good snorkelling trip starting at the beach of **Club Las Hadas** (see Sleeping, page 306), US$40 includes soft drinks and equipment. The water is clear and warm, with lots to see. The best beach is the lovely crescent of **Santiago**, 8 km north, but there are three others, all of which are clean, with good swimming, frequent buses serve these from the centre. There's a **tourist office** ⓘ *Blv Miguel de la Madrid 4960, T333-2277, Mon-Fri 0900-1500.*

Manzanillo centre

Southeast of Manzanillo

Southeast of Manzanillo is **Tecomán**, which has a delightful atmosphere but was hit by a major earthquake in January 2003, leaving several dead and some damage to buildings. To the west of Tecomán, the small coastal resort of **Cuyutlán**, on the fast highway between Colima and Manzanillo, has a pleasant, black-sand beach.The coast road continues southeast to the unspoilt fishing village of **Boca de Apiza** (no hotels but some seafood restaurants). There is abundant birdlife at the mouth of the river. Further south still the road reaches Playa Azul, Lázaro Cárdenas, Zihuatanejo and, eventually, Acapulco. For 80 km beyond Manzanillo it is good, then Route 200, although paved, is in poor condition in some parts and for long stretches you cannot see the ocean. In other places there are interesting coastal spots. About one hour south of Tecomán is the village of **San Juan de Lima**, on a small beach. Halfway between Tecomán and Playa Azul is another uncrowded beach, **Maruata**, where you can ask the restaurant owner if you can camp or sling a hammock (see page 283).

North of Manzanillo

San Patricio Melaque is in a bay which is one of the most beautiful on the Pacific coast, but it is very commercialized, crowded at holiday times and targets long-stay residents. The beach is long, shelving and sandy with a rocky coast at each end and pelicans diving for fish. The waves are not so big at **Playa San Patricio**. The week leading up to St Patrick's Day is **fiesta** time, when there are nightly fireworks, dances, rodeos, etc. There's a **tourist office** ⓘ *Sonora 15, T357-0100*, but it is better to visit Mari Blanca Pérez at **Paraíso Pacífico Tours** ⓘ *Hotel Barra de Navidad, T355-5122, May-Dec 0900-1400, Jan-Apr 0900-1800*, who is very helpful.

Manzanillo orientation

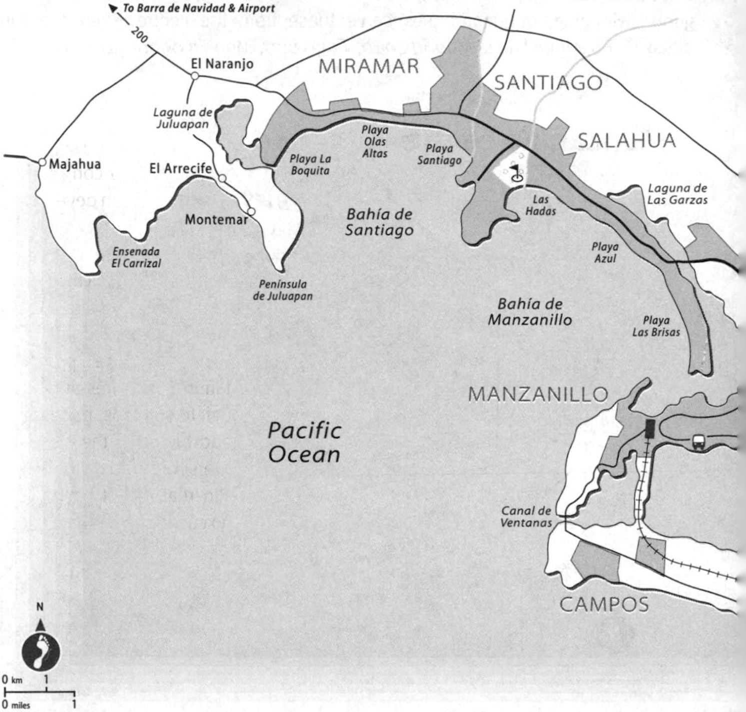

Barra de Navidad, just along the beach from Melaque, is commercial but still pleasant and has a monument to the Spanish ships that set out in 1548 to conquer the Philippines. Barra is one and a half hours from Manzanillo; the beach is beautiful, very good for swimming, but at holiday times it is very crowded and a lot less pleasant. The **Colorín** liquor store, opposite **Hotel Barra de Navidad**, changes money, sells stamps and has a mailbox. A friendly and useful resource is at **Ciber@net** internet café, one block from the bus terminal at Veracruz 212, where Pedro Flores can change money and offer friendly advice. There is a book exchange on Mazatlán between Sinaloa and Guanajuato. The **tourist office** ⓘ *Jalisco 67, T355-5100, www.barradenavidad.com, Mon-Fri 0900-1700, Sat and Sun 1000-1400*, is helpful and English is spoken.

La Manzanilla is quite a pretty seaside village 14 km north of the Routes 200/80 junction. Three kilometres north of the beach is Boca de Iguanas with two trailer parks: **Boca de Iguanas** and **Tenacatita**. For both places take the unpaved road from Highway 200 as far as the abandoned Hotel Bahía de Tenacatita; at the T-junction, turn right, pass the hotel, and the campsites are about 500 m further on the left. This place is nothing to do with the village of **Tenacatita**, which is further up the coast, and has a perfect beach complete with palm huts and tropical fish among the rocks; good for snorkelling (there are two sections of beach, the bay and oceanside).

Route 200, a little rough in places, links Barra de Navidad with Puerto Vallarta, the second largest resort in Mexico. There are beaches and hotels on this route and places to stay in Perula village at the north end of **Chamela** beach (see Sleeping, page 306). The Pemex station at Chamela is closed and there's no other for miles.

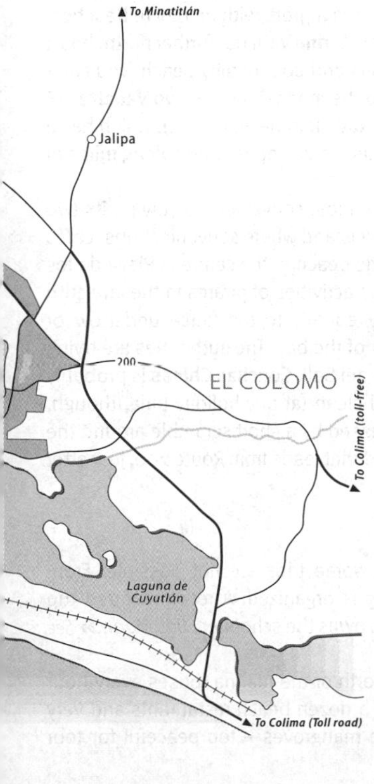

Puerto Vallarta and around

▸▸ *pp306-324. Colour map 3, B1.*

➔ *Phone code: 322.*

A highly commercialized sun-and-sand holiday resort marred by congestion and widespread condominium developments, Puerto Vallarta also has its advantages. For some, Puerto Vallarta occupies the most striking bay in Mexico topped off with dolphins cavorting in the clear waters. The stepped and cobbled streets of the old centre are picturesque, accommodation and restaurants are varied enough to suit most budgets, there is much good hiking in the surrounding hills and watersports and diving are easily accessible. Increasingly it has become a base for excursions and for special-interest trips including ornithology and whale watching. ▸▸ *See Activities and tours, page 317.*

Ins and outs

Getting there The Aeropuerto Internacional Ordaz (PVR), 6 km north of the town centre, is served by national and international airlines with flights to destinations in Mexico, the US and Europe (mostly package). Buses from the airport can be caught by taking the walkway to the other side of the street and walking to the main road and getting buses for the centre, US$0.40.

The long-distance bus station, almost directly opposite the airport, is a 30-minute ride from town, buses from the bus terminal may take the long way into the centre, it is worth changing buses on the main road to get a direct bus into the centre. Puerto Vallarta is on the Carretera Costera, Route 200, which runs south along the Pacific coast, all the way to the Guatemalan border. If you want to get a taxi into town they're half the price if you get them from across the main road outside the airport.

Getting around Taxis are expensive in Puerto Vallarta. Local buses operate on most routes north to Nuevo Vallarta and beyond, and south to Mismaloya and Boca de Tomatlán. Buses marked 'Centro' go through town, while those marked 'Túnel' take the bypass.

Tourist information The **tourist office** ⓘ *Independencia 123, T223-2500 ext 230, www.visitpuertovallarta.com*, is in the government building on the main square.

Sights

Greater Puerto Vallarta is drawn out along some 25 km of the west-facing curve of the deeply incised Banderas Bay. It can be split into six sections: **North Central** is the oldest, with the main plaza, cathedral and seafront Malecón as well as an uninviting strip of pebble/sand beach; **South Central**, across the Río Cuale, is newer but similarly packed with shops and restaurants and bordered by the fine, deep sand of Playa de los Muertos; **South Shore** is where the mountains come to the sea, there are several cove beaches and a scattering of big hotels; **North Hotel Zone** is a long stretch from town towards the cruise ship terminal and the airport, with mediocre beaches, many big hotels and several commercial centres; **Marina Vallarta**, further north, has a dazzling array of craft, a golf course, smart hotels and poor quality beach (you can't walk far because of condominiums built around the marina); and **Nuevo Vallarta**, 18 km north of centre, in the neighbouring state of Nayarit (time difference), which has a golf course and marina, along with modern, all-inclusive hotels strung along miles of white-sand beach, far from amenities.

Most travellers will find the central area the most convenient to stay in; its two halves are divided by the Río Cuale and a narrow island where souvenir shops, cafés and the museum are located. The most dramatic beach in the centre is Playa de los Muertos, apparently named after the murderous activities of pirates in the late 16th century, although the 'dead' tag could apply equally to the fierce undertow or possibly to the pollution that affects this corner of the bay. The authorities are trying to get people to use a sunnier sobriquet: 'Playa del Sol'. **Conchas Chinas** is probably the best beach close to town, being quiet and clean (at any holiday time, though, every beach is packed); this beach can be accessed by a short scramble around the rocky point to the south or by a cobblestone road that leads from Route 200, just after **Club Alexandra**.

Around Puerto Vallarta

During the rainy season, June to September, some trips are not possible. From November to April, humpback whale watching is organized. A recommended trip including snorkelling is with John Pegueros, who owns the schooner *Elías Mann*. ▸▸ *See also Tour operators, page 317.*

Playa de los Tomates, a 25-minute walk north of the marina (buses every hour from the marina), has good birdwatching, half a dozen beach restaurants and very few tourists. You can hire a boat to go to the mangroves – too peaceful for tour operators to get involved. On the way **Las Palmas**, 40 km northeast of Puerto Vallarta is the workers' *pueblo* of **Ixtapa**, established by the Montgomery Fruit Co in 1925. Near here are post-Classic stone mounds scattered over a wide area.

Ten kilometres south of Puerto Vallarta, along the coast road is **Mismaloya**, where John Huston made *Night of the Iguana* with Richard Burton. It is a lovely beach backed by a steep subtropical valley, even though the **La Jolla Mismaloya** hotel looms over the sands. The beach is clean and you can hire umbrellas and chairs for the day, US$1; beware of the undertow at low tide. The film set has been developed as **Iguana Park**. You can go horse riding up the valley with Victor, of **Rancho Manolo** ⓘ *beside the road bridge, T80018*.

Puerto Vallarta north to Tepic

Heading north from Puerto Vallarta the coast road continues to **Las Varas** and then veers eastwards to **Compostela** where it turns north again towards Tepic. From Puerto Vallarta to Las Varas the road passes some very attractive beach resorts, the first of which is **Bucerías**. **Los Veneros** ⓘ *between Bucerías and Punta de Mita, T(329) 291-0088, daily 1000-1800, entry US$10*, is a pretty cove with fairly safe sea bathing. There is a private beach club reached down a 7-km private road through woods to the beach. The resort is beautifully designed and clean with two restaurants, bar, café and gardens terraced towards the beach. The food is excellent and there's no extra charge for sunbeds/umbrellas. You can take a shuttle bus from Los Veneros bus station. **Punta**

Puerto Vallarta

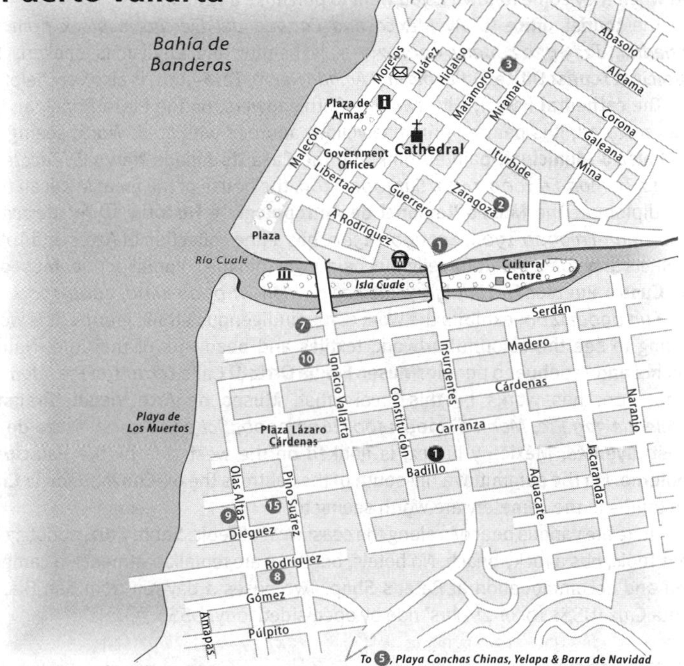

N

0 metres 200
0 yards 200

Sleeping
Casa Andrea 8
Casa del Puente 1
Casa Kimberley 2
Cuatro Vientos 3
Hacienda & Spa 4
La Jolla de Mismaloya 5
Las Palmas Beach Resort 6
Molina de Agua 7
Nautilus & Marina Club 12
Playa los Arcos 9
Posada Río Cuale 10
Rosita 11
Velas Vallarta 13
Yasmín 15

Eating
Café Catedral 1

 de Mita, a fishing village and beach resort at the tip of a peninsula, has fish restaurants, miles of beach and abundant birdlife. At **Playa Desileteros** there is an excellent restaurant (see Eating, page 312). **Medina** or **Pacífico** buses from Puerto Vallarta pass every 15 minutes. There are boat trips to the nearby **Islas Marietas**, where there are caves and birds. Camping is possible on the beach. Simple accommodation is also available (see Sleeping, page 306). North of Punta de Mita are beaches on the coast road include **Chacala**, a nice free beach lined with coconut palms, good swimming, cold showers and a restaurant; it is reached by an unsurfaced road through jungle.

❢ There is a time change between Nayarit and Jalisco; Jalisco is seven hours behind GMT, Nayarit and all the Pacific coast north of Jalisco is seven hours behind.

Tepic to Guadalajara » pp306-324.

Tepic → *Phone code: 311. Colour map 3, B1. Altitude: 900 m.*

Capital of Nayarit State, Tepic was founded in 1531 at the foot of the extinct volcano of Sangagüey. It is a clean but slightly scruffy town with many little squares, filled with trees and flowers.

The landscape around Tepic is wild and mountainous; access is very difficult. The Huichol and Cora people live in this region. Their dress is very picturesque; their craftwork – bags (carried only by men), scarves woven in colourful designs, necklaces of tiny beads (*chaquira*) and wall-hangings of brightly coloured wool – is available from souvenir shops. You may see them in Tepic but it is best to let them approach you when they come to town if you want to purchase any items.

The **tourist office** ⓘ *Av México and Calzada del Ejército, 1 block from the cathedral, T213-9203, daily 0900-2000*, is helpful and English is spoken. The **Municipal Tourist Office** ⓘ *Puebla and Amado Nervo, T216-5661*, is also very helpful.

The **cathedral** (1891), with two fine Gothic towers, on the Plaza Principal, has been restored; it is painted primrose yellow, adorned with gold. Worth seeing are the **Palacio Municipal**, painted pink and the **Casa de Amado Nervo** ⓘ *Zacatecas Norte 281, Mon-Fri 1000-1400, Sat 1000-1300*, the house of the great Mexican poet and diplomat. The **Museo Regional de Antropología e Historia** ⓘ *Av México 91 Norte, Mon-Fri 0900-1900, Sat 0900-1500*, has a fine collection of Aztec and Toltec artefacts and some beautiful religious paintings from the colonial period. **Museo de Los Cuatro Pueblos** ⓘ *Hidalgo y Zacatecas, Mon-Fri 0900-1400, 1600-1900, Sat and Sun 0900-1400*, exhibits the work of four indigenous ethnic groups. It is worth visiting to see the colourful artwork, textiles and beadwork of the Cora, Nahua, Huichol and Tepehuano people. **Museo Emilia Ortiz** ⓘ Calle *Lerdo 192 Pte, Mon-Sat 0900-1400*, has works by this local artist. **Museo de Arte Visual 'Aramara'** ⓘ *Allende 329 Pte, Mon-Fri 0900-1400, 1600-2000, Sat 0900-1400*. **Plaza de los Constituyentes**, México y Juárez, is flanked on the west side by the **Palacio de Gobierno.** On the summit of a hill south of the centre is the **ex-Convento de la Cruz**. The tombs in the cemetery are worth seeing too.

There are various beaches along the coast west of Tepic. **Santa Cruz**, about 37 km from Tepic, has a rocky beach. No hotels, but there are rental apartments, a camping area and accommodation at **Peter's Shop**. Two buses a day run from San Blas to Santa Cruz (US$1.10, or 2½ hrs' ride by open-sided lorry, US$0.75).

Huaynamota

You can visit **Cora** villages only by air, as there are no real roads, and it takes at least two days. However, it is possible to visit **Huichol** villages from the small town of Huaynamota in the mountains northeast of Tepic. Huaynamota has become much easier to reach with the opening of the Aguamilpa Dam. Boats leave from the west end of the dam at 0900 and 1400 (US$7), stopping at *embarcaderos* for villages along the way. The valley, despite being flooded, is still beautiful, particularly at the narrower parts of the dam where huge boulders hang precariously on clifftops. The *embarcadero* for Huaynamota is at the end of the dam where the Río Atengo feeds in. A community truck meets the launch (US$1.30). It is 8 km up a dirt road to the town, which is half populated by Huichol, some of whose traditional houses can be seen on its fringes. There are no hotels. For possible lodging, ask at the church or at the store (basic supplies) on the long south side of the plaza. There is a good view over the river valley from the large boulder beside the road at the edge of town. From Huaynamota ask around for guides to Huichol villages, four or more hours away. **Semana Santa** (Easter week) is famous, and many people from surrounding communities converge on Huaynamota at this time. Combis leave for the dam from Tepic at Avenida México just down from Zaragoza, US$3, one and a half hours.

San Blas and around → *Phone code: 328. Colour map 3, B1.*

This old colonial town, built as a fortress against piracy, is 69 km from Tepic and overcrowded during US and Mexican summer holidays. Founded in 1768, little is left of the old Spanish fortress, **Basilio.** It is from here that the Spanish set off to colonize Baja California and North America. Above the town are **La Contaduría** ⓘ *US$0.60*, the Spanish counting house (1773), and **La Marinera**, a ruined church. The views over the town, estuaries and mangrove swamps from beside an incredibly ugly statue on the battlements are superb.

Tepic

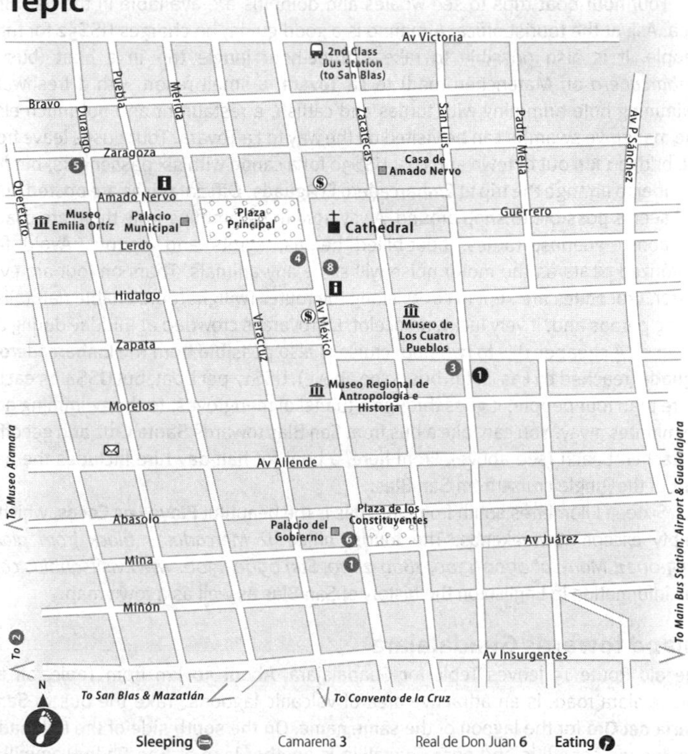

0 metres 100
0 yards 100

Sleeping
Altamirano 1
Bugamvillas 2
Camarena 3
Fray Junípero Serra 4
Ibarra 5
Real de Don Juan 6
Sierra de Alicia 8

Eating
Tiki Room 1

In town, near the harbour, is the old **Customs House** (1781-1785) and a stone and adobe church (1808-1878) on the plaza. Up to the mid-19th century, San Blas was a thriving port and it still has a naval base and a (smelly) harbour.

There are few tourists early in the year or in August when it becomes very hot and there are many mosquitoes, but not on the beach 2 km from the village. However, there are other biting insects, so take repellent anyway. The two worst bugs are *jejenes* or *no sees* during the dry season, and *sancudos*, the big black monsters, during the wet season. But don't be too put off, as they are diminishing year by year, and if you don't linger around vegetation and still water they are not so bad.

Quieter than the dirty town beach is the extensive and often-deserted **Playa El Rey** on the north side of the estuary of the same name, beyond the lighthouse. Take a boat across the river from just west of the harbour, US$0.60 each way; the boatman works until 1730, but stops at lunchtime. Tell him when you want to return so that he knows to look out for your frantic waving from the other bank. The best beach is **Playa de las Islitas** reached by bus marked 'Las Veras' from the bus station, or 'El Llano' from Paredes y Sinaloa, just off the plaza. There is some threat of resort development here. At the beach of **Matanchén**, 7 km from San Blas (taxi US$3), there is good swimming but, again, many mosquitoes. Good home-made fruitcakes and bread are sold here. Surfing can be done at these beaches, but rarely at any one time is the surf up at all of them. Check at **Juan Bananas** (see below, Activities and tours, page 317). San Blas also claims to be home to the world's longest wave. About three times a year it is possible to surf non-stop for over a mile, from town towards Las Islitas, relaying on a series of point breaks.

Four-hour boat trips to see whales and dolphins are available in the San Blas area. Ask at the tourist office. Armando is a good guide; he charges US$52 for three people. It is also possible to take a three-hour jungle trip in a boat (bus to *embarcadero* on Matenchén road) to **La Tovara**, a small resort with a freshwater swimming hole brimming with turtles and catfish, a restaurant and not much else. The mangrove swamps can be visited on the way to La Tovara. Tour buses leave from the bridge 1 km out of town and cost US$30 for a canoe with six passengers, but it is cheaper to arrange the trip at **Embarcadero El Aguada**. Official prices are posted but it still seems possible to shop around. Away from the swimming hole there are coatis, raccoons, iguanas, turtles, boat-billed herons, egrets and parrots. Avoid fast motorized boats as the motor noise will scare any animals. Tours on foot are even better. Crocodiles are kept in caves along the route. Twilight tours enable naturalists to see potoos and, if very lucky, an ocelot. La Tovara is crowded at midday during the summer. A cheaper 1½- to two-hour cruise is also possible from the **Embarcadero El Aguada** (reached by Las Islitas bus – see above), US$17 per boat, but US$4.25 each if more than four people; it goes through a tunnel of mangroves, to the swimming hole 20 minutes away. You can take a bus from San Blas towards Santa Cruz and get off at Matachén beach (see above). From here, a boat for half-day hire includes the best part of the jungle cruise from San Blas.

Sixteen kilometres south from San Blas is the beautiful **Playa Los Cocos**, which is empty except at weekends. The **tourist office** ⓘ *Mercado, 1 block from plaza, T255-0021, Mon-Sat 0900-1300, 1800-2000, Sun 0900-1300. www.visitsanblas.com,* has information in English on the history of San Blas as well as a town map.

Inland towards Guadalajara

The old Route 15 leaves Tepic for Guadalajara. About 50 km from Tepic, off the Guadalajara road, is an attractive area of volcanic lagoons. Take the bus to **Santa María del Oro** for the lagoon of the same name. On the south side of the toll road is the Laguna Tepetiltic and near Chapalilla is another lake at San Pedro Lagunillas. There is a turn-off at Chapalilla to Compostela and Puerto Vallarta. At **Ahuacatlán**, 75 km from Tepic, the 17th-century ex-Convento de San Juan Evangelista stands on

"A field of upright swords" – the making of tequila

The quote from Paul Theroux's *The Old Patagonian Express* describes the swathes of blue agave grown in the dry highlands of the state of Jalisco and a few neighbouring areas. Agave is the raw material for tequila and, although there are some 400 varieties of agave, only the blue agave is suitable. After eight years growing in the fields, the spiky leaves are hacked off and the central core, weighing around 45 kg, is crushed and roasted. The syrup extracted is then mixed with liquid sugar, fermented for 30-32 hours and then distilled twice. White tequila is the product of a further four months in vats. It can be drunk neat, with a pinch of salt on the back of your hand, followed by a suck on a wedge of lime, or mixed into cocktails such as the margarita. Gold tequila is a blend of white tequila and tequila aged in wooden casks. Añejo, aged tequila, is a golden brown from spending at least two years in oak casks. Special premium tequila has no sugar added.

In pre-Conquest times, the local people used the agave sap to brew a mildly alcoholic drink, pulque, still drunk today. The Spaniards, however, wanted something more refined and stronger. They developed mezcal and set up distilleries to produce what later became tequila. The first of these was established in 1795 by royal decree of King Charles IV of Spain. It is still in existence today: La Rojena, the distillery of José Cuervo, known by its black crow logo, is the biggest in the country.

In recent years tequila exports have increased but not without problems. Demand has oustripped supply – not enough blue agave was planted eight years ago.

Tequila, like many other spirits, is blended. While the best tequila is 100% *puro de agave*, a couple of distilleries appear to have been blending more than they would like to admit. In 2001 the Consejo Regulador del Tequila, whose job it is to check and monitor standards on the industry, made a couple of surprise calls on well-established distilleries and were denied entry – suggesting strongly they had something to hide.

Around the town of Tequila there are 12 distilleries, of which 10 produce 75% of the country's tequila. Tours of the distilleries can be arranged with a free sample at the end, and of course shopping opportunities. Tours are hourly 1000-1400, US$3.50, lasting about one hour. Some tours in English – check locally for precise times. **Tequila Cuervo**, T3634-4170, in Guadalajara, or T742-0076 in Tequila (contact Srta Clara Martínez for tours). At **Tequila Sauza**, T742-0244, or in Guadalajara on T3679-0600. Dating from 1873, you can see the famous fresco illustrating the joys of drinking tequila. **Herradura**, T3614-9657, 8 km from Tequila, is in an old hacienda outside Amatitlán village, which has adobe walls and cobblestone streets and is worth a visit.

If buying tequila most of the liquor available in town should be drunk quickly and kept off the palate as much as possible. If you're looking for quality there are a few things to look out for. Look for the stamp of CRT (the Consejo Regulador del Tequila mark), look for 100% agave and finally, for the very best, look for *reposada* (matured). If it has all three, it's a fine tequila – and you should sip it gently.

the Plaza Principal; handicrafts are on sale here. Nearby, the village of **Jala** has a festival mid-August. From here the **Ceboruco volcano** can be reached in a day. On the main road a lava flow from Ceboruco is visible at El Ceboruco, Parador Turístico, with restaurant, information, toilets and a shop.

Ixtlán del Río, 84 km from Tepic (one hour 15 minutes by bus), has a few souvenir shops, a Museo Arqueológico in the Palacio Municipal, and a *casa de cambio*. Harvest (maize) festival is mid-September. Two kilometres out of town are the ruins of **Los Toriles** ⓘ *US$2.35*, a Toltec ceremonial centre on a warm, wind-swept plain. The main structure is the Temple of Quetzalcoatl, noted for its cruciform windows and circular shape. The ruins have been largely restored and some explanatory notes are posted around the site. There is a caretaker but no real facilities. Two kilometres beyond the Los Toriles site is **Motel Hacienda**, with pool. The road climbs out of the valley through uncultivated land, where trees intermix with prickly pear and chaparral cactus.

The journey from Tepic to Guadalajara cannot easily be broken at Ixtlán for sightseeing since buses passing through in either direction tend to be full; the bus on to Guadalajara takes three hours.

Tequila → *Phone code: 374. Colour map 3, B2. Altitude: 1300 m.*

As the bus approaches Tequila the aroma of the blue agave, from which it is distilled, fills the air and then the plants in neat rows can be seen growing in the pleasant, hilly countryside. Tequila is the main place where the famous Mexican drink is distilled. Tours of the distilleries are available (see box, page 305) and stores will let you sample different tequilas before you buy. Often around 20 bottles are open for tasting. The town is attractive, a mix of colonial and more modern architecture. It is a pleasant place to stay but there is not much to do other than tour the distilleries and there is little in the way of nightlife other than imbibe the local produce and recover the following morning. Along Calle Sixto Gorjón, where the arriving buses drop you, there are several liquor stores selling tequila, restaurants where you can eat for under US$5, pharmacies, doctors, dentists and the **Rojo de los Altos** bus ticket office at No 126A. In the town centre there are two plazas next to each other. On one is the **Templo de Santiago Apóstol**, a large, pretty, old stone building, with a 1930s municipal market next to it. Also on this plaza is the post office and **Banamex**. About a block behind **Banamex**, where Sixto Gorjón ends, is the entrance to the **José Cuervo distillery**. Along Calle Ramón Corona is the **Sauza distillery**. Both provide tours – see box. The **Museo Nacional del Tequila** ⓘ *Calle Ramón Corona 34, Tue-Sun 1000-1700, US$1, 50% discount for students*, is full of the history of tequila, along with the origins, processes, cultivation and distilling of tequila. Apparently 100% agave tequila blends in well with the human metabolism to the extent that if it's good stuff you don't get a hangover. Years of personal experience suggests otherwise, but buy the best you can. The **Palacio Municipal** on the main square puts out a stall by the map, which supposedly offers tourist information. In reality, it just sells tours of the distilleries, which include trips to the fields.

A day trip from Guadalajara is possible, by car, bus or Tequila Express (see page 317).

Sleeping

Guadalajara *p290, map p290*
The smart business hotels are in the modern western part of the city, around the Plaza del Sol, roughly 2 km west of the Centro Histórico.
LL Presidente Intercontinental, López Mateos Sur and Av Moctezuma, T3678-1234, www.ichotelsgroup.com/h/d/icon/hd/gdlha. Some deluxe suites with private patio, high-rise tower with built-in shopping centre, cavernous lobby.
LL Quinta Real, Av México 2727 y López Mateos, T3615-0000. Designed as colonial manor, convenient location, good, 78 large, well-furnished rooms, original artwork, good restaurant.

AL Aranzazú, Av Revolución 110 Pte, T3942-4040, www.aranzazu.com.mx. Central, very good, full business services – see the bats departing from the top floor roof eaves at dusk. A little overpriced.

AL Plaza Génova (Best Western), Juárez 123, T3613-7500, www.hplazagenova.com. In the Centro Histórico, price includes continental breakfast and welcome cocktail. Clean, good service, good restaurant. Recommended.

A Francés, Maestranza 35, T3613-1190, www.hotelfrances.com. Colonial building with central patio, oldest hotel in the city, built in 1610, have a drink there at 'happy hour' 1800-1900, to enjoy the bygone atmosphere, disco and bar music noisy at night, some rooms small but very good-value penthouse suite , free parking underneath adjoining Plaza de la Liberación, 3 blocks away.

A Rotonda, Liceo 130, T/F3614-1017, central, near cathedral. Remodelled 19th-century building, attractive, dining area in courtyard, cheap set lunches, nice public areas, rooms OK, with TV, phones, covered parking.

B Azteca, Javier Mina 311, 1½ blocks east of Mercado Libertad, 3617-7465. Clean, very friendly, some rooms with good views, parking around the corner.

C Canadá, Estadio 77, ½ block west of old bus station, T3619-4014. All rooms with bath, hot water, some with TV, clean, good value.

D Janeiro, Av Obregón 95, 1 block south of Mercado Libertad, T3617-5063. Best value in the market area. A few rooms have balconies overlooking the busy market street, close to Plaza de los Mariachis. Ideal for people-watching or insomnia.

D La Hacienda, Circunvalación Pte 66, a long way from the centre of town, in Col Cd Granja, off Av Vallarta on left before you reach *periférico* and head to Tepic, T3627-1724, ext 117. Motel with shaded, pool, clubhouse, hook-ups.

D Posada San Pablo, Madero 429 (no sign), T3614-2811. A family home that's been welcoming backpackers for years. No sign, just ring the bell and Lilia will let you in if she thinks you look OK. Quiet, informal and friendly. A small charge for laundry and use of kitchen.

D Posada Tapatía, López Cotilla 619, T3614-9146. Colonial-style house, 2-3 blocks from Federalismo, one of the better budget places, although traffic can be a problem.

E Estación, Independencia Sur 1297, across the main boulevard beside train station, T3619-0051. Quiet, clean, safe, luggage store, hot water, small, limited restaurant. Recommended.

E Hostel Guadalajara, Maestranza 147, close to the centre, T3562-7520, www.hostelguadalajara.com. Youth Hostel-affiliated, with good facilities including kitchen, laundry, internet access and lounge area.

E León, Independencia Sur 557. Bath, towels, hot water, clean, staff friendly and helpful.

Tlaquepaque

Consider staying in Tlaquepaque if stocking up on gifts before heading home.

L El Tapatío, Blvd Aeropuerto 4275, Tlaquepaque, en route to airport, T3837-2929. Fine view of city, extensive grounds, very attractive and comfortable rooms.

L-AL La Villa del Ensueño, Florida 305, Tlaquepaque, T3635-8792, www.villadelensueno.com. 8 rooms, 2 suites, pool, including breakfast, no smoking, English spoken.

B La Posada de la Media Luna, off Juárez 1 block east of the Parián,Tlaquepaque, T3635-6054. Delightful rooms, with private bath, TV and telephone, includes breakfast on colourful patio. Excellent value.

Tonalá *p294*

D Hotel Tonalá, Madero 22, Tonalá. Plain but in good shape, some rooms with TV.

Chapala *p294*

A Villa Montecarlo, west edge of town on Av Hidalgo at Calle Lourdes, T765-2120.

Phone codes *Guadalajara 33; Tlaquepaque 33; Tonalá 33; Chapala 376; Ajijic 376; Jocotepec 387; Tapalpa 343; Colima 312; Manzanillo 314; Tecomán 313; San Patricio Melaque 315; Barra de Navidad 315; Puerto Vallarta 322; Tepic 311; San Blas 328; Tequila 374.*

Family rooms or suites available, very comfortable, in beautiful grounds with palms and mangoes.

B Chapala Haciendas, Km 40, Chapala-Guadalajara highway, T765-2720. Live music Wed and Sat. Unheated pool.

B Nido, Av Madero 202, close to lake, T765-2116. Brick building, old photos in reception hall, clean, cheaper without TV, accepts Visa and MasterCard, good restaurant, swimming pool, parking for motorcycles beside pool.

Camping

PAL, 1 km from the lake between Chapala and Ajijic, Apdo Postal 1-1470, Guadalajara, T766-0040. Trailer park, 1st class, pool, good.

Ajijic to Jocotepec *p295*

L-A Posada del Pescador, Miguel Arana 611, Jocotepec outskirts, T763-0028. *Cabañas* with bedroom, living room, kitchen and bathroom, set in a lovely garden.

AL La Nueva Posada, Donato Guerra 9, Ajijic, T766-1444. Breakfast included, vast rooms, Canadian management, horse riding, golf, tennis, theatre, gardens, swimming pool, restaurant, attractive outdoor seating in garden overlooking lake, colonial decor, delightful.

Tapalpa *p295*

B Posada Hacienda, Raul Quintero 120, T432-0193. Nice bungalows with fireplace and small kitchen.

D Hotel Tapalpa. With huge holes in the floor, but clean and fairly cheap.

Colima *p295*

AL-A Hotel América, Morelos 162, T312-9596. A/c, cable TV, phone, largest rooms in new section, pretty interior gardens, travel agency, steam baths, good restaurant, central, friendly.

A Ceballos, Torres Quintero 12, T312-4449, main square, www@hotelceballos.com. A fine building with attractive *portales*, some huge rooms with a/c, clean, good food in its 2 restaurants (pricey), secure indoor parking, very good value. Highly recommended.

C Gran Hotel Flamingos, Av Rey Colimán 18, near Jardín Núñez, T312-2525. Pleasant small rooms with fan, bath, simple, clean, breakfast expensive, disco below goes on till 0300 on Sat and Sun.

C-D La Merced, Hidalgo 188 (entrance at Juárez 82), T312-6969. Pretty colonial house with rooms around patio filled with plants, all rooms same price, TV, bath. Highly recommended for budget travellers.

E Núñez, Juárez 88 at Jardín Núñez, T312-7030. Basic, dark, with bath.

Manzanillo *p297, map p297*

AL La Posada, Calzada Lázaro Cárdenas 201, near the end of Las Brisas peninsula, T333-1899. American owned, beautifully designed rooms, some back into the very rock of an outcrop.

A Marlyn, at Santiago Beach, T333-0107. 3rd-floor rooms with balcony overlooking the beach. Recommended.

B Colonial, González Boncanegra 28 and México, at the port, T332-1080. Colonial building with good restaurant, good central location and friendly.

B Anita, at Santiago Beach, T333-0161. Built in 1940, has a certain funky charm, clean and on the beach.

C Azteca Centro, Madero 265, at the port, T332-7343. Fairly new, fan, TV, clean, opposite the market, good value.

D Emperador, Dávalos 69, at the port, T332-2374. Good value, friendly, fan, TV, cheap restaurant.

E Casa de Huéspedes Central, behind bus station, in town. With bath, fan, OK.

Camping

La Marmota trailer park, at junction of Highways 200 and 98, Manzanillo. Cold showers, bathrooms, pool, laundry facilities.

Trailer Park El Palmar, Miramar and Santiago beaches, 4½ km north of Manzanillo, T333-5533. With a large swimming pool, run-down, very friendly, coconut palms.

Southeast of Manzanillo *p298*

B Hotel Bucanero, Cuyutlán, near the north end of the seafront, T326-4005. Clean rooms, good restaurant, games room and souvenir shop. Swimming here is excellent and umbrellas and wooden walkways protect feet against the hot sun and sand.

C Gran Fénix, Javier Mina 460, Tecomán, T324-0791. Larger rooms have a/c, smaller rooms are noisier but hotel is recommended.

D-E Yeza, Lázaro Cárdenas 59, Tecomán. Very clean, spacious rooms in a quiet spot on the corner from the bus station, the owner's son speaks English.

North of Manzanillo *p298*

L-AL Villas Camino del Mar, San Patricio Melaque, T355-5207. Rooms or villas on beach, 2 pools, discounts for long stays.

AL Hotel Barra de Navidad, López de Legazpi 250, Barra de Navidad, T824-4043, www.hotelbarradenavidad.com. With balcony on beach, or bungalows where you can cook, pool.

AL-A Los Artistas Bed and Breakfast, Isla Navidad, reached by ferry, T355-6441, www.islanavidad.com/meson. Spectacular private mansion converted into an exclusive hotel, 27 golf holes, private beaches, pools, individualized service, good value.

A Delfín, Morelos 23, Barra de Navidad, T355-5068, http://hoteldelfinmx.com. Very clean, pool, gym, hot water, friendly. Recommended.

A Hacienda Melaque, Morelos 49, San Patricio Melaque, T355-5334. Tennis court, kitchen, pool.

B Monterrey, Gómez Farías 27, San Patricio Melaque, T355-5004, on beach. Clean, fan, bath, parking, superb view.

B Posada Pablo de Tarso, Gómez Farías 408, San Patricio Melaque, T355-5117, facing beach. Pretty, galleried building, tiled stairs, antique-style furniture.

B Santa María, Vallarta, San Patricio Melaque, opposite **Flamingo**, T357-0338. Friendly. Recommended.

C San Nicolás, Gómez Farías 54, San Patricio Melaque, T357-0066, beside **Estrella Blanca** bus station. Noisy but clean. Off season, very pleasant.

C San Lorenzo, Av Sinaloa 7, T355-5139, Barra de Navidad. Very clean, hot water, friendly staff, good restaurant opposite.

D Caribe, Sonora 15, Barra de Navidad. Fan, friendly, kitchen facilities, family-run.

D Posada Pacífico, Mazatlán 136, Barra de Navidad, T355-5359, 1 street behind bus terminal. Clean, fan, friendly, good restaurant opposite, good value.

E Posada Carmelita, Tomatlán, Km 103 south of Puerto Vallarta and 12 km inland (not to be confused with Boca de Tomatlán, on the coast), has a few modest hotels with bath, clean.

Camping

Melaque Follow the 'Melaque' signs and at the end of the main road is a free camping place on the beach at the bay, very good, easily accessible for RVs, popular for vehicles and tents.

Trailer Park La Playa, San Patricio Melaque, T357-0065, in the village, on beach. US$13 for car and 2 people, full hook-up, toilets, cold showers.

Tenacatita Take the unpaved road from Highway 200 north of Barra de Navidad as far as the abandoned **Hotel Bahía de Tenacatita**; at the T-junction, turn right, pass the hotel, and the following 2 campsites are about 500 m further on the left: **Tenacatita**, trailer park, hook-ups, cold showers, toilet, laundry facilities, restaurant. **Boca de Iguanas**, trailer park, vehicle free, hook-ups, cold showers, toilets, laundry facilities, clean, pleasant location.

Chamela Villa Polonesia Trailer Park, near Chamela, full hook-ups, hot showers, on lovely beach (follow signs from Route 200 on unmade road). Recommended. Restaurant on road to trailer park, clean, good food.

Puerto Vallarta *p299, map p301*

LL Sierra, Nuevo Vallarta, T297-1300. Colourful building-block hotel, smart, modern, all inclusive.

LL Velas Vallarta, Marina Vallarta, North Hotel Zone, T221-0091, www.velasvallarta.com. Rustic with Moorish touches, part timeshare hotel with verdant gardens, golf course opposite, all-inclusive options.

L Casa Kimberley, Zaragoza 445, North Central, T222-1336. Former home of Richard Burton and Elizabeth Taylor, 10 rooms full of memorabilia of the actors, breakfast included, bar, great views, pool, much cheaper in low season.

L Hacienda and Spa, Blv Francisco Medina Ascencio, North Hotel Zone, T224-6667. Modern, with colonial influence, gym, Temazcal treatments, pleasant pool, is nicest in zone but 100 m to beach and on main road, discounts out of season.

L Las Palmas Beach Resort, Blv Medina Ascencio, North Hotel Zone, Km 2.5, T226-1220. Castaway-on-a-desert-island theme, all rooms with sea view.

L Molina de Agua, Ignacio L Vallarta 130, South Central, T222-1957. Cabins in pleasant wooded glade on bank of river, a/c, good service, 2 pools. Recommended.

L Nautilus and Marina Club, Marina Vallarta, T221-1015. Olympic pool and dive tank in this resort. Most rooms have private balcony or patio.

L Playa Los Arcos, Olas Altas 380, South Central, T222-0583. Good location for restaurants, undersized pool terrace overflows to Playa Los Muertos.

AL Casa Andrea, Rodríguez 174, South Central, T222-1213, www.casa-andrea.com. Small hotel suites, close to cafés and restaurants, pleasant garden with bar, pool, owner operated, good friendly service with attention to detail. Reduced rates in low season.

AL Rosita, Paseo Díaz Ordaz 901, north end of Malecón, North Central, T223-2000, hrosita@zonavirtual.com.mx. Puerto Vallarta's original holiday hotel (1948) with pool, on town beach.g

AL-B Casa del Puente, North Central, by bridge opposite market, enter through the restaurant, T222-0749, www.casadelpuente.com. Suites with kitchen in a private villa suspended above river, delightful, book months ahead, cheaper in low season, good value.

A Casa Corazón, Amapas 326, South Central, T/F222-6364, corazon@zianet.com. US-owned hideaway on steep slope above southern end of Playa Los Muertos, overpriced but 3 big rooms on top terrace with spectacular views worth the premium, including big breakfast, beach access with bar and restaurant.

A Cuatro Vientos, Matamoros 520, North Central, T222-0161, www.cuatrovientos.com. Up steep cobbled street from church, spectacular views, good restaurant perched high above city, plunge pool, breakfast included, friendly and relaxed atmosphere. Recommended.

A Posada Río Cuale, Aquiles Serdán 242, South Central, near new bridge, T/F222-0450. Small pool in front garden, not very private, nice, colonial-style rooms.

B Bernal, Francisco I Madero 423, South Central, T222-3605. Friendly, large rooms, fan, good showers. Recommended.

B Posada de Roger, Basilio Badillo 237, South Central, T222-0836. Communal kitchen, pool, cable TV, a/c, great breakfast restaurant (**Freddy's Tucan**).

C-D Yasmín, Basilio Badillo 168, South Central, T222-0087. Plant-filled courtyard arrangement behind **Café Olla**, a/c, clean, restaurant, 1 block from the beach, noisy till at least 2300.

D-E El Castillo, Francisco I Madero 273, South Central. Fan, hot water, cable TV, cheaper without bath. Convenient for restaurants, a few blocks from the beach.

D-E Lina, Francisco I Madero 376, South Central, T222-1661. With bath, hot water, fan, run-down, rooms on street noisy.

Camping

Puerto Vallarta, north of centre, just north of bypass then east 2 blocks. Popular.

Tacho, 2 trailer parks, on road to Pitillal, opposite Marina. 60 spaces but spacious.

Around Puerto Vallarta *p300*

LL La Joya de Mismaloya, Mismaloya, Km 11.5, T228-0660. Romantic but over-developed setting on filmset beach.

LL Majahuitas Resort, between Quimixto and Yelapa beaches, only accessible by boat, transfers included, T221-2277, www.mexicoboutiquehotels.com/majahuitas, run by Margot and Lirio González. All-inclusive resort, 8 guesthouses, on cove, sandy beach, rustic furniture, solar energy, horse riding and snorkelling available portion of profits go to indigenous community of Chacala, good value.

B Lagunitas, Yelapa, www.hotel-lagunita.com. Cabin hotel with pool.

C Mateo and Elenita, Yelapa, breakfast included in price. Visit their waterfall.

Camping

Beto and Felicidad, camping available 30 mins' walk up valley from **Yelapa**, US$4 per person, in beautiful setting (Felicidad's home-made *tortillas*are 'the best in Mexico').

Also at fishing village of Yelapa, best reached by boat from **Hotel Rosita** at 1130: camp under *palapas* (shelters), about US$4 per person.

Puerto Vallarta north to Tepic *p301*

A Hotel and Trailer Park Piedras Blancas, Punta de Mita. Good, also camping, hook-ups US$12-14, restaurants.

C Coca, Rincón de Guayabitos, among several hotels and restaurants on a rocky peninsula to the south of the beach.

C Tía Adriana's bed and breakfast, Sayulita, T/F(329) 291-3029, www.tiaadrianas.com Nov-Jun, good, central, good value.
E Hotel Contreras, Las Varas. With fan and bath, clean, small rooms.

Camping

Trailer Park, Sayulita, 2½ km off Route 200, contact Apdo 5-585, CP 06500, Mexico City, T5572-1335. On beautiful beach, German owner, very friendly, also has bungalows. Highly recommended.

Tepic *p302, map p303*

AL Fray Junípero Serra, Lerdo Pte 23, T212-2525, main square. Comfortable, big rooms, clean, a/c, good restaurant, friendly, good service. A little noisy with the new road, but still recommended.
AL Real de Don Juan, Av México 105 Sur, on Plaza de Los Constituyentes, T/F216-1888. Charming, traditional style. With parking.
A Bugamvillas, Av Insurgentes y Libramiento Pte, T218-0225. Very comfortable rooms with a/c, TV, pool, restaurant with great food and good wine list.
A Sierra de Alicia, Av México 180 Norte, T212-0322. With fan, tiled stairways, friendly.
B Santa Fe, Calzada de la Cruz 85, near Parque La Loma, a few mins from centre, T213-1966. With TV, clean, comfortable, good restaurant.
C Ibarra, Durango Norte 297A, T212-3870. Luxurious rooms, with bath and fan (some rooms noisy) and slightly spartan, cheaper rooms without bath, very clean.
C-D Tepic, Dr Martínez 438, T213-1377, near bus station outside town. With bath, clean, friendly but noisy.
D Altamirano, Mina 19 Ote, T212-7131, near Palacio de Gobierno. noisy, good value. Parking.
E-F Camarena, San Luis Norte 63, 4 blocks southeast of Zócalo. Without bath, clean, friendly.
E-F Pensión Morales, Insurgentes y Sánchez, 4 blocks from bus station. Clean and friendly, hotel is now closed but family still put up backpackers in what is now a private house.

San Blas *p303*

Accommodation becomes scarce and more expensive around Semana Santa and other holidays.
L Garza Canela, Cuauhtémoc Sur 106, T285-0307, www.garzacanela.com. Very clean, excellent restaurant, small pool, nice garden. Highly recommended.
B Casa Mañana, Los Cocos beach. Austrian run, hotel and restaurant, good food. Many apartments for rent.
B Posada del Rey, Campeche, T285-0123. Very clean, swimming pool, excellent value.
C Marino Inn, Batallón, T285-0340. With a/c, friendly, pool, fair food.
C-D El Tesoro de San Blas, 50 m south of dock, 5 mins from centre. Rooms and villas, hot water, satellite TV, US owners.
D Posada Irene, Batallón 122, 4 blocks southwest of Zócalo. Basic with a fan, few rooms with a shower and hot water. Kitchen, friendly.
D-E Posada Azul, Batallón 126, 4 blocks from plaza towards beach, T285-0129. 3-bedded rooms with fan and hot water, cheaper for simple 2-bedded rooms without bath, cooking facilities.
E Hotel Delfín, Los Cocos beach. With bath, balcony, good view, good value but some beds a bit lumpy.

Camping

No camping or sleeping permitted on beaches but several pay campsites available. All trailer parks in the town centre are plagued by mosquitoes.
Playa Amor, Los Cocos beach. The best trailer park, good beach, on a narrow strip of land between road to Santa Cruz and cliff, good, popular, 16 km south of town.

Tepic to Guadalajara *p302*

D Hotel Colonial, Hidalgo 45 Pte, Ixtlán del Río. Very friendly. Recommended.
C-D Bungalows and Trailer Park Koala, La Laguna, Santa María del Oro. Bungalows accommodating up to 4 people, several trailer sites and a large campground. Good cheap meals available. Fishing and waterskiing on nearby lagoon.

Tequila *p306,*

C Abasolo, Abasolo 80, T742-0195. Well (over) decorated, rooms have TV.
C Posada del Agave, Sixto Gorjón 83, T742-0774. Excellent value with private bath, TV, very comfortable.

D Motel Delicias, Carretera Internacional 595, on the highway to Guadalajara about 1 km outside Tequila, T742-1094. Best available, TV, off-street parking.
E Colonial, Morelos 52, corner of Sixto Gorjón, T742-0355. Characterless, but central, clean and not run-down, some rooms with private bath. A good deal.

Eating

Guadalajara *p290, map p290*
As can be expected in a city of this size there is a wide variety of restaurants on offer, look in local tourist literature for the flavour of the month. There are also fast-food outlets, *pizzerías* and Mexican *cafeterías* and bars. The cheapest restaurants are in the streets near the old bus station, especially in Calle de Los Angeles, and upstairs in the large Mercado Libertad (San Juan de Dios) in the centre. There are also plenty of cheap *loncherías*.
TTT **Piaf**, Marsella 126. French cuisine, live music, friendly, closed Sun. Excellent.
TTT-TT **El Ganadero**, on Av Américas. Excellent beef, reasonable prices.
TTT-TT **El Mexicano**, Plaza Tapatía, Morelos 81. Rustic Mexican decor. Recommended.
TTT-TT **La Rinconada**, Morelos 86 on Plaza Tapatía. A beautiful colonial building, columned courtyard, carved wood doors, open until 2130, separate bar.
TTT-T **La Trattoria**, Niños Héroes 3051. Very good, reasonably priced Italian, very popular (queues form for lunch from 1400).
TT **Carnes Asadas El Tapatío**, Mercado Libertad (there are 3). Strictly for carnivores, try delicious *carne en su jugo* (beef stew with potatoes, beans, bacon, sausage, onion and avocado, garnished with salsa, onion and coriander).
TT **Carnes Asadas Rigo's**, Independencia 584A. Popular. Goat is a speciality, roasted each day and served with radish, onion and chilli.
TT **Cortijo La Venta**, Federación 725, T3617-1675. Daily 1300-0100. Invites customers to fight young bulls (calves) after their meal (the animals are not harmed, guests might be), restaurant serves meat, soups, salads.
TT **La Pianola**, Av México 3220 and several other locations. Good, reasonable prices, serves *chiles en nogada*. Excellent.
TT-T **Café Madoka**, Enrique González Martínez 78, T3613-3134, just south of Hidalgo. Excellent very early breakfasts, well known for the men who play dominoes there. Friendly, a Guadalajara institution.
T **Búfalo**, Calderón de la Barca and Av Vallarta. Tacos and cheap *comida corrida*, very friendly.
T **Café D'Osio**, around the corner from Hotel Hamilton, on corner of Prisciliano Sánchez and Ocampo. Excellent breakfast and delicious tortas, especially the roast pork, not expensive. Daily 0900-1800.
T **La Catedral del Antojito**, Pedro Moreno 130, a pedestrian street. Colonial-style house, restaurant upstairs above bridal gown shop, serves tacos, tortas etc, good meal for under US$2.
T **La Playita**, Av Juárez between Corona and Maestranza, also one at Morelos 99, by the tourist office. Very good; try *tortas de lomo doble carne con aguacate* (pork and avocado special).
La Bombilla, López Cotilla y Penitenciaría. Very good for *churros* and hot chocolate.

Zapopan
TT **El Asadero**, opposite the Basílica in Zapopan. Very good.

Tonalá *p294*
TT **El Rincón del Sol**, 16 de Septiembre 61, Tonalá. An attractive restaurant serving steaks and Mexican food.
TT **Restaurant Jalapeños**, Madero 23, Tonalá. Serves pizza, beer and regular meals.

Chapala *p294*
TTT-TT **La Langosta Loca**, Ramón Corona. Good seafood.
TT **La Leña**, Madero 236. Open air, serves *antojitos* and steaks, bamboo roof.
T **Café Paris**, Madero 421. Sidewalk tables, popular, *comida corrida* US$3, also breakfast and sandwiches.

Cafés and ice creams
Bing's, Madero, by the lake. Ice cream parlour. Try the *mamey* flavour!

Ajijic to Jocotepec *p295*
Jocotepec is famous for its ice cream.
TTT-TT **Posada Ajijic**, Morelos, Ajijic, opposite pier, T766-0744. Bar and restaurant, accept

credit cards; pier here with fish restaurant at the end, indoor and outdoor seating and bar, used to be over water but stilts are now over dry land.

ŦŦ **Ajijic**, pavement café on corner of plaza. Cheap drinks, Mexican snacks, hearty *parrillada* Sat, Sun.

ŦŦ **Los Girasoles**, 16 de Septiembre 18, Ajijic. Mexican food in walled courtyard.

Ŧ **Lonchería**, on plaza, Ajijic. Clean, good simple meals, cheap, grilled chicken, used by locals and Americans.

Tapalpa *p295*

The more expensive restaurants have tables on balconies overlooking the square and all are visited by *mariachis*.

ŦŦŦ-ŦŦ **Posada Hacienda**, overlooking the square (which has a US$1 cover charge) is well placed.

Colima *p295*

ŦŦ **El Vivero**, Constitución 61, Colima. Nice open-air plant-filled courtyard, moderately priced specialities including seafood, Mexican and Italian, live music Thu-Sun.

ŦŦ **La Troje**, on southeast of Colima heading to Manzanillo, T312-2680. Good, *mariachis*, very Mexican.

ŦŦ **Los Naranjos**, Gabino Barreda 34, ½ block north of Jardín Torres Quintero, Colima. Going since 1955, nice, well known.

Ŧ **El Trébol**, southwest corner of Zócalo. Probably the best of several restaurants on the Zócalo serving inexpensive meals.

Cafés, bakeries and ice cream parlours

Centro de Nutrición Lakshmi, Av Madero 265, Colima. Good yoghurt and wholemeal bread run by Hari Krishnas.

Around Colima *p297*

ŦŦ-Ŧ **Los Portales** and **Comala**, both in the town of Comala. Popular restaurants, with *mariachis* and local specialities; open until 1800. If you sit and drink you will usually be brought complementary food until you wilt from *mariachi* overload.

Manzanillo *p297, map p297*

ŦŦŦ-ŦŦ **Carlos 'n' Charlie's**, Blv M de la Madrid Km 6.9, on the beach. Seafood and ribs, great atmosphere.

ŦŦŦ-ŦŦ **Chantilly**, Juárez. Popular café serving big traditional meals and good coffee. Closed Sat.

ŦŦ **Portofino's Pizza**, Blv M de la Madrid, Km 13. Italian, very good pizza.

ŦŦ **Plaza de la Perlita**, next door to Portofino's Pizza. Good food, live music.

Ŧ **Johanna**, opposite bus station entrance Good food, cheap.

Ŧ **Mercados**. There are central markets with *fondas* for good cheap seafood, clean.

Southeast of Manzanillo *p298*

ŦŦŦ **Willy's Seafood Restaurant**, Playa Azul, on the beach. French owner, primarily seafood, some meat, very good.

North of Manzanillo *p298*

There are many restaurants on the beach at San Patricio Melaque but most close at 1900.

ŦŦŦ **Antonio's**, on grand bay, Barra de Navidad. Gourmet food, award-winning restaurant.

ŦŦŦ-ŦŦ **Ambar**, Veracruz 101, Barra de Navidad. Half menu vegetarian, real coffee, good breakfast and crêpes, closed lunchtime. Recommended.

ŦŦŦ-ŦŦ **Seamaster**, on the beach, Barra de Navidad. Best ribs.

ŦŦ **Koala's at the Beach**, Alvaro Obregón 52, San Patricio Melaque, 2 blocks from **Camino del Mar**. Small, good, great food in walled garden compound off dusty street. Canadian/Australian run.

ŦŦ **Maya Melaque**, on the beach, San Patricio Melaque, T355-6881. Fine inexpensive cuisine, Mediterranean style, open during high season, reservations recommended for beachside tables.

ŦŦ **Velero's**, Barra de Navidad Delicious snapper and good views.

ŦŦ-Ŧ **Banana's**, on the beach, Barra de Navidad. Good breakfast and coffee.

Puerto Vallarta *p299, map p301*

South Central

ŦŦŦ **Chez Elena**, Matamoros 520, T222-0161, up lots of steps but worth it. Beautiful view over town from large balcony, popular well-established restaurant, award-winning food. Recommended.

ŦŦŦ **Daiquiri Dick's**, Olas Altas 314, T222-0566. Restaurant and bar open for breakfast, lunch and dinner, opposite Playa

Los Muertos, excellent cooking, classical harp and guitar music Sun 1300-1500.

¥¥¥-¥¥ **Jazz Café/Le Bistro**, by the bridge on Insurgentes. Garden, bamboo, beside river, pleasant for coffee and classical music (piano or harp) in morning, crowded and expensive in evening, many vegetarian dishes, clean.

¥¥¥-¥¥ **Señor Ponchos**, Madero 260 and Vallarta. Authentic Mexican, typical breakfast, seafood and lobster, moderate prices.

¥¥ **A Page in the Sun**, Olas Altas opposite Los Arcos hotel on corner. Coffee is excellent, cakes home-made, 2nd-hand bookshop.

¥¥ **Café Catedral**, Basilio Badillo and Insurgentes. Very good breakfasts, fine coffee, good value.

¥¥ **Las Palapas**, on the beach near Playa de los Muertos. Good food, service, value, decor and atmosphere.

¥¥-¥ **Café Olla**, lower end Basilio Badillo. Good-value Mexican and barbecue in cramped open-fronted dining room, very popular.

¥¥-¥ **Fredy's Tucán**, Basilio Badillo 237. Good courtyard dining, mainly Mexican menu, good breakfast with bottomless coffee.

¥¥ **Los Arbolitos**, east end of Lázaro Cárdenas. 3 balconied floors above river. Mexican, good atmosphere.

North Central

¥¥ **Café Amadeus**, Miramar 271, up steps from Guerrero. Classical music, books, board games in delightful whitewashed rooms or balcony perched above old town, coffee, delectable cakes. Recommended.

¥¥ **Rico Mac Taco**, Av México, corner Uruguay. Busy, cheap and widely popular.

¥¥-¥ **Juanita's**, Av México 1067. Attracts locals as well as value-seeking gringos, good.

¥¥-¥ **Las Milagros**, Juárez and Pipila. Forget the queues at the popular gringo restaurants, this one is excellent, moderately priced, cosmopolitan, live music, colonial-style courtyard. Recommended.

¥ **Gaby**, Mina. Small, family-run, eat in garden, excellent food, cheap and clean.

¥ **Pepe's Tacos**, Calle Honduras, opposite Pemex at northern end of downtown. Cheap, ethnic and delicious in spartan pink/white dining room, open all night.

Tepic *p302, map303*

The restaurant in the bus terminal is overpriced. There are lots of fish stalls by market on Puebla Norte.

¥¥ **El Tripol**, in mall, near plaza. Excellent vegetarian.

¥¥ **Roberto's** and **Chante Clair**. Both good food and near Parque La Loma, closed Sun.

¥¥ **Tiki Room**, San Luis Norte opposite Hotel Camarena. Restaurant, art gallery, video bar, fun.

San Blas *p303*

On Sun women prepare delicious pots of stew *al fresco* on the plaza.

¥¥ **Las Islitas**. With a distinctly nautical feel, good-value seafood, also sells banana bread. Recommended.

¥¥ **Tumba de Yako**, on way to beach. Yoghurt and health foods, and the original version of *pan de plátano* (banana bread), advertised all over town.

¥¥-¥ **Las Olas**. One of many seafood restaurants on the beach. Good and cheap with good local dishes.

Tequila *p306*

¥¥ **El Marinero**, Albino Rojas 16B. Nice seafood restaurant with strolling musicians.

¥¥ **El Sauza**, Juárez 45, beside **Banamex**. Restaurant/bar, Mexican atmosphere.

¥¥-¥ **El Callejón**, Sixto Gorjón 105. Rustic Mexican decor, à la carte, *antojitos* and hamburgers.

Entertainment

Guadalajara *p290, map p290*

Bars and clubs

Just stroll down Maestranza south of Juárez from about 0830 and listen for the noise. **La Maestranza** is very popular, and brings out the *machismo* with distinctive themes of the matador. **La Maskara** and **La Jaula** are on the same block, and gay friendly. **La Mansión** is round the corner, and **Femina La Latina** offers an altogether more cultured approach to the whole drinking/socializing malarkey.

Cinema

Good-quality films, some in English, are shown at the *cine-teatro* in the **Instituto Cultural Cabañas** (see page 292), which also has a good *cafetería*.

Music
Concerts and theatre in the **ex-Convento del Carmen**. A band plays every Thu at 1800 in the **Plaza de Armas**, in front of the Palacio de Gobierno, free. Organ recitals in the **cathedral**. **Peña Cuicacalli**, Av Niños Héroes almost at corner of Av Chapultepec, T3825-4690, opens 2000, US$5, food and drink available, fills up fast; local groups perform variety of music including Latin American folk music Fri and Sat.

Theatre
Instituto Cultural Cabañas, see page 292. The Ballet Folklórico del Instituto Cultural Cabañas performs Wed 2030, US$5. The Instituto is also an art school, with classes in photography, sculpture, ceramics, literature, music, theatre and dance.
Teatro Degollado, Plaza de la Liberación, T3658-3812 . **Ballet Folklórico de la Universidad de Guadalajara**, performs every Sun at 1000, superb, highly recommended, prehispanic and Mexican-wide dances, and other cultural shows, US$2-10 (check before you go). The theatre is open to the public Mon-Fri 1000-1300, just to look inside. **Grupo Folklórico Ciudad de Guadalajara** performs here every Thu at 2000.

Chapala *p294*
Bars and clubs
Beer Garden, where Madero reaches the lake. Restaurant/bar with live amplified Mexican music, dancing, tables on the beach.

Around Colima *p297*
Bars and clubs
Botanero Bucaramanga, outside the town of Comala, on the Colima road. Bar with *botanas* (snacks) and more *mariachis*.

Puerto Vallarta *p299, map p301*
Bars and clubs
Carlos O'Brian's, Malecón and Andale, Olas Altas. Attracts a motley crowd of revellers and starts hopping after 2200. **Christine**, at Hotel Krystal. For spectacular light show, disco, expensive drinks and cover. Many clubs and late bars throughout central area.

Festivals and events

Guadalajara *p290, map p290*
21 Mar Benito Juárez's birthday; everything closes.
Jun-Oct In Jun, the **Virgen de Zapopan** (see page 294), leaves her home to spend each night in a different church where fireworks are let off. The virgin has a new car each year but the engine is not started; men pull it through the beautifully decorated streets with ropes. The climax is **12 Oct** when the virgin leaves the cathedral for home, there are great crowds along the route. **Oct** **Fiestas de Octubre**; throughout the month there is a great fiesta with concerts, bullfights, sports and exhibitions of handicrafts from all over Mexico.
Late Nov/early Dec **Feria Internacional del Libro**, the 3rd largest book fair in the world, is held in Guadalajara's Gran Salón de Exposiciones. As well as the usual gathering of publishers, there are round-the-clock readings of poetry and fiction, music, dance, theatre, games, food and drink. For information, write (in English or Spanish) to FIL Guadalajara, Francia 1747, Col Moderna, Guadalajara, Jal 44190, México, T523-8100331, www.fil.com.mx.

Chapala *p294*
2-3 Oct Fiesta de Francisco de Asís, with fireworks and excellent food served in the streets.

Ajijic to Jocotepec *p295*
11-18 Jan There is a local **fiesta** in Jocotepec.

Colima *p295*
Oct-Nov The annual **feria** of the region (agriculture, cattle and industry, with much additional festivity) runs from the last Sat of Oct until the 1st Sun of Nov. Traditional local potions (all the year round) include *jacalote* (from black maize and pumpkin seeds), *bate* (*chía* and honey), *tuba* (palm tree sap) and *tecuino* (ground, germinated maize).

Shopping

Guadalajara *p290, map p290*
The best shops are no longer in the centre, although a couple of department stores have

branches there. The best stores are in the shopping malls, of which there are many, small and large, mainly on the west side.

Bookshops

Librería La Fuente, Medellín 140, near Juan Manuel in the centre, T3613-5238. Sells used books and magazines in English and Spanish, interesting to browse in, some items quite old, from 1940s and 1950s.
Librería México, Plaza del Sol, local 14, area D, on Av López Mateos side, T3121-0114. Has US magazines and newspapers.
Sanborn's, several branches: Av Vallarta 1600 and Gen San Martín; Juárez and 16 de Septiembre; Plaza Bonita and López Mateos Sur 2718 (near Plaza del Sol). English books and magazines are available at a reasonable mark-up.

Crafts, furniture and textiles

The blue, green, amber and amethyst blown-glass articles are made at 2 glass factories. Many other crafts are available in Tlaquepaque, and you can watch the potters at work. Although you may sometimes find better bargains in Tonalá (see below), overall **Tlaquepaque** is the cheapest and most varied source of local crafts, with attractive shops set in old colonial villas; best buys are glass, papier-mâché goods, leather (cheapest in Mexico), and ceramics.
Antigua de México, Independencia 255, Tlaquepaque. Beautiful, expensive furniture in a lovely building, used to be a convent, the family has branches in Nogales and Tucson so furniture can be shipped to their shops there.
Casa de Artesanías de Jalisco, González Gallo 20, Parque Agua Azul, T3619-4664. Mon-Sat 1000-1900, Sun 1000-1400. High-quality display (and sale) of handicrafts, ceramics, paintings, hand-blown glass, dresses, etc (state-subsidized, reasonably priced but not cheap).
Casa de los Telares, Hidalgo 1378, some way from the main shopping area.Traditional textiles are woven on hand looms.
La Casa Canela, Independencia 258, near Cruz Verde, T3635-3717. Sells furniture and crafts, don't miss the colonial kitchen at the back of the house.
Museo Regional de la Cerámica, Independencia 237, Tlaquepaque.
See page 294.

Jewellery

Sergio Bustamante, Independencia 238. Zona Centro, Tlaquepaque. Good modern jewellery; expensive but well worth a look, a stream runs through this house with a colonial façade.

Markets

Mercado Libertad (also known as **San Juan de Dios**), Javier Mina, has colourful items for souvenirs with lots of Michoacán crafts including Paracho guitars and Sahuayo hats, leather jackets and *huaraches* (sandals). Delicious food is served upstairs on the 1st level (particularly goat meat, *birria*, also very sweet coconut called *cocada*), fruit juices and other soft drinks.

Tonalá *p294*

In Tonalá, market days are Sun and Thu. For shopping in the centre of town, **Aldana Luna**, Juárez 194, T3683-0302, sells wrought-iron furniture; **Plaza Juárez**, Juárez 141, is a large building with several craft shops in it. **Artesanías Nuño**, Juárez 59, T3683-0011, sells brightly painted wooden animals.

Puerto Vallarta *p299, map p301*

Shopping opportunities are endless, including armies of non-aggressive beach vendors. The **flea market** is grossly overpriced; the many shops often offer better value, but not much. Guadalajara is cheaper for practically everything. The **market**, by the bridge at the end of Insurgentes, sells silver, clothes and souvenirs as well as meat and fish. There's a large, well-stocked supermarket nearby.
Bookshops Rosas Expresso, Olas Altas 399. 2nd-hand books, English and some in German.
Jewellery Olas de Plata, Francisco Rodríguez 132. Plaza Malecón has 28 curio shops, restaurant, music etc.
Supermarket GR, Constitución 136, is reasonable for basics.

San Blas *p303*

Crafts Huichol Cultural Community store, Juárez 64. For Huichol art; it claims to be non-profit making. Great freehand beadwork with glass beads, yarn paintings, decorated masks and scented candles.

Activities and tours

Guadalajara *p290, map p290*

Golf

Rancho Contento, 10 km out on Nogales road; **San Isidro**, 10 km out on Saltillo road, noted for water hazards; **Santa Anita**, 16 km out on Morelia road, championship course.

Hiking

Club Colli, bulletin board Av Juárez 460, details from **Café Madrid**, Juárez 264 or T3623-3318.

Rafting

Expediciones México Verde, José Ma Vigil 2406, Col Italia Providencia, T/F3641-5598. Rafting specialists (Actopan, Jatate, Santa María, Antigua-Pescados, Filobobos and Usumacinta rivers).

Spectator sports

Baseball Apr-Sep.
Bullfights Oct-Mar. Plaza de Toros is on Calzada de la Independencia.
Charreadas (rodeos) are held in mid-Sep at Unión de San Antonio; *lienzo charro* near Parque Agua Azul at Aceves Calindo Lienzo, Sun at 1200.
Football is played all year round. The Estadio Jalisco is on Calzada de la Independencia.

North of Manzanillo *p298*

Tour operators

Donatours, Veracruz, next to bus terminal, Barra de Navidad. Travel agent.
Nautimar, Hamberto, Barra de Navidad, T355-5790. Snorkel, scuba diving and waterskiing.

Puerto Vallarta *p299, map p301*

Tour operators

Many agents and hotel tour desks offer boat trips, car hire and tours at big discounts if you accept a timeshare presentation. Worthwhile savings are to be made for those prepared to brazen out the sales pitch, and many do.
American Express, Morelos 660, esq Abasolo, T223-2955. Town guide available.
John Pegueros, Lázaro Cárdenas 27, Apdo Postal 73, Bucerías, Nayarit, CP63732, T(329) 298-0060. Whale watching and snorkelling trips on the schooner *Elías Mann*. Tickets from Marina Vallarta, US$60, includes some meals, starts 0800.
Open Air Expeditions, Guerrero 339, T222-3310, openair@vivamexico.com, Oscar and Isabel run hiking trips (mountain or waterfall), whale-watching (winter), kayaking, birdwatching and other trips from US$40, knowledgeable guides.
Vallarta Adventure, Av las Palmas 39, Nueva Vallarta, T/F297-1212, www.vallarta-adventures.com. Boat trips, whale-watching (US$65-80), Sierra Madre expedition (US$75), jeep safari (US$75), dolphin encounter (US$128), Las Caletas by night or by day (US$78), also scuba diving, PADI certificate.

Cycling

Bikemex Adventures, Guerrero 361, T223-1834. Offers trips for cyclists of varying grades of competence, from local environs up to 3-4 days in old silver towns of Sierra Madre, all equipment provided including good, front-suspension bikes, from US$45, also offers hiking adventures.

Horse riding

Rancho El Charro, T224-0114. Horse riding expeditions to jungle villages and Sierra Madre silver towns. Independent guides and horses congregate at lower end of Basilio Badillo; also occasionally at fishermen's wharf, by **Hotel Rosita** for short beach and mountain trips, agree price beforehand.

Tepic *p302, map p303*

Tour operators

Tovara, Ignacio Allende 30. **Viajes Regina**, tours to San Blas, Playas de Ensueño, and Tepic city tour.

San Blas *p303*

Tumba de Yako (see Eating, page 312) rents out **surf boards**. Owner, Juan Bananas, was coach to the Mexican surfing team, gives lessons, speaks English. **Mountain bike** and **kayak** hire (for estuaries) also available.

Transport

Guadalajara *p290, map p290*

Air

Miguel Hidalgo (GDL), 20 km from town; 3 classes of taxi (*especial*, *semi-especial* and *colectivo*) charge fixed rates for 3 city zones; no tip necessary. To reach the airport, bus No 176 'San José del 15' (grey) leaves from intersection of Corona and Calzada de la Independencia every 20 mins, US$0.25. **Autotransportes Guadalajara-Chapala** runs 2nd-class buses from old bus terminal every 15 mins, 0655-2125, US$0.35, stop at airport on way to/from Chapala.

Airline offices Mexicana, reservations T3678-7676, arrival and departure information T3688-5775, ticket office: Av Mariano Otero 2353, by Plaza del Sol, T3112-0011. **AeroMéxico**, reservations T3669-0202, airport information T3688-5098, ticket offices: Av Corona 196 and Plaza del Sol, Local 30, Zona A. **AeroCalifornia**, López Cotilla 1423, T3826-8850. **Air France**, Vallarta 1540-103, T3630-3707. **American**, Vallarta 2440, T3616-4090 for reservations, T3688-5518 at airport. **Continental**, ticket office Astral Plaza, Galerías del Hotel Presidente Intercontinental, Locales 8-9, T3647-4251 reservations, T3688-5141 airport. **Delta**, López Cotilla 1701, T3630-3530. **KLM**, Vallarta 1390-1005 T3825-3261. **United**, Plaza Los Arcos, Av Vallarta 2440, local A13, T3616-9489.

Bus

Local Tourist office in Plaza Tapatía has a full list of local and long-distance buses. If in doubt ask the bus driver. Regular buses cost US$0.20, *Línea Azul* 'luxury' bus US$0.45.

Some useful lines: **Route 275**, on 16 de Septiembre and Revolución, from **Zapopan**-Plaza Patria-Glorieta Normal-Av **Alcalde**-Av 16 de Septiembre-Av Revolución-**Tlaquepaque-new bus station-Tonalá** (there are different 275s, from A to F; most follow this route, check with the driver). **Route 707** also goes to Tonalá (silver-blue bus with Tur on the side). **Route 60** goes along **Calzada de la Independencia** from **zoo**, passing Estadio Jalisco, Plaza de Toros, **Mercado Libertad** and **Parque Agua Azul** to the old bus terminal and the railway station (if you are going to Parque Mirador, take bus 62 northbound. There is also a trolley bus that runs along the Calzada de la Independencia to the entrance to the Mirador, better than 60 or 62. For the **old bus station**, take minibus 174 south along Calzada de la Independencia from Mercado Libertad, or bus 110 south along Av Alcalde. **Route 102** runs from the **new bus terminal** along Av Revolución, 16 de Septiembre and Prisciliano Sánchez to **Mercado Libertad. Route 258 or 258A** from San Felipe (north of cathedral) or **258D** along Madero go to **Plaza del Sol. Route 371** runs from **Tonalá** to **Plaza del Sol**. A shuttle bus runs between the 2 bus stations.

There is a luxury bus service **Línea Azul** running from **Zapopan**, along Avila Camacho, past Plaza Patria shopping centre to the Glorieta La Normal, south down Av Alcalde, through **Tlaquepaque**, to the new bus station and ending in Tonalá. Another luxury bus service to the centre is **Línea Cardenal**. No buses after 2230.

Long distance The **old bus station**, Los Angeles and 28 de Enero, city centre, serves towns roughly within 100 km of Guadalajara. You have to pay 20 centavos to enter the terminal (open 0545-2215). It has 2 *salas* (wings): A and B, and is shaped like a U. The flat bottom of the U fronts Dr R Michel, where the main entrances are. There is a side entrance to Sala A from Los Angeles and to both A and B from 15 de Febrero via a tunnel. Taxi stands are on both sides of the terminal. By the entrances to the *salas* is a **Computel** outlet with long-distance and fax service. Shuttle buses to the new bus station leave from here, US$0.20. In Sala A there are 2nd-class buses to **Tepatitlán** and **Zapotlanejo** and *'La Penal'* (the prison), with **Oriente**. 1st-class buses to the same destinations leave from the new bus terminal. Buses to **Chapala** (every 30 mins, 0600-2140, US$1.60) and **Ajijic** (every 30 mins, 0700-2100, US$1.80) leave from here with **Autotransportes Guadalajara-Chapala**. Round trip package to the *balneario* at **San Juan Cosalá**, US$5.25 including admission to the baths. In Sala B, **Omnibus de Rivera** sells tickets to the same *balneario* for US$1.50 and at **La Alteña** booth for the *balnearios* **Agua Caliente** and **Chimulco**. A **Primera Plus/Servicios Coordinados** booth sells tickets to places served by the new bus terminal. Buses to **Tequila** every 30 mins, US$3. Both *salas* have several food stands serving *tortas*, etc, and there are toilets, luggage store and magazine stand.

The **new bus station** is 10 km from the centre, near the El Alamo junction; buses

102 and 275 go to the centre, US$0.25, frequent service (see Local transport, above), journey takes at least 30 mins.

In the centre of town bus information and tickets are available at 2 offices on Calzada de la Independencia underneath Plaza Tapatía (access from Independencia), daily 0900-1400, 1600-1900. Very handy because of the distance from the centre of town although it is worth getting your departure information at the bus station before you go into town. Most services sold are for the higher class travel.

The terminal is in the shape of a big U, with modules 1 to 7 evenly spaced around the outside. Buses enter the U at Module 1, following through to 7 at the other end of the U. Different companies have a presence in several modules and while they will sell you a ticket to any destination, you have to get to the correct module. So, shop around, preferably without your bag. Most terminals now have baggage storage, along with telephones, toilets, restaurants, shops and occasionally manned tourist information booths.

There are probably direct buses to every conceivable destination in Mexico. The schedules for the most commonly used are below, with modules. To **Acapulco**, 1730 and 1900, 17 hrs, US$57, Mod 7. To **Aguascalientes**, hourly 0500-2000, 4 hrs, US$15, Mods 1, 2, 6 and 7. To **Barra de Navidad**, every 2 hrs 0700-1500, and 2200 and 0100, 5 hrs, US$18, Mods 1 and 2. To **Chihuahua**, 8 between 0600 and 2000, 16 hrs, US$65, Mod 7. To **Colima**, hourly, 3 hrs, US$12, Mods 1, 2 and 6. To **Guanajuato**, hourly, 4 hrs, US$18, Mods 1, 2 and 7. To **Hermosillo**, every couple of hrs, 23 hrs, US$76, Mods 3 and 4. To **Lagos de Moreno**, very regular, 3 hrs, US$11, best service from Mod 5. To **León**, hourly, 4 hrs, US$15, Mods 1 and 2. To **Los Mochis**, almost hourly through the day, 15 hrs, US$60, Mods 3 and 4. To **Manzanillo**, hourly, more regular in the afternoon, 6 hrs, US$16, Mods 1, 2 and 3. To **Mazatlán**, every hr day and night, 8 hrs, US$32, Mods 3 and 4. To **Mexicali**, every hr day and night, 34 hrs, US$109, Mods 3 and 4. To **Mexico City** (North Terminal): every 15 mins, 8-9 hrs, US$33, most often at Mod 1. To **Morelia**, every 2 hrs, 4 hrs, US$16, Mods 1 and 2. To **Puerto Vallarta**, every 2 hrs in the morning, 6 hrs, US$27, Mods 1, 2, 3 and 4. To **Querétaro**, every 30 mins, 5 hrs, US$21, most often at Mod 1. To **San Luis Potosí**, every 2 hrs, 5 hrs, US$19, Mod 5. To **San Miguel de Allende**, 1300 and 1500, 6 hrs, US$26, Mod 1. To **Tepic**, every 30 mins, day and night, 3½ hrs, US$15, Mods 3, 4, 6 and 7. To **Tijuana**, hourly, day and night, 33 hrs, US$116, Mods 3 and 4. To **Uruapan**, every 2 hrs, 4½ hrs, US$13, Mods 1 and 2. To **Zacatecas**, roughly every 3 hrs, 5 hrs, US$20, Mods 6 and 7.

Car

Car hire Avis, at airport, T3688-5656. **Budget**, Av Niños Héroes, esq 16 de Septiembre, T3613-0027. **Hertz**, office at Hotel Quinta Real, other at airport, others scattered throughout city, T3614-6162. **National**, Niños Héroes 961, by Hotel Carlton, and other offices at the hotels Fiesta Americana, Holiday Inn Select, and the airport, T3614-7175. **Quick**, Av Niños Héroes, esq Manzano, T3614-2247.

Metro

The metro, or *tren ligero*, has **Línea 1** running under Federalismo from Periférico Sur to Periférico Norte. **Línea 2** runs from Juárez station westbound and passes Mercado Libertad. Fare US$0.40, 1-peso coins needed to buy tokens.

Taxis

No meters are used. A typical ride in town costs US$2-4. From the centre to the new bus station is about US$6; if the taxi ticket booths are open at the bus station it costs around US$4. A taxi to the airport costs US$10.

Horse-drawn carriages US$22 per hr from the Museo Regional de Guadalajara at the corner of Liceo and Hidalgo, or on Independencia just below Plaza Tapatía.

Train

For the Tequila Express, see page 321.

Tonalá *p294*

Bus Bus 275 from the centre goes through **Tlaquepaque** en route to the bus station and then, to Tonalá; it's a bumpy 45-min journey.

Chapala *p294*

Bus The station is on Av Madero at the corner of Miguel Martínez. Buses from **Guadalajara** every 30 mins, 0515-2030, 1 hr. 2 blocks south of bus station, minibuses leave every 20 mins for **Ajijic**, 2 pesos, and **San Juan Cosalá**, 3 pesos.

Taxi Stand on Zócalo and at the bus station.

Ajijic to Jocotepec *p295*

Bus From **Chapala** or **taxi** US$3.20. Jocotepec can be reached from Ajijic or from the Mexico-Guadalajara highway. Bus **Chapala**-Jocotopec US$2, every hr in each direction.

Colima *p295*

Air

Airport (CLQ) 19 km from centre, T314-4160. Flights to **Mexico City** and **Tijuana**.

Airline offices AeroCalifornia, Av San Fernando 533-1, Plaza Roma, T314-4850. Aeromar, T313-1340. AeroMéxico, T313-1340.

Bus

2 bus stations on the outskirts: 'Suburbana' for buses within Colima state – urban buses and combis run to centre, US$0.50; take Routes 1 or 19, or taxi, about US$1.40; and, 'Foránea' for buses out of state, take Route 4 or 5 from Jardín Nuñez. If going to **Uruapan** it is best to go to **Zamora** (7-8 hrs, although officially 4 hrs) and change there. To **Guadalajara**, hourly service, US$12, 2½-3 hrs; **Manzanillo**: 3 hrs, US$4.50; **Mexico City**: US$50.

Manzanillo *p297, map p297*

Air

Frequent flights from airport (ZLO), 19 km from town, to **Mexico City** and **Guadalajara**. Other domestic destinations include **Chihuahua**, **Monterrey**, **Puerto Vallarta** and **Saltillo**. US destinations: **Los Angeles**.

Airline offices Airlines Aeromar, T333-0151. **AeroCalifornia**, Blv Miguel de La Madrid Km 13.5, T334-1414. **Aerolitoral**, T333-2424. **Mexicana**, T332-1972.

Bus

To **Miramar**, US$0.45, leave from J J Alcaraz, 'El Tajo' and can be picked up anywhere along the Av Niños Héroes. Several to **Guadalajara**, 6 hrs, US$16. To **Mexico City**, 11 hrs, US$52. To **Barra de Navidad**, 1½ hrs, US$.3.50. To **Colima**, 3 hrs, US$4.70. Down the coast to **Lázaro Cárdenas** and crossroads for Playa Azul with **Autobus de Occidente** or **Galeana**, 7 hrs. To **Acapulco**, US$21. To **Zihuatanejo**, 2130, US$18. To **Puerto Vallarta**, 1st class with **Trans Cihuatlán** at 0800 and 1200, 4½ hrs. Bus terminal in Av Hidalgo outside centre, local buses go there. Taxi to centre US$1.50.

Car

Car hire **Budget**, Blv Miguel de la Madrid Km 10, T333-1445. **National**, Km 7, Carretera Manzanillo-Santiago, T333-0611.

North of Manzanillo *p299*

Barra de Navidad

Bus Buses from terminal on Calle Veracruz, to **Manzanillo**, 1st class, 1215, 1615, 1815 and 2000, US$4.50, 2nd class; hourly from 0745, US$3.70. To **Puerto Vallarta**, 1st class, 0915 and 1315, 4 hrs, US$15; 2nd class 0900, 1000, 1200, 1400, 1600 and 1800, 5½ hrs, US$13.

Puerto Vallarta *p299, map p301*

Air

International Ordaz airport (PVR), 6 km from centre, T221-1325. If you walk 100 m to the highway and catch a local bus to town, it will cost far less than the US$10 taxi fare. Excellent international connections to the USA, Europe, Central and South America.

Airline offices AeroMéxico, T224-2777. Aero California, T209-0645. Alaska Airlines, T95-800-426-033. American Airlines, T91-800-90460. America West, T800-235-9292, 800-533-6862. Continental, T91-800-90050. Delta, T91-800-90221. Mexicana, T224-8900. United, T911-800-00307, 800-426-5561.

Bus

Local **Mismaloya** to Marina, US$0.40, but complicated routing. The main southbound artery through town is México-Morelos-Vallarta; the main northbound is Juárez-Insurgentes. Plaza Lázaro Cárdenas is the main terminal in south of town and starting point for Mismaloya-Boca buses going south. Buses marked 'Olas Altas' go to South Central, those marked 'Hoteles' or 'Aeropuerto' go to North Hotel Zone and beyond. Buses are also marked for 'Marina' and 'Mismaloya/Boca' (Boca de Tomatlán). The ones marked 'Centro' go through town, those with 'Túnel' take the bypass. Buses to outlying villages with **Medina** bus line, terminal at Brasil, between Brasilia and Guatemala, regular (15-20 mins) service to **Nuevo Vallarta**, **San José**, **San Juan**, **Bucerías**, **Manzanilla**, **Punta de Mita** and others. Fares US$0.75-$1.50.

Long distance All buses leave from bus station almost opposite the airport (turn left when you exit from arrivals, then it's a short walk), 30 mins from centre depending on the route. Taxis from the airport to the main bus station charge inflated prices.

There are frequent services to **Guadalajara**, 6 hrs, US$26. To **Tepic**, every 20 mins, 3 hrs, US$11. To **Barra de Navidad,** 4 hrs, US$16, and **Manzanillo**, 4½ hrs, US$20, every couple of hrs. Other regular services to **Acapulco**, **Aguascalientes**, **Cd Guzmán**, **Cd Juárez**, **Colima**, **León**, **Mazatlán**, **San Patricio Melaque**, **Mexico City**, **Monterrey**, **Querétaro**, **Tecomán**, **Tijuana** and **Zihuatanejo**.

Around Puerto Vallarta *p300*

Water taxi To reach **Yelapa**, take the tourist water taxi from pier – Los Muertos – US$18 return, leaves 1030, 1100. From fisherman's quay on Malecón, by **Hotel Rosita**, opposite McDonald's, US$10 one way, leaves 1130. From **Boca de Tomatlán** (bus, US$0.40) water taxi from beach is US$4 one way, leaves 1030.

Tepic *p302, map p303*

Air

Airport Amado Nervo (TPQ) with flights to **Los Angeles**, **Mexico City**, **Tampico** and **Tijuana** daily with Aero California, T216-1636 or **AeroMéxico**, T213-9047.

Bus

Bus station is a fairly short walk from town centre, T213-6747; bus from centre to terminal from Puebla Norte by market. At bus station there are phones, post office, left-luggage and tourist information (not always open). Bus to **San Blas** from main bus terminal and from local bus station on park at Av Victoria y México, from 0615 every hr US$3.60. To **Guadalajara**, frequent departures, 3½ hrs, US$15. To **Mazatlán**, 4½ hrs, US$13. To **Los Mochis**, US$58. To **Puerto Vallarta**, every 20 mins, 3 hrs US$11. To **Mexico City**, 13 hrs, US$48.

San Blas *p303*

Bus Bus station on corner of Plaza. To **Tepic**, frequent from 0600, 1½ hrs, US$3.60. To **Guadalajara**, 8½ hrs, US$16.

Tequila *p306*

Bus

2nd class from the old terminal, Sala B, in **Guadalajara**, Rojo de los Altos, every 45 mins, up to 2 hrs, US$2.80. Return from outside **Rojo de los Altos** ticket office, Sixto Gorjón, 126A, every 20 mins, 0500-1400, then every 30 mins until 2030.

Taxi

To **Guadalajara** US$19, plus US$9 in tolls if you take the expressway.

Train

The **Tequila Express**, T3880-9099 (Guadalajara), www.tequilaexpress.com.mx, is a rather comfortable way of visiting the town from Guadalajara. It's all jazzed up and smart-looking – not how the Mexican rail industry used to be that's for sure – but you spend the day drifting towards the town, exploring one of the plantations and then returning with no fear of driving. Sat and/or Sun only, leaving about 1000, returning around 2000, US$60 for adults, US$32 for kids. Book from tour operators in Guadalajara (or see website for optopns).

Directory

Guadalajara *p290, map p290*

Banks

There are many *casas de cambio* on López Cotilla between Independencia and 16 de Septiembre and 1 in Plaza del Sol. **American Express**, Plaza Los Arcos, Local 1-A, Av Vallarta 2440, esq Francisco García de Quevedo, about 5 blocks east of Minerva roundabout, T3630-0200, daily 0900-1800 for the travel agency and 0900-1430,

1600-1800 to change money. Across Prisciliano Sánchez from the Jardín San Francisco is a **Banco Inverlat** with ATM. There are many others arouind town.

Cultural centres

Alliance Française, López Cotilla 1199, Sector Juárez, T3825-2140. **Instituto Cultural Mexicano-Norteamericano de Jalisco**, Enrique Díaz de León 300 (see below, Language schools). **Instituto Goethe**, Morelos 2080 y Calderón de la Barca, T3615-6147, library, nice garden, newspapers.

Dentists

Dr Abraham Waxtein, Av México 2309, T3615-1041, speaks English.

Doctors

Dr Daniel Gil Sánchez, Pablo Neruda 3265, 2nd floor, T3642-0213, speaks English (1st consultation, 2½ hrs, including thorough physical, US$50**Dr Virginia Rivera**, Eulogia Parra 2432, near López Mateos, T3616-6637, ophthalmologist. English-speaking, US$25 for 1st consultation, US$20 for subsequent consultations, consultations Mon, Wed and Fri 1600-1930.

Embassies and consulates

Australia, López Cotilla 2030, T3615-7418, 0800-1330, 1500-1800. **Austria**, Montevideo 2695, Col Providencia, T3641-1834, 0900-1330. **Belgium**, Metalúrgica 2818, Parque Industrial El Alamo, T3670-4825, Mon-Fri 0900-1400. **Canada**, trade officer and consul, Hotel Fiesta Americana, local 31, T3616-5642, 0830-1400 and 1500-1700. **Denmark**, Lázaro Cárdenas 601, 6th floor, T3669-5515, 0900-1300, 1600-1800. **El Salvador**, Fermín Riestra 1628, between Bélgica and Argentina, Col Moderna, T3810-1061, hrs for visas 1230-1400, normally visas will be received the same day. **France**, López Mateos Norte 484 entre Herrera y Cairo y Manuel Acuña, T3616-5516, 0930-1400. **Germany**, Corona 202, T3613-9623, 1130-1400. **Guatemala**, Mango 1440, Col del Fresno, T3811-1503, 1000-1400. **Honduras**, Ottawa 1139, Col Providencia, T3817-4998, 1000-1400, 1700-1900. **Israel**, Av Vallarta 2482 Altos, Sector Juárez, T3616-4554, 0930-1500. **Italy**, López Mateos Norte 790-1, T3616-1700, Tue-Fri 1100-1400. **Netherlands**, Lázaro Cárdenas 601, 6th floor, Zona Industrial, T3811-2641, 0900-1400, 1630-1900. **Nicaragua**, Eje Central 1024, esq Toreros, Col Guadalupe Jardín, behind Club Atlas Chapalita, T3628-2919, 1600-1800. **Spain**, Av Vallarta 2185, T3630-0450, 0830-1330. **Sweden**, J Guadalupe Montenegro 1691, T3825-6767, 0900-1400, 1600-1900. **Switzerland**, Av Revolución 707, Sector Reforma, T3617-5900, 0800-1400, 1600-1900. **UK**, Eulogio Parra 2539, T3616-0629, 0900-1500, 1700-2000. **US**, Progreso 175, T3825-2700.

Immigration

Mexican tourist cards can be renewed at the immigration office (1st floor) in the Palacio Federal on Av Alcalde between Juan Alvarez and Hospital, across the avenue from the Santuario de Guadalupe. The Palacio Federal also contains a post office and fax service.

Internet

Imprenta Rápida, Local J in the mall on Juárez 323, T3613-5258. **Futurama**, Pedro Moreno 570, Local 1, T3613-7318. **Cyber café**, López Cotilla, southwest corner of Parque Revolución, 1st floor, T3826-3771, also with pizza, snacks, beer and soft drinks. **Mr Ch@t**, Madero between Ocampo and Guerra, printers and scanners too. **Arrobba**, Av Lázaro Cárdenas 3286, just west of intersection with López Mateos, Mon-Sat 1000-2200, drinks, snacks, salads.

Language schools

Centro de Estudios para Extranjeros de la Universidad de Guadalajara, Tomás V Gómez 125, between Justo Sierra and Av México, T3616-4399, www.cepe.udg.mx, with or without homestay. The **Instituto Cultural Mexicano-Norteamericano de Jalisco**, at Enrique Díaz de León 300, T3825-5838, 5 levels of instruction, cultural lectures on Fri, homestays possible. The **Universidad Autónoma de Guadalajara (UAG)**, a private university, offers Spanish classes through their Centro Internacional de Idiomas, T3641-7051, ext 32251, 0800-1800, at Edificio Humanidades 1st floor, on the main campus at Av Patria 1201, Col Lomas del Valle, 3a sección, www.uag.edu, 7 levels of instruction, each lasting 4 weeks, homestays possible. **Vancouver Language Centre**, Av Vallarta 1151, Col América, T3826-0944 (T1-604-687-1600-Vancouver), www.study-mexico.com, 1 week intensive programmes. See also **National Registration Center for Study Abroad** under Learning Spanish in Essentials, page 25.

Laundry
Aldama 125 (walk along Independencia towards train station, turn left into Aldama).

Medical services
Hospitals Hospital del Carmen, Tarascos 3435, Fraccionamiento Monraz (behind Plaza México), T3813-0042, a good private hospital (take credit cards). **Hospital Angel Leaño,** off the road to Tesistán, T3834-3434, affiliated with the University (UAG). For those who cannot afford anything else there are the **Hospital Civil**, T3614-5501, and the **Nuevo Hospital Civil**, T3618-9362.

Pharmacies There are 3 big chains: Farmacias Guadalajara, Benavides and ABC. **Farmacia Guadalajara**, Av Américas and Morelos, has vaccines and harder-to-find drugs, T3615-5094.

Vaccinations For *antirrábico* (rabies), T3643-1917; to receive the vaccine you have to go to **Clinic 3 of the Sector Salud**, T3823-3262, at the corner of Circunvalación División del Norte and Federalismo, across the street from a Telmex office, near the División del Norte Station, Line 1, *tren ligero*; you can also get an HIV test here. **Sidatel** (AIDS), T3613-7546.

Post office
Main post office, V Carranza, just behind Palacio de Justicia, Mon-Fri 0800-1900, Sat 0900-1300. There are also branches at the Mercado Libertad (San Juan de Dios) and at the old bus station. To send parcels abroad go to Aduana Postal in same building as main post office, Mon-Fri 0800-1300, T3614-9002. **FedEx** has 3 outlets: Av Américas 1395; Plaza del Sol Locales 51-55; Av Washington 1129, next to Bolerama 2000, T3817-2502. **UPS**, Av Américas 981, Local 19, T01-800-902-9200.

Telephone

International collect calls can be made from any coin-box phone kiosk and direct dial calls can be made from LADA pay phones. You can also make long-distance calls and send faxes from **Computel** outlets: one in front of old bus station, one on Corona y Madero, opposite Hotel Fénix. **Mayahuel**, Paseo Degollado 55, has long-distance service, fax, sells Ladatel cards, postcards and maps. There is a credit card phone at Ramón Corona y Av Juárez, by the cathedral. 2 **USA Direct** phones, 1 within and 1 beyond the customs barrier at the airport.

Chapala *p294*,
Banks *Casa de cambio*, Av Madero near Beer Garden, Mon-Sat 0830-1700. **HSBC**, Madero 208, ATM taking Visa, MasterCard, and cards of Cirrus and Plus networks. Nearby is a **Banamex** with ATM. **Bancomer,** Hidalgo 212 near Madero, ATM taking Visa; across the street is a **Banca Serfín**, ATM. **Lloyds**, Madero 232, is a real estate office, *casa de cambio*, travel agency and *sociedad de inversión*; many Americans keep their money here. **Laundry** Zaragoza y Morelos. Dry cleaners at Hidalgo 235A, also repairs shoes and other leather items. **Medical services** IMSS clinic on Niños Héroes between Zaragoza and 5 de Mayo. **Centro de Salud**, Flavio Romero de V and Guerrero. **Red Cross**, Parque de la Cristina. **Postal services** The **post office** is at Hidalgo 223. Nearby is a **UPS** office. **Mail Box Etc**, Carretera Chapala-Jocotepec 155, opposite PAL Trailer Park, T766-0747. Shipping office at Hidalgo 236 uses FedEx and DHL. **Telephones Computel** on the plaza, long distance and fax, accepts Amex, MasterCard, AT&T. Also pay phones for long-distance calls on Zócalo and outside bus station.

Ajijic to Jocotepec *p295*
Banks Opposite taxi stand at Colón 29, Ajijic is a *casa de cambio*. On southwest corner of plaza is **Banco Promex** with 2 ATMs. **Immigration** Castellanos 4, Ajijic, T766-2042. **Laundry** About ½ block north at Colón 24A is a *lavandería*. **Medical services** Dentists: 2 dentists' offices on Colón, just south of plaza, Ajijic. **Doctors**: Dr

Alfredo Rodríguez Quintana, T766-1499 (home). Hospitals and clinics: Clínica Ajijic, Carretera Ote 33, T766-0662, with 24-hr ambulance service. **Postal services** Post office,1 block south of plaza, corner of Colón and Constitución. Ajijic Real Estate, Morelos 4, T766-2077, is an authorized UPS outlet. **Telephone** On the northwest corner of the plaza is a Computel booth for long-distance phone and fax, daily 0800-2100.

Colima *p295*
Banks Banco Inverlat, Juárez 32, on west side of Jardín Núñez, ATM takes Amex, Visa, Diner's Club. Casa de cambio at Morelos and Juárez on southwest corner of same park. Bacomer at Madero and Ocampo 3 blocks east of plaza, ATM takes Visa and Plus. Casa de cambio across the street. Banamex, one block south on Ocampo at Hidalgo, has an ATM. **Internet** Cyber café, Plaza Country, Av Tecnológico, 15 blocks north of centre, Mon-Fri 0900-2200, Sat and Sun 1000-2200. **Laundry** Lavandería Shell, 27 de Septiembre 134, daily 0900-2000, inexpensive, quick. **Medical services** Hospitals and clinics: Hospital Civil, T312-0227. Red Cross T312-1451. Pharmacy: Farmacia Guadalupana on northeast corner of Jardín Torres Quintero behind cathedral. Another pharmacy on northeast corner of Zócalo. **Post office** Av Francisco I Madero and General Núñez, northeast corner of Jardín Núñez. **Telephone** Computel, Morelos 234 on south side for long-distance phone and fax, and at bus station, daily 0700-2200, accepts Visa, MasterCard, Amex and AT&T cards. Fax not always in use.

Manzanillo *p297, map p297*
Medical services Hospital Civil, T332-4161. Red Cross, T336-5770.

North of Manzanillo *p298*
Internet Cybernet between beachfront and Gómez Farías, near Hotel Monterrey, San Patricio Melaque. **Medical services** Dra Herlinda Rubio, English speaking, Barra de Navidad. **Internet** Ciber@net, Veracruz 212, Barra de Navidad.

Puerto Vallarta *p299, map p301*
Banks *Casas de cambio* on nearly every street in tourist areas. Rates inferior to Guadalajara. Check Bancomer's *cambio* at Juárez 450, for good rates. Like most, it is open every day until late. Numerous banks offer slightly better rates (but slower service) and ATMs for Visa, MasterCard. **Embassies and consulates** Canada, Edif Vallarta Plaza, Zaragoza 160, 1st floor, interior 10, T222-5398, daily 1000-1400. USA, T222-0069. **Immigration** In front of the Marina terminal, T224-7970. **Internet** Numerous internet cafés normally charging around US$2 per hr. **Laundry** Practically 1 on every block in South Central; numerous throughout resort. **Medical services** Dra Irma Gittelson, Juárez 479, speaks French and English, very helpful. Emergency: T915-724-7900. **Post office** Mina between Juárez and Morelos. **Telephone** Long-distance phone (*casetas*) and fax at Lázaro Cárdenas 267, open daily to 2300, also in lobby of Hotel Eloisa. Many shops bear *Larga distancia* sign, check tariffs.

Tepic *p302, map p303*
Banks *Casas de cambio* at México 91 and 140 Norte, Mon-Sat 0900-1400, 1600-2000. **Telephones** Credit card phone at Veracruz Norte y Zapata Pte.

San Blas *p303*
Banks Banamex just off Zócalo, exchange daily 0830-1000 only. **Comercial de San Blas** on the main square will change money, plus commission. **Laundry** 2 blocks down toward the beach from La Familia. Will take your clothes and return them, very clean, later or the next day.

Tequila *p306*
Banks Banamex, corner of Sixto Gorjón and Juárez, 24-hr ATM accepts Visa and MasterCard. Many ATMs in town. *Casa de cambio*, Sixto Gorjón 73, daily 0900-1400, 1600-2000, change cash and Tcs.

State of Veracruz

Often overlooked by tourists, the State of Veracruz is off the usual beaten track. Maybe it hasn't got the best beaches in Mexico but for almost everything else it's hard to beat. Inland, there's adventure tourism with Mexico's highest mountain, deepest caves and fastest rapids. Temperatures rise as the land drops to the green, fertile coastal plain and the endless plantations. To the south, beyond the plains of the vast Río Papaloapan, the Tuxtla mountains, tropical and lush and a birdwatcher's paradise, contrast dramatically with the wilderness of the massive oil refineries at Minatitlán and Coatzacoalcos.

In the north, the Huastec people are best known for their traditional huapango *music and falsetto singing. In the vanilla-growing Papantla area, the spectacular* volador *ritual, an example of surviving Totonac traditions, is performed regularly in Papantla and outside the ruins of El Tajín, one of the most magnificent archaeological sites in all America. Xalapa, the lively state capital and an important university city, has one of the best museums in the whole country. But it's the rich cultural mix that makes Veracruz so special. For 300 years, the port was Spain's gateway to the riches of the New World. The arrival of black slaves profoundly influenced the people and culture – most notably the music – of this region. Veracruz is a popular destination for Mexican tourists who enjoy the famous hospitality of the Veracruzanos, known as* jarochos, *and the eternally festive, tropical-port atmosphere that crescendoes each spring during the liveliest carnival in all Mexico.* ▸▸ *For Sleeping, Eating and other listings, see pages 338-345.*

Mexico City to Veracruz ▸▸ *pp338-345.*

Much of the area east of Mexico City constituted the eastern tribute quarter conquered by the Mexica, formerly the Aztecs, who derived great wealth from those subject nations that stretched from the Basin of Mexico to the Guatamalan border.

By road, the principal route to the coast from Mexico City is paved all the way, a distance of about 150 km. A fast toll road runs all the way from Mexico City to Veracruz.

Orizaba → *Phone code: 272. Colour map 3, B5. Altitude: 1283 m.*

The favourite resort of the Emperor Maximilian, on the eastern edge of the mountains, lost much of its charm in the 1973 earthquake, when the bullring, many houses and other buildings were lost; the city is now heavily industrialized. The setting, however, is lovely. In the distance is the majestic volcanic cone of Orizaba. The town developed because of the natural springs in the valley, some of which are used by the textile and paper industries and others are dammed to form small pools for bathing beside picnic areas. The **Cerro del Borrego**, the hill above the Alameda park, is a favourite early-morning climb. On the north side of the Zócalo is the market, with a wide variety of local produce and local women in traditional dress, and the many-domed **San Miguel** church (1690-1729). There are several other interesting churches. The **ex-Palacio Municipal** is the actual cast-iron Belgian pavilion brought piece by piece from France after the famous 19th-century Paris Exhibition, an odd sight. The **Museo de Arte del Estado** ⓘ *4 Ote y 23 Sur, Tue-Sun 1000-1400, 1600-1900*, in the Oratorio de San Felipe Neri, has a delightful collection of colonial to contemporary paintings. The **tourist office** ⓘ *Pte 2, mornings only*, is across the river from the Zócalo.

Around Orizaba

A road leaves Orizaba southwards, up into the mountains of **Zongolica**, a dry, poor and isolated region, cold and inhospitable, inhabited by various indigenous groups who speak Nahuatl, the language of the Aztecs. Zongolica village is a good place to buy *sarapes* (shawls); take the early bus from Orizaba (ask for direct one) to get clear views of the mountains.

Beyond Orizaba, en route to the coast, the scenery is magnificent. The road descends to coffee and sugar-cane country and a tropical riot of flowers. It is pleasant except when a northerly blows, or in the heat and mugginess of the wet season.

Córdoba → *Phone code: 271. Colour map 3, B5. Altitude: 923 m.*

Eight kilometres beyond Fortín in the rich valley of the Río Seco, is the old colonial city of Córdoba, which is also crazy with flowers. Its Zócalo is spacious, leafy and elegant; three sides are arcaded; two of them are lined with tables. On the fourth is an imposing church with a chiming clock. There are several hotels in the Zócalo, which is alive and relaxed at night. In **Portal de Zavallos**, General Iturbide signed the Treaty of Córdoba in 1821, which was instrumental in freeing Mexico from Spanish colonial rule. There's a local **museum** ⓘ *Calle 3, No 303, daily 1000-1300, 1600-2000.* Córdoba has the highest rainfall in Mexico, but at predictable times.

Xalapa

▸▸ *pp338-345.* *Colour map 3, B5.*

→ *Phone code: 228. Altitude: 1425 m.*

The capital of Veracruz state since 1885 and 132 km from the port, Xalapa (also spelt **Jalapa**) is in the *tierra templada* and is a lively town in keeping with its climate. It is yet another 'City of Flowers', with walled gardens, stone-built houses, wide avenues in the newer town and steep, cobbled, crooked streets in the old.

A settlement called Xallac ('the place of the sandy waters') is known to have existed here in the 12th century. It has always been a good place to break the journey from the coast to the highlands and, in the 18th century, development was helped by the creation of a huge annual trading fair. There was a passion for building and renovation in the flamboyant Gothic style during the first part of the 19th century.

The excellent, modern **Anthropology Museum** ⓘ *Tue-Sun 1000-1800, US$1, Tue free, half price for students with ID, guided tours included in fee*, second only to the one in Mexico City, is in the northern suburbs of Xalapa, on the road out towards Mexico City. The museum concentrates on exhibits from the region's three major prehispanic civilizations, showing treasures of the Olmec, Totonac and Huastec coastal cultures. It has the best collection of Olmec monumental stone sculptures in all Mexico, including several of the magnificent colossal heads from the south of Veracruz and Tabasco, and the exquisite *Señor de las Limas*.

The **Pinacoteca Diego Rivera** ⓘ *Herrera 5 (Zócalo), Tue-Sun 1000-1800, free*, has a small permanent collection of Rivera's paintings. Pico de Orizaba is visible from hotel roofs or Parque Juárez very early in the morning, before the haze develops. The **tourist office** ⓘ *Blv Cristóbal Colón 5, T841-8500, www.xalapa.gob.mx*, is a long walk or short taxi ride from the centre.

Around Xalapa

The **Texolo** waterfalls are some 15 km southwest of Xalapa and 5 km from the pretty village of **Xico**, just beyond the town of Coatepec. There is a deep ravine and a good, cheap restaurant at the falls. The old bridge is still visible but a new bridge across the ravine has been built. It is a pleasant place for a cold swim, birdwatching and walking. The film *Romancing the Stone* used Texolo as one of its locations. To get there, take a bus from Xalapa (US$0.60, every 30 minutes).

The famous xalapeño (jalapeño) chilli originally comes from the Xalapa region.

Naolinco is 30 minutes' ride, 40 km northeast of Xalapa up a winding hilly road. Two waterfalls, with various pools, tumble several thousand feet over steep wooded slopes. **Restaurant La Fuente** serves local food and has a nice garden. **Las Cascadas** has a mirador to admire the falls from. Both restaurants are on the way into town.

Two hours northwest from Xalapa is the archaeological site of **Filobobos** ⓘ *US$2*. It includes El Cuajilote, a 400-m-wide ceremonial centre, and Vega de la Peña, an area of basalt rocks decorated with bas reliefs, a ball court and several pyramids by the river banks. Abundant wildlife here includes toucans, parrots and otters.

Route 140 towards the capital, renowned for being foggy, continues to climb to **Perote,** 53 km from Xalapa. The **San Carlos fort** here, now a military prison, was built in 1770-1777; there is a good view of Cofre de Perote volcano (known, in Aztec times, as *Nauhtecuhtli*, 'Four Times Lord'). A road branches north to Teziutlán, with a Friday market, where good *sarapes* are sold. A local fair, *La Entrega de Inanacatl*, is held in the third week in June. The old convent at **Acatzingo**, 93 km beyond Perote on Route 140, is worth seeing. Another 10 km and you join the road to Puebla and Mexico City.

Papantla

» *pp338-345. Colour map 3, B5.*

→ *Phone code: 784.*

Some 40 km inland from Tecolutla is Papantla ('Where banners abound'), built on the top of a hill overlooking the lush plains of northern Veracruz. It was the stronghold of a Totonac rebellion in 1836. **Traditional Totonac dress** is still seen: the men in baggy white trousers and sailor shirts and the women in lacy white skirts and shawls over embroidered blouses. Papantla is also the centre of one of the **world's largest vanilla-producing zones**, although production has decreased in recent years due to the proliferation of mass-produced synthetic vanilla. The vanilla is processed in **Gutiérrez Zamora**, a small town about 30 km east (close to Tecolutla), and a 'cream of vanilla' liqueur is also produced. The **Fiesta de la Vainilla** is held throughout the area in early June. The **tourist office** ⓘ *Palacio Municipal, on the Zócalo, T842-0026 ext 730, Mon-Fri 0900-1400, 1800-2100,* is helpful, with good information, maps and bus schedules; English spoken.

Sights

The Zócalo, formally known as **Plaza Téllez**, is bordered by Enríquez on its downhill north edge; on the south uphill side the **Catedral de Nuestra Señora de la Asunción** (1700) has a remarkable 50-m-long mural on its northern wall called *Homenaje a la Cultura Totonaca*, by Teodoro Cano García (1979), with the plumed serpent Quetzalcoatl along its entire length. *Voladores* perform in the church courtyard each Sunday at 1100, and as many as three times daily during the colourful 10 days of Corpus Christi (late May or early June), along with games, fireworks, artistic exhibitions, dances and cockfights. For a sweeping view of the area, walk up Reforma to the top of the hill where the giant **Monumento al Volador** was erected in 1988. Murals and mosaic benches in the Zócalo also commemorate Totonac history and their conception of creation. Northeast of the plaza is **Mercado Hidalgo** ⓘ *20 de Noviembre, daily 0600-2000*, off the northwest corner of the Zócalo, where traditional handmade clothing is sold amid fresh produce and livestock.

El Tajín

→ *Colour map 3. B5. 2 km from Papantla.*

ⓘ *Daily 0800-1800, except mid-Aug 0800-1900. US$2.80. Guidebook US$1.25, available in Museo de Antropología, Mexico City, rarely available on site. There is a* *small modern museum, a cafetería and souvenir shops. In the wet season beware of a large, poisonous creature like a centipede. El Tajín can be visited either from Papantla or from Poza Rica, see below.*

The great city of El Tajín once covered approximately 1050 ha at the heart of which are four major groupings of structures: **Tajín proper** covers the valley floor; most of the major temples are located here. This is also the location of most of the carved and plain ball courts as well as ceremonial and market plazas. This area was the religious and commercial centre of the city. **Tajín Chico** is a huge terraced acropolis dominated by an elaborate multi-storeyed palace and administrative structures for the city's elite. The largest buildings erected at El Tajín are on the upper levels of Tajín Chico. Along with its Annex, the **Building of the Columns** is the greatest architectural complex in the city. It was the special domain of the ruler 13 Rabbit, who governed at the city's zenith. The **West Ridge** is mostly an artificially tiered

El Tajín

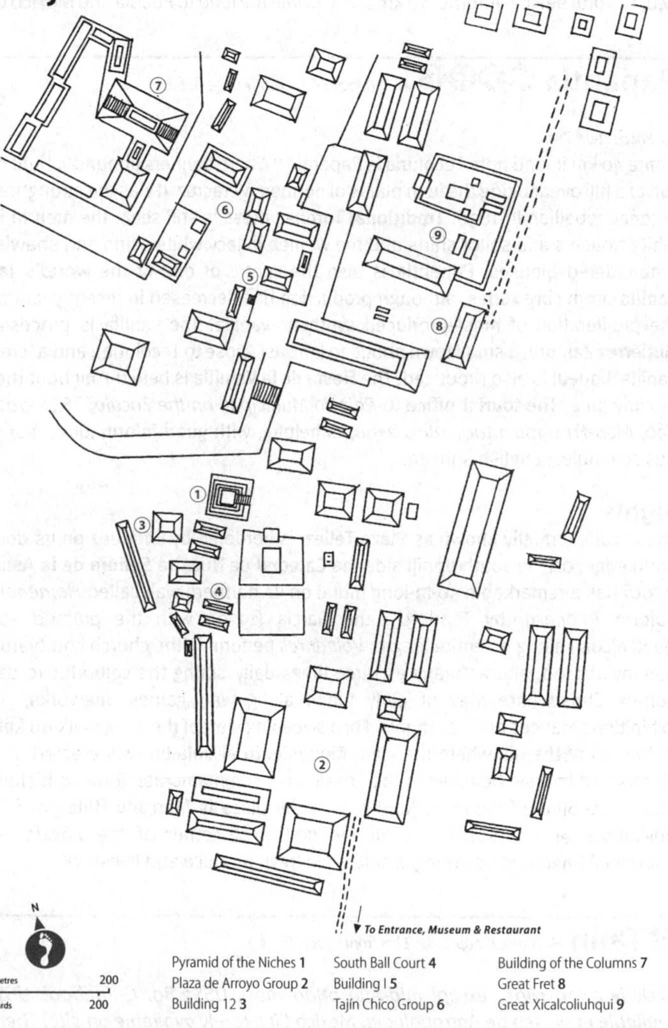

The voladores of El Tajín

Traditionally, on Corpus Christi, Totonac rain dancers erect a 30-m mast with a rotating structure at El Tajín. Four *voladores* (flyers) and a musician climb to the top of the surmounting platform. There, the musician dances to his own pipe and drum music, while the roped *voladores* throw themselves into space to make a dizzy spiral descent, head first, to the ground.

Voladores are now in attendance at El Tajín every day (during high season, other times just weekends), and fly if and when they think there are enough tourists (donations expected).

natural hill. The structures here are thought to be elite residences, modest temples and, perhaps, small ball courts. The **East Ridge** is very similar to the West Ridge but with fewer structures.

The suggested timescale for El Tajín's construction is AD 300-900, with a great surge of energy around AD 600, the time when Teotihuacán and Monte Albán were experiencing collapse and abandonment. Although impressive, the architecture of El Tajín is less informative than the rich corpus of iconography that decorated the Pyramid of the Niches, the North Ball Court, the South Ball Court and the Building of the Columns. Most of the imagery associated with these structures tells of conquest, ball games, the interplay between this existence and that of the gods, the dignified sacrifice of warriors and ball players and the undignified sacrifice of captive enemy lords. But the ball game was the single most important activity expressed in the imagery of El Tajín, as emphasized by the presence of at least 11 ball courts at the site. The obsession with the ball game and its related iconography suggests that the city was an immense academy where young men were trained in the skills and rules associated with the game. As yet, no evidence supports this suggestion, but it is tempting to speculate that the residences on the East and West Ridges were intended to house young trainees.

Associated almost exclusively with the ball game and players, the cult of the maguey, pulque and pulque deities at El Tajín presents a puzzle, perplexing because the maguey will not grow in the general area. The probability is that the city was the creation of a small enclave of Huastecs rather than the Totonacs who then inhabited and still inhabit the region. The maguey proliferates throughout the Highlands, and in the mythology of the Central Highlands it was a Huastec who drank more than the stipulated four cups, became drunk, stripped naked and had to return in disgrace to his homeland.

Pyramid of the Niches

The form of the pyramid, one of the earliest structures at El Tajín, is very distinctive, and said to have 365 niches, one for each day of the year. Dated approximately AD 600, it is crowned with a sanctuary that was lined with engraved panels, one of which shows a cacao plant bearing fruit. Cacao was precious and of great commercial value to the people of the area. There is some evidence that the rulers of El Tajín controlled its cultivation in the zones surrounding the site. Another trapezoidal panel depicts a priest or ruler adorned with ball game accoutrements and holding a knife ready to perform a ritual sacrifice, the scene being set within the confines of a ball court. The depiction of a skull at the foot of the executioner indicates sacrifice by decapitation.

North Ball Court

The imagery of the North Ball Court is only partially understood. Most of the problems associated with this zone derive from erosion and mutilation of the engravings. Men in bat costumes are a major theme in these panels and suggest influence from the Maya region where men dressed in this way were common images on ceramics of the Classic period. Also present in the North Ball Court is the imagery of the ball game and human sacrifice.

South Ball Court

The South Ball Court offers a fascinating glimpse into the philosophy that underpinned the whole ritual life of El Tajín. Central to the narrative is the role of the ball player who acts as an intermediary between this world and that of the gods. In the engravings, the ball player is presented to the executioner and decapitated while the gods look on. Two of the panels are bordered with the image of a laughing pulque deity with two bodies, and there are many Venus symbols. The death god, Mitlantecuhtli, emerges from an urn of pulque, and many of the known gods of the Mesoamerican pantheon are represented. In some of the painted books of the Central Highlands, the powerful gods Quetzalcoatl and Tezcatlipoca oppose each other in a ball game; at El Tajín, it is possible that the human players represented the earthly aspects of these gods. The imagery of the engravings of the South Ball Court is extremely complex, but it does imply that, through the ball game, humans can approach the realm of the gods by means of the decapitation of the principal players.

Tajín Chico

The Building of the Columns is another area with a very complex iconographical narrative. However, while the iconography of the South Ball Court expresses a communion between gods and men, the iconography of the Building of the Columns refers to themes that are much more mundane. The focus of attention is the ruler 13 Rabbit, whose glyph is repeated many times on the surface of the column drums, always with the image of a rabbit and the number 13 expressed by two bars, each counting as five, and three dots. 13 Rabbit has clearly been on a conquest campaign because a number of prisoners are lined up in preparation for the decapitation ritual. They have been divested of almost all their clothes and thus divested of their dignity. They are named by glyphs above or near their persons, which indicates that they were chiefs of opposing polities; the common warrior was rarely identified by name. Whereas the warrior/ball player of the South Ball Court approached his death with calm dignity, the prisoners of the Building of the Columns are forced toward the sacrificial block, some held by the hair. Two sacrificial sequences but two very different approaches to death. The narrative of 13 Rabbit is now in the site museum. Although seen and depicted as all-powerful, 13 Rabbit was not omnipotent enough to prevent the destruction of the city and probably the state of El Tajín, which occurred shortly after the engraving of the Building of the Columns was completed. The great centre of the ball game, like so many others, perished, but at whose hands has yet to be discovered.

Poza Rica and south to Veracruz

▸▸ *pp338-345. Colour map 3, B5.*

→ *Phone code: 782.*

Twenty-one kilometres northwest of Papantla is Poza Rica, a pretty ugly oil city formed out of four old *rancherías*, which happened to lie on top of the then second largest oil strike in the world. It has an old cramped wooden market and a simple mural by O'Higgins (*From Primitive Prehispanic Agricultural Works to the Present Day Oil Industry Development*, 1959) on the outside of the **Palacio Municipal**. The **tourist office** ⓘ *T822-1390 ext 129*, is at the back of the Palacio Municipal on the ground floor.

From Poza Rica you can head north to visit the **Castillo de Teayo**, a pyramid with the original sanctuary and interesting carvings on top (buses every 30 minutes, change halfway).

Coast road to Veracruz

East of Papantla, a side road branches off the main Route 180 to the coast at Tecolutla, a very popular resort on the river of that name, toll bridge US$2.50. The **fiesta** that takes place two days before the carnival (February to March) in Veracruz is recommended.

Forty-two kilometres further south, Route 180 passes through **Nautla**, a pleasant town. Three kilometres before Nautla, Route 131 branches inland to Teziutlán. **El Pital** (15 km in from the Gulf along the Nautla River, 80 km southeast of Papantla), was identified early in 1994 as the site of an important, sprawling pre-Columbian seaport (approximately AD 100-600), which lay hidden for centuries under thick rainforest. Now planted over with bananas and oranges, the 100 or more pyramid mounds (some reaching 40 m in height) were assumed by plantation workers to be natural hills. Little excavation or clearing has yet been done, but both Teotihuacán-style and local-style ceramics and figurines have been found.

The ruins of **Cempoala** ⓘ *US$1.40*, are 40 km north of Veracruz. Cortés was welcomed by the inhabitants of the coastal city who became his allies against the Aztecs. The ruins are interesting because of the round stones uniquely used in construction. Sundays can be very crowded. It is a pleasant site and setting and *voladores* are often in attendance. To get there take a second-class bus to Cardel, and then a micro to Cempoala.

Chachalacas is a fine uncrowded beach. There's a swimming pool and changing facilities (US$1 adults) in an expensive but spotless hotel of the same name. Local delicacies, including *robalito* fish, are sold from *palapas* on the beach. It is worth asking the restaurants on the beach to let you hang up your hammock, most have showers and toilets. They charge US$2 if you agree to eat at their restaurant.

La Antigua, the site of what was thought to be Cortés' house, is 1.5 km off the road to Cardel, some 30 km north of Veracruz. Take a Cardel bus from the second-class part of the bus station (US$0.40) and get off at La Antigua Caseta, the first toll booth the bus comes to. It is an easy 10- or 15-minute walk from there. The house is worth visiting just to see the large ceiba roots growing all over the walls.

Veracruz

» *pp338-345. Colour map 3, B5.*

→ *Phone code: 229.*

Veracruz is a mixture of the very old and the new; there are still many picturesque white-walled buildings and winding side streets. The centre is at the back of the harbour and has something of a 1950s feel about it. It is very much a port town, noisy and congested, but lively, full of music and dance, and with a definite Caribbean air.

Ins and outs

Getting there Aeropuerto Las Bajadas (VER) is 12 km from the city centre with a shuttle service into town. The bus terminals (first and second class) are about 3 km from the town centre, on Avenida Díaz Mirón (see Transport, page 343). Highways 150 and 150D (*supercarretera*) link Mexico City to the Gulf coast at the port of Veracruz. Route 180 runs north-south along the coast.

Getting around All places of interest are within easy walking distance of Plaza de Armas. Frequent buses run along the seafront to Mocambo or Boca del Río during the day, but at night you may have to take a taxi.

Tourist information The **tourist office** ⓘ *Palacio Municipal on the Zócalo, T932-9942*, is helpful but they have no hotel price lists or town maps. The **Federal Tourist Office** ⓘ *T932-1613, www.veracruz.gob.mx*, en route to Boca del Río, has more information.

Best time to visit It is generally hot. However, if planning to visit Veracruz or the hills inland (for example Xalapa) between July and September, check the weather forecast because many tropical storms, known as *nortes*, blow themselves out in this region, bringing heavy rain. From October to January the weather tends to be changeable, with cold, damp winds from the north. At this time the beaches and Malecón are empty and many resorts close, except over Christmas and New Year when the tourists flood in and all road transport is booked up five days in advance.

Background

The principal port of entry for Mexico lies on a low alluvial plain bordering the Gulf coast. Cortés landed near here at Isla de los Sacrificios on 17 April 1519. The first settlement was called Villa Rica de la Vera Cruz; its location was changed several times, including to La Antigua (see above). The present site was established in 1599.

Culturally, Veracruz is a Caribbean city, home to the *jarocho* costume, dance and music, which features harps and guitars. The most famous dances, accompanied by the *conjunto jarocho* dressed in white, are the *bamba* and *zapateado*, with much stamping and lashing of feet related to the flamenco of Andalucía in Spain. Mexico's version of the Cuban *danzón* music and the *música tropical* add to the cultural richness. Many cultural events can be seen at the **Instituto Veracruzano de Cultura**, a few blocks from the Zócalo, with a good, new café and library; a nice place to relax.

Sights

The heart of the city is **Plaza de Armas** (Zócalo). The square is white-paved, with attractive cast-iron lampstands and benches, and surrounded by the cathedral (with an unusual cross, depicted with hands), the **Palacio Municipal** and colonial-style hotels. The plaza comes alive in the evenings with an impressive combination of the crush of people, colour and marimba music, *danzón* or *son veracruzano* in the floodlit setting. From 15 July to the end of August there is jazz in the Zócalo from 1900. At night, too, the Malecón (seafront) is very lively, with performers entertaining the public.

Veracruz

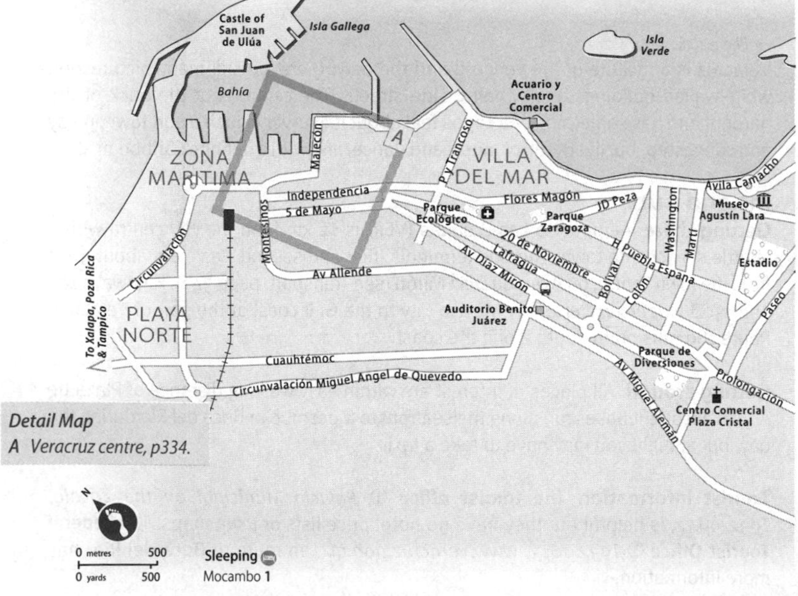

The city's two most interesting buildings are the very fine 17th-century **Palacio Municipal** (1627), on Plaza de Armas, with a splendid façade and courtyard, and the **Fortress of San Juan de Ulúa** (1565) ⓘ *Tue-Sun 0900-1700, US$1.80*, built on Isla Gallega to deter the buccaneers but now joined by a causeway to the mainland. It later became a political prison and Mexico's 'Robin Hood', Chucho el Roto, famously managed to escape three times. Benito Juárez was also incarcerated here between 1858 and 1861. In 1915, Venustiano Carranza converted it into a presidential palace. Take the bus marked Ulúa from Malecón/Avenida República. The **Baluarte de Santíago** ⓘ *Francisco Canal y Gómez Farías, Tue-Sun 1000-1630, US$2.10*, a bastion that once formed part of the city walls, contains a small prehispanic gold collection recovered from a wreck. The **market** on the Salvador Díaz Mirón triangle (Ignacio Allende/Miguel Alemán/Hernán Cortés) is a fascinating experience.

The **Museo de la Ciudad** ⓘ *Zaragoza 397, Mon-Sat 0900-1500, US$0.35*, has a good, well-displayed collection of photographs; it traces the history of Veracruz from the Conquest to 1910. Plazuela de la Campana, by Serdán and Zaragoza, is an attractive small square. The **Museo Carranza** ⓘ *Malecón, Tue-Sun 0900-1700, free*, has photos of the Revolution, the life of Carranza and his battles against the Huerta regime. The **Museo Histórico Naval** ⓘ *Gómez Farías and Morales, daily 0900-1700, free*, has an excellent and extensive collection of naval memorabilia, especially from the 1914 resistance to US invasion.

On the way to Mocambo beach, where Bulevar Avila Camacho meets Bulevar Ruiz Cortines, is the **Museo Agustín Lara** (**La Casita Blanca**) ⓘ *US$2, free on Sun*, a must for anyone interested in Mexican popular music. It was the home of the greatest 20th-century Mexican songwriter, Agustín Lara, who wrote more than 700 songs (*Solamente una vez*, *Veracruz*, *Granada* and *María Bonita* among the most famous), many of which still reverberate around the streets and squares of Veracruz. A pianist plays and sings Tuesday to Saturday 1100-1400, 1600-1900; at other times visitors are welcome to play Lara's piano.

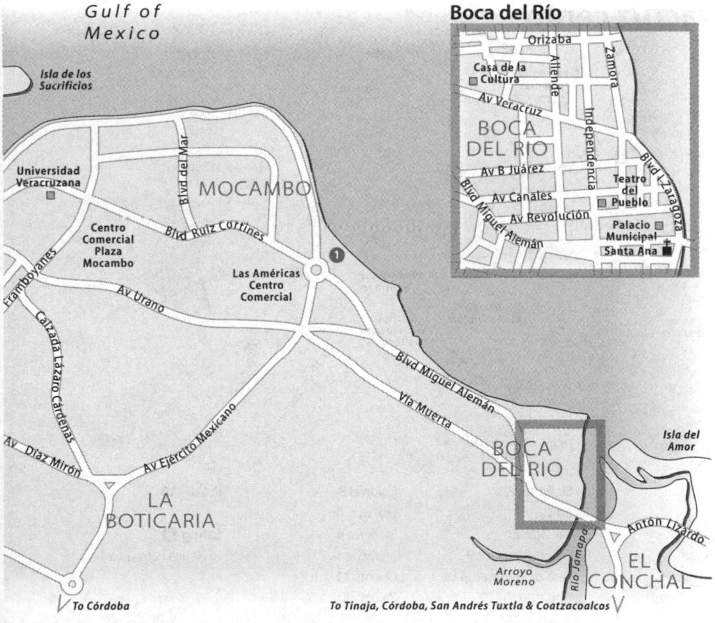

Around Veracruz

→ For the coast north of Veracruz, see page 331.

The beaches along the waterfront, and the sea, are polluted from the heavy shipping. A short bus ride from the fish market takes you to **Mocambo** beach, which has a superb, 50-m swimming pool (with restaurant and bar), beach restaurants, Caribbean-style beach huts and dirty sand; the water is quite a bit cleaner but still rather uninviting in colour. There are crabs and mosquitoes and much pestering by sellers. The beach is crowded, and at holiday time cars race up and down and there are loud radios, etc. To Mocambo take a bus marked 'Boca del Río' on Avenida Zaragoza.

Harbour trips are available from the Malecón. On Sunday, there are trips to **Mandinga** for cheap fresh seafood (big prawns) and local entertainment.

Some 6 km to the south of Veracruz (*colectivo* from Av Zaragoza) is **Boca del Río,** beyond Mocambo, on the left bank of the mouth of Río Jamapa. In 1518, the Spaniard Grijalva gave the already existing settlement the name of Río de Banderas as the inhabitants carried small flags in order to transmit messages. Worthy of a visit is the church of Santa Ana (1716). Modern buildings of interest include the Palacio Municipal, Teatro del Pueblo and the Casa de la Cultura, but most people come to Boca del Río to eat at one of its many fish restaurants.

A 10-minute bus ride from Boca del Río to the other side of the river is **El Conchal,** a small residential development overlooking picturesque lagoons with a number of attractive restaurants. The bus continues along a low sandy spit to Punta Antón Lizardo where there is a small village with a few beach restaurants and good sand and bathing.

Papaloapan region

» pp338-345. Colour map 3, C5/C6.

Route 180 heads southeast from the port of Veracruz along the flat, wet coastal plain through Alvarado and on the Tuxtla mountains and the Isthmus of Tehuantepec. An alternative route is to turn inland through the fertile Papaloapan region and on south into the state of Oaxaca. **Puerto Alvarado** is a modern fishing port 1½ hours south from Veracruz by bus, none too pleasant for women on their

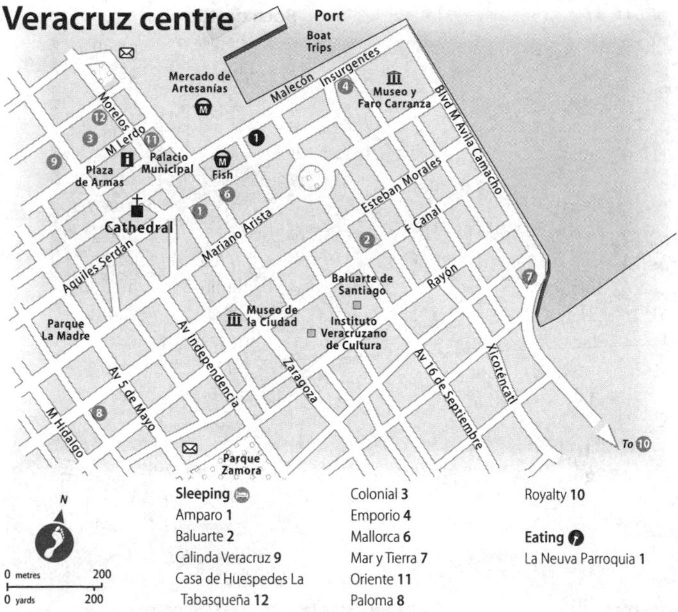

own as there are many bars and drunks. Crossing the **Río Papaloapan** (Butterfly River) by a toll bridge along Route 180 leads to the sugar-cane area around Lerdo de Tejada and Angel R Cavada. At **El Trópico** shop a dirt road turns left to some quiet beaches such as Salinas and Roca Partida.

Tlacotalpan → *Phone code: 288. Colour map 3, C6.*

About 15 km from Alvarado, Route 175 crosses the over the Río Papaloapan at Buenavista, and heads southwards to the town of Tlacotalpan where the Papaloapan and San Juan rivers meet. This small town, once the main town in southern Veracruz, and an important international port in the steamship era, is regarded as the **centre of Jarocho culture**. It has many **picturesque streets** with one-storey houses all fronted by stuccoed columns and arches painted in bright colours. There are two churches in the Zócalo, the Parroquia de San Cristóbal and the Capilla de la Candelaria, and a Casa de las Artesanías on Chazaro, 1½ blocks from the Zócalo. The **Museo Salvador Ferrando** ⓘ *US$0.50*, contains interesting local 19th-century paintings, furniture, artefacts and Jarocho costume. The **tourist office** ⓘ *T884-2050, Mon-Fri 0800-1400, 1500-1900, Sat and Sun 1000-1400*, is on the main plaza.

Otatitlán

Another 40 km, beyond Cosamaloapan, is a ferry to Otatitlán, also on the east bank of the river (US$0.25, it leaves whenever there are sufficient passengers). The town, also known as **El Santuario**, dates back to early colonial times. Its houses have tiled roofs supported by columns (not as impressive as Tlacotalpan), but most interesting is the church. The priest maintains that the gold-patterned dome is the largest unsupported structure of its kind in Mexico, measuring 20 m wide and 40 m high.

Tuxtepec » *pp338-345. Colour map 3, C5.*

→ *Phone code: 287.*

This is the natural place for a stay in the Papaloapan area. It is an important supply centre in the state of Oaxaca, a large commercial city, untouristed and tranquil; prices here are lower than in other parts of Oaxaca. The region has significant agricultural activity with local industries including a sugar mill, brewery and paper mill. The city is built on the left bank of the Río Santo Domingo. Avenida Independencia runs along the riverfront, has the market, shops and several miradors offering good views. A small ferry crosses the river from below the viewpoint next to **Hotel Mirador**. The people of Tuxtepec consider themselves more *jarochos* (ie from the state of Veracruz) than *oaxaqueños*; the mixture of the music and exuberance of Veracruz with the food and handicrafts of Oaxaca is fascinating. The **tourist office** ⓘ *Cámara Nacional de Comercio Serytour, Libertad esq Allende, opposite Parque Benito Juárez, T875-0886, Mon-Fri 0900-1400, 1700-2000, Sat 0900-1300*, has limited information.

Parque Benito Juárez, the main plaza, has a monument to the mother and child, an ample Palacio Municipal to the south, and a modern cathedral to the east. Further west is Parque Hidalgo, with a statue of the father of Mexico's Independence. The modern **Casa de la Cultura** is on Daniel Soto by Bulevar Benito Juárez.

Around Tuxtepec

The **Presa Miguel Alemán**, a lake formed by the Miguel Alemán and Cerro de Oro dams, is very scenic. There are several points of access, the most widely used being that of **Temascal**, a small town near the Alemán dam, with shops and a few places to eat.

The road west of Tuxtepec towards the state of Puebla is quite scenic; along it are a number of towns and villages that maintain an indigenous flavour, *huípiles* and crafts can be found here, especially on market day. The road is paved as far as

 Jalapa de Díaz and then continues to **San Bartolomé Ayautla** and **Huautla de Jiménez**. **San Lucas Ojitlán** is a Chinantec town, 42 km from Tuxtepec, with a hilltop church dominating the surroundings.

Jalapa de Díaz is 70 km from Tuxtepec, near the base of Cerro Rabón, a mountain with a spectacular 500-m sheer cliff face. The town is built on several small hills, with the church on the highest.

Tuxtepec to Oaxaca

The road from Tuxtepec to Oaxaca, Route 175, is a spectacular steep and winding route, cars need good brakes and it is reported to be difficult for caravans and cyclists; the latter are recommended to take a bus. It is mostly a paved road, but sections near the high passes can at times be badly potholed and rutted. The ride up from Tuxtepec to Oaxaca takes six to seven hours, a bit less in the opposite direction. From Tuxtepec, at 30 m above sea level, the road climbs 30 m gradually to Valle Nacional (see below). Just after crossing the Río Valle Nacional it climbs steeply into the Sierra Juárez, reaching the El Mirador pass (2900 m) in 2½ hours. The transition from lush lowland forest to pines is splendid, there are lovely views of the ridges and valley far below (sit on the right if travelling south to Oaxaca). From here the road drops in two hours to Ixtlán de Juárez and San Pablo Guelatao, the birthplace of Benito Juárez (gas station, restaurants). The route continues to drop to the dry valley of the Río Manzanillo, at 1500 m, before climbing again to La Cumbre pass (2700 m), from which there are fine views of Oaxaca below, one hour further.

Valle Nacional → *Colour map 3, C5. Altitude: 60 m.*

Set in the beautiful valley of the Río Valle Nacional, 48 km south of Tuxtepec, is the small town of Valle Nacional, which sees few visitors, but offers basic services and excellent opportunities for birding and walking in the surrounding hills. The town is laid out lengthwise along the main road; there is a gas station at the Tuxtepec end – fill up here on the way to Oaxaca. Nearby are several rubber plantations (for example just across the bridge on the road to Oaxaca) and tappers may be seen at work early in the morning, especially in the dry season. This area had a horrific reputation as the *Valle de los Miserables*, in the era of Porfirio Díaz, for political imprisonment and virtual slavery from which there was no escape.

Los Tuxtlas

» *pp338-345. Colour map 3, C6.*

Back on the coastal Route 180, southeast of Alvarado and the Papaloapan, is Tula where there is a spectacular waterfall, **El Salto de Tula**; a restaurant is set beside the falls. The road then climbs up into the mountainous volcanic area of Los Tuxtlas, known as the Switzerland of Mexico for its mountains and perennial greenness.

Santiago Tuxtla → *Phone code: 294. Colour map 3, C6.*

This pleasant town of colonial origin is set on a river. In the main square is the largest known Olmec head, carved in solid stone, and also a museum, **Museo Tuxtleco** ⓘ *Mon-Sat 0900-1800, Sun 0900-1500, tourist info available here,* containing examples of local tools, photos, items used in witchcraft (*brujería*), the first sugar-cane press used in Mexico and another Olmec head. There is dancing to *jarana* bands in the Christmas fortnight. In June and July, dancers wear jaguar masks to perform the *danza de los liseres.*

The archaeological site of **Tres Zapotes** lies to the west; it is reached by leaving the paved road south towards Villa Isla and taking either the dirt road at Tres Caminos (signposted) in the dry season (a quagmire from May-December), or in the wet season access can be slowly achieved by turning right at about Km 40, called Tibenal, and following the dirt road north to the site of the **museum** ⓘ *daily 0900-1700, US$1.65 (if it is closed, the lady in the nearby shop has a key)*. The site, once the centre of the Olmec culture, is a 1-km walk (the bus cannot reach Tres Zapotes if rain has swollen the river that the road has to cross). At the museum, there is an Olmec head, also the largest carved stela ever found and stela fragments bearing the New World's oldest Long Count Date, equal to 31 BC. In this region of Mexico there are other Olmec sites at Cerro de las Mesas, Laguna de los Cerros and San Lorenzo Tenochtitlán. The other major Olmec site is further east, at La Venta, in the neighbouring state of Tabasco (see page 397).

Travellers with little time to spare may find the trip to Tres Zapotes not worth the effort as there is little to see at the site.

San Andrés Tuxtla → *Phone code: 294. Colour map 3, C6.*

A further 15 km beyond Santiago lies San Andrés Tuxtla, the largest town of the area, with narrow winding streets, bypassed by a ring road. It has a well-stocked market with Oaxacan foods such as *carne enchilada* (spicy meat) and *tamales de elote* (cakes of maize-flour steamed in leaves). It is the centre of the cigar trade. One factory beside the main road permits visitors to watch the process and will produce special orders of cigars (*puros*) marked with an individual's name. The **tourist office** at the Palacio Municipal, is in office of the Secretariá de Relaciones Exteriores.

Catemaco

» pp338-345. Colour map 3, C6.

→ *Phone code: 294.*

Catemaco town is famed for its traditional *brujos* (sorcerers) who have become a great tourist attraction. It is a pleasant town with a large colonial church and picturesque setting on the lake, 13 km from San Andrés Tuxtla (irregular bus service). There are stalls selling handicrafts from Oaxaca, and boat trips out on the lake to see the shrine where the Virgin appeared, the spa at Coyamé and the Isla de los Monos (boat owners charge US$30-35 per boat). The **Isla de los Monos** is home to a colony of macaque monkeys introduced from Thailand for the University of Veracruz. Launches to the island charge US$12.50, or you can pay US$3.20 to be rowed there by local fishermen – cheaper and more peaceful.

For most of the year sleeping on the beach is not recommended (assaults and robberies), although at Easter time many people camp here.

Around Catemaco

The **Reserva Ecológica Nanciyaga** ⓘ *T943-0808*, 7 km round the northern shore of the lake, has rainforest with rich birdlife, including toucans. The film *Medicine Man*, with Sean Connery, was filmed using the ecological park as a 'jungle' backdrop.

Catemaco to Playa Hermosa

The Gulf coast may be reached from Catemaco along an 18km road to **Sontecomapan**, crossing over the pass at Buena Vista and looking down to the *laguna* where, it is said, Francis Drake sought refuge. The village of Sontecomapan (**Hotel Sontecomapan**) lies on an entry to the *laguna* and boats may be hired for the 20-minute ride out to the bar where the *laguna* meets the sea. A large part of the lagoon is surrounded by mangrove swamp, and the sandy beaches, edged by cliffs, are almost deserted except for local fishermen and groups of pelicans. Beaches, such as **Jicacal** and **Playa Hermosa**, are accessible to those who enjoy isolation.

Coatzacoalcos, Minatitlán and around

▸▸ *pp338-345. Colour map 3, C6.*

→ *Phone code: Coatzacoalcos 921, Minatitlán 922.*

The road from Catemaco heads south to Acayucan then east to Minatitlán and **Coatzacoalcos**. The latter is the Gulf coast gateway for the Yucatán Peninsula, 1.5 km from the mouth of its wide river. It is hot, humid and lacking in culture. The beach is dangerous at nights, do not sleep there or loiter. **Minatitlán**, the oil and petrochemical centre, is 39 km upriver. The road between the two towns carries very heavy industrial traffic and both cities are often under a pall of smog. There is a high incidence of lung disease. Not many foreigners visit either town, but there are hotels and restaurants in both places should you choose to stay.

Acayucan, at the junction of Highway 180 and 185, makes a great place to stop if you're driving from Mexico City to points south. There's not a great deal to do, apart from wander the streets, watch the municipal game of basketball, log on in an internet café, or watch a movie, but it's a decent town.

About 40 km east of Coatzacoalcos, on a side road off Route 180 is **Agua Dulce**, where there is a campground (see Sleeping, below). Further east along the Gulf coast is **Sánchez Magallanes** (turn off Route 180 at Las Piedras, 70 km from Coatzacoalcos, signposted), a pleasant, friendly town where you can camp safely on the beach.

Sleeping

Orizaba *p325*
B-C **Trueba**, Ote 6 and Sur 11, T724-2744, www.hoteltrueba.com. Resort facilities.
C **De France**, Ote 6, No 186, T725-2311. Charming building, clean, comfortable, shower, friendly, reasonable if uninspiring restaurant.
E **América**, Ote 6, No 269. Very friendly and good value.

Córdoba *p326*
A **Hotel Laifer**, Av 5 between Calle 9 y 11, T714-0099. 4-star hotel, swimming pool, gymnasium, video games room, a/c, secure parking, friendly. Highly recommended.
B **Mansur**, Av 1, No 301, y Calle 3, on square, T712-6000. Smart.
C **Gorbeña**, Calle 11, No 308, between Calle 3 y 5, T712-0777. Large rooms. Recommended.
C **Virreynal**, Av 1 No 309 and Calle 1, T712-2377. Good central spot on the main plaza.
E **La Nueva Querétana**, Av 4, No 508. Basic but cheap.

Xalapa *p326*
Cheaper hotels are up the hill from the market. Town centre hotels are generally noisy.
L **Misión Xalapa**, Victoria y Bustamante, T818-2222. Good restaurant, excellent bookshop, changes TCs.
A-B **Mesón del Alférez**, Zaragoza y Sebastián Camacho 2, T/F818-6351, www.pradodelrio.com. Charming, small rooms, free parking opposite, good food. Highly recommended.
B-C **Salmones**, Zaragoza 24, T817-5431. Excellent view of Pico de Orizaba from the roof, good restaurant. Recommended.
D **Araucarias**, Avila Camacho 60, T817-3433. With balcony and view, TV, fridge, good cheap restaurant.
D **Limón**, Av Revolución 8, behind the cathedral, T817-2204. Good clean rooms, with hot water bath, some with nice views.
D **Plaza**, Enríquez, T817-3310. All rooms with private bath and TV, some rooms airless, clean, safe, friendly, will store luggage, good view of Pico de Orizaba from the roof. Recommended.
E **El Greco**, Av Revolución, 4 blocks up from the cathedral. T817-1357. With bath, hot water, clean.

Around Xalapa *p326*
C **Hotel Central**, near plaza, in Perote, T825-1462. Quiet, friendly, with bath, TV.

E Gran Hotel, on plaza, in Perote. Basic, limited water.

Papantla *p327*

A Tajín, Dr Núñez and Domínguez 104, T/F842-0121, www.hoteltajin.com.mx. 59 rooms, restaurant with good-value breakfast and bar, fairly clean, hot water, phone, TV, parking, reasonable.
C-D Totonocapan, 20 de Noviembre y Olivo, T842-1220. Hot water, TV, a/c, bar/ restaurant, good value.
D México, Obispo de Las Casas y Núñez, opposite Cine Tajín), T842-0086. Basic, cheapest in town.

Poza Rica and south to Veracruz *p330*

AL Poza Rica, 2 Norte, Poza Rica, between 10 and 12 Ote, T822-0112. Friendly Best Western, fairly comfortable, good restaurant.
B-C Salinas, Blv Ruiz Cortines 1905 y Cazones, Poza Rica, T822-0706. Good, a/c, TV, restaurant, pool, secure parking.
C Nuevo León, Av Colegio Militar, Poza Rica, T822-0528, opposite market. Rooms quite spacious, fairly clean and quiet. Recommended.
D Fénix, 6 Norte (near Av Central Ote), Poza Rica, T822-3572. Basic, but one of the better cheap places.

Camping

Trailer Park Quinta Alicia, Km 84. Very clean, plenty of shade in the palms. Helpful and friendly.

Coast road to Veracruz *p331*

D Casa de Huéspedes Malena, Av Carlos Prieto, Tecolutla. Pleasant rooms, clean.
D Hotel Malinche, La Antigua. Quiet, laid-back and peaceful.
E Los Buhos, Tecolutla, close to the beach. Very good rooms with hot shower and TV.

Camping

D Torre Molina trailer park, 16 km from Nautla on coastal Route 180 (going towards Veracruz). Electricity, water and sewage disposal, hot showers, bathrooms, swimming pool, on beach. Recommended.

Veracruz *p331, maps p332 and p334*

The Zócalo is very lively at night, so rooms overlooking the square can be noisy.
AL Mocambo, Calzada Ruiz Cortines 4000, south of the port on Playa Mocambo, T922-0203. 1930s palace, good service and food. Highly recommended.
A Calinda Veracruz, Independencia and Lerdo, near Zócalo, T989-3800, www.hotelescalinda.com.mx. Probably the best in the centre.
A Emporio, Insurgentes Veracruzanos y Xicoténcatl (Malecón), T932 2222, www.hotelesemporio.com. Very good, with bath, swimming pool, inexpensive *comida corrida* and superb buffet breakfast Sat and Sun.
B Colonial, on Zócalo, T932-0193. Swimming pool, indoor parking. Recommended.
C Baluarte, opposite the small fort of Baluarte, Canal 265, T932-6042. Good, clean. Recommended.
C Mar y Tierra, Figueroa y Malecón, T/F932-6096. Cheaper in low season, some rooms with balconies overlooking the harbour, restaurant serving good breakfast.
C Royalty, Abasolo 34, T932-3988. Average, near beach, 20 mins' walk from Zócalo, but noisy as it caters mainly to student groups. Recommended.
D Impala, Orizaba 658, T937-0169. With bath, cold water, mosquitoes but clean, near bus station.
D Mallorca, Aquiles Serdán 424. T932-7549. With bath and fan, radio, newly furnished, very clean. Highly recommended.
D Oriente, M Lerdo 20, T/F931-2490. Secure parking, clean, friendly, balconies (noisy from street), good fans, some a/c.
E Amparo, Aquiles Serdán 482, T932-2738. With fan, insect screens, clean, hot water, good value. Recommended.
E Casa de Huéspedes La Tabasqueña, Av Morelos 325. Fan, new bathrooms, upper rooms less good, front rooms noisy, many others without windows, cheap, clean, safe, helpful.
E Paloma, Av Morales y Reforma, T932-4260. Clean, basic, fan, friendly, good value.
E Santander, Landero y Coss 123, T932-4529. With bath and TV, very clean.

***Phone codes** Orizaba 272; Córdoba 271; Xalapa 228; Papantla 784; Poza Rica 782 Veracruz 229; Tlacotalpan 288; Tuxtepec 287; Santiago Tuxtla 294; San Andrés Tuxtla 294; Catemaco 294; Coatzacoalcos 921; Minatitlán 922.*

Tlacotalpan *p335*

B **Tlacotalpan**, R Beltrán 35, T/F884-2063. Clean, a/c, restaurant, good value.

C **Posada Doña Lala**, Carranza 11, T884-2580. With a/c and TV, good restaurant.

D **Reforma**, Carranza 2 (sometimes known as **Viajero**), T884-2022. Good.

F **Jarocho**, Carranza 22. Seedy, but large rooms in old house, good view of town from roof.

Tuxtepec *p335*

B-C **El Rancho**, Avila Camacho 435, T875-0722, elrancho@prodigy.net.mx. With a/c, pool, restaurant, evening entertainment, parking. Recommended.

C **Hacienda**, Blv Benito Juárez 409, T875-1500. With a/c, restaurant, pool, gardens, parking.

C-D **Playa Bruja**, Independencia 1531, T875-0325. With a/c, pool, cafeteria, parking.

D **María de Lourdes**, 5 de Mayo 1380, T875-0410. A/c, cheaper with fan, hot water, good parking. Recommended.

D-E **Tuxtepec**, Matamoros 2 corner of Independencia, T875-0934. With a/c (cheaper with fan), hot water, restaurant, good value. Recommended.

E-F **Casa de Huéspedes Ocampo**, Ocampo 285 y Libertad. With bath, fan, friendly.

F **Catedral**, Guerrero, near Zócalo, T875-0764. Very friendly, fan and shower.

Santiago Tuxtla *p336*

C **Castellanos**, on Plaza, T947-0300. Hot shower, clean, swimming pool. Recommended.

D **Estancia Olmeca**, No 78 on main highway just north of ADO office, T947-0737. Clean, friendly, parking.

E **Morelos**, Obregón 13 and Morelos, T947-0474. Family-run, quiet, nicely furnished.

San Andrés Tuxtla *p337*

B **del Parque**, Madero 5, T942-0198. A/c, very clean, good restaurant.

C **Posada San José**, Belisario Domínguez 10, T942-1010, close to plaza. Run by nice family and staff, restaurant, pick-up truck for excursions, 2nd hotel at Monte Pío.

C-D **San Andrés**, Madero 6, just off plaza, T942-0604. Clean, a/c, restaurant, parking, laundry service.

D **Colonial**, Pino Suárez opposite **Figueroa**, T942-0552. With bath, hot water, clean.

D-E **Figueroa**, Pino Suárez 10. Hot water, friendly.

E **Juárez**, 400 m down street from ADO terminal, No 417, T942-0974. Clean, friendly.

Catemaco *p337*

There are a number of hotels at the lakeside.

A **La Finca**, just outside town, T943-0430. Pool, attractive grounds, beautiful setting beside lake, full at weekends, a/c, comfortable rooms, but poor food and service.

B-C **Juros**, Playa 14, T943-0084. Hot water, café, waterskiing on lake, will allow trailers and use of parking.

C **Catemaco**, on main square, T943-0203. A/c, excellent food and swimming pool.

D **Del Brujo**, Ocampo y Malecón, T943-0071. Fan, a/c, shower, nice clean rooms, balcony overlooking the lake. Recommended.

D **Los Arcos**, Madero 7, T943-0003. Clean, fan, good value.

E **San Francisco**, Matamoros 26, T943-0398. With bath, basic, but good and clean.

E-F **Acuario**, corner of plaza, T943-0418. Hot water and parking.

Camping

Trailer park at Solotepec, by the lake on the road to Playa Azul. US$6.50 per vehicle, very clean, hook-ups, bathrooms. Recommended.

La Ceiba, restaurant and trailer park, Av Malecón, 6 blocks west of Zócalo. By lakeshore, camping and hook-ups, bathrooms with hot water, restaurant and lakeside patio.

Coatzacoalcos, Minatitlán and around *p338*

B **Kinaku**, on the corner of Ocampo and Victoria, Acayucan, T245-0016. Clean, modern rooms, with a/c and TV. Restaurant and pool.

C **Ritz**, Acayucan, a better deal, has many new rooms, with good showers, a/c, TV, very clean, spacious and comfortable.

Camping

Rancho Hermanos Graham, Agua Dulce. Nice location, full hook-up, cold showers, US$6.50 for car and 2 people.

Eating

Orizaba *p325*
In the market, try the local morning snack, *memelita picadita.*
¥¥ **Radha's**, on Sur 5 between Ote 1 and 3. Indian vegetarian restaurant serving excellent *comida corrida.*
¥¥ **Romanchú**, main street. Excellent international cuisine.
¥ **Crazy Foods**, opposite **Hotel de France**. Good and cheap, nice sandwiches.

Córdoba *p326*
¥¥¥-¥¥ **Cantábrico**, Calle 3, No 9, 1 block from Zócalo, T712-7646. Excellent meat and fish dishes, fine wines and good service, 'worth a trip from Mexico City!'. Highly recommended.
¥¥¥-¥¥ **El Balcón**, enter through **Hotel Zevallos**. Balcony overlooking Zócalo. Recommended.
¥¥-¥ **Brujes**, Av 2, No 306. Good *comida corrida.*

Xalapa *p326*
There are several good cafés on Carrillo Puerto for good-value *comida corrida.*
¥¥¥-¥¥ **La Casona del Beaterio**, Zaragoza 20. Good atmosphere, tastefully restored house with patio and fountain, good breakfast.
¥¥ **La Champion**, Allende, going towards the bus terminal. Nice atmosphere, good-value *comida corrida* Mon-Sat.
¥¥ **La Churrería del Recuerdo**, Victoria 158. Superb, authentic Mexican food at very reasonable prices; real 'home' cooking. No alcohol. Highly recommended.
¥¥-¥ **Café Linda**, Primo de Verdad. Good service and good-value *comida corrida* every day, often live music in the evenings.
¥¥-¥ **La Parroquia**, Zaragoza 18, and another on Av Camacho, same menu and prices as famous restaurant of same name in Veracruz.
¥¥-¥ **Quinto Reyno**, Juárez 67, close to main plaza. Lunches only. Excellent vegetarian restaurant with health food shop, very good service.
¥ **La Sopa**, Diamante, an alleyway just off Enríquez. Great tapas, cheap.

Around Xalapa *p326*
In Coatepec there are several good cafés and restaurants around the main plaza.
¥¥¥-¥¥ **Casa Bonilla**, Cuauhtémoc 20, Coatepec. Award-winning restaurant renowned for its delicious and varied langoustine dishes. It's worth coming to Coatepec just to eat here.

Papantla *p327*
¥¥ **Las Brisas del Golfo**, Dr Núñez. Reasonable prices and very good.
¥¥-¥ **Catedral**, Núñez y Curado, behind cathedral. Plain, clean, cheap breakfasts and good 'fast' meals, 0630-2100.
¥ **Sorrento**, Zócalo. Covered in decorative tiles, good, cheap. Recommended.

Poza Rica and south to Veracruz *p330*
¥ **Café Manolo**, 10 Ote 60 y 6 Norte, Poza Rica. Good breakfast.
¥ **Lonchería El Petrolero**, Plaza Cívica 18 de Marzo y Av Central Ote, Poza Rica. Excellent bread baked on premises, popular with locals.

Veracruz *p331, maps p332 and 334*
In the main market, Cortés y Madero, there are cheap restaurants in the mezzanine. The fish market has excellent fish and shrimp cocktails. *Toritos* are a local drink made of egg, milk, fruit and alcohol, delicious and potent. Nearby **Boca del Río** is famous for its excellent and fairly cheap fish restaurants.
¥¥¥-¥¥ **Café de la Catedral**, Ocampo y Parque Zamora. Large, local, few tourists, try fish stuffed with shrimps.
¥¥ **Karen**, Arista 574 between Landero y Coss and Zaragoza. Good fish restaurant.
¥¥ **La Nueva Parroquia**, on Malecón, is famous throughout Mexico (it used to be called **Café La Parroquia**, on Plaza de Armas). Two coffee houses in same block, very popular, excellent coffee, good food and full of atmosphere. You haven't been to Veracruz until you've been here, or so they say.
¥¥ **La Paella**, Plaza de Armas, 138, has its name written into the concrete of the entrance floor as well as a sign. Good *comida corrida.*
¥¥ **La Quinta del Son**, on paved side street off Aquiles Serdán. Bar and restaurant, food nothing special but excellent Cuban-style *trova* band in afternoon.
¥¥ **Olímpica**, Zaragoza 250, near the fish market, 2 blocks from the Zócalo. A good local fish restaurant.

ΨΨ **Tano's** just off the Malecón, Mario Molina 20. Excellent fresh fish.

ΨΨ **Tiburón**, Landero y Coss 167, corner of Aquiles Serdán, 2 blocks from Zócalo. An interesting place, run by 'Tiburón' González, the 'Rey de la Alegría', or 'Rey Feo' of carnival; the walls are covered in pictures of him and his *comparsas*, dating back to at least 1945. The food is good and inexpensive too.

Ψ **El Tranvía**, General Prim corner of Rayón, opposite Parque Zamora. For good value unpretentious food (not just fish).

Ψ **Emir Cafetería**, Independencia 1520, near F Canal. Good breakfast.

Ψ **La Puerta del Sol**, on Molina, 1 block south of the Zócalo. Friendly bar, cheap beer.

Cafés and ice cream parlours

El Azteca de Cayetano, Mario Molina 94. *Mondongo de fruta* (a selection of all the fruits in season, plus fruit-flavoured ice) are prepared on a plate.

Le Blé, coffee house, on road parallel to Blv Avila Camacho, between F Canal and Rayón. Good decor, fine variety of coffees.

Mondongo de Fruta, M Molina 88. Not cheap but delicious for fruits, juices and ices.

Nevería y Refresquería Aparito, Aquiles Serdán and Landero y Coss, near fish market. Good for fruit and juices, try *mondongo de frutas*.

Tlacotalpan *p335*

ΨΨ-Ψ **Brisas de Tlacotalpan**, one of several good fish restaurants with terraces on the riverfront.

ΨΨ-Ψ **La Flecha**. Excellent *sopa de mariscos* and *jaiba a la tlacotalpina* (crab).

Tuxtepec *p335*

ΨΨ **El Estero**, Benito Juárez by Independencia. Fish dishes and local cuisine. Excellent.

ΨΨ **La Tablita**, Matamoros 2. Good *comida corrida* and à la carte. Long hours.

ΨΨ **Taquería Gambrinos**, 5 de Mayo 438, 1½ blocks from Parque Juárez. Excellent tacos, very popular, busy every evening.

ΨΨ **Villa de Carvajal**, Muro Blv esq Nicolás Bravo, on the riverfront. Seafood and grill.

ΨΨ-Ψ **Los Caporales**, Independencia 560. Good value *comida corrida* and à la carte.

Ψ **La Mascota de Oro**, 20 de Noviembre 891. Cheap, very friendly.

San Andrés Tuxtla *p337*

ΨΨ **La Carreta**, near the town centre, otherwise known as **Guadalajara de Noche**. It appears small from the outside but is large and pleasant inside. Well recommended. Sells *tepache*, a drink made from fermented pineapple, similar in flavour to cider, and *agua de jamaica* (hibiscus juice).

Catemaco *p337*

On the promenade are a number of good restaurants. The best value are those not directly on the lake. At the rear of the market are some inexpensive, good restaurants serving *comida corrida* for US$2-2.50.

ΨΨ-Ψ **María José**, on the promenade. The best of the bunch.

Coatzacoalcos, Minatitlán and around *p338*

Soyamar, Guerrero 23, Acayucan. Good vegetarian snack option if you're passing through.

Festivals and events

Veracruz *p331, maps p332 and 334*

Feb/Mar The **Shrovetide carnival** is said to be Mexico's liveliest. The carnival starts a week before **Shrove Tue** and ends on **Ash Wed**; Sat-Tue are the main days with parades. At this time of year it can be very difficult to find accommodation or transport.

Tlacotalpan *p335*

31 Jan There is a well-known **Candelmas** fiesta here when accommodation is impossible to find.

Tuxtepec *p335*

Jun The *fiestas patronales* in honour of **St John the Baptist** are held 24 and 25 Jun. There are fairs, fireworks and dances, including the *flor de piña* folk dance for which the Papaloapan region is well known.

Activities and tours

Xalapa *p326*

Tour operators

There are 4 travel agents on Camacho; the one nearest Parque Juárez is very helpful. Xalapa is a base for whitewater rafting on the Filobobos River.

Tuxtepec *p335*

Boating and fishing

The Papaloapan River and its tributaries, as well as the Presa Miguel Alemán, offer plenty of opportunities for watersports. Motor-boating and rowing are popular on the rivers and artificial lake; races are held in May.

The most common species found are *robalo* (sea bass), *mojarra* (carp), and on the Río Tonto (Puente de Caracol) *sábalo* (tarpon).

Rodeo

Tuxtepec has a *lienzo charro* with capacity for 5000 spectators, where rodeos are held; this is an important regional tradition.

Transport

Orizaba *p325*

Bus **Mérida**, 1 bus (ADO), US$55, 1st class. To **Veracruz**, many buses, 2½ hrs, US$6.

Córdoba *p326*

Bus Bus station is at the end of Av 6. Services to **Veracruz**, 2 hrs, US$7; **Puebla**, 3 hrs, US$11; **Mexico City**, hourly, 5 hrs, US$18; to **Coatzacoalcos**, US$25; **Oaxaca** and many others.

Xalapa *p326*

Air

There is a small airport serving a few national destinations, 15 km southeast of the city.

Bus

Local Buses marked 'Xalapa' or 'Museo' run north to the **Anthropology Museum**. To reach nearby towns of **Coatepec** and **Xico** take a bus from Av Allende, west of the city centre. **Long distance** Bus station, CAXA, is on the outskirts. Buses marked 'Centro' will take you into town. **Coatzacoalcos**, 8 a day, up to 6½ hrs, US$23-39. **Mexico City**, hourly, 5 hrs, US$17 (travelling to TAPO bus station). **Puebla**, hourly, 3½ hrs, US$10. **Veracruz**, frequent, 2½ hrs, US$5-7. **Villahermosa**, 10 a day, 8-10 hrs, US$372. Also buses to **Poza Rica** and **Papantla**.

Papantla *p327*

Bus

ADO terminal, Juárez 207, 5 blocks from centre, T842-0218. To **Mexico City**, 4 a day, 5 hrs via Poza Rica, US$12; **Oaxaca**, 5 a day, 7-9 hrs, US$20-29; **Poza Rica**, regular service, 45 mins, US$1.35; to **Xalapa**, 9 daily, 4½ hrs, US$13; **Veracruz**, 10 a day, 4 hrs, US$13. Many services to local destinations, including **El Tajín**, buses leave when full. Occasional minibus to El Tajín from southwest corner of Zócalo, unreliable schedule about every 1-1½ hrs. **Transportes Urbano-TUSPA** buses for El Tajín leave from office on 16 de Septiembre near Obispo de las Casas (US$0.50).

Taxi

Taxi rank on Enríquez between 5 de Mayo and Zócalo, and on Juárez.

Poza Rica and south to Veracruz *p330*

Air

Airport **El Tajín**, 3 km south of Poza Rica, T822-2119; several flights daily to Mexico City.

Airline offices Aeromar, T824-3001. AeroMéxico, Edificio Géminis, Parque Juárez, T822-6142.

Bus

All buses leave from new terminal referred to as ADO, about 1.5 km from centre. Take white bus from centre, or taxi. Terminal is divided into ADO (T822-0085, also office in centre, 6 Norte opposite **Hotel Fénix**, open daily, hours vary) and all others, good facilities, tourist office. **El Tajín**, buses leave every 20-30 mins 0700-2000 from behind Monumento de la Madre statue, marked Chote or Chote Tajín. Ask driver for Las Ruinas, US$0.50, 20-25 mins, most go to the entrance. **Barra de Cazones**, Transportes Papantla or Autotransportes Cazones, 1 hr, US$1.20 (often waits 30 mins in Cazones on way back until bus fills). It is not always necessary to go to bus station to catch your bus: buses to Barra de Cazones pass through the centre along Blv Cortines. **Mexico City** and **Tampico**, every 30 mins, 5 hrs, US$14-18. **Pachuca**, 4½ hrs, US$9.50. **Papantla**, 45 mins, US$1.35, bus may be caught on Av Central Ote by Plaza Cívico 18 de Marzo. **Tecolutla**, 1¾ hrs, US$3.40. **Veracruz**, almost hourly, 3-4 hrs, US$15-18. **Xalapa**, frequent, up to 5½ hrs, US$15-18.

Veracruz *p331, maps p332 and 334*

Air

At Las Bajadas (VER), 12 km from the centre, to the capital several flights daily and flights to coastal cities. Flights also to **Houston**,

San Antonio and **Havana**. AeroMéxico, García Auly corner of Simón Bolívar, between bus station and seafront.

Airline offices AeroMéxico, García Auly 231, T935-0142. **Mexicana**, Av 5 de Mayo y Aquiles Serdán, T932-2242.

Bus

The majority of buses are booked solid for 3 days in advance throughout summer and other holiday periods; at other times queues of up to 2 hrs possible at Mexico City booking offices of bus companies (best company: ADO). Book outward journeys on arrival in Veracruz, as the bus station is some way out of town and there are often long queues. Referred to as ADO. The bus station is divided into 1st and 2nd class; the 1st-class part, mostly ADO company, is on the main street, Díaz Mirón y Xalapa, T937-6790; **Autobuses Unidos**, mostly 2nd class, is on Lafragua y Xalapa (2 blocks from ADO), T937-2376. For local buses, get accurate information from the tourist office. Buses to the main bus station along Av 5 de Mayo, marked ADO, and from the station to the centre, blue and white or red and white buses marked Díaz Mirón, pass 1 block from the Zócalo, US$0.35, or *colectivos*, also US$0.35. Taxi to ADO terminal from centre, US$1.50.

Mexico City, frequent services round the clock, 5½ hrs, US$29. **Mérida**, 15 hrs, US$58-68. **Oaxaca**, a few services through the day, direct 7 hrs, local 8½ hrs, US$28. **Puebla**, every couple of hrs, 4 hrs, US$20; **Tapachula**, 3 a day, 9½-15 hrs, US$46; **Villahermosa**, almost hourly, 7 hrs, US$26-30. To **Xalapa**, frequent departures, 2 hrs, US$5-6.

Connections with Guatemala For Guatemala take bus to Tapachula and then from the border into Guatemala City; quicker than the much more mountainous route further north. Alternatively, take ADO bus to **Oaxaca**, then carry on to Tapachula.

Tlacotalpan *p335*

Bus To/from **Veracruz** via Alvarado (**Rápidos de Papaloapan** US$3.10, 2¼ hrs), to **Santiago Tuxtla**, **San Andrés Tuxtla** (Cuenca US$2.50, 1½ hrs) and **Villahermosa**.

Tuxtepec *p335*

Air

The airport is in Loma Bonita, 36 km east on the road to Sayula. Veracruz, 165 km to the north, has the main airport in the area.

Car

The Tuxtepec-Palomares road, Route 147, provides a shortcut to the Transístmica. The road via Sayula is 20 km longer, but much safer. AU buses covering the route from Tuxtepec to Tehuantepec, Juchitán and Salina Cruz, take only the Sayula road.

Bus

There is a joint bus station for **ADO**, **AU** and **Cuenca** at Matamoros by Blv Avila Camacho. Other 2nd-class companies have their own stations. 3 buses nightly to **Juchitán** (6 hrs, US$12.50), **Tehuantepec** (6½ hrs, US$14) and **Salina Cruz** (7 hrs, US$15) with AU. To **Oaxaca**, 12 daily, 7½ hrs, US$11.60. To **Mexico City**, frequent, 6½-9 hrs, US$24-7. To **Puebla**, 10 daily, 6 hrs, US$19. To **San Andrés Tuxtla**, frequent daily service, 4 hrs, US$8. To **Valle Nacional**, every 15 mins 0500-2100, 1 hr, US$2. To **Veracruz**, frequent daily service, 3 hrs, US$8.

Santiago Tuxtla *p336*

Bus AU bus from **Veracruz**, 2nd-class, 3 hrs, US$2.80, 1st class, US$7. **Tlacotalpan**, with Cuenca, every 2 hrs, 1¼ hrs, US$3. **Tres Zapotes** from Morelos (1 block from ADO), 0700, 0830, 1130, 1300, 1500, 1630.

San Andrés Tuxtla *p337*

Bus ADO to **Campeche**, 2315, 15 hrs, US$40. AU to **Catemaco**, frequent, US$0.80. **Mexico City**, evening departures, 9 hrs, US$28-32. **Tuxtepec**, 13 buses a day, 4 hrs, US$8 via Cosamaloapan. **Villahermosa**, regular service, 6 hrs, US$17.

Catemaco *p337*

Bus **Coatzalcoalcos**, regular service, 4 hrs, US$8. **Minatitlán**, US$4.50. **Santiago Tuxtla**, regular service, 50 mins, US$1.40. For **Tuxtepec**, change in San Andrés Tuxtla. **Veracruz**, every 10 mins, 3½ hrs, US$8. **Villahermosa**, 6 hrs, US$17.

Directory

Córdoba *p326*

Banks Casa de Cambio, on Av 3 opposite Bancomer.

Xalapa *p326*

Banks Banca Serfín on Enríquez will change TCs in dollars and other major currencies. Santander on Carrillo Puerto changes dollar TCs. American Express at Viajes Xalapa, Carrillo Puerto 24, T817-6535, in centre, sells cheques against Amex card. *Casa de cambio*, on right side of Zamora going down hill, English spoken. Rates vary enormously, so shop around. Quick service and good rates at Dollar Exchange, Gutiérrez Zamora 36. **Cultural centres** Centro de Recreación Xalapeño has exhibitions. El Agora, underneath Parque Juárez, cultural centre with live music, films and exhibitions. Plaza Cristal, 10-pin bowling, next to cinema. **Internet** Serviexpress, Zaragoza 14B. Café Chat, on Camacho opposite Parque Bicentenal, another in shopping arcade off Enríquez. Most charge US$2.50 per hr. **Laundry** Several on Allende and Ursulo Galván, all charge by weight, usually US$3 per 3 kg, some offer same-day service, others up to 3 days. **Medical services** There are 2 dentists on Ursulo Galván. The hospital is on Nicolás Bravo. **Post office** Letters can be sent to the Lista de Correos on Diego Leño. **Telephone** Long-distance phone in shop on Zaragoza, with a sign outside, others behind the government palace also on Zaragoza.

Papantla *p327*

Banks Bancomer and Banamex, on Zócalo, 0900-1300, change cash and TCs till 1200. Serfín, between the 2, does not change Tcs. **Medical services** Hospital Civil, Madero 518, T842-0094. Red Cross, T842-0126. Farmacia Aparicio, Enríquez 103, daily 0700-2200. **Post office** Azueta 198, 2nd floor, Mon-Fri 0900-1300, 1500 1800, Sat 0900-1200.

Poza Rica and south to Veracruz *p330*

Banks Bancomer, opposite Hotel Poza Rica. Serfín, 4 Norte y 2 Ote. **Cultural centres** Casa de la Cultura, Guatemala 502, T822-3185. **Medical services** Cruz Roja, Blv Lázaro Cárdenas 106, T823-6871. **Laundry** Yee del Centro, Prolongación 20 de Noviembre.

Veracruz *p331, maps p332 and 334*

Banks Bancomer, Independencia y Juárez, has its own *casa de cambio* for dollars and TCs, good rates, open Mon-Fri 0930-1730, Sat and Sun 1100-1400. Banca Serfín, Díaz Mirón, 2 blocks from bus station, changes US$ cash and TCs. Banamex is at Independencia esq Juárez. American Express agency is Viajes Olymar, Blv Avila Camacho 2221, T931-3406. La Amistad, Juárez 112 (behind the hotels on the Zócalo), *casas de cambio* rates not as good as the banks but much quicker; Hotel Veracruz changes money at similar rates. **Embassies and consulates** US Consular Agency, Víctimas del 25 de Junio 388, in centre. **Internet** Networld Café, Callejón Clavijero 173, near Francisco. Canal, Mon-Sat 0900-2100, US$1.25 per hr. Stationet, 5 de Mayo, between Lerdo and Zamora, Mon-Sat 0900-2100, US$1 per hr. Micro Café, Ruiz Cortines, 100 m on from Museo Agustín Lara, Mon-Sat 1000-2300, US$1.80 per hr. **Laundry** Madero 616, US$1.50 per 3 kg, open 0730-2300. **Post offices** Main post office by bridge to San Juan de Ulúa fortress, a fine building inaugurated in 1902 by Porfirio Díaz, Mon-Fri 0900-1200; also Palacio Federal, 5 de Mayo y Rayón, Mon-Fri 0800-1900.

Tuxtepec *p335*

Banks Bancomer, Independencia 437, cash and TCs, 0900-1400, complicated. HSBC, Independencia 895, cash and TCs. Agencia de Divisas Greco, Independencia 269, cash and TCs, poor rates, Mon-Fri 0900-1800, Sat 0900-1400. **Internet** Tuxcom, Guerrero esq Blv Muro, by riverfront, Mon-Sat 0800-2100, Sun 0900-1900, US$1.95 per hr. Tux-Net, Morelos 200, Mon-Sat 0900-2100, US$2.15 per hr. **Laundry** Lava Sec, Guerrero esq Blv Muro and Independencia 1683, wash and dry US$3.25 per 4 kg load.

Santiago Tuxtla *p336*

Banks Exchange at Banco Comermex on Plaza, TCs 0900-1330.

San Andrés Tuxtla *p337*

Internet 'Ri' Chat, Constitución Norte 106, near plaza.

Catemaco *p337*

Banks Bancomer, opposite cathedral, open Mon, Wed, Fri 0900-1400.

State of Guerrero

While Acapulco still retains something of its old mystique and promises of exotic encounters, there are many other resorts dotting the coastline of Guerrero. All the usual beach holiday activities are there for the taking: surfing, waterskiing, parascending and scuba diving or trips in glass-bottomed boats. And, if you want to avoid the crowds, there are still many beautiful offbeat beaches well away from the mega resorts. Inland, Guerrero is rugged and remote, until you come to the attractive university city and state capital, Chilpancingo. » *For Sleeping, Eating and other listings, see page 351-355.*

Chilpancingo → *Phone code: 747. Colour map 3, C4. Altitude: 1250 m.*

The journey from Mexico City to Acapulco and the Pacific coast often includes a stop-off at Cuernavaca, the 'city of eternal spring' (see page 143) and a detour to the silver town of Taxco (see page 147). Further south, beyond the Mexcala River, the road passes for some 30 km through the dramatic canyon of **Zopilote** to reach the university city of Chilpancingo, capital of Guerrero state at Km 302. There is a small but grandly conceived plaza with solid neoclassical buildings and monumental public sculptures commemorating the workers' struggle: *El hombre hacia el futuro* and *El canto al trabajo* by Victor Manuel Contreras. In the **Palacio de Gobierno** there is a museum and murals. The colourful reed bags from the village of Chilapa (see below) are sold in the market. The **Casa de las Artesanías** for Guerrero is on the right-hand side of the old main Mexico City-Acapulco highway. It has a particularly wide selection of Olinalá lacquer-ware. The local **fiesta** starts on 16 December and lasts a fortnight.

Around Chilpancingo

Olmec cave paintings can be seen at the **Grutas de Juxtlahuaca** ⓘ *3-hr tour US$25*, east of Chilpancingo. The limestone cavern is in pristine condition; it has an intricate network of large halls and tunnels, stalagmites and stalactites, a huge underground lake, cave drawings from about AD 500, a skeleton and artefacts. Take a torch, food and drink and a sweater if going a long way in. To reach the caves, drive to Petaquillas on the non-toll road then take a side road (paved, but poor in parts) through several villages to Colotlipa (*colectivo* from Chilpancingo, see Transport, US$1.50, 1½ hours). Ask at the restaurant on the corner of the Zócalo for a guide to the caves.

Mexico City to Acapulco

The four-lane toll freeway from Mexico City runs west of the old highway, bypassing Chilpancingo, continuing as far as **Tierra Colorada** (where there is an exit), and on to Acapulco. The completion of the highway is the third improvement: the first motor road was pushed over the ancient mule trail in 1927, giving Acapulco its first new lease of life in 100 years; when the road was paved and widened in 1954, Acapulco began to boom.

It takes about 3½ hours to drive from the capital to Acapulco on the 406-km four-lane highway, although the toll is very high.

Warning You are advised not travel by car at night in Guerrero, even on the Mexico City-Acapulco highway and coastal highway.

Acapulco » *pp351-355. Colour map 3, C3.*

→ *Phone code: 744.*

Acapulco is the most popular resort in Mexico, particularly in winter and spring. It does not fit everyone's idea of a tropical beach resort. The town stretches for 16 km in a series of bays and cliff coves and is invading the hills. The hotels, of which there are 250, are mostly perched high to catch the breeze, for by midday the heat is sizzling; they are filled to overflowing in January and February. While the party mood may suit some, with lots more competition along the coast you may find another option more suitable to your tastes. .

Ins and outs

Getting there Aeropuerto Alvarez Internacional (ACA) is 23 km east of Acapulco. The airport shuttle takes one hour to town; ticket office is outside the terminal. **Transportaciones de Pasajeros Aeropuerto** shuttle service charge the return trip (*viaje redondo*) when you buy a ticket, so keep it and call 24 hours in advance for a taxi. It is possible to find a microbus for Puerto Marquez, where you can connect with buses for Costera Miguel Alemán.

The long-distance bus terminals are on Avenida Ejido (**Estrella Blanca** second-class terminal), reached by bus from Costera Miguel Alemán; allow at least 45 minutes during peak time. Also **Estrella de Oro** buses leave from the bus station on Avenida Cuauhtémoc, east of Parque Papagayo, two blocks from the first-class **Estrella Blanca** terminal.

Getting around The most useful bus route runs the length of Costera Miguel Alemán, linking the older part of town to the different beaches and hotels. Bus stops are numbered, so find out which number you need to get off at.

Tourist information There are two tourist offices: the **State office** ⓘ *Costera Miguel Alemán 445, near the convention centre, T434-0170, www.sectur.guerrero.gob.mx*, is helpful and has brochures and maps; the **Municipal office** ⓘ *behind the Fuerte San Diego on Ornitos*, is less useful.

Sights and beaches

Acapulco has all the paraphernalia of a booming resort: swanky shops, nightclubs, red-light district, golf club, touts and street vendors and now also air pollution. The famous beaches and expensive hotels are a different world from the streets, hotels and crowded shops and buses of the city centre, which is only two minutes' walk away. The Zócalo is lively in the evenings.

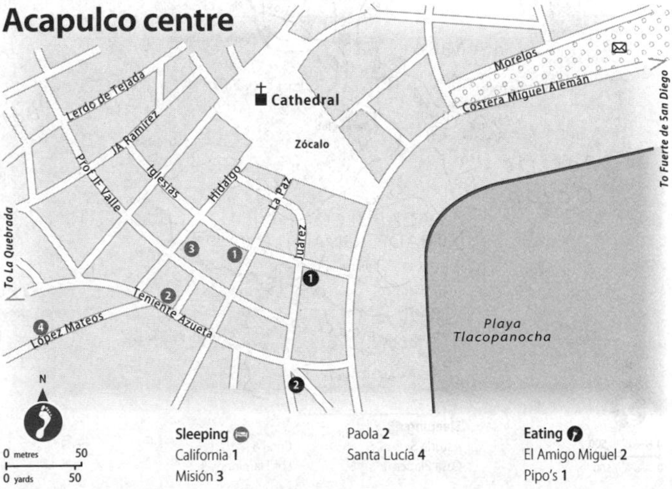

Acapulco in colonial times was the terminal for the Manila convoy. Its main defence, **Fuerte de San Diego** ⓘ *T482-3828, Tue and Sun, 0930-1830, 1000-1800, museum entrance US$3*, where the last battle for Mexican Independence was fought, has been transformed into an attractive museum of the history of Acapulco and of Mexico. It is well worth a visit.

There are some 20 beaches, all with fine, golden sand; deckchairs on all beaches (US$0.50); parachute skiing in front of the larger hotels at US$12 for five minutes. Every evening, except Monday, there is a waterskiing display opposite Fuerte de San Diego.

The two most popular beaches are the sickle-curved and shielded **Caleta**, with its smooth dirty water but clean sands, and the straight, surf-pounded beach of **Los Hornos**. Swimmers should look out for motorboats close in shore. **Mágico Mundo Marina** ⓘ *US$4*, is on Isla Yerbabuena, a little island off Caleta, with sharks, piranhas, eels and stingrays in an aquarium, and a swimming pool with waterchute, and breezy bar above. At **Playa Revolcadero** development is continuing, with new luxury hotels, new roads and landscaping; it is being called Acapulco Diamante. The hidden, sheltered beach of **Playa Angosta** offers a smaller, more secluded option a 15-minute walk from the centre.

The surf is dangerous on the beach west of the road and the beaches are unsafe at night.

At **Playa Icacos** there is a marineland amusement park **Ci-Ci** ⓘ *US$5.70 for whole day, daily 1000-1800*, with a waterslide, pool with wave-machine and arena with performing dolphins and sea-lions (nothing special). The boat trip across the beach to **Puerto Marqués** ⓘ *US$2 return (or 30 minutes by bus)*, is pleasant; you can hire small boats there for US$12 per hour. Bay cruises, 2½ hours, are available from Muelle Yates.

Acapulco Bay

0 metres 500
0 yards 500

Sleeping
Asturia **5**
Casa Blanca **1**
Coral **6**
Los Flamingos **3**

One sight that should not be missed in Acapulco is that of the amazing cliff divers at **La Quebrada** ⓘ *daily, US$2, at 1930, 2030, 2130 and 2230 for the best show at night diving with torches*, who plunge up to 45m into the water below, timing their dives to coincide with the incoming waves. **Hotel El Mirador Acapulco** offers a package including the show, drinks and food (US$15 at 1230 and US$18 in the evening).

A day trip south of Acapulco, east of the airport takes you to **Barra Vieja**, for great beaches and sunsets. Some *cabañas* and *palapas* are available, and the good **Sol y Mar** restaurant (try the *pescador a la talla,* BBQ fish with tropical herbs and spices) which also has a good pool. Other activities include horse riding, quad bikes and visiting a bird sanctuary with flamingoes. To get there take the bus from Costera Miguel Alemán to Puerto Marquez and connect with a bus US$0.40 or *colectivo* taxi US$0.80 to Barra Vieja, or take a taxi US$20, 30 minutes.

Coast northwest of Acapulco » *pp375-395.*

Pie de la Cuesta

Twelve kilometres northwest, Pie de la Cuesta is preferred by many budget travellers to Acapulco itself, but it is also commercialized. There are several bungalow-hotels and trailer parks (see Sleeping), a lagoon (six-hour boat trip US$5), and long, clean, sandy beaches. At Pie de la Cuesta you can swim and fish year round, drink *coco loco* (fortified coconut milk) and watch the sunset from a hammock.

Laguna Coyuca (also known as La Barra or Laguna Pie de la Cuesta), over 10 km long, 38 km northwest of Acapulco, has interesting birdlife, water hyacinths and tropical flowers and can be explored by motorboat. **Coyuca de Benítez,** near the Laguna Coyuca, is a market town selling exotic fruit, cheap hats and shoes. There is no bank but shops will change US dollars. Take a combi from town to La Barra on the lagoon. Pelicans fly by the lagoons, there are passing dolphins and plentiful sardines, and young boys seeking turtle eggs.

Zihuatanejo

→ *Phone code: 755. Colour map 3, C2.*

A beautiful fishing port with a good range of accommodation, and an increasingly popular alternative to the overdeveloped Cancún peninsula. It is 237 km northwest of Acapulco by Route 200, which goes via Barra de Navidad along the Pacific coast to Puerto Vallarta. Also more directly along the new highway from Mexico City through Ixtapa. The road to Ixtapa runs north through coconut plantations where the slightly alcoholic drink *tuba*, made from coconut milk fermented on the tree, is for sale.

Despite being spruced up, 'Zihua', as it is called locally, still retains much of its Mexican village charm. There is a handicraft market by the church, some beachside cafés and a small **Museo Arqueológico** ⓘ *Av 5 de Mayo, US$0.60,* in the old Customs and Immigration building. At sunset, thousands of swallows meet in the air above the local cinema in the centre of town and all settle for the night within the space of one minute on the telephone poles. The **Plaza de Toros** is at the town entrance with seasonal *corridas*. **Tourist information** ⓘ *T/F554-2001, www.ixtapa-zihuatanejo.com,* with bilingual assistance, is available from the Palacio Municipal.

There are five beaches in the bay, including **Playa La Madera**, near town and a bit dirty; better is **Playa La Ropa**, 20 minutes' walk from the centre, with the *Sotavento* and other hotels, and some beach restaurants. Also good is **Playa Las Gatas**, secluded, and a haven for aquatic sports. It can be reached by boat from the centre (US$3 return) or a 20-minute walk from La Ropa beach over fishermen-frequented

Zihuatanejo

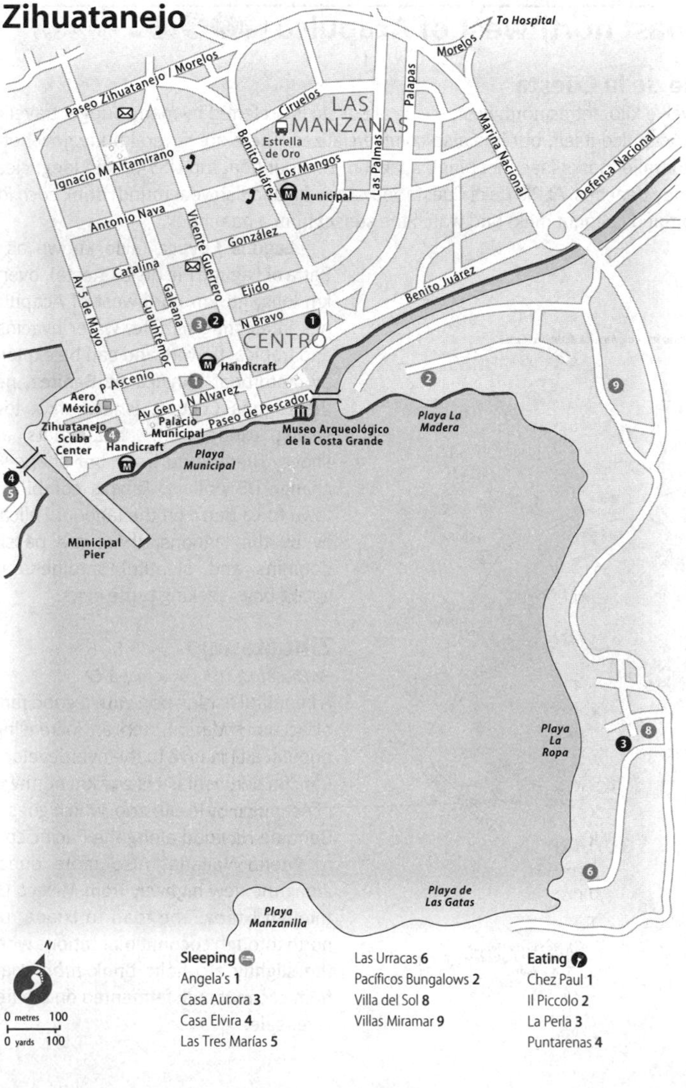

Sleeping
- Angela's 1
- Casa Aurora 3
- Casa Elvira 4
- Las Tres Marías 5
- Las Urracas 6
- Pacíficos Bungalows 2
- Villa del Sol 8
- Villas Miramar 9

Eating
- Chez Paul 1
- Il Piccolo 2
- La Perla 3
- Puntarenas 4

rocks. Off the coast there are rock formations, to which divers go, and **Isla Ixtapa**, a nature reserve with numerous restaurants. **Playa Linda**, to the north, is a beautiful beach (no hotels) easily reached by *colectivo* (30 minutes). The yacht, *Fandango Zihua*, takes bay cruises from the municipal pier.

Ixtapa → *Phone code: 755. Colour map 3, C2.*

From Zihuatanejo it's a short 7-km drive, bus journey (US$0.50 from Paseo Zihuatanejo/Morelos) or taxi (US$5), to Ixtapa, meaning 'where there are salt lakes'. The resort, developed on a large scale, boasts 14 beaches. There are turtles, many species of shellfish and fish, and pelicans at **El Morro de los Pericos**, which can be seen by launch. There is an island a few metres off **Playa Quieta**; boats go over at a cost of US$5. Ixtapa's large luxury hotels all obtain food supplies from Mexico City making food more expensive, as local supplies aren't guaranteed; there is also a shopping complex, two golf courses, waterski/parachute skiing and tennis courts and a a yacht marina. **Isla Grande** has been developed as a nature park and leisure resort. The **tourist office** ⓘ *T553-1967*, is in Ixtapa Shopping Plaza.

The beach can be dangerous with a strong undertow; small children should not be allowed in the sea alone. Also, there are crocodiles in the lagoons at the end of the beach.

Although paved Highway 134 leads directly from Mexico City and Toluca to Ixtapa, there is no fuel or other supplies after **Ciudad Altamirano** (188 km, pleasant motel on southwest edge of city with a/c). This road also runs through remote country, prone to landslides, and there is occasional bandit activity, with unpredictable army check-points (looking for guns and drugs).

After Ixtapa the coastal route continues northwest to Lázaro Cárdenas and Playa Azul in Michoacán (see page 283). The pleasant little beach town of **Troncones**, 20 km north of Ixtapa, has several restaurants and a hotel.

Sleeping

Acapulco *p346, map p347*
Most cheaper hotels are grouped around the Zócalo, especially on La Paz and Juárez. In the high season you should make reservations, at least for 1 night, before arriving. For the better hotels you can make reservations at the bus terminal in Mexico City. Take care with the numbering along the Costera Miguel Alemán; basically it means nothing, a better reference is to the beach names and major hotels.

LL Villa Vera Raquet Club, T484-0333, www.clubregina.com. A celebrity spot where Elvis once stayed.

AL El Mirador Acapulco, at the top next to the cliff divers, T482-1155, www.hotelelmiradoracapulco.com.mx. Hotel with a long tradition, great place to view the divers at La Quebrada, private seawater pool (no beach), a/c, some rooms with jacuzzi, restaurant and bar.

A Los Flamingos, Av López Mateos, T482-0690. One of the finest locations in Acapulco, glorious cliff-top views. In the 1950s it was a retreat for John Wayne, Johnny Weissmuller et al. Gardens, pool, restaurant, breakfast included.

B Casa Blanca, Cerro de la Pinzona, T483-5954. With swimming pool.

C Misión, Felipe Valle 12, close to Zócalo, T482-3643. Very clean, colonial.

D Acapulco, Benito Juárez 28, 3 blocks from Zócalo. Fan, TV, basic, more expensive with a/c and fridge, clean, friendly.

D Asturia, Quebrada 45, T483-6548. With bath, single rooms in low season, clean, very friendly, pool, free coffee, more expensive with a/c and TV, parking. Recommended.

D Coral, Quebrada 56, T482-0756. Good value, friendly, reasonably quiet, small pool.

D El Tropicano, Costera Miguel Alemán 150, on Playa Icacos, T484-1332. Clean, a/c, big garden, 2 pools, bars, restaurant, very friendly and helpful. Recommended.

D Olivieda, Costera Miguel Alemán 207, 1 block from Zócalo. Large 50s building, clean, fan, hot water, lift, great views from top rooms.

D-E California, La Paz 12, T482-2893, 1½ blocks west of Zócalo. English and French spoken, fan, hot water, pleasant rooms and patio, owner good source of information for sport fishing, good value.

E Acela, La Paz 29, T482-0661. With bath and fan, clean, safe, owner friendly and speaks English, family-run.

E Paola, Teniente Azueta, 2 blocks from Zócalo, T482-6243. Hot shower, fan, roof terrace with pool. Good staff and nice rooms, but cold showers and a bit noisy.

E Sagamar, Quebrada 51, T483-5053. With bath, basic, friendly, some English spoken, safe, clean, use mosquito coil.

E Santa Lucía, López Mateos 33, T482-0441. Family owned, will negotiate if not full, good value.

Camping

Acapulco West KDA, Barra de Coyuca. Beachfront, security patrol, pool, restaurant, hot showers, laundry, store, volleyball, basketball, Spanish classes, telephones.

Quinta Dora Pie de la Cuesta,13 km up the coast on Highway 200. *Palapas*, bathrooms, cold showers, hook-ups, US$12 for 2 plus car, US$4 just to sling hammock.

Trailer Park El Coloso, La Sabana. Small swimming pool, secure.

Trailer Park La Roca, on road from Puerto Marquez to La Sabana. Secure.

Pie de la Cuesta *p349*

B Puesta del Sol, Pie de la Cuesta, T460-0412. Pool and restaurant. Recommended.

C Villa Nirvana, Pie de la Cuesta. Canadian/Mexican owners (depending on season), with kitchen, clean, pool, good value. Recommended.

D Casa Blanca, Pie de la Cuesta. Rooms for 3; management are nice, food good.

D Centro Vacacional, Pie de la Cuesta. 0700-2400. The student organization **SETEJ** offers dormitory accommodation if you have a valid international student card.

Zihuatanejo *p349, map p350*

It's difficult to find accommodation in Mar and around Christmas and New Year.

LL Villa del Sol, Playa La Ropa, T555-5500, www.hotelvilladelsol.net. Beachfront suites, highly regarded award-winning hotel, 2 world-class restaurants, daily events, tennis courts, health and fitness centre and 4 pools.

AL Villas Miramar, Playa La Madera, T554-3350. Suites, 2 pools, lovely gardens.

A-B Pacíficos Bungalows, Zihuatenejo, T554-2112. Advance reservation necessary. Huge terrace with good views. Anita is very friendly, helpful and speaks English and German. Highly recommended.

B Las Urracas, Playa La Ropa, T554-2049. Cooking facilities, good value.

C Casa Aurora, Nicolás Bravo 42. Clean with bath and fan, more expensive with a/c and cable TV, not all rooms have hot water.

D Casa Elvira, Juan Alvarez, in older part of town on waterfront, T554-2061. Very basic hotel-restaurant, but clean, fan, with bath (cold water only), the restaurant is on the beachfront (the place to watch the world go by), good and reasonable.

D Las Tres Marías, La Noria 4, cross the wooden footbridge, T554-2191. Very pleasant with large communal balconies overlooking town and harbour, clean but sparsely decorated, tiny baths, nice plants, hotel has an **annexe** at Juan Alvarez 52, restaurant, similar rooms, slightly more expensive, best on 2nd floor, note that price doubles during Christmas holidays.

D Rosimar, Ejido, T554-2139. Quiet, hot water, TV, some with kitchen facilities.

E Angela's, Pedro Ascenio 10, T554-5084. New *hostal*, some dorm rooms, communal kitchen, fan, clean, owners Gregg and Angela Canadian/Mexican, friendly and helpful.

Ixtapa *p351*

LL-A Barcelo, Blv Ixtapa, T553-1858. With panoramic lift, reductions for AAA members. Recommended. Taxi between centre and main hotels, US$3.

LL-A Las Brisas, 5-min drive from downtown Ixtapa, T553-2121. Spectacular, in a small jungle.

Camping

Playa Linda Trailer Park, on Carretera Playa Linda at **Playa Linda Hotel**, just north of Ixtapa. 50 spaces, full hook-ups, restaurant, recreation hall, babysitters, on beach, US$14 for 2, comfortable.

Phone codes *Chilpancingo 747; Acapulco 744; Zihuatanejo 755; Iztapa 755.*

Eating

Acapulco *p346, map p347*

Fish dishes are a speciality of Acapulco. There are a number of variously priced restaurants along and opposite Playa Condesa, another group of restaurants along Playa Caleta walkway, and yet another group with mixed prices on the Costera opposite the **Costa Club Acapulco**. 250 or so to choose from. Many cheap restaurants in the blocks surrounding the Zócalo, especially along Juárez. As the coast road climbs south towards Las Brisas, there are a number of restaurants with truly spectacular views (particularly after dark) over the bay.

ΨΨΨ **Fairmont Acapulco Princess**. Sun lunch buffet, including champagne, seafood, goes until 1800, an event worth saving space for!

ΨΨΨ **Madeira**, Las Brisas. Recommended for its cuisine, its atmosphere and the view.

ΨΨΨ **Pipo's**, Almirante Breton 3 (off Costera near Zócalo). One of the first-established and best restaurants in Acapulco. Fine cuisine. There are 2 other branches: Costera and Plaza Canadá; and Calle Mahahual, Puerto Marquez.

ΨΨΨ-ΨΨ **El Amigo Miguel** (popular), Juárez 9, and across the road, near Zócalo. Fixed-menu lunch, good seafood.

ΨΨ **El Zorrito**, opposite the **Costa Club Acapulco**. Excellent local food with live music, a 2nd branch 1 block west (opposite the **Howard Johnson Hotel**) is open 24 hrs and very popular late after the clubs close.

ΨΨ **Italianissimo**. Near **Nachos**, decent pizza and garlic bread, average price for area.

ΨΨ **Su Casa**, Av Anahua 110. Moderately priced, with views, great margaritas under the stars.

ΨΨ-Ψ **El Mayab**, Costera Miguel Alemán 151. Good-value set meal. Recommended.

Zihuatanejo *p349, map p350*

Look out for cheaper dining near and in the market.

ΨΨΨ **Chez Paul**, Benito Juárez. International gourmet and sushi. Expensive but recommended.

ΨΨΨ-ΨΨ **El Patio**, 5 de Mayo, beside Catholic church. Excellent food and atmosphere, beautiful patio/garden, live music occasionally.

ΨΨ **Il Piccolo**, Nicolás Bravo 22. Restaurant and video bar, excellent value, good pizzas.

ΨΨ **Puntarenas**, close to **Hotel Las Tres Marías**. Excellent cooking, friendly, not expensive, popular, slow service.

ΨΨ **Stall 27** at marketplace. Very popular, cheap and good, try local lobster for about US$10; most meals cost around US$3.

ΨΨ-Ψ **La Perla**, Playa La Ropa. Very popular, good food, slow service.

Ixtapa *p351*

ΨΨΨ **Villa de la Selva**, T553-0362. Recommended for food and views, book in advance.

ΨΨ-Ψ **Two Fat & Tropical Boys**, Centro Comercial Los Arcos, T553-0160. A popular bar/restaurant, live music, varied menu.

Ψ **Super Tacos**, west of the commercial centre by the roundabout. Great hot sandwiches.

Entertainment

Acapulco *p346, map p347*

Bars and clubs

Acapulco has a superb, varied nightlife at the weekends, and every major hotel has at least 1 disco. Others worth trying include:

Baby O, towards the naval base on Costera Miguel Alemán.

Disco Beach, Costera Miguel Alemán, between the **Diana** and **Hotel Fiesta Americana Condesa**. By the beach, informal dress – open till 0500, good.

Close to the Zocaló a couple of options:

Karaoke, famous for its Les Girls-style show on Thu-Sat at 2300.

La Casa Blanca, La Paz 8. Bar popular with locals.

Las Puertas, behind the cathedral by stairs on Ramírez, disco and live music.

Mangos, Costera Miguel Alemán, American sports-style bar, popular, food.

Ixtapa *p351*

Bars and clubs

Every hotel without exception has at least 1 nightclub/disco and 2 bars.

Activities and tours

Zihuatanejo *p349, map p350*

See also Ixtapa, below.

Activities in the region are varied including **sailfishing**, with several operators found by the pier, and **scuba diving**. Hire of all equipment and guide from **Zihuatanejo Scuba Center**, T554-2147, www.divemexico.com, English spoken. Off Playa Las Gatas is an underwater wall built, according to one legend, by the Tarascan King Calzonzin, to keep the sharks away while he bathed; the wall is fairly massive and can be seen clearly while scuba diving. US$8 a day for mask, snorkel and fins. Other operators: **Zihua Scuba**, Juan Alvarez 41b, T554-8171, US$55 per tank, US$75 double dive, beginners course US$75. Also on the same street is **Nautilus Divers**, Juan N Alvarez 33, T554-9191, www.nautilus-divers.com, prices as above.

Ixtapa *p351*
Activities are numerous and much the same as for Zihuatanejo.
Adventours, Hotel Villas Paraíso, Ixtapa, T556-3322. Arranges walks, cycling, sea-kayaking, birdwatching and rappelling.
Ixtapa Aqua Paradise, Centro Comercial Los Patios, Local 137, T553-1510, www.ixtapa aquaparadise.com. Scuba diving; PADI diving courses, excursions and night dives.

Transport

Acapulco *p346, map p347*
Air
Direct international connections with many US cities, with charter flights from Europe in the summer. Good domestic connections including **Mexico City**, **Cd Juárez**, **Cuernavaca**, **Culiacán**, **Guadalajara**, **León**, **Monterrey**, **Puerto Vallarta** and **Tijuana**.

Airline offices AeroMéxico, T484-7009, and Mexicana, T484-1215, offices are in Torre Acapulco, Costera Miguel Alemán 1252. American, T466-9248. **Condor**, T800-524-6975. Delta, T800-902-2100. Taesa, T485-2488.

Bus
Local Several bus routes, with 1 running the full length of Costera Miguel Alemán linking the older part of town to the latest hotels, marked 'Caleta-Zócalo-Base', US$0.35, US$0.40 for the buses with a/c. Buses to **Pie de la Cuesta**, 12 km, US$0,40. From Ejido bus terminal to the Zócalo for the 'Zócalo-Caleta' bus.

Long distance There are 3 bus terminals. Grupo Estrella Blanca is on Av Ejido for **Puerto Escondido** and coastal destinations. Estrella Blanca's 1st-class terminal is 2 blocks from **Estrella de Oro**'s on Av Cuauhtémoc, behind Papagayo Park with buses for **Puebla**, **Cuernavaca**, **Guadalajara**, **Tijuana**, **Tampico** and Mexico City. **Mexico City**: 4-5 hrs (1st class or *plus*), 8 hrs (others); deluxe a/c express buses US$24 and super luxury US$37; ordinary bus, US$24 1st and US$26 *plus*. To **Zihuatanejo**: , every hr from 0420, 5 hrs, US$9. To **Taxco** US$14, 10 daily. To **Cuernavaca**, 6 hrs, US$14. To **Oaxaca**, no direct bus, change at Puerto Escondido or Pochutla (waiting room and luggage deposit at Pochutla); also via Pinotepa Nacional (at 2100) but worse road. Bus to **Puerto Escondido** every hr on the ½ hr from 0430-1630, plus 2300, 2400, 0200, 9½ hrs, US$21, and *directo* at 1330 and 2300, US$18, seats bookable, advisable to do so the day before, 7½ hrs. To **Tapachula**, take Impala 1st-class bus to **Huatulco**, arriving 1930; from there **Cristóbal Colón** at 2030 to **Salina Cruz**, arriving about midnight, then take 1st- or 2nd-class bus.

Taxi
US$20, 1 hr; sample fare: Zócalo to Playa Condesa US$2.50. Taxis are more expensive from bus terminal; walk ½ block round corner and catch one on the street, US$2 to Zócalo.

Zihuatanejo *p349, map p350*
Air
Ixtapa-Zihuatanejo international airport (ZIH), 20 km from town, T554-2070. Many direct domestic flights from **Mexico City** and **Guadalajara**, with other destinations by connection. International from **Houston**, **Los Angeles**, **Phoenix**, **San Francisco** and **Seattle**.
Airlines AeroMéxico, T554-2018; Delta (airport), T554-3386; **Mexicana**, Hotel Dorado Pacífico, Ixtapa, T322-0810.

Bus
Estrella de Oro operates its own terminal on Paseo Palmar, serving **Mexico City**, with services at 0640, 2000, 2210, 2300, 9 hrs, US$38. Services to **Acapulco** (4-5 hrs) calling at Petatlán and Tecpan de Galeana, at 0600,

0900, on the hour until 1800, US$11, and 0700, 0800 and 1300 (US$11.50). To **Lázaro Cárdenas**, 0630, 0830, 0930, 1200 then hourly until 2000, 2 hrs, US$4.50.
The **Central de Autobuses** is on the Zihuatanejo-Acapulco highway opposite Pemex station (bus from centre US$0.40); Estrella Blanca operates from here. The terminal is clean, with several snackbars and services.

To **Acapulco**, hourly, US$11-10. **Manzanillo**, US$22, **Colima**, US$45, 10 hrs, **Puerto Vallarta**, 1020 and 2235. To **Mexico City**, 0930, 1200, 2100, 2200 (superior class US$48), 2230, US$34. To **Laredo**, at 1730, 30 hrs, US$65. To **Lárazo Cárdenas**, hourly after 1230, US$4.70-5.50. To **Puerto Escondido** and **Huatulco**, at 1920, US$29 to US$34.

Car

Car hire Hertz, Nicolás Bravo and airport, T554-3050; several others with offices at the airport and in Ixtapa hotels including: **Avis**, **Budget**, **Dollar** and **Economy**.

Directory

Acapulco *p346, map p347*

Embassies and consulates Canada, T01-7-484-1305, Local 23, Centro Comercial Marbella, corner of Prolongación Farallón and Miguel Alemán, Mon-Fri 0900-1700. **France**, Av Costa Grande 235, T482-3394. **Germany**, Antón de Alaminos 46, T484-7437. **Holland**, El Presidente Hotel, T483-7148. **Norway**, Maralisa Hotel, T484-3525. **Spain**, Av Cuauhtémoc y Universidad 2, T485-7205. **Sweden**, Av Insurgentes 2, T485-2935. **UK** British Consul (Honorary), Lorraine Bajos, T484-1735. **USA**, Alexander Richard, Hotel Continental Emperial, T469-0505, 0900-1400.
Immigration Juan Sebastián el Cuno 1, Costa Azul el Lado, T484-9021, 0800-1400, take a 'Hornos Base' bus from Miguel Alemán, US$0.35, 30 mins, visa extensions possible.
Internet Cafés normally charge US$1 per hr, good speeds. **Laundry** Tintorería Bik, 5 de Mayo. **Lavadín**, José María Iglesias 11a, T482-2890, next to Hotel Colimense, recommended. **Post office** Costera, 2 blocks south of Zócalo. **Telephone** Public offices will not take collect calls; try from a big hotel (ask around, there will be a surcharge).

Oaxaca and the Isthmus

La Ciudad de Oaxaca is a lively, colourful and cosmopolitan city; a UNESCO World Heritage Site since 1987, where days can be spent wandering and very pleasant evenings can be spent people-watching from the terrace restaurants.

The Central Valleys, which surround the state capital, make a fine destination for several interesting day trips or overnight visits. The area features awe-inspiring archaeology (Monte Albán, Mitla and Yagul are but the best known of many sites), authentic native towns and villages, their people, markets, crafts and fiestas. And El Tule – the world's largest tree. There is good walking with impressive views throughout the region. The area has good public transport and excursions can easily be organized.

The 510 km of Oaxaca's Pacific coast, stretching from Guerrero to the west and Chiapas to the east, include some truly spectacular shoreline and provide varied opportunities for seaside recreation. Many beaches are still entirely virgin (accessible only on foot or by sea), while others are being developed for various tastes and to varying degrees; with one or two burnt out by overcrowding, pollution, drugs or crime. Huatulco is the best-known international resort on the Oaxaca coast, but there are many other popular areas including Puerto Escondido, Puerto Angel, Salina Cruz and their respective surroundings.

Travelling on to the Yucatán or Guatemala, you pass the Isthmus of Tehuantepec, a lowland region with a strong local culture, dominated by the Zapotecs. Often passed through, stop for a while if you like to visit the quieter spots. ▸▸ *For Sleeping, Eating and other listings, see page 375-395.*

Mexico City to Oaxaca

The express toll road from Mexico City to Oaxaca first runs generally eastwards to Puebla (see page 156), where it turns south to wind through wooded mountains at altitudes of between 1500 m and 1800 m, emerging at last into the warm, red-earth Oaxaca valley. It has been described as a stunning bus ride along a new motorway through cactus-filled valleys and plains. The route described here, however, avoids the new motorway in favour of the less sophisticated but equally attractive Route 190, which continues from Oaxaca to Tehuantepec. The road, although paved throughout and in good condition, serpentines unendingly over the sierras and is quite beautiful. The alternative coastal route is also very attractive and of special interest to visitors who wish to engage in the many watersports available. Buses on the new express toll road now take six hours from Mexico City to Oaxaca.

Atlixco → *Phone code: 244.*

Route 190 heads south from Puebla to Izúcar de Matamoros. A side road leads to **Huaquechula** where there's a 16th-century Renaissance and plateresque chapel. The road passes through Atlixco ('the place lying on the water'), which has interesting baroque examples in the **Capilla de la Tercera Orden de San Agustín** and **San Juan de Dios**. The annual **Atlixcayotl festival** is on San Miguel hill. Nearby are the curative springs of **Axocopán**.

Izúcar de Matamoros and around → *Phone code: 243. Colour map 3, C4.*

After Atlixco, Route 190 continues to the town of Izúcar de Matamoros (from *itzocan*, meaning his dirty face), famous for its clay handicrafts, the 16th-century convent of **Santo Domingo**, and two nearby spas, **Los Amatitlanes** (about 6 km away) and **Ojo de Carbón**.

A road leads southwest from Izúcar to **Axochiapan**, Morelos state and to a paved road to the village of **Jolalpan** with the baroque church of Santa María (1553). There are very few restaurants in Jolalpan; ask where you can get a meal. The bus from Axochiapan stops in front of the church in Jolalpan. The road (and bus) continues to **Atenango del Río** in Guerrero state, the last 20-30 km are unpaved.

Acatlán to Oaxaca

From Izúcar de Matamoros, Route 190 switchbacks to **Tehuitzingo**. Then the landscape is fairly flat to Acatlán, a friendly village where black and red clay figures, and palm and flower hats are made.

Carry on to Petlalcingo (restaurant), then ascend to **Huajuapan de León**, an important centre for palm products. To the southeast (12 km) is the Yosocuta Dam with fish farms and recreational facilities. Second-class bus from Oaxaca to Huajuapan, four a day, US$3.50.

After Huajuapan de León, Route 125 leads to **Pinotepa Nacional**. The next town on Route 190 is **Tamazulapan** with a 16th-century church and a pink stone arch in front of the city hall.

Yanhuitlán, 72 km northwest of Oaxaca on Route 190, has a beautiful 400-year-old church, part of the Santo Domingo monastery, built on a prehispanic platform; it is considered one of the best examples of 16th-century New World Hispanic architecture. Yanhuitlán is in the Sierra Mixteca, where Dominican friars began evangelizing in 1526. Two other important centres in the region were San Juan Bautista at **Coixtlahuaca** and the open chapel at Teposcolula. The scenery and the altars, the huge convents in such a remote area are a worthwhile day trip from Oaxaca. The new highway from **Nochixtlán** to Oaxaca (103 km) has been recommended for cyclists: wide hard shoulders and easy gradients.

Oaxaca city » pp375-395. Colour map 3, C5.

→ *Phone code: 951. Altitude: 1546 m.*

Founded by the Spanish as Antequera in 1521 on the site of a Zapotec and Mixtec settlement, Oaxaca gracefully combines its colonial and native roots. Fine stone buildings, churches, arcades and airy patios speak for its importance during the colonial period, while its markets, crafts, dances and feast days point to a more indigenous past. Relaxing with a coffee or beer on one of the many street cafés of Oaxaca, it's easy to while away the hours. Once you've explored the museums, catherdrals, markets and surrounding streets, you can sit down with another beer to plan your days exploring the surrounding hills and valleys.

Ins and outs

Getting there Aeropuerto Xoxocotlán (OAX) is 9 km south of the city. Airport taxis (*colectivos*) will take you into the city centre, US$9. The first-class bus terminal is northeast of the Zócalo on Calzada Niños Héroes (some second-class buses also leave from here). The second-class terminal is west of the Zócalo on Calzada Valerio Trujano, near the Central de Abastos market. **Autobuses Unidos** (AU) have its own terminal northwest of the Zócalo at Prolongación Madero.

Getting around Local town minibuses mostly charge US$0.20. For the first-class bus terminal, buses marked 'VW' leave from Avenida Juárez; for the second-class terminal, buses are marked 'Central'. Most of the important sites are in or near the city centre and can be reached on foot.

Tourist information **Sedetur Tourist Office** ⓘ *Murguía 206, T514-2548, daily 0800-2000, www.oaxaca.gob.mx*, with maps, posters, postcards and information; ask here about the **Tourist Yú'ù** hostel programme in local communities (see Sleeping, Route to Mitla, page 377). **Instituto Nacional de Estadística, Geografía e Informática (INEGI)** ⓘ *Emiliano Zapata No 316, corner of Escuela Naval Militar, T512-4823*, for topographic maps and information about the state. *Oaxaca Times*, English monthly, www.oaxacatimes.com; *Oaxaca*, monthly in Spanish, English and French; *Comunicación*, in Spanish, with a few articles translated into English and French; *Guía Cultural*, published monthly by the Instituto Oaxaqueño de las Culturas, has a complete listing of musical events, exhibitions, conferences, libraries, etc.

Safety Oaxaca is a generally safe city; however, sensible precautions are advised. The **Tourist police** ⓘ *Zócalo, near the cathedral*, are friendly and helpful; or you can contact the **Centro de Protección al Turista** ⓘ *T516-7280*.

Sights

The Zócalo with its arcades is the heart of town, a pleasant park with new paving around the central bandstand. It's a pleasant place to sit and watch the world from one of the street cafés, or take a stroll. It is always active, and the surrounding cafés and restaurants are always busy. Free music and dance events are often held in the evenings. In the daytime vendors sell food; in the evening they offer tourist wares. It is especially colourful on Saturday and Sunday nights when indigenous women weave and sell their goods.

The colourful markets and varied crafts of Oaxaca are among the main attractions of the region, see Shopping, page 384.

Avenida Independencia is the main street running east-west, the nicer part of the old city is to the north of it; a simpler area, housing the cheaper hotels, lies to the south. Independencia is also a dividing line for the north-south streets, which change names here. Calle Macedonia Alcalá is a cobbled pedestrian walkway, which joins the Zócalo with the church of Santo Domingo, many colonial buildings can be seen along this mall; this street and Calle Bustamante, its continuation to the south, are the dividing line for east-west streets, which change names here.

Oaxaca

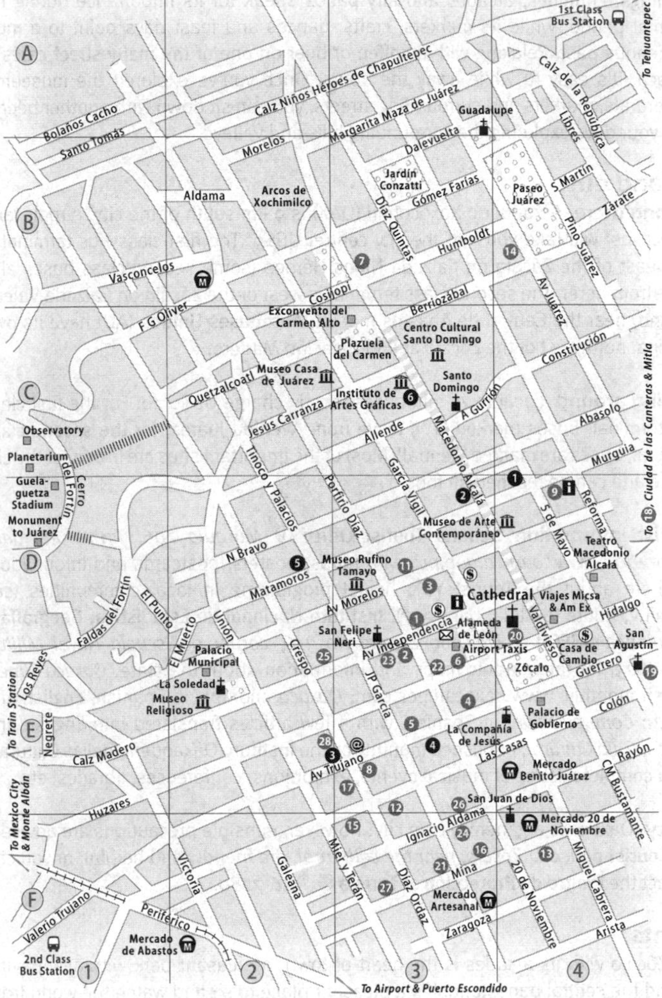

0 metres 200
0 yards 200

Sleeping
Antonio's **1** *D3*
Casa Cid de León **3** *D3*
Central **2** *E3*
Ferri **12** *E3*
Hostel Casantica **11** *D3*
La Cabaña **13** *F4*
La Casona del Llano **14** *B4*
Las Rosas **4** *E3*
Lupita **17** *E3*
Luz de Luna **18** *D4*
Magic Hostel **19** *E4*
Marqués del Valle **20** *D3*
Mesón del Rey **5** *E3*
Mina **16** *E3*
Monte Albán **6** *E3*
Palmar **21** *F3*
Parador San Andrés **22** *E3*
Parador Santo Domingo de Guzmán **7** *B3*
Paulina Youth Hostel **8** *E3*
Plata Gelatina **23** *E3*
Posada Catarina **24** *F3*
Posada del Centro **25** *E2*
Posada Don Matías **26** *E3*
Posada Las Casas **15** *F3*
Principal **9** *D4*
Rivera del Angel **27** *F3*
Valle de Oaxaca **28** *E2*

Eating
Café Alex **3** E2
El Naranjo **4** E3
Gaia **1** D4
Hostería de Alcalá **2** D3
La Crepe **2** D3
Manantial Vegetariano **5** *D2*
Pizza Nostrana **6** C3

Worth visiting is the **Palacio de Gobierno**, on the south side of the Zócalo; it has beautiful murals and entry is free. There are often political meetings or protests outside. The **Teatro Macedonio Alcalá** ⓘ *5 de Mayo with Independencia*, is an elegant theatre from Porfirio Díaz's times. It has a Louis XV-style entrance and white marble staircase; regular performances are held here. Visit also the **Arcos de Xochimilco** on García Vigil, starting at Cosijopi, some eight blocks north of the Zócalo. In this picturesque area are the remains of an aqueduct, cobbled passageways under the arches, flowers and shops. The house of the Maza family, for whom Benito Juárez worked and whose daughter he married, still stands at Independencia 1306 and is marked by a plaque. Porfirio Díaz birthplace is similarly remembered at the other end of Independencia, in a building that is now a kindergarten, near La Soledad. DH Lawrence wrote parts of *Mornings in Mexico* in Oaxaca, and revised *The Plumed Serpent*; the house he rented is on Pino Suárez. The bar **El Favorito**, on 20 de Noviembre, a couple of blocks south of the Zócalo, is supposedly the original that inspired Malcolm Lowry in his novel *Under the Volcano*.

There is a grand view from **Cerro de Fortín**, the hill to the northwest of the centre; here is the Guelaguetza amphitheatre; a monument to Juárez stands on a hillside below. Atop the hill are an observatory and **planetarium** ⓘ *shows Mon-Sat 1230 and 1900, Sun 1230, 1800 and 1900, US$20, students US$1*; best to take a taxi (about US$3.50) since the walk is dark and deserted. It is a pleasant walk from town to the hill as far as the planetarium and antennas, but muggings have been reported in the trails that go through the woods and the dirt road that goes beyond.

Ciudad de las Canteras, the quarries from where the stone for the city's monumental churches and public buildings was extracted, has been converted into a beautifully landscaped park. It is located on Calzada Niños Héroes de Chapultepec, at the east end of Calzada Eduardo Vasconcelos; several city bus lines go there. There is a small stadium here and the site of the **Expo Feria Oaxaca**, a fair with rides, craft exhibits, food and various live performances, held throughout the year (check in the tourist information office for details).

Churches

On the Zócalo is the 17th-century **cathedral** with a fine baroque façade (watch the raising and lowering of the Mexican flag daily at 0800 and 1800 beside the cathedral), but the best sight by far, about four blocks from the square up the pedestrianized Calle Macedonio Alcalá, is the church of **Santo Domingo** ⓘ *daily 0700-1300, 1700-2000, no flash photographs allowed*, with its adjoining monastery, now the Centro Cultural Santo Domingo (see below). The church is considered one of the best examples of baroque style in Mexico. It first opened to worship in 1608 and was refurbished in the 1950s. Its gold leaf has to be seen to be believed. The ceilings and walls, sculptured and painted white and gold, are stunningly beautiful.

The massive 17th-century **Basílica de La Soledad** (between Morelos and Independencia, west of Unión) has fine colonial ironwork and sculpture (including an exquisite Virgen de la Soledad). Its interior is predominantly fawn and gold; the plaques on the walls are painted like cross-sections of polished stone. The fine façade is made up of stone of different colours, pinks and greens; it is considered the best example of carved stonework in the city. The church was built on the site of the hermitage to San Sebastián; begun in 1582, it was recommenced in 1682 because of earthquakes. It was consecrated in 1690 and the convent was finished in 1697. The **Museo Religioso de la Soledad** ⓘ *Independencia 107, daily 1000-1745, US$0.35 donation requested*, at the back of the church, has a display of religious artefacts. In the small plaza outside the encircling wall, refreshments and offerings are sold. There are elaborate altars at the church of **San Felipe Neri** ⓘ *Av Independencia y García*. At **San Juan de Dios** ⓘ *20 de Noviembre y Aldama*, there is an indigenous version in paint of the conquistadors' arrival in Oaxaca and of an anti-Catholic uprising in 1700.

Guelaguetza or Lunes del Cerro

This impressive annual celebration in July is where all the colour and variety of Oaxaca's many different cultural groups come together in one place. For those with an interest in native costumes, music and dance, it must not be missed.

The word Guelaguetza originally means something like 'reciprocity' in Zapotec, the interchange of gifts or favours. Some elements of the celebration may well date from prehispanic times, however the contemporary event is a well-organized large-scale folklore festival.

The main event is a grand folk dance show held at the Guelaguetza stadium on the slopes of Cerro del Fortín, on Monday morning. The performance is lively and very colourful, with the city below serving as a spectacular backdrop.

Among the favourite presentations are always Flor de Piña, danced by women from the Tuxtepec area with a pineapple on their shoulder, and Danza de la Pluma, performed by men from the Central Valleys using enormous feather headdresses. The most elaborate costumes are those of the women from the Isthmus of Tehuantepec, including stiffly starched lace *resplandores* (halos) on their heads. At the end of each performance, gifts are thrown from the stage to the audience – watch out for the pineapples!

Los Lunes del Cerro are usually the last two Mondays in July. The performance begins 0900 ends around 1300. Tickets for seats in the lower galleries (A and B) are sold in advance through Sedetur and cost US$35. Details from the Oaxaca State Tourism Department, Murguía 206, Centro Histórico, Oaxaca, T(951) 514-8501, www.guelaguetza-oax.com. Advance tickets go on sale from early May. The upper galleries (C and D) are free, line up before 0600, gates open around 0700, the performance begins at 1000 and finishes around 1400. Take a sweater as it is chilly in the morning, but the sun is very strong later on. A sun hat and sun-screen are essential, a pair of binoculars is also helpful in the upper galleries. Drinks and snacks are sold.

In addition to the main event, there are scores of other happenings in Oaxaca at this time of year, ranging from professional cycling races to classical music concerts, a Feria del Mezcal, and several smaller celebrations in nearby villages. Many events are free and a complete programme is available from Sedetur.

On the Saturday before Lunes del Cerro, at around 1800, participating groups parade down the pedestrian mall on Macedonio Alcalá, from Santo Domingo to the Zócalo. This is a good opportunity to see their splendid costumes close up and to meet the participants. On Sunday is the election of the Diosa Centeotl (goddess of the new corn), who presides over the following week's festivities. Candidates are chosen based on their knowledge of native traditions.

On Monday night, following the Guelaguetza, the Donají legend is presented in an elaborate torchlight performance at the same stadium starting around 2000. Donají was a Zapotec princess who fell in love with a Mixtec prince, Nucano, and eventually gave her life for her people. Some claim that the two lovers are buried in the same grave in Cuilapan de Guerrero.

This was the first church in Oaxaca, originally dedicated to Santa Catalina Mártir. The church of **San Agustín** ⓘ *Armenta y López at Guerrero*, has a fine façade, with bas relief of St Augustine holding the City of God above adoring monks (apparently modelled on that of San Agustín in Mexico City, now the National Library). The church of **La Compañía de Jesús** ① *Trujano, diagonal to the Zócalo*, first built in 1579, has a wooden altarpiece; in the central niche is an image of the Virgin of the Immaculate Conception, hence it is also known as the **Iglesia de la Inmaculada**.

Museums

The **Centro Cultural Santo Domingo** is a cultural complex that includes a museum, exhibit halls, botanical garden, library, newspaper archives and bookstore; concerts are also performed here. It is housed in the former convent of Santo Domingo (Macedonio Alcalá y Gurrión), next to the Santo Domingo church. Construction of the convent started in 1575. It was occupied by the Dominican friars from 1608 to 1812. After the expulsion of the church it was occupied by the Mexican army between 1812 and 1972; later it housed the regional museum. Between 1994 and 1998, the convent was very beautifully restored, using only original materials and techniques. The **Museo de las Culturas de Oaxaca** ① *Tue-Sun, 1000-1900, US$3.80, use of video US$3*, housed in the Centro Cultural Santo Domingo, and sometimes referred to as 'the Louvre of Oaxaca', is a superb museum that requires at least four hours to visit; exhibits are beautifully displayed and explained in Spanish (with plans to implement a system of recorded explanations in other languages); highly recommended. Fourteen galleries cover the history of Oaxaca from prehispanic times to the contemporary period; the archaeology collection includes spectacular riches found in Tomb 7 of Monte Albán. There are also exhibits of different aspects of Oaxacan culture, such as crafts, cooking, traditional medicine etc, as well as temporary exhibits.

Also in the Centro Cultural is the interesting **Jardín Etnobotánico** ① *free guided tours in Spanish daily at 1300 and 1800, in English Tue, Thu and Sat at 1100 and 1600, 1 hr, sign up in advance*. This garden aims to preserve different species of plants that are native to southern Mexico and have played and continue to play a role in the lives of different ethnic groups in Oaxaca; you can learn about the different species of *agaves* used to make mezcal, pulque and tequila; the trees used to make crafts; the *grana cochinilla*, an insect that lives in certain cacti and is used to dye cloth; the plants used in folk medicine; and many more species.

The **Instituto de Artes Gráficas de Oaxaca** (IAGO) ① *Alcalá 507, 0900-2000, closed Tue, free, but a donation is appreciated*, housed in an 18th-century building, is almost opposite the Centro Cultural. It has interesting exhibition rooms, a very good reference library and beautiful courtyards filled with flowers.

The **Museo de Arte Contemporáneo** ① *Alcalá 202, 1030-2000, closed Tue, US$1*, a good exhibition with library and café is housed in a late 17th-century house with a stone façade. The **Museo de Arte Prehispánico Rufino Tamayo** ① *Morelos 503, Mon, Wed-Sat 1000-1400, 1600-1900, Sun 1000-1500, US$3* has an outstanding display of pre-Columbian artefacts dating from 1250 BC to AD 1100, donated by the Oaxacan painter Rufino Tamayo in 1974. Information is in Spanish only and is not comprehensive. The **Museo Casa de Juárez** ① *García Vigil 609, Tue-Sat 1000-1730, Sun 1000-1700, US$3* is where Benito Juárez lived. It contains some of his possessions, historical documents and some bookbinding tools. The **Museo de Filatelia** ① *Reforma 504, Tue-Sun 1000-1930, free*, has temporary exhibits, a philatelic library and tours by appointment.

Monte Albán

→ *Colour map 3, C5.*

① *Daily 0800-1800, US$4.50. A charge of US$3 is made to use video cameras; fees for the guides who hang around the site are variable, ask several of them and beware of overcharging. Monte Albán receives many visitors during high season. Most people go in the morning, so it may be easier to catch the afternoon bus.* »» *To get there, see Transport, page 390.*

Monte Albán is situated about 10 km (20 minutes) west of Oaxaca, on a hilltop dominating the surrounding valley. The ruins were declared a UNESCO World Heritage Site in 1987, and additional restoration was carried out between 1992 and 1994, when a museum and visitors' centre were built. Monte Albán features pyramids, walls, terraces, tombs, staircases and sculptures of the ancient capital of the Zapotec culture.

There are tri-lingual (Spanish, English and Zapotec) signs throughout the site. From the ruins at Monte Albán there are paths leading to the valleys below.

Although the city of Monte Albán extended far beyond the confines of the **Main Plaza**, it is this that archaeologists, art historians, historians and tourists have looked to, when assessing and interpreting the raison d'être of this fascinating site. Constructed 400 m up a steep mountain, without immediate access to water or cultivable land, the Main Plaza has at times been considered the site of a regional marketplace or ceremonial centre. The marketplace theory becomes less convincing when access to the site is considered: not only would the visitor have had to haul merchandise up the back-breaking hill, but entrance to the plaza was severely restricted. The modern access roads did not exist in ancient times and the only way into the site was through three narrow passageways, which could easily have been guarded to restrict entry. The modern ramp cuts across what was the ball court to the southeast of the **North Platform**. The space at the centre of the Main Plaza would seem ideal for religious ceremonies and rituals: the absence of religious iconography contradicts this interpretation. The imagery at Monte Albán is almost exclusively militaristic, with allusions to tortured captives and captured settlements.

To the right, before getting to the ruins, is **Tomb 7**, where a fabulous treasure trove was found in 1932; most items are in the Centro Cultural Santo Domingo in Oaxaca and the entrance is closed off by a locked gate. **Tomb 172** has been left exactly as it was found, with skeleton and urns still in place, but these are not visible. Tombs 7 and 172 are permanently closed.

If you're in reasonable shape consider hiring a bike for the day, and enjoy the ride down at least.

The site **museum** is good, exhibiting stone glyphs and sculptures as well as smaller artefacts; explanations are in Spanish only, and flash photography is prohibited. Informative literature and videos in several languages are sold in the bookstore in the visitors' centre, which also houses a small restaurant.

The Main Plaza

The Main Plaza at Monte Albán is delineated north and south by the two largest structures in the city, which have been interpreted as palace and/or public building (North Platform) and temple (South Platform). Apart from these two impressive structures, the ball court and the arrow-shaped building in front of the South Platform, the Main Plaza has 14 other structures, six along the west side of the Plaza, three in the middle and five along the east side. One structure, known as Edificio de los Danzantes (Dancers), has bas reliefs, glyphs and calendar signs (probably 5th century BC). During the period AD 450-600, Monte Albán had 14 districts beyond the confines of the Main Plaza: it has been proposed that each of the 14 structures located within the Main Plaza corresponded with one of the districts outside. Each pertained to a distinct ethnic group or polity, brought together to create a pan-regional confederacy or league. The arrow-shaped structure functioned as a military showcase; it also has astronomical connotations.

The Confederacy

The presence of a number of structures in or bordering the Main Plaza that housed representatives of distinct ethnic groups supports the theory that Monte Albán came into being as the site of a confederacy or league. Its neutral position, unrelated to any single polity, lends credence to this suggestion. The absence of religious iconography, which might have favoured one group over the others, emphasizes the secular role of the area, while the presence of the Danzantes sculptures suggests a trophy-gathering group. However, although Monte Albán may have served defensive purposes, the presence of the Danzantes and the captured town glyphs argues for an

Monte Albán

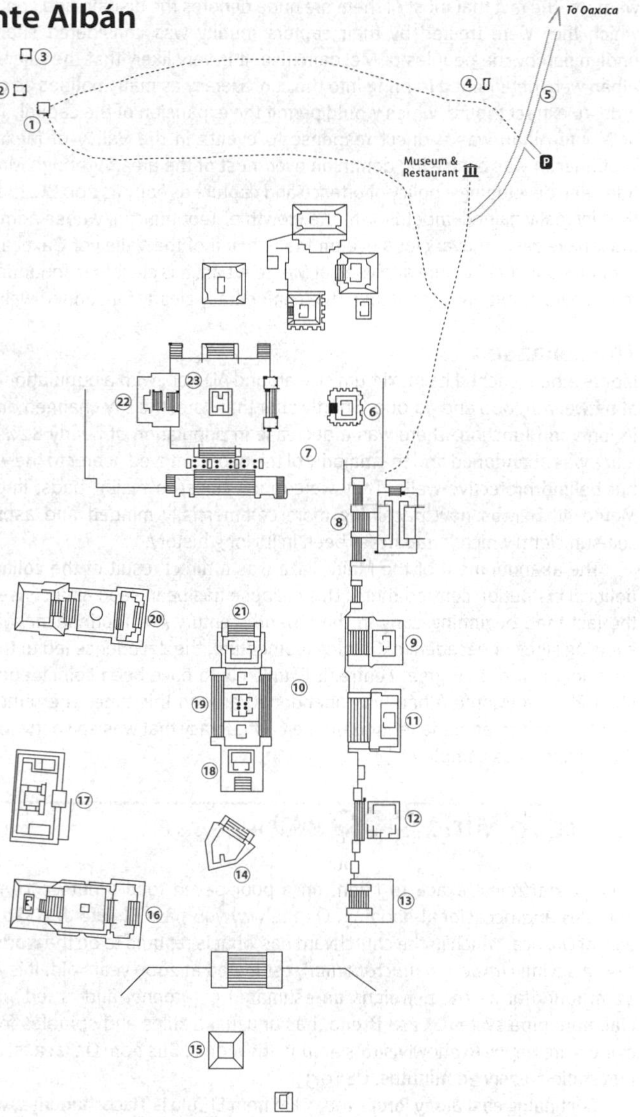

Tomb 104 **1**
Tomb 103 **2**
Tomb 172 **3**
Tomb 7 **4**
Tomb 105 **5**
Mound A **6**
North Platform **7**
Ball Court **8**
Building U **9**
Chapel **10**
Building P **11**
Palace (Building S) **12**
Building Q **13**
Observatory (Building J) **14**
South Platform **15**
Complex M **16**
Building of the Dancers (with Building L superimposed) **17**
Building I **18**
Building H **19**
Complex IV **20**
Building G **21**
Building B **22**
Sunken Patio **23**

N
0 metres 50
0 yards 50

offensive and expansionist role. In all, about 310 stone slabs depicting captives, some of whom are sexually mutilated with streams of blood (flowers) flowing from the mutilated parts, have been found. Some of these woeful captives are identified by name glyphs, which imply hostilities against a settlement and the capture of its warriors. The fact that most of them are nude denotes the disdain and contempt with which they were treated by their captors: nudity was considered shameful and undignified by the peoples of Mesoamerica. It is very likely that the rulers of Monte Albán were determined to bring into the confederacy as many polities as possible in order to extract tribute, which would permit the expansion of the capital. The growth of Monte Albán was a direct response to events in the Valley of Mexico, where Teotihuacán was exercising dominion over most of the area. Although Monte Albán had been developing a policy of offence and capture as early as 200 BC, the growth of the city really gained impetus with the growth of Teotihuacán, whose administrators must have cast an avaricious eye on the rich soil of the Valley of Oaxaca. From the ceramics and architecture analysed at Monte Albán, it is clear that Teotihuacán never realized its ambitions in that area; the confederacy clearly functioned well.

The collapse

Monte Albán reached its maximum size around AD 600, with a population estimated at between 15,000 and 30,000. Shortly after that date, the city changed dramatically in form and function. There was a decrease in population of nearly 82%, the Main Plaza was abandoned and the majority of the people moved nearer to the valley floor, but behind protective walls. They were much closer to major roads, implying that Monte Albán was now becoming more commercially minded and aspired to be self-sufficient, which it had never been in its long history.

The abandonment of the Main Plaza was a direct result of the collapse of the political institution centred there. This collapse has been seen as a consequence of the fact that, beginning early in the seventh century AD, Teotihuacán was already showing signs of decadence. Gaining momentum, the decadence led to the massive abandonment of that great centre. It is unlikely to have been coincidental that the Main Plaza at Monte Albán was abandoned around this time. The removal of the Teotihuacán threat made redundant the Confederacy that was so costly to maintain: the collapse was complete.

Route to Mitla » *pp375-395.*

It is 42 km from Oaxaca to Mitla, on a poor paved road (Route 190) with many potholes and occasional flooding. On the way you pass **El Tule** ⓘ *US$0.35*, 12 km east of Oaxaca, which in the churchyard has what is reputed to be the **world's largest tree**, a savino (*Taxodium mucronatum*), estimated at 2000 years old. It is 40 m high, 42 m round at its base, weighs an estimated 550 tonne, and is fed water by an elaborate pipe system. **Casa Breno**, has unusual textiles and spindles for sale, the owners are happy to show visitors around the looms. Bus from Oaxaca, second-class bus station, every 30 minutes, US$0.35.

Continuing east along Route 190, 5 km from El Tule is **Tlacochahuaya**, with a 16th-century **church** ⓘ *US$0.45*, and vivid indigenous murals; visit the cloisters at the back and see the decorated organ upstairs. Bus from Oaxaca second-class terminal, US$0.35.

Teotitlán del Valle

Another 5 km further, a paved road leads off Route 190 to Teotitlán del Valle, where wall hangings and *tapetes* (rugs) are woven, and which is now becoming rather touristy. There is an artesans' market near the church, and a **Museo Comunitario** ⓘ *Mon-Sat 1000-1800, US$0.50*. The best prices for weavings are to be had at the stores along the road as you come into town, but they may be even cheaper in Oaxaca where competition is stronger. Make sure you know whether you are getting all wool or a mixture and check the quality. A well-made rug will not ripple when unfolded on the floor. Buses leave every hour from 0700-2100, from second-class bus terminal (US$0.45); the second-class bus may provide the contacts you need to buy all the weavings you want! From the town of Teotitlán del Valle you can walk up to the nearby hills across the river or hike north to the town of Benito Juárez.

Tlacolula → *Colour map 3, C5.*

Tlacolula has a most interesting Sunday market and the renowned Capilla del Santo Cristo in the church. The chapel is similar in style to Santo Domingo in Oaxaca, with intricate white and gold stucco, lots of mirrors, silver altar rails and sculptures of martyrs in gruesome detail. Two beheaded saints guard the door to the main nave (**Fiesta**: 9 October). There is a pleasant walled garden in front of the church. A band plays from 1930 every evening in the plaza (take a sweater, cold wind most evenings). On the main street by Parque Juárez is **Casa de Cambio Guelaguetza**, cash only, fair rates. The townspeople are renowned for their mezcal preparation. The indoor market next to the church is very interesting. Between the church and the market you might see a local lady selling dried grasshoppers! Tlacolula can be reached by bus from Oaxaca, from the second-class bus station every 10 minutes, daily 0600-1900, US$1.10. Taxis stop by the church, except on Sunday when they gather on a street behind the church; ask directions. Tlacolula's bus station is just off the main highway, several blocks from the centre; pickpockets are common here, be especially careful at the Sunday market and in the scrum to board the bus.

Santa Ana del Valle

Quality weavings can be found at Santa Ana del Valle (3 km from Tlacolula). The village is peaceful and friendly with a small museum showing ancient textile

Around Oaxaca

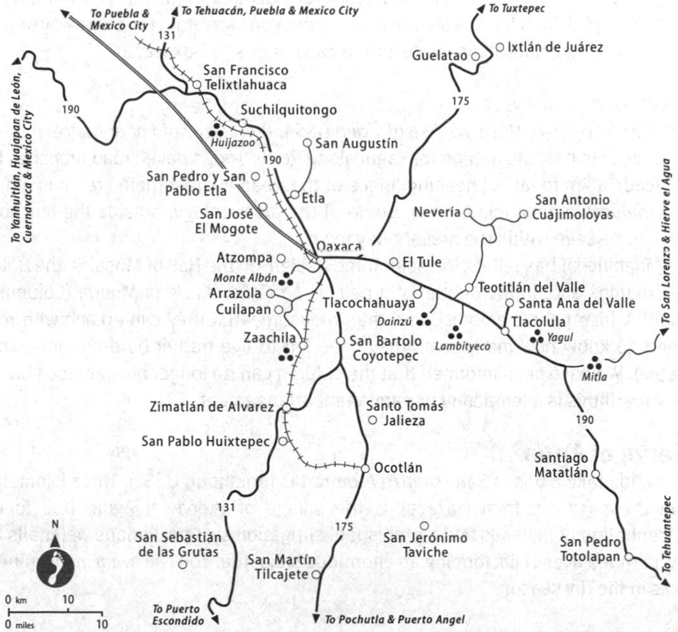

The Zapotecs

The Zapotec language is used by over 300,000 people in the state as a first or second language (about 20% of Oaxaca State population speaks only an indigenous language). The Zapotec people, who weave fantastic toys of grass, have a dance, the Jarabe Tlacolula Zandunga, performed by barefoot girls splendid in most becoming coifs, short, brightly coloured skirts, ribbons and long lace petticoats, while the men, all in white with colourful handkerchiefs, dance opposite them with their hands behind their backs. Only women, from Tehuantepec or Juchitán, dance the slow and stately Zandunga, costumes gorgeously embroidered on velvet blouse, full skirts with white pleated and starched lace ruffles and huipil.

techniques; ask any villager for the keyholder. There are two fiestas, each lasting three days. One takes place the second week of August, the other at the end of January. Buses leave from Tlacolula every 30 minutes.

Yagul

ⓘ *Daily 0800-1700, US$2.70. Tours in English on Tue, US$15, from Oaxaca agencies.*

Further east along Route 190 is the turn-off north for Yagul, an outstandingly picturesque archaeological site where the ball courts and priests' quarters are set in a landscape punctuated by candelabra cactus and agave. Yagul was a large Zapotec and later Mixtec religious centre. The ball court is said to be the second largest discovered in Mesoamerica; it also one of the most perfect discovered to date. There are fine tombs (take the path from behind the ruins, the last part is steep) and temples, and a superb view from the hill behind the ruins. Recommended. Take a bus to Mitla from the Oaxaca second-class terminal (see below) and ask to be put down at the paved turn-off to Yagul (five minutes after Tlacolula terminal). You will have to walk 1 km uphill from the bus stop to the site and you can return the same way or walk 3 km west to Tlacolula along Route 190 to catch a bus to Oaxaca.

Mitla → *Phone code: 951. Colour map 3, C5.*

ⓘ *Daily 0800-1700, US$2.70, use of video US$3, literature sold at entrance.*

A further 5 km past the turn-off for Yagul along Route 190, a paved road branches left and leads 4 km to Mitla (meaning 'place of the dead') where there are ruins of four great palaces among minor ones. Some of the archaeology, outside the fenced-in site, can be seen within the present-day town.

Magnificent bas-reliefs, the sculptured designs in the Hall of Mosaics, the Hall of the Columns and, in the depths of a palace, *La Columna de la Muerte* (Column of Death), which people embrace and then measure what they can't reach with their fingers to know how many years they have left to live (rather hard on long-armed people). We have been informed that the column can no longer be embraced but do not know if this is a temporary or permanent arrangement.

Hierve el Agua

From Mitla take a bus to San Lorenzo Albarradas (one hour, US$1). Three kilometres from there (57 km from Oaxaca) is the village of Hierve el Agua. Due to the concentration of minerals and a prehispanic irrigation system, various waterfalls are now petrified over a cliff, forming an enormous stalactite. You can swim in the mineral pools in the dry season.

South of Oaxaca

Along Route 175 to Pochutla are several towns that specialize in the production of different crafts. **San Bartolo Coyotepec**, 12 km southeast of Oaxaca, is known for its black pottery. Doña Rosa de Nieto accidentally discovered the technique for the black-glazed ceramics in the 1930s, and her family continues the tradition, as do many other potters in town. **San Martín Tilcajete**, 21 km from Oaxaca, 1 km west of the main road, is the centre for the *alebrije* production, animals carved from copal wood, painted in bright colours and often having a supernatural look to them. **Santo Tomás Jalieza** is the centre for cotton and wool textiles, produced with backstrap looms and natural dyes in the surrounding villages. Market day is Friday.

Cuilapan de Guerrero

In Cuilapan, 12 km southwest of Oaxaca, there is a vast unfinished 16th-century **convent** ⓘ *daily 0900-1700, US$2.20*, now in ruins, with a famous nave and columns, and an 'open chapel', whose roof collapsed in an earthquake. The last Zapotec princess, Donaji, daughter of the last ruler Cosijoeza, married a Mixtec prince at Tilantengo and was buried at Cuilapan. On the grave is an inscription with their Christian names, Mariana Cortez and Diego Aguilar. Reached by bus from Oaxaca from second-class bus station, on Calle Bustamante, near Arista (US$0.50).

North of Cuilapan and 6 km west of the main road is **San Antonio Arrazola**, another town where *alebrijes*, mythical animals made of copal wood are sold by the artisans. **Zaachila** ⓘ *daily 0800-1700, US$2.20*, 5 km beyond Cuilapan, was the last capital of the Zapotec empire. Today this town still maintains some of its ancestral traditions in the local cooking (several restaurants). There is black pottery production, and market day is Thursday. Here are the partially excavated ruins of Zaachila, with two Mixtec tombs; the outer chamber has owls in stucco work and there are carved human figures with skulls for heads inside. Take bus to Zaachila (US$0.60), which leaves every 30 minutes, then walk to unexcavated ruins in the valley.

Eighty kilometres south on Route 131 is **San Sebastián de las Grutas** ⓘ *guide obligatory, US$2*, about 10 km northwest of El Vado, off the main road, where there is a system of caves. One 400-m-long cave, with five chambers up to 70 m high, has been explored and is open to visitors. Ask for a guide at the Agencia Municipal next to the church. Take a **Solteca** bus bound for Sola de Vega or San Pedro del Alto, from the second-class terminal, leaves 0500, 0600, 1100, 1400 and returns 0600, 0700, 0800, 1200 – you may find that this will more than likely leave you high and dry! Also note there are no hotels but camping is possible.

North of Oaxaca ▸▸ *pp375-395.*

San Felipe del Agua

Oaxaca is a growing hotbed of ecotourism, with many options for tours. For good hikes, take local bus to San Felipe del Agua, north of the city. To the left of where the buses stop at the end of the line is a car parking area, just below it starts a dirt road; follow this road and in five minutes you will reach the San Felipe Park entrance and a booth where you register with the guard. Several trails fan out from here; one follows the river valley, it goes by some picnic areas and a swimming pool, continues upstream crossing the river several times before reaching a waterfall in about one hour. There are longer walks to the mountain to the north, crossing through several vegetation zones, from low dry shrub to pleasant pine forest; allow five or six hours to reach the summit.

Santa María Atzompa

At Santa María Atzompa, 8 km northwest of Oaxaca, at the foot of Monte Albán, green glazed and terracotta ceramics are produced. You can see the artisans at work; their wares are sold at **La Casa del Artesano**. Buses leave from the second-class terminal.

Etla Valley

The Etla Valley, along which Route 190 runs, had a number of important settlements in prehispanic times. Seventeen kilometres along this road and 2 km to the west is **San José el Mogote**, an important centre before the rise of Monte Albán; there is a small museum housing the artefacts found at this site. **San Pedro y San Pablo Etla**, 19 km from Oaxaca, has an important Wednesday market specializing in Oaxacan foods such as *quesillo* (string cheese), *tasajo* (dried meat) and different types of bread; the town has a 17th-century church and convent. At **Santiago Suchilquitongo**, 27 km from Oaxaca and atop a hill, are the ruins of **Huijazoo**, once an important centre that controlled the trade between the Central Valleys and the Cañada region; the local museum has a reproduction of a Huijazoo polychromatic mural, which has been compared to those at Bonampak (see page 412). The town of **San Agustín Etla** (turn-off east from Route 190 at Guadalupe Etla) was once an important industrial centre and in the 19th century it had two large cotton mills; with the introduction of synthetic fibres came a decline to this area. Since 1998, the town has found a new use for the cotton and other natural fibres available in the region, with the production of handmade paper for artists. Cotton, agave fibres, pineapple, nettle, ash, limestone and other raw materials are used in the workshop, which welcomes visitors. Further information from the Instituto de Artes Gráficas on Alcalá 507 in Oaxaca city.

Sierra Juárez

The Sierra Norte or Sierra Juárez is a region of beautiful landscapes and great biological diversity; seven of the nine types of vegetation that exist in Mexico can be found in this area. The region is starting to develop ecotourism with community participation; permits are required to camp on community land. The mountains gradually drop to the Papaloapan valley to the north. There are two access roads, Route 175 from Oaxaca to Tuxtepec, and the small roads that go north from Route 190, past Teotitlán and Santa Ana del Valle (see page 364). The Oaxaca-Tuxtepec road has been recommended as exhilarating for cyclists.

Oaxaca coast » *pp375-395.*

Puerto Escondido → *Phone code: 954. Colour map 3, B5.*

The town and its surroundings offer some stunningly beautiful beaches with world-class surfing, good facilities for visitors, and the town is a good base for various interesting excursions. Sadly, however, Puerto Escondido is at risk of becoming a case study in unsustainable tourism development. It was a small and sleepy fishing village as recently as the 1980s, until the population rapidly increased, perhaps in response to grandiose plans for Acapulco-style development. These never panned out and tourism instead developed low-rise and haphazardly, creating considerable environmental and social impact. The state tourist police now patrol both the main beach and tourist areas on quad bikes. They are English speaking and helpful.

At present, Puerto Escondido is a bustling and very commercial seaside resort. El Adoquín, the city's pedestrian tourist mall along Avenida Pérez Gasga near the beach teems with vacationing Mexican families in season, sunburnt foreigners and hard-core surfies throughout the year; December to January are the most crowded, May to June are the quietest (and hottest) months. A handful of luxury hotels and resorts are clustered above Playa Bacocho. Playa Zicatela, home to the Mexican Pipeline, is where surfers and their crowd hang out, with the majority of tourist facilities found in the vicinity of **El Adoquín**.

The real town, where prices are lower and there is less of a hard-sell atmosphere, is located up the hill on the other side of the highway. There is an ample selection of hotels and restaurants in all areas. Many fast-talking '*amigos*' are found at all the nearby beaches and other sites frequented by tourists offering an impressive array of goods and services for sale or hire; be polite and friendly (as are most of the vendors) but also wary, since there is no shortage of overpricing and trickery. **Sedetur information kiosk** ⓘ *at the west end of El Adoquín, ginainpuerto@yahoo.com*, is run by Gina Machorro, a very helpful, friendly person who is knowledgeable about the town and the region. She speaks English, Spanish and French, giving a two-hour walking tour of Puerto Escondido on Wednesday and Saturday, US$18.

Safety Even with the vast improvements in security, safety is an especially important issue in and around Puerto Escondido. A safe and pleasant stay here is possible with the appropriate precautions, but carelessness can have the most severe consequences. Never walk on any beach at night, alone or in groups. The ocean currents at Zicatela can be treacherous and although there are life guards now paid by the government, there are easier ways to meet them than getting drowned.

The **Playa Principal**, abutting El Adoquín pedestrian mall, has the calmest water but it is very close to the city and not clean. A few fishermen still bring in the catch of the day here and a small pier is being built for them and the tourist craft, which offer sport fishing and excursions to nearby bays and beaches. Immediately to the south is **Playa Marinero**, with slightly stronger surf (reportedly a good place for beginners), also built

Puerto Escondido

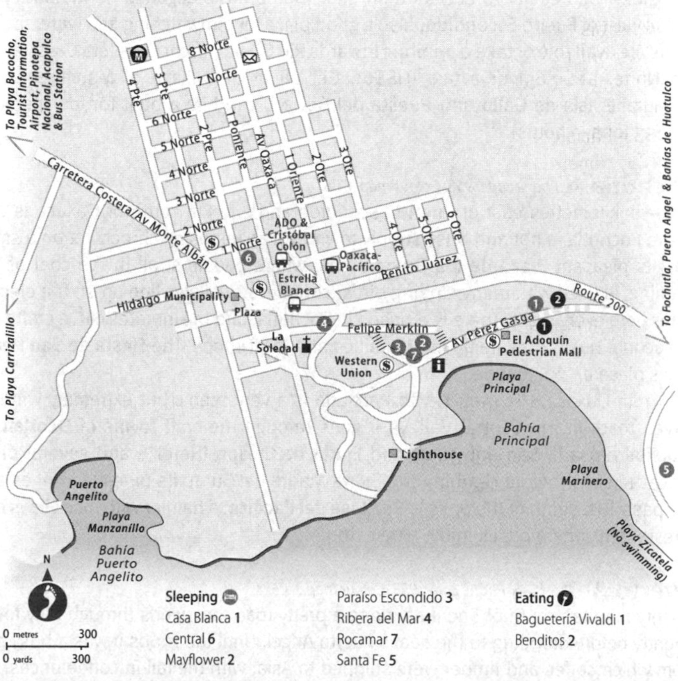

up with hotels, bars and restaurants. Further south, past a rocky point called Rocas del Morro, lies the long expanse of **Playa Zicatela**, which claims to be the best surfing beach in Mexico, with the Mexican Pipeline producing the fastest-breaking waves, at times over 12 foot high, anywhere in the world. It makes for breath-taking viewing. It is suitable only for experienced surfers and very dangerous for swimming. To the west of the main bay, past a lovely headland (being built up with condominiums) and a lighthouse, are a series of picturesque bays and beaches, all accessible by road or boat from town. **Playa Manzanillo** and **Puerto Angelito** share the Bahía Puerto Angelito and are the closest, an easy 15-minute walk; they are pretty with reasonably safe swimming but very commercial; every square millimetre of shade is proprietary here. Further west is **Playa Carrizalillo**, with swimming and more gentle surfing than Zicatela, accessible along a steep path, or by boat or taxi. **Playa Bacocho** is next, a long beautiful stretch of less developed beach, where the ocean, alas, is too dangerous for swimming.

Around Puerto Escondido

Seventy-four kilometres west of Puerto Escondido is the 140,000-ha **Parque Nacional Lagunas de Chacahua**, a wildlife refuge of sand dunes, interconnected lagoons, mangroves and forest. La Pastoría is the largest lagoon, connected to the sea by an estuary; it has nine islets that harbour thousands of birds, both resident and migratory. On the shores of the lagoon is the village of Chacahua, home to some of the area's small Afro-Mexican population. There is a crocodile hatchery nearby, aimed at preserving this native species. A tour is the easiest way to see the park and learn about its wildlife (see Activities and tours). To go independently you need two days; take a bus to Río Grande (from Carretera Costera and 3a Norte), then another one to Zapotalito from where there are boats (US$4.50 per person if there are enough passengers) to the village of Chacahua. If you plan to stay the night, take a mosquito net.

Closer and easier to access than Chacahua are the **Lagunas de Manialtepec**, 16 km west of Puerto Escondido, also a good place for birdwatching and watersports. Tours are available or take a minibus towards Río Grande (from Carretera Costera and 3ra Norte, US$0.65) or a taxi (US$6). Get off at the village of Manialtepec; at restaurants **Isla de Gallo** and **Puesta del Sol** you can hire a boat for four persons (US$33 for two hours).

Pochutla → *Phone code: 958. Colour map 3, C5.*

Sixty-six kilometres east of Puerto Escondido and 240 km south of Oaxaca is San Pedro Pochutla, a hot and busy supply town with an imposing church set on a small hill. Its pleasant **Plaza de las Golondrinas**, where people stroll in the cool of the evening, is filled with many singing birds; countless swallows line up on the electric wires here every night. There is a prison in Pochutla, and the inmates carve crafts out of coconut husks for sale by their families and local shops. The **Fiesta de San Pedro** takes place on 29-30 June.

From Oaxaca, Highway 175 to Pochutla is a very scenic but extremely winding paved road. In the Central Valleys it goes through the craft towns of **Ocotlán de Morelos** (**Posada San Salvador**) and **Ejutla de Crespo** (**Hotel 6** and several other places to stay), before climbing the Sierra Madre del Sur to its pine-clad ridges and the pass. Just south of the pass is **San José del Pacífico**, a hamlet with nice views and a restaurant where buses make a rest stop.

Puerto Angel → *Phone code: 958. Colour map 3, C5.*

Twenty minutes south of Pochutla along a pretty road that winds through hilly forest country before dropping to the sea is Puerto Angel. Until the 1960s it was a busy port from which coffee and timber were shipped to Asia; with the fall in coffee prices, the

Oaxacan cooking

The food of the state of Oaxaca is a fine representation of the complexity and variety of its cultures. The region's cuisine ranges from sublime to highly unusual.

A stroll through any of Oaxaca's markets will quickly bring you into contact with vendors selling *chapulines*. These small grasshopper-like creatures are fried, turning them bright red, and then served with lime. Another interesting ingredient in the diet is gusanito, a small red worm that is used to make a special sauce or ground with salt to accompany mezcal.

There are local curiosities for vegetarians as well. Flor de calabaza, squash flowers, are used in soup, empanadas, or as a garnish. Soup is also prepared from nopales, the young leaves of the prickly-pear cactus.

The most typical regional snacks are tlayudas, huge crispy tortillas, covered with a variety of toppings (beef, sausage, beans or cheese) and grilled over the coals. Oaxacan string cheese, known as quesillo, is also famous, as is the area's excellent chocolate, best enjoyed as a hot beverage. A slightly fermented drink made from corn flour is known as atole.

Barbacoa is a pork, lamb or beef dish combining several different types of chillies and special condiments such as avocado leaves. The colour of the resulting sauce is a very deep red, reminiscent of another platter appropriately called mancha manteles (tablecloth stain).

The essence of Oaxacan cooking, however, and the recipes for which the state is most famous, are its many moles, which come in all colours of the rainbow. They are served as sauces accompanying beef, chicken, turkey or pork. The most complex by far is mole negro (black), combining at least 17 different ingredients including cocoa beans and sesame seeds. Mole colorado (red), or just coloradito, is also very typical and quite spicy. Almendrado (also red) is milder and slightly sweet. Mole verde (green) is a bit tangy, while mole amarillo (yellow) rounds out Oaxaca's culinary chromatic spectrum.

local population turned to selling turtle skins until 1990, when this activity was banned in Mexico. Tourism and fishing are currently the main economic activities here. The town lies above a beautiful flask-shaped bay; unfortunately the turquoise water is polluted, but there are hopes for improvement if a planned sewage system is installed. Because of its lovely setting it has been described as 'the ideal place to rest and do nothing'. The beach, right in town, is an ideal spot to watch the activity of the small charming dock. A short walk away, either along the road or on a concrete path built on the rocks (not safe at night), is **Playa del Panteón**, a small beach in a lovely setting, but crowded with restaurants (touts await visitors on arrival) and many bathers in season. There are cleaner and more tranquil nearby beaches east of town. **Estacahuite**, with simple *cabañas*, 1 km from town, about a 20-minute walk, has good snorkelling (gear rental from hut selling drinks and snacks) but beware of strong waves, currents and sharp coral that can cut you; La Boquilla, with comfortable Canadian-run bungalows, is 3 km away, off a signed track on the road to Pochutla. There is a fiesta on 1 June to celebrate the **Día de la Marina** and another on 1 October, the **Fiesta de San Angel**.

Zipolite and San Agustinillo

Four kilometres west of Puerto Angel is Zipolite, one of the few nude beaches in Mexico and once an inspirationally beautiful spot that still attracts many foreign visitors. Sadly, a few years ago, it became a veritable Paradise Lost, notorious for drugs, crime and violence, including murder. Things seem to be cleaning up a little, and the interest is recovering. The beach here is very steeply shelved and there are dangerous undercurrents, especially near the rocks at the east end.

Another 3 km west lies **San Agustinillo**, a long, pretty beach, with an extraordinary cave in the cliffs. The western end is quite built up with private homes. Swimming is safest at the west end of the beach, surfing best near the centre. Nude bathing is prohibited.

Mazunte

One kilometre further west is Mazunte, perhaps the least developed major beach in the area but rapidly changing, so responsible tourism is especially important here (see Responsible tourism, page 38). The beach is on federal land and drug laws are strictly enforced here; nude bathing is prohibited, the safest swimming is at either end of the bay. At the east end of Mazunte is the **Centro Mexicano de la Tortuga** ⓘ *guided tours in Spanish and English, Tue-Sat 1000-1630, Sun 1000-1430, US$2, children under 12 US$1, crowded with tour buses from Huatulco 1100-1300 during high season; interested researchers may contact the director at http://centromexicanodelatortuga.org*, a government institute that studies sea turtles and works to conserve these frequently endangered species, as well as to educate visitors and the local population. There are interesting viewing tanks to observe many species of turtles underwater. A trail leads from the west end of the beach to **Punta Cometa**, a spit of land with lovely views of the thundering breakers below, a popular spot to view the sunset, well worth the 30-minute walk.

La Ventanilla

Two kilometres west of Mazunte is a signed turn-off for Ventanilla. It is 1.5 km from here to the village and visitors' information centre on the shores of a lagoon. Tours are run by local residents who are working on a mangrove reforestation project (in 1997 Hurricane Pauline wiped out part of the mangroves here) and have a crocodile farm to repopulate the area. The tour combines a rowing boat ride through the mangroves for up to 10 people, a visit to the crocodile farm and a walk on the beach, US$3.25 per person, many birds, crocodiles and iguanas may be seen; the guides speak Spanish only. Recommended. Horse riding tours along the beach are also available for US$5.40 per hour. Those wishing to spend the night can camp or stay with a family. Simple meals are available in the village.

Huatulco → *Phone code: 958. Colour map 3, C5.*

East of Pochutla (50 km, one hour), and 112 km west of Salina Cruz on the coast road is Huatulco, a meticulously engineered and environmentally aware resort complex surrounded by 34,000 ha of forest reserve and nine splendid bays (where pirate ships used to shelter). It offers golf, swimming pools, international and Mexican cuisine, nightlife, beaches, watersports, excursions into the forest and exploration of archaeological sites. The product is safe, clean, efficient, an international vacation resort in a lovely setting with a mild Mexican flavour. Huatulco's high seasons include Holy Week, July-August and November-March, with regular charter flights from the USA and Canada during the latter months; prices can as much as double during these periods.

The Sedetur tourist office ⓘ *Blv Benito Juárez, Tangolunda, T/F581-0176, sedetur6@oaxaca.gob.mx*, is near the golf course, helpful and informative. An auxiliary **information booth** ⓘ *Parque Central*, a *Crucecita*, run by Señor Cipriano, is a handy alternative source of information. Two other useful **websites** are *hotels.baysofhuatulco.com.mx* and *www.baysofhuatulco.com.mx*.

The Huatulco complex encompasses several interconnected towns and development areas; and there are many taxis (US$2), some of which operate as *colectivos* (US$0.40). **Tangolunda** (meaning beautiful woman in Zapotec), on the bay of the same name and also known as the Zona Hotelera, is set aside for large luxury hotels and resorts; it also has the golf course and the most expensive restaurants, souvenir shops and nightlife. **Chahué**, on the next bay west, where development only began in 1999, has a town park with spa and beach club, a marina and a few hotels. Further west (6 km from Tangolunda) is **Santa Cruz Huatulco**, once an ancient Zapotec settlement and Mexico's most important Pacific port during the 16th century (later abandoned). It has the marina where tour boats leave for excursions, as well as facilities for visiting yachts, several upscale hotels, restaurants, shops and a few luxury homes. An open-air chapel by the beach here, the Capilla de la Santa Cruz, is attractive; nearby is a well-groomed park.

La Crucecita, located 2 km inland, is the functional hub of the Huatulco complex, with housing for the area's employees, bus stations, banks, a small market, ordinary shops, bars, plus the more economical hotels and restaurants. It also doubles as a Mexican town, which the tourists can visit, more cosmetic by the manicured Plaza Principal, less so towards the highway. The old-looking but brand-new Templo de Guadalupe church stands on a small hill next to the plaza.

Huatulco's coastline extends for almost 30 km between the Río Copalita to the east and the Río Coyula to the west. Hills covered in deciduous forest – very green during the rainy season (June-September), yellow and parched in the dry – sweep down to the sea. Nine turquoise bays with 36 golden beaches line the shore, some bays have road access while others can only be reached by sea.

For boat trips and other activities, *see page 387.*

Around Huatulco

In the Huatulco area the **Sierra Madre del Sur** mountains drop from the highest point in the state of Oaxaca (3750 m) right down to the sea. There are ample opportunities for day-hiking, see Activities and tours. In the hills north of Huatulco are a number of coffee plantations that can be visited. Huatulco travel agencies arrange for full-day plantation tours, which include a meal with traditional dishes at the farm and bathing in fresh water springs or waterfalls; US$44 per person.

Take extra care in the sea as the currents are very dangerous. Also watch your belongings.

Day trips to the different coastal attractions to the west, including Puerto Angel, Mazunte and Puerto Escondido, are offered by travel agencies for US$20. Much ground is covered so it is a long day.

Bays of Huatulco

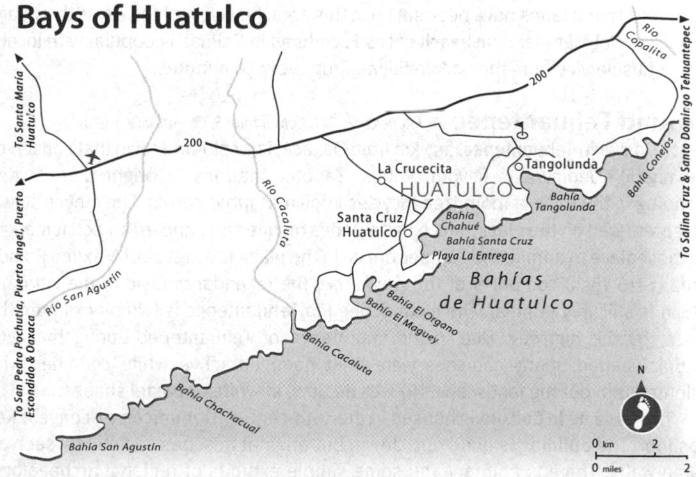

Isthmus of Tehuantepec

» pp375-395. Colour map 3, C6.

From the city of Oaxaca, Route 190 heads southeast, through the towns of **San José de Gracia** and **El Camarón** (see Sleeping, page 375), towards the Golfo de Tehuantepec and the Pacific.

Only about 210 km separate the Atlantic and the Pacific at the hot, once heavily jungled Isthmus of Tehuantepec, where the land does not rise more than 250 m. This narrowest point of Mexico is also the geographic boundary between North and Central America. There is the Trans-Isthmian Highway between Salina Cruz and Coatzacoalcos, the terminal cities on the two oceans. The regional airport at **Ciudad Ixtepec** has flights to Oaxaca and Mexico City.

The Isthmus has a strong cultural character all of its own. The people are *mestizo* and descendants of several different indigenous groups, but Zapotecs predominate. Once a matriarchal society, Zapotec women continue to play a very important role in local affairs. Their typical dress is most intricate and beautiful, and they are high-pressure saleswomen. The men, for the most part, work in the fields, or as potters or weavers, or at the Salina Cruz oil refinery.

The Isthmian region of Oaxaca is dominated by three neighbouring cities: **Salina Cruz** is a modern industrial city and port; **Tehuantepec** is the smallest and most authentic; while **Juchitán** has the largest and most interesting market. The climate throughout the area can be oppressive, very hot and quite humid, hence the region's cultural events usually take place late in the evening. Winds are very strong on and near the Isthmus, due to the intermingling of Pacific and Caribbean weather systems.

Salina Cruz

→ *Phone code: 971. Colour map 3, C6.*

A modern and industrial city and port, with broad avenues and a large central plaza. Salina Cruz is surrounded by hills and many poor neighbourhoods. Some of the nearby beaches are quite scenic but oil pollution, high winds, dangerous surf and sharks all conspire against would-be bathers. Do not park close to the beach, as your vehicle may be sandblasted.

Ten kilometres to the southeast is a picturesque fishing village with **La Ventosa** beach, which, as the name says, is windy. In 1528 the Spanish conquerors established a shipyard here; the old lighthouse, **El Faro de Cortés**, can still be seen. Buses go to the beach every 30 minutes from a corner of the main square.

The coast west of Salina Cruz is quite scenic, with several high sand dunes and lagoons; shrimp farms have been set up in this area. Just west of the city is the village of Salinas del Marquez; the beach of **Las Escolleras** in Salinas is popular with locals. Urban bus service from the park in Salina Cruz every 30 minutes.

Around Tehuantepec

→ *Phone code: 971. Colour map 3, C6. Altitude: 150 m.*

Santo Domingo Tehuantepec, 257 km from Oaxaca, is a colourful town that conserves the region's indigenous flavour. Robust Zapotec matrons in bright dresses ride standing in the back of motorized tricycles known as *moto-carros*. Life moves slowly here, centered on the plaza, which has arcades on one side, and an adjacent market, the best place to admire the Zapotec dress. In the plaza is a statue of Máximo Ramón Ortiz (1816-1855) composer of the *zandunga*, the legendary music of the Isthmus, which is still very popular. The meandering Río Tehuantepec is two blocks from the plaza, by the highway. Due to the importance of Tehuantepec during the early colonial period, many churches were built here; attractive white churches with coloured trim dot the landscape. Houses are low, in white or pastel shades.

The **Casa de la Cultura** is housed in the 16th-century Dominican ex-convent Rey Cosijopi. The building is quite run down, but original frescoes can still be seen on some walls. There is a library and some simple exhibits of regional archaeology, history and costumes. Ask the caretaker to open the exhibits for you. The **Museo Casa de la Señora Juana C Romero** is a chalet built entirely with materials brought from France; Señora Romero's great-granddaughter lives there today, ask for permission to visit the house.

There are two tourist offices, **SEDETUR** ⓘ *Carretera Transístmica 7, 2nd floor, opposite the petrol station, T715-1236*, the regional office for the Isthmus and the **Regiduría de Turismo** ⓘ *Palacio de Gobierno.*

Around Tehuantepec

To the northwest of town, off the road to Oaxaca, are the unrestored ruins of **Guiengola**, 'the Mexican Machu Picchu', so called because of its lonely location on a mountain. It has walls up to 3 m high, running, it is said, for 40 km; there are the remains of two pyramids and a ball court. This last fortress of the Zapotecs was never conquered (*guiengola* is the Zapotec word for fortress); Alvarado and his forces marched past it in 1522. Take the 0500 bus from Tehuantepec towards Oaxaca and get off at the Puente las Tejas bridge (8 km from Tehuantepec); this is the last place to buy water on the way to the ruins. Take the turning at the signpost 'Ruinas Guiengola 7 km'. Walk 5 km then turn left, uphill, to the car park. From here it is 1½ hours' walk to the ruins, there are no facilities or entry fees. Try to return before 0900 because it gets very hot; take plenty of water. Alternatively, take a taxi to the car park and ask the driver to return for you three hours later (US$5.50 each trip).

Juchitán and around → *Phone code: 971. Colour map 3, C6.*

Twenty-seven kilometres from Tehuantepec is the larger and more modern city of Juchitán de Zaragoza, an important commercial and cultural centre on the Isthmus. It has a nice plaza next to impressive colonial municipal buildings and many churches including that of **San Vicente Ferrer**, the city's patron saint. Many Zapotec women here still wear traditional costumes as everyday dress. The **tourist office** is at the Palacio de Gobierno. The **Mercado Central 5 de Septiembre** is the largest market on the Isthmus; traditional barter still takes place here. The meat and produce section is dirty, but the crafts section on the second floor is well worth a visit; this is the best place to see the elaborate embroidered Zapotec dresses which sell for up to US$600.

South of Juchitán and stretching for some 100 km to the east are three very large, shallow lagoons. On the shores of Laguna Superior, the closest one, 10 km south of the city, is the fishing village of **Playa Vicente**; across from here are several scenic islands. In Laguna Mar Muerto, the furthest one to the east, there are salt pans.

Sleeping

Oaxaca *p357, map p358*
There are over 160 hotels in Oaxaca in all price categories. If you wish to stay at a particular hotel reservations are recom mended during peak holiday periods (Easter, Jul-Aug, Christmas and New Year).

There are many cheap hotels in the block formed by the streets Mina, Zaragoza, Díaz Ordaz and JP García; also on Trujano 4 blocks from the Zócalo).

LL Casa Cid de León, Av Morelos 602, 2 blocks from the Zócalo, T514-1893, www.mexicoboutiquehotels.com/ciddeleo n.Intimate and charming with a fine terrace.

AL Casa Conzatti, Gómez Farías 218, T513-8500, www.oaxacalive.com/conzatti. 45 rooms in refurbished colonial house, a/c, safety deposit box, exchange, restaurant.

AL Hostel Casantica, Av Morelos 601, T516-2673, www.hotelcasantica.com. Beautifully restored former convent set around 2 elegant courtyards, the smaller of which has a modest pool. The café/restaurant serves good coffee, but service can be painfully slow.

AL Marqués del Valle, Portal de Clavería, right on the Zócalo by cathedral, T514-0688, www.hotelmarquesdelvalle.com.mx. Modern colonial style, clean, friendly, good restaurant on the plaza. Recommended.

A Parador Santo Domingo de Guzmán, Alcalá 804, T/F514-2171, www.paradorsto domingo.com.mx. An all-suite hotel with secure car parking, pool, cable TV. Suites have bedroom, sitting room and kitchen, daily maid included. Recommended.

A Posada Catarina, Aldama 325, T516-4270, www.hotelesdeoaxaca.com. Modern colonial, comfortable, parking. Good value.

B Ferri, Las Casas 405, T514-5290. Modern, comfortable, clean, spacious, secure parking. Recommended.

B La Casona del Llano, Juárez 701, T514-7719. Nice location across from Paseo Juárez, pleasant, restaurant.

B Las Rosas, Trujano 112. Old charm, nice patio, clean, excellent, quiet, friendly, good view from roof.

B Mesón del Rey, Trujano 212, 1 block from Zócalo, T516-0033. Clean, modern, fan, quiet except for street-facing rooms, good value, restaurant.

B Monte Albán, Alameda de León 1, T516-2777. Friendly, colonial style, opposite cathedral, daily folk dance performances (see Entertainment page 383).

B Parador San Andrés, Hidalgo 405, 2 blocks from the Zócalo, T/F514-1011, paradorsanandres@prodigy.net.mx. Comfortable, colonial style, nice courtyard, new in 1999, very pleasant.

B Rivera del Angel, Francisco Javier Mina 518, T516-6666. Large and busy hotel in good condition. Swimming pool and volleyball court. Popular with Mexicans.

B-C Antonio's, Independencia 601, 1 block from Zócalo, T516-7227. Colonial patio, hot water, spotless, good restaurant, but closed in evening.

C Posada del Centro, Independencia 403, T/F516-1874, posadabb@prodigy.net.mx. Modern colonial, nice, spotless, cheaper with shared bath.

C Posada Don Matías, Aldama 316, T/F501-0084. New, homely, beautiful patio, tastefully decorated, clean. Recommended.

C Principal, 5 de Mayo 208, 2 blocks from the Zócalo, T/F516-2535. Colonial house, very clean, private shower, morning coffee and cookies included. English spoken, very friendly, rooms overlooking street are a bit noisy but still heavily booked.

C-D Valle de Oaxaca, Díaz Ordaz 208, T516-3707, luivalle@prodigy.net.mx. Clean, comfortable, table soccer, good restaurant.

D Don Mario, Cosijopi 219 and Rufino Tamayo, T514-2012. Clean, former house of artist Rufino Tamayo, internet service, close to ex-convent of Santo Domingo.

D Hostal Pochon, Callejón del Carmen 102, T516-1322, www.hostalpochon.com. 6 dormitories and a couple of private rooms, just a couple of mins from the Zócalo. Use of kitchen, internet, good friendly atmosphere. Recommended.

D Palmar, JP García 504 y Mina, T516-4335. Cheaper without bath, convenient, friendly, family-run, hot water in morning, safe motorcycle parking.

D Posada Las Casas, Las Casas 507 y Díaz Ordaz, T516-2325. Clean, with bath, cheaper without bath, normally friendly, good value.

D-E Central, 20 de Noviembre 104, 1 block from the Zócalo, T514-9425. With bath, hot water, good value but very noisy, fills up early.

D-E La Cabaña, Mina 203, T516-5918. With bath, cheaper without, safe, clean but noisy, good value.

E Lupita, Díaz Ordaz 314, T516-5733. Large, pleasant rooms, upstairs rooms are bright with brilliant views across the city and mountains from the flat rooftop.

E Mina, Mina 304, T516-4966. Shared bath, hot water, clean, basic, good value.

E-F Luz de Luna, Juárez 101, T516-9576, www.geocities.com/luznuyoo. New and funky, kitchen, courtyard, dorm rooms, live music on occasion, hammocks and tents on terrace cheaper.

C-E Paulina Youth Hostal, Trujano 321, T516-2005, www.paulinahostel.com. Dorms and private rooms. Friendly and spotlessly gleaming with garden. Will store luggage, cheaper with Youth Hostal or ISIC cards. English spoken.

F Magic Hostel, Fiallo 305, T516-7667, www.magichostel.com.mx. Popular and full of tourists, friendly, kitchen and laundry facilities, stores luggage, internet access, purified water, good place to meet travellers. Good breakfast.

Phone codes *Atlixco 244; Izúcar de Matamoros 243; Oaxaca 951; Mitla 951; Puerto Escondido 954; Pochutla 958; Puerto Angel 958; Huatulco 958; Salina Cruz 971; Tehuantepec 971; Juchitlán 971.*

F Plata Gelatina, 1 block from Zócalo, Independencia 504, T514-9391. Funky atmosphere, clean, baggage storage, internet access, Mexican owned.

Camping

Oaxaca Trailer Park, Violeta 900, Col Reforma, north of town off the road to Mitla at a sign marked 'Infonavit' (corner of Pinos and Violetas). US$4.50 for a tent, US$6 for a camper van, secure; bus 'Carmen-Infonavit' from downtown.

Route to Mitla *p364*

In 13 towns, throughout the Central Valleys around Oaxaca, including Tlcolula, there are tourist accommodations known as **Tourist Yú'ù** run by local communities (**F** per person, US$2.70 to camp). Each house has a room with 6 beds, equipped kitchen, bathroom with hot water. For details contact the Sedetur office, see page 357.

D Hotel y Restaurante La Zapoteca, Mitla, before bridge on road to ruins, T958-0026. Private bath, hot water, parking, friendly, good food.

D Hotel y Restaurante Mitla, Mitla town square, T958-0112. Private bath, simple, clean, friendly, local food.

Puerto Escondido *p368, map p369*

Puerto Escondido and Playa Zicatela have more than 100 hotels in all categories.

L-AL Aldea del Bazar, Benito Juárez 7, T582-0508. A veritable Sultan's palace, complete with Middle Eastern dress for the staff, huge garden with palms, pool, large rooms, good restaurant. Recommended.

AL Santa Fe, Calle del Moro, Playa Zicatela, T582-0170. A/c, pool, very good food, including vegetarian.

A Paraíso Escondido, Unión 10, Centro, T582-0444. Away from beach, a/c, pool, colonial style; restaurant open in high season.

B Barlovento, Camino al Faro 3, Centro, T582-0220. Pool, fridge, very comfortable, on the way to the lighthouse.

B Casa Blanca, Av Pérez Gasga 905 (Adoquín), T582-0168. A/c in some rooms, fan, hot water, clean, well furnished, balconies and a pool.

B-C Bungalows Casa del Mar, Retorno A6, Fraccionamiento Bacocho, T/F582-2377. Equipped bungalows.

C Ben Zaa, 3a Sur 303, T582-0523, on hill climbing to the lighthouse. Fan, hot water, pool.

C Bungalows Acuario, Calle del Moro, Playa Marinero, T582-0357. Cheaper with shared bath, pool, gym, scuba diving centre, the first in the area to treat its waste water.

C Bungalows Zicatela, Calle del Moro, Playa Zicatela, T/F582-0798. A/c, cheaper with fan, fridge, pool, small restaurant.

C Inés, Calle del Moro, Playa Zicatela, T582-0792. Fan, hot water, pool, restaurant.

C Rincón del Pacífico, Av Pérez Gasga 900 (Adoquín), T582-0193. Hot water, beach bar, restaurant, very popular, always full.

C Rocamar, Av Pérez Gasga 601, T582-0339. Upper rooms with a/c and balcony, hot water, restaurant.

D Bungalows Villa Marinero, Carretera Costera, Playa Zicatela, T582-0180. On seafront, kitchen/eating area, pool, friendly.

D Casa Loma, Camino al Faro opposite Escuela Las Primeras Luces, on road to lighthouse. Cook prepares meals on request (including your catch).

D Castillo de Reyes, Av Pérez Gasga 210, T582-0442. Clean, nice rooms, hot water, quiet, good beds, friendly, good value. Highly recommended.

D Central, 2 Pte between 1 Norte and Hidalgo, in bus terminal area, T/F582-0116. Clean, friendly.

D Cocoa Beach, de los Fundadores s/n, also access from Felipe Merklin, T582-0428, behind the church. Small rooms, mosquito nets, family-run.

D Mayflower, Andador Libertad, T582-1755, on pedestrian walkway perpendicular to El Adoquín. With bath, fan, kitchen facilities, pool table (**F** per person in dormitory), friendly, good value, showers and luggage storage for non-guests. English and German spoken. Recommended.

E Casa de Huéspedes San Martín, 1a Oriente 106, Centro, T582-0883. Basic, private bath, fan, clean, close to bus stations.

E Girasol, Av Oaxaca 403, T/F582-1168, in bus station area. With bath, fan, parking. Many other economic hotels in the Centro, near the bus station as well as bungalows and cabins on Playa Zicatela.

E Ribera del Mar, Felipe Merklin 205, T/F582-0436, behind Iglesia de la Soledad.

Fan, hot water, clean, quiet, laundry facilities, some rooms with great views of the sea. Good value.

E **Rockaway**, Calle del Moro, Zicatela, T582-0668. Popular hangout with hippie twist and a well-maintained pool.

Camping

Trailer Park Neptuno, Av Pérez Gasga, T582-3668, on waterfront. Space for vehicles, tents and hammocks, pool, cold showers, electricity, run-down, US$5 per car with 2 people.

Trailer Park Palmas de Cortés, Av Pérez Gasga y Andador Azucena, T582-0774. Clean bathrooms, shade, US$3 per car, US$4 per person. Recommended.

Pochutla *p370*

C **Izala**, Lázaro Cárdenas 59, T584-0115. A/c, cheaper with fan, nice garden, clean, comfortable.

C-D **Costa del Sol**, Lázaro Cárdenas 47, T584-0318. A/c (cheaperwith fan), small pool, cable TV, parking.

D **Loma Real**, Mina 17 by entrance from Oaxaca, T584-0645. A/c, cheaper with fan, pool, garden, parking.

D **Santa Cruz**, Lázaro Cárdenas 88, across from Oaxaca terminal (shuttle to Oaxaca leaves from here), T584-0116. Cheaper with fan, basic.

E **Pochutla**, Francisco Madero 102, corner of plaza, T584-0003. Bath, ceiling fan, good value.

Puerto Angel *p370*

B-C **Soraya de Puerto Angel**, José Vasconcelos s/n, T584-3009. Beautiful views, clean, spacious terraces, a/c, good parking.

C **Cañón De Vata**, Playa del Panteón, T584-3137. Lovely garden setting, gets very booked, good restaurant. Recommended.

C **Villa Florencia**, Av Principal Virgilio Uribe across from town beach, T/F584-3044. A/c, no hot water, cheaper with fan, clean, comfortable, friendly, Italian-Mexican run, restaurant, bar, library with terrace.

D **Casa de Huéspedes Gundi y Tomás**, central and up the hill opposite old military base, T584-3068, www.puertoangel-hotel.com. Shared bath, clean, good value, popular, stores luggage, money exchange, breakfast and snacks served (cook prepares dinner every day for guests, but expensive).

D **Casas Penélopes**, on road to Zipolite and Mazunte. Friendly, beautiful location. Highly recommended.

D **El Rincón Sabroso**, T584-3095. Beautiful views, clean, quiet, friendly, hot water.

D **La Cabaña**, Playa del Panteón, T584-3105. Fan, clean, friendly, free morning coffee. Recommended.

D **Puesta del Sol**, on road to Playa del Panteón, T584-3096. Fan, cheaper with shared bath, clean, restaurant, very friendly, English and German spoken. Recommended.

E **Capy's**, on road to Playa del Panteón, T584-3002. Fan, clean, nice restaurant. Recommended.

E **Casa de Huéspedes Leal**, central, T584-3081. Shared bath, washing facilities, friendly. Recommended.

Camping

There is a campground halfway between Puerto Angel and Pochutla, very friendly, driveway too steep for large vehicles, US$8.50 for 2 in campervan. Recommended.

Zipolite and San Agustinillo *p371*

At Zipolite the shore is lined with *palapas* offering cheap meals and accommodation (beds from US$3.50 per night, hammocks from US$2.50, shared bath, basic facilities), with informal discos at night. At San Agustinillo there are simple *cabañas* (**E**) and restaurants.

B-E **Solstice**, Calle del Amor 94, Zipolite, www.solstice-mexico.com, price for up to 4 people at 4 *cabañas* around a palm-shaded courtyard (also dorms, **E**) including breakfast. According to the many readers who have written in, it's a quiet spot .

E **Posada San Agustín**, San Agustinillo. With private bath, ceiling fan, mosquito net, nice views, friendly.

Mazunte *p372*

Several *palapas* offer simple accommodation along the middle of the beach.

B **Posada Alta Mira**, on a wooded hillside overlooking the west end of the beach, T/F584-3104, www.labuenavista.com. 10 lovely *cabañas*, spacious, clean, comfortable, spectacular views, no electricity yet. Restaurant serves the best food in Mazunte.

B-D Balamjuyuc, next to Posada Alta Mira, balamjuyuc@hotmail.com. Simpler but in the same splendid setting, breakfast and drinks served.
D-E Posada Brisa Marina, Col Roca Blanca, F584-3070, brisamarinaca@yahoo.com. New large rooms on the beach. Friendly.
E Porfiria, next door to Ziga. Basic, friendly, kitchen facilities, small bar.
E Restaurant and Cabañas Yuri. Basic, friendly, fan, some with separate bath, (**F** in hammocks).
E Ziga, at the east end near the Centro Mexicano de la Tortuga. Semi-private bath, fan, mosquito net, clean, friendly, family-run, nice views, good value. Recommended.

Huatulco *p372*
Discounts of up to 50% can be expected in the low season.
LL Quinta Real, Blv Benito Juárez 2, Tangolunda, T581-0428, www.hotelesboutique.com/quintareal. Exclusive resort, perched overlooking the bays and golf club, beach club, pool, excellent restaurant and bar. Recommended.
L Marina Resort, Tehuantepec 112, Santa Cruz, T587-0963, www.hotelmarinaresort.com. Pools, restaurants, disco.
L-AL Plaza Huatulco, Blv Benito Juárez 23, Tangolunda, T581-0035. Small luxurious hotel with personalized service.
AL Gran Hotel Huatulco, Carrizal 1406, La Crucecita, at the entrance to town, T587-0115. A/c, pool.
AL Meigas Binniguenda, Blv Sta Cruz 201, Santa Cruz, T587-0077, binniguenda@prodigy.net.mx. Colonial style, gardens, pool, restaurant and beach club.
AL Posada Chahué Best Western, Mixie y Mixteco, Chahué, T587-0945, bwposadachaue@prodigy.net.mx A/c, pool, terrace restaurant.
A-C Misión de los Arcos, Gardenia 902 y Tamarindo, La Crucecita, T/F587-0165, www.misiondelosarcos.com. A/c, comfortable, elegant suites, cheaper with fan, well-equipped gym, good value.
B Busanvi I, Carrizal 601, La Crucecita, T587-0056. A/c and fan, hot water, apartments with kitchenette, pool.
C Posada de Rambo, Guarumbo 307, La Crucecita, near main plaza, T587-0958. With bath, fan, TV with cable.
C-D Posada del Carmen, Palo Verde 307, La Crucecita, T587-0593. Nice rooms, cold water, cheaper with 1 double bed.
D Benimar, Bugambilia and Pochote, La Crucecita, T587-0447. With bath, fan, hot water, simple rooms.
D Casa de Huéspedes Koly, Bugambilia 301, La Crucecita, near Plaza, T583-4887. With bath, fan, cable TV.
D San Agustín, Carrizal and Macuil, La Crucecita, T587-0368. Clean, basic, good value.

Salina Cruz *p374*
B Costa Real, Progreso 22, near Avila Camacho, T714-0293. A/c, restaurant, parking.
C-D María del Carmen, Manzanillo 17 and Tampico, T714-5625. A/c, modern, nice, cheaper with fan.
D Pacífico, Avila Camacho 709, T/F714-5552. A/c, cheaper with fan, restaurant.
D Posada del Jardín, Avila Camacho 108, T714-0162. A/c, bath (**E** with fan).
F Pensión, La Ventosa, at the top of the dirt road coming from Salina Cruz (on the right) and 200 m after the first path that leads down to the beach. Friendly family rents hammocks, US$1 a night, fried fish US$1. *Champas*, or hammocks, under thatch shelters by the beach, US$1 a night.

Tehuantepec *p374*
C Guiexhoba, on road to Oaxaca, T715-0416. A/c, mini-fridge, pool, restaurant, parking.
D-E Donají del Istmo, Juárez 10, T715-0064, in Centre. A/c, cheaper with fan, clean, friendly. Recommended.
D-E Oasis, Melchor Ocampo 8, T715-0008, 1 block from plaza. Good atmosphere, with bath and a/c, cheaper with fan, simple, safe parking, owner is helpful, good information on local history and traditions.
E Casa de Huéspedes Istmo, Hidalgo 31, 1½ blocks from the main plaza, T715-0019. Quiet, basic, with lovely patio.

Camping
Hotel Calli, on the south of town (see above), will let RVs use their backyard.

Isthmus of Tehuantepec *p374*
D El Mirador, San José de Gracia, Km 116 from Oaxaca. Clean, very friendly, noisy from passing trucks, overlooking a beautiful valley, parking in front.

D **Hotel Santa Elena**, El Camarón, Km 134 from Oaxaca. Clean, friendly, fan and TV.

Juchitán and around *p375*
The Casa de Cultura can help if you want to stay with local people and learn about their culture.
B **Santo Domingo**, Carretera Transístmica, Juchitán, T711-1959. A/c, restaurant, pool.
C-D **Don Alex Lena Real**, 16 de Septiembre 48, Juchitán, T711-1064. Modern comfortable rooms, a/c, clean. Cheaper in older wing and with fan, restaurant.
D **Alfa**, Carretera Panamericana Km 821, T711-0327. A/c, bath, cheaper with fan.
E **Casa de Huéspedes San Gerónimo**, Cd Ixtepec, close to train station and market. Clean, good.
E **Modelo**, 2 de Abril 64, T711-1241, Juchitán, near market. With bath, fan, basic.
E **San Juan**, 16 de Septiembre 127, Cd Ixtepec. Bath, some with a/c, acceptable.

Eating

Oaxaca *p357, map p358*
Around the Zócalo
Most restaurants on the main square cater for tourists, and are therefore pricey (efficiency and standards depend a bit on how busy they are, but generally they are good).
¶¶¶-¶¶ **Asador Vasco**, above **Bar Jardín**. Live Mexican music in the evening, good food and service.
¶¶ **Gaia**, Labastida 115. Organic meals, energizing juices and tarot card reading.
¶¶ **Portal de la Soledad**, on the north side of the Zócalo. Fine dining on the plaza with exciting adaptions of regional food.
¶¶-¶ **Café Amarantos** and **Mario's Terranova Restaurant**, Hidalgo, at east side of Zócalo. Great food, friendly and efficient service, pricey.
¶¶-¶ **La Primavera**. Good-value meals, international and traditional dishes, good snacks and espresso coffee, slow.
¶ **El Mesón**. Buffets 0800-1830, good at US$2.50, breakfast, *comida corrida* poor value, good tacos, clean, quick service.
Tartamiel, Trujano, ½ block east of Zócalo. Pastry shop.

North of Independencia
¶¶¶ **Café Bar Tapas & Pisto**, Macedonio Alcalá 403, upstairs. Artfully renovated colonial house, excellent view from top terrace, more pricey but worth visiting just for the bathroom.
¶¶¶ **Casa Oaxaca**, García Vigil 407. Where food is art, fine courtyard, excellent service and food, reservations very necessary, popular with artists and writers such as Gabriel García Márquez, excellent value.
¶¶¶-¶¶ **Hostería de Alcalá**, Macedonio Alcalá 307. Excellent food and quiet atmosphere in colonial courtyard, good service, expensive.
¶¶¶-¶ **Marco Polo**, 5 de Mayo 103. 0800-2300. Mexican and international dishes, good.
¶¶ **Arte y Tradición**, García Vigil 406. Craft centre with courtyard café, excellent service and food, Mon-Sat 1100-2200.
¶¶ **La Abeja**, Porfirio Díaz 610 y Carranza. Breakfast and lunch, set vegetarian meals, bakery, garden setting.
¶¶ **La Crepe**, Macedonio Alcalá 307. Lovely 1st-floor location with some tables overlooking the street. Good fresh salads, crêpes and cheap breakfast combos.
¶¶ **Los Olivos**, Calzada Madero. Good vegetarian menu and buffet.
¶¶ **Pizza Rústica**, Alcalá 804 and Murguia. Great pizza, popular and friendly.
¶¶-¶ **El Bicho Pobre II**, Calzada de la República. Lunch only, very popular and will serve platters of various dishes. Highly recommended.
¶¶-¶ **El Decano**, 5 de Mayo 210 and Murguia, 0800-2400. Serves *comida corrida* 1400-1500, Mexican dishes, good value. Also a good night spot.
¶¶-¶ **Flor de Loto**, Morelos 509, next to Museo Rufino Tamayo. Good value, clean, vegetarian and Mexican. *Supesteka* is delicious, also breakfast.
¶¶-¶ **Manantial Vegetariano**, Matamoros with Tinoco and Palacios. Excellent cheap vegetarian meals, buffet US$4.50, pleasant patio. Live music at weekends. Recommended.
¶¶-¶ **Pizza Nostrana**, corner of Allende close to Santo Domingo church, 1300-2300. Delicious Italian cuisine, specializing in vegetarian dishes.
¶¶-¶ **Tito's**, García Vigil No 116. Good food at very reasonable prices. Fantastic baguettes.
¶ **Bamby**, García Vigil 205. Good breakfast, good value.
¶ **Guidos**, Porfirio Díaz. Good for cheap *menú del día*. Popular, with cheap pasta and coffee.

¥ **La Verde Antequera**, Matamoros 3 blocks north of Zócalo. Good daily lunch specials, best *comida corrida* in town for US$1.
¥ **Trece Cielos**, Matamoros 101. Good, cheap daily *menú*.

Cafés and bakeries

Café y Arte Geono, Macedonio Alcalá 412. Nice garden, good coffee and cakes.
El Rincón del Libro, Jardín de la Soledad 1, on Independencia and Mier y Terán. Terrace, also internet, gallery and gift shop, plaza out front also great spot for ice cream (try tequila flavoured).
La Brew Coffee and Wafflehouse, García Vigil 409B, 4 blocks from the Zócalo, T514-9673. Great breakfast and delicious treats of fruit waffles, brownies, muffins, cookies, breads and bagels.

South of Independencia

The most popular place to eat *tlayudas* (oversized tortillas) and other local snacks in the evening is from stalls and restaurants along Aldama, between Cabrera and 20 de Noviembre.
¥¥¥ **Flor de Oaxaca**, Armenta y López 311. Pricey but excellent meals and delicious hot chocolate.
¥¥-¥ **Coronita**, Díaz Ordaz 208 below **Hotel Valle de Oaxaca**. Tasty lunches, traditional Oaxacan dishes.
¥¥ **El Naranjo**, Trujano 203. In courtyard of 17th-century house, traditional Oaxaca fare, expensive but good, known for its *moles*. If you like the food, why not join one of the cooking classes?
¥¥-¥ **Hipocampo's**, Hidalgo 505. Good-value set meals, popular with locals. Mon-Sat 0800-2200, Sun 1000-1900.
¥¥ **La Quebrada**, Armenta y López. Excellent fish, open only to 1800.
¥¥-¥ **Café Alex**, Díaz Ordaz 218 y Trujano. Good *comida corrida* and varied à la carte, coffee and breakfasts, delicious pancakes with fruit, good value. Recommended.
¥ **El Patio Grande**, Hidalgo 412, 2 blocks from Zócalo. Cheap *comida corrida*, Guelaguetza dancing.
¥ **María Cristina's**, in Mercado 20 de Noviembre. Excellent *caldos* and *comidas*.
¥ **Fiesta**, Las Casas 303. Good for breakfast or *comida corrida*.
¥ **El Shaddai**, Av Hidalgo 121 y Galeano. Family-run, good and cheap.
¥ **Girasoles**, 20 de Noviembre 102. Small, good vegetarian food. Recommended.
¥ **Comedores** Some of the most authentic Oaxacan food is found in the *comedores familiares,* such as **Clemente, Los Almendros, La Juchita**, but they are way out of town and could be difficult to get to, or in *comedores populares* in the market.
Hermanas Jiménez, Mercado de Abastos. Recommended for a local bread called *pan de yema*, made with egg yolk.

Route to Mitla *p364*

Teotitlán del Valle has 1 simple restaurant. **Tlacolula** has several simple restaurants. The market at El Tule, has good food.
¥ **María Teresa**, Mitla, 100 m from site towards village. Good *comida corrida.*
¥ **La Sonora**, on eastern edge of El Tule. Quite tasty food.

Puerto Escondido *p368, map p369*

¥¥¥ **Hotel Santa Fé**, Zicatela. Excellent vegetarian, but expensive. Worth it for the great views at sunset.
¥¥¥-¥¥ **La Galería**, in **Hotel Arcoiris**, Italian, good pizzas but pricey.
¥¥-¥ **Cappuccino**, Pérez Gasga Good coffee, fruit salads, some dishes pricey.
¥¥-¥ **El Cafecito**, Calle del Moro, Zicatela. Excellent breakfasts, chocolate bread, very popular. Highly recommended.
¥¥-¥ **El Jardin**, Zicoleta, Playa Marinero. Good vegetarian.
¥¥ **Cabo Blanco**, Calle del Moro, Zicatela. Popular relaxed dining, good BBQ fish and vegetarian food, does free dinner on Mon night party. Excellent breakfasts, chocolate bread.
¥¥ **El Tabachín**, Playa Marinero, behind **Hotel Santa Fe**. Vegetarian, café, breakfast and lunch.
¥¥ **Liza**, Playa Marinero, off Carretera Costera. Good food, nice location.
¥¥ **Super Café Puro**, off top flight of stairs of walkway that starts at the tourist information kiosk. Good for breakfast, pleasant terrace, Mexican, family-run.
¥¥-¥ **Baguetería Vivaldi**, Av Pérez Gasga. Good breakfast and sandwiches.
¥¥-¥ **Beniditos**, Av Pérez Gasga. *The* place for pizza, good value.

Cafés, bakeries and heladerías

Pepe's, 8a Norte, near market. Great sandwiches.

Carmen's Bakery, on a path to the beach from main road, Zicatela. Great pastries baked on the premises, also 2nd-hand books and magazines.

Gelatería Giardino, Av Pérez Gasga 609, just east of El Adoquín. Excellent Italian ice cream and fruit ices, made on the premises, also cappuccino coffee. Highly recommended (closed May-Jun).

Un Tigre Azul, Av Pérez Gasga on El Adoquín, upper floor. Bar, coffee and snacks, nice views and internet.

The market on 8 Norte and 3 Pte is another place to find good and economical eating. Clean with varied typical menus, *comida corrida* from US$2.50 is good value.

Puerto Angel *p370*

¥¥¥-¥¥ Cañón de Vata. Also good, mainly vegetarian.

¥¥-¥ Villa Florencia. Hotel with an excellent restaurant serving good Italian and Mexican dishes, charming place.

¥¥ Beto's by turn-off for Playa del Panteón. Good fish (fresh tuna) and cheap beer, nice views.

¥ Cangrejo, by Naval Base gate. Popular bar, also good breakfasts and excellent tacos.

¥ Mar y Sol. Cheap, good seafood.

¥ Sirenita. Popular for breakfast and bar, friendly.

Mazunte *p372*

The best food and view is at the **Posada Alta Mira**, see Sleeping, above.

¥¥-¥ La Dolce Vita, on main road at west end. Good Italian pizza and home-made pasta, pricey.

¥ El Paso, on main road west of the bridge. Inexpensive and friendly.

¥ Pizzería Iris, on track between the west end of the beach and the road.

Huatulco *p372*

Restaurants on the beach, out of town, tend to be the cheapest. There are luxury restaurants at the Tangolunda hotels. In La Crucecita, prices get cheaper as you get away from the plaza; there are several restaurants along Gardenia.

¥¥¥ Il Giardio del Papa, Flamboyán 204, La Crucecita. Italian chef was once the Pope's cook, expensive.

¥¥¥ Jardín del Arte, Paseo Mitla at **Hotel Marlín**, Santa Cruz. French and international, expensive.

¥¥¥ Las Cúpulas, Blv Benito Juárez 2 in **Hotel Quinta Real**, Tangolunda. Fine dining with panoramic view of the harbour, also popular breakfast venue. Recommended.

¥¥¥-¥ Oasis Café, Flamboyán 211 y Bugambilia, by main plaza, La Crucecita. Varied menu, grill, seafood, Oaxacan food, good value. Recommended.

¥¥ Café Dublin, Carrizal 504, La Crucecita. Irish pub, popular, good hamburgers, upstairs café, popular expat hangout.

¥¥ Don Porfirio, Blv Benito Juárez, Tangolunda. Fish and seafood specialities, also steak.

¥¥ La Crema, Carrizal and Flamboyán, La Crucecita. Popular bar restaurant, pizzas, bar food, games. Recommended.

¥¥-¥ El Sabor de Oaxaca, Guamuchil 206, La Crucecita. Regional cooking, Oaxacan *mole*, good value.

¥¥-¥ La Crucecita, Bugambilia and Chacah, La Crucecita. Breakfast, snacks, set meals, economical.

¥¥-¥ Los Portales, Bugambilia 603, Plaza Principal, La Crucecita. Breakfast, tacos and other snacks, open late.

¥ Café Huatulco, near the marina, Santa Cruz. Regional coffee and snacks.

¥ Mandinga, Flamboyán 101, La Crucecita. Chicken and seafood, some seriously cheap dishes.

¥ Mercado 3 Mayo, Guamuchil, La Crucecita. Market *fondas* serving typical dishes at very cheap prices, good value.

Salina Cruz *p374*

¥¥ Aloha, Wilfrido Cruz 13-A. Seafood and regional dishes.

¥¥ Restaurant, at the end of the road which crosses the village. Good restaurant under a high palm roof, excellent fish.

¥ El Lugar, corner of Acapulco and 5 de Mayo on 1st floor, opposite the plaza. Mexican food, good.

Tehuantepec *p374*

¥¥¥-¥ Restaurant Scaru, Leona Vicario 4. Good food, fish and seafood specialities, upscale, nice courtyard and mural,

🍴🍴 **Mariscos Angel**, 5 de Mayo No 1, by entrance from Salina Cruz. Seafood. Cheap food on top floor of market, here you can get the local speciality, pork or chicken, stuffed with potatoes. The local *quesadillas* made of maize and cheese are delicious; sold at bus stops.
🍴🍴-🍴 **Café Colonial**, Juana C Romero 66. Good *comida corrida* and à la carte, a variety of Mexican dishes, clean, friendly.

Juchitán and around *p375*
🍴🍴🍴-🍴 **Casa Grande**, Juárez 125, on the main square, Juchitán. In a beautifully restored colonial house, good food, live music.
🍴🍴🍴-🍴 **Deyaurihe**, 5 de Septiembre corner of Aldama, Juchitán. Mexican food, *comida corrida* and à la carte.
🍴🍴 **Los Chapulines**, 5 de Septiembre and Morelos, Juchitán. Regional and international food, *comida corrida* and à la carte, a/c.
🍴🍴 **La Manzana**, Nicolás Bravo 10, Cd Ixtepec. Seafood and international cooking.
🍴🍴 **La Tropicana**, 16 de Septiembre, Cd Ixtepec. Mexican cooking.
🍴🍴 **Pizzería La Vianda**, 5 de Septiembre 54-B, Juchitán. Pizza and seafood.

Entertainment

Oaxaca *p357, map p358*
Bars and clubs
Candela, Murguía 413 y Pino Suárez. Salsa, merengue, live music from 2200, restaurant, popular with visitors and locals, cover US$5.
Casa de Mezcal, in front of the market. Popular drinking hole.
La Tentación, Murguía, between Macedonio Alcalá and García Vigil. Salsa, merengue, live music starting 2230, open late, friendly atmosphere, cover US$4.
NRG, Calzada Porfirio Díaz 102. Wed-Sat 2230-0230, disco club, cover US$5, the current hotspot.

Cinemas
Ariel 2000, Juárez y Berriozabal, subtitled films for US$3, 2 for 1 on Wed.
Cinemas Geminis, Escuela Naval Militar 409; new centre, T515-6888, normally US$3.50.
Multimax, Plaza del Valle; new multi-screen complex (with shopping mall), 2 for 1 Wed, normally US$4.20.

Folk dancing
Guelaguetza-style shows, when there are enough people, at:
Casa de Cantera, Murguía 102, T514-9522. US$12, US$22 includes buffet dinner.
Monte Albán, nightly at 2030, US$8, photography permitted. Book if you can.

Puerto Escondido *p368, map p369*
Bars and clubs
It is not advisable to stay at bars and discos past 0300.
Barfly. Good music, regular screenings of films and videos.
El Son y la Rumba. Rooftop bar with live salsa and rumba at night. Restaurant serves *comida corrida* during the day.
El Tubo. Disco, popular with local surfers.
Los 3 Diablos, Av Pérez Gasga 604. New lively bar with pool table, nice friendly staff.
Tequila Sunrise, Av Marina Nacional, just west of El Adoquín. Open-air disco, varied music, international crowd.
Wipeout. Rock and techno music.

Zipolite and San Agustinillo *p371*
Livélula, Zipolite, a quiet little bar, open 0800-0200, Wed, Sat. Ping-pong, table foot ball, hammocks and plenty of time to relax.

Huatulco *p372*
Several luxury hotels have shows such as the **Barcelo's Fiesta Mexicana with Mariachis**, folk dancing, Mexican buffet, reservations T581-0055.
La Guelaguetza folklore show at **Noches Oaxaqueñas**, Blv Benito Juárez, Tangolunda, reservations T581-0001.
Latin dancing at **Magic Tropic**, Santa Cruz. Also **La Papaya**, Benito Juárez, Manzana 3, Lote 1, Bahía de Chahué, T583-4911. Popular, US$5 cover, European-style disco, big screen, human fish tank.

Festivals and events

Oaxaca *p357, map p358*
Jul Guelaguetza, also called **Los Lunes del Cerro**, is the city's most important festival. A festive atmosphere permeates the city for over 2 weeks at the end of Jul (see page 360).
Oct El Señor del Rayo, a 9-day event in the 3rd week of Oct, including excellent fireworks.

2 Nov Day of the Dead, a mixture of festivity and solemn commemoration, best appreciated at the Panteón General (main cemetery). Always ask before photographing. In recent years Oaxaca has hosted a rugby 'tournament of death' in conjunction with the festival, for information, www.planeta.com.
8-18 Dec **Fiesta de la Soledad**, patroness of Oaxaca, with fine processions centred around the Basílica and throughout the city.
Dec During the 9 days before Christmas, the **Novenas** are held. Groups of people go asking for shelter, *posada*, as Joseph and Mary did, and are invited into different homes. This is done in the centre as well as other neighbourhoods like San Felipe (5 km north) and at Xoxo, to the south. The *posadas* culminate on the night of 24 Dec with what is known as **Calendas**, a parade of floats representing allegories from the birth of Christ; every church in town prepares a float honouring its patron saint, the groups from all the parishes converge at the cathedral at 2300 (best seen from balcony of the restaurants around the Zócalo; go for supper and get a window table).
23 Dec **Noche de Rábanos**, outside the Palacio de Gobierno, is a unique contest of figures carved out of radishes. Stands made of flowers and corn stalks have been added in recent years to this old tradition.

Teotitlán del Valle *p364*
3 May **Fiesta de las Cruces**, when people climb to a cross on a beautiful summit above town (across the river); good hiking at any time of the year.
Jul Since 1999 a **Fiesta Antigua Zapoteca** is celebrated here to coincide with the Guelaguetza in Oaxaca.
8 Sep Feast of **Virgen de la Natividad**.

Puerto Escondido *p368, map p369*
Mar Long board tournament.
Aug Master World Surf Championship.
Nov The **city's festivities** are held throughout the month, along with a **surfing tournament**. In the middle of the month is the **Festival Costeño de la Danza**, with colourful, lively folk dances.

Huatulco *p372*
1st week Apr Fiesta del Mar
3 May Fiesta de la Santa Cruz.
1st week May International sail-fishing tournament.
12 Dec Fiesta de la Virgen de Guadalupe.

Tehuantepec *p374*
Festivals and traditions are very important in Tehuantepec. There are many colourful and ceremonious celebrations throughout the year, for which the women don their elaborate embroidered dresses and lace halos, known as *resplandores*. The town is divided into 15 wards; each one has a patron saint. **Fiestas patronales** are held in each neighbourhood for several days in honour of the local patron, these culminate on the saint's day. Another type of celebration are *velas*, which are very formal dances.
19 May Vela Zandunga.
1st week Aug Fiestas of Santo Domingo are held in the centre of Tehuantepec.
Mid-Aug **Velas de Agosto** are held throughout the Isthmus.
24 Jun Fiestas in honour of **St John the Baptist** in the San José neighbourhood.
26 Dec Vela Tehuantepec.

Juchitán and around *p375*
Although every birth and wedding is reason for a colourful celebration, best known are the *velas*, formal dances in a decorated setting resembling a European palace, for which the attendees wear traditional dress. There are *velas* throughout the year, the most important ones are held during **May** in honour of **San Vicente Ferrer**.

Shopping

Oaxaca *p357, map p358*
Crafts
Many crafts are produced throughout the state of Oaxaca. Crafts are sold in nearby villages or they may be purchased in the city of Oaxaca, at the markets listed below. There are endless shopping temptations, such as green and black pottery, baskets and bags made from cane and rushes, embroidered shirts, skirts, painted wooden animals called *alebrijes*, hammocks, tooled leather goods, woven wall hangings and rugs.
Alfarería Jiménez, Zaragoza 402, fine cream and purple-black pottery (Zapotec and Mixtec designs).

Instituto Oaxaqueño de las Artesanías, García Vigil 809, T516-9211. Government run, cheaper and better than most, service good, with very good small **market** nearby on junction of García Vigil and Jesús Carranza, for beautiful coloured belts and clothes.
Arte y Tradición, García Vigil 406, superior craft shops, offer excellent selection of quality rugs at good prices.
El Palacio de las Gemas, Alcalá 100 block, is recommended for gemstones, good selection at reasonable prices.
La Mano Mágica, Alcalá 203, for the highest quality rug collection.
Lo Mexicano, García Vigil, at end furthest from centre. Excellent selection of high-quality crafts at reasonable prices, run by young Frenchman.
Mercado Artesanal, JP García y Zaragoza, has a large selection of all kinds of crafts.
Mercado Benito Juárez, in the centre, has a sampling of different wares including a selection of leather bags and straw hats.
Mercado de Abastos, you are likely to find better prices; there is a selection of pottery and basketry used by locals and a section with other crafts.
Mujeres Artesanas de las Regiones de Oaxaca (MARO), 5 de Mayo 204, T516-0670, daily 0900-2000, a regional association of Oaxacan craftswomen with a sales and exhibition store.
Productos Típicos de Oaxaca, Belisario Domínguez 602, cheapest and largest selection of pottery plus a variety of fabrics and sandals (city bus near *ADO* depot goes there).
Yalalag, 5 de Mayo y Murguía. Good selection of jewellery, rugs and pottery, somewhat overpriced.

Bookshops

Amate, Alcalá 307, best selection of English-language books and magazines and a nice selection of books about Oaxaca and Mexico.
Proveedora Escolar, Independencia 1001 y Reforma, large, excellent selection on all subjects, cheaper.

Markets

The city has 4 main markets, all of which are worth a visit; polite bargaining is the rule everywhere.
Mercado de Abastos, also known as the **Central de Abastos**, near the 2nd-class bus station, is the largest; a cacophony of sights, sounds and aromas, busiest on Sat and not to be missed. Prices here tend to be lower than in the smaller markets. Try the grasshopper-like creatures called *chapulines* fried in huge vats on several of the stands.
Mercado 20 de Noviembre (Aldama on the corner of 20 de Noviembre), in the centre of town, has clean stalls selling prepared foods, cheese and baked goods. Next door, the larger **Mercado Benito Juárez** has a selection of household goods, fruits, vegetables, crafts and regional products, such as *quesillo* (string cheese), bread and chocolate.
Mercado Artesanal, Zaragoza and JP García, has a good selection of crafts intended for the tourist trade.

Photography

Centro Fotográfico Alvarez Bravo, Murguía 302, photo exhibits and sales.
Foto Rivas, Juárez 605, opposite Parque Juárez and 20 de Noviembre C-502, has an excellent collection of photographs of Oaxacan themes, new and old, also sells postcards and film.
Galería Nunduá, Nicolás Bravo 206, photo exhibits and sales.

Regional food and drink

On Mina and 20 de Noviembre, opposite the 20 de Noviembre market, are several mills where they grind cacao beans, almond, sugar and cinnamon into a paste for making delicious hot chocolate, the cacao smell permeates the air in this area. Some of the brands sold are **Mayordomo** (very good), **Guelaguetza** and **La Soledad**. These same outlets sell Oaxacan *mole*, a thick paste used for preparing sauces. *Mole* and *quesillo,* the regional string cheese, are sold at the Benito Juárez market, where **La Oaxaqueña** stalls are recommended. Also at Mina y 20 de Noviembre is **La Casa del Dulce** sweet shop. Mezcal is readily available throughout town.

Puerto Escondido *p368, map p369*

Crafts and souvenirs are available from shops all along **El Adoquín**, stalls on the main street, east of El Adoquín and on **Andador Libertad**, a walkway going uphill from about the middle of El Adoquín. Shop around, vendors on the beach are likely to ask for higher prices and you may find better value in shops north of the highway.

Ahorrara, 3a Pte y 5a Norte, large well-stocked supermarket.

Oasis, Adoquín, opposite the tourist kiosk, fine accessories and gifts.

Papi's souvenir shop has a small selection of foreign books for sale or trade.

Surfing gear and clothing are best bought from shops in Zicatela.

Huatulco *p372*

Mercado de Artesanías de Santa Cruz, Blv Santa Cruz, corner Mitla, has a variety of regional crafts.

Museo de Artesanías Oaxaqueñas, Flamboyán 216, Plaza Principal, La Crucecita, also exhibits and sells a variety of Mexican crafts.

Activities and tours

Oaxaca *p357, map p358*

Birdwatching

Almost 700 species of birds can be found in the state of Oaxaca. Its strategic location at the junction between North and Central America and its geographic diversity, spanning the Pacific and Atlantic watersheds, result in great diversity. There are birding opportunities in the Central Valleys, in the mountain range separating the Central Valleys from the Pacific coast, in the coastal lagoons, the thorn forests along Route 190, and in the cloud forests and lowlands of the Atlantic coast (see Valle Nacional).

Cooking classes

Susan Trilling, T508-0469, www.seasonsofmyheart.com. Recommended.

Many language schools also have cooking classes, see page 394.

Cycling

Zona Bici, García Vigil 406, T516-0953. New aluminium-frame bikes, front suspension, US$10 for 24-hr rental. Wonderful way to see surrounding countryside. Minimum 2 people, US$28 each, make reservations. Recommended.

Horse riding

La Golondrina, Borde del Río Atoyac 800, San Jacinto Amilpas, T452-7570, thoroughbred Andalucían horses.

Public baths

Baños Reforma, Reforma 407, daily 0700-1800, steam bath US$4, sauna US$4.

Baños San Rafael, Tinoco y Palacios 514, Mon-Sat 0600-1800, Sun 0600-1530, hot water.

Temazcal, Reforma 402, T516-1165, Indigenous ancient ceremonial steam bath with herbs, also offers massages and aromatherapy US$50.

Tour operators

There are many in town, most running the same tours, eg daily to Monte Albán; El Tule, Mitla and, sometimes, another village on this route; city tour; Fri to Coyotepec, Jalietza and Ocotlán; Thu to Cuilapan and Zaachila; Sun to Tlacolula, Mitla and El Tule. Basically, the tours tie in with local markets. Regular day tours cost US$11-13 per person; special tours on demand about US$22 per hr for 4 passengers.

Eugenio Cruz Castaneda, T513-4790, offers excellent guided trips to Monte Albán, other archaeological sites and can arrange custom itineraries throughout Oaxaca State.

Expediciones Sierra Norte, Manuel Bravo. T514-8271, www.sierranorte.org.mx, run hiking and mountain-bike tours in the Sierra Juárez, north of the town of Benito Juárez. Tours depart daily from office at 0930, call day before for reservations.

La Brujita Tours, labrujita_oax@yahoo.com Flamboyant and friendly Susan McGlynn organizes personalized tours that take you to the heart of Oaxacan markets, home-cooked meals with local families and to visit local artisans at work in their shops. New offices opening – drop her an email to find out where.

Judith Reyes at **Arte y Tradición**, García Vigil 406, runs good tours to outlying villages in her VW van, US$8 per hr.

Tierraventura, Abasolo 217 and Av Juarez, T501-1363, www.tierraventura.com, run tours to the highlands (Sierra Juárez, Sierra Mixteca, Hierve el Agua) and coast, US$20-30 per day.

Route to Mitla *p364*
Tours (1000-1300, rather rushed) to **Tule**, **Mitla** and **Tlacolula** from Oaxaca agencies, cost US$7.50, not including entry fees.

Sierra Juárez *p368*
Expediciones Sierra Norte, T/F513-9518.
Tierraventura, T/F514-3043. Oaxaca-run hiking and mountain biking tours in this region.

Puerto Escondido *p368, map p369*

Diving
The region's coastline offers good opportunities for snorkelling and scuba diving; snorkelling from the beach is easiest at Puerto Angelito. Tours and diving lessons with Jorge Pérez Bravo, **Aventura Submarina**, Av Pérez Gasga, at west end of El Adoquín, T/F582-2353. You are likely to see turtles and dolphins on the way to the snorkelling and diving sites. Snorkelling, 3 hrs, US$22 per person. Diving lessons, US$55 for 1 tank; if qualified, US$38 for 1 tank, US$55 for 2.

Fishing
Boats can be hired for fishing at Playa Principal or through travel agencies for approximately US$27 per hr for up to 4 passengers.

Horse riding
Horse riding, T582-1950. Meet at point of Zicoleta, 3 hrs minimum, US$10 per hr.

Kayaking
New to Puerto Escondido, US$6 per hr, enquire at Las Hamacas at Matialtepec Lagoon. Recommended.

Pelota Mixteca
A modern version of an ancient Mixtec ball game is played on Sat and Sun in Bajos de Chila, 15 mins from Puerto Escondido, on the road to Acapulco. In a 9-m 35-m court, teams of 5-7 players propel a rubber ball weighing almost 1 kg, using elaborately decorated leather mitts that weigh between 3.5 kg and 6 kg. A game can take up to 4 hrs.

Surfing
Playa Zicatela is a surfer's haven, but dangerous for the novice. Board rental from US$13 a day from 360 Surf Shop. Lessons from the lifeguards on the towers, US$28.

Tour operators
Ana's Ecotours (contact Ana Márquez at Tigre Azul, Av Pérez Gasga). Ana is a certified, recommended guide, speaks English and is very knowledgeable about the region and especially its birds. Tours to all the natural attractions in the area and cultural tours of her native Mixtec community, day trip, US$32 per person.
Gina Machorro (speaks English and French), offers a 2-hr walking tour of Puerto Escondido's local culture and history, US$16 per person (Wed and Sat only during the winter). Contact through the tourist information kiosk.
Michael Malone, a Canadian ornithologist, is another recommended guide who is in Puerto Escondido Nov-Mar (ask at tourism information kiosk).

Puerto Angel *p370*
Azul Profundo, next door to **Cordelia's** on Playa del Panteón, T584-3109. Scuba diving with experienced instructors, up-to-date equipment, PADI service available. Also runs snorkelling trips which visit beaches along the coast. English spoken.

Huatulco *p372*

Birdwatching
Aventura Huatulco, T044-958-589-3907 (mob), US$25, offers 3-hr birdwatching trips 0600-0900.

Cycling
A mountain bike is a good way to get around this area and to reach the high points with the many views of the bays. Bike rentals in La Crucecita from restaurants near the plaza, US$1.65 per hr. Rentals and cycling tours from **Motor Tours**, **Eco Aventuras**, **Adventuras Huatulco** and other agencies (see Tour operators).

Also **Scooter** hire and off-road motorbikes for rent, Blv Santa Cruz, local 1, T583-4766. Need credit card and licence.

Diving and snorkelling
There are good snorkelling areas on reefs by the beach at **La Entrega** (Bahía Santa Cruz), **Riscalillo** (Bahía Cachacual) and **San Agustín** (Bahía San Agustín). The islands of **Cacaluta**

(Bahía Cacaluta) and **La Montosa** (Bahía Tangolunda) are also surrounded by reefs with several species of coral, many different organisms can be seen here in relatively shallow water. Snorkel and fins at Santa Cruz marina, US$5 or through agencies who organize tours. There are good scuba diving opportunities and the cliffs that separate the different bays continue underwater an average of 30 m.

Diving lessons and tours from:

Action Sports Marina (Gala Hotel).

Buceo Sotavento, Punta Tangolunda, local 2, T581-0051.

Hurricane Divers Playa Santa Cruz, Manzana 19, Lote 8, T587-1107, www.hurricanedivers.com. Package diving tours if you have your certificate.

Fishing

Launches and yachts for deep-sea fishing charge US$100 per hr, minimal rental 3 hrs.

Coorporativo Tangolunda, T587-0081, Bahía Santa Cruz, cheaper option.

Golf

The Tangolunda golf course offers 18-hole, par-72 golf with nice views of the surroundings. Reservations T581-0037, green fee US$65, clubs and carts extra.

Health spa

Xquenda Huatulco Spa, Vialidad Lambda s/n, Bahía Chahué, T583-4448, www.huatulcospa.com. Massage, beauty salon, gym, 25m pool, temazcal treatments.

Hiking

There are opportunities for hiking in the forested hills to the north of Huatulco. Because part of the forest is deciduous, the experience is very different in the rainy season, when it is green, and in the dry season when the area is brown and even some cacti change from green to violet. The Río Copalita to the north and east of Huatulco is quite scenic. It has waterfalls and rapids, walking here can be combined with a visit to the Punta Celeste Zapotec archaeological site.

Horse riding

Rancho Caballo de Mar, on the shores of the Río Copalita, east of Huatulco and south of Route 200, T587-0530, offers riding tours along the river, on forested trails and on the beaches of Bahía de Conejos, US$25 for 3 hrs.

Rafting

Several companies run tours down the Copalita and Zimatán rivers. These can be as basic as a float down the river or as challenging as class 4-5 rapids; ask enough questions to find the tour that best suits you. Half-day tours US$33-40, full-day tours for US$65-76 per person. Note that from Feb-May there may not be enough water.

Providers include:

Aventuras Piraguas, Plaza Oaxaca Local 19, on Flamboyán across from the plaza, La Crucecita, T/F587-1333, canoe trips and rafting in up to class 5 rapids.

Copalita River Tours, Gardenia and Palo Verde (**Posada Michelle** lobby), La Crucecita, T/F587-0535, kayak and rafting tours.

Rock climbing

There are rock climbing opportunities at **Piedra de los Moros**, a few km north of Route 200, on the road to Pueblo Viejo, the turn-off is west of the Bahías de Huatulco entrance road; by the **Copalitilla waterfall**, on the Copalita river canyon, 65 km from Huatulco; and in **Punta Celeste**, at the Botazoo Park, 8 km from Huatulco.

Sailing

Luna Azul, day and evening sailing trips and private charter. Contact Jack Hennessey on T587-0945, or drop in at the **Hotel Posada Chahue**, Calle Mixie L 75, Sector R Bahía de Chahue, T587-0945, www.lunaazul.netfirms.com.

Tour operators

Full-day boat tours to see the different bays are offered by travel agencies for US$17-27 per person, with stops for swimming, snorkelling and a meal; there are catamarans, sail boats, yachts and small launches. Trips can also be arranged at the Santa Cruz marina directly with the boatsmen, they will probably speak Spanish only. Some of the bays can also be reached by land, and there are tours on all-terrain quad bikes (*cuatrimotos*).

Action Sports Marina, at Sheraton Resort, Tangolunda, T581-0055, ext 842, diving

lessons and tours, watersports.
Bahías Plus, Carrizal 704, La Crucecita, T/F587-0811, and at **Hotel Binniguenda**, Santa Cruz, T/F587-0216, airline reservations, tours, helpful, American Express reps on 2nd floor of La Crucecita office.
Eco Aventuras, La Crucecita, T587-0669, adventure tours, cycling, rock climbing, kayaking, birdwatching.
Jungle Tour, at Blv Chahué, Lote 22, Manzana 1, T587-1381, quad tours.
Motor Tours, at T587-1818, **Hotel Castillo Huatulco**, Santa Cruz, T583-0400, local and regional tours, motorcycles and quad bikes.

Watersports

Wind surfing, sailing, wave running and waterskiing equipment can be rented at the major hotels and beach clubs. **Zax Aventura Extrema**, Av Bahía San Augustín, Manzana 17, Lote 24, Coxula, T583-4426, tubing.

Transport

Oaxaca *p357, map p358*

Air

Xoxocotlán (OAX) airport is about 9 km south, direction Ocotepec. Airport taxis cost US$2.30 per person. Book at **Transportación Terrestre Aeropuerto** on Alameda de León No 1-G, opposite the cathedral in the Zócalo (T514-4350) for collection at your hotel to be taken to airport, office open Mon-Sat 0900-1400, 1700-2000.

To **Mexico City** with AeroMéxico, Mexicana, Aerocaribe and **Aviacsa**, several daily, US$180 one-way. To **Puerto Escondido** and **Huatulco**, with Aerocaribe, at 1030 and 1705, US$120 one way (US$85 advance booking), same price both destinations. To **Puerto Escondido** with **Aerotucán**, daily US$120, also **Aerovega** has flights US$96. To **Tuxtla Gutiérrez**, with **Aerocaribe** at 1210 and 1440, with **Aviacsa** at 1235, US$146 one way. To **Tapachula**, with **Taesa** at 1005, US$100. To **Cd Ixtepec** (Tehuantepec Isthmus), with **Aerocaribe**, at 0840, US$85 one way. For other destinations it is necessary to make a connection in Mexico City.

Airline offices For airline websites, see page 32. **Mexicana**, Fiallo 102 y Av Independencia, T516-8414, Mon-Fri 0900-1900, Sat and Sun 0900-1800. **Aerocaribe**, Fiallo 102 y Av Independencia, T516-0266. **AeroMéxico**, Av Hidalgo 513 Centro, T516-3229. **Aviacsa**, Pino Suárez 604, T518-4566. **Aerotaxi (Turoca)**, Calzada Porfirio Díaz 104, Col Reforma, T515-7270. **AeroTucán**, Alcalá 201, T501-0532. **AeroVega**, Hotel Monte Albán, Alameda de León 1, T516-2777.

Bus

Local Buses mostly charge US$0.35. To the 1st-class bus station, buses marked 'VW' go from Av Juárez. Many lines marked 'Central' go by the 2nd-class bus station. *Colectivos* from Bustamante 3rd block from the Zócolo, US$0.50 to airport.

Long distance For 1st-class buses, buy tickets in advanced at the Ticket Bus Office, 20 de Noviembre 103, T515-1214, Mon-Sat 0800-2200, Sun 0900-1600. 1st-class terminal, also referred to as **ADO** terminal is northeast of Zócalo on Calzada Niños Héroes de Chapultepec (no luggage office, taxi from centre US$3). **ADO, Cristóbal Colón, Sur** and **Cuenca** operate from here. Note that many 2nd class buses leave from here too. 2nd-class terminal is west of Zócalo on Calzada Valerio Trujano, just west of the Periférico, across from the Central de Abastos; it is referred to as the 'Central Camionera' (has left-luggage office, open until 2100). Some 2nd-class companies also offer superior service on some runs. The **Autobuses Unidos** (AU) terminal (2nd class, 2 levels of service, 1 is very good, modern buses but without a/c) is at Santa Rosa, near the Teatro Alvaro Carillo. 1st-class terminal is the only one for **Villahermosa** and the **Yucatán**. Tickets for **ADO, Cristóbal Colón, AU, Sur** and **Cuenca** can also be purchased at Periférico 152, T516-3222, by the pedestrian crosswalk across from the Mercado de Abastos. To **Mexico City**, most go to TAPO (Mexico City east bus terminal) but there are also services to the North and South terminals. Many buses throughout the day and night, prices from US$24 to US$49. To **Puebla**, 1st-class buses take the *autopista*, 4½ hrs, 2nd-class buses go on the old road, 5-6 hrs, good scenery in both cases, many buses throughout the day, US$21. To **Veracruz**, it is 7½ hrs via the *autopista* and Orizaba. Luxury service: **Cristóbal Colón Plus**, at 2330, US$15-26, **ADO**, at 0830 and 2030, US$22.70; 2nd class: **Cuenca** (1st-class terminal) at 2400, US$13.15; **AU** (AU terminal), at 2230, US$16.80; book early, alternatives are to change at Puebla or go via Tuxtepec. **Cristóbal Colón** to **Villahermosa**, daily at 1700 and 2100, US$22.70, 14 hrs, book well ahead. To **Mérida**, **Cristóbal Colón**, Sun at 0900, 16½ hrs.

The route to Chiapas from Oaxaca is via Tehuantepec, the 1st 2 hrs are on very windy roads. To **Tuxtla Gutiérrez** and **San Cristóbal de las Casas**, luxury service: **Cristóbal Colón Plus**, at 2000, US$26.40, 10½ hrs (Tuxtla); US$27, 12½ hrs (San Cristóbal); 1st class: **Cristóbal Colón**, at 1930 (both) and 2215 (Tuxtla only), US$20.30 (Tuxtla), US$23.50 (San Cristóbal). 2nd class to Tuxtla only: with **Oaxaca-Istmo** 4 daily, with **Fletes y Pasajes** 6 daily, several daytime departures, US$18, 10-11 hrs. To **Tapachula**, 1st class, **Cristóbal Colón**, US$24, 11 hrs; 2nd class, with **Fletes y Pasajes**. Book well in advance as buses often come almost full from Mexico City. To **Tehuantepec**, scenic, 1st class: **Cristóbal Colón**, 13 daily, US$9.60, 5½ hrs; 2nd class: with **Oaxaca-Istmo** and **Fletes y Pasajes**, every 30 mins 0600-2400, US$7.40, 5½ hrs. To **Cd Cuauhtémoc**, US$33, 12 hrs. To **Arriaga**, US$7, 6 hrs, 5 a day.

1st-class services to the Pacific coast go through Tehuantepec in the Isthmus, a long detour, but it avoids the switchback curves of the more direct route which occasionally suffers from landslides in the rainy season. To **Pochutla**, 1st class: **Cristóbal Colón**, via Isthmus, 4 daily, US$14.70, 11 hrs; 2nd class: direct route, very scenic, with **Oaxaca-Pacífico** and **Estrella del Valle**, direct serviceat 0945, 1415 and 2230, US$6.75, 6 hrs; regular service, same companies, every 30 mins throughout the day. Night bus to **Puerto Angel**, 2315, arrives 0600. To **Puerto Escondido**, 1st class: **Cristóbal Colón**, via Isthmus, 0100, 0930 and 2400, US$14.80, 12 hrs (night bus via Pochutla 7 hrs); 2nd class: via Pochutla, with **Oaxaca-Pacífico** and **Estrella del Valle**, direct service at 0945, 1415 and 2230, US$7.60, 7 hrs; with **Estrella Roja**, superior service at 2245, US$8.70, direct service 4 daily, US$7.60; with **Tran-Sol** via **Sola de Vega**, at 0600, 1300 and 2200, US$7.60, 7 hrs (Oaxaca-Sola de Vega US$2.70). To **Huatulco**, 1st class: **Cristóbal Colón**, via Isthmus, 4 daily, US$14.60, 9½ hrs; 2nd class: via **Pochutla**, with **Oaxaca-Pacífico** at 2200, 7 hrs, or take a day bus to Pochutla and transfer there.

Car

Car hire Phone ahead to book, a week before if possible. **Arrendadora Express**, 20 de Noviembre 204A, T/F516-6776, rents out cars motorcycles and bicycles; **Hertz**, La Bastida 115, T516-2434; **TTN**, 5 de Mayo 217-7 y Murguía, T516-2577.

Car park Safe parking at Estacionamiento La Brisa, Av Zaragoza y Cabrera, US$3.50 per night, closed Sun.

Taxi

Shuttle vans A new service running to **Pochutla**. **Auto Express de Turismo**, Atlántida. Reservations and tickets at Oficina Matriz, La Noria 101, T514-7077 and Suc Maihuatlán, 3 de Octubre 114, T572-0380, US$12. Comfortable vans and faster, worth booking ahead; 0700, 1100, 1500, 1700 and 2130.

Monte Albán *p361*

Bus **Autobuses Turísticos** depart from **Hotel Rivera del Angel**, Mina 518 near Díaz Ordaz (bus tickets available from hotel lobby), every ½ hr from 0830 to 1330, US$3 return, last bus back at 1800; 2 hrs at the site, allowing only just enough time to visit ruins before returning (you are permitted to come back on another tour on 1 ticket for an extra US$1 but you will not, of course, have a reserved seat for your return). Several buses from **Hotel Trébol**, 1 block south of Zócalo, US$1.30, 0930, 1030, returning 1330, 1400. Local city buses marked 'Colonia Monte Albán', US$0.20, pass along the street outside **Hotel Rivera del Angel**. You can also catch the same bus as it begins its route in front of the **Panadería México** next to the Mercado de Abastos. Either way you will be left at the end of the bus route in the Col Monte Albán neighbourhood at the foot of the hill of the Monte Albán ruins. There are a few friendly kiosks where you will be dropped off. Ask them for the way and you should find yourself walking or hitching up a somewhat steep, black paved road for about 4 km to the ruins. The hike offers nice views but it's best not to go alone. Take the tourist bus to Monte Albán, see the ruins at your leisure, then walk 4 km downhill from the ruins to Col Monte Albán and get a city bus back from there. Some people prefer to walk up and take the tourist bus back.

Route to Mitla *p364*
Bus From Oaxaca 2nd-class station every 10 mins, 0600-1900, US$1, 40 mins. The ruins are 10 mins' walk across the village from the bus stop on the main road (2 blocks from the square).

Taxi US$10 each to Mitla for 4 sharing, with time to take photographs at Tule and Mitla and to buy souvenirs at ruins, or approximately US$10 per hr for touring as you please. You can alternatively take a *colectivo* US$1.50 from beside the Mercado de Abastos on Mercaderes (close to the 2nd-class bus station).

Hierve el Agua *p366*
Bus 2nd-class buses from Oaxaca pass through Hierve El Agua twice daily, 0810 and 1400.

Puerto Escondido *p368, map p369*
Air
Airport (PXM) 10 mins' drive west of town. With **Aerocaribe**, T582-2023, daily from **Mexico City** at 1140, to Mexico City at 1300, 1 hr, US$87; daily from **Oaxaca** at 0955 and 1640, to Oaxaca at 1045 and 1820, 30 mins, US$70. With **Aerovega** (T/F582-0151) daily from Oaxaca at 0800, to Oaxaca at 0730, US$100. Also with **Aerotucán**, T582-1725, daily from Oaxaca, US$110. *Colectivo* from airport, US$2.80 per person, T582-0030.
Car hire Budget, Av Juárez at the entrance to Bacocho, T582-0312.

Bus
The terminal is about 10 blocks north of town.
Local To Pochutla, from corner Carretera Costera and Av Oaxaca, every 20 mins, 0500-1900, 1½ hrs, US$1.60. For **Puerto Angel**, **Zipolite** and other beaches: transfer in Pochutla to pick-up or *colectivo* taxi .

Long distance To **Acapulco**, with Estrella Blanca, a/c, semi-direct service every couple of hrs from 0400, 7½ hrs, US$18.50; regular service, hourly 0500-1730, 9 hrs, US$14. To **Mexico City**, with **Estrella Blanca**, 1st class at 1830, 1930 and 2030 to the Southern Terminal, US$40, 12 hrs via Acapulco; to travel during the day go to Acapulco and transfer there; **Oaxaca-Pacífico/Estrella del Valle**, 1st class, at 1745, US$33, 14 hrs via Oaxaca, arrives at **Fletes y Pasajes** terminal near TAPO (east terminal). To **Oaxaca**, with **Estrella del Valle**, Av Hidalgo 400 near Av Oaxaca, direct service at 0815, 1245, 2215, US$8.50, 1st class at 2230, US$10.50. **Cristóbal Colón**, 1a Norte 207, 3 daily via Tehuantepec, US$16.50, 12 hrs. To **Huatulco**, via Pochutla at 0730, 1130, 1530, 1900 and 0040, 2¼ hrs, US$5.20, 2nd class 1800, 2½ hrs, US$3.80. To **Puebla**, with **Oaxaca-Pacífico/Estrella del Valle**, 1st class, at 1745, US$25, 10 hrs via Oaxaca, leaves you by the highway, not CAPU. To **Salina Cruz**, with **Estrella Blanca**, Av Oaxaca, 4 a day, 5 hrs, US$6.50. To **Tapachula**, with **Cristóbal Colón**, 2000, 14-15 hrs, US$27. To **Tuxtla Gutiérrez** and **San Cristóbal de las Casas**, with **Cristóbal Colón**, 0845 and 2130, Tuxtla US$4, 12 hrs, San Cristóbal, US$29, 14 hrs. To **Zihuatanejo**, with Estrella Blanca, 1 direct bus daily.

Pochutla *p370*
Bus
To **Acapulco**, with Estrella Blanca, 0630, 1000, 1545, 1915, 2200, 8½ hrs, US$21. To **Huatulco** (La Crucecita), with **Oaxaca-Pacífico**, every 15 mins 0500-2000, 1 hr, US$1. To **Mexico City**, with **Estrella Blanca**, 1st class, via Acapulco, 1500, 1900, 12-13 hrs, US$37; with **Oaxaca- Pacífico**, via Oaxaca, 1800 and 1900, 13 hrs, US$24. To **Oaxaca**, with **Oaxaca-Pacífico/Estrella del Valle**, direct service 0945, 1415, 2300, 6 hrs, US$7. 2nd-class service, 14 daily, 9 hrs, US$6.20; with **Cristóbal Colón** via the Isthmus, at 1445 and 1930, US$14.70. To **Puerto Escondido**, with small buses from side street near church, every 20 mins 0500-1900, 1½ hrs, US$1.30; also with through buses coming from Oaxaca or Salina Cruz. To **San Cristóbal de las Casas**, twice daily, US$26, 13 hrs. To **Salina Cruz**, with **Cristóbal Colón**, 5 daily; with Estrella Blanca, 3 daily, 3-4 hrs, US$7. To **Tapachula**, with **Cristóbal Colón**, 2100, 12 hrs, US$24. To **Tuxtla Gutiérrez**, with Cristóbal Colón, 0945 and 2230, 10 hrs, US$19.

Taxi and colectivo
For **Puerto Angel**, **Zipolite** and other beaches, pick-up trucks with benches in the back and shared taxis (*colectivos*) do round trips on the coastal road in both directions; these taxis also offer private service (*carreras*); in Pochutla, wait at marked bus stops along the main road. To **Puerto Angel**, truck US$0.40, *colectivo* US$0.70 per person, taxi US$4. To **Zipolite**, truck US$0.45, *colectivo* US$1, taxi US$6. To **Mazunte**, truck US$0.50, *colectivo* US$1, taxi US$6. Beware of overcharging, which is especially common in this area.

Huatulco *p372*
Air
Aeropuerto Bahías de Huatulco (HUX), is located 17 km northwest of Huatulco along Route 200, T581-9099; airport van service T581-9014, US$27. Taxi US$12, 20 mins. From **Mexico City**, **Mexicana**, daily at 1005 and 1335, returning from Huatulco 1150 and 1520; discounts for advanced purchase. From **Oaxaca**, **Aerocaribe** daily at 0700 and 1705, returning from Huatulco at 0750 and 1755. All international flights are charters and run in the boreal winter only.

Airline offices Aerocaribe, Hotel Castillo Huatulco, Santa Cruz, T587-1220. **Mexicana**, Hotel Castillo Huatulco, Santa Cruz, T587-0223.

Bus
Local 2nd-class buses to **Pochutla** from Blv Chahué and Riscalillo, La Crucecita, every 15 mins 0500-2000, US$1.20, 1 hr. 2nd-class buses to **Salina Cruz** from Blv Chahué and Bugambilia, frequent departures, 3 hrs. *Colectivo* taxis run from Tangolunda and Crucecita (main plaza), US$0.40.

Long distance To **Acapulco**, with Estrella Blanca, 1st class, 4 daily, 9 hrs, US$23; 2nd class, 3 daily, 11 hrs, US$17. To **Mexico City**, with **Cristóbal Colón**, 1st class, 4 daily (arriving at various terminals), 14 hrs, US$44, via Isthmus and Oaxaca; with **Estrella Blanca**, 1st class, at 1800, 13 hrs, US$44, via Acapulco. To **Oaxaca**, 1st class with **Cristóbal Colón**, Gardenia corner Ocotillo, La Crucecita, 2 daily, US$18, via Isthmus 8 hrs; luxury **Plus** service at 2100, US$22. 2nd class with **Oaxaca-Pacífico**, Calle Jazmín, La Crucecita, 1 daily, 7 hrs, US$9, via Pochutla. To **Puerto Escondido**, with **Cristóbal Colón**, 1st class, 7 daily, US$5, 2 hrs; with **Estrella Blanca**, Gardenia corner Palma Real, La Crucecita, 1st class, 4 daily, 2½ hrs, US$5.30, 2nd class, 3 daily, US$3.90. To **Salina Cruz**, with **Cristóbal Colón**, 1st class, 8 daily continuing to Tehuantepec and Juchitán, 2½ hrs, US$6.50; with **Plus** service, 2 daily, US$6.50; with **Estrella Blanca**, 3 daily, 2½ hrs, US$5.80. To **Tapachula**, with **Cristóbal Colón**, 1st class, at 2215, 10 hrs, US$26. To **Tuxtla Gutiérrez**, with Cristóbal Colón, 1st class, 2045 and 2345, 8 hrs, US$20. To **Pochutla** from Blv Chahué and Riscalillo, La Crucecita, *microbuses* every 15 mins, 0500-2000, US$1.20. Make connections at the crossroads at Pochutla for *colectivos*, minibuses and taxis for **Puerto Angel**, **Mazunte**, **Puerto Escondido** and **Zipolite**.

Isthmus of Tehuantepec *p374*
Air There's an airport at Cd Ixtepec with flights to **Mexico City**, with **Aeromar**, 2 daily flights weekdays, 1 daily flight weekends, US$168-257. To **Oaxaca**, with **Aerocaribe**, 1 daily flight at 0935, US$8.

Salina Cruz *p374*
Air
Regional airport at Cd Ixtepec, transport to airport US$9 per person.

Bus
Regional service to **Tehuantepec** (US$0.65) and **Juchitán** (US$1.40) every 10 mins with **Istmeños**, 0500-2400, from Progreso west of Tampico, by train tracks. Frequent 2nd-class service to **Huatulco**, 3 hrs. There is a joint bus station for **Cristóbal Colón**, **ADO**, **AU** and **Sur** at the north end of town, by the Carretera Transístmica.

To **Coatzacoalcos**, 6 hrs, US$14.50. To **Oaxaca**, 1st class: **Cristóbal Colón**, 8 daily, 6 hrs, US$13; 2nd class: Oaxaca-**Istmo**, 3 daily, 6 hrs, US$10. To **Pochutla**, 1st class with **Cristóbal Colón**, 5 daily; 2nd class; with **Estrella Blanca**, 3 daily, 3-4 hrs, US$9. To **Puerto Escondido**, 2nd class, with **Estrella Blanca**, 4 daily, 5 hrs, US$6.50. To **Tapachula**, with **Cristóbal Colón** 2nd class, along the coast, 9-10 hrs, 0740 and 2030, US$17, 1st-class bus at 2000, US$21. To **Tuxtla Gutiérrez** and **San Cristóbal de las Casas**,

2 daily buses come from Oaxaca or Puerto Escondido and are very often full, book well in advance, US$15 (Tuxtla), US$18 (San Cristóbal); alternatively, take a 2nd-class bus to **Juchitán**, then to Arriaga and from there to Tuxtla and San Cristóbal.

Tehuantepec *p374*

Bus

Regional **Istmeños** buses leave from the highway (Carretera Cristóbal Colón), at the end of 5 de Mayo. To **Salina Cruz**, every 10 mins, 0500-2400, US$0.65, 45 mins. To **Juchitán**, every 10 mins, 0500-2400, US$0.80, 1 hr. There is a joint bus station for **Cristóbal Colón, ADO, AU** and **Sur** on the outskirts of town; taxi to Zócalo US$1, *moto-carro* US$0.50 or 15 mins' walk (walking not recommended at night).
To **Arriaga**, 0600, 0800, 1800 to connect to Tonalá (not confirmed). It is not always possible to get a reservation with **Cristóbal Colón** in Tehuantepec, for Chiapas destinations; you have a better chance from Salina Cruz or Juchitán, where more buses stop. To **Cancún**, with **ADO** at 1430, US$68. To **Coatzacoalcos**, with **ADO** and **Sur**, 1st class 5 daily, 6 hrs, US$13; 2nd class every 30 mins, US$10. To **Oaxaca**, **Pochutla**,and **Puerto Escondido**, with **Cristóbal Colón**, 1st class 4 daily, US$7.50 (Huatulco), US$10 (Pochutla), US$14 (Puerto Escondido). To **Huatulco**, 2nd class, 0600, 1330, US$6. To **Mexico City**, with **Cristóbal Colón**, *plus* service, 2030, US$42; 1st class, 2000, 2145, US$48. To **San Cristóbal de la Casas**, with **Cristóbal Colón**, 0030 and 1400, 6½ hrs, US$16. To **Tonalá** and **Tapachula**, with **Cristóbal Colón**, 2 nightly, US$9 (Tonalá), US$19 (Tapachula). To **Tuxtepec** and **Veracruz**, with **AU** via Sayula, 1040, 2140, US$14, 6 hrs (Tuxtepec), US$23 (Veracruz). To **Tuxtla Gutiérrez**, with **Cristóbal Colón**, 0030, 1400, 2200, 4½ hrs, US$13. To **Villahermosa**, with **Cristóbal Colón** 1st class, US$17, 8 hrs, 2nd class US$14.

Car

Tehuantepec is at the junction of the Carretera Transístmica (185) and Route 190, which connects it with Oaxaca, 257 km away.

Taxis

3-wheeled motorized rickshaws (*moto-carros*) take locals around town; you have to stand and hold on to the railing.

Juchitán and around *p375*

Bus

Regional bus service to **Tehuantepec** (US$0.80) and **Salina Cruz** (US$1.40). Every 15 mins with **Istmeños**, 0500-2400, from Prolongación 16 de Septiembre, by the highway to Tehuantepec. Joint bus station for **Cristóbal Colón**, **ADO**, **Sur** and **AU** at Prolongación 16 de Septiembre, just south of the highway to Tehuantepec. To **Huatulco**, with **ADO** 0600, US$8.60; with **Cristóbal Colón**, 5 daily, US$9; with **Sur**, 3 daily, US$5.55. To **Coatzacoalcos**, with **ADO** 13 daily, US$13; with **Sur**, every 20 mins, US$8. To **Mexico City**, with **ADO** luxury, at 2145, US$72; with **ADO** 1st class, 1900 and 2100, US$52; with **AU** 6 daily US$42. To **Oaxaca**, with **ADO** luxury, 3 daily, US$16; 1st class: **ADO** 3 daily, **Cristóbal Colón** 7 daily, 6 hrs, US$13. To **Pochutla** and **Puerto Escondido**, with **Cristóbal Colón**, 4 daily, US$14 (Puerto), US$12 (Pochutla); with **Sur**, 2330, US$12 (Puerto), US$9 (Pochutla). To **San Cristóbal de las Casas**, with **Cristóbal Colón**, 3 daily, US$16. To **Tapachula**, with **ADO** at 0230, US$23; with **Cristóbal Colón**, 2 nightly, US$19; with **Sur** 0230 and 1600, US$16. To **Tuxtepec**, with **AU** at 1115, US$13. To **Tuxtla Gutiérrez**, with **Cristóbal Colón**, 5 daily, US$14. To **Veracruz**, with **ADO** 0055 and 2130, US$215; with **AU** 1115, US$24.

Car

Juchitán is 26 km northeast of Tehuantepec. At La Ventosa, 14 km northeast of Juchitán, the road splits: the Carretera Transístmica (Route 185) continues north towards Coatzacoalcos on the Gulf of Mexico, and the Carretera Costera (Route 200) goes east to San Pedro Tapanatepec, where it splits again, one road going to Tuxtla Gutiérrez and the other to Tapachula.

Directory

Oaxaca *p357, map p358*

Banks **Bancomer**, on García Vigil, 1 block from Zócalo, exchanges TCs in own *casa de cambio*, 0900-1600, and Visa ATM. **Banco Santander Mexicano**, Independencia 605, cash and TCs, good rates, TCs changed

Mon-Fri 0900-1330. **Amex** office **Viajes Micsa**, Valdivieso 2, T516-2700, just off Zócalo. **Escotiabank**, Periférico near Mercado de Abastos, best rates. *Casa de cambio*, Abasolo 105, 0800-2000 changes TCs. *Casa de cambio* at Armenta y López, near corner with Hidalgo, Mon-Sat 0800-2000, shorter hrs on Sun. No problem to change TCs at weekends as there are many *casas de cambio* around the Zócalo. **Embassies and consulates** Canada, Pino Suárez 700 local 11B. **Italy**, Alcaclá 400, T516-5058. **USA** (Consular Agency), Alcalá 407, T514-3054, conagent@prodigy.net.mx **Immigration** Pensamientos 104, Col Reforma, Mon-Fri 0900-1400, 2nd floor. **Internet** Many cyber cafés and in the post office, Mon-Fri 0800-1900, with fairly good set-ups, charging US$1 per hr. **Language schools** There are many schools in the city most of which can normally offer family stays which can enhance your learning. The following have all been recommended: **Academia Vinigúlaza**, Abasolo 503, T513-2763, www.vinigulaza.com, small groups, US$83 per 15-hr week, good place to talk with Mexican students, also cooking and salsa classes. **Amigos del Sol**, Libres 109, T514-3484, www.oaxacanews.com/amigosdelsol.htm, small groups, US$85 per week, 3 hrs per day, or US$15 per day; accommodation can also be arranged, recommended. **Becari**, M Bravo 210, Plaza San Cristóbal, CP 68000, T/F514-6076, www.becari.com.mx, 4 blocks north of Zócalo, US$105 for a 15-hr week with fully qualified teachers, courses including culture, history, literature and politics, with workshops on dancing, cooking or art, flexible programmes, recommended. **Centro de Idiomas**, Universidad Autónoma Benito Juárez, Burgoa, 5 blocks south of Zócalo, weekly or monthly classes (US$200 per month), or private tuition, very professional and good value for money, recommended. **Español Interactivo**, Armenta and López 311-B, T514-6062, www.mexonline.com/esp-interactivo.htm, small groups, US$75 per week, 3 hrs per day, cooking, dancing. **Instituto Cultural Oaxaca**, Av Juárez 909, T515-3404, www.instculturaloax.com.mx, in addition to Spanish classes, local crafts and culture (including dance, cooking, weaving and pottery) are taught. 4 hrs of formal Spanish teaching are complemented with 2 hrs spent in cultural workshops and 1 hr of informal conversation with a native speaker; US$105 per week, US$400 per month. **Instituto de Comunicación y Cultura**, M Alcalá 307-12, 2nd floor, T/F516-3443, www.iccoax.com, cultural workshops and field trips included in the programme, US$150 per week, US$450 per month. **Instituto Johann Goethe**, JP García 502, T/F514-3516, wide variety of courses, eg 4 weeks, 2 hrs a day, US$160. **Soléxico Language and Cultural Center**, Abasolo 217 and Juárez, T/F516-5680, www.solexico.com, variable programme with options for homestay, excursions and volunteering. Have branch in Playa del Carmen. See also Learning Spanish in Essentials, page 25.
Laundry Lavandería Azteca, Hidalgo 404 between Díaz Ordaz y J P García, Mon-Sat 0830-2000, quick service, delivers to nearby hotels, 3.5 kg US$3.80. **Lavandería Hidalgo**, Hidalgo and J P García, Mon-Sat 0800-2000, 3.5 kg US$3.80. **ELA, Super Lavandería Automática**, Antonio Roldán 114, Col Olímpica, washes and irons. **Libraries Biblioteca Circulante Benedict Crowel Memorial**, Pino Suárez 519, English lending library with very good English books, a few French and Spanish, used books and magazines for sale (Mon-Fri 1000-1300, 1600-1900, Sat 1000-1300), US$13 per year plus US$13 returnable deposit. **Biblioteca Pública Central**, Alcalá 200 (no sign), has a lovely courtyard and a reading room with Mexican newspapers and magazines. Next door is the library of the **Museo de Arte Contemporáneo**. For the libraries at the **Centro Cultural Santo Domingo** and the **Instituto de Artes Gráficas**. **Luggage storage** Servicio Turístico de Guarda **Equipaje y Paquetería**, Av Tinoco y Palacios 312, Centro, T516-0432, open 24 hrs.
Medical services Dentist: **Dra Marta Fernández del Campo**, Armenta y López 215, English speaking, very friendly, recommended. **Doctor: Dr Víctor Tenorio**, Clínica del Carmen, Abasolo 215, T516-2612, close to centre (very good English). Dr Marco Antonio Callejo (English speaking), Belisario Domínguez 115, T515-3492, surgery 0900-1300, 1700-2000. **Pharmacy**: 20 de Noviembre and Ignacio Aldama, open till 2300. **Post office**, Alameda de León,

Independencia y 20 de Noviembre.
Telephone Public card phones are the easiest way to make long-distance calls, otherwise shop around for rates at long-distance phone establishments.

Puerto Escondido *p368, map p369*
Banks Some 11 banks have ATMs around town. **Bancomer**, 1a Norte y 2a Pte, cash and TCs 0800-1400. **HSBC**, 1a Norte y 3a Pte, cash and TCs, cash advance on Visa and MasterCard, Mon-Sat 0800-1900. **Banamex**, Av Pérez Gasga east of El Adoquín, 0900-1300. **Bannorte**, Oaxaca and Hildago, cash and TCs, reliable service. 2 *casas de cambio* on El Adoquín, open till 2000, poor rates. **Internet** Some 35 internet cafés about town all charge $2 per hr.
Laundry Lavandería at east end of El Adoquín, US$1 per kg or US$3.25 per load, self-service, Mon-Sat 0900-2100. Another one at Av Pérez Gasga by Hotel Nayar, US$2 per kg. **Medical services** Doctors: **Dr Francisco Serrano Severiano**, 1a Norte y 2a Pte, opposite Bancomer, speaks English, 0900-1300, 1700-2000. **Dr Max**, Av Oaxaca and 7a Norte, new office, no emergency service, recommended. **Hospitals and clinics: Clínica de Especialidades del Puerto**, Av Oaxaca, has been recommended. **Clínica de Loredes**, 1a Pte y 1a Norte, surgery and emergency. **Clínica Santa Fe**, Av 5a Pte. **Opticians: Optica Nuestra Señora de la Luz**, Hildago 101, T582-1844. Emergency prescription glasses, contacts. **Pharmacies: Farmacia La Moderna**, Av Pérez Gasga 203, T582-0214, has a physician in house, open 24 hrs. **Post office** 7a Norte by Av Oaxaca, good telegraph service to wire money (need transfer number from sender), Western Union office next door.

Pochutla *p370*
Banks All on main street: **Bancomer**, 0830-1400, cash and TCs. **Banorte**, 0830-1400, cash and TCs. **HSBC**, 0830-1700, cash and TCs. **Banomex**, opposite plaza, ATM and Western Union office. **Internet** Email in a couple of places on Lázaro Cárdenas. **Medical services** Public hospital just south of town.

Puerto Angel *p370*
Banks Cash and TCs changed at **Hotel Soraya**. Banks in Pochutla. **Internet** Caseta Puerto Angel, Calle José Vasconcelos 3 (next to **Hotel Soraya**), T584-3038.

Huatulco *p372*
Banks HSBC, Bugambilia corner Sabalí, La Crucecita, cash and TCs, cash advances through ATM only. **Bancomer**, Blv Santa Cruz y Otitlán del Valle, Santa Cruz, cash and TCs. **Inverlat**, Blv Santa Cruz, Santa Cruz, cash and TCs. **American Express**, Bahías Plus, Carrizal 704, La Crucecita, cash and TCs at good rates, Mon-Sat 0900-1400. *Casa de cambio*, Guamúchil near the Plaza, La Crucecita, poor rates. **Internet** Informática Mare, Guanacastle 203, 2nd floor, near market, US$3 per hr. **Laundry** Lavandería Abril, Gardenia 1403 y Pochote, La Crucecita, US$0.75 per kg. **Lavandería Estrella**, Flamboyán y Carrizal, La Crucecita, US$0.75 per kg, Mon-Sat 0800-2100. **Medical services** Especialidades Médicas Santa Cruz, Flamboyán at Plaza, La Crucecita, private, English spoken. **Central Médica Huatulco**, Flamboyán 205, La Crucecita, T587-0104, private. **IMSS**, social security hospital, Blv Chahué, just south of La Crucecita. **Post office** Blv Chahué, at south end of La Crucecita.

Salina Cruz *p374*
Banks Bancomer, Avila Camacho. **HSBC**, Avila Camacho and Coatzacoalcos. Both change cash and TCs. **Internet** Service from **Edtzin**, Tampico 40, and **Nautinet**, Tampico 15; both US$2.20 per hr. **Laundry** Alborada, Tampico and Guaymas, US$1.65 per kg.
Medical services Hospital Civil, Avila Camacho, Centre, T714-0110.

Tehuantepec *p374*
Banks HSBC, Juana C Romero, 0800-1700. **Bancomer**, 5 de Mayo. **Banorte**, 5 de Mayo. All change cash and TCs. **Internet** Service in Salina Cruz or Juchitán.

Juchitán and around *p375*
Banks Bancomer, 16 de Septiembre by the main plaza, Mon-Fri 0830-1400, cash and TCs. **HSBC**, 16 de Septiembre y Alvaro Obregón, Mon-Fri 0800-1900, Sat 0900-1400, cash and TCs. **Internet** Servitel, Efraín Gómez and 16 de Septiembre, US$4.35 per hr. **Istmored**, just north of town on the road to Ixtepec, US$3.25 per hr.

Tabasco and Chiapas

The states of Tabasco and Chiapas merge to form a geographical block that separates Mexico from Guatemala and the Yucatán Peninsula. Until recently, low-lying, jungly Tabasco was considered an oil state with little appeal for tourists, but oil wealth has brought Villahermosa, the state capital, a certain self-assurance and vibrancy, and the parks, nature reserves and huge meandering rivers in the eastern and southern regions of the state are beginning to attract visitors. Its lands once gave rise to the first great civilization of Mesoamerica, the Olmec, whose influence was felt through vast zones of Mexico and further afield.

In Chiapas, the land of the Classic Maya (whose descendants still inhabit the highland villages today), the attractions are better known: San Cristóbal de las Casas is the end of the line for many travellers who base themselves in this delightful colonial and indigenous town while they soak up the atmosphere and explore the jungle waterfalls; the dramatic Sumidero Canyon; the multi-coloured lakes, and – highlight of any trip to Mexico – the ruins at Palenque, with a jungle setting that is arguably the most atmospheric and beautiful of all the Maya sites. Chiapas is also a good entry point for Guatemala. You can head straight for northern Guatemala and the ruins of Tikal or take a more genteel entry through the western highlands and idyllic Lake Atitlán.

Although in some ways Chiapas has fallen victim to the progress bug, it nevertheless seems impervious to the intrusion of outsiders. The Lost World feeling is created by indigenous inhabitants and their villages which make everything seem timeless. The appalling treatment the inhabitants have suffered over centuries was the fundamental cause of the rebellion on 1 January 1994, which led to the occupation of San Cristóbal by the revolutionaries of the EZLN (Zapatista Army of National Liberation) and their continuing struggle in and beyond the boundaries of Chiapas. » For details of Routes to Guatemala, see page 414; for Sleeping, Eating and other listings, see pages 418-436.

Villahermosa

» pp418-436. Colour map 4, B1.

→ *Phone code: 993. Population: 275,000.*

Capital of Tabasco state, hot and humid Villahermosa is a busy, prosperous and attractive city on the Río Grijalva, which is navigable to the sea. Prices here tend to be high, although it is possible to find cheaper alternatives.

The **cathedral**, ruined in 1973, has been rebuilt, its twin steeples beautifully lit at night; it is not in the centre. There is a warren of modern colonial-style pedestrian malls throughout the central area. The **Centro de Investigaciones de las Culturas Olmecas** (CICOM) is set in a new modern complex with a large public library, expensive restaurant, airline offices and souvenir shops, a few minutes' walk south, out of town along the river bank. The **Museo Regional de Antropología Carlos Pellicer** ⓘ *Tue-Sun 0900-1900, US$1*, on three floors, has well laid-out displays of Maya and Olmec artefacts. Two other museums worth visiting are the **Museo de Cultura Popular** ⓘ *Zaragoza 810, Tue-Sun 0900-2000, free*, and the **Museo de Historia de Tabasco** ⓘ *Av 27 de Febrero corner of Juárez, Tue-Sun 0900-2000, Sun 1000-1700, US$0.50.* **Mercado Pino Suárez** ⓘ *Pino Suárez corner of Bastar Zozaya*, offers a sensory overload as every nook and cranny is taken up with a variety of goods; everything from barbecued *pejelagarto* to cowboy hats, colourful handmade fabrics, spices and dangling naked chickens en route to the kettle. The local drink, *pozol*, is believed to cure a hangover. You can watch it being made here as the *pozoleros* grind the hominy into a thick dough to then mix it with cacao and water; its grainy starchiness is somewhat of an acquired taste. Nonetheless it is popular, and the *pozoleros* will serve you the drink *al gusto*, that is, with as much or as little sugar as you want. The **Institute of Tourism** ⓘ *Av de los Ríos y Calle 13, T316-3633, daily 0800-2000, English spoken*, is good for maps and advice on Tabasco state.

Parque Nacional La Venta

ⓘ *Blv Adolfo Ruiz Cortines, T314-1652, Tue-Sun 0800-1600, US$2; it takes up to 2 hrs to do the park justice; excellent guides speak Spanish and English (US$6.65 for 1 hr 10 mins), recommended.*

In 1925 an expedition of archaeologists discovered huge sculptured human and animal figures, urns and altars in almost impenetrable forest at **La Venta**, 120 km west of Villahermosa, and once the centre of the ancient Olmec culture. In the 1950s the monuments were threatened with destruction by the discovery of oil nearby. The poet Carlos Pellicer got them hauled all the way to a woodland area near Villahermosa, now the Parque Nacional de La Venta, also called the Museo Nacional de la Venta. The park, with scattered lakes, next to a children's playground, is almost opposite the old airport entrance (west of downtown). There, the 33 exhibits are dispersed in various small clearings. The huge heads, one of them weighing 20 tonne, are Olmec, a culture that flourished about 1150-150 BC. The figures have suffered a certain amount of damage through being exposed to the elements (those in the Xalapa Anthropological Museum are in far better condition) but to see them here, in natural surroundings, is an experience not to be missed. There is also a zoo with creatures from the Tabasco jungle: monkeys, alligators, deer, wild pigs and birds. There is nothing to see at the original site of La Venta. Outside the park, on the lakeside, is an observation tower, **Mirador de las Aguilas** ⓘ *free*, with excellent views, but only for the fit as there are lots of stairs. Taxis charge US$1.50 to the Parque. Bus Circuito No 1 from outside second-class bus terminal goes past Parque La Venta. From Parque Juárez in the city, take a 'Fraccionamiento Carrizal' bus and ask to be let off at Parque Tomás Garrido, of which La Venta is a part.

Be sure to take insect repellent for the visit.

Parque Yumká

ⓘ *T356-0107, daily 0900-1600, US$2, most tour agencies offer round trips for about US$8*, a safari park containing 108 ha of Tabasco's three major habitats – jungle, savannah and lagoon, is a 'zoo without cages' offering walking, trolley and boat tours of each habitat. While the ecological park partly promotes the diversity of the region's flora and fauna, there are also animals from Asia and Africa. It's an easy day trip; take the *colectivo* to the airport and the park is next door.

South of Villahermosa

» *pp418-436. Colour map 4, B1.*

South of Villahermosa on Route 195 the nice, clean little town of **Teapa** has several hotels and beautiful surroundings. Also in Teapa are the **Grutas de Cocona**, which house a stunning array of stalagmites and beautiful displays of colour. The caves are approximately 500 m deep and a fresh and inviting river runs through them. There is a restaurant and campsite in the area.

Southwest of Teapa on Route 195 is **Pichucalco**, an affluent town with a lively and safe atmosphere. The Zócalo throngs in the evening with people on after-dinner *paseos*. Buses hourly to Villahermosa, US$4. There are hotels, restaurants and bars here. South of Pichucalco on Highway 195 on the way to Tuxtla Gutiérrez, is **Bochil**, an idyllic stopover.

Tuxtla Gutiérrez

» pp418-436. Colour map 4, B1.

→ *Phone code: 961. Altitude: 522 m.*

The street system here is as follows: Avenidas run from east to west, Calles from north to south. The Avenidas are named according to whether they are north (Norte) or south (Sur) of the Avenida Central and change their names if they are east (Oriente) or west (Poniente) of the Calle Central. The number before Avenida or Calle means the distance from the Centre measured in blocks. You know whether it's an Avenida or a Calle by the order of the address: Avenidas have their number, then Sur or Norte followed by east or west; Calles have the east or west position first. For example, 1 Norte Oriente is the eastern part of the first avenue north of Avenida Central; 2 Oriente Norte is the north part of the second street west of Calle Central. It all sounds very complicated, but as long as you check map and road signs very carefully, it is not difficult to navigate your way around the city.

To find your way around the complicated street-naming system, see Transport page 429.

The capital of Chiapas, Tuxtla Gutiérrez is a busy, shabby city with a couple of points of interest to the tourist. The main sights are a long way from the centre and too far to walk; the gem is the zoo. The feast of the Virgen de Guadalupe is celebrated on 12 December. To get to the **tourist office** ⓘ *Belisario Domínguez 950, Plaza Instituciones, T602-5127, www.turismochiapas.gob.mx, Mon-Fri 0900-2100, Sat 0900-2000, Sun 0900-1500*, take a *colectivo* from the junction of Avenida Central and Calle 2 Oriente. There is also an office in the ADO bus terminal on Calle 2 Poniente Norte and Avenida 2 Norte Poniente, which has more or less the same limited information as the main office.

Sights

In the Parque Madero at the east end of town (Calzada de los Hombres Ilustres) is the **Museo Regional de Chiapas** ⓘ *Tue-Sun 0900-1600, US$3.30*, with a fine collection of Maya artefacts, an auditorium and a library. Nearby is the **Jardín Botánico** (botanical garden) ⓘ *Tue-Sun 0900-1600, free.*

Tuxtla is best known for its superb **zoo** ⓘ *Tue-Sun 0830-1730; in Spanish only, the donations box is in front of the educational centre on the right as you enter*, some 3 km south of town up a long hill. It was founded by Dr Miguel Alvarez del Toro, who died in 1996. His philosophy was to provide a free zoo for the children and indigenous people of the area. The zoo is very large and many of the animals are in open areas, with plenty of room to run about. Monkeys are not in cages, but in areas of trees pruned back so they cannot jump out of the enclosure. Some birds wander along the paths among the visitors. The zoo makes for a very pleasant and educational afternoon. Recommended. Take mosquito repellent. *Colectivos* to 'Zoológico' and 'Cerro Hueco' from Mercado (Calle 1a Oriente Sur y 7 Sur Oriente), pass the entrance every 20

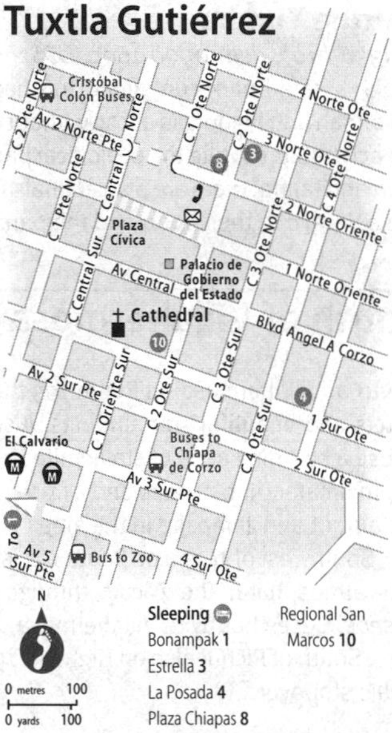

minutes; taxis charge US$2.50-3 from centre or town buses charge US$0.20. When returning, catch the bus from the same side you were dropped off as it continues up the hill to the end of the line where it fills up for the return journey.

Sumidero Canyon » pp418-436. Colour map 4, B1.

ⓘ *Daily 0600-1800, www.sumidero.com.*

An excellent paved road through spectacular scenery leads to the rim of the 1000-m-deep Sumidero canyon, now a national park. Native warriors, unable to endure the Spanish conquest, hurled themselves into the canyon rather than submit. Camping is permitted outside the gate (bus US$3; *colectivo* from San Cristóbal de las Casas bus terminal, US$2.50; taxi fare US$25 return; try to get a group together and negotiate with a combi driver to visit the viewpoints on the road into the canyon, US$15 per vehicle, leave from 1 Norte Oriente). To get to the first viewpoint only, take a *colectivo* marked 'Km 4', get out at the end and walk about 3 km up the road. With your own car, you can drive up to the last mirador (restaurant), a two- to three-hour trip, 20 km east of the city. At Cahuaré, 10 km in the direction of Chiapa de Corzo, it is possible to park by the river. If going by bus, US$1.50 each way, get out just past the large bridge on the Chiapa de Corzo road. Boat tours start from below this bridge, where there is also a car park and restaurant serving good seafood. A boat trip into the Sumidero Canyon costs US$6.50 per person for two hours; boats leave when full. It costs US$65 to hire a boat for private a group. Take a sweater as the boats go very fast and it can feel cool. Boat trips are excellent for birdwatching, and green iguanas, American crocodiles (including some real monsters over 4 m long) and howler monkeys are often spotted. From Tuxtla, a taxi to all miradores will charge US$18; first mirador only US$10. Or taxi to Chiapa de Corzo, US$5, then a *colectivo* boat from there. A licensed taxi service from Tuxtla to the Canyon can be booked at Avenida 1 Sur Poniente 1203, T613-7033.

❢ *Especially recommended at sunset.*

❢ *Ask locally about the pollution situation; the water is sometimes filthy although the canyon is still impressive.*

Tours from San Cristóbal including boat trip costs US$22-25. It is easier to find people to make up numbers in Chiapa de Corzo than in Cahuaré, as the former is a livelier place with more restaurants, launches and other facilities.

Chiapa de Corzo → *Phone code: 961. Colour map 4, B1. Altitude: 456 m.*

Fifteen kilometres beyond the canyon, Chiapa de Corzo, a colonial town on a bluff overlooking the Grijalva River, is more interesting than Tuxtla. In the centre is a fine 16th-century crown-shaped **fountain**; the 16th-century church of **Santo Domingo** with an engraved altar of solid silver; and craftsmen who work with gold, jewellery and lacquerwork. Chiapa de Corzo was a pre-Classic and proto-Classic Maya site and shares features with early Maya sites in Guatemala; the ruins are behind the Nestlé plant, and some unrestored mounds are on private property in a field near modern houses. There are one-and-a-half- and two-hour boat trips along the river to spot crocodiles, turtles, monkeys and hummingbirds, cost US$50 or US$60 for 12 passengers; wait by water's edge, boats soon fill up.

The waterfall at the **Cueva de El Chorreadero** is well worth a detour of 1 km. The road to the cave is 10 km past Chiapa de Corzo, a few kilometres after you start the climb up into the mountains to get to San Cristóbal. Camping is possible but there are no facilities; take a torch.

San Cristóbal de las Casas

▸▸ pp418-436. Colour map 4, B1.

➔ *Phone code: 967. Altitude: 2110 m.*

One of Mexico's most beautiful towns, San Cristóbal de las Casas is stunningly located in the fertile Jovel valley, with the mountains of Huitepec to the west and Tzontehuitz to the east. The city is a charming blend of colonial architecture and indigenous culture, laid out in the colonial period with 21 indigenous *barrios* on the city's perimeter, which were later integrated into the totally *mestizo* city that existed by the 18th century. The indigenous population is today an important part of San Cristóbal's atmosphere, many of them earning a living by selling handicrafts in the town's two markets. The centre is rich in architectural variety, with excellent examples of baroque, neoclassical and plateresque, a Mexican style characterized by the intricate moulding of façades, resembling the work of silversmiths, hence the name, which means 'like a silversmith's'. ▸▸ *For Sleeping, Eating and other listings, see page 418-436.*

For trips to the nearby villages, see page 402.

Ins and outs

Getting there There is a small airport (SZT) about 15 km from town. The first-class bus terminal services destinations all over Mexico, while the two second-class terminals are for local buses to destinations within Chiapas and to the Guatemalan border. Those travelling to Palenque by car will have fine views but should avoid night-time journeys because of armed robberies. ▸▸ *For details, see Transport, page 430.*

Getting around Most places are within walking distance of each other although taxis are available in the town and to the nearby villages; the cheaper *colectivos* run on fixed routes only.

Best time to visit Due to its altitude, San Cristóbal has a pleasantly mild climate compared to the hotter Chiapas towns such as Palenque and Tuxtla. During June, July and August, it is warm and sunny in the morning, while in the afternoon it tends to rain, with a sharp drop in temperature. Warm, waterproof clothes are needed, although the heavy rains conveniently stop in the evening, when you can enjoy San Cristóbal's many cheap restaurants and friendly bars and cafés.

Tourist information The **tourist office** ⓘ *Hidalgo 1, at the government offices, T678-6570, Mon-Sat 0800-2000, Sun 0900-1400*, is very helpful with all types of information and provides good maps; usually someone there speaks English. The **Municipal Office** ⓘ *on the main plaza, in the Palacio Municipal, T678-0665*, has a good free map of town and surroundings.

Sights

The main square, **Plaza 31 de Marzo**, has a gazebo built during the era of Porfirio Díaz. In front of the plaza is the neoclassical **Palacio Municipal**, built in 1885. A few steps away is the **Catedral de San Cristóbal**, built in the 16th century, painted in ochre, brown and white, with a baroque pulpit added in the 17th century. Adjacent to the cathedral is the church of **San Nicolás**, which houses the historical archives of the diocese. The building dates from 1613, and is believed to be the only church in Mexico to preserve its original design in the architectural style of indigenous people's churches. Just off the plaza, at the beginning of Insurgentes, is the former **Casa de la Sirena**, now the **Hotel Santa Clara**. Built at the end of the 16th century, this is a rare example of colonial residential architecture in the plateresque style. The interior has the four classic corridors of renaissance constructions. Heading off the plaza in the opposite direction, going north up 20 de Noviembre, you reach the **Church and Ex-Convento de Santo Domingo**. By far the most dramatic building in the city, it features an elaborate baroque façade in moulded mortar, especially beautiful when viewed in the late afternoon sun, which picks out the ornate mouldings with salmon pink hues. The church's altarpieces are covered in gold leaf, and the pulpit is intricately carved in a style peculiar to Mexico, known as churrigueresque, even more elaborate than the baroque style of Europe. Outside the market is the main handicraft market, with dozens of stalls selling traditional textiles, handmade dolls, wooden

San Cristóbal de las Casas

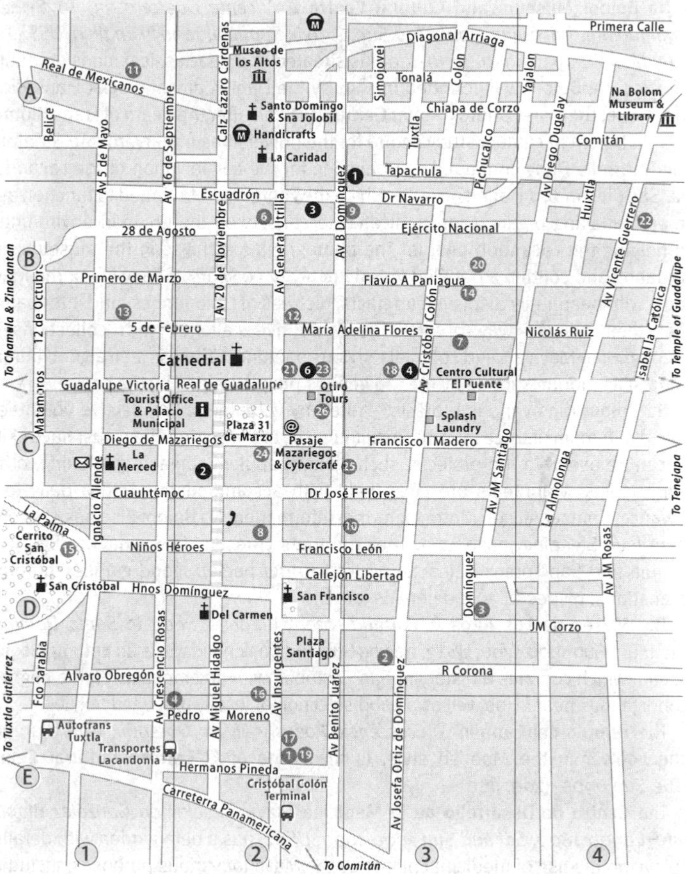

Sleeping
Barón de las Casas **26** *C2*
Capri **1** *E2*
Casa Babylon **2** *D3*
Casa de Huéspedes Chamula **3** *D3*
Casa de Huéspedes Santa Lucía **4** *E2*
Casa Mexicana **6** *B2*
Casa Vieja **7** *B3*
El Cerillo **9** *B3*
Fray Bartolomé de las Casas **8** *D2*
Palacio de Moctezuma **10** *D3*
Posada del Candil **11** *A1*
Posada Diego de Mazariegos **12** *B2*
Posada El Paraíso **13** *B1*
Posada Jovel **14** *B3*
Posada Los Morales **15** *D1*
Posada Lucella **16** *E2*
Posada Lupita **17** *E2*
Posada Margarita **18** *C3*
Posada Vallarta **19** *E2*
Posadita **20** *B3*
Real del Valle **21** *C2*
Rincón del Arco **22** *B4*
San Martín **23** *C2*
Santa Clara **24** *C2*
Youth Hostel **25** *C3*

Eating
El Gato Gordo **6** *C2*
La Casa del Pan **1** *A3*
La Paloma **2** *C2*
Las Estrellas **3** *B2*
Mayambé **4** *C3*

toys and jewellery. To the west of the centre, and up a strenuous flight of steps, is the **Templo del Cerrito**, a small church with fine views of the city and the surrounding mountains. The church is called *cerrito* (small hill) because it is set on an isolated, tree-covered hill. At the other end of the city, to the east, is another little church on a hill, the **Templo de Guadalupe**. This church is used by the indigenous people of the barrio de Guadalupe, the nearest to the centre of the 21 such indigenous neighbourhoods. Each neighbourhood is characterized by the dress of the local people, depending on which indigenous group they belong to, and by the handicrafts produced by them. Guadalupe is the barrio of candle makers, saddle makers, and wooden toy makers. The other barrios, such as Mexicanos, the oldest in the city, are further afield and not recommended for unguided visits.

Na Bolom Museum and Cultural Centre ⓘ *Vicente Guerrero 33, T678-1418, www.nabolom.org, guided tours Tue-Sun, 1130 in Spanish, 1630 in English, US$4.50; library Mon-Fri 0930-1330, 1630-1900*, is situated in a neoclassical mansion dating from 1891. **Na Bolom** was founded in 1951 by the Danish archaeologist Frans Blom and his wife, the Swiss photographer Gertrudis Duby. After the death of Frans Blom in 1963, Na Bolom became a study centre for the universities of Harvard and Stanford, while Gertrudis Duby continued campaigning for the conservation of the Lacandón area. She died in 1993, aged 92, after which the centre has continued to function as a non-profit-making organization dedicated to conserving the Chiapan environment and helping the Lacandón people. The photographic archives in the museum are fascinating and contain a detailed visual history of 50 years of daily life of the Maya people with beautifully displayed artefacts, pictures of Lacondones, and information about their present way of life. There are five galleries with collections of pre-Columbian Maya art and colonial religious paintings. There is also a good library. A shop sells products made by the indigenous people helped by the centre.

Na Bolom runs various projects, staffed by volunteers. Prospective volunteers spend a minimum of three months, maximum six, at the centre. They must have skills that can be useful to the projects, such as anthropology, organic gardening, or be multi-linguists. Volunteers are given help with accommodation and a daily food allowance. Contact Allison Motto for further information. **Na Bolom** also has 12 rooms to rent (see Sleeping, page 418). They run tours (Tuesday to Sunday) to San Juan Chamula and San Lorenzo Zinacantán; US$10 per person, good guides, thorough explanations, respectful to indigenous locals.

The **Museo de Los Altos** ⓘ *Calzada Lázaro Cárdenas, next to Santo Domingo church, Tue-Sun 1000-1700, US$3, free on Sun and bank holidays*, is an anthropological museum which contains a history of San Cristóbal, with an emphasis on the plight of the indigenous people, as well as a good selection of locally produced textiles.

The **Templo del Carmen** ⓘ *Crescencio Rosas y Alvaro Obregón*, with a unique archery tower in the Moorish style, is the home of **El Carmen Cultural Centre** ⓘ *Tue-Sun 0900-1700, free.*

The **Centro de Desarrollo de la Medicina Maya** ⓘ *Salomón González Blanco, Mon-Fri 0900-1800, Sat and Sun 1000-1600, US$2*, has a herb garden with detailed displays on the use of medicinal plants by the Maya for various purposes, including child delivery.

Villages near San Cristóbal

» *pp418-436.*

Travellers are strongly warned not to wander around in the hills surrounding San Cristóbal, as they could risk assault. Warnings can be seen in some places frequented by tourists. Remember that locals are particularly sensitive to proper dress (that is neither men nor women should wear shorts, or revealing clothes) and manners; persistent begging should be countered with courteous, firm replies.

You are recommended to call at **Na Bolom** (see above) before visiting the villages, to get information on their cultures and seek advice on the reception you are likely to get. **Photography** is resisted by some of the indigenous people because they believe the camera steals their souls, and photographing their church is stealing the soul of God; it is also seen as invasive and sometimes profiteering. Either leave your camera behind or ask your guide to let you know when you can and cannot take pictures. Cameras have been taken by villagers when photography has been inappropriate. Much of the population does not speak Spanish. You can visit the villages of San Juan Chamula, Zinacantán and Tenejapa. While this is a popular excursion, especially when led by a guide, several visitors have felt ashamed at going to look at the villagers as if they were in a zoo; there were many children begging and offering to look after private vehicles.

Zinacantán

Zinacantán is reached by VW bus from the market, US$0.75, 30 minutes' journey, sometimes with frequent stops while the conductor lights rockets at roadside shrines; taxi US$4. The Zinacantán men wear pink/red jackets with embroidery and tassels, the women vivid pale blue shawls and navy skirts. Annual festival days here are 6 January, 19-22 January, 8-10 August; visitors are welcome. At midday every day the women prepare a communal meal, which the men eat in shifts. The main gathering place is around the **church** ⓘ *US$0.40 for entering, official ticket from tourist office next door; photography inside is strictly prohibited*; the roof was destroyed by fire. There are two **museums** but both have recently closed because the community felt that they only benefited those most involved in them. Check before planning a visit. **Ik'al Ojov** ⓘ *off Calle 5 de Febrero, 5 blocks down Av Cristóbal Colón from San Lorenzo church, and 1 block to the left; donation requested*, includes two traditional *palapas* or huts that people used to live in and there is a small collection of regional costumes. It occasionally holds shows and there is an annual festival on 17 February. There is also a tiny gift shop. The second museum is the **Museo Comunitario Autzetik ta jteklum** ⓘ *1 block from San Lorenzo church*, which is run by women from Zinacantán and also has exhibits on local culture.

Above the municipal building on the right, creative, resourceful Antonia has opened **Antonia's House** ⓘ *Isabel la Católica 7*. There is a small crafts shop and she and her family will demonstrate back-strap weaving, the making of tortillas and many other aspects of life in the village. She usually has some *posh* on the go – it's strong stuff, and the red variant will set your throat on fire... Be ready with a couple of litres of water! Antonia is very easy going and she may not charge for a sample of *posh*, however bear in mind that she makes her living from the shop, so buy something or leave a contribution. Tours from San Cristóbal cost US$12.

San Juan Chamula → *Colour map 4, B1.*

Signs in Chamula warn that it is dangerous to walk in the area on your own; robberies have occurred between Chamula and both San Cristóbal and Zinacantán. (Seek full advice on any travel outside San Cristóbal de las Casas in the wake of events since early 1994.)

In this Tzotzil village 10 km northwest of San Cristóbal the men wear grey, black or light pink tunics, while the women wear bright blouses with colourful braid and navy or bright blue shawls. One popular excursion is to visit the brightly painted **church** ⓘ *a permit (US$1) is needed from the village tourist office and photographing inside the church is absolutely forbidden*. There are no pews but family groups sit or kneel on the floor, chanting, with rows of candles lit in front of them, each representing a member of the family and certain significance attached to the colours of the candles. The religion is centred on the 'talking stones' and three idols as well as certain Christian saints. Pagan rituals are held in small huts at the end of August. The pre-Lent festival ends with celebrants running through blazing harvest chaff. This happens just after Easter prayers are held, before the sowing season starts. Festivals in Chamula should *not* be photographed; if you wish to take other shots ask permission, people are not unpleasant, even if they refuse (although children may pester you to take their picture for a small fee). For reasons of cultural understanding and safety it is recommended that you visit Chamula on a tour.

There are many handicraft stalls on the way up the small hill southwest of the village. This has a good viewpoint of the village and valley. Take the road from the southwest corner of the square, turn left towards the ruined church then up a flight of steps on the left.

To get to Chamula, you can catch a VW bus from the market in San Cristóbal every 20 minutes, last at 1700, last one back at 1900, US$0.70 per person (or taxi, US$4). It is an interesting walk from San Cristóbal to Chamula along the main road to a point 1 km past the crossroads with the Periférico ring road (about 2.5 km from town centre); turn right on to an old dirt road, not signposted but it is the first fork you come to between some farmhouses. Then head back via the road through the village of Milpoleta, some 8 km downhill; allow five hours for the round trip (one hour for Chamula). Best not done in hot weather. Also, you can hike from Chamula to Zinacantán in 1½ hours: when leaving Chamula, take the track straight ahead instead of turning left onto the San Cristóbal road; turn left on a small hill where the school is (after 30 minutes) and follow a smaller trail through light forest. After about an hour you reach the main road 200 m before Zinacantán (but see warning, above).

Tenejapa → *Phone code: 967.*

Few tourists visit Tenejapa. The village is very friendly and many men wear local costume. Ask permission to take pictures and expect to pay. The Thursday market is traditionally for fruit and vegetables, but there are a growing number of other stalls. The market thins out by noon. Excellent woven items can be purchased from the weavers' cooperative near the church. They also have a fine collection of old textiles in their regional ethnographic **museum** adjoining the handicraft shop. The **cooperative** can also arrange weaving classes.

Other excursions from San Cristóbal

Two other excursions can be made, by car or local bus, from San Cristóbal. The first goes south on the Pan-American Highway (30 minutes by car) to **Amatenango del Valle**, a Tzeltal village where the women make and fire pottery in their yards, and then southeast (15 minutes by car) to **Aguacatenango**, a picturesque village at the foot of a

Around San Cristóbal de las Casas

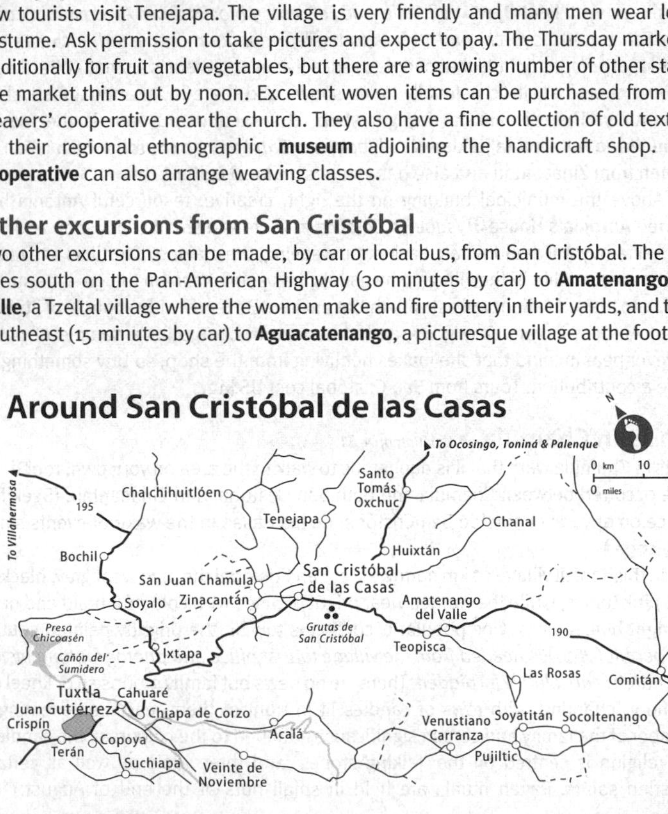

mountain. Continue one hour along this road past **Villa Las Rosas** (hotel) to **Venustiano Carranza**, where the women wear fine costumes, and there is an extremely good view of the entire valley. There is a good road from Las Rosas to Comitán as an alternative to the Pan-American highway. There are frequent buses.

Las Grutas de San Cristóbal ⓘ *US$0.30*, are caves 10 km southeast of the town, which contain huge stalagmites and are 2445 m deep but only lit for 750 m. Refreshments are available. Horses can be hired at Las Grutas for US$13 for a five-hour ride (guide extra) on beautiful trails in the surrounding forest. Some of these are best followed on foot. Yellow diamonds on trees and stones mark the way to beautiful meadows. Stay on the trail to minimize erosion. The land next to the caves is taken up by an army football pitch, but once past this, it is possible to walk most of the way back to San Cristóbal through woods and fields. Las Grutas are reached by **Autotransportes de Pasaje** '31 de Marzo' *colectivos* every 15 minutes (0600-1900, US$0.60) from Avenida Benito Juárez 37B, across the Pan-American Highway just south of the **Cristóbal Colón** bus terminal (or take a *camioneta* from Pan-American opposite San Diego church 500 m east of Cristóbal Colón). *Colectivos* are marked 'San Cristóbal, Teopisca, Ciudad Militar, Villa Las Rosas', or ask for minibus to 'Rancho Nuevo'. To the bus stop take 'San Diego' *colectivo* 1 block east of Zócalo to the end of Benito Juárez. When you get to Las Grutas, ask the driver to drop you at Km 94; the caves are poorly signed.

Tours from San Cristóbal to the **Sumidero Canyon** (see page 399) including boat trip cost around US$15 with numerous travel agencies, 0900-1600. San Cristóbal can also serve as a base for exploring the Maya ruins at **Palenque** (210 km away, see page 408), **Bonampak** and **Yaxchilán**, near the Guatelmalan border (see page 412).

Route to Palenque

» *pp418-436*.

Ocosingo

→ *Phone code: 919. Colour map 4, B1.*

Palenque (see page 408) can be reached by paved road from San Cristóbal de las Casas, a beautiful ride via Ocosingo, which has a local airport, a colourful market and several hotels. It was one of the centres of fighting in the Ejército Zapatista de Liberación Nacional (EZLN) uprising in January 1994.

Toniná

→ *Colour map 4, B1.*

ⓘ *0900-1600, US$1.30, drinks are available at the site; also toilets and parking.*

The Maya ruins at Toniná are 12 km from Ocosingo, with bus links to San Cristóbal de las Casas. A tour from San Cristóbal to Toniná costs US$15; it is possible to drive in an ordinary car, or take a taxi (US$6). There are also *colectivos* (15 minutes, US$1) running from the market, or you can walk from Ocosingo

Toniná is one of the last Classic Maya sites, with the palace high on a hill to your left. It is well worth visiting the ruins, which were excavated by a French government team. The temples are in the Palenque style with internal sanctuaries in the back room, but influences from many different Maya styles of various periods have been found. The huge pyramid complex, seven stone platforms making a man-made hill, is 10 m higher than the Temple of the Sun at Teotihuacán and is the tallest pyramidal structure in the Maya world. Stelae are in very diverse forms, as are wall panels, and some are in styles and of subjects unknown at any other Maya site. Ask the guardian to show you the second unrestored ball court and the sculpture kept at his house. He will show you round the whole site; there is also a small **museum**.

Agua Azul

ⓘ *Entry US$1.30, US$4 for cars. Entry price is not always included in day trips from Palenque, which allow you to spend up to 3 hrs at Agua Azul.*

Hardship for the Chiapanecos

For the visitor to Chiapas, the state's wonders are many: lush tropical jungle, quaint colonial villages, or the modern, prosperous capital, Tuxtla Gutiérrez. However, the peacefulness masks the troubles of the state's indigenous peoples. Their plight was splashed across the world's press with the Zapatista uprising of January 1994 and has remained a photogenic story ever since (see Recent politics, page 1215).

Chiapas, the southernmost state and one of Mexico's poorest, appears much like its neighbour, Guatemala, and shares many of the same problems. Subsistence has been a way of life for centuries, illiteracy and infant mortality are high, particularly among those who have retained their languages and traditions, shunning the Spanish culture. The Chiapas government estimates that nearly one million indigenous people live in the state, descendants ofthe great Maya civilization of AD 250-900. The indigenous Chiapanecos of today are not a monolith; they are spread out across the state, they do not speak the same language, nor dress alike, have the same customs nor the same types of tribal government.

The Tzotziles and Tzeltales total about 626,000 and live mainly on the plateau and the slopes of the high altitude zones. The Choles number 110,000 and live in the towns of Tila, Tumbalá, Salto de Agua, Sabanilla and Yajalón. The 87,000 Zoques live near the volatile Chichonal volcano. The 66,000 Tojolabales live in Margaritas, Comitán, La Independencia, La Trinitaria and part of Altamirano. On the high mountains and slopes of the Sierra Madre are the 23,000 Mames and the 12,000 Mochós and Kakchikeles. The Lacandones, named after the rainforest they occupy, number only 500 today. Along the border with Guatemala are 21,500 Chujes, Kanjobales and Jacaltecos, although that number includes some refugees still there from the Guatemalan conflict, which ended in a negotiated peace in late 1996.

A minority of the indigenous population speaks Spanish, particularly in the Sierra Madre region and among the Zoques. Many have dropped their traditional clothing. Customary positions of authority along with stewardships and standard bearers have been dropped from tribal governance, but medicine men continue to practise. They still celebrate their festivals in ways unique to them and they think about their ancestors as they have for centuries. Many now live in the large cities, but those who remain in *el campo* are, for the most part, poor. They get by, eating tortillas with salt, some vegetables and occasionally beans. Many who leave for the city end up as domestic servants, labourers or street pedlars. The scarcity of land for indigenous people has been a political issue for many decades and limited land reform merely postponed the crisis that eventually erupted in the 1990s, and continues to cause the government considerable difficulties.

The series of jungle waterfalls and rapids at Agua Azul run for 7 km and are breathtakingly beautiful. They are easily visited on a day trip from Palenque. All the travel agencies, and many hotels, offer a tour there for about US$10, including a visit to the waterfall at Misol-Há and Agua Clara (see below). Agua Azul's main swimming area has many restaurants and indigenous children selling fruit. Swimming is good, in clear blue water during good weather, in muddy brown water during bad (but still refreshing if very hot, which it usually is). Swimmers should stick to the roped areas where everyone else can see them; the various graves on the steep path up the hill alongside the rapids are testament to the dangers of swimming in those areas. One of the falls is called 'The Liquidizer', an area of white water in which bathing is extremely dangerous. On no account should you enter this stretch of water; many drownings have occurred. Even in the designated areas, the currents can be ferocious. Beware of hidden tree trunks in the water if it is murky.

Violent robberies have been reported at Agua Azul; never go alone; groups of at least four are best.

The path on the left of the rapids can be followed for 7 km, with superb views and secluded areas for picnics. There are also several *palapas* for hammocks, and plenty of space for free camping anf some rooms to rent.

Agua Clara and Misol-Há

Eight kilometres from Agua Azul along the river is Agua Clara, a nature reserve. At Misol-Há there is a stunning waterfall usually visited first on day trips from Palenque. A narrow path winds around behind the falls, allowing you to stand behind the immense curtain of water. Swimming is possible in the large pool at the bottom of the tumbling cascade of water, but it is usually better to wait until you get to Agua Azul for a good swim. However, during the rainy season swimming is reported to be better at Misol-Há, so go by bus or check with your tour operator, as some only allow a brief stop at Misol-Há.

Palenque town → *Phone code: 916. Colour map 4, B2.*

A friendly, colourful little town whose sole reason to exist is to accommodate the tourists heading for the famous archaeological site nearby. There is plenty of accommodation for every budget, with dozens of cheap *posadas* around the centre, and a new tourist barrio, **La Cañada**, with more expensive hotels, restaurants and bars. Souvenirs are available at lower prices than elsewhere on the Ruta Maya, making Palenque a convenient place to stop off en route to the southerly Chiapan towns of San Cristóbal and Tuxtla Gutiérrez. Travellers coming to Palenque from Mérida, Campeche and other cities in the Yucatán Peninsula will find it much hotter here, particularly in June, July and August. The **Fiesta de Santo Domingo** is held on the first week of August.

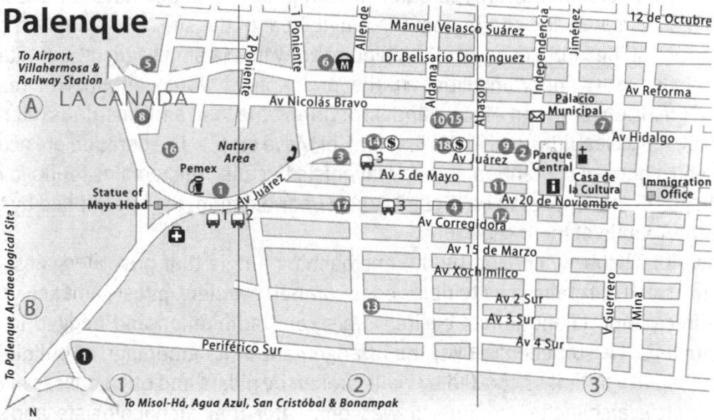

Sleeping
Avenida 1 *A1*
Chan Kah Centro 2 *A3*
Kashlan 3 *A2*
Lacroix 7 *A3*
La Posada 5 *A1*
La Selva 6 *A2*
Marantha 4 *A2*
Maya Tulipanes 8 *A1*
Misol-Há 9 *A3*
Naj K'in 18 *A2*
Posada Canek 11 *A3*
Posada Charito 12 *B3*
Posada San Juan 13 *B2*
Posada Shalom 14 *A2*
San Miguel 10 *A2*
Xajlel Jade 15 *A2*
Xibalba 16 *A1*
Yun-Kax 17 *A2*

Eating
La Selva 1 *B1*

Buses
ADO, Cristóbal Colón & Maya de Oro Bus Terminal 1 *A2*
Auto Transportes Rodolfo Figueroa Lacandonia 2 *A2*
Colectivo to Ruins 3 *A2/B2*

The **tourist office** ⓘ *daily 0800-2000*, is on Juárez, a block below the plaza and next to the craft market. They are very helpful and provide good free map of Palenque and the ruins. There's another **City Tourism Office** ⓘ *Independencia, daily 0800-1500, 1600-2000, www.palenque.com.mx*, in the Palacio Municipal. A **tourist police office** ⓘ *Av Reforma and Francisco Javier, T345-0788, T348-3406, Mon-Sat 0900-1500, 1600-2100*, works in conjunction with the tourist office.

Five kilometres from Palenque town, but 3 km before the ruins, **El Panchan** ⓘ *www.palenquemx.com/elpanchan*, is host to a fascinating mix of philosophies, foods and intellectual interests. Don Moisés, founder of El Panchan, first came to Palenque as an archaeologist and was one of the first guides to the ruins. He bought a plot of land, named it Panchan – Maya for 'heaven on earth' – and started to raise a family. Now he has divided lots among his children who run various businesses. It is about 10° cooler at Panchan than Palenque town due to the dense foliage cover. Although vastly different, all businesses at Panchan have intertwined themselves into the natural jungle that surrounds them, creating an almost Robinson Crusoe setting – if you don't want to stay in town and like the idea of being based in the forest, get a bus or taxi here soon after arriving in Palenque town. ›› *See Sleeping and Eating, pages 421 and 425.*

Palenque

›› *pp418-436. Colour map 4, B1.*

ⓘ *Daily 0800-1645, US$4; guided tours posible; expensive water and some basic food on sale; there are lots of souvenir stalls at the main entrance. Colectivos back to the town leave from outside the main entrance, US$1, every 6-18 minutes. From Palenque town, take a colectivo from either of the two points, see Transport, page 429.*

Water at the site is very expensive; bring your own. The cheapest food is the tacos from the stalls.

Built at the height of the Classic period on a series of artificial terraces surrounded by jungle, Palenque is one of the most beautiful of all the Maya ruins in Mexico. It was built for strategic purposes, with evidence of defensive apertures in some of the retaining walls. In the centre of the site is the Palace, a massive warren of buildings with an asymmetrical tower rising above them, and fine views to the north. The tower was probably used as an astronomical observatory and a watchtower. The outer buildings of the palace have an unusual series of galleries, offering shade from the jungle heat of the site.

From about the fourth century AD, Palenque grew from a small agricultural village to one of the most important cities in the prehispanic world, although it really achieved greatness between AD 600 and 800. During the long and illustrious reign of Lord Pacal, the city rapidly rose to the first rank of Maya states. The duration of Pacal's reign is still a bone of contention among Mayanists because the remains found in his sarcophagus do not appear to be those of an 81-year-old man, the age implied by the texts in the Temple of the Inscriptions.

Since its discovery, choked by the encroaching jungle that pushed against its walls and scaled the stairs of its temples once climbed by rulers, priests and acolytes, the architecture of Palenque has elicited praise and admiration and begged to be reconstructed. The corbelled vaults, the arrangement of its groupings of buildings, the impression of lightness created by walls broken by pillars and open spaces make Palenque-style architecture unique. It was only later that archaeologists and art historians realized that the architecture of Palenque was created mainly to accommodate the extraordinary sculptures and texts that referred not only to historical individuals and the important events in their lives, but also to mythological beings who endorsed the claims of dynastic continuity or 'divine right' of the rulers of this great city. The structures most illustrative of this function are the Palace, a group of buildings arranged around four patios to which a tower was later added, the Temple of the Inscriptions that rises above the tomb of Lord Pacal, and the temples of the Group of the Cross, used by Chan Bahlum, Pacal's successor, who made claims in the inscriptions carved on the tablets, pillars and balustrades of these exceptional buildings, claims which, in their audacity, are awe inspiring.

Warning The ruins are surrounded by thick, mosquito-infested jungle so wear insect repellent and make sure you're up to date with your tablets (May to November is the worst time for mosquitoes). It is extremely hot and humid at the ruins, especially in the afternoon, so it is best to visit early. Unfortunately, as well as mosquitoes, there have also been reports of criminals hiding in the jungle. As ever, try and leave valuables at home to minimize any loss.

The Palace

The Palace and Temple XI are located in the centre of the site. The Palace stands on an artificial platform over 100 m long and 9 m high. Chan Bahlum's younger brother, Kan Xul, was 57 when he became king. He devoted himself to enlarging the palace, and apparently built the four-storey tower in honour of his dead father. The top of the tower is almost at the level of Pacal's mortuary temple, and on the winter solstice the sun, viewed from here, sets directly above his crypt. Large windows where Maya

Palenque archaeological site

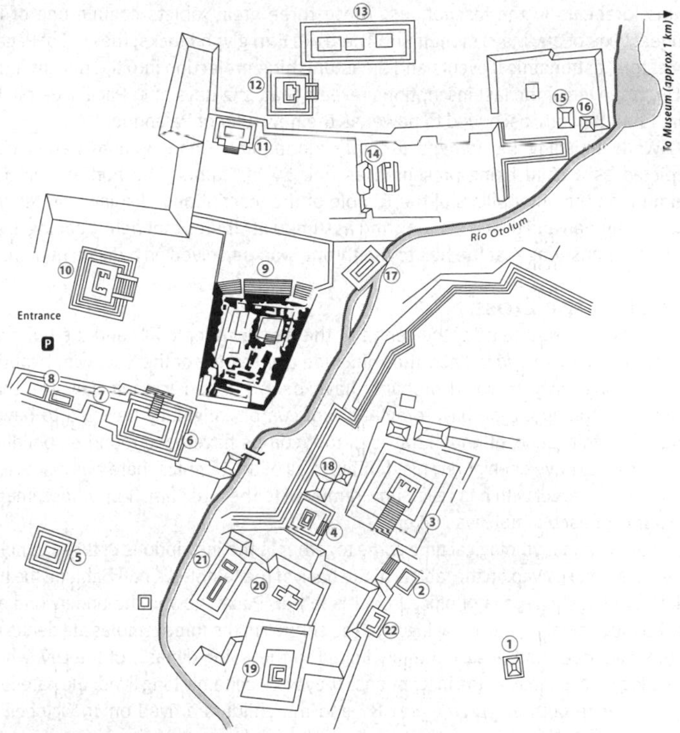

N

0 metres 50
0 yards 50

Mirador **1**	Palace **9**	Otolum Aqueduct **17**
Foliated Cross **2**	Temple XI **10**	Temple XIV **18**
Temple of the Cross **3**	Temple X **11**	Temple XX **19**
Temple of the Sun **4**	Temple of the Count **12**	Temple XXI **20**
Temple of the Lion **5**	North Group **13**	Temple XXII **21**
Temple of the Inscriptions **6**	Ball Court **14**	Temple XVII **22**
Temple XIII **7**	Encampment **15**	
Temple of the Skull **8**	Queen Baths **16**	

astronomers could observe and chart the movement of the planets, ancestors of the royal lineage of Palenque, pierce the walls of the tower. Kan-Xul reigned for 18 years before being captured and probably sacrificed by the rulers of Toniná. During his reign Palenque reached its greatest degree of expansion, although recent excavations at the site may prove differently.

Temple of the Inscriptions

The Temple of the Inscriptions, along with Temple XII and Temple XIII, lies to the south of the Palace group of buildings and is one of the rare Maya pyramids to have a burial chamber incorporated at the time of its construction. This building was erected to cover the crypt in which Lord Pacal, the founder of the first ruling dynasty of Palenque, was buried. Discovered in 1952 by Alberto Ruz-Lhuillier, the burial chamber measured 7 m long, 7 m high and 3.75 m across, an incredible achievement considering the weight of the huge pyramid pressing down upon it. According to the inscriptions, Lord Pacal was born in AD 603 and died in AD 684. Inside, Ruz-Lhuillier discovered his bones adorned with jade jewellery. Around the burial chamber were various figures carved in stucco, depicting the Bolontikú, the Nine Lords of the Night of Maya mythology. There was a narrow tube alongside the stairs, presumably to give Pacal spiritual access to the outside world. Pacal also left a record of his forebears in the inscriptions. These three great tablets contain one of the longest texts of any Maya monument. There are 620 glyph blocks; they tell of Pacal's ancestors, astronomical events and an astonishing projection into the distant future (AD 4772). One of the last inscriptions reveals that, 132 days after Pacal's death, his son, Chan Bahlum, ascended to power as the new ruler of Palenque.

The temple cannot be climbed and the sarcophagus is no longer on view.

While finishing his father's funerary monument, Chan Bahlum had himself depicted as a child being presented as heir by his father. The portraits of Chan Bahlum, on the outer pillars of the Temple of the Inscriptions, display features that are both human and divine. He took and assumed attributes that rightly belong to the gods, thus ensuring that the heir to the throne was perceived as a divine human.

Group of the Cross

To the extreme southeast of the centre of the site lie Temple XIV and the buildings known as the *Grupo de la Cruz*. These include the Temple of the Sun, with beautiful relief carvings, which would probably have been painted in their day. The three temples in this group all have dramatic roof-combs, originally believed to have a religious significance, although traces of roof-combs have been found on buildings now known to have been purely residential. In all of the temples there was discovered a huge stone tablet with bas-relief, now removed to the museum, from whose images the name of each temple was taken.

Human and mythological time come together in the inscriptions of these temples. In each tableau carved on the tablets at the back of the temples, Chan Bahlum, the new ruler, receives the regalia of office from his father, Pacal, now in the underworld and shown much smaller than his living son. The shrines in the three temples are dedicated to the Palenque Triad, a sacred trinity linked to the ruling dynasty of the city, whose genealogy is explained in the inscriptions. They were certainly long lived: the parents of the triad were born in 3122 or 3121 BC and the children arrived on 19 October, 23 October and 6 November, 2360 BC. It has been shown that these were dates of extraordinary astronomical phenomena: the gods were intimately related to heavenly bodies and events. They also provided a mythological origin for the dynasty which is detailed on the three main tablets from the Group of the Cross. Rulers died and gods were born in an impressive merging of historical and mythological events. At their completion, the three temples of the Group of the Cross housed the divine sanction for the dynasty as a whole and gave the rationale for its descent through females and males.

Sarcophagus

Pacal's sarcophagus, or coffin, is carved out of a solid piece of rock, with a carved slab covering it. Every element in the imagery of the sarcophagus lid is consistent with Maya iconography. It is exquisitely beautiful. The central image is that of Lord Pacal falling back into the fleshless jaws of the earth monster who will transport him to Xibalba, the realm of the dead. A cruciform world-tree rises above the under-world maw. The same world-tree appears on the tablets in the sanctuaries at the backs of the buildings known as the Group of the Cross. A long inscription runs around the edge of the lid, which includes a number of dates and personal names that records a dynastic sequence covering almost the whole of the seventh and eight centuries.

Four plugs in the corners of the lid filled the holes used with ropes to lower the lid into place; the plug in the southeast corner had a notch cut in it so that the channel, built into the stairway leading to the upper world, would allow spiritual communion between the dead king and his descendants above. Although the imagery of the sarcophagus lid refers to Pacal's fall into Xibalba, the location of the tower of the palace ensures that he will not remain there. The sun, setting over the crypt on the winter solstice, will have to do battle with the Nine Lords of the Night before re-emerging triumphantly in the east; the nine tiers of the pyramid represent the nine battles to be fought during his downward journey. Pacal, who awaits the sun at the point where the final battle had been fought, will accompany the sun as he re-emerges from Xibalba in the east. Palenque, the westernmost city of the Classic Maya, was in the 'dead zone', which placed it in the perfect position to accommodate the descent of the sun and Lord Pacal into the underworld.

On each set of balustrades, Chan Bahlum began his text with the birth of the patron god of each temple. On the left side of the stairs, he recorded the time elapsed between the birth of the god and the dedication of the temple. Thus, mythological time and contemporary time were fused. Each temple was named for the central image on its inner tablet. When Chan Bahlum died in 702 after ruling for 18 years, his younger brother and heir erected a fourth shrine to record the apotheosis of the departed king (Temple XIV). On these reliefs, Chan Bahlum emerges triumphantly from the underworld and dances towards his mother, Lady Ahpo-Hel.

The lengths to which the rulers of Palenque went to establish legitimacy for their claims of divine right could not guarantee the survival of Palenque after the collapse felt throughout the Classic Maya region, when the building of elite religious structures stopped and stelae where no longer engraved with the details of dynastic events. Toniná, the city that captured and probably sacrificed the Palenque ruler Kan-Xul, outlived the great centre made glorious by Pacal and Chan Bahlum. The last-known dated monument from the Maya region registers AD 909 at the lesser site; it is to be supposed that soon afterwards, Toniná went the way of the other centres of the Classic Maya world.

The **museum** ⓘ *Tue-Sun 0900-1630, free with ruins ticket*, is on the way back to the town, with an expensive restaurant and gift shop – buy water in town. Many of the stucco carvings retrieved from the site are here, as well as jade pieces of jewellery, funerary urns and ceramics. Readers wishing to learn more about the iconography and writing system of the Classic Maya are referred to: *A Forest of Kings*, L Schele and D Freidel, William Morrow and Company, NY 1990.

Yaxchilán, Bonampak and Lacanjá

▸▸ pp418-436. Colour map 4, B2.

ⓘ *Yaxchilán 0800-1600, US$3; Bonampak 0800-1645, US$3 (free for under 13s, students and over 60s) plus US$11.50 for compulsory transport with the Jach Winik coop to the site; this includes toilet and locker and entry to the small museum. It's a 1-hr journey from Frontera Corozal to Bonampak.*

Yaxchilán

Yaxchilán is a major Classic Maya centre built along a terrace and hills above the Río Usumacinta where there are more howler monkeys than people. The temples are ornately decorated with stucco and stone and the stone lintels are carved with scenes of ceremonies and conquests. Bonampak, originally under the political domination of Yaxchilán, was built in the late Classic period on the Río Lacanjá, a tributory of the Usumacinta. It is famous for its murals, dated at AD 800, which relate the story of a battle and the bloody aftermath with the sacrificial torture and execution of prisoners.

Take suitable footwear and rain protection for jungle walking, drinking water, insect repellent and passport (military checkpoints). Beware of mosquitoes and sandflies.

From around AD 200 to the early 10th century, the era known as the Classic Maya witnessed the growth of many small settlements into great centres noted for wonderful architecture, sculpture, painted ceramics, impressive advances in mathematics and hieroglyphic writings, and the growth of an elite who often created alliances with other polities through marriage. Wide causeways, *sacbés*, were built between centres enabling the inhabitants to maintain contact with those of other towns. All these great advances came to an end around AD 909, when the Classic Maya civilization collapsed. For many years Mayanists have postulated about the cause of the collapse: some have suggested land exhaustion, others have suggested invasion from the Central Highlands, while still others believe in a peasant revolt against the conspicuous consumption of an ever-expanding elite. The painted walls of Structure 1 at Bonampak illustrate well the extravagance indulged in by the elite of this centre on the margins of the Lacandón rainforest.

For information on the border crossing at Frontera Echeverría/Corozal, see page 642.

Bonampak

The murals at Bonampak are very realistic with an excellent use of colour and available space. Painted on the walls, vault rises and benches of three adjoining but not interconnecting rooms, they describe the rituals surrounding the presentation at court of the future ruler. Some of the rituals were separated by considerable intervals, which adds to the solemnity of the ceremony. It is very possible that the rituals illustrated were only a small selection of a far greater series of events. The people participating were mainly elite, including the royal family, and a strict hierarchy was observed in which eminent lords were attended by minor nobility.

In Room 1, the celebration opens with the presentation of the young prince, a simple act in which a porter introduces the child to an assembly of lords, dressed for the occasion in white robes. The king, dressed simply, watches from his throne. Also present are two representatives from Yaxchilán, one male and one female. It is probable that the female is the wife or consort of Chaan-Muan, the ruler of Bonampak. After this simple opening, the spectacle begins. Lords are represented dressing in sumptuous clothing and jewellery, musicians appear playing drums, turtle carapaces, rattles and trumpets and they all line up for a procession, which will bemuse the peasantry, labourers and artisans waiting outside. We never see the lower orders, but, open-mouthed, we can stand with them to observe the spectacle. The headdresses alone are enough to bedazzle us and the great diversity in the attire of the participants illustrates the wide spectrum of social functions fulfilled by those attending the ceremony.

The imagery and text of the sculptured lintels and stelae at nearby Yaxchilán proclaim the right of the heir to accede to the throne while emphasizing the need to take captives to be sacrificed in honour of the king-to-be. This need is echoed in the paintings of Room 2, Structure 1, at Bonampak. A ferocious battle is in progress in which the ruler, Chaan-Muan, proves his right to the throne. In the midst of battle, he shines out heroically. The local warriors pull the hair of those of the opposite side, whose identity is not known. Many captives were taken. In the ensuing scene, the full horror of the fate of those captured by the Maya is illustrated.

On a stepped structure, the ruler Chaan-Muan oversees the torture and mutilation of the captives taken in the recent battle. This event is clearly in the open air and surely witnessed by the inhabitants of Bonampak, whose loyalty is rewarded by admission to the bloody circus. The torture of the captives consisted of mutilation of the hands; some disconsolate individuals hold up their hands dripping blood, while one has clearly been decapitated, his head resting on a bed of leaves. It is to be supposed that the torture of the captives would be followed by death, probably by decapitation. The gods demanded sacrifice, which was provided by the rulers in an extravaganza of bloodletting. It must be understood that what appears to be outright bloodthirstiness was a necessary part of Maya ritual and probably accepted by all the polities throughout the Classic Maya region. It is very probable that the heir would not have been acceptable without this gory ritual.

The murals of the third room at Bonampak express the events that were meant to close the series of rituals designed to consolidate the claim to the throne by the son of the ruler. At first sight, the paintings that cover the walls of room three of Structure 1 appear to celebrate the sacrifices of the previous depictions in an exuberant public display of music, dance and perhaps song. The background is a pyramid, and ten elegantly dressed lords dance on different levels, colourful 'dance-wings' sprouting from their hips. The dominant dancer on the uppermost level is believed to be the ruler, Chaan-Muan. However, it has been noted that a very strong element of sacrifice accompanies the extrovert display. In a more private corner, the royal family is portrayed preparing to engage in blood sacrifice; a servant proffers them a container that the sacred bloodletting instruments. There are also indications that the male dancers had already drawn blood by means of penis perforation. As at Yaxchilán, blood endorsed the dynastic claims of the royal family.

The rituals portrayed on the walls of Structure 1 at Bonampak are thought to have been performed between 790 and 792, a time when the collapse of the Classic Maya was beginning to be felt. The extravagant use of enormous amounts of fine cloth, expensive jaguar pelts, jade beads and pectorals, elegant costumes, headdresses made from rare feathers, and spondylus shells was not enough to reverse the decadence of the civilization that had produced magnificent works in art, architecture, jewellery, mathematics, astronomy and glyphic writing: within a hundred years, the jungle was to claim it for its own.

Lacanjá

At Lacanjá (9 km from Bonampak) there is a community of Lacandones. For more details ask at **Na-Bolom** in San Cristóbal de las Casas. Local guides can be hired for hikes in the jungle and to the ruins of Bonampak. Lucas Chambor at the **Casa de Cultura** is a good source of advice. There have been some reports of hostility towards tourists. Lacanjá to Bonampak with locals costs US$6.50-9. The walk through the jungle is beautiful and crosses several streams. Another walk in the area is to the **Cascadas de Moctuniha** (one hour each way, US$6.50 with guide).

Routes to Guatemala » pp418-436.

There are two main border crossings into Guatemala: one at Ciudad Cuauhtémoc (La Mesillain Guatemala), reached via Route 190 from San Cristóbal de las Casas, and the other at Tapachula along the coastal Route 200 from the neighbouring state of Oaxaca. A third option is to cross the border by boat, east of Palenque, along the rivers San Pedro or Usumacinta. Note: if planning on returning to Mexico after an excursion to Guatemala, ensure you get an exit stamp, at the immigration office. Pick up your tourist card and a slip of paper, take this to any bank, pay US$18 and the slip is stamped. Not doing this can lead to problems when you try to leave Mexico again.

Tenosique and Río San Pedro route

The Río San Pedro route starts at Tenosique, a friendly place east of Palenque (money exchange at clothing shop, Ortiz y Alvarez at Calle 28 No 404, good rates for dollars to quetzales, poor for dollars to pesos). From here the route takes you by road to La Palma, boat to El Naranjo, in Guatemala, and then road to Flores.

From Tenosique to **La Palma** on the Río San Pedro, *colectivos* starting at 0600 from in front of the market, one hour, US$1, two hours by bus (from Tenosique bus station, which is outside town, take taxi, US$1.70 or *colectivo* to 'Centro', or walk 20 minutes). Taxi to La Palma US$7, shared by all passengers. From La Palma boats leave to El Naranjo (Guatemala) at 0800 (or when they have enough passengers), but timings are very irregular (they wait for a minimum of five passengers before leaving), at least 4½ hours, US$22 (to check boat times, T343-0811 Rural at the Río San Pedro). Be at the boat one hour early, it sometimes leaves ahead of schedule; if this happens ask around for someone to chase it, US$3-4 per person for three people. If there are fewer than five passengers, the boat may be cancelled, in which case you must either wait for the next one, or hire a *rápido* (US$125, maximum four people). You may be able to arrange a slower boat for up to six people for US$100. In La Palma, two restaurants are poor value; one restaurant will change money at weekends at a reasonable rate.

It is a beautiful boat trip, through mangroves with flocks of white herons and the occasional alligator, dropping people off at homesteads. There is a stop at the border post two hours into the journey to sign out of Mexico, a lovely spot with a lake and lilies. In the rain, your backpack will get wet; take waterproofs and a torch/flashlight. There are no officials on arrival at the jetty in El Naranjo; Immigration is a short way uphill on the right (entry will cost US$5 in quetzales or dollars, beware extra unofficial charges at Customs); bus tickets to Flores are sold here.

Río Usumacinta route

The Río Usumacinta route takes you by road to Benemérito (southeast of Yaxchilán and Bonampak), boat to Sayaxché, Guatemala and then road to Flores. **Autotransportes Comitán Lagos de Montebello** buses (Avenida Manuel Velasco Suárez, Palenque, three blocks from food market) run eight a day starting at 0400 until 1530 to **Benemérito**, on the Mexican side of the Usumacinta, 7-12 hours but will be quicker when the new paved road is completed; basic buses, dreadful road, crowded (it's about half the time in a *camioneta* if you can hitch a ride). You must visit immigration, about 3 km from Benemérito, to sign out of Mexico (the bus will wait).

Once in Benemérito where there is a 2100 curfew (two basic *pensiones*), hope for a boat to Guatemala; this may take a couple of days. The boat goes to Sayaxché and should stop at Pipiles for immigration. A trading boat takes two days, US$4-5; a motorized canoe eight hours, US$5-10. From Sayaxché, buses run to Flores.

Alternatively, take the bus Palenque-Frontera Echeverría, now more often known as Frontera Corozal, 1000, four hours by good road, US$5.50; or minibuses at 0730, 1100, 1400 from 5 de Mayo by **Restaurante El Caimito**, US$4.50 (many travel agencies in Palenque run minibuses on this route, leaving at 0600, to connect with the boat to Bethel, 35 minutes, and on to Flores as below). About an hour down this route at Km 61 is an excellent breakfast stop, Valle Escondido. Keep an eye out for hummingbirds. At Echeverría/Corozal there is an immigration post, two hotels and restaurants. It's a five-minute launch ride to La Técnica, see box, page 642.

San Cristóbal to the border

South of San Cristóbal and heading for Guatemala, follow the 170-km paved road via **Teopisca** (comfortable cheap *pensión*) to **Comitán de Domínguez**, a lively, attractive town with a large, shady plaza. The **tourist office** ⓘ *Mon-Fri 1000-1400, 1700-2000*, is on the main square, in the Palacio Municipal.

From Comitán the road winds down to the Guatemalan border at Ciudad Cuauhtémoc via La Trinitaria (near the turn-off to Lagunas de Montebello, restaurant but no hotel). **Ciudad Cuauhtémoc**, despite its name, is not a city, but just a few buildings; the **Cristóbal Colón** bus station is opposite Immigration, with an overpriced restaurant and an excellent hotel. Be sure to surrender your tourist card and get your exit stamp at Mexican Immigration in Ciudad Cuauhtémoc before boarding a pick-up for Guatemalan immigration; you will only have to go back if you don't. A pick-up to the Guatemalan border, 4 km, costs US$0.65 per person. Walk 100 m to Immigration and Customs (open until 2100). Beyond the Guatemalan post at La Mesilla, see Border essentials box, page 579, a beautiful stretch of road leads 85 km to Huehuetenango. This route is far more interesting than the one through Tapachula; the border crossing at Ciudad Cuauhtémoc is also reported as easier than that at Talismán.

Lagunas de Montebello and Chinkultic

Six kilometres south of Comitán take a right turn for the Maya ruins of **Tenán Puente** (5 km), situated in a forest; there is a shortcut on foot. In 1996 the tomb of a Maya nobleman (AD 1000) was discovered here. The buildings at Tenán are more restored than those at Chinkultic (see below). A road branches off the Pan-American Highway, 16 km further on, to a very beautiful region of vari-coloured lakes and caves, the **Lagunas de Montebello** (a national park). Off the road to Montebello, 30 km from the Pan-American Highway, lie the ruins of **Chinkultic** ⓘ *closes at 1600, US$3*, with temples, ball court, carved stone stelae and a *cenote* (deep round lake, good swimming) in beautiful surroundings; from the signpost the ruins are about 3 km along a dirt road. Watch and ask for the very small sign and gate where the road to the ruins starts (about 1 km back along the main road, towards Comitán, from **Doña María's**, see Sleeping, page 418, don't attempt any short cuts); worth visiting when passing. *Colectivo* from Comitán US$1.

Combi vans or buses marked 'Tziscao' or 'Lagos' to the Lagunas de Montebello National Park (60 km from Comitán, US$1.30 about one hour), via the **Lagunas de Siete Colores** (so called because the oxides in the water give varieties of colours), leave frequently from Avenida 2 Poniente Sur y Calle 3 Sur Poniente, four blocks from the plaza in Comitán; buses go as far as Laguna Bosque Azul, a one-hour journey. For those with their own transport there are several dirt roads from Comitán to the Lagunas; a recommended route is the one via La Independencia, Buena Vista, La Patria and El Triunfo (beautiful views), eventually joining the road west of the Chinkultic ruins.

Tziscao

Tziscao is 9 km along the road leading right from the park entrance, which is 3 km before Bosque Azul; five buses a day Comitán-Tziscao; the last bus and *colectivo* back connecting with the 1900 bus to San Cristóbal is at 1600. The last combi to Comitán is at 1700. A trip to the Lagunas de Siete Colores from Comitán can be done in a day (note that the less accessible lakes are hard to get to even if staying in the vicinity). It is also possible to hire a combi, which takes 12 people, to go to the Lakes and Chinkultic for

 US$15 per hour. A day trip to Chinkultic and the lakes from San Cristóbal de las Casas is also possible, if exhausting (take passport and tourist card). The **Bosque Azul** area is now a reserve. The area is noted for its orchids and birdlife, including the famous *quetzal*, but it gets very busy at weekends and holidays. There are small caves nearby.

Route to Tapachula » *pp418-436.*

Travelling from the neighbouring state of Oaxaca, Routes 190 and 200 merge to cross the Isthmus of Tehuantepec. Accommodation is available at **Zanatepec**, and **Tapanatepec**, which is where Highway 190 heads northeast to Tuxtla Gutiérrez and Highway 200 continues southeast along the coast of Chiapas to the Guatemalan border.

Arriaga → *Phone code: 966. Colour map 3, C6.*

Arriaga is a good stopping place just across the state border that separates Oaxaca from Chiapas; many banks around Zócalo for exchange. The road from Arriaga to Tapachula is a four-lane divided freeway.

From Arriaga, Route 200 continues to Tonalá, formerly a very quiet town but now noisy and dirty. Bus Tonalá-Tapachula, three hours, US$6.75; also buses to Tuxtla). This is by far the most direct road for travellers seeking the quickest way from Mexico City to Guatemala.

Puerto Arista → *Phone code: 961. Colour map 3, C6.*

Along the coast from Tonalá to Tapachula there are several fine-looking and undeveloped beaches, although waves and currents are dangerous. Puerto Arista (17 km south of Tonalá) is now being built up, but it is still a relatively peaceful area with 32 km of clean beach to relax on with no salespeople; bus/*colectivo* from Tonalá every hour, 45 minutes, US$0.60, taxi US$2; plenty of buses to Arriaga, US$0.75. Many hotels, motels and restaurants on the beach; hot and, in the wet season, sandflies.

Buses also from Tonalá to **Boca del Cielo** further down the coast, which is good for bathing and has *cabañas* with hammocks, and similarly **Cabeza del Toro**. **Paredón**, on the huge Laguna del Mar Muerto, 14 km west of Tonalá, has excellent seafood and one very basic guesthouse. You can take a local fishing boat out into the lagoon to swim; the shore stinks because fishermen clean fish on the beach among dogs and pigs. Served by frequent buses.

On the way to Tapachula you pass through **Pijijiapan** where there is the **Hotel Pijijilton**(!) next to the **Cristóbal Colón** bus station. From **Huixtla**, a good, scenic road winds off into the mountains parallel to the border, towards Ciudad Cuauhtémoc and Comitán (see above).

Tapachula and around » *pp418-436. Colour map 4, C1.*

→ *Phone code: 962.*

Tapachula is a pleasant, neat, but expensive and hot commercial town. **Avenidas** run north-south, **calles** east-west (Oriente-Poniente). Odd-numbered **calles** are north of Calle Central, odd **avenidas** are east of Avenida Central. It has an airport, and is the road and rail junction for Guatemala (road crossings at the Talismán bridge or at Ciudad Hidalgo). The **tourist office** ⓘ *4 Norte 35, Edificio del Gobierno del Estado, 3rd floor, between 3 and 5 Pte, T626-5470, Mon-Fri 0900-1500, 1800-2000*, is helpful.

Around Tapachula

Visit the ruins of **Izapa** (proto-Classic stelae, small museum) just off the road to Talismán; the part of the site on the north is easily visible but a larger portion is on the

Border essentials: Mexico-Guatemala

Ciudad Cuauhtémoc

Tourist cards and visas are available at the border; some reports say only 15 days are being given, but extensions are possible in Oaxaca or Mexico City. It is forbidden to bring in fruit and vegetables.

Drivers entering Mexico At the border crossing your vehicle is fumigated, US$7.25, get receipt (if re-entering Mexico, with documents from a previous entry, papers are checked here). Proceed 4 km to Migración to obtain tourist card or visa, or have existing visa checked. Then go to **Banjército** to obtain the necessary papers and windscreen sticker or, if re-entering Mexico, to have existing papers checked. Mon-Fri 0800-1600, Sat-Sun 0900-1400. Mexico is 1 hr ahead of Guatemala.

Talismán

It is 8 km from Tapachula to the 24-hour border at Talismán.

Immigration The Mexican Customs post is 200 m from the Guatemalan one. Exit tax US$0.45. Lots of pushy children offer to help you through border formalities; pay US$2-3 for one, which keeps the others away.The toilet at immigration at the crossing is dangerous, hold-ups have been reported day and night.

Guatemalan consulate
See Tapachula.

Crossing into Guatemala By car can take several hours. If you don't want your car sprayed inside it may cost you a couple of dollars. Do not park in the car park at the control post, as it is very expensive.

Driving into Mexico See Essentials, Motoring, on the temporary import of vehicles, page 70. Car papers are issued at the Garita de Aduana on Route 200 out of Tapachula. There is no other road; you can't miss it. Photocopies of documents must be made in town; there are no facilities at the Garita. Reported to be a frustrating procedure – be prepared and be patient.

Exchange Change money in town rather than with men standing around Customs on the Guatemalan side (check rates before dealing with them, and haggle; there is no bank on the Guatemalan side).

Ciudad Hidalgo

There is a border crossing south of Tapachula, at Ciudad Hidalgo, opposite Tecún Umán with connections to Coatepeque, Mazatenango and Retalhuleu. A few blocks from the town plaza is Mexican Immigration, at the foot of the 1-km-long bridge across the Río Suchiate; cycle taxis cross the bridge for about US$1, pedestrians pay US$0.15. You cannot change TCs here.

south side of the highway, about 1 km away, ask caretaker for guidance. These buildings influenced Kaminal Juyú near Guatemala City and are considered archaeologically important as a proto-Maya site. Some findings from the ruins are displayed in the **Museo Regional del Soconusco** on the west side of the Zócalo in Tapachula. To reach Izapa take combi from Unión Progreso bus station. Forty-five kilometres northeast of Tapachula, beyond the turning to Talismán, is **Unión Juárez**, where you can have your papers stamped and proceed on foot via Talquián to the Guatemalan border at Sibinal.

A worthwhile hike can be made up the **Tacaná volcano** (4150 m), which takes two to three days from Unión Juárez. Ask for the road to Chiquihuete; no cars. The Tapachula tourist office can help; in Unión Juárez ask for Sr Umberto Ríos at **Restaurante Montaña,** he will put you in touch with guide Moisés Hernández, who charges US$15 a day. It is possible to stay overnight in Don Emilio Velásquez's barn halfway up, US$2; he offers coffee and *tortillas*. At the top are some *cabañas* in which you sleep for free; sleeping bag essential.

Sleeping

Villahermosa *p396*
The price difference between a reasonable and a basic hotel can be negligible, so you might as well go for the former. Try to book hotel rooms in advance, especially during the holiday season (May onwards). Hotels tend to be full Mon-Thu; arrive before nightfall if you can.
L **Casa Inn**, Madero 418, T358-0102. Central, newly refurbished, some rooms with good views, clean, helpful, with good terrace restaurant overlooking Calle Madero. Nearby parking.
L-C **Maya-Tabasco**, Blv Ruiz Cortines 907, T312-1111. All services, ask for special offers.
AL **Cencali**, Juárez y Paseo Tabasco, T315-1999. Excellent breakfast. Highly recommended.
B **Provincia Express**, Lerdo 303, T314-5376. Recently refurbished and upgraded. Clean, modern with DirecTV and a/c. Good.
C **Chocos**, Lino Merino 100 and Constitución, T312-9644, near ADO terminal. Friendly, clean, a/c.
D **Madero**, Madero 301, T312-0516. Clean, better than many on Madero, some rooms cheaper for 4.
D **Oriente**, Madero 425, T312-0121. Clean, hot shower, fan, good restaurant. Recommended.
D **San Miguel**, Lerdo 315, T312-1426. Quiet, clean, shower, fan, very friendly, no windows, run-down.
E **Del Río**, Av Constitución 206 and Reforma, on plaza off Madero, T312-6055. Central with fan, bar below.

Tuxtla Gutiérrez *p398, map p398*
There is plenty of budget accommodation near the 1st-class ADO terminal, along Av 2 Norte Ote, beyond the plaza.
AL **Bonampak**, Blv Belisario Domínguez 180, T602-5916, hotbonam@prodigy.net.mx. Social centre of the city, clean, noisy at night, expensive restaurant.
AL **Flamboyant**, Blv Belisario Domínguez 1081, T615-0888. Comfortable with good swimming pool.
B-C **Palace Inn**, Blv Belisario Domínguez, 4 km from centre, T615-0574. Generally recommended, lovely garden, pool, noisy videobar.
C **Regional San Marcos**, 1 Sur y 2 Ote Sur 176, T613-1940. Cheaper without TV, close to Zócalo, bath, fan or a/c, clean.
D **Estrella**, 2 Ote Norte 322, T612-3827. With bath, friendly, clean, quiet, comfy, a bit run-down but safe, free drinking water. Recommended.
D **Plaza Chiapas**, Av 2 Norte Ote y 2 Ote Norte, T613-8365. Clean, with fan and hot shower, most rooms have balconies, good value, good restaurant, enclosed car park. Recommended.
E **La Posada**, Av 1 Sur Ote y 5 Ote Sur, T612-6827. With or without bath, laundry facilities, friendly.
E **Posada de Chiapas**, 2 Sur Pte 243, T612-3354. Small rooms with bath, TV, friendly.
F **Posada del Sol**, 3 Pte Norte, 1 block from Cristóbal Colón buses. With hot shower and fan, good service, good value and basic.

Camping
C **La Hacienda**, trailer-park-hotel, Belisario Domínguez 1197 (west end of town on Route 190), T615-0849. US$7-8 per tent, 4 spaces with hook-up, hot showers, restaurant, minipool, US$13.50 for car and 2 people, a bit noisy and not easily accessible for RVs over 6 m; owner speaks English.

San Cristóbal de las Casas *p400, map p401*
Look on the bulletin board outside the tourist office for guesthouses advertising cheap bed and breakfast.
AL **Casa Mexicana**, 28 de Agosto 1, T678-0698, www.hotelcasamexicana.com. Cable TV, indoor patio with fountain, very plush and comfy, same owner as **La Galería** restaurant. Highly recommended.
AL-A **Casa Vieja**, María A Flores 27, T678-2598, www.casavieja.com.mx. Elegant converted colonial house, relaxing, TV, good restaurant, hot water,

will heat rooms on request if weather cold, parking, laundry service.

AL-A Posada Diego de Mazariegos, 5 de Febrero 1, 1 block north of plaza, T678-0833, www.diegodemazariegos.com.mx. Comfortable, quiet, restaurant, live music regularly in the evening in bar **Tequila Zoo**. Recommended.

B Na Bolom, Vicente Guerrero 33, T678-1418, www.nabolom.org. Beautiful, 12-room guesthouse in cultural centre (see page 402), bath, fireplace, 3 meals available, lunch and dinner US$5 each. Recommended.

B Palacio de Moctezuma, Juárez 16, T678-0352, www.palaciodemoctezuma.com. Colonial style, good Mexican food. Rooms downstairs sometimes damp – 1st floor much better. Highly recommended.

B Posada El Paraíso, Av 5 de Febrero 19, T/F678-0085. Mexican-Swiss owned, impeccable rooms varying in size, many open onto pretty patio, excellent restaurant, nearby parking beneath cathedral. Highly recommended.

B Rincón del Arco, Ejército Nacional 66, 8 blocks from centre, T678-1313, www.rincondelarco.com. Friendly, bar, restaurant and nice garden. Recommended.

B Santa Clara, Insurgentes 1, on plaza, T678-1140. Colonial style, clean, some rooms noisy, good restaurant, swimming pool and pool bar. Highly recommended.

C Posada Jovel, Flavio Paniagua 28, T678-1734, hoteljovel@hotmail.com. Villa style, roof terrace, clean, quiet, hot water, extra blankets available, will store luggage, restaurant, horses for hire, laundry facilities.

C Real del Valle, Av Real de Guadalupe 14, next to plaza, T678-0680, hrvalle@mundo maya.com.mx. With breakfast, very clean, friendly, avoid noisy room next to kitchen, hot water, laundry, credit cards accepted, parking. Well maintained and good value.

C-D El Cerrillo, Belisario Domínguez 27, T678-1283. Lovely rooftop patio. Recommended.

C-D San Martín, Real de Guadalupe 16, in the centre of the city near the plaza, T678-0533, hotelsanmartin@prodigy.net.mx. Clean, hot water, left-luggage. Once excellent, standards falling.

D Barón de Las Casas, Belisario Domínguez 2, T678-0881. Clean and comfortable, good value. Recommended.

D Capri, Insurgentes 54, T678-3018, near **Cristóbal Colón** bus terminal. Clean, helpful. Recommended.

D Casa Babylon, on Josefa Ortiz and Ramón Corona. Newish place with private rooms and baths. Popular with backpackers, with use of kitchen, laundry, chill-out room and roof terrace. Very helpful and friendly place. Some beds a bit lumpy.

D Fray Bartolomé de las Casas, Insurgentes and Niños Héroes, T678-0932. Attractive courtyard, with bath, nice rooms (some dark) and patio with **Café Kate**, can be noisy, extra blankets available, hot water 0700-1000 and 1900-2000, safe parking.

D Posada Los Morales, Ignacio Allende 17, T678-1472. Cottages with open fires (wood US$0.80), kitchen (no pots or pans) and hot showers, beautiful gardens overlook city, parking possible (some cottages are very basic, with no water), beautiful bar/restaurant with live music. Owner is a collector and exporter of rustic-style Mexican furniture.

D Posada Lucella, Av Insurgentes 55, T678-0956, opposite Iglesia Santa Lucía (noisy bells!). Some rooms with bath, hot water, others shared, good value, clean, safe, quiet rooms around patio, large beds.

D Posada Vallarta, Hermanos Pineda, near Cristóbal Colón bus terminal, T678-0465. Clean, quiet, hot water, car parking. Recommended.

D Posada San Agustín, Ejército Nacional 7, T678-1816. Large rooms, shared bath, family-run, friendly. Recommended.

D-F Posada Media Luna, Hermano Domíngez 5, T631-5590, paint49@hot mail.com. Laundry service, hot water, internet, cable TV, pretty garden.

E Posada Lupita, near bus terminal on Insurgentes. Nice plant-filled courtyard, popular, often full.

E Posada Margarita, Real de Guadalupe 34, T678-0957. Private room without bath, spotless, washing and toilets, friendly, hot water, popular with backpackers, attractive restaurant (not cheap), wholefood.

Phone codes *Villahermosa 993; Teapa 932; Bochil 932; Tuxtla Gutiérrez 961; Chiapa de Corzo 961; San Cristóbal de las Casa 967; Tenejapa 967; Ocosingo 919; Palenque town 916; Arriaga 966; Puerto Arista 961; Tapachula 962.*

E Youth Hostel, Benito Juárez 2. 24-hr hot water, popular with backpackers.
E-F Posada Doña Rosita, Ejército Nacional 13, 3 blocks from main plaza, kitchen and laundry facilities, breakfast included. Slightly eccentric Doña Rosita is very knowledgeable about local affairs and herbal medicine and provides a course consisting of 4 hrs of classes, an introduction to vegetarian cooking and 5 meals, costing about US$35.
F Casa de Huéspedes Chamula, Julio M Corzo 18. Clean, hot showers, washing facilities, friendly, parking, noisy, with shared bath, some rooms without windows.
F Casa de Huéspedes Santa Lucía, Clemente Robles 21, 1 block from the bus terminal, T678-0315. Shared bath, ask for hot water, refurbished, one of the cheapest. Recommended.
F Los Camellos, Guadalupe 101, T678-0665. Youth hostel. Price includes breakfast, popular with backpackers.
F Magic Hostel, 47 Real de Guadalupe, comfortable dorm rooms, popular with backpackers. Friendly and recommended, although a little noisy at night.
F Posada del Candil, Real de Mexicanos 7, T678-2755. Hot shower, parking, clean, laundry facilities, good value.
F Posadita, Flavio Paniagua 30. With bath, clean, laundry facilities. Recommended.

Camping

Rancho San Nicolás, T678-0057, at end of Francisco León, 1.5 km east of centre. trailer park in a beautiful, quiet location, but do take warm blankets or clothing as the temperature drops greatly at night, hot showers, US$7 for room in *cabaña*, US$5 to camp, US$12 for camper van with 2 people (electricity hook-up), children free, laundry facilities. Recommended.
Trailer park Bonampak, Route 190 at west end of town. 22 spaces with full hook-up, hot shower, heated pool in season, restaurant, US$10 per vehicle, US$5 per person.

Agua Azul *p407*

There are 2 places with *cabañas* for hammocks (hammock rental US$1.50 and up, US$3.50 per person in beds in dormitory); if staying, be very careful of your belongings; thefts have been reported.

Camping

Camping Agua Azul is popular and reliable, opposite the parking lot; camping costs US$1.75, US$3.30 for 2 in camper van, and US$0.15 for use of toilets (100 m further on are free public toilets). You can also camp at the **Estación Climatológica at Paso del Cayuco (F)**, it's about 15-20 mins' walk up the falls to the wire fence station.

RVs can stay overnight at Agua Azul, using the facilities, without paying extra (as long as you do not leave the park). Follow the path up the falls to a 2nd campsite, cheaper, less crowded. There are more *cabañas* and nice places to sling a hammock further upstream, all cheaper and less touristy than lower down.

Palenque town *p408, map p407*

It is convenient to stay at hotels near the Pemex service station, as they are also nearer the ruins and the bus stations. Prices treble around fiesta time.
AL Maya Tucán, on road into town, T345-0290. Swimming pool, a/c, bar, restaurant, lovely views from rooms.
AL Maya Tulipanes, Cañada 6, T345-0201, www.mayatulipanes.com.mx. A/c, cable TV, rooms vary in size, price and quality, garage, pool, bar/restaurant next door. Recommended.
A-C Kashlan, 5 de Mayo 105, T345-0297, kashlan@palenque.com.mx. With bath, fan or a/c, hot water, quiet, clean, will store luggage, mosquito nets. Helpful owner Ada Luz Navarro offers tours to Agua Azul and Misol-Há falls, laundry opposite, restaurant with vegetarian food in same building, bus and boat tours to Flores in Guatemala offered, internet US$1.50 per hr. Recommended.
B Chan Kah Centro, corner of Juárez and Independencia, T345-0318. A/c, restaurant, street parking, terrace bar with happy hour.
B Xibalba, Merle Green 9, T345-0411. Spacious rooms, clean, hot water, a/c, fan. Recommended.
B-C Naj K'in, Hidalgo 72. With bath and fan, hot water 24 hrs, safe parking.
C La Posada, at La Cañada, T345-0437. Hot water, fans, basic, a little run-down but OK, 'designed for young travellers, international ambience', peaceful, luggage store.
C-D San Miguel, Hidalgo and Aldama, above **Union Pharmacy**, T345-0152, new, big clean rooms, balcony, hot water and fan, good value. Recommended.

D Lacroix, Hidalgo 30, T345-0014, next to church. With bath, fan, no hot water, some cheaper rooms, pleasant place.
D Posada Kin, Abasolo s/n, 20 de Noviembre y 5 de Mayo, very near Zócalo, T345-1714, posada_kin@hotmail.com. Clean and large doubles with bathroom, fan, tours available, safe and luggage store. Recommended.
D Posada Nacha'n Ka'an, 20 de Noviembre 25 and Allende, T345-4737. Hot water, fans, cheaper rooms in the dormitory. Recommended.
D Posada Shalom, Av Juárez 156, T345-0944. New, friendly, clean, noisy, stores luggage. Recommended.
D-E Marantha, 20 de Noviembre 19, T345-2348. Family-run, friendly service, hot water, some rooms have TV at no extra charge.
D-E Xajlel Jade, Hidalgo 61, T345-0463. Clean, comfortable rooms in quiet street, family-run, hot water. Recommended.
D-E Yun-Kax, Av Corregidora 87 (behind Santo Domingo), T345-0146. Quiet, clean, large rooms, hot water. Recommended.
E Avenida, Juárez 216, T345-0116. With restaurant, clean, large rooms with fan, parking, no hot showers, some rooms with balcony.
E La Selva, Av Reforma 69. Newly renovated, very good value, same owners as **Posada Charito**, clean.
E Misol-Há, at Juárez 12, T345-0092. Fan, with bath, hot water, clean, owner Susana Cuevas speaks English.
E Vaca Vieja, 5 de Mayo 42, T345-0388, 3 blocks from plaza. With bath, popular with gringos, good restaurant.
E-F Posada Canek, 20 de Noviembre. More expensive rooms have bath, all with fan and toilet, very clean, ground-floor dormitory near reception noisy, helpful staff, prices are per person, fills up early in peak time, arrive before 1000 check-out time.
E-F Posada San Juan, T345-0616 (from ADO go up the hill and 1st right, it's on the 4th block on the left). With bath, cheaper without, cold water, fan, clean, quiet, firm beds, secure locks, nice courtyard, very good for budget accommodation, safe parking available.
F Posada Charito, 20 de Noviembre 15B, T345-0121. Clean, friendly, family-run, very good value, basic, some rooms very airless, ground floor best, laundry service.
F Posada Kushul-ha, 20 de Noviembre 131, T345-0483. New, clean rooms with bath, fan, TV. Close to bus stations.

Road to the ruins

El Panchan is a collection of budget *cabañas* and room options, set in the rainforest. A very calming atmosphere and defintely worth a look.
D-E Margarita and Ed's, El Panchan, edcabanas@yahoo.com. The plushest cabins at El Panchan. Private thatched-roof cabins, very comfortable and clean, private bath, hot water; caretaker Pablo is friendly and helpful.
E Chato's, El Panchan, panchen@yahoo.com. Cabins with private or shared bath.
E Jaguar, over the road from El Panchan, but the philosophy is still the same.
E-F Rakshita, cabins, place to sling a hammock, Maya study area, meditation area, **Rakshita's Vegetarian Restaurant**, see below.
F Betos, El Panchan. Sling a hammock, prepare for loud dance music at night, outside bar.
F Elementos Naturales, on road to ruins, past Panchan, www.elementosnaturales.org. Youth hostel, can sling hammock US$3 or camp US$3. Includes breakfast. Pleasant outdoor feel.

Camping

Calinda Nututún, 3.5 km along Palenque-Ocosingo road, T345-0100. US$3.30 per person, vehicle free, US$2 per camping site per night, rather run-down, no tent rentals, rooms (**B**) are neglected, toilets and bath; beautiful lake and waterfall (good swimming).
Trailer Park Mayabell, on road to ruins, 2 km before entrance (bus from town US$0.30), T345-4271, www.mayabell.com.mx. For caravans and tents, US$13 per vehicle with 2 people. US$13 for tent or US$3 to sling hammock (an *ambulante* sells hammocks once a day, or you can hire them for an additional US$1.50), palmleaf huts, bathrooms, hot showers, good restaurant but not cheap, nice setting. Cabins for US$40 and US$55 with a/c available, popular so can be noisy, the place is not to everyone's taste; many mosquitoes and many ticks in long grass. At night, around 0100, you can often hear the howler monkeys screaming in the jungle; quite eerie.

Yaxchilán, Bonampak and Lacanjá *p412*
There is basic accommodation at Bonampak; take hammock and mosquito net. Thieving has been reported. **Camping** is restricted to the INAH site on the Usumacinta.
At Lacanjá there are 4 campsites where you can sling a hammock: **Kin Bor**, **Vicente K'in**, **Carlos Chan Bor** and **Manuel Chan Bor**.

Tenosique and Río San Pedro route *p414*
D **Rome**, Calle 28, 400, T342-2151. Clean, will change dollars for residents, bath, not bad.
E **Azulejos**, Calle 26, 416. With bath, fan, clean, hot water, friendly, helpful owner speaks some English, opposite church.
E **Casa de Huéspedes La Valle**, Calle 19. With bath, good, but a little grubby.

Río Usumacinta route *p414*
D **Centro Turístico and Grutas Tsolk'in,** T7861-1198 (community phone), www.ecoturlacandona.com. Clean, well kept rooms with communal bathrooms. Much more friendly and helpful than the nearby Escudo Jaguar (which is overpriced and unfriendly). Less than 5 mins' walk from the dock. Take a right turning opposite immigration office.

San Cristóbal to the border *p415*
In Comitán, accommodation is inferior in quality and almost twice the price of San Cristóbal.
B **Internacional**, Av Domínguez 22, Comitán, T632-0111, near plaza. Good, decent restaurant.
B **Los Lagos de Montebello**, Comitán, T632-0657. On Pan-American Highway, Km 1,257. Noisy but good.
D **Delfín**, Av Domínguez 19-A, Comitán, T632-0013, on plaza. Small rooms but hot water, helpful and clean.
E **Hospedaje Montebello**, Comitán, 1 block from **Delfín**. Clean, sunny courtyard, laundry, fax service, friendly. Recommended.
F **Hospedaje Primavera**, Calle Central Benito Juárez 42, ½ block off Plaza, Comitán. Room without bath.

Route to Tapachula *p416*
B **Galilea**, Av Hidalgo y Callejón Ote, Tonalá, T663-0239. With bath, a/c, good, basic cheap rooms on 1st floor, balconies, on main square, with good restaurants.
C **Hotel El Estraneo**, Av Central, Pijijiapan, T(918) 645-0264. Very nice, parking in courtyard.
C **Ik-Lumaal**, Arriaga, near Zócalo, T662-0895. A/c, clean, quiet, good restaurant.
C-D **Posada San Rafael**, Zanatepec. Motel. Very comfortable, safe parking.
D **Colonial**, Callejón Ferrocarril, Arriaga, next to bus station, T662-0856. Clean, friendly, quiet, limited free parking.
D **Motel La Misión**, Tapanatepec, on Highway 190 on northern outskirts, T(971) 717-0140. Fan, hot water, clean, TV, hammock outside each room, affiliated restaurant, very good.
E **Sabrina**, Pijijiapan. Nice, clean and quiet, safe parking.
F **Hotel Iris**, Callejón Ferrocarril, Arriaga, near bus station. Bath, fan, basic.

Camping
José's Camping Cabañas (ask *colectivo* from Tonalá to take you there, US$0.60 extra), at east edge of Puerto Arista, follow signs. Canadian run, well organized, clean, laundry, restaurant (including vegetarian), library.

Tapachula and around *p416*
AL **Loma Real**, Carretera Costera 200, Km 244, T626-1440, 1 km north of city, www.travelodge.com.mx. Operates as a 1st-class hotel, use of swimming pool, cold showers.
C **San Francisco**, Av Central Sur 94, T626-1454, 15 mins from centre. Good, a/c, large rooms, hot water, TV, restaurant, safe parking.
C **Santa Julia**, next to **Cristóbal Colón** terminal, in centre within 1 block of Plaza Central, T626-2486. Bath, phone, TV, a/c, clean, good.
E **Cinco de Mayo**, Calle 5 Pte y Av 12 Norte. With bath (cheaper without), not very clean, convenient for Talismán *colectivos*, which leave ½ block away.
E **Colonial**, Av 4 Norte 31. Attractive courtyard, about 1 block from central square, good value, clean, safe.
E **San Román**, Calle 9 Pte between Av 10 y 12 Norte. Shower, fan, safe motorcycle parking, clean, quiet, friendly, drinks for sale.

Eating

Villahermosa *p396*

¥¥¥-¥¥ Los Tulipanes, Malecón, south of Paseao Tabasco, typical food. Recommended.

¥¥ Hotel Madan, Madero 408, has a restaurant serving good breakfast, inexpensive fish dishes, a/c, newspapers, a pleasant and quiet place to escape from the heat.

¥¥ El Matador, Av César Sandino No 101a, local meat dishes, good value.

¥¥ Rodizio do Brasil, Parque la Choca, Stand Grandero. Speciality *espadas*, good Brazilian food.

¥¥-¥ Aquarius, Javier Mina 309, near Av Méndez. Vegetarian food, juice bar and health food store.

¥¥-¥ Café El Portal, Independencia 301, delicious typical food of the region with some exotic regional platter such as *empanadas* stuffed with *pejelargarto*, a strange-looking freshwater fish with an impressive set of alligator-type jaws and curiously leathery skin. Service is very friendly, artsy atmosphere.

¥¥-¥ El Torito Valenzuela, next to **Hotel Madero**. Mexican specialities, excellent and inexpensive. Highly recommended.

¥ Zona Luz, Aldama 615. Typical Mexican/ Tabasqueña food. Cheap, quaint, airy with a charming colonial feel about it.

Cafés

Café La Cabaña, Juárez 303-A, across the way from the Museo de Historia de Tabasco. Has outdoor tables where town elders congregate to debate the day's issues over piping cups of cappuccino. Very entertaining to watch. No meals.

El Café de la Calle Juárez, Juárez 513, indoor/outdoor café. Great for breakfast, good coffee, a new menu every month. Outdoor tables are great for people watching.

South of Villahermosa *p397*

¥¥ El Mirador, Teapa. Good restaurant on main square.

¥¥ Familiar, Teapa, main street 125. Friendly, not cheap but filling. Recommended.

Tuxtla Gutiérrez *p398, map p398*

¥¥ El Chato, opposite **Hotel San Marcos**. One of the few touristy places, *huaraches*, grilled meat, OK.

¥¥ Parrilla La Cabaña, 2 Ote Norte 250. Excellent tacos, very clean.

¥¥ Tuxtla, Av 2 Norte Pte y Central, near plaza. Good *comida corrida* and fruit salad.

¥¥-¥ Las Pichanchas. Av Central Ote 857. Pretty courtyard, typical food, dancing from Chiapas with *marimba* music 1400-1700 and 2000-2300.

¥¥-¥ Nah Yaxal, 6 Pte Norte, just off Av Central Pte. Vegetarian, popular with students.

¥ La Parcela, 2 Ote Sur, near **Hotel Plaza Chiapas**. Good, cheap, good breakfasts. Recommended.

¥ Las Delicias, 2 Norte Pte, close to **Cristóbal Colón** terminal. Good breakfasts and snacks.

¥ Los Gallos, Av 2 Norte Pte, 20 m from **Cristóbal Colón** terminal. 0700-2400, good and cheap.

¥ Maryen, 2 Ote Norte between 1 Norte and Av Central. Good, cheap tacos.

¥ Mina, Av Central Ote 525, near bus station. Good cheap *comida*.

Cafés and ice cream parlours

Bing, 1 Sur Pte 1480. Excellent ice cream.

Café Avenida, on Av Central just past **Aerocaribe** office. Good coffee shop, does cappuccino and espresso. Popular with locals.

Café Mesón Manolo, Av Central Pte 238. Good value, reasonably priced.

Coffee shop, Av Central Pte 224, below **Hotel Avenida**. Serves excellent coffee.

Chiapa de Corzo *p399*

There are good seafood restaurants by the riverside.

¥¥¥-¥¥ Jardín Turístico on main plaza, open until 2000. *Plato jardín* is a selection of different regional dishes.

San Cristóbal de las Casas *p400, map p401*

There are several cheap, local places on Madero east of Plaza 31 de Marzo.

¥¥¥ El Teatro, next to Teatro Municipal on 16 de Septiembre. Good quality French food.

¥¥ Capri, Insurgentes 16. Good food, set meals at reasonable prices.

¥¥ Cocodrilo Café & Bar, Plaza 31 de Marzo. Smart café / bar on the southside of the plaza.

¥¥ El Fogón de Jovel, Av 16 Septiembre No 11, opposite the Jade Museum. One of the best restaurants in town and a great place to experiment and try out a variety of local dishes. Try the local liquor, *posh*. Colourful vibe with 2 themed rooms – Revolution and Mask. Live music at night.

ƚƚ **El Puente**, Real de Guadalupe 55, has a restaurant with good food and a great atmosphere.

ƚƚ **La Paloma**, Hidalgo 3, a few doors from Zócalo. Inventive regional dishes at reasonable prices; international cuisine a little more. Popular with tourists, best coffee, good breakfast, good pasta, international (many German) newspapers, art gallery next door, live music at weekends.

ƚƚ **Madre Tierra**, Insurgentes 19 (opposite Franciscan church), T678-4297. Anglo-Mexican owned, European dishes, vegetarian specialities, good breakfasts, wholemeal breads from bakery (also takeaway), pies, brownies, chocolate cheesecake, Cuban and reggae music in the evenings, popular with travellers, not cheap.

ƚƚ **María Cartones**, Plaza 31 de Marzo, T631-6002. Old time favourite, with tables overlooking the plaza.

ƚƚ **París-México**, Madero 20. Smart, French cuisine, excellent breakfasts, reasonably priced *comida corrida*, classical music. Not cheap, apart from the 3 daily menus (very good). Highly recommended.

ƚƚ **Tuluc**, Insurgentes 5. Good value especially breakfasts, fresh *tamales* every morning, near plaza, popular, classical music, art for sale and toys on display.

ƚƚ-ƚ **Emiliano's Moustache**, Av Crescencio Rosas 7. *Taquería*, popular with Mexicans. Recommended.

ƚƚ-ƚ **La Margarita**, Real de Guadalupe 34. Open for breakfast at 0700. Live music in the evenings, flamenco, rumba and salsa, good tacos.

ƚƚ-ƚ **Mayambé**, Real de Guadalupe 66, T674-6278. Breakfast, lunch and dinner. Excellent selection of Thai, Arab and Indian dishes. Great service. A nice change from the usual beans, good value. Great atmosphere. Highly recommended.

ƚ **Craft market**, Insurgentes. The stalls here are the cheapest places for lunch in San Cristóbal. They do set meals for US$1.20, usually beef or chicken. Numerous stalls nearby sell punch, often made with *posh*, the alcoholic brew made by the people of Chamula.

ƚ **El Mirador II**, Madero. Next door to Flamingo. Good local and international food, excellent *comida corrida* US$3. Recommended.

ƚ **El Gato Gordo**, Real de Guadalupe 20, T678-8313. Cheap set breakfast, crêpes, *tortas*, vegetarian.

ƚ **Juguería Ana Banana**, Av Miguel Hidalgo 9, good cheap typical Mexican food and fresh juices.

ƚ **La Alpujarra**, corner of Madero and Juárez, a bakery-cum-pizzeria, with the best European-style crusty white bread in town.

ƚ **Las Estrellas**, Escuadrón 201. Good cheap food, including vegetarian, good brown bread, try the *caldo Tlalpeño*, nice atmosphere, Mexican/Dutch owned, very friendly and cheap. Recommended.

Cafés, juice stalls and bakeries

Café Centro, Real de Guadalupe. Popular for breakfast, good *comida*.

Café San Cristóbal on Cuauhtémoc. Good coffee sold in bulk too, chess hangout.

El Manantial, 1 de Marzo 11. Good *licuados* and juices.

La Casa del Pan, Dr Navarro 10 with B Domínguez. Excellent wholemeal bread, breakfasts, live music, closed Mon. Highly recommended but not cheap.

Lacteos Maya, Av J M Santiago, has excellent locally made yogurt.

La Fe Café, Diego Mazarriegos and 12 de Octobre. T678-9978. Cappuccinos and a sawdust floor (for that little extra fibre), express home delivery (for a coffee shop!) 1600-2230.

La Selva Café, Crescencio Rosas and Cuauhtémoc. 30 types of really delicious organic coffees, owned by growers' collective, art gallery, lively in evenings. Good healthy breakfast and cakes. Recommended.

Naturalísimo, 20 de Noviembre 4. Healthy, low-fat vegetarian food, fresh (delicious) yoghurt, fruit sherbet and juices, wholewheat bread and home-baked goodies, pleasant courtyard inside. Recommended.

Tortas Tortugas, Guadalupe Victoria, near corner of Av 20 de Noviembre. Excellent sandwiches.

Palenque town *p408, map p407*

The classier restaurants are in the barrio La Cañada, behind the Maya head as you enter town.

ŸŸŸ **El Tapanco Grill**, Av Juárez 65, 2 blocks below plaza above **Bing** ice cream shop. Good steak, balcony dining.

ŸŸŸ **La Selva**, Km 0.5 on Hidalgo (road to ruins). Excellent, smart dress preferred, live music at weekends, recommended.

ŸŸ **El Herradero**, Av Juárez 120. Breakfast and reasonably priced meals, fast service, open 24 hrs. Recommended.

ŸŸ **El Rodeo**, Juárez 116, near plaza. Does good breakfasts and meat dishes, popular with travellers. Recommended.

ŸŸ **Las Tinajas**, 20 de Noviembre 41 y Abasolo. Good, family-run, excellent food, huge portions, highly recommended.

ŸŸ **Pizzería Palenque**, Juárez 168 and Allende, T345-0332. Good pizzas and prices.

ŸŸ-Ÿ **Lakan-Há**, Juárez 20. Good tacos, fast, efficient.

ŸŸ-Ÿ **Mara's**, Juárez 1, by the Zócalo, cheap set menus.

ŸŸ-Ÿ **Restaurante Maya**, Hidalgo and Independencia. Very popular, fills up by 1900, set-menu lunches and à-la-carte dinner, mainly Mexican.

ŸŸ-Ÿ **Yunuen**, at **Hotel Vaca Vieja**. Generous portions at reasonable prices, good steaks, popular with local ranchers.

Ÿ **Mundo Maya**, Juárez 10, friendly, good and cheap Mexican fare.

Café de los Altos, opposite **Hotel Kashlan**, Good coffee.

Café de Yarra, Hidalgo 66. New café, stylish setting, good for breakfast, good prices.

Road to the ruins

ŸŸ **Don Mucho**, El Panchan. Completely outdoor restaurant, excellent Italian-Mexican food, fantastic breakfast, people come from Palenque town to eat here, often with fire dancing at night, quite exotic given the forest backdrop, will host 'passing through' travelling musicians.

ŸŸ-Ÿ **Rakshita's Vegetarian Restaurant**, El Panchan. Whimsical, doused in spirituality, staffed by a throng of belly-danceresque gals, good array of vegetarian platters. Deliciously original fruit shakes.

San Cristóbal to the border *p415*

ŸŸ **Helen's Enrique**, Comitán, on plaza opposite church. Good food in pleasant surroundings.

Ÿ **Buffalo Café**, Comitán, near plaza, Av Central y Calle Norte. Live music daily at 2030.

Cafés and ice cream parlours

Café Casa de la Cultura, Comitán, on the plaza. Sandwiches only.

Nevelandia, Comitán, Central Norte 1. Clean. Recommended.

Tapachula and around *p416*

ŸŸ **Viva Pizza**, Av Central. Good pizza, reasonable price.

Ÿ **Snoopy**, Av 4 no 19. Friendly, excellent *tortas*, breakfasts.

Good, cheap chicken on Central Norte.

Ice cream parlours

Helados Irma, Calle 13 Pte between Av 4 y 6. Good ice cream.

Entertainment

San Cristóbal de las Casas
p400, map p401

Bars and clubs

Bar Makia, Hidalgo, just off plaza, above a shop. Fri and Sat from 2200 until very late.

Blue Bar, Av Crescencio Rosas 2, live music after 2300, salsa, rock, reggae, pool table, good atmosphere.

Cocodrilo, Insurgentes 1, T678-0871. Cappuccinos, cocktails, beer and live music every night: reggae, *trova*, flamenco and rumba.

El Circo, 20 de Noviembre 7; couple of blocks north of the Zocalo. Live music.

Emiliano's Moustache (see page 424) has a bar open until 0100.

Las Velas, Madero, ½ block from plaza. Reggae, Honduran music, sometimes live, happy hour 2000-2200, open till dawn.

Revolución, 20 de Noviembre and 1 De Marzo. Café, bar with internet upstairs, happy hour 1500-1700, live soul, blues and rock music at 2000, good atmosphere.

Cinema and theatre

Centro Bilingüe at the Centro Cultural El Puente (see Cultural centres, page 435), Real de Guadalupe 55. Videos, usually about local issues, every day except Sun 3 good films in original version, US$1.25. Film schedules are posted around town.

La Ventana, Real de Guadalupe 46. Cinema club showing a good range of films.
Teatro Municipal Daniel Zebadúa, 20 de Noviembre and 1 de Marzo, film festivals each month, films at 1800 and 2100 US$2 (US$1.50 students).

Palenque town *p408, map p407*
Bars and clubs
Discoteca Kichan, 20 de Noviembre, varied music.
El Rocamar, Plaza Independencia and Av 5 de Mayo. Restaurant/bar. Watch your change.

Festivals and events

Villahermosa *p396*
Feb Ash Wednesday is celebrated from 1500 to dusk by the throwing of water bombs and buckets of water at anyone who happens to be on the street – get wet!

Chiapa de Corzo *p399*
The fiestas here are outstanding.
Jan Daylight fiestas, **Los Parachicos**, on 15, 17 and 20 Jan, and the **Chunta Fiestas**, at night, 9-23 Jan. The **musical parade** is on 19 Jan. All lead to the climax, 20-23 Jan, in honour of **San Sebastián**, with a pageant on the river.
25 Feb El Santo niño de Atocha.
25 Apr Festival de San Marcos, with various *espectáculos*.

San Cristóbal de las Casas *p400, map p401*
Early Nov Festival Maya-Zoque, which lasts 4 days, promoting the 12 different Maya and Zoque cultures in the Chiapas region, with dancing and celebrations in the main plaza.
Mar/Apr There is a popular **spring festival** on Easter Sun and the week after.
12 Dec La Fiesta de Guadalupe.

Shopping

San Cristóbal de las Casas *p400, map p401*
Bookshops
La Pared, Av Miguel Hidalgo 2, T678-6367, lapared9@yahoo.com, opposite the government tourist office. Open Tue-Sun, 1000-1400 and 1600-2000. Books in English and a few in other European languages, many travel books including **Footprint** guides, book exchange, American owner Dana Gay very helpful, also offers cheapest phone service in town (see Directory, page 434). **Soluna**, Real de Guadalupe 13B, has a few English guidebooks, a wide range of Spanish titles and postcards.
Pasaje Mazariegos (in the block bounded by Real de Guadalupe, Av B Domínguez, Madero and Plaza 31 de Marzo) has luxury clothes and bookshops, restaurants and travel agents.

Crafts
Part of the **Ex-Convento de Santo Domingo** has been converted into a cooperative, Sna Jolobil, selling handicrafts from many local villages especially textiles (best quality and expensive); also concerts by local groups.
La Casa del Jade, Av 16 de Septiembre 16. The shop, which sells top quality jade, also has a museum with replicas of jade relics and the Tomb of Pakal (Maya King of Palenque), which is now more difficult to visit at Palenque. **Taller Lenateros,** Flavio A Paniagua 54, T678-5174, conjuros@sancristobal.com.mx A paper-making workshop run primarily by a Maya group. Their paper and prints are made from natural materials and their profits help support around 30 Maya families. Also offers demonstrations and workshops US$6.50 per day. **Souvenir markets** on Utrilla between Real de Guadalupe and Dr A Navarro. **Amber Museum** in Plaza Sivan shop, Utrilla 10, T678-3507. There are many shops on Av Real de Guadalupe for amber and jade plus other *artesanías*. The market north of Santo Domingo is worth seeing as well. The **craft market** at Parque Fray Bartolomé de las Casas has stands offering an assortment of local sweets such as *cocada*, balls of sweetened and caramelized shredded coconut, as well as small, perfectly shaped animal figurines made, strangely enough, of sweetened hard-boiled egg yolks. Different, yet tasty. **Casa de Artesanías**, Niños Héroes and Hidalgo. Top-quality handicrafts. The shop is also a museum.

Palenque town *p408, map p407*
Av Juárez is lined with souvenir shops selling hammocks, blankets, Maya figurines and

hats. Sales staff are less pushy than in towns in the Yucatán Peninsula; bargain for the best prices.

Activities and tours

Tuxtla Gutiérrez *p398, map p398*

Tour operators

Carolina Tours, Sr José Narváez Valencia (manager), Av Central Pte 1138, T612-4281; reliable, recommended; also coffee shop at Av Central Pte 230.

Viajes Kali, Av Central Ote 507 corner of 4 Ote, T/F611-3175, heugenia@chis1.telmex.net.mx. Tours to Sumidero Canyon with English/French/Italian-speaking guide, also books national flights.

Viajes Miramar, in Posada del Rey, Calle 1 Ote Norte 310, T612-3983, viajesmiramar@infosel.net.mx Good, efficient service for national flight bookings.

San Cristóbal de las Casas *p400, map p401*

Horse riding

Horses can be hired from **Casa de Huéspedes Margarita**, prices US$16-20 for horse and guide, to Chamula, 5 hrs, US$9, reserve the day before. Also from **Sr José Hernández**, Calle Elías and Calle 10 (1 block from Av Huixtla and Chiapa de Corzo, not far from Na Bolom), US$10 for half a day, plus guide US$11.50; **Real de Guadalupe 51A**, to Chamula US$6.50, also to Rancho Nuevo and San José; **Francisco Ochón**, T678-5911, goes to Chamula, US$6.50. **Viajes Chincultik** (see Tour operators, below) offer horse riding tours to San Juan Chamula, US$11.

Rafting

There are several rivers in the San Cristóbal area that offer great rafting opportunities.

Explora-Ecoturismo y Aventura, T678-4295, www.prodigyweb.net.mx/explora. Eco-sensitive company with good recommendations offer rafting, caving, sea kayaking, river trips and multi-day camping expeditions on a variety of rivers. Price for a 6-day river and camping trip US$520.

Tour operators

There are many agencies to choose from. As a rough guide to prices: to San Juan Chamula and Zinacantán, US$12. Horse riding to San Juan Chamula, US$12. Sumidero Canyon, US$14, Montebello Lakes and Amatenango del Valle, US$18. Palenque Ruins, Agua Azul and Misol-Há, US$23. Toniná Ruins, US$26. There's also a 3-day jungle trip option taking in Agua Azul, Misol-Há, the ruins at Bonampak, Cedro River Falls, Yaxchilán and Palenque ruins. Camping in the jungle, US$175. Day trips to Bonampak and Yaxchilán are also possible, but they are much cheaper if booked in Palenque; take care to check what is included in packages.

Héctor Mejía, T678-0545, walking tour (Tue and Thu, 0900, from outside Santo Domingo, US$11, 4 hrs) around cottage industries, eg candy maker, doll maker, toy maker.

Mercedes Hernández Gómez, tours of local villages, starting at 0900 from kiosk on the Plaza 31 de Mayo (arrive early), returns about 1500, about US$12 per person. Mercedes, who is training as a shamen, speaks English, is very informative, but somewhat eccentric and has been known to expel people from tours if she gets a bad vibe.

Na Bolom Museum and Cultural Centre, Vicente Guerrero 33, T678-1418, www.nabolom.org (see page 402).

Raúl and Alejandro, T678-3741, chamul@hotmail.com. Offer tours to San Juan Chamula and Zinacantán. They depart from in front of the cathedral at 0930 and return at 1400, in blue VW minibus, US$11, in English, Spanish and Italian. Friendly, very good and highly recommended.

Tierra Maya, 20 Real de Guadalupe, www.TravelbyMexico.Com/chis/tierramaya. Friendly and reliable tour operator running shuttles to Panajachel, Guatemala, (US$37) as well as within Chiapas.

Viajes Chincultik, Real de Guadalupe 34, T/F678-0957, agchincultik@hotmail.com. Runs group tours to the Lagunas de Montebello, to the Sumidero Canyon, Palenque, Toniná and camping trips to Laguna Miramar; also to Yaxchilán, Bonampak, and Tikal in Guatemala, as well as good local village tours.

Viajes Pakal, Cuauhtémoc 6-A, T678-2818, www.pakal.com.mx. A reliable agency and culturally friendly tours, several branches in other cities. Good for flight bookings, though some require 4 days' notice.

Palenque town *p408, map p407*

Horse riding

Tours can be booked at the **Clínica Dental Zepeda**, Juárez s/n – the dentist owns the horses. Also through **Cabañas de Safari** in Palanque archaeological zone Km 1, T345-0026. **Gaspar Alvaro** also rents horses. He can be located at his house on the road to the ruins, directly in front of Mayabel. Gaspar will take you on a 3-hr ride through rainforested trails in the surrounding area of the ruins. Good chance of seeing monkeys and toucans. US$15 for 3 hrs. Tell him specifically that you want to go through the rainforest and not on the road.

Tour operators

Inter Travel, Juárez 48, T345-1566, domestic and international flight arrangements, hotel reservations, a new tour to Lagunas Catazajá (27 km from Palenque). Includes a 3-hr motor-boat ride and a visit to a bird sanctuary, US$45 per person, minimum 4 people.
Na Chan Kan, corner of Hidalgo and Jiménez, T345-0263, www.palenquemx.com/viajesnachan. Offer a wide selection of packages ranging from tours to Agua Azul to tours of the Yaxchilán and Bonampak ruins as well as transportation to Guatemala.
Shivalva (Marco A Morales), Merle Green 1, La Cañada, T345-0411, tours of Palenque, Yaxchilán, Bonampak, Tikal, Guatemala City, Belize, Copán.
Yax-Há, Av Juárez 123, T345-0798. English spoken. Recommended.

Guides

Alonso Méndez is a well-versed guide with extensive knowledge of flora, fauna, medicinal uses of plants and an intimate knowledge of the Palenque ruins. A respected authority on Chiapan ethnobotany, Alonso has a gift of academic and spiritual understanding of the rainforest. He speaks English, Spanish and Tzeltzal and can be found at his home in **El Panchan** camping site. Full-day hiking trips US$50 for a group of 6-8 people. Highly recommended.
José Luis Zúñiga Mendoza, T341-14736, tentzun@hotmail.com. Very easy going, José has excellent knowledge of the Palenque area and in addition to guided trips around the ruins offers jungle walks and stays with local communities.

Misol-Há *p407*

Tour operators

All the travel agencies in Palenque do a cheap tour to both Misol-Há and Agua Azul, about US$9 per person. Most tours allow about ½ hr at Misol-Há and 3-4 hrs at Agua Azul. Bring a swimsuit and plenty of drinking water. *Colectivos* from Hidalgo y Allende, Palenque, for Agua Azul and Misol-Há, 2 a day, US$9; *colectivos* can also be organized between Misol-Há and Agua Azul, in either direction. Taxi US$45 with 2 hrs at Agua Azul, or to both falls US$65. Several buses from Palenque daily (direction San Cristóbal de las Casas or Ocosingo), to crossroads leading to the waterfall, US$3.35, 2nd class, 1½ hrs. You can purchase bus tickets from **Transportes Figueroa**, about 100 m from the **ADO** bus station (in direction of the town centre) in Palenque. Bus time is approximately 1½ hrs from Palenque to the turn-off to the Agua Azul road. From the crossroads walk the 4 km downhill to the falls on a beautiful jungle-lined road (or hitch a ride on a minibus for US$1). If, after a long day at the falls, you have no desire to walk the 4 km back to the main road (steep) you can always catch a ride back to Palenque on tour buses that have extra space, US$4. They leave from the Agua Azul parking lot 1500-1800. Back from the junction 1400-1600 with **Transportes Maya** buses. There are buses between San Cristóbal de las Casas and Palenque (to 2nd-class bus station, **Transportes Maya**), which will stop there, but on a number of others you must change at Temo, over 20 km away, north of Ocosingo.

Yaxchilán, Bonampak and Lacanjá *p412*

Tour operators

Operators from Palenque offer a 1-day trip to Bonampak and Yaxchilán, US$58 per person all inclusive. Drive to Bonampak, breakfast included, drive and boat to Yaxchilán, lunch and back. Tough going for 13 hrs, but worth it. A 2-day road and river trip to Bonampak and Yaxchilán is also available from travel agencies, US$100 per person, all transport and food included. **Colectivos Chambala** at Hidalgo y Allende, Palenque, also run 2-day trips, slightly cheaper, again all inclusive, minimum 6 passengers.

For planes to Bonampak contact **Sr Quintero**, T342-0099.

Tenosique and Río San Pedro route *p414*
Hotel Kashlan, Palenque, offers 2-day and 3-day trips to Flores via Yaxchilán and Bonampak. Reliable and recommended. On Av Juárez several agencies offer tours to Flores by minibus and/or taxi, boat and public bus, via Tenosique, La Palma and El Naranjo. You probably won't meet any other travellers. Difficult to find enough people during the low season (otherwise you pay the whole trip yourself), about US$70 per person, 16-hr trip.

Tapachula and around *p416*
Tour operators
Viajes Tacaná, operated by Sr Adolfo Guerrero Chávez, Av 4 Norte No 6, T626-3502, trips to Izapa ruins, to mountains, beaches and can gain entry to museum when closed.

Transport

Villahermosa *p396*
Air
Airport Carlos R Pérez (VSA), 18 km from town – international flights from Havana and Houston, good national connections. VW bus to town US$3 each, taxi US$9.50 for 2.

Airline offices Aerocaribe, Javier Mina 301-A, T314-3202. **AeroMéxico**, Periférico Carlos Pellicer 511, T312-6991. **Aviacsa**, T316-5736. **Mexicana**, Av Madero 109, or Desarrollo Urbano Tabasco 2000, T316-3132.

Bus
Reserve your seat as soon as you can; buses to Mexico City are often booked up well in advance. 1st class, **ADO** bus terminal is on Javier Mina between Méndez and Lino Merino, 12 blocks north of centre, computerized booking system. The **Central Camionera** 2nd-class bus station is on Av Ruiz Cortines, near roundabout with fisherman statue, 1 block east of Javier Mina, opposite Castillo, 4 blocks north of **ADO** (ie 16 from centre).

Several 1st-class buses to **Mexico City**, regular departures, 10-12 hrs, US$54. To **Cancún**, 12 a day, 12 hrs, US$46-58. To **Catazajá**, 1½ hrs, US$4; **Chetumal**, 7 a day, 8 hrs, US$28; **Campeche**, 6 hrs, US$16.50; **Mérida**, many daily, 8 hrs, US$32; **Oaxaca**, via Coatzacoalcos and Tehuantepec, from ADO terminal at 1800, 1940 and 2125, 1st class, stops at about 7 places, US$37; **Palenque**. 8 a day from the ADO terminal, 14 a day 2½ hrs, US$7.50; **Puebla** ADO *'GL' plus* service via *autopista*, US$30, 1st class US$25.50; **San Andrés Tuxtla**, 6 hrs, US$12.50; **San Cristóbal de las Casas**, every couple of hrs, 6 hrs, US$9; also 2nd-class bus with 1 change at Tuxtla, leaves 0800, arrives 2100, fine scenery but treacherous road; **Tapachula**, 14 hrs, US$20; **Veracruz**, with ADO, 8 daily, 8 hrs, US$51 Primera Plus; **Xalapa**, with ADO, 7 a day, 8-10 hrs, US$32-53. To **Emiliano Zapata** and **Tenosique** (for Río San Pedro crossing into Guatemala, see page 433), buses 0700, 0800, 1330, 3-4 hrs.

Car
Car hire Hertz car rental is available from the airport. **Agrisa**, M Ocampo corner of Paseo Tabasco and Malecón, T312-9184, good prices, eg US$40 per day including taxes and insurance, but it is expensive to return the car to another city.

South of Villahermosa *p397*
Bus There are buses between Teapa and **Villahermosa**, 50 km, 1 hr, US$2.20. Also to **Chiapa de Corzo** at 0730, through lovely, mountainous landscape (see page 399).

Tuxtla Gutiérrez *p398, map p398*
Air
Terán airport is the main one. It is a military airport converted for civilian use. It has no facilities for bad weather, so if there is fog, flights are re-routed to Llano San Juan, further out of town. Good national connections.

Airline offices Aviacsa, Av Central Pte 1144, T612-6880, 40 mins.

Bus
Cristóbal Colón 1st-class bus terminal is at Av 2 Norte Pte 268 (opposite **UNO** and **Maya de Oro**). Left luggage at *Juguería* opposite bus station, and at **Maya de Oro** bus station, opposite the ADO (San Cristóbal) terminal.

To **Cancún**, 1230, US$42. To **Córdoba**, ADO, 1725, 1900, Cristóbal Colón 2130, US$38. To **Chetumal**, 1430, US$44. To **Cd Cuauhtémoc**, towards Guatemala, 7 a day, 0500-2230, including Altos, US$10. To **Comitán**, 0500 then each hr to 1900 and 1 at 2300, Altos, US$5.80. To **Mexico City**, 4 a day, 16 hrs, US$64, 1st class, US$42, 2nd class. To **Villahermosa**, at 1500, 2300, 8½ hrs, US$10.30, **Altos de Chiapas** 6 a day between 0700 and 2345. To **Mérida**, change at Villahermosa if no direct service at 1530 (**Altos**), US$26. The scenery between Tuxtla and Mérida is very fine, and the road provides the best route between Chiapas and the Yucatán. To **Oaxaca**, 1130, 1915, 10 hrs, US$24 1st class, US$18 2nd class. To **Palenque**, Altos, 6 a day, 0500-2300, 7 hrs, US$9.40, other buses pass through Palenque. To **Pochutla**, at 0935 and 2015, 10 hrs, US$24. To **Puebla**, ADO US$42, departs 1900, Cristóbal Colón 4 per day in the afternoon, **UNO** US$65, 14 hrs. **Oaxaca Pacífico** buses to **Salina Cruz**, from 1st-class bus terminal. Take travel sickness tablets for Tuxtla-Oaxaca road if you suffer from queasiness. Frequent buses 0500-2300 to **San Cristóbal de las Casas**, 2 hrs, US$3.60 (2nd class US$3), superb mountain journey; *colectivos* from near Av 2 Ote Sur y 2 Sur Ote do the journey for US$3. To **Tapachula**, 16 a day; there are more 1st class than 2nd class to the Talismán bridge (1st class is less crowded), US$16. To **Tonalá**, 1615, US$13. To **Tulum**, 1230, US$51. To **Veracruz**, 1930, US$34.

Taxis

Easy to flag down anywhere. US$2 within the centre, US$2.50-3 to the zoo, US$5 to Chiapa de Corzo (for Sumidero Canyon).

Chiapa de Corzo *p399*

Bus Buses from Tuxtla Gutiérrez, Calle 3 Ote Sur, US$0.50, frequent; several a day (1 hr) to **San Cristóbal de las Casas**, US$3.50. Cristóbal Colón to **Mexico City**, 1815, US$36.50.

San Cristóbal de las Casas *p400, map p401*

Air

San Cristóbal has a small airport (SZT) about 15 km from town; Aerocaribe flies to **Tuxtla Gutiérrez**. Charter flights available to see **Lacanjá**, **Bonampak** and **Yaxchilán** on the Río Usumacinta, 7 hrs in all (US$100 per person if plane is full, more if not). All with Aerochiapas at airport. Aeromar, T5133-1111, takes small planes to **Mexico City**, US$230 return.

Airline offices Aviacsa, in Xanav agency, Pasaje Mazariegos, local 2, Real de Guadalupe, T678-4441, although they do not fly from San Cristóbal.

Bicycle

Bike hire Los Pingüinos, Av Ecuador, T678-0212, www.bikemexico.com/pinguinos, 0915-1430, 1600-1900, rents mountain bikes for US$7 for 3 hrs or US$10 per day, US$14 for 24 hrs. Guided biking tours half or full days, English, German spoken, beautiful countryside and knowledgeable guides, highly recommended.

Rodada 28, on María Adelina Flores, opposite **Hotel Casa Vieja**, Mon-Sat 0900-1330, 1600-2000, US$2 per hr, US$8 per day.

Bus

Bus timetables and tickets available for first class travel from the ticket office, corner of Real de Guadalupe and Belisario Domínguez, T678-8503, for the following bus lines: **ADO, UNO, Cristóbal Colón, Sur, Altos, ETN, Primera Plus, Estrella de Oro** and **Maya De Oro**. The 1st-class bus terminal serves all destinations in the country. There are 2 other 2nd-class terminals across the road, only serving Chiapan destinations.

From the 1st-class terminal, on Allende: to **Campeche**, 0930, *servicio plus*, 2100, US$25. To **Cancún**, several daily, 17 hrs, US$42-51. To **Cárdenas**, ADO US$17. To **Chetumal**, 1430, 11 hrs, US$29. To **Arriaga**, at 1200 via **Tuxtla Gutiérrez**, US$6. To **Cd Cuauhtémoc**, several daily, 3 hrs, US$6.5 – see below for buses to Guatemala. To **Coatzacoalcos**, at 0630, US$14.80. To **Comitán**, 7 per day, 1½ hrs, US$3.60. To **Mérida**, 0930, 1730, 13 hrs, US$34. To **Mexico City**, 1350, 1530 and 1800, 18 hrs, US$50. To **Oaxaca**, 2 with Cristóbal Colón at 1700 and 2000, US$28, 1 with **Maya de Oro** at 2200, US$35. To **Palenque**, 10 daily, 5½ hrs, US$8. To **Playa del Carmen**, US$42. To **Pochutla**, 1815 and 2100, 13 hrs, US$26. To **Puebla**, 1530 and 1730, US$46. To **Puerto Escondido**, with

Cristóbal Colón, 1st class, 0745, 1815 and 2100, US$27. To **Tapachula**, 5 a day, 9 hrs, US$14.30. To **Tuxtla Gutiérrez**, 12 a day, US$3.60 (US$6 with UNO luxury 1st class – with seats that are practically beds, at 1800 and 1445). To **Tulum**, US$40. To **Veracruz**, 1840, US$35. To **Villahermosa**, 1125, 1830, 7 hrs, US$13.

Lacandonia 2nd-class bus to **Palenque** from 2nd-class bus station, also on Allende, 7 a day between 0100 and 2015, 4-5 hrs, US$9 (via Agua Azul, US$6); Cristóbal Colón, 1st-class service, up to 4 times daily (including at least 1 *servicio plus*) US$10, bookings 5 days in advance; Maya de Oro, from Cristóbal Colón terminal, 3 times daily, a/c, videos, non-stop; Rodolfo Figueroa, 5 times a day, US$4.50, a/c. (On reaching Ocosingo it is not uncommon to be told the bus is going no further; your onward fare to Palenque will be refunded but you will have to make your own way.) Autotransportes Tuxtla, F Sarabia, between Carretera Panamericana and Alvaro Obregón, 2nd class to Palenque, reserved seats, US$5. Minibuses to **Tuxtla Gutiérrez** leave from in front of 1st-class bus station, when full, US$2.

Bus to Guatemala Cristóbal Colón, south end of Av Insurgentes (left-luggage facilities Mon-Sat 0600-2000), clean station, direct 1st-class buses to the Guatemalan border at **Cd Cuauhtémoc**, 170 km, several daily from 0700, 3 hrs, US$3.50 (leave bus at border, not its final destination). 1 ADO bus a day to the border at 1900, book in advance. Altos to Cd Cuauhtémoc/ border, 3 a day, US$5. Cristóbal Colón to **Comitán** (if you can't get a bus to the border, take 1 to Comitán and get a pick-up there, US$0.50), hourly from 0700. 87 km (a beautiful, steep route). *Colectivos* also leave for Comitán from outside the Mexican Immigration building, US$2.50, departing when full, 1 hr. 2nd class to border with Autotransportes Tuxtla, US$2.75 (do not take 1430 ACL 2nd class, next to Trans Lacandonia, on Carretera Panamericana, as it arrives too late for onward transport). For details on crossing the border at La Mesilla see pages 417 and 579.

Several operators run run a shuttle to the Guatemalan border and beyond, including Viajes Chincultik (see Tour operators, above) Tue and Fri: **La Mesilla** (US$20), **Quetzaltenango** (US$40), **Panajachel** and **Lake Atitlán** (US$50) and **Antigua** (US$60).

Car

Car hire Budget, Mazariegos 36, T678-1871, in Hotel Mansión del Valle.

Scooters

Croozy Scooters, Belisario Domínguez 7, www.prodigyweb.net.mx/croozyscooters. Rents out small scooters, a good way of moving around. US$25 a day. They provide maps and suggested routes. Deposit and ID required. Recommended.

Taxi

US$1.60 anywhere in town, *colectivo* US$0.70.

Villages near San Cristóbal *p402*

Bus Get to outlying villages by bus or communal VW bus (both very packed); buses leave very early, and often don't return until next day, so you have to stay overnight; lorries are more frequent. To **Zinacantán** catch also VW bus from market. Buses and combis (US$1.50) from the market area to **San Andrés Larrainzar** (bus at 1000, 1100, 1400, with return same day, US$0.80 one way) and **Tenejapa**. Transportes Fray Bartolomé de las Casas has buses to **Chanal**, **Chenalhó** (US$15 with taxi, return, 1 hr stay), **Pantelhó**, **Yajalón** and villages en route to Ocosingo. Transportes Lacandonia on Av Crescencio Rosas also go to the villages of **Huixtán**, **Oxchuc** and **Yajalón**, on the way to Palenque and to **Pujiltic**, **La Mesilla** and **Venustiano Carranza**. If you are in San Cristóbal for a limited period of time it is best to rent a car to see the villages.

See also **Scooters**, under San Cristóbal, above.

Ocosingo *p405*

Many buses and *colectivos* to **Palenque**, 2½ hrs, US$3.30 and **San Cristóbal de Las Casas**.

Palenque town *p408, map p407*

Air

Aerocaribe flies daily during the high season to Palenque from **Cancún** via Flores, Guatemala – check with travel agents. There are also flights from **Huatulco**, **Mérida**, **Oaxaca** and **Tuxtla Gutiérrez**. For flights to Bonampak and Yaxchilán, see below.

Bus

Local Micro buses run back and forth along the main street, passing the bus station area, to and from the ruins, every 10 mins, US$0.80 (taxi US$6). All bus companies have terminals close to each other at west end of Av Juárez with 20 de Noviembre.

Long distance There are 3 bus terminals, 2 smaller 2nd-class ones serving destinations in Chiapas state, and the **ADO/Cristóbal Colón** terminal, with buses to Chiapas destinations as well as longer journeys, all on 1st-class buses. To **Cancún**, 1st-class terminal, 2000, 13 hrs, US$37; 2nd-class buses, 2345, US$26. To **Campeche**, 1st-class terminal, US$21, 0800 and 2100, 5 hrs, US$16 (ADO); 2nd-class buses, 2345, US$10. To **Escárcega**, 1st-class terminal, 1410, 1730, 3 hrs, US$10; 2nd class 2345, US$6. To **Mérida**, 1st-class terminal, 0800, 2100, 8 hrs, US$25. To **Mexico City**, 1st-class terminal, 1800, 2000, 16 hrs, US$51, also **Alto** at 2130, US$41. To **Oaxaca**, 1st-class terminal, 1730, 15 hrs, US$38 (ADO). To **San Cristóbal**, 1st-class terminal, 8 daily between 0500 and 2200, 5½ hrs, US$8 (also 1st-class service from **Lacandonia** terminal, 2 doors down, 8 a day, US$11); 2nd-class buses, 3 a day from 0730, US$5.50; from the **Lacandonia** terminal, next door to **Express Plus**, 0530, 0645, 0845, US$5. To **Tulum**, 1st-class terminal, 2000, 11 hrs, US$32. To **Tuxtla Gutiérrez**, 1st-class terminal, 0930, 1200, 1830, 6 hrs, US$9.40; 2nd class buses, 3 a day from 0730, US$7. To **Villahermosa**, 2nd-class buses, 6 per day from 0500, US$6.50.

Taxi

Taxis charge a flat rate of US$1.50 within the town, US$4 to the **Panchan** and nearby **Mayabel** camping areas.

Colectivos to the ruins run from 2 places, every 15 mins starting at 0600; last one passes by **El Panchan** at 1800. They run from 2 places: Allende between Hidalgo and Juárez, and from Allende between 20 de Noviembre and Corregidora. US$0.70. *Colectivos* to **Playas de Catazajá** (for Escárcega and Campeche) leave from Allende between 20 de Noviembre and Corregidora, US$0.80. There is also a *colectivo* service to **Santa Elena/Flores**.

Yaxchilán, Bonampak and Lacanjá

p412

Air

Flights from **Palenque** to Bonampak and Yaxchilán, in light plane for 5, about US$600 per plane, to both places, whole trip 6 hrs. Prices set, list available; **Viajes Misol-Há**, Juárez 48 at Aldama, T345-0911, run charter flights to Bonampak and Yaxchilán for US$150 per person return, minimum 4 passengers.

Boat

From **Bethel**, Guatemala, *lanchas* are charging US$93 per boat return to visit Yaxchilán. From **La Técnica**, Guatemala, US$53 return. From **Corozal**, Mexico, it is between US$50-60 per boat.

Bus

Autotransportes Comitán Lagos de Montebello (Manuel Velasco 48, 2 blocks west of plaza, Palenque) buses at 0300, 0430, 0630, 0900 and 2000 all pass the turn-off to Bonampak, US$5.50, check details in advance. Last *colectivo* returning from Echeverría/Corozal, to **Palenque** passing crossroads for Bonampak at 1500. Buses from Palenque from Chancalá bus terminal every 3 hrs or so, from 0730 to **San Javier**, 3 hrs; *colectivos* US$4. From San Javier, a jungle trail leads to Bonampak, easy to follow but several hours' walk with nowhere to stay en route.

Yaxchilán is reached by 1-hr boat journey from Echeverría; you must register at the immigration office here if you are continuing on to Guatemala. There is no problem finding a boat (max 10 people), but try to be there before 0900 to meet other travellers wanting to share launch, you may be able to share with tour parties who arrive from 0900 onwards. It is a beautiful ride, with rewarding ruins at the end of it. The custodian of the ruins is very helpful.

Car

Bonampak is over 30 km from Frontera Echeverría/Corozal and can be reached from the crossroads to Lacanjá on the road to Echeverría/Corozal.

Tenosique and Río San Pedro route *p414*

Bus You can get to Tenosique from **Villahermosa** by ADO bus (0430, 0700, 0800, 1330), 4 hrs, from **Emiliano Zapata** by frequent 1st- or 2nd-class bus, US$2. From **Palenque** minibuses **Libertad** leave from 20 de Noviembre y Allende from 0700 to **Emiliano Zapata**, 1 hr, US$2.50 (take 0700 to be sure of making the boat at La Palma); and from there to Tenosique at 0800 or 0900, 90 mins, US$2. ADO have a direct bus to Tenosique from **Palenque** at 0430, 2 hrs, US$3.25. Many travel agents in Palenque organize *colectivos* direct to **La Palma** at 1000, US$14 per person to connect with the boat to **El Naranjo** (4 passengers minimum). Alternatively, take a *colectivo* before 0645 to **Playas de Catazajá** from the stop just up from ADO (US$1.00, 30 mins); get off at the **El Crucero de la Playa** crossroads on the Villahermosa-Tenosique road and wait for the bus to pass at 0730 (2 hrs to Tenosique, US$2). Similarly, from Tenosique to Palenque, take the Villahermosa bus (every hour or so during the day) as far as El Crucero de la Playa, and then take one of the regular minibuses running to Palenque. Bus also from **Mexico City** with ADO, 16½ hrs,US$45.

Río Usumacinta route *p414*

Bus Coming from Guatemala you may well get stuck at the border as the 0600 Santa Elena-Bethel bus does not connect with buses to Palenque (you may be able to get a lift with a pick-up, or one of the tour buses, which start arriving around 1200; bargain hard). Passengers have to wait until 0400 next day. Bus from Frontera Echeverría/Corozal to **Palenque**, 0500, US$3, and at 1230, US$5. Many military checkpoints.

Boat

Yaxchilán lanchas are a coop of 3 (**Tikal y Yaxchilán, Nueva Alianza** and **Tikalchilán**), based in Corozal near the dock, T00502-6111224/1238605 and run all year. Rack prices but negotiate hard. 1-3 people, 6oo pesos; 4 people, 700 pesos; 5-7 people, 900 pesos; 8-10 people, 1200 pesos. 4 hrs round trip including site visit. If you're an independent traveller it's best to wait for the tour groups to arrive between 0900-1130 every day or ask around for groups at your hotel.

For *lanchas* to **Bethel**, the coop charges the following prices: 1-3 people, 350 pesos; 4 people, 450; 5-7 people, 550; 8-10 people, 700 pesos. Bargain hard though. 25 mins.

To **La Técnica** they charge 50 pesos per person. To Piedras Negras, the price is negotiable.

Comitán *p415*

Bus

Buses from **San Cristóbal de las Casas** with **Cristóbal Colón**, frequent between 0730 and 2030, US$3.75, 2 hrs, last bus back at 1930. And *colectivos* operated by **Balun Canan**, US$2.50, 1 hr, departing when full. One **Cristóbal Colón** bus goes on to Tuxtla (via San Cristóbal), US$3.50, 4 hrs. Minibuses from Comitán to **Tuxtla** leave from the Cristóbal Colón bus station. Buses, combis and pick-up trucks from Comitán run to the border at **Cd Cuauhtémoc**.

Ciudad Cuauhtémoc *p415*

Bus

Local Buses are *de paso* from San Cristóbal so no advance booking is possible. The **Cristóbal Colón** bus leaves Comitán 0800, 1100 (coming from San Cristóbal) and in the afternoon for the border at Cd Cuauhtémoc, fare US$2.75. **Autotransportes Tuxtla** leave from Comitán (on the main highway at approximately Av 2 Sur) at regular intervals for the border, 1½ hrs. There are at least 8 buses to Comitán 0800-1930 from Cd Cuauhtémoc, with 2nd-class buses during the evening.

Long distance Cristóbal Colón (terminal near the Pan-American Highway, Comitán) has 1st-class buses to **Mexico City** at 0900, 1100 and 1600 (which leave the border 2½ hrs earlier), fare US$40.75 (from Mexico City to Comitán at 1415 and 2040, fully booked 2 hrs in advance); to **Oaxaca** at 0700 and 1900, US$33; to **Tuxtla Gutiérrez** at 0600 and 1600, US$8, and to **Tapachula** (via Arriaga) at 1200 and 2000, US$20. Entering Mexico from Guatemala, to San Cristóbal, direct buses US$3.50, or take a minibus to Comitán, US$1.55; these connect with combis at the **Autotransportes Tuxtla** terminal for **San Cristóbal de las Casas**.

Taxi
Pick-ups charge US$1.55 per person Comitán-border; beware short-changing. From here take a taxi, US$1.65, or *colectivo*, to the Guatemalan side (4 km uphill, minimum 3 people) and get your passport stamped.

Arriaga

Bus To many destinations, mostly 1st class, to **Mexico City**, 1645, 12-13 hrs, US$42; **Tuxtla**, with **Fletes y Pasajes** at 1400 and 1600, 4 hrs, US$7; **Oaxaca**, 6 hrs, US$7.

Tapachula *p416*

Air
Flights from **Mérida**, **Mexico City**, **Tuxtla Gutiérrez**, **Veracruz** daily. Combis to airport from Calle 2 Sur No 40, T625-1287. From airport to border, minibuses charge US$26 for whole vehicle, so share with others, otherwise take *colectivo* to 2nd-class bus terminal and then a bus to Cd Hidalgo.

Airline offices Aviacsa, Calle Central Norte 52-B, T/F626-3159. **AeroMéxico**, Av 2 Norte 6, T626-3921. **Taesa**, T626-3702.

Bus
Cristóbal Colón bus **Mexico City**-Guatemala City takes 23 hrs, with a change at the border to **Rutas Lima**. **Transgalgos**, 7a Avenida, T230-5058, run a new direct service to Guatemala City and Antigua 0930 and 1330, US$45. Mexico City-Tapachula, 20 hrs (**Cristóbal Colón**, 1st class, Av 3 Norte y 17 Ote, T626-2880; 2nd class, Prolongación 9 Pte s/n, T626-1161). To/from Tapachula to **Mexico City**, US$40, 5 a day (frequent stops for toilets and food, also frequent police checks, no toilet or a/c on bus), much better to take *plus* service, 1915, US$58. Buses from Mexico City all leave in the afternoon; the 1545 and 1945 go on to Talismán. The 2nd-class bus station is at Av 3 Norte, Calle 9 Ote. **Oaxaca**, **Cristóbal Colón** and **Fipsa**(Calle 9 Ote, T626-7603), 14 hrs, US$19, many passport checks (**Fipsa** has 4 a day, continuing to Puebla and Córdoba, take 1830 to see sunrise over the Sierra Madre; also has 2 a day to Mexico City). To **Puebla**: 16 hrs, plus US$47; **UNO**, US$53. To **San Cristóbal de las Casas** and **Tuxtla Gutiérrez** at 1100. To **Tehuantepec** and **Salina Cruz**: 0915, 8 hrs, US$14.80.

Border with Guatemala: Talismán *p417*

Bus
There are few buses between the Talismán bridge and Oaxaca or Mexico City although they do exist); it is advisable therefore to travel to Tapachula for connection; delays can occur there at peak times.

Taxi
Combi vans run from near the Unión y Progreso bus station, about US$1; *colectivo* from outside **Posada de Calú** to Talismán, US$0.60, also from Calle 5 Pte between Av 12 y Av 14 Norte. Taxi Tapachula-Talismán, negotiate fare to about US$2.

A taxi from Guatemala to Mexican Immigration will cost US$2, but it may be worth it if you are in a hurry to catch an onward bus.

Hitchhikers should note that there is little through international traffic at the Talismán bridge.

Border with Guatemala: Ciudad Hidalgo *p417*

Bus From Calle 7 Pte between Av 2 Norte and Av Central Norte, Tapachula, buses go to 'Hidalgo', US$1.25

Directory

Villahermosa *p396*

Banks **American Express**, Turismo Nieves, Sarlat 202, T314-1818. **Banamex**, Madero and Reforma, Mon-Fri 0900-1700. **HSBC**, Suárez and Lerdo, changes TCs at good rates. **Cultural centres** **Centro Cultural**, Corner of Madero and Zaragoza, T312-5473. Presentations of local artists and photographers. Live music, workshops in literature, local handicrafts and musical interpretation, among others. **El Jaguar Despertado**, Saenz 117, T314-1244, forum for artists and local Villahermosino intellectuals. Hosts concerts, art exhibitions and book presentations. **Internet** C@fe internet, Aldama 404-C, lobby of the **Hotel Howard Johnson**. US$1.50 per hr. Many others scattered around town. **Post office** On Ignacio in the centre. **DHL**, parcel courier service, Paseo Tabasco.

Tuxtla Gutiérrez *p398, map p398*
Banks Bancomer, Av Central Pte y 2 Pte Norte, for Visa and TCs, 0900-1500. HSBC, Mon-Sat 0800, good rates and service. For cheques and cash: 1 Sur Pte 350, near Zócalo. There are ATMs in various branches of Farmacia del Ahorro, all over the city. **Immigration**, 1 Ote Norte. **Internet** Free at library of Universidad Autónoma de Chiapas, Route 190, 6 km from centre. Compucentro, 1 Norte Pte 675, upstairs. US$1 per hr. Various other internet cafés springing up, costing about US$1/hr. **Post office** On main square.
Telephone International phone calls can be made from 1 Norte, 2 Ote, directly behind post office, 0800-1500, 1700-2100 (1700-2000 Sun).

San Cristóbal de las Casas *p400, map p401*
Banks Banamex, Real de Guadalupe y Portal Oriental, changes cheques without commission, 0900-1300. Banca Serfín on the Zócalo, changes Euro, Amex, MasterCard, Tcs. Banca Serfín on the Zócalo, changes Euro, Amex, MasterCard, TCs. Bancomer, Plaza 31 de Marzo 10, charges commission, cash advance on Visa, American Express or Citicorp TCs, good rates and service. Casa Margarita will change dollars and TCs. Banks are usually open for exchange 0900-1600. HSBC, Diego de Mazariegos, good rates for cash and TCs (US$ only), fast, efficient, cash advance on MasterCard, open Sat afternoons. Casa de Cambio Lacantún, Real de Guadalupe 12, Mon-Fri 0900-1400, 1600-1900, Sat and Sun 0900-1300 (supposedly, may close early), no commission, at least US$50 must be changed and much lower exchange than at the banks. 24-hr ATM at Banorte, 5 de Febrero, adjacent to cathedral. Quetzales can be obtained for pesos or dollars in the *cambio* but better rates are paid at the border. **Cultural centres** The Casa de Cultura, opposite El Carmen church on junction of Hermanos Domínguez and Hidalgo, has a range of activities on offer: concerts, films, lectures, art exhibitions and conferences. Casa/Museo de Sergio Castro, Guadalupe Victoria 47 (6 blocks from plaza), T678-4289, 1800-2000 (but best to make appointment), entry free but donations welcome. Excellent collection of indigenous garments, talks (in English, French or Spanish) and slide shows about customs and problems of the indigenous population. El Puente, Real de Guadalupe 55, 1 block from the plaza, T678-4157, www.elpuenteweb.com, Spanish lessons with a restaurant, internet centre and a small cinema. Check their notice board for forthcoming events. A good place to meet other travellers. **Na Bolom Museum and Cultural Centre**, see page 402 and Sleeping, above. **Immigration** On Carretera Panamericana and Diagonal Centenario, opposite Hotel Bonampak. From Zócalo take Diego de Mazariegos west, after crossing bridge take Diagonal on the left towards Highway, 30-min walk. **Internet** There are many internet cafés all over town with rates around US$0.80 per hr. Service is generally good. **Language schools** Centro Cultural El Puente, Real de Guadalupe 55, Caja Postal 29230, T/F678-3723, www.elpuenteweb.com (Spanish programme), rates around US$10 per hr, homestay programmes available from US$230 per week, registration fee US$35. Mixed reports. Instituto Jovel, María Adelina Flores 21, Apdo Postal 62, T/F678-4069, www.institutojovel.com. Group or 1-to-1 classes, homestays arranged, said to be the best school in San Cristóbal as their teachers undergo an obligatory 6-week training course; very good reports from students, all teachers bilingual to some extent. Universidad Autónoma de Chiapas, Av Hidalgo 1, Dpto de Lenguas, offers classes in English, French and Tzotzil. **Laundry** Superklin, Crescencio Rosas 48, T678-3275, US$1.30 per kg, for collection after 5 hrs. La Rapidita, Insurgentes 9, new coin-operated machines for self-service or they will launder clothes for you 1-3 kg US$3.50. **Medical services** Doctors: Dra Carmen Ramos, Av Insurgentes 28, next to (south of) Templo de Santa Lucía, T678-1680, best to call ahead if possible or make an appointment through tourist office. Servicio Médico Bilingüe, Av Benito Juárez 60, T678-0793, Dr Renato Zarate Castañeda speaks English, is highly recommended and if necessary can be reached at home, T678-2998. Hospitals and clinics: Red Cross, Prolongación Ignacio Allende, T678-0772. Recommended. Pharmacies: Farmacia Bios, corner of

Cuauhtémoc and Hidalgo. Well-stocked pharmacy. **Post office** Cuauhtémoc 13, between Rosas and Hidalgo, Mon-Fri 0800-1900, Sat 0900-1300. **Telephone** Computel, Insurgentes 64B, fax, also guards luggage; El Paso, Av Insurgentes 79-C, T678-5685. Long distance calls, luggage storage, postal service, and handy location close to the bus station. Telmex, Niños Héroes and Hidalgo, also has 24-hr ATM. La Pared, Av Miguel Hidalgo 2, owner Dana Gay offers long-distance calling service, cheap rates, and a bookshop to browse. Long-distance phone calls can be made from the Boutique Santo Domingo on Utrilla, on corner of Paniagua, takes credit cards, collect call possible; and at shops at Av 16 de Septiembre 22, Madero 75 and Av Insurgentes 60. Phone and fax services available at the tourist office in the Plaza. International calls from 2nd-class bus station.

Palenque town *p408, map p407*

Banks Exchange rate only comes through at 1000, then banks open until 1200. Bancomer, changes TCs, good rates. Yax-Há Cambio on Juárez, daily 0700-2000, changes US$ cash and TCs. Next door at No 28, is Banamex, Mon-Fri 0930-1400, slow. Restaurante El Rodeo also changes TCs at bank rate. At weekends TCs can be changed at many travel agencies and other shops on Av Juárez; also, the owner at Farmacia Central will change US$ at a reasonable rate. ATMs at Bancomer and Banamex, but with long queues. **Internet** Several internet cafés along Juárez with good service and prices ranging from US$1-1.50 per hr. **Laundry** Opposite Hotel Kashlan, US$2 per 3 kg, 0800-1930. At the end of Juárez is a laundry, US$3 per 3 kg. **Post office** Independencia, next to Palacio Municipal, helpful, Mon-Fri 0900-1300. **Telephone** Long-distance telephones at ADO bus terminal, cheaper than many other telephone offices; at Mercería bookshop in Aldama near Juárez, and a shop by Hotel Palenque in the Zócalo.

Comitán *p415*

Banks Bancomer, on plaza will exchange Amex TCs; 2 others on plaza, none change dollars after 1200; also a *casa de cambio*. **Embassies and consulates** Guatemala, Calle 1 Sur Pte 26 y Av 2 Pte Sur, T672-0491. Mon-Fri 0800-1200, 1400-1700, Sat 0800-1400; tourist card US$10 (even for those for whom it should be free), valid 1 year, multiple entry.

Ciudad Cuauhtémoc *p415*

Banks Don't change money with the Guatemalan customs officials: the rates they offer are worse than those given by bus drivers or in banks (and these are below the rates inside the country). There is nowhere to change TCs at the border and bus companies will not accept cheques in payment for fares. 300 m after the border, however, you can get good rates for TCs at the Banco de Café. The briefcase-and-dark-glasses brigade changes cash on the Guatemalan side only, but you must know in advance what the quetzal rates are.

Tapachula *p416*

Banks Avoid the crowds of streetwise little boys at the border; exchange is rather better in the town, bus station gives a good rate (cash only). Banamex, Blv Díaz Ordaz, 0830-1230, 1400-1600, disagreement over whether TCs are changed. HSBC is the only bank open Sat, changes TCs. Casa de Cambio Tapachula, Av 4 Norte y Calle 3 Pte, changes dollars, TCs, pesos, quetzales and lempiras (open late Mon-Sat), but not recommended, poor rates. Very difficult to change money on Sun. Try the supermarket. **Embassies and consulates** Guatemala, Calle 2 Ote 33 and Av 7 Sur, T626-1252 (taxi from Cristóbal Colón terminal, US$1), Mon-Fri 0800-1600; visa US$10, friendly and quick, take photocopy of passport, photocopier 2 blocks away. **Immigration** Av 14 Norte 57, T626-1263. **Laundry** There is a laundry, at Av Central Norte 99 between Calle 13 y 15 Ote, US$3 wash and dry, 1 hr service, about 2 blocks from Cristóbal Colón bus station, open Sun. Also on Av Central Norte between Central Ote y Calle 1, opens 0800, closed Sun. **Telephone** Several long-distance phone offices, eg Esther, Av 5 Norte 46; La Central, Av Central Sur 95; Monaco, Calle 1 Pte 18.

Yucatán Peninsula

The Yucatán Peninsula, which includes the states of Campeche, Yucatán and Quintana Roo, is sold to tourists as the land of Maya archaeology and Caribbean beach resorts. And there's no denying it, the warm turquoise sea, fringed with fine white-sand beaches and palm groves of the 'Mayan Riviera' are second to none. And it would be a crime not to tread the beaten path to the sensational ruins at Chichén Itzá, Uxmal and Tulum. But it more than pays to explore beyond the main itineraries to visit some of the lesser known Maya sites such as Cobá, Edzná or Dzibilchaltún, or the imposing Franciscan monastery and huge pyramid at Izamal. There are flamingo feeding grounds at Celestún and Río Lagartos and over 500 other species of bird, many of which are protected in Sian Ka'an Biosphere Reserve, which covers 4500 sq km of tropical forest, savanna and coastline. Ever since Jacques Cousteau filmed the Palancar Reef in the 1960s, divers have swarmed to the clear waters of Cozumel, the 'Island of the Swallows', to wonder at the many species of coral and other underwater plants and creatures, at what has become one of the most popular diving centres in the world. Also popular and specialized is diving in the many cenotes *(sink holes), including the famous Nohooch Nah Chich, part of the world's largest underground cave system.*

History

After the Maya arrived in Yucatán about 1200 BC, they built monumental stone structures during the centuries leading up to the end of the pre-Classic period (AD 250). Later they rebuilt their cities, but along different lines, probably because of the arrival of Toltecs in the ninth and 10th centuries. Each city was autonomous, and in rivalry with other cities. Before the Spaniards arrived the Maya had developed a writing system in which the hieroglyphic was somewhere between the pictograph and the letter. Fray Diego de Landa collected their books, wrote a very poor summary, the *Relación de las Cosas de Yucatán*, and with Christian but unscholarly zeal burnt most of the codices, which he never really understood.

The Spaniards found little to please them when they first arrived in the Yucatán: no gold, no concentration of natives; nevertheless Mérida was founded in 1542 and the few natives were handed over to the conquerors in *encomiendas* (see page 1213). The Spaniards found them difficult to exploit: even as late as 1847 there was a major revolt, fuelled by the inhumane conditions in the *henequén* (sisal) plantations, and the discrimination against the Maya in the towns, but it was the expropriation of Maya communal lands that was the main source of discontent. In July 1847 a conspiracy against the *Blancos*, or ruling classes from Mexico, was uncovered in Valladolid and one of its leaders, Manuel Antonio Ay, was shot. This precipitated a bloody war, known as the *Guerra de Castas* (Caste War) between the Maya and the *Blancos*. The first act was the massacre of all the non-Maya inhabitants of Tepich, south of Valladolid. The Maya took control of much of the Yucatán, laying siege to Mérida, only to abandon it to sow their crops in 1849. This allowed the governor of Yucatán to counter-attack, driving the Maya by ruthless means into southern Quintana Roo. In Chan Santa Cruz, now called Felipe Carrillo Puerto, one of the Maya leaders, José María Barrera, accompanied by Manuel Nahuat, a ventriloquist, invented the 'talking cross', a cult that attracted thousands of followers. The sect, called Cruzob, established itself and renewed the resistance against the government from Mexico City. It was not until 1901 that the Mexican army retook the Cruzob's domain.

People

The people are divided into two groups: the Maya, the minority, and the *mestizos*. The Maya women wear *huípiles*, or white cotton tunics (silk for fiestas), which may reach the ankles and are embroidered round the square neck and bottom hem. Their ornaments are mostly gold. A few of the men still wear straight white cotton (occasionally silk) jackets and pants, often with gold or silver buttons, and when working protect this dress with aprons. Carnival is the year's most joyous occasion, with concerts, dances and processions. Yucatán's folk dance is the *jarana*, the man dancing with his hands behind his back, the woman raising her skirts a little, and with interludes when they pretend to be bullfighting. During pauses in the music the man, in a high falsetto voice, sings *bambas* (compliments) to the woman. The Maya are a courteous gentle people. They drink little, except on feast days, speak Mayan languages, and profess Christianity laced with a more ancient nature worship.

Access to sites and resorts

Many tourists come to the Yucatán, mostly to see the ancient **Maya sites** and to stay at the new coastal resorts. A good paved road runs from Coatzacoalcos through Villahermosa, Campeche and Mérida (Route 180). An inland road from Villahermosa to Campeche gives easy access to Palenque (see page 408). If time is limited, take a bus from Villahermosa to Chetumal via Escárcega, which can be done overnight as the journey is not very interesting (unless you want to see the Maya ruins off this road, see page 488). From Chetumal travel up the coast to Cancún, then across to Mérida. Route 307, from Chetumal to Cancún and Puerto Juárez is all paved and in very good condition. Air services from the US and Mexico City are given under Mérida, Cancún and Cozumel.

The state of Quintana Roo is on the eastern side of the Yucatán Peninsula and has recently become the largest tourist area in Mexico with the development of the resort of Cancún, and the parallel growth of Isla Mujeres, Cozumel and the 100-km corridor south of Cancún to Tulum. Growth has been such, in both Yucatán and Quintana Roo, that there are insufficient buses at peak times; old second-class buses may be provided for first-class tickets and second-class buses take far too many standing passengers. There is also a lack of information services. Where beaches are unspoilt they often lack all amenities. Many cheaper hotels are spartan.

Warning: So many of the tourists coming to the coastal resorts speak no Spanish so price hikes and short-changing have become very common, making those places very expensive if you are not careful. In the peak, winter season, prices are increased anyway, by about 50%.

Quintana Roo (and especially Cozumel) is the main area for **diving** and **watersports** in the Yucatán Peninsula, and the options are mentioned in the text. However, watersports in Quintana Roo are expensive and touristy, although operators are generally helpful; snorkelling is often in large groups. On the more accessible reefs the coral is dying and there are no small coral fish, as a necessary part of the coral life cycle. Further from the shore, though, there is still much reef life to enjoy.

A useful website on places and activities in the Yucatán is www.yucatantoday.com, the web version of the monthly *Yucatán Today* magazine.

State of Campeche

Take time out to explore the State of Campeche. Colonial architecture is plentiful, there are several fortified convents and Campeche city itself was fortified to protect its citizens from pirate attacks. There are many archaeological sites, most demonstrating influences of Chenes-style architecture. Relax at the resorts of Sihoplaya and Seybaplaya while watching pelicans dive and iguanas scurry. You can try the beaches at Ciudad del Carmen, eat delicious red snapper and buy a cheap, but sturdy, Panama hat. The exhibits at several museums reflect the seafaring nature of the area and the pre-Conquest civilization that occupied these lands. The official government website is at www.campeche.gob.mx » *For Sleeping, Eating and other listings, see page 446-450.*

Tabasco to Campeche » *pp446-450.*

There are two routes to Campeche from the neighbouring state of Tabasco: the inland Highway 186, via Escárcega, with two toll bridges (cost US$4.25), and the slightly longer coastal route through Ciudad del Carmen, Highway 180; both converge at Champotón, 66 km south of Campeche. Highway 186 passes Villahermosa's modern international airport and runs fast and smooth in a sweeping curve 115 km east to the Palenque turn-off at Playas del Catazajá; beyond, off the highway, is **Emiliano Zapata** (Fiesta: 26 October), a busy cattle centre, with Pemex station.

Francisco Escárcega → *Phone code: 982. Colour map 4, B2.*

Escárcega, a shortening of its full name Francisco Escárcega, is a major hub for travellers on their way south to the states of Tabasco and Chiapas, north to Mérida in the state of Yucatán, east to Maya sites in Campeche and Quintana Roo states, and further east to the city of Chetumal. The town itself is not particularly enticing, set on a busy highway with a dusty Wild West atmosphere. If stuck here overnight, all you need to know is that there are a couple of hotels, a bank and several cheap restaurants.

Coast road to Campeche » *pp446-450.*

Although Highway 180 via Ciudad del Carmen is narrow, crumbling into the sea in places and usually ignored by tourists intent on visiting Palenque, this journey is beautiful and more interesting than the fast toll road inland to Campeche. The road threads its way from Villahermosa 78 km north through marshland and rich cacao, banana and coconut plantations, passing turnings to tiny coastal villages with palm-lined but otherwise mediocre beaches. It finally leads to the river port of **Frontera**, where Graham Greene began the research journey in 1938 that led to the publication of *The Lawless Roads* and later to *The Power and the Glory*. The **Feria Guadalupana** is held from 3-13 December, with an agricultural show, bullfights, *charreadas* and regional dances.

The road briefly touches the coast at the Tabasco/Campeche state border. It then runs east beside a series of lakes (superb birdwatching) to the fishing village of **Zacatal** (93 km), at the entrance to the tarpon-filled **Laguna de Términos** (named for the first Spanish expedition, which thought it had reached the end of the 'island' of Yucatán). Just before Zacatal is the lighthouse of **Xicalango**, an important pre-Columbian trading centre. Cortés landed near here in 1519 on his way to Veracruz and was given 20 female slaves, including 'La Malinche', the indigenous princess baptized as Doña Marina who, as the Spaniards' interpreter, was to play an important role in the Conquest. A bridge crosses the lake's mouth to Ciudad del Carmen.

Ciudad del Carmen → *Phone code: 938. Colour map 4, B1.*

This is the hot, bursting-at-the-seams principal oil port of the region. The site was established in 1588 by a pirate named McGregor as a lair from which to raid Spanish shipping; it was infamous until the pirates were wiped out by Alfonso Felipe de Andrade in 1717, who named the town after its patroness, the Virgen del Carmen.

Most streets in the centre are numbered; even numbers generally run west-east, and odd south-north. Calle 20 is the seafront *malecón* and the road to the airport and University is Calle 31. Fishing excursions can be arranged through the **Club de Pesca** ⓘ *Nelo Manjárrez, T382-0073, at Calle 40 and Calle 61*. Coastal lagoons are rich in tarpon *(sábalo)* and bonefish.

The attractive, cream-coloured **cathedral** (Parroquia de la Virgen del Carmen), begun 1856, is notable for its stained glass. **La Iglesia de Jesús** (1820) opposite Parque Juárez is surrounded by elegant older houses. Nearby is the Barrio del Guanal, the oldest residential quarter, with the church of the **Virgen de la Asunción** (1815) and houses with spacious balconies and tiles brought from Marseilles.

There are several good **beaches** with restaurants and watersports, the most scenic being Playa Caracol (southeast of the centre) and Playa Norte, which has extensive white sand and safe bathing. The town's patroness is honoured with a cheerful **fiesta** each year between 15 and 30 June.

Maya ruins in south Campeche

Calakmul → *Colour map 4, B2.*

ⓘ *Daily 0800-1700, US$3.*

Three hundred kilometres southeast from Campeche town, and a further 60 km off the main Escárcega-Chetumal road, the ruins of Calakmul are only accessible by car. The site has been the subject of much attention in recent years, due to the previously concealed scale of the place. It is now believed to be one of the largest archaeological sites in Mesoamerica, and certainly the biggest of all the Maya cities, with somewhere in the region of 10,000 buildings in total, many of them as yet unexplored. There is evidence that Calakmul was begun in 300 BC, and continually added to until AD 800. At the centre of the site is the Gran Plaza, overlooked by a pyramid whose base covers five acres of ground. One of the buildings grouped around the **Gran Plaza** is believed, due to its curious shape and location, to have been designed for astronomical observation. The **Gran Acrópolis**, the largest of all the structures, is divided into two sections: **Plaza Norte**, with the ball court, was used for ceremonies; **Plaza Sur** was used for public activities. The scale of the site is vast, and many of the buildings are still under excavation, which means that information on Calakmul's history is continually being updated. To reach Calakmul, take Route 186 until Km 95, then turn off at Conhuás, where a paved road leads to the site, 60 km.

Xpujil → *Phone code: 983. Colour map 4, B2.*

ⓘ *Tue-Sun 0800-1700, US$3, US$3 to use a video camera.*

The name means a type of plant similar to a cattail. The architectural style is known as Río Bec, characterized by heavy masonry towers simulating pyramids and temples, usually found rising in pairs at the ends of elongated buildings. The main building at Xpujil features an unusual set of three towers, with rounded corners and steps that are so steep they are unscalable, suggesting they may have been purely decorative. The façade features the open jaws of an enormous reptile in profile on either side of the main entrance, possibly representing Itzamná, the Maya god of creation. Xpujil's main period of activity was AD 500-750; it began to go into decline around 1100. Major excavation on the third structure was done as recently as 1993, and there are still many unexcavated buildings dotted about the site. It can be very peaceful and quiet in the early mornings, compared with the throng of tourist activity at the more accessible sites such as Chichén Itzá and Uxmal. To get there, see Transport, page 448.

The tiny village of Xpujil, on the Chetumal-Escárcega highway, is conveniently located for the three sets of ruins in this area, Xpujil, Becán and Chicanná. There are two hotels and a couple of shops. Guided tours to the more remote sites, such as Calakmul and Río Bec, can be organized through either of the two hotels, costing about US$20-30 per person for the whole day.

Becán → *Phone code: 996. Colour map 4, B2.*

ⓘ *Daily 0800-1700, US$3.*

Seven kilometres west of Xpujil, Becán is another important site in the Río Bec style, its most outstanding feature being a moat, now dry, surrounding the entire city, believed to be one of the oldest defence systems in Mesoamerica. Seven entrance gates cross the moat to the city. The large variety of buildings on the site are a strange combination of decorative towers and fake temples, as well as structures used as shrines and palaces. The twin towers, typical of the Río Bec style, feature on the main structure, set on a pyramid-shaped base supporting a cluster of buildings, which seem to have been used for many different functions.

Chicanná → *Phone code: 981. Colour map 4, B2.*

ⓘ *Daily 0800-1700. US$3.*

Located 12 km from Xpujil, Chicanná was named upon its discovery in 1966 in reference to Structure II: chi – mouth, *can* – serpent, and *ná* – house, 'House of the Serpent's Mouth'. Due to its dimensions and location, Chicanná is considered to have been a small residential centre for the rulers of the ancient regional capital of Becán. It was occupied during the late pre-Classic period (300 BC-AD 250); the final stages of activity at the site have been dated to the post-Classic era (AD 1100). Typical of the Río Bec style are numerous representations of the Maya god Itzamná, or Earth Mother. One of the temples has a dramatic entrance in the shape of a monster's mouth, with fangs jutting out over the lintel and more fangs lining the access stairway. A taxi will take you from Xpujil bus stop to Becán and Chicanná for US$10, including waiting time.

Hormiguero → *Colour map 4, B2.*

Twenty kilometres southwest of Xpujil, Hormiguero is the site of one of the most important buildings in the Río Bec region, whose elaborate carvings on the façade show a fine example of the serpent's-mouth entrance, with huge fangs and a gigantic eye.

Río Bec

Río Bec is south off the main highway, some 10 km further along the road to Chetumal. Although the site gave its name to the architectural style seen in this area, there are better examples of it at the ruins listed above. Río Bec is a cluster of several smaller sites, all of which are very difficult to reach without a guide.

Champotón → *Colour map 4, A2.*

Back near the west coast of Campeche state, Route 261 runs 86 km due north from Escárcega through dense forest to the Gulf of Mexico, where it joins the coastal route at Champotón, a relaxed but run-down fishing and shrimping port spread along the banks of Río Champotón. In prehispanic times it was an important trading link between Guatemala and Central Mexico; Toltec and Maya mingled here, followed by the Spaniards; in fact blood was shed here when Francisco Hernández de Córboba was fatally wounded in a skirmish with the inhabitants in 1517. On the south side of town can be seen the remnants of a 1719 fort built as a defence against the pirates who frequently raided this coast. The Feast of the Immaculate Conception (8 December) is celebrated with a joyous festival lasting several days.

Sihoplaya and Seybaplaya → *Phone code: 982. Colour map 4, A2.*

Continuing north, Highways 180 and 261 are combined for 17 km until the latter darts off east on its way to Edzná and Hopelchen (bypassing Campeche, should this be desired).

A 66-km toll *autopista*, paralleling Highway 180, just inland from the southern outskirts of Champotón to Campeche, is much quicker than the old highway. Champotón and Seybaplaya are bypassed. But from the old Highway 180, narrow and slow with speed bumps, you can reach the resort of **Sihoplaya** (regular buses from Campeche US$1). A short distance further north is the larger resort of Seybaplaya. This is an attractive place where fishermen mend nets and pelicans dry their wings on posts along the beach. On the highway is the open-air **Restaurant Veracruz**, serving delicious red snapper (fresh fish at the seafront public market is also good value), but in general there is little to explore. Only the **Balneario Payucán** at the north end of the bay makes a special trip worthwhile; this is probably the closest decent beach to Campeche (33 km), although a little isolated, since the water and sand get filthier as one nears the state capital. Nevertheless, there is still much reef life to enjoy.

Campeche

» *pp446-450. Colour map 4, A2.*

→ *Phone code: 981.*

Campeche's charm is neatly hidden behind traffic blocked streets, but once inside the city walls it reveals itself as a good place to break your journey out to the Yucatán. At the end of the 20th century, the town of Campeche was declared a Cultural Heritage Site by UNESCO. The clean streets of brightly painted houses give the town a relaxed Caribbean feel. A hurricane in 1996 destroyed the Malecón, which has since been rebuilt and is now a beautiful promenade where people stroll, cycle, walk and relax in the evening in the light of the setting sun.

Ins and outs

Like many Yucatán towns, Campeche's streets in the Old Town are numbered rather than named. Even numbers run north/south beginning at Calle 8 (no one knows why) near the Malecón, east to Calle 18 inside the walls; odd numbers run east (inland) from Calle 51 in the north to Calle 65 in the south. Most of the points of interest are within this compact area. A full circuit of the walls is a long walk; buses marked 'Circuito Baluartes' provide a regular service around the perimeter.

The **state tourist office** ⓘ *T816-7364, www.campeche.gob.mx, 0800-2100 daily*, is on the Malecón in front of the Palacio de Gobierno (walk down Calle 61 towards the sea). There is another smaller **tourist office** on the northeastern corner of the Zócalo. Open daily 0900-2100. For a good orientation take the Centro Histórico tour, a regular **tourist tram** ⓘ *daily on the hour from 0900-1200 and 1700-2000, 45 mins, US$6,50, English and Spanish spoken*, running from the main plaza.

Background

Highway 180 enters the city as the Avenida Resurgimiento, passing either side of the huge **Monumento al Resurgimiento,** a stone torso holding aloft the Torch of Democracy. Originally the trading village of Ah Kim Pech, it was here that the Spaniards, under Francisco Hernández de Córdoba, first disembarked on Mexican soil (22 March 1517) to replenish their water supply. For fear of being attacked by the native population, they quickly left, only to be attacked later by the locals further south in Champotón, where they were forced to land by appalling weather conditions at sea. It was not until 1540 that Francisco de Montejo managed to conquer Ah Kim Pech, founding the city of Campeche on 4 October 1541, after failed attempts in 1537 and earlier in 1527. The export of local dyewoods, *chicle*, timber and other valuable cargoes soon attracted the attention of most of the famous buccaneers, who constantly raided the port from their bases on Isla del Carmen, then known as the Isla de Tris. Combining their fleets for one momentous swoop, they fell upon Campeche on 9 February 1663, wiped out the city and slaughtered its inhabitants. Five years later the Crown began fortifying the site, the first Spanish colonial settlement to be completely walled. Formidable bulwarks, 3 m thick and 'a ship's height', and eight bastions (*baluartes*) were built in the next 36 years. All these fortifications soon put a stop to pirate attacks and Campeche prospered as one of only two Mexican ports (the other was Veracruz) to have had the privilege of conducting international trade. After Mexican Independence from Spain, the city declined into an obscure fishing and logging town. Only with the arrival of a road from the 'mainland' in the 1950s and the oil boom of the 1970s has Campeche begun to see visitors in any numbers, attracted by its historical monuments and relaxed atmosphere (*campechano* has come to mean an easy-going, pleasant person).

Sights

Of the original walls, seven of the *baluartes* and an ancient fort (now rather dwarfed by two big white hotels on the seafront) remain. Some house museums (see below).

The heart of the city is the Zócalo, where the austere Franciscan **cathedral** (1540-1705) has an elaborately carved façade; inside is the Santo Entierro (Holy Burial), a sculpture of Christ on a mahogany sarcophagus with a silver trim. There is plenty of shade under the trees in the Zócalo, and a small pagoda with a snack bar.

Right in front of the Zócalo is the **Baluarte de Nuestra Señora de la Soledad** (see Museums, below), the central bulwark of the city walls, from where you can do a walking tour of the **Circuito Baluartes**, the remains of the city walls. Heading east, you will come to the **Puerta del Mar**, formerly the entrance for those permitted to enter the city from the sea, which used to come up to this point. Next along the *Circuito* is a pair

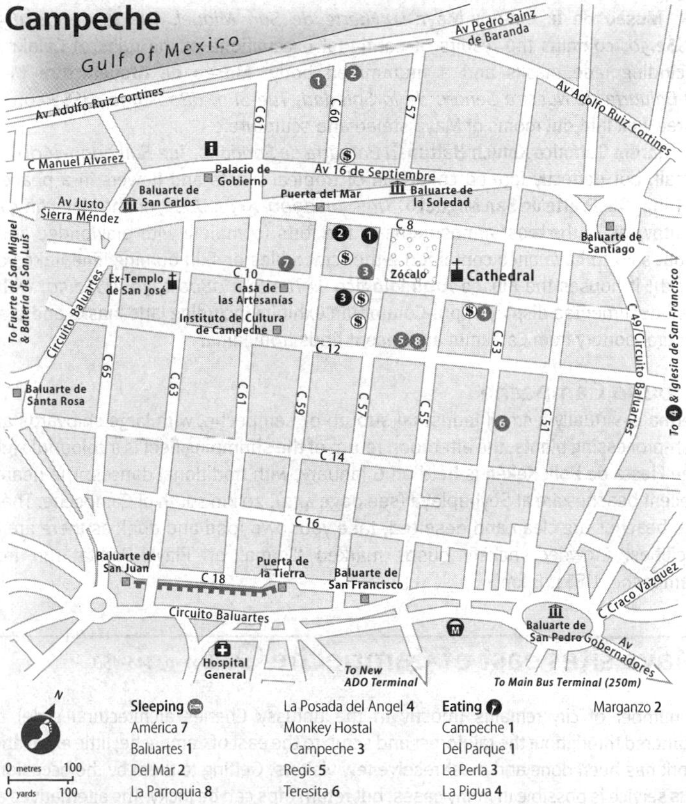

of modern buildings, the **Palacio de Gobierno** and the **Congreso.** The latter looks like a flying saucer, and makes for a bizarre sight when viewed with the 17th-century **Baluarte de San Carlos** in the background. Baluarte de San Carlos now houses a museum (see below). Heading west on the continuation of the *Circuito*, you will come to **Templo de San José**, on Calle 10, an impressive baroque church with a beautifully tiled façade. It has been de-consecrated, and is now an educational centre. Back on to the *Circuito*, you will next reach the **Baluarte de Santa Rosa**, now the home of the tourist information office. Next is **Baluarte de San Juan**, from which a large chunk of the old city wall still extends, protecting you from the noisy traffic on the busy road beyond it. The wall connects with **Puerta de la Tierra** ⓘ *Tue, Fri and Sat 2030 (for information, contact the tourist office)*, where a *Luz y Sonido* (Light and Sound) show takes place. The continuation of the *Circuito* will take you past the **Baluarte de San Francisco**, and then past the market, just outside the line of the city walls. **Baluarte de San Pedro** flanks the northeast corner of the city centre, and now houses a museum (see below). The *circuito* runs down to the northwest tip of the old city, where the **Baluarte de Santiago** houses the Botanical Gardens (see Museums, below).

Further from the city walls is the **Batería de San Luis**, 4 km south from the centre along the coast road. This was once a lookout post to catch pirates as they approached the city from a distance. The **Fuerte de San Miguel**, 600 m inland, is now a museum (see below). A 20-minute walk along Avenida Miguel Alemán from Baluarte de Santiago is the **San Francisco** church, 16th century with wooden altars painted in vermilion and white. Nearby are the **Portales de San Francisco**, a beautifully restored old entrance to the city, with several good restaurants in its shadow.

Museo de la Cultura Maya ⓘ *Fuerte de San Miguel, Tue-Sun 0800-1830, US$2.50*, contains the results of continual excavations at the ruins of Calakmul, including jade masks and a mummified body. **Museo de Arquetectura Maya** ⓘ *Baluarte de Nuestra Señora de la Soledad, Tue-Sun, 0800-1930, US$2.50*, has three well-laid-out rooms of Maya stelae and sculpture.

Jardín Botánico Xmuch'Haltun ⓘ *Baluarte de Santiago, Tue-Sun 0900-1600*, is a small, but perfectly formed collection of tropical plants and flowers in a peaceful setting. The **Fuerte de San Miguel** ⓘ *Tue-Sun 0900-1930, US$3*, on the Malecón 4 km southwest, is the most atmospheric of the forts (complete with drawbridge and a moat said to have once contained either crocodiles or skin-burning lime, take your pick!); it houses the **Museo Arqueológico** ⓘ *Tue-Sun 0800-1730, US$2.50*, with a well-documented display of pre-Columbian exhibits including jade masks and black funeral pottery from Calakmul and recent finds from Jaina.

Around Campeche

Lerma is virtually a small industrial suburb of Campeche, with large shipyards and fish-processing plants; the afternoon return of the shrimping fleet is a colourful sight. The **Fiesta de Polk Kekén** is held on 6 January, with traditional dances. The nearest decent beaches are at Seybaplaya (see page 442), 20 km south of Campeche. There, the beaches are clean and deserted; take your own food and drink as there are no facilities. Crowded, rickety buses marked 'Lerma' or 'Playa Bonita' run from Campeche, US$1, 8 km.

Maya sites east of Campeche » *pp446-450.*

A number of city remains (mostly in the unfussy Chenes architectural style) are scattered throughout the rainforest and scrub to the east of Campeche; little excavation work has been done and most receive few visitors. Getting to them by the occasional bus service is possible in many cases, but return trips can be tricky. The alternatives are one of the tours run by some luxury hotels and travel agencies in Campeche (see above) or renting a vehicle (preferably with high clearance) in Campeche or Mérida. Whichever way you travel, carrying plenty of drinking water is strongly advised.

Edzná → *Colour map 4, A2.*

ⓘ *Tue-Sun 0800-1700, US$3; local guides available.*

The closest site to the state capital is Edzná ('House of Grimaces'), reached by the highway east to Cayal, then a right turn onto Highway 261, a distance of 61 km. A paved shortcut southeast through China and Poxyaxum (good road) cuts off 11 km; follow Avenida Nacozari out along the railway track. Gracefully situated in a lovely, tranquil valley with thick vegetation on either side, Edzná was a huge ceremonial centre, occupied from about 600 BC to AD 200, built in the simple Chenes style mixed with Puuc, Classic and other influences. The centrepiece is the magnificent, 30-m-tall, 60-sq-m **Temple of the Five Storeys**, a stepped pyramid with four levels of living quarters for the priests and a shrine and altar at the top; 65 steep steps lead up from the Central Plaza. Opposite is the **Paal U'na**, Temple of the Moon. Excavations are being carried out on the scores of lesser temples by Guatemalan refugees under the direction of Mexican archaeologists, but most of Edzná's original sprawl remains hidden away under thick vegetation. Imagination is still needed to picture the network of irrigation canals and holding basins built by the Maya along the valley below sea level. Some of the site's stelae remain in position (two large stone faces with grotesquely squinting eyes are covered by a thatched shelter); others can be seen in various Campeche museums. There is also a good example of a *sacbé* (sacred roads). There is a small *comedor* at the entrance. Edzná is well worth a visit especially in July (exact date varies), when a Maya ceremony to honour Chac is held, to encourage or to celebrate the arrival of the rains. To get there see Transport, page 448.

Hochob

ⓘ *Daily 0800-1700, US$3.*

Of the more remote and even less-visited sites beyond Edzná, Hochob and Dzibilnocac are the best choices for the non-specialist. Hochob is reached by turning right at Hopelchén on Highway 261, 85 km east of Campeche. This quiet town has an impressive fortified 16th-century church but only one hotel. From here a narrow paved road leads 41 km south to the village of **Dzibalchén**. Don Willem Chan will guide tourists to Hochob (he also rents bikes for US$3.50 per day), helpful, speaks English. Directions can be obtained from the church here (run by Americans); you need to travel 18 km southwest on a good dirt road (no public transport, hopeless quagmire in the rainy season) to the village of Chenko, where locals will show the way (4 km through the jungle). Bear left when the road forks; it ends at a small *palapa* and, from here, the ruins are 1 km uphill with a magnificent view over the surrounding forest. Hochob once covered a large area but, as at Edzná, only the hilltop ceremonial centre (the usual Plaza surrounded by elaborately decorated temple buildings) has been properly excavated; although many of these are mounds of rubble, the site is perfect for contemplating deserted, yet accessible Maya ruins in solitude and silence. The one-room temple to the right (north) of the plaza is the most famous structure: deep-relief patterns of stylized snakes moulded in stucco across its façade were designed to resemble a mask of the ferocious rain god Chac. A door serves as the mouth. A fine reconstruction of the building is on display at the Museo de Antropología in Mexico City. Early morning second-class buses serve Dzibalchén, but, returning to Campeche later in the day is often a matter of luck.

The word 'cocktail' is said to have originated in Campeche, where 17th-century English pirates enjoyed drinks adorned with palm fronds resembling cocks' tails.

Dzibilnocac

ⓘ *Daily 0800-1700, US$4.35.*

Twenty kilometres northeast of Dzibalchén at Iturbide, this site is one of the largest in Chenes territory. Only three temples have been excavated here (many pyramidal mounds in the forest and roadside *milpas*); the first two are in a bad state of preservation, but the third is worth the visit: a unique narrow edifice with rounded corners and remains of a stucco façade, primitive reliefs and another grim mask of Chac on the top level. Much of the stonework from the extensive site is used by local farmers for huts and fences. A bus leaves Campeche at 0800, 3 hours, return 1245, 1345 and 1600, US$3.35. If driving your own vehicle, well-marked 'km' signs parallel the rocky road to Iturbide (no accommodation); bear right around the tiny Zócalo and its attendant yellow church and continue (better to walk in the wet season) for 50 m, where the right branch of a fork leads to the ruins. Other sites in the region require 4WD transport and appeal mostly to archaeologists.

Becal

Becal is the centre for weaving Panama hats, here called *jipis* (pronounced 'hippies') and ubiquitous throughout the Yucatán. Many of the town's families have workshops in cool, moist backyard underground caves, which are necessary for keeping moist and pliable the shredded leaves of the *jipijapa* palm from which the hats are made. Most vendors give the visitor a tour of their workshop, but are quite zealous in their sales pitches. Prices are better for *jipis* and other locally woven items (cigarette cases, shoes, belts, etc) in the **Centro Artesanal, Artesanías de Becaleña** ⓘ *Calle 30 No 210*, than in the shops near the plaza, where the hat is honoured by a hefty sculpture of three concrete *sombreros*! More celebrations take place on 20 May during the **Feria del Jipi**.

Sleeping

Francisco Escárcega *p439*

C **María Isabel**, Justo Sierra 127, T824-0045. A/c, restaurant, comfortable, back rooms noisy from highway.

C **Motel Akim Pech**, on Villahermosa highway. A/c or fans and bath, reasonable rooms, restaurant in motel, another across the street, also Pemex station opposite.

D-E **Escárcega**, Justo Sierra 86, T824-0188, around the corner from the bus terminal (turn left twice). Clean, bath, parking, hot water, good restaurant, small garden.

Coast road to Campeche *p439*

C **Chichén Itzá**, Aldama 671, Frontera, T332-0097. Not very clean, fan, shower, hot water.

D **San Agustín**, Pino Suárez, Frontera, T332-0037. Very basic, fan, no mosquito net.

Ciudad del Carmen *p439*

Hotel accommodation can be difficult to come by Mon-Thu; book in advance and arrive early.

AL **EuroHotel**, Calle 22 No 208, T382-3044, reganem@prodigy.net.mx. Large and modern, 2 restaurants, pool, a/c, disco, built to accommodate the flow of Pemex traffic.

C **Lino's**, Calle 31 No 132, T382-1766. A/c, pool, restaurant, also has 10 RV spaces with electricity hook-ups.

D **Hotel Playa Dorna**, on Playa Norte. Clean, friendly, pool, TV, hot water, 2 strip bars loud and late at weekends.

D **Zacarías**, Calle 24 No 58, T382-3506. Modern, some cheaper rooms with fans, brighter a/c rooms are better value. Recommended.

E **El Ancla**, Av Periférica. One of several hotels near the ADO bus station. Simple rooms, TV, a/c, good restaurant in spectacular waterside setting.

Campeche *p442, map p443*

In general, prices are high. Beware of over-charging and, if driving, find a secure car park.

AL **Del Mar**, Av Ruiz Cortines 51, T816-2233. 5-star hotel on the waterfront with pool, gym, good bar and restaurant.

A **Baluartes**, Av 16 de Septiembre 128, T816-3911. Recently remodelled, on the foreshore, very good restaurant, pool.

B América, Calle 10 252, T816-4588. Hot water, friendly, no safe deposit, clean, fans but hot, safe parking, with night watchman.
C Regis, Calle 12 148, between 55 y 57, T816-3175. Nice setting among cool colonial columns in the centre, good service.
D La Parroquia, Calle 55, between 10 y 12. Good sized rooms and dormitories looking into a pleasant courtyard. Internet available, includes breakfast.
D La Posada Del Angel, Calle 10 No 307, T816-7718 (on the side entrance of the cathedral). A/c, attractive, some rooms without windows, clean. Recommended.
D-E Monkey Hostal Campeche, Calle 57 and Calle 10 overlooking the Zócalo, T811-6500. Dormitory accommodation, with lockers, and private rooms. Also laundry, internet, bike hire, kitchen and book swap. Price includes breakfast and can arrange local tours.
E Teresita, Calle 53 No 31, 2 blocks east of plaza, T816-4534. Very basic rooms with fans, no hot water. Cheapest in town, but good if you're on a tight budget.

Camping

New facility being built in town as part of the watersport area north of town. Ask at tourist information for details.
Club Náutica, 15 km south of town. Big campsite with good facilities. Good spot for a few days' stay.

Eating

Francisco Escárcega *p439*

There are few places used to serving tourists, but there is a good and cheap *lonchería* opposite the bus terminal.
TT Titanic, corner of the main highway and the road to the train station (first turning on the right after turning right out of the bus terminal). For a more expensive meal with a/c.

Ciudad del Carmen *p439*

TT El Kiosco, in Hotel del Parque with view of Zócalo. Modest prices, eggs, chicken, seafood and Mexican dishes.
TT Pepe's, Calle 27 No 15. A/c, attractive seafood dishes.
TT Vía Veneto, in the EuroHotel (see Sleeping, above). Reasonable prices, good breakfasts.
TT-T La Fuente, Calle 20. 24-hr snack bar with view of the Laguna.
TT-T El Pavo, tucked away down Calle 36A, in Col Guadalupe. This superb, family-run restaurant serves excellent seafood dishes at cheap prices. Very popular with the locals.
T La Mesita, outdoor stand across from the old ferry landing. Well-prepared shrimp, seafood cocktails, extremely popular all day.

Cafés

There are several tiny cafés along the pedestrian walkway (Calle 33) near the Zócalo.
Café Vadillo, Calle 33. The 'best coffee in town'.
Mercado Central, Calle 20 y 37, not far northwest of Zócalo. Inexpensive snacks are available in the thriving market.

Campeche *p442, map p443*

Campeche is known for its seafood, especially *camarones* (large shrimps), *esmedregal* (black snapper) and *pan de cazón* (baby hammerhead shark sandwiched between corn tortillas with black beans). Food stands in the market serve *tortas*, tortillas, *panuchos* and *tamales* but hygiene standards vary widely; barbecued venison is also a marketplace speciality.
TTT-T La Parroquia, Calle 55 No 8. Open 24 hrs, good local atmosphere, friendly and clean. Recommended.
TT La Perla, Calle 10 between 57 and 59. Good fish, busy and popular, venison, squid, locals' haunt, erratic service.
TT La Pigua, Av Miguel Alemán, opposite Cine Estela. Seafood in pleasant garden setting.
TT Los Portales, Calle 10 No 86. Authentic local atmosphere, try the *sopa de lima*, 1900-midnight.
TT-T Marganzo, Calle 8. Upmarket, good breakfast and meals, excellent service, popular with locals.
TT-T Restaurant Campeche, almost next door to Restaurant del Parque, has an extensive menu, big portions and is very good value.
TT-T Restaurant del Parque, on the plaza opposite the cathedral. Good, cheap.

Phone codes *Francisco Escárcega 982; Ciudad del Carmen 938; Xpujil 983; Becán 996; Chicanná 981; Sihoplaya 982; Seybaplaya 982; Campeche 981.*

Festivals and events

Campeche *p442, map p443*
Feb/Mar Good **Carnival.**
7 Aug State holiday.
Sep Feria de San Román, 2nd fortnight.
4-13 Oct Fiesta de San Francisco.

Maya sites east of Campeche *p444*
13-17 Apr A traditional **Honey and Corn Festival** is held in Holpechén.
3 May Día de la Santa Cruz.

Shopping

Campeche *p442, map p443*
Excellent cheap **Panama hats** *(jipis)*, finely and tightly woven so that they retain their shape even when crushed into your luggage (within reason); cheaper at the source in Becal. Handicrafts are generally cheaper than in Mérida. There are souvenir shops along Calle 8, such as **Artesanía Típica Naval**, Calle 8 No 259, with exotic bottled fruit like *nance* and *marañón*, or **El Coral**, Calle 8 No 255, with a large variety of Maya figurines; many high-quality craft items are available from the **Exposición** in the Baluarte San Pedro. **Casa de Artesanía**, Calle 10, open 900-2000, daily. Good-quality handicrafts displayed on bizarre Maya dummies, with a mock-up hammock-making cave.

Camping and general supplies (and laundrette) at **Superdíaz** supermarket in Akim-Pech shopping area at Av Miguel Alemán y Av Madero, some distance north of the Zócalo, 0800-2100.

The **market**, from which most local buses depart, is beside Alameda Park at the south end of Calle 57. Plenty of bargains here. Try the ice cream, although preferably from a shop rather than a barrow. **Super 10** supermarket behind the post office has an excellent cheap bakery inside.

Activities and tours

Campeche *p442, map p443*
Tour operators
Intermar Campeche, Av 16 de Septiembre 128, T816-9006, aurea@travel2mexico.com. **Viajes Chicanná**, Av Augustín Melgar, Centro Comercial Triángulo del Sol, Local 12, T811-3503. Flight bookings to Cuba, Miami and Central America. **Viajes del Golfo**, Calle 10 No 250 D, T816-4044. Tours to Edzná, Calakmul.

Edzná *p445*
Tour operators
Picazh Servicios Turísticos, Calle 16 No 348 between 357 and 359, T816-4426, run transport to ruins, with or without guide, US$20. Recommended. **Viajes Programados**, Calle 59, Edificio Belmar, in Campeche, offers daily 2-hr tours at 1000, US$20; tours from the **Hotel Baluartes**.

Transport

Tabasco to Campeche *p444*
Bus Buses from Emiliano Zapata, all ADO: to **Tenosique**, almost hourly, 1½ hrs US$2.80 (plus 2, 2nd-class companies); to **Villahermosa**, 17 departures between 0600 and 2000, US$8; to **Mérida**, 5 a day between 0800 and 2100, US$29; to **Escárcega**, 5 between 0630 and 2100, US$7.50; to **Chetumal**, 2130, US$20.

Francisco Escárcega *p439*
Bus Most buses from Chetumal or Campeche drop you off at the 2nd-class terminal on the main highway. To buy tickets, you have to wait until the outgoing bus has arrived; sit near the ticket office and wait for them to call out your destination, then join the scrum at the ticket office. There is an ADO terminal west of the 2nd-class terminal, a 20-min walk. From there, 1st-class buses go to **Palenque**, several daily, 3 hrs, US$14; **Chetumal**, 4 a day, 4 hrs, US$13; **Campeche**, 5 a day, 2 hrs, US$8. From the 2nd-class terminal, there are buses to Campeche, 16 a day, 2½ hrs, US$5.60; **Chetumal**, 3 a day, 4 hrs, US$11; **Mérida**, 4 a day, 6 hrs, US$13.50; **Playas de Catazajá**, connecting with *colectivos* to Palenque, at 0830, 0930 and 1030, US$5; **Villahermosa**, 12 a day, 4 hrs, US$12.50. *Colectivos* to **Palenque** leave from outside the 2nd-class terminal at 1300, US$5.50.

Xpujil *p440*
Bus 2nd-class buses from **Chetumal** and **Escárcega** stop on the highway in the centre of Xpujil, some 800 m east of the 2 hotels. There are 4 buses a day to Escárcega, between

1030 and 1500, 3 hrs, US$6. 8 buses a day go to Chetumal, 2 hrs, US$5. Change at Escárcega for buses to Palenque or Campeche. 1st-class buses will not stop at Xpujil.

Ciudad del Carmen *p439*

Air

Carmen's efficient airport (CME, 5 km east of the plaza) has also benefited from the oil traffic, with flights daily to **Mérida**, **Mexico City**, **Poza Rica**, **Tampico**, **Veracruz** and **Villahermosa**.

Airline offices Mexicana, Calle 22 y 37, T382-1171.

Bus

ADO bus terminal some distance from centre. Take bus or *colectivo* marked 'Renovación' or 'ADO'; they leave from around the Zócalo. At least 8 ADO services daily to **Campeche**, 3 hrs, and **Mérida**, 9 hrs, US$19, includes 3 departures between 2100 and 2200 (worth considering if stuck for accommodation); hourly bus to **Villahermosa** via the coast, 3 hrs. A connection can be made to **Palenque** at 2330 or 0400, a slow but worthwhile trip. Buses also travel via **Escárcega**, where connections can be made for Chetumal and Belize.

Car

Car hire Auto Panamericana, Calle 22, T382-2326. Not cheap. Auto-Rentas del Carmen, Calle 33 No 121, T382-2376.

Campeche *p442, map p443*

Air

Modern, efficient airport (CPE) on Porfirio, 10 km northeast. Aero México direct daily to **Mexico City**, T816-5678. If on a budget, walk 100 m down service road (Av Aviación) to Av Nacozari, turn right (west) and wait for 'China-Campeche' bus to Zócalo.

Bus

Local Tourist buses run to **Edzná** from Puerta de la Tierra, in front of the market, 0900 and 1400, US$20 return, also cheaper combis from the same stop. Buses to **Calakmul** depart from Baluarte de San Pedro, weekends only at 1700. Buses to **Seybaplaya** leave from the tiny Cristo Rey terminal opposite the market, 9 a day from 0615, 45 mins.

Long distance The bus station is about 3km south of the centre. Buses from outside the terminal travel the *circuito* road. A taxi costs US$2. The 2nd-class bus terminal is about 1km east of the centre along Av Gobernadores, but services are steadily moving to the main terminal. To **Cancún**, 2300, 2330, US$25; to **Chetumal**, 1200, US$19; To **Cd del Carmen**, 9 a day from 0745, US$10; To **Escárcega**, hourly from 0200, 2 hrs, US$8; to **Cristóbal Colón**, 2210, US$7.50; to **Mérida**, 11 a day 0545-1930, 2½ hrs, US$10; with Maya de Oro, 0400, US$12; with Cristóbal Colón, 2030, US$8; to **Mexico City**, 1600, US$85; **Oaxaca**, 2155, 2400, US$60; **Palenque**, 1st class with ADO, 3 a day from 0030, 5-7 hrs, US$19; **San Cristóbal de las Casas**, with Maya de Oro, 2400, 14 hrs, US$36; with Cristóbal Colón, 2210, US$28; **Veracruz**, 1st class, 1030, 1300 and 2100, 14 hrs, US$54; **Villahermosa**, 5 a day from 0900, 6½ hrs, US$21.

Car

Car hire Next to Hotel del Mar, Av Ruiz Cortines 51, T816-2233. Hertz and Autorent car rentals at airport.

Edzná *p445*

Bus A tourist bus goes from **Campeche** town wall at 0900, US$10 per person. At weekends take a bus to Pich from Campeche marketplace at 0700, 1000 and 1030 (1-hr trip) but it may be hours late; return buses pass the site (5 mins' walk from the highway) at 0930, 1230 and 1300. In the week, the Pich bus leaves Campeche at 1400, only of any use if you are prepared to sleep rough as there is nowhere to stay in the vicinity; hitching back is difficult, but you may get a ride to El Cayal on the road to Uxmal.

Directory

Ciudad del Carmen *p439*

Banks Banco del Atlántico or Banamex, both at Calle 24 y 31. **Post office** Calle 29 y 20, 1 block from the plaza.

Campeche *p442, map p443*

Banks Banamex, Calle 10 No 15. Banco del Atlántico, Calle 50 No 406; Mon-Fri 0900-1300; all change TCs and give good service. Bancomer, opposite the Baluarte de la Soledad. American Express, T811-1010, Calle 59, Edificio Belmar, oficina 5, helpful for lost cheques, etc. Plenty of places to get cash on credit cards and ATMs. **Cultural centres** Casa del Teniente de Rey, Calle 59 No 38 between 14 and 16, houses the Instituto Nacional de Antropología e Historia (INAH), dedicated to the restoration of Maya ruins in the state of Campeche, as well as supporting local museums. INAH can be visited for information regarding any of the sites in the state, T811-1314, www.inah.gob.mx. Centro Manik, Calle 59 No 22 between 12 and 14, T/F816-2448, vegetarian restaurant, bookshop, handicrafts, art gallery, music lessons, conferences, concentrates on ecology, environmentalism and health, also developing ecotourism in southern Campeche. **Immigration** The Oficina de Migración at the Palacio Federal will extend Mexican visas. Take copies of your passport as well as the original. **Internet** Cybercafé Campeche, Calle 61 between Calle 10 and 12, 0900-1300, US$1.50 per hr, several others around but somewhat slower. **Laundry** Calle 55 between 12 and 14, US$0.60 per kg. **Medical services** Red Cross, T815-2378, emergency T815-2411. **Post office** Av 16 de Septiembre (Malecón) y Calle 53 in Edificio Federal (go to the right upon entry for telegraph service); Mon-Fri 0800-2000, Sat 0900-1300 for *Lista de Correos*, registered mail, money orders and stamps. **Telephone** Telmex, Calle 8 between Calle 51 y 53, free; Calle 51 No 45, between 12 and 14. Intertel, long-distance phones and fax, Calle 57 No 1 between 10 and 12.

State of Yucatán

The archaeological sites of Chichén Itzá, Oxkintoc, Uxmal, Kabah and Labná are just a few of the many strewn throughout the State of Yucatán. Try not to miss Dzibilchaltún; the intrusion of European architecture is nowhere more startling than here. The region's many cenotes *(deep pools created by the disintegration of the dry land above an underground river) were sacred to the Maya who threw precious jewels, silverware and even humans into their depths; many are perfect for swimming. On the coast, boat trips are organized to observe pelicans, egrets and flamingoes in their natural habitat. It is possible to visit some of the impressive* henequén *(sisal) haciendas in the more rural areas and admire the showy mansions that line the Paseo de Montejo in Mérida.* ▸▸ *For Sleeping, Eating and other listings, see pages 463-473.*

North to Mérida

At **Maxcanú,** the road to Muná and Ticul branches east; a short way down it is the recently restored Maya site of **Oxkintoc** ⓘ *US$3*. The Pyramid of the Labyrinth can be entered (take a torch) and there are other ruins, some with figures. Ask for a guide at the village of Calcehtoc, which is 4 km from the ruins and from the Grutas de Oxkintoc (no bus service). These, however, cannot compare with the caves at Loltún or Balankanché (see pages 455 and 460). Highway 180 continues north towards Mérida through a region of numerous *cenotes*, soon passing a turn-off to the turn-of-the-century Moorish-style *henequén* (sisal) hacienda at **San Bernardo,** one of a number in the state that can be visited; an interesting colonial museum chronicling the old Yucatán Peninsula tramway system is located in its lush and spacious grounds. Running beside the railway, the highway continues 47 km to its junction with the inland route at **Umán,** a *henequén* processing town with another large 17th-century church and convent dedicated to St Francis of Assisi; there are many *cenotes* in the flat surrounding limestone plain. If driving Highway 180/261 is a divided four-lane motorway for the final 18 km stretch into Mérida. There is a ring road around the city.

Mérida » pp463-473. Colour map 4, A2.

→ Phone code: 999.

The capital of Yucatán state and its colonial heart, Mérida is a bustling, tightly packed city full of colonial buildings in varying states of repair. There is continual activity in the centre, with a huge influx of tourists during the high season mingling with busy Meridanos going about their daily business. Although the city has been developed over many years for tourism, there is plenty of local flavour for the traveller to seek out off the beaten track. Attempts to create a sophisticated Champs Elysées-style boulevard in the north of the city at Paseo Montejo have not been quite successful; the plan almost seems to go against the grain of Mérida's status as an ancient city, which has gradually evolved into a place with its own distinct identity.

Ins and outs

Getting there All buses from outside Yucatán State arrive at the CAME terminal on Calle 70 between Calle 69 y 71, a few blocks from the centre. There is another bus terminal around the corner on Calle 69, where buses from local destinations such as Uxmal arrive. The airport is 8 km from the city, bus 79 takes you to the centre. Taxis to the centre from the airport charge US$9.

Getting around You can see most of Mérida on foot. Although the city is big, there is not much to concern the tourist outside a few blocks radiating from the main plaza. The VW Beetle taxis are expensive, due to their scarcity; fares start at US$3 for a short journey. *Colectivo* buses are difficult to locate; they appear suddenly on the bigger roads in the city, you can flag them down anywhere. They terminate at the market; flat fare US$0.25.

Tourist information The main **tourist office** ⓘ *Calle 60 y Calle 57 (just off Parque Hidalgo), daily 0800-2000*, is very helpful. There are other tourist offices on the main plaza by the Palacio Municipio and at the airport.

Mérida is a safe city, with its own **tourist police** ⓘ *T925-3200*, recognizable by their brown and white uniforms.

Best time to visit During July and August, although very hot, Mérida is subject to heavy rains during the afternoon.

Background

Mérida was originally a large Maya city called Tihoo. It was conquered on 6 January 1542, by Francisco de Montejo. He dismantled the pyramids of the Maya and used the stone as the foundations for the cathedral of San Ildefonso, built 1556-1559. For the next 300 years, Mérida remained under Spanish control, unlike the rest of Mexico, which was governed from the capital. During the Caste Wars of 1847-1855, Mérida held out against the marauding forces of indigenous armies, who had defeated the Mexican army in every other city in the Yucatán Peninsula except Campeche. Reinforcements from the centre allowed the Mexicans to regain control of their city, but the price was to relinquish control of the region to Mexico City.

Sights

The city revolves around the large, shady Zócalo, site of the **cathedral**, completed in 1559, the oldest cathedral in Latin America, which has an impressive baroque façade. It contains the Cristo de las Ampollas (Christ of the Blisters), a statue carved from a tree that burned for a whole night after being hit by lightning, without showing any damage at all. Placed in the church at Ichmul, it then suffered only a slight charring (hence the blistering name) when the church was burned to the ground. To the left of the cathedral on the adjacent side of the plaza is the **Palacio de Gobierno**, built 1892. It houses a collection of enormous murals by Fernando Castro Pacheco, depicting the struggle of the Maya to integrate with the Spanish. The murals can be viewed until 2000 every day. **Casa de Montejo** is on the south side of the plaza, a 16th-century

Mérida

N

0 metres 300
0 yards 300

Sleeping
Casa Becil **1** *E2*
Casa Bowen **2** *E2*
Casa San Juan **16** *E2*
Colonial **3** *C2*
Dolores Alba **4** *D4*
Gobernador **5** *C2*
Gran **6** *D3*
Hostal Zócalo **17** *D2*
La Misión de Fray Diego **7** *D2*
La Paz **8** *E2*
Las Monjas **9** *D2*
Latino **18** *D2*
Margarita **11** *D2*
Medio Mundo **19** *C2*
Mucuy **12** *C3*
Nómadas Youth Hostel **13** *C2*
Posada Toledo **14** *C3*
San José **15** *D2*
Trinidad **22** *C2*

Eating
Alberto's Continental **5** *C2*
Amaro **1** *C2*
Café La Habana **8** *C2*
Café Petropolis **2** *E1*
El Trapiche **3** *D2*
El Tucho **4** *C3*
Italian Coffee Company **9** *D2*
La Prosperidad **6** *C3*
Los Almendros **7** *C4*

palace built by the city's founder, now a branch of Banamex. Away from the main Plaza along Calle 60 is Parque Hidalgo, a charming tree-filled square, which borders the 17th-century **Iglesia de Jesús.** A little further along Calle 60 is the **Teatro Peón Contreras**, built at the beginning of the 20th century by an Italian architect, with a neoclassical façade, marble staircase and Italian frescoes.

There are several 16th- and 17th-century churches dotted about the city: **La Mejorada**, behind the Museum of Peninsular Culture (Calle 59 between 48 and 50), **Tercera Orden**, **San Francisco** and **San Cristóbal** (beautiful, in the centre). The **Ermita**, an 18th-century chapel with beautiful grounds, is a lonely, deserted place 10 to 15 minutes from the centre.#

Museo de Antropología e Historia ⓘ *Paseo de Montejo 485, Tue-Sun 0800-2000, US$2*, housed in the beautiful neoclassical Palacio Cantón, has an excellent collection of original Maya artefacts from various sites in the Yucatán state. The displays are very well laid out, and the explanations are all in Spanish. There are many examples of jade jewellery dredged from *cenotes*, and some examples of cosmetically deformed skulls with sharpened teeth. This is a good overview of the history of the Maya.

Museo Macay ⓘ *Calle 60, on the main plaza, daily 1000-1730, US$2*, has a permanent exhibition of Yucatecan artists, with temporary exhibits by contemporary local artists. **Museo de Arte Popular** ⓘ *Calle 59 esq 50, Barrio de la Mejorada, Tue-Sat 0900-2000, Sun 0800-1400, free*, has a permanent exhibition of Maya art, handicrafts and clothing, with a good souvenir shop attached. **Museo de la Canción Yucateca** ⓘ *Calle 57 between 50 and 48, Tue-Sat 0900-2000, free*, in the Casa de la Cultura, has an exhibition of objects and instruments relating to the history of music in the region. **Pinacoteca Juan Gamboa Guzmán** ⓘ *Calle 59 between Calle 58 and 60, Tue-Sat 0800-2000, Sun 0800-1400, US$1*, is a gallery showing old and contemporary painting and sculpture.

Around Mérida

» *pp463-473. Colour map 4, A2.*

Celestún

→ *Phone code: 988.*

A small, dusty fishing resort west of Mérida much frequented in summer by Mexicans, Celestún stands on the spit of land separating the Río Esperanza estuary from the ocean. The long beach is relatively clean except near the town proper, with clear water ideal for swimming, although rising afternoon winds usually churn up silt and there is little shade; along the beach are many fishing boats bristling with *jimbas* (cane poles), used for catching local octopus. There are beach restaurants with showers. A plain Zócalo watched over by a simple stucco church is the centre for what little happens in town. Cafés (some with hammock space for rent) spill onto the sand, from which parents watch offspring splash in the surf. Even the unmarked post office ⓘ *Mon-Fri 0900-1300*, is a private residence the rest of the week.

The immediate region is a biosphere reserve, created to protect the thousands of migratory waterfowl who inhabit the lagoons; fish, crabs and shrimp also spawn here, and kingfishers, black hawks, wood storks and crocodiles may sometimes be glimpsed in the quieter waterways. In the winter months Celestún plays host to the largest flamingo colony in North America, perhaps more than 20,000 birds – in the summer most of the flamingoes leave Celestún for their nesting grounds in the Río Lagartos area. Boat trips to view the wildlife can be arranged at the newly built visitors centre below the river bridge 1 km back along the Mérida road (US$60 for one six people, plus US$4 per person for the reserve entrance fees, 1½ hours). Make sure your boatman takes you through the mangrove channel and to the Baldiosera freshwater spring in addition to visiting the flamingoes. It is often possible to see flamingoes from the bridge early in the morning and the road to it may be alive with egrets, herons and pelicans. January-March is the best time to see them. It's important to wear a hat and use sunscreen. Hourly buses to Mérida 0530-2030, one hour, US$4.

Progreso and around → *Phone code: 969.*

Thirty-six kilometres north of Mérida, Progreso has the nearest beach to the city. It is a slow-growing resort town, with the facilities improving to service the increasing number of US cruise ships that arrive every Wednesday. Progreso is famous for its industrial pier, which at 6 km is the longest in the world. It has been closed to the public since someone fell off the end on a moped. The beach is long and clean and the water is shallow and good for swimming.

A short bus journey (4 km) west from Progreso are **Puerto Yucalpetén** and **Chelem**. Balneario Yucalpetén has a beach with lovely shells, but also a large naval base with further construction in progress.

Five kilometres east of Progreso is another resort, **Chicxulub**; it has a narrow beach, quiet and peaceful, on which are many boats and much seaweed. Small restaurants sell fried fish by the *ración*, or kg, served with tortillas, mild chilli and *cebolla curtida* (pickled onion). Chicxulub is reputed to be the site of the crater made by a meteorite crash 65 million years ago, which caused the extinction of the dinosaurs. (The site is actually offshore on the ocean floor.) The beaches on this coast are often deserted and, between December and February, 'El Norte' wind blows in every 10 days or so, making the water turbid and bringing in cold, rainy weather.

Dzibilchaltún

ⓘ *0800-1700, US$3, free with ISIC card.*

Halfway between Mérida and Progreso turn right for the Maya ruins of Dzibilchaltún. This unique city, according to carbon dating, was founded as early as 1000 BC. The site is in two halves, connected by a *sacbé* (sacred road). The most important building is the **Templo de Las Siete Muñecas** (Temple of the Seven Dolls), at the east end, which is partly restored. At the west end is the ceremonial centre with temples, houses and a large plaza in which the open chapel, simple and austere, sticks out like a sore thumb. The evangelizing friars had clearly hijacked a pre-Conquest sacred area in which to erect a symbol of the invading religion. At its edge is the **Cenote Xlaca** containing very clear water that is 44 m deep (you can swim in it, take mask and snorkel as it is full of fascinating fish); there's a very interesting nature trail starting halfway between the temple and the *cenote*; the trail rejoins the *sacbé* halfway along. The **museum** is at the entrance by the ticket office (site map available).

VW combis leave from Parque San Juan in Mérida, corner of Calle 62 y 67A, every one or two hours between 0500 and 1900, stopping at the ruins en route to **Chablekal**, a small village further along the same road. There are also five direct buses a day on weekdays, from Parque San Juan, marked 'Tour/Ruta Polígono'; the bus returns from the site entrance on the hour, passing the junction 15 minutes later, taking 45 minutes from the junction to Mérida (US$0.60).

The Convent Route » pp463-473.

The route takes in Maya villages and ruins, colonial churches, cathedrals, convents and *cenotes*. It is best to be on the road by 0800 with a full gas tank. Get on the Periférico to Ruta 18 (signs say Kanasín, not Ruta 18). At **Kanasín, La Susana** is known especially for local delicacies like *sopa de lima*, *salbutes* and *panuchos*. Clean, excellent service and abundant helpings at reasonable prices. Follow the signs to **Acanceh**. Here you will see the unusual combination of the Grand Pyramid, a colonial church and a modern church, all on the same small plaza (see Tlatelolco in Mexico

City; page 97). About four blocks away is the Temple of the Stuccoes, with hieroglyphs. Eight kilometres further south is **Tecoh**, with an ornate church and convent dedicated to the Virgin of the Assumption. There are some impressive carved stones around the altar. The church and convent both stand at the base of a large Maya pyramid. Nearby are the caverns of **Dzab-Náh**; you must take a guide as there are treacherous drops into *cenotes*. Next on the route is **Telchaquillo**, a small village with an austere chapel and a beautiful *cenote* in the plaza, with carved steps for easy access.

A popular day trip from Mérida, this tour unfortunately cannot be done on public transport, so a car is necessary.

Mayapán and around

ⓘ *US$3.*

A few kilometres off the main road to the right you will find the Maya ruins of Mayapán, a walled city with 4000 mounds, six of which are in varying stages of restoration. Mayapán, along with Uxmal and Chichén Itzá, once formed a triple alliance, and the site is as big as Chichén Itzá, with some buildings being replicas of those at the latter site. The restoration process is ongoing; the archaeologists can be watched as they unearth more and more new buildings of this large, peaceful, late-Maya site. Mayapán is easily visited by bus from Mérida (every 30 minutes from terminal at Calle 50 y 67 behind the municipal market, one hour, US$1 to Telchaquillo). It can also be reached from Oxcutzcab.

Thirty kilometres along the main road is **Tekit**, a large village containing the church of San Antonio de Padua, with many ornate statues of saints. The next village, 7 km further on, is called **Mama**, with the oldest church on the route, famous for its ornate altar and bell-domed roof. Another 9 km is **Chumayel**, where the legendary Maya document *Chilam Balam* was found. Four kilometres ahead is **Teabo**, with an impressive 17th-century church. Next comes **Tipikal**, a small village with an austere church.

Maní

Twelve kilometres further on is Maní, the most important stop on this route. Here you will find a large church, convent and museum with explanations in English, Spanish and one of the Maya languages. It was here that Fray Diego de Landa ordered important Maya documents and artefacts to be burned, during an intense period of Franciscan conversion of the Maya people to Christianity. When Diego realized his great error, he set about trying to write down all he could remember of the 27 scrolls and hieroglyphs he had destroyed, along with 5000 idols, 13 altars and 127 vases. The text, entitled *Relation of Things in Yucatán*, is still available today, unlike the artefacts. To return to Mérida, head for Ticul, to the west, then follow the main road via Muná.

Ticul and Oxkutzcab → *Phone code: 997. Colour map 4, A2.*

Eighty kilometres south of Mérida, Ticul is a small, pleasant little village known for its *huípiles*, the embroidered white dresses worn by the older Maya women. You can buy them in the tourist shops in Mérida, but the prices and quality of the ones in Ticul will be much better. It is also a good base for visiting smaller sites in the south of Yucatán state, such as Sayil, Kabah, Xlapak and Labná (see below).

Sixteen kilometres southeast of Ticul is Oxkutzcab, a good centre for catching buses to Chetumal, Muná, Mayapán and Mérida (US$2.20). It is a friendly place with a large market on the side of the plaza and a church with a 'two-dimensional' façade on the other side of the square.

Grutas de Loltún and around

ⓘ *Tue-Sun 0930, 1100, 1230 and 1400. US$3 with obligatory guide, 1 hr 20 mins. Recommended. Caretaker may admit tours on Mon, but no lighting.*

Know your hammock

Different materials are available for hammocks. Some you might find include **sisal**, which is very strong, light, hard-wearing but rather scratchy and uncomfortable, and is identified by its distinctive smell; **cotton**, which is soft, flexible, comfortable, not as hard-wearing but, with care, is good for four or five years of everyday use. It is not possible to weave cotton and sisal together, although you may be told otherwise, so mixtures are unavailable. **Cotton/ silk** mixtures are offered, but will probably be an artificial silk. **Nylon** is very strong and light but it's hot in hot weather and cold in cold weather.

Never buy your first hammock from a street vendor and never accept a packaged hammock without checking the size and quality. The surest way to judge a good hammock is by weight: 1500 g (3.3 lb) is a fine item, under 1 kg (2.2 lb) is junk (advises Alan Handleman, a US expert). Also, the finer and thinner the strands of material, the more strands there will be, and the more comfortable the hammock. The best hammocks are the so-called 3-ply, but they are difficult to find. There are three sizes: single (sometimes called *doble*), *matrimonial* and family (buy a *matrimonial* at least for comfort). If judging by end-strings, 50 would be sufficient for a child, 150 would suit a medium-sized adult, 250 a couple. Prices vary considerably so shop around and bargain hard.

Nearby, to the south, are the caverns and pre-Columbian vestiges at Loltún (supposedly extending for 8 km). Take pick-up (US$0.30) or truck from the market going to Cooperativa (an agricultural town). For return, flag down a passing truck. Alternatively, take a taxi, US$10 (can be visited from Labná on a tour from Mérida). The area around Ticul and Oxkutzcab is intensively farmed with citrus fruits, papayas and mangoes. After Oxkutzcab on Route 184 is **Tekax** with restaurant **La Ermita** serving excellent Yucatecan dishes at reasonable prices. From Tekax a paved road leads to the ruins of **Chacmultún.** From the top you have a beautiful view. There is a caretaker. All the towns between Muná and Peto, 14 km northeast of Oxkutzcab off Route 184, have large old churches. Beyond the Peto turn-off the scenery is scrub and swamp as far as the Belizean border.

The Puuc Route

Taking in the four sites of Kabah, Sayil, Xlapak and Labná, as well as Uxmal, this journey explores the hilly (or *puuc* in Maya) region to the south of Mérida. All five sites can be visited in a day on the 'Ruta Puuc' bus, which departs from the first-class bus station in Mérida every day at 0800, US$11, entry to sites not included. This is a good whistle-stop tour, but does not give you much time at each of the ruins, but five sites in one day is normally enough for most enthusiasts; if you want to spend longer seeing these sites, stay overnight in Ticul.

Kabah

ⓘ *0800-1700, US$3.*

On either side of the main road, 37 km south of Uxmal and often included in tours of the latter, are the ruins of Kabah. On one side there is a fascinating **Palace of Masks** (*Codz-Poop*), whose façade bears the image of Chac, mesmerically repeated 260 times, the number of days in the Almanac Year. Each mask is made up of 30 units of mosaic stone. Even the central chamber is entered via a huge Chac mask whose curling snout forms the doorstep. On the other side of this wall, beneath the figure of the ruler, Kabal, are impressive carvings on the door arches, which depict a man about to be killed, pleading for mercy, and two men duelling. This side of the road is mostly reconstructed; across the road the outstanding feature is a reconstructed arch marking the start of the *sacbé* (sacred road), which leads all the way to Uxmal, and several stabilized, but unclimbable mounds of collapsed buildings being renovated. The style is Classic Puuc.

Sayil, Xlapak and Labná

ⓘ *Entrance US$3 at each site.*

Sayil means 'The Place of the Ants'. Dating from AD 800-1000, this site has an interesting palace, which in its day included 90 bathrooms for some 350 people. The simple, elegant colonnade is reminiscent of the architecture of ancient Greece. The central motif on the upper part of the façade is a broad mask with huge fangs, flanked by two serpents surrounding the grotesque figure of a descending deity. From the upper level of the palace you can see a tiny ruin on the side of a mountain called the Nine Masks.

Thirteen kilometres from Sayil, the ruins of Xlapak have not been as extensively restored as the others in this region. There are 14 mounds and three partially restored pyramids.

Labná has a feature that ranks it among the most outstanding sites of the Puuc region: a monumental arch connecting two groups of buildings (now in ruins), which displays an architectural concept unique to this region. Most Maya arches are purely structural, but the one at Labná has been constructed for aesthetic purposes, running right through the façade and clearly meant to be seen from afar. The two façades on either side of the arch differ greatly in their decoration; the one at the entrance is beautifully decorated with delicate latticework and stone carving imitating the wood or palm-frond roofs of Maya huts.

Uxmal

▸▸ *pp463-473. Colour map 4, A2.*

→ *Phone code: 997.*

ⓘ *Daily 0800-1700, US$9. Son et Lumière shows, US$3, in Spanish; rental of translation equipment US$2.50. Shows are at 2000 in summer and 1900 in winter. Mixed reports. Guides available with 1½ hour tours. Tours in Spanish US$40, in English, French, German and Italian US$45.* ▸▸ *For transport to Uxmal, see page 471.*

Built during the Classic period, Uxmal is the most famous of the ruins in the Puuc region. The characteristic features of Maya cities in this region are the quadrangular layout of the buildings, set on raised platforms, and an artificially created underground water-storage system. The **Pyramid of the Sorcerer** is an unusual oval-shaped pyramid set on a large rectangular base; there is evidence that five stages of building were used in its construction. The pyramid is 30 m tall, with two temples at the top. The **Nunnery** is set around a large courtyard, with some fine masks of Chac, the rain god, on the corners of the buildings. The east building of the Nunnery is decorated with double-headed serpents on its cornices. There are some plumed serpents in relief, in excellent condition, on the façade of the west building. The **House of the Governor** is 100 m long, and is considered one of the most outstanding buildings in all of Mesoamerica. Two arched passages divide the building into three distinct sections that would probably have been covered over. A bove the central entrance is an elaborate trapezoidal motif, with a string of Chaac masks interwoven into a flowing, undulating serpent-like shape extending to the façade's two corners. The stately two-headed jaguar throne in front of the structure suggests a royal or administrative function. The **House of the Turtles** is sober by comparison, its simple walls adorned with carved turtles on the upper cornice, above a short row of tightly packed columns, which resemble the Maya *palapas*, made of sticks with a thatched roof, still used today. The **House of the Doves** is the oldest and most damaged of the buildings at Uxmal. What remains of it is still impressive: a long, low platform of wide columns topped by clusters of roof combs, whose similarity to dovecotes gave the building its name.

Izamal and around

» *pp463-473. Colour map 4, A3.*

→ *Phone code: 988.*

Sixty-eight kilometres east of Mérida is the friendly little town of Izamal. Once a major Classic Maya religious site founded by the priest Itzamná, Izamal became one of the centres of the Spanish attempt to Christianize the Maya.

Fray Diego de Landa, the historian of the Spanish conquest of Mérida (of whom there is a statue in the town), founded the huge **convent** and **church**, which now face the main **Plaza de la Constitución**. This building, constructed on top of a Maya pyramid, was begun in 1549 and has the second largest atrium in the world. If you examine carefully the walls that surround the magnificent atrium, you will notice that some of the faced stones are embellished with carvings of Maya origin, confirming that, when they had toppled the pre-Columbian structures, the Spaniards re-used the material to create the imported architecture. There is also a throne built for the Pope's visit in 1993. The image of the Inmaculada Virgen de la Concepción in the magnificent church was made the Reina de Yucatán in 1949, and the patron saint of the state in 1970. Just 2½ blocks away, visible from the convent across a second square and signposted, are the ruins of a great mausoleum known as the **Kinich-Kakmo pyramid** ⓘ *0800-1700, free, entrance next to the tortilla factory.* You climb the first set of stairs to a broad, tree-covered platform, at the end of which is a further pyramid (still under reconstruction). From the top there is an excellent view of the town and surrounding *henequén* and citrus plantations. Kinich-Kakmo is 195 m long, 173 m wide and 36 m high, the fifth highest in Mexico. In all, 20 Maya structures have been identified in Izamal, several on Calle 27. Another startling feature about the town is that the entire colonial centre, including the convent, the arcaded government offices on Plaza de la Constitución and the arcaded second square, is painted a rich yellow ochre, giving it the nickname of the 'golden city'.

From Izamal you can go by bus to **Cenotillo**, where there are several fine *cenotes* within easy walking distance from the town (avoid the one *in* town), especially **Ucil**, excellent for swimming, and **La Unión**. Take the same bus as for Izamal from Mérida. Past Cenotillo is Espita and then a road forks left to Tizimín (see page 462).

The cemetery of **Hoctún**, on the Mérida-Chichén road, is also worth visiting; indeed it is impossible to miss, there is an 'Empire State Building' on the site. Take a bus from Mérida (last bus back 1700) to see extensive ruins at **Aké**, an unusual structure. Public transport in Mérida is difficult: from an unsigned stop on the corner of Calle 53 y 50, some buses to Tixkokob and Ekmul continue to Aké; ask the driver.

Chichén Itzá

» *pp463-473. Colour map 4, A3.*

ⓘ *Daily 0800-1730, US$9, free bag storage, free for Mexicans on Sun and holidays, when it is incredibly crowded; you may leave and re-enter as often as you like on day of issue. Guided tours US$40 per group of any size; it is best to try and join one, many languages available. Best to arrive before 1030 when the mass of tourists arrives. Son et lumière (US$3 in English, US$1.35 in Spanish) at Chichén every evening, in Spanish* *at 1900, and then in English at 2000; not as good as at Uxmal. A tourist centre has been built at the entrance to the ruins with a restaurant and small museum, bookshop and souvenir shop with exchange facilities. Drinks, snacks and toilets are available at the entrance and at the* cenote. *The site is hot, take a hat, suncream, sunglasses, shoes with good grip and drinking water.*

Chichén Itzá means 'mouth of the well of the water-sorcerer' and is one of the most spectacular of Maya sites. The Castillo, a giant stepped pyramid dominates the site,

Chichén Itzá

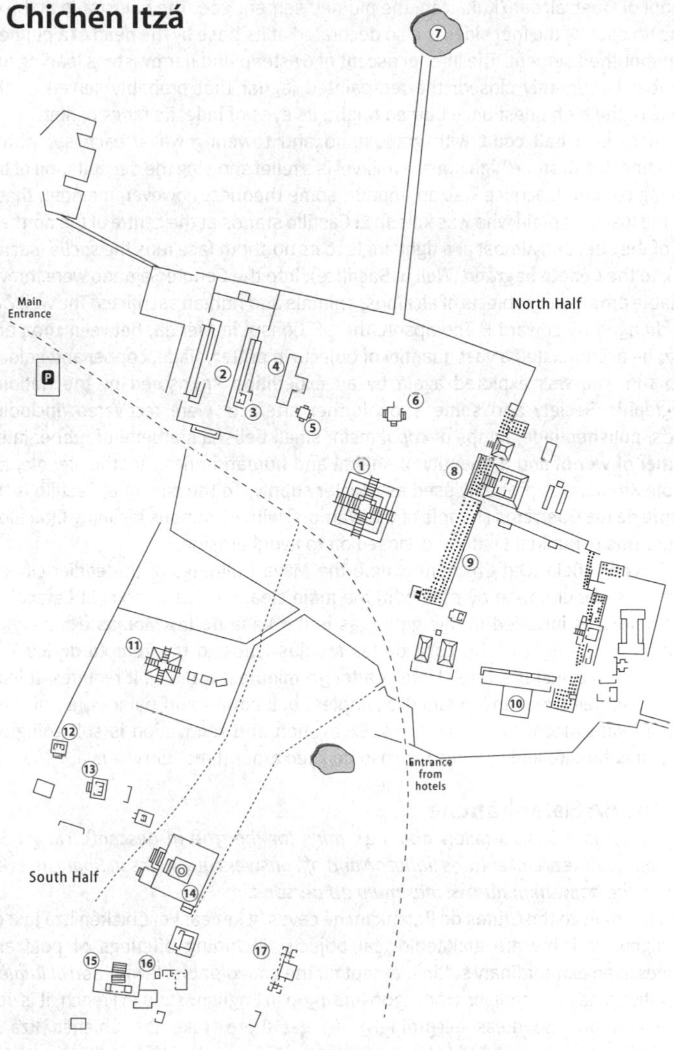

Castillo **1**
Ball Court **2**
Temple of the Jaguar **3**
Platform of the Skulls (Tzompantli) **4**
Platform of Eagles **5**
Platform of Venus **6**
Well of Sacrifice **7**
Temple of the Warriors & Chacmool Temple **8**
Group of a Thousand Columns **9**
Market **10**
Tomb of the High Priest **11**
House of the Deer **12**
Red House **13**
El Caracol (Observatory) **14**
Nunnery **15**
'Church' **16**
Akabdzilo **17**

 watched over by Chacmool, a Maya fertility god who reclines on a nearby structure. The city was built by the Maya in late Classic times (AD 600-900). By the end of the 10th century, the city was more or less abandoned. It was reestablished in the 11th-12th centuries, but much debate surrounds by whom. Whoever the people were, a comparison of some of the architecture with that of Tula, north of Mexico City (see page 136), indicates they were heavily influenced by the Toltecs of Central Mexico.

The major buildings in the north half display a Toltec influence. Dominating them is **El Castillo** ⓘ *1100-1500, 1600-1700, closed if raining*, its top decorated by the symbol of Quetzalcoatl/Kukulcán, the plumed serpent god. The balustrade of the 91 stairs up each of the four sides is also decorated at its base by the head of a plumed, open-mouthed serpent. The interior ascent of 61 steep and narrow steps leading to a chamber is currently closed; the red-painted jaguar that probably served as the throne of the high priest once burned bright, its eyes of jade, its fangs of flint.

There is a **ball court** with grandstand and towering walls, each set with a projecting ring of stone high up; at eye-level is a relief showing the decapitation of the winning captain (sacrifice was an honour; some theories, however, maintain that it was the losing captain who was killed). El Castillo stands at the centre of the northern half of the site, and almost at a right angle to its northern face runs the *sacbé* (sacred way), to the **Cenote Sagrado** (Well of Sacrifice). Into the Cenote Sagrado were thrown valuable propitiatory objects of all kinds, animals and human sacrifices. The well was first dredged by Edward H Thompson, the US Consul in Mérida, between 1904 and 1907; he accumulated a vast quantity of objects in pottery, jade, copper and gold. In 1962 the well was explored again by an expedition sponsored by the National Geographic Society and some 4000 further artefacts were recovered, including beads, polished jade, lumps of *copal* resin, small bells, a statuette of rubber latex, another of wood, and a quantity of animal and human bones. Another *cenote*, the Cenote Xtoloc, was probably used as a water supply. To the east of El Castillo is the **Templo de los Guerreros** (Temple of the Warriors) with its famous reclining **Chacmool** statue. This pyramidal platform is closed off to avoid erosion.

Chichén Viejo (Old Chichén), where the Maya buildings of the earlier city are found, lies about 500 m by path from the main clearing. The famous **El Caracol**, or Observatory, is included in this group, as is the **Casa de las Monjas** (Nunnery). A footpath to the right of the Casa de las Monjas leads to the **Templo de los Tres Dinteles** (Temple of the Three Lintels) after 30 minutes' walking. It requires at least one day to see the many pyramids, temples, ball courts and palaces, all of them adorned with astonishing sculptures. Excavation and renovation is still going on. Interesting birdlife and iguanas can also be seen around the ruins.

Grutas de Balankanché

ⓘ *0900-1700, US$4.70 (allow about 45 mins for the 300-m descent), closed Sat afternoons. The caretaker turns lights on and off, answers questions in Spanish, every hour on the hour, minimum 6, maximum 20 persons.*

Tours run daily to the Grutas de Balankanché caves, 3 km east of Chichén Itzá just off the highway. There are archaeological objects, including offerings of pots and *metates* in an extraordinary setting, except for the unavoidable, 'awful' *son et lumière* show (five a day in Spanish; 1100, 1300 and 1500 in English; 1000 in French; it is very damp and hot, so dress accordingly). To get there, take the Chichén Itzá or Pisté-Balankanché bus hourly at a quarter past, US$0.50, taxi US$15.

On the morning and afternoon of the spring and autumn equinoxes, the alignment of the sun's shadow casts a serpentine image on the side of the steps of El Castillo, see page 468.

Valladolid and around » pp463-473. Colour map 4, A3.

→ *Phone code: 985.*

Situated roughly halfway between Mérida and Cancún, Valladolid is a pleasant little town, until now untouched by tourism. Its proximity to the famous ruins of Chichén Itzá, however, means that Valladolid has been earmarked for extensive development by the Mexican government. Construction is underway of a new international airport at Kaná, in the deserted land near Chichén Itzá, which will open Valladolid's doors to a much larger influx of travellers than the trickle it receives at the moment, and two new luxury hotels are being built on the outskirts of the town.

Valladolid is set around a large plaza, flanked by the imposing Franciscan cathedral. Most of the hotels are clustered around the centre, as well as numerous restaurants catering for all budgets, favouring the lower end. There is a slightly medieval feel to the city, with some of the streets tapering off into mud tracks. The Vallisoletanos, as they are known, are friendlier than their Meridano neighbours, and Valladolid's location makes it an ideal place to settle for a few days, while exploring the ruins of Chichén Itzá, the fishing village of Río Lagartos on the north coast, and the three beautiful *cenotes* in the area, one of which is right in the town itself, on Calle 36 y 39.

The **tourist office** ⓘ *southeast corner of the plaza*, is not very helpful but they give a useful map. Much more helpful information can be obtained from **Antonio 'Negro' Aguilar** ⓘ *Calle 44 No 195*. Something of a local celebrity, he was a baseball champion in the 1950s and 60s, playing for the Leones de Yucatán and the Washington Senators. Now semi-retired, he runs a shop selling sports equipment, rents bicycles and rents very cheap accommodation (see Sleeping, page 465). He is glad to offer information on any of the tourist attractions in the area; if cycling around, he will personally draw you a map of the best route you should take. Antonio can also help organize tours in a minivan to the ruins at Ek-Balam, minimum four people, US$3 per person.

Cenote Zací ⓘ *Calle 36 between Calle 37 and 39, daily 0800-1800, US$2, half price for children*, right in town, is an artificially lit *cenote* where you can swim, except when it is occasionally prohibited due to algae in the water. There is a thatched-roof restaurant and lighted promenades. A small town **museum** ⓘ *Calle 41, free*, housed in Santa Ana church, shows the history of rural Yucatán and has some exhibits from recent excavations at the ruins of *Ek-Balam*.

Seven kilometres from Valladolid is the beautiful **Cenote X-Kekén** ⓘ *daily 0800-1800, US$2.50*, at **Dzitnup**, the name by which it is more commonly known. It

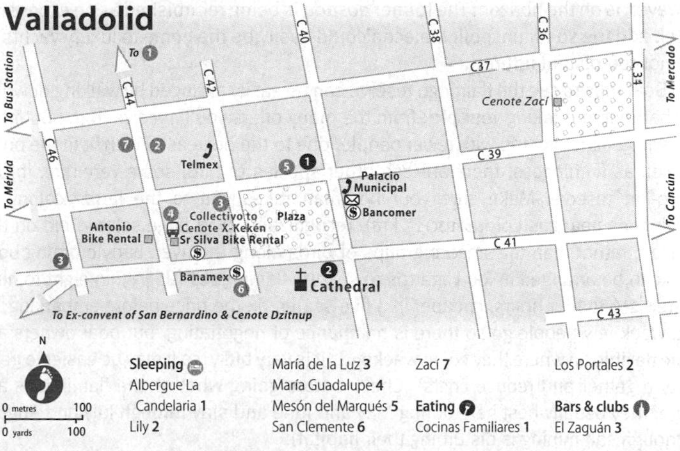

is stunningly lit with electric lights, the only natural light source being a tiny hole in the cavernous ceiling dripping with stalactites. Swimming is excellent, the water is cool and refreshing, although reported a little dirty, and harmless bats zip around overhead. Exploratory walks can also be made through the many tunnels leading off the *cenote*, for which you will need a torch. *Colectivos* leave when full from in front of **Hotel María Guadalupe,** US$1, they return until 1800, after which you will have to get a taxi back to Valladolid, US$4. Alternatively, hire a bicycle from Antonio Aguilar (see above) and cycle there, 25 minutes. Antonio will explain the best route before you set off. There is also the newly discovered, easily reached *cenote* close by, called **Samulá** ⓘ *US$2.25.*

Ek-Balam

ⓘ *Daily 0800-1700, US$2.*

Twenty-five kilometres north of Valladolid are the recently opened Maya ruins of Ek-Balam, meaning 'Black Jaguar'. The ruins contain an impressive series of temples, sacrificial altars and residential buildings grouped around a large central plaza. The main temple, known as 'The Tower', is an immaculate seven-tiered staircase leading up to a flattened area with the remains of a temple. The views are stunning, and because they are not on the tourist trail, these ruins can be viewed at leisure, without the presence of hordes of tour groups from Cancún. To get there by car, take Route 295 north out of Valladolid. Just after the village of Temozón, take the turning on the right for Santa Rita. The ruins are some 5 km further on. A recommended way for those without a car is to hire a bike, take it on the roof of a *colectivo* leaving for Temozón from outside the **Hotel María Guadalupe,** and ask to be dropped off at the turning for Ek-Balam. From there, cycle the remaining 12 km to the ruins. There are also minivans to Ek-Balam run by Antonio Aguilar (see page 461).

Río Lagartos and around → *Colour map 4, A3.*

Tizimín is a dirty, scruffy little town en route to Río Lagartos, where you will have to change buses. If stuck, there are several cheap *posadas* and restaurants, but with frequent buses to Río Lagartos, there should be no need to stay the night here.

Río Lagartos is an attractive little fishing village on the north coast of Yucatán state, whose main attraction is the massive biosphere reserve containing thousands of **pink flamingoes**, as well as 250 other species of bird. The people of Río Lagartos are extremely friendly and very welcoming to tourists. The only route is on the paved road from Valladolid; access from Cancún is by boat only, a journey mainly made by tradesmen ferrying fish to the resort. Development in Río Lagartos, however, is on the horizon. The former *posada* is being refurbished as an expensive hotel, and the so-far unspoilt Malecón could easily be the home to luxury yachts in the not-too-distant future.

Boat trips to see the flamingo reserve can be easily arranged by walking down to the harbour and taking your pick from the many offers you'll receive from boatmen. You will get a longer trip with fewer people, due to the decreased weight in the boat. As well as flamingoes, there are 250 other species of bird, some very rare, in the 47-sq-km reserve. Make sure your boatman takes you to the larger colony of flamingoes near **Las Coloradas** (15 km), recognizable by a large salt mound on the horizon, rather than the smaller groups of birds along the river. Early morning boat trips can be arranged in Río Lagartos to see the flamingoes (US$35, in eight to nine seater, 2½ to four hours, cheaper in a five-seater, fix the price before embarking; in mid-week few people go so there is no chance of negotiating, but boat owners are more flexible on where they go; at weekends it is very busy, so it may be easier to get a party together and reduce costs). Check before going whether the flamingoes are there; they usually nest here during May and June and stay through July and August (although salt mining is disturbing their habitat).

Sleeping

Mérida *p451, map p452*

The prices of hotels are not determined by their location with budget hotels close to the plaza and the better hotels often further away. If booking into a central hotel, always try to get a room away from the street side, as noise on the narrow streets begins as early as 0500.

LL Hacienda Xcanatun, Km 12, Carretera Mérida-Progreso, T/F941-0213, www.xcanatun.com. Carefully restored hacienda, 10 mins out of town, relaxed atmosphere with great attention to detail, full breakfast included, restaurant possibly the best in Mérida without an expensive price tag, located in a converted machine room with ceilings high enough to give you vertigo, live music every day. Highly recommended.

L La Misión de Fray Diego, Calle 61 No 524 between 64 and 66, T01-800-221-0599, www.lamisiondefraydiego.com. Very pleasant colonial-style hotel situated around 2 shady courtyards. Section nearest the road is original 17th century, formally connected to the convent behind. Mini-bar and TV in all rooms, small pool and restaurant.

AL Medio Mundo, Calle 55, No 533 between 64 and 66, T/F924-5472, www.hotelmediomundo.com. Renovated old home now a charming hotel with 10 high-ceiling rooms, garden patio and swimming pool. Great hosts. Recommended.

AL-L Gobernador, Calle 59 No 535, corner of 66, T930-4141, www.gobernadormerida.com.mx. Good clean hotel with 2 small pools. All rooms with a/c, cable TV and phone. 'Executive' rooms are better. Restaurant offers buffet breakfast. Highly recommended.

AL-A Colonial, Calle 62 No 476, on the corner of Calle 57, T923-6444, www.hotelcolonial.com.mx. Great location 2 blocks from the plaza. Small but comfortable rooms with TV and a/c, with small pool. Very friendly and efficient staff and restaurant serving good buffet meals, including a highly recommended breakfast.

A Gran Hotel, Parque Hidalgo, Calle 60 No 496, with Av 59, T923-6963. A/c, TV, hot water, phone, clean, helpful, owner speaks English. A great place to stay with a good atmosphere. Popular with the stars of film and stage, and politicians including Fidel Castro. Not all rooms have windows – ask if you want one. Pizza/pasta restaurant, free parking.

B Dolores Alba, Calle 63 No 464 between 52 and 54, T928-5650. Rooms with bath and fan, some with a/c, quiet, friendly, good breakfast for US$4.50, pool, safe parking in courtyard, will make reservations for sister establishment at Chichén Itzá.

B-C Posada Toledo, Calle 58 No 487 esq 57, T923-1690, hptoledo@finred.com.mx. Good value, central, a/c extra, in charming old house with lots of plants, cheap breakfast, has paperback exchange.

C Casa San Juan, Calle 62 No 545A between 69 and 71, T986-2937, www.casasanjuan.com. Restored 19th-century house with pleasant courtyard, large rooms with bath, some with a/c, includes breakfast.

C Trinidad, Calle 62 No 464 esq 55, T923-2033, www.hotelestrinidad.com. Old house, dorm rooms cheaper, hot water, clean bathrooms, tranquil, courtyard, lovely garden, sun roof, can use pool at the other hotel. Continental breakfast included in the price. Recommended.

D Casa Becil, Calle 67 No 550-C, between 66 and 68, T924-6764. Convenient for bus station, fan, bath, hot water, clean, safe, popular, quiet, friendly, owner speaks English, makes you feel at home. Rooms on first floor light and breezy. Recommended.

D Casa Bowen, restored colonial house (inside better than out), corner of Calle 66, No 521-B, esq 65, near ADO bus station, T928-6109. Often full at weekends, rooms on the main street noisy, bath, hot water but irregular supply, exchanges dollars, stores luggage. Good.

D La Paz, Calle 62 No 522 between 65 and 67, T923-9446. Tall, tired rooms in old colonial house, some noise in the morning from nearby bus station, but otherwise quiet.

D Las Monjas, Calle 66A No 509 between 61 and 63, T928-6632. Clean, quiet, luggage store, good value. Recommended.

Phone codes *Mérida 999; Celestún 988; Progreso 969; Ticul 997; Oxkutzcab 997; Uxmal 997; Izamal 988; Valladolid 985.*

D Margarita, Calle 66 No 506 and 63, T923-7236. With shower, clean, good, rooms a bit dark and noisy downstairs, cheaper rooms for 5 (3 beds), parking, friendly, excellent value.

D Mucuy, Calle 57 No 481, between 56 and 58, T928-5193, www.mucuy.com. Good, but 1st-floor rooms are very hot rooms with shower, use of fridge, washing facilities, nice gardens, efficient. Highly recommended.

D-F Nómadas Youth Hostal, Calle 62 No 433, end of Calle 51, 5 blocks north of the plaza, T924-5223, nomadashostel@hotmail.com. Private rooms, dorms and camping, hot water, full kitchen, drinking water, clean, friendly, owner Raúl speaks English and is very helpful, good value and a great place to meet other travellers. Free salsa classes on Fri.

E Latino, Calle 66 No 505 esq 63, T923-5087. With fan and shower, friendly and clean.

E San Clemente, Calle 58 No 586, T928-1795. Bath, hot water, basic, clean, good value.

E San José, west of plaza on Calle 63 No 503 with 62 and 64, T928-6657, san_jose92@latinmail.com. Bath, hot water, basic, clean, friendly, rooms on top floor are baked by the sun, one of the cheapest, popular with locals, will store luggage, good cheap meals available, local speciality *poc chuc*. Recommended.

E Hostal Zócalo, on the south of the plaza, T930-9562, hostel_zocalo@yahoo.com. New place, big clean, dormitory rooms. Kitchen for guests. Good spot.

Camping

Trailer Park Rainbow, Km 8, on the road to Progreso, US$5 for 1 or 2, hot showers, all facilities and good bus connection into town.

Celestún *p453*

LL Eco Paraíso, Km 10 off the old Sisal Highway, T916-2100, www.ecoparaiso.com In coconut grove on edge of reserve, pool, tours to surrounding area including flamingoes, turtle nesting, etc.

D Gutiérrez, Calle 12 (the Malecón) No 22. Large beds, fans, views, clean.

E San Julio, Calle 12 No 92, T916-2170. Large bright rooms and clean bathrooms, owner knowledgeable about the area.

Progreso and around *p454*

AL Casa Quixote, Calle 23 No 64, between 48 and 50, T935-2909, www.casaquixote.com. Selection of comfortable rooms and a pool.

B-C Tropical Suites, Av Malecón and Calle 20, T935-1263. Suites and rooms with cable TV, a/c, sea views.

C Progreso, Calle 29 No 142, T935-0039. Simple rooms in the centre.

Ticul and Oxkutzcab *p455*

D Trujeque, just south of main plaza, Oxkutzcab, T975-0568. A/c, TV, clean, good value, discount for stays over a week.

D-E Sierra Sosa, Calle 26, near Zócalo, Ticul, T972-0008. Cheap rooms that are dungeon-like, but friendly, clean and helpful.

E Casa de Huéspedes, near bus terminal, Oxkutzcab. Large rooms with bath, TV, fan, friendly. Recommended.

E Hotel Rosario, Oxkutzcab, turn right out of bus station then right again. Double room, shower, cable TV.

E Motel Buganvillas, on the edge of Ticul on the road to Mérida, T972-0761. Clean, basic rooms.

E San Miguel, Calle 28 near the market, Ticul, T972-0382. Quiet, good value, parking.

Uxmal *p457*

There is no village at Uxmal, just the hotels. For cheap accommodation, go to Ticul, 28 km away (see above).

L Hacienda Uxmal, T976-2013, 300-400 m from ruins. Good, efficient and relaxing (3 restaurants, 0800-2200), a/c, gardens, swimming pool.

L The Lodge at Uxmal, at entrance to ruins, T976-2102, www.mayaland.com. Same owners as **Hacienda Uxmal**. Comfortable, a/c, bath, TV, fair restaurant.

AL Misión Uxmal, 1-2 km from ruins on Mérida road, T976-2022, Km 78, www.hotelesmision.com.mx. Rooms a bit dark, pool.

A Club Méditerranée Villa Arqueológica, Mérida T928-0644. Beautiful, close to ruins, good and expensive restaurant, excellent service, swimming pool. Recommended.

C Rancho Uxmal, about 4 km north of ruins, T923-1576. Comfortable rooms, hot and cold water, camping for US$5, pool, reasonable food but not cheap (no taxis to get there).

D-F Sacbé Hostel, at Km 127 on Highway 261, T858-1281. A mix of private rooms (private bath), dormitories and campsite, with space for hammocks, and solar-powered showers, with breakfast and dinner for a little more.

Camping

No camping allowed at the site, but there is a campsite at **Sacbé Hostel**, see above. 2nd-class buses from Mérida to Campeche pass by, ask to be let out at the Campo de Baseball. French and Mexican owners, beautifully landscaped park, fastidiously clean and impeccably managed. 9 electric hook-ups (US$7-10 for motor home according to size), big area for tents (US$2.75 per person with tent), *palapas* for hammocks (US$2.65 per person), for cars pay US$1, showers, toilets, clothes-washing facilities, also 3 bungalows with ceiling fan (**E**), breakfast, vegetarian lunch and dinner available (US$2.65 each). Highly recommended.

Izamal and around *p458*

C Macan-Che, Calle 22 and Calle 33, T954-0287, www.macanche.com. 4 blocks north of the plaza, pleasant bungalows, breakfast. Recommended.

Chichén Itzá *p458*

L Hacienda Chichén, T924-4222, www.haciendachichen.com. Close to the ruins, with charming bungalows.

AL Villas Arqueológicas, T851-0034, Apdo Postal 495, Mérida. Close to the ruins. Pool, tennis, restaurant (expensive and poor). Both are on the other side of the fenced-off ruins from the bus stop; you cannot walk through ruins, either walk all the way round, or take taxi (US$1-1.50).

A Hotel Misión Chichén Itzá, Pisté. A/c, pool, disappointing, gloomy, poor restaurant, not easily seen from the road; it has staircases with plumed serpents and a big statue facing north on top.

B-C Stardust Posada Annex, Pisté, about 2 km before the ruins if coming from Mérida (taxi to ruins US$2.50). Good value, especially if you don't want TV or a/c (fans available), swimming pool, popular with German tour groups, average restaurant.

C Pirámide Inn, 1.5 km from ruins, at the Chichén end of Pisté, T851-0115. Clean but run-down, with good food, swimming pool, hammocks and *palapas*, friendly English-speaking owner, trailer park and camping US$6.50 for 2 plus car in front of hotel, US$4.50 in campground (owned by **Stardust**, see above) but still check in at hotel reception, cold showers.

D Dolores Alba, Km 123, T928-5650. Small hotel (same family as in Mérida, where you can make advance reservations, which is advisable in view of long walk from ruins), 2.5 km on the road to Puerto Juárez (bus passes it), in need of renovation, with shower and fan, clean, has swimming pool and serves good, expensive meals, English spoken, RVs can park in front for US$5.

D Posada Novelo, near **Pirámide Inn**. Run by José Novelo who speaks English, guest access to pool and restaurant at nearby **Stardust Inn**.

D Posada Olalde, 100 m from main road at end of Calle 6. Clean, quiet and friendly – good budget deal.

D-E Maya Inn, on main road to Chichén Itzá. With bath, cheaper without, also hammock space, clean.

Valladolid *p461, map p461*

A Mesón del Marqués, north side of Plaza Principal, T859-1985, www.mesondelmarques.com. A/c, with bath, pool, on square, with good but pricey restaurant, cable TV, excellent value. Recommended.

B-C Zací, Calle 44 No 191, T856-2167. A/c, cheaper with fan, TV, good pool, clean, quiet.

C María de la Luz, Calle 42 No 193-C, Plaza Principal, T856-1181, www.mariadelaluzhotel.com. Good, a/c, swimming pool (non-residents, US$0.50), excellent restaurant, buffet breakfast US$3.50, *comida corrida* US$5, closes at 2230. Takes Visa.

C San Clemente, Calle 42 No 206, T856-2208. With a/c, spacious, quiet, clean, has car park, TV, small swimming pool, restaurant, opposite cathedral, in centre of town. Recommended.

D Antonio 'Negro' Aguilar rents rooms for 2, 3 or 4 people. The best budget deal in the town for 2 or more, clean, spacious rooms on a quiet street, garden, volleyball/basketball court. The rooms are on Calle 41 No 225, before the **Maya Hotel**, but you need to book them at Aguilar's shop on Calle 44 No 195, T856-2125. If the shop is closed, knock on the door of the house next door on the right of the shop.

D María Guadalupe, Calle 44 No 198, T856-2068. Quiet, fan, clean, good value, hot water, washing facilities. Recommended.

E Albergue La Candelaria, Calle 35 No 201-F, T856-2267, candelaria_hostel@hotmail.com. Good cheap option, especially for solo travellers. Single-sex dorms with fan, clean, hot water, kitchen, washing facilities, hammocks out the back in the garden, TV room. Recommended.

E Lily, Calle 44 No 192. Hot shower, cheaper with shared bath, fan, basic, good location, laundry facilities, friendly.

Río Lagartos and around *p462*

E Tere and Miguel, near the harbour (ask at the bus terminal). 3 rooms for rent, very nicely furnished, double and triple rooms, 1 with an extra hammock, sea views.

Eating

Mérida *p451, map p 452*

There are a number of taco stands, pizzerías and sandwich places in Pasaje Picheta, a small plaza off the Palacio de Gobierno.

TTT Casa de Piedra 'Xcanantun', in Hacienda Xcanantun (see Sleeping, above). Km 12 Carretera Mérida-Progreso, T941-0213. Fine dining, best restaurant in the area (although a bit out of town). Popular with locals. Reserve if possible. Highly recommended.

TTT-TT Bologna, Calle 21 No 117a, Col Itzimná. Italian, great pizza and handmade pasta (pizza oven imported from Italy!), beautiful plaza with hanging pots, live music Fri and Sat at night. Recommended.

TTT-TT Pórtico del Peregrino, Calle 57 between 60 and 62. Dining indoors or in an attractive leafy courtyard, excellent food.

TTT-T Café La Habana, Calle 59 y Calle 62. International cuisine, a/c, nice atmosphere. Friendly, efficient service with good local dishes, open 24 hrs.

TT Alberto's Continental, Calle 64 No 482 esq Calle 57. Local, Lebanese and international food, colonial mansion. Recommended.

TT Café Continental, Calle 60 between 55 and 53. Buffet breakfast, nice setting, classical music. 0630-1400. Recommended.

TT El Tucho, Calle 60 near University. Good local dishes and occasional live music.

TT La Alameda, Calle 58 No 474 between Calle 57 and 55. Arabic and Mexican cuisine, lunch only, closes at 1800.

TT La Pérgola (both drive-in and tables), at corner Calle 56 and 43. Good veal dishes. Warmly recommended. Also in Col Alemán at Calle 24 No 289A.

TT La Prosperidad, Calle 53 y 56. Yucatecan food, live entertainment at lunchtime.

TT Los Almendros, Calle 50A No 493 esq 59, in high-vaulted, whitewashed thatched barn. For Yucatán specialities, first rate.

TT Los Balcones, Calle 61 on north side of plaza, T924-5499. Great 1st-floor location overlooking the plaza. Food can be some what hit and miss, but for a drink and snack this is a good spot, with internet as well.

TT Los Cardenales, Calle 69 No 550-A esq 68, close to bus station. Good value, open for breakfast, lunch and dinner.

TT-T Amaro, Calle 59 No 507 between 60 and 62, near the plaza. With open courtyard and covered patio, good food, especially vegetarian, try *chaya* drink from the leaf of the *chaya* tree; their curry, avocado pizza and home-made bread are also very good, Mon-Sat 1200-2200.

TT-T La Vía Olympo, on main plaza opposite cathedral. Good-value Mexican and Yucatecan dishes, good service and outdoor seating.

T Café/Restaurant Mérida, Calle 62 between 59 and 61. Full 3 course for US$2.50 – a bargain, and it's tasty food as well!

T El Escorpión, just off plaza on Calle 61. Good cheap local food.

T El Trapiche, near on Calle 62 half a block north of the plaza. Good local dishes, excellent pizzas and freshly made juices.

T Marys, Calle 63 No 486, between 63 and 58. Mainly Mexican customers. Recommended.

T Mily's, Calle 59 between 64 and 66. *Comida corrida* for under US$3.

T Paparazzi Pizza, Calle 62, just north of the plaza. Great for a quick snack – a huge slice of pizza and a drink for US$1.20.

Cafés, juices and ice cream parlours

Café Petropolis, Calle 70 opposite CAME terminal. Existed long before the terminal was built, family-run, sometimes staffed entirely by children, who do a very good

job, turkey a speciality, excellent quality, good *horchata* and herb teas.
El Colón Sorbetes y Dulces Finos, Calle 62 near Colón, 13 blocks from centre, serving ice cream since 1907, great sorbets, *meringue*, good menu with explanation of fruits in English. Highly recommended. About 30 different flavours of good ice cream.
Italian Coffee Company, Calle 62 between 59 and 61. A bit like a Mexican 'Starbucks', but nevertheless serves excellent coffee, decent panini-style baguettes, and tasty cakes for those feelin' a trifle decadent.
Jugos California, good fruit salads at Calle 65, at the main bus station and many other branches all over city.

Theres a good *panadería* at Calle 65 y 60, serving banana bread and orange cake, and another good bakery at Calle 62 y 61. Parque Santa Ana, is good for cheap street fare. Closed middle of day.

Celestún *p453*
Many beachside restaurants along Calle 12, but be careful of food in the cheaper ones; recommended is **La Playita**, for fried fish, seafood cocktails. Food stalls along Calle 11 beside the bus station should be approached with caution.
‡‡ **Chivirico**, across the road from **Playita**, offers descent fish, shrimp and other marine offerings.
‡‡ **El Lobo**, Calle 10 and 13, on the corner of the main square. Best spot for breakfast, with fruit salads, yoghurt, pancakes, etc. Celestún's best pizza in the evenings.

Progreso and around *p454*
The Malecón at Progreso is lined with seafood restaurants, some with tables on the beach. For cheaper restaurants, head for the centre of town, near the bus terminal.
‡‡-‡ **Las Palmas** and **El Cocalito** are 2 of several reasonable fish restaurants in Chelem.
‡ **Casablanca**, **Capitan Marisco** and **Le Saint Bonnet**, Malecón, Progreso, are all recommended.

Ticul and Oxkutzcab *p455*
‡‡ **Los Almendros**, Calle 23, Ticul. Nice colonial building with patio, good Yucatecan cuisine, reasonable prices.
‡‡ **Pizzería La Góndola**, Calle 23, Ticul. Good, moderately priced pizzas.
‡ **El Colorín**, near Hotel Sierra Sosa on Calle 26, Ticul. Cheap local food.

Uxmal *p457*
‡‡‡-‡‡ Restaurant at ruins, good but expensive.

Izamal and around *p458*
There are several restaurants on Plaza de la Constitución.
‡‡ **Kinich-Kakmó**, Calle 27 No 299 between 28 and 30. Near ruins of same name, local food.
‡‡ **Tumben-Lol**, Calle 22 No 302 between 31 and 33. Yucatecan cuisine.
‡ **El Norteño** at bus station. Good and cheap.
‡ **Wayane**, near statue of Diego de Landa. Friendly, clean.

Chichén Itzá *p458*
Mostly poor and overpriced in Chichén itself (cafés inside the ruins are cheaper than the restaurant at the entrance to the ruins, but they are still expensive). Restaurants in Pisté close 2100-2200.
‡ **Poxil**, Mérida end of town, for breakfast.
‡ **Sayil** in Pisté. Has good *pollo pibil* for US$2.60.

Valladolid *p461, map p461*
There is a well-stocked supermarket on the road between the centre and bus station.
‡‡ **La Sirenita**, Calle 34N, between 29 and 31, T856-1655, a few blocks east of main square. Highly recommended for seafood, popular and friendly, only open to 1800, closed Sun.
‡‡ **Plaza Maya**, Calle 41 No 235, a few blocks east of main square. Good *comida corrida*, step up from the rest below.
‡ **Cocinas Familiares**, northeast corner of Plaza Principal, next to **Mesón del Marqués**. Marginally cheaper Yucatecan food, pizzas, etc.
‡ **Los Portales**, on southeast corner of main square. Very good and cheap.
‡ **Mercado**, Calle 37, 2 blocks east of the Cenote Zací. Cheap meals in the market.

Cafés
There's a nice café on the corner of Calle 40 and 39, off the plaza. Open till late but doesn't serve alcohol.

Río Lagartos and around *p462*
For a fishing village, the seafood is not spectacular, as most of the good fish is sold to restaurants in Mérida and Cancún.

🍴 **Isla Contoy**, Calle 19 No 134, average seafood, not cheap for the quality.
🍴 **Los Negritos**, off the plaza, moderately priced seafood.

Entertainment

Mérida *p451, map p452*

Bars and clubs

There are several good bars on the north side of the plaza, beer is moderately priced at US$1.20, although food can be expensive. There are a number of live-music venues around Parque Santa Lucía, a couple of blocks from the main plaza.
Café Expresso, on Parque Hidalgo, is good for an early evening beer (if they aren't having liquor licence problems).
El Establo, 2 doors down from **El Tucho** towards the plaza, upstairs from the street, 2100-0230. Live local bands, plus occasional Cuban cabaret entertainers. Free entry, drinks US$2 and over.
El Tucho Calle 55 between Calle 60 and 58. A restaurant open till 2100 only, with live music, often guest performers from Cuba play.
Mambo Cafe, Plaza Las Americanas Shopping Mall, T987-7533. Big club in Mérida, mainly salsa but all kinds of music.
Panchos, Calle 59 between 60 and 62. Very touristy, staff in traditional gear, but lively and busy, live music, patio.

Cinema

There is a cinema showing subtitled films in English on Parque Hidalgo.
Teatro Mérida, Calle 62 between 59 and 61, shows European, Mexican and independent movies as well as live theatre productions. The 14-screen multiplex **Cinepolis** is in the huge Plaza de las Américas, north of the city; *colectivo* and buses take 20 mins and leave from Calle 65 between 58 and 60. See the free listings magazine *Yucatán Today,* available at hotels and the tourist office, for other evening activities.

Theatre

Teatro Peón Contreras, Calle 60 with 57. Shows start at 2100, US$4, ballet, etc. The university puts on many theatre and dance productions.

Valladolid *p461, map p461*

Bars and clubs

El Zaguán, Calle 41 and 41A, 2 blocks west of the plaza. One of the few places serving alcohol without a meal, nice setting in plant-filled courtyard, music, open until 0300.

Festivals and events

Mérida *p451, map p452*

Every **Thu** there is a cultural music and dance show in Plaza Santa Lucía. **Sat** brings En **El Corazón del Mérida**, with music and dance in bars, restaurants and in the street. Every **Sun** the central streets are closed off to traffic, live music and parades abound.
6 Jan Mérida celebrates its birthday.
Feb/Mar Carnival takes place the week before Ash Wed (best on Sat). Floats, dancers in regional costume, music and dancing around the plaza and children dressed in animal suits.

Río Lagartos *p462*

17 Jul A big local **fiesta**, with music, food and dancing in the plaza.
12 Dec **Virgen de Guadalupe**. The whole village converges on the chapel built in 1976 on the site of a vision of the Virgin Mary by a local non-believer, who suddenly died, along with his dog, shortly after receiving the vision.

Chichén Itzá *p458*

21 Mar and 21 Sep On the morning and afternoon of the spring and autumn equinoxes, the alignment of the sun's shadow casts a serpentine image on the side of the steps of El Castillo. The popularity of the occasion is growing and you'll be lucky to get close enough to see the action.

Shopping

Mérida *p451, map p452*

Bookshops

Librerías Dante, Calle 59, No 498 between 58 and 60. Calle 61 between 62 and 64 (near Lavandería La Fe), used books. Also **Libros Usados**, Calle 57, between Calle 60 y 62. Used English books, will buy, swap or sell.

Cameras and film

Repairs on Calle 53 y 62. **Mericolor**, Calle 67 y 58. Recommended for service and printing;

also **Kodak** on Parque Hidalgo. Many processors around crossing of Calle 59 y 60. Prices are high by international standards. **Camera repairs Fotolandia**, Calle 62 No 479G y 57, T924-8223.

Crafts and souvenirs

Many souvenir shops are dotted in the streets around the plaza. They all specialize in hammocks (see box, page 456). They also sell silver jewellery from Taxco, Panama hats, *guayabera* shirts, *huaraches* (sandals with car-tyre soles), baskets and Maya figurines. Always bargain hard, the salesmen are pushy, but they expect to receive about half their original asking price. The main **handicraft market** is on Calle 56 y 67. There is a smaller handicraft market on Calle 62, 1 block from the plaza. The **Mercado de Artesanías**, on Calle 67 between 56 and 58, has many nice things, but prices are high and the salespeople are also pushy.

There are several frequently recommended shops for hammocks (best to compare them). **El Mayab**, Calle 58 No 553 and 71, friendly, limited choice but good deals available; and **La Poblana**, Calle 65 between 58 and 60, will bargain, especially for sales of more than 1, huge stock; also **Jorge Razu**, Calle 56 No 516B between 63A and 63, very convincing salesman, changes TCs at good rates. Recommended. **El Aguacate**, Calle 58 No 604, corner of Calle 73. Good hammocks, no hard sell. Recommended. Helpful, bargaining possible if buying several items. **Santiago**, Calle 70 No 505 between 61 and 63. Very good value. **Tita**, Calle 59 between Calle 60 and 62. Enthusiastic hard sell, they only sell sisal hammocks, good selection, give demonstrations.

Good silver shops and several antique shops on Calle 60 between 51 and 53. **Bacho Arte Mexicano**, Calle 60 No 466 between Calle 53 and 55. Also sells other jewellery and ornaments. **Paty**, Calle 64 No 549 between Calle 67 and 69. Stocks reputable 'Kary' brand *guayaberas*, also sells hammocks. **Miniaturas**, Calle 59 No 507A, near plaza. Traditional folk art, Day of the Dead miniatures, wrestling masks. Calle 62, between Calle 57 y 61, is lined with *guayabera* shops, all of a similar price and quality. Embroidered *huipil* blouses cost about US$25. Good, cheap *guayabera* shop on northwest corner of Parque San Juan, prices half those of the souvenir shops in the centre. Clothes shopping is good along Calle 65 and in the **García Rejón Bazaar**, Calle 65 y 60. Good leather *huaraches* sandals, robust and comfortable, from the market, US$10. Excellent cowboy boots for men and women, maximum size 10, can be bought around the market for US$46.

Supermarkets

San Francisco de Assisi, on Calle 67 y 52. A big, well-stocked supermarket. Also at Calle 65, between Av 50 and 52.

Progreso and around *p454*

Worth a visit is **Mundo Marino**, Calle 80 s/n, 1 block from the beach, T915-1380. A souvenir shop whose friendly owner Luis Cámara once caught a great white shark. Many shark-related as well as other marine souvenirs are on sale.

Izamal and around *p458*

Market, Calle 31, on Plaza de la Constitución, opposite convent, closes soon after lunch. **Hecho a mano**, Calle 31 No 332 between 36 and 38. Folk art, postcards, textiles, jewellery, papier-mâché masks.

Activities and tours

Mérida *p451, map p452*

Tour operators

Most tour operators can arrange trips to popular local destinations including Chichén Itza, Uxmal, Celestún and nearby *cenotes*. **Yucatán Trails**, Calle 62, No 482, Av 57-59, T928-2582, yucatantrails@hotmail.com. Tours to all the popular local destinations, such as Uxmal, Celestún and Progreso. **Mayaland Tours**, in **Hotel Casa del Balam**, T926-3851, and **Fiesta Americana**, T925-0622, have their own hotel at Chichén Itzá. **Mayan Iniciatic Tours**, Paseo de Montejo 481, T920-2328, mayan@yuc1.
telmex.net.mx. **Carmen Travel Services**, **Hotel María del Carmen**, Calle 63 No 550 y Calle 68, T923-9133, 3 other branches. **Wilbert Torres Campos**, T922-3553 or through the Sindicato de Guías de Yucatán on T924-8656, is an excellent guide with well over 20 years' experience and is especially

knowledgeable regarding the Yucatán's Maya sites and can arrange transport to all sites.

Chichén Itzá *p458*

Tour operators

Recommended guide from Mérida: **Miguel Angel Vergara**, Centro de Estudios Maya Haltun-Ha, T927-1172, PO Box 97148.

Transport

Mérida *p451, map p452*

Air

Aeropuerto Rejón (MID), 8 km from town. From Calle 67, 69 and 60, bus 79 goes to the airport, marked 'Aviación', US$0.35, roughly every 20 mins. Taxi set price voucher systems US$8; *colectivo* US$2.50. Good domestic flight connections. International flights from **Belize City**, **Houston**, **Miami** and **Havana**. Package tours Mérida-Havana-Mérida are available (be sure to have a confirmed return flight). For return to Mexico ask for details at Secretaría de Migración, Calle 60 No 285.

Airline offices AeroCaribe, Paseo Montejo 500B, T928-6790. **Aerolínenas Aztecas**, T01-800-229-8322. **AeroMéxico**, Av Colón 451 and Montejo, T920-1260. **Aviacsa**, T926-9087. **Aviateca**, T926-9087. **Mexicana** office at Calle 58 No 500 esq 61, T924-6633, and Paseo Montejo 493.

Bus

Buses to destinations outside Yucatán state leave from the 1st-class terminal at Calle 70, No 555, between Calle 69 and 71 (it is called CAME). The station has lockers; it is open 24 hrs a day. About 20 mins' walk to centre, taxi US$3.50. Schedules change frequently. The ADO terminal, around the corner, is for Yucatán destinations, with the single exception of buses to Chichén Itzá, which depart from the CAME terminal.

To **Mexico City**, 6 a day, 20-24 hrs, several rest stops, US$81 (ADO, 5 a day); direct Pullman bus Mexico City 1400 and 1700. Regular 2nd-class buses to **Campeche**, with ATS (2½ hrs, US$5.50) also pass **Uxmal**, 6 a day between 0630 and 1900; 1st-class fare (not via Uxmal), ADO, every 30 mins, 2½ hrs, US$9. To **Celestún**, 2nd class, frequent departures, 2 hrs, US$3.50. **Chetumal**, at 1300, 1800 and 2300, 6 hrs, US$20. **Cd del Carmen**, 1st class, ADO, 18 a day, 6 hrs, US$21. **Coatzacoalcos**, 5 a day, 12 hrs, US$40. Buses to **Palenque**, 5 a day, 8 hrs, US$28 from ADO terminal, **Cristóbal Colón** luxury service US$28; alternatively take Villahermosa bus to Playas de Catazajá. US$18.50, 8½ hrs, then minibus to Palenque, or go to Emiliano Zapata, 5 buses a day US$23, and local bus (see page 448). Buses to **Progreso**, US$1.10 with **Auto Progreso**, leave from the bus station on Calle 62, between Calle 65 and 67, every 15 mins 0500-2100. **Puerto Juárez** and **Cancún** (**Autobuses de Oriente**), every hr 0600-2400, 2nd class, US$14, 1st class, US$19, *plus*, US$20, 4½ hrs. Buses to and from Cancún stop at Calle 50, between Calle 65 and 67. If going to **Isla Mujeres**, make sure the driver knows you want Puerto Juárez, as the bus does not always go there, especially at night. Buses to **Tulum**, via Chichén Itzá, Valladolid, Cancún and Playa del Carmen, several daily, from main terminal, 6 hrs, US$15, 2nd class, drops you off about 1 km from the ruins. For buses to Uxmal and Chichén Itzá see under those places. To **Valladolid**, US$8, 1st Express, US$6, 2nd class (9 a day). **Veracruz**, ADO, 1030, and 2100, 16 hrs, US$55. Many buses daily to **Villahermosa**, 1st class (several from 1030 to 2330) 8 hrs, US$32; **Tuxtla Gutiérrez**, 3 1st-class evening departures, 15hrs, US$42 with **Autotransportes del Sureste de Yucatán**, also with **Cristóbal Colón**, US$30. To **San Cristóbal de las Casas**, 1915 and 2100, 13hrs, US$38; also 2 a day with **Cristóbal Colón**, 1915 and 2345. Buses to **Celestún** and **Sisal** from terminal on Calle 71, between 64 and 66. To **Tenosique**, 2100, US$28. To **Tizimín**, **Cenotillo** and **Izamal**, buses leave from Calle 50 between Calle 65 and 67. Route 261, Mérida-Escárcega, paved and in very good condition.

To Guatemala Take a bus from Mérida to San Cristóbal and change there for Comitán, or to Tenosique for the route to Flores. A more expensive alternative would be to take the bus from Mérida direct to Tuxtla Gutiérrez (times given above), then direct either Tuxtla-Cd Cuauhtémoc or to Tapachula.

To Belize Paved all the way to Chetumal. Bus Mérida-Chetumal US$18.50, luxury, US$18, 1st class, takes 7 hrs (**Autotransportes del Caribe, Auto transporte Peninsular**), US$13, 2nd class.

Car

Car hire Car reservations should be booked well in advance wherever possible. All car hire firms charge around US$40-45 a day although bargains can be found in low season. All agencies allow vehicles to be returned to Cancún at an extra charge. **Alamo**, T946-1623 (airport). **Executive**, Calle 60, down from Gran Hotel. Good value. **Hertz**, Calle 55 No 479, esq 54, T924-2834. Most car hire agencies have an office at the airport and, as all share the same counter, negotiating usually takes place. **MeriCar**, Calle 41 No 504A between 60 and 62, T924-0949. **Maya Car**, Paseo Montejo 486, between 41 and 43, T924-0445. **World Rent a Car**, Calle 60 No 486A, between 55 and 57, T924-0587, US$40.

Car service Servicios de Mérida **Goodyear**, Calle 59, near corner of Av 68. Very helpful and competent, owner speaks English, serves good coffee while you wait for your vehicle. Honest car servicing or quick oil change.

Taxi

There are 2 types: the Volkswagens, which you can flag down, prices range from US$3.50-7; cheaper are the 24-hr radio taxis, T928-5328, or catch 1 from their kiosk on Parque Hidalgo. In both types of taxi, establish fare before journey; there are set prices depending on the distance, the minimum is an expensive US$3.50 even for a few blocks.

Celestún *p453*

Bus Buses leave every 1-2 hrs from the local bus station on Calle 67 between 50 and 52, in Mérida, 2-hr journey, 1st class US$3.50, 2nd class US$3.

Progreso and around *p454*

Boat Boats can be hired to visit the reef of **Los Alacranes** where many ancient wrecks are visible in clear water.

Bus Buses from **Mérida** leave from the small terminal on Calle 62 between 67 and 65, next to Hotel La Paz, every 10 mins. US$0.80 1-way/US$2 return. Return journey every 10 mins until 2200.

Ticul and Oxkutzcab *p455*

Colectivo There are frequent VW *colectivos* to Ticul from Parque San Juan, in **Mérida**, US$2.

Uxmal *p457*

Bus There are 6 buses a day from **Mérida**, from the terminal on Calle 69 between 68 and 70, US$1.80. Return buses run every 2 hrs, but if you've just missed 1, go to the entrance to the site on the main road and wait for a *colectivo*, which will take you to Muná for US$0.50. From there, many buses (US$1.70) and *colectivos* (US$1.40) go to Mérida.

Car Parking at the site costs US$1 for the whole day. Uxmal is 74 km from **Mérida**, 177 km from **Campeche**, by a good paved road. If going by car from Mérida, there is a new circular road round the city: follow the signs to Campeche, then Campeche via ruinas, then to Muná via Yaxcopoil (long stretch of road with no signposting). Muná-Yaxcopoil is about 34 km. Parking US$1.

Izamal and around *p458*

Bus Bus station is on Calle 32 behind government offices, can leave bags. 2nd class to **Mérida**, every 45 mins, 1½ hrs, US$1.50, lovely countryside. Bus station in Mérida, Calle 50 between Calle 65 and 67. 6 a day to/from **Valladolid** (96 km), about 2 hrs, US$2.30-3.

Chichén Itzá *p458*

Bus Chichén Itzá is easily reached from **Mérida** by ADO 2nd class, 2½ hrs, US$4, from 0500, bus station on Calle 71 between 64 and 66. 1st-class bus, US$5.80. Return tickets from the gift shop near entrance to site. Buses drop off and pick up passengers until 1700 at the top of the coach park opposite entrance to *artesanía* market. Many buses a day 0830-1630 go to **Cancún** and **Puerto Juárez**, US$8. The 1st bus from Pisté to Puerto Juárez is at 0730, 3 hrs. ADO bus office in Pisté is between **Stardust** and **Pirámide Inn**. Budget travellers going on from Mérida to Isla Mujeres or Cozumel should visit Chichén from Valladolid (see below), although if you plan to go through in a day you can store luggage at the visitors' centre. Buses from **Valladolid** go every hr to the site, the 0715 bus reaches the ruins at 0800 when they open, and you can return by standing on the main road 1 km from the entrance to the ruins and flagging down any bus going straight through. *Colectivo* entrance-Valladolid, US$2.30. Bus Pisté-**Valladolid** US$1.80; Pisté-**Tulum**, 1 bus only at 1300, US$9. Chichén Itzá-**Tulum**, bus at 0800, 1330, 1445 and 1630, 4 hrs, US$9, very crowded.

Hitchhiking to Mérida is usually no problem.

Valladolid *p461, map p461*
Bus The main bus terminal is on Calle 37 and Calle 54. **Cancún**: Express Oriente, 9 a day, 2½ hrs, US$9, Avante 3 a day, US$8. **Chichén Itzá**: 10 a day, 30 mins, US$2.50. **Izamal**: 2 a day, 2 hrs, US$3.80. **Mérida**: 9 buses a day with various companies, 2½ hrs, US$9 goes via Chichén Itzá. **Playa del Carmen**: 9 a day, 3½ hrs, US$12. **Tizimín** (for Río Lagartos): 10 a day, 2 hrs, US$2 (for some strange reason it costs the same for a return ticket to Tizimín, make sure you ask for it if planning to return to Valladolid). **Tulum**: 1400 and 1550, 2 hrs, US$5.

Río Lagartos and around *p462*
Bus There are 2 terminals side by side in Tizimín. If coming from Valladolid en route to Río Lagartos, you will need to walk to the other terminal. Tizimín-Río Lagartos, 7 per day, 1½ hrs, US$2. To **Valladolid**, 10 per day, 1 hr, US$1.50. To **Mérida**, several daily, 4 hrs, US$4. There are also buses to **Cancún**, **Felipe Carrillo Puerto** and **Chetumal**.

It is possible to get to Río Lagartos and back in a day from **Valladolid**, if you leave on the 0630 or 0730 bus (taxi Tizimín-Río Lagartos US$25, driver may negotiate). Last bus back from Río Lagartos at 1730.

Directory

Mérida *p451, map p452*
Banks Banamex, at Calle 56 and 59 (Mon-Fri 0900-1300, 1600-1700), ATM cash machine. Many banks on Calle 65, off the plaza. Most have ATM cash machines, open 24 hrs. **Cultural centres** Alliance Française, Calle 56 No 476 between 55 and 57. Has a busy programme of events, films (Thu 1900), a library and a *cafetería* open all day. **Embassies and consulates** Belize (also British Vice Consul), Major A Dutton (retd) MBE, Calle 58-53, No 450, T928-6152, 0900-1600. Canada, Av Colón, 309-D, T925-6419. Cuba, Calle 1-D, No 320, between 44 and 4D, T944-4215. Germany, T981-2676. France, T925-2886. Switzerland, T927-2905. US, Paseo Montejo 453 y Av Colón, T925-5011. **Internet** Multitude of internet cafés, most charging US$1-1.50. **Language schools** Instituto de Español, Calle 29, Col México, T927-1683. Modern Spanish Institute, Calle 29 No 128, between 26 and 28, Col México, T927-1683, www.modernspanish.com, courses in Spanish, Maya culture, homestays. **Laundry** Lavandería, Calle 69 No 541, 2 blocks from bus station, about US$4.50 a load, 3-hr service. La Fe, Calle 61, No 518, between Calle 62 and 64. US$4.50 for 3 kg. Highly recommended (shoe repair next door). Self-service hard to find. **Libraries** English library at Calle 53 between 66 and 68. Many books on Mexico, used book for sale, bulletin board, magazines, reading patio. Tue, Thu, Fri 0900-1300, 1400-1900; Mon, Wed, Sat 0900-1300. **Medical services** Hospitals: Centro Médico de las Américas (CMA), Calle 54 No 365 between 33A and Av Pérez Ponce, T926-2619, emergencies T927-3199, affiliated with Mercy Hospital, Miami, Florida, US. IDEM, Calle 66, between 67 and 65, open 24 hrs, specializes in dermatology. Red Cross, T924-9813. **Post office** Calle 65 and 56. Will accept parcels for surface mail to US only, but don't seal parcels destined overseas; they have to be inspected. For surface mail to Europe try Belize, or mail package to US, *poste restante*, for collection later if you are heading that way. An airmail parcel to Europe costs US$15 for 5 kg. Also branches at airport (for quick delivery) or on Calle 58. DHL on Av Colón offers good service, prices comparable to post office prices for air mail packages over 1 kg. **Telephone** International calls possible from central bus station, airport, the shop on the corner of Calle 59 and 64, or public telephones, but not from the main telephone exchange. Phone card and credit card phone booths on squares along Calle 60, but many are out of order. Collect calls can be made on Sat or Sun from the *caseta* opposite central bus station, but beware overcharging (max US$2). Telegrams and faxes from Calle 56, between 65 and 65A (same building as post office, entrance at the

back), Mon-Fri 0700-1900, Sat 0900-1300. **Tel World** offer long-distance fax service from offices on Calle 60 No 486, between 55 and 57.

Izamal and around *p458*
Banks Bank on square with statue to Fray Diego de Landa, south side of convent. **Post office** On opposite side of square to convent.

Chichén Itzá *p458*
Banks ATMs on the main street.
Telephone International calls may be placed from **Teléfonos de México**, opposite Hotel Xaybe. Internet available in Pisté.

Valladolid *p461, map p461*
Banks **Bancomer** on east side of square, changes TCs 0900-1330. **Banco del Atlántico**, corner of Calle 41 and 42, quick service for TCs, from 1000. **Banco del Sureste** has a branch in the shopping centre on Calle 39, 5 blocks west from the plaza. Mon-Fri 0900-2100, Sat and Sun 0900-1400, 1700-1930. **Internet** Internet café, corner of Calle 46 and 37, daily 1000-2100. **Modutel Communication**, Calle 42 No 197, on the plaza, Mon-Sun 0700-2200, US$1.50 per hr. There are many others. **Laundry** Teresita, Calle 33 between 40 and 42, US$6 for 5.5 kg. **Post office** On east side of plaza, 0800-1500 (does not accept parcels for abroad). **Telephone** Telmex phone office on Calle 42, just north of square; expensive **Computel** offices at bus station and next to Hotel San Clemente; **Ladatel** phonecards can be bought from *farmacias* for use in phone booths.

State of Quintana Roo

The burgeoning international destinations of Cancún, Playa del Carmen, Isla Mujeres and Cozumel overshadow the eastern coast of the Yucatán and the State of Quintana Roo. Resorts: you either love them, hate them or simply enjoy the beautiful beaches, package tours and reliable restaurants. If Cancún is your port of entry for a trip through Mexico and Central America, it will certainly make for a good contrast to other regions. Diving in the area is popular, either off the coast of Isla Mujeres or Cozumel, or in the underwater caves or cenotes found in the region. The Maya ruins of Tulum are gloriously located, and the quieter spot of Cobá is worth a trip, as is the wilderness reserve of Sian Ka'an. To the far south, Chetumal seems a world away from the tourist hot spots, but it is the stepping-off point for travel to Belize and Guatemala. ▸▸ *For Sleeping, Eating and other listings, see pages 490-506.*

Isla Holbox → *Phone code: 984. Colour map 4, A3.*

Also north of Valladolid, but in the neighbouring state of Quintana Roo, turn off the road to Puerto Juárez after Nuevo Xcan to Isla Holbox. Buses to **Chiquilá** for boats, three times a day; also direct from Tizimín at 1130, connecting with the ferry, US$2.20. The ferry leaves for Holbox 0600 and 1430, one hour, US$1, returning to Chiquilá at 0500 and 1300. A bus to Mérida connects with the 0500 return ferry. If you miss the ferry a fisherman will probably take you (for about US$14). You can leave your car in the care of the harbour master for a small charge; his house is east of the dock. Take water with you if possible. During 'El Norte' season, the water is turbid and the beach is littered with seaweed.

There are five more uninhabited islands beyond Holbox. Beware of sharks and barracuda, although very few nasty occurrences have been reported. Off the rough and mostly unpopulated bulge of the Yucatán coastline are several islands, once notorious for contraband. Beware of mosquitoes in the area.

Cancún

» pp490-506. Colour map 4, A3.

→ *Phone code: 998.*

In 1970, when Cancún was 'discovered' by the Mexican tourist board, it was an inaccessible strip of barren land with beautiful beaches; the only road went straight past Cancún to Puerto Juárez for the ferry to Isla Mujeres, which had been a national tourist destination since the 1950s. Massive international investment and government sponsorship saw the luxury resort of Cancún completed within 25 years. The 25-km hotel zone, set on a narrow strip of land in the shape of a number seven alongside the coast, is an ultra-modern American-style boulevard, with five-star hotels, high-tech nightclubs, high-class shopping malls and branches of McDonald's, Burger King and Planet Hollywood. It could have been viewed as man's domination of nature to his benefit until Hurricane Wilma bulldozed its way through the Hotel Zone of Cancún. After six months, Cancún has struggled back to its feet (see box, page 475).

Cancún

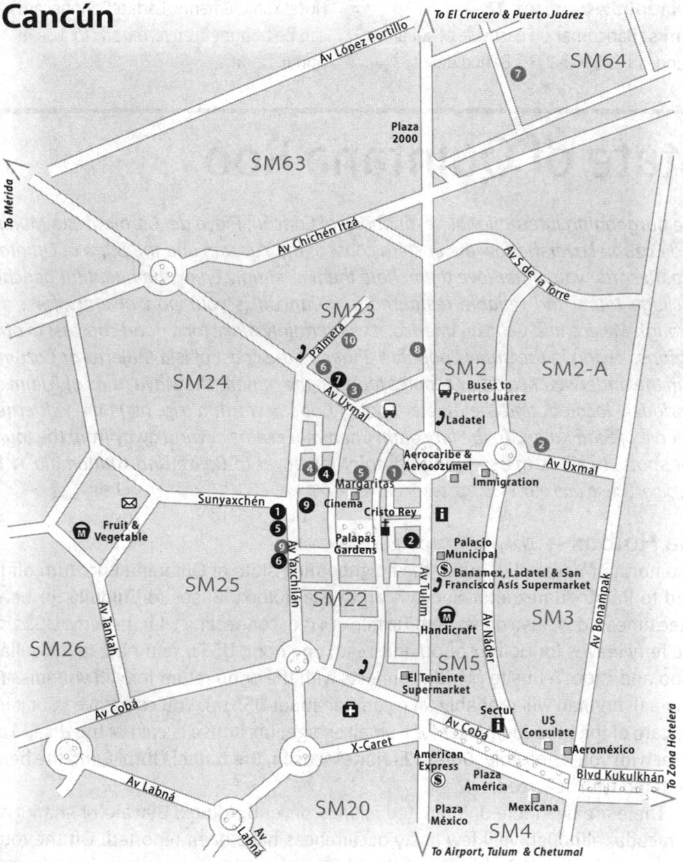

Sleeping
Cancún Rosa **1**
El Alux **3**
El Rey del Caribe **2**
Las Palmas **10**
Margaritas **4**
Mayan Hostel **5**
Mexico Hostel **6**
Piña Hermanos **7**
San Carlos **8**
Villa Rossana **9**

Eating
100% Natural **1**
El Pescalor **2**
La Habichuela **4**
Pastelería Italiana **5**
Pericos **6**
Rincón Yucateco **7**
Villa Rica **9**

Wilma devastates Cancún

On Friday 21 October 2005 Hurricane Wilma smashed into the Yucatán Peninsula. Thousands of tourists and local residents took shelter as winds up to 175 mph pounded the coast for three days.

Wilma hit land at Cozumal and damaged an area stretching from Tulum in the south to Isla Holbox in the north, killing at least six people and destroying thousands of homes and hotels in its path.

Shortly after the hurricane had moved on, Tourism Secretary Rodolfo Elizondo estimated the area would lose up to US$800 million in tourism revenue over the next two months.

Reconstruction began very quickly, as hotels tried to open for the official start of the tourism season; most failed to hit the December deadline. The rebuilding of the beach cost almost US$22 million and was completed in April 2006, by which time many of the resort's 28,000 hotel rooms were back in operation.

However, the low-lying jungle along the road between Cancún and Tulum will take at least five years to grow back. And that's not the end of the story. Several category five hurricanes are forecast for the 2006 season, and further destruction seems inevitable.

Love or hate Cancún, its presence on the international tourism market is indisputable. From all-in-one package tours to international government conferences, Cancún has an enviable record. It's worth a trip just to see what it's like. Jump on a Ruta 1 or Ruta 2 bus and ride it as far you like. You'll quickly see the international hotel chains with hundreds of rooms, packed along the sinuous sand bar. Spotted along the way Hotel Zone international shopping brands, restaurants and entertainment centres provide the complete holiday experience.

Ins and outs

Getting there Cancún airport is 16 km south of the city. A *colectivo* taxi to the **Hotel Zone** or the centre costs US$9; pay at the kiosk outside airport. Drivers go via the Hotel Zone, but must take you to whichever part of the city centre you want. If going to the centre, make sure you know the name and address of your hotel before you get in the taxi, or the driver will offer to take you to a budget hotel of his own choice. Buses go to the centre via Avenida Tulum every 30 minutes from the airport. Taxi to the airport from the centre, US$10. Buses go from several stops, marked 'Aeropuerto', along Avenida Tulum, catch the bus from the centre road, every 30 minutes, US$0.50. There is a tourist information kiosk in the airport, and a *casa de cambio*.

Getting around Ruta 1 and Ruta 2 buses go from the centre to the Hotel Zone, US$0.60; Ruta 1 runs 24 hours and goes via Avenida Tulum; Ruta 2 runs 0500-0330 and goes via Avenida Cobá to the bus terminal. Buses to the Hotel Zone can be caught from many stops along Avenida Tulum. Buses to **Puerto Juárez** for the boat to Isla Mujeres leave from outside **Cinema Royal**, across Avenida Tulum from the bus terminal, US$0.55. To get around in the centre, board a bus at Plaza 2000 and ask the driver if he's going to Mercado 28; those buses go along Avenida Yaxchilán; all others go to the Hotel Zone. Taxis are cheap and abundant in Cancún. Flat rate for anywhere within the centre is US$1-1.50; Hotel Zone from centre US$3; Puerto Juárez US$3. Many taxis stop at **El Crucero**, the junction of Avenida Tulum and Avenida López Portillo outside Plaza 2000, but there are often queues.

Downtown Cancún is a world apart from the Hotel Zone. It evolved from temporary shacks housing the thousands of builders working on the Hotel Zone, and is now a massive city with very little character. The main avenue is Tulum, formerly the highway running through the city when it was first conceived. It is now the location of the handicraft market, the main shops, banks and the municipal tourist office. There are also restaurants, but the better ones are along Avenida Yaxchilán, which is also the main centre for nightlife.

The cheaper end of the city, and a good area for budget travellers to base themselves, is around **El Crucero** (see above). The rest of the city is fairly expensive, but not as much as the Hotel Zone. The city is laid out in *supermanzanas* (SM), the blocks of streets between avenues, with smaller *manzanas* (M), or blocks, within them. Often the address you are given is, for example, SM24, M6, L3. L stands for *lote*, and is the precise number of the building within its *manzana*. This can lead to confusion when walking about, as the streets also have names, often not mentioned in the addresses. Look closely at street signs and you will see the SM and the M numbers. Taxi drivers generally respond better to addresses based on the *manzana* system.

Tourist information The **tourist office** ⓘ *Av Tulum 26, www.qroo.gob.mx, in a building that also houses local government offices*, is not very helpful; you'll get a glossy pocket guide to Cancún full of adverts for expensive restaurants. There is a new and well-equipped office at the **Conventions and Visitor Bureau** ⓘ *corner of Av Cobá and Av Bonampak, T884-6531*. Here the staff are helpful and friendly with information on new attractions, hotels and excursions.

Around Cancún

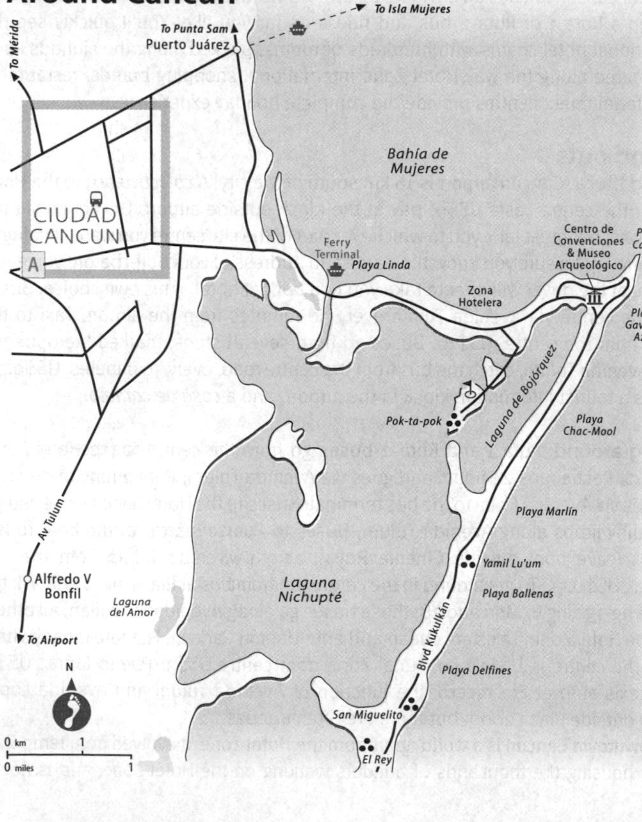

Cancún to Isla Mujeres

A strip of coastline north of **Punta Sam** is officially part of Isla Mujeres. It is being developed as a luxury resort, but without the high-rise buildings of Cancún's Hotel Zone.

Puerto Juárez, about 3 km north of Cancún, is the dock for the cheaper ferry services to Isla Mujeres; there is also a bus terminal, but services are more frequent from Cancún. There are many buses between Cancún and Puerto Juárez, for example No 8 opposite the bus terminal (US$0.70). A taxi from Puerto Juárez to Downtown Cancún should be no more than US$2.

Isla Mujeres

» *pp490-506. Colour map 4, A3.*

→ *Phone code: 998.*

A refreshing antidote to the urban sprawl of Cancún, Isla Mujeres is a good place to relax for a few days away from the hurly-burly of package tourism. The island is especially nice in the evening, when all the Cancún day trippers have gone. The town is strictly low-rise, with brightly coloured buildings giving it a Caribbean island feel. The island's laws prohibit the construction of any building higher than three floors, and US franchises such as **McDonald's** and **Walmart** are not allowed to open branches here.

There are several good beaches on Isla Mujeres, the best being **Playa Cocos** on the northwest coast, five minutes' walk from the town. Further south, there are several places to swim, snorkel and observe marine life. Restaurants and nightspots are plentiful, good quality and cheaper than those on the mainland, and the people are friendlier. There are several ways to explore the island: you can rent a golf cart, many of which chug around the streets all day, good for families; mopeds and bicycles are cheap and plentiful to rent, and a public bus runs all the way from the town to El Paraíso, almost at the southern tip of the island.

The name Isla Mujeres refers to the large number of clay female idols found by the Spaniards here in 1518. The island contains the only known Maya shrine to a female deity: Ixchel, goddess of the moon and fertility. The ruins of the shrine are at the southern tip of the island. The **tourist office** ⓘ *Rueda Medina, opposite the ferry dock, Mon-Fri 0900-2100, Sat 0900-1400, www.isla-mujeres.net*, is very helpful. The immigration office is next door.

In October there is a festival of music, with groups from Mexico and the US performing in the main square, and from 1-12 December, during the fiesta for the Virgin of Guadalupe, there are fireworks and dances until 0400 in the plaza.

Sights

Most of the sights south of the town can be seen in a day. The first of these, 5 km from the town, is the **Turtle Farm** ⓘ *T877-0595, daily 0900-1700, US$2*, with hundreds of sea turtles weighing from 170 g to 270 kg in a humane setting. To get there, take the bus to the final stop, Playa Paraíso, double back and walk five minutes along the main road.

At the centre of the island are the curious remains of a pirate's domain, called **Casa de Mundaca** ⓘ *daily 0900-1700, US$1*. A big, new arch gate marks its entrance. Paths have been laid out among the large trees, but all that remains of the estate (called Vista Alegre) are one small building and a circular garden with raised beds, a well and a gateway. Fermín Mundaca, more of a slave-trader than a buccaneer, built Vista Alegre for the teenage girl he loved. She rejected him and he died, broken-hearted, in Mérida. His epitaph there reads *Como eres, yo fui; como soy, tu serás* ('What you are I was; what I am you shall be'). See the poignant little carving on the garden side of the gate, *La entrada de La Trigueña* (the girl's nickname). To get there, get off the bus at the final stop, and turn the opposite way to the beach; the house is a short walk away.

El Garrafón ⓘ *T877-1100*, is a snorkelling centre 7 km from the town, being developed into a luxury resort in the style of Xcaret on the mainland. Snorkelling is still possible (US$15, lockers US$2, plus deposit, equipment rental available). There is a 12-m bronze cross submerged offshore, trips to snorkel around it cost US$13 (1½ hours, no lunch). There is an expensive restaurant and bar at El Garrafón, and a small beach. The snorkelling is good past the pier, along a reef with some dead coral. Large numbers of different coloured fish can be seen at very close range. If you want to walk to El Garrafón from the bus stop at Playa Paraíso, take the second path on the right to the beach from the main road. The first path leads through **Restaurant Playa Paraíso**, which charges US$1 for the privilege of walking through their premises to the beach. Playa Paraíso is an expensive mini-resort for Cancún day-trippers; there is a swimming-with-sharks option, during which harmless nurse sharks are treated cruelly so that tourists can have their picture taken with them. Once on the beach, you can walk all the way to El Garrafón along the coast, although it gets very rocky for the final part. It is easier to go as far as the cluster of beach villas, then cut through one of them (ask for permission) to the main road. The whole walk takes about half an hour. When you arrive at El Garrafón, turn right at the building site, go down the hill to **Hotel Garrafón** del Castillo, which is the entrance to the snorkelling centre.

A further 15 minutes' walk from El Garrafón, at the tip of the island, are the ruins of the Maya shrine **Santuario Maya a la Diosa Ixchel**, dedicated to Ixchel the goddess of fertility. Unfortunately, these are no longer free to visit. They have been bought and developed as part of the **El Garrafón 'National Park'** ⓘ *US$5.50*. A cultural centre has also been built here with large sculptures by several international artists.

South of Cancún

» pp490-506. Colour map 4, A3.

Puerto Morelos → *Phone code: 998.*

A quiet little village 34 km south of Cancún, Puerto Morelos is one of the few places that still retains some of the charm of an unspoilt fishing village (but not for much longer!), making it a good place to stop over en route to larger towns further south, such as Playa del Carmen. The village is really just a large plaza right on the seafront with a couple of streets going off it. If on arrival at Cancún airport you don't wish to spend the night in the city, you could get a taxi directly to Puerto Morelos. This is also the place to catch the car ferry to the island of Cozumel (see below). The **Sinaltur** office on the plaza offers a range of good snorkelling, kayak and fishing trips. **Goyos**, just north of the plaza, offers jungle adventures and rooms for rent, although erratic hours are maintained.

Playa del Carmen → *Phone code: 984.*

What used to be a pleasant little town on the beach has lost the charms of its former existence as a fishing village. Recent development for tourism has been rapid, but Playa, as it is known locally, has not had the high-rise treatment of Cancún. The beach is dazzling white, with crystal-clear shallow water, ideal for swimming, and further out there is good scuba diving. There is lodging for every budget, and plenty of good restaurants and bars of every type. Many travellers choose Playa as their base for trips to the ruins of Tulum in the south, and archaeological sites such as Cobá in the interior.

The town is laid out in a grid system, with the main centre of tourist activity based on Avenida 5 (pedestrianized in the central section at night between 1800 and 0200), one block from and parallel with the beach. This is where the more expensive hotels and restaurants are, as well as being the centre for nightlife. Cheaper accommodation can be found up Avenida Juárez and further north of the beach.

Tourist information is scant, although there is a new **tourism office** ⓘ *corner of Av Juárez and Av 15, T873-0263*, which has useful information and maps, and the kiosk on the main plaza will provide a copy of *Destination Playa del Carmen*, a useful guide with maps produced by US residents.

Cozumel

» pp490-506. Colour map 4, A3.

→ *Phone code: 987.*

The town, San Miguel de Cozumel, is a seedy, overpriced version of Playa del Carmen. Daily tour groups arrive on cruises from Miami and Cancún, and the town's services seem geared towards this type of tourist. But Cozumel is a mecca for scuba divers, with many beautiful offshore reefs to explore, as well as much interesting wildlife and birdlife. Travellers looking for a beach holiday with some nightlife will find the island disappointing compared to Playa del Carmen. There is only one nice beach on the west side, and the eastern, Atlantic coast is far too rugged and choppy for swimming.

Playa del Carmen

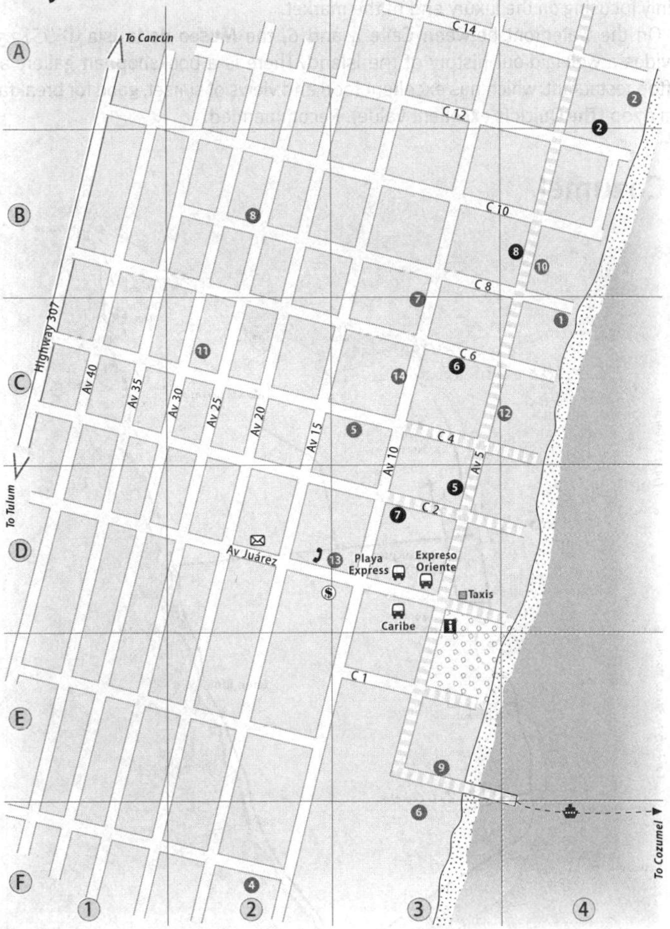

Sleeping
Alhambra 1 *C4*
Blue Parrot 2 *A4*
Cabañas Tuxatah 4 *F2*
Casa Tucán 5 *C3*
Continental Plaza Playacar 6 *F3*
Happy Gecko 7 *B3*
Hostel Playa 8 *B2*
Las Molcas 9 *E3*
Maya Bric & Tank-Ha Diving 10 *B4*
Mom's & Restaurant 11 *C2*
Posada Las Flores 12 *C4*
Posada Marinelly 13 *D2*
Urban Hostel 14 *C3*

Eating
Buenos Aires 6 *C3*
Da Gabi 2 *A4*
Le Bistro 7 *D3*
Media Luna 8 *B4*
Pez Vela 5 *D3*

N

0 metres 100
0 yards 100

Ins and outs

The airport is just north of San Miguel with a minibus shuttle service to the hotels. There are 10-minute flights to and from the airstrip near Playa del Carmen, as well as flights linking to Mexico City, Cancún, Chichén Itzá and Houston (Texas). The passenger ferry from Playa del Carmen runs every two hours (see above), and the car ferry leaves twice daily from Puerto Morelos (see page 478). There are no local buses, but Cozumel town is small enough to visit on foot. To get around the island, there are organized tours or taxis; otherwise, hire a jeep, moped or bicycle.

San Miguel de Cozumel

The island's only town has very little character, mainly due to the construction of a US air base during the Second World War, whose airfield has now been converted for civilian use. There is a variety of accommodation, with a few budget hotels, but mainly focusing on the luxury end of the market.

On the waterfront between Calle 4 and 6, the **Museo de la Isla** ⓘ *US$3.30*, provides a well-laid-out history of the island. There is a bookshop, art gallery and rooftop restaurant, which has excellent food and views of sunset, good for breakfast, from 0700 (**The Quick** is excellent value). Recommended.

Cozumel

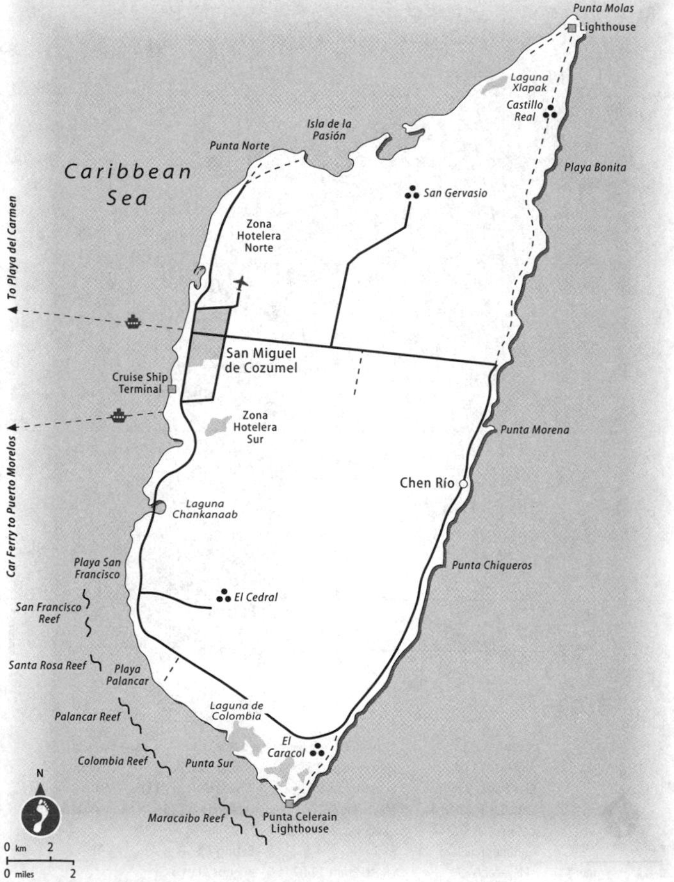

Beaches

In the north of the island the beaches are sandy and wide, although those at the Zona Hotelera Norte were damaged in 1989 and are smaller than they used to be. At the end of the paved road, walk up the unmade road until it becomes 'dual carriageway'; turn left for the narrow beach, which is a bit dirty. Cleaner beaches are accessible only through the hotels. South of San Miguel, **San Francisco** is good if narrow (clean, very popular, lockers at **Pancho's**, expensive restaurants), but others are generally narrower still and rockier. All the main hotels are on the sheltered west coast. The east, Caribbean coast is rockier, but very picturesque; swimming and diving on the unprotected side is very dangerous owing to ocean underflows. The only safe place is at a sheltered bay at **Chen Río**. Another bay with possibilities is **Punta Morena**, which is a good surf beach, there is good accommodation (contact Matt at **Deep Blue**, on Salas 200, for more information and transport) and seafood (try the *ceviche*). Three good (and free) places for snorkelling are: the beach in front of **Hotel Las Glorias**, 15 minutes' walk south from ferry (you can walk through the hotel's reception); **Playa Corona**, further south, is too far to walk, so hitch or take a taxi (there is a small restaurant and pier); and **Xul-Ha**, further south still, which has a bar and comfortable beach chairs.

The best public beaches are some way from San Miguel town.

Archaeological sites

There are some 32 archaeological sites on Cozumel; those on the east coast are mostly single buildings (thought to have been lookouts, navigational aids). The easiest to see are the restored ruins of the Maya-Toltec period at **San Gervasio** ⓘ *0700-1700, US$3.50, guides are on hand, or you can buy a self-guiding booklet at the bookshop on the square in San Miguel, or at the flea market, for US$1*. It is in the

San Miguel de Cozumel

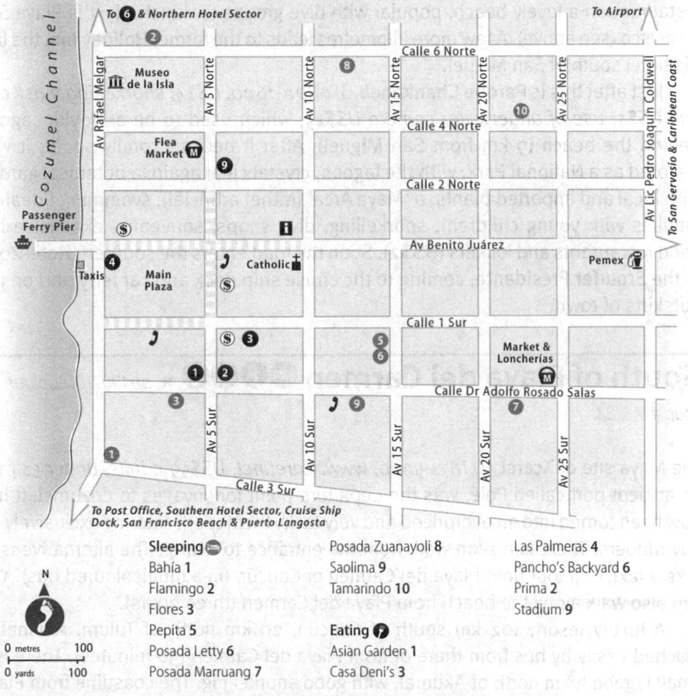

north of the island (7 km from Cozumel town, then 6 km to the left up a paved road, toll US$1), an interesting site, quite spread out, with *sacbés* (sacred roads) between the groups of buildings. There are no large structures, but a nice plaza, an arch, and pigment can be seen in places. It is also a pleasant place to listen to birdsong, see butterflies, animals (if lucky), lizards, landcrabs and insects. **Castillo Real** is one of many sites on the northeastern coast, but the road to this part of the island is in very bad condition and the ruins themselves are very small. **El Cedral** in the southwest (3 km from the main island road) is a two-room temple, overgrown with trees, in the centre of the village of the same name. Behind the temple is a ruin, and next to it a modern church with a green and white façade (an incongruous pairing). In the village are large, permanent shelters for agricultural shows, rug sellers and locals who pose with *iguanas doradas* (golden iguanas). **El Caracol**, where the sun, in the form of a shell, was worshipped, is 1 km from the southernmost Punta Celarain. At Punta Celarain is an old lighthouse.

Around the island

A circuit of the island on paved roads can easily be done in a day (see Local transport below). Head due east out of San Miguel (take the continuation of Avenida Juárez). Make the detour to San Gervasio before continuing to the Caribbean coast at **Mescalito's** restaurant. Here, turn left for the northern tip (road unsuitable for ordinary vehicles), or right for the south, passing Punta Morena, Chen Río, Punta Chiqueros (restaurant, bathing), El Mirador (a low viewpoint with sea-worn rocks, look out for holes) and Paradise Cove. At this point, the paved road heads west while an unpaved road continues south to Punta Celarain. Here there is the **Punta Sur Ecological Reserve** ⓘ *T872-0914, www.cozumelparks.com.mx*, an ecotourism development, with a variety of natural landscapes with lagoons and mangrove jungles. A snorkelling centre has opened here as well as a viewing platform. On the road west, opposite the turn-off to El Cedral, is a sign to **Restaurante Mac y Cía,** an excellent fish restaurant on a lovely beach, popular with dive groups for lunch. Next is Playa San Francisco (see above). A few more kilometres leads to the former **Holiday Inn,** the last big hotel south of San Miguel.

Just after this is **Parque Chankanab** ⓘ *0800-1600, US$4, snorkelling mask and fins US$5, use of underwater camera US$25,* which used to be an idyllic lagoon behind the beach (9 km from San Miguel). After it became totally spoilt, it was restored as a National Park, with the lagoon, crystal clear again, a botanical garden with local and imported plants, a 'Maya Area' (rather artificial), swimming (ideal for families with young children), snorkelling, dive shops, souvenirs, expensive but good restaurants and lockers (US$2). Soon the road enters the southern Hotel Zone at the **Stouffer Presidente,** coming to the cruise ship dock and car ferry port on the outskirts of town.

South of Playa del Carmen

» *pp490-506. Colour map 4, A3/B3.*

The Maya site of **Xcaret** ⓘ *T871-5200, www.xcaret.net, US$59 adults, under 5s free,* an ancient port called Polé, was the departure point for voyages to Cozumel. It has now been turned into an overpriced and very tacky themepark catering exclusively for day-trippers. There is a 1-km walk from the entrance to Xcaret. The alternative is to take a taxi, or a tour from Playa del Carmen or Cancún (in a multicoloured bus). You can also walk along the beach from Playa del Carmen (three hours).

A luxury resort, 102 km south of Cancún, 20 km north of Tulum, **Akumal** is reached easily by bus from there or from Playa del Carmen (30 minutes). There is a small lagoon 3 km north of Akumal, with good snorkelling. The coastline from Playa

Cenote diving

There are more than 50 *cenotes* in this area – accessible from Ruta 307 and often well signposted – and cave diving has become very popular. However, it is a specialized sport and, unless you have a cave diving qualification, you must be accompanied by a qualified dive master. A cave diving course involves over 12 hours of lectures and a minimum of 14 cave dives using double tanks, costing around US$600. Accompanied dives start at around US$60. Specialist dive centres offering courses are: Mike Madden's **CEDAM Dive Centres**, PO Box 1, Puerto Aventuras, T/F873-5129; **Aquatech**, Villas de Rosa, PO Box 25, **Aventuras Akumal No 35**, Tulum, T875-9020, www.cenotes.com; **Aktun Dive Centre**, PO Box 119, Tulum, T871-2311, www.aktundive.com, and **Cenote Dive Center**, Tulum, T871-2232, www.cenotedive.com, Norwegian owned.

Some of the best *cenotes* are 'Carwash', on the Cobá road, good even for beginners, with excellent visibility; 'Dos Ojos', just off Ruta 307 south of Aventuras, the second largest underground cave system in the world; it has a possible link to the Nohoch Nah Chich, the most famous cenote and part of a subterranean system recorded as the world's largest, with over 50 km of surveyed passageways connected to the sea.

A word of warning: *cenote* diving has a higher level of risk than open water diving – do not take risks and only dive with recognized operators.

del Carmen down to just short of Tulum to the south is known as the 'Riviera Maya' – a strip of upmarket, generally all-inclusive hotels. Two ferries run daily to Cozumel. Also just south of Akumal are **Chemuyil** (*palapas*, thatched shelters for hammocks, US$4, free shower, expensive restaurant, laundry facilities) and **Xcacel** (campground has water, bathrooms, cold showers and restaurant, very clean, US$2 per person, vehicles free, snorkel hire US$5 a day, beautiful swimming in the bay). Ask guards if you can go on turtle protection patrol at night (May-July).

Thirteen kilometres north of Tulum, 122 km from Cancún (bus from Playa del Carmen, 45 minutes), the beautiful clear lagoon of **Laguna Xel-Há** ⓘ *daily 0800-1630, US$10,* is full of fish, but fishing is not allowed as it is a national park. Snorkelling gear can be rented at US$7 for a day, but it is often in poor repair; better to rent from your hotel. Lockers cost US$1. Arrive as early as possible tó see fish as the lagoon is full of tourists throughout most of the day. Snorkelling areas are limited by fencing. Bungalows, first-class hotels and fast-food restaurants are being built. The food and drink is very expensive. There is a marvellous jungle path to one of the lagoon bays. Xel-Há ruins, known also as **Los Basadres** ⓘ *US$3.35,* are located across the road from the beach of the same name. Few tourists but not much to see. You may have to jump the fence to visit; there is a beautiful *cenote* at the end of the ruins where you can have a lovely swim.

Tulum → *Phone code: 984. Colour map 4, A3.*

ⓘ *Daily 0800-1800, entry US$3.50, parking US$1.50, students with Mexican ID free.*
The Maya-Toltec ruins of Tulum are perched on coastal cliffs in a beautiful setting above the azure sea. The ruins are 12th century, with city walls of white stone. The temples were dedicated to the worship of the Falling God, or the Setting Sun, represented as a falling character over nearly all the west-facing doors (Cozumel was the home of the Rising Sun). The same idea is reflected in the buildings, which are wider at the top than at the bottom.

The main structure is the **Castillo,** which commands a view of both the sea and the forested Quintana Roo lowlands stretching westwards. All the Castillo's openings face west, as do most, but not all, of the doorways at Tulum. Look for the alignment of the **Falling God** on the temple of that name (to the left of the Castillo) with the pillar and the back door in the **House of the Chultún** (the nearest building in the centre group to the entrance). The majority of the main structures are roped off so that you cannot climb the Castillo, nor get close to the surviving frescoes, especially on the **Temple of the Frescoes**.

Tulum is crowded with tourists (best time to visit is between 0800 and 0900). Take towel and swimsuit if you wish to scramble down from the ruins to one of the two beaches for a swim (the larger of the two is less easy to get to). The reef is from 600 m to 1000 m from the shore, so if you wish to snorkel you must either be a strong swimmer, or take a boat trip.

There is a tourist complex at the entrance to the ruins. Guide books can be bought in the shops, local guides can also be hired. About two hours are needed to view at leisure. The parking area is near Highway 307, and there's a handicraft market. A small train takes you from the parking area to the ruins for US$1, or it is an easy 500 m walk. The paved road continues down the coast to **Boca Paila** and beyond, access by car to this road from the car park is now forbidden. To reach the road south of the ruins, access is possible 1 km from Tulum village. Public buses drop passengers at El Crucero, a crossroads 500 m north of the car park for Tulum Ruinas (an easy walk) where there is an ADO bus terminal that is open for a few hours from 0800; at the crossroads are some hotels, a shop (will exchange traveller's cheques), on the opposite side of the road a naval base and airstrip, and a little way down Highway 307 a Pemex station.

If staying in the area, the beach running south of the ruins is dotted with quiet, isolated *palapas*, *cabañas* and hotels to fit most budgets. Alternatively the village of **Tulum** (as opposed to the ruins) is 4 km south of El Crucero. A taxi from the village to the ruins costs US$2.50. It is not very large but is growing rapidly and has a bus station, post office, bank (HSBC), several grocery shops, two bakeries, hotels and restaurants. There is a **tourist information office** in the village, next to the police station, two blocks north of the bus terminal. The information centre set up by the *Weary Traveller* backpacker centre has taken over as the primary source of information for this area. Located at the southern end of town a block away from the ADO bus terminal. Friendly and knowledgeable staff give fairly impartial information on hotels, excursions and restaurants. Another source of information is the **Sian Ka'an Information Centre** ⓘ *Av Tulum between Satélite and Géminis, Tulum, T/F871-2363, siankaan_tours@hotmail.com*, which has information about visiting the reserve (see below) and several other areas of interest.

! When arriving by bus, get off at El Crucero for the ruins and nearby accommodation.

Cobá → *Colour map 4, A3.*

ⓘ *Daily 0800-1700, US$3.50.*

An important Maya city in the eighth and ninth centuries AD, whose population is estimated to have been between 40,000 and 50,000, Cobá was abandoned for unknown reasons. The present-day village of Cobá lies on either side of Lago Cobá, surrounded by dense jungle, 47 km inland from Tulum. It is a quiet, friendly village, with few tourists staying overnight.

The entrance to the ruins of this large but little-excavated city is at the end of the lake between the two parts of the village. A second lake, **Lago Macanxoc**, is within the site. There are turtles and many fish in the lakes. It is a good birdwatching area. Both lakes and their surrounding forest can be seen from the summit of the **Iglesia**, the tallest structure in the **Cobá Group**. There are three other groups of buildings to visit: the **Macanxoc Group**, mainly stelae, about 1.5 km from the Cobá Group; **Las Pinturas**, 1 km northeast of Macanxoc, with a temple and the remains of other buildings that had columns in their construction; the **Nohoch Mul Group**, at least another kilometre from Las Pinturas. Nohoch Mul has the tallest pyramid in the northern Yucatán, a magnificent structure, from which the views of the jungle on all sides are superb. You will not find at Cobá the great array of buildings that can be seen at Chichén Itzá or Uxmal, nor the compactness of Tulum. Instead, the delight of the place is the architecture in the jungle, with birds, butterflies, spiders and lizards, and the many uncovered structures that hint at the vastness of the city in its heyday (the urban

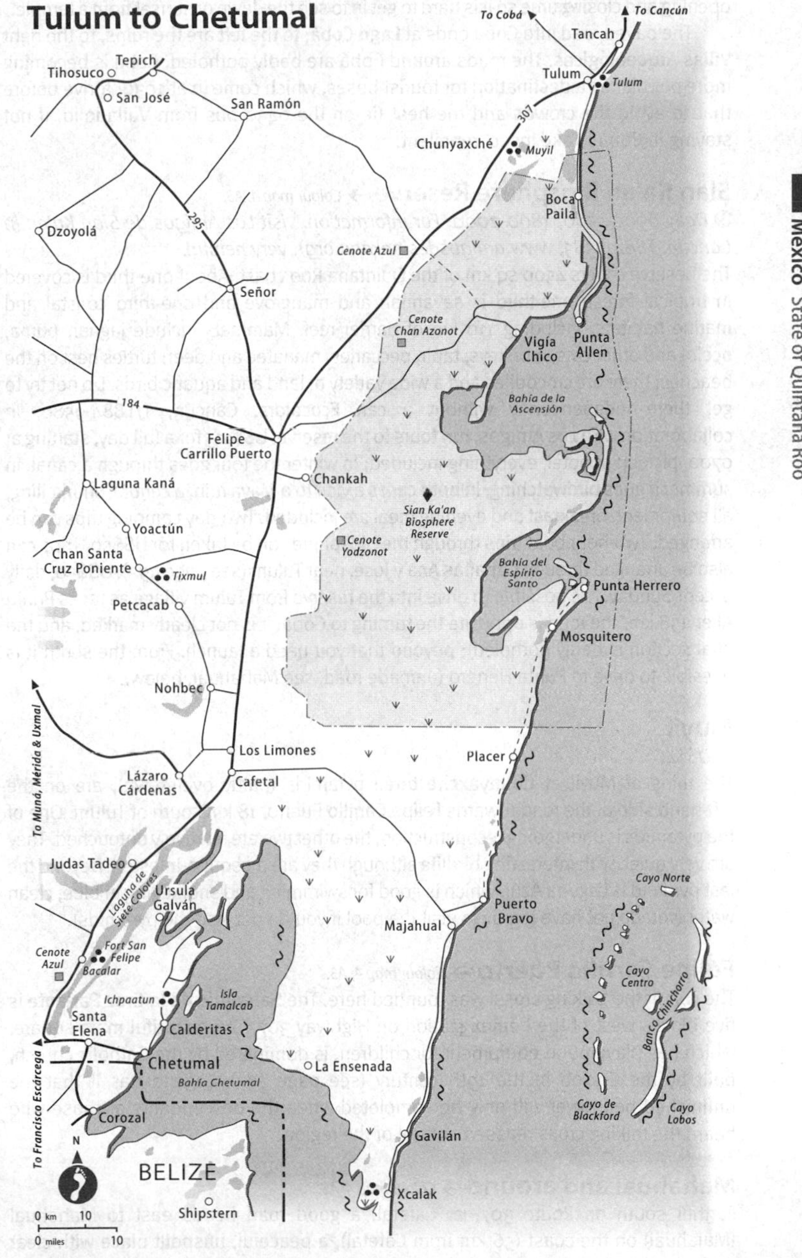

Tulum to Chetumal

extension of Cobá is put at some 70 sq km). An unusual feature is the network of ancient roads, known as *sacbés* (sacred roads), which connect the groups in the site and are known to have extended across the entire Maya Yucatán. Over 40 *sacbés* pass through Cobá, some local, some of great length, such as the 100-km road to Yaxuná in Yucatán state.

At the lake, toucans may be seen very early; also look out for greenish-blue and brown mot-mots in the early morning. The guards at the site are very strict about opening and closing time so it is hard to get in to see the dawn or sunset from a temple.

The paved road into Cobá ends at **Lago Cobá**; to the left are the ruins, to the right **Villas Arqueológicas**. The roads around Cobá are badly potholed. Cobá is becoming more popular as a destination for tourist buses, which come in at 1030; arrive before that to avoid the crowds and the heat (ie on the 0430 bus from Valladolid, if not staying in Cobá). Take insect repellent.

Sian Ka'an Biosphere Reserve → *Colour map 4, A3.*

ⓘ *Daily 0900-1500, 1800-2000. For information, visit Los Amigos de Sian Ka'an in Cancún, T884-9583, www.amigosdesiankaan.org); very helpful.*

The Reserve covers 4500 sq km of the Quintana Roo coast. About one-third is covered in tropical forest, one-third is savannah and mangrove and one-third coastal and marine habitats, including 110 km of barrier reef. Mammals include jaguar, puma, ocelot and other cats, monkeys, tapir, peccaries, manatee and deer; turtles nest on the beaches; there are crocodiles and a wide variety of land and aquatic birds. Do not try to get there independently without a car. **Ecocolors**, Cancún, T/F884-9580, in collaboration with **Los Amigos**, run tours to the reserve, US$115 for a full day, starting at 0700, pick up at hotel, everything included; in winter the tour goes through a canal, in summer it goes birdwatching, in both cases a visit to a Maya ruin, a *cenote*, snorkelling, all equipment, breakfast and evening meal are included. Two-day camping trips can be arranged. Two-hour boat trips through the biosphere can be taken for US$50. Trips can also be arranged through **Cabañas Ana y José**, near Tulum (see page 493), US$50, daily except Sunday. It is possible to drive into the reserve from Tulum village as far as Punta Allen (58 km; the road is opposite the turning to Cobá; it is not clearly marked, and the final section is badly potholed); beyond that you need a launch. From the south it is possible to drive to Punta Herrero (unmade road, see Mahahual, below).

Muyil

ⓘ *US$4.*

The ruins of Muyil at **Chunyaxché** three pyramids (partly overgrown), are on the left-hand side of the road towards Felipe Carrillo Puerto, 18 km south of Tulum. One of the pyramids is undergoing reconstruction; the other two are relatively untouched. They are very quiet, with interesting birdlife although they are mosquito-infested. Beyond the last pyramid is Laguna Azul, which is good for swimming and snorkelling in blue, clean water (you do not have to pay to visit the pool if you do not visit the pyramids).

Felipe Carrillo Puerto → *Colour map 4, A3.*

The cult of the 'talking cross' was founded here. The **Santuario de la Cruz Parlante** is five blocks west of the Pemex station on Highway 307. The beautiful main square, which has playground equipment for children, is dominated by the Catholic church, built by the Cruzob in the 19th century (see page 437). Legend has it that the unfinished bell tower will only be completed when the descendants of those who heard the talking cross reassert control of the region.

Mahahual and around → *Colour map 4, A3.*

Further south on Route 307, at Cafetal, a good road heads east to Mahahual (Majahual) on the coast (56 km from Cafetal), a peaceful, unspoilt place with clear water and beautiful beaches. The cruise ship dock gives a clue to the occassional interruption to the peace and calm with Mahahual welcoming cruise ships travelling up and down the Mexican and Central American coast. A combi leaves from downtown at 0600, and from the bus terminal in Chetumal at 0600 and 1515, returning at 0630, 0845 and 1600. An offshore excursion is possible to **Banco Chinchorro**, where there is a coral bank and a white-sand beach.

About 2 km before Mahahual a paved road to the left goes to **Puerto Bravo** and on to Placer and **Punta Herrero** (in the Sian Ka'an Biosphere Reserve, see above).

Just over 3 km along this road a right turn goes to the **Sol y Mar** restaurant, with rooms to rent, coconut palms and beach. Another 10.5 km along the Punta Herrero road, again on the right, is **Camidas Trailer Park**, see Sleeping, page 494.

Xcalak → *Colour map 4, B3.*

Across the bay from Chetumal, at the very tip of Quintana Roo, is Xcalak, which may be reached from Chetumal by private launch (two hours), or by the unpaved road from Cafetal to Mahahual, then turning south for 55 km (186 km by road from Chetumal, suitable for passenger cars but needs skilled driver). *Colectivos* from Chetumal, daily 0700-1900, 16 de Septiembre 183 y Mahatma Ghandi, check return times. Bus runs Friday 1600 and Sunday 0600, returning Saturday morning and Sunday afternoon (details from Chetumal tourist office). Xcalak is a fishing village with a few shops selling beer and basic supplies and one small restaurant serving Mexican food. A few kilometres north of Xcalak are two hotels, **Costa de Cocos** and **Villa Caracol**, both American run; the latter is good, with comfortable *cabañas*, although expensive. From here trips can be arranged to the unspoiled islands of Banco Chinchorro or to San Pedro, Belize. **Villa Caracol** has sport fishing and diving facilities. In the village you may be able to rent a boat to explore Chetumal Bay and Banco Chinchorro. Do *not* try to walk from Xcalak along the coast to San Pedro, Belize; the route is virtually impassable.

Chetumal

» *pp490-506. Colour map 4, B3.*

→ *Phone code: 983.*

The state capital of Quintana Roo, Chetumal, is a necessary stopover for travellers en route to Maya sites in the south of the peninsula, and across the frontier to Belize and Guatemala. Although attractions are thin on the ground, Chetumal does have the advantage of being a small Mexican city not devoted to tourism, and thus has a more authentic feel than other towns on the Riviera Maya. It is 240 km south of Tulum. The Chetumal bay has been designated a natural protected area for manatees, and includes a manatee sanctuary.

The avenues are broad, busy and in the centre lined with huge shops selling cheap imported goods. The main local activity is window-shopping, and the atmosphere is more like a North American city, with an impression of affluence that can be a culture shock to the visitor arriving from the much poorer country of Guatemala. The **tourist office** ⓘ *Av Miguel Hidalgo 22, 1st floor, esq Carmen Ochoa de Merino*, is mainly for trade enquiries. There is very little tourist information in Chetumal; it is usually best to go to a travel agent such as **Tu-Maya** (see page 500).

The *paseo* near the waterfront on Sunday night is worth seeing. The State Congress building has a mural showing the history of Quintana Roo. The **Museo de la Cultura Maya** ⓘ *Av Héroes de Chapultepec by the market, Tue-Thu and Sun 0900-1900, Fri and Sat 0900-2000, US$5*, is highly recommended. It has good models of sites and touchscreen computers explaining the Maya calendar and glyphs. Although there are few original Maya pieces, it gives an excellent overview; some explanations are in English, guided tours are available, and there's a good bookshop with English magazines.

Around Chetumal » pp490-506.

Towards Bacalar

Six kilometres north of Chetumal are the stony beaches of **Calderitas**, bus every 30 minutes from Colón, between Belice and Héroes, US$1.80, or taxi US$5, many fish restaurants. Camping at Calderitas, signposted, OK, US$2.75. Beyond are the unexcavated archaeological sites of **Ichpaatun** (13 km), **Oxtancah** (14 km) and **Nohochmul** (20 km). Sixteen kilometres north on Route 307 to Tulum is the **Laguna de los Milagros**, a beautiful lagoon for swimming. Further on, 34 km north of Chetumal, is **Cenote Azul**, over 70 m deep, with a waterside restaurant serving inexpensive and good seafood and regional food (but awful coffee) until 1800. There is also a run-down trailer park (Apartado 88, Chetumal), a relaxing place to camp; other *cenotes* in area. Both the *laguna* and the *cenote* are deserted in the week.

About 3 km north of Cenote Azul is the village of **Bacalar** (nice, but not special) on the **Laguna de Siete Colores**, which has swimming and skin-diving; *colectivos* from terminal (Suchaa) in Chetumal, corner of Miguel Hidalgo and Primo de Verdad, 0700-1900 every 30 minutes, US$1.60, return from plaza when full; also buses from Chetumal bus station every two hours or so, US$1.60. There is a Spanish fort there overlooking a beautiful shallow, clear, freshwater lagoon, and abundant birdlife on the lake shore. This is the fort of **San Felipe**, said to have been built around 1729 by the Spanish to defend the area from the English pirates and smugglers of logwood. There is a plaque praying for protection from the British and a small **museum** ⓘ *US$0.70*. The British ships roamed the islands and reefs, looting Spanish galleons laden with gold, on their way from Peru to Cuba. There are many old shipwrecks on the reef and around the Banco Chinchorro, 50 km out in the Caribbean (information kindly provided by Coral Pitkin of the **Rancho Encantado**, see page 494). There is a dock for swimming from north of the plaza, with a restaurant and disco next to it. North of Bacalar a direct road (Route 293) runs to Muná, on the road between Mérida and Uxmal. Gasoline is sold in a side-street.

Towards Francisco Villa

From Chetumal you can visit the fascinating Maya ruins that lie west on the way (Route 186) to Francisco Villa and Escárcega, if you have a car. There are few tourists in this area and few facilities. Take plenty of drinking water. About 25 km from Chetumal at **Ucum** (fuel), you can turn off 5 km south to visit **Palmara**, located along the Río Hondo, which borders Belize; there are swimming holes and restaurant.

Border essentials: Mexico-Belize

Chetumal

Customs and immigration
Procedure can be slow, particularly at peak holiday times when Belizeans come on charter buses for cheap shopping; over the bridge is Belizean passport control. For people entering Mexico, tourist cards are available at the border. It has been reported that only 15 days are given but you can get an additional 30 days at the Servicios Migratorios in Chetumal. Note that fresh fruit cannot be imported into Belize.

Driving Leaving Mexico by car, go to the Mexican immigration office to register your exit and surrender your vehicle permit and tourist card; very straightforward, no charges. Go to the office to obtain compulsory Belizean insurance (also money changing facilities here). Entering Belize, your car will be registered in your passport.

Exchange Money is checked on entering Belize. Excess Mexican pesos are easily changed into Belizean dollars with men waiting just beyond customs on the Belize side, but they are not there to meet the early bus. You can change US for Belizean dollar bills in the shops at the border, but this is not necessary as US$ are accepted in Belize. If you can get a good rate (dollars to pesos) in the bank, it is sometimes better to buy Belizean dollars with pesos in *casas de cambio* than to wait until you enter Belize where the US dollar/Belize dollar rate is fixed at 1:2.

Just before Francisco Villa (61 km from Chetumal), the ruins of **Kohunlich** ⓘ *0800-1700, US$2*, lie 8.5 km south of the main road, 1½ hours' walk along a sweltering, unshaded road; take plenty of water. Descriptions in Spanish and English. Every hour or so the van passes for staff working at **Explorer Kohunlich**, a luxury resort hotel halfway to the ruins, which may give you a lift, but you'll still have 4 km to walk. There are fabulous masks (early Classic, AD 250-500) set on the side of the main pyramid, still bearing red colouring; they are unique of their kind (allow an hour for the site). About 200 m west of the turning for Kohunlich is an immigration office and a stall selling beer; wait here for buses to Chetumal or Xpujil, which have to stop, but first-class buses will not pick up passengers. *Colectivos* 'Nicolás Bravo' from Chetumal, or bus marked 'Zoh Laguna' from bus station pass the turning.

Other ruins in this area are **Dzibanché** and **Knichná** ⓘ *both free*. Both are recent excavations and both are accessible down a dirt road off the Chetumal-Morocoy road. The remains of a Maya king have recently been disinterred (June 1999) at Dzibanché, which is thought to have been the largest Maya city in southern Quintana Roo, peaking between AD 300 and 1200. Its discoverer, Thomas Gann, named it in 1927 after the Maya glyphs he found engraved on the sapodilla wood lintels in Temple VI – *Dzibanché* means 'writing on the wood' in Maya. Later excavations revealed a tomb in Temple I, believed to have belonged to a king because of the number of offerings it contained. This temple is also known as the **Temple of the Owl** because one of the artefacts unearthed was a vase and lid carved with an owl figure. Other important structures are the **Temple of the Cormorants** and **Structure XIII**, known as 'The Captives', due to its friezes depicting prisoners. Knichná means 'House of the Sun' in Maya, christened by Thomas Gann in reference to a glyph he found there. The **Acropolis** is the largest structure. To reach these sights follow the Chetumal-Escárcega road, turn off at Km 58 towards Morocoy, 9 km further on. The road to Dzibanché is 2 km down this road, crossing the turning for Knichná.

Sleeping

Isla Holbox *p473*
AL Villa Delfines, on the beach, T875-2196, www.holbox.com. Romantic palm-roofed bungalows, pool and leading to the beach, expensive but nice.
A Faro Viejo, T875-2217, www.faroviejoholbox.com.mx. Large, breezy rooms looking over the beach. Some rooms with kitchens.
B Mawimbi, T875-2003, www.mawimbi.net. Stylishly decorated *cabañas* with kitchenette, stepping out onto the beach.
C La Palapa, T875-2121, www.hotellapalapa.com. Very clean cabins, leading onto the beach.

Camping
Best camping on beach east of village (north side of island).

Cancún *p474, maps p474 and 476*
Accommodation in the Hotel Zone starts at around US$75, rises quickly and is best arranged as part of a package holiday. The beaches are supposedly public so you don't have to stay in a hotel to hang out on the beach. The centre or Downtown area has many cheaper options, but prices are still higher than other parts of the Yucatán Peninsula.

Hotel Zone
Some of these hotels have special offers during Jul and Aug, listed in *Riviera Maya Hotels Guide*, available free at the airport. If circumstances find you in the market head along the strip and find 1 that takes your fancy – discounts can be considerable. 2 good options are are: **LL Le Meridien**, Retorno del Rey Km 14, T881-2200.
L Presidente Inter-Continental, Av Kukulcán Km 7.5, T883-0200.

Town centre
Many hotels, especially the budget ones, tend to be full during Jul. It is best to get to them as early as possible in the morning, or try to make a reservation if planning to return to Cancún after a trip to the interior or Isla Mujeres. El Crucero, location of some of the budget hotels, is said by locals to be safe during the day, but unsafe at night.
AL Margaritas, Yaxchilán y Jasmines, T/F884-9333. Modern, efficient service, outside restaurant, bar, pool, travel agent and care hire.
A El Rey del Caribe, Av Uxmal esq Náder, SM2A, T884-2028, reycarib@cancun.com.mx. A/c, gardens, parking, pool, jacuzzi.
B Cancún Rosa, Margaritas 2, local 10, T884-2873. Close to bus terminal. A/c, TV, phone, comfortable rooms.
C El Alux, Av Uxmal 21, T884-0662. Turn left and first right from bus station. A/c with bath, clean, TV, some rooms cheaper, good value. Recommended.
C María Isabel, Palmera 59, T884-9015, near bus station and Av Tulum. Fan and a/c, hot water, TV, small and clean, friendly, helpful, will store luggage, avoid rooms backing onto noisy air shaft.
C Villa Rossana, Av Yaxchilán opposite Mexhotel, Lotes 67, 68, 69, T884-1943. Popular, central and spacious, good location.
C-E Las Palmas, Palmeras 43, T884-2513. Huge rooms, clean with TV, a/c, fan, kitchen, cheaper in dormitory, good value. Recommended.
D Piña Hermanos, Calle 7 No 35, SM64, M6, L14, near El Crucero, T884-2150. Very clean, nice decor, restaurant, friendly staff. Highly recommended.
D San Carlos, Cedro 10 (2nd turning onto Cedro from bus terminal), T884-0786, near and handy for the bus terminal. Mixed bag of rooms, some cramped and shabby, the upper floor is OK and slightly more expensive.
E Mayan Hostel, Margaritas 17, round the corner from **Mexico Hostel**, T892-0103, www.cancunhostel.com. Simple dormitory accommodation, with laundry, internet, kitchen and good services.
E Mexico Hostel, Palmera 30, T887-0191. The best budget deal in Cancún, very clean, dormitories, breakfast included, TV, lockers, kitchen. Recommended and a good place to stop when just arriving.

Phone codes *Isla Holbox 984; Cancún 998; Isla Mujeres 998; Puerto Morelos 998; Playa del Carmen 984; Cozumel 987; Tulum 984; Chetumal 983.*

Camping
A big trailer park has been built opposite Punta Sam, 150 spaces, camping (**F** per person), shop selling basic commodities. Irregular bus service there, or hitchhike from Puerto Juárez. Check to see if restaurant is open evenings. Take mosquito repellent.

Isla Mujeres *p477*
AL Condominio Nautibeach, on Playa Los Cocos, T877-0606, www.nautibeach.com. 2-bed apartments, a/c, pool, right on beach facing the sunset.
AL María del Mar, Av Carlos Larzo 1, on the road down to the north beach, T/F877-0179, www.cabanasdelmar.com. Close to the best beach, restaurant, pool, *cabañas* and rooms, overlooks Coco beach. Lovely beach bar with hammocks and rocking chairs for 2.
B Rocamar, Nicolás Bravo y Zona Marítima, T/F877-0101, rocamar@mjmnet.net. On the eastern side, quiet, nice views.
C Isla Mujeres, next to church. With bath, renovated, run by pleasant Englishman.
C-F Pocna Hostel (price per person), top end of Matamoros on the northeast coast, T877-0090, www.pocna.com. Mixed-sex dormitories, 6-14 to a room, also 2 double rooms (**C**), sheets US$10 deposit, restaurant, bar, big screen TV with movies. **F** camping or in hammock. Busy, often booked up in summer and Dec. Recommended but sometimes dirty.
C Vistalmar, on promenade about 300 m left from ferry dock, T877-0209 (**D** for longer stays). Ask for rooms on top floor, bath, balcony, a/c, fan, TV, insect screens, good value.
D Isleño, Madero and Guerrero, T877-0302. Very clean, with bath, cheaper without, helpful.
D Las Palmas, Guerrero 20. Central, 2 blocks from north beach, good, clean.
D María José, Madero 25, T877-0130. Clean, fans, friendly, scooter hire.
D Osorio, Madero, 1 block from waterfront. Clean, fan, with bath and hot water, friendly, reception closes at 2100. Recommended.
E Urban Hostel, Hidalgo and Matamoros, T879-9342, urbanhostel@yahoo.com. Clean and tidy budget bunkhouse.

Puerto Morelos *p478*
A Rancho Libertad, next door to Caribbean Reef Club, T871-0181, www.rancholibertad.com. Thatched *cabañas*; the price includes breakfast, scuba diving and snorkelling gear for rent.
D Posada Amor, opposite the beach, T871-0033. Very pleasant, well-built *cabañas* with good mosquito nets, the cheaper ones have outdoor communal showers, there is also a good restaurant and prices are reduced considerably out of season.

Playa del Carmen *p478, map p479*
Prices quoted are for the high season – Jul-Aug and Dec; during the low season prices will drop by about 25%.
L Continental Plaza Playacar, T873-0100. A huge new luxury development just south of the ferry terminal, excellent in every respect, non-residents can use swimming pool.
AL Alhambra, Calle 8 Norte, on corner with the beach, T873-0735, www.alhambra-hotel.net. All rooms with balcony or sea view, family-run, French and English spoken. Recommended.
AL Las Molcas, T873-0070, near ferry pier. Pool, a bit shabby, friendly staff, interesting architecture, its open-air restaurant across the street is good and reasonable.
AL-B Blue Parrot, at the north end of town, on a popular stretch of beach between Calle 12 y 14, T873-0083. Price depends on type of room and facilities, has bungalows, no a/c, with excellent bar (happy hour 2200) and café, volleyball court, deep-sea fishing expeditions. Highly recommended.
B Maya Bric, Av 5, between Calle 8 and 10, T873-0011. Hot water, clean, friendly, pool, Tank-Ha dive shop (see Activities and tours, page 498).
B Mom's, Av 30 y Calle 4, T873-0315, about 5 blocks from bus station or beach. Clean, comfortable, small pool, good restaurant with Chinese home cooking and plenty of vegetables.
C Cabañas Tuxatah, 2 mins from sea, 2 blocks south from Av Juárez, T873-0025. German owner, Maria Weltin, speaks English and French. Bath, clean, comfortable, hot water, laundry service, beautiful gardens, breakfast US$4. Recommended.
C Posada Las Flores, Av 5 between Calle 4 and Calle 6. Popular, friendly, courtyard, near beach.
C-D Posada Marinelly, Av Juárez between Calle 10 and 15, T873-0140. Near the centre,

some rooms noisy, very clean, nice staff, family-run, good cheap café downstairs.
D **Casa Tucán**, Calle 4 Norte, between 10 and 15 Av Norte, T/F873-0283. Nice patio, small but clean rooms. Pool and good restaurant.
D **Posada Marixchel**, Calle 30 and 1 Sur, T873-0823. Shower, safe, fan, clean. Recommended.
E **Happy Gecko**, Av 10 between Calle 6 and 8, T873-2144, happygeckohotel@yahoo.com. Good rooms with kitchen, fan and bath, some with a/c. Provide *cenote* diving and snorkelling tours, and can arrange airport pick-up for a small charge.
E **Hostel Playa**, Av 25 with Calle 8, T803-3277, www.hostelplaya.com. Private and single sex dorm rooms with lockers. Use of kitchen and laundry facilities.
E **Urban Hostel**, Av 10 between 4 and 6, T879-9342, urbanhostel@yahoo.com Dormitories, hot water and fan, mosquito nets, kitchen facilities, lockers under the beds, curtains separate the rooms so watch out for wandering hands in the night.

Camping
Outback, small trailer park on beach at end of Calle 6. US$10 for car and 2 people.
Punta Bete, 10 km north, the right-hand one of 3 campsites at the end of a 5-km road, on beach. US$3 for tent, also 2 restaurants and *cabañas*.

Cozumel *p479, map p481*
Prices may rise by up to 50% around Christmas.
AL-A **Bahía**, Av Rafael Melgar y Calle 3 Sur, T872-1791. A/c, phone, cable TV, fridge, breakfast included, free internet, even-numbered rooms have balcony.
AL-C **Flamingo**, Calle 6 Norte 81, T872-1264, www.hotelflamingo.com. Showers, fan, clean, family-run, good value. Recommended.
A-B **Amaranto**, Calle 5 Sur, Av 15-20, T872-3219, amarantotamarindo@prodigy.net.mx. Bungalows, fridge, microwave, new, run by Eliane and Jorge, Spanish, English and French spoken, childcare on request. Recommended.
B **Tamarindo**, Calle 4 Norte 421, between 20 and 25, T/F872-3614. Bed and breakfast, 3 rooms, shared kitchen, hammocks, dive gear storage and rinse tank, purified drinking water, laundry, safe deposit box, TV, also run by Eliane and Jorge, Spanish, English and French spoken, childcare on request.
C **Pepita**, Av 15 Sur y Calle 1 Sur, T/F872-0098. Very pleasant rooms around a plant-filled courtyard, modern fittings, a/c, fridge in all rooms, free coffee and cookies in the morning. Recommended.
C **Posada Marruang**, A R Salas 440, between Av 20 Sur and Av 25 Sur, T872-1678. Very spick and span, large comfortable rooms set back from road; barking dog ensures occasional noise and total security.
C **Posada Zuanayoli**, Calle 6 Norte between Av 10 and Av 15 Norte, T872-0690. Tall, old building in quiet street, TV, modern facilities, fridge, fan, free coffee, drinking water.
D **Flores**, A R Salas 72, off plaza, T872-1429. 50 m from the sea, very cheap for central location. A/c, cheaper with fan.
D **Posada Edem**, Calle 2 Norte 124, T872-1166. Kitchen, a/c, fan, also apartments in B range, clean, very good value. Recommended.
D **Posada Letty**, Calle 1 Sur y Av 15 Sur, T872-0257. Hot water, clean, good value. Recommended.
E **Saolima**, A R Salas 260, T872-0886. Clean, fan, showers, hot water. Recommended.

Tulum *p483*
Tulum village
Many new hotels and restaurants have sprung up, turning Tulum Av into a lively spot, and worth a visit on any stay, and new budget accommodation makes it a good choice for backpackers. The only limitation is the mafia-like control of public transport by the strong taxi union. This means there are no public buses to the beach, a taxi will cost you US$3.50 or more. For places to stay in Sian Ka'an Biosphere Reserve, see page 493.
C **L'Hotel**, 1 block north of bus stop. A/c or fan, hot showers, new and clean.
D-E **Hotel Maya**, near bus stop, T871-1234. Fan, shower, reasonable, restaurant with slow service, small shop, parking in front.
D-E **Rancho Tranquilo**, far south end of town. *Cabañas*, nice setting, quiet as the name suggests.
F **Weary Traveller Hostel**, 1 block south of ADO, T871-2461. Bus terminal, backpackers' hostel, good meeting place, price includes basic breakfast and dinner, bunk rooms with

comfy beds, book exchange, information centre, internet (US$2.50 per hr).

Tulum beach

To reach the beach *cabañas* it is better to get off the bus in town and take a taxi (US$3-5 depending on season); otherwise the ruins are ½-hr walk from the bus stop. In high season *cabañas* are very popular.

L Posada Margherita, T876-3072, www.posadamargherita.com. Well-designed hotel with complete wheelchair access, runs scuba diving courses for the disabled. Good Italian restaurant. Recommended.

AL Dos Ceibas, 9 km from the ruins. Luxury cabins on the edge of the Sian Ka'an Biosphere Reserve.

A Ana y José, restaurant, 7 km south of ruins, T887-5470. *Cabañas* and rooms, some are right on the beach, with pool, very clean, comfortable and hospitable. Trips can be arranged to the Sian Ka'an Biosphere Reserve (see page 486). Recommended.

A Los Arrecifes, T879-7307, *cabañas*, live music and shows, restaurant.

B Cabañas Diamante K, on the beach quite near the ruins, T871-2283. Rustic with nice bar and restaurant, with hints of the Crystal Maze. Recommended.

C-D Don Armando, near the ruins, T871-2743, cabanasarmandos@yahoo.com.mx. *Cabañas* for up to 4, prices variable, popular, staff are friendly and helpful, but watch your gear. Cheap but limited restaurant with long queues, bar with noisy disco till 0200, certain bus tickets available.

E Mar Caribe, near the ruins. Smaller complex than its neighbour, **Don Armando**, but a friendly atmosphere, and much more peaceful, cheaper if you bring your own hammock.

E Playa Condesa, next door to **Diamante K**. Simple and pleasant, airy wooden *cabañas*. Electricity a few hours each evening.

E Santa Fe, near the ruins, T880-5854. Basic *cabañas*, new toilets and showers but only 4 and 2 of each, US$1 extra for mosquito net, hammocks or tents, water problems, reported insecure, watch your belongings. Has a restaurant, good breakfasts and fish dinners, reggae music; English, French and Italian spoken; laid-back atmosphere, but cheaper cabins are badly constructed and lack privacy; free camping possible further up the beach.

E-F El Mirador, nearest to the ruins (10 mins' walk). Small, quiet, *cabañas* (won't rent to singles), hammocks available, camping, 2 showers, use of restaurant toilets (clean), bar and restaurant with excellent views.

Cobá *p484*

B Villas Arqueológicas (Club Méditerranée), about 2 km from site on lake shore, T858-1527. Open to non-members, excellent, clean and quiet, a/c, swimming pool, good restaurant with moderate prices, but expensive beer. Don't arrive without a reservation, especially at weekends; and yet making a reservation by phone seems to be practically impossible.

E Hotel Restaurant El Bocadito, in the village, on the street leading to the main road. Run-down, spartan rooms with fan, intermittent water supply, poor security, good but expensive restaurant (which is popular with tour groups), books and handicrafts for sale. Recommended.

Sian Ka'an Biosphere Reserve *p486*

AL Cabañas Los Arrecifes, in the reserve, 8 km south of Tulum, quiet, pleasant, with smart chalets on the beach and others behind, cheaper, with good fish restaurant shaped like a ship (no electricity), limited menu.

A Centro Ecológico Sian Ka'an, T871-2499, www.cesiak.org. Environmentally considerate and sensitive accommodation in the heart of the Reserve.

A Rancho Sol Caribe, Punta Allen. 2 comfortable *cabañas*, with bath, restaurant. Recommended.

D Cabañas de Tulum, 100 m from **Cabañas Los Arrecifes**, also with good restaurant, clean cabins with shower, electricity 1730-2100; interesting fish in the *cenote* opposite, take taxi there (US$5-6 from ruins car park), empty white beaches.

Felipe Carrillo Puerto *p486*

C El Faisán y El Venado, 2 blocks northeast of main square. Mixed reports on cleanliness, but hot water and good-value restaurant, popular with locals.

D San Ignacio, near Pemex. Good value, a/c, bath, towels, TV, secure car park.

E Chan Santa Cruz, just off the plaza. Good, basic, clean and friendly (**Restaurante 24 Horas** is open, as you'd imagine, 24 hrs, OK).

F María Isabel, near the plaza. Clean, friendly, laundry service, quiet, safe parking.

Mahahual and around *p486*

There are plenty of options for sleeping with hammocks, camping and *cabañas*.

C-F Kabah-na,T838-8861, kabahna@ yahoo.com. *Cabañas* or space to hang a hammock, right on the beach.

D Sol y Mar restaurant, en route to Puerto Bravo, near Mahahual, with rooms to rent, bathrooms and spaces for RVs, also coconut palms and beach.

E-F Kok Hal, Mahahual, on the beach close to the old wharf. Shared bath and hot showers.

Camping

Camidas Trailer Park, Punta Herrero road, with palm trees, *palapas*, restaurant and space for 4 RVs, US$5 per person, car free.

Chetumal *p487, map p487*

AL Los Cocos, Héroes de Chapultepec 138, T832-0544. Reductions for AAA members, a/c, pool, restaurant. Recommended.

C Caribe Princess, Av Obregón 168, T832-0520. A/c, TV, good, very clean, no restaurant. Recommended.

C El Dorado, Av 5 de Mayo 42, T832-0315. Hot water, a/c, friendly and quiet. Recommended.

C Real Azteca, Belice 186, T832-0720. Cheerful, friendly, but no hot shower. 2nd-floor rooms best, but still not too good.

C Ucum, Gandhi 4, T832-0711. A/c, fan, bath, pleasant, quiet (rooms away from street), expensive laundry, parking in enclosed car park included in price, good value, restaurant next door recommended for *ceviche*.

C-D Jacaranda, Av Obregón 201, T832-1455. Clean, good, bath, safe parking.

D Big Ben, Héroes 48-A, T833-1710. Clean, shabby, safe, cheaper rooms for 4, with bath. Arabic restaurant downstairs.

D María Dolores, Alvaro Obregón 206, T832-0508. Bath, hot water, fan, clean, windows don't open, noisy, restaurant **Solsimar** downstairs good and popular. Recommended.

E Crystal, Colón y Av Belice. Fan, bath, parking.

F CREA, Calzada Veracruz y Alvaro Obregón, T832-3465, CP 77050. Youth hostel. No hot water, clean, run-down, friendly, camping US$2. Recommended.

Camping

Sunrise of the Caribbean, trailer park on the road to Calderitas. US$15 for car and 2 people, cold showers, electricity, laundry facilities, *palapas*, boat ramp.

Towards Bacalar *p488*

AL Rancho Encantado, 3 km north of Bacalar, on the west shore of the lagoon. Resort hotel, half-board available, Apdo 233, Chetumal, T/F894-7074, www.encan tado.com. With private dock, tour boat, canoes and windsurf boards for rent, private cabins with fridge and hammock, very good.

D Hotel América, Bacalar, 700 m north of the bus stop on the plaza (walk in the opposite direction to Chetumal). Recommended.

D Hotel Las Lagunas, about 2 km south of Bacalar (on left-hand side of the road going towards the village). It is very good, wonderful views, helpful, clean, comfortable, hot water, swimming pool and opposite a freshwater lake; restaurant is poor and overpriced.

Camping

Camping possible at the end of the road 100 m from the lagoon, toilets and shower, US$0.10, but lagoon perfect for washing and swimming.

Eating

Cancún *p474, maps p476 & 474*

The **Hotel Zone** is lined with expensive restaurants, with every type of international cuisine imaginable, but with a predominance of Tex-Mex and Italian. Restaurants in the centre are cheaper, and the accent is on local food.

The cheapest area for dinner is **SM64**, opposite **Plaza 2000**. Popular with locals, especially on Sun when it is hard to get a table; there are 4 or 5 small, family-run restaurants serving local specialities. *Comida corrida* for as little as US$2. **Mercado 28** is the best budget option for breakfast or lunch, with many cheap outdoor and indoor *loncherías* serving *comida corrida*, very popular with locals, quick service.

TTT **El Pescador**, Tulipanes 28. Good seafood, well established with excellent reputation but expensive.
TTT **La Habichuela**, Margaritas 25. Caribbean seafood, tropical garden setting, jazz music.
TT **100% Natural**, Av Yaxchilán y Sunyaxchén. Good choice for vegetarians, seafood, healthy breakfasts, big portions, great value.
TT **La Chiquita del Caribe**, Av Xel-Há at Mercado 28. Great seafood, good value. Recommended.
TT **Las Tejas**, Av Uxmal, just before Calle Laurel. Good food at reasonable prices.
TT **Pericos**, Av Yaxchilán 71. Themed Mexican, staff in fancy dress, very touristy and lively atmosphere but good food and great live band.
TT **Rincón Yucateco**, Av Uxmal 24, opposite Hotel Cotty. Good Mexican breakfasts, popular.
TT **Villa Rica**, Av Yaxchilán 35. Veracruz seafood specialities, live band, good service.
TT **Yamamoto**, Av Uxmal and Nader. Japanese food, popular, good quality.
T **Los Huaraches**, on Av Uxmal opposite Yaxchilán. Fast food, cheap *empanada* specials after 1300.
T **Mr Greek**, Av Uxmal 40 between Yaxchilán and Tulum. Outdoor stand with authentic Greek food and tacos.

Cafés

Pastelería Italiana, Yaxchilán, just before turning of Sunyaxchén. Excellent coffee and pastries, friendly. A few other cheap eateries along Yaxchilán, tucked away between the pricey themed restaurants, some open during the day only.

Isla Mujeres *p477*

The most popular street for restaurants is Hidalgo – meander down the street and take your pick.
TTT **Mesón del Bucanero**, Hidalgo, opposite Rolandis. Steak, seafood, terrace, classy.
TTT **Rolandis**, Hidalgo, T877-0700. Italian, terrace overlooking street, busy. Recommended.
TT **All Natural**, Plaza Karlita on Hidalgo. Speciality grilled fish, many varieties, some vegetarian dishes.
TT **El Balcón de Arriba**, Hidalgo 12, above souvenir shop. Varied menu, excellent fish and seafood, some vegetarian and tempura dishes, very friendly staff, large portions. Highly recommended.
TT **Isla Tequila**, Hidalgo 19a. Popular, steak, seafood, good bar, live music, helpful, friendly owners, who also have a bookstore next door.
TT **Manolos**, Juárez. Small, nice decor, seafood, barbecue, baked potatoes.
TT **Pizzería Los Amigos**, Hidalgo. Small, with 2 tables outside, excellent pizzas and pasta.
T **Lonchería La Lamita**, Juárez 25B. Nice and clean serving good-value, tasty food.
T **La Susanita**, next door to Poc-Chuc. Excellent home cooking, friendly locals' place; when closed it is the family's living room.
T **Loncherías**, at the northwest end of Guerrero, open till 1800. Good for breakfast, snacks and lunch. All serve the same local fare at similar prices.
T **Poc-Chuc**, Juárez y Madero. Very good local food, big portions, good *tortas*.

Cafés

Aluxes Café, Av Matamoros, next to **Al Forno** Pizza. Good café, with cappuccinos, lattes, tea, muffins, bagels and juices. Recommended.
Cafecito, Matamoros 42. Nice breakfast place, waffles, juice, sandwiches, 0800-1400.
Red Eye, Av Hidalgo Centro, north end. Open early, breakfast, coffee.

Puerto Morelos *p478*

TT **Johnny Cairo**, with good typical food.
TT **Pelícano**. Serves very good seafood.

Playa del Carmen *p478, map p479*

TTT **Jazzy Cat**, Calle 6 between Av 5 and Av 10. Rib roasts, oven-baked lasagne, home-made pasta.
TTT **Panchos**, Av 5 between Calle 10 and 12. Traditional Mexican food, speciality flambées and flaming Spanish coffee.
TT **Buenos Aires**, Calle 6 Norte between Av 5 and Av 10, on Plaza Playa. Speciality Argentine meats, run by Argentines, nice for a change from Mexican food.
TT **Da Gabi**, just up Calle 12 from Blue Parrot, good pastas, Mexican dishes, breakfast buffet (also has rooms in **C** range).
TT **La Choza**, Av 5 between Av Juárez and Calle 2. Great food, set menus, good breakfasts, Tex-Mex dinners.

ŸŸ **La Parrilla**, Av 5 y Calle 8. Large portions, good service, live music every night, popular.
ŸŸ **Le Bistro**, Calle 2. Good French cheese/ Caribbean chicken and wine. Recommended.
ŸŸ **Los Almendros**, Calle 6 and Av 10. Excellent Mexican food, friendly. Recommended.
ŸŸ **Media Luna**, Av 5 between Calle 8 and Calle 10. Excellent vegetarian and seafood.
ŸŸ **Pez Vela**, Av 5 y Calle 2. Good atmosphere, food, drinks and music (closed 1500-1700).
ŸŸ **Sabor**, Calle 4 and Av 5. Vegetarian and healthfood, bakery.
ŸŸ **Yaxche**, Calle 8 between Av 5 and Av 10. Traditional Maya cuisine.
Ÿ **Argentino Bar Restaurant**, Calle 12, between Av 5 and the **Blue Parrot**. Great BBQs, good breakfast cheap, good sports bar. Recommended.
Ÿ **Lonchería Maquech**, Calle 1 between Av 5 and 10. Set lunch daily, cheap, friendly. Recommended.
Ÿ **Tacos Senjansen**, Av Juárez between Calle 10 and 15. Nice open-air café under **Posada Marinelly**, for good breakfast and snacks.

Cafés and bakeries

Coffee Press, Calle 2 between Av 5 and the beach. Espresso, cappuccino, latte, breakfast.
Java Joe's, Av 5 between Calle 10 and 12. Italian and gourmet coffees, sandwiches, pastries.

Cozumel *p479, map p480*

There are few eating options for budget travellers. The cheapest places for breakfast, lunch or an early dinner are the *loncherías* next to the market on A R Salas, between Av 20 and 25. They serve fairly good local *comida corrida*, 0800-1930.
ŸŸŸ **Lobster's Cove**, Av Rafael Melgar 790. Seafood, live music, happy hour 1200-1400.
ŸŸŸ **Pancho's Backyard**, Rafael Melgar 27, in **Los Cinco Soles** shopping complex in big courtyard out the back. Mexican food and wine elegantly served, good food.
ŸŸŸ **Prima**, Salas 109. Northern Italian seafood, handmade pasta, brick oven pizzas, non-smoking area.
ŸŸ **Asian Garden**, 5 Av 148, between 1a Sur and Salas. Good Chinese food.
ŸŸ **Casa Deni's**, Calle 1 Sur 164, close to plaza. Open-air restaurant, very good, moderate prices.
ŸŸ **Las Palmeras**, at the pier (people-watching spot). Very popular for breakfast, opens 0700, always busy. Recommended.
ŸŸ **The Stadium**, Calle 2 Norte y Av 5. US style, breakfasts, burgers, steaks, lobster, satellite TV, money exchange, phones for USA.

Cafés and bakeries

Coffee Bean, Calle 3 Sur 9 near waterfront. Good coffee, great pies, cakes and brownies.

Tulum *p483*

Several chicken restaurants along Av Tulum.
ŸŸ **Bistro Nocturne**, Tex-Mex food, very good-value dining, nice decor (check out the bones on the ceiling above the bar).
ŸŸ **Charles** has beautiful, shell decor, nachos, good fish. Nice patio area out back.
ŸŸ **París de Noche**, French-Mexican food, lobster, outside garden setting, excellent food and open for breakfast, good value.
Ÿ **Doña Tinas**, good basic and cheap, in a grass hut at southern end of town.
Ÿ **El Mariachi**, taco bar with good *fajitas*, cheap.
Ÿ **El Tacontento**, 2 blocks north of **ADO** station. Good basic Mexican, cheap tacos.

Cobá *p484*

There are plenty of restaurants in the village, on the road to **Villas Arqueológicas** and on the road to the ruins, they are all quite pricey. There's also a grocery store by **El Bocadito** and souvenir shops.
ŸŸ **Pirámides**, on corner of track leading to **Villas Arqueológicas**. Highly recommended.
Ÿ **Nicte-Ha**, good and friendly.

Sian Ka'an Biosphere Reserve *p486*

ŸŸ-Ÿ **La Cantina**, Punta Allen, a good, non-touristy restaurant (US$3-4 for fish).

Felipe Carrillo Puerto *p486*

ŸŸ **Danburger Maya**, next door to hotel **San Ignacio**. Good food, reasonable prices, helpful.
Ÿ **Restaurant Addy**, on main road, south of town. Good, simple.

Chetumal *p487, map p487*

ŸŸŸ **Chicho's Lobster House**, Blv Bahía esq Vicente Guerrero, T832-7249. Expensive but good seafood, friendly.

ŦŦ Barracuda, about 4 blocks north of market, then 3 blocks west (another area with many restaurants). Good seafood.

ŦŦ Sergio Pizza, Obregón 182. Pizzas, fish, and expensive steak meals, a/c, good drinks, excellent service.

ŦŦ-Ŧ Arcada, Héroes y Zaragoza, open 24 hrs, with mini-market at the back.

Ŧ El Vaticano. Popular with locals, good atmosphere, cheap.

Ŧ Mercado. Cheap meals in the market at the top of Av Héroes, but the service is not too good and tourists will be stared at a lot.

Juice bars and ice cream parlours

Jugos Xamach, corner of Salvador y Quintana Roo. Good juices, friendly local spot.

Delicious yoghurt ice in shop opposite market.

Towards Bacalar *p488*

ŦŦ La Esperanza, 1 block north from plaza. Thatched barn, good seafood.

ŦŦ Punta y Coma, Orizaba, 3 blocks from Zócalo. Inexpensive, large menu including vegetarian. Recommended.

Entertainment

Cancún *p474, maps p476 and 474*

Bars and clubs

At the time of researching and writing this edition of **Footprint Mexico and Central America**, the availability of entertainment in the Hotel Zone had still not settled down. If seeking a good night out, get on the bus or catch a cab, and follow your instincts.

A night out in the Hotel Zone will set you back anywhere between US$20 and US$50. Many of the classic locations – **Señor Frogs**, **La Boom** and **Bum-Bum** – were destroyed in Hurricane Wilma. **Señor Frogs** will almost certainly rise again. Ask locally for the clubs that have opened in the Hotel Zone.

Cinemas

The main one, **Cine Royal**, is on Av Tulum near the bus terminal. **Multiplex**, showing mostly Hollywood blockbusters with Spanish subtitles, entry US$2.30. There are a couple of smaller cinemas near El Crucero; 1 of them, Calle 10, SM64, shows vintage Mexican gangster films in Spanish. Also a multiplex cinema in the Hotel Zone at **Plaza Kukulcán**.

Isla Mujeres *p477*

Bar and clubs

Most of the bars have a permanent happy hour, with 2 drinks for the price of 1. Not particularly good value, since the prices are double the usual. **Daniel's**, Hidalgo between Madero and Morelos. Very popular (and loudest) in the early evening, live music every night. **Kokonuts**, Hidalgo 65, towards beach from centre. Most popular in town, fills up after 2200, dance floor, happy hour, young crowd. Further along towards the beach is **Chile Locos**, more sedate than **Kokonuts**, with live marimba music. **La Palapa**, on Playa Los Cocos. Serves cocktails and snacks and is busy during the day until everyone leaves the beach, then fills up again after midnight. There is sometimes live music at **La Taverna**, on the harbour near the ferry dock. It has a nice location on wooden stilts in the sea, but the venue is having difficulty competing with the popularity of places in the centre like **Daniel's** and **Kokonuts**. **Mr Papas**, Hildago below Matamoros. Lively bar and nightclub with good variety of DJ music.

Playa del Carmen *p478, map p479*

Bars and clubs

The Blue Parrot Inn, Calle 12 y Av 1, next to beach. Live music every night, happy hour 1700-2000 and 2200-2400. **Bouron Street**, Av 5 between Calle 6 and 8. Live Louisiana blues and jazz, Cajun food, great, relaxed atmosphere earlier, draught beer. Owner Paul Anderson is friendly and helpful. **Buena Onda**, Av 5 between Calle 26 and Calle 28. Live music, salsa, funk, reggae. **Crocodillos**, Juárez, disco, small cover, popular with the locals, good at weekends. **Espiral**, Av 5 off the main plaza. House and techno. **Señor Frogs**, by the pier. Part of large chain, live reggae and karaoke, 2200-late. **Tequila Barrel**, Calle 5 between Av 10 and 12. Live blues music daily 2000-2400, Tex-Mex Bar and grill, friendly owner (Greco) and staff. **Fiesta Latina**, Calle 8 y Av 25. Live Latin music and ballet show.

Cozumel *p479, map p480*

Bars and clubs

The Stadium, see Eating, above. **Havana Club**, Av Rafael Melgar, north of the ferry. **Cigar Jazz Bar**, with live jazz, Wed and Fri

1330-1800. **Café Salsa**, 10 Av between Juárez and 2 Norte. Salsa bar, popular alternative and slightly more authentic. **Scaramouche**, Av Rafael Melgar y A R Salas. The best. **Neptuno**, Av Rafael Melgar y Calle 11, south of centre. The last 2 are state-of-the-art discos, as well as hotel nightclubs.

Shopping

Cancún *p474, maps p476 and 474*
There are several US-style shopping malls in the Hotel Zone. The main one, **Plaza Kukulcán**, has over 200 shops, restaurants, a bowling alley and video games. It is open from 1000-2200, and the prices are high for most things, including souvenirs. The main **craft market** is on Av Tulum near Plaza Las Américas; it is a huge network of stalls, all selling exactly the same merchandise: silver jewellery from Taxco, ceramic Maya figurines, hammocks, jade chess sets. Prices are hiked up to the limit, so bargain hard: most vendors expect to get half what they originally ask for. The market called **Mercado 23** (at the end of Calle Cedro, off Av Tulum) has cheaper souvenirs and less aggressive salesmen, but the quality is shoddy; *guayabera* shirts are available on one of the stalls. Several new smoking shops have appeared, cashing in on the craze for Cuban cigars; these are all located on or just off Av Tulum. Cheaper clothes shops than the Hotel Zone can be found at the north end of Av Tulum, near Plaza 2000. Pricey leather goods, clothes and jewellery can be bought in the **Plaza 2000** shopping mall.

Isla Mujeres *p477*
Books
Cosmic Cosas, Matamoros 82, T876-3495. New and used books bought, sold and exchanged, CDs, internet café, US-run, good place to meet fellow travellers.

Cigars
Tobacco & Co, Hidalgo 14. Cuban cigars and smoking paraphernalia. There are several other shops in the centre selling Cuban cigars.

Souvenirs
Av Hidalgo is lined with souvenir shops, most of them selling the same things: ceramic Maya figurines and masks; hammocks; blankets; and silver jewellery from Taxco. Bargaining is obligatory – try and get the desired item for half the original asking price, which is what the vendors expect to receive. There are more souvenir shops along the harbour front, where the salesmen are more pushy, and more shops along Av Morelos.

Playa del Carmen *p478, map p479*
Lots of expensive souvenir shops clustered around the plaza; cheaper shops, for day- to-day items, are on Av Juárez. There's a cheap *panadería* at the beginning of Av Juárez. For developing photos and buying film, there are several places along Av 5. **Joyería Cobá**, Av 5, recommended jewellers.

Chetumal *p487, map p487*
Shops are open 0800-1300, 1800-2000. Av Héroes is the main shopping street. Good for foreign foodstuffs – cheaper at the covered market in the outskirts than in the centre. A new commercial centre is being built at the site of the old bus station. **Super San Francisco** supermarket, near bus station, is better than the one behind **Arcada** restaurant.

Activities and tours

Cancún *p474, maps p476 and 474*
Boat trips and cruises
Trips to Isla Mujeres, with snorkelling, bar, shopping, start at US$27.50, or US$35 with meal. **M/V Aqua II**, T887-1909, has all-inclusive day cruises to Isla Mujeres starting from US$44. **Nautibus**, a vessel with seats below the waterline, makes trips to the reefs, 1½ hrs, a good way to see fish, Playa Linda dock, T883-3552. There are a number of other cruises on offer. **Atlantis submarines** offer trips in a 48-passenger vessel to explore natural and man-made reefs off Cancún. For more information contact Robert Theofel on T883-4963.

Bullfighting
Plaza de Toros, Av Bonompak south, has shows every Wed at 1530. Admission US$33, tickets available at travel agents and the ring.

Tour operators

Colors Travel, Av Yaxchilán 7C, SM24, T887-7929, colors@correoweb.com. Very friendly and helpful owner Martha Reyes Sangri; all-inclusive package deals to Río Lagartos and Ek-Balam with guides in various languages; overnight trip by plane to Tikal ruins in Guatemala; flights to Cuba, many other trips, reliable service. **Mayan Destinations**, Cobá 31, Edificio Monaco, SM22, T884-4308. All the usual destinations, such as Chichén Itzá, Xcaret, Tulum, as well as flights to Cuba. Many others in the centre and at larger hotels. Most hotels on the hotel zone have their own travel agency.
American Express, Av Tulum 208, esq Agua, SM 4, T884-5441.

Watersports

A variety of watersports can be organized on the beaches along the hotel zone, including parasailing, water-skiing, windsurfing and jet-skiing.

Isla Mujeres *p477*

Scuba diving and snorkelling

Touts along the seafront may tell you that the snorkelling centre at El Garrafón is closed. It is not. There are various reefs for diving and snorkelling, as well as a sunken cross specifically placed in deep water for divers to explore.
Coral, Av Matamoros13-A, T877-0763, www.coralscubadivecenter.com Over 25 years' experience, bilingual staff, good range of local dive sites.
Sea Hawk, Zazil-Ha (behind **Hotel Na-Balam**) T/F877-0296. Certified PADI instructors, 2-tank dive US$50, introductory course including shallow dive US$75. Also snorkelling trips and fishing trips.

Tour operators

Prisma Tours, Av Juárez 22, T/F877-0938. Tours to Tulum, Cobá, Chichén Itzá, Uxmal, Sian Ka'an in a/c vans. Also cheap and reliable airport transfer from Cancún Airport-Puerto Juárez. **Tercer Milenio**, Abasolo 46, between Juárez and Hidalgo, T877-0795. Tours to archaeological sites in Quintana Roo, airport transfer, high-class van rental, reservations for cruises, golf cart, moped and car rental, scuba diving, flights to Cuba, Belize, Guatemala.

Kitesurfing

Try kitesurfing or skateboarding with IKARUS, Av 5, Calle 16, T803-3490, www.ikaruskiteboarding.com. Good kit and instruction in this hair-raising sport, US$150.

Scuba diving

Abyss, Calle 12 and the beach, near the **Blue Parrot**, T873-2164, abyssdiveshop.com. Said to be the best. Run by fully certified American instructor David Tomlinson, PADI courses cost US$324; 1-tank dive costs US$40, 1-day introductory course US$69, also cavern dives and night dives.
Adventures Underwater, on plaza, T873-2647. Diving courses in English, French or Spanish, 3 certified instructors, 1-day beginner course US$60, open water PADI US$350, advanced refresher course US$250, cavern diving in 2 *cenotes* US$100.
Tank-Ha, in **Maya Bric Hotel**, T873-0302, www.tankha.com, and **Phocea Caribe**, Av 5 between Calle 12 and Calle 14, T873-1024, are also recommended.

Tour operators

Classique Travel, Calle 6 between Av 5 and Av 10, T/F 873-2598. Long-standing and reliable agency with a branch in Cancún, tours to Chichén Itzá US$72, including transport from hotel, guide, entry, food, also bookings for national and international flights, helpful staff. **Euro Latino**, Av 5 No 165B, Calle 6-8, T873-0549. An efficiently run agency with young European staff, 2 of their tours are: **Dawn in Tikal** (Guatemala) US$278, including flight, overnight stay in hotel, all meals, all transfers; **Weekend on Cozumel**, including dive (all levels) plus 2 nights and the ferry, US$72.

Cozumel *p479, map p480*

Scuba diving

See box, Cenote diving, page 483. The island is famous for the beauty of its underwater environment. The best reef for scuba diving is **Palancar**, reached only by boat. Also highly recommended are **Santa Rosa** and **Colombia**. For more experienced divers the reefs at **Punta Sur**, **Maracaibo** and **Baracuda** should not to be missed. There are at least 20 major dive sites. Almost all Cozumel diving is drift diving, so if you are not used to a current, choose an operator you feel comfortable with.

Dive centres There are 2 different types of dive centre: the larger ones, where the divers are taken out to sea in big boats with many passengers; the smaller, more personalized dive shops, with a maximum of 8 people per small boat.

The best of the smaller centres is said to be **Deep Blue**, A R Salas 200, esq Av 10 Sur, T/F872-5653, www.deepbluecozumel.com. Matt and Deborah, an English/Colombian couple, run the centre. All PADI and NAUI certifications, eg Open Water, US$360; 3-5-day dive packages US$165-250; cavern and *cenote* diving, including 2 dives, transport and lunch US$130.

Other small dive centres are: **Black Shark**, Av 5 between A R Salas and Calle 3 Sur, T/F872-5657; **Blue Bubble Divers**, Av 5 Sur, esq Calle 3, T872-1865; **Diving Adventures**, Calle 5 No 2, T872-3009.

Decompression centres **Buceo Médico Mexicano**, Calle 5 Sur No 21B, T872-2387, immediate localization (24-hr) VHF 16 and 21. It is suported by US$1 per day donations from divers with affiliated operators. **Cozumel Hyperbarics** in Clínica San Miguel, Calle 6 Norte No 135 between Av 5 and Av 10, T872-3070, VHF channel 65. **Nachicocom**, on the seafront and Calle 5 Sur, T872-1430. A new one.

Tour operators

Ferinco Travel Tours, T872-1781. Own airline with flights to all major Maya sites.

Tulum *p483*

Diving Several dive shops all along the Tulum corridor. See page 483 for cavern diving operators and specialist courses – highly recommended if you like diving. There are many untrained snorkelling and diving outfits, take care. **Aktun**, next to **Hotel El Mesón**, 1 km out of Tulum on main road, T871-2311, www.aktundive.com. German/Mexican-run, experienced NACD and IANTD instructor, very friendly, speaks English, French and Dutch. **Hidden World's Cenotes**, at Dos Ojos caverns (largest in the world), T877-8535, www.hiddenworlds.com.mx. Only technical fill station in Tulum, snorkel (US$40) diving trips (from US$50), several trips a day.

Chetumal *p487, map p487*

Tour operators

Tu-Maya, Av Héroes 165A, T832-0555. 1-day tours to Guatemala, Belize and Calakmul. **Explora Premier**, Av Juárez 83, esq Zaragoza, T832-3096, otocarybe@mpsnet.com.mx. Eco and adventure tours, car rental.

Transport

Cancún *p474, maps p476 and 474*

Air

International departure tax is US$22. Cancún airport (CUN) has expensive shops and restaurant, exchange facilities, double check your money, especially at busy times, poor rates too, 2 hotel reservation agencies (no rooms under US$45). 2 terminals: Main and South (or 'FBO' building), white shuttle minibuses between them. From Cancún there are domestic flights and connections throughout the country. For international connections see Getting there on page 31 and 66. For airline websites, see page 32.

Airline offices Aerocaribe and Aerocozumel, Av Cobá 5, Plaza América SM4, T884-2000. **AeroMéxico**, Av Cobá 80, SM3, T884-3571. **American Airlines**, Aeropuerto, T883-4460. **Aviacsa**, Av Cobá 37, SM4, T887-4211. **Aviateca**, Av Cobá 5, Plaza América SM4, T887-4110. **Continental**, Aeropuerto, T886-0006. **Cubana de Aviación**, Av Yaxchilán 23, T887-7373. **Iberia**, Aeropuerto, T886-0243. **Lacsa**, Av Cobá 5, Plaza América SM4, T887-3101. **Mexicana**, Av Tulum, T887-4444.

Bus

Local Regular buses to Cancún from outside the ferry dock, US$0.50. On the whole it is better to catch outgoing buses to more distant destinations in Cancún rather than in Puerto Juárez as there are more of them.

Long distance Cancún bus terminal, at the junction of Av Tulum and Uxmal, is small, well organized and handy for the cheaper hostels. The bus station is the hub for routes west to Mérida and south to Tulum and Chetumal, open 24 hrs, left luggage US$0.55 per hr. Many services to **Mérida**, 4 hrs, ranging from *Plus* with TV, a/c, etc US$28, to

1st class US$19, to 2nd class US$11; all services call at **Valladolid**, 2hrs, US$9, 1st class, US$7, 2nd class. To **Chichén Itzá**, many buses, starting at 0630, 3 hrs, US$7-10. Expreso de Oriente also has services to **Tizimín** (3 hrs, US$8), **Izamal**, **Cenotillo** and **Chiquilá**. To **Palenque**, US$40, and **San Cristóbal**, 7 a day between 1415 and 2030, 17 hrs, US$48-57. To **Villahermosa**, 1000, 1300 and 1845, 12 hrs, US$43. **Playa del Carmen** every 10 mins, US$2.25. Inter Playa Express every 30 mins to **Puerto Morelos**, US$1; to **Xcaret**, US$2.25; 3 times daily to **Puerto Aventuras**, US$2.50, **Xel-Há**, US$3.30, and **Tulum**, every 10 mins, 2 hrs, US$5.60. Other services to Playa del Carmen and Tulum are more expensive, eg 1st class Caribe Inter to Playa del Carmen US$3, 2nd class US$2.35, and US$4.75 to Tulum. Last bus to Playa del Carmen 2000, first bus to Tulum 0430. These services are en route to **Chetumal**, from 0500, then every 2 hrs until 0030, 5½ hrs, US$17. The 0800 departure for Chetumal arrives for connection to Flores and will get you to Belize City by around 2000. Several other services to Chetumal include Caribe Express, deluxe service with a/c.

Car

Car hire Budget Rent-a-Car in Cancún has been recommended for good service. A 4-door Nissan Sentra, a/c, can be hired for US$24 per day from Budget at the airport, insurance US$15. Avis, Plaza Caracol, cheapest but still expensive. There are many car hire agencies, with offices on Av Tulum, in the Hotel Zone and at the airport; look out for special deals, but check vehicles carefully.

Car parking Do not leave cars parked in side streets; there is a high risk of theft. Use the parking lot on Av Uxmal.

Ferry

The ferry to **Isla Mujeres** is much cheaper from Puerto Juárez (see below). The one from Cancún departs from Playa Linda Pier, at the mainland side of the bridge across Canal Nichupté, about 4 km from centre, opposite the **Calinda Quality Cancún Beach**. Playa Linda has shops, agencies for boat trips, a snack bar and Computel. The ferry leaves 9 times a day between 0900 and 1645, US$12.50 return, 20 mins' journey. Returns 7 times a day between 0900 and 1700.

Cancún to Isla Mujeres *p477*

Bus

Regular buses to Cancún from outside the ferry dock, Puerto Juárez, US$0.50. On the whole it is better to catch outgoing buses to more distant destinations in Cancún rather than in Puerto Juárez as there are more of them.

Ferry

There are 2 ferry departure points for Isla Mujeres. From **Puerto Juárez**, the more expensive ferry costs US$3.50 and leaves Puerto Juárez every 30 mins between 0600 and 2330 and takes 30 mins. Passengers are packed inside; badly functioning a/c makes for a hot and airless journey of 15 mins. The cheaper ferry is in an open-decked boat with cool breezes, much nicer but slightly slower journey, 40 mins, US$1.80, every 45-60 mins from 0600-1800. Car ferries leave from **Punta Sam** 5 times a day from 0800, US$7-8 per car, US$1.20 passengers, 45 mins. There is a luggage store, 0800-1800, and a tourist information desk at the jetty. There are also ferries leaving from the Hotel Zone in Cancún.

Isla Mujeres *p477*

Air

The small airstrip in the middle of the island is mainly used for private planes. Flights can be booked to Cancún and Chichén Itzá through **Mundaca Travel**, on Hidalgo, T877-0025. Charters with **Island Airtours**, contact T877-0331, Helena or Adriana. Also directly with Capt Joaquín Ricalde T9845-3038 (mob) for sightseeing trips to Isla Mujeres, Holbox, Cozumel, Tulum, Chichén Itzá.

Bicycle and moped

Many touts along Hidalgo offer moped rentals at similar rates: US$8 per hr, US$20 full day. **Sport Bike**, Av Juárez y Morelos, has good bikes. **Cárdenas**, Av Guerrero 105, T/F877-0079, for mopeds and golf carts. Bicycles are usually offered by the same places as mopeds for about US$8 per day.

Bus

A public bus runs from the ferry dock to Playa Paraíso every ½ hr, US$0.25.

Ferry

For information on ferries to and from the island, see Cancún to Isla Mujeres, above.

Taxi

A taxi from town to **El Garrafón** is US$3.40. For the return journey, sharing a taxi will work out marginally more expensive than the bus for 4 people. A taxi from El Garrafón to the bus stop at Playa Paraíso is US$1. Taxis charge an additional US$1 at night. There are several places renting **golf carts**, eg Ciros, on Matamoros near Playa Cocos. Rates are generally US$40-50 per day. A credit card is usually required as a deposit.

Puerto Morelos *p478*

Bus

There are buses to Cancún and Playa del Carmen every ½ hr. Buses depart from the main road, taxi to bus stop US$3.

Ferry

Car ferries to **Cozumel** depart twice a day at 0600 and 1500, the dock is 500 m south of the plaza. Taxi from Cancún airport to Puerto Morelos cost US$25-35.

Playa del Carmen *p478, map p479*

Air

There are also flights to **Cozumel** from the nearby airstrip; touts will mingle with the queues for the ferry to get passengers. Flights cost US12.50 1-way, 10 mins.

Bus

The ADO bus terminal is on Av Juárez between Av 5 and 10. All buses depart from here. The following prices and times are for ADO buses (1st class, a/c, usually showing a video on longer journeys); **Premier**, also 1st class; **Maya de Oro**, supposed to be 1st class but quality of buses can be poor; **Cristóbal Colón**, good 1st-class service. To **Cancún**, 8 per day, 1¼ hr, US$3. To **Mérida**, 4 per day, 7 hrs, US$10. To **Valladolid**, 0730 and 1115, 3½ hrs, US$8 (most buses going to Mérida stop at Valladolid. 2nd-class buses to Valla
dolid go via Tulum, US$6.50). To **Chichén Itzá**, 6 per day, 4 hrs, US$7. To **Tulum**, 5 per day, 1 hr, US$2. To **Xcaret**, frequent service, 10 mins, US$1. To **Xel Há**, 2 per day, 1 hr, US$2. To **Chetumal**, 8 per day, 5 hrs, US$10. To **Mexico City**, 3 per day, 24 hrs, US$54. To **San Cristóbal de las Casas**, 3 per day, 16 hrs, US$37.

Car

Car hire Caribetur, Av 10 No 128 between Calle 2 and 4 Norte, T873-2292. **Freedom**, Av 5, T873-1459. **Happy**, Plaza Tucán, Local 6, T873-1739. **Hertz**, T873-0703. **Budget**, T873-0100.

Ferry

Ferries to **Cozumel** depart from the main dock, just off the plaza, every hr on the hr, 0400-2200, ½ hr, US$8 1-way, buy ticket 1 hr before journey.

Taxi

Cancún airport US$25. Beware of those who charge only US$5 as they are likely to charge an extra US$20 for luggage. Tours to **Tulum** and **Xel-Há** from kiosk by boat dock US$30; tours to Tulum, Xel-Há and **Xcaret**, 5-6 hrs, US$60; taxi to Xcaret US$6.65. Taxis congregate on the Av Juárez side of the square (**Sindicato Lázaro Cárdenas del Río**, T873-0032).

Cozumel *p479, map p480*

Air

To **Mexico City** direct with **Mexicana**, or via Cancún; **Continental** to **Houston**; **Aerocaribe** to **Cancún** and **Chichén Itzá**. **Aerocaribe** and **Aerocozumel** have almost hourly flights to **Cancún**.

Airline offices Most are based at the airport, 2 km north of the town. **Aerocozumel**, T872-3456. **Continental**, T872-0847. **Mexicana**, P Joaquín between Salas and Calle 3 Sur, next to Pemex, T872-0263.

Bicycle and moped

There is no bus service, but taxis are plentiful. The best way to get around the island is by hired moped or bicycle. Mopeds cost US$25-30 per day, credit card needed as deposit; bicycles are around US$8 per day, US$20 cash or TC deposit. **Rentadora Cozumel**, Av 10 Sur No 172 between Salas y Calle 1 Sur, T872-1120. **Splash**, Calle 6 Norte, T872-3977.

Car

Car rental There are many agencies, including Less Pay, in Hotel Barracuda, T872-4744. **Budget Jeep and Auto**, Av 5 y Calle 2, T872-0903. **Aguila Jeep and Moto**, Calle 11 No 101, T872-0729.

Tulum *p483*

Bicycle

Bikes can be hired in the village at US$1 per hr, a good way to visit local centres (**Cristal** and **Escondido** are recommended as much cheaper, US$2, and less commercialized than **Xcaret**).

Bus

Regular buses go up and down the coastal road travelling from Cancún to Tulum en route to Chetumal, stopping at most places in between. Some buses may be full when they reach Tulum; very few buses begin their journeys here. **Felipe Carrillo Puerto**: several 0600-1200 and 1600-2200, 1 hr, US$4.70, continuing to **Chetumal**: 4 hrs, 2nd class, US$10, 1st class US$12. For **Cobá**: take the Playa del Carmen-Tulum-Cobá-Valladolid bus which passes El Crucero at 0600, 1100 and 1800 (in the other direction buses pass Tulum at 0715 and 1545, all times approximate, may leave 15 mins early). To **Cobá**, 45 mins, US$1.35. To **Mérida**, several daily, 6 hrs, US$10, 2nd class. To **Tizimín**, daily at 1400, via Cancún and Valladolid. To **Escárcega** and **Córdoba**, 0800, to **Palenque** US$34. To **San Cristóbal**, 1845, often late, US$45. To **Villahermosa**, 1630, 2100, US$35. To **Mexico City**, 0815, 1315, 2100, US$85. **Autobuses del Caribe** offices are next door to **Hotel Maya**. Buy tickets here rather than wait for buses at the crossroads, but this still does not ensure getting a seat. It may be better to go to Playa del Carmen (US$1.40) for more connections to nearby destinations. If travelling far, take a bus to Felipe Carrillo Puerto and transfer to **ADO** there.

Taxi

Tulum town to Tulum ruins US$3.50; to the *cabañas* US$3.50; to **Cobá** about US$25.

Cobá *p484*

Bus

Buses into the village turn round at the road end. There are 3 a day to **Valladolid**, coming from Playa del Carmen and Tulum, passing through at 0630, 1130 and 1830, 2 hrs to Valladolid, US$2.50; 2 buses a day to **Tulum** and **Playa del Carmen** at 0630 and 1500, US$1 to Tulum.

Taxi

A taxi to **Tulum** should cost you around US$25. If you miss the bus there is a taxi to be found at El Bocadito.

Felipe Carrillo Puerto *p486*

Bus

Bus station opposite Pemex. **Autotransportes del Caribe** (Playa Express) to **Cancún** daily from 0600, 1st and 2nd class to **Tulum**, US$2, and **Playa del Carmen** en route. To **Mérida**, via Muná, 4½ hrs, US$10; to **Valladolid**, 2nd class, 2 hrs, US$3.75; to **Chetumal**, 1st class, 2 hrs, US$3.35.

Chetumal *p487, map p487*

Air

Airport (CTM) 2.5 km from town. Flights to **Cancún**, **Mérida**, **Belize City** (Aerocaribe), **Mexico City**, **Monterrey** and **Tijuana**.

Airline offices Aerocaribe, Plaza Varudi, Av Héroes 125. **Aviacsa**, T832-7765.

Bus

Bus information T832-5110. The main bus terminal is 3 km out of town at the intersection of Insurgentes y Belice. Taxi into town US$1.20. There is a bus into the centre from Av Belice. **Left luggage** lockers cost US$0.20 per hr. If buying tickets in advance, go to the ADO office on Av Belice esq Ghandi, 0800-1600. There are often more buses than those marked on the display in the bus station. Always ask at the information desk. Many buses going to the border, US$0.30; taxi from Chetumal to border, 20 mins, US$6 for 2. Long-distance buses are often all booked a day ahead, so avoid unbooked connections. Expect passport checks on buses leaving for Mexican destinations. To **Mexico City** with **Autobuses del Caribe**, 2100, 20 hrs, US$70. To **Villahermosa**, 5 between 1830 and 2230, 9 hrs, US$25, the road is bad so the journey sometimes takes longer. To **Puebla**, 0630, 2200 and 2230, 16 hrs, US$62. To **Escárcega**, 5 departures, 1045-2230, 5 hrs, US$12. To **Palenque**, 2215, 14 hrs, US$21, or take bus to San Cristóbal. To **San Cristóbal**, 0130 and 1845, US$27, or the 2115, 13 hrs, US$30 calling at **Escárcega** (US$12), **Emiliano Zapata** (11½ hrs, US$19), **Palenque** (US$21) and **Ocosingo** (13½ hrs, US$26). To **Tuxtla Gutiérrez**, 2115, US$34. To **Mérida**, 0730, 1330, 1730 and 2330, luxury US$18, sleeper at 2330, US$31. To **Felipe Carrillo Puerto**, 1200 and 2300, 2 hrs, US$7. To **Cancún**, almost hourly, 6 hrs, 2nd class US$16, luxury at midnight US$20. To **Tulum**, 8 a day, 4 hrs, US$10. To **Playa del Carmen**, every couple of hrs, 5 hrs, US$10. To **Minatitlán**, 2000, 12 hrs, US$34. There are also buses to **Veracruz** (1045 and 1830, 10hrs, US$46), **Campeche** (1200, 6 hrs, US$18) **Villahermosa** (2200, US$25), **Córdoba** (2100, US$53) and **Xpujil** (5 a day, 2½ hrs, US$5). To **Bacalar** buses are very frequent (several per hr). To **Francisco Villa**(US$1.30) and **Xpujil** (US$4) at 1300 and 1600.

To Belize To **Corozal**, **Orange Walk** and **Belize City**, 3½-5 hrs on paved road, US$7, schedules change frequently. Money-changers in the bus terminal offer marginally poorer rates than those at the border. If intending to stay in Belize City, do not take a bus that arrives at night as you are advised not to look for a hotel in the dark. To **Orange Walk**, 2½ hrs, US$4.50. It is difficult to hitch to the Belizean border. To hitch once inside Belize, it is best to take the *colectivo* from in front of the hospital (1 block from the bus station, ask) marked 'Chetumal-Santa Elena', US$1.

To Guatemala San Juan Travel Agency, based at Chetumal bus station, T832-5110. Leaves 1500 for **Flores**, arriving 2100, returns 0500 connecting to 1400 bus to **Cancún**. US$35 one way plus US$3 at the Belize-Guatemala border. Direct daily buses to Flores in Guatemala, at 0620, 0700, 1400 and 1430, 8 hrs, US$17-22.

Car

There's a petrol/gas station just outside Chetumal on the road north at the beginning of the road to Escárcega, and another at Xpujil.

Garage Talleres Barrera, helpful, on Primo de Verdad; turn east off Héroes, then past the electrical plant.

Taxi

There are no city buses; taxis run on fixed-price routes, US$0.50 on average. Cars with light-green licence plates are a form of taxi.

Colectivos To **Bacalar** and **Francisco Villa** (for Kohunlich and Xpujil) depart from the junction of Av Miguel Hidalgo and Francisco Primo de Verdad.

Directory

Cancún *p474, maps p476 and 474*

Banks There are 11 Mexican banks along Av Tulum, all in SM4 and SM5. **American Express**, for changing their own TCs at better rates than anywhere else, is on Av Tulum, just south of Av Cobá. Many *casas de cambio* in the centre, mainly around the bus terminal and along Av Tulum. *Casas de cambio* in the Hotel Zone give slightly lower rates for TCs than those in the centre.
Cultural centres Casa Tabasco, Av Tulum 230, displays and handicrafts for sale from the state of Tabasco, a good place to go if bored of the same old souvenirs in Cancún.
Embassies and consulates Austria, Cantera 4, SM15, Centro, T884-7505. **Canada,** Plaza Caracol, 3rd floor, Hotel Zone, T883-3360. **France**, Hotel Casa Turquesa, Hotel Zone, T885-2924. **Germany**, Punta Conoco 36, SM24, Centro, T884-1898; **Italy**, Alcatraces 39, SM22, Centro, T884-1261. **Netherlands**, Hotel Presidente, Hotel Zone, T883-0200. **Spain**, Oasis Corporativo, Hotel Zone, T883-2466. **Sweden**, **Switzerland**, Hotel Caesar Park, Hotel Zone, T881-8013. **UK**, Hotel Royal Caribbean, Hotel Zone, T881-0100. **US**, Plaza Caracol, 3rd floor, Hotel Zone, T883-0272. **Immigration office** On the corner of Av Náder and Av Uxmal. There is also an office in the airport, T886-0492, where the staff are better trained and speak English. **Internet** Numerous cafés charging US$1-1.50 per hr. Generally good servers, open until around 2300. **Language schools** El Bosque del Caribe, Náder and Uxmal, T/F884-1065, www.cancun-language.com.mx. **Laundry** Alborada, Nader 5, behind tourist information building on Av Tulum. **Cox-boh**, Av Tankah 26, SM24.
Medical services American Hospital (24-hr), Viento 15, Centro, T884-6133. **Total Assist** (24-hr) Claveles 5, Centro, T884-1058. **American Medical Centre**, Plaza Quetzal,

Hotel Zone Km 8, T883-0113. **Post office** At the end of Av Sunyaxchén, near Mercado 28, Mon-Fri 0800-1900, Sat 0900-1300. **Telephone** Many public phones everywhere, phone cards available from general stores and pharmacies. Collect calls can be made without a card. Also many public phones designed for international calls, which take coins and credit cards. Fax at post office, Mon-Sat, and at San Francisco de Asís shopping mall, Mon-Sat until 2200.

Isla Mujeres *p477*

Banks Banco del Atlántico, Av Juárez 5. Banca Serfín, Av Juárez 3. Both can get very busy. Good rates, varying daily, are offered by several *casas de cambio* on Av Hidalgo. The one opposite Rolandis is open daily 0900-2100. **Internet** Several new internet cafés operate on the island US$2-2.50 per hr, but speeds can be a little slow. **Language school** Ixchel Language Institute, Matamoros 82, 1-wk survival courses, US$10 per hr, individual, US$5.50 group lessons. **Laundry** Tim Pho, Juárez y Abasolo. **Medical services** Doctors: Dr Antonio Salas, Hidalgo, next to *Farmacia*, T877-0477. 24 hrs, house calls, English spoken, air ambulance. Dr Antonio Torres, Av Matamoros esq Guerrero, T877-0050. 24 hrs, English and German spoken. **Post office** At the end of Guerrero towards the beach. **Telephone** Phone cards can be bought at some of the souvenir shops along Hidalgo. International calls and faxes at Gold & Silver, Av Hidalgo 58.

Puerto Morelos *p478*

Internet There is an internet café on the corner of the plaza opposite Posada Amor, US$2.50/hr, Mon-Sat 1000-1400, 1600-2100.

Playa del Carmen *p478, map p479*

Banks Bancomer, Av Juárez between Calle 25 and 30. Banamex, Av Juárez between Calle 20 and 25. A few doors down is Santander. Banorte, Av 5 between Av Juárez and the beach. Inverlat, Av 5 between Av Juárez and Calle 2. HSBC, Av Juárez between Calle 10 and 15, also at Av 30 between Calle 4 and 6. There are several *casas de cambio* along Av 5, which change TCs with no commission. Count your money carefully as short changing is not uncommon.

Immigration office Centro Comercial, Plaza Antigua, Av 10 Sur, T873-1884. **Internet** All the cybercafés in town charge between US$1.50-2 per hr. **Language schools** Playalingua,Calle 20 between 5 and 10, T873-3876, www.playalingua.com, weekend excursions, a/c, library, family stays, US$85 enrolment fee, US$185 per wk (20 hrs). Playa Spanish School 'El Estudiante', Av 15 between Calle 14 and 16, T/F879-3595, www.playaspanishschool.com. US$7.00/hr. Recommended. Also offer courses in English and German. Solexico Language and Cultural Center, Av 35 between 6 and 6 bis, T873-0755, www.solexico.com. Variable programme with workshops, also have a school in Oaxaca. **Laundry** Av Juárez, 2 blocks from bus station; another on Av 5. Maya Laundry, Av 5 between Calle 2 and Calle 4, Mon-Sat 0800-2100. Laundry in by 1000, ready in the afternoon. **Medical services** Dentist: Perla de Rocha Torres, Av 20 Norte between 4 and 6, T873-0021, speaks English. Recommended. International Medical Services, Dr Victor Macías Orosco, Av 35 between Calle 2 and 4, T873-0493. 24-hr emergency service, land and air ambulance, ultrasound, most major insurance accepted. Tourist Divers Medical Centre, Dr Mario Abarca, Av 10 between Av Juárez and Calle 2, T873-0512. Air and land ambulance service, hyperbaric and diving medicine, affiliated with South Miami Hospital, all insurance accepted. **Police** Av Juárez, next to the post office, T873-0291. **Post office** Av Juárez y Av 15, Mon-Fri 0800-1700, Sat 0900-1300. Telegraph office is around the corner on Av 15.

Cozumel *p479, map p480*

Banks 4 banks on the main square, all exchange money in morning only, but not at same hours: HSBC, on Juárez (all with ATM machines), Bancomer, Banamex, Atlántico. *Casas de cambio* on Av 5 Norte and around square, 3.5% commission, open longer hours. **Internet** Several internet cafés set up recently charging around US$1.50 per hr. **Laundry** Express, Salas between Av 5 and Av 10, T872-3655. Coin-op and service washes, US$9 medium load, collection service and dry cleaning. **Medical services** Dentist: Dr Hernández, T872-0656. Hospitals and clinics Red Cross,

A R Salas between Calle 20 and Calle 25 Sur, T872-1058. **Centro Médico de Cozumel**, Calle 1 Sur No 101, esq Av 50, T872-3545. English spoken, international air ambulance, 24-hr emergency service. **Pharmacy**: Salas between Av 12 and Av 20, 0700-2400. **Post office** Av Rafael Melgar y Calle 7 Sur, Mon-Fri 0900-1800, Sat 0900-1200. **Telephone** Ladatel phones (if working) on main square at corner of Av Juárez and Av 5, or on Salas, just up from Av 5 Sur, opposite **Roberto's Black Coral Studio.** For calls to the US, go to **The Stadium. Telmex** phone offices on the main square next to Restaurant Plaza Leza, 0800-2300, and on Salas between Av 10 and 15. There are also expensive **Computel** offices in town, eg at the cruise ship dock. **Telephone centre** for long distance on corner of Rafael Melgar and Calle 3 Sur. Also public telephone *caseta* at Av 5 esq Calle 2, 0800-1300, 1600-2100.

Tulum *p483*

Banks 4 money exchange booths near bus station in Tulum village. TCs can be changed at the offices of the GOPI Construction Company, although not at a very good rate. **Medical services** Malaria prophylaxis available from **Centro de Salud**, opposite hospital (request tablets for *paludismo*). **Telephone** Long-distance phones in ADO terminal in town.

Chetumal *p487, map p487*

Banks The banks all close at 1430. There are several ATMs. For exchange, **Banamex**, Obregón y Juárez, changes TCs. **Banco Mexicano**, Juárez and Cárdenas, TCs or US$ cash, quick and courteous service. Several on, or near, Av Héroes with ATMs. Banks do not change quetzales into pesos. Good rates at **Bodegas Blanco** supermarket beside bus terminal; will change US dollars and Belize dollars (only if you spend at least 15 of the total on their groceries!). Try also **Casa Medina**, L Cárdenas. Pemex stations will accept US and Belizean dollars, but at poor rates for the latter. **San Francisco de Assisi** supermarket changes TCs, next to bus station. **Embassies and consulates** **Guatemala**, Av Héroes de Chapultepec 354, T832-6565. Open for visas, Mon-Fri 0900-1700. It is best to organize your visa, if required, in your home country before travel. **Belize**, Hon Consul, Lic Francisco Lechón Rosas, Rotondo Carranza 562 (behind Super San Francisco) , T878-7728; visas can take up to 3 weeks to get, and many are only issued in Mexico City. **Internet** Eclipse, 5 de Mayo 83 between PE Calles and Zaragoza. 0930-1500, 1800-2100, not very friendly but cheap at US$3 per hr. **Los Cebollones**, Calzada Veracruz 452, T832-9145, also restaurant and cocktail bar. **Laundry** **Lavandería Automática 'Lava facil'**, corner of Héroes and Confederación Nacional Campesina. **Medical services** Malaria prophylaxis available from **Centro de Salud**, opposite hospital (request tablets for paludismo). **Post office** 16 de Septiembre y PE Calles. Mon-Fri 0800-1730, Sat 0900-1300. Packets to be sent abroad must be taken unwrapped to the bus terminal to have them checked by customs before taking them to the post office. Better to wait till another town. Parcel service not available Sat. **Western Union** office attached to post office, same hours.

Guatemala

Footprint features

Introduction

Guatemala has a monopoly on colour – from the red lava tongues of the volcanoes in the Western Highlands to the creamy shades of the caves in the southern Petén, and from the white sand of the Caribbean coast near Lívingston to the black sand and fabulous orange sunsets on the Pacific. And that's just nature's palette. Completing this work of art are traditional Maya fiestas, arcane religious rituals, where idol worship and Roman Catholicism merge, and jungle temples where ancient ruins tell of long-lost civilizations. Deep in Guatemala's northern jungle, the majestic cities of the Maya are buried. Temples, stelae and plazas have been discovered here, along with evidence of human sacrifice and astronomical genius, to reveal their dynastic history and traditions.

Antigua is the colonial centre of the New World. Gracefully ruined after an 18th-century earthquake, its cobbled streets are lined with columned courtyards, toppled church arches, preserved pastel-coloured houses, flowers and fountains galore. Formed by an explosion that blew the lid off the top of a volcanic mountain, Lake Atitlán and its three volcanoes are truly breathtaking. Further west, the bustling city of Quetzaltenango makes an excellent base from which to explore the volcanoes, markets and villages of the Western Highlands, such as the mountain community of Todos Santos, where the colourful clothes of the Maya and the All Saints' Day horse race are major attractions. In the Verapaces, rivers run through caves stuffed with stalagmites and stalactites. On the humid lower slopes of the Pacific, Olmec-influenced ruins are buried among coffee bushes and turtles nest on the shore, while on the Caribbean coast the Garífuna rock to the sound of the punta and dolphins frolic in the sea.

★ Don't miss...

1 **Antigua** Cobbled streets and pastel shades in this centre of linguistic learning, reborn from the rubble of devastating earthquakes; a good base for visits to nearby active volcanoes, page 534.

2 **Lake Atitlán** The most beautiful lake in the world, swathed in mystery, surrounded by volcanoes, page 551.

3 **Todos Santos Cuchumatán** Hidden in the mid-west mountains, the vibrancy, colour and culture of the Mam Indians erupts at the annual festival (15 November), page 582.

4 **Around Quetzaltenango** Explore the indigenous towns, markets and volcanoes of the western highlands, page 587.

5 **Lívingston and Río Dulce** The rediscovered Caribbean coast is a good place to chill, with rainforest hiking and waterfalls close to Río Dulce, pages 611 and 612.

6 **Tikal** One of the great Maya ruins in Central America, tribute to this ancient civilization; use the island of nearby Flores as your base, page 635.

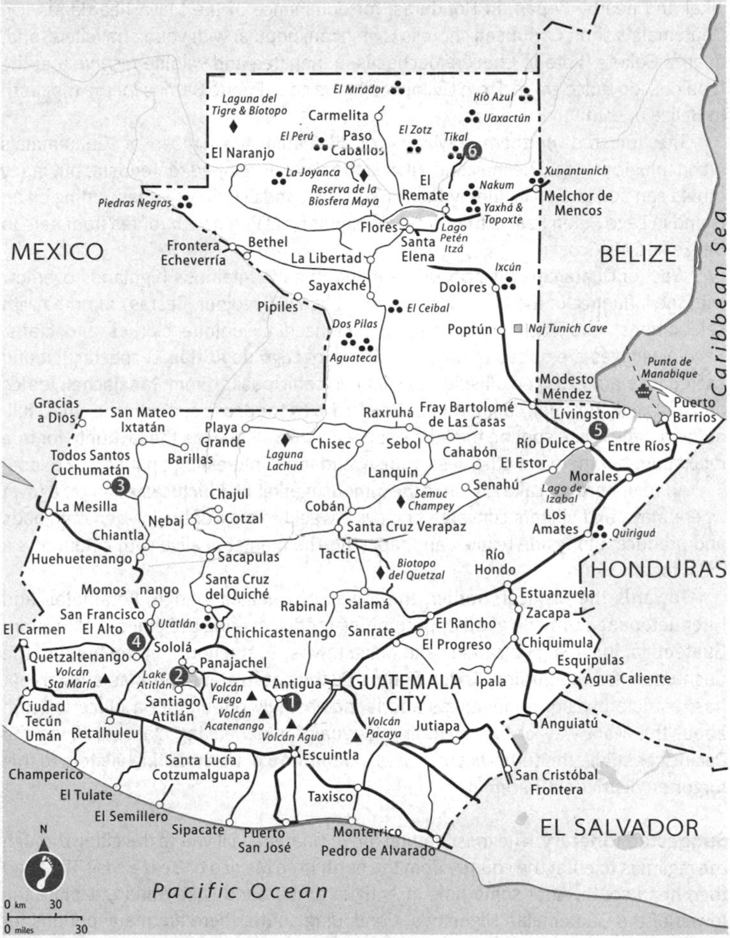

Planning your trip

Where to go

Guatemala City is a modern, polluted capital. It is the main entry point for travellers by air and long-distance bus. While there are some sites of interest and a couple of excellent museums in the city centre and some great nightlife, few stay long, preferring to head west to the clean air and relaxed atmosphere of **Antigua**. Once the capital, Antigua was built by the Spanish *conquistadores*. Later destroyed by several huge earthquakes, the grand ruins of colonial architecture remain and the dramatic location, at the foot of three volcanoes, as well as its prominence as a centre for Spanish studies, make Antigua a justifiably popular destination.

Heading northeast from Guatemala City, lie the highlands of the Verapaz region. **Cobán** is the main focus, with access to nearby traditional villages, the caves at Lanquín, the natural bridge of Semuc Champey and, at Purulhá, the Mario Dary Rivera Reserve which protects the habitat of the quetzal, the Guatemala's national bird. Skirting the northern shores of Lago de Izabal is the newly formed Bocas del Polochic Wildlife Reserve which is full of monkeys, avifauna and other wildlife.

South of the lake, the highway runs close to **Quiriguá**, which once competed with Tikal and nearby Copán, in Honduras, for dominance of the Maya heartlands. On Guatemala's short **Caribbean** shore is Lívingston, popular with young travellers, and, near El Golfete Biotopo Chocón-Machacas, a manatee and wildlife reserve and the fabulous Río Dulce gorge. From Lívingston boats go to Puerto Barrios for the trip north to Belize or south to Honduras.

The forested northern lowlands of **El Petén** hide most of Guatemala's archaeological sites. The majestic **Tikal** is the most developed for tourism, but many others can be reached including Uaxactún, Yaxhá and El Ceibal. **Flores**, sitting on an island in Lago Petén Itzá, is the centre for exploring El Petén with routes from here to Belize and Mexico.

West of Guatemala City, beyond Antigua, the mountainous highlands overflow with the influence of the Maya. Market days filled with colour, fiestas crammed with celebrations, and each community characterized by unique clothes and crafts. Several villages are dotted around the shores of **Lago de Atitlán**, a spectacular and sacred lake protected on all sides by silent volcanic peaks. From **Panajachel**, ferries and trails link the small communities. **San Pedro La Laguna** is currently the chief chill-out and hang-loose spot on the lake's shores, with **San Marcos** the favourite for true relaxation; but there are other less touristy and more interesting options to explore.

An hour north of Lake Atitlán is the famous market of **Chichicastenango**, a town where Maya and visitors converge in a twice-weekly frenzy of buying general goods and produce, alongside textiles and tapestry. The market is alive with colour and a must for any visitor.

Towards the Mexican border, the towns of Quetzaltenango, Retalhuleu and Huehuetenango provide good opportunities for discovering the charms of western Guatemala, including volcanoes and Maya towns. To the north, in the heart of the Cuchumatanes mountains, **Todos Santos Cuchumatán** stands firm as a town that has restricted western influences and is increasingly popular as a place to learn about the Mam way of life, including language and weaving classes. Along the Pacific coastline, the turtle-nesting sites of **Monterrico** are attracting visitors to this forgotten district of Guatemala.

Suggested itinerary The most natural trip in Guatemala if you're travelling through the region is to enter the country from the north from Mexico or Belize, visit Tikal and then head south. After some time in Antigua and around Lake Atitlán, explore the towns of the Guatemalan Highlands. Continuing south, there are many options for crossing the border. Head for El Florido, for best access to Copán, or out to the Caribbean and the crossing at Entre Ríos-Corinto. Three to four weeks is a good stay in Guatemala; any less and you'll have to rush around.

When to go

Climate is dependent upon altitude and varies greatly. Most of the population lives at between 900 and 2500 m, where the climate is healthy – with warm days and cool nights, so you'll need warm clothes at night. The majority of visitors spend most of their time in the highlands, where the dry season lasts from November to April. Some places enjoy a respite from the rains (the *canícula*) in July and August. On the Pacific and Caribbean coasts you can expect rain all year round, heaviest on the Pacific in June and September with a dry spell in between, but with no dry season on the Caribbean. In the lowlands of El Petén, the wet season is roughly May to October, when the mosquitoes are most active. December to February are cooler months, while March and April are hot and dry. In terms of festivals, the key events are Semana Santa at Easter in Antigua, see page 538 and All Saints' Day, in Todos Santos, see page 583.

Finding out more

Instituto Guatemalteco de Turismo (INGUAT), 7 Av, 1-17, Zona 4, Centro Cívico, Guatemala City, T2421-2800, www.visitguatemala.com. INGUAT provides bus times, hotel lists and road maps. Staff are helpful. The INGUAT airport office is open daily 0600-2100.

INGUAT tourist offices

If an address is not given, see Embassies, page 512.
Canada, T001-613-233-2349.
Germany, Joachim Karntaz-Alle 45-47, 10557, Berline Tiergarten.
Italy, Viale Prassilla 152, 00124, Rome, T390-6-5091-6626.
Mexico, T00-52-5202-1457, turismoembagua@prodigy.net.mx.
Spain, Calle Rafael Salgado 9, 4th Izquierda, 28036 Madrid, T/F34-91-457-3424.
USA, T001-202-518-5514.

Useful websites

Regional websites covering some of the more popular areas include **www.atitlan.com**, **www.mayaparadise.com** (Río Dulce/Lívingston), **www.cobanav.net** (Cobán) and **www.xelapages.com** (Quetzaltenango).

Of the several publications with websites, the *Revue*, **www.revuemag.com**, is probably the most useful to the visitor. Information on Guatemala and the Maya at **The Guatemalan Maya Centre**, 94A Wandsworth Bridge Rd, London SW6 2TF, T/F020-7371-5291, www.maya.org.uk. Library, video archive and textile collection.

Language

The official language is Spanish. Outside the main tourist spots few people speak English. There are more than 20 Mayan languages. Guatamala is one of the biggest centres for learning Spanish in Latin America.

Working in Guatemala

If you would like to **volunteer** it is best to try and make contact before arriving, if only by a few days. Such is the demand for positions that unskilled volunteers very often have to pay for board and lodgings. Work needs to be planned and, although there is always work to do, your time will be used most efficiently if your arrival is expected and planned for. In Antigua, **El Arco Volunteer Work Center** ⓘ *5 Av Norte 25 B, T/F7832-0162*, places people in short or long term positions. Helpful with plenty of contacts across the country. Also in Antigua is **Project Mosaic Guatemala** ⓘ *1 Av Sur 21, T7813-5758, www.promosaico.org*, an information centre and clearing house for volunteers, with access to opportunities all over the country. To help in local children's homes, contact **Casa Guatemala** ⓘ *14 Calle, 10-63, Zona 1, Guatemala City, T2232-5517, www.casa-guatemala.com*, which runs a project for abandoned and malnourished children at Río Dulce. See page 613. **Casa Alianza** ⓘ *Av Simeón Cañas 7-06, Zona 2, Guatemala City, T2433-9600, www.casa-alianza.org*, is a project that helps street kids. For more information see page 533. There are also opportunites to work in children's homes in Quetzaltenango (Xela). Two organizations are **Casa Hogar de Niños** and the **Asociación Hogar Nuevos Horizontes.** See page 598. Also check out Xela-based volunteering information organization **www.entremundos.org. Proyecto Ak 'Tenamit** ⓘ *11 Av 'A', 9-39, Zona 2, Guatemala City, T2254-1560; for further information ring Steve Dudenhoefer on T5908-3392, www.aktenamit.org,* is based at Clínica Lámpara, 15 minutes upriver from Lívingston. It was set up to help 7000 civil-war- displaced Q'eqchi' Maya who now live in the region in 30 communities. Also in Guatemala City is **UPAVIM** ⓘ *Calle Principal, Col La Esperanza, Mesquital Zona 12, T479-9061, www.upavim.org, Mon-Fri 0800-1800, Sat 0800-1200*. This project helps poor families, providing social services and education for the workers using fair trade principles.

Volunteers are welcomed by the **Fundación Mario Dary** ⓘ *17 Calle between 5 and 6 Av, Puerto Barrios, T7948-0944; or Diagonal 6, 17-19, Zona 10, Guatemala City, T2333-4957*, which operates conservation, health and education projects on the Punta de Manabique. Other projects involving working with nature and wildlife include the **Asociación de Rescate y Conservación de Vida Silvestre (ARCAS)** ⓘ *T/F2253-5329, arcaspeten@intelnet.net.gt*, which returns wild animals to their natural habitat.

Several language schools in Quetzaltenango fund community development projects and seek volunteers. Make enquiries in town or via www.xelapages.com. At **Quetzaltrekkers** ⓘ *T7765-5895, www.quetzaltrekkers.com*, volunteer hiking guides might be required. Also, the **Guatemala Solidarity Network** ⓘ *73 Blackshaw Rd, London, SW17 0BS, UK, www.guatemalasolidarity.org.uk*, can assist with finding projects that look at human rights issues. On Lake Atitlán is **Comité Campesino del Altiplano** ⓘ *T5804-9451, www.ccda.galeon.com*, 10 minutes from San Lucas. This Campesino Cooperative now produces Fair Trade organic coffee buying from small farmers in the region; long-term volunteers are welcome but Spanish is required.

Before you travel

Visas and immigration

Only a valid **passport** is required for citizens of: all Western European countries; USA, Canada, Mexico, all Central American countries, Australia, Israel, Japan and New Zealand. The majority of visitors will get 90 days on arrival.

Visa renewal This must be done in Guatemala City after 90 days, or on expiry. Passport stamp renewal on expiry for those citizens only requiring a valid passport to enter Guatemala must also be done at the immigration office at **Dirección General de Migración**, 6 Avenida, 3-11, Zona 4, Guatemala City, T2411-2411, Monday-Friday 0800-1600 (0800-1230 for payments). This office extends visas and passport stamps only once for a further period of time, depending on the original time awarded. These rules have been introduced to stop people leaving the country for 72 hours (which is the legal requirement) every six months and returning, effectively making them permanent residents.

Guatemala embassies and consulates

Australia and **New Zealand**, see Japan.

Belgium, Av Winston Churchill 185, 1180, Brussels, T2-345-9058 (also covers Holland and Luxembourg).

Belize, 8 A St, Belize City, T223-3150.

Canada, 130 Albert St, Suite 1010, Ottawa, Ontario, K1P 5G4, T613-233-7237.

Costa Rica, Del Gimnasio Fitsimons 100 metros sur, 50 metros oeste Sabana Sur, San José, T291-6208

El Salvador, 15 Av Norte, No 135, San Salvador, T2271-2225.
France, 73 rue de Courcelles, 75008, Paris, T42277863 (also covers Portugal and Switzerland).
Germany, Joachim-Karnatz-Allee 45-47 D-10557, Berlin, T30-206-4363.
Honduras, Calle Arturo López Rodezno 2421, Col Las Minitas, Tegucigalpa, T231-1543.
Israel, Medinat Hayeduim 103 Beit Ackerstein entry B, floor 2, Herzlia Pituach, T729-957-7335 .
Italy, Via Dei Colli della Farnesina 128, 00194, Rome, T3638-1143.
Japan, No 38 Kowa Bldg, 9th Floor, Room 905, Nishi-Azabu, Tokyo 106, T3-380-01830 (also covers Australia, Bangladesh, India, Iraq, New Zealand, Philippines and Thailand).
Mexico, Av Explanada No 1025, Lomas de Chapultepec, 11000 México DF, T5540-7520.
Nicaragua, Km 11.5 on road to Masaya, Managua, T799-609.
Panama, Calle Abel Bravo y Calle 57, Bella Vista, Edif Torre Cancún, Apt 14-A, Panama City, T269-3475.
Spain, Calle Rafael Salgado No 3, 4th Izquierda, 28036, Madrid, T1-344-1417 (also covers Morocco).
UK, 13 Fawcett St, London SW10 9HN, T020-7351-3042, embaguatelondon@btinternet.com.
USA, 2220 R St NW, Washington DC, 20008, T202-745-4952, www.guatemala-embassy.org.

Customs

You are allowed to take in, free of duty, personal effects and articles for your own use, two bottles of spirits and 80 cigarettes or 100 g of tobacco. Temporary visitors can take in any amount in quetzales or foreign currencies. The local equivalent of US$100 per person may be reconverted into US dollars on departure at the airport, provided a ticket for immediate departure is shown.

What to take

Most of the areas you are likely to visit in Guatemala are above 1500 m. While temperatures may well be comfortably warm in the day, it will be cold in the evening and at night. Bad weather may bring noticeable drops in temperature. In many tropical areas where mosquitoes and other biting insects are common, take long trousers and long-sleeved shirts for after dusk. The sun is strong everywhere at midday, so have a hat to hand.

Money

Currency → *US$1=7.50 quetzales.*

The unit is the quetzal, divided into 100 centavos. There are coins of one quetzal, 50 centavos, 25 centavos, 10 centavos, five centavos and one centavo. The paper currency is for five, 10, 20, 50 and 100 quetzales.

Banks

There are numerous banks in Guatemala and in cities and towns most have ATMs (*cajeros automáticos*). All will change US dollars cash into quetzales, the majority will change traveller's cheques and accept Visa to obtain cash. MasterCard is less commonly accepted.

Credit cards and traveller's cheques

Visa is the most widely recognized and accepted bank card. If you have a MasterCard try G&T Continental (which has a daily withdrawal limit of US$65) or Credomatic/Banco de América Central, which are few and far between.

There is often a shortage of small change – get small notes when you first change money to pay hotel bills, transport, etc.

Banks usually charge up to 2% per transaction to advance quetzales on a credit card. It is common for establishments to make a charge for use of credit cards – usually about US$3. Check before you sign. In the main it is only higher-class hotels and restaurants that accept cards. Amex cards are not very widely accepted. Visa assistance, T1-800-999-0115/T2331-8720; MasterCard T1-800-999-1480/T2334-0578. American Express T1-800-999-0245/T2470-4848. Citicorp and Visa traveller's cheques are easier to change outside the main cities than Amex. Your passport is required and in some cases the purchase receipt as well, especially in the capital.

Cost of living and travelling

Guatemala is one of the cheapest Central America countries, and those travelling on a tight budget should be able to get by on US$25 a day. With shorter distances, especially compared with Mexico to the north, travel becomes much less of a demand on your budget with the exception of the trip north to Tikal.

Getting there

Air

From the USA **American** (Atlanta; Chicago; Miami), **Continental** (Houston), **Delta** (Atlanta), **United** (Los Angeles), **Grupo Taca** (Miami). From Canada Connections are made through San Salvador, Los Angeles or Miami.

From Europe **Iberia** flies from Madrid via Miami, with connecting flights from other European cities. Long-haul operators from Europe will share between airlines, taking passengers across the Atlantic normally to Miami, and using **Taca**, for example, to link to Guatemala City. **Air France** daily from Paris.

From Central America Connections available throughout Central America, in most cases travelling through the capital city. There are exceptions with connections to Belize from Flores. **Tikal Jets** are planning a service from Mexico City. See page 41, for regional airpasses. From the **Caribbean** **Copa** from Santo Domingo and San Juan; **Copa** from Kingston and Montego Bay, Jamaica, and from Port au Prince via Panama. **Copa** and **Taca** from Havana.

From South America **Lacsa** from Bogotá via San José, **Copa** via Panama. For international flights to **Flores** see Flores Transport, page 648.

Road

There are good road crossings with all of Guatemala's neighbouring countries. Several crossing points to southern Mexico from western Guatemala with additional routes through the jungle from Palenque. From Belize it is possible to cross from Benque Viejo del Carmen. Links with Honduras are possible on the Caribbean near Corinto, and for the ruins at Copán the best crossing is El Florido. There are three road routes into El Salvador.

Touching down

Airport tax, entry and exit information

There is a 17% ticket tax on all international tickets sold in Guatemala. There is also a US$30 or quetzal equivalent, international departure tax, and a 20 quetzal domestic departure tax. There is sometimes an unofficial tourist tax charge (10-30 quetzales) at some borders, charged on leaving or entering overland (borders may not be open 24 hours). Bribery is now less common at border crossings. Ask for a receipt and, if you have time and the language ability, do not give in to corrupt officials. Report any problems to INGUAT.

Touching down

Business hours Mon-Fri 0800-1200, 1400-1800. Shops: 0900-1300 and 1500-1900, often mornings only on Sat. Banks: Mon-Fri 0900-1500, some city banks are introducing later hours, up to 2000; in the main tourist towns, some banks are open 7 days a week.
Official time 6 hrs behind GMT.
Telephone Country code T+502.
Voltage Generally 110 volts AC, 60 cycles. Electricity is generally reliable in the towns but can be a problem in more remote areas like Petén.
Weights and measures The metric system is obligatory on all customs documents; duties are levied by weight. US measures are widely used in commerce; most foodstuffs are sold by the pound.

Local customs and laws

Tipping Hotel staff (bell boys, US$0.25 for light luggage, US$0.50 for heavy); restaurants (10% in the better places; often added to the bill); airport porters (US$0.25 per piece of luggage).

Prohibitions Caught with drugs and you'll wind up in prison where the minimum penalty is five years. In the traditional laid-back travellers' drug haven of San Pedro on Lake Atitlán a number of police have been installed. Take care with gambling in public places and do not take photos of military installations.

Safety

Since the 1996 ceasefire between government and URNG forces, travellers should not encounter difficulties. In some parts of the country you may be subject to military or police checks. Local people can be reluctant to discuss politics with strangers. Do not necessarily be alarmed by 'gunfire' which is much more likely to be fireworks and bangers, a national pastime, especially early in the morning.

Robberies and assaults on tourists are becoming more common. Assaults on buses in Zone 1, Guatemala City have been reported. While you can do nothing to counter the bad luck of being in the wrong place at the wrong time, sensible precautions can minimize risks. Single women should be especially careful. Tourist groups are not immune and some excursion companies take precautions. Bus hijacks have reduced – try to travel by day, especially on the road between Flores and Tikal in El Petén, and Flores and the Belizean border.

National police T110; Tourist police in Antigua, T832-7290.

We have received a number of reports on out-of-control tourist shuttle bus (minibus) drivers. It is difficult to tell if a driver will be dangerous before the journey starts but you may want to ask other travellers before booking a trip or consider taking long-distance public buses on longer journeys.

Asistur, T1500/2421-2810 is a 24-hour, year-round tourist assistance programme for any problem or question. There is also a national tourist police force, **POLITUR**, T5561-2073.

Getting around

Air

Inter, part of **Grupo Taca**, links Guatemala City with Flores/Santa Elena, T361-2144), www.grupotaca.com. See under Flores/Santa Elena for services to Tikal. Private charters are on the increase. **Tikaljets**, www.tikaljets.com, and **TAG**, www.tag.com.gt, also fly this route.

Road

Bus There is an extensive network of bus routes throughout the country. The chicken buses are mostly in a poor state of repair and overloaded. Faster and more reliable Pullman services operate on some routes. Correct fares should be posted. We receive regular complaints that bus drivers charge tourists more than locals, a practice that is becoming more widespread. One way to avoid being overcharged is to watch for what the locals pay or ask a local, then tender the exact fare on the bus. Many long-distance buses leave very early in the morning. Make sure you can get out of your hotel/*pensión*. For international bus journeys make sure you have small denomination local currency or US dollar bills for border taxes. At Easter there are few buses on Good Friday or the Saturday and buses are packed with long queues for tickets for the few days before Good Friday. Many names on bus destination boards are abbreviated (Guate: Guatemala City; Chichi: Chichicastenango; Xela/Xelajú: Quetzaltenango, etc). Buses in the west and north are called *camionetas*. Regarding pronunciation in Guatemala, 'X' is pronounced 'sh', as in Xela (shay-la). On many tourist routes there are **minibus shuttles**, quick, comfortable, and convenient, they charge a little more than the regular buses, but can be useful. They can be booked through hotels and travel agencies and will pick you up from your hotel.

There are 13,100 km of roads, 27% of which are paved.

Car and motorcycle The paved roads have vastly improved in the past two years and are now of a high standard, making road travel faster and safer. Hurricane Stan in October 2005 has left some damage but this is steadily being repaired.) Even cycle tracks (*ciclovías*) are beginning to appear on new roads. However, a new driving hazard in the highlands is the deep gully (for rainwater or falling stones) alongside the road. High clearance is essential on many roads in remoter areas and a 4WD vehicle is useful.

Bringing a vehicle into Guatemala requires the following procedure: presentation of a valid International Driving Licence; a check by **Cuarantena Agropecuaria** (Ministry of Agriculture quarantine) to check you are not importing fruit or veg; at **Aduana** (Customs) you must pay 35 quetzales for all forms and a tourist vehicle permit for your vehicle. A motorcycle entry permit costs the same as a one for a car. The description of your vehicle on the registration document must match your vehicle's appearance exactly. You must own the car/motorcycle and your name must be on the title papers. When entering the country, ask the officials to add any important accessories you have to the paper. Car insurance can be bought at the borders.

On leaving the country by car or motorcycle, two stamps on a strip of paper are required: surrender of the vehicle permit at customs and the **Cuarantena Agropecuaria** (quarantine) inspection, which is not always carried out. It is better not to import and sell foreign cars in Guatemala as import taxes are very high.

Gasoline 'Normal' costs US$2.07, 'premium' US$2.12 for the US gallon. Unleaded (*sin plomo*) is available in major cities, at Melchor de Mencos and along the Pan-American Highway, but not in the countryside, although it is gradually being introduced across the country. Diesel costs US$1.30 a gallon.

Security Spare no ingenuity in making your car or motorbike secure. Try never to leave the car unattended except in a locked garage or guarded parking space. Lock the clutch or accelerator to the steering wheel with a heavy, obvious chain or lock. Street children will generally protect your car fiercely in exchange for a tip. Don't wash your car: smart cars attract thieves. Be sure to note down key numbers and carry spares of the most important ones. Try not to leave your fully laden motorbike on its own. An Abus D or chain will keep the bike secure. A cheap alarm gives you peace of mind if you leave the bike outside a hotel at night. Most hotels will allow you to bring the bike inside. Look for hotels that have a courtyard or more secure parking and never leave luggage on the bike overnight or whilst unattended. Also take a cover for the bike. Just about all parts and accessories are available at decent prices in Guatemala City at FPK, 5 Calle 6-75, Zona 9.

Border crossings From Mexico to Western Guatemala: **Tecún Umán/Ciudad Hidalgo** is the main truckers' crossing. It is very busy and should be avoided at all costs by car. **Talismán**, the next border crossing north, is more geared to private cars. **La Mesilla** is the simplest for private cars and you can do your own paperwork with ease. All necessary documents can be obtained here.

Car hire Average rates are US$50-80 per day. Credit cards or cash are accepted for rental. Local cars are usually cheaper than those at international companies; if you book ahead from abroad with the latter, take care that they do not offer you a different vehicle claiming your original request is not available. Cars may not always be taken into neighbouring countries (none are allowed into Mexico or Belize); rental companies that do allow their vehicles to cross borders charge US$15 for permits and paperwork. If you wish to drive to Copán, you must check this is permissible and you need a letter authorizing you to take the vehicle in to Honduras. **Tabarini** and **Hertz** do allow their cars to cross the border.

Cycling The scenery is gorgeous, the people friendly and colourful, but the hills are steep and sometimes long. The Pan-American Highway is OK from Guatemala City west; it has a shoulder and traffic is not very heavy. Buses are frequent and it is easy to load a bicycle on the roof; many buses do so, charging about two-thirds of the passenger fare. On the road, buses are a hazard for cyclists, Guatemala City is particularly dangerous. Look out for the cycle tracks (*ciclovías*) on a few main roads.

Hitchhiking Hitching is comparatively easy, but risky, especially for single women. Also beware of theft of luggage, especially in trucks. The best place to try for a lift is at a bridge or on a road out of town; be there no later than 0600, but 0500 is better as that is when truck drivers start their journey. Trucks usually charge US$1-1.50 upwards for a lift/day. Recently, travellers suggest it can be cheaper by bus. In remote areas lifts in the back of a pick-up are usually available; very crowded, but convenient when bus services are few and far between, or stop early in the day.

Sleeping

The tourist institute INGUAT publishes a list of maximum prices for single, double and triple occupancy of hundreds of hotels throughout the country in all price ranges, though the list is thin at the budget end. They will deal with complaints about overcharging if you can produce bills or other proof. Room rates should be posted in all registered hotels. Ask if taxes (*impuestos*) are included when you are given the room rate. INGUAT tax is 12% and service charge is usually an additional 10%. Busiest seasons: Easter, December and the European summer holiday (July-August). Most budget hotels do not supply toilet paper, soap or towels. There are no official campsites in Guatemala.

Eating

Traditional Central American/Mexican food such as tortillas, tamales, tostadas, etc are found everywhere. Tacos are less spicy than in Mexico. *Chiles rellenos*, chillies stuffed with meat and vegetables, are a speciality in Guatemala and may be *picante* (spicy) or *no picante*. *Churrasco*, charcoal-grilled steak, is often accompanied by *chirmol*, a sauce of tomato, onion and mint. *Guacamole* is also excellent. Local dishes include *pepián* (thick meat stew with vegetables) in Antigua, *patín* (tomato-based sauce served with *pescaditos*, small fish from Lake Atitlán wrapped in leaves), *cecina* (beef marinated in lemon and bitter orange) from the same region. *Fiambre* is widely prepared for families and friends who gather on All Souls' Day (1 November). It consists of all kinds of meat, fish, chicken, vegetables, eggs or cheese served as a salad with rice, beans and other side dishes. Desserts include *mole* (plantain and chocolate), *torrejas* (sweet bread soaked in egg and *panela* or honey) and *buñuelos* (similar to profiteroles) served with hot cinnamon syrup. For breakfast try *mosh* (oats cooked with milk and cinnamon), fried plantain with cream, black beans in various forms. *Pan dulce* (sweet bread), in fact bread in general, and local cheese are recommended. Try *borracho* (cake soaked in rum).

Drink

Local beers are good (Monte Carlo, Cabra, Gallo and Moza, a dark beer); bottled, carbonated soft drinks (*gaseosas*) are safest. Milk should be pasteurized. Freshly made *refrescos* and ice creams are delicious made of many varieties of local fruits; *licuados* are fruit juices with milk or water, but hygiene varies, so take care. Water should be filtered or bottled.

By law alcohol can't be consumed after 2000 on Sundays.

Festivals and events

1 Jan.
Holy Week (4 days). Easter celebrations are exceptional in Antigua and Santiago Atitlán.
1 May Labour Day.
15 Aug (Guatemala City only).
15 Sep Independence Day.
12 Oct Discovery of America.
20 Oct Revolution Day.
1 Nov All Souls' Day. Celebrated with abandonment and drunkeness in Todos Santos. In Santiago Sacatepéquez the Día de los Muertos is characterized by colourful kite-flying (*barriletas*).
24 Dec Christmas Eve (from noon).
25 Dec Christmas Day.
31 Dec (from noon).

12 Oct and **Christmas Eve** are not business holidays. During Holy Week, bus fares may be doubled. Although specific dates are given for fiestas there is often a week of jollification beforehand.

Shopping

Visiting a **market** in Guatemala can be one of the most enjoyable and memorable experiences of any trip. Bartering in the markets is the norm and is almost expected and unbelievable discounts can be obtained. You won't do better anywhere else in Central America. But getting the discount is less important than paying a fair price. Woven goods are normally cheapest bought in the town of origin. Try to avoid middlemen and buy direct from the weaver. Guatemalan **coffee** is highly recommended, although the best is exported; coffee sold locally is not vacuum-packed. Film for transparencies is hard to find but it is normally available in Guatemala City at 9 Calle, 6-88, Zona 1, and in other large cities.

Sport and activities

Archaeology

Archaeology is the big attraction. Consequently there is a huge number of organizations offering tours. Some companies operate out of Flores and Santa Elena in the Petén using local villagers to help with expeditions. Try **Maya Expeditions,** 15 Calle "A", 14-07, Zona 10, T2363-4955, www.mayaexpeditions.com, who offer trips to Piedras Negras (with archaeologists who worked on the 1990s excavation of the site), Río Azul, the Petexbatún area, El Mirador, led by Doctor Richard Hansen (the chief archaeologist of the site) and a brand new trip to the recently discovered Cancuén site, led by its chief archaeologist, Doctor Arthur Demarest. **Explorations**, 27655 Kent Road, Bonita Springs, Florida, FL 34135, T1-239-992-9660, www.explorationsinc.com, has tours led by archaeologist and Maya specialist Travis Doering.

Mountain biking

Mountain biking is an increasingly popular activity in Guatemala. There are numerous tracks and paths that weave their way across the country, passing hamlets as you go. One recommended operator in Antigua, which also deals in the gear, is **Old Town Outfitters**, 5 Avenida Sur, 12 "C", T7832-4171, www.bikeguatemala.com, who offer mountain bike tours starting at US$25 for a half day.

Mountain and volcano climbing

Guatemala represents a wealth of opportunity for climbers – with more than 30 volcanoes on offer. There are also the heights of the Cuchumatanes Mountains in the Highlands, which claims the highest non-volcanic peak in the country at 3837 m, and those of the relatively unexplored Sierra de Las Minas in eastern Guatemala close to the Río Motagua Valley. For climbing in the Sierra de las Minas, a biosphere reserve, contact **La Fundación de la Naturaleza**, 19 Avenida "B", 0-83, Zona 15, Vista Hermosa II, T2369-5151, to obtain a *permiso*. **Turismo Ek Chuah**, 3 Calle 6-24, Zona 2, www.exchuah.com, offer volcano specific tours. For volcano climbing around Guatemala City and Antigua see pages 530 and 547.

Nature tourism

The majority of tour operators listed in this guide will offer nature-oriented tours. There are several national parks, *biotopos* and protected areas in Guatemala, each with their highlights. **CECON** (Centro de Estudios Conservacionistas) and **INGUAT** have set up conservation areas (*biotopos*) for the protection of Guatemalan wildlife (the quetzal, the manatee, the jaguar, etc) and their habitats. Several other national parks (some including Maya archaeological sites) and forest reserves have been set up or are planned. Many of these are administered by the national parks and protected areas authority **CONAP** (Consejo Nacional de Areas Protegidas), 5 Avenida, 6-06, Zona 1, Guatemala City, T2238-0000, http://conap.online.fr. Another useful organization is the non-profit making project, **Proyecto Ecológico Quetzal**, 2 Calle, 14-36, Zona 1, Cobán, T/F7952-1047, www.ecoquetzal.org, run by David Unger.

Spiritual interest

There is a spiritual centre on the shores of Lake Atitlán that offers courses in accordance with the cycle of the moon: **Las Pirámides** is in San Marcos La Laguna and offers yoga, meditation as well as spiritual instruction year round (see also page 559 and page 567). At the **Takilibén Maya Misión** in Momostenango, day keeper Rigoberto Itzep offers courses in Maya culture. You can leave a message for him from Monday to Friday between 0800-1200, 1400-1700, T7736-5051. See also page 580.

Textiles and weaving

It is possible to get weaving lessons in many places across the Highlands. Weaving lessons can also be organized through Spanish schools.

Watersports

Diving You can dive in Lake Atitlán with **ATI Divers** at La Iguana Perdida in Santa Cruz, T7762-2621,www.laiguanaperdida.com. **Kayaking** Kayak tours (five days for US$350) are run by Old Town Outfitters, 5 Avenida Sur, 12 "C", T5399-0440, www.bikeguatemala.com **Waterskiing** Possible at Río Dulce from Hacienda Tijax, www.tijax.com, see page 617, and from **La Iguana Perdida** in Santa Cruz La Laguna, see under diving for the address. **Whitewater rafting** Possible on a number of rivers in Guatemala across a range of grades. However, none of the trips are turn-up-and-go – they have to be arranged in advance. In general, the larger the group, the cheaper the cost. The country's best outfitter is **Maya Expeditions**, see address under Archaeology. They raft the Río Cahabón in Alta Verapaz (Class III-V), the Río Naranjo close to Coatepeque (Class III), the Río Motagua close to Guatemala City (Class III-IV), the Río Esclavos, near Barbarena (Class III-IV), the Río Coyolate close to Santa Lucía Cotzumalguapa (Class II-III) and the Río Chiquibul in the Petén (Class II-III). They also run a rafting and caving tour in the Petén and a combined archaeology and rafting tour where you would raft through a canyon on the Río Usumacinta (Class II). For a little extra excitement **Maya Expeditions** also arrange bungee jumping at Río Dulce.

Health

Guatemala is healthy enough if precautions are taken about drinking water, milk, uncooked vegetables and peeled fruits; carelessness on this point is likely to lead to amoebic dysentery, which is endemic. In Guatemala City three good hospitals are: **Bella Aurora**, 10 Calle A Zona 14; **Centro Médico**, 6 Avenida 3-47, Zona 10, T2332-3555, and **Herrera Llerandi**, 6 Avenida, 8-71, Zona 10, T2384-5959, but you must have full medical insurance or sufficient funds to pay for treatment. English and other languages are spoken. Most small towns have clinics. At the public hospitals, which are seriously underfunded and where care for major problems is not good, you may have an examination for a nominal fee, but drugs are expensive.

Keeping in touch

Communications

Internet Internet cafés are found in all tourist destinations, ask around in the cities for the best rates. Rates vary between US$1 to US$5 an hour.

Post Airmail to Europe takes 10-14 days. Letters cost US$0.52 for the first 20 g and between US$5.85 for 100 g to US$48 for a maximum weight of 2 kg. Airmail letters to the US and Canada cost US$0.39 for the first 20 g. Airmail parcel service to US is reliable (four to 14 days) and costs US$3.76 for 100 g up to US$31.90 for 2 kg. Parcels over 2 kg may only be sent abroad from Guatemala City, Correos y Telégrafos, 7 Avenida y 12 Calle, Zona 1. See under Panajachel and Chichicastenango for alternative services.

Telephone There are two main service providers – **Telgua** and **Telefónica**. Telefónica sell cards with access codes, which can be used from any private or public Telefónica phone. Telgua phone booths are ubiquitous. They use cards sold in values of 20 and 50 quetzales. The price of a local call is US$0.05 per minute; a national call costs US$0.77 per minute. Most businesses offering a phone call service charge a minimum of US$0.13 for a local call, therefore it's a cheaper option to buy a phone card. International calls can be made from these booths, however unlike the local calls it is cheaper to find an internet café or shop which tend to offer better rates (eg in the popular tourist spots some companies offer calls through the internet at US$0.26 per minute to Europe). From a Telgua phone dial 147 before making an international call. Operator calls are more expensive. For calling card and credit card call options you need a fixed line in a hotel or private house. First you dial 9999 plus the following digits: For Sprint USA, dial 136; AT&T Direct: 190; Germany: 049; Canada: 198; UK (BT): 044; Switzerland: 041; Spain: 034,

All phone numbers in the country are on an 8-figure basis. No prefixes (eg 0 for numbers outside Guatemala City) are necessary. For directory enquiries, dial 1524.

Italy: 039. Collect calls may be made from public Telgua phones by dialling T147-120. International calls via the operator, T147-110. Comcel and PCS offer mobile phone services. Local sim cards can be bought for between 50 and 100 quetzales including some free calls from tiendas and supermarkets. Rates are around US$0.13 a minute for a national call, US$1.06 for international.

Media

Newspapers The main newspaper is *Prensa Libre* (www.prensalibre.com). The *Guatemala Post* is published in English online, www.guatemalapost.com. *Siglo Veintiuno* is a good newspaper, started in 1989 (www.sigloxxi.com). Mega popular is *Nuestro Diario*, a tabloid with more gory pics than copy. The *Revue*, www.revuemag.com, produced monthly in Antigua, carries articles, advertisements, lodgings, tours and excursions, covering Antigua, Panajachel, Quetzaltenango, Río Dulce, Monterrico, Cobán, Flores and Guatemala City.

Guatemala City

→ *Colour map 5, C2 . Altitude: 1500 m.*

Smog-bound and crowded, Guatemala City is the commercial and administrative centre of the country. It is a sprawl of industrial activity lightly sprinkled with architectural treasures and out-of-place tributes to urban sculpture. Rarely rated by visitors, this is the beating heart of Guatemala and is worth a couple of days if you have time and can bear the noise and pollution in Zona 1. Guatemala City is surrounded by active and dormant volcanoes easily visited on day trips. ▸▸ *See Sleeping, Eating and other listings, pages 526-534.*

Ins and outs

Getting there

The airport is in the south part of the city at La Aurora, 4 km from the Plaza Central, T2331-8392. It has banks, ATMs, internet, bars and restaurants and a Comcel kiosk. A taxi to Zona 10 Is US$7, Zona 1, US$9. The Zona 4 chicken bus terminal between 1-4 Avenida and 7-9 Calle serves the Occidente (west), the Costa Sur (Pacific coastal plain) and El Salvador. The area of southern Zona 1, contains many bus offices and is the departure point for the Oriente (east), the Caribbean zone, Pacific coast area towards the Mexican border and the north, to Flores and Tikal. First-class buses often depart from company offices in Zona 1 (see map). Note that some companies have been moved from Zona 1 and Zona 4 out to Zona 7 and 12. ▸▸ *For further details, see Transport, page 530.*

Getting around

Any address not in Zona 1 – and it is absolutely essential to quote zone numbers in addresses – is probably some way from the centre. Addresses themselves, being purely numerical, are usually easy to find. For example, 19 Calle, 4-83 is on 19 Calle between 4 Avenida and 5 Avenida at No 83. See also Trolley Tour, page 530.

Tourist information

INGUAT ⓘ *7 Av, 1-17, Zona 4 (Centro Cívico), 24 hrs T1801-464-8281, T2421-2800, www.visitguatemala.com, Mon-Fri 0800-1600.* English is sometimes spoken. They are very friendly and provide a hotel list, a map of the city, and general information on buses, market days, museums, etc. Also in the **airport arrivals hall** ⓘ *T2331-4256, 0600-2100*, where staff are exceptionally helpful and on the ball.

Background

Guatemala City was founded by decree of Carlos III of Spain in 1776 to serve as capital after earthquake damage to the earlier capital, Antigua, in 1773. Almost completely destroyed by earthquakes in 1917-1918, it was rebuilt in modern fashion, or in copied colonial, only to be further damaged by earthquake in 1976. Most of the affected buildings have been restored.

Sights

The old centre of the city is Zona 1. It is still a busy shopping and commercial area, with several good hotels and restaurants, and many of the cheaper places to stay. However, the main activity of the city has been moving south for some years, first to Zona 4, now to Zonas 9, 10 and 14. With the move have gone companies, commerce, banks, embassies, museums and the best hotels and restaurants. The best residential areas are in the hills to the east, southeast and west.

Around Zona 1

At the city's heart lies the **Parque Central**. It is intersected by the north- to south-running 6 Avenida, the main shopping street. The eastern half has a floodlit fountain; on the west side is **Parque Centenario**, with an acoustic shell in cement used for open-air concerts and public meetings. The Parque Central is popular on Sunday with many *indígenas* selling textiles.

To the east of the plaza is the **Catedral**. It was begun in 1782 and finished in 1815 in classical style with notable blue cupolas and dome. Inside are paintings and statues from ruined Antigua. Solid silver and sacramental reliquary are in the east side chapel of the Sagrario. Next to the cathedral is the colonial mansion of the Archbishop. Aside from the cathedral, the most notable public buildings constructed between 1920 and 1944, after the 1917 earthquake, are the **Palacio Nacional**, built of light green stone (the guards have keys and may show you round the state rooms), the Police Headquarters, the Chamber of Deputies and the Post Office. To the west of the cathedral are the **Biblioteca Nacional** and the Banco del Ejército. Behind the **Palacio Nacional** is the Presidential Mansion.

Detail maps
A Zona 1, p523
B Zona 9, 10 & 13, p525.

Guatemala City orientation

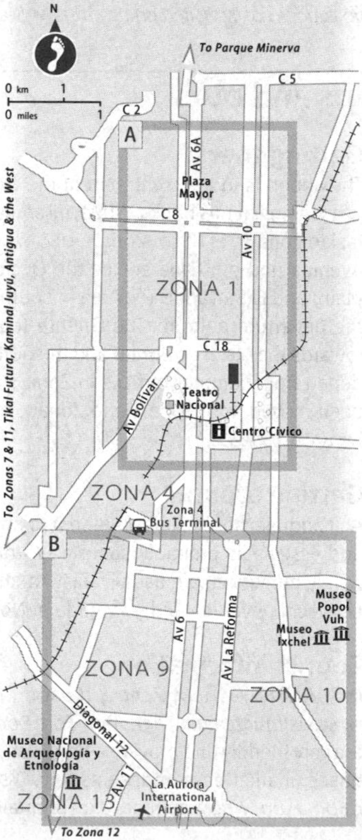

Zona 1

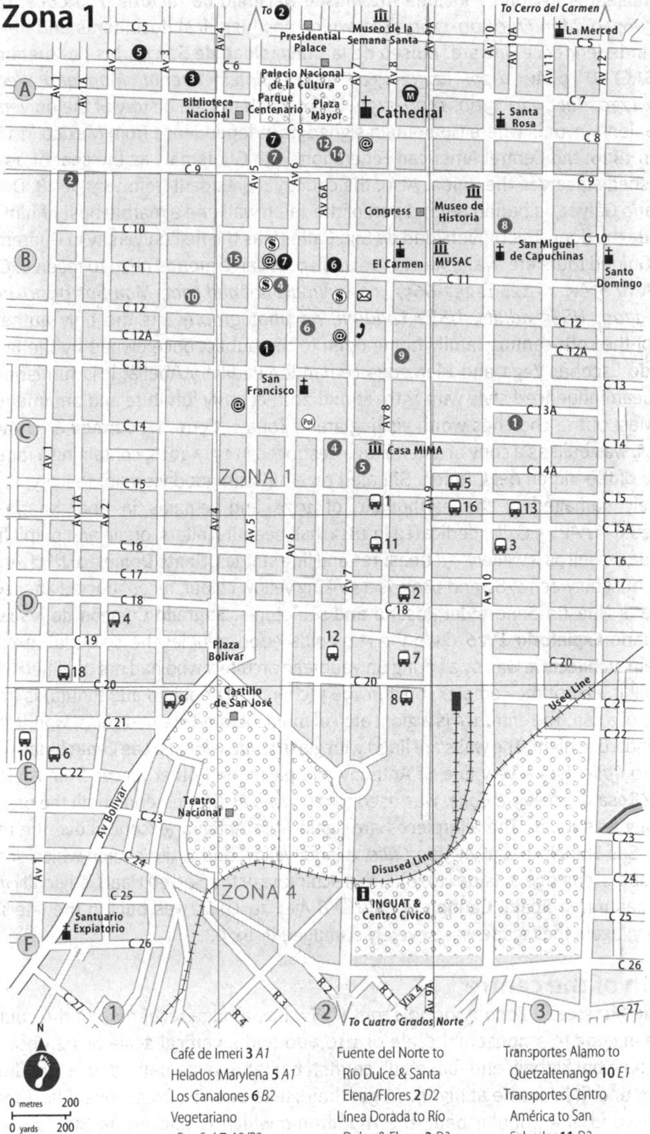

Sleeping

Casa San José **2** *B1*
Chalet Suizo **4** *C2*
Colonial **5** *C2*
Continental **6** *B2*
Pan American **7** *A2*
Pensión Meza **8** *B3*
Posada Belén **1** *C3*
Spring **9** *C2*

Eating

Altuna **1** *C2*
Arrin Cuan **2** *A2*
Café de Imeri **3** *A1*
Helados Marylena **5** *A1*
Los Canalones **6** *B2*
Vegetariano Rey Sol **7** *A2/B2*

Bars & clubs

El Portal **12** *A2*
Europa **4** *B2*
La Bodeguita del Centro **10** *B1*
Las Cien Puertas **14** *A2*
Tzijolaj **15** *B2*

Transport

ADN to Santa Elena **5** *C3*
Escobar y Monja Blanca to Cobán **1** *C2*
Fuente del Norte to Río Dulce & Santa Elena/Flores **2** *D2*
Línea Dorada to Río Dulce & Flores **3** *D3*
Líneas Américas to Quetzaltenango **4** *D1*
Marquensita to Quetzaltenango **6** *E1*
Rápidos del Sur **8** *E2*
Rutas Orientales to Chiquimula & Esquipulas **7** *D2*
Terminal for buses to Chimaltenango, Panajachel & Santa Cruz del Quiché **9** *E1*
Transportes Alamo to Quetzaltenango **10** *E1*
Transportes Centro América to San Salvador **11** *D2*
Transportes Galgos to Mexico **12** *D2*
Transportes Litegua to Puerto Barrios & Río Dulce **13** *C3*
Transportes Rosita to Santa Elena/Flores & Melchor de Mencos **16** *C3*
Transportes Velásquez to Huehuetenango & La Mesilla (Mexican border) **18** *D1*

Museums in Zona 1 include the **Museo Nacional de Historia** ⓘ *9 Calle, 9-70, T2253-6149, Mon-Fri 0800-1700, free*, which has historical documents and objects from Independence onward. **Museo de la Universidad de San Carlos de Guatemala (MUSAC)** ⓘ *9 Av, 9-79, T2232-0721, musac@intelnet.net.gt, Mon and Wed-Fri 0930-1730, Sat 0930-1300, 1400-1730, US$1.05*, charts the history of the university. The Salon Mayor is where Guatemala signed its independence from Mexico in 1823, and in 1826, the Central American Federation, with Guatemala as the seat of power, abolished slavery in the union. Also, the country's president from 1831-1838, Doctor Mariano Gálvez, is buried behind part of the salon wall and a marble bust of him sits outside the door. The Universidad de San Carlos was the first university in Guatemala City. Guided tours are available at 1100 and 1500. Large groups need to reserve. **Casa MIMA** ⓘ *8 Av, 14-12, T2253-6657, casamima@hotmail.com, Mon-Sat 0900-1230, 1400-1700, US$5 adults, US$2 children, no photography*, is the only authentic turn-of-the-19th-century family home open to the public, once owned by the family Ricardo Escobar Vega and Mercedes Fernandez Padilla y Abella. It is furnished in European-influenced style with 15th- to mid 20th-century furniture and ornaments.

Most of the churches worth visiting are in Zona 1. **Cerro del Carmen** ⓘ *11 Av y 1 Calle A*, was built as a copy of a hermitage destroyed in 1917-1918, containing a famous image of the Virgen del Carmen. Situated on a hill with good views of the city, it was severely damaged in the earthquake of 1976 and remains in poor shape. **La Merced** ⓘ *11 Av y 5 Calle*, dedicated in 1813, has beautiful altars, organ and pulpit from Antigua as well as jewellery, art treasures and fine statues. **Santo Domingo** ⓘ *12 Av y 10 Calle*, built between 1782 and 1807, is a striking yellow colour, reconstructed after 1917, image of Nuestra Señora del Rosario and sculptures. **Sagrado Corazón de Jesús,** or **Santuario Expiatorio** ⓘ *26 Calle y 2 Av*, holds 3000 people; the colourful, exciting modern architecture was by a young Salvadorean architect who had not qualified when he built it. Part of the complex, built in 1963 (church, school and auditorium) is in the shape of a fish. The entrance is a giant arch of multicoloured stained glass, wonderfully illuminated at night. The walls are lined with glass confessionals. **Las Capuchinas** ⓘ *10 Av y 10 Calle*, has a very fine St Anthony altarpiece, and other pieces from Antigua. **Santa Rosa** ⓘ *10 Av y 8 Calle*, was used for 26 years as the cathedral until the present building was ready. The altarpieces are again from Antigua (except above the main altar). **San Francisco** ⓘ *6 Av y 13 Calle*, a large yellow and white church which shows earthquake damage outside (1976), has a sculpture of the Sacred Head, originally from Extremadura, in Spain. **Carmen El Bajo** ⓘ *8 Av y 10 Calle*, was built in the late 18th century; again the façade was severely damaged in 1976.

North of the centre

Parque Minerva ⓘ *Zona 2, 0900-1700, US$2*, has a huge relief map of the country made in 1905 to a horizontal scale of 1:10,000 and a vertical scale of 1:2,000. The park has basketball and baseball courts, bar and restaurant and a children's playground (it is unsafe at night). To get there, take bus V21 from 7 Avenida, Zona 4. Just beyond is a popular park, the **Hipódromo** which is packed on Sundays with bumper cars and mechanical games, and a great little train for kids.

South of the centre: Avenida La Reforma

The modern **Centro Cívico**, which links Zona 1 with Zona 4, includes the Municipalidad, the Palacio de Justicia, the Ministerio de Finanzas Públicas, the Banco de Guatemala, the mortgage bank, the social-security commission and the tourist board. The curious **Teatro Nacional** ⓘ *Mon-Fri 0800-1630 for tours, free, but tips appreciated*, dominates the hilltop of the west side of the Centro Cívico. There is an excellent view of the city and surrounding mountains from the roof. An old Spanish fortress provides a backdrop to the Open Air Theatre adjoining the blue and white mosaic-covered Teatro Nacional.

Cuatro Grados Norte, located on Vía 5 between Ruta 1 and Ruta 2, is a pedestrianized area which has grown up around the IGA theatre and bookshop (a cultural centre which sometimes has interesting concerts and exhibitions). Cafés and bars have tables on the street and it's safe and fun to wander around at night. The **Centro Cultural de España** is located here with live music, films, exhibitions and conferences, there is also a branch of Sophos an excellent bookshop. On Saturdays there is a street market with craft and jewellery stalls, often cultural events in the street. On Sundays there are clowns and events for children. It's a strange mix of wealthy Guatemalans strolling with their poodles and alternative street-market types; sit back and enjoy watching the people.

To see the finest residential district go south down 7 Avenida to Ruta 6, which runs diagonally in front of Edificio El Triángulo, past the **Capilla de Yurrita** (Ruta 6 y Vía 8). Built as a private chapel in 1928 on the lines of a Russian Orthodox church, it has been described as an example of "opulent 19th-century bizarreness and over-ripe extravagance". There are many woodcarvings, slender white pillars, brown/gold ornamentation and an unusual blue sky window over the altar. Ruta 6 runs into the wide tree-lined Avenida La Reforma.

To the east, in Zona 10, are some excellent museums: **Museo Ixchel del Traje Indígena** ⓘ *Campus of Universidad Francisco Marroquín, 6 Calle Final, T2331-3638, Mon-Fri 0900-1700, Sat 0900-1300, US$2.60*, has a collection of indigenous dress.

Zona 9, 10 & 13

Sleeping
- Dos Lunas Guest House 1
- Holiday Inn 2
- Otelito 8
- San Carlos 5
- Residencial Reforma La Casa Grande 5
- Westin Camino Real 6

Eating
- Hacienda de los Sánchez 1
- Hacienda Real 2
- Inca Grill 3
- Kacao 5
- Los Alpes 6
- Sophos 7
- Tamarindos 12
- Tre Fratelli 8

Bars & clubs
- Cheers 9
- Kalua 10
- Shakespeare's Pub 11

In addition to the clothes there are photos from the early 20th century, paintings and very interesting videos. A shop sells textiles that aren't usually available on the tourist market, prices are fixed. **Museo Popol Vuh de Arqueología** ⓘ *6 Calle Final, T2361-2301, www.populvuh.ufm.edu.gt, Mon-Fri 0900-1700, Sat 0900-1300, US$2.60, US$2 charge to take photographs*, has an extensive collection of pre-Columbian and colonial artefacts, as well as a replica of the Dresden Codex, one of the only Maya parchment manuscripts in existence. **Museo de Historia Natural de la USAC y Jardín Botánico** ⓘ *Calle Mcal Cruz 1-56, T2334-6065, Mon-Fri 0800-1600, US$1.30*, has gardens, stuffed animals and live serpents.

In **Parque Aurora**, Zona 13, in the southern part of the city, are La Aurora International Airport, the Observatory, racetrack and **Parque Zoológico La Aurora** ⓘ *T2472-0507, http://laurorazoo.centroamerica.com, Tue-Sun 0900-1700, US$1.10*. The newer areas show greater concern for the animals' well-being. There are also several museums: **Museo Nacional de Antropolgía y Etnología** ⓘ *Salón 5, Parque Aurora, Zona 13, T2472-0478, Tue-Fri 0900-1600, Sat-Sun 0900-1200, 1330-1600, US$4, no photos*. Contains outstanding Maya pieces including stelae from Piedras Negras and typical Guatemalan dress, as well as good models of Tikal, Quiriguá and Zaculeu, and other Maya items. There are sculptures, murals, ceramics, textiles, a collection of masks and an excellent jade collection. Around the corner is the **Museo Nacional de Historia Natural** ⓘ *T2472-0468, Mon-Fri 0900-1600, Sat-Sun 0900-1200, 1400-1800, US$1.30*, which houses a collection of national fauna, including stuffed birds, animals, butterflies, geological specimens, etc. Opposite the archaeology museum, the **Museo de Arte Moderno** ⓘ *Salón 6, Parque Aurora, Zona 13, T2472-0467, US$1.30*, has a modest but enjoyable collection. Next door is the **Museo de los Niños** ⓘ *T2475-5076, Tue-Fri 0800-1200, 1300-1700, Sat-Sun 1000-1330, 1430-1800, US$4.50*, an interactive museum with a gallery of Maya history and the Gallery of Peace which houses the world's largest single standing artificial tree – a ceiba.

Sleeping

You can get better prices in the more expensive hotels by booking corporate rates through a travel agent or simply asking at the desk if any lower prices are available. Hotels are often full at holiday times, eg Easter and Christmas. At the cheaper hotels single rooms are not always available. There are many cheap *pensiones* near bus and railway stations and markets; those between Calle 14 and Calle 18 are not very salubrious.

Zona 1 *p522, map p523*

A Pan American, 9 Calle, 5-63, T2232-6807. Quiet and comfortable rooms with TV, but try to avoid rooms on the main road side. Parking, and breakfast included. Restaurant with good food in the mid-range price bracket.

A-B Posada Belén, 13 Calle "A", 10-30, T2232-9226, www.posadabelen.com. A colonial-style house run by the friendly Francesca and René Sanchinelli, who speak English. Laundry, email service, luggage store and good dining room. Parking. Tours available.

C Chalet Suizo, 14 Calle, 6-82, T2251-3786. In a good central position with constant hot-water showers (cheaper with shared bathroom). It is popular, so often crowded. There is a locked luggage store, safety box, and the rooms are secure. However, those rooms facing the main street are noisy. Also, avoid rooms 9-12 as a noisy pump will disturb sleep and 19-21 have very thin walls. Parking free.

C Colonial, 7 Av, 14-19, T2232-6722. Rooms are quiet with TV and nice dark cedar wood furniture. It's pleasant and friendly too.

C Continental, 12 Calle, 6-10, T2230-5814. 2 floors up with a very secure street entrance. It has vast, comfortable rooms, but they're spartan; some quadruples available. All are very clean with private bath, TV costs extra. Credit cards accepted.

C Spring, 8 Av, 12-65, T2230-2858. Bright rooms with TV (costs a little extra) in this quiet haven of tranquillity and flowers amid the pollution of Zona 1. Rooms without private shower are cheaper. Patio garden, good breakfasts, and parking near by. Free coffee, email service, phone calls, luggage store. Probably the best choice in Zona 1 at this price.

C-D Casa San José, 9 Calle 1-42, T2232-9350, casasanjose@latinmail.com. Doubles and rooms with 3, 4, 5 beds, well set up for groups, meals available, friendly and helpful with travel arrangements, popular with volunteers, TV/ video and meeting space. All rooms with shared bath.

D-E Pensión Meza, 10 Calle, 10-17, T2232-3177. A large ramshackle place with beds in dorms. It is popular, staff are helpful and English is spoken. It is reported as noisy and some rooms are damp. Other rooms are darker than a prison cell, but cheered by graffiti, poetry and paintings. There is a ping pong table and book exchange.

South of the centre: Avenida La Reforma *p524*

L-AL Westin Camino Real, Av La Reforma y 14 Calle, Zona 10, T2333-3000, www.caminoreal.com.gt. Excellent value, good restaurants open 0600-2330, gym, pool, spa, airport shuttle, piano bar and live Cuban music Fri and Sat at 2100.

AL Holiday Inn, 1 Av, 13-22, Zona 10, T2332-2555, www.caminoreal.com.gt. Good value with a pool, gym, bar, email centre, and free airport shuttle available.

AL Hotel San Carlos, Av La Reforma, 7-89, Zona 10, T2332-6055, www.hsancarlos.com. A small, charming hotel, with pool and plant-filled patio. Includes breakfast and free airport transfer.

AL Otelito, 12 Calle, 14-51, T2339-1811, www.otelito.com. 12 lovely rooms in this small, boutique hotel which changes its colour theme once a month. Includes breakfast, shuttle to hotel and limited internet. Restaurant Mon-Wed 0630-2100, Thu-Sat 0630-2230, Sun 0630-2030.

A Residencial Reforma La Casa Grande, Av La Reforma, 7-67, Zona 10, T/F2332-0914. Near US Embassy, with nicer rooms than the next door San Carlos. Colonial style, all rooms come with TV. Good, small restaurant, open 0630-2100, a bar and internet service. Good value.

B Hincapié Guest House, Av Hincapié, 18-77, Zona 13, T2332-7771, ruedapinillos@yahoo.com. On the far side of the airport runway. Continental breakfast included and free airport transport. Cable TV in the rooms.

B-C Hotel Aeropuerto Guest House, 5 mins' walk from the airport at 15 Calle "A", 7-32, Col Aurora 1, Zona 13, T2332-3086, www.aeropuertoguesthouse.com. Free transport to and from the airport. With or without bath, and is clean and safe, breakfast included. Free internet.

D Dos Lunas Guest House, 21 Calle, 10-92, Aurora II, Zona 13, T334-5264, www.hoteldoslunas.com. Price per person. A comfy B&B. Very close to the airport with free transport to or from the airport. There's storage service, free breakfast and water and tourist information. Lorena, the landlady, also organizes shuttles and taxis and tours. English spoken. Reservations advisable as often full.

Eating

Zona 1 *p522, map p523*

There are all kinds of food available in the capital, from the simple national cuisine to French, Chinese and Italian food. There is a plethora of fast-food restaurants and traditional *comedores* where you will get good value for money; a reasonable set meal will cost no more than US$2.50. The cheapest places to eat are at street stalls and the various markets – take the normal precautions.

TTT Altuna, 5 Av, 12-31. Serves tasty Spanish food in huge portions. Lobster available but expensive. Delicious coffee. This hotel has a beautiful traditional Spanish bar interior. There is a branch in Zona 10 at 10 Calle, 0-45.

TTT Hotel Pan American, 9 Calle, 5-63 (see Sleeping). Best lunchtime menu.

TT Arrin Cuan, 5 Av, 3-27. A famous local institution specializing in traditional food from Cobán (*subanik*, *gallo en chicha*, and *kak ik*). The restaurant is centred around a small courtyard with a little fountain and live lunchtime marimba music. Breakfast available. Also on the 16 Calle, 4-32, Zona 10.

TT Café de Imeri, 6 Calle, 3-34. Serves sandwiches, salads, soups and pastries in a patio garden. Set lunch and excellent cakes. It's popular with young professional Guatemalans. Try the *pay de queso de elote* (maize cheesecake). Its bakery next door has a rare selection of granary breads, birthday cakes, etc. Closed Sun.

TT **Los Canalones – Parrillada Argentina**, 6 Av A, 10-39, barbecue on the street outside, for serious meat eaters, Alejandro *El Argentino* does tasty chunks of meat and chorizo served with excellent salad, get there early, open 1200-1600. US$5.60 including soup, endless tortillas and *refresco*.

T **Restaurante Vegetariano Rey Sol**, 8 Calle, 5-36, is a prize vegetarian find – a wholesome food and ambience oasis amid the fumes of Zona 1, and popular with the locals. Delicious veggie concoctions at excellent prices served canteen-style by friendly staff. Breakfasts and *licuados* also available. Closed Sun. Newer, larger and brighter branch at 11 Calle, 5-51.

Ice cream parlours

T **Helados Marylena**, 6 Calle, 2-49. Not quite a meal but almost. This establishment has been serving up the weirdest concoctions for 90 years. From the probably vile – fish, chile, yucca and cauliflower ice cream – to the heavenly – beer and sputnik (coconut, raisins and pineapple). The *elote* (maize) is good too. This city institution is credited with making children eat their vegetables! Anyone travelling with fussy eaters should stop by here. Open daily 1000-2200.

South of the centre: Avenida La Reforma *p524*

Most of the best restaurants are in the '**Zona Viva**', within 10 blocks of the Av La Reforma on the east side, between 6 Calle and 16 Calle in Zona 10. **Zona 9** is just across the other side of Av La Reforma. Drinks, particularly wines, are expensive.

There are several options in the area around **Cuatro Grados Norte** providing tapas, sushi, churros and chocolate. Lively, especially on Fri and Sat nights.

TTT **Hacienda de los Sánchez**, 12 Calle, 2-25, Zona 10. Good steaks and local dishes, but seriously crowded at weekends, and so not the most pleasant of settings compared with other steakhouses in the vicinity.

TTT **Hacienda Real**, 13 Calle, 1-10, Zona 10, opposite **Holiday Inn**. An excellent steak selection. Candles and palms create a garden- like atmosphere. Nice little bar with Mexican leather chairs on one side.

TTT **Inca Grill**, 2 Av 14-32, Zona 10. Tasty Peruvian food, live Andean music.

TTT **Kacao**, 2 Av, 13-44, Zona 10. A large variety of delicious local and national dishes, which are attractively prepared and served in ample portions. The setting is fantastic – a giant thatched room, *huípiles* for tablecloths, beautiful candle decorations, some options are expensive.

TTT **Tamarindos**, 11 Calle, 2-19A, Zona 10, T2360-2815. Mixed Asian, sushi, Vietnamese rolls, mushrooms stuffed with almonds and crab are some of the tantalizing options at this very smart Asian restaurant with spiral shades and soothing bamboo greens.

TTT **Tre Fratelli**, 2 Av 13-25, Zona 10. Good Italian food, tasty bread and parmesan cheese, very lively and popular, some tables outside.

TT **Café Vienés**, in the **Camino Real**, Zona 10. One of the best places for German-style coffee and cakes, your chance to try a chocolate fondu.

TT **Los Alpes**, 10 Calle, 1-09, Zona 10. A Swiss/Austrian place with light meals, which also offers a smorgasbord of excellent cakes and chocolates. Popular with Guatemalan families. Closed Mon.

TT-T **Cafesa**, 6 Av, 11-64, Zona 9. 24-hr diner serving western and Guatemalan food with some seriously cheap options.

T **Sophos**, Av La Reforma, 13-89, El Portal 1, Zona 10, T2332-3242. An attractive indoor and outdoor café with the best bookshop in town. Literary events on Thu nights until 2300.

Cuatro Grados Norte

TTT **Café Rouge**, **Cuatro Grados Norte**, Vía 5 between Ruta 1 and Ruta 2. Good cappuccinos, chocolate things and apple pie.

TTT **L'Ostería**, Vía 5 between Ruta 1 and Ruta 2. Italian on the corner with leafy terrace, popular, brick pizza oven.

TT **Arguileh**, Vía 5 between Ruta 1 and Ruta 2. Eastern-style kebabs and *pan árabe*, wooden decor, looks good.

TT **Tarboosh**, Vía 5 between Ruta 1 and Ruta 2, not far from **L'Ostería**, T2385-9091. Mediterranean cuisine in a funky upstairs setting with loud live music acts.

Entertainment

Bars and clubs

Cheers, 13 Calle, 0-40, Zona 10. A basement sports bar with pool tables, darts, and large cable TV. Mon-Sat 0900-0100, Sun 1300-2400ish. Happy hour until 1800.
Colloquia, inside La Cúpula at 7 Av, 13-01, Zona 9. One of Guate's hotspots, and worth a visit. On Tue nights there are poetry meetings and on Thu nights there's techno, trance and house music. Tue-Sat 0900-2400.
El Portal, Portal del Comercio, 8 Calle, 6-30, Zona 1. This was a favourite spot of Che Guevara and you can imagine him sitting here holding court at the long wooden bar. A massive stuffed bull's head now keeps watch over drinkers. To get there, enter the labyrinths of passageways facing the main plaza at No 6-30 where there is a Coke stand. At the first junction bear round to the left and up on the left you will see its sign. *Comida típica* and marimba music, beer from the barrel. Mon-Sat 1000-2200.
Europa, 11 Calle, 5-16, Zona 1. Popular peace-corps/travellers' hangout, sports bar, shows videos, books for sale. Mon-Sat 0800-0100.
Kalua, 1 Av 15 Calle. Huge club opened in mid-2004, 3 floors with different tunes, stylish.
La Bodeguita del Centro, 12 Calle, 3-55, Zona 1, T2239-2976. The walls of this hip place in an old stockhouse are adorned with posters of Che Guevara, Bob Marley and murdered Salvadorean Archbishop Romero. There's live music Thu-Sat at 2100, talks, plays, films, exhibitions upstairs. Wooden tables are spread over 2 floors, free popcorn with drinks and seriously cheap nachos and soup on the menu. It's an atmospheric place to spend an evening. Call in to get their **Calendario Cultural** leaflet. Daily 0900-0100.
Las Cien Puertas, Pasaje Aycinea, 7 Av, 8-44, just south of Plaza Mayor, Zona 1. Has a wonderful atmosphere with political, satirical and love missives covering its walls. There's excellent food and outdoor seating and it's friendly. Daily 1600-2400.
Sabor Latino, 1 Av, 13 Calle, Zona 10. A club that's under **Rock and Salambo** on the same block as **Mi Guajira**. The night begins with salsa and graduates to a more hip-hop beat.
Shakespeare's Pub, 13 Calle, 1-51, Zona 10. English-style basement bar with a good atmosphere, American owner, a favourite with ex-pats and locals, safe for women to go and drink. Mon-Fri 1100-0100, Sat and Sun 1400-0100.
Tzijolaj, 11 Calle, 4-53, Zona 1, T220-3262. This place often has live singing and music.

Cinema and theatre

There are numerous cinemas and they often show films in English with Spanish subtitles.
La Cúpula, 7 Av, 13-01, Zona 9, T2334-2606, lacupula2001@hotmail.com. Contemporary plays, concerts, dance and alternative cinema; details in the press. Restaurant, bar, bookshop and shops in the same complex.
Teatro Nacional, Centro Cívico. Most programmes are Thu-Sun.

Shopping

Bookshops

Museo Popol Vuh bookshop has a good selection of books on pre-Columbian art, crafts and natural history. The Museo Ixchel also has a bookshop. **Librería del Pensativo**, La Cúpola, 7 Av, 13-01, Zona 9, has a large selection of books with helpful staff on hand. **Luna y Sol**, 12 Calle, 3-55, Zona 1, next to **Bodeguita del Centro**, good selection of books, cassettes, etc. **Sophos**, Av La Reforma, 13-89, El Portal 1, Zona 10, good selection including childrens books, literary magazines, a few classical music CDs.

Maps

Maps can be bought from the **Instituto Geográfico Nacional** (IGN), Av Las Américas, 5-76, Zona 13, T2332-2611. Mon-Fri 0900-1730. The whole country is covered by about 200 1:50,000 maps available in colour or photocopies of out of print sections. None is more recent than 1991. There is, however, an excellent 1996, 1:15,000 map of Guatemala City in 4 sheets. A general *Mapa Turístico* of the country is available here, also at INGUAT.

Markets and supermarkets

The **Central Market** operates underground behind the cathedral, from 7 to 9 Av, 8 Calle, Zona 1. One floor is dedicated to native textiles and crafts, and there is a large, cheap basketware section on the lower floor. Silverware is cheaper at the market than elsewhere in Guatemala City. Other markets include the **Mercado Terminal** in Zona 4, and the **Mercado de Artesanía** in the Parque Aurora, near the airport, which is for tourists. Large shopping centres have been opened in the last few years, which are good for a wide selection of local crafts, artworks, funky shoes, clothes and the local scene. Don't miss the *dulces*, candied fruits and confectionery.

The best shopping centres are **Centro Comercial Los Próceres**, 18 Calle and 3 Av, Zona 10, the **Centro Comercial La Pradera**, Carretera Roosevelt and Av 26, Zona 10. There is a large **Paiz** supermarket on 18 Calle and 8 Av and a vast shopping mall **Tikal Futura** at Calzada Roosevelt and 22 Av. *Artesanías* for those who shop with a conscience at the fair-trade outlet **UPAVIM**, Calle Principal, Col La Esperanza, Mesquital Zona 12, T479-9061, www.upavim.org, Mon-Fri 0800-1800, Sat 0800-1200.

Activities and tours

Tour operators

Aire, Mar y Tierra, Plaza Marítima, 6 Av, 20-25, Zona 10, T2337-0149. Recommended.
Clark Tours, 7 Av 14-76. Zona 9 Guatemala City, T470-4700, www.clarktours.com.gt, and several other locations, long-established, very helpful, tours to Copán, Quiriguá, etc.
Four Directions, 18, 6-03, Zona 11, T2474-3771, www.fourdirections.com.gt. Recommended for Maya archaeology tours. English spoken.
Maya Expeditions, 15 Calle "A", 14-07, Zona 10, T2363-4955, www.mayaexpeditions.com. Very experienced and helpful, with varied selection of short and longer river/hiking tours, whitewater rafting, bungee jumping, cultural tours, tours to Piedras Negras.
Setsa Travel, 8 Av, 14-11, Zona 1, T2230-4726, very helpful, tours arranged to Tikal, Copán, car hire.
Trolley Tour, T5907-0913, www.chiltepe.com. Tue-Sat 1000-1300, Sun 1000. Pick-ups from Zona 10 hotels for 3-hr city tours, US$20, children, US$10.
Tourama, Av La Reforma, 15-25, Zona 10, T2368-1820, tourama@guate.net. German and English spoken. Recommended.
Turismo Ek Chuah, 3 Calle 6-24, Zona 2, T2220-1491, www.ekchuah.com. Nationwide tours as well as some specialist and tailor-made tours.

Transport

Air

Flights to Flores and Petén, with **Tikal Jets**, **Grupo Taca** and **TAG** leave daily. See under Flores for more information, page 648.

Airline offices

Domestic airlines Grupo Taca at the airport and Av Hincapié, 12-22, T2279-8222, www.taca.com. **Tikal Jets**, Av Hincapié, 18-00, Zona 13, and at the airport, T2361-3342 www.tikaljets.com. **Tag**, Av Hincapié y 18 Calle, Zona 13, T2361-1180.
International airlines Air France, Av La Reforma, 9-00, Zona 9, Plaza Panamericana, T2334-0043. **American Airlines**, Av Las Américas, 18-81, Zona 14, T2337-1177. **Continental Airlines**, 18 Calle, 5-56, Zona 10, Edif Unicentro, T2385-9610. **Copa**, 1 Av, 10-17, Zona 10, T2385-5555. **Delta Air Lines**, 15 Calle, 3-20, Zona 10, Edif Centro Ejecutivo, T1800-300-0005. **Grupo Taca** (includes Aviateca, Lacsa, Nica and Inter), see above. **Iberia**, Av La Reforma, 8-60, Zona 9, Edif Galerías Reforma, T2332-7471/2332-0911. **KLM**, 6 Av, 20-25, Zona 10, T2367-6179. **Lufthansa**, Diagonal 6, 10-01, Zona 10, T2336-5526. **Mexicana**,13 Calle, 8-44, Zona 10, Edif Plaza Edyma, T2333-6001. **United**, Av La Reforma, 1-50, Zona 9, Edif La Reformador, 2nd floor, T2336-9923.

Bus

Local

Buses operate between 0600-2000 after which you will have to rely on taxis.

In town, US$0.13 per journey on regular buses and on the larger red buses known as *gusanos* (worms) except on Sun and public holidays when they charge US$0.16.) One of the most useful bus services is the **101**, which travels down 10 Av, Zona 1, and then cuts across to the 6 Av, Zona 4, and then across Vía 8 and all the way down the Av La Reforma, Zona 10. Bus No **V21** also goes to the Zona Viva (Zona 10) travelling down from the Plaza Mayor on the 6 Av, Zona 1. The **82** also travels from Zona 1 to 10 and can be picked up on the 10 Av, Zona 1 and the 6 Av, Zona 4. Bus **85**, with the same pick-up points, goes to the cluster of museums in Zona 13. Buses **37**, **35**, **32** all head for the INGUAT building which is the large blue and white building in the Centro Cívico complex. **40R** goes from the 6 Av, Zona 4, to the Tikal Futura shopping complex – a good spot to catch the Antigua bus, which pulls up by the bridge to the complex. Buses leaving the 7 Av, Zona 4, just 4 blocks from the Zona 4 bus terminal, for the Plaza Mayor, Zona 1, are *gusano* **V21, 35, 36, 82**, and **101**. The **T64** goes to the Botanical Gardens, Natural History Museum and the office of CECON, which are all next to each other.

Long distance

Watch your bags everywhere, but like a hawk in the Zona 4 terminal.

There are numerous bus terminals in Guatemala City. Many have changed in the last year. The majority of 1st-class buses have their own offices and departure points around Zona 1. Hundreds of chicken buses for the south and west of Guatemala leave from the Zona 4 terminal, as well as local city buses. International buses have their offices scattered about the city. (The cheaper Salvador buses leave from near the Zona 4 terminal.) The Zona 4 bus terminal has to be the dirtiest and grimmest public area in the whole of the city.

The main destinations with companies operating from Guatemala City are:

Antigua, 1 hr, US$0.66, until 2000 with **Transportes Unidos**, 1 Av corner of 3 and 4 Calle, Zona 7.

Biotopo del Quetzal and **Cobán**, 3½ hrs and 4½ hrs respectively, hourly from 0400-1700, US$2.66 and US$4, with **Escobar y Monja Blanca**, 8 Av, 15-16, Zona 1, T2238-1409.

Zacapa, **Chiquimula** (for **El Florido**, Honduran border) and **Esquipulas** with **Rutas Orientales**, 19 Calle, 8-18, Zona 1, T2253-7282, every 30 mins 0430-1800. To Zacapa, 3¼ hrs, to Chiquimula, 3½ hrs, to Esquipulas, 4½ hrs, US$5.33.

Huehuetenango, with **Los Halcones**, Calzada Roosevelt, 37-47, Zona 11, T2439-2780, 0700, 1400, 1700, US$5.33, 5 hrs, and **Transportes Velásquez**, 20 Calle, 1-37, Zona 1, T2221-1084, 0800-1700, hourly, 5 hrs, US$2.66.

Panajachel, with **Transportes Rebulí**, 1 Av, corner of 3 y 4 Calle, Zona 7, T2230-2748, hourly from 0530-1530, 3 hrs, US$1.60 also to **San Lucas Tolimán** 0500-1500, 3 hrs US$1.75.

Puerto Barrios, with **Transportes Litegua**, 15 Calle, 10-40, Zona 1, T2253-8169, www.litegua.com, 0430-1800, 21 a day, 5 hrs, US$5.33, 1st class US$10.70 and **Río Dulce**, 0600, 0900, 1130, 1300, 5 hrs, US$5.33.

El Petén with **Fuente del Norte** (same company as **Líneas Máxima de Petén**), 17 Calle, 8-46, Zona 1, T2251-3817, going to **Río Dulce** and **Santa Elena**. There are numerous departures from midnight to 2130; 5 hrs to Río Dulce, US$5.20; to Santa Elena, 9-10 hrs, US$10.70; buses vary in quality and price, breakdowns not unknown. The 1000 and 2130 departures are a luxury bus **Maya del Oro** with snacks, US$17 the advantage being it doesn't stop at every tree to pick up passengers. **Línea Dorada**, 16 Calle, 10-03, Zona 1, T2220-7990, www.tikalmayan world.com, at 0900, 2100 and 2200, US$24.00 to **Flores**, 8 hrs and on to **Melchor de Mencos**, 10 hrs. **Transportes Rosita**, 15 Calle, 9-58, Zona 1, T2253-0609, to **Santa Elena** and **Melchor de Mencos**, 1500, 1700, 2000 **especial** US$10, 1900 normal, US$6.50, 10 hrs. On to Melchor, 12 hrs, **normal** US$8.45, **especial** US$10.To **Santa Elena** ADN, 8 Av, 16-41, Zona 1, T2251-0050, luxury service, 2100, US$26.60, 2200 and 2300, US$14.70, toilets, TV and snacks. Also **Rápidos de Sur**, 20 Calle, 8-55, Zona 1, T225l-5383. 0600 and 2200, 7hrs, fast service US$12.50.

Quetzaltenango (Xela) and **San Marcos**. 1st-class bus to Xela with **Transportes Alamo**, 21 Calle, 0-14, Zona 1, T2251-4838, from 0800-1730, 6 daily Mon-Sat, 4 hrs, US$4. Manic drivers who go round corners on 3 wheels, not recommended. **Líneas Américas**, 2 Av, 18-47, Zona 1, T2232-1432, 0500-1930, 7 daily, US$4. **Galgos**, 7 Av, 19-44, Zona 1, T2253-4868, between 0530-1700, 5 daily, 4 hrs, US$4. **Marquensita**, 1 Av, 21-31, Zona 1, T2253-5871. From 0600-1700, 8 a day, US$3.75, to Xela and on to San Marcos US$4.40. To **Tecpán**, with **Transportes Poaquileña**, 1 Av corner of 3 and 4 Calle, Zona 7, 0530-1900, every 15 mins, 2 hrs, US$1.

Jalapa with **Unidos Jalapanecos**, 22 Calle 1-20, Zona 1, T2251-4760, 0430-1800, hourly, 3 hrs, US$2. **Chantla Gomerana**, 4 Calle y 8 Av, Zona 12, to **La Democracia**, every 30 mins from 0600-1630 via Escuintla and

Siquinala, 2 hrs. Transportes Cubanita to **Reserva Natural de Monterrico** (La Avellana), 4 Calle y 8 Av, Zona 12, at 1030, 1230, 1420, 3 hrs, US$2. To **Puerto San José** and **Iztapa**, from the same address, 0430-1645 every 15 mins, 1 hr 30 mins.

At 20 Calle and Av Bolívar, Zona 1, there is a small bus station, with chicken buses leaving for **Chimaltenango**, **Los Encuentros** and **Santa Cruz del Quiché**. Walk under the underpass (safe for all) and bear to the right, where you will emerge on 6 Av opposite the Centro Cívico.

From the Zona 4 bus terminal.
To **Chichicastenango** and **Santa Cruz del Quiché**, hourly from 0500-1800, with Veloz Quichelense. Delta y Tropicana, to **Escuintla** and **Taxisco**, every 30 mins, 0600-1830, 1½ hrs. Numerous buses to **Santa Lucía Cotzumalguapa**. To **Jalapa** with Transportes Melva Nacional, T2332-6081, 0415-1715, every 30 mins, 3 hrs 30 mins, US$2. **San Pedro Pinula** between 0500-1800.

International buses
Reserve the day before if you can. Taking a bus from Guatemala City as far as, say, San José is tiring and tiresome (the bus company's bureaucracy and the hassle from border officials all take their toll).

San Salvador King Quality and Confort Lines, 18 Av, 1-96, Zona 15, T2369-0404, daily at 0630, 0800, 1400, 1530, US$20. Tickets from all travel agencies in Guatemala City and Antigua. Melva Internacional and Pezzarossi, 3 Av, 1-38, Zona 9, are ½ block from the Zona 4 terminal, T2331-0874, hourly from 0515-1615, US$8. Both these companies have onboard toilets and TV. Pullmantuur, from the Holiday Inn, 1 Av, 13-22, Zona 10, T2332-9785, daily at 0700, 1300, and 1500, US$29 and US$48. Ticabus, 11 Calle, 2-74, Zona 9, T2361-1773 at 1230 daily(5 hrs, US$9), with connections to **Managua** (US$38), **San José** (US$49) and **Panama** (US$77). Transportes Centro América, 16 Calle, 7-75, Zona 1, T2232-0235, to Puerto bus terminal, San Salvador, 0730, 5hrs, US$7. Door to door, US$20.

One of the cheapest ways to get to San Salvador is with Mermes, 1 Calle, 4-59, Zona 9, T2334-3151, at 0900 and 1330, US$8.

Honduras Avoiding El Salvador, take a bus to Esquipulas, then a minibus to the border. Hedman Alas, 2 Av, 8-73, Zona 10, T2362- 5072, to Copán via El Florido, at 0500, 5 hrs, US$36, to San Pedro Sula, 8 hrs, US$46, to La Ceiba and Tegucigalpa, both 12 hrs and US$53.

Mexico Trans Galgos Inter, 7 Av, 19-44, Zona 1, T2253-9131, to **Tapachula** via **El Carmen**, 0730, 1330, 7 hrs, US$21. Línea Dorada, address above, to **Tapachula** at 0700 and 1600, US$35. Transportes Velásquez, 20 Calle, 1-37, Zona 1, T2221-1084, 0800-1100, hourly to **La Mesilla**, 7 hrs, US$4. Transportes Fortaleza del Sur, Calzada Aguilar Batres, 4-15, Zona 12, T2230-3390 to **Tecún Umán**, 0130, 0300, 0330, 0530 via **Retalhuleu**, 5 hrs, US$5.20.

To **Chetumal** via **Belize City** with Línea Dorada change to a minibus in Flores, watch out for overbooking. Leaves 1000 and 2100. Journey often takes longer than advertised due to Guatemala-Belize and Belize-Mexico border crossings.

Car
Avenidas have priority over *calles* (except in Zona 10, where this rule varies).

Car hire companies Hertz, 7 Av, 14-76, Zona 9, T2334-2540, also at Camino Real and the airport, www.hertz.com. Budget, at the airport T2331-0273, also at Av Hincapié 11-01, Zona 13, www.drive-budget.com. Tabarini, 2 Calle "A", 7-30, Zona 10, T2331- 2643, airport T2331-4755, www.tabarini.com. Tally, 7 Av, 14-60, Zona 1, T2232-0421, very competitive, have pick-ups. Recommended.

Car and motorcyle repairs Mike and Andy Young, 27 Calle, 13-73, Zona 5, T2331-9263, Mon-Fri 0700-1600. Excellent mechanics for all vehicles, extremely helpful. Honda motorcycle parts from FA Honda, Av Bolívar, 31-00, Zona 3, T2471-5232. Some staff speak English. Car and motorcycle parts from FPK, 5 Calle, 6-75, Zona 9, T2331-9777. David González, 32 Calle, 6-31, Zona 11, T5797-2486, for car, bike and bicycle repairs. Recommended.

Shuttles
Shuttles are possible between Guatemala City and all other destinations, but it's a case

of reserving them first. Contact shuttle operators in Antigua (see Transport, Antigua). Guatemala City-Antigua, US$7-8, Panajachel US$20, Chichicastenango US$20.

Taxi

If possible call a taxi from your hotel or get someone to recommend a reliable driver; there are more than 300 illegal taxis in the city which should be avoided.

There are 3 types of taxis – **Rotativos**, **Estacionarios** and the ones that are metered, called **Taxis Amarillos**. *Rotativos* are everywhere in the city cruising the length and breadth of all zones. You will not wait more than a few mins for one to come along. They are numbered on their sides and on their back windscreen will be written TR (*Taxi Rotativo*) followed by 4 numbers. Most of them have a company logo stamped on the side as well. *Estacionarios* also have numbers on the sides but are without logo. On their back windscreen they have, the letters TE (*Taxi Estacionario*) followed by 4 numbers. They are to be found at bus terminals and outside hotels or in other important places. They will always return to these same waiting points (good to know if you leave something in a taxi). Do not get in a taxi that does not have either of these labels on its back windscreen. *Rotativos* and *Estacionarios* are unmetered, but *Estacionarios* will always charge less than *Rotativos*. The fact that both are unmetered will nearly always work to your advantage because of traffic delays. You will be quoted an inflated price by *Rotativos* by virtue of being a foreigner. *Estacionarios* are fairer. It is about US$8 from the airport to Zona 1. From Zona 1 to 4 is about US$3.50-4. The metered *Taxi Amarillo* also moves around but less so than the *Rotativos*, as they are more on call by phone. They only take a couple of minutes to come. Taxis of the **Amarillo Express**, T2332-1515, are 24 hr.

Directory

Banks

The legal street exchange for cash may be found on 7 Av, between 12 and 14 Calle, near the post office (Zona 1), but be careful; don't go alone. Banks change US dollars into quetzales at the free rate, but actual rates and commission charges vary; if you have time, shop around. **Banco Industrial**, Av 7, opposite the central post office, Visa cards only, Mon-Fri 0900-1530. **Bancafé**, 18 Calle, 8-75, near the Zona 1 bus terminals, has a Visa ATM. **Bancared**, near Parque Centanario on 6 Calle and 4 Av has 24-hr ATM for Visa/Cirrus. **Lloyds Bank plc**, 6 Av, 9-51, Zona 9, Edif Gran Vía, also at 14 Calle and 4 Av, Zona 10, with ATM. Mon-Fri 0900-1500. **Banco Uno**, 10 Calle, 5-40, Visa and ATM. Mon-Fri 0930-1730, Sat 1000-1300. **Bancafé**, Av La Reforma, 9-30, Zona 9, T2331-1311, Mon-Fri until 2000. Quetzales may be bought with MasterCard at **Credomatic**, beneath the Bar Europa, at 11 Calle, 5-6 Av, Zona 1. Mon-Sat 0800-1900. MasterCard ATM also at: **Banco Internacional**, Av La Reforma and 16 Calle, Zona 10. **Western Union**, T2360-1737, collect 1-800-360-1737.

Embassies and consulates

Austria, 6 Av, 20-25, Zona 10, T2368-2324. Mon-Fri 0900-1200. **Belgium**, 6 Av, 16-24, Zona 10, T2385-5234. Mon-Fri 0900-1400. **Belize**, AV Reforma 1-50, Zona 9, Edif Reformador, 8th floor, office 803, T2334-5531. Mon-Fri 0900-1200, 1400-1600. **Canada**, 13 Calle, 8-44, Zona 10, T2365-1250. Mon, Thu, Fri 0800-1630. **Costa Rica** (consulate), 1 Av, 15-52, Zona 10, Edif Galerías Reforma, T2363-1685. Mon-Fri 0900-1400. **El Salvador**, 5 Av, 8-15, Zona 9, T2360-7670. Mon-Fri 0800-1400. **France**, 16 Calle, 4-53, Zona 10, Edif Marbella, 11th floor, T2337-4080. Mon-Fri 0900-1200. **Germany**, 20 Calle, 6-20, Zona 10, T2364-6700. Mon-Fri 0900-1200. **Honduras**, 19 Av "A", 20-19, Zona 10, T2363-5622. Mon-Fri 0900-1300 (takes 24 hrs to get a visa, quicker in Esquipulas). **Israel**, 13 Av, 14-07, Zona 10, T2333-6951. Mon-Fri 0900-1400. **Japan**, Av La Reforma, 16-85, Zona 10, Edif Torre Internacional, T2367-2244. Mon-Fri 0930-1200. **Mexico**, 2 Av, 7-57, Zona 10, T2420-3433. Mon-Fri 0900-1300, 1500-1800. **Netherlands** 11 Calle, 2-29, Zona 14, T2368-3026. Mon-Fri 0800-1630. **Nicaragua**, 10 Av, 14-72, Zona 10, T2368-0785. Mon-Fri 0900-1300, English spoken. **Panama**, 10 Av, 18-53, Zona 14, T2333-3835. Mon-Fri 0830-1430. **Spain**, 6 Calle, 8-48, Zona 9, T2379-3530. Mon-Fri 0900-1400. **Switzerland**, 16 Calle, 0-55, Zona 10, Edif Torre Internacional, 14th floor,

T2367-5520. Mon-Fri 0900-1130. **UK**, 16 Calle, 0-55, Zona 10, T2367-5425-29. Embassy open Mon-Thu 0800-1230, Fri 0800-1200. Consulate Mon-Thu 0830-1200, Fri 0830-1100. Now responsible for UK citizens in El Salvador, Honduras and Nicaragua. Australian/New Zealand citizens should report loss or theft of passports here. **USA**, Av La Reforma, 7-01, Zona 10, T2331-1541, usembassy.state.gov/guatemala, Mon-Fri 0800-1700.

Emergency

T128 for ambulance, T122 for the *bomberos*, the fire brigade who also get called to accidents. See page 520 for hospitals.

Immigration

Immigration office Dirección General de Migración, 6 Av, 3-11, Zona 4, T2411-2411. For extensions of visas. If you need new entry stamps in a replacement passport (ie if one was stolen), a police report is required, plus a photocopy and a photocopy of your passport. They also need to know your date and port of entry to check their records.

Internet

Mesón Don Quijote, 11 Calle, 5-27, opposite Bar Europa, Zona 1. **Café Internet**, opposite Telgua office. **Café Net**, in Centro Comercial Real del Parque on the corner of the Plaza Mayor where Wendy's is. Also inside Edificio Geminis in Zona 10.

Medical services

Doctors Dr Boris Castillo Camino, 6 Av, 7-55, Zona 10, Of 17, T2334-5932. 0900-1230, 1430-1800. Recommended. **Dentists** Centro Médico, 6 Av, 3-47, Zona 10, T2332-3555, English spoken by some staff. **Opticians** Optico Popular, 11 Av, 13-75, Zona 1, T2238-3143, excellent for repairs.

Post office

The main post office is at 7 Av and 12 Calle, Zona 1. Mon-Fri 0830-1700. This is the only post office in the country from which parcels over 2 kg can be sent abroad. See Essentials for postage rates. Poste Restante keeps mail for 2 months.

Antigua and around

→ *Colour map 5, C2.*

Antigua is rightly one of Guatemala's most popular destinations, overflowing as it is with colonial architecture and fine churches on streets that are linked by squat houses, painted in ochre shades and topped with terracotta tiles, that bask in the fractured light of the setting sun. Apart from the ruins, Antigua is a very attractive place. It is the cultural centre of Guatemala and arts flourish here. Maya women sit in their colourful clothes amid the ruins and in the Parque Central. In the late-afternoon light buildings such as Las Capuchinas are very attractive, and in the evening the cathedral is beautifully illuminated as if by candlelight. Around Antigua are a cluster of sites, highland villages and volcanoes to explore. *»» See Sleeping, Eating and other listings, pages 541-550.*

Ins and outs

Getting around *Avenidas* run north to south and *calles* run from east to west. House numbers do not give one any clue about how far from the Parque Central a particular place is. *»» For further details, see Transport, page 548.*

Tourist information INGUAT office ⓘ *corner of 5 Calle Ote and 4 Av Sur, 0800-1300, 1400-1700 Sat and Sun 0900-1300, 1400-1700, T7832-0763, info-antigua@inguat.gob.gt*, is very helpful, with lots of maps and information. Volunteer work information available. English, Italian and a little German spoken. The monthly magazine *The Revue* is a useful source of information with articles and advertisements in English, free.

Safety Unfortunately, despite its air of tranquillity, Antigua is not without unpleasant incidents. Take care and advice from the tourist office on where to go or not to go. There are numerous *tourist police* (green uniforms) who are helpful and conspicuous; their office is at 4 Avenida Norte at the side of the Municipal Palace. If you wish to go to Cerro de la Cruz (see Sights) or the cemetery they will escort you leaving 1000 and 1500 daily. Antigua is generally safe at night, but it's best to keep to the well-lit area near the centre. Report incidents to police and the tourist office. See also page 515. Tourist assistance 24 hours, T2421-2810.

Background

Until it was heavily damaged by an earthquake in 1773, Antigua was the capital city. Founded in 1543, after the destruction of an even earlier capital, Ciudad Vieja, it grew to be the finest city in Central America, with numerous great churches, a university (1676), a printing press (founded 1660), and a population of around 50,000, including many famous sculptors, painters, writers and craftsmen.

Antigua has consistently been damaged by earthquakes. Even when it was the capital, buildings were frequently destroyed and rebuilt, usually in a grander style, until the final cataclysm in 1773. For many years it was abandoned, and most of the accumulated treasures were moved to Guatemala City. Although it slowly repopulated in the 19th century, little was done to prevent further collapse of the main buildings until late in the 20th century when the value of the remaining monuments was finally appreciated. Since 1972 efforts to preserve what was left have gained momentum, and it is now a UNESCO World Heritage Site. The major earthquake of 1976 was a further setback, but now you will see many sites that are busy with restoration, preservation or simple clearing. If the city was not treasure enough, the setting is truly memorable. Volcán Agua (3766 m) is due south and the market is to the west, behind which hang the imposing peaks of Volcán Acatenango (3976 m) and Volcán Fuego (3763 m) which still emits the occasional column of ash as a warning of the latent power within.

Sights

In the centre of the city is the **Parque Central**, the old Plaza Real, where bullfights and markets were held in the early days. The present park was constructed in the 20th century though the fountain dates back to the 18th century. The **Cathedral** ⓘ *US$0.40*, to the east, dates from 1680 (the first cathedral was demolished in 1669). Much has been destroyed since then and only two of the many original chapels are now in use. The remainder can be visited. The **Palacio de los Capitanes Generales** is to the south. The original building, dates from 1558, was virtually destroyed in 1773 but was partly restored in the 20th century and now houses police and government offices. You can climb to the second floor to admire the view (Monday to Friday 0800-1600). The **Cabildo**, or Municipal Palace, is to the north and an arcade of shops to the west. You can climb to the second floor for a great view of the volacanoes (Monday to Friday 0800-1600). The **Museo de Santiago** ⓘ *Tue-Fri 0900-1600, Sat-Sun 0900-1200, 1400-1600, US$1.30*, is in the municipal offices to the north of the plaza, as is the **Museo del Libro Antiguo** ⓘ *same hours and price*, which contains a replica of a 1660 printing press (the original is in Guatemala City), old documents and a collection of 16th- to 18th-century books (1500 volumes in the library). The **Museo de Arte Colonial** ⓘ *Tue-Fri 0900-1600, Sat-Sun 0900-1200, 1400-1600, US$3.30*, is half a block from Parque Central at Calle 5 Oriente, in the building where the San Carlos University was first housed. It now has mostly 17th- to

Antigua

Sleeping

Aurora & La Fuente Restaurant **1** *C4*
Casa Capuchinas **3** *B4*
Casa de Santa Lucía 3 **4** *B3*
Casa de Santa Lucía 4 **5** *C2*
Casa Encantada **31** *F4*
Casa Florencia **6** *B2*
Casa los Cántaros **7** *E3*
Casa Santo Domingo **8** *C6*
Cloister **9** *C3*
Convento Santa Catalina **10** *C3*
El Descanso **11** *C3*
Estella López **29** *B2*
Internacional Mochilero **12** *B2*
Jungle Party Hostal **14** *C3*
La Casa de Don Ismael **15** *C2*
La Casa de los Sueños & Azafrán **16** *D5*
Las Camelias Inn **2** *C5*
La Tatuana **18** *D3*
Mesón de María **30** *C3*
Mesón Panza Verde **24** *F3*
Mochilero's Place **20** *D2*
Papaturro **21** *C4*
Porta Hotel Antigua **22** *E3*
Posada de Don Quijote **25** *B2*
Posada del Angel **23** *F4*
Posada Doña Luisa **26** *D2*
Posada Juma Ocag **13** *C2*
Posada Landivar **17** *D2*
Posada La Quinta **17** *D2*
Wanderer's Hostel **29** *B2*
Yellow House **28** *B2*

Eating

Barrocas **5** *D5*
Café Barroco **2** *C5*
Café Condesa **3** *D3*
Café Condesa Express **4** *C6*
Café Flor **6** *D4*
Café Rocio **27** *B3*
Café Sky **33** *D5*
Cafetería Alemana Charlotte **8** *A3*
Caffé Mediterraneo **20** *D3*
Comedor Antigüeño **9** *C2*
Doña Luisa Xicoténcatl **10** *C4*
El Portal **11** *D3*
El Sereno **12** *B4*
Epicure **13** *B3*
Fonda de la Calle Real **14** *C3*
Frida's **15** *B3*
Helas Taberna Griega **18** *C4*
La Casa de los Mixtas **38** *C2*

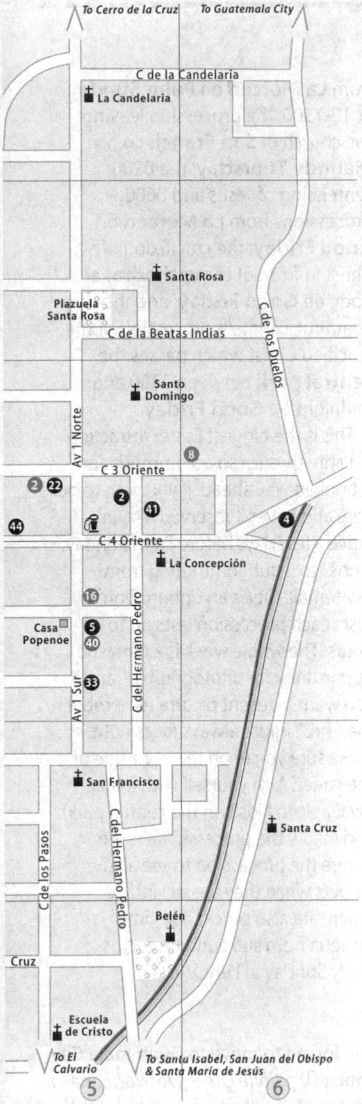

La Antigua Vinería **16** *E3*
La Casserole **41** *C5*
La Fuente **10** *C4*
New Bagel Barn **1** *D3*
Nicolás **44** *C5*
Ni-Fu Ni-Fa **22** *C5*
Peroleto **42** *B2*
Perú Café **24** *C4*
Quesos y Vino's **25** *B3*
Rainbow Café & Travel Center **26** *D2*
Tostaduría Antiqua **28** *D3*
Travel Menu **29** *D3*
Tre Fratelli **30** *D2*
Vivero y Café de la Escalonia **31** *F3*

Bars & clubs
Café 2000 **32** *D3*
Café No Sé **40** *D5*
Casbah **43** *B3*
La Chiminea **34** *C3*
La Sala **39** *D3*
Los Arcos Reds **35** *B3*
MonoLoco **36** *D3*
Reilly's Irish Pub **37** *B3*
Rikki's **19** *C4*
Torero's **45** *C1*

18th-century religious art, well laid out in large airy rooms around a colonial patio. The **Casa Popenoe** ⓘ *1 Av Sur, corner of 5 Calle, Mon-Sat 1400-1600, US$1.30*, is a restored colonial house (1632) containing many old objects from Spain and Guatemala.

Hotel Casa Santo Domingo is one of Antigua's most beautiful sights – a converted old Dominican church and also monastery property. Recent archaeological excavations have turned up some unexpected finds at the site. During the cleaning out of a burial vault in September 1996, one of the greatest finds in Antigua's history was unearthed. The vault had been filled with rubble, but care had been taken in placing stones a few feet away from the painted walls. The scene is in the pristine colours of natural red and blue, and depicts Christ, the Virgin Mary, Mary Magdalene and John the Apostle. It was painted in 1683, and only discovered by placing an ultraviolet light over it. Within the monastery grounds are the **Colonial Art Museum**, with displays of Guatemalan baroque imagery and silverware and the **Pre-Columbian Art Museum, Glass Museum, Museum of Guatemalan Apothecary** and the **Popular Art and Handicrafts of Sacatepequez Museum** ⓘ *3 Calle Ote 28, 0900-1600, US$5.30 for each museum* .

There are many fine colonial religious buildings: 22 churches, 14 convents and 11 monasteries, most ruined by earthquakes and in various stages of restoration. Top of the list are the cloisters of the convent of **Las Capuchinas** ⓘ *2 Av Norte y 2 Calle Ote, 0900-1700, US$3.90*, with immensely thick round pillars (1736) adorned with bougainvillea. The church and convent of **San Francisco** ⓘ *1 Av Sur y 7 Calle Ote, 0800-1200, 1400-1700, US$0.40*, with the tomb of Hermano Pedro, is much revered by all the local communities. He was canonized in 2002. The church has been restored and now includes the **Museo de Hermano Pedro** ⓘ *Tue-Sun 0800-1200, 1500-1700, US$0.40*. The convent of **Santa Clara** ⓘ *6 Calle Ote y 2 Av Sur, 0900-1700, US$3.90*, was founded in about 1700 and became

Semana Santa

This week-long event is a spectacular display of religious ritual and floral design. Through billowing clouds of incense, accompanied by music, processions of floats carried by purple- robed men make their way through the town.

The cobbled stones are covered in carpets of flowers known as *alfombras*, made up of coloured sawdust and flowers.

The day before the processions leave from each church, Holy Vigils (*velaciones*) are held, and the sculpture to be carried is placed before the altar (*retablo*), with a backdrop covering the altar. Floats (*andas*) are topped by colonial sculptures of the cross-carrying Christ. He wears velvet robes of deep blue or green, embroidered with gold and silver threads, and the float is carried on the shoulders by a team of 80 men (*cucuruchos*), who heave and sway their way through the streets for as long as 12 hours. The processions, arranged by a religious brotherhood (*cofradía*), are accompanied by banner and incense carriers, centurions, and a loud brass band.

The largest processions with some of the finest carpets are on Palm Sunday and Good Friday. Not to be missed are: the procession leaving from **La Merced** on **Palm Sunday** at 12-1300; the procession leaving the church of **San Francisco** on **Maundy Thursday**; the 0200 sentencing of Jesus and 0600 processions from **La Merced** on **Good Friday**; the crucifixion of Christ in front of the **cathedral** at noon on **Good Friday**; and the beautiful, candlelit procession of the crucified Christ which passes the **central park** between 2300 and midnight on **Good Friday**.

This is the biggest Easter attraction in Latin America so accommodation is booked way ahead. If you plan to be here and haven't reserved a room, arrive a few days before Palm Sunday. If unsuccessful, commuting from Guatemala City is an option. Don't rush: each procession lasts up to 12 hours. The whole week is a fantastic opportunity for photographs – and if you want a decent picture remember the Christ figure always faces right, so make sure you're on the right side of the street. Arm yourself with a map (available in kiosks in the central park) and follow the processional route before the procession to see all the carpets while they are still intact. (There are also processions into Antigua from surrounding towns every Sunday in Lent.)

one of the biggest in Antigua, until the nuns were forced to move to Guatemala City. The adjoining garden is an oasis of peace. **El Carmen** ⓘ *3 Calle Ote y 3 Av Norte*, has a beautiful façade with strikingly ornate columns, tastefully illuminated at night, but the rest of the complex is in ruins. Likewise **San Agustín** ⓘ *5 Calle Pte y 7 Av Norte*, was once a fine building, but only survived intact from 1761 to 1773; earthquake destruction continued until the final portion of the vault collapsed in 1976, leaving an impressive ruin. **La Compañía de Jesús** ⓘ *3 Calle Pte y 6 Av Norte, 0930-1700*, at one time covered the whole block. The church is closed for restoration but you can access the rest of the ruins from 6 Avenida Norte. The church and cloisters of **Escuela de Cristo** ⓘ *Calle de los Pasos y de la Cruz*, a small independent monastery (1720-1730), have survived and were restored between 1940 and 1960. The church is refreshingly simple and has some interesting original artwork. **La Recolección** ⓘ *Calle de la Recolección, 0900-1700, US$3.90*, despite being a late starter (1700), became one of the biggest and finest of Antigua's religious institutions. It is now the most awe-inspiring ruin in the city. **San Jerónimo** ⓘ *Calle de la Recolección, 0900-1700*,

US$3.90, was at first a school (early 1600s) for La Merced, three blocks away, but later became the local customs house. There is an impressive fountain in the courtyard. **La Merced** ⓘ *1 Calle Pte y 6 Av Norte, 0800-1700*, with its white and yellow façade dominates the surrounding plaza. The church (1767) and cloisters were built with earthquakes in mind and survived better than most. The church remains in use and the cloisters ⓘ *US$0.40*, are being further restored. Antigua's finest fountain is in the courtyard. **Santa Teresa** ⓘ *4 Av Norte*, was a modest convent, but the church walls and the lovely west front have survived. It is now the city's men's prison.

Other ruins including **Santa Isabel**, **Santa Cruz**, **La Candelaria**, **San José El Viejo** and **San Sebastián** are to be found round the edges of the city, and there is an interesting set of the Stations of the Cross, each a small chapel, from San Francisco to **El Calvario** church, which was where Pedro de Betancourt (Hermano Pedro) worked as a gardener and planted an esquisuchil tree. He was also the founder of the **Belén Hospital** in 1661, which was destroyed in 1773. However, some years later, his name was given to the **San Pedro Hospital**, which is one block south of the Parque Central.

There is a fabulous panorama from the **Cerro de la Cruz**, which is 15 minutes' walk from the northern end of town along 1 Avenida Norte.

Around Guatemala City and Antigua

▸▸ *pp541-550*

Ciudad Vieja – the former capital – is 5.5 km southwest of Antigua at the foot of Volcán Agua. In 1527, Pedro de Alvarado moved his capital, known then as Santiago de Los Caballeros, from Iximché to San Miguel Escobar, now a suburb of Ciudad Vieja. On 11 September 1541, after days of torrential rain, an immense mudslide came down the mountain and swallowed up the city. Alvarado's widow, Doña Beatriz de la Cueva, newly elected governor after his death, was among those drowned. Today Ciudad Vieja is itself a suburb of Antigua, but with a handsome church, founded in 1534, and one of the oldest in Central America. There's a **fiesta** on December 8. Between Ciudad Vieja and San Miguel de las Dueñas is the **Valhalla macadamia nut farm** ⓘ *T7831-5799, visits and nut tasting are free.*

About 3 km northwest of Ciudad Vieja is **San Antonio Aguas Calientes**. The hot springs unfortunately disappeared with recent earthquakes, but the village has many small shops selling locally made textiles. **Carolina's Textiles** is recommended for a fine selection, while on the exit road **Alida** has a shop. You can watch the weavers in their homes by the roadside. Local **fiestas** are 16-21 January, Corpus Christi and 1 November.

Beyond San Juan del Obispo, beside Volcán Agua, is the charming village of **Santa María de Jesús**, with its beautiful view of Antigua. In the early morning there are good views of all three volcanoes from 2 km back down the road towards Antigua. Colourful *huípiles* are worn, made and sold from a couple of stalls, or ask at the shops on the plaza. The local **fiesta** is on 10 January.

Five kilometers beyond San Lucas Sacatepéquez, at Km 29.5, Carretera Roosevelt (the Pan-American Highway), is **Santiago Sacatepéquez**, whose **fiesta** on 1 November, Día de los Muertos (All Souls' Day), is characterized by colourful kite-flying *(barriletas)*. They also celebrate 25 July. Market days are Wednesday and Friday.

Visiting a **coffee farm** is an interesting short excursion. **Tour Finca Los Nietos** ⓘ *San Lorenzo El Cubo, T7831-5438, www.fincalosnietos.com, by appointment only Mon-Fri 0830-1100*, is 6 km from Antigua. Thet conduct a 1½-hour tour of the cafetal including processing, roasting and tasting (US$6).

North of Guatemala City is **Mixco Viejo**, the excavated site of a post-Classic Maya fortress, which spans 14 hilltops, including 12 groups of pyramids. Despite earthquake damage it is worth a visit and is recommended. It was the 16th-century capital of the Pokomam Maya.

Volcanoes » pp541-550

The three volcanoes surrounding Antigua give incomparable views of the surrounding countryside and are best climbed on a clear night with a full moon, or after a very early morning start. Altitude takes its toll and plenty of time should be allowed for ascending. Take lots of water and fleeces, as the summits are cold. Climbing boots are recommended, especially on Fuego and Pacaya, to cope with the cinder. As a general rule, descents take from a third to a half of the ascent time. The tourist office in Antigua is helpful; enquire there about conditions before setting out. They also have a list of authorized independent guides if you would rather use one of them. Robberies have occurred even where large parties are climbing these volcanoes. None of these have been on Pacaya, since the security set-up was introduced more than six years ago.

Volcán Pacaya

ⓘ *Tours are available for US$5 upwards, with Gran Jaguar, Eco-Tour Chejo's and Tivoli. The popular and best time for organized trips is to leave Antigua at 1300 and return at 2100. Departures also 0600 returning 1300. In addition there is a US$3.25 fee to be paid at the entrance to the Volcán Pacaya National Park in San Francisco de Sales (where there are toilets).*

At 2552 m, the still-active Volcán Pacaya can't be missed. One of the highlights of this trip is surfing down the scree at high speed as the sun sets. The cone is covered in black basaltic rock shed from the crater. The rocks get warm and are lethally sharp. At the lip of the crater the sulphurous gases that are being belched out are chokingly disgusting, but the yellow, green and red colours blotched on the crater lip are striking. The roaring magma-filled mouth can be seen on the far side of the crater once the gaseous winds disperse. As the sun sets on the horizon, Agua is silhouetted in the distance, a weak orange line streaked behind it.

Pacaya has erupted about 20 times since 1565, but since the mid-1960s it has been erupting continuously. Should you be in Antigua when Pacaya erupts you may see some spectacular lava flows. Always check its alert status before signing up for a tour. It is about 1½ hours to the base of the crater, then a further 30 to 45 minutes scrambling up the scree and volcanic throw up – depending on how good you are at tackling the 'one step forward, two steps back' syndrome. The trick is to walk on your toes and not your heels. Try to avoid going on a mid-morning departure, which usually results in an arrival at the summit just as it is covered in cloud. Take torch/flashlight, refreshments and water and – it may sound obvious – wear boots or trainers, not sandals. Security officers go with the trips and police escorts ensure everyone leaves the area after dark. Check the situation in advance for **camping** (well below the crater lip, see Sleeping, below). Sunrise comes with awesome views over the desolate black lava field to the distant Pacific (airborne dust permitting) and the peaks of Fuego, Acatenango and Agua.

> ! *The most exciting volcano to climb is Pacaya because it's active and you can moon wander near the crater on rubble that is black, sharp and lifeless.*

Volcán Agua

ⓘ *Most organized tours with Antigua tour operators are during the day and cost about US$20 per person with guide and security, but less if there is a larger party. Trips normally leave Antigua about 0500.*

The easiest of the three Antigua volcanoes, at 3760 m, is climbed from **Santa María de Jesús**. Ask for directions in the village or speak to Aurelio Cuy Chávez at the **Posada El Oasis**, who offers a guide service. For Agua's history, see Ciudad Vieja. The crater has a small shelter (none too clean), which was a shrine, and about 10 antennae. There are great views of Volcán Fuego. It's a three- to five-hour climb if you are fit, and at least two hours down. Make sure you get good directions if you do it alone (although this is not recommended by INGUAT); there are several old avalanches you have to cross before regaining the trail. If you do not, you may get lost. To get the best views before the clouds cover the summit, it is best to stay at the radio station at the top. Climbing at night is recommended, either by torchlight or by the light of the moon; Saturday-Sunday is recommended for the ascent. Take an early bus from Antigua to Santa María de Jesús, which allows you to climb the volcano and return to Antigua in one day. Agua can also be climbed from **Alotenango**, a village between Agua and Fuego, south of Ciudad Vieja. It's 9 km from Antigua and its name means 'place surrounded by corn'. Looking at the market building in Alotenango, take the left route up; turn left at the T-junction, then first right and up. There are only two decision points: take the right fork, then the left. It is not advisable to descend Agua towards Palín in the southeast, as there is precipitous forest, steep bluffs, and dry watercourses, which tend to drop away vertically and a route is hard to plot. Alotenango has a **fiesta** from 18-20 January.

Volcán Acatenango

ⓘ *If you do this climb independently of a tour agency, ask for a guide in La Soledad. However INGUAT recommends authorized guides for all volcano climbs.*

Acatenango is classified as a dormant volcano and is the third-tallest in the country (3975 m) with two peaks to its name. Its first recorded eruption was in 1924. Two other eruptions were reported in 1924-1927 and 1972. The best trail (west of the one shown on the 1:50,000 topographic map) heads south at **La Soledad**, 2300 m (15 km west of Ciudad Vieja), which is 300 m before the road (Route 5) turns right to Acatenango (see sleeping). A small plateau, La Meseta on maps, known locally as **El Conejón**, provides a good camping site two-thirds of the way up (three or four hours). From here it is a further three or four hours' harder going to the top. There is a shelter, holding up to 15 people, on the lower of the two summits. Though dirty and in poor condition, this is the best place to sleep. The climb to the higher peak takes about 45 minutes. The views of the nearby (lower) active crater of Fuego are excellent and you can watch the activity of Pacaya at night.

Volcán Fuego

ⓘ *It is recommended by INGUAT that you take a guide.*

This volcano (3763 m) can be climbed via Volcán de Acatenango, sleeping on the col between the two volcanoes where there is a primitive shelter, then climbing for a further four hours over tiring loose ash to the crater. This one is for experienced hikers only. Do not underestimate the amount of water needed for the climb. It is a seven-hour ascent with an elevation gain of 2400 m – it's a very hard walk, both up and down, and easy to lose the trail. There are steep, loose cinder slopes, which are very tedious, in many places. It is possible to camp about three-quarters of the way up in a clearing. Fuego has had frequent dangerous eruptions in recent years though generally not without warning. Its last major eruption was in 1974. Check in Antigua before attempting to climb. If driving down towards the south coast you can see the red volcanic rock it has thrown up.

Sleeping

Antigua *p534, map p536*

In the better hotels, advance reservations are advised for weekends and Dec-Apr. During Holy Week hotel prices are significantly higher, sometimes double for the more expensive hotels. In the Jul-Aug period, find your accommodation early in the day.

LL Posada del Angel, 4 Av Sur 24 A, T7832-5244, www.posadadelangel.com. Breakfast included, dining room, exercise pool, fireplaces, 5 suites individually decorated, roof terrace, romantic, exclusive and private. Bill Clinton stayed here.

LL-AL Casa Santo Domingo, 3 Calle Ote 28, T7820-1220, www.casasantodomingo.com.gt. This is a beautifully designed hotel with 126 rooooms in the ruins of a 17th-century convent with prehispanic archaeological finds, with good service, beautiful gardens, a magical pool, good restaurant with breakfast included. Worth seeing just to dream. See also Sights, page 537.

LL-AL La Casa de los Sueños, 1 Av Norte 1, T/F7832-0802, www.lacasadelossuenos.com. A richly furnished, beautiful, colonial building, with friendly and helpful owners. Some rooms are grander than others so make sure you know what you're taking. Breakfast is included and served at a vast table, medieval-style. The gardens have a swimming pool and patio. Restaurant **Azafrán** on the premises.

LL-AL Mesón Panza Verde, 5 Av Sur 19, T7832-2925, www.panzaverde.com. Colonial indulgence at its height, breakfast included for the 12 rooms – 3 doubles, 9 suites. The bathrooms are pamper palaces in their own right. All with cupolas and arresting designs. There is a slither of a swimming pool for your morning work out. See also Eating.

L Casa los Cántaros, 5 Av Sur 5, T7832-0674. 5 rooms set around a gorgeous patio with flourishing orange and lemon trees, genuine colonial house. Very peaceful and intimate, breakfast included. Parking.

L-AL Casa Encantada, 9 Calle Pte, esq Av 4 Sur, T7832-7903, www.casaencantada-antigua.com. This sweet colonial boutique hotel with 10 rooms is a perfect retreat from the centre of Antigua. It has a small rooftop terrace where breakfast is served and a comfortable sitting room with open fire, books, lilies and textile-lined walls. 2 rooms are accessed by stepping stones in a pond. The suite, with jacuzzi, enjoys views of the 3 volcanoes.

L-AL The Cloister, 5 Av Norte 23, T7832-0712, www.thecloister.com. 7 big rooms around luscious patio garden, inviting sitting room, library, view of the clock tower, breakfast avaliable.

L-AL Porta Hotel Antigua, 8 Calle Pte 1, T7832-2801, www.portahotels.com. Has all the benefits associated with a hotel in this range as well as beautiful gardens and a pool, parking. It is some 4 blocks from the plaza on a quiet street. For US$6.25 non-residents can use the pool.

L-C Posada Landivar, 5 Calle Pte 23, close to the bus station, T7832-2962, www.merced-landivar.com. Rooms with private bathroom and a/c. It's safe and in a good position. Discounts for longer stays. Parking. Recommended.

AL Hotel Convento Santa Catalina, 5 Av Norte 28, T7832-3080, www.conventohotel.com. 12 rooms with lovely bedspreads, wooden ceilings and quarry tiled floors, 4 apartments in this converted convent. Good deal for longer stays. **Las Catalinas** restaurant on premises.

AL Hotel Mesón de María, 3 Calle Pte 8, T7832-6068, www.hotelmesondemaria.com. Great little place with a wonderful roof terrace. 20 stylish rooms are decorated with local textiles. Free internet and breakfast included at a local restaurant. Friendly and attentive service. Showers have large skylights.

AL-B Casa Capuchinas, 2 Av Norte 7, T7832-7941, www.casacapuchinas.com. This is a special place with 5 large, colonially furnished rooms, with fireplaces and massive beds, adjoining beautiful tiled bathrooms and special touches. A continental breakfast is included.

A Aurora, 4 Calle Ote 16, T/F7832-0217, www.hotelauroraantigua.com. The oldest hotel in the city with old plumbing (but it works) and 1970s features. Quieter rooms face a patio overflowing with beautiful flowers. Continental breakfast included, English is spoken.

B Casa Florencia, 7 Av Norte 100, T7832-0261, www.cflorencia.net. A sweet little hotel enjoying views towards Volcán Agua. 11 rooms with all the usuals including safety box and kitchen for guests. The balcony has *cola de quetzal* plants lining it. Staff are very welcoming, no credit cards. Recommended.

B La Tatuana, 7 Av Sur 3, T7832-1223, www.latatuana.com. Small hotel that's friendly, clean and safe; discounts are available off-season. Some rooms are a little dark. Choose carefully. (Allegedly Tatuana was a witch condemned to death by the Spanish Inquisition and burnt in the central plaza in the capital.)

B Papaturro, 2 Calle Ote 14, T7832-0445. Family atmosphere, rooms around attractive restaurant/bar area, run by El Salvadoranian couple, 5 rooms, 1 with bath and mini kitchen, breakfast included, full board available, good deals for longer stays.

C El Descanso, 5 Av Norte 9, T7832-0142. Rents 4 clean rooms on the 2nd floor, with private bath. There's a family atmosphere here and the place is extremely friendly and welcoming.

C La Casa de Don Ismael, 3 Calle Pte 6, lotificación 2a callejón, T7832-1932, www.casadonismael.com. Has a fabulous terrace with ringside views of Volcán Agua. It's worth staying there to enjoy this. 7 rooms, 3 shared bathrooms and free coffee and water for guests.

C Posada Doña Luisa, 7 Av Norte 4, T7832-3414, posadadoluisa@hotmail.com. Near the San Agustín church, good view of romantically lit ruins at night, a clean and very friendly place with a family atmosphere. It has 8 rooms with private bath and a small cafeteria. Parking.

C-D Las Camelias Inn, 3 Calle Ote 19, T/F7832-5780, www.cameliasinn.com. 16 rooms, some with bath. There's a small patio and balconies to hang out on. There's also an apartment with and a small kitchen for rent. Parking.

C-D Posada de Doñ Quijote 1 Calle Pte 22 A and B, T7832-0775, www.posadaquijote.com. Old colonial house, with of without bath, patio, friendly, good value.

D Casa de Santa Lucía No 3, 6 Av Norte 43A, T7832-1386. There are 20 standard clean rooms here all with private bathrooms, towels, soap, hot water and free drinking water. Beautiful views of La Merced and Volcán de Fuego. Parking.

D Casa de Santa Lucía No 4, Alameda Sta Lucía Norte 5, T7832-3302. Way more attractive than Nos 2 and 3, with 30 rooms for the same price. Only 14 years old, it has been built in a colonial style, with dark wood columns and is decorated with large clay bowls in the patio. Parking.

D Hotel Mochilero's Place, 4 Calle Pte 27, above **La Bodegona** supermarket, T7832-7743. Offers a warm welcome and 10 rooms, some with bath. Shared bathrooms are ultra clean with good showers. Free coffee, cable TV in reception. It is sometimes a little noisy from the street, but recommended. Safe luggage store for non-residents, US$0.60.

D Internacional Mochilero, 1 Calle Pte 33, T/F7832-0520. Internet, terrace with sofas and view, rooms with and without bath, clean, good value.

D Posada Juma Ocag, Calzada Santa Lucía Norte 13, T7832-3109. A small, but clean and nicely decorated hotel, using local textiles as bedspreads. It has an enclosed roof terrace, is quiet and friendly, shared bathrooms.

D-E Yellow House, 1 Calle Pte 24, T7832-6646. 8 clean rooms in this hostel run by the very welcoming Ceci. Breakfast included. Colonial style, laundry service, free internet use. 3 rooms with bath, kitchen, patio, parking. Recommended.

E Posada La Quinta, 5 Calle Pte 19, T7832-1713, basic. Some single rooms are cell-like but they have their own shower and are a good deal for single travellers who want their own bathroom. Luggage stored. Coffee and purified water available, small patio area.

E Jungle Party Hostal & Café, 6 Av Norte 20, T7832-0463, jungleparty2001@yahoo.com. Price per person. 32 beds spread across 6 rooms and 3 shared showers. Friendly management. Hot water, lockers, small patio, TV, free breakfast. BBQ on Sun at 1900.

E Primavera, 3 Callejón, off 3 Calle Pte near Alameda Sta Lucía, T7832-1479. 15 rooms with shared bathrooms that are clean. Good for the price though and in a quiet location. 2 rooms have private bathroom.

F Wanderers' Hostel, 7 Av 50, T7832-9578. Small, new hostel, cheapest in town. Good chilled-out communal area, decent breakfast. Rooftop terrace. Basic.

Apartments

Look on the notice boards in town. Rooms and apartments are available from about US$25 a week up to US$500 per month. One recommended family is **Estella López**, 1 Calle Pte 41A, T7832-1324, who offers board and lodging on a weekly basis. The house is clean, and the family friendly.

Around Antigua *p539*

E Restaurante Posada El Oasis, Santa María de Jesús. The owner hires horses and offers a guide service for volcano. Basic rooms, welcoming.

F Pensión, Volcán Acatenango. Basic, with good cheap meals.

Eating

Antigua *p534, map p536*

For the cheapest of the cheap go to the stalls on the corner of 4 Calle Pte and 7 Av Norte, and those at the corner of 5 Calle Pte and 4 Av Sur. During the Easter period, the plaza in front of La Merced is transformed into a food market. At all these places you can pick up *elote, tortillas, tostadas* and *enchiladas*.

TTT **Azafrán**, La Casa de los Sueños, 1 Av Norte 1, T/F7832-5215. Serves international cuisine with tables in the patio. Tue-Sun 1200-1500, 1900-2200. Recommended.

TTT **El Sereno**, 4 Av Norte 16, T/F7832-0501. Grand entrance with massive imposing heliconia plants in the courtyard. It has a lovely terrace bar up some stone steps and a cave for romantic dining; it's popular at weekends. International/Italian cuisine. 1200-1500, 1800-2300.

TTT **Hotel Casa Santo Domingo**, 3 Calle Ote 28, T7832-0140. Sun-Thu 0600-2200, Fri and Sat 0600-2400. A range of international and national food (mixed reports) in superb surroundings. Very good service and music.

TTT **La Casserole**, Callejón de Concepción 7, T7832-0219 close to **Casa Santo Domingo**. Mon-Sat 1200-1500, 1900-2200. Sun 1200-1500. Sophisticated French cooking with fresh fish daily served at tables set in a beautiful courtyard, exclusive. Rigoberta Menchú dined with Jacques Chirac here! Closed Mon.

TTT **Nicolás**, 4 Calle Pte 20, T7832-0471, www.nicolas.com.gt. Thu-Mon 1230-1500, 1900-2300. Thu and Fri Cuban jazz. New swish restaurant in lovely surrounds.

TTT **Tre Fratelli**, 6 Calle Pte 30, T/F7832-7730. Good Italian food, family atmosphere, romantic candlelit roof terrace, excellent bread with cumin seeds made on the premises for sale, delicious lasagna served with a mound of spinach cooked in garlic.

TTT-TT **Caffé Mediterráneo**, 6 Calle Pte 6A, T7832-7180. 1 block south of the plaza. Mouth-watering Italian cuisine with great candlelit ambience. Recommended. Wed-Mon 1200-1500, 1830-2200.

TTT-TT **Fonda de la Calle Real**, 5 Av Norte 5 and No 12, also at 3 Calle Pte 7 (which wins over the others for the setting). Its speciality is *queso fundido*. It also serves local dishes including *pepián* (and a vegetarian version) and *Kak-ik*, a Verapaz speciality.

TTT-TT **Ni-Fu Ni-Fa**, 3 Calle Ote 21, T7832-6579. Great Argentinian-style steaks, excellent salad bar included in price, candle-lit garden, good service.

TT **Frida's**, 5 Av Norte 29, Calle del Arco, T7832-0504. Daily 1200-0100. Ochre and French navy colours decorate this restaurant's tribute to Mexico's famous female artist. It is quite dark inside but Frida memorabilia and colander-like lampshades lighten the interior. Efficient service. 2nd floor pool table, Wed and Thu ladies' night.

TT **La Antigua Vinería**, 5 Av Sur 34A, T/F7832-7370. Mon-Thu 1800-0100, Fri-Sun 1300-0100. Owned by Beppe DÁngella, next door to San José ruins. Amazing photographic collection of clients in various stages of inebriation, excellent selection of wines and grappa, you name it. Very romantic, feel free to write your comments on the walls, very good food, pop in for a reasonably priced *queso fundido*/glass of wine if you can't afford the whole hog.

TT **Perú Café**, 4 Av Norte, T7832-9121. Daily 1200-2200. Distinctly fishy, *ceviche*, seafood, pretty courtyard, live music Sun lunch.

TT **Quesos y Vino's**, 5 Av Norte 32, T7832-7785. Wed-Mon 1200-1600, 1800-2200. Authentic Italian food and owners, good selection of wines, wood-fired pizza oven, sandwiches, popular.

TT-T **Café Flor**, 4 Av Sur 1, T7832-5274. Full-on delicious Thai/Guatemalan style and Tandoori food, delivered up between 1100-2300. The stir-fries are delicious, but a little overpriced. Discount offers sometimes available. Staff are friendly.

TT-T **Café Rocio**, 6 Av Norte 34. This is a palace of Asian food delight. Virtually everything on the menu is mouth-wateringly delicious. Don't leave without indulging in the *mora crisp*: hot blackberry sauce sandwiched between slices of vanilla ice cream! Highly recommended.

TT-T **Helas Taberna Griega**, 4 Av Norte 4, inside **La Escudilla**, see below. Open 1800-0100, from 1300 weekends, closed Wed. Delicious food including pitta bread stuffed with goodies, Greek olives, tzatsiki, all surrounded by a Greek ruin and sea mural, fishing net and shells.

¶¶-¶ Rainbow Café, 7 Av Sur, on the corner of 6 Calle Pte. Consistently delicious vegetarian food served in a pleasant courtyard surrounded by hanging plants, good filling breakfasts, indulgent crêpes, popular, live music evenings, book exchange. Bar at night with happy hour and ladies' nights. Recommended.

¶ Barrocas, 1 Av Sur 7, T5983-9462. Wed-Mon 1200-1500, 1800-2200. Sushi, spring rolls, Thai curry served up in a small restaurant with adjacent courtyard decorated in funky light shades. Open fire sometimes lit. Great for hanging out when there's a chill in the air.

¶ Comedor Antigüeño, Alameda Sta Lucía 4, near the PO, T7832-5995. This locally run place offers an absolute bargain of a *menú del día* (fish, chicken), which includes soup and sometimes a drink. It is extremely popular and can get ridiculously busy, so best to turn up before 1300 for lunch. Recommended.

¶ La Casa de los Mixtas, 3 Calle Pte 3 Callejón 2A. Cheap Guatemalan fodder with a few tables on the pavement next to **Casa de Don Ismael**, good breakfasts, set lunch way above average, friendly family. Recommended. Mon-Sat 0900-1900.

¶ Travel Menu, 6 Calle Pte 14. Big fat juicy sandwiches and tofu stir-fry, in candlelit place, friendly.

Cafés and delis

Café Barroco, Callejón de la Concepción 2, T7832-0781. Peaceful garden, stylish, delicious cakes, coffees, huge selection of English teas for the deprived.

Café Condesa, 5 Av Norte 4. West side of the main plaza in a pretty courtyard, popular, a little pricey for the portions, breakfast with free coffee fill-ups, desserts, popular Sun brunches. 0700-2100.

Café Condesa express, 4 Calle Ote 51, on the way out of town. 0600-1830, for those early morning starts. Takeaways, coffees, cakes. Also on Parque Central.

Café Sky, 1 Av Sur 15. Daily 0800-2300. Rooftop café-cum-bar with panoramic views over town, happy hour Tue-Sat.

Cafetería Alemana Charlotte, Callejón de los Nazarenos 9, between 6 and 7 Av Norte. Good breakfasts, cakes, good coffee, German books, newspapers, and films.

Doña Luisa Xicoténcatl, 4 Calle Ote 12, 1½ blocks east of the plaza. Popular meeting place with an excellent bulletin board, serving breakfasts, tasty ice cream, good coffee, good burgers, extensive menu, large portions. Good views of Volcán Agua upstairs. Shop sells good selection of wholemeal, banana bread, yogurts, etc; don't miss the chocolate and orange loaf if you can get it. 0700-2130.

El Portal, 5 Av Norte 6. Latest hangout for the young and beautiful, coffee from their own Finca Filadelfia, home-made cakes, pies, pasties, cappuccinos, expressos, *licuados*, take away. 0700-2100.

Epicure, 6 Av Norte 35-A, T7832-1414. This deli serves lovely sandwiches and renowned scotch eggs. All bread baked on the premises.

La Fuente, 4 Calle Pte 14 next to **Doña Luisa**, sandwiches, light meals and cakes at tables set around fountain, colourful and popular, excellent service. Amazing selection of *huíplies* and *cortes* for sale Sat.

New Bagel Barn, 5 Calle Pte 2. 0600-2200. Popular, breakfast, snack deals with bagels, videos shown no charge.

Peroleto, Alameda Sta Lucía 36. Run by a temperamental Nicaraguan owner, next to San Jerónimo church, stop by here for the wickedest *licuados* in town and you probably won't be able to bypass the cake cabinet either. It has a *ceviche* restaurant next door open until 1800.

Tostaduría Antigua, 6 Calle Pte/Av Sur Esquina. Roasts and brews good Antiguan coffee, many say the best in town. You can smell the coffee ½ a block away in each direction. 0900-1300,1430-1800.

Vivero y Café de La Escalonia, 5 Av Sur Final 36 Calle, T7832-7074. This is a delightful place, well worth the walk – a café admist a garden centre with luscious flowers everywhere, pergola, classical music, *postres*, herb breads, salads and cold drinks. Bird of paradise flowers and tumbergia. Daily 0900-1800.

Entertainment

Antigua *p534, map p536*

Bars and clubs

Café 2000, 6 Av Norte 8, between 4 and 5 Calle Pte. Daily 0800-0100. Happy hour Tue-Sat 1930-2300. Kicking most nights with indie music, and hard, cool lines in decor, but the free films or sports events shown on a giant screen can alter the balance in the bar between those on a bender and those glued to the screen. Good salads.

Cafe No Sé, 1 Av y 11 Calle. Small, dark lit bar which is proving popular on the travelling circuit.

Casbah, 5 Av Norte 30. Thu-Sat 1800-0100. Cover charge includes a drink. Gay night is Thu. Has a medium-sized dance floor with a podium. It plays a mix of good dance and Latin music, the closest place to a nightclub atmosphere in Antigua.

La Chiminea, 7 Av Norte 18. Mon-Sat 1700-2430. Happy hour every day seriously cheap, relaxed atmosphere, mixed young crowd, dance floor, salsa, rock.

La Sala, 6 Calle Pte, T5671-3008. Quiz, Wed nights. One of the most popular dancing and watering holes in town.

Los Arcos Reds Bar y Restaurante, 1 Calle Pte 3. Daily 0800-2400. All decorated in red, pool table, satellite TV fireplace, 100 things on the menu from Thai to steak. Good frozen licuados. Happy hour every day 1900-2400. Patio out back, free films.

MonoLoco, 5 Av Sur 6. Daily 1100-0100. Rooftop veranda, heaving at weekends, happy hour 1700-2000, also good food – huge plates of *nachos* go down well with the booze, excellent burritos, burgers, Wed ladies night.

Reilly´s Irish Pub/ Bar, 5 Av Norte 32, Daily 1400-0100, happy hour 1600-2000. Guinness available, popular, reasonably priced food.

Rikki's Bar, 4 Av Norte 4, inside **La Escudilla**. Usually packed full of gringos, but attracts a young Guatemalan crowd as well, popular with students and visitors and the gay fraternity. Good place to meet people. A good mix of music, including jazz.

Torero's, Av de la Recolección. Proving to be very popular with students and their teachers for salsa nights on Thu.

Cinemas

Antigua must be the home of the lounge cinema. All show films or videos in English, or with subtitles.

Café 2000, 6 Av Sur, shows free films daily.

Cinema Bistro, 5 Av Sur 14, food and film deal.

Cine Sin Ventura, 5 Av Sur 8. The only real screen in town, auditorium can get cold, and they could do with hitting the brightness button.

Festivals and events

Antigua *p534, map p536*

Mar/Apr Easter week: see box, page 538.

21-26 Jul for the feast of San Santiago.

31 Oct-2 Nov All Saints and All Souls, in and around Antigua.

7 Dec Quema del Diablo (burning of the Devil) by lighting fires in front of their houses and burning an effigy of the Devil in the Plazuela de La Concepción at night, thereby starting the Christmas festivities.

15 Dec The start of what's known as the Posadas, where a group of people leave from each church, dressed as Mary and Joseph, and seek refuge in hotels. They are symbolically refused lodging several times, but are eventually allowed in.

Shopping

Antigua *p534, map p536*

Antigua is a shopper's paradise, with textiles, furniture, candles, fabrics, clothes, sculpture, candies, glass, jade and ceramics on sale. The **main municipal market** is on Alameda Santa Lucía next to the bus station, where you can buy fruit, clothes and shoes. The *artesanía* market is opposite, next to the bus lane.

Art

Galería de Arte Antigua, 4 Calle Ote 27 y 1 Av. Tue-Sat. Large art gallery.

Bookshops

Numerous bookshops sell books in English and Spanish, postcards, posters, maps and guides including **Footprint**.

Un Poco de Todo, near Casa del Conde on 5 Av Norte on the plaza. **Casa del Conde**, 5 Av Norte 4; has a full range of books from beautifully illustrated coffee table books to guides and history books. **Rainbow Cafe**, 7 Av Sur 18, second-hand books. **Hamlin y White**, 4 Calle Ote 12A. Books on Guatemala are cheaper here than at **Casa del Conde**.

Crafts, textiles, clothes and jewellery

Many other stores sell textiles, handicrafts, antiques, silver and jade on 5 Av Norte between 1 and 4 Calle Pte and 4 Calle Ote.

Casa Chicob, Callejón de la Concepción 2. Beautiful textiles, candles, ceramics for sale, www.casachicob.com.

Casa de Artes, 4 Av Sur 11, www.casadeartes.com.gt, for traditional textiles and handicrafts, jewellery, etc. Very expensive.
Casa de los Gigantes, 7 Calle Ote 18, for textiles and handicrafts.
Diva, at 5 Av Norte 16 for western-style clothes and jewellery.
El Telar, Loom Tree, 5 Av Sur 7, all sorts of coloured tablecloths, napkins, cushion covers and bedspreads are sold here.
Huipil market held in the courtyard of La Fuente every Sat 0900-1400. The display is very colourful and if the sun is out this is an excellent place for photos.
Mercado de Artesanías, next to the main market at the end of 4 Calle Pte.
Nativo's, 5 Av Norte, 25 "B", T7832-6556. Sells some beautiful textiles from such places as Aguacatán.
Nim P'ot, 5 Av Norte 29, T7832-2681, www.nimpot.com, a mega-warehouse of traditional textiles and crafts brought from around the country. Excellent prices.
Textura, 5 Av Norte 33, T7832-5067 for lots of bedroom accessories.

Food

Doña María Gordillo, 4 Calle Ote 11. Famous throughout the country. It is impossible to get in the door most days but, if you can, take a peek, to see the *dulces*, as well as the row upon row of yellow wooden owls keeping their beady eyes on the customers.
La Bodegona, 5 Calle Pte 32, opposite **Posada La Quinta**, on 5 Calle Pte and below **Hotel Mochilero's** on 4 Calle Pte, large supermarket.
Tienda de Doña Gavi, 3 Av Norte 2, behind the cathedral, sells all sorts of lovely potions and herbs, candles and home-made biscuits. Doña Gaviota also sells Guatemala City's most famous ice creams in all sorts of weird and wonderful flavours (see **Helados Marylena**, page 528, for the story).

▲ Activities and tours

Antigua *p534, map p536*

Pampering parlours

Antigua Spa Resort, San Pedro El Panorama, lote 9 and 10 G, T7832-3960. Swimming pool, steam baths, sauna, gymnasium, jacuzzi, beauty salon. Daily 0900-2100. Reservations advised.
Mayan Spa, Alameda Sta Lucía Norte 20, T7832-3537. Massages and pampering packages, including sauna, steam baths and jacuzzi, are available. Mon-Sat 0900-1800.

Riding

Ravenscroft Riding Stables, 2 Av Sur 3, San Juan del Obispo, T7830-6669. You can also hire horses in Santa María de Jesús.

Swimming

Porta Hotel Antigua, non-residents may use the pool for a charge.
Villas de Antigua (Ciudad Vieja exit), T7832-0011-15, for buffet lunch, swimming and marimba band.

Tour operators

Adrenalina Tours, 5 Av Norte near 31 Portal Hotel Posada Asjemenou, T7832-1108, www.adrenalina tours.com. Xela's respected tour operator has opened up in **Posada Asjemenou**. As well as in-country shuttles, there are minibuses to San Cristóbal de las Casas, US$50. Also customized packages, week end trips to Xela and discounted Tikal trips.
Adventure Travel Center Viareal, 5 Av Norte 25B, T/F7832-0162, daily trips to Guatemalan destinations (including Río Dulce sailing, river and volcano trips), Monterrico, Quiriguá, El Salvador and Honduras.
Antigua Tours, Casa Santo Domingo, 3 Calle Ote 22, T7832-5821, www.antiguatours.net. Run by Elizabeth Bell, author of 4 books on Antigua. She offers walking tours of the city (US$18 per person), book in advance, Mon, Thu 1400-1700, Tue-Wed, Fri-Sat 0930-1230. During Lent and Holy Week there are extra tours, giving insight into the processions and carpet making.
Aventuras Naturales, Col El Naranjo No 53, Antigua, T7832-3328, www.aventurasnaturales.tripod.com. Specialized trips including guided birding tours.
Aventuras Vacacionales, end of 2 Av Sur, turn left for 20 m, on the right is Residencial San Jose, bell No 4, T7832-6056, www.sailing-diving-guatemala.com. Highly recommended sailing trips on *Las Sirenas* with Captain John Clark (see also under Río Dulce, page 619).
Eco-Tour Chejo's, 3 Calle Pte 24, T832-5464, ecotourchejos@hotmail.com. Well-guarded walks up volcanoes. Interesting tours are also

available to coffee *fincas*, flower plantations and nut plantation, etc, shuttle service, horse riding, very helpful.

Gran Jaguar, 4 Calle Pte 30, T7832-2712, www.guacalling.com/jaguar/. Well- organized volcano tours with official security, great fun. Also shuttles and trips to Tikal. Very highly recommended for the Pacaya trip.

Old Town Outfitters, 5 Av Sur, 12 "C", T5399-0440, www.bikeguatemala.com. Mountain bike tours (½-day tour, US$25), kayak tours (5 days, US$350), outdoor equipment on sale, maps, very helpful.

Rainbow Travel Center, 7 Av Sur 8, T7832-4202, www.rainbowtravelcenter.com. Full local travel service, specialists in student flights and bargain international flights, they will attempt to match any quote. It also sells ISIC, Go25 and teachers' cards. Manager Phillipa Myers is also the warden for the British Embassy in the area. English, French, German and Japanese spoken.

Sin Fronteras, 5 Av Norte 15 "A", T7832-1017, www.sinfront.com. Local tours, shuttles, horse riding, bicycle tours, national and international air tickets including discounts with ISIC and Go25 cards. Also sells travel insurance. Agents for rafting experts **Maya** Expeditions. Reliable and highly recommended.

Tivoli Travel, 4 Calle Ote 10, T7832-4274, antigua@tivoli.com.gt. Helpful with any travel problem, English, French, Spanish, German, Italian spoken, reconfirm tickets, shuttles, hotel bookings, good-value tours. Useful for organizing independent travel as well as tours. Recommended. Closed Sun.

ViaVenture, 2 Calle Ote 2, T7832-2509, www.viaventure.com. A professional tour operator offering special interest and tailor-made tours.

Vision Travel, 3 Av Norte 3, T832-3293, www.guatemalainfo.com. A wide range of tours. Frequently recommended. Also has guidebooks for reference or to buy, along with a water bottle-filling service to encourage recycling. Cheap phone call service. Shuttles and tours. Closed Sun.

Transport

Antigua *p534, map p536*

Bus

To **Guatemala City**. Buses leave when full between 0530 and 1830, US$0.65, 1-1½ hrs, depending on the time of day, from the Alameda Santa Lucía near the market, from an exit next to **Pollo Campero** (not from behind the market). All other buses leave from behind the market. To **Chimaltenango**, on the Pan-American Highway, from 0600-1600, every 45 mins, US$0.32, for connections to **Los Encuentros** (for **Lake Atitlán** and **Chichicastenango**), **Cuatro Caminos** (for **Quetzaltenango**) and **Huehuetenango** (for the Mexican border). It is possible to get to Chichicastenango and back by bus in a day, especially on Thu and Sun, for the market. Get the bus to Chimaltenango and then change. It's best to leave early. See Chimaltenango for connections. The only direct bus is **Rebuli** to **Panajachel** leaves at 0700, from 4 Calle Pte, in front of **La Bodegona** supermarket, US$4, 2½ hrs. Returning 1100. Other buses to Pana via Chimaltenango with **Rebuli** and **Carrillo y Gonzalez**, 0600-1645, US$2. To **Escuintla**, at 0530-1600, 1 hr, US$0.80.

International buses To **Copán**, direct with **El Condor**, 4 Calle Pte 34, T5498-9812. 0400, returns 1430, US$30 return.

Shuttles Hotels and travel agents run frequent shuttle services to and from **Guatemala City** and the **airport** (1 hr) from 0400 to about 2000 daily, US$7-10 depending on the time of day: details from any agency in town. There are also shuttles to **Chichicastenango**, US$20, **Panajachel**, US$10, **Quetzaltenango**, US$25, and other destinations, but check for prices and days of travel. Private shuttle to Guatemala City US$10-30, depending on the number of people.

Around Guatemala City and Antigua *p539*

Bus To **Ciudad Vieja**, US$0.16, every 30 mins, 20 mins. **San Miguel de las Dueñas**. Take a bus marked 'Dueñas', every 30 mins, 20 mins, US$0.20. To **San Antonio Aguas Calientes**, every 30 mins, 30 mins, US$0.20. To **Santa María de Jesús** every 30 mins, 45 mins, US$0.40. There are a few buses a day between **Mixco Viejo** and the Zona 4 terminal, Guatemala City. The bus goes to Pachalum; ask to be dropped at ruins entrance.

Learning the lingo

Antigua is overrun with language students and so some say it is not the most ideal environment in which to learn Spanish. There are about 70-plus schools, open year round. At any one time there may be 300-600 overseas students in Antigua. Not all schools are officially authorized by INGUAT and the Ministry of Education. INGUAT has a list of authorized schools in its office. Rates depend on the number of hours of tuition per week, and vary from school to school. As a rough guide, the average fee for four hours a day, five days a week is US$120-200, at a reputable school, with home-stay, though many are less and some schools offer cheaper classes in the afternoon. You will benefit more from the classes if you have done a bit of study of the basics before you arrive. There are guides who take students around the schools and charge a high commission (make sure this is not added to your account). They may approach tourists arriving on the bus from the capital.

All schools offer one-to-one tuition; if you can meet the teachers in advance, so much the better, but don't let the director's waffle distract you from asking pertinent questions. Paying more does not mean you get better teaching and the standard of teacher varies within schools as well as between schools. Beware of 'hidden extras' and be clear on arrangements for study books. Some schools have an inscription fee. Several schools use a portion of their income to fund social projects and some offer a programme of activities for students such as dance classes, Latin American film, tours, weaving and football. Before making any commitment, find some- where to stay for a couple of nights and shop around at your leisure. Schools also offer accommodation with local families, but check the place out if possible before you pay a week in advance. Average accommo-dation rates with a family with three meals a day are US$40-60 per week. In some cases the schools organize group accommodation; if you prefer single accommodation, ask for it.

Volcán Agua *p540*
Bus From Antigua to **Alotenango** from 0700-1800, 40 mins.

Volcán Acatenango *p541*
Bus To reach **La Soledad**, take a bus heading for Yepocapa or Acatenango village and get off at La Soledad.
Car Tabarini, 6 Av Sur 22, T7832-8107, also at the **Hotel Radisson Villa Antigua**, T7879-4444, www.tabarini.com.
Motorcycle hire La Ceiba, 6 Calle Pte 15, T7832-0077. **Bike hire** See Tour operators.
Taxi Servicio de Taxi 'Antigua'. Manuel Enrique Gómez, T5417-2180, has been recommended. **Horse-drawn carriage** Available at weekends and during fiestas around the plaza. **Tuc Tuc** Motobike taxis with a seat for 2 will whizz you around town for US$1.20.

Directory

Antigua *p534, map p536*
Banks
Banks are closed Wed-Sun of Holy Week and none change money between Christmas and New Year. Most banks are open Mon-Fri 0900-1800, some until 1900 and Sat 0900- 1300. **Bancafé**, on 4 Calle Pte on the edge of the plaza, with a 24 hr ATM for Visa, Plus. Fairly quick service. **Banco de América Central**, on the plaza, Visa and MasterCard ATM (Cirrus and Plus), but bank hours only. **Banco Industrial**, 5 Av Sur 4, near plaza, gives cash on Visa ATM (24 hr) and Visa credit card at normal rates, no commission. Extremely quick service. **Banquetzal** on plaza, good rates, no commission, MasterCard (Cirrus) ATM.

Internet
Some internet cafés offer discount cards, which are worth buying if you are in town for any length of time. The following are recommended: **Enlaces**, 6 Av Norte 1. **FunkyMonkeyNet**, Paseo de los Corregidores, 5 Av Sur 6.

Language schools
Footprint has received favourable reports from students for the following language schools: **Academia Antigüeña de Español**, 1 Pte 10, T/F7832- 7241. **Alianza Lingüística 'Cano'**, Av El Desengaño 21A, T7832-0370. Private classes are also available. **Amerispan**, 6 Av Norte 40 and 7 Calle Ote, T7832-0164, www.amerispan.com. In the US, Po Box 58129, 117 South 17th St, 14th floor, Philadelphia PA 19103. **Centro Lingüístico Maya**, 5 Calle Pte 20, T/F7832-1342, www.clmmaya.com. **CSA** (Christian Spanish Academy), 6 Av Norte 15, Aptdo Postal 320, T7832-3922, www.learncsa.com. **Don Pedro de Alvarado**, 6 Av Norte 39, T7832-4180. 20 years' experience. Proyecto Bibliotecas Guatemala (PROBIGUA), 6 Av Norte 41B, T/F7832-2998, www.probigua.conexion.com. Gives a percentage of profits towards founding and maintaining 14 public libraries in rural towns; frequently recommended. **Proyecto Lingüístico Fran- cisco Marroquín**, 7 Calle Pte 31, T7832-3777, www.plfm-antigua.org. **Sevilla Academia de Español**, 1 Av Sur 8, T/F7832-5101, www.sevillantigua.com. **Tecún Umán**, 6 Calle Pte 34A, T/F7832-2792, www.tecunuman.centramerica.com.

Private Lessons Check ads in **Doña Luisa's** and others around town and the tourist office. Recommended: **Julia Solís**, 5 Calle Pte 36, T7832-5497, julisar@hotmail.com (she lives behind the tailor's shop). **Armalia Jarquín**, Av El Desengaño 11, T7832-2377. There are, unbelievably, numerous No 11s on this road. Armalia's has a sign up and is opposite No 75, which has a tiled plaque.

Laundry
All charge about US$0.75 per kg and close Sun and half-day Sat. **Lavandería Gilda**, 5 Calle Pte between 6 and 7 Av, very good and can do a wash and dry in 2 hrs. **Central**, 5 Calle Pte 7B.

Medical services
Hospitals and clinics Casa de Salud **Santa Lucía**, Alameda Sta Lucía Sur 7, T7832-3122. Open 24 hrs, good and efficient service. Consultation prices vary. **Hospital Privado Hermano Pedro**, Av El Desengaño 12A, T7832-6419. **Opticians** Optica Santa **Lucía**, 5 Calle Pte 28, T7832-0384. Sells contact lens solution and accessories.

Police
Tourism police, 4 Av Norte, between 3 and 4 Calle Ote down the side of City Hall, T7832-7290. The office is open 24 hrs. Just knock on the door or ring their number. **National Police** are based in Antigua, in the Palacio de los Capitanes General, on the south side of the plaza.

Post office
At Alameda Sta Lucía and 4 Calle Pte, near the market. Mon-Fri 0800-1830, Sat 0830-1400; *Lista de correos* keeps letters for a month. **Courier services** There are several in town, including **DHL**, 6 Calle Pte and 6 Av Sur.

Telephones
Telgua, 5 Av Sur, corner of the plaza for international and local calls. There are public phone boxes inside the **Telgua** building, which are quieter to use than the couple under the arches on the west side of the square. Mon-Fri 0800-1800, Sat 0800-1200.

Lake Atitlán and around → *Map 4, C2.*

Beautiful scenery stretches west of the capital, through the Central Highlands amongst volcano landscapes dotted with colourful markets and the Maya wearing traditional clothes in the towns and villages. Aldous Huxley called Lake Atitlán "the most beautiful lake in the world" and attractive villages flank its shores. Further north you can explore the streets of Chichicastenango as the town fills with hawkers and vendors at the weekly markets serving tourists and locals alike. North of Chichicastenango, the Quiché and Ixil Triangle regions have small, very traditional hamlets set in beautiful countryside that is easily explored by bus. ▸▸ *For Sleeping, Eating and other listings, see pages 564-577.*

Ins and outs

The easiest way to get to the Lake Atitlán area is by the numerous buses that plough the Pan-American Highway changing at Los Encuentros or El Cuchillo junctions. Alternatively shuttles go to Panajachel from most big tourist centres. Villages around the lake are connected to Panajachel by boat services. Some are served by buses. Some Hurricane Stan damage from October 2005 is still visible and some small roads remain unrepaired. Access is not affected, though. The village that was completely destroyed behind Santiago Atitlán was declared a mass graveyard. ▸▸ *For further details, see Transport, page 574.*

Towards Lake Atitlán

The Pan-American Highway heads west out of the capital passing through Chimaltenango and on to Los Encuentros where it turns north for Chichicastenango, Santa Cruz del Quiché, Nebaj and the Ixil Triangle (see page 563), and south for Sololá and the Lake Atitlán region. It continues to the western highland region of Quetzaltenango (see page 587), Totonicapán, Huehuetenango and the Cuchumatanes Mountains (see page 582).

Chimaltenango and around

Chimaltenango is busy with traffic. Here, another road runs south, 20 km, to Antigua. This tree-lined road leads to Parramos where it turns sharp left. Straight on through the village, in 1.5 km, is a well-known inn and restaurant (see Eating). This road continues through mountains to Pastores, Jocotenango and finally to Antigua. At **San Andrés Itzapa** which is well worth a visit, there is a very interesting **chapel to Maximón** ⓘ *6 km south of Chimaltenango, open till 1800 daily*. Shops by the chapel sell prayer pamphlets and pre-packaged offerings. Beyond Chimaltenango is **Zaragoza**, a former Spanish penal settlement, and beyond that a road leads 13 km north to the interesting village of **Comalapa**. This is the best place to see *naïf* painting and there are plenty of galleries. There's a colourful market on Monday and Tuesday.

The routes west, Tecpán and Los Encuentros

Returning to the Pan-American Highway the road divides 6 km past Zaragoza. The southern branch, the **old Pan-American Highway**, goes through Patzicía and Patzún (see below) to Lake Atitlán, then north to Los Encuentros. The northern branch, the **new Pan-American Highway** which is used by all public transport, goes past Tecpán (see below) and then to Los Encuentros. From Los Encuentros there is only the one road west to San Cristóbal Totonicapán, where it swings northwest to La Mesilla/Ciudad Cuauhtémoc, at the Mexican border.

From Zaragoza the Pan-American Highway runs 19 km to near **Tecpán**, which is slightly off the road at 2287 m. It has a particularly fine church with silver altars, carved wooden pillars, odd images and a wonderful ceiling which was severely damaged by the 1976 earthquake. There is accommodation, restaurants and banks. Near Tecpán are the important Maya ruins of **Iximché** ⓘ *5 km of paved road south of Tecpán, 0800-1700, US$3.25*, once capital and court of the Cakchiqueles. The first capital of Guatemala after its conquest was founded near Iximché; followed in turn by Ciudad Vieja, Antigua and Guatemala City. The ruins are well presented with three plazas, a palace and two ball courts on a promontory surrounded on three sides by steep slopes.

The old and new Pan-American Highways rejoin 11 km from Sololá at the **El Cuchillo** junction. About 2 km east is **Los Encuentros**, the junction of the Pan-American Highway and the paved road 18 km northeast to Chichicastenango, see page 560.

To Lake Atitlán along the old Pan-American Highway

Rewarded by amazing views of Lake Atitlán and the surrounding volcanoes, travellers of the southern road from Zaragoza to Lake Atitlán encounter a much

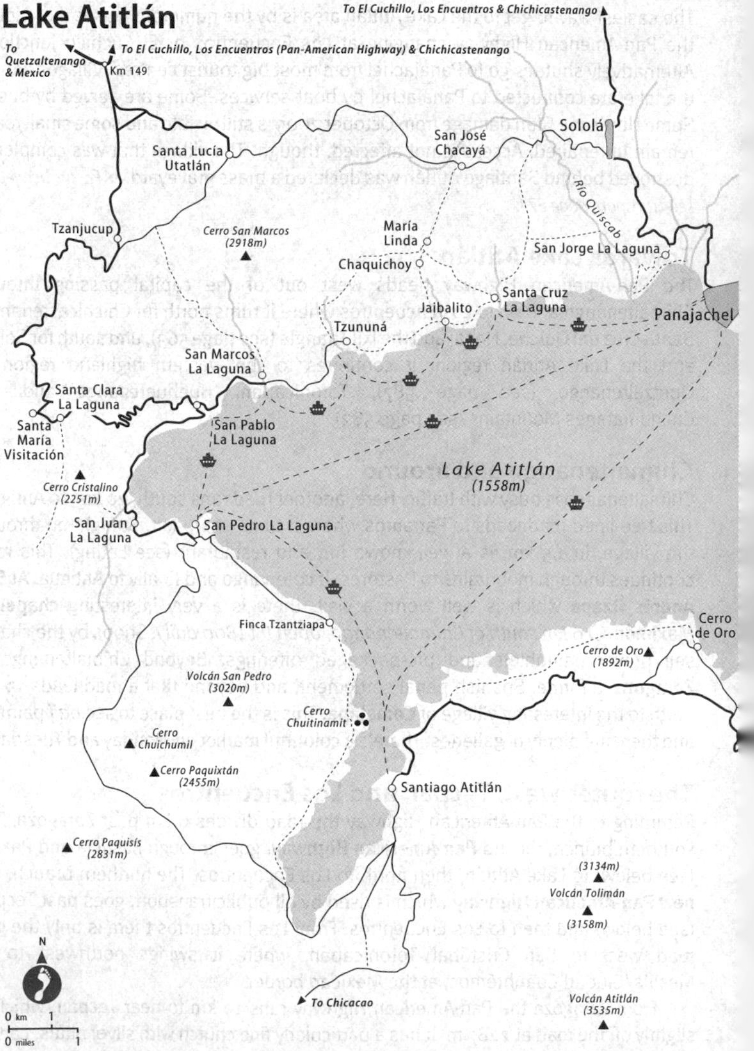

more difficult route than the northern option, with several steep hills and many hairpin bends. Nevertheless, if you have both the time and a sturdy vehicle, it is an extremely rewarding trip.

The route goes through **Patzicía**, a small Maya village founded in 1545 (no accommodation). Market days are Wednesday and Saturday and the local **fiesta** is 22-27 July. The famous church, which had a fine altar and beautiful silver, was destroyed by the 1976 earthquake. Beyond is the small town of **Patzún**; its church, dating from 1570, is severely damaged and, while it is still standing, it is not open to the public. There is a Sunday market, which is famous for the silk (and wool) embroidered napkins and for woven *fajas* and striped red cotton cloth; other markets are on Tuesday and Friday and the town **fiesta** is 17-21 May. For accommodation, ask at the *tiendas*.

The road leaves Patzún and goes south to Xepatán and on to **Godínez**, the highest community overlooking the lake. From Godínez, a good paved road turns off south to the village of San Lucas Tolimán and continues to Santiago Atitlán.

The main (steep, paved) road continues straight on for Panajachel. The high plateau, with vast wheat and maize fields, now breaks off suddenly as though pared by a knife. From a viewpoint here, there is an incomparable view of Lake Atitlán, 600 m below. The very picturesque village of San Antonio Palopó is right underneath you, on slopes leading to the water. It is about 12 km from the viewpoint to Panajachel. For the first 6 km you are close to the rim of the old crater and, at the point where the road plunges down to the lakeside, is **San Andrés Semetabaj** which has a beautiful ruined early 17th-century church. Market day is Tuesday. Buses go to Panajachel.

Sololá → *Colour map 5, C1. Altitude: 2113 m.*

On the road down to Panajachel is Sololá, which has superb views across Lake Atitlán. A fine, modern, white church, with brightly coloured stained-glass windows and an attractive clocktower dated 1914, dominates the west side of the plaza. Sololá is even more special for the bustling market that brings the town to life every Tuesday and Friday, when the Maya gather from surrounding commuities to buy and sell local produce. Women and particularly men wear traditional dress. While it is primarily a produce market, there is also a good selection of used *huípiles*. Even if you're not in the market to buy, it is a colourful sight. Markets are mornings only; Friday market gets underway on Thursday. There's a great **fiesta** 11-17 August.

From Sololá the old Pan-American Highway weaves and twists through a 550-m drop in 8 km to Panajachel. The views are impressive at all times of day, but particularly in the morning. Time allowing, it is quite easy to walk down direct by the road (two hours), you also miss the unnerving bus ride down.

Panajachel » pp564-577. Colour map 5, C1.

The old town of Panajachel is charming and quiet but the newer development, strung along a main road, is a tucker and trinket emporium. It's busy and stacked cheek by jowl with hundreds of stalls and shops along the main road. Some of the best bargains are here and textiles and crafts from across the country can be found. Panajachel is a gringo magnet, and if you want to fill up on international cuisine and drink then it's a good place to stay for a few days. » *For Sleeping, Eating and other listings, see pages 564-577.*

Ins and outs

Getting there and around The town centre is the junction of Calle Principal and Calle (or Avenida) Santander. The main bus stop is here, stretching south back down Calle Real, and it marks the junction between the old and the modern towns. *Tuc-tucs* will take you anywhere within town for US$1.25. It takes about 10 minutes to walk from the junction to the lake shore. Calle Rancho Grande is sometimes called Calle del Balneario and other streets have variants. » *For further details, see Transport, page 741.*

Tourist information **INGUAT** ⓘ *Calle Santander 1-87, T7762-1106, daily 0900-1700.* Helpful. Also www.atitlan.com, www.atitlantimes.com.

Safety There have been reports from travellers who have suffered **robbery** walking around the lake between San Juan and San Pablo and between San Marcos and Tzununá. Seek local advice from **INGUAT**, other travellers and local hotels/hostels before planning a trip.

Background

The original settlement was tucked up against the steep cliffs to the north of the present town, about 1 km from the lake. Virtually all traces of the original Kaqchikel village have disappeared, but the early Spanish impact is evident with the narrow streets, public buildings, plaza and church. The original Franciscan church was founded in 1567 and used as the base for the Christianization of the lake area. Later, the fertile area of the river delta was used for coffee production, orchards and many other crops, some of which are still grown today, and can be seen round the back of the tourist streets or incorporated into the gardens of the hotels. Tourism began here in the early 20th century with several hotels on the waterfront, notably the **Tzanjuyú** and the **Monterrey**, the latter originally a wooden building dating from about 1910, rebuilt in 1975. In the 1970s came an influx of young travellers, quite a few of whom stayed on to enjoy the climate and the easy life. Drugs and the hippy element eventually gave Panajachel a bad name, but rising prices and other pressures have encouraged this group to move on – some to San Pedro across the lake. Others joined the commercial scene and still run services today.

Sights

The old town is 1 km from the lake and dominated by the **church**, originally built in 1567, but now restored. It has a fine decorated wooden roof and a mixture of Catholic statues and Maya paintings in the nave. A block up the hill is the daily **market**, worth a visit on Sunday mornings especially for embroideries. The local **fiesta** runs from 1-7 October, the main days are at the weekend and on 4 October.

Panajachel

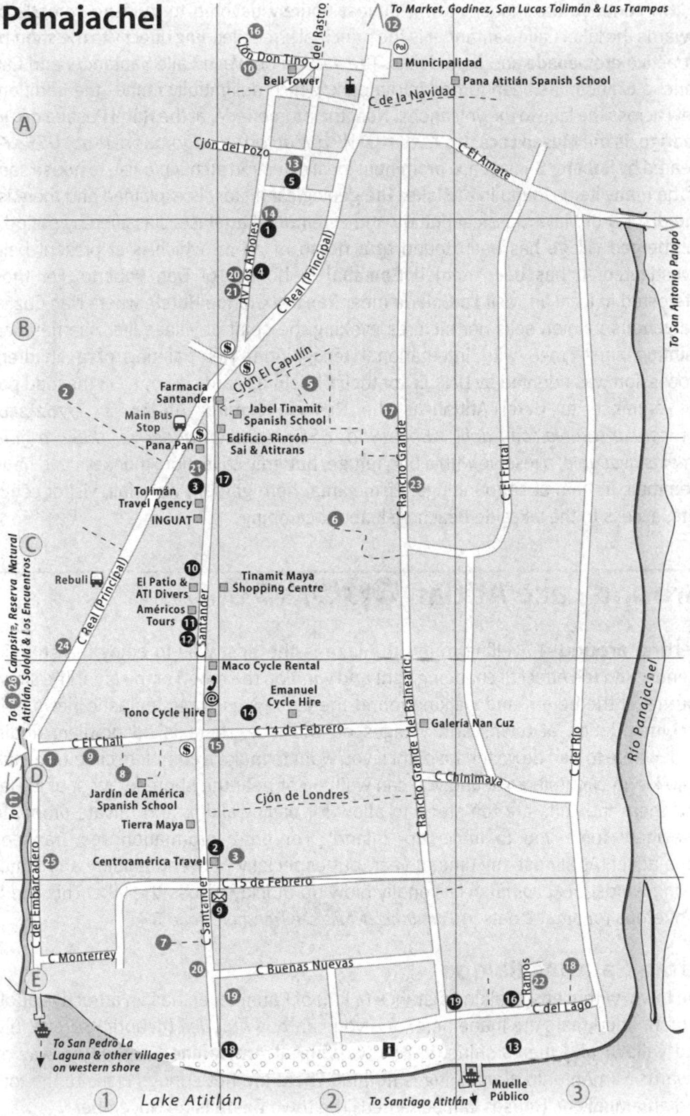

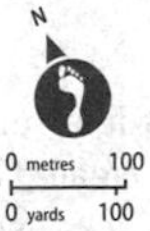

Sleeping
Atitlán 4 *C1*
Cacique Inn 1 *D1*
Casa de Huéspedes y Cafetería Las Hermanas 2 *B1*
Dos Mundos 3 *D2*
Hospedaje Casa Linda 5 *B2*
Hospedaje El Príncipe 6 *C2*
Hospedaje El Viajero 7 *E1*
Hospedaje Ramos I 22 *E3*
Hospedaje Sánchez 8 *D1*
Hospedaje Tommy 9 *D1*
Hospedaje Villa Lupita 10 *A2*
Las Casitas 12 *A2*
La Zanahoria Chic 13 *A2*
Los Arboles 14 *A2*
Mario's Rooms 15 *D1*
Montana 16 *A2*
Müllers Guest House 17 *B2*
Playa Linda 18 *E3*
Posada de Don Rodrigo 19 *E2*
Posada de los Volcanes 20 *E1*
Primavera 21 *C1*
Rancho Grande 23 *C2*
Riva Bella 24 *C1*
Santa Isabel 25 *D1*
Tzanjuyú 11 *D1*
Visión Azul 26 *C1*

Eating
Al Chisme 1 *B2*
Bombay 2 *D1*
Chez Alex 3 *C1*
Circus Bar 4 *B2*
Crossroads Café 5 *A2*
Deli Llama de Fuego 11 *C1*
El Pájaro Azul 9 *E2*
El Patio 10 *C1*
Guajimbo's 12 *C1*
Las Olas 13 *E3*
Last Resort 14 *D2*
Los Pumpos 16 *E3*
Pana Rock Café & Pana Arte 17 *C2*
Sunset Café 18 *E2*
Toyocal 19 *E2*

Bars & clubs
Discoteca Chapiteau 20 *B2*
El Aleph 21 *B2*

In contrast, the modern town, almost entirely devoted to tourism, spreads out towards the lake. Calle Santander is the principal street, leading directly to the short but attractive **promenade** and boat docks. The section between Calle Santander and Calle Rancho Grande has been turned into a park, which delightfully frames the traditional view across the lake to the volcanoes. Near the promenade, at the **Hotel Posada de Don Rodrigo**, is the **Museo Lacustre Atitlán** ⓘ *Wed-Mon 0900-1200, 1400-1800, US$4.60*, created by Roberto Samayoa, a prominent local diver and archaeologist, to house some of the many items found in the lake. The geological history is explained and there is a fine display of Maya classical pottery and ceremonial artefacts classified by period. A submerged village has been found at a depth of 20 m, which is at present being investigated. It has been named **Samabaj** in honour of Don Roberto. For those interested in local art, visit **La Galería** (near **Rancho Grande Hotel**), where Nan Cuz, an indigenous painter, sells her pictures evoking the spirit of village life. She has been painting since 1958 with international recognition. Her painting of a children's procession was adopted by UNICEF for their Christmas cards in 1971. On the road past the entrance to **Hotel Atitlán** is the **Reserva Natural Atitlán** ⓘ *T7762-2565, www.atitlanreserva.com, daily 0800-1800, US$4, children under 12, US$2, a guide (free) is available*, a reserve with a bird refuge, butterfly collection, monkeys and native mammals in natural surroundings. Picnic area, herb garden, waterfall, visitor centre, café, access to the lakeside beach. Ask about camping.

Around Lake Atitlán » *pp564-577.*

Getting around Travelling round the lake is the best way to enjoy the stunning scenery and the effect of changing light and wind on the mood of the area. The slower you travel the better, and walking round the lake gives some fantastic views. With accommodation at towns and villages on the way, there is no problem finding somewhere to bed down for the night if you want to make a complete circuit. The lake is 50 km in circumference and you can walk on or near the shore for most of it. Here and there the cliffs are too steep to allow for easy walking and private properties elsewhere force you to move up 'inland'. For boat information see Transport, Panajachel. At almost any time of year, but especially between January and March, strong winds (*El Xocomil*) occasionally blow up quickly across the lake. This can be dangerous for small boats. » *For further details, see Transport, page 574.*

Santa Catarina Palopó

The town, within easy walking distance (4 km) of Panajachel, has an attractive adobe church. Reed mats are made here, and you can buy *huípiles* (beautiful, green, blue and yellow) and men's shirts. Watch weaving at **Artesanías Carolina** on way out towards San Antonio. Bargaining is normal. There are hot springs close to the town and an art gallery. Houses can be rented. The town **fiesta** is 25 November.

San Antonio Palopó

Six kilometres beyond Santa Catarina, San Antonio Palopó has another fine 16th-century church. Climbing the hill from the dock, it lies in an amphitheatre created by the mountains behind. Up above there are hot springs and a cave in the rocks used for local ceremonies. The village is noted for the clothes and headdresses of the men, and *huípiles* and shirts are cheaper than in Santa Catarina. A good hike is to take the bus from Panajachel to Godínez, take the path toward the lake 500 m south along the road to Cocales, walk on down from there to San Antonio Palopó (one hour) and then along the road back to Panajachel via Santa Catarina Palopó (three hours). You can walk on round the lake from San Antonio, but you must eventually climb steeply up to the road at Agua Escondida. The local **fiesta** 12-14 June.

San Lucas Tolimán

San Lucas is at the southeastern tip of the lake. It is not so attractive as other towns. It is known for its fiestas and markets especially Holy Week with processions, arches and carpets on the Thursday and Friday, and 15-20 October. Market days are Tuesday, Friday and Sunday (the best). There are two banks and an internet centre. **Comité Campesino del Altiplano** is based in the small village of Quixaya, 10 minutes from San Lucas. This Campesino Cooperative now produces fair trade organic coffee buying from small farmers. You can visit its organic processing plant on a small coffee finca and learn about its *café justicia,* and political work ⓘ *T5804-9451, www.ccda.galeon.com,* long-term volunteers welcome, Spanish required.

Volcán Atitlán and Volcán Tolimán

ⓘ *Ask Father Gregorio at the Parroquia church, two blocks from the Central Plaza, or at the Municipalidad for information and for available guides in San Lucas. Father Greg has worked in the area for more than 40 years so has a vested interest in recommending safe and good guides. One such is Carlos Huberto Alinan Chicoj, leaving at 2400 with torches to arrive at the summit by 0630 to avoid early cloud cover.*

From San Lucas the cones of **Atitlán**, 3535 m, and **Tolimán**, 3158 m, can be climbed. The route leaves from the south end of town and makes for the saddle (known as Los Planes, or Chanán) between the two volcanoes. From there it is south to Atitlán and north to the double cone (they are 1 km apart) and crater of Tolimán. Though straightforward, each climb is complicated by many working paths and thick cover above 2600 m. If you are fit, either can be climbed in seven hours, five hours down.

❢ Cloud on the volcano tops is common, but least likely November-March. There have been reports of robbery so consider taking a guide, or at least local advice, when climbing the volcanoes.

Santiago Atitlán

Santiago is a fascinating town, as much for the stunningly beautiful embroidered clothing of the locals, as for the history and character of the place with its mix of Roman Catholic, evangelical and Maximón worship. There are 35 evangelical temples in town as well as the house of the revered idol Maximón. The Easter celebrations here rival Antigua's for interest and colour. These are some of the most curious and reverential ceremonies in the world. If you only visit Guatemala once in your lifetime and it's at Easter and you can't bear to leave Antigua, come to Santiago at least for Good Friday. Commemorative events last all week and include Maximón as well as Christ.

You will be taken to the house of Maximón for a small fee. The fine church, with a wide nave decorated with colourful statues, was founded in 1547. The original roof was lost to earthquakes. At certain times of the year, the square is decked with streamers gently flapping in the breeze. The women wear fine clothes and the men wear striped, half-length embroidered trousers (the most beautiful in Guatemala). There is a daily market, best on Friday and all sorts of art work and crafts can be bought. **Asociación Cojol ya weaving centre** ⓘ *T5499-5717, Mon-Fri 0900-1600, Sat 0900- 1300, free, weaving tours also.* As well as Holy Week, the local **fiesta** takes place 23-27 July.

Near town is the hill, **Cerro de Oro**, with a small village of that name on the lake. The summit (1892 m) can be reached from the village in 45 minutes. There are plans to reopen the medical centre in town. For more information on the **Lake Atitlán Medical project** and volunteer opportunities, see www.puebloapueblo.org.

San Pedro La Laguna

San Pedro is a small town set on a tiny promontory with coffee bushes threaded around tracks lined with hostels and restaurants on the lakeside fringes, and with the **Tz'utujil Maya** dominating the main part of the town up a very steep hill behind. San Pedro is now the favourite spot to hang out in for a couple of days or longer. It's a place to relax, to soak in hot baths, learn a bit of Spanish and horse ride. Some of the semi-permanent gringo inhabitants now run bars and cafés or sell home-made jewellery and the like. Grass is easily available and harder drugs can be found, however police have been drafted in for greater law enforcement. There's a **fiesta** 27-30 June with traditional dances. The cobbled road from the dock facing Panajachel (known as the *muelle)* climbs up to the centre and another goes down, more or less at right angles, to the other dock (known as the *playa* – beach) facing Santiago with the town arranged around.

The town lies at the foot of the **Volcán San Pedro** (3020 m), which can be climbed in four to five hours, three hours down. It is now in the Parque Ecológico Volcán San Pedro, www.parquevolcansanpedro.org, and all climbers now pay US$13.30 which

San Pedro La Laguna

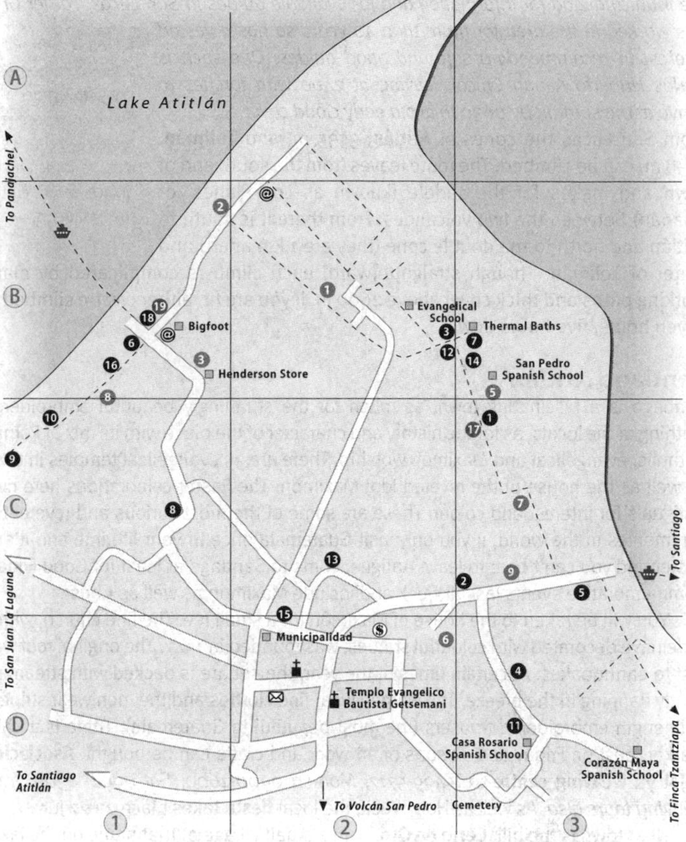

Sleeping
Hospedaje Buenas Nuevas 1 *B2*
Hospedaje Casa Elena 2 *B1*
Mansión del Lago 3 *B1*
Sak' Cari 5 *B3*
San Francisco 6 *D2*
Ti-Kaaj & Restaurant 7 *C3*
Valle Azul 8 *B1*
Villa Sol 9 *C3*

Eating
Arte Libre 1 *C3*
Café Arte 2 *C3*
Café Munchies 3 *B2*
Comedor del Viajero 4 *D3*
Comedor Santa Elena 5 *C3*
El Fondeadero 6 *B1*
El Otro Lado 7 B3
Emperador 8 *C1*
La Ultima Cena 15 *C2*
Luna Azul 9 *C1*
Maritza 10 *C1*
Nick's Place 18 *B1*
Pachanay 11 *D3*
Pinocchio 12 *B2*
Rosalinda 13 *C2*
Thermal Baths 7 *B3*
Tin Tin 14 *B3*
Vayavos 16 *B1*

Bars & clubs
Alegre 19 B1
D'noz 19 *B1*
Jorj's 17 *C3*

includes a guide. **Politur** also work in the park and there have been no incidents of robbery since the park's inauguration. Camping is possible. Go early (0530) for the view, because after 1000 the top is usually smothered in cloud; also you will be in the shade all the way up and part of the way down.

Evangelical churches are well represented in San Pedro, and you can hardly miss the pink and white **Templo Evangelico Bautista Getsemaní** in the centre. A visit to the rug-making co-operative on the beach is of interest and backstrap weaving is taught at some places. Market days are Thursday and Sunday (better). A visit to the **thermal baths** ⓘ *about US$3.20 a session, Mon-Sat 0800-1900*, is a relaxing experience. Note that the water is solar heated, they are not chemical hot springs. Massage also available. For general local information ask at **Bigfoot**, who will advise you on horse riding to neighbouring villages, guides for climbing Volcán San Pedro and whatever else you have in mind. Canoes are made in San Pedro and hire is possible.

San Juan La Laguna and Santa Clara La Laguna

The road north from San Pedro passes around a headland to San Juan La Laguna (2 km), a traditional lakeside town. Look for **Los Artesanos de San Juan** ⓘ *8 Av, 6-20, Zona 2, T5963-9803, sanjuanerme@yahoo.com.mx*, and another image of Maximón displayed in the house opposite the Municipalidad. **Rupalaj Kistalin** ⓘ *close to the textile store, LEMA, T5964-0040, daily 0800-1700*, is a highly recommended organization run by local guides. See under Activities and tours. **LEMA** ⓘ *T2425-9441, lemasociaion@hotmail.com*, the women weavers' association which uses natural dyes in their textiles, is also in town. Weaving classes are also possible (T7759-9126). On the road towards San Pablo there is a good viewpoint from the hilltop with the cross; a popular walk. A more substantial walk, about three hours, is up behind the village to Santa Clara La Laguna, 2100 m, passing the village of **Cerro Cristalino** with its attractive, large white church with images of saints around the walls.

Santa María Visitación and San Pablo La Laguna

A short distance (500 m) to the west, separated by a gully, is another smaller place, Santa María Visitación. As with Santa Clara La Laguna, this is a typical highland village, and unspoilt by tourism. San Juan is connected to San Pablo by the lakeshore road, an attractive 4 km stretch mainly through coffee plantations. San Pablo, a busy village set 80 m above the lake, is known for rope making from *cantala* (maguey) fibres, which are also used for bags and fabric weaving.

San Marcos La Laguna

San Marcos' location is deceptive with the main part of the community 'hidden' up the hill. The quiet village centre is set at the upper end of a gentle slope that runs 300 m through coffee and fruit trees down to the lake, reached by two paved walkways. The village has grown rapidly in the last few years with an explosion of a recommended kind – lots of **massage**, **yoga**, and all sorts of therapies can now be found here. It is the ideal place to be pampered. Beyond the centre, 300 m to the east is the main dock of the village down a cobbled road. Parts of the village still show mudslide damage from Hurricane Stan in October 2005. Down the pathways are the hotels, some with waterfront sites have their own docks. There is a slanting trail leaving the village up through dramatic scenery over to Santa Lucía Utatlán, passing close to Cerro San Marcos, 2918 m, the highest point in the region apart from the volcanoes.

If arriving by boat and staying in San Marcos, ask to be dropped at the Schumann or the Pirámides dock.

San Marcos to Santa Cruz

From the end of San Marcos where the stone track goes down to the dock, a rough track leads to **Tzununá**, passable for small trucks and 4WD vehicles, with views across the lake all the way. The village of Tzununá is along the tree-lined road through coffee plantations with a few houses up the valley behind. There is also a brand new hotel with wonderful views. See Sleeping. There is a dock on the lakeside but no facilities. From here to Panajachel there are no roads or vehicular tracks and the villages can only be reached by boat, on horse or on foot. Also from here are some of the most spectacular views of the lake and the southern volcanoes. **Jaibalito** is smaller still than Tzununá, hemmed in by the mountains. See Sleeping.

Arguably the best walk in the Atitlán area is from Jaibalito to Santa Cruz.

Santa Cruz La Laguna

Santa Cruz village is set in the most dramatic scenery of the lake. Three deep ravines come down to the bay separating two spurs. A stone roadway climbs up the left-hand spur, picks up the main walking route from Jaibalito and crosses over a deep ravine (unfortunately used as a garbage tip) to the plaza, on the only flat section of the right spur, about 120 m above the lake. The communal life of the village centres on the plaza. The hotels, one of them overflowing with flowers, are on the lake shore. Behind the village are steep, rocky forested peaks, many too steep even for the locals to cultivate. The **fiesta** takes place 7-11 May.

There is good walking here. Apart from the lake route, strenuous hikes inland eventually lead to the Santa Lucía Utatlán-Sololá road. From the left-hand (west) ravine reached from the path that runs behind the lake shore section, a trail goes through fields to an impossible looking gorge, eventually climbing up to Chaquijchoy, Finca María Linda and a trail to San José Chacayá (about four hours). In the reverse direction, the path southwest from San José leads to the Finca María Linda, which is close to the crater rim from where due south is a track to Jaibalito, to the left (east) round to the trail to Santa Cruz. Others follow the ridges towards San José and the road. These are for experienced hikers, and a compass (you are travelling due north) is essential if the cloud descends and there is no one to ask. From Santa Cruz to Panajachel along the coast is difficult, steep and unconsolidated, with few definitive paths. If you do get to the delta of the Río Quiscab, you may find private land is barred. The alternatives are either to go up to Sololá, about 6 km and 800 m up, or get a boat.

Chichicastenango

» *pp564-577. Colour map 5, B1.*

→ *Altitude: 2071 m.*

Chichicastenango is a curious blend of mysticism and commercialism. It is famous for its market where hundreds come for a bargain buy. On market mornings the steps of the church are blanketed in flowers as the women, in traditional dress, fluff up their skirts, amid baskets of lilies, roses and blackberries. But, with its mixture of Catholic and indigenous religion readily visible, it is more than just a shopping trolley stop. On a hilltop peppered with pine, villagers worship at a Maya shrine; in town, a time-honoured tradition of brotherhoods focuses on saint worship. Coupled with the mist that encircles the valley in the late afternoon, you can sense an air of intrigue.

» *For Sleeping, Eating and other listings, see pages 564-577.*

Ins and outs

Getting there Chichi is served by numerous chicken buses that head north from Los Encuentros or south from Santa Cruz del Quiché. There are direct buses from Xela and Guatemala City and shuttles from Antigua, the city and Pana. » *For further details, see Transport, page 574.*

Tourist information **Tourist office** ⓘ *7 Calle, half a block east of the main square, T/F7756-2022, Sun-Thu 0800-1800, Fri 0800-1200.*

Background

Often called 'Chichi' but also known as Santo Tomás, Chichicastenango is the hub of the Maya-K'iche' highlands. The name derives from the *chichicaste*, a prickly purple plant like a nettle, which grows profusely, and *tenango*, meaning 'place of'. Today the locals call the town 'Siguan Tinamit' meaning 'place surrounded by ravines'. The townsfolk are also known as *Masheños,* which comes from the word *Max*, also meaning Tomás. About 1000 *ladinos* live in the town, but 20,000 Maya live in the hills nearby and flood the town for the Thursday and Sunday markets. The town itself has winding streets of white houses roofed with bright red tiles, which wander over a little knoll in the centre of a cup-shaped valley surrounded by high mountains. The men's traditional outfit is a short-waisted embroidered jacket and knee breeches of black cloth, a woven sash and an embroidered kerchief round the head. The cost of this outfit, now over US$200, means that fewer and fewer men are wearing it. Women wear *huípiles* with red embroidery against black or brown and their *cortes* have dark blue stripes.

Sights

A large plaza is the focus of the town, with two white churches facing one another: **Santo Tomás** the parish church and **Calvario**. Santo Tomás, founded in 1540, is open to visitors, although photography is not allowed, and visitors are asked to be discreet and enter by a side door (through an arch to the right). Next to Santo Tomás are the cloisters of the Dominican monastery (1542). Here the famous *Popol Vuh* manuscript of the Maya creation story was found. A human skull wedged behind a carved stone

Chichicastenango

N

0 metres 100
0 yards 100

Sleeping
Chalet House 3
Chugüilá 4
El Salvador 6
Maya Lodge 7
Mayan Inn 8
Pensión Girón & Restaurante Las Brasas 9
Posada Belén 1
Posada El Arco 5
Santo Tomás 11

Eating
Caffé Tuttos 1
La Fonda de Tzijolaj 4
La Parrillada 2
La Villa de los Cofrades 4
Tu Café 5
Tziguan Tinamit 6

face, found in Sacapulas, can be seen at the **Museo Arqueológico Regional** ⓘ *main plaza, Tue, Wed, Fri, Sat 0800-1200, 1400-1600, Thu 0800-1600, Sun 0800-1400, closed Mon, US$0.70, photographs and video camera not permitted.* There's also a jade collection once owned by 1926-1944 parish priest Father Rossbach.

The Sunday and Thursday **markets** are both very touristy, and bargains are harder to come by once shuttle loads of people arrive mid-morning. Articles from all over the Highlands are available: rugs, carpets and bedspreads; walk one or two streets away from the main congregation of stalls for more realistic prices; nowadays prices are cheaper in Panajachel for the same items. You won't find anything here now that you can't find in Panajachel.

The idol, **Pascual Abaj**, a god of fertility, is a large black stone with human features on a hill overlooking the town. Crosses in the ground surrounding the shrine are prayed in front of for the health of men, women and children, and for the dead. Fires burn and the wax of a thousand candles, flowers and sugar cover the shrine. One ceremony you may see is that of a girl from the town requesting a good and sober husband. If you wish to undergo a ceremony to plead for a partner, or to secure safety from robbery or misfortune, you may ask the *curandero* (US$7 including photographs). To reach the deity, walk along 5 Avenida, turn right on 9 Calle, down the hill, cross the stream and take the second track from the left going steepest uphill, which passes directly through a farmhouse and buildings. The farm now belongs to a mask-maker whom you can visit and buy masks from. Follow the path to the top of the pine-topped hill where you may well see a Maya ceremony in progress. It's about half an hour's walk. The site can be easily visited independently, or an INGUAT-approved guide can take you there and explain the history and significance (US$6.50, one or two hours, identified by an INGUAT jacket and license in town).

Santa Cruz del Quiché and around → *Population: 7750. Altitude: 2000 m.*

Santa Cruz del Quiché, often simply called Quiché, is a quaint, friendly town, with a colourful daily market covering several blocks. There are few tourists here and prices are consequently reasonable. Its main attraction is **Utatlán**, the remains of the Maya K'iche' capital. The large Parque Central has a military garrison on the east side with a jail on the lower floor and a sinister military museum with reminders of recent conflicts above. The town's **fiesta** – about 14-20 August – varies around the Assumption.

Three kilometres away are the remains of temples and other structures of the former Quiché capital, **Gumarcaj**, sometimes spelt **K'umarkaaj**, and now generally called **Utatlán** ⓘ *0800-1700, US$1.30*. From the bus station, walk west along 10 Calle for 40 minutes, until you reach a small junction, with a blue sign (SECP). Take the right lane up through gates to the site. The city was largely destroyed by the Spaniards, but the stonework of the original buildings can be seen in the ruins, which can be reached on foot; the setting is very attractive and well maintained. There are two subterranean burial chambers (take a torch, as there are unexpected drops) still used by the Maya for worship and chicken sacrifices. The seven plazas, many temples, ball court, gladiator's archway and other features are marked.

There is a paved road east from Quiché to (8 km) **Santo Tomás Chiché**, a picturesque village with a fine, rarely visited Saturday market **(fiesta** 25-28 December). There is also a road to this village from Chichicastenango. Although it is a short-cut, it is rough and virtually impassable in any vehicle. It makes a good, three- to four-hour walk, however. Further east (45 km) from Chiché is **Zacualpa**, where beautiful woollen bags are woven. The church has a remarkably fine façade and there is an unnamed *pensión* near the plaza. Market days are Sunday and Thursday.

At **Joyabaj** women weave fascinating *huípiles* and there is a colourful Sunday market, followed by a procession at about noon from the church led by the elders with drums and pipes. This was a stopping place on the old route from Mexico to Antigua. There is good walking in the wooded hills around, for example north to Chorraxaj (two hours), or across the Río Cocol south to Piedras Blancas to see blankets being woven. Ask at the **Conalfa** office in Joyabaj for information or a guide. The **Centro Xoy** arranges tours (for the benefit of community development) and offers Spanish and K'iche' lessons. During **fiesta** week (9-15 August) Joyabaj has a *Palo Volador* and other traditional dances. There is a restaurant next to the Esso station on the Santa Cruz end of the plaza with a bank opposite (will change US dollars cash).

The road east to Cobán

The road east from Sacapulas is one of the most beautiful, and roughest, mountain roads in all Guatemala, with magnificent scenery in the narrow valleys. There is accommodation in **Uspantán** and this is the place to stay for the night enroute to Cobán. See Transport for all details. Coming from Huehuetenango via Aguacatán to Sacapulas, see page 586. It's a five-hour walk from Uspantán south to **Chimul**, the birthplace of **Rigoberta Menchú**, Nobel Peace Prize winner in 1992. The village was virtually wiped out during the 1980s, but the settlement is coming to life again. Only pick-ups go the village.

The Ixil Triangle

» pp564-577.

The Ixil Triangle is made of up of the highland communities of Nebaj, Chajul and Cotzal. The forested mountainous scenery provides great walking opportunities, although sadly, out of local necessity, many of the slopes have been badly deforested and the wood burnt for fires. The traditional dress of the Nebaj women – an explosion of primary colours – is spectacular. Much of this area was decimated during the Civil War and then repopulated with the introduction of 'model villages' established by the government. Evidence of wartime activities can still be seen and more remote Maya Ixil-speaking villages are gradually opening up to visitors with the introduction of hostel and trekking facilities.

Nebaj and around

→ *Colour map 5, B1.*

The town of Nebaj is high in the Cuchumatanes Mountains and its green slopes are often layered with mist. It is coloured by the beautiful dress worn by the local women, in an extravaganza of predominantly green, with red, yellow, orange, white and purple. The *corte* is mainly maroon with vertical stripes of black and yellow; some are bright red, and the *huipil* is of a geometric design. The women also wear a headdress with colourful bushy pom-poms on them. The men hardly ever wear the traditional costume; their jacket is red and embroidered in black designs. The main plaza is dominated by a large, simple white church. At the edge of the plaza there are weaving co-operatives selling *cortes, huípiles* and handicrafts from the town and the surrounding area – bargaining is possible. When you arrive, boys will meet you from incoming buses and will guide you to a *hospedaje* – they expect a tip. Nebaj has Sunday and Thursday markets and a **fiesta** on 12-15 August with traditional dancing.

There is an excellent website for Nebaj run by Solidaridad Internacional: www.nebaj.org, with useful phrases in Ixil and your daily Maya horoscope.

La tumba de la Indígena Maya is a shrine just outside Nebaj (15 minutes) where some of those massacred during the war were buried. Take the same route as to Ak'Tzumbal, but at the bottom of the very steep hill, immediately after the bridge over the river, take a left, walk straight on over a paved road, then you come to a small junction – carry straight on until you see a minor crossroads on a path with an orange house gate to your left. Look up and you will see a small building. This is the shrine. Walk to your right where you will see a steep set of stairs leading to the shrine.

There is a walk to **Ak'Tzumbal**, through fields, where rabbits can be seen, and through long, thin earth tunnels used by the military and guerrillas during the war.

You need a guide to walk this cross-country route. Alternatively you can take the road to Ak'Tzumbal, where the new houses still display signs warning of the danger of land mines. Walk down 15 Avenida de Septiembre away from the church, and take a left just before **El Triangulo** gas station past **El Viajero Hospedaje**, then left and then right down a very steep hill and keep walking (1½ hours). When you reach a small yellow tower just before a fork – take the right (the left goes to Salquil Grande) to reach the 'model village'. Above the village of Ak'Tzumbal is **La Pista**, an airstrip used during the war. Next to it bomb craters scar the landscape. Only a few avocado trees, between the bomb holes, survive, and the *gasolinera* to refuel planes, is still there, although it is now covered in corrugated iron. There are plans to erect a memorial here. Ask around for directions.

Chajul and Cotzal

Chajul, the second largest village in the Ixil Triangle, is known for its part in the Civil War, where Rigoberta Menchú's brother was killed in the plaza, as relayed in her book *I, Rigoberta Menchú*. According to the Nobel Peace Prize winner on 9 September 1979, her 16-year-old brother Petrocinio was kidnapped after being turned in for 15 quetzales. He was tortured in the plaza by the army along with numerous others. Villagers were forced to watch the torture under threat of being branded communists. People were set on fire, but the onlookers had weapons and looked ready to fight. This caused the army to withdraw. Chajul's main **festival** is the second Friday in Lent. There is also a pilgrimage to Christ of Golgotha on the second Friday in Lent, beginning the Wednesday before (the image is escorted by 'Romans' in blue police uniforms). Market day is Tuesday and Friday. It is possible to walk from Chajul to Cotzal. It is a six-hour walk from Nebaj to Chajul. A couple of very basic *hospedajes* are in town.

Cotzal is spread over a large area on a number of steep hills. The village's **fiesta** is 21-24 June, culminating in the day of St John the Baptist (24 June). Market days are Wednesday and Saturday. You can hire bikes from **Maya Tour** on the plaza next to the church. Nebaj to Cotzal is a pleasant four-hour walk. There's no accommodation or restaurants in other small villages and it is difficult to specify what transport is available in this area as trucks and the occasional pick-up or commercial van are affected by road and weather conditions. For this reason, be prepared to have to spend the night in villages.

Sleeping

Chimaltenango and around *p551*

A-B La Posada de Mi Abuelo, Carretera a Yepocapa, Parramos, T7849-5930. A delightful inn formerly a coffee farm, good restaurant. Packages with horse riding, biking and meals are available.

D Pixcayá, 0 Av, 1-82, Comalapa, T7849-8260. Hot water, parking.

Sololá *p553*

D Del Viajero, 7 Av, 10-45, on Parque Central (also annexe around the corner on Calle 11) T7762-3683. Rooms with bath, cheaper without, spacious, clean and friendly, good food in restaurant on plaza (El Cafetín).

E El Paisaje, 9 Calle, 5-41, 2 blocks from Parque Central, T7762-3820. Pleasant colonial courtyard, shared baths and toilets, clean, hot water, restaurant, good breakfast, family-run, laundry facilities.

Panajachel *p554, map p555*

L Atitlán, 1 km west of centre on lake, 2nd turning off the road to Sololá, T7762-1441, www.hotelatitlan.com. Full board available, colonial style, excellent rooms and service, beautiful gardens with views across lake, pool, private beach, top-class restaurant.

AL Posada de Don Rodrigo, Final Calle Santander, overlooks the lake, T7762-2326, www.posadadedonrodrigo.com. Pool, sauna, terrace, gardens, good restaurant, excellent food and service, comfortable and luxurious bathrooms, fireplaces.

AL Los Arboles (Apart-Hotel), Av de los Arboles 0-42, lakeside, T7762-0544/48. Fully equipped apartments for 2-3 people, swimming pool, gardens, TV, fireplace, colonial-style, parking.

A Cacique Inn, Calle del Embarcadero, Centro, T/F7762-1205, www.caciqueinn.com.gt. Large, comfortable rooms some with fireplace, credit cards accepted, swimming pool, magnificent house and spacious gardens, English spoken, good food.

A Rancho Grande, Calle Rancho Grande, Centro, T762-1554, www.ranchogrande inn.com. Cottages in charming setting, 4 blocks from beach, popular for long stay, good, including breakfast with pancakes. Pool with café in spacious gardens with good children's play equipment. Staff are helpful. Recommended.

A Visión Azul, on road to **Hotel Atitlán**, T/F7762-1426. Restaurant, pool, attractive gardens, campground on lakeside US$2 per person, US$4 per tent.

A-B Dos Mundos, Calle Santander 4-72, Centro, T7762-2078, www.hoteldos mundos.com. Pool, cable TV, some rooms surround pool, good Italian restaurant (**La Lanterna**). Breakfast included.

A-B Playa Linda, on main promenade, T7762-0096, www.hotelplayalinda.com. Nicely decorated large rooms, comfortable,TV, fireplaces, cheaper without lake view, pool and jacuzzi. Run by friendly US-Guatemalteco couple, good.

B Müllers Guest House, Calle Rancho Grande 1-81, Centro,T7762-2442. Comfortable, quiet, good breakfast included. Recommended.

B Primavera, Calle Santander, Centro, T7762-2052, www.primaveratitlan.com. Clean, bright rooms, with TV, cypress wood furniture, gorgeous showers, washing machine available, friendly. Recommended. Expensive restaurant **Chez Alex** serves French food but lovely patio setting at the back. Don't get a room overlooking the street at weekends.

B Tzanjuyú, first left on road to Sololá, T7762-1318. Superb position on bluff overlooking lake, in need of renovation but good value, flower gardens, restaurant, pool, romantic spot, quiet, camping US$13.50 per tent. Beds reportedbly uncomfortable.

B-C Posada de los Volcanes, Calle Santander, 5-51, Centro, T7762-0244, www.posadadelos-volcanes.com. 12 rooms with bath, hot water, clean, comfortable, quiet, friendly owners, Julio and Janet Parajón.

C Montana, Callejón Don Tino, near bell tower in the old town, T7762-0326. Comfortable, TV, hot water, parking, large patio.

C Riva Bella, Calle Real, 2-21, Centro, T7762-1348. Bungalows with parking, with bath, good, clean, nice garden. Recommended.

D Hospedaje El Príncipe, Callejón Los Yach, off Calle Rancho Grande (follow signs, worth the walk), T7762-0228. 14 rooms, hot water shower, clean, good budget option, garden.

D Hospedaje El Viajero, final Calle Santander, Centro, T7762-0128. With bath, comfortable large, clean rooms, hot water, friendly, laundry facilities, nice flower garden.

D Hospedaje Ramos I, close to public beach, T7762-0413. Run by Maya family, friendly, safe, loud music from nearby cafés, with bath, hot water, clean, good value, some rooms have TV. View from new 2nd floor.

D Las Casitas, Calle Real 1-90, old town, T7762-1224. Neat bungalows, breakfast available, with bath, hot shower, attractive gardens, friendly, next to police station and market, buses stop outside but it's quiet at night. Medical Lab at entrance for those travellers complaints.

D La Zanahoria Chic, 1 Av 0-46, Av de los Arboles, old town, T7762-1249. Restaurant, rooms above, clean, TV, hot water, colonial style, friendly, hot water, coffee, luggage store.

D Mario's Rooms, Calle Santander esq Calle 14 Febrero, Centro, T7762-1313. Cheaper without bath, with garden, clean, bright rooms, hot showers, good breakfast, but not included, popular and friendly.

D Santa Isabel, Calle del Embarcadero 8-86, Centro, T7762-1462. 2 rooms in large house, quiet, hot water, with bath, friendly, nice gardens, parking, also fully equipped bungalow available for longer rent. Recommended.

E-F Hospedaje Tommy, Calle El Chali 3-43, Centro, T7762-0799. Clean shared bathroom, small attractive garden, 6 rooms.

F Casa de Huéspedes y Cafetería Las Hermanas, Barrio Santa Elena 4-02, passageway about 10 m from where the bus stops (sign to Spanish School Mayan), T7762-0673. Pretty garden, 5 rooms, 1 with bath, family atmosphere, meals available, good value. Several other cheap hotels on this passageway.

E **Hospedaje Casa Linda**, Callejón El Capulín, Centro, T7762-0386. Hot shower, garden, friendly, clean and quiet. Good value. Recommended.

F **Hospedaje Sánchez**, Calle El Chali 3-65, Centro, T7762-2224. Clean, friendly, hot shower, family-run, quiet, comfortable. Recommended.

F **Hospedaje Villa Lupita**, Callejón Don Tino, old town, T7762-1201. Pretty courtyard, hot showers, clean, friendly, parking, good value, recommended.

Apartments

Ask around for houses to rent; available from US$125 a month for a basic place, to US$200, but almost impossible to find in Nov and Dec. Break-ins and robberies of tourist houses are not uncommon. Water supply is variable. **Apartamentos Bohemia**, Callejón Chinimaya, rents furnished bungalows.

Camping

Possible in the grounds of **Hotel Visión Azul** and **Tzanjuyú** – see above for details.

Santa Catarina Palopó *p556*

LL **Tzam Poc Resort**, Via Rural km 6.5, T7762-2680, www.tzampocresort.com. New resort on the slopes above Santa Catarina with an amazing infinity pool. Lovely villas and spa. There's also a bow and arrow range.

LL-L **Casa Palopó**, less than 1 km beyond Santa Catarina, on the left up a steep hill is T7762-2270, www.casapalopo.com. One of the finest hotels in the country, 9 beautiful rooms all richly furnished, flowers on arrival, excellent service, heated pool, spa, gym, top class restaurant overlooking the lake – reservations necessary.

AL **Villa Santa Catarina**, T7762-1291, www.villasdeguatemala.com. 36 comfortable rooms with balconies around the pool, most with view of lake. Good restaurant.

San Antonio Palopó *p556*

You can stay in private houses (ask around) or rent rooms (take sleeping bag).

A-C **Hotel Terrazas del Lago**, T7762-0157. On the lake with view, bath, clean, restaurant, a unique hotel built up over the past 30 plus years.

San Lucas Tolimán *p557*

AL-B **Toliman**, Av 6, 1 block from the lake, T7722-0033, www.atitlanhotel.com. 18 rooms and suites in lovely colonial-style washed in terracotta colours with some lovely dark wood furniture. Suite no 1 is very romantic with lit steps to a sunken bath, good but expensive restaurant (reservations), fine gardens, pool, partial lake views. Recommended.

D **Casa Cruz Inn**, Av 5 4-78, a couple of blocks from the park. Clean, comfortable beds, run by an elderly couple, garden, quiet, good value.

D **Hotel y Restaurante Don Pedro**, Av 6, on lakeside, T7722-0028. Unattractive building – a sort of clumsy rustic, 12 rooms which are a little rough around the edges, restaurant, bar.

D **La Cascada de María**, Calle 6, 6-80, T7722-0136. With bath, TV, parking, garden, restaurant, good.

Santiago Atitlán *p557*

Book ahead for Holy Week.

AL-D **Posada de Santiago**, 1.5 km south of town, T/F7721-7167, www.posadadesantiago.com. Comfortable stone cottages, some cheaper accommodation, restaurant with home-grown produce and delicious food, tours, massage and language classes arranged. Friendly and amusing management – David, Susie and his mum, Bonnie – quite a trio. Highly recommended. Has its own dock or walk from town.

A **Bambú**, on the lakeside, 500 m by road towards San Lucas, T7721-7332, www.ecobambu.com. 10 rooms, 2 bungalows and one *casita* in an attractive setting with beautifully tended gardens, restaurant, a secluded pool, a few mins by *lancha* from the dock. Kayaks available.

D-E **Chi-Nim-Ya**, walk up from the dock, take the first left and walk 50 m and it's there on the left, T7721-7131. Good, clean, comfortable and friendly, cheaper without bath, good value, good café, cheap, large helpings.

E **Tzutuhil**, on left up the road from the dock to centre, above **Ferretería La Esquina**, T7721-7174. With bath and TV, cheaper without, restaurant, great views, good.

Camping

Camping is possible near **Hotel Bambú**.

San Pedro La Laguna *p557, map p558*

Accommodation is mostly cheap and laid-back, your own sleeping bag, etc, will be useful.

E **Hospedaje Casa Elena**, along the path behind **Nick's Place** (see map), T5310-9243. With large bathrooms or shared bath (some are nicer than others), clean, excellent views of lake. Recommended.

E **Hotel San Francisco** (see map). Rooms with lake view, garden, cooking facilities, cold water, helpful owner, washing facilities, cheaper without bath, good value. Tours offered.

E **Mansión del Lago** (see map), T5811-8172, www.hotelmansiondellago.com. Up a hill with good views, with bath, hot water, TV costs more, very good value.

E **Sak' Cari** (see map), T7721-8096, www.hotelsakcari.com. With bath, hot water, lovely rooms with great garden – get those with fabulous lake views. Extremely good value. Recommended.

E **Ti-Kaaj**, uphill from Santiago dock, 1st right (see map). Simple rooms, hammock space, popular with backpackers, lovely garden and small pool; basic, but worth it for pool.

E **Villa Sol** (see map), T2334-0327. With bath, cheaper shared, but the rooms aren't as nice. The newer part is a lot nicer. There are 2 bungalows with kitchen facilities, friendly staff, nice rooms. Recommended.

F **Hospedaje Buenas Nuevas** (see map). Small, friendly, hot shower.

F **Valle Azul**, 100 m south of the Panajachel dock (see map), T7721-8152. Good value, nice view, good restaurant, but very run-down.

San Juan La Laguna *p559*

A **Hotel Uxlabil**, 11 Calle (15 Av final, 12-53, Zona 10, Oakland, Guatemala City, T2366-9555), www.uxlabil.com. This is an eco-hotel set up on the hill with its own dock, a short walk from the town centre. It's run by very friendly people with a small restaurant. It is a perfect, relaxing getaway, with Maya sauna and tended gardens, in this most unassuming and interesting of towns. It has links with the ecotourism association in town. Recommended.

San Marcos La Laguna *p559*

A-C **Las Pirámides**, Las Pirámides dock, a residential, meditation centre. See also page 519.

C **Posada Schumann**, 2nd dock, T5202-2216, www.posadaschumann.com. With waterfront and dock, bungalows in attractive gardens, some with kitchenettes, sauna, restaurant, comfortable.

C-F **Paco Real**, 2nd dock, first pathway, T5918-7215, elpacoreal@hotmail.com. Cabins with shared bath and rooms with private bath. Dorms also (F per person), clean, good restaurant. Sauna and massage and free yoga available.

D **Aaculaax**, Las Pirámides dock, on a path from the **Centro Holístico**, niecolass@hotmail.com. A Hansel-and-Gretel affair on the lake shore. It is a blend of cave work with Gaudí-type influence from the stained-glass work down to the sculptures and lamp shades. A corner of artistic Nirvana on Lake Atitlán – this place is highly recommended. Each of the 7 rooms, with private bathroom, is different, with quirky decor. In addition it is run on an eco-basis, compost toilets and all. It is run by the ever-so-lucky German, Niels. There is a restaurant, bar, bakery and massage room. Also glass and papier mâché workshops.

D **Hotel Jinava**, 2nd dock, left at the top of first pathway, T5299-3311. This is heaven on a hill. With fabulous views, it clings to a steep slope with lovely rooms, restaurants, terraces and a patio, books and games and solitude if you want it. Close to the lakeshore with its own dock. Only 5 rooms, breakfast included. German-owned. Recommended.

E **Casa Azul**, first dock, T7736-2316, www.lagodeatitlanyogacentre.com. It can also be reached from the centre of the village. This is a gorgeous little place offering yoga classes, reiki and massages. Vegetarian food every night. Eco-philosophy and so bathrooms are organic. Orthpaedic beds in the 3 rooms, use of kitchen, organic veg garden.

E **La Paz**, 2nd dock, first pathway, T5702-9168. Bungalows and 1 dorm (F per person), vegetarian restaurant, quiet with nice communal area, popular.

E **Unicornio**, Las Pirámides dock, 2nd pathway. With self-catering, bungalows, shared kitchen and bathrooms. Has a little post office.

F Quetzal, Las Pirámides dock, 2nd pathway, T5306-5039. Price per person. 4 bunk rooms, shared bath, restaurant.

San Marcos to Santa Cruz *p559*

AL Lomas de Tzununá, Tzununá, T7820-4060, www.lomasdetzununa.com. This hotel enjoys a spectacular position high up above the lake. The views from the restaurant terrace are magnificent. The 10 spacious rooms, decorated with local textiles, have 2 beds each with lake views and a balcony. The hotel, run by a friendly Belgian family offers walking, biking, kayaking and cultural tours. The restaurant (🍴🍴-🍴) uses home-made ingredients, the hotel is run on solar energy and the pool does not use chlorine. Board games, internet, bar and giant chess available. The family are reforesting a hill. Breakfast and taxes included.

A-C La Casa del Mundo, Jaibalito, T5204-5558, www.lacasadelmundo.com. Enjoys one of the most spectacular positions on the entire lake. Room No 15 has the best view followed by room No 1. Many facilities, standard family-style dinner, lakeside hot tub, a memorable place with fantastic views. Repeatedly recommended.

Santa Cruz La Laguna *p560*

AL-B Villa Sumaya, Paxanax, beyond the dock, about 15 mins' walk, T5810-7199, www.villasumaya.com. Including breakfast, with its own dock, sauna, massage and healing therapies, yoga, comfortable, peaceful.

C La Casa Rosa, to the right as you face the dock from the water, along a path, T5416-1251, la_casa_rosa@hotmail.com. Bungalows and rooms, with bath, cheaper without, home-made meals, attractive garden, sauna. Candlelit dinners at weekends.

D Arca de Noé, to the left of the dock, T5515-3712, thearca@yahoo.com. Bungalows, good restaurant, BBQ, lake activities arranged, nice atmosphere, veranda overlooking really beautiful flower-filled gardens and the lake, low- voltage solar power.

E-F La Iguana Perdida, opposite dock, T5706-4117, www.laiguanaperdida.com. All rooms and dorm with shared bath, lively, especially weekends, delicious vegetarian food, BBQ, popular, friendly, good atmosphere, **ATI Divers** centre (see page 572), water-skiing; kayaks US$0.65 per hr. Bring a torch.

Chichicastenango *p560, map p561*

You won't find accommodation easily on Sat evening, when prices are increased. As soon as you get off the bus, boys will swamp you and insist on taking you to certain hotels.

L Mayan Inn, corner of 8 Calle ,1-91, T7756-1176. A classic, colonial-style courtyard hotel, filled with plants, polished antique furniture, beautiful dining room and bar with fireplaces. The staff are very friendly and wear traditional dress. Secure parking.

AL Santo Tomás, 7 Av, 5-32, T7756-1061. A very attractive building with beautiful colonial furnishings. It is often full at weekends, pool, sauna, good restaurant and bar. Buffet lunch (US$13) on market days in stylish dining room. The attendants are in traditional dress. Bathroom use, US0.70.

B Maya Lodge, 6 Calle, 4-08, T7756-1167. 9 rooms with bath, courtyard, right on the corner of the plaza, quaint dining room, breakfast available.

C Chalet House, 3 Calle, 7-44, T/F7756-1360. A clean, guesthouse with family atmosphere, hot water. Don't be put off by dingy street.

C Chugüilá, 5 Av, 5-24, T/F7756-1134, hotelchuguila@yahoo.com. Some rooms with fireplaces. Avoid the front rooms, which are noisy, restaurant.

C Posada El Arco, 4 Calle, 4-36, T7756-1255. Clean, very pretty, small, friendly, garden, washing facilities, negotiate lower rates for stays longer than a night, some large rooms, good view, parking, English spoken.

D Pensión Girón, Edif Girón on 6 Calle, 4-52, T7756-1156. Clean rooms with bath, cheaper without, hot water, parking, 17 rooms.

D-E El Salvador, 10 Calle, 4-47. 50 large rooms with bath, a few with fireplace (wood available in market), good views over town, parking. Cheaper, smaller rooms without bath available.

E Posada Belén, 12 Calle, 5-55, T7756-1244. With bath, cheaper without, hot water, clean, will do laundry, fine views from balconies and hummingbirds in attractive garden, good value. Recommended.

Santa Cruz del Quiché and around *p562*

C Rey K'iché, 8 Calle, 0-9, 2 blocks from bus terminal. Clean, comfortable, hot water, parking, restaurant, TV.

D Maya Quiché, 3 Av 4-19, T7755-1667. With bath, hot water, restaurant.
D Posada San Rafael, San Andrés Sajcabaja, T7755-1742. Including full board, traditional adobe rooms, ecotourism project run by Guatemalan/French family, horse riding, hiking, visits to local Maya sites.
E-F San Pascual, 7 Calle, 0-43, T5555-1107. With bath, cheaper without, occasional hot water in morning only, dirty shared bathroom, quiet, locked parking.
F La Cascada, 10 Av, 10 Calle. Friendly, clean.

The road east to Cobán *p563*
There are a couple of *hospedajes* in town.
F Galindo, 4 blocks east of the Parque Central. Clean, friendly, recommended.

The Ixil Triangle *p563*
F Solidaridad Internacional supports 6 hostels in the villages of **Xexocom, Chortiz, Xeo, Cocop, Cotzol** and **Parramos Grande** where there is room for 5 people. Contact them at the PRODONT-IXIL office, Av 15 de Septiembre (www.nebaj.org).

Nebaj *p563*
D Ixil, 2 Av, 9 Calle, 1 block back up the slope from the bus terminal and 1 block to the left, T7756-0036. Cream building with maroon base, private bath, TV, cheaper without TV, quiet.
D-F Ilebal Tenam, bottom of Av 15 de Septiembre, road to Chajul, T7755-8039. Hot water, shared and private bath, very clean, friendly, parking inside, attractive decor.
E Hotel Turansa, 1 block from plaza down 5 Calle, T7775-8219. Tiny rooms, but very clean, soap, towels, 2nd-floor rooms are nicer, TV and parking, little shop in entrance, phone service.
F Hospedaje Esperanza, 6 Av, 2-36. Very friendly, clean, hot showers in shared bathroom, noisy when evangelical churches nearby have activities, hotel is cleaner than it looks from the outside.
F Hostal Ixil Don Juan, 0 Av A, 1 Calle B, Canton Simocol. Take Av 15 de Septiembre and take a left at **Comedor Sarita**, opposite grey office of PRODONT-IXIL, then it's 100 m to the right, on the right, T7755-4014/1529. Part of **Programa Quiché**, run with the support of the EU, there are 6 beds in 2 rooms, each bed with a locked strongbox, and hot showers. The colonial building has a traditional sauna, *chuj*.
F Ixil, 5 Av, 10 Calle, on the road in from Sacapulas. In a colonial house, clean, pleasant and comfortable, big rooms, hot water.

Cotzal *p564*
F Cafetería and Hospedaje Christian, alongside the church. Basic.
F Hostal Doña Teresa. Has a sauna, patio and honey for the face for sale.

Eating

Panajachel *p554, map p555*
TTT Al Chisme, Av Los Arboles 0-42, T7762-2063. Good food, try eggs 'McChisme' for breakfast, good fresh pasta, excellent banana cake, good atmosphere, popular, a bit pricey. Daily 0700-2300. Live piano music at weekends, friendly service.
TTT Chez Alex, Calle Santander, centre, T7762-0172. French menu, good quality, mainly tourists, credit cards accepted.
TTT Circus Bar, Av Los Arboles 0-62, T7762-2056. Has Italian dishes including good pizzas, good coffee, popular. Live bands at weekends, excellent atmosphere. Recommended. Open 1200-2400.
TTT Guajimbo's, Calle Santander. Good atmosphere, excellent steaks, fast service, popular, live music some evenings. Recommended.
TTT Los Pumpos, Calle del Lago (see map). Varied menu, bar, good fish and seafood dishes.
TTT Pana Rock Café with **Pana Arte** upstairs, Calle Santander 3-72. Buzzing around happy hour (2 for 1), salsa music, very popular, international food, pizza.
TTT Sunset Café, superb location on the lake. Open 1100-2400. Excellent for drinks, light meals and main dishes, live music evenings, but you pay for the view.
TTT Tocoyal, annexe to **Hotel del Lago**. A/c, groups welcome, buffet on request but tourist prices.
TTT-TT El Pájaro Azul, Calle Santander 2-75, T7762-2596. Café, bar, crêperie with gorgeous stuffed sweet or savoury crêpes, cakes and pies. Vegetarian options available. Reasonable prices, good for late breakfasts, occasional slow service. 1000-2200. Recommended.
TT Bombay, Calle Santander near Calle 14 Febrero, T7762-0611. Vegetarian recipes,

German beer, Mexican food, good food and wines, set lunch popular, good service. Very highly recommended. 1100-2130.

₸₸ Crossroads Café, Calle de Campanario 0-27. Global choice of quality coffee, but you can´t go wrong with Guatemalan! Excellent cakes, Tue-Sat 0900-1300, 1500-1900.

₸₸ El Patio, Calle Santander. Good food, very good large breakfasts, quiet atmosphere but perfect for people watching from the garden. Try the amaretto coffee.

₸₸ The Last Resort, Calle 14 de Febrero 2-88, T7762-2016. 'Gringo bar', classic spot, all-you-can-eat breakfasts, friendly, huge portions and reasonable prices, open all day, bar, table tennis, good information. Has open fire going in the colder months.

₸₸ Restaurante Las Olas, overlooking the lake at the end of Calle Santander, down by the dock. Serves the absolute best nachos, great for just before catching the boat.

₸ Deli Llama de Fuego, Calle Santander, T7762-2586. Thu-Tue 0700-2200. Sweet little café with a giant cheese plant as its focus. Breakfasts, muffins, bagels, pizzas, pasta, Mexican food and vegetarian sandwiches.

Bakeries

Don´t miss an evening treat a block down from **Orale**, on Calle Santander; you'll see the stall with cakes, pies, *tostadas, atoles*, hot chocolate and other treats for the seriously deprived.

Pana Pan, Calle Santander 1-61. Excellent wholemeal breads and pastries, banana bread comes out of the oven at 0930, wonderful, cinnamon rolls also recommended.

San Lucas Tolimán *p557*

₸ La Pizza de Sam, Av 7, 1 block down from the plaza towards the lake. Pizzas and spaghettis.

₸ Restaurant Jardín, orange building on corner of plaza. *Comida típica* and *licuados*.

Santiago Atitlán *p557*

There are many cheap *comedores* near the centre. The best restaurants are at the hotels.

₸₸₸ El Pescador, on corner 1 block before **Tzutuhil**. Full menu, good but expensive.

₸₸₸ Posada de Santiago, 1.5 km south of town, T/F7721-7167. Delicious, wholesome food and excellent service in lovely surroundings. Highly recommended.

₸ Restaurant Wach'alal, close to **Gran Sol**. A small yellow-painted café serving breakfasts, snacks and cakes. Airy and pleasant. Daily 0800-2000.

San Pedro La Laguna *p560*

Be careful of drinking water in San Pedro; both cholera and dysentery exist here.

₸₸ Arte Libre (see map). Little café in garden with basketware chairs serving up 100% pure veg and fruit juices and breakfasts. Closed Mon.

₸₸ El Fondeadero (on map). Good food, lovely terraced gardens, reasonable prices.

₸₸ El Otro Lado (on map). Shows movies every night and has a rooftop and sports bar.

₸₸ Pinocchio (on map). Italian, popular for breakfast, reasonable prices, closed Sun.

₸₸ Rosalinda, near centre of village (on map). Friendly, breakfasts (eg *mosh*), local fish and good for banana and chocolate cakes.

₸₸ Thermal Baths, along shore from *playa*. Good vegetarian food and coffee, expensive.

₸₸ Vayavos (on map). Run by Israelis, Italian dishes.

₸₸-₸ Café Arte, uphill from **Hotel San Pedro** (on map). All meals, vegetarian dishes, good value.

₸₸-₸ Café Munchies (on map), T206-9758. Breakfasts served up on painted tables plus rooms (**F**, basic) close by. Also thermal waters.

₸₸-₸ La Ultima Cena, opposite Municipalidad. Good pizzas, pancakes, very popular.

₸₸-₸ Luna Azul, along shore (on map). Popular for breakfast and lunch, good omelettes.

₸₸-₸ Nick's Place, on the left up from the *muelle*. Cheap, popular, comfy sofas, free films every night. Flies everywhere in the downstairs area, service is slow, looking pretty grotty now.

₸₸-₸ Pachanay, along the road opposite **Hotel San Pedro**. Lunch and dinner, cheap rice dishes, reggae music, chilled, gallery.

₸₸-₸ Restaurant Maritza (on map). With commanding views over lake. Chilled place to hang out with reggae music. Service is slow though. 5 rooms also to rent with shared bath. (**G**).

₸₸-₸ Ti Kaaj (on map). Good Italian and local dishes.

₸₸-₸ Tin Tin (on map). Good value, Thai food, delightful garden. Recommended.

ŧ **Comedor del Viajero** (on map). New and locally run, with roof top tables. Ultra cheap and friendly.
ŧ **Comedor Sta Elena**, near **Nick's Italian**. Seriously cheap and filling breakfasts.
ŧ **Emperador**, up the hill (on map). *Comedor* serving good local dishes.

San Marcos La Laguna *p559*
All hotels and hostels offer food.
ŧŧ **Il Giardino**, up the 2nd pathway. Attractive garden, Italian owners, good breakfasts.

Chichicastenango *p560, map p561*
The best food is in the top hotels, but is expensive. On market days there are plenty of good food stalls and *comedores* in the centre of the plaza which offer chicken in different guises or a set lunch for US$1.50. There are several good restaurants in the **Centro Comercial Santo Tomás** on the north side of the plaza (market).
ŧŧ **Caffé Tuttos**, 12 Calle, near **Posada Belén**. Good breakfast deals, pizzas, and *menú del día*, reasonable prices.
ŧŧ **La Fonda de Tzijolaj**, on the plaza. Great view of the market below, good meals, pizza, prompt service, reasonable prices.
ŧŧ **Las Brasas Steak House**, 6 Calle 4-52, T7756-2226. Nice atmosphere, good steak menu, accepts credit cards.
ŧŧ **Tziguan Tinamit**, on the corner of 5 Av, esq 6 Calle. Some local dishes, steaks, tasty pizzas, breakfasts, good pies but a little more expensive than most places, good.
ŧŧ-ŧ **La Villa de los Cofrades**, on the plaza. Café downstairs, breakfasts, cappuccinos, expressos, good value. There is a 2nd restaurant up the street and upstairs, more expensive, great people-watching location and an escape during market days, popular for breakfast.
ŧ **La Parrillada**, 6C 5-37, Interior Comercial Turkaj. Escape the market hussle, courtyard, reasonable prices, breakfast available.
ŧ **Tu Café**, 5 Av 6-44, on market place, Santo Tomás side. Snacks, budget breakfast, sandwiches, set lunch, good value. 0730-2000.

Santa Cruz del Quiché *p562*
Try *sincronizadas*, hot tortillas baked with cubed ham, spiced chicken and cheese.
ŧ **El Torito Steak House**, 4 Calle, ½ block west directly opposite church. Good meat and chicken dishes, a little dingy around edges.
ŧ **La Cabañita Café**, 1 Av, 1-17. Charming, small café with pinewood furniture, home-made pies and cakes, excellent breakfasts (pancakes, cereals, etc), eggs any way you want 'em, great snacks, for example *sincronizadas*. Recommended. Looks a little jaded from the outside, a favourite for tea with the military!
ŧ **La Casona**, 6 Av, 2-66, Zona 1. Old colonial house, very reasonable prices, nice atmosphere, also vegetarian, good quality. Recommended.
ŧ **La Toscan**, 1 Av just north of the church, same road as **Musicafé** and **La Cabañita**. A little pizza and *pastelería* with checked cloth covered tables. Lasagne lunch a bargain with garlic bread and pizza by the slice also.
ŧ **Musicafé**, 1 Av, 1-16. Good food, reasonable, with pleasant ambience.

The road east to Cobán *p563*
ŧ **Cafetería Kevin**. One of several cafés serving up decent food and vegetables.

Nebaj *p563*
Boxboles are squash leaves rolled tightly with *masa* and chopped meat or chicken, boiled and served with salsa and fresh orange juice.
ŧ **Cafetería y Restaurante Naabá**, Calzada 15 de Septiembre. Open 0700-2200. Traditional food and snacks.
ŧ **Campestre**, 1 block from the plaza. Serves up chicken dishes, *licuados* and the only place serving some western fare – cornflakes and hash browns for breakfast. 0730-2100.
ŧ **El Descanso**. Popular volunteer hang-out, good food and useful information about their other community- based projects (see www.nebaj.com) and **La Red Internet Café**.
ŧ **El Trigal**, Av 15 de Septiembre, just after gas station **El Triángulo**. Excellent bakery.
ŧ **Maya Inca**, on the plaza. Substantial food, run by Peruvians hence the name.
ŧ **Pizza del César**, opposite **Bancafé**. Breakfasts, mouth-watering strawberry cake. Daily 0730-2100.

Cotzal *p564*
ŧ **Comedor and Hospedaje El Maguey**. Bland meal, but decent size, plus drink, are served up for for US$1.70. Don't stay here, though, unless you're desperate.

Entertainment

Panajachel *p554, map p555*

Bars and clubs

Circus Bar, Av los Arboles. Good live music at weekends, daily 1700-0100.

Discoteca Chapiteau, Av los Arboles 0-69, nightclub Thu-Sat 1900-2400.

El Aleph, Av los Arboles. One of a number of bars, Thu-Sat 1900-0300.

San Pedro La Laguna *p557*

Bars and clubs

Nick's Place, overlooking the main dock, is popular, and well frequented in the evening. Nearby are **Bar Alegre**, a sports bar and **D'noz**. **Bar Jorji's** is another popular spot as is **Ti Kaaj**.

Shopping

Panajachel *p554, map p555*

Bartering is the norm. There are better bargains here than in Chichicastenango. The main tourist shops are on Calle Santander; the upmarket places are near the centre, eg: **El Güipíl**, with a selection of quality items available or at the bottom end. Part way down is **Tinamit Maya Shopping Centre**, Calle Santander, with many stalls for typical items, bargain for good prices. **Makki's**, opposite Banco Agromercanti, offers something different with its curios and furniture. Maya sell their wares cheaply on the lakeside; varied selection, bargaining is easy/expected. **Chalo's Tienda**, Calle Real, is the town's 'mini-supermarket'.

Chichicastenango *p560, map p561*

Chichicastenango's markets are on Sun and Thu. See page 562.

Festivals and events

Chichicastenango *p560, map p561*

1 Jan Padre Eterno.
20 Jan San Sebastián.
19 Mar San José.
Feb/Apr Jesús Nazareno and María de Dolores (both Fri in Lent).
Mar/Apr Semana Santa (Holy Week).
29 Apr San Pedro Mártir.
3 May Santa Cruz.
29 Jun Corpus Christi.
18 Aug: Virgen de la Coronación.
14 Sep: Santa Cruz.
29 Sep San Miguel.
30 Sep: San Jerónimo Doctor.
1st Sun of Oct Virgen del Rosario.
2nd Sun in Oct: Virgen de Concepción.
1 Nov San Miguel.
13-22 Dec Santo Tomás, with 21 Dec being the main day. There are processions, traditional dances, the *Palo Volador* (Dec 19, 20, 21) marimba music, well worth a visit – very crowded.

Activities and tours

Panajachel *p554, map p555*

Diving

ATI Divers, El Patio, Calle Santander, T7762-2621, www.laiguanaperdida.com. A range of options including PADI Open Water US$175, fun dive US$25, 2 for US$45. PADI Rescue and Dive Master also available. Altitude speciality, US$65. Dives are made off Santa Cruz La Laguna and are of special interest to those looking for altitude diving. Here there are spectacular walls that drop off, rock formations you can swim through, trees underwater, and because of its volcanic nature, hot spots, which leaves the lake bottom sediment boiling to touch. Take advice on visibility before you opt for a dive.

Fishing

Lake fishing can be arranged, black bass (*mojarra*) up to 4 kg can be caught. Boats for up to 5 people can be hired for about US$15. Check with INGUAT for latest information.

Hang-gliding (vuelo libre)

Rogelio, contactable through **Americo's** Tours, Calle Santander, and other agencies will make arrangements, at least 24 hrs' notice is required. Jumps, costing about US$50, are made from San Jorge La Laguna or from above Santa Catarina, depending on weather conditions.

Horse riding

Enquire locally round the lake. The best, though expensive, option is 10 km south of Santiago (see page 573).

Kayaking and canoeing

Kayak hire is around US$2 per hr. Ask at the hotels, INGUAT and at lakeshore. **Diversiones**

Acuáticos Balán, in a small red and white tower on the lakeshore, rent out kayaks. Watch out for strong winds that occasionablly blow-up quickly across the lake; potentially dangerous in small boats.

Tour operators

All offer shuttle services to Chichicastenango, Antigua, the Mexican borders, etc, and some to San Cristóbal de las Casas (see under Transport) and can arrange most activities on and around the lake. **Americo's Tours**, Calle Santander, T7762-2021, www.americosexport.com. **Atitrans**, Edif Rincón Sai, T7762-2336, www.atitrans.com. **Centroamericana Tourist Service**, Calle Santander, T/F7762-2496. Several others on Calle Santander. **Tierra Maya**, Calle Santander, T7725-7320, www.tierramayatravel.com. Friendly and reliable tour operator which runs shuttles to San Cristóbal de las Casas (US$37) as well as within Guatemala. **Toliman Travel**, Calle Santander, T7762 2455.

Waterskiing

Arrangements can be made with ATI Divers at Iguana Perdida in Santa Cruz.

Santiago Atitlán *p557*

Tour operators

Aventura en Atitlán, Jim and Nancy Matison, Finca San Santiago, T5515-3712, wildwest@amigo.net.gt. 10 km outside Santiago. Offer riding and hiking tours (US$30-50).

Francisco Tizná from the Asociación de Guías de Turismo, T7721-7558, is extremely informative. Ask for him at the dock or at any of the hotels. Payment is by way of a donation.

San Pedro La Laguna *p557*

Tour operators

Bigfoot, 0800-1700, until 2000 in high season. Run by the super-helpful Juan Baudilio Chipirs.

San Juan La Laguna *p559*

Tour operators

Rupalaj Kistalin,T5964-0040, rupalajkistalin@yahoo.es, offers interesting cultural tours of the town visiting painters, weavers, *cofradías* and traditional healers. As well as this cultural circuit there is an adventure circuit taking in Panan forest and a canopy tour at Park Chuiraxamolo' or a nature circuit taking in a climb up the Rostro de Maya and fishing and kayaking. Highly recommended. Some of the local guides speak English.

San Marcos La Laguna *p559*

Wellbeing

Centro Holístico San Marcos, up the 2nd pathway, beyond **Unicornio**, www.sanmholisticcentre.com. Mon-Sat 1000-1700. Offer iridology, acupuncture, kinesiology, Indian head massage, reflexology and massage. Classes in various techniques can also be taken.

Lago Atitlán Yoga Centre, www.lagoatitlanyogacentre.com, is run by **Casa Azul**, see Sleeping, above.

Las Pirámides, T205-7151, www.laspiramides.com.gt. The month-long course costs US$10 per person per day, accommodation included. Shorter courses can also be arranged for a little more per day. In the grounds are a sauna, a vegetarian restaurant with freshly baked bread and a library. This is a relaxing, peaceful place.

Chichicastenango *p560, map p561*

Tour operators

Chichi Turkaj Tours, 5 Av, 4-42, T2215-0731. Daily 0800-2000. Shuttles and tours.

Maya Chichi Van, 6 Av, 6-45, T7756-2187, mayachichivan@yahoovan.com. Shuttles and tours ranging from US$10-650.

Nebaj *p563*

Tour operators

Gaspar Terraza Ramos guides tourists to all the local places. He usually waits near the bus station or in the plaza and will probably find you. He can arrange horse hire.

Guías Ixiles (El Descanso Restaurant), T5311-9100, Felipe and Miguel Brito, contactus@nebaj.com. ½- to 3-day hikes, bike rental, new trek to Todos Santos.

Solidaridad Internacional, Av 15 de Septiembre, www.nebaj.org. Inside the PRODONT-IXIL (Proyecto de Promoción de Infraestructuras y Ecoturismo) office, in a grey building on the right 1 block after the Gasolinera El Triángulo on the road to Chajul. For further information call in to see the director Pascual, who is very helpful. 2-, 3-and 4-day hikes, horses available.

Trekking Ixil, T5418-3940, trekkingixil@hotmail.com. 1- to 4-day treks, mountain bike rental, horse riding.

Chajul and Cotzal *p564*
Tour operators
Ask Teresa at **Hostal Doña Teresa** about trips from the Cotzal or ask for Sebastián Xel Rivera who leads 1-day camping trips.

Transport

Chimaltenango *p560, map p561*
Bus Any bus heading west from Guatemala City stops at Chimaltenango. To **Antigua** leave from the corner of the main road and the road south to Antigua where there is a lime green and blue shop – **Auto Repuestos y Frenos Nachma**, 45 mins, US$0.32. To **Chichicastenango**, every 30 mins, 0600-1700, 2 hrs, US$1.70. To **Cuatro Caminos**, 2½ hrs, US$2. To **Quetzaltenango**, every 45 mins, 0700-1800, 2½ hrs, US$2.20. To **Tecpán** every 30 mins, 0700-1800, 1 hr.

The routes west, Tecpán and Los Encuentros *p551*
Bus From Tecpán to **Guatemala City**, 2¼ hrs, buses every hr, US$1.05; easy day trip from Panajachel or Antigua.

To Lake Atitlán along the old Pan-American Highway *p552*
Bus To and fro m **Godínez** there are several buses to Panajachel, US$0.35 and one bus daily Patzún-Godínez. To **San Andrés Semetabaj**, bus to Panajachel, US$0.30.

Sololá *p553*
Bus To **Chichicastenango**, US$0.40, 1½ hrs; to **Panajachel**, US$0.33, every 30 mins, 20 mins, or 1½-2 hrs' walk; to **Chimaltenango**, US$1.05; to **Quetzaltenango**, US$1.50. *Colectivo* to **Los Encuentros**, US$0.15; to **Guatemala City** direct US$1.50, 3 hrs.

Panajachel *p554, map p555*
Bicycle Several rental agencies on Calle Santander, eg **Maco Cycle Rental** and **Tono Cycle Rental**. Also **Alquiler de Bicicletas Emanuel**, on Calle 14 de Febrero. The cost is US$0.65 up per hr or about US$5 for 8 hrs, US$7 per 24 hrs.

Boat
There are 2 types of transport – the scheduled ferry service to Santiago Atitlán and the *lanchas* to all the other villages. The tourist office has the latest information on boats. The boat service to **Santiago Atitlán** runs from the dock at the end of Calle Rancho Grande from 0600-1630, 8 daily, US$2.70 one way, US$2 return, 1¼ hrs in the large **Naviera Santiago** ferry, T7762-0309 or 20-35 mins in the fast *lanchas*. Some *lanchas* to all the other villages leave from here, but most from the dock at the end of Calle Embarcadero run by **Tzanjuyú** from 0630-1700 every 45 mins or when full (min 10 people). If you set off from the main dock the *lancha* will pull in at the Calle Embarcadero dock as well. These *lanchas* call in at **Santa Cruz**, **Jaibalito**, **Tzununá**, **San Marcos**, **San Pablo**, **San Juan** and **San Pedro**, US$1.30, then US$2 to San Marcos and beyond. To **San Pedro** US$2.70. The first boat of the day is direct to San Pedro. If there is a demand, there will almost always be a boatman willing to run a service but non-official boats can charge what they like. Virtually all the dozen or so communities round the lake have docks, and you can take a regular boat to any of those round the western side. Note that, officially, locals pay less. The only reliable services back to Panajachel are from Santiago or San Pedro up to about 1600. If you wait on the smaller docks round the western side up to this time, you can get a ride back to Panajachel, flag them down in case they don't see you, but they usually pull in if it's the last service of the day. Only buy tickets on the boat – if you buy them from the numerous ticket touts on the dockside you will be overcharged. There are no regular boats to Santa Catarina, San Antonio or San Lucas: pick-ups and buses serve these communities, or charter a *lancha*, US$30 return to Santa Catarina and San Antonio. Bad weather can, of course, affect the boat services. Crossings are generally rougher in the afternoons, worth bearing in mind if you suffer from sea-sickness.

Boat hire and tours *Lanchas* can be hired to go anywhere round the lake, about US$37 round trip, maximum passengers about 10 (negotiable). For round trips to San Pedro and Santiago and possibly San Antonio Palopó, with stopovers, go early to the lakefront and bargain. Trip takes a full day, eg 0830-1530, with stops of 1 hr or so at each, around US$6-7, if the boat is full. If on a tour, be careful not to miss the boat at each stage – if you do, you will have to pay again.

Bus

Rebuli buses leave from opposite Hotel Fonda del Sol on Calle Real, otherwise, the main stop is where Calle Santander meets Calle Real. **Rebuli** to **Guatemala City**, 3½ hrs, US$2.50, crowded, hourly between 0500 and 1500. To **Guatemala City via Escuintla** south coast, 8 a day plus 3 **Pullman** a day. Direct bus to **Quetzaltenango**, 7 a day between 0530 and 1415, US$2.10, 2½ hrs. There are direct buses to **Los Encuentros** on the Pan-American Highway (US$0.50. To **Chichicastenango** direct, Thu and Sun, 0645, 0700, 0730 and then hourly to 1530. Other days between 0700-1500, US$1.40, 1½ hrs. There are direct buses to **Cuatro Caminos**, US$1.30 (see page 578) from 0530, for connections to Totonicapán, Quetzaltenango, Huehuetenango, etc. To **Antigua** take a bus up to Los Encuentros through Sololá. Change for a bus to **Chimaltenango** US$1.40, and change there for Antigua. There is also a direct bus (**Transpopeye**) to **Antigua** leaving 1030-1100, daily, US$4.60, which leaves from opposite the bank. To **Sololá**, US$0.20, 20 mins, every 30 mins. You can wait for through buses by the market on Calle Real. The fastest way to southern **Mexico** is probably by bus south to Cocales, 2½ hrs, 5 buses between 0600 and 1400, then many buses along the Pacific Highway to Tapachula on the border. For La Mesilla take a bus up to Los Encuentros, change west for Cuatro Caminos. Here catch a bus north to La Mesilla. Some travel agencies go direct to San Cristóbal de las Casas via La Mesilla, daily at 0600. See Tour operators.

Motorcycle

Motorcycle hire About US$6 per hr, plus fuel and US$100 deposit. Try **Maco Cycle** near the junction of Calle Santander and 14 de Febrero, T7762-0883. Bikes generally poor, no locks or helmets provided.
Motorcycle parts **David's Store**, opposite **Hotel Maya Kanek**, has good prices and also does repairs.

Shuttles

Services are now available, run jointly by travel agencies, to **Guatemala City**, **Antigua**, **Quetzaltenango**, **Chichi** and more. Around 4 a day. Chichicastenango US$10, Quetzaltenango US$15 and the Mexican border US$35. See under Tour operators.

Santa Catarina Palopó *p556*

Pick-up There are frequent pick-ups from Panajachel and boat services.

San Antonio Palopó *p556*

Pick-up Frequent pick-ups from Panajachel. Enquire about boats.

San Lucas Tolimán *p557*

Boat Enquire about boats. Private *lancha*, US$35. **Bus** To **Santiago Atitlán**, hourly and to **Guatemala City** via **Panajachel**.

Santiago Atitlán *p557*

Bus To **Guatemala City**, US$2.15 (5 a day, first at 0300). Two **Pullmans** a day, US$2.80. To **Panajachel**, 0600, 2 hrs, or take any bus and change on main road south of San Lucas.
Boat 4 sailings daily to Pana with *Naviera*, 1¼ hrs, US$1.30, or by *lancha* when full, 20-35 mins, US$1.30-2. To **San Pedro** by *lancha* at 0800, 0900, 1030, 45 mins, US$1.30.

San Pedro La Laguna *p557*

Boat Up to 10 *lanchas* to **Panajachel**. To **Santiago**, leave when full (45 mins, US$1.30). To **San Marcos**, every 2 hrs. Private *lanchas* (10 people at US$2 each).
Bus There are daily buses to **Guatemala City**, several leave in the early morning and early afternoon, 4 hrs, US$2.50 and to **Quetzaltenango**, in morning, 3½ hrs, US$2.

San Marcos La Laguna *p559*

Boat Service roughly every ½ hr to **Panajachel** and to **San Pedro**. Wait on any dock. Fare US$1.30 to either. **Bus** San Pedro to Pan-American Highway can be boarded at San Pablo. **Pick-up** Frequent pick-ups from the village centre and anywhere along the main road. To **San Pedro**, US$0.40, less to villages en route.

Chichicastenango *p560, map p561*

Bus Buses passing through Chichi all stop at 5 Av/5 Calle by the **Hotel Chugüilá**, where there are always police and bus personnel to give information. To **Guatemala City**, every 15 mins from 0200 to 1730, 3 hrs, US$2.70. To **Santa Cruz del Quiché**, at least every ½ hr between 0600-2000, US$0.70, 30 mins or 20 mins, depending on whether the bus driver is aiming for honours in the graduation from the School of Kamikaze Bus Tactics. To **Panajachel**, 1 hr, US$1.70, 0700, 0900, 1200, 1300, or take any bus heading south and change at Los Encuentros (US$0.70). Same goes for **Antigua**, where you need to change at Chimaltenango. To **Quetzaltenango**, 5 between 0430-0830, 2½ hrs, US$2. To **Mexico**, and all points west, take any bus to Los Encuentros and change. To **Escuintla** via **Santa Lucía Cotzumalguapa**, between 0300-1700, 3 hrs, US$2. There are additional buses to local villages especially on market days.

Shuttle **Chichi Turkaj Tours**, 5 Av, 4-42, T5215-0731, daily 0800-2000. Shuttles to the capital, Xela, Panajachel, Huehuetenango and Mexican border. **Maya Chichi Van**, 6 Av, 6-45, T7756-2187. Shuttles and tours ranging from US$10-650.

Santa Cruz del Quiché and around *p562*

Bus Terminal at 10 Calle y 1 Av, Zona 5. To **Guatemala City**, at 0300 until 1700, 3 hrs, US$2. To **Nebaj** and **Cotzal**, 8 a day, US$1.30, 3 hrs; a rough but breathtaking trip, arrive in good time to get a window seat (may leave early if full). Buses leave, passing through Sacapulas (1 hr, US$0.90), at 0800, 0900, 1000, 1030, 1400, 1500, 1600, 1700. To **Uspantán**, via **Sacapulas**, for **Cobán** and **San Pedro Carchá** at 0930, 1300, 1500, 1530, 3 hrs, US$1.30. To **Joyabaj**, several daily, via Chiché and Zacualpa, US$0.50, 1½ hrs. First at 0800 with buses going on to the capital. Last bus back to Quiché at 1600. It is possible to get to **Huehuetenango** in a day via Sacapulas, then pick-up from bridge to **Aguacatán** and bus from there to Huehuetenango. Last bus to Huehue from Aguacatán, 1600. Daily buses also to **Quetzaltenango**, **San Marcos**, and to **Panajachel**. To **Joyabaj**, Joyita bus from **Guatemala City,** 10 a day between 0200 and 1600, 5 hrs, US$1.50. There are buses from **Quiché** to **San Andrés Sajcabaja.**

The road east to Cobán *p563*

Bus and trucks Several trucks to Cobán, daily in the morning from **Sacapulas**; US$1.25, 7 hrs if you're lucky, usually much longer. Start very early if you wish to make it to Cobán the same day. There is no direct bus to Cobán; instead, take 1 of the 3 Quiché-Uspantán buses (0930, 1300, 1500), passing Sacapulas at about 1030, 1400, 1600, there is also a departure from Sacapulas around midday or a truck to **Uspantán**. There have been occasional reports of robberies on the road between Uspantán and Cobán. Then take the early morning bus at 0300 from Uspantán to Cobán. Truck to Cobán 0800-0900. Hitchhiking to Cobán is also possible. (Truck Uspantán-San Cristóbal Verapaz, US$1.25.) Buses to Quiché: 0300, 2200, other early morning departures.

Nebaj *p563*

Bus The bus ride to Quiché is full of fabulous views, hair-raising bends, and bus drivers who seem hell-bent on leaving the unpaved road for the tarmac from Sacapulas south, at which point they up the speed even more. There is at least 1 rusting bus roof down a chasm to be viewed. Buses to **Quiché** (US$1.30, 3 hrs) passing through **Sacapulas** (1¾ hr from Nebaj, US$0.78) leave 2400, 0100, 0200, 0300, 0400, 0530, 0630-0700, 0800, 1100. You can travel to **Cobán** in a day by getting a truck or pick-up from outside the village or earliest bus to Sacapulas, get off at the junction to **Cunén** (1 hr from Nebaj) and hitch or bus it from there. There is a lone bus shelter on the mountain road at this junction and you may not wish to wait there if you are on your own, in which case continue to Sacapulas to pick the bus up there (another 40 mins from the junction.)

Chajul and Cotzal *p564*

Bus Buses to Chajul and Cotzal do not run on a set schedule. It is best to ask the day before you want to travel, at the bus station. There are buses and numerous pick-ups on Sun when villagers come to Nebaj for its market, which would be a good day to visit the villages. There is a definite 0500 bus to Chajul on Tue returning 1200. Alternatively, bargain with a local pick-up driver to take you on a trip.

Directory

Panajachel *p554, map p555*

Banks Banco Industrial, Calle Santander (TCs and Visa ATM), Banco de Comercio, Calle Real, US$TCs and cash, Visa ATM opposite. Banco Industrial and Banco Inmobilario do not provide cash on cards inside the bank. There is a *cambio* on the street near Mayan Palace for US$ cash and TCs, good rate. **Internet** Many in centre, shop around for best prices; standard is US$1 per hr. Cheaper in the old town. **Medical services** Centro de Salud Calle Real, just downhill from the road to San Antonio Palopó. Farmacia Santander, top end of Calle Santander, very good and helpful. **Post office** Calle Santander. Difficult but not impossible to send parcels of up to 1 kg abroad as long as packing requirements are met. Get Guated Out, Centro Comercial, Av Los Arboles, T/F7762-0595, good but more expensive service, they use the postal system but pack and deal with formalities for you. DHL, Edif Rincón Sai, Calle Santander. **Telephone** Telgua, Calle Santander. **Language schools** Jardín de América, Calle 14 de Febrero, T7762-2637, www.jardindeamerica.com. US$80 for 20 hrs per week tuition, lodging with family, US$60 per week. Jabel Tinamit, behind Edif Rincón Sai, T7762-0238, www.jabeltinamit.com. Similar tariff. Pana Atitlán Language School, Calle de la Navidad, 0-40, T7762-1196.

San Lucas Tolimán *p557*

Banks Banrural and Corpobanco. **Internet** Available in the plaza.

Santiago Atitlán *p557*

Banks G&T Continental, opposite the church. **Internet** Next to Chim-ni-ya.

San Pedro La Laguna *p559*

Banks Banrural changes cash and TCs only. **Internet** There are several internet and phone offices. **Language schools** This is a popular place for learning Spanish. Tuition for 1 week/20 hrs about US$50. Here most students make their own accommodation arrangements. Casa Rosario, www.casarosario.com, offers classes from US$57 a week; homestays offered. Corazón Maya, T7721-8160, www.corazonmaya.com, from US$43 for 5 days' tuition and homestay. Tz'utujil classes also. Run by the welcoming Marta Navichoc. San Pedro, T5715-4604, www.sanpedrospanish-school.org, from US44 per week; homestays possible. School has a great location with gardens close to the lakeshore. **Medical services** Centro Médico opposite Educación Básica school has a good doctor who does not speak English.

San Juan La Laguna *p559*

Banks Banrural, diagonally opposite Nick's Place. Changes cash and TCs only. **Internet** There are a couple of places in town.

San Marcos La Laguna *p559*

Language schools Casa Rosario, T5613-6401. La Escuela, close to Hotel Jinava, San Marcos La Laguna, run by a Québécois couple above their own-designed dream home. They have the best house in one of the most glorious spots in Guatemala. Teaching in *palapas* on the terraces above.

Chichicastenango *p560, map p561*

Banks There are a number of banks in town (see map) taking Visa and MasterCard. Bancafé, corner 5 Av/6 Calle, also has 24 hr Visa ATM. Mayan Inn will exchange cash. **Internet** There is occasional connection at Aces, inside Hotel Girón, 6 Calle, 4-52, expensive. **Post office** 7 Av, 8-47. Cropa Panalpina, 7 Av opposite post office, T7756-1028, cropachi@amigo.net.gt Will pack and ship your purchases back home by air cargo. **Telephone** Telgua, 6 Calle between 5 y 6.

Santa Cruz del Quiché *p562*

Banks Banco Industrial, 3 Calle y 2 Av, top corner of Parque Central, cash on Visa cards and TCs; G&T Continental, 6 Calle y 3 Av, Visa and MasterCard TCs. **Internet** Megatel, 1 Av and 3 Calle, Zona 5. **Post office** 3 Calle between 1 Av and 0 Av, Zona 5. Telgua: 1 Av/2 Calle, Zona 5.

Nebaj *p563*

Banks Bancafé and Banrural, TCs only, north side of park. **Internet** There are 2 email services in town. **Language schools** The Nebaj Language School, www.nebaj.org. Call in at the offices of Solidaridad Internacional, 20 hrs a week US$75 plus US$45 for homestay. **Post office** Behind Bancafé.

The Western Highlands

Just before the volcanic highlands reach their highest peaks, this part of the western highlands divides into scores of small market towns and villages, each with its own character – the loud animal market at San Francisco El Alto, the extra-planetary landscape at Momostenango, and its Maya cosmovision centre, and the dancing extravaganzas at Totonicapán. The modern ladino town of Huehuetenango sits at the gateway to the Sierra de los Cuchumatanes, within which hides, in a cold gash in a sky-hugging valley, the indigenous town and weaving centre of Todos Santos Cuchumatán. ▸▸ *For Sleeping, Eating and other listings see pages 583-587.*

Ins and outs

This area is well connected by buses from the Cuatro Caminos junction, Quetzaltenango or Huehuetenango. The road from Cobán is another access option, although a much slower one. ▸▸ *For further details, see Transport, page 585.*

Nahualá and Cuatro Caminos

Before the major four-way junction of Cuatro Caminos, the Pan-American Highway runs past Nahualá, a Maya village at 2470 m. The traditional *traje* is distinctive and best seen on market days on Thursday and Sunday, when finely embroidered cuffs and collars are sold, as well as very popular *huípiles*. The **Fiesta de Santa Catalina** is on 23-26 November (main day 25). There is an unpaved all-weather road a little to the north and 16 km longer, from Los Encuentros (on the Pan-American Highway) through Totonicapán (40 km) to San Cristóbal Totonicapán. The route from Chichicastenango to Quiché, Xecajá and Totonicapán takes a day by car or motorcycle, but is well worth taking and recommended by cyclists. There are no buses. **Cuatro Caminos** is a busy junction with roads, east to Totonicapán, west to Los Encuentros, north to Huehuetenango and south to Quetzaltenango. Buses stop here every few seconds so you will never have to wait long for a connection. There is a petrol station and lots of vendors to keep you fed and watered. Just north of Cuatro Caminos is **San Cristóbal Totonicapán**, noted for its *huípiles*.

Totonicapán → *Colour map 5, B1. Altitude: 2500 m.*

The route to San Miguel Totonicapán, the capital of its department, passes through pine-forested hillsides, pretty red-tiled roofs and *milpas* of maize on the road side. The 18th-century beige church stands on one of the main squares, unfortunately now a parking lot, at 6 y 7 Avenida between 3 and 4 Calle. The market is considered by Guatemalans to be one of the cheapest, and it is certainly very colourful. Saturday is the main market noted for ceramics and cloth, with a small gathering on Tuesdays. There is a traditional dance **fiesta** on 12-13 August, music concerts and a chance to see *cofradía* rituals. The annual **feria** is on 24-30 September in celebration of the Archangel San Miguel, with the main **fiesta** on 29 September. The **Casa de Cultura** ⓘ *8 Av, 2-17, T7766-1575, www.larutamayaonline.com/aventura.html, Mon-Fri 0800-1200, 1400-1630*, run by Carlos Humberto Molina, displays an excellent collection of fiesta masks, made on site at the mask factory, and for sale. It has a cultural programme with a number of tour options. You need to reserve in advance.

San Francisco El Alto

San Francisco stands high on a great big mound in the cold mountains at 2640 m above the great valley in which lie Totonicapán, San Cristóbal and Quetzaltenango. It is famous for its market, which is stuffed to capacity, and for the animal market

Border essentials: Guatemala-Mexico

La Mesilla-Ciudad Cuauhtémoc The Pan-American Highway runs west from the junction to Huehuetenango to La Mesilla.
Guatemalan immigration Open 0600-2100. You may be able to pass through out of hours for a surcharge. The Mexican border post is in Ciudad Cuauhtémoc (just a few buildings, not a town), about 4 km from the Guatemalan border. If you are crossing into Mexico and will be there less than 7 days there will be no departure fee. If you stay more than 7 days the charge is 210 pesos and must be paid at a bank listed on the immigration papers before departure. There are pick-ups during the day. Crossing by private vehicle is reported to be fairly simple.
Sleeping There are a couple of *pensiones* at the border inside Guatemala including **Hotel Mily's** (**F**), 10 rooms, hot water.
Transport Buses La Mesilla-Huehuetenango run 0330-1800, 2 hrs, US$1.05. Express buses run by **Transportes Velásquez** go to Guatemala City (US$5, 7 hrs).
Banks Rates are not usually favourable at the border in either currency. **Banrural** in La Mesilla with ATM and at the border, or haggle in the street.
Entering Guatemala A tourist card for Guatemala can be obtained at the border (see page 28). For visas, also see this section and for border 'charges'. Guatemalan immigration are currently charging an unofficial 30-quetzal fee to enter Guatemala. Point out that this is not official and insist on a receipt; this should throw them and they should wave you through.
Crossing by private vehicle Full details under Getting around by car, page 516.
Mexican consulates: Mexican visas are available at the border. See also Quetzaltenango, Embassies and consulates.
Car insurance For Mexico and Guatemala, arranged at Banco G&T Continental's agent, Edif Villa Rosa opposite Mi Tierra Café Internet.

held above town, where creatures from piglets to kittens to budgies are for sale. The town's **fiesta** is on 1-6 October in honour of St Francis of Assisi.

The **market** is packed to bursting point on Fridays with locals buying all sorts, including woollen blankets for resale throughout the country. It's an excellent place for buying woven and embroidered textiles of good quality, but beware of pickpockets. Go early to see as much action as possible. Climb up through the town for 10 minutes to see the animal market (ask for directions all the time as it's hard to see 5 m ahead the place is so chocka).

The **church** on the main square is magnificent; notice the double-headed Hapsburg eagle. It is often full on market days with locals lighting candles, and their live purchases ignoring the 'Silencio' posters. The white west front of the church complements the bright colours of the rest of the plaza, especially the vivid green and pink of the Municipalidad.

Momostenango → *Colour map 5, B1.*

Momostenango is set in a valley with ribbons of houses climbing higgledy-piggledy out of the valley floor. Momostenango, at 2220 m, represents *Shol Mumus* in K'iche', meaning 'among the hills', and on its outlying hills are numerous altars and a hilltop image of a Maya god. Some 300 medicine men are said to practise in the town. Their insignia of office is a little bag containing beans and quartz crystals. Momostenango is the chief blanket-weaving centre in the country, and locals can be seen beating the blankets (*chamarras*) on stones, to shrink them. There are also weird stone peaks known as the *riscos* – eroded fluted columns and draperies formed of volcanic ash – on the outskirts of town.

The town is quiet except on Wednesday and Sunday **market days**, the latter being larger and good for weaving, especially the blankets. On non-market days try **Tienda Manuel de Jesús Agancel** ⓘ *1 Av, 1-50, Zona 4, near Bancafé*, for good bargains, especially blankets and carpets. There is also **Artesanía Paclom** ⓘ *corner of 1 Calle and 3 Av, Zona 2*, just five minutes along the road to Xela. This family have the weaving looms in their back yard and will show you how it's all done if you ask.

The **Feast of Wajshakib Batz' Oj** (pronounced 'washakip'), is celebrated by hundreds of *Aj Kij* (Maya priests) who come for ceremonies. New priests are initiated on this first day of the ritual new year; the initiation lasting the year. The town's very popular **fiesta** is between 21 July and 4 August, with the town's patron saint of Santiago Apóstol celebrated on 25 July. The **Baile de Convites** is held in December with other dances on 8, 12 and 31 December and 1 January. At **Takilibén Maya Misión**, Chuch Kajaw (day keeper) Rigoberto Itzep welcomes all interested in learning more about Maya culture and cosmology. He offers courses in culture and does Maya horoscope readings . He also has a **Maya sauna (Tuj)** ⓘ *Tue and Thu 1400-1700, US$6.50; you can leave a message for him on T7736-5051, Mon-Fri 0800-1200, 1400-1700. He can be found just after the Texaco garage on the right on the way in from Xela at 3 Av, 6-85, Zona 3.*

Just outside town are three sets of *riscos* (eroded columns of sandstone with embedded quartz particles), creating a strange eerie landscape of pinnacles that look like rocket lollipop ice creams. To get there, take the 2 Calle, Zona 2, which is the one to the right of the church, for five minutes until you see a sign on a building pointing to the left. Follow the signs until you reach the earth structures (five to 10 minutes).

Huehuetenango and around

▸▸ *pp583-587. Colour map 5, B1.*

→ *Altitude: 1905 m.*

Huehuetenango – colloquially known as Huehue – is a pleasant, large town with little to detain the visitor. However, it is a busy transport hub serving the Cuchumatanes Mountains and the Mexican border. Its bus terminal, 2 km from town, is one of the busiest in the country. There are Maya ruins near the town, which were badly restored by the infamous **United Fruit Company,** and new adventure tourism opportunities opening up nearby. Trips, including horse rides, to more remote spots in the Huehuetenango region to see forests, haciendas and lakes are organized by **Unicornio Azul.**

There is a useful website at www.interhuehue.com.

The neoclassical **cathedral** was built between 1867-1874, it was destroyed by earthquake in 1902, and took 10 years to repair. In 1956, the image of the patron saint, the Virgen de la Concepción was burnt in an altar fire. Then, during the 1976 earthquake, 80% of it was damaged, save the bells, façade and cupola. The skyline to the north of the city is dominated by the Sierrra de los Cuchumatanes, the largest area over 3000 m in Central America.

The ruins of **Zaculeu** ⓘ *0800-1800, free*, the old capital of the Mam Maya, are 5 km west of Huehuetenango on top of a rise with steep drops on three sides – a site chosen because of these natural defence measures. Its original name in Mam was *Xinabajul*, meaning 'between ravines'. In K'iche' it means 'white earth'. It was first settled in the Early Classic period (AD 250-600), but it flourished during the late post-Classic (AD 1200-1530). In July 1525, Gonzalo de Alvarado, the brother of Guatemala's conqueror, Pedro de Alvarado, set out for Zaculeu with 80 Spaniards, 40 horses and 2000 indigenous fighters, passing Mazatenango and Totonicapán on the way. The battle lasted four months, during which time the soldiers and residents of Zaculeu were dying of hunger, and eating their dead neighbours. The weakened Kaibil Balam, the Zaculeu *cacique* (chief), called for a meeting with Gonzalo. Gonzalo told the Mam chief that peace was not on the cards. Negotiations followed with the outcome being that Kaibil Balam be instructed in Christianity, obey the Spanish king and leave the city, whereupon Gonzalo de Alvarado would take possession of the Mam kingdom settlement in the name of the Spanish crown.

Aguacatán → *Colour map 5, B1. Altitude: 1670 m.*

The women of Aguacatán wear the most stunning headdresses in the country. On sale in *tiendas* in town, they are a long, slim belt of woven threads using all the colours of the rainbow. The women also wear beautiful clothes – the *cortes* are dark with horizontal stripes of yellow, pink, blue and green. The town **fiesta** is 40 days after Holy Week, Virgen de la Encarnación.

Towards Todos Santos Cuchumatán

To get to Todos Santos, you have to climb the front range of the Cuchumatanes Mountains above Chiantla by a steep road from Huehuetenango. **Chiantla** has the **Lunas Café** with art gallery and the nearby paleontological site of **El Mamutz**. Looking down on a clear day the cathedral at Huehuetenango resembles a blob of orange blancmange on the plain. At the summit, at about 3300 m, there is **El Mirador**. The new paved road continues over bleak moorland to Paquix where the road divides. The unpaved road to the north continues to Soloma. The other to the west goes through

Huehuetenango

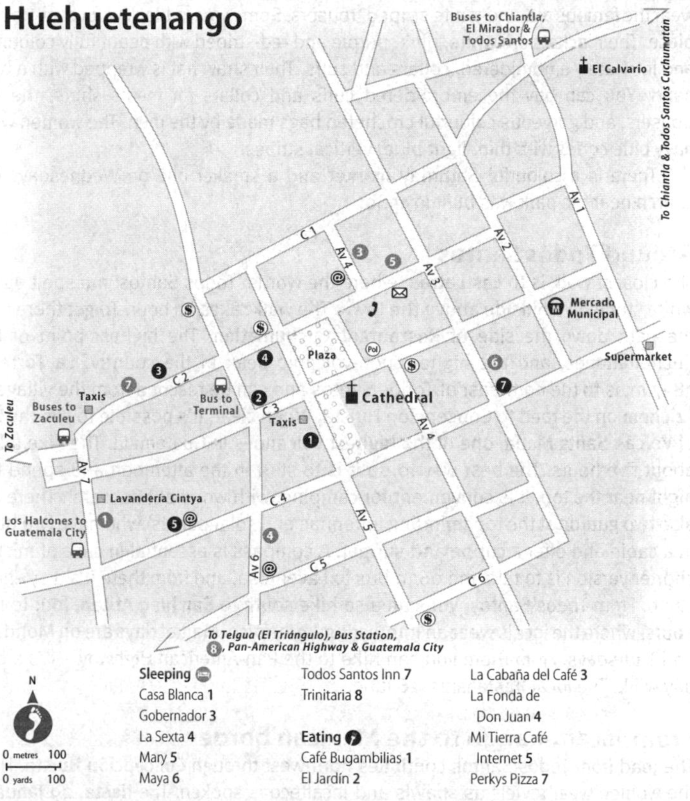

Sleeping
Casa Blanca 1
Gobernador 3
La Sexta 4
Mary 5
Maya 6
Todos Santos Inn 7
Trinitaria 8

Eating
Café Bugambilias 1
El Jardín 2
La Cabaña del Café 3
La Fonda de Don Juan 4
Mi Tierra Café Internet 5
Perkys Pizza 7

 Aldea Chiabel, noted for its outhouses, more obvious than the small dwellings they serve. Here, giant agave plants appear to have large pom-poms attached – reminiscent of the baubles on Gaudí's Sagrada Familia in Barcelona. On this journey you often pass through cloud layer, eventually surfacing above it. On cloudier days you will be completely submerged until descending again to Huehuetenango. The road crosses a pass at 3394 m before a difficult long descent to Todos Santos, about 50 km from Huehuetenango. The walk northwest from Chiantla to Todos Santos Cuchumatanes can be done in around 12-14 hours, or better, two days, staying overnight at **El Potrillo** in the barn owned by Rigoberto Alva. This route crosses one of the highest parts of the sierra at over 3500 m. Alternatively, cycle the 40-km part-gravel road, which is steep in places, but very rewarding.

Todos Santos Cuchumatán

▸▸ *pp583-587. Colour map 5, B1.*

→ *Altitude: 2470 m.*

High in the Cuchumatanes, the Mam-speaking Todos Santeros maintain a traditional way of life with their striking, bright, traditional dress and their adherence to the 260-day Tzolkin calendar. The town is hemmed in by 3800-m-high mountains either side that squeeze it into one long, 2-km street down the valley. The town is famous for its weaving, and even more famous for the **horse race** held on 1 November, see box page 583.

Some of Guatemala's best weaving is done in Todo Santos. Fine *huípiles* may be bought in the co-operative on the main street and direct from the makers. The men wear the famous red-and-white striped trousers. Some wear a black wool over-trouser piece. Their jackets are white, pink, purple and red-striped with beautifully coloured, and intricately embroidered, collars and cuffs. Their straw hat is wrapped with a blue band. You can buy the embroidered cuffs and collars for men's shirts, the red trousers, and gorgeous colourful crocheted bags made by the men. The women wear navy blue *cortes* with thin, light blue, vertical stripes.

There is a colourful Saturday **market** and a smaller one on Wednesday. The **church** near the park was built in 1580.

Around Todos Santos

The closest walk is to **Las Letras**, where the words 'Todos Santos' are spelt out in white stone on a hillside above the town. The walk takes an hour. To get there take the path down the side of **Restaurant Cuchumatlán**. The highest point of the Cuchumatanes, and the highest non-volcanic peak in the country, **La Torre** at 3837 m, is to the northeast of Todos Santos and can be reached from the village of **Tzichem** on the road to Concepción Huista. When clear, it's possible to see the top of Volcán Santa María, one of the highest volcanoes in Guatemala. The hike takes about five hours. The best way to do it is to start in the afternoon and spend the night near the top. It is convenient for camping, with wood but no water. There are also two guards at the top (minding antennae and solar panels) who have two beds in a cabin and offer a cuppa and supper. A compass is essential in case of mist. A shorter version is to take the 0630 bus to Laventosa, and from there it's a 1½-hour climb. From Todos Santos, you can also hike south to **San Juan Atitán**, four to five hours, where the locals wear an interesting *traje típico*. Market days are on Mondays and Thursdays. From there you can hike to the Pan-American Highway – it's a one day walk. The local **fiesta** is 22-26 June.

From Jacaltenango to the Mexican border

The road from Todos Santos continues northwest through **Concepción Huista**. Here the women wear towels as shawls and Jacalteco is spoken. The **fiesta**, 29 January-

Todos Santos Festival

The horse racing festival of Todos Santos is one of the most celebrated and spectacular in Central America – it is also a frenzied day that usually degenerates into a drunken mess. Quite simply riders race between two points, having a drink at each turn until they fall off.

According to Professor Margarito Calmo Cruz, the origins of the fiesta lie in the 15th or 16th century with the arrival of the *conquistadores* to Todos Santos. They arrived on horseback wearing large, colourful clothes with bright scarves flowing down their backs and feathers in their hats. The locals experimented, imitating them. They enjoyed it and the tradition was born.

When the day begins, the men are pretty tipsy, but sprightly and clean. The race is frantic and colourful with scarves flying out from the backs of the men. As the day wears on, they get completely smashed, riding with arms outstretched – whip in one hand and beer bottle in the other. Their faces are mudspattered, they look dishevelled and are moaning and groaning from the enjoyment and the alcohol which must easily have reached near comatose level.

At times the riders fall, and look pretty lifeless on the track. They are dragged by the scruff of the neck, regardless of serious injury or death, to the edge of the fence as quickly as possible, to avoid trampling.

The men guzzle gallons of beer and the aim is to continue racing all day. A fall means instant dismissal from the race. There are wardens on the side lines with batons, whose primary job is the welfare of the horses, changing them when they see necessary. But they also deal with protesting fallen riders, who try and clamber back onto their horses. By the end of the day the spectacle is pretty grotesque. The horses are drenched with sweat and wild-eyed with fear. The men look hideous and are completely paralytic from booze. The edge of the course and the town is littered with bodies.

The race takes place on the road that winds its way out of town, not the incoming road from Huehue. It starts at 0800. There are about 15 riders on the course at any one time. It continues until noon, stops for *cerveza* guzzling and begins again at 1400, ending at 1700.

3 February, has fireworks and dancing. The hatmaker in Canton Pilar supplies the hats for Todos Santos, he welcomes viewers and will make a hat to your specifications (but if you want a typical Todos Santos leather *cincho*, buy it there).

Beyond Jacaltenango, is **Nentón,** and **Gracias a Dios** at the Mexican border. When the road north out of Huehue splits at Paquix, the right fork goes to **San Mateo Ixtatán,** with ruins nearby. The road crosses the roof of the Cuchumatanes, before descending to **San Juan Ixcoy, Soloma** and **Santa Eulalia,** where the people speak O'anjob'al as they do in Soloma. East along a scenic route is **Barillas.** There are several *pensiones* in these places and regular buses from Huehue.

Sleeping

Totonicapán *p578*

D-E Hospedaje San Miguel, 3 Calle, 7-49, Zona 1, T7766-1452. Rooms with or without bath, hot water, communal TV.

F Pensión Blanquita, 13 Av and 4 Calle. 20 rooms, hot showers, good. Opposite this *pensión* is a Shell station.

San Francisco El Alto *p578*

D-E Vista Hermosa, 2 Calle, 2-23, T7738-4010. 36 rooms, cheaper without bathroom, hot water, TV.

F Hotel Vásquez, 4 Av, 11-53, T7738-4003. Rooms all with private bathroom, but the owner is unwelcoming. Parking available.

Momostenango *p579*

E Ixcel (Estiver), downhill away from plaza at 1 Calle, 4-15, Zona 4, T7736-5036. 12 rooms, hot water, cheaper without bath, clean.

E-F La Villa, 1 Av, 1-13, Zona 1, below Bancafé, T7736-5108. 6 rooms, warm water only, clean and nicely presented.

F Hospedaje y Comedor Paclom, close to central plaza, at 1 Calle, 1-71, Zona 4. Pretty inner courtyard with caged birds and plants, hot water in shared bathrooms.

Huehuetenango *p580, map p580*

C Casa Blanca, 7 Av, 3-41, T7769-0777. Comfortable, good restaurant in a pleasant garden, buffet breakfast, set lunch, very popular and good value, parking.

C-D Maya, 3 Av, 3-55, T7764-0369. This former basic hotel has been remodelled with spa facilities, offering free coffee in reception, hot water and cable TV in rooms. It is ultra-clean, but some rooms are a little small, accepts credit cards add 7%.

D Mary, 2 Calle, 3-52, T7764-1618. With bath, cheaper without, good beds, hot water, cable TV, parking, clean, quiet, safe, well maintained, good value. Recommended.

D-E La Sexta, 6 Av, 4-29, T7764-6612. With bath, cheaper without, cable TV, restaurant, good for breakfast, clean, good value, phone call facility, stores backpacks without charge, home to 3 happy parrots.

D-E Trinitaria, Cda Kaibil Balam 9-30, Zona 5, near bus terminal, T7764-3922. 13 rooms with bath, cheaper without, hot water.

E Todos Santos Inn, 2 Calle, 6-74, T7764-1241. Shared bath and private bath available, hot water, TV, helpful, clean, laundry, some rooms a bit damp, luggage stored. Recommended. Better value for single travellers than Mary.

F Hotel Gobernador, 4 Av 1-45, T7764-1197. Garden, parking, with bath cheaper without, clean, good value.

Todos Santos Cuchumatán *p582*

Reservations necessary in the week before the Nov horse race, but even if you turn up and the town is full, locals offer their homes.

F Casa Familiar, up the hill, close to central park, myearth@c.net.gt. Run by the friendly family of Santiaga Mendoza Pablo. Hot shower, sauna, breakfast, dinner, but slow service (chase them up), delicious banana bread, spectacular view, popular. The Mendoza family make and sell *típicas* and give weaving lessons.

F Casa Mendoza. Basic, hot shower is some way from the rooms, free sauna.

F Hospedaje El Viajero, around the corner and then right from Hotelito Todos Santos, 5 rooms, 2 shared baths with hot water.

F Hotelito Todos Santos, above the central park. Hot water, clean, small café, but beware of boys taking you to the hotel quoting one price, and then on arrival, finding the price has mysteriously gone up!

F Hotel La Paz. Friendly, great view of the main street from balconies, excellent spot for the 1 Nov fiesta, shared showers have seen better days, enclosed parking.

F Hotel Mam, above the central park, next to Hotelito Todos Santos. Friendly, clean, hot water, but needs 1 hr to warm up, not too cold in the rooms as an open fire warms the building, good value.

San Juan Atitán *p582*

F Hospedaje San Diego. Only 3 beds, basic, friendly, clean, food.

Eating

Totonicapán *p578*

Comedor Brenda 2, 9 Av, 3-31. Good, serving local food.

Comedor Letty, 3 Calle, 8-18. Typical Guatemalan fare.

Momostenango *p579*

Comedor Santa Isabel, next door to Hospedaje y Vomedor Paclom. Friendly, cheap and good breakfasts.

Flipper, 1 Calle y 2 Av A. Good *licuados* and a range of fruit juices.

Hospedaje y Comedor Paclom, close to the central plaza and where buses arrive from Xela, 1 Calle, 1-71, Zona 4. Cheap meals, including snacks in a pretty inner courtyard.

Huehuetenango *p580, map p580*

Casa Blanca, 7 Av, 3-41. Try the breakfast pancake with strawberries and cream. The plate of the house is a meat extravaganza, fish and good salads served, set lunch good value. Open 0600-2200.

La Cabaña del Café, 2 Calle, 6-50. Log cabin café with to-die-for cappuccino, snack food and good *chapín* breakfasts, good atmosphere, but service is lamentably slow. Live guitar music on Sat. Mon-Sat 0800-2100. Recommended.

Café Bugambilias, 5 Av 3-59, on the plaza. large, unusual 4-storey building, most of which is a popular, cheap, restaurant, very good breakfasts, *almuerzos*, sandwiches, 0700-2200. Recommended.

El Jardín, 6 Av 2-99, Zona 1. Meat dishes, breakfasts, good pancakes and local dishes. It's worth eating here just to check out the toilets, which are right out of the 3rd-and-a-half floor of the office in the movie *Being John Malkovich*! Daily 0600-2200.

La Fonda de Don Juan, 2 Calle, 5-35. Italian restaurant and bar (try the *cavatini*), sandwiches, big choice of desserts, *licuados*, coffees, good pizzas, also *comida típica*, with reasonable prices all served in a bright environment with red and white checked tablecloths. Daily 0600-2200.

Mi Tierra Café Internet, 4 Calle, 6-46, T764-1473. Good drinks and light meals, Mexican offerings – try the *fajitas*, nice setting, popular with locals and travellers, recommended. Daily 0700-2100.

Perkys Pizza, 3 Av 4 Calle esquina. Wide variety of pizzas, eat in or takeaway, modern, clean, good value. Open 0700-2200.

Todos Santos Cuchumatán *p582*

There are *comedores* on the 2nd floor of the market selling very cheap meals.

Comedor Katy. Will prepare vegetarian meals on request, good value *menú del día*.

Cuchumatlán. Has sandwiches, pizza and pancakes, and is popular at night.

Mountain Muse. Run by American Rebecca who serves up veggie curry, pastas and breakfasts, with a book swap. www.stetson.edu/~rsitler/TodosSantos.

Patz Xaq, signposted 100 m down a track opposite and just before **Hotel La Paz** on the right. Serves *comida típica* from 0700-2100, great view.

Tzolkin. Good food, the most popular gringo hangout, can also arrange local tours.

Festivals and events

Todos Santos Cuchumatán *p582*

1 Nov Horse race. The festival begins on 21 Oct. See box, page 583.

2 Nov Day of the Dead, when locals visit the cemetery and leave flowers and food.

Shopping

Todos Santos Cuchumatán *p582*

The following shops all sell bags, trousers, shirts, *huípiles*, jackets and clothes. Prices have more or less stabilized at the expensive end, but the best bargains can be had at the **Tienda Maribel**, further up the hill from Casa Familiar and the **Cooperativa Estrella de Occidente**, on the main street. **Casa Mendoza**, just beyond Tienda Maribel, is where Telésforo Mendoza makes clothes to measure. A pair of trousers including material costs US$20. His young daughter, Isabela, is a keen businesswoman, and will offer you items in exchange for your watch or some jewellery, her parents unaware! **Domingo Calmo** also makes clothes to measure. A pair of trousers will cost US$3.90 plus material. Takes 4-5 hrs. His large, brown house with tin roof is on the main road to the Ruinas (5 mins) – follow the road up from Casa Familiar. Ask for the Casa de Domingo.

Activities and tours

Huehuetenango *p580, map p580*

Tour operators **Unicornio Azul**, based in Chancol, T5205-9328, www.unicornioazul.com. Horse riding trips in the Cuchumatanes.

Todos Santos Cuchumatán *p582*

Horse riding Horses can be hired from Casa Mendoza.

Transport

Totonicapán *p578*

Bus Every 15 mins from **Quetzaltenango**, US$0.32, 45 mins. Last bus returns 2000. Bus to **Los Encuentros**, US$1.50. From **Cuatro Caminos**, 30 mins, US$0.20.

San Francisco El Alto *p578*

Bus 2 km along the Pan-American Highway heading north from Cuatro Caminos is a paved road, which runs to San Francisco El Alto (3 km) and then to Momostenango (19 km). Bus from **Quetzaltenango**, 50 mins on Fri, US$0.33. The last bus back is at 1800.0

Momostenango *p579*

Bus From **Cuatro Caminos** (US$0.40) and **Quetzaltenango**, US$0.52, 1-1½ hrs. Buses to Xela every 30 mins from 0430-1600, US$0.52, 1½ hrs.

Huehuetenango *p580, map p580*

Bus

Local From the terminal to town, take 'Centro' bus (minibus), which pull up at cathedral, US$0.08, 5 mins. Taxis from behind the covered market building for US$2.60. To walk takes 20-25 mins. Bus leaves Salvador Osorio School, final Calle 2, every 30 mins, US$0.13, 15 mins, to **Zaculeu**, last return 1830. Taxi, US$7, including waiting time. To walk takes about 1 hr – either take 6 Av north, cross the river and follow the road round to the left, through Zaculeu modern village to the ruins, or go past the school and turn right beyond the river. The signs are barely visible.

Long distance To **Guatemala City**, 5 hrs, US$3.75, **Los Halcones**, 7 Av, 3-62, Zona 1 (they do not leave from the terminal) at 0430, 0700, 1400, reliable. From the bus terminal there are 12 a day to the capital from 0215-1600 via **Chimaltenango**, 5 hrs, US$3.70. Via **Mazatenango** there are 5 daily.

Heading north To **Todos Santos Cuchumatán**, 0300, 0500, 1200, 1400, 1500, 1600, 2-3 hrs, US$1.25. To **Barillas**, via **San Juan Ixcoy** (2½ hrs), **Soloma** (3 hrs), and **San Mateo Ixtatan** (7 hrs), 10 daily from 0200-2330, US$1.50. There are also buses to **San Rafael la Independencia** passing through Soloma and **Sta Eulalia**, US$3.25.

Heading northwest To **La Mesilla** for Mexico: frequent buses between 0330-1700, US$1.05, 2½ hrs, last bus returning to Huehue, 1800. To **Nentón**, via La Mesilla at 0530, 0930. To **Gracias a Dios**, 0500, 1230.

Heading south To **Quetzaltenango**, 13 a day from 0600-1600, US$1.05, 2-2¼ hrs. To **Cuatro Caminos**, US$1, 2 hrs; to **Los Encuentros**, for Lake Atitlán and Chichicastenango, 3 hrs, US$2.60.

Heading east To **Aguacatán**, 12 daily, 0600-1900, 1 hr 10 mins, US$0.52. To **Nebaj** you have to get to Sacapulas via Aguacatán as the 1130 direct bus no longer runs as far as Nebaj, although it is still advertised; to **Sacapulas**, 1130, 1245; to **Cobán**, take the earliest bus to Aguacatán and then Sacapulas and continue to Uspantán.

Aguacatán *p581*

Bus From **Huehue**, 1 hr 10 mins, US$0.52. It is 26 km east of Huehuetenango on a semi-paved route (good views). Returning between 0445 and 1600. Buses and pick-ups for **Sacapulas** and for onward connections to Nebaj and Cobán leave from the main street going out of town. Wait anywhere along there to catch your ride. A bus leaves between 1030-1100 to Sacapulas and there are meant to be more buses until 1400, after which you will have to rely on pick-ups. It is 1½ hrs, US$0.65 from Aguacatán to Sacapulas. To **Guatemala City** at 0300, 1100. See also Sacapulas.

Todos Santos Cuchumatán *p582*

Bus To **Huehuetenango**, 2-3 hrs, crowded Mon and Fri, 0400, 0500, 0600, 0615-30, 1145, 1230, 1300. Possible changes on Sat so ask beforehand. For petrol, ask at **El Molino**.

From Jacaltenango to the Mexican border *p582*

Bus From **Huehuetenango** at 0330, 0500, returning at 1130 and 1400, also pick-ups.

Directory

San Francisco El Alto *p578*

Banks G&T Continental, 2 Av, 1-95, takes MasterCard and changes TCs; **Banco de Comercio**, 2 Calle, 2-64, cashes TCs, takes Visa cards. **Bancafé**, 2 Calle, 3-23. Takes Visa and TCs.

Momostenango *p579*

Banks Banrural, on plaza, TCs only. **Bancafé**, esq 1 Av y 1 Calle, Zona 2, takes Visa.
Language schools Patzite, 1 Calle, 4-33, Zona 2, T7736-5159, www.patzite.20m.com.

Huehuetenango *p580, map p580*

Banks Many local banks taking Visa and MasterCard, some open Sat morning. The

bigger banks change TCs. Mexican pesos can be got from **Camicard,** 5 Av, 6-00.
Internet The cheapest is just outside the centre opposite El Triángulo shopping mall: Los Angeles 2, phone calls also. Several places around the centre, eg **Mi Tierra Café Internet**. **Post office** 2 Calle, 3-54. **Telephone** Telgua, Edif El Triángulo, 9 Av, 6-142, on main road out of town.
Language schools Some operate in the summer months only (see box, Learning the lingo, page 549). Huehuetenango would be a good spot to learn Spanish, as there are fewer chances of meeting gringos and conversing in your own tongue. **Señora de Mendoza**, 1 Calle, 1-64, Zona 3, T7764-1987. **Rodrigo Morales** (at Sastrería La Elegancia), 9 Av, 6-55, Zona 1. Recommended. **Spanish Academy Xinabajul**, 6a Av 0-69, Zona 1, T7764-1518, www.worldwide.edu/guatemala/xinabaj/. **Abesaida Guevara de López**, 10 Calle 'A', 10-20, Zona 1, T7764-2917. Recommended. Information on schools and other tourist information is posted in **Mi Tierra Café Internet**.

Todos Santos Cuchumatán *p582*
Bank Banrural TCs and dollars cash only. **Post office** Central park. **Language schools** All the local co-ordinators are on friendly terms with each other but all are competing for your business. Take your time and visit all 3 schools. **Hispano Maya**, opposite Hotelito Todos Santos, www.hispanomaya.org, US$115 with homestay. **Nuevo Amanecer**, escuela_linguistica@yahoo.com; US$115 with homestay. **Proyecto Lingüístico de Español**, US$115 with homestay, food reported as basic. **Working** There is also volunteer project to teach English in a nearby village where food and board is provided. Weaving can be taught.

Quetzaltenango and around

➔ *Colour map 5, C1. Altitude: 2335 m.*

Quetzaltenango (commonly known as Xela – pronounced 'shayla') is the most important city in western Guatemala. The country's second city is set among a group of high mountains and volcanoes, one of which, Santa María, caused much death and destruction after an eruption in 1902. The bulk of the city is modern, but its 19th-century downtown revamp and its narrow streets give the centre more of an historical feel. There are breathtaking views and a pleasant park with its beautifully restored façade of the colonial church. It is an excellent base from which to visit nearby hot springs, religious idols, volcanoes and market towns. ▸▸ *For Sleeping, Eating and other listings see pages 593-598.*

Ins and outs

Getting there Most visitors arrive by bus, a 30-minute (14.5 km) journey southwest of Cuatro Caminos, US$0.13. Buses pull into the Zona 3 Minerva Terminal. To get a bus into the city centre, take a path through the market at its far left or its far right, which brings you out in front of the Minerva Temple. Watch out for very clever pickpockets walking through this market. Buses for the town centre face away (left) from the temple. All Santa Fe services go to Parque Centro América, US$0.10. Alternatively take a taxi, US$2.60. ▸▸ *For further details, see Transport, page 596.*

Getting around The town centre is compact and all sites and most services are within walking distance. The Santa Fe city bus goes between the terminal, the *rotonda* and the town centre. Out of town destination buses stop at the *rotonda* and it is quicker to get here from the town centre than to the terminal. City buses for the terminal leave from 4 Calle and 13 Avenida, Zona 1, and those straight for the *rotonda* leave from 11 Avenida and 10 Calle, Zona 1, US$0.10. A taxi within Zona 1, or from Zona 1 to a closer part of Zona 3, is between US$1.30-2.

 Tourist information INGUAT ⓘ *7 Calle, 11-35, on the park, T7761-4931, Mon-Fri 0900-1600, Sat 0900-1300*. Utterly useless. Try the recommended tour operators for information. General information can be found at www.xelapages.com.

Background

The most important battle of the Spanish conquest took place near Quetzaltenango when the great K'iche' warrior Tecún Umán was slain. In October 1902 the Volcán Santa María erupted showering the city with half a metre of dust. An ash cloud soared 8.6 km into the air and some 1500 people were killed by volcanic fallout and gas. A further 3000 people died a short while later from malaria due to plagues of mosquitoes which had not been wiped out by the blast. Some 20 years on a new volcano, which was born after the 1902 eruption, began to erupt. This smaller volcano, Santiaguito, spews clouds of dust and ash on a daily basis and is considered one of the most dangerous volcanoes in the world. The city's prosperity, as seen by the grand neoclassical architecture in the centre, was built on the back of the success of the coffee *fincas* on the nearby coastal plain. This led to the country's first bank being established here. The town's **fiestas** are 9-17 September, Holy Week and October fiesta of La Virgen del Rosario.

Sights

The central park, **Parque Centro América,** is the focus of the city. It is surrounded by the cathedral, with its beautifully restored original colonial façade, and a number of elegant neoclassical buildings, constructed during the late 19th and early 20th century. The modern cathedral, **Catedral de la Diócesis de los Altos,** was constructed in 1899 and is set back behind the original. The surviving façade of the 1535 **Catedral del Espíritu Santo** is beautiful, intricately carved and with restored portions of murals on its right side. On the south side of the park is the **Casa de la Cultura**. Inside are the **Museo de la Marimba** with exhibits and documents relating to the 1871 Liberal Revolution. On the right-hand side of the building is the totally curious **Museo de Historia Natural** ⓘ *Mon-Fri 0800-1200, 1400-1800, US$0.90*. Deformed stuffed animals are cheek by jowl with pre-Columbian pottery, sports memorabilia, fizzy drink bottles, a lightning-damaged mirror and dinosaur remains. It satisfies the most morbid of curiosities with its displays of a two-headed calf, Siamese twin pigs, an eight-legged goat, and a strange sea creature that looks like an alien, known as *Diabillo del Mar* (little sea devil). On the park's southwest side is the **Museo de Arte**, with a collection of contemporary Guatemalan art, and the **Museo del Ferrocarril Nacional de los Altos** ⓘ *7 Calle and 12 Av, Mon-Fri 0800-1200, 1400-1800, US$0.90*, recounting the story of an electric railway between Xela and the Pacific slope. The **Banco de Occidente,** founded in 1881, and the first bank to opened in Guatemala, dominates the northern edge of the park. The overly wired up **Municipalidad** straddles the eastern edge of the park with its neoclassical columns. Its first building blocks were laid in 1881, but it wasn't completed until 1897. The stately **Teatro Municipal** (1892-1896) is on 14 Avenida y 1 Calle and can be visited outside of performance hours. Restored at a cost of four million quetzales it has an imposing presence. To its left, on Avenida 14 "A", is the Teatro Roma. Building began in 1898, but was not completed until 1931, when it became the first cinema to open in Guatemala. It was restored in 2000 as a theatre with a capacity for 1400 and is open for performances. See page 595.

There is a sickly green modern church, the **Sagrado Corazón**, on the Parque Benito Juárez near the market. Inside is a gigantic, free-standing, Chagall-influenced painting with swooping angels, and Christ in a glass box, built into the picture. The church of **La Transfiguración** ⓘ *near the corner of 11 Calle and 5 Av, Zona 1*, houses he largest crucified Christ figure (San Salvador del Mundo) to be found in Central America – it is almost 3 m in height and now housed behind glass. At 20 Avenida and 4 Calle is the city's **Cementerio** ⓘ *0700-1900*. Inside are the remains of the

Quetzalteco President, Estrada Cabrera (1898-1920) in a small cream neoclassical temple. Behind his tomb are the unmarked graves of a large number of cholera victims wiped out in a 19th-century epidemic. Manuel Lisandra Barillas (Guatemalan President 1885-1892) is also entombed here. There is a small patio area known as Colonia Alemana lined with graves of German residents; a large area where those that died as martyrs in the civil war lie; and a memorial to those that perished in the September Revolution of 1897.

North of Quetzaltenango » pp593-598.

Heading south to Quetzaltenango from Cuatro Caminos you pass the small *ladino* town of **Salcajá**, where *jaspé* skirt material has been woven since 1861. If you fancy a taste or a whiff of some potent liquor before bracing yourself for an entry into Quetzaltenango then this is the place to halt. It is worth a visit not only for the booze but its famous church – the oldest in Central America – and for its textiles, often seen being produced in the streets. In 1524 the first church in Central America was founded

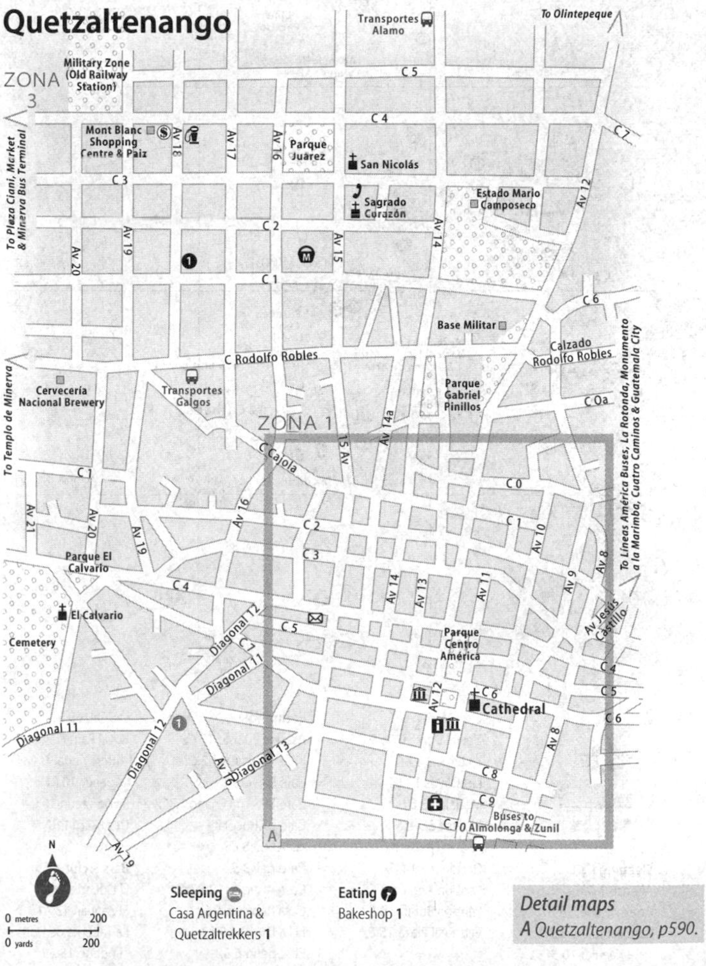

by the conquering Spaniards. **San Jacinto** is a small church on 6 Avenida y 2 Calle, the church is being restored and may not always be open. *Caldo de frutas*, a highly alcoholic drink with quite a kick, is not openly sold but is made in the town and drunk on festive occasions. It is illegal to drink it in public places. It is a concoction of *nances*, cherries, peaches, apples and *quinces* and is left to ferment in rum. There is also *rompope*, a drink made with eggs. **Salcajá** is a town that also revolves around textiles with shops on every street. Yarn is tied and dyed, untied, and wraps are then stretched around telephone poles along the road or on the riverside. One of these can be seen outside San Jacinto church. **Market day** is Tuesday.

San Andrés Xecul is a small village in stunning surroundings with an extra- ordinarily lurid coloured church, 8 km north of Xela. Painted a deep-mustard yellow in 1900, its figurines, including angels, have been given blue wings and pastel-pink skirts. Climb the

Quetzaltenango centre

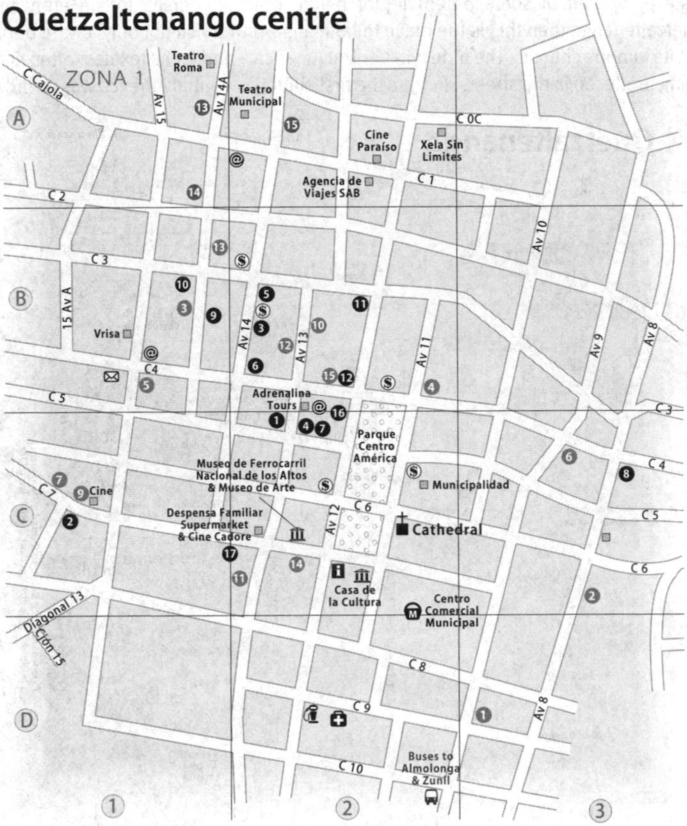

N

0 metres 100
0 yards 100

Sleeping
Altense 1 *D3*
Anexo Modelo 3 *B1*
Casa Iximulew 5 *B1*
Casa Kaehler 10 *B2*
Casa Mañen 6 *C3*
Hostal Don Diego 9 *C1*
Kiktem-Ja 11 *C2*
Los Olivos 12 *B2*
Modelo 13 *B1*
Moets Coffee & Guest House 7 *C1*
Occidental 14 *C2*
Pensión Andina 2 *C3*
Pensión Bonifaz 4 *B2*
Villa Real Plaza 15 *B2*

Eating
Asados Puente 17 *C2*
Blue Angel Café 2 *C1*
Café Baviera 1 *C2*
Café Taberna Enanos 7 *C2*
Café y Chocolate La Luna 8 *C3*
Cardinali 3 *B2*
Casa Antigua 12 *B2*
Casa Babylon 4 *C2*
El Delí Crepe 5 *B2*
El Kopetín 6 *B2*
Las Calas 9 *B1*
Royal París & Guatemaya Intercultural Travel Agency 10 *B1*
Salón Tecún 16 *C2*
Ut'z Hua 11 *B2*

Bars & clubs
El Duende 14 *A1*
El Zaguán 13 *A1*
La Taberna de Don Rodrigo 15 *A2*

hill a bit above the town and catch a glimpse of the fantastic dome – mulitcoloured like a beach ball. With your back to the church climb the cobbled street leading up the right-hand side of the plaza to a yellow and maroon chapel peering out across the valley. The view from here is spectacular. Market day is Thursday, opposite the church. The town's **fiestas** are on 21 November, 30 November and 1 December.

South of Quetzaltenango » *pp593-598.*

Souteast of Xela is **Cantel** which has the largest and oldest textile factory in the country. Sunday is **market** day and the town's **fiesta** is 12-18 August (main day 15). At Easter a passion play is performed. A little further on, on the outskirts of town, on the right-hand side (one minute on the bus), is the white **Copavic glass factory** ⓘ *T7763-8038, www.copavic.com, Mon-Fri 0500-1300, Sat 0500-1200*, where you can watch and photograph the workers blow the recycled glass.

Zunil

Pinned in by a very steep-sided valley is the town of Zunil, 9 km from Quetzaltenango. It is visited for the nearby hot thermal baths that many come to wallow in, and for its worship of its well-dressed idol San Simón (Maximón). The **market** is held on Mondays. The town's **fiesta** is 22-26 November (main day 25) and there is a very colourful Holy Week. The **church** is striking both inside and out. It has a large decorated altarpiece and a small shrine to murdered Bishop Gerardi at the altar. The façade is white with serpentine columns wrapped in carved ivy and decorated with dangling large coloured bulbs.

San Simón (Maximón) is worshipped in the town and is often dressed in different clothes at different times. A small charge is usually made for the upkeep. To the left of the church is the **Santa Ana Co-operative** which sells beautiful *huípiles*, shirt and skirt materials, as well as bags and bookmarks.

The nearby extinct **Volcán Pico Zunil**, rises to 3542 m to the southeast of the town. On its slopes are the **thermal baths of Fuentes Georginas** ⓘ *0700-1900, US$2, 70, children US1.30*, which you'll know you're approaching by the wafts of sulphurous fumes that come your way. There are several different-sized pools set into the mountainside surrounded by thick, luscious vegetation and enveloped in the steam that continuously rises up in wafts from the hot pools. There are spectacular views on the way to the baths.

The thermal baths of **Aguas Amargas** ⓘ *0800-1700, US$2, children, US$1.30*, are on Zunil Mountain below Fuentes Georginas. They are reached by following the road south and heading east (left) by Estancia de La Cruz. This road passes fields of flowers and would make a great trip on a bike.

El Viejo Palmar

This is Guatemala's Pompeii. The river that cuts through here flows directly down from the active Santiaguito volcanic cone following a series of serious lahars (mudflows of water and volcanic material) that took place in the 1990s. The small town of 10,000 was evacuated leaving an extraordinary legacy. In August 1998, the whole south end of the ghost town was destroyed by a massive lahar which crushed the church. This also shifted the course of the Río Nimá I which began to flow directly through the centre of the church remains. Very heavy erosion since has left the west front and the altar separated by a 30-m deep ravine – an unbelievable sight.

Volcán Santa María and Santiaguito

Santiaguito's mother is Santa María (3772 m), a rough 5½-hour climb (1500 m). You can see Santiaguito (2488 m) below, erupting mostly with ash blasts and sometimes lava flows. It is possible to camp at the summit, or on the saddle west of the summit, but it is cold and windy, but worth it because dawn provides views of the entire country's volcanic chain and an almighty shadow is cast across the area by Santa Maria's form. **Santiaguito** is a fairly new volcano that formed after the eruption of Santa María out of its crater. It erupts continuously on a daily basis throwing up ash. To see it erupting you need to climb Santa María where you will look down on this smaller volcano.

Do not attempt to climb Santiaguito – it is considered one of the most dangerous volcanoes in the world.

Laguna Chicabal

San Martín is where the two-hour climb to Laguna Chicabal ⓘ *0700-1800, US$2*, starts. This is a jelly-green lake, at 2712 m, in the crater of the extinct volcano (2900 m) of the same name, with wild white lilies, known as *cartucho,* growing at the edges. The Maya believe the waters are sacred and it is thought that if you swim in the lake you will become ill. The highlight of a trip here is the sight of the clouds tumbling down over the circle of trees that surround the lake, and then appearing to bounce on the surface before dispersing. Ceremonies of Maya initiation are held at the lake in early May, known as *Jueves de la Ascensión*. The walk from San Martín takes about two hours.

West of Quetzaltenango » *pp593-598.*

To Mexico from Quetzaltenango

It takes half an hour to reach **San Juan Ostuncalco**, 15 km away. It's a pleasant, prosperous town with a big white church noted for its good weekly **market** on Sunday and beautiful sashes worn by men. Its **fiesta**, Virgen de la Candelaria, is held on 29 January to 2 February. The road, which is paved, switchbacks 37 km down valleys and over pine-clad mountains to a plateau looking over the valley in which are San Pedro and San Marcos. **San Marcos** has a few places to stay and eat. It is a transport hub with little to see. **San Pedro Sacatepéquez** has a huge **market** on Thursday. The Maya women wear golden-purple skirts.

The extinct **Volcán Tajumulco**, at 4220 m, is the highest in Central America. Start very early in the day if you plan to return to San Marcos by nightfall. It's about a five-hour climb and a three-hour descent. Once you have reached the ridge on Tajumulco, turn right along the top of it; there are two peaks, the higher is on the right. The peak on the left (4100 m) is used for **shamanistic rituals**.

Dormant **Volcán Tacaná** (4093 m) on the Mexican border may be climbed from the village of Sibinal. Its last eruption was 1949, but there was activity in 2001, so check before climbing. It is the second-highest volcano in Guatemala with a 400-m wide crater and fumaroles on its flanks. Take a bus to Sibinal from San Marcos. It is a six-hour difficult climb to the summit and it's recommended that you ask for a guide in the village. About 15 km west of San Marcos the road begins its descent from 2500 m to the lowlands. In 53 km to **Malacatán** it drops to 366 m. It is a winding ride with continuous bends, but the scenery is attractive. There is accommodation.

The road to the coastal plain from San Juan Ostuncalco (see page 592) is the most attractive of all the routes down from the highlands, bypassing most of the small towns through quickly changing scenery as you lose height. After San Juan, go south for 1.5 km to **Concepción Chiquirichapa**, with a bright blue and yellow church, which is one of the wealthiest villages in the country. It has a small **market** early every Thursday morning and a **fiesta** on 5-9 December. About 6 km beyond is **San Martín Sacatepéquez**, which used to be known as San Martín Chile Verde, and is famous for its hot chillies. This village appears in Miguel Angel Asturias' *Mulata de Tal*. It stands in a windy, cold gash in the mountains. The slopes are superbly steep and farmed, giving fantastic vistas on the climb up and down from Laguna Chicabal

Border essentials: Guatemala-Mexico

El Carmen-Talismán
The international bridge over the Río Suchiate at Talismán into Mexico is 18 km west of Malacatán. The last staging post in Guatemala is El Carmen.
Guatemalan immigration Open 24 hrs. It is a 200-m walk between the 2 border posts. If entering by car, especially a rented car, be prepared for red tape, miscellaneous charges, vehicle fumigation and frustration.
Sleeping Hospedaje El Paso (B-C), T7776-9474, 13 rooms with bath, TV, a/c, cheaper without.
Transport For long-distance travel see Transport, Guatemala City. Travelling by bus to Mexico is quicker from Quetzaltenango than from San Marcos. Most traffic seems to go via Coatepeque and not via San Marcos. However, from Quetzaltenango, there are frequent buses to Talismán via San Marcos or Coatepeque; buses from Xela marked 'Talismán' usually involve a change in Malacatán, 40 mins from the border. From San Pedro Sacatepéquez , there are frequent local buses from 0430-1630 to Malacatán, from where *colectivos*, often crowded, will get you to the border. Or, take a bus from Quetzaltenango to Retalhuleu, 1½ hrs, US$0.78, and then another to the border, 2 hrs, US$1.85. **Línea Dorada**, www.tikanmayaworld.com, goes from Guatemala City to Tapacuhula at 0800, US$20. This border is not used much by heavy transport. Hitchhikers will find Tecún Umán better.

(see below). The men wear very striking long red and white striped tunics, beautifully embroidered around the hem. **Market** day is Sunday. The **fiesta** runs from 7-12 November (main day November 11).

Sleeping

Quetzaltenango *p587, map p590*
At Easter, 12-18 Sep and Christmas, rooms need to be booked well in advance.
L-A **Pensión Bonifaz**, 4 Calle, 10-50, T7765-1111, Zona 1. 75 clean, comfortable rooms with TV. Pool (noisy at times) which is occasionally heated. Good restaurant and bar. Parking.
A **Casa Mañen**, 9a Av, 4-11, Zona 1, T7765-0786, www.ComeSeeIt.com. Reports are consistently good, serves great breakfasts and friendly staff offer a very warm welcome. Room 2 is a great option with a bed on a mezzanine. Some rooms have microwave, fridge and TV. All are comfortable, and furnished with attractive wooden accessories. There is a small, pretty courtyard area, secure parking.
B **Modelo**, 14 Av "A", 2-31, Zona 1, T7761-2529. Friendly hotel with 20 rooms with TV, some set around a garden patio. Hot showers, restaurant and bargain breakfasts from 0715. Safe parking.
B **Villa Real Plaza**, 4 Calle, 12-22, Zona 1, T7761-4045. Dignified colonial building, 58 rooms with TV. Restaurant has good vegetarian food, and is good value. Parking.
C **Anexo Hotel Modelo**, 14 Av "A", 3-22, Zona 1, T7761-2606. 9 rooms with private bath and TV, good value. Part of Modelo.
C **Kiktem-Ja**, 13 Av, 7-18, Zona 1, T7761-4304. A central location with 16 colonial-style rooms, nicely furnished, locally made blankets on the beds, wooden floors, all with bath, hot water, open fires, car parking inside gates.
C **Los Olivos**, 13 Av, 3-22, T7761-0215, Zona 1. 26 pleasant rooms above parking area with private bathroom, TV and a restaurant with cheap breakfasts and meals.
D **Casa Kaehler**, 13 Av, 3-33, Zona 1, T7761-2091, www.casakaehler.com. 6 very nice old rooms, clean, hot water all day in private bathrooms, 1 room with bath, some rooms are very cold though. Breakfast included.

D Occidental, 7 Calle, 12-23, Zona 1, T7765-4069. 10 rooms, 1 of the cheapest budget rooms right in the town centre. Rooms lack natural light, but there's hot water and the town's on your doorstep.

D-E Altense, 9 Calle, 8-48, Zona 1, T7765-4648. 16 rooms with bath, hot water, parking, secure and friendly. However, if your room is on the 9 Av side, you'll be woken by rush-hour traffic. This is a good town centre deal for single travellers. Recommended.

E Casa Iximulew, 15 Av, 4-59, Zona 1, www.xelapages.com/iximulew/index.htm. 1 twin room, and 1 single room, hot water at low pressure.

E Moets Coffee & Guest House, 7 Calle 15-24, T5585-4213. 4 single (F per person) and 1 double room. Long stay discounts possible. Restaurant and bar.

E Pensión Andina, 8 Av, 6-07, Zona 1, T7761-4012. Private bathrooms, hot water, friendly, clean, sunny patio, restaurant, good value, parking.

E-F Hostal Don Diego, 7 Calle, 15-20, Zona 1, T7761-6497, dondiegoxela@hotmail.com. Sweet hostel, set about an interior courtyard with rooms with shared bathroom. Hot water and breakfast included. Bright and clean. Weekly and monthly rents available.

F Casa Argentina, Diagonal 12, 8-37, Zona 1, T7761-0010, lemovi@yahoo.com. 25 clean rooms, hot water, 10 shared bathrooms, cheaper in 18-bed dorm, new rooms with private bath, cooking facilities with purified water, friendly, laundry service. Monthly room rates, US$100.

Zunil *p591*

C Turicentro Fuentes Georginas, 6 cold bungalows with 2 double beds and 2 bungalows with 3 single beds. They have cold showers, fireplaces with wood, electricity from 1700-2200 and barbecue grills for guests' use near the baths. Guests can use the baths after public closing times. Reasonably priced restaurant with breakfasts, snacks and drinks, 0800-1800.

C-D Las Cumbres Eco Saunas y Gastronomía, T5210-3062. Daily 0700-1800. Just beyond Zunil on the left-hand side of the road heading to the coast (Km 210). This is just the place for some R&R with saunas emitting natural steam from the geothermal activity nearby. There are 12 rooms, with sauna, cheaper without sauna. There are separate saunas and jacuzzis for day visitors, and a restaurant serving wholesome regional food and natural juices. Highly recommended.

Eating

Quetzaltenango *p587, map p590*

TTT-TT Cardinali, 14 Av, 3-25, Zona 1. Owned by Benito, a NY Italian, great Italian food, including large pizzas with 31 varieties: 2 for 1 on Tue and Thu; tasty pastas of 20 varieties, extensive wine list. Recommended. Also does home delivery in 30 mins (T7761-0924).

TTT-TT El Kopetín, 14 Av, 3-51, Zona 1. Friendly, good, meat and seafood dishes, try the fish cooked in garlic.

TTT-TT Las Calas, 14 Av "A", 3-21, Zona 1. Breakfasts, salads, soups, paella and pastas served around a courtyard with changing art hanging from walls. The food is tasty with delicious bread to accompany, but small portions are served. The breakfast service is far too slow. Adjoining bar. Mon-Sat.

TTT-TT Restaurante Royal París, 14 Av "A", 3-06, Zona 1. Delicious food (try the fish in a creamy mushroom sauce), excellent choices, including vegetarian. Also cheap options. Run by Stéphane and Emmanuelle. Recommended. Live music from 2000 on Fri. French and Italian films on Tue.

TT Salón Tecún, Pasaje Enríquez, off the park at 12 Av y 4 Calle, Zona 1. Bar, local food, breakfasts also, TV, always popular with gringos and locals. They are often looking for bar workers.

TT Ut'z Hua, Av 12, 3-02, Zona 1. This prettily decorated restaurant with purple tablecloths does typical food, which is always very good and filling. Don't miss the *pollo con mole* or fish. Recommended.

TT-T Asados Puente, 7 Calle, 13-29. Lots of veggie dishes witH tofu and tempeh. Also ceviche. Popular with expats. Run by Ken Cielatka and Eva Melgar. Some profits go towards helping ill children.

TT-T Casa Antigua, 12 Av, 3-26. Savoury and sweet crêpes, baguettes and light meals served up in an 1814 house in a courtyard or inside. Bar available.

Café Taberna Enanos, 5 Calle near Av 12 and Parque Central, Zona 1. Good cheap breakfast, also has *menú del día*. Mon-Sat 0715-2000.

El Deli Crepe, 14 Av, 3-15, Zona 1. Good tacos, *almuerzo* with soup, great milkshakes, savoury and sweet crêpes, juicy *fajitas* that arrive steaming, but the restaurant is a little dirty around the edges.

Cafés and bakeries

Bakeshop at 18 Av, 1-40, Zona 3. A Mennonite bakery that is Xela's answer to *dulce* heaven. They bake a whole range of cookies, muffins, breads and cakes and sells fresh yoghurt and cheeses. Tue and Fri 0900-1800 so get there early as the goodies go really fast.

Blue Angel Café, 7 Calle, 15-79, Zona 1. Great salads, light meals, service a little slow though, movies shown on a monthly rotation, useful noticeboard.

Café Baviera, 5 Calle, 13-14, Zona 1. Open 0700-2000. Good cheap meals and excellent pies, huge cake portions (try the carrot cake) and coffee in large premises, with walls lined from ceiling to floor with old photos and posters. Good for breakfasts, but a little on the expensive side. Popular, but lacks warmth.

Café y Chocolate La Luna, 8 Av, 4-11, Zona 1. Delicious hot chocolate with or without added luxuries, good cheap snacks, also top chocolates and *pasteles* (the strawberry and cream pie is recommended), pleasant atmosphere in a colonial house decorated with moon symbols, fairy lights, and old photos (and a bed pan in the women's toilet!), a good meeting place.

Casa Babylon, 13 Av y 5 Calle, Zona 1. Enormous sandwiches (with veggie options) and crêpes. Recommended. Daily 1230-2230.

Entertainment

Quetzaltenango *p587, map p590*

Bars and clubs

El Duende, 14 Av "A", 1-42, Zona 1. Popular café-bar, 1800-2330. A favourite among Guatemalans and gringos.

El Zaguán, 14 Av "A", A-70, Zona 1. A disco-bar Wed, Thu 1900-2430, Fri, Sat 2100-2430, US$3.25, drink included; plays salsa music.

La Taberna de Don Rodrigo, 14 Av, Calle C-47, Zona 1. Cosy bar, reasonable food served in dark wood atmosphere, draught beer.

Salón Tecún, Pasaje Enríquez, 12 Av y 4 Calle, Zona 1. See Eating, above, for more details.

Cinemas

Cine Sofía, 7 Calle 15-18. Mon-Fri 1800, US$1.35. **Cadore**, 13 Av and 7 Calle, next to Despensa Familiar, Zona 1. **Cinema Paraíso Café**, 1 Calle, 12-20, art house, some in Spanish only, 2 showings daily, 3 at weekends, US$1.30.

Dance

Tropica Latina, in the **Marilyn Monroe Mansion**, 13 Av 5-38, T5892-8861. Classes Mon-Sat US$4-9, US$3.25 per hr.

Theatre

Teatro Municipal, 14 Av and 1 Calle, main season May-Nov, theatre, opera, etc, tickets US$7.

Shopping

Quetzaltenango *p587, map p590*

Bookshops

Bellas Letras, 3 Calle, 12-31 and Vrisa, 15 Av, 3-64, T7761-3237, has a good range of English-language second-hand books.

Markets

The **main market** is at Templo de Minerva on the western edge of town (take the local bus, US$0.10); at the southeast corner of Parque Centro América is the **Centro Comercial Municipal**, a shopping centre with craft and textile shops on the upper levels, food, clothes, etc below. There is another **market** at 2 Calle y 16 Av, Zona 3, south of Parque Benito Juárez.

Supermarkets

Centro Comercial Mont Blanc, Paiz, 4 Calle between 18-19 Av, Zona 3. **La Pradera**, near the Minerva Terminal. **Despensa Familiar**, 13 Av, 6-94.

North of Quetzaltenango *p589*

The smallest bottle of bright yellow *rompope* is sold in various shops around Salcajá, including the **Fábrica de Pénjamo**, 2 Av, 4-03, Zona 1, US$1.55, and it slips down the throat very nicely!

Activities and tours

Quetzaltenango *p587, map p590*

Tour operators

When taking a tour up any of the volcanoes make sure your guides stay with you all the time; it can get dangerous when the cloud rolls down.

Adrenalina Tours, inside Pasaje Enríquez, T7761-4509, www.adrenalinatours.com. Numerous tours are on offer including bike, fishing, rafting, horse riding, rock climbing and volcano tours as well as packages to Belize, Honduras and the Petén and trips to Huehue and Todos Santos. Highly recommended. Also offers Central American packages via **Andamos Travel**, www.andamostravel.com.

Agencia de Viajes SAB, 1 Calle, 12-35, T7761-6402. Good for cheap flights.

Guatemaya Intercultural Travel Agency, 14 Av "A", 3-06, T/F7765-0040, www.xela pages.com/guatemaya. Very helpful.

Mayaexplor, T7761-5057, www.maya explor.com. Run by Thierry Roquet who arranges a variety of trips around Xela and around the country. He can also arrange excursions into Mexico, Belize and Honduras and treks, eg Nebaj-Todos Santos. French-speaking. His website offers useful information for travellers. A proportion of funds goes towards local development projects. Recommended.

Quetzaltrekkers, based inside **Casa Argentina** at Diagonal 12, 8-37, T7765-5895, www.quetzaltrekkers.com. This recommended, established, non-profit agency is known for its 3-day hike (Sat am-Mon pm) from Xela across to Lake Atitlán. Proceeds go to the **Escuela de la Calle School** for kids at risk, and a dorm for homeless children. Also trek from Nebaj-Todos Santos, 5 days, 1st Mon of the month. Full-moon hike up Santa María. Day hikes possible. Hiking volunteers are also needed for a 3-month minimum period: hiking experience and reasonable Spanish required.

Zunil *p591*

See **Las Cumbres Eco Saunas y Gastronomía**, T5210-3062, under Sleeping, above.

Transport

Quetzaltenango *p587, map p590*

Bus

Local City buses run between 0630 and 1900. Between the town centre and **Minerva Terminal**, bus No 6, Santa Fe, US$0.10, 15-30 mins, depending on traffic. Catch the bus at the corner of 4 Calle and 13 Av by Pasaje Enríquez. Buses to the Rotonda leave from the corner of 11 Av and 10 Calle, US$0.10, or catch bus No 6, 10 or 13, from Av 12 y 3 Calle as they come down to the park, 15 mins. To catch buses to **San Francisco El Alto**, **Momostenango**, the **south coast** and **Zunil**, get off the local bus at the Rotonda, then walk a couple of steps away from the road to step into a feeder road where they all line up.

Long distance To **Guatemala City**, Galgos, Calle Rodolfo Robles, 17-43, Zona 1, T7761-2248, 1st-class buses, 6 a day from 0300-1615, US$3.90, 4 hrs, will carry bicycles (mixed reports on services to the city); **Marquensita** several a day (office in the capital 21 Calle, 1-56, Zona 1), leaves from the Minerva Terminal, US$3.90, comfortable, 4 hrs. **Líneas América**, from 7 Av, 3-33, Zona 2, T7761-2063, US$3.60, 4 hrs, between 0515-2000, 7 daily. **Transportes Alamo** from 14 Av, 5-15, Zona 3, T7763-5044, between 0430 and 1430, 5-7 a day, US$3.90, 4 hrs. For **Antigua**, change at Chimaltenango (Galgos, US$2 to Chimaltenango, **Marquensita**, US$2.90). The following destinations are served by buses leaving from the Minerva Terminal, Zona 3 and the Rotonda. To **Almolonga**, via **Cantel**, every 30 mins, US$0.20, 10 mins. (Buses to Almolonga and Zunil not via Cantel, leave from the corner of 10 Av and 10 Calle, Zona 1.) To **Chichicastenango** with **Transportes Veloz Quichelense de Hilda Esperanza**, at 0500, 0600, 0930, 1045, 1100, 1300, 1400, 1530, US$1.05, 2½ hrs. To **Cuatro Caminos** US$0.18, 30 mins. To **Huehuetenango** 0500-1730, every 30 mins, US$1.05, 2.5 hrs, and **Transportes Velásquez** to Huehuetenango, every 30 mins 0500-1730, US$1.05, 2½ hrs. To **La Mesilla** at 0500, 0600, 0700, 0800, 1300, 1400 with **Transportes Unión Fronteriza**, US$1.60, 4 hrs. To **Los Encuentros**, US$1.30. To **Malacatán**, US$2, 5 hrs. To **Momostenango**, every 2hrs, US$0.52, 2 hrs. To **Panajachel**, with Transportes Morales, at 1000, 1200, 1500, US$1.60, 2½-3 hrs. To **Retalhuleu**, US$0.90, 1½ hrs. To **Salcajá**, every 30 mins, US$0.20, 15 mins. To **San Andrés Xecul** every 2 hrs, US$0.26, 1 hr. To **San Cristóbal Totonicapán**, every 30 mins, US$0.26, 20 mins. To **San Francisco El Alto** every 1 hr, US$0.40. To **San Marcos**, every 30 mins, US$0.80, 1 hr. To **San Martín Sacatepéquez/ San Martín Chile Verde**, US$0.40, 1 hr. To **Santiago Atitlán**, with Ninfa de Atitlán at 0800, 1100, 1230, 1630, 4½ hrs. To **Tecún Umán** every 30 mins, 0500-1400, US$1.60, 4 hrs. To **Totonicapán**, every 20 mins, US$0.33, 1 hr. To **Zunil**, every 30 mins, US$0.26, 20-30 mins.

International: Adrenalina Tours, see Tour operators, runs a shuttle to and from San Cristóbal de las Casas, Mexico, US$35.

Car

Car hire **Tabarini Renta Autos**, 9 Calle, 9-21, Zona 1, T7763-0418.
Mechanic José Ramiro Muñoz R, 1 Calle, 19-11, Zona 1, T7761-8204. Also Goodyear Taller at the Rotonda and for motorbikes Moto Servicio Rudy, 2 Av, 3-48, Zona 1, T7765-5433.

Taxi

Found all over town, notably lined up along Parque Centro América. A journey within town is US$2.60. **Taxis Xelaju**, T7761-4456.

North of Quetzaltenango *p589*

Bus See also Transport, Quetzaltenango, above. All buses heading to Quetzaltenango from Cuatro Caminos pass through **Salcajá**, 10 mins. Buses from Xela to **Olintepeque**, US$0.13. From Xela to **San Andrés Xecul**, US$0.22, 30 mins. Or take any bus heading to Cuatro Caminos and getting off at the Esso station on the left-hand side, and then almost doubling back on yourself to take the San Andrés road. There are pick-ups from here, US$0.65. From Xela to **Almolonga**, US$0.13.

South of Quetzaltenango *p591*

Bus See also Transport, Quetzaltenango. **Cantel** is 15 mins by bus (11 km), and US$0.13 from Xela on the way to Zunil, but you need to take the bus marked for Cantel Fábrica and Zunil, not Almolonga and Zunil.

From **Zunil** to Xela via Almolonga leaves from the bridge. Walk down the left-hand side of the church to the bottom of the hill, take a left and you'll see the buses the other side of the bridge, US$0.20.
Fuentes Georginas. Reached either by walking the 8 km uphill just to the south of Zunil, 2 hrs (300 m ascent; take the right fork after 4 km, but be careful as robbery has occurred here), by pick-up truck in 15 mins (US$10 return with a 1 hr wait), or hitch a ride. If you come by bus to Zunil and are walking to the Fuentes, don't go down into town with the bus, but get off on the main road at the Pepsi stand and walk to the entrance road, which is visible 100 m away on the left.

El Viejo Palmar *p591*

Bus Just before San Felipe, and just before the Puente Samalá III, if you're heading south, is the turn to the right for El Viejo Palmar. Take any bus heading to the south coast, and asked to be dropped off at the entrance and walk. Or, take a pick-up from San Felipe park. Ask for Beto or Brígido.
Taxi From Xela round trip is US$20.

Volcán Santa María and Santiaguito *p591*

Bus To reach the volcano take the bus to **Llano del Pinal**, 7 km away, from the Minerva Terminal (every 30 mins, last bus back 1800). Get off at the crossroads and follow the dirt road towards the right side of the volcano until it sweeps up the right (about 40 mins) where you should take the footpath to the left (where it is marked for some distance); bear right at the saddle where another path comes in from the left, but look carefully as it is easily missed.

Laguna Chicabal *p592*

Bus/car The last bus to **Quetzaltenango** leaves at 1900, 1 hr. Parking at the entrance, US$1.30. It is a 40-min walk from the car park (and you'll need a sturdy vehicle if you attempt the steep first ascent in a car).

To Mexico from Quetzaltenango *p592*

Bus Volcán Tajumulco can be reached by getting to the village of **San Sebastián** from San Marcos. There are buses from San Marcos that take about 2 hrs.

Directory

Quetzaltenango *p587, map p590*
Banks Many banks on Parque Centro América. Non American Express TCs are difficult to change here. Maestro can't be used in ATMs. There is a Bancared, 24 hr Visa ATM on the park next to Banrural. Banco Industrial, corner of 5 Calle y 11 Av, 24 hr Visa ATM, Visa accepted. G&T Continental, 14 Av, 3-17. You can take out up to US$65 on MasterCard here. For more of an advance against MasterCard go to the Hyper Paiz shopping mall, beyond the Templo de Minerva. **Embassies and consulates** Mexico, 21 Av, 8-64, Zona 3, T7767-5542, Mon-Fri 0800-1100, take photocopies of your passport. **Emergencies** Police: T7761-5805; Fire: T7761-2002; Red Cross: T7761-2746. **Internet** Internet, 15 Av, 3-51, international phone calls also. Lots of places around town. **Language schools** See also the box on page 549. Many of Xela's schools can be found at www.xelapages.com/schools.htm. There are many schools, which offer individual tuition, accommodation with families, extra-curricular activities and excursions. Some also offer Mayan languages. Several schools fund community development projects, and students are invited to participate with voluntary work. Some, but not all, schools are non-profit making; enquire carefully. Extra-curricular activities are generally better organized at the larger schools. Prices start from US$130 per week including accommodation, but rise in Jun-Aug to US$1150 and up. The following have been recommended: Centro de Estudios de Español Pop Wuj, 1 Calle, 17-72, T/F7761-8286, www.pop-wuj.org. Guatemalensis, 19 Av, 2-14, Zona 1, T7765-1384, www.geocities.com/spanland/. Instituto Central América (ICA), 19 Av, 1-47 Calle, Zona 1, T/F7763-1871. INEPAS (Instituto de Estudios Español y Participación en Ayuda Social), 15 Av, 4-59, T7765-1308, www.inepas.org. Keen on social projects and has already founded a primary school in a Maya village, extremely welcoming. International Language School English Club, Diagonal 4, 9-71, Zona 9, T7767-3506. Harry Danvers is an expert on indigenous culture, worth a visit. You can also learn K'iche' and Mam. Juan Sisay Spanish School, 15 Av, 8-38, Zona 1, T7761-1586, www.juansisay.com. Kie-Balam, Diagonal 12, 4-46, Zona 1, T7761-1636, kie_balam@hotmail.com. Offers conversation classes in the afternoon in addition to regular hours. La Paz, Diagonal 11, 7-36, T/F7761-2159, escuela_lapaz@hotmail.com. Latin Arts, 10 Av, C-09, T/F7761-0424. Minerva Spanish School, 24 Av, 4-39, Zona 3, T7767-4427, www.xelapages.com/minerva. Proyecto Lingüístico Quetzalteco de Español, 5 Calle, 2-40, Zona 1, T/F7765-1061, www.hermandad.com. Recommended. Proyecto Lingüístico 'Santa María', 14 Av "A", 1-26, T/F7765-1262. Volunteer opportunities and free internet access. Ulew Tinimit, 7 Av, 3-18, T/F7761-6242.Sakribal, 6 Calle, 7-42, Zona 1, T7763-0717, www.sakribal.com. Community projects are available. Utatlán, 12 Av, 14-32, Pasaje Enríquez, Zona 1, T7763-0446, www.xelapages.com/utatlan. Voluntary work opportunities, one of the cheaper schools. **Laundry** Minimax, 14 Av, C-47. Lavandería Pronto, 7 Calle, 13-25, good service. Lavandería El Centro, 15 Av, 3-51, Zona 1, very good service. **Medical services** San Rafael Hospital, 9 Calle, 10-41, T7761-2956. Hospital Rodolfo Robles, a private hospital on Diagonal 11, Zona 1, T7761-4229. Hospital Privado Quetzaltenango, Calle Rodolfo Robles, 23-51, Zona 1, T7761-4381. **Post office** 15 Av y 4 Calle. **Telephone** Telgua, 15 Av "A" y 4 Calle. Kall Shop, 8 Av, 4-24, Zona 1. **Voluntary work** Asociación Hogar Nuevos Horizontes, nhcoordinadoras@hotmail.com, or Aida T7761-6122. Entre mundos, T7761-2179, www.entremundos.org, puts people in touch with opportunities. Hogar de Niños, Llanos de Urbina, Cantel, T7761-1526, hogardeninos@hotmail.com.

Southern Guatemala

The southern coastal plain of Guatemala supports many plantations of coffee, sugar and tropical fruit trees and its climate is unbearably hot and humid. Amid the fincas *some of the most curious archaeological finds have been unearthed, a mixture of monument styles such as Maya and Olmec, including Abaj Takalik, the cane field stones at Santa Lucía Cotzumalguapa and the big 'Buddhas' of Monte Alto.*

On the coast are the black-sand beaches and nature reserves of the popular and laid-back Monterrico and Sipacate resorts, where nesting turtles burrow in the sand and masses of birds take to the skies around. Casting a shadow over the coast, the Central Highland volcanoes of Lake Atitlán, and the Antigua trio of Fuego, Acatenango and Agua, look spectacular, looming on the horizon above the lowlands. ▸▸ *For Sleeping, Eating and other listings, see pages 603-607.*

Ins and outs

Numerous buses travel from Guatemala City and along the CA2 Highway that runs through the transport hub of Escuintla and through towns either side to the Mexican and El Salvadorean borders. ▸▸ *For further details, see Transport, page 605.*

Guatemala City to the Pacific coast

The main road from the capital heads to Escuintla, which connects Guatemala City with all the Pacific ports. There is also a direct route to Escuintla from Antigua. South of Guatemala City is **Amatitlán** on the banks of the lake of the same name. The lake is seriously polluted. The main reason for coming here would be for the **Day of the Cross** on 3 May when the Christ figure is removed from the church and floated out of a boat amid candles and decorations. A new *teleférico* has opened on the lake. **Palín** has a Sunday **market** in a plaza under an enormous ceiba tree. The textiles are exceptional, but are increasingly difficult to find. There are great views of Pacaya to the east as you head down to the coast, Volcán Agua to the northwest, and the Pacific lowlands to the west. An unpaved road runs northwest from here to Antigua via **Santa María de Jesús**. The town's **fiesta** is on 24-30 July. **Escuintla** is a large, unattractive provincial centre in a rich tropical valley. It is essentially a transport hub for travellers in the area.

Puerto San José, Chulamar and Iztapa

South of Escuintla the fast tarmacked highway heads to Puerto San José. Puerto San José used to be the country's second-largest port and first opened for business (especially the coffee trade) in 1853. The climate is hot, the streets and most of the beaches dirty, and at weekends the town fills up with people from the capital. Fishing is available (see under Iztapa below), and there are swimming beaches near by, but beware of the strong undercurrent. Some 5 km to the west of Puerto San José is Chulamar, a popular beach at weekends with good bathing. Iztapa is world renowned for deep-sea fishing, so much so that Guatemala's sailfish sport fishing was ranked as the best in the world in 1995. Sail fish, bill fish, marlin, tuna, dorado, roosterfish, yellowfin and snapper are to be found in large numbers. See Tour operators, page 605 for further details. The **Chiquimulilla Canal** runs either side of Puerto San José parallel to the coast, for close to 100 km. From here a trip can be taken through the canal by *lancha* to the old Spanish port of Iztapa, now a bathing resort a short distance to the east.

Monterrico

» pp603-607. Colour map 5, C2.

Monterrico is a small, black-sand resort where the sunsets are a rich orange and the waves crash spectacularly on to the shore. If you are in the area between September and January you can sponsor a baby turtle's waddle to freedom by taking part in a competition. The baby turtles are lined up just before sunset for a race to the sea.

Ins and outs

The landing stage is 10 minutes' walk from the ocean front, where you'll find the main restaurants and places to stay. When you step off the dock take the first left, and keep left, which heads directly to the main cluster of beach hotels. This road is known as Calle del Proyecto or Calle del Muelle. Walking straight on from the dock takes you to the main drag in town. When you get to the main drag and want to walk to the main group of hotels, take a left along the beach or take the sandy path to the left one block back from the beach where the sand is a tiny bit easier to walk on.

Sights

Monterrico's popularity is growing fast but mainly as a weekend and holiday resort with views that are undisturbed by high-rise blocks. All the hotels, mostly rustic and laid-back, are lined up along the beach, and there are a few shops and *comedores,* not linked to hotels, in the village of just 1500 people. The village is surrounded by canals carpeted in aquatic plants and mangrove swamps with bird and turtle reserves in their midst. These areas make up the **Monterrico Nature Reserve**. Anteater, armadillo, racoon and weasel live in the area. It is worth taking a boat trip at sunrise or sunset, to see migratory North and South American birds, including flamingo. However, the real stars in this patch are the olive ridleys – *Parlama blanca* and *Parlama negra* turtles, which lay eggs between July and October, and the Baule turtle, which lays between between October and February. There is a **turtle hatchery** ⓘ *daily 0800-1200, 1400-1700, US$1.* Just behind the hatchery there are 300 breeding crocodiles, 150 turtles and iguanas. The turtle liberation event takes place every Saturday during the aforementioned period at 1700.

Santa Lucía Cotzumalguapa

» pp603-607. Colour map 5, C2.

Amid the sugar-cane fields and *fincas* of this Pacific town lie an extraordinary range of carved stones and images with influences from pre-Maya civilizations, believed mostly to be ancient Mexican cultures, including the Izapa civilization from the Pacific coast area of Mexico near the Guatemalan border. The town is just north of the Pacific Highway where some of the hotels and banks are.

Ins and outs

You can visit all the sites on foot. However, you are advised not to go wandering in and out of the cane fields at the Bilbao site as there have been numerous assaults in the past You can walk along the tarmacked road north to the El Baúl sites (6 km and 8 km respectively from town), but there is no shade, so take lots of water. Ask for directions. There is an occasional 'Río Santiago' bus, which goes as far as Colonia Maya, close to the El Baúl hilltop. Only workers' buses go to **Finca El Baúl** in the morning, returning at night. To get to the museum, walk east along the Pacific Highway and take a left turn into the *finca* site. Alternatively, take a taxi from town (next to the plaza) and negotiate a trip to all four areas. They will charge around US$20.

Border essentials: Guatemala-Mexico

Tecún Umán-Ciudad Hidalgo
The Pacific Highway goes west from Escuintla to the Mexican border at Ciudad Tecún Umán, some 200 km away, passing Siquinalá, where there is a brand new bypass that emerges the other side of Santa Lucía Cotzumalguapa (buses run through the centre of these places), and on to Mazatenango (see page 602) and Retalhuleu (see page 602). The border is separated by the Río Suchiate from the Mexican town of Ciudad Hidalgo.

Guatemalan immigration
The 1 km bridge over the river separates the 2 border posts. For a fee, boys will help you with your luggage. Normally open 24 hrs.

Mexican consulates See Quetzaltenango and Reu.

Sleeping **Hotel Don José** (**D**), Calle Real del Comercio, T7776-8164, rooms with bath. **Hotel Villazul** (**D**), 3 Av, 5-28, T7776-8827. Rooms with bath and a/c.

Transport Buses run from the Mexican side of the border to Tapachula, 30 mins. To Guatemala City, US$5.20, run by **Fortaleza**, 4 direct buses daily, 5 hrs. Frequent slower buses via Reu and Mazatenango. *Colectivo* from Coatepeque, US$0.52. See also Talismán, page 593, for crossing into Mexico.

Directory There are numerous banks and money changers.

Sights

There is considerable confusion about who carved the range of monuments and stelae scattered around the town. However, it is safe to say that the style of the monuments found in the last 150 years is a blend of a number of pre-Columbian styles. Some say, that the prominent influence is Toltec, the ancestors of the Maya K'iche', Kaqchikel, Tz'utujil and Pipiles. It is thought the Tolteca-Pipil had been influenced in turn by the Classic culture from Teotihuacán, a massive urban state northeast of the present Mexico City, which had its zenith in the seventh century AD. However, some experts say that there is no concrete evidence to suggest that the Pipiles migrated as early as AD 400 or that they were influenced by Teotihuacán. All in all, the cultural make-up of this corner of Guatemala may never be known.

Do not believe any taxi driver who tells you that Las Piedras (the stones) have been moved from the cane fields to the museum because of the increasing number of assaults.

Four main points of interest entice visitors to the area. Bilbao, El Baúl, Finca El Baúl and the Museo de Cultura Cotzumalguapa. The remnants at **Bilbao**, first re-discovered in 1860, are mainly buried beneath the sugar cane but monuments found above ground show pre-Maya influences. It is thought that the city was inhabited between 1200 BC-AD 800. There are four large boulders – known locally as *Las Piedras* – in sugar-cane fields, which can be reached on foot from the tracks leading from the end of 4 Avenida in town. **El Baúl** is a Late Classic ceremonial centre, 6 km north of Santa Lucía, with two carved stone pieces to see; most of its monuments were built between AD 600-900. **Finca El Baúl** has a collection of sculptures and stelae gathered from the large area of the *finca* grounds. The **Museo de Cultura Cotzumalguapa** ⓘ *Finca Las Ilusiones, Mon-Fri 0800-1600, Sat 0800-1200, US$1.30, ask the person in charge for the key,* displays numerous artefacts collected from the *finca* and a copy of the famous Bilbao Monument 21 from the cane fields. It is less than 1 km east of town.

From Santa Lucía Cotzumalguapa to the Mexican border

Beyond Santa Lucía Cotzumalguapa is **Cocales**, where a good road north leads to Patulul and after 30 km, to Lake Atitlán at San Lucas Tolimán. The Pacific Highway continues through San Antonio Suchitepéquez to **Mazatenango** (where just beyond are the crossroads for Retalhueleu and Champerico) and on to Coatepeque and Ciudad Tecún Umán for the border with Mexico. Mazatenango is the chief town of the Costa Grande zone. While it is not especially attractive, the Parque Central is very pleasant with many fine trees providing shade. There is a huge **festival** in the last week of February, when hotels are very full and double their prices. At that time, beware of children carrying (and throwing) bags of flour.

Retalhuleu

→ *Colour map 5, C1.*

Retalhuleu, normally referred to as 'Reu' (pronounced 'Ray-oo') is the capital of the department. The entrance to the town is grand with a string of royal palms lining the route, known as Calzada Las Palmas. It serves a large number of coffee and sugar estates and much of its population is wealthy. The original colonial church of **San Antonio de Padua** is in the central plaza. Bordering the plaza to the east is the neoclassical **Palacio del Gobierno**, with a giant quetzal sculpture on top. The **Museo de Arqueología y Etnología** ⓘ *Tue-Sat 0830-1300, 1400-1800, Sun 0900-1230, US$1.30* next to the *palacio*, is small. Downstairs are exhibits of Maya ceramics.

Abaj Takalik

ⓘ *Daily 0700-1700, US$3.25, guides are volunteers so tips are welcomed.*

One of the best ancient sites to visit outside El Petén is Abaj Takalik, a ruined city that lies, sweltering, on the southern plain. Its name means 'standing stone' in K'iche'. The site was discovered in 1888 by botanist Doctor Gustav Brühl. It is believed to have flourished in the late pre-Classic period of 300 BC to AD 250 strategically placed to control commerce between the highlands and the Pacific coast. There are some 239 monuments, which include 68 stelae, 32 altars and some 71 buildings, all set in peaceful surroundings. The environment is loved by birds and butterflies, including blue morphos, and by orchids, which flower magnificently between January and March. The main temple buildings are mostly up to 12 m high, suggesting an early date before techniques were available to build Tikal-sized structures.

Towards the Mexican border

The main road runs 21 km east off the Pacific Highway to **Coatepeque**, one of the richest coffee zones in the country. There is a bright, modern church in the leafy Plaza Central. The local **fiesta** takes place from 11-19 March. There are several hotels, *hospedajes* and restaurants. **Colomba,** an attractive typical village east of Coatepeque in the lowlands, has a basic *hospedaje*.

Routes to El Salvador

Three routes pass through Southern Guatemala to El Salvador (see box, page 603, for border information). The main towns are busy but scruffy with little to attract the visitor. If travelling by international bus to El Salvador, see page 530.

Route 1 The Pan-American Highway: The first route heads directly south along the paved Pan-American Highway from Guatemala City (CA1) to the border at San Cristóbal Frontera. **Cuilapa,** the capital of Santa Rosa Department, is 65 km along the Highway. About 9 km beyond Los Esclavos is the El Molino junction. Beyond, just off the Pan-American Highway, is the village of **El Progreso**, dominated by the imposing Volcán Suchitán, at 2042 m, now part of the Parque Regional Volcán Suchitán run by La Fundación de la Naturaleza. There is accommodation. The town **fiesta** with horse racing is from 10-16 November. From El Progreso, a good paved road goes north 43 km to Jalapa (see page 608) through open, mostly dry country, with volcanoes always in view. There are several crater lakes including **Laguna del Hoyo** near **Monjas** that are worth visiting. The higher ground is forested. Beyond Jutiapa and El Progreso the

Border essentials: Guatemala-El Salvador

Frontera-San Cristóbal
This is the principal crossing. Heavy transport and international buses favour this route.
Guatemalan immigration Open 0600-2000 but it is usually possible to cross outside these hours with additional charges.

Valle Nuevo/Las Chinamas
Since the construction of the Santa Ana bypass, this has become a popular route for lighter traffic.

Guatemalan immigration
Officially open 0800-1800.

Ciudad Pedro de Alvarado/ La Hachadura
This is becoming a busier crossing as roads on both sides have improved.
Sleeping There are several cheap *hospedajes* (all **G**, basic), but it is not recommended that you plan to stay here.
Transport The last bus for Sonsonate in El Salvador leaves at 1800.

Pan-American Highway heads east and then south to Asunción Mita. Here there is a turning left to Lago de Güija. Before reaching the border at **San Cristóbal Frontera** (see box) the Pan-American Highway dips and skirts the shores (right) of **Lago Atescatempa**, with several islands set in heavy forest.

Route 2 Via Jalpatagua: The second, quicker way of getting to San Salvador is to take a highway which cuts off right from the first route at El Molino junction, about 7 km beyond the Esclavos bridge. This cut-off goes through El Oratorio and Jalpatagua to the border at **Valle Nuevo** (see above), continuing then to Ahuachapán and San Salvador.

Route 3 El Salvador (La Hachadura) via the border at Ciudad Pedro de Alvarado: This coastal route goes from Escuintla to the border bridge over the Río Paz at La Hachadura (El Salvador). It takes two hours from Escuintla to the border. You pass **Auto Safari Chapín** ⓘ *Km 87.5, T2363-1105, Tue-Sun 0900-1700, US$3.25*, east of Escuintla, an improbable wildlife park, but busy at weekends and holidays. **Taxisco** is 18 km beyond and just off the road. It's a busy place, which has a white church with a curious hearts and holly design on the façade. To the east is Guazacapán which merges into **Chiquimulilla**, 3 km to the north, the most important town of the area, with good quality leather goods available. Accommodation is available. A side excursion can be made from Chiquimulilla up the winding CA 16 through coffee *fincas* and farmland. About 20 km along there is a turning to the left down a 2- to 3-km steep, narrow, dirt road which goes to **Laguna de Ixpaco**, an impressive, greenish-yellow lake that is 350 m in diameter. It is boiling in some places, emitting sulphurous fumes and set in dense forest. This trip can also be made by heading south off the Pan-American Highway after Cuilapa (just before Los Esclavos) towards Chiquimulilla on the CA 16, with old trees on either side, some with orchids in them, where you will reach the sign to Ixpaco, after 20 km. Thirty kilometres beyond on the Pacific Highway is **Ciudad Pedro de Alvarado** on the border. See above.

Sleeping

Puerto San José, Chulamar and Iztapa *p599*
LL-L Villas del Pacífico, Chulamar, T2362-6030. The usual luxuries available. A day pass costs US$40 per person, but the food is reported to be extremely bad value.
AL-A Hotel y Turicentro Eden Pacific, Barrio El Laberinto, Puerto San José, T7881-1605. 17 a/c rooms with TV, private beach and pools.

B Club Vacacional Agua Azul, Km 106.5, Puerto San José, T/F7881-3445. 32 rooms, with TV, a/c and pools, reasonable food.
B Santa María del Mar, Chulamar, T7881-1287. Pools, restaurant and a private beach with changing facilities.
C Hotel Club Sol y Playa Tropical, 1 Calle, 5-48, on the canal, Iztapa, T7881-4365. With pool, friendly staff and standard rooms with fans. Good food at restaurant. There are a number of *comedores* in town.
D Papillon, Barrio Miramar, Puerto San José, T7881-1064. On beach, restaurant and pool.

Monterrico *p600*
Most hotels are fully booked by Sat midday and prices rise at weekends – book beforehand if arriving at the weekend.
A-C San Gregorio, Calle del Proyecto, behind El Kaimán, T/F2238-4690. 22 modern rooms with bath, fan and mosquito nets. There is a large part-shaded pool, a restaurant set around the pool. Non-guests can use the pool for a fee.
B Hotel Pez de Oro, at the end of main strip to the east, T2368-3684, pezdeoro@intelnett.com. 11 spacious bungalows attractively set around a swimming pool. All rooms have private bathroom, mosquito lamps, pretty bedside lights and fan. Some with a/c. Recommended.
C Eco Beach Place, 250 m west of the main drag, T5611-6637, ecobeachplace@hotmail.com. Facing the ocean, take a right off Calle Principal down the path opposite Las Margaritas, on the beach. This cosy place has 10 rooms with bath, mosquito nets and fans. There is a pool, and restaurant. Breakfast included in the room price. There is a discount on stays of 3 nights or more.
C-D El Baule Beach, 300 m left up the beach, T5418-6155. With 20 rooms that are nearly clean, with bath, and mosquito nets. Fans cost extra. There are 2 pools and restaurant. Organizes shuttles. Not as popular as it used to be.
C-D El Mangle, main strip, T5514-6517. Rooms with fans, bathrooms, and mosquito nets (some are a little dark), centred around a nice, clean pool, set a little back from the beach front. It's quieter than some of the others and gets more pleasant by the year. Recommended.
C-D Hotel Restaurante Dulce y Salado, some way away from the main cluster of hotels and a 500-m hard walk east through sand if you are on foot, T5817-9046, www.dulceysalado.com. The compensations are the sea view and the fantastic uninterrupted view of the highland volcanoes behind. Run by a friendly Italian couple, Fulvio and Graziella, the hotel has 8 clean and nice rooms, with bath, fans and mosquito nets, set around a pool. Breakfast included, good Italian food.
C-D Johnny's Place, main strip, T5812-0409, www.playademonterrico.com. Owned by a super-friendly US and Kiwi couple, Sid Eschenbach and Jan Clarke. There are 7 equipped bungalows, rooms with bath, cheaper without, and a dorm. All windows have mosquito netting. Internet, table tennis; swimming pools, fishing and a restaurant with free coffee fill-ups. Recommended.
D Hotel y Restaurant Kaiman, on the beach side, T5617-9880, big bar (1000 'til you're done at the weekends) and restaurant. The rooms are very clean, with bath, fan, and mosquito nets. There are 2 pools for adults and children, but not in top shape. Discounts for longer stays.
D-E El Delfín, T5702-6701, eldelfin99@yahoo.com. Bungalows, with mosquito nets, fans and private bathroom and rooms. Although the hotel is on the beach, most people hang out in the courtyard and by the pool at the back. Restaurant with vegetarian food. Organizes shuttles at any hour. Recommended.
D-F Café del Sol, 250 m west of the main drag next to Eco Beach Place, T5810-0821, www.cafe-del-sol.com. 9 rooms, roadside pool. Rooms across the road in an annexe are much more spartan. There is a pleasant bar area.

Santa Lucía Cotzumalguapa *p600*
B Santiaguito, Pacific Highway at Km 90.4, T7882-5435. A/c, TV and hot and cold water, pool and restaurant. Non-guests can use the pool for US$2.60.
C-D Hotel El Camino, diagonally opposite Santiaguito across the highway at Km 90.5, T7882-5316. Rooms with bath, tepid water, fan, some rooms with a/c (more expensive). All have TV. Good restaurant.

E Hospedaje La Reforma, stone's throw from the park on 4 Av, 4-71. Large number of dark box rooms and dark shared showers. Clean though.

Retalhuleu *p602*
B La Colonia, 1.5 km to the north at Km 180.5, T7772-2048. Rooms with a/c and TV, pool, and good food.
B Posada de Don José, 5 Calle, 3-67, T7771-4177, donjose@terra.com.gt. Rooms with a/c and fan, TV. There is a very good restaurant serving such mouthwatering temptations as lobster sautéed in cognac. Restaurant and café are set beside the pool. Non-guests can use the pool for US$1.30.
B Siboney, 5 km northwest of Reu in San Sebastián, Km 179, T7771-0149. Rooms are with bath, a/c and TV, set around pool. Try the *caldo de mariscos* or *paella* in the excellent restaurant. Non-guests can use the pool for a fee.
C Astor, 5 Calle, 4-60, T7771-2559, hotelastor@intelnett.com. A colonial-style place with with 27 rooms, a/c, hot water, TV, set around a pretty courtyard where there's a pool and jacuzzi. Parking and restauarant. Bar La Carreta is inside the hotel with MTV on the go all the time. Non-guests can use the pool and jacuzzi here (nicer than the one at Posada de Don José) for a fee.
D Modelo, 5 Calle, 4-53, opposite the **Astor**, T7771-0256. Run by a friendly old couple, with rooms like barns set around a basic patio, with bath and fan. Those with windows on the main street suffer from noise.
F Hilman, 7 Av, 7-99. Rooms have fans and are clean, basic but acceptable.

Eating

Monterrico *p600*
Be careful especially with *ceviche*: bad stomachs are not unknown. There are lots of local *comedores* along Calle Principal, which leads to the beach.
TT Restaurant Italiano, at the end of the main strip to the east, at **Hotel Pez de Oro**, T7368-3684. It is popular and consistently good. Recommended.

Santa Lucía Cotzumalguapa *p600*
T Pastelería Italiana, Calzada 15 de Septiembre, 4-58. Open early for bakery.

Retalhuleu *p602*
TT Restaurante La Luna, 5 Calle, 4-97, on the corner of the plaza. Good *típico* meals served.
T El Patio, corner of 5 Calle, 4 Av. *Menú del día* US$1.60, cheap breakfasts. Limited.
T El Volován, on the plaza, delicious cakes and pies.

Entertainment

Monterrico *p600*
Bars and clubs
El Animal Desconocido, on beach close to Johnny's Place. Open from 2000 in the week.
El Caracol, T5918-3632, 1000-2400, with live music every Sat and cinema.

Activities and tours

Monterrico *p600*
Fishing
Along the coast will provide rich pickings including tuna, dolphin fish, roosterfish and mackerel.

Tour operators
Those preferring to stay on land can rent horses for a jaunt on the beach. *Lancha* and turtle-searching tours are operated by a couple of agencies in town.
El Arco de Noé, run by the friendly Noé Orantes, an INGUAT-registered guide, T5703-3781. His blue-painted house is just a couple of mins up from the dock on the way to the beach on Calle del Proyecto. He runs tours along the canals at 0600 and 1800 daily for US$5 per person.
Iguana Tours, 1 block from the dock on Calle Principal, T/F7885-0688, and with a rep at the sanctuary, runs a number of trips. Office hours are 0800-1900 daily.

Transport

Guatemala City to the Pacific coast *p599*
Bus From Guatemala City to **Amatitlán** (every 30 mins, US$0.26) from 0700-1900 from 20 Calle and 2 Av, Zona 1. From **Escuintla** (1½ hrs), to the capital from the 8 Calle and 2 Av, Zona 1, near the corner of the plaza in Escuintla. However, buses that have come along the Pacific Highway and are going on to the capital pull up at the main

bus terminal on 4 Av. From the busy terminal there are buses direct to **Antigua** at 0700, 1200, 1300, 1500, 1630, 1800 1½ hrs, US$0.65. See page 548. To **Taxisco** every 30 mins, 0700-1700, 40 mins, US$1.05 for La Avellana, for boats to Monterrico. There are frequent buses to **Iztapa** with the last bus departing at 2030.

If you are changing in Escuintla for **Santa Lucía Cotzumalguapa** to the west, you need to take a left out of the bus terminal along the 4 Av up a slight incline towards the police fortress and take a left here on its corner, 9 Calle, through the market. Head for 3 blocks straight, passing the **Cinammon Pastelería y Panadería** on the right at 9 Calle and 2 Av. At the end here are buses heading to Santa Lucía and further west along the Pacific Highway. It is a 5- to 10-min walk. Buses leave here every 5 mins. To **Santa Lucía Cotzumalguapa** (the bus *ayudantes* shout 'Santa'), 35 mins, US$0.45. On the return, buses pull up at the corner of the 8 Calle and 2 Av, where Guatemala City buses also pass.

Puerto San José, Chulamar and Iztapa *p599*

Bus Regular buses from the capital passing through **Escuintla**, 2 hrs, US$1.30. From Puerto San José to Iztapa, US$0.13. If you are heading further east by road from Iztapa along the coast to **Monterrico** (where the road is lined with loofah plantations), you need to cross the canal to **Pueblo Viejo** by ferry, 5 mins (US$2.20 per car and US$0.40 per foot passenger from 0600 to 2045 daily). There are regular buses between Iztapa and Escuintla.

Monterrico *p600*

Bus and boat

The **first route** to Monterrico involves heading direct to the Pacific coast by taking a bus from the capital to **Puerto San José**, 1 hr, and changing for a bus to **Iztapa**. Or take a direct bus from Escuintla to Iztapa. Then cross the inlet by ferry to **Pueblo Viejo** for US$2.20 per car, and US$0.40 per foot passenger, from 0600 to 2045 daily, 5 mins. Then take a bus to Monterrico, about 25 km east, 1 hr, US$0.65. Buses run to and from Pueblo Viejo between 0600-1500, from the corner of main street and the road to Pueblo Viejo to the left, 3 blocks north of the beach, just past the Catholic church on the right.

The **second route** involves getting to Taxisco first and then La Avellana. Antigua to **Escuintla** by bus is 1-1½ hrs, US$0.65. From there, there are regular departures to **Taxisco**, 40 mins, US$1.05. From Taxisco to La Avellana, buses leave hourly until 1800, US$0.40, 20 mins. If you take an international bus from Escuintla (45 mins, US$1.30), it will drop you off just past the Taxisco town turnoff, just before a bridge with a slip road. Walk up the road (5 mins) and veer to the right where you'll see the bus stop for La Avellana. Direct **Cubanita** buses from Guatemala City to **La Avellana** via Taxisco at 1030, 1230 and 1420, 3 hrs, US$3. At La Avellana take the **motor boats** through mangrove swamps, 20-30 mins, US$0.40 for foot passengers, cars US$6.50, from 0630 and then hourly until 1800. The journey via this route from Antigua to Monterrico uses 3 public buses and the boat, and takes about 3¼ hrs if your connections are good. Return boats to **La Avellana** leave at 0330, 0530, 0700, 0800, 0900, 1030, 1200, 1300, 1430, 1600. Buses leave La Avellana for Taxisco hourly until 1800, US$0.40. Buses pull up near the **Banco Nor-Oriente** where numerous buses heading to Guatemala and Escuintla pass.

Shuttles

Alternatively, numerous travel agencies in Antigua run shuttles, US$10-12 one way. You can book just a return shuttle journey for US$5-12 in Monterrico by going to the Don Quijote office at the **ALM School** (see below) on the road that leads to the dock, Calle del Proyecto, Antigua T611-5670, donquijotetravel@yahoo.com.

From Santa Lucía Cotzumalguapa to the Mexican border *p601*

Bus 5 a day **Cocales-Panajachel**, between 0600 and 1400, 2½ hrs, US$1.05. Frequent buses to **Mazatenango** from Guatemala City, US$1.56; to the border at Tecún Umán US$1.56.

Santa Lucía Cotzumalguapa *p600*

Bus Regular departures to the capital. Buses plying the Pacific Highway also pass through, so if you are coming from Reu in the west or Escuintla in the east you can get off here.

Car If you are driving, there are a glut of 24-hr Esso and Texaco gas stations here. See under Guatemala City to the Pacific coast for catching transport from **Escuintla**.

Retalhuleu *p602*
Bus Services along the Pacific Highway to Mexico leave from the main bus terminal, which is beyond the city limits at 5 Av 'A' on the right-hand side, just before a *tienda* sign saying 'Caseta Sonia'. To **Coatepeque** (0600-1800), **Malacatán, Mazatenango** and **Champerico** (0500-1800). Buses also leave from here to **El Asintal**, 30 mins, US$0.13, every 30 mins from 0600-1830, last bus back to Reu 1800). Or catch them before that from the corner of 5 Av 'A' and the Esso gas station as they turn to head for the village. Leaving from a smaller terminal at 7 Av/10 Calle, there are regular buses to **Tecún Umán, Talismán** and **Guatemala City** via the Pacific route, and to Xela (1¾ hrs, US$0.80, every hr 0500-1800).

Abaj Takalik *p602*
Bus Take a bus to El Asintal from **Retalhuleu** and walk the hot 4 km to the site entrance. Or, take any bus heading along the Pacific Highway and get off at the **El Asintal** crossroads. A pick-up from here to El Asintal is US$0.52. Then, take a pick-up from the town square to Abaj Takalik. If the pick-up is almost full, which would be rare, it should cost you only US$0.40. However, since there are only *fincas* along this road, you will probably be on your own, in which case it is US$3.90 to the site or US$6.50-7.50 round trip, including waiting time. Bargain hard though.

Taxi A taxi from central plaza in Reu to the site and back including waiting time is US$13.

Towards the Mexican border *p602*
Bus From Quetzaltenango to **Coatepeque**, US$0.40, or catch any bus heading to Cd Tecún Umán from Reu.

Directory

Monterrico *p600*
Language school Proyecto Lingüístico Monterrico, T5978-4492. **Medical services** There is a clinic behind El Delfín open at weekends. **Post office** near Hotel Las Margaritas on the Calle Principal.

Santa Lucía Cotzumalguapa *p600*
Banks Banco G&T Continental, on the highway, accepts MasterCard. Banco Industrial, accepts Visa, 3 Av between 2 and 3 Calle. There's a Bancared Visa ATM on the plaza. **Telephone** Telgua, Cda 15 de Septiembre near the highway.

Retalhuleu *p602*
Banks There are plenty of banks in town taking Visa and MC. ATMs also. **Embassies and consulates** Mexico, inside the Posada de Don José. Mon-Fri 0700-1230, 1400-1800. **Internet** La Casona, 4 Calle, 4-58, daily 0830-1230, 1500-1800. **Medical services** Hospital Nacional de Retalhuleu, Blv Centenario, 3 Av, Zona 2, 10 mins along the road to El Asintal, T7771-0116. **Post office** on the plaza. **Telephone** 5 Calle, 4-18.

Guatemala City to the Caribbean

From the capital to the Caribbean the main road passes through the Río Motagua Valley, punctuated by cacti and with the Sierra de Las Minas mountains rising abruptly in the west. Dinosaur remains, the black Christ and the Maya ruins of Quiriguá can be found on or close to the highway. The banana port of Puerto Barrios is a large transport and commercial hub and jumping off point for the Garífuna town of Lívingston, and trips down the lush gorge of the Río Dulce with some great places to see and stay on its banks as well as those of Lago de Izabal. ▸▸ *For Sleeping, Eating and other listings, see pages 614-622.*

Ins and outs

Getting there The Carretera al Atlántico or Atlantic Highway, stretches from Guatemala City all the way to Puerto Barrios on the Caribbean coast in the department of Izabal. Most of the worthwhile places to visit are off this fast main road, along the Río Motagua valley, where cactus, bramble, willow and acacia grow. There are numerous buses. ➧ *For further details, see Transport, page 619.*

Along the Atlantic Highway

Before Teculután is **El Rancho** at Km 85, the jumping-off point for a trip north to Cobán (see page 625). There are a few places here to stay. Geologists will be interested in the **Motagua fault** near Santa Cruz, between Teculután and Río Hondo. Just before Río Hondo (Km 138), a paved road runs south towards Estanzuela. Shortly before this town you pass a monument on the right commemorating the 1976 earthquake, which activated a fault line that cut across the road. It can still be seen in the fields on either side of the road. The epicentre of this massive earthquake, which measured 7.5 on the Richter scale, and killed 23,000 people, was at **Los Amates**, 65 km further down the valley towards Puerto Barrios.

Estanzuela

Estanzuela is a small town fronting the highway. Its **Museo de Palaeontología, Arqueología y Geología** ⓘ *daily 0800-1700, free*, displays the incredible reconstructed skeletal remains of a 4 m prehistoric giant sloth found in Zone 6, Guatemala City and a giant armadillo among others. Take a minibus heading south from Río Hondo and ask to be dropped at the first entrance to the town on the right, where there is an Orange Crush Caseta Ana No 2. Then walk right, into the town, and continue for 600 m to the museum, 10 mins. When you reach the school, walk to the right and you will see the museum.

Chiquimula, Volcán de Ipala and the Honduran border

Chiquimula is a stop-off point for travellers who stay here on their way to or from Copán Ruinas, Honduras, if they can't make the connection in one day (see page 610 for border crossing). The **fiesta**, which includes bullfighting, is from 11-18 August.

An alternative route to Chiquimula and Esquipulas is from the southeast corner of Guatemala City (Zona 10), where the Pan-American Highway heads towards the Salvadorean border. After a few kilometres there is a turning to **San José Pinula** (**fiesta**: 16-20 March). After San José, an unpaved branch road continues for 203 km through fine scenery to Mataquescuintla, Jalapa (several *hospedajes*, good bus connections; **fiesta**: 2-5 May), San Pedro Pinula, San Luis Jilotepeque, and Ipala to Chiquimula (see page 608). Southwest of Chiquimula, the extinct Volcán de Ipala (1650 m) can be visited. The crater lake is cool and good for swimming.

At **Vado Hondo**, 10 km south of Chiquimula on the road to Esquipulas, a smooth dirt road branches east to the Honduran border (48 km) and a further 11 km to the great Maya ruins of Copán. The border is 1 km after the village. See box, opposite.

Esquipulas → *Colour map 5, C3.*

Esquipulas is dominated by a large, white basilica, which attracts millions of pilgrims from across Central America to view the image of a Black Christ. The town has pulled out the stops for visitors, who, as well as a religious fill, will lack nothing in the way of food, drink and some of the best kitsch souvenirs on the market. If it's possible, stop at the mirador, 1 km from the town, for a spectacular view on the way in of the basilica, which sits at the end of a 1.5-km main avenue. The history of the famous *Cristo Negro* records that in 1735 Father Pedro Pardo de Figueroa, suffering from an incurable chronic illness, stood in front of the image to pray, and was cured. A few years later, after becoming Archbishop of Guatemala he ordered a new church to be built to

Border essentials: Guatemala-Honduras

Entre Ríos-Corinto

Guatemalan immigration

You can get your exit stamp at the Guatemalan immigration in Puerto Barrios or Lívingston if you are leaving by boat to Honduras. If you arrive in Guatemala by boat, go straight to either of these offices.

Honduran consulate If you need a visa, you must obtain it in Guatemala City, or at Esquipulas.

Transport Minibuses leave the market on 8 Calle in Puerto Barrios for Entre Ríos every 15 mins between 0630-1800, US$0.40. They pull up at the immigration post beyond Entre Ríos at El Cinchado and wait for you to complete formalities. The minibus continues the journey (15 mins) over a bridge over the Río Motagua. There is nothing here except a handful of moneychangers and pick-ups to take you the 30 mins, to Honduran immigration.

Honduran immigration In Corinto. Pick-up to Tegucigalpita (1½ hrs). From the border to Tegucigalpita, US$3. This Corinto-Tegucigalpita road, via Cuyamelito, is also covered by an hourly bus service with **Línea Costeños**. If you take a pick-up, it leaves you at the bus stop heading for Omoa (US$0.40, 1¼ hrs) and on to Puerto Cortés (US$0.80, 2 hrs). With swift connections the journey is just under 4 hrs from Puerto Barrios to Omoa. It would not be wise to leave Puerto Barrios later than 0800 for this crossing due to pick-up connections. In the rainy season, start even earlier.

house the sculpture. The **basilica** ⓘ *open until 2000*, was completed in 1758 and the *Cristo Negro* was transferred from the parish church shortly after that. Inside the basilica, the Black Christ is on a gold cross, elaborately engraved with vines and grapes. It was carved by Quirio Cataño in dark balsam wood in 1595. The image attracts over 1,000,000 visitors per year, some crawling on their hands and knees to pay homage. The main **pilgrimage times** are 1-15 January (with 15 January being the busiest day), during Lent, Holy Week and 21-27 July.

Quiriguá

ⓘ *Daily 0730-1630, US$4. Take insect repellent. There are toilets, a café and you can store your luggage with the guards. There is no accommodation at the site, but you can camp. The site is reached by a dirt road from the Atlantic Highway. The village of Quiriguá is about half way between Zacapa and Puerto Barrios on the highway, and about 3 km from the entrance road to the ruins.*

The remarkable Late Classic ruins of Quiriguá include the tallest stelae found in the Maya world. The UNESCO World Heritage Site is small, with an excavated acropolis to see, but the highlight of a visit is the sight of the ornately carved tall stelae and the zoomorphic altars. The Maya here were very industrious, producing monuments every five years between AD 751-806, coinciding with the height of their prosperity and confident rule. The earliest recorded monument dates from AD 480.

It is believed that Quiriguá was an important trading post between Tikal and Copán, inhabited since the second century, but principally it was a ceremonial centre. The Kings of Quiriguá were involved in the rivalries, wars and changing alliances between Tikal, Copán and Calakmul. It rose to prominence in its own right in the middle of the eighth century, around the time of Cauac Sky who ascended to the throne in AD 724. Cauac Sky was appointed to the position by 18 Rabbit, powerful ruler of Copán (now in Honduras), and its surrounding settlements. It seems that he was fed up with being a subordinate under the domination of Copán, and during his reign, Quiriguá attacked Copán and captured 18 Rabbit. One of the stelae tells of the beheading of the Copán King in the plaza at Quiriguá as a sacrifice after the AD 738

Border essentials: Guatemala-Honduras

El Florido
Open 0700-1900. If you are going to Copán for a short visit, the Guatemalan official will give you a 72-hr pass, stapled into your passport. You must return through this border within this period, but you will not require a new visa. Exit fees of US$1.30 are being charged.
Honduran consulate If you need a visa to enter Honduras, go to the lobby of the **Hotel Payaquí**, Esquipulas, where there is a consulate office, manned by very helpful staff. It's reportedly quicker to get your Honduran visa here than in the capital.
Transport See page 619. Taxi Chiquimula-border US$18. Chiquimula-Copán and back the same day in a taxi costs US$35. It is impossible to visit Copán from Guatemala City by bus and return the same day; travel agents do 1-day or overnight minibus trips.
Crossing by private vehicle
If crossing by car make sure you have all the right paperwork. If you are in a Guatemalan hire car you will need a letter of authorization from the hire company allowing you to take the car across the border to Honduras. You can leave your car at the border and go on to Copán by public transport, thus saving the costs of crossing with a vehicle. If leaving Honduras for Guatemala with a vehicle, you need 3 stamps on your strip from Migración, Tránsito (where they take your *Proviso Provisional*), and Aduana (where they take your *Pase Fronterizo* document and cancel the stamp in your passport).

For a better road to Honduras from Chiquimula, see Agua Caliente, page 612.
Border with Guatemala
There are many money changers but for US$ or TCs, change in Copán, better rates.
Honduran immigration
At El Florido on the border. They charge a small entry and exit fee.
Transport Pick-up trucks run all day every day when full until 1700 between Copán Ruinas and the border, 30 mins, connecting with buses to Guatemalan destinations. The cost is around US$2.50. Bargain for a fair price. They leave from one block west of the park, near the police station. See Chiquimula, Transport. There is a direct minibus service Copán-Antigua, run by **Monarcas Travel**, with offices in Antigua and Copán Ruinas.

battle. After this event 18 Rabbit disappears from the official chronicle and a 20-year hiatus ensues in the historical record of Copán. Following this victory, Quiriguá became an independent kingdom and gained control of the Motagua Valley, enriching itself in the process. And, from AD 751, a monument was carved and erected every five years for the next 55 years. The tallest stelae at Quiriguá is **Stelae E**, which is 10.66 m high with another 2.5 m or so buried beneath. It is 1.52 m wide and weighs 65 tonnes. One of its dates corresponds with the enthronement of Cauac Sky, in AD 724, but it's thought to date from AD 771. All of the stelae, in parkland surrounded by ceiba trees and palms, have shelters, which makes photography difficult. Some monuments have been carved in the shape of animals, some mythical, all of symbolic importance to the Maya.

Thirteen kilometres from Quiriguá is the turn-off for **Mariscos** and Lago de Izabal (see page 614). A further 28 km on are the very hot twin towns of Bananera/Morales. From Bananera there are buses to Río Dulce, Puerto Barrios and the Petén.

Puerto Barrios → *Colour map 5, B3.*

Puerto Barrios, on the Caribbean coast, is a hot and dusty port town, still a central banana point, but now largely superseded as a port by Santo Tomás. The launch to the Garífuna town of Lívingston leaves from the municipal dock here. While not an unpleasant town, it is not a destination in itself, but rather a launch pad to more beautiful and happening spots. On the way into town, note the cemetery on the right-hand side, where you will pass a small, Indian mausoleum with elephant carvings. During the 19th century, *culi* (coolies) of Hindu origin migrated from Jamaica to Guatemala to work on the plantations. The **fiesta** is 16-22 July.

Lívingston and around

▸▸ *pp614-622. Colour map 5, B3.*

Lívingston, or La Buga, is populated mostly by Garífuna blacks, who bring a colourful flavour to this corner of Guatemala. With its tropical sounds and smells, it is a good place to hang out for a few days, sitting on the dock of the bay, or larging it up with the locals, *punta*-style. *Coco pan* and *cocado* (a coconut, sugar and ginger *dulce*) and locally made jewellery are sold in the streets. The town is the centre of fishing and

Lívingston

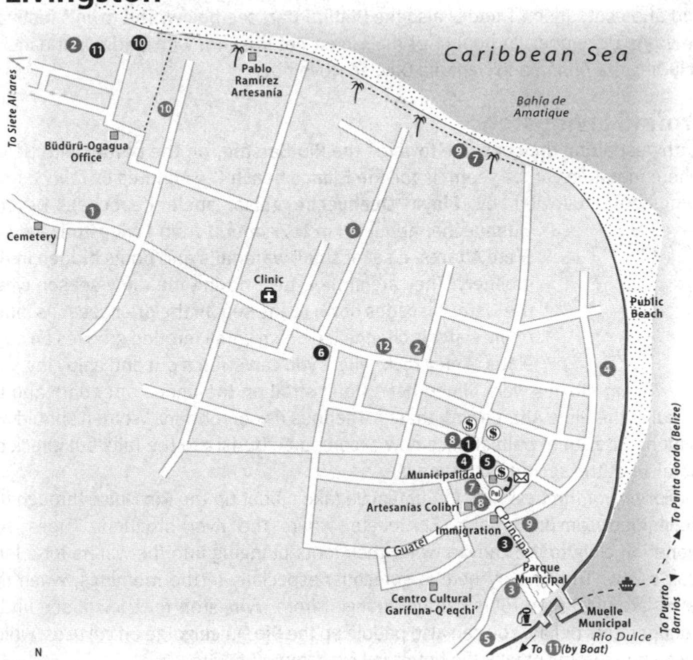

N

0 metres 100

0 yards 100

Sleeping
African Place **1**
Blanco **2**
Casa Rosada **3**
El Viajero **5**
Garífuna **6**
Hospedaje Doña Alida **4**
Las Hamacas **11**
Río Dulce **7**
Ríos Tropicales **8**
Villa Caribe
Tucán Dugú **9**
Waba **10**

Eating
Bahía Azul **1**
El Malecón **3**
Happy Fish **4**
McTropic **5**
Ubouhu **6**

Bars & clubs
Beluba Ñuruba **7**
Black Sheep **8**
Büdürü **2**
Cocobongo **9**
Happy Fisherman's Place **10**
Lugudi Barana **11**
Tropicool **8**
Ubafu **12**

Border essentials: Guatemala-Honduras

Agua Caliente
Guatemalan immigration Open 0600-1900.
Honduran consulate In Hotel Payaquí, Esquipulas, very helpful, 0930-1800, T7943-1143.
Transport Minibuses run from Esquipulas, US$0.65, 15 mins. By taxi US$6.50. From Chiquimula, US$1.80, every 10 mins.

shrimping in the Bay of Amatique and only accessible by boat. It is nearly 23 km by sea from Puerto Barrios and there are regular daily boat runs which take 35 minutes in a fast *lancha*. The bulk of the town is up a small steep slope leading straight from the dock, which is at the mouth of the Río Dulce estuary. The other part of town is a linear spread along the river estuary, just north of the dock and then first left. The town is small and everything is within walking distance. The Caribbean beach is pretty dirty nearer the river estuary end, but a little further up the coast, it is cleaner, with palm trees and accommodation. Closer to the town are a couple of bars and weekend beach discos. The town's **Centro Cultural Garífuna-Q'eqchi'** is perched on a hillock, and has the best views in the whole of Lívingston. At the other side of town, near the hotel **African Place**, is the **Asociación Garífuna Guatemalteca Büdürü-Ogagua** ⓘ *T7947-0105, 0800-1200, 1400-2000*, which focuses on dance, music, *artesanía*, food and ecotourism. There is also the **Büdürü Bar**, see below. The town's **festivals** are 24-31 December, in honour of the Virgen del Rosario, with traditional dancing including the *punta*, and Garífuna Day, 26 November.

Around Lívingston

Northwest along the coastline towards the Río Sarstún, on the border with Belize (where manatee can be seen), is the **Río Blanco beach** (45 minutes by *lancha* from Lívingston), followed by **Playa Quehueche** (also spelt Keueche). Beyond Quehueche, about 6 km (1½ hours) from Lívingston, are **Los Siete Altares**, a set of small waterfalls and pools hidden in the greenery. They are at their best during the rainy season when the water cascades down to the sea. In the drier seasons much of the water is channelled down small, eroded grooves on large slabs of grey rock, where you can stretch out and enjoy the sun. Early *Tarzan* movies were filmed here. Don't stroll on the beach after dark and be careful at the Siete Altares end; there's a serious risk of robbery. Women should not go alone or even in pairs. Police now accompany tourists to the falls but check on arrival what the security situation is.

Boats can be hired in Lívingston to visit beaches along the coast towards San Juan and the Río Sarstún.

For one of the best trips in Guatemala take a boat up the **Río Dulce** through the sheer-sided canyon towards El Golfete, where the river broadens. Trees and vegetation cling to the canyon walls, their roots plunging into the waters for a long drink below. The scenery here is gorgeous, especially in the mornings, when the waters are unshaken.Tours can be arranged from Lívingston for US$10, see under Tour operators below. You can also paddle up the Río Dulce gorge on *cayucos*, which can be hired from some of the hotels in Lívingston.

The **Biotopo Chocón Machacas** ⓘ *0700-1600, US$5*, is one place where the elusive manatee (sea cow) hangs out, but you are unlikely to see him munching his way across the lake bottom, as he is very shy and retreats at the sound of a boat motor. (The manatee is an aquatic herbivore, which can be up to 4 m long when adult, and weigh more than 450 kg. It eats for six to eight hours daily and can consume more than 10% of its body weight in a 24-hour period.) Administered by CECON, the reserve is a mangrove zone, half way between Río Dulce town and Lívingston, on the northern

Border essentials: Guatemala-El Salvador

Anguiatú
This border is 19 km from the Padre Miguel Junction on the main road and 33 km from Esquipulas.
Immigration Open 0600-1900.
Transport There are *colectivos* to/from Padre Miguel junction connecting with buses to Chiquimula and Esquipulas. From Esquipulas, minibuses run every 30 mins, 0600-1720, US$1.05, 40 mins. By taxi, US$30. From Chiquimula there are minibuses every 30 mins from 0515-1700, 1½ hrs, US$1.20.

shore of **El Golfete** – an area where the Río Dulce broadens into a lake that is 5 km across. Four Q'eqchi' communities of 400 people live on land within the 6245-ha reserve. Within the reserve are carpets of water lilies, dragonflies, blue morpho butterflies, pelicans and cormorants. On land spot army ants, crabs, mahogany trees and the *labios rojos* ('hot lips') flower.

Proyecto Ak' Tenamit ⓘ, *www.aktenamit.org*, meaning 'new village' in Q'eqchi', is 15 minutes upriver from Lívingston. It was set up to help 7000 Q'eqchi' Maya displaced by the civil war. Volunteers are needed for a minimum of a month's work (board and transport, and weekends off). A working knowledge of Spanish is required. Near here is the **Río Tatin tributary** and the wonderfully sited **Finca Tatín**, see Sleeping. **Reserva Ecológica Cerro San Gil**, with its natural pools, karstic caves and biostation, can be visited from here, or from Río Dulce. Contact **FUNDAECO** ⓘ *T7948-5487, Guatemala City T2440-4609, fundaeco@quetzal.net*, or call in to see them at their offices next to the **Hotel Henry Berrisford.**

Lago de Izabal

» *pp614-622. Colour map 5, B3.*

The vast Lago de Izabal narrows to form a neck at the town of Fronteras. Better known as Río Dulce, it is famed for its riverside setting and there are some beautiful places around the lake and river in which to stay. Just south of Río Dulce on the lake is the Castillo de San Felipe. On the northern shore of the lake is the town of El Estor, and on its southern shore the smaller town of Mariscos. Further east, beyond Río Dulce, the river broadens out to El Golfete, where there is the Biotopo Chacón Machacas. It then narrows into one of the finest gorges in the world, and opens out at its estuary, with Lívingston at its head (see page 612). This area can be wet in the rainy season, but it experiences a lull in July, known as the *canícula*.

Fronteras/Río Dulce and around

Río Dulce is a good place to stop and kick back for a couple of days. Allow yourself to be tempted to laze on a boat for the afternoon, walk in the nearby jungle, or eat and drink at one of several dockside restaurants. Río Dulce, www.mayaparadise.com, is 23 km upstream from Lívingston at the entrance to Lago de Izabal, is easily accessible from Puerto Barrios by road, and is the last major stop before the Petén. It's also a good place to collect information about the area stretching from El Estor to Lívingston.

On the shore of Lago de Izabal is **Casa Guatemala** ⓘ *14 Calle, 10-63, Zona 1, Guatemala City, T2232-5517, www.casa-guatemala.com, or the Hotel Backpacker's*, an orphanage where you can work in exchange for basic accommodation and food. At the entrance to Lago de Izabal, 2 km upstream, is the old Spanish fort of **Castillo de San Felipe** ⓘ *0800-1700, US$1.30*. The fortification was first built in 1643 to defend the coast against attacks from pirates. Between Río Dulce and El Estor is **Finca El Paraíso**, a hot waterfall with waters that plunge into a cool-water pool below.

Border essentials: Guatemala-Belize

Puerto Barrios/ Lívingston-Punta Gorda

Guatemalan immigration
Offices are in Puerto Barrios and Lívingston, both open 24 hrs. Exit fees to leave Guatemala by boat are US$10. You must have your exit stamp from immigration before you can buy a ticket. If you come to Guatemala by boat you must go straight to the Puerto Barrios or Lívingston immigration offices.

El Estor and around → *Colour map 5, B3.*

El Estor enjoys one of the most beautiful vistas in Guatemala. It is strung along the northwest shore of Lago de Izabal, backed by the Santa Cruz mountain range, and facing the Sierra de las Minas. The lake is the largest in Guatemala at 717 sq km. It is a great place to relax, swim (down a nearby canyon), go fishing and spot manatee. It is so laid back that young guys bicycle right through the doors of some restaurants screeching to a halt at the bar, and local men come round with buckets stuffed full of freshly plucked strawberries for sale. The town dates back to the days when the Europeans living in the Atlantic area got their provisions from a store situated at this spot, now the **Hotel Vista al Lago.** Briton Skinner and Dutchman Klee used to supply the region from *el store* from 1815 to 1850. Nickel-mining began just outside town in 1978, but was suspended at the **Exmibal plant** after the oil crisis of 1982, because the process depended on cheap sources of energy.

You can hire a boat from Río Dulce to El Estor for about US$65, passing near the hot waterfall, inland at **Finca El Paraíso** (see page 613), which can be reached by a good trail in about 40 minutes. The Río Sauce cuts through the impressive **Cañón El Boquerón,** where you can swim with the current all the way down the canyon, which is brilliant fun. It's a deep canyon with lots of old man's beard hanging down, strange rock formations and otters and troops of howler monkeys whooping about. One of the locals will paddle you upstream for about 800 m (US$1). Exploring the Río Zarco, closer to town, also makes for a good trip, with cold swimming. The **Refugio de Vida Silvestre Bocas del Polochic** (Bocas del Polochic Wildlife Reserve) is a 23,000-ha protected area on the western shores of the lake. Howler monkeys are commonly seen. In addition to over 350 bird species, there are iguanas, turtles and the chance of sighting crocodiles and manatees. The NGO **Defensores de la Naturaleza** ⓘ *2 Calle and 5 Av, T/F5949-7237, www.defensores.org.gt*, has a research station at Selempim with bunk beds (F per person), food, showers and kitchen. Its a two- or three-hour boat ride from El Estor to Ensenada Los Lagartos.

Mariscos is on the southern shore of Lago de Izabal. The best reason to come here is the nearby **Denny's Beach.** See Sleeping, below.

Sleeping

Chiquimula *p608*

C **Hotel Posada Don Adán**, 8 Av, 4-30, T7942-0549. All rooms with private bathroom, a/c, TV. Run by a friendly, older couple.

D **Posada Perla del Oriente**, 2 Calle between 11 and 12 Av, T7942-0014. All rooms with TV, some with a/c, parking, pool, quiet. Restaurant. Recommended.

D-E **Victoria**, 2 Calle, 9-99, next to the bus station (so ask for rooms away from street), T7942-2732. All rooms have bath, cold water, fan, cable TV, towels, soap, shampoo, some rooms have a/c, drinking water provided, good restaurant, good value, will store luggage. Recommended.

E **Hernández**, 3 Calle, 7-41, T7942-0708, hotel@guate.net. Cheaper without bathroom, fans. TVs in rooms and a pool add to its attractions. It's family-run, quiet and friendly, but not such a good deal for single travellers (although you can't usually get the use of a pool at this price).

EHotel Palmeras, 10 Av, 2-00, close to bus terminal, T7942-467. Clean rooms with private bathroom, fan, a/c and TV.

Esquipulas *p608*

There are plenty of hotels, *hospedajes* and *comedores* all over town, especially in and around 11 Calle, also known as Doble Vía Quirio Cataño. Prices tend to double before the Jan feast day. They also rise at Easter and at weekends. When quiet, midweek, bargain for lower room prices.

AHotel Chortí, on the outskirts of town at Km 222, T7943-1148. All 20 rooms have a/c, TV, phone and *frigobar*. There are 2 pools, a restaurant and bar.

BLegendario, 3 Av and 9 Calle, T7943-1824. Built around garden, 2 pools, restaurant, parking.

CHotel El Peregrino, just up from the Hotel Esquipulao, T7943-1054. Clean rooms in a newer part.

CHotel Villa Zonia, 10 Calle, 1-84, T7943-1133. Looking a little Alpine and very nice.

CHotel y Restaurante Esquipulas, 2 Av, 11-68, T7943-2023. Rooms with TV and hot water. A few unpleasant insects in the rooms though and some staff aren't too friendly.

DLos Angeles, 2 Av, 11-94, T7943-1254. Spotless rooms with bath, TV and fans, parking, friendly service. Recommended.

DPayaquí, 2 Av, 11-26, T7943-1143, www.payaqui.com. The 40 rooms are extremely nice, with *frigobars,* full of beers for the pilgrims to guzzle, hot-water showers and free drinking water, swimming pool, parking, restaurant, bar; credit cards, Honduran lempiras and US dollars accepted.

EHotel Calle Real, 3 Av, 10-00, T7943-2405. Rooms all with private bathroom, with TV, hot water, clean.

EPensión Casa Norman, 3 Av, 9-20, T7943-1503. Rooms with bath and hot water.

FSan Carlos 2, used to be known as **París**, 2 Av, 10-48, T7943-1276. 28 very clean rooms. Cheaper without bath, hot-water showers.

Quiriguá *p609*

D-EHotel y Cafetería Edén, T7947-3281. Helpful, cheaper with shared bath, basement rooms are very dark, clean. The bus comes as far as here, which is where the back route walk to the ruins starts.

EHotel Restaurante Santa Mónica, in Los Amates, 2 km south of Quiriguá village on the highway, T2421-2800. 17 rooms all with private bath, TV and fan, pool, restaurant. It is opposite a 24-hr Texaco gas station. Convenient if you don't want to walk the 10-15 mins into Quiriguá village for the 2 hotels there. There are a couple of shops, banks, and *comedores* here.

EHotel y Restaurante Royal, T7947-3639. With bath, cheaper without, clean, mosquito netting on all windows, good place to meet other travellers, restaurant.

Camping

You can camp in the car park of the ruins for free, but facilities are limited to toilets and very little running water.

Puerto Barrios *p611*

A-DHotel del Norte, at the end of the 7 Calle, T/F7948-0087. A rickety, old wooden structure with sloping landings on the seafront side. All rooms have bath, some with a/c. There is a pool and expensive restaurant, but worth it for the English colonial tearoom atmosphere, no credit cards, but will change US$ cash.

BHotel Valle Tropical, 59 rooms on 12 Calle between 5 and 6 Av, T7948-7084, www.hotel vablletropical.com. All rooms with a/c and private bathroom, inviting pool, gym and restaurant, parking. Non-guests can use pool.

CEl Reformador, 16 Calle and 7 Av 159, T7948-5489, reformador@intelnet.net.gt. 51 rooms with bathroom and TV, some with a/c, some with fan, restaurant, laundry service, clean, quiet, accepts credit cards. Recommended. The same management run the **Oguatour** travel agency across the road.

C-EHotel Europa, 8 Av, between 8 and 9 Calle, T7948-0127. 23 clean rooms, with bath, fan, 2 more expensive rooms with a/c, good restaurant, parking, friendly Cuban management. Next door is **Restaurant La Habana Vieja**.

D-EHotel y Restaurante La Caribeña, 4 Av, between 10 and 11 Calle, T7948-0384. 43 rooms, some with a/c and TV, parking, close to boat and bus terminals, popular restaurant serving fish dishes.

E Hotel Lee, 5 Av, between 9 and 10 Calle, T7948-0830. Convenient for the bus station and dock, 24 rooms with fan and TV, with private bath, cheaper without. Noisy restaurant opposite. Friendly service.
E-F Hotel Xelajú, 8 Av, between 9 and 10 Calle, T7948-1117. 15 rooms, with bath, cheaper without, fans, quiet, and ultra-clean shared bathrooms.

Lívingston *p611, map p611*
AL **Hotel Villa Caribe Tucán Dugú**, up Calle Principal from the dock on the right, T2334-8136. Cheaper in low season. All rooms have sea view and baths. There is a swimming pool (available to non-guests when the hotel is not busy for US$3.25), and a large restaurant overlooking the sea.
C-E **Hospedaje Doña Alida**, 150 m to the right beyond **Tucán Dugú**, in a quiet location, T7947-0027. It has direct access to the beach and some rooms with great sea views and balconies, with restaurant.
D **Casa Rosada**, a pastel pink house set on the waterfront, 600 m from the dock, T7947-0303, www.hotelcasarosada.com. 10 bungalows furnished with attractive hand-painted furniture. There's a large 10-bedded dorm upstairs for families only, overlooking the bay. Meals are set for the day, ranging from pasta to delicious shrimps bathed in garlic, for the evening meal. Often full, so reservations are advisable.
D **Las Hamacas**, on the beach, T5692-9738, caracol173@hotmail.com. Lovely 2-storey bungalows, with fridge, in quiet setting with probably the largest dog kennel in the world nearby! Boat access only on the Río Dulce. Diving and other watersports organized.
D-E **Hotel Ríos Tropicales**, T7947-0158. This place has some nice touches to distinguish it from the majority of other places in town, like funkily designed mirror frames and terracotta-tiled floors. There are 8 rooms, with fans, 2 with private bath, a laundry, book exchange and an 8% discount on meals at the **McTropic** restaurant up the road.
E **Garífuna** (see map), T7947-0183. 10 comfortable, ultra-clean rooms with private bath, laundry. Recommended.
E **Hotel Río Dulce**, main street, T7947-0764, An early 19th-century wooden building, with a seriously sloping landing on the 1st floor, a good place from which to watch life pass by. Try and get a room upstairs rather than behind the old building. Rooms with or without bathrooms. There is a restaurant on the ground floor with some tables directly on the street. See Eating.
E **Waba**, barrio Pueblo Nuevo, T7947-0193. Run by a friendly family offering upstairs rooms with a balcony and sea views. Rooms with private bath are clean and cool, with fan. *Comida típica* is served at a little wooden restaurant (0700-2130) on site. Good value and recommended.
E-F **African Place**, right at the end of the main street, so quite a walk from the dock, T7947-0218. Built in Moorish style (the owners are Spanish) with beautiful tile work and a garden, but it looks very out of place in Lívingston. There are 24 clean rooms with bath, cheaper without, but some are a little musty.
F **El Viajero**, popular, clean and friendly, rooms with fans. Some have private bath, cheaper without. If the front desk is unmanned take a walk down the garden, where you'll probably find those in charge having a nap!
F **Hotel Blanco**, T7947-0267, labocadela buga@yahoo.com. Rooms with or without private bathrooms, upstairs with balcony and hammocks. Book exchange.

Around Lívingston *p612*
C-G **Denny's Beach**, T5709-4990, dennysbeach@hotmail.com. With its gorgeous lakeside location, accessible by *lancha* from Río Dulce, or from Mariscos, or call in at **Shop-N-Go** in Mariscos to arrange for a pick-up. Tours, wake boarding and horse riding arranged. Internet service. A remote and complete get away.
D **Restaurante El Viajero**, opposite Ak'Tenamit in Barra de Lampara, T5902-7059. Serves fish food (0700-2000) and offering rooms right on the water. There are 4 rooms, some with terrace.
E **Hotel Ecológico Salvador Gaviota**, along the coast, towards Siete Altares, beyond **Hotel Ecológico Siete Altares**, T5514-3275, hotelsgaviota@hotmail.com. Rooms are with shared bath, but the bungalows for 2 or 4 people have private bath. Rooms available for monthly rent. All set in lush surroundings. There is a bar and restaurant (0730-220), and free *lancha*

service – just ring beforehand. Tours available. The beach here is lovely, hummingbirds flit about and the owner Lisette is friendly. Highly recommended.
E-F Finca Tatin, Río Tatin tributary, with great dock space to hang out on, T5902-0831, www.fincatatin.centro america.com. It's B&B, whether you opt for a room with private bath, or a dorm bed. Spanish classes (20 hrs), and 7 days lodging is US$120 a week. Take a *lancha* from Lívingston (US$6) to get there.
G Hotel Ecológico Siete Altares, on the beach, on the way to Siete Altares, T2220-9067. 4 *cabañas*, fantastically located, although the owner has the best-sited one. The others are quite some way back from the beach, up a hill.

Camping

Biotopo Chocón Machacas, 400 m from the entrance, next to a pond, with grills for cooking on, and toilets, but no food or drink for sale.

Fronteras/Río Dulce *p613*

A Catamaran Island Hotel, T7930-5494, www.catamaranisland.com. Finely decorated *cabañas*, 40 rooms set around the lake edge, an inviting pool, large restaurant with good food, lancha from Río Dulce, 10 mins down- stream, or call for a pick-up. Recommended.
A-F Hacienda Tijax, T7930-5505, www.tijax.com. 2 mins by *lancha* from the dock, jungle lodges, and other simpler accommodation; camping facilities. There is a beautiful jungle trail, a rubber plantation, bird sanctuary, pool with whirlpool and jacuzzi, natural pools to swim in, horse riding, rowboat hire and a medicine trail. Excellent food in the riverside bar and restaurant, tranquil and beautiful. Highly recommended.
A-F Hotel La Ensenada, Km 275, 500 m to the right at the Shell station, T7930-5240. Riverside location, breakfast included, restaurant, pool, nice gardens, camping and campervan facilities.
C-F Bruno's, on the lake, and a stone's throw from the where the buses stop, T7930-5174, www.mayaparadise.com/brunoe.htm. Best rooms overlook the lake, also dorms, camping, campervan parking, pool, restaurant. Non-guests can pay to use pool. The marina has 28 berths. Restaurant service is consistently not up to scratch.
D Posada del Río, under the bridge with river views, across the road and behind Bruno's, T7930-5167. 6 standard rooms with private bath and fan, some with TV.
D-E La Cabaña del Viajero, 500 m from the castle, T7930-5062. Small place with pool, traditional cabañas as well as larger family-style *cabañas* with private bathroom and some cute little attic rooms as well.
D-E Tortugal Marina, T5306-6432, www.tortugal.com. 5 beautifully presented bungalows with gorgeous soft rugs on the floor. Bathrooms are shared. Plentiful hot water. There is also the *ranchito* which is cheaper. There is a riverside restaurant and bar, pool table in a cool upstairs attic room with books, satellite TV, internet, phone and fax service. Very highly recommended.
D-F Hotel Backpacker's, by the bridge on the south bank of the river, T7930-5169, www.hotelbackpackers.com. Restaurant and bar, dorms with lockers, internet and telephone service, profits go to **Casa Guatemala** (see below). Recommended.
E Café Sol, 500 m north of the bridge on the road to Tikal, T7930-5143. Friendly, clean, fans, good-value rooms, cheaper without bath, TV costs a bit extra. Useful if you have to catch an early bus.

El Estor *p614*

C Marisabella, 8 Av and 1 Calle on the waterfront, T7949-7215, urlich@internetde telgua.com.gt. Large rooms with tiled private bathrooms, some with TV, internet service.
D Hotel Vista al Lago, 6 Av, 1-13, T7949-7205. 21 clean rooms with private bath and fan. Ask for the lakeview rooms, where there is a pleasant wooden balcony on which to sit. Friendly owner Oscar Paz will take you fishing, and runs ecological and cultural tours.
E Hotel Central, facing the park, T7949-7244. Lake views from the 2nd floor. Family-run, it's very good value with 12 rooms with private bath and fan, and there's a communal TV.
E Villela, 6 Av, 2-06, T7949-7214. 9 big rooms with bath, clean, some quite dark though. Flower-filled garden with chairs to sit out in. Recommended.

Eating

Chiquimula *p608*

ΨΨ**El Patio**, behind **Hotel Chiquimulja**. A great thatch-roofed, open-air wooden restaurant with wicker furniture. Good breakfasts and *fajitas* on the main menu. It's popular and recommended.

Ψ**Magic**, corner of 8 Av and 3 Calle. A good place from which to watch the world go by, and most of what's on offer is seriously cheap. Sandwiches, *licuados* and burgers.

Ψ**Pastelería Las Violetas**, 7 Av, 4-80, and another near **Hotel Victoria**. An excellent cake shop with a fine spread, good-value sandwiches too, plus great cappuccino, and a/c. Next door is its bakery.

Esquipulas *p608*

There are plenty of restaurants, but prices are high for Guatemala.

ΨΨΨ**La Hacienda**, 2 Av, 10-20. Delicious barbecued chicken and steaks. Kids' menu available, breakfasts available, probably one of smartest restaurants in town.

ΨΨ**Restaurante Payaquí**, 2 Av, 11-26, inside the hotel of the same name. Specialties include turkey in *pipián*, also lunches and breakfasts. A poolside restaurant makes a pleasant change.

Ψ**Café Pistachos**, close to **Hotel Calle Real**. Clean, cheap snack bar with burgers, hotdogs, etc.

Puerto Barrios *p611*

ΨΨΨ-ΨΨ**Restaurante Safari**, at the north end of 5 Av and 1 Calle, overlooking the bay with views all around. Basically serving up oceans of fish, including whole fish plus *ceviche* and fishburgers.

ΨΨ**La Fonda de Quique**, an orange and white wooden building at 5 Av and corner of 12 Calle. Nicely a/c with handmade wooden furniture, serving lobster, fish and meats, plus snacks.

Ψ**La Habana Vieja**. Run by a Cubano serving Cuban food, among other things, plus a café serving bagels and fast food. The bar serves *mojitos* too. Recommended.

Lívingston *p611, map p611*

Fresh fish is available everywhere, ask for *tapado* in restaurants – a rich soup with various types of seafood, banana and coconut. Women sell *pan de coco* on the streets.

ΨΨ**Bahía Azul**, Calle Principal. Excellent breakfasts, but dreadful coffee. Tables on the street as well as a dining-room. Specializes in salsas, *camarones* and *langosta*. There is a tourist service and the **Exotic Travel Agency**.

ΨΨ**Happy Fish**, just along from the **Hotel Río Dulce**. A popular restaurant with internet café. Serves a truckload of fish (not quite so happy now) with good coffee. Occasional live music at weekends.

ΨΨ**Hotel Río Dulce** (on map). The restaurant serves delicious Italian food prepared with panache by the hospitable Italian chef, Fernando Capelli. Recommended.

Ψ**El Malecón**, 50 m from the dock on the left. Serves *chapín* and western-style breakfasts, seafood and chicken *fajitas*, all in a large, airy wooden dining area.

Ψ**McTropic**, opposite the **Hotel Río Dulce**. Street tables, great breakfasts, and cocktails. Good service and popular.

Ψ**Ubouhu**, near the **Ubafu**. With street tables outside, this Garífuna-run place, meaning 'world', has chicken, steak and shrimps on the menu, as well as drinks. It's one of the popular local gossip exchanges.

Fronteras/Río Dulce and around *p613*

ΨΨ**Restaurante y Pizzería Río Bravo**, dockside. Friendly management serving breakfasts, seafood, chicken, pastas and pizzas. Open 0700-2300.

El Estor *p614*

ΨΨ-Ψ**Restaurante Típico Chaabil**, lakeside. A thatched restaurant with plenty of fish to eat. Cheap breakfasts.

Ψ**Dorita**. A *comedor* serving seafood, very good meals, excellent value and popular with the locals.

Ψ**Marisabella**, 8 Av and 1 Calle. Good and cheap spaghetti, as well as fish and chicken, with lake views.

Ψ**Restaurant Elsita**, 2 blocks north of the market on 8 Av. This is a great people-watching place. There's a large menu and the food is good.

Ψ**Restaurante Hugo's**. Parque Central. *Mariscos, comida rápida*, vegetarian food and ice cream.

Entertainment

Lívingston *p611, map p611*

Bars and clubs

Beluba Ñuruba and **Cocobongo** are happening bars down on the beach.

Black Sheep Cinema and Bar is a popular Bob Marley shrine with happy hour as well as a cinema showing afternoon movies. Open 1400 until dawn.

Büdürü Bar y Restaurante, at Barrio París, 15 mins along the beach from town (see also under Tour operators).

Happy Fisherman's Place, next to the **Hotel Bahía Caribe** on the beach, is popular and mellow. Open all day.

Lugudi Barana, a disco that's also on the beach and popular with visitors and locals. Sun only, 1500-0100.

Tropicool, around the corner from **Bahía Azul**, is one of the most popular hang-outs from 0800-0100, with happy hr until 2100.

Ubafu, on the road down to **African Place**, is unmissable. It is heaving most nights as locals and travellers dance the *punta*. A live band plays nightly from about 2100 with drums, a conch shell and turtle shells, the *punta*'s instrument ensemble. This large, wooden bar, decked out in Bob Marley posters and Rastafarian symbols, is definitely worth a visit. Try the *coco loco*, rum and coco milk served up in a coconut. At the week ends the place is a little less packed as it vies for attention with the beach bars and discos.

Puerto Barrios *p611*

Bars and clubs

The Container, just past the **Hotel del Norte** overlooking the sea, an unusual bar constructed from the front half of an old ship equipped with portholes, and a number of banana containers from the massive banana businesses just up the road. Open 0700-2300.

Mariscos de Izabal, one of the most popular spots in Puerto Barrios. A thatched bar that is mostly a drinking den but with tacos, tortillas and burgers served amid beating Latin rhythms. You can hang out until here 0100.

Activities and tours

Lívingston *p611, map p611*

Tour operators

Büdürü Bar y Restaurante, on the beach at Barrio París 15 mins from town, offers guided tours in English and Spanish on Garífuna culture, US$7-10, T7947-0603.

Exotic Travel Agency, in the Bahía Azul restaurant, T7947-0049, exotictravelagency@hotmail.com

Happy Fish, T7947-0661, www.happyfishresort.com

Ixchel Tours, near the former **Pizzería Rigoletto**.

You can also contract any of the *lancheros* at the dock to take you anywhere. They charge US$10, US$16 round trip to Río Dulce; to Playa Blanca, US$10; to Siete Altares, US$26, 4 people maximum.

Fronteras/Río Dulce *p613*

Sailing

Captain John Clark's sailing trips on his 46-ft Polynesian catamaran, *Las Sirenas*, are highly recommended. Food, taxes, snorkelling and fishing gear, and windsurf boards included. Contact **Aventuras Vacacionales SA**, Antigua, www.sailing-diving-guatemala.com

Tour operators

Atitrans Tours, on the little road heading to the dockside. To **Finca Paraíso** for US$20.

Otiturs, next to Tijax Express, T5219-4520. Run by the friendly and helpful Otto Archila. Offers a minibus service as well as tours to local sites, internal flights and boat trips.

Tijax Express, opposite Atitrans, T7930-5505, info@tijax.com, which also has internet.

Lancheros offer trips on the river and on Lago de Izabal. They can be contacted at the muelle principal, under the bridge. Ask for César Mendez, T5819-7436, or ask at **Atitrans** for collection.

Transport

Estanzuela *p608*

Bus From **Guatemala City** to Zacapa, US$2.25 with **Rutas Orientales**, 0500-1830, every 30 mins, 2¾-3 hrs. To **Esquipulas** with same service that continues from Zacapa, US$1, 1½ hrs. To **Puerto Barrios**, US$2, 3¼ hrs. With **Vargas** 0430-1730, every 30 mins, 3½ hrs, US$2.35. Minibus leaving from next to church, 0700-0730 and 1200-1230, for the turn-off to the Quiriguá ruins, 2 hrs, US$1.05. To **Estanzuela**, 10 mins, US$0.26.

Chiquimula, Volcán de Ipala and the Honduran border *p608*

Bus Take an early bus to **Ipala**; stay on the bus and ask the driver to let you off at Aldea El Chaparroncito (10 mins after Ipala). From here it's a 1½-hr ascent, following red arrows every now and then. Another ascent goes via Municipio Agua Blanca. Take a minibus to **Agua Blanca** from Ipala and get out at the small village of El Sauce, where the trail starts. The last bus from Ipala to Chiquimula is 1700.

Chiquimula *p608*

Bus There are 3 small terminals in Chiquimula, all within 50 m of each other. To **Guatemala City**, **Transportes Guerra** and **Rutas Orientales**, hourly, US$3, 3¼-3½ hrs, leave from 11 Av between 1 and 2 Calle, as do buses for **Puerto Barrios**, several companies, every 30 mins, between 0300-1500, 4 hrs, US$2.60. To **Quiriguá**, US$1.55, 1 hr 50 mins. Take any Puerto Barrios-bound bus. On to **Río Dulce** take the Barrios bus and get off at La Ruidosa junction and change, or change at Bananera/Morales. To **Flores** with **Transportes María Elena**, 8 hrs, 0400, 0800, 1300. Buses to **Ipala** and **Jalapa** also leave from here; 4 buses daily to Jalapa between 0500-1230, 4½ hrs, US$1.80; to Ipala, US$0.65. Supplemented by minibuses 0600-1715 to Ipala, US$0.65. To **Zacapa**, US$0.52, 25 mins, from the terminal inside the market at 10 Av between 1 and 2 Calle. Same for those to **Esquipulas**, every 10 mins, US$1.05, until 1900. To and from **Cobán** via El Rancho (where a change must be made), US$1.65. Buses to **El Florido** (Honduras border) leave with **Transportes Vilma** from inside the market at 1 Calle, between 10 and 11 Av, T942-2253, between 0530-1230 on the hour, and then 1320, 1345, 1430, 1500, 1530, 1630, US$1.05, 1½ hrs. Buses return from the border at 0530, 0630 and then hourly 0700-1700. See page 610, Border with Honduras.

Esquipulas *p608*

Bus From the capital every 30 mins, 0400-1800 (see also page 530), US$3.60, 4-4½ hrs, with **Rutas Orientales**. Leaving Esquipulas, 1 Av "A" and 11 Calle, T943-1366, for **Guatemala City** every 30 mins from 0200-1700, 4½ hrs, US$3.60. To **Chiquimula** by minibus, every 30 mins, 0430-1830, US$1.05. To **Agua Caliente** (Honduran border) and **Anguiatú** for El Salvador, see below. **Transportes María Elena**, 12 Calle, between 5 and 6 Av, to **Santa Elena, Petén** at 0300, 0700, 1200, 9 hrs.

Quiriguá *p609*

Bus Emphasize to the bus driver you want Quiriguá *pueblo*, not the *ruinas*. Countless travellers have found themselves left at the ruins and having to make a return journey to the village for accommodation.

To get to the **ruins** directly, take any bus heading along the highway towards Puerto Barrios and ask to be let off at the *ruinas*. At this ruins crossroads, take a pick-up (very regular), 10 mins, US$0.40, or bus (much slower and less regular) to the ruins 4 km away. Last bus back to highway, 1700. You can walk, but take lots of water, as it's hot and dusty with little shade. To get to the **village** of Quiriguá, 3 km south from the ruins entrance road, it is only a 10-min walk to the **Hotel Royal**. Keep to the paved road, round a left-hand bend, and it's 100 m up on the left. Or take a local bus heading from the highway into the village (US$0.13). The **Hotel Edén** is a further 5 mins on down the hill. There is a frequent daily bus service that runs a circular route between Los Amates, Quiriguá village and then on to the entrance road to the ruins, US$0.13. You can also walk through the banana plantations from Quiriguá village to the ruins as well. From **Hotel Royal** walk past the church towards the old train station and the **Hotel Edén**, and follow the tracks branching to the right, through the plantation to the ruins.

Puerto Barrios *p611*

Boat It's a 10-min walk to the municipal dock at the end of Calle 12, from the **Litegua** bus station. Taxi, US$0.65 per person. Ferries *(barca)* leave for Lívingston at 1030 (1½ hrs, US$1.30). *Lanchas* also leave when a minimum of 12 people are ready to go, 35 mins, US$3.25. The only scheduled *lanchas* leave at 0630 and 0730, and the last will leave, if there are enough people, at 1800.

Transportes El Chato, 1 Av, between 10 and 11 Calle, T7948-5525, pichilingo2000@ yahoo.com, also does trips from here to

Punta de Manabique, and other places near and far, from US$25 up to US$325 from between 1-10 people.

To Belize *Lanchas* leave for **Punta Gorda** at 1000 with **Transportes El Chato**, address above, returning at 1600, 1 hr, US$13. There is also one at 1400. To the **southern Belize Cayes**, US$325 for 1-10 people. To **Placencia**, US$390. To **Puerto Cortés, Honduras** Minimum 6 people in *lancha*, US$300.

Bus To **Guatemala City**, with **Litegua**, 6 Av between 9 and 10 Calle, T7948-1002, www.litegua.com. 18 a day, 5 hrs, US$5.20. Bus to **El Rancho** (turn-off for Biotopo del Quetzal and Cobán), 4 hrs, take any bus to Guatemala City. To **Quiriguá**, 2 hrs, US$2, take any capital-bound bus. To **Chiquimula**, operated by **Carmencita**, 4 hrs, US$3. Alternatively, catch a bus to Guatemala City, getting off at Río Hondo, and catch a *colectivo* or any bus heading to Chiquimula. For **Río Dulce**, take any bus heading for Guatemala City and change at **La Ruidosa** (15 mins). For minibuses to **Entre Ríos**, for the El Cinchado border crossing to **Honduras (Corinto)**, with connections to Omoa, Puerto Cortés and La Ceiba, see page 609.

Lívingston *p611, map p611*

Boat Ferry from **Puerto Barrios** to Lívingston (22.5 km), daily at 1000 and 1700, 1½ hrs, US$1.30. Returning to Puerto Barrios, 0500 and 1400 daily (to connect with the last bus to Guatemala City). Private *lanchas* taking 16-25 people also sail this route, 35 mins, US$3.25. They leave at 0630 and 0700 from Lívingston to Puerto Barrios and then when full. Lívingston to **Río Dulce**, with short stops at Aguas Calientes and the Biotopo Chacón Machacas, US$9.10 one way, US$15.60 round trip. *Lanchas* definitely leave at 0900 and 1300 for Río Dulce, but these make no stops. To **Honduras** (Omoa, Puerto Cortés, La Ceiba), *lanchas* can be organized at the dock: to Omoa, US$32.50 per person, minimum 7 people. With **Bahía Azul**, for US$35 per person including exit tax (see Immigration below), 6 people minimum. With the same company to **Utila**, US$90, 2 days. To **Belize** (Punta Gorda, Placencia, Cayos Zapotillos), there is no regular ferry service from Lívingston. Anyone who takes you must have a manifest with passengers' names, stamped and signed at the immigration office. Most days fast *lanchas* make the trip to Punta Gorda. Enquire at the dock and negotiate a fare with the *lanchero* association, US$13 per person, min 8 people. To the cayes, US$39 per person round trip, max 8 people. Boats to Placencia, with **Bahía Azul**, for US$50 per person, 4 people minimum. Boats to Zapotilla cayes, US$35 per person, 6 people minimum with the same company. **Happy Fish**, runs boat/shuttle to **Antigua**, Quirigúa, and **San Pedro Sula**.

Fronteras/Río Dulce and around *p613*

Boat

Lanchas colectivas leave for **Lívingston** from 0900 and 1300, US$10. Private *lanchas* can be arranged at the dock to any of the river or lakeside hotels.

Bus

Local To get to **Castillo de San Felipe**, take a boat from Río Dulce, or *camioneta* from the corner of the main road to Tikal, and the first turning left after the bridge by **Pollandia**, US$0.26, 5 mins, or a 5-km walk. From Río Dulce to **Finca El Paraíso**, take a bus from the corner of the main street and a road turning left at **Pollandia** north of the bridge, 45 mins, US$0.90. Ask to be dropped at the entrance: US$0.65. Buses to Río Dulce pass the *finca* between 40 and 50 mins past the hour. To **El Estor**, US$1.30, 1½ hrs on a partially paved road, 0500-1600, hourly, returning 0500-1600. These buses leave north of the bridge, from the corner of the first road to the left, where there is a Pollandia restaurant. To **Puerto Barrios**, take any bus to **La Ruidosa** and change, 35 mins, US$0.65 to junction then a further 35 mins and US$0.65.

Long-distance To **Guatemala City** and **Flores**: through buses stop at Río Dulce. To **Guatemala City** with **Litegua**, T7930-5251, www.litegua.com, 0300, 0545, 0745 and 1200, US$3.90, 6 hrs. **Fuente del Norte**, T5692-1988, 23 services daily, 0700, then virtually hourly on the ½ hr from 1030 until 0230, US$5. Luxury service 1300, 2400, US$13. **Línea Dorada**, at 2400 and 1300, luxury service, 5 hrs, US$30. To **Flores** from 0630-0300, 20 buses daily, 4½ hrs with

Fuente del Norte, US$6.40. Luxury service, 1430, US$13. This bus also stops at **Finca Ixobel** and **Poptún**, US$3.90. **Línea Dorada**, to Flores, 2400, 1430, 3½ hrs, luxury service with a/c, TV and snacks, US$30, and on to **Melchor de Mencos** for Belize and returning. Fuente del Norte, also to **Melchor de Mencos**, US$11, at 1230, 2030, 2230-0300, **Sayaxché** at 2200 and one to **Naranjo** at 2100.

Shuttles

Atitrans, T7930-5111, www.atitrans.com, runs a shuttle service at 1500 to **Antigua**, minimum 2 people, US$40, 4½ hrs. To Río Dulce from Antigua, 0430. Also express minibus to **Flores** for US$115.

El Estor and around *p614*

Bus

The ferry from Mariscos no longer runs, but a private *lancha* can be contracted.

El Estor-Río Dulce, 0500-1600, hourly, 1¼ hrs, US$1.30. For routes from El Estor to Cobán, via either Panzós and Tactic, or Cahabón and Lanquín, see page 630. For the **Cañón El Boquerón**, take the Río Dulce bus and ask to be dropped at the entrance. Or hire a bike from town (8 km) or a taxi, US$6.50, including waiting time.

To **Cobán**, with **Transportes Valenciana**, 1200, 0200, 0400 and 0800, 8 long and dusty hrs, with no proper stop, US$2.60. The 0800 leaves its terminal and does a massive tour of the town before leaving from the park at 0900, but it's best to be there for 0800, because you will be swinging from the side wing mirror by the time it leaves, it's so packed. To **Guatemala City**, 0100 direct, via Río Dulce, 7½ hrs, or go to Río Dulce and catch one. At 2400 and 0300 via Río Polochic Valley. Bus to **Santa Elena, Petén** at 0500.

Directory

Chiquimula *p608*

Banks There are several banks accepting MasterCard and Visa, and ATMs. **Internet** 2 internet centres. **Post office** Close to the bus terminal inside the market. **Telephone** Office on the plaza.

Esquipulas *p608*

Banks There are a number of banks and ATMs in town close to the park, Visa and MasterCard accepted. There are money changers in the centre if you need *lempiras*. Better rates than at the borders. **Post office** End of 6 Av, 2-43.

Puerto Barrios *p611*

Banks Lloyds, 15 Calle and 7 Av, handles MasterCard only. Bancafé, 13 Calle and 7 Av, with Visa ATM. Banco G&T Continental, 7 Calle and 6 Av, it's possible to withdraw up to US$65 on MasterCard and Visa. TCs. Banco Industrial, 7 Av, 7-30, 24-hr Visa ATM and cash on Visa cards. **Immigration** corner of 12 Calle and 3 Av, open 24 hrs. **Internet** Café Internet, opposite gas station, corner of 6 Av and 13 Calle. **Post office** Corner of 6 Calle and 6 Av. **Telephone** Telgua, corner of 10 Calle and 8 Av.

Lívingston *p611, map p611*

Banks Bancafé, cash advance on Visa and MasterCard, TCs and cash changed. Has a 24-hr Visa-only ATM. Banco de Comercio will change Amex and MasterCard TCs and cash. There is also a Banrural. Some hotels will change cash, including Casa Rosada. **Immigration** Calle Principal, opposite Hotel Tucán Dugú, is open 24 hrs daily, T7947-0240. Just knock if the door is shut. **Internet** Black Sheep Cinema and Bar has internet. **Post office** Next to Telgua, behind the Municipalidad, take the small road to the right. **Telephone** Telgua, behind the Municipalidad, 0800-1800. **Laundry** Lavandería Doña Chila, opposite the Casa Rosada.

Fronteras/Río Dulce *p613*

Banks There are 2 banks: Visa, TCs and cash only. 2 ATMS. **Internet** Captain Nemo's Communications behind Bruno's, and phone call service and Tijax Express. Hotel Backpacker's has internet as does Información Río Dulce, near the dock (also phone service). **Post office** Near the banks.

El Estor *p614*

Banks Corpobanco and Banrural accept TCs and cash. **Post office** On the park.

The Verapaces

Propped up on a massive limestone table eroded over thousands of years, the plateau of the Verapaz region is riddled with caves, underground tunnels, stalagtites and stalagmites. Cavernous labyrinths used by the Maya for worship, in their belief that caves are the entrances to the underworld, are also now visited by travellers who marvel at the natural interior design of these subterranean spaces. Nature has performed its work above ground too. At Semuc Champey, pools of tranquil, turquoise-green water span a monumental limestone bridge; beneath the bridge a river thunders violently through. The quetzal reserve also provides the opportunity to witness a feather flash of red or green of the elusive bird, and dead insects provide curious interest in Rabinal, where their body parts end up on ornamental gourds. The centre of this region – the imperial city of Cobán – provides respite for the traveller with a clutch of museums honouring the Maya, coffee and orchid, and a fantastic entertainment spectacle at the end of July with a whirlwind of traditional dances and a Maya beauty contest. *»» For Sleeping, Eating and other listings, see pages 627-631.*

Ins and outs

The principal road entrance to the Verapaces leaves the Atlantic Highway at El Rancho heading up to Cobán. This junction is one hour from Guatemala City. *»» For further details, see Transport, page 629.*

Background

Before the Spanish conquest of the region, Las Verapaces had a notorious reputation – it was known as Tezulutlán (land of war) for its aggressive warlike residents, who fought repeated battles for years with their neighbours and rivals, the K'iche' Maya. These warring locals were not going to be a pushover for the Spanish conquerors and they strongly resisted when their land was invaded. The Spanish eventually retreated in despair and the weapon was replaced with the cross. Thus, Carlos V of Spain gave the area the title of Verdadera Paz (true peace) in 1548. The region's modern history saw it converted into a massive coffee- and cardamom-growing region. German coffee fincas were established from the 1830s until the Second World War, when the Germans were invited over to plough the earth by the Guatemalan government. Many of the *fincas* were expropriated during the war, but some were saved from this fate by naming a Guatemalan as the owner of the property. The area still produces some of Guatemala's finest coffee – served up with some of the finest cakes! The Germans also introduced cardamom to the Verapaces, when a *finquero* requested some seeds for use in biscuits. Guatemala is now the world's largest producer of cardamom.

Baja Verapaz *»» pp627-631.*

The small region of Baja Verapaz is made up of a couple of Achi'-Maya speaking towns, namely Salamá, Rabinal, San Jerónimo and Cubulco. The department is known for the quetzal reserve, the large Dominican *finca* and aqueduct, and the weird decorative technique of the crafts in Rabinal.

Sierra de las Minas Biosphere Reserve → *Colour map 5, A2.*

ⓘ *To visit, get a permit in San Augustín from the office of La Fundación de Defensores de la Naturaleza, Barrio San Sebastián, 1 block before the Municipalidad, T7945-1477. The contact is Claudia Paíz. Alternatively, contact the* **Fundación** *offices in Santa Elena, Péten, at 5 Calle, 3 Av "A", Zona 2, T7926-3095, or in the capital at 19 Av B, 0-83, Zona 15, Vista Hermosa II, T2369-5151.*

Just north of El Rancho, in the department of El Progreso, is **San Agustín Acasaguastlán**, an entrance for the Sierra de las Minas Biosphere Reserve, one of Guatemala's largest conservation areas with peaks topping 3000 m and home to the quetzal, harpy eagle and peregrine falcon. Puma, jaguar, spider monkey, howler monkey, tapir and pizote also roam its mountains.

Biotopo del Quetzal

ⓘ *Daily 0700-1600, US$2.60, parking available, disabled entrance. Run by CECON (Centro de Estudios Conservacionistas), Av Reforma, 0-63, Zona 10, Guatemala City, T2331-0904.*

The Biotopo del Quetzal, or **Biosphere Mario Dary Rivera**, is between Cobán and Guatemala City at Km 160.5, 4 km south of Purulhá and 53 km from Cobán. There are two trails. Increasing numbers of quetzals have been reported in the Biotopo, but they are still very elusive. Ask for advice from the rangers.

Salamá, Rabinal and Cubulco

Shortly before Salamá is **San Jerónimo**, where there is a Dominican church and convent, from where friars tended vineyards, exported wine and cultivated sugar. There is an old sugar mill (*trapiche*) on display at the *finca* and a huge aqueduct of some 124 arches to transport water to the sugar cane fields and the town. Salamá sits in a valley with a colonial cathedral, containing carved gilt altarpieces as its centrepiece. The town also has one of a few remaining Templos de Minerva in the country; it was built in 1916. Behind the Calvario church is a hill – Cerro de la Santa Cruz – from where a view of the valley can be seen. Market day is Monday and is worth a visit. The village of **Rabinal** was founded in 1537 by Fray Bartolomé de las Casas. It has a 16th-century church, and a busy Sunday **market**, where lacquered gourds, beautiful *huípiles* and embroidered napkins are sold. The glossy lacquer of the gourd is made from the body oil of a farmed scaly insect called the *niij* (*Llaveia axin*). The male *niij* is boiled in water to release its oil, which is then mixed with soot powder, to create the lacquer used to decorate the gourds. The **Museo Rabinal Achí** ⓘ *2 Calle y 4 Av, Zona 3, T5311-1536, museoachi@ hotmail.com*, displays historical exhibits and has recently produced bilingual books about the Achí culture. West of Rabinal, set amid maize fields and peach trees, **Cubulco** is known for its tradition of performing the pole dance, *Palo Volador*, which takes place every 20-25 July. Men, attached to rope, have to leap from the top of the pole and spiral down, accompanied by marimba music. There are three basic *hospedajes* in town.

Alta Verapaz » pp627-631.

The region of Alta Verapaz is based on a gigantic mountain, Sierra de Chamá. Dinosaurs roamed the area more than 65 million years ago before it was engulfed by sea. It later emerged, covered with limestone rock, which over millions of years has left the area riddled with caves, and dotted with small hills. In the far northwest of the department are the mystical, emerald-green waters of Laguna Lachuá.

Santa Cruz Verapaz and around

Santa Cruz Verapaz has a fine, white, 16th-century church and a **festival** between 1-4 May when you can see the wonderful Danza de los Guacamayos (scarlet macaws). **Poqomchi' Maya** village is 15 km northwest of Tactic, see below, at the junction with the road to Uspantán. To get there, take the San Cristóbal Verapaz bus, 25 minutes (see below), or take any bus heading to the capital, get off at the junction and walk the couple of hundred metres into the town. The local **fiestas** are 15, 20 January, 21-26 July with the *Palo Volador*. 8 December when the devil-burning dance can be seen. Six kilometres west towards Uspantán is **San Cristóbal Verapaz**, which has a large, white, colonial church. From the church, a 1-km long, straight, road (Calle del Calvario) slopes down and then curves upwards to a hilltop **Calvario Church**. At Easter, the entire road is carpeted in flowers that rival those on display in Antigua at this time of year. There is **Museo Katinamit** ① *T7950-4039, cecep@intelnet.net.gt, Mon-Fri 0900-1200, 1500-1700*, run by the Centro Comunitario Educativo Poqomchi', dedicated to the preservation and learning of the Poqomchi' culture.

Cobán and around

» *pp627-631. Colour map 5, B2.*

→ *Altitude: 1320 m.*

The cathedral and centre of the Imperial City of Cobán (www.cobanav.net), is perched on a long, thin plateau with exceptionally steep roads climbing down from the plaza. To the south the roads are filled with the odd, well-preserved colonial building and a coffee finca. There is year-round soft rainfall, known as *chipi-chipi*, which is a godsend to the coffee and cardamom plants growing nearby. Most visitors use the city as a base from which to visit the sights around. There's an unofficial **tourist office** on the Parque Central run by the helpful people at **Access Computación**, in the same building as **Café Tirol** (see page 629). English is spoken, they have lots of information and can help organize tours. For information on northern Alta Verapaz and the southern Petén, check www.puertamundomaya.com.

Sights

The **cathedral** is on the east side of the Parque Central and dates from the middle of the 16th century. The chapel of **El Calvario**, in the northwest, has its original façade still intact. On the way up to the church are altars used by worshippers who freely blend Maya and Roman Catholic beliefs. Its worth climbing the 142 steps to get a bird's-eye view of Cobán. The **Museo El Príncipe Maya** ⓘ *Mon-Sat 0900-1300, 1400-1800, US$1.30, 6 Av, 4-26, Zona 3*, is a private museum of pre-Columbian artefacts. The **Parque Nacional Las Victorias** ⓘ *just west of El Calvario, daily 0700-1800, US$0.80*, has two little lagoons in its 84 ha. There are paths and you can picnic and camp, loos but no showers, but check with the tourist office about safety before going. The daily **market** is near the bus terminal. **Starbucks** coffee fans can check out where their mug of the old bean comes from – direct from **Finca Santa Margarita** ⓘ *on the edge of town, gustavg@intelnet.net.gt, Mon-Fri 0800-1230, 1330-1700, Sat 0800-1200, 45-min tour, US$2.50, 3 Calle, 4-12, Zona 2*. Don't miss a visit to the flower-filled world of **Vivero Verapaz** ⓘ *Mon-Sat 0700-1800, US$1.30, 2.5 km southwest of town, 40-min walk, or taxi ride, US$1.30*, an orchid farm with more than 23,000 specimens, mostly flowering from December to February – the best time to go – with the majority flowering in January.

Around Cobán

Southeast of Cobán (8 km) is **San Juan Chamelco** with an old colonial church. A one-hour walk from here is **Aldea Chajaneb** (see Sleeping). Along this road are the caves of **Grutas Rey Marcos** ⓘ *US$1.30*, and **Balneario Cecilinda** ⓘ *Sat and Sun 0800-1700*. **San Pedro Carchá** is 5 km east of Cobán on the main road and used to be famous for its pottery, textiles, wooden masks and silver, but only the pottery and silver are available now. The local food speciality here is *kaq Ik*, a turkey broth.

Parque Nacional Laguna Lachuá

ⓘ*US$5.20*

Near **Playa Grande**, northwest of Cobán, is Parque Nacional Laguna Lachuá. The deep velvet-green lake, formed by a meteor impact, is 5 sq km and 220 m deep in places. It is surrounded by dense jungle, which is virtually unspoilt, and the chances of seeing wildlife at dawn and dusk are high. There is a guided nature trail and camping (see Sleeping). In this area is the **Río Ikbolay**, a green river that runs underground through caves. When it emerges the other side it is blue. The river has changed its course over time leaving some of its run-through caves empty, making it possible to walk through them. The **Proyecto**, see page 629, runs jungle hikes in this area.

Lanquín and Semuc Champey

▸▸ *pp627-631.Colour map 5, B2.*

Lanquín is surrounded by mountainous scenery reminiscent of an Alpine landscape. It nestles in the bottom of a valley, where a river runs through it. With a hammock bar at the village entrance, caves and the clear water pools at Semuc Champey, it is worth kicking back for a few days and inhaling the high altitude air. Lanquín is 56 km east of Cobán, 10 km from the Pajal junction. Just before the town are the **Grutas de Lanquín** ⓘ *0800-1600, US$2.60, 30-min walk from town*. The caves are lit for 200 m and strange stalactite shapes are given names, but it's worth taking a torch as well. The cave, whose ceiling hangs with thousands of stalactites, is dangerously slippery, although handrails will help you out. The sight of the bats flying out at dusk is impressive. Outside the cave you can swim in the river and camp for free.

From Lanquín you can visit the natural bridge of **Semuc Champey** ⓘ *0600-1800, US$2.60, parking US$0.65*, a liquid paradise stretching 60 m across the Cahabón

Gorge. The limestone bridge is covered in stepped, clear blue and green water pools, that span the length and breadth of it. Upstream you can see the water being channelled under the bridge. As it thunders through, it is spectacular. At its voluminous exit you can climb down from the bridge and see it cascading. You can swim in all the pools and little hot flows pour into some of them.

North of Cobán and the southern Petén crossroads

About 100 km northeast of Cobán is **Sebol**, reached via Chisec (www.visitchisec.com with information on the Grutas de Candelaria and Laguna Lachuá, see page 626) and Raxruja. From here roads go north to Sayaxché and east to Modesto Méndez via Fray Bartolomé de las Casas. West of Raxruja are the **Grutas de Candelaria** ⓘ *US$5.35 including a guided tour*, an extensive cavern system with stalagmites. Take the road to Raxrujá and look for a sign saying 'Escuela de Autogestión Muqbilbe' and enter here to get to the caves and eco-hotel (A). Camping is possible. North of Raxruja is the Maya site of Cancuén ⓘ *www.puertamundomaya.com, US$8*, reached by *lancha* in 30 minutes (US$40 for 1-12 people), from the village of La Unión (camping and meals are available at the site). Ten kilometres east of Sebol, and 15 minutes by bus, is **Fray Bartolomé de las Casas,** a town that is just a stop-off for travellers on the long run between Poptún and Cobán or Sayaxché. A rough dirt road (currently being tarmacked) links Fray Bartolomé de las Casas, Sebol and Sayaxché via unappealing **Raxrujá.** The scenery is beautiful with luscious palms, solitary sheer-sided hills and thatched-roofed homes.

Sleeping

Sierra de las Minas *p623*
D **La Cabaña de Los Albores**, Chilascó. A 130-m-high waterfall is near this ecotourism project.

Biotopo del Quetzal *p624*
B **Posada Montaña del Quetzal**, at Km 156, T2331-0929. Bungalows or rooms with private bathrooms, hot water, café, bar, swimming pool and gardens.
E-F **Hospedaje Los Ranchitos**, next to Biotopo entrance. Clean rooms, hot water, and dorms, which are fairly basic, *comedor*. This is an excellent spot from where to see the quetzal in the early morning (0600) , especially Jul-Nov.

Salamá, Rabinal and Cubulco *p624*
D **Tezulutlán**, Ruta 4, 4-99, Zona 1, just off the plaza, Salamá, T7940-1643. One of the best in town with bath, cheaper without, restaurant, some rooms have hot water. It's clean and quiet.
E **San Ignacio**, 4 Calle "A", 7-09, Salamá, T7940-0186. Behind the Telgua building, with bath and TV, clean and friendly.
E-F **Posada San Pablo**, Rabinal. Clean and friendly, will do the laundry, but there are hard beds and the *posada* has no hot water.

Santa Cruz Verapaz and around *p624*
B-C **Hotel Park**, on the main road south of the junction to the Poqomchi' Maya village, Santa Cruz, Verapaz, T/F7950-4539, rooms of varying prices with TV, restaurant, bar, gym, excellent gardens and a small zoo.
D **Chi' Ixim**, Km 182.5, just beyond Tactic, T7953-9198. Rooms with private bath, hot water and fireplaces, restaurant.
E-F **Hotel El Portón Real**, 4 Av, 1-44, Zona 1, Santa Cruz Verapaz, T7950-4604. Dreary from the outside, but inside this hotel is lovely with lots of wood furnishings. It's run by a very friendly *señora*. Rooms, with bath, cheaper without, hot water and free drinking water. The hotel closes its doors at 2130.

Cobán *p625, map p625*
Accommodation is extremely hard to find on the Fri and Sat of **Rabin Ajau** (last week of Jul) and in Aug. For Rabin Ajau you need to

be in town a few days beforehand to secure a room, or ring and reserve.

A La Posada, 1 Calle, 4-12, Zone 2, T7952-1495, www.laposadacoban.com. 14 attractively decorated rooms all with private tiled bathrooms and fireplaces, colonial hotel with well-kept flourishing gardens, credit cards accepted, stylish restaurant with terrace and fireplace, stop by for a drink if nothing else. Café too, see Eating.

B Alcazar Doña Victoria 1, 1 Av 5-34, Zona1 T7952-1143. More expensive than the original **Doña Victoria** (see below), modern colonial style, handy for the bus.

B-C Hotel Posada de Don Juan Matalbatz, 3 Calle, 1-46, Zona 1, T/F7952-1599. This is a colonial-style hotel with rooms set around a courtyard. Despite the nearby bus terminal it is very quiet and safe. All rooms have TV and there's a restaurant and pool table, parking. Tours offered.

C Hotel de Posada Carlos V, 1 Av 3-44, Zona 1, T7951-1133, victormoino@hotmail.com. Lantern-lined entrance, Swiss-chalet style, eclectic, Italian family, fireplace in lounge, restaurant, bar, cosy, modern annex not as nice.

C-F Hostal de Doña Victoria, 3 Calle, 2-38, Zona 3, T7951-4213. In a 400-year-old former Dominican convent with colonnaded gallery, attractive gardens and a good restaurant (see below). Also cheap dorm room. Excursions arranged, recommended.

D Central, 1 Calle, 1-79, T/F7952-1442, heinemann@terra.com.gt. Next to **Café San Jorge**, a stone's throw from the cathedral. There are 15 very clean large rooms, around a patio, with hot shower. Rooms with TV cost a little extra.

D Monja Blanca, Diagonal 4, 6-37 Zona 2 T7951-1712. All rooms are set around a pretty courtyard, very peaceful, old-fashioned dining room, breakfast good value. The place is run by a slightly eccentric *señora* and looks shut from the outside. Recommended.

D-E Hotel Posada de Don José, 6 Av, 1-18, Zona 4, T7951-4760. 14 rooms with private bathroom, TV, cheaper without, clean general bathrooms, laundry, friendly, courtyard, good budget option.

E La Paz, 6 Av, 2-19, T7952-1358. Hot water, safe parking, pleasant, 38 rooms, cheaper without bath, laundry, café, garden, popular.

E-F Casa D'Acuña, 4 Calle, 3-11, Zona 2, T7951-0482, casadeacuna@yahoo.com. 2 bunk beds to a room, ultra-clean bathrooms with hot water, laundry service, internet, excellent meals, tempting goodies and coffee in **El Bistro** restaurant in a pretty courtyard (see Eating). The owners run a tourist office, shop and tours. Recommended.

Around Cobán *p626*

B Don Jerónimo's, Km 5.3, carretera a Chamil, Aldea Chajaneb T/F5301-3191, www.dearbrutus.com/donjeronimo. Bungalows to rent, with full board including 3 vegetarian meals a day. All-inclusive, hiking, swimming and tubing, massage, great for relaxation. From Cobán in a taxi, 30 mins, about US$6. Or, take a bus from Cobán to Chamelco, then bus or pick-up to Chamil and ask to be let off at **Don Jerónimo's**.

Parque Nacional Laguna Lachuá *p626*

E National park accommodation. Price per person. Bunk beds with mosquito netting or camping (tents available). Bring your own food and rubbish bags. There are fireplaces, showers and toilets.

E-G Finca Chipantun, on the borders of the national park on the bank of the Río Chixoy, T7951-3423. With rooms, hammocks or camping space. 3 meals a day are provided at extra cost but at excellent value – the most expensive is dinner at US$3.

Lanquín and Semuc Champey *p626*

C El Recreo, Lanquín, at the village entrance, T7952-2160. Clean, good meals, friendly, pool, but this isn't always filled with water.

F El Retiro, 5 mins from Lanquín on the road to Cahabón. Campsite, *cabañas*, dorm beds and restaurant, in a gorgeous riverside location. There's an open fire for cooking, hammocks to chill out in, and tubes for inner tubing the river. To get there don't get off in town, continue for 5 mins and ask to be dropped off. Highly recommended.

F Hospedaje El Centro, Lanquín, close to the church. Friendly, good simple dinner, basic.

Camping

It is possible to camp for as long as you want at Semuc Champey once you've paid the entrance fee. There are toilets and cooking areas. Take insect repellent, a mosquito net, and all food and water.

See also **El Retiro**, above.

North of Cobán and the southern Petén crossroads *p627*

E Las Diamelas, Fray Bartolomé de las Casas, just off park, T5810-1785. Cleanest rooms in town. Restaurant food is OK and cheap.

F Rancho Ríos Escondidos, near Grutas de Candelaria, on the main road. Camping possible at this farmhouse. Ask for Doña América.

Eating

Cobán *p625, map p625*

TTT El Bistro, in Casa D'Acuña (see Sleeping). Excellent menu and massive portions. Try the blueberry pancakes, great yogurt, do not walk through the restaurant without putting your nose into the cake cabinet! Recommended.

TT El Refugio, 2 Av, 2-28, Zona 4, T952-1338. Excellent waiter service and substantial portions at good value prices – steaks but also fish, chicken and snacks, good-value set lunch, cocktails, big screen TV, bar, 1030-2300.

TT Hostal de Doña Victoria, restaurant inside on 3 Calle, 2-38, Zona 3. Serves up breakfast, lunch and supper in a semi-open area with a pleasant, quiet ambience. Good Italian food, including vegetarian options, is the speciality of the house. Also mini cellar bar **El Estable**, romantic venue, cubas and candlelight.

T Cafetería San Jorge, next to **Hotel Central**. Local delights tacos, *tostadas, pay de queso*, cheap breakfasts, set lunch and snacks, friendly service, shut Sun.

T Tropikuba, 2C 8-24, Zona1. Family atmosphere, bamboo and salsa music, excellent meaty options, good-value beer and food. Recommended. Open 1830-2230.

Cafés

Café El Tirol, 1 Calle, 3-13, on the main park. Good meals, 52 coffee concoctions, 17 teas and 9 hot chocolate options, home-made wholemeal bread, good cakes. 0700-2200. Recommended.

Café La Posada, part of La Posada (see Sleeping). Has divine brownies and ice cream, sofas with a view of the Parque Central and, unfortunately, some very ugly satellite dishes. Open afternoons.

Lanquín and Semuc Champey *p626*

There are *tiendas* in Lanquín selling good fruit and veg, and there are a couple of bakeries, all open early, for stocking up for a trip to Semuc Champey.

T Comedor Shalom, Lanquín. Excellent value, if basic, including drink.

T Rancho Alegre, Lanquín, at the entrance to the village. Relaxing hammock bar ideal for a chilled beer.

Entertainment

Cobán *p625, map p625*

Bars and clubs

Milenio, 3 Av 1-11, Zona 4, 5 rooms, dance floor, live music weekends, beer by the jug, pool table, big screen TV, week ends minimum consumption US$3, popular place with a mature crowd.

Soluna Café Bar, 12 Av, 1-12, Zona 2, relaxed atmosphere, popular with Cobaneros, Wed-Sat 1730-2400.

Festivals and events

Cobán *p625, map p625*

Mar/Apr Holy Week.

Last week of Jul Rabin Ajau, the election of the Maya Beauty Queen. Around this time the Paa banc is also performed, when the chiefs of brotherhoods are elected for the year.

1-6 Aug Santo Domingo, the town's fiesta in honour of its patron.

Activities and tours

Cobán *p625, map p625*

Tour operators

Aventuras Turísticas, 1 Calle, 3-25, Zona 1, T7951-1358, also offers tourist information.

Interconti, 2 Calle, 6-01, Zona 2, T7951-3191. Offers travel agency services and local tours. Very helpful. **Proyecto Ecológico Quetzal**, 2 Calle, 14-36, Zona 1, Cobán, T/F7952-1047, www.ecoquetzal.org. Contact David Unger. Trips are organized to the multicoloured Río Ikbolay, northwest of Cobán, see page 626, and the mountain community of Chicacnab.

Transport

Biotopo del Quetzal *p624*

Bus From **Guatemala City**, take a Cobán bus with Escobar-Monja Blanca and ask to be let out at the Biotopo, hourly from 0400-1700, 3½ hrs, US$3.90; **Cobán**-Biotopo,

1 hrs, US$1.05, take any capital-bound bus; bus **El Rancho**-Biotopo, US$1.30, 1¼ hr. Cobán-Purulhá, local buses ply this route between 0645-2000 returning until 1730, US$0.52, 1 hr 20 mins.

Salamá, Rabinal and Cubulco *p624*
Bus Salamá-Rabinal, US$0.50, 1-1½ hrs. Rabinal is reached by travelling west from Salamá on a paved road. From **Guatemala City**, 5½ hrs, a beautiful, occasionally heart-stopping ride, or via El Progreso, and then Salamá by bus. Buses leave 0330-1600 to Guatemala City via Salamá from **Cubulco**. There is a bus between Rabinal and Cubulco, supplemented by pick-up rides.

Santa Cruz Verapaz and around *p624*
Bus From **Cobán** between 0600-1915 every 15 mins, US$0.26, 40 mins. All capital-bound buses from Cobán run through **Tactic**, or take a local bus between 0645-2000, returning between 0500-1730, 40 mins, US$0.32. Bus from Cobán to **Senahú**, 6 hrs, from opposite INJAV building, from 0600-1400, 4 daily, US$2.35. If you are coming from El Estor, get off at the Senahú turn-off, hitch or wait for the buses from Cobán. Trucks take this road, but there is little traffic, so you have to be at the junction very early to be in luck.

Cobán *p625, map p625*
Bus To **Guatemala City** with Transportes Escobar-Monja Blanca, T7951-1793, hourly from 0130-1730, 4 hrs, US$4, from its own offices near the terminal. From the main Cobán terminal: to **El Estor**, 10 daily, first at 0400, and mostly morning departures, but check in the terminal beforehand, 8 hrs, US$2. To **Fray Bartolomé de las Casas**, between 0600-1600 by bus, pick-up and trucks, every 30 mins. Route **Raxrujá-Sayaxché-Flores** there are minibuses micro buses del norte that leave from 1 Av 3 Calle, T7952-1086 via Raxruha-Sayaxché from 0630-1730 buses direct to Sayaxché leave at 1100 and 1400. 4 hrs, US$3.15. In Sayaxché you take a passenger canoe across the river (there is also a car ferry) where minibuses will now whisk you to Flores on a tarmacked road in 45 mins. To **Uspantán**, 1000 and 1200, 5 hrs, US$1.40. Cobán can be reached from **Santa Cruz del Quiché** via Sacapulas and Uspantán, and from **Huehuetenango** via Aguacatán, Sacapulas and Uspantán. To **Salamá**, minibus, US$1.75, 2¼ hrs.

Car **Ochoch Pec**, at the entrance to town, T7951-3474.

Around Cobán *p626*
Bus Every 15 mins from Cobán to **San Juan Chamelco** between 0530-1900, US$0.13 and leave from 5 Av and 3 Calle. Buses leave Cobán for **San Pedro Carchá**, every 10 mins, US$0.13, 15 mins, between 0600-1820. Heading for **Playa Grande** from Cobán, also known as **Ixcan Grande**, ask the bus driver to let you off before Playa Grande at 'la entrada del parque', from where it's a 4.2-km (1-hr) walk to the park entrance. Buses leave Cobán at 0500, 1000 and 1230, the first 2 via Chisec, 4½ hrs, US$3.90. There are also minibuses that leave when full for US$5.20.

Lanquín and Semuc Champey *p626*
Bus From **Cobán** there are minibuses El Cahabonero that leave from the 2 Av 2-25, Zona 4 from 0900 a total of 15 per day, 9 that only go as far as **Cahabón** (US$2.50, 2hrs) and 6 that go onto Lanquín (US$3.15, 3hrs) There are now 2 that go direct to Semuc Champey at 1015 and 1500. From **Cahabón** to **El Estor** at 0400, 3-3½ hrs. From Lanquín to **Flores**: take the 0400 or 0600 Cobán bus to **Pajal**, 1 hr, US$0.30, then any passing bus or vehicle to **Sebol**, 2-2½ hrs (there are Las Casas-Cobán buses passing hourly in the morning only) and then pick-up, hitch or bus to Sayaxché and then Flores Semuc Champey is a 10-km walk to the south from Lanquín, 3 hrs' walking along the road, which is quite tough for the first hour as the road climbs very steeply out of Lanquín. If planning to return to Lanquín the same day, start very early to avoid the midday heat. To get there in a pick-up start early (0630), US$0.65, or ask around for a private lift (US$13 return). Transport is very irregular so it's best to start walking and keep your fingers crossed. By 1200-1300 there are usually people returning to town to hitch a lift with. If you are on your own and out of season, it would be wise to arrange a lift back.

Car There is a gas station in Lanquín near the church.

North of Cobán and the southern Petén crossroads *p627*

Bus Local transport in the form of minibuses and pick-ups connects most of these towns before nightfall.
Bus to **Poptún** leaves at 0300 from the central park, 5¾ hrs, US$3.25. This road is extremely rough and the journey is a bone-bashing, coccyx-crushing one. Buses to **Cobán** at 0400 until 1100 on the hour. However, do not be surprised if one does not turn up and you have to wait for the next one. To **Flores** via Sebol, Raxrujá and Sayaxché at 0700 (3½ hrs, US$3.90 to Sayaxché) a further ½-1 hr to Flores. The road from **Raxrujá** via Chisec to Cobán is very steep and rocky. **Chisec** to Cobán, 1½ hrs. The Sayaxché-Cobán bus arrives here for breakfast and continues between 0800 and 0900. You can also go from here to Sebol to Modesto Méndez to join the highway to **Flores**, but it is a very slow, killer of a journey. Buses leave from Cobán for Chisec from the market terminal at 0500, 0800, 0900. The 1000 Cobán-Playa Grande bus also passes through Chisec.

Directory

Cobán *p625, map p625*

Banks Most banks around the Parque Central will change money. MasterCard accepted at G&T Continental, corner of 1 Calle and 2 Av. Visa ATM at Bancafé, just down from the cathedral on 1 Av. **Internet** Access Computación, same building as Café Tirol. Fax and collect-call phone service only. Infocel, 3 Av, between 1-2 Calle, Zona 4. **Language schools** Active Spanish School, 3 Calle, 6-12, Zona 1, T7952-1432 (Nirma Macz). La Escuela de Español Muq'bil' B'e, 6 Av, 5-39, Zona 3, T7951-2459 (Oscar Macz), muqbilbe@intelnet.net.gt Offers Spanish and Q'eqchi'. **Laundry** Lavandería Providencia, opposite Café Tirol. **Medical services** Policlínica y Hospital Galen, a private institution on 3 Av, 1-47, Zona 3, T7951-2913. **Post office** Corner of 2 Av and 3 Calle. **Telephone**, you can make international calls from Telgua and Access Computación (see above).

El Petén

Deep in the lush lowland jungles of the Petén lie the lost worlds of Maya cities, pyramids and ceremonial centres, where layers of ancient dust speak of ancient tales. At Tikal, where battles and burials are recorded in intricately carved stone, temples push through the tree canopy, all wrapped in a mystical shroud. Although all human life has vanished from these once-powerful centres, the forest is humming with the latter-day lords of the jungle: the howler monkeys that roar day and night. There are also toucans, hummingbirds, spider monkeys, wild pig and coatimundi. Jaguar, god of the underworld in Maya religion, stalks the jungle but remains elusive, as does the puma and the tapir. Penetrating further into the undergrowth away from Tikal, the adventurous traveller can visit El Mirador, the largest Maya stronghold, as well as El Zotz, El Perú, El Ceibal and Uaxactún all by river, by foot and on horseback. » *For Sleeping, Eating and other listings, see pages 644-650.*

Ins and outs

Best time to visit The dry summer months and wet winter months offer different advantages and disadvantages. In the summer months of November through to early May, access to all sites is possible as tracks are bone-dry. There are also less mosquitoes and if you are a bird lover, the mating season falls in this period. In the rainy winter months, from May-November, tracks become muddy quagmires making many of them impassable, also bringing greater humidity and mosquitoes. Take plenty of repellent, and reapply frequently. It's also fiercely hot and humid at all times in these parts so lots of sun screen and drinking water are essential.

Background

Predominatly covered in jungle, the Petén is the largest department of Guatemala although it has the smallest number of inhabitants. The northern area was so impenetrable that its Maya settlers, the Itza's, were not conquered by the Spaniards until 1697. In 1990 21,487 sq km of the north of the Petén was declared a Reserva de la Biósfera Maya (Maya Biosphere Reserve), by CONAP, the National Council for Protected Areas. It became the largest protected tropical forest area in Central America. Inside the boundaries of the biosphere are the Parque Nacional Tikal, Parque Nacional Mirador-Río Azul and Parque Nacional Laguna del Tigre.

Poptún → *Colour map 5, B3.*

Poptún is best known for its association with **Finca Ixobel**, see Sleeping. Otherwise, it is just a staging-post between Río Dulce and Flores, or a stop-off to switch buses for the ride west to Cobán.

Flores and Santa Elena » *pp644-650. Colour map 5, A2.*

Flores is perched on a tiny island in Lake Petén Itzá'. Red roofs and palm trees jostle for position as they spread up the small hill, which is topped by the white twin-towered cathedral. Some of the streets of the town are lined with houses and restaurants that have been given lashings of colourful paint, giving Flores a Caribbean flavour. *Lanchas*, drifting among the lilies and dragonflies, are pinned to the lake edges. Santa Elena is the dustier, less elegant and noisier twin town on the mainland where the cheapest hotels, banking services and bus terminal can be found.

Ins and outs

Getting there and around Flores is 2 km from the international airport on the outskirts of Santa Elena. The airport departures hall has an internet place. Tour operator and hotel representatives are based in the arrival halls. A causeway links Flores with Santa Elena. A taxi from the airport into Santa Elena or Flores, US$1.30, 5 minutes, but bargain hard. If you arrive by long-distance bus from Guatemala City, Mexico or Belize, the new terminal is 10 blocks south of the causeway. There are hotels in Santa Elena and Flores across the causeway (10 to 15 minutes from Santa Elena). Chicken buses run between the two, US$0.26. *Tuc-tucs* charge US$0.70 for journeys between the two.

Tourist information INGUAT ⓘ *in the airport, T7956-0533, daily 0700-1200, 1500-1800; there are also 2 offices on the road to Tikal at Km 5 and Km 8, Mon-Fri 0800-1600 and daily 0700-1500, respectively.* **ProPetén** ⓘ *Calle Central, T7926-1370, www.propeten.org*, associated with **Conservation International. CINCAP** (Centro de Información sobre la Naturaleza, Cultura y Artesanía de Petén) ⓘ *on the plaza, T7926-0718, www.alianzaverde.org*, has free maps of Tikal, and other local information. Housed in the same building is the **Alianza Verde** ⓘ *closed Mon*, an organization promoting sustainable eco-tourism. If you wish to make trips independently to remote Maya sites, check with **ProPetén** to see if they have vehicles making the journey.

Safety There have been no minibus hold-ups for 18 months on the road to Tikal. There has been one robbery on the road to Yaxhá. Get independent, up-to-date advice before visiting these places and leave all valuables at your hotel. **Asistur**, see page 515, can assist and have a base at Tikal.

Background

This jungle region was settled by the Maya Itza' Kanek in about AD 600, with their seat then known as La Isla de Tah Itza' (Tayasal in Spanish), now the modern-day Flores. The Itza's were untouched by Spanish inroads into Guatemala until the Mexican conquistador Hernán Cortés and Spanish chronicler Bernal Díaz del Castillo dropped by in 1525 on their way from Mexico to Honduras. In 1697 Martín Urzua y Arismendi, the governor of the Yucatán, fought the first battle of the Itza's, crossing the lake in a galley killing 100 indigenous people in the ensuing battle, and capturing King Canek. He and his men destroyed the temples and palaces of Tayasal and so finished off the last independent Maya state.

Sights

The **cathedral**, Nuestra Señora de los Remedios y San Pablo del Itzá, is plain inside. The cathedral houses a Cristo Negro, part of a chain of Black Christs that stretches across Central America, with the focus of worship at Esquipulas. **Paraíso Escondido** is home to the **zoo** ⓘ *US$2.70*. A dugout to the island costs US$16 round trip. Near the zoo is **ARCAS** (Asociación de Rescate y Conservación de Vida Silvestre) ⓘ *visitors US$2, T2478-4096, www.arcasguatemala.com*, where they care for rescued

Flores

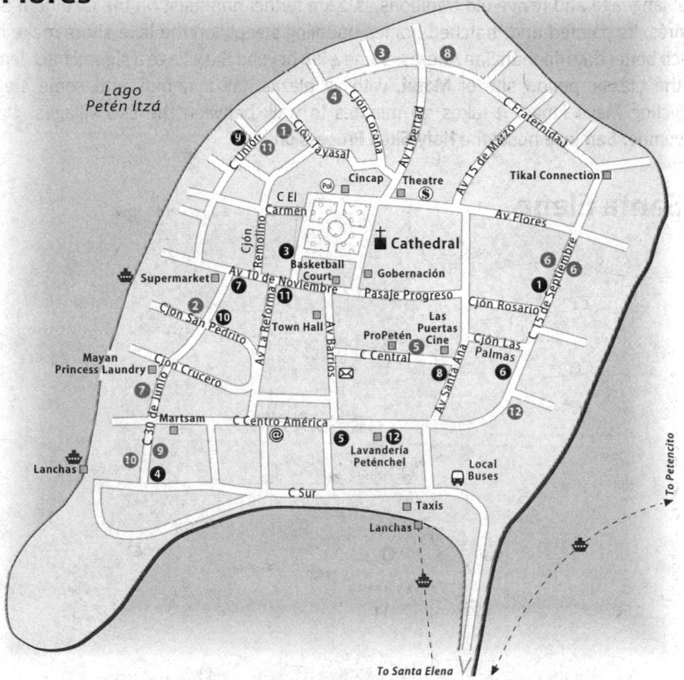

Sleeping
Casa Aurora 1
Casazul 3
Doña Goya 4
La Casona de la Isla 2
Mirador del Lago & Annexe 6
Petén 7
Sabana 8
Santana 10
Santa Rita 9
Tayasal 11
Villa del Lago 12
Youth Hostel Los Amigos 5

Eating
Café Arqueológico Yax-há 1
El Mirador 3
Hacienda del Rey 4
La Albahaca 10
La Canoa 5
La Galería del Zotz 6
La Luna 7
Las Puertas Café Bar 8
La Unión 9
Mayan Princess Café Bar & Cinema 11
Naomi's Café 12

animals with the purpose of releasing them back into the wild. Volunteers are welcome. There is a new centre and interactive trails at the site, Boat tours of the whole lake cost about US$10 per boat, calling at the zoo and **El Mirador** on the Maya ruin of **Tayasal** ⓘ*US$2.70*. **Actún Kan caves** ⓘ*0800-1700, US$2.70*, are a fascinating labyrinth of tunnels where, legend has it, a large serpent lived. They are 3 km south of Santa Elena and a 30 to 45 minutes' walk. To get there take the 6 Avenida out of Santa Elena to its end, turn left at a small hill, then take the first road to the right where it is well marked. South of Santa Elena is **Parque Naturual Ixpanpajul** ⓘ*T2336-0576, www.ixpan pajul.com*, where Tarzan tours and more are on offer. Local **fiestas** include 12-15 January, the Petén *feria*, and 11-12 December in honour of the Virgen de Guadalupe.

Around Lake Petén Itzá'

San Andrés, 16 km by road from Santa Elena, enjoys sweeping views of Lake Petén Itzá', and its houses climb steeply down to the lake shore. There is a language school. Adonis, a villager, takes good-value tours to El Zotz and El Mirador and has been recommended. Ask around for him; his house is close to the shoreline. You can also now volunteer in the village with **Volunteer Petén** ⓘ*Parque Nueva Juventud, T5711-0040, www.volunteerpeten.com*, a conservation and community project. The attractive village of **San José**, a traditional Maya Itza' village, where efforts are being made to preserve the Itza' language and revive old traditions, is 2 km further northeast on the lake from San Andrés. Its painted and thatched homes huddling steeply on the lake shore make it a much better day trip than San Andrés. Some 4 km beyond the village a signed track leads to the Classic period site of **Motul**, with 33 plazas, tall pyramids and some stelae depicting Maya kings. It takes 20 minutes to walk between the two villages. On 1 November San José hosts the **Holy Skull Procession**.

Santa Elena

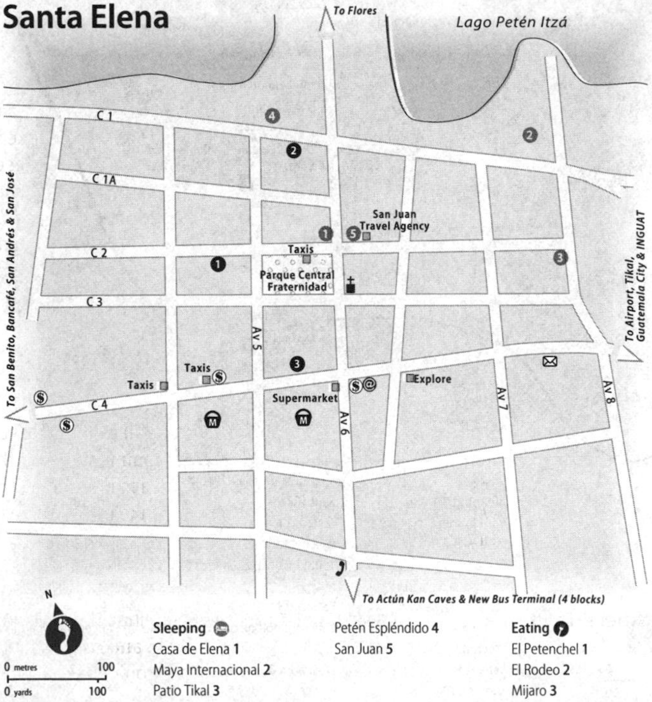

Sleeping
Casa de Elena 1
Maya Internacional 2
Patio Tikal 3
Petén Espléndido 4
San Juan 5

Eating
El Petenchel 1
El Rodeo 2
Mijaro 3

Border essentials: Guatemala-Belize

Melchor de Mencos-Benque Viejo
Border open 0600-2100. There is a 37.50 BZ dollar fee to leave Belize. If you need a visa for either Belize or Mexico obtain it at their consulates in Guatemala City. As a back-up there are 72-hr transit visas available at the border, which will cover you to the Mexican border at Chetumal, but not into Mexico. If you intend to stay in Belize, you may be able to get a visa at the border but there could be extra charges when you leave the country.
Transport The road is semi-paved. There are several buses from Santa Elena to Melchor de Mencos, starting at 0500, 2-3 hrs. Also *colectivos* from new station in Santa Elena, 1½ hrs, US$2. On the return to Santa Elena there there are regular *colectivos* and Rosita buses at 1100, 1400, 1600, 18OO, US$1.30. For Tikal, alight at Ixlu cruce. Heading to Belize: if you catch the 0500 bus from Santa Elena you can be in Belize City by 1200 having caught a bus from Benque de Viejo bus station. In addition, there is a non-stop minibus service from Santa Elena to Belize City, with **San Juan Travel Agency**, see page 648. This service terminates at the Marine Terminal in Belize, from where boats to the cayes leave. Also **Línea Dorada** at 0600, US$19, 4 hrs, returning 0900 to Flores. Between Melchor de Mencos and Benque Viejo, the first town in Belize, there are taxis to take you the couple of kilometres, BZ$1.50, but rip-offs are common – so bargain hard. To Mexico through Belize: there is a bus from Flores direct to Chetumal, Mexico, with San Juan Travel Agency and with **Línea Dorada**. This bus connects with an **ADO** bus to Playa del Carmen.
Exchange There are good rates for quetzales, Belizean dollars and Mexican pesos on the street; or try Banrural at the border (0700-2000).

At the eastern side of Lake Petén Itzá' is **El Remate**. The sunsets are superb and the lake is flecked with turquoise blue in the mornings. You can swim in the lake in certain places away from the local women washing their clothes and the horses taking a bath. There are many lovely places to stay, see Sleeping. West of El Remate is the 700-ha **Biotopo Cerro Cahuí** ⓘ *daily 0800-1600, US$2.70, administered by CECON*. It is a lowland jungle area where three species of monkeys, deer, jaguar, peccary, ocellated wild turkey and some 450 species of bird can be seen. If you do not wish to walk alone, you can hire a guide. Ask at your *posada*.

Parque Nacional Tikal

» *pp644-650. Colour map 5, A2.*

With its Maya skyscrapers pushing up through the jungle canopy, Tikal will have you transfixed. Steep-sided temples for the mighty dead, stelae commemorating the powerful rulers, inscriptions recording the noble deeds and the passing of time, and burials that were stuffed with jade and bone funerary offerings, make up the greatest Maya city in this tropical pocket of Guatemala.

Ins and outs

Getting there From Flores, it's possible to visit Tikal in a day. San Juan Travel Agency minibuses leave hourly between 0500 and 1000, one at 1400 and return hourly between 1400 and 1800, one hour, US$5 one way. Several other companies also run minibuses. If you have not bought a return ticket you can often get a discounted seat on a returning bus if it's not full. Minibuses also meet Guatemala City-Flores flights. A taxi to Tikal costs US$35 one way. You can also visit Tikal with a package tour from Guatemala City or Antigua. Prices for one-day excursions start at about US$140 return (including flights and transfers), two days US$180.

If you enter after 1500 your ticket is valid the following day. It is best to visit the ruins after 1400, or before 0900, as there are fewer visitors. An overall impression of the ruins may be gained in four or five hours, but you need at least two days to see it properly.

Getting around Open daily 0600-1800, US$7 (Q50) per day, payable at the national park entrance, 18 km from the ruins. (Park administration, T7920-0025). If you stay the night in the park hotels, you can enter at 0500 once the police have scoured the grounds. This gives you at least a two-hour head start on visitors coming in from Flores. At the visitor centre there is a post office, which stores luggage, a tourist guide service here (see below), exchange facilities, toilets, a restaurant and a few shops that sell relevant guidebooks. Take a hat, mosquito repellent, water and snacks with you as it's extremely hot, drinks at the site aren't cheap and there's a lot of legwork involved.

Tikal

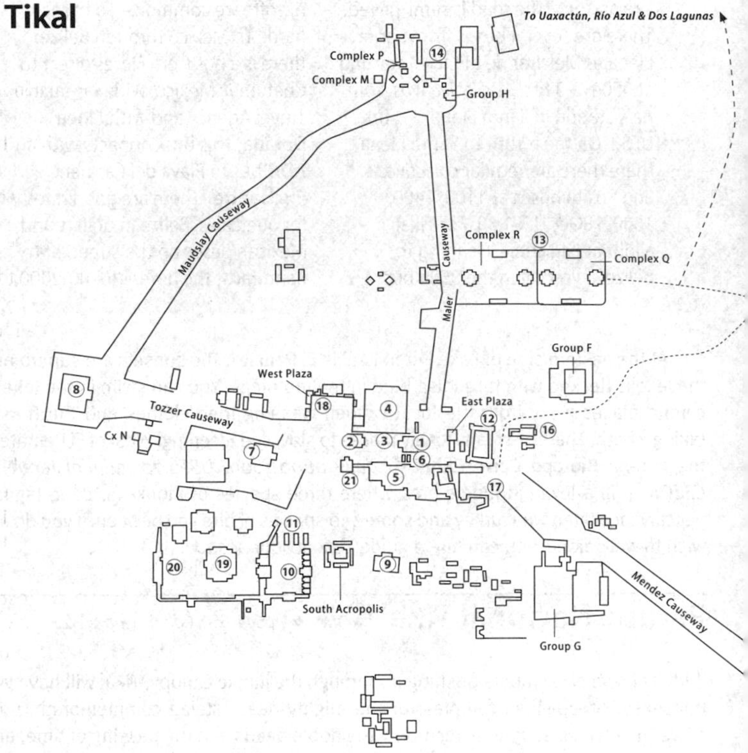

Sights ◯
Temple I (Temple of the Great Jaguar) **1**
Temple II (Temple of the Masks) **2**
The Great Plaza **3**
North Acropolis **4**
Central Acropolis **5**
Ball Court **6**
Temple III (Temple of the Jaguar Priest) **7**
Temple IV (Temple of the Double-Headed Serpent) **8**
Temple V **9**
Plaza of the Seven Temples **10**
Triple Ball Court **11**
Market **12**
Twin Pyramid Plazas **13**
North Group **14**
Temple VI (Temple of Inscriptions) **15**

From April to December it rains every day for a while; it is busiest November to January, during the Easter and summer holidays and most weekends.

Tourist information A guide is highly recommended as outlying structures can otherwise be missed. The official **Tourist Guide Association** offers tours of varying natures and in different languages. For one to five people tours of four hours are available, US$40. These are in Spanish, English or Italian. German and French tours are done for a minimum of US$50. The guidebook *Tikal*, by W R Coe, in several languages, has an excellent map.

History

At its height, the total 'urban' area of Tikal was more than 100 sq km, with the population somewhere between 50,000 and 100,000. The low-lying hill site of Tikal was first occupied around 600 BC during the pre-Classic era, but its buildings date from 300 BC. It became an important Maya centre from AD 300 onwards, which coincided with the decline of the mega power to the north, El Mirador. It was governed by a powerful dynasty of 30-plus rulers between about the first century AD until about AD 869, with the last known named ruler being Hasaw Chan K'awill II.

Tikal's main structures, which cover 2.5 sq km, were constructed from AD 550 to AD 900 during the Late Classic period. These include the towering mega structures of temples – shrines to the glorious dead – whose roof combs were once decorated with coloured stucco figures of Tikal lords. Doorways on the temple rooms were intricately carved – using the termite-resistant wood of the sapodilla tree – with figures and symbols, known as lintels. Tikal's stelae tell of kings and accessions and war and death. Its oldest stela dates from AD 292. Many Central Mexican influences have been found on the stelae imagery, in burial sites at Tikal and in decorative architectural technique, which led archaeologists to conclude that the city was heavily influenced from the west by forces from the great enclave of Teotihuacán, now just outside Mexico City. This war-like state bred a cult of war and sacrifice and seemed intent on spreading its culture. After the collapse of Teotihuacán in AD 600, a renaissance at Tikal was achieved by the ruler Ah Cacao (Lord Cocoa, Ruler A, Moon Double Comb, Hasaw Chan K'awil I, Sky Rain) who succeeded to the throne in AD 682 and died sometime in the 720s. However, in the latter part of the eighth century the fortunes of Tikal declined. The last date recorded on a stela is AD 889. The site was finally abandoned in the 10th

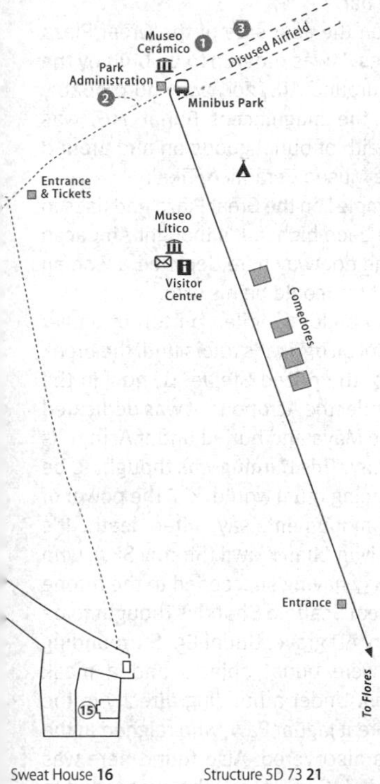

Sweat House **16**
Structure 5D 38 **17**
Structure 5D II **18**
Great Pyramid 5C 54 **19**
El Mundo Perdido (Lost World) **20**
Structure 5D 73 **21**

Sleeping
Jaguar Inn **1**
Jungle Lodge **2**
Tikal Inn **3**

century. Most archaeologists now agree the collapse was due to warfare with neighbouring states, over population, which resulted in environmental destruction, and drought. Tikal's existence was first reported by Spanish monk Andrés de Avendaño, but its official discovery is attributed to Modesto Méndez, Commissioner of the Petén, and Ambrosio Tut, Governor of the Petén, in 1848. They were both accompanied by an artist – Eusebio Lara.

Wildlife

Tikal is a fantastic place for seeing animal and bird life of the jungle. Wildlife includes spider monkeys, howler monkeys, three species of toucan (most prominent being the keel-billed toucan), deer, foxes and many other birds and insects. Pumas have been seen on quieter paths and coatimundis (*pizotes*), in large family groups, are often seen rummaging through the bins. The ocellated turkeys with their sky-blue heads with orange baubles attached are seen in abundance at the entrance, and at **El Mundo Perdido**.

The ruins

The **Great Plaza (3)** is a four-layered plaza with its earliest foundations laid around 150 BC and its latest around AD 700. It is dwarfed by its two principal temples – Temples I and II. On the north side of the plaza between these two temples are two rows of monuments. It includes Stela 29, erected in AD 292, which depicts Tikal's emblem glyph – the symbol of a Maya city – and the third century AD ruler Scroll Ahau Jaguar, who is bearing a two-headed ceremonial bar.

Temple I (Temple of the Great Jaguar) (1) on the east side of the Great Plaza rises to 44 m in height with nine stepped terraces. It was ordered to be built by the ruler Ah Cacao, who ruled between AD 682 to around AD 720-724, who probably planned it for use as his shrine. His tomb, the magnificent Burial 116, was discovered beneath Temple I in 1962 with a wealth of burial goods on and around his skeleton. The display is reconstructed in the Museo Cerámico/Tikal.

Temple II (Temple of the Masks) (2) faces Temple I on the Great Plaza and rises to 38 m, although with its roof comb it would have been higher. It's thought Ah Cacao ordered its construction as well. The lintel on the doorway here depicted a woman wearing a cape, and experts have suggested that this could be his wife.

The **North Acropolis (4)** contains some 100 buildings piled on top of earlier structures in a 1-ha area and is the burial ground of all of Tikal's rulers until the break with royal practice made by Ah Cacao. In 1960, the prized Stelae 31, now in the Museo Cerámico/ Tikal, see below, was found under the Acropolis. It was dedicated in AD 445. Its base was deliberately burnt by the Maya and buried under Acropolis buildings in the eighth century. This burning was thought to be like a 'killing', where the burning ritual would 'kill' the power of the ruler depicted on the monument, say, after death. It's thought to depict the ruler Siyah Chan K'awil (Stormy Sky), who died sometime around AD 457 having succeeded to the throne in AD 411. Yax Moch Xok (Great Scaffold Shark) is thought to be entombed in the first century AD grave, Burial 85. Surrounding the headless male body were burial objects and a mask bearing the royal head band. Under a building directly in the centre of this acropolis Burial 22 – that of ruler Great Jaguar Paw, who reigned in the fourth century, and died around AD 379 – was discovered. Also found here was Burial 10, thought to be the tomb of Nun Yax Ayin I (Curl Nose), who succeeded to the throne in AD 379 after Great Jaguar Paw. Inside were the remains of nine sacrificed servants as well as turtles and crocodile remains and a plethora of pottery pieces. The pottery which was laid out in this tomb had Teotihuacán artistic influences, demonstrating Tikal's links to the powers of Teotihuacán and

December to April is the best time for bird tours with November to February being the mating season. Mosquitoes can be a real problem even during the day if straying away from open spaces.

Teotihuacán-influenced Kaminal Juyú. Burial 48 is thought to be the tomb of Curl Nose's son, Siyah Chan K'awil (Stormy Sky).

Central Acropolis (5) is made up of a complex of courts connected by passages and stairways, which have expanded over the centuries to cover 1.6 ha. Most of the building work carried out took place between AD 550-900 in the Late Classic era. The **East Plaza** behind Temple I is the centre of the highway junctions of the Maler Causeway in the north, and the Méndez caseway heading southeast.

On the western side of the **West Plaza** is structure 5D II under which Burial 77 was brought to light. The skeleton was adorned with a jade pendant, which was stolen from the site museum in the 1980s.

Temple III (Temple of the Jaguar Priest) (7) is so called because of the scene of a figure in a glamorous jaguar pelt on a lintel found on the temple. Some experts believe this figure is Ah Chitam (Nun Yax Ayin II, Ruler C), son of Yax Kin, and grandson of the great Ah Cacao, and so propose that this is his shrine, although there has been no confirmation of this.Temple III was constructed around AD 810 and is 55 m tall.

Temple IV (Temple of the Double-Headed Serpent) (8) is the highest building in Tikal at 70 m. It was built in the Late Classic period around AD 741, as proven by hieroglyphic inscriptions and carbon dating. It's thought it was built to honour Yax Kin, the son of Ah Cacao, who became ruler in AD 734. A date on the lintel is AD 741, the same year that Temple I was dedicated.

Temple V (9) constructed between AD 700-750 during the reign of Yax Kin, is 58 m high. It is the mortuary temple of an unknown ruler.

El Mundo Perdido (The Lost World) (16) The Great Pyramid is at the centre of this lost world. At 30 m high, it is the largest pyramid at Tikal. It's flat topped and its stairways are flanked by masks. From the top a great view over the canopy to the tops of other temples can be enjoyed. Together with other buildings to the west, it forms part of an astronomical complex. The Lost World pyramid is a pre-Classic structure, but was improved upon in the Early Classic. East of el Mundo Perdido isthe Plaza of the **Seven Temples (10)**, constructed during the Late Classic period (AD 600-800). There is a triple court ball court lying at its northern edge.

Temple VI (Temple of the Inscriptions) (15) was discovered in 1951. The 12 m-high roof comb is covered on both sides in hieroglyphic text and is the longest hieroglyphic recording to date. It was carved in AD 766, but the temple was built under the rule of Yax Kin some years before. Altar 9 is at the base of the temple as is Stela 21, said to depict the sculptured foot of the ruler Yax Kin to mark his accession as ruler in AD 734. Unfortunately because of the location of this temple away from the rest of the main structures it has become a hideout for robbers and worse. Some guides no longer take people there. Take advice before going, if at all.

The North Group There are several twin pyramid complexes at the site, including Complexes Q and R, marking the passing of the *katun* – a Maya 20-year period.

The **Museo Cerámico** (**Museo Tikal**) ⓘ *near the Jungle Lodge, Mon-Fri 0900-1700, Sat and Sun, 0900-1600, US$1.30*, has a collection of Maya ceramics, but its prize exhibits are Stela 31 with its still clear carvings, and the reconstruction of the tomb of Tikal's great ruler, Ah Cacao. The **Museo Lítico** ⓘ *in the visitor centre, Mon-Fri 0900-1700, Sat and Sun, 0900-1600, US$1.30*. There are stelae and great photographs of the temples as they were originally found, and of their reconstruction, including the 1968 rebuild of the Temple II steps.

Photography is no longer allowed in either of these museums.

Other Maya ruins » *pp644-650.*

There are literally hundreds of Maya sites in the Petén. Below are a handful of sites, whose ruins have been explored, and of whose histories something is known.

Uaxactún

→ Colour map 5, A3.

In the village of Uaxactún (pronounced Waash-ak-tún) are ruins, famous for the oldest complete Maya astronomical complex found, and a stuccoed temple with serpent and jaguar head decoration. The village itself is little more than a row of houses either side of a disused airstrip. Uaxactún is one of the longest-occupied Maya sites. Its origins lie in the Middle pre-Classic (1000 BC-300 BC) and its decline came by the early post-Classic (AD 925-1200) like many of its neighbouring powers. Its final stelae, dated AD 889, is one of the last to be found in the region. The site is named after a stela, which corresponds to Baktun 8 (8 x 400 Maya years), carved in AD 889 – *uaxac* means 8, *tun* means stone. South of the remains of a ball court, in **Group B,** a turtle carving can be seen, and Stela 5, which marks the takeover of the city, launched from Tikal. Next door to this stela under Temple B-VIII were found the remains of two adults, including a pregnant woman, a girl of about 15 and a baby. It is believed this may have been the governor and his family who were sacrificed in AD 378. From Group B, take the causeway to **Group A**. In Group A, Structure A-V had 90 rooms and there were many tombs to be seen. The highest structure in the complex is Palace A-XVIII, where red paint can still be seen on the walls. In **Group E** the oldest observatory (E-VII-sub) ever found faces structures in which the equinoxes and solstices were observed. When the pyramid (E-VII) covering this sub-structure was removed, fairly well preserved stucco masks of jaguar and serpent heads were found flanking the stairways of the sub-structure. The ruins lie either side of the village, the main groups **(Groups A and B)** are to the northwest (take a left just before **Hotel El Chiclero** and follow the road round on a continuous left to reach this group). A smaller group **(Group E)** with the observatory is to the southwest (take any track, right off the airstrip, and ask. This group is 400 m away. The site is 24 km north of Tikal on an unpaved road. It is in fairly good condition taking less than one hour in any vehicle.

El Zotz

El Zotz, meaning bat in Q'eqchi', is so called because of the nightly flight from a nearby cave of thousands of bats. There is an alternative hiking route as well (see below). Incredibly, from Temple IV, the highest in the complex at 75 m, it is possible to see in the distance, some 30 km away, Temple IV at Tikal. The wooden lintel from Temple I (dated AD 500-550) is to be found in the Museo Nacional de Arqueología y Etnología in the capital. Each evening at about 1850 the sky is darkened for 10 minutes by the fantastic spectacle of tens of thousands of bats flying out of a cave near the camp. The 200-m-high cave pock marked with holes is a half-hour walk from the camp. If you are at the cave you'll see the flight above you and get doused in falling excrement. If you remain at the campsite you will see them streaking the dark blue sky with black in straight columns. It's also accessible via Uaxactún. There is some basic infrastructure for the guards, and you can camp.

One of the best trips you can do in the Petén is a three-day **hike to El Zotz and on through the jungle to Tikal**. The journey, although long, is not arduous, and is accompanied by birds, blue morpho butterflies and spider monkeys chucking branches at you all the way.

El Perú and the Estación Biológica Guacamayo

A visit to El Perú is included in the **Scarlet Macaw Trail**, a two- to five-day trip into the **Parque Nacional Laguna del Tigre**, through the main breeding area of the scarlet macaw. There is little to see at the Maya site, but the journey to it is worthwhile. In 2004 the 1200 year old tomb and skeleton of a Maya queen were found. A more direct trip involves getting to the Q'eqchi'-speaking isolated community of **Paso Caballos** (1¾ hours). Here, the **Comité de Turismo** can organize transport by *lancha* along the Río San Pedro. From Paso Caballos it is one hour by *lancha* to the El Perú campsite and path. It's possible to stop off at the **Estación Biológica Guacamayo** ⓘ *US$1.30,*

Border essentials: Guatemala-Mexico

El Naranjo - La Palma
Immigration Near the landing stage, 0700-1800.
Sleeping **Posada San Pedro** (**C**) has simple *cabañas* with mosquito nets, restaurant, T2334-8136/39, reservations in Guatemala City.
Transport **Fuente del Norte** from the Santa Elena bus station to El Naranjo 0300, 1400, 5 hrs, US$3.30. Return the same. **Transportes Pinita** buses leave from **Hotel San Juan** at 0500, 0900, 5 hrs, US$3.25, returning 1400-1500, 1700-1800. Naranjo Frontera at 0300-1830, every 30 mins returning 0430-1730. Rosío buses to El Naranjo at 0500, 0700, 0900. From El Naranjo, daily boats at 0600 and around 1300-1400, for La Palma, Mexico, US$22, cheaper to pay in quetzales, 4-5 hrs, including Mexican border crossing, from where buses go to Tenosique and on to Palenque. The 1300 boat will often get you to La Palma just in time to miss the last bus to Tenosique; be prepared to stay the night. If there are fewer than 5 passengers for the boat, it may be cancelled and your alternatives are to wait for the next boat, or hire a rápido, US$125. Return from La Palma to El Naranjo at 0800. Bus La Palma-Tenosique at 1700, also *colectivos*; it is not possible to get to Palenque the same day unless you hire a taxi in La Palma. Mexican tourist cards can be obtained at the border.
Exchange You can change money at the grocery store opposite immigration at a better US dollar-quetzal rate than the Mexican side of the border.

volunteers may be needed, contact Propeten, T7926-1370, www.propeten.org, where there is an ongoing programme to study the wild scarlet macaws (*ara macao*). The chances of seeing endangered scarlet macaws during March, April and May in this area is high because that's when they are reproducing. A couple of minutes upriver is the landing stage, where it's a 30-minute walk to the campsite of El Perú; howler monkeys, hummingbirds, oropendola birds and fireflies abound. From there, it is a two-hour walk to the El Perú ruins. Small coral snakes slither about, howler monkeys roar, spider monkeys chuck branches down on the path. White-lipped peccaries, nesting white turtles, eagles, fox and kingfishers have also been seen. The trip may be impossible between June and August because of rising rivers during the rainy season and because the unpaved road to Paso Caballos may not be passable. Doing it on your own is possible, though you may have to wait for connections and you will need a guide, about US$20 per day.

El Mirador, El Tintal and Nakbé → *Colour map 5, A2.*

El Mirador is the largest Maya site in the country. It dates from the late pre-Classic period (300 BC-AD 250) and is thought to have sustained a population of tens of thousands. It takes five days to get to El Mirador. From Flores it is 2½-three hours to the village of Carmelita by bus or truck, from where it is seven hours walking, or part horse riding to El Mirador. It can be done in four days – two days to get there and two days to return. The route is difficult and the mosquitoes and ticks and the relentless heat can make it a trying trip. Organized tours are arranged by travel agents in Flores – get reassurance that your agents have enough food and water. If you opt to go to El Mirador independently, ask in Carmelita for the **Comité de Turismo**, which will arrange mules and guides. Take water, food, tents and torches. It is about 25 km to El Tintal, a camp where you can sling a hammock, or another 10 km to El Arroyo, where there is a little river for a swim near a *chiclero* camp. It takes

There are paintings and treasures; guards will show you around if no one else is on hand.

Border essentials: Guatemala-Mexico

Bethel/La Técnica-Frontera Echeverría (Corozal)

Bethel immigration Open 24 hrs. You are advised to get your visa or Mexican tourist card in advance if you need one. You can get your Mexican immigration stamp at Corozal (24 hrs).

Transport Take a bus from Santa Elena via La Libertad to Bethel. **Transportes Pinita** bus, 0500, 3½-4 hrs, US$4, returns 1100. With **Fuente del Norte** at 0600, 5 hrs, US$3.30. Return the same time. At 0500 to La Técnica with **Pinita**, returning at 0400. (Buses return to Flores at 0400, 1100, 1700, but ask at the immigration point to be sure). The bus will then continue to the *lancha* point for the boat ride, 30 mins, US$33-40 per boat. However, if the bus does not wait you will have to walk 10-15 mins to the river. A further 12 km from Bethel, 25 mins, is La Técnica where the boat ride to Corozal is only US$2.90 per person, 3 mins. However, apparently the Bethel *lancha* coop does not like the La Técnica *lanchas* taking its trade and robberies on the road to La Técnica have reportedly taken place. At Corozal a paved road leads up 18 km to the Frontier Highway (35 km to the San Javier junction for Lacanjá and Bonampak). From the border it is 4 hrs by bus to Palenque. To get to Palenque in 1 day, take the 0500 bus from Santa Elena and catch a pick-up, bus or tour bus. There is also a daily shuttle service to Palenque, Mexico, 0500, US$30. Contact **San Juan Travel Agency** (see Tour operators, page 648). **Línea Dorada** also plies this route for US$30, 0600, 7 hrs.

Sleeping In Corozal you can choose between the unfriendly **Escudo Jaguar** and the **Centro Turístico & Grutas Tsolk'in**.

Pipiles-Benemérito

Immigration and transport Get to Sayaxché, 60 km, and then take a boat down the Río de la Pasión to the military post at Pipiles (exit stamps must be given here – if you need a Mexican tourist card it's advisable to get it in advance to avoid paying bribes at the border) and on to the town of Benemérito. There are trading boats which take 8 hrs, US$5; motorized cargo canoe US$5-10, 8 hrs; private launch US$100, 4 hrs.

Sleeping At Benemérito, there are a couple of basic *hospedajes*.

Transport From Benemérito, buses at 0600, 0700, 0800 and 1300 to immigration just past the Río Lacantún (or hitch in a truck); buses wait here before continuing to Palenque on an unpaved road; 7-12 hrs by bus Benemérito-Palenque (more in the wet). Take a hammock, mosquito net, food and insect repellent; the only accommodation between Sayaxché and Palenque are these few rooms in Benemérito, and dollars cannot be exchanged.

another day to El Mirador, or longer, if you detour via Nakbé. You will pass *chiclero* camps on the way, which are very hospitable, but very poor. In May, June and July there is no mud, but there is little chance of seeing wildlife or flora. In July to December, when the rains come, the chances of glimpsing wildlife is much greater and there are lots of flowers. It is a lot fresher, but there can be tonnes of mud, sometimes making the route impassable. The mosquitos are also in a frenzy during the rainy season. Think carefully about going on the trip (one reader called it "purgatory"). The site, which is part of the Parque Nacional Mirador-Río Azul, is divided into two parts with the **El Tigre Pyramid** and complex in the western part, and the **La Danta** complex, the largest in the Maya world, in the east, 2 km away. The larger of two huge pyramids – La Danta – is 70 m high; stucco masks of jaguars and birds flank the stairways of the temple complex. The other, El Tigre, is 55 m in height and is a wonderful place to be on top of at night, with a view of endless jungle and other sites, including Calakmul, in Mexico. In **Carmelita** ask around for space to sling your hammock or camp. There is a basic *comedor*. **El Tintal**, a day's hike from El Mirador, is said to be the second largest site in Petén, connected by a causeway to El Mirador, with great views from the top of the pyramids. **Nakbé**, 10 km southeast of El Mirador, is the earliest known lowland Maya site (1000-400 BC), with the earliest examples of carved monuments.

Northwest Petén and the Mexican border

An unpaved road runs 151 km west from Flores to **El Naranjo** on the Río San Pedro, near the Mexican **border**. At **Posada San Pedro** there are guides and arrangements for travel as far as Palenque. Close by is **La Joyanca** is a newly opened site where the chance of wildlife spotting is high. You can camp at the *cruce* with the guards.

Parque Nacional Laguna del Tigre and Biotopo

The park and biotopo is a vast area of jungle and wetlands north of El Naranjo. The best place to stay is the CECON camp, across the river below the ferry. This is where the guards live and they will let you stay in the bunk house and use their kitchen. Getting into the reserve is not easy and you will need to be fully equipped, but a few people go up the Río Escondido. The lagoons abound in wildlife, including enormous crocodiles and spectacular bird life. Contact CECON.

Sayaxché → *Colour map 5, B2.*

Sayaxché has a frontier town feel to it as its focus is on a bend on the Río de la Pasión. It is a good base for visiting the southern Petén including a number of archaeological sites, namely El Ceibal. You can change US dillar bills and traveller's cheques at **Banoro**.

El Ceibal

This major ceremonial site is reached by a 45-minute *lancha* ride up the Río de la Pasión from Sayaxché. It is about 1.5 km from the left bank of Río de la Pasión hidden in vegetation and extending for 1.5 sq km. The height of activity at the site was from 800 BC to the first century AD. Archaeologists agree that it appears to have been abandoned in between about AD 500 and AD 690 and then repopulated at a later stage when there was an era of stelae production between AD 771 and 889. It later declined during the early decades of the 10th century and was abandoned. You can sling a hammock at El Ceibal and use the guard's fire for making coffee if you ask politely – a mosquito net is advisable, and take repellent for walking in the jungle surroundings. Tours can be arranged in Flores for a day trip to Sayaxché and El Ceibal (around US$50) but there is limited time to see the site. From Sayaxché the ruins of the **Altar de los Sacrificios** at the confluence of the Ríos de la Pasión and Usumacinta can also be reached. It was one of the earliest sites in the Péten, with a founding date earlier than that of Tikal. Most of its monuments are not in good condition. Also within reach of Sayaxché is **Itzán**, discovered in 1968.

Piedras Negras

Still further down the Río Usumacinta in the west of Petén is Piedras Negras, a huge Classic period site. In the 1930s Tatiana Proskouriakoff first recognized the periods of time inscribed on stelae here coincided with human life spans or reigns, and so began the task of deciphering the meaning of Maya glyphs. Advance arrangements are necessary with a rafting company to reach Piedras Negras. **Maya Expeditions** (address on page 518) run expeditions, taking in Piedras Negras, Bonampak, Yaxchilán and Palenque. This trip is a real adventure. The riverbanks are covered in the best remaining tropical forest in Guatemala, inhabited by elusive wildlife and hiding more ruins. Once you've rafted down to Piedras Negras, you have to raft out. Though most of the river is fairly placid, there are the 30-m **Busilhá Falls**, where a crystal-clear tributary cascades over limestone terraces and two deep canyons, with impressive rapids to negotiate, before reaching the take-out two days later.

Petexbatún

From Sayaxché, the Río de la Pasión is a good route to visit other Maya ruins. From **Laguna Petexbatún** (16 km), a fisherman's paradise can be reached by outboard canoe from Sayaxché. Excursions can be made from here to unexcavated ruins which are generally grouped together under the title Petexbatún. These include **Arroyo de la Piedra**, Dos Pilas and Aguateca. **Dos Pilas** has many well-preserved stelae, and an important tomb of a king was found here in 1991 – that of its Ruler 2, who died in AD 726. Dos Pilas flourished in the Classic period when as many as 10,000 lived in the city. There are many carved monuments and hieroglyphic stairways at the site, which record the important events of city life. **Aguateca**, where the ruins are so far little excavated, gives a feeling of authenticity. The city was abandoned in the early ninth century for unknown reasons. Again, a tour is advisable. It's a boat trip and a short walk away. The site was found with numerous walls (it's known the city was attacked in AD 790) and a chasm actually splits the site in two. The natural limestone bridge connects a large plaza with platforms and buildings in the west with an area of a series of smaller plazas in the east. These places are off the beaten track and an adventure to get to.

Sleeping

Poptún *p631*

C-G Finca Ixobel, T5410-4307, www.fincaixobel.com. A working farm owned by Carole Devine, widowed after the assassination of her husband in 1990. This highly acclaimed 'paradise' has become the victim of its own reputation and is frequently crowded especially at weekends. However, you can still camp peacefully and there are great treehouses, dorm beds and private rooms. Private rooms, tree-houses, dorm beds, camping. One of the highlights has to be the food. The *finca* offers a range of trips that could keep you there for days.

Flores *p632, map p633*

AL Hotel Casona del Lago, overlooking the lake, T7952-8700, www.hotelesdepeten.com. 32 spacious rooms, some with balcony, in this lovely duck-egg blue and white hotel. Pool, restaurant, internet and travel agency.

A-B Hotel Casazul, Calle Fraternindad, T7926-0692, www.corpetur.com. 9 rooms, all blue and most with lakeside view. All with cable TV, a/c and fan. Friendliness of staff seems to have improved.

A-B La Casona de la Isla, Callejón San Pedrito, on the lake, T7926-0523, www.hotelesdepeten.com. Elegant rooms, fans, TV, clean, friendly, good restaurant, nice breakfasts, bar, garden, pool.

A-B Petén, 30 de Junio, T/F7926-0692, www.hotelesdepeten.com. Lake view, clean, pool inside the foyer area, luggage stored, ask for new rooms at the front. All with a/c and TV. Internet service.

B Hotel Santana, Calle 30 de Junio, T/F7926-0662, www.santanapeten.com. Lakeside restaurant, pool, clean rooms, all with their own terrace and TV.

B Sabana, Calle Fraternindad, T/F7926-1248, www.hotelsabana.com. Huge, spartan rooms, good service, clean, pleasant, good view, caters for European package tours, lakeside pool and restaurant.

D Casa Aurora, Calle Unión, T7926-3540, tikal@itelgua.com. 15 spartan rooms with bath and a/c. 6 have lake view and TV. Gaudí-esque roof terrace but no shade.

D Doña Goya, Calle Unión, T7926-3538. 6 clean rooms, 3 with private bath, cheaper without, 3 with balcony, terrace with superb views, friendly family which run the place.

D Santa Rita, Calle 30 de Junio, T7926-3216. Bath, clean, excellent service. 3rd-floor rooms have view of the lake, but rooms can get quite stuffy, despite the fans.
D Tayasal, Calle Unión, T7926-0568. Rooms of various sizes, fan, showers downstairs, some with private bath, roof terrace, very accommodating, can arrange a Tikal trip. Travel agency in reception.
D Villa del Lago, 15 de Septiembre, T7926-0629. Very clean, cheaper with shared bath. There's a terrace with lake view where breakfast is served, but the service is excruciatingly slow. The breakfast menu is open to non-guests, but avoid it in high season unless you don't mind a long wait.
D-F Youth Hostal Los Amigos, Calle Centro América and Av Barrios, T5584-8795, amigoshostel@gmail.com. Dorms with 20 beds and 2 private rooms and hammocks with a funky courtyard. Good, cheap restaurant; bar and internet available. Very helpful and friendly. Highly recommended. They rent out hammocks and mosquito nets for tours to Tikal.
E Doña Marta's. For a different experience find **La Unión** restaurant (Calle Unión) and call Marta and Oscar who live across the small stretch of water behind Flores, T7926-1452. They will pick you up and take you 2 mins across the lake to their house on the water's edge where you can swim. Peaceful, with views across to Flores. Recommended.
E El Tucán, on the lakeside, T926-0536, eltucan2@elsitio.com. 4 internal rooms only, fan, shared bathroom, comfortable. It's OK here, but can be very noisy because of the restaurant, and the shared bathroom means walking by some of the punters and cooks.
E Mirador del Lago, Calle 15 de Septiembre, T7926-3276. Beautiful view of the lake and a jetty to swim from. All with private bathrooms and (irregular) hot water. One of the better budget hotels and it has lake access. New annexe opposite, quiet. All with fan.

Santa Elena *p632, map p634*

AL-A Maya Internacional, lakefront, T926-2083, www.villasdeguatemala.com. Bungalows and rooms beautifully situated and with all services. Room 52 is particularly delightful. Restaurant and pool open to non-guests, 0630-2100.
L-A Petén Espléndido, 1 Calle, T7926-0880, www.petenesplendido.com. A great lake-front restaurant setting (0600-2200), with beautiful pool on the lake. Pool open to non-guests, US$4. Full range of business services available.
A Hotel del Patio Tikal,corner of Calle 2 and Av 8, T7926-0104. Clean, modern rooms with a/c, TV, expensive restaurant, beautiful pool and gym. It's best booked as part of package for cheaper rates.
C Casa de Elena, Av 6, just before the causeway, T926-2238, www.casaelena.com. With a beautiful tiled staircase, rooms have cable TV, pool, restaurant 0630-2100.
D-F San Juan, Calle 2, close to the Catholic church, T7926-0562, sanjuanttravel@hotmail.com.gt. Full of budget travellers in the older rooms, cheaper with shared bath, not always spotless. Some remodelled rooms with a/c and TV. Exchanges US dollars and Mexican pesos and buys Belizean dollars. It's not the nicest place to stay but it's safe, there's a public phone inside and parking. Note that the Tikal minibuses leave from 0500 so you will probably be woken early.

Around Lake Petén Itzá'*p635*

To reach the lodgings along the north shore of the lake can be up to a 2-km walk from El Remate centre, depending on where you stay (turn left, west on the Flores-Tikal main road). Turismoremate@hotmail.com can be used to contact all the hotels. There is street light up to the Biotopo entrance until 2200.
LL-AL La Lancha, T7928-8331, www.blancaneaux.com. Francis Ford Coppola's attractive, small hotel has 10 rooms, 4 of which have lake views. There's a pool and terrace restaurant and local arts and crafts have been used to decorate the rooms. Quiet and friendly in a lovely setting.
L Camino Real, 1.8 km from the western entrance of the Biotopo Cerro Cahuí, T7926-0204, www.quetzalnet.com/caminoreal/CR-Tikal.html. All rooms have views, good restaurant, a/c, cable TV, etc, lovely pool in an attractive setting.
AL Bahía Taitza Hotel and Restaurant, T7928-8125, www.taitza.com. 8 lovely cute rooms decorated with local furnishings set behind a beautiful lawn which sweeps down to the lakeshore. Rates include breakfast and transfer.

AL Hotel Ni'tun, 2 km from San Andres on the Santa Elena road, T5201-0759, www.nitun.com. Luxury *cabañas* on a wooded hillside above the lake, run by friendly couple Bernie and Lore, who cook fantastic vegetarian meals and organize expeditions to remote sites.

A-B La Casa de Don David, 20 m from the main road, on the El Remate side, T7928-8469, www.lacasadedondavid.com. Clean and comfortable, but a little overpriced, all rooms with private bath and some with a/c. Great view from the terrace restaurant with cheap food, bike hire free. Transport to Tikal. Helpful advice offered.

C-E Hotel y Restaurante Mon Ami, on the El Remate side, T7928-8413, www.hotelmon amicom. Guided tours to Yaxhá and Nakum organized with the owner who is a conservationist. Lovely new bungalows and hammocks for sleeping. English, French and Spanish spoken. Restaurant 0700-2130, with wines and seriously cheap chicken, pastas and other dishes served.

D Sun Breeze Hotel, exactly on the corner, on the El Remate side, T7928-8044. Run by the very friendly Humberto Castro. Little wooden rooms with views over the lake. Fans and *mosquiteros* in each room. 2 rooms now have private bathroom. He runs a daily service to Tikal and can run other trips.

E-F La Casa Doña Tonita, on the El Remate side, T5701-7114. One of the most chilled out places along the shore and popular, with a friendly, warm family running the place. Shared bathroom, rooms and a dorm. Enormous portions of good food. Highly recommended.

E-G La Casa Roja, on the El Remate side, T5909-6999. A red house with a tranquil, oriental feel. Rooms are under thatched roofs, with separate bathrooms in attractive stone and wood design. The rooms don't have doors but there are locked trunks. Hammock space and camping possible. Kayaks for rent and trips arranged. Recommended.

F El Mirador del Duende, on the main Flores-Tikal road in El Remate Village, T7926-0269, miradordelduende@gmail.com. Overlooks lake, camping, cabins, veg food, jungle trips, canoes, boat trips, mountain bikes, horses and guides are available.

F La Casa de Don Juan, on the main Flores-Tikal road in El Remate Village, T5309-7172. Rooms out the back behind the restaurant. Owner Don Juan offers tours.

Camping

Campsite with hammock facilities at El Sotz, just before El Remate.

Parque Nacional Tikal *p635*

You are advised to book when you arrive; in high season, book in advance. Take a torch: 24-hr electricity is not normally available.

AL-C Jungle Lodge, T5361-4098, www.quik.guate.com/jltikal/index.html. Spacious, comfortable bungalows, with bath, 24-hr hot water and fan (electricity 0700-2100), pool, cheaper without bath. They will cash TCs, full board available (Consistent reports of unsatisfactory food, and service is slow and portions small), **Jungle Lodge's** Tikal tours have been recommended.

A-B Tikal Inn, T/F7926-0065, hoteltikalinn@itelgua.com. Bungalows and rooms, hot water 1800-1900, electricity 0900-1600, 1800-2200, beautiful pool for guests' use only. Natural history tours at 0930 for US$10, minimum 2 people, helpful.

A-D Jaguar Inn, T7926-0002, www.jaguartikal.com. Full board, less without food. They will provide a picnic lunch, electricity 1800- 2200, hot water in the morning or on request Mar-Oct and Nov-Feb, 0600-2100. Will store luggage. There is also a dormitory with 6 beds. Hammocks with mosi nets and lockers.

Camping

F Camping Tikal, run by the **Restaurante del Parque**, reservations T2370-8140, or at the **Petén Espléndido**, T7926-0880. If you have your own tent or hammock it is US$3.25. If you need to rent the gear it is US$6.50. There are also *cabañas* with mattresses and mosquito nets for US$6.50 per person. They also do deals which include breakfast, lunch and dinner ranging from US$13-US$27 for a double. Communal showers available. Take your own water as the supply is very variable.

Uaxactún *p640*

E El Chiclero, T7926-1095, chiclero@ecotourism-adventure.com. Neat and clean, hammocks and rooms in a garden, also good food by arrangement.

F **Posada Aldana**, T5801-2588, edeniaa@yahoo.com. Little white *casitas*, tent and hammock space behind **El Chiclero**. Just before El Chiclero take a left on the road to the ruins and then first right until you see a whitewashed *casitas* on the right (2-min walk). Clean and run by a friendly family.

Sayaxché *p643*

C-D **Guayacán**, close to ferry, T7928-6111. Owner Julio Godoy is a good source of information.

E-F **Hotel Posada Segura**, turn right from the dock area and then first left, T7928-6162. Some rooms with bath, TV, clean, one of the best options in town.

Petexbatún *p644*

AL **Chiminos Island Lodge**, T2335-3506, www.chiminosisland.com. Remote, small eco-lodge close to a Maya site on a peninsula on the river. Great for exploring local sites, fishing and wildlife spotting. Includes all food.

B **Posada Caribe**, T/F7928-6114, including 3 meals, comfortable *cabañas* with bathroom and shower, excursion to **Aguateca** by launch and a guide for excursions.

Camping

Camping is possible at Escobado, on the lakeside.

Eating

Flores *p632, map p633*

ΨΨ-Ψ **La Albahaca**, Calle 30 de Junio. 1st-class home-made pasta and chocolate cake.

ΨΨ-Ψ **Café Arqueológico Yax-há**, Calle15 de Septiembre. Cheap daily soups and home-made nachos. Offers tours to little-known Maya sites and works with local communities to protect them.

ΨΨ-Ψ **Hacienda del Rey**, Calle Sur. Expensive Argentinian steaks are on the menu, but the breakfasts are seriously cheap.

ΨΨ-Ψ **La Luna**, Av 10 de Noviembre (on map). Refreshing natural lemonade, range of fish, meat and vegetarian dishes. The restaurant has a beautiful courtyard with blue paintwork set under lush pink bouganvillaea, recommended. Closed Sun.

ΨΨ **La Unión**, Calle Unión. Deceptive from the outside, it has a gorgeous little thatched wooden terrace on the lake with great views. Try the fish. Recommended more for the setting than the food.

ΨΨ **The Mayan Princess Restaurant Café Bar and Cinema**, Reforma and 10 de Noviembre. Has the most adventurous menu on the island including daily specials, many with an Asian flavour, relaxed atmosphere, with bright coloured textile cloths on the tables. Internet and free films. Closed Sun.

Ψ **El Mirador**, overlooking the lake but view obscured by restaurant wall. Seriously cheap food and snacks but service slow.

Ψ **La Canoa**, Calle Centro América. Good breakfasts (try the pancakes), dinners start at US$1.50, with good *comida típica*, very friendly owners.

Ψ **La Galería del Zotz**, 15 de Septiembre. A wide range of food, delicious pizzas, good service and presentation, and popular with the locals.

Ψ **Las Puertas Café Bar**, Av Santa Ana and Calle Central. Seriously cheap breakfasts, huge menu, good large pasta portions. It's popular with locals and travellers and is in an airy building, chilled atmosphere, games available. Popular at night. Closes at 2300 for food and 2400 completely. Closed Sun. Also Cine Las Puertas, opposite, with videos at 1930.

Ψ **Naomi's Café**, Calle Centro América. Filling breakfasts and meals. Open from 0600.

Santa Elena *p632, map p634*

ΨΨ **El Rodeo**, 1 Calle. Excellent, reasonable prices but occasional slow service, classical music and sometimes impromptu singing performances.

Ψ **El Petenchel**, Calle 2. Vegetarian food served here as well as conventional meats and meals. Excellent breakfasts. Good-value *menú del día*. Music played and prompt service.

Ψ **Restaurante Mijaro**, Calle 2 and Av 8. Great filling breakfasts and a bargain *menú del día* at US$1.70, all in a thatched-roofed roadside location.

Uaxactún *p640*

Ψ **Comedor Imperial**, at village entrance. Bargain *comida típica* for US$1.30.

Sayaxché *p643*

¥¥¥ **El Botanero Café Restaurante and Bar**, straight up from the dock and 2nd left. A funky wooden bar with logs and seats carved from tree trunks.

¥ **Restaurant La Montaña**, near dock. Cheap food, local information given.

¥ **Yakín**, near dock. Cheap, good food; try the *licuados*.

Activities and tours

Flores and Santa Elena *p632, maps p633 and 634*

Tour operators

Conservation Tours Tikal, Calle 15 de Septiembre, opposite Oficina Contable Tayasal, run by Lucía Prinz, T7926-0670, lprinz@rarecenter.org (or ask at Las Puertas). This organization, funded by UNESCO, employs people from Petén communities to take visitors on tours to local sites. English and Spanish spoken. Also walking tours in the jungle, birdwatching, horse and kayak tours also. 5% of profits go to conservation.

Explore, Calle Principal, Sta Elena, T7926-2375, www.exploreguate.com. Very helpful, reliable and professional operator offering tours to Tikal, Aguateca, Dos Pilas, Ceibal and Yaxhá.

Martsam Travel, Calle Centroamérica, T7926-0346, www.martsam.com. Guided tours to Tikal, US$40, El Zotz, El Mirador, El Peru, Yaxhá, US$25 and Nakum. Guides with wildlife and ornithological knowledge in addition to archaeological knowledge. Highly recommended.

San Juan Travel Agency, T/F7926-0042, sanjuantravel@hotmail.com.gt, offers transport (US$6.70) to Tikal, US$60 including tour. Excursions to Ceibal, US$40, and Uaxactún, US$40, but US$60 with a guide. Same prices for Yaxhá. Service to Belize, US$20, 0500 and 0700, 5 hrs. Also to Chetumal, Mexico, at 0500, US$25, 7 hrs. To Palenque at 0500, US$30, 7 hrs. Also see local guide under San Andrés, page 634.

Tikal Connection, Calle 15 de Septiembre, T7926- 4981, info@tikalcnx.com, used to be **EcoMaya**, runs tours to El Perú, El Mirador, Nakbé, El Zotz, Yaxhá, Dos Aguadas, Uaxactún. It also sells bus tickets.

Viajes de Tivoli, Calle Centroamerica, T5554-0433, www.tivoli.com.gt. Trips to local sites as well as general agency services.

Uaxactún *p640*

Tour operators

For guided walks around the ruins ask for one of the trained guides, US$10. For expeditions further afield, contact Elfido Aldana at **Posada Aldana**. Neria Baldizón at **El Chiclero**, has high-clearance pick-ups and plenty of experience in organizing both vehicle and mule trips to any site. She charges US$200 per person to go to Río Azul.

Sayaxché *p643*

Tour operators

Viajes Don Pedro, on the river front near the dock, T7928-6109, runs launches to El Ceibal (US$35 for up to 3), Petexbatún and Agua - teca (US$60 for up to 5), Dos Pilas (US$50 for small group). Trip possible by jeep in the dry season, Altar de los Sacrificios (US$100 min 2) and round trips to Yaxchilán for 3 days (US$400). Mon-Sat 0700-1800, Sun 0700-1200.

Transport

Poptún *p631*

Bus Take any **Fuente del Norte** bus or any bus heading to the capital from **Flores**, US$2.60, 2 hrs. To **Flores** 0830, 0930, 1030, or any Flores-bound buses from the capital. Bus Poptún-**Río Dulce**, 2 hrs, US$3.90. Buses will drop you at the driveway to **Finca Ixobel** if that's your destination, just ask. To **Guatemala City** there are plenty daily, 7-8 hrs, US$8-10. There is a local bus to **San Luis**, at 0930. The only bus that continues to **Fray Bartolomé de las Casas** (Las Casas on the bus sign) leaves at 1030, 5¾ hrs, US$4.

Flores and Santa Elena *p632, maps p633 and p634*

Air

Be early for flights, as overbooking is common. **Tikal Jets** closes its check-in 45 mins before departure from Santa Elena. The cost of a return flight is between US$116-180, shop around. **Grupo Taca**, T7926-0295, www.flyinter-taca.com, leaves **Guatemala City** daily at 0630, 1010, 1725, 1 hr 10 mins, returns 0815 and 1855. **Tikal Jets**, T7926-0386, www.tikaljets.com, to Flores 0630 daily, returning 1730; 40 mins.

Tag, also flies, T7926-0653. To **Cancún**, Grupo Taca. To **Belize City**, Tropic Air, T7926-0348, www.tropicair.com, with **Maya Island Air** and with **Tikal Jets**.

Boat

Lanchas moor along Calle Sur, Flores; behind the **Hotel Santana**; and from the dock behind **Hotel Casona de Isla** and beside the new arch on the causeway.

Bus

Local Local buses (chicken buses), US$0.26, Flores to Santa Elena, leave from the end of the causeway in Flores.

Long distance All long-distance buses leave from the new bus terminal, 6 blocks south of the Calle Principal in Santa Elena. It has a snack bar, toilets, seating and ATM. Opposite are restaurants, *comedores*, and a bakery. Banrural is down the side. Services from **Guatemala City**, see page 530. To **Guatemala City**, Línea Dorada, daily office hours 0500-2200, www.tikalmayanworld.com.com, leaves 1000, 2100, 1st class, US$24; 2200, US$16, 8 hrs. Buses also to **Tikal**. **Autobuses del Norte** (ADN), T7924-8131, luxury service, 2100, US$26.60, 2200 and 2300, US$14.70. **Fuente del Norte**, T7926-0666, office open 24 hrs, buses every 45 mins-1 hr, 0330-2230, US$11.30, 9 hrs. At 1000, 1400, 2I00, 2200, US$20, 7-8 hrs. 2nd-class buses, **Rosita**, T7926-5178 and **Rápidos del Sur**, T7924-8072, also go to the capital, US$10.70-13.30. If you are going only to **Poptún**, 2 hrs, or **Río Dulce**, 3½-4 hrs, make sure you do not pay the full fare to Guatemala City. To **Sayaxché** with **Pinita**, T9926-0726, at 1100, returns next day at 0600, US$2. With **Fuente del Norte** at 0600, US$1.33, returning 0600. There are also *colectivos* which leave every 15 mins 0530-1700, US$ 1.90. Buses run around the lake to **San Andrés**, with one at 1200 with **Pinita** continuing to **Cruce dos Aguadas,** US$2 and **Carmelita,** US$2.70 for access to El Mirador. Returning from Carmelita at 0500 the next day. To **Belize City**, see page 635. To **Copán**, Honduras, take **Transportes María Elena**, T5550-4190, to Chiquimula at 0400, 0800, 1300, US$10.70 then from Chiquimula to El Florido (see page 610) and finally on to Copán. Alternatively, take any bus to the capital and change at Río Hondo. The **María Elena** bus continues onto **Esquipulas**, 9 hrs, US$11. **Fuente del Norte** to **Cobán**, 0530. 0630, 1230, 1330, 5 hrs, US$ 8. To Jutiapa, 0500, 0530, 7hrs, returning 0900, US$11.30. To **Mexico**, see to Mexico through El Petén, and fast transport to Palenque on page 641. To **Melchor de Mencos** at the Belize border, 0500, 0600, 1630, 2300, 1½ hrs, US$ 2.70. Returning 0200, 0500, 0600, 1630, 2300. To **San Salvador**, 0600. 8 hrs, US$26.70. Returning 0600.

Car

There are plenty of agencies at the airport, mostly Suzuki jeeps, which cost about US$65-80 per day; **Hertz**, at the airport, T7926-0332. **Garrido** at Sac-Nicte Hotel, Calle 1, Santa Elena, T7926-1732.

Petrol is sold in Santa Elena at the 24-hr Texaco garage on the way to airport.

Around Lake Petén Itzá' *p635*

Bus and boat Minibus shuttles leave every 30 mins for San Andres, US$0.70, 30 mins and go on to San José. Public *lanchas* from San Benito have virtually come to a stop. Visitors can still charter a *lancha* from Flores for about US$10.

Bus There's a bus ticket and internet office opposite the turning to El Remate. Any bus/minibus heading for Tikal can stop at El Remate. Returning to **Flores**, pick up any minibus heading south (this is a lot easier after 1300 when tourists are returning). There is a bus service heading to **Flores** from El Remate at 0700, 0800, 0930, 1300 and 1400. **Semuc Tour** leaves El Remate at 1345 passing the **Grutas de Candelaria** at 1630, US$16, arriving **Cobán** at 1830, US$24.70. Also on to Lanquín, US$31.

Uaxactún *p640*

Bus To Uaxactún from Flores at 1200 arriving between 1600-1700, US$2.15, returning 0500 with **Transportes Pinita**. Foreigners have to pay US$2 to pass through Parque Nacional Tikal on their way to Uaxactún, payable at the main entrance to Tikal.

El Mirador, El Tintal and Nakbé *p641*

Bus 1 bus daily with **Transportes Pinita** to **Carmelita**. See under Flores, above, for information.

Northwest Petén and the Mexican border *p643*
Bus To **El Naranjo** at 0500 and 1000, returng at 0500, 1100 and 1300, US$3.30. Or hire a *lancha* from Paso Caballos.

Sayaxché *p643*
Bus There are buses to **Flores**, 0600, 0700, 1-2 hrs, and microbuses every 30 mins. To Raxrujá and on to **Cobán** via **Chisec** at 0400, US$4, 6½ hrs direct to Cobán. There are pick-ups after that. For **Lanquín** take the bus to Raxrujá, then a pick-up to Sebol, and then a pick-up to Lanquín, or the Lanquín *cruce* at Pajal, and wait for onward transport. See also under Transport Around Lake Petén Itzá. If you are heading to **Guatemala City** from here it could be quicker to head north to Flores rather than take the long road down to Cobán. However, this road has now been entirely tarmacked.

Petaxbatun *p644*
It is 30-40 mins in *lancha* from Sayaxché to the stop for **Dos Pilas** to hire horses. It's 50 mins-1 hr to **Chiminos** lodge and 1 hr 20 mins to the **Aguateca** site. To Dos Pilas and Aguateca from Chiminos, US$27 return to each site.

Directory

Flores and Santa Elena *p632, maps p633 and 634*
Banks **Banrural**, Flores, next to the church. TCs only. **Banco del Café**, Santa Elena, best rates for Amex TCs. Do not use its ATM: it eats cards by the dozen. **Banco de los Trabajadores**, MasterCard accepted. **Banco Agromercantil**, open until 1800. **Banquetzal**, MasterCard only. The major hotels and travel agents change cash and TCs. There's a bank oppostite the bus terminal. **Immigration** at the airport, T7926-0984. **Internet** There are plenty of places. Hotel internet terminals tend to have fairer prices than the internet shops. **Post office** In Flores and in Santa Elena. **Telephone** Telgua in Santa Elena. **Language schools** See under San Andrés and San José. **Laundry** Lavandería Petenchel, wash and dry. Open 0800-1900. **Medical services** Hospital Nacional, in San Benito, T7926-1333, open 24 hrs. **Centro Médico Maya**, 4 Av 335, Santa Elena, T7926-0810, speaks some English. Recommended. **Volunteer work** See ARCAS, page 512. Also www.volunteerpeten.com, and **Women's Association for the Revival of Traditional Medicine**, T5514-8889.

Around Lake Petén Itzá' *p635*
Language schools **Eco-Escuela de Español**, San Andrés, T7928-8106, www.ecoescuelaespanol.org. 20 hrs of classes and homestay for a week, US$150. The **Escuela Bio-Itzá**, San José, T7928-8142, www.bioitza.org, run by Martsam travel agency offers classes, homestay and camping (20 hrs per week with homestay US$150, camping, US$125).

Belize

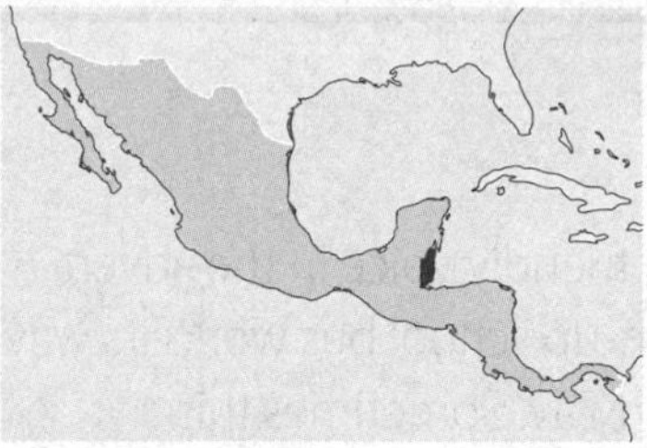

Footprint features

Introduction

"Be kind to tourists", says the big friendly voice in the advert on Belize's *Love FM*, as the beaten-up school bus works its way down the old Hummingbird Highway. Sometimes this smallest of countries appears innocent, naïve and relaxed.

Belize is a smorgasbord of landscapes, from mountainous, tropical rainforests with abundant wildlife to fertile subtropical foothills where sugar, rice, cattle and fruit trees are cultivated, and bird-filled coastal wetlands and small islands – known as cayes – with beautiful beaches.

Measuring 174 miles north to south and just 80 miles across, the country nestles on the coast between Mexico and Guatemala, with a land area of about 8860 sq miles, including hundreds of cayes. The reefs and cayes form a 184-mile barrier reef with crystal-clear water and are a major attraction for world-class diving, snorkelling and sport fishing. And hidden beneath the depths is the magnificent Blue Hole, one of the world's best dives.

Inland, rivers and rainforest invite you to head out, trekking, paddling and biking, to visit the ancient ruins of the Maya, or to cave in their spiritual underworld. For the beginner and the specialist bird-watching is an endless pleasure.

With a Caribbean history and a Central American geography, Belize is a subtle blend of cultures that encourages the laid-back attitude of the small (just 250,000) but ethnically diverse population, who paint an intriguing picture in this culturally different, English-speaking Central American nation.

★ Don't miss...

1. **Northern cayes** Scuba dive in the depths of the Blue Hole, pages 673.
2. **Crooked Tree Wildlife Sanctuary** One of Belize's premier birding sites, page 683.
3. **Actun Tunichil Muknal Cave** Explore the mysterious underworld of the Maya and tramp through the rainforest, page 692.
4. **Caracol** Visit the hidden ruins that once ruled over Tikal in neighbouring Guatemala, page 695.
5. **Cockscomb Basin Wildlife Sanctuary** Explore the only conservation area in the world working exclusively to protect the jaguar, page 704.
6. **The Black Hole Drop** Survive the exhilharating 200-ft rappel of Actun Loch Tunich cave, page 708.

Belize

Planning your trip

Where to go

The reputation of **Belize City** is not good but the authorities are working hard to clean it up and present a better face to tourists. Special tourist police have been introduced and crime is much less widespread than it was in the mid-1990s. That said, you may still be offered drugs on the streets – just be sensible. It is worth spending a day or two having a look around Belize City and getting a feel for the old town – it's not possible to really know Belize if you haven't spent some time in the city. Generally, the longer people stay the better they like it and resident Belizeans are friendly and welcoming. The short journey to visit **Belize Zoo** is definitely worthwhile. A little further on is the tiny capital of **Belmopan**, an hour from Belize City.

The **northern cayes**, a series of paradise islands with crystal-clear waters, palm-fringed beaches and mangroves, are the main hub of tourism. **Ambergris Caye**, more upmarket, and **Caye Caulker**, popular with budget travellers, are the two most-developed cayes, from where you can take trips to the smaller cayes and marine parks. They attract a wide range of travellers wishing to sample the delights of a Caribbean island. The atmosphere is laid-back with plenty of watersports for the active, spectacular diving and snorkelling on the barrier reef and outlying cayes and the world-famous **Blue Hole**.

On the mainland, the Northern Highway leads from Belize City to the Mexican border through some of the most productive farmland in the country. There is still plenty of room for wildlife at the **Community Baboon Sanctuary**, for black howler monkeys; the **Crooked Tree Lagoons and Wildlife Sanctuary**, for birds. The archaeological remains of **Lamanai** with a 112-ft temple (the tallest known pre-Classic Maya structure) is easily visited from Orange Walk, and **Altún Ha**, once a major Maya ceremonial site, are essential visits for 'Maya-philes'. The largest town in the north, **Orange Walk**, is a multi-racial city of Mennonites, Creoles, Maya and other Central Americans making their living from agriculture.

The Western Highway leads from Belize City, skirting the capital Belmopan, to **San Ignacio** and the Guatemalan border. San Ignacio and its twin town Santa Elena have a pleasant climate and are in a beautiful setting of wooded hills straddling the Macal River. A side trip to the **Mountain Pine Ridge** area offers great hiking, amid spectacular broadleaf forests, rivers, rapids, waterfalls and caves, making a worthwhile excursion with much to be enjoyed along the entire route to Caracol. There are several Maya sites, notably **Cahal Pech**, on the edge of town; **El Pilar**, north through Bullet Tree Falls; **Xunantunich**, across the Mopan River by hand-cranked ferry at San José Succotz with plazas, temples, ball court and *castillo*; and **Caracol**, the country's largest site to date rivalling Tikal in size, where the Sky Palace pyramid reaches a height of 138 ft.

The Southern Highway runs along the eastern edge of the Maya Mountains, through sparsely populated countryside dotted with indigenous settlements, to Dangriga and Hopkins Village and then past the world-famous **Cockscomb Basin Wildlife (Jaguar) Sanctuary**. The coastal area around **Placencia** offers idyllic palm-fringed beaches, diving and sport fishing, with plenty of accommodation choices for all budgets. Offshore cayes are reached by boat from **Dangriga** or Mango Creek. In the far south is **Punta Gorda** with the ruins of **Lubaantun**, a late-Maya ceremonial site where the infamous Crystal Skull was discovered. You can stay at guesthouses in Maya villages nearby as part of a community tourism project.

When to go

The high season runs from mid-December to March and pushes into May with clear skies and warm temperatures (25-30°C). Inland, in the west, day temperatures can reach 38°C, but the nights are cooler and usually pleasant. Between November and January there are cold spells during which the temperature at Belize City may fall as low as 13°C. Humidity is normally high, making it 'sticky' most of the time in the lowlands.

There are sharp annual variations in rainfall. From 1270 mm in the north and around 1650 mm in Belize City, there is a huge increase up to 4310 mm down in the south. The driest months are April and May; in June and July there are heavy showers followed by blue skies. Around August the *mauger* occurs, a mini-dry season of about six weeks. September to November tend to be overcast and there are more insects during these months.

Hurricanes threaten the country from June to November along the coast. An efficient warning system was put in place after Hurricane Mitch (1998) and most towns and large villages have hurricane shelters. 'Hurricane Preparedness' instructions are issued annually. Do not ignore local instructions about what to do following a forecast.

Suggested itineraries There are two simple options: coming from Mexico head south into Belize City, pop out to the Cayes then make your way south through Placencia to Punta Gorda and on to Guatemala or Honduras, or go west through San Ignacio visiting the caves of the highlands, and then to Tikal in Guatemala. If coming from Guatemala, visit San Ignacio, Belize City and the Cayes before heading south. You can get a good feel for Belize in a fortnight or less, but you could spend much longer if you have the time.

Finding out more

Belize tourist offices

Belize Tourism Board, Lower Flat, New Horizon Investment Building, 3½ miles Northern Highway, Belize City, T223-1913, www.travelbelize.org, also with an office in the Tourism Village, provides information on hotels and a variety of handouts on parks and reserves. (It is moving to 2 13th St.)

Useful websites

Given its size, the amount of information about Belize on the internet is phenomenal.

www.belizenet.com, **www.belize.net** and **www.belize.com** Good search engines with general information.

www.belize.gov.bz The government site on the country, packed with information on the official angle.

www.belizeaudubon.org and **www.pfbelize.org** Cover most of the protected areas of interest and support Belize's strong conservation focus.

www.ambergriscaye.com, **www.gocayecaulker.com**, **www.placencia.com** and **www.southernbelize.com** Speak for themselves.

belizex.com Covers much of the Cayo area.

www.belizereport.com The online version of the *Belize Report*.

www.belizenews.com Local news and links to the local newspapers (*Amandala, The Belize Times, The Reporter* and *The Guardian*).

www.belizeweb.com For when you're back at home and want to listen to a bit of Belizean radio.

Language

English is the official language, but Spanish is very widely used, especially in border areas. Creole is spoken by some throughout the country. Mennonite settlers in the north speak a Low German dialect. Several Mayan languages and Garífuna are spoken by ethnic groups to the south.

Before you travel

Visas and immigration

All nationalities need passports, as well as sufficient funds and, officially, an onward ticket, although this is rarely requested for stays of 30 days or less. Visas are not usually required by nationals from countries within the EU, Australia and New Zealand, most Caribbean states, the USA and Canada. Citizens of India, Israel, Austria and Switzerland do need a visa. There is a Belizean Consulate in Chetumal, Mexico, at Armada de México 91, T+52-983-8321803, US$25. If you do require a visa it is best to obtain one in Mexico City or your home country before arriving at the border.

Belize embassies and consulates

Canada (changes frequently), 1800 McGill College, Suite 2480, Montreal, Quebec H3A 3J6, T514-288-1687, F514-288-4998.
El Salvador, Calle El Bosque Norte, Block P, Casa, Col La Cima IV, San Salvador, T/F273-6744.
European Communities, Blvd Brand Whitlock 136, 1200 Brussels, Belgium, T/F+32-2-7326246, embelize@skynet.be
Germany, Lindenstrasse 46-48 7120, Beitigheim, Bissingen, T7142-3924, F7142-33225.
Guatemala and Central America, Edificio El Reformador 8th Floor, Suite 803, Av Reforma 1-50 Zone 9, Guatemala City, T2334-5531, F2334-5536.
Israel, Asia house, 4 Weizman St, Tel Aviv 4329, T3-6954142, F3-255816.
Mexico (Cancún), Nader 34, Cancún, Quintana Roo, T998-8878631.
Panama, El Dorado, T/F236-4132.
UK, High Commission, 22 Harcourt House, 19 Cavendish Sq, London, W1G 0PL, T/F020-74914139.
USA, 2535 Massachusetts Av, NW Washington DC 20008, T/F202-332-6888.

For the latest information, see www.belize.gov.bz and click on diplomat link.

Customs

Clothing and articles for personal use are allowed in without payment of duty, though laptop computers, video cameras, cellular phones and CD players and radios that you bring may be stamped on your passport to ensure they leave with you. Other import allowances are: 200 cigarettes or ½ lb of tobacco; one litre of alcohol; one bottle of perfume. Visitors can take in an unspecified amount of other currencies. No fruit or vegetables may be brought into Belize; searches are infrequent, but can be thorough. Pets must have proof of rabies inoculations and a vet's certificate of good health.

Money

Currency → *US$1=Bz$2 (stabilized).*

The monetary unit is the **Belizean dollar**, stabilized at Bz$2=US$1. Currency notes issued by the **Central Bank** are in denominations of 100, 50, 20, 10, 5 and 2 dollars, and coinage of 2 dollars and 1 dollar; 50, 25, 10, 5 and 1 cent coins are in use. The American expressions **quarter** (25c), **dime** (10c) and **nickel** (5c) are used, although 25c is sometimes referred to as a shilling. US dollars are accepted everywhere. A common cause for complaint or misunderstanding is uncertainty about which currency you are paying in. The price tends to be given in US$ when the hundred Belizean dollar mark is breached; make sure it is clear from the start whether you are being charged in US or Belizean dollars.

Exchange

See under Banks, Belize City, page 671. The government has recently restricted the exchange of foreign currency to government-licensed **casas de cambio**, but these only operate in major towns. You can still find some money changers at the borders, but the exchange rate is not as high as it has been, and there is a risk of both you and the money changer being arrested and fined.

Cost of living and travelling

The cost of living is high, compared to neighbouring countries, because of the heavy reliance on imports and extra duties. Budget travellers will still be able to get by on about US$35-40 per person per day if travelling in twos. Budget travellers can find exploring the interior difficult because public transport is limited to main highways and car hire is beyond the means of many. VAT has been replaced by a 9% sales tax which is charged on all services, but should **not** be charged on top of the 9% hotel tax charged on your room. A 1% 'Environmental Tax' is levied on all goods brought into the country.

Getting there

Air

From North America and Europe With the exception of neighbouring countries, international services to Belize go through the USA, with **American Airlines, Continental, Grupo Taca** and **US Airways**. There are no direct flights from Europe. Most flights from Europe go through the US and require an overnight stop in Miami or Houston.
From Central America There are daily connections to San Salvador with **Grupo Taca** and Flores (Guatemala) and San Pedro Sula (Honduras) with **Maya Island Air**, www.mayaislandair.com, and **Tropic Air**, www.tropicair.com.

Road

The most commonly used routes are with the Petén Department of Guatemala at Benque Viejo del Carmen and, to the north, at the border with Chetumal on Mexico's Yucatán Peninsula. Both immigration offices have recently been remodelled, reducing the waiting times. A less widely used crossing, for non-vehicular travellers, is at La Unión, where there are immigration facilities.

Sea

Boat services link the south of the country with Honduras and Guatemala. From Puerto Barrios, Guatemala, there is a boat service to Punta Gorda; from Puerto Cortés, Honduras, a boat goes to Placencia, via Mango Creek. Obtain all necessary exit stamps and visas before sailing – see under each town for details.

Touching down

Airport information

The main international airport and point of arrival is at Ladyville, 10 miles northwest of Belize City. For airport details, see page 664. When leaving by air you'll pay US$31.50 (payable in US dollars only) including PACT conservation tax (see page 662) plus a US$1.50 security bag fee per person. Departing overland costs US$18.75; by boat, US$3.75.

Tourist information

The quality and quantity of tourist information in Belize varies greatly. In the popular centres of the cayes, Placencia and the developed sections of Cayo there is a steady supply of information available. Moving away from these popular areas the information is less reliable.

There is an ID card system to validate official tourist guides which works well in the popular areas. Off the main routes there is less government checking of guides so a more ad hoc system works.

Maps of the country are limited and topographical maps have not been readily available for several years. The best internationally available maps are from ITMB.

Touching down

Business hours Shops are open 0800-1200, 1300-1600 and Fri 1900-2100, with half day on Wed. Small shops open additionally most late afternoons and evenings, and some on Sun 0800-1000. **Government** and commercial office hours are Mon-Fri 0800-1200, 1300-1600.
Official time Six hours behind GMT.
Telephone Country code T+501. Information T113. International operator T115.
Voltage 110/220 volts single phase, 60 cycles for domestic supply. Some hotels use 12 volt generators.
Weights and measures Imperial and US standard weights and measures.

Local customs and laws

Tipping In restaurants, 10% of the bill; porters in hotels US$2; chambermaids US$1 per day. Taxi drivers are tipped depending on the length of the transfer, whether 'touring' took place or for extra stops, from US$1-10.

Safety

A US student was strangled in Belize City in November 2005 – while this kind of incident is extremely rare, precautions are still advised, particularly if travelling alone or at night or in deserted areas. Beware of becoming intoxicated, or risk being a victim of theft or 'date rape'. Crimes against travellers are harshly punished, but despite the apparent availability of illegal drugs, the authorities are keen to prevent their use. The penalties for possession of marijuana are six months in prison or a US$3000 fine, minimum.

Getting around

Air

Maya Island Air and **Tropic Air** (see page 670) both provide in-country flights to the cayes, Corozal, Dangriga, Placencia and Punta Gorda; both have good safety records and regular schedules. It costs less to fly from the Municipal Airport in Belize City than from the International Airport to the same destination. There is one exception: if making a connection for an international flight, it is cheaper to arrive at the International Airport, obviously, than to take a taxi from the Municipal to the International Airport.

Road

Bus Public transport between most towns is by bus and, with the short distances involved, there are few long journeys to encounter. Trucks carry passengers to many isolated destinations. Most buses are ex-US school buses with small seats and limited legroom. There are a few ex-**Greyhounds**, mostly used for 'express' services and charters. It is recommended to buy tickets for seats in advance at the depot before boarding the bus. Most bus companies were acquired by **Novelos**, which went bust and is now called the **National Transportation Company**. Bus services are in a state of flux. Always seek local advice and information. Most buses have no luggage compartments so bags that do not fit on the luggage rack are stacked at the back. Get a seat at the back to keep an eye on your gear, but rough handling is more of a threat than theft.

Car Motorists should carry their own driving licence and certificate of vehicle ownership. Third-party insurance is mandatory and can be purchased at any border (Bz$25 a week,

Bz$50 a month, cars and motorbikes are the same, cover up to Bz$20,000 from the **Insurance Corporation of Belize,** 7 Daly Street, Belize City, T224-5328). Border offices are open Monday-Friday 0500-1700, Saturday 0600-1600. There are also offices in every district. Valid International Driving Licences are accepted in place of Belize driving permits. Fuel costs Bz$9.87, a Bz$3 recent rise for a US gallon but can be more in remote areas. Unleaded gasoline is now available in Belize.

Car hire Only one car rental company (**Crystal** – see page 671) will release registration papers to enable cars to enter Guatemala or Mexico. Without obtaining them at the time of hire it is impossible to take hire cars across national borders. Car hire cost is high in Belize owing to the heavy wear and tear on the vehicles. You can expect to pay between US$65 for a Suzuki Samuri and US$125 for an Isuzu Trooper per day. Cautious driving is advised in Belize as road conditions, although improving steadily, are constantly changing and totally unpredictable, with speed bumps, cyclists and pedestrians appearing around every bend. When driving in the Mountain Pine Ridge area it is prudent to check carefully on road conditions at the entry gate; good maps are essential. Emory King's annually updated *Drivers' Guide to Belize* is helpful when driving to the more remote areas.

Hitchhiking While practised freely by locals, hitchhiking is risky and not recommended for travellers. If, however, this is your preferred mode of travel, be prepared for long waits and break the journey down into smaller legs.

Sea

Boats Several boats ferry passengers to the most popular cayes of Caye Caulker and Ambergris Caye, with regular daily services from the Marine Terminal by the swing bridge in Belize City. Further south, boat transport is available at Dangriga to nearby cayes, with a service to Puerto Cortés, Honduras, also stopping at Placencia, as well as from Punta Gorda, with service to Puerto Barrios and Lívingston, Guatemala. In the north there is a daily service between Corozal and San Pedro, Ambergris Caye.

Sleeping

Accommodation throughout the country varies greatly. For the budget traveller there are options in most towns of interest, although prices are higher than in neighbouring countries. While standard hotel options exist, the area around San Ignacio offers several secluded hideaways of varying price and to the south there are options for staying in Maya communities which helps to maintain the cultural identity of the region. The Belize Tourist Board promotes good hotels under US$60 a night through the **Toucan Trail,** www.toucantrail.com. All **hotels** are subject to 9% government hotel tax (on room rate only) and 10% service charge is often added. **Camping** sites are gaining in popularity, and there are private camping facilities to be found in most tourist areas, with a variety of amenities offered. Camping on the beaches, in forest reserves or in any other public place is not allowed. Butane gas in trailer/Coleman stove-size storage bottles is available in Belize, and white gas for camp stoves is available at **Brodies** in Belmopan.

Eating

Dishes suffer a wonderful preponderance of rice'n'beans – a cheap staple to which you add chicken, fish, beef and so on. For the cheapest meals, order rice which will come with beans and (as often as not) banana or plantain, or chicken, vegetables or even a blending of beef with coconut milk. Belize has some of the best burritos in Central America but you have to seek them out, normally in hidden-away stalls in the markets. Along the coastal region and on the cayes seafood is abundant, fresh and reasonably cheap, but avoid buying lobster between 15 February and 14 June (out of season) as stocks are worryingly low. (Conch is out of season between 1 July and 30 September; Nassau grouper, between 1 December and 31 March.) Better restaurants offer a greater variety and a break from the standards, often including a selection of Mexican dishes; there are also many Chinese restaurants, not always good and sometimes overpriced.

Belikin beer is the local brew, average cost US$1.75 a bottle. Many brands of local rum are available too. Several local wines and liqueurs are made from available fruit. One favourite, called *nanche*, is made from *crabou* fruit and is very sweet, as is the cashew wine, made from the cashew fruit rather than the nut. All imported food and drink is expensive. A 9% sales tax is added to meals and a 10% service charge may be added as well.

Entertainment

In Belize City you will find a mix of bars, restaurants and clubs. Elsewhere, entertainment in Belize is limited somewhat to the weekend disco that gets going after the bars have closed. Demand is not great enough to require anything beyond the latest international dance classics. Come festival time and the mood changes, with the national music of punta rock coming to the fore.

Festivals and events

1 Jan New Year's Day.
Feb Weekend before or after Valentine's Day, Annual Sidewalk Arts Festival, Placencia.
9 Mar Baron Bliss Day; see also box, page 691.
Early Mar San José Succotz Fiesta.
Mar/Apr Good Fri and Sat and Easter Mon.
Late Apr or May National Agricultural and Trade Show (Belmopan).
1 May Labour Day.
May (variable) Cashew Festival (Crooked Tree), Cayo Expo (San Ignacio), Coconut Festival (Caye Caulker).
24 May Commonwealth Day.
23-25 Jun Lobster Fest, Placencia.
Early to Mid-Jul Benq ue Viejo Fiesta.
Aug International Costa Maya Festival (San Pedro, Ambergris Caye).
10 Sep St George's Caye Day.
21 Sep Belize Independence Day.
11 Oct Pan-American Day.
19 Nov Garífuna Settlement Day, festival normally over the weekend.
25 Dec Christmas Day.
26 Dec Boxing Day.

Most services throughout the country close down Good Friday to Easter Monday; banks close at 1300 on the Thursday, buses run limited services Holy Saturday to Easter Monday, though local flights and boats to the cayes are available. Christmas and Boxing Day are also limited in terms of services. Many shops will open for a few hours on holiday mornings, but still may have limited choices for food. Independence Celebrations begin on St George's Caye Day, 10 September, and there are events occurring daily through to Independence Day, 21 September. The 'September Celebrations', as they are locally called, often start two or three days in advance and require a lot of energy. The most colourful of Belizean festivals is Garífuna Settlement Day in November with celebrations concentrated around Dangriga, Seine Bight and Placencia. The tone of the festival varies greatly with a more public celebration of music and dance in Dangriga, with a more spiritual and quieter ambience in Seine Bight.

Shopping

Indigenous arts and crafts are noticeable primarily for their absence. Carved hardwood objects are widely available. Jewellery made of black coral is occasionally offered but should not be bought. There are some fine Belikin/diving T-shirts. If you want to buy music, Andy Palacio is one of the best punta rock artists.

Sport and activities

Archaeology

The protection of Belize's Maya heritage and its development into tourism sites is high on the agenda. Further excavation and protection of sites, better access, construction of tourist facilities like visitor centres and small souvenir shops, the availability of brochures and knowledgeable guides are all part of the plan. For information contact the **Archaeology Department**, T822-2106, in Belmopan, where there are plans underway for a new Museum of Archaeology.

Caving

Belize has some of the longest caving systems in the world. Main attractions in caves are crystal formations, but most of the caves in Belize were also used by the Maya, and in some Maya artefacts have been found. While government permission is required to enter unexplored systems, simple cave exploration is easy. The best one-stop shop for all levels is the **Caves Branch Jungle Lodge** (see page 707) on the Hummingbird Highway close to the entrance to the Blue Hole National Park. From San Ignacio tours also go to Chechem Ha, Barton Creek and Actun Tunichil Muknal Cave, known for their Maya artefacts.

Diving

The shores are protected by the longest barrier reef in the Western Hemisphere. The beautiful coral formations are a great attraction for scuba diving, with canyons, coves, overhangs, ledges, walls and endless possibilities for underwater photography.

Lighthouse Reef, the outermost of the three north-south reef systems, offers pristine dive sites in addition to the incredible Blue Hole. Massive stalagmites and stalactites are found along overhangs down the sheer vertical walls of the Blue Hole. This outer reef lies beyond the access of most land-based diving resorts and even beyond most fishermen, so the marine life is undisturbed. An ideal way to visit is on a live-aboard boat. An exciting marine phenomenon takes place during the full moon each January in the waters around Belize when thousands of the Nassau groupers gather to spawn at Glory Caye on Turneffe Reef.

Note There are decreasing numbers of small fish – an essential part of the coral lifecycle – in the more easily accessible reefs, including the underwater parks. The coral reefs around the northerly, most touristy cayes are dying, probably as a result of tourism pressures, so do your bit to avoid further damage.

Fishing

Belize is a very popular destination for sport fishing, normally quite pricey but definitely worth it if you want to splash out. The rivers offer fewer and fewer opportunities for good fishing, and tilapia, escaped from regional fish farms, now compete with the catfish, tarpon and snook for the food supply. The sea still provides game fish such as sailfish, marlin, wahoo, barracuda and tuna. On the flats, the most exciting fish for light tackle – the bonefish – is found in great abundance.

In addition to the restrictions on turtle and coral extraction, the following regulations apply: no person may take, buy or sell crawfish (lobster) between 15 February and 14 June, shrimp from 15 March to 14 July, or conch between 1 July and 30 September.

Fishing seasons Billfish: blue marlin, all year (best November to March); white marlin, November to May; sailfish, March to May. **Oceanic**: yellowfin tuna, all year; blackfin tuna, all year; bonito, all year; wahoo, November to February; sharks, all year. **Reef**: kingfish, March to June; barracuda, all year; jackfish, all year; mackerel, all year; grouper, all year; snapper, all year; bonefish, November to April; tarpon, June to August. **River**: tarpon, February to August; snook, February to August; snapper, all year. **Operators** In Belize City: **Belize River Lodge**, 8 miles Airport Rd, T225-2002, www.belizeriverlodge.com, excellent reputation. **Seasports Belize**, 83 North Front Street, T223-5505, www.seasportsbelize.com.

Nature tourism

Conservation is a high priority in Belize, with tourism vying for top spot as foreign currency earner in the national economy, and being the fastest-growing industry. Nature reserves are supported by a combination of private and public organizations including the Belize Audubon Society, the government and international agencies.

The **Belize Audubon Society** (PO Box 1001, 12 Fort Street, Belize City, T223-5004, www.belizeaudubon.org) manages seven protected areas including **Half Moon Caye Natural Monument** (3929 ha), **Cockscomb Basin Wildlife Sanctuary** (41,800 ha – the world's only jaguar reserve), **Crooked Tree Wildlife Sanctuary** (6480 ha – swamp forests and lagoons with wildfowl), **Blue Hole National Park** (233 ha), **Guanacaste National Park** (20.25 ha), **Tapir Mountain Nature Reserve** (formerly known as Society Hall Nature Reserve (2731 ha – a research area with Maya presence) and the **Shipstern Nature Reserve** (8910 ha – butterfly breeding, forest, lagoons, mammals and birds, contact BAS or the **International Tropical Conservation Foundation**, www.papiliorama.ch, Box 31, CH-2074 Marin-Neuchatel, Switzerland).

The **Río Bravo Management and Conservation Area** (105,300 ha) bordering Guatemala to the northwest of the country, covers some 4% of the country and is managed by the **Programme for Belize**, T227-5616, www.pfbelize.org, PO Box 749, 1 Eyre Street, Belize City.

Other parks include the **Community Baboon Sanctuary** at Bermudian Landing, **Bladen Nature Reserve** (watershed and primary forest), **Hol Chan Marine Reserve** (reef eco-system). Recently designated national parks and reserves include: **Five Blue Lakes National Park**, based on an unusually deep karst lagoon, and a maze of exotic caves and sinkholes near St Margaret Village on the Hummingbird Highway; **Kaax Meen Elijio Panti National Park**, at San Antonio Village near the Mountain Pine Ridge Reserve; **Vaca Forest Reserve** (21,060 ha); and **Chiquibul National Park** (107,687 ha – containing the Maya ruins of Caracol). There's also **Laughing Bird Caye National Park** (off Placencia), **Glovers Reef Marine Reserve**, and **Caye Caulker** now has a marine reserve at its north end.

Belize Enterprise for Sustained Technology (BEST) ⓘ *PO Box 35, Forest Drive, Belmopan, T802-3043, F802-2563*, is a non-profit organization committed to the sustainable development of Belize's disadvantaged communities and community-based ecotourism, for example Gales Point and Hopkins Village.

On 1 June 1996 a **National Protected Areas Trust Fund** (PACT), www.pactbelize.org, was established to provide finance for the "protection, conservation and enhancement of the natural and cultural treasures of Belize". Funds for PACT come from a Bz$7.50 conservation fee paid by all foreign visitors on departure by air, land and sea, and from 20% of revenues derived from protected areas entrance fees, cruise ship passenger fees, etc.

Visitors pay only one PACT tax every 30 days, so if you go to Tikal for a short trip from Belize, show your receipt in order not to pay twice.

Health

Those taking standard precautions find the climate pleasant and healthy. There are no mandatory inoculations required to enter the country unless coming from a country where yellow fever is a problem. Malaria prophylaxis is necessary only if staying in rural areas with poor medical care. Dengue fever is also rare but possible for travellers, and using insect repellent for mosquitoes is the best prevention for both diseases. Insect bites should be carefully scrutinized if not healing or if odd symptoms occur, as the possibilities of Chagas, leishmaniasis, or botfly larvae are all present. HIV has increased over the past few years and has been transmitted both by sexual contact and blood transfusions. **Medical services** have improved in recent years with the completion of the **Karl Heusner Memorial Hospital** in Belize City, though many Belizeans still seek medical care for serious ailments in Mérida or Guatemala City. The **British High Commission** in Belmopan (T822-2146) has a list of doctors and dentists.

Keeping in touch

Communications

Internet The relatively high cost of telephone calls makes internet surfing and cafés prohibitive. With the exception of San Ignacio, Ambergris Caye and Caye Caulker, internet cafés are less common than in neighbouring countries. When you do find one, the cost is upwards of US$2 per hour.

Post Airmail postage to Europe takes eight days and costs US$0.38 for a letter, US$0.20 for a postcard. A letter to USA costs US$0.30 and a postcard costs US$0.15. A letter to Austrailia costs US$0.50 and a postcard costs US$0.30, and takes two to three weeks. **Parcels**: US$3.50 per 0.5 kg to Europe, US$0.38 per 0.5 kg to USA. The service to Europe and USA has been praised, but surface mail is not reliable. Belize postage stamps are very attractive, much in demand, and a trip to the **Philatelic Bureau** in Belize City may provide you with your most treasured souvenir.

Telephone The much-maligned Belizean telephone system is steadily modernizing. There was a big overhaul in 2002 when telephone numbers were changed to seven digit and regional codes were removed. Most problems created by the switch are sorted, but if the number you are calling is not working contact **information** (T113) for help.

All towns have a telephone office and in most villages visitors can use the community phone. Payphones and card phones are fairly commonplace in Belize City and elsewhere. Most areas of the country, with a few exceptions, are covered by cellular phone service.

For information, dial T113; for the international operator, T115.

If you have many calls to make, a card phone works out much cheaper. There is a direct-dialling system between the major towns and to Mexico and USA. Local calls cost US$0.25 for three minutes, US$0.12 for each extra minute within the city, US$0.15-0.55 depending on zone. **BTL (Belize Telecommunications Ltd)** Church Street, Belize City, Mon-Sat 0800-1800, Sun and holidays 0800-1200, has an international telephone, telex and internet service.

Media

Newspapers, magazines and radio There are no daily newspapers in Belize. News is available in the weeklies, which generally come out on Friday morning, with the forthcoming Sunday's date: *The Belize Times* (PUP supported), *The Guardian* (UDP supported), *The Reporter* and *Amandala*. Good coverage of Ambergris Caye is provided by *The San Pedro Sun*, likewise *Placencia Breeze* covers Placencia. Small district newspapers are published sporadically. *Belize First!*, www.belizefirst.com, a quarterly magazine published in the USA (**Equator Travel Publications Inc**, 287 Beaverdam Road, Candler, NC 28715, USA, F828-667-1717), has articles on travel, life, news and history in Belize. Radio station **Love FM** (95.1FM) is the perfect summary of Belize on the airwaves. Try www.belizeweb.com for Belizean internet radio.

Belize City and Belmopan

Hardly large enough to warrant the title 'city', in any other country Belize City would be a dusty backwater, but in Belize it is the centre of the country, a blend of Latin American and Caribbean influences. Clapboard houses line dusty streets while people huddle in groups as the world drifts idly by. Born of the Belize River when the logs used to float downstream, it is still the main hub for maritime communications with boat services to the cayes. Nearby Belize Zoo is a model for zoos throughout the world. The capital, Belmopan, enjoys the cursed pleasure of being a planned city. Founded after a devastating hurricane struck Belize City, it has survived as the country's political centre, and has recently grown after several hurricanes have hit the country. » *For Sleeping, Eating and other listings, see page 667-672.*

Belize City » *pp667-672. Colour map 6, A1.*

→ *Population: 59,050.*

Belize City is the old capital and the largest town in Belize. Most of the houses are wooden, often of charming design, with galvanized-iron roofs. Most stand on seven-ft-high piles – signs of a bygone age when the city used to experience regular flooding. The city has improved greatly in recent years with the cleaning of the canals. Reclaimed land and a spate of building around the Eyre Street area, the new Museum of Belize, renovation of the Bliss Institute and the House of Culture suggest plans to improve the city are well underway. The introduction of tourist police has had a marked effect on crime levels, and the situation now requires sensible caution rather than paranoia. Just under a quarter of the total population live here, with the African strain predominant. Humidity is high, but the summer heat is offset by the northeast trades.

Belize City and the country escaped Hurricane Mitch in 1998 as it literally 'walked round Belize' turning south offshore hitting Honduras and the Bay Islands, before working its way through Guatemala. Hurricane Keith hit Ambergris Caye in October 2000 and Hurricane Iris in 2002, both acted as reminders of the inherent risks of Belize City's location.

Ins and outs

Getting there International flights arrive at **Phillip Goldson International Airport**, 10 miles from Belize City along the northern highway. Facilities in the check-in area include toilets, a restaurant, internet, bank (daily 0830-1200 and 1230-1800), viewing deck and duty-free shop. There are no facilities on the arrivals side but you can just walk round to the check-in area. Taxi fares to town are US$20, 30 minutes; taxi drivers strongly discourage sharing so team up, if need be, before getting outside. Make sure your taxi is legitimate by checking for the green licence plates. Taxis all operate on a fixed rate, so you should get the same price quoted by every driver. Ask to see a rate sheet if you have doubts about the price. Any bus going up the Northern Highway passes the airport junction (US$1), then it's a 1½-mile walk. For details of internal flights, see page 670.

Belize City

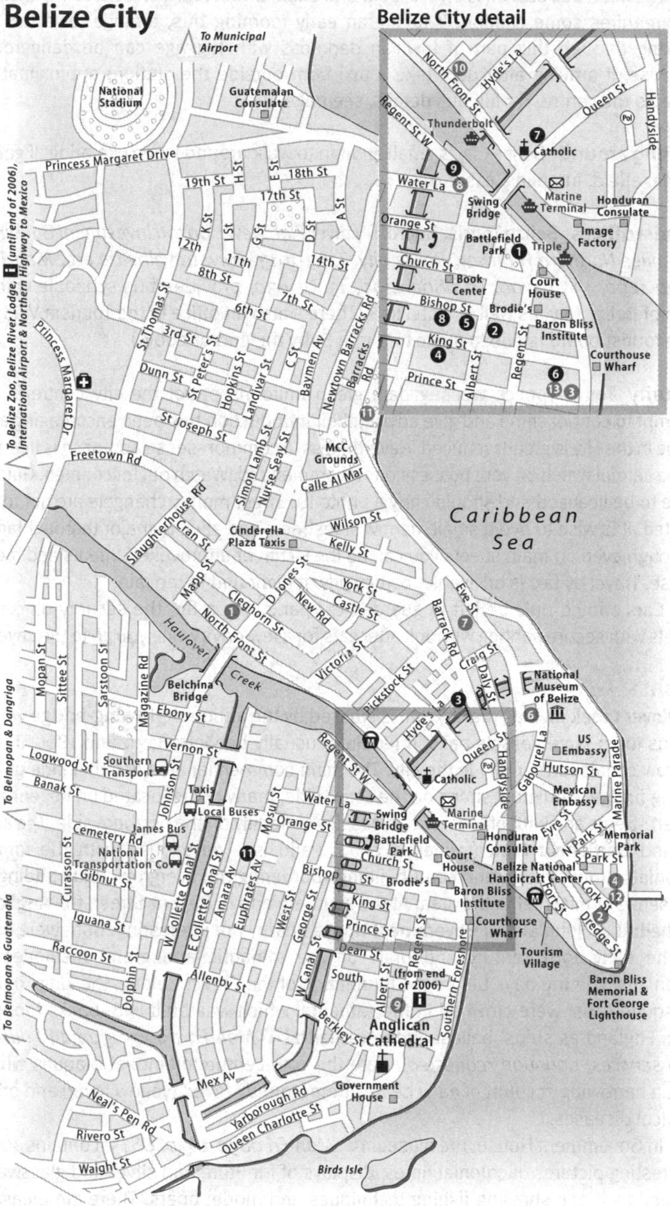

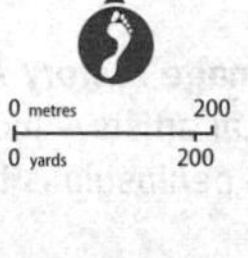

Sleeping

Bakadeer Inn 12
Bellevue 3
Chateau Caribbean 4
Freddie's 7
Great House 2
Isabel Guest House 8
Ma Ma Chen 6
Mopan 9
North Front Street Guest House 10
Princess 11
Radisson Fort George 12
Seaside Guest House 13

Eating

Big Daddy's 1
Blue Bird Café 2
Dario's 3
DIT's 4
El Centro 5
Jambel's Jerk Pit 6
Judith's Pastries 7
Macy's 8
Marlin 9
New Chon Saan 11

The main **bus station** is on West Collette Canal Street to the west of town, an area that requires some caution. If taking an early morning bus, arrange for a taxi as walking through this part of town in darkness with luggage can be dangerous. Likewise, if arriving after dark take a taxi from outside the station; approximately US$3 to the centre. For full bus details, see page 670.

Getting around Belize City is small enough to walk around when exploring. If going further afield, jump in a cab.

Tourist offices **Belize Tourist Board** ⓘ *Lower Flat, New Horizon Investment Building, 3½ miles Northern Highway, Belize City, T223-1913, www.travelbelize.org, Mon-Thu 0800-1200, 1300-1700, Fri 0800-1200, 1300-1630*, provides bus schedule with a map of Belize City, as well as hotel lists. There's also an office in the Tourism Village. (The tourist board is due to move to 2 13th St by the end of 2006.)

Security **Tourist police** wearing dark green uniforms patrol the city centre in an attempt to control crime and give advice; their introduction has been encouraging and crime in the city is greatly reduced. Nevertheless, a common-sense approach is needed and a careful watch on your possessions recommended. Watch out for conmen. Guides have to be licensed and should carry a photo ID. Street money changers are not to be trusted. It is wise to avoid small, narrow sidestreets and stick to major thoroughfares, although even on main streets you can be the victim of unprovoked threats and racial abuse. Travel by taxi is advisable, particularly at night and in the rain.

Cars should only be left in guarded car parks. For a tip, the security officer at hotels with secure parking will look after cars for a few days while you go to the cayes.

Sights

Haulover Creek divides the city and is crossed by the antiquated **swing-bridge** which opens to let large vessels pass, if required, usually between 1730 and 1800. Three narrow canals further divide the city. The main commercial area is either side of the swing-bridge, with most shops on the south side, many being located on Regent and Albert streets and with offices and embassies generally on the northern side. The area around **Battlefield Park** (formerly Central Park) is always busy, with the former colonial administration and court buildings bordering the overgrown park adding to the sense of mischief in the area. At the southern end of Regent Street, the **Anglican Cathedral** (St John's) and **Government House** nearby are interesting. Both were built in the early 19th century and draw on the romantic and grand memories of colonialism. In the days before the foundation of the Crown Colony, the kings of the Mosquito coast were crowned in the cathedral which was built with bricks brought from England as ships' ballast. In the **cathedral** ⓘ *Mon-Fri 0900- 1500 and during Sun services, donation requested*), note the 19th-century memorial plaques which give a harrowing account of early deaths from 'country fever' (yellow fever) and other tropical diseases.

In Government House, the **museum** ⓘ *Mon-Fri 0830-1630, US$5*, contains some interesting pictures of colonial times, displays of furniture and silver and glassware, as well as a one showing fishing techniques and model boats. There are pleasant gardens surrounding the museum if you are looking for somewhere quiet.

The **jail building** (1857) in front of the Central Bank on Gabourel Lane has been beautifully renovated and is now the new **National Museum of Belize** ⓘ *T223-4524, www.museumofbelize.org, Mon-Fri 0830-1700, US$10*, with exhibits on the history of Belize City and a permanent exhibit on the Maya sites of Belize.

Continuing to the right on North Front Street, pop into the **Image Factory Art Foundation** ⓘ *Mon-Fri 0900-1700*, for a peek at exhibitions by local artists – more grassroots than the other galleries. Moving towards the end of the peninsula is the new **Tourism Village** consisting of souvenir and gift shops and snack bars, along with several handicraft shops. This new development caters to tourists arriving from cruise ships. A little further on, at the tip of the peninsula, is **Memorial Park** on Marine Parade with a small obelisk, two cannon and concrete benches peppered with the holes of land crabs. The views across the bay can be quite spectacular in the early morning. The small park by the **Fort George Lighthouse** has a children's play area and is a popular meeting place. Baron Bliss' tomb is also here.

Belize Zoo (see page 690) is definitely worth a visit and not far from Belize City. The trip is very easy with buses from the Belize City passing the entrance every half hour.

Belmopan and around

» *pp667-672. Colour map 6, A1.*

→ *Population: 8130.*

As capital of Belize, Belmopan has been the seat of government since August 1970. It is 50 miles inland to the west of Belize City, near the junction of the Western Highway and the Hummingbird Highway to Dangriga (Stann Creek Town). Following the devastation caused in Belize City by Hurricane Hattie in 1961, plans were drawn up for a town which could be a centre for government, business and study away from the coast: Belmopan is the result.

The near-direct hit of Hurricane Mitch in 1998 and other hurricanes in recent years have prompted a renewed interest in plans to develop the capital, and several government organizations are in the process of relocating to the city, injecting a desperately needed 'heart' to this most eerie of capitals. One possible site of interest would be the **Department of Archaeology**, in the government plaza, which has a vault containing specimens of the country's artefacts. Unfortunately, the vault is currently closed and there are no plans to open it in the near future, although there is a small display and plans to build a museum. Part of the collection is displayed in the **Museum of Belize** (see Belize City, page 664).

Belmopan has been described as a disaster for the budget traveller.

Belmopan has the National Assembly building, two blocks of government offices (with broadly Maya-style architecture), the national archives, police headquarters, a public works department, a hospital, over 700 houses for civil servants, a non-governmental residential district to encourage expansion and a market. The Western Highway from Belize City is now good (a one-hour drive), continuing to San Ignacio, and there is an airfield (for charter services only).

Guanacaste National Park

One very good reason for stopping nearby is Guanacaste National Park, just outside Belmopan, which is well worth a visit. As Belmopan's accommodation is so expensive it may be better to take an early bus to the park from Belize City or San Ignacio rather than go from the capital. See also page 690.

Sleeping

Belize City *p664, map p665*

On the north side of the swing-bridge, turn left up North Front St for some of the cheaper hotels.

LL Radisson Fort George, 2 Marine Parade, T223-3333, www.radisson.com/belizecitybz. In 3 wings (**Club Wing**, where rooms have marble floors and panoramic views of the Caribbean; the **Colonial** Section with balconies overlooking the sea and **Villa**), rooms with partial sea view or pool view. Rooms are excellent with a/c, TV, and bathtubs. The staff are helpful and service is good. Good main restaurant (and **Stonegrill Restaurant** where food is cooked on hot, volcanic stones.) 2 lovely pools, fitness room and small garden. Fri pm live music. Bar with large TV screen, open until 2400 at weekends. **Le Petit Café** also on the premises.

LL-A **Bellevue**, 5 Southern Foreshore, T227-7051, bellevue@btl.net. A/c, private bath, good laundry service, restaurant (nice atmosphere, good lunches, steaks), leafy courtyard pool, nice bar with live music Fri nights, karaoke/music during the weeknights, good entertainment. The reception, however, stinks of damp and staff would rather watch TV than assist customers.

LL-A **Princess**, King's Park, T223-2670, www.princessbelize.com. On seafront (but not central), marina facilities, casino and bowling, cinema, a/c, good food and service in restaurant and bar (a/c with sea views, expensive), good business facilities, informal calypso bar near the dock is lively at night, nice pool and children's play area.

L **The Great House**, 13 Cork St, T223-3400, www.greathousebelize.com. A beautifully maintained white colonial building with 16 rooms furnished in homey style. 2 rooms have ocean view. Ask to read about its interesting history from 1927.

AL **Chateau Caribbean**, 6 Marine Parade, by Fort George, T223-0800, www.chateau caribbean.com. Main building is colonial. Rooms looking a little dated with a/c, good bar, restaurant (excellent Chinese and seafood), sea view, good service, parking.

A-B **Mopan**, 55 Regent St, T227-7351, www.hotelmopan.com. 14 rooms with bath, a/c, cheaper with fan, TV, in historic house, has restaurant and bar, new management very keen to help.

A-D **Bakadeer Inn** , 74 Cleghorn St, T223-0659, www.bakadeerinn.com. Private bath, a/c, TV, fridge, friendly. Recommended.

B-C **Isabel Guest House**, 3 Albert St, above Matus Store, T207-3139. 3 double rooms, 1 huge triple room, fans and fridges, quiet except when nearby disco operating at weekends, private shower, clean, friendly, safe, Spanish spoken. Isabel is very friendly. Highly recommended.

B-D **Seaside Guest House**, 3 Prince St, T227-8339, seasidebelize@btl.net. 6 rooms with private and shared baths, very clean, pleasant veranda with view out to the bay, a great place to stay and meet other travellers. Breakfast, drinks, book swap, credit cards accepted, internet access on site. Consistently recommended.

C **Freddie's**, 86 Eve St, T223-3851, freddies@btl.net. With shower and toilet, fan, hot water, clean, very nice, secure, very small.

C-D **Ma Ma Chen**, 5 Eve St, T223-4568, jessicachen1222@hotmail.com. 6 clean rooms with a/c or fan and private and shared bath. Run by quiet Chinese family with restaurant next door. Used to be Downtown but this burnt down.

D **North Front Street Guest House**, 124 North Front St, T227-7595. 1 block north of post office, 4 rooms, no hot water, some have fans, friendly, good information, keep windows closed at night and be sure to lock your door, on street and a bit noisy. Laundry and internet across street.

Belmopan and around *p667*

L-AL **Belmopan Hotel**, Constitution Drive, opposite bus stop and market, T822-2130. A/c, hot water, swimming pool, restaurant, bars.

A **Bull Frog**, 25 Half Moon Av, a 15-min walk east of the market through the parliament complex or a short taxi ride from the bus station, T822-2111. A/c, good, reasonably priced, laundry, karaoke nights on Thu (popular with locals).

C **El Rey Inn**, 23 Moho St, T822-3438, hibiscus@btl.net. Big rooms with fan, hot and cold water, basic, clean, friendly, laundry on request, central.

Eating

Belize City *p664, map p 665*

It can be difficult to find places to eat between 1500-1800.

TTT **Harbour View Restaurant**, Customs House, Fort St, T223-6420. Mon-Fri 1000-2200, Sat and Sun 1700-2200. With fine views of the bay and some tasty dishes but overpriced for the portions.

TTT **Jambel's Jerk Pit**, 2 King St, T227-6080. Excellent variety of Belizean and Jamaican dishes, including fresh seafood and vegetarian dishes. Outdoor patio.

TT **El Centro**, 4 Bishop St, T227-2413. Local dishes and burgers. A/c dining room and delivery available.

TT **Macy's**, 18 Bishop St, T227-3419. Recommended for well-prepared local game, Creole cooking, different fixed menu daily, charming host.

Marlin, 11 Regent St West, overlooking Belize River, T227-3913. Varied menu, good seafood.
Big Daddy's, on 2nd floor of market building, Church St, opposite BTL office. Good food, with pleasant view over the harbour. Closes when the food runs out.
Blue Bird Cafe, Albert St. Cheap fruit juices, specialities, basic, clean, reasonable. Inside tables are perfect for people watching.
Dario's, 33 Hyde's Lane. Classic Belizean hot meat pies, try 1 and then buy in bulk if you like them.
DIT's, 50 King St. Good for pastries, rice'n'beans and desserts.
Judith's Pastries, south end of Queen St. Good cakes and pastries.
New Chon Saan, 55 Euphrates Av, T227-2709. Best Chinese in town, pleasant atmosphere (taxi ride), takeaway. A thriving Chinese community means most Chinese food in Belize City is authentic.

Belmopan and around *p667*
Eating options are limited in Belmopan. There are several cheap *comedores* at the back of the market and a couple of bakeries near Constitution Drive. Cafés are closed on Sun.
Caladium, next to market, limited fare, moderately priced, small portions.
El Rey Inn, see Sleeping, above.
Aloha Café, next to **Scotiabank**. Friendly staff, good for breakfast or lunch, coffee, snacks, ice cream. Local newspapers to read.

Entertainment

Belize City *p664, map p665*
Bars and clubs
Lots of bars, some with jukeboxes, poolrooms and karaoke nights. Try the local drink, anise and peppermint, known as 'A and P'; also the powerful 'Old Belizeno' rum. The local beer, Belikin, is good, as is the 'stout', strong and free of gas. Guinness is also served, but is expensive.

Fri night is the most popular night for going out in Belize. Clubs often have a cover charge of US$5 and drinks are expensive once inside. Happy hour on Fri starts at 1600 at **Radisson Fort George** and continues at **Biltmore**, **Calypso** and elsewhere. The best and safest bars are found at major hotels, **Fort George**, **Biltmore Plaza**, **Bellevue** and **Princess**.
Bellevue Hotel Bar, see Sleeping, above, has multiple entertainment options for Fri nights, including 1 or 2 live bands and karaoke.
Club Calypso, at the **Princess Hotel**, see Sleeping, above, has top bands at weekends.
Eden Nightclub, 190 Newtown Barracks, T223-6888, DJs or live music from 2200 Thu-Sat nights.
The Wet Lizard, near the Tourism Village, has good American/Creole fare, reasonable prices, great view.

Casino
Princess Hotel, see Sleeping, above, has bowling lanes Tue-Sun, with large games room. The casino has slot machines, table games, with free drinks while you're gambling, a floor show with Russian dancers and a free buffet at 2330.

Cinema
Princess Hotel, see Sleeping, above, has a 2-theatre modern cinema, showing recent movies for US$7.50.

Shopping

Belize City *p664, map p665*
The whole city closes down on Sun except for a few shops open in the morning, eg **Brodies** in the centre of town. Banks and many shops and offices are also closed on Sat afternoons.

Books
Book Center, 4 Church St, T227-7457, books@btl.net, above **Thrift Center**. Excellent selection of books including second- hand books and back issues of some US magazines.
Brodies, Albert St, has decent selection of books on Belize and some paperback novels.

Markets and supermarkets
The **market** is by the junction of North Front St and Fort St.
Brodie's has widest grocery selection, though prices are slightly higher. Closed Sun.
Thrift Center, 2 Church St. Good food store, especially for dry goods at competitive prices.

Souvenirs
Handicrafts, woodcarvings and straw items are all good buys.

Zericote (or Xericote) wood carvings can be bought at **Brodies Department Store**, Central Park end of Regent St (which also sells postcards), the **Fort George Hotel**, see Sleeping, above, or **Egbert Peyrefitte**, 11a Cemetery Rd. Such wood carvings are the best buy, but to find a carver rather than buy the tourist fare in shops, ask a taxi driver. The wood sculpture of **Charles Gabb**, who introduced carving into Belize, can be seen at the Art Centre, near Government House. Wood carvers sell their work in front of the main hotels.

National Handicraft Center, South Park St. The Belize Chamber of Commerce's showcase promotes craftspeople from all over Belize; come here first for an overview of Belizean art and crafts.

Belize Audubon Society, across from the Tourist Village near the lighthouse, has a small but good selection of posters, T-shirts, gifts, and jewellery, all locally made in villages, and all at very reasonable prices.

Activities and tours

Belize City *p664, map p665*

Diving

Hugh Parkey's **Belize Dive Connection**, www.belizediving.com, is based at the Radisson's dock and is a professional outfit.

Tour operators

Discovery Expeditions, 5916 Manatee Drive, Buttonwood Bay, T223-0748, www.discoverybelize.com. An efficient and professional outfit offering interesting cultural and adventure tours out of the city and across the country. Recommended.

Island Expeditions Co, 1767 Magoon St, Southern Foreshore, T522-3328, www.islandexpeditions.com. Adventure and multi-sport wilderness, rainforest and reef trips.

Maya Travel Services, 42 Cleghorn St, T223-1623, www.mayatravelservices.com. Has received positive reports.

S&L Guided Tours, 91 North Front St, T227-7593, www.sltravelbelize.com. Recommended group travel (minimum 4 persons for most tours, 2 persons to Tikal). Office staff are disinterested and unfriendly. If booking tours in Belize from abroad it is advisable to check prices and services offered with a reputable tour operator in Belize first.

Transport

Belize City *p664, map p 665*

Air

The International Airport is 10 miles from Belize City (see page 664). The municipal airstrip for local flights is 15 mins' drive from the centre on the northern side of town, taxi, US$5, no bus service. Domestic services with **Tropic Air** and **Maya Island Air**, flights every 30 mins, 0700-1630. Flights to and from the islands can be taken from the international airport and companies link their flights to international arrivals and departures; flights from the international airport cost about US$15 more each way. **Maya** and **Tropic** also have services to Flores, Guatemala.

Airline offices American Airlines, San Cas Plaza, T223-2522 (reservations), Mon-Fri 0800-1800, Sat 0800-1200. **Continental Airlines**, 80 Regent St, T266-3822. **Belize Global Travel Services**, 41 Albert St, T227-7364, www.belizeglobal.com, provides services for **Grupo Taca** and **US Airways. Maya Island Air**, Municipal Airstrip, Belize City T233-1140, www.mayaislandair.com **Tropic Air**, Albert St, Belize City, T224-5671, www.tropicair.com.

Boat

Boats to **Caye Caulker** continuing to **San Pedro** (Ambergris Caye) leave from the Marine Terminal on North Front St with the **Caye Caulker Water Taxi Association**, T223-5752, www.cayecaulkerwatertaxi.com. Departures at 0800, 0900, 1030, 1200, 1330, 1500, 1430 and 1730 (latter to Caye Caulker only), Caye Caulker US$10, return US$15, to San Pedro, US$15, return US$25. Check website for changes in the schedule. Departures also with **Triple J** from its terminal at Courthouse Wharf, T223-3464, office hours 0700-1630, boats at 0800, 1030, 1200, 1500, 1630 to **Caye Caulker** and then **San Pedro**. To Caye Caulker, US$15, return US$25, to San Pedro US$20, US$40 return, Caye Caulker to San Pedro, US$15. Its boats are covered.

Bus

Within the city the fare is US$0.50 run by Belize **in Transit** services. They originate next to the taxi stand on Cemetery Rd.

There are bus services to all the main

towns. The **National Transportation Co operates Northern Transport** from West Collette Canal St, T228-2025 (can store luggage US$0.50). Heading north to **Chetumal** (see Mexico, page 487), about 15 daily each way, roughly every 30 mins, starting at 0500 until 1800, 3 hrs, US$2.50, express buses from 0600 stopping at **Orange Walk** and **Corozal** only, US$6.50, 2½ hrs. If taking a bus from Chetumal which will arrive in Belize City after dark, decide on a hotel and go there by taxi.

Heading west towards **Guatemala** by bus to **Belmopan** and **San Ignacio**, express bus 0900, US$3, with a/c and refreshments, ordinary bus every 30 mins, Mon-Sat frequent 0600-1900, Sun 0630-1700. **National Transport Co**, T227-2025, run until 2000. The 0600, 0630 and 1015 buses connect at the border with services to Flores, Guatemala. To **San Ignacio**, **Benque Viejo** and the **Guatemalan border** via Belmopan, **National Transportation Co**, US$2.50 to Belmopan, US$4.50 to Benque, US$4 to San Ignacio, hourly Mon-Sat, 1100-1900. The last possible bus connection to **Flores** leaves the border at 1600, but it is better to get an earlier bus to arrive in daylight. Many buses leave for **Melchor de Mencos**, 0600-1030. To **Flores**, Guatemala, minibuses leave the Marine Terminal on Front St, make reservation the previous day.

1st-class express buses from Belize City to **Flores/Tikal** with **Mundo Maya/Línea Dorada**, www.tikalmayanworld.com, leave from Belize City daily at 1000 and 1700, with buses connecting to Guatemala City and beyond. Also with services heading north to **Chetumal**. Check the **Mundo Maya** counter in the Marine Terminal on North Front St.

Heading south to **Dangriga**, via Belmopan and the Hummingbird Highway. **Southern Transport** (T227-3937), from the corner of Vernon and Johnson St near the Belchina Bridge, several daily on the hour 0800-1600, plus Mon 0600, US$5. **James**, to **Punta Gorda** via **Dangriga**, **Cockscomb Basin Wildlife Sanctuary** and **Mango Creek**, daily 0530, 1000 and 1445, 6-8 hrs, US$11.

Car

Car hire Cars start at US$60 plus insurance of around US$15 a day. Most rental firms have offices in Belize City and opposite the international airport terminal building. **Avis**, T203-4619, avisbelize@btl.net. **Budget**, 2½ miles, Northern Highway, T223-2435, www.budget-belize.com. **Crystal Auto Rental**, Mile 4¾ Northern Highway, T223-1600, www.crystal-belize.com, cheapest deals in town, but not always most reliable, wide selection of vehicles, will release insurance papers for car entry to Guatemala and Mexico. **Pancho's**, 5747 Lizarraga Av, T224-5554, www.panchos rentalbelize.com, locally owned rental company. **Hertz**, 11a Cork St, beside Radisson Fort George Hotel, T223-5395, safari@btl.net, and International Airport, T225-3300.

Taxis

Official cabs have green licence plates (drivers have ID card); within Belize, US$4 for 1 or 2 people; slightly more for 3 or more. There is a taxi stand on Central Park, another on the corner of Collet Canal St and Cemetery Rd, and a number of taxis on Albert St, Queen St and around town. Outside Belize City, US$1.75 per mile, regardless of number of passengers. Belize City to the resorts in Cayo District approximately US$100-125, 1-4 people. No meters, so beware of overcharging and make sure fare is quoted in Bz$.

Belmopan and around *p667*

Bus

To **San Ignacio**, hourly on the hour 0500-2100, 1 hr, US$2.50. To **Belize City**, Mon-Sat, every 30 mins, 0600-1900, hourly on Sun, 1 hr, US$3.50. Heading south hourly buses Mon-Sat 0830-1630 (fewer on Sun) to **Dangriga**, 1 hr, US$3, **Mango Creek**, 3 hrs, US$8 and **Punta Gorda**, 4½ hrs, US$9. James Bus leaves for **Belize City** and **Punta Gorda** from opposite the **National Transportation Co** bus station. To **Orange Walk** and **Corozal** take an early bus to Belize City and change.

Directory

Belize City *p664, map p665*

Banks

All banks have facilities to arrange cash advance on Visa. It is easy to have money wired to Belize City. Guatemalan quetzales and Mexican pesos are best bought at the border. There are several ATMs in Belize City **Atlantic Bank**, 6 Albert St, quick efficient service, small charge for Visa/MasterCard, smaller queues than **Belize Bank Belize Bank**, 60 Market Square, is particularly efficient and modern, US$0.50 commission on Amex cheques but a big charge for cash against Visa and MasterCard.

Cultural centres

Audubon Society, see page 662. **Baron Bliss Institute**, public library, temporary exhibitions; has 1 stela and 2 large discs from Caracol on display. **The Image Factory**, 91 Front St, has exhibitions of contemporary art, Mon-Fri 0900-1800. **The Belize National Handicraft Center** sales room on South Park St has a good supply of books about Belize culture. **Programme for Belize**, 1 Eyre St, T227-5616, www.pfbelize.org, is a conservation organization which manages land reserves including Río Bravo. **Society for the Promotion of Education and Research (SPEAR)**, 5638 Gentle Av, T223-1668, www.spear.org.bz, with a great reference library for everything Belizean.

Embassies and consulates

(See also Belmopan Directory, below) **Canada** (consulate), 80 Princess Margaret Drive, T223-1060. **Costa Rica**, 11A Handyside, T223-6525. **France**, covered by San Salvador. **Guatemala**, 8A St, T223-3150, 0900-1300, will not issue visas or tourist cards here; will tell you to leave it till you reach your exit point. **Honduras**, 22 Gabourel Lane, T224-5889, . **Italy** (consulate), 18 Albert St, T227-8449. **Mexico**, 18 N Park St, T223-0194. **Nicaragua**, 124 Newtown Barracks, T/F223-2666. **Panama**, Princess Margaret Drive, T223-4282. **USA**, 29 Gabourel Lane, T227-7161; consulate is round the corner on Hutson St, office hours, Mon-Fri, 0800-1200, 1300-1700.

Internet

Service at **BTL** and in some hotels, prices around US$4 per hr. Keep an eye out for cheaper options. **Mailbox**, on Front St.

Laundry

Northside Laundromat, North Front St, 0900-2000, US$4 for 6 kg wash and dry. **Belize Dry Cleaners and Launderomat**, 3 Dolphin St.

Post office

The main post office is at Queen St and North Front St, 0800-1700 (1630 Fri). Letters held for a month. Beautiful stamps for collectors around the corner on Queen St.

Telephone

Belizean Telecommunications Ltd (BTL), 1 Church St, just off Central Park, Mon-Sat, 0800-1800, Sun 0800-1200. Also public fax and booths for credit card and charge calls.

Belmopan and around *p667*

Banks

Scotia Bank 1915 Constitution Dr and **Belize Bank**, Constitution Dr, also provide cash advances.

Embassies and consulates

Costa Rica (consulate), 7 Shopping center, T822-3801. **El Salvador**, 49 Nanche St, T822-3404. **UK High Commission**, North Ring Rd, next to the Governor's residence, T822-2146, www.britishhighbze.com, Mon-Thu 0800-1200 and 1300-1600, Fri 0800-1400. Has a list of recommended doctors and dentists.

Internet

Techno Hub at bus station, US$4.5 per hr.

Post office

The post office is next to the market (opposite the immigration office).

Northern Cayes

The cayes off the coast are attractive, relaxing, slow and very 'Caribbean' – an excellent place for diving, sea fishing or just lazing about. Palm trees fringe the coastline, providing day-long shade for resting in your hammock looking out at the stunning azure seas. They are popular destinations, especially in August and between December and May.

There are some 212 sq miles of cayes. The cayes and atolls were home to fishermen and resting points to clean the catch or grow coconuts. But they have always been valued. The Maya built the site of Marco Gonzalez on the southwestern tip of Ambergris Caye, the largest and most populated of the islands. Nearby Caye Caulker is a popular destination for the more budget-minded visitor, while serious divers head for the Turneffe Islands. Other, smaller cayes are home to exclusive resorts or remain uninhabited, many being little more than mangrove swamps. St George's Caye, 9 miles northeast of Belize, was once the capital and the scene of the battle in 1798 which established British possession. ▸▸ *For Sleeping, Eating and other listings, see pages 676-682.*

Ins and outs

Most boats to Caye Caulker and Ambergris Caye leave from the Marine Terminal or the Triple J terminal. Boats leave regularly from 0630 to 1730 if you're just turning up. Otherwise check at your hotel as timetables change frequently.

For southern cayes, see under Southern Belize, page 700.

Ambergris Caye

▸▸ *pp676-682. Colour map 6, A2.*

➔ *Population: 4499.*

This island (pronounced Am-*ber*-gris), along with the town of **San Pedro**, has grown rapidly over the last couple of years, with over 50 hotels and guesthouses on the island. Buildings are still restricted to no more than three storeys in height, and the many wooden structures retain an authentic village atmosphere. The very helpful **Ambergris Tourist Information office** ⓘ *Mon-Sat 1000-1300, 1400-1900*, is next to the the town hall.

Although sand is in abundance, there are few beach areas around San Pedro town. The emphasis is on snorkelling on the nearby barrier reef and **Hol Chan Marine Park**, and the fine scuba diving, sailing, fishing and board sailing. The main boat jetties are on the east (Caribbean Sea) side of San Pedro. It can be dangerous to swim near San Pedro as there have been serious accidents with boats. Boats are restricted to about 5 miles per hour within the line of red buoys about 25 yards offshore, but this is not always adhered to. There is a 'safe' beach in front of the park, just to the south of the government dock. A short distance to the north and south of San Pedro lie miles of deserted beach front, where picnic barbecues are popular for day-tripping snorkellers and birders who have visited the nearby small cayes hoping to glimpse rosets, spoonbills or white ibis. If you go north you have to cross a small inlet with hand-pulled ferry, US$0.50 for foreigners. **Note** Only very experienced snorkellers should attempt to swim in the cutting between the reef and the open sea.

You cannot, in practice, walk north along the beach from San Pedro to Xcalak, Mexico.

Excursions from Ambergris Caye

Just south of Ambergris Caye, and not far from Caye Caulker, is the **Hol Chan Marine Park** ⓘ *US$10 entry fee; the park office (with reef displays and information on*

 Bacalar Chico National Park to the north) is on Caribeña St, T226-2247. This underwater natural park is divided into three zones: Zone A is the reef, where fishing is prohibited; Zone B is the seagrass beds, where fishing can only be done with a special licence (the **Boca Ciega** blue hole is here); Zone C is mangroves where fishing also requires a licence. Only certified scuba divers may dive in the reserve. Fish feeding, although prohibited, takes place at Shark Ray Alley, where about 15 sharks and rays are fed for the entertainment of tourists. Not the most natural of experiences but fascinating to see these creatures close up.

San Pedro is well known for its diving. Long canyons containing plenty of soft and hard coral formations start at around 50-60 ft going down to 120 ft. Often these have grown into hollow tubes which make for interesting diving. **Tackle Box, Esmeralda, Cypress, M & Ms** and **Tres Cocos** are only some of the dive sites. The visibility in this area is usually over 100 ft. There is a recompression chamber in San Pedro and a US$1 tax on each tank fill insures treatment throughout the island.

Although offshore, Ambergris Caye airport makes arranging tours to visit places on the mainland very easy (for example Altún Ha US$60 per person; Lamanai US$125 per person) while still being able to enjoy other water experiences (catamaran sailing, deep-sea fishing, manatee and Coco Solo).

Caye Caulker

» pp676-682. Colour map 6, A2.

On Caye Caulker, a thin line of white sandy beach falls to a sea of turquoise blue and green, while the reef can be seen a mile and a half from the shore. By day on this laid-back island, it's diving and snorkelling, sea and sand; at dusk everyone heads up to the 'split' to watch the sunset; by night it's eating, drinking and dancing. A quiet lobster-fishing island (closed season 15 February to 14 June) until fairly recently, its extremely relaxing atmosphere, gentle climate, postcard-perfect views and the myriad small restaurants and bars have drawn increasing numbers of tourists.

If swimming in the 'split', beware of fishing and powerboats which use it as a route from the ocean to the west side; serious accidents have occurred.

The caye is actually two islands separated by a small channel known as the 'split' with all the services on the southern island and, in the north, a **marine reserve** ⓘ *free for school parties, tourists are asked for a US$2 donation to help expansion and to increase the work in ecology education*. In the south, next to **Shirley's** is the **Caye Caulker Mini Reserve.**

Tour operators and hotels on the island have worked hard to improve services for visitors. The atmosphere is friendly and easy-going, but the usual common sense rules apply with regards to personal safety. Drugs are readily available, but they are illegal and you shouldn't expect any sympathy should you get into difficulties. Some think the atmosphere is more relaxed out of high season. Sandflies can be ferocious in season (December to February); take long trousers and a good repellent. Make sure you fix prices before going on trips or hiring equipment and, if you pay the night before, get a receipt.

A walk south along the shore takes you to the new airstrip, the Caye Caulker Mini Reserve and to mangroves where the rare black catbird can be seen and its sweet song heard.

Excursions from Caye Caulker

Reef trips are the same as those found on Ambergris Caye; for more details see under San Pedro (page 673) and under Activities and tours (page 680).

Generally all trips are offered at the same price by agreement between tour operators, eliminating the need to shop around for a good price. Tour operators share clients if numbers are not sufficient. This means that you can be certain there is always a trip, but make sure that the boat operator is reliable. Tour organizers must be licensed by the **Belize Tourist Board** and should have a licence to prove it. To encourage high standards, and for your own safety, insist on seeing proof that your guide is licensed.

Protect against sunburn on reef trips, even while snorkelling. For more information on all the trips and watersports available see Activity and tours, page 680.

Tours are slightly cheaper from Caye Caulker than Ambergris Caye. See Tour operators, page 681.

The Cayes

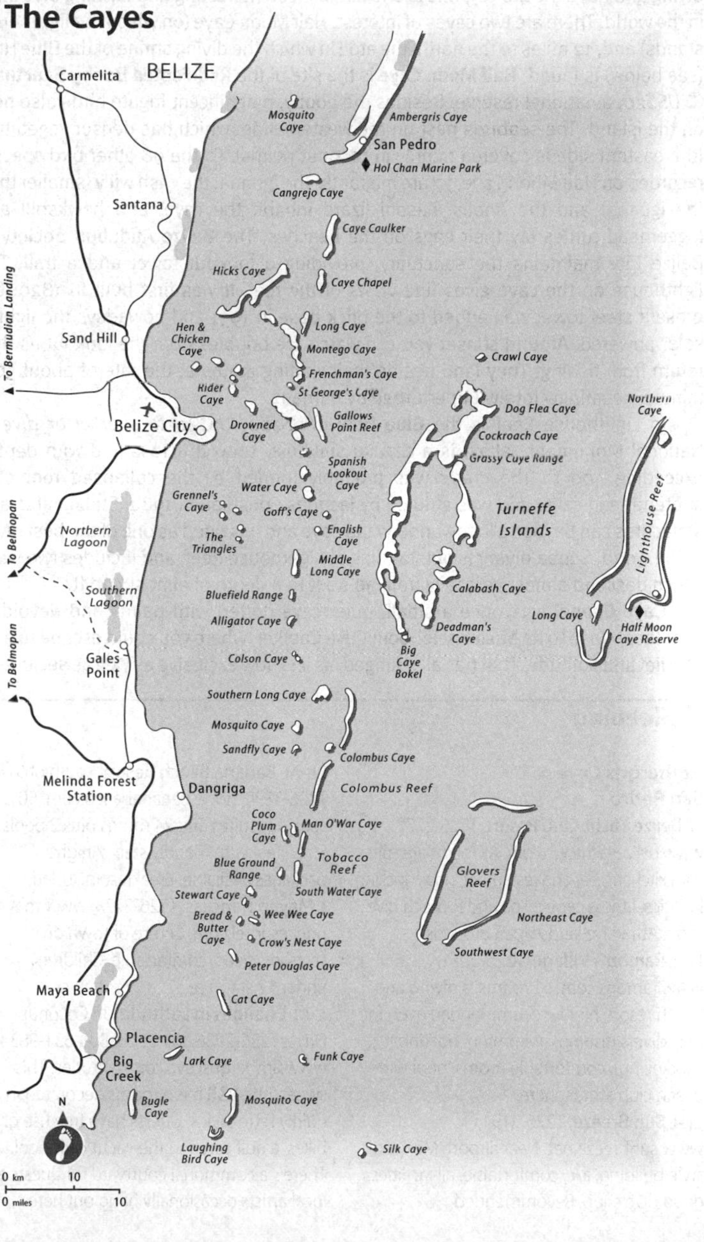

Lighthouse Reef, Turneffe Islands and the smaller cayes

» » pp676-682. Colour map 6, A2.

ⓘ *On arrival you must register near the lighthouse with the warden who will provide maps and tell you where you can camp.*

Lighthouse Reef is the outermost of the three north-south reef systems off Belize and is some 45 miles to the east of Belize City. Trips out here are not cheap, but if you like diving and have the money, this is one of the most interesting and exciting dive sites in the world. There are two cayes of interest: Half Moon Caye (on which the lighthouse stands) and, 12 miles to the north, the atoll in which the diving shrine of the Blue Hole (see below) is found. **Half Moon Caye** is the site of the **Red-Footed Booby Sanctuary** ⓘ *US$20*, a national reserve. Besides the booby, magnificent frigate birds also nest on the island. The seabirds nest on the western side, which has denser vegetation (the eastern side is covered mainly in coconut palms). Of the 98 other bird species recorded on Half Moon Caye, 77 are migrants. The iguana, the wish willy (smaller than the iguana) and the Anolis allisoni lizard inhabit the caye, and hawksbill and loggerhead turtles lay their eggs on the beaches. The **Belize Audubon Society** in Belize City maintains the sanctuary, providing a lookout tower and a trail. The lighthouse on the caye gives fine views of the reef. It was first built in 1820: the present steel tower was added to the brick base in 1931 and nowadays the light is solar powered. Around sunset you can watch the boobies from the lookout as they return from fishing. They land beside their waiting mates at the rate of about 50 a minute, seemingly totally unperturbed by humans.

In Lighthouse Reef is the **Blue Hole** ⓘ *US$20, US$40 to snorkel or dive*, a National Monument, which is a circular sinkhole, 1000 ft across and with depths exceeding 400 ft. The crater was probably formed by the collapsed roof of a subterranean cave, and was studied by Jacques Cousteau in 1984. Stalagmites and stalactites can be found in the underwater cave and it is rated as one of the best dives in the world. Scuba diving is outstanding at Lighthouse Reef, and includes two walls which descend almost vertically from 30-40 ft to a depth of almost 400 ft.

Caye Chapel was once a small, quiet caye dotted with palms and devoid of sandflies, close to its busier neighbour Caye Caulker, where you could escape to a bit of quiet and solitude. That has all changed, as it is now exclusive as well as secluded.

Sleeping

Ambergris Caye *p673*

San Pedro

LL **Belize Yacht Club Resort**, T226-2777, www.belizeyachtclub.com. All rooms are suites with kitchens, bar and restaurant, pool, docking facilities, fitness centre, spa and **Protech** dive shop. Attractive landscaped grounds.

LL-L **Ramon's Village**, T226-2071, www.ramons.com. 61 rooms, a diving and beach resort, highly recommended even for non-divers (fishing, swimming, boating, snorkelling), comfortable rooms, pool with beach club atmosphere.

LL-L **Sun Breeze**, T226-2191, www.sunbreeze.net. Near airport, Mexican-style building, a/c, comfortable, all facilities, good dive shop. Recommended.

LL-AL **Banana Beach Resort**, south of town, T226-3890, www.bananabeach.com. 50 spacious suites and 24 rooms plus 2 pools. Small feel with friendly staff. 7 night packages available. Breakfast included.

L **Mayan Princess**, T226-2778, www.mayanprinceshotel.com. Centre of town on seafront, clean, comfortable. Children under 12 stay free.

L-AL **Changes in Latitude**, 36 Coconut Drive, T226-2986, toll free 1-800-631-9834, www.ambergriscaye.com/latitudes. This sweet little B&B has 6 rooms decorated in quirky retro styles. Guests have free use of bikes, a golf cart and the yacht club pool. There's a communal courtyard for guests and local artists occasionally hang out here.

L-AL Paradise Resort Hotel, T226-2083. Wide selection of rooms and villas, good location, villas better value, cheaper summer rates, all watersports.

L-AL San Pedro Holiday Hotel, T226-2014, www.sanpedroholiday.com. 16 rooms and a suite in good central location, fun atmosphere with good facilities. Children 2-12 US$10.

AL-A Coral Beach, T226-2013, www.coralbeachhotel.com. Central location and good local feel.

AL-A Hotel San Pedrano, T226-2054, sanpedrano@btl.net. Another small hotel with a/c and fan rooms with private bathrooms. Children 6-12 years, US$5.

AL-A Lily's Caribbean Lodge, T206-2059, www.ambergriscaye.com/lilys. 6 rooms with sea view, 2 with partial view and 3 without view, all with a/c, clean and friendly.

AL-A Spindrift, T226-2018, www.ambergriscaye.com/spindrift. 24 rooms, 4 apartments, unattractive block but central location, good bar and restaurant, popular meeting place, a/c, comfortable.

B Tomas, 12 Barrier Reef Drive, T226-2061. 7 airy rooms with a/c, cheaper with fan, bath, drinking water, clean, friendly and family-run. Children under 6, free.

B-D Ruby's, San Pedro Town on the beach, T226-2063, www.ambergriscaye.com/rubys. 26 a/c or fan rooms, with private or shared bath, good views, central. Recommended as best value in town.

D Pedro's Inn, T226-1825, pedroback2000@yahoo.com. The island's only real budget place with onsite bar, BBQ and pool. Rooms have shared bathroom.

Outside San Pedro

Several resort-style complexes outside the town offer seclusion and an ambience that borders on paradise.

LL Capricorn Resort, 3 miles north of town, T226-2809, www.ambergriscaye.com/capricorn. Wooden cabins on beach with great restaurant.

LL Mata Chica Resort, 4 miles north, T226-5010, www.matachica.com. European owned and managed, beautiful and stylish stucco and thatched *cabañas* on a lovely beach, fantastic **Mambo** restaurant.

LL Victoria House, San Pedro, T226-2067, www.victoria-house.com. This stunning resort, 2 miles south of town, offers 4 different types of stylishly decorated rooms. There are also fully fitted villas in the grounds. Excellent facilities, lovely pool, good dive shop and watersports. Highly recommended.

LL-L Captain Morgan's Retreat, 3 miles north of town, T226-2567, www.belizevacation.com. Access by boat, thatched roofed *cabañas* with private facilities, pool, dock, secluded. Recommended.

LL-L El Pescador, on Punta Arena beach 3 miles north, Belize City, T/F226-2398, www.elpescador.com. Access by boat, specialist fishing lodge with good reputation, a/c, good food and service.

Caye Caulker *p674*

In all accommodation take precautions against theft. The arrival pier is just about in the centre of town, with all the accommodation on or within a 15-min walk of the main street. The southern end of town is slightly quieter and has a smattering of mangrove and bird life, but it's quite a walk from the 'split' for swimming or snorkelling. Camping on the beach is forbidden.

LL-L Rainbow Hotel, T226-0123, rainbowhotel@btl.net. 17 rooms and 1 apartment, with shower, hot water, good. Good street front location facing the beach and the popular **Rainbow Grill** and **Triple J** dock.

L Iguana Reef Inn, T226-0213, www.iguanareefinn.com. Probably the best place on the island, relaxing and quiet as it's on the back side. With 13 rooms and a bar.

L-AL Seaside Cabañas, first place you reach off the boat, T226-0498, www.seasidecabanas.com. 16 comfortable rooms and cabins in Mexican style with Moroccan furnishings – some with their own roof terraces set around the island's only pool. Excellent tours and very helpful.

L-B Vega Inn, T226-0142, www.vega.com.bz. Suites, houses and budget rooms, camping (**E** per person) and credit cards accepted. All doubles, with ceiling fan, fresh linen and hot showers. Camping ground is guarded, hot water, clean toilets.

AL Anchorage Resort, to the south, near **Ignacio's**, T226-0304, www.anchorageresort.com. 3-storey building with 18 comfortable, tiled rooms with private bathrooms, pleasant atmosphere, friendly family, drinks served under shade on the beach.

AL-A Shirley's Guest House, T226-0145, www.shirleysguesthouse.com, south end of the village on the beach. Very relaxing with 5 green and white raised cabins, with private and shared bath. No kids. Will pick up from boat terminal. Recommended.

AL-B Tree Tops, T226-0240, www.treetopsbelize.com. Spotless, spacious rooms and suites, comfortable beds with beach views, German spoken, powerful fan, cable TV, friendly, good value. Children must be over 10. Recommended.

AL-C Tropical Paradise Resort, T226-0124, www.tropicalparadise.biz. Cabins with hot showers, clean, restaurant, good excursions.

AL-C Tropics Hotel, on the main street, T226-0374, www.startoursbelize.com. OK rooms, with private bath and hot water. Cheaper for longer stays.

C-D Sandy Lane, 1 block back from main street, T226-0117. Bungalow-type accommodation, clean, private and cheaper shared bathrooms, hot showers, run by Rico and Elma Novelo. Also more expensive rooms with kitchen and TV for longer stays. Recommended.

D Daisy's, T226-0150. Clean, friendly, safe, cheaper rooms downstairs. Rooms with communal bathroom, hot water. Reductions for longer stays, will store valuables, cashes TCs.

D Edith's, 2 blocks from the beach and close to the **I and I Bar**. T206-0069. 11 rooms with bath, hot water, fan. Recommended.

D Ignacio Beach Cabins, T226-0175. 18 small purple huts raised very high on the beach just outside town to the south. Cheaper rooms are smaller with cold water bathrooms. Quiet and clean. Book exchange and bike rental. Recommended.

D Lorraine's Guest House, south end of the village, on the beach, T206-0162. A handful of simple yellow cabins, basic and a little tatty with fans and tables, but friendly and quiet.

D Marin's, 1½ blocks from the beach at the southern end, T226-0444. Good-sized rooms with private and shared facilities in green and white wooden cabins on stilts in a small compound.

D Mira Mar, 2front St, 2 blocks up from the dock, T226-0307. 2nd-floor rooms best, clean showers, helpful owner Melvin Badillo.

D-E Tina's Backpackers, T226-0351, rastatinabz@yahoo.com. Cheapest on the caye, with dorms, 1 private room, or sling a hammock. Very popular and noisy – great for meeting people, but not the place if you want peace and quiet. Dirty at times.

E Albert's, Front St, 1½ blocks north of dock, T226-0277. A dependable cheapie, very clean shared bathroom, OK for the first night. Above a minimart in the centre of the main strip.

Lighthouse Reef, Turneffe Islands and the smaller cayes *p676*

Many cayes have package deals for a few days or a week.

LL Caye Chapel Golf Resort, Caye Chapel, T226-8250, www.cayechapel.com. 22 deluxe villas with tennis courts, private airstrip and golf.

LL Turneffe Flats, Turneffe Islands (56 Eve St, Belize City), T220-4046, T1-800-815-1304 (USA), www.tflats.com. In a lovely location, offers week-long packages for fishing and scuba; takes 20 guests.

LL Turneffe Island Lodge, Big Caye Bokel, Turneffe Islands, T220-4142, www.turneffelodge.com. Can accommodate 16 guests for week-long fishing and scuba packages.

LL-L Blackbird Caye Resort, Turneffe Islands (c/o Blackbird Caye Co, 8 Front St, Belize City), T223-2767, T713-6581142 (USA), www.blackbird.com. This ecologically oriented resort on the 4000-acre island is used by the **Oceanic Society** and is a potential site for a biosphere reserve underwater project. Weekly packages arranged. Diving or fishing packages available, no bar, take your own alcohol.

L Calypso Beach Retreat, Long Caye, Lighthouse Reef Atoll, T523-8156, www.calypsobeachretreat.com. Small eco-friendly B&B with 4 beachfront rooms, packages available.

AL Cottage Colony, St George's Caye. Contact PO Box 428, Belize City, T227-7051, fins@btl.net. Colonial-style *cabañas* with dive facilities, price varies according to season, easy access from Belize City.

A Moonlight Shadows Lodge, Middle Long Caye, T822-3665. Still being developed but offering complete isolation.

Eating

Ambergris Caye *p673*

Celi's, behind **Holiday Hotel**. Good seafood. Recommended. Closed Wed when there is a beach BBQ.

ŦŦŦ **Elvi's Kitchen**, popular, upmarket, live music and roof built around flamboyant tree, can be very busy, won international award in 1996.
ŦŦŦ **Jade Garden Restaurant**, south of town. Chinese, sweet and sour everything, drinks expensive.
ŦŦŦ **Wild Mango's**, south of main strip, T226-2859. Closed Mon. Run by Amy Knox, former chef at **Victoria House**. Rustic setting over looking the sea. Try the rum-soaked bacon wrapped shrimp. All the delicious meals are tastefully presented. Recommended.
ŦŦŦ-ŦŦ **Ambergris Delight**, 35 Pescador Drive, pleasant place serving up Belizean cuisine and burgers. Closed Tue.
ŦŦŦ-ŦŦ **Fido's Courtyard**, towards north end of Front St. Lively bar-restaurant often with live music, good lunch and dinner. New sushi bar upstars.
ŦŦ **El Patio**, south of town, beyond Belize Yacht Club. Good, Mexican-style food, live music in evenings.
ŦŦ **Estel's Dine by the Sea** on the beach close to water taxi terminal. Good food and 1940s-50s music.

Caye Caulker *p674*
Beer is sold by the crate at the wholesaler on the dock by the generator; ice for sale at Tropical Paradise.
ŦŦŦ **Coco Plum Gardens**, at the southern end of the island, with art gallery. Pricey for Caye Caulker but worth it. Open for breakfast and dinner, Mon-Sat.
ŦŦŦ **Habanero's**, very close to main dock. Excellent and tasty food, the best in Belize according to some. Recommended.
ŦŦŦ **Marin's**, 3 blocks south 1 west of the dock. Good seafood all day everyday, cable TV, expensive but worth it.
ŦŦŦ-ŦŦ **Happy Lobster**, on main street. Good food with majority fish dishes and pasta. Recommended.
ŦŦŦ-ŦŦ **Tropical Paradise**, on the beach . Excellent seafood, varied menu, slightly more expensive than others.
ŦŦ **Glenda's**, old time island favourite. Good breakfast and lunches. Mornings only.
ŦŦ **Oceanside**, most popular bar on the island. Food OK, music and dancing until midnight.
ŦŦ **Popeye's**, on the beach. Live music some nights, opens at 0600 for breakfast.
ŦŦ **Rainbow Bar and Restaurant**, with the restaurant on its own jetty. Delicious burritos good value, beautiful view.
ŦŦ **Sandbox** , T226-0200. Not so popular as it used to be. With a good atmosphere and sandy floors for that complete beach experience.
ŦŦ-Ŧ **Romie's Sidewalk Restaurant and Bar**. Closed Thu. Good, cheaper seafood options than some of the island restaurants and very popular, especially in the evenings. Bagels and granola for breakfast. Recommend by locals.
Ŧ **Cafe Coco Loco**, next door to the **Lighthouse**. Delicious bagels, brownies and coffee. Try the fruit sorbet cooler made with ginger ale.
Ŧ **Lighthouse**. Real ice cream in cones.

Bars and clubs

Ambergris Caye *p673*
Big Daddy's Disco, open evenings but cranks up at midnight. For entertainment, try 'Chicken Drop' in Pier Lounge at **Spindthrift Hotel** on a Wed night: you bet US$1 on which square the chicken will leave its droppings. **Jaguar's Temple** and **Barefoot Iguana** are current popular nightspots .

Caye Caulker *p674*
Many of the restaurants become bars in the evenings. Try the **I and I Bar**, used to be the Swing Bar and still has the swings. **Oceanside** and the **Sunset** which cranks up big style after **Oceanside** closes at 2400 and is a lot of fun.

Shopping

Ambergris Caye *p673*
Island Supermarket, across from Ramon's, has a good range of supplies. There are many gift shops in the centre of town. Try Fidos which has Belizean Arts (paintings and prints by local artists) and Ambar Jewelry. **Kasbah and Orange** sell local crafts and jewellery.

Caye Caulker *p674*
There are at least 4 small 'markets' on the island where a variety of food can be bought; prices are 20-50% higher than the mainland. **Chan's Supermarket**, 1 street back from main street, open daily including Christmas and New Year's Day. There are a couple of gift shops and a gallery in the same building as **Coco Loco**.

Activities and tours

Ambergris Caye *p673*

Diving and snorkelling

Park fees are not included in prices quoted. US$10 for Hol Chan, US$20 for Blue Hole, US$20 Half Moon Caye and US$10 for Bacalar Chico. Also be clear on what's included. You will likely be charged extra for equipment. Instruction to PADI open water level available, from US$350. Local 2-tank dive US$60, Turneffe US$140-160, Blue Hole US$185. Many operators practice chumming to attract fish and sharks. Divers should discourage operators from doing this. Accommodation and dive packages at some hotels are very good value. All the dive operators offer **snorkelling** trips from US$25 for **Shark Ray Alley** to US$125 for the **Blue Hole**.

Ambergris Divers, T226-2634, www.ambergrisdivers.com, will collect divers from Caye Caulker for Blue Hole trip. Very good value dive and accommodation packages with **Spindthrift Hotel**.

Amigos del Mar, T226-2706, www.amigosdive.com, opposite Lily's, gets a lot of return customers and has been repeatedly recommended, but practices chumming at the Blue Hole.

Protech, at the **Belize Yacht Club**, T226-3008, www.protechdive.com, is the only operator offering overnight trips to the Blue Hole, US$275.

Ramon's Village, www.ramons.com. A bit more expensive than other operators. Check the diving shop's recent safety record before diving.

Fishing

Freedom Tours, T603-0357, hillyboo1991@yahoo.com, run by Gilbert 'Hilly Boo' Lara, has been recommended.

Other watersports

Board Crazy Watersports, T226-2283, wakeboarding, skiing, sumo tubing.

Karibbean Water Sports, behind **Spindrift Hotel**, T226-3205, rents out the jet-skis for US$100/hr.

Parasail Fun Sports, T226-3513, www.ambergriscaye.com/watersports.

Sailing Overnight tours on Nepenthe, www.belize-sailing.com, T600-2302, have been recommended.

Sailsports, Holiday Hotel, T226-4488, www.sailsportsbelize.com. Windsurfing, sailing, kitesurfing lessons and rentals.

Therapies

Asian Garden Day Spa, T622-5788, www.asiangardendayspa.com, **The Art of Touch**, T226-357, www.touchbelize.com, **Sol Spa**, T226-2410 and **Spa Shangri-La**, T226-3755, are new additions to the scene.

Tour operators

Travel and Tour Belize in town, T226-2031. Helpful, all services and can arrange flights, with a request stop at Sarteneja (for the Shipstern Nature Reserve).

Tanishas Tour. Daniel Núñez, does trips to the Maya sites on the north of the caye in the new Bacalar Chico National Park with his company.

Caye Caulker *p674*

Diving and snorkelling

Mask and snorkel hire from several dive and tour operators normally US$2.50 per day.

Belize Diving Services, T226-0143, www.belizedivingservices.com, is a dive shop on the island, with similar prices to Frenchie's, does not do the Blue Hole, but will refer divers to San Pedro.

Big Fish Dive Center, T226-0450, www.bigfishdive.com, go to the Blue Hole, US$160, Lighthouse Reef and Turneffe. It also works with **Frenchie's**.

Frenchie's Diving, T226-0234, www.frenchiesdivingbelize.com, charges US$250 for a 4-day PADI course, friendly and effective, 2-tank dive US$90, also advanced PADI instruction. Day excursion diving Blue Hole, etc, US$175, snorkellers welcome.

Paradise Down Scuba Center, T226-0437, www.paradisedown.com. Offers a range of courses and rents underwater cameras.

Fishing

Fishing can be arranged through tour operators.

Kayaking

Tour agencies along the main street rent kayaks.

Manatee watching

Available with most tour operators.

Sailing
Several full- and half-day and sunset sailing trips. **Raggamuffin Tours**, T226-0348, www.raggamuffintours.com, do a fun sunset cruise, US$25, with booze and music on a sail boat as well as offering a 3-day all-inclusive sailing tour to Placencia leaving Tue and Fri, US$277.50, minimum 8 people including all food and 2 nights' camping on Rendezvous Caye and Tobacco Caye. Beats travelling by bus and is an increasingly popular excursion! See also **Ras Creek** and **E-Z Boy Tours** below for their sailing trips.

Tour operators
Prices are consistent across all operators so find someone you connect with and feel you can trust. The main excursion is snorkelling in Hol Chan Marine Park and visiting Shark Ray Alley and San Pedro US$125, equipment included. Further afield there are other snorkelling trips, river and Maya site tours. Manatees and Goff Caye (a paradise perfect circular island with good snorkelling around), US$60; fishing trips US$175. Snorkelling excursions to the Turneffe Islands, Half Moon Caye, Bird Sanctuary and Blue Hole on request. **Sunset Tours** are popular with snorkelling until dusk, US$25.
E-Z Boy Tours, on main street, T226-0349. As well as the usual snorkelling tours, **E-Z** offers kayaking, seahorse and mangrove tours and an unusual 'Celestial Bodies' star-gazing/Maya mythology and croc spotting tour.
Raggamuffin, see above, do tours to the Caye Caulker Marine Reserve and Hol Chan. It can also arrange fishing tours with local fishermen, full day, US$275.

Guides Recommended guides include **Ras Creek**, 'a big man with a big heart', in his boat, based at the water taxi dock, US$27.50 including lunch and entrance fee to the Caye Caulker Marine Reserve; seahorse trips, fishing trips, US$37.50, booze cruise, US$10 per person; canoe and snorkel rental. **Neno Rosado**, of **Tsunami Adventures**, has been approved by the association and is reliable and knowledgeable.

Lighthouse Reef, Turneffe Islands and the smaller cayes *p676*
Tour operators
Dive operators on Ambergris and on Caye Caulker run trips to Half Moon Caye, the Blue Hole and Turneffe Islands, see Tour operators, above.

It's also possible to go from Belize City with **Hugh Parkey's Belize Dive Connection**, based at the Radisson's dock, www.belizediving.com. The main dive in the Blue Hole is very deep, at least 130 ft; the hole itself is 480 ft deep. Check your own qualifications as the dive operator probably will not – you should be experienced and it is advisable to have at least the Advance Open Water PADI course, although an Open water qualification is fine if you feel confident and don't have major problems equalizing.
Sunrise Travel, Belize City, T227-2051 or T223-2670, helps arrange trips, advance book.

Transport

Ambergris Caye *p673*
Air
Tropic Air, T226-2012, and **Maya Island Air**, T226-2435, have flights to/from both **Belize City** airports, many hourly, to **Caye Caulker** and **Corozal**. Charter services are available.

Bicycle and car
Bicycles US$2.50 per hr, negotiate for long-term rates.
Vehicle hire: golf carts from US$15 per hr and up to US$300/week, battery or gas powered, driver's licence needed.

Boat
More interesting than going by air are the boats. All these call at **Caye Caulker** (and **Caye Chapel** and **St George's Caye** on request). **Caye Caulker Water Taxi Association** to Caye Caulker and **Belize City** at 0700, 0800, 0930, 1130, 1300, 1430, 1530, 1630 (weekends and holidays to Caye Caulker only). With **Triple J** at 0700, 0900, 1030, 1300, 1430. Many regular boats between Ambergris Caye and Caye Caulker. There are boats to **Corozal** leaving from the lagoon side with *Thunderbolt*, T226-2904, 1500, returning 0700, US$45 one way. The *Island Ferry*, T226-3251, from Fido's dock, services the north of the island every 2 hrs from 0700-1700 then hourly 1800-2200. Also at 2400 and 0200 on Wed, Fri and Sat. Returns 0600-2200 every 2 hrs, US$10-25.

Caye Caulker *p674*
Bicycle and car Island Boy Rentals, T226-0229. Golf cart rental for US$10 per hr also bike hire for US$7.50 per day .

Air
Maya Island Air flies to/from **Belize City, Corozal** and **San Pedro**, several daily. Also flights with Tropic Air, T226-2439.

Boat
Boats leave from the main dock in front of Seaside Cabañas to **Belize City** with the Caye Caulker Water Taxi Association at 0630, 0730, 0830, 1000, 1200, 1330, 1500, 1600, 1700 (weekends and holidays), 45 mins 1 way (can be 'exciting' if it's rough). To **San Pedro** 0700, 0845, 1000, 1130, 1300, 1430, 1600 and 1715. Triple J leave from the Rainbow Hotel dock. See Transport, page 670, for more details.

Directory

Ambergris Caye *p673*
Banks Atlantic Bank and Bank of Belize, Mon-Thu 0800-1500, Fri 0800-1630. ATMs. Small denominations of US currency in regular use. **Internet** Caribbean Connection, Barrier Reef Dr. **Medical services** San Pedro Polyclinic II, T226-2536. Emergencies 226-2555. Hyperbaric chamber, T226-2851.

Caye Caulker *p674*
Banks Rates for cash and TCs are reasonable. **Atlantic Bank** Visa advances; US$5 commission and now with 24-hr ATM with Visa and MasterCard, Mon-Fri 0800-1500, Sat 0830-1200, and many other places for exchange. Gift shops will charge a commission. **Internet** **Caye Caulker Cyber Café**, 0700-2200, US$6 per hr. **Laundry** . There are 2 laundries with self-service options, ½ block back from the Seaside Cabañas. Ruby's on the left-hand side is recommended, US$6 for one load. **Post office** ½ block west of Big Fish Dive Center. **Telephone** International service from the telephone exchange (0900-1230, 1400-1630); cardphone outside the BTL office can be used for international calls. Collect calls possible at least to North America at no charge.

Northern Belize

Northern Belize is notable for the agricultural production of sugar, fruit and vegetables and for providing much of the country's food. But among the fields of produce are some well-hidden sights and wildlife magnets. The Maya ruins of Lamanai are just about visible in the spectacular setting of the dense jungle. Wildlife can easily be seen at the Community Baboon Sanctuary, the Crooked Tree Wildlife Sanctuary – home to thousands of beautiful birds – and the wildlife reserves of Shipstern near Sartaneja. The vast Río Bravo Conservation Area nudges up to the Guatemalan border and contains the truly isolated ruins and lodge of Chan Chich.

Heading north out of Belize City, the Northern Highway leads to the Mexican border. You can do the journey in just a few hours, passing through Orange Walk and Corozal, but you won't see a thing. It's definitely worth stopping off if you have time. ›› *For Sleeping, Eating and other listings, see page 686-689.*

Bermudian Landing and the Community Baboon Sanctuary

About 15 miles out of Belize City a road heading west leads to the small settlement of Bermudian Landing (12 miles on a rough road from the turn-off) that has been thrust into the global conservation spotlight. The small Creole village was once a transfer point for the timber that floated down the Belize River, but now there's a local wildlife museum – sponsored by the WWF – and the Community Baboon Sanctuary.

Crooked Tree Wildlife Sanctuary

ⓘ *US$4; you must register at the visitors' centre, drinks are on sale, but take food. There is a helpful, friendly warden, Steve, who will let you sleep on the porch of the visitors' centre. It is easy to get a lift to the sanctuary, and someone is usually willing to take visitors back to the main road for a small charge.*

The Northern Highway continues to **Sand Hill**, and a further 12 miles to the turn-off for the Crooked Tree Wildlife Sanctuary, which was set up in 1984 and is a rich area for birds. The network of lagoons and swamps attracts many migrating birds and the dry season, October to May, is a good time to visit. You may see the jabiru stork, the largest flying bird in the Western Hemisphere at a height of 5 ft and a wingspan of 11-12 ft, which nests here, as well as herons, ducks, vultures, kites, ospreys, hawks, sand pipers, kingfishers, gulls, terns, egrets and swallows. In the forest you can also see and hear howler monkeys. Other animals include coatimundi, crocodiles, iguanas and turtles. Glenn Crawford is a good guide as is Sam Tillet (see Sleeping, page 687).

The turn-off to the sanctuary is signposted but keep an eye out for the intersection which is 22 miles from Orange Walk and 33 miles from Belize City. There is another sign further south indicating the sanctuary but this just leads to the park boundary, not to the Wildlife Sanctuary. The mango and cashew trees in the village of Crooked Tree are said to be 100 years old. Birdwatching is best in the early morning but, as buses do not leave Belize City early, for a day trip take an early Corozal bus, get off at the main road (about 1¼ hours from Belize City) and hitch to the sanctuary. The village is tiny and quaint, occupied mostly by Creoles. Boats and guides can be hired for approximately US$70 per boat (maximum four people). It may be worth bargaining as competition is fierce. Trips include a visit to an unexcavated Maya site.

Altún Ha → *Colour map 6, A1.*

ⓘ *Daily 0900-1700, US$1.50, insect repellent necessary.*

The Maya remains of Altún Ha, 31 miles north of Belize City and two miles off the Old Northern Highway, are worth a visit. Altún Ha was a major ceremonial centre in the Classic period (AD 250-900) and also a trading station linking the Caribbean coast with Maya centres in the interior. The site consists of two central plazas surrounded by 13 partially excavated pyramids and temples. What the visitor sees now is composite, not how the site would have been at any one time in the past. The largest piece of worked Maya jade ever found, a head of the Sun God Kinich Ahau weighing 9½ lb (4.3 kg), was found here in the main temple (B-4) in 1968. It is now in a bank vault in Belize City. Nearby is a large reservoir, now called **Rockstone Road**.

Orange Walk → *Colour map 6, A1. Population: 13,483.*

The Northern Highway runs to Orange Walk (66 miles), the centre of a district where Creoles, Mennonites and Maya earn their living from timber, sugar planting and general agriculture. Nearby, the impressive ruins of Lamanai make a good day trip – see below. This is also the departure point for Sartaneja and the Shipstern Peninsula and for the long overland trip to Río Bravo Conservation Area, Chan Chich and Gallon Jug.

There is little to draw the visitor for an extended stay in Orange Walk. An agricultural centre and the country's second city, it is busy with the comings and goings of a small town. Orange Walk is a truly multicultural centre with inhabitants coming from all over Central America which makes Spanish the predominant language. Originally from Canada, Mennonites live in nearby colonies using the town as their marketing and supply centre. The only battle fought on Belizean soil took place here, during the Yucatecan Caste Wars (1840-1870s): the Maya leader, Marcus Canul, was shot in the fighting in 1872. A recently opened **House of Culture** ⓘ *Main St*, shows a history of the town's development.

Buses plying the route from Belize City to the Mexican border stop on Queen Victoria Avenue, the main street, close to the town hall. While a few pleasant wooden

Border essentials: Belize-Mexico

Santa Elena-Chetumal
Eight miles north of Corozal is the Mexican border at Santa Elena, where a bridge across the Río Hondo connects with Chetumal, 7 miles into Mexico. The border can be very busy, and therefore slow, especially at holiday times when chartered coaches bring shoppers to Mexico.

Border crossing formalities are relatively relaxed. The border is open 24 hrs a day and there is an exit tax including PACT (see page 662) of US$13.75.

Mexican tourist cards for 30 days are available at the border. To extend the tourist card beyond 30 days, go to immigration in Cancún. The Mexican Embassy is in Belize City if you need a visa.

If driving to Belize, third party insurance is obligatory. It can be purchased from the building opposite the immigration post. The Northern Highway is in good condition and driving time to the capital is roughly three hours. There are frequent buses from the border and Corozal to Belize City, see under Corozal. All northbound buses from Belize City go to Chetumal.

Money changers are on the Belize side of the border. You can buy pesos at good rates with US and Belizean currency. Rates for Belizean dollars in Mexico will be lower. Coming from Mexico, get rid of pesos at the border – changing them in Belize can be difficult.

buildings remain on quiet side streets, most are worn out and in bad need of repair. Many have been pulled down and replaced by the standard concrete box affairs, which lack either inspiration or style.

A toll bridge now spans the New River a few miles south of the town at Tower Hill. A market, which overlooks New River, is well organized, with good food stalls and interesting architecture.

West and south of Orange Walk

From Orange Walk a road heads west, before turning south, running parallel to the Mexican and then Guatemalan border, where it becomes unpaved. Along this road are several archaeological sites. First is **Cuello**, 4 miles west on San Antonio road, behind Cuello Distillery (ask there for permission to visit); taxi about US$3.50. The site dates back to 1000 BC, but, although it has yielded important discoveries in the study of Maya and pre-Maya cultures, there is little for the layman to appreciate and no facilities for visitors. At **Yo Creek** the road divides, north to San Antonio, and south through miles of cane fields and tiny farming settlements as far as **San Felipe** (20 miles via San Lázaro, Trinidad and August Pine Ridge). At August Pine Ridge there is a daily bus to Orange Walk at 1000. You can camp at the house of Narciso Novelo or 'Chicho' (T323-3019), a little-known secret and a relaxing place to stay set amongst bananas, pine tres, bushes and flowers; no fixed cost, just pay what you think. Chicho will meet you off the bus if you call ahead. At San Felipe, a branch leads southeast to Indian Church/Lamanai, 35 miles from Orange Walk (one hour driving, 4WD needed when wet). Another road heads west to Blue Creek Village on the Mexican border (see below).

Lamanai → *Colour map 6, A1.*

ⓘ *US$5.*

Near **Indian Church**, one of Belize's largest archaeological sites, Lamanai is on the west side of New River Lagoon, 22 miles by river south of Orange Walk. Difficult to get to and hidden in the jungle, it is a perfect setting to hide the mysteries of the Maya and definitely worth a visit. While the earliest buildings were erected about 700 BC, culminating in the completion of the 112-ft major temple, N10-43, about 100 BC (the tallest known pre-Classic Maya structure), there is evidence the site was occupied as long ago as 1500 BC. As a Maya site, it is believed to have the longest history of continuous occupation and, with the Spanish and British sites mentioned below and the present-day refugee village nearby, Lamanai's history is impressive. The Maya site has been partially cleared, but covers a large area so a guide is recommended. The views from temple N10-43, dedicated to Chac, are superb; look for the Yin-Yang-like symbol below the throne on one of the other main temples, which also has a 12-ft-tall mask overlooking its plaza. Visitors can wander freely along narrow trails and climb the stairways. There is a very informative museum housing the only known stela found at the site. There is also a fine jungle lodge. See Sleeping.

At nearby Indian Church, a Spanish mission was built over one of the Maya temples in 1580, and the British established a sugar mill here last century. The remains of both buildings can still be seen. The archaeological reserve is jungle and howler monkeys are visible in the trees. There are many birds and the best way to see them is to reach Lamanai by boat, easily arranged in Orange Walk or by taking a day trip from Belize City, see Tour operators, page 670. The earlier you go the better, but the trips from Orange Walk all leave at pretty standard times. The mosquitoes are vicious in the wet season (wear trousers, take repellent). The community phone for information on Indian Church, including buses, is T309-3015.

Blue Creek and around → *Colour map 6, A1.*

West of San Felipe is Blue Creek (10 miles), the largest of the Mennonite settlements. Many of the inhabitants of these close-knit villages arrived in 1959, members of a Canadian colony which had migrated to Chihuahua, Mexico, to escape encroaching modernity. They preserve their Low German dialect, are exempt from military service, and their industry now supplies the country with most of its poultry, eggs, vegetables and furniture. Some settlements, such as Neustadt in the west, have been abandoned because of threats by drug smugglers in the early 1990s. In 1998 Belize and Mexico signed an agreement to build an international bridge from Blue Creek across the river to La Unión, together with a river port close to the bridge. It is not known when work will start; at present there is a canoe-service for foot passengers across the Blue Creek.

A vast area to the south along the **Río Bravo** has been set aside as a conservation area (see page 662). Within this, there is a study and accommodation centre near the Maya site of **La Milpa**. The site is at present being excavated by a team from the University of Texas and Boston University, USA.

A good road can be followed 35 miles south to **Gallon Jug**, where a jungle tourism lodge has been built in the **Chan Chich** Maya ruin, See Sleeping. The journey to Chan Chich passes through the Río Bravo Conservation Area, is rarely travelled and offers some of the best chances to see wildlife. Chan Chich is believed to have the highest number of jaguar sightings in Belize, and is also a birdwatchers' paradise. Another road has recently been cut south through Tambos to the main road between Belmopan and San Ignacio, but travel in this region is strictly a dry-weather affair.

Sartaneja and northeast of Orange Walk

From Orange Walk a complex network of roads and tracks converge on **San Estevan** and Progresso to the north. The Maya ruins near San Estevan have reportedly been 'flattened' to a large extent and are not very impressive. Ten miles from San Estevan is a road junction; straight on is **Progresso**, a village picturesquely located on the lagoon of the same name. The right turn, signposted, runs off to the Mennonite village of **Little Belize** and continues (in poor condition) to **Chunox,** a village with many Maya houses of pole construction. In the dry season it is possible to drive from Chunox to the Maya site of Cerros (see below).

Three miles before Sarteneja is the visitor centre for Shipstern Nature Reserve, which covers 22,000 acres of this northeastern tip of Belize. Hardwood forests, saline lagoon systems and wide belts of savannah shelter a wide range of mammals (coatis and foxes, and all the fauna found elsewhere in Belize, except monkeys), reptiles and 200 species of bird. Also, there are mounds of Maya houses and fields everywhere. The most remote forest, south of the lagoon, is not accessible to short-term visitors. There is a botanical trail leading into the forest with trees labelled with Latin and local Yucatec Maya names; a booklet is available. At the visitors' centre is the **Butterfly Breeding Centre** ⓘ *daily 0900-1200, 1300-1600, except Christmas and Easter, US$5 including excellent guided tour.* Mosquito repellent is essential. There is dormitory accommodation at the visitors' centre, rather poor, US$10 per person. A day trip by private car is possible from Sarteneja or Orange Walk.

Choose a sunny day for a visit if possible; on dull days the butterflies hide themselves in the foliage.

Leaving the Northern Highway a road heads east to **Sarteneja**, a small fishing and former boat-building settlement founded by Yucatán refugees in the 19th century. The main catch is lobster and conch. On Easter Sunday there is a popular regatta, with all types of boat racing, dancing and music. There are the remains of an extensive Maya city scattered throughout the village, and recent discoveries have been made and are currently being explored to the south around the area of Shipstern Lagoon.

Corozal and around

→ *Colour map 5, B3.* *Population: 7888.*

The Northern Highway continues to Corozal (96 miles from Belize City), formerly the centre of the sugar industry, now with a special zone for the clothing industry and garment exports. Much of the old town was destroyed by Hurricane Janet in 1955 and it is now a mixture of modern concrete commercial buildings and Caribbean clapboard seafront houses on stilts. Like Orange Walk it is economically depressed but Corozal is much the safer place. It is open to the sea with a pleasant waterfront where the market is held. There is no beach but you can swim in the sea and lie on the grass. You can check out the local website at www.corozal.com.

Between Orange Walk and Corozal, in San José and San Pablo, is the archaeological site of **Nohmul**, a ceremonial centre whose main acropolis dominates the surrounding cane fields (the name means 'Great Mound'). Permission to visit the site must be obtained from Sr Estevan Itzab, whose house is opposite the water tower.

From Corozal, a road leads 7 miles northeast to **Consejo**, a quiet, seaside fishing village on Chetumal Bay. No public transport, taxi about US$10.

Six miles northeast of Corozal, to the right of the road to Chetumal, is **Four Mile Lagoon**, about a quarter of a mile off the road (buses will drop you there). Clean swimming, better than Corozal bay, some food and drinks available; it is often crowded at weekends.

Across the bay to the south of Corozal stand the mounds of **Cerros,** once an active Maya trading port whose central area was reached by canal. Some of the site is flooded but one pyramid, 69-ft high with stucco masks on its walls, has been partially excavated. Take a boat from Corozal, walk around the bay (a boat is needed to cross the mouth of the New River) or do the dry-season vehicular trail from Progresso and Chunox (see above). Trips can be arranged with **Hotel Maya** and **Hok'Ol K'in Guest House,** from US$60 for a water taxi carrying up to six people.

Sleeping

Bermudian Landing and the Community Baboon Sanctuary *p682*

A-B **Howler Monkey Lodge**, 400 m from museum, T/F220-2158, www.howlermonkeylodge.com. Screened windows, fans, cheaper with shared bath, discounts for students, TCs, Visa, MasterCard accepted, camping US$5 per person, bring tent, river tours US$25 per person, recommended. Transport from Belize City in pick-up add

US$40, 1-4 people, on request. Breakfast, lunch and dinner, US$5-9. Many good tours available including night-time crocodile adventures US$40. Canoe rentals in Burrell Boom for trips on Belize River to see birds, howler monkeys, manatee, hicatee.
C **Cabañas** are available alongside the visitors' centre, bath, hot water. Basic lodging is also available with families in the village which can be arranged through the Baboon Sanctuary office.

Crooked Tree Wildlife Sanctuary *p683*

AL-A Paradise Inn, T225-7044, advcam@aol.com. Run by the Crawfords, cabins with hot showers, restaurant, well maintained, friendly, boat trips, fishing, horse riding and tours.
AL-B Bird's Eye View Lodge, T203-2040, www.birdseyeviewlodge.com (owned by the Gillett family; in USA T/F570-588-0843). Single and double rooms, shower, fan, meals available, boat trips, horse riding, canoe rental, nature tours with licensed guide, ask for information at the **Belize Audubon Society** (see page 662).
AL-B Sam Tillet's Hotel, in centre of village, T220-7026, samhotel@btl.net. Wood and thatch cabin, tiny restaurant, great trips. Cabins may be rented , up to 4 people. Also cheap rooms and camping (**F**) can also be arranged if requested.

Orange Walk *p683*

AL-A Mi Amor, 19 Belize-Corozal Rd, T302-2031. With shared bath, with bath and fan, or with a/c, nice, clean, restaurant.
A St Christopher's, 12 Main St, T/F302-1064. Beautiful clean rooms and bathrooms, highly recommended and the best in town.
A-C D'Victoria, 40 Belize Rd (Main St), T322-2518, www.dvictoria hotel.com. A/c, shower, hot water, parking, quite comfortable, pool, but somewhat run-down.
C-D Akihito Japanese Hotel, 22 Belize Corozal Rd, T302-0185, akihitolee@ hotmail.com. An affordable place in the centre of town.
D-E Lucia's Guest House, 68 San Antonio Rd, T322-2244, www.luciasbelize.com. A new budget place that's getting recommendations, 5-mins west of town.
E Jane's, 2 Baker's St, T302-2293 (**Jane's II** on Market Lane). Large house in pleasant location. Upgraded to include hot water, but still scruffy.
E La Nueva Ola, 73 Otro Benque Rd, T322-2104. Large car park, run-down, probably the cheapest.

Neither **Jane's** nor **La Nueva Ola** is recommended but there are not many 'budget' options to choose from. Parking for vehicles is very limited at hotels.

Lamanai *p684*

AL Lamanai Outpost Lodge, at Indian Church,T/F223-3578, www.lamanai.com. Run by the incredibly friendly Howells, this beautiful lodge is a short walk from Lamanai ruins, overlooking New River Lagoon, package deals available, day tours, thatched wooden cabins with bath and fan, hot water, 24-hr electricity, restaurant, excellent and well-informed guides. Juvenile crocodile study under way and guests are invited to participate.

Camping

Nazario Ku, the site caretaker, permits camping or hammocks at his house, opposite path to Lamanai ruins, good value for backpackers.

Blue Creek and around *p685*

LL Chan Chich, Chiun Chah, T/F223-4419, or in the USA and Canada 1-800-343-8009, www.chanchich.com. A beautifully sited lodge in the midst of Maya ruins with an extensive trail system in the grounds, delicious food, fantastic birdwatching and wildlife-watching opportunties; very good guides; pool. Recommended. Phone before setting out for Chan Chich for information on the roads.
AL La Milpa Field Station, La Milpa, for information call T323-0011, or contact the Programme for Belize in Belize City (T227-5616, www.pfbelize.org). Makes a good base for exploring trails in the region and birdwatching. To reach La Milpa, go 6 miles west from Blue Creek to Tres Leguas, then follow the signs south towards the Río Bravo Escarpment. The reserve is privately owned and you will need proof of booking to pass the various checkpoints. 4 double *cabañas*, spacious, comfortable, with a thatched roof overhanging a large wooden deck, or a dormitory sleeping up to 30.
C Hill Bank Field Station, on the banks of the New River Lagoon. Also a good base for exploring trails in the region and

birdwatching, and with a dormitory sleeping up to 30. See **La Milpa Field Station**, above, for contact details.

Sartaneja and northeast of Orange Walk *p685*

AL **Krisami's Bay View**, T423-2283, www.krisamis.com. Rooms with private bath, a/c and TV.

B-C **Fernando's Guest House**, on seafront near centre of Sartaneja, T423-2085, sartenejabelize@hotmail.com.

D **Diani's**, on the seashore. Restaurant, seems to be undergoing eternal refurbishment. Houses can be rented for longer stays.

Corozal and around *p686*

AL-B **Tony's**, South End, T422-2055, www.tonysinn.com. With a/c, clean, comfortable units in landscaped grounds. Recommended, but restaurant overpriced.

A **Copa Banana**, 409 Corozal Bay Rd, T422-0284, www.copabanana.bz. Newest place in town, with 5 suites all with private bathrooms. US-owned so complimentary coffee each morning. Ask the bus driver to drop you off.

A **Hok'Ol K'in Guest House**, 4th Av and 4th St South, T422-3329, www.corozal.net. Immaculate rooms. Runs tours to Cerros.

A-B **Las Palmas Hotel (formerly Nestor's)**, 123, 5th Av South, T422-0196, www.nestorshotel.com. With bath and fan, OK, *refrescos* available, good food, lively bar downstairs. Big renovation underway, so expect a price hike.

C **Corozal Guest House**, 22 6th Av, T422-2358, www.corozal.bz. Basic, clean rooms, shared area with TV, lots of information about Belize and the area. Close to the bus terminal.

D **Caribbean Village Resort**, South End, T422-2045. Hot water, US$5 camping, US$12 trailer park, restaurant, recommended.

F **Papa's Guest House**, 5th Av South, next door to **Nestor's**. Very basic but cheap.

Camping

Caribbean Motel and Trailer Park, see **Caribbean Village Resort**, above. Camping possible but not very safe (US$4 per person), shaded sites, restaurant.

Eating

Orange Walk *p683*

Most restaurants in town are Chinese.

¶¶ **King Fu**, Baker's St. Chinese, excellent and filling.

¶¶-¶ **Juanita's**, 8 Santa Ana St (take road beside Shell station). Open 0600 for breakfast and all meals. Good, inexpensive Creole cooking. Same at **Julie's**, near police station.

¶ **Central Plaza Restaurant**, behind the main bus terminal. A popular choice in a handy location.

¶ **The Diner**, Clarke St, behind the hospital. Good meals, very friendly, taxi US$4 or walk.

¶ **Golden Gate**, Baker's St. Cheap Chinese.

¶ **Hong Kong II**, next to **Mi Amor**. Chinese.

Corozal and around *p686*

There are many Chinese restaurants in town.

¶¶¶ **Café Kela**, in a beachfront palapa on the shore. Best restaurant in town, intimate setting, fine food, good value, just sit back and enjoy.

¶¶ **Cactus Plaza**, 5th Av South. A loud bar with lots of fluorescent lighting and great a/c. Worth trying if you're stuck in town for the night.

¶¶ **Purple Toucan**, No 52, 4th Av North. Good restaurant and lively bar with pool table and good music. Opposite is **Marcelo's** which serves good pizza.

¶ **Border**, 6th Av South. Friendly Chinese, good food.

¶ **Corozal Garden**, 4th Av, 1 block south. Good, quick local food.

¶ **Gongora's Pastry**, southwest corner of main square. Hot pizza pieces, cakes and drinks.

¶ **Newtown Chinese**, 7th Av, just north of the gas station on the other side of the main road. Large portions, good quality, slow service.

Activities and tours

Orange Walk *p683*

Tour operators

Jungle River Tours, 20 Lovers Lane, T302-2293, lamanaimayatour@btl.net, in Lovers' Café on the southeastern corner of the park. Organizes and runs trips to Lamanai (US$45 plus entrance of US$5 including lunch departing 0900 returning 1600), Altún Ha and New River area, regular trips, *the* specialists on the region and consistently recommended. It also provides trips to any destination in Belize with a minimum of 4 people.

Transport

Bermudian Landing and the Community Baboon Sanctuary *p682*
Bus From **Belize City**: Mcfadzean Bus from corner of Amara Av and Cemetery Rd at 1215 and 1715 Mon-Fri; 1200 and 1400 Sat. **Rancho** Bus (Pook's Bus) from Mosul St, 1700 Mon-Fri, 1300 Sat, check details, US$1.50-2, 1 hr. Alternatively, any bus travelling the Northern Highway can drop you off at the turn-off to Bermudian Landing where you can wait for a bus, or hitch a ride. A day trip giving any meaningful time in the sanctuary is difficult by public transport, so it is best to stay the night.

Crooked Tree Wildlife Sanctuary *p683*
Bus Buses from **Belize City** with JEX (1035); return from Crooked Tree at 0600-0700.

Altún Ha *p683*
Bus With little transport on this road, hitching is not recommended – best to go in a private vehicle or a tour group. Vehicles leave **Belize City** for the village of **Maskall**, 8 miles north of Altún Ha, several days a week, but same-day return is not possible.

Orange Walk *p683*
Bus Bus station is on street beside the fire station, on the main road. All buses travelling from Belize City to Corozal and beyond to Chetumal stop in Orange Walk; **Belize**-Orange Walk, US$3. **Corozal**-Orange Walk, US$1.50, 50 mins. For **Lamanai** take bus to Indian Church (Mon, Wed, Fri 1600). Buses to **Sarteneja** outside **Zeta's Store** on Main St, 5 between 1300 and 1900, US$2.50. Also to Progresso at 1100 and 1130.

Lamanai *p684*
Boat See Tour operators, Orange Walk, above. For transport to Lamanai, also see Orange Walk.

Blue Creek and around *p685*
Air Flights to Chan Chich from Belize City can be chartered.

Sartaneja and northeast of Orange Walk *p685*
Air Sarteneja is 40 miles from **Orange Walk**; 1-hr drive. Private charters from **Corozal** cost about US$75 for the 30-min journey (compared with 3 hrs by road).

Boat The Thunderbolt service linking San Pedro and Corozal will stop at Sartaneja on request at no extra charge. The service departs **Corozal** at 0700, and leaves **San Pedro** at 1500, full trip cost is US$20. For enquiries call T226-2904, thunderbolttravels@yahoo.com.

Bus Bus from **Belize City** at 1200, US$4.50, from the corner of Victoria and North Front St. Buses also leave from **Corozal** (1400), via Orange Walk (1530).

Corozal and around *p686*
Air Maya Island Air, daily from Belize City via Caye Caulker and San Pedro (Ambergris Caye); **Tropic Air** daily from San Pedro. Airstrip 3 miles south, taxi US$1.50.

Boat See Boat, Sartaneja and northeast of Orange Walk, above.

Bus Heading south, buses leave every 30 mins, starting at 0400 running until 1830. Regular service 3 hrs, US$2.50, faster express service, 2½ hrs, US$3.50, leaves at 0600, 0700, 1200, 1500 and 1800. If heading north, buses from **Belize City** continue north to **Chetumal** terminal, with stopping time to allow for immigration procedures.

For those coming from Mexico who are interested in **Tikal** in Guatemala, it is possible to make the journey border to border in a day, with a change of bus in Belize City.

Taxi Leslie's Taxi Service, T422-2377. Transfers from Corozol to the Mexican frontier, US$22 for a 4-person taxi. Ask for a quote for other services. Reliable and professional.

Directory

Orange Walk *p683*
Banks Belize Bank on Main St (down Park St from Park, turn left) . **Scotia** Bank on Park, US$0.50 commission. Shell Station will change TCs. **Internet** K&M, on Main St.

Corozal and around *p686*
Banks Atlantic Bank (charges US$2.50 for Visa cash advances), **Bank of Nova** Scotia, and Belize Bank . For exchange also ask at the bus station. **Internet** Charlotte's Web, 5th Av between 5th and 6th St South, cyber café and book exchange.

Western Belize

Impressive sights – man-made and natural – line the route from Belize City to the Guatemalan border, starting with Belize Zoo – a pleasant break from the norm. Monkey Bay Wildlife Sanctuary and Guanacaste National Park are both worth a visit. From the bustling town of San Ignacio, there are canoe trips down the Macal River and dramatic cave systems, journeys into the impressive limestone scenery of Mountain Pine Ridge, and the spectacular Maya ruins of Caracol, Xunantunich and Cahal Pech to explore. Day-trippers can also cross the border for a quick visit to Tikal in Guatemala.

» *For Sleeping, Eating and other listings, see page 695-700.*

Belize City to San Ignacio » *pp695-700.*

The Western Highway leaves Belize City past the cemetery, where burial vaults stand elevated above the boggy ground, running through palmetto scrub and savannah landscapes created by 19th-century timber cutting. At Mile 16 is **Hattieville**, originally a temporary settlement for the homeless after Hurricane Hattie in 1961. The highway roughly parallels the Sibun River, once a major trading artery where mahogany logs were floated down to the coast in the rainy season; the place name 'Boom' recalls spots where chains were stretched across rivers to catch logs being floated downstream.

The small but excellent **Belize Zoo** ⓘ *daily 0900-1700, US$7.50, www.belizezoo.org, take any bus from Belize City along the Western Highway (1 hr)*, is at Mile 28½, watch out for the sign or tell the driver where you're going. It is a wonderful collection of local species (originally gathered for a wildlife film), lovingly cared for and displayed in wire-mesh enclosures amid native trees and shady vegetation, including jaguar and smaller cats, pacas (called gibnuts in Belize), snakes, monkeys, parrots, crocodile, tapir (mountain cow), peccary (wari) and much more. Highly recommended, even for those who hate zoos. Get there early to miss the coach party arrivals. Tours by enthusiastic guides, T-shirts and postcards sold for fundraising.

At Mile 31½, the **Monkey Bay Wildlife Sanctuary** protects 1070 acres of tropical forest and savannah between the highway and the Sibun River (great swimming and canoeing). Birds are abundant and there is a good chance of seeing mammals.

Forty-seven miles from Belize City, a minor road runs 2 miles north to **Banana Bank Lodge** and **Jungle Equestrian Adventure** (see Sleeping, page 695).

A mile beyond the **Banana Bank Lodge** and **Jungle Equestrian Adventure** turning is the highway junction for Belmopan and Dangriga. At the confluence of the Belize River and Roaring Creek is the 50-acre **Guanacaste National Park** ⓘ *US$2.50*, protecting a parcel of 'neotropical rainforest' and a huge 100-year-old *guanacaste* (tubroos) tree, which shelters a wide collection of epiphytes including orchids. Many mammals (jaguarundi, kinkajou, agouti etc) and up to 100 species of bird may be seen from the 3 miles of nature trails cut along the river. This is a particularly attractive swimming and picnicking spot at which to stop or break the journey if travelling on to Guatemala. It has a visitors' centre, where luggage can be left. To get there, take an early morning bus from Belize City, see the park in a couple of hours, then pick up a bus going to San Ignacio or Dangriga.

Soon after the junction to Belmopan is **Roaring Creek**, once a thriving town but now rather overshadowed by the barely illuminated capital nearby. At Camelote, a dirt road southwards takes you to **Roaring River** (see Sleeping, page 695). At Teakettle, turn south along a dirt road for 5 miles to **Pook's Hill Reserve** (see Sleeping, page 695).

The important but unimpressive **Floral Park** archaeological site is just beyond the bridge over **Barton Creek** (Mile 64). Two miles further is **Georgeville**, from where a

Paddling the Great Macal River

Time it right and you can paddle down the length of the Macal River taking part in La Ruta Maya canoe race. It's a gruelling three-day open canoe race, starting in San Ignacio covering 170 miles along the river before ending in Belize City on Baron Bliss Day (early March). All food and water is provided for the trip, but you'll need to be fit and healthy. You'll struggle to compete at the racing end of the field unless you're a top athlete and have a canoe of modern design, but plenty of people enter the race for the challenge and with a bit of luck it's possible to turn up, talk with people around town and find yourself a place on a boat. For information visit www.larutamayabelize.com.

gravel road runs south into the Mountain Pine Ridge Forest Reserve (see below). The highway passes the turn-off at Norland for **Spanish Lookout**, a Mennonite settlement area 6 miles north (**B & F Restaurant**, Centre Road, by Farmers' Trading Centre, clean, excellent value). The **Central Farm Agricultural College**, the village of **Esperanza** and other small settlements along the way keep the road interesting until it reaches **Santa Elena**. Formerly only linked by the substantial Hawkesworth suspension bridge to its twin town of San Ignacio, it now has a small, one-lane 'temporary bridge' you must take to cross the river to San Ignacio.

San Ignacio

Colour map: 6, A1. Population: approx 13,260 (including Santa Elena.

Sixty-eight miles from Belize City and 10 miles from the border, San Ignacio (locally called **Cayo**) is the capital of Cayo District and Western Belize's largest town, an agricultural centre serving the citrus, cattle and peanut farms of the area, and a good base for excursions into the Mountain Pine Ridge and Western Belize. It stands amid attractive wooded hills at 200-500 ft, with a good climate, and is a nice town to rest in if coming from Guatemala. The town is on the eastern branch of the Old, or Belize River, known as the Macal. The 185-mile river journey down to Belize City is internationally famous as the route for the annual 'Ruta Maya Belize River Challenge', a gruelling three-day canoe race held the weekend of Baron Bliss Day, 9 March, see box above.

A short walk from San Ignacio (800 m from **Hotel San Ignacio**) is **Cahal Pech** ⓘ *daily 0600-1700, US$5*, an interesting Maya site and nature reserve on a wooded hill overlooking the town, with a visitor centre and small museum.

Four miles west of San Ignacio on a good road is **Bullet Tree Falls**, a pleasant cascade amid relaxing surroundings on the western branch of the Belize River, here in its upper course known as the Mopan River.

Twelve miles north of San Ignacio is **El Pilar**, an archaeological site which straddles the border with Guatemala. Although it is a large site (about 94 acres), much of it has been left intentionally uncleared so that selected architectural features are exposed within the rainforest. The preserved rainforest here is home to hundreds of species of birds and animals. There are five trails – three archaeological, two nature – the longest of which is 1½ miles. There are more than a dozen pyramids and 25 identified plazas. Unusually for Maya cities in this region, there is an abundance of water (streams and falls). Take the Bullet Tree Road north of San Ignacio, cross the Mopan River Bridge and follow the signs to El Pilar. The reserve is 7 miles from Bullet Tree on an all-weather limestone road. It can be reached by vehicle, horse or mountain bike (hiking is only recommended for the experienced; carry lots of water).

The caretakers, who live at the south end of the site in a modern green-roofed house, are happy to show visitors around. The **Cayo Tour Guides Association** works in association with the **Belize River Archaeological Settlement Survey** (**BRASS**) and can take visitors. See also *Trails of El Pilar: A Guide to the El Pilar Archaeological Reserve for Maya Flora and Fauna* (published 1996).

Dr Rosita Arvigo, a Maya healer, sells a selections of herbs (the jungle salve, US$5, has been found effective against mosquito bites) and a book on medicinal plants used by the Maya. The herbs and books are also sold in most local gift shops. She also runs the **Ix Chel Wellness Center** offering herbology and traditional Maya healing, 25 Burns Av, T804-0264, by appointment only. For local medicines you could also talk to the García sisters (see San Antonio, page 694.)

The **San Ignacio Resort Hotel** houses the **Green Iguana Exhibit and Medicinal Jungle Trail** ⓘ *0700-1600, US$5.45 for a guided tour of the medicinal trail*, where you will learn about the life and habits of this vibrantly coloured reptile. Entrance fees are used to provide school scholarships for local pupils.

Local tour operators (see below) generally offer similar tours at similar prices. Canoe trips up the **Macal River** are worthwhile. They take about three hours upstream, 1½ hrs on return. Hiring a canoe to go upstream without a guide is not recommended unless you are highly proficient as there are Class II rapids one hour from San Ignacio. Another trip is to **Barton Creek Cave**, a 1½-hour drive followed by a 1½-hour canoe trip in the cave. The cave vault system is vast, the rock formations are beautiful, the silence is eerily comforting and all can be explored for a considerable distance by canoe (US$30 per person minimum three people). Tours can be arranged at almost every place in San Ignacio.

For a more adventurous caving tour, you shouldn't leave without going to **Actun Tunichil Muknal Cave** (the Cave of the Stone Sepulchre), a one-hour drive from San Ignacio to the Tapir Mountain Nature reserve, a 45-minute jungle hike in the reserve and then 3½-hours of adventurous, exhilarating caving. Besides the beautiful rock

formations, this cave is full of Maya artefacts and sacrificial remains (photography no longer allowed). To preserve this cave and the artefacts from any damage, only two companies are allowed to guide tours. Highly recommended are the guides from **Emilio Awe's Pacz Tours**; also **Mayawalk**, which offers many of the standard tours and a few innovative ones as well. See Activities and tours, page 698.

Maya artefacts can be seen in **Che Chem Ha Cave** ⓘ *T820-4063*, on the private property of the Moralez family on the Vaca Plateau, south of San Ignacio (Benque). In contrast to Barton Creek and Actun Tunichil Muknal this is a so-called dry cave. The family offers trips into the cave, a half-hour hike to the entrance, followed by a one- to 1½-hour walk in the cave. The view from the property is stunning and the family serves lunch. Tours start at 0900 and 1300. If you go by private transport be there in time for the tour and call the family in advance or, better still, book a tour with an agency in San Ignacio.

Trips to the nearby ruins of **Xunantunich** (see below) are very easy by bus, regular traffic going to the Guatemalan border. Tours of **Mountain Pine Ridge** are available (see below), but shop around carefully – if you decide to go with a taxi you probably won't get far in the wet season. Trips to **Caracol** are best arranged from San Ignacio, see page 698, and if you only want to visit Tikal in Guatemala, you can arrange a day trip which will maximize your time spent at the ruins. On a good road 9 miles west of San Ignacio is the tranquil town of **Benque Viejo del Carmen**, near the Guatemalan border. Many of the inhabitants are Maya Mopan. For information on the Benque Viejo-Melchor de Mencos border crossing, see page 635.

South of San Ignacio, halfway between Clarissa Falls turn-off and Nabitunich is Chial Road, gateway to adventure. A half-mile down the road is a sharp right turn that takes you through Negroman, the modern site of the ancient Maya city of **Tipu** which has the remains of a Spanish Mission from the 1500s. Across the river from here is **Guacamallo Camp**, rustic jungle camping and starting point for canoe trips on the Macal River. Two miles further up, also across the river, is **Ek Tun** (see Sleeping, page 696). **New Belize Botanic Gardens** ⓘ *T824-3101, www.belizebotanic.org, daily 0700-1700, US$2.50, guided walks 0730-1500, US$7.50*, on 50 acres of rolling hills, is next to the du Plooys' lodge (see Sleeping, page 696) with hundreds of orchids, dozens of named tree species, ponds and lots of birds. Recommended.

Xunantunich → *Colour map 6, A1.*

ⓘ *Daily 0730-1600, US$5; a leaflet on the area is available from the site for US$4. Apart from a small refreshment stand, there are no facilities for visitors, but a new museum has been built and a couple of stelae have been put on display in a covered area. It is an extremely hot walk up the hill, with little or no shade, so start early. Last ferry (free) back is at 1630.*

At Xunantunich ('Maiden of the Rock') there are Classic Maya remains in beautiful surroundings. The heart of the city was three plazas aligned on a north-south axis, lined with many temples, the remains of a ball court, and surmounted by the Castillo. At 130 ft this was thought to be the highest man-made structure in Belize until recent measurement of the Sky Palace at Caracol. The impressive view takes in the jungle, the lowlands of Petén and the blue flanks of the Maya Mountains. Maya graffiti can still be seen on the wall of Structure A-16 – friezes on the Castillo, some restored in modern plaster, represent astronomical symbols. Extensive excavations took place in 1959-1960 but only limited restoration work has been undertaken.

Just east of the ferry, **Magaña's Art Centre** and the **Xunantunich Women's Group** sell locally made crafts and clothing in a shop on a street off the highway. About 1½ miles further north are the ruins of **Actuncan**, probably a satellite of Xunantunich. Both sites show evidence of earthquake damage.

Mountain Pine Ridge

» pp695-700. Colour map 6, A1.

Mountain Pine Ridge is a Forest Reserve (146,000 acres) which covers the northwest section of the Maya Mountains, an undulating landscape of largely undisturbed pine and gallery forest, and valleys of lush hardwood forests filled with orchids, bromeliads and butterflies. (The devastation to large swathes of the pine forest was caused by a beetle in 2001.) There's river scenery to enjoy, high waterfalls, numerous limestone caves and shady picnic sites; it's a popular excursion despite the rough roads. The easiest way of visiting is on a trip from San Ignacio. Hitching is difficult but not impossible. Try contacting the **Forestry Conservation Officer** ⓘ *T824-3280*, who may be able to help.

Note the frequent changes of colour of the soil and look out for the fascinating insect life. If lucky you may see deer.

Two roads lead into the reserve: from Georgeville to the north and up from Santa Elena via Cristo Rey. These meet near **San Antonio**, a Mopan Maya village with many thatched-roof houses and the nearby Pacbitun archaeological site (where stelae and musical instruments have been unearthed). At San Antonio, the García sisters have their workshop, museum and shop where they sell carvings in local slate, and guesthouse (D). You can sample Maya food and learn about the use of medicinal plants. This is a regular stop on tours to the Mountain Pine Ridge. A donation of US$0.50 is requested; US$12.50 is charged to take photos of the sisters at work. Two buses a day from San Ignacio, 1000 and 1430, from market area; check times of return buses before leaving San Ignacio.

1000-ft Falls

The main forest road meanders along rocky spurs, from which unexpected and often breathtaking views emerge of jungle far below and streams plunging hundreds of feet over red-rock canyons. A lookout point, small charge, has been provided to view the impressive falls, said to be 1000 ft high (often shrouded in fog October to January). On a clear day you can see Belmopan from this viewpoint. It is quite a long way from the main road and is probably not worth the detour if time is short, particularly in the dry season when the flow is restricted. Eighteen miles into the reserve the road crosses the **Río On**. Here, where the river tumbles into inviting pools over huge granite boulders, is one of Belize's most beautiful picnic and swimming spots. The rocks form little water slides and are good for children.

At the driest time of year, February to May, there is an ever-present danger of fire. Open fires are strictly prohibited and you are asked to be careful.

Augustine

Five miles further on is the tiny village of Augustine (also called Douglas D'Silva or **Douglas Forest Station**), the main forest station where there is a shop, accommodation in two houses (bookable through the Forestry Dept in Belmopan, the area Forestry Office is in San Antonio) and a camping ground ⓘ *US$1, no mattresses (see rangers for all information on the area), keep your receipt, a guard checks it on the way out of Mountain Pine Ridge*. A mile beyond Augustine is a cluster of caves in rich rainforest. The entrance to the **Río Frío Cave** (in fact a tunnel) is over 65 ft high, and there are many spectacular rock formations and sandy beaches where the river flows out. Trees in the parking area and along the Cuevas Gemelas nature trail, which starts one hour from the Río Frío cave, are labelled. It's a beautiful excursion and highly recommended.

Forestry roads continue south further into the mountains, reaching **San Luis** (6 miles), the only other inhabited camp in the area, with post office, sawmill and forest station, and continuing on over the granite uplands of the Vaca Plateau into the **Chiquibul Forest Reserve** (460,000 acres).

The four forest reserves which cover the Maya Mountains are the responsibility of the Forestry Department, who have only about 20 rangers to patrol over a million acres of heavily forested land. A hunting ban prohibits the carrying of firearms. Legislation, however, allows for controlled logging; all attempts to have some areas declared national parks or biosphere reserves have so far been unsuccessful. You can stay in the area at **Las Cuevas Research Station and Explorers Lodge** – see accommodation, page 697.

Caracol ▲▲ ▸▸ *pp695-700. Colour map 6, A1.*

ⓘ *US$7.50.*

About 24 miles south-southwest of Augustine, Caracol (about one hour by 4WD) is a rediscovered Maya city. The area is now a National Monument Reservation. Caracol was established about 300 BC and continued well into the Late Classic period (glyphs record a victorious war against Tikal). Why Caracol was built in such a poorly watered region is not known, but Maya engineers showed great ingenuity in constructing reservoirs and terracing the fields. The **Sky Palace** (*Caana*) pyramid, which climbs 138 ft above the site, is being excavated by members of the University of Central Florida. Excavations take place February-May but there are year-round caretakers who will show you around. Currently very knowledgeable guides escort groups around the site twice daily and a new information centre and exhibition hall has been built. The road has been improved and is passable for much of the year with normal vehicles and year-round with 4WD. It is an interesting journey as you pass through the Mountain Pine Ridge, then cross the Macal River and immediately enter a broadleaf tropical forest. Take your own food as there is none at the site. Otherwise **Pine Ridge Lodge, Five Sister's Lodge** or **Blancaneaux Lodge** are open for lunch (see page 697).

Sleeping

Belize City to San Ignacio *p690*

L **Jaguar Paw Jungle Resort**, near Belize Zoo on curve of Caves Branch River on road south at Mile 31, enquiries T820-2023, www.jaguarpaw.com, with meals.

L-A **Pook's Hill Lodge**, Pook's Hill Reserve, T820-2017, www.pookshill belize.com. A 300-acre nature reserve on Roaring Creek, 6 *cabañas*, horses and rafting.

AL **Banana Bank Lodge and Jungle Equestrian Adventure**, Guanacaste National Park, T/F820-2020, www.bananabank.com. Resort accommodation, with meals, horse riding on river side and jungle trails, with birding and river trips.

A **Caesar's Place**, Mile 60, San Ignacio, T824-2341, www.blackrock lodge.com. Under same ownership as **Black Rock Lodge** see page 697. 4 rooms with bath, 4 full hook-ups for RVs, with showers and bath-room facilities, restaurant and bar, gift shop, swimming.

A-D **Roaring River**, Roaring Creek, T820-2037, www.roaringriverbelize.com. New owners, run by a friendly Belgian couple. Nice lodge along the river, *cabañas*, quiet, swimming pool, bar and tours.D for camping or lodge room.

C-E **Tropical Education Centre**, at Belize Zoo. Basic-style accommodation.

E **Monkey Bay Wildlife Sanctuary**, Mile 31 Western Highway, Belmopan, T820-3032, www.watershedbelize.org. Dormitory accommodation or you can camp on a wooden platform with thatched roof, swim in the river, showers available, take meals with family (there are plans to provide cooking facilities in the future).

San Ignacio and around *p691, map p692*

San Ignacio

Some hotels in town and on Cahal Pech Hill may be noisy at weekends from loud music, and during the day from traffic and buses.

LL-L **San Ignacio Resort Hotel**, 18 Buena Vista Rd, T824-2125, www.sanignacio belize.com. Southern end of town, on the road to Benque Viejo. Rooms with bath, a/c, hot water, and some with balconies. Clean, helpful staff, swimming pool, tennis court, excellent restaurant. Live music every weekend at the Stork Club. **Green Iguana Exhibit** on site, see Sights, and tour agency.

A Martha's Guest House, 10 West St, T804-3647, www.marthasbelize.com. 10 comfortable rooms, 2 with balcony, TV, a/c, cheaper without, lounge area, good restaurant, friendly, clean, kitchen facilities, the family also runs **August Laundromat**.

A-C Casa Blanca Guesthouse, 10 Burns Av, T824-2080, www.casablancaguesthouse.com. 8 clean rooms with 2 beds in each, private shower, fan or a/c, TV, use of kitchenette, free coffee, friendly.

B Elvira's Dinner & Guest House, 6 Far West St, T804-0243. Good clean rooms, with traditional Belizean food in the restaurant.

B-C Plaza, 4a Burns Av, T824-3332. Rooms in family house run by friendly elderly couple. All 8 rooms have 2 beds, balconies, TVs, a/c, cheaper without, all with bath, parking. Free coffee.

C Aguada Hotel, Santa Elena, across the river, T824-3609, www.aguadahotel.com. Full-service hotel, 12 rooms, private baths, a/c costs more, fresh water pond and heart-shaped swimming pool, quiet part of town, excellent restaurant and bar.

C-D Hi-Et, 12 West St, T824-2828, thehiet@yahoo.com. Lovely, red and cream old wooden building with 10 rooms and private shower, cheaper without. Reportedly noisy, nice balcony, friendly, helpful, family-run, stunning orchids in patio. Free coffee.

C-D Pacz Guesthouse, 4 Far West St, T824-4538, www.paczguesthouse.com. 5 good, clean, spacious and tidy rooms, most with fridge. Near the centre, but quiet.

D-E Max's Place, 49 Burns Av, T621-0556, maxcaballeros@yahoo.com. 5 basic rooms including a bunk room with shared bath room above family home. Communal TV. Shuttles and guided tours offered. Bike rental.

E Central, 24 Burns Av, T824-3134, easyrider@btl.net. Clean, secure, fans, shared hot showers, book exchange, friendly, veranda with hammocks, uncomfortable beds but recommended.

Around San Ignacio

In the area surrounding San Ignacio there are many jungle hideaways. Ranging from secluded and exclusive cottages to full activity resorts, and covering a wide range of budgets, these places are normally an adventure on their own. But before going, make sure you know what costs are included; food is often extra.

LL The Lodge at Chaa Creek, on the Macal River, south of San Ignacio off the Chial Rd, after the turn to Ix Chel Farm, T824-2037, www.chaacreek.com, or hotel office at 56 Burns Av, San Ignacio. In 20 years of operation this place has evolved from jungle cottages at the riverside on a working farm, to upscale accommodation, amenities and tours, with a spa, conference centre, morpho butterfly breeding centre, natural history movement and an adventure centre. Strong supporters of environmental groups and projects. Tours and excursions to all local attractions offered.

LL Blancaneaux Lodge, Mountain Pine Ridge Rd, east of San Ignacio, Central Farm, Cayo District, T/F824-3878, www.blancaneauxlodge.com. Once the mountain retreat of Francis Ford Coppola and his family, now one villa and wonderful, huge *cabañas* decorated in Guatemalan textiles, horse riding, croquet lawn, spa, hot pool, overlooking a stream that flows through the property, private air strip. Access to Big Rock Falls. Italian restaurant and bar. Recommended.

L Du Plooys', south of San Ignacio, past the Chaa Creek road, then follow (including one steep hill) to its end above the Macal River, T824-3101, www.duplooys.com. Several choices of accommodation and packages are available, enjoy the 'Hangover Bar' with cool drinks on the deck overlooking trees and river. The New Belize Botanic Gardens (see page 693) is also run by the du Plooy family.

L Ek Tun, south of San Ignacio, T820-3002, in USA T303-4426150, www.ektunbelize.com. A 500-acre private jungle retreat on the Macal River with access by boat only, with 2 very private deluxe thatched guest cottages, excellent food, spectacular garden setting, secluded sandy river beaches, birdwatching, caving, mineral pool for swimming, miles of hiking trails, canoeing and tubing down the river. Highlights include cave tours, adventure and a special Tikal Extension. Advance reservations only, no drop-ins, adults only and 3-night minimum.

L-A Green Heaven Lodge, south of San Ignacio, just past the Negroman turning on the Chial Rd, T820-4034, www.ghlodge belize.com. 4 cabins, excellent swimming pool, French restaurant and bar, close alternative to dining at the area resorts.
AL Five Sisters Lodge, east of San Ignacio, 2½ miles beyond **Blancaneaux Lodge** (see above), T/F820-4005, www.fivesisters lodge.com. Rustic cottages lit by oil lamps, great views, good-value restaurant. Recommended.
AL Las Cuevas Research Station and Explorer's Lodge, in the Chiquibul Forest, T824-3779, www.mayaforest.com. Isolated research station now open to non-researchers. Rivers, caves, archaeological sites nearby with a genuine wilderness experience.
AL Mountain Equestrian Trails, Mile 8, Mountain Pine Ridge Rd (from Georgeville), Central Farm PO, Cayo District, T820-4041, in USA T1-800-838-3913, www.metbelize.com. Accommodation in 4 double *cabañus* with bath, no electricity, hot water, mosquito nets, good food in *cantina*, offers ½-day, full-day and 4-day adventure tours on horseback in Western Belize, 'Turf' and 'Turf 'n' Surf' packages, and other expeditions, excellent guides and staff, birdwatching tours in and around the reserve.
AL Pine Ridge Lodge, east of San Ignacio, on the road to Augustine, just past turning to Hidden Valley Falls, T606-4557, www.pineridgelodge.com. *Cabañas* in the pinewoods, including breakfast.
AL Windy Hill Resort, 2 miles west of San Ignacio, on Graceland Ranch, T824-2017, www.windyhillresort.com. 14 cottage units, all with bath, dining room, small pool, nature trails, horseriding and river trips can be arranged, expensive.
AL-A Mopan River Resort, Benque Viejo, T823-2047, www.mopanriverresort.com. Belize's first all-inclusive, luxury resort on the Mopan River, opposite Benque Viejo, accessible only by boat, 12 thatched *cabañas* with verandas nestled in a lush coconut grove, swimming pool, water garden, minimum stay 7 nights.
AL-B Black Rock Lodge, T824-2341, www.blackrocklodge.com. South of San Ignacio, Mile 60. Road sometimes requires 4WD depending on weather, own transportation recommended. Another spectacular setting, though clearing and barbed wire fences detract, 6 *cabañas*, solar-powered electricity and hot water, hiking, riding, canoeing, birdwatching, excursions.
AL-B Maya Mountain Lodge (Bart and Suzi Mickler), ¾ mile east of San Ignacio at 9 Cristo Rey Rd, Santa Elena, San Ignacio, T824-2164, www.mayamountain.com. Welcoming, special weekly, monthly and family rates. Restaurant, expensive excursions, self-guided nature trail, swimming, hiking, riding, canoeing, fishing can be arranged.
B Cahal Pech Village, south of town, near Cahal Pech, T824-3740, www.cahalpech.com. Thatched cabins or a/c rooms, restaurant, bar, meeting facilities.
C Parrot Nest, near village of Bullet Tree Falls, 3 miles north of San IgnacioT820-4058, www.parrot-nest.com. Small but comfortable tree houses in beautiful grounds by the river, breakfast and dinner included, canoeing, birdwatching, horseriding available.
C-D Clarissa's Falls, on Mopan River, down a signed track on the Benque road, around Mile 70, T824-3916, www.clarissafalls.com. Owned by Chena Galvez, thatched cottages on riverbank by a set of rapids, also bunkhouse with hammocks or beds, camping space and hook-ups for RVs, rafting, kayaking and tubing available, wonderful food in the restaurants.

Camping

D-E Inglewood Camping Grounds, west of San Ignacio at Mile 68¼, T824-3555, www.ingelwoodcampingground.com. Palapas, camping, RV hook-ups, hot and cold showers, maintained grounds, some highway noise.
F Mida's, ½ mile from town on Branch Mouth Rd, near river, T824-3172, www.midas belize.com. Go down Burns Av, turn right down unpaved road after wooden church, after 200 yd turn left, campground is 300 yd on right. Hot showers, electricity, water, restaurant, very helpful, good value, cabins available (**B-C**) and they also organize trips to Tikal.
F-G Cosmos Camping, ½ mile beyond Mida's (see above). Tents for rent, washing and cooking facilities, run by friendly Belizean family, good breakfasts, canoe and bikes for hire, good. Cabins available (**E**).

Eating

San Ignacio and around *p691, map p692*

San Ignacio

ΨΨΨ **Running W**, in the San Ignacio Resort Hotel. One of the best restaurants in town. Also live music every 2nd Sat in the bar of the same hotel.

ΨΨ **Cafe Sol**, between Burns Av and West St. Serves coffee and pastries, with vegetarian, chicken and seafood dishes for lunch and dinner. Also has bookstore and gift shop.

ΨΨ **Erva's**, 6 Far West St, T824-2556. Vegetarian available, reasonable prices.

ΨΨ **Eva's Bar**, 22 Burns Av, T804-2267. Mon-Sat 0800-1500, 1800-late. Good diner-style restaurant, local dishes, helpful with good local information, bike rental, internet facilities, tours.

ΨΨ **The Green Dragon**, 8 Hudson St, T824-4782. Friendly Dutch-English owners, great for coffee, espresso, tea and smoothies. Also has internet, books, tours and healthfood store. Sells different herbal remedies made in Belize, like Ix Chel Farm's, Harry Guy and Rubby Dub.

ΨΨ **Hanna's**, 5 Burns Av. Popular with locals and foreigners, very good Indian-Belizean food, as well as currys, vegetarian and excellent fish. Many of the ingredients come fresh from their own farm, good value, open daily 0600-2100. Friendly staff and highly recommended.

ΨΨ **Sanny's Grill**, several blocks down the hill off the Western Highway past the Texaco station. Serves the 'world's best conch ceviche', full dinner menu, charming setting.

ΨΨ **Serendib**, 27 Burns Av. Good food and good value, Sri Lankan owners, Indian-style food, Mon-Sat, 1030-1500, 1830-1100.

ΨΨ-Ψ **Martha's Kitchen**, below Martha's Guest House. Very good breakfasts and Belizean dishes, plus pizzas and burger. Garden patio.

Ψ **Hode's Place**, Branch Mouth Rd, facing the basketball field, just outside town. Popular with locals and good value, Belizean food arriving in huge portions, open daily, pleasant yard to sit outside.

Ψ **Maxim's**, Bullet Tree Rd and Far West St. Chinese, good service, cheap, very good food, popular with locals, noisy TV at the bar.

Ψ **Old French Bakery**, JNC building. Good pastries for days out exploring.

Around San Ignacio

Ψ **Terry's**, north of San Ignacio, near the village of Bullet Tree Falls. Restaurant with limited menu but good food.

Ψ **Long Luck Chinese restaurant**, George Price, up the hill on the left, just after the Hydro road, Benque Viejo. The best Chinese in town.

Bars and clubs

San Ignacio and around *p691, map p692*

Cahal Pech, on a hill, with TV station, beside the road to Benque Viejo before the edge of town. Music and dancing at weekends, *the* place to be, live bands are broadcast on TV and radio all over Belize, good views. On a hill across the track from the club is Cahal Pech archaeological site.

Culture Club, same building as Pitpan, upstairs, live reggae Thu-Sat night, popular with foreigners and the local Rasta crowd.

Legends 200, Bullet Tree Rd. Disco, popular with locals.

Pitpan, right turn off King St to river. The open-air bar is at the back of the building, popular spot, open daily.

Stork Club, San Ignacio Resort Hotel, see Sleeping, above, live music every 2nd Sat in the bar.

Shopping

San Ignacio and around *p691, map p692*

Black Rock Gift Shop, near Eva's, linked to Black Rock Lodge, luggage can be left here if canoeing from Black Rock to San Ignacio, arts and crafts, workshop. **Celina's Supermarket**, Burns Av, next to the bus station. Not the cheapest but wide selection. Open Mon-Sat 0730-1200, 1300-1600, 1900-2100. **Maxim's**, West St, small, cheap supermarket. Fruit and veg market every Fri and Sat morning. Book exchange at **Snooty Fox**, Waights Av (opposite Martha's).

Activities and tours

San Ignacio and around *p691, map p692*

Many of the resorts and lodges in this area organize a variety of tours and expeditions (see Sleeping and Tour operators, above).

Therapies
See Dr Rosita Arvigo, page 692. Therapeutic Massage Studio, 38 West St, T604-0314. Mon-Fri 0800-1200, 1300-1630. Sat 0830-1200.

Tour operators
David's Adventure Tours, near bus terminal, T804-3674, www.davidadventuretours.com. Recommended for visits to Barton's Creek Cave, US$37, Mountain Pine ridge and Barton, US$67, Caracol, US$75, or guided canoe trips along the Macal River, including the medicinal trail and overnight camping, US$127. Always gets a good report.
Easy Rider, Bullet Tree Rd, T824-3734, for horse riding. Full-day tours for US$40 including lunch.
Pacz Tours, T824-2477/ 610-2477, www.pacztours.net, based out of **Eva's Bar**, offers truly great trips to Actun Tunichil Muknal Cave, US$75 including lunch and reserve fee of US$30. Excellent guides. Bob from the UK, who runs the bar, is the best starting point for information on any of the trips although your hotel will also have details and suggestions. Canoe trips on the Macal River, with bird and wildlife watching, medicinal plant trail, good value, US$20; Barton Creek Cave, US$35 for ½-day tour, Mountain Pine Ridge, US$30, Caracol and trip to pools, US$60, Tikal, US$85. Highly recommended. Bob is very helpful.
The Green Dragon, 8 Hudson St, T824-4782, www.greendragonbelize.com, is very helpful and will arrange hotel bookings all over Belize as well as tours around San Ignacio.
Mayawalk Tours, 19 Burns Av, across the street from **Pacz Tours**, T824-3070, www.mayawalk.com, has received good recommendations.
Maya Mystic Tours, Savannah St, T804-0055. Run by the friendly Omar Kantum. All trips organized including El Pilar, US$45 per person and river canoeing. Shuttles arranged.

Caracol *p695*
Tour operators
Many companies in the San Ignacio area offer trips to Caracol, see above.

Transport

San Ignacio and around *p691, map p692*
Bus National Transport Company Bus Station is on Burns Av. To **Belize City**, Mon-Sat 0430-1800 every hr, Sun hourly 0700-1800, 3½ -4 hrs, US$2.50. To **Belmopan**, same schedule as Belize City, 1 hr, US$1.70. To **Benque**, every 2 hrs, Mon-Sat 0730-2300 (less on Sun), 30 mins, US$0.75. Change at Belmopan for Danriga and the south.

The **San Ignacio Shuttle**, T823-2265, www.sanignacioshuttle.com, leaves from Café Sol at 0830 to the international airport/ municipal airport/marine terminal, US$30, 2 hrs. Ring the night before to reserve. Shuttle to Placenia, T605-8141, www.belizeweb.com, US$35. Call Tito or Max.

Taxi Savannah Taxi Drivers' Co-op, T824-2155, T606-7239 (Manuel, 24 hrs). To **Guatemalan border**, US$10 (*colectivo* US$2.50, on the road, but US$12.50 if you pick them up from their base opposite David's. To **Xunantunich** US$30 return, to **Belize City** US$75, to Tikal US$175 return, to Mountain Pine Ridge, US$75, Chaa Creek, US$30, Caracol, US$175 return. **Minibuses**: also run to **Tikal**, making a day trip possible. Organized tours cost about US$70.

Around San Ignacio
Bus and taxi National Transport Company run many daily buses from Belize City to **Benque Viejo**, and frequent buses from San Ignacio to Benque Viejo. Taxi US$10, or *colectivo* from central square, US$2.50. From the bus station at Benque, you need to get a taxi to the immigration post at **Melchor de Mencos**, US$1.25, 2 mins.

Xunantunich *p693*
Bus Bus from San Ignacio towards the border as far as **San José Succotz** (7 miles), US$0.75, where a hand-operated ferry takes visitors and cars across the Mopan River (0800-1600, free); it is then a 20-min walk uphill on an all-weather road. Return buses to San Ignacio pass throughout the afternoon.

Mountain Pine Ridge *p694*
Taxi Mountain Pine Ridge has no public transport. Apart from tours, the only

alternatives are to take a taxi or hire a vehicle or a mountain bike. Everything is well signposted. The private pick-ups which go into San Ignacio from Augustine are usually packed, so hitching is impossible.

Taxis charge around US$75-80 for 5 people. Roads are passable but rough Jan-May, but after Jun they are marginal and are impossible in the wet (Sep-Nov); essential to seek local advice at the time.

Directory

San Ignacio and around *p691, map p692*

Banks Banks open Mon-Fri 0830-1500, Sat 0830-1300, they are all neatly bunched together at the southern end of Burns Av, **Belize Bank** offers full service, TCs, Visa and MasterCard cash advance plus ATM. **Atlantic Bank**, Burns Av, also does cash advances and has an ATM. Both charge commission for cash advances. **Scotia Bank**, opposite Atlantic Bank, doesn't charge for cash advances. **Western Union**, has a branch in Celina's (supermarket), Burns Av, Mon-Thu 0800-1200 1300-1600, Fri and Sat also 1900-2100. **Eva's Bar** and **Martha's** both change TCs at good rates. Changers in the town square give better rates of exchange for dollars cash and TCs than you can get at the border with Guatemala. The best place to change dollars into quetzales is in Guatemala. **Internet** High charges from BTL mean internet services come and go. Cheapest place in town are **Cayo Community Computer Centre**, Hudson St, Mon-Sat 0800-2100, Sun 1000-1800 and Tradewinds **Eva's Bar**, US$3 for 30 mins. **Laundry** **August Laundromat** at Martha's and Mike's, and **Laundromat** at Burns Av. **Post office** Hudson St, reliable parcel service, Mon-Thu 0800-1200 and 1300-1700, Fri 0800-1200 and 1300-1600. **Telephone** BTL office at further end of Burns Av, opposite Venus Hotel, long-distance calls and fax service.

Southern Belize and the Southern Cayes

Southern Belize is the most remote part of the country and has poor roads, but it is worth exploring. Dangriga is the largest of several Garífuna settlements that burst into life every year on Settlement Day. The paradise beaches of Hopkins and Placencia are perfect for watersports and relaxing. Cockscomb Basin Wildlife (Jaguar) Sanctuary offers one of the best chances of seeing a big cat in the wild, while the sparsely populated far south around Punta Gorda has many Maya settlements to visit in a region dotted with impressive Maya ruins. ▸▸ *For Sleeping, Eating and other listings, see page 707-718.*

South to Dangriga

▸▸ *pp707-718. Colour map 6, A1.*

About 2 miles beyond the Belize Zoo on the Western Highway, the Coastal Highway (a good dirt road) runs southeast to **Gales Point**, a charming fishing village on a peninsula at the south end of Manatee Lagoon, 15 miles north of Dangriga. The villagers are keen to preserve natural resources and there are still significant numbers of the endangered manatee and hawksbill turtles. Boat tours of the lagoon are recommended.

Along the Hummingbird Highway

The narrow Hummingbird Highway branches off the Western Highway 48 miles west of Belize City, passes Belmopan and heads south. Skirting the eastern edge of Mountain Pine Ridge, the newly surfaced highway meanders through lush scenery of cohune palms, across vast flood plains filled with citrus trees which provide a spectacular backdrop for the 52-mile journey southeast to Dangriga.

The Hummingbird Highway climbs through rich tropical hardwood forest until reaching Mile 13, where a visitor centre marks a track leading off to **St Herman's Cave**. Two paths, with good birdwatching, lead through shady ferns before descending in steps to the cave entrance with its unique microclimate. You can walk for more than a mile underground but it can be slippery if wet; torch and spare batteries essential. There is a 3-mile trail to a campsite from the visitor centre.

Two miles further on is the **Blue Hole National Park**ⓘ *daily 0800-1600, US$6,* an azure blue swimming hole fringed with vines and ferns, fed by a stream which comes from St Herman's Cave. This is typical karst limestone country with sinkholes, caves and underground streams. After its long journey underground, the water here is deliciously cool until it disappears again into the top of a large underwater cavern. Eventually this joins the Sibun River which enters the sea just south of Belize City. There is a rough 2½-mile trail, through low secondary forest, between St Herman's Cave and the Blue Hole; good hiking boots are required. A sign on the roadway warns visitors against thieves; lock your car and leave someone on guard if possible when swimming. An armed guard and more wardens have been hired to prevent further theft and assaults. There is a visitor centre at the entrance.

The peaks of the mountains dominate the south side of the highway until about Mile 30, when the valley of Stann Creek begins to widen out into Belize's most productive agricultural area, where large citrus groves stretch along the highway.

Canoeing or tubing trips can be organized down Indian Creek, visiting the imaginatively named Caves Five, Four and Three and then Daylight Cave and Darknight Cave, from **Over-the-Top Camp** on the Hummingbird Highway, or **Kingfisher/Belize Adventures** in Placencia. Vehicle support is brought round to meet you on the Coastal Highway near Democracia.

Turn east at Mile 32 for 4 miles along a gravel road to **Tamandua**, a wildlife sanctuary in **Five Blue Lakes National Park**ⓘ *Friends of 5 Blues, PO Box 111, Belmopan, T809-2005, or the warden, Lee Wengrzyn, a local dairy farmer, or else Augustus Palacio (see Sleeping, below).* Follow the track opposite **Over-the-Top Camp**, turning right and crossing the stream for Tamandua, then for another 2 miles or so straight on following the signs for the national park, 1½ miles, where there is camping.

Dangriga » pp707-718. Colour map 6, A1.

→ *Population: 8814.*

The chief town of the Stann Creek District is on the seashore, which has the usual Belizean aspect of wooden clap-board houses elevated on piles, and is a cheerful and busily commercial place with a population largely of Black Caribs (Garífuna). North Stann Creek meets the sea at Dangriga, coming alive with flotillas of boats and fishermen. There are several gas stations, a good hospital and an airfield with regular flights. The beach has been considerably cleaned up and extended, being particularly nice at the far north of town at the **Pelican Beach Hotel,** where it is raked and cleaned daily. Palm trees have been planted by **Pal's Guest House** where the beach has been enlarged. Dangriga means 'standing waters' or 'sweet water' in Garífuna.

To understand a little more about the Garífuna culture, visit the newly opened **Gulisi Garífuna Museum**ⓘ *Stann Creek Valley Rd, T502-0639, www.ngcbelize.org, Tue-Sun 0900-1700, US$5.* The museum includes information about the origins of the Garífuna people, history and customs, with music and a working garden of traditional plants and herbs.

Cayes near Dangriga

Tobacco Cayeⓘ *US$15, 35 mins by speedboat from Dangriga,* is a tiny and quite heavily populated island, but has lots of local flavour and charm and, though becoming a little commercialized, still has an authentic feel. It sits right on the reef and you can snorkel from the sandfly-free beach although there are no large schools of fish; snorkelling gear for rent. Boats go daily, ask at **Riverside Café** ⓘ *US$12-15 per person.*

South Water Caye, the focus of a new marine reserve, is a lovely palm-fringed tropical island with beautiful beaches, particularly at the south end.

South of Dangriga → *Colour map 6, A1.*

The Southern Highway, now completely paved except for a stretch of a mile or so, connects Dangriga with Punta Gorda in the far south. Six miles inland from Dangriga the road branches off the Hummingbird Highway and heads south through mixed tropical forests, palmettos and pines along the fringes of the Maya Mountains. West of the road, about 5 miles from the junction with the Hummingbird Highway, a track leads to **Mayflower**, a Maya ruin. Some minimal work has begun on opening it up and some say it will eventually be the biggest archaeological site in southern Belize.

Fifteen miles from Dangriga, a minor road forks off 4 miles east to the Garífuna fishing village of Hopkins. Watch out for sandflies when the weather is calm. The villagers throw household slops into the sea and garbage on to the beach.

Turning east towards the Caribbean just before Kendal a road leads down the Sittee River to **Sittee River Village** and **Possum Point Biological Station**.

Glover's Reef

Glover's Reef, part of North East Cay and about 45 miles offshore, is an atoll with beautiful diving and has been a Marine Reserve since 1993, US$10. The reef here is pristine and the cayes are generally unspoilt, but yellow blight has hit the area killing most of the existing palm trees – especially on **Long Caye**. The combination of Hurricane Mitch and high water temperatures in recent years has damaged the coral, and the snorkelling is not as good as it once was.

Placencia

» pp707-718. Colour map 6, A1.

Placencia, a former Creole fishing village 30 miles south of Dangriga, is a small seaside community on a thin sandy peninsula promoting the delights of the offshore cayes and marinelife and is a good base for inland tours too. Continuing down the Southern Highway a couple of hotel signs indicate a turning (nothing official, look carefully) to a road that heads east to Riversdale (after 9 miles) turning south to follow the peninsula to **Maya Beach**, **Seine Bight** and, eventually, **Placencia**. The peninsula road is very rough from Riversdale to Seine Bight, with sand mixed with mud; 4WD is advisable.

Placencia was hit hard by Hurricane Iris in October 2001, but nevertheless is still becoming more and more popular among people looking for an 'end of the road' adventure. It's a relaxing combination of palm trees, relaxing on the beach, fishing, snorkelling and diving. If you time the trip right or get lucky, your visit may coincide with the migrations of the whale shark – the largest fish in the world at up to 55 ft – that passes through local waters from March to May. And, between January and March, hundreds of scarlet macaws gather at nearby Red Bank. Also worth hitting if you can time it right is the **Lobster Fest**, 23-25 June, with two days of music, dancing and lobster and the Sidewalk Arts Festival held the weekend before or after Valentine's Day. Placencia is a natural base for one- and two-day trips to **Cockscomb Basin Wildlife Sanctuary** – see page 704. **Big Creek**, on the mainland opposite Placencia, is 3 miles from Mango Creek (see below).

There are no streets, just a network of concrete footpaths connecting the wooden houses that are set among the palms. Rebuilding of the main sidewalk through the centre of the village, reported to be in the *Guiness Book of Records* as the world's narrowest street, has been completed after it was ripped out by Hurricane Iris in 2002. The atmosphere has been described as laid back, with lots of Jamaican music, particularly after Easter and Christmas celebrations.

The local **Placencia Tourism Center**ⓘ *T523-4045, www.placencia.com, Mon-Fri 0900-1700, closed public holidays*, is next to the petrol station, with lots of useful information. It also produces the local monthly news-sheet, *Placencia Breeze* (www.placenciabreeze.com).

Around Placencia

Trips can be made to local cayes and the **Barrier Reef**, approximately 18 miles offshore. Day trips include snorkelling, with a beach BBQ lunch of lobster and conch. Offshore cayes indude **Laughing Bird Caye**. **Gladden Spit** and **Silk Cayes Marine Reserve** (reserve fee US$10), also protected by **Friends of Nature.** Whale sharks visit the spit in March, April. May and June for 10 days after the full moon to feed on the spawn of aggregating reef fish.

Several hotels and guide services have kayaks that can be rented to explore some of the nearer islands or the quieter waters of the **Placencia Lagoon**. Those who want to keep their feet dry can go mountain biking on the peninsula or use it as a base for trips to **Cockscomb Basin Wildlife Sanctuary** and Maya ruins.

Placencia

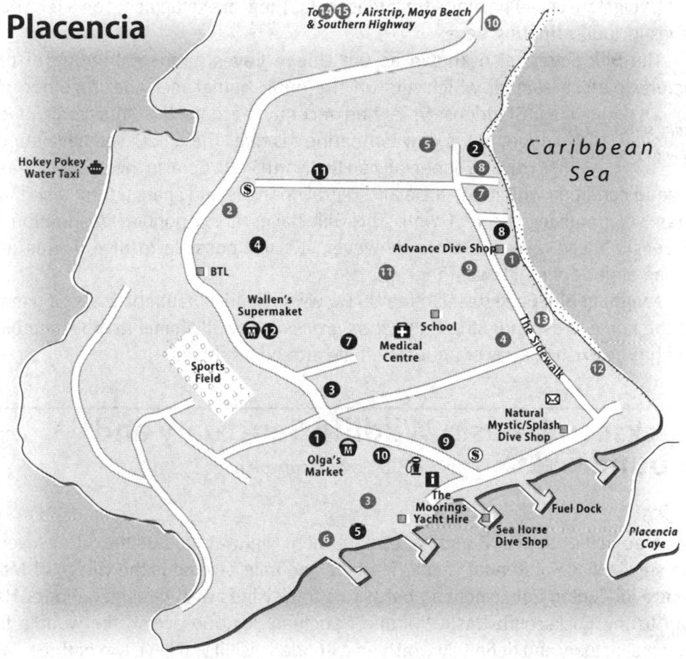

Sleeping
Cozy Corner 1
Deb & Dave's Last Resort 2
Dianni's Guest House 3
Easy Living Apartments 4
Inn at Robert's Grove 14
Lydia's Guesthouse 5
Omar's Guest House 13
Paradise Vacation 6
Ranguana Lodge 7
Seaspray 8
Serenade Guest House 9
Serenity Resort 15
Trade Winds 12
Turtle Inn 10
Yellow House 11

Eating
BJ's 1
Daisy's 11
De Tatch Café 2
Garden Brew Coffee House 12
John the Bakerman 4
Merlene's 5
Pickled Parrot Bar & Grill 7
Purple Space Monkey Village 3
Trattoria 8
Tutti-frutti Ice Cream Parlour 9
Wendy's Creole 10

Day tours by boat south along the coast from Placencia to **Monkey River** and **Monkey River Village**, www.monkeyrivermagic.com, are available. Monkey River tours, US$20 per person, feature howler monkeys, toucans, manatees and iguanas. Monkey River Village can be reached by a rough road, which is not recommended in wet weather. The road ends on the north side of the river and the town is on the south side, so call over for transport. Trips upriver can also be arranged here with locals but kayaking is best organized in Placencia. Trips can be arranged to Red Bank for the scarlet macaws which gather in their hundreds between January and March.

For information on travelling to Puerto Cortés, Honduras, see page 717.

North of Placencia is the Garífuna community of **Seine Bight** (see Sleeping, page 711).

Cayes near Placencia

Ranguana Caye is a private caye reached from Placencia (US$5). Getting there is free if it fits in with one of the regular trips, otherwise it costs US$150 each way for up to four people. Divers must bring their own scuba equipment. Day trips for diving, snorkelling or just relaxing cost US$45-50, and include lunch. For longer stays, see Sleeping, page 711.

At the southernmost end of the Mesoamerican Barrier Reef are the **Sapodilla Cayes**, US$10. Tours are arranged from Guatemala (for example see under Río Dulce and Lívingston) or can be made from Placencia. There are settlements on a few of the Cayes including **Hunting Caye**.

The **Silk Cayes**, also known as the **Queen Cayes**, is a small group of tiny, picture- perfect islands, which sits on the outer barrier reef and, together with Gladdens Spit, has recently become the core zone of the country's newest marine reserve. The Silk Cayes have superb diving, especially on the North Wall. Coral in the deeper areas is in good condition with many tube and barrel sponges and sharks, turtles and rays often seen cruising the reef wall. The Silk Cayes are a popular destination for Placencia-based dive operators, however, it's not possible to dive in this area during periods of rough weather.

The rainy season lasts from June to January.

Laughing Bird Caye (reserve fee US$4, www.friendsofnaturebelize.org), used to be the home of the Laughing Gull (*Larus articilla*), now it's home to other sea birds and has an exciting array of underwater life around its shores.

Cockscomb Basin Wildlife Sanctuary and around

» *pp707-718. Colour map 6, A1.*

ⓘ *US$5.*

Some 20 miles south of Dangriga, the Southern Highway crosses the Sittee River at the small village of **Kendal** (ruins nearby). One mile beyond is the village of **Maya Centre** (or Center) from where a poor 7-mile track winds west through Cabbage Haul Gap to the Cockscomb Basin Wildlife Sanctuary (21,000 acres), the world's first jaguar sanctuary and definitely worth an extended visit if you have two or three days. The sanctuary was created out of the Cockscomb Basin Forest Reserve in 1986 to protect the country's highest recorded density of jaguars (*Panthera onca*), and their smaller cousins the puma (red tiger), the endangered ocelot, the diurnal jaguarundi and that feline cutey, the margay. Many other mammals share the heavily forested reserve, including coatis, collared peccaries, agoutis, anteaters, Baird's tapirs and tayras (a small weasel-like animal). There are red-eyed tree frogs, boas, iguanas and fer-de-lances, as well as over 290 species of bird, including king vultures and great curassows. The sanctuary is a good place for relaxing, showering under waterfalls, tubing down the river, or listening to birds – hundreds of bird species have been spotted and there are several types of toucan, hummingbirds and scarlet macaws to be seen by early risers. The reserve is sponsored by the Belizean government, the **Audubon Society**, the **Worldwide Fund For Nature** and various private firms. Donations are very welcome.

Park HQ is at the former settlement of Quam Bank (whose milpa-farming inhabitants founded the **Maya Centre** outside the reserve). Here there is an informative visitors' centre. An 18-mile network of jungle trails spreads out from the centre, ranging in distance from a few hundred yards to 2½ miles. Walkers are unlikely to see any of the big cats as they are nocturnal, but if you fancy a walk in the dark you may be lucky. Note that the guards leave for the day at 1600. You will see birds, frogs, lizards, snakes and spiders. Longer hikes can be planned with the staff. Nearby is one of Belize's highest summits, **Victoria Peak** (3675 ft), which is an arduous four- or five-day return climb and should not be undertaken lightly. There is virtually no path, a guide is essential; February to May are the best months for the climb (for guides, see Activities and tours, page 716).

Punta Gorda

» *pp707-718. Colour map 6, B1.*

→ *Population: 4329.*

The turn-off from the Southern Highway for Mango Creek, Independence and Big Creek comes 15 miles after the Riversdale turn-off, and the road runs 4 miles east through the **Savannah Forest Reserve** to the mangrove coast opposite Placencia. About 35 miles beyond the junction, 10½ miles north of the T-junction for Punta Gorda, half a mile west of the road, is the **Nim Li Punit** archaeological site which has a new visitors' centre and clean spacious housing for the stelae. Nim Li Punit ('The Big Hat') was only discovered in 1974. A score of stelae, 15-20 ft tall, were unearthed, dated AD 700-800, as well as a ball court and several groups of buildings. The site is worth visiting – look for the sign on the highway. Day trips also offered from Placencia. A short distance beyond, the highway passes **Big Falls Village**, almost completely destroyed by Hurricane Iris. Take a short hike back to the hot springs for a swim, camp or sling a hammock, but first seek permission from the landowner, Mr Peter Aleman. Four miles from Big Falls, the Highway reaches a T-junction, know locally as the 'Dump', marked by a Shell station; the road to San Antonio branches right (west), the main road turns sharp left and runs down through a forest reserve for 13 miles to Punta Gorda. The road is paved from Big Falls to Punta Gorda.

> *Rainfall in this region is exceptionally heavy, over 170 inches annually, and the vegetation consequently luxuriant.*

Punta Gorda is the southernmost town of any size in Belize, a marketing centre and fishing port with a varied ethnic makeup of Creoles, Q'eqchi', Mopan, Chinese, East Indians and descendants of the many races brought here over the years as labourers in ill-fated settlement attempts. Three miles north of **Toledo** are the remains of the sugar cane settlement founded by Confederate refugees after the American Civil War. The coast, about 10 ft above sea level, is fringed with coconut palms. The seafront is clean and enjoyable – once you get away from Front Street, where the lively and colourful market on Wednesday, Friday and Saturday comes with the associated smells of fish and rotting vegetables. The *Voice of America* has an incongruous antenna complex to the south of town.

Toledo Visitors' Information Center, also called **Dem Dats Doin** ⓘ *in booth by pier, PO Box 73, T722-2470, demdatsdoin@btl.net, free, irregular opening hours*, Alfredo and Yvonne Villoria, provide information on travel, tours, guiding, accommodation with indigenous families (Homestay Programme), message service and book exchange, for the whole of Toledo district. **Tourist Information Centre** ⓘ *Front St, T/F722-2531, Mon-Sat 0800-1200 and 1300-1700*, provides a wealth of information about the area, including bus schedules to local Maya villages, and can organize reservations for flights and for hotels, tours and boat trips to Honduras. The **Toledo Ecotourism Association** has an office in the same building. Information on the **Village Guesthouse** and **Ecotrail** programme, as well as booking and transport to the villages.

Around Punta Gorda

There are many tours that can be enjoyed on the numerous rivers in the Toledo District. Countless species of birds make their homes along the rivers, as do troops of howler monkeys and other wildlife. Kayaking is a good way to view wildlife on the rivers. There are many white-sand beaches on the cayes off Punta Gorda for the beachcomber, or camper. Fly fishing is becoming a popular sport and sport fishing, snorkelling and scuba diving are available. **Toledo** is off the beaten path and has some of the most spectacular views, waterfalls, rainforest, cayes and friendly people.

South of Punta Gorda

» *pp707-718. Colour map 6, B1.*

San Pedro Columbia

Inland from Punta Gorda there are several interesting villages in the foothills of the Maya Mountains. Take the main road as far as the 'Dump', the road junction with the Southern Highway. Take the road west to San Antonio. After nearly 2 miles, there is a branch to San Pedro Columbia, a Q'eqchi' village. The Q'eqchi' are a group of Maya who speak the Q'eqchi' language. The women wear colourful costumes, including Guatemalan-style *huípiles*. There are many religious celebrations, at their most intense on **San Luis Rey Day** (5 August).

Lubaantun

ⓘ *0800-1600 daily, a caretaker will point out things of interest. Take refreshments.*
Beyond San Pedro, continuing left around the church, then right and downhill to the concrete bridge, then left for a mile, is the road to the remains of Lubaantun ('Fallen Stones'), the major ceremonial site of southern Belize. The site has a new visitor centre and has undergone extensive work to restore a large part of the ruins. It was found to date from AD 800-900, late in the Maya culture and therefore unique. A series of terraced plazas surrounded by temples and palaces ascend along a ridge from south to north. The buildings were constructed with unusual precision and some of the original lime-mortar facings can still be discerned. Excavation revealed whistle figurines, iron pyrite mirrors, obsidian knives, conch shells from Wild Cane Caye, etc. One of the great controversies of the site was the discovery in 1927 of the Crystal Skull by the daughter of the explorer FA Mitchell-Hedges (see box below).

This whole region is a network of hilltop sites, mostly unexcavated and unrecognizable to the layman.

Blue Creek

Blue Creek is another attractive indigenous village which has a marked trail to **Blue Creek Caves** ⓘ *US$12.50 per person, the caretaker is the guide*, and their Maya drawings. The trail leads through forest and along rock-strewn creeks. Swimming nearby is good swimming but choose a spot away from the strong current. Turn off 3 miles before San Antonio at **Roy's Cool Spot** (good restaurant; daily truck and all buses pass here).

Pusilhá

Pusilhá is one of the most interesting Maya cities, only accessible by boat. Many stelae have been found here dating from AD 573-731, and carvings are similar to

The Crystal Skull of Lubaantun

In 1927, a young woman by the name of Anna Mitchell-Hedges woke for her 17th birthday. For her it proved more eventful than most as she explored the recently excavated Maya site of Lubaantun to discover a finely crafted crystal skull made of pure quartz – setting off a tale of intrigue that remains to this day.

The size of a small watermelon, the translucent skull of reflected light weighs just over 5 kg. The skull is one of only two ever found in Central America. Its date of manufacture is unknown – but some put it at over 3600 years old – and its purpose is equally curious. Local Maya people gave the Skull of Doom to Anna's father, the British explorer FA Mitchell-Hedges as a gift, saying it was used for healing and, more sinisterly, for willing death.

Dating the skull precisely is difficult because of the purity of the crystal, but the details of the finding are equally mysterious, with speculation that the skull was 'placed' to make that birthday so special.

Today the skull is reported to be an ornament in the house of the ageing Anna who has promised, one day, to reveal the truth about the discovery.

those at Quiriguá, Guatemala. Rare features are a walled-in ball court and the abutments remaining from a bridge which once spanned the Moho River. Swimming in the rivers is safe. There are plenty of logging trails and hunters' tracks penetrating the southern faces of the Maya Mountains but, if hiking in the forest, do not go alone.

San Antonio

» pp707-718. Colour map 6, B1.

San Antonio (21 miles from Punta Gorda) was founded by refugees from San Luis in Guatemala in the late 19th century. Nearby there are Maya ruins of mainly scientific interest. There's a community phone for checking buses and other information, T702-2144. **Dem Dats Doin** in Punta Gorda (see page 705) will also be able to give information. There's a medical centre in the village.

There are no roads to the southern border with Guatemala along the Sarstún River. The newly created **Sarstoon-Temash National Park** is a wilderness of red mangroves and unspoilt rainforest. There are no visitor facilities at present. At **Barranco**, the only coastal hamlet south of Punta Gorda, there is a village guesthouse (part of TEA, see box, page 713). A dirt road goes to Barranco through the village of Santa Ana, or you can go by boat.

Sleeping

South to Dangriga *p700*

LL Manatee Lodge, Gales Point, T/F220-8040, in the US T1-877-462-6283, www.manateelodge.com. Resort on the shores of the Southern Lagoon, with trips to all local areas. Prices include transfers, meals and tours.

E Gales Point Bed and Breakfast Association, contact Hortence Welch on arrival or call T220-9031 in advance. Basic accommodation, no indoor plumbing, meals available.

Along the Hummingbird Highway *p700*

LL-E Caves Branch Jungle Lodge, ½ mile past St Herman's Cave, T/F822-2800, www.cavesbranch.com. Reached along ½-mile track, signed on the left, any bus between Belmopan and Dangriga will stop. A secluded spot on the banks of Caves Branch River, comfortable *cabañas* with private baths or **E** per person in the bunkhouse, camping US$5 per person, good, clean, shared bathrooms, great 'jungle showers', delicious meals served buffet style. More than just accommodation, this is very much an activity centre. Great trips through caves, 7-mile underground floats, guided jungle trips, overnight trips as well, tubing, kayaking, mountain biking and rappelling, including the adrenalin-busting **Black Hole Drop**. Excellent guides, pricey for some budgets starting at around US$60 but highly recommended. See also page 661.

A-D Palacios Mountain Retreat, Mile 31, Augustus Palacio, St Martha, Hummingbird Highway, T822-3683, www.palacios retreat.com. Good for relaxing, *cabañas*, bunk rooms and camping. Friendly, helpful, family atmosphere, safe, good local food, swimming in river, tours to waterfall in forest, caves and lagoon, Five Blue Lakes National Park, beware sandflies.

Dangriga *p701*

LL Bonefish, Mahogany St, on seafront near post office, T522-2243, www.bluemarlin lodge.com. A/c, US cable TV, hot water, takes Visa. Restaurant, diving and fishing. Packages are all inclusive.

L-AL Pelican Beach, outside town, on the beach north of town, T522-2044, www.pelicanbeachbelize.com. With private bath, hot water and a/c, verandah, pier with hammocks, 20 rooms, restaurant, bar, games lounge, gift shop, tours arranged, helpful (taxi from town, or 15-min walk from North Stann Creek).

B-D Pal's Guest House, 868 A Magoon St, Dangriga, T522-2095, www.palsbelize.com. 19 units on beach, all with balconies, sea views, bath, fan, cable TV, cheaper rooms in main building, shared bath downstairs, private upstairs. **Dangriga Dive Centre** runs from next door (see Activities and tours, below).

C-D Bluefield Lodge, 6 Bluefield Rd, T522-2742, bluefield@btl.net. Bright hotel, owner Louise Belisle very nice, spotless, comfortable beds, very helpful, secure. Highly recommended.

C-D Chaleanor, 35 Magoon St, T522-2587, chaleanor@btl.net. Fairly large rooms, some with TV and fan and a/c some with sea views, rooftop restaurant.

E Catalina, 37 Cedar St, T522-2390. Very small, not that clean, but family-run and friendly, store luggage.

Cayes near Dangriga *p701*

Tobacco Caye

There is no electricity on the island, but it's a good family atmosphere and great fun.

AL-A Ocean's Edge Fishing Lodge, T614-9633, USA T281-8940548, www2.symet.net/beltex. Full board, 7 cabins on stilts joined by elevated walkways, run by Raymond and Brenda Lee, excellent food, diving and fishing can be arranged.

AL-B Lana's on the reef, T522-2571, USA T909-9434556. Has its own fishing pier, snorkelling equipment hire, good Caribbean-style food, mosquito net, shared and private shower. Recommended.

AL-B Reef's End Lodge, T522-2419, www.reefsendlodge.com. Basic, small rooms, boat transfer on request from Dangriga.

C Island Camps, PO Box 174 (51 Regent St, Belize City, T227-2109). Owner Mark Bradley will pick up guests in Dangriga, A-frame huts and campground, meals on request, reef excursions, friendly, good value. Recommended.

South Water Caye

LL Blue Marlin Lodge, T522-2243, www.bluemarlinlodge.com. An excellent dive lodge offering various packages, small sandy island with snorkelling off the beach, good accommodation and food, runs tours.

LL Pelican's Pouch, which has rooms in a 2-storey colonial building, and 3 secluded cottages. **Pelican University** is ideal for groups housing up to 23 people at US$60 per person per day including 3 meals.

South of Dangriga *p702*

LL Hamanasi, Sittee Point, T/F520-7073, www.hamanasi.com. 17-acre resort, 18 rooms and suites with a/c. Swimming pool, full dive operation.

LL-L Jaguar Reef Lodge, south of Hopkins, just north of Sittee River, T520-7040, www.jaguar reef.com. 18 a/c rooms with refrigerators. Central lodge on sandy beach, swimming pool, diving, snorkelling, kayaking, mountain bikes, birdwatching and wildlife excursions.

L-AL Beaches and Dreams, Sittee Point, T/F523-7078, www.beachesanddreams.com. 4 extremely well-furnished beachfront rooms. Room rate includes full breakfast, Dangriga transfer, use of bikes and kayaks.

Border essentials: Belize-Guatemala

Punta Gorda-Puerto Barrios

Crossing to Guatemala A boat service goes to Puerto Barrios in Guatemala from Punta Gorda. **Requena Water Taxi**, 12 Front St, T722-2070, has fast skiffs daily 0900 leaving from main dock in front of immigration, returning at 0200, one hour. **Pichilingo** leaves daily at 1600, returning from Puerto Barrios at 1000. **Pichilingo** also provides a service to **Lívingston** on Tue and Fri, leaving 1000 and returning from Lívingston at 0700. Both companies provide services to Puerto Barrios and Lívingston by request. **Requena** also offers charters and trips to the cayes as well. Bike and motorbike transportation has been reported as difficult. Officials in Lívingston do not have the authority to issue vehicle permits to anything other than water craft.

Exchange There are money changers at both ends of the crossing but it is better to buy quetzales in Guatemala. Neither side changes TCs. Try to get rid of any Bz$ in Belize.

Transport can sometimes be arranged from **Pueblo Viejo** along a road to Jalacté (also reached by trail from Blue Creek and Aguacate), from where it is a 30-min hike to Santa Cruz del Petén (often muddy). From here trucks can be caught to San Luis on the highway near Poptún.

Belizean immigration Exit stamps for people and vehicles can be obtained at the Customs House next to the pier on Front St. Be there at least 1 hr before departure, or 2 hrs if loading a motorcycle. PACT exit tax payable, see page 662.

Guatemalan consulate If you need a visa it must be obtained in Belize City. Tourist cards are available in Puerto Barrios.

Although locals cross to shop in Guatemala, it is illegal to cross this southern land border between Guatemala and Belize. There is no Guatemalan government presence and entry stamps cannot be obtained. The area has been the focal point for border disputes locally and visitors to the area should take local advice before travelling. Maps are inaccurate.

AL Lillpat Resort, T/F520-7019, lillpat@btl.net. 4 a/c rooms on the Sittee River, pool, restaurant, bar, very convenient for Cockscomb, birdwatching and fishing. Specializes in river and sea fishing.

AL-A Hopkins Inn, on beach south of centre, T523-7013, www.hopkinsinn.com. White cabins with private bathroom, very clean and friendly, German spoken. Room rates include breakfast, owners are knowledgeable about the area.

AL-E Toucan Sittee, T523-7039, www.toucansittee.info. 400 yds down river from **Glover's**. Run by Neville Collins, lovely setting, rooms with screens and fans, bunkhouse, hot water, or fully-equipped riverside apartments, grow most of their own fruit and veg, also over 50 medicinal plants.

C-D Sandy Beach Lodge, 20-min walk south of village, T522-2023, T523-7006. A women's cooperative, run by 14 women who work in shifts, arrive before 1900 or they will have gone home, 6 thatched beachside *cabañas*, quiet, safe, friendly, clean.

C-D Tipple Tree Beya Inn, just before **Sandy Beach Lodge**, T20-7006, www.tippletree.com. English/American run, 4 rooms in a wooden house and small cabin apartment, camping possible.

E Swinging Armadillos Bunk House, on the pier, T522-2016. 5 rooms, outdoor shower, seafood restaurant, bar, usually the best in the village.

E-F Glover's Guest House, on river bank, T802-2505. 5 rooms, restaurant, camping, jungle river trips, run by Lomont-Cabral family and starting point for the boat to their **North East Caye** (see below). Price per person.

Glover's Reef *p702*

Glover's Reef Atoll

LL-AL Manta Reef Resort, Glover's Reef Atoll, 3 Eyre St, Belize City, T223-1895, F223-2764. 9 individual cabins with full facilities, in perfect desert island setting, 1-week packages available only, reservations essential, excellent diving and fishing, good food (E6 photo lab available). Highly recommended.

North East Caye

B-E Glover's Atoll Resort, T614-7177, www.glovers.com.bz. No reservations needed, 8 cabins with wood-burning stoves, US$99-249 per person per week (ranging from camping to cabins; nightly prices also). Weekly rates include round-trip transportation from Sittee River. Occasional rice and seafood meals, bring food, some groceries and drinking water (US$1.50 a gallon) available. A new beach was created by Hurricane Mitch in 2002. Best to bring everything you will need including food, torch, soap, candles, sun screen, toilet paper, alcoholic and/or soft drinks, allowing for possible supply shortages or bad weather when boats stop running. Facilities are simple, don't expect luxury and guests are invited to help out occasionally.

Placencia *p702, map p703*

Rooms may be hard to find in the afternoon (after arrival of the bus from Dangriga). Usually several houses to rent, US$200-550 per week, see the ads at the tourist information centre.

LL The Inn at Robert's Grove, north of the air strip and Rum Point Inn, T523-3565, www.robertsgrove.com. A luxury resort with two pools, massage service, sail boats and roof top Jacuzzis set on a white sand beach shaded by the odd palm tree. Rooms are spacious, comfortable and quiet and the restaurant serves good, filling food. Meal plans and full packages are available. Entertainment and tours, including PADI diving from its own marina, are organized. Friendly bar staff.

LL Turtle Inn, on beach close to airstrip, T523-3244, www.turtleinn.com. Completely destroyed by Hurricane Iris, owner Francis Ford Coppola rebuilt this impressive resort in local and Balinse style set around a circular pool with restaurant and spa.

L-AL Easy Living Apartments, T523-3524, www.easyliving.bz. Well-appointed roomy apartments with space for up to 4, at which point they represent good value – TV, fully equipped kitchen, good location at the centre of town, on the sidewalk.

AL Serenity Resort, just north of Rum Point Inn, just north of the airstrip, T523-3232. 10 a/c hotel rooms, 12 cottages, good beach, 2 bars – 1 on Placencia Lagoon – and restaurant.

AL Ranguana Lodge, T/F523-3112, www.ranguanabelize.com. Wooden cabins on the ocean, very clean.

AL-B Cozy Corner, on the beach, close to **Serenade and Yellow House**, T523-3450, cozycorner@btl.net. 10 rooms with fridge, TV, some cheaper rooms without a/c and good restaurant (Tue-Sun) in front.

AL-B Trade Winds Hotel, South Point, T523-3122, trdewndpla@btl.net. 9 very colourful cabins in a spacious private plot on the south beach, completely rebuilt after Hurricane Iris.

AL-B Serenade Guest House, T523-3380, hotelserande@btl.net. Spacious and airy rooms, all with a/c and private bath. Upstairs rooms are more expensive. The owners are very welcoming. Restaurant next door. Parking available.

A-B Dianni's Guest House, T/F523-3159, diannis@btl.net. Spacious rooms with a/c, most with 1 double and single bed. Fridge, coffee and tea provided, nice balcony with hammocks, internet available.

A-C Seaspray, T/F523-3148, www.seasprayhotel.com. Very nice, comfortable and friendly. Good-value rooms across a range of prices from beachside *cabañas* to small doubles in original building. Popular **De Tatch** restaurant on the beach, see Eating.

B-D Paradise Vacation Hotel, down by the piers, T523-3179, www.paradisevacationbelize.com. 12 rooms with private baths and 4 rooms with shared.

C Deb and Dave's Last Resort, on the road, T523-3207, www.toadaladventure.com. 4 very good budget rooms with shared bathroom, hot water, kayak and bike rental. Walk-ins only, no advance reservations. Also runs tours in local area.

C The Yellow House, T523-3481, www.ctbelize.com. A bright yellow building, directly behind Serenade, with 4 very comfortable rooms with communicating doors, so excellent for a family or group of friends. Front rooms have microwave, coffee machines and fridges. Excellent value. Also runs**B-C Garden Cabanas**, www.garden cabanas.com, and**A-C Mahogany Beach**.

D **Lydia's Guesthouse**, T523-3117, lydias@btl.net. 8 double rooms with shared toilet and shower, situated across the sidewalk on a quiet part of the beach. Kitchen facilities. Simple, but very chilled. Recommended.

D **Omar's Guest House**, on the sidewalk, T609-3135. Has rooms above his diner which could be a good choice.

E **Lucille's Rooms**. Run by Lucille and her family, private bath, fans, meals by arrangement.

Camping

Camping is possible on the beach or under the coconut palms.

Around Placencia *p703*

Seine Bight

LL **Luba Hati**, T523-3402, www.lubahati.com. A little bit of Tuscany flavoured with Belizean spices, in a positively peaceful setting, each room uniquely decorated and with a/c.

LL **Rum Point Inn**, T523-3239 (Toll free T1-888-235-4031, www.rumpoint.com. Owned by an American entomologist, well-respected dive shop, very spacious units (some with a/c) and some unusual architecture, swimming pool and library.

Maya Beach

L **Green Parrot Beach Houses**, T523-2488, www.greenparrot-belize.com. Beach houses on stilts, all with sea view, sleep up to 5, kitchenettes, open-air restaurant and bar.

L **Singing Sands Inn**, T/F520-8022, www.singingsands.com. 6 thatched cabins with bathrooms, hot water, fans, ocean view, snorkelling in front of the resort at False Caye, restaurant and bar on the beach.

L-AL **Maya Breeze Inn**, T523-8012, www.mayabreezeinn.com. 4 cottages on the beach, 2 with a/c, restaurant across the road.

AL-A **Barnacle Bill's**, T523-8010, www.goto belize.com/barnacle. 2 *cabañas*, complete with queen-sized bed, sleeper/sofa in the living/ dining area, full kitchen, private bath and fans.

Monkey River

Accommodation at or near Monkey River is under renovation after the destruction in the village caused by Hurricane Iris.

Mango Creek/Independence

A-B **Hello Hotel**, Independence, T503-2028, hotelhello@yahoo.com. Run by Antonio Zabaneh at the shop where the bus stops, clean, comfortable, helpful.

C-D **Ursella's Guest House**, T503-2062, 9 simple rooms with shared or private bath, TV.

F **Hotel above People's Restaurant**. Very basic, ask to borrow a fan and lamp, shower is a bucket of water in a cabin, basic restaurant.

Cayes near Placencia *p704*

L **Frank's Caye**, reservations through Serenade Guesthouse, T523-3380, www.belizecayes.com. 3 *cabañas* with private baths, restaurant and bar.

L-AL **Ranguana Caye**, reservations through Robert's Grove,T523-3565, www.roberts grove.com. 3 *cabañas*, each with a double and single bed and gas stove. Private hot showers and toilet in separate building. BBQ pits are provided so bring food, but meals are also available at US$35 per person.

Camping

Lime Caye (tent camping – crowded). Very good fishing at certain times of the year (contact local guides for information).

Cockscomb Basin Wildlife Sanctuary and around *p704*

There is usually space on arrival, but to guarantee accommodation, travellers can contact the **Belize Audubon Society**, see page 662.

L **Mama Noots Backabush Resort**, T422-3666, www.mamanoots.com. Electricity from solar, wind and hydro system, most fruits and vegetables grown organically on the grounds of the resort. 6 double rooms and 1 duplex thatched *cabaña* that sleeps up to 6. Private baths.

A-E **Mejen Tz'il's Lodge**, T520-3032; lsaqui@btl.net. Owned by Liberato and Araceli Saqui, screened rooms with double beds or bunk beds, verandah, private hot water showers and toilets in a separate building, restaurant on premises.

B-E Park HQ. New purpose-built cabins, and dormitories (**D-E** per person). Drinking water is available, also earth toilets, but you must bring all your own food, drinks, matches, torch, sheet sleeping bag, eating utensils and mosquito repellent. There is a picnic area, but the nearest shop is at Maya Centre.
D Nu'uk Che'il Cottages, Maya Centre, T520-3033, nuukcheil@btl.net. Simple thatched rooms in a garden next to the forest, take the botanical trail and learn about Maya medicine from Aurora Saqui; Ernesto, her husband, can arrange transport to the Park HQ.

Punta Gorda *p705*
AL Traveller's Inn, near **Southern Transport** bus terminal, T702-2568. Including breakfast, bath, a/c, restaurant, bar, clinical atmosphere, information on tours.
AL-B Punta Caliente, 108 José María Nuñez St, T605-0377, puntacal@btl.net. Private bath, hot water, fan and cable TV, good value, restaurant.
AL-C Tate's Guest House, 34 José María Nuñez St, T722-0147. A/c, cheaper without, clean, hot water, bathroom, TV, parking, friendly, breakfast before 0730, laundry.
AL-C Circle C, 117 West St, 1 block from bus terminal. 7 rooms. OK.
B Sea Front Inn, 4 Front St, T722-2300, www.seafrontinn.com. 14 rooms with private bath, hot water, a/c and TV, restaurant with great views and international menu. **Maya Island Air** and **Tropic Air** agents.
C Mahung's Inn, corner North and Main St, T722-2044, mahungsinn@hotmail.com. Reasonable, private bath, cable TV, also rents mountain bikes, US$5 per day.
C-D Nature's Way Guest House, 65 Front St, T702-2119, thfec@btl.net. Clean, friendly, good breakfast, camping gear for rent. Recommended.
C-D Pallavi, 19 Main St, T702-2414, gracemcp@hotmail.com. Tidy, balcony, clean, friendly.
C-D St Charles Inn, 23 King St, T722-2149, stcharlespg@btl.net. With or without bath, spacious rooms, fan, cable TV, good.
D-E Wahima, on waterfront, T722-2542. Clean and safe, all rooms with private bath, owner Max is local school teacher, friendly and informative. Also rents kitchenettes per week.
F Airport Hotel. Price per person, quiet, OK, communal bathrooms, clean, spartan. You can flag down the 0500 bus to Belize in front of **Wahima** or **Pallavi**, buy a ticket the night before to get a reserved seat.

San Pedro Columbia *p706*
L Fallen Stones Butterfly Ranch, 3 miles beyond the village, up some very steep, rocky hills, leave messages at Texaco in Punta Gorda, T722-2167, www.fallenstones.co.uk. Excellent site and ideal for visiting the nearby ruins of Lubaantun. Owned by an Englishman, working butterfly farm exporting pupae. Price includes tax, service and breakfast, jungle tours, laundry, airport transfers.
C-D Dem Dats Doin, Alfredo and Yvonne Villaria, T722-2470, demdatsdoin@btl.net (see Punta Gorda, Tourist offices, page 705).
E Guesthouse. Dormitory beds. You can buy drinks and get breakfast at the large yellow stone house.

Blue Creek *p685*
There's very basic accommodation at the house at the beginning of the trail to the caves. Blue Creek is one of the villages participating in the **TEA guesthouse** programme, see page 713.
E Roots and Herbs, halfway to Blue Creek; turn left at **Jim's Pool Room** in Manfredi Village, then continue about 5 miles. A couple of simple cabins with mosquito nets, Pablo is an excellent guide, good food. Price per person.

San Antonio *p707*
D Bol's Hilltop Hotel. Showers, toilets, meals extra, clean.

Eating

Dangriga *p701*
Starlight near **Cameleon**, towards bridge. Chinese food.
Ritchie's Dinette, on main street north of police station. Creole and Spanish food, simple, large portions, popular for breakfast.
Riverside Café, south bank of river, just east of main road. Nicer inside than it looks, good breakfast, good service and food, best place to get information on boats to Tobacco Caye.

Guesthouse Programme

An interesting alternative to Punta Gorda is to stay in indigenous villages as part of the Guesthouse Programme is run by villagers and the non-competitive cooperative the Toledo Ecotourism Association (TEA).

A number of villages have joined together and developed a visitor scheme which benefits all the villages. Each has built a well-appointed guesthouse, simple, but clean, with sheets, towels, mosquito nets, oil lamps, ablutions block, and a total of eight bunks in two four-bunk rooms. Visitors stay here, but eat in the villagers' houses on strict rotation, so each household gains equal income and only has to put up with intrusive foreigners for short periods. Villages taking part include **San Miguel**, **San José** (Hawaii), **Laguna**, **Blue Creek**, **Santa Elena**, and **Pueblo Viejo** are isolated villages beyond the Dump towards San Ignacio. **Medina Bank** is more accessible as its location is just off the southern highway. **Barranco** is a Garífuna village south of Punta Gorda, accessible by boat or poor road.

Local attractions include: San Antonio waterfall; caves at San José (Hawaii); Uxbenka ruins and caves 2½-hour walk from San Antonio (turn right just before Santa Cruz), with commanding view from ruins; and Río Blanco waterfalls, 10 minutes beyond the village. For Uxbenka and Santa Cruz, take Chun's bus on Wednesday and Saturday at 1300 from San Antonio and arrange return time. Do not take Cho's bus, it does not return. Many village men and children speak English. The local indigenous people have been relearning old dances from elderly villagers and are trying to rescue the art of making and playing the harp, violin and guitar for evening entertainments. Home-made excursions are arranged; these vary from a four-hour trek looking at medicinal plants and explaining agriculture, to seeing very out-of-the-way sights like caves and creeks (take boots, even in dry season). The village tour could be skipped, although by doing this on your own you deprive the 'guide' of income.

One night for two people, with a forest tour and two meals, costs nearly US$50 but all profits go direct to the villages, with no outsiders as middlemen. Dormitory accommodation is US$9 per person. Gross profits from the guesthouse are ploughed back into the villages' infrastructure, schools and other community projects. The scheme is co-ordinated by the TEA Office at the Tourist Information Center (BTB Building) in Punta Gorda, T722-2096, www.southernbelize.com/tea.html. The staff provide information about the participating villages, the key attractions, tours and courses, and take bookings and arrange transport. You may have to arrange your own transport, or a vehicle can be hired. Staff at the TEA will be able to advise. Hitching is not recommended as some villages are remote and may have only one car a day visiting. The 'market' buses leave Punta Gorda every Monday, Wednesday, Friday and Saturday at 1130 or 1200 depending on the village. They come from the villages on the morning of the same days departing early at 0400, 0500 or 0600, again depending on the village.

The **Homestay Programme** is a similar scheme that involves actually staying with the family in their house. Several villages in the area participate. As you are living with the family, privacy is generally less and the experience more intense. Details can be discussed with **Dem Dats Doin** in Punta Gorda, who will also help you arrange transport if required. Both programmes are a unique way to explore the Maya villages; you are unlikely to find such an experience elsewhere.

Ruby's Rainforest Café, past the Riverside Café, on the beach. Open sporadically but good food. Be prepared for Ruby – she's quite a character, very friendly, and you'll get the full family history. No good if in a hurry!

South of Dangriga *p702*

Ronnie's Kitchen, turquoise house on stilts north of the police station in Hopkins (follow the road left from the bus stop). Excellent food, friendly service, open 0630-2100, lunch includes burritos and chicken, Ronnie also runs a library and gives good local advice.

Placencia *p702, map p703*

Merlene's, in the Bakeder area south of the Placencia Village dock. One of the best, opens early for good breakfast.

Trattoria, directly on the beach just north of **Tipsy Tuna Sports Bar**. The only Italian restaurant in the village. Closed Sun.

BJ's Restaurant, near Olga's Market, see map. Good fried chicken and traditional Creole food. Recently owners Percy and Betty have begun to experiment and now they offer good Asian stir-fries and pizza – inexpensive and popular with locals.

Cozy Corner, on the beach. Very nice beachside bar and restaurant. Good, mid-priced barbecue and grilled seafood.

De Tatch Café, just before the north end of the sidewalk. Said to be the the best coffee in town, certainly is hugely popular with excellent seafood specials at night and snappy service; a winner.

The Garden Brew Coffee House, in a little garden next to **Wallen's Hardware**. Nice coffee and home made muffins.

Pickled Parrot Bar and Grill, close to **Wallen's Hardware**. Good pizza, chicken and seafood. Closed Sun.

Purple Space Monkey Village, on main road just west of the Placencia docks. Very good US-style breakfasts and burgers for lunch, excellent espresso, cappuccino and lattes, dinner menu features local seafood, internet.

Daisy's, sidewalk, close to **De Tatch**. Cheap meals and good ice cream.

John the Bakerman, follow the signs (see map. Freshly baked bread and cinnamon buns each afternoon at 1800 (takeaway only).

Miss Lilly's, set back from the sidewalk, opposite **Omar's Diner**. Lunch only, authentic Creole food cooked by Miss Lilly, a village elder and local comedienne.

Omar's Diner, on the sidewalk. Fish, meat, burgers, burritos, good cheap breakfasts.

Tutti-frutti Ice Cream Parlour, just before the Shell gas station on the opposite side of the main road. Great Italian ice cream, made by real Italians!

Wendy's Creole Restaurant and Bar, close to the gas station. Good food but service can be very slow so leave plenty of time if you're meeting transport.

Excursions from Placencia *p703*

Goyo's Inn/Restaurant Independence, Mango Creek. Family-owned, good food.

Lola's Café and Art Gallery, sign at south end of Seine Bight. For an entertaining evening with dinner, run by local artist Lola Delgado.

White house with green shutters, Mango Creek, behind **People's**. Better than at **People's**. Book 2 hrs in advance if possible.

Punta Gorda *p705*

Several cafés around the market area with good views over the bay.

Bobby's Main St. Serves excellent fish dishes, Bobby is a local fishing guide and arranges trips.

Earth Runnings Café and Bukut Bar, Main Middle St. Also with tourist info.

Emery Restaurant, Main St. Local dishes and seafood, popular with locals, reasonable prices, friendly.

Gomier's, behind the **Sea Front Inn**. For vegan meals and soya products.

Marenco's Ice cream Parlour, Main St. Serves good ice cream and food as well.

San Antonio *p707*

Theodora or **Clara**, next to hotel. Both do meals with advance notice. Local specialities are *jippy jappa/kula*, from a local plant, and chicken *caldo*.

Bars and clubs

Dangriga *p701*

Listen for local music 'Punta Rock', a Garífuna/ African-based Carib sound, now popular throughout Belize. **Local Motion Disco**, next to Cameleon, open weekends, punta rock, reggae, live music. **Riviera Club**, between bridge and **Bank of Nova Scotia**, popular nightclub at weekends (see Eating, above). Home-made instruments are a Garífuna speciality, especially drums. Studios can be visited.

Placencia *p702, map p703*
Tipsy Tuna Sports Bar, popular sports and karaoke beachside bar, from 1900. **Barefoot Beach Bar** at Tipsy Tuna is a very popular joint on the beach with happy hour 1700-1800. Closed Mon.

Festivals and events

Dangriga *p701*
18-19 Nov Garífuna, or Settlement Day, re-enacting the landing of the Black Caribs in 1823, having fled a failed rebellion in Honduras. Dancing all night and next day; very popular. Booking is advisable for accommodation. Private homes rent rooms, though. At this time, boats from Puerto Barrios to Punta Gorda (see below) tend to be full, but launches take passengers for US$10 per person.

Activities and tours

South to Dangriga *p700*
Tour operators
There's a wide variety of day and overnight excursions, from US$30 per boat holding 6-8 people. Contact Kevin Andrewin of **Manatee Tour Guides Association** on arrival. **Community phone**, T02-12031, minimum 48 hrs notice is advisable, ask for Alice or Josephine.

Dangriga *p701*
Diving
Dangriga Dive Centre, T522-3262. Derek Jones arranges fabulous trips to the cayes.

Tour operators
Pelican Beach Hotel runs tours to Cockscomb Basin, Gales Point and citrus factories. **Rosado's Tours**, T522-2119, 35 Lemon St Government Services.
Treasured Travels, 64 Commerce St, T522-2578, is very helpful, run by Diane.

South of Dangriga *p702*
Diving
Second Nature Divers, T/F523-7038, divers@btl.net, or enquire at **Hamanasi**. English owned, good guides and equipment, recommended spot to visit is Sharks' Cave.

Glover's Reef *p702*
Diving
Off The Wall Dive Center, Dangriga, Belize, T614-6348, www.offthewallbelize.com, offers dive courses. Friendly owners Jim and Kendra Schofield offer packages that include transport, accommodation, meals and diving.

Placencia *p702, map p703*
Diving and snorkelling
Full PADI scuba diving courses are available at most local dive shops, around US$350. Some dive operators listed below base themselves out of high-end resorts. Of the in-town operators **Seahorse, Advance** and **Splash** enjoyed solid reputations. However, environmental standards and genuine concern for the reef is somewhat lacking – something that could be improved with a little 'customer encouragement'. Prices are from about US$70, plus 9% sales tax, for 2-tank dives, US$105 to outer reef (gear extra). Seahorse Dive Shop, T523-3166, www.belizescuba.com, ask for Brian Young. Good selection of gear, including underwater photography equipment. **Advance Dive Centre**, T523-74037, advancdive@btl.net, owned by Vance Cabral, good solid operation. **Rum Point Dive Shop**, T523-3239, www.rumpointinn.com, **Splash**, T/F523-3345, splashbelize@yahoo.com. Owners helpful – specialize in dive training and courses. **Naudi Dive Shop**, T523-3595, www.nauticalinn belize.com, and **Robert's Grove Dive Shop**, T523-3565, www.roberts grove.com. **Ocean Motion Guide Service**, T523-3363, www.oceanmotionplacencia.com, is a reputable snorkelling tour operator. Snorkel trips generally cost US$45-50, including gear. Whale shark snorkelling, US$65. There is a whale shark and snorkelling fee of US$15 in operation from 1 Mar-3 Jul charged by Friends of Nature.

Fishing
Fishing, especially saltwater fly-fishing, is excellent in the Placencia area, with

recognized world-class permit fishing. Flats are hard-bottomed and good for wade fishing. Reputable licensed guides and tour operators include **Egbert Cabral**, T523-3132, info@destinationsbelize.com, **Kurt Godfrey**, T523-3277, and **Earl Godfrey**, T523-3433, lgodfrey@btl.net. **Destinations Belize**, offers combination cayes camping and fishing/snorkelling trips, plus whale shark interaction tours, T523-4018, www.destinationsbelize.com. **Bruce Leslie**, from **Tutti-frutti**, T523-3370. Rates for a full day of light tackle and fly fishing, including lunch, average US$275, maximum 2 anglers per boat for fly-fishing.

Kayaking

Toadal Adventures, T/F523-3207, www.toadaladventure.com, is a reputable tour operator for multi-day kayaking trips to cayes and Monkey River.

Sailing

Next Wave Sailing, T523-3391, www.nextwavesailing.com. Sunset cruises, US$45 and day sails, US$80. Booking out of **Purple Monkey**.

Cockscomb Basin Wildlife Sanctuary and around *p704*

Tour operators

The **Belize Audobon Society**, see page 662, runs the reserve. The most knowledgeable guides to the reserve live in Maya Centre; contact **Julio Saqui**, of **Julio's Cultural Tours**, T608-4992, www.cockscombmayatours.com, who runs the village shop and can look after any extra luggage. At **Greg's Bar**, on the main road in the middle of the village, you can contact **Greg Sho**, an experienced river and mountain guide who can arrange kayak trips.

Full-day Mopan Mayan cultural tours of Maya Centre Village are available including visits to workshops on traditional Mayan cooking, crafts, language and natural tropical medicines. Contact **Liberato** or **Araceli Saqui** at Maya Centre Village. Tour operators in Placencia run day trips for US$65.

Punta Gorda *p705*

Tour operators

Green Iguana Eco Adventures, T722-2475, provides a wide range of tours and services. **Tide Tours**, Main St, T722-2129, www.tidetours.org, organizes eco-tours.

Transport

South to Dangriga *p700*

Boat Gales Point can be reached by inland waterways from **Belize City**, but buses have largely superseded boat services.

Bus At least 2 daily **Southern Transport** buses run between **Belize City** and Dangriga on the coastal road.

Dangriga *p701*

Air **Maya Island Air** and **Tropic Air**, T522-2129, from **Belize City** several daily, also from **Punta Gorda** via Placencia. Tickets from the airstrip, or **Pelican Beach Hotel**.

Boat A fast skiff leaves 0900 (be there at 0800) on Sat for Puerto Cortés, Honduras, US$50. The service is irregular. When it runs it departs from north bank of river by bridge, T522-3227, ask for Carlos. Check in advance procedures for exit formalities. You can hire a boat for around US$25 per person in a party to Belize City, enquire locally.

Bus From **Belize City**, **Southern Transport**, Magazine St, several daily from 0800, returning daily from 0530, US$5, 3½-4 hrs (bus passes entrance to the Blue Hole National Park); also via Coastal Highway, 2 hrs. Bus to **Placencia** daily at 1200 and 1700, 3 hrs, US$5, via Hopkins and Sittee River, US$4; to **Belmopan**, 2½ hrs, US$4.50. The **Southern Transport** bus terminal is at the junction at the south end of town.

South of Dangriga *p702*

Bus From Dangriga or Placencia, **Southern Transport** around 0700, 1500, 1530 and 1800, which travel on to Placencia or Dangriga depending where you are going. **James Bus** from Dangriga to Placencia around 1130 and 1700, Placencia to Dangriga around 0600 and 1400.

To North East Caye, 4 daily **Southern Transport** buses (T522-2160) from **Dangriga** to Sittee River and **Glover's Guest House** at Sittee River Village (see above). Also 3 daily buses from **Placencia**. Alternatively, take any bus going south to the Sittee junction and take a ride to the guesthouse. If you get lost, phone ahead for help. At 0800 on Sun a sailing boat leaves for the reef, 5 hrs, US$20 per person 1 way (price included in accommodation package), returns Sat. At other times, charter a boat (skiff or sailing boat, US$200 1 way, up to 8 people, diesel sloop US$350, up to 30 people).

Placencia *p702, map p703*
Air Placencia has its own airstrip. **Maya Island Air** and **Tropic Air** (T523-3410) fly several times a day to **Belize City** (international and municipal), also to **Dangriga**, **Punta Gorda**.

Boat The **Hokey Pokey Water Taxi**, T523-2376, leaves from the gas station behind the **M'nM** store, across the lagoon to **Independence/Mango Creek** at 0630, 0730, 0800, 1430 and 1630, 15 mins, US$5. Returning 0630, 0730, 0830, 1100, 1215, 1430, 1630, 1730. From here buses depart for Punta Gorda and Belize City, see below.

The **Gulf Cruza**, T523-4045, provides a regular weekly service linking Placencia and Puerto Cortés in Honduras. The journey can be quite choppy so take motion sickness pills if required. From Placencia the boat leaves the dock near the petrol station at 0930 every Fri, passing Big Creek at to complete immigration formalities. It arrives in Puerto Cortés at 1200, US$50. Buy tickets in the Tourism Center.

Return service leaves Puerto Cortés on Mon at 1100 arriving 1330.

Bus **Placencia Peninsula Shuttle**, T607-2711, runs from the Placencia dock to the **Zeboz Hotel** 5 times daily each way, US$2.50-5. See the tourist office for schedule. Buses to **Dangriga** direct at 0600, 0630, 1400, 3 hrs, US$5. Express, US$6. Direct busess to **Punta Gorda**, from Placencia with **Southern Transport** or **James Buses**. Alternatively take the **Hokey Pokey Water Taxi**, see Boat above, to catch the **James Bus Line** buses from Independence Village, at 0930, 1045, 1500, 1630, 1645, 1½-2½ hrs. For buses to **Dangriga**, 1 hr, **Belmopan**, 2½ hrs and **Belize City**, 3½ hrs, also catch the boat to Independence. Buses leave at 0715, 0815, 1015, 1415 and 1645. Check times and fares at the Placencia tourist centre at the dock next to the Shell gas station.

Excursions from Placencia *p703*
Bus Belize City-Mango Creek, **Southern Transport**, or the less regular **James Bus Service**, from Pound Yard Bridge, US$8.50. Mango Creek-Belmopan, US$10.50.

Boat Regular service from Mango Creek to **Puerto Cortés**, Honduras, departs around 1100, but arrive earlier to be safe; ask Antonio Zabaneh at his store, T503-2428, to check times, US$50 1 way, 7-9 hrs. Remember to get an exit stamp, normally obtainable at the police station in Mango Creek if you arrive with enough time. See Placencia above for details.

Cockscomb Basin Wildlife Sanctuary and around *p704*
Bus Can be booked at time of reservation, or locals will drive you from Maya Centre, otherwise it is a 6-mile, uphill walk from Maya Centre to the reserve – allow 2 hrs for the walk to Maya Centre. If you leave early in the morning going either way you are likely to see quite a lot of wildlife. All buses going south from **Dangriga** go through Maya Centre, 40 mins, US$4; and north from Placencia, return buses from 0700 onwards to Dangriga. If walking, leave all unwanted gear in Dangriga in view of the uphill stretch from Maya Centre, or you can leave luggage at Julio's little store in Maya Centre for a daily fee.

Taxi A taxi from **Dangriga** will cost about US$50, it is not difficult to hitch back.

Punta Gorda *p705*
Air Airstrip 5 mins' walk east of town. Daily flights with **Maya Island Air** and **Tropic Air**, T722-2008, from Dangriga, Placencia, Belize City (both airports). Tickets at **Alistair King's** (at Texaco station), **Bob Pennell's** hardware store on Main St, the **Sea Front Inn** on Front St or the offices alongside the airstrip. Advance reservations recommended.

Bus From **Belize City**, 8 hrs (longer in heavy rain), US$11, **Southern Transport**, Mon-Sat 0600, 0800, 1200 and 1400, Sun 0800, 1200 and 1400, ticket can be bought day before, beautiful but rough ride. **Southern Transport** bus to Belize City Mon-Sat 0300, 0400, 0500 and 1000, Sun 0400, 0500 and 1000 stopping at **Mango**

Creek, **Dangriga** and **Belmopan** (schedules change on holidays). **Southern Transport** terminal is at very south end of José María Núñez St; lobby of **Traveller's Inn** serves as ticket office. **James** bus line to Belize City daily, 0600, 0800, 1100 and 1200; departs from government buildings near ferry dock. **James** bus returns from Belize City daily, leaving at 0500, 0900, 1000, 1500. To **San Antonio** from square, see below for schedules; buses to **San Pedro Columbia** and San José, Wed and Sat 1200, return Wed and Sat morning. Buses can be delayed in the wet season. For the latest information on schedules contact the Tourist Information Centre or **Dem Dats Doin** at the pier by the Customs House.

San Antonio *p707*
Bus and car From **Punta Gorda**, 1-1½ hrs, US$1.50, Mon, Wed, Fri, Sat 1230, from west side of Central Park, also 1200 on Wed and Sat, continuing to **Santa Cruz**, **Santa Elena** and **Pueblo Viejo** (1 hr from San Antonio). Alternatively, hire a pick-up van in **Dangriga**, or get a ride in a truck from the market or rice cooperative's mill in Punta Gorda (1 leaves early afternoon); or go to the road junction at Dump, where the northern branch goes to Independence/Mango Creek, the other to San Antonio; 6 miles, either hitch or walk. Bus from San Antonio to **Punta Gorda**, Mon, Wed, Fri and Sat 0530, also 0500 Wed and Sat (having left Pueblo Viejo at 0400). If going to **Dangriga**, take the 0500, get out at Dump to catch 0530 **Southern Transport** bus going north. This area is full of places to explore and it is well worth hiring a vehicle.

Directory

Dangriga *p701*
Banks Bank of Nova Scotia, MasterCard and Visa, and ATM. **Belize Bank** (Visa cash advances). **Immigration office** South end of Commerce St. **Internet** Val's laundry and **Pelican Beach Hotel**. **Laundry** Val's, Mahogany Rd near Bonefish, also has internet access. **Medical services** New Southern Regional Hospital, T522-2078, dannhis@btl.net. **Post office** Mahogany Rd. **Telephone** BTL office is on the main street.

Placencia *p702*
Banks Atlantic Bank south end of the village witn ATM. Also ATM opposite Wendy's. **Internet** On the main road is **Purple Space Monkey Village**, and **Placencia Office Supplies**, on the main road near the centre. Good machines, fast access. also at De Tatch. **Medical services** Basic medical care available at **Placencia Medical Center**, T223-3292, behind St John's Memorial School on the sidewalk. **Post office** Mon-Fri 0800-1200, 1330-1600. **Telephone** BTL office in the centre where you can make international calls. Payphones here, at the gas station and the ballfield.

Excursions from Placencia *p703*
Banks Belize Bank, Mango Creek/Independence, is open Fri only 0900-1200.

Punta Gorda *p705*
Banks Belize Bank, at one end of the park, will change excess Bz$ for US$ on production of passport and ticket out of the country. They do not change quetzales and charge US$5 for advancing cash against Visa and MasterCard, changes TCs. Mon-Thu 0800-1300, Fri 0800-1630. You can change Bz$ for quetzales at Customs in Punta Gorda (ask for Emilio from **Grace** restaurant) and Puerto Barrios. **Western Union**, is run by Mahung's, corner North and Main St, Mon-Sat 0800-1200, 1330-1700. **Internet** Punta Graphics, acapps@btl.net, round the back of the Texaco station. **Internet** , next door to Sea Front Inn. **Carisha's**, by clock tower. **Laundry** Sony's Laundry Service near airstrip. **Telephone** The BTL office on Main St and King St.

El Salvador

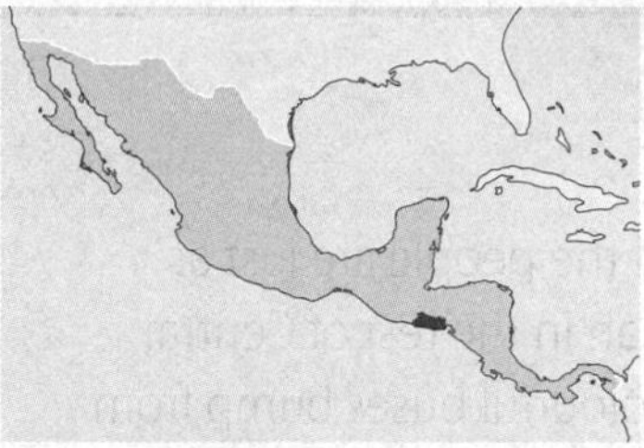

Footprint features

Introduction

El Salvador is a lively country and the people are just as friendly – some say more so – than in the rest of Central America. Ornately painted and colourful buses bump from place to place, just as they do in Guatemala and Honduras, but route numbers on the buses and the chaos of the bus station seem to clash. While the rest of Central America relies on tortillas, Salvadoreans fill them with beans, cheese or meat and call them *pupusas*. Pinning it down is difficult but there's a slightly different feel here from neighbouring countries.

Guidebooks tend to urge caution, but in reality El Salvador is no more dangerous than other Central American countries. During the civil war, Salvadoreans sought refuge abroad; now they're returning, bringing with them a gang culture and other less-than-favourable imports from the United States.

Despite the high rate of gang-related crime, frequent natural disasters and a tourist infrastructure less developed than its neighbouring countries, there are some compelling reasons why you should visit El Salvador: dramatic volcanic landscapes, blue-green lagoons, horizon-filling panoramas and golden beaches. In the northern hills around El Poy and Perquín the trekking is divine, with far-reaching views across staggered horizons. The stark cinder cone of Volcán Izalco offers a challenging but rewarding trek from the slopes of Cerro Verde, while El Impossible National Park provides adventurers with the chance to visit a forest newly accessible to visitors. Along the coast, choose from surfing, diving or simply lazing around and watching the endless display of Pacific sunsets.

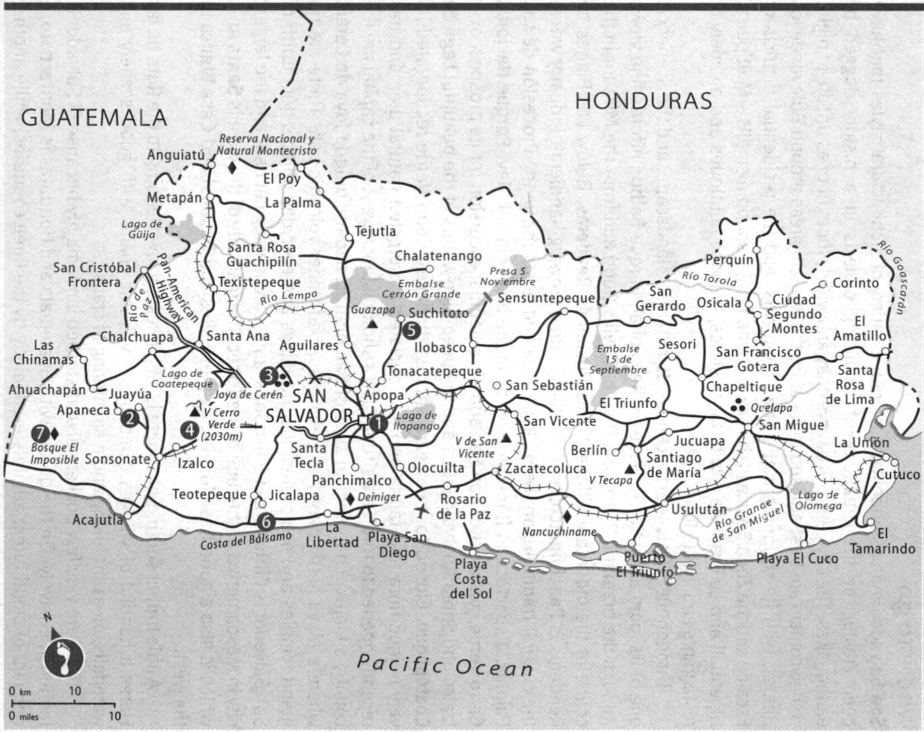

★ Don't miss...

1 **Puerta del Diablo** An easy trip from the capital for impressive views to the coastal lowlands through the Devil's Door, page 735.

2 **Ruta de las Flores** A string of picturesque villages offering stunning volcano vistas, coffee country, arts and crafts, page 745.

3 **Joya de Cerén** Suddenly engulfed by volcanic ash, El Salvador's Pompeii (although much smaller) is fascinating for Maya enthusiasts, page 747.

4 **Cerro Verde** Climb to the volcano summit of Cerro Verde for impressive views and scrabble through the cinder slopes of smoking Izalco nearby, page 747.

5 **Suchitoto** A treasured colonial town, buzzy centre of culture and great for hiking to nearby waterfalls, page 758.

6 **El Zonte, Tunco and Sunzal Beaches** Great spots for surfing and relaxing on black volcanic beaches, page 773.

7 **Reserva Nacional Bosque El Imposible** Hidden in the mountains of the southwest, one of Central America's most secluded and least visited national parks, page 774.

Planning your trip

The smallest of the Central American republics, El Salvador's tiny territory of Pacific beaches, volcanic peaks and mountains holds a population just shy of seven million – equal to Honduras with a land mass just one-sixth that of her northern neighbour. El Salvador's main attractions have not been promoted compared to those in neighbouring countries, and the lack of a developed tourist infrastructure stops many travellers from passing through. But visitors that do take the time, always leave with memories of a friendly people, warm and helpful, and the increasingly rare experience of occasionally being the only traveller in town. The devastating earthquakes of early 2001 literally brought the country to its knees. For the visitor, the most visible sign of damage is the destruction and damage caused to hundreds of the nation's colonial churches.

Life in El Salvador focuses strongly on San Salvador. All roads lead towards the capital with just a few exceptions. Consequently, planning your trip will involve either a visit to San Salvador or at least travelling through it. Fortunately the country is so small that the capital can make a convenient base, thus avoiding the hassle of dragging your bags across the country.

Where to go

San Salvador is a cosmopolitan city with a variety of architectural styles that have been created by the multitude of rebuilding projects in a history dogged by earthquakes. The city centre is always busy and widely thought of as unsafe at night, so newcomers are best advised to head for the western areas around Bulevar de los Héroes, with its shopping malls and restaurants, and the residential districts of Escalón and the Zona Rosa with its newly opened major shopping malls – Multiplaza, Hipermall and La Gran Vía – with fancy stores, branded boutiques and a variety of restaurants and night clubs.

Throughout El Salvador volcanoes dominate the landscape, and the scenery is one of its main attractions. Close to the capital, **Parque Balboa** affords fine views through the dramatic Puerta del Diablo (Devil's Door) and from the Mirador in the centre of the mountain village of **Los Planes de Renderos**. Below Los Planes de Renderos is **Panchimalco**, an old village with a growing handicraft industry where the cultural traditions are being kept alive and hosts the yearly Procesión de Las Palmas, a spectacular floral procession in the beginning of May. **Parque Nacional Cerro Verde**, just west of San Salvador, is a popular excursion for its prospect over Izalco and Santa Ana volcanoes and the deep-blue waters of the beautiful **Lago de Coatepeque**. Closed for two years after earthquakes, Cerro Verde recuperated its very unique flora and fauna and was declared a protected natural area and has recently opened to foreign visitors. Also a short distance west of the capital are the country's main archaeological sites of **San Andrés**, and the unique **Joya de Cerén**, where a Maya settlement has been preserved under volcanic ash. There are no grand temples and sculptures, just dwellings and everyday objects. Just north of San Salvador is **Cihuatán**, El Salvador's largest archaeological park and the largest city in Mesoamerica at the time of the Toltec. The main city of the west is **Santa Ana**, which is also a good base for visiting these sites and **Tazumal** and **Casa Blanca** to the west.

A little further south, **Sonsonate** is an interesting town leading to the **Ruta de las Flores** a handful of villages climbing the volcanic chains with good scenery and waterfalls, pleasant hiking and a smattering of crafts.

There are very few pockets of undisturbed land, mainly because El Salvador is farmed intensively. On the border with Guatemala and Honduras is **Montecristo**, a remnant of cloud forest administered jointly by the three countries, while another such survivor is **El Imposible**, one of the largest national parks in Central America. Just south of El Imposible is the **Barra de Santiago** protected natural area, home to a wide variety of species in the best preserved mangrove in the country.

North of San Salvador, near the Honduran border, are the towns of **La Palma** and **San Ignacio**, where handicrafts of brightly painted wood and other styles are made. Also north, but heading more to the east, is **Suchitoto**, one of the best-preserved colonial towns currently enjoying a revival that takes advantage of the beautiful scenery around Cerrón Grande resevoir. In eastern El Salvador are the cities of **San Vicente** and **San Miguel**, the port of La Unión/Cutuco and many small traditional towns. Those interested in the recent civil war can visit **Perquín**.

The Pacific coast at **La Libertad** is only a short trip from the capital and is a good place to start exploring the Balsam coast to the west, the surfing beaches and to get a feel for the country as a whole. The beaches of the **Costa del Sol** are definitely worth a stop for their long stretches of sand and estuaries. The **Gulf of Fonseca** has islands with secluded beaches which you can explore. In some parts of the country the infrastructure for tourism is quite rudimentary, but in others (such as the capital and nearby places of interest and some of the beach resorts) it is well developed.

Suggested itinerary With so many crossings and borders, the options for travel in and around El Salvador are very flexible. Points of interest are spread throughout the country so there is no natural route to travel. If you want to visit **Reserva Nacional El Imposible**, go for the La Hachadura crossing, drift through **Apaneca** and on to **San Salvador** before heading north to **Suchitoto**. If you're going to Honduras, head to **El Poy** if you want to drop into Santa Rosa de Copán or Gracias, or **Perquín** if you want Gracias or Tegucigalpa. For Nicaragua head to El Amatillo. El Salvador is subtly different to the other Central American nations. While you could shoot through the main highlights in 10 days, hang out for two to three weeks and soak up the nuisances. If you've got the time, you'll enjoy the difference.

When to go

The most pleasant months are from November to January. El Salvador is fortunate in that temperatures are rarely excessively high. The average for San Salvador is 28°C with a variation of only about 3°C. March to May are the hottest months; December to February the coolest. There is one rainy season, from May to October, with April and November being transitional periods; there are only light rains for the rest of the year: the average annual rainfall is about 1830 mm. Highest temperatures and humidity will be found on the coast and in the lowlands, with the heat at its greatest from March to May.

Finding out more

Corporación Salvadoreña de Turismo (Corsatur), Av El Espino 68, Urbanización Madreselva, Santa Elena, San Salvador, T2243-7835, www.elsalvadorturismo.gob.sv. rovides information locally and on the web.
Revue, www.revuemag.com. English-language magazine published in Guatemala, with a section on El Salvador. Look out for sister magazine *Pashalua*, www.pashalua.com, in Spanish with a useful monthly cultural agenda complete with list of events and directory.

Useful websites

www.buscaniguas.com.sv Gives access to lots of useful information.
www.elsalvador.com Site of *El Diario de Hoy*– look in 'Otros Sitios' for tourist info.
www.diariocolatino.com Site of the leftist *Co Latino* newspaper.
www.laprensa.com.sv Site of *La Prensa Gráfica* newspaper.
www.utec.edu.sv Site of Centre for Investigation of El Salvadorean Public Opinion (CIOPS) with information in Spanish on El Salvadorean political and social issues.
www.turismo.com.sv Lists of hotels, restaurants and interesting places to visit.

Language

Spanish is the official language and English is widely understood in business and travel industry-related circles.

Before you travel

Visas and immigration

Every visitor must have a valid passport. No visas are required for European, US, Canadian, Australian or New Zealand nationals. But check before travelling. Overstaying the limit on a tourist card can result in fines. Immigration officials can authorize up to 90 days stay in the country; extensions may be permitted on application to Migración, Centro de Gobierno (see under San Salvador).

Always check at a Salvadorean consulate for any changes to the rules.

El Salvador embassies and consulates

Belgium, Av de Tervuren 171, 2nd floor, 1150 Brussels, T733-0485.
Canada, 209 Kent St K2P 1Z8, Ottawa, Ontario, T613-238-2939, also in Montreal and Vancouver.
Germany, Joachin-Karnatz-Allee 47, 10557, Berlín (Tiergarten), T30-206-4660.
Israel, 4 Avigail, Apto 4, Abu-Tor, Jerusalem, Israel. 93551, T267-28411.
Italy, Via Gualtiero Castellini 13, Scala B int, 3, 00197 Roma, T06-807-6605.
Japan, Kowa 38, Building 803, Nishi Azabu 4 Ch, Tokyo, Japan 106, T33499-4461.
Spain, Calle Serrano 114, 2° Edif Izquierda, 28006 Madrid, T91-562-8002.
UK, Mayfair House, 3rd floor, 39 Great Portland St, London, W1N 7JZ, T020-7436 8282.
US: 1400 Sixteenth N.W. Washington, DC 20036, T202-387-6511; with consulates in several other large cities.
Information on more embassies at **www.rree.gob.sv**

Customs

All personal luggage is allowed in free. Also permitted: 50 cigars or 200 cigarettes, and 2 litres of liquor, two used cameras or a video recorder, one personal stereo, one portable computer and new goods up to US$500 in value (best to have receipts). No restrictions on the import of foreign currency; up to the amount imported and declared may also be exported.

Money

Currency → *US$1=8.75 colones.*

El Salvador adopted the dollar on 1 January 2001 and the national currency is being phased out slowly. All US coinage and notes are widely used, although you may have problems with US$20 bills and above. Most stores still price their products in colones or both currencies – be prepared by learning your 8.75 times table.

Exchange

Do not find yourself in the countryside without cash; traveller's cheques and credit cards are of limited use outside the capital and major cities. See under San Salvador, Banks, regarding exchange of traveller's cheques. Be aware that some banks will want to see your original purchase receipt. Credit cards are widely accepted in the better establishments but transactions are subject to 5% commission and are charged at the official rate. There are international Visa and MasterCard ATMs in El Salvador and larger cities throughout the country. For cash advances on Visa or MasterCard, go to **Aval-Visa** or **Banco de America Central de El Salvador**.

Touching down

Business hours Mon-Fri 0800-1200, 1400-1730; Sat 0800-1200. Banks: Mon-Fri 0900-1700, Sat 0900-1200. Banks are closed 29-30 Jun and 30-31 Dec. Government offices: Mon-Fri 0800-1600.
Official time 6 hrs behind GMT.
Telephone Country code T+503.
Voltage 110 volts, 60 cycles, AC (plugs are American, two flat pin style). Supply is far from stable; important electrical equipment should have surge protectors.
Weights and measures The metric system is used alongside certain local units such as the *vara* (836 mm), *manzana* (7000 sq m) and the *quintal* (45 kg). Some US weights and measures are also used; US gallons are used for gasoline and quarts for oil.

Cost of living and travelling

El Salvador is reasonably priced and two people should be able to travel for US$30 per person per day. However, the range of services open to the foreign tourist is still limited (although growing) so the quality of hotels is not as good as in neighbouring hotels for the same money.

Getting there

Air

From Europe To Miami with any transatlantic carrier, then to San Salvador with **American** or **Taca. Iberia** flies from Barcelona and Madrid via Miami.

From USA and Canada The main connection is with Miami. Other cities with flights to San Salvador are Atlanta, Dallas/Fort Worth, Houston, Los Angeles, Montreal, New Orleans, New York, Orlando, Phoenix, San Diego, San Francisco, Washington and Toronto.

From Central America and Mexico From all capitals and many larger cities in Mexico.

From South America Good connections to Colombia with a few flights to Barranquilla and Bogotá. Also connections with Buenos Aires, Cali, Caracas, Cartagena, Cucutá, Guayaquil, Quito, Lima, Medellín, Santa Marta and Santiago. Some flights via San José or Panama City.

Road

Several border crossings with neighbouring countries. To the west the Pan-American Highway arrives from Guatemala at San Cristóbal through Santa Ana, Las Chinamas (to the south) and La Hachadura, which is handy for El Imposible National Park. To the northwest the crossing is at Anguiatú. Also to the northwest the crossing at El Poy leads to southern Honduras, as does the crossing to the northeast at Perquín and to the east at El Amatillo.

Touching down

Airport information and departure taxes

The international airport is at Comalapa, 62 km southeast of San Salvador off the Coastal Highway, reached by a four-lane toll highway. There is a tourist information desk at the airport which is open sporadically. If closed, you can still pick up some useful leaflets. Taxis and buses provide regular links to the capital. » *For transport details see page 740.*

There is a 13% tax on international air tickets bought in El Salvador and an airport departure tax of US$27 for anyone staying more than six hours. The airport has offices for all the main car rental companies and there are two banks, a tourist office and **Grupo Taca** and **American Airline** offices. Border formalities tend to be relatively brief although searches maybe carried out. Entry and an exit tax of about US$0.65.

Local customs and laws

Most Salvadoreans are friendly and eager to practise English. So far San Salvador has few places where foreigners gather, although **Ximena's Guest House** off Bulevar de Los Héroes is one of the recognized hotels where backpackers meet up.

Tipping In upmarket restaurants: 10%, in others, give small change. Nothing for taxi drivers except when hired for the day; airport porters, *boinas rojas* (red berets), US$1 per bag.

Safety

Traditionally El Salvador has a reputation for violence and crime. In part this is a legacy of many years of civil war although this has been improved through a more active role of the police in later years. The reality is that most people visiting El Salvador return with reports of friendly, open people. Locals will talk incessantly about the country's problems and dangers but few actual examples materialize. Be cautious until you find your own level of comfort and always ask local advice. Statistically El Salvador has the unenviable distinction of having the worst levels of violent crime in the continent. This derives from Salvadoreans gang culture (*maras*) and most visitors will see nothing of this activity. Since March 1996, the army and the civil police (PNC) have been patrolling the highways in an effort to reduce crime. Do not stop for lone gunmen dressed in military-looking uniforms. If renting a car, buy a steering lock. Visitors to San Salvador should seek advice on where is not safe both inside and outside the city.

Getting around

Road

Bus Bus services are good and cover most areas, although the buses are usually crowded. The best time to travel by bus is 0900-1500; avoid Friday and Sunday afternoons. All bus routes have a number, some also have a letter. Strange as it may seem, the system works and the route numbers don't change. Buses are brightly painted, particularly around San Miguel.

Transport is not difficult for the budget traveller as nearly all buses have luggage racks. For bigger bags there is space at the back where a couple of seats have been removed so sit there if you want to stay close to your bag. However, when problems on buses do occur they are usually at the back of the bus. The cheaper alternatives to the **Pullman** buses, that cross to Guatemala and Tegucigalpa from **Puerto Bus** Terminal in San Salvador, have luggage compartments beneath them and the luggage is tagged.

Car At the border, after producing a driving licence and proof of ownership, you are given a *comprobante de ingreso* (which has to be stamped by immigration, customs and quarantine), US$12 to stay for 60 days. You receive a receipt, vehicle permit and vehicle check document. Under no circumstances may the 60 days be extended, even though the driver may have been granted 90 days in the country. Other fees for bringing a car in amount to US$6. A few kilometres from the border the *comprobante* will be checked. When you leave the country a *comprobante de ingreso* must be stamped again and, if you don't intend to return, your permit must be surrendered; total cost US$2. Do not overstay your permitted time unless you wish to be fined. Leaving the country for a few days in order to return for a new permit is not recommended as customs officials are wise to this and may demand bribes. To bring a vehicle in permanently involves a complex procedure costing thousands of dollars.

Maps A good map, both of the republic and the capital, can be obtained from Texaco, Esso, or from the Tourist Institute. **Petrol** costs per US gallon US$2.90 (*sin plomo*, unleaded), US$3.15 (super), US$2.90 (regular), US$2 (diesel). **Roads** are generally good throughout the country, but look out for crops being dried at the roadside or in central reservations. Take care of buses which travel very fast. **Insurance**, third-party, is compulsory in El Salvador and can be arranged at the border (enquire first at consulates). Under the 1996 law, **seat-belts** must be worn; the fine for not doing so is US$34. The fine for **drink-driving** is US$55. Do not attempt to bribe officials.

Sleeping and eating

As the most industrialized of the Central American states El Salvador has an impressive selection of international-standard business hotels in San Salvador. The country also has a good selection of more expensive hotels for those taking weekend breaks from the capital. At the lower end there is no shortage of cheap accommodation, but there is a shortage of **good**, cheap accommodation. If you have the time, shop around, don't check into the first hotel you come to.

If travelling at holiday times book accommodation in advance.

Eating

Pupusas, stuffed tortillas made of corn or ricemeal, are the quintessential Salvadorean dish. They come in several varieties including *chicharrón* (pork crackling), *queso* (cheese) and *revueltas* (mixed), and are typical, tasty and cheap. They are sold at street stalls, and are better there than at restaurants, but beware stomach infection from the accompanying *curtido* (pickled cabbage). On Saturday and Sunday nights people congregate in *pupuserías*. *Pavo* (turkey sandwiches) is common and good, as are *frijoles* (red beans). A *boca* is an appetizer, a small dish of yucca, avocado or chorizo, served with a drink before a meal.

Apart from in San Salvador, restaurants tend to close early, around 2000.

Coffee makes an excellent souvenir and is good value and delicious. **Beers** Suprema is stronger than Pilsener, while Golden Light is a reduced-alcohol beer. *Chaparro* is El Salvador's *chicha* or *agua dulce*. Although it is illegal to sell it, everyone has their source. *Chaparro curado* contains fruit or honey. It is a favourite at election times when alcohol sales are banned. Water bottles are emptied and filled with the clear *chaparro* for illegal swigging on the streets.

Festivals and events

1 Jan New Year's Day.
Mar/Apr Holy Week (3 days, government 10 days).
1 May Labour Day.
10 May Mothers' Day.
First week of Aug Corpus Christi (½ day).
15 Sep (½ day).
2 and **5 Nov** (½ day).
24 Dec (half day) and Christmas Day.

Government offices are also closed on religious holidays. Look in newspapers for details of regional fiestas and other fairs. There are many craft fairs, for example at San Sebastián and San Vicente.

Shopping

The best place to buy arts and crafts is in the village where the items are originally made; **Ilobasco** for ceramics, **San Sebastián** for hammocks and **La Palma** for painted wooden boxes, **Nahuizalco** for baskets and furniture of wicker and jute. If you cannot go there in person, the markets in **San Salvador** (Mercado Ex-Cuartel and Mercado de Artesanía) sell many of these items at a slightly higher prices. Branches of Nahanché have outlets in the major shopping malls with good quality handicrafts from all over the country.

Sport and activities

El Salvador has been a popular **surfing** destination for several decades, from La Libertad heading west. Beyond this there is some diving in the coastal area and volcano lagoons.

National parks provide opportunities for trekking and nature walks in particular at Parque Nacional Cerro Verde close to San Salvador and in the more remote parks of Montecristo and El Imposible.

Health

Gastroenteritic diseases are most common. Visitors should take care over what they eat during the first few weeks, and should drink *agua cristal* (bottled water) or bags of water sold in the street. Precautions against malaria should be taken if a night is spent on the coast, especially in the east of the country. Cases of dengue are on the increase. For diarrhoea, mild dysentery and parasitic infections get *Intestinomicina* tablets from any chemist or large supermarket. For amoebic dysentry take *Secnidal* tablets. El Salvador has one of the best health systems in Central America, so the capital is a good place to sort out problems. You can get a stool sample taken at the **Pro-Familia Hospital** ⓘ *25 Av Norte, near Metro Centro*, which gives you the result in about 12 hours.

Keeping in touch

Internet

Internet cafés are widespread in the capital and continuously popping up in smaller places outside San Salvador. A few hotels will offer online access where internet cafés are not available; in San Salvador most hotels and guesthouses have an internet connection.

Post

Air mail to and from Europe can take up to a month, but is normally about 15 days, US$0.35; from the USA, one week. Certified packets to Europe cost US$9.40, good service; swifter, but more expensive, is **EMS** (US$23 to Europe). Courier services are much quicker, but cost more. The correct address for any letter to the capital is 'San Salvador, El Salvador, Central America'.

Telephone

Since privatisation in 1998, competition has opened up the national telephone network. There is a network of public phones for these companies – all use prepaid phone cards that only work in the company's particular machines. Available at most street corners, super markets, gas stations to small stores they can be used for local and international calls, but make sure the card is from the same company as the public phone, if not you can not use it. The cards come in several denominations (US$3, US$5, US$10, US$25 etc).

There are no local area codes within El Salvador

In April 2005, Salvadorean telephone numbers were made 8 digit. Landlines had a 2 added in front, mobiles a 7. Some hotels will provide direct dialling – by far the easiest option. Dial T114 for **Information** (English spoken) and details of new phone numbers in capital. **Emergency: Police:** 911 (In capital), **Fire service:** T2271-2227, **Red Cross:** T2222-5155, **Hospital:** T2225-4481, **Maternity:** T2271-2555.

Media

Newspapers In San Salvador: *Diario de Hoy* (right wing), www.elsalvador.com, and *La Prensa Gráfica* (centre) every morning including Sunday, www.laprensagrafica.com; both have the most complete listings of cultural events in San Salvador. *Co Latino* is a left-wing newspaper. *El Mundo* in the afternoons except Sunday. US newspapers and magazines available at leading hotels.

Radio Of the 80 radio stations: one is government owned and several are owned by churches.

Television There are four commercial television stations, all with national coverage, and one government-run station with two channels. There are three cable channels, all with CNN news, etc. Luxury and first-class hotels and some guesthouses in San Salvador have cable.

San Salvador

➔ *Colour map 6, C1.* *Population: 1,000,000 (2.3 million including suburbs). Altitude: 680 m.*

Surrounded by a ring of mountains in a valley known as 'Valle de las Hamacas', San Salvador has suffered from both natural and man-made disasters. El Salvador's capital is a bustling cosmopolitan city with a rich blend of architectural styles; modern, yet retaining the charm of the Spanish era with the privilege of being one of the first European cities in the New World. Today, crumbling buildings await renovation and restoration, or the arrival of the next earthquake to deliver the final death knell. As always, some areas speed to recovery, and the shopping malls and wealthy suburbs to the west stand out in the pollution-filled valley. The further northwest you get from the city centre the higher you climb and the cleaner the air becomes.

San Salvador itself does not have many natural attractions, but there are several day trips to nearby volcanoes, crater lakes and beauty spots such as Los Planes de Renderos, the Puerto del Diablo and San Salvador's own volcano, Boquerón, which has a newly inaugurated paved road all the way to the top. While San Salvador is no beauty spot, there are, surprisingly, many green areas and trees planted alongside the streets giving the city a refreshing atmosphere. If you spend a few days in the city and surrounding area you could be pleasantly surprised by how easy it is to get around and how much there is to do. ➺ *For Sleeping, Eating and other listings, see pages 736-744.*

Ins and outs

Getting there The **international airport** (SAL) is at **Comalapa**, 62 km southeast of San Salvador towards Costa del Sol beach, reached by a four-lane, toll highway. Some domestic flights use the old airport at **Ilopango**, 13 km east of the capital. Most **international buses** arrive at the Puerto Bus terminal, although luxury services and **Ticabus** have their own terminals. Domestic bus lines use terminals at the east, south and west ends of the city. ➺ *For further details, see page 740.*

Getting around The main focal points of the city are the historical centre, the commercial district some 3 km to the west around Bulevar de los Héroes, and the residential and commercial districts of Escalón and Zona Rosa another 2 km further west. City buses and taxis are needed to get between the three (see page 741).

Four broad streets meet at the centre: Avenida Cuscatlán and its continuation Avenida España run south to north; Calle Delgado and its continuation Calle Arce, with a slight blip, from east to west. This principle is retained throughout: the *avenidas* run north to south and the *calles* east to west. The even-numbered *avenidas* are east of the central *avenidas*, odd numbers west; north of the central *calles*, they are dubbed Norte, south of the central *calles* Sur. The even-numbered *calles* are south of the two central *calles*, the odd numbers north. East of the central *avenidas* they are dubbed Oriente (Ote), west of the central *avenidas* Poniente (Pte). Sounding more complicated than it is, the system is straightforward and quickly grasped.

Tourist information Corporación Salvadoreña de Turismo (Corsatur) ⓘ *Av El Espino 68, Urbanización Madreselva, T2243-7835, www.elsalvadorturismo.gob.sv, Mon-Fri 0800-1230, 1330-1730.* Good information on buses, archaeological sites, beaches and national parks. Texaco and Esso sell good maps at some of their service

San Salvador

stations. The best maps of the city and country (US$3 and US$2 respectively) are available from the **Instituto Geográfico Nacional** ⓘ *1 Calle Pte y 43 Av Norte 02310, Col Flor Blanca, T2260-8000*. The **Instituto Salvadoreño de Turismo**, or **ISTU** ⓘ *Calle Rubén Darío 619, San Salvador Centre, T2222-8000*, has useful information about the 13 government-run **Turicentros** recreation and water parks in the country and on Cerro Verde and Walter T Deininger national parks.

Best time to visit The climate is semi-tropical and healthy, the water-supply relatively pure. Days are often hot, especially in the dry season, but the temperature drops in the late afternoon and nights are usually pleasantly mild. Since it is in a hollow, the city has a very bad smog problem, caused mainly by traffic pollution. Efforts are being made to reduce vehicle emissions.

Detail map
A San Salvador centre, p732.

Eating
Pueblo Viejo **2**

Bars & clubs
La Luna **3**

Security The city centre is considered by many to be dangerous after dark, but the area north of Bulevar de los Héroes up to around San Antonio Abad is quite safe. As a general rule stay out of poorly lit areas and keep to main roads where there are more people around. At night, taxis are a sensible alternative if you don't know where you're going exactly.

Armed security personnel are commonplace. There is a heightened atmosphere of tension in some areas. In downtown markets, don't carry cameras, don't wear watches or jewellery and don't flash money around.

Background

San Salvador was first established by Gonzalo, brother of the conquistador Pedro de Alvarado, in 1525. The settlement was named in honour of Christ the Saviour who, Pedro believed, had saved him from death in his first attempt to conquer the peoples of **Cuscatlán**, as the region was then known. In 1528 the town was moved to a site near present-day Suchitoto, only to be relocated 20 years later to its present location. Over the next three centuries it developed into the capital of the province of San Salvador. The city has been destroyed by earthquakes 14 times since 1575, the last being in 1986. Nowadays the buildings are designed to withstand seismic shocks, and most stood up well to the earthquake of 2001.

Sights

A number of important buildings are near the intersection of the main roads in the historic centre. On the east side of Avenida Cuscatlán is the **Plaza Barrios**, the heart of

the city. A fine equestrian statue looks west towards the renaissance-style **Palacio Nacional** (1904-1911). To the north is the **new cathedral**, which was left unfinished for several years after Archbishop Romero suspended its construction to use the money to reduce poverty. Work was resumed in 1990 and completed in 1999, the last consecration of a cathedral of the millennium. It now stands as a beacon of tranquillity amid the dirt and noise of the downtown capital. It commands a striking presence, gleaming white and modern, its façade flanked by two giant murals vividly splashed with the colourful work of the country's most famous artist, **Fernando Llort**. Inside it is quite bare, but for the fabulous circular stained-glass window of a dove surrounded by a hundred shards of brilliant yellow glass, which in turn is framed by yellow stars set in deep lapis lazuli-blue glass. Beneath the cathedral, a new chapel has been created to house the tomb of assassinated **Archbishop Oscar Romero**.

East of Plaza Barrios, on Calle Delgado, is the **Teatro Nacional**, whose interior has been magnificently restored. If you walk along 2 Calle Oriente you pass, on the right, **Parque Libertad** with the rebuilt church of **El Rosario** on the eastern side where José Matías Delgado, father of the Independence movement, lies buried. The interior, decked out in modern sculpture, is fascinating, although knocked slightly by the earthquake. The **Palacio Arquiepiscopal** is next door. Not far away to the southeast, on 10 Avenida Sur, is another rebuilt church, **La Merced**, whose belltower rang out Father Delgado's tocsin call to Independence in 1811.

One block north, across Calle Delgado, is the **Teatro Nacional** on Plaza Morazán, with a monument to General Morazán. Heading east along Delgado is the **Mercado Ex-Cuartel**, and the expected confusion of sounds and smells that besiege the senses. Nearby are some of the cheapest hotels in the city. Running west from the Teatro Nacional, Calle Arce leads to **Hospital Rosales** and its own gardens. On the way to the hospital is the great church of **El Sagrado Corazón de Jesús**, which is well worth a visit; don't miss the stained-glass windows. Turn left (south) here and after one block you come to the **Parque Bolívar**, with the national printing office to the south and the Department of Health to the north.

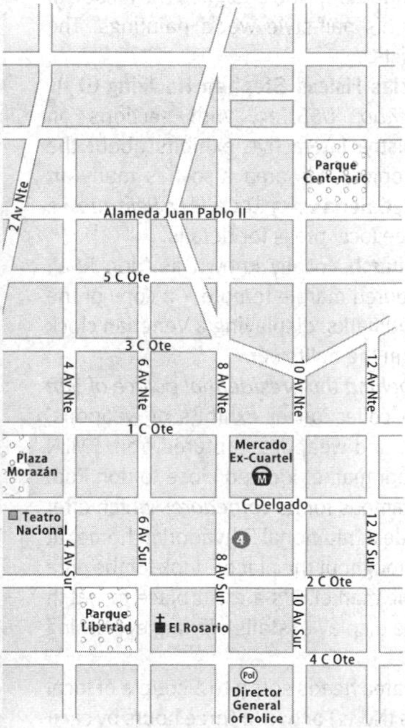

Four streets north of Calle Arce is the Alameda Juan Pablo II, an important road for bus transport, on which stands **Parque Infantil**, where you will find the Palacio de los Deportes. One block west is the **Centro de Gobierno**, with many official buildings.

The north side of Parque Bolívar is Calle Rubén Darío (2 Calle Poniente), which becomes Alameda Roosevelt, then Paseo General Escalón as it runs through the commercial and residential districts west of the centre. Heading west this boulevard first passes **Parque Cuscatlán**. A major junction is with 49 Avenida: to the south this avenue soon passes the national stadium, **Estadio Olímpico Flor Blanca**, before becoming the main highway to the international airport. To the north, 49 Avenida crosses Alameda Juan Pablo II beyond which it changes name to **Bulevar de los Héroes**, home to the fashionable shopping centres, **Metrocentro** and the newer **Metrosur**, the **Hotel Real Intercontinental**, some of the city's better restaurants and a glut of fast-food places, which is a busy area at all times, especially at night. At the Shell station by Metrocentro, mariachis and other musicians gather each evening, waiting to be hired; others wander around the restaurants, playing to diners.

Continuing west along Alameda Roosevelt, the next landmark at the Plaza Las Américas is the **Monumento al Salvador del Mundo**, a statue of Jesus standing on the Earth atop a column. From this junction the Pan-American Highway heads southwest to **Santa Tecla**. Straight ahead is **Paseo General Escalón**, Parque Beethoven and an area with many restaurants, shops and the Colonia Escalón residential district.

Another important residential and entertainment region is the **Zona Rosa** and **Colonia San Benito**, reached either from the Pan-American Highway or from Escalón. In this leafy suburb, some of the most elegant restaurants and the **Hotel Sheraton Presidente** and **Hotel Hilton Princess** (where former US president Clinton stayed while on his Central America tour) are found. **Museo Nacional de Antropología David J Guzman** ① *Feria Internacional, Av de la Revolución y Carretera a Santa Tecla, T2243-3750, Tue-Sun 0900-1700, US$1.50*, is a brand new museum worth visiting showcasing exhibits on the country's archaeological and historical past as well as numerous cultural events. Just north of the museum at the end of Avenida Revolución is **MARTE (Museo de Arte de El Salvador)** ① *T2243-6099, Tue-Sun 1000-1800, US$1.50, café and shop in lobby*. This new, privately run modern arts museum has permanent exhibits depicting the history of Salvadoran painters with temporary exhibits of artists from Latin America and other parts of the world.

A little further north is **El Arbol de Dios** ① *La Mascota y Av Masferrer, T2224-6200, Mon-Sat 1000-2200*, an arts and crafts store, restaurant, museum and garden, operated by the famed Salvadorean artist Fernando Llort, who designed the façade of the Metropolitan Cathedral and is known for his naïf-style wood paintings. The display here also includes the work of other artists.

In Colonia San Benito is **Museo de Ciencias Físicas Stephen Hawking** ① *Av Reforma 179, T2223-3027, Mon-Sat 1000-1400, US$1.25*, with sections on astronomy, ecology, electronics and biochemistry. Interactive exhibits about the sciences with monthly lectures on scientific topics. This area also has many art galleries such as **Galería Espacio** ① *Av La Capilla*, **Galería 1-2-3** ① *Calle La Reforma*, **La Pinacoteca** ① *Blv Hipódromo*, to name a few. See local press for details.

Worth visiting is the **María Auxiliadora church**, locally known as 'don Rua', situated in Barrio San Miguelito. This multi-coloured marble temple – a copy of the cathedral in Turin (Italy) – is one of the city's landmarks, displaying a Venetian clock tower and with a spectacular view of the city from the belltower.

Museo Militar de las Fuerzas Armadas ① *behind the presidential palace of San Jacinto at the former Cuartel El Zapote*, has a collection of exhibits of weapons, uniforms and decorations of the armed forces, and weapons captured from FMLN guerrillas. **Mercado de San Miguelito** is an indoor market located close to don Rua. Safer than many of the other city markets and famous for its *comedores* which offer typical Salvadoran dishes (difficult to find outside a traditional Salvadorian home) at economic prices. There are several food stalls throughout the place – look for the area decicated just to *comedores* at the far end of the market. It's a great place to watch people go about their shopping and to enjoy the display of stalls offering everything from herbal medicine to tropical birds.

A good sightseeing tour of the surrounding area heads south to a couple of local places of interest. Lasting most of the day by bus (No 12) or two to three hours by car it starts a few blocks southwest of the main square on the eastern side of the Mercado Central. It includes the **San Salvador Zoo** ① *Tue-Sun 0900-1600, US$0.60*, which though small, is quiet and attractive. Just three blocks away is the newly restored

Museo de Historia Natural ⓘ *Parque Saburo Hirao*, with interesting displays on prehistoric findings and a herbal medicine garden. To get there, take bus No 2 ' Zoo', and No 12 from the centre. You then pass the **Casa Presidencial** and go on up to the new residential district in the mountain range of **Planes de Renderos**. This place is crowned by the beautiful **Parque Balboa** ⓘ *daily 0800-1800*, and there's a good view of the city from El Mirador at the foot of the park. Parque Balboa is a **Turicentro**, with cycle paths, playground and gardens. From the park a scenic road runs to the summit of **Cerro Chulo**, from which the view, seen through the Puerta del Diablo (Devil's Door), is even better. There are local buses to Puerta del Diablo and Parque Balboa (No 12, US$0.35 from eastern side of Mercado Central and No 12-MC marked 'Mil Cumbres') almost hourly. Bus No 17 goes from the same location to Panchimalco through Los Planes de Renderos so you can get off at the junction there and take the No 12 to Parque Balboa and Puerta del Diablo.

The **Puerta del Diablo** consists of two enormous, nearly vertical rocks which frame a magnificent view of the Volcán San Vicente. The rocks are very steep but the sides can be climbed on reasonable paths for an even better view. A little beyond the car park and drinks stands at the Puerta del Diablo is a path climbing up a further summit, from which there are 360° views: to the coast, Lago Ilopango, the capital and volcanoes, including San Salvador, Izalco and Cerro Verde and San Vicente.

In the past there were reports of mugging. Incidences appear to have reduced making a visit a popular trip. However take sensible precautions during the daytime, take advice from vendors at the bottom of the hill, don't make the trip alone and do not stay after dark. At the foot of Cerro Chulo is **Panchimalco** (see page 735). The route to Panchimalco (No 17 from Mercado Central) and the coast branches off the road to Parque Balboa at the village of **Los Planes**, a few kilometres before the park.

Around San Salvador » pp736-744.

Many places can be visited in a day from San Salvador either on the frequent bus services or by car. Closest to the city is south to the indigenous village of **Panchimalco**, heading east are the beautiful setting and views around **Lago de Ilopango**; and to the southwest the crater of **Volcán San Salvador** (see Santa Tecla, below).

Heading west towards Santa Ana, but still manageable in a day, are the archaeological sites of **Joyo de Cerén**, El Salvador's Pompeii, and **San Andrés** and the peaks of **Volcán Izalco** and **Cerro Verde** (see page 748) with the deep blue waters of **Lago de Coatepeque** in the crater below. The limits of a comfortable weekend trip will take you to the garden park of **Ichanmichen**, which is restful (see Zacatecoluca), and the pyramid of **Tazumal** (west of Santa Ana) also worth a visit (page 749). At weekends the coast around La Libertad (see below) is very popular. Bus 495 from the Terminal del Occidente goes to the seaside resort of Costa del Sol (see page 775).

Panchimalco → *14.5 km south by a paved road.*

This small town and the surrounding area is home to the Pancho, descendants of the Pipil tribes, one of the region's dominant indigenous groups prior to conquest. This is one of the few places in El Salvador where you can still see indigenous people in traditional dress. Streets of large cobbles, with low adobe houses, thread their way between huge boulders at the foot of Cerro Chulo. A very fine baroque colonial church, Santa Cruz, has a white façade with statues of eight saints. Inside are splendid woodcarvings and wooden columns, altars, ceilings and benches. There is a bell inscribed with the cipher and titles of the Holy Roman Emperor Charles V, and a colourful cemetery. The Casa de La Cultura in the main street has frequent cultural events and crafts stores. The **Fiesta de Santa Cruz de Roma** is held on 12-14 September, with music and traditional dances; on 3 May (or the second Sunday of the month) there is the procession of **Las Palmas.** Bus 17 from Mercado Central at 12 Calle Poniente, San Salvador, every 45 minutes, 45 minutes, or minibus from near Mercado Central, very crowded but quicker (30 minutes), and cheaper (US$0.35).

Lago de Ilopango

Beyond the four-lane highway to Ilopango airport (14.5 km east) lie the deep waters of Lago de Ilopango. Surrounded by mountains, the views around El Salvador's largest and deepest crater lake are impressive. Before the conquest local people used to appease the harvest gods by drowning four virgins here every year. Private chalets make access to the lake difficult, except at clubs and the **Turicentro Apulo,** but it is well worth a visit. There are a number of lakeside cafés and bathing clubs, some of which hire dug-outs by the hour. The cafés are busy in the dry season (try **Teresa's** for fish dishes), but often closed in the middle of the year. **Hotel Vista del Lago** ⓘ *T2446-9511*, 3 km from Apulo turn-off on the highway, is on a hill top. Bus 15, marked Apulo, runs from the bus stop on Parque Hula Hula to the lake (via the airport), 1¼ hours, US$0.30. Entrance to the Turicentro camping site costs US$0.60.

> *The eastern shore is less polluted and is reached from Cojutepeque.*

Volcán San Salvador

This large massif has an impressive crater, more than 1.5 km wide and 543 m deep, known as **El Boquerón.** About 2 km to the east is the equally dramatic peak of **El Picacho** (1960 m) which dominates the capital. Buses leave a block from Plaza Merliot. By car you turn right just after the Plaza Merliot Mall and continue to the end of the road where a newly paved road take you up the volcano. A walk clockwise round the crater takes about two hours; the first half is easy, the second half rough. The views are magnificent, if somewhat spoilt by TV and radio towers and litter. **La Laguna** botanical garden is near the summit. The inner slopes of the crater are covered with trees, and at the bottom is a smaller cone left by the eruption of 1917.

You can follow the road north and then turn right through extensive coffee plantations and forest to reach the summit of **El Picacho**. This also makes an excellent climb from the Escalón suburb of San Salvador, in the early morning preferably, which takes about three to four hours return trip (take a guide). The easy access, great views and fresh climate has made the Volcano of San Salvador a popular destination for people in the capital, and as a result new restaurants have opened their doors in recent years. See Eating, page 737.

Sleeping

In the downtown area, some hotels lock their doors very early. Many cheap *hospedajes* near **Terminal de Oriente** are of dubious safety and not recommended for single women. Foreigners are advised not to be out in the city centre after dark.

13% VAT (IVA) is added to bills at major hotels. Most of the cheaper hotels are around the Centro Histórico.

LL Hotel Real Intercontinental San Salvador, Blv de los Héroes and Av Sisimiles, in front of the Metrocentro, T2211-3333, www.gruporeal.com. A useful landmark, smart, formal atmosphere (popular with business visitors), **Avis** car hire, **Taca** desk, shop selling souvenirs, postcards, US papers and magazines.

AL Radisson Plaza, 89 Av Norte and 11 Calle Pte, Col Escalón, T2257-0700, www.radisson.com. Elegant, a/c, cable TV, good value, parking.

B Alameda, 43 Av Sur and Alameda Roosevelt 2305, T2267-0800, www.hotelalameda.com. Good service, tour information and parking.

B Alicante Guest House, Calle las Rosas y Av Los Laureles 1, Col La Sultana, T2243-0889, www.alicante.com.sv. Telephone, cable TV, internet access for guests, breakfast included. Discounts for extended stays.

B Internacional Puerto Bus, Alameda Juan Pablo II y 19 Av Norte, at Puerto Bus terminal, T/F2221-1000. A/c, TV, wake-up service, etc.

B Mariscal, Paseo Escalón 3658, T2283-0220, www.hotelmariscal.com. Good apartments, a good deal for long-term stay.

B-C Good Luck, Av Los Sisimiles 2943, Col Miramonte (turn left at **Real Intercontinental** and go uphill 200 m), T2260-1666. TV, shower, cheaper without a/c, hot water, bright but simple, restaurant, secure parking.

B-C Grecia Real, Av Sisimiles 2922, Col Miramontes, 50 m west of **Hotel Real Intercontinental**, T2261-0555, www.greciareal.com. With good Greek restaurant. Recommended.

C American Guest House, 17 Av Norte 119 between Calle Arce y 1 Calle Pte, 3 blocks from Puerto Bus, T2271-8789. With bath (cheaper without), hot water, fan, helpful, will store luggage, accepts credit cards, discounts for groups. Oldest guest house downtown, run by the young at heart Irma Custodio in her 70s, weekly rates, **Cafetería La Amistad**, parking nearby, good.

C Florida, Pasaje Los Almendros 15, Urbanizacón Florida and Blv de los Héroes, T2260-2540, hotelflorida@navegante.com.sv. All rooms with bath, fan, laundry service, secure, proprietor speaks English, thin walls but good value. Recommended.

C Happy House, Av Sisimiles 2951, Col Miramonte, T/F2260-1568, www.hotelhappyhouse-elsalvador.com. Good, friendly, often full, parking, restaurant, good breakfast.

C-E International Guest House, 35 Av Norte 9 bis, Repato Santa Fe, T2226-7343. Private baths, breakfast included.

C-E Ximena's Guest House, Calle San Salvador 202, Col Centroamérica, T2260-2481, www.ximenasguesthouse.com. With cable TV, a variety of rooms with private bath and hot shower, cheaper in 4-6-bed dormitory, discounts for long stay, clean, pleasant, kitchen, breakfast US$2.50, lunch and dinner, fruit shakes with purified water and organic coffee. Internet, US$2/hr. Friendly and knowledgeable staff. Variety of economic tours as well as transport to their beach house **Capricho** and **Lisa Guest House** at organic farm. Conveniently located, but not easy to find (behind the Esso station on Blv de los Héroes). Recommended.

D Casa Clementina, Av Morazán y Av Washington 34, Col Libertad, T2225-5962. Very friendly, clean, pleasant, garden.

D Centro, 9 Av Sur 410, T2271-5045. A bit box-like, checkout 0900, TV, phone, friendly, washing facilities, clean, safe, recommended.

D Centro Histórico, 1 Calle Pte 124 y 1 Av Norte, 2 blocks from cathedral, T2208-6499, hotel.centro.h@integra.com.sv. A/c, TV, parking, good choice.

D El Palacio, 4 Calle Pte115, next to National Palace, T2222-2243, A/c, TV, parking, good central location.

D Nuevo Panamericano, 8 Av Sur 113, T2221-1199. Cold shower, safe, closes early (but knock on the door), will do laundry, meals from US$2 and parking space. Recommended.

D San Carlos, Calle Concepción 121, T2222-8975. With bath, early morning call (extra charge), doors locked 2400, cold drinks available, good, resident cockroaches but otherwise clean, **Ticabus** leaves from outside (ticket reservations in lobby office hours), owner arranges evening tours of the city US$6.

E Imperial, Calle Concepción 659, T2222-4920. Reasonable meals, car park, more expensive with toilet and shower.

F Emperador, Calle Concepción. With bath, friendly, good value, clean, laundry facilities on roof, recommended.

F Hospedaje España, 12 Av Norte 123. Fan, clean, bright, good value.

Eating

In the older **downtown** area few places are open to eat after 1830. Restaurants are open later in the western sections of the city. Along **Blv Hipódromo**, San Benito, restaurants are generally very good, but expensive. On **Blv de los Héroes** there are many restaurants, including US-style fast-food places. The strip along **Calle San Antonio Abad** has several local eateries.

TTT Acajutla Restaurant and Coctelería, Residencial Cumbres de Escalón, Av Maferrer Norte 8, T2263-1722. Great seafood.

TTT Al Pomodoro, Paseo Escalón 3952, Col Escalón, T2257-2544, also delivery – alessandrovizia@hotmail.com. Popular, good Italian.

TTT China Palace, Alameda Roosevelt 2731, T2298-4313. Excellent value, the oldest Chinese restaurant in San Salvador.

TTT Daruma, Blv El Hipódromo 428, Col San Benito, T2243-9416. Japanese gourmet food with home delivery.

TTT **Dynasty**, Blv Hipódromo 738-B, T2263-9955. Known for serving the best Chinese food in the city.

TTT **El Bodegón**, Paseo Escalón 3956 and 77 Av Norte, T2263-5283. The proprietor is Spanish and the food likewise. Excellent.

TTT **H'ola Beto's Escalón**, Pasaje Dordelly 4352 between 85 and 87 Av Norte (above Paseo Escalón). Best seafood in the city, also Italian, great service, parking. Recommended.

TTT **Hunan**, Paseo Escalón and 99 Av Norte, Plaza Villaviciencio, T2263-9911. Chinese restaurant with specialities from Hunan, Szechuan, Pekin and Shanghai.

TTT **Kamakura**, 93 Av Norte 617, Col Escalón T2263-2401. Japanese food.

TTT **La Pampa Argentina**, Blv Constitución 550, T2263-6550. Highly recommended for steaks, popular.

TTT **La Panetière**, Plaza Villaviciencio, local 5, Paseo Escalón. Delicious French pastry, crêpes, cappuccinos, popular with foreigners, a bit pricey but worth it.

TTT **Ostería dei Cualtro Galti**, Calle La Reforma 232, T2223-1625. Italian, good.

TTT **Paradise**, corner of Reforma, Col San Benito, in front of **Pizza Hut**, T2224-4201. Good for steak and lobster, excellent food and service. Expensive but worth it.

TTT **Pasquale Pasta e Pizza**, Paseo Escalón 3931, Col Escalón T2263-5445. Great Italian.

TTT **Señor Tenedor**, Av Olímpica, T2298-1766, www.senortenedor.com, and branch in **La Gran Vía**. Gourmet deli and restaurant.

TTT **Sushi Itto**, Blv Hipódromo, Col San Benito T2243-1166, and in shopping mall **La Gran Vía**. Sushi, expensive but good.

TTT **Tony Romas**, Blv de los Héroes (Metrocentro) and Zona Rosa, T2298-5500. Specializes in imported ribs.

TT **Basilea**, Centro Comercial Basilea, T2223-6818, www.restaurantebasilea.com. Nice garden atmosphere and small shopping centre, restaurant and excellent cakes (from **Shaw's Bakery,** next door; see Cafés, below).

TT **Café Café**, Calle El Tanque, 99 Av Norte y 7 y 9 Calle Pte bis 130, T2263-4034, www.cafecafe.com.sv. Locally popular Peruvian restaurant. Recommended.

TT **Coconut Grove**, 79 Av Sur y Calle La Mascota, 7 y 8, Col Escalón, T2264-2979. Seafood.

TT **El Zócalo II**, 71 Av Norte, just in front of Galerías mall. Excellent Mexican food.

TT **Felipe's**, 27 Calle Pte 743, Col Layco, off Blv de los Héroes. Popular Mexican restaurant, good value. Also with a branch by the US Embassy.

TT **Kalpataru**, Calle La Mascota 928 and Calle Maquilishuat, just below **Arbol de Dios**. Open until 2230, full restaurant service and lunch buffet, nice atmosphere. Best vegetarian place in town.

TT **KREEF**, new location at Plaza Kreef, Calle and Col Maquilishuat, T2264-7094. Restaurant and deli, specialities meat and juicy chicken filets, imported cheese, beer and wine.

TT **Pueblo Viejo**, in Metrosur, T2260-3545. Open 1100-2000, popular for lunch, local and steak dishes, including *parrillada*, and seafood.

TT **Restaurante Sol y Luna**, Blv Universitario, in front of **Cines Reforma**, T2225-6637. Delicious vegetarian food.

TT **Rosal**, 93 Av Norte y Calle El Mirador, Col Escalón, near **Hotel Radisson**, T2263-2391. Italian, good.

TT **Sopón Típico**, 71 Av Norte and 1 Calle Pte 3702, Col Escalón, T2298-3008 and Blv de Los Héroes, Pasaje Las Palmeras 130, Urbanización Florida T2260-2671. Typical Salvadorean soups and other dishes.

TT-T **Mercadito Merliot**, Antiguo Cuscatlán. Famous food market with fresh seafood dishes (among others).

T **The Brother**, Calle San Antonio Abad. Meats grilled on outdoor BBQ, large dishes and low prices.

Cafés, delis and juice stalls

There are numerous *cafeterías* serving cheap traditional meals such as *tamales*, *pupusas*, *frijoles*, rice with vegetables, etc. Often these places can be found around the major hotels.

Café de Don Pedro, Roosevelt y Alameda, next to Esso filling station. Good range of food, mariachi groups, open all night, another branch in Chiltiuapan, near Plaza Merliot Mall, also 24 hrs.

Oh-la-la, 1 Calle Ote and 69 Av Norte 168, just around the corner of Galerías mall, T2223-0161. Fine pastries.

Shakes, 3 Calle Pte 5254, Lomas Verdes, Col Escalón, T2263-4533. Juice bar and delicious fresh cakes. Recommended.

Shaw's, Paseo Escalón, 1 block west of Plaza Beethoven, Zona Rosa (see above) and at Metrocentro. Good coffee and chocolates, also sell US magazines and greetings cards.

Entertainment

Bars and clubs

Check for gigs in *La Prensa Gráfica* and *El Diario de Hoy*. All leading hotels have their own nightclub. All discos have ladies' night on Wed and Thu when women enter free and get a discount on drinks; go in a group. Zona Rosa, Col San Benito, has many bars/discos/open-air cafés in a 5-block area, well-lit, crowded Fri-Sat night (discos' cover charge is US$7), take bus 30B from near Esso/Texaco/Mundo Feliz on Blv de los Héroes before 2000, taxi thereafter. Just beyond Zona Rosa the new shopping malls of Multiplaza and La Gran Vía are the new favourite places for going out with both having strips of night clubs and bars where youngsters gather at the weekends.

Club 'M', Calle José Martí 7, San Benito, T2223-9321, trendy. **El Arpa** Av A 137 Col San José, run by Gerry from Ireland. **La Luna**, Calle Berlín 228, off Blv de los Héroes, Urbanización Buenos Aires 3, T2260-2921, www.lalunacasayarte.com. Great food and atmosphere, live music some nights, decor and furniture designed by local artists. Popular and fashionable place to hang out. Reasonably priced drinks and snacks, closed Sun, open for lunch Mon-Fri 1200-1500, set menu about US$2.50, no cover except Fri Salsa nights, US$6; take taxi late at night.

On Calle San Antonio Abad, good places for live music are **3 Diablos**, **Highland Bistro**, **Bar-bar-o** and **Café La T**, all opposite Centro Comercial San Luis. **El Atrio**, Calle San Antonio Abad, at Calle Alvarado 30, Urbanización Buenos Aires T2226-5411, is a café bar with library and theatre scene. Great cultural events throughout the month.

Cinema

A few older-style cinemas in the centre are being overshadowed by the multiplexes along the Blv de los Héroes. Look in local press for listings. 'Arthouse' films are shown at **La Luna**, **El Atrio** and **Café La T** (see Bars, above) on Tue 1800, free. **Alliance Française** arranges film seasons, T2223-8084.

Music, dance and theatre

Ballet and theatre at the **Teatro Nacional de Bellas Artes**, and music or plays at the Teatro Cámera.

Spectator sports

Check *La Prensa Gráfica* and *El Diario de Hoy*.

Baseball On the field opposite Mercado Nacional de Artesanías, Tue-Fri 1700, Cuban and US coaches, local teams, entrance US$1.25.

Boat racing **Club Náutico**, at the Estero de Jaltepeque, is famous for its boat races across the mud flats at low tide.

Motor racing At the new El Jabalí autodrome on lava fields near Quetzaltepeque.

Football Sun and Thu at the Cuscatlán and/or Flor Blanca stadiums.

Festivals and events

Mar/Apr Holy Week.

July/Aug Celebrations of El Salvador del Mundo are held the fortnight preceding **6 Aug**. As a climax, colourful floats wend their way up the Campo de Marte (the park encompasssing Parque Infantil and Palacio de Deportes; 9 Calle Pte and Av España).

On **5 Aug**, an ancient image of the Saviour is borne before the large procession, before church services the next day, celebrating the Feast of the Transfiguration.

12 Dec Día del Indígena; there are colourful processions honouring the Virgen de Guadalupe (take bus No 101 to the Basílica de Guadalupe, on the Carretera a Santa Tecla).

Shopping

Visa and MasterCard are increasingly accepted.

Art and antiques

Try **Casa de Antiguedades**, 3 Calle Pte entre 9 y 11 Av Norte 620, T2222-6203, Jorge Antonio Sibrian, T2260-6380. Antiques, frames, odd articles, recommended. Several small galleries and antique shops around Escalón (side streets north of Paseo Escalón); nice gallery/antique store **Sol y Luna**, 7 Calle Pte, Polish/Salvadorean-owned.

Bookshops

Magazines and newspapers in English can be bought at leading hotels and many shops sell US magazines. At the Universidad de El Salvador (UES) and the Universidad Centroamericana (UCA), www.libreriauca.com.sv. **Cervantes**, 9 Av Sur 114 in the Centre and Edif El Paseo 3, Paseo Escalón. **Clásicos Roxsil**, 6 Av Sur 1-6, Santa Tecla, T2228- 1212. **Editorial**

Piedra Santa, Av Olímpica 3428, Av 65-67 Sur, T2223-5502. **Etc Ediciones** in Centro Comercial Basilea, San Benito. Some English books at **Librería Cultural Salvadoreña** in Metrosur. **Olivos**, also café and restaurant, just below **Hotel Princess**, Zona Rosa, T2245-4221, www.olivoscafe.com, has a wide selection of books, specializing in alternative medicine and health.

Crafts

For a one-stop craft shop, visit the **Mercado Nacional de Artesanías**, opposite the Estado Mayor on the road to Santa Tecla (buses 101A, B or C, 42B, 79, 34, 30B), at prices similar to the Mercado Ex-Cuartel. Good cross section of items even if not that well presented. Some of the cheapest prices, daily 0800-1800. **El Arbol de Dios**, La Mascota y Av Masferrer, T2224-6200, see page 734. **La Cosecha**, Centro Cultural La Mazoroca, San Antonio Abad 1447, T2226-5219, exhibitions and workshop producing T-shirts, posters, etc relating to the Civil War, also wholesale prices. **Mercado Ex-Cuartel**, 8 Av Norte, 1 Calle Ote, crafts market, a few blocks east of the Teatro Nacional, rebuilt after a disastrous fire in 1995. **Tienda de Artesanías La Cosecha**, in Casa Cultural La Mazorca, Calle San Antonio Abad 1447, 100 m north of entrance to university, on left, good prices, large selection (bus 30B, 26, 44). You can buy fair trade arts and crafts at **Café La T**, Calle San Antonio Abad, and **Nahanché**, Metrocentro, Centro Comercial Basilea and Multiplaza, has a great selection of handicrafts from all over the country.

Markets and malls

Metrocentro, large shopping mall on the Blv de los Héroes, northwest of the city centre. Together with Metrosur this is the largest shopping mall in Central America. Another shopping centre, **Villas Españolas**, is on the Paseo Escalón, 1 block south of the Redondel Masferrer; it is more exclusive, with expensive boutiques. **Galerías Escalón**, Col Escalón, has department stores and cybercafés.

Activities and tours

Tour operators

Amor Tours, Alameda Manuel Enrique Araujo, carretera a Santa Tecla, T2224-2529, www.amortours.com.sv.

Agencia Internacional de Viajes Morales, Calle Loma Linda 1A Plt Locs 1A, 2A y 3A, Col San Benito, T2209-5100, is the American Express agents.

OTEC Turismo Joven, Paseo Escalón, T2264-0200, www.otec.com.sv, official ISIC office in El Salvador and STA Travel representative, offering travel assistance, resissue of lost tickets, date changes and rerouting. Special prices for student, teacher and youth with ISIC card.

Pullmantur, Av La Revolución, T2243-1300, www.pullmantur.com, besides luxury bus service to Guatemala, excellent package tours to Antigua.

Salva Natura, 33 Av Sur 640, Col Flor Blanca, T2279-1515, www.salvanatura.org, for information about Reserva Nacional Bosque El Imposible on the coast near Guatemala.

Suchitoto Tours, T2514-1345, 7848-3438 (mob) , www.suchitoto-tours.com. Run by knowledgeable and reliable locals who can offer tours to various parts of the country in minibus or 4WD, organize hotels, rent cars and do tours to Nicaragua, Honduras and Guatemala. It will also offer tourist information about the country.

Turinter, travel agency at Centro Comercial Plaza Jardín, Edificio A, Carretera Santa Tecla, T2223-0166, good rates and helpful staff.

Turismo, T2211-8580, www.turismo.com.sv, CORSATUR-certified, English-, French- and German-led tours emphasizing local history, traditions, archaeology and ecology.

Watersports

El Salvador Divers, Paseo Escalón 3 Calle Pte 5020, Col Escalón, T2264-0961, www.elsalvadordivers.com, offer weekly excursions and classes. Located behind the Villavicencio Mall.

Ríos Aventuras, Final 73 Av Sur B1, Col Escalón, T2298-0335, www.riosaventuras.com.sv. Bilingual guides organize rafting trips to Río Paz on the Guatemalan border.

Transport

Air

The international airport (SAL), T2339-9455, at Comalapa is 62 km southeast from San Salvador towards Costa del Sol beach. Acacya minibus to airport, from 3 Calle Pte y 19 Av Norte, T2271-4937, airport

T2339-9182, at 0600, 0700, 1000, 1400 (be there 15 mins before), US$3 one-way (leaves from airport when full, on right as you go out). **Acacya**, T2271-4937, also has a taxi service, US$20, the same as other radio taxi companies; ordinary taxis charge US$18, US$25 at night. Taxi to **La Libertad** beach US$20-30; to **Costa del Sol** US$20. There is a post office, a tourist office, 2 exchange desks, including **Banco Cuscatlán**) and duty-free shopping for both departures and arrivals.

The old airport is at Ilopango, 13 km east of the city and is primarily used by the air force and for some domestic flights.

Airline offices American Airlines, Alameda Roosevelt, Edificio Centroamericana, 3107, T2298- 0777. **Copa Airlines**, T2260-3399, www.copaair.com. **Delta**, 81 Av Norte y Calle El Mirador, Edif WTC, local 107, piso 4, Col Escalón T2275- 9292, www.delta.com. **Grupo TACA** , Oficinas Centrales Plaza Las Americas, T2267- 8222 , www.taca.com. **Mexicana**, Edificio Mejicana de Aviación, 2 nivel, Km 4.5, Carretera Sta Tecla, T2211- 9999, 9901, www.mexicana.com, **United Airlines**, Centro Comercial Galerías, local 14, 3700 Paseo Escalón, T2279- 3900, www.united.com.

Bus

Local Most buses stop running at 2100. City buses charge US$0.20 and microbuses charges US$0.25 within the city – have the right change or a small bill to hand. Most run 0500-2000, after which use taxis.

Some useful routes: 29 from Terminal de Oriente to Metrocentro via downtown; **30** Mercado Central to Metrocentro; **30B** from Mundo Feliz (100 m up from Esso station on Blv de los Héroes) to Escalón, 79 Av Norte, Zona Rosa (San Benito), Alameda Roosevelt and back to Metrocentro along 49 Av; **34** San Benito-Mercado de Artesanías-Terminal de Occidente-Mercado Central-Terminal Oriente; **52** 'Paseo' Parque Infantil- Metrocentro-Plaza Las Américas-Paseo Escalón-Plaza Masferrer; **52** 'Hotel' Parque Infantil-Metrocentro-Hotel Copa Airlines-Plaza Masferrer. Route **101** buses to/from Santa Tecla are blue and white for either class of service.

Domestic services go from **Terminal de Occidente**, off Blv Venezuela, T2223-3784 (take city buses 4, 7C, 27, 44 or 34); **Terminal de Oriente**, end of Av Peralta in Centro Urbano Lourdes (take city buses No 29 from Metrocentro, 42 from Alameda, or No 4, from 7 Calle), T2281-3086, very crowded with buses and passengers, keep your eyes open for the bus you want; and **Terminal Sur**, San Marcos, Zona Franca, about 9 km from the city (take city bus No 26 from Universidad Nacional area or Av España downtown, take taxi to city after 1830). Routes and fares are given under destinations.

Long distance and international

Heading south Ticabus departs from Hotel San Carlos, Calle Concepción 121, T2222-4808, www.ticabus.com, runs to **Guatemala**, 0600, 5hrs, US$11, **Tegucigalpa**, 0530, 6½ hrs, US$15, **San Pedro Sula**, 0530, 12 hrs, US$23, **Managua**, 0500, 12 hrs, US$25, **San José**, 33 hrs including overnight in **Managua**, US$37, **Panama City**, 0500, arriving 2200 the next day, US$62. Also with an office in Blv del Hipódromo, Zona Rosa, T2243-9764. **King Quality**, T2271-3330, to **Nicaragua** leave at 0530 and 1130, US$28. Departures for **Costa Rica** at 0330, US$48.

Puerto Bus terminal, Alameda Juan Pablo II y 19 Av Norte; T2222-3224 or T2221-1000, have departures to **Guatemala**, **Honduras**, **Nicaragua**, **Costa Rica** and **Panamá**. You can walk there from city centre, but not advisable with luggage; take bus 101D from Metrocentro, or bus 29, 52 to 21 Av Norte, 2 blocks south of terminal (city buses don't permit heavy luggage). The terminal has a *casa de cambio*, good rates, open daily and a restaurant.

Standard service to Guatemala **Pezzarossi**, **Taca**, **Transesmer**, **Melva**, **Vencedora**, **Daniel Express** and **Centro América** all operate services to Guatemala City more or less hourly (5½ hrs, US$10). **Tucan** buses, with a/c and bathrooms, has departures at 610 and 1630, US$13.

Luxury service to Guatemala **Confort Lines**, departures at 0730 and 1300, buses have a/c, meals, drinks, hostess, bathroom, TV, video, US$22. **King Quality**, T2271-3330, has departures at 0600 and 1530, with a bit more luxury, US$26. Branch office in Blv del Hipódromo, Zona Rosa, but departures times are different and tickets have to be bought in advance. **Pullmantur**, T2243- 1300, runs a 0700 service Mon-Sat, 0830 Sun, and a daily 1500 service from **Hotel Presidente** for US$26, luxury service, with a/c, film, drinks and meals.

Service to Honduras King Quality, T2271-3330, daily departures to **San Pedro Sula**, 0500 and 1230 and **Tegucigalpa**, 0600 and 1400, both US$28. **Pullmantur** T2243-1300, daily to **Tegucigalpa** at 0215, US$27.

Alternatively, take local services from Terminal de Oriente, Ruta 306 to Santa Rosa de Lima, 4 hrs, US$2.20, faster by express US$2.50, then Ruta 346 to the border at **El Amatillo**, 30 mins, US$0.40, last bus to border 1730; see Honduras chapter for onward transport.

Service to Mexico Also from **Terminal de Occidente**, El Cóndor goes to **Talismán**, Mexico via Sonsonate, La Hachadura and Escuintla, US$12, 0330, 9½ hrs, also 0700-0800 to Guatemala City. **Transgalgos** has direct departures to Mexico from Puerto Bus. **Ticabus** goes to **Tapachula**, via Guatemala, 0600, 11hrs, US$26.

Car

Car hire Local insurance (about US$10-15 per day plus a deductible US$1,000 deposit) is mandatory and 13% IVA applies: rentals from **Avis**, 43 Av Sur 137, T2261-1212. **Budget**, Calle Pte 2765 between 57 and 49 Av Norte, T2264-3888, www.budget.com. **Hertz**, Av Olímpica y 73 Av Sur Local 21, T2264-2818, www.hertz.com. **Sandoval & Co**, T2235-4405, sub compact late model cars from US$10 per day, English spoken. **Euro Rent-Cars**, 29 Calle Pte and 7 Av Norte 1622, T2235-5232, chamba_r@hotmail.com, cheap daily rates from US$10.

Car repairs Modern service centres of Record and **Impressa**, are found throughout the capital. Good source of spare parts found at **Super Repuestos**, T2221-4440.

Insurance **Asesuiza** is widely used for car insurance T2209-5025 as is **La Centroamericana**, T2298-6666.

Car papers Ministerio de Hacienda, T2226-1900, 'Tres Torres', turn left on Blv de los Héroes 300 m past Texaco station.

Taxi

Plenty (all yellow), don't have meters, ask fare before getting in. Trips within San Salvador will have a miminum cost of US$3 and most trips will be between US$4 and US$6. Airport is approximately US$18.-Few drivers speak English. They will charge more in the rain. More expensive radio taxis may be hired through **Acacya**, T2271-4937.

Directory

Banks

Most banks (except Cuscatlán, see below) open Mon-Fri 0900-1700, Sat 0900-1200; *casas de cambio* keep the same hrs but most close 1300-1400 for lunch. The banks have branches in all the shopping malls and in large hotels such as **Princess, Radisson.** ATMs only give US dollars. **Banco Agrícola Comercial de El Salvador**, Paseo Escalón 3635, T2279-1033, English spoken. **Banco Salvadoreño**, Calle Rubén Darío 1236, good rates for TCs and Visa card advances. Never change money with the street changers in Parque Infantil, in front of the *casas de cambio*. Quetzals, Mexican pesos and lempiras may be changed at **Casa de Cambio El Quetzal**, Alameda Juan Pablo Segundo y 19 Av Norte (Puerto Bus terminal), Mon-Fri 0800-1700, Sat 0800-1200. Accounts in dollars may be opened at **Citibank**, Edif Palic, CL Nueva 1, Alam Dr M E Araujo, Col Escalón, T2245-1850. **Aval-Visa**, Av Olímpica y 55 Av Norte (in Centro Comercial, behind Credomatic), does cash advances on Visa, T2279-3077. In emergency, for Visa International or MasterCard, T2224-5100; Visa TCs can only be changed by Visa cardholders. Visa ATMs can be found at Aval card 24-hr machines, the majority at Esso and Shell service stations (eg Esso, Blv de los Héroes), but also at Metrocentro, 8th floor food court, and Centro de Servicio, Av Olímpica. See also Yellow Pages. To replace lost or stolen **American Express TCs**, contact Agencia de Viajes Morales in Centro Comercial Loma Linda, in front of Canal 2 along Carretera Santa Tecla, T2209-5100, Mon-Fri 0800-1800. Otherwise call toll free T-800-6059 for assistance in both English and Spanish. **Western Union** for money transfers, c/o **Banco Salvadoreño** branches, T2225-2503 (48 other branches throughout the country, look out for the black and yellow sign), head office Alameda Roosevelt 2419 between 45 y 47 Av Sur, T2298-1888, Mon-Fri 0800-1700, Sat 0800-1200, take passport and photographic ID (30 mins if from USA/Canada, 2-3 hrs from Europe). **Banco de América Central** (Ex-Credomatic), next to Siman in Metrocentro and CC San Luis gives cash advances on credit cards.

Cultural centres

Alianza Francesa, 5 Av Norte 152, Col Escalón, T2260-5807. **American Society**, T2224-1330, Chester Stemp, Mon-Fri 0800-1600, at International School (Union Church), Calle 4 Final, Col La Mascota, T2263-8246, English-speaking Interdominational International Church, weekly church services and bible studies, people-helping opportunities. **Centro de Intercambio y Solidaridad (CIS)**, Blv Universitario 4, next to Cine Reforma, T2226-2623, www.cis-elsalvador.org, for language classes, brigade work, FMLN (Frente Farabundo Martí para la Liberación Nacional) programmes and schools. **Instituto para el Rescate Ancestral Indígena Salvadoreño (RAIS)**, Av Santiago 20, Col San Mateo, has programmes for local aid to indigenous communities and the Nahual language and customs.

Embassies and consulates

Belize, Calle el Bosque Ote y Calle Lomas de Candelaria No I, Block "P", Col Jardines de la 1a Etapa, T2248-1423. **Costa Rica**, Calle Cuscatlán 4115, between 81 and 83 Av Sur, Col Escalón, T2264-3863. **Canada**, Centro Financiero Gigante and Alameda Roosevelt y 63 Av Sur Lobby 2, local 6, T2279-4659. **France**, 1 Calle Pte 7380, Col Escalón, T2298-4260. **Germany**, 77 Av Norte y 7 Calle Pte 3972, T2263-2099. **Guatemala**, 15 Av Norte 135 between 1 Calle Pte and Calle Arce, T2271-2225. **Holland**, I Calle Pte 3796. **Honduras**, 89 Av Norte 561, between 7 and 9 Calle Pte, Col Escalón, T2263-2808. **Israel**, Centro Financiero Gigante, Torre B, 11 piso, Alameda Roosevelt y 63 Av Sur, T2211-3434. **Italy**, La Reforma 158, Col San Benito, T2223-4806. **Mexico**, Pasaje 12 y Calle Circunvalación, San Benito, behind Hotel Presidente, T2248-9906. **Nicaragua**, Calle Mirador and 93 Av Norte 4814, Col Escalón, T2263-8849. **Norway**, Calle Cuscatlán 133 between 83 and 81 Av Sur, Col Escalón, T2263-8257. **Panama**, Ed Gran Plaza Piso 2, Local 203, Blv del Hipódromo, Col San Benito, T2245-5410. **Spain**, Calles la Reforma 164, Col San Benito, T2257-5700. **Sweden**, Alameda Manuel E Araujo y 67 Av Sur 3515, T2281-7901. **Switzerland**, Pastelería Lucerna, 85 Av Sur y Paseo Escalón 4363, T2263-7485. **USA**, Blv Santa Elena, Antiguo Cuscatlán, T2278-4444, outside the city, reached by bus 101A.

Emergency

Ambulance/rescue (Comandos de Salvamento), T2222-0817. **Red Cross** Av Henry Dunat y 17 Av Norte, T2224-1330, emergency 24-hr, T2222-5155.
Police Emergency T911, T123, or T2228-1156, no coin needed from new coin phones. In San Salvador, metropolitan police respond to tourist complaints.

Immigration

Departamento de Inmigración, Centro de Gobierno, T2221-2111, Mon-Fri 0800-1600. They will consider extending tourist visas, but be prepared with photos and plenty of patience. **Migración y Extranjería**, Plaza Merliot and Hipermall Cascadas saves the trip to Centro de Gobierno and have quicker service.

Internet

Cafés (roughly US$1/hr) are found throughout the city especially at shopping malls.

Language schools

Centro de Intercambio y Solidaridad, Blv Universitario 4, T2226-2623, www.cis-elsalvador.org. Spanish school in the mornings 0800-1200, English school in the afternoons 1700-1900 – volunteer English teachers needed for 10-week sessions.
Cihuatan Spanish Language Institute (Ximena's), Calle San Salvador 202, Col Centro América (near Hotel Real Intercontinental), T2260-2481, ximenas@navegante.com.sv; rates are US$7 per hr.

Libraries

The **UCA** library (Universidad Centro-americana), José S Cañas, Autopista Sur, is said to be the most complete collection. US information library at **American Chamber of Commerce**, 87 Av Norte 720, Apto A, Col Escalón, Apdo Postal (05) 9, Sr Carlos Chacón, speaks English, helpful. **Centro Cultural Salvadoreño**, Av Los Sisimiles, Metrocentro Norte, T2226-9103, 0800-1100, 1400-1700, English library, excellent. **Intercambios Culturales de El Salvador**, 67 Av Sur 228, Col Roma, T2245-1488, extensive Spanish and English reference library, local artistic exhibitions, computer school.

Medical services

Hospitals and clinics Hospital de la Mujer, between 81 and 83 Av Sur y Calle Juan José Cañas, Col Escalón (south of Paseo, bus 52 Paseo), T2223-8955. Hospital Pro-Familia, 25 Av Norte 483, 11 blocks east of Metrocentro, T2225-6100, clinics and 24-hr emergency, reasonable prices. Hospital Rosales, 25 Av Norte y 3 Calle Pte, long waits. Clínicas Médicas, 25 Av Norte 640 (bus 3, 9, 44 centro from Universidad Nacional), T/F225-5233. If you contract a serious stomach problem, the doctor will send you for tests, which will cost US$5-6. **Doctors** Dr Cesar Armando Solano, at Av J J Cañas below Hotel Terraza, T2283-4651, is a surgeon with excellent equipment and reasonable rates. English spoken. Medicentro, 27 Av Norte is a good place to find doctors in most specialist fields, afternoons mostly after 1500. Dr Jorge Panameno, T2225-9928, English-speaking, makes house calls at night for about US$35.

Post office

Central Post Office at the Centro de Gobierno with EMS, T2271-4036. Good service to Europe. Mon-Fri 0730-1700, Sat 0730-1200. Lista de Correos, Mon-Fri 0800-1200, 1430-1700, good service for mail collection. Branches through the city.

Telephone

At the Centro de Gobierno, Metrocentro (daily 0700-1930, 1830 for fax), and other locations. Phone boxes throughout the city, card only, available at fast-food stores such as Pollo Campero; direct dialling to anywhere in the world, also collect calls.

Work

UCA University Simeon Cañas, Blv Los Próceres San Salvador, T2210-6600, www.uca.edu.sv. An English-language programme always needing certified English teachers.

Western El Salvador

Compact and with good transport links, Western El Salvador combines the dramatic volcanic landscapes of Cerro Verde, Volcán Izalco and Lago de Coatepeque – essential for any visitor to the country – with the serene beauty and majesty of countless waterfalls and the colourful Ruta de las Flores around Sonsonate. Little indigenous villages and pre-Columbian ruins contrast with the vibrancy of Santa Ana, El Salvador's second largest city. Three routes lead to Guatemala, the northernmost passing close to the impressive cloud forests of Parque Nacional Montecristo on the border with Honduras. » *For Sleeping, Eating and other listings, see pages 753-757.*

Izalco to Sonsonate » pp753-757.

From the junction with the Pan-American Highway, just west of Colón, route CA 8 heads west, past Armenia, to the town of Izalco at the foot of Izalco volcano (8 km from Sonsonate, bus 53C, US$0.10). The town has evolved from the gradual merging of the *ladino* village of Dolores Izalco and the indigenous village of Asunción Izalco. In colonial times this was an important trading centre and experienced a communist rebellion in 1932. Today the town is experiencing a tourist revival with good colonial architecture, a prominent and active indigenous population and rich heritage of religious imagery which blends indigenous and Roman Catholic beliefs which produces regular processions and festivals. Local **festivals** run 8-15 August and during the Feast of St John the Baptist from 17-24 June.

Note The town of Izalco and Izalco volcano are not directly connected by road. A paved road branches off the highway 14 km before the turning for Izalco town (about 22 km from Sonsonate) and goes up towards Cerro Verde, Volcán Izalco and Lago de Coatepeque (see page 747).

Sonsonate and around » pp753-757. Colour map 5, C6.

→ *Population: 120,000. Altitude: 225 m.*

Sonsonate, 64 km from the capital, is the country's chief cattle-raising region. It also produces sugar, tobacco, rice, tropical fruits, hides and balsam. The city was founded in 1552 and is hot, dirty and crowded, but worth checking to see the colonial architecture in the city centre. The beautiful **El Pilar** church (1723) is strongly reminiscent of the church of El Pilar in San Vicente. The **Cathedral** has many cupolas (the largest covered with white porcelain) and was badly damaged in the 2001 earthquake but is now fully restored. The old church of **San Antonio del Monte** (completed 1861), 1 km from the city, draws pilgrims from afar (**fiesta** 22-26 August). There is a small **railway museum**; look for the locomotive at the entrance to the city on the highway from San Salvador (Km 65). An important market is held each Sunday. The market outside the church is quite well-organized. In the northern outskirts of the city there is a waterfall on the Río Sensunapán. Legend has it that an indigenous princess drowned there, and on the anniversary of her death a gold casket appears below the falls. The main annual event is **Feria de Candelaria** in February. Easter Week processions are celebrated with particular fervour and are probably the most impressive in the whole country. On Easter Thursday and Holy Friday the streets are filled with thousands of members of the *cofradías* (brotherhoods).

Around Sonsonate

Route CA 8, northwest to Ahuachapán (see page 750), has spectacular scenery along the **Ruta de las Flores**, with frequent buses from Sonsonate (bus 249 and 285, US$0.50, two hours) covering the 40-km paved route. The road goes through the indigenous village of **Nahuizalco**, bus 205. Some of the older women here still wear the *refajo* (a doubled length of cloth made of tie-dyed threads worn over a wrap-round skirt), and various crafts are still made, including wood and rattan furniture. Although use of the indigenuos language is dying out you do still encounter people who speak Nahuat. The night market, unique in El Salvador, opens at dusk and has traditional local food on sale. There's a **religious festival** 19-25 June, with music, **Danza de los Historiantes** (see page 1237) and art exhibitions; also 24-25 December, with music and **Danza de los Pastores**. Take Bus 53 D from Sonsonate (US$0.10.)

Salcoatitán and Juayúa

A little further up the mountainside at Km 82 is Salcoatitán, a colonial village with a beautiful park in front of the colonial church. Further along, the road branches off to Juayúa with Los Chorros de la Calera 2 km further north (bus 249 from Sonsonate). The pretty town decorated with flowers – the name means 'River of Purple Orchids' in the local Nahuatl dialect – sits nestling in a valley dominated by volcanoes. It's a peaceful spot where you can watch people at work and kids playing in the semi-cobbled street. The surrounding region is blanketed in coffee groves; the bean was introduced to the area in 1838 and today the town produces about 10% of the coffee exported from El Salvador. Its church houses an image of the **Cristo Negro** (Black Christ) carved by Quirio Cataño at the end of the 16th century. **Tourist information** is available from Jaime Salgado, at **Juayutur** ⓘ *Restaurante Las Colinas, desvío Salcoatitán and Juayúa, T2469-2310, juayutur@navegante.com.sv*, who can provide good information about the activities available in the region including rappelling waterfalls, the hike of the seven waterfalls and the mountain lagoon with wild horses. Guides are trained local youngsters. Also check out the Casa de la Cultura, on the corner next to the park for information on Juayúa. The owners of **Akwaterra Tours** and the mountain cabin **La Escondida**, Gaby and Julio Vega, have a small store named **Terracotta** a block from the park. They are fluent in English and have travel tips for the region. They also offer tours.

There are a number of excursions you can do in the area to see wildlife including river otters, toucans, butterflies and many other animals. In the dry season **Laguna de las Ranas** (Laguna Seca) dries up attracting numerous reptiles as it shrinks. There are also trips to the 30-m high waterfall at **Salto el Talquezal**, the 50-m high **Salto de la Lagunilla Azul** and several other waterfalls in the region seven in one day if you take a tour, with swimming and picnics on the way (see below). Every weekend Juayúa celebrates the Feria Gastronómica, an opportunity to try a variety of traditional dishes, often accompanied by local events, music and shows.

The **Feria Gastrónomica Internacional** is in January and celebrates with dishes from all over the world; other festivals include **Día de los Canchules** (31 October), when people ask for candies and **Día de las Mercedes** (17 September), when the houses are decorated with branches and candles leading up to the procession of the Virgen de la Merced. Another local attraction is the newly opened **Museo del café**, of the coffee cooperative **La Majada** ⓘ *T2467-9008, www.cafemajadaoro.com.sv*, located in San José La Majada, just outside Juayua on the road to Los Naranjos. Tours include information on coffee processing and a trip to the processing plant. A coffee shop offers local brews and iced coffee.

Los Naranjos and around

Moving northeast of Juayúa, swirling up a scenic mountain road connecting Juayúa with Santa Ana you arrive at Los Naranjos, a small traditional coffee village located at the mountain pass between Santa Ana and the Pilón volcanoes. The lines of windbreaking trees preventing damage to coffee trees are particularly beautiful, while the high altitude makes the climate cool with the scent of cypress forests.

At Km 82 on the Carretera Salcoatitán to Juayúa is **Parque y Restaurante La Colina** ⓘ *T2452-2916*, with hammocks, arts and crafts, and horse riding available. The town has a tiny colonial church and an orchid greenhouse. **Apaneca** is a short distance uphill from Sonsonate – see under Ahuachapán page 750.

Several **waterfalls** and other sites of natural beauty can be found in the Sonsonate district. To the west, near the village of **Santo Domingo de Guzmán** (bus 246 from Sonsonate), are the falls of **El Escuco** (2 km north), **Tepechapa** (1.5 km further) and **La Quebrada** (further still up the Río Tepechapa), all within walking distance of both Santo Domingo and each other. Walk through the town, then follow the river, there are several spots to swim. Santo Domingo de Guzman is also known for its *alfarería* (pottery) of *comales*, clay plates used to create torillas and *pupusas* over open fire, and its many Nahuat speaking habitants. There's a festival in Santo Domingo, 24-25 December, with music and dancing. A short distance north is **San Pedro Puxtla** (bus 246), with a modern church built on the remains of an 18th-century edifice. From here you can visit the **Tequendama Falls** on the Río Sihuapán. Bus 219 goes east to **Cuisnahuat** (18th-century baroque church, where the **Fiesta de San Judas** takes place 23-29 November. From there it is 2 km south to the Río Apancoyo, or 4 km north to **Peñón El Escalón** (covered in balsam trees) and **El Istucal Cave**, at the foot of the Escalón hill, where indigenous rites are celebrated in November.

Santa Tecla to Santa Ana » *pp753-757.*

The new Pan-American Highway parallels the old one, continuing northwest to the border with Guatemala at San Cristóbal. Santa Ana, acting as a transport hub, has routes out to Ahuachapán to the west and the border at Las Chinamas, as well as north to Metapán and beyond to the border crossing of Anguiatú.

Fifteen kilometres from Santa Tecla, 7 km beyond the junction with the Sonsonate road, there is a junction to the right. This road forks immediately, right to **Quezaltepeque**, left (at **Joya de Cerén** café) to **San Juan Opico**. After a few kilometres on

Routes to Guatemala

The four roads which cross into Guatemala are **La Hachadura** (see under Sonsonate), **San Cristóbal** (via the Pan-American Highway, page 752), **Las Chinamas** (see under Santa Ana) and **Anguiatú** (beyond Metapán, page 752).

the San Juan road, you cross the railway by the Kimberley-Clark factory. At the railway is **Restaurante Estación Sitio del Niño** (seafood, steak, local dishes, in an old station).

Joya de Cerén

ⓘ *US$2.90, parking US$1.20.*

After the girder bridge crossing the Río Sucio there is a grain store beside which is Joya de Cerén (32 km from the capital). This is a major archaeological site, not for spectacular temples, but because this is the only known site where ordinary Maya houses have been preserved having been buried by the ash from the nearby Laguna Caldera volcano in about AD 600. Buildings and construction methods can be clearly seen; a painted book and household objects have been found. All the structures are covered with protective roofing. The site has a small but good museum, café, toilets and car park. For Transport information, see page 756.

San Andrés

ⓘ *Tue-Sun 0900-1700, US$2.90, popular for weekend picnics, otherwise it's quiet, café.*

Back on the main road, heading west is the excavated archaeological site of San Andrés, halfway between Santa Tecla and Coatepeque on the estate of the same name (its full name is **La Campana de San Andrés**). It is located at Km 32.5 on the Pan-American Highway, just after the Hilasal towel factory. A new museum at the site displays some of the ceramics found at the site, others can be seen at the Museo Antrpológico David J Guzmán in San Salvador. The museum also features a special indigo section with information about this natural dye. El Salvador was the number one producer of indigo in the world in colonial times. A large indigo *obraje* (processing basin) – probably the largest found in Latin America – was found at San Andrés during an archaeological excavation and has been preserved. A group of low structures stands in the valley (Structure 5, the furthest from the entrance, is closed because of erosion). There are good views of the nearby hills. To get there, take bus No 201 from Terminal de Occidente, US$0.80 (same bus from Santa Ana).

Lago de Coatepeque

At El Congo, 13 km before Santa Ana, a branch road leads south to the northern shore of the beautiful Lago de Coatepeque, a favourite weekend resort, with good sailing, watersports and fishing, near the foot of Santa Ana volcano. Many weekend homes line the north and east shores, making access to the water difficult, but there are public *balnearios*: **Casa Blanca** and **Recreativa El Jordán** ⓘ *US$0.05 per person, parking US$0.25*. There are two islands in the lake – **Anteojos** which is close to the hotels, and **Teopán** on the far side. The local **Fiesta del Santo Niño de Atocha** runs from 25-29 June.

Cerro Verde and Volcán Izalco

ⓘ *Park entrance US$1.50, passport or photocopy required, car park US$1. Guided tour to summit included, leaving from the entrance at 1100 daily. The park is run by the Instituto Salvadoreño de Turismo, for information T2222-1800, www.istu.gob.sv.n Ask park guards for advice on climbing Izalco.*

Climbing Izalco

Izalco, as can be seen from the lack of vegetation, is a geologically young volcano. Historical records show that activity began in the 17th century as a sulphurous smoke vent but, in February 1770, violent eruptions formed a cone which was more or less in constant activity until 1957. There was a small eruption in 1966 through a blowhole on the southeast slope testified by two 1000-m lava flows. Since that time it has been quiescent.

A path leads off the road (signposted) just below the car park on Cerro Verde. In 20-30 minutes, descend to the saddle between Cerro Verde and Izalco, then it's 1-1½ hours up (steep but manageable). The contrast between the green forest of Cerro Verde and the coal-black lava around Izalco is impressive.The climb is three hours from base. Beware of falling rocks when climbing. There's a spectacular view from the top. For a quick descent, find a rivulet of soft volcanic sand and half-slide, half-walk down in 15 minutes, then it's about one hour back up the saddle. This 'cinder running' requires care, strong shoes and consideration for those below. Try to ensure that low cloud is not expected before planning to go.

In October 2005 the Santa Ana volcano erupted for the first time in more than 100 years. The area of Santa Ana and Cerro Verde has been closed for safety reasons as the authorities fear a new eruption. The park was closed, but the area is being monitored and is likely to be opened at some point in 2006. Contact ISTU for information.

From El Congo another road runs south, around the east shore of Lago Coatepeque. This road is locally known as Carretera Panorámica, due to the fantastic view of Coatepeque on one side and the mountains and valleys beyond the ridge. After reaching the summit, the paved road branches right, climbing above the south end of the lake to **Parque Nacional Cerro Verde** (2030 m) with its fine and surprising views of the Izalco volcano (1910 m), and Santa Ana volcano (2381 m), the highest volcano in the country. The road up to Cerro Verde is lined with beautiful flowers and half way up there is a mirador with a great view of Lago Coatepeque. Cerro Verde is probably one of the most beautiful places in El Salvador due to the special flora and fauna, breathtaking views and fine volcano trekking.

A 30-minute walk along a nature trail leads you around the crater ridge, to a series of miradors with views of Lago Coatepeque and Santa Ana volcano. For the best view of Izalco, go in the morning, although the afternoon clouds around the cone can be enchanting. » *For information on climbing Volcán Izalco, see box above.*

Volcán Santa Ana

Three quarters of the way to Cerro Verde, a track branches off to the right to *Finca San Blas* (also can be reached on foot from Cerro Verde car park, 20 minutes). Accommodation is available in the cabins at **Casa de Cristal** run by the San Blas coffee cooperative.

It was possible to hike up the impressive Volcán Santa Ana, 2381 m – the highest point in El Salvador apart from two places on the Honduran frontier – after the October 2005 eruptions seek local advice. There are four craters inside one another; the newest has a turquoise-coloured lake and fuming columns of sulphur clouds. The views are spectacular, but it can be hazy in the dry season.

Izalco was known as the 'Lighthouse of the Pacific' because sailors approaching the port of Acajutla used the flares of its eruption as a reference point to get safely to harbour.

Santa Ana and around

» pp753-757. Colour map 5, C6.

→ *Population: 400,000. Altitude: 776 m.*

Santa Ana, 55 km from San Salvador and capital of its department, is the second largest city in the country. On the foothills of Santa Ana volcano, the basin in which it lies is exceptionally fertile, producing large amounts of coffee, with sugar cane coming a good second. The city, named Santa Ana La Grande by Fray Bernardino Villapando in 1567, is the business centre of western El Salvador. There are some fine buildings: the neo-Gothic **cathedral**, and several other churches, especially **El Calvario**, in neoclassical style. Of special interest is the classical **Teatro Nacional** ⓘ *on the north side of the plaza, a guide (small charge) will show you round on weekdays, watch local press for performances*, originally completed in 1910, now in the latter stages of interior restoration and one of the finest theatres in Central America. A donation from the Organization of American States is being used to replace the seating. The **Fiestas Julias** take place from 1-26 July.

Chalchuapa

→ *Population: 34,865 Altitude: 640 m.*

About 16 km west of Santa Ana, on the road to Ahuachapán, lies Chalchuapa. President Barrios of Guatemala was killed in battle here in 1885, while trying to reunite Central America by force. There are some good colonial-style domestic buildings. The church of Santiago Apóstol is particularly striking; almost the only one in El Salvador which shows strong indigenous influences (restored 1997-98). **Fiestas** 18-21 July, Santiago Apóstol, and 12-16 August, San Roque. **Tazumal** ruins next to the cemetery in Chalchuapa, are the tallest and probably the most impressive in El Salvador. Built about AD 980 by the Pipil, with its 14-step pyramid now, alas, restored

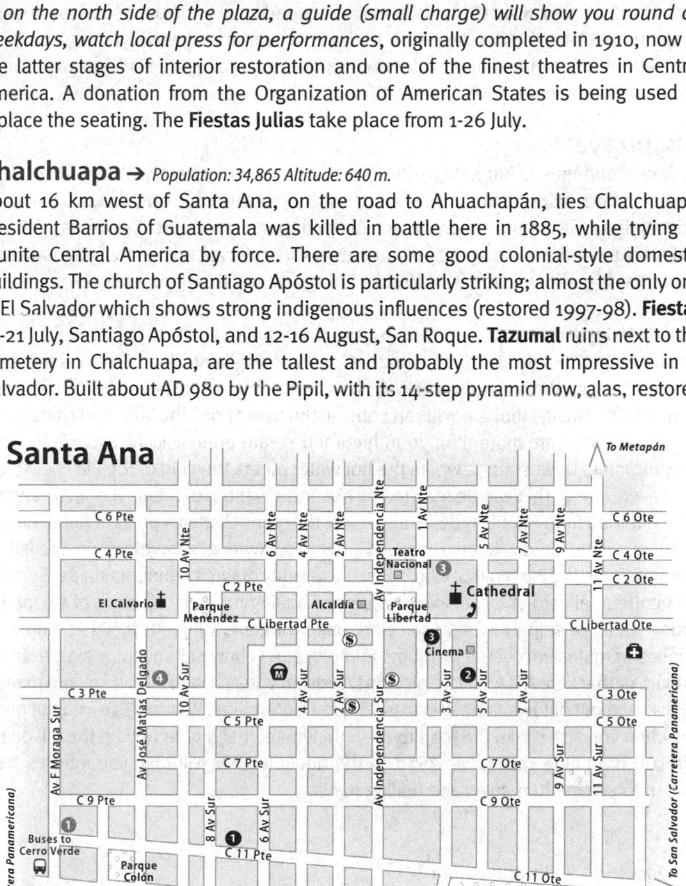

in concrete. The site has been occupied since 5000 BC and in the **Museo Regional de Chalchuapa** ⓘ *Tue-Sun 0900-1200, 1300-1700, US$3, bus 218 from Santa Ana, 30 mins, US$0.20*, are the artefacts that were found in the mud under the lake. There are some very interesting bowls used for burning incense, intricately decorated with animal designs. Some of the exhibits from the Museo de Arqueología in San Salvador, damaged in the 1996 earthquake, are on show here. The ruin is only five minutes' walk from the main road. On the main road near the ruins is a souvenir shop, **Tienda Tazumal** ⓘ *11 Av Sur 31, T2444-0803*, selling good reproductions and jewellery. It is run by Elida Vides de Jaime, whose husband can act as a guide to Tazumal and other nearby ruins. He is helpful and speaks some English.

Casa Blanca ⓘ *T2444-0892, ddpatrimonio@telemovil.net, daily, Km 78 Pan-American Highway, US$4*, is a newly opened archaeological site just outside Chalchuapa along the Pan-American Highway. There are several pyramids, ongoing excavations and a museum provides an insight to the archaeological past of this area and a section on indigo (*añil*) production.

Atiquizaya

The road continues 12 km west to Atiquizaya, a small, quiet town with one *hospedaje*, several good *pupuserías* (1600-2100) and **Restaurante Atiquizaya**, 1 km at intersection with main highway to Ahuachapán, good. At **Cataratas del Río Malacachupán** there is a beautiful 50-m high waterfall cascading into a lagoon; it's a 1-km hike to get there. Nearby is **Volcán Chingo** on the Guatemalan border.

Ahuachapán → *Colour map 5, C6. Population: 80,000. Altitude: 785 m.*

A quiet town with low and simple houses, 35 km from Santa Ana. Coffee is the main product. It draws the mineral water for its bathhouse from some hot springs close to the nearby falls of Malacatiupán. You can bathe in the river above the falls, and camp in the vicinity. The falls are more than 70 m high and steam impressively, especially in the early morning. Downstream, where the hot water meets the cold of the Río Frío, steam rises everywhere. This can be reached by bus (hourly most of the day) or 4WD along a 5-km dirt road from Atiquizaya (see above), or the same distance north of Ahuachapán. Pick-ups can be hired with driver for US$9 per day. Power is generated from the falls of Atehuezián on the Río Molino, which cascade prettily down the mountainside. See also the geothermal field of *los ausoles*, geysers of boiling mud with plumes of steam and strong whiffs of sulphur. The *ausoles* are used for generating electricity and only the smallest remains uncovered by drums and pipes. A yellow school bus leaves from the market, or there are **ATLA** private pick-ups/taxis, or you can walk. It is 3 km and marked on the road out of town to Apaneca as 'Planta Geotérmica'. You can't go into the plant, but when you arrive take the road to the right where, just a little way up the hill on the left, you hit a little *casita*. For US$0.50 the house owner will take you into his back garden to see the fumaroles and boiling pools.

Tacuba

ⓘ *0900-1600, look for the guard.*

Tacuba is an indigenous town, around 850-m above sea level, and 15 km west of Ahuachapán. Tacuba means 'the village of the football game', probably relating to the *juego de pelota* of the Maya, and the existence of many pre-Columbian mounds in the surrounding area suggest the region was heavily populated in the past. At the entrance to the town are the largest colonial church ruins in El Salvador, torn down by the earthquake of Santa Marta, the same tremors that ruined large parts of Antigua, Guatemala, in 1773. You can also visit the Casa de la Cultura office, **Concultura** ⓘ *3 km on main street north, 0900-1230, 1330-1600*, to see an interesting display of photos. The town is near the northern entrance of Reserva Nacional Bosque El Imposible, which is accessed by hiking or 4WD in the dry season.

Santa Ana blows her top

In October 2005 Volcán Santa Ana awoke from a sleep of more than 100 years. The eruption killed two and forced thousands to flee the area. A fumarole rose 10 km into the air and rocks were thrown a distance of 1.5 km. Shortly after, satellite photographs showed the ash cloud covering most of western El Salvador and parts of Guatemala. The danger has now passed, but check locally for access to the area.

The surrounding area offers a wide range of opportunities including waterfalls, pristine rivers, mountain hikes and panoramic views. **Ceiba de los Pericos,** 15 mins out of Tacuba by car, a 600-year-old ceiba tree where thousands of parrots flock together at dusk to sleep in its branches, ending the day with a deafening noise before resting for the night. In Tacuba centre the **Ceiba de las Garzas** is the rendezvous of hundreds of *garzas* (herons).

Local tour company **Manolo Tours,** led by Tacuba native Manolo Gonzalez, provide tours of the Tacuba area and to Reserva El Imposible. The dirt road leading from Tacuba to the cordillera, is steep and spectacular and provides impressive views; it is recommended although a 4WD is required.

Apaneca → *Population: 12,000 Altitude: 1450 m, the highest town in the country.*

Between Ahuachapán and Sonsonate is Apaneca (91 km from San Salvador, 29 km from Las Chinamas on the border) an extremely peaceful town with small cobbled streets, marking the northern end of the **Ruta de las Flores.** Founded by Pedro de Alvarado in 1543, Apaneca is known for its cool climate and winds – *apaneca* means *river of winds* in Nahuat. The town has a colonial centre, a traditional *parque* and a municipal market selling fruit, flowers and handicrafts. One of the oldest parochial churches in the country used to corner the central park but was demolished after damage caused by the 2001 earthquake. A new artisans market has opened – a great place to observe the local arts and crafts. Other local industries include coffee, flowers for export and furniture. Have a look at the topiary creations outside the police station. Check out the Casa de la Cultura in the centre of town. There are two small lakes nearby to the north, **Laguna Verde** and **Laguna Las Ninfas,** whose crater-like walls are clothed in tropical forest and cypress trees. A swim, according to local legend, is meant to be very beneficial to your health. This is the Cordillera de Apaneca, part of the narrow highland belt running southeast of Ahuachapán (see Sleeping). The lakes are popular with tourists. It is possible to swim in the former, but the latter is too shallow and reedy. There is also a beautiful natural pool called the **Balneario de Azumpa**. A local guide named **Walter Alberto Calderón Jr** ⓘ *T2433-0016, wal_calderon@hotmail.com,* at weekends has a team of young guides and provides tours to the local sights.

Santa Leticia

ⓘ *Archaeological site US$2; 2-hr coffee tour US$20; both combined US$35.*

Close by, and 10 minutes by bus No 249 from Juayúa, is the Santa Leticia archaeological site. The site is believed to be 2600 years old and was rediscovered in 1968 by the farm owner. Three huge monuments are buried among the coffee groves and you feel like a first-time discoverer, especially as it is a winding route to get there. There are three stone spheres with human characteristics weighing between 6000 and 11,000 kg.

South of Apaneca is the **Cascada del Río Cauta**. To get there, take bus 216 from Ahuachapán towards Jujutla, alight 3 km after the turn-off to Apaneca, then walk300 m along the trail to the waterfall.

Border essentials: El Salvador-Guatemala

San Cristóbal
The border with Guatemala is 30 km northwest from Santa Ana along the paved Pan-American Highway at San Cristóbal. This is the Carretera Panamericana crossing to Guatemala taken by the international buses and much heavy traffic.
Sleeping **F** El Paso, basic, friendly.
Salvadorean immigration The border is open 0600-2000.
Transport To Santa Ana, bus 201, US$0.80, 1½ hrs, 0400-1800.

Anguiatú
This is normally a quiet border crossing except when there are special events at Esquipulas in Guatemala.
Salvadorean immigration
The usual requirements apply; relaxed crossing.
Transport To Santa Ana, bus 235A, US$0.80, 1¾ hrs. To **Metapán** 40 mins, US$0.25. This is the best route from San Salvador to northwest Guatemala, Tikal and Belize, but there is an alternative through Honduras (see under El Poy, page 762). There is a road of sorts from Metapán to El Poy and two buses a day, four hours, US$1.80, but the poor state of the road is more than compensated for by spectacular scenery.

Las Chinamas
This is a busy crossing as it is the fastest road link from San Salvador to Guatemala City. The road to the border is being widened and repaved for its entire length, except where it passes through Chalchuapa at Km 78 and Ahuachapán at Km 100.
Salvadorean immigration
A straightforward crossing; quick service if your papers are ready.
Crossing by private vehicle
If driving with non-Central American licence plates, expect about 45 mins for formalities; you can hire a *trámite* (young boy) to hustle your papers through, US$2-3. Your vehicle will probably be searched by anti-narcotics officers (DOAN); do not refuse as your papers will be checked again 300 m into El Salvador. PNC (police) are courteous and efficient.
Transport 300 m above immigration, frequent buses to **Ahuachapán**, No 265, US$0.45, 25 mins. Change there to a No 202 to **San Salvador**. Between 0800 and 1400 you may try for a space on one of the international Pullmans, negotiate with driver's aide, about US$3.50 to the capital.
Exchange Coming from Guatemala, cash your quetzals at the border, check what you are given. Change money with the women in front of the ex-ISTU office next to Customs. Good quetzal-dollar rate, cash only.

Taking the northern road from Ahuachapán, 9 km west of town near the village of **Los Toles** are the Tehuasilla Falls, where the Río El Molino falls 60 m (bus 293 from Ahuachapán to Los Toles, then walk 1 km). The road continues northwest through the treeless **Llano del Espino**, with its small lake, and across the Río Paz into Guatemala.

North of Santa Ana

Texistepeque, 17 km north of Santa Ana on the road to Metapán, has an 18th-century baroque church, with **fiestas** on 23-27 December and 15 January. The town was one of the main areas for indigo (*añil*) production and colonial processing plants known as *obrajes* exist all around the area. Visit the indigo workshop and museum of Licenciado Marroquín just out of town.

Metapán is about 10 km northeast of Lago de Güija and 32 km north of Santa Ana. Its colonial baroque Catedral de San Pedro, completed by 1743, is one of the very few to have survived in El Salvador. The altarpieces have some very good silver work, using silver from local mines, and the façade is splendid. The **Fiesta de San Pedro Apóstol** runs from 25-29 June. There are lots of easy walks with good views towards **Lago de Metapán** and, further on, **Lago de Güija**. There are many lime kilns and a huge cement plant.

If planning to walk in the hills near Metapán, seek local advice and do not walk alone.

Reserva Nacional y Natural Montecristo

➔ *Colour map 5, C3.*

ⓘ *Park employees escort visitors, best Mon-Fri. Admission is paid 5 km before the park, US$1.25 per person, plus US$3 for vehicle. 4WD is necessary in the wet season (mid-May to mid-Oct). Camping is permitted. To hire 4WD and driver costs US$45 return, 7 hrs eg Sr Francisco Xavier Monterosa, Calle 15 de Septiembre Casa 40, T2402-2805, c/o Isaac Monterosa. In San Salvador ask at Salva Natura (see page 740) for details on visiting the park.*

A mountain track from Metapán gives access to El Salvador's last remaining cloud forest. Here there is an abundance of protected wildlife and it now forms part of El Trifinio, or the International Biosphere 'La Fraternidad', administered jointly by Guatemala, Honduras and El Salvador. Near the top of **Cerro Montecristo** (2418 m), which is the point where the three borders meet, there is an **orchid garden** with over 100 species (best time to see them in flower is early spring), an orchard and a camping ground in the forest. The views are stunning as is the change in flora and fauna with the altitude.

It is 20 km from Metapán to the park. It takes 1½ to two hours to go up, less to return. The trails to the summit take 1½ hours.

Sleeping

Izalco *p744*

C El Chele, Final Av Roberto Carillas, Calle La Violeta, Caserío Texcalito, T2453-6740. Some 800 m north of Izalco at a *finca* surrounded by forest – free transport available, call. Great view of Volcán Izalco. Escorted hikes and horse rides available to Cerro Verde and Izalco with visits to 2 barely investigated pre-Columbian ruins nearby.

Sonsonate *p745*

B Plaza, Calle 9 Oriente, Barrio del Angel, T/F2451-6626. A/c rooms, good restaurant, pool, recommended.

B-C Agape, Km 63 on outskirts of town, take old road through Sonsonate, the hotel is on the exit street to San Salvador, just before the main roundabout on the right side, T2451-1456, hotelplaza_sonsonate@yahoo.com. Converted convent, gardens, suites and rooms, a/c or fan, safe parking, fine restaurant, cable TV, pool, laundry service, recommended.

E Castro, on main street 3 blocks from Parque. With bath, fan, good, safe, friendly, some rooms with bed and hammock.

F El Brasil, 4 Av Norte. Basic, clean and friendly.

F Hospedaje Blue River, near bus station. with bath, large, clean rooms.

Salcoatitán and Juayúa *p745*

B Posada El Encanto, Col La Esmeralda 7677, Juayúa, T2452-2187, www.hotelencanto.com. Rooms have private bathroom, a/c and TV. Parking.

C-D Doña Mercedes, 29 Av Sur, 6 Calle Oriente 3-6, Juayúa, 1 block south of Farmacia Don Bosco, T2452-2207. Friendly owner Doña Paty offers discounts for longer stays, recommended.

C-D La Escondida, 6 km north of Juayúa at Finca El Portezuelo, T7888-4552, www.akwaterra.com. B&B in an exceptionally beautiful location, cradled between Laguna Verde and forest-clad mountains, with a view over to

Ahuachapán to the north. You can use this as a base for hikes, mountain biking, horse riding and coffee tours. Fireplace, DVD, equipped kitchen. Contact Julio and Gaby at Terracotta in Juayúa.

D-E Anahuac, 1 Calle Pte and 5 Av Norte, Juayúa, T2469-2401, hotelanahuac@tikal.dk. Dormitories for backpackers and tours.

D-E El Mirador, a block from the park, Juayúa, T2452-2232. A 3-storey building with restaurant on top.

Lago de Coatepeque *p747*

B Torremolinos, on pier out above the lagoon, T2441-6037. Pool, good rooms (a couple with hot showers), restaurant and bar, boating trips, popular at weekends with music, lively. Discounts for longer stays.

D-F Amacuilco, 300 m from Telecom, T2441- 6239. Very helpful manager (Sandra). 6 rooms (but avoid those which overlook the kitchen). Discounts for longer stays, art gallery, marimba classes and Spanish and Nahuatl lessons, all meals available, live music Fri and Sat night, pool, great view with jetty over the lake, secure, recommended, boat excursions on lake, tours arranged from US$30-40 per day (US$100 per week includes breakfast and dinner).

F Ecoturismo Lajamaya, final Calle los Planes, T2448-9718, laslajas@navegante.com.sv. Several cabins along lake shore, very nice and quiet park with pool, basic but safe.

Santa Ana *p749, map p749*

Many hotels close their doors from 2000 arrive early if you can.

B-C Sahara, 3 Calle Pte y 10 Av Sur, T2447-8865, hotel_sahara@yahoo.com. Good service, but a little overpriced.

C-D Internacional, 25 Calle Pte y 10 Av Sur, T2440-0810. With bath, restaurant in same building, safe parking for motorcycles, TV, laundry; not the most conventional of hotels.

C-D La Libertad, near cathedral, 4 Calle Ote 2, T441-2358. With bath, good-value budget choice, friendly, clean, helpful, safe car park across the street, US$2 for 24 hrs.

D-E Casa Frolaz, 29 Calle Pte 42-B between 8 and 10 Av Sur T2440-5302, www.casafrolaz.com. Beautiful and clean hostel with art, paintings, history books and a friendly reception, hot showers, tropical garden with hammocks and barbecue.

D-E El Faro, 14 Av Sur 9 entre 9 y 11 Calle Pte, T2447-7787. Clean rooms, good price.

E La Posada del Rey, 10 Av Sur 71, between 13 and 15 Calle Pte, east side of Mercado Colón and 50 m from bus terminal, T2440-0787, hotellaposadadelrey@hotmail.com. Low prices and nice rooms, friendly and helpful owners, good backpacker choice, highly recommended.

F Hospedaje Tikal, 10 Av Sur y Calle 9. Clean, quiet, large rooms, free chilled drinking water, popular with the 1-hr crowd.

Ahuachapán *p750*

B Casa Blanca, 2 Av Norte y Calle Gerardo Barrios, T/F2443-1505. 2 rooms a/c, clean, good, recommended (owner's husband is a doctor).

B-C El Parador, Km 102.5 Carretera a Guatemala, 1.5 km west of town, T/F2443-0331. Hotel and restaurant, a/c, good service, motel-style, relaxing, helpful owner, Sr Nasser, recommended. (Buses to border stop outside, T2443-1637.)

E San José, 6 Calle Pte, opposite the park, T2413-0033. With bath, clean, friendly, parking.

F Hospedaje Granada, 3 blocks down from plaza by market. Shared bath, clean.

F Hospedaje Milagro, near bus station. Clean, basic.

Tacuba *p750*

C Juanimar Suites, Av Cuscatlán 23, T2417-4204. In colonial house in Tacuba centre.

C-D La Cabaña de Tacuba, 50m west of Alcaldía, T2417-4332, hotellacabana@yahoo.com. Nice hotel with large park grounds, access to river pools, swimming pools, a/c, cable TV. Great food at restaurant.

D-F Hostal de Mama y Papa, Barrio El Calvario, 1 Calle 1, T2417-4268, www.imposibletours.com. Home of González family with dorm and private rooms with private bath available. Excellent, cheap food available. Son Manolo runs **Manolo Tours**.

Apaneca *p751*

AL Santa Leticia, Carretera Sonsonate Km 86.5, south of Apaneca, T2433-0357, www.coffee.com.sv. 11 comfortable double rooms, decorated in locally carved wood, pool, gardens, live music on Sun, restaurant, close to Santa Leticia archaeological site.

A-B **Las Cabañas de Apaneca**, T2433-0500, cabanasapaneca@navegante.com.sv. 12 cabins, many with good views, in pleasant gardens, more expensive with full board.
B **La Posada de Don Oli**, Ataco, a few kilometres west of Apaneca, oogomezduarte@yahoo.com.mx, T2450-5155. Hotel and restaurant in a colonial setting with traditional dishes owned by the local mayor, Oscar Gómez. Guides available to visit the local sights.
B **Villas Suizas**, at entrance to Apaneca, T2433-0193. Several log cabins with kitchen and living room and lovely gardens.
C **Hotel Laguna Verde Guest House**, T2260-2481. A nice small domo house located at the rim of a deep secondary crater with spectacular view. Located 250 m from Laguna Verde and 3 km from Apaneca makes it a perfect departure point for hiking in the area.
C-D **Las Orquídeas**, Av Central Sur 4, T2433-0061. Clean rooms, although the top ones are a little overpriced. Also offer accommodation in a family home.

North of Santa Ana *p752*

B-C **San José**, Carretera Internacional Km 113, Metapán, near bus station, T2442-0556. A/c, quiet, cable TV, safe parking, good, restaurant on ground floor (Sra García, the manager, will help with transport to Montecristo).
F **Hospedaje Central**, 2 Av Norte y Calle 15 de Septiembre. With bath, clean friendly, popular.

Eating

Izalco *p744*

ΨΨ **Casa de Campo**, across from Turicentro Atecozol, T2453-6530. The old *casco* of the *finca* Cuyancúa has been restored with beautiful gardens making it a good spot for a meal.
Ψ **Mariona**,in the centre, T2453-6580. One of several *comedores*. They serve a 55-year-old recipe for *sopa de gallina* (Creole chicken soup) famous all over Izalco.

Sonsonate *p745*

ΨΨ **Doña Laura**, located inside Hotel Agape (see Sleeping, above). Open 0730-2100. A/c. Highly recommended.
ΨΨ **Nuevo Hilary**, Av Rafael Campos 1-3. Local and Chinese food, generous servings, moderate prices.
Ψ **Burger House Plaza**, Pasaje Francisco Chacón. Open 0900-2000. Hamburgers, fried chicken with potato salad.

Salcoatitán and Juayúa *p745*

ΨΨ **Pollo Rico**, close to park, Juayúa, T2452-2385. Good mix of dishes as well as the traditional ones.
Ψ **La Terraza**, on corner of the park, Juayúa. A café and convenience store with a tourist kiosk nearby.
Ψ **Laura's**, 1 block from the park on 1 Av Sur, Juayúa. 'The best in town' according to one reader, serving *comida a la vista*.

Cafés

Pastelería y Cafetería Festival, 4 Calle Pte and 1 Av Sur, T2452-2269. Bakery and coffee shop – try the *pastelitos de ciruela* (plum pie) or the traditional *semita* with good view overlooking the park.

Santa Ana *p749, map p749*

Restaurants close quite early, between 2000 and 2100. *Comedores* are usually cheap and good value or try the food stalls beside the plaza or in front of the cathedral. Look for excellent pineapples in season.
ΨΨ **Kiyomi**, 4 Av Sur between 3 and 5 Calle. Good food and service, clean, reasonable prices.
ΨΨ **Los Horcones**, on main plaza next to the cathedral. Like a jungle lodge inside, with pleasant balcony dining, good cheap meals.
ΨΨ **Lover's Steak House**, 4 Av Sur y 17 Calle Pte, T2440-5717. Great value, recommended.
ΨΨ **Parrillada Texana**, Av Independencia Sur. Good grilled chicken, garlic bread and salads, good value.
ΨΨ **Talitunal**, 5 Av Sur 6. Mon-Sat 0900-1900. Vegetarian, attractive, good lunch, owner is a doctor and expert on medicinal plants.
Ψ **Expresión**, 11 Calle Pte 20, between Av 6 and 8, T/F440-1410, expresioncultural@yahoo.com. A great little coffee bar, restaurant, bookshop and internet café, with occasional art exhibitions. Cheap.
Ψ **Kikos**, Av Independencia Sur, near 5 Calle. Good chicken and pizza.
Ψ **Pupusería Memita**, 25 Calle Pte. Recommended for fresh *pupusas* made to order.
Ψ **Veras Pizza**, Av Independencia Sur. Good salad bar.

Chalchuapa *p749*
Several cheap and informal eateries with good quality meals around the newly renovated and charming central park.
¥¥ **Acajutla**, 7 Calle Ote 9, T2440-3517. High-quality seafood, popular, not cheap; accepts credit cards.
¥¥ **Los Antojitos**, Calle Ramón Flores 6, T2444-0722. Good meals.

Ahuachapán *p750*
¥¥ **Restaurant El Paseo**, **Restaurant Tanya** and **El Parador**, on the Las Chinimas road. All serve good meals.
¥ **Mixta's Restaurante**, good and cheap meals.

Cafés
Pastelería María, good cakes and biscuits.

Tacuba *p750*
¥ **Casa Grande** and **Mis Abuelas**, on the main park. Both serve typical food.

Apaneca *p751*
Stalls in the municipal market offer cheap meals and typical dishes.
¥¥¥-¥¥ **La Cocina de Mi Abuela**, in town, T2433-0100, and **Cabañas de Apaneca**, on the main highway. The 2 largest restaurants and most popular spots that attract people from far and wide.
¥¥ **El Viejo Pescador**, a couple of blocks southeast of the plaza, T2433-0463. Good food, pleasant garden patio dining.
¥ **Artesanías y Comedor Rosita**. Range of local dishes as well as arts and crafts.

North of Santa Ana *p752*
Just before entering Metapán, 50 m off the highway, at the rim of the Lagunita Metapán, there are a few places offering good fish from the lake, international menu, both with a/c.
¥¥ **Rincón del Pelón**. Best restaurant in town, helpful, friendly.
¥ **Comedor Carmencita**, 2 Av Norte. Clean, popular, basic meals.

Activities and tours

Ahuachapán *p750*
Tour operators
Tours & Aventuras, at Agencia de Viajes Morales, 2 Av Norte 2-4, T2413-2002. Talk to Beatriz Contreras.

Tacuba *p750*
Tour operators
Manolo Tours. See Hostal de Mama y Papa, see page 754.

Transport

Sonsonate *p745*
Bus No 248 to **Santa Ana**, US$1 along CA 12 north, 39 km, a beautiful journey through high, cool coffee country, with volcanoes in view. To **Ahuachapán**, bus 249, 2 hrs, slow, best to go early in the day; **San Salvador** to Sonsonate by bus 530, US$0.80, 1½ hrs, very frequent. To **Barra de Santiago**, bus 285. To **Los Cobanos** bus 259. Take care at the bus terminal and on rural routes (eg in Nahuizalco area).

Joya de Cerén *p747*
Bus No 108 from San Salvador Terminal de Occidente to San Juan; US$0.45, 1 hr. Bus 201 from Santa Ana, US$0.60, 1 hr, ask the bus driver to drop you at Desvío Opico from where you can catch another bus to Joya de Cerén.

Lago de Coatepeque *p747*
Bus From **Santa Ana**, bus 220 'El Lago' to the lake every 30 mins, US$0.35; from **San Salvador**, bus 201 to El Congo (bridge at Km 50) on Pan-American Highway, US$1, then pick up the No 220 bus to the lake, US$0.45. Other buses to Guatemala may also stop at El Congo, check. **Taxi** from Santa Ana US$10.

Cerro Verde and Volcán Izalco *p747*
Bus From **Santa Ana**, bus 248 goes to Cerro Verde, with the first bus at 0730, last at 1530, 1½ hrs, returning at 1000, 1100, 1300 and 1500. If you travel from **San Salvador** take the bus towards Santa Ana (No 205). Get off at the Shell gas station at El Congo, cross the bridge that goes over the highway and catch the No 248 at the junction from Santa Ana. If you come from the west take the bus from Esso gas station beween Izalco and Ateos that leads to Santa Ana and get off at junction 14 km below Cerro Verde summit and wait for No 248 that comes from El Congo.

Santa Ana *p749*
Bus No 201 from Terminal del Occidente, San Salvador, US$1, 1 hr, every 10-15 mins,

0400-1830. To **La Libertad**, take 'autopista' route bus to **San Salvador** and change buses in Nueva San Salvador. Buses (**Melva**, **Pezzarossi** and others) leave frequently from 25 Calle Pte y 8 Av Sur, T2440-3606, for **Guatemala City**, full fare as from San Salvador, 4-4½ hrs including border stops. Alternatively there are local buses to the border for US$0.45; they leave from the market. Frequent buses to **Metapán** and border at **Anguiatú**. No 238 follows a beautiful route to **Juayúa**.

Atiquizaya *p750*

Bus There are frequent buses to the river from the central park in Atiquizaya; buses 202 and 456 from Terminal Occidente in **San Salvador**, 2 hrs, US$0.90. From **Santa Ana**, 45 mins, US$0.40. All Ahuachapán buses stop in the Parque Central.

Ahuachapán *p750*

Bus Ahuachapán is 100 km from **San Salvador** by bus 202 (US$0.90), every 20 mins 0430-1830 to the capital, 2 hrs via **Santa Ana**. Microbuses to border from northwest corner of parque, US$0.45, 25 mins, slower buses same price. Frequent buses and minivans to the border at Km 117, **Las Chinamas**.

Tacuba *p750*

Bus Buses leave the terminal in **Ahuachapán** every 30 mins, 0500-1530, return 1630-1700, via **Ataco**; US$0.60, 45 mins, rough road.

Apaneca *p751*

Bus Local buses stop by the plaza, others pass on the main road, a few blocks north, leaving you with a fairly long walk. **Laguna Verde** can be reached by walking from Apaneca to Cantón Palo Verde and Hoyo de Cuajuste, then a further 1 km from where the road ends.

North of Santa Ana *p752*

Bus From Santa Ana bus No 235, US$0.80, 1 hr. If driving **San Salvador**-Metapán, a bypass skirts Santa Ana. Bus No 211 to border at **Anguiatú**.

Directory

Salcoatitán and Juayúa *p745*

Banks Banco de Comercio, 2 blocks behind the church on the road into Juayúa, 0830-1630. **Internet** Mini Librería, 4 Calle Ote, ½ block from main square, Juayúa.

Santa Ana *p749*

Banks Banks will change TCs. Banco Salvadoreño, and several other banks Av Independencia Sur, between Calle 3 and 7. **Internet** Expresión, has a couple of computers on the go in a very comfortable setting. **Laundry** Lavandería Solución, 7 Calle Pte 29, wash and dry US$2.50 per load, ironing service, recommended. **Police** Emergency T911. **Post office** 7 Calle Pte, between 2 Av and Av Independencia Sur.

Northern El Salvador

The route from San Salvador to western Honduras heads north, skirting the vast arm of the Cerrón Grande reservoir with volcanoes in the distance. Small villages are interspersed with brand new settlements tucked amongst the fields and hills as the road winds through mountainous landscape – a snapshot of the old way of life, and the emergence of the new. Currently enjoying a cultural revival, the charming colonial town of Suchitoto on the southern shore of the reservoir is definitely worth a visit.

▸▸ *For Sleeping, Eating and other listings, see pages 762-764.*

North from San Salvador

The old highway, Troncal del Norte (CA 4) used to be the only acess to the north from the capital, but has been replaced with a new and modern highway. This can be accessed from Bulevar Constitución, in the northeastern part of San Salvador, and swirls west around the Volcán de San Salvador towards the Pan-American Highway and branches out to Nejapa, Quezaltepeque and Apopa to the north. Another advance in the northern road system is the newly improved road that connects Aguilares with Suchitoto. It is 2½ hours by car from San Salvador to La Palma, then 11 km to the border at El Poy.

Apopa and Tonacatepeque

Apopa is a friendly town with a good market and a new shopping centre. It is the junction with a road to Quezaltepeque (12 km). (Bus 38B from San Salvador to Apopa, US$0.15.) A paved road runs east from Apopa to Tonacatepeque, an attractive small town on a high plateau. It has a small textile industry and is in an agricultural setting – check out the charming park and the colonial church. There has been some archaeological exploration of the town's original site, 5 km away. A paved road from Tonacatepeque runs 13 km south to the Pan-American Highway, some 5 km from the capital. In the other direction, a dry-weather road runs north to Suchitoto. Three kilometres beyond Apopa, on CA 4 Km 17, is **Finca Orgánica Las Termópilas** where **Lisa's Guest House,** is located (see page 762). There is also a Spanish-language school and they arrange volunteers for the 'Working Farm' project at Termópilas organic farm. Tours are available to the archaeological site Cihuatán (see below) as well as to Suchitoto and to Volcán Guazapa on horseback, which played a prominent part in the civil war. The panoramic views are amazing and you can visit the old guerrilla hide outs. Contact Lena and René Carmona at **Ximena's** (see page 737) or T2205-6320. All buses from Terminal de Oriente to Aguilares pass the entrance (US$0.25).

Aguilares

From Apopa, it's 21 km to Aguilares, 4 km beyond which are the ruins of **Cihuatán** ⓘ *0800-1600, FUNDAR map available from Lisa's Guest House or at Ximena's Guest House (see page 737); alternatively, contact chief archaeologist Paul Amaroli at FUNDAR in San Salvador, T2235-9453*. The name means 'place of women' and was presided over by female royalty. This was the largest city in Mesoamerica during the Toltec period and the city was surrounded by extended fortification measuring more than 10 sq km. This is the largest archaeological site in the country holding several tall pyramids, ball courts and *temazcales* (ritual saunas).

A newly improved road goes from Aguilares heading west to Suchitoto. If heading north, see page 760.

Suchitoto

Suchitoto, meaning 'the place of birds and flowers' in Nahuatl, was founded by the Pipil more than 1000 years ago. In 1528 the capital was moved to Suchitoto for 15 years as the villa of San Salvador suffered attacks from local tribes. In 1853 an earthquake destroyed much of San Salvador and many affluent families moved to Suchitoto leaving a lasting impression on the town. Today it is a small, very attractive colonial town with cobbled streets, balconied houses and an interesting church, and one of the favourite tourist spots in the country with cultural traditions kept alive by the many artists living and working in the town. Several hotels and restaurants in the town offer fantastic views towards Suchitlán and Volcán Guazapa. More than 200 species of bird have been identified in the area, and white-tailed deer inhabit the local woods.

The town was almost completely deserted in the early 1990s after 12 years of civil war which severely affected the region – 90% of the population left, leaving Suchitoto virtually a ghost town. A population and cultural revival has stimulated a range of activities and events, and the town is now considered the cultural capital of the country. Life centres on the main plaza which every evening becomes a bustle of people just wandering the streets. Suchitoto's telegraph poles have been decorated by artist Paulo Rusconi, and Parque San Martín, to the west end of town, is dotted with modern sculptures, some made using ex-war materials. Arts and cultural **festivals** take place every February, with internationally renowned artists on the menu. Another local festivity is the Palo Encebado, a competition involving attempts to clamber to the top of long greasy poles, and the cerdo encebado where a pig smeared with lard is chased through town and is kept by the first person who manages to grab it.

The **Teatro de Las Ruinas** is almost fully restored and hosts converts and events. **Iglesia de Santa Lucía** ⓘ *Mon-Sat 0800-1200, 1400-1600, all day Sun*, built in 1858 with wooden and hollow columns, has also been restored with a lot of stencil work inside. There is a splendid view from the church tower. **Casa Museo de Alejandro Cotto** ⓘ *daily 0800-1700, US$4, guided tour in Spanish but ask for an English tour with Sr Cotto (T2335-1140)*, home of movie director Alejandro Cotto, is an interesting museum with more than 132 paintings of El Salvador's most renowned artists, collections of books and music instruments.

Tourist office ⓘ *Calle Francisco Morazán 7, next to the telephone office, T2335-1782, daily 0800-1700*. They offer daily tours of the city centre, to Los Tercios waterfall and to Lake Suchitlán.

Around Suchitoto

A 30-minute walk north of town leads to the **Embalse Cerrón Grande** (also know as **Lago de Suchitlán**). **Proyecto Turístico Pesquero Puerto San Juan** is the newly opened harbour with boat shuttle services and, soon to open, restaurants and cafés on the lake shore. There will be an area for events, parking and arts, crafts and souvenir sales. This is the departure point for boat excursions across to remote areas in neighbouring Chalatenango, ask around and negotiate prices. Trips are available to five islands including **Isla de Los Pájaros**, which makes an interesting trip, 1-1½ hours, US$10-15.

Ferries cross the Embalse Cerrón Grande for San Luis del Carmen (25 minutes to San Luis, frequent departures all day), where there is *Comedor Carmen*, and buses linking to Chalatenango. The ferry also makes a stop at the small village of **San Francisco Lempa**.

Los Tercios, a waterfall with striking, gigantic, black, hexagonal-shaped basaltic columns, can be reached by car, foot and by *lancha*. It is at its most impressive in the wet season when the full force of nature is on show. Walk 10-15 minutes from town down the very steep road towards the lake known as Calle al Lago de Suchitlán. Lifts

 can be had for about US$2-3 if you can't face the steep climb back to town afterwards. Ask around. At the lake shore, where there are *comedores*, ask for a *lanchero*. A *lancha* to the base of the trail to Los Tercios is US$5-6 (negotiable) and takes 10 minutes (ask the *lanchero* to point out the trail). There are thousands of flies on the lake shore, but they don't bite. Walk upwards for 10-15 minutes in a straight line till you reach the road. You will see *flor de fuego* trees, vultures, fish eagles, blue morpho butterflies and lizards. Turn right and walk for two minutes to the third basic house on the right; take a right just before the house, through their property (if the family is there, say *'con permiso'*, payment is not required). A path leads to a mirador looking out over the lake. Veering to the right on the path descends steeply down black boulders where arching to the right, you will see these impressive hexagonal structures. You can also walk from the bus terminal south along Av 6 de Noviembre. Take the first gravel road on your left until you see the town rubbish dump (*el basurero municipal*) on your left. You need to pass through the next property on your left.

La Ciudad Vieja, one-time site of the capital, is 10 km from Suchitoto. An original Pipil town, it was taken over by the Spanish who made it their central base for 17 years before electrical storms, lack of water, and cholera forced them to flee. It is a private site but can be visited. There are plans for a museum and a café.

Boat trips go to lakeside villages associated with the FMLN in the civil war. Twelve kilometres away, on the road to Aguilares, a **Parque de la Reconciliación** is being developed at the foot of Cerro de Guazapa. Contact **CESTA** in San Salvador at T2220-0046, or the park directly on T7887-1129 and talk to Walter. Also, 3 km along this road is **Aguacayo** and a large church, heavily damaged in the war.

Chalatenango → *Colour map 5, C6. Population: 80,000. Altitude: 450 m.*

Highway 4 continues north from **Aguilares** passing the western extremity of the **Cerrón Grande** reservoir. A branch to the east skirts the northern side of the reservoir to Chalatenango, capital of the department of the same name. Rural Chalatenango is mainly agricultural, with many remote villages and many non-governmental organizations working in the area. Chalatenango is a delightful little town with annual fairs and **fiestas** on 24 June and 1-2 November. It is the centre of an important region of traditional livestock farms. Good market and several craft shops, for example **Artesanías Chalateca**, for bags and hammocks. The weekly horse fairs where horses, saddles and other equipment are for sale are very popular.

La Palma and around → *Colour map 5, C6. Population: 20,000. Altitude: 1100 m.*

The main road continues north through Tejutla to La Palma, a charming village set in pine-clad mountains, and well worth a visit. It is famous for its local crafts, particularly brightly painted wood carvings and hand-embroidered tapestries. Also produced are handicrafts in clay, metal, cane and seeds. There are a number of workshops in La Palma where the craftsmen can be seen at work and purchases made (see box). The **Fiesta del Dulce Nombre de María** takes place mid- or late February.

The picturesque village of **San Ignacio**, 6 km north of La Palma, has two or three small *talleres* producing handicrafts (20 minutes by bus, US$0.10 each way).

San Ignacio is the departure point for buses leading up a new safe but steep road leading up to the highest mountain of El Salvador, El Pital (2730 m). As you reach the pass below the mountain top, the road branches to **Las Pilas** to the left and **Miramundo** to the right. Both Miramundo and Las Pilas have small agricultural communities, specializing in organic crops. The extensive cabbage fields make beautiful vistas combined with the pine-clad mountains.

If you take the road from the summit to the right you end up in Miramundo which gives a view of pretty much all El Salvador. On clear days you can see almost all the volcanoes in the country, including Volcán Pacaya and Volcán Agua in Guatemala. Best view in the country no doubt!

Handicrafts of El Salvador

The artists' village of **La Palma**, in a pine-covered valley under Miramundo mountain, is 84 km north of the capital 10 km south of the Honduran frontier. Here, in 1971, the artist **Fernando Llort** "planted a seed" known as the copinol (a species of the locust tree) from which sprang the first artists' cooperative, now called **La Semilla de Dios** (Seed of God). The copinol seed is firm and round; on it the artisans base a spiritual motif that emanates from their land and soul.

The town and its craftspeople are now famous for their work in wood, including exotically carved *cofres* (adorned wooden chests), and traditional Christmas *muñecas de barro* (clay dolls) and ornamental angels. Wood carvings, other crafts and the designs of the original paintings by Llort, are all produced and exported from La Palma to the rest of El Salvador and thence worldwide.

In 1971 the area was almost exclusively agricultural; today 75% of the population of La Palma and neighbouring San Ignacio are engaged directly or indirectly in producing handicrafts. The painter **Alfredo Linares** (born 1957 in Santa Ana, arrived in La Palma 1981 after studying in Guatemala and Florence) has a gallery in La Palma, employing and assisting local artists. His paintings and miniatures are marketed abroad, yet you will often find him working in the family pharmacy next to the gallery. Many of La Palma's images are displayed on the famous Hilasal towels. If you cannot get to La Palma, visit the shop/gallery/workshop of Fernando Llort in San Salvador, **Arbol de Dios**.

Twenty kilometres from the capital is the indigenous town of **Panchimalco**, where weaving on the loom and other traditional crafts are being revived. Many Nahuatl traditions, customs, dances and the language survived here as the original indigenous people hid from the Spanish conquistadors in the valley beneath the Puerta del Diablo (now in Parque Balboa). In 1996 the painter Eddie Alberto Orantes and his family opened the **Centro de Arte y Cultura Tunatiuh**, named after a nahuat deity who is depicted as a human face rising as a sun over a pyramid. The project employs local youths (from broken homes, or former addicts) in the production of weavings, paintings and ceramics.

In the mountains of western El Salvador, villages in the coffee zone, such as **Nahuizalco**, specialize in weaving henequen, bamboo and reed into table mats and wicker furniture. There are also local artists like Maya sculptor **Ahtzic Selis**, who works with clay and jade. East of the capital, at **Ilobasco** (60 km), many ceramic workshops produce items including the famous *sorpresas*, miniature figures enclosed in an egg shell. In the capital there are crafts markets in which to bargain for pieces, while throughout the country, outlets range from the elegant to the rustic. But everywhere artists and artisans welcome visitors into their workshops.

Border with Western Honduras

The road continues north to the border at **El Poy**, for Western Honduras. From Citalá, a small town with colonial church and strong history from the war (you still see bullet holes in walls of the houses on street corners) 1 km west off the highway just before El Poy, an adventurous road goes to Metapán. Two buses daily take three hours for the 40 km, rough but beautiful journey.

Border essentials: El Salvador-Honduras

El Poy
The crossing between northern El Salvador and southwest Honduras at El Poy is straightforward in both directions. But best to arrive early if looking to travel far beyond the border area. The border posts are 100 m either side of the border.

Transport To San Salvador, Terminal de Oriente, bus 119, US$1.35, 3-4 hrs, often crowded, hourly; last bus from the capital 1600. The same bus to La Palma US$0.15, 30 mins.
Exchange Bargain with money changers at the border for the best rate for Honduran lempiras.

Sleeping

Apopa and Tonacatepeque *p758*
D-F **Lisa's Guest House**, Finca Orgánica Las Termópilas, 3 km beyond Apopa, on CA 4 Km 17. Same owners as **Ximena's Guest House** in San Salvador, see page 737. Budget lodging in dorms with shared bath and spacious family rooms with TV and private bath.

Suchitoto *p, map p759*
A-B **El Tejado**, 3 Av Norte 58, Barrio Concepción, T2335-1769. Beautifully restored colonial house with just 3 rooms, pools and beautiful view of Lake Suchitlán.
B-C **Los Almendros de San Lorenzo**, 4 Calle Pte, next to police station, T2335-1200, www.hotelsalvador.com. In a restored colonial house with exclusive rooms and delightful gardens. Delicious meals in the restaurant – people come from the capital to lunch here at weekends.
B-C **Posada de Suchitlán**, Final 4 Calle Pte, at the western end of town, T2335-1064, www.laposada.com.sv. Colonial-style, beautifully tiled and decorated, excellent hotel and restaurant, stunning view.
B-D **Posada Alta Vista**, on Av 15 de Septiembre near the square, T2335-1645. Good rooms, although the cheaper ones can be hot. Helpful, friendly staff. Rooftop terrace with great view of the town.
D **La Fonda El Mirador**, Calle 15 de Septiembre, Barrio Concepción, on the road that leads to the lake, T2335-1126, quintanilladavid@yahoo.com. Next to restaurant of same name, with superb views of lake and good food too.
D-E **Hostal 2 Gardenias**, 3 Av Norte 48, Barrio Concepción, T2335-1868, hostal2gardenias@hotmail.com. 5 rooms surrounding a gorgeous cobbled courtyard dominated by a flourishing mango tree, run by a group of artists who have added their touch. Inside is the **Zuka Fe & Bar** where you can enjoy a wide range of international beers. Great ambience, recommended. Offers guides to places of interest including Los Tercios.
E **Hacienda La Bermuda 1525**, Km 34.8 Carretera a Suchitoto, www.labermuda.com. Hotel and restaurant with frequent cultural activities located just outside Suchitoto.
E **Villa Balanza**, in front of Parque San Martín, T2335-1408. 2 rooms in the restaurant of same name. Beautiful and artistically decorated.

Chalatenango *p760*
D **La Ceiba**, behind the military fort, T2301-1080. With shower and bath. A nice, new 2-storey house.

La Palma and around *p760*
AL **Entre Pinos**, San Ignacio, T2335-9312, www.hotelentrepinos.com. 1st-class resort complex, a/c, pool, cable TV, sauna and small shop.
C **La Posada de Reyes**, San Ignacio, T2352-9223. Just behind the park offer nice private rooms with private bath and restaurant.
C-D **Paseo El Pital**, La Palma, T2305-9344. Restaurant and hotel, bit over priced but pleasant.
D **Hotel Maya**, Km 77.5 Troncal del Norte, T2305-0008. Motel with amazing panoramic view, at the entrance of La Palma,
D-E **Hotel La Palma**, Troncal del Norte, 84 km Carretera, La Palma, T/F2335-9012. 32 large

rooms, clean, with bath, friendly, good restaurant, beautiful gardens, nice pool, ceramics workshop, parking. Recommended.

D-E Las Praderas de San Ignacio, San Ignacio, a couple of kilometres before the border, T2350-9330. Cabins, beautiful gardens and economic restaurant.

D-F Hostal Miramundo, Miramundo, T2230-0437, www.hotelmiramundo.com. Nice rooms with hot water and a restaurant, great food and great views, recommended.

E-F Hotel Cayahuanca, San Ignacio, across the street at Km 93.5, T2335-9464. Friendly, good but expensive restaurant.

F Casa de Huéspedes Las Orquídeas, Las Pilas. Run by a local farming family (ask for a guided trip to the mountain top nearby – unrivalled panoramic view and free peaches!).

Eating

Apopa and Tonacatepeque *p758*

La Posada de John Paul, Finca Orgánica Las Termópilas. Serves natural foods, vegetarian meals with own-grown produce, also meat dishes and natural fruit juices.

Suchitoto *p758, map p759*

Local specialities include *salporitas* (made of corn meal) and *chachamachas*. Try the *pupusas* in the market and at the corner near *Telecom*. Several eating options around the main plaza.

El Dorado, by Lake Suchitlán, T2225-5103, www.gaesuchitoto.com. Bar and restaurant. Frequent concerts with invited artists.

Estancia La Bermuda, just out of Suchitoto, Km 34.8 Carretera a San Salvador, T2389-9078, www.labermuda.com. B&B, colonial-style restaurant with pool and cultural events.

Típicos El Portal, Parque Centenario, T2335-1679. The current hot spot, open until midnight.

Café Billard-Sanchez, 4 Calle Pte, by El Cerrito, Barrio Santa Lucía, T2335-1464. Bar and disco.

Café El Obraje, next to Santa Lucía church, T2335-1173. Renovated building, clean, reasonably priced, good breakfast variety.

Pupusería La Bella Esquina, on 15 de Septiembre and 4 Calle Ote. Very good, cheap food.

Pupusería Vista al Lago, Av 15 de Septiembre 89, T2335-1134. Good food.

Chalatenango *p760*

Several restaurants to choose from including **Rinconcitos**, next to the military fort, à la carte menu as well as *pupusas*, good.

La Palma and around *p760*

In Ignacio, there are many local *comedores*, including **Comedor Elisabeth**, which offer delicious *comida a la vista* including fresh milk, cheese and cream.

El Poyeton, Barrio San Antonio, 1 block from church, La Palma. Reliable, simple dishes.

La Estancia, on Calle Principal, La Palma, T/F2335-9049, 0800-2000, good menu, bulletin board.

Shopping

La Palma and around *p760*

Handicrafts The numerous arts and crafts producers of La Palma have come together and formed a **Placita Artesanal** – an artisans market, which is located by the Catholic church at the central plaza. **Artesanías El Tecomate**, Carlos Alfredo Mancía, T2335-9068, also good work in wood. Many of these products are also sold in San Salvador, but are much more expensive. **Artesanías El Típico**, Blanca Sola de Pineda, Calle Principal, good. **Cerámica San Silvestre**, opposite Hotel La Palma, wholesale/retail, good. **Cooperativa La Semilla de Dios**, Plaza San Antonio, T2335-9098, the original cooperative founded by Fernando Llort in 1971, huge selection of crafts and paintings, helpful. **Gallery Alfredo Linares**, T2335-9049 (Sr Linares' house), well-known artist whose paintings sell for US$18-75, daily 0600-1800, friendly, recommended. (If gallery is unattended, ask in the pharmacy). **Palma City**, Calle Principal behind church. Sra Alicia Mata is very helpful with finding objects, whether she stocks them or not, wood, ceramics, *telas*, etc.

Transport

Suchitoto *p758, map p759*

Bus To **Aguilares**, every 30 mins, No 163 between 0500 and 1800, 30 mins on newly paved road. Regular buses (No 129) from Terminal Oriente, **San Salvador**, beginning at 0330. The bus stops at the market and leaves town for the capital from 3 Av Norte, near the

Hostal 2 Gardenias. To **Ilobasco** by dirt road, 0800 and 1000, returning 1230 and 1430.

Ferry Cross the Embalse Cerrón Grande (Lago de Suchitlán) for **San Luis del Carmen** (25 mins to San Luis, frequent departures throughout the day) where there is Comedor Carmen, and buses linking to **Chalatenango**.

Chalatenango *p760*
Bus No 125 from Oriente terminal, San Salvador, US$1.10, 2½ hrs.

La Palma and around *p760*
Bus From **San Salvador**, Terminal de Oriente, No 119, US$2.25, 3 hrs, last return leaves at 1630.

Directory

Suchitoto *p758, map p759*
Banks Western Union available. Mon-Fri 0800-1600, Sat 0830-1200. Will cash TCs. No credit card facilities. **Internet** Cybercafé El Gringo, Barrio San José, and at 2 places on the main square either side of Típicos El Portal.

Eastern El Salvador

A primarily agricultural zone, the central region is lined with dramatic volcanoes, impressive scenery and the small towns of the Lempa Valley. Along the coast, quiet beaches and islands can be found on the way to the stunning Gulf of Fonseca to the east. In the north, an area of fierce disputes between the army and guerrillas during the civil war, small communities are slowly rebuilding and opening up to visitors. There are two border crossings to Honduras: to the north at Perquín, and the east at El Amatillo. ▸▸ *For Sleeping, Eating and other listings, see pages 770-772.*

East from San Salvador ▸▸ *pp770-772.*

There are two roads to the port of La Unión/Cutuco on the Gulf of Fonseca: the Pan-American Highway, 185 km through Cojutepeque and San Miguel (see below); and the **coastal highway**, also paved, running through Santo Tomás, Olocuilta, Zacatecoluca and Usulután (see page 772).

The **Pan-American Highway** is dual carriageway out of the city, but becomes single carriageway for several kilometres either side of Cojutepeque – sections that are twisty, rough and seem to induce some very bad driving.

At San Martín, 18 km from the capital, a paved road heads north to Suchitoto, 25 km on the southern shore of the Embalse Cerrón Grande, also known as Lago de Suchitlán. At Km 34.8 is Estancia La Bermuda, see page 763.

Cojutepeque → *Colour map 6, C1. Population: 46,000.*

The capital of Cuscatlán Department, 34 km from San Salvador, is the first town on the Pan-American Highway encountered heading east. Lago de Ilopango is a short trip to the southwest and there is a good weekly market. The town is famous for cigars, smoked sausages, *quesadillas* and tongue, and its annual **feria** on 29 August has fruits and sweets, saddlery, leather goods, pottery and headwear on sale from neighbouring villages, and sisal hammocks, ropes, bags and hats from the small factories of Cacaopera (Department of Morazán). There is also a **sugar cane festival** on 12-20 January.

Cerro de las Pavas, a conical hill near Cojutepeque, dominates **Lago de Ilopango** and gives splendid views of wide valleys and tall mountains. Its shrine of **Our Lady of Fátima** draws many pilgrims (religious ceremonies take place here on 13 May).

Ilobasco → *Population 80,100.*

From **San Rafael Cedros**, 6 km east of Cojutepeque, a 16 km paved road north to Ilobasco has a branch road east to Sensuntepeque at about Km 13. The surrounding area, devoted to cattle, coffee, sugar and indigo, is exceptionally beautiful. Many of Ilobasco's population are workers in clay; although some of its decorated pottery is now mass-produced and has lost much of its charm this is definitely the best place to buy pottery in El Salvador. Check out miniature *sorpresas*, delicately shaped microscopic sceneries the size of an egg (don't miss the naughty ones). Try **Hermanos López** ⓘ *entrance to town*, or **José y Víctor Antino Herrera** ⓘ *Av Carlos Bonilla 61, T2332-2324*, look for the 'Kiko' sign, fine miniatures for sale. The annual **fiesta** is on 29 September.

San Sebastián → *Population 26,000.*

Four kilometres from the turning to Ilobasco, further south along the Pan-American Highway at **Santo Domingo** (Km 44 from San Salvador), a paved road leads for 5 km to San Sebastián, where colourfully patterned cloth hammocks and bedspreads are made. You can watch them being woven on complex looms of wood and string. Behind **Funeraria Durán** there is a weaving workshop. Sr Durán will take you past the caskets to see the weavers. The **Casa de Cultura**, about 50 m from the plaza, will direct you to weaving centres and give information on handicrafts. Before buying, check prices and beware of overcharging. Market day is on Monday. To get there, bus No 110 from the Oriente terminal runs from San Salvador to San Sebastián (1½ hours, US$0.80). There are also buses from Cojutepeque.

San Vicente → *Colour map 6, C1. Population: 80,000.*

Founded in 1635, San Vicente is 61 km from the capital, and lies a little southeast of the Highway on the Río Alcahuapa, at the foot of the double-peaked **Volcán San Vicente** (or **Chinchontepec**), with very fine views of the Jiboa valley to the west. The town enjoys a lovely setting and is a peaceful place to spend a night or two. Its pride and joy is **El Pilar** (1762-69), the most original church in the country. It was here that

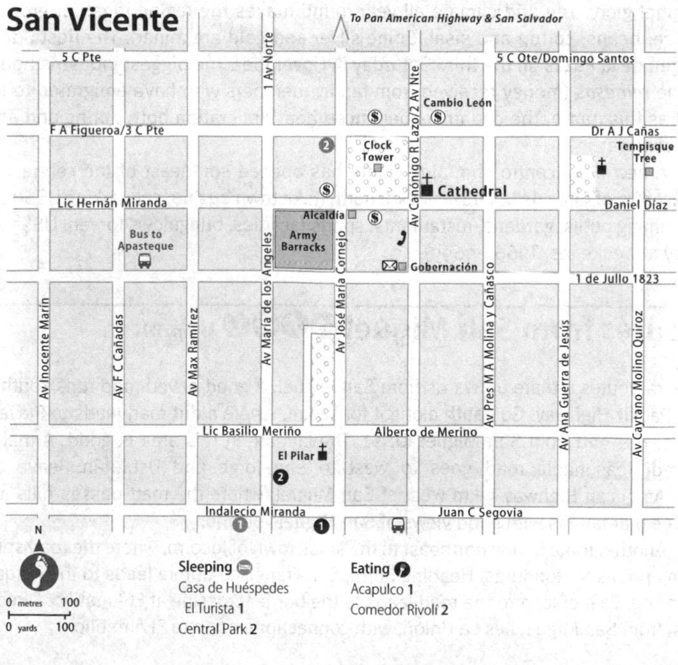

 the local chief, **Anastasio Aquino**, took the crown from the statue of San José and crowned himself King of the Nonualcos during the rebellion of 1832.

El Pilar stands on a small square 1½ blocks south of the Parque Central. On the latter is the cathedral, whose nave is draped with golden curtains. In the middle of the main plaza is a tall, open-work clock tower, quite a landmark when descending the hill into the city. Three blocks east of the main plaza is the *tempisque* tree under which the city's foundation charter was drawn up. The tree was decreed a national monument on 26 April 1984. An extensive market area can be found a few blocks west of the centre and hammock sellers are on nearby streets. An army barracks takes up an entire block in the centre. There's a small **war museum**; ask the FMLN office here or in San Salvador. **Carnival day** is on 1 November.

Around San Vicente

Three kilometres southeast of the town is the Balneario **Amapulapa** ⓘ *T2393-0412, US$0.60 entry and US$0.60 parking charges*, a Turicentro. There are three pools at different levels in a wooded setting. Unfortunately the site has a bad litter problem and a reputation for petty crime. Women should not walk there alone. Reached by buses No 158, 177 and 193 from San Vicente bus station, US$0.10. **Laguna de Apastepeque** ⓘ *T2389-7172*, near San Vicente off the Pan-American Highway, is small but picturesque. Take bus No 156 from San Vicente, or 499 from San Salvador. Ask in San Vicente for guides for climbing the San Vicente volcano.

San Miguel → *Colour map 6, C2. Population: 380,000 (approx).*

Set at the foot of the **Volcán San Miguel (Chaparrastique)**, which erupted in 1976, and **Chinameca**, San Miguel is the third largest city in El Salvador, 136 km from San Salvador. The capital of its department, the town was founded in 1530 as a military fortress by Don Luis de Moscoso. It now has one of the fastest growing economies in Central America, some pleasant plazas and a bare 18th-century cathedral. The city's theatre dates from 1909, but since the 1960s it has been used for various purposes other than the arts. After several years of restoration it reopened in 2003 in all its original glory. The arid climate all year round makes the region ideal for growing maize, beans, cotton and sisal. Some silver and gold are mined. The **fiesta de la Virgen de la Paz** is on the third Saturday in November. The biggest industry though is the *remesas* (money received from family members who have emigrated to the US) as this part of the country experienced heavy migration both during and after the civil war.

A new Metrocentro shopping centre has opened southeast of the centre. The **Turicentro of Altos de la Cueva** is 1 km north (take town bus 60, car parking US$0.60, swimming pools, gardens, restaurants, sports facilities, bungalows for rent US$3.45, busy at weekends, T2669-0699).

Routes from San Miguel » pp770-772.

Several routes radiate outwards from San Miguel. A good paved road runs south to the Pacific Highway. Go south along it for 12 km, where a dirt road leads to Playa El Cuco. Bus 320 from San Miguel, US$1. The climate in this area is good. A mainly paved, reasonable road goes to west to San Jorge and Usulután: leave the Pan-American Highway 5 km west of San Miguel, where the road passes hills and coffee plantations with good views of San Miguel volcano.

Another route heads northeast to the small town of Jocorro, where the road splits with options to Honduras. Heading north, San Francisco Gotera leads to the Perquín crossing. East of Jocorro the road leads to the border crossing at El Amatillo. Directly east from San Miguel lies La Unión, with connections north to El Amatillo.

San Francisco Gotera and around

The capital of Morazán Department can be reached directly from the Oriente terminal in San Salvador, or from San Miguel (bus 328). There are places to stay (see Sleeping).

Beyond San Francisco, the road runs to **Jocaitique** (there is a bus) from where an unpaved road climbs into the mountains through pine forests to **Sabanetas**, near the Honduran border. Accommodation is available at Jocaitique and Sabanetas.

Northeast of San Francisco is **Corinto** ⓘ *20 mins north of the village on foot, just east of the path to the Cantón Coretito, open daily*, which has two rock overhangs showing faint evidence of pre-Columbian wall paintings. Take an early bus, No 327, from San Miguel, US$1.

Ciudad Segundo Montes and around

Eight kilometres north of San Francisco Gotera is Ciudad Segundo Montes, a group of villages housing 8500 repatriated Salvadorean refugees (the community is named after one of the six Jesuit priests murdered in November 1989). If you wish to visit contact **PRODETUR** ⓘ *T2680-4088* for information. No formal accommodation is available.

Fourteen kilometres north of San Francisco is **Delicias de la Concepción**, where fine decorated hammocks and ceramics are made. The prices are good and they are helpful; worth a visit. Buses every 20 minutes from San Francisco.

Perquín and around → *Colour map 6, C2. Population: 5000 Altitude: 1200 m.*

Perquín – meaning 'Road of the Hot Coals' – is 205 km from San Salvador and was the guerrillas' 'capital', and the scene of much military activity. War damage used to be visible around the town, but all is now peaceful and the scenery is very beautiful,

surrounded by pine-topped mountains. There is a small central square with a Casa de la Cultura, post office and a PRODETUR **tourist information office** ⓘ *T2680-4086*. Opposite is the plain Iglesia Católica Universal Progresista.

The **Museo de la Revolución** ⓘ *T2610-6737, Tue-Sun 0830-1630, US$1.20, no photos or filming allowed, guided tours in Spanish, camping permitted, US$1*, clearly signposted from the plaza, has temporary exhibits as well as one on Archbishop Romero and all the gory details of his murder – nothing is spared. The museum, run by ex-guerrillas, is badly lit, but fascinating with photographs, propaganda posters, explanations, objects, pictures of the missing, and military paraphernalia. In the garden is the wreckage of an American-made helicopter, shot down by guerrillas in 1984. Sprawled like a piece of modern art, it could look at home in a contemporary art gallery.

Behind the town is the **Cerro de Perquín** ⓘ *US$0.25 to climb*. The views are fantastic with the town below nestling in the tropical scenery, green parrots flying through the pine trees, and the mountains stretching towards the border with Honduras. It is advisable to bring a guide. The **Festival de Invierno**, 1-6 August, is a mixture of music, exhibitions and film. Book accommodation ahead if planning to come for this festival. The **Festival de San Sebastián** is on 21-22 January, and for the **Virgen del Tránsito**, the patron saint of the church, on 14-15 August.

Nearby villages such as Arambala and El Mozote can be visited, or you can take a walking tour. At **El Mozote** is a memorial to a massacre in 1981. Five kilometres west of Perquín is **Arambala** which is slowly reconstructing. Locals will give you a tour of the town and church, destroyed by fire in the 1980s and now being rebuilt. Massacres took place here in the 1980s. Near Perquín, turn-off 2 km south, are the park and trails of **Cerro Pelón**. Nearby is **El Llano del Muerto**, a tourist area of naturally heated pools and wells. North of Perquín, straddling the new border with Honduras, is one of the few unpolluted rivers in the country. The people of Morazán are more reserved with strangers than in the rest of El Salvador. If travelling on your own, 4WD is advised.

Ruta de la Paz run by **PRODETUR** ⓘ *T2680-4086, daily 0730-1630 (0800-2100 during the winter festival)*, provides walks, culture and adventure tourism and can organize accommodation. Tours are anything between 25 minutes and five hours, one to 10 people, US$1.30 an hour. One-and-a-half-hour walking tours to Llanos, three hours to El Mozote.

Santa Rosa de Lima → *Population: 27,300.*

The shortest route from San Miguel to the Honduran border takes the Ruta Militar northeast through Santa Rosa de Lima to the Goascarán bridge at El Amatillo, a total of 58 km on newly paved road.

Santa Rosa is a charming little place with a wonderful colonial church set in the hillside. There are gold and silver mines, a market on Wednesday, and a curiously large number of pharmacies and shoe shops. The FMLN office has details about the **Codelum Project**, a refugee camp in Monte Barrios. The **fiesta** is on 22-31 August.

La Unión/Cutuco » *pp770-772. Colour map 6, C2.*

→ *Population: 43,000.*

It is another 42 km from San Miguel to the port of La Unión/Cutuco, on the Gulf of Fonseca. The spectacular setting on the west shore of the gulf does little to offset the heat and the faded glory of this port town which handles half the country's trade. Shortly before entering the town, the Pan-American Highway turns north for 33 km to the Goascarán bridge at **El Amatillo** on the border with Honduras (see box, opposite). A new project to make El Cutuco a modern port is underway. This mega project includes foreign investments such as a large Spanish tuna fish processing plant, with supporting infrastructure including new roads and hotels.

Border Essentials: El Salvador-Honduras

Perquín
The Honduran border has been moved, by treaty, to less than 3 km north of Perquín; this area has been the subject of disputes and definition problems for many decades. It was one of the basic causes of the 'Football War' of 1969 (see page 1212) and there were military confrontations between El Salvador and Honduras before the boundary disagreement was finally and completely resolved in April 2006. There is a border crossing 5 km past the frontier here and the route to Marcala and La Esperanza Honduras, is open. There is a bus service from Marcala to San Miguel, five hours, US$3.50, using this route, but be aware that the road may be impassable after heavy rains.

El Amatillo
Río Goascarán is the border, with El Amatillo on both sides of the bridge.
Salvadorean immigration The border closes at 1700 and may close for two hours at lunchtime. This is a very busy crossing, but is easy for those going on foot.
Crossing by private vehicle You will be hounded by *tramitadores* offering to help, but there's no need to use their services as it's a fairly relaxed crossing. Car searches are thorough at this crossing.
Sleeping Near the border are 2 *hospedajes*, both basic: **Anita** (with *comedor*) and **Dos Hermanos** (without).
Transport To San Miguel, bus No 330, 1 hour 40 mins, US$1.50. See also Santa Rosa de Lima.

Around la Unión

Conchagua is worth visiting to see one of the few old colonial churches in the country. The church was begun in 1693, after the original Conchagua had been moved to its present site, following repeated attacks on the island settlements by the English. **Fiestas**: 18-21 January and 24 July. (Good bus service from La Unión, No 382, US$0.10.) **Volcán Conchagua** (1243 m) can also be climbed and is a hard walk, particularly near the top where protective clothing is useful against the vegetation. It's about four hours up and two hours down. You will be rewarded by superb views over Volcán San Miguel to the west and the Gulf of Fonseca, which is bordered by El Salvador, Honduras and Nicaragua (where the Cosigüina volcano is prominent) to the east. **Turismo** ⓘ *based in San Salvador, T2211-8583, www.turismo.com.sv*, does tours to Volcán Conchagua on request. Or contact Eduardo on T7810-6612.

In the Gulf of Fonseco are the Salvadorean islands of **Isla Zacatillo, Isla Conchagüita** and, the largest, **Isla Meanguera** (about 4 km by 7 km). English and Spanish pirates occupied the island in the late 1600s, and international claims remained until the International Tribunal of the Hague awarded the island to El Salvador in preference to claims from Honduras and Nicaragua.

A *lancha* leaves La Union for the town of **Meanguera del Golfo**, on Meanguera. The journey across the gulf is beautiful – tranquil waters, fishing boats and views to the surrounding mountains. The island has secluded beaches with good bathing, for example Marahual (45-minute walk), with fringed with palm trees. About 5000 people live on the carefree island where painted boats float in the cove surrounded by small *tiendas* and *comedores* that serve fish, shark and prawns. The highest point on the island is Cerro de Evaristo at 512 m. Launches leave La Unión daily at 1000 but times change so ask locally, two hours, US$3. It's possible to arrange transport with a local boatman for transport to Coyolito (Honduras) and Isla Amapala for immigration, but make sure the price is set beforehand. You can travel to Honduras or Nicaragua if you have visited immigration in La Unión first to get the necessary paperwork.

Sleeping

San Vicente *p765, map p765*

D-E **Central Park**, on Parque Central, T2393-0383. With bath, TV, a/c, phone, good, clean, cheaper with fan, cheaper still without TV; café and restaurant downstairs.

F **Casa de Huéspedes El Turista**, Indalecio Miranda and Av María de los Angeles, T2393-0323. Well kept, fan. Shuts the door around 2130, early check-out, but good for the price.

San Miguel *p766, map p767*

Most hotels are on the entrance roads, although there are plenty of cheap places near the bus station.

A **Trópico Inn**, Av Roosevelt Sur 303, T2661-1800, tropicoinn@yahoo.com. Clean, comfortable, reasonable restaurant, swimming pool, garden, safe parking for motorbikes, recommended.

B **El Mandarín**, Av Roosevelt Norte, T2669-6969. A/c, pool, good Chinese restaurant.

C **Motel Millián**, Panamericana Km 136, T2669-5052. Pool, good value, recommended, good restaurant.

D **China House**, 15 Av Norte, Panamericana Km 137.5, T/F2669-5029. Clean, friendly.

E **King Palace** (ex **Hotel La Terminal**), opposite bus station. Good breakfast.

E-F **Caleta**, 3 Av Sur 601, T2661-3233. Basic, inexpensive, ample parking, fan, popular with local business travellers.

F **Migueleña**, 4 Calle Ote 610. Basic but good value, clean, large rooms, towels, bath, fan.

San Francisco Gotera *p767*

C-E **Hospedaje San Francisco**, Av Morazán 29, T2654-0066. Nice garden and hammocks.

Perquín and around *p767*

B **Hotel Perkin Lenca**, Km 205.5 Carretera a Perquín, T/F2680-4080, www.perkin lenca.com. Swiss cabins with restaurant **La Cocina de Ma'Anita**, daily 0700-1900.

D **Casa de Huéspedes Gigante**, 5 mins from Perquín at the bottom of the hill, CTE Perquín T2680-4037. Countless partitioned rooms which would probably be noisy if full, but rarely is, clean, cold showers, friendly, meals.

Camping

It's possible to camp in the grounds of the Museo de la Revolución, near a crater formed by a 227-kg bomb dropped in August 1981. Ask in the nearby *tiendas*.

Near the Río Zapo, PRODETUR has a great camping ground equipped with bathrooms and guides who can give you a tour of the area. Great for both trekking and hiking. There is also a simple cabin for rent here.

Santa Rosa de Lima *p768*

F **Florida**, Ruta Militar, T2641-2020. Helpful, fairly clean, basic, 3 parking spaces (arrive early).

F **Hospedaje Mundial**, near market. Rooms OK, with fan, basic, friendly, lots of parking.

F **Recreo**, 2 blocks from town centre in front of police station and Telecom, 4 Av Norte, Barrio el Recreo, T2641-2126. Friendly, fan, noisy, basic, recommended.

La Unión/Cutuco *p768*

E **San Francisco**, Calle General Menéndez 6-B, Barrio Concepción, T2604-4159. Clean, friendly, some rooms with hammocks and fan, safe parking, noisy, but OK. Some water problems.

Around la Unión *p769*

D **Hotel Paraíso**, Meanguera del Golfo. Has rooms with TV, private bath and hot water. Recommended.

Eating

Ilobasco *p765*

ŸŸ **Restaurante Ricky**, at 3 Av Sur. The town's only real restaurant with à la carte dining.

There are also 2 pizzerias, several local *comedores*, a **Pollo Campero** and a **Taco Hut**.

San Vicente *p765, map p765*

Ÿ **Acapulco**, by the central market. Good.

Ÿ **Casablanca**, next to the park, T2393-0549. Good shrimps, steaks, and you can swim in their pool for US$1.15.

Ÿ **Comedor Rivoli**, Av María de los Angeles Miranda. Clean, good breakfast and lunches.

Close to Hotel Central Park are **Pops** and **La Nevería**, for good ice cream.

San Miguel *p766, map p767*

Try *bocadillos de totopostes*, maize balls with either chilli or cheese; also *tustacos*, which are like small tortillas with sugar or honey. Both are delicious and traditional in San Miguel.

Ÿ **El Gran Tejano**, 4 Calle Pte, near cathedral. Great steaks.
Ÿ **Hotel & Restaurante Perquín Lenca**. The only real restaurant in town.

Perquín and around *p767*

Ÿ **Artesanía y Comedor 'La Muralla'**, on the corner of the park and main road out of Perquín. Cosy, very friendly and popular.
Ÿ **Comedor El Comal**, 1 block from the town hall in the centre of Perquín. 0600-2100. Basic, simple food.
Ÿ **Las Colinas**, at the top of the hill behind the Casa de la Cultura, near the entrance to the museum. Good *comidas típicas*.

Santa Rosa de Lima *p768*

ŸŸ **Martina**, near the bridge. Good food including *sopa de apretadores* at US$7.
Ÿ **Chayito**, Ruta Militar. Buffet, popular *comedor*.

La Unión/Cutuco *p768*

Bottled water is hard to find, but *agua helada* from clean sources is sold (US$0.05 a bag).
ŸŸ **Amanecer Marino**, on the waterfront. Beautiful view of the bay, good for watching the world go by. Mainly seafood.
Ÿ **Restaurante Puerto Viejo**, 3A Av Sur y 4 Calle Ote, T2604-3013. Best seafood in town, big portions, cheap, nice place on the terrace – try *tazón de sopa de pescado*.
Ÿ There are several cheap *comedores* to choose from, try **Comedores Gallego** and **Rosita**, recommended. **Comedor Tere**, Av General Menéndez 2.2, is fairly good.

Transport

Cojutepeque *p764*

Bus No113 from Oriente terminal in **San Salvador**, US$0.55; buses leave from Cojutepeque on the corner of the plaza, 2 blocks from the main plaza.

San Vicente *p765, map p765*

Bus No116 from Oriente terminal, **San Salvador**, every 10 mins or so, 1½ hrs, US$0.90. Returning to the capital, catch bus at bus station (Av Victoriano Rodríguez y Juan Crisóstomo Segovia), or outside the cathedral, or on the road out of town. To **Zacatecoluca**, bus 177, US$0.40 from bus station. Buses to some local destinations leave from the street that goes west-east through the market (eg 156 to **Apasteque**). You have to take 2 buses to get to **San Miguel** (see below), 1st to the Pan-American Highway (a few km), where there is a bus and food stop, then another on to San Miguel, US$1.30 total.

San Miguel *p766, map p767*

Air Airport 5 km south of the centre, taxi US$4. Regular daily flights to the capital, see under San Salvador.

Airline offices Taca, Condominio San Benito, opposite **Hotel Trópico Inn**, Av Roosevelt, T2661-1477.

Bus No 301, 306 and 346 from Oriente terminal, **San Salvador** (US$2.50, every 30 mins from 0500 to 1630, 2½ hrs). There are also 3 comfortable, express buses daily, US$5, 2 hrs. There are frequent buses to the Honduran border at **El Amatillo**, US$1. 4 buses (No 332A) daily to **Perquín**, from 0600-1240, US$1.35, 2¾ hrs.

Perquín and around *p767*

Bus From **San Miguel**, 332A, 2¾ hrs, US$1.50. Bus from Terminal Oriente in **San Salvador** takes 4½ hrs, very crowded, luggage a hindrance. Bus or truck from **Cd Segundo Montes**. Transport back to CSM or San Miguel may be difficult in the afternoons. If you're driving fill your tank before getting to Perquín because the last petrol station is 20 mins from the city and closes at 1700.

Santa Rosa de Lima *p768*

Bus To the Honduran border every 15 mins, US$0.50. Direct buses also to **San Salvador**, No 306, US$3 from 0400 until 1400, 3½ hrs.

La Unión/Cutuco *p768*

Bus Terminal is at 3 Calle Pte (block 3); to **San Salvador**, bus 304, US$2, 4 hrs, many daily, direct or via San Miguel, one passes the harbour at 0300. (Bus 320 to **San Miguel** US$0.45). Bus to Honduran border at **El Amatillo**, No 353, US$1.65.

Directory

San Vicente *p765, map p765*

Banks Banco Hipotecario on main plaza, exchange counter at side, 'leave guns and mobile phones with the guard, please'. Also branches of Banco Salvadoreño, Banco

Cuscatlán, and **Banco Agrícola Casa de Cambio León**, Calle Dr Antonio J Cañas, off northeast corner of main plaza. **Post office** In Gobernación, 2 Av Norte y Calle 1 de Julio 1823. **Telephone** Telecom, 2 Av Norte/Av Canónigo Raimundo Lazo, southeast of plaza.

San Miguel *p766, map p767*
Banks 0830-1200, 1430-1800. Banco Cuscatlán will change TCs, but you must produce receipt of purchase otherwise TCs are difficult to change. Banco Agrícola and Banco de Comercio are both next to Tropíco Inn. Casa de Cambio Lego, 2 Calle Pte, overlooking market. **Police** Emergency T911.

Santa Rosa de Lima *p768*
Banks Banco de Comercio will change TCs and Visa cash advances, also Servicambio near the church.

La Unión/Cutuco *p768*
Banks Exchange at Cafetín Brisas del Mar, 3 Av Norte y 3 Calle Ote. Banco Agrícola Comercial for US$ cash and TCs. Black market sometimes in centre. **Customs** 3 Av Norte 3.9. **Immigration** Av General Cabañas and 1 Av Norte. **Internet** Infocentro, 1 Calle Pte, 2-4 Av Norte, Mon-Fri. **Police station** Opposite Immigration office.

Pacific coast

Running the length of the country to the south, the Pacific coastline is a blend of stunning views, quiet beaches and private resorts. If basking in the sun isn't enough, the coast is a big hit with the surf crowd. For a little more activity, you can go west and visit the impressive Parque Nacional El Imposible. Heading east, towards Nicaragua, the islands of the Gulf of Fonseca are equally cut off. ▸▸ *For Sleeping, Eating and other listings, see pages 776-778.*

La Libertad ▸▸ *pp776-778. Colour map 6, C1.*

→ *Population: 22,800.*

Just before Santa Tecla, a branch road turns south for 24 km to the small fishing port of La Libertad, 34 km from San Salvador and just 25 minutes from the Comalpa International Airport. This is a popular laid-back seaside resort in the dry season, but is not very clean. The pier is worth seeing for the fish market awnings and, when the fleet is in, for the boats hauled up out of the water along its length. The cemetery by the beach has tombstones painted in the national colours, blue and white. On the seafront are several hotels and restaurants. At a small plaza, by the **Punta Roca** restaurant, the road curves left to the point, for fine views of La Libertad bay and along the coast. The market street is two blocks inland. The coast to the east and west has good fishing, surfing and bathing. The beaches are black volcanic sand (which can get very hot).

La Libertad gets very crowded at weekends and holidays. Service can be off-hand. Don't stay out alone late at night. For overnight stays the beaches to the west of La Libertad are better. Dedicated surfers may wish to stay for a while though, as the breaks at Punta Roca in Puerto La Libertad are rated amongst the best in the world. Surf season is November to April and the surf is excellent. Watch your belongings on the beach.

The town holds an annual **Gastronomic Festival** in early December and has resurrected the tradition of *lunadas* – full-moon parties in the dry season. Bonfires are lit on the beach, restaurants stay open late offering *comida típica* and some places provide live music and themed nights.

Around La Libertad

The **Costa del Bálsamo** (Balsam coast), running west from La Libertad and Acajutla, gave its name to the pain-relieving balsam, once a major export of the region. On the steep slopes of the departments of Sonsonate and La Libertad, scattered balsam trees are still tapped for their aromatic juices. Buses travel along the coast to Sonsonate (0600 and 1300, about four hours) offering stunning views of the rugged volcanic coast.

The eastern end of La Libertad is **Playa La Paz**, 2 km beyond which is **Playa Obispo**. About 1 km east of La Curva, on the right towards San Diego is the **Fisherman's Club** ⓘ *T2262-0302, entry US$6*, with pool, tennis courts and a good restaurant. The beach is good too, but beware of the rip tide; it's only advisable for surfers.

West of La Libertad » pp776-778.

Continuing west from Playa Conchalío at Km 38 you reach **Playa El Majahual** (see Sleeping) which does not have a safe reputation, nor is it very clean. A little further on, at Km 42, **Playa El Tunco** (bus 80 from La Libertad getting off at the turn-off where all the surfer hotels signs are posted (**Roca Sunzal** is the most visible one) is one of the best surfing beaches in this area with the two breaks of Sunzal and La Bocana both easily accessible. **Club Salvadoreño** and the **Automobile Club** also have their beach premises here. There is a short walk from the turn-off (couple of blocks) to the beach front. El Tunco has several hotels and restaurants (see Sleeping/Eating).

Further up the road at Km 43.5 is Sunzal. Although the breaks are amazing at Sunzal the small hotels at this beach are not as safe as they are at El Tunco and there are reports of burglary at the beach at dusk, so choose lodging at El Tunco. The exception in Sunzal is the brand new luxury hotel **Casa de Mar** which is located just in front of the breaks and is an option if you want a splurge or to use their gourmet seafood restaurant **Café Sunzal** which has great bites and panoramic views of the beach.

At Km 49.5 is **Playa Palmarcito**. This tiny and inviting beach is great for escaping the crowds, and good for beginners surfing as the breaks are not as violent as on other beaches. Located just in front of the beach is **Restaurante Las Palmas**, great meals and low prices. Crested atop a cliff next to Palmarcito is the **Atami Beach Club** ⓘ *T2223-9000*, a beautiful place with large pool, private beach, expensive restaurant, two bars, gardens. Access to **Club Atami** for US and other non-Central American passport-holders US$7, including a *cabaña* for changing. At the turn-off to the beach along the highway (next to police station) is the **Hotel Bosques del Río** (same owner as **Restaurante Las Palmeras**) ask for discounts for longer stays.

Just a couple of kilometres out of La Libertad on the Carretera Litoral is **Parque Nacional Walter Deininger** ⓘ *run by the Instituto Salvadoreño de Turismo, no permit required – simply present your passport at the gate; for more information contact ISTU on T2222-8000, www.istu.gob.sv*. There's great hiking, rivers, caves and a seed bank for endgangered tree species, medicinal plants and a nursery (guides are available). The views are fantastic and it's a good way to learn more about the flora and fauna.

At Km 53.5 is **Playa El Zonte** which has become a favourite especially among foreign tourists. It's a bit safer and quieter than El Tunco, due to its location further away from La Libertad, and top-notch surf breaks has made El Zonte a place people stay longer than anticipated. There are three hotels which all provide restaurant service and several informal cheap cafés down at the beach.

The Carretera Litoral continues for a further 40 km or so to Acajutla past rocky bays, remote black-sand beaches and through tunnels. Take great care with the sea if you bathe along this coast.

Acajutla and around → *Colour map 5, C6. Population: 36,000.*

At the junction of San Julian, a short journey south from Sonsonate, the coastal road heads south to the lowlands city of Acajutla, El Salvador's main port serving the western and central areas, 85 km from San Salvador (the port is 8 km south of the

 Coastal Highway). It is a popular seaside resort during the summer for Salvadorians but lodging in the village is not considered safe for foreigners.There are some good seafood restaurants with great panoramic views which are great for visits during daytime.

The rocky beach of **Los Cóbanos** (14 km south of Acajutla via San Julian, bus from Sonsonate) is very popular with weekending Salvadoreans and has one of only two coral reefs along the entire Central American Pacific coast making it a popular dive spot. Fishermen arrange boat trips, negotiate a price. José Roberto Suárez at **Los Cobanos Village Lodge** ⓘ *T2420-5248, sas_tun@hotmail.com*, speaks English and can be of assistance for renting boats and diving equipment.

The newly paved coastal road heads west running along the coast for 43 km before reaching the Guatemalan frontier at **La Hachadura**.

The black-sand beaches northwest of Acajutla at **Metalío** (safe for camping, but no formal place to stay) and **Barra de Santiago** are recommended, although there are few public facilities. At Barra de Santiago, 30 km west of Acajutla, the beach is reached along a 7 km compact dirt road or across a beautiful lagoon. A bird sanctuary is being developed on the estuary and nearby is a turtle farm and museum. The entire area is in the process of being declared an ecological reserve to protect endangered species including turtles and sea falcons. This beach has an island named **El Cajete** which has an archaeological site dated from around AD 900. There are several pyramids but the area has not been excavated. **El Capricho Beach House** ⓘ *T2205-6320* (same owners as **Ximena's** in San Salvador, see page 737), rent rooms here (see Sleeping, below).

Reserva Nacional Bosque El Imposible

ⓘ *Park entrance is US$6, payable at the gate. For more info contact Salvanatura office, 33 Av Sur 640, Col Flor Blanca, San Salvador, T2279-1515, www.salvanatura.org. Trained naturalist guides from the nearby community of San Miguelito accompany visitors into the park, helping to identify trails and routes for the specific conditions of the year and pointing out interesting plants, animals and other attractions along the trails. Voluntary donation of US$4-5 a day.*

So called because of the difficulty of getting into it, this 'impossibility' has also helped preserve some of the last vestiges of El Salvador's flora and fauna on the rocky slopes and forests of the coastal **Cordillera de Apaneca**. Traders used to travel through the region, navigating the steep 'impossible' passes from which the park takes its name.

Among the mammals are puma, ocelot, agouti and ant bear, and birds include black-crested eagle, white hawk and other birds of prey, black and white owl, and woodpeckers. There is also a great variety of reptiles, amphibians and insects, the greatest diversity in the country. There are eight different strata of forest, with over 300 species of tree that have been identified. While small in size at just 3130-ha the improving facilities at the park make it worth visiting if you have the time.

To get to the park, take the San Salvador-Sonsonate bus, and then the No 259 to Cara Sucia. Pick-ups leave for the park at 1100 and 1400. From Guatemala and the border regular buses heading for San Salvador pass through Cara Sucia from where you catch the 1100 and 1400 pick-ups.

East of La Libertad » *pp776-778.*

The second route to La Unión/Cutuco, runs east through the southern cotton lands. It begins on a four-lane motorway to the airport at Comalapa. The first place of any importance is (13 km) **Santo Tomás** where there are prehispanic ruins at **Cushululitán**, a short distance north. A new road to the east, rising to 1000 m, runs south of Lago de Ilopango to join the Pan-American Highway beyond Cojutepeque. Ten kilometres on from Santo Tomás is **Olocuilta**, an old town with a colourful market on Sunday under a great tree, famed for its church and rice dough *pupusas*. Both

Santo Tomás and Olocuilta can be reached by bus 133 from San Salvador. The highway to the airport crosses the Carretera Litoral (CA 2) near the towns of San Luis Talpa and Comalapa. The coastal road goes east, through Rosario de la Paz, across Río Jiboa and on to Zacatecoluca.

Costa del Sol

Just after Rosario, a branch road to the south leads to **La Herradura** (bus 153 from Terminal del Sur to La Herradura, US$0.90, 1½ hours) and the Playa Costa del Sol on the Pacific, which is being developed as a tourist resort. The beach is on a narrow peninsula, the length of which are private houses which prevent access to the sand until you reach the **Turicentro** ⓘ *0800-1800*. Here *cabañas* can be rented for the day, or for 24 hours (not suitable for sleeping), admission and car parking US$0.80 each, US$1.60 overnight (camping and *cabaña* rental may be refused). It is crowded at weekends and on holidays. There are extensive sandy beaches, but the sea has a mild undertow; go carefully until you are sure. There is also a great water park, **Atlantis Water Park** ⓘ *Km 51, carretera Costa del Sol, T2354-4557, www.atlantis.com.sv, bus routes 495 and 143 (every 15 mins).*

Isla Tasajera

At the southeast end of the Costa del Sol road, near the **Pacific Paradise** hotel, a ferry (US$1.75) leaves for Isla Tasajera in the Estero de Jaltepeque (tidal lagoon). For boat excursions, take Costa del Sol bus to the last stop and negotiate with local boatmen. Boat hire for the day costs US$75, including pilot. It's a great trip into the lagoon, with mangroves, dolphin watching and trips up the Río Lempa.

Zacatecoluca → *Colour map 6, C1. Population: 81,000. Altitude: 201 m.*

The capital of La Paz Department is 56 km from San Salvador by road and 19 km south of San Vicente. Good place to buy hammocks, eg nylon 'doubles', US$13. José Simeón Cañas, who abolished slavery in Central America, was born here. There is a cathedral in the Moorish style and an excellent art gallery.

Ichanmichen

ⓘ *Admission and car parking each US$0.75, bungalow rental US$4.*

Near the town is the garden park and Turicentro of Ichanmichen ('the place of the little fish'). It is crossed by canals and decorated with natural spring pools where you can swim. It is very hot but there is plenty of shade.

Usulután, Playa El Espino and Laguna El Jocotal → *Colour map 6, C2.*

About 110 km from the capital is Usulután, capital of its department. It's large, dirty and unsafe, and only useful as a transit point. Bus 302 from San Salvador, US$1.40. The coastal highway goes direct from Usulután to La Unión/Cutuco.

Playa El Espino can be reached from Usulután, by car (4WD) pick-up or slow bus; it is very remote but lovely. Some small hotels and restaurants operate but mostly during weekends. To visit the reserve, enquire at the entrance; hire a boat to see more.

Beyond Usulután, the impressive silhouette of **Volcán Chaparrasque** rises out of the flat coastal plain. Two roads go northeast to San Miguel, the first from 10 km along at El Tránsito, the second a further 5 km east, which keeps to the low ground south and east of Volcán San Miguel. Two kilometres beyond this turning on the Carretera Litoral is a short road to the right leading to Laguna El Jocotal, a national nature reserve supported by the World Wildlife Fund, which has an abundance of birds and snakes.

Playa El Cuco

About 12 km from the junction for San Miguel there is a turn to the right leading in 7 km to Playa El Cuco, a popular beach with several cheap places to stay near the bus

Border Essentials: El Salvador-Guatemala

La Hachadura
The border is at the bridge over the Río Paz, with a filling station and a few shops nearby.
Salvadorean immigration The immigration facilities are on either side of the bridge; a relaxed crossing.
Crossing by private vehicle The border crossing is quite straightforward but a private vehicle requires a lot of paperwork (about 2 hrs).
Sleeping **El Viajero, La Hachadura,** is safe, clean, good value, with fans.
Transport To San Salvador, Terminal de Occidente, bus No 498, 3 hrs; to Ahuachapán, by market, bus No 503, US$0.75, 50 mins.

station (bus 320 to San Miguel, US$0.45, one hour last bus 1600). The main beach is liable to get crowded and dirty at weekends and holidays, but is deserted mid-week. Single women should take care here; locals warn against walking along the beach after sunset. Another popular beach, **El Tamarindo,** is reached by following the coastal road a little further before taking a right turn.

Cases of malaria have been reported from El Cuco.

Sleeping

La Libertad *p772*

B Pacific Sunrise, at the entrance of La Libertad, T2346-2000, www.hotelesel salvador.com. A brand new hotel with pool, restaurant and rooms overlooking the Obispo beach which can be accessed via an ingenious pedestrian overpass. Best hotel in La Libertad and good rates if more people share the rooms.

C Rick, behind Punta Roca. With bath, clean, friendly, restaurant, good value.

C-D Puerto Bello, 2 Calle Pte, on the main avenue. With bath, run-down, small rooms.

D Hotel Surf Club, 2 Calle Pte 22-9, T2346-1104. Big rooms, a/c, kitchen area. Supermarket downstairs.

D Mango's Lounge and Shop, 4 Calle Pte. Playa La Paz, T2335-3782, www.punta mango.com. Great meals, comfortable lodging and surf gear for rent and sale. Owned by Rodrigo Barraza who runs the **Surfing Tour Company Punta Mango**, an authority in surf trips all over the country, very experienced, recommended. Good, safe budget option especially for single travellers. Boards for hire, used boards: US$12.00 per day, new and long board, US$16 – cheaper for 3 days or more. Will buy used boards.

D-F La Posada Familiar, 5 Av Sur, just up from the beach front. Cheaper without bath, popular with surfers and backpackers, basic, meals, clean, good value, hammocks, parking.

F Comedor Margoth, next to La Posada Familiar. Run-down but clean.

Around La Libertad *p772*

C Los Arcos, Playa Conchalío, T2335-3490. A/c, TV, 300 m from beach, safe, quiet, with pool, garden and restaurant.

West of La Libertad *p773*

All reached on bus No 80 from La Libertad.

A Atami Beach Club, Palmarcito, T2223-9000, www.atami.com.sv. Good rooms. Swimming pool and water slide. Seafood restaurant. In the grounds of the club is a private *rancho* .

B Hotel El Pacífico, Playa El Majahual, T2310-6504. Pool, restaurant.

C Roca Sunzal, Km 42, T2389-6126, www.rocalsunzal.com. Best hotel in El Tunco, beautifully located in front of beach, great view and pool, good value, good food in restaurant.

C-D Tortuga Surf Lodge, Tunco beach, T2389-6185. Cosy little cabin house, surfing lessons available.

D El Tubo, next to Papayas. Cheap rooms and board rental.

D Hotel y Restaurante Santa Fe, at the northern side of the entrance to the

Majahual beach, T2310-6508. Safe and nice, with pool, recommended.

E Casa de Frida Hotel, T2302-6068, www.lacasadefrida.com. Lodging in cabins behind restaurant with beachfront garden, cozy place with hammocks, Spanish owner Manuel is friendly and hospitable.

E Esencia Nativa, T7737-8879, esencianativa@yahoo.com. Run by surfer Alex Novoa with cheap rooms, pool, vegetarian and other original meals (popular restaurant, especially weekends). Surf classes and rental. Popular with surfers.

E Horizonte Surf Camp, El Zonte, T2323-0099, saburosurfcamp@hotmail.com. Simple bungalows, some with a/c, nice garden, pool, restaurant, board rental, clean, good service. Good choice for surfers.

E Papayas Lodge, Playa El Tunco, Carretera el Litoral Km 42, T2389-6231, papayadeltunco@hotmail.com. Family-run surf hostel. Clean rooms with fans, use of kitchen and safe. Owned by Salvadorean surf legend Papaya. Board sales and repair.

Acajutla and around *p773*

B Los Cóbanos Village Lodge, Carretera Acajutla, turn right at **Restaurant Marsolie**, T2260-5785, www.loscobanos.com. Beach-front cabin, pool, restaurant service, scuba diving, surfing, fishing.

B-E El Capricho Beach House, Barra de Santiago (same owners as **Ximena's**, see page 737), contact through T2260-2481. Private rooms with bath and a/c, cabin with dorms and ceiling fan, Clean and safe, beautiful beach. Located in wildlife reserve, close to mangroves and tip of peninsula. Tours in mangroves, fishing, surf classes, board rental available. Transport from the capital and tours to El Imposible National Reserve available. Take direct bus 285 to La Barra de Santiago which departs twice daily from Sonsonate, or bus towards border and pick-up from turn-off.

Reserva Nacional Bosque El Imposible *p774*

B Hostal El Imposible, T2411-5484. With restaurant/bar area, swimming pool and small trail. Cabins sleeping 2-6 people have private bath, hot water and small terrace, also restaurant service. Information from **Salvanatura** in San Salvador, T2279-1515. www.salvanatura.org. Dormitory cabins sleep 4.

Costa del Sol *p775*

Cheaper accommodation can be found 1 km east at Playa Los Blancos and in La Herradura.

A Izalco Cabaña Club. Good value, 30 rooms, pool; seafood a speciality.

D Miny Hotel y Restaurant Mila, Km 66, opposite police station. Very friendly, owner Marcos speaks English. Clean, simple, fan, pool, good food, beach access. Take bus 495 from Terminal Sur, San Salvador; buses are very crowded at weekends, but the resort is quiet during the week.

Playa El Cuco *p775*

A Hotel Pacific Paradise, El Cuco, 500 m before the estuary, T2502-2678, www.hotelpacificparadise.com. Full resort, with cabins around a pool, access to the beach and a restaurant.

A Torola Cabaña Club, Km 175, Playa Torola, El Tamarindo, run by **Izalco Club** at Costa del Sol, T2681-5528. Pool looking out to sea, great open air bar/restaurant, friendly, welcoming owner, recommended.

B Trópico Club, 2.5 km along the coast from Playa El Cuco, T2661-1800, tropicoinn@yahoo.com. Several cabins, pool and open-air dining. Leads directly to the beach. Run by the **Trópico Inn** in San Miguel, see page 770, which can provide information.

D Cucolindo, 1 km along the coast, T2619-9012, hotelcucolindo@hotmail.com. Cabin for 4, basic, cold water, mosquitos.

D Hotel La Tortuga, El Cuco. Cheap, good for backpackers.

D Los Leones Marinos, El Cuco, T2619-9015, with bath, clean and tidy.

Eating

La Libertad *p772*

There are cheap restaurants near the pier, in the market and around Playa La Paz and Playa El Obispo.

₸₸ El Nuevo Altamar, 4 Calle Pte, Playa La Paz, T2335-3235. Good for seafood, steaks and fowl.

₸₸-₸ Punta Roca, 5 Av Sur, T2335-3261. Mon-Fri 0800-2000, Sat and Sun 0800-2300. Try the shrimp soup. American-owned by Robert Rotherham, whose son Lonnie offers advice for travellers.

🍴🍴 **La Dolce Vita**, Playa Las Flores, 200 m east of the Shell gas station, T2335-3592. Excellent seafood and pasta restaurant.
🍴🍴 **Mariscos Freddy** and **La Marea**, on the beach at Playa Obispo. Good-value seafood restaurants.

West of La Libertad *p773*
🍴🍴 **Café Sunzal**, Playa Sunzal, T2389-6019, cafesunzal@navegante.com.sv. Great seafood and steak house, exquisite international cuisine, Km 43.5 Carretera El Litoral.
🍴🍴-🍴 **La Bocana**, Tunco beach, in front of the Tunco (pig). Great view from 2nd storey, good seafood, great-value prices.
🍴 **La Casa de Frida**, El Zonte, T2302-6068, www.lacasadefrida.com. Owned by Manuel, super-friendly Spaniard. A great restaurant located in large garden dotted with tables and hammocks just in front of the beach.

Costa del Sol *p775*
🍴 **Restaurante Kenny Mar**, Km 60, Carretera Costa del Sol, Playa San Marcelino, T2338- 2578. Delicious seafood with beach front view.

Activities and tours

La Libertad *p772*
Watersports
A surfing guide to El Salvador can be found at www.puntamango.com. Look for small surf rentals and surf classes at hostals on the coast west of Puerto La Libertad.
Atami Beach Club, see Sleeping, above.
Automobile Club of El Salvador has a chalet for bathing at La Libertad.
Hospital de Tablas, 5 Av Sur, for surfboard hire and repair.
Punta Rock, restaurant in La Libertad, owner Robert Rotherham (and 2 sons), surfboard rental US$15 per day, kayak rental, windsurfing lessons, excursions arranged, also deep-sea fishing US$180 up to 6 people, English spoken, equipment for sale; also has mountain bike rental.
Punta Mango Surf Trips, T2236-0025, www.puntamango.com (see also **Mango's Lounge** in La Libertad), run by Rodrigo Barraza, very experienced, does surf trips for the day or several days, even to surf beaches in the east.

Transport

La Libertad *p772*
Bus No 102 from **San Salvador** leaves from 4 Calle Pte, between 13 and 15 Av Sur, 1 hr via **Santa Tecla**, US$0.45. To **Zacatecoluca** at 0500, 1230 and 1530. La Libertad bus terminal is on 2 Calle Ote, east of the pier. Minibuses to La Flores and **Conchalío** leave from 4 Av Norte, Calle Gerardo Barrios, every 10 mins.
Car repairs Good workshop on 7 Av Sur. Francisco is helpful, good-quality work.
Taxi From **San Salvador** US$15-20 one-way, US$30 return, negotiate. A mini-van will take groups on tour anywhere in the country. Contact Robert Rotherham at **Punta Roca**, T2335-3261.

Acajutla and around *p773*
Bus No 207 from Terminal Occidente, **San Salvador**, US$2.80, or No 252 from **Sonsonate** US$0.30. 58 km from **Santa Ana**.

Zacatecoluca *p775*
Bus No133 from Terminal Sur, **San Salvador**. Direct bus to **La Libertad** 1540, US$0.65, or take San Salvador bus, change at Comalapa, 2 hrs.

Playa El Cuco *p775*
Boat Boat from El Tamarindo across the bay leads to a short cut to **La Unión**.
Bus From **La Unión**, 20 mins.

Directory

La Libertad *p772*
Banks There are no credit card bank facilities or ATMs in La Libertad. **Banco de Fomento Agropecuario**, Mon-Fri 0800-1600, Sat 0800-1200. Also has **Western Union**. Banco Desarollo, takes TCs. **Internet** Infocentros, in main street close to Puerto Bello, cheap. **Language school** 5 Av Norte, close to Punta Roca restaurant, T2449-0331, salvaspanischool@mailcity.com. **Police** Calle Gerardo Barrios and 1 Av Sur. Tourism police, based here, patrol the town and beach areas at weekends. A tourist kiosk is planned for the entrance to town. **Post office** Up the side of the Telecom office, 0800-1200, 1400-1700. **Telephone** Telepunto, next to Hotel Puerto Bello, 2 Calle Pte (0630-0830). Cheap rates. **Telecom** on same road.

Honduras

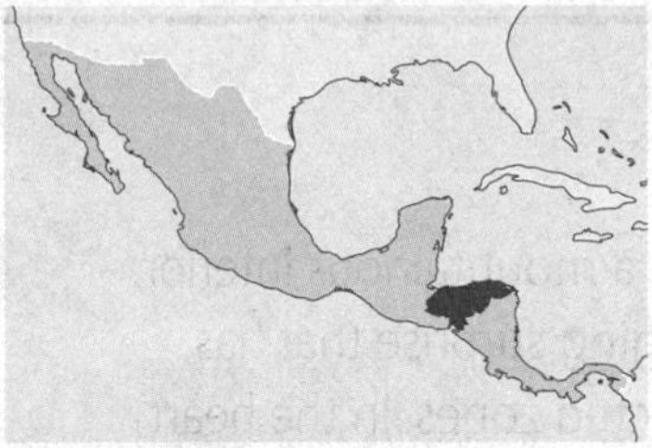

Footprint features

Introduction

Sliced, spliced and spread across a mountainous interior, Honduras is a pleasantly challenging surprise that has developed in curiously disconnected zones. In the heart of the mountains Tegucigalpa epitomizes the Latin city – a chaotic celebration of colonial architecture divided by steeply sloping cobbled streets. By contrast, the republic's second and more modern city, San Pedro Sula, on the coastal lowland plain, has a neat matrix of *calles* and *avenidas* that seem rather dull by comparison.

A world away, the Bay Islands bask in sunny skies. Utila thrives on a throw-it-together-and-see-if-it-works existence. It's easily the cheapest place to learn to dive in the western hemisphere.

Honduras is the second largest Central American republic after Nicaragua, but its population is smaller than that of neighbouring El Salvador, the smallest country. Bordered by Nicaragua, Guatemala, El Salvador and a narrow coastal Pacific strip, it is the northern Caribbean coast and beautiful Bay Islands that are a natural focus and a prime destination for visitors.

Inland, the mountainous terrain creates natural obstacles to easy, direct travel round the country. It also means that, for trekking and hiking, there are great swathes of beautiful hillside, many of which are dotted with small communities, largely disinterested in the comings and goings of the few travellers who venture so far off the beaten track.

In October 1998 Hurricane Mitch deluged Honduras with torrential rain causing great loss of life and damage to almost all parts of the country. While the physical damage has been cleaned up, a decade on the economic and social impact continues to ripple through the country.

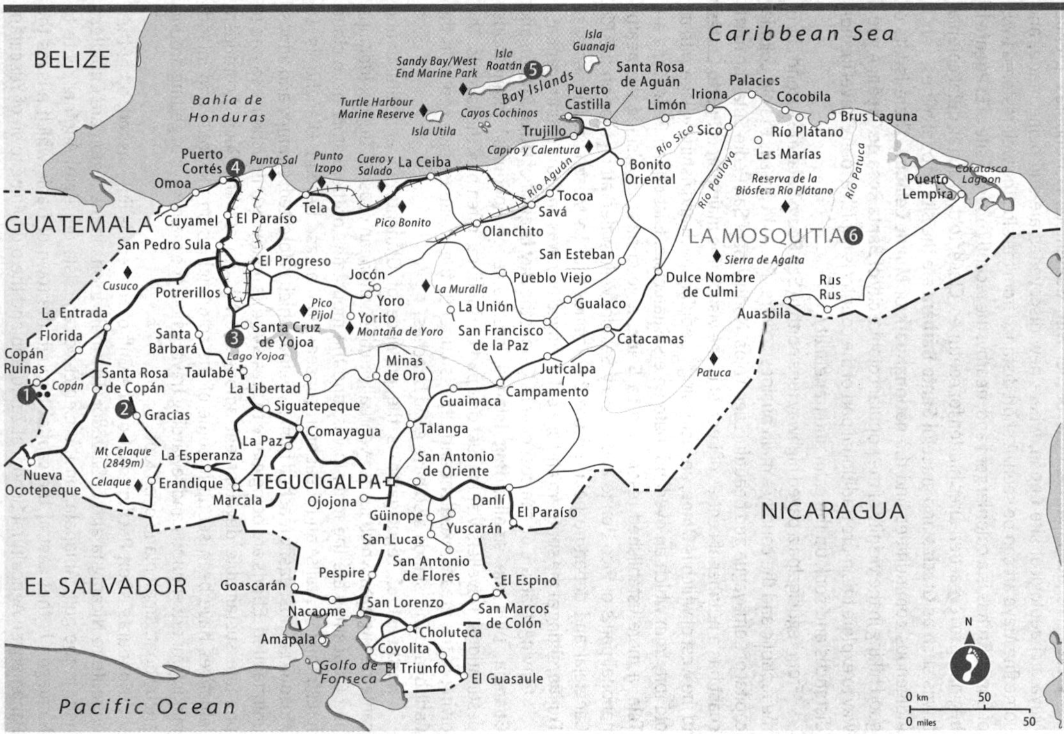

★ Don't miss...

1 **Copán** The serene and beautiful setting of the Maya ruins and the inscriptions of the stelae, page 805.

2 **Gracias** Colonial charm with the heights of Mount Celaque, a day's hike uphill, page 811.

3 **Lago Yojoa** The beautiful lakeside and the crashing cascades of nearby Pulhanpanzak waterfall, page 825.

4 **North coast beaches** Caribbean rhythms and thriving market towns, page 835.

5 **Bay Islands** Scuba diving, snorkelling or just chilling on the islands, page 856.

6 **La Mosquitia** The isolated rainforest wilderness of Central America's Little Amazon, page 874.

Planning your trip

Where to go

With the popularity of the Bay Islands as a diving destination, mainland Honduras is often missed in the frenzied rush to hit the water. And, while the beauty of the islands cannot be overstated, picking a route that takes in some of the smaller towns of Honduras gives a far better understanding of the country as a whole.

The capital and administrative centre is **Tegucigalpa**, which has an old, colonial sector and a new section with modern hotels, shops and businesses. Across the Río Choluteca is Tegucigalpa's twin city, **Comayagüela**, the working heart of the city with the markets and bus terminals. Around the capital, there are colonial villages, old mining towns, handicraft centres and good hiking areas, including **Parque Nacional La Tigra**, which will make ideal trips for a day or two.

West of Tegucigalpa, near the border with Guatemala, is Honduras' premier Maya archaeological site **Copán**, where new discoveries are still being made, and some fine Maya art can be seen. A short distance from the site, the well-restored town of **Copán Ruinas** is a colonial gem and, nearby, the recently opened site of **El Puente** is beginning to reveal treasures hidden for centuries. Closer to the capital, quiet colonial towns such as **Gracias** and graceful **Santa Bárbara** are the site of opal mines, Lenca indigenous communities and the **national park** of **Mount Celaque**. There is lots of good hiking in the vicinity of the popular colonial city of **Santa Rosa de Copán**. A good way to explore this more traditional part of the country is to pick a route, travel in short distances and soak up the calm and tranquillity.

From Tegucigalpa a paved highway runs north to **San Pedro Sula**, the second city of the republic and the country's main business centre. The road passes the old colonial capital of Comayagua and beautiful Lago Yojoa. Northwest of San Pedro Sula, the **north coast** has a number of centres of interest to the visitor. The main port is **Puerto Cortés**, to the west of which is **Omoa**, an increasingly popular beach and fishing village with an old fort, from which an overland route enters Guatemala. East of San Pedro Sula are **Tela**, a more established resort, and **La Ceiba**, a good base for visiting the nearby national parks of Pico Bonito and Cuero y Salado, whitewater rafting trips on the Río Cangrejal and departure point for the Bay Islands and La Mosquitia. Further east, **Trujillo**, sitting at the southern end of a palm-fringed bay, was once the country capital.

Curving in an arc off the cost near La Ceiba, the **Bay Islands** of **Utila**, **Roatán** and **Guanaja**, plus the smaller **Hog Islands**, are some of Honduras' main tourist destinations. Travellers visiting just one part of Honduras often pick the islands. The diving in the area is excellent and Utila is currently the cheapest dive centre in the Caribbean. The islands also have good beaches.

Northeast of Tegucigalpa is the province of Olancho, an agricultural and cattle-raising area which leads eventually to the Caribbean coast at Trujillo. Juticalpa and Catacamas are the main towns, and the mountains of the district have cloud forest, hiking trails and beautiful conservation areas. Beyond Olancho is **La Mosquitia**, most easily reached from La Ceiba, which is forested, swampy and almost uninhabited. Efforts are being made to preserve this relatively untouched area and to promote sustainable development among the Miskito and the Pech. Ecotourism initiatives have been set up in some of the communities on the coast and inland, making for adventurous and rewarding travel where the main ways of getting around are by boat, small plane or on foot.

Honduras' short **Pacific coast** on the Gulf of Fonseca is little visited, other than en route to Nicaragua and El Salvador. The main towns in the region are Choluteca and, in the gulf, Amapala, on the extinct volcanic Isla del Tigre. Another route to Nicaragua is that **east of the capital** through the town of Danlí, which passes the Panamerican Agricultural School at Zamorano and the old mining town of Yuscarán.

Suggested itineraries The Honduran trail is pretty straightforward. Most people arrive from Guatemala and visit **Copán** with its nearby ruins and growing range of activities. From Copán it's a bus to San Pedro Sula and a quick change to continue to **Tela** or **La Ceiba**, both close to national parks. From La Ceiba the ferry leaves for **Roatán** and **Utila**, the budget travellers' favourite for diving, snorkelling and island life. That trip will take about 10 days. If you have more time, a circular route goes to **Santa Rosa de Copán**, through **Gracias** to **Tegucigalpa**, and then from the capital to **Comayagua, Lago Yojoa** and **San Pedro Sula**. That will make your stay in Honduras close to three weeks – add one more if you want to visit **La Mosquitia**.

When to go

Altitude is the main impact on climate. In Tegucigalpa, at 1000 m, the temperatures range from 4-33°C, lowest in January-March, highest in April and May. In the lowlands to the north, temperatures in San Pedro Sula range from 20-37°C with the coolest months, November to February. On the Caribbean the dry season stretches from February-June, while the heaviest rains fall August to December. Inland, rain falls throughout the year, with the drier months being November to April. Some of the central highland areas enjoy a delightful climate, with a freshness that makes a pleasant contrast to the humidity and heat of the lowland zones.

Finding out more

Ministerio Hondureño de Turismo, main office is at Edificio Europa, Av Ramón E Cruz and Calle República de México, Col San Carlos, Tegucigalpa, T222-2124. Also an office at Toncontín Airport and several regional offices.

www.hondurastips.honduras.com A reliable favourite with lots of information about Honduras and links to national newspapers. The biannual publication, *HONDURAS Tips*, edited by John Dupuis in La Ceiba, Edificio Gómez, Local No 2, 4 Calle, T/F440-3383, is full of interesting and useful tourist information, in English and Spanish, free (available in Tegucigalpa from Ministerio Hondureño de Turismo).

www.letsgohonduras.com The official guide on the internet.

www.netsys.hn Good for business links.

Several regional guides are being developed – these are mentioned within the text.

Language

Spanish is the main language, but English is often spoken in the north, in the Bay Islands, by West Indian settlers on the Caribbean coast, and in business communities.

Before you travel

Visas and immigration

Neither a visa nor tourist card is required for nationals of Western European countries, USA, Canada, Australia, New Zealand, Japan, Argentina, Chile, Guatemala, Costa Rica, Nicaragua, El Salvador, Panama and Uruguay. Citizens of other countries, including Israelis, need either a tourist card, which can be bought from Honduran consulates for US$2-3, occasionally less, or a visa, and they should enquire at a Honduran consulate in advance to see which they need. The price of a visa seems to vary depending on nationality and where it is bought. Extensions of 30 days are easy to obtain (up to a maximum of six months' stay, cost US$5). There are immigration offices for extensions at Tela, La Ceiba, San Pedro Sula, Santa Rosa de Copán, Siguatepeque, La Paz and Comayagua, and all are more helpful than the Tegucigalpa office.

For embassies and consulates in Honduras see page 802.

Honduran embassies and consulates

Belize, 22 Gabourel Lane, Belize City, T02-245-889.
Canada, 151 Slater St, Suite 805-A, Ottawa, Ontario K1P 5H3, T613-233-8900.
El Salvador, 89 Av Norte between 7 and 9 Calle Pte 561, Col Escalón, San Salvador, T263-2808.
France, 8 rue Crevaux, 75116 Paris, T4755-8645.
Germany, Cuxhavener Str 14, D-10555 Berlín, T30397497-10.
Guatemala, 19 Av "A", 20-19, Zona 10, T2363-5622.
Israel, Calle Zohar Tal No 1, Herzlya Pituach, CP46741, T9957-7686.
Japan, 38 Kowa Bldg, 8F No 802, 12-24 Nishi Azabu 4, Chome Minato Ku, Tokyo 106, T03-3409-1150.
Mexico, Alfonso Reyes 220, Col Condesa, México DF, T55-211-5747.
Netherlands, Nassauplein 17, 2585 EB, La Haya, T70-364-1684.
Nicaragua, Reparto San Juan, del Gimnasio Hércules 1 cuadra al Sur, 1 cuadra al Este, Calle San Juan 312, Managua, T/F278-3043.
Spain, Paseo de la Castellana 164, Segunda Planta Derecha , Madrid, T91-579 02 51.
Sweden, Stjarnvagen 2 , 7th floor, Stockholm, T8731-5084.
UK, 115 Gloucester Place, London W1H 3PJ, T020-7486-4880.
USA, 3007 Tilden St NW, Pod 4M, Washington, DC 20008, T202-966-7702.
For information on visa requirements and embassies look on the web at www.sre.hn

Customs

There are no customs duties on personal effects. You are allowed to bring in 200 cigarettes or 100 cigars, or ½ kg of tobacco, and two quarts of spirit.

Money

Currency → *US$1=19.69 lempiras.*

The unit of currency is the **lempira** (written La and referred to as lemps within a few days of arrival,) named after a famous indigenous chief that lost his life while fighting the invasion of the Spaniards. It is reasonably stable against the US dollar. Divided into 100 centavos, there are nickel coins of 5, 10, 20 and 50 centavos. Bank notes are for 1, 2, 5, 10, 20, 50, 100 and 500 lempiras. No one has change for larger notes, especially the 500. Any amount of any currency can be taken in or out of the country.

Credit cards and traveller's cheques

Acceptance of credit cards in Honduras is patchy and commissions can be as high as 6%. Most businesses will try to tack on a service charge to credit card purchases which is illegal. If feeling particularly righteous ask the manager to call BAC and check if the charge is permitted. It is advisable to have traveller's cheques available and US dollars in cash as well.

MasterCard and Visa are accepted in major hotels and most restaurants in cities and larger towns. American Express is accepted in more expensive establishments. Cash advances are available from BAC, Banco Atlántida, Aval Card and Honducard throughout the country. BAC represents American Express and issues and services Amex credit cards. Cash advances using MasterCard cost US$10 in banks.

Cost of living and travelling

Honduras is not expensive for the visitor (two people can travel together in reasonable comfort for US$25 per person per day – less if on a tight budget), but prices for tourists fluctuate greatly. Transport, including domestic flights, is still the cheapest in Central America. Diving will set you back a bit, but at US$150 or so for a PADI course, it is still the cheapest in Central America.

Touching down

Business hours Mon-Fri 0900-1200, 1400-1800; Sat 0800-1200, some open in the afternoon. **Banks** in Tegucigalpa Mon-Fri 0900-1500; 0800-1100 only along the north coast on Sat. **Post offices**: Mon-Fri 0700-2000; Sat 0800-1200.
Official time 6 hrs behind GMT.

Telephone Country code T+504; Local operator T192; General information T193; International operator T197.
Voltage Generally 110 volts but, increasingly, 220 volts is being installed. US-type flat-pin plugs.
Weights and measures The metric system is official.

Getting there

Air

Tegucigalpa, La Ceiba, San Pedro Sula and Roatán all have international airports. There are no direct flights to Tegucigalpa from Europe, but connecting flights can be made via Miami, then with **American Airlines** or **Taca.** There are flights to Tegucigalpa, San Pedro Sula and Roatán from Houston with **Continental**, with services to Tegucigalpa from New York and Phoenix. Taca flies daily from Guadalajara, Guatemala City, Mexico City, Monterrey (Mexico), San Salvador, and San José (Costa Rica).

Iberia flies to San Pedro Sula via Miami from Madrid and Barcelona five days a week. **American Airlines** fly daily from Miami, as do Taca and Iberia. Taca also flies once a week from New Orleans. Taca flies from San José to San Pedro Sula direct, with flights from Belize City, Guatemala City, Panama City, San José and San Salvador. **Sol Air** have introduced daily flights from Miami to San Pedro Sula and Tegucigalpa – with flights as low as US$150, Miami-San Pedro Sula. There are twice-weekly flights from Grand Cayman Island to La Ceiba.

Road

There are numerous border crossings. With Guatemala to the west you can cross near Copán Ruinas at El Florido, on the Caribbean coast at Corinto or to the south at Agua Caliente. For El Salvador there are crossings at El Poy, leading to Suchitoto and the west of the country, and Perquín leading to San Miguel and the east of the country. For Nicaragua the border post town of Guasale in the south leads 116 km on a very bad road to the Nicaraguan town of León, while the inland routes at Las Manos and El Espino guide you to Estelí and Matagalpa, in the northern hills. Crossing to Nicaragua through the Mosquitia coast is not possible – officially at least.

Sea

A regular weekly service departing Mondays at 1100 links Puerto Cortés with Mango Creek and Placencia, in Belize – see page 852 for details. There are weekly boats from Lívingston in Guatemala in high season. Contact **Gunter's Dive School**, Utila, for details see page 868.

Touching down

Airport information and departure taxes

Airport Airport departure tax is US$27 (not charged if in transit less than nine hours). There is a 10% tax on all tickets sold for domestic and international journeys.

Land borders Taxes are charged on entry and exit at land borders, but the amount charged varies from border to border, despite notices asking you to denounce corruption. Entry is 20 lempiras (or US$2) and exit is 10 lempiras. Double is charged on Sunday. If officials make an excess charge for entry or exit, ask for a receipt. Do not attempt to enter Honduras at an unstaffed border crossing. When it is discovered that you have no entry stamp you will either be fined US$60 or escorted to the border, and you will have to pay the guard's food and lodging (you may be able to defray some of this cost by spending a night in jail).

Local customs and laws

Clothing On the north coast, where the climate is much hotter and damper, dress is less formal. **Tipping** Normally 10% of the bill but more expensive places add a service charge to the bill. **Identification** It is advisable to carry some form of identification at all times, because spot checks have increased, especially when entering or leaving major towns.

Safety

Unfortunately we are forced to report greater concerns over general security in Honduras. At the time of Hurricane Mitch in 1998 predictions suggested social problems would be prevalent in a few years. Reports of muggings and theft increased but there is now a Tourist Police in place – in Copán Ruinas, Roatán, La Ceiba, Tela and San Pedro Sula – that has reduced the problem. Take local advice and be cautious when travelling alone or off the beaten track. But remember, the vast majority of Hondurans are honest, friendly, warm and welcoming, and the general perception is that crime is now reducing.

Getting around

Air

There are airstrips in all large towns and many of the cut-off smaller ones. Airlines that make internal flights are: **Isleña**, **Sosa** and **Atlantic Air**. **Atlantic Air** serves La Ceiba, San Pedro Sula, Teguc, Roatán, Utila, Guanaja, Puerto Lempira, Caquira and Ahuas. **Sosa**, the largest domestic carrier, serves Roatán, Utila, Guanaja, Palacios, San Pedro Sula, Tegucigalpa and other destinations in Honduras. It is worth checking the price for longer flights as they are occasionally discounted to levels that compete with bus travel. La Ceiba is the main hub for domestic flights, especially for **Sosa** and **Atlantic**, and most flights to and from the islands stop there. The cheapest way to the islands is to get a bus to La Ceiba and then catch a flight. **Sol Air** ① *T/F232-5005, www.solair.net*, provides economical flights within Central America and to Miami, occasionally with very good promotional offers.

Road

The road system throughout the country has improved rapidly in recent years and Honduras probably has the best roads in Central America. However, many roads were built and maintained with US money when Honduras was supporting the contras in Nicaragua and are now showing signs of lack of maintenance. Traffic tends to travel fast on these apparently good roads, and road accidents are second only to Costa Rica in Latin America. If driving, take care and avoid driving at night. Total road length is now 15,100 km, of which 3020 km are paved, 10,000 km are all-weather roads and the remainder are passable in the dry season.

Buses There are essentially three types of service: local (*servicio a escala*), direct (*servicio directo*) and luxury (*servicio de lujo*). Using school buses a *servicio a escala* is very slow, with frequent stops and detours, and is uncomfortable for long periods. *Servicio directo* is faster, slightly more expensive and more comfortable. *Servicio de lujo* has air-conditioned European and Brazilian buses with videos.

Buses set out early in the day, with a few night buses running between major urban centres. Try to avoid bus journeys after dark as there are many more accidents and even occasional robberies.

If you suffer from motion sickness, the twisty roads can become unbearable. Avoid sitting at the back of the bus, take some water and sit by a window that will open. Minibuses are faster than buses, so the journey can be quite hair-raising. Pick-ups which serve out-of-the-way communities will leave you covered in dust (or soaked) – sit near the cab if possible.

Driving Regular **gasoline/petrol** costs US$3.10 per US gallon. Diesel US$2.50. On entering with a car (from El Salvador at least), customs and the transit police give a 30-day permit for the vehicle. This must be renewed in Tegucigalpa (anywhere else authorization is valid for only one Department). Charges for motorists appear to be: on entry, US$30 in total for a vehicle with two passengers, including provisional permission from the police to drive in Honduras, US$1 (official minimum) for car papers, fumigation and baggage inspection; on exit, US$2.30 in total. Motorcyclists face similar charges. These charges are changing all the time and differ significantly from one post to another (up to US$40 sometimes). They are also substantially higher on Saturday, Sunday and holidays and by bribery. You will have to pass through Migración, Registro, Tránsito, Cuarentena, Administración, Secretaría and then a police vehicle check. At each stage you will be asked for money, for which you will not always get a receipt. On arriving or leaving with a vehicle there are so many checks that it pays to hire a *tramitador* to steer you to the correct officials in the correct order (US$1-2 for the guide). No fresh food is allowed to cross the border. The easiest border crossing is at Las Manos. The **Pan-American Highway** in Honduras is in bad condition in parts. One reader warns to "beware of potholes that can take a car. They suddenly appear after 20 km of good road without warning".

! If hiring a car, make sure it has the correct papers, and emergency triangles which are required by law.

Cycling Bicycles are regarded as vehicles but are not officially subject to entrance taxes. Bicycle repair shops are difficult to find, and parts for anything other than mountain bikes may be very hard to come by. Some buses and most local flights will take bicycles. Most main roads have hard shoulders and most drivers respect cyclists. It is common for cars to blow their horn to signal their approach.

Hitchhiking is relatively easy. Travel is still by foot and mule in many rural areas.

Train

The **Ferrocarril Nacional de Honduras** has downgraded its one remaining passenger service between Tela and Puerto Cortés to a twice-weekly *ferrobus*.

Maps

The **Instituto Geográfico Nacional** produces two 1:1,000,000 maps (1995) of the country, one a tourist map which includes city maps of Tegucigalpa, San Pedro Sula and La Ceiba, and the other a good road map although it does not show all the roads. Both maps are widely available in bookshops in major cities and some hotels. **International Travel Maps** (**ITM**) has a 1:750,000 map of Honduras.

Sleeping

Accommodation in Honduras varies greatly. In Tegucigalpa and San Pedro Sula you will find the mix ranges from business-style hotels of international standards down to simple, but generally clean rooms. In popular tourist spots the focus is more on comfort and costs rise accordingly. Get off the beaten track and you'll find some of the most basic and cheapest accommodation in Central America – complete with accompanying insect life, it can be unbearable or a mind-broadening experience depending on your mood. There is also a 4% extra tax on hotel rooms.

Eating

The cheapest meals are the *comida corriente*, or the sometimes better prepared and more expensive *comida típica*, which usually contain some of the following: beans, rice, meat, avocado, egg, cabbage salad, cheese, bananas, potatoes or yucca, and always tortillas. *Carne asada* is charcoal-roasted meat and served with grated cabbage between tortillas; it is good, although rarely prepared hygienically. Make sure that pork is properly cooked. *Tajadas* are crisp, fried *plátano* chips topped with grated cabbage and sometimes meat; *nacatamales* are ground, dry maize mixed with meat and seasoning, boiled in banana leaves. *Baleadas* are soft flour tortillas filled with beans and various combinations of butter, egg, cheese and cabbage. *Pupusas* are thick corn tortillas filled with *chicharrón* (pork scratchings), or cheese, served as snacks with beer. *Tapado* is a stew with meat or fish, plantain, yucca and coconut milk. *Pinchos* are meat, poultry, or shrimp kebabs. *Sopa de mondongo* (tripe soup) is very common.

Cheap fish is found on the beaches at Trujillo and Cedeño. While on the north coast, look out for *pan de coco* (coconut bread) made by Garífuna (Black Carib) women, and *sopa de camarones* (prawn soup) which are prepared with coconut milk and lemon juice.

Drink

Soft drinks are called *refrescos*, or *frescos* (the name also given to fresh fruit blended with water, make sure you check that bottled water is used as tap water is unsafe); *licuados* are fruit blended with milk. Bottled drinking water is readily available in most places. Orange juice, usually sweetened, is available in cartons everywhere. *Horchata* is morro seeds, rice water and cinnamon. Coffee is thick and sweet. The main brands of **beer** are Port Royal Export, Imperial, Nacional and Salva Vida (more malty than the others). Local **rum** is cheap, try Flor de Caña white, or seven-year-old amber. Twelve-year-old Flor de Caña Centenario is regarded as the best.

Holidays and festivals

Most Roman Cathlic feast days are celebrated.
1 Jan New Year's Day.
14 Apr Day of the Americas.
Semana Santa Thu, Fri and Sat before Easter Sun.
1 May Labour Day.
15 Sep Independence Day
3 Oct Francisco Morazán.
12 Oct Columbus' arrival in America
21 Oct Army Day.

Shopping

The best articles are those made of wood. Straw items are also highly recommended. Leather is cheaper than in El Salvador and Nicaragua. As a single stopping point, the region around Santa Bárbara is one of the best places, with outlets selling handicrafts from nearby villages. Alternatively you can explore the villages yourself and see the goods being made. Coffee is OK, but not great.

Sales tax is 12%, often only charged if you ask for a receipt; 15% on alcohol and tobacco.

Sport and activities

Adventure and nature tourism

Adventure tourism is taking off with the usual array of activities. Mountain biking is increasingly popular as is horse riding around Copán. Hardcore adventure can be found in the swamp wetlands of Mosquitia, usually by taking an organized tour.

Nature trips take advantage of the wide variety of national parks in Honduras (see below). Birders have for years known about the treasures of the country, but hikers and trekkers are beginning to venture out through the valleys and across the hills that are often shrouded in cloud forest.

National parks → *See colour map 6 at the back of the book.*

The extensive system of national parks and protected areas provides the chance to enjoy some of the best scenery Honduras has to offer, much of it unspoilt and rarely visited. The National Parks' Office, **Conama**, is next to the Instituto Nacional Agrario in Tegucigalpa; chaotic but friendly and a good source of information. **Cohdefor** ⓘ *10 Av 4 Calle NO, San Pedro Sula, T253-4959*, the national forestry agency, is also much involved with the parks. The parks system has been in existence legally since a congressional decree was passed in 1987. Parks have different levels of services – see individual parks for details. Natural reserves continue to be established and all support and interest is most welcome. Parks in existence are **La Tigra**, outside Tegucigalpa (page 795), and the **Río Plátano** (page 875). Under development since 1987 are **Monte Celaque** (page 811), **Cusuco** (page 828), **Punta Sal** (page 837), **Capiro y Calentura** (page 843), **Montaña Cerro Azul-Meámbar** (page 825), **Montaña de Yoro** (page 844) and **Pico Bonito** (page 841). These parks have visitors' centres, hiking trails and primitive camping. The following have been designated national parks by the government: **Montecristo-Trifinio** (page 815), **Santa Bárbara** (page 826), **Pico Pijol** (Yoro, page 844), **Agalta** (Olancho, page 874) and **Montaña de Comayagua** (page 824). Wildlife refuges covered in the text are **Punto Izopo** (page 837), **Cuero y Salado** (page 841), **Las Trancas** (page 814) and **La Muralla-Los Higuerales** (page 873). For information on protected areas in the **Bay Islands**, see page 856.

Watersports

Diving off the Bay Islands has for a long time been the number one attraction, whether seeking some of the best and most varied diving in Central America, or looking to kickstart your scuba skills with some of the cheapest PADI courses on the planet. Snorkelling is also excellent off the Bay Islands if you've reached your dive limits or simply find the whole thing just a little too unnatural.

Whitewater rafting is growing steadily in Honduras with the hotspot being the River Cangrejal, close to La Ceiba, where Class II, III and IV rapids test both the novice and experienced paddler. The sport is relatively new to the country and more sites are certain to be found in the coming years.

Health

Dysentery and stomach parasites are common and malaria is endemic in coastal regions, where a prophylactic regime should be undertaken and mosquito nets carried. Inoculate against typhoid and tetanus. There is cholera, so eating on the street or at market stalls is not recommended. Tap water is definitely not safe; drink bottled water which is available almost everywhere. Ice and juices are usually made with purified water. Otherwise boil or sterilize water. Salads and raw vegetables are risky. There are hospitals and private clinics in Tegucigalpa, San Pedro Sula and all the larger towns.

Keeping in touch

Communications

Internet Internet cafés are widely available in the capital and in popular locations. Prices and connections vary greatly; in cities good speeds are at about US$1 per hour. On the islands, speeds are erratic and prices expensive.

Post Air mail takes four to seven days to Europe and the same for the USA. Letters up to 20 g cost US$0.40 to all parts of the world. Small packages – 500 g to 1 kg – cost US$3 to USA or Europe.

Telephone and fax **Hondutel** provides international telephone and fax services from stations throughout the country. The system is the most basic and most expensive in Central America. Telephone service between Honduras and Europe costs about US$4.81 per minute; calls to the USA cost US$2.70 per minute. Collect calls to North America, Central America and some European countries (not possible to Netherlands, Australia, Switzerland or Israel) can be made from the Hondutel office in Tegucigalpa. Fax charges per page, plus 12% tax, are US$1.80 to North America, US$1.80 to Europe, US$2 to South America and the Caribbean and US$3 to the rest of the world. To receive a fax at Hondutel costs one lempira per page.

Media

Newspapers The principal newspapers in Tegucigalpa are *El Heraldo* and *La Tribuna*. In San Pedro Sula they are *El Tiempo* and *La Prensa* (circulation about 54,000). Links on the net at www.honduras.com. The English weekly paper *Honduras This Week*, Centro Comercial Via Mare, Boulevard Morazán, T/F232-8818, available throughout the country, comes out on Saturday, US$0.35. Online edition at www.marrder.com/htw.

Television There are six television channels and 167 broadcasting stations. Cable TV is available in large towns and cities.

Tegucigalpa and around

→ Colour map 6, C2. Population: 819,876. Altitude: 1000 m.

Genuinely chaotic, Tegucigalpa – or Tegus as it is called by locals – is cramped and crowded, but still somehow retains a degree of charm in what remains of the colonial centre. If you can bear to stay away from the Caribbean for a few days, it has much more history and charisma than its rival San Pedro Sula, to the north. Surrounded by sharp, high peaks on three sides, the city is built on the lower slopes of El Picacho. The commercial centre is around Boulevard Morazán, an area known as 'zona viva', full of cafés, restaurants and shops. For contrast to the modern functional city, you can visit some of the centuries-old mining settlements set in forested valleys among the nearby mountains that are ideal for hiking. ▸▸ *For Sleeping, Eating and other listings, see pages 797-803.*

Getting there

The international airport, Toncontín, is 6½ km south of the centre, US$7-8 in a taxi to the centre. The airport is in a narrow valley creating difficult landing conditions: morning fog or bad weather can cause it to close. The Carretera del Sur (Southern Highway), which brings in travellers from the south and from Toncontín Airport, runs

Toncontín Airport, runs through Comayagüela into Tegucigalpa. It goes past the obelisk set up to commemorate 100 years of Central American Independence, and the Escuela Nacional de Bellas Artes, with its decorated Maya corridor and temporary exhibitions of contemporary paintings and crafts. There is no central bus station and bus companies have offices throughout Comayagüela. On arrival it is very much easier to take a taxi to your hotel until you get to know the city.

Getting around

The winding of streets in the city means that moving around in the first few days is as much about instinct as following any map. There are cheap buses and taxis for city transport. The Tegucigalpa section of the city uses both names and numbers for streets, but names are used more commonly. In Comayagüela, streets designated by number are the norm. Addresses tend not to be very precise, especially in the colonias around Boulevard Morazán east and south of the centre of Tegucigalpa.

Tourist information

Ministerio Hondureño de Turismo ⓘ *Edif Europa, Av Ramón E Cruz and Calle República de México, 3rd floor, Col San Carlos, T238-3974, also at Toncontín Airport, open 0830-1530*, provides lists of hotels and sells posters, postcards and slides. Information on cultural events around the country from **Teatro Nacional Manuel Bonilla** is better than at regional tourist offices. **El Mundo Maya** ⓘ *behind the cathedral next to the Parque Central, T222-2946*, is a private tourist information centre.

Best time to visit

The city's altitude gives it a reliable climate: temperate during the rainy season from May to November; warm, with cool nights in March and April; and cool and dry with very cool nights from December to February. The annual mean temperature is about 23°C (74°F).

Security

Generally speaking, Tegucigalpa is cleaner and safer (especially at night) than Comayagüela. If you have anything stolen, report it to **Dirección de Investigación Criminal (DIC)** ⓘ *5 Av, 7-8 Calle (next to Edificio Palermo), T237-4799*.

Background

Founded as a silver and gold mining camp in 1578, Tegucigalpa means silver hill in the original indigenous tongue; miners first discovered gold at the north end of the current Soberanía bridge. The present city is comprised of the two former towns of Comayagüela and Tegucigalpa which, although divided by the steeply banked Río Choluteca, became the capital in 1880 and are now united administratively as the Distrito Central.

Being off the main earthquake fault line, Tegucigalpa has not been subjected to disasters by fire or earthquake, unlike many of its Central American neighbours, so it has retained many traditional features. The stuccoed houses, with a single, heavily barred entrance leading to a central patio, are often attractively coloured. However, the old low skyline of the city has been punctuated by several modern tall buildings, and much of the old landscape changed with the arrival of Hurricane Mitch.

The rains of **Hurricane Mitch** in October 1998 had a devastating effect on the Distrito Central. But the damage caused by the Choluteca bursting its banks is hard to see these days, with the exception of the first avenue of Comayagüela, where abandoned homes and buildings remain empty. Bridges washed away by the floodwaters have now been replaced, power supplies are back and, in some respects, traffic is actually better now, since many routes were diverted from the heart of downtown. Today, Hurricane Mitch lives on as painful memory.

Sights

Crossing the river from Comayagüela by the colonial Mallol bridge, on the left is the old Casa Presidencial (1919), now the **Museo de la República de Honduras** (formerly the Museo Histórico) ⓘ *Mon-Sat 0830-1630, US$1.20, concessions for children and students,* which has better exhibits on the 19th than the 20th century. Visitors can see the President's office and the Salón Azul state room. (The new Palacio Presidencial is a modern building on Boulevard Juan Pablo II in Colonia Lomas del Mayab.)

Calle Bolívar leads to the Congress building and the former site of the University, founded in 1847. The site adjoining the church in Plaza La Merced is now the **Galería Nacional de Arte** ⓘ *Tue-Sat 1000-1700, Sun 1000-1400, US$5, bookshop and cafetería with a permanent art exhibition,* a beautifully restored 17th-century building, housing a very fine collection of Honduran modern and colonial art, prehistoric rock

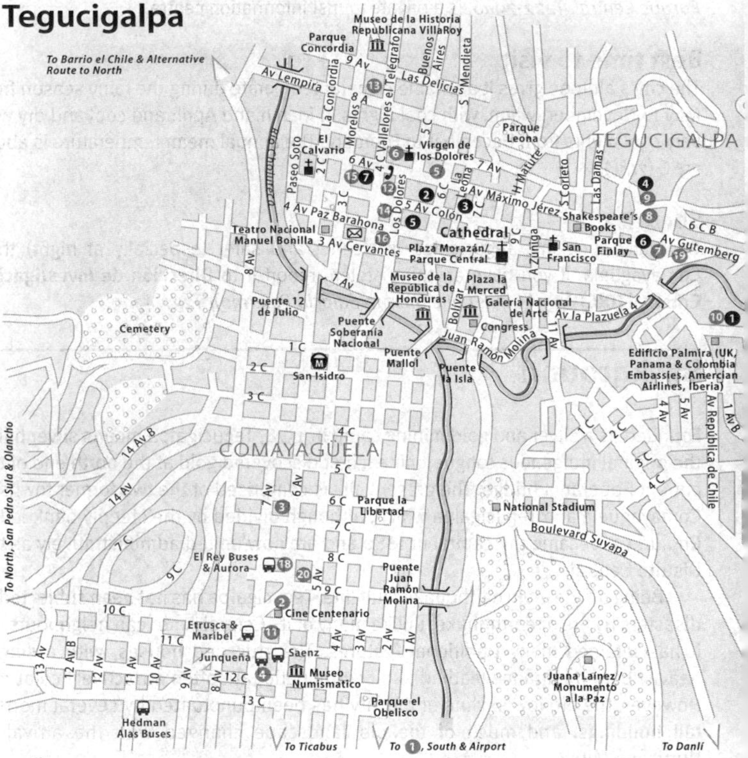

carvings and some remarkable pre-Colombian ceramic pieces. There are useful descriptions of exhibits, and explanations of the mythology embodied in the prehistoric and pre-Colombian art.

Calle Bolívar leads to the main square, Plaza Morazán (commonly known as Parque Central). On the eastern side of the square are the **Palacio del Distrito Central**, and the domed and double-towered **cathedral**, built in the late 18th century. See the gilt colonial altarpiece, the fine examples of Spanish colonial art, the cloisters and, in Holy Week, the ceremony of the Descent from the Cross.

Avenida Miguel Paz Barahona, running through the northern side of the square, is a key avenue. On it to the east is the church of **San Francisco**, with its clangorous bells, and (on 3 Calle, called Avenida Cervantes) the old **Spanish Mint** (1770), now the national printing works.

From Plaza Morazán, heading west towards the river to Avenida Miguel Paz Barahona and then right along 5 Calle (Calle Los Dolores), is the 18th-century church of **Iglesia de Nuestra Señora de los Dolores**. Two blocks north and three blocks west of the church is the beautiful Parque Concordia with good copies of Maya sculpture and temples. On a hilltop one block above Parque Concordia, on Calle Morelos 3A, is **Museo de la Historia Republicana Villa Roy** ⓘ *Mon-Sat 0900-1630, US$1.50*, the former site of the Museo Nacional and, in 1936, home of the former president, Julio Lozano. The building was restored, reconstructed and reopened in 1997. There are seven main rooms presenting Honduras' history from Independence in 1821 up to 1963, as well as cultural and temporary exhibits.

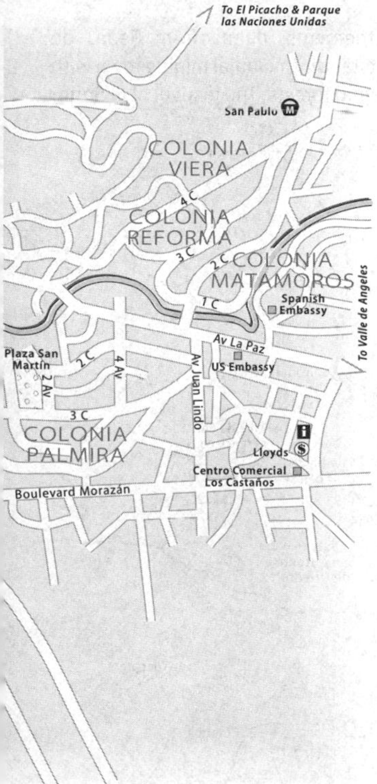

Ticamaya **20**

Eating
Alondra **1**
Bar Mediterráneo **2**
Duncan Maya **3**
Eliza **4**
Pastelería Francesa **5**
Taiwan **6**
Veracruz **7**

Back on Avenida Miguel Paz Barahona, and further west, are the **Teatro Nacional Manuel Bonilla**, with a rather grand interior (1915) inspired by the Athenée Theatre in Paris and, across the square, the beautiful old church of **El Calvario**. Built in elegant colonial style, El Calvario's roof is supported by 14 pillars.

In Colonia Palmira, to the southeast of the city, is Boulevard Morazán, with shopping and business complexes, embassies, banks, restaurants, *cafeterías* and bars. You can get a fine view of the city from the **Monumento a La Paz** ⓘ *open till 1700*, on Juana Laínez hill, near the Estadio Nacional (National Stadium), but don't walk up alone.

The backdrop to Tegucigalpa is the summit of **El Picacho**, with the Cristo del Picacho statue looming up to the north (see Excursions, below), although this can be hard to see at times. From Plaza Morazán go up 7 Calle and the Calle de la Leona to **Parque La Leona**, a small handsome park with a railed walk overlooking the city and safer than Monumento a La Paz. Higher still is the reservoir in El Picacho, also known as the

United Nations Park, which can be reached by a special bus from the No 9 bus stop, behind Los Dolores church (in front of Farmacia Santa Bárbara, Sunday only, US$0.15); alternatively, take a bus to El Piligüin or Corralitos (daily at 0600) from the north side of Parque Herrera in front of the Teatro Nacional Manuel Bonilla.

Comayagüela

Crossing the bridge of 12 de Julio (quite near the Teatro Nacional Manuel Bonilla, see above) you can visit Comayagüela's market of San Isidro. In the Edificio del Banco Central, is the **Pinacoteca Arturo H Medrano** ⓘ *12 Calle entre 5 y 6 Av*, which houses approximately 500 works by five Honduran artists and the **Museo Numismático** ⓘ *Mon-Fri 0900-1200, 1300-1600*, which has a collection of coins and banknotes from Honduras and around the world. Funds have been set aside to restore the older parts of Comayagüela which should make the place more enjoyable to explore.

Around Tegucigalpa

» pp797-803.

Heading north out of Tegucigalpa on the Olancho road, you come to **Talanga,** with a post office and Hondutel near the market on the main road. From Talanga it is a short trip to the historic and beautiful settlements of Cedros and Minas de Oro. From the Parque Central an unpaved road leads south to the Tegucigalpa-Danlí road making a triangular route possible back to the capital.

Cedros is one of Honduras' earliest settlements, dating from Pedro de Alvarado's mining operations of 1536. It is an outstanding colonial mining town with cobbled streets, perched high on an eminence amid forests. The festival of El Señor

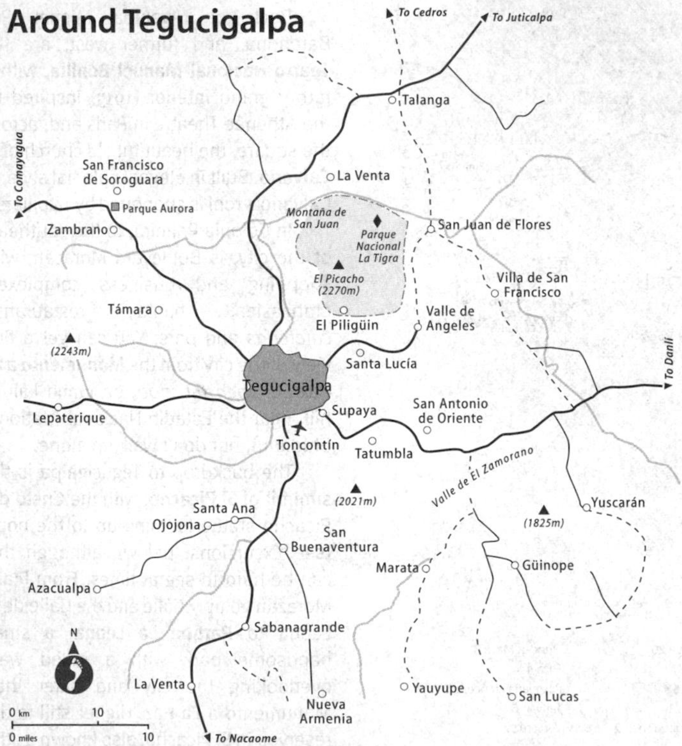

del Buen Fin takes place in the first two weeks of January. Buses to Talanga, Cedros and nearby San Ignacio leave from Reynita de San Ignacio in Mercado Zonal Belén, Comayagüela, T224-0066.

Santa Lucía → *Population: 4230. Altitude: 1400- 1600 m.*

Northeast of Tegucigalpa, on the way to Valle de Angeles, a right turn goes to the quaint old mining village of Santa Lucía which is perched precariously on a steep mountainside overlooking the valley with Tegucigalpa below. The town has a colonial church with a Christ staue given by King Felipe II of Spain in 1592. There is a charming legend of the Black Christ which the authorities ordered to be taken down to Tegucigalpa when Santa Lucía lost its former importance as a mining centre. Every step it was carried away from Santa Lucía it became heavier. When it was impossible to carry it any further they turned round, and by the time they were back in Santa Lucía, it was as light as a feather.

The town is lively with parties on Saturday night, and there is a festival in the second and third weeks of January. There are souvenir shops in the town, including **Cerámicas Ucles** just past the lagoon, second street on left, and another ceramics shop at the entrance on your right. There are good walks up the mountain on various trails, with fine views of Tegucigalpa.

A good circuit is to descend east from the mountain towards San Juan del Rancho through lovely landscapes on a good dirt road, then connect with the paved road to El Zamorano. From there continue either to El Zamorano, or return to Tegucigalpa (see below for opposite direction).

Valle de Angeles → *Population: 6635. Altitude: 1310 m.*

About 30 minutes' drive from Tegucigalpa, **Valle de Angeles** is on a plain below **Monte San Juan**, with **Cerro El Picacho** (2270m) and **Cerro La Tigra** nearby. It is a popular spot for trips from the city, with a cool climate year round and is surrounded by pine forests. There are tracks going through the forests, old mines to explore, a picnic area and a swimming pool; consequently it is crowded on Sundays. At the top of Cerro El Picacho there is a stunning view of the city, and if so inclined you can visit the **zoo** ⓘ *daily, 0800-1500, US$0.20*, of mostly indigenous animals including jaguar, spider monkeys and other animals and birds.

Parque Nacional La Tigra

ⓘ *US$10 entry. Go first to the Amitigra office, Edificio Italia, 6th floor, about 3 blocks southwest of Amex office in Av República de Panamá, T232-6771; helpful. Book a visit here in advance.*

Continue to San Juan de Flores (also called Cantarranas) and San Juancito, an old mining town. From here you can climb in the La Tigra cloud forest and even walk along the top before descending to El Hatillo and then to Tegucigalpa.

There are good climbs to the heights of Picacho and excellent hikes in the Parque Nacional La Tigra cloud forest. Only 11 km from Tegucigalpa, this cloud forest covers 238 sq km and is considered one of the richest habitats in the world with a great diversity of flora and fauna – bromeliads, orchids, arborescent ferns and over 200 species of birds. Single hikers must have a guide. There are two approach routes: go to **El Piligüin** (see below) for the Jutiapa entrance, from where you can start hiking, or to Gloriales Inn, in El Hatillo. You can also walk 24 km from Tegucigalpa to the Jutiapa entrance. Then hike to the visitors' centre of La Tigra at El Rosario (10 km, three hours, easy hiking, superb). Alternatively, go to **San Juancito**, above which is the national park (well worth a visit, a stiff, one-hour uphill walk to El Rosario visitor centre, park offices and six trails ranging from 30 minutes to eight hours, bring insect repellent).

A recommended hike is the **Sendero La Esperanza**, which leads to the road; turn right then take the **Sendero Bosque Nublado** on your left. The whole circuit takes about one hour 20 minutes. A few quetzal birds survive here, but you will need a good eye. In the rainy season (June, July, October and November) there is a spectacular 100-m waterfall (Cascada de la Gloria) which falls on a vast igneous rock. Do not leave paths when walking as there are steep drops. Also get advice about personal safety, as robberies have occurred.

From Parque Herrera in Tegucigalpa, buses throughout the day go to the village of **El Piligüin**, north of Santa Lucía. A delightful 40-minute walk down the pine-clad mountainside leads to **El Chimbo** (meals at *pulpería* or shop, ask anyone the way), then take bus either to Valle de Angeles or Tegucigalpa.

At Km 24 on the road to Danlí, there are climbs to the highest peak through the Uyuca rainforest. Information is available from the Escuela Agrícola Panamericana in the breathtaking **Valle del Zamorano**, or from the **Amitigra** office in Tegucigalpa (see above). The school has rooms for visitors. Visits to the school are organized by some tour operators. On the northwest flank of Uyuca is the picturesque village of **Tatumbla**.

Suyapa

Southeast of Tegucigalpa, the village of Suyapa attracts pilgrims to its big church, home to a tiny wooden image of the Virgin, about 8 cm high, set into the altar. A **fiesta** is held 1-4 February, during which they hold a televised *alborada* with singers, music and fireworks, from 2000-2400 on the second evening. Take a bus to the University or to Suyapa from 'La Isla', one block northwest of the city stadium.

Sabanagrande

Further south (40 km) is Sabanagrande, just off the main highway. This typical colonial town, complete with cobbled streets, is a good day trip from Tegucigalpa. There is an interesting colonial church (1809), Nuestra Señora del Rosario 'Apa Kun Ka' (the place of water for washing), with the **fiesta** of La Virgen de Candelaria from 1-11 February. At 1000 m it has a mild climate, beautiful scenery with pleasant walks, including views to the Pacific and the Gulf of Fonseca. The town is famous for its *rosquillas* (a type of biscuit).

Ojojona

→ *Population: 6670. Altitude: 1400 m.*

Ojojona is another quaint, completely unspoiled, old village about 30 minutes (24 km) south of Tegucigalpa; turn right off the Southern Highway. The village pottery is interesting but make your selection carefully as some of it is reported to be of poor quality. La Casona del Pueblo offers the best handicrafts in town, including fine rustic ceramics. **Fiesta** 18-20 January. There are two well-preserved colonial churches in Ojojona, with fine paintings, plus two more in nearby Santa Ana which is passed on the way from Tegucigalpa.

North of Tegucigalpa

Sleeping

Tegucigalpa *p790, map p792*
There is a 4% tax on hotel bills, plus 12% sales tax; check if it is included in the price.
LL Honduras Maya, Av República de Chile, Col Palmira, T220-5000, www.hondurasmaya.hn. Rooms and apartments, casino, swimming pool US$3.50, bars (the main bar is relaxed and has US TV channels), *cafeterías* (**Black Jack's Snack Bar, Cafetería 2000**), restaurant (**El Candelero**), conference hall and convention facilities for 1000, view over the city from uppermost rooms. Excellent travel agency in the basement that can book your flights to Roatán for no extra charge.
L Plaza San Martín, on Plaza San Martín (near **Honduras Maya**), Col Palmira, T232-8268, hpsmresv@ns.gbm.hn. Good *cafetería*, nice bar, great views of the city from the top terrace.
AL Humuya Inn, Col Humuya 1150, 5 mins from airport, T239-2206, www.humuyainn.com. Rooms and service apartments, US owner. Recommended.
A Plaza, on Av Paz Barahona, in front of post office, T237-2111. Good, **Papagayo** restaurant good for breakfast and set lunch.
C MacArthur, Av Lempira and Telégrafo, T237-5906. A/c, TV, private bath, cheaper without a/c. Recommended.
C-D Crystal, Máximo Jerez y S Mendieta, T237-8804. TV, a/c, good rooms, not very welcoming, parking, restaurant for 1000 (special events only), rooftop bar.
D Granada 1, Av Gutemberg 1401, Barrio Guanacaste, T222-2654. Hot water on 2nd floor only, good, clean, safe, TV lounge, table tennis.
D Granada 2, T237-7079 and **D Granada 3**, T237-0843, on the street leading uphill (to Barrio Casamate) from northeast corner of Parque Finlay. Good beds, hot water in all rooms, safe parking, both can be noisy from passing traffic so try to get a room away from the street. Recommended.
D Nuevo Boston, Av Máximo Jerez 321, T237-9411. Good beds, spotless, cable TV, hot water, central. Good value, no credit cards, rooms on street side noisy, friendly, free coffee, mineral water and cookies in lounge, stores luggage, well run. Repeatedly recommended.
E Marichal, Los Dolores y Colón, T237-0069. Ask for a back room, noisy but clean, centrally located.
E-F Iberia, Peatonal Los Dolores, T237-9267. Cold showers, clean, friendly, refurbished, stores luggage, cheaper without fan.
F Fortuna, Av P Valledores, beside Virgin de Los Dolores church. Without bath, blanket, towel, soap or toilet paper (more expensive with bath), good, clean, friendly, basic, stores luggage; there are several other cheap hotels in this area.
F Tegucigalpa, Av Gutemberg 1645. Basic but OK.

Comayagüela *p794*
Convenient for buses to the north and west and there are many cheap *pensiones* and rooms. It is noisier and dirtier than Tegucigalpa, and many establishments are unsuitable for travellers. If you are carrying luggage, take a taxi.
C-D Centenario, 6 Av, 9-10 Calle, T222-1050. Safe parking. Recommended.
D-E Real de Oro, Av Cabañas, 11 and 12 Calle. Clean, friendly.
E Condesa Inn, 7 Av, 12 Calle. Clean, hot shower, a/c, TV, *cafetería*, very friendly, a bargain. Recommended.
E-F San Pedro, 9 Calle, 6 Av, with bath, cheaper without or with private cold shower, popular, restaurant.
F California, 6 Av, 22-23 Calle. Private bath, friendly, close to Mi Esperanza bus station for Nicaragua.
F Colonial, 6 y 7 Av, 6 Calle 617, T237-5785. With bath, hot water, clean, secure (but unsafe area), front desk unhelpful, otherwise good service and value, restaurant next door (serves breakfast).
F Hotelito Latino, 6 Av, 8 Calle. Very basic, friendly, safe, *cafetería*.
F Hotelito West, 10 Calle, 6-7 Av. Towels and soap, hot water all day, very friendly, changes TCs. Recommended.
F Ticamaya, 6 Av, 8 Calle. Soap, towels and clean sheets daily, quiet, friendly, restaurant.

Valle de Angeles *p795*
B-D Villas del Valle, 500 m north of town, T766-2534, www.villasdelvalle.com. Selection of rooms, cabins and suites. Honduran and European food in the restaurant.

C **Hotel y Restaurante Posada del Angel**, northeast of centre, T766-2233, hotelposadadelangel@yahoo.com. swimming pool, indifferent service, moderate prices.

Parque Nacional La Tigre *p795*

E **Eco Albergue La Tigra**, in the old hospital of the mining company. Price per person. Rooms named after local birds, capacity for 50.

F **Hotelito San Juan**, San Juancito. 6 rooms with shared bathroom.

Eating

Tegucigalpa *p790, map p792*

For hotel restaurants, see above.

Most places are closed on Sun. There are good Chinese restaurants on Calle del Telégrafo in centre, enormous helpings at reasonable prices.

TTT **Alondra**, Av República de Chile on east side of **Honduras Maya**. One of the best.

TTT **El Arriero**, Av República de Chile, near **Honduras Maya**. Very good steaks and seafood.

TTT **El Trapiche**, Blv Suyapa, opposite National University. Colonial ranch atmosphere, good steaks and national dishes. Recommended.

TTT **Roma**, Av Santa Sede, Calle Las Acacias 1601, 1 block off Av República de Chile. The oldest Italian restaurant in the city, good pizzas.

TT **Casa María**, Av Ramón E Cruz, Col Los Castaños, 1 block off Blv Morazán. Colonial building, good food.

TT **China Food**, 2 blocks before the easternmost bridges on Blv Morazán, ½ block to the right. Good-value Chinese.

TT **Daymio**, Plaza Benito Juárez, Col Palmira. One of several Japanese restaurants in this part of town.

TT **Duncan Maya**, Av Colón 618, opposite central **Pizza Hut**. Good and reasonably priced.

TT **El Gachupín**, off Blv Morazán, Col El Castaño Sur. Superb, Mediterranean-style food, garden setting.

TT **El Ganadero**, Calle La Isla, behind Congress building. Steaks, chicken, seafood, good.

TT **El Padrino**, 1 block off Blv Morazán, Col Montecarlo behind **Popeye's**. Very good pizzas and other dishes.

TT **El Pórtico**, near Blv Morazán, T236-7099. Good food but don't be in a hurry.

TT **José y Pepe's**, Av República de Panamá, near the **Honduras Maya**. Excellent steaks, good service, good value. Warmly recommended.

TT **Mei-Mei**, Pasaje Midence Soto, central. Chinese. Recommended.

TT **Rojo, Verde y Ajo**, 1 Av B, Col Palmira. Good food, reasonable price, closed Sun.

TT **Sushi Bar** in the **Bakery Center**, 1 Av B, Col Palmira. Sushi and tempura.

TT **Taco Loco**, Paseo Argentina behind Blv Morazán. Mexican fast food.

TT **Tito**, ½ block off Blv Morazán on Av Juan Lindo. Good pizzas.

TT **Tony's Mar**, Blv Juan Pablo II y Av Uruguay, Col Tepeyac, T239-9379. Seafood, good, simple, New Orleans style.

T **El Patio 2**, easternmost end of Blv Morazán. Excellent traditional food and kebabs, good service and atmosphere, good value for the hungry. Recommended.

T **Taiwan**, round corner from **Hotels Granada 2 and 3**, on Av Máximo Jerez. Chinese food, huge portions, good value.

T **Veracruz**, Calle del Telégrafo between Máximo Jerez and Colón, near hotels **Boston** and **Fortuna**. Good breakfast, closed Sun.

Bakeries

Basilio's Repostería y Panadería, Calle Peatonal between Los Dolores and S Mendieta. Good cakes, bread and pastries.

Eliza, next door to **Hotel Granada 3**. Convenient, easiest place to eat in the immediate neighbourhood.

Pastelería Francesa, opposite French embassy. Recommended.

Salman's bakeries, several outlets in the centre. Good bread and pastries.

Cafeterías

Al Natural, Calle Hipólito Matute y Av Miguel Cervantes. Some vegetarian, some meat dishes, huge fresh fruit juices, antiques, caged birds, nice garden atmosphere.

Bar Mediterráneo, Calle S Mendieta, between Máximo Jerez and Colón. Delicious goat meat, and cheap set meals.

Cafetería Típica Cubana, Parque Finlay. Open 0700-1800 (1200 Sun). Good breakfast, good service.

Café y Librería Paradiso, Av Paz Barahona 1351. Excellent coffee and snacks, good library, paintings, prints and photos to enjoy, newspapers and magazines on sale, good meeting place.
Chomy's Café, Centro Comercial Asfura, Av Cervantes and 2 branches in Col San Carlos (Calle Ramón Rosa and Calle San Carlos). Good quiches, desserts, coffee, tea.
Don Pepe's Terraza, Av Colón 530, upstairs, T222-1084. Central, cheap, live music, but typical Honduran atmosphere. Recommended.
Stacolosal, Paseo de Panamá y Paseo Argentina off Av República de Chile, Col Palmira. Good cheap eating place, classical music and friendly owner. Open 0700-1900.

Comayagüela *p794*

Cafeterías

Bienvenidos a Golosinas, 6 Av, round corner from Hotel Colonial. Friendly, basic meals, beer.
Cafetería Nueva Macao, 4 Av No 437. Large portions, Chinese.
Comedor Tulin, 4 Av between 4 and 5 Calle. Good breakfasts.

Santa Lucía *p795*

¶¶ **Miluska**. A Czech restaurant serving Czech and Honduran food. Recommended.
¶ **Comedor**, next to the plaza/terrace of the municipality. On Sun food is available on the streets.

Valle de Angeles *p795*

¶¶ **La Casa de las Abuelas**, 1 block north of Parque Central, T766-2626. Has a pleasant courtyard with wine bar, café, library, satellite TV, video, email, fax and phone service, tourist information and art gallery.
¶¶ **Las Tejas**, opposite the Centro Turístico La Florida. A Dutch-owned restaurant.
¶ **Restaurante Turístico de Valle de Angeles**, on top of hill overlooking town. Good.

Parque Nacional La Tigra *p795*

¶ **Grocery store**, next door to Hotelito San Juan, San Juancito. Sells fuel, drinks and can prepare *comida corriente*; same owners as hotel, T766-2237.
¶ **Señora Amalia Elvir**, before El Rosario. Meals are available at Señora Amalia's house.

Entertainment

Tegucigalpa *p790, map p792*

Bars and clubs

In front of the Universidad Nacional on Blv Suyapa is **La Peña**, where every Fri at 2100 there is live music, singing and dancing, entrance US$1.40. Blv Morazán has plenty of choice in nightlife including **Taco Taco**, a good bar, sometimes with live mariachi music; next door **Tequila**, a popular drinking place only open at weekends. **Tobacco Road Tavern**, a popular gringo hang-out, in the downtown area on Calle Matute. **Iguana Rana Bar** is very popular with locals and visitors, similarly **Confettis** disco. Blv Juan Pablo II has discos with various types of music. **La Puerta del Alcalá**, 3½ blocks down from Taca office on Blv Morazán, Col Castaño Sur. Pleasant open setting.

Cinemas

Plazas 1 to 5, in Centro Comercial Plaza Miraflores on Blv Miraflores. **Regis**, **Real**, and **Opera**, at Centro Comercial Centroamérica, Blv Miraflores (all have good US films). **Multiplaza**, Col Lomas del Mayab, has 6-screen cinema. In city centre, 2-screen cinemas **Lido Palace**, and **Variedades**. Tauro and Aries, 200 m up Av Gutemberg leading from Parque Finlay to Col Reforma (same street as **Hotel Granada** 2 and 3), tickets US$1.65.

Shopping

Tegucigalpa *p790, map p792*

Bookshops

Metromedia, Edif Casa Real, Av San Carlos, behind Centro Comercial Los Castaños, Blv Morazán, English books, both new and secondhand, for sale or exchange. **Librería Paradiso** (see under *Cafetería* above). For books in Spanish, **Editorial Guaymuras**, Av Miguel Cervantes 1055. Second-hand bookstalls in Mercado San Isidro (6 Av y 2 Calle, Comayagüela), good value.

Markets

Mercado San Isidro, 6 Av at 1 Calle, Comaya-güela. Many fascinating things, but filthy; do not buy food here. Sat is busiest day. **Mercado de Artesanías**, 3 Av, 15 Calle, next to Parque El Soldado. Good value.

Good supermarkets: **La Colonia**, in Blv Morazón, **Más y Menos**, in Av de la Paz. Supermarket on Calle Salvador, 1 block south of Peatonal, near the post office in the centre, open until 2000.

Photography
Kodak on Parque Central and Blv Morazán for professional standard development of slides. **Fuji** in front of the cathedral and on Blv Morazán.

Activities and tours

Tegucigalpa *p790, map p792*
Tour operators
Columbia, Calle Principal between 11 y 12 Av, Blv Morazán, T232-3532, columbiatours@sigmanet.hn. Excellent for national parks, including Cusuco, Pico Bonito and Cuero y Salado, as well as Punta Sal and Bay Islands.
Explore Honduras Tour Service, Ed Paseo del Sol, 2 Av, 1. Calle NO San Pedro Sula, T552-6242, www.explorehonduras.com. Copán and Bay Islands tours.
Gloria Tours across from north side of Parque Central in Casa Colonial, T/F238-2232. Information centre and tour operator.
Trek Honduras, Av Julio Lozano 1311, T239-9827. Tours of the city, Bay Islands, Copán, San Pedro Sula, Valle de Angeles and Santa Lucía.

Transport

Tegucigalpa *p790, map p792*
Air
Toncontín Airport opens at 0530. Check in at least 2 hrs before departure; snacks, souvenir shops, several duty-free stores and internet. Buses to airport from Comayagüela, on 4 Av between 6 and 7 Calle, or from Av Máximo Jerez in downtown Tegucigalpa; into town US$0.19, 20 mins from left-hand side outside the airport; yellow cabs, US$7-8, smaller *colectivo* taxis, US$5 or more.

Airline offices Atlantic Airline, T440-2346, www.atlanticairlines.com.ni; **Air France**, Centro Comercial Galería, Av de la Paz, T237-0229; **Alitalia**, Col Alameda, 5 Av, 9 Calle No 821, T239-4246; **American**, Ed Palmira, opposite Honduras Maya, 1st floor, T232-1414; **British Airways**, Edif Sempe, Blv Comunidad Económica Europea, T225-5101; **Continental**, Av República de Chile, Col Palmira, T220-0999; **Grupo Taca**, Blv Morazán y Av Ramón E Cruz, T239-0148 or airport T233-5756; **Iberia**, Ed Palmira, opposite Honduras Maya, T232-7760; **Isleña Airlines**, Galerías La Paz, Av de la Paz, at Toncontín Airport, T443-0179, www.flyislena.com; **Japan Airlines**, Edif Galería La Paz, 3rd floor, Local 312, 116 Av La Paz, T237-0229; **KLM**, Ed Ciicsa, Av República de Chile y Av República de Panamá, Col Palmira, T232-6410; **Lufthansa**, Edif Plaza del Sol, No 2326, Av de la Paz, T236-7560. **Sol Air** in Tegucigalpa on T235-3737; **Sosa Airline**, at the airport, T233-7351.

Bus
Local Fares are US$0.08-0.12; stops are official but unmarked.
Long distance To **San Pedro Sula** on Northern Highway, 3¼-4 hrs depending on service. Several companies, including: **Sáenz**, Centro Comercial Perisur, Blv Unión Europea, T233-4229, and **Hedman Alas**, 11 Av, 13-14 Calle, Comayagüela, T237-7143, www.hedmanalas.com, both recommended; **El Rey**, 6 Av, 9 Calle, Comayagüela, T237-6609; **Viajes Nacionales** (Viana), terminal on Blv de Las Fuerzas Armadas, T235-8185. To **Tela** and **La Ceiba**, **Viana Clase Oro**, and **Etrusca**, 8 Av, 12 y 13 Calle, T222-6881. To **Choluteca**, **Mi Esperanza**, 6 Av, 23-24 Calle, Comayagüela, T225-1502. To **Trujillo**, **Cotraibal**, 7 Av, 10-11 Calle, Comayagüela, T237-1666. To **La Esperanza**, **Empresa Joelito**, 4 Calle, No 834, Comayagüela. To **Comayagua**, most going to San Pedro Sula and **Transportes Catrachos**, Col Torocagua, Blv del Norte, Comayagüela. To **Valle de Angeles** and **Santa Lucía**, from stop on Av La Paz (near filling station opposite hospital). To **Juticalpa** and **Catacamas**, **Empresa Aurora**, 8 Calle, 6-7 Av, Comayagüela, T237-3647. For **Danlí** and **El Paraíso**, for the Nicaraguan border at Las Manos, see under those towns in East of Tegucigalpa, see page 884.

For travellers leaving Tegucigalpa, take the Tiloarque bus on Av Máximo Jerez, by Calle Palace, and get off in Comayagüela at Cine Centenario (Av 6) for nearby **Empresa Aurora** buses (for **Olancho**) and **El Rey** buses (for **San Pedro Sula**). 3 blocks northwest is Cine Lux, near which are **Empresas Unidas** and **Maribel** (8 Av, 11-12 Calle, T237-3032) for **Siguatepeque**. Tiloarque bus continues to Mi Esperanza bus terminal (for **Choluteca** and **Nicaraguan border**). Take a 'Carrizal' or 'Santa Fe' bus ascending Belén (9 Calle) for **Hedman Alas** buses to **San Pedro Sula** and for Comayagua buses. The **Norteño** bus line to San Pedro Sula is alongside Mamachepa market, from where there are also buses for **Nacaome** and **El Amatillo** border with El Salvador.

International Ticabus, 16 Calle, 5-6 Av, Comayagüela, T222-0590, www.ticabus.com, to **Managua** 0915 (US$20, 9 hrs), **San José** (US$35), **San Salvador** (US$15), **Guatemala City** (US$26) and **Panama** (US$60) daily. Make sure you reserve several days ahead. Visa ATM near to offices. **Hedman Alas** have a service to **Guatemala City** and **Antigua** that leaves Tegucigalpa for San Pedro Sula, 0600, 12 hrs, US$52. Alternatively to **Nicaragua**, take **Mi Esperanza** bus to San Marcos de Colón, then taxi or local bus to El Espino on border. To **San Marcos**, 4 a day from 0730, and direct to border at 0400, US$2.50, 5 hrs (0730 is the latest one that will get you into Nicaragua the same day). Or **Mi Esperanza** bus to Río Guasaule border, several daily, 4 hrs, US$2. To **San Salvador**, **Cruceros del Golfo**, Barrio Guacerique, Blv Comunidad Económica Europea, Comayagüela, T233-7415, US$18, at 0600 and 1300, 6 hrs travelling, 1 hr or more at border. Connections to **Guatemala** and **Mexico**; direct bus to border at El Amatillo, US$2.50, 3 hrs, several daily; alternatively from San Pedro Sula via Nueva Ocotepeque and El Poy. To **San Salvador** and **Guatemala**, with **King Quality** from Tegucigalpa (T225-5415) from **Cruceros del Golfo** terminal, 0600 and 1300 and San Pedro Sula (T553-4547) at 0630. Alternatively, to Guatemala go to San Pedro Sula and take **Escobar, Impala** or **Congolón** to Nueva Ocotepeque and the border at **Agua Caliente**, or via **Copán** (see page 610).

Car

Car hire Avis, Edif Palmira and airport, T232-0088. **Budget**, Blv Suyapa and airport, T/F235-9531. **Hertz**, Centro Comercial Villa Real, Col Palmira, T239-0772. **Maya**, Av República de Chile 202, Col Palmira, T232-0992. **Molinari**, 1 Av, 2 Calle, Comayagüela and airport, T237-5335. **Thrifty**, Col Prados Universitarios, T235-6077. **Toyota**, T235-6694.

Car repairs Metal Mecánica, 1 block south of Av de los Próceres, Col Lara. Volkswagen dealer near Parque Concordia, good.

Taxi

About US$2-3 per person, but you can often bargain down to around US$1.50 a trip in the city. More after 2200, cheaper on designated routes, eg Miraflores to centre.

Santa Lucía *p795*

Bus To Santa Lucía from Mercado San Pablo, **Tegucigalpa**, hourly service, US$0.30, past the statue of Simón Bolívar by the Esso station, Av de los Próceres.

Valle de Angeles *p795*

Bus To Valle de Angeles every 45 mins, US$0.40, 1 hr, leaves from San Felipe, near the hospital. To **San Juan de Flores** 1000, 1230, 1530.

Parque Nacional La Tigra *p795*

Bus Buses leave from Mercado San Pablo, **Tegucigalpa**, for **San Juancito** from 1000, 1½ hrs, on Sat and Sun bus at 0800 packed with people visiting their families, US$0.75; passes turn-off to Santa Lucía and goes through Valle de Angeles. Return bus from San Juancito at 1500 from across the river and up the hill, opposite the park. On Sat, buses return at 0600 and 1200 from church, board early. For return journey double check local information. Alternatively, from behind Los Dolores church in Tegucigalpa you can take a bus to **El Piligüin/Jutiapa** at 0600; it passes through beautiful scenery by El Hatillo and other communities. From El Piligüin, it is a long, hot walk up to the park entrance.

Ojojona *p796*

Bus Buses leave **Comayagüela** every 15-30 mins from Calle 4, Av 6, near San Isidro market, US$0.40, 1 hr. From same location, buses go west to **Lepaterique** ('place of the jaguar'), another colonial village, over 1-hr drive through rugged, forested terrain. Distant view of Pacific on fine days from heights above village.

Directory

Tegucigalpa *p790, map p792*

Banks

There are many ATMs in the city centre. All banks have several branches throughout the city; we list the main offices. Branch offices are unlikely to change TCs, only US dollars cash. **BGA**, 5 Calle (Av Colón) in the centre and at 5 Calle in front of Plaza Morazán. **Banco Atlántida**, 5 Calle in front of Plaza Morazán (may agree to change money on Sat up to 1200). **Banco de Honduras (Citibank)**, Blv Suyapa. **Banco del País**, Calle Peotonal in the centre, changes TCs. **Banco de Occidente**, 3 Calle (Cervantes) y 6 Av (S Mendieta) in the centre.

Visa, MasterCard and American Express cash advances (no commission) and TCs at **BAC**, Blv Morazán, and at **Honducard**, Av de la Paz y Ramón E Cruz, and at **Aval Card**, Blv Morazán. Banks are allowed to trade at the current market rate, but there is a street market along the Calle Peatonal off the Parque Central, opposite the post office and elsewhere. Exchange can be difficult on Sat, try **Coin**, a *casa de cambio* on Av de la Paz, inside **Supermercado Más y Menos**, same rates as banks, no commission, Mon-Fri 0830-1730, Sat 0900-1200, changes TCs but will photocopy cheques and passport; another branch of **Coin** on Calle Peatonal, good rates. Recommended.

Cultural centres

Alianza Francesa, Col Lomas del Guijarro, T239-6163, cultural events Fri afternoon, French films Tue 1930. **Centro Cultural Alemán**, 8 Av, Calle La Fuente, T237-1555, German newspapers to read, cultural events. **Instituto Hondureño de Cultura Interamericana** (IHCI), Calle Real de Comayagüela,T237-7539, has an English library and cultural events.

Embassies and consulates

Argentina, Col Rubén Darío 417, T232-3376. **Belize Consulate**, T220-5000, Ext 7770. **Brazil**, Col La Reforma, Casa 1309, T236-5223. **Canada**, Ed Financiero Banexpo, Local 3, Col Payaqui, Blv Juan Bosco II, T232-4551. **Chile**, Av Las Minitas, Casa 501, T232-2114. **Colombia**, Ed Palmira No 200, opposite Honduras Maya, 4th floor, T232-1709. **Costa Rica**, Col El Triángulo, 1a Calle, opposite No 3451, T232-1768, bus to Lomas del Guijarro to last stop, then walk up on your left for 300 m. **Ecuador**, Av Juan Lindo 122, Col Palmira, T236-5980. **El Salvador**, 2 Av Calzada República de Uruguay, Casa 219, Col San Carlos T236-8045. **France**, Col Palmira, 3 Calle, Av Juan Lindo, T236-6432. **Germany**, Ed Paysen, 3rd floor, Blv Morazán, T232-3161. **Guatemala**, Col Las Minitas 4 Calle, Casa 2421, T232-9704, Mon-Fri 0900-1300, take photo, visa given on the spot, US$10. **Italy**, Av Principal 2602, Col Reforma, T236-6391. **Japan**, Col San Carlos, between 4 and 5 Calle, 2 blocks off Blv Morazán and Av de la Paz, T236-6828, behind Los Castaños Shopping Mall. **Mexico**, Av República de México, Paseo República de Brasil 2402, Col Palmira, T232-6471, opens 0900, visa takes 24 hrs. **Netherlands** (Consulate), Edif Barahona, Col Alameda, next to INA, T231-5007. **Nicaragua**, Av Choluteca 1130, bloque M-1, Col Lomas del Tepeyac, T232-9025 daily, 0800-1200, US$25, visa can take up to 2 days. **Norway**, consular services in front of Residencial el Limonar, T557-0856. **Panama**, Ed Palmira No 200, opposite Honduras Maya, 2nd floor, T239-5508. **Peru**, Calle La Reforma 2618, Col La Reforma, T221-0596. **Spain**, Col Matamoros 801, T236-6589, near Av de la Paz and US Embassy. **Sweden** (Consulate), Av Altiplano, Retorno Borneo 2758, Col Miramontes, T/F232-4935. **UK**, Edif Banexpo, 3rd floor, Col Payaqu, T232-0612. **USA**, Av La Paz, Mon-Fri 0800-1700, take any bus from north side of Parque Central in direction 'San Felipe', T236-9320. **Venezuela**, Col Rubén Darío 2116, T232-1879.

Immigration

Dirección General de Migración, Av Máximo Jerez, next to Hotel Ronda, Tegucigalpa.

Internet

Café Don Harry, Av República de Chile 525, Edif Galerías TCB, T220-6174. **@ccess Cyber Coffee**, Centro Commercial La Ronda, Av Máximo Jerez next to Super Donuts, Mon-Sat 0800-1900, US$1.50 for 30 mins. **Café Cyberplace**, Barrio La Plazuela, Av Cervantes 1215, opposite Souvenirs Maya, T220-5200, open 0900-1830, US$2 for 30 mins. **Cyberiada Internet Café**, Plaza Brezani, Av Máximo Jerez, Calle H Matute, open 24 hrs,

US$1.80 per hr with free coffee. **Multinet**, 1 Av B, Galerías Maya, Col Palmira, T232-3181, 0800-2100, US$4.45 per hr, also at Mall Multiplaza, local 114, Blv Juan Pablo II, Col Lomas del Mayab. **PC Cyber**, Edif Paz Barahona, Calle Peatonal, Mon-Fri 0830-1700, Sat 0830-1400.

Laundry

La Cisne, 1602 Calle La Fuente/Av Las Delicias, US$2.50 up to 5 kg, same-day service. **Lavandería Italiana**, Barrio Guadalupe, 4 blocks west of Av República de Chile 300 block. **Lavandería Super Jet**, Av Gutemberg, about 300 m east of Hotel Granada, US$0.20 per kg. **Mi Lavandería**, opposite Repostería Calle Real, 3 Calle, 2 Av, Comayagüela, T237-6573, Mon-Sat 0700-1800, Sun and holidays 0800-1700.

Medical services

Dentist Dra Rosa María Cardillo de Boquín, Ed Los Jarros, Sala 206, Blv Morazán, T231-0583. Recommended. **Dr Roberto Ayala**, DDS, C Alfonso XIII 3644, Col Lomas de Guijarro, T232-2407. **Hospitals** Hospital y **Clínica Viera**, 11 y 12 Av, 5 Calle, Tegucigalpa, T237-7136. **Hospital la Policlínica** SA 3 Av, 7 y 8 Calle, Comayagüela, T237-3503. **Centro** Médico Hondureño, 3 Av, 3 Calle, Barrio La Granja, Comayagüela, T233-6028.

Pharmacies Farmacia Rosna, in pedestrian mall off Parque Central, T237-0605, English spoken. Recommended. **Regis Palmira**, Ed Ciicsa, Av República de Panamá, Col Palmira. **El Castaño**, Blv Morazán.

Post office

Av Paz Barahona/C del Telégrafo, Lista de Correos (Poste Restante) mail held for 1 month, US$0.20 per letter. Mail boxes in main supermarkets. Pack books separately from clothes, etc when sending packages. The post office will send and receive faxes.

Telephone

Hondutel, Calle del Telégrafo y Av Colón, has several direct AT&T lines to USA, no waiting. Phone, fax and telegrams; open 24 hrs for phone services only. Also at 6 Av, 7-8 Calle, Comayagüela, with post office.

Work

Peace Corps, opposite Edif Ciicsa, on Av República de Chile, uphill past Hotel Honduras Maya.

Western Honduras

Close to the Guatemalan border, the serene ruins of Copán are Honduras' major Maya attraction. Treasured for its exceptional artistry when compared to other Maya sites, the ruins enjoy a calm and pleasant setting. The quiet town of Copán Ruinas nestles among hills nearby. In fact, the whole area is sprinkled with interesting towns and villages, mostly in delightful hilly surroundings; some with a colourful colonial history, others with their foundations in the Lenca communities, and many producing handicrafts. The ruins of Copán aside, one of the enjoyable aspects of western Honduras is that there are no 'must-sees' – just pick a route, take your time and enjoy the scenery and whatever else you may find. ▸▸ *For Sleeping, Eating and other listings, see page 815-823.*

San Pedro Sula to Copán ▸▸ *pp815-823.*

The Western Highway runs parallel to the border from San Pedro Sula southwest along the Río Chamelecón to Canoa (58 km), from where there is a paved road south to Santa Bárbara (a further 53 km). Continuing along the Western Highway, the road from Canoa towards Guatemala runs southwest to La Entrada (115 km from San Pedro), where it forks again left for Santa Rosa (see below) and right for an attractive 60-km road through deep green scenery to Copán Ruinas.

The regular bus is recommended rather than the dangerous minibus service, which can be a bit hair-raising. The road is paved throughout and in good condition.

La Entrada is a hot, dusty town and the place to change buses. Going south takes you to Santa Rosa and towards El Salvador, west to Copán and Guatemala. **Banco Sogerín** will cash traveller's cheques.

El Puente ⓘ *0800-1600, US$5*, is a national archaeological park reached by taking a turn-off, 4½ km west from La Entrada on the Copán road, then turning right on a well-signposted, paved road 6 km to the Visitors' Centre. It is near the confluence of the Chamelecón and Chinamito rivers and is thought to have been a regional centre between AD 600 and 900.

Copán Ruinas

» *pp815-823. Colour map 6, B1.*

➔ *www.copanhonduras.org.*

A charming town set in the hills just to the east of the border with Guatemala, Copán Ruinas – to give the town its full name – thrives and survives on visitors passing through to visit the nearby ruins. Nevertheless, it is arguably the best-preserved and

Western Honduras

one of the most pleasant towns in Honduras. Close to the border with Guatemala, it's a good place to stop for a few days before heading straight to San Pedro Sula (172 km) and the Bay Islands or Tegucigalpa (395 km), with the impressive ruins of Copán, good attractions, coffee plantation tours, hiking, caving, hot springs, horseback riding, language schools and volunteer opportunities.

The **Museo Copán** ⓘ *Mon-Sat 0800-1600, US$2*, on the town square has good explanations in Spanish of the Maya empire and stelae. There is a good selection of artefacts, a burial site and a tomb that was recently unearthed during a road-building project. It is a good idea to visit the museum before the ruins. **Enchanted Wings Butterfly House** ⓘ *2 blocks west of the cemetery on the road to Guatemala, T651-4133, daily 0800-1700, US$5.50*, is run by Bob 'The Butterfly Guy' Gallardo, specialist in Honduran butterflies. The garden, complete with restaurant, is beautiful and has exhibits of rare butterflies, a new orchid garden and birdwatching tours can be arranged. Recommended.

Copán archaeological site

ⓘ *Daily, 0800-1600, US$10 entry to ruins and Las Sepulturas, admission valid for 1 day; US$5 to enter the museum with entrance to the tunnels an additional pricey US$12. Guided tours available (US$20, 2 hrs), recommended; Antonio Ríos, T898-3414, owner of restaurant/shop opposite the ruins is recommended. The Copán Guide Association has a kiosk in the parking area where qualified bilingual guides can be hired at a fixed rate. Photographs of the excavation work and a maquette of the site are located in a small exhibition room at the ruins' visitors' centre. There is a cafetería by the entrance to the ruins, and also a handicrafts shop, in the Parque Arqueológico, next to the bookshop, with local and country maps, and a Spanish/English guide book for the ruins, which is rather generalized. Useful recent books are:* Scribes, Warriors

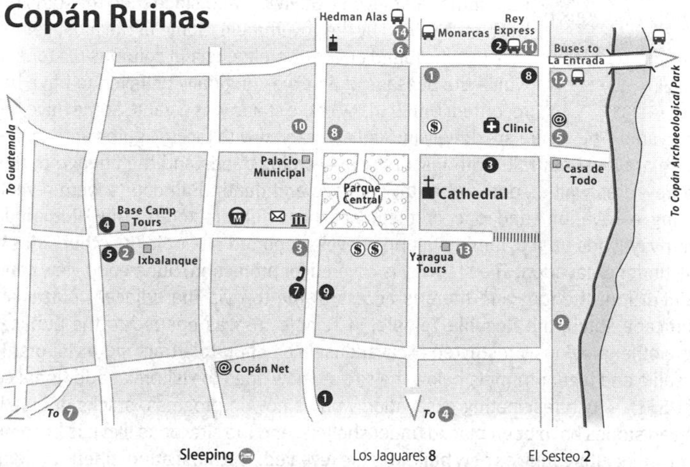

Sleeping
Brisas de Copán **1**
Café ViaVía Copán **2**
Camino Maya **3**
En La Manzana Verde **14**
Hacienda San Lucas **4**
Hospedaje Los Gemelos **5**
Hostel Iguana Azul **7**
Hotelito Yaxpac **6**
La Casa de Café **7**
Los Jaguares **8**
Madrugada **9**
Marina Copán **10**
Patty **11**
Posada Honduras **12**
Yaragua **13**

Eating
Café Vamos a Ver **7**
Carnitas Nía Lola **1**
El Sesteo **2**
Licuados Express **3**
Llama del Bosque **4**
Picame **8**
Pizza Copán **9**
Tunkul **5**

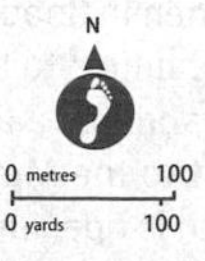

 and Kings: City of Copán, *by William and Barbara Fash (1991), and* History Carved in Stone, a guide to Copán, *by William Fash and Ricardo Argucía (3rd edition, 1998, US$3), published locally and available at the site. Luggage can be left for no charge.*

The magnificent ruins of Copán are one of Central America's major Maya sites, certainly the most significant in Honduras, and they mark the southeastern limit of Maya dominance. Just 1 km from the village, there is a signposted path beside the road from Copán to the ruins which passes two stelae en route. Get to the ruins as early as possible, or stay late in the day so you have a chance to be there without hordes of people.

Museo de Escultura Maya

ⓘ *US$10, ticket from main ticket office not at the museum.*

The impressive and huge two-storey Museo of Maya Sculpture and sculpture park houses the newly excavated carvings. In the middle of the museum is an open-air courtyard with a full-size reproduction of the Rosalila temple, found intact buried under Temple 16 with its original paint and carvings (see below). A reproduction of the doorway to Temple 16 is on the upper floor. The new museum houses the original stelae to prevent weather damage, while copies will be placed on site. More than 2000 other objects found at Copán are also in the museum. It is essential to visit the museum before the ruins. Good explanations in Spanish and English. The exit leads to the ruins via the nature trail.

Archaeological site

When John Lloyd Stephens and Frederick Catherwood examined the ruins in 1839, they were engulfed in jungle. (Stephens, a lawyer, and Catherwood, an architect, were the first English-speaking travellers to explore the regions originally settled by the Maya. They are credited with recording the existence of many of the ruins in the Maya area.) In the 1930s, the Carnegie Institute cleared the ground and rebuilt the Hieroglyphic Stairway, and since then the ruins have been maintained by the government. Some of the most complex carvings are found on the 21 **stelae**, or 3-m columns of stones on which the passage of time was originally believed to have been recorded. Under many of the stelae was a vault; some have been excavated. The stelae are deeply incised and carved with faces, figures and animals. There are royal portraits with inscriptions recording deeds and the lineage of those portrayed as well as dates of birth, marriage and death. Ball courts were revealed during excavation, and one of them has been fully restored. The **Hieroglyphic Stairway** leads up a pyramid; its upper level supported a temple. Its other sides are still under excavation. The stairway is covered for protection, but a good view can be gained from the foot and there is access to the top via the adjacent plaza. After Hurricane Mitch, the **Rosalila Temple**, in Temple 16, was opened to the public, as were other previously restricted excavations, in an effort to attract more visitors. The Rosalila and Jaguar tunnels below the site are now open to visitors at additional cost of US$12. Much fascinating excavation work is now in progress, stacks of labelled carved stones have been placed under shelters, and the site looks like it is becoming even more interesting as new buildings are revealed. The most atmospheric buildings are those still half-buried under roots and soil. The last stela was set up in Copán between AD 800 and 820, after less than five centuries of civilized existence. The nearby river has been diverted to prevent it encroaching on the site when in flood.

Some of the finest examples of sculpture from Copán are now in the British Museum in London, or at Boston.

Also near the ruins is a **sendero natural** (nature trail) through the jungle to the minor ball court; take mosquito repellent. The trail takes 30 minutes and has a few signposts explaining the plants, animals and spirituality of the forest to the Maya. After 1600 is the best time to see animals on the sendero natural, which is open until

1700. About 4 km from the main centre is the ceremonial site known as **Los Sapos** ⓘ *entry US$2* (The Toads), a pre-Classic site with early stone carvings. The toad was a Maya symbol of fertility. East of the main ruins near Los Sapos is a stone, **Estela 12**, which lines up with another, **Estela 10**, on the other side of the valley at sunrise and sunset on 12 April every year. Horse rides to Los Sapos can be arranged through **Yaragua Tours** (US$15, three hours, see Activities and tours, page 820).

Copán archaeological site

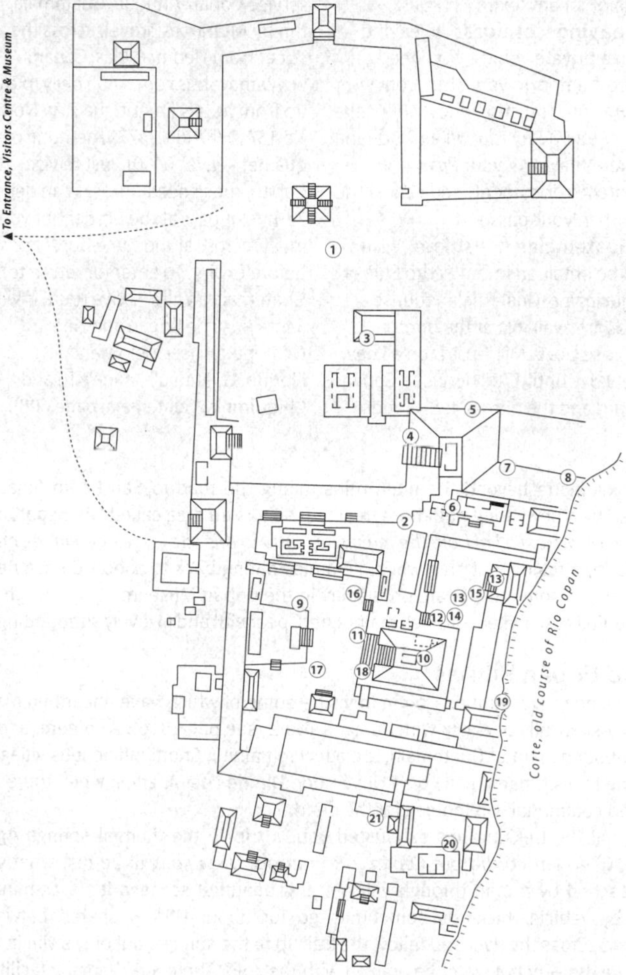

Main Plaza with Stelae **1**
Acropolis **2**
Ball Court **3**
Hieroglyphic Stairway **4**
Structure 26 **5**
Council House, Temple 22A **6**
Temple of Meditation/ Temple 22 **7**
House of Knives **8**
Structure 13 **9**
Structure 16 **10**
Altar Q **11**
Rosalila Building (within Structure 16) **12**
Entrance to Rosalila & Jaguar tunnels **13**
Hunal Building (beneath Rosalila) & Tomb of Founder **14**
East Court/Plaza de los Jaguares **15**
Plaza Occidental **16**
Altar I **17**
Altar H **18**
Temple 18 **19**
Structure 32 **20**
Zona Residencial **21**

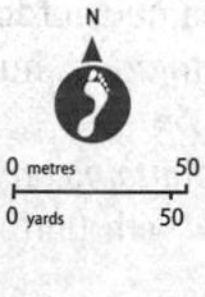

Border essentials: Honduras-Guatemala

El Florido

Honduran immigration The office is on the border at El Florido and you get stamps there. They charge entry and exit fees (see Touching down, page 786); ask for a receipt for any 'extra' charges.

Leaving Honduras If leaving with a private vehicle, you need three stamps on your strip from Migración, Tránsito (where they take your *Proviso Provisional*) and Aduana (where they take your *Pase Fronterizo* document) and cancel the stamp in your passport.

Guatemalan consulate Visas can be obtained in San Pedro Sula or Tegucigalpa. Guatemalan tourist cards are available at the border.

Transport Minibuses run all day every day until 1700 between Copán Ruinas and the border at El Florido, 30 mins, connecting with buses to Guatemalan destinations (see below). Catch the buses behind the municipal market. The cost should be about US$2.50. If heading for Antigua, there is a direct minibus service Copán-Antigua, Guatemala, run by **Monarcas Travel**, across the street from Hedman Alas, Copán, www.mayabus.com, 1400 daily, pick up from hotels (in Antigua 7 Av Norte No 15A, T/F7783-24779, geotours@gua.net, leaves 0400). Just to visit Copán, those needing visas can get a 72-hr exit pass at the border but you must recross at the same border post before expiry. To enter (or return to) Guatemala an alternative route is via Santa Rosa de Copán and Nueva Ocotepeque (see below and El Florido, Guatemala, page 610 and Chiquimula, Guatemala, page 608).

One kilometre beyond the main ruins, along the road to San Pedro Sula, or connected by a new stone path from the main site, is an area called **Las Sepulturas** ⓘ *entrance is almost 2 km from the main site, entry to this site is included in the main Copán ticket,* a residential area where ceramics dating back to 1000 BC have been found. Exhibits from the site are on display in the Copán Museum. It is a delightful site, beautifully excavated and well maintained, peaceful and in lovely surroundings.

Around Copán Ruinas

There are many caves around Copán to visit – some of which have unearthed Maya artefacts. Ask locally or check with Yaragua Tours (see page 820). Also here, and in the neighbouring part of Guatemala, are a few remaining Chorti indigenous villages, interesting to visit, particularly on 1 November, Día de Los Muertos, when there are family and communal ceremonies for the dead.

After all the trekking has exhausted you, a trip to the thermal springs **Agua Caliente,** ⓘ *20 km north from Copán, 0800-2000, US$1.50,* will be just what you need. Reached by a road through villages and beautiful scenery, it's a 45-minute journey by vehicle, pick-ups sometimes go for about US$17, shared between passengers. Cross the river and follow the trail up to the springs, but only swim in the river where the very hot water has mixed with the cold. There are changing facilities and toilets in the park. Take all food and water. Also on the road to Guatemala is the **Enchanted Wings Butterfly House** ⓘ *0800-1700, US$3.*

Nine kilometres east of Copán is **Santa Rita**, a small colonial town on the Copán River with cobblestones and red roofs (**Hospedaje Santa Rita** and unnamed outdoor restaurant recommended, off main road next to Esso; speciality *tajadas*, huge portions, cheap).

Also try the new **Macaw Mountain** ⓘ *T651-4245, www.macawmountain.com,* a unique ecotourism project incorporating Honduras' largest bird park with parrots, toucans and macaws. Tour of the coffee finca, coffee processing, riverside restaurant serving good, hearty food, visitors' centre, river swimming, highly recommended. Located 10 minutes from the town centre.

Santa Rosa de Copán and around

» pp815-823. Colour map 6, B1.

→ *Population: 35,000. Altitude: 1160 m.*

Santa Rosa is an important regional town with a colonial atmosphere of cobbled streets and some of the best colonial architecture in Honduras. Originally known as Los Llanos, it was made a municipality in 1812 and became capital of the Department of Copán when it was split from Gracias (now Lempira). The town is set in some of the best scenery in Honduras and the fine weather makes it ideal for hiking, horses and mountain biking.

Santa Rosa owes its wealth to the fact that it's an agricultural and cattle-raising area. Maize and tobacco are grown here, and visitors can see traditional hand-rolling at the **Flor de Copán cigar factory** ⓘ *3 blocks east of the bus terminal, Mon-Fri until 1700, closed 1130-1300, tours in Spanish at 1000 and 1400, US$2 per person – ask the guard at the gate.* The central plaza and church are perched on a hilltop. There is a quieter plaza, the **parque infantil** (playground) ⓘ *Calle Real Centenario y 6 Av SO*, which is fenced and a nice place to relax. The main **market** ⓘ *1 Calle and 3 Av NE*, has good leather items. **Farmers' markets** are held daily in Barrio Santa Teresa (take 4 Calle SE past 5 Avenida SE), and at 4 Calle SE and 5 Avenida SE on Sunday 0500 to 1000.

Santa Rosa de Copán

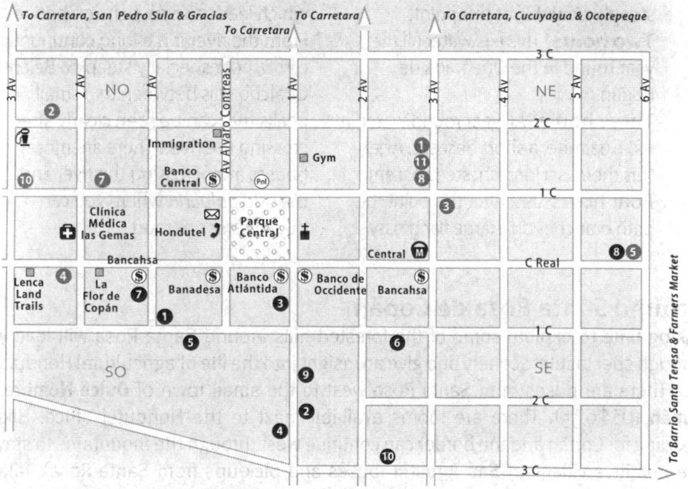

Sleeping
Blanca Nieves 1
Continental 2
Elvir 4
Hospedaje Calle Real 5
Hospedaje Santa Eduviges 7
Hospedaje Santa Rosa 8
Maya Central 10
Rosario 11
VIP Copán 3

Eating
Chiky's 1
El Rodeo 2
Flamingos 3
Las Haciendas 4
Las Haciendas II 5
Las Haciendas III 6
On Fu 7
Pizza Pizza 8
Rincón Colonial 9
Well 10

Walking from San Manuel Colohuete to Belén Gualcho

There is a well-defined, well-used and easy to follow mule trail linking these two villages, which makes a good one- or two-day hike. Maps are not essential as there are communities at many points along the way where advice can be sought. If required, a map of the area is available from the Lenca Cultural Centre in Gracias.

The path leading away from the village leaves from opposite the *pulpería* and *comedor* where the bus drops you, heading west and downhill into a valley. The path is used by 4WD vehicles and continues to San Sebastián. Just after the community of San José, after passing the last house, the path to Belén branches off. A smaller path leaves the 4WD track and climbs steeply up to your right and more northwest.

One hour Just after Peña Blanca, the path direction becomes unclear after it crosses an area of white chalky rocks. There are several other paths here. The main path heads north and steeply downhill at this point.

Two hours There is water all the year round in the Quebrada de Rogán.

Three hours All year round water in Río Gualmite, a short descent. After this there is a longish, steep ascent.

Four hours Just after this point the path branches on a large flat grassy area. Both paths lead to Belén Gualcho. The one to the left drops and crosses the river and then you are faced with a long, arduous and very steep ascent. We would recommend taking the path to the right, which exits to the far right of a grassy area by three small houses.

Five hours The path climbs as it skirts around the Cerro Capitán. Just after passing the steepest part, a small landslide forces the path into a descent almost to the river. From here, only 2 m above the river, you can walk steeply down off the path to the river bank where there is the most perfect camp site. Flat sandy soil in some shade on the edge of a coffee plantation and 2 m from the river.

Six hours From the camping site there is a long, continuous climb before dropping down sharply to cross the river. It is possible, but difficult, to cross the river at the point the path meets it. Take a small path off to the right just before the river, which leads to a suspension bridge. From the river it is a long continuous climb, not especially steep, to Belén Gualcho. It is between two small peaks that can be seen clearly after crossing the river. There are more houses after crossing the river and the odd *pulpería* where you can buy *refrescos* or food.

Around Santa Rosa de Copán

Taking time to explore some of the forested hills around Santa Rosa will lead you through spectacular scenery and give an insight into the life of agricultural Honduras.

There are buses from Santa Rosa west to the small town of **Dulce Nombre de Copán** (US$0.55). There are rooms available next to the Hondutel office. Hikers heading for Copán and the border can continue west through the mountains to stay at the primitive village of **San Agustín** (buses and pick-ups from Santa Rosa), take a hammock or sleeping bag, continuing next day through Mirasol you reach the Ruinas road at El Jaral, 11 km east of Copán ruins (see Copán Excursions above).

South of Santa Rosa, buses pass through **Cucuyagua**, with a scenic river, good swimming and camping on its banks, and **San Pedro de Copán**, an attractive village and an entry point into the **Parque Nacional Celaque**, see below.

A mule trail (see box, page 810) connects **Belén Gualcho**, a Lenca village in the mountains and a good base for exploring the surrounding area, with **San Manuel de**

Colohuete (1500 m), which has a magnificent colonial church whose façade is sculpted with figures of saints. Buses to San Manuel from Gracias at 1300, four hours, and usually a pick-up returning in the evening. There are no hotels so you must ask villagers about places to stay. There is an equally fine colonial church 30 minutes by 4WD vehicle to the southwest at **San Sebastián Colosuca** (1550 m). The village has a mild climate (two *hospedajes*; or try Don Rubilio; food at Doña Clementina García or Doña Alicia Molina). The Feria de San Sebastián is on 20 January. An hour's walk away is the Cueva del Diablo and 6 km away is Cerro El Alta with a lagoon at the top. From San Sebastián, a mule trail goes via the heights of **Agua Fría** to reach the route near the border at **Tomalá**.

Gracias

» *pp815-823. Colour map 6, B1.*

→ *Population: 19,380. Altitude: 765 m.*

One of the oldest and most historic settlements in Honduras, dominated by Montañas de Celaque, Puca and Opulaca – the country's highest peaks – Gracias is a charming, friendly town. Just 50 km from Santa Rosa, both the town and the surrounding countryside are worth a visit. Gracias was the centre from which Francisco de Montejo, thrice Governor of Honduras, put down the great indigenous revolt of 1537-38. Alonso de Cáceres, his lieutenant, besieged Lempira the indigenous leader in his impregnable mountain-top fortress at Cerquín, finally luring him out under a flag of truce, ambushed him and treacherously killed him. When the Audiencia de los Confines was formed in 1544, Gracias became for a time the administrative centre of Central America.

The helpful **tourist office** in the middle of the Parque Central can store luggage and arrange transport to Parque Nacional Celaque.

There are three colonial churches, **San Sebastián, Las Mercedes** and **San Marcos** (a fourth, Santa Lucía, is southwest of Gracias), and a restored fort, with two fine Spanish cannon, on a hill five minutes' walk west of the centre. The fort, **El Castillo San Cristóbal**, has been well restored, and at the foot of the northern ramparts is the tomb of Juan Lindo, President of Honduras 1847-1852, who introduced free education through a system of state schools.

Around Gracias

» *pp815-823.*

Balneario Aguas Termales

ⓘ *daily 0600-2000, US$1, rental of towels, hammock, inner tube, restaurant/bar.*

Some 6 km from Gracias along the road to Esperanza (side road signposted), are hot, communal thermal pools in the forest for swimming (one hour by a path, one hour 20 minutes by road). To find the path, walk 2 km beyond the bridge over Río Arcagual to a second bridge before which turn right by a white house. Climb the hill and take the first path on the left (no sign), cross the river and continue for about 15 minutes to the pools. Good place to barbecue.

Parque Nacional Celaque

It takes at least a day to climb from Gracias to the summit of **Monte Celaque** (2849 m, the highest point in Honduras). Most people allow two days to enjoy the trip. The trail begins from behind the visitors' centre of the Parque Nacional Celaque (1400 m), which is 8 km from Gracias, two hours' walk. There are several intersections, best to ask at each. You can also enjoy a day walk to **Mirador La Cascada** ⓘ *entry fee US$3 plus US$3 per night camping in the mountain*, about three hours from the visitors' centre, 1½ hours downhill going back. Transport can be arranged with the tourist office in the Plaza Central (US$10 per vehicle for up to four people). **Comedor Doña Alejandrina** just before the visitors' centre, provides excellent breakfasts. Not much of the 8-km road from Gracias to the park is passable when wet, without a high-clearance or 4WD vehicle. Transport can be arranged through the Lenca Centre. Armando Mondragon (Texaco station, T898-4002) does trips, including lunch. At the centre there are seven beds, shower and cooking facilities, US$1, drinks available, well maintained. There is another cabin nearby with 10 beds. Take a torch and sleeping bag. Behind the centre is a trail going down to the river where a crystal-clear pool and waterfall make for wonderful bathing. Ask the guide the exact way or pay US$6 for the guide. There is a warden, Miguel, living nearby who can supply food and beer but it is safer to take supplies from Gracias. Contact Cohdefor in Gracias before leaving for full information. There is a trail all the way to the summit (trees are marked with ribbons) which takes at least six hours: the first three are easy to a campsite at 2000 m (Campamento Don Tomás) where there is small hut, the rest of the way is steep. A better campsite if you can make it is Campamento Naranjo, with water, at about 2500 m – but you'll need a tent. Between these two sites, the climb is particularly steep and in cloud forest. Look out for spider monkeys. Above 2600 m quetzals have been seen. Many hikers don't bother with the summit as it is forested and enclosed; it's four hours down to the visitors' centre. Don't forget good hiking boots, warm clothing, insect repellent and, given the dense forest and possibility of heavy cloud, a compass is also recommended for safety. Also, beware of snakes. There is a trail westward from the summit to Belén Gualcho which is steep towards Belén. It takes a couple of days and a guide might be a good idea.

Visiting the other peaks around Gracias is more complicated but interesting. Information, maps that you can photocopy, camping gear and guided tours can be found at the Lenca Cultural Centre.

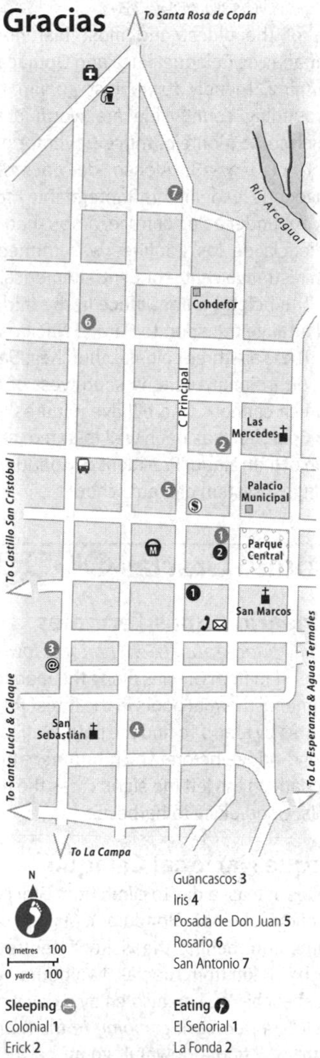

Gracias to Erandique

After Gracias, the road runs 52 km to **San Juan del Caite** (two *hospedajes*, Lempira and Sánchez, two restaurants nearby, helpful people and Peace Corps workers). From here a dirt road runs 26 km south to the small town of Erandique. Founded in 1560 and set high in pine-clad mountains not far from the border with El Salvador, it is a friendly town, and very beautiful. Lempira was born nearby, and was killed a few kilometres away. The third weekend in

Border essentials: Honduras-El Salvador

Perquín
South of Marcala the road crosses into El Salvador, 3 km before Perquín. There have been several confrontations with the Honduran military in the area but the border dispute has been settled by treaty. Recent reports suggest there is no Salvadorean immigration post; entering the country is possible, but illegal. In addition to the US$10 tourist card, you will be fined US$8 for US citizens, US$12 for Europeans. Ask locally for security conditions and the situation with regards to crossing here. There are buses along the very rough road from Marcala to San Miguel, El Salvador, and from Perquín to the border in the early morning. The rustic border crossing office is about 5 km inside Honduras.

El Poy
Take a bus from Nueva Ocotopeque to El Poy on the border, 15-20 mins, US$0.30. The exit tax is US$5.50. Buses leave El Poy for San Salvador regularly, 3-4 hrs.

January is the local **Fiesta de San Sebastián**. Best time to visit is at the weekend. Market days are Friday and Sunday. Each of the three *barrios* has a nice colonial church. Ask around as there are lakes, rivers, waterfalls, springs and bathing ponds in the vicinity. Nearby is San Antonio where fine opals (not cut gems, but stones encased in rock) are mined and may be purchased. The many hamlets in the surrounding mountains are reached by roads that have been either resurfaced or recently built and the landscapes are magnificent.

There are several roads radiating from Erandique, including one to **Mapulaca** and the border with El Salvador (no immigration or customs or bridge here, at the Río Lempa), a road to San Andrés and another to Piraera (all passable in a car).

La Esperanza → *Colour map 6, C2. Altitude: 1485 m.*

Beyond San Juan del Caite the main, but still rough and stony, road winds through beautiful mountain pine forests to La Esperanza. It is 43 km from San Juan del Caite and another 98 km on a good road to Siguatepeque. Capital of Intibucá Department, La Esperanza is an old colonial town in a pleasant valley. It has an attractive church in front of the park. There is a grotto carved out of the mountainside west of the town centre, a site of religious festivals. Good views. There is a market on Thursdays and Sundays when the Lenca from nearby villages sell wares and food but no handicrafts. Nearby is the indigenous village of **Yaramanguila**. It's an excellent area for walking in forested hills, with lakes and waterfalls, although very cold in December to January. You can hike to **Cerro de Ojos**, a hill to the northwest and visible from La Esperanza. It is forested with a clearing on top littered with many cylindrical holes; no one knows how they were formed, and they are a strange phenomenon. The turning to this hill is on the La Esperanza to San Juan road. Ask for directions.

Marcala and around » pp815-823. Colour map 6, C2.

→ *Population: 10,770. Altitude: 1300 m.*

From La Esperanza, an unpaved road runs southeast to Marcala in the Department of La Paz (a paved road goes to La Paz). During the hotter months from March to May, a cooler climate can be found in the highlands of La Paz, with pleasant temperatures during the day and cold (depending on altitude) at night. Ideal for hiking and with beautiful scenery and dramatic waterfalls in the surrounding area,

Border essentials: Honduras-Guatemala

Agua Caliente
You can cross into Guatemala at Agua Caliente, 16 km from Nueva Ocotepeque. There are 3 banks, a tourist office on the Honduran side, the **Comedor Hermanos Ramírez** for food, and one *hospedaje*. This can be a busy crossing but is quicker, cheaper and more efficient than the one at El Florido.

Honduran immigration All formalities completed at the border, daily 0700-1800. There are money changers outside the Honduran immigration building, keep lempiras for exit stamp and minibus ride Agua Caliente–Esqiupulas.

Guatemalan consulate The nearest is in San Pedro Sula.

Transport There are several buses a day from San Pedro Sula to Agua Caliente, the first at 0300, US$4.45, six to seven hours. Buses from Nueva Ocotepeque to Agua Caliente every 30 minutes from 0630, US$0.60. Money changers get on the bus between Nueva Ocotepeque and the border, good rates for US$ cash. Minibuses go to Esquipulas, US$0.25, with connections to destinations in Guatemala, see page 608.

Marcala is a good base from which to visit Yarula, Santa Elena, Opatoro, San José and Guajiquiro. The Marcala region is one of the finest coffee-producing areas of Honduras and a visit to 'Comarca', at the entrance to town, gives a good idea of how coffee is processed. Semana Santa is celebrated with a large procession through the main street and there is a **fiesta** in honour of San Miguel Arcángel in the last week of September.

Around Marcala

Near Marcala is Balneario **El Manzanal,** 3 km on the road to La Esperanza; it has a restaurant, two swimming pools and a boating lake, open weekends only. For panoramic views high above Marcala, follow this hike (one hour): head north past **Hotel Medina,** turn right (east) after the hotel and follow the road up into hills. After 2 km the road branches. Take the left branch and immediately on the left is a football field. A small path leaves from this field on the west side taking you through a small area of pine trees then out onto a ridge for excellent views. The track continues down from the ridge back to town, passing an unusual cemetery on a hill.

Estanzuela is an area next to a small village of the same name. A favourite spot to visit at weekends, it is a large grassy area next to a river where a dam has been built to provide an area for bathing, excellent camping (no food or drinks sold here). Best visited in the rainy season as the river is higher and the area greener. Take the road to La Esperanza from the Marcala to La Paz road. After 20 minutes (by car) take a right hand turning to Estanzuela. It is a one-hour walk from the turn-off passing the village of Estanzuela to the area.

There are caves nearby on **Musula** mountain, the Cueva de las Animas in Guamizales and Cueva de El Gigante and El León near La Estanzuela with a high waterfall close by. Other waterfalls are El Chiflador, 67 m high, Las Golondrinas, La Chorrera and Santa Rosita. Transport goes to La Florida where there is good walking to the village of **Opatoro** and climbing **Cerro Guajiquiro**. Between Opatoro and Guajiquiro is the Reserva las Trancas, a heavily forested mountain where quetzales have been seen.

Yarula and **Santa Elena** are two tiny municipalities, the latter about 40 km from Marcala, with beautiful views (bus Marcala–Santa Elena 1230 returns 0500 next day, 2¾ hours, enquire at Gámez bus office opposite market; truck daily 0830 returns from Santa Elena at 1300). Sometimes meals are available at *comedores* in Yarula and Santa Elena. The dirt road from Marcala gradually deteriorates, the last 20 km being terrible, high clearance essential, 4WD recommended. In **La Cueva Pintada**, south of Santa Elena, there are pre-Columbian cave paintings (*pinturas rupestres*) of snakes, men and dogs; ask for a guide in Santa Elena. Ask also in this village about the **Danza de los Negritos**, performed at the annual **fiesta** of Santiago, 24-25 March, in front of the church. A special performance may be organized, the dancers wearing their old wooden masks, if suitable payment is offered.

The village of **San José** (altitude: 1700 m) is a Lenca community where the climate can be cool and windy even in the hottest months. The scenery is superb. Good hill walking (see box above for two examples; there are many others), also rivers for swimming. Frequent pick-ups from Marcala, and two daily minibuses at about 0815 and 0900; from San José to Marcala minibuses depart at 0615 and 0645, one hour, US$1.

Nueva Ocotepeque

» *pp815-823. Colour map 6, B1.*

Heading south from Santa Rosa, Nueva Ocotepeque gives access to good hiking and leads to the borders with Guatemala and El Salvador. The old colonial church of La Vieja (or La Antigua) between Nueva Ocotepeque and the border, is in the village of Antigua Ocotepeque, founded in the 1540s, but destroyed by a flood from Cerro El Pital in 1934.

The **Guisayote Biological Reserve** protects 35 sq km of cloud forest, about 50% virgin and is reached from the Western Highway, where there are trails and good hiking. Access is from El Portillo, the name of the pass on the main road north. El Portillo to El Sillón, the park's southern entrance, three to five hours. Twice daily bus from El Sillón to Ocotepeque. **El Pital**, 3 km east of Nueva Ocotepeque, but 2 km vertically above the town, 2730 m is the third highest point in Honduras with several square kilometres of cloud forest. The park has not been developed for tourism.

The **Parque Nacional Montecristo** forms part of the Trifinio/La Fraternidad project, administered jointly by Honduras, Guatemala and El Salvador. The park is quite remote from the Honduran side, two to three days to the summit, but there are easy-to-follow trails. Access is best from Metapán in El Salvador. From the lookout point at the peak you can see about 90% of El Salvador and 20% of Honduras on a clear day. The natural resources office, for information, is opposite Texaco, two blocks from **Hotel y Comedor Congolón** at the south end of town. Raymond J Sabella of the US Peace Corps has written a very thorough description of the natural and historical attractions of the Department, including hikes, waterfalls and caves.

Sleeping

San Pedro Sula to Copán *p803*

C-E **San Carlos**, La Entrada, at junction to Copán Ruinas, T898-5228. A/c, modern, cable TV, bar, swimming pool, restaurant (T/F661-2187), excellent value.

E-F **Central**, by Shell, La Entrada. With 2 beds (cheaper with 1), bath, cold water, fans.

F **Hospedaje Golosino Yessi**, La Entrada. Parking, small rooms, OK.

F **Hospedaje María**, La Entrada. Good, limited food.

Copán Ruinas *p804, map p805*

Hotels are generally expensive here compared with other places in Honduras.

AL **Hacienda San Lucas**, south out of town, T651-4495, www.haciendasanlucas.com. Great spot for calm and tranquillity. 8 rooms with hot water bath, restaurant, renovated hacienda home, lovely views of Copán river valley and hiking trails.

AL **Posada Real de Copán**, on hill over-looking Copán, T651-4480, www.posadareal decopan.com. Full-service hotel, restaurant and very nice pool, US$5 for non-guests.

AL-C Marina Copán, on the plaza occupying almost an entire block, T651-4070, www.hotelmarinacopan.com. Swimming pool, sauna, restaurant, bar, live marimba music at weekends, also caters for tour groups, large rooms with TV, suites, very tasteful and spacious, friendly, nice atmosphere. Recommended.

B Camino Maya, corner of main plaza, T651-4646, hcmaya@david.intertel.hn. With bath, good restaurant, rooms bright and airy, cable TV, fans, rooms on courtyard quieter than street, English spoken, nice patio garden with parrot, balconies on some upstairs rooms.

B La Casa de Café, 4½ blocks west of plaza, T651-4620, www.casadecafecopan.com. Renovated colonial home, with breakfast, coffee all day, library, good information, beautifully designed garden, lovely views, friendly and interesting hosts, English spoken, very popular so best to reserve in advance, protected parking. Recommended.

B Los Jaguares on plaza opposite **Marina**, T651-4451. 10 rooms, with bath, TV, a/c, hot water, friendly staff, locked parking, no restaurant.

B Madrugada, T651-4092, take street from southeast corner of Parque, go down steps and turn right, by the river. Unprepossessing exterior but nice colonial-style interior, 15 rooms (upstairs best).

B-C Bella Vista, on hill by former police barracks, T445-1036. Clean, safe but poorly situated, good value.

C Brisas de Copán, T651-4118. Terrace, modern rooms with bath, hot water, quiet, limited parking. Recommended.

C-D Yaragua, ½ block east of the plaza, T651-4147, www.yaragua.com/hotel_esp.htm. With bath, hot water, safe, clean, friendly.

D Patty (see map), T651-4021. Fan, bath, no meals, good value, lots of parking. Recommended.

D-E Café VíaVía Copán, next to **Tunkul**, T651-4652, www.viaviacafe.com. Great rooms, newly decorated, part of a worldwide Belgian network of cafés, breakfast US$2.75, special price for students with card and discounts for more than one night, hot water, good beds, bar and great vegetarian food.

E Hotelito Yaxpac, 1 block north of Parque Central, T651-4025. 4 rooms with bath, cold water, nice view of countryside from balcony.

E-F Hostel Iguana Azul, next to La Casa de Café and under same ownership, T651-4620, www.iguanaazulcopan.com. Dormitory-style bunk beds in 2 rooms, shared bath, also 3 more private double rooms, hot water, laundry facilities, garden patio, colonial decor, clean, comfortable, common area, books, magazines, travel guides (including *Footprint*), maps, garden, fans, safe box, English spoken. Good for backpackers.

F En la Manzana Verde, near Hedman Alas, T651-4652, en_la_manzana_verde@yahoo.com. Great shared bunk rooms, shared bath, kitchen, same owners as **Vía Vía**. Good budget choice.

F Hospedaje Los Gemelos, 1 block down from **Banco de Occidente**, T651-4315. With shared bath, clean, fans, good value, friendly, pleasant patio, good for single women, also laundry facilities, internet, phone and fax service. Recommended.

F Posada Honduras, near the bus stops, T651-4082. Simple, with a small patio. Not great, but the cheapest in town.

Apartments

Casa Jaguar Rental Home, just 5 blocks from Parque Central, T651-4620, www.casajaguarcopan.com. Comfortable village residence with 2 double bedrooms, newly decorated and fully equipped for self-catering. Available for the night, week or month. Contact **La Casa de Café**, see above.

Santa Rosa de Copán and around

p809, map p809

A-B Elvir, Calle Real Centenario SO, 3 Av SO, T/F662-0805. Overpriced, safe, clean, quiet, all rooms have own bath, TV, hot water, drinking water, good but pricey meals in *cafetería* or restaurant.

B Continental, 2 Calle NO y 2-3 Av, T662-0801, on 2nd floor. Good value with bath, hot water, fan, cable TV, friendly management.

C VIP Copán, 1 Calle, 3 Av, T662-0265. With bath, TV, cheaper without, cell-like rooms but clean, safe, hot water in morning.

E Hospedaje Santa Eduviges, 2 Av NO y 1 Calle NO. Good beds, clean, pleasant, good value but some rooms damp.

E Maya Central (not to be confused with Hospedaje Maya), 1 Calle NO y 3 Av NO, T662-0073. With bath, cold shower, pleasant.

E-F Rosario, 3 Av NE No 139, T662-0211. Cold water, with bath, cheaper without, friendly.
F Blanca Nieves, 3 Av NE, Barrio Mercedes, T662-1312. Safe, shared bath with cold water, laundry facilities. Going down hill but worth a look.
G Hospedaje Calle Real, Real Centenario y 6 Av NE. Clean, quiet, friendly, best of the cheaper places but sometimes water failures.
G Hospedaje Santa Rosa, 3 Av NE No 42, Barrio Mercedes, T662-1421. Basic, clean, safe, cold water, laundry facilities, welcoming.

Around Santa Rosa de Copán *p810*
In Belén Gualcho hotels fill up quickly on Sat as traders arrive for the Sun market.
F Pensión, Corquín. Good *pensión* with a charming garden. Recommended.
G Hospedaje, east of Santa Rosa de Copán Lepaera, opposite market. Very basic.
G Hospedaje Doña Carolina, Belén Gualcho. Electricity goes off at 2130 so take a torch and candle. Films are shown every evening at 1930, ask anyone, US$0.10.
G Hotelito El Carmen, Belén Gualcho, 2 blocks east down from the church in the plaza. Friendly, clean, good views. Recommended.

Gracias *p811, map p812*
D Guancascos, at the west end of Hondutel road, T656-1219, www.guancascos.com. Bath, hot water, TV, also rents 2-room cabin at **Villa Verde** adjacent to Monte Celaque visitors' centre.
D Hotel Rosario, T656-1447. Hot water, private bath, clean and friendly.
D-E Posada de Don Juan, Calle Principal opposite **Banco de Occidente**, T/F656-1020, hotelposadadedonjuan@yahoo.com. Dutch-owned, good beds, great hot showers, nice big towels, laundry, some rooms have TV, parking. Recommended.
E Colonial, 1 block south of **Erick**, T656-1258. With bath, fan, bar, restaurant, very good.
F Erick, same street as bus office, T656-1066. With bath, cheaper without (cold shower), TV, comfortable beds, fresh, bright, clean, good value with helpful, friendly owners. Laundry facilities, stores luggage, shop selling basic supplies and can arrange transport to Mt Celaque. Very convenient and recommended.
F Finca Bavaria, new, quiet place at the edge of town. Good breakfasts. German/Honduran owned. Parking.
F Hospedaje Corazón de Jesús, on main street by market. Clean, OK.
F Hospedaje El Milagro, north side of market. Basic.
F Iris, 3 blocks south of Plaza, 1 block west, opposite San Sebastián church, T656-1086. Clean, cold water, closes at 2200, disco Sat.
F San Antonio, main street, 2 blocks from Texaco station (no sign) T656-1071. Clean, pleasant, friendly, good.

La Esperanza *p813*
Simple but pleasant *pensiones*.
E La Esperanza, T898-2068. With bath, cheaper without, warm water, clean, TV, friendly, good meals.
F El Rey, in Barrio La Morera, T898-2078. Clean, friendly.
F Hotel Mina, 1 block south of east side of market, T898-2071. Good beds, clean, very friendly, food available.
F Mejía Batres, ½ block from Parque Central. With bath, clean, friendly, excellent value.
F Rosario, on road to Siguatepeque. Basic.

Marcala and around *p813*
D-E Medina, on main road through town, T898-1866. The most comfortable, clean, modern with bath, *cafetería*, free purified water. Highly recommended.
F Hospedaje Edgar, main street, beginning of town. Clean, basic, no sheets.
F Hospedaje Jairo, 2 blocks east of main square. With bath.

Around Marcala *p814*
F Unnamed hotel, San José. Run by British man, Nigel Potter, or Nayo, basic but comfortable and clean, with meals. He also takes groups to stay in Lenca villages, US$5 per person plus US$10 per person for accommodation in a village; ask for the house of Doña Gloria, Profe Vinda, Nayo or Ruth. At least one of these will be present to meet visitors.

Camping
There is camping 10 mins' walk away from the hotel. Contact Nigel Potter – see above.

Nueva Ocotepeque *p815*
C **Sandoval**, opposite Hondutel, T653-3098. Rooms and suites, breakfast included, private bath, hot water, cable TV, mini-bar, phone, room service, restaurant attached, good value.
D **Maya Chortis**, Barrio San José, 4 Calle, 3 Av NE, T653-3377. Nice rooms with bath, double beds, hot water, fan, TV, mini-bar, phone, room service, quieter rooms at back, including breakfast, good restaurant, good value.
E-F **San Antonio**, 1 Calle, 3 Av, T653-3072. Small rooms but OK.
F **Gran**, about 250 m from town at the junction of the roads for El Salvador and Guatemala, just north of town, at Sinuapa. With bath, cold water, pleasant, clean, single beds only.
F **Ocotepeque**, by Transportes Toritos. Clean but noisy.

Eating

Copán Ruinas *p804, map p805*
¥¥¥ **Café Welchez** in Hotel Marina Copán. Good cakes but expensive and coffee 'unpredictable'.
¥¥¥ **Hacienda San Lucas**, south out of town, T651-4106. Set menu by reservation, with 5-course meal, local ingredients, candlelight – great place for a special meal.
¥¥¥ **Tunkul**, opposite Llama del Bosque. Good food includes vegetarian meals, large portions, not cheap, happy hour 2000-2100, large outdoor patio, nice for relaxing breakfast, helpful. Recommended.
¥¥ **Café Vamos a Ver**, 1 block from plaza. Lots of vegetables, good sandwiches and snacks, complete dinner US$5, pleasant, good value, daily 0700-2200.
¥¥ **Café ViaVia Copán** (see Sleeping, above). Food, fresh bread, bar, lodging.
¥¥ **Elisa's** at Camino Maya. Excellent food at reasonable prices, pleasant, good service.
¥¥ **Llama del Bosque**, 2 blocks west of plaza. Open for breakfast, lunch and dinner, pleasant, large portions of reasonable food, try their *carnitas típicas*. Recommended.
¥¥ **Pizza Copán**, US expat Jim cooks up good old US of A fare: chicken grilled over wood fire, BBQ steaks, burgers and good pizza.
¥¥ **Yaragua**, next to the hotel. Good home-cooked Honduran country food, huge, portions, a/c, attentive service, recommended. A new restaurant run by Tanya from the UK. Popular with travellers, good food, good bar.
¥ **Carnitas Nía Lola**, 2 blocks south of Parque Central, at end of road. Good view over river and valley, popular meeting place, daily 0700-2200, *comida típica*, inexpensive, busy bar, relaxed atmosphere and book exchange.
¥ **El Sesteo**, next to **Hotel Patty**. Typical lunch US$3, dinner US$3-4.50, friendly but rather nondescript atmosphere.
¥ **Licuados Express** (see map). Healthy juices, good coffee and bagels, 0630-1700, closes early on Sun.
¥ **Picame** (see map). Light meals, best rotisserie chicken in town, burgers, recommended.
¥ **Pupusería y Comedor Mari**, ½ block from market. The best cheap, typical food in town. Clean, decent service, very popular with locals at lunchtime. Daily specials like seafood soup. Zero decor, but it doesn't matter for the good hearty food.

Santa Rosa de Copán and around *p809, map p809*
¥¥¥ **Flamingos**, 1 Av SE, off main plaza, T662-0654. Relatively expensive but good pasta and chop suey, popular with locals.
¥¥¥ **Lily's**, Calle Real Centanario, ½ block from Parque Central. Expensive but very good food, nice garden, good wine list and cigars for sale.
¥¥ **Chikys**, 1 Calle SO y 1 Av SO. Mexican, good food, atmosphere, music and beer. Recommended.
¥¥ **El Rodeo**, 1 Av SE. Good menu, specializes in steaks, nice atmosphere, plenty of dead animals on the walls, pricey.
¥¥ **La Gran Villa**, on the *carretera*. Some of the tastiest meats and meals in Santa Rosa, run by Garífuna family. Recommended.
¥¥ **Las Haciendas**, 1 Av Calle SE. Steak and seafood, varied menu, filling *comida corriente*, and an attractive patio bar. Recommended. **Las Haciendas II**, 1 Calle SO, smaller, more intimate, same menu. The 3rd and for some the best is **Las Haciendas III**, at 1 Calle 2-3 Av SE, same ownership, menu, and prices, in a pleasantly restored home.
¥¥ **On Fu**, 1 Av SO, near Chikys, 2nd floor. Chinese and local dishes, large servings, good vegetables, attentive service.
¥¥ **Well**, 3 Calle 2 Av SE, Chinese, a/c, huge portions, good value and service.

Merenderoa El Campesino, at the bus terminal. Good *comedor*.

Pizza Pizza, Real Centenario 5 Av NE, 4½ blocks from main plaza. One of the best in town, good pizza and pasta, pleasant surroundings in old colonial house, great coffee, best meeting place, US owned, good source of information, book exchange. Recommended.

Rincón Colonial, 1 Av SE. Typical local cuisine, good, less expensive than its neighbours.

Around Santa Rosa de Copán *p810*

In Belén Gualcho there are 2 *comedores* on south side of plaza and east side on corner with store.

Comedor Mery, Belén Gualcho. 1 block northwest of plaza. Good food in a welcoming family atmosphere.

Las Haciendas, Belén Gualcho. Good.

Gracias *p811, map p812*

For breakfast, try the *comedores* near the market or, better, the restaurant at Hotel Iris (good *comida corriente* too) or Guancascos.

Comedor Graciano and **Pollo Gracianito**, main street. Good value.

La Fonda (see map). Good food, good value, attractively decorated, but no written menu – good practice for your Spanish. Recommended.

El Señorial, main street. Simple meals and snacks, once house of former president Dr Juan Lindo.

Rancho de Lily, 3 blocks west of Hondutel. Good value, rustic cabin, bar service, good snacks.

La Esperanza *p813*

Pizza Venezia, on edge of town towards Marcala. Good Italian dishes.

Café El Ecológico, corner of Parque Central. Home-made cakes and pastries, fruit drinks, delicious home-made jams.

Restaurant Magus, 1 block east of plaza, Good food in a formica video bar atmosphere.

Unnamed restaurant in front of church. Very good *comida corriente*.

Marcala and around *p813*

Riviera Linda, opposite Hotel Medina. Pleasant atmosphere, spacious, a little pricey but good food.

Café Express, beside Esso. Good breakfast and *comida corrida*. Recommended.

Darwin, main street in centre. Cheap breakfasts from 0700. Recommended.

El Mirador, on entering town by petrol station. Nice views from veranda, good food. Recommended.

Jarito, opposite market entrance. Good.

Around Marcala *p814*

Comedor, 500 m before plaza on main road. Good, clean and cheap.

Nueva Ocotepeque *p815*

Sandoval and **Don Chepe**, at Maya Chortis. The best options. Excellent food, small wine lists, good value. Recommended.

Comedor Nora, Parque Central, and

Merendera Ruth, 2 Calle NE, just off Parque Central. Both offer economical *comida corriente*, preferable to *comedores* around bus terminal.

Entertainment

Santa Rosa de Copán and around *p809, map p809*

Bars and clubs

Extasis, shows videos Mon-Thu night.

Luna Jaguar, at 3 Av, between 1 Calle SE and Calle Real Centenario, is the hottest disco in town, but proper dress required.

Manzanitas, is on the corner of 3 Av SE and Calle Real Centenario, if you fancy singing your heart out to a little karaoke.

Cinema

Plaza Saavedra, opposite Blanca Nieves, nightly at 1900.

Festivals and events

See also under each town and village.

Santa Rosa de Copán and around *p809, map p809*

21-31 Aug Festival de Santa Rosa de Lima; the 'Tobacco Queen' is crowned at the end of the week.

La Esperanza *p813*

3rd week in Jul Festival de la Papa.

8 Dec Fiesta de la Virgen de la Concepción.

Shopping

Copán Ruinas *p804, map p805*
Selling all sorts of local crafts are **La Casa de Todo**, just down the street from **Banco de Occidente**, is Copán's best crafts shop, with a popular café for light meals and snacks. **Arte Acción** is across the street from Casa de Todo, and has childrens art exhibits, runs art projects for kids. Stop in for information.
Mercado Artesenal, in the old *colegio* on the Parque Central, also home to a new interactive kids museum about the Maya. Tue-Sun 0900-1200, 1300-1800. The **El Jaral** shopping centre is 6 km from town on the road to San Pedro Sula.

Santa Rosa de Copán and around
p809, map p809
Supermercadeo Manzanitaz, Calle Centenario.

Activities and tours

Copán Ruinas *p804, map p805*
Animal and birdwatching
Birding guide and naturalist **Bob Gallardo** (T651-4133, rgallardo32@hotmail.com) is the owner of the Butterfly Garden and an expert on Honduran flora and fauna. He leads birding trips, **natural history tours**, orchid and serpent tours around Copán and other parts of Honduras, including La Mosquitia.

Horse riding
You will probably be approached with offers of horse hire which is a good way of getting to nearby attractions. Riding trips are available to Los Sapos and Las Sepulturas, US$10 for 4 hrs.
Finca El Cisne, T651-4695, www.fincaelcisne.com, full-day tours to the coffee plantation high in the mountains including horse riding, lunch and transport. Accommodation (**AL**) . Good trip.
Yaragua Tours, next to hotel of same name, T651-4050, www.yaragua.com, horse riding and coffee *fincas*. Daily 0700-2100. Recommended.

Tour operators
Base Camp Tours, T651-4695, nature hikes US$8, treks, motocross tours US$40, horse riding, expedition hikes US$20 and transport including shuttles to Guatemala City, Antigua US$12, San Salvador US$25, Gracias US$15, Santa Rosa de Copán US$15 and Río Dulce US$15. Base Camp has the best horses in town. Information at Tunkal.
MC Tours, across the street from **Hotel Marina**, T651-4453, www.mctours-honduras.com, local and countrywide tours.
Monarcas Travel, T651-4361, for shuttle service to Guatemala City and Antigua, www.mayabus.com, daily 0800-1800.
Horses for hire (but look around and bargain).

Santa Rosa de Copán and around
p809, map p809
Tour operators
Lenca Land Trails, at **Hotel Elvir**, T/F662-1375, lenca@hondutel.hn, run by Max Elvir, organizes cultural tours of the Lenca mountain villages in western Honduras, hiking, mountain biking, the lot, excellent source of information about the region.
Guide Ask at **Flor de Copán** cigar factory for **José Pineda** who runs tours to tobacco plantations at weekends, informative, only 30 mins from town, lovely countryside.

Gracias *p811, map p812*
Tour operators
Celaque Aventuras Tours, run by Christophe Condor is based in Guancascos, T656-1219, has walking tours, visits to La Campa, the national park, thermal baths, horse hire, US$8, includes horse riding, visit to thermal pools day or night, visiting natural caves. Hot springs only, US$4.
Guancascos Tourist Centre at the **Guancascos Hotel** arranges tours and expeditions to Monte Celaque Parque Nacional, local villages and other attractions.

Around Marcala *p814*
For trips to visit Lenca villages see Sleeping, page 817.

Transport

San Pedro Sula to Copán *p803*
Truck
From **La Entrada** the cheapest transport is by truck. From **Copán** ask about a truck by **Hotel Patty** and negotiate for the 60-km,

1-hr ride, about US$25 for 2 includes 1½ hrs at the site and a stop at **Las Lagunas** to see the roosting cattle egrets (recommended).

Copán Ruinas *p804, map p805*

Air

While there are occasional charter flights into Copán's new airstrip, there is no regular service. Information at **MC Tours**, see above. You canfly to Tablones in Guatemala, then cross the border to Copán.

Bus

Heading inland you normally have to go to San Pedro Sula before heading for the coast or south to the capital.

A new 1st-class direct service to **San Pedro Sula** with connections to **Tegucigalpa** and **La Ceiba** with **Hedman Alas** (T651-4106, www.hedmanalas.com), leaves at 0515 and 1030 daily, and 1430 Fri-Mon, 3 hrs to San Pedro (US$14). Also daily connection to Tela and San Pedro Sula Airport. To **Guatemala City** (US$35) and **Antigua** (US$41) at 1320. **El Rey Express**, located next to Hotel Patty, www.reyexpress.net. To **San Pedro Sula** departs at 0610, 0800, 1300, US$5, one way, with connections in San Pedro for Tegucigalpa and La Ceiba. Also Copán-Guatemala City daily. **Casasola-Cheny Express** for San Pedro Sula (T651-4078) at 0530, 0600, 0700 and 1400. Both services are comfortable, efficient, good value and with reclining seats.

If heading for **Santa Rosa de Copán** or **Gracias** get a bus to the junction at La Entrada and change there. Buses for **La Entrada** leave Copán Ruinas every 30 mins, 1 hr, US$1.80. Express minibus service to **San Pedro Sula**, airport and **Tela** from **Hotel Patty** – price depends on numbers. Numerous boys greet you on arrival to carry bags or offer directions for a small fee, while most are good kids, some will tell you hotels are closed.

For Guatemala direct – **Antigua** service leaves 1400, arriving 2000, **Monarcas Travel**. Return journey leaves Antigua 0400, minibuses to the border leave from behind Hotel Marino. Also with **Hedman Alas** to **Guatemala City** daily at 1430, and 1530 on Fri and Sat, US$35 one way.

If coming from **San Pedro Sula**, and returning, it is possible to see the Copán site in 1 day if you get the first and last buses.

Santa Rosa de Copán and around

p809, map p809

Bus Depart from city bus station on Carretera Internacional. **Local**: 'El Urbano' bus to centre from bus station (on Carretera Internacional, 2 km below town, opposite Hotel Mayaland), US$0.15, 15 mins; taxi US$1.40. **Long distance**: If coming from the Guatemalan border at Nueva Ocotepeque, the bus will stop at the end of town near Av Centenario, 2 km below town, opposite **Hotel Mayaland**. To **Tegucigalpa** (lovely scenery, lush pine forests, colonial villages), **Toritos** leaves at 0400 from terminal Mon-Sat 0400 and 1000 Sun, US$6, 10 hrs. Alternatively, take an express bus to San Pedro Sula and an express bus on to Tegucigalpa (US$5, 6 hrs). To **Gracias**, **Transportes Lempira**, several 0630-1800, 1½ hrs, US$1.30. To **San Pedro Sula**, US$2.50, 4 hrs, every 45 mins 0400-1730, express service daily 2½ hrs, US$3.50 (**Empresa Torito**). Bus to **La Entrada**, 1 hr, US$1. To **Copán Ruinas**, 4 hrs on good road, US$2.90, several direct daily 1100, 1230 and 1400. Alternatively, take any bus to La Entrada, 1 hr, US$1, and transfer to a Copán Ruinas bus. South on paved road to **Nueva Ocotepeque**, 6 daily, US$1.80, 2 hrs. There you change buses for El Salvador and Guatemala (1 hr to border, US$1, bus leaves hourly until 1700).

Around Santa Rosa de Copán *p810*

Bus Numerous buses head south daily from Santa Rosa to **Corquín** (US$0.75, 2 hrs). **Belén Gualcho** to **Santa Rosa** daily at 0430 (Sun at 0930). To **Gracias** from main plaza at 0400, 0500 and 1330.

Gracias *p811, map p812*

Bus A mail car goes to **La Esperanza** Tue, Thu, Sat 0400, or take bus to Erandique, 1315, get off at San Juan from where bus goes to La Esperanza the next day, or hitch, or rides can be taken on very dusty and bumpy pick-up trucks for US$3 – beware overcharging (0700 or earlier from south end of main street on highway). The road is much improved as far as San Juan. You can easily find a pick-up this far, 1½ hrs, US$1.50. Thereafter it is all-weather and can be rough. There is a bus service to **Santa Rosa de Copán**, US$1.30, from 0530 to 1630, 5 times a day, 1½ hrs; beautiful journey through majestic scenery. Also to **San Pedro Sula** at 0500 and 0800, US$3, 4 hrs. Daily bus service to **Lepaera** 1400, 1½ hrs, US$1.50; daily bus to **San Manuel de Colohuete** at 1300. **Cotral** bus ticket office is 1 block north of Parque Central. **Torito** bus, a few metres from the main terminal, has buses to the Guatemalan border at **Agua Caliente**, one at 1000, change buses at Nueva Ocotepeque.

Gracias to Erandique *p812*
Bus There are minibuses to **Erandique** from the bridge on the road to La Esperanza, 1100 daily, although most people go by truck from Gracias (there is sometimes a van service as far as San Juan) or La Esperanza (change trucks at San Juan intersection, very dusty). Return minibus to Gracias at 0500 daily, which connects with the bus to La Esperanza in San Juan. Trucks leave Erandique 0700 daily, but sometimes earlier, and occasionally a 2nd one leaves around 0800 for Gracias, otherwise be prepared for a long wait for a pick-up.

La Esperanza *p813*
Bus To **Tegucigalpa** several daily, 1½ hrs (**Cobramil**, also to **San Pedro Sula**, and **Joelito**, 4 hrs, US$2.60); to **Siguatepeque** 0700, 0900, last at 1000, US$1.20, 2 hrs; also bus to **Siguatepeque**, **Comayagua** at 0600; and to the **Salvadorean border**; bus stops by market. Hourly minibuses to **Yaramanguila**, 30 mins. Daily bus to **Marcala**, 2 hrs at 1230 (but check), US$0.80 (truck, US$1.20, 2¼ hrs). Minibus service at 1130, US$1.50. Daily minibus service to **San Juan**, departs between 1030-1200 from a parking space midway between the 2 bus stops, 2½ hrs, pick-ups also do this journey, very crowded; for **Erandique**, alight at Erandique turn-off, 1 km before San Juan and wait for truck to pass (*comedor* plus basic *hospedaje* at intersection). If going to Gracias, stay on the La Esperanza-San Juan bus until the end of the line where a pick-up collects passengers 15 mins or so later, 1 hr San Juan-Gracias. Buses to **Lake Yojoa** (see page 825), 2 hrs, US$2.50.

Marcala and around *p813*
Bus To **Tegucigalpa** 0500, 0915 and 1000 daily via La Paz, 4 hrs, US$2.40 (bus from Tegucigalpa at 0800 and 1400, **Empresa Lila**, 4-5 Av, 7 Calle, No 418 Comayagüela, opposite Hispano cinema); bus to **La Paz** only, 0700, 2 hrs, US$1; several minibuses a day, 1½ hrs, US$1.50. Bus also from Comayagua. Pick-up truck to **San José** at around 1000 from market, ask for drivers, Don Santos, Torencio, or Gustavo. Bus to **La Esperanza** at about 0830, unreliable, check with driver, Don Pincho, at the supermarket next to where the bus is parked (same street as Hotel Medina), 1½-2 hrs, otherwise hitching possible, going rate US$1.20. Bus to **San Miguel**, El Salvador, **Transportes Wendy Patricia**, 0500, 1200, 7 hrs, US$3.50.

Nueva Ocotepeque *p815*
Bus **Transportes Escobar** daily service **Tegucigalpa** to Nueva Ocotepeque/Agua Caliente, via La Entrada and Santa Rosa de Copán (12 Av entre 8 y 9 Calle, Barrio Concepción, Comayagüela, T237-4897; **Hotel Sandoval**, T653-3098, Nueva Ocotepeque). Buses to **San Pedro Sula** stop at La Entrada (US$1.70), 1st at 0030, for connections to Copán. There are splendid mountain views. From **San Pedro Sula** there are regular buses via Santa Rosa south (6 hrs, US$4.50); road is well paved.

Directory

Copán Ruinas *p804, map p805*
Banks **Banco Atlántida** with an ATM and **Banco de Occidente** are both on the plaza and change TCs and take Visa. **BAC**, has similar services and an ATM for MasterCard and AmEx. Guatemalan currency can be changed at Copán; it is possible to change quetzales near where buses leave for the border or with money changers behind Hotel Marina. **Internet** **Copán Net**, 1 block southwest of Parque Central, daily 0800-2100 (but Sat morning is for local children), La 2 per min. **Maya Connections**, next to Los Gemelos, US$1.50/ hr, daily 0730-1800. **Language schools** **Academia de Español Guacamaya**, T/F651-4360, www.guacamaya.com, classes US$130 a week, with homestay US$200, recommended. **Ixbalanque**, T/F651-4432, www.ixbalanque.com, 1-1 teaching plus board and lodging with local family, US$135 for 4 hrs teaching a day for 4 days, US$210

for classes and 7 days homestay. **Post office** Next to the market, Mon-Fri 0800-1200, 1300-1700, Sat 0800-1200, beautiful stamps available. Max 4 kgs by airmail. **Telephone** Phone calls can be made from the office of Hondutel 0800-2100.

Santa Rosa de Copán and around *p809, map p809*

Banks Atlántida (has Visa ATM, maximum withdrawal US$30) and Banco de Occidente both have ATMs and are on main plaza. **Cultural centre** ½ block south of Parque Central with live music and singing, sculpture and picture galley. **Immigration** Av Alvaro Contreras y 2 Calle NO, helpful, extensions available. **Internet** Pizza Pizza, has email at US$4 per hr, good machines. Prodigy, C Centenario, US$1 per hr, also across the road from the Hotel Copán, US$2 per hr. **Laundry** Lavandaría Florencia, Calle Centenario. **Medical services** Dentist: Dr Wilfredo Urquía, at Calle Real Centenario 3-4 Av NE, speaks English. Recommended. Doctors: Clínica Médica Las Gemas, 2 Av NO, near Hotel Elvir, T666-1428, run by Dr Soheil Rajabian (speaks English among other languages), 1st-class attention. Hospital: Médico Quirúrgico, Barrio Miraflores, Carretera Internacional, T/F662-1283, fast and efficient, but not cheap. **Post office and telephone** The post office and Hondutel are on the park, opposite side to the cathedral. **Voluntary work** Hogar San Antonio, run by nuns across the street from the Parque Infantil (city playground), welcomes volunteers, as does the Cultural Centre.

Gracias *p811, map p812*

Banks Bancafé, Bancrecer and Banco de Occidente, but none take Visa yet. **Cultural centres** Music lessons including marimba and flute, available from Ramón Alvarenga, 2 blocks west of the Parque Central on the same side as Iglesia San Marcos. **Post office and telephone** Hondutel and post office 1 block south of Parque Central, closes 1100 on Sat.

La Esperanza *p813*

Banks Banco de Occidente, Banco Atlántida and Banadesa. **Internet** Couple of new places, one near the cathedral, US$4 per hr.

Marcala and around *p813*

Banks Banco de Occidente, Bancafé and Banco Sogerín.

Nueva Ocotepeque *p815*

Banks Banco de Occidente will change TCs. Banco Atlántida has Visa facilities.

Tegucigalpa to San Pedro Sula

The main road connecting Tegucigalpa and the country's second largest city, San Pedro Sula, heads north through beautiful scenery along the shore of Lago Yojoa, skirting villages of the Lenca communities. Alhough the tendency is to head north for the warmth and beauty of the beaches, a slow gentle journey along the road can be very rewarding. » *For Sleeping, Eating and other listings, see page 828-835.*

Támara and Zambrano → *See Around Tegucigalpa map, page 794.*

The Northern Highway between Tegucigalpa and San Pedro Sula leaves the capital and enters the vast valley of Támara, with the village of the same name. A turning leads to the **San Matías waterfall**, in a delightful area for walking in cool forested mountains.

The road climbs to the forested heights of **Parque Aventuras** ⓘ *open at weekends*, at Km 33, good food, swimming pools, horses, bikes, then to **Zambrano** (altitude: 1450 m) at Km 34 and, at Km 36, midway between Tegucigalpa and Comayagua, **Parque Aurora** ⓘ *camping US$0.50 per person, admission US$0.70, food supplies nearby*. It has a small zoo, good swimming pools and a picnic area among pine-covered hills, a lake with rowing boats (hire US$1 per hour), a snack bar and lovely scenery. The birdwatching is good too.

Before descending to the Comayagua Valley, the Northern Highway reaches another forested mountainous escarpment. A track leads off to the right (ask for directions), with about 30 minutes' climb on foot to a tableland and the natural fortress of **Tenampua**, where the indigenous put up their last resistance to the conquistadores, even after the death of Lempira. It has an interesting wall and entrance portal.

Comayagua and around » pp828-835.

Colour map 6, B2.

→ *Population: 59,535. Altitude: 550 m.*

Founded on 7 December 1537 as Villa Santa María de Comayagua on the site of an indigenous village by Alonzo de Cáceres, Comayagua is a colonial town in the rich Comayagua plain, 1½ hours' drive (93 km) north from the capital. On 3 September 1543, it was designated the Seat of the Audiencia de los Confines by King Felipe II of Spain. President Marco Aurelio Soto transferred the capital to Tegucigalpa in 1880.

There are many old colonial buildings in Comayagua, reflecting the importance of Honduras' first capital after Independence in 1821. The city is looking a little jaded these days, but is still worth a visit for the impressive architecture. Comayagua was declared a city in 1557, 20 years after its founding. Within a couple of centuries a rash of civic and religious buildings were constructed. The former university, the first in Central America, was founded in 1632 and closed in 1842 (it was located in the Casa Cural, Bishop's Palace, where the bishops have lived since 1558). Others include the churches of **La Merced** (1550-1558) and **La Caridad** (1730), **San Francisco** (1574) and **San Sebastián** (1575). **San Juan de Dios** (1590 but destroyed by earthquake in 1750), the church where the Inquisition sat, is now the site of the Hospital Santa Teresa. **El Carmen** was built in 1785. The wealth of colonial heritage has attracted funds for renovation which have produced a slow transformation in the town. The most interesting building is the **cathedral** in the Parque Central, inaugurated in 1711, with its plain square tower and façade decorated with sculpted figures of the saints, which contains some of the finest examples of colonial art in Honduras (closed 1300-1500). Of the 16 original hand-carved and gilded altars, just four survive today. The clock in the tower was originally made over 800 years ago in Spain and is the oldest working clock in the Americas. It was given to Comayagua by Felipe II in 1582. At first it was in La Merced when that was the cathedral, but it was moved to the new cathedral in 1715. Half a block north of the cathedral is the **ecclesiastical museum** ⓘ *daily 0930-1200, 1400-1700, US$0.60*. One block south of the cathedral, at the corner of 6 Calle and 1 Avenida NO, is the **Museo de Arqueología** ⓘ *Wed-Fri 0800-1600, Sat and Sun 0900-1200, 1300-1600, US$1.70* (housed in the former Palacio de Gobernación), small scale but fascinating, with six rooms each devoted to a different period. Much of the collection came from digs in the El Cajón region, 47 km north of Comayagua, before the area was flooded for the hydroelectricity project.

There are two colonial plazas shaded by trees and shrubs. A stone portal and a portion of the façade of **Casa Real** (the viceroy's residence) still survives. Built in 1739-41, it was damaged by an earthquake in 1750 and destroyed by tremors in 1856. The army still uses a quaint old fortress built when Comayagua was the capital. There is a lively market area.

Parque Nacional Montaña de Comayagua is only 13 km from Comayagua, reached from the villages of San José de la Mora (4WD necessary) or San Jerónimo and Río Negro (usually passable). Contact **Fundación Ecosimco** ⓘ *0 Calle y 1 Av NO in Comayagua, T772-4681*, for further information about the trails which lead through the cloud forest to waterfalls. The mountain (2407 m) has about 6000 ha of cloud forest and is a major watershed for the area.

Siguatepeque → *Colour map 6, B2. Population: 39,165. Altitude: 1150 m.*

The Northern Highway crosses the Comayagua plain, part of the gap in the mountains which stretches from the Gulf of Fonseca to the Ulúa lowlands. Set in forested highlands 32 km northwest of Comayagua is the town of Siguatepeque, which has a cool climate. It is the site of the Escuela Nacional de Ciencias Forestales (which is worth a visit) and, being exactly halfway between Tegucigalpa and San Pedro Sula (128 km), is a collection point for the produce of the Intibucá, Comayagua and Lempira departments. The Cerro and Bosque de Calanterique, behind the Evangelical Hospital, is a 45-minute walk from the town centre. The Parque Central is pleasant, shaded by tall trees with the church of San Pablo on the north side and the cinema, **Hotel Versalles** and Boarding House Central on the east; **Hondutel** and the post office are on the south side.

Southwest from Siguatepeque, the route to La Esperanza is a beautiful paved road through lovely forested mountainous country, via **Jesús de Otoro**, where there are two basic *hospedajes* and **Balneario San Juan de Quelala** ⓘ *US$0.30*, which has a *cafetería* and picnic sites. North from Siguatepeque, the highway goes over the forested escarpment of the continental divide, before descending towards Lago Yojoa. Just south of Taulabé on the highway are the illuminated **caves of Taulabé** ⓘ *daily, US$0.40, guides available*, with both stalactites and bats. North of Taulabé, and 16 km south of the lake is the turn-off northwest of a paved road to Santa Bárbara.

Lago Yojoa → *Colour map 6, B2. Altitude: 635 m.*

ⓘ *For local information contact Enrique Campos or his son at Motel Agua Azul (see below). For more information, contact Proyecto Humuya, behind Iglesia Betel, 21 de Agosto, Siguatepeque (T773-2426), or Proyecto de Desarrollo Río Yure, San Isidro, Cortés, Apdo 1149, Tegucigalpa.*

Sitting pretty among the mountains is the impressive Lake Yojoa, 22½ km long and 10 km wide. To the west rise the Montañas de Santa Bárbara which include the country's second highest peak and the **Parque Nacional de Santa Bárbara** (see page 826). To the east is the **Parque Nacional Montaña Cerro Azul-Meámbar**. Pumas, jaguars and other animals live in the forests, pine-clad slopes and the cloud forest forming part of the reservoir of the Lago Yojoa basin. The national parks also have many waterfalls. The 50-sq-km Azul-Meámbar park is 30 km north of Siguatepeque and its highest point is 2047 m. To get to any of the entry points (Meámbar, the main one, Jardines, Bacadia, Monte Verde or San Isidro) a 4WD is necessary. A local ecological group, **Ecolago** ⓘ *Edificio Midence Soto, Parque Central (Tegucigalpa), T237 9659*, has marked out the area and is to offer guided tours of the park. **Ecolago** has guides who are expert in spotting regional birds; at least 373 species have been identified around the lake. At one time the lake was full of bass, but overfishing and pollution have decimated the stocks. Efforts are being made to clean up the lake and limited fishing is possible.

The Northern Highway follows the eastern margin to the lake's southern tip at **Pito Solo**, where sailing and motor boats can be hired. On the northern shore of Lago Yojoa is a complex of pre-Columbian settlements called **Los Naranjos**, which are believed to have had a population of several thousand. It is considered to be the country's third most important archaeological site spanning the period from 1000 BC to AD 1000, and includes two ball courts. The site is slowly being developed for tourism by the Institute of Anthropology and History but it may take several years for the site to open to the public. For the time being there is a forest walking trail. Excavation work is currently in progress and you can visit the site, but be warned that all you will see is work in progress. The local office of the institute (T557-8197) is at the **Hotel Brisas de Lago**. From the lake it is 37 km down to the hot Ulúa lowlands.

A paved road skirts the lake's northern shore for 12 km via Peña Blanca. A road heads southwest to **El Mochito**, Honduras' most important mining centre. A bus from

2 Avenida in San Pedro Sula goes to Las Vegas-El Mochito mine for walks along the west side of Lago Yojoa. Buses will generally stop anywhere along the east side of the lake. Another road heads north from the northern shore, through Río Lindo, to Caracol on the Northern Highway. This road gives access to the Pulhapanzak waterfall, with some unexcavated ceremonial mounds adjacent, and to Ojo de Agua, a pretty bathing spot near Caracol. **Peña Blanca** is, according to one reader, a 'very ugly town' on the north side of the lake. Almost makes you want to stay.

Pulhapanzak waterfall

ⓘ *US$1. The caretaker allows camping for US$0.85.*

The impressive 42-m waterfall at Pulhapanzak is on the Río Lindo. The waterfall is beautiful during, or just after the rainy season, and in sunshine there is a rainbow at the falls. There is a picnic area, a small *cafetería* and a good *comedor* 15 minutes' walk away down in the village, but the site does get crowded at weekends and holidays.

Santa Bárbara and around → *Colour map 6, B2. Population: 23,000. Altitude: 290 m.*

Santa Bárbara, surrounded by high mountains, forested hills and rivers, lies in a hot lowland valley 32 km west of Lago Yojoa. One of the nicest main towns in Honduras, it has little of architectural or historical interest compared with Gracias, Ojojona or Yuscarán, but it is here that you will find Panama hats and other goods made from junco palm. The majority of the population is fair-skinned (some redheads) and the people are vivacious. In addition to being a pleasant place to stay, Santa Bárbara is also a good base for visiting villages throughout the Santa Bárbara Department. Nearby, the ruined colonial city of **Tencoa** has recently been rediscovered. A short local trek behind the town climbs the hills to the ruined site of **Castillo Bogran**, with fine views across the valley and the town. Heading south out of Santa Bárbara, the paved road joins the Northern Highway south of Lago Yojoa.

The Department of Santa Bárbara is called the Cuna de los Artesanos (cradle of artisans), with over 10,000 craftspeople involved in the manufacture of handicrafts. The main products come from the small junco palm, for example fine hats and baskets. The main towns for junco items are **La Arada**, 25 minutes from Santa Bárbara on the road to San Nicolás, and then branching off south, and **Ceguaca**, on a side road off the road to Tegucigalpa. Flowers and dolls from corn husks are made in Nueva Celilac. Mezcal is used to make carpets, rugs and hammocks, which are easy to find in towns such as **Ilama**, on the road to San Pedro Sula, which has one of the best small colonial churches in Honduras (no accommodation). People here also make *petates* (rugs) and purses.

Between Santa Bárbara and Lago Yojoa is the **Parque Nacional de Santa Bárbara** which contains the country's second highest peak, Montaña de Santa Bárbara at 2744 m. The rock is principally limestone with many subterranean caves. There is little tourist development as yet, with just one trail, and you can track down a guide in Los Andes, a village above Peña Blanca and Las Vegas. The best time to visit is the dry season, January to June. For more information contact **Asociación Ecológica Corazón Verde** ⓘ *Palacio Municipal, Santa Bárbara*. There is a **Cohdefor** office just below the market (look for the sign) but they are not helpful.

San Pedro Sula and around

⏩ *pp828-835. Colour map 6, B2.*

→ *Population: 483,384. Altitude: 60-150 m.*

San Pedro Sula is the second largest and most industrialized city in the country and a centre for the banana, coffee, sugar and timber trades. It is a distribution hub for northern and western Honduras with good road links. Its business community is mainly of Arab origin, and it is considered the fastest-growing city between Mexico and Panama. By Central American standards, San Pedro Sula is a well-planned, modern city, but it's not a city you'll be inclined to stay in for long.

Ins and outs

Getting there San Pedro Sula is a more important international gateway than Tegucigalpa. Its airport, Ramón Villeda Morales (SAP) is 15 km from the city centre along a good four-lane highway. There is no bus station; companies have their own terminals, mostly in the southwest part of the city. See also Transport, page 833.

Getting around The city is divided into four quadrants: Noreste (Northeast, NE), Noroeste (Northwest, NO), Sudeste (Southeast, SE) and Sudoeste (Southwest, SO), where most of the hotels are located, although newer hotels, shopping malls and restaurant chains are in the Noroeste. There are buses, minibuses and taxis for getting around town.

Best time to visit Although pleasant in the cooler season from November to February, temperatures are very high for the rest of the year. It is, nevertheless, a green city, clean and the traffic is not too bad.

Background

The city was founded by Pedro de Alvarado on 27 June 1536 in the lush and fertile valley of the Ulúa (Sula) River, beneath the forested slopes of the Merendón

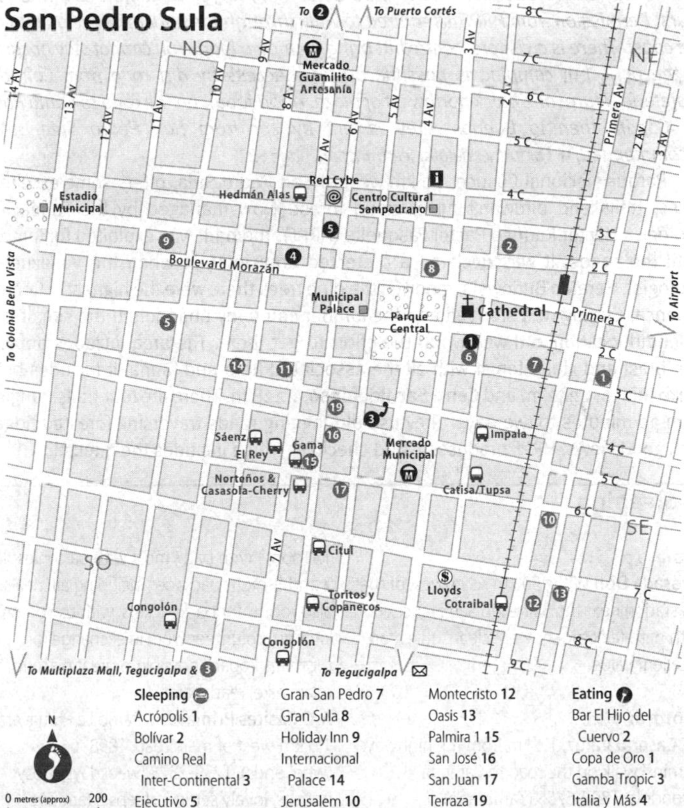

Sleeping
Acrópolis 1
Bolívar 2
Camino Real Inter-Continental 3
Ejecutivo 5
El Nilo 6
Gran San Pedro 7
Gran Sula 8
Holiday Inn 9
Internacional Palace 14
Jerusalem 10
Manhattan 11
Montecristo 12
Oasis 13
Palmira 1 15
San José 16
San Juan 17
Terraza 19

Eating
Bar El Hijo del Cuervo 2
Copa de Oro 1
Gamba Tropic 3
Italia y Más 4
La Fortuna 5

N
0 metres (approx) 200
0 yards (approx) 200

mountains. The flooding that accompanied Hurricane Mitch all but wiped out the banana plantations in the Ulúa Valley, east and north of San Pedro Sula. Now they have been replanted and exports have recommenced.

Sights

The large neocolonial-style **cathedral** was completed in the 1950s. **Museo de Antropología e Historia** ⓘ *3 Av, 4 Calle NO, Mon, Wed-Sat 0900-1600, Sun 0900-1500, US$0.75, first Sun of the month is free*, has displays of the cultures that once inhabited the Ulúa Valley up to Spanish colonization and, on the first floor, local history since colonization. There is a museum café in the adjacent garden with fine stelae and a good set lunch. **Museo Jorge Milla Oviedo** ⓘ *3 Av 9 Calle NE, Barrio Las Acacias, T552-5060*, is run by the foundation which cares for the Cuero y Salado wildlife reserve. **Expocentro** ⓘ *Av Junior, off boulevard to Puerto Cortés*, has temporary exhibitions, conferences and fairs. For train enthusiasts there is an old steam engine on display next to the train station. A taxi ride up the mountain behind the city has good views and costs US$2-2.50.

The higher and cooler suburb of Bella Vista, with its fine views over the city, affords relief from the intense heat of the town centre.

Parque Nacional Cusuco

ⓘ *Entrance is US$15 which includes a guided trip; you cannot go on your own. Contact the HRPF at 5 Av, 1 Calle NO, San Pedro Sula, T552-1014. Also contact* **Cohdefor**, *10 Av, 5 Calle NO, Barrio Guamilito, San Pedro Sula, T553-4959, or Cambio CA, who run tours. Permission from HRPF is required to walk through the park to Tegucigalpita on the coast. There is a visitors' centre but bring your own food. You cannot stay or camp in the park, but camping is possible outside. Access by dirt road from Cofradía (Cafetería Negro, one block northwest of plaza, good food), on the road to Santa Rosa de Copán, then to Buenos Aires: 2 hrs by car from San Pedro Sula, 4WD recommended.* » *For further details, see Transport, page 833.*

Parque Nacional Cusuco, 20 km west of San Pedro Sula, offers some excellent hikes, trails and birdwatching in cloud forest. Now managed by the Fundación Ecológica Héctor Rodrigo Pastor Fasquelle (HRPF), the park was exploited for lumber until the 1950s. It was declared a protected area in 1959 when the Venezuelan ecologist, Geraldo Budowski, reported the pine trees there were the highest in Central America. Cutting was stopped and the lumber company abandoned the site. It is a splendid location and well worth the effort to get there. The area includes tropical rainforest and cloud forest with all the associated flora and fauna. It includes both **Cerro Jilinco**, 2242 m, and **Cerro San Ildefonso**, 2228 m. There are four trails, ranging from 30 minutes to two days. They use old logging roads traversing forested ridges with good views. HRPF produces a bird checklist which includes the quetzal.

Sleeping

Támara *p823*

F Posada Don Willy, 500 m southwest of the toll station near the Balneario San Francisco. With bath (electric shower), clean, quiet, fan, excellent value.

Zambrano *p823*

L-E Caserío Valuz, 1½ km from the highway, 20 mins' walk on the road to Catarata Escondida, T898-6755 (Zambrano), T996-4294 (mob), www.caseriovaluz.com. 15 rooms with bath, most with balconies, 1, 2 and 3-night packages including all meals, also rooms for backpackers, with use of kitchen, volunteer work in exchange for room and board possible, a great place to relax, hike, read, paint.

A-C Casitas Primavera, Barrio La Primavera, 1½ km west of main road, T898- 6625 (weekends), T239-2328 (weekdays). Cosy houses, lovely setting, sleeps 6 (arrangements can be made for 1 or 2 people, **E**).

Comayagua and around *p824*
A-B Santa María, Km 82 on the Tegucigalpa highway, T772-7872. Private bath, a/c, cable TV. Best hotel in town, although not in the centre.
C Quan, 8 Calle NO, 3 y 4 Av, T772-0070, hquan@hondutel.hn. Excellent, with private bath, popular.
D América Inc, 2 Av y 1 Calle NO, T772-0360. A/c, hot water, private bath, TV, cheaper with fan.
D Imperial, 3 Av SO, Barrio Torondón, opposite **Norymax**, T772-0215. With bath, fan, TV, clean, friendly, good value, parking.
D-E Emperador, Calle Central y 4 Av SO, Barrio Torondón, T772-0332. Good, a/c, cable TV, cheaper with fan.
D-E Norymax, Calle Central y 3 Av SO, Barrio Torondón, T772-1210. Bath, a/c and TV, hot water, cheaper rooms available and car park.
E Honduras, 2 Av NO, 1 Calle. Clean, friendly, some rooms with bath.
E Libertad, south side of Parque Central. Nice courtyard, much choice of room size, clean apart from the toilets, cold water shower outside, helpful, good restaurant 2 doors away.
F Galaxia, Miramar, Primavera, Terminal and **Tío Luis**, are *pensiones*, all within a couple of blocks of the bus stop on the Panamericana.

Siguatepeque *p825*
D Zari, T773-2015. Hot water, cable TV, own generator, parking.
E-F Internacional Gómez, 21 de Junio, T773-2868. With bath (cheaper without), hot water, clean, parking.
F Boarding House Central, Parque Central, T773-2108. Very basic but good value; beware of the dog which bites.
F Mi Hotel, 1 km from highway on road into town. With bath, parking, restaurant.
F Versalles, on Parque Central. Excellent, with restaurant, use of kitchen on request.

Lago Yojoa *p825*
L Gualiqueme, cottage at edge of lake, for information contact Richard Joint at Honduyate, T882-3129. 4 bedrooms in main house, 2 in annexe, daily, weekly, monthly rental, weekend packages include ferry and fishing boat.
A-C Brisas del Lago, close to Peña Blanca at the northern end of the lake, T553-4884. Large hotel, good restaurant but overpriced, launches for hire.
B Finca Las Glorias, close to Peña Blanca, T566-0462, www.hotellasglorias.com. Bath, a/c, hot water, TV, bar, good restaurant, pool, great views – currently being restored.
B-C Oasi Italiana, on San Pedro Sula Highway in Yoya Cortés, some 20 km from the lake, T991-1195. Motel rooms with fans or a/c, swimming pool and great Italian food.
C Los Remos, Pito Solo, at the south end of the lake, T557-8054. Has cabins and camping facilities (**G**) and rooms in **E** range, clean, beautiful setting, good food, nice for breakfasts, no beach but swimming pool, boat trips, parking US$3.
C-D Hotel Agua Azul, at north end of lake, about 3 km west from junction at Km 166, T/F991-7244. Basic clean cabins for 2 or more persons, meals for non-residents, but food and service in restaurant is poor, beautiful gardens, manager speaks English, swimming pool, fishing, horse riding and boating, launches for hire, mosquito coils. Good reduction in low season. Recommended (except when loud karaoke is in full swing).
E D&D Brewery and Guesthouse, T994-9719, dndbrew@yahoo.com. Good rooms, with a garden with a small pool, book exchange and home brewed beer.
F Hotel Maranata, Peña Blanca. Clean, near bus stop, friendly.

Santa Bárbara and around *p826*
C-E Boarding House Moderno, Barrio Arriba, T643-2203. Rooms with fan better value than with a/c, with hot shower, quiet, parking. Recommended.
C-E Gran Hotel Colonial, 1½ blocks from Parque Central, T643-2665. Fans in all rooms, some with a/c, cold water, sparsely furnished, friendly, clean, good view from roof. Recommended.
F Ruth, Calle La Libertad, T643-2632. Rooms without windows, fan.
G Pensión, near the church, Colinas. Basic.

San Pedro Sula and around *p826, map p827*
LL Camino Real Inter-Continental, Blv del Sur at Centro Comercial Multiplaza,

T553-0000, sanpedrosula@interconti.com. Full service, new and the best in town.

AL **Gran Hotel Sula**, north side of the plaza, T552-9999, www.bestwestern.com. Excellent bargains at weekends.

AL **Holiday Inn**, Blv Morazán, 1a Calle between Av 10 and 11, T550-8080, www.holiday-inn.com. Best location in town, walking distance to the main square and restaurants.

A-B **Internacional Palace**, 3 Calle 8 Av SO, Barrio El Benque, T550-3838. A/c, helpful staff, internet service, parking, pool, bar, restaurant OK.

B-C **Ejecutivo**, 2 Calle 10 Av SO, T552-4289, www.hotel-ejecutivo.com. A/c, cable TV, café/bar, phone, own generator.

C **Acrópolis**, 3 Calle 2 y 3 Av SE, T/F557-2121. A/c, cable TV, parking, café, comfortable, friendly, good value.

C **Bolívar**, 2 Calle 2 Av NO, T553-3224. Recently redecorated (but not all rooms), a/c, TV, own generator, pool, restaurant, OK but reception unhelpful.

C **Manhattan**, 7 Av 3-4 Calle SO, T550-2316. A/c, a bit run-down.

C-E **Gran Hotel San Pedro**, 3 Calle 2 Av SO, T550-1513, www.hotelsanpedrosa.com. Private bath, a/c, cheaper with fan, popular, clean, good value, rooms overlooking street are noisy, stores luggage, secure parking.

D **Oasis**, 2 Av 7-8 Calle, T558-1502. Simple rooms in the market area.

D **Palmira 1**, 6 Calle 6 y 7 Av SO, T557-6522. Clean, very convenient for buses, large parking area.

D-E **Terraza**, 6 Av 4-5 Calle SO, T550-3108. Dining room dark, friendly staff, cheaper without a/c.

E **El Nilo**, 3 Calle 2 Av SO, T553-4689. Nice rooms, friendly.

E **Oasis**, 7 Calle 2 Av SE, T552-2650. Private bath, a/c or fan, double or twin beds, clean, but noisy.

F **Jerusalem**, 6 Calle 1 Av SE, T946-8352. Safe, good value.

F **Montecristo**, 2 Av 7 Calle SE, T557-1370. Noisy, not very clean, fan, safe.

F **San José**, 6 Av 5 y 6 Calle SO, just round corner from **Norteños** bus station, T557-1208. Friendly, clean, safe, cheap and cheerful.

F-G **San Juan**, 6 Calle 6 Av SO, T553-1488. Modern building, very noisy, clean, helpful, good value.

Eating

Comayagua and around *p824*

Parque Central is surrounded by restaurants and fast-food establishments.

₸₸₸ **Villa Real**, behind the cathedral, T772-0101. Mixes colonial atmosphere with good international and Honduran cuisine.

₸₸ **Hein Wong**, Parque Central. Chinese and international food, good, a/c, reasonable prices.

₸₸ **Las Palmeras**, south side of Parque Central, T772-0352. Good breakfasts, open for dinner and lunch, good portions, reasonable prices.

₸ **Fruty Tacos**, 4 Calle NO, just off southwest corner of Parque Central. Snacks and *licuados*.

₸ **Juanis Burger Shop**, 1 Av NO 5 Calle, near southwest corner of Parque Central. Friendly, good food, OK.

₸ **Venecia**, in front of **Supermercado Carol**, T772-1734. Popular café-style restaurant.

Siguatepeque *p825*

₸₸ **Granja d'Elia**, one of several restaurants on the Northern Highway. Open all day, lots of vegetables, also meat, all-you-can-eat buffet, French chef, veg from own market garden and bread on sale outside.

₸₸ **Juanci's**, also on main street. US-style hamburgers, good steaks and snacks, open until 2300.

₸ **Bicos**, southwest corner of Parque Central. Nice snack bar/patisserie.

₸ **Cafetería Colonial**, 4 Av SE (just behind the church). Good pastries and coffee, outside seating.

₸ **Pollos Kike**, next door. Pleasant setting, fried chicken.

₸ **Supermercado Food**, south side of plaza. Has a good snack bar inside.

Lago Yojoa *p825*

Roadside stalls near Peña Blanca sell fruit.

₸₸ **Brisas del Canal**, Peña Blanca, local food. Recommended, but small portions.

₸₸-₸ **Comedores**, on the roadside. Serve bass fish caught in the lake, with **Atenciones Evita** being a popular choice.

₸ **Comedor Vista Hermosa**, Peña Blanca. Has good, cheap food.

Cafés and bakeries

Panadería Yoja, one block from **Hotel Maranata**, Peña Blanca, good juices and pastries.

Santa Bárbara and around *p826*

🍴🍴 **Doña Ana**, 1 block above Parque Central. No sign but restaurant in Ana's dining room, crammed with bric-a-brac, only meat, rice, beans and bananas, plentiful and good food if a little boring.

🍴🍴 **El Brasero**, ½ block below Parque Central. Extensive menu of meat, chicken, fish, Chinese , good food, well prepared. Recommended.

🍴🍴 **Pizzería Don Juan**, Av Independencia. Very good pizzas.

🍴 **Comedor Everest**, by bus stop on Parque Central. Friendly, good *comida corriente*.

🍴 **Las Tejas**, near **Rodríguez**. Friendly, good pizzeria.

🍴 **McPollo**, main street. Clean, smart, good.

🍴 **Repostería Charle's**, Parque Central. Excellent cakes, pastries, about the only place open for breakfast.

San Pedro Sula and around *p826, map p827*

International restaurants in all the top hotels.

🍴🍴🍴 **Bar El Hijo del Cuervo**, 13 Calle 7-8 Av NO, Barrio Los Andes. Mexican cuisine, informal setting of *champas* in tropical garden with fountain, à la carte menu, tacos, quesadillas.

🍴🍴🍴 **La Huerta de España**, 21 Av 2 Calle SO, Barrio Río de Piedras, 4 blocks west of Av Circunvalación. Supposedly best Spanish cuisine in town. Daily until 2300.

🍴🍴🍴 **Las Tejas**, 9 Calle 16 y 17 Av, Av Circunvalación. Good steaks and fine seafood, as also at nearby sister restaurant **La Tejana**, 16 Av 19 Calle SO, Barrio Suyapa, T557-5276.

🍴🍴🍴 **Pamplona**, on plaza, opposite **Gran Hotel Sula**. Pleasant decor, good food, strong coffee, excellent service.

🍴🍴 **Applebees**, Circunvalación. Good food, good service, good prices. Highly recommended.

🍴🍴 **Chef Mariano**, 16 Av 9-10 Calle SO, Barrio Suyapa, T552-5492. Garífuna management and specialities, especially seafood, Honduran and international cuisine, attentive service, a/c, not cheap but good value, open daily for lunch and dinner.

🍴🍴 **Gamba Tropic**, 5 Av 4-5 Calle SO. Delicious seafood, good wine, medium prices, a/c.

🍴🍴 **La Espuela**, Av Circunvalación, 16 Av 7 Calle. Good grilled meats. Recommended.

🍴🍴 **La Fortuna**, 2 Calle 7 Av NO. Chinese and international, very good, not expensive, smart, good service, a/c.

🍴🍴 **Sim Kon**, 17 Av 6 Calle NO, Av Circunvalación. Arguably the best Chinese in town. Enormous portions. Try *arroz con camarones* (prawns with rice).

🍴 **Copa de Oro**, 2 Av 2 y 3 Calle SO. Extensive Chinese and western menu, a/c, pleasant. Recommended.

🍴 **Italia y Más**, 1 Calle 8 Av NO. Genuine Italian food, pizza, home-made ice-cream, very good.

🍴 **Shanghai**, 4 Av, Calle Peatonal. Good Chinese, popular on Sun, a/c.

Cafés

Café del Campo, 5 Calle 10 Av NO. Best coffee in town, 20 varieties, good à la carte breakfasts, big sandwiches, fish and prawn specialities US$6-8; bartender is cocktail specialist, smart, a/c, good service, very nice.

Café Nani, 6 Av 1-2 Calle SO. Very good *pastelería*.

Café Skandia, ground floor, **Gran Hotel Sula**. Open 24 hrs, best place for late night dinners and early breakfasts, good club sandwiches, good service.

Café Suisse, Blv los Próceres, across the street from **Frogs**, Swiss specialities.

Café Venecia, 6 Av 4-5 Calle. Good juices, cheap.

Espresso Americano, 2 branches, in Calle Peatonal, 4 Av, off southwest corner of Parque Central, and in Megaplaza shopping mall. Closed Sun, great coffee, cookies.

La Fuente de Salud y Juventud, Av 8 SO y Calle 5 and 6. Vegetarian lunch counter, generous portions, nice outside patio, get there early (1130-1200), popular, and food goes fast.

Entertainment

San Pedro Sula and around *p826, map p827*

Bars and clubs

A thriving nightlife exists beyond the casinos. **Frogs Sports Bar**, Blv Los Próceres, just above **Don Udo's**. 3 different bars, a/c, pool tables, 2nd-storey open deck overlooking their own beach volleyball court, giant TV screens showing US sports, snack bar, disco at weekends (karaoke), open 1700 until late, happy hr 1800-1900. **Mango's**, 16 Av 8-9 Calle SO, Barrio Suyapa. Open 1900 onwards, open terrace, pool tables, dance floor, rock music, snacks. Other nightclubs include **Henry's** and **Confetis**, both on Av Circunvalación NO; more exclusive is **El Quijote**, 11 Calle 3-4 Av SO, Barrio Lempira, cover charge.

Cinemas

There are 8 a/c cinemas, all showing Hollywood movies, look in local press for details.

Theatre

The Círculo Teatral Sampedrano stages occasional amateur productions (see below, Cultural centres). The **Proyecto Teatral Futuro**, is a semi-professional company presenting contemporary theatre of Latin American countries and translations of European playwrights, as well as ballet, children's theatre, and workshops. Offices and studio-theatre at 4 Calle 3-4 Av NO, Edif INMOSA, 3rd Flr, T552-3074.

Festivals and events

San Pedro Sula and around *p826, map p827*

End Jun Feria Juniana, the city's main festival.

Shopping

Siguatepeque *p825*

Leather goods A good leatherworker is Celestino Alberto Díaz, Barrio San Antonio, Casa 53, 2 Calle NE, 6 Av NE. 1 block north of Celestino's is a good shoemaker, leather shoes made for US$25.

San Pedro Sula and around *p826, map p827*

Bookshops

La Casa del Libro, 1 Calle 5-6 Av SO. Comprehensive selection of Spanish and English-language books, good for children's books and game, just off Parque Central. **Librería Atenea**, Edif Trejo Merlo, 1 Calle 7 Av SO. Wide choice of Latin American, US and British fiction, philosophy, economics and so on. **Librería Cultura**, 1 Calle 6-7 Av SO. Cheap paperbacks, Latin American classics. **Librería Editorial Guaymuras**, 10 Av 7 Calle NO. Wide range of Hispanic authors.

Food

Gourmet Foods, Blv Los Próceres, between Don Udo's and Frogs, T553-3106 (home delivery). Delicatessen with lots of expensive goodies, eg French and Dutch cheeses, caviar, smoked salmon, Italian sausages, champagne, etc. **Supermercado Los Andes**, good supermarket, strategically located at the intersection of Calle Oeste and Av Circunvalación.

Handicrafts

Large artisan market, **Mercado Guamilito Artesanía**, 6 Calle 7-8 Av NO. Typical Honduran handicrafts at good prices (bargain), with a few imported goods from Guatemala and Ecuador; also good for fruit and vegetables. Daily 0800-1700. **Danilo's Pura Piel**, factory and shop 18 Av B/9 Calle SO. **Honduras Souvenirs**, Calle Peatonal No 7, mahogany woodcraft. The **IMAPRO Handicraft School** in El Progreso has a retail outlet at 1 Calle 4-5 Av SE, well worth visiting, fixed prices, good value, good mahogany carvings. The **Museum Gift Shop**, at the Museo de Antropología e Historia has lots of cheap *artesanía* gifts open during museum visiting hours.

Activities and tours

Comayagua and around *p824*

Tour operators

Cramer Tours in Pasaje Arias. **Inversiones Karice's**, 4 Av NO, very friendly and helpful. **Rolando Barahona**, Av Central.

San Pedro Sula and around *p826, map p827*

Tour operators

Javier Pinel, PO Box 2754, T/F557-4056, local and regional tours, also offers bed and breakfast. **Maya Tropic Tours** in lobby of Gran Hotel Sula, T552-2405, www.mtthonduras.com, run by helpful Jorge Molamphy and his wife. **Mesoamerica Travel**, Col Juan Lindo, No 709 8 C and 32 Av

NO 710, T557-8447, www.mesoamerica-travel.com. Individual and group tours arranged, recommended for quality of service and reliability.

Transport

Zambrano *p823*

Bus From the capital take any bus going north to Comayagua, Siguatepeque or La Paz and tell the driver where you want to get off.

Comayagua and around *p824*

Bus To **Tegucigalpa**, US$1.10, every 45 mins, 2 hrs (Hmnos Cruz, Comayagua, T772-0850). To **Siguatepeque**, US$0.55 with Transpinares. To **San Pedro Sula**, US$1.50, 3 hrs, either catch a bus on the highway (very crowded) or go to Siguatepeque and change buses there. Incoming buses to Comayagua drop you on the main road outside town. From here you can walk or taxi into town. Buses depart from Torocagua: *colectivo* from Calle Salvador y Cervantes in town.

Siguatepeque *p825*

Bus Bus to **San Pedro Sula**, from the west end of town every 35 mins, US$1.35. **Tegucigalpa** with **Empresas Unidas** or **Maribel**, from west plaza, south of market, US$1.50, 3 hrs. Alternatively take a taxi, US$0.50, 2 km to the highway intersection and catch a Tegucigalpa-San Pedro Sula bus which passes every ½ hr. To **Comayagua**, Transpinares, US$0.50, 45 mins; to **La Esperanza** buses leave from near Boarding House Central, 1st departure 0530, several daily, taxi from town centre US$0.50.

Lago Yojoa *p825*

Bus To lake from **San Pedro Sula**, US$1, 1½ hrs; bus from lake to **Tegucigalpa** with Hedman-Alas, US$3, 3-5 hrs, 185 km.

Pulhapanzak waterfall *p826*

Bus By car it's a 1½-hr drive from San Pedro, longer by bus. There is a bus from **Peña Blanca** every 2 hrs to the falls, or take a Mochito or Cañaveral bus from **San Pedro Sula** from the bus station near the railway (hourly 0500-1700) and get off at the sign to the falls, at the village of Santa Buena Ventura, US$0.95. Alternatively stay on the bus to Cañaveral (take identification because there is a power plant here), and walk back along the Río Lindo, 2 hrs past interesting rock formations and small falls. Last bus returns at 1630 during the week.

Santa Bárbara and around *p826*

Bus To **Tegucigalpa**, 0700 and 1400 daily, weekends 0900, US$3, 4½ hrs with Transportes Junqueños (passing remote villages in beautiful mountain scenery); to **San Pedro Sula**, 2 hrs, US$1.90, 7 a day between 0500 and 1630. Bus to **San Rafael** at 1200, 4 hrs. Onward bus to **Gracias** leaves next day.

San Pedro Sula and around *p826, map p827*

Air

A taxi to the airport costs US$12 per taxi, but bargain hard. Yellow airport taxis cost US$18. Free airport shuttle from big hotels. Buses and *colectivos* do not go to the airport terminal itself; you have to walk the final 1 km from the La Lima road (bus to this point, US$0.18). Duty free, Global One phones, banks, restaurant on 2nd floor. Flights to **Tegucigalpa** (35 mins), **La Ceiba**, **Utila** and to **Roatán**. See Essentials for international flights.

Airline offices American, Ed Firenze, Barrio Los Andes, 16 Av 2-3 Calle, T558-0524, airport T668-3241. **Atlantic**, airport, T668-7309. **Continental**, Plaza Versalles, Av Circunvalación, T557-4141, airport T668-3208. **Grupo Taca** 13 Av NO corner of Norte de la Circunvalación, Barrio Los Andes, T557-0525, airport T668-3333. **Isleña**, Edif Trejo Merlo, 1 Calle 7 Av SO, T552-8322, airport T668-3333. **Sosa**, 8 Av 1-2 Calle SO, Edif Román, T550-6548, airport 668-3128.

Bus

Local Local buses cost US$0.10, smaller minibuses cost US$0.20.

Long distance **Heading south**, buses pass **Lago Yojoa** for **Tegucigalpa**, very regular service provided by several companies, 4½ hrs, 250 km by paved road. Main bus services with comfortable coaches and terminals in the town centre are: **Hedman Alas**, 7-8 Av NO, 3 Calle, T553-1361, 0830, 1330 and 1730, US$7; **Transportes Saenz**, 8 Av 5-6 Calle SO, T553-4969, US$7; **El Rey**, 7 Av, 5 y 6 Calle, T553-4264, or **Express**, 10 Av 8-9 Calle, Barrio Paz Barahona,

T557-8355; Transportes Norteños, 6 Calle 6-7 Av, T552-2145, last bus at 1900; **Viana**, Av Circunvalación, T556-9261.

Heading west from San Pedro the road leads to **Puerto Cortés**, a pleasant 45-min journey down the lush river valley. With **Empresa Impala**, 2 Av, 4-5 Calle SO No 23, T553-3111, from 0430 until 2200, US$1, or **Citul**, 6 Av, 7-8 Calle, and also on to **Omoa** (3 Calle East from 0600).

Heading east buses go to **La Lima**, **El Progreso**, **Tela** and **La Ceiba** (Tupsa and Catisa, 2 Av SO, 5-6 Calle, very regular to El Progreso, hourly to La Ceiba from 0600 and 1800, 3 hrs, US$3), some with a change in El Progreso, others direct. Also first class to La Ceiba with **Viana** at 1030 and 1730, and with **Hedman Alas** at 1000, 1400 and 1800. To **Trujillo**, 3 per day, 6 hrs, US$5, comfortable, **Cotraibal** departs from 1 Av, 7-8 Calle SE.

Heading southwest buses go to **Santa Rosa de Copán** through the Department of Ocotepeque, with magnificent mountain scenery, to the **Guatemalan border**. **Congolón**, 9 Av, 9-10 C SO, and **Empresa Toritos y Copanecos**, 6-7 Av, 11 Calle SO, serve **Nueva Ocotepeque** (US$8) and **Agua Caliente** on the Guatemalan border with 7 buses a day; **Congolón**, 8 Av 10 Calle SO, T553-1174, Torito, 11 Calle 7 Av SO, T557-3691,1 block apart.

To **Santa Rosa de Copán**, with connections at La Entrada for **Copán Ruinas**, with **Empresa Toritos y Copanecos**, T563-4930, leaving from 6-7 Av 11 Calle SO, every 20 mins, 0345-1715, 3 hrs, US$2. Take a bus to the junction of La Entrada and change for connection to Copán Ruinas if you're not going direct. 1st-class bus to **Copán Ruinas** with **Hedman Alas**, T553-1361, daily at 0950 and 1430, 3 hrs, US$14 with a/c, movie and bathrooms. Also direct service with **Casasola-Cheny Express** at 0800, 1300 and 1400.

Car

Car rentals Avis, 1 Calle, 6 Av NE, T553-0888; **Blitz**, Hotel Sula and airport (T552-2405 or 668-3171); **Budget**, 1 Calle 7Av NO, T552-2295, airport T668-3179; **Maya Eco Tours**, 3 Av NO, 7-8 Calle, and airport (T552-2670 or 668-3168); **Molinari**, Hotel Sula and airport (T553-2639 or 668-6178); **Toyota**, 3 Av 5 y 6 Calle NO, T557-2666 or airport T668-3174.

Car repairs Invanal, 13 Calle, 5 y 6 Av NE, T552- 7083, excellent service from Sr Víctor Mora.

Train

Enquire to see if services on the Tela-Puerto Cortés line continue to San Pedro Sula.

Parque Nacional Cusuco *p828*

Bus San Pedro Sula-Cofradía, 1 hr, US$0.15, from 5 Av, 11 Calle SO (buses drop you at turn-off 1 km from town); pick-up Cofradía-Buenos Aires 1½ hrs, US$1.75, best on Mon at 1400 (wait at small shop on outskirts of town on Buenos Aires road); the park is 12 km from Buenos Aires.

Directory

Comayagua and around *p824*

Banks Only BGA near Parque Central changes TCs, but others for cash include Banco Atlántida, Banco de Occidente, Banco Sogerín, Bancafé, Ficensa, Banadesa, Bamer and Banffaa. **Immigration** Migración is at 6 Calle NO, 1 Av, good place to get visas renewed, friendly. **Medical services** Dentist: Dr José de Jesús Berlioz, next to Colegio León Alvarado, T772-0054.

Siguatepeque *p825*

Banks BGA, Banco Atlántida, Banco de Occidente and Banco Sogerín.

Santa Bárbara and around *p826*

Banks Banadesa, Bancafé, Banco Atlántida, Banco de Occidente and Banco Sogerín.

San Pedro Sula and around *p826, map p827*

Banks BGA, has a beautiful mural in its head office, 5 Av, 4 Calle SO and a branch at 5 Av, 6-7 Calle SO, changes TCs. **Banco Atlántida**, on Parque Central, changes TCs at good rates. **Banco de Honduras** (Citibank). **Banco Continental**, 3 Av, 3-5 Calle SO No 7. **Banco de Occidente**, 6 Av, 2-3 Calle SO. **Bancafé**, 1 Calle, 1 Av SE and all other local banks. **BAC** for Visa, MasterCard and Amex is at, 5 Av y 2 Calle NO. These are also at **Aval Card**, 14 Av NO y Circunvalación, and **Honducard**, 5 Av y 2 Calle NO. **Cultural centres** Alianza Francesa, on 23 Av 3-4 Calle SO,

T/F553-1178, b.espana@publinet.hn, offers French and Spanish classes, has a library, films and cultural events. **Centro Cultural Sampedrano**, 3 Calle, 4 Av NO No 20, T553-3911, USIS-funded library, cultural events, concerts, art exhibitions and theatrical productions. **Embassies and consulates** Belize, Km 5 Blv del Norte, Col los Castaños, T551-0124, 551-0707. **El Salvador**, Edif Rivera y Cía, 7th floor, local 704, 5 y 6 Av 3 Calle, T/F553-4604. **France**, Col Zerón, 9 Av 10 Calle 927, T557-4187. **Germany**, 6 Av NO, Av Circunvalación, T553-1244. **Guatemala**, 8 Calle 5-6 Av NO, No 38, T/F553-3560. **Mexico**, 2 Calle 20 Av SO 201, Barrio Río de Piedras, T553-2604. **Nicaragua**, Col Trejo, 23 Av A entre 11 Calle B y 11 Calle C No 145, T/F550-3394. **Spain**, 2 Av 3-4 Calle NO 318, Edif Agencias Panamericanas, T558-0708. **Italy**, Edif La Constancia, 3rd floor, 5 Av 1-2 Calle NO, T552-3672. **Netherlands**, 15 Av 7-8 Calle NE, Plaza Venecia, Local 10, T557-1815. **UK**, 13 Av 10-12 Calle SO, Suyapa No 62, T557-2046. **Immigration** Calle Peatonal, just off Parque Central, or at the airport. **Internet** Internet cafés are found throughout town. **Internet Café**, Multiplaza centre, T550-6077, US$1/ hr. **Red Cybe Café**, Calle 3, 1 block east of the Hedman Alas bus terminal, US$1/hr. **Laundry** Excelsior, 14-15 Av Blv Morazán. **Lava Fácil**, 7 Av, 5 Calle NO, US$1.50 per load. **Lavandería Almich**, 9- 10 Av, 5 Calle SO No 29, Barrio El Benque. **Rodgers**, 4a Calle, 15-16 Av SO, No 114. **Medical services** Dentist: **Clínicas Dentales Especializadas**, Ed María Antonia, 3a Calle between 8 and 9 Av NO, apartamento L-1, Barrio Guamilito, T558-0464. **Post office** 3 Av SO between 9-10 Calle. **Telephone** Hondutel, 4 Calle 4 Av SO. Collect calls can be made from lobby of Gran Hotel Sula.

North coast

Honduras' Caribbean coast has a mixture of banana-exporting ports, historic towns and Garífuna villages that depend on their role as ports. Working from west to east the main towns of interest are Omoa, Puerto Cortés, Tela, La Ceiba and Trujillo. Hurricane Mitch dealt many of these communities a hard blow in 1998. In between the towns you will find isolated beaches and resorts, and national parks like Pico Bonito, which are perfect for hiking and whitewater rafting. The route west takes in the 'Jungle Trail' to Guatemala – which you can now do by bus.

Running parallel to the coast, a route from El Progreso runs south of the coastal mountain chain Cordillera Nombre de Dios leading to rarely visited national parks, pristine cloud forest and an alternative route to La Ceiba. » *For Sleeping, Eating and other listings, see page 845-855.*

Puerto Cortés → *Colour map 6, B2. Population: 65,000.*

Stuck out on the northwestern coast of the country and backed by the large bay of Laguna de Alvarado, Puerto Cortés is hot, tempered by sea breezes and close to many beautiful palm-fringed beaches nearby. The success of the place is its location and most Honduran trade passes through the port which is just 58 km from San Pedro Sula by road and rail, and 333 km from Tegucigalpa. It has a small oil refinery, a free zone and, being two days' voyage from New Orleans, is arguably now the most important port in Central America.

The Parque Central contains many fine trees but focuses on a huge Indian poplar, planted as a sapling in 1941, in the centre that provides an extensive canopy. The park was remodelled in 1996-1997 with new flower beds, a fountain and bronze statues.

Omoa → *Colour map 6, B2. Population: 2500.*

Omoa, 15 km from Puerto Cortés, is set in the beautiful Bahía de Omoa where the mountains, lusciously carpeted in jungle, tumble towards the sea. You can watch fine purple sunsets from the quiet laid-back bars on the beach. It has an 18th-century castle, Fortaleza de San Fernando, now renovated and worth a visit. It was built by the Spaniards to protect the coast and shipments of silver from British pirates. There is a **visitors' centre** and a small, interesting **museum** ⓘ *Tue-Sun 0800-1700, US$1.40, tickets on sale at gate, guides available.*

During the week Omoa is a quiet, friendly fishing village, but at weekends it gets a little busier with Hondurans from San Pedro, and the place becomes littered, followed by a grand clean-up the following Monday morning. Near Omoa are two waterfalls (**Los Chorros**), with lovely walks to each, and good hiking in attractive scenery both along the coast and inland.

East of San Pedro Sula

» *pp845-855.*

Tela → *Colour map 6, B2. Population: 67,890.*

Tela used to be an important banana port before the pier was partly destroyed by fire. Easily reached from San Pedro Sula with a bus service via El Progreso, it is pleasantly laid out with a sandy but dirty beach. Tela Viejo to the east is the original city joined by a bridge to Tela Nuevo, the residential area built for the executives of the American banana and farming company **Chiquita**. There is a pleasant walk along the beach east to Ensenada, or west to San Juan (see Around Tela; see also Security, below).

A **Garífuna Museum** ⓘ *at the river end of Calle 8 (also known as J Calle del Valle), T448-2856, www.tela-honduras.com, Mon-Sat 1700-1200, 1400-1700*, is an interesting and colourful introduction to Garífuna history and culture, with special emphasis on the contribution made by Honduran and Belizean Garífunas to contemporary music in the form of the frenetic rhythms of punta, a blend of rock, Afro-Caribbean and Spanish influences. Also with an art gallery of the local **Tela Artists Association**, and a museum selling *artesanía* and oil paintings.

Security In the last few years, Tela has suffered a law and order crisis, made worse by Hurricane Mitch-related problems. As of March 2002, Tela was the first place in Honduras to receive a contingent of the new specially trained Tourist Police – local reports say the changes for the better have been dramatic. Nevertheless, for the time being, express caution when walking alone and after dark.

Puerto Cortés

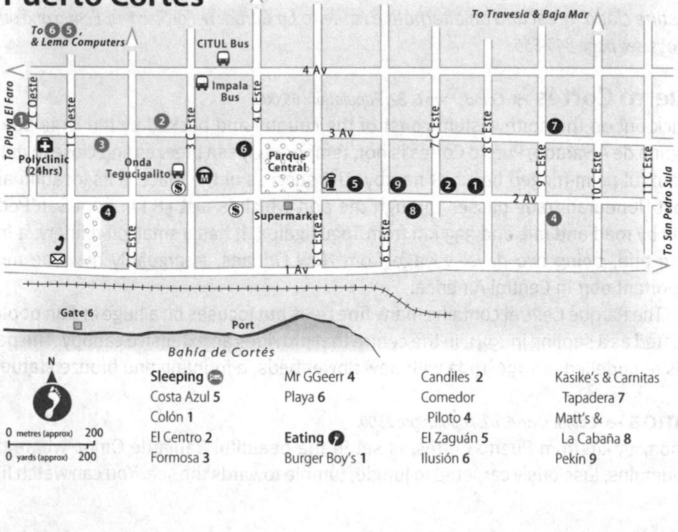

Border essentials: Honduras-Guatemala

Corinto

Honduran immigration
Immigration is now available at Corinto if crossing to Guatemala on the former 'Jungle Trail'. If taking a boat get your exit stamp from the Oficina de Migración in Puerto Cortés (see under Puerto Cortés), or Omoa.

Entering Honduras The immigration office just beyond Entre Ríos in Guatemala where the buses drop you. After crossing the border into Honduras, a pick-up will take you to Honduran immigration in Corinto. If you enter Honduras by boat you must go to immigration in Puerto Cortés as soon as possible. You may be asked for an entry tax of US$1.50. If you come from Guatemala by car you have to get a police escort from Corinto to Puerto Cortés. **Guatemalan consulate** See San Pedro Sula.

Entering Guatemala Buses leave Puerto Cortés for **Omoa** and **Corinto** on the border every hour or so (**Línea Costeños**, Ruta 3 or 4). A road now connects Puerto Cortés (Honduras) and Puerto Barrios (Guatemala), with a new bridge over the Motagua river, although one section of the journey is track. Take a bus to Corinto (as above) or, from Omoa, take a bus to Tegucigalpita (30 km) and from there a bus or pick-up to Corinto (20 km). After completing immigration at Corinto, take a pick-up from Tegucigalpita to the border crossing. The road goes through **Cuyamelito** where there is a *hospedaje* (see Sleeping, page 845), behind the bridge. From Corinto a pick-up goes 10 km to the suspension bridge at the border (a new concrete bridge is being built 800 m upriver). Across the bridge is Finca Arizona, from where there is an hourly bus to Puerto Barrios. From Cuyamelito it is still possible to go overland: it is a 2-km walk to the wharf from where a dug-out takes you through the swamps to the border, US$1.50, first at 0600, no controls. Another boat, US$2.50, on the Guatemalan side (Río Tinto) takes you to the Barra de Motagua and on to Finca la Inca banana plantation where you have to wait for a bus or hitch to Puerto Barrios. Take protection against the sun and mosquitoes, and be prepared for delays in wet season.

Around Tela

Local buses and trucks from the corner just east of the market go east to the Garífuna village of **Triunfo de la Cruz**, which is set in a beautiful bay. Site of the first Spanish settlement on the mainland, a sea battle between Cristóbal de Olid and Francisco de Las Casas (two of Cortés' lieutenants) was fought here in 1524.

Beyond Triunfo de la Cruz is an interesting coastal area that includes the cape, **Parque Nacional Punta Izopo** (1½-hour walk along the beach, take water – 12 km from Tela) and the mouth of the Río Leán. This, and its immediate hinterland, are a good place to see parrots, toucans, turtles, alligators and monkeys as well as the first landing point of the Spanish conqueror Cristóbal de Olid. For information contact **Prolansate** (see box, page 840). To get right into the forest and enjoy the wildlife, it is best to take an organized tour (see Tour operators, page 851). A trip to Punta Izopo involves kayaking through mangrove swamps up the Río Plátano, Indiana Jones style.

Further northwest, along palm-fringed beaches is **Parque Nacional Punta Sal 'Jeannette Kawas'** ⓘ *US$2*, contact **Prolansate** for information, a lovely place now protected within the park's 80,000-ha boundaries. It is one of the most important parks in Honduras and has two parts, the peninsula and the lagoon. During the dry season some 350 species of birds live within the lagoon, surrounded by forest, mangroves and wetlands. Once inhabited only by Garífuna, the area has recently suffered from the immigration of cattle farmers who have cleared the forest, causing erosion, and from a palm oil extraction plant on the Río San Alejo, which has dumped waste in the river and contaminated the lagoons. Conservation and environmental protection programmes are now under way.

Jardín Botánico at Lancetilla ⓘ *T448-1740, www.lancetilla.org, not well signposted – a guide is recommended, ask at the Cohdefor office; guide services daily 0800-1530, US$6; good maps available in English or Spanish US$0.30*, is 5 km inland, and was founded (in 1926) as a plant research station. Now, it is the second largest botanical garden in the world. It has more than 1000 varieties of plants and over 200 bird species have been identified. It has fruit trees from every continent, the most extensive collection of Asiatic fruit trees in the western hemisphere, an orchid garden, plantations of mahogany and teak alongside a 1200-ha virgin tropical rainforest. But be warned, there are many mosquitoes.

La Ceiba and around

» *pp 845-855. Colour map 6, B3.*

→ *Population: 126,721.*

La Ceiba, the capital of Atlántida Department and the third largest city in Honduras, stands on the narrow coastal plain between the Caribbean and the rugged Nombre de Dios mountain range crowned by the spectacular Pico Bonito (2435 m) – see page 841. The climate is hot, but tempered by sea winds. Once the country's busiest port, trade has now passed to Puerto Cortés and Puerto Castilla, but there is still some activity, mainly serving the Bay Islands. The close proximity to Pico Bonito National park, Cuero y Salado Wildlife Refuge and the Cayos Cochinos Marine Reserve gives the city the ambitious target of becoming an important ecotourism centre. While the opportunities aren't immediately obvious, there is definitely a buzz about town – watch out for developments. The main plaza is worth walking around to see statues of various famous Hondurans including Lempira and a couple of ponds.

A **butterfly and insect museum** ⓘ *Col El Sauce, 2a Etapa Casa G-12, T442-2874, www.hondurasbutterfly.com, Mon-Sat 0800-1200, 1300-1600, closed Wed afternoon, US$1, student reductions*, has a collection of over 10,000 butterflies,

Northwestern coast

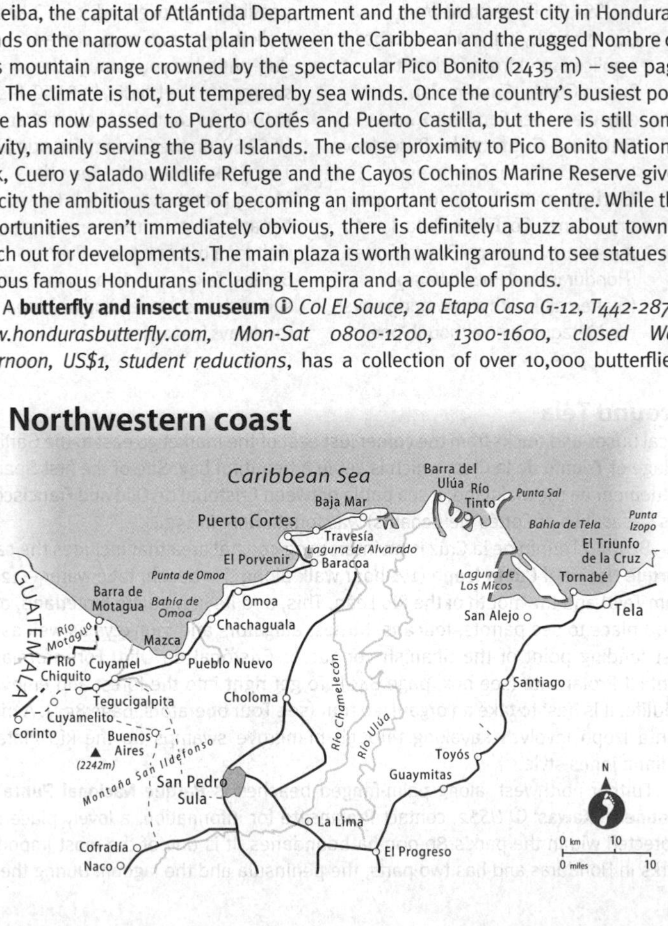

roughly 2000 other insects and snakes. Good for all ages, you get a 25-minute video in both Spanish; English and Robert and Myriam Lehman guide visitors expertly through the life of the butterfly. There is also a **Butterfly Farm** ⓘ *daily 0800-1630, entry US$6*, on the grounds of **The Lodge** at Pico Bonito.

Around La Ceiba » *See map, La Ceiba and the coast, page 840.*

Fig Tree Medical Centre ⓘ *T440-0041 (in La Ceiba), 25 km east of La Ceiba*, on the highway to Jutiapa, is a famous centre for alternative medicine. Operated by Dr Sebi, this facility is treating cancer and diabetes utilizing vegetarian diet, medications and the local hot springs. For more information or to visit call in advance. **Jutiapa** is a small dusty town with a pretty little colonial church. Contact Standard Fruit Company, Dole office in La Ceiba (off main plaza) to visit a local pineapple plantation. **Corozal** is an interesting Garífuna village near La Ceiba, at Km 209.5, with a beach, Playas de Sambrano and a hotel (see Sleeping, page 845). **Sambo Creek**, another Garífuna village, has nice beaches and a couple of hotels. Near the towns of **Esparta** and **El**

La Ceiba

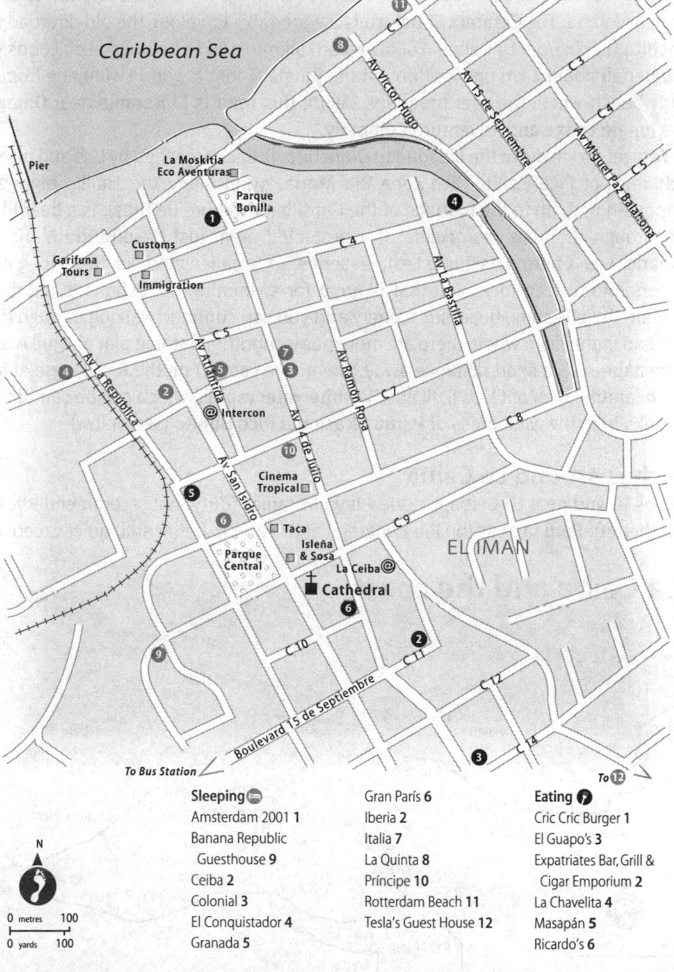

Sleeping
Amsterdam 2001 **1**
Banana Republic Guesthouse **9**
Ceiba **2**
Colonial **3**
El Conquistador **4**
Granada **5**
Gran París **6**
Iberia **2**
Italia **7**
La Quinta **8**
Príncipe **10**
Rotterdam Beach **11**
Tesla's Guest House **12**

Eating
Cric Cric Burger **1**
El Guapo's **3**
Expatriates Bar, Grill & Cigar Emporium **2**
La Chavelita **4**
Masapán **5**
Ricardo's **6**

Environmental challenge

The **Fundación Para la Protección de Lancetilla**, Punta Sal y Texiguat (Prolansate) is a non-governmental, apolitical, non-profit organization based in Tela. Originally set up by Peace Corps volunteers, it is now operated by local personnel and is involved in environmental programmes to protect and educate in conjunction with community development and ecotourism. It manages four protected areas: Parque Nacional 'Jeannette Kawas' (Punta Sal), Jardín Botánico Lancetilla, Refugio de Vida Silvestre Texiguat and Refugio de Vida Silvestre Punta Izopo. The Prolansate visitors' centre, Calle 9 Avenida 2-3 Northeast, T448-2035, www.prolansate.org, organizes trips to Punta Sal, Punta Izopo and Lancetilla, with guides, and provides information about other national parks, wildlife refuges and bird sanctuaries.

Porvenir thousands of crabs come out of the sea in July and August and travel long distances inland. The **Catarata El Bejuco** is a waterfall 7 km along the old dirt road to **Olanchito** (11 km from La Ceiba). Follow a path signposted to Balneario Los Lobos to the waterfall about 1 km upriver through the jungle. There is good swimming from a pebbly beach where the river broadens. Along this road is **El Naranjo** near **Omega Tours Jungle Lodge and Adventure Company.**

Yaruca, 20 km down the old road to Olanchito, is easily reached by bus and offers good views of Pico Bonito. **Eco-Zona Río María**, 5 km along the Trujillo highway (signposted path up to the foothills of the Cordillera Nombre de Dios), is a beautiful walk through the lush countryside of a protected area. Just beyond Río María is **Balneario Los Chorros** (signposted), a series of small waterfalls through giant boulders into a deep rock pool that is great for swimming (refreshments nearby). Upstream there is some beautiful scenery and you can continue walking through the forest and in the river, where there are more pools. Another bathing place, Agua Azul, with restaurant is a short distance away. The active can get on the **Río Cangrejal** for the exhilarating rush of Class II, III and IV **whitewater rapids**, which can be combined with treks in to the wilderness of **Parque Nacional Pico Bonito** (see below).

Beaches around La Ceiba

Beaches in and near La Ceiba include **Playa Miramar** (dirty, not recommended), **La Barra** (better), **Perú** (across the Río Cangrejal at Km 205.5, better still, quiet except at

La Ceiba and the coast

weekends, deserted tourist complex, restaurant, access by road to Tocoa, 10 km, then signposted side road 1.5 km, or along the beach 6 km from La Ceiba) and **La Encenada** (close to Corozal).

The beaches near the fishing villages of Río Esteban and Balfate are very special and are near Cayos Cochinos (Hog Islands) where the snorkelling and diving is spectacular. The Hog Islands (see page 861) can be reached by *cayuco* from **Nuevo Armenia**, a nondescript Garífuna village connected by road to Jutiapa. Take whatever you need with you as there is almost nothing on the smaller cayes. However, the Garífuna are going to and fro all the time.

Parque Nacional Pico Bonito

ⓘ *For further information on the park contact Leslie Arcantara at FUPNAPIB, at Calle 19, Av 14 de Julio, across from Suyapita Catholic church, Barrio Alvarado, T442-0618, www.picobonito.org. Maps are being prepared by Curla, see below, but are not yet available. Take care if you enter the forest: tracks are not yet developed, a compass is advisable. Tour companies in La Ceiba arrange trips to the park. A day trip, horse riding through the park, can be arranged through Omega Tours, see operators. Trip includes food and guide, US$25. Recommended. Access to Public Trails in Pico Bonito is US$6.*

Early morning is the best time for views of the Parque Nacional Pico Bonito, and for its birdlife and howler monkeys.

Pico Bonito (674 sq km) is the largest national park in Honduras and home to Pico Bonito (2435 m). The Río Cangrejal, a mecca for whitewater rafting, marks the eastern border of the park. It has deep tropical hardwood forests which shelter, among other animals, jaguars and three species of monkey, deep canyons and tumbling streams and waterfalls (including Las Gemelas which fall vertically for some 200 m).

Pico Bonito National Park has two areas open for tourism. The first is the Río Zacate area, located past the community of El Pino, 10 km west of La Ceiba; the second is on the Río Cangrejal, near the community of El Naranjo, about 7½ km from the paved highway.

A hanging bridge over the Río Cangrejal has recently been completed opening access to a new visitors' centre and El Mapache Trail up to the top of El Bejuco waterfall. Further up the road in Las Mangas, Guaruma (T442-2693) there is a very nice trail with beautiful swimming holes in a pristine creek. The trail is well maintained and local guides are available.

For the Río Zacate area, access is just past the dry stream (*quebrada seca*) bridge on the main La Ceiba to Tela highway from where the road leads to the entrance through pineapple plantations to a steep trail leading up to the Río Zacate waterfall, about one hour 20 minutes' hiking.

Good price range of accommodation available in both areas (see page 845).

Development of the park by **Curla** (Centro Universitario Regional del Litoral Atlántico) continues under the supervision of **Cohdefor**, the forestry office, and the **Fundación Parque Nacional Pico Bonito (FUPNAPIB)** ⓘ *Calle 19, Av 14 de Julio, La Ceiba, T442-0618.*

Cuero y Salado Wildlife Reserve

ⓘ *US$10 is made to enter the reserve, which you can pay at Fucsa, keep the receipt, plus US$5 per person for accommodation. The reserve is managed by the Fundación Cuero y Salado (Fucsa) Refugio de Vida Silvestre, 1 block north and 3 blocks west of Parque Central (see map) to the left of the Standard Fruit Company, La Ceiba, T/F443-0329, Apartado Postal 674. The foundation is open to volunteers, preferably those who speak English and Spanish.*

Near the coast, between the Cuero and Salado rivers, 37 km west of La Ceiba, is the Cuero y Salado Wildlife Reserve, which has a great variety of flora and fauna, including manatee, jaguar, monkeys and a large population of local and migratory birds. It extends for 13,225 ha of swamp and forest.

Nilmo, a knowledgeable biologist who acts as a guide, takes morning and evening boat trips for those staying overnight, either through the canal dug by Standard Fruit, parallel to the beach between the palms and the mangroves, or down to the Salado lagoon. Five kayaks are available for visitors' use. In the reserve are spider and capuchin monkeys, iguanas, jaguar, tapirs, crocodiles, manatee, hummingbirds, toucans, ospreys, eagles and vultures. A five-hour trip will take you to Barra de Colorado to see the manatees. Fucsa's administration centre, on the banks of the Río Salado, has photos, charts, maps, radio and a two-room visitors' house (see Sleeping, page 845). There is also a new visitor centre, with a full-service cafeteria and bilingual guides.

Trujillo and around

▸▸ *pp 845-855. Colour map 6, B3.*

➔ *Population: 45,000. www.trujillohonduras.com.*

Once a major port and the former capital, Trujillo sits on the southern shore of the palm-fringed Bay of Trujillo. It is a quiet, pleasant town with clean beaches nearby and calm water that is ideal for swimming. Christopher Columbus landed close to the area on his fourth voyage to the Americas and the town was later founded in 1525 by Juan de Medina making it the oldest town in Honduras. Hernán Cortés arrived here after his famous march overland from Yucatán in pursuit of his usurping lieutenant, Olid. Filibuster William Walker (see under Nicaragua) was shot near here in 1860; a commemorative stone marks the spot in the rear garden of the hospital, one block east of the Parque Central, and the old cemetery (near Hotel Trujillo) is his final resting place.

Fortaleza Santa Bárbara ⓘ *US$1*, a ruined Spanish fortress overlooking the bay, is worth a visit. Most of the relics found there have been moved to the museum of Rufino Galán, but there are still a few rusty muskets and cannon balls. Twenty minutes' walk from Trujillo plaza is the **Museo y Piscina Rufino Galán Cáceres** ⓘ *US$1, US$0.50 for swim*, which has a swimming pool filled from the Río Cristales with changing rooms and picnic facilities. Close by, the wreckage of a US C-80 aircraft which crashed in 1985 forms part of Sr Galán's museum. Inside the museum is more information and memorabilia about the accident. The rest of the collection is a mass of curios, some very interesting. The cemetery is rather overgrown, with collapsed and open tombs, but it does give a feel of the origins of early residents. The **Fiesta de San Juan Bautista** is in June, with participation from surrounding Garífuna settlements.

West of Trujillo, just past the football field on the Santa Fe road, is the **Río Grande**, which has lovely pools and waterfalls for river bathing, best during the rainy season. Take the path on the far side of river, after about 10 minutes cut down to the rocks and follow the river upstream along the boulders.

Beaches

Good beaches are found both on the peninsula and around Trujillo Bay. Before setting out ask which beaches are safe. Take a bus from near the Parque Central towards Puerto Castilla and ask the driver to let you off at the path about 1 km beyond the bridge over the lagoon. Other beaches around Puerto Castilla are separated by mangroves, are littered and have sandflies. The beaches in town tend to be less clean. If you're tempted to walk to find a cleaner stretch of sand don't walk alone; tourists here have been assaulted and robbed.

West of Trujillo

There are interesting Garífuna villages west of Trujillo. The road is rough, often impassable in wet weather, and jeeps are needed even in the dry season. **Santa Fe**, 10 km west of Trujillo , is a friendly place with several good Garífuna restaurants, for example **Comedor Caballero** and **Las Brisas de Santa Fe,** on the endless white sandy beach. The bus service continues to **San Antonio** (good restaurant behind the beach) and **Guadalupe.** Walk in the morning along the beach to Santa Fe and then get a bus back to Trujillo, taking plenty of water and sun block. This stretch of beach is outstanding, but watch out for *marea roja*, a sea organism which colours the water pink and can give irritating skin rashes to bathers. Also, be warned, local people consider this walk unsafe. It's best to go in a large group.

Santa Rosa de Aguán

One of the largest Garífuna communities, Santa Rosa de Aguán is an interesting coastal town, some 40 km east of Trujillo, with 7000 hospitable English- and Spanish-speaking inhabitants. The spreading settlement lies at the mouth of the Río Aguán, the greater part on the east of the bay. A white-sand beach stretches all the way to Limón, and the thundering surf is an impressive sight. Take drinking water, insect repellent, mosquito coils and high factor sun screen. To get there, see Transport, page 852.

Parque Nacional Capiro y Calentura

The Parque Nacional Capiro y Calentura encompasses these two mountains overlooking Trujillo. The four- to six-hour walk to the summit gives spectacular views and on a clear day Isla Roatán can be seen in the distance. The walk is best done early in the morning when the forest is alive with the sounds of birds, monkeys and other wildlife. The path can be reached by walking (or taking a taxi) up the hill past the **Villa Brinkley Hotel.** The road to the summit is in poor condition from the entrance of the park and can only be driven in a 4WD. Insect repellent is needed if you pause. The park is run by the **Fundación Capiro Calentura Guaimoreto (FUCAGUA)** ⓘ *Parque Central, Trujillo, Mon-Fri.* They have information on all the reserves in the area and also on hiking and tours. Until a new office is built in the park, entry tickets must be bought here before going to Capiro y Calentura. They are opening up new trails, improving old ones and organizing guided tours through parts of the forest. The hike along the

> *As with all walking in this area, it is best to go in a group to avoid attacks.*

Trujillo & the coast

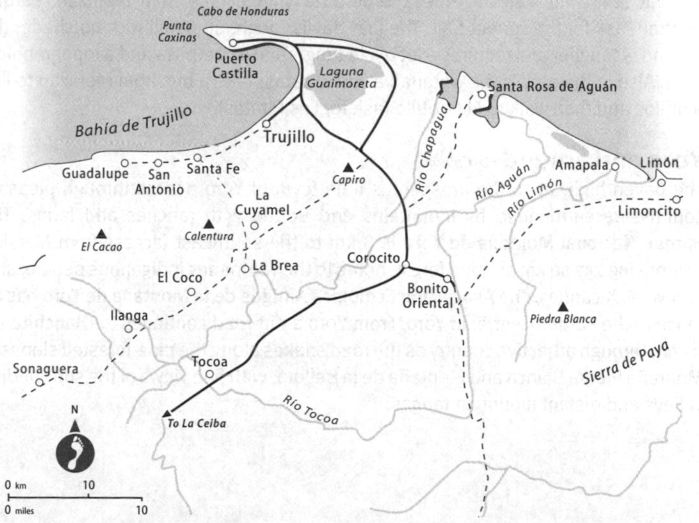

 Sendero de la Culebrina uses the remnants of a colonial stone road used to transport gold from the mines in the Valle de Aguán. Halfway up the Cerro de las Cuevas, 7 km beyond Cuyamel, are impressive caves showing traces of occupation by pre-Columbian Pech indigenous people.

Refugio de Vida Silvestre, Laguna de Guaimoreto (RVSLG)

FUCAGUA, see above, also administers the Refugio de Vida Silvestre, Laguna de Guaimoreto (RVSLG), northeast of Trujillo, where there is a bird island (Isla de los Pájaros), monkeys and good fishing. To visit, either arrange a trip with Fucagua, a tour agency such as Turtle Tours, or take a bus from Trujillo towards Puerto Castilla, get off just after the bridge which crosses the lagoon, then walk away from the lagoon for about 200 m to a dirt track on the left. Follow this and cross a low bridge and on the left is the house of a man who rents dug-out canoes. The Isla de los Pájaros is about 3 km up the lagoon, a bit too far for a dug-out. Another alternative is to go down to the wharf and hire out a motorized canoe or launch(price depends on the number of passengers and length of trip). There are no roads, paths or facilities in the area.

El Progreso and east

» *pp 845-855.*

El Progreso, an important but unattractive agricultural and commercial centre on the Río Ulúa, is 30 minutes' drive on the paved highway southeast of San Pedro Sula, en route to Tela. While most people make straight for the coast at Tela, heading east from El Progreso leads through mountain scenery up to the small town of Yoro, beyond to Olanchito and a link to La Ceiba. With everyone else rushing to the Bay Islands, you could well have the place to yourself.

Parque Nacional Pico Pijol

→ *Colour map 6, B2.*

This park protects the 2282-m summit of primary cloud forest that is home to many quetzales. It is 32 km from the town of **Morazán** in the Yoro Department, which is 41 km from Progreso (bus from Progreso or Santa Rita). In Morazán are **Hospedaje El Corazón Sagrado**, several restaurants and a disco. The lower slopes of Pico Pijol have been heavily farmed. Access by vehicle is possible as far as Subirana. A guide is needed from there to a large cave nearby and access is difficult. Another trail to the summit (2282 m) starts at **Nueva Esperanza** village (bus from Morazán, Parque Central); ask for the correct trail. The first day is tough, all uphill with no shade; the second is tougher and requires a lot of clearing. Take a compass and a topographical map. Also in the park is the waterfall at **Las Piratas**; take a bus from Morazán to Los Murillos and then walk to El Ocotillo (ask for Las Piratas).

Yoro and around

→ *Colour map 6, B2.*

The paved highway to the prosperous little town of Yoro passes through pleasant countryside surrounded by mountains and dotted with ranches and farms. The **Parque Nacional Montaña de Yoro** is 8 km to the southeast (access from Marale), comprising 257 sq km of cloud forest, home to the Tolupanes indigenous people, also known as Xicaques. The **Asociación Ecológica Amigos de la Montaña de Yoro** has an office in the Parque Central in Yoro. From Yoro a dirt road continues to **Olanchito** via **Jocón**, through attractive country as the road snakes along the pine-forested slopes of Montaña Piedra Blanca and Montaña de la Bellota, with fine views of the surrounding valleys and distant mountain ranges.

Sleeping

Puerto Cortés *p835, map p836*
Avoid 4 Calle between 1 and 2 Av and the area on 1 Av opposite the dockyards, it's unpleasant by day and dangerous at night.
AL **Playa**, 4 km west at Cienaguita, T665-1105. Hotel complex, directly on beach, cable TV, good fish dishes in restaurant. Mountain bikes for rent, available to non-guests.
B **Costa Azul**, Playa El Faro, T665-2260. Restaurant, disco-bar, billiards, table tennis, pool, horse riding, volley ball, good value.
C **Costa Mar**, Playas de la Coca Cola, T665-1367. Pleasant, with private bath, swimming pool and restaurant.
C **Mr GGeerr**, 9 Calle, 2 Av E, T665-0444. No hot water, very clean, a/c, bar, video, satellite TV. Recommended.
C-E **El Centro**, 3 Av 2-3 Calle, T665-1160. With bath, a/c, hot water, cable TV, parking, garden, café, pleasant, well furnished.
D **Frontera del Caribe**, Playas de Camaguey, road to Travesía, T665-5001. Very friendly, quiet, safe, on beach, restaurant on 1st floor, open, airy, good food, 7 rooms on 2nd floor, private bath, cold water, linen changed daily, fan. Recommended.
F **Colón**, 3 Av 2 Calle O. Diagonally opposite Hotel Puerto Limón in clapboard building, clean, safe, basic.
F **Formosa**, 3 Av 2 Calle E. With bath (some without), no towel, but soap and toilet paper provided, clean, fan, good value, friendly Chinese owner.

Omoa *p835*
C **Gemini B**, on main access road to beach, T658-9137. Bath, fan, *cafetería*, parking, lawn, comfortable.
C-D **Bahía de Omoa**, on beach, T658-9076. With bath, a/c, English, German and Dutch spoken, use of washing machine, comfortable and clean, owner Heinz has motor launch for fishing or scuba diving, sleeps 4.
D-E **Tatiana**, on beach. With bath, clean and quiet.
E **Ron's Backpackers**, about 300 m from the beach. Clean, double rooms, with screens and fans. Laundry, vegetarian and seafood restaurant with good, cheap food.
F **Hospedaje Champa Julita**, on beach, T658-9174/. Friendly, fan, basic, run-down.
F **Pia's**, on the beach, T658-9076 (same owners as **Bahía de Omoa**). Popular backpacking stop, with living room, small porch with hammocks and laundry facilities.
F **Roli's Place**, T/F658-9082, www.yaxpactours.com. 100 m from beach, clean rooms with private bath and hot water, more planned, good information here of the region, email, fax and phone service, bikes and kayaks for guests' use, games, garden and campground. Roli will change TCs, quetzales and dollars.
F **The tienda**, where the bus stops. Has cheap, basic rooms, shared bathroom, OK.

Tela *p836*
During Easter week, the town is packed; room rates double and advance booking is essential.
AL-A **Telamar**, T448-2196, www.telamar.com. A complex of wooden bungalows, set on a palm-fringed beach, rooms and villas available, restaurant, bar, golf club, swimming pool, conference centre.
B **César Mariscos**, on beach, T448-2083, www.hotelcesarmariscos.com. A/c, large rooms, restaurant.
B **Gran Central**, just south of the centre of town, T/F448-1099, www.grancentral.com. French-owned, beautifully restored historic banana port era hotel. 5 apartments, kitchen, hot water, cable TV, a/c, security, safe box in each room. Highly recommended.
B **Sherwood**, T448-1065, www.hotelsherwood.com. On waterfront, some cheaper rooms, a/c, TV, hot water, upper rooms have balconies and are airy, new pool, English-speaking owner, TCs or credit cards accepted, staff friendly and honest, restaurant busy at weekends.
B-C **Maya Vista**, top of hill, steep flight of steps starting opposite **Preluna**, T/F448-1497, www.mayavista.com. Canadian owned, French and English spoken, bath, a/c, hot water, bar, restaurant, delicious French-Canadian cuisine, fantastic views. Very highly recommended.
C **Bahía Azul**, on western end of beach, 11 Calle, 6 Av NE, T448-2381. With a/c or fan, avoid rooms on road side, good restaurant overlooking the sea, fine location.

C Ejecutivos, 8 Calle 3 Av NE, T448-1076. A/c, hot water, TV, 8 rooms with kitchenette.
C-D Tela, 9 Calle, 3-4 Av NE, T448-2150. Clean, airy, fans, hot water, will do laundry, with restaurant, but meagre breakfast, otherwise very good.
D Mango B&B, 8 Calle, 5 Av, T448-0338, www.mangocafe.net. A/c, hot water, TV, comfortable, well-furnished rooms, friendly, efficient, excellent restaurant.
E Bertha's, 8 Calle, 9 Av NE, T448-1009. Near bus terminal, new brick building, with bath, a/c, cheaper with fan, clean. Recommended.
E Mar Azul, 11 Calle, 5 Av NE, T448-2313. With fan and bath, charming helpful owner.
E Mundo Unido, Col 4 de Enero, dirección San Juan. 5 mins out of town by bus or taxi (US$1), French owned, helpful, cabins, mosquito nets, hammock space, cooking facilities, advanced horse riding US$25-30 per day. Recommended.
E-F La Posada del Sol, 8 Calle 3 Av NE, opposite **Ejecutivos**, T448-2111. With bath (cheaper without), clean, laundry facilities, nice garden.
F Sara, 11 Calle, 6 Av, behind the restaurant **Tiburón Playa**, T448-1477. Basic in a rickety old building, with bath, or without, poor sanitation. Cheapest in town, popular with backpackers, friendly, noisy especially at weekends from all-night discos.

Camping

El Retiro, out of town, 3 km on highway to La Ceiba, set back from the road by a small river, attractive setting, camping in vehicle allowed.

Around Tela *p837*

There are cheap houses and *cabañas* for rent in Triunfo de la Cruz. There is a small hotel in Río Tinto, near Parque Nacional Punta Sal; accommodation is also available in private houses.
A-B Caribbean Coral Inn, Triunfo de la Cruz, T448-2942, www.globalnet.hn/caribcoralinn. With bath, fan.
A-B The Last Resort, Tornabé, T/F984-3964. 8 bungalows for rent, some a/c, some fan, hot water, with breakfast, run by the Pacheco family, several cabins for different size groups, a great place to relax, full board available, good restaurant.
D-F Hotel El Triunfo, Triunfo de la Cruz. Rooms with bath or furnished apartments.

La Ceiba and around *p838, map p839*

La Ceiba

Electricity is irregular; have candles/torches at the ready.
AL La Quinta, at the Zona Viva, right on the beach, T440-3311, quintarealhotel.com. By far the best hotel in La Ceiba. Swimming pool, a/c, cable TV, beach, restaurant and bars.
B Gran Hotel París, Parque Central, T/F443-2391, hotelparis@psinet.hn. A/c, own generator, swimming pool, parking, good value.
B Tesla's Guest House, Calle Montecristo 212, Col El Naranjal, opposite Hospital La Fe, T/F443-3893. 5 rooms, private bathrooms, hot water, a/c, pool, phone, minibar, BBQ, laundry, friendly family owners speak English, German, French and Spanish, airport collection.
C Ceiba, Av San Isidro 5 Calle, T443-2737. With fan or a/c and bath, restaurant and bar, uncomfortable, but good breakfast.
C Iberia, Av San Isidoro, next door to **Ceiba**, T443-0401. A/c, windows without screen. Recommended.
C Italia, Av Ramon Rosas, T443-0150. Clean, a/c, good restaurant with reasonable prices, swimming pool, parking in interior courtyard.
C Paraíso, Calle 4 E, Barrio La Isla, T443-3535. Bath, a/c, hot water, TV, restaurant, 4 blocks from beach, bar, restaurant.
C-E Posada Don Giuseppe, Av San Isidro at 13 Calle, T/F442-2812. Bath, a/c (cheaper with fan), hot water , TV, bar, restaurant, comfortable.
D Banana Republic Guesthouse, Av Morazón, near Hospital d'Anthony, T440-1282, www.jungleriverlodge.com. Good, central location, clean and spacious rooms. Free internet, TV in common area. Same owners as **Jungle River Lodge**.
D Colonial, Av 14 de Julio, between 6a and 7a Calle, T443-1953. A/c, sauna, jacuzzi, cable TV, rooftop bar, restaurant with varied menu, nice atmosphere, tourist office, tours available. A bit run-down.
D El Conquistador, Av La República, T443-3670. Cheaper with fan, shared bath, safe, clean, TV.
D Príncipe, 7 Calle between Av 14 de Julio and Av San Isidro, T443-0516. Cheaper with fan and shared bath, bar/restaurant, TV.
E Amsterdam 2001, 1 Calle, Barrio La Isla, T443-2311. Run by Dutchman Jan (Don

Juan), good for backpackers, dormitory beds or rooms, with laundry, bit run-down, **Dutch Corner Café** for great breakfasts.

E **Granada**, Av Atlántida, 5-6 Calle, T443-2451, hotelparis@psinet.hn. Bath, a/c, clean, safe, cheaper with fan.

E **Rotterdam Beach**, next door to Amsterdam 2001 at 1 Calle, Barrio La Isla, T440-0321. On the beach, with bath, fan, clean, friendly, pleasant garden, good value. Recommended.

E **Tropical**, Av Atlántida between 4 y 5 Calle, T442- 2565. With bathroom, fan, basic, small rooms, noisy, sell cold drinks and water.

F **Las 5 Rosas**, Calle 8 near Av La Bastilla, opposite Esso. Clean, simple rooms, bath, fan, laundry, good value.

F **Pelican's Beat Beach Camp and Trailer Park** on Bonitillo Playa some 6 km west of La Ceiba on the road to Tela, T995-4122. Camp or sling a hammock, both available for rent. Food available, trips to nearby cayes, sea kayaking and horse riding. Regular buses from La Ceiba to Bonitillo from outside **Gran Hotel París**.

Around La Ceiba

B **Villa Rhina**, near the turn-off from the main road, Corozal, T443-1222, www.honduras.com/villarhina. With pool and restaurant.

C **Hotel Canadien**, Sambo Creek, T440-2099, www.hotelcanadien.com. With double suite, great pool and restaurant and extremely good value for money. Can arrange trips to Hog Islands for US$80 per boat. Enjoy it before the price goes through the roof.

E **Cabañas del Caribe**, in Dantillo, 5 mins out of town on the road to Tela, T441-1421, T997-8746 (mob). 6 big cabins, some with jacuzzi, and 7 rooms on the beach, restaurant serving breakfast. Video screen in restaurant. Great place to relax. Call 1 day ahead to collect from town. Buses from La Ceiba for Dantillo every 30 mins.

E **Hermanos Avila**, Sambo Creek, simple hotel-restaurant, clean, food OK.

E **Finca El Edén**, in Santa Ana, 32 km west of La Ceiba, bertiharlos@yahoo.de. Rooms, dorms, hammocks and mattresses. Good views to the sea and good food.

Beaches around La Ceiba *p840*

E **Chichi**, Nuevo Armenia. 3 small rooms, fan, mosquito net, clean, good food available.

Parque Nacional Pico Bonito *p841*

Río Cangrejo area

LL **Las Cascadas Lodge**, Km 5 Cangrejal road, T419-0030, www.lascascadaslodge.com. Exclusive lodge with just 3 rooms.

B-E **Omega Tours Jungle Lodge and Adventure Company**, El Naranjo, T440-0334, www.omegatours.hn. With wide range of options from simple rooms to comfortable cabañas and good food. Rafting and kayaking are available on the Río Cangrejal and trips to La Moskitia (see page 851).

D **Jungle River Lodge**, on Río Cangrejal overlooking Pico Bonito, T440-1282, www.jungleriverlodge.com. Private rooms and dorms, natural swimming pools, restaurant and breathtaking views. Rafting, canopy, hiking and mountain biking tours available. Activities include a free night's accommodation. Take Yaruka bus from main bus terminal, get off at Km 7; blue kayak marks entrance on river side of the road, call for arranged transport or join a tour at 0800 or 1300 from **Banana Republic Guesthouse**.

D-E **Cabañas del Bosque**, up the road from Jungle River at Las Mangas. Nice rustic cabins with spectacular views in rooms and dorms.

Río Zacate area

L **The Lodge**, Pico Bonito, T440-0388, T954-472-3881 (in the USA), www.picobonito.com. Honduras' first world-class ecolodge at the base of Parque Nacional Pico Bonito. 2 rooms, full-service nature lodge, swimming pool, gourmet restaurant, tours, guides, butterfly farm.

D **Natural View Ecoturism Center**, in El Pino, T386-9678. Very rustic cabins with access to trails in the vicinity. Cabins are built of adobe walls and thatched room, with a private bath, mosquito screens, but no power. Set in the middle of a plant nursery with a nice restaurant on premises. Efraín can help arrange several good trips nearby including a boat trip down the lower Río Zacate through mangroves to a farm located next to the beach, adjacent to Cuero y Salado.

D **Posada del Buen Pastor**, T950-3404. 4 rustic rooms on the upper story of a private home with private bath, Cable TV, and fan.

Cuero y Salado Wildlife Reserve *p841*

D-E **Refuge**, Fucsa's administration centre, on the banks of the Río Salado. Has photos, charts, maps, radio and a 2-room visitors' house, sleeping 4 in basic bunks, electricity from 1800-2100. No mosquito nets, so avoid Sep and Oct if you can. Don't wear open footwear as snakes and yellow scorpions can be found here. The refuge is becoming increasingly popular, so book lodging in advance, see page 841. Food available.

Camping There's tent space at the refuge.

Trujillo and around *p842*

L-B Christopher Columbus Beach Resort, outside town along the beach, drive across airstrip, T434-4966. 72 rooms and suites, a/c, cable TV, swimming pool, restaurant, watersports, tennis, painted bright turquoise.

B Resort y Spa Agua Caliente Silin, Silin, on main road southeast of Trujillo, T434-4249. *Cabañas* with cable TV, pool, thermal waters, restaurant, massage given by Pech Lastenia Hernández, very relaxing.

B-C Villa Brinkley (known locally as Miss Peggy's), on the mountain overlooking the bay, T434-4444. Swimming pool, good view, large rooms, wooden furniture, big bathrooms, sunken baths, fan, cheaper rooms in annex, full of character and friendly, motorbike rental, restaurant good for dinner.

C Campamento, Río Grande, Trujillo, 2 km along the road, T434-4244. Has a bar, good food, and 10 rooms, lovely setting, mountain backdrop, showers, palm trees, shade, basic but clean, ask about camping.

C Colonial, on plaza, T434-4011. With bath, hacienda style, restaurant (**El Bucanero**, see below), a/c, safe and clean.

C O'Glynn, 3 blocks south of the plaza, T434-4592. Smart, clean, good rooms and bathrooms, a/c, TV, fridge in some rooms.

D Trujillo, up the hill from the market, T434-4202. Fan, clean sheets daily, rooms with shower and toilet, TV, good value. Ask for a corner room, cockroaches in ground floor rooms, nice breeze.

E Mar de Plata, up street west, T434-4174. Upstairs rooms best, with bath, fan, friendly and helpful, beautiful view from room.

E-F Casa Kiwi, in Puerto Castilla, out of town, T/F434-3050, www.casakiwi.com. A 5-km, 15-min bus journey from town. Private rooms and dormitories, with kitchen and restaurant facilities. On a secluded beach with the benefits of internet, book swap, boat rides, horse riding, local trips and perfect for true relaxation. Buses to Puerto Castilla from the bus station every couple of hours, US$0.40. Watch when riding bikes in the area, especially at night.

E-F Catracho, 3 blocks south of church, then a block east, T434-4439. Basic, clean, noisy, no water at night, wooden cabins facing a garden, camping space US$1.50, parking.

F Buenos Aires, opposite Catracho, T434-4431. Monthly rates available, pleasant, clean, peaceful, but cabins damp and many mosquitos, organizes tours to national park.

F Coco Pando, Barrio Cristales, behind beach, T434-4748. Garífuna-owned, clean, bright airy rooms, restaurant serving typical Garífuna dishes, runs popular weekend disco nearby.

Yoro and around *p844*

D Hotel Olanchito, Barrio Arriba, Calle La Palma, Olanchito, T446-6385. A/c.

E Nelson, Yoro. Comfortable rooms with bath, fan, modern, good restaurant/bar and nice outdoor swimming pool on 3rd floor, bar/disco on roof with marvellous views. Warmly recommended.

E Valle Aguán y Chabelito, 1 block north of Parque Central, Olanchito, T446-6718. Under same management as **Hotel Olanchito**. Single rooms, with a/c, double rooms with fan, all rooms with cable TV, best in town, with best restaurant.

E-F Palacio, on main street, Yoro. All rooms with bath and fan and a good resaurant.

F Aníbal, corner of Parque Central, Yoro. Excellent value, private or shared bath, clean, pleasant, wide balcony, restaurant.

F Colonial, Calle del Presidio, Olanchito. Good value, bath, fan, cheaper with shared bath, restaurant, parking.

F Hospedaje, Jocón. Clean, basic and other accommodation, ask around.

Eating

Puerto Cortés *p835, map p836*

ΨΨ Candiles, 2 Av, 7-8 Calle. Good grills, reasonable prices, open-air seating.

ΨΨ Pekín, 2 Av, 6-7 Calle. Chinese, a/c, excellent, good service, a bit pricey but recommended. **Supermercado Pekín** next door.

Ψ Burger Boy's, 2 Av 8 Calle. Lively, popular with local teenagers.

Comedor Piloto, 2 Av 1-2 Calle. Mon-Sat 0700-1800, clean, satellite TV, fans, good value and service, popular.
El Zaguán, 2 Av 5-6 Calle, closed Sun, popular with locals, good for refreshments.
Ilusión, 4 Calle E opposite Parque. Pastries, bread, coffee, nice for breakfast.
Kasike's Restaurant-Bar-Peña, 3 Av y 9 Calle and **Carnitas Tapadera**, on same block. Recommended.
Matt's, on same block as **La Cabaña**, a/c, nice bar, good food, not expensive.
Wendy's, on the Parque. With inside play centre for children.

Cafés and ice cream parlours
Repostería y Pastelería Plata, 3 Av and 2 Calle E, near Parque Central. Good bread and pastries, excellent cheap *almuerzo*, buffet-style, kids' playroom. Recommended.

Omoa *p835*
Cayuquitos, on beachfront. Good-value meals all day, but service is very slow.
Fisherman's Hut, 200 m to right of pier. Clean, good food, seafood, recommended. Don't expect early Sun breakfasts after the partying the night before.
La Macarela, northwest end of beach. Good food, owner Silvia speaks English, good view.

Cafés and juice bars
Stanley, on the beach next door to **Cayuquitos**. Good value, with good shakes and juices.

Tela *p836*
The best eating is in the hotel restaurants.
Casa Azul, Barrio El Centro. Italian restaurant and bar, good food and nice atmosphere, French-Canadian owners, helpful.
César Mariscos (see Sleeping, above). Nice location on the beach, serves good seafood, open from 0700, very good breakfast menu.
Iguana Sports Bar, on road between 2 town bridges leading out of town. Open-air and music.
La Cueva, on the pedestrian mall. Smart, big menu includes steak, chicken, seafood, pricey.
Luces del Norte, of Doña Mercedes, 11 Calle, 2 Av NE, towards beach from Parque Central, next to **Hotel Puerto Rico**. Delicious seafood and good typical breakfasts, very popular, also good information and book exchange.
Mango Café Restaurant, by the river at the Garífuna Tours dock with views of the river, T448-2856, www.mangocafe.net. Italian, seafood and Garífuna specialities, run by owner of **Garífuna Tours**, Spanish school and internet on premises. Great place to eat before or after tours, **Garífuna Museum** on premises, and good place to meet travellers.
Maya Vista, in hotel (see Sleeping, above). Run by Québécois Pierre, fine cuisine, one of the best in Tela. Highly recommended.
Merendero Tía Carmen, at the hotel. Good food, Honduran specialities, good *almuerzo*.
Comedor Acuario, near Sara. Local food, cheap. Recommended.
Garífuna, at river end of 8 Calle. With *champas* at river's edge, typical Garífuna fare, conch soup, *tapado* (fish stew with coconut and yuca).
Iguana, 11 Calle 1 Av NE, close to old bridge. A la carte menu, pork chops speciality, open until midnight, good, disco Fri-Sun.
La Cascada, on the pedestrian mall, modest *comedor* in clapboard shack, cheap, home cooking, good, open early until late.
Los Angeles, 9 Calle, 2 Av NE. Chinese, run by Hong Kong owners, large helpings, good.
Pizzería El Bambino, 11 Calle, 50 m from new bridge. Good pasta, pizza, open-air eating on terrace, nice children's playground.
Sherwood, see Sleeping, above. Good food, popular, enjoy the view from the terrace, also opens 0700 and serves excellent breakfast.
Tuty's Café, 9 Calle NE near Parque Central. Excellent fruit drinks and good cheap lunch specials, but slow service.

Cafés and ice cream parlours
Repostería y Baleadas Tía Carmen, across the boulevard from the Merendero. Same excellent Honduran specialities, very good.

La Ceiba and around *p838, map p839*
Ricardo's, Av 14 de Julio, 10 Calle. Very good seafood and steaks, garden setting and a/c. Cracking wine list if you're looking to splash out. Recommended.

ǂǂ **Cafetería Cobel**, 7 Calle between Av Atlántida and 14 de Julio, 2 blocks from Parque Central. Could be the best *cafetería* in the entire country, very popular with locals, always crowded, good fresh food, daily specials, highly recommended. Unmissable.
ǂǂ **El Guapo's**, corner of 14 de Julio and 14 Calle. Open daily for dinner. US-Honduran owned, good combination of international and typical Honduran cuisine
ǂǂ **La Chavelita**, end of 4 Calle E, overlooking Río Cangrejal. Seafood, popular. Open daily, lunch and dinner
ǂǂ **La Plancha**, Calle 9, east of the cathedral. Best steak house in La Ceiba, with good seafood dishes. Open daily for lunch and dinner.
ǂ **Mango Tango**, on 1 Calle. The best Ceibeño cuisine in the Zona Viva. Menu includes fish, pork, chicken and beef dishes, and the best salad bar in town! Open daily for dinner from 1730. They also have a nice sports bar.
ǂǂ **Toto's**, Av San Isidro, 17 Calle. Good pizzería.
ǂ **Cric Cric Burger**, Av 14 de Julio, 3 Calle, facing attractive Parque Bonilla. Good fast food, several branches. Recommended.
ǂ **Expatriates Bar, Grill and Cigar Emporium**, at Final de Calle 12, above Refricón, 3 blocks south, 3 blocks east of Parque Central. Thu-Tue 1600-2400. Honduran-American owners, very affordable, with good steak and shrimps. Free internet service for clients. Also have a branch open at the Cangrejal River, Km 9.
ǂ **Gallo Pinto**, Calle 9, east of the cathedral. Affordable typical Honduran cuisine in a nice informal setting.
ǂ **Masapán**, 7 Calle, Av San Isidro-Av República. Self-service, varied, well-prepared choice of dishes, fruit juices, good coffee, daily 0630-2200. Recommended.
ǂ **Palace**, 9 Calle, Av 14 de Julio. Large Chinese menu, surf 'n' turf. Recommended.
ǂ **The Palm Restaurant**, centrally located, ½ a block from Parque Central in the **Banco de Occidente** building. American-style food open daily for breakfast, lunch and dinner. TVs with international news and sports. Free internet service for clients.
ǂ **Paty's**, Av 14 de Julio between 6 and 7 Calle. Milkshakes, wheatgerm, cereals, donuts, etc, purified water, clean. Opposite is an excellent pastry shop. There are 2 more Paty's, at 8 Calle E and the bus terminal.

Around La Ceiba *p839*
ǂǂ **Kabasa**, Sambo Creek. Seafood Garífuna-style, bar, delightful location.

Trujillo and around *p842*
Don't miss the coconut bread, a speciality of the Garífuna.
ǂǂ **Galaxia**, 1 block west of plaza. Good seafood, popular with locals.
ǂǂ **Oasis**, opposite BGA. Outdoor seating, Canadian owned, good meeting place, information board, good food, bar, English books for sale, book exchange, local tours.
ǂ **Bahía Bar**, T434-4770, on the beach by the landing strip next to **Christopher Columbus**. Popular with expats, also Hondurans at weekends, vegetarian food, showers, toilets.
ǂ **Don Perignon**, uphill from **Pantry**. Some Spanish dishes, good local food, cheap.
ǂ **El Bucanero**, on main plaza. A/c, video, good breakfast, *desayuno típico*.
ǂ **Pantry**, 1½ blocks from the park. Garífuna cooking and standard menu, cheap pizzas, a/c.

Entertainment

La Ceiba and around *p838, map p839*
Bars and clubs **La Casona**, 4a Calle. Most popular nightspot in town. Karaoke bar, good music, open Thu-Sat, 2000-0400. **Monaster**, 1 Calle, Thu-Sat 2000-0400. Nice setting, good a/c. Several others along 1 Calle.

Trujillo and around *p842*
Bars and clubs Head to **Rincón de los Amigos** or **Rogue's** if you're looking for drink at the end of the day. Also try the **Gringo Bar** and **Bahía Bar**. In Barrio Cristales at weekends there's punta music and a lively atmosphere. Recommended.
Cinema The cinema shows current US releases.

Festivals and events

Puerto Cortés *p835, map p836*
Aug Noche Veneciana on 3rd Sat.

Tela *p836*
Jun Fiesta de San Antonio.

La Ceiba and around *p838, map p839*
15-28 May San Isidro La Ceiba's patron saint's celebrations continue for 2 weeks, the

highlight being the international carnival on the 3rd Sat in May, when La Ceiba parties long and hard to the Afro-Caribbean beat of punta rock.

Shopping

Puerto Cortés *p835, map p836*
There is a souvenir shop, **Marthita's**, in the customs administration building (opposite Hondutel). The market in the town centre is quite interesting, 3 Calle between 2 and 3 Av. **Supertienda Paico** is on the Parque.

La Ceiba and around *p838, map p839*
Carrion Department Store, Av San Isidro with 7A Calle. **Deli Mart** late-night corner store on 14 de Julio, round corner from internet café, shuts at 2300. **El Regalito**, good-quality souvenirs at reasonable prices in small passage by large **Carrión** store. **T Boot**, store for hiking boots, Calle 1, east of Av San Isidro, T443-2499. **Supermarket Super Ceibena**, 2 on Av 14 de Julio and 6A Calle.

Trujillo and around *p842*
Garí-Arte Souvenir, T434-4207, in the centre of Barrio Cristales, is recommended for authentic Garífuna souvenirs. Owned by Ricardo Lacayo and open daily. **Tienda Souvenir Artesanía** next to Hotel Emperador, handicrafts, hand-painted toys. 3 supermarkets in the town centre.

Activities and tours

Puerto Cortés *p835, map p836*
Tour operators
Bahía Travel/Maya Rent-a-Car, 3 Av, 3 Calle, T665-2102. **Irema**, 2 Av 3-4 Calle, T665-1506. **Ocean Travel**, Plaza Eng, 3 Av 2 Calle, T665-0913.

Tela *p836*
Tour operators
Galaxia Travel Agency, 9 Calle 1 Av NE, near river, T448-2152, for reservations and confirmations of national and international flights. **Garífuna Tours**, southwest corner of Parque Central and in the **Mango Café**, T448-2904, www.garifunatours.com, knowledgeable and helpful with mountain bike hire, US$5 per day and internet service. Day trips to Punta Sal (US$22), Los Micas lagoon (US$24) and Punta Izopo (US$18). Also trips further afield to La Ceiba, Mosquita and a shuttle service between San Pedro Sula and La Ceiba, US$10 per person. Also La Ceiba to Copán, US$29. Good value. Highly recommended.

Around Tela *p837*
Tour operators
Garífuna Tours (address above) in Tela, run recommended tours for US$15 to Parque Nacional Punta Sal, food extra. Alternatively, take a motorized *cayuco* from Tela to Río Tinto beyond Punta Sal, and explore from there.

La Ceiba and around *p838, map p839*
Tour operators
Ask around to find a tour that suits your needs and to verify credentials.
Caribbean Travel Agency, run by Ann Crichton, Av San Isidro, Edif Hermanos Kawas, Apdo Postal 66, T/F443-1360, helpful, shares office with **Ríos Honduras**, T443-0780, office@rioshonduras.com, offering whitewater rafting, trips on the Río Cangrejal, spectacular, reservations 1 day in advance. **Garífuna Tours**, Av San Isidro 1 Calle, T440-3252, www.garifunatours.com. Day trips into Pico Bonito National Park (US$19 per person), Cuero y Salado (US$34), rafting on the Cangrejal (US$26), trips out to Cayos Cochinos (US$29) and a shuttle service to Tela (US$6). **Junglas River Rafting**, T440-1268, www.junglerivelodge.com. **La Ceiba Ecotours**, Av San Isidro, 1st block, 50 m from beach, T/F443-4207, hiking and riding in Parque Nacional Pico Bonito, visits to other nearby reserves, whitewater rafting, trips to La Mosquitia. **La Moskitia Eco Aventuras**, Av 14 de Julio at Parque Manuel Bonilla, T/F442-0104, www.honduras.com/moskitia, Jorge Satavero, very knowledgeable, enthusiastic and flexible. Specializes in trips to Mosquitia. Recommended. **Omega Tours**, T440-0334, www.omegatours.hn, runs rafting and kayaking trips on the Río Cangrejal, jungle hikes, and own hotel 30 mins upstream. Also tours to La Mosquitia ranging from easy adventure tours of 4 days from US$780 per person for 2, up to 13-day expeditions from US$1600. Prices drop dramatically with more people.

Cuero y Salado Wildlife Reserve *p841*

Tour operators

Although it is possible to go to the Salado and hire a villager and his boat, a qualified guide will show you much more. It is essential to bring a hat and sun lotion with you. Travel agencies in La Ceiba run tours there, but **Fucsa** arranges visits and owns the only accommodation in the reserve. Before going, check with **Fucsa** in La Ceiba. Although the office only has basic information, the people are helpful and there are displays and books about the flora and fauna to be found in the park. A guide and kayak for a 1-hr trip costs about US$10. Boatmen charge about US$20 for a 2-hr trip or US$40 for 5 hrs (6-7 persons maximum), US$6-7 for the guide.

Trujillo and around *p842*

Tour operators

Hacienda Tumbador Crocodile Reserve is privately owned, accessible only by 4WD and with guide, US$5 entry.

Turtle Tours at Hotel Villa Brinkley (see Sleeping, page 845, agency at **Oasis Café**, see Eating above), run trips to Río Plátano, 6 days, 5 nights from US$600, also to beaches, jungle hikes, etc. Very helpful even if you want to travel independently to Mosquitia, German, English, Spanish spoken, T/F434-4431, www.turtletours.de

Transport

Puerto Cortés *p835, map p836*

Bus

Virtually all buses now arrive and leave from 4 Av 2-4 Calle. Bus service at least hourly to **San Pedro Sula**, US$0.75, 45 mins, **Citul** (4 Av between 3 and 4 Calle) and **Impala** (4 Av y 3 Calle, T255-0606). **Expresos del Caribe, Expresos de Citul** and **Expresos del Atlantic** all have minibuses to **San Pedro Sula**. Bus to **Omoa** and **Tegucigalpita** from 4 Av, old school bus, loud music, very full, guard your belongings. **Citral Costeños** go to the Guatemalan border, 4-5 Av, 3C E.

Sea

If entering Puerto Cortés by boat, go to Immigration immediately. Coming from Belize there is an Immigration 'hut' on the dockside. Passports are often collected on the boat, handed in and returned as they are processed. US$1.50 entry fee, make sure that you have the stamp. This is the only official payment; if asked for more, demand a receipt.

To Guatemala Information from **Ocean Travel** at 3 Av, 2 blocks west of plaza.

To Belize Boats connecting to Belize leave from beside the bridge over the lagoon (Barra La Laguna), buy tickets at the blue wooden shack next to *joyería* near **Los Coquitos** bar just before bridge. Daily 0800-1700. The **Gulf Cruza** launch leaves Puerto Cortés on Mon at 1100, for **Mango Creek** and on to **Placencia**, 4 hrs arriving around 1340, US$50. Remember to get your exit stamp. To be sure of getting an exit stamp go to Immigration in town (address below). If arriving from Belize and heading on straight away you don't need to go into town to catch a bus. Get on to the bridge, cross over the other side and keep walking 200 m to the main road. Buses streaming past are going to San Pedro Sula and beyond.

Train

The railway station is near the harbour entrance to La Laguna de Alvarado. There are 3 trains a week (Fri, Sat and Sun) on the slow but enjoyable route to **Tela**, 0900, 4 hrs, US$1, returning at 1300 arriving at 1900. Timetables change, so check locally. Good way to travel if it fits in with your schedule.

Omoa *p835*

Boat Boats leave Omoa for **Lívingston**, Guatemala, on Tue and Fri around 1000. Ask around to confirm. Ask at **Fisherman's Hut** for Sr Juan Ramón Menjivar.

Bus A bus leaves **Puerto Cortés** at 0700 passing Omoa at 0730 to get to **Corinto** at the Guatemalan border. Buses also leave Omoa for the border at 1000, 1400 and 1700.

Tela *p836*

Bike Hire from **Garífuna Tours**, 9 Calle y Parque Central (see page 851).

Bus Catisa or **Tupsa** lines from San Pedro Sula to **El Progreso** (US$0.50) where you must change to go on to **Tela** (3 hrs in total) and **La Ceiba** (last bus at 1900). On Catisa bus ask to be let off at the petrol station on the main road, then take a taxi to the beach, US$0.50. Bus from Tela to **El Progreso** every 30 mins, US$1; to **La Ceiba**, every 25 mins, from 0410 until 1800, 2 hrs, US$1. Direct to **Tegucigalpa**, Traliasa, 1 a day from Hotel Los Arcos, US$4.50, same bus to **La Ceiba** (this service avoids San Pedro Sula); to **Copán**, leave by 0700 via El Progreso and San Pedro Sula to arrive same day. **Garífuna Tours**, see page 851, also offers a shuttle service direct to San Pedro, US$16 and Copán Ruinas, US$39.

Train The very basic, slow and enjoyable railway service to **Puerto Cortés** runs Fri, Sat and Sun at 1300, 4 hrs, US$1. Check locally for schedule. Good alternative way to travel.

Around Tela *p837*

Bus To **Triunfo de la Cruz**, US$0.40 (about 5 km, if no return bus, walk to main road where buses pass).

To get to the Parque Nacional Punta Sal you need a motor boat, or take a bus (3 a day) to Tornabé and hitch a ride 12 km, or take the crab truck at 1300 for US$0.40 (back at 1700), on to Miami, a small, all-thatched fishing village (2 hrs' walk along beach from Tornabé), beer on ice available, and walk the remaining 10 km along the beach. There are also pick-ups from Punta Sal to Miami, contact Prolansate for information.

From Río Tinto it is possible to walk west along the beach to Puerto Cortés; it is about 20 km from Río Tinto to Baja Mar (4-5 hrs' walk), from where buses run to Puerto Cortés. This would be quicker than taking buses Tela-Progreso-San Pedro Sula-Puerto Cortés, but not quicker than the train. Cayucos arrive in Tela early morning for shopping, returning to Río Tinto between 1000 and 1200, very good value.

For Lancetilla and the Jardín Botánico, either take employees' bus from town centre at 0700, or take a taxi from Tela, US$1.55, but there are few in the park for the return journey in the afternoon, so organize collection in advance.

La Ceiba and around *p838, map p839*

For La Mosquitia see page 874.

Air

Golosón (LCE), 10 km out of town. See Getting there, page 785, for international services. For full details of flights to Bay Islands, see next section. **Isleña** (T443-0179 airport), flies to **San Pedro Sula**, **Trujillo**, **Puerto Lempira**, **Roatán** and **Guanaja**; Taca and Lacsa fly to **Tegucigalpa** and **San Pedro Sula**. Sosa, the most reliable domestic airline flies to **Utila**, **Roatán**, **San Pedro Sula**, **Tegus** and others. Office on Parque Central, T443-1399. **Atlantic Air**, T/F440-2347, atlantic@caribe.hn, have the cheapest services. Standard fare to Roatán on **Sosa** or **Atlantic**. Slightly more on **Isleña**. At weekends there are some charter flights which may be better than the scheduled flights. Taxi to town US$8 per person or walk 200 m to the main road and share for US$2 with other passengers, also buses from bus station near Cric Cric Burger at end 3 Av, US$0.15. Intercity buses pass by the entrance.

Boat

Ferry schedules from the Muelle de Cabotaje, T445-1795 or T445-5056, with daily services as follows: **La Ceiba-Utila** 0815, 0930 and 1630, **Utila-La Ceiba**, 0630, 0945 and 1430, US$9. **La Ceiba-Roatán**, 1130 and 1615, **Roatán-La Ceiba**, 0600 and 1345, US$10. Boats leave from the new dock (Muelle de Cabotaje). Too far to walk, about 15-min taxi ride from town, US$2-3 per person if sharing with 4 people, buses available from centre of town.

Trips to the Hog Islands can be arranged, call T441-5987 or through **Mango Tango** restaurant. US$65 for a boat load.

Bus

Taxis from centre to bus terminal, which is a little way west of town (follow Blv 15 de Septiembre), cost US$1 per person, or there are buses from Parque Central. Most buses leave from here. **Traliasa**, **Etrusca** and **Cristina** bus service to **Tegucigalpa** via Tela several daily, US$6, avoiding San Pedro Sula (US$1 to Tela, 2 hrs); also hourly service to **San Pedro Sula**, US$2 (3-4 hrs). **Empresa Tupsa** direct to **San Pedro Sula** almost hourly from 0530 until 1800. Also 1st class with **Hedman Alas** – take taxi to separate terminal. To **Trujillo**, 3 hrs direct, 4½ hrs local (very slow), every 1½ hrs or so, US$3; daily bus La Ceiba-Trujillo-Santa Rosa de Aguán; to **Olanchito**, US$1, 3 hrs; also regular buses to **Sonaguera**, **Tocoa**, **Balfate**, **Isletas**, **San Esteban** and other regional locations.

Car

Car rental Maya Rent-a-Car, Hotel La Quinta, T443-3071. **Dino's Rent-a-Car**, Hotel Partenon Beach, T443-0404. **Molinari** in Hotel París on Parque Central, T/F443-0055.

Beaches around La Ceiba *p840*

Bus To **Nuevo Armenia** from La Ceiba at 1100 US$0.75, 2½ hrs. At the bus stop is the office where boat trips are arranged to **Cayos Cochinos**, US$10, trips start at 0700.

Cuero y Salado Wildlife Reserve *p841*

Bus To get there independently, take a bus to **La Unión** (every hr, 0600 until 1500 from La Ceiba terminus, 1½ hrs, ask to get off at the railway line, *ferrocarril*, or Km 17), an interesting journey through pineapple fields. There are several ways of getting into the park from La Unión. Walking takes 1½ hrs. Groups usually take a *motocarro*, a dilapidated train which also transports the coconut crop. From near Doña Tina's house (meals available), take a *burra*, a flat-bed railcar propelled by 2 men with poles (a great way to see the countryside) to the community on the banks of the Río Salado.

To return to La Unión, it is another *burra* ride or a 2-hr walk along the railway, then, either wait for a La Ceiba bus (last one at 1500), or ask for the short cut through grapefruit groves, 20 mins, which leads to the main La Ceiba-Tela road where there are many more buses back to town.

Trujillo and around

Boat Cargo boats leave for **Mosquitia** (ask all captains at the dock, wait up to 3 days, see page 874), the **Bay Islands** (very difficult) and Honduran ports to the west. Ask at the jetty. The trip to **Puerta Lempira** costs about US$15.

Bus Trujillo can be reached by bus from San Pedro Sula, Tela and La Ceiba by a paved road through Savá, Tocoa and Corocito. From **La Ceiba** it is 3 hrs by direct bus, 4 hrs by local. 3 direct **Cotraibal** buses in early morning from Trujillo, buses every 1½ hrs, 6 hrs, US$5. Bus from **Tegucigalpa** (Comayagüela) with **Cotraibal**, 7 Av between 10 and 11 Calle, US$6, 9 hrs; some buses to the capital go via La Unión, which is not as safe a route as via San Pedro Sula. To **San Pedro Sula**, 5 daily 0200-0800, US$5. Public transport also to **San Esteban** and **Juticalpa** (leave from in front of church at 0400, but check locally, arriving 1130, US$5.20 – see page 873). Bus to **Santa Fe** at 0930, US$0.40, leaves from outside **Glenny's Super Tienda**; to **Santa Rosa de Aguán** and **Limón** daily.

Santa Rosa de Aguán *p843*

Bus From **Trujillo**'s Parque Central Mon-Sat. Also bus service from **La Ceiba**. If driving from Trujillo, turn left at Km 343, 20 km along the highway, where a good gravel road runs another 20 km to Santa Rosa. From where the road ends at the west bank, take a canoe ferry across to the east side.

Yoro and around *p844*

Bus Hourly bus service to **El Progreso**, several daily to **Sulaco**.

Directory

Puerto Cortés *p835, map p836*

Banks All banks open Mon-Fri 0800-1700, Sat 0830-1130. BGA, 2 Av, 2 Calle. **Banco de Comercio** cashes TCs. **Banco de Occidente**, 3 Av 4 Calle E, cashes Amex TCs, accepts Visa/MasterCard. **Banco Ficensa** has ATM for MC and Amex only, 2 Av, 2C. Banks along 2 Av E, include **Atlántida** (2 Av, 3-4 Calle, has Visa ATM), **Bamer**, **BGA**, **Sogerín**. **Immigration** Migración is on 5 Av y 3-4 Calle next to Port Captain's office, daily 0800-1800. **Internet** Lema Computers, 5-6 Av, 2C, open Mon-Sat. **Medical services** Policlínica, 3 Av just past 1 Calle, open 24 hrs. **Post office** next door to **Hondutel**. **Telephone** Hondutel, at dock entrance, Gate 6, includes fax and AT&T. Direct to USA.

Omoa *p835*

Banks Banco de Occidente does not take credit cards, but will cash TCs. Some shops will change dollars. Ask around.

Immigration Migración has an office on the main road opposite Texaco. If you come from Guatemala by car you have to get a police escort from Corinto to Puerto Cortés.

Tela *p836*

Banks Banco Atlántida (with ATM), BGA, 9 C 3 Av, Visa and MasterCard cash advances and changes TCs. Also try Banadesa and Bancahorro. Casa de Cambio La Teleña, 4 Av, 9 Calle NE for US$, TCs and cash. Exchange dealers on street outside post office. **Immigration** Migración is at the corner of 3 Av and 8 Calle. **Internet** Service at the Mango Café. **Language classes** Mango Café Spanish School, US$99 for 4 hrs a day, Mon-Fri with a local tour on Sat, T448-2856, www.mangocafe.net.
Laundry El Centro, 4 Av 9 Calle, US$2 wash and dry. Lavandería Banegas, Pasaje Centenario, 3 Calle 1 Av. Lavandería San José, 1 block northeast of market. **Medical services** Centro Médico CEMEC, 8 Av 7 Calle NE, T/F448-2456. Open 24 hrs, X-rays, operating theatre, smart, well equipped.
Post office and telephone Both on 4 Av NE. Fax service and collect calls to Europe available and easy at Hondutel.

La Ceiba and around *p838, map p839*

Banks BGA, 9 Calle, Av San Isidro, and Banco Atlántida, Av San Isidro and 6-7 Calle, have ATM that accepts Visa and they will cash TCs at good rates. Cash advances on Visa and MasterCard from BAC on Av San Isidro opposite Hotel Iberia between 5 and 6 Calle; also American Express. Honducard, Av San Isidro for Visa, next to Farmacia Aurora. Better rates for US$ cash from *cambistas* in the bigger hotels (and at travel agency next door to Hotel Príncipe). Money exchange, at back of Supermercado Los Almendros, 7 Calle, Av San Isidro with Av 14 de Julio, daily 0800-1200, 1400-1800, T443-2720, good rates for US$ cash and TCs. **Internet** Hondusoft, in Centro Panayotti, 7A Calle between San Isidro and Av 14 de Julio, Mon-Fri 0800-2000, Sat 0800-1800, discount 1800-2000 when US$3 instead of US$6 per hr. La Ceiba Internet Café, Barrio El Iman, 9 Calle, T440-1505, Mon-Sat 0900-2000, US$3 per hr. **Iberia**, next to Hotel Iberia, US$0.80 per hr. **Intercon Internet Café**, Av San Isidro, opposite Atlántida ATM. **Language school** Best to do some research and look at the options. Worth considering are: Centro Internacional de Idiomas, T/F440-1557, www.hondurasspanish.com, provides a range of classes 5 days for US$150, with hotel option US$290, with branches in Utila and Roatán. Central America Spanish School, Av San Isidro No 110, Calle 12 y 13, next to Foto Indio, T/F440-1707, www.ca-spanish.com, US$150 for the week, homestay also an option adding US$70, just opened a branch on Utila. **Medical services** Doctors: Dr Gerardo Meradiaga, Edif Rodríguez García, Ap No 4, Blv 15 de Septiembre, general practitioner, speaks English. Dr Siegfried Seibt, Centro Médico, 1 Calle and Av San Isidro, speaks German. Hospital: Vincente D'Antoni, Av Morazán, T443-2264, private, well equipped. **Post office** Av Morazán, 13 Calle O. **Telephone** Hondutel for international telephone calls is at 2 Av, 5 y 6 Calle E.

Trujillo and around *p842*

Banks Banco Atlántida on Parque Central and BGA, both cash US$, TCs and handle Visa. Banco de Occidente also handles MasterCard and Western Union. **Immigration** opposite Mar de Plata. **Internet** Available in town. **Laundry** Next to Disco Orfaz, wash and dry US$2.50. **Libraries** Library in middle of square. **Medical services** Hospital on main road east off square towards La Ceiba. **Post office and telephone** Post office and Hondutel, F434-4200, 1 block up from church.

Yoro and around *p844*

Banks Banco Atlántida on Parque Central. **Post office and telephone** Post office and Hondutel 1 block from Parque Central.

Bay Islands

A string of islands off the northern coast of Honduras, the Bay Islands are the country's most popular tourist attraction. Warm, clear Caribbean waters provide excellent reef diving – some of the cheapest in the Caribbean. Equally enjoyable are the white-sand beaches, tropical sunsets and the relaxed atmosphere which positively encourages you to take to your hammock, lie back and relax. The culture is far less Latino than on the mainland. English is spoken by many and there are still Black Carib descendants of those deported from St Vincent in 1797. *►► For Sleeping, Eating and other listings, see page 862-872.*

Ins and outs

Getting there Transport to the Bay Islands is easy and there are regular and flights with **Isleña, Sosa** and **Atlantic Airlines** from La Ceiba and San Pedro Sula to Utila and Roatán. **Taca** has an international service from Miami to Roatán. There is also a daily boat service from La Ceiba to Roatán and Utila.

The islands → *www.caribbeancoast.com/bayislands/index.cfm*

The beautiful Bay Islands (**Islas de la Bahía**), of white sandy beaches, coconut palms and gentle sea breezes, form an arc in the Caribbean, some 32 km north of La Ceiba. The three main islands are **Utila**, **Guanaja** and, the largest and most developed, **Roatán**. At the eastern end of Roatán are three smaller islands: **Morat, Santa Elena**, and **Barbareta**, with many islets and cayes to explore. Closest to the mainland are the small, palm-fringed **Hog Islands**, more attractively known as **Cayos Cochinos**.

The underwater environment is one of the main attractions and is rich and extensive; **reefs** surround the islands, often within swimming distance of the shore. **Caves** and caverns are a common feature, with a wide variety of **sponges** and the best collection of **pillar coral** in the Caribbean. There are many protected areas including the **Marine Parks** of Turtle Harbour on Utila, and Sandy Bay/West End on Roatán, which has permanent mooring buoys at the popular dive sites to avoid damage from anchors. Several other areas have been proposed as marine reserves by the Asociación Hondureña de Ecología: the Santuario Marino de Utila, Parque Nacional Marino Barbareta and Parque Nacional Marino Guanaja. The Bay Islands have their own conservation association (see under Roatán, below).

The traditional industry is fishing, mostly shellfish, with fleets based at French Harbour; but the supporting boat-building is a dying industry. Tourism is now a major source of income, particularly because of the scuba diving attractions. English-speaking blacks constitute the majority of the population, particularly on Roatán. Utila has a population which is about half black and half white, the latter of British stock descended mainly from the settlers from Grand Cayman who arrived in 1830. Columbus anchored here in 1502, during his fourth voyage. In the 18th century the islands were the base for English, French and Dutch buccaneers. They were in British hands for over a century, but were finally ceded to Honduras in 1859. Latin Hondurans have been moving to the islands from the mainland in recent years.

The islands are very beautiful, but beware of the strong sun (the locals bathe in T-shirts), sandflies and other insects. Basic etiquette for snorkelling and diving applies. Snorkellers and divers should not stand on or even touch the coral reefs; any contact, even the turbulence from a fin, will kill the delicate organisms.

Utila

» pp862-872. Colour map 6, B3.

→ *Area: 41 sq km.*

Utila is the cheapest and least developed of the islands and has a very laid-back ambience. Only 32 km from La Ceiba, it is low lying, with just two hills, Pumpkin and the smaller Stewarts, either side of the town known as **East Harbour**. The first inhabitants were the Paya and there is scant archaeological evidence of their culture. Later the island was used by pirates; Henry Morgan is reputed to have hidden booty in the caves. The population now is descended from Black Caribs and white Cayman Islanders with a recent influx from mainland Honduras. Independence Day (15 September) festivities, including boxing and climbing greased poles, are worth staying for.

The **BICA Visitor Centre** ⓘ *in front of Mermaid's Restaurant*, has information on Honduran national reserves and sells Utila T-shirts. Marion Howell is the current President of BICA.

Around Utila

There are no big resorts on the island, although a couple of small, lodge-style, upmarket places have opened, otherwise the accommodation is rather basic. Sunbathing and swimming is not particularly good – people come for the diving. **Jack Neal Beach** has white sand with good snorkelling and swimming. **Chepee's White Hole** at the end of Blue Bayou peninsula has a beach for swimming. Snorkelling is also good offshore by the Blue Bayou restaurant, a 20-minute walk from town, but you will be charged US$1 for use of the facilities. There are hammocks and a jetty which is great for fishing at sunset, and the only place to get away from the terrible sandflies. There is also sandfly relief at **Big Bight**, **Redcliff** and **Rocky Point**.

You can hike to **Pumpkin Hill** (about 4 km down the lane by **BGA**, bikes recommended) where there are some freshwater caves with a beach nearby (watch out for sharp coral). It is also possible to walk on a trail from the airfield to Big Bight and the iron shore on the east coast, about 2 km, exploring tidal pools; nice views and beach but it is rocky so wear sandals.

You can visit the **Iguana Station** ⓘ *Mon, Wed and Fri 1400-1700, free*, a short walk up hill from the fire station – follow the signs.

Utila's cayes

A 20-minute motorboat ride from East Harbour are the cayes, a chain of small islands populated by fisherfolk off the southwest coast of Utila, which are known as the

Utila

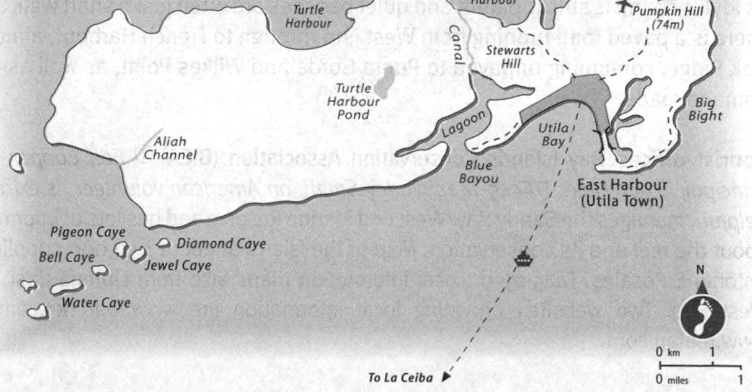

Utila's dive sites

There are currently around 50 dive sites around Utila, where permanent moorings have been established to minimize damage to the coral reef. Although the reef is colourful and varied, there are not a lot of fish, and lobster have almost disappeared. The dive sites are close to shore at about 20 m depth but they are all boat dives. Diving off the north coast is more spectacular, with drop-offs, canyons and caves. Fish are more numerous, helped by the establishment of the **Turtle Harbour Marine Reserve and Wildlife Refuge**.

Recently there have been improvements in conservation with the arrival of Coral Caye Conservation to investigate Utila. **Project Utila** started with a dive shop survey in October 1999 using 10 weeks of diving records to assess diving intensity on Utila's reefs. The project is mapping the reefs to check their health and plans to establish a programme of coral reef monitoring which can eventually be maintained by Honduran scientists. The project's aims are broad, including providing information for the management of Turtle Harbour Marine Reserve and the proposed Raggedy Caye Marine Reserve, and assessing the status of some of the marine species which are exploited for commercial and subsistence use. The long-term aim is to promote conservation of the marine ecosystems of Utila through education, training and the dissemination of information. Work on studying the migratory patterns of the whale shark, which passes through Honduran waters, has also begun on Utila.

Cayitos de Utila. **Jewel Caye** and **Pigeon Caye** are connected by a bridge and are inhabited by a fishing community which reportedly settled there to get away from the sandflies on Utila. Diamond Caye is privately owned and is looking for a new owner – in the meantime, the snorkelling offshore is excellent. **Water Caye** is a coconut island with 'white hole' sandy areas and with wonderful bathing in the afternoons. It is the only place where you can camp, sling a hammock or, in an emergency, sleep in or under the house of the caretaker; take food and fresh water, or rent the caretaker's canoe and get supplies from Jewel Caye.

Roatán

» *pp862-872. Colour map 6, B3.*

→ *Area:127 sq km.*

Roatán is the largest of the islands and has been developed quite extensively. But its idyllic charm is still apparent and quiet beaches are often just a short walk away. There is a paved road running from West End through to French Harbour, almost to Oak Ridge, continuing unpaved to Punta Gorda and Wilkes Point, as well as other unmade roads.

Tourist offices **Bay Islands Conservation Association (BICA)** ⓘ *Edif Cooper, Calle Principal, Coxen Hole, T/F445-1424 (Farley Smith, an American volunteer, is extremely helpful)*, manages the Sandy Bay/West End Marine Reserve and has lots of information about the reef and its conservation. Map of the island at about 1:50,000 supplied by Antonio E Rosales, T445-1559. Local information maps also from Librería Casi Todo, West End. Two websites providing local information are www.roatanet.com and www.roatan.com.

Coxen Hole

The capital and administrative centre of the department, Coxen Hole, or Roatán City, is on the southwest shore. Planes land and boats dock here and you can get transport to other parts of the island. It is a scruffy little town with not much of tourist interest but some souvenir shops are opening. Besides being the seat of the local government, it has immigration, customs and the law courts. There is a post office, supermarket, handicraft shops, photo shops, banks, travel agents, a bookshop and various other stores. Buses leave from outside the supermarket. All public transport starts or ends here. If taxis are shared, they are *colectivos* and charge the same as buses.

Sandy Bay

A short journey from Coxen Hole, en route to West End, is Sandy Bay, one of the quieter towns on the island. The **Carambola Botanical Gardens** ⓘ *daily 0700-1700, US$3, guided tours or nature trails*, created in 1985, contain many flowering plants, ferns and varieties of trees which can be explored on a network of trails – it is well worth a visit. The **Roatán Museum** ⓘ *US$4*, has displays covering the history of the island, with plenty of information about the pirates who called Roatán home, and a collection of artefacts. The **Institute of Marine Sciences** ⓘ *Anthony's Key Resort, Sandy Bay, Mon-Fri 1000 and 1500, Sat and Sun 1000, 1300 and 1600, US$4, free for guests*, has a dolphin pool and performances twice a day. Swimming with dolphins arranged.

West End

Five minutes by road beyond Sandy Bay, the popular community of West End is at the western tip of the island and is the most popular place to stay. It's a narrow beach on a palm-fringed bay with a distinctly relaxed and laid-back atmosphere. The **Sandy Bay/West End Marine Park** protects marine life in the area and large numbers of fish have flourished along the coast creating spectacular images for snorkellers. There are numerous good foreign and local restaurants with lots of pizza/pasta places, as well as hotels, *cabañas* and rooms to rent for all budgets. It is a stiff walk from Coxen Hole over the hills (three hours) to West End, or take the bus on the paved road (US$1, 20 minutes).

West Bay

A beautiful clean beach with excellent snorkelling on the reef, particularly at the west end, where the reef is only 10-20 m offshore and the water is shallow right up to where the wall drops off 50-75 m out and scuba diving begins. Paradise comes at a price and the sandflies here are a nightmare, but there are a couple of jetties where you can escape the sandflies which lurk in the powdery white sand. Take your own food and

Roatán

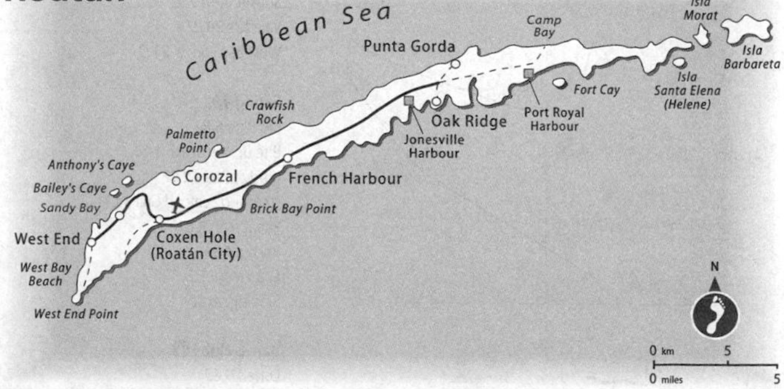

 drinks, and insect repellent. Developers have recently discovered the delights of West Bay and the atmosphere is changing fast. Apartments, hotels, bars and restaurants are springing up.

East of Coxen Hole

French Harbour, on the south coast, with its shrimping and lobster fleet, is the main fishing port of Roatán. There is no beach and there are two seafood packing plants. The road passes Coleman's (Midway) Bakery, where you can buy freshly baked

Roatán - West End & West Bay

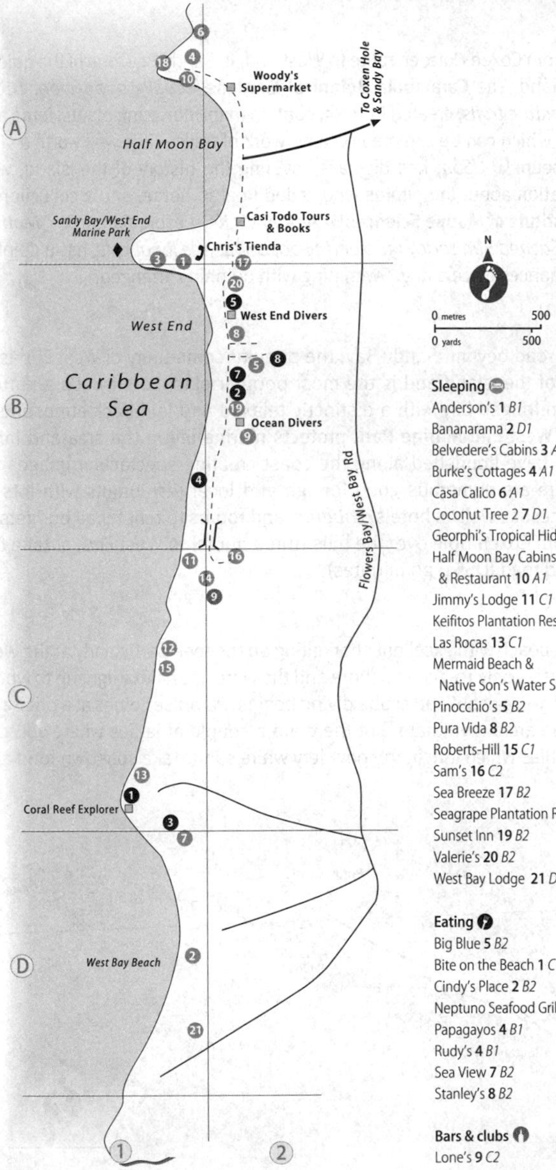

Sleeping
Anderson's **1** *B1*
Bananarama **2** *D1*
Belvedere's Cabins **3** *A1*
Burke's Cottages **4** *A1*
Casa Calico **6** *A1*
Coconut Tree 2 **7** *D1*
Georphi's Tropical Hideaway **9** *B2*
Half Moon Bay Cabins & Restaurant **10** *A1*
Jimmy's Lodge **11** *C1*
Keifitos Plantation Resort **12** *C1*
Las Rocas **13** *C1*
Mermaid Beach & Native Son's Water Sports **14** *C2*
Pinocchio's **5** *B2*
Pura Vida **8** *B2*
Roberts-Hill **15** *C1*
Sam's **16** *C2*
Sea Breeze **17** *B2*
Seagrape Plantation Resort **18** *A1*
Sunset Inn **19** *B2*
Valerie's **20** *B2*
West Bay Lodge **21** *D1*

Eating
Big Blue **5** *B2*
Bite on the Beach **1** *C1*
Cindy's Place **2** *B2*
Neptuno Seafood Grill **3** *C1*
Papagayos **4** *B1*
Rudy's **4** *B1*
Sea View **7** *B2*
Stanley's **8** *B2*

Bars & clubs
Lone's **9** *C2*

products. The bay is protected by the reef and small cayes which provide safe anchorage. Roatan Dive and Yacht Club and Romeos Marina (at Brick Bay) offer services for visiting yachts. Several charter yachts are based here. There are a few cheap, clean places to stay, as well as expensive hotels and dive resorts. Eldon's Supermarket is open daily and has a range of imported US food. **Gios Restaurant** and **Casa Romeos** serve top-quality seafood.

Across the island

The main road goes across the mountain ridge along the island with side roads to Jonesville, Punta Gorda and Oak Ridge. You can take a bus on this route to see the island's hilly interior, with beautiful views from coast to coast. Alternatively, hire a small 4WD, which is almost as cheap if shared between four people and allows you to explore the dirt roads and empty bays along the island's northern tip. **Jonesville** is known for its mangrove canal, which is best reached by hiring a taxi boat in Oak Ridge. **Oak Ridge**, situated on a caye (US$0.40 crossing in a dory from the bus stop), is built around a deep inlet on the south coast. It is a charming little fishing port, with rows of dwellings on stilts built on the water's edge (bus Coxen Hole-Oak Ridge, one hour depending on passengers, US$1.10).

Guanaja

→ *Colour maps 6,A3.* *Area: 56 sq km.*

Columbus called Guanaja the Island of Pines, but Hurricane Mitch swept most of them away. Since then, a great replanting effort has started and, until the new pines have grown, there are many flowering and fruiting plants thriving on the island. The island was declared a forest reserve in 1961, and is now designated a national marine park. Good (but sweaty) clambering on the island gives splendid views of the jungle and the sea and there are several attractive waterfalls, which can be visited on the hills rising to the summit of 415 m. The first English settler was Robert Haylock, who arrived in 1856 with a land title to part of the island, the two cayes which now form the main settlement of Bonacca and some of the Mosquito coast. He was followed in 1866 by John Kirkconnell who purchased Hog Caye, where the Haylocks raised pigs away from the sandflies. These two families became sailors, boat builders and landowners, and formed the basis of the present population.

Much of Guanaja town, locally known as **Bonacca** and covering a small caye off the coast, is built on stilts above sea water, with boardwalks and concrete pathways, hence its nickname: the 'Venice of Honduras'. There are three small villages, **Mangrove Bight**, **Savannah Bight** and **North East Bight**, on the main island. Much of the accommodation is all-inclusive resorts, but you can visit independently as well. Sandflies and mosquitoes cannot be escaped on the island, and none of the beaches offer respite (coconut oil, baby oil or any oily suntan lotion will help to ward off sandflies).The cayes are better, including Guanaja town. South West Caye is especially recommended.

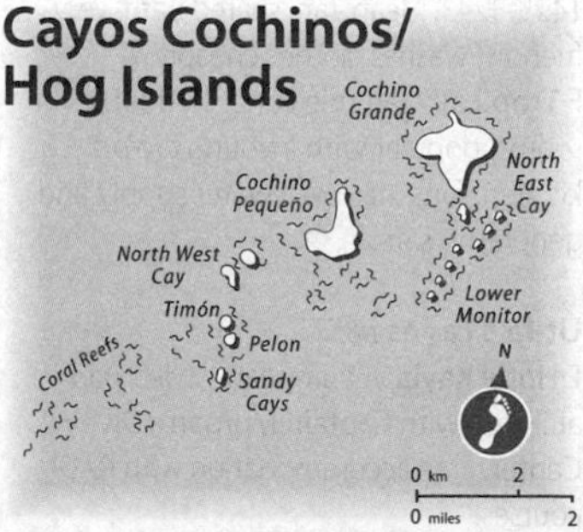

Cayos Cochinos (Hog Islands)

» pp862-872. Colour map 6, B3.

The Hog Islands, 17 km northeast of La Ceiba, constitute two small islands and 13 palm-fringed cayes. **Cochino Grande** is the larger island, rising to an altitude of just 143 m, and **Cochino Pequeño** is the smaller. Both have lush tropical vegetation with primeval hardwood forests and there are fewer biting insects than in the Bay Islands. There are Garífuna fishing villages of palm-thatched huts at Chachauate on Lower Monitor Cay, and East End Village on Cochino Grande. Transport to the Hog Islands can be sought on the supply *cayuco* from Nuevo Armenia (see page 841), or by chartering a boat from Utila. There is a small dirt airstrip. Dug-out canoes are the local form of transport. The islands are privately owned and access to most of the cayes is limited, being occupied only by caretakers. The Cayos Cochinos and surrounding waters are now a National Marine Reserve.

Sleeping

Utila *p857, map p857*
Cheaper hotels are along the main street.
L-AL Laguna Beach Resort, on point opposite Blue Bayou, T/F668-68452, www.utila.com. Comfortable lodge, with bungalows each with own jetty, 8-day package includes meals and diving US$970, non-diver US$840. Fishing offered, can accommodate maximum 40.
L-AL Utila Lodge Resort, T425-3143, www.utilalodge.com. An all-wooden building with decks and balconies, harbour view, a/c, 8 rooms, clean and modern, meals only when they have guests, dive shop (Bay Islands College of Diving) on site.
A-C Mango Inn, T425-3326, www.mango-inn.com. With bath, cheaper without, fan, spotless, helpful, roof terrace, reduction for students with **Utila Dive Centre**, good restaurant and coffee bar. Recommended.
B Utila, on water next to **Lodge**, T425-3340. Cheaper rooms downstairs, very clean, 24-hr water and power, fan, nice view, secure.
C-D Freddy's, off the boat and turn right and it's a long walk to just over the bridge, T425-3142. Good rooms, kitchens, quiet end of town.
D Bay View, T425-3114, 100 m from **Utila Lodge**. With or without bath, pier, family-run.
D-F Margaritaville, at very end of the village, T425-3366. Very clean, big rooms with 2 double beds, private bathroom, friendly.
E Blueberry Hill, T425-3141. Cheap and very basic rooms and houses for rent, lots of signs along the road.
E Celena, main street, T425-3228. With bath, clean with fan. Recommended.
E Countryside, 10 mins' walk out of town, T425-3216. Shared bath, rooms and apartments, quiet, clean, friendly, fan, porch, ask in town for Woody and Annie.
E Harbour View, right on water, T425-3159. **Parrot's Dive** on site, cheaper rooms with shared bathrooms upstairs, rooms with private bath downstairs, hot water, own generator, cleaning done only on arrival, TV, fans, run by Roger and Maimee.
E Laguna del Mar, opposite and owned by Trudy's, T425-3103. Terrace, clean, fans, mosquito nets, diving offered.
E Seaside, opposite Gunter's Dive School, T425-3150, hotelseaside@yahoo.com. Including private bathroom, very popular with budget travellers, laundry service, noisy in the mornings from cockerels and locals' music.
E Trudy's, 5 mins from airport, T/F425-3103. With and without bath, very clean, comfortable. Recommended. **Underwater Vision** dive shop on site.
E-F Cross Creek (see also Diving, below), T425-3334, www.ccreek.com. Good, clean rooms, with shower and shared toilets, discount for divers on courses.
F Coopers Inn, 5 mins' walk from the dock, T425-3184. Cheaper if you dive with **Captain Morgan's**, very clean and friendly, Danish cook. Recommended.
F Loma Vista, up rpad opposite the dock, T425-3243. Clean, fan, shared bath, very friendly, washes clothes cheaply.
F Tropical, Mammie Lane. 15 double rooms, popular with a young crowd, kitchen, fans, has own water supply and generator, safe.

Utila's cayes *p857*
F Hotel Kayla. A European- style hotel affiliated with **Captain Morgan's Dive Center**. Free accommodation with PADI courses.

Roatán *p858, maps p859 and p860*

Coxen Hole

C **Caye View**, Calle Principal, T445-1222. A/c, bath, TV, phone, laundry, restaurant, bar, overlooks water, overpriced.

C-E **Mom**, on main road into Coxen Hole, above pharmacy, next to hospital. Private or shared bath, modern, clean, a/c, TV.

E **El Paso**, next door to **Caye View**, T445-1367. Shared bath, restaurant.

F **Naomi Allen**, near the bus depot. Fan, clean, good.

Sandy Bay

LL **Anthony's Key Resort**, T445-1003, www.anthonyskey.com. Glorious location, accommodation in small cabins, launch and diving facilities (only open to resident guests), the owner, Julio Galindo, is very serious about helping the environment and local community. Dolphin pool at the resort looked after by the Institute of Marine Sciences.

A **Ocean Side Inn**, T445-1552, www.roatanet.com/oceanside_f.htm. Full board, friendly owners Joseph and Jenny, nice deck with view of bay, superb restaurant, diving packages offered, but no beach nearby, otherwise recommended.

B-C **Caribbean Seashore Bed and Breakfast**, on the beach at West Sandy Bay, T445-1123, www.roatanet.com/caribbeanbnb. Hot water, private bath, cooking facilities, friendly management.

West End

AL **Half Moon Bay Cabins**, Half Moon Bay, T445-1075. Bungalows and cabins with bath, restaurant with excellent seafood.

AL-B **Coconut Tree**, West End, T445-1648, www.westbaycoconuttree.com. Private cabins (3 double beds) owned by Vincent Bush, a/c, kitchen, balcony, hot water, fan, fridge, clean, friendly, discounts in low season.

A-B **Mermaid Beach**, West End, T445-1335, www.roatanet.com/mermaid. Clean, quiet, with bath, fan or a/c, dive shop next door.

A-B **Pura Vida**, T/F445-1141, www.puravidaresort.com. A/c, cheaper with fan, hot water, restaurant/bar/pizzeria open all day.

A-D **Sunset Inn**, West End, above **Ocean Divers**, T445-1925. Rooms in main hotel more expensive, private bath, some with kitchen and up to 5 beds, some with a/c, hot water, friendly; cheaper above **Ocean Connections** dive shop, shared bathroom, recommended, good discounts with diving in low season, Italian seafood restaurant.

A-E **Seagrape Plantation Resort**, Half Moon Bay, T445-1429, www.seagraperoatan.com. Cabins, rooms with private bath and budget options with shared bathroom, hot water, family atmosphere, friendly, Visa accepted, nice location on rocky promontory, no beach, snorkelling, full-service restaurant and bar, inclusive packages available. Shoredives for US$15 with equipment.

B **Casa Calico**, north of Half Moon Bay, T445-1946, www.casacalico.com. Comfortable, cable TV, videos, rooms and apartments, fan, 2 rooms with a/c, garden, huge balconies, apartments sleep 4 or more with kitchen, hot water, noisy in morning, owned by Frances Collins, friendly, helpful.

B **Georphi's Tropical Hideaway**, West End, T445-1794, www.roatangeorphis.com. 9 cabins, kitchens, coffee shop under trees with excellent cookies and pancakes, open all day.

B **Pinocchio's**, West End, behind **Sea View Restaurant**, T445-4466, www.roatanpinocchios.com. Comfortable rooms with good views of the ocean.

B **Posada Arco Iris**, Half Moon Bay, T445-1264, www.roatanposada.com. Apartments with kitchen, hot water, fan, large balcony, friendly owners. New restaurant on premises specializing in grilled meats. Highly recommended.

B-C **Keifitos Plantation Resort**, on hillside above beach, T978-4472, www.keifitos.com. Bungalows in a beautiful setting, short walk from village, mosquitoes, bar, good breakfasts to 1300, champagne breakfasts Sun, horses for rent with guide, friendly owners, very quiet, very clean. Recommended.

B-D **Roberts-Hill**, West End, T445-1176. Basic rooms with bath and fan, 2-storey *cabaña* and new cabins on the beach next to **Keifitos**.

C **Belvedere's cabins**, West End beach behind **Chris's Tienda**, T445-1171. Private bath, restaurant serving steaks, seafood, pasta and salad.

C **Dolphin Resort**, centre of Half Moon Bay, T445-1280. Private bathroom, a/c and fan. Recommended.

 drinks, and insect repellent. Developers have recently discovered the delights of West Bay and the atmosphere is changing fast. Apartments, hotels, bars and restaurants are springing up.

East of Coxen Hole

French Harbour, on the south coast, with its shrimping and lobster fleet, is the main fishing port of Roatán. There is no beach and there are two seafood packing plants. The road passes Coleman's (Midway) Bakery, where you can buy freshly baked

Roatán - West End & West Bay

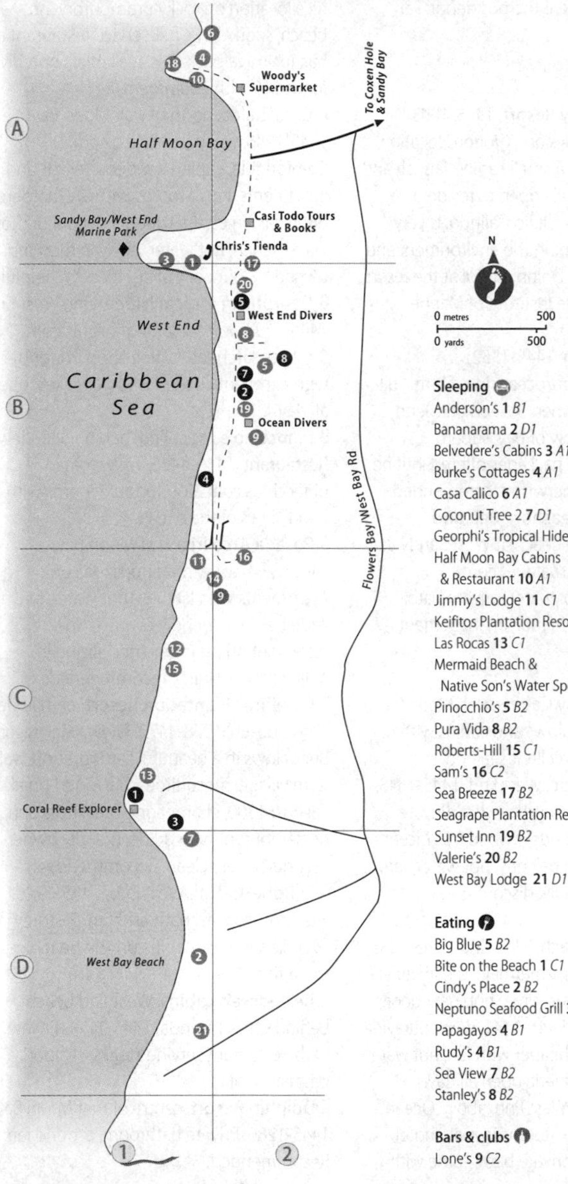

Sleeping
Anderson's **1** *B1*
Bananarama **2** *D1*
Belvedere's Cabins **3** *A1*
Burke's Cottages **4** *A1*
Casa Calico **6** *A1*
Coconut Tree 2 **7** *D1*
Georphi's Tropical Hideaway **9** *B2*
Half Moon Bay Cabins & Restaurant **10** *A1*
Jimmy's Lodge **11** *C1*
Keifitos Plantation Resort **12** *C1*
Las Rocas **13** *C1*
Mermaid Beach & Native Son's Water Sports **14** *C2*
Pinocchio's **5** *B2*
Pura Vida **8** *B2*
Roberts-Hill **15** *C1*
Sam's **16** *C2*
Sea Breeze **17** *B2*
Seagrape Plantation Resort **18** *A1*
Sunset Inn **19** *B2*
Valerie's **20** *B2*
West Bay Lodge **21** *D1*

Eating
Big Blue **5** *B2*
Bite on the Beach **1** *C1*
Cindy's Place **2** *B2*
Neptuno Seafood Grill **3** *C1*
Papagayos **4** *B1*
Rudy's **4** *B1*
Sea View **7** *B2*
Stanley's **8** *B2*

Bars & clubs
Lone's **9** *C2*

equipment, disorganized, wooden deck over sea, local food, bar, friendly, safe parking.

Guanaja *p861*
LL Posada del Sol, on an outlying caye, T/F668-3347, www.posadadelsol.com. Includes meals, launch trips, diving, fitness studio, 1st class, has a good underwater photographic and video facility for divers.
C-D Harry Carter, T455-4303, ask for fan, clean.
E Miss Melba, just before **Hotel Alexander** sign on left, house with flowers. 3 rooms in boarding house, run by friendly old lady with lots of island information, shared bathroom, cold water, great porch and gardens.

Cayos Cochinos (Hog Islands) *p861*
AL Plantation Beach Resort, Cochino Grande, T/F442-0974. VHF 12. Rustic cabins on hillside, hot water, fans, diving offshore, yacht moorings, good steep walk up to lighthouse for view over cayes to mainland, music festival end-Jul, local bands and dancers, they charge US$30 for the trip from La Ceiba.
E Cayo Timón (also known as **North Sand Cay**) can be visited from Utila, 1¼ hrs by boat; you can rent the caye (price per person), minimum 6, 8 is comfortable, A-frame, Polynesian style, do overnight diving trips, very basic, quiet, peaceful. Phone Roy and Brenda at **Thompson's Bakery**, Utila, T425-3112, for information.

Eating

Utila *p857, map p857*
Menus are often ruled by the supply boat: on Tue restaurants have everything, by the weekend some drinks run out.
TTT Jade Seahorse. 1100-2200, closed Thu. Good seafood, excellent vegetarian food and *licuados*, coolest decor in town, includes the Treetanic bar, high up in the trees 1700-2400.
TT Bundu Café. Excellent food, quiche, salads, sandwiches, juices and other drinks, run by friendly couple Steve and Fran, good book exchange, also has a video cinema, with movies nightly at 1930, US$1.50, also runs trips to Water Cay, popular hangout. Recommended.
TT Capt Jack's, next to **Gunter's Dive Shop**. Good, 0630-2100.
TT Delaney's Island Kitchen. 1730-2200 for pizza, lasagne and veg dishes, Danish cook, good specials nightly.
TT Golden Rose, opposite **Utila Lodge**. Superb food, reasonable prices, Mon-Sat 1000-2200, Sun 1400-2200. Highly recommended.
TT Las Delicias. 0800-2400. Local food, lively bar with music, live music Tue and Fri.
T Mermaid's Corner. Breakfast from 0700, huge pizza (US$6) and pasta, good value and popular. Nightly movies.
T Munchie's, near the dock. Nice snacks and good service. Also organize trips to the cayes.
T RJ's BBQ and Grill House. "Absolutely the best top-notch food in town", barbequed meat and fish, with generous portions. Wed, Fri and Sat from 1730. Very highly recommended.
T Thompsons Bakery. Open 0600-1200, best place for breakfast, very informal, friendly, good cakes, lots of information. Good yogurt and cakes.

Utila's cayes *p857*
There are a few restaurants, a Sat night disco and little else.

Roatán *p858, maps p859 and p860*
Evening meals cost US$4-10. There is a good seafood restaurant on **Osgood Caye** a few mins by free water taxi from wharf.

Coxen Hole
TT El Paso, next to the **Caye View**. Good seafood soup.
TT Qué Tal Café, on road to West End. Good coffee, herbal teas, sandwiches and pastries, shares space with bookstore.
T HB Warren. Large well-stocked supermarket (best place on island for fresh fruit) with *cafetería*, mainly lunch and snacks, open 0700-1800.
T Hibiscus Sweet Shop. Home-made fruit pies, cakes and biscuits.
T Pizza Rey, opposite Warren's. Pizza slices.

West End
TTT Deja Blue. Asian and Middle East specialities, good location, salad buffet, expensive but worth it.
TTT Half Moon Bay Restaurant, Half Moon Bay. Nice location to sit on terrace overlooking sea, more expensive than most, excellent food, service can be very slow.

₸₸₸ **Punta del Ovest music village**, 200 m along path behind **Bamboo**. Hut, exotic, clay-oven pizzas, one of the best in town. Shows a film every night.

₸₸ **Belvedere's**, on water, West End. Nice setting, tasty Italian food, Fri-Sun1900-2100. Recommended.

₸₸ **Big Blue**, above **West End Divers**, serves good Thai food.

₸₸ **Brick Oven**, about 15 mins out of West End (follow the signs), with good food and movies every night.

₸₸ **Cannibal Café**, in the **Sea Breeze**, excellent Mexican food, large helpings, good value.

₸₸ **Cindy's Place**, next to **Sunset Inn**, local family breakfast, lunches and dinner in garden, fish caught same morning, also lobster and king crab. Recommended.

₸₸ **The Cool Lizard**, Mermaid Beach. Seafood, vegetarian and chicken, home-made bread, salads, nice atmosphere, good.

₸₸ **Keifito's Hangout**, West End. Good breakfasts, champagne on Sun, reasonable prices.

₸₸ **Lighthouse**, on the point after Belvedere's, local dishes, good coffee and breakfasts, fried chicken and seafood. A bit run-down.

₸₸ **Papagayos**, Half Moon Bay, on a jetty, T445-1008. Good atmosphere for pre-prandial tipple, reggae music, basic meals, no sandflies, great sundeck, Thu is band/dance/party night, also rooms to rent (**B**).

₸₸ **Pinocchio's**, West End, along same path as the **Lighthouse**, www.roatanpinocchios.com. Excellent pasta, great stir fry and delicious salads, run by Patricia and Howard.

₸₸ **Pura Vida**, next to **West End Divers**, Italian, restaurant and pizzeria, good atmosphere.

₸₸ **Rick's American Café**, Sandy Bay. Tree top bar, shows all sports events, best steaks on Roatán. Open from 1700, except Wed.

₸₸ **Rudy's**. Good pancakes and cookies for breakfast, sandwich combos, good atmosphere but pricey, open all day.

₸₸ **Salt and Pepper Club**, entrance to West End. Supermarket, BBQ and live music.

₸₸ **Sea View Restaurant**, West End. Italian chef/manager, extensive menu, pasta, fish, chicken, pizza, good salads.

₸₸ **Tony's Pizzeria**, in the **Sunset Inn**. Fresh fish, good food, big portions.

₸₸ **Twisted Toucan**, West End. The place for drinking and dancing, happy hr 1600-1900.

₸₸ **Tyll's Kitchen**, in Tyll's Dive Shop, now open for breakfast, happy hour for rum and beer goes on all day.

₸₸ **Velva's Place**, at the far end of Half Moon Bay. Island-style seafood and chicken dishes, try the conch soup, good prices.

₸ **Stanley's**, up hill about 50 m north of **Sunset Inn**, small sign up path. Island cooking, menu changes daily, evening meal only, at 1900, cheap, good food, try their coconut dinner, friendly.

Tartines and Chocolate, Half Moon Bay. French bakery/patisserie, good bread and pastries.

West Bay

₸₸₸ **The Bite on the Beach**, on the point over West Bay. Wed-Sun brunch, huge deck in gorgeous position excellent, fresh food and great fruit punch. Recommended and very much what Roatán is about.

₸₸ **Neptuno Seafood Grill**, between **Fosters** and **Coconut Tree 2**. Seafood, paella, barbecued crab, extensive bar, open daily for lunch and dinner.

₸₸ **West Bay Lodge**, see Sleeping. Serves a good breakfast on a nice balcony with sea view.

East of Coxen Hole

There is a *taquería* close to BGA on the main road in French Harbour serving good tacos, burritos and hamburgers.

₸₸₸ **Gios**, French Harbour. Seafood, king crab speciality.

₸₸₸ **Roatan Dive and Yacht Club**, French Harbour. Daily specials, pizza, salads, sandwiches, usually very good.

₸₸ **BJ's Backyard Restaurant**, Oak Ridge, at the harbour. Island cooking, fishburgers, smoked foods, reasonable prices. There is a pizzeria and, next door, a supermarket.

₸₸ **Iguana Grill**, French Harbour. International cuisine and suckling pig.

₸₸ **Pirate's Hideaway**, at Calabash Bay, east of Oak Ridge. Seafood, friendly owner.

₸₸ **Romeo's**, French Harbour. Romeo, who is Honduran-Italian, serves good seafood, and continental cuisine.

₸₸ **Tres Flores**, French Harbour, on the hill. Good views, Mexican specialities, they pick up groups from West End, T245-0007.

Guanaja *p861*
Harbour Light, through Mountain View nightclub. Good food reasonably priced for the island.

Entertainment

Utila *p857, map p857*
Bars and clubs
Bar in the Bush, is the place to go, 100 m beyond the Mango Inn, very popular, lots of dancing and always packed, Wed 1800-2330, Fri and Sun 1800-0300. **Club 07**, opens Sat, free rum 2200-2300, good dancing. **Coco Loco**, on jetty at harbour front near Scuba Libre sign, popular in the evenings at sunset and late into the night, 1600-0000, closed Sun. **Las Delicias** and **Casino** are busy on Sat nights.

Cinema
Reef Cinema, opposite Bay Islands Originals shop, shows films at US$2 per person, they also do cash advances on Visa, MC and American Express. See also **Bundu Café**, page 865.

Roatán *p858, maps p859 and p860*
Bars and clubs
Most clubs come alive about midnight, play reggae, salsa, punta and some rock.
Coxen Hole: **Harbour View**, Thu-Sun nights, late, US$0.50 entrance, very local, usually no problem with visitors but avoid local disputes. Hot and atmospheric.
Sundowners Bar, popular happy hr from 1700-1900, Sun quiz followed by BBQ.
West End: **Bahía Azul**, Fri is party night, DJ, dancing. **C-bar**, fantastic location on beachfront near Seagrape Plantation.
Foster's, the late night hotspot, dance music Thu night as well as band nights. **Lone's Bar**, Mermaid Beach, nightly BBQ, reggae music.
East of Coxen Hole: **Al's**, Barrio Las Fuertes, before French Harbour, closed Sat night, salsa and plenty of punta.
Bolongas, French Harbour, weekends, late, US$1 entrance, upmarket, modern building, sometimes live Honduran bands and classy stripshow.

Festivals and events

Utila *p857, map 857*
Aug Sun Jam on Water Caye at a weekend at the beginning of Aug – watch out for details locally. They charge a La50 entrance fee to the island; bring your own tent/hammock, food and water.

Shopping

Utila *p857, map p857*
Arts and crafts **Bay Islands Original Shop** sells T-shirts, sarongs, coffee, hats, etc. Mon-Fri 0900-1200 and 1300-1800, Sat and Sun 0900-1200. Also **Annie Maude Gift Shop** and **Utila Lodge Gift Shop**. **Gunter Kordovsky** is a painter and sculptor with a gallery at his house, good map of Utila, paintings, cards and wood carving.

Roatán *p858, maps p859 and p860*
Supermarkets Best to buy supplies in Coxen Hole. **Coconut Tree** at West End expensive. **Woods** is cheaper. **Eldon** in French Harbour is also expensive. **Ezekiel**, West End, opposite church, fruit and vegetables, selection varies.

Activities and tours

Utila *p857, map p857*
Diving
Dive with care for yourself and the reef at all times; www.roatanet.com, has plenty of information about Utila and its dive sites.

Utila is a very popular dive training centre. Learning to dive is cheaper here than anywhere else in the Caribbean, especially if you include the low living expenses. It is best to do a course of some sort; students come first in line for places on boats and recreational divers have to fit in. In recent years Utila has developed a reputation for poor safety and there have been some accidents requiring emergency treatment in the recompression chamber on Roatán. Serious attempts have been made to change this by the diving community of Utila. Michel Bessette, manager and owner of Paradise Divers and a committee member of the Utila Clinic, says that the 3 or 4 accidents that happen annually are a result of cowboy divers and drug or alcohol abuse.
Instructors Choose an instructor who you get on with, and one who has small classes and cares about safety; follow the rules on alcohol/drug abuse and pay attention to the dive tables. There is a rapid turnover of

instructors; many stay only a season to earn money to continue their travels, and some have a lax attitude towards diving regulations and diving tables. Check that equipment looks new and well maintained. Boats vary, you may find it difficult to climb into a dory if there are waves. While a dive shop has a responsibility to set standards of safety, you also have a responsibility to yourself to know about diving times. If you don't, or are a beginner, ask.

Price There is broad price agreement across dive shops in Utila. Out of the revenues the **Utila Dive Supporters' Association** can budget for spending, facilities and eventually conservation. Whatever you may think of the idea, one benefit, according to Bessette, is greater safety and better organized protection of the reef. Whether this works remains to be seen, but the price of saving a few dollars could end up costing lives. Dive insurance at US$3 per day for fun divers, US$9 for students (advanced, or open water), US$30 for divemasters is compulsory and is available from the BICA office. It covers air ambulance to Roatán and the recompression chamber. Treat any cuts from the coral seriously, they do not heal easily.

PADI courses A PADI Open Water course costs US$199 (including certificate) with 4 dives, an Advanced course costs US$159 with 5 dives. Credit cards, if accepted, are 8% extra. Competition is fierce with over 15 dive shops looking for business, so you can pick and choose. Once qualified, fun dives are US$25 for 2 tanks, US$125 for 10 tanks. Most schools offer instruction in English or German; French and Spanish are usually available somewhere, while tuition handbooks are provided in numerous languages including Japanese. A variety of courses is available up to instructor level. If planning to do a diving course, it is helpful but not essential to take passport-sized photographs with you for the PADI card.

Dive operators

Bay Islands College of Diving, on main street close to **Hondutel** tower, T425-3192, info@dive-utila.com, www.dive-utila.com. 5-star PADI facility, experienced and well qualified staff, good boats ranging from 50 ft, for large parties to skiff for smaller ones, environmentally sound. Only dive shop on the island with a trauma centre and recompression chamber.

Captain Morgan's, T425-3349, www.diving utila.com, has been recommended for small classes, good equipment, friendly staff.

Cross Creek, T425-3134, www.crosscreek utila.com, 2 boats, maximum 8 people per instructor, 2-3 instructors, new equipment, 8 kayaks for hire (US$10 per day), accommodation on site for students, 18 rooms, can also arrange transfers from the mainland.

Deep Blue Divers, T/F425-3211, www.deepblueutila.com. New operator on the island, which means new gear and the friendly owners are getting good feedback through word of mouth.

Gunter's dive school based at Sea Side Inn, T/F425-3350, www.riconet.com/ecomarine, run by Roland from Austria and Miri, an

Israeli. The instructor, Pascal Floss, is experienced, has been on the island a long time and is recommended as the best person for finding fish and other aquatic life on the reef. **Gunter's** also offers trips to Water Caye and is the contact for trips to Lívingston, Guatemala.

Paradise Divers, on the seafront, T425-3148, www.todomundo.com/paradisedivers. Relaxed and friendly.

Utila Watersports, T/F425-3239, run by Troy Bodden; quality of instructors varies. Troy also hires out snorkelling gear, photographic and video equipment and takes boat trips. Good reports.

Utila Dive Centre, Mango Inn, T/F425-3326, www.utiladivecentre.com, www.mango-inn.com. Chris Phillips runs very professional courses, well-maintained equipment, sometimes takes divers to north coast in fast dory, recommended but no shade, surface interval on cayes.

Tour operators

Robinson Crusoe Tours, run by Shelby McNab who takes visitors on half-day tours around the island (US$10 per person) explaining his theory that Daniel Defoe based his famous book on Utila (not Alexander Selkirk off Chile), fascinating.

Tropical Travel Agency, for flights and clothes, Mon-Fri 0800-1100 and 1400-1700.

Roatán *p858, maps p859 and p860*

Diving

If you don't want to dive, the snorkelling is normally excellent. The creation of the Sandy Bay/West End Marine Park along 4 km of coast from Lawson Rock around the southwest tip to Key Hole has encouraged the return of large numbers of fish in that area and there are several interesting dive sites. Lobsters are still rare, but large grouper are now common and curious about divers. If the sea is rough off **West End** try diving around **French Harbour** (or vice versa) where the cayes provide some protection. There are more mangroves on this side, which attract the fish. **Flowers Bay** on the south side has some spectacular wall dives, but not many fish, and it is calm during the 'Northers' which blow in Dec-Feb. Few people dive the east end except the liveaboards (**Bay Islands Aggressor, The Aggressor Fleet**, Romeo Tower, French Harbour, T445-1518) and people on camping trips to Pigeon Cay, so it is relatively unspoilt. Because fishing is allowed to the east, tropical fish are scarce and the reef is damaged in places. In addition to a few stormy days from Dec to Feb, you can also expect stinging hydroids in the top few feet of water around Mar and Apr which bother people who are sensitive to stings (with friends like these, who needs anemones?). Vinegar is the local remedy.

Courses As on Utila, the dive operators concentrate on instruction but prices vary (since Dec 1994 the municipal government has set minimum prices). You can normally find a course starting within 1 or 2 days. There is more on offer than in Utila; not everyone teaches only PADI courses. Prices for courses and diving vary with the season. In low season good deals abound. Open water US$225, advanced US$160, fun dives US$25. Despite the huge number of dive students, Roatán has a good safety record but it still pays to shop around and find an instructor you feel confident with at a dive shop which is well organized with well-maintained equipment. As in other 'adventure' sports, the cheapest is not always the best. Dive insurance is US$2 per day, and is sometimes included in the course price. If you do not have dive insurance and need their services, the hyperbaric chamber charges a minimum of US$800.

Dive operators

Aquarius Divers, West End. PADI courses, fun dives, excursions to the south walls in conjunction with Scuba Romance dive shop, Brick Bay.

Native Son's Water Sports, next to Mermaid cabins, West End. Run by Alvin, local instructor, PADI and PDSI courses and fun dives.

Ocean Connections at Sunset Inn, West End, T/F445-1925, run by Carol and Phil Stevens with emphasis on safety and fun, good equipment, multilingual instructors, PADI courses, BSAC, the only shop with nitrox instruction, fast boats, also rooms and restaurant, dive/accommodation packages available. Recommended.

Sueño del Mar Divers, good, inexpensive, American-style operation, tends to dive the sites closest to home, T445-1717.

Tyll's Dive, West End, T403-8852, www.tyllsdive.com, multilingual instructors, PADI, SSI courses, accommodation also available.

West End Divers, West End, www.westendivers.com, Italian owned, competent bilingual instructors, PADI Dive Centre.

Bananarama, West Bay, in centre of beach, next to **Cabana Roatana**, small, friendly, run by young German family, boat and shore diving.

The Last Resort, Gibson Bight, T445-1838 (in USA T305-893-2436). Mostly packages from the USA.

Anthony's Key Resort, Sandy Bay. Mostly hotel package diving, also swim and dive with dolphins, see above.

Scuba Romance, Dixon Cove. New shop and equipment, large diesel boat and compressor, diving the south wall and the reef at Mary's Place, overnight trips to Barbareta, 6 dives, US$80, sleeping on the boat, work with Palm Cove Resort, cabin-style accommodation, home cooking.

Tour operators

At **Belvedere's Lodge** on the headland at Half Moon Bay, Dennis runs snorkelling trips to secluded bays beyond Antony's Key in a glass-bottomed yacht. He also takes charters and sunset cruises all along the coast. Horse riding available from **Keifitos** or **Jimmy's** in West End. Alex does day trips to Punta Gorda and 2/3-day trips in his sailboat *Adventure Girl*. His boat is moored at **Ocean Divers** dock, contact here or at Tyll's. **Far Tortugas** charters, trimaran *Genesis*, does sailing trips with snorkelling and reef drag (snorkellers towed behind slow moving boat), US$45 per day, US$25 per ½ day, contact **Casi Todo**, West End, T445-1347. **Coconut Tree** have a rainforest tour to Pico Bonito, US$112 including guide, transport, lunch and snorkelling.

Boat trips Kayak rentals and tours from **Seablades**, contact Alex at Casi Todo, 3-7 day kayak tours, US$150-250. Full and half-day rental US$20 and US$12 (with instruction), kayaks available at **Tyll's**. From Rick's American Café, **Casablanca** charters on yacht *Defiance III*, sunset cruises, party trips, full-day snorkelling, also can be arranged through **Casi Todo**. At West Bay beach is a glass-bottomed boat, **Caribbean Reef Explorer**, US$20 per 1½ hrs, unfortunately includes fish feeding, which upsets the reef's ecological balance. Glass-bottomed boat and 3-person submarine tours from the dock at Half Moon Bay, US$25 per person.

Fishing Trips can be arranged through Eddie, contact at **Cindy's** next to Ocean Divers, West End, small dory, local expert, good results, US$30 per hr, but prices can vary. Alternatively, go fishing in style from French Harbour, **Hot Rods** sports fisher, US$500 per day charter, T445-1862. See **Casi Todo**, above, for the Jimni fishing tours, half and full day. Fishing trips also available on **Flame** , contact Darson or Bernadette, T445-1616, US$20 per hr.

Travel agents

Airport travel agency at the airport, has information on hotels, will make bookings, no commission. **Bay Islands Tour and Travel Center**, in Coxen Hole (Suite 208, Cooper Building, T445-1585) and French Harbour. **Casi Todo 1** in West End or **Casi Todo 2** in Coxen Hole can arrange tours, locally and on the mainland, including fishing, kayaking, island tours, trips to Barbareta and Copán. Local and international air tickets also sold here as well as new and 2nd-hand books, Mon-Sat, 0900-1630. **Columbia Tours**, Barrio El Centro, T445-1160, good prices for international travel, very helpful. **Tropical Travel**, in Hotel Caye View, T445-1146. **Carlos Hinds**, T445-1446, has a van for trips, reasonable and dependable.

Guanaja *p861*

Diving and sailing

The most famous dive site off Guanaja is the wreck of the *Jado Trader*, sunk in 1987 in about 30 m on a flat bottom surrounded by some large coral pinnacles which rise to about 15 m. Big black groupers and moray eels live here, as does a large shy jewfish and many other fish and crustaceans.

End of The World, next to **Bayman Bay Club**, T/F991-1257, www.guanaja.com, diving instruction, beachfront bar, restaurant, cabins, kayaks, canoes, hobie cats, white-sand beach, fishing. Highly recommended resort.

Jado Divers, beside **Melba's**, T453-4326. US$26 for 2 dives, run by Matthew from US.

Preston Borden will take snorkellers out for US$25 per boat load (4-6 people), larger parties accommodated with larger boat, or for customized excursions, very flexible, .

Transport

Utila *p857, map p857*

Air

Sosa and **Atlantic Air**, have daily flights to **La Ceiba**, US$19, 3 times a day Mon-Sat. Also to **Roatán** (US$40), **San Pedro** (US$51) and **Tegucigalpa** (US$64). There is local transport between airport and hotels.

Bike

Bike hire about US$5 per day. **Delco Bike** or **Utila Bike Rental** below Howell's Internet.

Boat

Passenger services going to Utila, operated by **Safeway Maritime**, T445-1795. Fare is US$9 1-way, with a La10 dock fee charged when leaving Utila. **La Ceiba**-Utila 0815, 0930 and 1630, Utila-La Ceiba 0630, 0945 and 1430.

Boats from Utila to **Roatán** can be chartered for about US$70. Occasional freight boats, eg **Utila Tom**, take passengers from Utila to Roatán. It's a 3-hr journey and you and your possessions are liable to get soaked. Irregular boats go to **Puerto Cortés**, times posted in main street, 7 hrs, US$7.50, ask at public dock.

A boat service from Utila to **Omoa** (US$65) and **Lívingston** (US$135) in Guatemala runs almost weekly in high season, and fortnightly in low season. Food included. See Gisela and Tom at **Gunter's Dive Shop**, T905-7800, solvelamar@hotmail.com.

Roatán *p858, maps p859 and p860*

Air

If travelling to or from the mainland, check fares available on the day of travel, it may be cheaper to fly than to go by sea. The airport is 20 mins' walk from Coxen Hole, or you can catch a taxi from outside the airport for US$1.50. There is a hotel reservation desk in the airport, T445-1930. Change in Coxen Hole for taxis to West End. US$1 per person for *colectivos* to West End, US$2 to Oak Ridge. If you take a taxi from the airport they charge US$10 per taxi; if you pick one up on the main road you may be able to bargain down to US$5. **Isleña, Sosa** and **Atlantic Air** fly from **La Ceiba**, US$20 one-way (fewer Sun); flights also to and from **Tegucigalpa**, US$60, via **San Pedro Sula** (Isleña), US$50, frequency varies according to season. No other direct flights to other islands, you have to go via La Ceiba (to Utila US$38.50, to Guanaja US$51). Always buy your ticket in advance (none on sale at airport), reservations are not always honoured.

From the USA, **Taca** flies on Sat from **Houston**, on Sun from **Miami**. From Central America, daily flights from **Belize City** (Isleña), Sat from **San Salvador** (Taca).

Airlines Taca, at airport T445-1387; Isleña, airport T445-1088; Sosa, airport T445-1154. **Casi Todo** sells all flights within Honduras at same price as airlines.

Boat

Galaxy II sails from **La Ceiba** to Coxen Hole. Roatán-La Ceiba 0700, La Ceiba-Roatán 0930, T445-1795. No sailings in bad weather. At times the crossing can be rough, seasick pills available at ticket counter. Irregular boats from **Puerto Cortés** and **Utila**. Cruise ships visit from time to time, mostly visiting **Tabayana Resort** on West Bay.

Bike and moped

Captain Van's Rentals, West End; also from **Ole Rentavan**, T445-1819.

Bus

From Coxen Hole to Sandy Bay is a 2-hr walk, or a US$1 bus ride, hourly 0600-1700; taxi drivers will try to charge much more.

Car

Car rental **Captain Van**, West End, vans, also mopeds and bicycles, good information about the islands; **Roatan Rentals**, West End, range of vehicles, pick-ups and vans for rent; **Sandy Bay Rent-A-Car**, US$42 per day all inclusive, jeep rental, T445-1710, agency also in West End outside Sunset Inn; **Toyota**, opposite airport, have pick-ups, US$46, 4WD, US$65, Starlets US$35 per day, also 12-seater bus, US$56 per day, T445-1166.

Taxi

If you take a private taxi, *privado*, negotiate the price in advance. The official rate from the airport to Sandy Bay/West End is US$8 per taxi regardless of the number of passengers.

Guanaja *p861*

Air

The airport is on Guanaja but you have to get a water taxi from there to wherever you are staying; there are no roads or cars; Sosa and Isleña (T453-4208) fly daily from **La Ceiba**, 30 mins. Other non-scheduled flights available.

Boat

The *Suyapa* sails between Guanaja, La Ceiba and Puerto Cortés. The *Miss Sheila* also does this run and on to George Town (Grand Cayman). *Cable Doly Zapata*, Guanaja, for monthly sailing dates to Grand Cayman (US$75 one way). Irregular sailings from Guanaja to Trujillo, 5 hrs.

Directory

Utila *p857, map p857*

Banks Dollars are accepted on the island and you can pay for diving courses with dollars, TCs and credit cards, although the latter carry an 8-10% charge. **BGA** and **Banco Atlántida** Mon-Fri 0900-1600, Sat 0830-1130. **BGA** changes dollars and gives cash against a Visa, but not MasterCard. **Thompson's Bakery** will change dollars and TCs. **Ronald Janssen** at Cross Creek Divers does Amex, Visa and MasterCard advances plus 8%, so will Michel Bessette, owner of **Paradise Divers.** Other establishments do the same. Donations welcomed for conservation efforts. **Internet** Howell's Internet, near the dock, 0800-1730, closed Sat, extortionate at US$0.15 a min. **Seaside Internet**, next to Seaside Inn, Mon-Fri 0900-1400 and 1600-1800. Also **Internet Café** on road to Mango Inn, Mon-Sat 0900-1700. **Medical services** Utila Community Clinic (Mon-Fri 0800-1200), has a resident doctor. There was a case of malaria in early 1999, and a spate of dengue fever cases in late 1999. Sandflies are not carriers. **Post office** There is a post office at the pier opposite Captain Morgan's Dive Centre, Mon-Fri 0800-1200, 1400-1600, Sat 0800-1100. **Telephone** Hondutel office, Mon-Fri 0700-1100 and 1400-1700, Sat 0700-1100, is near Utila Lodge. The main service is reported as unreliable. **Hondutel** sends (and receives) faxes. **Ronald Janssen** also runs **Intertel**, an international phone service: North America US$4 per min, Europe US$7.50 (2 mins minimum), Mexico and Central America US$2, South America US$7, elsewhere US$8.50; incoming fax US$1.

Roatán *p858, maps p859 and p860*

Banks Banco Atlántida, BGA, Banco Sogerín and **Banffaa** in Coxen Hole. There is also a **BAC** office where you can get a cash advance on your Visa/MasterCard, upstairs, before Caye View Hotel on the main street. 5 banks in French Harbour; **BGA** in Oak Ridge, T245-2210, MasterCard for cash advances. No banks in West End. No exchange facilities at the airport. Dollars and lempiras can be used interchangeably for most services. **Internet** Available at the **Sunset Inn**. The **Lucky Lemp**, opposite Qué Tal coffee shop, main street Coxen Hole, phone, fax and email services. **Monoloco** reported to have very cheap packages. **Paradise Computer**, Coxen Hole, 10 mins' walk down road to West End. **Medical services** Dentist: upstairs in the Cooper building for emergency treatment, but better to go to La Ceiba or San Pedro Sula. **Doctor: Dr Jackie Bush** has a clinic in Coxen Hole, no appointment necessary, for blood or stool tests, etc. **Ambulance and Hyperbaric Chamber**, Anthony's Key with full medical service. **Local hospital**, Ticket Mouth Rd, Coxen Hole, T445-1499. **Post office** In Coxen Hole, stamps not always available, bring them with you or try **Librería Casi Todo** in West End. **Telephone** Very expensive, you will be charged as soon as a call connects with the satellite, whether or not the call goes through. **Hondutel** in Coxen Hole, fax is often broken. **Supertienda Chris**, West End, T/F445-1171, 1 min to Europe US$10, USA, Canada US$5. Both **Librería Casi Todo** and **Rudy's Cabins** in West End have a fax, US$10 per page to Europe, US$5 to USA. Rudy's charges US$2 a min to receive phone calls.

Guanaja *p861*

Banks BGA and Banco Atlántida.

The Northeast

Through the agricultural and cattle lands of Olancho State, a road runs near to the Parque Nacional Sierra de Agalta and beyond to Trujillo on the Caribbean coast. To the west, accessible only by air or sea, is the Mosquitia coast – a vast expanse of rivers and swamps, coastal lagoons and tropical forests filled with wildlife but very few people. From February to May you can taste the vino de coyol *which is extracted from a palm (a hole is made at the top of the trunk and the sap which flows out is drunk neat). With sugar added it ferments and becomes alcoholic* (chicha)*; it is so strong it is called* patada de burro *(mule kick).* ▸▸ *For Sleeping, Eating and other listings, see page 879-882.*

Tegucigalpa to the northeast coast

▸▸ *pp879-882.*

The Carretera de Olancho runs from the capital northeast to the Caribbean coast. It passes through **Guaimaca** and **San Diego**, **Campamento**, 127 km, a small, friendly village surrounded by pine forests, and on to the Río Guayape, 143 km.

By the river crossing at **Los Limones** is an unpaved road north to **La Unión** (56 km), deep in the northern moutains passing through beautiful forests and lush green countryside. To the north is the **Refugio de Vida Silvestre La Muralla-Los Higuerales** ⓘ *US$1*, where quetzales and emerald toucanettes can be seen between March and May in the cloud forest. For those that have made the effort to get to this spot, if you're camping you may experience the frissonic pleasure of jaguars 'screaming' during the night. The park comprises the three peaks of La Muralla, 1981 m, Las Parras, 2064 m, and Los Higuerales, 1985 m. Cohdefor has an office on the main plaza for information, closed weekends. You are now required to take a guide with you on the trail. Cost is US$4, arrange in La Unión. Four trails range from 1-10 km and are recommended. There are two campsites in the forest (contact Cohdefor on T/F222-1027 for prior arrangements), or there is accommodation for one or two at the visitors' centre.

Juticalpa → *Colour map 6, B3. Altitude: 420 m.*

The main road continues another 50 km from Los Limones to Juticalpa, the capital of Olancho department, in a rich agricultural area for herding cattle and growing cereals and sugar cane. There is a paved road northeast through the cattle land of Catacamas, continuing to just beyond Dulce Nombre de Culmí.

Catacamas and around → *Colour map 6, B4. Altitude: 400 m.*

Catacamas lies at the foot of Agalta mountain in the Río Guayape valley in the Department of Olancho, 210 km from Tegucigalpa. The Río Guayape (named after an indigenous dress, *guayapis*) is famous for its gold nuggets.

The town was established by the Spaniards and the colonial church dates from the early 18th century. It is an agricultural and cattle-raising district. The National School of Agriculture (ENA) is based here, ask if you wish to visit their agricultural demonstration plots in the Guayape valley, 5 km south of the town.

Hiking in the mountains behind Catacamas is beautiful. From Murmullo there are trails to coffee farms. **Río Talgua**, 4 km east of Catacamas, is interesting with caves in which significant pre-Columbian remains have been found. The area and caves are worth a visit. Hiking to **El Boquerón**, stop off at the main road near Punuare, 17 km west of Catacamas, and walk up **Río Olancho**, which has nice limestone cliffs and a pretty river canyon. Through much of the canyon the stream flows underground.

Beyond Catacamas, a rough road continues northeast up the Río Tinto Valley to **Dulce Nombre de Culmí**. Further on is Paya where the road becomes a mule track but, in three to four days in the dry season, a route can be made over the divide (Cerro de Will) and down the Río Paulaya to Mosquitia (see next section). Local police say that there is a path in the dry season from Dulce Nombre to San Esteban (about 30 km).

Juticalpa to Trujillo

There is a fine scenic road from Juticalpa to Trujillo. From Juticalpa head northeast and turn left where the paved road ends, to **San Francisco de la Paz**. Beyond San Francisco is **Gualaco**, which has an interesting colonial church (there are several places to stay, see Sleeping, page 879).

The town of **San Esteban** is 23 km from Gualaco. On the way you pass Agalta mountain, and some of the highest points in Honduras, and several waterfalls on the Río Babilonia.

After San Esteban the road continues to **Bonito Oriental** (via El Carbón, a mahogany collection point with the Paya communities in the vicinity). There are four hotels here. The final 38 km from Bonito Oriental to Trujillo are paved, through Corocito. There are many dirt roads between San Francisco and Trujillo. If driving, ask directions if in any doubt. Fuel is available in the larger villages but there is none between San Esteban and Bonito Oriental.

Parque Nacional Sierra de Agalta

Between the roads Juticalpa-Gualaco-San Esteban and Juticalpa-Catacamas-Dulce Nombre de Culmí lies the cloud forest of the Parque Nacional Sierra de Agalta, extending over 1200 ha and reaching a height of 2590 m at Monte de Babilonia, a massif with a number of interesting mountains. Several different ecosystems have been found with a wide variety of fauna and flora: 200 species of bird have been identified so far. There are several points of entry. Contact Cohdefor in Juticalpa, Culmí, Gualaco, San Esteban or Catacamas for information on access, maps, guides, mules and lodging. There is no infrastructure in the park, but a base camp is being built. A good trail leads to **La Picucha** mountain (2354 m). Access is from El Pacayal, 750 m, a short distance towards San Esteban from Gualaco (bus at 0700 which goes on to Tocoa). There are two campsites on the trail, the first at 1060m is just short of **La Chorrera** waterfall which has a colony of white-collared swifts that nest in the cave behind the falls. Four to six hours above is the second campsite at 1900 m. The final section is mainly dwarf forest with low undergrowth on the summit. There is much wildlife to be seen and a good viewpoint 1 km beyond at the site of two abandoned radio towers. Hiking time two days.

La Mosquitia

» *pp 879-882. Colour map 6, B4-5 and Eastern Honduras map, page 876.*

Forested, swampy and almost uninhabited, Mosquitia is well worth visiting if you have the time and energy. In the the Central American Little Amazon, you can hope to see rainforest wildlife including monkeys and incredible birdlife as you drift through the varied habitat that includes lowland tropical rainforest, coastal lagoons, undisturbed beaches, mangroves, grasslands and patches of pine savannah. Home to members of the Miskito and Pech tribes as well as the Garífuna ethnic group who live in small communities on the coast and along the major rivers. The Río Plátano Biosphere Reserve, a UN World Heritage Site, covers an area over 5200 sq km – one of the largest protected areas in Central America.

Ins and outs

While certainly a challenging environment, many backpackers visit the reserve either alone or with professional guides. For those travelling alone, as long as you have basic Spanish and are a reasonably confident traveller this is the cheapest option. With access by air, sea and recently by road you can visit anytime of the year but it is usually best to avoid the heavy rains during November, December and January. The driest months are March to May and August to October.

What to take It's a tough environment and you should go prepared. Take a mosquito net and repellent, clothing for rain and also for cooler temperatures at night, good walking shoes and a first aid kit. Also enough cash in small denominations for your stay (there are no banks in the area) and plastic bags to keep things dry.

For study of the region **MOPAWI (Mosquitia Pawisa)** is the best source of information and provides the main means of access for travellers to communities in Mosquitia. It is a non-profit-making, non-sectarian organization dedicated to the development of the region and the conservation of the biodiversity of its flora and fauna. The head office is in Puerto Lempira, T898-7460, with an office in Tegucigalpa (Residencias Tres Caminos 4b, lote 67, Apartado 2175, T235-8659). It also has offices in several other villages.

MOPAWI is concerned with the protection of natural and human resources throughout Mosquitia and the Department of Gracias a Dios. Among its many programmes is the conservation of marine turtles and the green iguana. The Reserva Biósfera Río Plátano (525,100 ha) with the Reserva Antropólogica Tawakha, the Reserva Nacional Patuca and together with Mosquitia Nicaragüense, constitute one of the largest forest reserves north of the Amazon.

Coastal villages

A narrow strand of land divides the inland waterway and Ibans lagoon from the Caribbean. Along this pleasant setting lie a number of small native villages starting with the Garífuna village of Plaplaya and continuing through the Miskito villages of Ibans, Cocobila, Raistá, Belén, Nueva Jerusalem and Kuri. Trails connect all of these villages making exploration easy with vast expanses of unspoiled, white-sand beaches providing an easy route for getting from place to place, with the sea providing a wonderful way to cool off during the heat of the day.

Apart from generally relaxing in the slow-paced life along the coast there are several interesting things to do in the area. In **Raistá**, the butterfly farm was a pilot project, focusing on raising the colourful butterfly species of the area to sell to live butterfly exhibition houses throughout the world.

In **Plaplaya**, a community-run Sea Turtle Project aims to protect the leatherback and loggerhead turtles that nest along the coast. Each night during the breeding season (March-June) members of the village patrol the beaches to find nesting turtles, carefully gathering the eggs and re-burying them in a guarded area where they are watched over until they hatch. The newborn turtles are then released into the sea. Visitors can accompany the beach patrols for a small donation to the program. There are two traditional dance groups in Plaplaya that can provide an interesting evening's entertainment for visitors.

The Miskito village of **Kuri**, 1½ hours along the beach from Belén, is worth a visit. Here the traditional wooden and thatch houses sit behind the beach, sheltered from the sea breezes by the 'Beach Grape' and palm trees along the sand dunes.

Reserva de la Biósfera Río Plátano

The reserve was established by the Honduran government in 1980 to protect the outstanding natural and cultural resources of the Río Plátano valley and its environs. In 1982 the UN declared the reserve a World Patrimony site. The tropical jungles here shelter a number of endangered birds, mammals and fish, among them **scarlet macaws** and **harpy eagles**, **jaguars** and **tapirs**, and the *cuyamel*, a prized food fish fast becoming extinct throughout Honduras. In addition, there are a number of **archaeological sites** about which little is known, and the fabled lost White City of the Maya is said to be hidden somewhere in the thick jungles of the Plátano headwaters. (The Society for the Exploration and Preservation of American History is in the process of preparing an expedition to find the city known as 'Kaha Kamasa'.)

The Miskito and the Pech living along the lower Plátano cultivate yuca, bananas, rice, corn and beans, and also feed themselves by hunting and fishing. The upper (southern) portion of the Plátano watershed was virgin jungle until quite recently, but is being quickly populated by mestizo immigrants from the poverty-stricken south of Honduras. These new residents are cutting down the forest to plant crops, hunting wildlife mercilessly, and using home-made dynamite in a very destructive form of fishing. The government's intention in 1995 officially to allow settlers into the Sico and Paulaya valleys, on the western edge of the reserve, was roundly criticized. It was feared that the agrarian reform programme would lead to the desertification of the Río Plátano. Given the pressure the reserve is under, it is recommended to visit it sooner rather than later.

Eastern Honduras

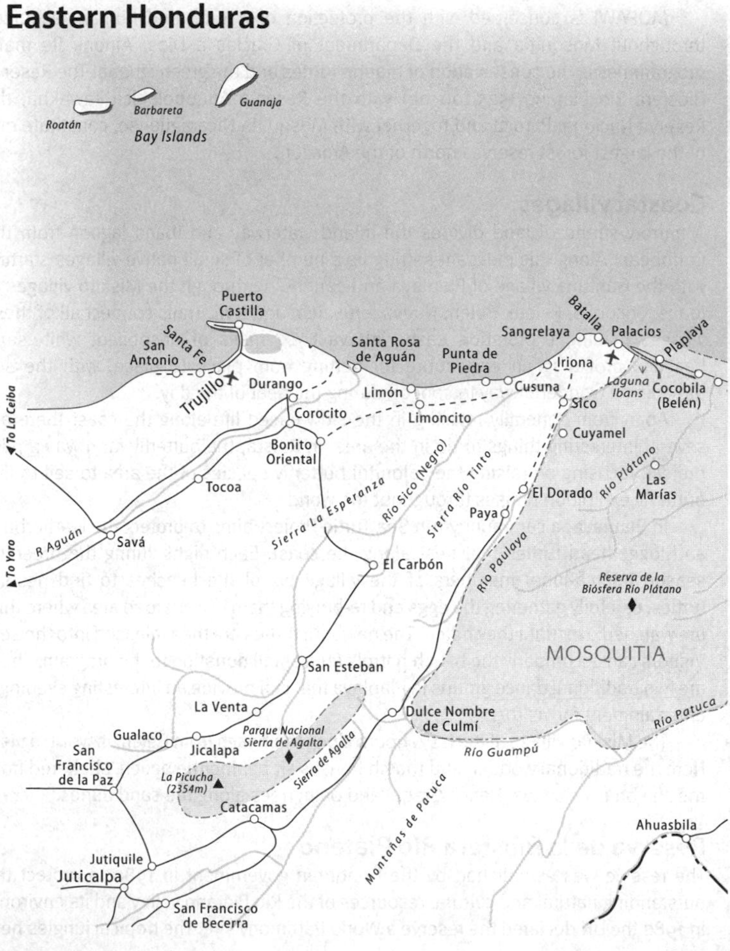

Along the Río Plátano

For those in search of a little more rugged adventure you should find a boat to take you up the Río Plátano to Las Marías, a small Miskito and Pech village that is the last outpost of civilization in this part of the reserve. Local boatman are trying to organize themselves with a view to regulating minimum standards, a fair price for the passage and a rotation system to ensure the work is shared more evenly between them.

Most people stay the night in Raistá before and after visiting Las Marías. Gasoline is very expensive in La Mosquitia and this is reflected in the high cost of transportation. The ride to Las Marías costs about US$130 so put together a group of four or five people to share the cost. That price should get you a boat and boatman for three days to take you on the round trip (four to six hours each way) from the coast with a day in Las Marías to look around. If you stay longer you should negotiate a fair price with the boatman to cover his extra time. Bring food and water for the trip as well as other jungle gear. The journey upstream to Las Marías, although beautiful, can become very tedious and uncomfortable. Birdwatching can provide a diversion; there are three species of toucan as well as tanagers, herons, kingfishers, vultures, hawk eagles and oropendolas. If you are lucky you might see crocodiles or iguanas. On arrival in Las Marías, arrange return at once.

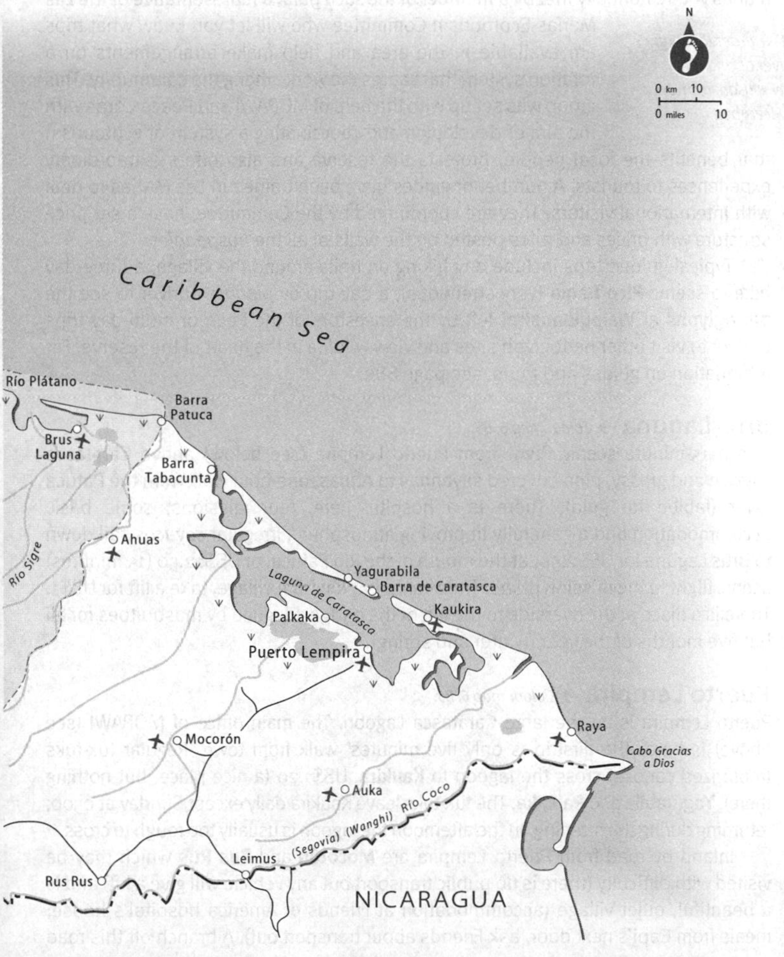

Border essentials: Honduras-Nicaragua

Leimus

Honduran immigration If you wish to cross here, obtain your exit stamp in Puerto Lempira. The immigration office is open Mon-Fri until 2300. This office is helpful and a good source of information.

An alternative route to Las Marías is by boat across Ibans Lagoon, 45 minutes by tuk-tuk, then 6½ hours' walk through jungle (rough path, hot, mosquitoes, take lots of water and insect repellent, and wear good hiking boots). This is only recommended for fit walkers in drier weather. Expect to pay around US$30 for the guide, and if returning from Las Mariás by boat you'll probably still have to pay the return fare even if you're only travelling one way.

Las Marías

This Miskito-Pech village is the furthest limit of upstream settlement. Once in Las Marías you're normally met by a member of the *saca guia*, a representative of the Las Marías Ecotourism Committee who will let you know what trips are available in the area and help make arrangements on a rotation system that shares the work among the community. This group was set up with the help of MOPAWI and Peace Corps with the aim of developing and coordinating a system of ecotourism that benefits the local people, protects the reserve and also offers extraordinary experiences to tourists. A number of guides have been trained in Las Marías to deal with international visitors. They are coordinated by the Committee, have a set price structure with prices and rules posted on the walls of all the *hospedajes*.

It is harder to advance upriver during the rainy season, from June to December.

Typical guided trips include day hiking on trails around the village, a three-day hike to scenic **Pico Dama** (very strenuous), a day trip by *pipante* upriver to see the **petroglyphs** at **Walpulbansirpi** left by the ancestors of the Pech or multi-day trips upriver to visit other petroglyph sites and view wildlife in the heart of the reserve. For information on guides and tours, see page 880.

Brus Laguna → *Colour map 6, B5.*

It is a 15-minute scenic flight from Puerto Lempira (see below) above Caratasca Lagoon and grassy, pine-covered savannas to **Ahuas**, one-hour walk from the Patuca River (fabled for gold). There is a hospital here, four missions, some basic accommodation and a generally improving atmosphere. Irregular *cayucos* sail down to Brus Laguna for US$2.50, at the mouth of the Río Patuca, or US$12.50 (15 minutes) scenic flight in the mission plane. The airstrip is 4 km from village, take a lift for US$1. There is a disco at the riverside to the left of the bridge. Plagued by mosquitoes for all but five months of the year (winter and spring).

Puerto Lempira → *Colour map 6, B5.*

Puerto Lempira is on the large Caratasca Lagoon. The main office of MOPAWI (see above) is here. The airstrip is only five minutes' walk from town. Regular tuk-tuks (motorized canoes) cross the lagoon to **Kaukira**, US$1.20 (a nice place, but nothing there), **Yagurabila** and **Palkaka**. The tuk-tuks leave Kaukira daily except Sunday at 0500, returning during the morning. In the afternoon the lagoon is usually too rough to cross.

Inland by road from Puerto Lempira are **Mocorón** and **Rus Rus** which may be visited with difficulty (there is no public transport but any vehicle will give a lift) and is a beautiful, quiet village (accommodation at Friends of America hospital's house; meals from Capi's next door, ask Friends about transport out). A branch off this road leads southeast to **Leimus** on the Río Coco and the border with Nicaragua. Ask for Evaristo López (at whose house you can get breakfast) who can arrange transport to Leimus, most days, three to four hours for about US$3.50. He is also knowledgeable about area safety. See also box, opposite.

The road continues south to the small town of **Ahuashbila** on the upper river of the Río Coco which marks the border with Nicaragua.

Sleeping

Tegucigalpa to the northeast coast *p873*

F **Hospedaje Santos**, Campamento. Basic.

F **Hotel**, on plaza, Guaimaca, above restaurant Las Cascadas. Good value, clean, friendly.

F **Hotelito Granada**, Campamento. Basic.

F **Hospedaje San Carlos**, La Unión. Serves good vegetarian food.

Juticalpa *p873*

D **El Paso**, 1 Av NE y 6 Calle NO, 6 blocks south of Parque (on way to highway), T885-2311. Quiet, clean, bath, fan, laundry facilities. Highly recommended.

D **Las Vegas**, 1 Av NE, T885-2700, central, ½ block north of Parque. Clean, friendly, with *cafetería*.

D-F **Antúñez**, 1 Calle NO y 1 Av NO, a block west of Parque Central, T885-2250. With bath (cheaper without), friendly, clean, also annex in same street.

F **Familiar**, 1 Calle NO between Parque and Antúñez. With bath, clean. Basic but recommended.

F **Fuente**, 5 mins from bus station on left side of main road to town centre. Basic but large and clean rooms.

F **Regis**, 1 Calle NO. Balcony, good value.

Catacamas and around *p873*

E **Central**, in Barrio El Centro, T899-4276. With bath, cheaper without, big mango tree in front.

E **Juan Carlos**, Barrio José Trinidad Reyes, T899-4212. Good restaurant. Recommended.

E **La Colina**, T899-4488. With bath, hot water, fan, TV, parking.

F **Hospedaje Tania**, on the main street, Dulce Nombre de Culmí. Very basic.

Juticalpa to Trujillo *p874*

F **Centro**, San Esteban. Very clean, nice family, best.

F **Hotel Hernández**, San Esteban. Cheapest.

F **Hotel San Esteban**, San Esteban. Very friendly, clean.

G **Calle Real**, Gualaco, near Parque Central. Basic, friendly, will store luggage.

G **Hotelito Central**, Gualaco. Similar to Calle Real.

Coastal villages *p875*

F **In Plaplaya** Doña Yohana, close to the village centre, **Doña Sede**, east of village centre with good meals, or **Basilia**, traditional and the cheapest, 15 mins west of centre.

F **In Raistá and Belén** Choose between **Eddie and Elma Bodden** on the lagoon and **Doña Cecilia Bodden**, just up from the lagoon towards the sea. Try the food at **Elma's Kitchen** in Raistá, thought by some to be the best food on the coast. Near the lagoon between Raistá and Belén is **Doña Exe**, and in Belén there is **Doña Mendilia**, near the grass airstrip.

Las Marías *p878*

Balancing the benefits of tourism are difficult in such a sensitive area. Sharing the benefits is 1 way of off-setting the negative impact of tourism and, whenever possible, the Ecotourism Committee tries to share tourists between the 4 basic but clean *hospedajes* (all F) of **Ovidio**, **Justa**, **Tinglas** or **Diana**, with meals available for US$3.

Brus Laguna *p878*

D-E **Estancia** and **Paradise**. Rooms with a fan and optional private bath.

Puerto Lempira *p878*

D **Gran Hotel Flores**. Some rooms with bath. Recommended.

E **Villas Caratascas**. Huts with bath, restaurant, disco.

F **Charly's restaurant**, Mocorón. Rooms available. Price per person.

F **Pensión Moderno**. Good, friendly, with electricity 1800-2230.

Eating

Juticalpa *p873*
Casa Blanca, 1 Calle SE. Quite smart with a good cheap menu, good paella.
Comedor Any, 1 Av NO. Good value, friendly.
El Rancho, 2 Av NE. Specializes in meat dishes, wide menu, pleasant.
El Tablado, 1 Av NE entre 3 y 4 Calle NO. Good fish, bar.

Cafés
Helados Frosty, near Parque Central. Ice creams.
La Galera, 2 Av NE. Specializes in *pinchos*.
Tropical Juices, Blv de los Poetas. Good fruit juices.

Catacamas and around *p873*
As de Oro, Catacamas. Good beef dishes, Wild West decor.
Asia, Catacamas. Chinese.
Comedor Ejecutivo, Catacamas. Buffet-style meals US$2, local craft decorations.
Continental, Catacamas. Chicken dishes, pizza, US beer.

In Dulce Nombre de Culmí, there are several *comedores* on the main plaza

Juticalpa to Trujillo *p874*
Comedor Sharon, Gualaco. One of several places to eat.

There are 3 nice *comedores* in San Esteban near the Hotel San Esteban.

Puerto Lempira *p878*
Delmy, 3 blocks north of main street. Chicken and other dishes, noisy.
Doña Aida, north side of main road to landing bridge. Fresh orange juice.
La Mosquitia, Centro Comercial Segovia in main street. Breakfasts and cheap fish.

Entertainment

Catacamas and around *p873*
Bars and clubs
Fernandos and **Extasis**. **Montefresco** is outside town towards Tegucigalpa, pool (US$1.20), live music 2 evenings a week.

Cinema
Cine Maya, Barrio El Centro.

Puerto Lempira *p878*
Bars and clubs
Hampu, by landing bridge.

Shopping

Juticalpa *p873*
From 0600 Sat the market in Parque Central has a good selection of food, fruit, vegetables and souvenirs, said to be the best outdoor market in Olancho.

Activities and tours

Mosquitia *p874*
Tour operators
Several commercial guides organize trips into the Río Plátano Biosphere Reserve and may be a good option for those with limited Spanish. All-inclusive packages range from 3-14 days and cost about US$100 per day. In order to support ecotourism in the reserve you are encouraged to check out the tour operator you are considering to be sure they are working with local people in their operations. For other options, see under San Pedro Sula, La Ceiba and Trujillo.
La Moskitia Eco Aventuras, with Jorge Satavero, office in La Ceiba, T442-0104, www.honduras.com/moskitia, who specializes in trips to La Mosquitia.
Mesoamerica Travel and **Fundación Patuca** (Hauke Hoops), see page 832, also specialize in travel in this region. Mesoamerica is the only company to run tours to the Zona Arriba of the Río Patuca (5 or 10 days).
Bob 'The Butterfly, Bird and Bug Guy' Gallardo, based in Copán Ruinas, rgallardo32@hotmail.com, leads highly regarded birding and other specialized nature trips to La Mosquitia.

Las Marías *p878*
Tour operators
The services of the *saca guía* are US$3.50. Guides are required even for day hikes due to the possibility of getting lost or injured on the faint jungle trails. The cost for a guide is US$6 per day for groups up to 5. Overnight hikes require 2 guides. River trips in a *pipante*, a shallow dug-out canoe manoeuvered with poles (*palancas*) and paddles (*canaletes*), require 3 guides plus

US$4.20 for the canoe. Two visitors and their gear will fit in each boat with the guides.

Transport

Tegucigalpa to the northeast coast *p873*

Bus From **Comayagüela** to La Unión, daily, take 4 hrs. To get to the park, hire a truck from La Unión for about US$18. There's little traffic so it's difficult to hitchhike. If driving from **San Pedro Sula**, take the road east through Yoro and Mangulile; from **La Ceiba**, take the Savá-Olanchito road and turn south 13 km before Olanchito.

Juticalpa *p873*

Bus Bus station is on 1 Av NE, 1 km southeast of Parque Central, taxis US$0.50. Hourly to **Tegucigalpa** from 0330 to 1800; bus to **San Esteban** from opposite Aurora bus terminal at 0800, 6 hrs, US$2.25. Bus to **Trujillo** departs 0400, 9 hrs, US$5.20. Bus to **Tocoa** at 0500.

Catcamas and around *p873*

Bus From **Tegucigalpa** to Juticalpa/ Catacamas, **Empresa Aurora**, 8 Calle 6-7 Av, Comayagüela, T237-3647, hourly 0400-1700, 3¼ hrs, US$2 to Juticalpa, 4 hrs US$2.75 to Catacamas. **Juticalpa**-Catacamas, 40 mins, US$0.60. Catacamas-**Dulce Nombre de Culmí** (see below), 3 hrs, US$1.35, several daily.

Juticalpa to Trujillo *p874*

Bus To Juticalpa and to the north coast (Tocoa and Trujillo) are fairly frequent.

La Mosquitia *p874*

Air

Alas de Socorro fly to **Ahuas**, T233-7025. This company charters planes for US$565, but per person it is US$60 one way to Ahuas (see Hospital, below). SAMi flies to various villages from Puerto Lempira, eg **Ahuas**, **Brus Laguna**, **Belén**. There are expensive express flights to places like **Auka**, **Raya**, **Kaukira**.

Airline offices Sosa, T898-7467.

Boat

Coastal supply vessels run between La Ceiba and the coastal villages of La Mosquitia. The *Corazón* and *Mr Jim* make the trip weekly and their captains can be found at the harbour east of La Ceiba. Prices vary (US$10-20); be prepared for basic conditions. There are no passenger facilities such as beds or toilets on board and the journey takes a good 24 hrs.

Rivers, lagoons and inland waterways are the highways in the reserve and dug-out canoes provide the public transportation. Once in Palacios, you can catch *colectivo* boat transport at the landing near the **Río Tinto Hotel** to travel along the inland passage to coastal villages in the reserve such as Plaplaya, Raistá and Belén (about US$3.50 for a 1 or 2-hr trip). There is usually a boat to meet the planes that arrive in the morning and information on prices to different locations is posted in the airline offices. If you miss the *colectivo* you will usually have to pay extra for a special trip (about US$20).

Land

The cheapest and most favoured route by locals, a recently upgraded road means you can now make the journey by road. Take a bus from La Ceiba to Tocoa (US$2). From the market in Tocoa take a series of pick-ups (US$16 per person) along the beach to Batalla, crossing the various creeks that block the way in launches that wait to meet the cars. The journey to **Batalla** takes about 5½ hrs. From Batalla cross the lagoon in a boat to **Palacios** (US$0.70) and continue from there. The trip is not possible in the wetter months of the year (Jul, Oct and Nov). Some may suggest the possibility of catching a truck from Limón to Sangrilaya then walking along the beach and wading across rivers for 1-2 days to get to Batalla. While this is possible it is not recommended because of the heat, bugs and general safety issues.

Directory

Juticalpa *p873*

Banks BGA (the only one that will change TCs), Banco Atlántida, Bancahorro, Banco de los Trabajadores, Banco de Occidente, Banco Sogerín and Bancafé. **Post office** 2 blocks north from Parque Central, opposite Shell station. **Telephone** Hondutel on main street, 1 block from Parque Central.

Catacamas and around *p873*
Banks Banco Atlántida, Banco de Occidente, Banco El Ahorro Hondureño, Banco Sogerín, all in Barrio El Centro.
Medical services Dentist: Elvia Ayala Lobo, T899-4129.

Mosquitia *p874*
Medical services Hospitals: Alas de Socorro operates from Ahuas to collect sick people from villages to take them to Ahuas hospital. Contact the Moravian church (in Puerto Lempira Reverend Stanley Goff, otherwise local pastors will help).

Puerto Lempira *p878*
Banks Banco Nacional de Desarrollo Agrícola changes dollars at poor rates, bad reputation.

Tegucigalpa to the Pacific

From the capital to the Golfo de Fonseca the route twists through mountain valleys down to the volcanic islands and Honduras' Pacific ports of San Lorenzo and Amapala. Near the coast the Pan-American Highway leads west to El Salvador and east though the hot plains of Choluteca to the quiet but popular beaches of Cedeña and Ratón and ultimately to Nicaragua. An alternative route to Nicaragua heads east, through the agricultural town of Danlí, to the border at Las Manos. Short detours from the highway lead to picturesque colonial villages and old mining centres in the hills. » *For Sleeping, Eating and other listings, see pages 884-888.*

Tegucigalpa to Goascarán

From the capital a paved road runs south through fine scenery. Beyond Sabanagrande (see page 796) is **Pespire**, a picturesque colonial village with the beautiful church of San Francisco, which has triple domes. Pespire produces small, delicious mangoes. At **Jícaro Galán** (92 km) the road joins the Pan-American Highway, which heads west through **Nacaome**, where there is a colonial church, to the border with El Salvador at **Goascarán**. At Jícaro Galán, Ticabus and other international buses from San Salvador, Tegucigalpa and Managua meet and exchange passengers.

San Lorenzo → *Colour map 6, C2. Population: 21,025.*

The Pan-American Highway continues south from Jícaro Galán, to the Pacific coast (46 km) at San Lorenzo, a dirty town on the shores of the Gulf of Fonseca. The climate on the Pacific litoral is very hot.

Amapala → *Colour map 6, C2.*

A 31-km road leaves the Pan-American Highway 2 km west of San Lorenzo, signed to Coyolito. It passes through scrub and mangrove swamps before crossing a causeway to a hilly island, around which it winds to the jetty at **Coyolito** (no *hospedajes* but a *comedor* and *refrescarías*).

The Pacific port of Amapala, on Isla del Tigre, has been replaced by Puerto de Henecán in San Lorenzo, and is reached by a road which leaves the Pan-American Highway at the eastern edge of San Lorenzo. The **Isla del Tigre** is yet another place reputed to be the site of hidden pirate treasure. In the 16th century it was visited by a number of pirates, including Sir Francis Drake. Amapala was capital of Honduras for a brief period in 1876 when Marco Aurelio Soto was president. Today, in addition to a naval base, Amapala is 'a charming, decaying backwater'. The 783-m extinct Amapala volcano has a road to the summit where there is a US army unit and a DEA contingent. You can walk round the island in half a day. There is a ferry service from

Border essentials: Honduras-El Salvador

Goascarán
The Santa Clara bridge over the Río Goascarán is the border with El Salvador. A temporary pass can be purchased on the Honduran side for US$1.50 for a visit to the Salvadorean town of **El Amatillo**; many Hondurans cross to purchase household goods and clothes.
Honduran immigration The border closes at 1700. Try to avoid lunchtime when there may be a two-hour break. This border is very relaxed.
Crossing by private vehicle Expect to be besieged by young *tramitadores* touting for your business. They wear a black and white uniform of sorts with name badges, carry an identity card issued by the border station, and will take the strain out of the three- to four-hour border crossing. Expect to pay about US$25 to the various officials on both sides.
Salvadorean consulate See Choluteca, page 883.
Sleeping Two cheap *hospedajes*, San Andrés and Los Arcos on the Honduran side.
Transport Bus Tegucigalpa-El Amatillo, hourly, US$1.50, four hours. El Amatillo-Choluteca, US$1, three hours, every 30 minutes, microbuses.
Exchange Moderate rates of exchange from money changers.

Coyolito, but fishermen will take you to San Lorenzo for a small fee, not by motor launch, and the trip takes half a day. The deep-sea fishing in the gulf is good. It is possible to charter boats to La Unión in El Salvador.

Choluteca and around » pp884-888. Colour map 6, C3.

Choluteca is expanding rapidly on the back of the local industries of coffee, cotton and cattle which flourish despite the hot climate. The town was one of the earliest settlements in Honduras (1535) and still has a colonial centre. The church of **La Merced** (1643) is being renovated and is due to be reconsecrated. The **Casa de la Cultura** and **Biblioteca Municipal** are in the colonial house of José Cecilio del Valle on the corner of the Parque Central. A fine steel suspension bridge crosses the broad river at the entrance into Choluteca from the north (it was built in 1937). The social centre of **San José Obrero** ⓘ *3 Calle SO*, where handicrafts, in particular carved wood and chairs, can be bought. The **Mercado Municipal** ⓘ *7 Av SO, 3 Calle SO*, is on outskirts of town.

The city was heavily damaged by floods during Hurricane Mitch. The suspension bridge still stands, but both banks of the Río Choluteca suffered badly.

Cedeño beach, on the eastern side of the Gulf of Fonseca 40 km from Choluteca, is a lovely though primitive spot, with clean sand stretching for miles and often thundering surf. Avoid public holidays, weekend crowds and take a good insect repellent. Spectacular views and sunsets over the Gulf of Fonseca south to Nicaragua and west to El Salvador, and of the volcanic islands in the bay. Hourly bus from Choluteca (US$0.60, 1½ hours). A turn-off leads from the Choluteca-Cedeño road to Ratón beach, more pleasant than Cedeño. Bus from Choluteca at 1130; returns next morning.

East of Tegucigalpa

» pp884-888. Colour map 6, C3.

A good paved road runs east from Tegucigalpa through the hills to Danlí, 92 km away in the Department of El Paraíso. There are no signs when leaving Tegucigalpa so ask the way. Some 40 km along, in the Zamorano Valley (see page 796), is the Escuela Agrícola Panamericana which is run for all students of the Americas with US help: it has a fine collection of tropical flowers (visits should be booked in advance at the office in Tegucigalpa – see page 796).

Yuscarán

→ Colour map 6,C3. Population 9270. Altitude: 1070 m.

At Km 47.5, a paved road branches south to Yuscarán, in rolling pineland country preserved by the **Reserva Biológica de Yuscarán** which protects much of the land around Montserrat mountain. The climate here is semi-tropical. Yuscarán was an important mining centre in colonial days and is a picturesque village, with cobbled streets and houses on a steep hillside. Ask to see the museum near the town plaza, you have to ask around to find the person who has the key, antiques and photographs are displayed in a restored mansion which belonged to a mining family. There is a Casa de Cultura in the former Casa Fortín, open Monday-Saturday. The Yuscarán distilleries, one in the centre, the other on the outskirts, are considered by many to produce the best *aguardiente* in Honduras (tours possible). The Montserrat mountain which looms over Yuscarán is riddled with mines. The old Guavias mine is close to Yuscarán, some 4 km along the road to Agua Fría. About 10 km further along, a narrow, winding road climbs steeply through pine woods to the summit of **Pico Montserrat** (1891 m).

Danlí

→ Colour map 6, C3. Altitude: 760 m.

Danlí, 102 km from Tegucigalpa, is noted for sugar and coffee production, a large meat-packing company (Orinsa), and is a centre of the tobacco industry. There are four cigar factories. The **Honduras-América SA factory** ⓘ *right-hand side of Cine Aladino, Mon-Fri 0800-1200, 1300-1700, Sat 0800-1200.* produces export quality cigars at good prices. Also **Placencia Tabacos**, on the road to Tegucigalpa, where you can also watch cigar-making. Better prices than at Santa Rosa. From Danlí to the north is **Cerro San Cristóbal** and the beautiful **Lago San Julián**.

El Paraíso

→ Colour map 6, C3.

A paved road goes south 18 km to El Paraíso, and beyond to the Nicaraguan border at Las Manos/Ocotal. El Paraíso is a pretty town in an area producing coffee, bananas and rice.

Sleeping

Tegucigalpa to Goascarán *p882*

There are very basic hotels with restaurants at the border in Goascarán.

C Oasis Colonial, Jícaro Galán, T881-2220. nice rooms, good restaurant and pool and an unnamed basic guesthouse.

D Perpetuo Socorro, Barrio el Centro, Jícaro Galán, T895-4453. A/c, TV.

F Intercontinental, in centre, Jícaro Galán. Basic, tap and bucket shower, friendly.

F Suyapa, Jícaro Galán. Basic, cheap.

San Lorenzo *p882*

D Miramar, Barrio Plaza Marina, T881-2038. 26 rooms, 4 with a/c, good restaurant, overpriced, in rough dockside area, best not to walk there.

E-F Perla del Pacífico, on main street. Fan, bath, comfortable, clean, friendly, central, charming. Recommended.

Amapala *p882*

Ask for **Doña Marianita**, who rents the 1st floor of her house.

Border essentials: Honduras-Nicaragua

Las Manos

This is recommended as the best of the three routes from Tegucigalpa to Nicaragua.

Honduran immigration Border crossing open daily 0800-1600.

Crossing by private vehicle Whether entering or leaving Honduras, you will find *tramitadores* will help you through the paperwork, and are recommended. Total costs are about US$25 and the receipts may not quite tally with what you have paid.

Transport Direct bus Las Manos to Tegucigalpa, 0930, US$2.

Exchange Buy and sell your córdobas in Nicaragua.

El Espino

Border formalities can be particularly tedious at El Espino.

Honduran immigration Immigration is 100 m from the border, open daily 0800-1600 (till 1630 on Nicaraguan side). Beware of taxis offering to take you to the border after 1600.

Nicaraguan consulate In Tegucigalpa.

Transport Taxis/minibuses run from Choluteca and San Marcos (10 km) to the border. From San Marcos they only leave when full, US$1, US$0.50 for locals. To Tegucigalpa, there is a direct bus through Choluteca with **Empresa Esperanza**, 4 hrs.

Exchange This is easy at this crossing for dollars and córdobas, but the rate for córdobas is better on the Nicaraguan side.

Río Guasaule

The other route from Choluteca to Nicaragua goes through El Triunfo to the border at the bridge over the Río Guasaule. This route is preferred by the international buses as the road is better. It may be worth choosing one of the many 'helpers' to steer you to the correct officials. Fix price beforehand.

Honduran immigration Open daily 0800-1600. On Ticabus, passengers' passports are collected by an official as the bus enters Honduras. Entry tax is paid to the official, who returns passports after sniffer dogs have checked the bus for drugs. No other customs checks.

Transport Bus Choluteca-Guasaule, US$1, 45 mins.

Exchange There is a bank, but lots of money changers offer rates slightly worse than in the capital. Watch out for children who try to distract you while changing money.

B **Hotel Villas Playa Negra**, Aldea Playa Negra, T898-8534. 7 rooms with a/c, 7 with fan, pool, beach, restaurant, isolated, lovely setting.

F **Al Mar**, above Playa Grande. Fan, scorpions, lovely view of mountains and sunset.

F **Pensión Internacional** on the harbour. Very basic, otherwise only local accommodation of low standard.

Choluteca and around *p883*

B **La Fuente**, Carretera Panamericana, past bridge, T882-0253. With bath, swimming pool, a/c, meals.

D **Camino Real**, road to Guasaule, T882-0610. Swimming pool, good steaks in restaurant. Recommended.

D **Centroamérica**, near La Fuente, T882-3525. A/c, good restaurant, bar, pool, good value.

D **Escuela de Español Mina Clavo Rico**, El Corpus, Choluteca 51103 (east of Choluteca), T/F887-3501. Price per person, US$90 per week, full board, living with local families, language classes (US$4 per hr), riding, craft lessons, work on farms, excursions.

D-E **Pierre**, Av Valle y Calle Williams, T882-0676. With bath (ants in the taps), a/c or fan, TV, free protected parking, *cafetería* has good breakfasts, very central, credit cards accepted. Recommended.

E Brabazola, Barrio Cabañas, T882-5535. A/c, comfy beds, TV, good.

E Pacífico, near Mi Esperanza terminal, outside the city. Clean, cool rooms, fan, cable TV, hammocks, quiet, safe parking, fresh drinking water, breakfast US$1.50.

F Hibueras, Av Bojórquez, Barrio El Centro, T882-0512. With bath and fan, clean, purified water, *comedor* attached, good value.

F San Carlos, Paz Barahona 757, Barrio El Centro. With shower, fan, very clean, pleasant.

F Santa Rosa, 3 Calle NO, in the centre, just west of market, T882-0355. Some with bath, pleasant patio, laundry facilities, clean, friendly. Recommended.

East of Tegucigalpa *p884*

B Escuela Agrícola Panamericana. Rooms are available, but there is nowhere to eat after 1700.

Yuscarán *p884*

D-E Hotel, T892-7213. Owned by Dutchman Freek de Haan and his Honduran wife and daughter, private or dormitory rooms, beautiful views of Nicaraguan mountains in the distance.

F Hotel Carol. 6 modern rooms with bath and hot water, annex to owner's fine colonial house, safe, family atmosphere, good value.

Danlí *p884*

C-D Gran Hotel Granada, T883-2499. Bar, cable TV, accepts Visa, restaurant and swimming pool, locals pay half price.

D-E La Esperanza, Gabriela Mistral, next to Esso station, T883-2106. Bath, hot water, fan (more expensive with a/c), TV, drinking water, friendly, parking.

F Apolo, El Canal, next to Shell station, T883-2177. With bath, clean, basic.

F Danlí, El Canal, opposite **Apolo**. Without bath, good.

F Eben Ezer, 3½ blocks north of Shell station, T883-2655. Basic, hot showers.

F Las Vegas, next to bus terminal. Noisy, restaurant, washing facilities, parking.

F Regis, 3 blocks north of Plaza Central. With bath, basic.

El Paraíso *p884*

E-F 5a Av Hotel y Restaurant, 5 Av y 10 Calle, T893-4298. Bath, hot water, parking, restaurant specializes in Mexican-American food.

F Lendy's, Barrio Nuevo Carmelo, by bus station, T893-4461. Clean, prepares food.

Eating

San Lorenzo *p882*

¥¥ Restaurant-Bar Henecán, on Parque Central. A/c, good food and service, not cheap but worth it.

Amapala *p882*

¥ Mercado Municipal. Several clean *comedores*.

¥ Restaurant-Bar Miramar by the harbour. Overlooking the sea, pleasant, very friendly, good meals, hamburgers and *boquitas*, and you can hang your hammock.

Choluteca and around *p883*

¥¥ Alondra, Parque Central. Old colonial house, open Fri-Sun only.

¥ Comedor Central, Parque Central. *Comida corriente* daily specials, *licuados*, sandwiches, good for breakfast. Local specialities are the drinks *posole* and *horchata de morro*.

¥ El Burrito, Blv Choluteca between 4 and 5 Av N. With good-value meals and fast service.

¥ El Conquistador, on Pan-American, opposite **La Fuente**. Steaks, etc, outdoor seating but you have to eat inside, good but slow service. Will change money for customers. Recommended.

¥ Frosty, on main street. Owned by **Hotel Pierre**, good food and juices.

¥ Tico Rico, Calle Vincente Williams. Has been highly recommended.

Yuscarán *p884*

¥ Cafetería Colonial, opposite Banco de Occidente. Serves excellent *desayuno típico* and *comida corriente*.

Danlí *p884*

¥ Comedor Claudio. Good *comida corriente*, good information from locals.

¥ El Gaucho and **España**, town centre. Good.

¥ El Paraíso de las Hamburguesas. Cheap, good, owner very friendly.

Pizzería Picolino, 2 blocks southwest of Parque Central. Good pizzas.
Rancho Típico, El Canal, near **Hotel Danlí**. Excellent.

El Paraíso *p884*
Comedor Edith, on a small square on main road, after Parque Central towards border. US$0.85 for a meal.

Festivals and events

Choluteca and around *p883*
8 Dec The feast day of the **Virgen de la Concepción**, a week of festivities, followed by the **Festival del Sur, 'Ferisur'**.

Danlí *p884*
3rd week Aug **Fiesta del Maíz** lasts all week, with cultural and sporting events, all-night street party on the Sat; it gets very crowded with people from Tegucigalpa.

Transport

San Lorenzo *p882*
Bus Frequent *busitos* from **Tegucigalpa** to San Lorenzo (US$1) and **Choluteca** (US$1.50).

Amapala *p882*
Boat Motorized *lanchas* run between **Coyolito** and Amapala, US$0.35 per person when launch is full (about 10 passengers), about US$4 to hire a launch (but you will probably have to pay for the return trip as well). First boat leaves Amapala at 0700 to connect with first Coyolito-San Lorenzo bus at 0800; next bus from Coyolito at 0900.

Choluteca and around *p883*
Bus To **El Espino** (Nicaraguan border) from Choluteca, US$1.15, 1 hr, 1st at 0700, last at 1400. Also frequent minibuses to **El Amatillo** (El Salvador border) via San Lorenzo, US$1, from bus stop at bridge. Buses to Choluteca from Tegucigalpa with **Mi Esperanza**, **Bonanza** and **El Dandy**; **Bonanza** continues to San Marcos and departs Tegucigalpa hourly from 0530, 4 hrs to Choluteca, US$1.90. The municipal bus terminal is about 10 blocks from the new municipal market, about 8 blocks from cathedral/Parque Central; **Mi Esperanza** has its own terminal 1 block from municipal terminal.

Yuscarán *p884*
Bus Frequent buses to **Zamorano** and **Tegucigalpa**; from the capital buses leave from Mercado Jacaleapa. For information, ask anyone in the Parque Central in Yuscarán.

Danlí *p884*
Bus From **Tegucigalpa**, US$2, from Blv Miraflores near Mercado Jacaleapa (from left-hand side of market as you face it), Col Kennedy, Tegucigalpa, hourly, 2 hrs, arrive 1½ hrs before you want to leave, long queues for tickets (take 'Kennedy' bus from C La Isla near the football stadium in central Teguci-galpa, or taxi, US$1.20, to Mercado Jacaleapa). **Express** bus from Col Kennedy, 0830, 1230 and 1700, US$2. One road goes east from Danlí to **Santa María** (several buses daily), crossing a mountain range with great views.

El Paraíso *p884*
Bus Minibuses from **Danlí** terminal to El Paraíso, frequent (0600 to 1740), US$0.40, 30 mins, don't believe taxi drivers who say there are no minibuses. **Emtra Oriente**, Av 6, Calle 6-7, runs 4 times a day from **Tegucigalpa** to El Paraíso, 2½ hrs, US$1.50. Buses from El Paraíso to **Las Manos**, about every 1½ hrs, US$0.35, 30 mins, or taxi US$4, 15 mins.

Directory

San Lorenzo *p882*
Banks **Bancahorro** (changes US$ cash and TCs), **Banco Atlántida**, and **Banco de Occidente** (no exchange); Chinese grocery gives good rates for US$ cash.

Amapala *p882*
Banks Banco El Ahorro Hondureño.

Choluteca and around *p883*
Banks Of the many banks in town, **Banco Atlántida** has a Visa ATM, and only **Banco de Comercio** changes TCs. Can be difficult to exchange money in Choluteca.
Embassies and consulates **El Salvador**, to south of town, fast and friendly, daily 0800-1500. **Post office** Mon-Fri 0800-1700, Sat 0800-1200, US$0.15 per letter for Poste Restante.
Telephone Collect calls to Spain, Italy, USA only.

Danlí *p884*

Banks Banco Atlántida changes TCs without problems. Cash on Visa card, maximum US$50. Other banks as well.

Medical services Dentist: Dr Juan Castillo, Barrio El Centro, T883-2083.

El Paraíso *p884*

Banks Several branches in town including BGA, Banco Atlántida, Banadesa, Bancaféand Banco Sogerín.

Nicaragua

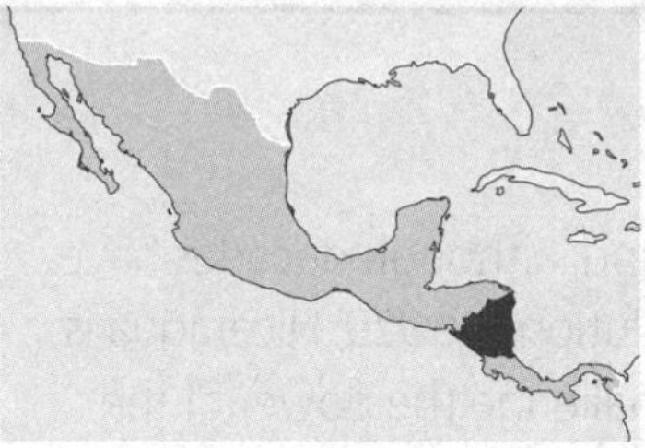

Footprint features

Introduction

Losing a reputation takes years and, although decades have passed since the Sandinista revolution of 1979, Nicaragua is still the country that fought to challenge the power of the Somoza dictatorship and suffered the political wrath of the US as a result. The memory of the conflict is prominent in the dark silhouette of Sandino that looks across Managua from the summit of Tiscapa Hill, and in a handful of museums and monuments in the northern towns of the country. Beyond these images and memories, talk of revolution has not disappeared, just receded. Nicaraguans are convinced that politicians – whether Somoza, Sandinistas or former president Arnoldo Alemán, imprisoned for 20 years for embezzlement – will always say one thing and do something completely different. In such a context, Nicaragua's beauty and charm reveals itself just occasionally.

Life is tough in a country dependent on agriculture that brings minimal wealth. Managua, beyond being the capital city, has little to attract the visitor. To the north, León has enough colonial churches to provide a one-stop guide to ecclesiastical architecture, and the hills around Matagalpa and Estelí provide great trekking opportunities.

But most travellers head south for for the hip Central American hang-out of Granada, or Masaya and nearby artisan centres. The island of Ometepe is the heart of Nicaragua, offering the chance to climb monkey-filled volcanic slopes. Alternatively, drift down the Río San Juan on the Costa Rican border to San Juan del Norte, or take the Rama Express to Bluefields and on to the Corn Islands for a spot of Caribbean diving. With surfing beaches and nesting turtles to the south near San Juan del Sur, and the open wilderness of the Miskitia heartland to the north, you'll find yourself a world away from the revolution.

★ Don't miss...

1 **Volcán Masaya** One of Central America's most active volcanoes, page 935.
2 **Laguna de Apoyo** Beautiful by day, spectacular by night with a full moon rising. Night swimming anyone? page 938.
3 **Granada** Charming city with cobbled streets and a bustling gringo life; one of Latin America's oldest towns, page 938.
4 **San Juan del Sur** The new surf spot in Central America – whisper it quietly, page 948.
5 **Isla Ometepe** Swim in the murky waters of Lake Nicaragua and visit the volcanic slopes of Ometepe Island, page 954.
6 **Río San Juan** From San Carlos to San Juan the river makes a fascinating trip, and it's a great route to Costa Rica, page 960.
7 **Corn Islands** Island life in the Caribbean; still quiet, but for how much longer? page 965.

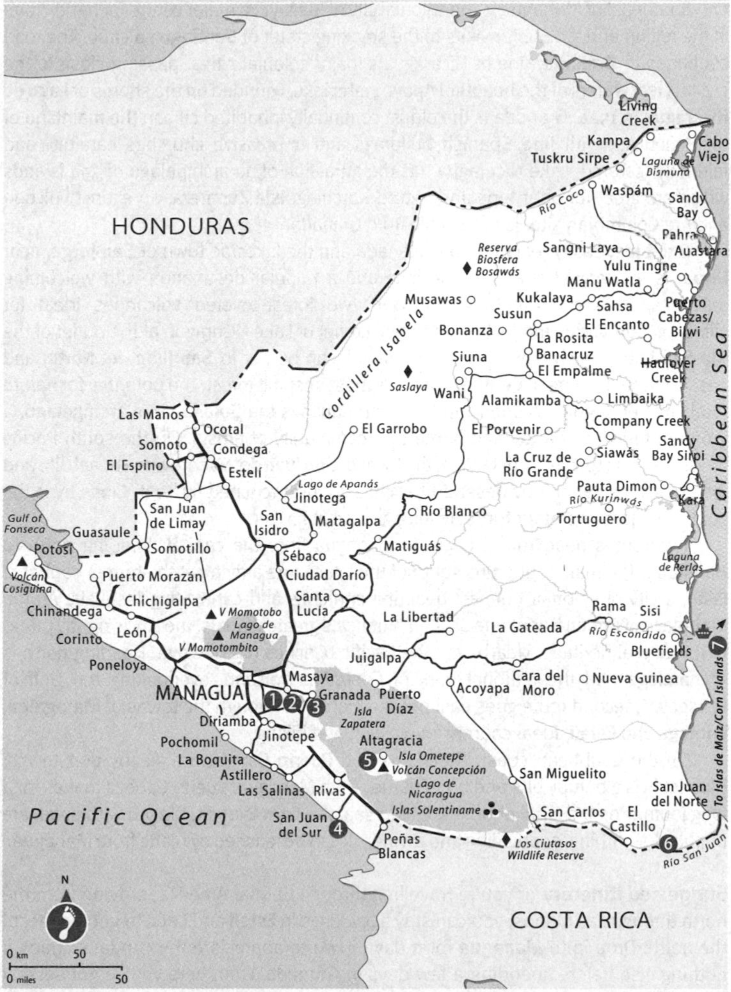

Planning your trip

Where to go

The largest of the Central American republics, Nicaragua is located at the junction of three continental plates. Earthquakes and volcanic eruptions frequently shake the country – at times to its foundations.

The people and most of the economic activity are concentrated in the western highlands, around the two great lakes of Managua and Nicaragua, and to the west of the volcanic chain which runs parallel to the Pacific shore. Stretching inland from the Caribbean coast, the largely unpopulated lowlands are challenging country for travelling and a nature paradise for those with the energy and time to spare.

Dramatic evidence of tectonic power can be seen in the capital, **Managua**, where the centre was destroyed by an earthquake in 1972. The old cathedral stands open to the skies, preserved as a museum. Other sites in the old colonial centre, close to the shores of **Lago de Managua**, reflect Nicaragua's recent civil war. Within easy reach of the capital are the Pacific beaches of **Pochomil** and **Masachapa**.

Southeast of Managua is the colonial city of **Masaya**, a major centre for handicrafts in the region and a base for visits to the smoking crater of **Santiago** volcano. The road continues to **Granada**, one of Nicaragua's major colonial cities, passing close to the crystal clear waters of the beautiful Apoyo crater lake. Founded on the shores of **Lago de Nicaragua** in 1524, Granada is the oldest continually inhabited city on the mainland of the Americas, with fine Spanish buildings and impressive churches carefully and faithfully restored. Lake Nicaragua has the attraction of an archipelago of 354 islands which are great for boat trips and nature watching. **Isla Zapatera**, an extinct volcano and pre-Columbian site, is accessible from Granada.

Ometepe, easily reached from Granada and the lakeside town of **San Jorge**, near **Rivas**, is the largest island in the lake and a popular destination with welcoming residents, indigenous petro-glyphs and two forest-covered volcanoes ideal for climbing. **San Carlos** marks the southeast corner of Lake Nicaragua at the outlet of the **Río San Juan**, which flows along the Costa Rican border to **San Juan del Norte**, and passes through some of Central America's most unspoilt forest; the potential for nature tourism is enormous. A short trip from San Carlos is the **Solentiname archipelago**, a group of forested islands and home to a community of artists. On the south Pacific coast, heading towards Costa Rica, the town of **San Juan del Sur** provides beach life and fabulous sunsets; nearby deserted beaches are best reached by boat. Close by is the country's most important turtle nesting ground at **La Flor**.

Two routes head round Lago de Managua from the capital, heading north to **Honduras**. The main route runs south of the lake shore arriving at the former capital of **León**, a city of colonial houses, beautiful churches and captivating festivals. As the birthplace of Rubén Darío, one of Latin America's greatest poets, the city is rightly proud of its cultural heritage. Nearby are the Pacific beaches of **Poneloya**. Heading north is **Chinandega** and the national park of **Cosigüina** volcano, overlooking the Gulf of Fonseca. A second route goes east of Lake Managua through the towns of **Matagalpa**, **Jinotega** and **Estelí**, ideal country for walking and hiking.

On the Caribbean coast, **Bluefields** and **Puerto Cabeza** are sleepy port towns. Bluefields is a bumpy bus and boat journey from Managua, Puerto Cabeza makes for a long journey on a couple of buses. Out to sea, the **Corn Islands**, fringed with coral, are popular for bathing, snorkelling and diving. All can be reached by plane from Managua.

Suggested itinerary If you're travelling through Central America, arriving from the north through Las Manos, you can stay a few days in **Estelí** and **León** to get the feel of the north. Drop in to **Managua** for a day or two to appreciate the capital's chaos if nothing else before spending a few days in **Granada**. From here you've got several options. Backtrack a bit for a few days in the isolated **Corn Islands**, or head round the southwest side of **Lake Nicaragua** and **Isla Ometepe. San Juan del Sur** on the Pacific coast is worth a stop before heading to Costa Rica. There are two options: straight down through **Peñas Blancas** which is good for the Nicoya Peninsula, or through **San Carlos**, good for Caños Negro Wildlife Reserve, Fortuna and Volcán Arenal.

When to go

The dry season runs from December to May, with temperatures becoming unbearably hot towards the end of the season. The wettest months are June to October. The most popular time to visit is just after the rainy season in November.

Finding out more

The Institute of Tourism in Managua (see page 899) has a wide range of brochures and information packs, www.intur.gob.ni.
In the **USA**, contact PO Box 140357, Miami, FL 33114-0357, T1-800-737-7253.

Useful websites

www.centramerica.com Has a search engine with news links and information.
www.nicanet.org For activist issues.
www.nicaragua.com Website with an e-community.
www.vianica.com Good general information, with details on hotels, transportation and itineraries.
www.toursnicaragua.com Has a good selection of photographs and images.

Language

A basic knowledge of Spanish is essential for independent travel in Nicaragua. On the Caribbean coast English is widely spoken, but in the rest of the country it's Spanish only.

Working and volunteering in Nicagua

Volunteer work in Nicaragua is not as common as it was during the Sandinista years. Foreigners now work in environmental brigades supporting the **FSLN**, construction projects, agricultural co-operatives and environmental organizations. Certain skills are in demand, as elsewhere in the developing world; to discover the current situation, contact non-governmental organizations in your home country, eg **Nicaraguan Network** ⓘ *1247 East St, SE, Washington, DC 20003, T202-544-9355, www.nicanet.org*; twin town/sister-city organizations and Nicaraguan Solidarity Campaigns, eg **NSC/ENN Brigades** ⓘ *129 Seven Sisters Rd, London N7 7QG, T020-7272-9619, www.nicaraguasc.org.uk*, or **Dutch Nicaragua Komitee** ⓘ *Aptdo Postal 1922, Managua.*

Casa Danesa ⓘ *T267-8126 (Managua)*, may be able to help find volunteer work, usually for three months, but shorter times are sometimes acceptable. An excellent short-term non-profit volunteer experience can be had with **El Porvenir** ⓘ *48 Clifford Terrace, San Francisco, CA 94117, T415-566-3976, www.elporvenir.org*, an outgrowth of **Habitats for Humanity**. Work is on drinking water, latrine and re-forestation projects.

Before you travel

Visas and immigration

Visitors need a passport with a minimum validity of six months and may have to show an onward ticket and proof of funds in cash or cheques for a stay of more than a week in the country. In reality this is rarely checked. No visa is required by nationals of European Union countries, the USA, Canada, Australia or New Zealand.

Visa rules are changing frequently, so check before you travel (www.cancilleria.gob.ni). If you need a visa it can be bought before arriving at the border, it costs US$25, is valid for arrival within 30 days and for a stay of up to 30 days;

 two passport photographs are required. A full 30-day visa can be bought at the border, but it is best to get it in advance. Visas take less than two hours to process in the embassies in Guatemala City and Tegucigalpa, but have been known to take 48 hours elsewhere. When consultation with Managua is required it takes longer. **Extensions** can be obtained at the **Dirección de Migración y Extranjería** ⓘ *Semáforo Tenderí, 1½ c al norte, Managua, T244-3989 ext 3 (Spanish only), www.migracion.gob.ni*. Arrive at the office before 0830. From the small office on the right-hand side you must obtain the *formulario* (3 córdobas). Then queue at the *caja* in the large hall to pay US$18 for your 30-day extension or US$37 for 90 days. This can take hours. In the meantime you can complete the forms. With the receipt of payment you queue at the window on the right. With luck you will receive the extension stamp by midday; you should get it the same day. There is a small Migración office in Metrocentro shopping mall where you can obtain a visa extension. Another possibility is to leave the country for at least 72 hours and re-enter on a new visa.

Nicaraguan embassies and consulates

Belgium, 55 Av de Wolvendael, 1180 Brussels, T375-6500.
Canada, contact Embassy in USA
Costa Rica, Av Central 2540, Barrio La California, San José, T223-1489.
El Salvador, Calle El Mirador y 93 Av Norte, No 4814, Col Escalón, San Salvador, T263-2292.
France, 34 Av Bugeaud, 75116 Paris, T4405-9042.
Germany, Joachim-Karnatz-Allee 45 (Ecke Paulstr) 10557 Berlin, T206-4380.
Honduras, Col Tepeyac, Bloque M-1, No 1130, DC T239-5225.
Italy, Via Brescia 16, 00198 Roma, T841-4693.
Japan, Kowa Bldg 38, Rm 903, 4-12-24, Nishi-Azabu, Minato-Ku, Tokyo 106, T3499-0400.
Mexico, Prado Norte 470, Col Lomas de Chapultepec, esq Explanada, 5540-5625.
Spain, Paseo de la Castellana 127, 1°-B, 28046 Madrid, T555-5510.
Sweden, Sandhamnasgatan 40,-6 tr, 11528, Stockholm, T667-1957.
UK, Vicarage House, 58-60 Kensington Church St, London W8 4DB, T020-7938-2373.
USA, 1627 New Hampshire Av NW Washington, DC 20009, T202-939-6570.

For the latest information on visa requirements and embassies look at www.cancilleria.gob.ni

Customs

Duty-free import of ½ kg of tobacco products, three litres of alcoholic drinks and one large bottle (or three small bottles) of perfume is permitted.

Money

Currency → *US$1=17.89 córdobas.*

The unit of currency is the **córdoba** (C), divided into 100 centavos. Any bank in Nicaragua will change US$ to córdobas and vice-versa. US dollars are accepted almost everywhere but change is given in córdobas.

Bank queues can be very long and you should allow plenty of time, especially on Monday mornings and the 15th and 31st of every month. When changing money take some ID or a copy. It is not possible to change currencies other than US dollars and Euros (**BanCentro** only) in Nicaragua. Money changers on the street (*coyotes*) during business hours are legitimate and their rates differ little from banks.

Exchange

Visa and MasterCard are accepted in nearly all restaurants and hotels, and in many shops. This applies to a lesser extent to Amex, Credomatic and Diners Club. But don't rely exclusively on credit cards. For cash advances the most useful bank is **Banco de América Central** (BAC). BAC offers credit card advances, uses the Cirrus debit system and changes all traveller's cheques with a 5% commission. In Managua ATM machines are found in the airport (Visa only), at the Metrocentro and Plaza Inter shopping malls and in many gas station convenience stores. Outside the capital ATMs are increasingly common in the main towns and at gas stations. Traveller's cheques often carry a commission of 5% so use your credit/debit card or cash if you can. Traveller's cheques can only be changed in Managua at **Multicambios** in Plaza España and around the country at branches of **Banco de Finanzas** (American Express cheques only) and **Banco de America Central.** Purchase receipts may be required when changing traveller's cheques in banks. It is best to carry US dollar notes and sufficient local currency away from the bigger towns.

ATMs are hard to find outside the capital. Try 24-hour petrol convenience stores.

Cost of living and travelling

Nicaragua is not an expensive country as far as hotel accommodation is concerned, and public transport is also fairly cheap. For food, a *comida corriente* costs about US$1.40 (meals in restaurants US$6-13, breakfasts US$2.50-3.50). However, on the islands or in out of the way places where supplies have to be brought in by boat or air, you should expect to pay more. A tight daily budget would be around US$20-25 a day.

Getting there

Air

From Europe Take any transatlantic flight to Miami or Houston and connect to **American, Continental** or **Grupo Taca.**

From USA Regular daily flights from Miami, Atlanta and Houston with either **American, Continental, Delta, Iberia** or **Taca**. Also from several US cities connecting through El Salvador.

From Latin America Good connections to Barranquilla, Bogotá, Buenos Aires, Cali, Cancún, Caracas, Cartagena, Guatemala City, Guayaquil, Havana, La Paz, Lima, Medellín, Mexico City, Panama City, Quito, San José, San Salvador, Santiago, Santo Domingo and São Paulo.

River

In San Carlos there is an immigration post linking with the boat journey on the Río Frío connecting to Los Chiles in Costa Rica. There is no official border crossing between San Juan del Norte and Costa Rica.

Road

The main road links to the north are at El Guasaule (page 930) and further inland on the Pan-American Highway at Las Manos (page 918) with a third option at the border north of Somoto at El Espino in Honduras (page 918). Crossing the border to Costa Rica in the south, the most commonly used crossing is at Perlas Blancas (page 949), although it is also possible to leave from San Carlos for Los Chiles (page 959), connecting with Fortuna and Lake Arenal.

Touching down

Airport information

All passengers arriving by air pay an entry tax of US$5, while departing passengers must pay an airport tax of US$32, payable in US dollars. All passengers have to pay a

Touching down

Business hours Mon-Fri 0800-1200, 1430-1730. Banks: Mon-Fri 0830-1200, 1400-1600, Sat 0830-1200/1300.
Official time 6 hrs behind GMT.
Telephone Country code T+505.
Voltage 110 volts AC, 60 cycles, US-style plugs.
Weights and measures The metric system is official, but in practice a mixture is used of metric, imperial and old Spanish measurements, including the *vara* (about 1 m) and the *manzana* (1.73 acres). Petrol is measured in US gallons, liquids in quarts and pints, speed in kph, fabric in yards, with centimetres and metres for height, pounds for weight and Celsius for temperature.

sales tax of US$5 on tickets issued in and paid for in Nicaragua; a transport tax of 1% is levied on all tickets issued in Nicaragua to any destination. For information on Managua airport, see page 910. The cost of entry overland is US$8, although this may be less on weekdays. Exit tax for foreigners is US$2 in cash, US$5 at weekends. If in the slightest doubt about charges, insist on being given a receipt and go to the Immigration Department in Managua to verify the charge. Officials in Las Manos are reported to try and overcharge – be firm. Motorists, see below.

Local customs and laws

Tipping US$0.50 per bag for porters; no tip for taxi drivers. Restaurants add 10%.

Safety

Visitors to Nicaragua must carry their passports with them at all times. If you carry a photocopy, make sure to have a copy of your visa or entrance stamp as well. They may inspect luggage on entering and leaving Nicaragua. Pickpocketing and bag slashing occur in Managua in crowded places, and on buses throughout the country. Apart from Managua at night, most places are generally safe. Reports of robberies and assaults in northern Nicaragua indicate that care should be taken in this area; ask about conditions before going, especially if proposing to leave the beaten track.

Getting around

Air

La Costeña ⓘ *T263-1228*, operates internal air services to Bluefields, Corn Island, Minas (Bonanza/Siuna/Rosita), Puerto Cabeza, San Carlos and Waspám (see text for details). **Atlantic Airlines** ⓘ *T270-5355*, *www.atlanticairlinesint.com*, provide similar coverage and connections to Tegucigalpa and other cities in Honduras.

Domestic flights should be reconfirmed as soon as possible. There is a 9 kg hand luggage limit. Stowed luggage 13.5 kg free, maximum 45 kg. Domestic departure tax is 30 córdobas in Managua and usually 15 córdobas in outlying airports.

Road

The road network has been greatly extended and improved in recent years. The Pan-American Highway from Honduras to Costa Rica is paved the whole way (384 km) as is the shorter international road to the Honduran frontier via Chinandega. The road between Managua and Rama (for Bluefields) is also paved.

Bus Local buses are the cheapest in Central America and often the most crowded. Baggage loaded on to the roof or in the luggage compartment may be

charged for, usually at half the passenger rate or a flat fee of US$0.50. International
Ticabus buses link Nicaragua with Central America from Panama to southern Mexico.

Car and motorcycle Motorists and motorcyclists must pay US$20 in cash on arrival at the border (cyclists pay US$2, and up to US$9 at weekends, though this tends to vary from one customs post to the next). There are no exit fees. For **motorcyclists**, the wearing of crash helmets is compulsory. Motorists pay the same entry tax as other overland arrivals (see above). Make sure you get all the correct stamps on arrival, or you will encounter all sorts of problems once inside the country. Do not lose the receipts, they have to be produced when you leave; without them you will have to pay again. Vehicles not cleared by 1630 are held at customs overnight. Up to four hours of formalities are possible when entering Nicaragua with a vehicle. On leaving, motorists pay five córdobas, as well as the usual exit tax. For procedures at each border, see the relevant sections of text. Petrol is sold by the gallon. Regular petrol costs US$2.60 per gallon, US$2.90 for super, diesel US$2.30 super - all are unleaded. There are 24-hour service stations in the major cities, elsewhere they close at 1800. Be careful when driving at night, few roads are lit and there are many people, animals and holes in the road.

Car hire costs around US$30 a day for a basic car, rising to US$85 for a jeep. Weekly discount rates are significant and if you want to cover a lot of sites quickly it can work out to be worthwhile. A minimum deposit of US$500 is required along with an international drivers' licence or a licence from your country of origin. Insurance is US$10-23 depending on cover. Before signing up check insurance and what it covers and also ask about mileage allowance. Most agents have an office at the international airport and offices in other parts of Managua.

Cycle Several cyclists have said that you should take a 'proof of purchase' of your cycle or suggest typing out a phoney 'cycle ownership' document to help at border crossings.

Hitchhiking Hitching is widely accepted, but not easy because so many people do it and there is little traffic – offer to pay a small contribution.

Sea

The main **Pacific ports** are Corinto, San Juan del Sur and Puerto Sandino. The two main **Atlantic ports** are Puerto Cabezas and Bluefields.

Sleeping

Most hotel accommodation is run by independent operators with a few international chains beginning to enter the top end of the market. Standards vary greatly but there is plenty of competition in the mid- to low-budget range in most towns. In smaller towns cheaper hotels tend to be better value.

Eating

Try *nacatamales*, cornflower dumplings stuffed with pork or chicken and vegetables, and boiled in banana leaves, an excellent value meal. *Gallo pinto* – rice and beans – is another tasty dish. Fizzy drinks are known as *gaseosas* in Nicaragua as in neighbouring countries. Fresh fruit-based drinks and juices are *frescos*. Coffee can be terrible as most good Nicaraguan beans go for export and locals drink instant – ask for *café percolado*. Restaurant bills attract a 15% tax and 10% service is added or expected as a tip.

Shopping

Masaya is the centre for *artesanía*, selling excellent crafts, high-quality cotton hammocks, leather goods and colourful woven rugs often used as wall hangings and wicker furniture. Ceramics are produced in many parts of the country.

Festivals and events

1 Jan New Year's Day.
Mar or Apr Holy Week from midday on Wed to Easter Sun.
1 May Labour Day.
19 Jul Revolution of 1979.
14 Sep Battle of San Jacinto.
15 Sep Independence Day.
2 Nov All Souls' Day (Día de los Muertos).
7 and 8 Dec Immaculate Conception (La Purísima).
25 Dec Christmas Day.

Businesses, shops and restaurants all close for most of Holy Week; many companies also close down during the Christmas-New Year period. Holidays which fall on a Sunday are taken the following Monday. Local holidays are listed under the towns.

Sport and activities

The national game is baseball, with a season running from November to February. Football comes a poor second, breaking the trend in most Latin countries.

Opportunities for **nature tourism** are growing rapidly, with the lowlands of the Caribbean coast and the highlands around Matagalpa attracting keen **nature watchers**. The islands of Lake Nicaragua and the Maribios volcanoes of León and Chinandega are popular destinations for **trekking**. Granada is experiencing a steady rise in interest and activities like **mountain biking** are growing rapidly. **Hot-air balloon** rides are available with flights over Managua and volcanoes. The Pacific coast has a few good swimming beaches and there are excellent **surfing** opportunities to the south. Out on the Corn Islands, **snorkelling** and **diving** are possible on nearby coral reefs.

Health

Take the usual tropical precautions with food and drink. Tap water is not recommended for drinking outside Managua, León and Granada and avoid uncooked vegetables and peeled fruit. Intestinal parasites abound; if requiring treatment, take a stool sample to a laboratory before going to a doctor. **Malaria** risk exists especially in the wet season; high risk areas are east of the great lakes, take regular prophylaxis. **Dengue fever** is increasingly present, including in Managua; avoid being bitten by mosquitoes.

Keeping in touch

Communications

Internet Widely available in the main cities and many smaller towns.

Post Airmail to Europe takes seven to 10 days, US$0.80; to USA, 18 days, US$0.55; to Australia, just over US$1.

Telephone and fax **Country code**: T505. Phone lines are owned by the **Enitel**. Automatic national and international telephone calls are possible from any phone.

Phone numbers in Nicaragua have seven digits. If you are phoning from inside the prefix zone you need to dial the seven digits, but if you are dialling a different zone you put 'o' in front. For example, to call Managua from Masaya it would be T0266-8689. Phone cards are available from gas stations, supermarkets and some shops.

International or national calls can be made at any **Enitel** office, 0700-2200. All phone calls paid for in córdobas. To the USA, US$3 for the first minute, US$1 for each following minute. Collect calls (*por cobrar*) to the USA and Europe are possible. For SPRINT, dial 171; AT&T 174 and MCI 166. To connect to phone services in Germany dial 169, Belgium 172, Canada 168, Spain 162, Netherlands 177, UK 175.

If phoning from inside the prefix zone, dial the seven digits; if dialling a different zone, put '0' in front. For example, to call Managua from Masaya it would be T0266-8689.

Media

Newspapers All newspapers are published in Managua, but many are available throughout Nicaragua: **Dailies**: *La Prensa*, centre, the country's best, especially for coverage of events outside Managua; *El Nuevo Diario*, centre-left and sensationalist; *La Noticia*, right, government paper. **Weeklies**: *El Seminario*, left-leaning, well-written with in-depth analysis; *7 Días*, pro-Government; *Tiempo del Mundo*, owned by Rev Moon, good coverage of South America, not much on Nicaragua. **Monthlies**: *El País*, pro-Government, good features. *Between the Waves*, tourist magazine in English.

Managua

→ *Colour map 7, A1. Population: 1,328,695. Altitude: 40-200 m.*

Managua, the nation's capital and commercial centre since 1852, was destroyed by an earthquake in March 1931 and then partially razed by fire five years later. Rebuilt as a modern, commercial city, the centre was again decimated by an earthquake in December 1972 when just a few modern buildings were left standing. Severe damage from the Revolution of 1978-1979 and flooding of the lakeside areas as a result of Hurricane Mitch in 1998 added to the problems. It's a tribute to the city's resilience that it still has the energy to carry on. ▸▸ *For Sleeping, Eating and other listings, see pages 905-913.*

Ins and outs

Getting there The airport is 12 km east of the city, near the lake. Buses and taxis (US$15 to Barrio Martha Quezada) run from the airport to the city. International bus services arrive at several terminals throughout the city. Conveniently **Ticabus** and **King Quality** are in Barrio Martha Quezada, where most of the cheap hotels are to be found. Provincial bus services have three main arrival/departure points. City buses and taxis serve the provincial terminals. ▸▸ *For further information see Transport, page 910.*

Getting around Managua is on the southern shores of Lake Managua (Lago Xolotlán), 60 km from the Pacific. Since 1997, the old centre has become a garden monument consisting mainly of open spaces, ageing buildings and lakeside cafés and restaurants. Despite lying over 14 seismic faults and the warnings of seismologists, some important new buildings have been built in the old centre, including a presidential palace between the ruins of the old cathedral and the lake front, the epicentre of the 1972 earthquake.

Directions are given according to landmarks; instead of cardinal points, the following are used: al lago *(north),* arriba *(east),* al sur *(south),* abajo *(west). This applies to the whole country, although* al norte *(north) is used outside Managua; even where there are street names or numbers, Nicaraguans give direction by landmarks.*

Two areas now lay claim to being the heart of Managua and both have multi-level shopping centres. The older of the two is based around the **Hotel Crown Plaza** (formerly the Hotel Intercontinental and is still referred to as old or 'viejo Intercontinental'), with a shopping and cinema complex, complete with US-style 'food court' and, to the west, **Barrio Martha Quezada** with many mid-range and budget hotels, and international bus services. Nearby, to the south, **Plaza España** has the country's best supermarket and numerous shops, banks, travel agents, tour companies and nearly every airline office in the country. The other heart of the city is based on the **Carretera a Masaya**, running from the new cathedral to Camino de Oriente. This stretch of four-lane highway includes the **Rotonda Rubén Darío**, the **Metrocentro** shopping complex, numerous restaurants, the new Pellas family business centre with the **BAC** and **Credomatic** headquarters, and the cinema, disco and offices of **Camino de Oriente**. You'll need to take a bus or taxi to get there or to the provincial bus terminals. **Buses** are cheap, crowded and infamous for their pickpockets. Their routes can be hard to fathom (some of the main ones are given on page 910). **Taxis** must have red number plates. Taxi-sharing in Managua is standard for non-radio taxis, so don't be surprised if the driver stops to pick someone up on roughly the same route. » *For further information see Transport, page 910.*

Tourist office Instituto Nicaragüense de Turismo (Intur) ⓘ *1 block west of the Hotel Crown Plaza, enter by the side door, T222-3333, information service T112, www.intur.gob.ni, Mon-Sat 0800-1700*, provides standard information, including information on all types of transport in the country.

Information on national parks and conservation should be obtained from **Sistema Nacional de Areas Protegidas (Sinap)** ⓘ *Ministerio de Medio Ambiente y Recursos Naturales (Marena), Km 12.5 Carretera Norte, T263-2617.*

Security Nicaraguans are incredibly friendly and, although Managua is one of the safest cities in Latin America, a few simple guidelines may be useful. Never walk at

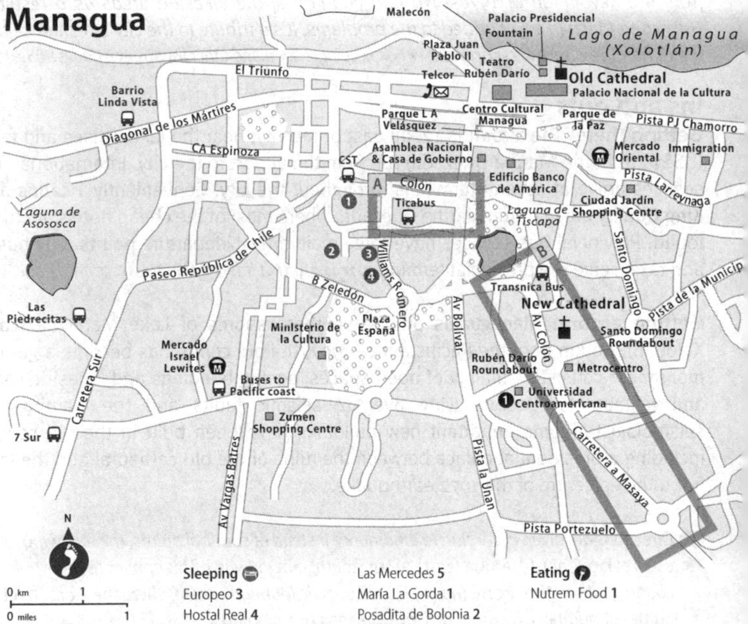

Sleeping
Europeo 3
Hostal Real 4
Las Mercedes 5
María La Gorda 1
Posadita de Bolonia 2

Eating
Nutrem Food 1

night unless you are in a good area or shopping centre zone. If you find yourself in a very poor neighbourhood simply take the next radio taxi. Arriving in Managua at night is not a problem, but choose your hotel in advance and take a taxi straight there. Long-distance buses are fine, but be careful in the market when you arrive to take the bus. If you prefer to avoid the bus terminals all together, get off the bus before you reach the market. When you arrive at the **Ticabus** station, make sure you know where you want to go before setting out. The **Mercado Oriental** (not to be confused with the Camino de Oriente which is safe and fun), said to be the largest informal market in Latin America, and its barrio, Ciudad Jardín, should be avoided at all costs.

Sights

In the old centre of Managua near the lake shore, the attractive neoclassical **Palacio Nacional de la** Cultura, previously the Palacio de los Héroes de la Revolución, has been beautifully restored and houses the **Museo Nacional de Nicaragua** ⓘ *Mon-Fri 0800-1200, 0200-1800, Sat 0800-1200, US$2, includes a 20-min introductory guided tour in English and French*, as well as the Archivo Nacional and the Biblioteca Nacional.

Damaged by earthquake, the **Catedral Vieja** (old cathedral) now has a roof of narrow steel girders and side-window support bars to keep it standing, the atmosphere is of a sad, old building past its prime, left in ruins, but still worth a look. The **Centro Cultural Managua**, next to the Palacio Nacional de Cultura, has a good selection of before and after photos of quake-struck Managua in 1972. The centre is also home to the national art school and the national music school. There are some art exhibits in galleries downstairs.

The garishly painted **Palacio Presidencial** is in front of the Palacio de la Cultura on the opposite corner to the old cathedral. These buildings are situated on the **Parque Central** and provide a striking contrast with the modern **Teatro Rubén** Darío ⓘ *on the lake shore, US$1.50-US$20 depending on show*, which hosts good plays, folkloric dances and musical events. There are usually temporary exhibitions in the theatre so, during the day, ask at the window to view the exhibit and you can probably look at the auditorium as well. The **Parque de la Paz**, just southeast of the Parque Central, is part of the rebuilding programme for the old centre. The park is a graveyard for weapons and a few dozen truckloads of AK-47s are buried there, some seen sticking out of the cement. Three blocks south of the Parque Central are the offices of the Asamblea Nacional (Nicaraguan parliament), which include the city's only high-rise building, once the Bank of America, now the offices of the *diputados* (parliamentary members).

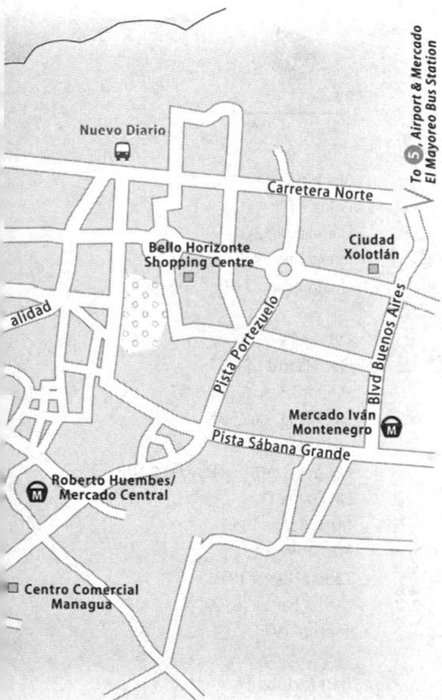

A significant landmark is the **Hotel Crown Plaza**, which has a distinctive design similar to a Maya pyramid. It used to be the **Hotel Intercontinental** and is likely to be referred to as the *Inter* by locals for several years. Just in front is the Plaza Inter shopping centre with cinemas, restaurants and shops. The Bolívar-Buitrago junction, at the northwest corner of Plaza Inter, is on a number of important bus routes.

Metrocentro

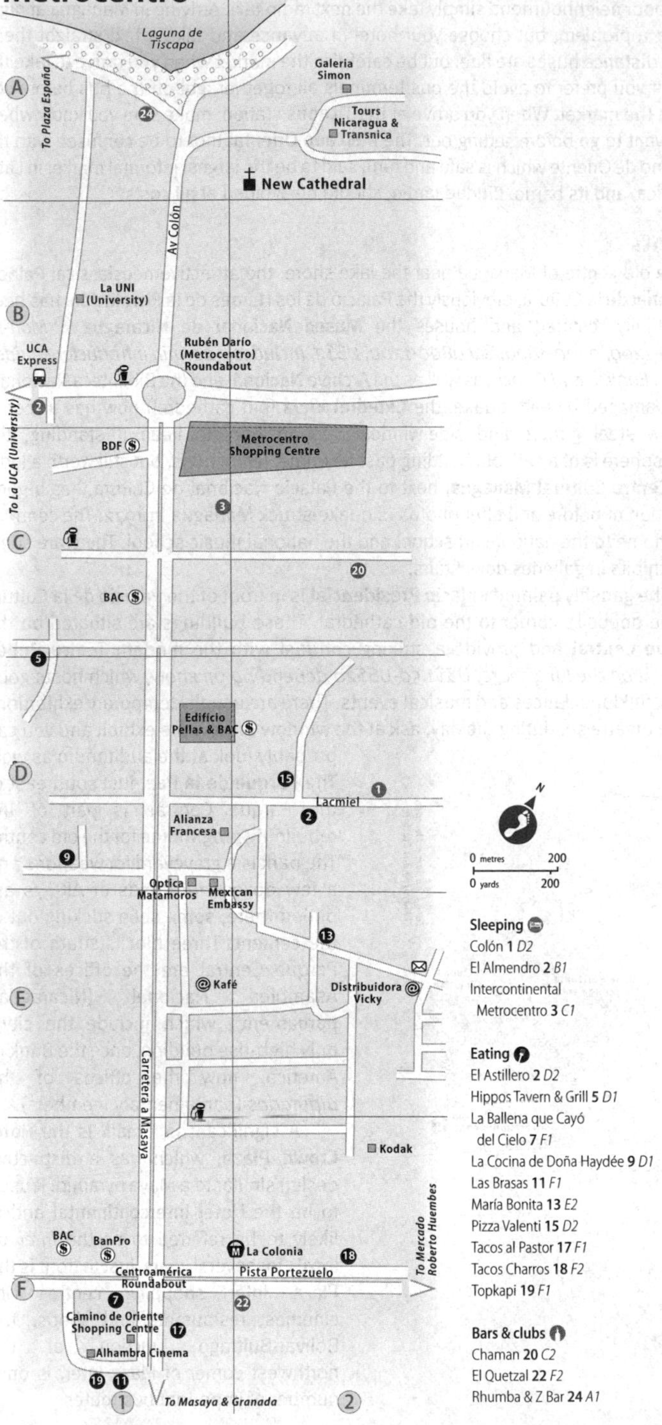

From the hilltop behind the Hotel Crown Plaza the **Parque Nacional de la Loma de Tiscapa** provides the best views of the capital and of the **Laguna de Tiscapa** on the south side of the hill. From the top, a giant black silhouette of **Sandino** stands looking out over the city. The spot has historical significance as it is the site of the former presidential palace; it was here that Sandino signed a peace treaty with Somoza and was abducted (and later killed) at the entrance to the access road. Underneath the park facing the *laguna* (now blocked by a fence) are the **former prison cells of the Somoza regime** ⓘ *daily 0800-1630*, where inmates were said to have been tortured before being tossed into the lake. To get there, take the road behind the Crown Plaza to the top of the hill using an access road for the Nicaraguan military headquarters. Guards at the park are nervous about photography; ask permission and photograph only downtown and towards the stadium – do not take photos on the access road up to the park.

From Tiscapa hill, the **Catedral Nueva** (new cathedral), inaugurated in 1993, can be seen 500 m to the south of the lake. Designed by the Mexican architect Ricardo Legoreto, comments on the exterior range from 'strikingly beautiful' to 'sacreligious'. The interior, which is mostly unadorned concrete, has been described as 'post-nuclear, with an altar resembling a futuristic UN Security Council meeting room' Many visitors are fascinated by the Sangre de Cristo room, where a life-size bleeding Christ is encased in a glass and steel dome, illuminated by a domed roof with hundreds of holes for the sun to filter through. At night, the dome sparkles with the glow of lightbulbs in the holes. Pedestrian access is possible from the Metrocentro junction, while vehicles need to approach from the east.

Barrio Martha Quezada, a mixture of well-to-do housing alongside poorer dwellings, is to the west of the Crown Plaza. South again, through the Bolonia district, is **Plaza España** by the Rotondo El Güengüense roundabout. Plaza España is reached either by continuing over the hill behind the Crown Plaza and branching right at the major junction, or by going south on Williams Romero, the avenue at the western edge of Barrio Martha Quezada (bus No 118).

Around Managua » pp905-913.

Laguna de Xiloá

ⓘ *Take bus No 113 to Las Piedrecitas for Xiloá, Sat and Sun only (US$0.35), US$1.60 for cars, US$0.30 for pedestrians.*

There are several volcanic-crater lakes close to Managua, some of which have become centres of residential development, with swimming, boating, fishing and picnicking facilities for the public. Among the more attractive of these lakes is Laguna de Xiloá, 16 km from Managua just off the new road to Léon. On Saturday and Sunday, the only days when buses run, Xiloá gets very crowded. It is quiet during the week and you can camp there, but without public transport you will have to walk or take a taxi. Other lakes within a 45-minute drive of Managua are the **Laguna de Masaya** and **Laguna de Apoyo** (see page 937).

Museo Las Huellas de Acahualinca

ⓘ *Along the lake, 2 km due west of the Museo Nacional, T266-5774, Mon-Fri 0800-1700, Sat 0800-1600, US$2 with an additional US$2 charged to take photographs and US$3 to use video cameras; all explanations in Spanish; taxi recommended as it is hard to find.*

These ancient prehistoric animal and human footprints, preserved in the sedimentary tufa and discovered when stone was being quarried to build homes in the area, represent some of the oldest evidence of human occupation in Nicaragua. A museum has been created around the original site and the 6000-year-old footprints have been left exactly as they were found in excavation. The museum also has a small display of ceramic artefacts found at the site (the oldest ceramics date from 1000 BC, 3000 years later than the footprints) and an illustration of the estimated height of the people who made the footprints.

Buses Nos 102, 12 or 6 pass the site; look for a concrete tower and a huge stone slab by a small red footbridge. Off the main road there are no signs. If you are driving, take the street that leads west (*abajo*) from the old centre. Turn right immediately before López Richardson; the pavement becomes a dirt road and the museum is on the right.

Mateare and Momotombito

Thirty kilometres northwest of Managua, **Mateare** is a pleasant fishing and agricultural town with some of the finest lake fish in Lake Managua (eat at your own risk). Distanced from the capital by a large peninsula, the lake is much cleaner here than on the Managua side. The fishermen can take you to the small volcanic island of **Momotombito**. The best time of year to visit is during the rainy season, when the island is green and the swell on the lake small. Price about US$60 for the day. There are other small islands in the shadow of the smoking Momotombo volcano, which appears to loom over the lake from the mainland shore. Momotombito is a nature reserve, and has much bird and reptile life and a legendary family of albino crocodiles. There is a small military outpost on the calm side of the island. Stop there to check in if you wish to hike on the islands. Bring drinks or food as gifts for the (non-uniformed) guards, who are very friendly and usually quite bored. They might take you hiking for a small fee.

! Beware of snakes when hiking around the island.

Pacific beaches near Managua

There are several beaches on the Pacific coast, about an hour's drive from Managua. Because of their proximity to the capital, they get very crowded during the high season (January to April). The nearest are **Pochomil** and **Masachapa** (54 km from Managua, bus service from terminal in Israel Lewites market every 35 minutes, US$1 to Pochomil). Pochomil is deserted in the week out of season; it gets cleaner the further south you go, but there are rock and strong waves here, so swim with care. It is a tourist centre with a few hotels and many small family owned restaurants.

! Don't sleep on the beach, mosquitoes will eat you alive.

At the entrance to Masachapa is the access road to the **Montelimar Resort**. Just before the gates of the resort is the dirt access road to the area's nicest public beach, **Montelimar Gratis** or **El Muelle de Somoza**, which is a long deserted stretch of clean sand running from the crumbling, old Somoza family pier to the rocky point that separates the resort from the rest of Masachapa. Take a bus to Masachapa and walk from main highway on the entrance road or drive to the pier, then walk north.

La Boquita is the nearest beach to the villages south of Managua and is visited by turtles from August to November. At **Casares** (69 km from Managua), south of La Boquita, the beaches are just south of the village. Access is a long hike or journey by 4WD and lodging is available.

Heading north from Managua, a visit to the broad, sandy **El Velero** beach ⓘ *US$3.50*, is recommended, despite the entry fee and poor road. Facilities are controlled by the INSSBI for the benefit of state employees and weekends are fully booked for weeks in advance.The beach is beautiful, and the sea is ideal for surfing and swimming. To get there, turn off at Km 60 on the old road to León and then follow signs. **El Tránsito** is another lovely, undeveloped Pacific beach. Buses from Managua leave at 1200, 1315 and 1500 (from Terminal Lewites) and return at 0600 or 0700, US$0.70.

Sleeping

Managua *p899, maps p900, p902 and p905*
15% tax is added to hotel bills. The government stipulates a small charge for rooms with a telephone (used or not).

Choose a central hotel (ie near the **Crown Plaza** or **Plaza España**) since transport to the outskirts can be difficult. There are many hotels west of the **Crowne Plaza** in Barrio Martha Quezada and near the **Casino Royale**. To get from the **Crown Plaza** to the **Casino Royale**, go west to the main north-south road (10 mins' walk, or take taxi), Av Williams Romero; **Casino Royale** is just south.

Most budget travellers stay in Barrio Martha Quezada (or else in Granada or Masaya, visiting Managua on regular minibuses). Don't always believe children touting for hotels if they say a place is full. Most hotels in the lower range have very thin walls and can be noisy!

LL Intercontinental Metrocentro, next to Metrocentro shopping centre, T278-4545, www.icmanagua.gruporeal.com. Managua's finest hotel, excellent service and location, very good restaurant, 157 rooms with all the amenities of a 5-star hotel. Discount rates with some tour operators.

L Crowne Plaza, Av Bolívar, 8a Calle Sur Oeste 101, Centro de Managua (in front of the Plaza Inter shopping centre), T228-3530, www.crowneplaza.com. Some rooms with lake view, rooms small for the price, slow service, sauna, use of swimming pool for non-residents on Sun for US$18, bookshop, handicraft shop, buffet, breakfast and lunch (see Eating, below), Visa cards accepted.

L-AL Las Mercedes, Km 11 Carretera Norte, outside the airport, T233-2010, www.lasmercedes.com.ni. Best Western hotel, handy if arriving late at night or passing through. The outdoor café is the best place to kill time near the airport.

AL Hotel El Almendro, 2 blocks west and ½ block south of Rotonda Rubén Darío (Metrocentro), T270-1260, www.hotelel almendro.com. 9 rooms with private bath, cable TV, a/c and kitchen, parking, breakfast included, very nice, small but pleasant patio.

AL-A Hostal Real, Av Bolonia 1001, opposite German Embassy, T268-1438, www.hostalreal.com.ni. Private bath with hot water, breakfast included, internet, cable TV, interesting and airy rooms decorated with

Barrio Martha Quezada

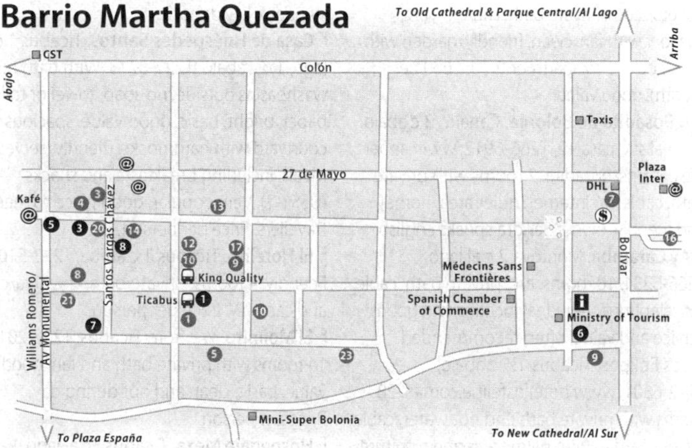

N

0 metres 100
0 yards 100

Sleeping
Casa de Huéspedes Castillo **3**
Casa de Huéspedes Santos **4**
Casa Gabrinma **5**
Crowne Plaza **16**
El Conquistador **7**
El Dorado **8**
El Hotelito **9**
El Molinito **10**
Hospedaje Carlos **12**
Hospedaje Meza **13**
Hospedaje Quintana **14**
Jardín de Italia **17**
Los Cisneros **20**
Los Felipes **21**
Sultana **1**
Travel House **23**

Eating
Comedor Sara **1**
Las Cazuelas **3**
Little Italy **5**
Malibu **6**
Mirna's **7**
Típicos Doña Pilar **8**

Bars & clubs
Jaro Kafé **9**
Shannon Irlandés **10**

antiques and art, 'the most beautiful hotel interior in Nicaragua', central, very clean and popular, reserve in advance.

A **El Conquistador**, Plaza Inter 1 c al sur, 1 c abajo, T222-4789, www.hotelelconquistador.com. 18 rooms, a/c, private bath, cable TV, refrigerator, lake view terrraza, good value and location.

B **Europeo**, Bolonia, Canal 2, 75 m abajo, T268-2130, www.hoteleuropeo.com.ni. A/c, private bath, hot water, cable TV, includes continental breakfast, restaurant, bar, fax, secure parking, laundry service, internet, very clean, each room is different, very friendly and helpful staff, hotel proceeds go to a drug rehabilitation programme, quiet but central location. Highly recommended.

B **María La Gorda**, Iglesia El Carmen, 1 c al sur, ½ c arriba, ½ c al sur, T268-2455, mgorda@ibw.com.ni. 8 rooms, a/c, private bath with hot water, email access, cable TV, telephone, just west of Martha Quezada,good value.

B-C **Colón**, Km 4.5 Carretera a Masaya, del Lacmiel 2 c arriba, T278-2490, hcolon@ibw.com.ni. With bath and a/c, cheaper with fan, cable TV, secure, clean, good restaurant.

B-C **Los Cisneros**, Bolonia, Casa del Obrero 2 c al sur, ½ c al este, T222-3535, www.hotelloscisneros.com. Private bath, cable TV, a/c, cheaper with fan, clean, friendly, garden with hammocks, also apartments (US$600 per month), good value.

B-C **Posadita de Bolonia**, Canal 2, 3 c abajo, 75 m al sur, casa 12, T266-6912, www.angelfire.com/ns/posadita. 7 rooms with private bath, cable TV, internet, quiet area, homey and friendly, owner Sandra speaks English.

C **Ay Caramba**, Montoya 2 c al lago, T266-6284. 10 rooms, a/c, private bath, cable TV, telephone, not ideal location but good service and value, often recommended.

C **Los Felipes**, Ticabus 1½ c abajo, T222 6501, www.hotellosfelipe.com.ni. 28 rooms with private bath and hot water, cable TV, big garden with palm trees and furniture for relaxing, internet access and friendly staff.

D **Casa Gabrinma**, Ticabus 1 c al sur, ½ c arriba, frente a radio La Primerísima, T222-6650. 4 rooms with fan, cable TV, cheap food, group discounts, friendly.

D **Travel House**, Residencia Bolonia, Mansión Teodolinda, 2 c abajo, 1 c al lago, 30 m abajo, T222-2199. Arranges transfers to Nicabus terminal, breakfast or dinner included, cable TV, a/c extra, clean, friendly.

E **Casa de Huéspedes Castillo**, Casa del Obrero 1 c arriba, 1½ c al sur (2 blocks from Ticabus), T222-2265. Also known as Casa Ramiro, with bath, fan, clean, quiet, safe, courtyard.

E **El Pueblo**, Intercontinental 3 c al lago, 2 c arriba. Simple, old house, big rooms, private bath, friendly.

E **Hospedaje Carlos**, Ticabus ½ c al lago, T222-2554. Rooms on left at the back are better than on the right, cold shower, fan, some with private bath and a/c extra, good value, clean. Price per person.

E **Hospedaje Quintana**, Ticabus 1 c al lago, ½ c abajo, T254-5487. Rooms with fan, shared shower (cold), laundry, clean, good value, family-run, friendly, internet. Recommended for longer stays or groups.

E **Jardín de Italia**, Ticabus 1 c arriba, ½ al lago, T222-7967, www.jardindeitalia.com. Some rooms with a/c (B), with bath, clean, garden with chairs, internet, friendly. Mixed reports. Take care of your belongings. Price per person.

E-F **El Dorado**, turn left 1½ c out of Ticabus station, T222-6012. Clean, with or without private bath, small rooms of varying standard, key deposit.

F **Casa de Huéspedes Santos**, Ticabus 1 c al lago, 1½ c abajo, T222-3713. With bath but washbasins outside, no soap, towel or toilet paper, bright, basic, good value, spacious courtyard with hammocks, friendly, serves meals, including breakfasts and snacks (US$1-2). Very popular, good place to meet travellers. Price per person.

F **El Hotelito**, Ticabus 1 c arriba, T222-5100. Friendly, 4 rooms, private bath, D with a/c and cable TV. Price per person.

F **El Molinito**, ½ c from Ticabus, T222-2013. 14 rooms with private bath and fan, good value, basic, clean and hot during day. Price per person.

F **Hospedaje Meza**, Ticabus 1c al lago, ½ c arriba, T222-2046. 15 rooms with private and shared bath and fan, colourful but run-down and rather shabby, TV.

F **Sultana**, at the Ticabus terminal. Dormitory accommodation, friendly, clean, fan, handy if you have an early bus, otherwise. noisy from 0500 and overpriced. Price per person.

Pacific beaches near Managua *p904*
LL Montelimar Resort, near Pochomil and Masachapa, T269-6769, www.barcelo montelimarbeach.com. This expensive resort is becoming popular with package tours and is often booked solid Nov-Apr. It has a broad, unspoilt sandy beach ideal for bathing and surfing. The nearest public transport is 3 km away at Masachapa, taxi from Managua US$30 (70 km), or hire a car.
A Ticomo Mar, on the nicest part of Pochomil beach, T265-0210. A/c and bath, best hotel in the region apart from Montelimar, but still poor value.
B Hotel Palmas del Mar, La Boquita, centre of beach, T552-8715. Beach front, private bath, a/c or fan, a bit noisy.
B Villas del Mar, just north of Pochimal centre, T266-6661. Crowded, overpriced food, party atmosphere, use of swimming pool US$5 per person.
C-E Centro Vacacional de Trabajadores, El Tránsito. Has good-value beach flats for 4-6 people at north end, normally available mid-week. Good meals available from Senora Pérez on the beach; possible accommodation too.
D Suleyka, Centro Turístico La Boquita, T552-8717. Shared baths and fan, 6 rooms, good restaurant with fresh fish dishes.

Eating

Managua *p899, maps p900, p902 and p905*
The Metrocentro shopping centre has several good ¶¶-¶ restaurants in its food court. Along with US, Guatemalan and Nicaraguan (**Rostipollo**, **Tip-Top**, **Quick Burger** and others) fast-food chains, it has cheaper versions of good Nicaraguan restaurants like **Doña Haydée**, and **María Bonita**. Branches of **La Plancha**, T278-2999, are good value and very popular (good beef, very generous portion).

Most restaurants will make a big salad or a rice, banana and bean dish for veggie lovers.
¶¶¶ Crowne Plaza, see Sleeping, above. Serves enormous buffet breakfasts (0600-1100) for US$11 (plus 15% tax and service charge), and an excellent lunch, Mon-Fri 1200-1500, US$14; *frijolada* buffet on Sat, US$16; and brunch and use of the pool on Sun for US$19. Open to non-residents (dress smartly); major credit cards accepted.
¶¶¶ El Astillero, across from Pizza Valenti in Colonial Los Robles, T267-8110. Daily 1200-0000. Very good *mariscos a la plancha*, and various other excellent seafood dishes in casual setting.
¶¶¶ El Muelle, Hotel Metrocentro ½ c arriba, T278-0056. Lunch and dinner, seafood, try *pargo al vapor* (steamed snapper), closed Mon.
¶¶¶ Harry's Grill Argentino, Km 8 Carretera a Masaya, contiguo a Texaco Las Colinas, T276-1067. Argentine beef grill in 7 different cuts, daily 1130-2330, very good.
¶¶¶ Hotel César, Km 8½ Carretera Sur, T265-2728. Good, try duck in orange sauce, best place for those craving real Euro-food, cheeses, wines, etc.
¶¶¶ Las Delicias del Bosque, Colegio Centroamericana 5 Km al sur, T088-30071. Restaurant for the Nicaraguan power brokers, lovely setting in hills, good food, Wed-Sat only.
¶¶¶ María Bonita, Altamira, de la Vicky 1½ c abajo, T270-4326. Mexican, closed Mon, popular on weekend nights with live music and a noisy, happy crowd, good food and service, fun.
¶¶¶-¶¶ La Cocina de Doña Haydée, opposite Pastelería Aurami, Planes de Altamira, T270-6100, www.lacocina.com.ni. A once-popular, family kitchen eatery that has gone upscale, traditional Nicaraguan food at higher prices than elsewhere, very popular with foreign residents, try the *surtido* plate for 2, US$6, Mon-Sun 0730-2230, and the carrot/orange *fresco*.
¶¶¶-¶¶ Malibu, Plaza Inter 2 c al sur, 15 m abajo, Plaza España/Barrio Martha Quezada area. Seafood, thatched roof, daily 1200-2200.
¶¶ Casa del Café, Metrocentro, outside the food court (1 level higher). Daily 0900-2100, great (Nicaraguan) coffee, smoothies, breakfast and salads, good pastries, pleasant.
¶¶ El Guapinol, Metrocentro. Very good grilled meat dishes, chicken, fish and a hearty veggie plate (US$4.50). Try *Copinol* dish with grilled beef, avocado, fried cheese, salad, tortilla and *gallo pinto* US$4, from 1100 daily.
¶¶ Hippos Tavern and Grill, Colonial los Robles ½ c al sur, T2671346. Grilled food, good salads, nice ambience, a/c, music, very popular for people-watching.
¶¶ La Ballena que Cayó del Cielo, next to Camino de Oriente, T277-3055. Nicaragua's best hamburgers, good grilled chicken, salsa and merengue videos.

ΨΨ **Las Brasas**, in front of Cine Alhambra, Camino de Oriente. Best value in town, good cheap Nicaraguan fare, traditional, outdoors, great atmosphere, sea bass, *churrasco* steak, best deal to drink rum with friends, ½ bottle comes with bowl of ice, limes, a coke and 2 plates of food.

ΨΨ **Tacos al Pastor**, Carretera a Masaya across from Camino de Oriente, T278-2650. Budget Mexican, *burritos* and *enchiladas*, popular with young crowd.

ΨΨ **Tacos Charros**, Plaza el Café, 1 c abajo. Cheap, large servings. Highly recommended.

ΨΨ-Ψ **Anada**, Estatua de Montoya 10 m arriba T228-4140. Daily 0700-2100. Nicaragua's first non-meat eatery and still the best, also good fruit juices.

ΨΨ-Ψ **Pizza Valenti**, Colonial Los Robles, T278-7474. Best cheap pizza, US$4.50, home delivery, very popular.

Ψ **China Bien Bien**, 27 de Mayo, near Santos, Plaza España/Barrio Martha Quezada area. Excellent fast food, Chinese.

Ψ **Comedor Sara**, next to Ticabus, Plaza España/ Barrio Martha Quezada area. Cheap, popular with gringos, serves breakfast, has notice board.

Ψ **Healthy Food**, Plaza El Sol, 4 c al sur, Casa 211, T270-4091. Low calorie breakfast and lunch buffets, vegetarian dishes, whole grain and soy galore, fruit juices. Mon-Fri 0700-1900 and Sat 0700-1500.

Ψ **Las Cazuelas**, CST (Central Sandinista de los Trabajadores), 2 c al sur, 1 c arriba, opposite **Casa de Huéspedes Santos** in the Plaza España/Barrio Martha Quezada area, T228-6090. Great cheap breakfasts (US$1.5), big portions, always music on, lunch and dinner as well (US$6).

Ψ **Mirna's**, Barrio Martha Quezada (No 7 on map). Open 0700-1500. Good cheap breakfasts and *comidas*, lunch buffet 1200-1500 popular with travellers and Nicaraguans, friendly service.

Ψ **Nutrem Food**, Portón principal de la UCA, 150 m abajo. Soy-based foods, vegetarian menu. Mon-Sat 0700-1800.

Ψ **Restaurant Little Italy**, Ticabus 1 c al lago, 2 c abajo, next to **Las Cazuelas**, Plaza España/ Barrio Martha Quezada area. Gringo food, cheap drinks, friendly owner, 1200-2300.

Ψ **Rincón Cuscalteco**, Plaza España roundabout, 1 c al lago, T266-4209. Good cheap *pupusas salvadoreñas*, also *vigorón* and *quesillos*, daily 1200-2200.

Ψ **Rincón Salvadoreño**, Enel Central 2 c al lago, T0886-7584. *Pupusas*, *tamales* and *quesadillas*, very cheap, simple and good.

Ψ **Típicos Doña Pilar**, ½ c from Santos on Santos Vargas Chávez, Plaza España/Barrio Martha Quezada area. Cheap buffet-style Nicaraguan food, very good, from 1700.

Ψ **Tonalli Café**, Ticabus 3 c arriba, ½ c al sur. Wholemeal breads, with breakfast and vegetarian dishes. Mon-Fri 0700-1900, Sat 0700-1500.

Ψ **Topkapi**, Camino de Oriente, across from Alhambra cinema. Pizza (US$2.50), tacos, Nicaraguan food, good people-watching, outdoor seating. Recommended.

Entertainment

Managua *p899, maps p900, p902 and p905*

Bars and clubs

There are several god places on Lacmiel (and it's safe to walk at night as well).

Bar Chaman, Colonial Los Robles. US$2 entrance, young, wild crowd, salsa, rock and disco on tape, lots of dancing and sweating.

El Quelite, Enitel Villa Fontana 5 c abajo, T267-0126. Open-air, typical Nicaraguan dance bar with good food; try the *corvina a la plancha* (sea bass) US$5, lots of dancing, live acts Thu-Sun.

El Quetzal, Rotonda Centro América, 1 c arriba, opposite Galería Simón, T278-1733. Fun crowd who fill big dance floor and dance non-stop, entrance free, live music, ranchera, salsa, merengue.

Jaro Kafé , Plaza Inter 2 c al sur, 15 m abajo, T268-6230. Salsa, reggae, Brazilian hiphop, rock, pop rock, socca, jazz and more world music, Wed-Sat 1900-0100.

La Casa de Los Mejía Godoy, Plaza El Sol 2 c al sur, T278-4913. Thu-Sat from 2130, reservations recommended, live music in small setting of the legendary folk/ revolutionary singers Carlos (Sat) and Luis Enrique Mejía Godoy (Fri), US$17 reserved seats on Fri and Sat, cheaper Thu, well worth the experience.

La Ruta Maya, de Montoya 150 m arriba. Entry US$5, good Nicaraguan bands Thu-Sat.

Rhumba & Z Bar, Carretera a Masaya Km 3.5, opposite **Galería Simon**, T278-1733. Lots of dancing, popular, weekends only.

Shannon Bar Irlandés, 1 block east and 1 block south of **Ticabus**, T222-6683, www.shannonbar.com. Excellent food, whisky and Guinness (which often runs dry due to popularity), open 1700-0200. Recommende. Some rooms with shared bath (F) with breakfast available for those early-morning **Ticabus** departures.

Cinemas

Alhambra 1, 2 & 3, Camino de Oriente. US films, Spanish subtitles, US$3, bring sweater for polar a/c.
Alianza Francesa, Altamira, 1 block north of Mexican Embassy. Fri 1900, free, shows French films and has art exhibits during the day.
Metrocentro. 4 screens, small theatres with steep seating, arrive early, US$3.

Dance and theatre

Ballet Tepenahuatl, folkloric dances at the Teatro Rubén Darío.
Doña Haydée, opposite **Pastelería Aurami**, Planes de Altamira, T270-6100. Folkloric dance on Tue.
Intermezzo del Bosque, Colegio Centroamericano 5 Km al sur, T088-30071. On Wed, food, dances, US$40, check with **Delicias del Bosque**, or **Grayline Tours**, www.graylinenicaragua.com.
Teatro Nacional Rubén Darío, Frente al Malecón de Managua, T222-7426.

Festivals and events

Managua *p899, maps p900, p902 and p905*

1-10 Aug The **Festival de Santo Domingo** (Managua's patron saint) is held at El Malecón church: ceremonies, horse racing, bullfights, cockfights, a lively carnival; proceeds go to the General Hospital. **1 Aug** (½ day) and **10 Aug** are local holidays.

Shopping

Managua *p899, maps p900, p902 and p905*

Bookshops

Hispamer, UCA, 1 c arriba, 1 c al sur. Best Spanish-language bookstore in the country, selling maps, postcards, badges, stickers and other tourist items.

Handicrafts

Mercado Oriental is not recommended, see Security page 900.
Mercado Ricardo Huembes (also called **Mercado Central**), Pista Portezuelo, take bus No 110 or 119. The best place to buy handicrafts, and just about anything else. Artesanía from all parts of the country at the northeast end of the parking lot.
Metrocentro, in Plaza Inter and in Centro Comercial Managua. Some handicrafts (goldwork, embroidery) and good general shopping.
Mi Pueblo at Km 9.5 on Carretera Sur, T882-5650. Handicrafts and plants and there's also a good restaurant.
Takesa, del Intercontinental 2 c al sur, ½ abajo, Edif Bolívar 203, T268-3301. A smart shop selling Nicaraguan arts and crafts, high quality and high prices.

Imported goods

Galería Simón, opposite **Z-Bar** on Carretera a Masaya. Imported goods, take your passport, accepts dollars and TCs (to the value of purchase).

Activities and tours

Managua *p899, maps p900, p902 and p905*

Spectator sports

The national sport and passion is **baseball**, with games on Sun mornings at the Estadio Denis Martínez. The season runs from Nov-Feb and tickets cost US$1-4. Other popular sports include **basketball** and **football** although none have a regular venue and season. Nicaragua has had 4 lightweight world champion **boxers** but the big fights are staged outside the country. There is also **cockfighting** and **bullfighting** (but no kill).

Tour operators

Careli Tours, Edificio Invercasa, Planes de Altamira, Frente al Colegio Pedagógico La Salle, www.carelitours.com. Guided tours through western Nicaragua and down the Río San Juan.
Globoaventuras, Villa Fontana, Colegio Centroamérica 200 m al lago, T277-4000, www.globoaventuras.com. Hot-air balloon flights over Managua and volcanoes. Prices from US$115 per person.
Grayline Nicaragua, Rotunda El Güegüense, 250 m al sur, contiguo a **Viajes América**, PO Box 91, Edificio Central Correos de Nicaragua, T883-6994, www.graylinenicaragua.com. Day trips, tours packages, hotels, car rentals.

Otec, Antigua Terminal de Nicabua, Calle 27 de Mayo, 3 c arriba, T222-2619, www.otectours.com.
Schuvar Tours, Plaza España Edif Bamer No 4, T266-3588, schuvar@ibw.com.ni.
Tours Nicaragua, Plaza Barcelona, Módulo '5, next to the Galería Internacional, T270-8417, www.toursnicaragua.com. A wide variety of tours to all parts of the country in vans, 4WD, boats and small plane, English-, German- and French-speaking guides. Contact Mike Newton, helpful.
Va Pues Tours, T611-8784, Apdo Postal LM-297, Managua, www.vapues.com. Tour operator and travel agency, Dutch owner, multilingual guides (English, French, German, Dutch, Italian), helpful, reservations for domestic flights, car rental, specializes in half- to 1-day tours (US$20-30) around León.

Transport

Managua *p899, maps p900, p902 and p905*

Air

For **Managua International Airport** (MGA), take any bus marked 'Tipitapa' from Mercado Huembes, Mercado San Miguel or Mercado Oriental (near Victoria brewery), US$0.16. Alternatively, take a taxi (US$9). Be early for international flights – formalities are slow and thorough. Artisan stalls and cheap food in between arrivals and departures. Duty free shops, café, toilets through immigration. You are not allowed to stay overnight in the airport. The bank (**Banpro**) at the airport (Mon-Fri 0830-1630, Sat 0830-1200), does not change TCs but does have an ATM machine accepting Visa.

Airline offices Air France, Plaza España, T266-2612, **Alitalia**, de Los Pipitos 1½ c abajo, T266-6997, **American Airlines**, Plaza España, T266-3900, **Atlantic Airlines**, Carretera a Masaya Km 4 donde fue el Lacmiel, T222-3037, www.atlanticairlines.com.ni, **British Airways**, in the Grupo Taca office, T266-3136, **Continental** (T270-3403), Carretera a Masaya Km 4. **Copa**, Carretera a Masaya, Sorbet Inn 1 c abajo, T267-5438, **Grupo Taca**, Plaza España, T266-3136, **Iberia**, Plaza España T266-4440, **Japan Airlines**, Plaza España, T266-3588, **LanChile**, Plaza España, T266-6997, **La Costeña** (for the Atlantic coast), at the airport, T263-1228, **LTU**, Rotonda Güegüense, 2½ c arriba, T266-7734.

Bus

Local Beware of pickpockets on the crowded urban buses, particularly on tourist routes. City buses run every 10 mins 0530-1800, every 15 mins 1800-2200, when last services begin their routes; buses are frequent but routes are difficult to fathom. Tickets cost about US$0.15.

The main bus routes are: **No 101** from Las Brisas, passing CST, Hotel Intercontinental, Mercado Oriental, then on to **Mercado San Miguel** and **El Mayoreo**; **No 103** from 7 Sur to Mercado Lewites, Plaza 19 de Julio, Metrocentro, **Mercado San Miguel** and **Villa Libertad**; **No 109** from Teatro Darío to the Bolívar/Buitrago junction just before Intercontinental turns east, then southeast to **Mercado Huembes/bus station**; **No 110** runs from 7 Sur to **Villa San Jacinto** passing en route Mercado Lewites, Plaza 19 de Julio, Metrocentro, Mercado Huembes/bus station and Mercado San Miguel; **No 113** runs from Ciudad Sandino, Las Piedrecitas, CST, Intercontinental, to **Mercado Oriental**; **No 116** runs east-west below Inter-continental, on Buitrago, also passing CST; **No 118** takes a similar route but turns south on Williams Romero to Plaza España, thence to **Israel Lewites bus station**; **No 119** runs from Plaza España to **Mercado Huembes/ bus station** via Plaza 19 de Julio; **No 123** runs from Mercado Lewites via 7 Sur and Linda Vista to near Palacio Nacional de Cultura, and **Nuevo Diario**.

Long distance From La UCA express inter-city buses leave for **Diriamba**, **Jinotepe**, **San Marcos**, **Masaya** (Plaza San Miguelito) and **Granada**, no set schedule, most leave when they are full.

South of Managua: buses leave from Mercado Huembes (also called **Mercado Central**). **Masaya**, every 15 mins, 0530-2140, 1 hr, US$0.40; **Express** from La UCA, every 30 mins, 0500-2100, 40 mins, US$0.80. **Granada**, every 15 mins, 0520-2140, 1½ hrs, US$0.70; **Express** from La UCA, every 30 mins, 0500-2200, 1 hr, US$1. **Rivas**, every 25 mins, 0330-1900, 2 hrs, US$1.60; **Express**, 1½ hrs, US$2.25. **San Jorge** (dock), 6 between 0830 and 1500, 2½ hrs, US$2 or take bus to Rivas and change there. **San Juan del Sur**, 6 daily 0930-1600, 3½ hrs, US$2.25. **Peñas Blancas**, 0400, 3½ hrs, US$3.50.

East and then north or south: buses leave from **Mercado El Mayoreo** east of town. **Boaco**, every 30 mins, 0400-1900, 2 hrs, US$1.50. **Juigalpa**, every 15 mins, 0500-1800, 3 hrs, US$2.30. **El Rama**, every 2 hrs, 0400-2200, 8 hrs, US$7. **San Carlos**, 4 daily 0500-1300, 9½ hrs, US$7. **Matagalpa**, every 30 mins, 0500-2000, 2½ hrs, US$2.60. **Jinotega**, every hr, 0500-1800, 3½ hrs, US$3.50. **Estelí**, every 30 mins, 0400-2100, 2 hrs, US$2.60; **Express luxury**,1315 and 1515, 2 hrs, US$3. **Ocotal**, every hr, 0510-1700, 3 hrs, US$3.70. **Somoto**, hourly, from 0400-2000, 3 hrs, US$3.50.

West and northwest: buses leave from the **Mercado Israel Lewites** (also called **Mercado Boer**). Besides the regular and express busses, small vans (*compartidos*) go to most of the places mentioned below, often faster than the bus, but there's not a lot of room for luggages. **Pochomil**, every 30 mins, 0600-1900, 2½ hrs; **Express** 1¾ hrs, US$0.90. **Diriamba**, every 20 mins, 0530-2130, 1¼ hr, US$0.80. **Jinotepe**, every 20 mins, 0500-1930, 1½ hr, US$1.50. **León**, every 30 mins, 0500-1800, 2 hrs, US$1.20. Buses taking the new highway through La Paz Centro are faster than those using the 'carretera vieja', ask before leaving. **El Sauce**, 0745, 1445, 1545, 3 hrs, US$2.50. **Chinandega**, every 40 mins, 0500-1930, 2½ hrs, US$2.20. **Corinto**, every hr, 0500-1715, 3 hrs, US$3. **Guasaule**, 0600, 4 hrs, US$3.50.

International buses The cheap and efficient international buses are often booked up many days in advance and tickets will not be sold until all passport/visa documentation is complete. The best known is **Ticabus**, which parks in Barrio Martha Quezada, from Cine Dorado, 2 c arriba, T222-3031, www.ticabus.com, with services throughout Central America. Next door are the **King Quality** buses, T228-1454. **Transnica** is a long-haul bus option, de la Rotonda de Metrocentro 300 m al lago, 50 m arriba, T277-3133, www.transnica.com.

Costa Rica **Ticabus** leaves at 0545, 0700 and 1200, 10 hrs, US$12.50. **King Quality** 1300, US$15. **Transnica** 0530, 0700, 1000 and 1500 'ordinario', US$20 round trip, 'ejecutivo' 1200, US$40. The cheapest way of travelling to San José is to take a bus Managua-Rivas, then a *colectivo* to the border (Peñas Blancas), another between the border posts, then take local bus to San José; takes 15 hrs altogether and costs about US$8.

El Salvador **Transnica** leaves at 0500, 11 hrs, US$25. **Ticabus** at 0500 and 1230, US$25, US$50 return. **King Quality** at 0400 and 1100, US$26.

Guatemala City **Ticabus** leaves at 0500 travelling via El Salvador, 25 hrs including overnight in El Salvador, US$33 (plus overnight costs). **King Quality** leaves at 0430, US$53 (plus overnight costs in El Salvador).

Honduras **Ticabus** leaves at 0600, 7 hrs, US$20 for Tegucigalpa, continuing at 1400 for San Pedro Sula, 3 hrs, total cost US$28. **King Quality** leaves at 0400 and 1100, US$23. The cheapest way of travelling to Tegucigalpa, using local buses, will cost you about US$5.

Mexico For Tapachula, same as for Guatemala City, continuing at 1200 and arriving in Tapachula at 1700, total cost US$51.

Panama **Ticabus**, same as for Costa Rica, leaving San José at 2200, then 18 hrs to Panama City, total price US$37.50.

Car

Car hire Given the poor public transport and the decentralized layout of Managua, you may find that renting a car is the best way to get around, especially if you're part of a group. **Alamo**, Edif Delta Km 5 Carretera Masaya, T270-1939. **Budget**, Barrio Altagracia, Estatua Montoya 1 c al sur, 1 c abajo, T266-6226, www.budget.com.ni, or Intercontinental, T222-2336. **Dollar Rent a Car**, T266-3620, www.dollar.com, also at Intercontinental. **Hertz** , at the airport, Hotel Intercontinental (T222-2320, www.hertz.com.ni), or Edif Caribe Motors, Km 4 Carretera Sur, T266-8399. **Leo's**, southwest side of Rotonda Güegüense, T266-3719. **Lugo**, T277-0582, www.lugorentacar.com.ni. Rates from US$25 per day up to US$63 for a small bus, unlimited mileage, US$12 per day accident protection, tax not included, discounts for 2 weeks or more.

Taxis

Taxis – the best method of transport for foreigners in Managua – can be flagged down along the street; verify the fare before entering. Fares range from US$1-US$1.50 for a short trip, US$1.50-US$2.50 across town,

US$9 to airport. Fares are always per person, not per car. After telling the driver your destination, if travelling far or in a different direction to other passengers he may decide not to take you. If he agrees, ask how much (*¿por cuánto me lleva?*) then get in. If the front seat is empty take it as the back seat will be filled en route. Street names and numbers are not universal in the city and the taxi driver may not know your destination; it may be handy to have the telephone number of your hotel with you. If heading for Barrio Martha Quezada, ask for the **Ticabus** if you do not know your exact destination.

Recommended, more expensive, radio taxis for early flights or late night transport are **Co-op 25 de Febrero**, T222-5218, or **Co-op 2 de Agosto**, T263-1512, get price quote on the phone (normally 80-100% more expensive).

❶ Directory

Managua *p899, maps p900, p902 and p905*

Banks

Any bank in Nicaragua will change US$ to córdobas and vice-versa. TC purchase receipts may be required in banks when changing TCs. The best 2 banks for foreigners are **Banco de América Central (BAC)** and **Banco de Finanzas (BDF)**. **BAC** offers credit card advances, uses the Cirrus debit system and changes all TCs with a 5% commission. **BDF** changes American Express TCs only, also with a 5% commission. In Managua ATM machines are found in the airport (Visa only), at the Metrocentro and Plaza Inter shopping malls and in many gas station convenience stores ('Red Total'). There are several money changers at the road junction in Altamira by the restaurant **Casa del Pomodoro** and outside **La Colonia** shopping centre in Plaza España. After 1800 and on Sun they are usually tricksters. On Sun you can change money at the **Intercontinental**, major hotels or banks inside **Metrocentro**. See page 894 for more details.

Embassies and consulates

Canada, costado este de Casa Nazaret, 1 c arriba, C El Nogal No 25, T268-0433, Mon-Thu 0900-1200. **Costa Rica**, Montoya 1½ c arriba, Calle 27 de Mayo, T266-3986, Mon-Fri 0900-1500. **Denmark**, Rotonda El Güegüense 1 c abajo, 2 c al lago, ½ c abajo, T268-0250, Mon-Fri 0800-1400. **Netherlands**, del Canal 2, 1 c al lago, 1 c abajo, Apdo 3534, T266-6175, Mon-Fri 0800-1600. **France**, Iglesia El Carmen 1½ c abajo, T222-6210, Mon-Fri 0800-1600. **Germany**, Plaza España 200 m al lago, T266-3917, Mon-Fri 0900-1200. **Guatemala**, Km 11 Carretera a Masaya, T279-9609, Mon-Fri 0900-1200 only. **Honduras**, Reparto San Juan del Gimnasio Hércules, 1 c al sur, 1 arriba, Calle San Juan 312, 15 mins' walk from the Hotel Intercontinental Metrocentro, T278-3043, Mon-Fri 0900-1200. Visas in a couple of hours, US$10. **Italy**, Rotonda El Güegüense 1 c al lago, T266-6486, Mon-Fri 0900-1200. **Mexico**, Carreta a Masaya Km 4.5, take the 2nd street on the left and it's at the 1st crossroads on your right, in Altamira, T277-5886. **Panama**, Col Mantica, el Cuartel General de Bomberos, 1 c abajo, casa 93, T266-8633, Mon-Fri 0830-1300. **Sweden**, Plaza España, 1 c abajo, 2 c al lago, ½ c abajo, Apdo Postal 2307, T266-0085, Mon-Fri 0800-1200. **Switzerland**, Restaurante Marseillaise 2 c al lago, Apdo Postal 166, T277-3235. **UK**, closed in 2003, contact British Embassy in Costa Rica, Aptdo 815-1007, Ed Centro Colón, 11th floor, San José, T258 2025, www.britishembassycr.com. **US**, Km 4.5 Carretera del Sur, T266-6010, Mon-Fri 0730-0900. **Venezuela**, Km 10.5 Carretera a Masaya, T276-0267.

Emergencies

Police T118 in an emergency; the local police station number will depend on what *distrito* you are in. Start with the Metrocentro area number, T265-0651. **Fire** T115 in an emergency; the central number is T265-0162. **Red Cross** T128 in an emergency.

Immigration and customs

Immigration, near Ciudad Jardín, Antiguo Edif del Seguro Social (bus No 101, 108) Mon-Fri 0800-1600, T244-3989. **Customs:** Km 5 Carretera del Norte (bus No 108).

Internet

Lots of places, especially in and around Plaza Inter, María Quezada and Metrocentro. Most internet cafés are open daily, charge around US$0.60 per hr and also offer internet calls.

Language school
Casa Nicaragüense de Español, Km 11.5 Carretera Sur, Spanish classes and a thorough introduction to Nicaragua, accommodation with families. **Huellas**, Col Centroamérica, Callejón El Ceibo G-414, T277-2079, intensive classes, private classes and regular classes (0880-1200). **Nicaragua Spanish School**, Rotonda Bello Horizonte, 2 c al sur, 2 c arriba, T244-4512, regular and private classes. **Universidad Americana**, Centro de Idiomas Extranjeros, T278-3800 ext 301, open course with flexible hrs and regular 5-month course. **Universidad Centroamericana (UCA)**, Centro de Idiomas Extranjeros, T278-3923, ext 242-351, 5-week regular classes of all levels and open classes with flexible hrs.

Libraries
Casa Ben Linder Library, Estatua Monseñor Lezcano 3 c al sur, 1½ c arriba, also good book exchange, T266-4373.

Medical services
Dentists Dr Claudia Bendaña, T277-1842 and Dr Mario Sánchez Ramos, T278-1409, T278-5588 (home). **Doctors** Internal medicine, Dr Enrique Sánchez Salgado, T278-1031, Dr Mauricio Barrios, T266-7284. Gynaecologists, Dr Walter Mendieta, T278-5186, Dr Edwin Mendieta, T266-6591. Paediatricians, Dr Alejandro Ayón, T268-3103, Dr César Gutiérrez Quant, T278-6622, T278-5465 (home). **Hospitals** Generally crowded, with very long queues. The best are **Hospital Bautista**, near Mercado Oriental, T249-7070; **Hospital Militar**, south from Intercontinental and take 2nd turning on left, T222-2172; and **Hospital Alemán-Nicaragüense**, Km 6 Carretera Norte Siemens, 3 c al sur, 249-3368, operated with German aid. Phone for appointment first if possible. **Private clinics** are an alternative. **Policlínica Nicaragüense**, consultation US$30. **Med-Lab**, Plaza España 300 m al sur, recommended for tests on stool samples, the director speaks English.

Post office
21 locations around Managua, the main office for the country is 1 block west of Parque Central. Wide selection of beautiful stamps. Poste Restante (*Lista de Correos*) keeps mail for 45 days, US$0.20 per letter. There is another post office in the Centro Comercial Managua and at the airport.

Telephone
Enitel, same building as post office, open 0700-2230. There is a small office in the international airport. Telephone offices are spreading around Managua.

To the Northern Highlands

A couple of routes to the Honduran border use the Pan-American Highway heading north of Lake Managua. The road rises and winds through hilly country, with fields set aside for agriculture and coffee growing, giving way to mining and pine forests. Damage from the Revolution is evident in the small town of Estelí, as it is throughout the region. A short detour south of Estelí takes a paved road to good walking and wildlife country in Matagalpa and Jinotega. North of Estelí the road splits, leading to Somoto and Ocotal, and completing the 214-km paved road from the capital to Honduras. » *For Sleeping, Eating and other listings, see pages 918-922.*

Tipitapa and further north → *Colour map 7, A1.*

Heading east out of Managua along the southern shore of the lake is Tipitapa (21 km). The resort has reopened and you can swim in clean water in the baths. The air-conditioned restaurant attached to the thermal baths is good. There is a colourful market, and the **Fiesta del Señor de Esquipulas** takes place on 13-16 January.

The Pan-American Highway goes north through Tipitapa to **Sébaco,** passing through **Ciudad Darío,** where the poet Rubén Darío was born. You can see the house, which is maintained as a **museum** ⓘ *Mon-Fri 0800-1200, 1400-1700*. There is an arts festival for the week of his birthday, 18 January. Sébaco and the surrounding area was badly affected by Hurricane Mitch. East of the highway is **Esquipula**, 2½ hours by bus, a good place for hiking, fishing and riding.

Matagalpa and around

▸▸ *pp918-922. Colour map 6, C4.*

➔ *Altitude: 672 m.*

From Sébaco a road leads to Matagalpa, and some of the best walking country in Nicaragua. Matagalpa has an old church, and while it is about the only colonial-style building left, the town retains a simple agrarian charm. It was badly damaged in the Revolution but all war damage has now been repaired. A coffee boom in the late 1990s benefitted the region greatly, but the crash in coffee prices in 2001 has subsequently decimated the fragile local economy. The local festival and holiday on 26 September celebrates the **Virgen de las Mercedes**.

Matagalpa is a small town, the main focus of the surrounding agricultural land and the birthplace of Carlos Fonseca, one of the founder members of the FSLN. The house he was born in, now the **Museo Carlos Fonseca** ⓘ *1 block east of Parque San José*, looks certain to remain closed for the foreseeable future, but the local FSLN office has the keys. It's a busy town with just the **cathedral** and the **Galería de los Héroes y Mártires**, in the main square to the north, to consider as sights. The **Centro Popular de la Cultura** is 2½ blocks north, four blocks east from the northeast corner of the cathedral plaza. The **tourist office** ⓘ *near the Iglesia Molagüina, Mon-Fri 0800-1200, 1400-1700, English spoken*, has useful information. Coffee, the region's main source of employment, is harvested from November to February and can be seen drying in the sun at the southern edge of town. There is also some cattle ranching in the area and the chief industry is the Nestlé powdered-milk plant.

A 32-km road runs from Matagalpa east to the Tuma valley. Matagalpa, with its beautiful mountains and diverse scenery, is one of the best hiking areas of Nicaragua. A nice way to discover the area on your own is with *Treasures of Matagalpa*, a brochure describing five one-day hikes ranging from four to eight hours, including a detailed map, instructions and a description of the history of the area. You can buy it (US$1.75) at **Centro Girasol** ⓘ *2 blocks south and 1 block west of Terminal Sur, T612-6030*. All profit goes to supporting families with disabled children. You should also visit the centre if you're interested in volunteer opportunities.

Jinotega and around ➔ *Colour map 6, C4. Population: 33,000. Altitude: 641 m.*

A rough road spirals north from Matagalpa to Jinotega rising out of the valley and into one of the most scenic paved highways in the north, lined by highland farms, virgin cloud forest and breathtaking views of the surrounding valleys and mountains. At Km 143, **Diparate de Potter** ⓘ *T612-6228, daily 0900-2100*, serves beef and chicken dishes and is worth a stop to enjoy the scenery.

Jinotega is a pleasant, friendly town which has famous images in the church; if closed, ask around. The jail which was used in the years of the Somoza dictatorship has been converted into a youth centre. There are several banks near the main plaza and an **INTUR tourist office** ⓘ *Banco Caley Dagnal, 25 m al este, T632-4552*. A beautiful hike, which starts from behind the cemetery, leads up to the cross above the city (one and a half hours' round trip). As with Matagalpa, excellent coffee is grown in the region. One road leads from Jinotega to El Tuma power station (18 km); another, which is unpaved and picturesque, goes to Estelí, through La Concordia, but there's very little transport from La Concordia to Estelí.

Eight kilometres east of Jinotega is the beautiful **Lago de Apanás** (buses every hour from Jinotega, 20 minutes, US$0.25), an artificial lake created by the damming of the

Río Tuma. The lake is used to produce energy in a hydroelectric plant and is great for fishing, full of *guapote* (perch) and *tilapia*. Small enterprises lining the lake will fry fish for visitors and it's possible to rent a small boat and fish on the lake; ask the locals.

The paved highway north of Jinotega leads to **San Rafael del Norte**. There are some good murals in the local church, and a chapel on the hill behind, at Tepeyak, built as a spiritual retreat. The town was involved in the Sandinista struggle and its recent history is very interesting. The **Museo General Sandino** ⓘ *Casa Museo Ejército Defensor de La Soberanía Nacional; if locked, ask for the key at the mayor's house across the street*, is where Sandino used to send off telegrams to his troops in different parts of the northern hills. The young woman to whom he dictated his messages became his wife and the town has claimed him as their native son ever since.

North of Sébaco

From Sébaco (see page 913) a 134-km journey to the border at El Espino takes you through sharp hills with steep climbs and descents, but it's smooth and quite well banked. A reasonable road leads off the Pan-American Highway 10 km northwest of

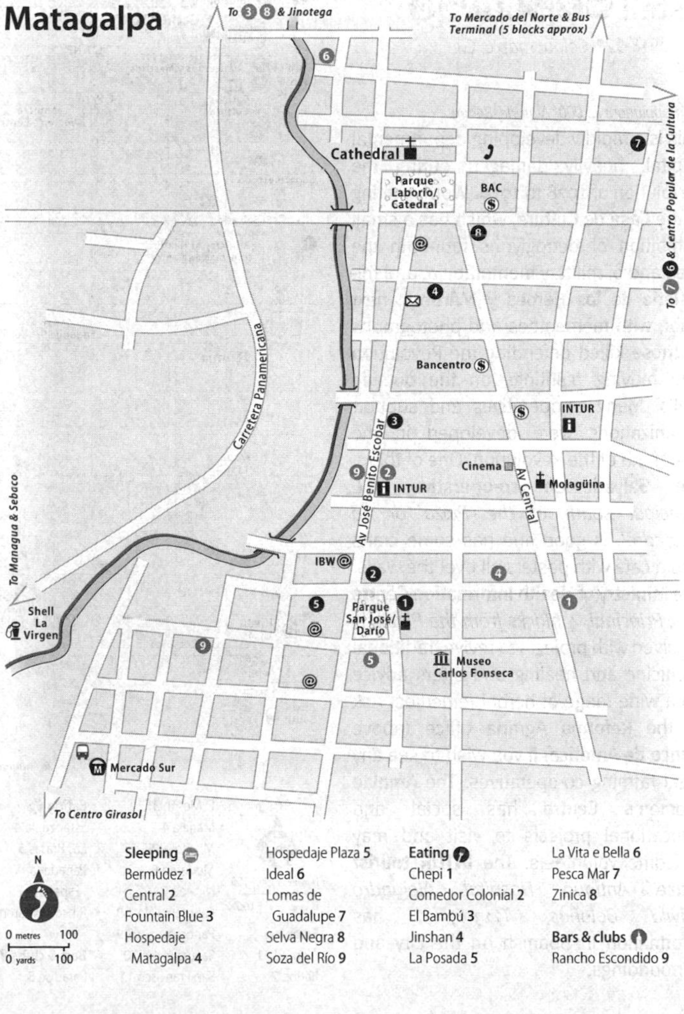

Sébaco, near **San Isidro**, to join the Pacific Highway near León (110 km). If travelling south, this is an attractive route to Managua through the Chinandega cotton-growing area, past the chain of volcanoes running west from Lake Managua, and through León. Buses run from Estelí to San Isidro every 30 minutes (two hours, US$0.50), and San Isidro to León every 30 minutes (three to four hours, US$1.50.)

After San Isidro, the Pan-American Highway continues through **La Trinidad**, an attractive mountain village set in a canyon, before reaching Estelí.

Estelí

⏩ *pp918-922. Colour map 6, C3.*

➔ *Population: 73,000 Altitude: 844 m.*

This is a rapidly developing departmental capital, heavily damaged during the Revolution of 1978 to 1979. Worth visiting is the **Casa de Cultura,** which has a small exhibition of petroglyphs found in the area and of military memorabilia, and the **Galería de los Héroes y Mártires**, next door, with mementoes and photographs of those killed defending the Revolution and moving paintings on the outside walls. Many co-operatives and support organizations were developed in the aftermath of the Revolution. One of them, the **Salvadorean co-operative** ⓘ *C Principal south of the Plaza de la Cathedral*, is good and has some crafts and a café with posters all over the walls. The **Ministry of Health Information Centre** ⓘ *C Principal, 4 blocks from the Plaza*, is involved with projects to revive traditional medicine and healing and offers advice on a wide range of herbal remedies. Ask at the **Reforma Agraria** office (above **Banco de América**) if you wish to see any local farming co-operatives. The **Amnlae Women's Centre** has social and educational projects to visit and may welcome volunteers. The **INTUR tourist office** ⓘ *Antiguo Hospital Alejandro Dávila Bolaños, T713-6799*, has information in Spanish on the city and surroundings.

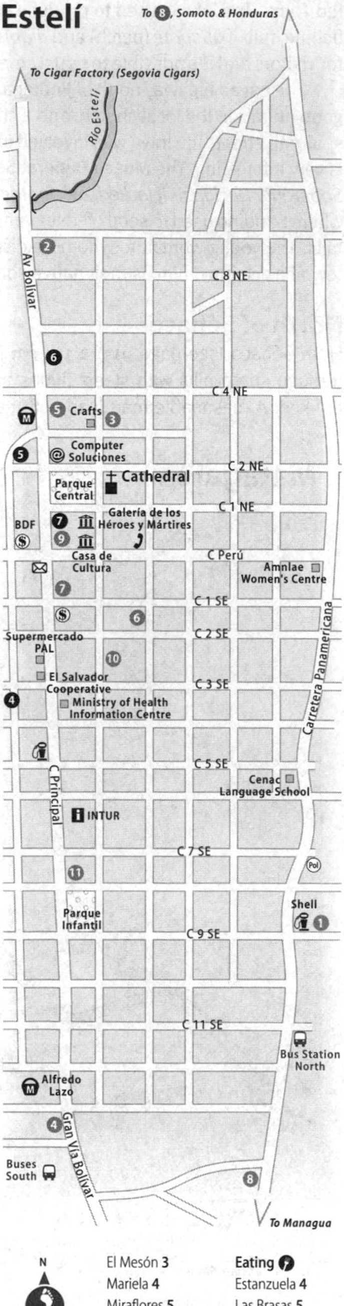

Sleeping 🛏
Alameda 1
Barlop 2
El Mesón 3
Mariela 4
Miraflores 5
Moderno 6
Nicarao 7
Panorama No 1 8
Panorama No 2 9
Sacuanjoche 10
San Francisco 11

Eating
Estanzuela 4
Las Brasas 5
Panadería España 6
Rincón Pinareño 7

Bars & clubs
Paradise 8

Around Estelí » pp918-922.

Miraflor → *Colour map 6, C3. Altitude: 800-1500 m.*

Miraflor is a 5675-ha nature reserve 28 km northeast of Estelí in the Department of Jinotega. It contains the **Laguna de Miraflor** and has a wide range of flora and fauna (including the quetzal). The **Unión de Cooperativas Agropecuarias Héroes y Mártires de Miraflor** ⓘ *contact Porfirio Zepeda (speaks English), contiguo a Talleres del Mingob, Estelí, T713-2971, www.miraflor.org, or Katharina Pförtner and Gene Hinz, T713-4041*, operates in the reserve, has a tourism project and is in charge of environmental protection. The co-operative can provide wooden huts, basic facilities and accommodation (C-F), meals, horse hire (US$2 for two hours) and guided walks (US$20 per person). It is recommended for a visit to see rural life and is a beautiful area for riding. Travelling to the region at night is not recommended due to reported crimes, although police have been installed at the entrance to the Miraflor reserve.

El Sauce and around

A very poor gravel road just north of Estelí runs to El Sauce where there is a large 16th-century church (burnt down in 1997 and refurbished in 2002). It's a place of pilgrimage and people come from all over Central America to visit the black **Christ of Esquipulas**, celebrated in a giant festival which culminates 15-18 January. After 20 km, an equally rough road branches north to Achuapa, beyond which an unmade road continues through the *artesanía* town of **San Juan de Limay** (one *hospedaje*), famous thoughout Nicaragua for its great **soapstone carvings**. The artists are happy to invite you into their house to watch them carve (average sculpture costs US$8 or less). Further on, **Pueblo Nuevo** (two basic *hospedajes*) is near an archaeological site. From here the road goes on to join the Pan-American Highway just east of Somoto.

Condega → *Population: 8000. Altitude: 561 m.*

From Estelí, the Pan-American goes north to Condega, a quiet town producing agricultural goods. Its name means 'pottery makers' and the indigenous village was once known for its ceramics. Some of the country's most beautiful pottery is still made here and visitors are welcome at the **Ducuale Grande Ceramic Co-operative** ⓘ *opposite Colegio Ana Velia de Guillén, T752-2374*, a women's co-op that makes attractive red-clay earthenware; there's a small shop attached. Condega has a small and well-kept **archaeological museum** ⓘ *Casa de Cultura de Condega, Plaza Central, Julio C Salgado, opposite the Policía Nacional, T752-2221, Tue-Sun 0800-1200, 1400-1800*, with permanent expositions of discoveries from the region.

Somoto → *Population: 14,000. Altitude: 700 m.*

Continuing along the highway you reach Somoto, a pleasant town in a lovely setting. Recent excavations have uncovered unusual pre-Columbian remains which are on display at the **Museo Arqueológico de Somoto** ⓘ *in the mayor's office, opposite the old Banco del Café, Mon-Fri 0800-1200*. The town is also famous for the best *rosquillas* in Nicaragua, a traditional toasted food, dry but tasty, made of egg, cheese, cornmeal and butter. Try the *viejita* which also has pure cane sugar in the centre. There are many road-side stands en route from Estelí to Somoto.

Ocotal → *Colour map 6, C3. Population: 27,000. Altitude: 606 m*

A road turns off right to Ocotal (18 km), a clean, cool, whitewashed town on a sandy plain and well worth a visit. It is near the Honduran border, to which a road runs north (bus marked Las Manos), and the scenery is wonderful. From Ciudad Sandino – formerly Jícaro – 50 km east from Ocotal, you can get to **San Albino**, where there are many gold mines and the nearby Río Coco is used to wash the gold.

Border essentials: Nicaragua-Honduras

El Espino/Somoto
There's nowhere to stay in El Espino. There's a duty-free shop and a food bar on the Nicaraguan side and several cafés on the Honduran side.
Nicaraguan immigration 20 km beyond Somoto is El Espino, 5 km from the Honduran border at La Playa. The Nicaraguan side is open 24 hrs.
Crossing by private vehicle
Motorists leaving Nicaragua should enquire in Somoto if an exit permit has to be obtained there or at El Espino. This applies to cyclists too.
Transport Minibuses run between Somoto and the border every hour 0615-1710, US$1, with at least 2 buses daily Somoto-Estelí (0610 and 1410) continuing to Managua, US$2.15, 5 hrs; Managua-Somoto hourly from 0400-2000, 3 hrs, US$3.50. On the Nicaraguan side taxis wait to take you to Somoto, they may try to overcharge; pay no more than US$8. On the Honduran side, taxis go between the border and the Mi Esperanza bus stops, when full, US$1 for foreigners, less for locals.
Directory Banks: no money changers on Nicaraguan side but locals will oblige.

Las Manos/Ocotal
This is recommended as the best route from Tegucigalpa to Managua.
Nicaraguan immigration Open 24 hrs. All those arriving must fill in an immigration card, present their luggage to the customs authorities and obtain a receipt, and then present these to the immigration authorities with passport and entry fees. Leaving the country, fill out a card, pay the tax and get your passport stamped.
Crossing by private vehicle After completing immigration procedures, go to Tránsito to pay for the vehicle permit, obtain clearance from Revisión, and get your vehicle permit from Aduana (Customs).
If it is busy, you could go first to Customs and get your number in the queue. On leaving the country, complete the immigration requirements, then go to Tránsito to have the vehicle checked, and to Customs to have the vehicle stamp in the passport cancelled. Surrender the vehicle permit at Customs and take another form back to Tránsito; this will be stamped, signed and finally handed over at the exit gate.
Transport Las Manos-Ocotal bus, every 30 mins or when full, 0615-1730, US$0.80, 45 mins.
Taxis also available, US$7-8 set fare before boarding.
Directory Money changers operate on both sides. Rates for cash and TCs are usually better in Estelí.

Sleeping

Tipitapa and further north *p913*
D El Valle, Sébaco, on the highway towards Ciudad Darío. Quiet, with fan and shower, patio with pool, English and Italian spoken. With restaurant.
F Hospedaje El, Ciudad Darío, 1½ blocks before the bridge on left. Basic but friendly.
F Hotel Oscar Morales, Esquipula. Clean, with shower.

Matagalpa and around *p914, map p915*
Many places shut their doors by 2200-2300. The town has an erratic water supply and possible shortages Mar-Apr.
A Lomas de Guadalupe, 500 m east of INAA, T612-7505. 26 rooms, private bath with hot water, cable TV, telephone, internet, new and pretty view, but not central.
B-E Ideal, Tienda Rosalinda ½ c al oeste, T612-2483. With bath and TV (cheaper without), better rooms are upstairs, beware

overcharging, good but expensive restaurant, disco on Sat.
D **Fountain Blue**, Colegio Santa Teresita, ½ c al este, T612-2733. Private bath with hot water, fan, cable TV.
D **Wanpani**, Shell La Virgen, ½ c al sur, 20 m al este, T612-4761. 12 rooms, *cafetería*, private bath and fan.
E **Central**, Av José Benito Escobar. Looks nice, clean rooms, good value, good reports.
E **Hospedaje Matagalpa**, 1 block east of Parque San José, T612-3834. With bath, clean, light and airy.
E **Soza del Río**, Av José Benito Escobar. With bath, nice patio, good value, opposite river, basic, meals available.
F **Bermúdez**, 2 blocks east of Parque San José. Some rooms with bath, poor, run- down, but popular, good car parking, helpful, meals.
F **Hospedaje Plaza**, on south side of Parque San José. Small rooms with thin walls and peepholes, poor beds, mosquitoes, basic.

Around Matagalpa

L-C **Selva Negra**, 10 km on road to Jinotega at Km 139.5, at 1200 m, T772-3883, www.selva negra.com. Cabins in a private cloud forest reserve. Good, expensive restaurant (book at weekends), good starting point for walks, private rainforest reserve, with self-guided trails, ask at the hotel for a map.
B **Campestre San Ramón y Finca Esperanza Verde**, San Ramón east of Matagalpa, T612-5003. Built for ecotourism and specifically for observation of butterflies, 2 rooms, private bath, fan, telephone, internet access. Also guesthouses in the area – call for details.
C **Hacienda San Rafael**, on the road to La Dalia, T612-2229. This lovely organic coffee farm is the producer of the fine **Café de los Reyes**. Lodging is in an attractive wooden lodge that affords some spectacular views of surrounding mountains above well-manicured gardens. The 270-ha farm has short nature paths, 1 leading to a small waterfall. Rooms have 1 shared bath, meals are available, reservations only.

Jinotega and around *p914*

B **Sollentuna Hem**, del Batazo 5 c al norte, T632-2334. 23 rooms, private bath with hot water, fan, restaurant, garage, best in town.
C **La Colema**, Banco Mercantil ½ c al este, T632-2017. Rooms with private bath and TV.
D **Bolper**, south side of Shell El Carmen, T632-2966. 10 rooms, private bath with hot water, cable TV, simple and friendly.
E **Cubulcan**, barrio Centroamérica, frente a taller Luna, T632-2727. 5 rooms with private bath, cheap food, parking.
F **Hotel Tito**, Banco Caley Dagnal 1½ c al este, T632-2607. 7 rooms, some with shared bath, clean, friendly and helpful owners, very good value, cheap food and fresh fruit drinks.
F **Hotel y Soda La Tica**, next to bus station. Motel-type, beware of overcharging.

San Rafael del Norte

F **Hospedaje Rocío**, just south of the petrol station, T652-2313. Small, homely and very clean, good value, with bath and set meals.

Estelí *p916, map p916*

B **Alameda**, Shell Esquipulas 1 c al este, 1½ c al sur, T713-6292. A/c, private bath with hot water, cable TV, pool, restaurant, secure parking.
B **Alpino**, Texaco ½ al este north of town, T713-2828. 18 rooms and 4 apartments, private bath, a/c or fan, cable TV.
B **Moderno**, T713-2378, east corner of cathedral, 2½ c al sur. Hot water, clean, friendly.
B **Panorama No 1**, on Pan-American Highway, T713-3147. Private bath, hot water, a/c, cable TV, noisy but convenient for buses.
B-C **Los Arcos**, costado noroeste de Catedral, 1 c al norte, T/F713-3830, hotelosarcos@hot mail.com. Cable TV, private bath with hot water, laundry service and secure parking. Cheaper with fan. Profits go towards social projects of the **Fundación Familias Unidas**.
C **Panorama No 2**, in city centre close to Casa de Cultura, T713-5023. Same features as No 1, better rooms upstairs, but much quieter at night with good acess to town centre and restaurants, secure parking.
D **Barlop**, 5 blocks north of main square, T713-2486. 12 rooms, 6 good, 6 basic, all with private bathroom, good, friendly.
D **El Mesón**, Av 1a NE Calle 3a NE, 1 block north of cathedral, T713-2655, barlan@ ibw.com.ni. With shower, fan, restaurant, TV, changes TCs. Thin walls but friendly service.
D **Mariela**, south of market Alfredo Lazo, T872-7460. Clean, safe, very small rooms, washing facilities, parking inside gates, basic.
D **Nicarao**, 1½ blocks south of main plaza, Av Bolívar/C Principal, T713-2490. With

shower (cheaper without), restaurant in leafy courtyard with good breakfasts, ideal for sitting around and relaxing, closes at 2200.

E **Sacuanjoche**, Enitel 2½ c al sur, T713-2482. 13 rooms, bath, breakfasts, good location.

F **San Francisco**, Calle Principal, T713-3787. Clean and simple.

F **Miraflores**, ½ block north of the plaza. Restaurant, private bathroom, hot water, TV in restaurant, basic, but OK if others are full.

F **Rizo**, Ferretería Briones 75 m al sur, T713-2862. 7 rooms with shared bath and fan.

Around Estelí *p917*

D **Bel Rive**, near Ocotal, across from Shell Ramos on Pan-American Highway, T732-2146. Cable TV, fan, private bath with hot water, restaurant, good value noisy locale.

D **Benmoral**, Ocotal, opposite **Enel** at entrance to town off highway, T732-2824. Private bath with hot water, fan, cable TV, good restaurant, best value in town.

D **Hotel Colonial**, Somoto, just north of main plaza. Very smart rooms in family-run hotel.

D-E **Panamericano**, on main plaza, Somoto, T722-2355. Quiet, landlord helpful, speaks English. 20 rooms, TV and private bath in newer ones, which are much nicer, great value, unparalleled artisan store with rare crafts from the entire northern region. Highly recommended.

D-F **El Viajero**, Esso 3½ c al oeste, Ocotal, T732-2040. With shared bath and fan, more expensive with private bath, cheap set meals.

E **El Bambú**, Profamilia 1 c al este, Somoto, T722-2330. 24 rooms, a/c, private bath, simple and nice, good restaurant.

E **Hotel Restaurant Mirador**, opposite bus station, Ocotal. Clean, friendly, with bath.

E-F **Pensión Baldovinos**, frente al Parque, Condega, T752-2222. 6 rooms, cheaper with shared bath, fan, group discounts.

F **Baghal**, Centro de Salud 1½ c al sur, Somoto, T722-2358. 7 rooms, shared bath, fans, TV, breakfast, helpful. Recommended.

F **Hospedaje Diana**, around El Sauce. Clean, basic.

F **Hospedaje El Castillo**, Ocotal. Basic, quiet, close to bus, candles provided for blackouts.

F **Hospedaje Framar**, on main plaza next to Casa de Cultura, Condega, T752-2393. 14 very clean and pleasant rooms, cold showers, nice garden, safe, friendly, owner speaks English, excellent value. Safe parking for motorcycles.

F **Internacional**, 1 block from Plaza Central, Somoto. Clean and basic.

F **Pensión Wilson**, Ocotal. Good, friendly.

F **Viajero**, near El Sauce. Noisy, fan, friendly, good food.

Eating

Tipitapa and further north *p913*

ΨΨ **El Sesteo**, Banco del Café, 2 c al oeste, Ciudad Darío, T622-2242, Chicken, shrimp, onion steak, clam cocktail, fried fish.

ΨΨ **Los Gemelos**, next to **ENEL**, Ciudad Darío, T622-2004. Seafood and good steaks.

Ψ **Entre Ríos**, Tipitapa, main street opposite Texaco, T295-3245. Very good lake perch, sweet and sour shrimp in nut sauce, daily, 1000- 2100.

Matagalpa and around *p914, map p915*

ΨΨ-Ψ **Comedor Colonial**, Parque San José/Darío. Good in evenings.

ΨΨ-Ψ **La Posada**, Parque Darío ½ c al norte, T612-2330. Fish *à la Tipitapa*.

ΨΨ-Ψ **La Vita e Bella**, an Italian-run restaurant at the north end town. It's up an alleyway, well worth the effort, reasonable. Has received strong praise from a couple of readers.

Ψ **Chepi**, Parque San José/Darío. Large portions, excellent value, popular.

Ψ **El Bambú**, Av José Benito Escobar. Popular with locals.

Ψ **Jinshan**, 1 block south of Parque Laborio. Chinese, good.

Ψ **Pesca Mar**, Cancha del Brigadista 3 c al este, T612-3548. Shrimp in garlic butter, red snapper in onions, daily until 2200.

Ψ **Vi Pay**, Parque San José/Darío. Daily 0900-2000, good.

Ψ **White House Pizza**, 1½ c al norte, T612-7575. Open daily, delivers in local area.

Ψ **Zinica**, opposite Casa Pellas, T612-5921. Daily 0900-2100, tacos, sandwiches and chicken. Very cheap.

Jinotega and around *p914*

Ψ **El Rincón de Don Pancho**, next to Esso, T632-3413. Tue-Sun 1030-2230. Cheap, good local food, mariachi music Sat and Sun nights.

Ψ **Jinocuba No 1**, Alcaldía 5 c al norte, T632-2607. *Mojito cubano, pollo habanero.* Daily 1200-2400.

Estelí *p916, map p916*
TT-T Rincón Pinareño, across from Panorama No 2, T713-4369. daily 1100-2200, smoked chicken, *vaca frita, sandwich cubano*, cheap, good, excellent deserts.
T Estanzuela, Supermercado Las Segovias 75 m al norte, T713-4522. Daily 0730-1830. Good tacos, *enchiladas, nacatamales* and sandwiches.
T Las Brasas, just off northwest corner of parque central, T713-4985. Tue-Sun 1130-2400. Very good Nicaraguan food, try *cerdo asado* (grilled pork), very popular, liveliest during the week. Recommended.
T Panadería España, about 3 blocks north of Parque Central on Av Bolívar. Good but pricey.
T Soda La Confianza, 1 block south of Parque Central. Cheap, good food.
T Sopas El Carao, Almacén Sony 1 c al sur, 1 c al oeste, T713-3678. Daily 0900-2000. Chicken, crab and iguana soups, grilled meats, very *Nica*.

Around Estelí *p917*
TT-T La Llamarada del Bosque, on Parque Central, Ocotal, T732-2643. Mon-Sat 0630-2000. Good-value buffet for breakfast, lunch and dinner, delivery available.
TT-T La Llanta, Petronic 100 m al oeste, Somoto, T722-2291. Daily 1000-2200. Good pork and chicken dishes, jalapeño steak.
TT-T La Quinta, Petronic 200 m abajo, Ocotal, T732-3420. Shrimp, sea bass, *filete miñón*. Open until 0400, live music on Fri.
T El Almendro, parque central ½ c al sur, Somoto, T722-2152, daily 1100-2200, beef.
T La Cabaña, opposite Enel, Ocotal, T732-2415, 1000-2300, soups, seafood and grilled meats.
T Tepecxomoth, Farmacia El Pueblo 25 m al este, Somoto, T722-2667. Daily 1000-2200, grilled rabbit and venison, beef ribs.

Entertainment

Matagalpa and around *p914, map p915*
Bars and clubs
Centro Popular de la Cultura, see page 914. Sat live music, Fri movie night, theatre.
Disco Luz de la Luna, 4 km out of town on the road to Managua. The most popular spot.
La Licor, near Rancho Escondido. Another popular hang-out.
Rancho Escondido, south end of town. Popular with locals, live music at weekends.

Estelí *p916, map p916*
Paradise, on highway at Km 154. Decent food, great atmosphere, open-air dance floor, good fun Thu-Sat nights.
Villa Vieja, also known as **El Brujito**, ½ block north of Parque Central on Av Bolívar. Good atmosphere, live music at weekends.

Shopping

Matagalpa and around *p914, map p915*
Mercado del Norte, close to northern highway, is filthy.
Mercado Sur, across from Terminal Sur, is busy and not the healthiest; look for fine black pottery made in local co-operatives.

Estelí *p916, map p916*
There are 2 small markets, 1 north, 1 south of Parque Central. Big **Supermercado PAL**, on C Principal.
La Esquina, opposite **Hotel El Mesón**craft shop located.

Activities and tours

Estelí *p916, map p916*
Tour operators
Tisey, next to **Hotel El Mesón** and run by same management. Apdo Postal No 63, T713-2655.

Transport

Tipitapa and further north *p913*
Bus From **Managua**, Plaza Mayoreo, via La Fanisa, Waspan, La Subasta, Aeropuerto and Zona Franca, every 10 mins, 0530-2100, 45 mins, US$0.25. Bus to **Estelí**, US$1.40, pick-up on the road coming from Managua, every 30 mins, 0455-1755. Bus to **Masaya**, US$0.35, every 20 mins, 0500-1900, 1 hr, change there for Granada.

Matagalpa and around *p914, map p915*
Bus Terminal Sur, by Mercado del Sur is used for destinations north, south and west including Managua, Estelí and Jinotega. **Estelí**, every 30 mins, 0515-1800, 1½ hrs, US$1. **Jinotega**, every 30 mins, 0500-1800, 1½ hrs, US$1. **León**, express, 0600 and 1500, 3 hrs, US$2.30, alternatively take the bus to Estelí, get off at San Isidro (junction) where buses leave for León every 30 mins.

Managua, every 30 mins, 2½ hrs, US$2.60. **Masaya**, 0700, 1400 and 1530, 4 hrs, US$2. **Tipitapa**, every 30 mins, 2 hrs, US$2, also when heading for Masaya or Granada (change in Tipitapa).

Terminal Norte, by Mercado del Norte, is for destinations within Matagalpa department, ie **San Ramón** and **El Tuma**. **Taxi** between terminals US$0.75.

Jinotega and around *p914*

Bus Most destinations will require a change of bus in Matagalpa. **Matagalpa**, every ½ hr, 0500-1800, 1½ hrs, US$0.90. **Managua**, every hr, 0400-1700, 3½ hrs, US$3350. **San Rafael de Norte**, every 15 mins, 0600-1700, 1 hr, US$0.70. Trucks from Jinotega market to San Rafael del Norte at 0700, 0800 and 0900, thereafter regular buses; trucks to **Estelí** at 0700, US$1, 3 hrs.

Estelí *p916, map p916*

Bus There are 2 terminals in town. **South terminal**, next to the southern market, serves all routes to the south including destinations that are accessed via Sébaco: **León**, 0625 and 1500, 3 hrs, US$2. Alternatively, take any bus going south on the Panamericana and change at **San Isidro**, ½ hr, US$0.50; from here wait by the roadside for buses south to León. **Managua**, every 30 mins, 0445-1515, 2 hrs, US$2.60; Express 0545 and 0645, US$3, 2 hrs.

North terminal (with small shops and cheap places to eat) serves northern destinations: **El Sauce**, 0900, 3 hrs, US$1.25. **Jinotega**, every hr, 0730-1530, 2 hrs, US$1.50. **Ocotal**, for border crossing at **Las Manos**, hourly, 0600-1730, 2 hrs, US$1. **Matagalpa**, every hr, 0620-1730, 1½ hrs, US$1.50. **San Juan de Limay**, 0915 and 1215, 4 hrs, US$2.25. **Somoto**, for border crossing at **El Espino**, every ½ hr, 0530-1800, 1½ hrs, US$1.

Around Estelí *p917*

Bus The **Ocotal** bus station is on the highway, 1 km south of town centre, 15-20 mins' walk from Parque Central.

Ciudad Antigua, 1 daily, 1200, 1 hr, US$1. **Estelí**, leaves the city market every hr, 0600-1700, 2 hrs, US$1. **Las Manos/ Honduras border**, every 30 mins, 0545-1730, 45 mins, US$0.50. **Managua**, every hr, 0510-1515, 4 hrs, US$3.25. **Somoto**, every 45 mins, 0600-1600, 2½ hrs, US$1.50.

Directory

Matagalpa and around *p914, map p915*

Banks Bancentro, Av Central, changes cash and TCs. **Credomatic**, hidden behind the Toyota dealer off the main plaza, cash advances on Visa and MC. Several other banks close to Bancentro, and money changers near the cathedral (varying rates). **Internet** CompuacSer internet, Av José Benito Escobar, 1 block north of Parque San José.

Estelí *p916, map p916*

Banks Bancentro, 1 street west of Calle Principal. **Banpro**, Parque Central, Visa cash advance, US$3 commission, efficient. **Agencia de Viajes Tisey** in Hotel El Mesón changes TCs at the official rate; many street changers, for cash only, on Av Bolívar. **Internet** Computer Soluciones, on northwest corner of plaza, US$0.60 per hr. **Language schools** Cenac (Centro Nicaragüense de Aprendizaje y Cultura), Apdo 10, Estelí, T713-5437, cenac@ibw.com.ni, 500 m north of the north bus terminal, 20 hrs of Spanish classes, living with a family, full board, travelling to countryside, meetings and seminars, opportunities to work on community projects, US$140 per week. Also welcomes volunteer tutors for teaching English to Nicaraguans and others. Also **Movimiento de Mujeres**, Casa Nora Astorga, Apdo 72, Estelí, which occupies one of the Cenac buildings and offers classes. **Los Pipitos- Sacuanjoche Escuela de Español**, ½ block south of Teatro Nancy, Apdo 80, T713-5511, www.lospipitosesteli.org.ni, all profits go to disabled children and their families, excursions to local co-operatives, social projects and nature reserve are part of the course, staying with families, US$120-175 per week, flexible. **Horizonte Nica**, INISER 2 c al este, ½ c al norte, T713-4117, 4-week intensive course, Mon-Fri 800-1200 and 1400-1700, horizont@ibw.com.ni

Around Estelí *p917*

Banks Several banks around Parque Central. The Shell petrol station changes dollars.

León and the west

A third route to Honduras leaves the capital heading through the Pacific lowlands to the Gulf of Fonseca in the shadow of Los Maribios, a chain of volcanoes from Momotombo on Lake Managua to Cosigüina overlooking the gulf. This route takes in León, a city influential in shaping Nicaraguan history since colonial times. On the Pacific coast are the beaches at Poneloya and the major port of Corinto. From León, 88 km from Managua, the Pacific Highway continues north to the industrial town of Chinandega. From here, routes lead west to the port of Corinto, north to the Gulf of Fonseca and east to Guasaule and the Honduran border. For the adventurous traveller, León is a good base to climb one of the volcanoes of Los Maribios: Momotombo is known for its perfect shape and incredible views from the top; Cerro Negro is the youngest volcano in Central America, erupting every four to five years; Volcán Telica has bubbling mudholes at the base and glowing lava in the crater; San Cristóbal is the tallest volcano in Nicaragua and highly active; Cosigüina is surrounded by beautiful nature and famous for its huge crater lake and spectacular views. ▸▸ *For Sleeping, Eating and other listings, see pages 930-935.*

Towards Léon

The old paved road to León crosses the Sierra de Managua, offering fine views of the lake. It is longer than the new Pacific Highway and not in good condition. About 60 km down the new road to León lies the village of **La Paz Centro**, with several truck-stop restaurants and accommodation. There is a good range of cheap, handmade pottery here, and you can ask to see the potters' ovens and production of bricks. Try the local speciality *quesillo*, mozzarella cheese, onions and cream wrapped in tortilla, available all along the highway. From here you can reach **Volcán Momotombo**, which dominates the Managua skyline from the west. It is possible to camp on the lakeside with great views of the volcano.

You need a permit to climb Momotombo from the south as they have built a geothermal power station on the volcano's slopes. We understand no permit is required to climb the volcano from the north but one reader has urged us to remove that information after a gruelling 11-hour climb which, at times got "extremely dangerous". It is best to use a professional guide – ask at **Va Pues** or **Quetzaltrekkers** in León (see Tour operators, page 934).

León Viejo

ⓘ *US$2 entrance fee includes Spanish-speaking guide.*

At the foot of the volcano lies León Viejo destroyed by earthquake and volcanic eruption on 31 December 1609 and now being excavated. It was here that the brutal first Spanish governor of Nicaragua Pedrarias and his wife were buried in La Merced church next to Francisco Hernández de Córdoba, the country's founder who had been beheaded under order of Pedrarias. Archaeological excavations have revealed the **cathedral**, the **Convento de la Merced**, the **Casa del Gobernador**, as well as the bodies of Hernández de Córdoba and Pedrarias, which have been placed in a special tomb in the Plaza Mayor. The ruins themselves are little more than low walls and probably only of serious interest to archaeologists, but you can see the ground plan of the old Spanish town and from the ruins of the old fortress there are breathtaking views of Volcán Mombotombo, Lake Managua and Momotombito Island and the Maribios Volcanoes Range. To get to León Viejo, take the 0830 bus from Managua to La Paz Centro, then another to León Viejo, and walk 1 km to the ruins. The return bus is at 1400.

León

» pp930-935. Colour map 6, C3.

→ *Population: 184,792. Altitude: 50 m.*

León has a colonial charm unmatched elsewhere in Nicaragua, except perhaps by Granada. It has narrow streets, red-tile roofs, low adobe houses and time-worn buildings everywhere. Founded by Hernández de Córdoba in 1524 at León Viejo, 32 km from its present site, it was moved here after the devastating earthquake of 1609. The existing city was founded in 1610. In recent years, economic factors have taken precedence over the cleaning up of old buildings, but the work continues slowly.

Descriptions of León's fight against the Somoza régime can be found in the book Fire from the Mountain: The Making of a Sandinista, *by Omar Cabezas.*

As the capital, León was the dominant force in Nicaragua until Managua took control in 1852. Today, it is still thought of as the 'intellectual' capital, with a university (Universidad Nacional Autónoma de Nicaragua, UNAN) founded in 1804, religious colleges, the largest cathedral in Central America, and several colonial churches. It is said that Managua became the capital, although at the time it was no more than an indigenous settlement, because it was halfway between violently Liberal León and equally violently Conservative Granada.

Ins and outs

Getting there Regular buses to León run from Managua and Chinandega, with frequent routes from Estelí and Matagalpa. International buses will drop you off, if asked, at the entrance to town. The bus terminal is at the northeastern end of town, a 20-minute walk, or short taxi ride from the centre.

Getting around Most attractions are within a few blocks of the centre so choosing a fairly central hotel will make it an easy city to explore on foot. Local buses will take you to the terminal and a network of *colectivos* work as cheap taxis (US$0.15). Taxis cost US$0.60 during the day, US$0.70 at night.

Tourist office INTUR ⓘ *Parque Rubén Darío 2½ c al norte, T311-1325, www.leononline.net*, has maps for sale, reference books and friendly staff.

Sights

Legend has it that the plans for the **Basílica de la Asunción** (to give the cathedral its full name) were switched with those of Lima (Peru) by mistake. However, the enormous size of the building, designed by Guatemalan architects, may be explained by the need to withstand the area's heavy seismic activity. Construction was begun in 1746 and was not completed for 113 years. Its famous shrine – 145 cm high, covered by white topazes from India given by Felipe II of Spain – is, sadly, kept in a safe in the vestry, to which the bishop holds the key. The cathedral also houses a very fine ivory Christ, the consecrated Altar of Sacrifices and the Choir of Córdoba, the great Christ of Esquipulas (in bronze with a cross of very fine silver) and statues of the 12 Apostles. At the foot of one of these statues is the tomb of Rubén Darío, the 19th-century Nicaraguan poet, and one of the greatest in Latin America, guarded by a sorrowful lion. All the entrances to the cathedral are guarded by lions said to come alive after midnight to patrol the old church. The old Plaza de Armas, in front of the cathedral, is now **Parque Jerez**, but is usually referred to as **Parque Central**; it contains a statue of General Jerez, a mid-19th century Liberal leader.

To see inside the cathedral, visit 0700-0900, or 1600-1800.

León has the finest **colonial churches** in Nicaragua, more than 12 in all, and they are the city's most significant attraction. **La Recolección**, with a beautiful baroque Mexican façade, built in 1786, has a neoclassical interior with mahogany woodwork.

Memories of a Revolutionary

During the 1978-1979 Revolution, León was the centre of heavy fighting. There are many monuments from that time in the city. In the city centre a plaque marks the spot where the first President Somoza was assassinated in 1956 by poet Rigoberto López Pérez. Visitors can also see **El Fortín** (from the cathedral, go west about 10 blocks, then south), the ruined last stronghold of Somoza's national guard. It's best to go early in the morning for the great views of town and several volcanoes. A commemorative march goes there each 7 July. **El Veinte Uno**, the national guard's 21st garrison, was also ruined, and the scene of an important battle in April 1979; the jail around the corner (three blocks south of cathedral) has been converted into a garden with a statue to *El Combatiente Desconocido* (the unknown warrior). In the Barrio San Felipe, 7-8 blocks north of the market behind the cathedral, a statue of **Luisa Amanda Espinoza** remembers the first woman member of the FSLN to die (in 1970).

Across the street from the north side of the cathedral is an interesting mural covering the history from pre-Columbian times to the Sandinista Revolution, completed in 1990. Sadly it seems many of the murals are being painted over as the images of the Revolution are gradually removed and replaced. It surrounds a commemorative park, the **Mausoleo Héroes y Mártires**. There is also the **Galería Héroes y Mártires** (Calle 1 NO, between Av 1 and 2), which sells handicrafts and houses the twinning office with New Haven (US).

La Merced, which was built in 1615 and burned by pirates in 1685, is notable for its seven different altars. It is one of the oldest churches in León and has fine woodwork inside and a restored exterior. **San Felipe** was built at the end of the 16th century for the religious services of the black and mulatto population of the city. It was rebuilt in the 18th century in a manner true to its original form, a mixture of baroque and neoclassical. **El Calvario**, constructed during the same period, is notable for its neoclassical façade attributed to the growing French influence in Spain at the time. The **Iglesia y Convento de San Francisco** ⓘ *US$1.50*, founded in 1639, is the oldest convent with a church in León. It still has two plateresque altars from Spain and its original pillars. In 1830, after the expulsion of the Franciscans from Nicaragua, it was used by various civic organizations and is now a gallery. The **Iglesia de San Nicolás de Laborío**, was founded in 1618 for the local indigenous population, and is the most modest of the León churches, constructed of wood and tiles over adobe walls with an unostentatious façade and a simple altar, 10 m tall. The celebration for San Nicolás is 10 September. The **Iglesia de Nuestra Señora Pilar de Zaragoza** was built from 1884-1934 and has two unusual octagonal turrets and an arched doorway with tower above. There is a pleasant walk south across the bridge, past the **church of Guadalupe**, to the cemetery.

The house of poet Rubén Darío, the famous 'Four Corners' in Calle Rubén Darío, is now the **Museo-Archivo Rubén Darío** ⓘ *Tue-Sat 0900-1200, 1400-1700, Sun 0900-1200, entry and guided tour free but donations accepted.* It has an interesting collection of personal possessions, photographs, portraits and a library with a wide range of books of poetry in Spanish, English and French. Darío died in 1916 in another house in the northwest sector (marked with a plaque). Alfonso Cortés – another of Nicaragua's finest poets who wrote a famous poem while chained to the bars in front of Rubén's old bed – went insane while living in Darío's house in 1927 and spent the rest of his years in a Managuan asylum until his death in 1969, leaving behind the *museo-archivo*.

Two blocks west of La Merced church is the **Centro Popular de la Cultura** which has frequent exhibitions and events, and is the only place in León to see live folk concerts (schedule on the front door). The **Museo de Leyendas y Tradiciones** has handcrafted life-size models depicting the rich legends of León. The **Museo Ortiz Guardián** ⓘ *Mon-Fri 1100-1900, US$2*, is a colonial home and art museum. **Museo Archivo Alfonso Cortés** ⓘ *Mon-Sat 0800-1200, 1400-1700*, has dusty displays of the great poet's manuscripts. **CIMAC** ⓘ *Costado sur del Puente Martínez, ½ c arriba, 1 c al norte,*

León

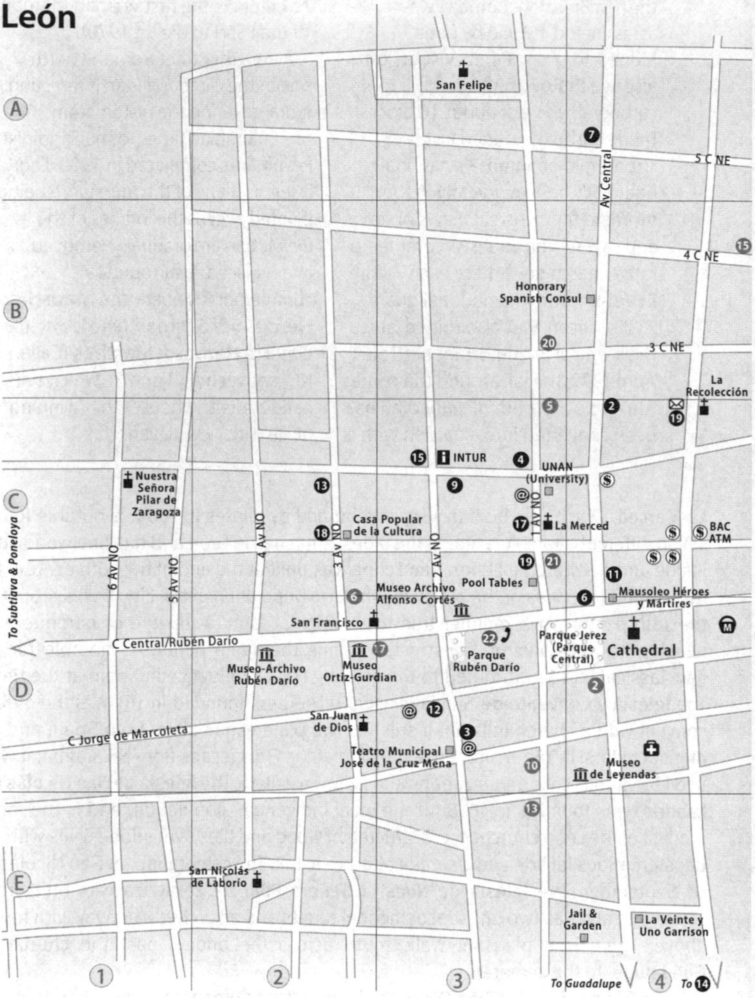

Sleeping
América 1 *D4*
Austria 2 *D4*
California 3 *A6*
Casa Vieja 4 *B5*
Colonial 5 *C3*
El Convento 6 *D2*
El Parcador de Don Gonzalo 7 *C5*
Europa 8 *B6*
Grand 9 *A6*
Hostal Clínica 10 *D3*
La Avenida 11 *A6*
La Cabaña 12 *A5*
La Casona 13 *E3*
La Casona Colonial 14 *B5*
La Posada del Doctor 15 *B4*
Los Balcones 16 *C5*
Mi Pueblo 17 *D3*
Primavera 18 *A5*
San Juan D'Leon 19 *B5*
Vía Vía 20 *C5*

Eating
Buen Gusto 1 *D5*
Café Pizza Roma 2 *C4*
Café Taquezal 3 *D3*
Cafetín Puerto Café Benjamin Linder 4 *C3*
Comedor Tealí 5 *B6*

T311-0752, cimac@ibw.com.ni, Mon-Fri 0800-1100, 1400-1700, Sat 0800-1100, which used to be a garbage plant, has been transformed into a centre for urban environmental initiatives, with a self-guided trail and further information available at site.

Sutiava

The western end of the city is the oldest, and here is the oldest of all the churches, the parish church of **San Juan Bautista** in Sutiava (1530). Las Casas, the Apostle of the Indies, preached here several times. It has a fine façade, the best colonial altar in the country and an interesting representation of *El Sol* (the sun), carved in wood on the ceiling. The church has been beautifully reconstructed. Just south of the church on the dirt plaza is a new **museum** ⓘ *daily 0800-1100, 1400-1700, Sat 0800-1000, US$0.50,* housing many colonial period relics.

On the main street north of the church is a small **Museo de la Comunidad Indígena Sutiava** or **Museo Adiac** ⓘ *T311-5371, Mon-Fri 0800-1200, 1400-1700, Sat 0800-1200, donations greatly appreciated,* with an anthropological and historical museum. The ruins of the nearby parish churches of Vera Cruz and Santiago are both crumbling and unapproachable. Also in the suburb of Sutiava is the **Casa de Cultura** with several interesting murals adorning the walls. Inside there are a few cafés, information about prominent Nicaraguan cultural figures and the offer of a free history and cultural lesson on Thursdays (1500) in basic Spanish.

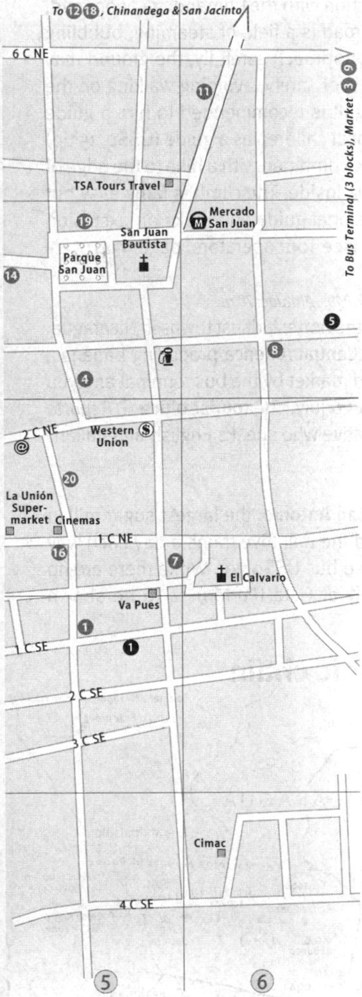

El Oasis **7** *A4*
El Sesteo **6** *C4*
Flor de Sacuanjoche **9** *C3*
Italian Pizza **11** *C4*
Jala la Jarra **12** *D3*
La Casa Vieja **13** *C2*
Lacmiel **14** *E4*
Mi Tierra **15** *C3*
Payitas **17** *C3*
Subway *C2* **18**
White House Pizza **19** *C3/C4*

Bars & clubs
Divino Castigo **20** *B3*
Don Señor **21** *C3*
Las Ruinas **22** *D3*

Around León

» *pp930-935.*

Poneloya and Las Peñitas beaches

A bumpy road from León heads west to **Poneloya** and **Las Peñitas**, a couple of relaxed and very friendly beach communities 19 km from León. Both contain long beautiful stretches of sand and a mixture of humble houses and rich vacation homes. Most of the coast has big waves and strong currents (swim here with great caution – there are drownings every year). The south end of Las Peñitas and Puerto Mántica, at the north end of Poneloya, are the best for swimming, with good surfing in between, but there are no boards available to rent. During the week you will have the beaches to yourself so be prepared to fend for yourself, but at weekends people come from León and in Semana Santa it's sardine time. It is possible to rent quadbikes from the *pulpería* at the intersection of the road to Las Peñitas and Poneloya, called **Licorería Estela de los Mares** (US$10 per hour, you must also show a driving licence, sign a release form and pay a US$10 deposit).

San Jacinto

On the road to Estelí, 12 km north of the intersection with the Chinandega-León road, is **San Jacinto**. About 200 m to the west of the road is a field of steaming, bubbling **mud holes**, which is worth visiting. You should approach carefully, the ground may give and scald your legs; follow other footmarks for safety, avoiding walking on the crystallized white sulphur and listen for hissing. It is recommended to hire a guide (ask tour operators in León) or trust one of the local children as a guide (US$0.25 tip) to show you where it is safe to walk. A visit can be combined with a hike to the edge of the spectacular crater of Telica with glowing lava inside. The climb is fairly easy but trails can be hard to find. Best to use a professional guide and make an excursion from León – ask at **Va Pues** or **Quetzaltrekkers** (see Tour operators, page 934).

Chinandega → *Colour map 6, C3. Population: 137,940. Altitude: 70 m.*

About 40 km beyond León, Chinandega is one of the hottest, driest towns in Nicaragua. Agriculturally, this is one of the richest areas in Central America producing bananas, peanuts, sugar cane and shrimps. There's a good market by the bus terminal and you can hire horse-drawn cabs. The local fiesta is on 26 July. The **tourist office** ⓘ *Reparto Los Angeles, T341-2040*, has a helpful representative who speaks English and Italian.

Chichigalpa

Not far away, near Chichigalpa, is the **Ingenio San Antonio**, the largest sugar mill in Nicaragua, with a railway between the town and the mill (five trains a day each way May-November, passengers taken, US$0.10; also bus US$0.30). While there are no official tours of the installations, you can apply at Gate (*Portón*) 14 to be shown

León & Los Maribios volcanic chain

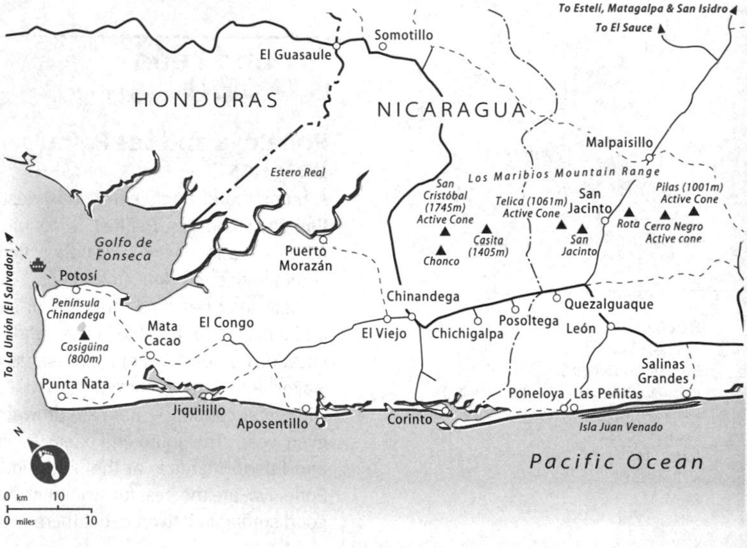

around. On the edge of Chichigalpa itself is the **Flor de Caña distillery**, maker of what many believe to be the finest rum in the world, aged up to 21 years and made in over 15 flavours. On leaving you will recognize the picture on the bottle labels, a palm-shaded railway leading towards Chichigalpa with volcanoes in the background.

Corinto → *Colour map 6, C3. Population: 17,414. Altitude: 3 m.*

Twenty-one kilometres from Chinandega, Corinto is the main port and the only one at which vessels of any considerable size can berth. About 60% of the country's commerce passes through here. The town itself is on a sandy island, **Punto Icaco**, connected with the mainland by long railway and road bridges. There are beautiful old wooden buildings with verandas, especially by the port. Entry to the port is barred to those without a permit.

On the Corinto-Chinandega road is **Paseo Cavallo beach** (**Restaurante Buen Vecino**). The sea is treacherous here and people drown every year. There are no facilities in Corinto's barrier islands, but they are beautiful with crashing surf on one side, calm and warm swimming water on the other. The journey can be negotiated with any fisherman. A *panga* can be rented for the whole day for US$40 so you can explore the numerous islands and mangroves. You'll see lots of birdlife but also lots of sandflies, so bring repellent.

North of Chinandega

The road north to Puerto Morazán passes through the village of **El Viejo**, US$0.20 by bus from Chinandega, 5 km, where there is an old church, **La Basílica del Viejo**, famous throughout the country for its celebration on 6 December called *La Lavada de la Plata*, which consists of devotees washing all silver parts of the altar. The Basílica has la Virgen del Hato, which leaves the altar every December in a major pilgrimage to visit Corinto, Chinandega, León and Managua.

From Chinandega there are six buses a day to **Potosí** (at least three hours, US$1.20). In the centre of the village there are warm thermal springs in which people relax each afternoon. There are also pleasant black-sand beaches; the sea, although the colour of coffee, is clean. The passenger ferry from Potosí to La Unión (El Salvador) has been suspended. Ask around for an ad hoc service or ask in Chinandega before setting out to the peninsula. There are some suggestions that there may be a service from Corinto to La Unión.

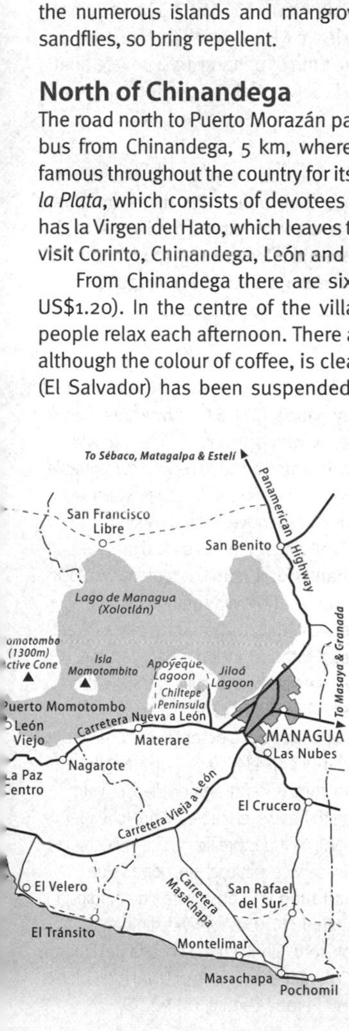

It is a four-hour hike to the cone of **Volcán Cosigüina**. The path is overgrown and very difficult to follow, so you may need a guide (see Tour operators, page 934) There is plenty of wildlife in the area, including poisonous snakes. On 23 January 1835, one of the biggest eruptions in history blew off most of the cone, reducing it from 3000 m to its present height of 800 m, throwing ash as far as Colombia, and leaving an enormous crater lake. From the cone there are beautiful views of the Golfo de Fonseca shared by Nicaragua, Honduras and El Salvador. The volcano and the surrounding dry tropical forest are a Reserva Natural, administered by the Ministry of the Environment and Natural Resources in Managua.

Border essentials: Nicaragua-Honduras

Guasaule

Nicaraguan immigration The distance between the border posts is 500 m. Open 24 hrs. To enter Nicaragua costs are US$7 plus a US$1 Alcaldía charge; to exit it is US$2 plus the US$1 immigration charge.

Transport Buses run every 30 mins from the border to Chinandega, US$1.40. Express bus to Managua, 1130, 1230 and 1700, 4 hrs, US$3.50 via Somotillo and León. From Managua to Río Guasaule at 1810.

Directory Money changers offer the same rates for córdobas to lempiras as on the Honduran side. Banco de Crédito Centroamericano, beside immigration, is recommended, good rates, no commission, and will accept photocopy of passport if yours is being checked by immigration.

Potosí

Nicaraguan immigration and customs Open 0800-1700, but closed for lunch. Exit is US$2 and Nicaraguan immigration entrance is US$7. Transport Buses from Potosí-Chinandega, 0230, 0345, 0500, 0620, 0710, 1000, 1500, US$2, 3 hrs. If trying to leave Nicaragua, there is no ferry at the time of printing; try a private boat to El Salvador, from US$100.

Jiquilillo beach, 42 km from Chinandega, is reached by a mostly paved road branching off the El Viejo-Potosí road. Lying on a long peninsula, there are a few lodgings and small restaurants. From Chinandega a rough paved road goes to the Honduran border on the **Río Guasaule** near **Somotillo** (where the road improves) heading to Choluteca, Honduras. The bus from Chinandega takes 1¾ hours (US$1.25).

Sleeping

Towards León *p923*

F **Hospedaje El Buen Gusto**, La Paz Centro. Friendly, fairly clean, basic.

F **Hospedaje El Caminante**, close to the highway, La Paz Centro. Basic, friendly, cheap.

León *p924, map p926*

L **El Convento**, connected to San Francisco church, T311-7053, www.hotelelconvento.com.ni. A/c, cable TV, includes breakfast, beautiful colonial design decorated by antiques with a lovely interior garden, restaurant, Nicaragua's most charming colonial hotel and León's best.

A **Los Balcones**, esquina de los bancos, 3 blocks from cathedral, T311-0250, www.hotelbalcones.com. Private bath, hot water, a/c, cable TV, colonial building, pleasant courtyard, bar and restaurant.

B **Austria**, Costado Oeste de la Catedral 1 c al sur, ½ abajo, T311-1206, www.hotelaustria.com.ni. Central with hot water, a/c, cable TV, clean, secure parking, often fully booked, breakfast US$3.

B-C **Europa**, 3 Calle NE, 4 Av, 2 blocks south of railway station, T311-6040, www.hoteleuropaleon.com. With bath and a/c (cheaper with fan), cold water, brusque service, comfortable patios with bar and shade, coffee available, restaurant expensive, limited parking inside, guard will watch vehicles parked on street.

B-C **Grand Hotel**, from bus terminal ½ block south, T311-1327, www.grandhoteldeleon.com. With bath, hot water, cable TV, a/c (cheaper without), includes breakfast, clean, garden, safe parking, breakfast US$4, other meals US$5, book ahead.

B-C **La Posada del Doctor**, 20 m from Parque San Juan, T311-4343, www.laposadadeldoc tor.com. Recently remodelled, private bath with hot water, cable TV, a/c (cheaper with fan), includes breakfast, use of kitchen, laundry service, patio, clean, good value.

B-C **San Juan D'León**, weste side of Iglesia San Juan, T311-0547, www.hsanjuandeleon.com. Similar to **La Posada del Doctor**.

B-D **Colonial**, 50 m north of UNAN, 2½ blocks north of Parque Central, T311-2279,

www.hotelcoloniadeleon.com. Pleasant, fine old building and patio, rooms and in need of refurbishment, a/c and bath, cheaper without, good views from upstairs, front rooms with balcony can be noisy at weekends.
D América, Av Santiago Argüello, 2 blocks east of cathedral, T311-5533. With bath and fan, clean, good value, friendly, nice patio and garden, breakfast US$2, other meals US$3, cold drinks, internet, convenient location, secure garage nearby.
D La Casona Colonial, Parque San Juan ½ c abajo, T311-3178. Private bath, fan, pleasant garden, colonial decor, friendly.
D-E Primavera, Desmotadora Gurdián on exit road to Chinandega (so used by truck drivers), T311-4216. With bath and a/c, cheaper with fan, helpful and friendly, secure parking, breakfast US$1.50, other meals US$3.
E California, across from the bus station and new market, T311-5074. Friendly, family-run, with nice patio and TV. Handy for bus station, but early check-out (0900). Price depends on how long you stay.
E Hostal Clínica, 1 ½ blocks south of Parque Central on 1 Av NO, T311-2031, mary mergalo2000@yahoo.com. Family-run place, with single and double rooms with private or shared bathroom. Very friendly, washing facilities, breakfast and drinks available – good early reports.
E La Cabaña, Ermita de Dolores 1 c al sur, ½ c al este, T311-0467. Clean simple rooms with shared bath and fan.
E Mochilas Inn, Parque San Juan, 80 m al Oeste, T311-2976, mochilasinn@hotmail.com. Good backpackers' choice with dormitory rooms, friendly atmosphere, a bar and a living room with TV, close to the city centre.
E-F La Casona, 2 blocks south of Teatro González, T311-5282, lacasonahostal@ hotmail.com. Double rooms with private or shared bath, fan (cheaper per person for dorm), spacious house with lots of places to relax, garden with hammocks, pool (not always filled), use of kitchen, laundry service or washing facilities, recommended, popular with volunteers.
E-F Vía Vía, del Servicio Agrícola Gurdián 75 m al sur, T311-6142, www.viaviacafe.com. comfortable, friendly, fan, shared bath, cheaper per person for dorm, garden, laundry service, café with cheap food, dance, Spanish classes and trips to local places of interest. Part of a worldwide network of Belgian cafés. Recommended.
F Casa Vieja, 1½ blocks south of Parque San Juan. Friendly, clean, quite social, family feel, large rooms with fans, communal bathroom and kitchen (pay extra when using gas), discounts for longer stays or for shared room.
F El Parcador de Don Gonzalo, Fernández de Oviedo (sign on the door only says *Hospedaje*), in front of Iglesia El Calvario, T311-6750. Family-run *hostal* with 1 spacious dorm (6 beds) and private fan, basic but very clean, safe, secure, friendly, use of kitchen and laundry facilities, running water might be gone in the afternoon (buckets available), cheap, recommended.
F La Avenida, north of Mercado San Juan, T311-2068. With bath, family-run, fan, breakfast available US$1-2, friendly, laundry facilities. Far from centre but a good choice.
F Mi Pueblo, Calle Rubén Darío opposite San Francisco, T843-7025. With bath and fan, partitioned walls, fridge, washing machine. Also cyber café, Spanish classes and tour agency. Price is per person.

Poneloya and Las Peñitas *p927*
C-D La Montaña, Playa Las Peñitas, T317-372. 4 rooms with a/c and private bath (cheaper with fan) and shared bath, restaurant.
C-D Suyapa Beach Hotel, Playa Las Peñitas, T854-2699 (León), www.suyapabeach.com. Best in region, a/c (cheaper with fan), ask for an upstairs room with ocean view and a breeze, all with private bath, very clean, swimming pool in season and outdoor beach shower, group discounts. Good mid-range restaurant with great view, try *pescado a la suyapa*, fresh snapper in a tomato, pepper and onion sauce, excellent. Recommended.
D Posada de Poneloya, opposite Lacayo, Poneloya, T311-4612. Cabinas with bath, fan, parking.
E-F Lacayo, on the beach. Great location, dusty rooms, basic, bats in the roof and beware of insects at night, bring coils. Cheap dorm, good, cheap food, restaurant has good *repochetas*, great place to sling a hammock and relax.
F Barca de Oro, T317-0275, www.barca deoro.com. Good, cheap and simple accommodation, with tours arranged by locals to see nesting turtles on nearby Juan Venado Island.

Chinandega *p928*

A Los Volcanes, Km 129 Carretera a Chinandega, at entrance to town, T341-1000. Hot water, a/c, cable TV, phone, bar, restaurant, clean, good service. Recommended.

C-D Glomar, Mercado Central 1 c al sur, T341-2562. Cheaper with shared bath. Owner will change dollars, but mistrusts foreigners, his son is friendly, good food, cold beer, bar and restaurant may be closed Sun evening.

E Aniram, Shell 1½ c al este, T341-4519. Private bath, cable TV, fan or a/c, cheap meals, parking, good value.

E California, Esso El Calvario 1 c al este, 1½ c al sur, T341-0936. Private bath, a/c or fan, cable TV, homely and friendly.

C-E Casa Granada, antiguo Interbank ½ c al oeste, T341-0325. Private bath with fan (more expensive with a/c) and cable TV, fax and laundry, restaurant, trips to San Cristóbal volcano.

F Chinandega. Basic, fan, shared bath.

Corinto *p929*

D Central, in front of Port Buildings. Clean, a/c.

F Hospedaje Luvy, 2 blocks from plaza. Fan, dirty bathrooms.

North of Chinandega *p929*

E Las Vegas, Somotillo. Small rooms, fan, not too clean, restaurant.

Eating

León *p924, map p926*

Few restaurants have signs so you'll have to be standing outside the door before you know you're there. Many are closed on Sun. There are good *panaderías* 2 blocks east of cathedral, Mon-Sat from 0800.

¶¶ Bar/Restaurant Las Balcones, esquina de los bancos, 3 blocks from cathedral, T311-0250. In a colonial building, good atmosphere, open daily for breakfast, lunch and dinner, bar 1900-2200.

¶¶ Café Pizza Roma, 2½ c north of the cathedral, T311-3568. Wed-Mon 1200-2300, good pizzas, recommended.

¶¶ Café Taquezal, across the street from Teatro Municipal, T311-7282. Pleasant atmosphere, dishes of shrimp, calamari, pastas, very good. Mon-Sat 1800-0200.

¶¶ Cafetín Puerto Café Benjamín Linder, next to UNAN (northern corner), T311-0548. Daily 0800-2400, good place for food, coffee, a few beers. Internet access.

¶¶ El Sesteo, next to cathedral on Parque Central, T311-5327. Renovated, excellent food and *the* place for watching the world go by. Daily 1800-2400.

¶¶ Flor de Sacuanjoche, northeast corner of UNAN, 75 m abajo, T311-1121. Best vegetarian meals, meat dishes, lunch and breakfast. Daily 1800-2300.

¶¶ Jala la Jarra, 1c al sur, T867-5894. Colourful bar/restaurant, small terrace, fish and meat dishes. 1100-2300.

¶¶ Lacmiel, 5 blocks south of cathedral, T311-4992. Good food, live music, open air. Recommended.

¶¶ Subway, Noreste del Hotel Convento, Daily 1000-2200, combos for US$3.5.

¶¶ White House Pizza in front of church La Recolección or ½ block north of the Parque, T311-7010, daily 1100-2200, cafeteria style, good cheap pizza, home delivery as well.

¶¶-¶ Restaurante Italian Pizza, ½ c north of cathedral, T311-0857. Daily 0900-2130, serves pizzas as well as Lebanese food.

¶ Buen Gusto, Parque los Poetas 1c al sur. Closed Sun, very cheap, buffet-style *comedor*.

¶ Casa Popular de Cultura, 1 block north of plaza central, 2½ blocks west. Sandwiches and hamburgers, nice atmosphere.

¶ Central, Calle 4 Norte. Good *comida corriente*.

¶ Comedor Tealí, same street as **Hotel Europa**, 2 blocks south of railway staion. Daily 0700-2030, cheap, good Nicaraguan food, great natural fruit drinks, friendly.

¶ El Barcito, northwest of Parque Central. Popular, soft drinks, milkshakes, slow service.

¶ El Oasis, Calle 5 and Av Central. Good value, limited menu, popular.

¶ La Casa Vieja, 1½ blocks north of San Francisco church, T311-3701. Mon-Sat 1600-2300, pleasant bar, good-quality snacks, good value. Highly recommended.

¶ Mi Tierra, 2 blocks north of Parque Rubén Diarío (close to **Flor de Sacuanjoche**). Cheap Nicaraguan-style buffet, nice atmosphere. Mon-Sat 1200-2200, Sun 1200-1900.

¶ Payitas, across from Parque La Merced, T311-5857. Jalapeño steak, hamburgers, sandwiches. Daily 0900-2400.

Sutiava *p927*

¶¶ **Caña Brava**, on the Carretera Circunvalación, T311-5666. Best food in town, try their *pollo deshuesado* (boneless chicken).

¶¶ **Los Pescaditos**, Iglesia de Sutiava 1 c al sur, 120 m al oeste, near Sutiava church, T311-2684. Excellent fish at reasonable prices. Daily 1200-2230. Recommended.

¶ **Caperas**, on the Carretera Circunvalación. Good, cheap Nicaraguan food.

¶ **Montezerino**, Km 91 on the bypass, T311-2638. Outdoor, good meat and fish, pleasant.

Poneloya *p927*

¶ **Cáceres**. Good *comida corriente*.

¶ **La Peña del Tigre**. Good restaurant, huge portions (great *repochetas*), friendly, open air, good views. It's near a tall rock on the beach where bathing is dangerous and prohibited.

Chinandega *p928*

¶ **Chiles Café**, Shell Central 1½ c al norte, T341-0520. Good tortilla soup, Mexican fare. Daily 1200-2300.

¶ **Corona de Oro**, Iglesia San Antonio 1½ c al este, T341-2539. Good for chicken curry, shrimp skewers.

¶ **El Mondongazo**, south side of Colegio San Luis, T341-4255. Traditional Nicaraguan foods, *sopa mondongo* (tripe soup), beef, chicken and meatball soup.

¶ **El Refugio**, Esso El Calvario ½ c al sur, T341-0834. Great beef specialities, try the breaded tongue.

¶ **Hungaro**, Copepach ½ c arriba, far from the centre, T341-3824. Hungarian-style sweetbreads, beef fillet in paprika sauce, friendly staff. Daily 1100-2300.

¶ **Parador**, Texaco Los Encuentros 300 m al norte, T341-0885. Cheap sandwiches, hamburgers and fruit drinks. Daily 1100-2300.

Corinto *p929*

¶¶-¶ **Meléndez**, on main plaza. Good but can be pricey.

North of Chinandega *p929*

¶ **Comedor Adela**, Potosí. 24-hrs.

¶ **Tezoatega**, Basílica 1½ c al norte, El Viejo, T344-2436. Chicken and beef dishes, very good. Daily 1200-2300.

Entertainment

León *p924, map p926*

Bars and clubs

Next to La Merced park is a small disco upstairs, in a brown wooden house, unsigned and unnamed, but very popular.

Bar El Alamo, 1 block north of Plaza, T311-1212. Daily 1000-2400, good atmosphere, cheap draught beer.

Discoteca Dilectus, south entrance to city. Wed-Sun, upmarket crowd, a/c, parking, US$5 entrance, drinks and food expensive.

Divino Castigo, 1 block north of UNAN. Daily 1700-0100, good atmosphere, concerts on Tue, cultural nights on Thu. Look at the *mesa maldita* (cursed table) where old newspaper articles tell you the cruel history of this house, in which a Guatemalan killed 13 women. Or ask for Sergio Ramírez's book from which the bar derives its name.

Don Señor, across from Parque La Merced, T311-1212. Wed-Sun from 2000, karaoke Wed and Fri, place to see Nicaraguans cut loose.

Las Ruinas, by Parque Rubén Darío, T311-4767. Dancing in the bombed-out ruins of the 1979 Revolution, Thu-Sun from 1900.

Video Luna, across the street from **Hotel Colonial**. Entrance US$1, Sat and Sun only.

Cinema

Next to La Unión supermarket, 1 block north and 1 block east of El Sesteo in Plaza Siglo Nuevo, T311-7080/ 83. Films shown in English with Spanish subtitles.

Pool tables

½ block north of Parque Central (next to **Hong Kong**). Daily 1000-0100, popular with locals.

Chinandega *p928*

Bars and clubs

Monserrat, main entrance Reparto Monserrat 2 c al este, T341-3465. Thu-Sun after 2000, has a big dance floor, appetizers, rum and cold beer, dance music.

Festivals and events

León *p924, map p926*

Mar/Apr Holy Week ceremonies are outstanding with sawdust street-carpet, similar to those in Guatemala, especially in Sutiava on Good Fri after 1500.

20 Jun Liberation by Sandinistas.
1 Nov All Saints' Day.
Dec Santa Lucía is celebrated in Sutiava; there are processions, religious and cultural events, sports and Pepe Cabezón (a giant head on legs) accompanies La Gigantona (an impossibly tall princess) through the city.
7 Dec Día de la Concepción, festivities including singing, dancing and fireworks.

Shopping

León *p924, map p926*
The old **market** (dirty) is near the centre, behind the cathedral, and the **new market** is at the bus terminal, 5-6 blocks east of the old railway station, which itself is now **Mercado** San Juan, not touristy, good local atmosphere.
La Unión, Calle 1 Norte, 1 block north of central market, good supermarket.
Libro Centro Don Quijote, next to Hotelito Calle Real, second-hand books, some in English.

Activities and tours

León *p924, map p926*
Tour operators
Quetzaltrekkers, 1½ blocks east of Iglesia la Recolección (opposite Unión Fenosa) T311-6695, www.quetzaltrekkers.com. A non-profit organization raising money for streetkids through tourism. It offers adventurous (multiday) hikes to the volcanoes and lakes around León (Momotombo, Telica, Cerro Negro, Cosigüina), US$16-US$58, includes all (local) transport, food, water, camping equipments. Also has volunteer opportunities (working with streetkids and guiding tours).
TSA Tours Travel, Esso, 75 m abajo (oeste), T311-1806, sells tickets for Ticabus (leaving Managua), Mon-Fri 0730-1800, Sat 0730-1500.
Va Pues Tours, opposite El Calvario Church, from Cathedral 3 blocks east, T611-8784, www.vapues.com. Open daily, English, French, Spanish in office, German-, Italian- and Dutch- speaking guides, helpful, reservations for domestic flights, car rental, specialized in half- to full-day tours (US$20-30) around León, like Juan Venado Island at the Pacific coast, San Jacinto mud springs and iguana farm, Momotombo and Cerro Negro (also volcano surf, only for experienced boarders, US$55 for ½ day includes private transport, boards and protection gear, guide), recommended.

Transport

Towards León *p923*
Bus Frequent bus service to **La Paz Centro** from Managua, Terminal Lewites, every 30 mins.

León *p924, map p926*
Bus The bus terminal is in the far eastern part of town, a long walk or short taxi ride from the centre. Small trucks also ferry people between the bus terminal and town for US$0.25. Besides the regular and express buses, small vans (called *compartidos*) go to most places below, often faster than the bus.

El Guasaule, 0415, 2½ hrs, US$2. **El Sauce**, every hr, 0615-1545, 2½ hrs, US$1.50. **Chichigalpa**, every 15 mins, 0400-1630, 30-45 mins, US$0.75. **Chinandega**, every 15 mins, 0430-1800, 1¼ hrs, US$0.60. **Corinto**, every 15 mins, 0500-1630, 2 hrs, US$1. **Estelí**, 0520, 1240 and 1510, 3 hrs, US$2. **Matagalpa**, direct bus at 0430 and 1425, 3 hrs, US$2.30, or take any bus to San Isidro (see below) and change there to Matagalpa. **Managua**, every 15 mins, 0500- 2000, 2½ hrs, US$1.50 (the ones taking the new Highway through La Paz Centro are faster than those using the *carretera vieja*, ask before leaving). **Salinas Grandes**, 0600 and 1200, 1½ hrs, US$0.40. **San Isidro**, every 30 mins, 0420-1730, 2½ hrs, US$1.50. Every 30 mins buses from San Isidro to Estelí and Matagalpa.

Taxi Taxis around town charge US$0.40 in the day and US$0.80 at night.

Around León *p927*
Bus Take No 101 from **León**'s Terminal Interurbana, or the central market west to the bus stop near Sutiava church on Calle Rubén Darío, **Poneloya**, then walk 3 mins to Terminal Poneloya outside the market, from where a small bus leaves every hr or so for **Las Peñitas** (0600-1700, 45 mins, US$0.5) at the south end of Poneloya beach.

Taxi From León costs around US$8.

Chinandega *p928*
Bus Most buses leave from the new market at the southeast edge of town. **Corinto**, every 20 mins, 0600-2100, 30 mins, US$0.30. **Guasaule**, every 2 hrs, 0600-1600, 2 hrs, US$2.

León, every 15 mins, 0600-1700, 1¼ hr, US$0.60. **Managua**, every 30 mins, 0600-1600, 3 hrs, US$2.25. **Somotillo**, every 3 hrs, 0900-1500, 2 hrs, US$2. Buses for **Potosí**, **El Viejo** and **Puerto Morazán** leave from the Mercadito at northwest of town. A local bus connects Terminal, Mercado and Mercadito.

Directory

León *p924, map p926*
Banks Most of the country's banks are represented in the blocks north of the cathedral. **Bancentro**, Calle 1 NE between Central y 1 E will change dollars and all TCs, 5% commission. **Banpro** changes dollars. Cash advances from **Banco de América Central (BAC)**, which houses **Credomatic**, next to La Unión supermarket, they all change TCs, T311-7848. ATMs can be found inside La Unión supermarket (visa), at BAC next to La Unión (MC, Cirrus, Maestro) and in the cinema also next to La Unión. **Interbank** is behind El Sesteo. **Western Union**, 2 blocks south of Iglesia San Juan, T311-2426. **Internet** Several places in town, reasonably fast connection, most offer internet calls as well. **Language classes** Nicaragua Spanish School León, Iglesia La Merced, 1½ c abajo, T311-2116, http://pages.prodigy.Net/nss-pmc/ index.htm, regular classes and private tutors, with cultural interaction and trips to beach, theatre, etc. **Hotel Vía Vía**, Servicio Agrícola Gurdián 75 m al sur, T311-6142, tutored study with flexible hrs. US$5 per hr, US$400 per month. **Academia Europea**, Iglesia Recolección ½ c al sur, ex-edificio Banic, T311-7324, www.academia-europea.com, US$15 per hr, flexible hours. **Hostal Mi Puebo**, Catedral 2½ c abajo, US$7 per hr, or package (US$100) includes homestay, 2 hrs per day and 2 tours (Cerro Negro and León Viejo). **Post office** opposite the Recolección church, 0800-1200, 1300-1630. **Telephone** Enitel (Telcor), Parque Central, opposite cathedral. International calls possible. Small **Enitel** office on Darío, on road to Sutiava, about 10 blocks from main plaza, open till 2200, and another in the bus terminal.

Around León *p927*
Consular offices Costa Rica, Chinandega, Banpro 20 m al norte, T341-1584, Mon-Fri 0800-1200, 1300-1530. **Honduras**, Chinandega, frente a Enitel, T341-0949, Mon-Fri 0830-1630. **El Salvador**, Chinandega, corner opposite La Curacao, T341-2049, Mon-Fri 0800-1400. **Post office and telephone** in Enitel building opposite Caprax Pizza.

Towards Granada → *Colour map 7, A1.*

The journey from Lago de Managua to Lago de Nicaragua passes several volcanoes including Volcán Santiago whose crater spews out tonnes of sulphurous gases over Parque Nacional Volcán Masaya. Nearby Masaya town is a centre for handicrafts near a coffee-growing zone. The blasted remains of Mombacho are near the historical city of Granada. The perfect cone of Concepción, on Isla de Ometepe, rises out of the waters of Lago de Nicaragua which has a number of other islands that can be visited by boat. ▸▸ *For Sleeping, Eating and other listings, see pages 941-947.*

Parque Nacional Volcán Masaya

ⓘ *Entrance at Km 23 on the road from Managua. Soft drinks, bottled water and sometimes fresh coconut water are available at the summit of Santiago crater. Getting there: ask bus driver to drop you off at Km 23 on the Managua-Masaya route. It's easy to hitchhike from either city, especially on Sun. At the entrance, park rangers might be available to drive you up to the summit, US$0.70.*

Created in 1979, Parque Nacional Volcán Masaya is the country's oldest national park. It covers an area of 54 sq km, contains 20 km of trails leading to and around two volcanoes rising to around 400 m. **Centro de Interpretación Ambiental (Visitor Centre)** QUERY ⓘ *1.5 km in from the entrance, Mon-Fri 0900-1700, Sat and Sun 0900-1900, US$4 per person.* Shortly after is a beautiful area with toilets, picnic facilities and barbecues (*asadores*) for the use of visitors. **Camping** is possible here but there are no facilities after the visitor centre closes.

The dramatic **Santiago crater** of Volcán Masaya is a spectacular sight and definitely worth visiting. Two volcanoes are within the perimeter of the park. Volcán Nindirí last erupted in 1670. The more active Volcán Masaya burst forth in 1772 and again in 1852, forming the Santiago crater between the two peaks; this in turn erupted in 1932, 1946, 1959 and 1965 before collapsing in 1985, and the resulting pall of sulphurous smoke made the soil uncultivable in a broad belt to the Pacific. Take drink, a hat and hiking boots if planning much walking. If walking to the summit, leave early as there is little shade along the road.

Santiago's most recent eruption was on 23 April 2001. Debris pelted the parking area of the park with flaming rocks at 1427 in the afternoon, shooting tubes of lava onto the hillside just east of the parking area and setting it ablaze. Today the cone remains highly irregular with large funnels of sulphuric acid being followed by periods of little or no smoke. A larger eruption can be expected soon.

Although research into the activity of Volcán Masaya is limited, gaseous emissions range from 500 to 3000 tonnes a day, making the volcano one of the largest natural polluters in the world.

Volcán Masaya was called *Popogatepe* or 'mountain that burns' by the Chorotega people who believed that eruptions were a sign of anger from the goddess of fire, Chacitutique. To appease her they made sacrifices to the lava pit, which often included children and young women. In the 16th century Father Francisco de Bobadilla planted a cross on the summit of Masaya to exorcize the *Boca del Infierno* (Mouth of Hell); the cross visible today commemorates the event.

The biggest natural heroes of the park are the unique **parakeets** (*chocoyos*) who nest in the active Santiago crater. These orange- or crimson-fronted parakeets are best spotted just before the park closes between March and October. They lay two to four eggs per nest in the interior cliffs of the crater in July and after incubation and rearing lasting roughly three months, leave their highly toxic home for the first time.

From the visitor centre, a short path leads up to Cerro El Comalito, with good views of Mombacho, the lakes and the extraordinary volcanic landscapes of the park; longer trails continue to Lake Masaya and the San Fernando crater.

Masaya » *pp 941-947. Colour map 7, A1.*

→ *Population: 140,000. Altitude: 234 m.*

Masaya lies 29 km southeast of Managua, and is the folkloric and crafts centre of Nicaragua, home to more artisans than any other place in the country. The town is in almost constant celebration with religious festivals, including Central America's longest party, the **San Jerónimo** festival. Running for three months from September 30, the festival includes many traditional dances, countless processions and music. Smaller festivals happen every Thursday with the **Jueves de Verbena** which has local dancing, music, food and drinking late into the night. The **tourist office** in the craft market near the music stage is helpful (mostly Spanish spoken).

Local handicrafts are sold in the market near the bus station and in the new **Centro de Artesanías** (closed Sundays) in the old market (also called the Centro Cultural Antiguo Mercado de Masaya). The newly restored 19th-century market was ruined during the Revolution. The 'new' market is very popular with Nicaraguans and sells excellent hammocks, nice leather work, colourful woven rugs and furniture. The artisan market has concerts every Thursday night with food, free admission and a range of musical and dance acts. This is the best place to see one of Masaya's more than 30 professional folkloric dance troops. The 'old' market, close to the bus park, is marginally cheaper but crowded, dirty and not recommended. Masaya is also the centre for Nicaraguan rocking chairs, which can be bought packed for transporting by air. The best place for local craftwork is the barrio of **Monimbo**. On Avenida los Leones you find several **guitar shops**, where you can order a guitar made just for you. Try a little shop (in the backyard) 75 m east of Parque los Leones (T522-2479), where they'll charge you US$40-50 for a new guitar.

Around Masaya

Fifteen minutes from Masaya is **Nindirí**, named after its former chief represented by a statue in the Parque Central. Known as the city of myths and legends, it is one of the oldest settlements in Nicaragua with evidence of over 3000 consecutive years of habitation. It is so rich in ceramic history that its small museum, the privately owned **Museo Nindirí** ⓘ *1 block north of the Rubén Darío library, Tue-Sat, donation of US$1-2 requested*, has one of the country's most impressive pre-Columbian collections and Spanish colonial relics. It is run by the wife of the founder who will show you around. The town suffered in the Revolution of 1978 to 1979 and in Masaya you can visit the **Museo de Héroes y Mártires** ⓘ *open daily*. Another museum, 45 minutes' walk from Plaza Central (ask directions), is that of **Camilo Ortega**, which has exhibits on recent history.

The small **Laguna de Masaya** is at the foot of Volcán Masaya; water is too polluted for swimming, but it's a good view from the town. **Volcán Santiago** is also nearby.

Just outside Masaya to the north, on the road from Managua, is an old hilltop fortress, **Coyotepe** ⓘ *US$0.50*, also called La Fortaleza, built in the 19th century to protect Masaya. Once a torture centre used first by the Somozistas, later by the Sandinistas, it is now a clubhouse for the boy scouts. It is deserted and eerie (take a torch, or offer a boy scout US$1-2 to show you around). Even if you don't want to see the fort, the view from the top of the hill is spectacular.

The nearby village of **Niquinohomo** is Sandino's birthplace (see Background), and the house where he lived from the age of 12 is opposite the church in the main plaza.

San Juan de Oriente is a charming colonial village with an interesting school of pottery (products are for sale). Nearly 80% of the inhabitants are engaged in the ceramic arts. To visit an artisan family workshop walk from north entrance of the village towards the church. Just before the church and next to the women's co-op is the house of Dulio Jiménez, who is very happy to show visitors his operation. Buses from Granada cost US$0.30. It is a short walk to neighbouring **Catarina** (famous for

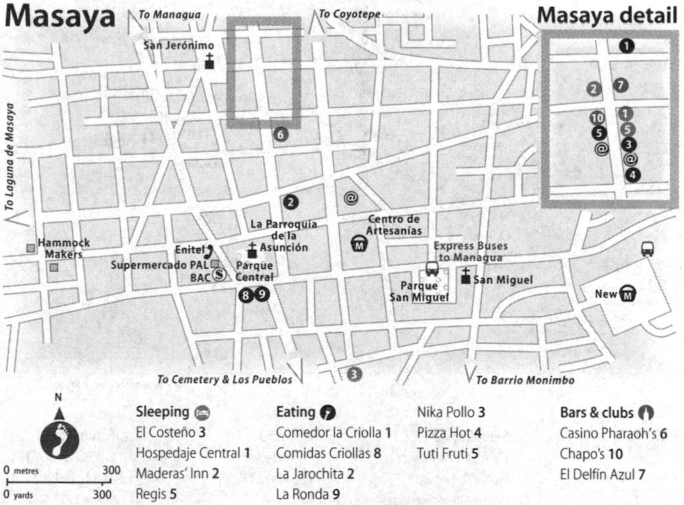

ornamental plants), and a 1-km walk or drive uphill to **El Mirador,** with a wonderful view of Laguna de Apoyo (Granada and Volcán Mombacho too on a clear day).

Laguna de Apoyo ⓘ *US$0.20, US$1 in a car,* is very clean, beautiful for swimming and well worth a visit. It's quiet during the week but busy at weekends. Without your own transport it's probably easiest to visit the lagoon from Granada with transport provided by **The Bearded Monkey**, see page 942. There is also accommodation on the lake shore. Transport out to Laguna de Apoyo leaves **The Bearded Monkey** in Granada 1030, Monday, Wednesday and Friday, returning 1800, US$6.

Granada

pp 941-947. Colour map 7, A1.

➔ *Population: 111,506. Altitude: 60 m.*

Situated on the northwest shore of vast Lake Nicaragua, and at the foot of Volcán Mombacho, Granada is increasingly popular and currently the place to hang out in Nicaragua. Founded in 1524 by Hernández de Córdoba on the site of the indigenous village of Xalteva, it is the oldest city to be continually inhabited and in its original location in continental Latin America. The prosperous city was attacked on at least three occasions by British and French pirates coming up the San Juan and Escalante rivers, and much of old Granada was burnt by filibuster William Walker in 1856; but Granada, the third largest city of the republic, still retains many beautiful buildings and has preserved its Castilian traditions.

Ins and outs

Getting there Very regular and quick bus and minibus service to Managua makes this a good base even if your interest is the capital. International buses pass the western side of town.

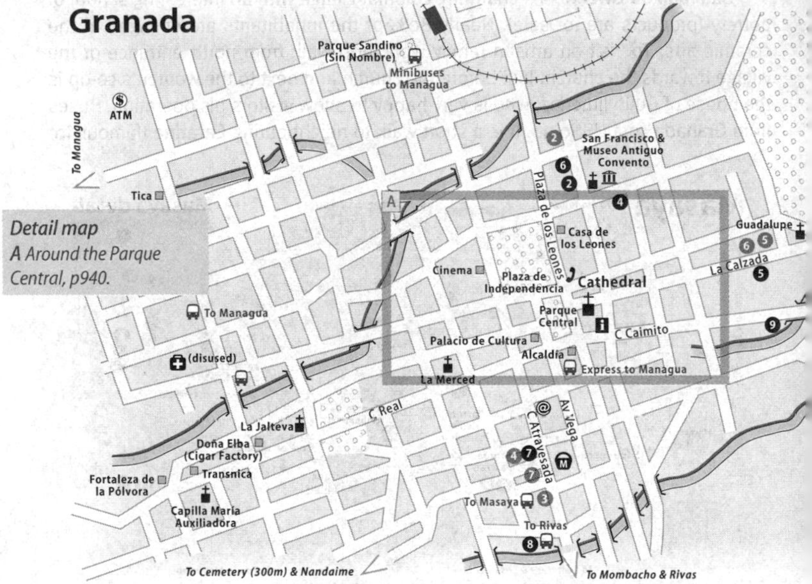

Sleeping
Casa San Francisco **2**
Hostal Esfinge **3**
Hostal Oasis Granada **4**
Italiano **5**
La Calzada **6**
Posada del Rey **7**

Eating
Café Chavalos **1**
Cambalache **2**
El Ancla **3**

Getting around Small and manageable on foot, the focal point of the town is the Parque Central. Heading east takes you to Lake Nicaragua and the Complejo Turístico (tourist centre). South of the Parque is the working heart of the city with the market and many bus departure points. East, west and north of the park, the streets are a bit quieter. Horse-drawn carriages available for hire if you want to rest your feet.

Tourist office The local **INTUR** office ⓘ *east side of Parque Central next to the cathedral (on the corner of Calle Caimito), www.granada.com.ni,* has good maps of Nicaragua and information on the country.

Sights

The centre of the city, about 10 blocks from the lake, is the **Parque Central**, with many trees and food stalls selling Granada's famous *vigorón*, a popular dish of fried pork skins, yucca, and cabbage salad served on a big banana leaf. Bordering the park are many civic buildings, the landmark **Hotel Alhambra**, the cathedral and the local tourist office (southeast corner). In between the red house of the Bishop and the cathedral is the century cross with a time capsule of belongings from 1899 buried underneath in the hope of a peaceful 20th century. This practice was repeated in 1999 with another cross and time capsule in front of the La Merced church in the hope of a peaceful 21st century (let's hope they have better luck!). The **cathedral**, rebuilt in neoclassical style, is simpler in design and ornamentation than the church of **La Merced** to the west, which was built in 1781 to 1783, half destroyed in the civil wars of 1854, restored in 1862 and is currently undergoing another restoration. Its interior is painted in pastel shades, predominantly green and blue. It has some unusual features and interesting lighting. Away from the centre, beyond La Merced, is the church of **La Jalteva** (or *Xalteva* – the indigenous name of Granada), which faces a park with formal ponds. Not far from La Jalteva is **La Pólvora** ⓘ *donations to the caretaker*, an old fortress that has been partially restored and opened to the public. There's a nice rooftop with views of the church and volcano east from the turrets. The chapel of **María Auxiliadora** ⓘ *open to public at 1600*, where Las Casas, Apostle of the Indies, often preached, is hung with local lace and needlework. Heading southwest from Jalteva, the cemetery is worth a visit as the resting place of key figures from Nicaraguan history. Heading towards the Managua bus terminal from Jalteva, you pass the beautiful, now-dilapidated **Hospital** which was built in 1886.

❢ To view the interiors of Granada's churches you must time your visit from 0600-0800 or 1500-1700.

Directly north of Parque Central is the restored **Casa de Los Leones** ⓘ *T552-4176, www.c3mundos.org, free during the day, check bulletin board for events*, restored and run by the international foundation **Casa de los Tres Mundos**. It is a beautiful colonial house, with art exhibits and concerts. Heading west is the **fortress-church of San Francisco**, Nicaragua's oldest, though

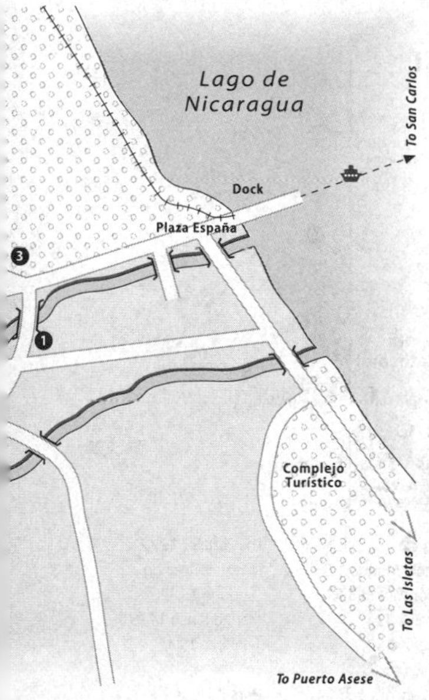

El Tercer Ojo **4**
Frutti D' Mare **5**
Mister Pizza **6**
Tasa Blanca **7**
Tito Bar **8**
Vivaldi **9**

burned many times and now only the front steps are from 1524; inside there are wonderful sculptures. Next door is the **Museo del Convento de San Francisco** ⓘ *0800-1800, US$2, US$2.50 extra for photography*. Originally a convent (1524), then a Spanish garrison, William Walker's garrison, a university and more recently an institute, the cloister surrounds about three dozen tall palms. Restoration is now complete and it is the country's most interesting pre-Columbian museum, housing 28 sculptures from Isla Zapatera in the lake. They date from AD 800-1200, note especially the double sculptures of standing or seated figures bearing huge animal masks, or doubles, on their heads and shoulders (lizard, tortoise, jaguar, etc). The museum also contains several galleries with changing exhibits of Nicaraguan art and there's a snack bar.

A road runs from the Parque Central to Plaza España by the dock on Lake Nicaragua; the **church of Guadalupe** is on this road. From Plaza España it is a 30-minute walk along the lakeshore to the **Complejo Turístico** ⓘ *US$0.12*, an area with restaurants, bars, paths and benches. The lake beach is popular, having been cleaned up and built into a nice park; marimba bands stroll the beach and play a song for you for a small fee. At night everyone decants to the club and bars of the *complejo*.

Horse-drawn carriages are for hire and are used here as taxis by the locals. The drivers are happy to take foreigners around the city (US$4.50 for 30 minutes, US$9 per hour). You can see most of the city's sites in a half-hour rental. A nice walk, or carriage ride, starts from La Pólvora and continues down Calle Real, past La Capilla María Auxiliadora, La Jalteva, La Merced to Parque Central. From the cathedral you can then continue to La Virgen de Guadalupe and to the lake front along La Calzada.

The latest additon to things to do is the **Canopy Tour** provided by **Mombotour** on the east slope of Mombacho or by **Mombacho Canopy Tour** on the west slope. Or ask for crater diving at Tierra Tour. The latter also make reservations for the **Butterfly reserve** ⓘ *towards Laguna Apoyo, cabins US$25, tents on platforms US$10 per person*. See Tour operators, page 945.

Around the Parque Central

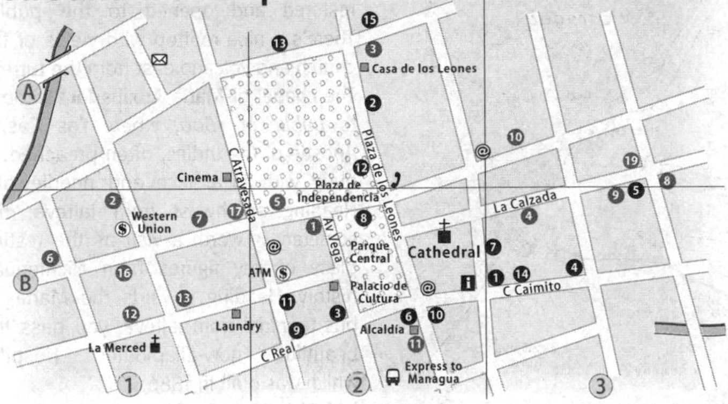

N

0 metres 50
0 yards 50

Sleeping
Alhambra 1 *B2*
Bearded Monkey 2 *B1*
Central 4 *B3*
Colonial 5 *B2*
El Club 6 *B1*
Hospedaje Calif 7 *B1*
Hospedaje Cocibolca 8 *A3*
Hospedaje Granada 9 *B3*
Hospedaje Sevilla 10 *A3*
La Casona de los Estrada 3 *A2*
La Gran Francia 11 *B2*
Nuestra Casa 12 *B1*
Posada Don Alfredo 13 *B1*

Eating
Al Piccolo Mundo 1 *B3*
Café don Simon 3 *B2*
Cafemail 2 *A2*
Don Daffa 6 *B2*
Don Luca's 5 *B3*
Doña Conchi's 4 *B3*
El Zaguán 7 *B3*
Kiosko la Gata 8 *B2*
La Cueva del Dragón 9 *B2*
La Gran Francia 10 *B2*
Los Bocaditos 11 *B2*
Los Portales 12 *A2*
Maverick Reading Lounge 13 *A2*
Mediterráneo 14 *B3*
TelePizza 15 *A2*

Bars & clubs
Café Nuit 16 *B1*
Flamingo & Leidy's 17 *B1*
Zoom 19 *A3*

A trip out to Laguna de Apoyo is a great day trip. **Nicaragua Libre,** on the main road between Granada and Nandaime, reached by bus from Granada, is a cooperative project offering accommodation (E) and options for trekking and climbing Mombacho volcano. Contact UCA – see Tour Operators.

Sleeping

Parque Nacional Volcán Masaya *p935*
B **Hotel Volcán Masaya**, Km 23 Carretera a Masaya, close to the park entrance, T522-7114. Bath, a/c, fridge, and lobby area for relaxing, very comfortable. Great view of the volcano and park.

Masaya *p936, map p937*
B-C **El Costeño**, Ministerio Publico 2½ c al Sur, T522-3057. Private bath, a/c. Cheaper with fan.
C-D **Maderas' Inn**, Cuerpo de Bomberos 1½ c al sur, T522-5825, hmaderas@ibw.com.ni. Private bath with fan (more expensive with a/c). Clean comfortable rooms although some a little small. Airport-hotel transport available. Very friendly owners also own a house that sleeps 10 in Laguna de Apoyo (available for rent, US$ 10 per person).
E **Regis**, La Curacao (main street) 40 m al norte, T522-2300, cmolinapalma@hotmail.com. Shared bath, fan, clean, very good breakfast (other meals if ordered), fruit juices, helpful owner who is very knowledgeable about the town and surrounding area. Highly recommended.
F **Hospedaje Central**, next door to **Hotel Regis**, T522-2867. Small rooms with bath and TV.
F **Masayita**, 2 blocks west of Parque Central, T605-1995. Clean, basic and cheapest place in town, but reports of theft.

Around Masaya *p937*
A-B **Norome**, on lake shore, Laguna de Apoyo, T867-7304, www.noromevillas.com. Accessed by the shore road to the east, charming lakefront lodge with 8 rooms, a/c, bar, restaurant, very clean, smartly decorated , great views and setting, jacuzzi and small dock.
E-F **The Monkey Hut**, bottom of the lake access road to Laguna de Apoyo, 100 m west, T887-3546 (**Bearded Monkey** in Granada), www.thebeardedmonkey.com/monkeyhut.htm. Can be booked with transfer from Granada, dorm (US$9) and private rooms (US$20 double), kitchen available, canoe, kayak and sailboat rentals and lots of other watery activities.

Granada *p938, maps p938, p940*
There is a shortage of hotels and restaurants in Granada. Try not to arrive too late at night.
AL **Colonial**, 25 m north of Parque Central, T552-7299. 37 rooms, private bath with hot water, a/c, cable TV, telephone, 2 pools, very nice, French owned and operated.
AL **La Gran Francia**, esquina sureste del Parque Central, T552-6000, www.lagranfrancia.com. Traditional colonial decor, classic rooms with private bath, cable TV, a/c, minibar, internet access.
AL-C **Casa San Francisco**, Corrales 207, T552-8235, csfgranada@yahoo.com. 2 colonial houses with 6 rooms that greatly vary. 1 houses a suite and 2 comfortable rooms with private bath, cable TV, a/c, pool, a modern kitchen and includes breakfast. The other location (**B-C**) has 3 smaller, but nice rooms and a restaurant. Very friendly, clean, quiet, home-style.
A **Alhambra**, Parque Central, T552-4486, www.hotelalhambrani.com. Pleasant, comfy rooms although 1st-floor ones are a bit run-down, with bath, large restaurant, good fruit breakfasts, high prices, terrace is nice place for a beer overlooking Plaza Central, parked cars guarded by nightwatchman.
A **Kekoldi de Granada**, Calle El Consulado, 3½ blocks west of Parque Central, T248-0804, www.kekoldi.com. 12 rooms, all with private baths with hot water, a/c, queen-size beds and cable TV.
A **La Casona de los Estrada**, 50 m west of the Convento San Francisco, T552-7393, www.casonalosestrada.com. Pleasant well-lit rooms, most luxurious in Granada, decorated with antiques and charm, expensive restaurant, English spoken.
B **El Club**, Calle de la Libertad and Av Barricada, 3½ blocks west of Parque Central, T552-4245, www.elclub-nicaragua.com. Dutch owned, very nice, pleasant modern rooms with private bath, a/c, cable TV and some with internet access, friendly and helpful staff, good value, restaurant and bar.

C Italiano, La Calzada, next to Iglesia Guadalupe, T552-7047. Italian owned, bath and a/c, nice patio, drinks available, good value.
D Hospedaje Cocibolca, La Cazada, T552-7223, www.hotelcocibolca.com. Good and friendly, clean, bath, use of kitchen, family-run, friendly, internet access. Also have the new, very comfortable **Hotel Cocibolca**.
D Hospedaje El Maltese, Plaza España 50 m al sur, opposite *malecón* in the Complejo Turístico, T552-7641. 11 very clean rooms with private bath, a/c, nice furnishings, Italian spoken, also restaurant **La Corte Del Maltese**, Tue-Sun 1200-2100.
C Hospedaje Sevilla, from Enitel office (Parque Central) 1½ blocks towards the lake, T552-6117. Llooks faded from the outside, but nice, clean and spacious rooms with private bath, a/c, cable TV, quiet and friendly.
D Nuestra Casa, de Porto Banco ½ c al lago, T861-0791. Rooms with and without bath, fan, TV, bar and restaurant (🍴🍴🍴) serving Italian and barbeque food (1800-0000). There's also a bar with live music in the weekend (open until 0200).
D-E Hostal Oasis Granada, Calle Estrada 109, south of the centre, T552-8006. Mix of dormitory (US$7), shared and private rooms (US$25-32), with breakfast available. Laundry service and washing facilities. Full range of facilities from book exchange and swimming pool, through to free coffee and internet (and internet calls to Canada and USA) and DVDs. Popular and gets good reports.
E Central, La Calzada, T552-7044, friendly, clean, laundry facilities, quirky mix of rooms and corridors, dorm (**F**), mixed reports; still popular with backpackers, good restaurant.
E Posada del Rey, Calla la Concepcion, ½ block west of the market, T841-8229. Simple but clean, partitioned walls, TV in common area, internet access (US$1.50).
F The Bearded Monkey, Calle 14 de Septiembre, near the fire station, T552-4028, www.thebeardedmonkey.com. Dormitory accommodation with footlockers and shared bath, and a few private rooms. Also the **Monkey Suite** (**E**) complete with 4-poster bed. Relaxed common areas, vegetarian and non-vegetarian food served all day and excellent breakfasts, bar, cable TV, internet access and cheap calls, films in the evening, great atmosphere, comfortable and friendly. Use lockers since everybody is able to walk in and out. Storage while you're away.
F Hospedaje Calif, ½ block west of Cine Karawala, T552-2101, dorm-style rooms with bunk beds, basic. Price per person.
F La Calzada, La Calzada near Guadalupe church, T522-6815, guesthouselacalzada @yahoo.com. Big rooms some with bath (**E**), fan, friendly, great breakfasts.
F-G Hostal Esfinge, opposite market, T552-4826, esfingegra@hotmail.com. Rooms with character, 50 years old, Those in the newer building are smaller and warmer but some with bath (**E**), patio with washing facilities, friendly, clean, motorcycle parking in lobby, kitchen, safe. Recommended.

Eating

Masaya *p936, map p937*
There are 2 *fuentes de soda* near the northeast corner of the Parque Central. Many places have congregated on the southwest corner of the main plaza. There's a supermarket on the west side of the park.
🍴🍴 **La Jarochita**, 1½ north of park, T522-4831. Mexican, excellent, try chicken *enchilada* in *mole* sauce.
🍴🍴 **La Ronda**, south side of the Parque Central. Closed Mon, bar, restaurant.
🍴🍴-🍴 **Nika Pollo**, 3½ blocks north of the park (next to **Regis**). Serves (roasted) chicken with tortilla and chile (US$7.25 for a whole chicken, US$2,25 for ¼).
🍴 **Comedor la Criolla**, 1½ blocks north of **Hotel Regis** (1 block south of the fire dept), T522-7610. Daily 0700-2000, has good *comida corriente* (cheap US$2 buffet).
🍴 **Comidas Criollas**, south side of the plaza, T522-6696. *Comida corriente* US$2, natural drinks. Packed with locals for lunch.
🍴 **Golden Pizza**, ½ block south of park, T522-4601. Home delivery, daily 1100-2200.
🍴 **Panadería Corazón de Oro**, 2-3 blocks towards highway from the church. Excellent *pan de queso*(cheese bread), US$0.50 a loaf.
🍴 **Pizza Hot**, 3 blocks north of the park. Wed-Mon 1000 -2200, whole pizza or slice.
🍴 **Sacuanjoche**, inside artisan's market, between the bus terminal and town. Serves chicken tacos.
🍴 **Tuti Fruti**, in front of **Regis**. For smoothies, fruit shakes or salads and cheap fast food. Daily 0800-2200.

Granada *p938, maps p938, p940*
Most restaurants close on Mon. Hotel restaurants (eg ¥¥ **The Bearded Monkey** and ¥¥ **Central**) are popular meeting places. Several good mid-range places can be found around Convento San Francisco. There are good breakfasts at the market.

Granada's most famous dish is the cheap, filling and messy *vigorón* – a large banana leaf filled with fried pork skin, yucca and tomato, covered in cabbage salad, a mixture of chilli peppers and lime juice.The best place to find a good *vigorón* is on Parque Central.

In the **Complejo Turístico** on the lakeshore there are many places for dancing and eating (flying insects can make it miserable at the start of the rainy season).

¥¥¥ **El Zaguán**, behind cathedral, T552-2522. Great grilled meats cooked on wood fire, best beef dishes in Granada, friendly service, nice setting in colonial home on quiet street, excellent. Mon-Fri 1200-1500, 1800-2200, Sat and Sun 1200-2200.

¥¥¥ **La Gran Francia**, corner of Parque Central. Historic house, classic setting, expensive French cuisine, tavern, bar, excellent espresso with pleasant views from upper-floor balcony. Daily 1100-2300.

¥¥¥ **Mediterráneo**, Calle Caimito, T552-6764. Lovely colonial house, quiet garden setting, expensive but worth it and popular with foreigners, Spanish owners and menu, very good seafood. Daily 0800-2300.

¥¥¥-¥¥ **Doña Conchi's**, Calle Caimito, T552-7376, laconchis@hotmail.com. Beautiful restaurant with Spanish, Mediterranean and seafood, home-made bread, small *artesanía* shop. Recommended but a bit pricey and wear something tidy. Wed-Sun 0900-2200.

¥¥¥-¥¥ **Frutti D'Mare**, opposite **Hostal la Calzada** on La Calzada, T552-6441. Daily 1100-2300. Italian restaurant specializing in *mariscos* (US$5) and fish (US$12).

¥¥ **Al Piccolo Mundo**, Calle el Caimito, 1 block east of the cathedral, T851-7208. Thu-Tue 1200-2230. Excellent pizza Napolitana from wood fire oven (US$4 medium pizza).

¥¥ **Cambalache**, opposite the Convento San Francisco, T860-4729. Thu-Mon 1700-2200. Friendly Argentinian owners serve good international, mainly Italian and Spanish dishes, with fresh ingredients. The menu varies and there's a good selection of wines. Home-made desserts and liquors as well.

¥¥ **Casa San Francisco**, Calle Corrales, north corner of the Convent, T552-8235, www.csf-hotel-granada.com. Colonial-style restaurant, Latin (Mexican) cuisine, Tue-Sat 1800-2300, Sun with brunch 1000-1300.

¥¥ **Charly's Bar,** de Petronic 5 c al oeste y 25 m al sur, T552-2942, www.charlys-bar.com. Mon-Fri 1100-1500, 1800-2300, Sat and Sun 1100-2300. Specializes in BBQ and German dishes, good but a bit out of town.

¥¥ **El Tercer Ojo**, Calle El Arsenal, south corner of Convento San Francisco, T552-6451. Tue-Sun 1000-0000. Lounge restaurant and tapas bar, French crêpes, vegetarian food, Tue sushi night, colourful, pleasant courtyard, relaxed atmosphere. Range of activities includes book exchange, reading room, Cine Euro (Wed), cultural nights (Thu).

¥¥ **El Volcán**, Calle Estrada, Iglesia La Merced 1c al sur, T552-2878. Daily from 1000, shish kebabs, *quesillos* and sandwiches.

¥¥ **La Terrazza La Playa**, in Complejo Turístico. Great *cerdo asado* and *filete de guapote*.

¥¥ **Mister Pizza**, opposite Convento San Francisco (next to **Cambalache**), T552-7869. Daily 1100-2200. A good choice, with cheap pasta and pizza, helpful information.

¥¥ **Vivaldi**, Calle el Caimito, 4½ blocks to the lake, T522-7567. Italian restaurant, pasta, meat and fish, popular for its swimming pool (US$3). Restaurant 1200-2200, pool 0800-2200, closed Mon.

¥¥-¥ **Los Bocaditos**, Calle el Comercio. Mon-Sat 0800-2200, Sun 0800-1600. Buffet from 1100-1500, breakfast and dinner menu.

¥¥-¥ **Los Portales**, opposite **Cafemail** on Plaza de los Leones, T552-4115. Simple Mexican food, cheap *comida económica*, good. Daily 0700-2200.

¥¥-¥ **Maverick Reading Lounge**, Calle El Arsenal 104, ½ block left from north end of Los Portales. Relaxed atmosphere, English and Spanish magazines, excellent coffee and pies.

¥ **Café Chavalos**, La Calzada towards the lake, past the Guadalupe church and **Hotel Granada**, ½ block to the right, www.building newhope.com/Cafe_Chavalos. A training program for 'would-be gang members' (*chavalos* is Spanish slang for 'kids') who, under supervision of chef Sergio, learn to prepare international cuisine, only US$6 for a complete 5-course dinner, in a small, colourful restaurant. Recommended. Tue-Fri 1830-2100.

Café Don Simón, Parque Central. Coffee, good pastries, breakfast and sandwiches. 0700-2100.

Cafemail, next to La Casa de Los Leones, T552-6847. Daily 0700-2000. Coffee, sodas, beer, fast food, internet, very good, great outdoor and indoor setting.

Don Daffa, next to mayor's office on Parque Central, in the corner house. Daily 1100-2200. Live music Fri-Sun from 1600, seriously cheap lunch buffet with some very fresh food, great value.

Don Luca's, La Calzada, near **Hospedaje Cocibolca**. Excellent pizza, pasta, cheap, nice setting.

El Ancla, La Calzada, across from **Hotel Granada**. Wed-Mon 1000-2230. Fresh outdoor setting, decent food and service, Nicaraguan dishes.

Kiosko La Gata, on Parque Central, daily 1000-1900, offers traditional *Nica* drinks like *chicha* and *cacao con leche*.

Restaurant Querube's, near the market. Popular with locals, set lunch menu (US$1.50).

Tasa Blanca, near market. Mon-Sat 0600-2100, Sun 0600-1400. Friendly, good coffee.

TelePizza, Calle Caimito, ½ block from Parque Central, T552-4219. Daily 1000-2200. Great pizzas and quick service.

Tito Bar, near Shell station. Good local place, with cheap typical Nicaraguan food.

Tropi Fruta, next to **Hostal La Calzada**. Daily 0730-2000. Breakfast, *jugos naturales*, fruit salads.

Entertainment

Masaya *p936, map p937*

Bars and clubs

Casino Pharaoh's, 3 blocks north of the park, T522-5222.

Chapo's, Bomberos 2 ½ c al sur.Mon-Fri 1200-0200, Sat and Sun 1400-0300. A trendy bar/club, good for a beer and hamburger with cable TV.

Coco Jambo, 4-5 blocks west of the Parque Central on the Malecón Masaya. Busy at weekends.

El Delfín Azul, 1½ Calle south of the fire department. Fri-Sun.

La Ronda, south side of the Parque Central. Locals also gather here.

Dance

Every Thu folkloric dances behind the Mercado Artesanía in Masaya.

Granada *p938, maps p938, p940*

Bars and clubs

The street behind the **Hotel Alhambra**, Calle Atravesada, has, or is close to, most of Granada's nightlife and restaurants.

Café Nuit, opposite **La Fábrica**, in Calle La Libertad. Fri-Wed 1900-0200. With garden and patio, live music 2100-0000. Small cover charge on Fri and Sat.

César, on waterfront (Complejo Turístico). Fri and Sat only. Recommended for dancing and drinking. Very popular, inexpensive bar, merengue and salsa music.

El Club, ½ block from **La Fábrica** and **Café Nuit**, Mon-Thu open until 2400, Fri-Sun until 0200. Very nice, popular with Nicaraguans and foreigners.

Flamingo, Calle Atravesada, next to the cinema. *Cantina* with cheap beer and a diverse clientele. Very popular. Upstairs is Leidy's Bar, dancing and karaoke.

La Fábrica, 2 blocks west of the Parque Central. Daily 1900-0200. An old colonial-style, modern bar, nice patio, young crowd, cheap beer, rock music, full of foreigners. Thu ladies night (free drinks 2000-2300).

Nuestra Casa, 1 block north of La Merced, Fri-Sun 1800-0200, bar with live music.

Zoom Bar, La Calzada 3 c al lago, across from **Hospedaje Cocibolca**, Mon-Fri 1200-0000, Sat and Sun 1200-0300, next to beer, vodka, whisky and more, *zoomburgers* (US$3.50).

Cinema

1 block behind **Hotel Alhambra**, good, modern, 2 screens.

Bearded Monkey plays DVDs every night.

El Tercer Ojo, Calle El Arsenal (across from Convento San Francisco), with 'Cine Euro' every Wed 1500-1700.

Festivals and events

Granada *p938, maps p938, p940*

Mar Folklore, Artesanía and Food Festival for 3 days (check locally for dates).

Mar/Apr Holy Week.

14-30 Aug Assumption of the Virgin.

Aug La Hípica takes place 2nd weekend of Aug. The Sun preceding La Hípica is La

Fiesta de Toros with bulls running in the streets of Granada.
25 Dec **Christmas** celebrated with masked and costumed performers.

Shopping

Granada *p938, maps p938, p940*
Market (large green building south of Parque Central) is dark, dirty and packed; lots of stalls on the streets outside, also horse cab rank and taxis. Main shopping street runs north-south, west of plaza.
Supermercado Lacayo, Calle Real Xalteva, ½ block towards the lake from Iglesia La Merced, large choice, a bit expensive.
Supermercado Pali, next to the outdoor market, cheaper than Lacoyo.

Activities and tours

Granada *p938, maps p938, p940*
Tour operators
Auxiliadora Travel Agent, Calle Estrada, (next to Oasis), T899-9290. Helpful and efficient.
Island Kayaks, in the same office as Mombotour, offer sea kayaking in Lake Nicaragua, classes given in Las Isletas.
Mombacho Canopy Tour, on the road up to the Mombacho cloud forest reserve, T0888-2566. The views are not as spectacular as the other canopy, but it is fun and only US$25, US$10 student discount. Tue-Sun 0830-1730.
Mombotour, Cutirre Canopy Tour, Centro Comercial Granada, 2 contiguo al BDF, T552-4548, www.mombotour.com. 17 platforms located between 3 m and 30 m above the ground on the lake side of Volcán Mombacho, coffee tours, birding walks, 2 trips per day to the ranch from their office, canopy US$35, includes transfers to the site.
Oro Travel, Convento San Francisco ½ c al norte, T552-4568, www.orotravel.com. Owner Pascal speaks French, English and German, friendly, generally helpful, tours of Mombacho volcano reserve.
Tierra Tour, La Calzada, Cathedral 2 blocks towards the lake, T862-9580, www.tierra tour.com. Dutch-Nicaraguan owned, knowledgeable and very helpful, good free tourist information, budget tours (from US$10) like birding, islands (including Zapatero), Ometepe, kayaking and diving in a crater lake, good reports.

UCA Tierra y Agua, Trips to Isla Zapatera, and to Nicaragua Libre on the lower slopes of Mombacho. T880-5848, ucatierrayagua@yahoo.es.

Transport

Masaya *p936, map p937*
Bus Buses leave from the new market or you can also catch a non-express bus from the Carretera a Masaya towards **Granada** or **Managua**. Express buses leave from Parque San Miguel to La UCA in **Managua** when full or after 20 mins, 0600-2000.

Granada, every 30 mins, 0600-1800, 45 mins, US$0.40. **Jinotepe**, every 30 mins, 0500-1800, 1½ hrs, US$0.40. **Managua**, every 30 mins, 0400-1800, 1 hr, US$0.40. Express to **Managua**, every 30 mins, 0400-2100, 40 mins, US$0.80. **Matagalpa**, 0600 and 0700, 4 hrs, US$2.25. Or take a bus to **Tipitapa**, 0300-1800, 45 mins, US$2, change for Matagalpa.

Buses run to Valle de Apoyo for **Lago de Apoyo** from Masaya 3 times a day (0530, 1040 and 1620, 45 mins, US$0.50) then walk down the road that drops into the crater. The bus returns to Masaya at 0630, 1130 and 1650. You will have to get off at Km 37.5 and walk down the 5-km access road (it's very dusty in the dry season, so bring a bandana). Hitching is possible though traffic is sparse on weekdays.

Taxi Fares around **Masaya** are US$0.30-0.80. **Granada**, US$15; **Managua** US$20; **airport** US$25. Horse-drawn carriages (*coches*) US$0.30.

From **Granada** to Laguna de Apoyo, US$15-20, or from **Managua**, US$35-40.

Granada *p938, maps p938, p940*
Air Nature Air flies from Granada to San José and Liberia (**Costa Rica**), www.nature air.com, book with tour operators.

Bicycle Rental available from several places in town (US$10 per day) and **kayak** (tours from US$25) rental also at several tour companies.

Bus Express minibuses to **Managua** leave every 20 mins from Parque Sandino and from a small lot just south of BAC on Parque Central, arriving in Managua at UCA, 0500-2000, 45 mins, US$1.

Leaving from the Shell station, 1 c south of the Mercado: **Masaya**, every 30 mins,

0500-1800, 40 mins, US$0.40; **Rivas**, 0540, 0630, 0800, 0930, 1130, 1230, 1330 and 1510, 1½ hrs, US$1; **Niquinohomo**, every 20 mins, 0550-1750, 45 mins, US$1, use this bus for visits to Diriá, Diriomo, San Juan de Oriente, Catarina; or **Jinotepe**, 0550, 0610, 0830, 1110, 1210 and 1710, 1½ hrs, US$0.80, for visits to **Los Pueblos**, including Masatepe and San Marcos.

From the bus terminal next to the old hospital to the west of town: **Managua**, regular bus to Mercado Roberto Huemges, every 20 mins, 0400-1900, 1½ hrs, US$0.75. **Nandaime**, every 20 mins, 0500-1800, 1 hr, US$0.70.

International Tica, Transnica and King Quality buses heading to **San José** and **Costa Rica** all pass through Granada and have offices on Calle Real Xalteva.

Ticabus, T552-4301, US$10, daily at 0700 and 1300. **Transnica**, US$10, daily at 0620, 0800 and 1100.

Ferry For boat travel, see Lago de Nicaragua.

The Granada-**San Carlos** ferry leaves the main dock on Mon and Thu at 1500 and passes **Altagracia**, Ometepe after 3½ hrs (US$3.5 1st class, US$1.5 2nd class), **Morrito** (7 hrs, US$4 1st class, US$2 2nd class), **San Miguelito** (9 hrs, US$4.75 1st class, US$2.50 2nd class). It stops in San Carlos after 15 hrs (US$7 1st class, US$3 2nd class). This journey is tough, take your own food and refreshments. The ferry returns from San Carlos on Tue and Fri.

For **Altagracia** you can also take a cargo boat with passenger seats on Wed and Sat (1200, 4½ hrs, US$1.50). Alternatively go to San Jorge, the main departure point for Ometepe, with boats leaving daily almost every hr between 0730-1730 (1hr) to Moyagalpa. Take the bus to Rivas (1½ hrs, US$1) and then a taxi or *colectivo* to San Jorge (US$0.20). See also San Jorge, page 958.

Taxi Granada taxi drivers are useful for finding places away from the centre, US$0.35 during the day, US$0.70 at night. **Managua** US$25, but check taxi looks strong enough to make the journey.

Directory

Masaya *p936, map p937*

Banks Bancentro and Banco de América Central (BAC), on Parque Central change TCs and cash at good rates. Street changers around market and plaza. **Internet** Intecomp, is south of the main plaza. Mi PC a colores, on Sergio Delgadillo. **Medical services** Dr Gerardo Sánchez, next to town hall, speaks some English. Dr Freddy Cárdenas Ortega, near bus terminal, is a recommended gynaecologist. **Post office** On Sergio Delgadillo. **Telephone** Enitel office on Parque Central.

Around Masaya *p937*

Language schools Apoyo Intensive Spanish School, Laguna de Apoyo, T882-3992, www.guegue.com.ni/eco-nic, groups of 4, 5 hrs' tuition per day. 5-day programme, US$190 for a week including accommodation and food or US$690 per month, family stays available. It is also possible to stay in the lodge without enrolling in the school, from US$16 plus meals, contact the Proyecto for information.

Granada *p938, maps p938, p940*

Banks Banco de Centro América (BAC) on Parque Central, T552-3352, will change TCs and you can buy US$ using Visa. ATM (Visa only) at BDF, Calle Atravesada, 1 block west of Parque Central. ATM at Esso Station, 15-min walk from town centre, accepts Visa, Cirrus, Maestro and MasterCard. Western Union, from fire station ½ block south, Mon-Sat 0800-1300, 1400-1700. **Internet** Internet cafés can be found all over town, while most *hostales* and hotels also offer internet access, including international calls. **Language schools** Casa Xalteva, Calle Real Xalteva 103, T552-2436, www.casaxalteva.com, small Spanish classes for beginners and advanced students, 1 week to several months, US$125 a week, homestays arranged, US$75 a week, voluntary work with children, recommended. Nicaragua Spanish School, Palacio de la Cultura, frente al Parque Central, T552-7114, http://pages.prodigy.net/nss-pmc/index.htm, classes daily 0800-1200, US$195 per week includes homestay, US$7 per hr. Full range of activities like volunteering, cultural program and afternoon/weekend excursions. One on One, La Calzada 450, T552-6771, www.1on1tutoring.net, flexible classes, on an hourly basis, US$7 per hr, packages available with homestays and volunteer opportunities. Vanessa Mercado offers private individual classes, T888-6567, or ask at El Club, 3 blocks west of Parque Central. ABC, English-language school now also offering Spanish classes, Calle Arellano, Sultana radio ½ c al sur, T862-4958, US$140 per week. Also see Apoyo Intensive Spanish School, on Laguna de Apoyo, page 938. **Laundry** Laundry service 1½ blocks west of the park, T522-6532, US$3 for the machine, daily 0700-1900.

Medical services Dr Francisco Martínez Blanco, Clínica de Especialidades Piedra Bocona, ½ block west of Cine Karawale, T552-5989, f_mblanco@ yahoo.com, general practitioner, speaks good English, consulta- tion US$10. **Telephone** (Enitel) on corner northeast of Parque Central. **Post office** From fire station ½ block east, ½ block north.

Managua to Costa Rica

Travelling towards Costa Rica, the Pan-American Highway passes through agricultural land, with branches heading east to Granada and west to the Pacific coast. Rivas makes a good stopping place for trips to Lago de Nicaragua and Isla de Ometepe, or you can head for the coast and the spectacular sunsets and surf beaches of San Juan del Sur, or the turtle nesting sites of Astillero and La Flor. The Pan-American Highway has bus services running all the way to the border with Costa Rica (148 km). The road runs into the Sierra de Managua, reaching 900 m at Casa Colorada, 26 km from Managua. Further on, at El Crucero (a cool and pleasant place), a paved branch road goes through the Sierra south to the Pacific beaches of Pochomil and Masachapa (see page 904). ➤➤ *For Sleeping, Eating and other listings, see pages 950-953.*

Diriamba ➤➤ *pp950-953. Colour map 7, A1.*

→ *Population: 57,682. Altitude: 580 m.*

The highway continues through the beautiful scenery of the sierras to Diriamba, in a coffee-growing district 42 km from Managua. In the centre of the town is the **Museo Ecológico de Trópico Seco** ⓘ *Tue-Sat 0800-1200, 1400-1700, Sun 0800-1200, US$1*, with displays of local flora and fauna, including coffee and turtles, and a section on volcanoes. The local **fiesta** is on 20 January. There is a 32-km dirt road direct to the beach at Masachapa (no buses, see page 904).

Five kilometres north of Diriamba a paved road branches off the main highway and runs east through **San Marcos,** Masatepe (famous for wooden and rattan furniture) and Niquinohomo to Catarina and Masaya. A road also leads to **La Concepción**, a small, industrious village in the highlands, very typical of this part of Nicaragua, where few travellers go. The area is rich in pineapple, pitaya, coffee, mandarins and oranges and the people are welcoming. Access is by bus from Jinotepe, every 20 minutes, US$0.50, or from Managua's Roberto Huembes terminal, every half an hour, US$0.75.

Jinotepe and around → *Population: 42,566. Altitude: 569 m.*

Five kilometres beyond Diriamba is Jinotepe, capital of the coffee-growing district of Carazo. It has a fine neoclassical church with modern stained-glass windows from Irún, in Spain. 'Liberation Day' is celebrated on 5 July here, while the **fiesta** in honour of St James the Greater runs from 24-26 July.

From **Nandaime,** 21 km south of Jinotepe, a paved road runs north to Granada (bus US$0.50). Nandaime has two interesting churches, El Calvario and La Parroquia (1859-1872). The annual **fiesta**, 24-27 July, features masked dancers.

At Km 85 is the signed turn off that leads down a long dirt road to the private reserve and lodge of **Domitila** (see Sleeping, below).

Rivas » pp950-953. Colour map 7, A2.

→ *Population: 41,764. Altitude: 139 m.*

About 45 km beyond Nandaime (US$0.40 by bus) is Rivas. The Costa Rican national hero, drummer Juan Santamaría, sacrificed his life here in 1856 when setting fire to a building captured by the infamous William Walker (see Background, page) and his men. On the town's Parque Central is a lovely old basilica (in need of repair). In the dome you can see the fresco of the sea battle against the ships of Protestantism and Communism. The Parque has some old, arcaded buildings on one side, but also some new buildings.

Rivas is a good stopping place if in transit by land through Nicaragua. The bus station, adjacent to the market, is on the northwest edge of town about eight blocks from the main highway. The road from the lake port of San Jorge joins this road at Rivas; 11 km beyond Rivas, at La Virgen on the shore of Lake Nicaragua, it branches south to San Juan del Sur. The **tourist office** (**INTUR**) ⓘ *75 m west of the Texaco station (in front of Hospedaje Lidia), T453-4914 (ask for Sr Francisco Cárdenas)*, has good maps of Nicaragua and general information.

Refugio de Vida Silvestre Río Escalante Chacocente

ⓘ *US$0.70*

Between Nandaime and Rivas are various turnings south which lead eventually to the Pacific coast (all are rough; high clearance is better than 4WD). One of these turnings (89 km from Managua if going via Diriamba and Jinotepe; 61 km from Peñas Blancas), just south of the Río Ochomogo bridge, is signposted Refugio de Vida Silvestre Río Escalante Chacocente. This 4800-ha reserve of forest and beach is the second most important turtle nesting site in the country and one of the biggest tracts of tropical dry forest in the Pacific basin. The forest is full of mammal, reptile and birdlife and the beach is long and empty. Bring your own hammock and shade. The rough dirt road to the coast (45 km) goes to Las Salinas. Turn right here to **Astillero**, which has a fishing co-operative, and continue to the reserve. You will probably have to ask directions to the reserve several times and cross a number of rivers, the last of which is very wide (it can't be crossed after rain without a very strong 4WD, lots of speed and bravado). Camping is safe and you can buy fish from the co-op. At **Chacocente**, there is a **Marena** office, a government-sponsored **turtle sanctuary** (the only signs after Astillero say 'authorized personnel only'; don't be put off, they welcome visitors, but ask for directions). The **Marena** wardens protect newly hatched turtles and help them make it to the sea (a magnificent sight during November and December). Unfortunately, newly laid turtle eggs are considered to have aphrodisiac properties and are used as a dietary supplement by the locals. **Marena** is virtually powerless to prevent egg theft, although for two months a year the place is protected by armed military personnel.

San Juan del Sur » pp950-953. Colour map 7, A2.

→ *Population: 14,521. Altitude 4 m.*

San Juan del Sur on the Pacific coast has a beautiful bay which is slowly developing, and the sunsets have to be seen to be believed. A sandy beach and some rocky caves can be reached easily by walking round the point opposite the harbour. The town is 28 km from Rivas south along the Pan-American Highway and then right to the coast along a road which is in good condition. There is also a direct dirt road from Rivas going through beautiful countryside, but it is only good when dry.

The town beach is cleaned daily, but at weekends and on holidays, especially Semana Santa, San Juan is busy; otherwise the beaches are quiet during the week. The

Border essentials: Nicaragua-Costa Rica

Peñas Blancas
This is the only road crossing between Nicaragua and Costa Rica.
Nicaraguan immigration
0800-1200 and 1300-1745. When entering Nicaragua, complete Costa Rican exit formalities and then walk the 500 m to the new border controls. International bus passengers have to disembark and queue for Immigra- tion to stamp their passports. Then unload your baggage and wait in a line for the customs official to arrive. You will be asked to open your bags, the official will give them a cursory glance and you reload. Passports and tickets will be checked again back on the bus. If you are not on a bus, there are plenty of helpers on hand. Allow 45 mins to complete the formalities. You will have to pay US$5-8 to enter Nicaragua plus a US$1 Alcaldía charge. If you come before 0800 or after 1700 Mon-Fri or at any time at the weekend, you will have to pay US$12 plus the Alcaldía charge.

When leaving Nicaragua, pay US$1 Alcaldía charge to enter the customs area and then complete formalities in the new customs building where you pay US$2 to have your passport checked Mon-Fri 0800-1700, US$4 0600-0800 and after 1700, or any time on Sat and Sun. Then walk the 500 m to the Costa Rican border and simply have your passport stamped. Buses and taxis are available from the border; hitching is difficult.
Crossing by private vehicle
There is no fuel going into Nicaragua until Rivas (37 km). Arriving: After you have been through Migración, find an inspector who will fill out the preliminary form to be taken to Aduana. At the Vehículo Entrando window, the vehicle permit is typed up and the vehicle stamp is put in your passport. Next, go to Tránsito to pay for the car permit. Finally, ask the inspector to give a final check.

Leaving: First pay your exit tax in the office at the end of the control station (receipt given). Then return for your exit stamp and complete the Tarjeta de Control Migratorio. Motorists must then go to Aduana to cancel vehicle papers; exit details are typed on to the vehicle permit and the stamp in your passport is cancelled. Find the inspector in Aduana who has to check the details and stamp your permit. If you fail to do this you will not be allowed to leave the country; you will be sent back to Sapoá by the officials at the final Nicaraguan checkpoint.
Transport Buses to Rivas, every ½ hr, 0600-1800, US$0.60, 1 hr. From here buses connect to Managua, every ½ hr, 0330-1800, US$1.50, 2 hrs 45 mins or to Granada, every 45 mins, 0530-1625, US$1, 1 hr 45 mins, try to board an express bus from Rivas to your destination. Express buses from Peñas Blancas to Managua, every 30 mins, 0700- 1800, US$3.50, 3½ hrs. There can be long waits when international buses are passing through. If you are travelling independently, a good time to cross is around 0900, before the buses arrive.

INTUR tourist office ⓘ *between the beach and the market in front of Joxi, www.sanjuandelsur.org.ni, Mon-Fri 0900-1200, 1300-1700, Sat 0900-1200*, is helpful, sells maps and a guide of San Juan del Sur. Alternatively, try www.sanjuandelsur.info.

South of San Juan del Sur

You can take a boat to more pristine beaches such as **Playa del Coco** on the poor road to Ostional. Or ask around for a bus leaving to Ostional (1300 at the market, two hours). The surfing on nearby beaches is good.

Refugio de Vida Silvestre La Flor ⓘ *US$7, US$2.50 student discount, access by 4WD or on foot*, covers 800 ha of tropical dry forest, mangroves, estuary and beach. A beautiful, sweeping cove with sand and many trees, it is the most important and most visited beach by nesting sea turtles from August to November. During the high season armed guards protect the arrival of the turtle (sometimes in their thousands and usually lasting a period of three days). The rangers are very happy to explain the creatures' reproductive habits. Many birds live in the protected mangroves at the south end of the beach. Camping is provided (one tent only) during the turtle arrivals, US$10 per night, first come, first served. Bring a hammock and mosquito netting as insects are vicious at dusk. The ranger station sells soft drinks and will let you use their outhouse. To get there, the exit for the dirt path south is 200 m before the entrance to San Juan del Sur, 21 km from the highway. Several rivers, most of which have firm beds, must be crossed.

Sleeping

Diriamba *p947*

B Hotel and Restaurante Lagos y Volcanes, 1½ km from Instituto Guillermo Ampié, T277-3399. 20 rooms, with a/c, jacuzzi, TV, restaurant and pool, parking, great views, lots of orange trees.

E Diriangén, Shell 1 c al este, ½ c al sur, T422-2428. Private bath with fan, parking.

Jinotepe *p947*

AL-A Domitila, Km 85, T881-1786, www.domitila.org. This tropical dry forest reserve near the shores of Lake Nicaragua and Isla Zapatera has some very fine forests with simple, rustic lodging, with private bath, sawdust toilets offered at a high price with meals included. All hiking trails are charged at additional high rates; visits to Isla Zapatera can be arranged and are better value.

C Montreal, Esso 3 c al sur, T412-2847. 8 rooms with private bath and hot water, fans.

C-D Brisas del Mombacho, Km 66.5 Carretera a Rivas, T452-2312. Private bath with a/c and TV, cheaper with fan.

D Hotel Casa Grande, Enitel, 1 c norte, 1 c abajo, T532-3512. Private bath, hot water, cable, some rooms with a/c, nice building, central location, very clean.

Rivas *p948*

C Cacique Nicarao, 2 blocks west of Parque Central, next to the cinema (3 blocks south and 2 east from bus terminal), T453-3234. Rooms have a/c, cheaper with fan, comfortable, slow service, shower, cold water, best in town, clean, well equipped, good restaurant, Visa accepted, secure parking.

F El Coco, on Pan-American Highway near where bus from border stops. Noisy, basic, small rooms, shower, interesting bar, *comedor* with vegetarian food, nice garden.

F Hospedaje Internacional, near the Texaco station. Good breakfast.

F Hospedaje Lidia, Texaco, ½ c abajo near bus stop, T453-3477. Clean, noisy, private or shared bath, family-run.

San Juan del Sur *p948*

Hotel prices in San Juan del Sur double for Semana Santa, Christmas and New Year.

LL-L Morgan´s Rock, Playa Ocotal, T296- 9442, www.morgansrock.com. Luxury hacienda on a secluded beach with options for activities and wildlife trips in the surrounding area.

L-AL Piedras y Olas, de la parroquia 1½ c al este, T568-2110, www.piedrasyolas.com. Beautiful luxurious *casas* with everything included, private bath, a/c, cable TV, small living room, kitchen or kitchenette, terrace or balcony, peaceful, excellent service. Sailing trip on *Pelican Eyes* can be arranged.

A Casablanca, opposite Bar Timón, T568-2135, casablanca@ibw.com.ni, a/c. Restored house on beach, cable TV, private bath, clean, friendly, small swimming pool, laundry service, secure parking, transfers to San Jorge or Peñas Blancas US$25 per person.

A Villa Isabella, north corner of church, T568-2568, www.sanjuandelsur.org.ni. 17 rooms, includes breakfast and coffee or tea, a/c, and fan, private bath, very clean, lovely wooden house, well decorated with ample windows and light, video library, disabled access, English spoken, very helpful.

B **Encanto del Sur**, 50 m south of the church, T568-2222. Spacious, new, clean rooms with private bath, a/c and TV.
B **Gran Ocean**, ½ block from the beach, T568-2219, www.hotelgranoceano.com.ni. Private bath, a/c, cable TV, breakfast, clean but lacks atmosphere.
B **Royal Chateau**, from the church 2 blocks north, T0458-2551. Cheaper without a/c, big rooms, cable TV, clean, secure parking, bar and restaurant, breakfast US$2.50, other meals to order, 4 blocks from beach.
C **Joxi**, 1½ blocks west from the market (towards the beach), T458-2348, casajoxi@ibw.com.ni. Friendly, clean, a/c, bath, bunk beds, Norwegian run, restaurant, bar, can arrange sailing trips on the boat *Pelican Eyes*.
D-E **Costa Azul**, 1 block west of the market (towards the beach), T458-2294. 4 rooms with a/c (cheaper with fan), shared bath, clean, hammocks, kitchen, parking area.
E **Bahía Majagual Eco-lodge**, just past Playa Marsella, 10 km from San Juan del Sur, T0886-0439, www.sanjuandelsur.org.ni. This is one of the area's most beautiful beaches, noisy but festive foreign crowd, daily shuttles for San Juan (leave from San Juan market at 1100), camping dorms and private rooms, bar and restaurant.
E **Estrella**, on same street as **Joxi** (see below), T045-82210. With meals, balconies, sea view, partitioned walls, shared shower, take mosquito net and towel, clean, mixed reports on service, popular.
F **Casa Oro Youth Hostel** , 1 block from beach on church street (corner house), T568-2415, www.casaeloro.com. 2 dormitories (US$5), 4 double rooms (with and without bath) and plenty of hammocks, free use of fully equipped kitchen, beautiful garden, popular, but some strict rules like lights turning off at 1000 and you're not allowed to bring your own drinks.
F **Gallo de Oro**, 500 m north of town. Very basic but friendly, nice setting at end of beach.
F **Hospedaje Casa No 28**, 40 m from beach, near minibus stop for Rivas. Big airy rooms, shared showers, laundry facilities, clean, friendly owners, good.
F **Hospedaje La Fogata**, south side of market, T045-82271. Clean, friendly, with and without bath, family-run, good cheap food, keep an eye on your things.

Camping
Customs Office may give permission for camping and to park motor-caravans and trailers on the wharves if you ask them nicely.

Motor-caravans and trailers may be parked on Marsella beach: coming south, turn right on entering San Juan, by shrimp-packing plant.

South of San Jan del Sur *p949*
L-E **Parque Marítimo El Coco**, 18 km south of San Juan del Sur, T892-0124, www.playaelcoco.com.ni, apartments, bungalows and houses for 4-10 people, some on beach, others ocean view, very nice and closest lodging to La Flor Wildlife Refuge.

Eating

Diriamba *p947*
ꝉ **El Patio de Don Pedro**, before Diriamba on the Carretera Sur, just after the turning to Masatepe at Las Esquinas, mostly Mexican food, nice decor, sleepy service.

Jinotepe *p947*
ꝉ **Pizza Danny's** is very good, 50 m north of municipal building (try their special, small but delicious, US$7).

Rivas *p948*
ꝉ **Comedor Lucy**, on street leaving Parque Central at corner opposite **Banco de Nicaragua**, *comidas corrientes* and vegetarian food.
ꝉ **El Mesón**, behind San Francisco. Buffet-style.
ꝉ **Restaurant Chop Suey**, in the arcade in Parque Central.
ꝉ **Restaurante Mariscazo**, Del estadio Yamil Rios Ugarte, 800 metros al Sur, on the Pan American Highway, T563-1077, mariscazo@hotmail.com, seafood and meat menu, good seafood soup. Highly Recommended.

San Juan del Sur *p948*
There's a good *panadería* 1 block from beach and cafés along the beach for breakfast and drinks. The beachfront restaurants all serve good fish (about US$4 a meal). The restaurants popular with the locals are along the beach front near the **Hotel Estrella**.
ꝉꝉꝉ **La Cascada**, 1½ blocks east of Parque, at Piedras y Olas. Palm-thatched restaurant, excellent location overlooking the harbour.
ꝉꝉꝉ-ꝉꝉ **Bar Timón**, by the beach, T045-82243. Lobster (US$12) and prawns are specialities,

most popular place, good fish, slow service, very laid back and Nicaraguan.

¶¶¶-¶¶ Big Wave Daves, 200 m west of Texaco, T458-2203, bwds@ibw.com.ni. Tue-Sun 0830-0000. Popular with foreigners, good food, some meals overpriced (check prices for meals that are not on the menu). Ask here about full moon parties (they leave from Daves, US$20 includes transport, punch and food, bring your own hammock).

¶¶¶-¶ Pizzería San Juan, T458-2295, Tue-Sun 1700-2130. Very good pizza and pasta, recommended.

¶¶ Iguana Beach, next door to **Timón**. Fri-Tue 0730-1430. European dishes, friendly.

¶¶ O Sole Mio, 500 m north of **Hotel Casa blanca**, Italian, pizza and pasta. Recommended.

¶¶ Ranchos, 200 m north of the market, opposite **Las Flores**, T899-4588. Thu-Tue 0815-0000, bar and restaurant, chicken (US$5) or lobster (US$8).

¶¶ Ricardo's Bar, north of **Bar Timón** on beach. Thu-Mon 1500-0000, Sun from 1000. Popular with foreigners, good chicken salad, movies on Mon and Thu night, good maps of the town.

¶ Brisas Marinas, **Hotel Estrella** 20 m al oeste, T458-2176. Seafood soup, *ceviche*. From 0700 daily.

¶ The Chicken Lady, on the west side of the park. Popular and cheap *comedor*, good Nica food (*gallo pinto*, chicken or meat, banana and salad) for US$1.50, friendly.

¶ El Globo, **Hotel Estrella** 75 m al sur. Chicken and beef burgers, cold beer from 0900 until dawn.

¶ Eskimo, **Hotel Estrella** 75 m al sur. Daily 0930-2300. Sundaes, banana splits, and malt drinks.

¶ La Fogata, south side of market, T458-2271. Daily from 0700, fried fish, sandwiches.

¶ Las Flores, Mercado 1½ c al norte, T458-2284. Daily 1600-0200, with bar.

¶ Lago Azul, **Hotel Estrella** ½ c al sur, T458-2325. Daily 0800-2300. Garlic shrimp, sandwiches.

Activities and tours

San Juan del Sur *p948*

Canopy tours

Canopy Tours Da' Flying Frog Nicaragua, T568-2351, tiguacal@ibw.com.ni. US$25, close to San Juan del Sur with 17 platforms.

Diving

Escuela de Buceo San Juan del Sur, 50 m west of Texaco, T279-8628, www.abucear.com. Padi courses, boat trips, diving and fishing tours, US$50, 2 tanks.

Sailing

Pelican Eyes, **Hotel Piedras y Olas**, T458-2110. Sails to the beach at Brasilito (US$60 per person, minimum 10 people, leaves San Juan at 0900, return 1700).

Surfing

The coast north and south of San Juan del Sur is among the best in Central America for surfing, all access is by boat or long treks in 4WD. The **Annual Championship** at Playa Madera take place in the last week of Jul (only locals compete).

The town's best surf guide is **Sergio Calderón**, known as Chelo, he is also the manager of **Hotel Colonial**, Frente al antiguo Cinema Piñeda, T458-2539, hotel.colonial@ ibw.com.ni, and **Nica Surf International** (NSI), which specializes in outer sea surf. Week package (US$650) includes accommodation, food, material, instructor and transport. Or US$20 per person (minimum of 3) for an instructor, board and transport. Contact Chelo (or Euclides) at **Hotel Colonial**. They also arrange tours like kayak surfing, canopy tours, snorkelling or fishing.

Arena Caliente, ½ block north of the market, T839-7198. Also arrange boards and transport, US$7 per day, wetsuit US$5, transport US$6 (return trip, supposed to leave twice a day at 0900 and 1200), instructor US$6 per hr. Also for fishing trips (US$75, 5 hrs). Owner Byron López also rents some rooms with shared bath (US$6).

Transport

Jinotepe *p947*

Bus For **Managua** leave from the terminal in the northeast corner of town, every 20 mins, US$0.55; to **Nandaime** every 30 mins, US$0.35; to **Diriamba-Masaya** every 20 mins.

Rivas *p948*

Bus **Managua**, every ½ hr, 0400-1800, 2 hrs, US$1.60. **Granada**, every 1-1½ hr, 0615-1625, 1½ hr, US$1. **Jinotepe**, every

1-1½ hr, 0550-1710, 1¾ hr, US$1. **San Juan del Sur**, every ½ hr, 0600-1730, 45 mins, US$0.70 (taxi US$1 per person). **Peñas Blancas/ Sapoá – Costa Rica**, every ½ hr, 0500-1730, 1 hr, US$.60. **Las Salinas**, several 0910-1630, 2hrs, US$1.25.

Taxi To **San Jorge**, the best way to get to the dock, US$0.70, *colectivos* US$0.20. Ticabus office is close to Texaco.

San Juan del Sur *p948*
Bus **Managua**, several during the day, 0500-1530, 3½ hrs, US$2.25. Or take a bus/taxi to Rivas and change here. **Rivas**, every ½ hr, 0500-1700, 40 mins, US$0.70. Ticabus tickets are available opposite Joxi.

Taxi To **Rivas** US$1. Taxi to **San Jorge** US$15, better take taxi to Rivas and change at the market or the roundabout at the entrance of the town (all buses and taxis from Rivas to San Jorge pass here).

For the **border**, take any bus to Rivas, get off when it hits the Pan-American Highway (this crossing is also know as 'La Virgen'); all buses heading south from here will go to **Peñas Blancas** (every 30 mins). Taxi to the border is US$10.

The *H2O* **watertaxi** leaves from the beach, in front of Hotel Estrella at 1100 (return 1700) to the **northern beaches** like Mishal, Marsella, Madera, Bahía Majagual and Costa Blanca, US$6.50 per person (minimum of 3).

Directory

Rivas *p948*
Banks Banco de Finanzas for changing cash and Amex TCs, from the fire station, 1 c south, 75 m east, T453-0743. Banco de Centro América (BAC), 4 blocks from the market/bus terminal, ATM (Visa, MasterCard, Cirrus), changes TCs, Mon-Sat 0830-1630, Sat 0830-1100. ATM at Texaco only uses Visa. Western Union, 1 block from Market, Mon-Fri 0830-1600, Sat 0830-1200. **Internet** Gaby Cyber, from bus terminal 5 blocks south, ½ block east, US$1 per hr, Mon-Sat 0800-2000, Sun 0900-1900. **Telephone** Enitel is 3 blocks south of Parque Central, or 7 blocks south and 3 blocks east from bus terminal.

San Juan del Sur *p948*
Banks There is no bank. Hotels Casablanca and Joxi and some shops, like Pulpería Sánchez (Mon-Sat 0800-2200, Sun 0800-1900), will change money. **Internet** Several places in town (connections can be very slow). Casa Joxi (US$2/hr, daily 0630-2030), Leo's (US$2/hr, daily 0800-2100) and at Supercyber Internet Service (US$2/hr, 0800-2200, internet calls as well). **Language schools** Casa Escuela Rosa Silva , 2 blocks south past Hotel Villa Isabella, www.spanishsilva.com, private lessons, 'dynamic' classes. Escuela Integral de San Juan del Sur, frente a la Bahía, T568-2432, http://pages.prodigy.net/nss-pmc/SJDS/sjds.htm, regular morning classes, tutoring with flexible hours, US$195 for o1 week of 20 hrs. Playas del Sur Spanish school, frente al mar en la casa de la Cultura, T458-2115, escuelaplayasdelsur@yahoo.com, packages range from US$95 (only classes) to US$170 (clases, homestay and activities), 10 female experienced instructors, flexible hours, one-to-one instruction. Karla Cruz, 1½ blocks south of park (3rd house to the right after the road turns right), T607-2833, karlacruzsjds@yahoo.com, private instructor also gives Spanish classes, US$5/hr, discount for longer periods, additional US$40 for home-stay in her house, recommended. **Laundry** Most of the mid to upper-range hotels will do laundry for their guests on request. Near Soya Restaurant (ask there), hand wash, line dry. **Post office** 150 m left (south) along the seafront from the main junction.

Lago de Nicaragua → *Colour map 7, A2.*

The 'Gran Lago de Nicaragua' or Lago Cocibolca, is a freshwater lake full of saltwater fish which have swum up the Río San Juan from the sea and adapted to the fresh water. These fish exist in no other lake in the world, like the sawtooth fish and the shark brought to fame by the author Edward Marriott in his novel, Savage Shore. *Seen regularly on the east side of Isla Ometepe is a rare freshwater member of the bull shark family* (Carcharhinus nicaragüensis). *Terrapins can be seen sunning themselves on the rocks and there are many interesting birds. The lake has three major archipelagos (over 400 islands) as well as the largest lake island in the world, Ometepe. Created by a massive eruption of Volcán Mombacho 3000 years ago, Las Isletas Archipelago, just southeast of Granada, consists of 354 islands covered with lush vegetation, most of which are uninhabited. The Zapatera Archipelago is the most significant pre-Columbian sites in Nicaragua and a national reserve (for tours, see page 958). In the southeastern part of the lake is the Solentiname Archipelago.* ▸▸ *For Sleeping, Eating and other listings, see pages 956-959.*

The lake is 148 km long by 55 km at its widest point (8264 sq km).

San Jorge → *Colour map 7, A2.*

San Jorge, on the southwestern shore of Lake Nicaragua close to Rivas, is the main departure point for Ometepe Island, but on Sundays in summer the town itself is very lively with music, baseball, swimming and lots of excursion buses.

Isla Ometepe ▸▸ *pp956-959. Colour map 7, A2.*

→ *Population: 32,000. Altitude: 60-1610 m.*

The largest freshwater island in the world, Ometepe is a highlight of any trip to Nicaragua and is definitely worth a visit. It has two volcanoes, one of them, **Concepción**,

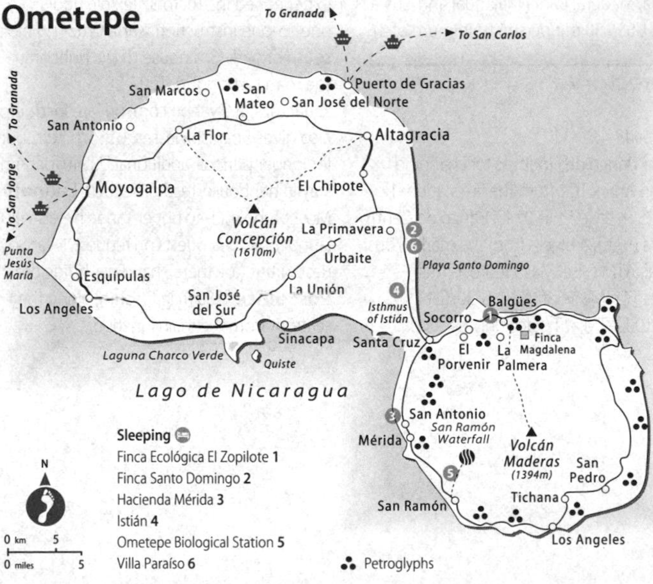

a perfect cone rising to 1610 m; the other, **Volcán Maderas**, rises to 1394 m. There are two main villages on the island on either side of Volcán Concepción: **Moyogalpa** and **Altagracia**, which are connected by bus. Moyogalpa has the atmosphere of a tourist port and there is not much to hold you in town unless you're catching an early boat the following day. Altagracia, like other small villages on the island, is more charming. The people of Ometepe are said to be the kindest in Nicaragua, partly because the Revolution and Civil War were never waged here. There are many indigenous **petroglyphs** in several locations on the island, the best being near Finca Magdalena.

Altagracia

Pick-ups meet boats arriving at Altagracia to provide transport for the 2-km ride into town. In the main plaza there is a **sculpture park** of pre-Columbian-style ceramics with some large basalt statues, similar to those housed in the San Francisco museum in Granada. The **Museo de Ometepehas** ⓘ *half a block from the Parque Central, US$1, guide in Spanish*, has displays covering local ethnographic and environmental themes. Ask for the birdwatching site about 3 km from Altagracia; birds fly in the late afternoon to nest on offshore islands.

You can stroll to the base of **Volcán Concepción** (which had its last major eruption in 1954), for good views of the lake in the company of many birds and howler monkeys. To climb the volcano, leave from Cuatro Cuadros, 2 km from Altagracia, and make for a cinder gully between forested slopes and a lava flow. There are several *fincas* on the lower part of the volcano. The ascent takes about five hours (take water), with alpine vegetation, heat from the crater and howler monkeys as attractions. It gets very steep near the summit. It's recommended that you get a guide as visibility is often restricted by clouds and it is easy to get lost, especially in the final stages (US$15 per person, minimum of three). Ask for guides near the pier; otherwise contact Eduardo Ortiz and his son José, of **Cuatro Cuadros**, or Eduardo Manzanares or Berman Gómez from **Exploring Ometepe**, who helped with the BBC programme *Beyond Boundaries* in 2005. There is an alternative route up Volcán Concepción from behind the church in Moyogalpa. Again, a guide is recommended for safety in jungle sections (machete useful) and cloud (eight hours up). Camping is possible near the top. South of Volcán Concepción is Charco Verde lagoon (see below).

Around Isla Ometepe

For **Volcán Maderas** ⓘ *US$1.50 to climb, US$3.50 with a guide*, take an early bus (0430 or 0530) from Altagracia to Balgües (or stay overnight there), ask for **Finca Magdalena** (20 minutes' walk), go up through banana plantations and forest to the top, beautiful lagoon in the crater, two to three hours up (can be very muddy, boots recommended). This is one of the country's finest Pacific basin cloud forests with howler monkeys accompanying your journey to the top. The climb to the summit of Volcán Maderas is not technical, but a guide may be helpful. Guides can be found at the coffee co-operative in Balgües, **Finca Magdalena** and in Moyagalpa at **Exploring Ometepe** or at **Hotel Ometepetl**. On the southwest flank of Volcán Maderas is **Salto San Ramón**, a 110-m waterfall. Take water on all hikes and climbs.

Other activities on the island include the **Laguna Charco Verde** (ask around for the legend on Chico Largo who is still said to watch the lagoon), the waterfall at San Ramon or the underground spring and water eye of **La Presa** ⓘ *close to Santo Domingo, privately owned, US$1*. The island does not offer a lot in terms of entertainment besides some local dancing at weekends (ask around). Every month there is the *Fiesta de la Luna Llena* (full-moon party) at Charco Verde (ask around for directions and times). **Fiestas patronales** are held year-round in different villages, the festivities 22-26 July in Moyogalpa and 12-18 November in Altagracia include both religious processions and bull riding.

Islas Solentiname » pp956-959. Colour map 7, A2.

One hour by fast boat (two or more hours by public boat) from San Carlos on the southeastern shore of Lake Nicaragua is the 36-island **Archipiélago de Solentiname**. These sparsely populated islands are covered with humid tropical forest and are home to many birds and a unique school of painting and balsa wood sculptures.

On **Isla San Fernando**, many locals carve and paint balsa wood figures. The diet on the island is somewhat limited but there is lots of fresh fruit. Ask for Julio Pineda or his sister Rosa, one of the local artists. The island has a new **museum** ⓘ *US$1*, with a variety of natural and cultural history exhibits as well as a spectacular view of the archipelago, especially at sunset; if closed ask in the village if it can be opened. Apart from at the hotel (see below), there is no electricity on the island, so take a torch.

Isla La Venada, named for its plentiful population of deer (*venado*), is also home to artists, in particular the house of Rodolpho Arellano who lives on the south side of the island. He is one of the region's best painters and his wife, daughters and grandson all paint tropical scenes and welcome visitors to see and purchase their works. On the north side of the island is a series of semi-submerged caves with some of the best examples of petroglyphs from the pre-Columbian Guatuso tribe. **Isla El Padre** is privately owned and the only island inhabited by howler monkeys. If you circle the island in a boat they can usually be spotted in the trees.

Isla Mancarrón is the largest in the chain, with the highest hill at 250 m. This is where the famous revolutionary/poet/sculptor/Catholic priest/Minister of Culture, Ernesto Cardenal, made his name by founding a school of painting, poetry and sculpture, and even decorating the local parish church in naïve art. There is a monument to the Sandinista flag outside the church. Hiking is possible on the island where many parrots and Moctezuma oropendolas make their home. The island's hotel of the same name is part of the local folklore as its founder Alejandro Guevara was a hero of the Sandinista Revolution; his widow Nubia and her brother Peter now look after the place.

Sleeping

Lago de Nicaragua *p954*

AL Finca Preciosa, on the lake in front of Mombacho, T897-0262, alfredhorsberg @sopris.net. Small ecolodge, bed and breakfast, 1 room in the owner's house and *cabañas*. Friendly owner arranges pick-up from Granada and boat tours (Zapatera, Ometepe, Río San Juan). Good report.

A Nicarao Lake Resort, on the island of La Ceiba, T266-1694, www.nicaraolake.com.ni. Includes all meals, a/c, good beds, part-time generator, delightful setting, restaurant.

San Jorge *p954*

D Mar Dulce, 300 m south of dock, bath, TV and parking.

F Nicarao, left off the Rivas-San Jorge road, near the dock, basic meals, friendly.

Isla Ometepe *p954, map p954*

Altagracia

F Castillo, Altagracia. Friendly, good food, slow service, water problems, trips can be organized to rock carvings on the volcano, US$4 per person or US$12 for a group guide.

F Central, Altagracia, on main street to Moyogalpa. Attractive courtyard and dining room (with great food in large portions), good friendly service, with bath, nice patio, *cabañas* in garden. Recommended.

F Don Kencho, Altagracia. Basic, option of shower.

Around Isla Ometepe

B-C Villa Paraíso, Playa Santo Domingo, T563-4675, www.villaparaiso.com.ni. *Cabañas* with bath and fan or in lodge without bath, Austrian owner, German spoken, clean, lake view, friendly, peaceful, lovely setting, best food on the island (but won't permit you to bring own food), good birdwatching. Highly recommended.

C Finca Santo Domingo, Playa Santo Domingo, T552-8787. 16 rooms with private bath and a/c (cheaper with fan), bar restaurant (dinner US$4-5), nice, relaxed, day trips by boat and horse.

C Ometepe Biological Station, San Ramón, T453-0875, www.lasuerte.org. Mainly for biology students, the station manages about 325 ha of conservation land in the San Ramón area. Includes mountain bikes, kayaks, meals. Rooms are simple with shared bath. Price is for full board.

C-E Finca Playa Venecia, San José de Sur, 250 m from the road, T887-0191. 1 cabin for 2 and another for 4 people, a/c. Cheaper for 3 double rooms with outside toilet. Meals available, horse rental, trips to Charco Verde.

C-F Hotel Charco Verde Inn, almost next to the lagoon, San José de Sur, T887-9302. Pleasant *cabañas* with private bath, a/c, terrace (US$25-30), doubles with private bath and fan (US$15-20), shared rooms (US$5 per person), restaurant.

C-F La Isla, del Puerto 1 c arriba, Moyogalpa, T459-4258. Private bath and a/c (cheaper with shared bath and fan), friendly, clean, kitchen, boat, bicycle rental.

D Ometepetl, on main street from dock, Moyogalpa, T459-4276, ometepetlng@hotmail.com. A/c (cheaper without), some rooms a bit dirty, friendly and very helpful, food (US$4), best rental cars on the island.

D-E Istián, Playa Santo Domingo, south of Villa Paraíso, across the beach (reservations through Ometepetl). Basic, fan, bath (cheaper without), views of both volcanoes, friendly but not very clean, transport from Moyogalpa US$20 (up to 12), tours and car rental.

D-F Finca Magdalena, www.fincamagdalena.com, T880-2041. A working co-operative farm run by 27 families, with accommodation in a small cottage, *cabañas* (US$15-30) double (US$5), single, dorms (US$2.25) and hammock space. Camping possible. Friendly, basic, very popular with travellers. Good meals around US$2; the food, much of it locally and organically produced, is very good. You can work in exchange for lodging.

E Casa Familiar, del Puerto 2 c al este, 20 m al sur, Moyogalpa, T459-4240. Private bath, a/c and good restaurant (US$3.75) with vegetarian or fried fish. Daily 0600-2100, recommended.

E Los Ranchitos, on same street as telephone company, Moyogalpa, T459-4112. Basic rooms, excellent food (0730-2130), reasonable prices, highly recommended.

E-F Hospedaje Central, from the dock 1 block right, 3 blocks up the hill, Moyogalpa, T459-4262, hospedajecentralometepe@hotmail.com. Private bath and fan, dorm (US$2), hammocks, TV, bar and restaurant, good food (US$3), washing machine, very attentive friendly service, same concept as **Hospedaje Central** in Granada.

F El Puerto, next to La Portuaria, Moyogalpa, T459-4194. Shared bath with fan.

F Finca Ecológica El Zopilote, about 1 km west of Balgües. With dormitory, hammock and camping accommodation. Use of kitchen and free track up to the volcano.

F Hacienda Mérida, near San Ramón. This former ranch of Somoza García was confiscated by the Sandinistas and the given to the Institute of Tourism by ex-president Violeta Chamorro. Simple hostel beds or camping, seriously cheap food (sometimes buffet-style dinners US$3.50) well prepared with fresh ingredients from the island. Popular. Mountain bike and kayak rentals (priced in dollars so watch the budget).

F Hotel Bahía, on main street from dock, Moyogalpa, T459-4273. Clean, with bath, balcony and restaurant (0700-2200). Good food (pasta US$1.75). Recommended.

F Hotel Buenavista, Playa Santo Domingo, 50 m down the road from**Villa Paraíso**. Has rooms with private or shared bath, friendly and relaxed atmosphere, laundry possible.

F Pensión Aly, opposite Shell, Moyogalpa, T459-4196. Price per person. Clean, uncomfortable beds, rooms with private and shared bath, helpful, but poor value and service in restaurant.

F Pensión Jade, Moyogalpa. Very basic, good atmosphere, friendly, water problems, meals available good value.

F Playa Volcán, from Catholic church in Mérida 150 m to the lake, T871-8303, www.playavolcan.tk. With simple *cabaña*, hammock and camping, good cheap food, good reports. Local tours arranged, bike hire.

Islas Solentiname *p956*

It's possible to stay in basic but generally very clean private homes.

L Refugio Mancarrón, Mancarrón, up the hill from the dock and church, T265-2716 (Managua). Includes 3 meals per day. Good spot, ideal for wildlife, hiking, with good rooms and food.

C **Hotel Celentiname or Doña María**, San Fernando. With meals, safe, pretty grounds. Shared baths, tiny rooms with weak beds and no windows. 2 new cabins with private bath and spectacular lake views. Owners Daniel and María are very friendly and helpful, no advance booking.

D **Albergue de la Comunidad de Solenti name/Doña Esperanza**, Mancarrón, T283-0083. Low-ceiling cabins in need of care, big grassy grounds, food available, library. Turn right before church and yell at gate (*¡Buenas!*), rustic cabins with full board included, some with private bath, some with shared, owned by the famed priest Ernesto Cardenal (can be booked through his **Galería** de Los Tres Mundos, in Managua, T278-5781).

Activities and tours

Lago de Nicaragua *p954*

Guided tours to the Archipiélago Zapatera are available from tour operators in Managua and Granada. There's also a range of tours and activities with accommodation available (**B**). Boats run 3 times a week (US$3 per person). There's a new tourism project from the UCA cooperative **Tierra y Vida**, T880-5848, ucatierrayagua@yahoo.

Isla Ometepe *p954, map p954*

Tour operators

Exploring Ometepe, 75 m from the port in Moyogalpa (in front of **Hotel Ometepetl**), T569-4132, ometepeisland@hotmail.com. Local guides can be found here, a tour guide association with experienced, knowledge able, helpful and English-speaking guides offering island tours (US$15 per person), Volcán Concepción (US$10) or Maderas (US$15). Recommended are Horacio Galán, T895-5521, Bermán Gómez, T836-8360 and Eduardo Manzanares, T873-7714, at the office of **Exploring Ometepe** or when making rounds at several hotels (at night).

Ometepe Tours, in Moyogalpa, ½ block north of BND, T459-4242, sells a useful booklet with maps and information.

Transport

Lago de Nicaragua *p954*

Boat The islands can be visited either by hired boats or motor launches, from the restaurant at the end of the road beyond the Complejo Turístico, US$10 per hr for the whole boat, US$50 per hr for 6 in a motor launch, or US$10 per hr for 2 in a rowing boat.

Another option is to take the morning bus (or taxi US$3.50) from Granada to **Puerto Asese**, 3 km further south, a tranquil town at the base of the Asese Peninsula at the head of the Ensenada de Asese. Boats can be hired at US$10-12 per hr for 2 people.

Trips to various lake destinations (**Zapatera**, **El Muerto**, **Islas Solentiname**, **Río San Juan**) can be arranged through various tour companies, up to 15 people on day trips, 8 for overnight voyages. See San Jorge, below, for the most frequently used service to Ometepe.

San Jorge *p954*

Boat A boat leaves for **Ometepe** almost every hr, 0745-1730, 1 hr, US$1.50 (*lancha*), US$2 (ferry). Return journeys from 0530-1600.

Taxi From San Jorge a road runs from the shore through Rivas (see page 948) to the port of San Juan del Sur (see page 948). Taxi to **Rivas**, US$0.75 (per person), *colectivos* US$0.20.

From Rivas, the Pan-American Highway runs along the west coast of the lake to Sapoá and the Costa Rican border.

Direct from San Jorge to **San Juan del Sur** costs US$15. It is a lot cheaper to take a taxi to Rivas and another one from Rivas to San Juan (US$1). Rivas also has connections with **Granada**, **Masaya** and **Managua**.

Isla Ometepe *p954*

The lake can have very big wind swells.

Boat The best access route to the island is from San Jorge on the lake's southwest shore to Moyogalpa. The ferry (US$1.75) and boat (US$1.25) offer regular services with one of them leaving every hr 0730-1730. Cars are transported with the ferry. **Roman Lake Lines Ferry** runs a fast boat service (½ hr), schedule and boat not reliable.

From Moyogalpa to **San Jorge** boat or ferry every 30 mins between 0530-0700 and 1100-1330. Also at 0900 and 1600.

Launches sail from Granada to **Altagracia** Mon and Thu at 1500, ticket office open 0900. 3½-4 hrs to Altagracia, US$1.50. Boats leave Altagracia for Granada on Tue and Fri. Things left on deck will get wet. As it can be very crowded, a good spot for sleeping is on the

Border essentials: Nicaragua-Costa Rica

San Carlos to Los Chiles

This is a frequently used crossing point between Nicaragua and Costa Rica, providing good access to and from Fortuna; it's normally quick and hassle free. There is a track of sorts from the south side of the Río San Juan, but most travellers go by boat up the Río Frío.

Nicaraguan immigration Border is now open 0800-1600 daily. Exit stamp (US$2), must be obtained in San Carlos Mon-Fri only. If travelling into Costa Rica the exit stamp must be obtained in San Carlos. Entrance stamps into Costa Rica (US$8) are only available on arrival in Los Chiles. Check with the police in advance for the latest position.

Transport 3 launches a day San Carlos-Los Chiles, at 1030, 1330 and 1500, 2 hrs, US$7.

Note The Nicaragua-Costa Rica border runs along the southern bank of the Río San Juan but has been the subject of government tension and debate with regards to Costa Rica's rights to navigate the river. The Costa Rican border reaches the south banks of the Río San Juan 2 km downriver from El Castillo but the river in its length is Nicaraguan territory. It is best to travel in Nicaraguan boats on the river, as Costa Rican boats could be detained or turned back.

San Juan del Norte

This area of the Caribbean coast is a narcotics zone, with drugs being landed from San Andrés (Colombia). Before attempting to crossthe border, seek information on safety.

Nicaraguan immigration There is no official immigration in San Juan del Norte. Travellers have reported being able to get stamps from the authorities here but this is not recommended. It's better to go to Bluefields or to one of the posts up the Río San Juan. Take advice on what to do on arrival in Costa Rica; the official entrance is Limón.

Transport Boats go from San Juan del Norte to Barra del Colorado in Costa Rica, but it is very expensive – ask about fishing boats and canoes.

cabin roof. Snacks and soft drinks are sold on board. Ticket office in Granada is at the dock; ENAP T552-2745.

Bus On the island, almost hourly 0600- 1830 from Moyogalpa to **Altagracia** (1 hr, US$0.50) and 3 extra using the northern road at 0830, 1430 and 1630. From Moyogalpa to: **Balgüe** (1030 and 1530, 1 hr, US$0.75). **Mérida** (1430 and 1630), Mérida and **San Ramón** (0800, 3 hrs, US$1). Reduced service on Sun.

Taxi (US$0.75) and *colectivo* (US$0.20) to **Rivas** with connections to San Juan del Sur, the Costa Rican border, Granada, Masaya and Managua.

Islas Solentiname *p956*

Boat Private transfers from San Carlos to **Solentiname** 1-1½ hr, US$55-85 per boat. The public boat goes Tue and Fri only at 1100 from **San Carlos**, 0300 from **Mancarrón**, 3½ hrs, US$2.15.

Directory

Isla Ometepe *p954, map p954*

Banks In Moyogalpa, change money (no TCs) in the 2 biggest grocery stores (1 opposite Hotel Bahía), or in hotels. **Comercial Hugo Navas** also gives cash advances on credit cards (MasterCard and Visa). **Western Union**, 3 blocks up the hill from the dock, Mon-Fri 0830-1200, 1300-1630, Sat 0830-1130. **Internet** Tienda Fashion in Altagracia, 1 block from Hotel Central towards the plaza (US$2.90/hr) and will change TCs (at a poor rate). **Comercial Arcia** in Moyogalpa (US$2/hr), very slow, Mon-Sat 0800-1900, Sun 0800-1200.

Río San Juan

The Río San Juan, running through deep jungles, drains Lake Nicaragua from its eastern end into the Caribbean at San Juan del Norte. Over 190 km long and with more than 17 tributaries, it runs the length of the southern border of the Indio Maíz Biological Reserve and connects the Atlantic and Pacific Oceans. It is the best area in Nicaragua to spot wildlife. This great river has played an integral part in Nicaragua's colonial and post-colonial history and is one of the most accessible of the country's many pristine nature-viewing areas. ▸▸ *For Sleeping, Eating and other listings, see pages 962-963.*

Background

First sailed by the Spanish in 1525, the complete length of the river was navigated on 24 June 1539, the day of San Juan Bautista, hence its name. In colonial times it was a vital link between the Spanish Caribbean and the port of Granada. After three attacks by Caribbean pirates on Granada, the Spanish built a fortress at El Castillo in 1675. The English tried to take the fort twice in the 18th century, failing the first time thanks to the teenage Nicaraguan national heroine Rafaela Herrera, and then succeeding with Lord (then Captain) Nelson, who later had to withdraw owing to tropical diseases. Later it became the site of many aborted canal projects. It is still a most rewarding boat journey.

San Carlos → *Colour map 7, A2. Altitude: 39 m.*

San Carlos is the capital of Río San Juan Department and the jumping-off point for excursions to Islas Solentiname (see page 956), Río Frío to Los Chiles in Costa Rica and the Río San Juan itself, with irregular launches to the river from the lakeside. Nearby are the two great nature reserves of Los Guatusos and Indio Maíz. In the wet it is very muddy. At San Carlos there are the ruins of a fortress built for defence against pirates.

Los Guatusos Wildlife Reserve

Known as the cradle of wildlife for Lake Nicaragua, Los Guatusos is home to many exotic and varied species of bird and reptile. It is also heavily populated by monkeys, especially howlers. The reserve is crossed by three rivers, Guacalito, Zapote and Papaturro, most popular for boat touring. It is essential to be at the park for sunrise to see the best of the wildlife. After 1030 the river often becomes busier with the immigration traffic of labourers heading to Costa Rica. A new **research centre** ⓘ *explanations in Spanish only, US$4, ask for Armando who is an enthusiastic expert on orchids,* built by Friends of the Earth and the Spanish Government has a collection of over 90 orchids native to the region and a butterfly farm. Visitors are welcome. Lodging is also possible in the research centre (E per person, bunkbeds with mosquito netting and shared bath). There is a public boat from San Carlos to Papaturro (Monday-Saturday 1100 and 1400, US$1, 1½ hrs; check return schedule locally).

El Castillo to the Caribbean

Some 60 km downriver is El Castillo, built around the restored ruins of the 18th-century Spanish fort called **La Fortaleza de la Inmaculada Concepción**. The old fort has a good history **museum** ⓘ *closes at 1200 for lunch, US$1*. The **tourist office** on the quay has a leaflet about the fort and town. It was here that Nelson did battle with the Spanish forces. There are great views of the river from the fortress. The town is on a wide bend in the river where some shallow but tricky rapids run the whole width. Horseriding is possible (about US$6 per hour). El Castillo is a good place to pick up food on the river.

Reserva Biológica Indio Maíz

A few kilometres downstream is the Río Bartola and the beginning of the Reserva Biológica Indio Maíz, 3000 sq km of mostly primary rainforest and home to over 600 species of bird, 300 species of reptile and 200 species of mammal including many big cats and howler, white-faced and spider monkeys. Sleeping is possible in **Refugio Bartola**, see page 962, a research station and training ground for biologists; it has a labyrinth of well-mapped trails behind the lodge. The hotel guides are very knowledgeable. They will also take you down the Río Bartola in canoe for great wildlife viewing and birding. Neglect in recent years has made turning up without booking a bit of a gamble, so make sure you book in advance. Camping is possible: ask the park ranger where; his guard house is across the Río Bartola from the **Refugio Bartola** lodge.

Bartola and further east

The river past Bartola becomes more beautiful. Here the Costa Rican border reaches to the south bank of the river. The Costa Rican side is partially deforested; the Nicaraguan side with the Indio Maíz Reserve is almost entirely intact. Watch out for turtles, birds and crocodiles. Two hours downriver is the Río Sarapiquí and immigration check-points for both Costa Rica and Nicaragua (no stamps available though).

If coming from the Río San Juan to Río Sarapiquí you will need to check in with the Costa Rican guard station if you want to spend the night, or even if you want to pick up something at the store. If continuing down the river without stopping you only need to check in at the Nicaraguan station on the Río San Juan.

Past the Sarapiquí, the San Juan branches north, and both sides of the river (heavily forested) become part of Nicaragua again as the Río Colorado heads into Costa Rica. Two hours or so later, the San Juan reaches the Caribbean via a series of magnificent forest-wrapped lagoons. The Río Indio must be taken to reach the isolated but surprisingly wealthy village of San Juan del Norte.

San Juan del Norte → *Colour map 7, A3.*

One of the wettest places on the American continent at over 5000 mm of rain per year, San Juan del Norte (also called Santa Isabel) is also one of the most beautiful, with primary rainforest, lagoons, rivers and the Caribbean Sea. It is settled by a small population (estimated at 275), though it was once a boom town in the 19th century, when the American industrialist Cornelius Vanderbilt was running his steamship line between New York and San Francisco. Then called Greytown, San Juan del Norte was the pick-up point for the steamship journey to the Pacific via the Río San Juan, Lake Nicaragua to La Virgen and then by mule overland to San Juan del Sur. This service was quite popular during the 'gold rush' of San Francisco. The town remained in its location on the Bahía San Juan del Norte, actually a coastal lagoon, until the 1980s, when fighting caused its population to flee. Re-established in its current location on the the east bank of the Río Indio, the village is separated from the Caribbean Sea by 400 m of rainforest. The population is a mix of Miskito, Creole, Rama and Hispanic.

Mark Twain made the crossing as a young man from San Francisco to New York via San Juan del Norte. He recounted the journey in his book Travels with Mr Brown.

There is no land route from here to Bluefields and the boat takes about three hours, US$600. Due to its proximity to Limón, in Costa Rica, colones are the standard currency here as all the food and supplies are bought easier there than in San Carlos. In Sarapiquí and San Juan del Norte córdobas, colones and dollars are all accepted.

If coming in your own boat (chartered), a trip further down the **Río Indio** is recommended, with lots of wildlife, virgin forest and Rama (please respect their culture and privacy). A visit to the ruins of old **Greytown** is also interesting, with a well-marked trail that leads through various cemeteries buried in the forest and to the town centre where only foundations and the church bell remain. It has been described as 'incredibly atmospheric' with amazing wildlife and is great for birding in the morning. Note names on tombstones, which include sailors from around the world. Most of the year the entrance is underwater so rubber boots are of great use here as for the rest of the region. Swimming is best in the **Blue Lagoon**; the Caribbean is also accessible, but with many sharks. If coming on the public boat from San Carlos, Melvin can arrange tours with one of his *pangas* (expect to pay around US$15-20 for a boat).

Sleeping

San Carlos *p960, map p960*

All hotels are basic. If yours has no running water, there is a bathhouse by the pier.

B-D **Cabinas Leyka**, Policía Nacional 2 c al oeste, T283-0354. With bath, a/c, cheaper with fan, balcony with view of the lake, serves breakfast, best in town.

F **Casa de Protocolo**, top of town on park opposite church. Clean, nets, private bath.

F **Costa Sur**, Consejo Supremo Electoral 50 m al sur, T283-0224. 10 rooms with shared or private bath and fan, meals.

F **Hospedaje Yuri**, by lake, near new dock. Nice room, cheap, friendly.

F **Hotelito San Carlos**, by jetty. With fan, basic, breakfast US$1.25.

El Castillo *p961*

C **Albergue El Castillo**, next to fortress above city dock, T892-0174. Oddly designed, comfortable rooms with shared balcony overlooking river, shared bath and good restaurant downstairs. Best room are Nos 1 and 10 for ventilation, but in No 10 you get noisy bats for company! Good food, great view of river from deck, good *camarones del río* (river shrimp) in garlic butter.

C **Hotel Richardson**, from the dock 1 block downriver and ½ a block away. Very small rooms with private bath, seemingly abandoned, but the only private bath in town.

F **Universal**, left from the dock and follow signs on your left. On the river with beautiful views, small rooms, clean, friendly owners.

Reserva Biológica Indio Maíz *p961*

B **Refugio Bartola**, T289-7924. Price (per person) includes 3 meals (**C** without food), fruit juices, simple rooms with solid beds, ask for mosquito netting. Excellent meals, great *camarones del río, cerdo a la plancha.*

Bartolo and further east *p961*

D **Paraíso de la Frontera(Doña Adilia's Place)**, on the Sarapiquí. Private bath, simple, friendly, Nicaraguan-owned lodge. Not terribly clean, shared bath, fan, restaurant with set meals, US$3.

San Juan del Norte *p961*

D **Hotel Lost Paradise** (or **Melvin's Place**), left out of the ferry and follow the river about 500 m. Price per person. Ceiling fan, private bath, clean, bring coils or mosquito netting, owner Melvin speaks some English and is very helpful. There's a bar, restaurant, hammocks on gazebo by the river, highly recommended. Tell the kitchen in advance if you want meals.

F **Greytown Lodge**, no sign, near Melvin's. Basic and friendly accommodation with cooking facilities.

Eating

San Carlos *p960, map p960*

¥¥-¥ **El Mirador**, west end of town in ruins of fort. Lovely view of lake, Río Frío and Río San Juan, decent food with dishes from US$3.

¥ **Comedor Londras** on the jetty next to BDF and also in the covered market. 1 of several good, cheap *comedores*.

Félix Dining Room, main street. 2 plastic tables on the street but good meals, US$1.50.
Kaoma, Río San Carlos. Fresh fish caught by the owner, good food with occasional live music. Recommended.
Miralago, by the lake. Painted pink and purple, good grilled meat and salad, but nasty mosquitoes in the evening.

El Castillo *p961*
Bar Cofalito, on the jetty. Good view and even better *camarones de río* (crayfish), considered by many the best in town, occasional fresh fish. Owner has river kayaks and can organizeexpedition on the Río San Juan, rents motorboat (US$10 per hr) for tarpon and snook fishing.

San Juan del Norte *p961*
Simple food, fresh lobster if in season, if not the fried snook is recommended. There is a pleasant bar upriver from Doña Ester's Place with a big palm ranch and cold beer, card-playing locals and friendly Rama. It can be hard to find someone in San Juan to cook a meal, so bring snacks and arrange meals at Doña Ester's or Melvin's Place in advance.

Entertainment

San Juan del Norte *p961*
Bars and clubs
There is a disco which is full of festive locals at weekends dancing to reggae, salsa, rap and merengue. If staying at Melvin's Place he will take you to the disco to make sure you have a good time and get home safely. It's a short walk but a ride in his *super-panga*, if offered, is not to be missed. There are no police in San Juan and while the locals are very honest, be aware that this is border country and care should be taken, particularly at night.

Transport

San Carlos *p960, map p960*
Air La Costeña has daily flights from Managua Mon-Sat, US$76 return, sit on right on way to San Carlos for views of Ometepe's volcanoes. Flight at 1000, except Sun and Fri, 1300. There is a maximum weight for flights – you will be asked your body weight. Flights land and take off within 5 mins, so early arrival is advised. Taxi from airstrip to dock US$1.

Boat *Pangas* are small motor boats; *botes*, long, narrow ones; *planos*, big broad ones.

San Carlos-**Granada** ferry leaves from main dock Tue and Fri, 1400, 15 hrs, US$4.

Solentiname Archipelago, stopping at islands La Venada, San Fernando and Mancarrón from San Carlos, and in reverse en route to San Carlos. San Carlos-**Solentiname**, Tue and Fri 1300, 2½ hrs, US$4. Solentiname-**San Carlos**, Tue, Fri 0400. **Los Guatuzos Wildlife Refuge**, stopping at village of Papaturro, San Carlos-**Río Papaturro**, Tue and Fri 0800, 5½ hrs, US$5. Río Papaturro-**San Carlos**, Mon, Thu 0500. San Carlos-**El Castillo**, 0800 (daily except Sun) and 1400 (daily), 3-4 hrs, US$5. El Castillo-**San Carlos**, daily 0430, 0500, 0600. San Carlos-**San Juan del Norte**, Thu 0800, 12-14 hrs, US$15. San Juan del Norte-**San Carlos**, Sun 0330, 13-15 hrs.

Crossing to **Costa Rica** from **San Carlos-Los Chiles**, 1000 (daily), 2 hrs, US$4. **Los Chiles-San Carlos**, 1600 (daily).

Private boats are expensive but are faster. Ask at docks, restaurants, taxi drivers or at tourism office. Average round-trip rates: **El Castillo** US$190-250, **Solentiname** US$75-100. Group tours are available from tour operators in Managua.

Bus **Managua**-San Carlos is a brutal ride, but locals prefer it to the ferry trip. There are some lovely views during the early part and pure pain in the kidneys at the end. San Carlos- **Managua**, daily at 0200, 0600, 0800 and 1100, 9½ hrs, US$7. Returning from Mercado El Mayoreo at 0500, 0600, 0700 and 1300.

El Castillo to the Caribbean *p961*
Boat There are about 4 daily boats from San Carlos to **El Castillo** (2½ hrs, US$1.50), schedules seem to change frequently. Other boats do the trip but without fixed schedules. If you plan to continue beyond El Castillo, it can only be done by prior arrangement in San Carlos or Managua, or with lots of patience and cash.

Directory

San Carlos *p960, map p960*
Banks BDF, next to dock for Solentiname. No exchange for TCs and you can only change cash with street changers.

Eastern lowlands

→ Colour map 7, A3.

Nicaragua's eastern tropical lowlands make for a striking change from the rest of the country. Gone are the volcanoes, hills and valleys, and in their place is lush, tropical rainforest drenched between May and December with heavy rainfall. Most of the population are the African-influenced Miskito people who live in the northern lowlands, mainly around Puerto Cabezas. Their economy is based on timber, fishing and mining. To reach the Caribbean port of Bluefields and the idyllic and peaceful Corn Islands, you can fly or take the famous 'Bluefields Express' downriver. English is widely but not universally spoken. »» *For Sleeping, Eating and other listings, see pages 967-970.*

Background

This area, together with roughly half the coastal area of Honduras, was never colonized by Spain. From 1687 to 1894 it was a British Protectorate known as the Miskito Kingdom. It was populated then, as now, by the Miskito, whose numbers are estimated at 75,000. There are two other indigenous groups, the Sumu (5000) and the Rama, of whom only a few hundred remain, near Bluefields. Also near Bluefields are a number of Garífuna communities. Today's strong African influence has its roots in the black labourers brought in by the British to work the plantations and in Jamaican immigration. The Afro-Nicaraguan people call themselves *criollos* (Creoles). The largest number of inhabitants of this region are Spanish-speaking *mestizos*. The Sandinista Revolution, like most other political developments from the Spanish-speaking part of Nicaragua, was met with mistrust. Although the first Sandinista junta recognized the indigenous peoples' rights to organize themselves and choose their own leaders, many of the programmes initiated failed to encompass the social, agricultural and cultural traditions of eastern Nicaragua. Relations deteriorated and many engaged in fighting for self-determination. A low point was reached when the Sandinista Government ordered forced resettlement of many Miskito villages, burning to the ground what was left behind. About half the Miskito population fled as refugees to Honduras, but most returned after 1985 when a greater understanding grew between the Sandinista Government and the people of the east coast. The Autonomous Atlantic Region was given the self-governing status in 1987; it is divided into Región Autonomista Atlántico Norte (RAAN) and Región Autonomista Atlántico Sur (RAAS).

In Nicaragua, the Caribbean coast is almost always referred to as the Atlantic coast.

Managua to Rama

»» pp967-970.

At **San Benito**, 35 km from Managua on the Pan-American Highway going north, the Atlantic Highway branches east, paved all the way to Rama on the Río Escondido. Shortly after Teustepe, a paved road goes northeast to Boaco. A turn-off, unpaved, goes to **Santa Lucía**, a village inside a crater, with a women's handicraft shop. There is also a co-operative here with an organic farming programme (information from **Unag** in Matagalpa). **Boaco** (84 km from Managua) is called the city of two floors because of its split-level nature. The upper floor has a nice square with good views of the countryside.

Juigalpa and around

→ *Colour map 7, A2.* *Population: 41,000.*

The Atlantic Highway continues through Juigalpa, a pleasant town with one of the best museums in Nicaragua, housing a collection of idols resembling those at San Agustín, Colombia: **Museo Gregorio Aguilar Barea** ⓘ *Mon-Fri, US$0.25, T812-0784.* The bus terminal is in the town centre near the market, up the hill. Banks on main plaza accept dollars in cash only.

Rama

The main road continues east to **Santo Tomás** and smaller villages (including La Gateada, turn-off to **Nuevo Guinea**, centre of cacao production, connected by air from Managua via San Carlos on Friday with **La Costeña**, T285-0160), then to **Cara de Mono**, on the Río Mico, and finally to Rama, 290 km from Managua.

Bluefields

» *pp967-970. Colour map 7, A3.*

→ *Population: 42,665.*

Dirty, chaotic yet curiously inviting, Bluefields, the most important of Nicaragua's three Caribbean ports, gets its name from the Dutch pirate Abraham Blaauwveld. It stands on a lagoon behind the bluff at the mouth of the Bluefields River (Río Escondido), which is navigable as far as Rama (96 km). In May there is a week-long local festival, **Mayo-Ya!** with elements of the British maypole tradition, local music, poetry and dancing. The local **Fiesta de San Jerónimo** is on 30 September. The **tourist office** (**INTUR**) ⓘ *T822-1111*, is next door to the old Migración building. There are bars, a couple of reggae clubs, *comedores*, restaurants and an **Almacén Internacional**. Prices are about the same as in Managua. Be prepared for frequent power and water cuts.

Laguna de Perlas

The lagoon itself is some 50 km long with mostly Creole villages round its shores, like Pearl Lagoon, Haulover, Brown Bank, Marshall Point and San Vicente. La Fe and Orinoco are Garífuna villages and Raitipura and Kakabila are indigenous villages. In Raitipura there is a Danish housing project, run by Mogens Vibe who takes on volunteers for a minimum of one week (recommended). At **Pearl Lagoon village** there is a very friendly hostel, **Miss Ingrid's**. Within walking distance is the swimming beach of **Awas** (basic accommodation). Larger vessels may be available for transport to Puerto Cabezas, but there is no transport south of Bluefields.

Outlying areas of the Región Autonomista Atlántico Sur

The **Río Kurinwás** area north of Bluefields is a fascinating, largely uninhabited jungle area, where it is possible to see monkeys. It might occasionally be possible to get a boat to **Tortuguero** (also called Nuevo Amanecer) a *mestizo* town which will really give you a taste of the frontier. Tortuguero is about a six-hour speedboat ride from Bluefields up the Kurinwás River; several days by regular boat. The **Río Grande** is the next river north of the Kurinwás, connected to the Pearl Lagoon by the Top-Lock Canal. At its mouth are five interesting villages: the four Miskito communities of Kara, Karawala, Sandy Bay Sirpi and Walpa, and the Creole village of La Barra. **Sandy Bay Sirpi** is situated on both the river and the Caribbean and has a nice beach.

Travelling upriver, the Río Grande is noticeably more settled than the Río Kurinwás. Quite a bit upriver (also about a six-hour speedboat ride from Bluefields, several days by regular boat), you reach the *mestizo* town of **La Cruz de Río Grande**. It was founded in about 1922 by Chinese traders to serve workers from a banana plantation (now disused) further upriver. La Cruz has a very pretty church. The adventurous can walk between La Cruz and Tortuguero; it takes about 10 hours each way in the dry season, 12 hours in the rainy season.

Islas de Maíz/Corn Islands

» *pp967-970. Colour map 5, A2.*

The Corn Islands are two small islands fringed with white coral and slender coconut trees, perfect for relaxation. **Little Corn**, the smaller of the two and far more idyllic, escaped serious damage in the 1988 hurricane and can be visited by boat from the larger island, **Big Corn**, a one-hour ride by *panga*. On Little Corn Island there is no electricity and no phones, just pristine white-sand beaches and some of the Caribbean's finest undisturbed coral reefs. Big Corn is a popular Nicaraguan holiday resort (the best months are March and April). The nicest beaches on Big Corn are on **Long Bay** (walk across the island from Playa Coco)and **Brig Bay**, by the dock.

If you climb the mountain, wear long trousers as there are many ticks. On Little Corn you can climb the lighthouse for fantastic views of the whole island (not recommended if you are uncomfortable with heights). The language of the islands is English. The islanders are very friendly but petty thievery has been reported. Be wary of touts who greet you at the airport, posing as impartial guides; they may charge you for their services. Make sure you take enough money with you to the island as credit cards are not accepted; dollars are widely used. There is only one bank (**Caley Dagnall**), or you can change cash and TCs at the **Western Union**. There is a **post office** about 100 m south of the airport shack.

Everything is more expensive than on the mainland.

Northeast Nicaragua » pp967-970.

Puerto Cabezas → *Colour map 6, B6. Population: 50,941.*

Puerto Cabezas, capital of the Región Autonomista Atlántico Norte, has a distinctly different atmosphere from Bluefields. It is principally a large Miskito village and offers an excellent introduction to the Miskito area. You can arrange to stay in small Miskito villages, for example near Haulover, a few hours by boat south of Puerto Cabezas. There are significant minorities of *mestizos* (referred to on the coast as *españoles* or the Spanish) and Creoles, many of whom came to 'Port' by way of Las Minas. Spanish is a second language for the majority of residents; many speak at least some English, and for some, English is their native language. The local name for Puerto Cabezas is **Bilwi**, although the name is of Sumo origin. The Miskitos conquered the Sumos to obtain the town some time in the last century. There are two main roads, the only paved streets, which run parallel to each other and to the sea. At the southern end of the town is the port area; a walk along the pier at sunset is highly recommended. The airport is at the northern end. The main market occupies the central part of town. Traveller's cheques can be changed by Augusto Chow; ask for 'El Chino'.

Waspám and the Río Coco → *Population: 38,701.*

The Coco River (called *Waspán* in Spanish and *Wanghi* in Miskito) is the heart of Miskito country. There is a road from Puerto to Waspám; during the dry season the 130-km trip should take about three hours by 4WD vehicle, several hours longer by public bus (leaves Puerto at 0700, Monday-Saturday and, with luck, returns from Waspám at 1200). The bus can be boarded at several points in Puerto along the road out of town, US$5 to Waspám. The trip takes you through the pine forests, red earth, and north of Puerto towards the Coco River (the border with Honduras), and you will pass through two Miskito villages, **Sisin** and **Santa Marta**. Hitching is possible; if you cannot get all the way to Waspám, make sure you are left at Sisin, Santa Marta or La Tranquera. You can take lifts from the military; never travel at night.

Parque Nacional Saslaya → *Colour map 6, B4.*

Saslaya was the first national park in Nicaragua, located within the **Reserva Biosfera Bosawás** which contains the largest tropical cloud forest in Central America. The **Proyecto Ecoturístico Rosa Grande**, supported by Nature Conservancy and the Peace Corps involves the community of **Rosa Grande**, 25 km from Siuna, near an area of virgin forest with a trail, waterfall on the River Labú and lots of wildlife including monkeys and large cats. One path leads to a lookout with a view over the **Cerro Saslaya**; another circular path to the northwest goes to **Rancho Alegre Falls**. Guides can be hired for US$7 a day plus food. Excursions cost US$13 per person for guide, food and camping equipment. You may have to pay for a camp guard while hiking. Contact Don Trinidad at the *comedor* in Santa Rosa. In Siuna, contact **Proyecto Bosawás** ⓘ *200 m east of airstrip; Mon-Fri 0800-1700*. Groups of five or more must reserve in advance; contact the **Amigos de Saslaya** ⓘ *c/o Proyecto Bosawás, Siuna, RAAN*, by post or telegram.

Tourism is in its infancy here and you may find little things 'added on' to your bill. Be certain you have enough supplies for your stay.

Sleeping

Managua to Rama *p964*

E **Boaco**, Boaco, on the 1st level, opposite Cooperativa San Carlos, T842-2434. Small beds, private and shared baths, friendly owners who include one of the country's finest archaeologists, Edgar Espinoza, the current director of the Museo Nacional de Nicaragua. It may be possible at the weekend to convince Edgar to guide you to hidden petroglyph sites in the hills; call ahead.
F **Casa de Soya**, Santa Lucía. Good food, friendly owners, single room for rent, basic. Good views from nearby mountains.
F **Sobalvarro**, Boaco, on the square. Simple and clean.

Juigalpa *p964*

D **La Quinta**, on main road at the east end of town. A/c or fan, bath, clean, friendly, restaurant has good food and a fine view of surrounding mountains.
E-F **Rubio**, on main north road, clean, friendly, with bath (cheaper without), TV, laundry.

Rama *p965*

Limited accommodation; best to wait until you get to Bluefields.

Bluefields *p965*

Hotels may be full if you arrive late or are last off the ferry.
B **Bluefields Bay Hotel**, Barrio Pointeen, T822-2838. A/c, with bath, clean. Rooms upstairs are better. Excursions offered to surrounding areas. Highly recommended.
B **La Casona**, Barrio Central, opposite disco Bacchus, T822-2436. With breakfast, private bath, cable TV, a/c.
C **Caribbean Dreams**, opposite Hollywood T822-0107. With bath, water erratic, basic but clean, owners helpful.
C **South Atlantic**, near central square. Run by Fanny Chambers (native English speaker), with bath, safe, a/c, cable TV, fridge, clean, friendly, excellent food.
C **South Atlantic II**, T822-2265. New annex in main street, with sports bar looking across the bay.
D **Marda Maus**, on the dock near central market, T822-2429, 1 of the nicer places in its price range with bath and fan, dark, not too clean, no restaurant, near market.
E **El Bluff**, in El Bluff. With bath, cheaper without, fan, limited water, friendly, restaurant, pleasant.
E **El Dorado**, 1 block from the main steet. Quiet spot, may offer floor space to late arrivals.
E **Hollywood**, Barrio Punta Fría, Mercado Teodoro Martínez ½ c arriba, T822-2282. 12 rooms, some with fan others more expensive with a/c and cable TV. Has its own well and generator, friendly, restaurant, clean.
F **Airport**, above **Costeña** office at airport. Clean and friendly.
F **Las Brisas**, Barrio Central, Muelle de las Pangas, T822-1471. 12 basic rooms with fan and shared baths.
F **Pearl Lagoon**, Barrio Central, frente a UNAG, T822-2411. Private bath, laundry service, restaurant, good value.

Islas de Maíz/Corn Islands *p965*

Rats are a problem in all the hotels; they aren't dangerous, but aren't pleasant either.

Big Corn

B **Bayside Hotel**, T285-5001. All rooms with a/c and cable TV, a bit run-down but ocean-front on the best snorkelling reef on the island.
B **El Paraíso Club Cabinas**, Briggs Bay, T285-5077. With bath, porch with hammock, clean, bar, restaurant, slow service, horses, bicycles and snorkelling gear for rent, noisy

part of the island but popular. Some misunderstandings with restaurant bills have been reported, keep track of your tab.

C Panorama, close to beach. Clean, simple, with private bath.

D Beachview, next to **Panorama**. Some rooms with bath, a bit run-down but good views from the balcony.

D Nautilus Guest House, at the north end of town, T285-5077. Has good rooms with screened windows, fans, kichen and refrigerator available and meals. Pleasant gardens.

E Brisas del Mar, Playa Coco. Good, simple, friendly and good breakfast, restaurant.

E Estrella, Enitel 80 m east, 73 m south, T822-0523. Shared bath with fan.

E Sweet Pearly, Barrio Central del Muelle 8 m south, T822-0512. 24 rooms, private and cheaper shared baths, fan, laundry.

Little Corn

B Casa Iguana, on a 3-ha bluff overlooking the sea, www.casaiguana.net. US-owned, friendly, helpful, 4 smart cabins with bath, 2 cabins with shared bath. Have opened a dive shop (**Dive Little Corn**) and also hire out snorkelling equipment and arrange fishing trips. TCs accepted.

B Hotel Los Delfines, T258-5239 (in Managua), hotellosdelfines@hotmail.com. Cabins very close to a nice beach, with restaurant, some rooms with a/c and private bath. Owner Bonnie is a native of the island and very proud of his kitchen, which serves good seafood cocktails and fresh lobster. He will take visitors in his boat around the island for snorkelling US$40 or, when it's calm, to Pearl Keys.

E Derek's, on beach. Beautiful remote setting, price per person in 4-bed cabins. You can also camp for a small fee.

F Bridget's, in village. Very basic (stifling heat at night) but good food.

Puerto Cabezas *p966*

C El Cortijio, Calle Comercio, Barrio San Pedro, T282-2223. 6 rooms with bath, a/c, cable TV, parking, fax, laundry.

D Cayos Miskitos, 2 blocks east of the plaza. Good, comfortable rooms with bath, clean, friendly, arrangement breakfast in advance.

D El Viajante, central. Clean, very friendly, basic rooms with fan, singles only, shared baths, *comedor* serves breakfast.

Parque Nacional Saslaya *p966*

E Chino, Siuna. The best and most expensive.

F Bosawás Field Station, on the river Labú. Has hammocks but not many, clean but simple, locally produced and cooked food about US$1.25.

F Costeño, Siuna,100 m east of airstrip. Basic.

Eating

Managua to Rama *p964*

Boaco is cattle country and there are many good places to enjoy a local steak.

TT La Casona, Boaco, next to Texaco, T842-2421. Daily 0800-2300. Try their *lomo de costilla* or *plato típico*.

TT La Cueva, Boaco, south side of the Parroquia Santiago church, T842-2438. Very good steaks.

Bluefields *p965*

TT Bay View Restaurant, next to Tía Irene. Beautiful spot on the water to watch the world go by with a drink, popular.

TT Restaurant Flotante, built over the water at the end of the main street. Average prices, slow service, great view.

Islas de Maíz/Corn Islands *p965*

Steer clear of baby lobsters as the harvesting can threaten the local population.

Big Corn

Ask around for where meals are available; the restaurants serve mainly chicken and chop suey, but in private houses you can find much better fare. Try fresh coconut bread (from family stores), banana porridge and sorrel drink (red, and ginger-flavoured). The main market area is near **Will Bowers Wharf** and is a cheap place to eat.

TT Sevva's Place, 500 m past **Bayside Hotel**, T285-5058. Great seafood, chicken, fine location, good food, try breakfast on rooftop. Beach in front is good for swimming.

T Nautilus Restaurant, at the north end of town. Serves healthy fruit and juices.

T Sunset Restaurant, at the north end of the bay. Serves excellent fish and lobster.

Little Corn

All the hotels have restaurants, though you should book.

Comedor Isleta/Miss Rosie's in village, next to Bridget's. Has simple good food.

Puerto Cabezas *p966*
There are numerous cheap *comedores*. Prices are much higher than elsewhere in Nicaragua because almost everything has to be brought in by air.
Pizzería Mercedita, near the harbour. Very good, expensive, wide liquor selection, good service. Recommended.

Parque Nacional Saslaya *p966*
Comedor Jassy, La Rosita, near the entrance of town on the Siuna side. Recommended.
Comedor Melania, Rosa Grande. A meal costs about US$1.
Comedor Siuna, opposite **Hotel Costeño**, Siuna, has good *comida corriente*.
Desnuque, Siuna. There are 2 *comedores* Desnuque, 1 in the market and the other on a hill near the baseball stadium and airstrip, the latter has good pizza as well as typical Nicaraguan food. Recommended.

Activities and tours

Islas de Maíz/Corn Islands *p965*
Activities on the islands include snorkelling, mountain biking, horse riding and hiking.

Diving is increasingly popular off the islands. Both **Nautilus** and **Casa Iguana's Dive Little Corn** (www.divelittlecorn.com) have equipment for hire. 2 dives cost around US$55, night dives cost around US$45. **Casa Iguana** offers PADI Open Water Course for US$315.

Fishing Contact **Ernie Jenkie** (US$5 per hr), Big Corn.

Transport

Managua to Rama *p964*
Bus 2 trucks a day to **Santa Lucía** from Boaco, US$1, 1 bus a day to and from **Managua**.

From Boaco, unpaved roads go north to **Muy Muy** and **Matagalpa**, and south to **Comoapa**. **Managua**-Boaco goes every 40 mins from Plaza Mayoreo (2 hrs 10 mins, US$1.50).

Juigalpa *p964*
Bus Every 15 mins from **Managua**, US$2.30, 3 hrs.

Rama *p965*
Bus From **Managua** buses leave from the Mercado Mayoreo. **Managua**-Rama, every hr, 0400-1130, 8 hrs, US$7. To Managua, hourly from 0400-1130. To **Juigalpa**, every hr, 0800-1500, 6 hrs, US$3.75. **Juigalpa**-El Rama, hourly from 0800-1500.
Ferry The ferry from Rama to Bluefields – the **Bluefields Express** – is packed with hundreds of people, assorted animals and goods. The journey passes through the sparsely populated eastern region of Nicaragua. The wide, fast flowing river passes land that is mostly cultivated, with the occasional subsistence farmer's dwelling. The **express boat** schedule appears to be Rama-**Bluefields**, Tue, Thu, Sat, Sun at 1700, Bluefields-Rama at 0500, 1½ hrs; ordinary boat Rama-Bluefields, Mon, Wed and Fri in the early morning (around 0800 when the bus has arrived), from Bluefields-Rama between 1100 and 1300, 5 hrs, US$8. Food and soft drinks sold on the ferry. **Fast boats**, *pangas*, can be hired for US$12-15 per person Rama- Bluefields, taking 1½ hrs, or hitch a ride on a fishing boat. There is usually 1 waiting when the bus arrives.

Bluefields *p965*
Air The airport is 3 km from centre; either walk (30 mins) or take a taxi jeep (US$0.80). **La Costeña** (Managua T263-1228, Bluefields T822- 2500) and **Atlantic Airlines** (Managua T233-2791, Bluefields T822-1299) share the service to **Bluefield**, US$45 1-way, US$78 return. **Costeña** has 3 flights a day (Mon-Sun 0700, 0830, 1600). **Atlantic**, 3 daily flights (Mon- Sun 0645, 1030, 1410). Flights connect to flights to **Puerto Cabezas** and the **Corn Islands**.

Managua airlines offices are in the domestic terminal. Bring passport, it is sometimes asked for in the departure lounge. There is a customs check on return to Managua. Flights are sometimes early.
Boat Several wharves near the market provide access to the port. *Pangas* can be rented for trips. From the main wharf small boats leave irregularly for villages on the coast and Laguna de Perlas, such as Tasbapounie (*hospedaje*); food may be scarce in all settlements. A boat leaves daily 0800 to **Laguna de Perlas** (Pearl Lagoon), 80 km north of Bluefields 3-6 hrs, US$4.35.

Islas de Maíz/Corn Islands *p965*
Air La Costeña from **Managua** and **Bluefields** to the Corn Islands, daily at 0630 and 1400 from Managua, 0700 and 1535 from Corn Islands (0845 and 1535 on Sun), US$105 return. The same advice on passport and customs applies as under Bluefields. Air services are suspended from time to time because of the poor state of the runway on Big Corn. Book well in advance and book return immediately on arrival.

Boat A boat leaves Big Corn for **Little Corn**, if the weather's OK, 0900 and 1600. It runs to coincide with the plane timetable, 45 mins. Starts in Little Corn first, leaving for Big Corn 0630 and 1400. Not for the faint-hearted if it's choppy. US$5 each way.

Passenger-carrying cargo boats leave Bluefields for the **Corn Islands** from the docks of **Copesnica**, north of town, around a small bay and past the ruined church: Wed, Fri, Sun 0700-1000, return Thu, Sun, Tue, US$4.35 one way, 5 hrs. The water around Bluefields is dirty, muddy brown, but soon becomes a clear, sparkling blue.

There is usually a boat from **Bluefields** (the Lynx Express), via El Bluff on Wed at 0830, 4 hrs, but there is no guarantee. Boats back to Bluefields leave from Will Bowers Wharf; tickets are available in advance from nearby office. You may be able to find a fishing boat that will take you but make sure the boat is properly equipped and seaworthy. Check with the **Capitanía** in Bluefields, or in El Bluff and with anyone you can find who has information. Trips take 5-8 hrs. Hire a boat from (ask around), normal charge US$40 one way, US$80 for the *panga* for a full day.
Bus Buses and *colectivos* travel clockwise and anti-clockwise round Big Corn. US$0.70 per person regardless of distance all day.

Puerto Cabezas *p966*
Air The airstrip is 3 km from the town. Taxis will charge US$1 to any point in Puerto (it is also possible to walk).

La Costeña (T263-1281) flies daily from **Managua** in small 20-seater planes. There are also daily flights via **Bonanza**, **Siuna** and **Rosita**. Frequent cancellations so it's best to make reservation and pay just before plane leaves. Bring your passport: there are 'immigration' checks by the police in Puerto, and sometimes in the waiting lounge in Managua; also, there is a customs check when returning from the coast by air to Managua.
Car It is not possible to rent a vehicle or bicycle in Puerto, but arrangements for a car and driver can be made (ask a taxi or at your *hospedaje*). Public bus service is available between Puerto and **Waspám** (see below) and from **Matagalpa** (14 hrs). Furthermore, Puerto is connected by road to **Managua**; however, this 559-km trip should only be attempted in the dry season (early Jan to mid-May) in a 4WD vehicle. With luck, it will take only 2-3 days (the road, almost all of it unpaved, is not bad from Managua to Siuna, but becomes very difficult after that); do not drive at night. If you drive back from Puerto to Managua, take the road out of town and turn left at the sign, SW Wawa.

Parque Nacional Saslaya *p966*
Air La Costeña flies daily to Siuna, reservations in Siuna, T263-2142.
Bus Daily from Siuna market to the park at 0500 and 0730, sometimes at 1100, US$2.25.
Car There are 2 road links from **Managua**: 1 through Matagalpa and Waslala; the other through Boaco, Muy Muy, Matiguás and Río Blanco, a very scenic 330-km drive, about 7 hrs by 4WD in the dry season; check on the security situation before starting out.

La Rosita is 70 km east of Siuna, and it is also possible to drive on through to **Puerto Cabezas**, although the road is in poor shape.

❶ Directory

Bluefields *p965*
Banks There are branches of Caley Dagnall and Banco de Nicaragua.

Puerto Cabezas *p966*
Hospital On the outskirts of town.

Costa Rica

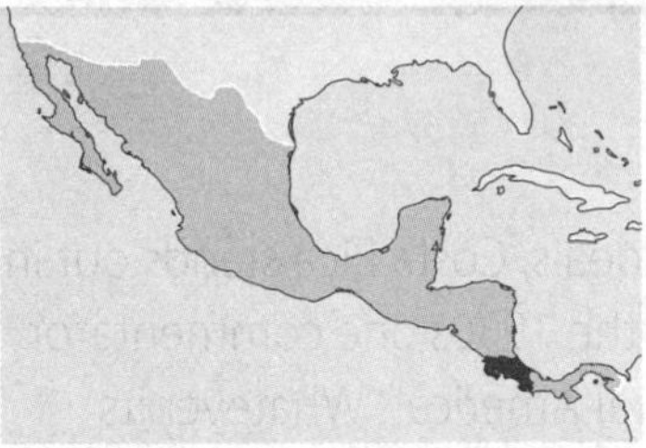

Footprint features

Introduction

A beacon of neutral democratic ideals, Costa Rica stands out in a turbulent region; as far back as the 1930s one commentator called it the "Switzerland of Central America". Whatever its political credentials and claims to neutrality, this country is undeniably a nature-lovers' paradise: you'll find moss-draped cloud forest on the slopes of Monteverde, where the red and green, sacred quetzal bird hides in the treetops and hummingbirds congregate to drink nectar; there's rainforest wilderness on the Osa Peninsula and remote turtle-nesting beaches on the north Atlantic and Pacific coasts. The country's volcanic peaks range from the gentle steaming lagoons of Irazú and Poás to the explosive Arenal, just outside Fortuna, where red-hot lava lights up the night sky.

Travellers looking to combine nature and comfort should head to the endless sand and surf beaches of the Nicoya Peninsula, Quepos and Parque Nacional Manuel Antonio, or to the off-beat strands of the Caribbean. For adrenaline junkies there's whitewater rafting, trekking and coast-to-coast mountain biking, and the chance to climb the barren *páramo* savannahs to the peak of Cerro Chirripó.

Historically Costa Rica has avoided the extremes of external influences. The Spanish found no mineral wealth here or compliant indigenous labour to work the land. Hard conditions and poverty forced both conquerors and conquered to work and live side by side. It was only with the arrival of wealth from the magic coffee bean in the Central Highlands that a landed gentry arose to conflict with the interests of a liberal merchant class. As a result, Costa Rica's architectural highlights are somewhat limited compared to much of the region, concentrated in the churches that dot the Central Highlands.

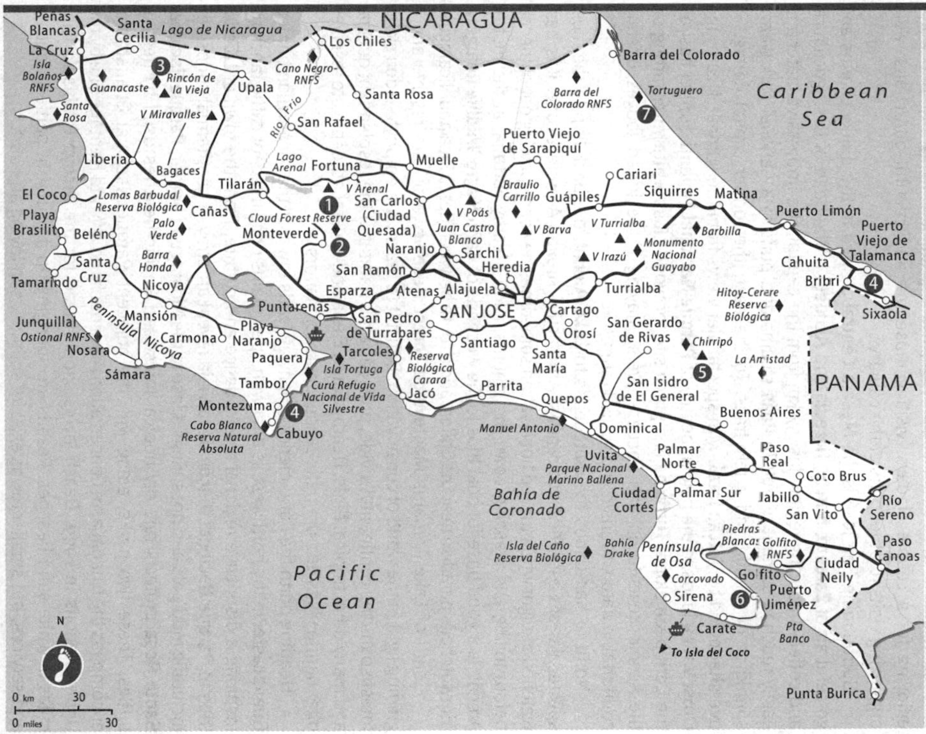

★ Don't miss...

1 **Volcán Arenal** Central America's most active volcano is an easy trip from nearby Fortuna, page 1020.

2 **Monteverde** Visit the cloud forests of Monteverde and Santa Elena: it's pleasant walking, the tropical birdlife is incredible and you can fly through the forest on the Sky Trek zip wire, page 1029.

3 **Parque Nacional Rincón de la Vieja** Spluttering mud and hot sulphur pools amidst dry tropical forest; great hiking, page 1034.

4 **Beachlife** Pick from either side: most popular Montezuma on the Nicoya Peninsula or Puerto Viejo de Talamanca on the Caribbean side, pages 1048 and 1093.

5 **Cerro Chirripó Grande** Hike to Costa Rica's highest point, page 1071.

6 **Puerto Jiménez and the Península de Osa** Wild West atmosphere and the most affordable way to get to the rainforest wilderness of the Osa Peninsula, page 1080.

7 **Parque Nacional Tortuguero** Explore the beach looking for nesting turtles at night and rainforest wildlife on the waterways by day, page 1091.

Planning your trip

Geographically Costa Rica is the smallest but two of the Central American republics (after El Salvador and Belize) and only Panama and Belize have fewer inhabitants. Despite these diminutive tendencies, the 'Rich Coast' has carved out a niche market as the nature destination in Central America with a well-developed network of national parks and biological reserves protecting large tracts of unspoilt tropical wilderness. Adventure activities are an option to sap untapped adrenaline and there are plenty of glorious beaches for lazing around and soaking up the perfect climate. Known throughout Latin America as the continent's purest democracy, Costa Rica celebrated a centenary of democracy in 1989. For Ticos, as the citizens are known, the country has the highest standard of living in Central America, the highest literacy rate (95%), the second-lowest birth rate (after Panama) and the greatest degree of economic and social advancement.

Where to go

Costa Rica's main attractions are its countryside, nature and wildlife. Although the country has a colourful history, most of the colonial heritage has been lost in earthquakes over the centuries. **San José**, the capital, is a lively city, and worth enjoying for a couple of days, visiting museums and cultural attractions while organizing visits to other parts of the country.

Surrounding San José is the **Meseta Central** draped in the quirky charms and graceful air of **Zarcero**, **Sarchí**, **Heredia** and **Alajuela** in the heart of this agricultural and coffee-producing region. Just 57 km from the capital, the impressive crater and easily reached summit of **Volcán Poás** steams and puffs in a national park with a sprinkling of wildlife and a few trails. To the east, the former capital Cártago is overshadowed by **Volcán Irazú**, with spectacular views from the summit. Nearby the **Orosí Valley** leads to the hidden beauty of **Parque Nacional Tapantí**. Further east on the Caribbean slope, **Turrialba** is a prime site for world-class **whitewater rafting** on the scenic Reventazón and Pacuare rivers, staying in secluded lodges offering comfortable nature tourism and guided tours.

North to San Carlos the route leads to **Lake Arenal**, the backdrop to the most spectacular of Costa Rica's volcanoes – the active **Arenal**. A perfect cone, it is best watched at night when the red hot lava can sometimes be seen spewing out of the top before rolling and crashing down the mountainside. Nearby **Fortuna**, at the foot of Arenal, is a good base for boat trips to the wetlands of **Caño Negro Wildlife Refuge**, a birdwatcher's paradise near **Los Chiles**, and a route between Costa Rica and Nicaragua.

South of Lake Arenal is **Monteverde Forest Reserve**, a private reserve and a guiding light in the world of conservation. Difficult to reach, the epiphyte-laden cloud forest spans the continental divide, protecting the habitat of the resplendent quetzal and many other tropical birds. Nearby **Santa Elena** and several other private reserves offer nature visits and dramatic canopy tours for visitors.

Heading north the Pan-American Highway leads towards the Nicaraguan border. **Guanacaste**, in the northwest, is drier with open plains once used for cattle ranching inspiring a distinctive regional music, dance and culture. From the town of **Liberia**, trips to **Parque Nacional Rincón de la Vieja** reveal an array of geothermal curiosities including mud pots and hot springs. Close to the Nicaraguan border, **Parque Nacional Santa Rosa** protects rare dry tropical forest and Pacific beaches used by nesting turtles. These two parks, along with the adjacent Parque Nacional Guanacaste, encompass the Guanacaste Conservation Area, declared a World Heritage Site by the United Nations in 1999. Beach lovers should head for the **Nicoya Peninsula** with miles of white-sand beaches. Resorts are springing up if you want parties, dancing and services, but smaller towns exist for solitude, sun loving and surf.

On the southern Pacific, beautiful beaches fringe the coast from the transport hub of **Puntarenas** through the surf hangout of **Jacó**, to the justifiably popular **Quepos** with nearby **Parque Nacional Manuel Antonio**, and the quieter spots around **Dominical** and **Playa Hermosa**. In the far south, the **Osa Peninsula** draws naturalists to the beauty of **Parque Nacional Corcovado**'s protected primary rainforest. It's tough, hot, sweaty and not for the faint hearted but you won't regret the effort.

The Pan-American Highway takes the high road down the southern spine of the country from San José to Panama through the spectacular mountain scenery of the Cordillera Talamanca. The country's highest mountain, **Cerro Chirripó** (3820 m), is climbed from **San Gerardo** near **San Isidro de El General**. Throughout the area, lodges catering for all budgets offer birdwatching and guided tours in the mountains, where the **Parque Nacional Chirripó** and neighbouring **Parque Internacional La Amistad** protect the country's largest area of virgin forest with the greatest biological diversity.

Puerto Limón is the main town on the Caribbean with a vibrancy and rhythm that shines through at carnival each October. While much of the region is used for banana cultivation, on the coast towards the Nicaraguan border is **Parque Nacional Tortuguero**, reached through a network of inland canals and waterways full to bursting with tropical birdlife, basking crocodiles, noisy monkeys and beaches used by nesting turtles.

South of Puerto Limón the road leads to Panama through the towns of **Cahuita, Puerto Viejo** and **Manzanillo.** Strong local cultures, a proud expatriate community and protected tropical rainforest attract backpackers and the discerning traveller to this forgotten corner of Costa Rica. It's also the best route to Bocas del Toro in Panama.

Suggested itinerary All traffic goes through San José so your visit will inevitably involve a few days in the capital. If travelling from Nicaragua, you have two options. Cross by land at Peñas Blancas to travel down the **Nicoya Peninsula** for a few days on the beach, or to **Liberia** to spend time clambering around the volcanic **Rincón de la Vieja**. The second option is to cross to Los Chiles for a trip to **Caño Negro Wildlife Reserve** before moving on to **Fortuna** and the explosive **Arenal**. The next stop might be a few days in Santa Elena to visit **Monteverde Cloud Forest.** From here, you could spend 10 days travelling down the Pacific coast, stopping at **Manuel Antonio National Park** and the **Osa Peninsula** in the south before heading to Panama. Alternatively, head to **San José** and after a few days, continue east to **Tortuguero** before heading south to **Cahuita, Puerto Viejo de Talamanca** and the border with Panama. At a push you would need two or three weeks in Costa Rica; four to five weeks would be much more relaxing.

When to go

In general, the best time to visit December to February. This is during the dry season (December to April), but before the temperatures really rise (March and April). Two main factors contribute to the local climatic conditions: altitude and location. The climate varies from the heat and humidity of the Caribbean and Atlantic lowlands, usually around the mid-20°Cs, falling to the warm temperate Meseta Central with chilly temperatures at greater heights – in the Cordillera Talamanca, the average temperature is below 16°C. On the Pacific side there is a well-defined wet season (May-November). The wetter Atlantic side has no specific dry season but there is less rainfall between March and September. Festivals are spread throughout the year, but the two biggest are Independence Day (September) and Día de la Raza (October).

Finding out more

Tourist offices

Instituto Costarricense de Turismo (**ICT**), underneath the Plaza de la Cultura, Calle 5, A Central-2, T223-1733, toll free 800-222-1090, www.visitcostarica.com. Mon-Fri 0900-1700. All tourist information is given here along with a good free map of San José and the country. See page 987 for more details. There is also an office in the main post office.

Useful websites

www.centralamerica.com Costa Rica's Travelnet, contains general information on tourist-related subjects. Recommended.

www.infocostarica.com A Yahoo-style search engine with information, links and maps for all things Costa Rican.

Language

Spanish is the first language, but you will always find someone who can speak some English in almost every place you visit. In the Caribbean the Afro-Caribbean population speak a regional creole dialect with elements of English.

Before you travel

Visas and immigration

Nationals of most EU nations, the US, Canada, Israel and Japan do not need visas for visits of up to 90 days. Nationals of Ireland, Australia and New Zealand do not need a visa, but visits are limited to 30 days. For more information check www.migracion.go.cr.

If you overstay the 30- or 90-day permitted period, you must report to Immigration before leaving the country. For longer stays ask for a Prórroga de Turismo at Migración (Immigration) in San José. For this you need four passport photos, an airline or bus ticket out of the country and proof of funds (for example traveller's cheques); you can apply for an extension of one or two months, at 300 colones per month. The paperwork takes three days. If you leave the country, you must wait 72 hours before returning, but it may be cheaper and easier to do this to get a new 30-day entry. Travel agents can arrange all extension and exit formalities for a small fee.

Monetary fines for overstaying your visa or entry permit have been eliminated; if you plan to stay longer, be aware that immigration officials have said that tourists who overstay their welcome more than once will be denied entry into the country on subsequent occasions – part of government efforts to crack down on 'perpetual tourists'.

An onward ticket (a bus ticket, which can be bought at the border immigration office or sometimes from the driver on Tica international buses, or a transatlantic ticket) is asked for, but can be refunded in San José with a loss of about US$3 on a US$20 ticket. Cashing in an air ticket is difficult because you may be asked to produce another ticket out of the country. Also, tourists may have to show at least US$300 in cash or traveller's cheques before being granted entry (especially if you have no onward ticket).

Costa Rican embassies and consulates

Australia, De la Sala House , 11th floor, 30 Clarence St , Sydney NSW: 2000, T9-261-1177.

Belize, 7 Shopping Center, Belmopan, T822-3801.

Canada, 325 Dalhouise St, Suite 407, Ottawa, ON, K1N 7G2, T613-562-2855.

El Salvador, 85 Av Sur y Calle Cuscatlán, 4415 Col Escalón, SS, T264-3865.

France, 78 Ave Emile Zola, 75015 Paris, T4-578-9696.

Germany, Dessauerstrasse 28-29 D-10963 Berlin, T30-2639-8990.

Guatemala, 1 Av 15-52, Zona 10, Guatemala City, T2363-1685.

Honduras, Residencial El Triángulo Lomas del Guijamo, Calle 3451, Tegucigalpa, T232-1768.

Israel, Rehov Diskin 13 Apt 1, Kiryat Wolfson, Jerusalem, 92473, T2-566-6197.

Italy, Via Bartolomeo Eustachio 22 Interno, 600161 Roma, T4425-1046.

Japan, Kowa Building, No 38, 9th floor, 901 4-12-24 Nishi Azabu Minato, Ku Tokio, 106-0031, T3-486-1812.

Mexico, Calle Río Poo 113, Col Cuauhtémoc between Río Pánuco and Lerma, México DF, T5525-7765.

Netherlands, Laan Copes van Cattenburch 46, 2585 GB, Den Haag, T70-354-0780.

Nicaragua, de la Estatua de Montoya, 2 c al lago y ½ c arriba (Callejón Zelaya), Managua, T266-2404.

Norway (covers **Sweden** and **Denmark**), Skippergat 33, 8th floor, 0154 Oslo, Noruega, T2233-0408.
Panama, Calle Samuel Lewis Edificio Plaza Omega, 3rd floor, Contiguo Santuario Nacional Panamá, T264-2980.
Spain, Paseo de la Castellana 164, 17-A, 28046 Madrid, T9-1345-9622.
Switzerland, Schwarztorstrasse 11, 3007 Berna, T031-372-7887.
UK (covers **Portugal**), Flat 1, 14 Lancaster Gate, London W2 3LH, T020-7706-8844.
USA, 2112-S St, North West Washington DC 20008, T202-234-2945.
More embassy addresses are listed at www.rree.go.cr.

What to take

Climate is generally very comfortable in Costa Rica limiting the need for specialist clothing. If choosing to go to the higher altitudes, Chirripó for example, be sure to take warm clothing and rain gear. For jungle treks take long-sleeved shirts and trousers that will protect you from insect bites.

Customs

Duty-free allowances are 500 g of manufactured tobacco, 2 kg of chocolate and 5 litres of liquor. Any amount of foreign or local currency may be taken in or out, but amounts over US$10,000 must be declared. Cameras (up to six rolls of film), binoculars, camping equipment, laptop computers and other portable items of personal/professional/leisure use are free of duty.

Money

Currency → *US$1–425 colones.*

The unit is the colón which devalues annually at a rate of about 10%. Small, golden-coloured coins are minted for 5, 10, 25, 50, 100 and 500 colones. Notes in use are for 1000, 2000, 5000 and 10,000 colones. US dollars are widely accepted but don't depend on being able to use them.

Exchange

US dollars can be exchanged in most banks. For bank drafts and transfers commission may be charged. Banks may charge whatever commission they please on traveller's cheques (some private banks charge commission on US dollars cash) and other services; shop around for the best deal. General opening times: Monday to Friday 0900-1500, although more banks are starting to stay open later and several open on Saturdays. Most tourist and first-class hotels will change dollars and traveller's cheques for guests only; the same applies in restaurants and shops if you buy something. Hardly anyone will change damaged US dollar notes. All state-run banks and some private banks will change euro, but it is almost impossible to exchange any other major currency in Costa Rica. Most banks will process cash advances on Visa/MasterCard. ATMs which accept international Visa and/or MasterCard are widely available at most banks, and in shopping malls and at San José airport. However, travellers report that Visa is more acceptable than MasterCard. Credomatic handles all credit card billings; they will not accept a credit card charge that does not have the imprint of the borrower's card plus an original signature. This is the result of fraud, but it makes it difficult to book tours or accommodation over the phone.

For card loss or theft: MasterCard/Visa T0800-011-0184; AMEX T0800 012-3211.

Cost of living and travelling

Costa Rica is more expensive than countries to the north. While transport is reasonably cheap, you get less for your money in the hotels. You will be able to survive on US$30 a day, but that does not allow for much in the way of activities.

Getting there

Air

From Europe From most European cities flights connect in the US at Miami, Houston, Dallas and many others with **American Airlines, Continental** and **Grupo Taca.** There are direct charter flights in season from several European cities including Frankfurt (**Condor**), with plans for direct flights from Madrid and Milan.

From North America Flights from North America are many and varied (more than 20 each week), again some stop in Miami so check if a direct flight is important. Departure points include: Atlanta, Boston, Chicago, Dallas, Houston, Los Angeles, Miami, New York, Orlando, San Francisco, Toronto, Washington DC.

Daniel Oduber International Airport, near Liberia, receives flights throughout the year and is conveniently located just 30 minutes from some of Guanacaste's finest beaches. Charter specials, available from time to time, include New York-Costa Rica US$99. Enquire at travel agents for details.

From South America Flights from South American cities include Bogotá (**Copa, Grupo Taca**), Cali (**SAM, Grupo Taca**), Caracas (**Grupo Taca**), Cartagena (**SAM**), Guayaquil (**Grupo Taca**), Lima (**Grupo Taca**), Quito (**Grupo Taca**) and Santiago (**Grupo Taca**).

From Central America The **Grupo Taca** alliance provides connections with all capitals and several of the more popular tourist destinations including Cancún, Guatemala City (also **United** and **Copa**), Managua (**Copa**), Mexico City (also **Mexicana, United**), Panama City (**Copa**), San Pedro Sula, San Salvador (**Copa**) and Tegucigalpa.

From the Caribbean There are a couple of flights a week to Havana (**Cubana, Grupo Taca**) and regular charters to San Andrés, Colombia (**SAM**). Also flights to Santo Domingo (**Copa**).

Road

Road links to the north are on the Pan-American Highway at Peñas Blancas with immigration services and buses connecting to and from Nicaragua. It is possible to cross the northern border close to Los Chiles making the journey by land or boat to San Carlos. Crossing the border on the North Pacific is possible but immigration services are non-existent and transportation is irregular.

The main crossing to Panama at Paso Canoas is straightforward and problem free. On the Caribbean coast Sixaola links with the Panamian town of Guabito over the old banana bridge. Immigration services on both sides but only in normal office hours.

Sea

The main ports for international cargo vessels are **Puerto Limón,** with regular sailings to and from Europe, and **Caldera,** on the central Pacific coast. Contact shipping agents, of which there are many, in Puerto Limón and San José for details. Cruise vessels arrive at Caldera, Puntarenas and Puerto Limón, normally stopping for little more than 24 hours.

Touching down

Airport information and departure tax

The main international airport is at San José (see page 986). Departure tax is a flat rate of US$26 per person, regardless of nationality or immigration status, when leaving by

Touching down

Business hours Mon-Fri 0900-1200, 1400-1730 (1600 government offices), Sat 0800-1200. Shops: Mon-Sat 0800-1200, 1300-1800 (most stay open during lunch hour).
Emergency numbers Police: T117/127. Fire: T118. Medical (Red Cross): T128. (Police, Fire, Red Cross emergencies/bilingual operators: T911). Information about national parks: T192.
Official time 6 hrs behind GMT.
Telephone Country code T+506.
Voltage 110, 60 cycles, AC (US-syle flat-pin plugs).

air. Exit taxes, by air or land, and legislation regarding visa extensions, are subject to frequent change and travellers should check these details as near to the time of travelling as possible.

Local customs and laws

You must carry your passport (or a photocopy) with you at all times.

Tipping A 10% service charge is automatically added to restaurant and hotel bills, as well as a 13% sales tax.

Safety

Generally speaking, Costa Rica is very safe but, as ever, there are some problem areas. Look after your belongings in hotels – use the safe. If hiring a car do not leave valuables in the vehicle and leave nothing unattended on beaches or buses. Theft (pickpockets, grab-and-run thieves and muggings) is on the increase in San José, especially in the centre, in the market, at the Coca Cola bus station, in the barrios of Cuba, Cristo Rey, México, 15 de Setiembre and León XIII. Keep away from these areas at night and on Sunday, when few people are around as we have received reports of violent robberies. Street gangs, known as *chapulines*, are mostly kids. The police do seem to be trying to tackle the problem but help yourself by avoiding potentially dangerous situations.

Getting around

Air

Airports There are domestic airports, with scheduled services provided by **Sansa** or **NatureAir** at Barra Colorado, Carate, Carrillo-Sámara, Coto 47, Drake Bay, Golfito, Liberia, La Fortuna, Limón, Nosara Beach, Palmar Sur, Puerto Jiménez, Punta Islita, Quepos, Tamarindo, Tambor and Tortuguero. Several charter companies also operate out of San José. ▸▸ *For details see page 998.*

Road

Costa Rica has a total of 35,700 km of roads of which 7500 km are paved. The Pan-American Highway runs the length of the country, from the Nicaraguan to the Panamanian borders. A new bridge over the Tempisque River has drastically reduced travel time to the beaches of the Nicoya Peninsula. A highway has been built from Orotina to Caldera, a new port on the Gulf of Nicoya, which has replaced Puntarenas as the principal Pacific port, and a highway is being built from Orotina to Ciudad Colón. Another road from Orotina to Quepos has improved access to the Pacific beaches. This is yet to be extended as far as Domincal, but continuing further south from Dominical to Ciudad Cortés, the road is generally good. All four-lane roads into San José are toll roads. It is illegal to ride in a car or taxi without wearing seatbelts.

Bus The good road network supports a regular bus service that covers most parts of the country. Frequency declines with popularity but you can get to most places with road access eventually. San José is the main hub for buses, although you can skip down the Pacific coast by making connections at Puntarenas. Coming from Nicaragua, direct to Arenal, requires cutting in and travelling through Tilaran.

Two new shuttle bus companies, **Interbus**, T283-5573, www.interbusonline.com, and **Fantasy Tours/GrayLine**, T220-2126, www.graylinecostarica.com, offer transport from the capital to dozens of beach and tourism destinations in comfortable a/c minibuses, bilingual drivers, hotel pick-up, tickets US$17-38 one way.

Car With a few precautions, driving in Costa Rica allows for greater flexibility when travelling. Many of the nature parks are in remote areas; 4WD and high-clearance is recommended and sometimes essential; in the wet season some roads will be impassable. Always ask locals or bus drivers what the state of the road is before embarking on a journey. Do not assume that if the buses are running, a car can get through too.

Tourists who enter by car or motorcycle pay US$10 road tax, including mandatory insurance, and can keep their cars for an initial period of 90 days. This can be extended for a total period of six months, for about US$10 per extra month, at the **Instituto Costarricense de Turismo**, or at the **Customs office** ⓘ *Av 3, Calle 14*, if you take your passport, car entry permit, and a piece of stamped paper (*papel sellado*) obtainable at any bookshop. If you intend to drive in the country for more than three months, you are required to apply for a Costa Rican Driver's Licence at Avenida 18, Calle 5, San José. Cars are fumigated on entry: exterior US$8. If you have an accident while in the country do not move the vehicle and immediately contact **Policía de Tránsito** ⓘ *San José, T800-TRANSITO, 222-9330 or 222-9245.*

Driving at night is not recommended.

Car hire Renting a car can be a surprisingly economical way to travel if you can form a group and split the costs. As with all rentals, check your vehicle carefully as the company will try to claim for the smallest of 'damages'. Most leases do not allow the use of a normal car off paved roads. Always make sure the spare tyre is in good order, as holes are frequent. You can have tyres fixed at any garage for about US$2 in 30 minutes. Guideline prices: smallest economy car US$33-47 per day includes unlimited mileage or US$198-294 per week; 4WD vehicle costs US$48-150 per day, US$288-900 per week, including unlimited mileage. Driver's licence from home and credit card generally required. Collision damage waiver (CDW) insurance is mandatory and costs an extra US$10-17 per day; excess is between US$750 and US$1500. Cash deposits or credit card charges range from US$800 to US$1800, so check you have sufficient credit. If you plan to drop off a hired car somewhere other than where you picked it up, check with several firms for their charges: **Elegante**, **Ada** and **National** appear to have the lowest drop-off fees. Insurance will not cover broken windscreens, driving on unsurfaced roads or damaged tyres.

Discounts are available during the 'Green Season', (May-November).

Security Never leave anything in a hired car and never leave your car on the street, even in daylight. Secure parking lots are available in most cities, roughly US$1.25 per hour. Regular reports of break-ins at national parks and other popular tourism areas.

Fuel Main fuel stations have regular (unleaded) US$1.15 and diesel US$0.65 per litre; super gasoline (unleaded) is available throughout the country, US$0.69 (264 colones) per litre. Prices are regulated by the government.

Road tolls for passenger cars are between US$0.20 and US$0.40. The following are 75 colones: San José-San José airport; San José-Santa Ana; San José-Cártago. All have a voluntary 'fast' lane for motorists to pay with 100-colón coin; the 25-colón 'donation' goes towards road repairs. 150 colones: San José-Guápiles. The San José-Cártago and San José-Santa Ana toll booths have automatic machines accepting 5, 10, 20 colón coins (silver ones only).

Cycling Cycling is easier in Costa Rica than elsewhere in Central America; there is less heavy traffic and it is generally more 'cyclist friendly'. However, paving is thin and soon deteriorates; look out for cracks and potholes, which bring traffic to a crawl. The prevailing wind is from the northeast so, if making an extensive tour, travelling in the direction of Panama is slightly more favourable.

Recommended reading for all users: Baker's *The Essential Road Guide to Costa Rica*, with detailed strip maps, kilometre by kilometre road logs, motoring information plus San José map and bus guide (Bill Baker, Apdo 1185-1011, San José). Cycle shops have sprung up around the country offering parts and repair services.

! Motorcyclists must wear helmets by law.

Hitchhiking Generally easy and safe by day, but take the usual precautions.

Sea

Ferries serve the southern section of the Nicoya Peninsula from Puntarenas. The Osa Peninsula has a regular ferry service linking Golfito and Puerto Jiménez, and Bahía Drake is reached on boats from Sierpe. Boats travel to Tortuguero from Moín, close to Puerto Limón, and from Cariari, north of Guápiles.

Train

All commercial lines are closed. For the truly devoted there is talk of reintroducing a tourist 'banana' train from Siquirres to Matina on the Caribbean side. Ask locally for details. A tourist train (weekends) from San José to the Pacific, departing from Estación del Pacífico, 600 m south of Parque Central, at 0600, travelling to Caldera with a stop in Orotina; returns at 1500. Tickets (US$25 return) must be purchased Monday-Wednesday for following weekend. The tours are in refurbished 1940s German wagons. Contact **America Travel,** T233-3300, www.ticotraintour.com.

Maps

The **Instituto Geográfico Nacional,** Calle 9, Avenida 20-22, at the Ministry of Public Works and Transport in San José, supplies good topographical maps for walkers, 0730-1600. **ITM** has a 1:500,000 travel map of Costa Rica, available at bookstores throughout the country. Maps are also available in San José at **7th Street Books,** Calle 7, Avenida 1 and Central, T256-8251, **Universal,** Avenida Central, Calle 1 and Central, T222-2222, and **Lehmann,** Avenida Central, Calle 1-3, T223-1212.

Sleeping

Accommodation in Costa Rica favours couples and groups – the price of a single room is often the same as a double, and the price of a room for four is often less than double the price for two. So if you can get in a group, the cost per person falls considerably. Accommodation prices during the 'green' season (May to November), are generally much lower. A 13% sales tax plus 3.39% tourism tax (total 16.39%) are added to the basic price of hotel rooms. A deposit is advised at the more expensive hotels in San José, especially in the high season (December to April), to guarantee reservations. If you arrive late at night in the high season, even a guaranteed reservation may not be kept.

The **Costa Rica Bed & Breakfast Group**, which has 300 bed and breakfast inns and small hotels around the country in its membership, helps with reservations. The **Costa Rican Chamber of Hotels** ⓘ *T248-0990, www.costaricanhotels.com*, provides information about its members (mostly larger hotels) and an online reservation system. The **Costa Rican Tourist Board** ⓘ *www.turismo-sostenible.co.cr*, has introduced a fledgling eco-rating system for hotels, an encouraging indicator of progress.

Camping opportunities in Costa Rica are limited with few offical campsites. It is possible to camp in some national parks. Conact the Fundación de Parques Nacionales in San José for details (see Nature tourism, below).

Eating and drinking

Local cuisine

Sodas (small restaurants) serve local food, which is worth trying. Very common is *casado*, a cheap lunch which includes rice, beans, stewed beef or fish, fried plantain and cabbage. *Olla de carne* is a soup of beef, plantain, corn, yucca, *ñampi* and *chayote* (local vegetables). *Sopa negra* is made with black beans, and comes with a poached egg in it; *picadillo* is another meat and vegetable stew. Snacks are popular: *gallos* (filled tortillas), *tortas* (containing meat and vegetables), *arreglados* (bread filled with the same) and *empanadas*. *Pan de yuca* is a speciality, available from stalls in San José centre. For breakfast, try *gallo pinto* (rice and beans) with *natilla* (a slightly sour cream). Best ice cream can be found in Pops shops. In general, eating out in Costa Rica is more expensive than elsewhere in Central America.

Sales tax of 13% plus 10% service charge are added to restaurant bills.

Drink

There are many types of cold drink, made either from fresh fruit, or milk drinks with fruit (*batidos*) or cereal flour whisked with ice cubes. Drinks are often sugared well beyond North American or European tastes (ask for *poco azúcar*). The fruits range from the familiar to the exotic; others include *cebada* (barley flour), *pinolillo* (roasted corn), *horchata* (rice flour with cinnamon), *chan*, which according to Michael Brisco is 'perhaps the most unusual, looking like mouldy frogspawn and tasting of penicillin'. All these drinks cost the same as, or less than, bottled fizzy products. Excellent coffee. Local beers are Bavaria, Pilsen, Imperial, Rock Ice and Kaiser (which is non-alcoholic).

Festivals and events

1 Jan New Year's Day.
19 Mar St Joseph.
Mar/Apr Nearly everyone is on holiday at Easter; everywhere is shut on Thu, Fri and Sun, and many shops close on Sat and most of the previous week as well.
11 Apr Battle of Rivas.
1 May Labour Day.
Jun Corpus Christi.
29 Jun St Peter and St Paul.
25 Jul Guanacaste Day.
2 Aug Virgin of Los Angeles.
15 Aug Mothers' Day.
15 Sep Independence Day.
12 Oct Día de la Raza (Columbus Day). The main festival is Carnival in Puerto Limón, the week before and after Columbus Day, when the focus of the country for once dwells on the country's largest Caribbean town. There's music, dance, street processions and general festivities. Hotels book up, but it's definitely worth making the effort to go.
8 Dec Immaculate Conception.
25 Dec Christmas Day.
28-31 Dec San José only.

Shopping

The best buys are wooden items, ceramics and leather handicrafts. Many wooden handicrafts are made of rainforest hardwoods and deforestation is a critical problem. Coffee should have 'puro' on the packet or it may contain sugar or other additives.

Sport and activities

Nature tourism

Tourists particularly enjoy the many well-kept and well-guarded national parks and nature reserves which protect some samples of the extraordinarily varied Costa Rican ecosystems. The variety is daunting and includes some of the last patches of dry tropical forest in the Parque Nacional Santa Rosa, the cloud forest of Monteverde and the Talamanca Mountains and nine active volcanoes including Rincón de la Vieja, Poás, Irazú and of course Arenal. There is a standard entrance fee of US$7 for all national parks. Birdwatchers and butterfly lovers have long flocked to Costa Rica to see some of the 850 or so species of birds (the whole of the US counts about 800) and untold varieties of butterflies. All of these can best be seen in the parks, together with monkeys, deer, coyotes, armadillos, anteaters, turtles, coatis, raccoons, snakes, wild pigs, and, more rarely, wild cats and tapirs.

Manuel Antonio is closed on Monday; Cabo Blanco is closed on Monday and Tuesday.

Although the national parks and other privately owned reserves are a main tourist attraction, many are in remote areas and not easy to get to on public transport; buses or coaches that do go tend to stay for a short time. There is a tendency for tour companies to dominate the National Park 'market' to the exclusion of other public transport. For tight budgets, try making up a party with others and sharing taxis or hiring a car.

The **Sistema Nacional de Areas de Conservación** (SINAC) ⓘ *T283-8000, PO Box 10104-1000, San José, www.costarica-nationalparks.com*, administers the National Park System (write in advance or call). For information and permits to visit and/or camp or conduct research in the parks apply to **Fundación de Parques Nacionales** (**FPN**) ⓘ *Av 15, San José, T257-2239, Mon-Fri 0800-1200, 1300-1700*, 300 m north and 150 m east of Santa Teresita Church, Barrio Escalante, between Calles 23-25. Check in advance if your trip depends on gaining entrance. If you want to work as a volunteer in the parks, at US$12 per day for lodging and food, contact the **Asociación de Voluntarios** (**ASVO**) ⓘ *Av 1, Calle 10-12, San José, T233-4989, www.asvocr.com*. Bilingual tourist information and/or telephone numbers for individual national park offices is available by dialling T192.

Watersports

The rivers of Costa Rica have proved to be highly popular for **whitewater rafting**, kayaking and canoeing, both for the thrill of the rapids and the wildlife interest of the quieter sections. The five most commonly run rivers are the Reventazón (and the Pascua section of it), Pacuare, Corobicí, Sarapiquí and El General. You can do a day trip but to reach the Class IV and V rapids you usually have to take two to three days. The Reventazón is perhaps the most accessible but the Pacuare has been recommended as a more beautiful experience. The Corobicí is slow and popular with birdwatchers. **Ríos Tropicales** (see page 998) has been recommended.

For reasons of safety heavy rain may cause cancellations, so you need flexibility in your plans.

There is **swimming** on both Atlantic and Pacific coasts. Offshore, **sea kayaking** is increasingly popular. **Snorkelling** and **scuba diving** are offered by several hotels and most beach tour offices, but you have to pick your spot carefully. Anywhere near a river will suffer from poor visibility and the coral reef has died in many places because of agricultural pollutants washed downstream, particularly on the Caribbean coast. Generally, on the Caribbean side, you can see wrecks and coral reefs, particularly in the southeast towards the Panamanian border, while on the Pacific side you see large pelagics and sportfish. Liveaboard dive boats head for the islands of Caño and Isla del Coco. Divers are not permitted in national parks or reserves, nor within 500 m of the protected sea turtle zone north of Parque Nacional Tortuguero. **Windsurfing** is good along the Pacific coast, particularly in the bay close to La Cruz and world class on Lake Arenal, particularly the west end. Lots of hotels have equipment for hire and operators in San José will know where the best conditions prevail at any time. Be careful of obstacles in the water along rocky coastlines and near river mouths. **Surfing** is popular on the Pacific and southern Caribbean beaches, attracting professionals who follow storm surges along the coast. Beginners can take classes in some resorts like Tamarindo, Jacó and Dominical, and proficient surfers can get advice on waves from surf shops in these areas.

For **sport fishing**, sailfish and marlin are targeted off the Pacific; snook and tarpon are caught in the Caribbean, the largest snook being found in September and October, mostly north of Limón (where there are fishing lodges), but also towards Panama. Exciting it may be, cheap it is not. Anglers can save money in groups, since it is usually the same cost to rent a boat for one or four.

Other sports

Football (soccer) is the national sport (played every Sunday at 1100, September to May, at the Saprissa Stadium). **Mountain biking** is popular throughout most parts of the country with options to simply rent the bike and push out on your own, or join a guided trip. There are several **golf** courses close to the capital, and a growing number on the Nicoya Peninsula and at **Los Sueños Marriott**, near Jacó. The Meseta is good country for **horse riding**; horses can be hired by arrangement directly with owners. Most fiestas end with **bullfighting** in the squares, with no horses used. Bullfights are held in San José during the Christmas period. There is no kill and spectators are permitted to enter the ring to chase, and be chased by, the bull. If you're looking for a last big-spending celebration, **hot-air balloon rides** take you over the trees near Arenal Volcano and also the Turrialba region. Contact **Serendipity Adventures** ⓣ *T635-2325, www.serendipity adventures.com.* And the final suggestion is to jump off a bridge... **Bungee jumping**, that is, off the Colorado bridge, close to Grecia in the Meseta Central (see page 997).

Health

Drinking water is safe in all major towns; elsewhere it should be boiled, but bottled water is widely available. Intestinal disorders are prevalent in the lowlands although Chagas disease is now rare. Malaria is on the increase; malaria prophylaxis is advised for visitors to the lowlands, especially near the Nicaraguan and Panama border. If visiting jungle areas be prepared for insect bites with repellent and appropriate clothing. Dengue fever has been recorded throughout the country, mostly in coastal cities. Uncooked foods should not be eaten. The standards of health and hygiene are among the best in Latin America.

Keeping in touch

Communications

Internet Internet cafés are popular and connections in the towns tend to be good. Prices vary but a rough guide is US$1 for one hour in the Central Valley; twice that in beach towns and tourism areas. Rates are lower around colleges and universities.

Post Airmail letters to **Europe** cost 130 c, postcards 115 c; to **North/South America**, letters 110 c, 95 c for postcards; to **Australia**, **Africa** and **Asia**, letters 170 c, postcards 140 c. *Expreso* letters, 140 c extra, several days quicker to USA and North Europe. Registered mail, 400 c. Airmail takes 5 to 10 days. All parcels sent out of the country by foreigners must be taken open to the post office for clearance. *Lista de Correos*, charges 75 c per letter and will keep them for four weeks. For information call **Correos de Costa Rica** ⓘ *T800-900-2000.*

Telephone Long-distance telephone services are handled by the state-run **Instituto Costarricense de Electricidad** (ICE) and its subsidiary **Radiográfica Costarricense SA** (RACSA) ⓘ *Telecommunications Centre, A 5, Calle 1, San José, Mon-Fri 0800-1900, Sat 0800-1200, closed Sun.*

Standard rates to **US**, **Canada**, **Mexico** and **South America** are US$0.45 a minute; **Panama** is US$0.40 and **Europe** and the rest of the world (except Central America and Belize) US$0.60 a minute if you dial direct; operator-assisted calls cost up to US$3.12 a minute. Only variable rates are to **Central America**: standard rates between 0700 and 1900 (US$0.40 a minute), reduced between 1900 and 2200 (US$0.35) and reduced again between 2200 and 0700 and during the weekend (US$0.28). Add 13% sales tax.

Public phones are maddening to use, various kinds available: some use 10 and 20 colón silver coins, others use 50 colón gold coins, and still others employ at least two types of calling cards, but not interchangeably. The 199 cards are recommended, but it's often easiest to call collect inside (T110) and outside (T116) the country. Assistance for hearing impaired (Spanish only) is T137.

Phone cards with 'Personal Identification Numbers' are available for between US$0.80 and US$10. These can be used for national and international direct dialling from a private phone. Calls abroad can be made from phone booths; collect calls abroad may be made from special booths in the RACSA office, or from any booth nationwide if you dial T116 for connection with the international operator (T175 for collect calls to the USA). Phone cards can be used. Dial T124 for international information. Country Direct Dialling Codes are: To the **USA**: **MCI/World Phone** 0800-012-2222, **AT&T** 0800-0114-114, **Sprint/GlobalOne** 0800-013-0123, **Worldcom** 0800-014-4444.

Call T911 for emergencies; operator T113, international operator T116.

Media

Newspapers and magazines The best San José morning papers are *La Nación* (www.nacion.co.cr) and business-orientated *La República* (www.larepublica.net); there is also *Al Día*, *El Heraldo*, *Diario Extra* (the largest circulating daily) and *La Prensa Libre* (www.prensalibre.co.cr). *La Gaceta* is the official government daily paper. The *Tico Times* (www.ticotimes.net) is out on Fridays, San José, which is great for news in English with classifieds.

Television and Radio Six local TV stations, many MW/FM radio stations throughout the country. Local **Voz de América** (VOA) station. **Radio Dos** (95.5 FM) and **Rock Radio** (107.5 FM) have English-language DJs and music. Many hotels and private homes receive one of the four TV stations offering direct, live, 24-hour satellite TV from the USA. All US cable TV can be received in San José.

San José

→ Colour map 7, B3. Population: 968,367. Altitude: 1150 m.

Nestled in a broad, fertile valley producing coffee and sugar-cane, San José was founded in 1737 and became capital in 1823 after struggles for regional ascendency between competing towns of the Central Valley. Frequent earthquakes have destroyed most of the colonial buildings and the modern replacements do little to inspire. But, like any city, if you can get under the skin, the mix of museums and general attractions make it worth a couple of days stay. ▸▸ *For Sleeping, Eating and other listings, see pages 991-1003.*

Ins and outs

Getting there

Aeropuerto Internacional Juan Santamaría is 16 km from the centre along a good *autopista*. A taxi costs US$10-12 and efficient buses running every 10 minutes leave from outside the terminal building for San José city centre. Long-distance buses have their terminals scattered round town (see map) but the majority are close to the Coca Cola Terminal, in the central west of the city. Bus connections in Costa Rica and with other Central American countries are very good.

Getting around

For the most part the city conforms to a grid systems – avenidas run east-west; calles north-south. Avenidas to the north of Avenida Central are given odd numbers; those to the south even numbers. Calles to the west of Calle Central are even-numbered; those to the east are odd-numbered. The three main streets, Avenida Central, Avenida 2 and the intersecting Calle Central, encompass the business centre. The main shops are along Avenida Central, a pleasant downtown stroll in the section closed to traffic.

Some people find the narrow streets too heavily polluted with exhaust fumes preferring to stay in the suburbs of Escazú, Alajuela or Heredia using regular bus services to make the journey to town. It's probably a good choice if you've already visited San José, but if it's your first time in the capital you should give it a try for a

San José

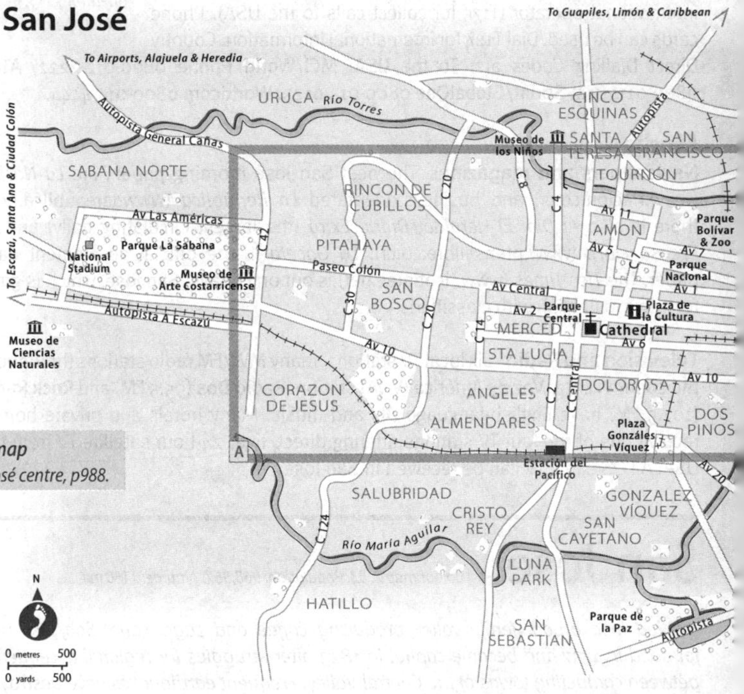

Detail map
A San José centre, p988.

couple of days at least. A circular bus route travels along Avenida 3 out to La Sabana and back making a useful circuit and an impromptu city tour. Taxis can be ordered by phone or hailed in the street; they are red are legally required to have meters and use them. Traffic is congested especially between 0700 and 2000, so driving in the city centre is best avoided. If you do drive, watch out for no-parking zones. Seven blocks of the Avenida Central, from Banco Central running east to Plaza de la Cultura, are closed to traffic and most of the streets downtown are one-way streets.

Few buildings have numbers, so find out the nearest cross-street when getting directions; 200 m means two blocks.

Tourist information

Instituto Costarricense de Turismo ⓘ *under Plaza de la Cultura, Calle 5, Av Central-2, T223-1733, Mon-Fri 0900-1700*. Also at Juan Santamaría airport (very helpful, will check hotels for you), the main post office and at borders. Free road maps of Costa Rica, San José and the metropolitan area and public transport timetables available. **Otec** ⓘ *Calle 3, Av 1-3, Edif Ferenz, T256-0633, www.otec.co.cr, Apdo 323-1002 San José*, the youth and student travel office, is extremely helpful, and offers good special discounts for ISTC and FIYTO members.

Student cards give reductions in most museums.

Best time to visit

The climate is comfortable, with temperatures between 15° and 26°C, though the evenings can be chilly. The rainy season lasts roughly from May to November; the rest of the year it's mainly dry.

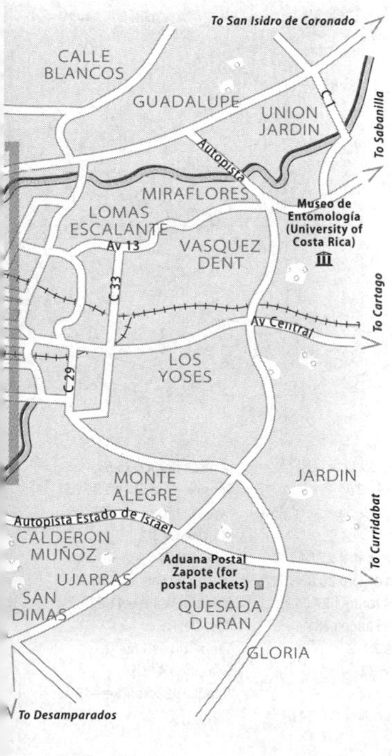

Sights

Many of the most interesting public buildings are near the intersection of Avenida Central and Calle Central. The **Teatro Nacional** ⓘ *just off Av 2, on Calle 3, T221-1329 (tours), T221-5341 (event and ticket information), Mon-Sat 0900-1700, US$3*, built in 1897, has marble staircases, statues, frescoes and foyer decorated in gold with Venetian plate mirrors. It has a coffee bar run by **Café Britt** and guided tours. Nearby is **Plaza de la Cultura** ⓘ *Av Central, Calle 3-5*, which, in addition to being a great place for people-watching, hosts public concerts. The recently renovated **Museo de Oro** ⓘ *entrance is off Calle 5, T243-4202, www.museosdelbancocentral.org, Tue-Sun 0930-1700, US$6, children US$1*, has a booty of golden treasure buried beneath the Plaza de la Cultura. Fine golden figures of frogs, spiders, raptors and other creatures glisten in this spectacular Pre-Columbian gold museum sponsored by the **Banco Central**. Also here is the **Museo Numismático** with an exhibition on the history of Costa Rican money.

The **Museo Nacional** ⓘ Calle *17, Av Central-2, T257-1433, Tue-Sat 0830-1600, Sun 0900-1600, US$4, children and students with ID free*, east from the Plaza de la Cultura, has interesting displays on archaeology, anthropology, national history, some gold and ex-President Arias' Nobel Peace Prize. Information is in Spanish and English. Facing it is the **Plaza de la Democracia**, a concrete cascade built to mark the November 1989 centenary of Costa Rican democracy. The **Palacio Nacional** ⓘ *Av Central, Calle 15*, is home of the Legislative Assembly; any visitor can attend debates, sessions start at 1600.

Two blocks north of the Museo Nacional is the **Parque Nacional**, with a grandiloquent bronze monument representing the five Central American republics ousting the filibuster William Walker (see Nicaragua, History section) and the abolition of slavery in Central America. There is also a statue donated by the

San José centre

Sleeping 🛏
Aurola Holiday Inn **2** *B5*
Avenida Segunda **3** *C5*
Bienvenido **5** *B3*
Boston **6** *C4*
Britannia **7** *A5*
CACTS **8** *B2*
Casa Ridgway **9** *C6*
Centroamericano **10** *B4*
Cinco Hormigas Rojas **11** *B6*
Costa Rica Backpackers **13** *C6*
Del Rey **14** *B5*
Diana's Inn **15** *B5*
Don Carlos **17** *B5*
Fleur de Lys **20** *C5*
Fortuna **21** *C4*
Galileo Backpackers' Hostel **22** *B1*
Gaudy's Backpackers' Hostel **23** *A1*
Gran Imperial **25** *B4*
Grano de Oro **26** *B2*
Hostal Toruma **27** *C6*
Hostel Pangea **28** *A5*
Joluva **29** *A5*
Marlyn **32** *A4*
Otoya **33** *B4*
Pensión América **34** *B4*
Pensión Boruca **35** *B3*
Pensión de la Cuesta **36** *B5*
Pensión Musoc **37** *B3*
Príncipe *C4* **38**
Rialto **39** *B4*
Rincón de San José **40** *B6*
Ritmo del Caribe **41** *B2*
Rosa del Paseo **42** *B2*
Santo Tomás **1** *B5*
Tica Linda **44** *C5*
Tranquilo Backpackers **45** *A5*

Sandinista Government of Nicaragua to the people of Costa Rica. To the north of the park is the **Biblioteca Nacional**. East of the library is the new **Museo de Formas, Espacio y Sonidos** ⓘ *Calle 17, Av 3-7, T222-9462, Tue-Fri 0930-1600, US$1, students and children free, wheelchair accessible, signs in Braille*, housed in the old Atlantic Railway Station. In the old liquor factory west of the Biblioteca Nacional, now the Centro Nacional de la Cultura, is the **Museo de Arte y Diseño Contemporáneo** ⓘ *Av 3, Calle 15-17, T257-7202, Tue-Sat 1000-1700, US$3, students with ID US$0.50.*

One of the best museums in the city is the recently renovated **Museo del Jade Fidel Tristan** ⓘ *INS building 11th floor, Av 7, Calle 9-13, T287-6034, Mon-Fri 0830-1530, US$3*, with the largest collection of jade carvings in Central America, pottery and sculpture. With explanations in Spanish and English, and topped off with a beautiful view over the city, it's a fascinating museum and shouldn't be missed.

Eating

Ana Italiana **1** *B2*
Café Mundo **2** *B6*
Café Parisienne **3** *B5*
Churrería Manolo **4** *B4*
El Cuartel de la Boca del Monte **19** *B6*
Gran Diamante **5** *B4*
La Bastille **6** *B2*
La Esquina del Café **7** *A5*
La Puriscaleña **8** *B4*
La Vasconia **9** *B5*
Lubnan **10** *B2*
Machu Picchu **11** *B2*
Morazán **12** *B5*
Pollo a la Leña **13** *B5*
Soda Tapia **14** *B1*
Tin Jo **15** *C5*
Vishnu **16** *B5*

Bars & clubs

Chelle's **17** *B5*
Disco Salsa 54 **18** *B5*
Nashville South **20** *B5*
Risas **21** *B4*

Buses

Alajuela & Airport Buses **1** *B3*
Heredia Buses **2** *B3/B4*
Liberia Buses **3** *B3*
Panaline Bus **4** *B3*
San Isidro Buses **5** *D4*
Ticabus **6** *C5*
Transnica Bus **7** *B3*
Terminal Alfaro **8** *A3*
Terminal Atlántico Norte **9** *A3*
Terminal Caribe (Sixaola) **10** *A4*
Terminal Cartago **11** *D5*
Terminal Coca Cola **12** *B3*
Terminal Los Santos **13** *D6*
Terminal Puntarenas **14** *C3*
Terminal Turrialba **15** *C5*

 Along Calle Central, west of the Teatro Nacional, is **Parque Central**, with a bandstand in the middle among trees, again with occasional performances. East of the park is the monumental architecture of the **Catedral Metropolitana**; to the north is the **Teatro Melico Salazar** ⓘ *see press for details or call T221-4952*, with a good mix of performances throughout the year.

Further west, in **Parque Braulio Carrillo**, opposite the eclectic neo-Gothic design of **La Merced** church, is a huge carved granite ball brought from the Diquis archaeological site near Palmar Norte. There are other such designs at the entrance to the Museo de Ciencias Naturales.

At the end of Paseo Colón, at Calle 42, **Parque La Sabana** was converted from the former city airport in the 1950s; the old airport building on the east side is now the **Museo de Arte Costarricense** ⓘ *T222-7155, Tue-Sat 1000-1600, US$5, US$1 for students, Sun 1000-1400, free,* with a small but interesting display of paintings and sculptures. At the west end of the park is the **Estadio Nacional**, with seating for 20,000 spectators at (mainly) football matches, basketball, volleyball and tennis courts, a running track, lake and swimming pool.

Opposite the southwest corner of Parque Sabana are the impressive natural displays of the **Museo de Ciencias Naturales** ⓘ *Colegio La Salle, T232-1306, Mon-Sat 0730-1600, Sun 0900-1700, US$1.50, children US$1*, next to the Ministry of Agriculture; take 'Sabana Estadio' bus from Avenida 2, Calle 1 to the gate.

North of Avenida Central, on Calle 2, is the **Unión Club**, the principal social centre of the country. Opposite is the **Correo Central**, general post and telegraph office which also houses an internet café, pastry shop and the **Museo Postal, Telgráfico y Filatélico** ⓘ *upstairs, Mon-Fri 0800-1700, free.*

A couple of blocks to the west is the hustle and bustle of the **Mercado Central**, dating back to 1881, rich with the shouts, cries, smells and chaos of a fresh produce market. Good cheap meals for sale as well as some interesting nick-nacks for the passing tourist. Often crowded; watch for thieves.

The Disneyesque building on the horizon to the north of the city is the **Centro Costarricense de Ciencias y Cultura** (Scientific and Cultural Centre) in the old city penitentiary with the **Galería Nacional, Biblioteca Carlos Luis Saénz,** the **Auditorio Nacional** and **Museo de Los Niños** ⓘ *Calle 4, Av 9, T258-4929, Tue-Fri 0800-1530, Sat-Sun 0930-1630, US$1.60, children US$1.* Interesting as much for the well-restored building as for the exhibits using former prison cells and spaces to good effect.

Along Avenida 3, north of the Plaza de la Cultura, are the four gardens of the remodelled **Parque Morazán**, with another bandstand at the centre. A little to the northeast, **Parque España**, cool, quiet, and intimate, has for neighbours the **Casa Amarilla** (Yellow House), seat of the Ministry of Foreign Affairs, and the **Edificio Metálico**, imported from Europe to become one of the country's first schools.

To the north of Parque Morazán is **Parque Simón Bolívar**, now a recreation area, with **Simón Bolívar National Zoo and Botanical Gardens** ⓘ *Av 11, just east of Calle 7 (go down Calle 7 about 3 blocks from Av 7), T233-6701, Mon-Sun 0900-1630, US$2.* It's been remodelled and much improved, with all native plants numbered and listed in a brochure; animals' cages are small. There's also a restaurant and souvenir shop.

To the north of town, a reasonable walk or a short taxi ride, is **Spirogyra** ⓘ *100 m east, 150 m south of Centro Comercial El Pueblo (near Hotel Villa Tournón), T222-2937, daily 0800-1700, guided tours for more than 10 people (reservations required), US$6, US$5 students, US$3 children*, a fascinating butterfly farm close to the city but filled with life. To get there, take 'Calle Blancos' bus from Calle 3 and Avenida 5 to El Pueblo.

Around San José »pp991-1003.

San José is a good base for excursions into the beautiful Meseta Central. Excursions to the spectacular **Orosí Valley** and **Irazú Volcano** are given under Cártago (see page 1012). **Volcán Poás** gently simmers and steams from its elevated position at the northern limit of the Central Highlands and can be visited from San José (**TUASA** bus departs from Avenida 2, Calle 12-14 at 0830, returns 1430, US$4.75 round trip, T442-6900) Heredia or Alajuela (see page 1004). To reach **Volcán Barva** in Parque Nacional Braulio Carrillo, take a bus to San José de la Montaña (see page 1007). Enquire first about the likely weather when planning a visit to Poás, Irazú or Barva as cloud will limit the views; early morning visits recommended.

San Antonio de Escazú, a western suburb of San José popular with the expatriate community, hosts the Día del Boyero (National Oxcart Drivers' Day) on the second weekend in March. Festivities culminate on the Sunday in a colourful oxcart parade from the school to the centre, accompanied by typical *payasos* (clowns). Open-air dancing in the evening to music played on a marimba.

In La **Guácima,** 35 minutes west of San José, 20 minutes south of Alajuela, is a **Butterfly Farm** ⓘ *daily 0830-1700, US$15 adults, US$10 students, US$7.50 children under 12, includes guided tour every 2 hrs, last one at 1500*, dedicated to rearing and exporting over 120 species of butterflies. The first such farm in Latin America, now with over 100 associated farmers throughout Costa Rica, it is believed to be one of the second largest exporters of farm-bred butterflies in the world (the largest is in Taiwan). Created by Joris Brinckerhoff, a former Peace Corp volunteer and his wife in 1984, the farm opened to the public in 1990. All visitors receive a two-hour guided tour. Visit in the morning as butterflies require heat from the sun for the energy to fly so when it is cool or cloudy, there may be less activity. The Butterfly Farm offers round trip minibus transportation from San José hotels (US$15, US$10 students, US$8 children, reservations required, T438-0400). The public bus for La Guácima, leaves from Calle 10, Avenida 2-4, behind La Merced Church in San José (0800, 1100 and 1400, returns at 1230, 1530 and 1730, 1 hour, US$0.55); at the last stop walk 300 m from the school south to the butterfly sign. From Alajuela take a bus marked 'La Guácima abajo' which departs 100 m south, 100 m west of **Tikal Supermarket** (40 minutes, at 0620, 0900, 1100 and 1300; returning at 0945, 1145, 1345, 1545 and 1745).

From San José you can take a tour of **Café Britt's coffee farm** ⓘ *near Barva de Heredia, T260-2748, www.coffeetour.com, 1100, 1½ hrs, US$30*, where you can see the processing factory, tasting room and a multi-media presentation using professional actors of the story of coffee. You can arrange to be picked up at various points and hotels in San José. The new **Teatro Dionisio Chaverría** at **Café Britt** hosts weekend theatre and a children's show on Sunday afternoons.

Sleeping

San José *p985, maps p986 and p988*
There are cheap hotels between the Mercado Central, Mercado Borbón and the Coca Cola terminal. Cheaper hotels usually have only wooden partitions for walls, making them noisy. Hotels in the red light district, Calle 6, Av 1-5, near Mercado Central, charge on average US$10 with toilet and shower for a night.

LL-AL Grano de Oro, Calle 30, Av 2, T255-3322, www.hotelgranodeoro.com. Exquisite converted 19th-century mansion, 35 rooms and suites, beautiful terrace gardens, renowned restaurant, friendly, tasteful, good value.

L Aurola Holiday Inn, Av 5 between Calle 5-7, pool, T222-2424, www.aurola-holiday inn.com. Mainly business clientèle, casino, good view of city from casino.

L-AL Britannia, Calle 3, Av 11, T223-6667, www.hotelbritanniacostarica.com. 1910 Spanish-style beautifully restored mansion, high standard, antique furniture, very good service, excellent restaurant, worth the money.

L-AL Del Rey, Av 1, Calle 9, Apdo 6241-1000, T257-7800, www.hoteldelrey.com. Nice single, double, triple rooms, standard or deluxe, suites. Landmark hotel, centre of casino and upmarket red-light district, not recommended for families, walls a bit thin, restaurant.

L-AL Fleur de Lys, Calle 13, Av 2-6, T223-1206, www.hotelfleurdelys.com. Restored Victorian mansion house, good restaurant, bar. Stylishly elegant. Recommended.

AL Rosa del Paseo, Paseo Colón, Calle 28-30, T257-3225, www.rosadelpaseo.com. Beautifully restored mansion, breakfast included. Good location for access to the city centre but not in the heart of town.

AL Don Carlos, Calle 9, Av 7-9, T221-6707, www.doncarloshotel.com. 36 rooms, interesting traditional building, much artwork and statuary, sun deck, free coffee, Annemarie's giftshop with good selection, credit cards accepted, airport shuttle.

AL Santo Tomás, Av 7, Calle 3-5, T255-3950, www.hotelsantotomas.com. French Victorian mansion, 20 rooms, pool, garden, internet access, secure parking, Restaurant El Oasis next door, tours arranged.

A Rincón de San José, formerly Edelweiss, Av 9, Calle 13-15, 100 m east of Condovac offices, T221-9702, www.hotelrinconde sanjose.com. English, Dutch and Spanish spoken, clean, comfortable, native hardwood furniture and carved doors, pleasant courtyard bar, helpful, friendly.

A-B CACTS, Av 3 bis, Calle 28-30, 3 blocks north of Pizza Hut, Paseo Colón, T221-2928, www.hotelcacts.com. Safe, good service, breakfast and taxes included, TV, friendly, pets allowed. Recommended.

A-C Joluva, Calle 3b, Av 9-11, T223-7961. With breakfast, old house, friendly, safe, good laundry service, good value. A relaxing and gay-friendly hotel.

B Cinco Hormigas Rojas, Calle 15, Av 9-11, T255-3412, www.cincohormigasrojas.com. Nice decor, small house. Prices includes taxes.

B Diana's Inn, Calle 5, Av 3, Parque Morazán, near Holiday Inn, T223-6542, dianas@rac sa.co.cr. An old building formerly used by the president, now restored, includes breakfast and taxes, discounts available, a/c, TV, hot water, noisy, free luggage storage, safe box.

B Ritmo del Caribe, Paseo Colón and Calle 32, diagonal from KFC restaurant, T256-1636, www.ritmo-del-caribe.com. Simple, good rooms and friendly atmosphere, free airport shuttle, good value, breakfast and taxes included. German owner Tomas also runs Wild Rider Motorcycles and rents 4WD vehicles at 'backpacker rates' (see Motorcycle rental, page 1000).

C Centroamericano, Av 2, Calle 6-8, T221-3362, ghcmejer@racsa.co.cr. Includes taxes, private bath, clean small rooms, very helpful, will arrange accommodation in other towns, free shuttle (Mon-Fri) to airport, laundry facilities.

C Fortuna, Av 6, Calle 2 y 4, T223-5344, hfortuna@infoweb.co.cr. Quiet, helpful.

C Pensión de la Cuesta, Av 1, Calle 11-15, T256-7946, www.suntoursandfun.com. A little off the wall in style with artwork all over this old colonial home. Shared bath, use of the kitchen and internet, includes breakfast.

C-D Hostel Pangea, Av 11, Calle 3 bis, T221-1992, www.hostelpangea.com. Friendly, clean spot, use of kitchen. Good local information, with free coffee, internet, breakfast and pool, good spot.

C-D Tranquilo Backpackers, Calle 7, Av 9-11, T222-2493, www.tranquilobackpackers.com. Dormitory and private rooms with great, relaxed atmosphere, but not very helpful.

C-E Casa Ridgway, Calle 15, Av 6-8, T233-6168, www.amigosparalapaz.org. 1-4 beds in room, shared bath, use of kitchen, very helpful, friendly, laundry possible, group rates and facilities.

D Avenida Segunda, Av 2 No 913, Calle 9-11, T222-0260, acebrisa@racsa.co.cr. Includes taxes, shared or private bath, friendly, stores luggage.

D Bienvenido, Calle 10, Av 1-3, T233-2161. Clean, hot shower, near centre and airport bus, best hotel near Coca Cola bus terminal.

D Boston, Av 8, Calle Central-2, T221-0563. With or without bath, good, very friendly, but noisy, will store luggage.

D Marlyn, Av 7-9, Calle 4, T233-3212. More with bath, hot showers, good security, will store luggage, parking for motorcycles (just).

D Otoya, Calle 1, Av 3-5, T221-3925, erickpensionotoya@24horas.com. Close to the centre, cleanish, friendly and quite popular, you're allowed to use the telephone which can be a bonus (free local calls). Hot water throughout and some rooms with private bath, includes taxes. Luggage store, laundry service and English spoken.

D Pensión Musoc, Calle 16, Av 1-3, T222-9437. With or without private bath, very clean, hot water, luggage stored, will do laundry, friendly, near bus stations so somewhat noisy, but recommended.
D Príncipe, Av 6, Calle Central-2, T222-7983, with bath, hot water, TV, top rooms best, quiet, friendly, includes taxes.
D-E Costa Rica Backpackers, Av 6, Calle 21-23, T221-6191, www.costaricabackpackers.com. Top billing at these prices with a pool, good dormitory and private rooms, kitchen and laundry services, free coffee and internet. Parking possible.
D-E Gaudy's Backpackers' Hostel, Av 5, Calle 36-38, T258-2937, www.backpacker.co.cr. Good backpacker choice, with dormitory accommodation, kitchen, communal areas and internet access. Good location and quieter than the other cheap options.
D-E Gran Imperial, on the western side of the Central Market, Calle 8, Av 1-Central, T222-8463. Mixed reports, small rooms, thin walls, clean, sometimes noisy, with or without private bath, limited hot showers, includes taxes, restaurant with good prices, best to reserve, good for meeting other travellers with balcony overlooking Central Market. A great spot for relaxing, locked luggage store, TV.
D-E Hostal Toruma, Av Central, Calle 29-31, T234-9186, www.hicr.org. 93 beds, clean, hot water, crowded but safe, lockable storage in each room, includes breakfast, cheaper for ISIC or YHA members; free use of internet and kitchen for guests; a good place for meeting other travellers to arrange group travel, and for booking other hostels in the country. Members can leave bags. There are 20 affiliated hostels throughout Costa Rica.
E Galileo Backpackers' Hostel, 100 m east of SodaTapia, T248-2094, www.galileohostel.com. Friendly place and faces, charming property with dorm beds, free internet.
E Pensión Boruca, Calle 14, Av 1-3, near Coca Cola terminal, T223-0016. Shared bath, hot water, laundry service, rooms a bit dark but friendly owner.
E Rialto, Av 5, Calle 2, 1 block north of Correos, T221-7456. Shared or private bath, hot water, safe, friendly but can be very noisy.
F Pensión América, Av 7, Calle 4. Clean, large rooms, good value.
F Tica Linda, Av 10, Calle 7-9. Dormitory accommodation, use of kitchen, hot water and laundry, TV in communal area. Will store luggage, popular with travellers. No sign, just a notice on the front. Moves often which makes finding the place a problem, but popular. Ask locally.

Near the airport

See Alajuela, page 1007.

Around San José *p991*

A Pico Blanco Inn, San Antonio de Escazú, T228-1908. All rooms with balconies and views of Central Valley, several cottages, English owner, restaurant with English pub, Costa Rican flavour, airport pick-up can be requested. Recommended.
A-B Costa Verde Inn, 300 m south of the 2nd San Antonio de Escazú cemetery, T228-4080, www.costaverdeinn.com. A secluded and charming country home with 14 imaginatively decorated rooms – a popular choice away from the centre of town.

Camping

Belén, San Antonio de Belén, 2 km west of intersection at Cariari and San Antonio, 5 km from airport, turn off Highway 1 on to Route 111, turn right at soccer field then 1st left for 1 km, T239-0421. US$10 per day, American-owned trailer park, shade, hot showers, laundry, friendly, recommended, good bus service to San José.

Eating

San José *p985, maps p986 and p988*

Traditional dishes, feasting on a steady supply of rice and beans, tend to be a little on the heavy side but are definitely worth trying.

At lunchtime cheaper restaurants offer a set meal called a *casado*, US$1.50-2.50, which is good value. There are several cheap Chinese places along Av 5. For reliable and seriously cheap places, try the **Mercado Central**, around the **Coca Cola** bus terminal and the area to the southwest of **Parque Central**. *Autoservicios* do not charge tax and service and represent the best value. There are plenty of fast-food outlets dotted throughout the city.
TTT **Ana Italiana**, T222-6153, Paseo Colón, Calle 24 y 26. Good Italian and friendly. Closed Mon.
TTT **Café Mundo**, Av 9, Calle 13-15, opposite **Hotel Rincón de San José**, T222-6190. Old

mansion tastefully restored, good salads, great pasta, wonderful bread, a stylish joint.

ΨΨΨ **El Chicote**, on north side of Parque Sabana, T232-0936. Reliable favourite, country style, good grills.

ΨΨΨ **El Cuartel de la Boca del Monte**, Av 1, Calle 21-23, T221-0327. Live music at night but a good and popular restaurant by day.

ΨΨΨ **Jurgen's**, Calle 41 and Paseo Rubén Darío, Barrio Dent in Los Yoses, T224-2455. 1st-class service, excellent international menu in a sophisticated atmosphere. Closed Sun.

ΨΨΨ **La Bastille**, Paseo Colón, Calle 22, T255-4994. Stylish French food in elegant surrounds. Closed Sun.

ΨΨΨ **La Cocina de Leña**, north of the centre in El Pueblo, Barrio Tournón, T255-1360. Excellent menu of the very best in Tico cuisine, upmarket, pricey, but warm, friendly ambience.

ΨΨΨ **La Esquina del Café**, Av 9, Calle 3b. Speciality coffee roasters with good restaurant, souvenir shop, live music twice a month. Daily 0900-2200.

ΨΨΨ **La Masia de Triquell**, Edif Casa España, Sabana Norte, T296-3528. Catalan, warmly recommended. Closed Sun.

ΨΨΨ **Le Chandelier**, 50 m west and 100 m south of the main entrance of the ICE building in Los Yoses, T225-3980. One of the best French restaurants in town, reservations required. Closed Sun.

ΨΨΨ **Los Ranchos Steak House**, Sabana Norte near **Hotel TRYP Meliá**. Reliable, good food.

ΨΨΨ **Lubnan**, Paseo Colón, Calle 22-24, T257-6071. Authentic Lebanese menu, vegetarian selections, great service.

ΨΨΨ **Marbella**, out beyond San Pedro mall, T224-9452. Fish, paella specialities, packed on Sun, very good.

ΨΨΨ **Morazán**, Calle 9, Av 3, facing Parque Morazán. Not touristy, popular with locals, friendly, excellent breakfast, delicious blackberry juice.

ΨΨΨ **Tin Jo**, Calle 11, Av 6-8, T221-7605. Probably the best Asian cuisine in town.

ΨΨ **Gran Diamante**, Av 5, Calle 4-6. With a 'lively kitchen' where you can watch the food being prepared.

ΨΨ **La Vasconia**, corner of Av 1, Calle 5, great little restaurant combining a passion for football and food. Basic in style, good traditional dishes.

ΨΨ **Los Antojitos**, on Paseo Colón, on Pavas Highway west of Sabana, in Tibás, San Antonio de Escazú and in Centro Comercial Cocorí (road to suburb of San Pedro), T232- 2411. Serves excellent Mexican food at fair prices.

ΨΨ **Machu Picchu**, Calle 32, Av 1-3, T222-7384. Open from 1700, closed Sun. Great Peruvian food, good service in homely atmosphere.

ΨΨ **México Bar**, north of the Coca Cola district in Paso de la Vaca, T221-8461. Dead by day comes out at night with a flurry of music and good Mexican food.

ΨΨ **Vishnu**, Av 1, Calle 1-3, also on Calle 14, Av 2. Daily 0800-2000. Best-known vegetarian place in town, good quality, cheap and good *plato del día*. Try their soya cheese sandwiches and ice cream, sells good wholemeal bread.

Ψ **Chicharronera Nacional**, Av 1, Calle 10-12. *Autoservicio* and very popular.

Ψ **China Bonita** at Av 5, Calle 2-4. One of the cheapest Chinese options in town.

Ψ **Comedor**, Calle 8, Av 4-6, beneath 'Dorado' sign. Very cheap.

Ψ **Corona de Oro**, Av 3, Calle 2-4 (next to Nini). An excellent *autoservicio*.

Ψ **Don Sol**, Av 7b No 1347. Excellent 3-course vegetarian lunch , run by integral yoga society (only open for lunch).

Ψ **El Merendero**, Av 6, Calle Central-2. *Autoservicio* serving cheap local food, popular with Ticos.

Ψ **La Puriscaleña**, on the corner of Calle Central and Av 5, is a good, local *comedor*. The *menú del día* is a tasty bargain.

Ψ **Pollo a la Leña**, Calle 1, Av 3-5, which has seriously cheap chicken, popular with locals.

Ψ **Popular**, Av 3, Calle 6-8. Good *casado*.

Cafés sodas and ice cream parlours

Bagelman, Paseo Rubén Darío (Av Central), Calle 33, just east of **Hostal Toruma** in Barrio Escalante, T224-2432. Smart and tasty fast-food bagel heaven, delivers to area hotels. Also in San Antonio de Escazú, T228-4460.

Café del Teatro, Av 2, Calle 3, in foyer of National Theatre. Pricey but worth it for the sheer style and sophistication of the belle époque interior. Mon-Sat.

Café Parisienne on the Plaza de la Cultura , the street café of the **Gran Hotel Costa Rica**. Food a little overpriced, but have a coffee and watch the world go by.

Churrería Manolo, Av Central, Calle Central- 2 (new restaurant upstairs), open 24 hrs. Simple, quick food with takeaway options on the street, good sandwiches and hot chocolate.

Helados Boni, Calle Central, Av 6-8. Home-made ice cream.
Helados Rena, Calle 8, Av Central. Excellent.
La Esquina del Café, Av 9, Calle 3b, Barrio Amón, T257-9868. Daily 0900-2200. Specialty coffee roasters with beans from 6 different regions to taste, also a good restaurant with a souvenir shop. Live music twice a month.
La Nutrisoda, Edif Las Arcadas. Home-made natural ice cream. 1100-1800.
Macrobiótica, Calle 11, Av 6-8. Health shop selling good bread.
Musmanni, has several outlets throughout the country, varying quality, best in the large cities and in the morning.
Pops, with several branches throughout town and the country, has excellent ice cream too.
Ruiseñor, Paseo Rubén Darío and Calle 41-43, Los Yoses, T225-2562. The smart place to take coffee and snacks in east San José.
Soda El Parque, Calle 2, Av 4-6. Open 24 hrs. A popular spot for business people by day and relaxing entertainers by night.
Soda La Luz, Av Central, Calle 33, east towards Los Yoses. Good filling cheap meals.
Soda Nini at Av 3, Calle 2-4. Cheap and cheerful.
Soda Tapia, Calle 42, Av 2-4, east side of Parque Sabana. Classic stopping place for Josefinos, with good food, served quickly.
Soda Vegetariana, next to **Librería Italiana**. Vegetarian with good juices and food.
Spoon has a central bakery at Av Central, Calle 5-7. Good coffee and pastries to take-out or eat in, also light lunches.

Around San José *p991*

🍴 **Taj Mahal**, San Antonio de Escazú, from Centro Comercial Paco, 1 km west on the old highway, T228-0980. Indian food for a change.

Entertainment

San José *p985, maps p986 and p988*

Bars and clubs

The *Tico Times* has a good listings section.
Beatles, Calle 9, Av Central. Good music, popular with ex-pats.
Calle de la Armagua, San Pedro. Happening street for young Ticos from 2230 onwards.
Centro Comercial El Pueblo, north of town in Barrio Tournón, with a cluster of fine restaurants, bars and discos. This is where Ticos party the night away literally until dawn. **Cocoloco** is the liveliest of the discos, **Infinito** gets a slightly older crowd and **La Plaza** outside the centre, is often not as busy.
Chelle's, Av Central, Calle 9, T221-1369. Excellent 24-hr bar and restaurant which changes its mood through the day, and its clientele. Great snacks and people watching.
Disco Salsa 54, Calle 3, Av 1-3. The place to go for salsa.
El Cuartel de la Boca del Monte, Av 1, Calle 21-23, T221-0327. Live music at weekends, popular with students, hip young things but without the flashy dress. Recommended.
Key Largo, Parque Morazan. Live music, very popular with the **Hotel del Rey** crowd.
La Avispa, Calle 1, Av 8-10, and **Déjà vu**, Calle 2, Av 14-16. Both are gay-friendly discos, but not exclusively so.
Nashville South, Calle 5, Av 1-3. A popular Country-and-Western-style gringo bar.
Risas, Calle 1, Av Central, T223-2803. Bars on 3 floors, good, popular with locals.
Terrau, out in San Pedro on Calle de la Armagua. The most popular of many clubs along this street. The area gets going around 2300 and keeps going till dawn. You'll need photo ID to get into the clubs.

Cinemas

Excellent modern cinemas showing latest releases are located throughout the metropolitan area, see *La Nación* for listings:
Cine Universitario at the UCR's Abelardo Bonilla law school auditorium in San Pedro, T207-4717, shows good films at 1700 and 1900 daily, US$3-4.
El Semáforo in San Pedro shows films made in Latin America and Spain.
Cine Omni, Av 1, Calle 3-5, T221-7903 and **Variedades**, Calle 5, Av Central-1, T222-6108 are a couple of CCM theatres in the centre. Others can be found in Los Yoses, T223-0085, San Pedro, T283-5716, Rohrmoser, T232-3271 and Heredia, T293-3300.
Sala Garbo, Av 2, Calle 28, T222-1034, shows worldwide independent art house movies.

Theatre

More than 20 theatres offer live productions in the San José area; check the *Tiempo Libre* entertainment supplement every Thu in *La Nación* for show times, mostly weekends.
Teatro Nacional, Av 2, Calle 3-5 T221-5341 (recommended for the productions, the

architecture and the bar/café), US$3 for guided tour, T221-1329, behind it is La Plaza de la Cultura, a large complex.
Teatro Melico Salazar, Parque Central, T221-4952, www.teatromelicosalazar.go.cr, for popular, folkloric shows.
Teatro del Angel, Av Central, Calle 13-15, T222-8258, 3 modern dance companies.

Festivals and events

San José *p985, maps p986 and p988*
Dec-Jan Christmas/New Year: festivities last from mid-Dec to the first week of Jan, with dances, horse shows and much confetti throwing in the crowded streets. The annual El Tope horse parade starts at noon on 26 Dec and travels along the principal avenues of San José. A **carnival** starts next day at about 1700 in the same area. Fairs, firework displays, food and music at El Zapote, frequent buses from the centre.
Mar The International Festival of Culture assembles musicians from throughout Central America in a week of performances in the Plaza de Cultura around the 2nd week of Mar, although concern over the future of the event exists due to lack of funding.
2nd Sun in Mar Día del Boyero (Day of the Oxcart Driver) is celebrated in San Antonio de Escazú. Parades of ox-drawn carts, with music, dancing and blessings from the priesthood.
Mar/Apr Street parades during Easter week.
Sep 15 Independence Day: bands and dance troupes move through the streets, although activities start to kick-off the night before with the traditional nationwide singing of the National Anthem at 1800.

Shopping

San José *p985, maps p986 and p988*
Crafts and markets
Market on Av Central, Calle 6-8, 0630-1800 (Sun 0630-1200), good leather suitcases and wood. **Mercado Borbón**, Av 3-5, 8-10, fruit and vegetables. More and more *artesanía* shops are opening: **Canapi**, Calle 11, Av 1 (a co-operative, cheaper than most), **Mercado Nacional de Artesanía**, Calle 11, Av 4, T221-5012, Mon-Fri 0900-1800, Sat 0900-1700, is a good one-stop shop with a wide variety of goods on sale. **La Casona**, Calle Central, Av Central-1, daily 0900-1900, a market of small *artesanía* shops, is full of interesting little stalls. **Galería Namu**, opposite the Alianza Francesa building on Av 7 and Calle 5-7, T256-3412, www.galerianamu.com, is the best one-stop shop for home-grown and indigenous art, with the distinctly bright coloured ceramics of Cecilia Figueres. Items can be shipped if required. At the **Plaza de la Democracia** in front of the National Museum, tented stalls run the length of a city block, great place to buy hammocks, arts and crafts at competitive prices. Don't be afraid to negotiate. **Centro Comercial El Pueblo**, near the Villa Tournón Hotel, also has a number of stalls but mainly for upmarket products and prices, built in a traditional 'pueblo' style.

In **Moravia** (8 km northeast of San José with stops often included on city tours) the block-long **Calle de la Artesanía** includes various souvenir stores, including well-known **La Rueda**, T297-2736, good for leatherworks.

Bookshops
Casa de la Revista, Calle 5, Av 1-3, T256-5092. Mon-Fri 0900-1800, Sat 0800-1700. Good selection of maps, newspapers, magazines and some books (mostly paperbacks) in English. Other locations include Escazú, San Pedro, Rohrmoser, Curridabat, Moravia, Alajuela, Cártago and Heredia, for information call main office of Agencia de Publicaciones de Costa Rica, T283-9383. **Librería Lehmann**, Av Central, Calle 1-3, T223-1212, has a large and varied selection of Spanish and English books and magazines. They also stock several maps including the 1:50,000 topographical maps produced by the Instituto Geográfico Nacional de Costa Rica (IGN). **Mora Books**, Av 1, Calle 3-5, T255-4136, in Omni building above Pizza Hut, Mon-Sat 1100-1900. Large selection of used books, reasonable prices. **7th Street Books**, Calle 7, Av Central, T256-8251, marroca@racsa.co.cr. A wide range of new and used books covering all topics of interest to visitors to Costa Rica, including *Footprint*. Mon-Sat 0900-1800, Sun 1000-1700.

Photography
1-hr colour processing available at all IFSA (Kodak) branches. Fuji processing in 1 hr at Universal stores. **Taller de Equipos Fotográficos**, 120 m east of kiosk Parque Morazán, Av 3, Calle 3-5, T223-1146 (Canon

repairs – authorized workshop). **Tecfot**, Av 7, Calle Central, T221-1438, repairs all cameras, authorized Minolta dealer, good service, reasonable rates.

Shopping malls

Shopping malls are popping up in different parts of town including San Pedro, on the eastern ring road, complete with cinema. Newly expanded **Multiplaza Mall**, near **Camino Real**, Escazú, has great shops and lots of cinemas. Across the highway toward San José is **Plaza Itskatzú**, a colonial-style shopping centre with restaurants and shops. Another is the **Terra Mall** in Curridabat.

Activities and tours

San José *p985, maps p986 and p988*

If you're planning on staying in or around San José for a while, look in the Calendar pages of the *The Tico Times* for clubs and associations.

Bungee jumping

After Rafael Iglesias Bridge (Río Colorado), continue on Pan-American Highway 1.5 km, turn right at Salón Los Alfaro, down track to Puente Colorado. **Tropical Bungee** operates 0900-1600 daily in the high season, US$65 1st jump, US$30 for the 2nd (same day only) includes transportation from San José, reservations required, T248-2212, www.bungee.co.cr. Exhilarating.

Cycling

Coast to Coast Adventures, T280-8054, www.ctocadventures.com, run trips in the local area.

Swimming

The best public pool is at **Ojo de Agua**, 5 mins from the airport in Alajuela, 15 mins from San José. Daily 0800-1600, US$1.55, T441-2808. Direct bus from Calle 10, Av 2-4 (behind La Merced Church) in San José or take bus to Alajuela and then another to San Antonio de Belén. There is also an open-air pool at **Plaza González Víquez**, in the southeast section of San José, crowded. Weekends only, US$1, T256-6517.

Tour operators

For independent travel to Tortuguero, see pages 1091 and 1105.

Aventuras Naturales, Av Central, Calle 33-35, T225-3939, www.toenjoynature.com. Specialists in whitewater rafting with their own lodge on the Pacuare which has a canopy adventure tour. Also several other trips. **COOPRENA (Simbiosis Tours)**, Apdo 6939-1000, San José, T248-2538, www.turismoruralcr.com. A group supporting small farmers, broadly working to the principle of sustainable tourism. It offers tours and has accommodation available around the country. **LA Tours**, PO Box 492-1007, Centro Colón, T221-4501. Kathia Vargas is extremely helpful in rearranging flights and reservations. **Swiss Travel Service**, is one of the biggest tour operators with branches in many of the smarter hotels, T282-4898, www.swisstravelcr.com. Can provide any standard tour, plus several specialist tours for birdwatchers. Good guides and warmly recommended. **Super Viajes**, American Express representative, Oficientro Ejecutivo La Sabana, Edif 1 Sabana, PO Box 3985, T220-0400.

Those specializing in naturalist tours include **Aguas Bravas**, T292-2072, www.aguas-bravas.co.cr, whitewater rafting on rivers around the Central Valley, also horse riding and biking. **Costa Rica Expeditions**, Av 3, Calle Central 3, T257-0766, www.costaricaexpeditions.com, Upmarket wildlife adventures include whitewater rafting (US$95 for 1-day trip on Río Pacuare, includes lunch and transport, good; other rivers from US$69-95) and other options. They own **Tortuga Lodge, Corcovado Lodge Tent Camp** and **Monteverde Lodge**. Daily trips, highly recommended. **Ecole Travel**, lobby of Gran Hotel , T223-2240, www.ecoletravel.com. Chilean-Dutch, highly recommended for budget tours to Tortuguero, Corcovado and tailor-made excursions off the beaten track. **Green Tropical Tours**, Calle 1, Av 5-7, T229-4192, www.greentropical.com, with options outside the norm including tours to Guayabo National Monument, Los Juncos and cloud forest. **Horizontes**, Calle 28, Av 1-3, T222-2022, www.horizontes.com. One of the big operators in Costa Rica, high standards, educational and special interest, advice given and arrangements made for groups and individuals. **Mitur**, T296-7378, www.mitour.com. A range of tours throughout the country, including Ilan Ilan in Tortuguero US$215, 3-days, 2 nights. **Real**

Places, Real People, T810-4444, www.realplaces.net. 1- and 3-day tours visiting rural Costa Rica for baking, ceramics, mask making and other traditional activities. **ACTUAR**, T248-9470, www.actuarcosta rica.com, is an association of 26 community-based rural tourism groups spread across the country. **Ríos Tropicales**, Calle 38, between Paseo Colón and Av 2, 50 m south of Subway, T233-6455, www.rios tropicales.com. Specialists in whitewater rafting and kayaking, good selection and careful to assess your abilities, good food, excellent guides, US$250 for 2-day trip on Río Pacuare, waterfalls, rapids, including camping and food. Many other options throughout the country. **Typical Tours**, Las Arcadas, next to the **Gran Hotel Costa Rica**, T233-8486, city tours, volcano tours, nature reserves, rafting, cruising.

Several companies focus on trips to **Tortuga Island** off the southern tip of Nicoya Peninsula. Try **Bay Island Cruises**, T258-3536, bayislan@racsa.co.cr, daily tours to Tortuga Island, US$79 includes lunch and transport from San José area.

Transport

San José *p985, maps p986 and p988*

Air

The much-improved Aeropuerto Internacional Juan Santamaría (SJO) is at El Coco, 16 km from San José along the Autopista General Cañas (5 km from Alajuela). Airport information, T443-2622 (24 hrs). The **Sansa** terminal for domestic flights is next to the main terminal. **Sansa** runs a free bus service to the airport for its passengers. There is another terminal, about 1 km west of the main terminal, used by charter flights and private planes. Buses to city centre from main street outside ground-floor terminal. Buses to airport, continuing on to Alajuela from Av Central-2, Calle 10, every 10 mins from 0500-2100; 45 mins, US$0.50 (good service, plenty of luggage space). Taxi to and from airport, US$12. Taxis run all night from the main square. For early flights you can reserve a taxi from any San José hotel the night before. All taxi companies run a 24-hr service. Bank at the airport 0800-1600, with ATM available as well. ICT, open in the day time, has a helpful tourist office in the main terminal for maps, information and hotel reservations.

Internal flights Sansa and Nature Air (from Tobias Bolaños, 8 km west of San José, in Pavas) operate internal flights throughout the country. **Sansa** T221-9414, www.fly sansa.com, check-in is at office on Av Las Americas and Calle 42, free bus to and from airport. Check schedules on **Nature Air**, T299-6000, www.natureair.com If you made reservations before arriving in Costa Rica, confirm and collect tickets as soon as possible after arrival. Book ahead, especially for the beaches. In Feb and Mar, planes can be fully booked 3 weeks ahead. On all internal scheduled and charter flights there is a baggage allowance of 12 kg. Oversized items such as surfboards or bicycles are charged at US$15 if there is room in the cargo hold.

From San José you can fly to **Barra del Colorado**, **Coto 47**, **Drake Bay**, **Golfito**, **Liberia**, **Limón**, **Nosara**, **Palmar Sur**, **Puerto Jiménez** (with a connecting flight to **Carate**, on the border of Corcovado National Park), **Punta Islita**, **Quepos**, **Carrillo-Sámara**, **Tamarindo**, **Tambor**, **Tortuguero** and **Granada** in Nicaragua and **Bocas del Toro** in Panama.

Airline offices

International carriers **Air France**, Condominio Vista Real, 1st floor, 100 m east of POPs, Curridabat, T280-0069; **Alitalia**, Calle 24, Paseo Colón, T295-6820; **American**, Sabana Este, opposite Hotel TRYP Meliá, T257-1266; **Avianca**, Edif Centro, p 2, Colón, Paseo Colón, Calle 38-40, T233-3066; **British Airways**, Calle 13, Av 13, T257-8087; **Condor Airlines**, Calle 5, Av 7-9, T256-6161; **Continental**, Oficentro La Virgen No 2, 200 m south, 300 m east and 50 m north of American Embassy, Pavas, T296-4911; **Copa**, Av 5, Calle 1, T223-2672; **Delta**, 100 m east of Toyota and 50 m south, T257-2992; **Grupo Taca**, see **Sansa** above; **Iberia**, Paseo Colón, Calle 40, T257-8266; **KLM**, Sabana Sur, behind Controlaría General Building, T220-4111; **Lloyd Aéreo Boliviano**, Av 2, Calle 2-4, upstairs, T255-1530; **LTU International Airways** (German charter airline), Condominio da Vinci, Oficina No 6, Barrio Dent, T234-9292; **Lufthansa**, Calle 5, Av 7-9, T243-1818; **Martinair**, Dutch charter airline – subsidiary of KLM, see above; **Mexicana**, Paseo Colón Torres Mercedes, T295-6969, Mexican Tourist Card available here; **SAM**, Paseo Colón, Calle 38-40, Edif

Centro Colón, 2nd floor, T233-3066; **Singapore Àirlines**, Edificio Isabella San Pedro, T234-2223; **Servivensa**, Edif Centro Colón, 2nd floor, Paseo Colón, Calle 38-40, T257-1441; **Swissair**, Calle Central, Av 1-3, T221-6613; **United Airlines**, Sabana Sur, behind Controlaría General Building, T220-2027; **Varig**, Sabana West 150 m south of Canal 7, T290-5222.

National and charter airlines Nature Air (see above); Sansa (see above); **Aerobell**, T290-0000, www.aerobell.com, at Pavas; **Alfa Romeo Aéreo Taxi**, in Puerto Jiménez, T735-5112 ; **Paradise Air**, T296-3600, www.flywithparadise.com, based in Pavas; **Helicópteros del Norte**, helicopter charters and sightseeing tours out of San José, US$350 per hr, T232-7534.

Bus

Local Urban routes in San José cost US$0.50 or less. Hand baggage in reasonable quantities is not charged. A cheap tour of San José can be made on the bus marked 'periférico' from Paseo Colón in front of the Cine Colón, or at La Sabana bus stop, a 45-min circuit of the city. A smaller circuit is made by the 'Sabana/ Cementerio' bus, pick it up at Av 2, Calle 8-10.

Long distance In the majority of cases, buses start or finish their journey at San José so there are services to most towns; see under relevant destination for details of times and prices. Check where the bus stops at your destination, some routes do not go to the centre of towns, leaving passengers some distance away. Up-to-date timetables are in a free leaflet *Hop on the Bus*, giving times but no prices, distributed by **Ecole Travel**.

Bus stations are scattered around town: **Alajuela** (including airport) from Av 2, Calle 12-14; **Cahuita**, **Limón**, **Manzanillo**, **Puerto Viejo de Talamanca**, **Sixaola** all served from Gran Terminal del Caribe (**Guapileños**, **Caribeños**, **Sixaola**); **Jacó**, **Carará**, **Quepos**, **Manuel Antonio**, **Uvita** all depart from from Terminal Coca Cola; **Santa Cruz** (½ block west), **Peñas Blancas** (100 m north) from outside Terminal Coca Cola; **Cártago** from Terminal Cártago during the day, after 2030 from **Gran Hotel Costa Rica**, Av 2, Calle 3-5; **Cd Quesada (San Carlos)**, **Fortuna**, **Guápiles (Braulio Carrillo)**, **Los Chiles**, **Caño Negro**, **Monteverde** (outside terminal), **Puerto Jiménez** (outside terminal), **Puerto Viejo Sarapiquí**, **Tilarán** (½ block north) from Terminal Atlántico Norte at Av 9, Calle 12; **Playa del Coco**, **Liberia** from Calle 14, Av 1-3; **Golfito**, **Nicoya**, **Nosara**, **Palmar Norte**, **Paso Canoas**, **Sámara**, **San Vito**, **Tamarindo** from Terminal Alfaro; **San Isidro de El General** (2 companies, **Musoc** and **Tuasur**), new terminal down on Av 22-24, Calle Central, **Heredia** from Terminal Heredia or a minibus from Av 2, Calle 10-12; **Volcán Irazú** from Av 2, Calle 1-3, opposite **Gran Hotel Costa Rica**; **Volcán Poás** from Av 2, Calle 12-14; **Puntarenas** from Terminal Puntarenas, Calle 16, Av 10-12; **Santa María de Dota** from Terminal Los Santos; **Turrialba** from Terminal Turrialba.

Two new shuttle bus companies offer transport from the capital to dozens of beach and tourism destinations, see Getting around, page 980.

International buses If the timing of your journey is important book tickets; in Dec-Jan, buses are often booked 2 weeks ahead, while at other times of the year outside holiday seasons there are plenty of spaces. **Ticabus** terminal at Calle 9-11, Av 4, T221-8954, www.ticabus.com, office open Mon-Sun 0600-2200. **Ticabus** to **Guatemala City**, 0600, 0700, 1230, 60 hrs, US$44, with overnight stay in Managua and San Salvador. To **Tegucigalpa**, 0600, 0700 and 1230, 48 hrs, US$31, overnight stay in Managua. To Managua at 0600, 0700 and 1230, US$11, 10 hrs including 1 hr at Costa Rican side of border and another 2 hrs on Nicaraguan side while they search bags. To **Panama City** leaves at 2200 daily, US$25 one-way, 18 hrs (book in advance). To get a Panamanian tourist card you must buy a return ticket – you can get a refund in Panama but with a discount of 15%. The **Ticabus** from Panama City tends to arrive between 0400 and 0500 and you are left on the street. There is a 24-hr café nearby if you wish to avoid the expense of a hotel. **Transnica**, Calle 22, Av 3-5, T223-4242, www.transnica.com, runs new buses with TV, video, a/c, snacks, toilet, to **Managua** daily at 0400, 0530, 0700 and 0900, US$20 return. Before departure have your ticket confirmed on arrival at the terminal; when buying and confirming your ticket, you must show your passport. When boarding the bus you are given an immigration form.

Panaline goes to **Panama City** daily at 1300 from Calle 16, Av 3, T256-8721, US$22 one way, US$41 return, reduction for students, arrives 0700; a/c, payment by Visa/MasterCard accepted. To **David**, from Terminal Alfaro, US$18 (buses daily at 0730 and 1200, 9 hrs); book in advance. They are modern, comfortable buses, although there is not much room for long legs, but they have the advantage of covering a scenic journey in daylight. A bus to **Changuinola** via the Sixaola-Guabito border post leaves San José at 1000 daily, 8 hrs, US$8, from opposite Terminal Alfaro, T556-1432 for information, best to arrive 1 hr before departure; the bus goes via Siquirres and is the quickest route to **Limón**.

Car

Car hire Most local agencies are on or close to Paseo Colón, with a branch or drop-off site at or close to the airport and other locations around the country.

Adobe, Av 12, Calle 28, T258-4242, www.adobecar.com; **Alamo**, Av 18, Calle 11-13, north of Plaza Víquez, T233-7733, www.alamocostarica.com, also on Paseo Colón, T221-4700, with branches in La Fortuna, San Carlos, Quepos, Liberia and Tamarindo; **Avis**, offices in San Antonio de Belén and Sabana Norte, T293-2222, www.avis.co.cr; **Budget**, Calle 30, Paseo Colón, T255-4750, www.budget.co.cr, also at international airport, T440-4412; Alajuela, Liberia, Tamarindo and Jacó Beach; **Dollar**, Paseo Colón, Calle 34-36, T257-0671, www.dollarcostarica.com; **Economy**, downtown on Paseo Colón, T231-5410, www.economyrentacar.com, also at San José, Liberia, Flamingo Beach, Tamarindo, Jacó and Manuel Antonio ; **Hertz**, Calle 38, Paseo Colón, T221-1818, www.costaricarentacar.net; **Hola**, west side of Best Western Irazú Hotel in La Uruca, T231-5666, service@hola.net; **National**, Calle 36, Av 7, T290-8787, www.natcar.com, also to Alajuela, airport, Liberia and Jacó Beach; **Payless** (formerly **Elegante**), Calle 10 Av 13-15, T257-0026, www.paylesscr.com, also in Liberia, Tamarindo, Jacó, and Quepos; **Thrifty**, Calle 3, Av 13, T257-3434, thrifty@racsa.co.cr; **Solid**, T442-6000, www.rentacarcostarica.com, several offices around town including **Hostal Toruma**, most competively priced in town; **Toyota**, Paseo Colón, T258-5797, www.toyotarent.com, good cars, also at the airport and in Liberia; **Tricolor**, on Paseo Colón, reservations T440-3333, www.tricolorcarrental.com, English and German spoken; **Wild Rider Motorcycles**, also rents cheap 4WD vehicles (see below).

Motorcycle and bike

Rental Wild Rider Motorcycles, Paseo Colón, Calle 32 diagonal Kentucky, next to Ritmo del Caribe Hotel, T258-4604, www.wild-rider.com, Honda XR250s, Yamaha XT600s and Kawasaki KLR650s available for rent from US$45-75 a day, US$600 deposit required. 4WD vehicles also available, US$240-320 per week, monthly discounts.

Cycle repairs Cyclo Quiros, Apartado 1366, Pavas, 300 m west of US Embassy. The brothers Quiros have been repairing bikes for 20 years, good place for general info and repairs, highly recommended.

Taxis

Minimum fare US$0.57 for 1st km, US$0.31 additional km. Taxis used to charge more after 2200, but that rule has been rescinded. Taxis are red and have electronic meters called 'marías'; if not, get out and take another cab. For journeys over 12 km price should be negotiated between driver and passenger. Radio cabs can be booked in advance. To order a taxi, call **Coopeguaria**, T226-1366, **Coopeirazu**, T254-3211, **Coopemoravia**, T229-8882, **Coopetaxi**, T235-9966, **Taxi San Jorge**, T221-3434, **Taxis Guaria**, T226-1366, **Taxis Unidos SA**, which are the official taxis of the Juan Santamaría International Airport and are orange instead of red, T222-6865, or look in the classified adverts of *The Tico Times* for car and driver hire.

Directory

San José *p985, maps p986 and p988*

Banks

Queues in state-run banks tend to be long; using privately run banks is recommended. The 15th and end of the month (pay day for government employees) are especially bad. Visa and MasterCard ATMs are widespread and the best option in the capital. Queues tend to be shorter outside San José. Money can be sent through **Banco de San José** or **Banco de Costa Rica** at 4%. Credit card holders can obtain cash advances from **Banco de San José** (Visa, MasterCard) and **Credomatic Los Yoses** in colones (MasterCard ATM) and **Banco Popular** (Visa ATM) minimum cash advance: US$50 equivalent. ATMs which will accept international Visa/MasterCard are available at most banks, shopping malls and San José airport. **Banco Crédito Agrícola de Cártago**, state-run, 9 branches, also makes advances on Visa, no commission, no limits. **Banco de Costa Rica**, Av 2, Calle 4, state-run, changes TCs, open 0830-1500, long queues, 1% commission. **Banco de San José**, Calle Central, Av 3-5, private, commission 2.5%. **Banco Nacional**, head office, Av 1-3, Calle 2-4, state-run, will change TCs into dollars but you pay a commission, accepts Visa credit cards as do most of the bigger banks in San José and other major towns. Many private banks are open late and Sat, including **Banco Cuscatlán**, with 12 branches around the country, Mon-Fri 0800-1800, Sat 0800-1200, T299-0299.

An alternative to the banks for getting money is the money transfer services: **Western Union**, T283-6336, www.westernunion.com, which operates out of many pharmacies and other locations and **Moneygram**, T295-9055, www.moneygram.com. Quicker than banks but you pay a price premium. **Interbank**, transfers are cheaper and you don't need an account, but take several days or more. Ask at a bank's information desk for details.

Cultural centres

Alianza Francesa, Av 7, Calle 5, French newspapers, French films every Wed evening, friendly; **Centro Cultural Costarricense Norteamericano**, Calle 37, Av 1-5, Los Yoses, T207-7500, www.cccncr.com, good films, plays, art exhibitions and English-language library, open to 1930, free.

Embassies and consulates

Belgium, Barrio Dent, T280-4435, 0800-1330; **Canada**, Building 5 (3rd floor) of Oficentro Ejecutivo La Sabana, Sabana Sur, T242-4400, Mon-Thu 0800-1630, Fri 0800-1330; **El Salvador**, Paseo Colón, from Toyota 500 m north and 25 m west, T257-7855; **France**, Curridabat, 200 m south, 25 m west of Indoor Club, T234-4167, 0830-1200; **Germany**, Rohrmoser, 200 m north and 75 m east of Oscar Arias' house, T232-5533, 0900-1200; **Guatemala**, 500 m south, 30 m east of POPs, Curridabat, T283-2557, 0900-1300; **Honduras**, Rohrmoser, T291-5143, 0900-1230; **Israel**, Edificio Colón, 11th floor, Paseo Colón, Calle 38-40, T221-6444, 0900-1200; **Italy**, Los Yoses, Av 10, Calle 33-35, T234-2326, 0900-1200; **Japan**, Oficentro building No 7, La Sabana, T296-1650; **Mexico**, Consulate, Av 7, Calle 13-15, T225-7284, 0830-1230; **Netherlands**, Oficentro Ejecutivo La Sabana, Sabana Sur, T296-1490, Mon-Fri 0900-1200; **Nicaragua**, Av Central, Calle 25-27, opposite Pizza Hut, T222-2373, 0830-1130 and 1330-1500, 24-hr wait for visa, US$25, dollars only, passport photo; **Norway**, Centro Colón, 10th floor, T283-8222. Mon-Thu 1400-1700; **Panama**, San Pedro, T281-2442, strict about onward ticket, 0900-1400, you need a photograph and photocopy of your passport, visa costs US$10 cash and takes up to 24 hrs; **Spain**, Paseo Colón, Calle 32, T222-1933; **Sweden**, honorary consul at Almacén Font, 100 m east of La Pozuelo, La Uruca, T232-8549; **Switzerland**, Centro Colón, p 10, Paseo Colón, Calle 38, T221-4829, 0900-1200; **UK**, Centro Colón, p 11, end of Paseo Colón with Calle 38 (Apdo 815-1007), T258-2025, 0900-1200; **USA**, in the western suburb of Pavas, opposite Centro Comercial, catch a ruta 14 bus to Pavas, Zona 1 from Av 1 and Calle 16-18, T220-3939, 0800-1630; **Venezuela**, Los Yoses, de la 5a entrada, 100 m south, 50 m west, T225-8810, 0830-1230, visa issued same day, US$30, helpful.

Immigration

The immigration office is on the airport highway, opposite Hospital México. You need to go here for visas extensions, etc. Queues can take all day. To get there, take bus 10 or 10A Uruca, marked 'México', then cross over highway at the bridge and walk 200 m along highway – just look for the queue or ask the driver. Better to find a travel agent who can obtain what you need for a fee, say US$5. Make sure you get a receipt if you give up your passport.

Internet

Cybercafé, in the basement of Edificio Las Arcadas, next to the Gran Hotel Costa Rica, daily 0700-2300, very helpful and friendly staff, US$0.65, 10 mins, US$1.50, 1 hr. Terrace café outside serving excellent coffee and pizzas, newspapers, good atmosphere. If that's not enough, also self-service laundry. A genuine and complete internet café. **Internet Café**, 4th floor, Av C, Calle 4, 0900-2200. A better way to spend less money as it is just c400 for full or part hr, but not a café. Several branches around town including at the western end of Paseo Colón in Edifico Colón, Calle 38-40, and if you want to tap all night there is a 24-hr café in San Pedro, close to Banco Popular.

Language schools

The number of schools has increased rapidly. Listed below are just a selection recommended by readers. Generally, schools offer tuition in groups of 2-5 for 2-4 weeks. Lectures, films, outings and social occasions are usually included and accommodation with families is encouraged. Many schools are linked to the university and can offer credits towards a US course. Rates, including lodging, are around US$1,200 a month. **Academica Tica de Español**, in San Rafael de Coronado, 10 km north of San José, T229-0013, www.academiatica.com; **AmeriSpan**, 117 South 17th St, Ste 1401, Philadelphia, PA 19103, www.amerispan.com, has affiliated schools in Alajuela, Heredia, San José and 6 others locations; **Costa Rican International Language Academy** , Barrio California, T233-8914, www.crilang.com, run by Aída Chávez, offers language study and accommodation with local families, and instruction in Latin American music and dancing as well; **Costa Rica Spanish Institute**, Zapote in San Pedro district, T234-1001, www.cosi.co.cr, US$280 per week, US$400 with homestay in San José, also branch in Manuel Antonio; **Instituto Británico** in Los Yoses, Apdo 8184, 1000 San José, T225-0256, www.institutobritanico.co.cr, teaches English and Spanish; **Instituto de Español Costa Rica**, A 1, Calle Central – Calle 1, Apartado 1405-2100, Guadalupe, T283-4733, www.professionalspanish.com. Close to the centre of San José, and complete with its own B&B. English, French and German spoken; **Universal de Idiomas**, in Moravia, T223-9662, www.universal-edu.com, stresses conversational Spanish; **Intercultura**, Apdo 1952-3000, Heredia, T260-8480, www.interculturacostarica.com. Intensive courses with excursions to beaches, volcanoes, rainforest. Volunteer programmes.

Laundry

Washing and dry cleaning at Centro Comercial San José 2000, 0730-2000, US$3.75 for large load; **Lavandería Costa Rica**, Av 3, Calle 19-21, US$5 for a large load; **Lavandería Lavamex**, below Hotel Gran Imperial at Calle 7, Av 1-Central, US$4 to wash, US$4 to dry, quick service and very friendly. Book swap, very popular with travellers, much more than a laundry thanks to the helpful owners Karl and Patricia.

Libraries

Biblioteca Nacional, opposite Parque Nacional, Mon-Fri 0830-1630, also has art and photography exhibitions; **Centro Cultural Costarricense Norteamericano**, C 37, Av 1-5, www.cccncr.com, T207-7500, has a good English-language library.

Medical services

Dentists Clínica Dental Dr Francisco **Cordero Guilarte**, Rohrmoser 300 m east of Plaza Mayor, T223-8890; **Dra Fresia Hidalgo**, Uned Building, San Pedro, 1400-1800, English spoken, reasonable prices, recommended, T234-2840; **Fernando Baldioceda** and **Silvia Oreamuno**, 225 m north of Paseo Colón on the street which intersects at the Toyota dealership: both speak English; **Alfonso Villalobos Aguilar**, Edif Herdocía, p 2, Av 3, Calle 2-4, T222-5709. **Doctors** **Dr Jorge Quesada Vargas**, Clínica Internacional, Av 14, Calle 3-5, speaks German. **Hospitals and clinics** Social Security hospitals have a good reputation (free to social security members, few members of staff speak English), free ambulance service run by volunteers: **Dr Calderón Guardia**, 257-7922, **San Juan de Dios**, T257-6282, **México**, T232-6122; **Clínica Bíblica** Calle 1, Av 14, 24-hr pharmacy, T257-5252, frequently recommended and the one most used by the local expatriate community and offers 24-hr emergency service at reasonable charges with staff who speak English, better than the large hospitals, where queues are long; **Clínica Católica**, northeast of San José, another private hospital with 24-hour pharmacy, T246-3000; **Hospital CIMA**, T208-1000, on the highway toward Escazú, country's newest and most modern private hospital, bilingual staff, expensive rates, 24-hr pharmacy, T208-1080.

Police
Thefts should be reported in San José to **Recepción de Denuncias**, Organismo de Investigación Judicial (OIJ), Calle 19, Av 6-8, T295-3643. Call for nearest OIJ office in outlying areas.

Post office
Calle 2, Av 1-3, open for sale of stamps Mon-Fri, 0700-1700, Sat-Sun 0700-1800. Stamp vending machine in main post office. Lista de Correos, Mon-Fri 0800-1700, quick service. **Couriers** DHL, Pavas, Calle 34, T209-0000, www.dhl.com; **Fed Ex**, main office is in Barreal de Heredia, T293-3157, www.fedex.com; **UPS**, 50 m east of Pizza Hut central office, Pavas, San José, T290-2828, www.ups.com.

Telephone
Faxes and internal telegrams from main post office. Fax abroad, internet access and email from **RACSA**, Av 5, Calle 1, 0730-2200 (see also Essentials, page 985). **ICE (Instituto Costarricense de Electricidad)**, Av 2, Calle 1, for phone calls (phone card only), and fax service, 0700-2200, 3-min call to UK US$10, friendly service (cheaper than **Radiográfica**, but check). Collect/reverse charge telephone calls can be made from any public telephone. English-speaking operators are available. See also page57.

Meseta Central West

Hilly and fertile with a temperate climate, the Central Highlands is a major coffee-growing area. Fairly heavily populated, picturesque and prosperous towns sit in the shadows of active volcanoes. Exploring the towns and villages of the region – each with its own character and style – gives good insight into the very heart of Costa Rica.

From San José, the Pan-American Highway heads east through the Meseta Central for 332 km along good roads to the Nicaraguan border. While CA1 will take you north, by sticking to it you'll miss visiting the remnants of colonial architecture found in Alajuela, Heredia and the countless smaller towns that enjoy the spring-like temperatures of the highlands. Although it's easier to explore the region in a private vehicle, frequent public buses and short journeys make hopping between towns fairly straightforward – if stepping out from San José it's probably worth dumping most of your luggage in the city and travelling light. ▸▸ *For Sleeping, Eating and other listings, see pages 1007-1011.*

Northwest of San José ▸▸ *pp1007-1011.*

Alajuela → *Colour map 7, B3. Population: 53,430. Altitude: 952 m.*

The provincial capital of Alajuela has a very slightly milder climate than San José making it a popular weekend excursion for Josefinos. Famous for its flowers and market days (Saturday market is good value for food), regular buses from San José make it an easy day trip. Alternatively, stay in Alajuela, and use the regular buses to visit the capital.

Alajuela, 5 km from the international airport, is handy for early flights and late arrivals.

The town centres on the Parque Central with the 19th-century domed church on the eastern side. The unusual church of La Agonía, five blocks further east, is an interesting mix of styles. One block to the south, Juan Santamaría, the national hero who torched the building in Rivas (Nicaragua) in which William Walker's filibusters were entrenched in 1856, is commemorated by a monument. One block north of the Parque Central, the **Museo Histórico Juan Santamaría** ⓘ *Av 3, Calle 2, Tue-Sun 1000-1800*, tells, somewhat confusingly, the story of this war.

Parque Nacional Volcán Poás → *Colour map 7, B3.*

ⓘ *Daily 0800-1530, 1 hr later Fri-Sun, Dec-Apr, US$7, good café next door, and toilets further along the road to the crater. If you wish to get in earlier you can leave your car/taxi at the gates, walk the 3 km up the hill and pay on your way out. The volcano is very crowded on Sun – go in the week if possible.*

Volcán Poás (2708 m) sits in the centre of the Parque Nacional Volcán Poás (6506 ha), where the still-smoking volcano and bubbling turquoise sulphur pool are set within a beautiful forest. The crater is almost 1.5 km across – the second largest in the world. The park is rich with abundant birdlife given the altitude and barren nature of the terrain and home to the only true dwarf cloud forest in Costa Rica.

> *Arrive early – clouds often hang low over the crater after 1000 obstructing the view. Wear good shoes, a hat, and suncream.*

From Alajuela two paved roads head north for 37 km to the volcano. The first through San Pedro de Poás and Fraijanes, the second follows the road to San Miguel, branching left just before the town of Vara Blanca. In the park, trails are well marked to help guide you from the Visitors' Centre to the geysers, lake and other places of interest. The main crater is 1 km along a road from the car park. There is a visitors' centre by the car park with explanations of the recent changes in the volcano. There is also a good café run by **Café Britt**; alternatively, bring your own food and water.

From **Vara Blanca** the road runs north past the popular La Paz waterfall, round the east side of the volcano through Cinchona and Cariblanco. **La Paz Waterfall Gardens** ⓘ *5 km north of Vara Blanca, T225-0643, www.waterfallgardens.com, US$25, students with ID US$15*, has forest trails past five huge falls and one of the world's largest butterfly and hummingbird gardens, a restaurant and the **Peace Lodge Hotel** (LL). The road is twisty, winding through lush forest, with several waterfalls down to the lowlands at **San Miguel**. Here the road leads either northeast heading to La Virgen and eventually Puerto Viejo de Sarapiquí (see page 1088), or northwest to Venecia (see below).

Meseta Central - west

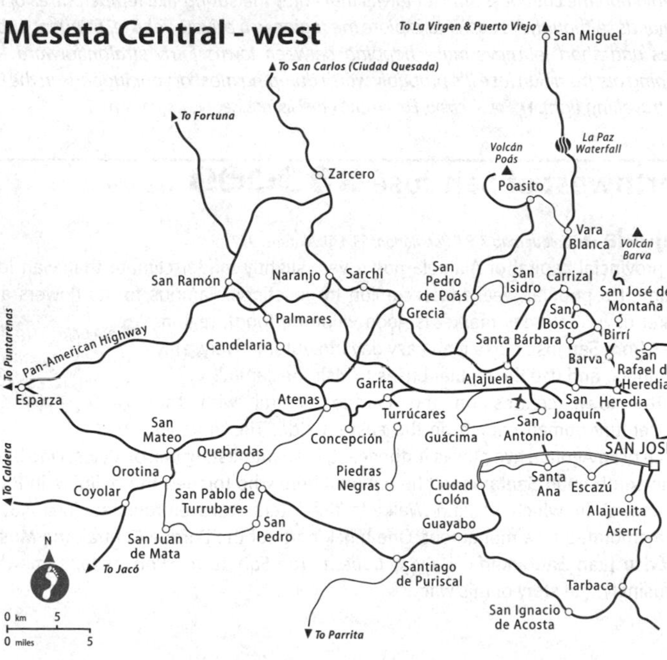

La Virgen

Ten kilometres northeast of San Miguel is La Virgen, near the Río Sarapiquí, a good spot for Class I, II and III rafting which is organized by the hotel **Rancho Leona**. From San José, take the Río Frío bus which passes through San Miguel, or a bus from San Carlos, and ask to get off at **Rancho Leona**. Juan Carlos in La Virgen has been recommended as a guide for rafting, T761-1148, from US$25 per person.

Venecia and around

Heading west from San Miguel, Venecia (three buses daily from San José, 4½ hours, US$4) has an interesting church. Near Venecia are the pre-Columbian tumuli of **Ciudad Cutris**. A good road goes to within 2 km of Cutris, from where you can walk or take a 4WD vehicle; get a permit to visit from the local finca owner.

West of Venecia is Aguas Zarcas where the road splits. Heading directly north, the roads descends into the jungle lowlands, following the Río San Carlos towards the Nicaraguan border, passing through several small towns. After about 40 km, in Boca Tapada, is **La Laguna del Lagarto Lodge** (see page 1008).

Grecia

The road from Alajuela to San Carlos (see page 1017) passes through Grecia and several towns of the Meseta Central, with good paved roads leading to others. With coffee as the mainstay of the region, the hills are covered with green coffee bushes, interspersed with other plants for shade. Grecia is also a major pineapple producer, and has an interesting church made entirely of metal. The **Museo Regional de Grecia** ⓘ *Mon-Fri 0900-1700, free*, is in the Casa de la Cultura. A short distance along the road to Alajuela is **El Mundo de los Serpientes** ⓘ *T494-3700, snakes@racsa.co.cr, 0800-1600, US$11, reductions for biology students*, a snake farm with more than 50 species. On the old road about 10 km towards Tacares is **Los Chorros Recreational Park** ⓘ *US$4*, with two massive waterfalls and picnic spots .

Sarchí and Naranjo → *Colour map 7, B3.*

Heading west is the town of Sarchí, the country's artisan centre, where you can visit the *fábricas* that produce the intricately geometric and floral designs painted on ox-carts, which are almost a national emblem. The town is divided in two, Sarchí Norte and Sarchí Sur, separated by some 4 km. The green church (until they paint it again) in Sarchí is especially attractive at sunset. Travel agents in San José charge around US$55 for a day trip to Sarchí usually combined with a trip to Volcán Poás.

The road continues north to Naranjo, a quiet agricultural town with an exquisite bright white church undergoing restoration, and a shocking post-modern pyramidal structure in the main square.

Zarcero

Frequent bus services from San José/Alajuela pass through Zarcero, on the lip of the continental divide, en route to San Carlos (Ciudad Quesada). The town is famous for vegetable farming, dairy products and notable for the topiary creations of Evangelista Blanco Breves that fill the main plaza. Bushes are clipped, trimmed and shaped into arches leading up to the white church with twin towers, with shapes of animals, dancing couples, a helicopter, many designs of Henry Moore-like sculptures and a small grotto. The interior of the quaint church, overshadowed somewhat by the plaza, is made entirely of wood, even the pillars, painted cream and pale grey with patterns in blue, brown, green and pink; cartouches, emblems and paintings.

San Ramón and Los Angeles Cloud Forest Reserve

West of Naranjo along the Pan-American Highway is the town of San Ramón, 76 km from San José. A clean town, known locally as the City of Poets, with an attractive

 Parque Central, and a street market on Saturday mornings. The **Museo de San Ramón** ⓘ *opposite the park, Tue-Fri 1300-1700*, records the history and culture of the local community. There's good walking in the surrounding area. You can visit the coffee processing plant (in season) at the **Cooperativa de Café** ⓘ *US$15-39*, in San Ramón.

Twenty kilometres north of San Ramón is the private 800-ha Los Angeles Cloud Forest Reserve (see **Hotel Villablanca**, page 1009) which offers hiking, guided tours, horse riding and canopy ascents. The local **fiesta** is around the day of San Ramón, 30 August, when local saints are carried on litters to the town's church.

Palmares and Atenas → *Colour map 7, B3.*

Palmares, 7 km southeast of San Ramón, has a pretty central park with lovely tall trees, where sloths are occasionally spotted. The quiet town comes alive in January for the annual **Fiestas de Palmares**, with food, carnival rides and parades.

After Palmares you can pick up the Pan-American Highway and head to the coast or return to San José, or continue south to Atenas. The church and main plaza in Atenas lie on an earthquake fault. The local speciality, *toronja rellena*, is a sweet-filled grapefruit. Atenas is reputed to have the best climate in the world, with stable temperatures of between 17 and 32°C year round (plus rain, of course).

North of San José »pp1007-1011.

Heredia → *Colour map 7, B3. Population: 30,968. Altitude: 1200 m.*

Ten kilometres north of San José, Heredia is capital of the province of the same name and an important coffee centre. It is a convenient and pleasant place to stay, away from the pollution of San José but close to the capital and the airport, and with good public transport. The town is mostly new with only the main square maintaining a colonial atmosphere in its architecture. The short squat **Basílica de la Inmaculada Concepción**, built in 1797, has survived countless earthquakes. To the north of the central plaza, with a statue to the poet Aquileo Echeverría (1866-1909), is the solitary defensive structure of **El Fortín**. Across the street the **Casa de la Cultura** is a fine colonial home that now hosts concerts and exhibitions. The School of Marine Biology at the Universidad Nacional campus has a **Museo Zoológico Marino**.

Around Heredia

One of the largest coffee *beneficios* is **La Meseta**. The bus from Heredia to Santa Bárbara will drop you at the gate and you can ask for a guided tour. A more popular tour is of **Café Britt's** coffee farm ⓘ *US$30, tours 1100, 1½ hrs, T260-2748, www.coffeetour.com*, near Barva de Heredia where you can see the processing factory, tasting room and multimedia presentation of the story of coffee. You can be picked up from Heredia or at various points in San José. The new **Teatro Dionisio Chaverria** at Café Britt hosts weekend theatre, and a children's show on Sunday afternoons.

North of Heredia is the historic town of **Barva**, on the slopes of Volcán Barva; frequent buses to/from Heredia (**Los Jardines B&B**, T260-1904). At Barva, the **Huetar Gallery** is recommended for arts, crafts and delicious food. There is also a **Museo de Cultura Popular** ⓘ *Mon-Fri 0900-1600, US$1.50*, 500 m east of the Salón Comunal de Santa Lucía de Barva. Beyond Barva is **Santa Bárbara**, good seafood at the **Banco de los Mariscos**, 500 m west from the central plaza. Five kilometres west of Heredia is **San Joaquín de Flores**, a small rural town with views of Barva and Poás volcanoes.

A short distance south of Heredia on the road to **Santo Domingo** is **INBio Parque** ⓘ *T507-8107, www.inbio.ac.cr, Tue-Sun 0800-1800, US$15, under-12s US$8*, an educational and recreational centre which explains and gives insight into Costa Rica's biological diversity. In a small area you can visit the ecosystems of central highland forest, dry forest and humid forest, with trails set out for bromelias and *guarumo*.

Volcán Barva

Parque Nacional Braulio Carrillo ⓘ *park entry US$7, no permit needed* (see page 1086), to the north of Heredia, includes Volcán Barva, at 2906 m. This section of the park is ideal for hiking with a good trail leading up to the summit with three lagoons nearby, and excellent views and wildlife encounters for the few that make the effort. The really enthusiastic can hike all the way down to the lowlands arriving close to La Selva Biological Station near Puerto Viejo de Sarapaqui, but careful planning is required. There is a ranger station and camp site near the entrance, 4 km north of Sacramento, from where it's a 3-km easy climb to the top – still a treasure and, amazingly, a well-kept secret from the hordes.

San José de la Montaña to Sacramento

From San José de la Montaña it is four hours' walk to Sacramento but some buses continue towards Sacramento halving the walk time (otherwise walk, hitchhike, or arrange a ride with the park director). Taxi Heredia-Sacramento, US$7.

South of San José

Aserrí to San Pablo de Turrubares

Ten kilometres south of San José is Aserrí, a village with a beautiful white church. On Friday and Saturday evenings, street bands begin the fiesta with music from 2000, followed by marimbas. Extremely popular among locals, the dancing is fabulous, with *chicharrones*, tortillas and plenty of other things to eat and drink. Further along the same road is **Mirador Ram Luna,** a restaurant with a fine panoramic view. At the end of the road is **San Ignacio de Acosta**, again with a good church containing life-size Nativity figures. Buses from San José (Calle 8, Av 12-14 in front of the Baptist church) via Aserrí hourly from 0500 to 2230, return 0430 to 2100, one hour. The unpaved road continues to **Santiago de Puriscal**, which was the epicentre for many earthquakes in 1990. Although the church is now closed as a result, there are excellent views from the town and the road. From here it is possible to take a dirt road to the Pacific coast, joining the coastal road near Parrita (see page 1061). Alternatively, take the road to **San Pablo de Turrubares**, from where you can either head west for Orotina, via an unpaved road through San Pedro and San Juan de Mata, or for Atenas via Quebradas, then east to Escobal, next stop on railway, then 4WD necessary to Atenas.

Sleeping

Alajuela *p1003*

LL Xandari, T443-2020, www.xandari.com. Once an old coffee finca overlooking the Central Valley, now, this architectural treasure has 16 private villas, health restaurant, organic gardens, new spa treatments and many facilities. One of the best hotels in Costa Rica.

L Hampton Inn Airport, T436-0000, www.hamptoninn.com. 100 rooms, double glazing, a/c, free form outdoor pool, bar, fast food places nearby, children free and discounts for 3 or 4 adults sharing.

L Hampton Inn and Suites, T442-3320, www.grupomarta.com. Luxury suites, conference rooms and facilities for business travellers. The 2 Hampton Inns are the closest place to stay near the airport, 2 km east of Juan Santamaría on the main highway.

A Viña Romántica, up in the hills near Alajuela on road to Poás volcano, 10 mins from airport, T847-8610, www.vinaromantica.com. Great spot, gourmet meals.

A-C Hotel 1915, Calle 2, Av 5-7, 300 m north of park central, T440-7163, www.1915.com. Old family home smartly refurbished with stylish garden patio café. Very good service. Rooms have cable TV, mini fridge, telephone, some with a/c, price includes breakfast. Best in town for the price.

B Hotel Alajuela, on corner across from central park at Av Central and Calle 2,

T441-1241, alajuela@racsa.co.cr. 50 generally good rooms and apartments all with private bathrooms. Helpful staff, garden patio and large restaurant for relaxing.

B Islands B&B, Av 1, Calle 7-9, 50 m west of La Agonía church, T442-0573, islandsbb@hotmail.com. A small family-run Tico-owned B&B with 8 comfortable rooms. Some rooms have cable TV, free local calls. Airport pick-up available, very secure and 24-hr parking.

B-D Charly's Place, a couple of blocks north of the central park on Av 5, Calle Central-1, T440-6853, lilyhotel@latinmail.com. Popular place, with 14 rooms most with private bathrooms, cheaper without, some with TV. Also new cheap backpackers' area. Credit cards accepted.

C Mango Verde Hostel, Av 3, Calle 2-4, T441-6630, mirafloresbb@hotmail.com. 6 clean rooms with private bath and hot water, close to the centre of town. Courtyard, kitchen and communal area create a relaxing atmosphere. Parking.

C Pensión Alajuela, Av 9, Calle Central-2, opposite the court house, T441-6251, www.pensionalajuela.com. Mixed bag of 10 simple rooms, some with private bath, some without. Small bar downstairs, laundry and fax service. 24-hr parking next door.

D-E Central Alajuela, Av Central, Calle 8, close to the bus terminal, T443-8437. Pretty basic rooms, shared bathrooms have cold water but it is reasonably clean. Popular with Ticos arriving from out of town.

D-E Cortez Azul, Av 3, Calle 2-4, 100 m west of Museo Juan Santamaría, T443-6145, www.aventurasencostarica.com. Popular spot with a handful of good, clean rooms.

D-E Villa Real, Av 3, Calle 1, T441-4022, www.aventurasencostarica.com. Claims of cleanliness largely unjustified, but it is popular with travellers and you can use the kitchen and wash clothes. Probably the cheapest place in town.

Parque Nacional Volcán Poás *p1004*

Camping in the park is not permitted but there are several places advertising cabins on the road up to Poás and nearby.

L-A Poás Volcano Lodge, west of Poasito, 200 m from Vara Blanca junction on road to Poasito, at El Cortijo farm, sign on gate, 1 km to house, T482-2194, www.poasvolcanolodge.com. English owned, includes breakfast, dinner, wholesome food, rooms in converted buildings with bath, or in farmhouse with shared bath, jungle trail, good walking, 25 mins to volcano by car, 1½ hrs from San José.

C Alberque Ecológica La Providencia, near Poás NP (2 km from green entrance gate to volcano), T232-2498. Private reserve, beautiful horse riding tour US$25-30 including lunch.

La Virgen *p1005*

A La Quinta de Sarapiquí Lodge, Bajos de Chilamate on the Río Sardinal, T761-1052, www.laquintasarapiqui.com. Costa Rican-owned, family-run lodge, 23 rooms with bath and fan, bar and restaurant overlooking the rainforest, very popular with birdwatchers with bird list available. Also a frog and butterfly garden.

B Albergue Ecológico Islas del Río, T292-2072 in San José, T766-6524, in Chilamate, www.aguas-bravas.co.cr. Price per person. The operational centre of Aguas Bravas close to Puerto Viejo de Sarapiquí, includes meals, rooms with private and shared bathroom, ideal for groups. Río Sarapiquí trips arranged. If continuing to Puerto Viejo de Sarapiquí, see p1088.

C-E Finca Pedro y el Lobo, T761-1406, www.fincapedro.com. Beautiful rustic accommodation, also options for camping, kayaking, rafting and exploring waterfalls.

D-E Rancho Leona, T761-1019, www.rancholeona.com. Basic dormitories, kayaking also original stained-glass windows for sale.

Venecia and around *p1005*

A La Laguna del Lagarto Lodge, Boca Tapada, T289-8163, www.lagarto-lodge-costa-rica.com. 12 rooms with bath, 6 with shared bath, friendly, 500 ha of forest, good for watching animals, boat trips down Río San Carlos to Río San Juan.

C-F Recreo Verde, Marsella, near Venecia, T472-1020. A good choice in a recreational and ecological conservation park. There are hot springs, primary forest, a few trails going to nearby caves and helpful, friendly staff.

Grecia *p1005*

A-B Posada Mimosa, Apdo 135-4100, Costa Rica, T494-5868, www.mimosa.co.cr. B&B, rooms, suites and a couple of cabins set in beautiful tropical gardens.

Sarchí and Naranjo *p1005*
A Rancho Mirador, on the Panamericana, 1 km west of the turn-off for Naranjo, T451-1302. Good-value *cabañas*, good restaurant with local food, a spectacular view of coffee fincas and San José in the distance. Owner Rick Vargas was formerly a stunt pilot in the US.
B Hotel Villa Sarchí Lodge, 800 m north of Sarchí, T454-3029. 11 rooms with private bath, hot water, cable TV and pool.
D Cabinas Daniel Zamora, Sarchí, T454-4596. With bath, fan, hot water, very clean and extra blankets if cold at night.
E Cabinas Sarchí, opposite Banco Nacional, Sarchí, T454-4425. With bath. You may have to call owner if unattended.
F La Bamba, Naranjo, down the hill by the football pitch. May muster up enough energy to let you stay in one of their simple rooms.

Zarcero *p1005*
B-C Don Beto, by the church, T463-3137. With bath, very friendly, clean.

San Ramón and Los Angeles Cloud Forest Reserve *p1005*
L Hotel Villablanca, north of town set in the 800-ha Los Angeles Cloud Forest Reserve, T461-0300, www.villablanca-costarica.com. Naturalist hikes, some up to 8 hrs, canopy tour, horse riding and the famous La Mariana Chapel with handpainted ceiling tiles – you don't have to stay to visit.
A-B La Posada, T445-7359, www.posada hotel.com. 400 m north of the cathedral, parking, 27 good rooms, with private bath, hot water. Use of kitchen, laundry, parking and small patio for relaxing.
D Hotel Nuevo Jardín, 5 blocks north of the central park, T445-5620. Simple, clean, friendly.
D San Ramón, 100 m east of Banco de Costa Rica, T447-2042. 30 spotless rooms (but pretty garish decor), with private bathroom, hot water and cable TV. Parking.
E Gran Hotel, 150 m west of post office, T445-6363. Big rooms, private bathrooms, hot water, OK, friendly, communal TV area.

Palmares and Atenas *p1006*
AL El Cafetal Inn, out of Atenas, in St Eulalia, 4.7 km towards Grecia, T446-5785, www.cafetal.com. Nice seting on a coffee plantation, private house, large pool, 10 rooms, recommended.

Heredia *p1006*
AL Valladolid, Calle 7, Av 7, T260-2905, valladol@racsa.co.cr. 11 spacious rooms and suites, all with a/c, private bath, telephone and cable TV. 5th floor has sauna, jacuzzi and **Bonavista Bar** with fine views overlooking the Central Valley.
A-B Apartotel Vargas, 800 m north of Colegio Santa Cecilia and San Francisco Church, T237-8526, apartotelvargas@ yahoo.com. 8 large, well-furnished apartments with cooking facilities, hot water, laundry facilities, TV, enclosed patio with garage and nightwatchman, English-speaking staff. Sr Vargas will collect you from airport. Excellent choice if taking language classes and in a group. Best option in town.
D Hotel Heredia, Calle 6, Av 3-5, T238-0880. 10 rooms, some quite dark, but all have private bath and hot water.
D Las Flores, Av 12, Calle 12-14, T261-8147. With bath, clean, quiet and recommended.
F Colonial, Calle 4-6, Av 4, T237-5258. Clean, friendly and family-run, will park motorcycles in restaurant.
F El Verane, Calle 4, Av 6-8, next to central market, T237-1616. Rooms on street side are slightly better, close to bus terminal.

Around Heredia *p1006*
LL Finca Rosa Blanca, 1.6 km from Santa Bárbara de Heredia, T269-9392, www.finca-rblanca.co.cr. Deluxe suites in an architectural explosion of style and eloquence, romance and exclusivity at the extremes of imagination and fantasy. Restaurant and bar for guests only.
AL Bougainvillea de Santo Domingo, just west of Santo Domingo, T244-1414, www.bougainvillea.co.cr. Includes breakfast, excellent service, pool, spectacular mountain setting, free shuttle bus to San José. Highly recommended.

Eating

Alajuela *p1003*
Finding something to eat in Alajuela is not difficult, most restaurants, cafés and sodas are within 1 or 2 blocks of the Parque Central and down Calle Central.
ΨΨ La Mansarda, central plaza. Good, wholesome Tico dishes.
Ψ Café Almibar, Av Central, Calle 1-3. Another snacking stop popular with locals.

Ψ **La Cocina de Abuelita**, Av Central, Calle 1-3. Simple lunchtime, buffet menu.
Ψ **Trigo Miel**, Av 2, Calle Central-2. One of a couple of patisserie cafés in Alajuela serving divine snacks and good coffee.

Venecia and around *p1005*
Ψ **El Parque**, near church, Venecia. Good local food.

Zarcero *p1005*
The town is known for cheese and fruit preserves.
Ψ **Soda/Restaurant El Jardín**, 1st floor, overlooking the plaza. Local lunches and breakfasts. Good view of topiary.

San Ramón *p1005*
Ψ **Tropical**, near northwest corner of the Parque. Excellent ice cream parlour.

Heredia *p1006*
ΨΨΨ-Ψ **La Rambla**, Calle 7, Av 7. Services a good mix of *comida típica* and international dishes.
ΨΨ **Café Azzura**, 50 m from southwest corner of the main plaza, T260-9083. Great ice cream, cakes, shakes, cappuccino and people watching.
ΨΨ **Cowboy Restaurant**, Calle 9, Av 5. Grill option where the Mid-West meets Costa Rica. Lively bar in the evenings. Credit cards accepted.
ΨΨ **El Gran Papa**, Calle 9, Av 3. Open for dinner only, with a good range of *bocas*, pastas and cocktails.
ΨΨ **La Luna de Valencia**, a few kilometres north of Barva, T269-6665. Authentic paella restaurant, vegetarian options, friendly service, recommended.
ΨΨ **Le Petit Paris**, Calle 5 and Av Central-2, T262-2564. A little piece of France simply oozing style in the heart of Heredia. The ambience shifts between the bar, restaurant and patio café. The food is French, divine and there is live music on Thu, closed Sun.
ΨΨ-Ψ **Baalbek Bar & Grill**, San Rafael de Heredia, on the road to Monte de la Cruz, T267-6482. Good Mediterranean food, live music.
ΨΨ-Ψ **Bulevar Bar**, Av Central, Calle 5-7. One of the happening places with a lively balcony bar upstairs and fast food and *bocas* available.
ΨΨ-Ψ **Fresas**, Calle 7, Av 1, T262-5555. Diner-style restaurant serving everything you could possible want including snacks, sandwiches, breakfast, full meals, fresh fruit juices and strawberries; bar upstairs.
ΨΨ-Ψ **Las Espigas**, southwest corner of Parque Central. Good for coffee, pastries and lunch specials.
Ψ **Vishnu Mango Verde**, Calle 7, Av Central-1, T237-2526. Good wholesome vegetarian served fast food style out front or a little more leisurely out back.

Festivals and events

Alajuela *p1003*
11 Apr Juan Santamaría Day, a week of bands, concerts and dancing in celebration of the life of the town's most famous son.
Mid-Jul the fruitful heritage comes to the fore with a Mango Festival of parades, concerts and an arts and crafts fair.

Shopping

Sarchí and Naranjo *p1005*
One of the largest *artesanías* is **Fábrica de Chaverri** in Sarchí Sur. **Taller Lalo Alfaro**, the oldest workshop, is in Sarchí Norte and worth a visit to see more traditional production methods. Both sell hand-made furniture, cowhide rocking chairs and wooden products as well as the ox-carts, which come in all sizes.

Heredia *p1006*
Bookshop **Brian's Books**, 50 m east of courthouse in Zona Rosa plaza. Used books in English.

Transport

Alajuela *p1003*
Bus Service to **San José**. Depart Alajuela from main bus terminal Calle 8, Av Central-1, or Av 4, Calle 2-4 every 10 mins, 30 mins, US$0.55, with both services arriving on Av 2 in the capital. To **Heredia** from 0400 until 2200, 30 mins, US$0.40. Buses to the Butterfly Farm at **La Guácima** marked 'La Guácima abajo' leave from Av 2 between Calle 8-10, US$0.30. 1 block south of the terminal buses depart for several small villages in the area including **Laguna de Fraijanes** and **Volcán Poás**.

Parque Nacional Volcán Poás *p1004*
The volcano can be reached by car from **San José**. A taxi for 6 hrs with a side trip will cost

about US$50-60. There is a daily excursion bus from the main square of Alajuela right up to the crater, leaving at 0915 (or before if full), connecting with 0830 bus from San José (from Av 2, Calle 12-14); be there early for a seat; although extra buses run if necessary, the area gets very crowded, US$3.50 return, T237-2449. The bus waits at the top with ample time to see everything (clouds permitting), returning at 1530. Daily bus **Alajuela-Poasito** 1200 (US$1) will take you part way to the summit. From **Poasito** hitch a lift as it is a 10-km walk. Other options include taking the 0600 or 1600 bus from Alajuela to **San Pedro de Poás**, hitch/taxi to Poasito and stay overnight, hiking or hitching up the mountain next morning. Taking a 0500 bus from Alajuela to Poasito arrives 2 hrs before the park gates open.

Sarchí and Naranjo *p1005*
Bus Express bus from **San José** to Sarchí, Calle 16, Av 1-3, 1215, 1730 and 1755, Mon-Fri, returning 0530, 0615, 1345, Sat 1200, 1½ hrs, US$0.80. **Tuasa** buses every 30 mins, 0500-2200 from Alajuela bus station, 1½ hrs, US$0.50.

Transportes Naranjo, T451-3655, have buses to and from **San José**'s Coca Cola terminal every 40 mins. Buses connect other towns and villages in the area.

San Ramón and Los Angeles Cloud Forest Reserve *p1005*
Heading north the road forks, left to **Zarcero** (20 km) and finally to **Cd Quesada**. The right fork heads north to **La Tigra** and **Fortuna** passing the Los Angeles Cloud Forest Reserve.
Bus Many buses going to San Ramón continue to **Puntarenas**. They originate at the Empresarios Unidos stop in **San José** at Calle 16, Av 10-12, 10 a day, every 45 mins or so, US$1.40. There is also a service via **Alajuela**. Buses run to surrounding villages and towns.

Palmares and Atenas *p1006*
The library on the plaza in Atenas also serves as the bus office, Cooptransatenas, T446-5767. Many daily buses to **San José**, either direct or via **Alajuela**, US$0.60.

Heredia *p1006*
Bus From **San José** from Av 2, Calle 12-14, buses every 10 mins daily, 0500-0015, then every 30 mins to 0400, 25-min journey, US$0.40. Return buses from Av 4, Calle Central. Local buses leave from Av 8, Calle 2-4, by market.

Volcán Barva *p1007*
Accessible from **Heredia**, there is no route from the San José-Limón Highway. Buses leave from the market at 0630, 1230 and 1600, returning at 0730, 1300, 1700. Arriving at Porrosati. Some continue as far as Sacramento, otherwise walk 6 km to park entrance, then 4 km to lagoon. Be careful if leaving a car, there are regular reports of theft from rental cars.

Directory

Alajuela *p1003*
Banks No shortage of banks, all within 3 blocks of each other and most with AMT, including Banco Nacional, Calle 2, Av Central-1, facing central park, Banco Interfin, next door. 1 block south of central park is Banco Crédito Agrícola de Cártago, Calle 2, Av Central-2, and 2 blocks north is Banco de Santa Cruz, Calle 2, Av 3, which is also the office of Credomatic. **Emergency** T911. **Internet** Southside of main plaza, Mon-Sun 0900-2200, US$0.60/hr. Also with pool tables. Interplanet, across from La Agonía church on Av Central and Calle 9, stands out largely due to the fluorescent lighting, daily 0830-2200. **Medical services** Hospital San Rafael, Av 9, Calle Central-1, north end of town, T440-1333, can help in a crisis. **Post office** Corner of Av 5 and Calle 1, Mon-Fri 0730-1700, Sat mornings.

Sarchí and Naranjo *p1005*
Banks Banco Nacional has branches in Sarchí Sur and Sarchí Norte, and on the north side of the plaza in Naranjo, with Visa and MasterCard ATM. **Post office** Services are found in both villages.

Heredia *p1006*
Language schools Centro Panamericano de Idiomas, San Joaquín de Flores, T265-6306, www.cpi-edu.com. Accommodation with local families. Also have schools in Monteverde and Playa Flamingo. Intercultura Language and Cultural Center, Heredia, T260-8480, www.interculturacostarica.com. Small classes, also with a campus at Playa Samara.

Meseta Central East

The eastern Central Highlands offer relative quiet, despite being close to San José. The former capital and pilgrimage site of Cártago sits meekly at the bottom of the fuming Irazú volcano before it falls away to the beautiful Orosí Valley. The thundering Río Reventazón leads the next step down the Atlantic slope, beginning its journey to the Caribbean, passing Turrialba, a good base for whitewater adventure. Meanwhile, the slopes of nearby Turrialba volcano hide the country's main archaeological site of Guayabo and good hiking opportunities to its summit. » *For Sleeping, Eating and other listings, see pages 1014-1017.*

Cártago and around » *pp1014-1017. Colour map 7, B3.*

→ *Population: 33,539. Altitude: 1439 m.*

Cártago, at the foot of the Irazú Volcano and 22.5 km from San José on a toll road (US$0.75), is encircled by mountains. Founded in 1563, it was the capital of Costa Rica for almost 300 years until San José assumed the role in 1823. Since then the town has failed to grow significantly and remains small, though densely populated. Earthquakes in 1841 and 1910 destroyed many of the buildings and ash from Irazú engulfed the town in 1963. While colonial-style remnants exist in one or two buildings, the town feels as if it is still reeling from the impact of so much natural devastation and is keeping quiet waiting for the next event.

The most important attraction in town, and the focal point for pilgims from all over Central America, is the **Basílica de Nuestra Señora de Los Angeles**, the patroness of Costa Rica, on the eastern side of town. Rebuilt in 1926 in Byzantine style, it houses the diminutive **La Negrita**, an indigenous image of the Virgin under 15 cm high, worshipped for her miraculous healing powers. The basilica houses a collection of finely made silver and gold images, no larger than 3 cm high, of various parts of the human anatomy, presumably offered in the hope of being healed. The most important date in the pilgrims' calendar is 2 August, when the image of La Negrita is carried in procession to churches in Cártago with celebrations throughout Costa Rica.

Also worth seeing is **La Parroquia** (the old parish church), roughly 1 km west of the basilica, ruined by the 1910 earthquake and now converted into a delightful garden retreat with flowers, fish and hummingbirds.

Around Cártago

Aguas Calientes, 4 km southeast of Cártago and 90 m lower, has a warm-water *balneario* ideal for picnics. On the road to Paraíso, 8 km from Cártago, is an orchid garden, the **Jardín Lankester** ⓘ *10 mins' walk from the main road, T552-3247, daily 0830-1500, US$3.10*, run by the University of Costa Rica. The best displays are between February and April. While off the beaten track, the gardens are worth a visit. The Cártago-Paraíso bus departs every 30 minutes from the south side of central park in Cártago (15 minutes); ask the driver to let you out at Campo Ayala. Taxi from Cártago, US$5.

Volcán Irazú → *Colour map 7, B3. Altitude: 3432 m.*

ⓘ *US$7, 0800-1530 most of the year.*

Irazú's crater is an impressive half-mile cube dug out of the earth, surrounded by desolate grey sand, which looks like the surface of the moon. President Kennedy's visit in 1963 coincided with a major eruption and, in 1994 the north wall of the volcano was destroyed by another eruption that sent detritus down as far as the Río Sucio, within sight of the the San José-Limón Highway. The views are stupendous on a clear day and the main reason for the trip. But the clouds normally move in enveloping the lower peaks and slopes by 1300 (sometimes even by 0900 or 1000 between July and November), so get there as early as you can to have a greater chance of a clear view of the mountains and the sun shining on the clouds in the valley below. There's little wildlife other than the ubiquitous Volcano Junco bird and the few plants which survive in this desert, but ongoing colonization is attracting more birds.

It's definitely worth the trip and an early start. As one traveller wrote: "In the afternoon the mountain top is buried in fog and mist or drizzle, but the ride up in the mist can be magical, for the mountainside is half displaced in time. There are new jeeps and tractors, but the herds of cattle are small, the fields are quilt-work, handcarts and ox-carts are to be seen under the fretworked porches of well-kept frame houses. The land is fertile, the pace is slow, the air is clean. It is a very attractive mixture of old and new. Irazú is a strange mountain, well worth the ride up."

The Orosí Valley

Further east from Cártago a trip round the Orosí Valley makes a beautiful circular trip, or a fine place to hang out for a while in a valley that is often overlooked as the crowds rush to the more popular spots on the coast. The centrepiece of the valley is the artificial Lake Cachí used for hydro-electric generation. Heading round the lake counter-clockwise, the road passes through Orosí, clips the edge of Parque Nacional Tapantí, continuing to the Cachí Dam and completes the circuit passing through Ujarrás. Along the way there are several miradors which offer excellent views of the Reventazón Valley. For transport see each destination. Day trips can be easily arranged from San José.

In **Orosí** there is an 18th-century **mission** ⓘ *closed Mon*, with colonial treasures, and just outside two **balnearios** ⓘ *US$1.60*, with restaurants serving good meals at fair prices. It's a good place to hang out, take some low-key language classes, mixed with mountain biking and trips to the national park and other sites of interest.

Parque Nacional Tapantí-Macizo de la Muerte

ⓘ *Daily 0700-1700, US$7.*

Twelve kilometres beyond Orosí is the Parque Nacional Tapantí-Macizo de la Muerte, one of the wettest parts of the country (some parts reportedly receiving as much as 8 m of rain a year). Approached from Orosí, and just 30 km from Cártago, the national park is suprisingly easy to reach and packs in the interest.

Covering 58,000 ha, Tapantí-Macizo includes the former Tapantí National Park and much of the Río Macho Forest Reserve. The park protects the Río Orosí basin which feeds the Cachí Dam hydro power plant. Strategically, the southern boundary of the park joins with Chirripó National Park, extending the continuous protected area that makes up La Amistad Biosphere Reserve. The park incorporates a wide range of life zones with altitudes rising from 1220 m to over 3000 m at the border with Chirripó. The diverse altitudes and relative seclusion of the park has created an impressive variety of species – 260 bird species, 45 mammals, lizards, snakes – a list which is currently incomplete due to the recent creation of the park. There are picnic areas, a nature centre with slide shows (ask to see them) and good swimming in the dry season (November-June), and trout fishing season (1 April-31 October).

From June to November/December it rains every afternoon.

Cachí

Continue around the lake to Cachí and the nearby **Casa del Soñador** (Dreamer's House) which sells wood carvings from the sculpture school of the late Macedonio Quesada. The road crosses the dam wall and follows the north shore to Ujarrás, then back to Cártago. The **Charrarra tourist complex** ⓘ *30-mins' walk from Ujarrás*, has a good campsite, restaurant, pool, boat rides on the lake and walks. It can be reached by direct bus on Sunday. Buses leave from Cártago one block north of the Cártago ruins.

Ujarrás

Ujarrás (ruins of a colonial church and village) is 6.5 km east of Paraíso, on the shores of the artificial Lago Cachí. There is a bus every 1½ hours from Paraíso that continues to Cachí. Legend has it that in 1666 English pirates, including the youthful Henry Morgan, were seen off by the citizens of Ujarrás aided by the Virgin. The event is now celebrated annually in mid-March when the saint is carried in procession from Paraíso to the ruined church.

Turrialba and around

» *pp1014-1017. Colour map 7, B3.*

→ *Population: 20,000. Altitude: 646 m.*

Turrialba (62 km from San José) bridges the Central Valley highlands and the Caribbean lowlands, and was once a stopping point on the old Atlantic railway between Cártago and Puerto Limón. The railway ran down to Limón on a narrow ledge poised between mountains on the left, and the river to the right, but no longer operates. The **Centro Agronómico Tropical de Investigación y Enseñanza (CATIE** – T558-2000 ext 2275, www.catie.ac.cr) about 4 km southeast of Turrialba covers more than 800 ha of this ecologically diverse zone (with many fine coffee farms), has one of the largest tropical fruit collections in the world and houses an important library on tropical agriculture; visitors and students are welcome for research or birdwatching. Past CATIE on the south side of the river, a large sugar mill makes for a conspicuous landmark in Atirro, the centre for macadamia nuts. Nearby, the 256-ha **Lake Angostura** has now flooded some of the whitewaters of the Río Reventazón. What has been lost as world-class whitewater is believed, by some, to be a Lake Arenal in the making. A glimpse of the vegetation covered lake will convince you otherwise.

Around Turrialba

Many whitewater rafting companies operate out of Turrialba, with trips to the **Río Reventazón** and **Río Pacuare**. The rafting is excellent; the Pascua section of the Reventazón can be Class V at rainy times. The Pacuare is absolutely perfect with divine scenery. By contacting the guides in Turrialba you can save about 30% on a trip booked in San José, provided they are not already contracted.

Volcán Turrialba (3329 m) may be visited from Cártago by a bus from Calle 4 y Avenida 6 to the village of San Gerardo. From Turrialba take a bus to Santa Cruz. From both, an unpaved road meets at **Finca La Central**, on the saddle between Irazú and Turrialba.

Monumento Nacional Guayabo

ⓘ *Tue-Sun 0800-1530, US$4, local guides available, water, toilets, no food.*

About 19 km north of Turrialba, near Guayabo, is a 3000-year-old ceremonial centre excavated with paved streets and stone-lined water channels. The archaeological site, 232 ha and 4 km from the town of Guayabo, is now a national monument, and dates from the period 1000 BC-AD 1400. There are excellent walks in the park, plenty of birds and wildlife can be seen. Worth a trip to see Costa Rica's most developed ancient archaeological site but small in comparison to the great sites of the Maya.

Sleeping

Cártago *p1012*

B Los Angeles Lodge B&B, near the Basílica at Av 4, Calle 14-16, T551-0957. Clean, nice rooms.

D Dinastia, Calle 3, Av 6-8, close to the old railway station, at the Las Ruinas end of town, T551-7057. Slightly more expensive with private bath. The rooms are small although better with a window. Safe hotel but in lively area north of the central market. Credit cards accepted.

Volcán Irazú *p1012*
D Hotel Gestoria Irazú, on the slopes of Irazú on the way up, in **San Juan de Chicúa**, T253-0827. Simple rooms with private bath, hot water and extra blankets to get you through the cold winter nights.

Orosí Valley *p1013*
B Orosí Lodge, T533-3578, www.orosilodge.com. 7 rooms with balcony overlooking the valley towards Volcán Irazú each with private bath, hot water and kitchenette. Just about everything you could want; divine home-baked cookies, mountain bikes, kayaks and horses for rent and an internet service. Credit cards accepted. Excellent value.
B-C Cabinas Media Libra, T533-3838. Rather stark and characterless rooms, with telephone, TV, fridge. But clean and friendly service, and good local knowledge. Credit cards accepted.
C-F Montaña Linda, T533-2153 (international), T533-3640 (local), www.montanalinda.com. A classic and well- run backpackers' place, with a range of options. Dormitory rooms, camping, and B&B service if you just can't get out of bed! Toine and Sara are friendly and know their patch very well, organizing trips to local sights.
D Río Palomo, in Palomo, just south of Orosí, T533-3128. Cabins, pool, laundry facilities, good restaurant.

Parque Nacional Tapantí-Macizo de la Muerte *p1013*
L Monte Sky Mountain Retreat, near Tapantí, T228-0010. Cabins with shared bath, cold water, includes meals, hiking trails through forest. **Camping** platforms also available.
B Kiri Lodge, 1.5 km from the park entrance, T533-2272, www.kirilodge.com. Excellent lodging and food, breakfast included, peaceful, very friendly, good trails on 50-ha property.

Camping
No camping is allowed at the park, but visitors can stay in the rustic park-run lodge near the entrance. Bring your own blankets and food, reservations required, US$3, contact regional park office T551-2970. See also **Monte Sky Mountain Retreat**, above.

Turrialba *p1014*
AL Wagelia, Av 4, entrance to Turrialba, T556-1566. 18 rooms, bath, some a/c, restaurant.
B-C Interamericano, facing the old railway station on Av 1, T556-0142, www.hotelinteramericano.com. Price per person. Very friendly place run by mother-daughter team, popular with kayakers. Clean, private or shared bath. Safe for motorbikes. Internet service, bar and communal area with TV and books.
C **Alcázar**, Calle 3, Av 2-4, 25 m north of **Banco Norte**, T393-0767. Small terrace upstairs, each room has cable TV, telephone, fan and a private bath with hot water. Small, cheap bar/restaurant downstairs with frightening colour schemes.
C-D Central, next to **Interamericano**, T556-0170. Price per person, with bath, restaurant, basic.
D Hotel Turrialba, Av 2, Calle 2-4, T556-6396. Clean simple rooms with private bath, hot water and TV. There are also a couple of pool tables and drinks for sale.
E Laroche, north of Parque Central on Calle 1. Simple and basic rooms but friendly with comfortable beds. Small bar downstairs.
F Whittingham, Calle 4, Av 0-2, T550-8927. 7 fairly dark but OK rooms, some with private bath – an option if other places are full.

Around Turrialba *p1014*
LL Casa Turire, 14 km southeast of Turrialba, follow the signposts, T531-1111, www.hotel casaturire.com. Overlooking Lake Angostura, 12 luxury rooms with bath, 4 suites, cable TV, phone, restaurant, pool, library, games room, in the middle of a 1620-ha sugar, coffee and macadamia nut plantation. Virgin rainforest nearby, trails, horses, bike rental, excursions.
A Turrialtico, on road to Siquirres, T538-1111, www.turrialtico.com. On top of hill with extensive views. Rooms are clean with private bath, comfortable, friendly. Going northeast from Turrialba, the main road follows the Río Reventazón down to Siquirres (see page 1089).
C Albergue Mirador Pochotel, Pavones, T538-1010. 10 basic cabins, a popular spot.
E San Agustín, Vereh, some 25 km southeast of Turrialba (take bus via Jicotea), www.costaricabackpacker.com. Truly isolated for a real rural Costa Rica experience. Candlelight camping, river bathing, hiking and horse riding in surrounding area – basic, and a very pure rainforest experience.

Monumento Nacional Guayabo *p1014*
D **Albergue y Restaurant La Calzada**, T559-0023. Call in advance to make a r reservation and check they're open.

Eating

Cártago *p1012*
¥ **Auto 88**, east of public market. *Cafetería*-style, with beer-drinking room adjoining dining room.
¥ **Soda Apollo**, on northwest cornerof parque, opposite La Parroquia. 24-hr snack option.

Volcán Irazú *p1012*
¥¥-¥ **Restaurante Linda Vista**. Spectacular views, as you'd expect from Costa Rica's highest restaurant, serving good food and drinks. But most people stop to post, stick, pin or glue a business card, or some other personal item, to the wall.

Turrialba *p1014*
¥¥¥-¥¥ **Kingston**, out of town heading south, T556-1613. The locally popular restaurant.
¥¥-¥ **Pizzería Julián**, on the square. Popular.
¥ **La Garza**, on main square. Cheap, local good food.
¥ **Nuevo Hong Kong**, just east of the main square. Good, reasonable prices.
¥ **Soda Burbuja**, a block south of square on Calle Central. Local dishes, excellent portions, very good value.

Activities and tours

Cártago *p1012*
Tour operators
Mercatur, next to Fuji at Av 2, Calle 4-6, provides local tourist information.

Around Turrialba *p1014*
Tour operators
See also the companies in San José (ie **Ríos** Tropicales, page 998).
Tico's River Adventures, T556-1231, www.ticoriver.com. With recommended local guides.
Serendipity Adventures, T507-1358, www.serendipityadventures.com. Canyoning rappelling and hot-air ballooning. Recommended
Loco's Tropical Tours, T556-6035, www.whiteh2o.com. A small locally owned operator, providing custom rafting trips on the Reventazón and Pacuare rivers, 2-day trips, also horse riding tour to Laguna Bonilla.

Transport

Cártago *p1012*
Bus A good bus service supplies the surrounding area. To **San José** every 10 mins from Av 4, Calle 2-4. Arrives and departs San José from Calle 5, Av 18-20 for the 45-min journey. After 2030 buses leave from **Gran Hotel Costa Rica**, Av 2, Calle 3-5. **Orosí/Río Macho**, for **Parque Nacional Tapantí** every 30 mins from Calle 6, Av 1-3, 35-55 mins. **Turrialba**, every hr from Av 3, Calle 8-10, 1 hr direct, 1 hr 20 mins *colectivo*. **Cachí**, via **Ujarrá** and **Paraíso** from Calle 6, Av 1-3, every 1½ hrs, 1 hr 20 mins. **Paraíso**, every 5 mins from Av 5, Calle 4-6. **Aguacalientes**, every 15 mins from Calle 1, Av 3-5. **Tierra Blancas** for **Irazú**, every 30 mins from Calle 4, Av 6-8.

Closest bus for **Irazú** rides to San Juan de Chichua, still some 12 km from the summit. The bus leaves Cártago from north of the central market, Av 6, Calle 1-3, at 1730, returning at 0500 the next day, so you have to spend at least 2 nights on the volcano or in a hotel if you can't get a ride. To visit **Volcán Turrialba** take a bus from Calle 4 y Av 6 to the village of San Gerardo.

Volcán Irazú *p1012*
Bus It is possible to get a bus from Cártago to Tierra Blanca (US$0.33) or San Juan de Chicúa (which has 1 hotel) and hitch a ride in a pick-up truck. Alternatively you can take a bus from Cártago to Sanatorio. Ask the driver to drop you at the crossroads just outside Tierra Blanca. From there you walk 16 km to the summit. If you're looking for a day trip from San José a yellow 'school' express bus run by **Buses Metropoli SA**, T272-0651, runs from **San José**, Sat, Sun and holidays, 0800 from Gran Hotel Costa Rica, stops at Cártago ruins 0830 to pick up more passengers, returns 1215 with lunch stop at **Restaurant Linda Vista**, US$6.

Taxi From **Cártago** is US$32 return. A taxi tour from **Orosí** costs US$10 per person, minimum 3 people, and stops at various places on the return journey, eg Cachí dam and Ujarrás ruins. Since it can be difficult to find a decent hotel in Cártago, it may be easier to take a guided tour leaving from **San José**, about US$35, 5½ hrs includes lunch, transport from San José. If driving from San José, take the turn off at the Ferretería San Nicolás in Taras, which goes directly to Irazú, avoiding Cártago.

Orosí Valley *p1013*
Bus From **Cártago** to Orosí/Río Macho from Calle 6, Av 1-3, every 30 mins, journey time of 35-55 mins. US$0.50.

Parque Nacional Tapantí-Macizo de la Muerte *p1013*
Bus 0600 bus from Cártago to Orosí gets to Puricil by 0700, then walk (5 km), or take any other Cártago-Orosí bus to Río Macho and walk 9 km to the refuge. Alternatively take a taxi from **Orosí** (US$7 round trip, up to 6 passengers), or **San José**, US$50.

Turrialba *p1014*
Bus From **San José** every hr 0530-2200 from Terminal Turrialba, Calle 13, Av 6-8, 1½ hrs, US$1.60; from **Cártago**, 1 hr, US$0.80, runs until about 2200. Service to **Siquirres**, for connections to Caribbean lowlands, hourly, 40 mins, US$1.50.

Monumento Nacional Guayabo *p1014*
Bus From **Turrialba**, there are buses at 1100 (returning 1250) and 1710 (returning 1750), and on Sun at 0900, return 1700 (check times, if you miss it is quite difficult to hitch as there is little traffic), US$0.45 to Guayabo. If you can't get a bus all the way to Guayabo, several buses each day pass the turn-off to Guayabo, the town is a 2-hr walk uphill (taxi US$10, easy to hitch back). Tour operators in **San José** offer day trips to Guayabo for about US$65 per person (minimum 4 people), cheaper from Turrialba.

Directory

Cártago *p1012*
Banks No shortage of banks, most with ATMs. Banco de Costa Rica, Av 4, Calle 5-7. Banco Interfin, Park Central at Av 2, Calle 2. Banco Nacional, Av 2, Calle 1-3.
Emergencies Call T911. **Internet** Café Línea, Av 4, Calle 6-8, the only internet place in town, looks decidedly temporary.
Medical services Dr Max Peralta, entrance on Calle 3, Av 7. The pharmacy is along Av 4 between Calle 1-6.

Orosí Valley *p1013*
Language schools Montaña Linda Language School uses local teachers to get you *hablando español* with a homestay option if you want total submersion. Recommended – see Sleeping, above.

Northern Costa Rica

The Cordillera de Tilarán and the Cordillera de Guanacaste stretch to the Nicaragua border. Tucked in the eastern foothills is the vast man-made Lago Arenal, resting calmly beneath the highly active Volcán Arenal. A number of quieter spots can be found in the area with fine opportunities for fishing and seeing the wildlife, while the more active can go rafting, windsurfing, horse riding and trekking. ▸▸ *For Sleeping, Eating and other listings, see pages 1022-1027.*

San Carlos and around → *Colour map 7, B3.*

Also known as **Ciudad Quesada,** San Carlos is the main town of the northern lowland cattle and farming region and is a hub of communications. True to form, the town has a frontier feel with an air of bravado and a pinch of indifference. Situated on the downside of the northern slopes of the central highlands mountain region, the temperature rises and the speed of life slows down. In a town without major sights, the huge church overlooking the main plaza stands out. The cavernous interior is matched for style by modern stained-glass windows and an equally massive sculpture of Christ above the altar. As a regional centre San Carlos is served by frequent buses from San José, and

Border essentials: Costa Rica-Nicaragua

Los Chiles
This crossing point is now open to foreigners but the road link is a dirt track, and San Carlos on the Nicaraguan side is remote from the rest of that country.

Costa Rican immigration All formalities are in Los Chiles which is a few kilometres short of the border. The office is close to the river and leaving procedures are normally straightforward. Daily 0800-1600, usually closed for lunch. If entering Costa Rica, officials can be more difficult, mainly because they are sensitive about the many Nicaraguan immigrants wishing to enter the country. Crossing purely overland is possible. It is some 4 km to the border post, and a total of 14 km to San Carlos with no regular transport. See Nicaragua – San Carlos and San Juan del Norte/Greytown for details on the Río San Juan border, page 949.

Transport Boat A regular launch goes down the Río Frío across the Río San Juan to San Carlos, 0800 or when full, 45 minutes, US$5. There are other launches if demand is sufficient. You can follow the track north to the Río San Juan and then find a ferry to cross, but enquire before trying this route.

has good connections to La Fortuna and Los Chiles. The new bus terminal, about 1 km north of town, is close to a shopping centre and a new cinema. From San Carlos a paved road runs northwest to **Florencia** (service station). At Platanar de San Carlos, at **Hacienda Platanar**, are a couple of sleeping options, see page 1022.

Los Chiles and Refugio Natural de Vida Silvestre Caño Negro → *Colour map 7, B3.*

Heading through the northern lowlands, a good road carves through rich red laterite soils in an almost straight line for 74 km through flat land where the shiny leaves of orange and citrus fruit plantations have replaced forest. Just short of the Nicaraguan border is Los Chiles, where boat trips head through dense, tropical vegetation into the 10,171-ha Caño Negro Natural Wildlife Refuge and Caño Negro Lake, spanning about 800-ha in the rainy season. Birdwatchers flock to the northern wetlands to see the amazing variety of birdlife which feasts at the seasonal lake created by the flood waters of the Río Frío. The lake slowly shrinks in the dry season (January to April). The variety of habitats in the refuge makes a rewarding trip for anyone interested in seeing alligators, turtles and monkeys. Fishing trips for snook and tarpon are easily arranged.

Los Chiles is a small town on the banks of the Río Frío, a few hundred metres west of Highway 35. The central plaza is also a football pitch, and most places of interest are within a block or two. The days pass slowly as children chuck themselves off the dockside in the heat of the afternoon sun. Ask about **guides** at **Restaurant Los Petates, Restaurant El Parque** or **Rancho Eco-Directa.** A three-hour tour with **Esteban, Oscar Rojas** (T471-1414) and **Enrique**, who have all been recommended, costs about US$60. Alternatively, **Aventuras Arenal** in Fortuna run trips to Caño Negro (see below) approximately US$35-40. It is cheaper to get a boat from Los Chiles to the park (US$60 for a boat, up to four people) rather than taking a tour from elsewhere (ie Fortuna) and convenient if you are going on to Nicaragua, but there are not always boats available nor sufficient numbers to fill one economically. Call the **Caño Negro park administration** ⓘ *T460-4164*, for information and reservations for food and lodging.

Fishing trips are likely to be beyond the budgets of many, but then what price do you put on catching a 2-m-long tarpon! A full day's fishing on the Río Frío, Río

San Juan or Lago de Nicaragua (boat, rods and drinks included) can range from US$95 to US$500 with **No Frills Fishing Adventures** (see page 1022), depending on the boat and destination.

Fortuna

→ Colour map 7, B3. Population: 7658. Altitude: 254 m.

The small town of Fortuna, is an ideal base for exploring the Arenal region with the ominous silhouette of the active Volcán Arenal looming above the town. Reached on a paved road running west from San Carlos/Ciudad Quesada or along the northern shore of Lake Arenal from Tilaran, it's worth a few days of your travels.

Once a quiet town that shuddered in the shadow of the volcano's power, Fortuna is growing rapidly to accommodate the regular influx of visitors keen to see the active volcano. The place is busy with visitors and coach parties in the day but becomes strangely quiet in the evenings, with the streets often pretty empty by around 2100.

Around Fortuna

About 6 km south of Fortuna are the impressive **Río Fortuna Waterfalls** ⓘ *US$6, drinks available at the entrance*, plunging 70 m into the cloud of swirling mist and spray. It's a pleasant walk down the road for a couple of kilometres before heading uphill through yucca and papaya plantations. From the entrance, a steep and slippery path leads to the falls, so take shoes with a good tread. Bathing is possible, so take swimming clothes, but safer 50 m downstream. If you don't want to walk, there are several options. You can drive, but 4WD is necessary. Bicycle hire (US$3 per hour, US$15 per day) is one option and hard work, or you can hire a horse for the day at around US$35. Two to three hours' climb above the falls is the crater lake of Cerro Chato. The top (1100 m) is reached through mixed tropical/cloud forest, with a good view (if you're lucky) but beware of snakes on the path. A guide, if you need one, will charge US$9.

Safari river floats down the Río Peñas Blancas (US$40) and whitewater rafting, best in the wet season (from US$69 for a one-day trip including all food and transport) are available through several tour operators. **Horse riding** through the forest to Monteverde costs around US$65 per person for the day trip. Luggage is taken on pack animals or by vehicles. Some operators seem to change the route once underway due to some 'unforeseen problem', so agree the route and try to arrange compensation if there are major changes. Due to competition for business, many horses are

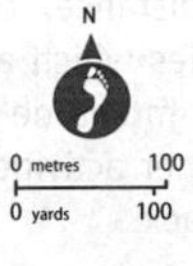

Sleeping
Cabinas Guacamaya 1
Cabinas Hervi 2
Cabinas La Amistad 3
Cabinas Monte Real 4
Carmela 5
Fortuna 6
Gringo Pete's 7
La Posada Inn 8
Las Colinas 9
San Bosco 11
Sissy 12

Eating
Choza de Laurel 2
El Jardín 3
La Casa de Hara 4
Las Brasitas 5
Lava Rocks 6
Nene's 7
Pizza Luigi's 8
Rancho La Cascada 9

 overworked on this route. Although difficult when on a budget, try not to bargain down the price, and ask to see the horses before beginning the journey. The journey is also possible by jeep-boat-jeep (US$30-35).

A small **snake farm** ⓘ *a few kilometres west of Fortuna, US$2*, with 40 specimens is a good opportunity to get up close and personal with these rather cool creatures.

Almost 5 km north of Fortuna is the **Baldi Thermae complex** ⓘ *T479-9651, daily 1000-2200, US$14*, with four thermal pools ranging from 37° up to 63°C – the limits of endurance without being poached. Poolside drinks, looks good, feels great (taxi from town US$2, bus US$1).

Ten kilometres northwest of Fortuna is **Balneario Tabacón** ⓘ *T256-1500, daily 1000-2200, day guests welcome, entry US$29*, a kitsch complex of thermal pools, waterfalls and (for residents) beauty treatments, with three bars and a restaurant. The water is hot and stimulating; there are a pools at descending heights and temperatures as well as waterslides and a waterfall to sit under. The food is good and the fruit drinks thirst quenching. The resort (L) is popular with evening coach tours from San José. Taxi from Fortuna to Tabacón US$4.50. There are cheaper hot springs across the road for US$6. Cheaper still are the hot waters about 4 km further along the road at **Quebrada Cedeña**, which are clean and safe. There is no sign but look for local parked cars.

Also near Fortuna are the limestone **Cavernas del Venado**. Tours from Fortuna with all equipment can be arranged through **BoBo Adventures** ⓘ *T479-9390, US$35*. Buses from San Carlos en route to Tilarán daily, return transport to Fortuna at 2200.

Volcán Arenal → *Colour map 7, B3.*

Skirting the slopes of the 1633-m Volcán Arenal, the road travels north around the base to the man-made **Lago Arenal** and hydroelectric dam. The highly active volcano is beautiful, a classic Stromboli-type cone shape characterized by explosions sending out hot grey clouds of sulphurous gases, which can descend the slopes at alarming speeds. The lava streams have moved from the west side to the northeast following activity in recent years. Although the side facing Fortuna is green, the side facing the lake is grey and barren, and the lava flows are clearly visible. There are three active craters and several fumaroles, with activity particularly impressive at night, as the red hot lava crashes, smashes and tumbles down the hillside accompanied by rumbles and intermittent roars (rather like someone moving furniture upstairs). The activity is fuelled by a magma chamber that vulcanologists believe is just 5 km below the surface.

Some people say there is greater volcanic activity around full moon.

Arenal has been continuously active since July 1968, when an eruption killed 78 people and more or less destroyed three villages including Tabacón which is situated above the *balneario*. The most recent continuous major activity was in May 1998, but in August 2000 a small group travelled beyond the permitted area, and were engulfed by a pyroclastic avalanche and the guide later died of third degree burns. Arenal has been reasonably active in 2006 – you can see the latest images at www.arenal.net/arenal-volcano.htm.

If you are visiting between May and December you may not see much as the volcano is usually obscured by clouds and rain and there can be bad weather for weeks on end. Clouds and rain are common in the afternoons all year round, but the clouds do break and you may be lucky. If you can hire a taxi for a trip at about 0400-0500 – and you can get up – the sky is often clearer.

On no account walk up the volcano beyond the level of the vegetation – it's dangerous. However, there is good hiking on the lower slopes from Fortuna.

To the east, the vast Lago Arenal reflects the moods of the volcano perfectly: smooth and calm from a distance, but whipped up to a waved frenzy by strong easterlies which are squeezed by the hills on either side. The surrounding area offers a multitude of opportunities for hiking, mountain biking, windsurfing and many other activities. There is also access to Santa Elena and Monteverde on foot or horseback.

Park information Much of the area surrounding the volcano is a national park which most people visit as part of a tour. The most common entrance is through **Hotel Los Lagos** (see page 1024), costing US$25 including a trip to Baldi Thermae baths. Following the eruption in 2000, the area was closed until considered safe again; if it has not reopened, tours will be developed to view lava flows from another point. Alternatively **Aventuras Arenal** will provide dependable advice.

Tour operators offer trips to view the volcano at night followed by a visit to the thermal baths; a typical four-hour tour, costing US$25 per person, leaves Fortuna at about 1815 and returns by 2200. Make sure the entry fee to the baths is included.

You can also visit the park on your own. The entrance is on the western flank of the volcano, on the other side to Fortuna, 2 km down a bumpy road signposted to Arenal Observatory Lodge. Four interesting trails, taking up to 1½ hours each, lead through the national park going through a mixture of terrains, that flourish in the microclimate of heavy rainfall bought on by the volcano.

North to Upala

A quiet route north leads from Fortuna to **San Rafael de Guatuso**. There is a 'voluntary' toll of US$1 between Jicarito and San Rafael for reconstruction work on this road. You can come back to the lake either by turning off before San Rafael through **Venado** (where there are caves), or from San Rafael itself, where there are a couple of basic hotels. If you continue along the road from San Rafael northwest towards the Nicaraguan border you come to **Upala** and a poor road east to **Caño Negro**. There is a direct bus from San José to Upala (from Avenida 3-5, Calle 10 at 1445, four hours).

Around Lago Arenal

A mostly paved road twists and winds round the northern shore of Lake Arenal, leading to Tilarán via Nuevo Arenal. Whether travelling by bus or car, you can get from Fortuna to Monteverde via Tilarán in a day, but set out early to make your connection with the 1230 bus in Tilarán or to avoid driving after dark. The lakeside road has improved greatly in recent years, but some sections are still unpaved. The main hazard is the winding road and some seriously pot-holed sections.

There is plenty of good accommodation around the lake shore, much of it in the higher price brackets. With only a couple of buses a day, and limited traffic, getting off the bus for a look will almost certainly delay you for a day.

If you do stop, an excellent café for a meal and drink with great views over the lake is **Toad Hall** ⓘ *T692-8020*, towards the northeastern end, which has an excellent souvenir shop with a good mix of Costa Rican crafts, some modern, some traditional, most desirable.

Along the north coast of Lago Arenal, **Arenal Botanical and Butterfly Gardens** ⓘ *4 km east of Arenal town, T694-4273, www.exoticseeds.com, 0900-1600 (closed Oct), US$8*, is a delightful place (still under development along with the surrounding area), with more than 2500 species of plants from around the world, birds, an enclosed butterfly sanctuary and a new serpentarium (guide leaflet and soft drinks included).

With a head count of just over 2500 (**Nuevo**) **Arenal** is a small town with not much to see. The town is new, because it moved from its original location which now lies deep below the surface of the lake.

Continuing west towards Tilarán, the western side of the lake is popular with **windsurfers** throughout the year, and between December and April the conditions are world class. A batch of hotels cater for windsurfers of all levels; there are many other options in the area so take your pick if you want to stop.

Tilarán → *Colour map 7, B2.*

Tilarán would not appear on the list of destinations for travellers were it not for its role as a small regional transport hub for people journeying between Fortuna, Santa

 Elena/Monteverde and Cañas on the Pan-American Highway. In town there is pretty much nothing to do, and with luck, the connecting buses will be timed perfectly to avoid you having to wait too long. But if you do, there are several places to catch a bite to eat, and several good places to stay if you need a bed for the night.

Sleeping

San Carlos and around *p960*
AL Hotel La Garza, Platanar de San Carlos, 8 km from Florencia, T475-5222, www.hotellagarza.com. 12 charming bungalows with bath and fan, overlooking river. Idyllic spot with good views of Arenal. Guided tours, boat trips, fishing, 230 ha of forest and cattle ranch.
AL Tilajari Resort Hotel, Muelle San Carlos, 13 km north of Platanar de San Carlos, T469-9091, www.tilajari.com. Luxury rooms, and suites, a/c, private bath, tennis courts, two pools, sauna, bar, restaurant, horses. Excursions. Justifiably popular with luxury groups.
C Don Goyo, San Carlos, T460-1780. A baker's dozen of clean, well-lit rooms, with private bathrooms, fans, cable TV – best value in town.
C La Central, on west side of park, San Carlos, T460-0301, www.hotellacentral.net. Private bath, hot water, fan, TV and phone in room.
C-D El Retiro, on the north side of the park, San Carlos, T460-0463. Bath, hot water, clean and comfortable, popular with local business people.
D del Valle, Av 3, Calle 0-2, San Carlos, T460-0718. Nothing special but friendly and secure, a good deal at this price.
E Cabinas Kimbara, on the main road 800 m north of the Muelle gas station, T469-9100. Basic rooms, private bath, fan, includes taxes, pool.
E-F Fernando, Av 1 Calle 2-4, around corner from **Banco Popular**, T460-3314. Probably the best of several basic *pensiones* if you can get one of the new rooms.

Los Chiles *p1018*
A No Frills Fishing Lodge, on the main highway just before town, T471-1410, nofrills@racsa.co.cr, set on a 40-ha property, clean modern rooms, restaurant and bar, 8 boats for fishing expeditions (see page 1019).
C Rancho Tulipan, 1 block west of the parque central opposite the immigration offices, T471-1414, cocas34@hotmail.com. New, good restaurant, 8 clean well-appointed rooms with a/c, TV, bath and hot water, breakfast and taxes included. Can arrange a wide variety of tours in the area including river safaris and fishing trips. The manager Oscar Rojas is useful for information on travelling to Nicaragua.
D-E Cabinas Jabirú, 100 m from the bus stop, a few blocks from the central park, T471-1496. Cheaper price for Youth Hostel members. Good, but simple rooms, with private bathrooms, fan, some with TV and parking. Postal service, fax and laundry and a range of interesting tours. Cheapest to **Caño Negro** (US$20 per person, minimum 3) and to El Castillo de la Concepción in Nicaragua.
D-F Hotel Carolina, close to main highway, T471-1151. Clean and well maintained – the best of the budgets. Accommodation ranges from small, fairly dark rooms with shared bath to a/c cabins with TV.
F Onassis, southwest corner of main plaza, T471-1001. Your best bet of the strip facing the football pitch. Basic rooms, clean, shared bath.

Fortuna *p1019, map p1019*
Generous discounts in the green/low season are common.
L-AL Las Cabañitas, 1.5 km east of town, beyond **Villa Fortuna**, T479-9400. 30 cabins with private baths, a couple of pools, observatory for viewing Arenal volcano, restaurant. Recommended.
AL Arenal Country Inn, south of town, T479-9670, www.arenalcountryinn.com. A former working hacienda with 20 large, fully equipped *cabinas* set in pleasant tropical gardens. After eating in the dining room – once a holding pen – you can rest by the pool before heading out to explore.
A Hotel Arenal Rossi, T479-9023, www.hotelarenalrossi.com. 1 km west, towards the volcano, with breakfast, friendly owner, hot water, fan, watch the volcano from the garden, horses rented, good value.
A-B Cabinas Monte Real, 1 block from the main plaza, T479-9357. Close to the centre, quiet and friendly, big rooms with private

bath and hot water, next to the river and also close to centre. Parking.

A-B San Bosco, town centre, T479-9050, www.arenal-volcano.com. All rooms with private bath, quiet, signs on main road, clean, friendly, nice gardens with terrace, pool and view of the volcano, excellent service and attention to detail, slightly less without a/c, also rents a few houses.

B Cabinas Guacamaya, town centre, T479-9393, www.cabinasguacamaya.com. 10 good-sized rooms sleeping 3 or 4, all with private bath and hot water, fridge and a/c. Clean and tidy, with plenty of parking.

B Cabinas Villa Fortuna, 500 m south of the bridge, 1 km east from the central plaza, T479-9139. 10 bright and tidy cabins, with neat bathrooms, fans or a/c, nice pool and simple gardens.

B Hotel Carmela, on the south side of the church, T479-9010. Newly renovated, 12 rooms with private bath, floor and ceiling fans, some with fridge. Very central, hot showers, can arrange tours. Apartment sleeping 5 available (**E** per person).

B Las Colinas, southeast of the central park, T479-9305, hcolinas@racsa.co.cr. 20 tidy rooms, with private bathroom, some with excellent views. Friendly management, good discounts in the low season. Internet access. Recommended.

C Cabinas La Amistad, central, T479-9364. Clean, friendly, hot water, hard beds.

C Cabinas Las Flores, west of town, 2 km on road towards the volcano, T479-9307. Clean, basic, but a little overpriced. Camping possible.

C-E Arenal Backpacker's Resort, T479-7000, www.arenalbackpackersresort.com. New hostel a short distance out of town. Dorm and private rooms, pool in the garden with view of Arenal.

D Cabinas Hervi, south of church on road to the river, T479-9430. Bright rooms, private bath with hot water, a/c or fan. Balcony with view of the church, good discounts in the green season.

D Fortuna, 1 block southeast of the central park, T479-9197. Simple rooms, but very clean. Price includes breakfast.

E Sissy, office is 100 m south and 100 m west of church, T479-9256. Price per person. Quiet spot beside the river, basic rooms with private bathroom; others have shared bath, and there's access to a kitchen and camping spaces (US$3 per person); simple but friendly. Recommended.

F Albergue Ecoturístico La Catarata, 2 km from town, rough road, T479-9522, www.turismoruralcr.com. Price per person. Reservations essential for these 8 cabins in co-operative with organic garden, home-made soaps and shampoos, good fresh food, butterfly farm, taxi US$2, hot water, laundry, all meals. Run by community association and supported by WWF Canada and CIDA Canada.

F Gringo Pete's, east end of town, T479-8521, gringopetes2004@yahoo.com. New place in town, dormitory and private rooms, clean and tidy. Kitchen facilities and communal area for relaxing. Good notice board and tours arranged. Recommended.

F La Posada Inn, a couple of blocks east of the parque central, T479-9793. Price per person. 4 simple, but spotless rooms, shared bath with hot water, fans but mosquitoes reported. Small communal area out front, and the friendly owner Thadeo is very helpful.

Volcán Arenal *p1020*

Fortuna is the easiest place to stay if you don't have your own transport (see page 1022), but the whole area from Fortuna all along the shores of the lake is littered with hotels and eating options, each taking advantage of superb views and relative seclusion. Hotels on the southern side of the lake are slightly cut off but have fantastic views.

LL-L Arenal Observatory Lodge, on the northwestern side of the volcano, 4 km after El Tabacón, a turn towards the lake down a (signposted) gravel road, T290-7011, www.arenal-observatory.co.cr. 4WD recommended along this 9-km stretch (taxi -jeep from Fortuna, US$12). Set up in 1973, the observatory was purely a research station but it now has 42 rooms varying from cabins with bunk beds and bath, to newer rooms with queen-size beds. The service is excellent and there are stunning views of the volcano (which is frighteningly close), Lake Arenal, and across the valley of Río Agua Caliente. The lava flows on the other side of the volcano, but the trails are beautiful and the service excellent.

L Volcano Lodge, 6 km from Fortuna, T460-6080, www.volcanolodge.com. With open-air restaurant good for viewing the volcano.

L-AL Montaña de Fuego, T460-7340, www.montanadefuego.com. 66 bungalows and rooms, with the stylish (and pricey) **Acuarelas** restaurant.

L-C Los Lagos, T461-1818, www.hotellos lagos.com. 27 comfortable cabin rooms sleeping up to 4, day visits US$12, excellent food and spectacular views of the volcano over the lake with a campsite (US$10 per night), with good facilities and small café. There are 3 marked footpaths towards the lava fields and lakes through the forest.

AL Arenal Vista Lodge, T382-2565. 25 rooms with bath, arranges boat trips, riding and hiking, close to hanging bridges and canopy tour, also butterfly garden.

AL-A Linda Vista del Norte Lodge, on the gravel road, taking the right fork (not to the **Arenal Observatory Lodge**), near **Arenal Vista Lodge**, T380-0847. Nice views, several good, unspoilt trails in the area, horse riding tours, hot water. Recommended.

A Cabañas Arenal Paraíso, 7.5 km from Fortuna, T460-5333. 12 nice houses with bath, fridge and terrace views of the volcano.

Camping

About 4 km from Fortuna on the road to Lake Arenal, turn at sign on left side of the road '*Bienvenidos a Junglas y Senderos Los Lagos*'. Site is 2 km uphill, very steep, good facilities, tours to hot springs at night. This is one of the best places to watch volcanic activity at night.

There is a small campsite just before the park entrance with hook-ups for vehicles, US$2.50 per person. Great views of the volcano and a good spot for walking.

Camping is also possible on the edge of the lake, no services, but good view of volcano at night.

North to Upala *p1021*

L Magil Forest Lodge, 3 km from Col Río Celeste, near San Rafael de Guatuso, T221-2825. Set in 240 ha on the foothills of the 1916-m **Volcán Tenorio** (now a national park of 12,871 ha with thermal waters, boiling mud and unspoilt forest). 10 rooms with private bath, price includes meals.

F Pensión Buena Vista, Upala. Basic, food available.

North coast of Lago Arenal *p1021*

LL La Mansión Marina and Club, T692-8018, www.lamansionarenal.com. On the lake, beautiful pool, very relaxing.

LL-AL Arenal Lodge, travelling round the lake from Fortuna, just north of the dam wall up 2.5-km steep road, T460-1881, www.arenallodge.com. Stunning views to the north and south. Rooms, suites, meal extra in excellent restaurant.

AL Hotel Tilawa, 8 km north of Tilarán, T695-5050, www.hotel-tilawa.com. With great rooms, restaurant, tennis and excellent opportunities for wind surfing, kayaking and birdwatching. Equipment for rent for US$55 a day. Guaranteed beginner lesson – if it's not fun it's free; try not to laugh and you've got a good deal. Good discounts off season.

AL La Ceiba, 6 km from Arenal, T692-8050. Overlooking Lake Arenal, Tico owned and run, good, helpful, great panoramic views, good breakfast.

A Aurora Inn B&B (Nuevo) Arenal, T694-4245, www.hotelaurorainn.com. With private bath, pool and jacuzzi overlooking Lake Arenal. Breakfast included.

A Chalet Nicholas, west end of lake, T694-4041, www.chaletnicholas.com. Bed and breakfast (a speciality), run by retired North Americans, hot water, non-smokers only, friendly. Recommended.

A Hotel Los Héroes (Pequeña Helvecia), 10 km from Arenal towards Tilarán, T692-8012, www.hotellosheroes.com. Delightful Swiss owners with inspiring energy and a superb hotel, complete with Swiss train service.

A Rock River Lodge, on the road skirting the lake, T692-1180, www.rockriverlodge.com. Rooms and bungalows, with bathroom, good restaurant. Excellent activity spot with day options for surfing (US$35) and fishing (US$55) and good mountain biking with bikes available for hire.

B La Alondra, west of **La Mansión Marina and Clubs**, T692-8036. With simple, basic rooms sleeping up to 4 and great Tico restaurant from US$5.

Tilarán *p1021*

B-C Naralit, on the south side of the church, T695-5393. Clean, new buildings.

C Cabiñas El Sueño, 1 block north of bus terminal/central park, T695-5347. Clean rooms around central patio, hot water, fan, TV, friendly and free coffee. Good deal.

D Hotel Restaurant Mary, south side of church, T695-5479. Bath, small pleasant rooms, newly renovated, upstairs recommended.

E Central, round the back of the church, 1 block south, T695-5363. With shared bath (more with own bath), noisy.

Eating

San Carlos and around *p960*
Variety of sodas in the central market offer *casados*, check out the great sword collection displayed at La Ponderosa.
ΨΨΨ Coca Loca Steak House, next to Hotel La Central, T460-3208. Complete with Wild West swing door.
ΨΨ Los Geranios, Av 4 and Calle 0. Popular bar and restaurant serving up good *bocas* and other dishes.
ΨΨ Restaurant Crystal, on the western side of the plaza. Sells fast food, snacks, ice cream and good fruit dishes.

Los Chiles *p1018*
Ψ Los Petates, on road running south of the central park. Has good food, cheap with large portions but check the bill.
Ψ El Parque on the main plaza. With good home cooking.

Fortuna *p1019, map p1019*
ΨΨΨ Las Brasitas, at west end of town (see map), T479-9819. Open-air restaurant serving abundant authentic Mexican fare with a laid-back European-café style.
ΨΨΨ La Vaca Muca, out of the town on the way to Tabacón, T479-9186. Typical Latino food.
ΨΨΨ Lava Rocks, south side of the church, T479-8039. Smooth open-air café restaurant serving excellent coffee and good food with chilled music. Travel agency on site for any questions. Definitely worth a visit.
ΨΨ Choza de Laurel, west of the church, T479- 9231. Typical food in a rustic setting, serving breakfast, lunch and dinner, US$2-US$4.50, occasionally greeted by passing hummingbirds.
ΨΨ Coco Loco, south of town, T468-0990. Fast food, sandwiches, plate of the day, gallery and souvenirs.
ΨΨ El Jardín, on the main street opposite the gas station, T479-9360. Good menu with a mix of local and fast food, pizza, *menú del día* US$2.25, good place to watch the world go by.
ΨΨ Nene's, 1½ blocks east of the main square, T479-9192. Good food, pleasant service, not expensive. Recommended.
ΨΨ Pizza Luigi's, west end of town (see map), T479-9898. Formal, open-air restaurant with distinctly Italian pretensions toward pizza and pasta. Good wine list for Fortuna.
ΨΨ Rancho La Cascada, corner of Parque with high conical thatched roof, T479-9145. Good *bocas*, films sometimes shown in evenings.
ΨΨ Steakhouse Arenal next to **Hotel Las Flores**. Mid-priced steak house with Texan tendencies.
ΨΨ Vagabondo, west end of town, T479-9565. Reasonably priced pizza and pasta, also rooms with breakfast (**B-C**).
Ψ La Casa de Hara, round the side of **Hotel Fortuna**. Very good local food, fast service and normal prices – where the locals eat.

North coast of Lago Arenal *p1021*
ΨΨΨ-Ψ Willy's Caballo Negro, a couple of km west of (Nuevo) Arenal, T694-4515. The best restaurant for miles, serving vegetarian, Swiss and seasonal fish dishes with organic salads. Warm family atmosphere.
ΨΨ Pizzería e Ristorante Tramonte (Nuevo) Arenal, T694-4282. For Italian cuisine, excellent food, salad bar and very friendly.
ΨΨ Restaurante Lajas (Nuevo) Arenal, T694-4385. Tico and vegetarian fare.
ΨΨ Típico Arenal (Nuevo) Arenal, T694-4159. Good local dishes with seafood and vegetarian options. Large room upstairs (**C**) with private bath and hot water, the best cheap place in town.
ΨΨ Toad Hall, northeast of the lake, T692-8020. Café, restaurant and gift shop.

Tilarán *p1021*
ΨΨ Restaurant La Carreta, at the back of the church, T695-6593. The place to go and relax if you have time to kill. Excellent pancakes, coffee and good local information.
Ψ Stefanie's, out of the bus station to the left on the corner of the main plaza. Good and quick if you need a meal between buses.
Heladería Baloons serves great ice cream.

Activities and tours

Fortuna *p1019, map p1019*
Tour operators
Aventuras Arenal, on the main street, T479-9133, www.arenaladventures.com. Provides all tours in the area, and has been

around for many years. Can help with enquiries about other parts of Costa Rica.

Canopy Tour, east down the main street, T479-9769, www.crarenalcanopy.com. Offer a short horse riding journey from Fortuna, US$45, as well as quad tours, mountain bike rental and general tours.

Desafío, just off main square by thatched restaurant, T479-9464, www.desafiocostarica.com. Full range of tours, and with office in Monteverde.

Eagle Tours, T479-9091, www.eagletours.net. Helpful, with usual tours.

Sunset Tours, T479-9800, www.sunsettourcr.com. Reliable, long-standing company with a selection of tours. Recommended.

Transport

San Carlos and around *p960*

Bus Direct bus from Terminal Atlántico Norte, **San José**, 2¼ hrs, hourly, from 0645-1815, US$2.20, return 0500-1930. From San Carlos buses go northwest to **Tilarán** via **Fortuna** and **Arenal** (0630 and 1400), other buses go to **Fortuna** through El Tanque (6 daily, 1½ hrs), **San Rafael de Guatuso** and **Upala**, north to **Los Chiles** (hourly, 3 hrs), northeast to towns on the Río San Carlos and Río Sarapiquí, including **Puerto Viejo de Sarapiquí** (5 a day, 3 hrs), and east to the Río Frío district.

Los Chiles *p1018*

Bus Going into Costa Rica, there are direct buses to **San José** daily 0500, 1500, 5 hrs, from San José Atlántico Norte Terminal, Calle 12, Av 7-9, to Los Chiles at 0530, 1530, US$4 with **Auto Transportes San Carlos**, T255-4318. Alternatively take one of the hourly buses from the same terminal in San José to **San Carlos** (**Cd Quesada**) from where there are hourly services, 2 hrs, US$2.20. From **Fortuna**, take the bus to San Carlos, get off at Muelle and wait for a connection.

Fortuna *p1019, map 1019*

Bus There are daily returning buses every hr from 0500-1930 from Terminal Atlántico Norte, **San José**, Auto Transportes San José-San Carlos, T255-4318, 4½ hrs, via San Carlos, US$2.50; 6 buses a day from **San Carlos**, 1 hr, US$1, 4 different routes. 2 buses a day to **Tilarán**, 0800 (connecting to 1230 bus Tilarán-Santa Elena/Monteverde and 1300 bus Tilarán-Puntarenas) and 1700, US$2.90, 4 hrs. Subject to demand, there are direct minibuses to **Monteverde** and **Tamarindo** (US$25 per person, min 6). Taxis in the area overcharge. Agree on price before travelling.

Car hire Alamo, T479-9722, has an office in town.

Tilarán *p1021*

Bus If heading for Santa Elena and Monteverde see page 1028. Direct bus from **San José**, 4 daily, 4 hrs, from Terminal Atlántico Norte. 2 daily buses to **San Carlos** via Fortuna at 0700 and 1230. To **Fortuna**, 3 hrs, US$2.00. Daily bus to **Santa Elena** (for Monteverde), 1230, 2½ hrs, US$1.65, return 0700 daily. Tilarán-**Puntarenas** 0600, 1300, 3 hrs, US$3. 5 daily buses to/from **Cañas** (at 0500, 0730, 1000, 1230 and 1530, 40 mins, US$1.25), where buses head north and south along the Pan-American. If you get the 1230 Tilarán-Liberia bus you can get from there to the Nicaraguan border before it closes.

Directory

San Carlos and around *p960*

Banks Banco Nacional, Av Central, west of the church, T461-9200. Banco de Costa Rica, east side of park and another near the market, T461-9006, both have ATMs. Others nearby, include Banco Popular, T460-0534. **Internet** Ask around or try Café Internet, Av 5, Calle 2-4, 400c/hr, Mon-Fri 0800-2100, Sat 0800-1800. **Post office** Av 5, Calle 2-4.

Los Chiles *p1018*

Banks Banco Nacional, with ATM, on central park. **Post office** Services provided by Cabiñas Jabirú, 25 m north of market.

Fortuna *p1019, map p1019*

Banks Banco Nacional de Costa Rica, T479-9022, will change TCs, US$1 commission, ATM . Banco Popular, T479-9422, Visa ATM. Coocique, open Sat mornings 0800-1200, Visa ATM. **Internet** Prices in Fortuna are quite expensive. Try Eagle Tours, T479-9091 or Destiny Tours. **Laundry** Lavandería La Fortuna, Mon-Sat 0800-2100, US$5 wash and dry 4 kg. **Pharmacy** Farmacia Dr Max, east down the main street, Mon-Sat 0730-2030, Sun

0800-1200. **Post office** Down main street, shares building with the police.

North coast of Lago Arenal *p1021*
Banks Banco Nacional (Nuevo) Arenal, beside the football pitch.

Tilarán *p1021*
Banks Banco Cootilaran, a couple of blocks north of the Parque Central, has a Visa and MasterCard ATM, and there is also a Banco de Costa Rica in town. **Internet** Café across from bus station.

Northwest Costa Rica

The route of the Pan-American Highway heads north passing near the world-renowned Monteverde Cloud Forest in the Cordillera de Tilarán, the marshes of the Parque Nacional Palo Verde, the active Volcán Rincón and the dry tropical forest of the Parque Nacional Santa Rosa on the Pacific coast, as it crosses the great cattle haciendas of Guanacaste before reaching the Nicaraguan border. *» For Sleeping, Eating and other listings, see pages 1036-1044.*

San José to Esparza and Barranca

The Pan-American Highway from San José descends from the Meseta Central to Esparza, an attractive town with a turbulent early history, as it was repeatedly sacked by pirates in the 17th century, belying its peaceful nature today.

The stretch of the highway between San Ramón and Esparza (31 km) includes the sharp fall of 800 m from the Meseta Central, often shrouded in mist and fog making conditions treacherous for road users. Beyond Esparza is the **Bar/Restaurant Mirador Enis**, a popular stopping place for tour buses breaking the journey at a service station with fruit stalls nearby, before a left turn at Barranca for Puntarenas, 15 km.

Puntarenas and around → *Colour map 7, B3. Population: 22,009.*

Puntarenas fills a 5-km spit, thrusting out into the Gulf of Nicoya, east to west, but no wider than six avenues. Although popular with locals, most visitors pass through, using it as a transport hub with links to the southern Nicoya Peninsula or to get a bus north or south to other parts of the country without returning to San José. If heading for Nicoya, see page 1047. If heading to Santa Elena/Monteverde see below, and page 1042. It is also the Pacific destination for the bright white, cruise palaces that float through the Central American ports, and dock at Muelle de Cruceros on the Calle Central.

Once the country's main Pacific port with rail links to the Central Highlands, it has since been superseded by Caldera a short distance to the south. The northern side of the peninsula, around Calle Central with the market, banks, a few hotels and the fishing docks, is run-down and neglected, typical of small tropical ports. The southern side is made up of the **Paseo de los Turistas**, drawing crowds to the hot, sometimes dirty beach, especially at weekends. There are several hotels along the strip, as well as restaurants, bars and a general seafront beach atmosphere. There is a public swimming pool at the western end of the point (US$1 entrance), close to the ferries, and good surfing off the headland. There is a **Museo de la Historia Marina** ⓘ *T661-5036, Tue-Sun 0945-1200, 1300-1715, US$1.80*, in the Cultural Centre by the main church and tourist office. Across the gulf are the hills of the Nicoya Peninsula. The new **Puntarenas Marine Park** ⓘ *T661-5272, daily 0900-1700, US$7*, offers 28 large aquariums showing Costa Rica's marine life. In the gulf are several islands including the **Islas Negritas**, a biological reserve reached by passenger launches.

Monteverde and Santa Elena » pp1036-1044

Monteverde Cloud Forest Reserve is one of the most precious natural jewels in Costa Rica's crown, and an opportunity to see plants, insects, birds and mammals in grand profusion – well in theory, at least. Protected by law, this private preserve is also protected by appalling access roads on all sides (the nearest decent road is at least two hours from the town). Santa Elena and Monteverde, although separate, are often referred to as the same place; most sites of interest are between the town of Santa Elena at the bottom of the hillside and Monteverde Cloud Forest Reserve at the top.

Ins and outs

From the Pan-American Highway northwest to Km 149, turn right just before the Río Lagarto. Continue for about 40 km on mostly gravel road (allow 2½ hours) to Santa Elena. Parts of the road are quite good, but in wet weather 4WD is recommended for the rough parts. If driving, check that your car rental agreement allows you to visit Monteverde. A 33-km shorter route is to take the Pipasa/Sardinal turn-off from the Pan-American Highway shortly after the Río Aranjuez. At the park in Sardinal, turn left, then go via Guacimal to the Monteverde road.

Buses comes from Puntarenas via the Km 149 route. There are also buses from Tilarán to the north, linked with Fortuna by Volcán Arenal, and Cañas on the Pan-American Highway. There are two daily buses from San José.

Alternatively you can make the journey from Tilarán by bus or private transport. It's an equally poor road – a journey that takes a couple of hours, but, if driving, you can visit the quiet and dramatic **Cataratas de Viento Fresco**, some 11 km from Tilarán, 800 m down a very steep road, followed by a 400-m walk. It's a bit hairy if it's raining but worth the effort.

Santa Elena and around

Santa Elena is a rugged and busy place, often packed with visitors exploring the options or just passing time. It is cheaper to stay in town than along the single, unpaved road that twists and turns for 5 km through the village of Monteverde, with hotels and places of interest situated along the road almost to the reserve itself. **Santa Elena Reserve, Sky Trek** and **Sky Walk** are to the north of Santa Elena, all other places of interest are east, heading up the hill.

Five kilometres north of Santa Elena, off the road to Tilarán, **Sky Walk** ⓘ *T645-5238, www.skywalk.co.cr, daily 0700-1600, US$17, student US$13, child US$8*, uses six suspension bridges to take you through the cloud forest at canopy level, the highest being 42 m above the ground. **Sky Trek** ⓘ *T645-5238, www.skywalk.co.cr, daily 0700-1500, US$44, student US$35, child US$31*, is even more popular and a breathtaking experience, as you fly through the air on a system of cables strung out from giant forest trees. On clear days the view from the highest tower is unbelievable.

Very close to Santa Elena, at the start of the climb to Monteverde, is the **Serpentarium** ⓘ *T645-5238, daily 0800-1700, US$7, US$5 students*, with specimens of snakes and amphibians found in the nearby cloud forest.

One hundred metres beyond **Hotel Sapo Dorado** is the **Orchid Garden** ⓘ *T645-5510, daily 0800-1700, US$5, US$3 students*, with about 400 species collected by Gabriel Barboza.

A dirt road opposite the **Hotel Heliconia** leads to the **Monteverde Butterfly Garden** ⓘ *wolfej@racsa.co.cr, daily 0930-1600, US$7, US$5 students, including guided tour, best time for a visit 1100-1300*, a beautifully presented large garden planted for breeding and researching butterflies. Near the Butterfly Garden is **Finca Ecológica**, ⓘ *T645-5554, 0700-1700 daily, US$7, night tours US$14, free map*, with three trails totalling around 5 km with bird lists for birdwatching and varied wildlife in this transitional zone between cloud and tropical dry forest, guides available. Good night tours. Down the same path is **Aerial Adventures** ⓘ *daily 0700-1800, US$15, T645-5960*, a ski-lift-style ride travelling slowly through the treetops. Ideal for birdwatching.

Santa Elena Cloud Forest Reserve

ⓘ *0700-1600, entrance US$9, students US$4.50, guided day/night tours US$15, T645-5390, www.monteverdeinfo.com/reserve, for information. It is a long, steep hike from the village; alternatively hire a taxi, US$6.50 (car load).*

One kilometre along the road north from Santa Elena to Tilarán, a 5-km track is signposted to the reserve, managed by the **Centro Ecológico Bosque Nuboso de Monteverde.** It is 83% primary cloud forest and the rest is secondary forest at 1700 m, bordered by the Monteverde Cloud Forest Reserve and the Arenal Forest Reserve. There is a 12-km path network and several lookouts where, on a clear day, you can see and hear Volcán Arenal. The 'canopy tour' is recommended: you climb inside a hollow strangler fig tree then cross between two platforms along aerial runways 30 m up, good views of orchids and bromeliads, then down a 30-m hanging rope at the end. There are generally fewer visitors here than at Monteverde. The **Centro Ecológico Bosque Nuboso** is administered by the local community and profits go to five local schools. It was set up by the Costa Rican government in 1989 with collaboration from Canada. The rangers are very friendly and enthusiastic. There is a small information centre where rubber boots can be hired and a small café open at weekends. Hand-painted T-shirts are for sale.

Monteverde and around → *Colour map 7, B3.*

Strung out along the road to the cloud forest, the settlement at Monteverde – between Santa Elena and the reserve – was founded by American Quakers in the 1950s. Without a centre as such, it started life as a group of dairy farms providing milk for a co-operative cheese factory. The cheese factory ⓘ *shop closes 1600*, now privately owned, still operates selling excellent cheeses of various types, fresh milk, ice cream, milkshakes to die for and *cajeta* (a butterscotch spread).

Today, Monteverde maintains an air of pastoral charm, but tourism provides more revenue for the town than dairy produce ever could. It was the vision of the dairy farmers that led to the creation of the reserve to protect the community watershed. When George Powell and his wife spent time in the region studying birds they realized the importance of protecting the area. Working with local residents they created the reserve in 1972 – foresight that has spawned the creation of many other natural attractions locally and throughout the country.

Reserva Sendero Tranquilo ⓘ *daily, T645-5010, entry restricted to 12 people at any one time*, is a private 200-ha reserve near the Monteverde cheese factory. Reservations and guides should be arranged through **El Sapo Dorado** hotel.

Just before the entrance to Monteverde Cloud Forest is the **Hummingbird Gallery** ⓘ *T645-5030, 0930-1700, slide shows several times a week at 1630, US$4*, where masses of different hummingbirds can be seen darting around a glade, visiting feeding dispensers filled with sugared water. Outside the entrance is a small shop/photo gallery which sells pictures and gifts, as well as Bromeliads Nature Bookstore and Café. There is also a slide show at **Hotel Belmar, The Hidden Rainforest** ⓘ *1930 daily except Fri*, by Bobby Maxson.

Adjoining the Monteverde Cloud Forest is **El Bosque Eterno de los Niños (Children's Eternal Rainforest)** ⓘ *T645-5003, acmmcl@racsa.co.cr*, established in 1988 after an initiative by Swedish schoolchildren to save forests. Currently at 22,000 ha, the land has been bought and is maintained by the **Monteverde Conservation League** with children's donations from around the world. The **Bajo Tigre** trail takes 1½ hours, parking available with notice, a guide can be arranged, but no horses are allowed on the trail. Groups can arrange trips to the **San Gerardo** and **Poco Sol Field stations** ⓘ *0800-1600, entrance US$5, students US$2, contact* *the Monteverde Conservation League for reservations at San Gerardo or Poco Sol, T645-5003, www.acmcr.org*, one of Costa Rica's best kept secrets.

Monteverde Cloud Forest Reserve

ⓘ *www.cct.or.cr. The reserve entrance is at the field station at the top of the road. Bus from Santa Elena heads up the hill leaving at 0600 and 1100 returning at 1400 and 1700. The total number of visitors to the reserve at any one time is 150, so be there before 0700 to make sure of getting in during high season (hotels will book you a place for the following day). Tour buses come in from San José daily. Entrance fee US$13 (students with ID half-price) valid for multiple entry during the day, cannot be purchased in advance. Office open 0700-1630 daily; the park opens at 0700 and closes at 1700. A small shop at the office sells various checklists, postcards and APS film, gifts and excellent T-shirts, the proceeds of which help towards the conservation project.*

Monteverde & Santa Elena

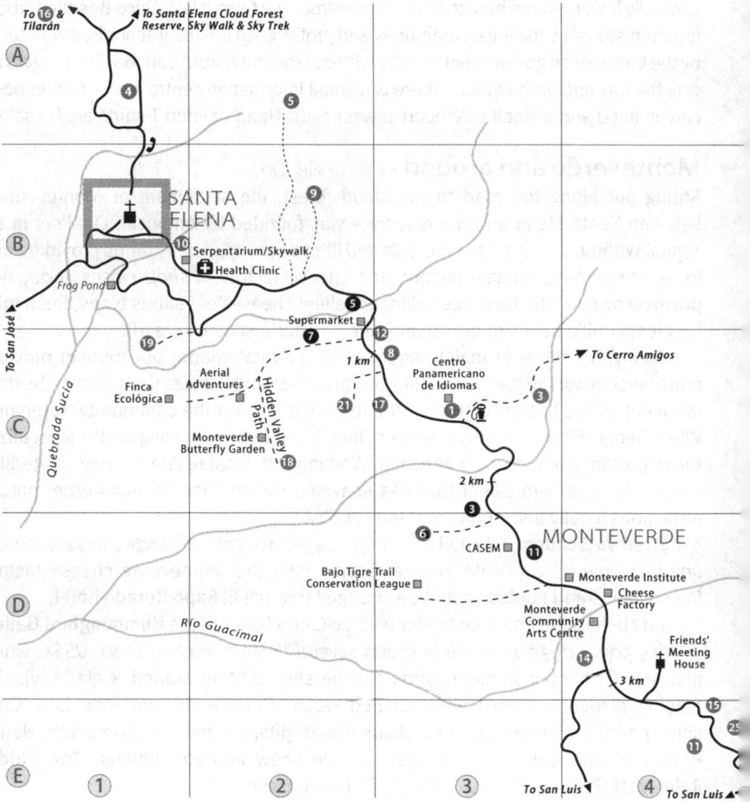

Sleeping

Albergue Bellbird 1 *C3*
Arco Iris 2 *Santa Elena detail*
Belmar 3 *C3*
Cloud Forest Lodge 5 *A2*
El Bosque 6 *D3*
El Colibrí 7 *Santa Elena detail*
El Establo 8 *C3*
El Sapo Dorado 9 *B2*
Finca Valverde 10 *B1*
Fonda Vela 11 *E4*
Heliconia 12 *C3*
Hospedaje El Banco 13 *Santa Elena detail*
La Colina Lodge 14 *D4*
Mariposa 15 *E4*
Miramontes 16 *A1*
Montaña Monteverde 17 *C3*
Monteverde Inn 18 *C2*
Monteverde Lodge 19 *C1*
Pensión Cabinas Marín 4 *A1*
Pensión El Sueño 20 *Santa Elena detail*
Pensión Manakin 21 *C2*
Pensión Santa Elena 22 *Santa Elena detail*

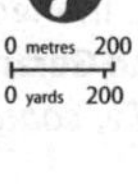

Straddling the continental divide, the 10,500-ha Monteverde Cloud Forest Reserve is privately owned and administered by the Tropical Science Centre – a non-profit research and educational association. The reserve is mainly primary cloud forest and spends much of the year shrouded in mist, creating stunted trees and abundant epiphytic growth. It contains more than **400 species of bird**, including the resplendent quetzal, best seen in the dry months between January and May, especially near the start of the Nuboso trail, the three-wattled bellbird with its distinctive 'bonk' call and the bare-necked umbrella bird. There are more than **100 species of mammal**, including monkeys, Baird's tapir and six endangered cats – jaguar, jaguarundi, margay, ocelot, tigrillo and puma – reptiles and amphibians. But be warned, travellers have told us there is little chance of seeing much wildlife. The reserve also includes an estimated 2500 species of plant and more than 6000 species of insect.

The best months are January-May, especially February, March and April.

The entrance is at 1500 m, but the maximum altitude in the reserve is over 1800 m. Mean temperature is between 16° and 18°C and average annual rainfall is 3000 mm. The weather changes quickly and wind and humidity often make the air feel cooler.

The commonly used trails are in good condition and there are easy, short and interesting walks for those who do not want to hike all day. Trail walks take from two hours but you could easily spend all day just wandering around. Trails may be restricted from time to time if they need protection. There is a trail northwards to the Arenal volcano that is increasingly used, but it is not easy. There are three refuges for people wishing to spend the night within the reserve boundaries, see Sleeping. Free maps of the reserve are available at the entrance. Follow the rules, stay on the paths, leave nothing behind, take no fauna or flora out; no radios or tape recorders are allowed.

Guides Natural history walks with biologist guides, every morning and afternoon, 3-4 hrs, US$16 (children half price); advance reservations at the office or through your hotel are strongly recommended. If you use a private (non-reserve) guide you must pay his entrance fee too. An experienced and recommended guide is **Gary Diller** ⓘ *T645-5045, cicadadesigms2002@yahoo.com*; he also does night tours. There are 25 others operating, of varying specialization and experience. Excellent night tours in the reserve are available normally with **Ricardo Guindon** or call

Santa Elena detail

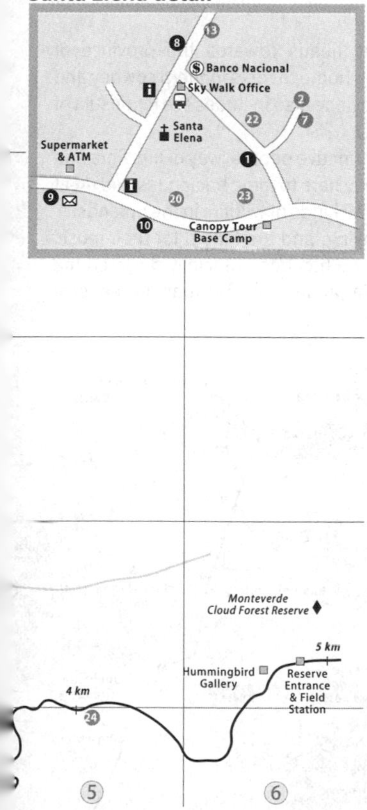

Pensión Tucán **23** *Santa Elena detail*
Trapp Family Lodge **24** *E5*
Villa Verde **25** *E4*

Eating
Chunches **1** *Santa Elena detail*
El Bosque **3** *C3*
Johnny's Pizza **5** *B2*
Lucia's **7** *C2*
Marisquería El Márquez **8** *Santa Elena detail*
Morphos **9** *Santa Elena detail*
Pollo Asado El Campesino **10** *Santa Elena detail*
Stella's Bakery **11** *D3*

Monteverde Reserve ⓘ *T661-1008, US$13*, at 1900 prompt. Day or night, a guide is recommended if you want to see wildlife, since the untrained eye misses a lot.

Donations and volunteer work Donations are welcomed for purchasing additional land and maintaining and improving existing reserve areas. If you are interested in volunteer work, from non-skilled trail maintenance to skilled scientific assistance work, surveying, teaching or studying on a tropical biology programme, contact the reserve (US$14 per person, board and lodging, two weeks minimum). The Conservation League works with schools in the area on education regarding conservation. Donations can be made at the **Monteverde Cloud Forest Reserve** office or **Tropical Science Centre** ⓘ *San José, T253-3267, www.cct.or.cr*, or the **Monteverde Conservation League** ⓘ *Apdo Postal 124-5655, San José, Costa Rica, T645-5003, www.acmcr.org.*

North to Guanacaste Province

➡ *pp1036-1044*

North of Barranca, the Pan-American Highway heads towards the province of Guanacaste – the cultural heartland of Costa Rica, home to the *sabanero* cowboy and the rolling plains of the northern ranches. The province also includes the Peninsula of Nicoya and the lowlands at the head of the gulf.

Guanacaste, with its capital Liberia, has a distinctive people, way of life, flora and fauna. The smallholdings of the highlands give way here to large haciendas and great cattle estates. The rivers teem with fish; there are all kinds of wildlife in the uplands.

The people are open, hospitable and fun-loving, and are famed for their music and dancing, and in fact, the Punto Guanacasteco has been officially declared the typical national dance. There are many fiestas in January and February in the local towns and villages, which are well worth seeing.

Guanacaste Conservation Area

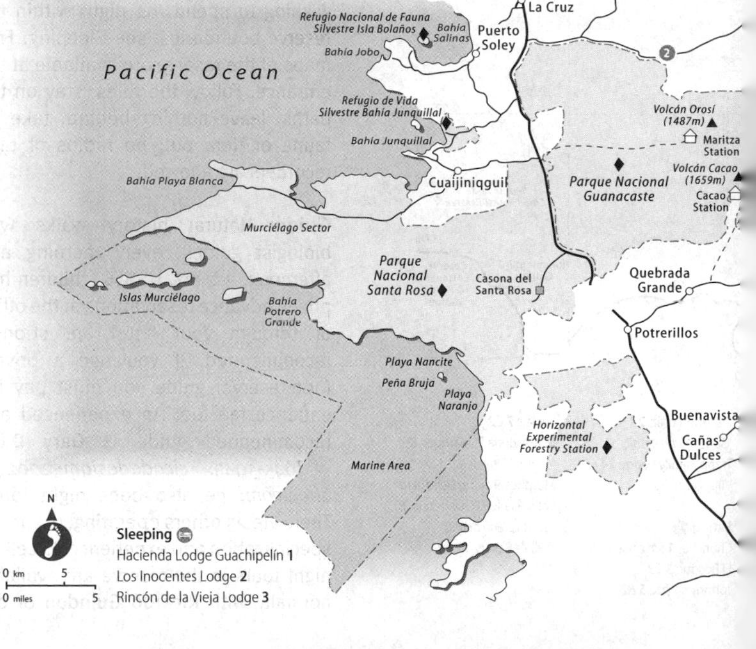

Heading northwest on the Pan-American Highway, turn right just after the Río Aranjuez at Rancho Grande (or just south of the Río Lagarto at Km 149) to access a dramatic and at times scenic route to Santa Elena-Monteverde (see page 1032).

Forty-three kilometres north of Barranca is the turn-off for **Las Juntas**, an alternative route to Monteverde for those using the Tempisque ferry or arriving from Guanacaste; a third of it is paved. After Las Juntas, there is a mining ecomuseum at **La Sierra de Abangares** ⓘ *daily 0600-1800, US$1.80*, with mining artefacts from a turn-of-the-20th-century gold mine.

Four kilometres north, the long-awaited bridge over the Tempisque River finally opened in April 2003, ending the long waits for the car ferry. After about 6 km a road to the right at San Joaquín leads to the **Hacienda Solimar Lodge**, a 1300-ha cattle farm with dry tropical virgin forest bordering Parque Nacional Palo Verde (see below) near Porozal in the lower Tempisque River basin. The freshwater Madrigal estuary on the property is one of the most important areas for waterbirds in Costa Rica (only guests staying at the Hacienda can visit). Also surrounded by gallery forest, it is recommended for serious birdwatchers. Reservations essential, contact **Birdwatch** ⓘ *T228-4768, www.birdwatchcostarica.com, see also page 1043.*

Rainfall is moderate: 1000-2000 mm a year; there is a long dry season which makes irrigation important, but the lowlands are deep in mud during the rainy season.

Sixty-seven kilometres north of Barranca, **Cañas** has little to keep the visitor for long. There are a number of interesting sights nearby and, for the traveller arriving from the north, this is the cut-through to Tilarán and connecting buses to Arenal or Fortuna. **Las Pumas** ⓘ *behind Safaris Corobicí, Cañas, free but donations welcome and encouraged*, is a small, private, Swiss-run animal rescue centre which specializes in looking after big cats, including jaguar. It's an unmissable if rather sad experience.

Parque Nacional Palo Verde

At the south of the neck of the Nicoya Peninsula is Parque Nacional Palo Verde, currently over 18,650 ha of marshes with many water birds. Indeed, in the *laguna* more than 50,000 birds are considered resident. The views from the limestone cliffs are fantastic. **Palo Verde Biological Station** ⓘ *T661-4717, www.ots.ac.cr*, is a research station run by the Organization for Tropical Studies. It organizes natural history walks and basic accommodation (ordinary visitors US$60 with three meals and a guided walk, cheaper for researchers; make advance reservations). Turn off the Pan-American Highway at **Bagaces**, halfway between Cañas and Liberia. There is no public transport. The **Palo Verde Administration offices** ⓘ *T661-4717*, are in Bagaces, next to the service station. Camping US$2 per person and lodging US$12 in park, meals available. There are two ranger stations, Palo Verde and Catalina. Check roads in wet season.

Liberia and around → *Colour map 7, B2. Population: 40,000.*

Known as the 'White City', Liberia is a neat, clean, cattle town with a triangular, rather unattractive modern church, and single-storey colonial houses meticulously laid out in the streets surrounding the central plaza. A well-paved branch road leads southwest to the Nicoya Peninsula.

There is a **tourist office** ⓘ *3 blocks south of the plaza on Calle 1, Av 6, T666-1606*, which is helpful, English is spoken; leave a donation as the centre is not formally funded (and information is not always accurate). In the same building is the **Museo del Sabanero** (**Cowboy Museum**) ⓘ *museum and tourist office Mon-Sat 0800-1200, 1300-1600, US$0.45*, a poorly presented display of artefacts. You can also get some tourist information across the plaza from the church.

Twenty kilometres north of Liberia is Costa Rica's first commercial **ostrich farm** ⓘ *T666-0950 for information on tours*, with blueneck and black breeds. A further 3 km north is the turn-off northeast to **Quebrada Grande**.

Parque Nacional Rincón de la Vieja

ⓘ *Park entry US$6. There are 2 ways into the park: the southern route, which has less traffic, goes from Puente La Victoria on the western side of Liberia and leads, in about 25 km, to the Santa María sector, closest to the hot springs. In this part, you can stay for US$2.50 per person in the old, spacious, and basic refurbished Santa María Hacienda 2 km inside the park. Bring your own food and bedding, or camp. From the old hacienda you can hike 8 km to the boiling mud pots (Las Pailas) and come back in the same day; the sulphur springs are on a different trail and only one hour away. The northern route turns right off the Pan-American Highway 5 km*

Liberia

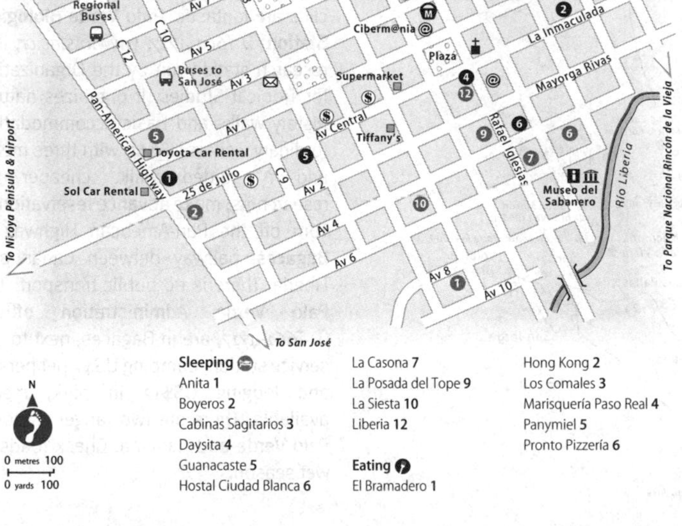

Sleeping
Anita 1
Boyeros 2
Cabinas Sagitarios 3
Daysita 4
Guanacaste 5
Hostal Ciudad Blanca 6
La Casona 7
La Posada del Tope 9
La Siesta 10
Liberia 12

Eating
El Bramadero 1
Hong Kong 2
Los Comales 3
Marisquería Paso Real 4
Panymiel 5
Pronto Pizzería 6

Border essentials: Costa Rica-Nicaragua

Peñas Blancas

Immigration Office hours 0800-1800 (Nicaragua 0800-1200 and 1300-1745). On leaving Costa Rica you have to go to Migración to surrender your passport to be stamped and to give in your immigration form. At another window you pay 75 colones for a 'Cruz Roja' stamp and to get your passport back. 'Helpers' may try and sell you the form before you arrive at the office – you do not have to buy it from them. Trolley pullers charge US$0.50 to carry bags between these posts, a short distance. Across the border, passports are inspected on the Nicaraguan side. Crossing to Nicaragua may be a slow process; if you arrive when a Tica, Sirca or other international bus is passing through this is especially true. When leaving Nicaragua you pay US$1 for the 'right to leave', another US$2 at customs and there are reports of a US$1 bus station tax on the Nicaraguan side. Visa stamps are given at the border. If you have no outward ticket for Costa Rica, and are challenged, you can buy a cheap bus ticket back to Nicaragua at the border (valid for one year).

Crossing by private vehicle

Entering Costa Rica by car, first pay your entrance stamp, then go to Aduana Permiso de Vehículo for your vehicle permit (state how long you want); get insurance at the 'Seguro Obligatorio' window. Your vehicle is then briefly inspected before you can depart. Fumigation cost US$3 for cars, US$4 for pick-ups. Leaving by car, hand over the printed vehicle permit you got on arrival. For documents and other requirements, see page 980.

Transport There are several express or ordinary buses a day from/to San José, 100 m north of Coca Cola terminal, 4 hrs or 6 hrs, US$5; only the earliest (0430 and 0500) from San José will get you to the border before it closes. Bus from the border to Liberia, US$1.25, 1½ hrs. Only a few buses from La Cruz, US$0.60, taxi costs US$4-5.

Banks There is a bank in Customs (usually changes cash, does not change TCs, open 0800-1200, 1300-1600) and money changers to ease your passage. Good rates if you shop around; there's no great difference between rates on either side.

northwest of Liberia, through Curubandé (no public transport on this route). Beyond Curubandé, you cross the private property of Hacienda Lodge Guachipelin (US$2 to cross), beyond which is Rincón de la Vieja Lodge, see Sleeping.

Most easily visited from Liberia, Parque Nacional Rincón de la Vieja (14,161 ha) was created to preserve the area around the Volcán Rincón de la Vieja, to the northeast of the town. It includes dry tropical forest, mud pots, hot sulphur springs and several other geothermal curiosities. The volcanic massif reaches to 1916 m and can be seen from a wide area around Liberia when not shrouded in clouds. The area is cool at night and subject to strong, gusty winds and violent rains; in the day it can be very hot, although always windy. These fluctuations mark all of the continental divide, of which the ridge is a part. From time to time the volcano erupts, the last eruption being in November 1995, when it tossed rocks and lava down its slopes.

The park is home to over **350 recorded species of bird** including toucans, parrots, three-wattled bellbirds and great curassows, along with howler monkeys, armadillos and coatis, ticks and other biting insects. It also has the largest density of Costa Rica's national flower the *guaria morada* or **purple orchid**. Horses can be rented in the park from some of the lodges. If you want to climb the volcano you will need to camp near the top, or at the warden's station, in order to ascend early in the morning before the clouds come in. Trails through the park lead to most sights of interest, including beautiful waterfalls and swimming holes. There are several accommodation options in or near the park, and shorter trips easily arranged from Liberia.

Parque Nacional Santa Rosa

About half-way to the Nicaraguan border from Liberia, is Parque Nacional Santa Rosa (38,673 ha). Together with the Murciélago Annex, the peninsula to the north of the developed park, it preserves some of the last dry tropical forests in Costa Rica, and shelters abundant and relatively easy-to-see wildlife. During the dry season, the animals depend on the water holes, and are thus easy to find until the holes dry up completely. Conservation work in the area is also trying to reforest some cattle ranches in the area – helped by the fact that cattle have not been profitable in recent years.

Close to the park headquarters and research buildings, the historically important **La Casona** was an essential visit for every Tico child as it is from here that the patriots repelled the invasion of the filibuster Walker in 1856, who had entrenched himself in the main building. Unfortunately the old hacienda building, once the Museo Histórico de Santa Rosa, was almost completely destroyed by fire in May 2001. The newly rebuilt La Casona was reopened in 2002. There are several good trails and lookouts in the park, the easiest of which is close to La Casona. Lasting a couple of hours, it leads through dry tropical forest with many Indio Desnudo (naked Indian) trees, which periodically shed their red flaky bark.

Deeper in the park, **Playa Naranjo** (12 km, three hours' walk or more, or use 4WD, park authorities permitting) and **Playa Nancite** (about the same distance from the entrance) are major nesting sites of **leatherback** and **Olive Ridley sea turtles**. The main nesting season is between August and October (although stragglers are regularly seen up to January) when flotillas of up to 10,000 Ridley turtles arrive at night on the 7-km long Playa Nancite. Females clumsily lurch up the beach, scoop out a deep hole, deposit and bury an average of 100 ping-pong-ball sized eggs before returning exhausted to the sea (see also Ostional). Playa Nancite is a restricted-access beach; you need a written permit to stay plus US$2 per day to camp, or US$15 in dormitories. Permits from **SPN** in San José, and the **Park Administration building** ⓘ *Santa Rosa, T666-5051. Make sure you have permission before going.* Research has been done in the Playa Nancite area on howler monkeys, coatis and the complex interrelation between the fauna and the forest. Playa Naranjo is one of the most attractive beaches in the country. It is unspoilt, quiet and very good for surfing. There is good camping, drinking water (although occasionally salty) and BBQ facilities.

The incoming tidal surge is very dangerous, be off the island before the tide comes in.

La Cruz and Isla Bolaños → *Colour map 7, B2.*

The last town before the border, La Cruzhas a bank (for cash, traveller's cheques or credit card transactions), a handful of hotels and absolutely incredible sunsets from the hilltop overlooking the Bahía de Salinas. Down in the bay the Islas Bolaños Wildlife Refuge and some of the best conditions for windsurfing in Costa Rica.

Isla Bolaños is a 25-ha National Wildlife Refuge protecting the nesting sites of the brown pelican, frigate bird and American oystercatcher. The island is covered with dry forest and you can only walk round the island at low tide. No camping is allowed.

Sleeping

San José to Esparza and Barranca *p1027*
A Finca Daniel, 14 km off the Inter-American highway at Miramar, T639-9900, www.finca-daniel.com. Memorable sunsets, wildlife, canopy tour, horse riding, waterfalls and spring-fed pool on 27 ha.

C Hotel Río Mar, Barranca, T663-0158. With bath, restaurant, good.
D Hotel Castanuelas, close to the highway, T635-5105. A/c, quiet, cooler alternative to Puntarenas.

Puntarenas and around *p1027*
Accommodation is difficult to find from Dec-Apr, especially at weekends.
AL-A Tioga, on the beach front with Calle 17, T661-0271, www.hoteltioga.com. 52 rooms; those with balconies are much better with good views. All with private bath, a/c, TV and telephone. Restaurant, swimming pool, casino, very good.
A La Punta, Av 1, Calle 35, T661-0696. Good spot 1 block from car ferry, with bath, friendly, clean, hot water, restaurant, secure parking, good pool, American-owned, big rooms.
B-C Las Hamacas on beach front between Calle 5-7, T661-0398. Rooms are OK, but noisy when the bar is in full flow. Small pool. Could do with a lick of paint; for now it is overpriced.
C Cayuga, Calle 4, Av Central-1, T661-0344. 31 rooms with private bathroom, a/c, pretty dark rooms, restaurant. There is a small garden patio but it's hardly paradise.
C Gran Imperial, on the beach front, in front of the Muelle de Cruceros, T661-0579. Pleasant rooms, although a little dark, but clean with private bath and fan. Small garden patio, and a very chilled atmosphere. Good spot and handy for buses.
C-D Gran Hotel Chorotega, on the corner of Calle 1, Av 3 near the banks and market, T661-0998. Clean rooms with private bath, cheaper with shared. Efficient and friendly service. Popular with visiting business people. A good deal.
D Cabezas, Av 1, Calle 2-4, T661-1045. 23 rooms, some with private bath, cheaper without. Simple rooms with no frills but bright and clean. Good deal.
D Río, Av 3, Calle Central-2 near market, T661-0331. Private bath, fans, good rooms. Friendly Chinese owners keen to help, lively, sometimes noisy, but popular place.
F Monte Mar, Av 3, Calle 1-3, T661-2771. Very basic, some rooms with fan, but bearable on a budget.

Around Puntarenas
B Casa San Francisco, at Roble, 10 km east of Puntarenas, on the coast, T663-0148. Near regional hospital, run by 2 Canadian women, with breakfast, pool, clean, laundry facilities, friendly and helpful. Recommended.
B Villa del Roble, at Roble, 10 km east of Puntarenas, by the sea, T663-0447. 5 rooms, quiet, small pool, charming.

Santa Elena *p1028, map p1030*
A Arco Iris, 100 m north of **Banco Nacional**, T645-5067, www.arcoirislodge.com. Rooms with bath, restaurant with good healthy breakfast, horses for rent, plenty of parking.
A Finca Valverde, 300 m east of **Banco Nacional** up hill on road to the reserve, T645-5157, www.monteverde.co.cr. Rooms with bath, nice gardens for birdwatching, bar, restaurant.
A Miramontes, leading into Santa Elena from the north, T645-5152, www.swisshotel miramontes.com. 6 comfortable rooms in a quiet spot, Swiss-run, with a wonderful restaurant.
C Hospedaje El Banco, T645-5204. Price per person. Family-run, friendly, hot shower, clean, good information, English spoken.
C Pensión El Sueño, T645-5021. Very friendly, hot shower, small but nice rooms, clean, pricey meals, car park. Run by Rafa Trejos who does horse-riding trips into the mountains to see quetzals, etc, US$35.
C-D Pensión Santa Elena, T645-5051, www.monteverdeinfo.com/pension.htm. Very popular, clean, good food, kitchen available.
C-E El Colibrí, T645-5682, clean, friendly, timber built, with balconies.
D Pensión Tucán, T645-5017, bargain for lower price in low season, with bath in nice rooms, or **E** in basic cabins with shower (supposedly hot), friendly management, good breakfast and restaurant recommended but closed for Sun lunch. It's also a travel agency.
F Pensión Cabinas Marín, 500 m north of the centre past the Agricultural College. Spacious rooms (room 8 has a nice view), good breakfasts, friendly.

Monteverde *p1029, map p1030*
LL-AL El Establo, next to **Heliconia**, T645-5110, www.establo.com. 80 carpeted rooms with private bathroom, restaurant, 50-ha farm with 50% cloud forest, own nature guide, good birdwatching, riding stables, 35 horses, family-run, very accommodating. Recommended.

L Monteverde Lodge, T645-5057, www.costaricaexpeditions.com. Restaurant, jacuzzi, daily slide shows 1815. Recommended.

L-AL Heliconia, T645-5109, www.hotelheliconia.com. Private bathrooms, restaurant, very comfortable, excellent food, private reserve and nature rails. Highly recommended.

AL Belmar, 300 m behind service station, T645-5201, www.hotelbelmar.net. Swiss chalet-style, beautiful views of Nicoya, restaurant, good; transport from San José available.

AL Cloud Forest Lodge, 300 m north of Sapo Dorado, T645-5058, www.cloudforestlodge.com. 18 rooms with bath, restaurant, beautiful views (**Canopy Tours**, T645-5243, offer tours of 5 platforms, connected by steel cables, to explore the forest canopy, US$45 per person, US$35 for students at **Cloud Forest Lodge**).

AL El Sapo Dorado, 30 suites, 10 with fireplaces, T645-5109, www.sapodorado.com. Good but expensive restaurant, 0700-2100.

AL Fonda Vela, T645-5125, www.fondavela.com. Private bathroom, hot water, 40 beautiful rooms and suites spread around 5 buildings, 25-min walk, 5-min drive to the reserve, on a 14-ha farm with forest and trail system, good birding, 2 excellent restaurants (open to public), bar, TV room, art gallery and conference room.

AL Hotel de Moñtana Monteverde, T645-5046, monteverde@ticonet.co.cr. Comfortable, set meals, good, wholesome food, sauna, jacuzzi, horses for hire, good views of Nicoya, excellent birdwatching on 15-ha reserve, transport from San José available. Recommended.

AL San Luis Biological Station and Ecolodge, 40-min drive south from Monteverde, down a spur road near the top of the hill, T645-8049 (call ahead to book), www.ecolodgesanluis.com. On 65 ha of farmland and cloud forest in the San Luis Valley, adjoining Monteverde Cloud Forest. Price per person. 5 cabins, horse riding, swimming in river and other options.

AL Trapp Family Lodge, closest to the reserve, T645-5858, www.trappfam.com. Tidy rooms, upstairs with balconies, downstairs with terraces, friendly and helpful hosts.

AL Villa Verde, 1.5 km from reserve, T645-5025, www.villaverdehotel.com. Rooms with hot showers, others with shared bath, some with kitchenette, includes breakfast, restaurant, clean, nice, excellent views. Good package rates for students.

B Mariposa, T645-5013. 3 rooms in a single block sleeping up to 3 people, with private bath. A family atmosphere with breakfast included in the price.

B-D El Bosque, next to restaurant of same name, T645-5158. 26 rooms, hot showers, comfortable, clean, fine views, beautiful gardens and short trail, safe parking.

B-D La Colina Lodge, between Monteverde and reserve, T645-5009. Private bath, balconies with some rooms, cheaper in dormitory, helpful, luggage stored, small area for camping, one of the original houses of Monteverde with some nice touches. Marvin Rockwell, the former owner and one of the original Quaker settlers, pops in to give talks when requested.

B-E Pensión Manakin, just beyond **Establo**, along a short road on the right, T645-5080, www.manakinlodge.com. 10 simple rooms, a few with private bath, cheaper with shared bath, also fully equipped cabins. Filling breakfast and evening meals are available, in a family atmosphere great for sharing stories with other guests. A small balcony at the back makes a calm place to sit and relax. The Villegas are very knowledgeable about the area, and will help arrange tours and transport up to the reserve if required.

D Monteverde Inn, down track opposite **Heliconia**, T645-5156. Price per person, private bathroom, quiet, but run-down.

D-E Albergue Bellbird, just before the gas station, T645-5518. Half a dozen rooms in mainly dormitory-style accommodation, with shared bathrooms, new restaurant with typical food.

Monteverde Cloud Forest Reserve *p1030*

Shelter facilities throughout the reserve cost US$3.50-US$5 a night, reserve entry fee for each night spent in the park, plus key deposit of US$5. Bring sleeping bag and flashlight. You can make your own meals. Dormitory- style accommodation for up to 30 people at entrance, **Albergue Reserva Biológica de Monteverde**, T645-5122, US$23 full board only. Reservations only for all reserve accommodation (usually booked up by groups).

North to Guanacaste Province *p1032*
A **Hacienda Solimar Lodge**. 8 rooms with private or shared bathroom, includes meals, minimum 2 nights, transport on request, local guide, horse riding. Recommended for serious birdwatchers, reservations essential, contact **Birdwatch**, T228-4768, www.birdwatchcostarica.com, see page 1033.
B-C **Capazuri B&B**, 2.5 km north of Cañas, T669-6280. Also camping US$5 per person.
C **Cañas**, Calle 2, Av 3, Cañas, T669-0039. With bath, clean, pleasant.
C **El Corral**, Pan-American, Cañas, T669-1467. With bath and restaurant.
E **Cabinas Corobicí**, Cañas, T669-0241. 11 good rooms with bath and parking available. Price per person.

Liberia and around *p1034, map p1034*
A **Las Espuelas**, 2 km south of Liberia, T666-0144, www.bestwestern.com. Good, a/c, satellite TV, swimming pool, round trip bus service from San José.
B **Boyeros**, on Pan-American Highway with Av Central, T666-0722. Pool, bath, restaurant.
B **Hostal Ciudad Blanca**, Av 4, Calle 1-3, from Gobernación 200 m south, 150 m east, T666- 3962. 12 nice but dirty rooms, a/c, hot water, phone, TV, restaurant/bar, parking, rooster wake up call.
B **Hotel del Aserradero**, Pan-American Highway and Av 3, T666-1939. 16 big rooms with bath, parking and fans.
B **Santa Clara Lodge**, 4 km from Quebrada Grande, T666-4054. 4 rooms shared bath, 1 room with bath, cattle farm, riding, dry forest.
C **Guanacaste**, Calle 12, Av 3, just round corner from bus stations, T666-0085. Clean, bath, friendly, restaurant, safe parking, money exchange, **Ticabus** agency, transfers and tours, camping area, English spoken, group discount, 15% student discount, affiliated youth hostel. Recommended.
C **La Siesta**, Calle 4, Av 4-6, T666-0678. With bath, restaurant, clean, swimming pool, helpful owner who speaks English.
C-E **Hotel Daysita**, Av 5, Calle 11-13, T666-0197. Restaurant, pool, quiet, not central. Cheaper to share 6-bedded room with bath.
D-E **La Casona**, Av 6, Calle Central, T666-2971. Rooms for up to 4 people, shared bath, washing facilities, rooms facing street get very hot; more expensive in new annex with private bath.
D-E **Liberia**, ½ block south of main square, T666-0161. With bath, cheaper with shared bath, fans, clean, friendly, good information board and breakfast only restaurant, laundry facilities. Recommended.
E **Cabinas Sagitarios**, Av 11, Calle 2, T666-0950. With bath, run by Dutchman and Costa Rican, breakfast and dinner available on request, friendly, tours to Ostrich Farm.
F **Anita**, Calle 4 y Av 8, T666-1285. Bath, clean, family-run, friendly, café, shop, parking, best of the range.
F **La Posada del Tope**, Rafeal Iglesias, 1½ blocks south from cathedral, T666-3876. Price per person, cold shower, laundry facilities, clean, friendly, helpful, parking, bike rentals, baggage storage, the owner Dennis has a telescope for star gazing.

Parque Nacional Rincón de la Vieja *p1034*
AL **Hacienda Lodge Guachipelin**, accessed through the northern route, T666-8075, office 442-2818, www.guachipelin.com. Meals available, 18 rooms, internet, canopy tour, camping US$1.70 but no fires, naturalist guides, riding, hot springs, sulphur springs, mud pools, waterfalls (transport from Liberia arranged, US$25 per person round trip).
AL-A **Rincón de la Vieja Lodge**, accessed through the northern route, T200-0238, www.rincondelaviejalodge.net. Canopy tour, sulphur hot springs, tennis and butterfly garden, internet. Also packages including transport from San José. The lodge is on the edge of the park and there are horses for rent, guides and tours. From there it is 3¼ hrs to the volcano, 30 mins to Las Pailas, 45 mins to the thermal springs, Azufrales, and 2¼ hrs to the Hidden Waterfalls.
A-B **Buena Vista Mountain Lodge**, accessed through the Santa María sector, T661-8158. Rooms, waterslide, canopy tour, spa, internet, restaurant/bar.
F **Miravieja Lodge**, accessed through the Santa María sector, T662-2004. Rustic lodge in citrus groves, meals, transport and tours available.

Parque Nacional Santa Rosa *p1036*
Camping
There is a pleasant campground at Park Administration, T679-9692, about 7 km from the entrance with giant strangler figs that

shade your tent from the stupendously hot sun, and very adequate sanitary facilities, picnic tables, and so forth for US$2.15 per person per night. There is a small *comedor* for meals (breakfast 0600-0630, lunch 1100-1200, evening 1700-1800, good) and drinks near the campground but it is advised you bring some of your own supplies; a tent is useful: essential in the wet season. You may be able to sleep on the veranda of one of the scientists' houses. Bring a mosquito net and insect repellent. If the water is not running, ask at Park Administration.

La Cruz and Isla Bolaños *p1036*

LL-AL Ecoplaya Beach Resort, Bahía Salinas, T228-7146, www.ecoplaya.com. All-inclusive resort, well maintained with nice restaurant.

AL-A Los Inocentes Lodge, on slopes of Volcán Orosí, 16 km east of La Cruz, T679-9190, www.losinocentesranch.com. Price per person, meals extra, 11 rooms with bath in beautiful former working hacienda, pool, horse riding on the lower slopes of the volcano, forest trails and guides. Day trips possible for US$30 – call ahead.

B Amalia's Inn, 100 m south of Parque Central, T679-9181. Stunning views, small pool, very friendly and excellent local knowledge. Extra person US$5, and 1 room sleeps 6. Excellent value for groups and recommended.

B Hostal de Julia, on road out to the Pan-American Highway, T/ F679-9084. Clean, tidy rooms, ample parking.

C-D Cabinas Santa Rita, 150 m south of Parque Central, T679-9062. Nice, clean, secure with good parking. Cheaper with fan. Would be great in any other town not competing with Amalia's.

D Hotel Bella Vista, ½ block northwest of the plaza, T679-8060. Rooms, restaurant/bar, great view.

F Cabinas Maryfel, opposite bus terminal (but no obvious sign), T679-9534. Price per person, dark and basic, but OK for the price.

Camping

Playa Morro Trailer Park y Cabinas, west of La Cruz, on Bahía Salinas looking over to Isla Bolaños, T382-2989. Drinking water, showers, toilets, tennis, barbecue, fishing boats and horses to rent, 1-km beach.

Eating

Puntarenas and around *p1027*

There are many bars and a couple of discos along the Paseo de los Turistas. A number of Chinese restaurants on Av Central and Calle 1 and there is good, cheap food from market stalls, eg *sopa de carne* (meat soup).

TT **Aloha**, on the seafront on Calle 17, T661-2375. Worth checking out.

TT **Casa de Mariscos**, Calle 7-9, T661-1666. On the beach front, good seafood, reasonable prices, closed Tue.

TT **Jardín Cervecero Bierstube**, on the seafront at Calle 23-25, T661-0330. Good for sandwiches, hamburgers and a beer.

TT **Kayte Negro**, north side of the peninsula on Av Badillo, Calle 17. Good local food.

TT **La Yunta**, on the beachfront at Calle 19, T661-3216. A popular steak house.

TT **Mariscos Kahite Blanco**, near launch. Excellent and locally renowned seafood.

TT **Soda Brisas del Mar**, on Calle Central, Av 2-4. Good for a snack.

T **Soda Macarena**, opposite the Muelle de Cruceros (dock). Handy while waiting for buses.

Around Puntarenas

TT **María Vargas**, Roble, 10 km east of Puntarenas. Bar and restaurant, friendly, good food, reasonable prices.

Santa Elena *p1028, map p1030*

TTT **Chunches**, opposite **Pensión Santa** Elena, T645-5147. A very useful place with good expresso bar and snacks, used books, magazines, laundromat, fax service.

TT **Marisquería El Márquez** (see map), T645-5918. Seafood and *casados*.

TT **Morphos**, (see map), T645-5607. Typical and international fare, recommended, with a good atmosphere, but not cheap.

T **Pollo Asado El Campesino** (see map). Tico soda, early breakfast special.

Monteverde *p1029, map p1030*

TTT-TT **Johnny's Pizza**, on main road between Santa Elena and Monteverde, T645-5066. Good wood oven-cooked pizzas in a relaxed atmosphere, café, souvenir shop. Tables outside give extra chance to see wildlife.

ŸŸŸ-ŸŸ **Restaurant Lucia's**, down road opposite Heliconia, T645-5337. Tasty lasagne, international and vegetarian fare.
ŸŸ **Restaurant El Bosque**, on road to reserve, next to Casem. Shop, good food, clean, open from 0630.
Ÿ **Stella's Bakery**, opposite Casem, T645-5560. Excellent wholemeal bread, cakes and good granola – there's a café if you want to eat in.

North to Guanacaste Province *p1032*
ŸŸŸ **Rincón Corobicí**, next to La Pacífica, Cañas, T669-6191. Clean and pleasant, with a small zoo and offers rafting down Río Corobicí, T669-0544.
ŸŸ **Restaurant Panchitos**, main square, Cañas. Good and inexpensive.
ŸŸ **Central**, main square. Good Chinese restaurant.

Liberia and around *p1034, map p1034*
ŸŸŸ **Marisquería Paso Real**, south side of main square. Great ceviche and seafood.
ŸŸ **Chop Suey**, Calle Central. Chinese, big helpings.
ŸŸ **Copa de Oro**, next to Hotel Liberia. Chinese, huge servings, good value.
ŸŸ **El Bramadero**, part of the Hotel Bramadero on the Pan-American Highway. Popular, breakfast from 0630, lively bar in the evenings.
ŸŸ **Jardín de Azúcar**, just off plaza, T666-3563. Self service, good variety and tasty.
ŸŸ **Pronto Pizzería**, Calle 1, Av 4. Good food (not just pizzas) in a charming colonial house.
ŸŸ-Ÿ **Hong Kong**, 1½ blocks east of church. Chinese, cheap and cheerful.
Ÿ **Los Comales**, Calle Central , Av 5-7. Traditional Guanacaste dishes prepared with maize, run by women's cooperative.
Ÿ **Panymiel**, Av Central, Calle 8-9, and Av 3, Calle 2. Bakery, snacks and drinks, good value.

La Cruz and Isla Bolaños *p1036*
Ÿ **La Orchidea**, La Cruz, T679-9316. Seafood, cheap, daily 0630-2200.
Ÿ **Restaurant Telma**, La Cruz, T679-9150. Tico food, cheap.
Ÿ **Soda Estadio**, La Cruz. Good, cheap.
Ÿ **Soda Marta**, La Cruz, T679-9347. Cheap Tico fare.

Festivals and events

Puntarenas and around *p1027*
Jul Fiesta de la Virgen del Mar, on the Sat closest to the 16 Jul, with a week of festivities leading to a carnival and regatta of decorated fishing boats and yachts.

Monteverde *p1029, map p1030*
Dec-Mar Monteverde Music Festival, T645-5053, classical and jazz concerts at sunset, local, national and international musicians. Programme from local hotels, US$10.

Liberia and around *p1034, map p1034*
25 Jul, Guanacaste Day sees dancing, parades and cattle related festivities.

Shopping

Monteverde *p1029, map p1030*
Casem, a co-operative gift shop, is located just outside Monteverde on the road to the reserve next to El Bosque restaurant, T645-5190. It sells embroidered shirts, T-shirts, wooden and woven articles and baskets. Next door, there's a shop selling Costa Rican coffee.

Liberia and around *p1034, map p1034*
Tiffany's, Av C-2, Calle 2, general gifts, cigars.
Mini Galería Fulvia, on the main plaza, sells Tico Times, English papers and books. English spoken and helpful.

Activities and tours

North to Guanacaste Province *p1032*
Tour operators
CATA Tours, Cañas, T296-2133, rafting tours and full-day tours to Parque Nacional Palo Verde. **Safaris Corobicí** is 4 km past Cañas on the Pan-American Highway, 25 m before the entrance to **Centro Ecológico La Pacífica**, T669-6191. Float tours down the Río Corobicí and Río Tenorio, US$35 per person for 2 hrs rafting, US$60, ½-day.

Liberia and around *p1034, map p1034*
Tour operators
Hotel Liberia can organize tours, rent out bikes and assist with enquiries. A recommended guide for the nearby national parks is **Alejandro Vargas Rodríguez**, who lives in front of the Red Cross, T666-1889.

Puntarenas and around *p1027*

Tour operators

See under San José Tour operators, page 997, for Gulf of Nicoya cruises.

Transport

San José to Esparza and Barranca *p1027*

Bus If going from **San José** to Monteverde it is possible to change buses in Barranca, rather than going all the way to Puntarenas, if you leave the capital before 1230.

Puntarenas and around *p1027*

Bus Terminal for San José is at Calle 2, Av 2-4. Buses every 40 mins 0415-1900 to **San José**, 2 hrs, US$2.50. Buses from San José leave from Terminal Puntarenas Calle 16, Av 10-12, 0600-1900. Daily bus to **Santa Elena** for Monteverde, 1315 and occasionally at 1415. Buses south to **Quepos** from main bus station, 0500, 1100 and 1430 (high season) via **Jacó**, US$2.70, 4 hrs, return 0430, 1030, 1630. To **Liberia** with **Empresa Arata**, 5 a day, first at 0530, last 1500, 2½ hrs, US$1.50. To **Tilarán** via **Cañas** at 1130 and 1630. Good café at bus terminal where you can wait for your bus.

Ferry Check which dock your ferry leaves from. For the **Nicoya Peninsula** see page 1044. To southern Nicoya Peninsula from the dock at Calle 35. To **Playa Naranjo** at 0600, 1000, 1420,and 1900, returning at 0730, 1250, 1700 and 2100, 1½ hrs. T661-1069 for exact times. Pedestrians US$1.60, motorbikes US$3, cars US$12. The ferry dock is about 1 km from Puntarenas bus station, local buses run between the two, otherwise walk or get a taxi. Buses meet the ferry for **Nicoya** (through Carmona, 40 km unpaved, 30 km paved road, crowded, noisy, frequently break down, US$1.25, 2¼ hrs), **Sámara** (US$1.30), **Coyote**, **Bejuco** and **Jicaral**.

From the same dock a car ferry goes to **Paquera** at 0630, 1030, 1530 and 2030, returning at 0430, 0830, 1300 and 1730, 1½ hrs. T641-0118 to check the times. On arrival, get on the bus (which waits for the ferry) as quickly as possible (to **Cóbano**, 2-3 hrs, US$1.25, bad road, to **Montezuma** US$2.60, 1½ hrs at least), pay on the bus, or get a taxi. **Hotel Playa Tambor** also runs a car ferry to **Paquera** at 0500, 1230, 1700, leaving Paquera 0800, 1430 and 2030. A bus to **Tambor** will be waiting at Paquera on your arrival. T661-2084 for information.

Launch **Paquera**-Puntarenas leaves from behind the central market, directly north of the bus stop at 0600, 1100 and 1515, returning at 0730, 1230 and 1700. Pedestrians US$1.50, motorbikes US$1.80, Tickets are sold when the incoming boat has docked.

Santa Elena *p1028, map p1030*

Bus From **Puntarenas**, Terminal Empresarios Unidos, daily at 1415, occasionally at 1315 as well, 2½-4 hrs, returns 0600, US$2.20. This bus arrives in time to catch a bus to **Quepos** for Manuel Antonio. See Monteverde Transport, below, for buses from **San José**. For an alternative route to Santa Elena from **Arenal**, see p.

To **Tilarán** the 0700 (US$1.80, 3 hrs) connects with the 1230 bus to **Fortuna** and others to **Cañas** for the Pan-American Highway, Liberia and Nicoya Peninsula.

Car There is a service station, Mon-Sat 0700-1800, Sun 0700-1200.

Horse Several places rent horses; look for signs between Santa Elena and Monteverde or ask at your hotel. Try not to hire horses that look overworked.

Taxi Santa Elena-**Monteverde**, US$6, and Monteverde-the reserve, US$5.75 (hunt around for good prices). Not so easy to find a taxi for return trip, best to arrange beforehand.

Monteverde *p1029, map p1030*

Bus From **San José** a direct bus runs from Av 9, Calle 12, just outside Terminal Atlántico Norte (4½ hrs, US$4) daily at 0630 and 1430. Leaves Monteverde from **Hotel Villa Verde** also at 0630 and 1430, picking up through town, stopping at Santa Elena bus stop (be early). Check times in advance, Sat bus does not always run in low season (T645-5159 in Santa Elena, T222-3854, in San José). This service is not 'express', it stops to pick up passengers all along the route, and is not a comfortable ride. Keep your bag with you at all times; several cases of theft reported. Alternatively, get a bus to **Puntarenas** and change there for Santa Elena, see above.

North to Guanacaste Province *p1032*

Bus The Cañas bus station is 500 m north of the centre, where all buses depart from except for those to San José, which leave from the terminal 300 m west of Parque Central on the Pan-American Highway. To **San José**, Transportes La Cañera, T669-0145, 8 daily from 0400, 3½ hrs, arriving and departing from Calle 16, Av 1-3. To **Liberia**, 10 daily from 0530. To **Puntarenas**, 8 daily from 0600. To **Upala**, for Bijagua and Volcán Tenorio, 7 daily from 0500, 13/4 hrs, US$1.50. To **Tilarán**, 7 daily from 0600. Buses to Tilarán for **Nuevo Arenal**, past the volcano and on to **Fortuna**, or for connections to **Santa Elena** and **Monteverde**. If going by road, the turn-off for Tilarán is at the filling station, no signs. For a description of this route in reverse see page 1017.

Liberia and around *p1034, map p1034*

Air The Aeropuerto Internacional Tomás Guardia, about 13 km from Liberia (LIR) on the road to the Nicoya Peninsula was reopened in 1992, revamped in 1995 and renamed Aeropuerto Daniel Oduber Quirós, after the former president who came from Guanacaste. The new runway can handle large jets and charter flights, and direct daily flights to **Miami**. Lacsa, T666-0306; Sansa, T221-9414; Nature Air, T220-3054. There is a direct weekly flight to **New York** arriving Sat, through Air-Tech, www.airtech.com, Wed, Sat and Sun. Delta flights from **Atlanta**. American flights from **Miami**, Continental from **Houston**.

Bus To **San José** leave from Av 5, Calle 10-12, with 14 a day, US$4.25, 4 hrs. Other buses leave from the local terminal at Calle 12, Av 7-9. Liberia to **Playa del Coco**, 6 a day, 0530-1815, **Playa Hermosa** and **Panama**, 1130 and 1900, **Puntarenas**, 7 a day, 0500- 1530, **Bagaces/Cañas**, 4 a day, 0545-1710, **Cañas Dulces**, 3 a day, 0600-1730, **La Cruz/ Peñas Blanca**, 8 a day 0530-1800. **Filedefia- Santa Cruz-Nicoya**, 0500-2020, 20 a day.

Car Car rental Sol and Toyota car rental agencies (see map) offer same prices and allow you to leave the vehicle at San José airport for US$50.

Parque Nacional Rincón de la Vieja *p1034*

A taxi costs US$30 one-way from Liberia. Most hotels will arrange transport for US$15 per person, minimum 6 passengers. Departure at 0700, 1 hr to entrance, return at 1700; take food and drink. You can also hitch; most tourist vehicles will pick you up. If you take your own transport a 4WD is best, although during the dry season a vehicle with high clearance is adequate.

Parque Nacional Santa Rosa *p1036*

Parque Nacional Santa Rosa is easy to reach as it lies west of the Pan-American Highway, about 1 hr north of Liberia. Any bus going from Liberia to Peñas Blancas on the Nicaraguan border will drop you right at the entrance (US$0.70, 40 mins), from where it's a 7-km walk, but you may be able to hitch a ride. Last bus returns to Liberia about 1800. Coming from the border, any bus heading south will drop you off at the entrance.

La Cruz and Isla Bolaños *p1036*

Bus Regular buses to **San José** from 0545 until 1630, 5 hrs. To **Liberia**, 5 daily 0700-1730, 1½ hrs. To **Peñas Blancas**, 5 daily 0730- 1730, 1 hr. To **Playa Jobo** in Bahía Solanos, at 0530, 1030 and 1500, from main plaza.

Directory

Puntarenas and around *p1027*

Banks Banco Nacional and Banco de Costa Rica, on Av 3, Calle 1-3 near the Central Market, changes TCs, and with ATM. **Internet** Millennium Cyber Café, on the beach front with Calle 15, T661 4759, only one in town so popular, 1000-2200, 600c per hr. Free coffee if you're lucky. **Post office** Av 3, Calle Central-1, close to Central Market. **Telephone** ICE and Radiográfica, Av C, Calle 2-4.

Santa Elena *p1028, map p1030*

Banks Banco Nacional, 0900-1500, to change TCs with commission and advance cash against Visa. ATM machine for Visa in the supermarket opposite the post office. **Internet** Several places are opening up, but with poor communication links are charging a exorbitant prices. Try **Tranquilo Communications** at Pensión Santa Elena, US3 per hr.

Monteverde *p1029, map p1030*
Cultural centres Galería Extasis, 250 m south of La Cascada, T645-5548, exhibits sculptures by the Costa Rican artist, Marco Tulio Brenes. **Language schools** A branch of the Centro Panamericano de Idiomas, in Heredia, has opened a school on the road up to the reserve, T645-5026. Accommodation is with local families.

Liberia and around *p1034, map p1034*
Banks Banco Popular and Bancrecer both have Visa ATMs. **Banco de Costa Rica** is on the main plaza. **Credomatic**, Av Central, MasterCard ATM. For money exchange, try *casa de cambio* on Calle 2 or ask around, eg Restaurant Chun San, behind the cathedral. **Internet** ½ block south of the church, cheap, good machines, 1000-2200. Ciberm@nia, north side of main plaza, T666-7240, US$1.25 per hr. **Medical services** Enrique Baltodano Hospital, T666-0011. Pharmacies close to main plaza.

Península de Nicoya

Fringed by idyllic white-sand beaches along most of the coastline, the Nicoya Peninsula is hilly and hot. There are few towns of any size and most of the roads not connecting the main communities are in poor condition. While several large hotel resorts are increasingly taking over what were once isolated coves, they are generally grouped together and there are still many remote beaches to explore. A few small areas of the peninsula are protected to preserve wildlife, marine ecosystems and the geological formations of Barra Honda. ▸▸ *For Sleeping, Eating and other listings, see pages 1049-1059.*

Ins and outs

Getting there There are several ways of getting to the Nicoya Peninsula. The recently opened **Taiwan Friendship Bridge** over the Tempisque saves time and gas money getting to the peninsula, eliminating the ferry. Just across the river is **Hotel Rancho Humo,** T255-2463 (L) with boat trips on the Tempisque and Bebedero rivers, visits to Palo Verde and Barra Honda national parks.

A second route takes the **Salinero car ferry** from Puntarenas across the Gulf of Nicoya to Playa Naranjo. See page 1027. Buses meet the ferry for Nicoya (US$1.25, 2¼ hours), Sámara (US$1.30), Coyote, Bejuco and Jicaral. A fourth route also departs from Puntarenas to Paquera from the dock at Calle 35. See page 1027. On arrival, get on the bus (which waits for the ferry) as quickly as possible (to Cóbano, two to three hours, US$1.25, bad road, to Montezuma US$2.60, 1½ hours at least), pay on the bus, or get a taxi. **Hotel Playa Tambor** also runs a ferry service, **Naviera-Tambor SA,** between Puntarenas and Paquera, with a bus running between Paquera and the hotel in Tambor.

Getting around All the beaches on the Nicoya Peninsula are accessible by road in the dry season. Most places can be reached by bus from Nicoya. However, the stretch from Paquera to Montezuma and the Cabo Blanco Reserve is connected to Playa Naranjo and the north only by very poor roads. There is no bus connection between Playa Naranjo and Paquera and the road is appalling even in the dry season.

Beaches Even in high season, you will be able to find a beautiful beach which is uncrowded. There are so many of them, just walk until you find what you want. You will see plenty of wildlife along the way, monkeys, iguanas and squirrels as well as many birds. There can be dangerous undertows on exposed beaches; the safest bathing is from those beaches where there is a protective headland, such as at Playa Panamá in the north.

Santa Cruz and around

Heading from Liberia by road, the first town you reach is Santa Cruz, known as Costa Rica's National Folklore City for its colourful fiestas, dancing and regional food. January is the month for the fiesta dedicated to Santo Cristo de Esquipulas, when it can be difficult to find accommodation. There is also a rodeo fiesta in January. But for the rest of the year, it's a quiet little town, with a charming modern church, providing supplies for the beach tourism industry. If you need to buy food, Santa Cruz is a good place to stock up.

In **Guaitil**, 9 km east of Santa Cruz and 19 km north of Nicoya, local artisans specialize in reproductions of indigenous Chorotegan pottery. They work with the same methods used by the indigenous long ago, with minimal or no use of a wheel and no artificial paints. Ceramics are displayed at the local *pulpería*, or outside houses. At **San Vicente**, 2 km southeast of Guaitíl, local craftsmen work and sell their pottery.

West coast beaches » *pp1049-1059.*

A number of beaches are reached by unpaved roads from the Santa Cruz-Liberia road. Many can be accessed by bus from the Liberia bus station, others may require you to change buses at Santa Cruz. Each of the beaches has its appeal – Tamarindo and Playa del Coco for partying, Flamingo to the north and Junquillal for their greater seclusion, and Grande for nesting turtles and surfing.

Playa del Coco and around

After the town of **Comunidad**, a road leads east to Playa del Coco and Playa Hermosa, and the ever-pending resort development of Playa Panamá, see below.

Playa del Coco is a popular resort some 8 km from the highway, set in an attractive islet-scattered bay hemmed in by rocky headlands. It's a good place to chill out, with a mix of good services without being too developed. The best beaches are to the south. All activities concentrate on the beach and fishing. Coco is the starting point for surf trips to Santa Rosa spots by boat, such as **Witch's Rock**. Snorkelling and diving are nothing special, but for a diving expedition to the **Islas Murciélago**, see page 1057.

There are bars, restaurants and a few motels along the sandy beach. It is too small to get lost. To reach it, leave the road at Comunidad (road paved). Be wary of excursions to secluded Playa Verde, accessible by boat only, as some boatmen collaborate with thieves and reap the rewards later. A 2½-km road heads southwest from Playa del Coco to **Playa Ocotal**.

Sightings of manta rays and bull sharks are common around Islas Catalinas and Islas Murciélago.

Playa Hermosa and Playa Panamá

A spur road breaks from the main road to Playa del Coco heading north to Playa Hermosa. This is one of the nicest resorts and served by a paved road. Accommodation is mixed, but it's a good quiet alternative to other beaches in the region. Walking either to the left or the right you can find isolated beaches with crystal-clear water.

The big **Papagayo** tourist complex near Playa Panamá, which once planned to provide as many as 60,000 hotel rooms, started in 1993. Objections from many quarters have delayed construction, but the project continues at a slower pace.

Playa Tamarindo and around

South of Filadefia, close to Belén, a mostly paved but poor road heads east to the beach and popular surf spot of Playa Tamarindo, www.tamarindobeach.net, and other nearby beaches. Looking directly out to the west, the sunsets are incredible and while most make their way to the beach for that magic moment, the strong beach culture makes this a popular place to hang out.

Either side of the sunset, Tamarindo is a flurry of activity. The beach is attractive – although not stunning – with strong tides in places so take care if swimming. Three good breaks provide a variety of options for the surf crowd. Beyond surf and sun, the most popular excursion is an evening trip to Playa Grande and the leatherback turtle nesting sights from October to March. While the town is driven by surfing, there's a good blend of hotels and bars to make it a good beach stop – not too busy, but not so quiet that it's dead.

Playa Flamingo and beaches to the north

North of Tamarindo and Playa Grande are the beaches of **Conchal, Brasilito, Flamingo** and **Potrero**. It's a collection of beaches with subtle changes of atmostphere. Conchal is a beautiful 3-km beach full of shells, but with only luxury accommodation; most budget travellers stay at Brasilito and walk along the beach. Further north, the bay around Playa Flamingo has white sand, although the actual beach has some fairly intrusive developments with a grab-all approach to beachfront properties; in fact, the beach is now polluted and not as beautiful as it once was. But several other smaller beaches retain a relaxed atmosphere where life is governed by little more than the sunrise and beautiful sunsets. Further north is the isolated beach of Potrero with pockets of visitors largely enjoying their own company.

Playa Grande

North of Playa Tamarindo is Playa Grande and the **Parque Nacional Marino Las Baulas de Guanacaste** (485 ha terrestrial, 22,000 ha marine), well known as a nesting site for **leatherback turtles** (October-February). Organized trips to the beaches are possible

Península Nicoya

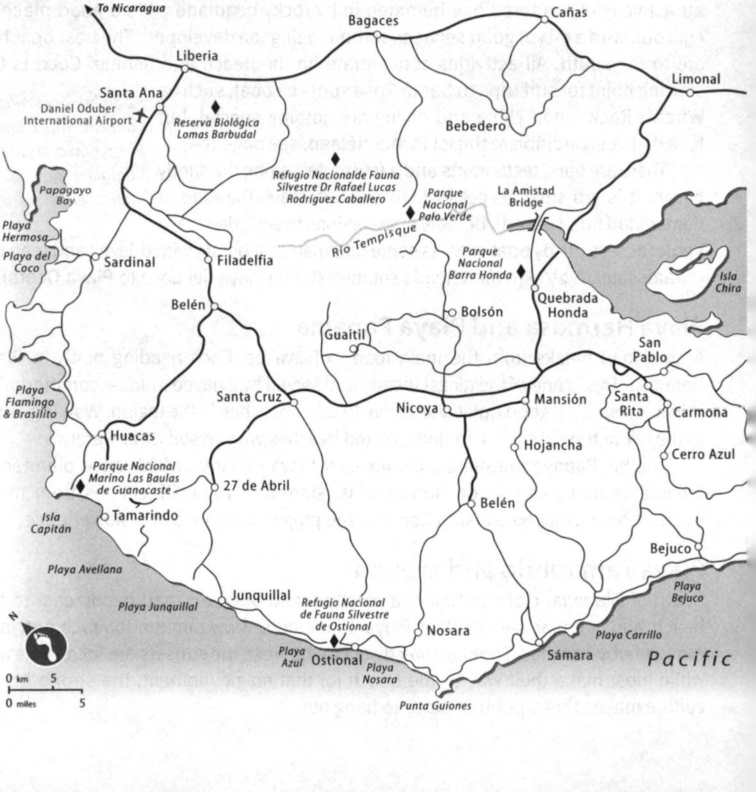

from Tamarindo. Also in town is **El Mundo de La Tortuga** ⓘ *T653-0471*, an unusual turtle museum. The road from the main highway at Belén leads directly to Playa Grande, a sleepy town with almost no transport and no way of getting around.

Playa Junquillal → *Colour map 7, B2.*

South of Tamarindo, Playa Junquillal is one of the cleanest beaches in Costa Rica and is still very empty. Completely off the beaten track with almost no tourist facilities, it does have a selection of stylish hotels, most of which are quite pricey, but there is also camping if you have a tent.

Nicoya → *Colour map 7, B2.*

Nicoya, at the heart of the peninsula, is a pleasant little town distinguished by possessing the country's second oldest church, the 17th-century church of San Blas. Damaged by earthquake in 1822 it was restored in 1831, and is currently undergoing renovations. The Parque Central, on Calle and Avenida Central, is leafy and used for occasional concerts. Buses arrive at Avenida 1, Calle 3-5. Most hotels and banks are within a couple of blocks of the central park. The area **Conservation Offices** (**ACT**) are on the northern side of central park. There is no general information for visitors, but they can assist with specific enquiries.

Parque Nacional Barra Honda → *Colour map 7, B2.*

ⓘ *Entry US$6, no permit required.*

A small park in the north of the Nicoya Peninsula (2295 ha), Barra Honda National Park was created to protect a mesa with a few caves and the last remains of dry tropical forest in the region. The **park office** is near Barra Honda at **Santa Ana**, at the foot of the mesa, and there are two different trails to the top; two hours' hiking.

Sámara and Playa Carrillo

→ *Colour map 7, B2.*

Sámara, samarabeach.com, is a smallish Tico village that has maintained some of its regular way of life alongside tourist development. The beautiful beach at Sámara, 37 km from Nicoya on a paved road, is probably the safest and one of the best bathing beaches in Costa Rica. Playa Carrillo is 5 km away at the south end of the beach. The litter problem is being tackled with rubbish bins, warning signs, refuse collections and bottle banks. Both places have airstrips served by scheduled services from San José.

Nosara → *Colour map 7, B2.*

Nosara, www.nosara.com, is a small village about 26 km north of Sámara without much to see or do in it – which makes it ideal if you like lying around on beaches. Indeed most come for the three unspoiled beaches which are not particularly close to the village.

Playa Nosara is north of the village across the Río Nosara where you may see turtles (see Ostional below); Peladas is the prettiest and smallest, south of the river, and Guiones is safe for swimming and good for surfing. Expatriates have formed the Nosara Civic Association to protect the area's wildlife and forests and prevent exploitation.

Playa Ostional

North of Nosara is Playa Ostional where **Olive Ridley turtles** lay eggs in July-November along the coastal strip of the Refugio Nacional de Vida Silvestre Ostional. The turtles arrive for nesting at high tide. The villagers are allowed to harvest the eggs in a designated area of the beach, the rest are protected and monitored. Outside the egg-laying period it is exceptionally quiet. Contact the MINAE (Ministry of Environment and Energy) ranger station for details.

Southern Península de Nicoya

pp1049-1059.

The southern Nicoya Peninsula is almost completely cut off from the north. Roads are appalling and those that exist are frequently flooded in part. For this reason most access the region by ferry from Puntarenas. Arriving at **Playa Naranjo** there are several expensive eating places by the dock and a gas station. Beaches and stopping points are dotted along the southern shore of the peninsula passing through low key coastal centres of Tambor, Montezuma, Cabuya, Mal País and Playa Santa Teresa.

Paquera

Paquera is a small village 22 km along the coast from Playa Naranjo. There are a few shops and some simple lodgings, for example **Cabinas Rosita** on the inland side of the village. It is separated from the quay by 1 km or so; apart from a good soda, a restaurant, a public telephone and a branch of **Banco de Costa Rica**, there are no facilities.

Tambor, Curú National Wildlife Refuge and Cóbano

The small village of **Tambor**, 19 km from Paquera, has a dark sand beach, some shops and restaurants. The beach is beautiful, 6 km long with rolling surf; 1½ hours on a bone-shaking road from the ferry. However cruise ships from Puntarenas come here, and part of the beach has been absorbed by the large and controversial **Hotel Playa Tambor**. Built around a cattle farm by the Barceló group of Spain, the resort is alleged to have encroached on the public beach and drained a swamp which was a wildfowl habitat. A second stage is planned at Punta Piedra Amarilla, with a 500-boat yacht marina, villas and a total of 1100 rooms. Buses travelling from Paquera to Montezuma, pass through Tambor, connecting with the car ferry arriving from Puntarenas, US$2.60, two hours.

North of Playa Tambor is the **Curú National Wildlife Refuge** ⓘ *T661-2392 in advance and ask for Doña Julieta.* Only 84 ha, but with five different habitats and 110 species of bird. Access is through private land.

Cóbano, near Montezuma, can be reached by bus from Paquera ferry terminal, and buses for Tambor, Cóbano and Montezuma meet the launches from Puntarenas (there is an airstrip with flights from San José). Roads north, west and south out of Cóbano, require 4WD. Cóbano has a petrol/gas station.

Montezuma → *Colour map 7, B2.*

No longer a quiet sleepy hamlet, Montezuma is a very popular small village on the sea. It is a well-liked backpacking destination and at busy periods hotels fill up every day, so check in early. Although it gets crowded, there are some wonderful beaches; many are rocky, with strong waves making it difficult to swim, but it's very scenic. There are beautiful walks along the beach, sometimes sandy, sometimes rocky, always lined with trees that visit impressive waterfalls. There is a tourist office at **Aventuras Montezuma**, which is very helpful and often knows which hotel has space; ask here first before looking around. The once-popular **Cabinas Karen** are now closed. Prior to her death in 1994, Doña Karen donated her land to the National Parks in memory of her late husband creating what was to become Reserva Natural Absoluta Cabo Blanco (see below). **Cabinas Karen** now house park guards.

Montezuma can be reached in four hours from Puntarenas if you get the early launch.

Around Montezuma

Close to the village, 20 minutes up the Río Montezuma, is a beautiful, huge **waterfall** with a big, natural swimming hole, beyond which is a smaller waterfall. Intrepid walkers can carry on up to further waterfalls but it can be dangerous and accidents have been reported. There's another waterfall, 6 km north of Montezuma, with a pool right by the beach – follow the road out to the beach at the north end of town and keep going past three coves for about half an hour until you reach the trail off to the left (you can't miss it). » *For organized tours and expeditions, see Tour operators, page 1057.*

You can use Montezuma as a base for exploring the **Reserva Natural Absoluta Cabo Blanco** ⓘ *Wed-Sun 0800-1600, US$6, jeep/taxi from Montezuma US$7, first at 0700, returns 1600.* The 1172-ha reserve is 11 km from Montezuma. The marine birds include frigate birds, pelicans and brown boobies; there are also monkeys, anteaters, kinkajou and collared peccary. You can bathe in the sea or under a waterfall. At the beautiful **Playa Balsitas**, 6 km from the entrance, there are pelicans and howler monkeys.

At **Cabuya**, 2 km from Cabo Blanco Reserve, the sea can be cloudy after rough weather. Cabuya Island can be visited on foot at low tide. On the road west out of Cabuya, **Cafetería El Coyote** specializes in local and Caribbean dishes. On the west coast of the peninsula is the little village of **Mal País**. The coast here is virtually unspoilt with long white beaches, creeks and natural pools, and few facilities stretching further to the beach of **Santa Teresa**, which is perfect for relaxing and increasingly popular with surfers.

You can also arrange tours to **Isla Tortuga**. Many businesses rent horses. check the horses are fit and properly cared for. Recommended for horses are **Cocozuma Traveller** and **Aventuras Montezuma**.

Sleeping

Santa Cruz *p1045*
B Diria, on the main road, T680-0080. Bath, restaurant, pools.
B-C La Pampa, 25 m west of Plaza de los Mangos, T680-0586. A/c, cheaper without, near parque, good, clean.
D-E Anatolia, 200 m south, 100 m west of plaza, T680-0333. Plywood partitions, dirty bathrooms.
F Pensión Isabel, behind the church, T680-0173. Price per person, simple box rooms.

Playa del Coco and around *p1045*
Good discounts (up to 40%) in green season. At Playa Ocotal, only top end accommodation, but good diving services.
LL-AL El Ocotal Resort Hotel, Playa Ocotal, T670-0321, www.ocotalresort.com. Rooms, suites and bungalows, PADI dive shop on beach, sport fishing, surfing, tennis, 3 pools, car hire, excursions.
AL Villa Casa Blanca, Playa Ocotal, T670-0518. 15 idyllic rooms, with breakfast, friendly and informative, family atmosphere, small pool. Pricey but very good.
AL-A La Puerta del Sol, north of Playa del Coco, T670-0195. Great little family-run hotel. Good food in Italian restaurant, small

At the end of December 2005, a deformed, two-headed Olive Ridley sea turtle hatchling was found on the beach at Ostional. Although the turtle was in good health, experts at the World Wildlife Fund believe that ocean pollution and climate change could be to blame.

pool and gym, friendly atmosphere and free scuba lesson in hotel pool.

A **Ocotal Inn B&B**, Playa Ocotal, T670-0835, www.ocotalinn.com. Large rooms, excellent Peruvian seafood restaurant.

A **Villa del Sol**, at northern end of Playa del Coco, T670-0085, www.villadelsol.com. Canadian-owned (from Quebec), with pool, clean, friendly, safe, big garden with parrots. Recommended.

B **Coco Palms**, Playa del Coco, beside football pitch, T670-0367. German-run, large pool, gringo bar and parking.

B **Pato Loco Inn**, Playa del Coco, T670-0145. Airy rooms, Italian restaurant, internet for guests.

B-D **Cabinas Chale**, north of Playa del Coco, T670-0036. Double rooms and villas, with private bath. Pretty quiet, small resort-style spot, small pool, 50 m from beach. Good deal, especially villas which sleep up to 6.

C **Cabinas El Coco**, just north of the pier right on the beach, T670-0110. With bath and good reasonable restaurant.

C **Witch's Rock Surf Camp**, Playa del Coco, T670-1138. Simple rooms.

C-D **Luna Tica**, Playa del Coco, south of the plaza, T670-0127. Also with an annex over the road (friendly, clean), both usually full at weekends.

Playa Hermosa and Playa Panamá *p1045*

The Playa Panamá area has several all-inclusive resort-style hotels (**L**), including: **El Nakuti Resort**, **Hotel Costa Blanca**, **Hotel Esmeralda** and the **Four Seasons**.

AL **El Velero**, Playa Hermosa, T672-1017, www.costaricahotel.net. With an airy villa feel, nice rooms with a/c and bathrooms, pool, clean, good restaurant.

AL **Villa del Sueño**, southern end of Playa Hermosa, T672-0026, www.villadelsueno.com. Canadian-owned, with big rooms, good restaurant, pool and live music. Apartments for longer stays.

B **Hotel Playa Hermosa** , southern end of Playa Hermosa, T672-0046. Italian-run, 22 clean rooms, better prices for groups, very good Italian restaurant overlooking gardens. Recommended.

B **Iguana Inn**, 100 m from the beach, T672-0065. 9 rooms, some with kitchen. Relaxed, laid-back spot, with use of kitchen, and laundry.

Playa Tamarindo and around *p1045*

Book in advance at Christmas and New Year.

LL **Capitán Suizo**, a long way south of the centre towards Playa Langosta, T653-0075, www.hotelcapitansuizo.com. 8 bungalows, 22 rooms with patio or balcony, a/c, pool, restaurant, kayaking, scuba diving, surfing, sport fishing available, riding on hotel's own horses, Swiss management. One of Costa Rica's distinctive hotels.

L-AL **Tamarindo Diria**, near centre of town, T653-0032, www.eldiria.com. Full range of services, good restaurants, beautiful pool, expensive tours offered with good guide, now with a golf course nearby.

A-B **Cabinas Hotel Zullymar**, at the southern end of town, T653-0140, www.zullymar.com. Rooms with a/c and cheaper cabins, good beach bar. Recommended.

B **Cabinas Marielos**, near the bus stop, T653-0141, www.cabinasmarieloscr.com. Clean basic rooms, with bath, use of kitchen, popular, book ahead.

B **Pozo Azul**, at the northern entrance to town, T653-0280. Cabins, a/c, cheaper in low season, cooking facilities, clean, good, swimming pool.

C **Frutas Tropicales**, just south of **Tamarindo Vista Best Western**, T653-0041. 3 simple, spotless and quiet rooms.

C **Villas Macondo**, 1 block back from the beach, T653-0812, www.villasmacondo.com. Rooms with shared kitchen, and apartments. Swimming pool, washing machine, safety boxes, fridge and friendly people too!

D **Botella de Leche**, at the southern end of town, T653-0189, www.labotellade leche.com. Hostel rooms, very clean, use of kitchen, big communal lounge. Good choice.

E **Rodamar**, 50 m from **Tamarindo Vista**, T653-0109. No a/c or fan, no mosquito nets, but clean, helpful, kitchen, shared bath. Family atmosphere and cheapest good deal.

F **Tsunami**, at the northern end of town. Basic, tidy rooms, private bath and use of the kitchen. Turn up and see if there's free space – probably full of surfers more interested in water than comfort – great value.

Playa Grande *p1046*

AL-A **Hotel Las Tortugas**, right on the beach in the centre of town, T653-0423, www.cool.co.cr/usr/turtles. 11 rooms with bathroom, pool, restaurant, meals included, tours arranged.

B-C Playa Grande Inn, T653-0719, www.playagrandeinn.com. Formerly Rancho Diablo. 10 rooms with fan. A good set up for surfers.

E Cabinas/Restaurante Playa Grande, 500 m before beach at the entrance to town, T354-7661 (mob). Price per person, 8 cabins with bath and kitchen, also **camping**.

Playa Flamingo and beaches to the north *p1046*

AL Mariner Inn, Playa Flamingo, T654-4081. 12 new rooms with bath, a/c, free camping on the beach.

A Bahía Potrero Beach Resort, Playa Potrero, T654-4183. Bar, pool, 10 rooms with bath.

A-B Cabinas Bahía Esmeralda, Playa Potrero, T654-4480. Garden, pool, hot water, roof ventilator. Italian restaurant.

A-B Cabinas Isolina, Playa Potrero, T654-4333, www.isolinabeach.com. 250 m from beach, nice garden, roof ventilator.

B-C Hotel Brasilito, Playa Brasilito, close to beach on plaza, T654-4237, www.brasilito.com. Good rooms, also with horses, kayaks and bikes to rent, now includes the **Los Arcades Restaurant**, run by Charlie and Claire, mixing Thai and local dishes. Closed Mon.

C Cabinas Mayra, Playa Potrero, T654-4213. On beach, friendly, with pretty, basically equipped cabins. Camping on the beach.

C Ojos Azules, Playa Brasilito, T654-4343. Run by Swiss couple, 18 cabins, good breakfasts with home-baked bread, nightmare decor.

F Brasilito Lodge, Playa Brasilito, right on the beach, T654-4452, www.brasilito-conchal.com. Price per person, big rooms, good beds, bit of a bargain really. Internet service, several tours available. Also camping.

Playa Junquillal *p1047*

A-AL Iguanazul, T658-8124, www.iguanazul.com. 24 different sizes of tiled-roof cabins on a cliff, great spot, hot water, fan or a/c, pool, restaurant, bar, sport fishing on 27-ft *Marlin Genie*, close to good surfing.

A El Lugarcito, T658-8436, ellugarcito@racsa.co.cr. B&B, ocean views, restaurant/bar, tours, diving, boutique.

A Tatanka, T658-8426, tatanka@racsa.co.cr. 10 cabins with a pool, good restaurant serving Italian, French and Tico dishes.

A-C Guacamaya Lodge, T658-8431, www.guacamayalodge.com. Immaculate bungalows and one fully equipped house with pool, ocean views, Swiss cuisine.

B El Castillo Divertido, T658-8428, www.costarica-adventureholidays.com. Castle rooms, restaurant, gardens, rooftop star-gazing deck, music.

B Playa Junquillal, on the beach, T653-0432. Sleeping 2-4. Ideal for surfers and beach lovers.

B-C Hibiscus, close to the beach, T658-8437. Big rooms with big windows, seafood restaurant with German specialities, garden, 50 m to beach, German-run.

Camping

Camping Los Malinches, after **Iguanazul** at the northern entrance to town off main road down a dirt track, spectacular location, clean bathroom provided. Worth the effort, but bring all your own food.

Nicoya *p1047*

A-AL Hotel Turístico Curime, 500 m south of the centre on road to Sámara, T685-5238. Fully equipped bungalows, 3-m-deep pool.

D Jenny, or **Yenny** as the sign says, on the corner of Calle 1, Av 4, T685-5050. Spotless, with bath, a/c, towels, soap and TV. Cavernous rooms – book in with a friend and play hide and seek. Recommended.

D Las Tinajas, opposite Liberia bus stop on Av 1, T685-5081. With bath, modern, clean, good value.

D-E Pensión Venecia, opposite old church on square, T685-5325. Squidgy beds but good value for the price. Recommended.

E-F Chorotega, Calle Central, Av 4-6, T685-5245. With bath (cheaper without), very good value, clean, quiet. Rooms at back have windows. Clothes-washing facilities (good Chinese soda opposite).

Sámara *p1047*

AL Hotel Fénix, on beach about 2 km east of the village, T656-0158, www.fenix hotel.com. 6 slightly cramped double units with fans, kitchenettes, hot water, small pool, friendly. Internet for guests.

AL Mirador de Sámara Aparthotel, rising up the hill above the village, T656-0044, www.miradordesamara.com. Very friendly, German-owned. 6 large, cool and comfortable suites with bath and kitchen. Recommended.

A-B **Belvedere**, sloping up the hill, T656-0213. Very friendly German owners. A cosy hotel with 10 small rooms, very clean. Recommended.

B **Marbella**, inland, road going south, T656-0362. German-run, beautiful grounds, pool, good service, close to beach. Recommended.

B-C **Casa Valeria**, on the beach near the supermarket, T656-0511. Friendly and good value, especially for 3 sharing, breakfast included, various different rooms, some with sea view, all nicely decorated, most with bath, hot water, kitchen and laundry available, small bar, tours, tickets and car rental arranged. Recommended.

D **Arenas**, at the western end of town, T656-0320. Comfortable, cheaper for longer stays, good restaurant opposite, pleasant bar next door.

Camping

Camping Coco, near the beach, T656-0496. With toilets, electricity until 2200. The same family own **Camping San Martín**, T656-0336, same deal, also offers **La Tigre Tours** kayak, snorkel, diving, trips to see dolphins.

Camping Los Mangos, slightly further from the beach.

Nosara *p1047*

A **Villaggio**, Punta Guiones de Garza, close to Nosara, 17 km north of Sámara, T654-4664, www.flordepacifico.com. An upmarket yet simply furnished beach hotel with vacation ownership plan, 30 bungalows, international restaurant, club house, bars, pool, disco, good packages arranged in San José, T233-2476.

B **Blew Dog's Surf Camp**, near Playa Guiones, T682-0080, www.blewdogs.com. Comfortable cabins, also flop house for US$10 per person, pool table, pool, videos, full service reggae bar/restaurant.

B **Rancho Suizo Lodge**, Playa Pelada, T682-0057, www.nosara.ch. Swiss-owned bungalows, restaurant, credit cards accepted, whirlpool, hiking, riding, bird and turtle watching.

C **Casa Río Nosara**, on the road to the airstrip, T682-0117. Rancho-style house with cabins and nice garden, clean, friendly, camping, canoe tours and horse riding arranged, German owners.

D **Cabinas Agnell**, in the village, T682-0142. With bath, good value.

E **Cabinas Chorotega**, in the village near the supermarket, T682-0129. 8 simple, clean rooms, shared or own bath. Bar and restaurant downstairs so can be noisy.

Playa Ostional *p1048*

You can camp on the beach.

F **Cabinas Guacamaya**, T682-0430. Price per person, with bath, clean, good food on request.

F **Cabinas Ostional**, next to the village shop. Very basic accommodation in cabins with bath, clean, friendly.

Playa Naranjo *p1048*

A-B **Oasis del Pacífico**, on beach, T661-0209. A/c, old building, clean, quiet, pool, good restaurant, free transport from ferry. Recommended.

C **El Paso**, north of ferry, T641-8133, with bath, cheaper without, cold water, clean, restaurant and pool.

E **Cabinas Maquinay**, 1.3 km towards Jicaral, T661-1763. Simple rooms with a pool and the attached **Disco Maquinay**.

Tambor, Curú National Wildlife Refuge and Cóbano *p1048*

LL **Tango Mar**, 3 km from Tambor, T683-0001, www.tangomar.com. All services including golf course and its own spectacular waterfall.

C **Dos Lagartos**, Tambor, T683-0236. Cheap, clean, good value.

C-D **Cabinas Cristina**, on the beach, Tambor. With bath, T683-0028, cheaper without, good food.

Montezuma *p1048*

Montezuma is a very small place; hotels furthest from the centre are a 10-min walk.

L-A **El Jardín**, T642 0074 www.hotelel jardin.com. 15 rooms and 2 fully equipped villas located on the hill overlooking the town and ocean beyond. Rooms come with private shower, hot water, and a/c, private terraces and hammocks. In the grounds is a pool with a little waterfall, very restful and great views, superb spot.

AL El Tajalín, T642-0061, www.tajalin.com. Very smart hotel, spotlessly clean, rooms come with private hot water shower and a/c, located in a quiet out of the way spot and yet moments from the high street. Hammock terrace for relaxing.

AL-B Los Mangos, a short walk south of the village, T642-0076, www.hotellosmangos.com. Large site comprising 9 bungalows, each accommodating 3 people, with bath, hot water and fan. Also 10 rooms, some with shared bath, some for 4 people. Yoga classes run from an open-sided pagoda on the grounds. Different and fun and lots of free mangos (when in season).

AL-C Amor de Mar, T642-0262, www.amordemar.com. This well-loved hotel has the feeling of a special place. Rooms are pristine with private bath and hot water. Breakfast and brunch is served on a very pretty terrace that joins well-manicured gardens, where visitors can recline in hammocks and stare out to sea.

AL-E Hotel Moctezuma, in the centre of town, T642-0058, www.playamontezuma.net/ecotours/hotel.htm. Rooms on 3 sides of the central junction. The cheapest are located above **Chico's Bar** and **Moctezuma Bar** – hence they can be very loud at night. Cheaper rooms are basic and come with shared cold water bathroom; there are also midrange rooms upstairs with private bath and hot water, some have sea view and there is a terrace overlooking the sea on one side, the town on the other. Across the street to the beach side, all rooms have private hot water showers and sleep 1-4; on the other side of the street – over the shops – they offer fully equipped rooms with small kitchen, fridge, stove etc. They have been recently renovating their cheaper lodgings, so call in advance to check changing prices.

A Horizontes, on road to Cóbano, T642-0534, www.horizontes-montezuma.com. Language school, restaurant, pool, hot water. Highly recommended.

B Pargo Feliz, T642-0065, elpargofeliz@costarricense.cr. Cabins with bath. Serves good food in a peaceful atmosphere – something the owners are keen on.

B Cabinas Mar y Cielo, on the beach, T642-0261. 6 rooms, sleeping 2-5 people, all with bath, fan and sea view. Recommended.

B Montezuma Paradise, 10 mins' walk out of town, on the road to Cabuya, past the waterfall entrance, T642-0271. Very friendly owners have rooms with shared bath and 1 with private, overlooking the ocean and minutes from a secluded beach cove.

B-C La Cascada, 5 mins' walk out of town, on the road to Cabo Blanco, close to the entrance to the waterfalls, T642-0057. Lovely hotel with pretty, well-kept rooms and a wide hammock terrace overlooking the ocean for relaxing. Restaurant serves local food for breakfast, lunch and dinner.

B-C Montezuma Pacific, 50 m west of the church, next to El Tajalin, T642-0204. With private bath, hot water and a/c.

D Lucy, follow road south past **Los Mangos**, T642-0273. One of the oldest hotels in town and one of the most popular budget options, due to its location on the sea. 10 rooms with fans, some with sea view. Shared bath, pleasant balcony, recently renovated. Ultra-friendly Tica owner. Restaurant next door opens during high season. Recommended.

D-F El Tucán, at the top of the road down to the beach, T642-0284. Wooden hotel on stilts, clean, small wood-panelled rooms, shared shower and toilet, fan, mosquito net on window. Recommended.

E El Parque, behind **El Parque Restaurant**, on Playa Montezuma. Budget accommodation on the beach – basic rooms, clean but tatty, but location and price more than make up for it. Internet café behind the hotel.

E Hotel El Capitán, on the main street, T642-0069. Old wooden house with an endless variety of rooms, most with shared cold water bath, but some with private. Very friendly owners and good location, can get a little noisy, good for backpackers.

E Pensión Arenas, on the beach, T642-0308. Run by Doña Meca, rustic small rooms, with fan, shared bath, no frills but pleasant balcony and sea view. Free camping. Laundry service.

E Pensión Jenny, at the end of the track by the football field, T642-0306. Basic lodging with shared bath, cheap and clean, nice out of the way location. Laundry service.

Around Montezuma *p1049*

L Milarepa, Playa Santa Teresa, on beach, T640-0023, www.milarepahotel.com. Nice bamboo bungalows, open-air bathroom.

AL Celaje, Cabuya, on beach, T642-0374. Very good Italian restaurant. Pool, rooms with bath, hot water, good.

AL-A Los Caballos, 3 km north on road to Cóbano from Montezuma, T642-0124. 8 rooms with bath, pool, outdoor restaurant, ocean views, gardens, 5 mins from beach, horses a speciality.

AL-C Mal País Surf Camp, Mal País, T640-0031, www.malpaissurfcamp.com. Restaurant, pool, also **camping**.

AL-D Funky Monkey Lodge, Santa Teresa, T640-0317, www.funky-monkey-lodge.com. The same very friendly and hospitable owners have extended their relaxed and very attractive resort. They now have one bungalow sleeping 8 people, 3 private bungalows and two apartments, sleeping 2/4 and a suite with a large balcony overlooking the ocean. They also have a rather upmarket dormitory with individual beds. The apartments have a/c, ocean view, access to the kitchen and face the swimming pool. They have a restaurant, bar, TV, DVD, ping-pong table, surfboard rental and organise surf lessons, local tours, car or ATV rental. Recommended.

A-C Cabinas Las Rocas, 20 mins south of Montezuma, T642-0393, www.caboblanco park.com. Good but quite expensive meals, small, seashore setting, isolated.

A-E Frank's Place, Mal País, the road junction, T640-0096, www.frankplace.com. Set in tropical gardens. Wide variety of rooms with private or shared bath, and self-catering options available. Good range of services and local advice.

B-C Cabañas Bosque Mar, Mal País, T640-0074. Clean, large rooms, hot water shower, attractive grounds, good restaurant on beach nearby, 3 km to Cabo Blanco Reserve.

B-C Cabañas Playa Santa Teresa, Playa Santa Teresa, T640-0137. 150 m from beach, surfboard rental, horses, German-run.

C Cabinas Mar Azul, Mal País, T642-0298, Run by Jeannette Stewart, camping possible, delicious fried fish, shrimp, lobster.

C Linda Vista, on the hill over Montezuma, T642-0274. Units sleep 6, with bath (cold water) and fan, ocean views.

C Mochila Inn, 300 m outside Montezuma, T642-0030. *Cabinas* from US$30, also houses and apartments for around US$350 per month.

C-E Cabinas y Restaurante El Ancla de Oro, Cabuya, T642-0369. Some cabins with bath, others shared bathroom, seafood restaurant, lobster dinners US$10, filling breakfasts, owned by Alex Villalobos, horses US$20 per day with local guide, mountain bike rental, transport from Paquera launch available. **El Delfín** restaurant at crossroads, friendly, good-value local food.

D Casa Zen, Santa Teresa. Smart, budget accommodation with shared bath and one fully furnished apartment. Camping area also available. Close to the beach, restaurant onsite.

E-F Cabañas Playa El Carmen, Playa Santa Teresa, T683-0281. Basic cabins and camping, shared bath and kitchen. **Jungle Juice**, vegetarian restaurant, smoothies, meals from US$4.

Camping

Rincón de los Monos, 500 m along the beach from the centre of Montezuma, T643-0048. Clean, well organized, lockers for rent, many monkeys.

Eating

Santa Cruz *p1045*

¶ **Coopetortilla**, 3 blocks east of the church. A local institution– a women's cooperative cooking local dishes. Very cheap and enjoyable.

Playa del Coco and around *p1045*

¶¶¶ **Mariscos la Guajira**, on southern beach. Popular and beautiful beach-front location.

¶¶¶ **Papagayo**, near the beach, T670-0298. Good seafood, recommended.

¶¶ **Bananas**, on the road out of town. The place to go drinking and dancing until the early hours.

¶¶ **Cocos**, on the plaza, T670-0235. Bit flashy and pricey for the area, good seafood.

¶¶ **El Roble**, beside the main plaza. A popular bar/disco.

¶¶ **Playa del Coco**, on beach. Popular, open from 0600.

¶ **Jungle Bar**,on road into town. Another lively, slightly rougher option.

Playa Tamarindo and around *p1045*

¶¶¶ **Fiesta del Mar**, on the loop at the end of town. Large thatched open barn, good food, good value.

TTT Ginger, at the northern end of town, T672-0041. Tue-Sun. Good Thai restaurant.
TTT Iguana Surf restaurant on road to Playa Langosta. Good atmosphere and food.
TT Coconut Café, on beach near **Tamarindo Vista**. Pizzas, pastries and good fish. Check the sodas for good breakfasts and cheap evening meals.
TT El Arrecife, on roundabout. Popular spot to hang out, with Tico fare, good chicken and pizzas.
TT The Lazy Wave, on road leading away from the beach, T653-0737. Menu changes daily, interesting mix of cuisine, seafood.
TT Portofino, at end of road by roundabout. Italian specialties and good ice cream.
TT Stellas, on road leading away from the beach. Very good seafood, try dorado with mango cream. Recommended.
T Arco Iris, on road heading inland. Cheap vegetarian, great atmosphere.
T Frutas Tropicales, near Tamarindo Vista. Snacks and breakfast.

Playa Flamingo and beaches to the north *p1046*

TT La Casita del Pescado, Playa Brasilito. Some reasonably priced fish dishes which you have to eat quickly because the stools are made of concrete.
TT Marie's Restaurant, Playa Flamingo, T654-4136. Breakfast, seafood, *casados* and international dishes.
TT Pizzeria Il Forno, Playa Brasilito. Serves a mean pizza.
TT Restaurant La Boca de la Iguana, Playa Brasilito. Good value.
TT-T Las Brisas, at the northern end of Playa Potrero. A great spot for a beer and a snack, and surprisingly popular – well, 5 people – for its cut-off location.
T Costa Azul, Playa Potrero, by the football pitch. One of several restaurants in the area, popular with locals.
T Cyber Shack, Playa Brasilito. Internet, coffee, breakfast and UPS service.
T Hillside Café, Playa Flamingo, T654-4226. Breakfast.

Playa Junquillal *p1047*

TTT La Puesta del Sol, T658-8442. The only restaurant along the strip, but then nothing could compete with the dishes from this little piece of Italy. Spectacular setting. Very popular so reservations required.

Nicoya *p1047*

TT Café de Blita, 2 km outside Nicoya towards Sámara. Good.
TT Soda El Triángulo, opposite **Chorotega**. Good juices and snacks, friendly owners.
TT Teyet, near **Hotel Jenny**. Good, quick service.
T Daniela, 1 block east of plaza. Breakfast, lunches, coffee, *refrescos*, good.

Sámara *p1047*

There are several cheap sodas around the football pitch in the centre of town.
TTT Restaurant Delfín, on the beach. Very good value and French owned. They also have *cabinas*.
TT El Ancla Restaurant, on the beach, T656-0716. Seafood.
TT Las Brasas, by the football pitch, T656-0546. Spanish restaurant and bar.
TT Restaurant Acuario, on the beach. Serves Tico and other food.
T Soda Sol y Mar, on the road to Nosara. Costa Rican and western food.

Nosara *p1047*

TTT Gilded Iguana, Playas Guiones. Gringo food and good company.
TTT La Dolce Vita, south along the road out of town. Good but pricey Italian food.
TT Casa Romántica, Playas Guiones. The European restaurant.
TT Corky Carroll's Surf School, T682-0385. Surf lessons and a good Mexican/Thai restaurant (closed Sun).
TT Giardino Tropicale, in the middle section. Pizza.
TT Hotel Almost Paradise , Playas Guiones, T682-0173. Good food with a great view.
TT La Luna, slightly up the hill. Good food and ambience.
TT Olga's, Playa Peladas. Seafood on the beach.
T Soda Vanessa, Playas Guiones. One of several sodas in the village. Good and very cheap.

Playa Ostional *p1048*

TT-T Mirador de los Tortugueros, 1 km south of **Cabinas Guacamaya**. A good restaurant, serving coffee and pancakes. Great atmosphere. Recommended.

Montezuma *p1048*

TTT Congo Azul Restaurant and Bar. Pricey buffet- style restaurant, mainly seafood with salads and sides. Guests can choose their cuts, cooked on a grill in the spacious garden and brought to the table.

TTT Playa de Los Artistas/Cocina Mediterránea, about 5 mins south of town on the road to Cabuya. Best restaurant in town.

TT Bakery Café, north end of town. Great for breakfast, with bread, cakes and excellent vegetarian food.

TT Chico's Playa Bar, on the beach. Popular hangout, great sushi. They stop serving food in the low season.

TT Cocolores, on the beach behind **El Pargo Feliz**, T642-0096. Closed Mon. Good for seafood and nice veggie options.

TT El Sano Banano, on the road to the beach. Health food restaurant, good vegetarian food, large helpings, daily change of menu, milkshakes, fresh fruit and yoghurt, owned by Dutch/Americans, free movies with dinner.

TT Pizza Romana, opposite **El Capitán**. Good Italian food cooked by Italians, pizzas, pesto, fresh pastas, etc.

TT-T Rico Rico, behind **Las Gemelas**. Great pizza, Italian owned, attractive restaurant off the main street.

T El Parque, on the beach. Good typical food, *casados*, sandwiches and best breakfast *pinto* in town. Lovely place for a coffee, or drinks and snacks in the afternoon, or watching the boatmen first thing in the morning – they open early.

T Soda El Caracol, located by the football field. One of several sodas around town serving good Tico food, very cheap.

T Soda Monte Sol, on the road to Cabo Blanco. Recommended for good Mexican burritos, good value, big helpings.

T Soda Las Gemelas, on the beach. Good simple local food.

Entertainment

Sámara *p1047*

Bars and clubs

Bar La Góndola is popular and has a dart board. Opposite is **Bar Colocho**. **Dos Lagartos** disco is on the beach near **Al Manglar** and the disco at **Isla Chora** is the place to be during the season if you like resort discos.

Nosara *p1047*

Bars and clubs

Some of the nightlife is in the village as well – **Bambú, Disco Tropicana** and various others line the football pitch.

Montezuma *p1048*

Bar Moctezuma, usually open the latest, but not so loud as the others.

Chico's Bar and **Chico's Playa Bar**, the latter for a relaxing cocktail by the beach, the former for late night salsa dancing or very loud reggaeton parties.

Congo Azul Bar runs a house and electronic night on Thu – a nice break from the local salsa and reggaeton, which is very popular, although they often use the same DJ who plays great music but a very similar set each week.

Around Montezuma *p1049*

Bar Tabu, Santa Teresa. Probably the most popular bar in the area, great location on the beach, good music, always lively, open late.

La Llora Amarilla, Santa Teresa, now very popular, large venue that hosts regular disco and party nights.

Mal País Surf Camp, Mal País. Bar open every night, live jam night on Wed.

Shopping

Sámara *p1047*

The **supermarket**, near **Casa del Mar**, is well stocked and you can get fresh bread and croissants from **Chez Joel**. **Free Radical** super/soda on main road, 1 km east of town centre, offers fresh *ceviche*, delightful pastries, beer, wine, natural juices, local honey and unusual hand-blown glass products.

Montezuma *p1048*

There are now a number of rather pricey, boutique-style souvenir and clothes shops in Montezuma, most sell a very similar range.

Librería Topsy, T642-0576, sells books and maps and will take postcards and small letters to the post office for you. Mon-Fri 0800-1400, Sat 0800-1200.

TÁKALÁ, T642-0667. Italian-owned glass shop, beautiful hand-blown objects and artwork, including beads and jewellery. Glass blowing classes are available.

Activities and tours

Playa Hermosa and Playa Panamá *p1045*

Diving

Diving Safari, based at the Sol Playa Hermosa Resort on Playa Hermosa, T453-5044, www.billbeardcostarica.com. One of the longest-running diving operations in the country, offering a wide range of options in the region.

Playa del Coco and around *p1045*

Tour operators

Agua Rica Charters, T670-0473, www.aguaricacharters.com, or contact them through the internet café. Can arrange transport to Witch's Rock for surfers, approx US$400 for up to 10. **Deep Blue Diving**, beside Hotel Coco Verde, T670-1004, www.scuba-diving-in-costa-rica.com, has diving trips to Islas Catalinas and Islas Murcielago, where sightings of manta rays and bull sharks are common. 2-tank dive from US$55. Will also rent gear. Also **Rich Coast Diving**, TT670-0176, www.richcoastdiving.com.

Playa Tamarindo and around *p1045*

Diving

Try the **Pacific Coast Dive Center**, T653-0267, or **Agua Rica Dive Center**, T653-0094.

Tour operators

Many tours to see the turtles nesting at night in Playa Grande. **Iguana Surf Tours**, T653-0148, rent surfboards, they have one outlet near the beach, opposite the supermarket, the other in the restaurant of the same name. **Hightide Adventures and Surfcamp**, T653-0108, www.tamarindoadventures.net, offers a range of tours.

Sámara *p1047*

Tour operators

Most hotels will arrange tours for you. You can rent bikes from near the *ferretería* on the road to Cangrejal. Recommended, though, is the newer **Tip Top Tours**, T656-0650, run by a very nice French couple, offering dolphin tours (from US$45 per person), mangrove tours (US$43 per person) and waterfall tours (US$20 per person). Naturalist guided tours to Barra Honda and Isla Chora (US$70 per person), as well as slightly more unusual trips like *Journée Cowboy* where you spend a day on the ranch roping cattle and eat with a Tico family. **Wing Nuts Canopy Tour**, T656-0153 US$40, kids US$25, family-run, friendly service, spectacular ocean views from the treetops, newly expanded to 12 platforms, lots of wildlife close up, great photo opportunity, 1st-class equipment.

Nosara *p1047*

Tour operators

Casa Río Nosara for horse or river tours, and **Gilded Iguana** for kayaking and fishing. For turtle tours, try **Rancho Suizo**, T682-0057, or **Lagarta Lodge**, T682-0035, who are both sensitive to the turtles and don't exploit or bother them.

Montezuma *p1048*

Tour operators

Aventuras en Montezuma, T642-0050, avenzuma@racsa.co.cr. Offers a similar range, snorkelling to Tortuga Island, canopy, sunset and wildlife tours for similar prices, also taxi boat to Jacó, US$35, minimum 5 people. Ivan and his staff are also exceptionally helpful as a tourist office and can advise on hotels and other matters locally and nationally. They also book and confirm flights. **Cocozuma Traveller**, T642-0911, www.cocozumacr.com. Tico-owned company, now one of the best in Montezuma. Runs all the usual tours including horse rides and Isla Tortuga. Their boat taxi now runs to Jacó (US$35), Sámara (US$50) and Puntarenas (US$40). They will also arrange hotels, transfers, car rental and have quadbikes for hire. Very helpful staff are happy to give information about the area. **Eco Tours Montezuma**, T642-0058, on the corner opposite Soda Monte Sol, offer a wide range of tours, including shuttle to Cabo Blanco (US$3), kayaking/ snorkelling at Isla Cabuya (US$25 per person), day trip to Isla Tortuga (US$40 per person), horse rental (US$25) and bike rental (US$5 per day). Also boat/road transfers to Jacó/Tamarindo for around US$150 for up to 6 people.

Montezuma Expeditions, top of the high street, T642-0919, www.montezuma expeditions.com. Very efficient set up – organize private and group transport around the country, most trips average around US$35 per person, these include, Tamarindo, San José and Jacó and locations on the Caribbean side.

Zuma Tours, Cóbano, T642-0024, www.zumatours.net. Lots of information available on their website.

Transport

Santa Cruz *p1045*

Bus Buses leave and arrive from terminals on Plaza de los Mangos. From **San José**, 9 daily, 0700-1800, 4½ hrs, US$5, Calle 18-20, Av 3, ½ block west of Terminal Coca Cola, return 0300-1700; to **Tamarindo**, 2030, return 0645, US$1, also to **Playa Flamingo** and nearby beaches, 0630, 1500, return 0900, 1700, 64 km; to **Liberia** every hr, US$1, 0530-1930; to **Nicoya** hourly 0630-2130, US$0.35.

Taxi To **Nicoya**, US$10.50 for 2 people.

Playa del Coco and around *p1045*

Bus From **San José** from Calle 14, Av 1-3, 0800, 1400, 5 hrs, return 0800, 1400 US$4.50. 6 buses daily from **Liberia** 0530-1815, return 0530-1800.

Playa Hermosa and Playa Panamá *p1045*

Bus From **Liberia**, Empresa Esquivel, 0730, 1130, 1530, 1730, 1900, return 0500, 0600, 1000, 1600, 1700, US$0.80.

Playa Tamarindo and around *p1045*

Air Several daily flights from **San José** with Sansa (US$78 one way) and **NatureAir** (US$90) from **San José**. Daily flight from **Fortuna** with Sansa.

Bus From **Santa Cruz**, 0410, 1330, 1500 daily. Tamarindo to Santa Cruz first bus at 0600, US$1. Express bus from **San José** daily from Terminal Alfaro, 1530, return 0600 Mon-Sat, 0600, Sun 1230, 5½ hrs. Bus back to San José, can be booked through Hotel Tamarindo Diria, US$5.

Playa Flamingo and beaches to the north *p1046*

Bus From **San José** to Flamingo, Brasilito and Potrero, daily from Av 3, Calle 18-20, 0800, 1000, 6 hrs, return 0900, 1400. From **Santa Cruz** daily 0630, 1500, return 0900, 1700, 64 km to Potrero.

Playa Junquillal *p1047*

Bus Daily from **Santa Cruz** departs 1030, returns to Santa Cruz at 1530.

Nicoya *p1047*

Bus From **San José**, 8 daily from Terminal Alfaro, 6 hrs; from **Liberia** every 30 mins from 0430-2200; from **Santa Cruz** hourly 0630-2130. To **Playa Naranjo** at 0500 and 1300, US$1.45, 2¼ hrs. 12 buses a day to **Sámara**, 37 km by paved road, 1 to **Nosara**.

Sámara *p1047*

Air Daily flights from **San José**, Sansa US$78, Nature Air, US$90.

Bus From **Nicoya**, 45 km, US$1.15, 1½ hrs, 0800, 1500, 1600, return 0530, 0630, 1130, 1330, 1630. Express bus from Terminal Alfaro, **San José** daily at 1230, return Mon-Sat 0430, Sun 1300, 5-6 hrs. School bus to **Nosara** around 1600 – ask locally for details. It is not possible to go from Sámara along the coast to Montezuma, except in 4WD vehicle; not enough traffic for hitching.

Taxis Official and others stop outside bus station (US$20 to **Nosara**, US$10 to **Nicoya**).

Nosara *p1047*

Air Sansa has daily flights to **San José**, US$78, Nature Air, US$90.

Bus Daily from **Nicoya** to Nosara, Garza, Guiones daily from main station, 1300, return 0600, US$2, 2 hrs, 65 km; from **San José** daily from Terminal Alfaro at 0600, 6 hrs, return 1245.

Playa Ostional *p1048*

Bus There is 1 a day at 0500 to **Santa Cruz** and **Liberia**, returns at 1230 from Santa Cruz, 3 hrs, US$1.75.

Montezuma *p1048*

Bus To **Paquera** daily at 0530, 0815, 1000, 1215, 1400 and 1600, connecting with the car and passenger ferry to **Puntarenas** central docks. Tickets available in advance from tourist information centre; be at bus stop outside Hotel Moctezuma, in good time as the bus fills up quickly, US$2.60, 1 hr (the road has been paved). To **Cabuya** US$1, buses run 4 times a day. Change at Cóbano for **Mal País** – 2 buses run daily from Cóbano, 1100 and 1400 (check as times can change).

Taxi To **Cóbano** US$5; to **Paquera** US$20.

Directory

Santa Cruz
Banks Banco Nacional, with ATM, on main road. **Post office** 400 m west of Plaza de los Mangos.

Playa del Coco and around
Banks Banco Nacional, closed Sat. **Internet** Café Internet 2000, on road out of town, also try E-Juice Bar, T670-05563 and Leslie Café.

Playa Tamarindo and around *p1045*
Banks Banco Nacional, opposite Hotel Diria. **Internet** Tamarindo Internet, T653-0404.

Nicoya *p1047*
Banks With ATMs on main square and Calle 3, with very welcome a/c. **Post office** On corner of main square.

Sámara *p1047*
Banks There is no bank in Sámara, although hotels may change money. **Internet** Tropical Latitudes Internet Café in centre of town, and hotels may offer access. **Post office** Almost on the beach.

Nosara *p1047*
Internet and telephone **Nosara Office Centre**, offering email, fax, photocopies and international calls. **Language schools** **Rey de Nosara** language school is in the village, T682 0215, www.reydenosara.itgo.com. Classes from US$15 per hr. They can often advise about other things to see and do in the area and arrange tours and homestays.

Montezuma *p1048*
Banks Change money at Hotel Moctezuma, Aventuras en Montezuma and Cocozuma Traveller (otherwise go to the Banco Nacional in Cóbano, T642-0210). **Internet** There is an internet café in Pizz@net next to the Hotel Moctezuma, US$2 per hr. Sano Banano has an all-Macintosh internet, a little pricey at US$3 per hr and can be slow. Another is located behind El Parque Hotel. **Laundry** Laundrette in Pensión Jenny and Hotel Arenas (on the beach). **Medical services** If you need a pharmacy, you will have to go to Cóbano.

Central Pacific coast

West of the Central Highlands lies a slim lowland strip of African palm with just the occasional cattle ranch. But, for the visitor, it is the miles of beaches stretching from Jacó almost continuously south to Uvita that are the real attraction. Parque Nacional Manuel Antonio is a major destination with developed services. Further south, the beaches are quieter and the Parque Nacional Marino Ballena, which is harder to get to, is barely developed; but it's of interest to divers and whalewatchers. » *For Sleeping, Eating and other listings, see pages 1064-1069.*

Esparza to the Pacific Coast

From Esparza on the Pan-American Highway a road runs 21 km southeast to **San Mateo** (from where a road runs northeast to Atenas and the Central Highlands – see Meseta Central section). Just before San Mateo, at Higuito de San Mateo, is **Las Candelillas** ⓘ *T428-9157*, a 26-ha farm and reforestation project with fruit trees and sugar cane. There is a day use recreational area with showers, pool and riding, trails and bar/restaurant.

From San Mateo a road runs south to **Orotina**, which used to be an important road/rail junction on the San José-Puntarenas route. Today the area is home to **Original Canopy Tour** at **Mahogany Park** ⓘ *T257-5149*, which charges US$45 to fly through the trees; transportation is available.

West of Orotina the road forks northwest to the port of **Caldera,** via Cascajal, and southwest to the Pacific coast at Tárcoles.

The Costanera to Quepos

» *pp1064-1069.*

The Costanera or coastal road passes through Jacó, Manuel Antonio and Quepos and on to Dominical before heading inland to San Isidro de El General or continuing south to Palmar Norte. If you want a popular beach, pick somewhere before Manuel Antonio. Beyond, although not deserted, you'll find things a lot quieter. If driving yourself, check the state of the roads and bridges before setting out to San Isidro. Just because buses are getting through, it doesn't mean cars can. The road is paved as far as Quepos and with few potholes. Thereafter it is a good, but dusty, gravel road, paved in villages until Paquita, just before Quepos. After Quepos the road is unpaved to Dominical. From Dominical the road inland through Barú to San Isidro is paved but landslides can make this section hazardous. High clearance is needed if a bridge is down. South from Dominical, the Costanera drifts through small expat communities which are only just being explored by visitors. They cover a range of budgets, but all are for people seeking a little solitude... while it lasts.

If travelling by car, leave nothing of value in your vehicle; thefts, robberies and scams are regularly reported in the area.

Reserva Biológica Carara

ⓘ *0700-1600, US$7.*

Between Orotina and Jacó the Carara Biological Reserve (5242 ha) is rich in wildlife. Three trails lead through the park: one lasting a couple of hours leaves from close to Tarcoles bridge; the others lasting a little over one hour from the ranger station to the south. The reserve protects a transitional zone from the dry north coast of the country to the very humid region of the southeast. Spider monkeys, scarlet macaws and coatis can all be seen in the reserve.

One of the most popular free experiences in Costa Rica is to peer over the side of the Río Tárcoles bridge to see the opaque sediment-filled waters broken by the bony backs of the somnolent crocodiles below. It's easy to find the spot to stop, as cars cram the roadside, especially at dawn and dusk when scarlet macaws can be seen returning to their roosts from Carara Biological Reserve on the southern banks of the river.

You can get a closer look by taking a boat tours with **Jungle Crocodile Safari** ⓘ *T292-2316*, or **Crocodile ECO Tour** ⓘ *T637-0426*, US$25 per person from the dock in Tárcoles, US$35 round trip from Jacó.

Next to Carara is **La Catarata** ⓘ *T236-4140, 0800-1500, 15 Dec-15 Apr, US$7.50*, a private reserve with an impressive waterfall with natural pools for bathing; take the gravel road up the hill beside **Hotel Villa Lapas**: it's 5 km to the entrance, and a 2½-km hike to falls and pools, but it's worth the effort. There are signs on the main road. **Bijagual Waterfall Tours** ⓘ *T661-8263*, offer horse riding or 4WD to the falls.

Jacó

A short distance from Carara is Jacó, a large stretch of sandy beach, with a lively, youthful energy. It is popular with surfers, weekenders from San José and comes with a rough'n'ready, earthy commercial appeal. If you want to learn to **surf**, this is as good a place as any, with several surf shops offering courses and boards for rent. If you want to party with crowds on their annual holiday, it's a great spot. If you're looking for peace and quiet, go elsewhere.

Jacó to Quepos

From Jacó the potholed road runs down the coastline with lovely views of the ocean. The beaches are far quieter and, if you have a car, you can take your pick. A few kilometres south is **Playa Hermosa**, which is right on the main road and has a popular surfing beach. If travelling by car, 20 km further and a few kilometres off the road is **Playa Bejuco**, **Esterillos Centro** and **Playa Palma**, near Parrita; definitely worth exploring. Beyond **Parrita** (Banco Nacional, Banco de Costa Rica, a gas station and a few stores) the road travels through a flat landscape of endless African palm plantations. Many of the plantation villages are of passing interest for their two-storey, balconied houses laid out around a central football pitch, a church of some denomination and the obligatory branch of AA. The carriageway narrows to single track on bridges along this road so take care if you're driving, especially at night.

Quepos → *Colour map 7, B3. Population: 14,674.*

Developed as a banana exporting port by United Brands, Quepos was forced to recreate itself following the devastation of banana plantations in the region overwhelmed by Panama disease, in the early 1950s. Endless rows of oil-producing African Palm have replaced the bananas and Quepos has long since shrugged off the portside image, to the extent that few even bother to explore the dock at the southern end of town.

South of Quepos, a winding road, lined with hotels, bars, restaurants and stores rises and falls for 7 km before reaching the beautiful coastline of Parque Nacional Manuel Antonio (see below) and nearby beautiful beaches. The impact on what was once an attractive stretch of jungle-clad coastline is indisputable. For some it is an environmental catastrophe, for others it is a demonstration of the importance of planning to protect. Quepos plays an important role as a service town for local and foreign tourists. It is cheaper than the Manuel Antonio road, there is no shortage of restaurants, bars and shops, and regular buses make the journey to the national park.

❢ Quepolandia *is a locally produced free magazine, www.quepolandia.com.*

Parque Nacional Manuel Antonio

ⓘ *Tue-Sun 0700-1600, closed Mon, US$7. Guides available, but not essential, at entrance. Early and late are the best times to see the wildlife. Breakfast and other meals available from stalls just before the river, where cars can be parked and minded for US$1 by the stallholders. Basic toilets, picnic tables and drinks available by the beaches, cold water showers at Manuel Antonio and Espadilla Sur beaches.*

From the southeastern corner of Quepos, a road winds up, over and round the peninsula of Punta Quepos, passing the flourishing hotels, restaurants, bars and stores along the length of this rocky outcrop. Travelling the road for the first time, you can't fail to be impressed by the beauty of the views. And at night, you can't help being blinded by the neon lights that speckle the hillside – evidence of the vibrant tourist trade. At times it is difficult to believe a national park flourishes on the other side of the watershed.

With 683 ha of mangrove swamps and beaches, home to a rich variety of fauna and flora, Manuel Antonio National Park can rightly claim to be one of Costa Rica's most popular protected areas – second only to Volcán Poás. Just 7 km south of Quepos on a paved road, three beautiful, forest-fringed beaches stretch along the coastline and around the headland of Punta Catedral: **Espadilla Sur**, **Manuel Antonio** and **Puerto Escondido**. Iguanas and white-faced monkeys often come down to the sand.

In addition to enjoying the beaches, hiking is also good in the park. A 45-minute trail, steep in places, runs round the Punta Catedral between Espadilla Sur and Manuel Antonio beaches. If you're early, and quiet, it is possible to see a surprising amount of wildlife. A second walk to Puerto Escondido, where there is a blow hole, takes about 50 minutes. The map sold at the entrance shows a walk up to a mirador, with good views of the coastline.

Manuel Antonio has been a victim of its own success with some of the animals becoming almost tame. But for all the criticism of recent years, it is still beautiful and highly enjoyable. Overdevelopment outside the park and overuse within has led to problems of how to manage the park with inadequate funds. In 1992 the National Park Service (SPN) threatened to close it and a number of tour operators removed it from their itineraries. You are not allowed to feed the monkeys but people do, which means that they can be a nuisance, congregating around picnic tables expecting to be fed and rummaging through bags given the chance. Leave no litter and take nothing out of the park, not even seashells.

The range of activities in the area outside the park is slightly bewildering. Sea kayaking is possible, as is mountain biking, hiking, canopy tours, canyoning, deep-sea fishing and even quad biking. Most hotels can assist with booking trips, and there are agencies in Quepos that can also advise. The beaches in the park are safer than those outside, but rip tides are dangerous all along the coast. Beaches slope steeply and the force of the waves can be too strong for children.

Quepos to Palmar Norte

Playa Matapalo

Beaches, beaches, endless stretches of sandy beaches. Thirty kilometres southeast from the congestion of Quepos towards Dominical the unpaved coastal road drifts

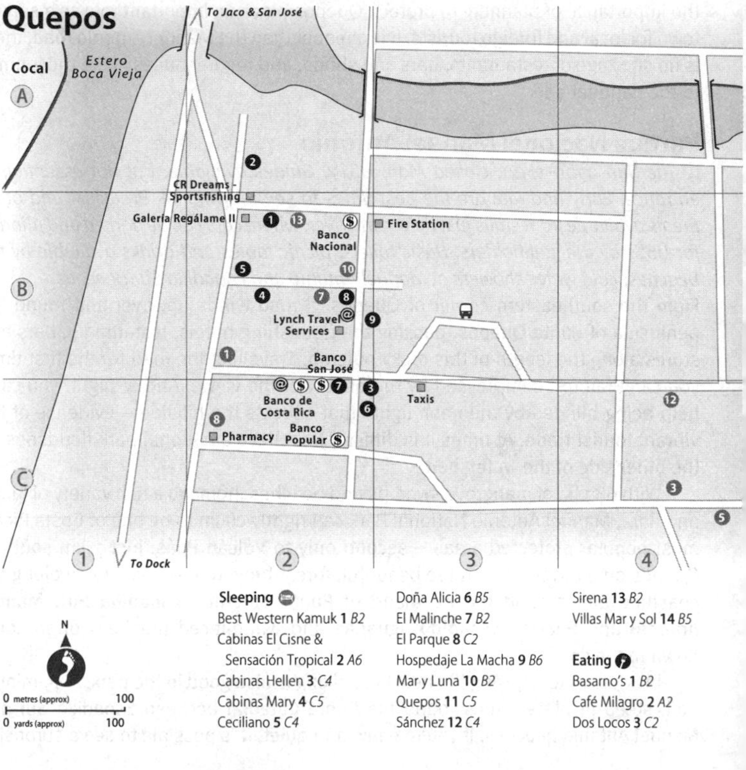

almost unnoticed through Playa Matapalo, where you'll find an expansive, beautiful sandy beach recommended for surfing, relaxing and playing with your ideas of paradise. Other activities, in an overwhelmingly Swiss community, include fishing, horse riding and hiking to mountain waterfalls.

Dominical → *Colour map 7, B2.*

Twelve kilometres further on, at the mouth of the Río Barú, is Dominical (www.dominical.net), a small town with a population of a few hundred. No more than 500 m from one end to the other it's popular with surfers and often busy. It's a great spot for surfing. Hotel prices soar in high season and most hotels are close to noisy bars. Treks and horse riding trips to waterfalls are possible if the beach is too much to bear. Just north of the town **Hacienda Barú** has a **national wildlife preserve**, with activities like abseiling, canopy tours and nature walks (see below). If you want to touch up your Spanish try the **Adventure Education Center** ⓘ *T787-0023, www.adventurespanishschool.com*, with an immersion Spanish school. Most people come here for the surfing; if you want to learn visit the **Green Iguana Surf Camp** ⓘ *T825-1381, www.greeniguanasurfcamp.com*, who provide board hire, group lessons, individual lessons and package deals.

Punta Dominical is 4 km south of town (no transport). A poor dirt road follows a steep path inland up the Escaleras (stairs) to some secluded accommodation blending beach and rainforest.

Uvita

If you get the impression the southern Pacific coast is about beaches, you'd be right. The village of Uvita, 18 km south of Dominical, has beautiful beaches all along the coastline. You can walk in the nearby forests, swim in nearby waterfalls or at the beach, take a boat trip and watch birds. Ballena National Marine Park (see below) protects over 5000 ha of Pacific coral reef, and humpback whales can be sighted at nearby Isla Ballena between December and April.

❢ Tell the bus driver where you are going and he will drop you off at the closest point to your chosen hotel.

The road south from Uvita is being repaved as far as Ciudad Cortés, and access to the beaches of Playa Ballena and Playa Bahía is getting easier with consequent development of the area.

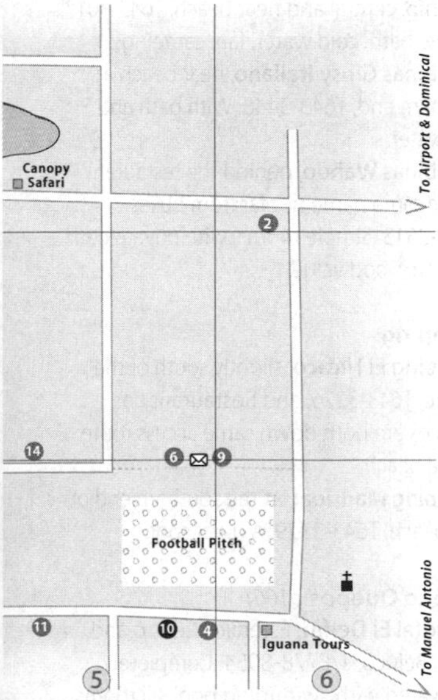

El Banco Sports Bar **4** *B2*
El Gran Escape **5** *B2*
Escalofrío **6** *C2*
L'Angolo **7** *C2*
Pan Aldo **10** *C5*
Pizza Gabriels **8** *B2*
Pueblo **9** *B2*

Parque Nacional Marino Ballena

The vast majority of Ballena (Whale) Marine National Park is coastal waters – 5161 ha against 116 ha of protected land – which may go some way to explaining why there isn't a lot to see at this least-developed national park. The underwater world is home to coral reefs and abundant marine life that includes common and bottle-nosed dolphins as well as occasional visits from humpback whales at times seen with their calves.

Although there is a rarely staffed **rangers station** ⓘ *T786-7161*, in Bahía, and signposts line the Costanera, the infrastructure in the park is non-existent. There is a nominal entrance fee of US$6 which is rarely collected. Along the beach at Bahía is a turtle-nesting project administered by the local community. As with the park itself, the organization is very ad hoc – visitors and volunteers are welcome. Beachcombing is good, as is snorkelling when the tides are favourable. Boat trips to the island can be arranged from Bahía, and diving is starting up with the most recommended local being Máximo Vásquez, or Chumi as he is known. The coastal road continues south beside **Playa Tortuga**, passing small communities of foreigners hiding and enjoying one of the quietest spots near a beach in Costa Rica, to join the Pan-American Highway at Palmar Norte (see page 1072).

Sleeping

Esparza to the Pacific coast *p1059*

AL El Rancho Oropéndola, San Mateo, T428-8600. Cabins with private bath or rooms with shared bath, rustic and peaceful, pool, nature trails.

C Cabinas Kalim, Orotina, near plaza, T428-8082.

Reserva Biológica Carara *p1060*

L Villa Caletas, Punta Leona, to the south of the reserve, T637-0505, www.hotelvillacaletas.com. One of the distinctive hotels of Costa Rica. French owned, 8 rooms, 20 bungalows, atop a mountain with amazing views, spectacular sunsets, lush gardens, pool, restaurant, boat and nature tours.

Jacó *p1060*

Accommodation in Jacó is overpriced; look for discounts May-Nov.

AL Cocal, on beach near the centre of town, T643-3067, www.hotelcocalandcasino.com. 2 pools, hammocks, German-owned, restaurant. Highly recommended.

AL-B Cabinas Las Palmas, northern end of town, T643-3005. Neat rooms, some with kitchenette, all with bath and fan, clean. Pretty gardens.

A-B Alice, south of centre, T643-3061. Tidy rooms with private bath, small terrace and pool.

A-B Los Ranchos, central and close to the beach, T643-3070. 4 bungalows and 8 rooms sleeping 4-8 people, lively spot.

A-B Pochote Grande, northern end of town, T643-3236, www.hotelpochotegrande.net. Beautiful German-owned hotel with bar and restaurant. Good rooms, free-form pool and a superb 500-year-old *pochote* tree shading the grounds. Good value.

B Cabinas La Cometa, central, T643-3615. With fan and hot water, very clean.

B El Jardín, at northern end of town, close to the beach, T643-3050. 10 rooms in quiet spot, friendly with small pool.

B Hotel Paraíso Escondido, 150 m east of the Catholic church on calle Los Cholos, T643-2883, www.hoteljaco.com. All rooms with a private bath, patio and a/c, rooms cheaper with fan. Swimming pool and laundry service. The owner often meets arriving buses. Good spot and worth the price.

C Bohío, central and near beach, T643-3017. Private bath, cold water, fan, camping.

D Cabinas Gipsy Italiano, near beach at northern end, T643-3448. With bath and hot water.

D Cabinas Wahoo, behind the restaurant of the same name not far from buses, T643-3513. Simple rooms, with private bath and fan. Good value.

Camping

Camping El Hicaco, slightly south of the centre, T643-3226, and **Restaurant Los Hicacos** are both down same access route to the beach.

Camping Madrigal, at the southern end of the beach, T643-3329. A quiet spot.

Jacó to Quepos *p1061*

AL Hotel El Delfín, Esterillos Centro and Playa Bejuco, T/F778-8054. Completely renovated with swimming pool, all rooms with breezy balcony, secluded, clean, good restaurant, considered by many to be one of the best beach hotels in Costa Rica. Recommended.

AL La Isla, Playa Palo Seco, T779-9016. Bar, pool, horse and canoe trips, hot water, a/c.

A Beso del Viento, Playa Palo Seco, 5 km, T779-9674, www.besodelviento.com. Swimming pool, French owners, stylish rooms.
A Vista Hermosa, Playa Hermosa, T643-3422. Pool, simple rooms with a/c, restaurant, secure parking.
A-B Auberge du Pelican, Esterillos Este, T778-8105, www.aubergepelican.com. Café, French-Canadian owners, restaurant. Great spot, private airstrip out back, beach out front.
A-B Hotel Sandpiper Inn, T643-1042, www.sandpipercostarica.com. Spacious cabins, pool, restaurant, sportfishing.
B La Felicidad Country Inn, Esterillos Centro and Playa Bejuco, T778-6824, wwwlafelicidad.com. Oceanfront, pool and restaurant.
B-C Cabinas Maldonado, Playa Palma, T227-5400. Rooms sleeping 4, with bath, cold water, kitchen.
D Finca Don Herbert, Playa Palma. With bath, clean, parking.
D Rooms/Restaurant Alex, Playa Palma, T779-6667. 2.6 km south, with bath, fan. Recommended.
D-E Jungle Surf Café, Playa Hermosa. Basic cabins with a Tex-Mex burger bar.
E Rancho Grande, Playa Hermosa, T643-3529. Large wooden house with communal kitchen, popular with surfers, great atmosphere. Small store for supplies.
F Las Brisas, Playa Palma. Simple rooms near beach.

Quepos *p1061, map p1062*

It's difficult to find accommodation on Sat Dec-Apr, and when schools are on holiday.
A Best Western Kamuk, central, near the bus terminal, T777-0811, www.kamuk.co.cr. Shower, TV, a/c, some ocean views, bar and restaurant with large-screen videos.
A Hotel Sirena, near bus station, T777-0528. 14 quite good rooms with private bathroom, a/c. Restaurant and pool.
B Cabinas El Cisne and Sensación Tropical, 75 m north of Catholic church and football pitch, T777-0719. Safe, family-run, secure parking, bigger rooms on left. Recommended.
B-C El Malinche, close to bus station, T777-0093. 27 clean and good rooms, simply decorated, some with a/c much cheaper without.
C Cabinas Pedro Miguel, towards Manuel Antonio, T777-0035, www.cabinaspedromiguel.com. Simple rooms, a small pool and very friendly Tico owners. Next door is the **Centro de Idiomas del Pacífico**, see page 1069.
C Villas Mar y Sol, towards the eastern side of town, T777-0307. 8 rooms with private bath and hot shower. Relaxed spot, parking.
C-D Ceciliano, towards the eastern side of town, on the road leading to Manuel Antonio, T777-0192. Family-run, quiet, small rooms, with bath, hot.
C-D Hotel Quepos, eastern side of town, T777-0274. With bath, cheaper without, simple, recommended.
D Cabinas Hellen, eastern side of town, T777-0504. Quite small rooms with private bath and fan, but clean and plenty of parking.
D Cabinas Mary, by football pitch close to Iguana Tours, T777-0128. Clean, friendly, OK.
D-E Wide Mouth Frog, short distance from the bus terminal, T777-2798, www.widemouthfrog.org. Private rooms and dorms.
D-F Hospedaje La Macha, next to post office on walkway by the football pitch, T777-0216. Includes the cheapest beds in town. Very basic but clean.
E Cabinas Kali, 200 m northeast of bus station, T777-1491. Nice rooms, family-run, clean, friendly, safe but noisy.
E Doña Alicia, on walkway by football pitch, T777-0419. Big cabin with bath, friendly, quiet, parking, can wash clothes.
E El Parque, on waterfront road, T777-0063, Price per person, friendly, clean, a bit run-down but good value, private bath, fan.
E Mar y Luna, central, T777-0394. With or without bath, quiet, clean, friendly, popular.
E Sánchez, a couple of blocks east of the bus terminal, T777-0491. Without bath, OK.

Parque Nacional Manuel Antonio *p1061*

There are hotels all along the road from Quepos to Manuel Antonio, many of them expensive. Many shut in the low season; in high season, it's best to book ahead. The area is full to bursting at weekends with locals camping on the beach. The parked Second World War plane – decked out as a bar – marks the start of the downhill to the beach.
LL El Parador, 2 km from the main road, T777-1414, www.hotelparador.com. 80 rooms, all facilities, stunning views of the ocean, in style of Spanish parador, helicopter landing pad – just in case! (**AL** in low season).

LL Makanda by the Sea, down a dirt road leading to Punta Quepos from opposite **Café Milagro**, T777-0442, www.makanda.com. 11 villas and studios with superb open design. An idyllic and romantic paradise spot.
LL Sí Como No, T777-0777, www.sicomo no.com. A superb hotel with beautiful touches of design using stunning stained glass, all the comforts you would expect, and service par excellence plus a cinema.
LL-L Byblos, on the main road, T777-0411. All-in bungalows in a resort, sleeping 1-4, French restaurant, pizzería, pool (**AL** in low season).
L-AL Costa Verde, at the train carriage restaurant and reception, T777-0584, www.costaverde.com. Apartments for 2-4 people, with kitchenette and bath, 2-bedroom villas available, well-appointed, pool and a couple of restaurants. Several nature trails out the back. Recommended.
L-AL Karahé, along the main road towards the beach, on private road, T777-0170, www.karahe.com. Includes breakfast, cabins on a steep hillside with lovely view, sleep 3-4, recommended, fridge, bath, a/c or fan, good restaurant, swimming pool across the road, access to beach, walk to park along the beach.
L-A La Arboleda, T777-1056, www.hotel arboleda.com. Cabins on hillside leading down to beach sleep 2-3, bath, fan, Uruguayan restaurant, 8-ha wood. Beware snakes, crabs and monkeys in the yard at night. Recommended.
L-A Plinio, on hillside, T777-0055, www.hotelplinio.com. 13 rooms, award-winning restaurant, plus bar and pool. 7-km nature trail with an 18-m observation tower. Recommended.
AL Villa de la Selva, overlooking the bay, T777-0434. 5 simple rooms, some with kitchenettes. Up above most of the activity, this is a charming spot away from the mêlée. Recommended.
A Hotel del Mar, on the main road towards Quepos, T777-0543, www.hoteldelmarcostarica.com. Rents surfboards, sells drinks and light meals and has a collection of English novels to read in the bar.
A Hotel Manuel Antonio, T777-1237, restaurant, good breakfast, camping possible nearby, ask in the restaurant. Handy, just minutes from the national park and the beach.
A Vela Bar, T777-0413, www.velabar.com. Large rooms with bath, fans, safes, very good restaurant, fishing and other trips, also has a fully equipped house to rent.
A-B B&B Casa Buena Vista, T777-1002. Offers a breathtaking view and wonderful breakfast terrace, friendly owner.
B Mono Azul, T777-1954, monoazul@ racsa.co.cr. 20 rooms, conference rooms, library, internet, 2 nightly movies, international headquarters of **Kids Saving the Rainforest** and souvenir store with profits going to save the rainforest, friendly place with a couple of pools, and a good restaurant.
C Cabinas Ramírez, towards the end of the road, T777-5044. With bath, food and bar, free hammocks and camping, guests can help with cooking in exchange.
D Vista Serena Hostel, at the start of the road, T777-5132, vistaserena2003@ yahoo.com. Good quality but budget option on the Manuel Antonio strip. Good rooms, private or dorms, and balconies with hammocks looking out to the coast.
E Costa Linda, up the side road just before the park, T777-0304. Double rooms or 4-bedded room, fan, water shortage, watch out for racoons raiding the outdoor kitchen in the night, good breakfasts; dinner rather pricey.

Dominical *p1063*

Booking hotels is slightly easier in the Dominical and Uvita area using regional specialists and booking service **Selva Mar**, T771-4582, www.exploringcostarica.com.
L Villas Escaleras, Punta Dominical, T385-1526, www.villas-escaleras.com. Beautifully equipped villas sleeping up to 10 people, spectacular views, a great spot to hide away.
AL Diuwak, back from the beach, T787-0087, www.diuwak.com. Rooms and suites, sleeping up to 4 people, with private bath. Mini supermarket and (pricey) internet service, new pool.
AL Hotel/Restaurant Roca Verde, on the beachfront about 1 km south of Dominical, T787-0036, www.rocaverde.net. Tropical rooms with a/c. Small balcony or terraces, with a pool. Big bar and restaurant. Recommended.

AL Villas Río Mar Jungle and Beach Resort, out of town, 500 m from beach, T787-0052, www.villasriomar.com. 40 bungalows with bath, fridge and fan, pool, jacuzzi, tennis court, trails, riding, all inclusive.
AL-B Hotel Pacífico Edge, Punta Dominical, T771-4582, www.exploringcostarica.com. Selva Mar service. 4 large cabins with great views of ocean and rainforest.
A Hacienda Barú, about 2 km north of Dominical, T787-0003, www.hacienda baru.com. A 332-ha reserve that began life as a private reserve in 1972. Cabins sleeping 3 or more with private bath, hiking, riding. So much to see and do in such a small area. There is a canopy observation platform, tree climbing, night walks in the jungle and several self-guided trails and a butterfly garden.
B Bella Vista Lodge, Punta Dominical, T388-0155 or T771-4582 (through the Selva Mar reservation service). Great view, good large meals, owned by local American 'Woody Dyer', organizes trips in the area. There are also houses to rent.
B Posada del Sol, 100 m from beach, T787-0085. Owned by local historian Mariela Badilla, 20-odd rooms, bath, fan, patio with hammocks, also 2-bedroom apartment with kitchen for US$150 per week. Rooms vary.
B-C Río Lindo, at the entrance to town, T787-0028. Clean, tidy rooms with a balcony or terrace. Private bath with fan or a/c. Pool and bar area.
B-C Tortilla Flats, formerly Cabinas Nayarit right on the sea front, T787-0033. Rooms sleeping up to 3 people, with private bath and hot water. A bit overpriced if just for 2.
B-E Cabinas San Clemente, on beach, T787-0026. Clean, with or without a/c, friendly, US-owned, restaurant, also cheaper, basic dorm rooms, shared bath, fan; San Clemente Bar and Grill, under same ownership, good, big portions.
C-E Cabinas El Coco, at end of main street, T787-0235. With or without bath, negotiate price, unfriendly, noisy, a last option. Camping possible.

Uvita *p1063*
The central booking service Selva Mar, T771-4582, www.exploringcostarica.com, makes booking a hotel in this area easier.
AL Canto de Ballenas, 6 km south of Uvita, close to Parque Nacional Marino Ballena, T248-2538, www.turismoruralcr.com. Rustic, but fine, wooden cabins in a simple landscaped garden. Great spot in a quiet location.
AL Villa María Luisa Lodge, Bahía Uvita, T743-8094. Simple cabins sleeping up to 6.
B Cabinas El Chamán, 2 km south on the beach, T771-2555. Nice location, 8 simple *cabinas* with private bathroom, camping US$4 per person.
C-D Coco Tico Ecolodge, Uvita village, T743-8032. 6 clean *cabinas*, sleep 3, with private bathroom and trails outback.
D Cabinas Las Gemelas, Playa Bahía Uvita, T743-8009. Simple rooms, with showers and bathrooms. Quiet spot with gardens for camping.
D Cabinas Los Laureles, Uvita village, 200 m turn on the left from the main road, T771-8008. Nice location, 3 *cabinas* with private bathroom, simple and quite good.
D Roca Paraíso, near Cabinas El Chamán, T220-4263 for information. Basic.
E Cabinas Punta Uvita, opposite Restaurant Los Almendros close to the beach. Simple, basic *cabinas* with private bathroom.
E-F Cascada Verde, Uvita village, up the hill, www.cascadaverde.org. *Hostal*, educational retreat and organic farm, German-run, vegetarian food, yoga and meditation workshops available. Pay for a bed, hammock or camp, or work for your lodgings. Long-term lodgings preferred, great spot if you take to the place.
F Steve's Toucan Hotel, Uvita village, just off the main road, T743-8140, www.tucan hotel.com. Low-key and pleasant spot in Uvita. Dormitory and private rooms, kitchen available, and advice on local travel options.

Parque Nacional Marino Ballena *p1063*
AL Hotel Villas Gaia, Playa Tortuga, 200 m to the beach, T244-0316, www.villasgaia.com. 12 spacious cabins with private bathrooms (hot water), fan and terrace. Swimming pool and restaurant serving Swiss, international and vegetarian dishes. Ocean view, diving school, horses. Several other quiet secluded options opening up.
A Posada Playa Tortuga, Playa Tortuga, T384-5489. Run by Gringo Mike, a great spot and place to stay, and Mike knows everything there is to know about the area.

Eating

Jacó *p1060*

There are lots of *sodas* in Jacó.

Sunrise Grill Breakfast Place, centre of town. Breakfast from 0700, closed Wed.

Wishbone, on the main street. Big plates of Mexican food, from US$6.

Chatty Cathy's, on the main drag. A popular dining spot.

La Ostra, centre of town. Good fish in this pleasant open-air restaurant open all day.

Wahoo, just within the centre to the north. Good Tico food, mainly fish.

Jacó to Quepos *p1061*

Doña María's Soda, small central market, Parrita, T842-3047. Tasty *casados*.

Quepos *p1061, map p1062*

There are many good restaurants along the road towards Manuel Antonio.

Basarno's, near the entrance to town. Bar, restaurant, club, daily 1000-0100. Good mix of snacks and a lively spot later in the night.

El Gran Escape, central, T777-0395. Lively collection of restaurants and bars offering Tex Mex, pizza and sushi. Good food and service, recommended.

Dos Locos, central, T777-1526. Popular with Mexican and Tico fare, open to the street, occasional live music.

El Banco Restaurant and Sports Bar, near El Gran Escape, T777-0478. Newly remodelled long bar with bright neon, good Tex Mex food and will cook your catch.

Escalofrío, next to Dos Locos. Pizza, pasta and ice cream to die for from US$4.

Gardin Gourmet, opposite Escalofrío. Great new deli with lots of imported treats.

Pizza Gabriels, central, T777-1085. Popular little spot with a lively undercurrent. Fine pizza and pasta from US$6.

Cafés, snacks and bakeries

The municipal market (for fruit and bread) is at the bus station.

Café Milagro, on the waterfront, T777-0794, www.cafemilagro.com. Best expresso, cakes, pies, Cuban cigars, souvenirs, freshly roasted coffee for sale; another branch on the road to Manuel Antonio.

L'Angolo, opposite Dos Locos. Serves a divine mix of breads, olives, hams and everything you'd need for self-catering or picnicking in style.

La Buena Nota, on road near the beach in Manuel Antonio, T777-1002. Sells English-language newspapers. A good place to seek local information, run by Anita Myketuk, who has initiated publicity on rip tides.

Pan Aldo, right in front of the soccer pitch, T777-2697. Italian specialties, wholewheat sourdough, pastries, croutons, great bread and pastries.

Dominical *p1063*

Jazzy's River House, down the main (er, only) street. More an open-house cum cultural centre, occassionally have meals followed by an open mike set up on Wed.

Restaurant El Coco, in town. Serves good food and rents budget rooms.

San Clemente, in town. A good mix of Tex Mex with big servings.

Thrusters, in town. A hip spot for the surf crowd, with sushi in the front restaurant.

Soda Nanyoa, Dominical, offers Costa Rican specialities.

Entertainment

Jacó *p1060*

Bars and clubs

Discos in town include **Central**, close to the beach, T643-3076, **Los Tucanes**, **El Zarpe Sports Bar**, T643-3473, **Club Olé**, T643-1576, restaurant, bar, disco and games.

Activities and tours

Quepos *p1061, map p1062*

Tour operators

Amigos del Río, opposite the football pitch, T777-0082, amigorio@racsa.co.cr, river rafting, kayaking, canopy and horse riding tours, good guides. **Iguana Tours**, close to the church on the football pitch, T777-1262, www.iguanatours.com. Excellent local knowledge with many tours available. Friendly and helpful. **Lynch Travel Services**, right in the centre of town, T777-0161, www.lynchtravel.com.

Transport

Jacó *p1060*

Bus From **San José** Coca Cola bus station, 3 daily, 3½ or 4½ hrs, US$3.80 or US$4.60, arrive at Plaza Jacó-Complex terminal at north end of town, next to **Pizza Hut**. Also several buses to **Quepos**.

Quepos *p1061*
Air There are several daily flights from **San José**, with **Sansa** and **Nature Air** (US$50 one way). The Sansa office is under Hotel Quepos, T777-0683.

Bus There are 3 express buses a day leaving **San José** Coca Cola bus station, T223-5567, at 0600, 1200 and 1800, returning at 0600, 0930, 1200 and 1700, 3½ hrs, US$4.50, book a day in advance, 6 regular buses, 4½ hrs, US$4. There are buses northwest along the coast to **Puntarenas**, 3½ hrs, 0430, 1030, and 1500, return 0500, 1100, 1430, US$2.10. 2 daily buses via **Dominical** to **San Isidro de El General**, T771-4744, 0500, and 1330, 3½ hrs, US$2.00, connections can be made there to get to the Panamanian border, return 0700, 1330.

Taxi Taxis congregate opposite the bus terminal, just up from **Dos Locos** restaurant. Minibuses meet flights.

Parque Nacional Manuel Antonio *p1061*
Bus There are 3 express buses a day (see Quepos, Transport, above), direct from **San José**, 4 hrs, US$4.50. At weekends buy ticket the day before; buses fill to standing room only very quickly. Roads back to San José on Sun evening are packed. A regular bus service runs roughly ½-hourly from beside **Quepos** market, starting at 0545, to Manuel Antonio, last bus back at 1700, US$0.35.

Car If driving, there is ample guarded parking in the area, US$6.

Taxi From **Quepos**, approximately US$10. Minibuses meet flights from San José to the airport at Quepos (see above), US$2.25.

Dominical *p1063*
Bus to **Quepos** 0545, 0815, 1350 (Sat and Sun) and 1450. To **San Isidro**, 0645, 0705, 1450, 1530, 1 hr. To **Uvita** at 0950, 1010, 1130 (weekends) 1710 and 2000. To **Cd Cortés** and **Cd Neily** 0420 and 1000. To **San José**, 0545, 1340 (Sat and Sun), 7 hrs.

Uvita *p1063*
Bus From **San José** Terminal Coca Cola, Mon-Fri 1500, Sat and Sun 0500, 1500, return Mon-Fri 0530, Sat and Sun 0530, 1300, 7 hrs. From **San Isidro** daily 0800, 1600, return 0600, 1400. From **Dominical**, last bus 1700 or 1800.

Directory

Jacó *p1060*
Banks Banco Nacional in centre of town. **Internet** Iguana Mar, Centro de Computación and Mexican Joe's Internet Café. **Language schools** City Playa Language Institute, T643-2244, www.ipailanguageschool.com, offers Spanish classes with or without homestay, and the novel option of free surfing lessons. **Post office** Near Municipalidad offices.

Quepos *p1061, map p1062*
Banks Several branches in town including Banco Nacional which has a Visa ATM as does Banco Popular and Banco San José. The best place to exchange TCs or US$ cash is at Distribuidora Puerto Quepos, opposite Banco de Costa Rica, 0900-1700, no paperwork, no commission, all done in 2 mins, same rate as banks. **Immigration** On the same street as the Banco de Costa Rica. **Internet** Access available from Internet Quepos, fast machines, good service, US$1.50/hr. Several others in town including Arte Net, Quepos Diner & Internet Café, Internet Tropical, CyberLoco and Internet Cantina. **Language schools** Escuela D'Amore, in a great setting overlooking the ocean, halfway between Quepos and the national park, T777-1143, www.escueladamore.com. Believes in the immersion technique, living with local families. Pacífico Spanish School, T777-0805, www.pacificospanishschool.com, US$350 per week including lodging in owners' hotel, good classes. Costa Rica Spanish Institute, T234-1001, www.cosi.co.cr. **Laundry** Lavanderías de Costa Rica, near the football pitch, good. **Medical services** The hospital is out of town, T777-0922. Red Cross, T777-0118. **Police** T777-0196. **Post office** On the walkway by the football pitch, 0800-1700.

San José to Panama

Heading through the Talamanca mountains, the Pan-American Highway reaches its highest point at Cerro de la Muerte (Peak of Death) and passes El Chirripó, Costa Rica's highest peak at 3820 m, as the scenic road drops down through the valley of the Río de El General to the tropical lowlands of the Pacific coast and the border with Panama. Private reserves along the route are ideal for birdwatching – here the resplendent quetzal enjoys a quieter life than his Monteverde relations – and mountain streams are stocked with trout providing both sport and food. Lodges and hotels are usually isolated, dotted along the highway. Towards Costa Rica's most southerly point, the Península de Osa is a nature haven of beautiful pathways, palm-fringed beaches and protected rainforest – well worth the effort if you have the time. » *For Sleeping, Eating and other listings, see pages 1075-1080.*

Travelling the Pan-American Highway

» *pp1075-1080.*

From San José the Pan-American Highway runs for 352 km to the Panama border. It's a spectacular journey but challenging if you're driving, with potholes, frequent rockslides during the rainy season, roadworks and generally difficult conditions.

From Cártago, the route heads south over the mountains, beginning with the ascent of **Cerro Buena Vista** (3490 m), a climb of almost 2050 m to the continental divide. A little lower than the peak, the highest point of the road is 3335 m at Km 89 which travels through barren *páramo* scenery. Those unaccustomed to high altitude should beware of mountain sickness brought on by a too rapid ascent, see Health, page 82. For 16 km the road follows the crest of the Talamanca ridge, with views of the Pacific 50 km away, and on clear days of the Atlantic, 80 km to the east.

Four and a half kilometres east of Km 58 (Cañón church) is **Genesis II**, a privately owned 40-ha cloud forest **National Wildlife Refuge**, at 2360 m, bordering the **Tapantí-Macizo de la Muerte National Park**. Accommodation is available here and at several other places along the way, see Sleeping, page 1075. At Km 78 is **Casa Refugio de Ojo de Agua**, a historic pioneer home overlooked but for a couple of picnic tables in front of the house. At Km 80 a steep, dramatic road leads down the spectacular valley of the Río Savegre to **San Gerardo de Dota**, a birdwatchers' paradise. The highest point is at Km 89.5, where temperatures are below zero at night.

San Isidro de El General → *Colour map 7, B3. Population: 45,145. Altitude: 702 m.*

The drop in altitude from the highlands to the growing town of San Isidro passes through fertile valleys growing coffee and raising cattle. The huge **cathedral** on the main plaza is a bold architectural statement, with refreshing approaches to religious iconography inside. The **Museo Regional del Sur** ⓘ *Calle 2, Av 1-0, T771- 5273, Mon-Fri 0800-1200, 1330-1630, free*, is in the old marketplace, now the Complejo Cultural. The 750-ha **Centro Biológico Las Quebradas** ⓘ *7 km north of San Isidro, T771-4131, Tue-Fri 0800-1400, Sat and Sun 0800-1500, closed Oct*, has trails and dormitory lodging for researchers. San Isidro de El General is also the place to stock up for a trip into Parque Nacional Chirripó and to climb Cerro Chirripó Grande (3820 m), see page 1071.

Parque Nacional Chirripó

ⓘ *US$7, crowded in season, make reservations in Oficina de los Parques Nacionales (OPN), Calle 4, Av Central-2, San Isidro de El General, T771-3155, open*

Climbing the Chirripó peaks

The early morning climb to the summit of Cerro Chirripó, Costa Rica's highest mountain, is a refreshing slog after the relative comforts often encountered in Costa Rica. The hike takes you through magnificent cloud forest draped in mosses and ephiphytes before entering a scorched area of *paramo* grasslands with incredible views to the Pacific and Atlantic coastlines on clear days. The widlife – birdlife in particularly – is incredible and, even if you don't see it, you will certainly hear it. The trek itself is not difficult but it is tiring being almost consistently uphill on the way and a knee-crunching, blister-bursting journey down.

From the *refugio* inside the park, you can also explore the nearby Crestones, a volcanic outcrop that has been etched on to the minds of every Costa Rican, and the creatively named Sabana de los Leones and Valle de los Conejos.

If you wish to climb the 3820m Cerro Chirripó, Costa Rica's highest mountain, you must make advance reservations by calling the park service office in San Gerardo, T771-3155, located to the east of San Isidro de El General. After phoning for reservations you are given a couple of days to pay by bank deposit to guarantee your space. Visitors are not allowed into the park without reservations at the *refugio*. During the dry season it's often full, so it's a good idea to make arrangements as soon as possible. Start in the early morning for the 8- to 10-hour hike to the *refugio*. The cost is US$7 entry for each day spent in the park, plus US$6 shelter fee per night. The *refugio* has simple but adequate accommodation, with space for about 80 people and a large kitchen area.

The cold – often frosty in the morning – is a bit of a shock in contrast to the rest of Costa Rica, but you can rent blankets and sleeping bags from the *refugio* (US$1 each). Gas cookers are also available for hire (US$2). There are sufficient water supplies en route so you will need only to carry your food supplies. Electrical power at the *refugio* is only for a couple of hours each night, so be sure to bring a flashlight. The top of Chirripó is located another 5.1 km from the Crestones base camp.

In addition to the high camp there is a shelter about half way up, **Refugio Llano Bonito** (2500 m), which is simple and occasionally clean, with wooden floor, two levels to sleep on, no door but wind protection, drinking water and toilet. It's about four hours' walk from San Gerardo and three hours' walk on to **Refugios Base Crestones**. Plan for at least two nights on the mountain – although you can do it with only one night if you want. While nights can be cold, daytime temperatures tend to be warm to hot, so go prepared with sunscreen and hat. In the rainy season, trails up the plateau are slippery and muddy, and fog obscures the views. Time your descent to catch the afternoon bus back to San Isidro.

0600-1700. If you want to walk or climb in the park, get food in San Isidro and book accommodation at the OPN. Take the 0500 Pueblo Nuevo bus from northwest corner of Parque Central, or the 1400 from the new bus station to San Gerardo de Rivas (US$1.05, 1½ hrs, return at 0700 and 1600), which passes the entrance to the park. Interesting trip up the Río Chirripó valley.

San Isidro de El General is west of Costa Rica's highest mountain Cerro Chirripó Grande (3820 m) in the middle of Parque Nacional Chirripó (50,150 ha). Treks starts from San Gerardo de Rivas (see below). The views from the hilltops are splendid and the high plateau near the summit is an interesting alpine environment with lakes of glacial origin and diverse flora and fauna. The park includes a considerable portion of cloud forest and the walk is rewarding.

Parque Nacional Chirripó neighbours **Parque Internacional La Amistad** (193,929 ha), established in 1982, and together they extend along the Cordillera de Talamanca to the Panamanian border, comprising the largest area of virgin forest in the country with the greatest biological diversity.

San Gerardo de Rivas

Situated in a cool, pleasant spot, San Gerardo de Rivas is at the confluence of the Río Blanco and the Río Pacífico Chirripó. Close to Parque Nacional Chirripó entrance, it is the starting point for the climb up **Cerro Chirripó Grande** (3820 m). If you haven't booked accommodation at the refugio in San Isidro you can book it at the **MINAE office** (see box, page 1071).

Handy for weary legs after the climb, there are **hot springs** ⓘ *entrance US$1*, in the area. Before crossing the new concrete bridge turn left to 'Herradura' for 10 minutes then look for the sign after Parque Las Rosas; go down to the suspension bridge, cross the river and continue for 10 minutes to the house where you pay.

Buenos Aires to Paso Real

Continuing southeast, a good road sinks slowly through the Río General valley where the Talamanca Mountains dominate the skyline. At Km 197 (from San José), the change from coffee to fruit is complete; at the junction for **Buenos Aires** is the huge **Del Monte** cannery. The town, a few kilometres off the Pan-American Highway, has some simple accommodation.

Heading 17 km east towards the mountains is the **Reserva Biológica Durika**, a privately owned reserve of roughly 800 ha, aiming to create a self-sustained community in the Talamanca mountains. Accommodation is available in some rustic cabins.

South along the highway, the small towns of Térraba and Boruca are the most prominent remains of the nation's indigenous population. The community of **Boruca**, with a small hostal (F), has a small, poorly maintained museum, but every year the **Fiesta de los Diablitos** on the last day of December and first two days of January and the last day of January and the first two days of February in **Rey Curre** see the culture come alive in a festival of music, dance and costume. Daily bus to Boruca from Buenos Aires, 1130, 1½ hours.

At **Paso Real** the highway heads west to Palmar Norte, with a turn heading towards San Vito (see below) and the Panamanian border.

Palmar Norte and Palmar Sur

Taking a sharp turn at Paso Real (straight on for San Vito – see below), the Pan-American Highway heads west to Palmar Norte (Km 257 – with gas station) from where a paved road leads to Ciudad Cortés. A new road heads northwest to Dominical (see page 1063).

Crossing the Río Grande de Terraba leads to Palmar Sur, 90 km from the Panamanian border. There are several stone spheres in the area. A banana plantation close to town has stone spheres – 1.5 m in diameter and accurate within 5 mm – of pre-Columbian manufacture, though their use is a matter of conjecture. Recent theories are that they were made to represent the planets of the solar system, or that they were border markers.

From Palmar Sur the Pan-American Highway heads southeast to Chacarita (33 km) where a road turns off to the Osa Peninsula, to Río Claro (another 26 km) where a road leads to Golfito, another 15 km leads to Ciudad Neily which is 16 km from the border at Paso Canoas.

Border essentials: Costa Rica-Panama

Paso Canoas
Shops sell luxury items brought from Panama at prices considerably lower than those of Costa Rica (for example sunglasses, stereo equipment, kitchen utensils, etc).
Immigration Border open 0600-2200 (Costa Rica time).
Costa Rica is 1 hr behind Panama. For information on entering Panama, see Visas and immigration on page 1114.
Customs No fruit or vegetables can be taken into Panama. **Crossing by private vehicle**: Those motoring north can get insurance cover at the border for US$17 ensuring public liability and property damage.

Sierpe

Through a matrix of cooperative banana and African plantations, a road leads to Sierpe, on the Río Sierpe, where there are several small hotels and the departure point for boats to Bahía Drake, see page 1081.

Paso Real to San Vito

pp1075-1080. Colour map 7, B4.

The road from Paso Real to San Vito is now paved and has lovely views. **La Amistad International Park** has few facilities for visitors at present, but one lodge is found way up in the hills beyond Potrero Grande, just south of the Paso Real junction on the way to San Vito. Near the border is **San Vito**. Originally built by Italian immigrants among denuded hills, it is a prosperous but undistinguished town.

On the road from San Vito to Ciudad Neily at Las Cruces are the world-renowned **Wilson Botanical Gardens** ⓘ *T773-4004, www.ots.ac.cr, US$6, good self-guide booklet for the principal trail US$2.20*, owned by the **Organization for Tropical Studies**, 6 km from San Vito. In 360 ha of forest reserve over 5000 species of tropical plants, orchids, other epiphytes and trees with 331 resident bird species. It is possible to spend the night here if you arrange first with the **OTS** ⓘ *T240-6696, in San José: AL per person all inclusive, US$18 per person for day visits with lunch*). On the same road is **Finca Cántaros** ⓘ *T773-3760*, specializing in local arts and crafts, owned by Gail Hewson Gómez. It's one of the best craft shops in Costa Rica – worth a look even if you don't buy anything.

Border with Panama-Sabalito

The road from San Vito to Ciudad Neily is paved, in good condition and offers some of the best coastal views in the country as the road rapidly falls through the hills. From San Vito a good gravel road, paved in places, runs via Sabalito (Banco Nacional) to the Panama border at Río Sereno. There are buses from Sabalito to San José. See Panama chapter for details of this border crossing.

Golfito and around

pp1075-1080. Colour map 7, B4.

Thirty-one kilometres north of the border a road branches south at Río Claro (several pensiones and a fuel station) to the former banana port of Golfito, a 6-km long linear settlement bordering the Golfo Dulce and steep forested hills. While elements of hard sweat and dock labour remain, Golfito's prominence today comes from being Costa

Rica's only free port, set up in 1990, selling goods tax free at about 60% of normal prices. Popular with shoppers from throughout the country, it can be difficult to get a hotel room at weekends. Check out www.golfito.info for information on lodging and activities in the area.

Golfito also provides boat and ferry access to Puerto Jiménez and the Osa Peninsula, and popular fishing and surfing beaches to the south of the town.

Entering the town from the south heading north there are a few hotels where the road meets the coast. In 2 km is the small town centre of painted buildings with saloon bars, open-fronted restaurants and cheap accommodation – probably the best stop for budget travellers. Nearby is the dilapidated *muellecito* used by the ferries to Puerto Jiménez and water taxis. A further kilometre north are the container port facilities and the **Standard Fruit Company**'s local HQ, though many of the banana plantations have been turned over to oil palm and other crops. Beyond the dock is the free port, airstrip and another set of hotels.

The **Refugio Nacional de Fauna Silvestre Golfito**, in the steep forested hills overlooking Golfito, was created to protect Golfito's watershed. Rich in rare and medicinal plants with abundant fauna, there are some excellent hikes in the refuge. Supervised by the University of Costa Rica, they have a field office in Golfito.

Thirty minutes by water taxi from Golfito, you can visit **Casa Orquídeas** ⓘ *T775-1614, tours last about 2½ hrs, US$5 per person, US$20 minimum, closed Fri*, a family-owned botanical garden with a large collection of herbs, orchids and local flowers and trees, that you can see, smell, touch and taste.

To the north of Golfito is the **Parque Nacional Piedras Blancas** tropical wet forest. The area was being exploited for wood products, but has been steadily purchased since 1991 with help from the Austrian government and private interests, notably the classical Austrian violinist Michael Schnitzler. All logging has now ceased and efforts are devoted to a research centre and ecotourism, concentrated in an area designated **Parque Nacional Esquinas**. Near the village of **La Gamba** a tourist lodge has been built (see Sleeping, below). La Gamba is 6 km along a dirt road from Golfito, or 4 km from Briceño on the Pan-American Highway between Piedras Blancas and Río Claro.

Beaches around Golfito

Playa de Cacao is about 6 km (1½ hour walk) north of Golfito round the bay, or a short trip by water taxi. Further north is the secluded beach of **Playa San Josecito** with a couple of adventure-based lodges.

About 15 km by sea south of Golfito, and reached by water taxi or a long bus journey (US$2 by *colectivo* ferry from the small dock; 0600 and 1200, return 0500, 1300), **Playa Zancudo** is a long stretch of clean golden sound, dotted with a few rustic hotels ideal for relaxing and lazing away the days. Still further south is **Pavones**, where a world record left-hand wave has elevated the rocky beach to the realm of surfing legend. South of Pavones, towards the end of the peninsular and at the mouth of the Golfo Dulce is **Punta Banco**.

Ciudad Neily, Paso Canoas and the Panama border

Ciudad Neily is an uninspiring town providing useful transport links between San Vito in the highlands and the coastal plain, and is roughly 16 km from Paso Canoas on the border with Panama. Paso Canoas is a little piece of chaos with traders buying and selling to take advantage of the difference in prices between Costa Rica and Panama. With little to hold you, there is little reason to visit unless heading to Panama. If misfortune should find you having to stay the night, there are some reasonable options.

Sleeping

Travelling the Pan-American Highway *p1070*

A **Hotel de Montaña Savegre**, San Gerardo de Dota, T740-1028, www.savegre.co.cr. Waterfalls, trout fishing, prices include meals.

A-B **Genesis II Lodge**, National Wildlife Refuge, T381-0739, www.genesis-two.com. In rooms with shared bath, for birders and naturalists. The trees are literally dripping with epiphytes in this cloud forest and it is a worthwhile stopover. **Camping (G)** with bath and shower provided, tents available for rent. There is plenty to do including a Treescape canopy system, a suspension bridge, 3 platforms and a couple of zips (US$25 for guests, US$35 for day visitors) There is also a **volunteer programme** – minimum duration 4 weeks at US$150 per week. Contact Steve and Paula Friedman, Apartado 655, 7050 Cártago, or SJO 2031, Unit C-101, PO Box 025216, 1601 NW 97th Av, Miami FL33102-5216.

A-B **Trogón Lodge**, San Gerardo de Dota, T740-1051, www.grupomawamba.com. 23 fine wooden cabins with private bathroom, set amongst beautiful gardens connected by paths used by dive-bombing hummingbirds.

B **Finca Eddie Serano Mirador de Quetzales**, Km 70, T381-8456. Price per person. 43-ha forest property at 2650 m. Eddie Serrano has passed away, but one of his sons will show visitors quetzals (almost guaranteed but don't tell anyone at Monteverde Cloud Forest) and other endemic species of the highlands, 10 cabins, sleeping 2-5, with wonderful views, private bath, price includes breakfast, dinner and guided hike.

D **Hotel and Restaurant Georgina**, Km 95, T770-8043. At almost 3300 m, Costa Rica's highest hotel, basic, clean, friendly, good food (used by southbound **Tracopa** buses), good birdwatching; ask owners for directions for a nice walk to see quetzals.

Camping

Los Ranchos, San Gerardo de Dota, at the bottom of the hill, T771-2376. Camping in perfect surroundings. No transport down here, but pick-ups from the highway can be arranged.

See also **Los Genesis II Lodge**, above.

San Isidro de El General *p1070*

A **Rancho La Botija**, out of town on the road to San Gerardo, T770-2146, www.ranchola botija.com. Restaurant, pool, hiking to nearby petroglyphs, open 0900 at weekends, great restaurant littered with fragments of *botijas*. Recommended.

B **Talari Mountain Lodge**, 10 mins from San Isidro on the road to San Gerardo, T771-0341, www.talari.co.cr. 8-ha farm, with bath, riverside cabins, known for birdwatching, rustic.

C **Hotel Los Crestones**, in town, T770-1200. Big rooms, wheelchair accessible.

C-D **Astoria**, on north side of square, T771-0914, expansive hallway, tiny but clean rooms.

D **El Valle**, Calle 2, Av Central-2, T771-0246. Cleanish, one of the better cheapies.

D **Hotel/Restaurant Amaneli**, in town, T771-0352. 41 quite good rooms with private bathroom, fan, some noisy.

D **Hotel Iguazu**, Calle Central, Av 1, T771-2571. Hot water, cable TV, clean, safe with parking.

D-E **Hotel Chirripó**, south side of Parque Central, T771-0529. Private or shared bath, clean, very good restaurant, free covered parking, recommended.

E **Lala**, Calle Central, Av 1, T771-0291. Basic and simple.

San Gerardo de Rivas *p1072*

Most accommodation options can be reached on the community telephone: T771-1866; all are on the road up to the park.

D **El Uran**, at the very top, closest to the park entrance, T771-1669, www.hoteluran.com. Simple, clean rooms, lots of blankets and a restaurant that will feed you early before setting out.

D **Marín**, next to MINAE office, T308-6735. Basic but friendly and good value.

D **Pelícano**, T382-3000. 10 rooms with great views, a bar and restaurant. Beautiful setting with countless birds.

E **Cabinas Bosque**, T771-4129. With a small bar and restaurant. Looks a bit scruffy from the outside, but spotless rooms and great views over the valley from some rooms. (Over the bridge you arrive at the home of **Sr Francisco Elizondo Badilla** (the local 'champion' speed climber and his family who have a small cabin.)

E Cabinas El Descanso, T771-7962, eldescanso@ecotourism.co.cr. Price per person, with 7 bunks, bathroom, hearty meals available, gas stove for hire, horses for rent and guide services offered, recommended.
E Cabinas/Restaurant Elimar, 500 m out of village. Swimming pool, simple restaurant, 4 quite good *cabinas* with private bathroom, hot water.
D-E Roca Dura, opposite the football pitch, T771-1866. Built on a huge boulder, hot showers, good *comedor*, nice view, shop next door, friendly owners.

Camping

You can camp at or near the park office, in San Gerardo near the bus stop. Check in first and pay US$0.30.

Buenos Aires to Paso Real *p1072*

B-C Cabañas, Durika Biological Reserve, T730-0657, www.durika.org. Rustic cabins. Includes 3 vegetarian meals a day, with a wide range of activities including walks, hikes to the summit of Cerro Durika and cultural tours. Around US$10 per person on top of the daily rate.
E Cabinas Violeta, Buenos Aires, next to the fire station, 200 m west of the plaza, T730-0104. Clean, simple, central and OK if you're stuck for the night.
F Cabinas Mary, Buenos Aires, 800 m south of the centre close to the **Aridikes** office, T730-0187. Quiet spot which tries to be clean.

Palmar Norte and Palmar Sur *p1072*

C-E Hotel y Cabinas Casa Amarilla, 300 m east of bus station on the plaza, T786-6251. With fan, cabins are more expensive than the hotel rooms, rooms at back quieter, rooms over restaurant noisy but cheaper.
D Cabinas Tico-Alemán, on the highway near the gas station, T786-6232. 25 *cabinas* with private bathroom. Best in town.
F Hotel Xinia, 150 m east from bus station, T786-6129. 26 rooms, very basic but OK, shared bathroom.

Sierpe *p1073*

A Río Sierpe Lodge, T384-5595. All-inclusive plan with an emphasis on fishing.
B Oleaje Sereno, T786-7580. Good rooms, with restaurant on river bank.
E-F Margarita, T786-7574. 13 good rooms, friendly owners. Good value.

Paso Real to San Vito *p1073*

B El Ceibo, just down from main plaza, T773-3025. With bath, hot water and TV, good restaurant.
C-D Cabinas Rino, right in the centre of town, T773-3071. Clean and well maintained. Good deal.
D Cabinas Las Huacas, near Cabinas Firenze, T773-3115. 13 OK cabinas with private bathroom, hot water, TV, which were looking very run-down when visited.
E Las Mirlas, 500 m out of town on road to Sabalito, T773-3714. In same location as Hotel Pitier, but more attractive.
F Cabinas Firenze, close to the gas station, on the road from San Isidro, T773-3741. 6 basic *cabinas*, sleep 5, with private bathroom.
F Colono, plaza area, T773-4543. Cheap and central.
F Hotel Pitier, 500 m out of town on road to Sabalito, T773-3027. Clean, with bath.

Golfito *p1073*

AL Esquinas Rainforest Lodge, near La Gamba, 6 km from Golfito, T775-0901, www.esquinaslodge.com. Full board, private baths, verandas overlooking the forest, tours, all profits to the local community.
B Las Gaviotas, next to El Gran Ceibo, T775-0062, lasgaviotas@hotmail.com. 21 cabins and rooms, with bath, a/c and with excellent restaurant looking out over the waterfront.
B Sierra, at the northernmost part of town, near the airport and free zone, T775-0666. 72 double rooms, a/c, a couple of pools, restaurant. Rooms are better than the place looks from the outside.
C Golfo Azul, T775-0871. 20 comfortable large rooms, with bath and a/c, good restaurant.
C La Purruja Lodge, 4 km south of Golfito, T775-5054, www.purruja.com. 5 duplex cabins with bath, plus camping US$2 per tent.
D Delfina, town centre, T775-0043. Shared bath, fan, friendly, basic. Some rooms with private bath much better. Rooms on street are noisy, parking available.
D Mar y Luna, T775-0192. 8 rooms sleeping 2-4, with bath, fan, restaurant on stilts above the sea, quiet spot, good deal.

D Melissa, behind **Delfina**, T775-0443. 4 simple rooms, with private bath, clean and quiet, great spot overlooking bay. Parking and recommended.
D-E Del Cerro, close to the docks, T775-0006. 20 simple rooms sleeping 1-6, private bathroom, laundry services, fishing boat rentals.
D-E Golfito, central, T775-0047. Quiet, with a couple of rooms overlooking the bay and an apartment at US$30. A little run-down but OK.
E Costa Rica Surf, T775-0034. 25 dark rooms, most with private bath. Big bar downstairs. Not the best in town but OK.
F El Uno, above Chinese restaurant of same name, T775-0061. Very basic and mildly amusing if you fancy pretending to be a banana in a packing case, but friendly.

Beaches around Golfito *p1074*
L Tiskita Jungle Lodge, Punta Banco, T296-8125, www.tiskita-lodge.co.cr. A 162-ha property including a fruit farm, with excellent birdwatching, 14 cabins overlooking ocean. Overlooks beach, cool breezes, waterfall, jungle pools, trails through virgin forest – great spot.
L-A Cabinas La Ponderosa, Pavones, T824-4145 (T954-771-9166 in USA), www.cabinaslaponderosa.com. Owned by 2 surfers, large cabins, fan or a/c, with bath (hot water), walking, horse riding, fishing, diving and surfing; also house for rent (sleeps 6), restaurant.
A-B Oasis on the Beach, Playa Zancudo, T776-0087, www.oasisonthebeach.com. Cabins and apartments with kitchenettes, internet and tours. Great spot and atmosphere.
A Latitude 8, Playa Zancudo, T776-0168, www.latitude8lodge.com. A couple of secluded, tranquil cabins with full kitchen and hot water.
A Los Cocos, Playa Zancudo, Apdo 88, Golfito, T776-0012, www.loscocos.com. Beach front cabins at the ocean with private bathroom, hot water, mosquito net, fan, kitchenette, refrigerator, veranda. Also provide boat tours and taxi service. Discounts for longer stays. Heavenly.
B Pavones Surf Lodge, Pavones, T222-2224 (San José). Includes meals, 2 cabins with bath, 6 rooms with shared bath.
B-C Coloso Del Mar, Playa Zancudo, T776-0050, www.coloso-del-mar.com. Great little spot with 4 simple cabins overlooking the beach, Tico/Caribbean restaurant.
B-C Mira Olas, Pavones, T393-7742. Cabins with kitchen and fan, low monthly rates, jungle trail.
B-C Sol y Mar, Playa Zancudo, T776-0014, www.zancudo.com. 4 screened cabins, hot water, fan, 3-storey rental house, US$700 per month, 50 m from ocean, bar/restaurant, meals 0700-2000, home-baked bread, great fruit shakes, volleyball with lights for evening play, badminton, paddleball, boogie boards, library. Highly recommended.
E Pensión Fin del Mundo, Playa Zancudo, over **Restaurant Tranquilo**. 6 simple rooms with fan, mosquito net, clean, shared bathroom. English book exchange at Tienda Buen Precio.
E Rancho Burica, Pavones. With thatched cabins, horse riding, fishing, tours to Guaymí indigenous reserve.

Ciudad Neily, Paso Canoas and the Panama border *p1074*
Ciudad Neily
C Cabinas Andrea, T783-3784. 18 clean *cabinas* with private bathroom, a/c or fan, TV. Popular with Ticos coming through town, handy for main bus terminal.
D-E El Rancho, just off the highway, T783-3060. 50 resort-style cabins with bath, TV, much cheaper without, restaurant opens at 1600.
E Cabinas Heileen, north of plaza, T783-3080. Simple *cabinas* with private bathroom, fan.
E Hotel Musuco, just off the Pan-American Highway, T783-3048. With bath, cheaper without, fan, clean and quiet. Good deal.
F Hotel Villa, north of **Hotel Musoc**, T783-5120. Cheapest and last option in town.

Paso Canoas
D Cabinas Interamericano, T732-2041. With bath and fan, some with a/c, good value upstairs, restaurant.
E Cabinas Jiménez, T732-2258. Quite good *cabinas* with private bathroom, fan. Very clean, good deal.
E Cabinas Jiménez Annexe, T732-2258. OK if all else is full.
E Hilda, south of town, T732-2873. Good rooms, very clean, restaurant over the road. Recommended.

F **Cabinas El Paso**, T732-2740. OK rooms with shower.

Eating

San Isidro de El General *p1070*

‡‡ **La Cascada**, Av 2 and Calle 2, T771-6479. Balcony bar where the bright young things hang out.
‡‡ **Restaurant Crestones**, south of the main plaza, T771-1218. Serves a good mix of snacks, drinks and lively company.
‡‡ **Restaurant El Tenedor**, Calle Central, Av Central-1, T771-0881. Good food, friendly, big pizzas, recommended.
‡‡ **Soda Chirripó**, south side of the main plaza. Gets the vote from the current gringo crowd in town.
‡ **La Marisquería**, corner of Av 0 and Calle 4. Simple setting but great *ceviche*.
‡ **Soda J&P**, indoor market south of the main plaza. The best of many.

Paso Real to San Vito *p1073*

‡‡ **Lilianas**, San Vito. Still showing homage to the town's Italian heritage with good pasta dishes and pizza.
‡ **Restaurant Nelly**, San Vito, near Cabinas Las Huacas. Good wholesome truck drivers' fayre.

Golfito *p1073*

Many seafood places along the seafront.
‡‡ **Cubana**, near post office. Good food. Try the *batidos*.
‡‡ **El Uno**, near Cubana. Good, reasonably priced seafood.
‡‡ **La Dama del Delfín Restaurant**, downtown. Breakfast from 0700, snacks (hamburger, sandwiches, spaghetti), home-baked goods, closed for dinner and Sun.
‡ **Le Eurekita**, centre. Serves a mean breakfast of *huevos rancheros*.

Beaches around Golfito *p1074*

‡‡ **Bar y Restaurant Tranquilo**, Playa Zancudo. A lively spot between Zancudo Beach Club and Coloso del Mar.
‡‡ **Macondo**, Playa Zancudo. A new Italian restaurant which also has a couple of rooms.
‡ **Soda Katherine**, Playa Zancudo, T776-0124. From US$4, great Tico fare; also simple cabins.

Activities and tours

San Isidro de El General *p1070*

Tour operators

Ciprotur, Calle 4, Av 1-3, T771-6096, www.ecotourism.co.cr. Good information on services throughout the southern region.
Selvamar, Calle 1, Av 2-4, T771-4582, www.exploringcostarica.com, general tours and the main contact for out of the way destinations in the southern region.

Golfito *p1073*

Tour operators

Land Sea Tours, T775-1614, landsea@racsa.co.cr, know everything there is to know about the area. They can organize almost anything including national and international flights, and can advise on the minimal opportunities for crewing on yachts heading up and down the coast.

Transport

San Isidro de El General *p1070*

Bus Terminal at Av 6, Calle Central-2 at the back of the new market and adjacent streets but most arrive and depart from bus depots along the Pan-American Highway. From **San José** (just outside Terminal Coca Cola), hourly service 0530-1700, US$3.30, 3 hrs (buses to the capital leave from the highway, Calle 2-4). To **Quepos** via **Dominical** at 0500 and 1330, 3 hrs. However, **Tracopa** buses coming from **San José**, going south go from Calle 3/Pan-American Highway, behind church, to **Palmar Norte**, US$2.25; **Paso Canoas**, 0830-1545, 1930 (direct), 2100; **David** (Panama) direct, 1000 and 1500; **Golfito** direct at 1800; **Puerto Jiménez**, 0630, 0900 and 1500. Waiting room but no reservations or tickets sold. **Musoc** buses leave from the intersection of Calle 2-4 with the Pan-American Highway.

Local buses tend to leave from the newish bus terminal to the south of the main plaza. Buses to **San Gerardo de Rivas** and **Cerro Chirripó** leave at 1400, returning at 1600. There is an early morning bus to San Gerardo leaving at 0500.

Palmar Norte and Palmar Sur *p1072*

Air Daily flights with Sansa (US$72)and Nature Air, **San José**-Palmar Sur (US$73 one way).

Bus Express bus to **Palmar Norte** from Terminal Alfaro, with **Tracopa** from **San José**, 7 daily 0600-1800, 5 hrs, via **San Isidro de El General**, 5 buses return to the capital 0445-1300. 5 buses daily to **Sierpe** for the boat to **Bahía Drake** (page 1081) 45 mins. Also buses north to **Dominical**, and south to the **Golfito** and the Panamanian border.

Sierpe *p1073*
Bus and Boat 5 buses daily to **Palmar Norte**, 0530-1530, 45 mins. Boats down Río Sierpe to **Bahía Drake**, 1½ hrs, US$70 per boat. Many hotels in Drake have boats that pick up guests, you may be able to get a lift, US$15 per person.

Paso Real to San Vito *p1073*
Bus Direct buses **San José** to San Vito, 4 daily, 0545, 0815, 1130 and 1445, from Terminal Alfaro, Calle 14, Av 5; direct bus San Vito-San José 0500, 0730, 1000, 1500, 6 hrs, corriente buses take 8 hrs. Alternative route, not all paved, via Cd Neily (see below); from San Vito to **Las Cruces** at 0530 and 0700; sit on the left coming up, right going down, to admire the wonderful scenery; return buses pass Las Cruces at 1510.

Golfito *p1073*
Air Several daily flights to **San José**, with Sansa (US$75 one way). Runway is all weather, tight landing between trees; 2 km from town, taxi US$0.50.

Bus From **San José** 0700 (8½ hrs) and 1500 (6 hrs express) daily from Terminal Alfaro, return 0500 (express), 1300, US$6; from **San Isidro de El General**, take 0730 bus to Río Claro and wait for bus coming from Cd Neily. To **Paso Canoas**, US$1.25, hourly from outside Soda Pavo, 1½ hrs. To **Pavones** at 1000 and 1500, and return at 0430 and 1230, 3 hrs, US$2.50. A spit of land continues south to Punta Burica with no roads and only a couple of villages.

Sea Water taxis in and around Golfito, Froylan Lopex, T824-6571, to Cacao Beach, Punta Zancudo, Punta Encanto or to order, US$20 per hr up to 5 persons. **Docks** Land Sea Tours (see Tour operators, above) and Banana Bay Marina (T775-0838, www.bananabaymarina.com) accommodate boats up to 150 ft – either of these places might be an option if heading south on a boat, but you'll need to ask nicely and be a bit lucky.

Ciudad Neily, Paso Canoas and the Panama border *p1074*
Bus The terminal in Cd Neily is at the northern end of town, beside the Mercado Central. Daily bus to **San José**, with **Tracopa**, from main square (6 daily, US$6, 7 hrs, on Sun buses from the border are full by the time they reach Cd Neily). Buses arrive at Av 5 and Calle 14 in San José. Services to **San Vito** inland, and to **Palmar**, **Cortés** and **Dominical** (0600 and 1430, 3 hrs). Also to **Puerto Jiménez** at 0700 and 1400, 4 hrs. Bus for **Golfito** leaves from the centre of town every 30 mins. The Pan-American Highway goes south (plenty of buses, 20 mins, US$0.35) to Paso Canoas on the Panamanian border. *Colectivo* US$1.10, very quick.

San José-Paso Canoas, US$9, 8 hrs from Terminal Alfaro at 0500, 1100 (direct), 1300, 1800, return 0400, 0730, 0900, 1500 (T223-7685). Not all buses go to the border. International buses that reach the border after closing time wait there till the following day. Hourly buses to Cd Neily, ½ hourly to Golfito.

❶ Directory

San Isidro de El General *p1070*
Banks Banco Nacional, on north side of plaza, Mon-Fri, 0830-1545. **Internet** Bruncanet, on north side of plaza, and MS Internet Café. **Post office** 3 blocks south of the church. **Telephone** ICE office on Calle 4, Av 3-PAH.

Paso Real to San Vito *p1073*
Banks There are branches of Banco Nacional and Banco Popular in San Vito. **Post office and internet** The post office is at the northern end of town.

Golfito *p1073*
Banks Banco Nacional near dock, Mon-Fri 0830-1535, T775-1622. **Internet** Internet café, on ground floor below Hotel Golfito. Good set up, good machines.

Península de Osa – rain, snakes and mosquitoes

Avoid the rainy season. Bring umbrellas (not raincoats, too hot), because it will rain, unless you are hiking, in which case you may prefer to get wet. Shelters can be found here and there, so only mosquito netting is indispensable. Bring all your food if you haven't arranged otherwise; food can only be obtained at Puerto Jiménez and Agujitas in the whole peninsula, and lodging likewise. The cleared areas (mostly outside the park, or along the beach) can be devastatingly hot. Chiggers (*coloradillas*) and horseflies infest the horse pastures and can be a nuisance, similarly sandflies on the beaches; bring spray-on insect repellent. Another suggestion is vitamin B1 pills (called thiamine, or *tiamina*). Mosquitoes are supposed to detest the smell and leave you alone, but see Health, page 53. Get the Instituto Geográfico maps, scale 1:50,000. Remember finally that, as in any tropical forest, you may find some unfriendly wildlife like snakes (fer-de-lance and bushmaster snakes may attack without provocation), and herds of peccaries. You should find the most suitable method for keeping your feet dry and protecting your ankles; for some, rubber boots are the thing, for others light footwear which dries quickly.

Ciudad Neily, Paso Canoas and the Panama border *p1074*
Banks In Cd Neily, there are branches of Banco Nacional and Banco de Costa Rica. At Paso Canoas, banks on either side of border close at 1600 local time. Slightly better dollar rate for colones on the Costa Rican side. No difficulty in getting rid of surplus colones with money changers.
Internet Planet Internet at the northern end of Cd Neily.

Península de Osa

Across the Golfo Dulce is the hook-shaped appendage of the Osa Peninsula. Some distance from most other places of interest in the country, the journey is worthwhile as the peninsula is world famous for the diversity of flora and fauna in Parque Nacional Corcovado, with some of the best rainforest trekking and trails in the country. » *For Sleeping, Eating and other listings, see pages 1084-1086.*

Ins and outs

Getting there Getting to the peninsula is getting easier. There is a daily ferry service from Golifito arriving at the small dock in Puerto Jiménez. There are also bus services from San José, passing through San Isidro de El General and Palmar North, and from the south at Ciudad Neily. Boats ply the coastal route from Sierpe to Bahía Drake and you can fly from San José.

Puerto Jiménez → *Colour map 7, B4. Population: 2500.*

Once the gold-mining centre of the Osa Peninsula, Puerto Jiménez still has the feel of a frontier town although most miners were cleared from the Parque Nacional Corcovado area in 1985.

Today, Puerto Jiménez is a popular destination with its laid-back, occasionally lively atmosphere, reasonable beaches nearby and, of course, the beautiful national park on the Pacific side of the peninsula. A particular charm of Puerto Jiménez, barely five blocks square, is its relative freedom from road traffic – Scarlet macaws can be seen roosting in the trees around the football pitch. There are good local walks to the jungle, where you will see monkeys and many birds, and to beaches and mangroves. There is a seasonal migration of humpbacks between October and March.

Look out for El Sol de Osa, *www.soldeosa.com, an up-to-date community information service.*

Geological treasures can be seen at the gold mine at **Dos Brazos** about 15 km west of town; ask for the road which goes uphill beyond the town, to see the local gold mines. Several *colectivo* taxis a day to Dos Brazos, last bus back at 1530 (often late); taxi US$7.25. You can also take a long walk to **Carate** (see below) which has a gold mine. Branch to the right and in 4 km there are good views of the peninsula. A topographical map is a big help, obtainable from Instituto Geográfico in San José. At **Cabo Matapalo** on the tip of the peninsula, 18 km south of Puerto Jiménez, are several expensive sleeping options.

Bahía Drake

Arriving by boat from Sierpe, Bahía Drake provides a northern entrance point to the Osa Peninsula and Parque Nacional Corcovado. In March 1579, Sir Francis Drake careened his ship on Playa Colorada in Bahía Drake. A plaque commemorating the 400th anniversary of the famous pirate's nautical aberration was erected in Agujitas. Life in the bay is not cheap, and combined with transport, costs can quickly mount up. Bahía Drake, which continues south merging seamlessly with Agujitas, is a popular destination for **divers** with Isla Caño nearby. Open water PADI courses (US$325) are available at **Cabinas Jinetes de Osa** or through **Caño Divers** at Pirate Cove.

Puerto Jiménez

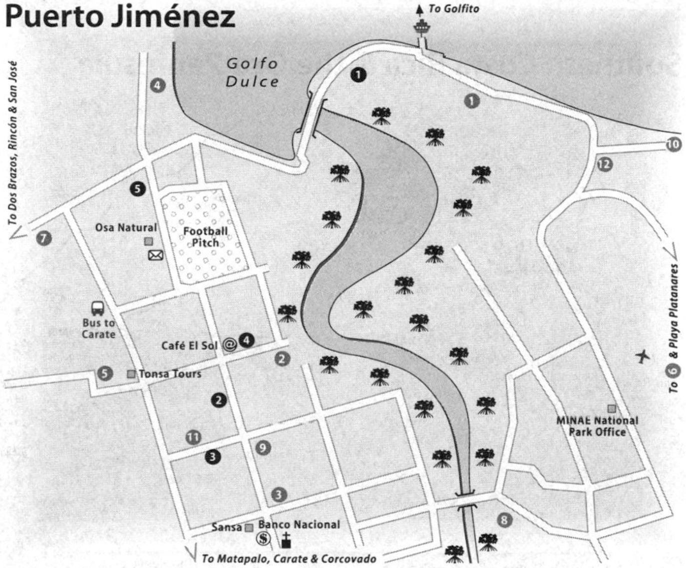

Sleeping
Agua Luna **1**
Cabinas Bosque Mar **2**
Cabinas Marcelina **3**
Cabinas Puerto Jiménez **4**
Cabinas Thompson **5**
Crocodile Bay Lodge **6**
Iguana Iguana **7**
La Choza del Manglares **8**
Oro Verde **9**
Parrot Bay Village **10**
Pensión Quintero **11**
Puerto Jiménez Yacht Club **12**

Eating
Agua Luna **1**
Carolina & Escondido Trex **2**
Il Giardino **3**
Juanita's Mexican Bar & Grille **4**
Pizza Rock **5**

Parque Nacional Corcovado

▸▸ *pp1084-1086. Colour map 7, C4.*

Corcovado National Park, including **Reserva Biológica Isla del Caño** (84 ha), comprises over 42,469 ha – just under half the Osa Peninsula. Consisting largely of tropical rainforest, swamps, miles of empty beaches, and some cleared areas now growing back, it is located on the Pacific Ocean at the western end of the peninsula. An ideal spot for just walking along endless beaches, the park is also filled with birds, mammals and six species of cat.

Ins and outs

If short of time and/or money, the simplest way to the park is to take the pick-up truck from outside **Tonsa Tours** in Puerto Jiménez to Playa Carate (most days at 0600 and 1400, 2½ hrs, US$7 one way, returning at 0800 and 1600, ask in advance about departure). Or call **Cirilo Espinosa** (T735-5075), or **Ricardo González** (T735-5068), for a 4WD jeep taxi. It is possible to book a flight from Puerto Jiménez to Carate or La Sirena in the park for US$99 per person, minimum five people. Ask at the airstrip or call T735-5178. The **MINAE office** ⓘ *Puerto Jiménez, near the airport, T735-5036, daily 0830-1200, 1300-1700*, will give permits for entering the park (US$7) and will book accommodation at **La Sirena** in dormitories, maximum 20 people, (F) for bed (reservation essential), take sheets/sleeping bag, camping (F), no reservation needed, three meals available. Bring mosquito netting.

> *Hiking boots and sandals are useful if you are walking any distance in the park.*

Southern Costa Rica & the Osa Peninsula

Around the park

At **Carate** there is a dirt airstrip and a store, run by Gilberto Morales and his wife Roxana (they rent rooms, but they are often full of gold miners; they also have a tent for hire, but take a sleeping bag). There are several luxury options here and a couple more lodges 30 minutes' walk west along the beach.

Five minutes' walk further down the beach is **La Leona** park wardens' station and entrance to the park. To go beyond here costs US$7 per day, whether you are walking along the beach to La Sirena (18 km, six hours, take sun protection), or just visiting for the day. Lodging is available (see page 1085). Beyond here to the end of **Playa Madrigal** is another 2½-hours' walk, partly sandy, partly rocky, with some rock pools and rusty shipwrecks looking like modern art sculptures. The shore rises steeply into the jungle, which grows thickly with mangroves, almonds and coconut palms. Check with wardens about high tide so you don't get stuck. There are a couple of rivers along the beach, the first, Río Madrigal, is only about 15 minutes beyond La Leona (lovely and clear, deep enough for swimming about 200 m upstream, a good place for spotting wildlife). The best place for seeing wildlife, though, is La Sirena, where there are paths inland and the terrain is flatter and more isolated.

You can head inland from Sirena on a trail past three conveniently spaced shelters to **Los Patos**, after passing several rivers full of reptiles (20 km, six to nine hours depending on conditions). The wooden house is the ranger station with electricity and TV, and four beds available at US$1.75 per night; meals possible if you do not bring your own food. Its balcony is a great observation point for birds, especially the redheaded woodpecker. From Los Patos you can carry on to the park border then, crisscrossing the **Río Rincón to La Palma** (small *hostal*), a settlement on the opposite side of the peninsula (13 km, six more hours), from which there are several 'taxis' making the one-hour trip to Puerto Jiménez (see above). An offshoot of this trail will lead you to a raffia swamp that rings the **Corcovado Lagoon**. The lagoon is only accessible by boat, but there are no regular trips. Caymans and alligators survive here, sheltered from the hunters.

From Sirena you can walk north along the coast to the shelter at Llorona (plenty of waterfalls), from which there is a trail to the interior with a shelter at the end. From Llorona you can proceed north through a forest trail and along the beach to the station at **San Pedrillo** on the edge of the park. You can stay here, camping or under roof, and eat with the rangers, who love company. From San Pedrillo you can take the park boat (not cheap) to Isla del Caño, a lovely manned park outpost. See under Quepos for Taximar boat service from Quepos and Dominical to Isla del Caño or Bahía Drake.

Isla del Coco

This has to be one of the world's most distant island destinations: the steep-sided and thickly wooded island and national park of 24 sq km lies 320 km off the Osa Peninsula, on the Cocos Ridge, which extends some 1400 km southwest to the Galápagos Islands. There is virtually nothing on the island, apart from a few endemic species, but you can visit for some of the world's best diving. The BBC/Discovery Channel shot some dramatic silhouetted images of tiger sharks here for their *Blue Planet* series. Historically, though, it was a refuge for pirates who are supposed to have buried great treasure here, though none has been found by the 500 or so expeditions looking for the 'x' that marked a spot. Travel by chartered boat can be made in Puntarenas, after a government permit has been obtained, or you can take a scuba diving cruise on the **Okeanos Agressor** ⓘ *T232-0572 ext 60 (in US: PO Drawer K, Morgan City, LA 70381, T504-385-2416)*. The twice-monthly 10-day trips are understandably expensive (about US$3,095 for 10 days).

Sleeping

Puerto Jiménez *p1080, map p1081*

LL Crocodile Bay Lodge, south of town, T735-1115, www.crocodilebay.com. All comforts including pool, swim-up bar, massage and luxury sportfishing.

L Parrot Bay Village, left from the pier, T735-5180, www.parrotbayvillage.com. Fully equipped wooden cabins sleeping 1-5, restaurant, beautiful spot, almost private beach. Cheaper in groups.

A La Choza del Manglares, right beside the mangrove on the river, T735-5002, www.manglares.com. Clean, well-maintained cabins with private bath. In the day regular visits from monkeys, scarlet macaws and the occasional crocodile in the grounds by the river. Completely renovated.

A-B Agua Luna, facing pier, T735-3593, agualu@racsa.co.cr. New rooms sleeping 2-4 with bath, good, although pricey; restaurant next door.

A-B Cabinas Puerto Jiménez, on the gulf shore with good views, T735-5090. New owners of remodelled big rooms, many with private decks looking out to the gulf, spotless.

B-C Cabinas Marcelina, down main street, T735-5007. With bath, big clean, friendly, nice front yard, totally renovated, small discount for youth hostelling members.

D Hotel Oro Verde, down main street, T735-5241. Run by Silvia Duirós Rodríguez, 10 clean, comfortable rooms, with bath and fan, some overlooking the street.

D Iguana Iguana, on road leading out of town, T735-5158. Simple rooms with private bath, restaurant, small bar, pool in high season.

E Cabinas Bosque Mar, T735-5681. Clean, large rooms and restaurant.

E Pizzería Cabinas Mariel, T735-5071. Simple cabins.

F Cabinas Thompson, 50 m from the centre, T735-5910. With bath, fan, clean but dark.

F Pensión Quintero, just off main street, T735-5087. Price per person. Very simple wooden building, but clean and good value, will store luggage. Ask for Fernando Quintero, who rents horses and has a boat for up to 6 passengers, good value; he is also a guide, recommended.

F Puerto Jiménez Yacht Club, turn left off the ferry, T735-5313. Camping pushing up to the beach, with showers and bathrooms. Great spot and a wide range of tours.

Around Puerto Jiménez

LL Lapa Ríos Wilderness Resort, at Cabo Matapalo, T735-5130, www.laparios.com. The cream of the crop. Includes meals. 14 luxury palm-thatched bungalows on private 400-ha reserve (80% virgin forest, US owners Karen and John Lewis), camping trips, boats can be arranged from Golfito. Idyllic, fantastic views, recommended.

AL-A El Remanso Rainforest Beach Lodge, Cabo Matapalo, T735-5569, www.elremanso.com. Houses and cabins for rent, all fully equipped and with ocean views, an oasis of peace.

A Iguanal Lodge, 5 km southeast of Puerto Jiménez behind the airstrip, T829-5865, www.iguanalodge.com. 4 cabins, good swimming and surfing.

Bahía Drake *p1081*

LL Aguila de Osa Inn, the normal landing point, T296-2190, www.aguiladeosa.com. Includes meals; fishing, hiking, canoeing and horse riding available, comfortable cabins made with exotic hardwoods. Recommended.

LL La Paloma Jungle Lodge, T239-0954, www.lapalomalodge.com. Price per person includes meals, 9 cabins with bath, guided tours with resident biologist, pool. Packages available.

L Drake Bay Wilderness Camp, opposite **Aguila de Osa Inn**, T770-8012, www.drakebay.com. Price per person, with meals, cabins, tents available, pleasant family atmosphere, pool, 2 restaurants. Great views. Wide ranges of tours available.

AL Cabinas Jinete de Osa, T236-5637, www.costaricadiving.com. Good hotel, run by 2 brothers from Colorado. Diving a speciality – PADI courses offered. Spacious and airy rooms, all with bath, hot water, fan. Recommended.

AL-A Pirate Cove, northern end of the beach, T786-7845, www.piratecove.com. Very nice tent-like cabins emulate an outdoor experience minus the mud. US$55 per person shared bath, US$70 with bath, 3 meals included.

B Rancho Corcovado Lodge, in the middle of the beach, T786-7059. Price per person. Simple, rustic rooms, many with view, all with bath. Friendly Tico owners, nice open-air restaurant on beach serves *comida típica*. Camping permitted.

D Bella Vista Lodge, on the beach at the southern end of town, T770-8051. The only budget option in town and disappointing. Basic rooms, 2 with bath, 3 shared (even more basic), meals (US$3-5) not included.

Camping

Camping is allowed outside **Rancho Corcovado** (use of electricity and bathrooms included) or outside **Pirate Cove** (north end of beach), no fixed price, small charge for baths.

Parque Nacional Corcovado *p1082*

MINAE office, facing the airstrip, Puerto Jiménez, T735-5036. For booking dormitory accommodation and camping facilities in Corcovado National Park.

LL Casa Corcovado Jungle Lodge, along the coast from San Pedrillo, T256-3181, www.casacorcovado.com. Outside the park in the forest, but with 500 m of beach more or less opposite Isla del Caño, 14 bungalows, many facilities, packages from 2 nights full board with boat transport (2 hrs) from Sierpe.

L-AL Corcovado Lodge, 30 mins' walk west of Carate along the beach, T257-0766, www.costaricaexpeditions.com. 20 walk-in tents with 2 campbeds in each, in a beautiful coconut grove with hammocks overlooking the beach; walk-ins are possible but to be sure of space book through **Costa Rica Expeditions** in San José. Clean showers and toilets; good food, take a flashlight. Behind the camp is a trail into the jungle with a great view of the bay from a clearing; many birds to be seen, plus monkeys and frogs.

A La Leona Eco-Lodge, 30 mins' walk west of Carate along the beach, T735-5705, www.laleonalodge.com. Rustic tent cabins, crocodile spotting, rappelling, yoga and night hikes. Price per person.

F La Leona park wardens' station, at entrance to the park. Maximum 12 people in basic rooms or camping, meals available. Book in high season through SINAC (see page 983).

Eating

Puerto Jiménez *p1080, map p1081*

TTT Agua Luna, on the seashore near the dock, T735-5033. Stylish setting , beautifully presented but pricey.

TTT Il Giardino, just off the main street. Quiet little Italian, with the odd piece of sushi thrown in for good measure, intimate setting, and good food.

TTT-TT Carolina, down the main street, T735-5185. Highly recommended for fish (everything actually), good prices. **Escondido Trex** office at back of restaurant.

TT Juanita's Mexican Bar and Grille, central, T735-5056. Happy hr, crab races, good Mexican fare, seafood from US$4.

T Pollo Frito Opi Opi, north end of town, T735-5192. Fried chicken, hamburgers, fries.

T Soda Bosquemar, on main street, T735-5681. Good food at good prices.

Activities and tours

Puerto Jiménez *p1080, map p1081*

Tour operators

Escondido Trex, in the back of **Carolina**, T735-5210, www.escondidotrex.com. running since 1992, excellent local information, treks, kayaking and jungle trips, from one-day upwards.

MINAE office, facing the airstrip, T735-5036, for booking dormitory lodging and camping facilities in Corcovado National Park.

Aventuras Tropicales, opposite the football pitch, T735-5195, www.osanatural.com. Can book accommodation and has a couple of internet machines.
Tonsa Tours, run by the quiet Jaime, provides many of the normal tours, and also jungle treks across to Carate. Not for the faint-hearted, but certain to be fascinating.

Transport

Puerto Jiménez *p1080, map p1081*
Air There are daily flights between Puerto Jiménez and Golfito with Sansa(US$78) and Nature Air (US$65 one way) from San José.

Bus 1 block west of the main street. A café by the bus terminal is open Sat 0430 for a cheap and reasonable breakfast. From **San José**, just outside Terminal Atlántico Norte (C 12, Av 9-11), there are 2 buses daily to Puerto Jiménez at 0600 amd 1200 via San Isidro, US$7, 8 hrs, return 0500, T735-5189. There are also buses from **San Isidro**, leaving from the Pan-American Highway at 0930 and 1500 daily, US$4.50, returns at 0400 and 1300, 5 hrs. To **Cd Neily** at 0500 and 1400, 3 hrs, US$3. A few *colectivos* to **Carate** depart from outside Restaurant Carolina daily 0530 and 0600, cost US$7. Service may be restricted in the wet season.
coast
Car To reach Puerto Jiménez from the Pan- American Highway (70 km), turn right about 30 km south of Palmar Sur; the road is newly paved to Rincón, thereafter it is driveable with many bridge crossings. There is a police check point 47 km from the Pan-American Highway.

Sea 1 boat leaves from the dock in **Golfito** at 1130, US$2.50, 1½ hrs, return 0600, or you can charter a taxi boat for about US$60, up to 8 passengers.

Directory

Puerto Jiménez *p1080, map p1081*
Banks Branch of Banco Nacional, T735-5155. **Internet** Café El Sol, on main street, 0700-1900, US$8 per hr. **Post office** Opposite the football pitch.

San José to the Atlantic

Heading east from San José the Central Highlands quickly fall away to the sparsely populated flat Caribbean lowlands. The tropical rainforest national parks of Tortuguero and Barra del Colorado, leading through coastal canals and waterways, are a nature lover's paradise with easily arranged trips, normally from San José, into the rainforest. South of the distinctly Caribbean city of Puerto Limón, coastal communities have developed to provide comfortable hangouts and laid-back beach life for all budgets.
▸▸ *For Sleeping, Eating and other listings, see pages 1095-1108.*

There are two routes from San José to Puerto Limón on the Atlantic coast. The newer main route goes over the Cordillera Central, through the Parque Nacional Braulio Carrillo down to Guápiles and Siquirres. This highland section is prone to fog and if driving yourself, requires extra care. The second, more scenic but considerably longer, route follows the old Atlantic railway to Cártago, south of Irazú volcano to Turrialba, joining the main highway at Siquirres.

Parque Nacional Braulio Carrillo → *Colour map 7, B3.*

The third largest of Costa Rica's national parks Parque Nacional Braulio Carrillo was created to protect the high rainforest north of San José from the impact of the new San José-Guápiles-Puerto Limón highway. It extends for 47,583 ha, and encompasses five different types of forest with abundant wildlife including hundreds of species of bird, jaguar, ocelot and Baird's tapir. Various travel agencies offer naturalist tours, approximately US$65 from San José. San José to Guápiles and Puerto Limón buses go through the park.

The entrance to the **Quebrada González centre** ⓘ *daily 0800-1530 US$7*, on the highway is 23 km beyond the Zurquí tunnel, just over the Río Sucio at the Guápiles end. It has a new administration building. To get there, take any bus to the Atlantic and ask to be dropped off. There are three trails: **Las Palmas**, 1.6 km (you need rubber boots); across the road are **El Ceibo**, 1 km, circular; and **Botarrama**, entry 2 km from Quebrada González (El Ceibo and Botarrama are to be joined). The trail has good birdwatching and the views down the Río Patria canyon are impressive. The Zurquí centre near the tunnel has been closed but may open again soon so ask at headquarters. It has services and the 250-m Los Jilqueros trail to the river.

Beyond Quebrada González (1.5 km) is **Los Heliconios** ⓘ *entry US$7*, butterfly garden with an insect museum and amphibians. Adjoining it, **Reserva Turística El Tapir** ⓘ *entry US$7*, has a 20-minute trail and others of one to two hours.

Parque Nacional Braulio Carrillo & Puerto Viejo loop

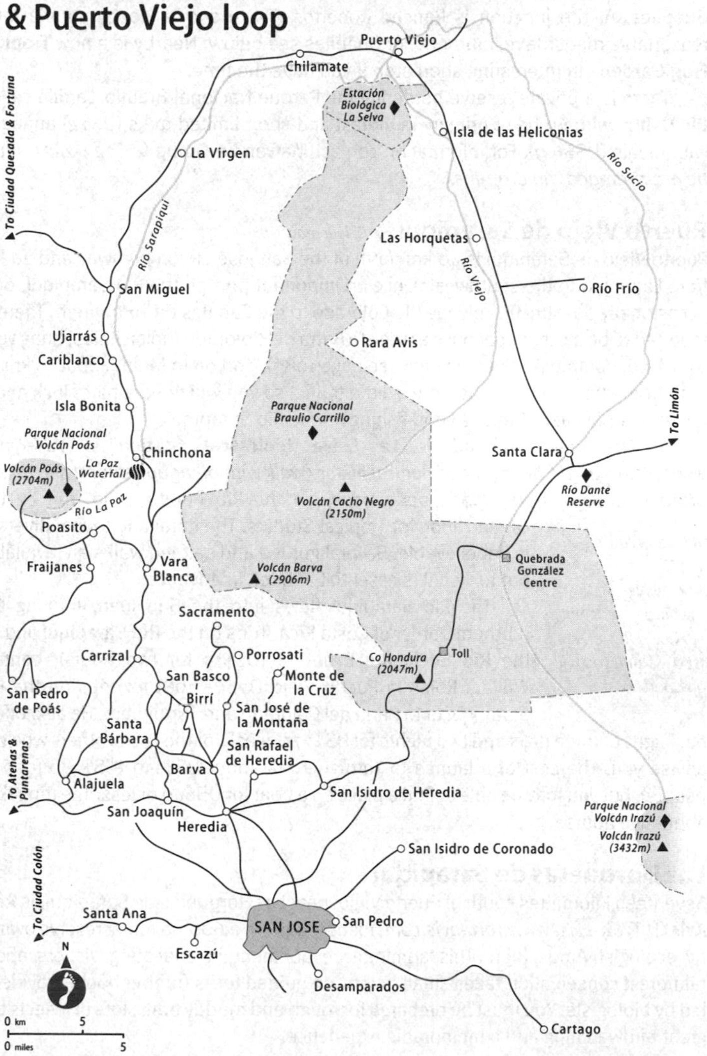

An ingenious **Rainforest Aerial Tram** (*teleférico*) ⓘ *Tue-Sun 0630-1600, Mon 0900-1530, 90 mins' ride costs US$49.50, students with ID and children half price, children under 5 not allowed*, lifts visitors high up into the rainforest, providing a fascinating up-close and personal view of the canopy life and vegetation. The price includes a guided nature walk. It's best to go as early as possible for birds. Tourist buses arrive 0800. There's a guarded car park for private vehicles and restaurant for meals in the park. It can be difficult to get reservations during the high season. There's a **Rainforest Aerial Tram office in San José** ⓘ *Av 7, Calle 7, behind Aurola Holiday Inn, T257-5961; there's an all-inclusive package from San José leaving around 0800 daily, US$78.50, students and under 11s US$53.75, with pick-ups at most major hotels.*

Further on, at the Soda Gallo Pinto is the **Bosque Lluvioso** ⓘ *T224-0819, 0700-1700, entry US$15*, a 170-ha private reserve. It is at Km 56 on the Guápiles highway (**Rancho Redondo**), with a restaurant and trails in primary and secondary forest.

The turn-off at Santa Clara to Puerto Viejo de Sarapiquí is 13 km before Guápiles. At the junction is Rancho Robertos (T711-0050, a good, popular and reasonable roadside restaurant). For Guápiles see below. Nearby is a new **Tropical Frog Garden**, an interesting short stop if you have the time.

There is a private reserve bordering the Parque Nacional Braulio Carrillo called **Río Danta**, with 60 ha of primary rainforest and short limited treks (US$4) arranged with meals (US$6-9). For information contact **Mawamba Group** ⓘ *T223-2421; must be pre-arranged; no drop-ins.*

Puerto Viejo de Sarapiquí → *Colour map 7, B3.*

Puerto Viejo de Sarapiquí is 40 km north of the San José-Limón highway and 20 km from La Virgen to the southwest. Once an important port on the Río Sarapiquí, only occasionally do launches ply the Río Colorado to the Canales de Tortuguero. There is reported to be a cargo boat once a week to Barra del Colorado (no facilities, bring your own food, hammock, sleeping bag; see page 1089), and on to Moín, about 10 km by road from Puerto Limón. But there is little traffic, so you will need a bit of luck and a fair amount of cash. There is good fishing on the Río Sarapiquí.

In the neighbourhood is **La Selva Biological Station** ⓘ *T766-6565, www.ots.ac.cr, 3½ hour guided natural history walk with bilingual naturalists daily at 0800 and 1330-1600, US$25 per person,* on the Río Puerto Viejo, run by the Organization for Tropical Studies. The floral and faunal diversity is unbelievable. Several guided and self-led walks are available but to visit it is essential to book in advance.

The Río San Juan is wholly in Nicaragua, so you technically have to cross the border and then return to Costa Rica. This will cost US$5 and you will need passport/visa.

The Río Sarapiquí flows into the San Juan, forming the northern border of Costa Rica. Trips on the **Río Sarapiquí** and on the **Río Sucio** are beautiful (US$15 for two hours); contact William Rojas in Puerto Viejo (T766-6108) for trips on the Río Sarapiquí or to Barra del Colorado and Tortuguero. He also offers packages of three days and two nights for US$275 or ask for the Lao brothers who will advise you. The cost of a launch to Tortuguero is about US$150 (US$350 for four people), but you may be able to find a place on a boat for US$40 or less. The trip takes about five hours.

Las Horquetas de Sarapiquí

Seventeen kilometres south of Puerto Viejo, near Las Horquetas de Sarapiquí, is **Rara Avis** ⓘ *T764-1111, www.rara-avis.com*, rustic lodges in a 600-ha forest reserve owned by ecologist Amos Bien. This admirable experiment in educating visitors about rainforest conservation takes small groups on guided tours (rubber boots provided), led by biologists. You must be prepared for rough and muddy trails, lots of insects but great birdwatching and a memorable experience.

Border essentials: Costa Rica-Nicaragua

Barra del Colorado

Costa Rican immigration This is not a regular border crossing and there are no formal facilities on the Costa Rican side. Do not leave for Nicaragua by boat or on foot without checking with the Guardia Civil in Barra del Colorado or Tortuguero, who are very helpful. Similarly, check with them if arriving from Nicaragua.

Transport Transport, mostly by boat, is costly, typically US$30 for a ½-day. There are several fishermen who will take you up the coast on their way to fish in Nicaraguan waters, US$20-30. You can go by irregular boat from Barra up the Río Colorado, Río San Juan and Río Sarapiquí to Puerto Viejo, 5-6 hours. A small boat for 4 without roof costs US$150 (or US$50 per person), a larger boat with roof (recommended) costs US$185 for 4; you see caimans, turtles and lots of birds. There are several border checkpoints. Foreigners travelling along Río San Juan must pay US$5 entry and exit tax at Nicaraguan checkpoint and receive stamp in passport. If you have arrived from Nicaragua, an alternative to going south along the coast to Puerto Limón, is to take a bus from the river bank opposite Isla Buena Vista 25 km up the Río Colorado, daily except Sun, leaves 0600, by dirt track to Cariari and then to Guápiles.

Guápiles, Guácimo and Siquirres → *Colour map 7, B3-B4.*

One hour from San José (bus US$1.45), Guápiles is the centre of the Río Frío banana region. It is another 25 km from Guácimo to Siquirres, a clean, friendly town and junction for roads from Turrialba with the main highway and former railways.

Matina

Twenty-eight kilometres beyond Siquirres, heading north at the 'techo rojo' junction is Matina, a small, once-busy town on the railway but off the highway. Today, it is an access point to Tortuguero and the less well-known private **Reserva Natural Pacuare**, 30 km north of Puerto Limón, which is accessible by canal from Matina. Run by Englishman John Denham, it has a 6-km stretch of **leatherback turtle nesting beach**, protected and guarded by the reserve. Volunteers patrol the beach in May and June, measuring and tagging these magnificent marine turtles (US$50 per person per week, includes good meals and accommodation). For volunteer working, contact Carlos Fernández, **Corporación de Abogados** ⓘ *Av 8-10, Calle 19, No 837, San José, T233-0508, fdezlaw@racsa.co.cr.*

Puerto Limón and the Atlantic coast

» *pp1095-1108.*

On a rocky outcrop on an almost featureless coastline, Puerto Limón is the country's most important port. Between Puerto Limón and the Río San Juan on the Nicaraguan border, the long stretch of Atlantic coastline and its handful of small settlements is linked by a canal system that follows the coastline. The region encompasses Parque Nacional Tortuguero, famed for its wildlife and turtle nesting beaches, and Refugio Nacional de Fauna Silvestre Barra del Colorado. The Río San Juan forms the border between Costa Rica and Nicaragua, however the border is not mid-river, but on the Costa Rican bank. English is widely spoken along the coast.

Puerto Limón→ *Colour map 7, B4. Population: 61,494.*

Built on the site of the ancient indigenous village of Cariari, Columbus dropped anchor at Punta Uvita, the island off the coastline, on his fourth and final voyage. The climate is very humid and it rains almost every day. With a mainly black population, and a large Chinese contingent, the town has a distinctly Caribbean feel expressed particularly during carnival each October, but in most bars every weekend.

Parque Vargas and the seafront promenade at the rocky headland are popular places for social gatherings and killing time, making for ideal people-watching territory, especially in the evening. Parque Vargas, sadly rather run-down, is an impressive botanical display with a colourful mural depicting the history of Limón and a bandstand.

On the upside, the nightlife is good, particularly for Caribbean music and dancing, culminating in carnival every October, Costa Rica's largest festival. There is a small **Museo Etnohistórico de Limón** ⓘ *Calle 2, Av 2, Mon-Fri 0900-1200, 1300-1600*, featuring material relating to Columbus' arrival in Limón. The cargo docks are still active with international crews making regular journeys, as well as being the landing point for pristine floating palaces cruising the Caribbean. The **carnival**, which lasts a few days leading up to 12 October, is Costa Rica's biggest; it's crowded, prices rise, but is definitely worth seeing if you can get a room.

Around Puerto Limón

Playa Bonita and **Portete** have pleasant beaches about 5 km along the coastal road from Puerto Limón. **Moín**, a further 1.5 km east along the road, is the sight of the new international docks which exports some 2.8 million bunches of bananas annually. The docks are also the departure point for barges to Tortuguero and Barra del Colorado (eight hours). Boats also run from Moín to Tortuguero (see below) and may be hired at the dockside. Buses run to Moín every 40 minutes from 0600-1740, 30 minutes, US$0.10. If shipping a vehicle check which dock. Some simple accommodation options are available if you end up waiting here.

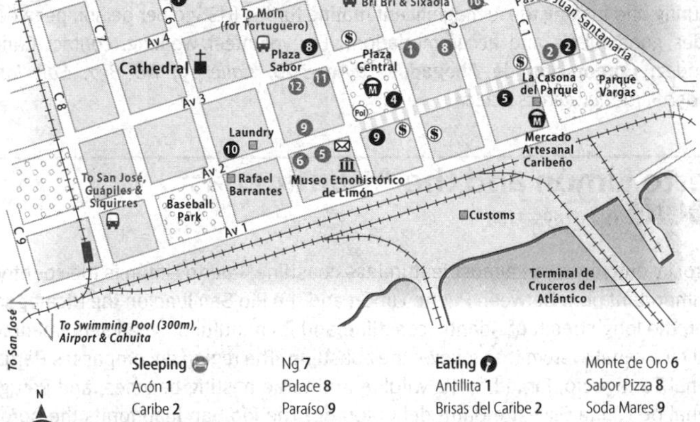

Sleeping
Acón 1
Caribe 2
Continental 3
International 4
King 5
Miami 6
Ng 7
Palace 8
Paraíso 9
Park 10
Tete 11
Wilson 12

Eating
Antillita 1
Brisas del Caribe 2
Diplo's 3
Doña Toda 4
Marisquería El Cevichito 5
Monte de Oro 6
Sabor Pizza 8
Soda Mares 9
Soda Yans 10
Springfield 11

Parque Nacional Tortuguero

▸▸ pp1095-1108. Colour map 7, B4.

ⓘ *Tortuguero Information Centre, T833-0827, safari@racsa.co.cr.* ▸▸ *For transport details and tour operators, see pages 1105 and 1107.*

Tortuguero is a 29,068-ha national park, with a marine extension of over 50,000 ha, protecting the Atlantic nesting sites of the green and leatherback turtle and the Caribbean lowland rainforest inland. As with much of Costa Rica, getting the timing right to see this natural phenomenon is essential. The green turtles lay their eggs at night on the scrappy, rather untidy beach from June to October, with the hatchlings emerging from the depths of their sandy nests until November at the latest. Leatherbacks can be seen from March to June. Hawksbill and loggerheads also nest at Tortuguero but numbers are minimal. Trips to look for nesting turtles are carefully monitored and you must be accompanied by a licensed guide at all times.

While your visit may not coincide with those of the turtles, the canals of jungle fringed waterways, teeming with bird and insect life, behind the beach are a pleasure throughout the year.

A **visitor centre**, close to the village of Tortuguero, has information on the park and the turtles. Round the back of the headquarters there is a well-marked 1.4-km nature trail, recommended. In the centre is a small gift shop. To the northern end of the village is the **Caribbean Conservation Corporation**, which has played a fundamental role in the creation and continued research of the turtle nesting grounds. There's an interesting and very informative **natural history museum** ⓘ *T224-9215 (San José), www.cccturtle.org, 1000-1200, 1400-1730, donation US$1.*

A guide is required for trips along the beach at night and recommended for trips through the waterways. If travelling with a lodge, tours will be arranged for you. If organizing independently, contact the information kiosk in the village for instructions and to link up with a registered guide. To visit the turtles at night you must pay US$7 park entrance fee, and US$5 each for a guide. A guide and tour in no way guarantees you will see a turtle or hatchlings.

Tours through the water channels are the best way to see the rainforest, ideally in a boat without a motor. The canal, bordered with primary rainforest, gives way to smaller channels, and, drifting slowly through forest darkened streams, the rainforest slowly comes alive with wildlife including birds – over half of those found in Costa Rica – monkeys, sloths and, for the lucky, alligators, tapirs, jaguars, ocelots, peccaries, anteaters and even manatees. You can hire a canoe and guide for about US$6 per hour per person in a boat without motor, US$12 with a motor, minimum 4. Night tours, US$15 per person per hour. Fishing tours, all equipment included are US$35 per person, minimum two. (See Directory, below, for tour operators and guides.) Take insect repellent.

> ! *Do not swim at Tortuguero as there are sharks.*

Barra del Colorado

▸▸ pp1095-1108.

The canals are part artificial, part natural; originally they were narrow lagoons running parallel to the sea separated from it by .75 km of land. Now the lagoons are linked, and it is possible to sail as far as Barra del Colorado, in the extreme northeast of Costa Rica, 25 km beyond Tortuguero. They pass many settlements. The town is divided by the river, the main part being on the northern bank. Secluded and difficult to get to, the Refugio Nacional de Fauna Silvestre Barra del Colorado (81,213 ha) is a national wildlife refuge. The reserve and the Parque Nacional Tortuguero share some boundaries, making for a far more effective protected zone. The fame of the region's fauna extends to the waters which are world renowned for fishing.

Once across the Río Colorado (which in fact is the south arm of the Río San Juan delta), you can walk to Nicaragua (see under Nicaragua, San Juan del Norte) along the coast, but it is a long 30-km beach walk, take food and lots of water. Most hikers overnight en route. Seek advice before setting out.

South from Puerto Limón » *pp1095-1108.*

Penshurst

South of Limón, a paved road shadows the coastline normally separated by little more than a thin line of palms. Beyond Penshurst is the **Hitoy Cerere Biological Reserve**. If you have time, camping is easy in the hills and there are plenty of rivers for swimming. Further south the road leads to Cahuita, Puerto Viejo and on towards Manzanillo – all sleepy beach towns, with lively centres, comfortable hideaways, and coastal and nature opportunities to explore. If heading for the border, heading inland just north of Puerto Viejo takes you through Bri Bri and on to Sixaola.

From Penshurst it is 11.5 km to **Cahuita**; this stretch of the road is paved to the edge of Cahuita.

Cahuita and Parque Nacional Cahuita → *Colour map 7, B4.*

ⓘ *Entry to the park US$7. The official entrance to the park is at Puerto Vargas, about 5 km south of Cahuita, where there are the park headquarters, a nature trail, camping*

Cahuita

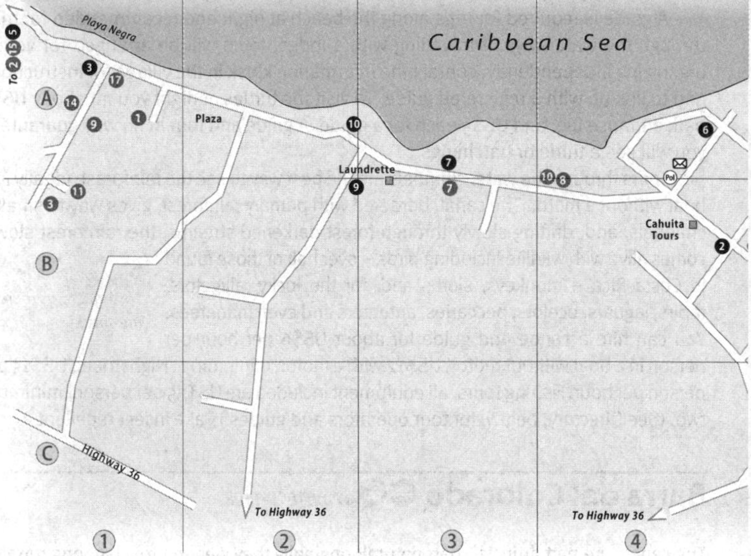

Sleeping

- Atlántida Lodge 1 *A1*
- Bobo Shanti 21 *B5*
- Bungalows Aché 4 *C6*
- Cabinas Atlantic Surf 16 *C6*
- Cabinas Iguana 3 *B1*
- Cabinas Palmar 5 *B6*
- Cabinas Safari 6 *B5*
- Centro Turístico Brigitte's 9 *A1*
- El Encanto B&B Inn 7 *B3*
- Jardín Tropical & Cabinas Mambo 11 *B1*
- Jenny's Cabinas 12 *B6*
- Kelly Creek 13 *C6*
- Kontiki 14 *A1*
- La Diosa 2 *A1*
- Magellan Inn 15 *A1*
- National Park 20 *C6*
- Reggae Rest & Cabinas 17 *A1*
- Restaurant & Bungalows Bluspirit 8 *B4*
- Safari Cabinas Ocean View 10 *B4*
- Spencer Seaside Lodging 18 *B6*
- Vaz Cabañas 19 *C6*

Eating

- Beach House 15 *B5*

facilities and toilets. Take the bus to Km 5, then turn left at the sign. There is a tourist complex in the area, and the restaurant Marisquería, at Puerto Vargas park entrance, Italian, with a jovial host, who also has rooms. You can enter the park for free from the southern side of Cahuita, which is ideal for relaxing on the beach, but leave a donation. If you have the option, visit during the week when it is quieter.

The small town of Cahuita hides 1 km back from the main road, and enjoys a sleepy feel accordingly. A laid-back community, it's a good place to hide away in one of the secluded spots or to party in the centre of town. North of the town there is a beautiful black-sand beach ideal for swimming or just lazing about in a hammock, while to the south is the national park. Most people stay in Cahuita to explore the park.

Cahuita National Park (1068 ha) is a narrow strip of beach protecting a coral reef off shore and a marine area of 22,400 ha. The length of the beach can be walked in about three hours, and passes endless coconut palms and interesting tropical forest, through which there is also a path. It is hot and humid, so take drinking water, but a wide range of fauna can be seen, including howler monkeys, white face monkeys, coatis, snakes, butterflies and hermit crabs. Over 500 species of fish inhabit the surrounding waters and reef tours are available. An old Spanish shipwreck can be seen and reached without a boat. Snorkellers should take care to stay away from the coral which is already badly damaged by agricultural chemicals and other pollutants. The park extends from the southern limit of Cahuita town southeast to Puerto Vargas.

Note: Cahuita and Puerto Viejo have suffered from what locals believe is a lack of support and investment from central government. An undercurrent of problems, partially based on the perception that everyone on the Caribbean coast takes drugs, does mean that you may be hassled for drugs. If you are not interested, just say no.

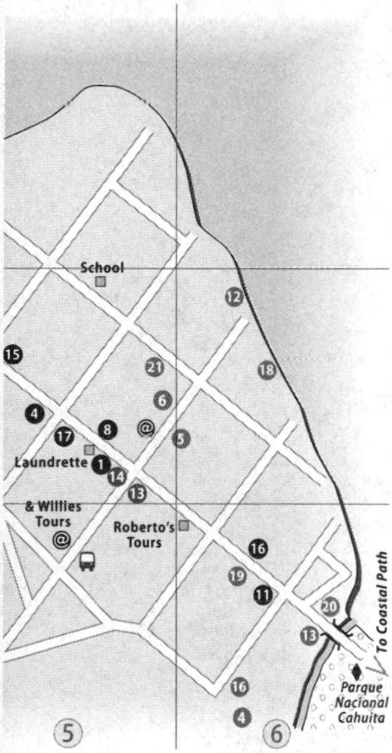

Cha Cha Cha **2** *B5*
Chao's Paradise **3** *A1*
Coral Reef **1** *B5*
La Casa Creole **5** *A1*
La Fe **8** *B5*
Mango Tango Pizzeria **17** *B5*
Miss Edith's **6** *A4*
Palenque Luisa **4** *B5*
Pastry Shop **7** *B3*
Pizzería El Cactus **9** *B2*
Sobre las Olas **10** *A2*
Soda Priscilla **16** *C6*
Sol y Mar **11** *C6*
Vista del Mar **12** *C6*

Bars & clubs
Cocos **14** *B5*
Rikki's **13** *B5*

Puerto Viejo de Talamanca

➔ *Colour map 7, B4.*

Puerto Viejo is a good base and a quietly happening party town, with a number of good beaches stretching out to the south. There is reef diving nearby, or you can head south to Mandoca for lagoon diving from canoes. Surfers seek out the glorious **Salsa Brava** wave which peaks from December to February. Away from the beach nature trips range from tough treks in Gandoca-Manzanillo Wildlife Refuge (see below) through to gentle strolls around the self-guided botanical gardens to the north of town. There are also several cultural trips to KeKöLdi and BriBri indigenous reserves and the newest offering takes dug-outs to the inland town of Yorkin. The **Asociación Talamanqueña de Ecoturismo y Conservación** ⓘ *ATEC, T750-0191, greencoast.com/atec.htm*, provides tourist information, sells locally made

Activities in the area are numerous and you could spend many days exploring the options.

 crafts and T-shirts, and also offers guide services, rainforest hikes, snorkelling and fishing trips. The **South Caribbean Music Festival** takes place in the months leading up to Easter.

Around Puerto Viejo

There are a number of popular beaches southeast along the road from Puerto Viejo. Traffic is limited, buses occasional, but it is walkable. About 4 km away is **Playa Cocles** which has some of the best surfing on this coast, and 2 km further on is **Playa Chiquita** with many places to stay. Next is **Punta Uva**, beyond which, after another 5 km, you arrive in **Manzanillo,** followed by white-sand beaches and rocky headlands to **Punta Mona** and the **Gandoca-Manzanillo Wildlife Refuge** ⓘ *ANAI, T224-6090*, a celebration of Costa Rican diversity largely left alone by prospectors and tourists alike. Among other projects, marine scientists are studying protecting the giant leatherback turtle. Volunteer work is possible.

Puerto Viejo de Talamanca

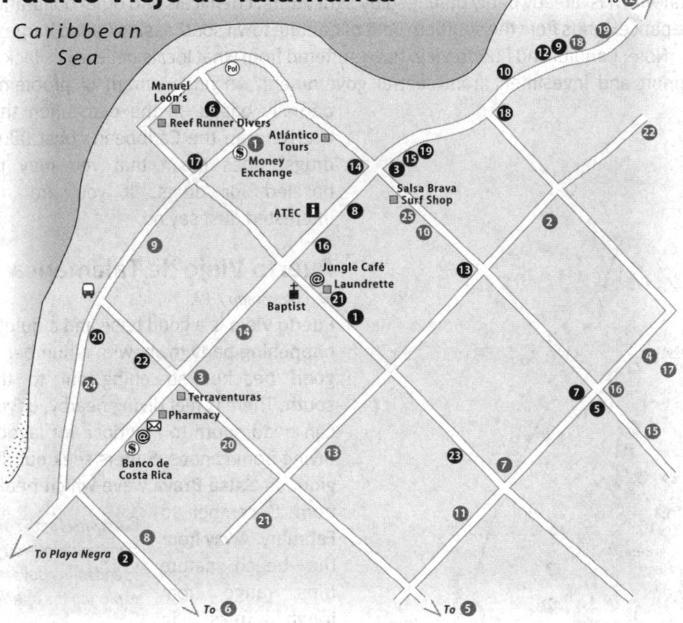

0 metres 50
0 yards 50

Sleeping
Bull Inn **20**
Cabinas Casa Verde **2**
Cabinas Grant **3**
Cabinas Lika **21**
Cabinas Los Almendros **1**
Cabinas Popular **17**
Cabinas Rolando **15**
Cabinas Soda Mitchell **16**
Cabinas Tropical **4**
Cabinas Yucca **19**
Cashew Hill **5**
Coco Loco Lodge **6**
Fortaleza **14**
Guaraná **13**
Jacaranda **7**
Las Olas Camping & Cabinas **18**
Los Sueños **8**
Maritza **9**
Puerto Viejo **10**
Pura Vida **11**
Rocking J's **12**
Tamandua Lodge **22**

Eating
Amimodo **9**
Bread and Chocolate **1**
Chili Rojo **16**
El Loco Natural **2**
El Parquecito **3**
Hot Rocks **14**
Jammin Juices & Jerk Chicken **17**
La Terraza **15**
Lidia's Place **5**
Monchies **23**
Pan Pay **6**
Peace & Love Coffee **22**
Pizza Boruca **21**
Pizzeria Rusticone **13**
Pollo Frito **18**
Red Stripe Café **20**
Salsa Brava **12**
Soda Miss Sam **7**
Soda Palmer **19**
Stanford's **10**
Tamara **8**

Bars & clubs
Baba Yaga **25**
Sunset **24**

Border essentials: Costa Rica-Panama

Sixaola

Costa Rican immigration The border is open 0700-1700. The immigration office is just before the railway bridge, over the river Sixaola, which marks the border with Panama. Advance watches by 1 hr on entering Panama.

Sleeping At the entrance to town is E **Imperio**, 8 basic cabins with ventilator, shared bath.

E **Cabinas Sánchez**, T754-2105, clean and tidy, best option.

F **Doris**, T754-2207, basic rooms with fan, partitions; friendly.

Transport A railway runs to Almirante (Panama) from Guabito, on the Panamanian side. If crossing to Panama take the earliest bus possible to Sixaola (see Panama, Northwestern Caribbean coast, page 1187). Direct San José-Sixaola bus from Terminal del Caribe, Autotransportes Mepe (T221-0524), 5 hrs, US$6.30, 0600, 1000, 1330, 1530, plus 0800 on Sat, return 0700, 0830, 1300, 1530; also 6 daily from Puerto Limón (Radio Casino), 4 hrs.

Banks There are no banks in Sixaola, but you can change money in the supermarket. Rates, especially to the US dollar, are very poor. Shops near the border in Panama will accept colones but shops in Changuinola and beyond do not.

Bribri

At **Hotel Creek**, north of Puerto Viejo, the paved road heads through the hills to the village of Bribri, at the foot of the Talamanca Range Indigenous Reserve. Halfway between is **Violeta's Pulpería**. From Limón, **Aerovías Talamaqueñas Indígenas** fly cheaply to **Amubri** in the reserve (there is a *casa de huéspedes* run by nuns in Amubri). Villages such as Bribri, Chase, Bratsi, Shiroles and San José Cabécar can be reached by bus from Cahuita. Several buses daily to Bribri from Limón. Continuing south from Bribri is Sixaola, on the border with Panama (see box).

Sleeping

Puerto Viejo de Sarapiquí *p1088*

AL **Selva Verde Lodge**, out of town, heading west a few km towards La Virgen, T766-6800, www.holbrooktravel.com. On over 200 ha of virgin rainforest reserve, 40 double rooms, 5 bungalows for 4, includes meals, caters mainly for tour groups. Sensitively set in amongst the rainforest, evening lectures by biologists, excellent for birdwatchers and naturalists with extensive trail system, rafting, canoeing and riding through property; tours with biologists organized.

AL-B **El Gavilán Lodge**, on the southern bank of the Río Sarapiquí, reached by taxi, T234-9507, www.gavilanlodge.com. Includes breakfast, set in 100-ha private reserve by the river pier, good restaurant, good jungle paths, riding and river tours, 12 rooms private bath, garden jacuzzi, special group and student/reseacher rates, day trips and overnight trips from San José.

A **El Bambú**, in centre north of park, T766-6359, www.elbambu.com. Bath, fan, TV, pool, gym, including breakfast, very nice.

South Caribbean Coast

B Posada Andrea Cristina, just out of town near the main road junction, T766-6265, www.andreacristina.com. Comfortable small cabins, set amongst tropical gardens. Good local knowledge.
C Mi Lindo Sarapiquí, overlooking park, T766-6074. 6 spotless rooms with bath, fan, hot water and restaurant downstairs. Recommended.
E Cabinas Monteverde, next to El Bambú, T766-6236. With bath, restaurant, but pretty dirty.
E Hospedaje Gonar, on road to the dock above hardware store (*ferretería*) without signpost, T844-4677. Basic rooms, ones with windows slightly better. Shared bath, pretty dirty.

Las Horquetas de Sarapiquí *p1088*
AL River-Edge Cabin, T764-3131, www.rara-avis.com. Deep in the rainforest. There is also treetop accommodation and rates for backpackers at the **Las Casitas**.
AL Waterfall Lodge, T764-3131, www.rara-avis.com. A beautiful jungle lodge in an idyllic setting, includes meals, private bath.

Guápiles, Guácimo and Siquirres *p1089*
A Casa Río Blanco, Guápiles, about 6 km west of Guápiles look out for the big yellow road sign on, take first right before the Río Blanco bridge and follow signpost for 1 km, T710-4124, www.casarioblanco.com. Accommodates 12 guests in comfortable cabins, with breakfast, run by Herbie and Annette from Amsterdam. Beautiful gardens and a great spot for people interested in the environment. Recommended.
B Río Palmas, Guácimo, 1 km past EARTH School, T760-0330. 30 rooms, private bathroom, pool, restaurant. The 200-ha property includes ornamental plant farm and rainforest.
C Cabinas Car, Guápiles, 50 m west of church, T710-0035. 10 clean and tidy rooms, with private bath, hot water, fan and TV.
C Centro Turístico Pacuare, Siquirres, T768-6482. Renovated, with large pool.
C Centro Turístico Río Blanco, Guápiles, on main road at entrance to town, T710-7857. With bath, fan. Recommended.
D Alcema, Siquirres, 50 m east of market, T768-6004. Some dark rooms, with fan, clean, shared bath.
D Cabinas de Oro, Guápiles, northeast of bus terminal, T710-6663. Clean rooms, private bath with hot water, cheaper without. Restaurant nearby.
D Don Quito, 3.5 km towards Siquirres, T768-8533. Pleasant, good restaurant.
E Hotel Alfaro (El Tunél), Guápiles, 50 m west of bus terminal, T710-6293. Simple rooms, no frills, but clean. Open 24 hrs, with a rather funky aluminium stairway. Good value.

Puerto Limón *p1090, map p1090*
Beware of theft at night, and remember it is a port; there are a lot of drunks roaming the streets.
A-B Park, Av 3, Calle 1-2, T798-0555. Neat little hotel with 34 rooms, sea facing rooms quiet and cool, recently renovated, restaurant good.
B-C Acón, on corner of main square, Calle 3, Av 3, T758-1010. Big rooms with private bath, a/c, clean, safe, good restaurant, a bit run-down, popular daily disco **Aquarius** except Mon.
B-C Caribe, facing Parque Vargas, Av 2, Calle 1-2, T758-0138. Big, immaculate rooms with private bath, hot water and big fan. Good deal.
C-D Miami, next to **King** on Av 2, Calle 4-5, T758-0490. 35 rooms, all with private bath, some with a/c, others with fans. Secure and efficient. Credit cards accepted.
C-D Tete, 1 block west of main square, Av 3, Calle 4-5, T758-1122. Clean rooms, bright and good beds. Some rooms sleeping up to 6 and some with balconies overlooking square.
D Palace, 1 block north of bus stops, Calle 2-3, Av 2. Family-run hotel, with 33 mostly big rooms. Pretty clean, balcony overlooking street, popular with travellers and good place to make up groups for Tortuguero.
D-E International, opposite the **Continental**, Av 5, Calle 2-3, T758-0434. Private bath, some with a/c other with fan, good deal.
E Continental, a little north of the centre, Av 5, Calle 2-3, T798-0532. 25 big, good and clean rooms with ceiling fans.
E King, next to post office near main square on Av 2, T758-1033. Simple rooms, pretty dark, but clean and secure.

F Hotel Wilson, on street west of main square, Av 3, Calle 4-5, T758-5028. Clean, tidy and central, OK.
F Ng, Calle 4, Av 5-6, T758-2134. 15 basic rooms some with bath, cheaper without. Basic and a bit untidy, but friendly. Price per person. Good for the price.
F Paraíso, Av 2, Calle 4-5. Plyboard partitions divide a once-beautiful house into tiny, dark, box rooms. Hard core roughing it and a little sad.

Parque Nacional Tortuguero *p1091*
Top-end hotels normally target package deals; walk-in rates given where available. There are many cheap *cabañas* in town; the boatmen or villagers will help you find them. Staying in town is better for the truly local economy.

In town
B Casa Marbella, in front of the Catholic Church, T709-8011, www.casamarbella.tripod.com. B&B with 4 small rooms, with private bath. Run by local guide Daryl Loth. Good source of information and in centre of village.
B Miss Junie's, T709-8102. 12 good cabins at the north end of town.
D Cabinas Tortuguero, T709-8114, tinamon@racsa.co.cr. 5 little cabins, each sleeping 3 with private bath, pleasant little garden with hammocks. Nice spot.
D Yoruki Lodge, T709-8068. Clean simple rooms looking over the river.
D-E Cabinas Sabina's, T709-8069. Winding down, the end of an era, with just 16 rooms remaining. Good views looking out over to the Caribbean.
D-E Mary Scar, T711-0671. Basic stuff: foam mattresses, but friendly enough if things elsewhere are full.

Out of town
Places out of town, best visited as part of a package, include:
LL Jungle Lodge Hotel, north end of the lagoon, T233-0133, www.grupopapagayo.com. 50 big, wooden panelled rooms, complete with pool, wet bar, games room and disco.
L Tortuga Lodge, T257-0766 (San José), www.costaricaexpeditions.com. Price per person includes meals. Very comfortable accommodation, in big rooms each with veranda or balcony.
AL Mawamba Lodge, T293-8181, www.grupomawamba.com. Comfortable cabins with fans, pool, walking distance to town. Turtle beaches are behind property.
AL Pachira Lodge, across the canal from the town, T223-1682, www.pachiralodge.com. 3-day/2-night package includes transport, food, tours with bilingual guide, US$239.
AL Turtle Beach Lodge, T248-0707, www.turtlebeachlodge.com. 2- to 7-day packages from US$175 in 48 ha of beautifully landscaped tropical grounds.
A Laguna Lodge, T225-3740, www.lagunatortuguero.com. 50-odd cabins, with bath and fan, restaurant, bar, beautiful gardens, pool and conference room.
B Caribbean Paradise, one channel back from Tortuguero, T223-0238 (difficult to reach, try going direct when you arrive). Run by Tico Carlos and his wife Ana, includes 3 meals. 16 simple rooms, no set itinerary, personal service, activities as you want them. A refreshing change from the general offering and very enjoyable.
B El Manati, T534-7256. Tico family-run, simple rooms with a terrace. Relaxing spot, work with Ecole Travel in San José. Price includes breakfast, good value.
B-E Tortuguero Caribe Lodge, near **Ilan Ilan**, T385-4676. 10 simple cabins, friendly Tico-run and owned. Book direct or as package through **Ecole Travel** in San José. More expensive price includes breakfast and dinner.
D Ilan Ilan, through the **Agencia Mitur** in San José, T296-7378, www.ilan-ilanlodge.com. All-inclusive packages, simple rooms in a line, with small terrace. Pool, jacuzzi and riverside bar. Recommended.
F Caño Palma Biological Station, 6 km north of Tortuguero, administered by the **Canadian Organization for Tropical Education and Rainforest Conservation** (in Canada T905-683-2116). Basic rooms for volunteer staff. Price per person, includes meals. A good place for serious naturalists or just for unwinding, accommodation for up to 16 in wooden cabin, freshwater well for drinking and washing. Minimum stay 2 weeks.

Camping
You can sometimes camp at the national park office for US$2.50.

Barra del Colorado *p1091*

L Silver King Lodge, T711-0708, www.silverkinglodge.com. Price per person. Deluxe sport-fishing hotel, 5-night packages includes flights, meals, rooms with bath, a/c, hot water, pool.

D Tarponland Lodge, T710-2141. Cabins, run by Guillermo Cunningham, very knowledgeable and helpful. If you have a tent you may be able to camp at **Soda La Fiesta**, lots of mosquitoes.

Penshurst *p1092*

AL Los Aviarios del Caribe, 30 km south of Limón just north of Penshurst, T750-0775, www.ogphoto.com/aviarios. A sloth rescue sanctuary with a small nature reserve. The friendly owners offer canoe trips in the Estrella river delta and there's a volunteer programme if you have time to spare. They also have a number of comfortable rooms. Recommended.

AL Selva Bananita Lodge, 20 km from Puerto Limón at Cerro Mochila heading inland at Bananito, T253-8118, www.selvabananito.com. 7 cabins on secluded farm, solar heating, primary rainforest tours, tree climbing, horses and bikes to rent.

Cahuita and Parque Nacional Cahuita *p1092, map p1092*

Beware of theft on the beach, and drug pushers who may be undercover police.

L-AL El Pizote Lodge, Playa Negra, T750-0227/0088. Rooms, bungalows and fully equipped houses in private gardens. Nice family feel, swimming pool.

L-A La Diosa, Playa Grande, past Playa Negra, T755-0055, www.hotelladiosa.net. Colourful bungalows with luxury jacuzzi, a/c, private hot water bath, hammocks, pool, gym, massage, games room, internet, surf/kayak equipment – all this and on the beach – cheaper out of season.

AL Magellan Inn, 2 km north of Cahuita, T755-0035, www.magellaninn.toposrealestate.org. Includes breakfast, 6 beautifully decorated rooms with bath and fan, and 10,000-year-old pool (honestly) set in peaceful gardens and with renowned French Creole restaurant.

AL-A Bunglalows Malu, Playa Negra, T755-0114. Extremely well-built bungalows in manicured gardens, a/c, private bath, hot water, one with kitchen. Swimming pool and jacuzzi for guests, bar and breakfast.

AL-A El Encanto Bed and Breakfast Inn, Playa Negra, T755-0113, www.elencantobedandbreakfast.com. Attractive place built by very stylish French owners, among shady gardens with pool. 3 bungalows with private bath, hot water, fan, mosquito net, terrace and hammocks and 1 3-bedroom apartment. Yoga and massage are available.

AL-C Kayas Place, Playa Negra, T750-0690, www.kayasplace.com. Beautifully hand built with reclaimed wood, each room is a little different and accommodation ranges from simple to more luxurious *cabinas*. Opposite the beach, a nice chilled spot.

A Resort style Atlántida Lodge, Playa Negra, north of Cahuita, on the main road, T755-0115, www.atlantida.co.cr. With private bath and ceiling fan. Pleasant gardens, pool, jacuzzi, massage, safe parking for cars and motorcycles. Bar and restaurant onsite.

A-B Bungalows Aché, by the entrance to the national park, T755-0119, www.bungalowsache.com. A little off the beaten track in a very tranquil and attractive location. Well-kept bungalows with private hot water bath, mosquito nets, coffee maker, fridge and hammocks, friendly owners.

A-C Chimuri Beach Cottages and **Jungle Lodge**, Playa Negra, T750-0119, www.greencoast.com/chimuri.htm. Rustic, painted wooden cottages in private gardens, close to the beach. Cottages sleep 1-4 and all have fully equipped kitchens. Owners can organize tour to the Keköldi Indigenous Reserve and birdwatching tours in their own reserve – see www.ecohostel.com.

A-C Jardín Tropical and Cabinas Mambo, Playa Negra, north of Cahuita, T755-0033, jardintropical@racsa.co.cr. 2 decent bungalows sleeping 2-4, or a house with kitchen for 5. Poison dart frogs in the gardens.

B Kelly Creek, within a couple of blocks of the centre of town, by entrance to national park, T755-0007, kellycr@racsa.co.cr. Large rooms with veranda, ceiling fan to assist fresh sea breezes, good service and great spot.

B-C Cabinas Iguana, 800 m north of Cahuita, T755-0005, www.cabinas-iguana.com. Swiss-owned, very friendly, cabins or houses to rent, kitchen, fan, mosquito netting, balcony, clean, waterfall-fed pool, nice location. Big 2-for-1 book swap. Very good value. Recommended.

C Cabinas Palmar, down a little road from the bus stop which goes straight to the seafront, T755-0243. Tico-run, clean, good, friendly and very helpful. Internet café.
C-D Restaurant and Bungalows Bluspirit, just out of town on the road to Playa Negra. Gorgeous split-level bungalows with private bath, hot water and hammocks, by the beach. Run by a very friendly couple who also serve fresh fish and Italian home-cooked meals in their bar and restaurant.
C-D Safari Ocean View, towards Play Negra, T755-0393. 5 decent *cabinas* with private bath and hot water, also terrace and hammocks, great location a short amble to the shore and good value for the price.
C-D Cabinas Atlantic Surf, south end of town near the beach, T755-0116. Wooden hotel with communal balconies and hammocks and relaxed vibe. Rooms come with private hot water bath, fan and mosquito nets.
C-D Centro Turistico Brigitte's, Playa Negra, north of Cahuita, down a small track, T755- 0053, www.brigittecahuita.com. Friendly, quiet, Swiss-run, good restaurant, wildlife, 2 small cabins sleeping 2 – one with kitchen, excellent local information, internet, laundry service, bike rentals, horse riding and many different tours. Recommended.
C Jenny's Cabinas, heading to the beach, T755-0256. Balconies with view, Canadian owned, bath, fan, breakfast available, running water, close to the sea but surrounding area a bit scruffy.
C-D Reggae Rest and Cabinas, near Chao's Paradise in Play Negra, T755-0515. Basic *cabinas* all with private bath in nice location by the beach.
C-D Hotel National Park, opposite Kelly Creek, by entrance to national park, T755-0244. Bright rooms, fan, just about friendly but the beach front restaurant makes it a good spot.
D Cabinas Nirvana, towards Playa Negra, T755-0110, nirvana99@racsa.co.cr. Wooden rooms in a very tranquil spot, hot water private bath, swimming pool in gardens.
D Cabinas Mina, main street. Very friendly owners offer very basic rooms with private bath and cold water.
D Cabinas Belo Horizonte, Playa Negra, north of Cahuita, T755-0206. Newly renovated, a couple of good rooms, quite simple but on the beach, rent for US$200 per month or US$20 per day.
D Cabinas Surf Side, facing the school, T755-0246. Clean, good value and with parking.
C Cabinas Tito, Playa Negra, north of Cahuita, T755-0286. Clean, quiet cabins sleeping 2-3, good for families, good value.
D Coco Congo, Playa Negra, T750-0652. Rather overpriced rooms which are dark and tatty, but pleasant owners, in front of beach, restaurant on site, 5-min walk to town.
D New Cabinas Arrecife, right on the coast close to **Miss Edith's**, T755-0081. OK rooms, but great spot and view from restaurant.
D Sol y Mar, on the road to parque nacional, T755-0237. Friendly owners have rooms that sleep 2-6 people, with private hot-water bath. Rooms are a little tatty, but fine and some very spacious. Their local restaurant is good for breakfast.
D Vaz Cabañas, towards the park entrance, T755-0218. Friendly, cold shower, some fans, quite clean, good restaurant, safe parking. Recommended.
D Villa Delmar, close to national park entrance, T755-0392. Recently built rooms with private shower, cold and hot water. Bicycle rental, laundry service and parking.
D-E Bobo Shanti, around the corner from Cabinas Safari. Colourfully painted in red, green and gold, a rasta-relax. Rooms have private bath, hot and cold water. Chilled vibes.
D-E Cabinas Margarita, Playa Negra, north of Cahuita, down a 200-m path, T755-0205. Simple rooms, quiet spot, nice atmosphere, clean.
C Spencer Seaside Lodging, on beach close to **Jenny's Cabinas**, T755-0027, beachfront basic rooms, internet, community kitchen. Price per person. Recommended.
D Cabinas Safari, opposite **Cabinas Palmar**, T755-0405, simple rooms with fan and shared bath and hot water, friendly owner Wayne Palmer, clean, price per person, good value.

Camping

It's possible to camp in Cahuita National Park.
Kontiki, near Playa Negra, T755-0261. With laundry, showers and toilets, also a few cabins.
Colibrís Paradise, out of village close to Playa Negra.

Puerto Viejo de Talamanca *p1093, map p1094*
Discounts are often available May-Nov.
L-AL **Samasati Lodge & Retreat Center**, near Hone Creek on junction halfway between Cahuita and Puerto Viejo, T750-0315, www.samasati.com. Beautiful mountain location with 100-ha reserve, vegetarian restaurant, meditation courses, reservation recommended.
AL-A **Cabinas Los Almendros** (see map), T750-0235, flchwg@racsa.co.cr. 3 fully equipped apartments and a complex of conventional rooms with private hot water bath, a/c and cable TV in the more expensive ones. None of the Caribbean charm but good facilities, especially for families. Cash exchange, credit card advances, tour advice, good, friendly service.
A **Escape Caribeño**, 500 m along road to Punta Uva, T750-0103. German-run, well-furnished cottages, fully equipped, some a/c.
A **Lizard King**, out of town, heading north, T750-0614/0630. Smart *cabinas* located upstairs at their Mexican restaurant, not always open. Swimming pool.
A-B **Bungalows Calalú**, on the road to Cocles, T750-0042, www.bungalowscalalu.com. Bungalows with and without kitchen, also swimming pool and beautiful butterfly garden in the grounds.
A-B **Cabinas Casa Verde**, central, T750-0015, www.cabinascasaverde.com. Comfortable rooms with hammocks, private bath, cracked tile showers in beautiful gardens. A pool and open-air jacuzzi add to the relaxation. The owner collects Central American poison dart frogs and keeps them in tanks dotted around the grounds; ask to take a look, even if you are not a guest. Very nice owners and staff, recommended spot.
A-C **Cashew Hill**, south of town, T750-0256, www.cashewhilllodge.co.cr. Re-developed in the last few years, although retaining rustic charm. 6 family-orientated rooms, with both private and shared bath, fans and mosquito nets. Set in 1 ha of beautiful gardens on the rolling hills above the town, mirador looks out over the jungle tops to the sea. Yoga massage retreats and classes available. Quiet, very chilled atmosphere.
A-C **Coco Loco Lodge**, south of town, T750-0281, www.cocolocolodge.com. Quiet spot in expansive garden south of town, nice thatched wooden and stone cabins, some fully equipped with kitchen and cable TV. Popular. English, German and Spanish spoken.
B **Guaraná**, opposite **Lulu Berlu Gallery**, T750-0244, www.hotel guarana.com. Very attractive hotel if a little pricey, well kept. All rooms with private, hot water bath, fans, mosquito nets, private balconies and hammocks. They also have a communal kitchen and parking space.
B **Maritza**, central, T750-0003. In cabins, with bath, clean, clean, friendly. Affiliated to International Youth Hostel Association, English spoken. A map in the bar shows all the hotels and *cabinas* in the area. Highly recommended.
B-C **Cabinas David**, just out of town past **Lizard King**, T750-0542, cabinas_david@yahoo.com. *Cabinas* with private, hot water shower, individual terrace with hammocks.
B-C **Jacaranda**, a few blocks back (see map), T750-0069, www.greencoast.com/jacaranda.htm. A very relaxed spot away from the beach set in beautiful gardens, with coloured mosaic pathways and private areas to read and relax. Rooms are fixed with colourful throws and side lights, showers are spacious. A very attractive place, hot water throughout, fans and mosquito nets. Communal kitchen. Massages can be booked to take place in a pagoda in their flower garden.
C **Cabinas Grant**, on the road out of town (see map), T752-2845, New local ownership but all the same set up. Large clean rooms, with private bath and fan. Each with a small terrace. Restaurant upstairs is now a seafood eatery.
C **Cabinas Tropical**, on the coast, T750-0283, www.cabinastropical.com. 8 spotless rooms, some with fridges, with good mattresses, private bath and hot water. Pleasant gardens with shaded garden house for relaxing, small bar/café. Recommended. The German owner, Rolf Blancke, is a tropical biologist and runs tours. Recommended.
C **Cabinas Yucca**, north of town, T750-0285. 5 *cabinas* with private hot water showers, good value and great spot, nice beach garden, parking, friendly, German-run.

C Hotel Fortaleza, on main street, T750-0028. New establishment in the middle of town. Rooms with private hot water bath, not a particularly special building, but fine, clean and a very relaxed friendly atmosphere with communal terrace for watching street life.
C-D Cabinas Dolce Vida, past Carlos Pool Bar. Rooms with private showers.
C-D Cabinas Rolando, in the side street behind Soda Lidia. Well recommended *cabinas*, private shower, hot water.
C-D Cabinas Soda Mitchell, close to Soda Lidia. 3 sparkling new rooms sleeping 2/3, with private shower and (usually) hot water. Very pleasant owner and quiet out of the way location.
C-D Café Rico, north end of town. Coffee shop with a couple of rooms with private shower and hot water. Very friendly English owner and probably the best coffee in town.
C-D Pura Vida, a few blocks back from the main street (see map),T750-0002, German-Chilean run, friendly, very clean, hammocks, lacking in character. Recommended.
C-E Puerto Viejo, just off the main street (see map), T750-0620. Great management make the place the most chilled in town. 78 basic rooms sleeping 1 to 5, 3 have private hot-water bath, the rest are shared hot and cold water showers. There is a communal kitchen and large areas to eat, chat and be social. One fully equipped apartment for monthly rental (approx. US$500). Owners are all surfers and they offer board rental, buy and sell, also wave info. Scooter rental available. Restaurant onsite. Popular with surfers.
C-F Las Olas Camping and Cabinas, next to Salsa Brava Restaurant. Basic for the price – camping from US$6, rooms from US$25 – rooms with private bath and hot water, but great spot on the beach and friendly local owners. Showers and toilet facilities for campers.
D Bull Inn, first left after new **Harbor Supermarket**. Locally owned, very clean and bright rooms with private bath, hot water, and a communal balcony.
D Los Sueños, main steret (on map), T750-0369, www.costaricaguide.info/lossuenos.htm. Laid-back and very relaxing, just 4 colourful and bright rooms.
D-E Cabinas Popular, opposite the back entrance of Casa Verde. Nicely located at the back of the town – very peaceful with rural backdrop – rather basic rooms and a little dark, but extremely good value, private shower, but cold water.
D-F Rocking J's, on the beach out of town, towards Cocles, T750-0657, www.rockingjs.com. A sprawling multi-coloured campers' paradise. Huge covered hammock hotel and area for tents – bring your own or rent one of theirs . They also have a 'tree house' room, with one double bed under a retractable ceiling so you may watch the stars, also a music system and fridge (you need never come down) and the 'King Suite', an open-sided, colourful room, with private bath. Coloured mosaic murals are spreading the floors, walls, communal kitchen, toilets and restaurant, all done by guests. They also offer kayak, surfboard and bike rentals, and the occasional full moon party.
E Cabinas Lika, southern end of town (see map). Friendly back backers set up with private rooms, dorms and hammocks, shared kitchen and laid-back vibe.
E Cabañas Yoli, 250 m from bus stop. Clean, basic, fan, OK – one of the last Tico-owned places.
E Hotel Oro, central, T750-0469. Budget rooms with private shower.
E Sol y Sombre, at entrance to town, with the style of the French. 5 clean rooms, with fan and mosquito nets. Small restaurant downstairs.
F Cabinas Salsa Brava, popular with surfers.
F Tamandua Lodge, behind Cabinas Dolce Vida. Very basic budget accommodation, shared rooms, shared bathroom, shared kitchen.

Around Puerto Viejo *p1094*

LL-A Aguas Claras, 4.5 km from Puerto Viejo on road to Manzanillo, T750-0131, www.aguasclaras-cr.com. 5 beautiful cottages each painted a different colour with pretty white wooden gables and balconies. All fully equipped and very close to the beach. **Restaurant Miss Holly** serves gourmet breakfast and lunch. Recommended.
L Tree House Lodge, Punta Uva, T750-0706, www.costaricatreehouse.com. Dutch owner Edsart has 3 apartments – 2 of which are the

most unusual in Costa Rica: the treehouse and the beach suite (there is also a beach house). All are fully equipped with kitchen facilities and hot water, and all are equally luxurious.

L-AL Shawandha, Playa Chiquita, T750-0018, www.shawandhalodge.com. Beautiful bungalows in the jungle with a calm and private feel and fantastic mosaic showers. Massages now available. Very stylish restaurant serving French Caribbean fusion, pricey.

AL Hotel Kasha, Playa Chiquita, T750-0205, www.costarica-hotelkasha.com. 14 bungalows in lush gardens on the beach, beautiful pool, jacuzzi and restaurant.

AL Hotel Las Palmas, Playa Uva, T759-0303, www.laspalmashotel.com. Cabins, 26 rooms, pool, snorkelling, rainforest, tours, transport from San José on Wed, Fri, Sun, US$30 return, US$20 one way.

AL-A Cariblue Bungalows, Playa Cocles, TT750-0035, www.cariblue.com. Nice natural complex with palm roofs, set in beautiful garden. Restaurant and bar on site along with a games room and library.

A Almonds and Corals Tent Camp, Playa Uva, T272-2024, www.geoexpediciones.com. Luxury camping with bath and hot water in tents on platforms in the forest, pool, restaurant, trips arranged to Punta Mona, snorkelling, bike hire, breakfast and dinner included. Sleeping in the wild, with some comfort thrown in.

A Playa Chiquita Lodge, Playa Chiquita, T750-0408, www.playachiquitalodge.com. The lodge labels itself a beach jungle hotel and that's exactly what it feels like. They have eleven rooms and three houses (monthly rentals accepted) all with hot water, hammocks and plenty of space, easy beach access and breakfast included.

A Totem Cabinas, Playa Cocles, T750-0758, www.totemsite.com. Surf-orientated hotel heavy on the bamboo furniture. Luxury rooms with lounge areas, private shower, hot water, cable TV and private balconies overlooking Playa Cocles. Italian bar and restaurant, internet room and swimming pool. Surf board rental and surf and Kite school.

A-B La Costa de Papito, Playa Cocles, T750-0080, www.lacostadepapito.com. 11 beautifully designed bungalows with all the style you'd expect from Eddie Ryan (**Carlton Arms Hotel**, New York). Rooms withfan and bath. Great owners who love to make their guests happy, recommended. **Costa de Papito** now host **Pure Jungle Spa**, T750-0536, www.purejunglespa.com, Tue to Sat, or by appointment. Treatments are organic and handmade and sound good enough to eat… they range from chocolate facials to banana body wraps.

A-B Miraflores Lodge and Restaurant, Playa Chiquita, T750-0038, www.miraflores lodge.com. 10 rooms (2 with kitchen), a/c, breakfast included, with bath, fan, gardens, lots of wildlife. English and French spoken. Cheaper rates in low season.

B Azania, Playa Cocles, T750-0540, www.azania-costarica.com. Beautiful thatched-roof bungalows with great facilities in garden setting, restaurant, pool and jacuzzi, parking.

B Cabinas Pangea, Manzanillo, behind **Aquamor**, T759-0604. 2 nice rooms with bath, also house on beach with kitchen.

B Playa Chiquita Lodge, Playa Chiquita, T750-0062, www.playachiquitalodge.com. 12 cabins with private bathroom, German-Tico restaurant and bar, 500 m from beach, naturalist guides available.

C-D Cabinas Something Different, T759-9014, Manzanillo. 10 very clean rooms, 6 with a/c, all with private bath and hot water, big parking area and kitchen use available, nice local people.

E Cabinas Las Veraneras, Manzanillo. Rooms with shared bath.

E Cabinas/Restaurant Maxi, Manzanillo, T754-2266. Basic rooms, highly respected seafood restaurant.

E Selvin Cabins and restaurant, Playa Uva. With room and dormitory accommodation.

Eating

Puerto Limón *p1090, map p1090*

Cheap food is available in and around the Central Market. *Casados* in market in the day, outside it at night, good, cheap food. Try *pan bon*, spicy bread from Creole recipe, sold near bus stop for San José.

ΨΨΨ **Springfield**, north of town opposite the hospital. Stylish with a mix of Tico and international dishes. Best restaurant in town.

TT Antillita, Calle 6, Av 4-5. Caribbean rice and beans, meat, open evenings only.
TT Brisas del Caribe, facing Parque Vargas, Av 2, Calle 1, T758-0138. Cheap noodles, meat, seafood, and good service.
TT Marisquería El Cevichito, Av 2, Calle 1-2, T758-1380. Good fish, steaks and *ceviche* and good spot for people-watching.
TT Monte de Oro, Av 4, Calle 3-4. Serves good local dishes, in a rough and ready atmosphere.
TT Park Hotel, Av 3, Calle 1-2. Does good meals overlooking the sea.
TT Sabor Pizza, corner of Av 3 and Calle 4. Good pizza.
TT Soda Yans, Av 2, Calle 5-6. Popular spot.
T Diplo's, Av 6, Calle 5-6. The best, and cheapest, Caribbean food in town.
T Doña Toda, near market on main square. Good.
T Milk Bar La Negra Mendoza, at the central market. Good milk shakes and snacks.
T Samkirson, Calle 3, Av 3-4. One of several Chinese restaurants. Good value.
T Soda Mares, overlooking market square. 0700-1400, good food.

Parque Nacional Tortuguero *p1091*

TT Café Caoba, Tortuguero village. Cheap and has excellent pizza, sandwiches and shrimp.
TT Miss Junie's, north end of Tortuguero village. Very popular, has good local dishes, reservation necessary.
TT The Vine, Tortuguero village. Pizzas and sandwiches.
T El Dolar, Tortuguero village. Simple restaurant, small menu, good *casado*.
T Restaurant El Muellecito, Tortuguero village, T710-6716. Also 3 simple cabins.

Cahuita and Parque Nacional Cahuita *p1092, map p1092*

If the catch is good restaurants have lobster.
TTT La Casa Creole, Playa Negra, by the Magellan Inn, 2 km north of Cahuita, T755-0104 (for reservations). A culinary feast of French and Creole creations, from US$8. Mon-Sat 0600-0900. Recommended.
TT Cha Cha Cha, Cahuita, T755-0191. International menu, great food and service, refreshing chic decor, very good pasta from US$4. Opens at 1700, closed Mon.
TT Chao's Paradise, T755-0421, Playa Negra. Typical Caribbean food and seafood specials, good little reggae bar, with oropendula nests overlooking the beach.
TT Restaurant Palenque Luisa , Cahuita. Has the distinctly tropical feel with split-bamboo walls, sand floors and a good *menú típico* .
TT Miss Edith's, Cahuita, T755-0248. Almost legendary. Delicious Caribbean and vegetarian food, nice people, good value, no alcohol licence, take your own, many recommendations for breakfast and dinner, but don't expect quick service. Open daily until 2130.
TT Restaurant Banana, top of Playa Negra. A good restaurant and bar away from the crowds. Recommended.
TT Sobre las Olas, Playa Negra, T755-0109. On the beach serving Tico and Mexican, popular bar in the evening. Closed Tue.
TT Sol y Mar, Cahuita. Open 0730-1200, 1630-2000, need to arrive early and wait at least 45 mins for food. Red snapper and volcano potato especially wicked, US$5; also good breakfasts, try cheese, egg and tomato sandwich, US$2. Good value.
TT Coral Reef, next to Coco's Bar, Cahuita. Very accommodating local management can cook to your tastes, great local food with seafood specialties.
TT-T Rest Le Fe, opposite Coco's Bar, Cahuita. Large variety of dishes all centered round rice and beans, good typical food.
TT Mango Tango Pizzeria, Cahuita. Great home-made pasta with a wide variety if Italian sauces, quite a rarity in these parts, good pizza, good restaurant.
TT-T 100% Natural Coffee Shop, Cahuita. Snacks, tapas and cocktails, and of course, natural coffees. Internet.
TT-T The Beach House, Cahuita. Bar and restaurant, cocktails served, laid-back establishment on the high street. Surf lessons and info available.
T Soda Priscilla, opposite Sol y Mar, Cahuita. Good budget breakfast pinto, eggs and fresh juices.
T Ice Cream Shop, high street, Cahuita. Ice cream and juice kiosk.
T The Pastry Shop, Playa Negra, T755-0275. Delicious breads, brownies and pies.

ΨΨΨ Amimodo, north end of town, overlooking the beach, beyond **Standord's**. Fine Italian restaurant with prices to match. Reputedly fantastic. Weekend Latin nights. Doesn't always come with a smile.

ΨΨΨ-Ψ Stanford's, Upstairs restaurant has a rather pricey, but good menu in arty surroundings.

ΨΨ Chili Rojo, main street (see map). Thai, Eastern and vegetarian food including humous and falafel platters and coconut curries and delicious home-made ice cream.

ΨΨ El Loco Natural, main street (see map, T750-0233. Healthy foods, live music weekends and a boutique.

ΨΨ El Parquecito, facing sea in the centre. Nice breezy atmosphere, specializes in pizza and Italian dishes.

ΨΨ Grant Seafood, main street. New seafood restaurant located over **Cabinas Grant**.

ΨΨ Jammin Juices and Jerk Chicken, by the coast. Roasted chicken with a variety of home-made sauces and salsas, also great vegetarian selection, open for breakfast, lunch and early dinners. Recommended.

ΨΨ La Terraza, main street, above **Frutería Ivone**. New Italian. Lovely owner and chef, will cook to your requirements – ravioli, lasagne, pastas and seafood and tiramisu for afters.

ΨΨ Peng Peng restaurant, in **Hotel Puerto Viejo**. New Chinese and Asian food restaurant, run by very friendly crew, in the vibrant and very lively **Hotel Puerto Viejo**. Serves sushi, soups, stir fries, curries, tasty cream cheese won tons, saki and 'bubble teas', good food, good prices. Recommended.

ΨΨ Pizzeria Rusticone, 1 block back from main street (see map). Best pizzas in town cooked in original ovens, excellent pastas including home-made ones, all at good prices, recommended.

ΨΨ Salsa Brava, north end of town (see map). Spanish food, closed Sun. Recommended.

ΨΨ Tamara, on main street, T750-0148. Open 0600-2100. Local good fish dishes, popular throughout the day and packed at weekends.

ΨΨ-Ψ Bread and Chocolate, centre of town (see map). A breakfast café run by a special American family who drove to Costa Rica from Texas in a school bus run on vegetable oil. They pride themselves on home baking and their morning menu is filled with good, home-made choices, ranging from eggs, bacon and fresh bread to oatmeal with apple and cinnamon. Breads and cakes, mint and nut brownies and divine chocolate truffles are home-made and the café is well recommended.

ΨΨ-Ψ Hot Rocks, main street. American joint that serves steak, nachos and pizzas, cocktails and beers served in front of cinema-size movie screen – they show 3 films a night, free with dinner or drinks.

Ψ Carlos Pool Bar, 1 block from the main street, behind **Pollo Frito**. Locally owned bar that serves cheap and large *casados*, soda included in the price. Pool tables and sometimes a movie showing.

Ψ Lidia's Place, south of centre. Good typical food and to-die-for chocolate cake that does not hang round.

Ψ Peace and Love Coffee, south end of town. Ex-**Bambú** owners. Italian crew making fantastic home-made breads and pizzas, lasagnas and other mouthwatering delicatessen items at surprisingly reasonable prices.

Ψ Pizza Boruca, opposite the church (see map). Best pizza slices in all Costa Rica, cheap and delicious – this man is always busy.

Ψ Pollo Frito, north end of town, opposite **Stanford's** (see map). Affectionately named the 'fried chicken place' – no one ever remembers its real name. A late-opening café, perfect for late-night snacking, serves mainly (as you would guess) fried chicken and yucca, but also rice and beans, *casados* and sandwiches.

Ψ Soda Miss Sam, south of the centre, good local food piled high, good value.

Ψ Soda Palmer, north end of town (see map). Cheap Chinese food, big plates, nice people.

Ψ Red Stripe Café, south end of town, opposite the bus stop (see map). Snacks and smoothies.

Cafés and bakeries

Monchies, 2 blocks off the main street (see map). Delicious baked goods.

Pan Pay, beachfront. Good bakery. Also serve great breakfasts: eggs with avocado, fresh bread and tomato salsa, omelets, pastries, etc. A good place to read the paper and nod at the locals – a very popular spot in the morning.

Around Puerto Viejo *p1094*

🍴🍴 **El Living**, Playa Cocles. Pizza, drinks and music, very laid back, and good prices.

🍴🍴 **La Isla Inn**, Playa Cocles. Serves Japanese Caribbean fusion, including sushi, soups, salads, and stir-fry.

🍴🍴 **Magic Ginger**, Hotel Kasha, Playa Chiquita. Restaurant and bar serving gourmet French cooking, seafood specials and exotic salads.

🍴🍴 **Rest Maxi**, Manzanillo. Reggae-style restaurant serving typical Caribbean food and seafood specials.

🍴 **Aguas Dulce**, Playa Cocles. Ice creams, pastries and sandwiches.

Entertainment

Cahuita and Parque Nacional Cahuita *p1092, map p1092*

Bars and clubs

Rikki's Bar and **Cocos Bar** in the centre of Cahuita; the latter is the livelier of the 2 and hosts reggae nights on Fri and live music.

Coffee Bar, on the shore near **Cabinas** Jenny, is a good reggae spot.

Puerto Viejo de Talamanca *p1093, map p1094*

Bars and clubs

Puerto Viejo is still lamenting the loss of Bambu Bar, which was burnt down in 2005. Puerto probably has the most lively nightlife on Costa Rica's entire Caribbean coast and has always run on an unspoken rota – each bar having a particular night, and this is still (loosely) the case. Various bars have bid for Bambu's Mon and Fri reggae nights, which now run between **Sunset Bar** (by the bus stop) and **Baba Yaga** (next to **Hotel Puerto Viejo**). Sunset has live events and pool tables, they have also taken over **Jam Night** on Wed (that used to be held at **Tesoro** in Cocles). Baba Yaga is smaller and more intimate; and they run the occasional dance music event.

Jhonny's Bar (or **Mike's Playground**, depending on how local you are – Jhonny's is the original) is perhaps the best night now in town on Thu, Sat and Sun. Right on the beach, with Puerto's reggae/dancehall best.

Stanford's Disco, tends to be the quietest, despite being one of the orginals.

Bar In and In, over Rest Tamara in the high street is a much more laid-back reggae bar for pre-party drinks and cocktails. There is a small bar at **Café Puerto Viejo**, with olives and expensive cocktails – ambient and chilled music makes a change from the reggae everywhere else.

Activities and tours

Parque Nacional Tortuguero *p1091*

Tour operators

Most people visit Tortuguero as part of a 2- or 3-day package tour from San José flying into the airport, or catching an agency bus and boat from Matina. It is possible to travel to Tortuguero independently (see Transport, below). Tours from San José include transport, meals, 2 nights' lodging, guide and boat trips for US$219-252 per person (double occupancy).

Mawamba, T223-2421, www.grupomawamba.com. Minimum 2 people, 3 days/2 nights, daily, private launch so you can stop en route, with launch tour of national park included. Accommodation at **Mawamba Lodge**, 3-day/2-night package, Tue, Fri, Sun US$260, using **Ilan Ilan Lodge**, T255-3031. **Tortuga Lodge** and **Laguna Lodge** also offer similar packages.

OTEC (see page 987) runs 3-day/2-night tours for US$180, with small student discount; a trip to see the turtles in Jul-Sep costs extra. Tours from Puerto Viejo de Sarapiquí, including boat trip to Tortuguero, meals, 2 nights' lodging, guide and transport to San José cost US$275-400 per person (double occupancy). *Riverboat Francesca*, T226-0986, www.tortuguerocanals.com, costs US$190 per person 2 day-1 night trips exploring the canals for exquisite wildlife, sportfishing. Longer packages are also available.

Caño Blanco Marina, 2 Av, 1-3 C, San José, T256-9444 (San José), T710-0523 (Tortuguero). Runs a daily bus-boat service San José-Tortuguero at 0700, US$50 return, Book in advance – if you miss the boat, there is nothing else in Caño Blanco Marina.

Organizing a package trip from **Puerto Limón** is more difficult. **Viajes Tropicales Laura**, T758-2410, have been highly recommended, daily service, open return

US$60 if phoned direct, more through travel agencies, pick-up from hotel, will store luggage, lunch provided, excellent for pointing out wildlife on the way. An inclusive 2-day, 1-night package a from Puerto Limón with basic accommodation, turtle-watching trip and transport (no food) costs from US$99 per person.

Guides Several local guides have been recommended, including **Johnny Velázquez**; **Alberto**, who lives next to Hotel Mary Scar; **Rubén Bananero**, who lives in the last house before you get to the National Park office, sign on pathway, recommended for 4-hr tour at dusk and in the dark; **Chico**, who lives behind Sabina's Cabinas, US$2 per hr, and will take you anywhere in his motor boat; **Ernesto**, who was born in Tortuguero, and has 15 years' experience as a guide, contact him at Tropical Lodge or through his mother, who owns Sabina's Cabinas; **Rafael**, a biologist who speaks Spanish and English (his wife speaks French), and lives 500 m behind Park Rangers' office (ask rangers for directions); he also rents canoes. **Ross Ballard**, a Canadian biologist who can be contacted through Casa Marbella.

Daryl Loth lives locally and runs **Tortuguero Safaris**, T833-0827, safari@racsa.co.cr. **Barbara Hartung** of **Tinamon Tours**, T709-8004, www.tinamontours.de, a biologist who speaks English, German and Spanish, is recommended for boat, hiking and turtle tours in Tortuguero (US$5 per person per hr; all-inclusive trips from Limón 3-days, 2-nights, US$150). Both Daryl and Barbara are strong supporters of using **paddle power**, or at most electric motors.

There are several **boats for rent** from Tortuguero, ask at the *pulpería*. The use of polluting 2-stroke motors is outlawed in Tortuguero, and the use of 4-stroke engines is limited to 3 of the 4 main water channels.

Cahuita and Parque Nacional Cahuita *p1092*

Snorkelling equipment and surfboards available for rent. **Horses** can be hired, but try to ensure they are in good shape. **Bicycles** can be hired for about US$7 per day and you can cycle to Puerto Viejo and the Panamanian border through some beautiful scenery.

Tour operators

Wide range of activities available including water sports and nature tours.

Cahuita Tours, T755-0232, exotica@racsa.co.cr, excursions by jeep and glass-bottomed boat tours over the reefs, bike, diving and snorkelling equipment rental, international telephone service (ICE) and Western Union money transfer. GrayLine bus travel can be arranged here.

Roberto's Tours, office located at his restaurant (**Roberto's**) on the main street. Very nice people run all the usual tours of the area including snorkelling and diving.

Willies Tours, T843-4700, www.willies-costarica-tours.com. Willie is most helpful and knows everything about Cahuita and surrounding areas. He runs tours to Tortuguero, Panama, Bri Bri indigenous reserve and whitewater rafting in the Pacuare river. The office is located opposite the bus stop, where he also runs an internet café.

Puerto Viejo de Talamanca *p1093, map p1094*

Tour operators

Tours in Puerto Viejo include canopy, snorkelling, boat trips and diving in Cahuita and Manzanillo, trips to an indigenous reserve, rafting in Pacuare, kayaking, bird watching, etc. ATEC is the easiest source of information but you can also try **Canopy Tour** and **Terraventuras**, T750-0750, www.terraventuras.com, **Exploradores Outdoors**, T750-6262, www.exploradoresoutdoors.com, **Atlántico Tours**, T750-0004, offer several trips. **Reef Runner Divers**, T750-0480, Yuppi & Tino, T750-0621, **Dragon Scooter Rental**, T750-0728, in Puerto Viejo, and **Aguamar Adventures**, in Manzanillo, who have been operating since 1993, offer diving courses and local trips. Prices from US$35.

Transport

Puerto Viejo de Sarapiquí *p1088*

Bus Buses stop on north side of park. From **San José** 7 daily from Gran Terminal del Caribe, 1½ hrs through PN Braulio Carrillo, or through Heredia, 4 daily, 3½ hrs. From **Cd Quesada**, 5 daily, 2½ hrs.

Car To get there by car from **San José**, after passing through the PN Braulio Carrillo take

Route 4, a paved road which turns off near Santa Clara to Puerto Viejo; it bypasses Río Frío and goes via Las Horquetas. A more scenic but longer route leaves from Heredia via San Miguel and La Virgen, and on to Puerto Viejo.

Guápiles, Guácimo and Siquirres *p1089*
Bus In Guápiles, buses leave from a central terminal a block to the north of the church. Regular buses to **San José** and **Puerto Limón**. Buses to **Puerto Viejo de Sarapiquí** ever 2½ hrs, and to **Río Frío** every 1½ hrs.

For Siquirres, at least 1 bus per hr leaves Gran Terminal del Caribe in **San José**, 2½-hr journey.

Puerto Limón *p1090, map p1090*
Bus Town bus service is irregular and crowded. Service from **San José** with **CoopeLimón**, T233-3646 and **Caribeño**, T222-0610, at least every hr, 0500-2000, daily. Arrive and depart from Calle 2, Av 1-2, US$3, 2½ hrs. Also services to **Guápiles** and **Siquirres**. From same stop buses to Siquirres/Guápiles, 13 daily, 8 direct. Near Radio Casino on Av 4, Calle 3-4, buses leave for **Sixaola**, first 0500, last 1800, US$2.50, stopping at **Cahuita**, Puerto Viejo and Bri Bri en route. To **Manzanillo**, at 0600, 1430, returning 1130, 1900, 1½ hrs, US$1.50. To **Moín** from Calle 5, Av 3-4, every 30 mins between 0600-2200.

Parque Nacional Tortuguero *p1091*
Air Daily flights from **San José** with Nature Air (US$$70).

Bus and boat It is quite possible to travel to Tortuguero independently, but more challenging than the all-inclusive packages. There are a couple of options. From **Limón**, regular vessels leaves from the Tortuguero dock in **Moín**, north of Limón, US$50 return. It is a loosely run cooperative, but boats generally leave by 1000. If possible, book in advance through the Tortuguero Information Centre (check the times; they change frequently). If you are in a group,you may be able to charter a boat for approximately US$200.

From **Limón**, the bus/boat combination is the cheapest option and a mini-adventure in itself. Take the 0900 bus to Cariari from the Terminal Gran Caribe, arriving around 1045. Walk 500 m north to the ticket booth behind the police station where you can buy you bus/boat ticket to Tortuguero. Take the 1200 bus to **La Pavona**, arriving around 1330. Take one of the boats to Tortuguero, which will arrive about 1500. The journey is about US$10 one way. Don't be talked into a package if you're not interested – there are plenty of services to choose from in Tortuguero. The return service leaves at 0830 and 1330 giving you 1 or 2 nights in Tortuguero. (There appears to be an attempt to monopolize this service but for the time being at least, there are a couple of boats in operation.)

It is also possible to take a bus from Siquirres to **Freeman** (unpaved road), a Del Monte banana plantation, from where unscheduled boats go to Tortuguero; ask around at the bank of the Río Pacuare, or call the public phone office in Tortuguero (T710-6716, open 0730-2000) and ask for **Johnny Velázquez** to come and pick you up, US$57, maximum 4 passengers, 4 hrs. Sometimes heavy rains block the canals, preventing passage there or back. Contact **Willis Rankin** (Apdo 1055, Limón, T798-1556) an excellent captain who will negotiate rampaging rivers. All riverboats for the major lodges (see below) leave from Hamburgo or Freeman. If excursion boats have a spare seat you may be allowed on.

Barra del Colorado *p1091*
Air Flights to **San José** daily with Sansa (US$63).

Boat To **Tortuguero** takes 1½ hr and costs US$50. A motorized canoe can take 8 people and costs up to US$80, 2 hrs. Try and arrive in a group as boats are infrequent.

Cahuita and Parque Nacional Cahuita *p1092, map p1092*
Bus Service direct from **San José**'s Terminal del Caribe, **Sixaola**, 0600, 1530, return 0730, 0930, 1100, 1630, US$4, T257-8129, **Transp Mepá**, 4 hrs, US$4.50, and from **Puerto Limón**, in front of Radio Casino, 0500-1800, return 0630-2000, 1 hr, US$0.80, T758-1572,

both continuing to Bribri, and Sixaola (dirt road) on the Panamanian border (US$1, 2 hrs). The bus drops you at the crossing of the 2 main roads in Cahuita.

Puerto Viejo de Talamanca *p1093, map p1094*
Bus Daily service from **San José** from Gran Terminal del Caribe, 0600, return 0700, 0900, 1100, 1600, 4½ hrs, US$4.65; from **Limón** daily from Radio Casino, 0500-1800, return 0600-2000, 1½ hrs; 30 mins from **Cahuita**, US$0.45. To **Manzanillo** at 0700, 1530, 1900, returning 0500, 0830, 1700, ½ hr, US$0.80. To **Sixaola** 5 daily, 0545 until 1845, 2 hrs, US$1.80.

Penshurst *p1092*
Bus Small buses leave **Limón** (Calle 4, Av 6) for Valle de Estrella/Pandora, 7 a day from 0500, at 2-hourly intervals, last at 1800, 1½ hrs (returning from Pandora at similar times).

Around Puerto Viejo *p1094*
Express bus to **Manzanillo** from Terminal Sixaola, **San José**, daily, 1600, return 0630. From **Limón** daily 0600, 1430, return 1130, 1900, 1½ hrs.

Directory

Puerto Limón *p1090, map p1090*
Banks Usual hours and services, all with ATMs at Banco de Costa Rica, Av 2, Calle 1, Mon-Fri 0900-1400; Banco Nacional, Av 2, Calle 3, with ATM; Banco Popular, Calle 3, Av 1-2, with ATM. Banco de San José, Av 3, Calle 3-4, with ATM. **Internet** Edutec Internet, on 2nd level above Plaza Caribe, US$2.30 per hr. Also 24-hour access at Internet, 1 block from Mas X Menos, US$1 per hr. **Laundry** Av 2, Calle 5-6, price per item, not that cheap, but 2-hr turnaround. **Medical services** Red Cross, Calle 3, Av 1-2, T758-0125. **Hospital**, on road to Moin, T758-2222. **Post office** Opposite central for international calls at Av 2, Calle 5-6 and at Calle 3, Av 4-5, Mon-Thu 0800-1700, Fri 0800-1600.

Cahuita and Parque Nacional Cahuita *p1092, map p1092*
Banks There are none. Money exchange is difficult except occasionally for cash dollars (Cahuita Tours changes dollars and TCs). Take plenty of colones from Limón. Nearest banks are is in Puerto Viejo and Bribri (20 km) but several places accept credit cards. **Internet** Cyberbet, part of Cabinas Safari , US$1.60 per hr. Willies Tours has internet, opposite the bus station. **Post office** Next to police station at northern end of town.

Puerto Viejo de Talamanca *p1093, map p1094*
Banks Banco Nacional is 3 blocks south of ATEC, with ATM machine, but only take Visa or Plus (not MasterCard of Cirrus). The bank in Bribri does accept MasterCard credit card. You can change TCs and cash at Manuel León's general store on the beach. Cabinas Los Almendros changes TCs, euros and US dollars, and give credit card advance. **Internet** From ATEC, US$2.50 per hr. Also Jungle Café, fastest internet in town, but pricey and pre-pay cards only. Books, Librería & Bazar Internet, also fast, US$2.50 per hr. Internet next to Hot Rocks, slow, but open late. **Medical services** Chemist at the new shopping area by the bank. **Police** On sea front. **Post office** At the new shopping area by the bank. US$2 to send, US$1 to receive, atecmail@racsa.co.cr. **Telephone** There is a public telephone outside the ATEC office.

Panama

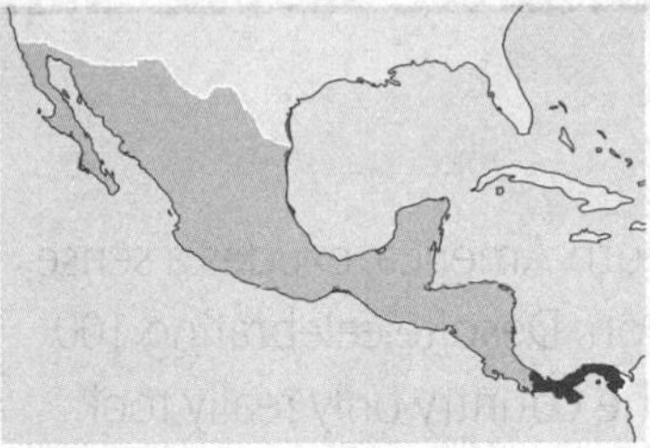

Footprint features

Introduction

Panama, the crossing point to South America, exudes a sense of self-discovery and determination. Despite celebrating 100 years of independence in 2003, the country only really took control of itself in January 2000 when, after years of wrangling, the US finally handed over the running of the inter-oceanic Panama Canal. The 'Big Ditch' has always been at the heart of Panama, but now the country has begun to tell the world about its other claims to fame. Around Bocas del Toro beaches, coral and tiny coloured frogs are pulling in the crowds, while the islands of the San Blas archipelago continue to draw visitors to this distant corner of the country. The cool highlands around Boquete are ideal for hiking and have enough whitewater to satisfy river rafters. Beyond and between these extremes, the opportunities for exploration remain largely unexploited. To the west is the expansive rainforest of the Darién Gap, where even the great Pan-American Highway is forced to give way to the power of nature.

Until a century ago Panama was part of Colombia, linked by the ominous and daunting Darién Gap. Its strategic importance as a bridge between two oceans has given Panama a global role but even today it is not thought of as part of Central America by others in the region. Secretive banking practices made it an important international finance centre, while impressive standards of living made it the destination of choice for a handful of high-profile asylum seekers and a useful dumping ground for the international community. However, since the ousting of former US ally and president Manuel Noriega, Panama has started to change, letting go of its past and exploring new ground as a destination for adventurous travellers.

★ Don't miss...

1 **Panamá Viejo** The sacking of Golden Panama in 1519 is the stuff of pirate legend; explore the ruins and take a trip back in history, page 1131.
2 **The Canal** Affectionately known as the 'Big Ditch', the canal is one of the world's engineering marvels and greatest short cuts, page 1148.
3 **San Blas** The Caribbean archipelago offers a great insight into the autonomous lifestyle of the Kuna people, page 1160.
4 **Isla de Coiba** Dive the sites around this untouched Pacific island, page 1170.
5 **Chiriquí Highlands** Explore the western highlands on foot or plummet down the whitewater in a raft, page 1177.
6 **Bocas del Toro** Beautiful, isolated beaches and coral reefs; hardly surprising this is the fastest-growing destination in Central America, page 1188.
7 **Darién** Trying hard to shake off the dangerous image, parts of the rainforest wilderness are opening up to visitors and trips are always memorable, page 1198.

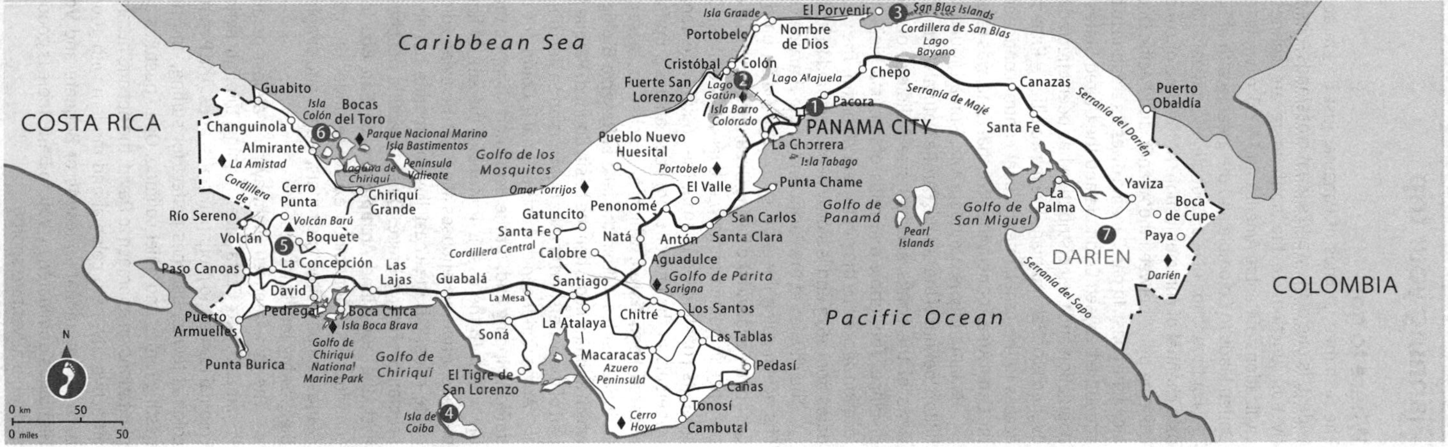

Planning your trip

Where to go

The S-shaped isthmus of Panama, just 80 km at its narrowest and 193 km at its widest, is one of the world's great crossroads – its destiny has been entirely shaped by this junction. To the north there are connections and links with the great civilizations of Central America and Mexico, while to the south, the wilderness of the Darién leads to Colombia and the great wealth of South America.

For thousands of years people and animals have used the Panamanian corridor as a channel of communication. At the time of conquest, the Spaniards used it as a crossing point between the Atlantic and Pacific Oceans and forays north and south along the coast. In part Panama owes its creation to this positioning (the outcome of a squabble between Colombia and the United States in 1903), and the make-up of its population and their distribution has been effected by this corridor ever since. Today, over 40% of Panamanians live in two cities – Panama City and Colon – which control access to the canal. International control continued until 31 December 1999, when the Canal Area, formerly the US Canal Zone, was returned to Panamanian jurisdiction.

Panama City is a modern city, spread round the Bahía de Panamá. From the hilltop lookout of the unique Parque Natural Metropolitano, visitors enjoy spectacular views of the banks and high-rise buildings of the capital with the Canal in the distance. The rubble and ruins of Panamá Viejo lie to the east, the city's original location sacked by the pirate Henry Morgan. The younger replacement of Casco Viejo dates from 1673 and is slowly being restored to its former glory.

The city lies at the Pacific end of the **Panama Canal**, a feat of engineering which lifts ocean-going liners 26 m to Lago Gatún on the 67.5-km voyage between the Caribbean Sea and the Pacific Ocean. The financial cost of the canal was staggering; the price in human terms was over 22,000 lives. Owned and operated by the USA since its construction in 1914, the 16-km wide Canal Zone reverted to Panamanian ownership at the end of 1999. The Canal is surprisingly beautiful, consisting of the river-fed **Lago Gatún**, which is reached by a series of locks on the Pacific and Caribbean sides. Within the lake is **Reserva Biológica de la Isla Barro Colorado**, to which animals fled when the basin flooded. **Parque Nacional Soberanía**, which forms part of the watershed of Lake Gatún, is an easier trip, just 30 minutes from the capital.

At the Caribbean end of the Canal is **Colón**, the country's major port for container traffic, shipping and, for the dedicated shopper, the second largest tax-free zone in the world. To the east is **Portobelo**, the site of flamboyant 16th- and 17th-century markets, where warehouses filled with Peruvian gold and silver were guarded against pirate raids. Off the coast lies the marine burial site of the British buccaneering seaman Sir Francis Drake. Quiet, beautiful beaches await the visitor today. Further east, the 365-island **Archipiélago de San Blas** of crystalline waters and palms continues its autonomous existence under the guidance of the Kuna nation. The islands can be visited and hotels, lodges and simple cabinas are opening to cater for the growing tourist interest.

The Pan-American Highway runs almost parallel to the Pacific coastline from Panama City to Costa Rica, running through agricultural zones, Pacific beaches, colonial towns and mountain landscapes. The **Península de Azuero** is dotted with old colonial towns, beaches perfect for surfing, and nature reserves of wetland birds, nesting turtles and quiet solitude. Open pastures and savannahs give way to sugar plantations on approach to **David**, the hot and humid third city of the Republic. It is an attractive city, both colonial and modern with good communications and an ideal base for the mountain resorts of **Boquete** and **Volcán**. Up in the cooler **Chiriquí Highlands** dominated by **Volcán Barú**, there is good hiking, horse-riding, river rafting and other adventure sports.

North of the **Talamanca Mountains**, banana plantations stretch across the northern Caribbean lowlands that surround **Laguna de Chiriquí**. The offshore islands of **Bocas del Toro** and the **Parque Nacional Marino Isla Bastimentos** are home to nesting turtles, birds and other wildlife. Once cut off and difficult to reach, the islands are growing in popularity. If lying around relaxing on idyllic beaches isn't appealing enough, the snorkelling and diving on the unspoilt reefs is excellent.

Darién in the east is the most inhospitable part of Panama where all roads, including the Pan-American Highway, eventually just peter out. With no land links between Panama and Colombia, the fit and adventurous are tempted to cross one of the world's last great wildernesses by foot or boat to the border and Colombia beyond. While not impossible, several high-profile kidnappings have occurred and it is extremely dangerous.

Suggested itinerary Most people arrive in Panama and head straight for **Bocas del Toro** - it's chilled, relaxed and there's a lot going on. From there it's a long haul to **Panama City**. A short trip to see or to travel the **Panama Canal** is essential. From **Colón** on the Caribbean it's a short trip out to the **San Blas Islands**. A couple of weeks should cover the main areas. If you're heading to South America, you can improvise a journey working along the coast to **Puerto Obaldía** or catch a boat to Cartagena from Colón. The overland journey through the **Darién Gap** is possible but not to be undertaken lightly. If in any doubt, fly.

When to go

The most popular time to visit is in the dry season from mid-Dec to mid-April. Temperatures vary little throughout the country ranging year-round temperatures from 30°-32°C (85°-90°F) in the day dropping to 21°-22°C (70°-72°F) at night. Above 500 m temperatures fall making the highland towns attractive spots to cool off.

Rainfall, however, varies greatly. The Caribbean side of the central Cordillera is soaked with around 4000 mm annually. On the Pacific slope, it is much lighter with an average of 1700 mm. Both areas have pronounced seasonal variations. Rainfall begins to taper off sometime in December for the dry season. At this time rainfall on the Pacific side is scarce, or absent altogether, though on the Atlantic side you can expect a downpour 365 days a year. Even in the rainy season, however, the downpours, though heavy, usually last only an hour or two, and almost always come in mid-afternoon.

Finding out more

Instituto Panameño de Turismo (IPAT) toll-free T1-800-231-0568 from the US or Canada, www.visitpanama.com, or contact your nearest embassy. Once in country, IPAT have an office in Panama City (see page 1125).

Useful websites

www.businesspanama.com Economic and political information.

www.panama-guide.com Expatriate community forum, news, chat and information.

www.panamainfo.com An excellent site in English with good general information on Panama and links to several other national sites including newspapers, government organizations and tourist services.

www.panamatours.com A pure tourism site with a good overview of the country.

www.stri.org The Smithsonian Tropical Research Institute, whose headquarters are in Panama.

Language

Spanish is the national language, but English is widely understood. The older generation of West Indian immigrants speak Wari-Wari, a dialect of English incomprehensible to most other English speakers. In rural areas indigenous people use their own languages and many are bilingual.

Before you travel

Visas and immigration

Visitors must have a passport, and in most cases a tourist card (issued for 90 days and renewable for another 90 at the Immigration Office in Panama City, David or other provincial offices, eg Changuinola) or a visa (issued for 90 days, extendable for a further 90 days). Tourist cards are available at borders, from Panamanian consulates, *Ticabus* or airlines. To enter Panama officially you must have an onward flight ticket, travel agent confirmation of the same, or be able to demonstrate that you have sufficient funds (in cash, credit card or valid traveller's cheques) to cover your stay and departure. Recent travellers report these are asked for on the land frontier with Costa Rica and at Puerto Obaldía (Darién); generally officers are not very strict unless they fear you may be destitute.

You can check visas requirements at www.panaconsul.com.

Citizens from most European (including the United Kingdom) and Central American countries do not need a tourist card or a visa. Citizens from the United States, Canada, most Caribbean, South American and some Asian countries need a tourist card (US$5) available at airlines and travel agencies. Citizens of the following countries require a visa: Egypt, Peru, Dominican Republic, many African, Eastern European and Asian countries – check before travelling with you're the nearest Consulate office.

Nationals not requiring visas can renew their 90-day tourist cards once for a total of 180 days, after which you must leave the country for three days. The necessary documents must all be obtained in advance: a photo-ID card (*carnet*), to be surrendered when you return for an exit visa, will be issued; allow one to two hours for this. Requirements are two passport photos, a ticket out of the country or proof of sufficient funds, a brief letter explaining why you wish to extend your stay, a letter from a permanent resident accepting legal and financial responsibility for you during your extra days in Panama, and two photocopies of the name page and the entry stamp page of your passport. All papers must be presented at *Prórrogas* in the immigration office and a fee of US$11 paid for each 90-day extension before the photo ID card is issued. Requirements for renewing a visa are similar, but include two photocopies of the original visa.

Panama embassies and consulates

Australia, 39 Wardell Rd, Earlwood, Sydney NSW 2206, T9558-2500.
Austria, Elisabethstr 4/5/4/10, A-1010 Vienna, T587-2347.
Belgium, Av Louise 390-392, 1050 Brussels, T649-0729.
Canada, 130 Albert St, Suite 300 Ottawa, ON, Kip 564, T236-7177.
Costa Rica, Calle 38, Av 7 y 9, San José, T257-3241.
France, 145 Av de Suffren, 75015 Paris, T4566-4244.
Germany, Joachim-Karnatz-Allee 45, 3 OG, 10557 Berlín, T30-226-05811.
Israel, Rehov Hei Be´iyar 10/3, Tel Aviv 62998, T696-0849.
Italy, Viale Regina Margherta No 239, Cuarto Piso, Interno 11, 00198 Roma, T1156-60707.
New Zealand, Shortland St, Auckland, T379-8550.
Nicaragua, del Cuartel de Bomberos 1 cuadra abajo, Managua, T266-2224.
South Africa, 832 Duncan St, Brooklyn, Pretoria, 0181, T/F1236-22629.
Spain, Claudio Coello 86, 1° 28006, Madrid T576-7668.
Sweden, Ostermalmsgatan 59, 114 50, 102 04 Stockholm, T662-6535.
UK, 40 Hertford St, London W1Y 7TG, T020-7493-4646.
USA, 2862 McGill Terrace NW, Washington DC 20008, T202-483-1407.

Embassies/consulates in these and other countries can be checked at www.mire.gob.pa.

Customs and duty free

Panamanian Customs are strict; drugs without a doctor's prescription may be confiscated.

Cameras, binoculars, etc, 500 cigarettes or 500 g of tobacco and three bottles of alcoholic drinks for personal use can be taken in free of duty. However, passengers leaving Panama by land are not entitled to any duty-free goods.

Money

Currency → *US$1=1 balboa.*

The unit of currency in Panama is the balboa (B/.), but Panama is one of the few countries in the world which issues no paper money; US banknotes are used exclusively, and US notes and coins are legal tender. There are 'silver' coins of 50c (called a *peso*), 25c (called *cinco reales* or *cuara*, from US 'quarter'), 10c, nickel of 5c (called a *real*) and copper of 1c. All coins are used interchangeably with US equivalents, which are the same in size and composition. There is great reluctance in Panama to accept US$50 and US$100 dollar notes because of counterfeiting. Do not be offended if asked to produce ID and sign a register when spending them. You can take in or out any amount of currency. If travelling north remember that US dollar notes, especially smaller denominations, are useful in all Central American countries and may be difficult to obtain in other republics. Stocking up on a supply of US$5 and US$1 notes greatly facilitates border crossings and traffic problems in Central America where 'fees' and 'instant fines' can become exorbitant if you only have a US$20 note.

Credit cards

Visa ATMs are available at branches of **Telered** ⓘ *T001-800-111-0016*, if card is lost or stolen. MasterCard/Cirrus ATMs are available at **Caja de Ahorros** offices and others in the Pronto system. **MasterCard emergency number** ⓘ *T001-800-307-7309*; **Western Union** ⓘ *T269-1055*. See Panama City Directory, page 1146, for other ATMs and for credit card phone numbers.

Cost of living and travelling

Prices are somewhat higher than in the rest of Central America, although food costs much the same as in Costa Rica. The annual average increase in consumer prices fluctuates in line with US trends.

Getting there

Air

From Europe No direct services. Connecting flights go to Miami, then by **American Airlines** or **Copa** to Panama City. **Iberia** goes from Madrid via Miami. From Frankfurt, Paris, Madrid and London, there is a connection via Bogotá with **Avianca** and **SAM**.

From USA Direct flights from Atlanta, Baltimore, Houston, Los Angeles, Miami, New York (some change planes in San José), Orlando and Portland. For other US cities, connections are made in Miami or Houston.

From Central America Direct flights to Cancún and Mexico City, Guatemala City, Managua, San José and San Salvador. No direct flights to Tegucigalpa, but connections with **Lacsa** through San José or **Taca** in San Salvador.

From South America Lots of flights from Colombia with **Copa** (Barranquilla, Bogotá, Cartagena, Cali, Medellín) and **SAM** (Bogotá). One-way tickets are not available from Colombia to Panama on **SAM** or **Copa**, but a refund on an unused return portion is possible, less 17% taxes, on **SAM. LAB** fly from Santa Cruz (Bolivia). From Guayaquil and Quito, **Continental, Ecuatoriana** and **Copa. Copa** from Santiago de Chile and Lima. From Caracas, **Mexicana, Copa** and **Aeropostal.**

From the Caribbean **Copa** has flights from Havana, Kingston, Port-au-Prince, San Juan and Santo Domingo.

Road

Overland passage to Panama from Costa Rica on the Pacific side is at Paso Canoas, where crossing is straightforward, simple and fast. International buses make the journey from Costa Rica to David and on to Panama City stopping briefly for paperwork at the border (see page 1172). A less popular but more entertaining crossing point is Sixaola/Guabito on the Caribbean coast, made significantly more straightforward by a new road between Almirante and Chiriquí Grande linking the region to the rest of the country. Passengers and vehicles (car or motorcycle) are given 30 days at the border. US$1 is payable for fumigation, US$3 for minibus. Rental vehicles may not leave Panama.

Overland routes to Colombia are possible through the Darién Gap where the purist has a difficult, but not impossible challenge. Alternatively it is possible to hop, skip and jump your way along the Caribbean coast taking canoes, but the cost can be considerable. For details see the Darién section, page 1198 .

Sea

The Panama Canal is on the itineraries of many shipping services from Europe and the USA which take passengers but charges are high.

There are several boats that make the journey from Isla Grande on the Caribbean across to **Cartagena**, charging US$150-200 for the journey. It is also possible to travel by sea to/from **Colombia**. See page 1163 for San Blas connections. A couple of boats travel weekly from Colón to **San Andrés Island**, Colombia, from where there are connections to Cartagena; the **Johnny Walker** takes 30 hours, but the service is very irregular and travellers have sometimes had to wait over a week in vain. There are (contraband) boats from Coco Solo, Colón, to the Guajira Peninsula, Colombia. The uncomfortable three-day journey is undertaken entirely at your own risk and you may have to wait days for a sailing. You have to bargain for your fare on these boats and accommodation is a little primitive.

Staying closer to the coastline it is possible to cross the border to Colombia on the Caribbean side close to **Puerto Obaldía**, and on Pacific coast via Jaqué and possibly La Palma. These routes are not cheap and can take several days (see page 1202).

Touching down

Airport information

Tocumen International Airport is 27 km east of the city centre. Taxis (US$25) and buses run to Panama City. For a lower price, take a shared cab (compartivo), and while you may wait a little longer the price becomes US$10-15 for two or three people respectively. An airport exit tax of US$20 has to be paid by all passengers (cash only). There is a US$4 tax on air tickets over US$100 purchased in Panama.

Local customs and laws

Tipping In restaurants tip 10% of the bill, often added to the bill in Panama City. Porters would expect US$1 for assistance at the airport. Taxi drivers don't expect tips, see Panama City Directory, page 1146.

Touching down

Business hours Government departments Mon-Fri 0800-1200, 1230-1630. Banks open at different times, but usually open all morning, and often on Sat. Shops: Mon-Sat 0700/0800-1200, 1400-1800/1900.

Official time 5 hrs behind GMT.

Telephone Country code T+507.

Voltage 110 volt, 60 Hz AC. US-style plugs. 220 volt is occasionally available in homes and hotels.

Weights and measures Metric and imperial systems are both used.

Getting around

Air

There are local flights to most parts of Panama by several airlines. The most reliable is **Aeroperlas** (T315-7500, www.aeroperlas.com), the **Grupo Taca** subsidiary, with destinations throughout the country. Other services include: **Mapiex** (T315-0344, www.mapiex.com) offering charter flights between Bocas del Toro, David and Panama City. **Air Panama** (T315-0279, www.turismoaereo.com) offers a wide range of domestic services. **Ansa** (T226-7891) which flies to San Blas; **Parsa** (T226-3883) provides a charter service; **Transpasa** (T236-0842) has charter flights to San Blas; **Chitreana** (T226-4116) flies to Chitré, Los Santos, Las Tablas and Guararé, and **Aerotaxi** (T226-7891) operates a service to San Blas and charter flights.

On internal flights passengers must present their identity documents and have their luggage weighed. As excess baggage charges are frequent, ask if it is cheaper to ship excess as air freight (*carga*) on the same flight.

Road

There are now about 9700 km of roads, of which 3100 km are paved. The highway running from Colón to Panama City, widened to four lanes in 1999, is the only fully paved road crossing the isthmus. A well-maintained scenic road traverses the isthmus from Gualaca in Chiriquí to the town of Chiriquí Grande in Bocas del Toro, crossing the Swedish-built Fortuna hydroelectric dam. In 1999 construction was completed to extend the road from Chiriquí Grande to Almirante and the regional centre of Changuinola, opening up a beautiful new route along the Caribbean. The Pan-American Highway, usually called the *Interamericana* in Panama, runs east from Panama City to Chepo and into the province of Darién, and west to the Costa Rican border. It is paved throughout (as far east as the Panama/Darién provincial border) and is being improved. There is a modern toll road between Panama City and La Chorrera, and the section between David and La Concepción is a modern, four-lane highway. Expressways were built in 1999 to ease traffic congestion in and around Panama City.

Bus The bus network covers the entire country, generally with efficient, timely services. Some of the long-distance buses are small 'mini' buses, normally modern and comfortable, but large, modern air-conditioned buses are being introduced. They are more expensive than elsewhere in Central America. Slower 'regular' buses run in country areas. 'Express' buses with air conditioning operate between Panama City and Colón and to David and the border with Costa Rica.

Car **Car hire:** On average rates range from US$24 per day for a small saloon to US$65 for four-wheel-drive jeep, free mileage, insurance US$8 per day, 5% tax, US$500 deposit (can be paid by credit card), minimum age 23, home driver's licence acceptable. If you require a 4WD it is better to book a few days in advance. If planning to rent from an international company, consult them before leaving home. Sometimes very good deals are available that cannot be made at the Panama office. Rental cars are not allowed out of the country; they are marked by special licence plates.

Driving: Super grade gasoline (called *super*) costs about US$1.90 per US gallon (3.78 litres); unleaded is available in larger towns. Low octane (*regular* or *normal*) costs about US$1.80; diesel is about US$1.30. For motorcyclists, note that a crash helmet must be worn.

Taking a car with Panamanian plates to Costa Rica requires a permit from the Traffic Police (*Tránsito*) obtainable on presentation of the ownership certificate and a document from the Judicial Police (*PTJ*) indicating that the vehicle has not been reported stolen. A travel agency, for example **Chadwick's** in Balboa, will arrange this for you for US$30. Exit calls for four papers which cost US$4.20 (obtainable from customs in Paitilla Airport).

Sea

Boats and comfortable yachts provide tours all or part way through the canal. Contact tour operators in Panama City or Colón for details. It is also possible to travel through as a linehandling if you have sailing experience and turn up at the right time.

A regular ferry makes the journey to the island of Bocas del Toro from Almirante and Chirquí Grande on the western Caribbean coast. To the east, canoes serves the archipelago of San Blas.

Access to and from Colombia is possible by sea, along the Caribbean or Pacific coasts, although the journey takes several days and can be costly, see page 1202 .

Shipping a vehicle Taking a vehicle to Colombia, Venezuela or Ecuador is not easy or cheap. The best advice is to shop around the agencies in Panama City or Colón to see what is available when you want to go. Both local and international lines take vehicles, and sometimes passengers, but schedules and prices are very variable.

To Panama, recommended agency is **Panalpina**, Los Andes 2, Ojo de Agua, Vía Transmística, Panama City, T273-7066, www.panalpina.com. Jürgen Lahntaler speaks German, English and Spanish. **Panalpina** can also arrange shipment of vehicles to Ecuador, Venezuela and Chile.

To Colombia, agents include: **CSAV**, PO Box: 0832-2775, Edificio Frontenac, Local 2-B, Calle 50 y esq 54 Este, Ciudad de Panamá, T269-1613, www.csav.com, who also sail to other countries in South America on both the Atlantic and Pacific side.

To Barranquilla, **Vicente Simones' Colón**, T195-1262, beeper 270-0000, code 700283, will arrange all paperwork for US$25: car passage US$800, motorcycle US$50, plus US$50 per passenger, no accommodation on ship other than hammock space, take food and drink for a week (even though voyage should be three days).

To Cartagena, **Captain Newball**, Edificio Los Cristales, Piso 3, Calle 38 y Avenida Cuba, Panama City. On the same route **Central American Lines** sail once a week, agent in Panama, Colón T441-2880, Panama City T236-1036. Also, **Géminis Shipping Co SA**, Apdo Postal No 3016, Zona Libre de Colón, República de Panamá, T441-6269, F441-6571. Mr Ricardo Gil is helpful and reliable. Another agent, **Barwil**, Galerías Balboa Suite 35, Av Balboa, Panama City, T263-7755, www.barwil-panama.com, arranges shipments to Colombia (Cartagena) and elsewhere in Latin America from Balboa or Cristóbal.

Customs formalities at the Colombian end will take up to three days to clear (customs officials do not work at weekends). Cartagena is the best port because it is privately run, more secure and more efficient. Go first to customs: **DIAN**, Manga CL27 A 24-83, Diagonal DIAN, Jefe División de Servicio al Comercio Exterior. Here you will receive, free, the necessary documents to enter the port (takes about 24 hours).

To Ecuador, weekly (sometimes more often) sailings with combined services of **Maersk Line**, Plaza Credicorp Bank Panama, 22nd Floor, Suite 2201-2202, Panama City, T206-2200, www.maerskline.com, visit the website to find your nearest office.

Hapaglloyd agents are **AGENCO**, Edif Eurocentro, PB, Avenida Abel Bravo, Urbanización Obarrio, Panama City, T300-1400, www.hapag-lloyd.com, about US$900 for a 6-m container. Shipping to Guayaquil from Panama's new container port of Manzanillo, next to Colón, is the best choice, preferable to Colombia or Venezuela. **TNE (Transportes Navieros Ecuatorianos**, T269-2022) ship vehicles to Guayaquil; agent in Cristóbal, Agencia Continental SA, T445-1818. Another agent recommended in Cristóbal is **Associated Steamships**, in Balboa, T211-9400, www.shipsagent.com. Customs agents cost US$60 in Colón, US$120 in Guayaquil; 12 days from starting arrangements in Panama to leaving Guayaquil docks. Seek advice on paperwork from the Ecuadorean consul in Panama. **Barwil** (see above for Colombia) will ship vehicles to Arica, Chile.

To Venezuela, In addition to those mentioned above, agents include: **Cia Transatlántica España**, T269-6300, to La Guaira. **Vencaribe** (a Venezuelan line), agent in Cristóbal: **Associated Steamship (Wilford and McKay** – see above), T252-1258 (Panamá), T445-0461 (Cristóbal). There are several agencies in Colón/ Cristóbal across the street from the Chase Manhattan Bank and next door to the YMCA building. Formalities before leaving can be completed through a travel agency – recommended is **Continental Travel Agency**, at the Hotel Continental, T263-6162. In Venezuela there are customs complications (without carnet) and this route is not really recommended.

Maps

Topographic maps and aerial photos are sold by the **Instituto Geográfico Nacional Tommy Guardia (IGNTG)** ⓘ *Vía Simón Bolívar, opposite the National University (footbridge nearby, fortunately), T236 2444, take Transístmica or Tumba Muerto bus, Mon-Fri 0800-1530*, with physical maps of the country in two sheets at US$4 each. Other maps US$3.50 per map, eg 1:250,000 sheets covering Panama in sections, or 1:12,500 of Panama City. **ITM** (www.itmb.com) have a 1:480,000 travel map of Panama.

Sleeping

The very best in five-star luxury is available in Panama City and several comfortable lodges are found in the larger towns and mountain and jungle hideaways. If travelling further afield, accommodation in our C category and below is available in most towns of interest. Camping is generally tolerated.

Eating

In Panama City the range of food available is very broad with a profusion of restaurants and well-stocked supermarkets. In the interior tastes are simpler and available ingredients less varied. Most food is boiled or fried in vegetable oil (usually soybean oil). Virtually every restaurant will have a *comida corriente* (meal of the day) which will include a serving of meat, chicken or fish, white rice and a salad, a dish of boiled beans garnished with a *tajada* (slice) of fried ripe plantain. It will cost about US$2 in towns, perhaps more in the city, less in villages. A bowl of *sopa de carne* (beef broth with vegetables) or *de pescado* (fish chowder) is usually available as a first course for US$0.50. Breakfast normally consists of eggs, a small beefsteak or a slice of liver fried with onions and tomatoes, bread and butter and some combination of *frituras*.

The staple of Panamanian food is white rice, grown not in paddies but on dry land, and usually served at every meal, often with the addition of chicken, shrimp, vegetables, etc. Meat is usually fried (*frita*) or braised (*guisada*), rarely grilled except in the better restaurants. Beef is common; pork, chicken and the excellent fish are usually a better choice.

The national dish is *sancocho de gallina*, a stew of chicken, yuca, *ñame* (dasheen), plantain, cut-up pieces of corn on the cob, potatoes and onions and strongly flavoured with *culantro*, an aromatic leaf similar in flavour to coriander (*cilantro*). *Ropa vieja* ('old clothes') is beef boiled or steamed until it can be shredded, then sautéed with onions, garlic, tomatoes and green or red peppers, often served with yellow rice (coloured with *achiote*). Piquant *ceviche*, eaten as a first course or a snack with cold beer, is usually raw corvina or shellfish seasoned with tiny red and yellow peppers, thin slices of onion and marinated in lime juice; it is served very cold with crackers (beware of the bite). A speciality of the Caribbean coast is *sao*, pigs' feet pickled with lime and hot peppers. Also try *arroz con coco*, coconut rice, or the same with *tití*, tiny shrimp; also *fufú*, a fish chowder with coconut milk. *Mondongo* is the stewed tripe dish called *menudo* in Mexico; the Panamanian version is less spicy, but very well seasoned.

Sweets Most *panaderías* sell good pastries: in Panama City most of the European standards are available; in the country, try *empanadas* (see above), *orejas*, *costillas* or *ma'mellena* ('fills me up more', a sweet bread-pudding with raisins); *dulces* (of coconut, pineapple, etc), are cakes or pastries, not sweets/candies as elsewhere (the latter are *confites*). Among the items sold at the roadside you may see bottles stopped with a corncob, filled with *nance*, a strong-flavoured, yellow-green fruit packed with water and allowed to ripen and ferment slightly; *pifá/pixbae*, a bright orange fruit which, when boiled, tastes much like sweet potato (two or three will see you though to your next meal); *níspero*, the tasty, acidic yellow fruit of the chicle tree.

There are dozens of sweetened fruit drinks found everywhere in the country, making excellent use of the many delicious tropical and temperate fruits grown here: *naranja* (orange), *maracuyá* (passion fruit), *guayaba*, *zarzamora* (blackberry), *guanábana*, etc. The generic term is *chicha dulce* which also includes drinks made with rice or corn. Most common carbonated canned drinks are available. Panamanian beer tends to be low in alcohol, *Panamá* and *Soberana* are the most popular locally. *Chicha fuerte* is the alcoholic form of corn or rice drink fermented with sugar, brewed mostly in the countryside. Sample with care. The local rum, for example *Carta Vieja*, is not bad. *Seco*, a harsh brand of 'white lightning' made from the juice of sugar cane, brand name *Herrerano*, deserves considerable respect.

Festivals and events

1 Jan New Year's Day.
9 Jan Martyrs' Day.
Feb/Mar Shrove Tuesday Carnival.
Mar/Apr Good Friday.
1 May Labour Day (Republic).
15 Aug Panama City only.
1 Nov National Anthem Day.
2 Nov All Souls' Day.
3 Nov Independence Day.
4 Nov Flag Day
5 Nov Independence Day (Colón only).
10 Nov First Call of Independence.
28 Nov Independence from Spain.
8 Dec Mothers' Day.
25 Dec Christmas Day.

The fiestas in the towns are well worth seeing. Panama City at **Carnival** time, held on the four days before Shrove Tuesday, is the best. During carnival, women who can afford it wear the voluminous *pollera* dress, a shawl folded across the shoulders, velvet slippers, tinkling pearl and polished fish-scale hair ornaments (called *tembleques* from their quivering motion) in spirited shapes and colours. The men wear a *montuno* outfit: round straw hats, embroidered blouses and trousers sometimes to below the knee only, and carry the *chácara*, or small purse.

School holidays are December-March when holiday areas are busy; make reservations in advance.

At the **Holy Week** ceremonies at Villa de Los Santos the farces and acrobatics of the big devils – with their debates and trials in which the main devil accuses and an angel defends the soul – the dance of the 'dirty little devils' and the dancing drama of the Montezumas are all notable. The ceremonies at **Pesé** (near Chitré) are famous all over Panama. For other festivals in this region, see page 1167. At **Portobelo**, near Colón, there is a procession of little boats in the canals of the city. See under Portobelo for the *Congos*, page 1159. **Bullfights**, where the bull survives, are an important part of rural fairs, as are rodeo events.

The indigenous Ngöbe-Bugle (Guaymí) of Chiriquí province meet around 12 February to transact tribal business, hold feasts and compete for brides by tossing balsa logs at one another; those unhurt in this contest, known as *Las Balserías*, are viewed as heroes.

Shopping

More traditional Panamanian crafts include the colourful *molas* embroidered by the Kuna people of the San Blas islands. Masks, costumes, ceramics and woven hats can be found in several small villages dotted around the Azuero Peninsula. These are on sale in many places. Straw, leather and ceramic items are also available, as are carvings of wildlife made from wood, nuts and other natural materials. And of course, don't forget the quintessential **Panama hat**. Good ones are expensive. Duty-free imported goods including stereos, photographic equipment, perfume and clothes are cheap in the Colón Free Zone on the Caribbean coast. Most items are cheaper than at point of origin.

Sport and activities

Panama's tourism potential for special interest travel is only now being truly appreciated. It is a paradise for fishermen and birders alike; there are fine beaches and beautiful islands along both Atlantic and Pacific coasts; several indigenous as well as colonist communities provide considerable cultural interest; ecotourists can find a variety of challenging activities; and there are few routes as appealing to the long-distance traveller as crossing the Darién Gap (should this become safe again). Although visitor facilities in Panama are well developed for those engaged in international commerce, off-shore banking and for bargain-hunting shoppers, many other aspects of tourism are developing quickly.

Birdwatching

Birdlife is particularly abundant and varied in Panama and the country is an important destination for many birdwatchers. The Darién jungle, both coastlines, the forest fringe along the Canal, and the Chiriquí highlands (where quetzales, among many other species, may be seen) all provide their own special attractions for the birder. Those interested are referred to *A Guide to the Birds of Panama*, by R S Ridgely and J A Gwynne Jr (Princeton University Press, 1992.)

Diving

Diving is the best locally developed sport. The Caribbean coral reefs are similar to those of Belize and Honduras, extending southeast for 100 km along from the Costa Rica border and then from Colón 300 km to the border with Colombia. For information on these areas, see under Bocas del Toro, Portobelo and the San Blas Islands. The Pacific has quite different ecosystems owing to the much greater tidal ranges, differing water temperature and density. Places to go include Taboga, the Pearl Islands, Iguana Island and Parque Nacional Coiba. A third, and perhaps unique experience, is diving in the lakes of the Panama Canal, mainly to visit wrecks, submerged villages and the odd train left behind by the filling of the canal. **Scuba Panama** have a good website, www.scubapanama.com.

Hiking

Volcán Barú, Panama's highest peak at 3475 m, and nearby Cerro Punta are the two best climbs in the country but there are several excellent long walks. The hike from Cañita on the Darién road over the continental divide to Cartí is an alternative to flying to San Blas. The Caminos de Cruces and Real are jungle walks that follow in the steps of the Conquistadors crossing the continental divide and, if combined into an ocean-to-ocean hike, take eight days. A good range for hiking is the Serranía de Majé east of Panama City, visiting Embera villages and its howler monkey population. Closer is the Parque Nacional Chagres and a three-day walk from Cerro Azul to the coast.

Nature tourism

Some 43% of Panama remains forested and a quarter of the land has protected status that includes 14 national parks, wildlife refuges and forest reserves that are home to over 900 recorded bird species – more than neighbouring Costa Rica – including the endangered great green macaw and the spectacular harpy eagle, the national bird. Most national parks can be visited without hindrance if you can get there – there is supposed to be a US$3 entry fee but it is rarely charged. Transport can be very difficult and facilities non-existent; the largest, Darién National Park, is a good example. But slowly the value of the National Park system to tourism is being realized and some parks now have accommodation in huts for US$5 a bed. Contact **Asociación Nacional de Conservación de la Naturaleza** (ANCON) ⓘ *Amelia Denis de Icaza, Cerro Ancón, Quarry Heights, Apdo 153, T314-0060, www.ancon.org*, or **ANAM** who have their headquarters near the domestic terminal at Albrook.

Surfing

Surfing is best Isla Grande, Playa Venado on the Azuero Peninsula, Santa Catalina on the Pacific coast of Veraguas and Bocas del Toro. In the capital, **Kenny Myers** ⓘ *T6671-7777, www.panamasurftours.com*, offers tours to the more out of the way beaches. Check out **Riomar beach** ⓘ *near San Carlos, just 1.5 km from Panama City, T240-9128, www.riomar surf.com*. Options range from turn-up-and-surf to rooms, boards, classes and transport.

Whitewater rafting and river running

Whitewater rafting is best in the Chiriquí river system near David – classes III to IV on the Río Chiriquí (all year round) – and the Chiriquí Viejo Palón section (December to April) when the river is not in full speight. Also in the Parque Nacional Chagres area, north of Panama City, with grades II and III which some consider better for tubing – floating downriver on an inflated inner tube (generally best August to December).

Health

No particular precautions are necessary. Water in Panama City and Colón is safe to drink. Drink bottled water outside the cities, especially in Bocas del Toro where the expanding water system is not as clean as desired. In smaller towns, it is best to drink bottled or boiled water to avoid minor problems. Yellow fever vaccination is recommended before visiting Darién. Travelers to Darién Province and San Blas Province in Panama (including the San Blas Islands) should treat these as malarial areas in which there is resistance to chloroquine. Treatment is expensive; insurance underwritten by a US company would be of great help.

Keeping in touch

Communications

Internet The web has spread extensively throughout the country. Charges average out at about US$1.50-2 an hour. Details of cybercafés are given in the Directory text.

Post When sending mail, great care should be taken to address all mail as 'Panama' or 'RP' (Republic of Panama). Airmail takes up to 10 days, sea mail three to five weeks from Europe. Example rates for airmail (up to 15 g) are as follows: Central, North and South America and Caribbean, 35c; Europe, 45c up to 10 g, 5c for every extra 5 g; Africa, Asia, Oceania, 60c. Parcels to Europe can only be sent from the post office in the El Dorado shopping centre in Panama City (bus from Calle 12 to Tumba Muerto). Post offices, marked with blue and yellow signs, are the only places permitted to sell stamps.

Telephone Collect calls are permitted, three minutes minimum, rates are higher than direct, especially to USA. **Cable & Wireless** now run the telephone system and have offices in most towns. Cost of direct dialled calls, per minute, are between US$1-3.20. Calls are roughly 20-30% cheaper for most, but not all destinations from 1700-2200. Lowest rates apply Sunday all day. Many cheap international call centres in Panama City, check the the internet cafés on Vía Veneto, off Vía España for the best offers.

Dial T102 for the local operator and T106 for an international operator.

Public payphones take 5, 10 and sometimes 25 cent coins. Phone cards are available in denominations of US$3, 5, 10, 20 and 50, for local, national and international calls. There are prepaid *Aló Panamá* cards – dial 165 for connection in US$10, US$20, US$30 and US$50 denominations, but they are 50% more expensive than payphone cards. For **AT&T** dial T109. For *SPRINT* (collect calls only) T115 and for **MCI** T108. **BT Chargecard** calls to the UK can be made through the local operator.

Media

Newspapers *La Prensa*, www.prensa.com, is the major local daily newspaper. Others are *La Estrella de Panamá*, *El Universal de Panamá*, *El Panamá América*, www.epasa.com, and two tabloids, *Crítica Libre*, www.critica.com.pa, and *El Siglo*. *Colón News* is a weekly publication in Spanish and English. In English is the bi-weekly *Panama News*, www.thepanamanews.com.

The international edition of the *Miami Herald* is printed in Panama and many other US newspapers are widely available in the capital.

Panama City

→ *Colour map 8, B1.*

Panama City is a curious blend of old Spain, US-style mall developments and the bazaar atmosphere of the east. Hardly surprising then that it has a polyglot population unrivalled in any other Latin American city.

Beyond the new developments and skyscrapers which mushroomed along the southern end of the Canal, the palm-shaded beaches, islands in the bay and encircling hills still constitute a large part of Panama City's charm. And its cabarets and nightlife are an added attraction for any self-respecting hedonist. ▸▸ *For Sleeping, Eating and other listings, see pages 1134-1147.*

Ins and outs

Getting there Tocumen International Airport is 27 km from the city centre. For flights see page 1115. Set price taxis (US$25), cheaper if shared (*compartido*) and buses are available for getting into Panama City. The bus journey should take one hour but can take up to three in the rush hour. Car rental companies also have offices at the airport. The city is well served by international buses from countries throughout Central America, with offices in the centre of town. ▸▸ *For further details, see Transport, page 1143.*

Getting around The old part of the city, Casco Viejo, can easily be toured on foot. There are old, usually crowded and very cheap buses for getting to other districts. The reasonably-priced taxis charge on a zone system and can be shared if you wish to economize. Taxis can be hired by the hour for a city tour. At night, radio taxis are preferable. Many *avenidas* have both names and numbers, although locals are most likely to use the names, so asking for directions can be a bit complicated. Also, because there is no postal delivery to homes or businesses, few buildings display their numbers, so try to find out the nearest cross street.

The wider metropolitan area has a population of approximately 720,000. Adjacent to the city, but constituting a separate administrative district, is the town of San Miguelito, a residential area for over 330,000 people. Once a squatter community, every available square inch of hillside has been built on and it is increasingly considered to be a part of greater Panama City.

Panama City

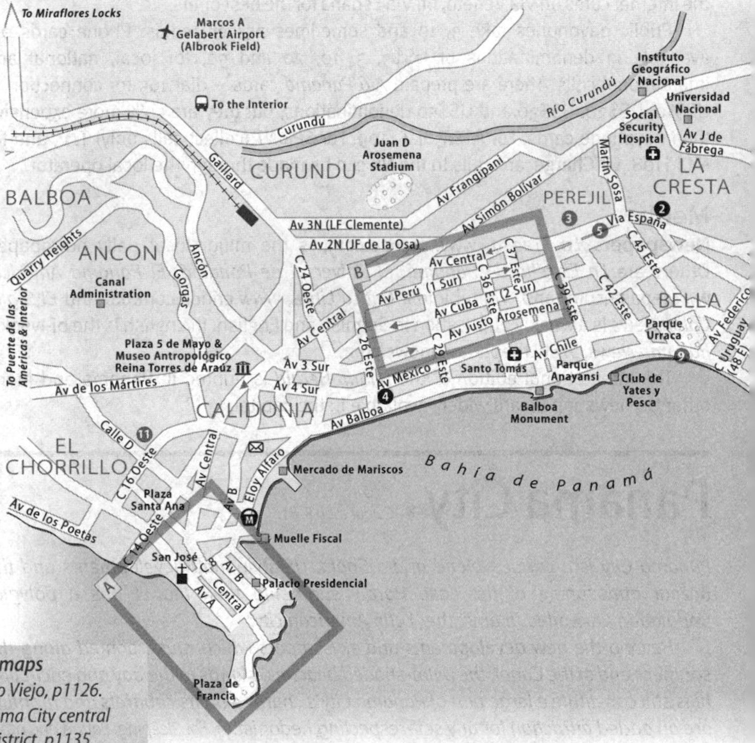

Detail maps
A Casco Viejo, p1126.
B Panama City central hotel district, p1135.

Sleeping
Apartotel Plaza **2**
Bella Vista **3**
Caesar Park **4**
California **5**
El Panamá **6**
Hostel la Casa de Carmen **7**
Hostel Voyager **8**
Miramar Intercontinental **9**
Riande Aeropuerto **14**
Riande Continental **10**
Riazor **11**

Tourist offices Information office of the **Instituto Panameño de Turismo** (IPAT) ⓘ *Atlapa Convention Centre, Vía Israel opposite Hotel Caesar Park, Apdo 4421, Panamá 5, T226-4614, www.visitpanama.com, or www.ipat.gob.pa, 0900-1600,* issues good list of hotels, *pensiones*, motels and restaurants, and a free *Focus on Panama* guide (also available at airport and major hotels). There are other **IPAT kiosks** ⓘ *Tocumen Airport in Panamá Viejo, Tue-Sun 0800-2200; on the pedestrian mall on Av Central, Mon-Fri 0900-1700; and opposite Hotel Continental on España.*

Security Tourist police on mountain bikes are present in the downtown areas of the city, recognizable by their broad armbands. Panamanians are generally very friendly and helpful. Accustomed to foreigners, they are casual about tourists. However, as in any large city with many poor people, certain areas can be dangerous after dark and reasonable precautions should be taken at all times. Attacks have been reported in Casco Viejo (although this area is now well patrolled by police during the daytime) and Panamá Viejo. Marañón (around the market), San Miguelito (on the way in from Tocumen Airport) and Calidonia can all be dangerous; never walk there at night and take care in daylight, too. Poor districts like Chorillo, Curundú and Hollywood are best avoided altogether. Probably the safest area for budget travellers to stay is Bella Vista, although it is deserted after dark and street crime can take place here at any hour. Taxis are the safest way to travel around the city and drivers will give you good advice on where not to go. If concerned, lock the doors of the taxi.

Eating
Caffé Pomodoro **1**
Calypso **2**
El Trapiche **3**
Gran China **4**
Jimmy's **5**
Manolo **6**
Niko's Café **7**

Background

Modern Panama City was founded on its present site in 1673. The capital was moved from Old Panama (Panamá Viejo), 6.5 km to the east, after Henry Morgan looted the South American treasure chest depot of Golden Panama in 1671. Today, it is a thoroughly modern city complete with congested streets and noisy traffic. Uncollected trash mouldering in the tropical heat and the liberal use of razor-wire are other eyesores but, despite its blemishes, the city does possess considerable charm. The old quarter, called Casco Viejo or San Felipe, massively fortified by Spain as the era of widespread piracy was coming to an end, lies at the tip of the peninsula at the eastern end of the Bay of Panama.

Sights

The principal districts of interest to vistors include El Cangrejo, Campo Alegre, Paitilla, and Coco del Mar, where the international banks, luxury hotels and restaurants are located. Calidonia, Bella Vista and Perejil are bustling with commerce, traffic, and mid-price hotels.

Casco Viejo

Casco Viejo (the 'Old Compound' or San Felipe), which occupies the narrow peninsula east of Calle 11, is an unusual combination of beautifully restored public buildings, churches, plazas, monuments and museums alongside inner-city decay which, after decades of neglect, is now gradually being gentrified. Several budget hotels are found here, some very badly run-down but not without their faded glory. Created in 1673 after the sacking of old Panama, Casco Viejo is a treasure trove of architectural delights, some restored, others in a desperate state of repair, but most demanding a gentle meander through the shady streets. In 1992 local authorities began reviving some of the area's past glory by painting the post-colonial houses in soft pastels and their decorations and beautiful wrought-iron railings in relief. New shops and restaurants are moving into restored buildings in an attempt to make Casco Viejo a tourist attraction.

At the walled tip of the peninsula is the picturesque **Plaza de Francia**, with its bright red poinciana trees and obelisk topped by a cockerel (symbol of the Gallic nation), which has a document with 5000 signatures buried beneath it. Twelve large narrative plaques and many statues recall the French Canal's construction history and personalities; the work of Cuban doctor Carlos Finlay in establishing the cause of yellow fever is commemorated on one tablet. Facing the plaza is the French Embassy, housed in a pleasant early 20th-century building; it stubbornly refused to relocate during the years when the neighbourhood declined and is now one of the main focus points in the area's renaissance. Built flush under the old seawalls around the plaza are **Las Bóvedas** (The Vaults), the thick-walled colonial dungeons where prisoners in tiny barred cells were immersed up to their necks during high tides. Nine 'vaults' were

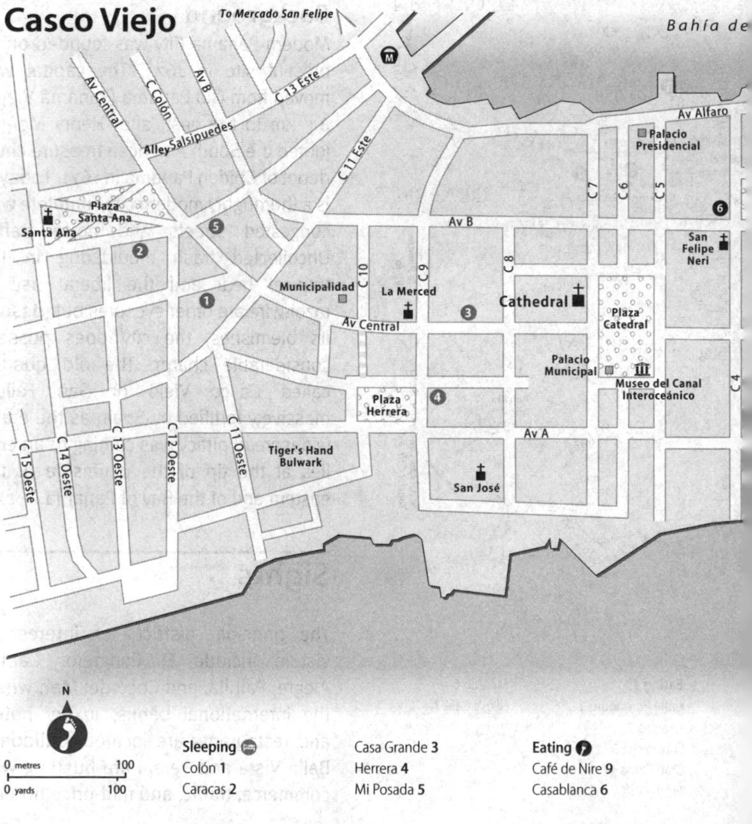

restored by the Instituto Panameño de Turismo (IPAT) in 1982 and converted into an art gallery – **Galería Las Bóvedas** ⓘ *Tue-Sun 1100-1900; students offer walking tours of the Casco Viejo from here during these hours,* copies of *Focus on Panama* are available here – and handicraft centre. The French restaurant **Las Bóvedas** occupies another two 'vaults' next to the former Palacio de Justicia, partly burned during 'Operation Just Cause' and now housing the **Instituto Nacional de Cultura** (INC), with an interesting mural by Esteban Palomino on the ground floor.

Steps lead up from the Plaza de Francia to the **Paseo de las Bóvedas** promenade along the top of the defensive walls surrounding the peninsula on three sides. This is a popular place for an evening stroll; it is ablaze with bougainvillea and affords good views of the Bahía de Panamá, the Serranía de Majé on the Panama/Darién provincial border (on a clear day), Calzada Amador (known during the Canal Zone era as the Causeway) and the islands beyond.

Two blocks northwest of the Plaza (Avenida A and Calle 3) are the restored ruins of the impressive **Church and Convent of Santo Domingo** (1673, later destroyed by fires in 1737 and 1756), both with paired columns and brick inlaying on their façades. The famous 15-m-long flat arch, **Arco Chato**, which formed the base of the choir was built entirely of bricks and mortar with no internal support. When the great debate as to where the Canal should be built was going on in the United States Congress, a Nicaraguan postage stamp showing a volcano, with all its implications of earthquakes, and the stability of this arch – a supposed proof of no earthquakes – are said to have played a large part in determining the choice in Panama's favour. A chapel on the site has been converted into the interesting **Museo de Arte Colonial Religioso** ⓘ *Tue-Sat 0830-1630, admission US$0.75, students and seniors US$0.25, T228-2897,* whose treasures include a precious golden altar, a delicate snail staircase, silver relics and wooden sculptures from Lima and Mexico, 19th-century engravings of the city, and the skeleton of a woman found during excavation of the church.

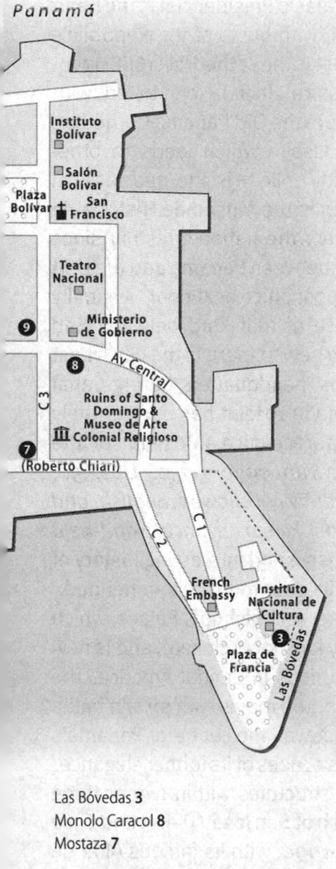

Not far from Santo Domingo, across Avenida Central, the neoclassical **Teatro Nacional** ⓘ *T262-3525, Mon-Fri 0800-1600,US$0.50,* with 850-seat capacity, opened in 1908 with Verdi's *Aida* being performed in what was then considered the state of the art in acoustics. French-influenced sculptures and friezes enliven the façade, while Roberto Lewis' paintings depicting the birth of the nation adorn the theatre's dome. The ballerina Dame Margot Fonteyn, who married a member of the prominent Arias family and was a long-time resident of Panama until her death in 1991, danced at the theatre's re-inauguration in 1974.

Diagonally opposite the Teatro Nacional (Avenida B and Calle 3) is the peaceful **Plaza Bolívar**, with a statue of the liberator Simón Bolívar, draped in robes, standing below a large condor surrounded by plaques of his deeds.

 Around the square are the former **Hotel Colombia**, the **Church of San Felipe Neri**, and many 19th-century houses still displaying roofs of red-clay tiles bearing the stamp 'Marseilles 1880'. On the east side stand **San Francisco Church** ⓘ *Mon-Sat 1430-1800, Sun all day*, colonial but 'modified' in 1917 and modernized in 1983, and the **San Francisco Convent** (1678), the largest of all the religious buildings, which was restored by Peruvian architect Leonardo Villanueva. The Bolivarian Congress of June 1826, at which Bolívar proposed a United States of South America, was also held in the Chapter Room of the Convent, now known as the **Salón Bolívar**, and the 1904 Constitution was also drafted here. This northern wing was dedicated as the **Instituto Bolívar** in 1956; its wood panelling, embossed leather benches and paintings (restored in part by the government of Ecuador) may be viewed with an authorized guide from the Bolivarian Society, T262-2947. The adjacent Colegio Bolívar, built on a pier over the water, is due to become the new Cancillería (Ministry of Foreign Affairs).

Another long block west of Plaza Bolívar, and one block north on the seafront (Avenida Eloy Alfaro) between Calles 5 y 6, is the **Palacio Presidencial**, the most impressive building in the city, built as an opulent residence in 1673 for successive colonial auditors and governors, enlarged and restored under President Belisario Porras in 1922.

A few blocks west, Avenida Alfaro curves north around the waterfront to the colourful **Central Market**, Mercado San Felipe (see Shopping, page 1140) and the **Muelle Fiscal** wharf where coastal vessels anchor and small cargo boats leave for Darién and sometimes Colombia. Two blocks further north, where Avenida Alfaro meets Avenida Balboa by the pier, is the modern **Mercado de Mariscos** (fish and seafood market), where fishermen land their catch.

Returning to Casco Viejo, two blocks south of the Palacio Presidencial is the heart of the old town, the **Plaza Catedral** or **Independencia**, with busts of the Republic's founders, and surrounding public buildings. On the west is the **cathedral** (1688-1794, refurbished in 1999), its twin towers, domes, classical façade encrusted with mother-of- pearl and three of the tower bells brought from the Old Panama Cathedral. To the right of the main altar is a subterranean passage which leads to other *conventos* and the sea. On the southwest corner with Calle 7 is the neoclassical **Palacio Municipal** (City Hall), on the first floor of which is the **Museo de Historia de Panamá** ⓘ *Mon-Fri 0800-1600, US$0.50*, which covers the nation's history since European landfall, and includes highlights of the treaty between Panama and the USA which led to the construction of the Canal. The former post office next door, originally built in 1875 as the **Grand Hotel** ("the largest edifice of that kind between San Francisco and Cape Horn" according to a contemporary newspaper), is the city's best example of French architecture. It became de Lesseps' headquarters during Canal excavations in the 1880s and was sold back to Panama in 1912. It has been entirely gutted and converted into the **Museo del Canal Interoceánico** (Museum of the Panama Canal) ⓘ *Plaza Catedral, T/F211-1650, Tue-Sun 0930 -1730, US$2.50, concessions US$0.75, free on Sun 0930-1730 Photography not allowed. English- and French-speaking guides available, other languages if booked in advance. Hand-held English audio commentaries US$5*. It has a comprehensive and interesting history of Panama – mainly the central provinces – as shaped by its pass route, recommended.

The east side of the Plaza is dominated by the former **Archbishop's Palace**, which was later occupied by a university, a shelter for runaway kids (now closed), and is now the run-down **Central Hotel** (1884), once the most luxurious in Central America. The interior featured a palm garden, restaurants, barber shop, 100 rooms with private baths and a wooden staircase imported from New York, and it was the centre of Panama's social life for decades. Today it is decrepit but still retains echoes of its former elegance.

There are a number of other interesting religious structures within two or three blocks of the cathedral, but the most-visited is the **Church of San José** ⓘ *Av A and Calle 8, 1 block west and 2 south of the Plaza Catedral, T228-0190*, with its famous Altar de

Oro, a massive baroque altar carved from mahogany and, according to common belief, veneered with gold. This was one of the few treasures saved from Henry Morgan's attack on Old Panama in 1671 and legend records different versions of how it was concealed from the buccaneers: whitewashed by the priest, or even covered in mud by nuns; however, a remark attributed to Morgan hints that he was not deceived!

A block to the south on Calle 9 is the run-down **Plaza Herrera**. French influence is evident in the windows and flower-filled cast-iron balconies of the green and pale pink houses and *pensiones*. Behind Plaza Herrera are the ruins of the **Tiger's Hand Bulwark**, where the defensive wall ended and the landward-side moat began. The strongpoint held a 50-man military post and 13 cannon; it was demolished in 1856 as the town expanded but restored in 1983. Portions of the moat can still be detected.

Avenida Central and Calidonia

From Calle 10 heading north, Avenida Central, Panama City's main commercial street, enters the 'mainland', curves northwest then sweeps northeast running almost parallel with the shore through the whole town. En route its name changes to Vía España – although signs reading 'Avenida Central España' exist in parts – on its course northeast to Tocumen Airport. At its crossing with Calle B, close to Casco Viejo, is the small **Plaza Santa Ana** with a colonial church (1764), a favourite place for political meetings; the plaza has many restaurants and is a good place to catch buses to all parts of the city. Nearby, running towards the Central Market between Avenida Central and Calle B (officially known as Carrera de Chiriquí), is an exotic, narrow alley called **Salsipuedes** – 'Get out if you can' – where crowded stalls sell everything from fruit to old books and medicinal plants. Over 75 of the street's residents in 1892 were Chinese merchants, but the city's Chinatown (**Barrio Chino**) is now largely confined to nearby Calle Juan Mendoza and adjacent Calle B with a typical Chinese archway at the entrance, good Chinese restaurants and general shops.

The next section of Avenida Central is a pedestrian precinct called **La Peatonal**, with trees and decorations, modern department stores and wandering street vendors. **Plaza 5 de Mayo**, at Calle 22 Este, is another busy bus stop from which buses leave for the Canal. In the centre of the Plaza is an obelisk honouring the firemen who died in a gunpowder magazine explosion on the site in May 1914. Housed in the old railway station (1913-1946), almost opposite the Plaza de Lesseps, on Avenida Central south side of Plaza 5 de Mayo (although expected to move to Curundu in 2006), is the **Museo Antropológico Reina Torres de Araúz** ⓘ *Tue-Sun 1000-1600, T262-4138, US$2*. It has five salons (partly looted during 'Operation Just Cause') exhibiting Panamanian history, anthropology and archaeology, rare collection of pre-Columbian gold objects and ceramics (Profesora Torres de Araúz, a renowned anthropologist and founder of the museum, died in 1982). It was renovated in 1999 and hosts occasional performances. One block east of Plaza 5 de Mayo is the **Museo Afro-Antillano** ⓘ *Justo Arosemena and Calle 24, T262-5348, Tue-Sat 0900-1600, Sun 1500-1800, US$0.50*, which features an illustrated history of Panama's West Indian community and their work on the Canal. There's a small library.

Ancón

Ancón curves round the hill of the same name north and east and merges into Panama City. It has picturesque views of the palm-fringed shore. The following **walk** takes in the sights of Ancón: walk to the top of the hill in the morning for views of the city, Balboa and the Canal (toilets and water fountain at the top – you may have to climb part of the radio tower to see anything); the entrance is on Avenida de los Mártires (formerly Avenida de Julio and briefly Avenida Presidente Kennedy). From Avenida de los Mártires take a clockwise route around the hill, bearing right on to Balboa Road (Avenida Estado de Jamaica), you will soon come upon the **Kuna Artesans** market on your left where the Kuna sell their

Take care on Ancón Hill, robberies sometimes occur.

 multicolored *molas*. Further on down and to the left is the **Mercado Artesanal** where a wider variety of handicrafts, woven baskets from the Wounaan-Embera people, as well as Ecuadorian sweaters can be found. You will come upon **Chase Manhattan** and **Citibank** shortly after passing the Mercado Artesanal. The post office and a café follow. Then walk down the Prado lined with royal palms to the **Goethals Memorial** ⓘ *free, identity must be shown to the guards*, in honour of the engineer George Washington Goethals, behind the building of the Canal. The steps lead to the administration building to see the recently restored murals of the Construction of the Canal. Follow Heights Road until it becomes Gorgas Road where you will pass the headquarters of the **Smithsonian Tropical Research Institute** ⓘ *opposite Plaza 5 de Mayo, Mon-Fri 0900-1700, Sat 0900-1200, T212-8113, changyau@tivoli.si.edu*, an English-language scientific research library where applications to visit Barro Colorado Island are made. The café/bookshop (Mon-Fri 1000-0430) sells environmental books and nature guides, including national park maps.

A little further, among trees and flowers, is the former **Gorgas Army Community Hospital**. Named after William Crawford Gorgas, the physician who is credited with clearing the Canal Zone of the more malignant tropical diseases before construction began in the beginning of the 20th century. Gorgas Road leads back to Avenida de los Mártires, but look out for the sign to the **Museo de Arte Contemporáneo** ⓘ *Av de los Mártires, entrance on Av San Blas, T262-8012, Mon-Fri 0900-1600, Sat 0900-1200, free but donations welcomed (privately owned)*. Housed in a former Masonic Lodge (1936), the permanent collection of national and international modern paintings and sculptures has special exhibitions from time to time, with marquetry, silkscreen and engraving workshops, and a library of contemporary visual art open to students. At the foot of Ancón Hill the **Instituto Nacional** stands on the four-lane Avenida de los Mártires. At **Mi Pueblito** ⓘ *north of Av de los Mártires, east of the Quarry Heights entrance, open till 2200, small admission charge*, you'll find nostalgic replicas of three different villages: one colonial from the Central Provinces, one Afro-Antillian and one indigenous. It's on a busy road so best to take a taxi. To continue further west into Balboa see page 1144.

La Exposición

East of Plaza 5 de Mayo, along the oceanside Avenida Balboa (a popular stretch for jogging), on a semi-circular promontory jutting out into the water by Calle 34, is a great monument to **Vasco Núñez de Balboa**, who stands sword aloft as he did when he strode into the Pacific on 15 September 1513. The 1924 statue stands on a white marble globe poised on the shoulders of a supporting group representing the four races of Man. To the east is **Parque Anayansi**, a pleasant shady park, popular with local couples and flocks of parrots in the late afternoon; this waterfront area was nicely refurbished in 1998.

Two more pleasant plazas, Porras and Arias, can be found west of Hospital Santo Tomás across Avenida 3 Sur (Justo Arosemena). This central part of the city is known as La Exposición because of the international exhibition held here in 1916 to celebrate the building of the Canal. There are two museums nearby: **Museo de Ciencias Naturales** ⓘ *Av Cuba y Calle 30, T225-0645, Tue-Sat 0900-1530, Sun 1300-1630, US$1, students and seniors US$0.25*, which has good sections on geology, palaeontology, entomology and marine biology, and **Museo Casa del Banco Nacional** ⓘ *Calle 34 between Av Cuba and Av Justo Arosemena, Mon-Fri 0800-1230, 1330-1630, free*, which, although not widely known, is worth a visit. It contains a large numismatic and stamp collection and a history of banking from the 19th century, old postal and telephone items and historic photos.

Further east, as Avenida Balboa begins to curve around the other end of the Bay of Panama to Punta Paitilla, is **Bella Vista**, once a very pleasant residential district and site of many hotels in our B and C ranges. It includes the neighbourhood of

Perejil ('parsley'), originally called Perry Hill. Bordering this on the north, where Vía España passes the Iglesia del Carmen, is **El Cangrejo** ('the crab') apartment and restaurant district, with many upmarket stores and boutiques. The University City is on the Transisthmian Highway. Opposite the campus is the Social Security Hospital. All these areas are evidence of Panama City's sensational growth since the post-war economic boom and the spread of the centre eastwards; the attractive residential suburb of Punta Paitilla was an empty hill where hunting was practised as recently as the 1960s.

The 265-ha **Parque Natural Metropolitano** ⓘ *between Av Juan Pablo II and the Camino de la Amistad, west of El Cangrejo along the Río Curundú, T232-5552, www.parquemetropolitano.org, Tue-Sun 0800-1600, park open 0730-1800*, has a mirador (150 m) with a great view over the city and a glimpse of the Canal, as well as two interpretive walking trails from which *tití* monkeys, agoutis, coatis, white-tailed deer, sloths, turtles and up to 200 species of bird may be glimpsed (go early morning for best viewing); green iguanas sun themselves on every available branch. To get there, take the bus marked 'Tumba Muerto', from Avenida Central, and ask to be dropped at the Depósito. The park is signposted from here, otherwise make for the crane and the tree-covered hill. The **Smithsonian Institute** has installed a unique construction crane for studying the little-known fauna in the canopy of this remnant of tropical semi-deciduous lowland forest, which can be visited while walking the paths of the Metropolitan Park. Researchers and students wishing to use the crane need to apply through the Smithsonian Institute. The Visitors' Centre ⓘ *Av Juan Pablo II, T232-5516*, runs guided one-hour tours and holds regular slide shows. No ANAM permit is required; it's a recommended, easy excursion.

Parque Municipal and Botanical Summit Gardens ⓘ *Carretera Gaillard towards Gamboa, 20 mins from Panama City, Mon-Fri 0800-1600, Sat/Sun 0800-1800, T232-4854/4007, there is a nominal entrance fee.* There is a small zoo in the gardens with most of the animals found in Panama. The cages are reported to be a bit small. There is a harpy eagle at the zoo providing an opportunity to see and appreciate the size of these incredible birds. There is also information on their conservation in the small visitors centre.

Around Panama City

» pp 1134-1147.

Panamá Viejo

ⓘ *www.panamaviejo.org, free. Getting there: taxi from the city centre, US$1.80; buses from Vía España or Avenida Balboa, US$0.20. Panamá Viejo also makes a good excursion for passengers with a little time to kill at nearby Tocumen Airport; taxis can be as much as US$5 but still reasonable, especially if this is the only chance you'll have to see Panamá. Alternatively, take any bus marked Vía España, get off at Vía Cincuentenario, then take a bus to Panamá Viejo, total cost US$0.45.*

A recommended short trip is to the ruins of Panamá Viejo, 6.5 km northeast along the coast. A wander among the ruins still gives an idea of the site's former glory, although many of the structures have been worn by time, fungus and the sea. The narrow **King's Bridge** (1620) at the north end of the town's limits is a good starting point; it marked the beginning of the three trails across the isthmus and took seven years to build. Walking south brings you to the **Convento de San José**, where the Golden Altar originally stood (see page 1127); it was spared by the great fire that swept the town during Morgan's attack (which side started the fire is still debated). Several blocks further south is the main plaza, where the square stone tower of the **cathedral** (1535-1580) is a prominent feature. In the immediate vicinity are the Cabildo, with imposing arches and columns, the remnants of **Convento de Santo Domingo**, the **Bishop's Residence**, and the **Slave Market** (or House of the

 Genovese), whose gaol-like structure was the hub of the American slave trade. There were about 4000 African slaves in 1610, valued at about 300 pesos apiece. Beyond the plazas to the south, on a rocky eminence overlooking the bay, stand the **Royal Houses**, the administrative stronghold including the **Quartermaster's House**, the **Court** and **Chancellery**, the **Real Audiencia** and the **Governor's Residence**.

Further west along the Pacific strand are the dungeons, kitchens and meat market (now almost obliterated by the sea); a store and refreshment stands cluster here on the south side of the plaza, and handicrafts from the Darién are sold along the beach. Across Calle de la Carrera stands another great complex of religious convents: **La Concepción** (1598) and the **Compañía de Jesús** (1621). These too were outside the area destroyed by the 1671 fire but are today little more than rubble. Only a wall remains of the Franciscan **Hospital de San Juan de Dios**, once a huge structure encompassing wards, courtyards and a church. Another block west can be seen part of the **Convento de San Francisco** and its gardens, facing the rocky beach. About 100 m west is the beautiful **Convento de La Merced**, where Pizarro, Almagro and their men attended Mass on the morning they sailed on their final and momentous expedition to Peru. Decades later Morgan stored his plunder here until it could be counted, divided up and sent back to the Atlantic side. At the western limit of Panamá Viejo stands **La Navidad Fort** (1658). Its purpose was merely to defend the **Matadero (Slaughterhouse) Bridge** across the Río Agarroba but its 50-man garrison and half-dozen cannon were no match for the determined force of privateers; it is also known as Morgan's Bridge because it was here that the attack began.

There is a new **visitors' centre**, with exhibitions in Spanish, as well as maps, pictures and models of how Panama's first city would have looked. There are also opportunities for students to volunteer in future excavations (check the website). By the ruins is **Museo de Panamá Viejo** ⓘ *Vía Cincuentenario, T226-89156, Mon-Sun 0900-1700, US$2.*

The whole area (unfenced) is attractively landscaped, with plenty of benches to rest on, and floodlit at night. Late afternoon when the sun is low is an especially nice time to visit, although at least two hours should be allowed to appreciate the site

Panamá Viejo

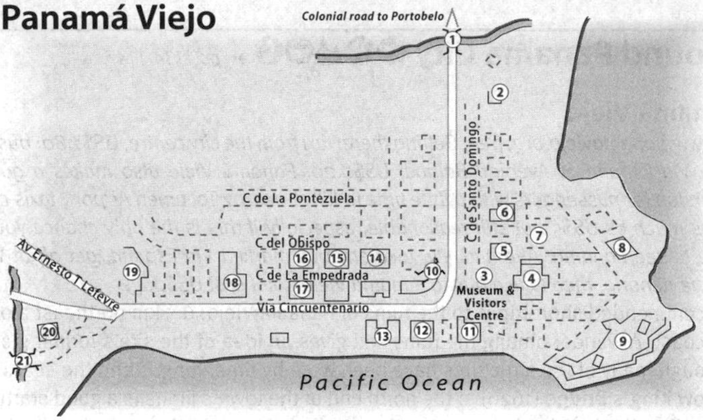

1 King's Bridge
2 Convento de San José
3 Main Plaza
4 Cathedral
5 Cabildo
6 Convento de Santo Domingo
7 Bishop's Residence
8 Slave's House/ House of the Genovese
9 Royal Houses
10 Emperor's Bridge
11 Dungeons
12 Kitchens
13 Meat Market
14 Convento de Compañía de Jesús
15 Convento La Concepción
16 Church of La Concepción
17 Hospital de San Juan de Dios
18 Convento de San Francisco
19 Convento de la Merced
20 La Navidad Fort
21 Matadero/ Slaughterhouse Bridge

fully. The main ruins are patrolled by police and reasonably safe. **Dame Margot Fonteyn**, the ballerina, is buried alongside her husband Roberto Arias Guardia in the Jardín de la Paz cemetery behind Panamá Viejo. IPAT organizes free folklore events and local dance displays on Saturdays in the dry season (*verano*), which are worth seeing. The tourist office in Panama City (T226-7000) has a list of programmes and can supply professional guides if required.

Balboa → *Colour map 8, B1.*

The town and docks of Balboa are just over 3 km west of Panama City (10 minutes by taxi) and stand attractively between the Canal quays and Ancón Hill. It has been described as efficient, planned and sterilized – a typical American answer to the wilfulness and riot of the tropics.

The Canal administration building (with fine murals on the ground floor) and a few other official residences are on Balboa Heights. At the foot of the Heights is the town of Balboa, with a small park, a reflecting pool and marble shaft commemorating Goethals, as well as a long palm-flanked parkway known as the Prado. At its eastern end is a theatre, a service centre building, post office and bank.

Fuerte Amador

Before the Puente de las Américas crosses the Panama Canal the long peninsula of Fuerte Amador stretches into the Pacific, formerly the HQ of the Panamanian Defence Force, seized by US forces in 1989 and returned to Panama in 1994. Beyond Fuerte Amador are the formerly fortified islands of Naos, Perico and Flamenco, linked by the 4-km causeway (**Calzada Amador**) built of rubble excavated from the Canal. There are many interesting buildings in this area bearing the marks of the conflict, and some attractive lawns and parkland. The Calzada has been extensively developed over recent years. As you enter the Causeway you pass the Figali Convention Centre, built and inaugurated in 2003 for the Miss Universe competition and centennial celebrations. The Figali Centre now hosts major music and sports events. It has fine views of the Puente de las Américas and the ships lined up to enter the Canal. There are small charges for entry and for swimming at Solidaridad beach on **Naos** (crowded at weekends and the water is polluted – not recommended). There is a small marine park with local marine life on show. At Punta Culebra on Naos is the new **Marine Exhibition Center** ⓘ *T212-8171, Tue-Fri 1300-1700, Sat-Sun 1000-1800, US$1* (of the Smithsonian Tropical Research Institute), with interesting aquaria and exhibitions on marine fauna. As the road reaches **Isla Perico**, there is a newly built block of restaurants, bars and some shops underneath what is set to be an apartment-style hotel. A 'mega resort' is in process at Naos Harbour – a 300 room hotel, 114 room apartment-hotel, casino, shops, condos and new beach and there is a proposal for a cable car to the Causeway descending from the top of Ancón Hill. **Flamenco**, the last of the islands, is headquarters for the National Maritime Service and home to the Flamenco Yacht Club, a large duty-free store and a pristine mall of boutiques, expensive souvenir shops and lively range of restaurants, bars and clubs. Most popular between Wednesday and Saturday nights.

Taboga Island

There are launch services to Taboga Island (**Calypso Queen**, T226-1991/1551, **Canal & Bay Tours**, T314-1349), about 20 km offshore. The island is a favourite year-round resort, and produces delicious pineapples and mangoes, and has one of the oldest churches in the Western hemisphere. Admission to the beach at **Hotel Taboga** is US$10, redeemable in tokens to buy food and drink (covered picnic huts cost extra). There are other good places to swim around the island, but its south side is rocky and sharks visit regularly.

All items are expensive on Taboga Island; bring plenty of cash as there is no bank.

The trip out to Taboga is very interesting, passing the naval installations at the Pacific end of the Canal, the great bridge linking the Americas, tuna boats and shrimp fishers in for supplies, visiting yachts from all over the world at what remains of the Balboa Yacht Club, and the Calzada Amador. Part of the route follows the channel of the Canal, with its busy traffic. Taboga itself, with a promontory rising to 488 m, is carpeted with flowers at certain times of year. There are few cars in the meandering, helter-skelter streets, and just one footpath as a road.

Pearl Islands → *Colour map 8, B2.*

A longer trip, 75 km southwest by launch, takes you to the Pearl Islands, visited mostly by sea anglers for the Pacific mackerel, red snapper, corvina, sailfish, marlin and the other species which abound in the waters around. High mountains rise from the sea, and there is a little fishing village on a shelf of land at the water's edge. There was much pearl fishing in colonial days. **Contadora**, one of the smallest Pearl Islands (three-hour boat trip), has become quite famous since its name became associated with a Central American peace initiative. It was also where the last Shah of Iran, Mohammed Rezá Pahlaví, was exiled, in a house called Puntalara, after the Iranian Revolution. Contadora is popular with Canadian, Spanish and Italian holidaymakers and is becoming crowded, built-up and consequently is not as peaceful as it once was. Lack of drinking water is now harming the tourist development. There are beautiful beaches with crystal-clear water, good skin-diving and sailing, and lots of sharks.

Sleeping

Panama City *p1123, maps p1124, p1126 and p1135*

There is a 10% tax on all hotel prices. Most hotels are a/c, all others have fans. Cheaper accommodation can be found in pensiones and there are cheap places on Av México.

LL Miramar Intercontinental, Av Balboa, T206-8888, www.miramarpanama.com. On the seafront with excellent views. 3 restaurants, huge pool, gym and exclusive marina (US$100 per night). Broadband internet available, US$15 per day. President Bush stayed here on his 2005 visit to Panama, hiring 120 rooms.

LL-L Caesar Park , Vía Israel y Calle 77, T270-0477, www.caesarparkpanama.com. 4 restaurants, 1 with excellent view over bay, another offering Southeast Asian cuisine, casino and sports bar, outdoor swimming pool.

L El Panamá, Vía España 111, T215-9000, www.elpanama.com. Tropical art deco style, vast rooms, good pool and vast 'Vegas' style casino, a bit inefficient but generally good.

L Euro Hotel, Vía España 33, opposite the Bella Vista, T263-0802. A/c, private bath, cable TV, pool, restaurant and bar on busy street.

AL Riande Aeropuerto, near Tocumen Airport (5 mins), T290-3333, www.hoteles riande.com. A/c, clean, free transport to airport, good breakfasts, pool (loud music all day), tennis, casino.

AL Riande Continental, Vía España and Ricardo Arias, T263-9999. Sister hotel to the Riande Aeropuerto and a landmark in the modern city centre. Good value with prices including buffet breakfast. Casino on site.

A Roma Plaza, Av Justo Arosemena y Calle 33, T227-3844, www.hotelromaplaza.com. Rooms are clean and airy but expensive given stiff competition in the area, rooftop pool. Restaurant with Italian emphasis offers a good-value buffet breakfast for US$5.25.

A-B Costa Inn, Av Perú y Calle 39, T227-1522, www.hotelcostainn.com. Very good value, sparklingly clean, rooftop pool with great views of the city. Double rooms feature 2 bathrooms. Italian Garden Restaurant with smoking and non-smoking areas. Breakfast included.

B California, Vía España y Calle 43, Bella Vista, T263-7736, www.hotel-california.ws. With bath, a/c, modern, good value and with discounts for longer-stay clientele, TV, nice restaurant, friendly, safe.

B Caribe Av Perú y Calle 28, T225-0404, caribehotel@hotmail.com. 153 very large rooms, one of the city's older hotels, rooftop pool and bar, casino, restaurant.

B Hostal La Casa de Carmen, Calle 1, Urbanización El Carmen Casa 32, Vía Brasil, 1 block back from Vía España, T/F263-4366, www.lacasadecarmen.com. Good, cheap place close to the business centre of town.

B **Hotel Internacional**, Plaza 5 de Mayo, T262-4933, hinterpan@cwpanama.net. Spacious rooms with a/c and cable TV, although a little tatty for the price, the views of the city and ocean are almost worth it.

B-C **Hotel Vía España**, Calle Martín Sosa (on the corner of Vía España), T264-0800. Fairly new hotel with clean rooms and comfy beds, a/c, private bath, telephone, TV with cable. A few suites have a jacuzzi for an very good price. Restaurant on site and internet (US$1 per 30 mins) available. Friendly, recommended.

C **Acapulco**, Calle 30 Este y Av Perú, T225-3832. A/c, clean, TV, private bath, some rooms a little musty but ones with balcony are better, excellent restaurant, safe parking, conveniently located. Recommended.

C **Andino**, Calle 35 off Av Perú, beside Parque Parades, T225-1162, andino@sinfo.net. Large rooms and all mod cons including TV, fridge and telephone. Some rooms a little smoky. Family run, friendly, free interent access, laundry quiet street. Highly recommended.

C **Bella Vista**, Vía España 31 y Calle 42, T223-1785. A/c, cable TV, private bath, safe deposit. Recommended.

C **Covadonga**, Calle 29, Av Perú, T225-5275. Small rooms but good rooftop terrace pool with views over the bay.

C **Hotel Latino**, Av Cuba y Calle 36 Este, T227-2994, hlatino@cableonda.com. Slightly dingy rooms, a/c, private bath, cable TV.

C **Hotel Marbella**, Calle D (between Calle 55 and Calle Eusebio A Morales), El Cangrejo, T263-2220, hmarbella@cableonda.net. Plush rooms with a/c, cable TV and private bath in safe, central area of town.

C **Lisboa**, Av Cuba y Calle 31, T227-5916. Modern, a/c, TV, restaurant, good value. Decoration is very 'red', so if you like your accommodation fiery, you'll love this place.

C **Veracruz**, Av Perú y Calle 30, T227-3022, www.hotelveracruz.com.pa. Very good restaurant, helpful staff and elegant reception area, but rooms in need of decoration and noisy next to the street.

C-D **Centro Americano**, Av Justo Arosemena y Av Ecuador, T227-4555, www.hotelcentroamericano.com. Very clean, hot water, good reading lights, TV, restaurant and ice machine on every floor, good value. Discounts for longer stays. Recommended.

C-D **Residencial La Alameda**, Calle 30 Este, Av Cuba, T225-1758. Clean, modern, a/c, hot water, cable TV, parking.

C-D **Venecia**, Av Perú, between Calle 36 and 37, T227-7881, hotelvenecia@hotmail.com. Small, box-like rooms, some smelly, others are much better. Range of prices for rooms.

Panama City central hotel district

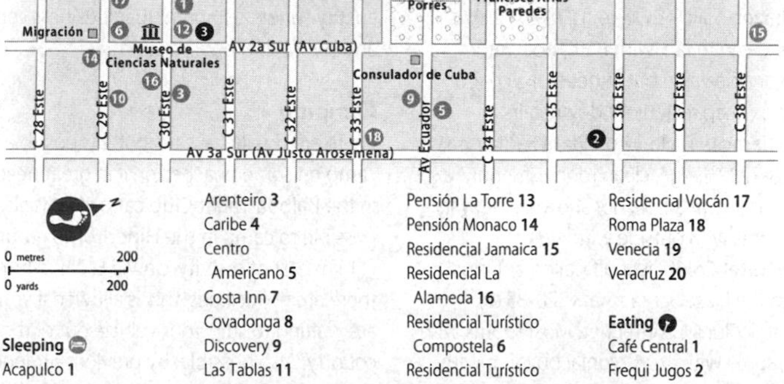

0 metres 200
0 yards 200

Sleeping
Acapulco **1**
Andino **2**
Arenteiro **3**
Caribe **4**
Centro Americano **5**
Costa Inn **7**
Covadonga **8**
Discovery **9**
Las Tablas **11**
Lisboa **12**
Pensión La Torre **13**
Pensión Monaco **14**
Residencial Jamaica **15**
Residencial La Alameda **16**
Residencial Turístico Compostela **6**
Residencial Turístico El Edén **10**
Residencial Volcán **17**
Roma Plaza **18**
Venecia **19**
Veracruz **20**

Eating
Café Central **1**
Frequi Jugos **2**
Rincón Tableño **3**

D Arenteiro, Calle 30 Este y Av Cuba, T227-5883. Hot water, TV, modern, very clean, excellent value. New bar and restaurant.
D Discovery, Av Ecuador, T225-1140. Clean, fairly quiet, safe parking and free airport pick-up, very good value. Bar.
D Dos Mares, Calle 30 between Perú and Cuba, T/F227-6150. A/c, bath but rooms in need of renovation, hot water, pool on roof, good restaurant, TV, phone. Recommended.
D Pensión Manhatten, 5 de Mayo (situated on Av Central), T212-1312. Private bath, TV. Good rooms for the price, although the area can be risky at night.
D-E Hostel Voyager, Ed Di-Lido Apt 3 and Apt 8, Calle Manuel Maria Icaza, close to Jimmys Restaurant, T260-5913, www.voyagerhostelpanama.com. Dormitory rooms (US$8 per person), price includes continental breakfast, laundry service, TV, use of kitchen and free internet service for guests – great place to meet other travellers, but mixed reports on the rooms. Recommended.
D Ideal, Calle 17 Oeste just off Av Central, between Plaza Santa Ana y Plaza 5 de Mayo, T262-2400. A/c (cold), shared hot shower, pool, cable TV, internet at US$1/hr, safe.
D Pensión Monaco, Av Cuba y Calle 29, T225-2573. Unfriendly staff but very well appointed rooms with TV and a/c.
D Residencial Jamaica, Av Cuba and Calle 38, T225-9870. Smart-looking building with very clean rooms, colour TV, a/c. Good.
D Residential Turístico Compostela, Av Cuba and Calle 29, T227-6394. Stylishly decorated rooms with good beds, TV, a/c, even dimmer switches on the lights. Better than many far more expensive options.
D Residential Turístico El Edén, Calle 29 Este between Av Cuba and Justo Arosemena, T225-2946. TV, a/c, hot water. Clean, very good value.
D Riazor, Calle 16 Oeste, T228-0777. A/c, cheaper with fan, with bath, hot water, reasonable value but in need of a coat of paint, cheap restaurant downstairs.
D-E Caracas, Calle 12 on Plaza Santa Ana, T228-7232. Large, clean rooms, friendly, a/c (cheaper with a fan), hot showers, be wary of rooms with outside windows.
D-E Hotel Colón, just off Calle 12, 1 block from the Plaza Santa Ana, T228-8510, elhotelcolon@pa.inter.net. Most rooms with fan, some with a/c. Colonial building with lovely tiling downstairs. Beds soft but clean.
D-E Pensión La Torre Av Perú (south side), Calle 39, T225-0172. A/c (cheaper without), TV, cleanish, cheap, but this is a real by-the-hour place, rooms dark.
D-E Residencial Volcán, Calle 29 and Av Perú, T225-5263, opposite Migración, next to Museo de Ciencias Naturales. Fan, a/c extra, with shower, friendly, safe, clean. Very good value and popular with backpackers.
E Casa Grande, Av Central, Calle 8-9, T211-3316, 1 block behind the cathedral. Good location but basic rooms with shared bath.
E Hotel Herrera, Calle 9, Plaza Herrera, T228-8994. Handsome colonial building, slowly decaying, faded grandeur. Some beds very soft. Try to get a room overlooking the plaza. Lovely airy 2nd-floor lounge, friendly.
E Las Tablas, Av Perú 2830 y Calle 29 Este, T227-3699. With bath, cheaper without, cold water, fan, safe, quiet except for rooms overlooking street. Opposite is El Machetazo supermarket, food for cheap meals.
E Mi Posada, Calle 12 y Av Central (Plaza Santa Ana). Basic, mixed reports.
E Sevilla, Av Justo Arosemena 46-40, T227-2436. With bath and a/c, cheaper without, good.

Apartments

All have kitchenette, colour and cable TV, some with pool.
L-AL Las Huacas Hotel and Suites, Calle 53 El Cangrejo, T213-2222, www.lashuacas.com. Interesting apartments designed around various Panamanian cultural themes – the choice includes Kuna, Azuero Peninsula, Darién Rainforest and French Canal. Larger suites with space for 4 are available. The 2nd-floor Boca Town Suite is very cool – have a look.
A Crystal Suites Hotel, Vía Brasil y Samuel Lewis, T263-2644, www.crystalsuites.com. Luxury suites, restaurant, bar, business centre and swimming pool.

Camping

There are no official sites but it is possible to camp on some beaches or, if in great need, in the Balboa Yacht Club car park. It is also possible to camp in the Hipódromo grounds (11 km east of the city, on Vía España) but there are no facilities; this is allowed if you are waiting to ship your vehicle out of the country. Also possible, by previous arrangement, at La Patria swimming pool nearby, and at the Chorrera (La Herradura) and La Siesta beaches on the Pan-American Highway.

Taboga Island *p1133*
You may be able to find locals to stay with, ask around.
A Taboga, T250-2122, htaboga@sinfo.net. Apdo 550357, Paitilla, Panamá, 300 m east of wharf. A/c, TV, restaurant, café, pool, beach, tropical birds.
C Chu, on main street, 200 m left of wharf, T250-2036. Wooden colonial style, thin walls, shared bath, beautiful views, own beach, terrace restaurant serving traditional fish and chicken dishes.

Pearl Islands *p1134*
L Contadora Resort, T264-1510, www.hotelcontadora.com. Same ownership as **El Panamá** in Panama City, chalet complex, nice location on beach, but reportedly run-down.

Eating

Panama City *p1123, maps p1124, p1126 and p1135*
There is a wide range of international restaurants in all styles and price ranges. There are also good restaurants in most of the more expensive hotels.
TTT **Casablanca**, Plaza Bolívar in Casco Viejo. Long-established reputable restaurant with tables al fresco in the picturesque plaza in Casco Viejo.
TTT **Casco Viejo**, Calle 50, Mansión Dante. Excellent French food, interesting decor, closed Sun. Expensive but recommended.
TTT **Sushi Itto**, between Av Samuel Lewis y Calle 55, at the back of Plaza Obarrio building, T265-1222. Mexican owned, mixing sushi and Japanese dishes with Latin food.
TTT **Gauchos Steak House**, Calle Uruguay y Calle 48. Choose your own steak, a must for meat lovers. Good.
TTT **La Cocotte**, Uruguay 138, T213-8250. In former private house, excellent French cuisine, expensive, Hilary Clinton slipped out of the embassy to eat here – but not on a Sun as it closes.
TTT **Las Bóvedas**, in converted dungeons at seaward end of Casco Viejo (take a taxi), T228-8068. Good French food, art galleries adjoining, live jazz Thu-Sat, closed Sun.
TTT **Limoncillo**, Calle 47 y Uruguay, Marbella, T263-5350, www.limoncillo.com. Contemporary award-winning international cuisine, with good reviews over the years.
TTT **Matsui**, Av Eusebio A Morales A-12. Japanese, excellent all you can eat 1200-2000.
TTT **Miraflores Restaurant**, Miraflores Visitor Centre. Mon-Sat 1200-2300. A little out of town, but thoroughly different. Classy dining with an up-close view of passing ships. Great salads, North American style meats and pastas, and buffet. Used as a location in the movie *The Tailor of Panama*.
TTT **Rendezvous**, at the **Riande Continental**. Open 24 hrs, superb Sun brunch.
TTT-TT **Monolo Caracol**, Av Central, Casco Viejo, across from Palacio Nacional de Gobierno y Justicia. Excellent food, tapas and seafood, can get noisy.
TTT-TT **Mostaza**, Calle A opposite Arco Chato. One of the best restaurants in Casco Viejo, with large portions and live music at weekends.
TT **Athen's**, corner of Av Uruguay and Av 4 Sur, Obarrio, behind the Delta petrol station. Excellent pizza, also Greek and Middle Eastern food including stuffed pitta breads and good salads, lively atmosphere, young crowd, very good.
TT **Café de Nire**, Av Central y Calle 3. Offers a covered outside dining area, popular place, food reportedly average.
TT **Caffé Pomodoro**, Av Eusebio A Morales, north of Calle 55, in patio of **Apartotel Las Vegas**. Garden setting, also a/c, North Italian pasta and sauces, informal, moderately priced.
TT **Calypso**, Vía España y Calle 46, La Cresta, T223-0749. French restaurant and bar.
TT **Dalí**, Av Samuel Lewis y Santa Rita. Dali-esque decor, French and Italian food.
TT **El Mesón del Prado**, Edif Alcalá, Tumba Muerto, T260-9466. Informal, Spanish, seafood, snacks, moderate prices.
TT **El Trapiche**, Vía Argentina 10, T221-5241. Many dishes including *empanadas* (meat filled fritters) and *mondongo* (seasoned tripe), also in Panamá Viejo, Vía Cincuentenario, Panamanian food with traditional music and dance programmes, call for information.
TT **Gran China**, Av Balboa, between Calle 26 y 27. Good-value Chinese.
TT **Jimmy's**, Paseo Cincuentenario just beyond Atlapa Centre, T226-1096. Panamanian, good grills, seafood, fast food and fish, served under a thatched roof, very

popular, also on Av Samuel Lewis opposite **Riande Continental**, a/c, self service, good for breakfast and lunch.

¶¶ **Korea House**, Calle 52, block north of Vía España opposite **Cine Aries**. Sushi bar, Japanese and Korean.

¶¶ **La Cascada**, Av Balboa y Calle 25. Beef, pork, seafood, enormous helpings, open air, 'doggy bags' given, kitsch decor but good service, menus in charming English to takeaway. Highly recommended. Closed Sun, credit cards not accepted.

¶¶ **La Tablita**, Transisthmian Highway, Los Angeles district, T260-1458. Good steaks, reasonable prices.

¶¶ **Las Américas**, Av 1 Sur, Calle 57/58, 1 block south of Vía España, T223-4676. Elegant Italian, good cellar.

¶¶ **Las Costillitas** on Vía Argentina. Same management as **La Cascada**, same huge menu (which takes 30 mins to read), same reasonable prices, and closed on Sun.

¶¶ **Las Tinajas**, on Calle 51, near **Ejecutivo Hotel**, T263-7890. Panamanian, traditional entertainment Tue and Thu-Sat from 2100, craft shop, closed Sun. Recommended.

¶¶ **Le Sandwich de Paris**, Calle 51, just before **EcoMargo Tours** on the opposite side of the road. French. Good crunchy baguettes and crêpes at reasonable prices; good for lunch.

¶¶ **Manolo**, Vía Argentina, sidewalk terrace. A favourite for politicians and young people in evenings and Sun morning, draught beer served with Spanish *tapas*, *churros* a speciality, also on Vía Venetto y Calle Eusebio A Morales, tables or counter, same menu, prices and service.

¶¶ **Marbella**, Av Balboa y Calle 39. Spanish seafood, *cazuela de mariscos, paella*, good.

¶¶ **Nápoli**, Calle 57, Obarrio, 1½ blocks south of Vía España. Big, family-style, good Italian pizzas with real Italian dough, also by Plaza 5 de Mayo.

¶¶ **Ozone Café**, Calle Uruguay. Food from all over the world, upmarket, good and popular, many other restaurants in same area.

¶¶ **Parrillada Martín Fierro**, Calle Eusebio A Morales, T264-1927. Surf 'n'turf.

¶¶ **Pavo Real**, Calle 51, just west of Calle Ricardo Arias, Campo Alegre, T269-0504. Upmarket English pub with restaurant, darts, good food, ex-pat hangout, Mon-Tue 1200-2400, Wed-Sat 1200-0330, live music from 2200, closed Sun.

¶¶ **Pencas**, Amador Causeway, in front of Plaza de las Banderas, T211-3671, www.pencas.com. Panamanian food and live 'Panamanian Expressions' – folkloric nights with music and dancing on Wed nights. Call ahead and make a reservation as it gets busy.

¶¶ **Piccola Pizza**, Calle 50 y Elvira Méndez, below **Hilton** and **Ancón Expeditions**. Italian, decent pizza but not the friendliest service.

¶¶-¶ **Restaurant y Pizzeria Sorrento**, Vía Ricardo Arias 11, T269-0055. One of best meal deals in town. Excellent pizza, pasta and more traditional Panamanian dishes at good prices.

¶¶-¶ **Siciliano's Café**, Calle Manuel M Icaza, in front of **Bancafé**. Excellent Sicilian and Mediterranean food of pizzas, pastas, soups and pittas, at great prices, best served outside in their quiet fan-cooled terrace.

¶ **Angel**, Vía Argentina 68, T263-6411. Spanish, seafood, imported mussels, eel, *bacalao* (cod), closed Sun.

¶ **Angie's Pasao Cincuentenario**, opposite Jimmy's. Buffet style with huge portions and low prices. Very popular around lunchtime.

¶ **Benihana**, Calle 60, Obarrio. Favoured by Japanese locals, closed Sat.

¶ **Casa Vegetarian Kuan Yin**, Ricardo Arias, just before the **Continental Hotel**. Chinese orientated vegetarian buffet; very cheap.

¶ **Centolla's Place**, Vía España, Río Abajo, T221-7056. Caribbean seafood, catering to Antillean community, friendly, worth a taxi ride. Recommended.

¶ **Frequi Jugos**, Av Justo Arosemena, Edificio Hatillo, between Calle 35 and 36. Not entirely vegetarian, but a good place for a fresh fruit juice/fruit salad. Has a good lunch buffet. Convenient for the hotel district.

¶ **Govinda's**, Calle 47, No 24, Marbella. Many vegetarian specialities.

¶ **La Victoria**, Av Central, next to **Minimercado Teresa** . Open 1100-2300. Very cheap (US$1 a meal) with juke box and a/c. Recommended. Also recommended is the unnamed restaurant opposite, very popular with locals.

¶ **Mango's Pub & Grill**, Calle Uruguay 1-24, T269-4856. US-style bar and food, many imported beers, best hamburger south of Houston, live music Tue and Sat, recommended for lunch and evening.

¶ **Mireya**, Calle Ricardo Arango y Ricardo Arias, near **Continental Hotel**, T269-1876. Health food bakery, good value, recommended, also Calle 39 y Av Balboa, Bella Vista.

¥ **Mi Salud**, Calle 31 y Av México 3-30. Owned by dietary specialist Carlos Raúl Moreno, vegetarian options, Mon-Sat 0700-1900.
¥ **Niko's Café** with 4 locations at Vía España near El Rey supermarket, T264-0136; El Dorado Shopping Centre, T260-0022; Paitilla, past old airport T270-2555; and behind the former Balboa High School in the Canal Zone T228-8888. Very good, cheap, self-service.
¥ **Palacio Imperial**, Calle 17 near **Ticabus** office. Good and cheap Chinese.
¥ **Riazor**, Calle 16, 15-105, T228-2541. Just as it was 40-50 years ago, cheap local food with style. Recommended. Take a taxi at night.
¥ **Rincón Tableño**, Av Cuba No 5 y Calle 31. Panamanian. Several locations, good *comida criolla*, lunchtimes only. Recommended.
¥ **Tang**, Calle A y Cenbule, off Plaza Santa Ana. Cheap, friendly, Chinese. Recommended.

Cafés and snacks
Café Coca Cola, Av Central and Plaza Santa Ana, not the safest area. Pleasant, friendly, reasonably priced – US$3 for set lunch.
Café Central, Av Central, between Calle 28 and 29, Calidonia. Basic and cheap food, OK.
Café Jaime, corner of Calle 12 and Av Central. Good *chichas* (natural drinks).
Dulcería Panadería La Gran Vida, Av Central 11-64 (between Calle 11 y 12). Good *chicha* juice, good cheap ice cream, *empanadas* and cakes. Recommended.
Groovy Café, Vía Venetto, Edificio Torres de Alba. A bit hit and miss, and not quite as groovy as its name suggests, generally decent filled potatoes, salads and sandwiches. Not much in the way of coffee.
Markany, Av Cuba y Av Ecuador. Good snacks.
Panadería y Dulcería Río de Oro, opposite **Rey Supermarket** on Vía España, lower level of the shopping center. Good place for a cheap snack with good cakes and pastries.

Fuerte Amador *p1133*
¥¥¥ **Café Barko**, Calzado de Amador. One of the most established restaurants in Flamenco, specializing in seafood and Panamanian dishes, beautifully prepared.
¥¥ **Crêpes and Waffles**, located upstairs at the Flamenco Mall. Pleasant, light dishes.
¥¥-¥ **Mi Ranchito**, by Naos Isla, T228-4909. The charming, simple, outdoor restaurant is highly recommended in the evening for seeing the skyline, as well as for good, cheap traditional food and drink.

Pearl Islands *p1134*
¥¥ **Gallo Nero**, by runway. Good seafood especially lobster, pizza and pasta, at reasonable prices. Run by German couple, Gerald and Sabine.
¥ **Fonda Sagitario**, near **Gallo Nero** , café, cheap; also supermarket and a duty-free shop.
¥ **Michael's**, opposite **Gallo Nero**, good pizzas, ice cream.

Entertainment

Panama City *p1123, maps p1124, p1126 and p1135*
Bars and clubs
La Chiva Parrandera is an open-sided bus that tours the hot-spots 2000-2400, T263-3144, for information, US$25 per person.

Many late night haunts are concentrated in the Marbella district such as **La Cantina, Galerías Marbella**, Calle 5 East, T264-4958, Wed-Sat, ladies nights and live music, **Mangos, Café Dalí** and **Fonda Antioqueña**.

Café Bolívar, Plaza Bolívar, Casco Viejo. Small, snug bar with outside tables.
Casablanca, Plaza Bolívar, Casco Viejo. Fancy, hip bar and restaurant offering Provençale/Thai cuisine, mixed reports on the food, a/c.
Deep Room, Calle Uruguay area of Bella Vista. An excellent club. Tribal house and electronica. Late start, sometimes 0400.
Las Molas, entrance to **Chase Manhattan** Bank, Vía España, Los Angeles district. Small bands, rural decor, drinks US$1.50.
La Parrillita, Av 11 de Octubre, Hato Pintado. Restaurant/disco in a railway carriage.
Las Bóvedas, Plaza de Francia, Casco Viejo, T228-8068. Jazz on the weekends from 2100-0100.
Next, Av Balboa, T265-8746. Wed-Sat, commercial disco, pricey cover charge.
Panamá Viejo, T221-1268. Colombian restaurant, bar and disco, open 24 hrs.
Peach Monkeys Lounge, **Hotel Caeser Park** Lobby, T270-5170. Mon-Sat. Chic.
Unplugged, Calle 48, Bella Vista. Mon-Sat, rock 'n' roll club.
Voodoo Lounge, Plaza Pacífica, Punta Pacífica, T215-1581. Fri house music, live DJs Sat electronic music.

Wasabi Sushi Lounge, Marbella, T264-1863, Electronic music and sushi, ladies nights, sangria and live DJs.

Cabarets, casinos and gambling

There are more than 20 state-managed casinos, some in the main hotels with profits intended for charitable public institutions. Most offer blackjack, baccarat, poker, roulette and slot machines (*traganikles*). Winnings are tax-free and paid without deductions. The **National Lottery** is solemnly drawn (televized) Wed and Sun at 1300 in Plaza de la Lotería between Av Perú y Cuba; 4-digit tickets, called *billetes* or *pedazos*, cost US$1, a win pays up to US$2000; 'chance' tickets, with only 2 digits cost US$0.25, and pay up to US$14.
Josephine's, Calle 50 y Av Uruguay, El Cangrejo. Cover charge US$20, continuous show Mon-Sat 2100-0400.
Le Palace, Calle 52, opposite **Hotel El Ejecutivo**, T269-1844. No cover, shows from 2030.

Cinema and theatre

La Prensa and other newspapers publish daily programming (*cartelera*) of cultural events. Cinemas cost US$2.50 except **Cine Balboa** near Steven's Circle, US$2; by law all foreign films must be subtitled in Spanish. **MultiPlaza Mall** at Punta Pacífica, **Albrook Mall**, www.albrookmall.com, and **Multi Centro** in Paitilla, have large multi-screen cinemas.
Anayansi Theatre, in the Atlapa Convention Centre, Vía Israel, San Francisco, has a 3000-seat capacity, good acoustics, regular recitals and concerts.
Balboa Theatre, near Steven's Circle and post office in Balboa, with folkloric groups and jazz concerts sponsored by National Institute of Culture.
Cine Universitario, in the National University, T264-2737, US$1.50 for general public, shows international and classic movies, daily (not holidays) at 1700, 1900 and 2100.
Guild Theatre, in the Canal Area at Ancón mounts amateur productions mainly in English.
Teatro Nacional, see page 1127, occasionally has shows and performances. There are regular folklore sessions every other Sun and monthly National Ballet performances when not on tour, check press for details.

Live music

Café El Aleph, Vía Argentina north of Vía España, T264-2844. Coffee house atmosphere, snacks and full meals, internet facilities, occasional art shows, live jazz at weekends, phone for programme.
Café Gardel, Vía Argentina, T269-3710. Small restaurant, tiny bar, perfect atmosphere for jazz.
Giorgio's, 1 block south of Vía Porras.
Hotels Granada and **Soloy** (Bar Maitai, T227-1133) are recommended for live Latin music at weekends.
Las Bóvedas, on Plaza de Francia, T228-8068. Jazz on weekends 2100-0100.
Nottingham, Fernández de Córdoba, Vista Hermosa, T261-0314. Live salsa at weekends, no cover charge, restaurant.
Vino's Bar, Calle 51 y Colombia, Bella Vista, T264-0520. Live salsa at weekends, cover charge, restaurant.

Festivals and events

Panama City *p1123, maps p1124, p1126 and p1135*

Feb/Mar **Carnival** activities include a parade on Shrove Tue and have become more elaborate in recent years.
3 Nov **Independence Day**, practically the whole city – or so it seems – marches in a colourful and noisy parade through the old part of the city lasting over 3 hrs. Another parade takes place the following day.
Dec Annual **Christmas parade**, with US influence much in evidence, rather than the Latin American emphasis on the *Nacimiento* and the Three Kings.

Shopping

Panama City *p1123, maps p1124, p1126 and p1135*

Duty-free imported luxuries of all kinds are an attraction at the Zona Libre in Colón, but Panama City is a booming shopping centre where bargains are not hard to find; anything from crystal to cashmere may be cheaper than at their point of origin.

The smartest shops are along **Calle 50** (Av 4 Sur) in Campo Alegre, and **Vía España** in Bella Vista and El Cangrejo, but **Av Central** is cheaper, the best and the most popular.

Of the various commercial centres, with banking, entertainment and parking facilities, the largest is **Los Pueblos**, on Vía Tocumen, with buses leaving from 5 de Mayo, or take a taxi for US$5. It's a huge complex of mega stores drawing in large numbers. **Multi Plaza** is a new mall located at Punta Pacífica, close to Atlapa, with department stores, shops, restaurants, banks and an 8-screen cinema. **Multi Centro** is at Punta Paitilla and easily accessible from the centre of town. **Albrook**, by the national bus terminal, have a mall that includes a large cinema.

Arts and crafts

Traditional Panamanian *artesanía* includes *molas* (see page 1165), eg Emma Vence, T261-8009; straw, leather and ceramic items; *chunga nawala* (palm fibre) canasters; the *pollera* circular dress, the *montuno* shirts (embroidered), the *chácara* (a popular bag or purse), the *chaquira* necklace made by Ngöbe-Buglé (Guaymí) people, and jewellery. Indigenous Darién (Embera) carvings of jungle birds and animals from cocobolo wood or *tagua* nut (small, extremely intricate, also *tagua* necklaces) make interesting souvenirs (from US$10 up to US$250 for the best, museum- quality pieces). The tourist office has a full list of *artesanía* shops, including those in the main hotels.

Artesanías Nacionales Several indigenous co-ops selling a good selection direct from open-air outlets, eg in Panamá Viejo, Canal Area at Balboa and along road to Miraflores Locks at Corozal (daily if not raining).

Colecciones, Vía Italia opposite **Hotel Plaza Paitilla Inn**, has a wide selection. Plenty of straw articles available, including baskets, bags, traditional masks and Panama hats (US$150 for the best quality).

Flory Salzman on Vía Venetto at the back of **El Panamá Hotel**, T223-6963. The best place outside San Blas Islands for *molas*, huge selection, sorted by theme, ask for discounts.

Inovación, or **Indutípica**, Av A y Calle 8 Ote (opposite San José Church) for reproductions of pre-Columbian ceramics and jewellery, necklaces, Kuna *molas* (prices starting from US$2.50) from the Darién, and Ngöbe-Buglé dresses from Bocas del Toro.

Mercardo Artesanal de Cinco de Mayo, behind the old Museo Antropológico Dra Reina. Stalls selling Kuna, Ngöbe-Buglé and Embera crafts as well as local Panamanian work. They also have a selection of hammocks and artefacts from neighbouring countries.

Reprosa, Av Samuel Lewis y Calle 54, T269-0457. A unique collection of pre-Columbian gold artefacts reproduced in sterling silver vermeil; David and Norma Dickson make and sell excellent reproductions (**Panamá Guacas**, T266-6176).

Books and music

Gran Morrison, Vía Espana, T269-2211, and 4 other locations around the city. Books, travel guides and magazines in English.

La Garza, Av José de Fábrega y Calle 47, near the University. Bookshop with good supply of Latin American literature (Spanish only).

Legends, Calle 50, San Francisco, diagonal to the Iglesia de Guadalupe de Panamá, T270-0097. A cultural oasis – CDs, books, T-shirts and posters.

Librería Argosy, Vía Argentina north of Vía España, El Cangrejo, T223-5344. Very good selection in English, Spanish and French, also sells tickets for musical and cultural events. Recommended.

National University Bookshop, on campus between Av Manuel Espinosa Batista and Vía Simón Bolívar, T223-3155. For excellent range of specialized books on Panama, national authors, social sciences and history, Mon-Fri 0800-1600. Highly recommended.

The campus **Simón Bolívar Library** has extensive Panamanian material, only for registered students but visitors engaged in special research can obtain a temporary permit from the director, Mon-Fri 0800-2000, Sat 0900-1300.

Librería Cultural Panameña, SA, Vía España, Perejil, T223-5628, www.libreria cultural.com. Mon-Fri 0900-1800, Sat 0900-1700. Excellent, mostly Spanish bookshop with obscure Panamanian prints as well as regular titles and very helpful staff.

The Smithsonian Tropical Research Institute (see page 1130), Edif Tupper, Av de los Mártires (opposite National Assembly), has a bookshop and the best English- language scientific library in Panama, Mon-Fri 0800-1600.

Camping equipment

Army-Navy store, Av Central near Plaza 5 de Mayo, for various pieces of camping and hiking equipment.

Army Force, east end pedestrianized section of Av Central, west of Plaza 5 de Mayo.

Markets and supermarkets

Bargain hard as prices are extremely competitive. The central **Mercado San Felipe**, close to the docks and Palacio Presidencial, is the place for fresh produce (pigs, ducks, poultry and geese) and pets. The most interesting part is the chaotic shopping area along Calle 13 and the waterfront (Terraplen). It's the best place to buy 2nd-hand jungle and military supplies (eg powerful insect repellents, machetes and cooking equipment) for a trek into the forested interior. The nearby **fish market** is clean and has the best prices.

Supermercado El Rey has a branch on Vía España just east of **Hotel Continental**, at El Dorado, and at several other locations. **Super 99, Farmacias Arrocha, Casa de la Carne** (expensive) and **Machetazo**, also a department store (on Av Central, Calidonia) are said to be the city's best.

Newspapers and magazines

The international edition of the *Miami Herald* is widely available at newsstands and hotels, as are leading US papers and magazines. Spanish and English magazines at branches of **Farmacias Arrocha, Super 99** and **Gago** supermarkets/drugstores.

Photography

There are many places for equipment and developing such as **Foto Decor** and **Foto Enodi**, Vía Porras. **Relojería**, Calle Medusín, off Av Central in Calidonia. Watch shop for camera repairs.

Activities and tours

Panama City *p1123, maps p1124, p1126 and p1135*

Beaches

Many are within 1½ hrs' drive of the city. **Fort Kobbe** beach (US$7.50, with vouchers given for drinks and hot dogs, bus from Canal Area bus station US$0.75, 30 mins) and **Naos beach** (US$1, Amador bus from same station, US$0.30, then 2-km walk along causeway) have been recommended. Veracruz beach is not recommended as it is both dirty and dangerous. All are dangerous at night.

Cockfights

Club Gallístico, Vía España near junction with Vía Cincuentenario, T221-5652, most Sun, same bus as for race track, but get out at crossing with Calle 150.

Golf

Panama Golf Club, T266-7436.
Coronado Beach Golf Club, part of the Hotel Coronado Club Suites Resort (open to tourists who get guest cards at Coronado office on Calle 50).
Summit Golf and Resort, 20 mins out of the city along Carretera Gaillard, T232-4653, www.summitgolfpanama.com. Tourists welcome, green fees and rented clubs.

Horse races

President Ramón racetrack, Juan Díaz. Thu, Sat, Sun and holidays. Entry from US$0.50-2.50. Take a bus to Juan Díaz.

Swimming

Piscina Patria (the Olympic pool), San Pedro or Juan Díaz bus, US$0.15.
Piscina Adán Gordón, between Av Cuba and Av Justo Arosemena, near Calle 31, 0900-1200, 1300-1700 (except weekends to 1700 only). Admission US$0.50 (take ID) Women must wear bathing caps; take a padlock for locker.

Tour operators

Airemar, Calle 52 y Ricardo Arias 21, T269-2533. Highly recommended for flights to South America.
Ancon Expeditions, Calle Elvira Méndez, next to **Marriott Hotel**, T269-9415, www.ancon expeditions.com. This is the tour operator for the environmental agency ANCON. Excellent guides and service, with especially recommended programmes in the Darién region (Cana Valley and Punta Patiño), but can arrange programmes to most of Panama's wilderness areas. Trans- Darién treks and specialist birding programmes available.
Arco Iris, Apdo. 6-2544 El Dorado, T227-3318, www.arcoirispanama.com. Full range of local tours.
Cinco Continentes, Av Principal La Alameda, Edif Plaza San Marcos, T260-8447. Helpful with shipping a car. Recommended.
EcoMargo Tours, Calle 51 Bella Vista, local 24, next to **Las Tinajas** restaurant, T264-8888, www.margotours.com. Specializes in ecotourism for small groups with emphasis on using local guides, can book various lodges and excursions.

Adventures in Panama, Av La Amistad, Plaza Psari, Local 1, next to Blockbuster Video, El Dorado, www.adventuresinpanama.com. Specialist in hiking, rock climbing, canyoning, very knowledgeable about Darién and the old colonial roads, very active on looking for new opportunities. Many trips focus on the nearby Chagres National Park including the 'Jungle Challenge' which involves rappelling off a series of waterfalls – great fun! Good store of equipment with the unusual option of naturist hiking if the mood takes you and weather suits
Eco Circuitos, T314-1586, www.eco circuitos.com. Expertly run with conservation an utmost priority. Good range of creative tours include hiking, diving, cultural exchange and educational programs.
Aventuras Panama, Edif Celma, El Paical, T260-0044, www.aventuraspanama.com. Good adventure options.
Panama Travellers, Vía Argentina, in front of El Parque Andres Bello, Edif Yolanda, T214-7345, www.panamatravellers.com. The usual tours, Canal, eco-exploring, birdwatching, jungles, kayaks, etc.
Panama Jones, T/F428-3476, www.panamacanal.com. English spoken, specialists in adventure tourism. Their 11-night Panama Explorer tour gives a good look at the diverse aspects of the country.
Panama Star Tours, Calle Ricardo Arias, Edif Comi PB, T265-7970, www.panamastar.com. Arranges itineraries and books accommodation throughout the country.
Riande, Calle Elvira Méndez (next to the Continental hotel), T263-9999, turismo@ hotelesriande.com. English spoken, helpful.
Scubapanama, Urbanización El Carmen, Av 6 Norte y Calle 62a No 29-B, T261-3841, www.scubapanama.com. Respected local dive operator. Offers dives in the Caribbean (near Portobelo), Pacific and the Canal. One option includes all 3 areas in 1 day! Longer trips can be arranged on request, including options in Pearl Islands and Isla Coiba. Given sufficient numbers all-inclusive multi-day trips to Isla Coiba start at around US$450-500. Certification courses up to dive master available.
Shirley Tours, T314-1301. Trips arranged through the www.panamacanal2000.com. Broad range of activities including hiking and trekking the Camino Real, good for ecotourism options. Owner Charles Shirley is very helpful and has a good knowledge of Panama.

Pearl Islands *p1134*
Argonaut Steamship Agency, Calle 55 No 7-82, Panama City, T264-3459. Launch cruises.

Transport

Panama City *p1123, maps p1124, p1126 and p1135*

Air

Airport information T238-4160, T238-4322 or T226-1622.
Tocumen International Airport (PTY), 27 km. Official taxi fare is US$25 to or from Panama City, maximum 2 passengers in same party, US$14 each sharing with 1 other, or US$10 per person if you share making it a *colectivo*. US$2 extra if you go by the toll road – much quicker. Bargaining is possible with regular cabs but not with tourist taxis at the airport.

From airport to city, walk out of the terminal and across the main road to the bus shelter. Another option is to walk 300 m to the traffic circle where there is a bus shelter (safe but hot during the day). For about US$3 (should only be US$1.20) driver takes you by Panamá Viejo, just off the main airport road.

Buses to the airport are marked 'Espana-Tocumen', 1 hr, US$0.35, but if going at a busy time, eg in the morning rush hour, allow 1½-3 hrs.

There is a 24-hr **left-luggage** office near the **Budget** car rental desk for US$1 per article per day (worth it, since theft in the departure lounge is common). The official IPAT tourist office at the airport remains open to meet late flight arrivals. There are duty-free shops at the airport with a wide selection and good prices. Most facilities are found in upper level departure area **Banco Nacional de Panamá**, **Cable & Wireless** office for international phone, fax and internet access); car rental is downstairs at Arrivals.

Domestic flights operate from Marcos A Gelabert airport at Albrook in the Canal Area. There is no convenient bus service, taxis charge US$1-2. Good self-service café especially for fried breakfast before early flight to San Blas. **Aeroperlas** operates daily flights to 17 destinations throughout the country (eg from Panama City to Colón US$26, David US$65, Bocas del Toro US$66, Yaviza/El Real US$55, all fares one-way). **Mapiex Aéreo** and **Aviatur** also fly to several destinations throughout the country, and there are charter flights to many Darién outposts. Sample hourly rates for private hire: Twin Otter 20 passenger, US$630. Rodolfo Causadias of **Transpasa**, T226-0842 is an experienced pilot for photographic work.

Airline offices For international airline websites see page 32. **Aerolíneas Argentinas**, Vía Brasil y Av Ramón Arias, T269-3815; **AeroMéxico**, Av 1BNorte, El Cangrejo, T263-3033; **Aeroperlas**, reservations T315-7500, www.aeroperlas.com; **Air France**, Calle Abel Bravo y 59 Obarrio T269-7381; **Alitalia**, Calle Alberto Navarro, T269-2161; **American Airlines**, Calle 50 Plaza New York, T269-6022; **Avianca**, 223-5225; **Aviatur**, T315-0311; **Cathy Pacific**, Av 1-B Norte, El Cangrejo, T263-3033; **Continental**, Av Balboa y Av 4, Ed Galerías Balboa, Planta Baja, T263-9177; **Copa**, Av Justo Arosemena y Calle 39, T217-2672; **Cubana**, Av Justo Arosamena, T227-2291; **Delta**, Edif World Trade Centre, Calle 53E, Marbella, T214-8118; **Grupo Taca**, Centro Comercial Camino de Cruces, Local 2, Vía Ricardo J Alfaro, T360-2093; **Iberia**, Av Balboa y Calle 34, T227-3966; **KLM**, Av Balboa y Calle Uruguay, Edif Plaza Miramar, T264-6395; **LAB**, Calle 50 No 78, Ed Bolivia, T263-6771; **LanChile**, Calle 72, San Francisco, T226-7119; **Lufthansa**, Calle Abel Bravo y 59 Obarrio, Ed Eurocentro, T269-1549; **Mapiex Aéreo**, T315-0344; **Mexicana**, Vía Argentina, Ed Torre el Cangrejo oficina 64, T264-9855; **United Airlines**, Bella Vista, L-1, T225-6519;

Bus

Local The traditional small buses known as *chivas*, consisting of locally made wooden bodies grafted onto truck chassis, have all but disappeared. Most buses in urban areas are 2nd-hand US school buses brightly painted in fanciful designs, but poor condition. They are known as *diablos rojos* (red devils) and are notorious for roaring engines and aggressive drivers. Most outbound (east) buses travel along Av Perú, through Bella Vista, before fanning out to their various destinations. Inbound (west) buses travel along Vía España and Av Central through the Calidonia shopping district. Basic fare US$0.25, usually paid to the driver upon descending; if there is a fare box, deposit upon entering. To stop at the next authorized stop, call out '*parada*' to the driver.

Long distance All buses apart from the Orange buses leave from the bus terminal in Albrook, near the domestic airport. Taxi US$2 to centre. Facilities at terminal include ATMs, internet access, clothes shops, luggage shops, bakeries and basic restaurants.

Most long-distance buses are fairly modern and in good condition. Except for the longest routes, most are 24-seater 'Coaster'-type minibuses. Check if a/c on next bus out is functioning. Offices are arranged in long line from right to left in the terminal.

Orange buses to all **Canal Area** destinations (Balboa, Miraflores, Paraíso, Kobbe, etc) leave from SACA terminal near Plaza 5 de Mayo; from the Plaza, walk past the National Assembly tower and turn left.

From the Albrook bus terminal (T232-5803): **Chitré (Los Santos)**, 20 per day, 0600-2300, 4½ hrs, US$6; **Tonosi (Los Santos)**, 0745 and1300, 5½ hrs, US$8.50; **Macaracas (Los Santos)**, 0830 to 1530 every couple of hours, 5 hrs, US$7; **Las Tablas (Los Santos)**, 13 per day, 0600-1900, 5 hrs, US$6.50; **Calobre (Las Palmas)**, 0800-1700 every 1½ hrs, 4½ hrs, US$8; **Las Palmas**, 0830, 4½ hrs, US$8; **Cañaza (Las Palmas)**, 0845 and 1045, 4½ hrs, US$7; **Santiago**, 21 per day, 0300-2400, 4 hrs, US$7, with Expreso Veraguense 16 per day, 0100-2300; **Ocú (via Las Minas)** 8 per day, 0700-1700, 5½ hrs, US$6; **Pesé (Las Minas)**, 4½ hrs, US$6; **Yaviza**, 7 per day, 8-10 hrs (delays possible during rainy season) US$14; **Agua Fría**, 15 per day, 0600-1530, US$7; **Colón**, many buses, less frequent at weekends, express buses leave every 20 mins, peak weekends book or be prepared to wait, 1½ hrs, US$2, pay on bus; **David** and on to **the border** with (Trans 5 Estrellas) 1030, 1930 and 2330 (express), 3 hrs, US$10.60 or US$15 to David), and further down terminal – with **Padafront**, T225-3690 – 11 per day, 0700-2400, US$11, express buses at 2300 and 2400 (US$15), also with Utranschiri US$10.60; **Cañita** (Utracasa) 17 per day, 0640-1740, 2½ hrs, US$2.50; **San Carlos-Chamé**, 1½ hrs, US$2.50; **El Valle de Antón**, US$3.50; **Penonomé**, 20 buses daily, 2½ hrs US$3.70; **El Copé** and **La Pintada** (Utracopa) 0600-1800, 3½ hrs US$5; **Aguadulce** (Utasa), many buses, 3 hrs, US$4.70; **Olá**, calling at Río Hato, daily at 1500, US$4.50. Almirante and Changuinola, 1 night bus daily at 2000, 9 hrs, US$23-24.

International buses Buses going north through Central America get booked up so reserve a seat in advance and never later than the night before departure. **Ticabus**, with office in the main terminal, Calle 17 Ote, T314-6385, www.ticabus.com, run a/c buses to **San José**, daily at 1100, arriving at 0300 the next day, US$25 1-way (but check times and prices which change at regular intervals); continuing to **Managua**, US$36; **Tegucigalpa**, US$56, and on as far as **Tapachula** on the Mexico-Guatemala Pacific coast border, US$84, via **Guatemala City**, US$69 (3½ days, overnight in Managua and El Salvador). Tickets are refundable; they pay on the same day, minus 15%. **Panaline** to **San José** from the Hotel Soloy, Av Peru y Calle 30, T227-1133, and the main terminal leaves daily at 1300. You can also travel with **Padafront** Panama City-Paso Canaos then change to **Tracopa** or other Costa Rican buses for San José and other destinations.

Car

Several major downtown arteries become one-way during weekday rush hours, eg Av 4 Sur/Calle 50, one-way heading west 0600-0900, east 1600-1900. The Puente de las Américas can be used only to go into or out of town depending on time and day, mostly weekends; these directions are not always clearly signed. Puente Centenario, at the entrance to the Culebra Cut, was opened in Aug 2000 to lighten the load over the Puente de las Américas.

Car rental **At the airport**: Avis, T238-4056; Budget, T238-4068; **Dollar**, T238-4032; Hertz, T238-4081 and **National**, T238-4144. **In El Cangrejo**: **Avis**, Vía Venetto, T264-0722; **Barriga**, Edif Wonaga 1 B, Calle D, T269-0221; **Budget**, T263-9190; **Dollar**, T269-7542. **Gold**, Calle 55, T264-1711; **Hertz**, Hotel Caesar Park, T226-4077 ext 6202, Calle 50, T264-1111, El Cangrejo T263-6663; **International**, Vía Venetto, T264-4540.

Cycling

Almacén The Bike, Calle 50 opposite Telemetro. Good selection of cycle parts.

Taxi

Service is generally good, but can be scarce during peak hours and many drivers have little clue where many streets are – it's good to have a rough idea of the address location; voluntary sharing is common but not recommended after dark. Most newer taxis have a/c. If a taxi already has a passenger, the driver will ask your destination to see if it coincides with the other passenger's. If you do not wish to share, waggle your index finger or say '*No, gracias*'. Similarly, if you are in a taxi and the driver stops for additional passengers, you may refuse politely. Zone system: US$1 for 1 passenger within 1 zone, US$0.25 for each additional zone (US$2 is a common overcharge in zone 1). Additional passengers US$0.25 each regardless of zones; sharing passengers each pay full fare. Panamanians rarely tip, but foreigners may add US$0.25 or US$0.50 to the fare. Hourly hire, advised for touring dubious areas, US$7 per hr, US$8 with a/c. Radio taxis summoned by telephone are highly recommended. They are listed in yellow pages under 'Taxis'. Add US$0.40 to fare for pick-up. 'Tourist taxis' at major hotels (aged, large American cars with 'SET' number plates) have a separate rate structure: they are more expensive than those you flag down.

Train

Station on Carretera Gaillard. A luxury train now runs daily to **Colón** US$20 one way, US$35 return, 0700, returns 1730, 1¼ hrs. Aventuras 2000, T227-2000, www.colon 2000.com, operate the service.

Taboga Island *p1133*

Boat Taboga is reached in 1-1½ hrs from Pier 17-18 in **Balboa** (check the times in advance, office T228-4348, or pier T232-5395); taxi **Bella Vista**, Pier 18, US$3-4 per person. There are 2 boats daily during the week (0830 and 1500 or 1700 Thu) and 3 boats on Sat, Sun and holidays (0830, 1130 and 1600). Return boats Mon-Wed and Fri 1000 and 1630 or 1830; Thu 1000; weekends 1430 and 1700. From Nov to Jan there are 3 boats daily. Return fare US$7. You can charter a boat for US$120 per day including fishing. Ask at the Balboa Yacht Club office.

Pearl Islands *p1134*

Air Return air ticket to **Contadora** from Paitilla, US$59 by **Aeroperlas**, T250-4026. **Mountain bike hire** by entrance to Caesar Park, US$5 per hr.

Directory

Panama City *p1123, maps p1124, p1126 and p1135*

Banks

See also Money, page 1115. Try to avoid 15th and last working day of the month, pay days. Panamanian banks' hours vary, but most open Mon-Fri 0800-1500, Sat 0800-1200. **Visa** T264-0988; **MasterCard** T263-5221; **Diners** T263-8195. **Algemene Bank Nederland** changes Thomas Cook TCs. **American Express**, Agencia de Viajes Fidanque, Av Balboa, Torre Banco BBVA, Piso 9, T225-5858, Mon-Fri 0800-1715, does not exchange TCs. International Service Center, T001-800-111- 0006. ATM for withdrawals at **Banco Continental** near hotel of same name. **Banistmo**, Calle 50, Mon-Fri 0800-1530, Sat 0900-1200, changes TCs, no commission on AMEX, US$5 per transaction for other TCs. **Banco General** takes American Express, Bank of America and Thomas Cook TCs, 1% commission, minimum US$2 per transaction. Branch at Av Central y 4 Sur (Balboa) can be used for cash advances from ATMs on Visa. **Bank of America**, Vía José de la Cruz Herrera, Calle 53 Este, no commission on own TCs, US$0.10 tax. You can buy AMEX TCs at **Banco Mercantil del Istmo** on Vía España (they also give cash advances on MasterCard). **Banco Nacional de Panamá**, Vía España opposite the Hotel Continental, T205-2000, changes AMEX TCs with 1% commision. **Banco Sudameris** will also change Thomas Cook TCs. **Chase Manhattan Bank**, US$0.65 commission on each TC, Visa advances. **Citibank** has plenty of ATMs for cash withdrawals for its own debit or credit card-holders, also Visa cash advances. **Lloyds Bank**, Calle Aquilino de la Guardia y Calle 48, Bella Vista, T263-6277, T263-8693 for foreign exchange, offers good rates for sterling (the only bank which will change sterling cash, and only if its sterling limit has not been exhausted). It is possible to change South American currencies (poor rates) at **Panacambios**, ground floor, Plaza Regency, behind Adam's Store, Vía España, near the Banco Nacional de Panamá and opposite Hotel Riande Continental (it also has postage stamps for collectors).

Conservation

Asociación Nacional de Conservación de la Naturaleza (ANCON), Calle Amela Dennis de Icaza, Ancón Hill, past Panama's Supreme Court, in former Quarry Heights, Casa 153, T314-0060, www.ancon.org, for comprehensive information on the country's natural attractions and environmental matters. They also run a chain of lodges throughout the country eg in Darién and Bocas.

Embassies and consulates

Canada, World Trade Centre, Galería Comecial, piso 1, Marbella, T264-9731; **Chile**, Vía España, Edif Banco de Boston, T223-9748, 0900-1200, 1400-1600; **Colombia**, MM Icaza 12, Edif Grobman, 6th floor, T264-9266, 0800-1300; **Costa Rica**, Calle Samuel Lewis, T264-2980, 0900-1600; **Cuba**, consular services at Av Cuba y Ecuador, frente a Parque Porras, T227-5277; **Denmark**, Vía Cincuentenario 28, T270-0944, 0800-1200, 1330-1630; **Ecuador**, Edif Grobman, 3rd floor, T264-7820, 0830-1300; **El Salvador**, Av Manuel Espinoza Batista, Edif Metropolis 4A, T223-3020, 0900-1300; **France**, Plaza de Francia, Zona 1, T211-6200, www.amba france-pa.org; **Germany**, Edif Bank of America, Calle 50 y 53, T263-7733, 0900-1700; **Guatemala**, Edif Altamira, 9th floor, 9-25, Vía Argentina, T269-3406, 0800-1300; **Honduras**, Av Justo Arosemena y Calle 31, Edif Tapia, 2nd floor, T225-8200, 0900-1400; **Israel**, Edif Grobman, Calle MM Icaza, 5th floor, PO Box 6357, T264-8022; **Italy**, Av Bal boa Edif Banco Exterior, T225-8948, 0900-1200; **Japan**, Calle 50 y 60, Edif Don Camilo, Urbanización Obarrio, T263-6155, 0830-1200, 1400-1700; **Mexico**, Edif Credicorp, Calle 50, T210-1523, 0800-1200; **Netherlands**, Altos de Algemene Bank, Calle MM Icaza, 4, T264-7257, 0830-1300, 1400-1630; **Nicaragua**, Edif de Lessep's, 4th floor, Calle Manuel María Icaza, T264-3080; **Norway**, Edif Comasa, 5th floor, Av Samuel Lewis, T263-1955, 0900-1230, 1430-1630; **Spain**, Plaza Porras, entre Av Cuba y Av Perú, Calle 33A, T227-5122, 0900-1300; **Sweden**, consulate at Av Balboa y Calle Uruguay, T264-3748, 0900-1200, 1400-1600; **Switzerland**, Av Samuel Lewis y Calle Gerardo Ortega, Edif Banco Central Cancellería, 4th floor, T264-9731, PO Box 499 (Zona 9A), 0845-1145; **UK**, Torre Swiss Bank, Calle 53, Zona 1, T269-0866; **USA**, Av Balboa y 40, Edif Macondo, 3rd floor, T207-7000, 0800-1700. Consulate in new Miramar building, Calle 39 y

Av Balboa, ground floor; **Venezuela**, Edif Hong Kong Bank, 5th floor, Av Samuel Lewis, T264-2524, 0830-1100.

Immigration

Migración y Naturalización, Av Cuba (2 Sur) y Calle 29, T225-8925; visa extensions and exit permits issued Mon-Fri 0800-1530. **Ministerio de Hacienda y Tesoro**, Av Perú/Calle 36, T227-4879, for tax compliance certificate (*paz y salvo*) required for exit visa (*permiso de salida*) if you stay more than 30 days. **Customs** For renewal of permits and obtaining exit papers for vehicles at Paitilla airport.

Internet

Internet cafés are everywhere in Panama City, and are especially concentrated in the commercial centre around Vía España. Rates can be as low as US$0.50 per hr. New places are constantly opening, with many offering perks to clients, such as free coffee.

Language schools

ILERI , 42G Vía La Amistad, El Dorado T/F 260-4424, www.ileripanama.com. Small school offering homestays, US$380 per wk 1-to-1 tuition. **Laundry** **Lavamático Lavarápido**, Calle 7 Central No 7-45, ½ block from Plaza Catedral, Mon-Sat 0800-2000, Sun 0900-1400, US$0.75 with hot water, US$0.60 cold, soap and drying extra. Many around Plaza Catedral; wash and dry US$2. **Lavandería** y Lavamático America, Av Justo Arosemana and Calle 27. Self service was and dry only US$1.50. Very convenient for the hotel district.

Medical services

Hospitals and clinics The US Gorgas **Army Community Hospital** has closed and US medical facilities have moved to the Howard Air Force Base, across the Puente de Las Américas. Private clinics charge high prices; normally visitors are treated at either the **Clínica San Fernando**, T229-2004, or the **Clínica Paitilla**, T269-6060, which both have hospital annexes. For inoculations buy vaccine at a chemist and ask them to recommend a clinic; plenty in La Exposición around Parque Belisario Porras.

Dentist Balboa Dental Clinic, El Prado, Balboa, T228-0338, good, fair price. **Dr Daniel Wong, Clínica Dental Marbella**, Edif Alfil (ground floor), near Centro Comercial Marbella, T263-8998. **Dr D Lindo**, T223-8383, very good but fix price before treatment.

Post office

There is no **home** postal delivery service in Panama. Recipients either have a post office box (*apartado*), or receive mail via General Delivery/Poste Restante (*Entrega General*). The new main post office is close to Casco Viejo at the west end of Av Balboa at Av B, opposite the Mercado de Mariscos, Mon-Fri 0700-1745, Sat 0700-1645; 'Poste Restante' items are held for a month. Official name and zone must be included in the address: **Main Post office**: 'Zona 1, Central, Av Balboa opposite Mercado de Mariscos'; **Calle 30 East/Av Balboa**: 'Zona 5, La Exposición'; **El Dorado Shopping Centre**, Tumba Muerto: 'Zona 6A, El Dorado'; **Vía España, Bella Vista** (in front of Piex store): 'Zona 7, Bella Vista'. Parcels sent 'poste restante' are delivered either to **Encomiendas Postales Transístmicas** at the El Dorado Centro Comercial or the main post office if there is no duty to pay on the goods. The post office operates a courier system called **EMS** to most Central and South American countries, Europe, US and some Asian countries. Packages up to 20 kg: 2 to 3 days to USA (500 g documents to Miami US$13); 3 to 4 days Europe US$20; Asia US$25. Also private courier services, eg **UPS**, Edif Fina, Calle 49, El Cangrejo, ½ kg to London or Paris, 3-4 days, US$30; **Jet Express (Federal Express)**, Edif Helga, Vía España y Av 4 Sur/Calle 50, ½ kg to Miami, 2 days, US$19.

Telephone

Cable & Wireless has its main office in Vía España, on the ground floor of Banco Nacional building. It offers excellent but expensive international telephone, telex, fax and modem (use Bell 212A type) facilities. Collect calls to 21 countries, dial T106. For cost of phone cards and international calls, see Essentials, page 1123. Local calls in Panama City, US$0.10 for 3 mins, US$0.05 for each additional min; anywhere else in the country, US$0.15 per min.

Balboa *p1133*

Banks Chase Manhattan Bank and Citibank. **Post office** Av Balboa and El Prado. **Telephone** Cable & Wireless.

The Panama Canal area

→ *Colour map 8, B1.*

Whether travelling through the Canal, or just standing at its side, watching the vast ocean-going vessels rise and fall as they pass through the huge canal locks is a spectacular sight. In the middle of Lago Gatún is Parque Nacional Isla Barro Colorado, a popular destination for nature lovers and birdwatchers. On the eastern side of the canal, 2 km after Miraflores Lock, is the entrance to the Parque Nacional Camino de Cruces which has several designated hiking trails including the Camino de Cruces colonial gold route which continues through Parque Nacional Soberanía as far as the Chagres River. ▸▸ *For Sleeping, Eating and other listings, see pages 1150-1151.*

Background

The Panama Canal was created from the artificial, river-fed Lago Gatún, 26 m above sea level which supplies the water for the lock system to function. Ships sail across the lake after having been raised from sea level by a series of locks on either the Atlantic or the Pacific approach. They are then lowered by the locks on the opposite side. As the crow flies, the distance across the isthmus is 55 km. From shore to shore the Canal is 67.5 km, or 82 km (44.08 nautical miles) from deep water to deep water. It has been widened to 150 m in most places. The trip normally takes eight or nine hours for the 30 to 40 ships passing through each day. On the Atlantic side there is a normal variation of 30 cm between high and low tides, and on the Pacific of about 380 cm, rising sometimes to 640 cm.

From the Pacific, the Canal channel goes beneath the Puente de las Américas and passes the port of Balboa. The waterway has to rise 16.5 m to Lago Miraflores. The first stage of the process is the Miraflores Locks, 1.5 km before the lake. A taxi to the locks from the city costs US$10. At the far end of the lake, ships are raised another 9.5 m by the single-step Pedro Miguel Locks, after which the 13 km Gaillard, or Culebra Cut is entered, a narrow rock defile leading to Lago Gatún. Opposite Miraflores Locks, there is a swing bridge. Gaillard Cut can be seen from Contractor's Hill, on the west side, reached by car (no buses) by turning right 3 km past Puente de las Américas, passing Cocolí, then turning as signed. The road beyond Cocolí goes on to Posa, where there are good views of the locks, the cut and former Canal Zone buildings.

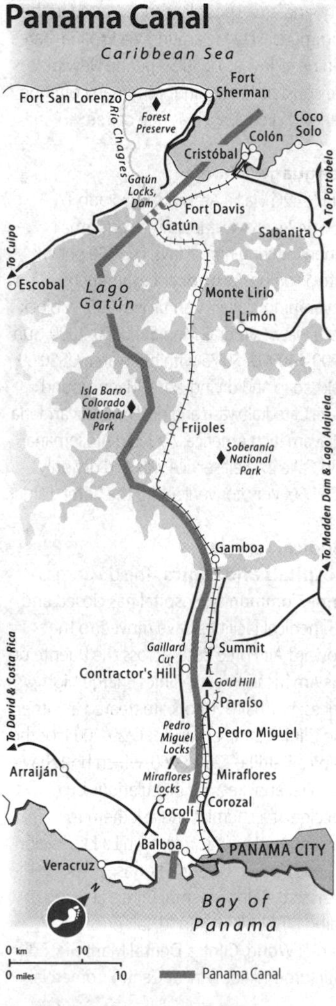

Barro Colorado

For 37 km the Canal passes through Lago Gatún. Enough water must be accumulated in the reservoir during the rainy season to operate the locks throughout the three to four month dry season, since a single ship's transit can use up to 50 million gallons. (A high level reservoir, Lago Alajuela, formerly Madden Lake, feeds the lake and maintains its level; see below.) In the lake is **Barro Colorado Island**, to which animals fled as the basin slowly filled. It is a formally protected area called the **Barro Colorado Nature Monument** and has been a site of scientific research for over 70 years. The excursion is highly recommended for seeing wildlife, especially monkeys, and includes a walk around a guided trail with over 50 points of interest.

Gatún Locks

Continuing north, 10 km southwest of Colón are the Gatún Locks (*Esclusas de Gatún*) with their neat, attendant town. The observation point here ⓘ *open 1000-1630*, is perhaps the best spot in the Canal area for photographing the passage of ships. The most magnificent of the Canal's locks, Gatún integrates all three lock 'steps' on the Atlantic side, raising or lowering ships to or from 26 m in one operation. The flights are in duplicate to allow ships to pass in opposite directions simultaneously. Passage of the locks takes about one hour.

After crossing the lock, the road forks with the left-hand branch bridging the Chagres River just downstream from the graceful Gatún Dam – the largest earth dam in the world when it was built in 1906. Opposite the power plant is the **Tarpon Club**, T443-5316, a fishing club which has a very nice restaurant, disco and bar. A short distance further south is an attractive lakeside picnic area and small boat-launching area. The road goes on down the lake to Escobal and Cuipo through lovely scenery, good for birding. There are no hotels in Cuipo but there are plenty of buses to/from Colón (US$1.60, two hours, US$0.25 to the locks). A bus from Colón to Gatún Locks costs US$0.75.

Canal tours

Most people are surprised by the stunning beauty of the scenery around the Canal, and it is also interesting to see the mechanics of the passage. One way of seeing the Canal is on the luxury daily train that runs to Colón (US$20 one way, US$35 return, 0700, returns 1730, 1¼ hrs. **Aventuras 2000** ⓘ *T227-2000, www.colon2000.com*, operate the service. Alternatively, contact T317-6070, www.panarail.com.

It's also possible to visit the **Miraflores Locks**. The Miraflores Visitor Centre ⓘ *Mon–Sun, 0900-1700, www.pancanal.com, US$8 entrance to the museum and Canal viewing platform, US$5 for platform only*, was constructed as part of Centenial celebrations at a cost is US$6 million. The museum is spread over four floors and includes a training stimulator originally used for pilots transiting vessels through the Canal. The entrance price includes a documentary film in English and Spanish. There is a café and restaurant on site, the latter, **The Miraflores** (ΨΨΨ-ΨΨ) was used in the movie *The Tailor of Panama*. It is open from 1200-2300, serving steaks, salads, pastas, buffet à la carte.

Lago Alajuela

It is a two-hour drive through picturesque jungle to Lago Alajuela, formerly Madden Lake, east of the Canal. The lake, used to generate electricity as well as to maintain the level of Lago Gatún, covers 50 sq km and is within **Parque Nacional Chagres**. The park can be reached by bus from Panama City, first to Las Cumbres and then a second

Everything that crosses the Canal pays by weight, although there are plans to introduce a flat fee. The record for the smallest sum is held by Richard Halliburton, who swam from ocean to ocean between 14 and 23 August 1928, paying US$0.36 for his 150 lbs.

bus to Caimitillo. After that it is a 3½- to four-hour walk to Nuevo Caimitillo. Dugout canoe will take you to Emberá indigenous villages at Parara Puru (15 minutes) and Embera Drua (30-40 minutes). The Emberá in this area are friendly and seem to be coping well with the impacts of tourism on their lives – they also make excellent quality crafts which are sold at very reasonable prices. It may be possible to stay within the village of Parara Puro for a small fee and with the permission of community, giving a greater insight into village life. The Chagres area has great potential for wildlife watching and jungle adventure. Multi-day trekking trips into wildlife rich parts of the forest can be arranged with some companies in Panama City, as can tubing, rafting and abseiling within the watershed – see Tour operators in Panama City, page 1142. If visiting the villages on the Chagres River on an organized tour make sure your company pays the correct visitation fee to the community in question – there have been several incidents of payment being withheld. On a similar note all trips made in the area should involve the employment of Emberá guides/assistants to ensure that these villages benefit from tourism on their lands. The Camino Real passes through the park. There is another refuge at Cerro Azul, marking the start of a challenging three-day hike to the north coast, guide essential. Take a bus for Chepo from Panama City and get off at Vista Hermosa, then walk the 6 km to the ranger hut.

The canal drive runs from Balboa along the Gaillard Highway. Beyond Fort Clayton there is a fine view of the Miraflores and Pedro Miguel locks. Beyond Pedro Miguel town a road branches off to the left to Summit (Las Cumbres), where there are experimental gardens containing tropical plants from all over the world (closed Monday) and a good, small zoo containing native wildlife. **La Hacienda** restaurant serves native dishes. The alternative road to Lago Alajuela (37 km) crosses the Las Cruces trail (an old cannon marks the spot), and beyond is deep jungle. If walking the trail, take machete and compass. Halfway along the Las Cruces trail (1¼ hours) a gravel track, the Plantation Road, turns left, emerging after 1¼ hours on the Gamboa highway 1.5 km north of Summit.

A large area of rainforest between Lago Gatún and Lago Alajuela has been set aside as **Parque Nacional Soberanía** with many walking trails. The park is very popular with birdwatchers with just under 400 species recorded to date, and is reputedly one of the finest observation areas for birds in the world. The park has two fabulous trails for wildlife observation and also has an aviary for harpy eagles. Plantation Trail begins right at the entrance of the road that leads to the Canopy Tower and Pipeline Road is about 17 km long in total, accessed from the Gaillard highway running along the canal, just north of Gamboa, the old American dredging port. The now-abandoned coast-to-coast pipeline was built during the Second World War by the United States and hidden in the jungle as a guarantee of oil supply should the canal be sabotaged. The park has an information centre at the Summit Garden.

Sleeping

Lago Alajuela *p1149*

LL-L Canopy Tower Ecolodge and Nature Observancy, signposted from just beyond Summit Gardens on the Transisthmus Highway, T264-5720, www.canopytower.com. A hotel and ecolodge that rises to the rainforest canopy in a converted old communications tower. 7 quirky little rooms, with private bath, price includes meals and guided walks. Some cheaper rooms available off season. Excellent for wildlife. Day trips and guided tours also welcome.

LL-L Gamboa Rainforest Resort, on the hill above Gamboa overlooking the Chagres River, T314-9000, www.gamboaresort.com. This looming green and white resort built on old American golf course has a reception area like a huge greenhouse, restaurant (a bit

The Parque Nacional Soberanía once held the world record for the most birds counted in a 24-hour period.

soulless) and swimming pool. There is an ancient tree dividing the complex. Cheapest rooms are in apartments formerly occupied by US dredging engineers. An **aerial tramway** runs silently through the canopy to a mirador with good views of the canal (at US$35 not cheap but an easy way to see monkeys, sloths and crocodiles). Orchid, butterfly, fish and crocodile exhibits are also part of this tour available to non-residents too. They also run tours to see crocodiles at night and birding trips to the Pipeline Rd.

C **Cabañas Flotantes** in the Chagres River. Interesting place to stay with thatched 'floating cabins' moored between Lago Alajuela and the Canal. For further information, **Panama Paradise**, T269-9860.

Activities and tours

Barro Colorado *p1149*

Visitors without permits will be turned away on arrival.

Smithsonian Institute, at the Tupper Building in Ancón, US$40, T212-8026, visitstri@tivoli.si.edu. Arrange daily trips which last 4-6 hrs, including boat, audiovisual display and lunch, but take water. Take a Gamboa Summit bus from next to Plaza 5 de Mayo (0600 and 0615) to the Dredging Division dock at Gamboa (US$0.65), from where the boat leaves. Make arrangements with the Institute in Ancón. Tours don't go Mon or Thu, maximum 12 people Tue and Wed, 15 on Fri, 25-30 Sat and Sun – book in advance, especially at weekends. ID required when booking.

Gatún Locks *p1149*

Agencia Giscomes, T/F264-0111. Offers trips through the canal every 2nd and 4th Sat or Sun of the month, leaves at 0730. Partial boat trips are also offered on the canal, through Miraflores Locks as far as Pedro Miguel locks.

Aerotours, T262-8710, fly Piper J3 Cub trips, 30 mins US$60 per person, full coast to coast, 2 hrs, US$200.

Transport

Gatún Locks *p1149*

Orange bus from Panama City to **Miraflores Locks** leaves from the bus station next to Plaza 5 de Mayo (direction Paraíso), 20 mins, US$0.35. Ask driver to let you off at the stop for 'Esclusas de Miraflores', from where it's a 10-min walk to the locks. Taxi to the locks, US$10 per hr. Another good way to see the **Panama Canal area** is to rent a car.

Lago Alajuela *p1149*

The trip to **Summit** may be made by train on Sun or buses marked Gamboa, every 1-1½ hrs, from bus station next to Plaza 5 de Mayo, US$0.45, 1½-hr ; the Paraíso bus will also take you to the **Miraflores** and **Pedro Miguel** locks.

Colón and Cristóbal

→ Colour map 8, B1.

Landfall on the Caribbean side for the passage of the Canal is made at the twin cities of Cristóbal and Colón, the one merging into the other almost imperceptibly and both built on Manzanillo Island at the entrance of the Canal in Bahía Limón. The island has now been connected with the mainland. Colón was founded in 1852 as the terminus of the railway across the isthmus; Cristóbal came into being as the port of entry for the supplies used in building the Canal.

Avenida del Frente is the main commercial street and is quite active but has lost its past splendour: the famous Bazar Francés closed in 1990, the curio shops are not noteworthy and the railway station stands virtually deserted except for the movement of a few freight trains. Nevertheless, there is talk of declaring the whole of Colón a free zone (the Zona Libre being the city's main attraction), the authorities are moving to give the city new housing and employment (residential estates like 'Rainbow City' and 'Puerto Escondido' are being extended on the landward side to relocate entire neighbourhoods of slums), and the demands on Cristóbal's busy port facilities (200 million tons of cargo a year) continue to increase. It is to be hoped that, if these plans are realized, Colón may become a pleasant place again. ▸▸ For Sleeping, Eating and other listings, see pages 1157-1159.

Ins and outs

At Cristóbal ships usually dock at Pier No 9, five minutes from the shops of Colón. Vehicles wait at the docks for those wanting to visit Colón and other places.

Security Mugging, even in daylight, is a real threat in both Colón and Cristóbal. The situation has improved now that the two main streets and some of the connecting ones are guarded by police officers; you are still strongly recommended not to stray too far from their range of sight. Keep a few dollars handy for muggers if the worst happens.

Tourist office IPAT tourist office ⓘ *Calle 13 between Central y Domingo Díaz (just before Ley supermarket, opposite Silenciadores Colón), T441-4460, Mon-Fri 0830-1630*, helpful. Also try **Cámara de Comercio** ⓘ *Plaza 5 de Mayo*, if your tourism involves business.

Colón

Colón was originally called Aspinwall, after one of the founders of the Transisthmian Railway. The French-influenced **cathedral** ⓘ *C 5 y Av Herrera,1400-1745 daily*, has an attractive altar and good stained-glass windows. **The Washington Hotel** ⓘ *on the seafront at the north end of the town*, is the town's most historic structure and is worth a look. The original wooden hotel was built in 1850 for employees of the Railroad Company. President Taft ordered a new fireproof hotel to be built in 1912 and the old one was later razed. Although remodelled a number of times, today's building, with its broad verandas, waving palms, splendid chandelier, plush carpets and casino, still conjures up a past age, while the café provides an excellent view of ships waiting to enter the Canal.

Next door is the **Casa de Lesseps**, home of the Suez Canal's chief engineer during the 1880s (not open to the public). Across from the **Washington** is the **Old Stone Episcopal Church**, built in 1865 for the railway workers; it was then the only Protestant church in Colombia (of which Panama was a province).

Running north through the centre of Colón is the palm-lined **Avenida Central**, with many statues (including one of *Columbus and the Indian Girl*, a gift from the Empress of France). The public market is at the corner of Calle 11. Avenida del Frente, facing the Bahía de Limón, has many old wooden buildings with wide verandas.

The main reason to come to Colón is to shop at the **Zona Libre** ⓘ *Mon-Fri 0800-1700 (a few places retail on Sat morning), if you have a car, pay a minder US$1 to watch it while in the zone*. It's the second-largest free zone in the world, an extensive compound of international stores and warehouses established in 1949 and surrounded by a huge wall – pick up a free map from hotels or tourist office showing who sells what. A passport or official ID must be shown to gain entry to the zone.

The 30-minute beach drive around Colón's perimeter is pleasant and cool in the evening; despite the slums at the south end there are some nice homes along the east shore of the peninsula. Permission from the Port Authority security officer is required to enter the port area, where agents for all the world's great shipping lines are located in colonial Caribbean-style buildings dating from 1914. Almost lost in a forest of containers is the **Panama Canal Yacht Club** ⓘ *T441-5882*, whose open-air restaurant and historically decorated bar offer very good food (seafood and Chinese). This is the place to ask about sailing boat charters to the San Blas Islands or shorter trips aboard visiting yachts.

Around Colón and Cristóbal

A well-paved road branches off the Transisthmus Highway at Sabanitas, 14 km east of Colón, and runs northeast along the coast for 33 km to the historic Spanish garrison port of **Portobelo** (see below). The rocky **Costa Arriba** is very attractive, with a number of lovely white-sand beaches (crowded at weekends). Playa María Chiquita (14 km) has a bathing pavilion, toilets, bar and restaurant managed by the government tourist bureau. A local speciality is *sao*, Jamaican-style pig's feet pickled with lime and chillies, sold from roadside stalls. Playa Langosta, also with swimming, bar and restaurant, is 3 km further on. There are plenty of small restaurants along this road serving fresh seafood. A group of people can rent a boat at Puerto Pilón, close to Sabanita (US$100-150 a day) for a ride to Portobelo, seas are often rough, take precautions. In **Buenavista**, just before entering Portobelo, a cannon marks the spot where Henry Morgan landed for his devastating 15-day sack of the town in 1668.

Colón

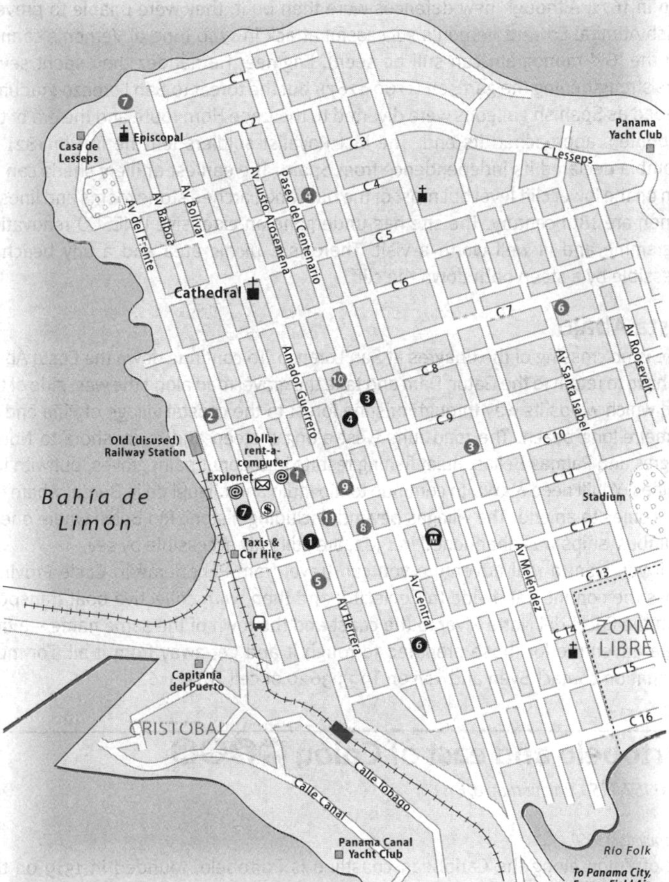

Sleeping
Andros 1
Astor 2
Carlton 3
García 4
Internacional 5
Meryland 6
Nuevo Washington 7
Pensión Acrópolis 8
Pensión Anita 9
Pensión Plaza 10
Sotelo 11

Eating
Antonio 1
Fenix 3
La Cabaña Avila 4
Recession 6
Veteranos 7

N
Not to scale

West of Colón » pp1157-1159.

From Colón the Caribbean Costa Abajo, stretching west of the Canal, can also be visited. The road leaves Colón through new housing developments (on the left is the modern city of Margarita) and runs 10 km southwest to the Gatún Locks (see above).

Fuerte San Lorenzo → *Colour map 8, B1.*

Perched on a cliff-top promontory overlooking the mouth of the Río Chagres with great views of the coast, Fort San Lorenzo is one of the oldest and best-preserved Spanish fortifications in the Americas. Construction had begun the year before Drake launched a 23-ship attack on the post (1596) and proceeded up the Chagres in an unsuccessful attempt to reach Panama City. The following century, Morgan fought a bloody 11-day battle to take the fort as a prelude to his decisive swoop on Panamá Viejo in 1671. Although new defences were then built, they were unable to prevent British Admiral Edward Vernon's successful attack in 1740 (one of Vernon's cannon with the 'GR' monogram can still be seen). Engineer Hernández then spent seven years strengthening the garrison (1760-1767), but the threat to San Lorenzo gradually receded as Spanish galleons were diverted to the Cape Horn route and the era of the freebooters approached its end. The last Royalist soldiers left the fort in 1821 as Colombia declared its Independence from Spain. The earliest artillery sheds can be seen on the lower cliff level but most of the bulwarks, arched stone rooms and lines of cannon are 18th century. The site has undergone an extensive UNESCO renovation programme and is well worth a visit. There is a picnic area and a tiny beach is accessible by a steep path down the cliff.

Costa Abajo

There is no crossing of the Chagres at San Lorenzo. To continue down the Costa Abajo you have to return to the Gatún Dam and take the gravel road along the west side of the river, which winds its way through pristine forest to the coastal village of Piña and its kilometre-long beach. The road runs west along a steep and rocky shore to Nuevo Chagres and Palmas Bellas, quiet fishing resorts in coconut palm groves, but with few facilities. You'll need a 4WD to continue to Río Indio and Miguel de la Borda, where the road comes to an end. The villages beyond, including historic Río Belén where one of Columbus' ships was abandoned in 1502, are still only accessible by sea.

If you want a real adventure you can travel from Penonemé in Coclé Province across the continental divide to Coclecito, and then, with collective boat transport, down the Coclé del Norte River to the coast and the town of the same name – a true jungle adventure for those prepared to rough it and get away from it all. For more information contact Sven and Vivi on T993-3620 or cell T674-1162.

Portobelo and east of Colón

» pp1157-1159. *Colour map 8, B1.*

→ *Population: 5850.*

East of Colón along the Caribbean coastline is Portobelo, founded in 1519 on the protected bay in which **Columbus** sought shelter in 1502. Researchers believe they have now located the wreck of the *Vizcaíina*, abandoned by Columbus, in shallow waters somewhere off the coast of Portobelo. Now little more than a large village, the 'Beautiful Port' was once the northern terminus of the **Camino Real**, where Peruvian treasure, carried on mule trains across the isthmus from Panama City, was stored in fortified warehouses. The gold moved on when the periodic arrival of the

The nearby beach of La Huerta can only be reached by boat.

Exploring the Camino Real and surrounding area

Although little of the Camino Real remains, its two branches from Madden Lake/Lago Alajuela across the mountains to Nombre de Dios (30 km) and Portobelo can still be hiked.

The trail starts at the old manganese mining zone (Mina 1, on the dirt road that runs from the Transístmica to a little way up the Río Boquerón). Buses run occasionally from the Transístmica to Salamanca, roughly where the Río Boquerón empties into Madden Lake. The trail follows the Río Boquerón up to the continental divide and the Río Nombre de Dios down the northern watershed to the coast near the present-day town.

This historic trek is easy for anyone with reasonable fitness, as one can drive to entry and exit points. Guides are not really necessary, the rivers are beautiful (and carry little water in the dry season) and the jungle is almost untouched; the trail is straight-forward and rises only to 330 m at the divide. Allow about three days for the Boquerón-Nombre de Dios trek. The trail to Portobelo branches off the Boquerón trail at the Río Diablo or Río Longue. After you leave the Boquerón you will need to navigate by compass. The Diablo takes the trekker higher into the divide (700 m) than the Longue (350 m, the route that the treasure-laden mules followed) and the terrain is more broken; both lead to the Río Cascajal (higher reaches are strewn with large boulders), which descends to the Caribbean.

The highest point in the region, Cerro Brujo (979 m), is passed en route. There are jaguars in this forested refuge, but they are unlikely to present any danger to hikers – indeed, you'd be lucky to see one. The Cascajal reaches the road about 1 km east of Portobelo. The Boquerón-Portobelo hike is more demanding than the other and takes four days maximum, a good machete is essential, and solitude guaranteed for at least two days.To the south and east of the Camino Real are the rivers of the Chagres system which flow into Lago Alajuela. Some of these are now being exploited for rafting. Check with tourist agencies in Panama City for Camino Real treks. Also see page 1156 for description of part of the Camino Real.

Spanish Armada created famed fairs where the wealth of the New World was exchanged for goods and supplies from Europe. The fair of 1637 saw so much material change hands that, according to the Englishman Thomas Gage, it took 30 days for the loading and unloading to be completed. In the **Royal Contaduría**, or Customs House, bars of gold and silver were piled up like firewood. Such riches could hardly fail to attract foreign pirates. Portobelo was one of **Francis Drake**'s favourite targets but it was also his downfall; he died here of dysentery in 1596 and was buried in a lead-lined coffin in the bay off Isla Drake. Divers are currently attempting to discover the exact spot, intending to return Drake's body to his home city of Plymouth. By the beginning of the 17th century several *castillos* (Santiago, San Gerónimo and San Fernando) had been built of coral stone quarried nearby to protect the harbour. Attacks continued, until in 1740 the treasure fleets were rerouted around the Horn and the Portobelo Fairs ended. The fortifications were rebuilt after Vernon's attack in 1744 but they were no longer seriously challenged, leaving the fortresses visible today. The largest, the aptly named 'Iron Castle', was largely dismantled during Canal construction. But there are many other interesting ruined fortresses, walls, rows of cannon and remains of the town's 120 houses and public buildings still to be seen standing along the foreshore amid the present-day village. In 1980 the remains of the colonial structure, known as the **Monumental Complex** ⓘ *US$1, closed Sun*, was declared a World Cultural Heritage monument by UNESCO. The Contaduría (1630) has been restored, with similar plans for the Plaza, Hospital Chapel and the Fernández House. There is a small museum with a collection of arms.

In **San Felipe Church** (1776) is the 17th-century cocobolo-wood statue of the Black Christ, about whose origin there are many legends. One tells of how fishermen found it floating in the sea during an epidemic of cholera in the town. It was brought ashore and immediately the epidemic began to wane. Another says that the life-size image was on its way to Cartagena when the ship put in to Portobelo for supplies. After being thwarted five times by rough weather to leave port, the crew decided the statue wished to remain in Panama. It was thrown overboard, floated ashore and was rescued by the locals.

The Tourist office (IPAT) ⓘ *just west of the square behind the Alcadía, T448-2073, Mon-Fri 0830-1630*, can provide guides, schedules of Congos and other performances, as well as comprehensive information about the many local points of interest, including the surrounding 34,846-ha **Portobelo National Park**, which has 70 km of coast line with beautiful beaches, superb scuba diving sites and boat rental to visit secluded beaches nearby. Services in town are limited with no bank or post office and just one minimart.

Isla Grande

» *pp1157-1159. Colour map 8, B1.*

A paved road continues northeast from Portobelo to Isla Grande, and another heads east to Nombre de Dios (25 km) and Palenque. Scuba diving is offered at several places along the way. The road passes through **Garrote** and **La Guaira**, from where *pangas* can be hired (US$1, although they might try and charge US$2 if you take the boat on your own) at the car park to cross to **Isla Grande**. The island is a favourite because of its relaxed lifestyle, fishing, scuba diving and snorkelling, windsurfing and dazzling white palm-fringed beaches. The best beaches are enclosed in front of the two expensive hotels, but you should be able to use them. A good, more public beach, is on a spit before **Hotel Isla Grande**. The island's 300 black inhabitants make a living from fishing and coconut cultivation, and a powerful French-built lighthouse crowns the small island's northern point, where there is a mirador, reached by steep path. There are a number of colourful African-tinged festivals held here throughout the year, particularly on 24 June, 16 July and the pre-Lenten Carnival with *Congos*. The part of the village to the right of the landing stage is more lively with competing salsa sounds.

Nombre de Dios

» *pp1157-1159. Colour map 8, B1.*

The beautiful, deserted mainland beaches continue as the 'road' heads east to Nombre de Dios. The historic town (1520) near the present village was once the thriving trading port which first hosted the famed fairs, located at the end of the stone-paved Camino Real from the capital. By the 1550s more than half the trade between Spain and its colonies was passing through its lightly defended harbour, but in 1594 the decision was made to move operations to the more sheltered site of Portobelo. The Camino Real was diverted and Nombre de Dios was already dying when Drake captured and burnt it two years later, so that William Dampier could describe the site some years later as "only a name...everything is covered by the jungle with no sign that it was ever populated." Excavations have taken place revealing the Spanish town, parts of the Camino Real, a broken cannon and other objects, most of which are now in the National Museum.

The modern village is built on either side of a freshwater channel, a footbridge links the two. The church is built on a plaza on the west side, the main square is on the east. It has few facilities, one hotel and a restaurant on the square, but there's a beautiful beach for the few who get this far. A *cayuco* (US$3 per person, 12 minutes) can be taken to Playa Damas, an unusual beach where alternating patches of red and white sand resemble a chess board. The beach is owned by an amateur ecologist who has built some rustic huts and a campsite (**Costa El Oro,** T263-5955) on a small island here, he also offers expert guidance on local fishing and diving spots. Buses come into the centre en route to Portobelo or Cuango; while most go as far as the main square before coming back the same way, some turn round before this at the little plaza beside the police station.

The track staggers on for another 25 km linking the peaceful fishing villages of the Costa Arriba. Locals eagerly await the paved road's eventual extension through the succession of seaside villages to the Golfo de San Blas opposite El Porvenir, the capital of the Kunas' self-governed area of **Kuna Yala** (Kuna Earth).

Not far beyond Nombe de Dios, near Viento Frío, is **Diver's Haven,** T448-2248, recommended for diving tours. The next village is **Palenque,** unspoilt, with a good beach, very rudimentary huts being built for visitors. **Miramar** is the cleanest of all the *pueblitos* along this coastline. The occasional smuggling boat puts in here and a few Panama City tourists come to stay in the three houses on the tiny **Isla Bellavista** (ask Niano at **Bohio Miramar** bar/restaurant to rent – US$70 for house with three double beds, no beach but you can swim off the jetty). Boats can take you on to **Santa Isabel** (beyond the reach of the dirt road), US$35 for the boat, or to **San Blas** US$25 each, minimum eight people. The village at the end of the road is **Cuango,** a bit run-down and dusty between rains, with a littered beach.

Sleeping

Colón and Cristóbal *p1150, map p1153*

AL Meryland, Calle 7 y Santa Isabel, T441-7128. New with restaurant.

AL Nuevo Washington, Av del Frente Final, T441-7133, nwh@sinfo.net. Art deco style, guarded enclave, clean, restaurant, good view of ships entering the canal, also the small Pharaoh casino and the 24-hrs **Los Piratas** bar.

B Carlton, Calle 10 y Av Meléndez, T447-0112. A good choice and one of the better hotels.

C Andros, Av Herrera, between Calle 9 y 10, T441-0477. Modern, clean, fan or a/c, bath, TV, good restaurant, *cafetería*.

C Internacional, Av Bolívar, y Calle 11, T441-8879. Well furnished, bar, restaurant.

C Sotelo, Guerrero y Calle 11, T441-7702. Small but clean rooms.

D-E García, Calle 4, 75 m east of Av Central, T441-0860. Basic, but airier than some others in this category, pay a little more and get a/c.

D-E Pensión Plaza, Av Central y Calle 7, T441-3216. Clean and cheap, more expensive rooms have a/c and TV.

E Astor, Frente, between Calle 7 y Calle 8, T441-0233. Big airy rooms – best at front, with plant-filled balcony. Recommended.

E Pensión Acrópolis, Av Amador Guerrero y Calle 11, opposite Sotelo, T441-1456. Shared bath.

E Pensión Anita, Amador Guerrero y Calle 10, TT441-2080. Dark rooms, basic.

Fuerte San Lorenzo *p1154*

D Las Bahías, on the edge of the roadless Golfo de los Mosquitos, 4 km west of Coclé del Norte and 60 km from Colón. A small rustic lodge. 4 *cabañas* on the beach with 1 double and 2 single beds in each. Las Bahías is only accessible by boat, either by collective *cayuco* from Gobea or Río Indio (US$8) or from Muelle de Calle 5 in Colón.

Portobelo and east of Colón *p1154*

B Cabañas el Mar, in Buenaventura, 5 km west on road to Colón, T448-2102. With a/c, cheaper with fan, quiet location by the sea.

B Scuba Portobelo, also in Buenaventura, T448-2147 or T261-3841. Scuba gear available for hire.

D Aquatic Park, on road towards Colón. Dormitory accommodation, expensive.

E Hospedaje La Aduana, in town on main square. Somewhat noisy bar.

Isla Grande *p1156*

On holidays and dry season weekends, make reservations in advance; prices often double during high season. All hotels have bars and simple restaurants.

LL Bananas Village Resort, north side of the island, usually accessed by boat but also by path over the steep hill, T263-9510, www.bananasresort.com. Relatively discreet luxury hotel, on the best beach on the island, with a good but expensive bar.

B Damaris, 300 m to right of the dock, T687-8202. **Turquesa** bar/restaurant, popular with Panamanians.

B Isla Grande, T225-6722. US$45 for 4 beds, with a/c. Bungalows scattered along an excellent sandy beach. Popular with Panamanians, restaurant, pool table, ping pong, a little bit run-down but good value.

B Villa Ensueño, right at the landing stage, T/F448-2964. Large lawns (big enough to play football) with gardens and a hammock on each balcony.

D Cabañas Jackson, immediately behind main landing stage, T441-5656. Many huts/bungalows available.

D Cabañas Monte Carlos, La Guaira, T441-2054.

Nombre de Dios *p1156*

C Diver's Haven, not far beyond Nombe de Dios, near Viento Frío, T448-2248. Recommended for diving tours.

E Casa de Huéspedes, on main square. With restaurant. A beautiful beach can be enjoyed by those few who get this far. A *cayuco* (US$3 per person, 12 mins) can be taken to Playa Damas, an unusual beach where alternating patches of red and white sand resemble a chess board. The beach is owned by an amateur ecologist who has built some rustic huts and a campsite (**Costa El Oro**, T263-5955) on a small island here, also offers expert guidance on fishing and diving spots.

E Bohio, to left of road, on beach 50 m before the quay. 2 small but light rooms with TV and fan; the restaurant at the back of the jetty rents out 2 dark rooms. Boats can take you on to Santa Isabel (beyond the reach of the dirt road), US$35 for the boat, or to San Blas US$25 per person, minimum 8 people.

F Nameless hospedaje, Cuango. Ask for María Meneses at 1st house on the left on east side of square. There is also one restaurant and store here.

Eating

Colón and Cristóbal *p1150, map p1153*

See Sleeping for **Panama Canal Yacht Club**. Hotels **Carlton** and **Washington** also have good restaurants (¥¥). There are several fast food outlets.

¥¥ Hotel Andros, Av Herrera y Calle 9, T441-0477. Modern, self-service, open until 2000, except Sun – check out the mirrors, news is you just have to be there.

¥¥ Veteranos, Calle 9 y Av del Frente, T441-v3563. Popular with visiting business men, port officials and lately with younger clientele.

¥ Antonio, Av Herrera y Calle 11. Unremarkable but decent.

¥ Fenix, Central y Calle 8. Basic local fare.

¥ La Cabaña Avila, Av Central y Calle 8, Caribbean food.

¥ Nacional, esquina Guerrero y Calle 11. Popular with locals, good for breakfast.

¥ Recession, Calle 13 y Central. Good soups, Chinese and other dishes, cheap.

Portobelo and east of Colón *p1154*

A number of small *fondas* serving coconut rice with fresh shrimps, spicy Caribbean food with octopus or fish, or *fufú* (fish soup cooked with coconut milk and vegetables).

¥¥ Los Cañones, in Buenaventura, 5 km west on the road to Colón, good food in a lovely setting by the water, not cheap.

¥ El Hostal del Rey, corner of Parque Central, Portobelo. Good meals and value.

¥ La Torre, T448-2039, in La Escucha, 3 km before the town. Good food.

Isla Grande *p1156*

¥¥ Kiosco Milly Mar, just west of landing pier. Excellent fish dishes, moderate prices.

¥ Candy Rose. Serves drinks with a special octopus cooked in coconut milk.

Festivals and events

Portobelo and east of Colón *p1154*

21 Oct The miraculous reputation of the Black Christ is celebrated annually, when purple- clad pilgrims come from all over the country and the statue is paraded through the town at 1800 on a flower- and candle-covered litter carried by 80 men (who take 3 steps forward and 2 steps back to musical accompaniment); feasting and dancing till dawn.

Jan-Mar/Apr Other fiestas in the Portobelo region – for example **Carnival, Patron Saint's Day** (20 Mar) – are opportunities to experience the *congos*. Unlike the dance of the same name found elsewhere on the Caribbean coast, the *congo* here is the name given both to the main, male participants and a slowly unfolding ritual which lasts from the **Día de los Reyes** (6 Jan) to **Easter**. Among the various explanations of its symbolism are elements of the people's original African religions, their capture into slavery, their conversion to Catholicism and mockery of the colonial Spaniards. Members of the audience are often 'imprisoned' in a makeshift palisade and have to pay a 'ransom' to be freed.

Transport

Colón and Cristóbal *p1150, map p1153*

Air

Former US France Field AFB has replaced Colón's old airstrip as the busy local airport, on the mainland east of the city, taxi under US$1 but bargain. **Aeroperlas** has daily flights Mon-Thu to **Panama City**; T430-1038, US$26 one way. Flights are hectic with Free Zone executives; no reservations so allow plenty of time or plan to stay the night in Colón.

Bus

Bus station on Av del Frente and Calle 12. Express (a/c) US$2.25, and regular buses, US$1.75, daily to **Panama City** every 20 mins, less frequent at weekends, about 2 hrs. Hourly to **Portobelo** daily, US$2, 1 hr.

Boat

Shipping a vehicle: to **South America**, see page1118. For **San Blas** try asking at Coco Solo pier, T430-7327.

Taxi

Tariffs vary but not expensive, US$0.75 in Colón, US$1.25 to outskirts, US$5-7/hr. Car rental and taxis on Av del Frente facing Calle 11; most drivers speak some English and can advise on 'no-go' areas.

Train

US$20, one way, US$35 return, to **Panama City**, leaves 1730, station on west side of town just off the centre.

Portobelo and east of Colón *p1154*

Bus Buses from **Colón**, every hr from 0700 from the bus station on Av del Frente y Calle 13, 1 hr, US$1; **María, Chiquita**, 40 mins, US$0.80. Portobelo can be visited from Panama City in a day without going into Colón by taking an early bus to the Sabanitas turn-off (US$1) and waiting for a Colón-Portobelo service (US$1).

To villages further east, take buses marked 'Costa Arriba' from stop at back of square: **Nombre de Dios**, 45 mins US$1; **Palenque**, 70 mins, US$1.50; **Miramar**, 80 mins US$3, **Cuango**, 1½ hrs, US$3.50. Road paved until just beyond Nombre de Dios.

Boat Launch to **Santa Isabel** (beyond the reach of Costa Arriba road), 2 hrs, to **San Blas** 3 hrs .

Isla Grande *p1156*

On Sun the last bus from La Guaira back to **Portobelo** leaves at 1500 and is always packed. Hitching with Panamanian weekenders is possible, all the way to **Panama City** if you're lucky!

Directory

Colón and Cristóbal *p1150, map p1153*

Banks Banco Nacional de Panamá. Caja de Ahorros. **Chase Manhattan Bank. Citibank. Lloyds Bank** agency in Colón Free Zone, at Av Santa Isabel y Calle 14, T445-2177. Mon-Fri 0800-1300. **Internet** Explonet, Frente, between Calle 9 y Calle 10, Mon-Sat 0800-2300, Sun 1300-2000, US$2.50/hr. **Dollar Rent-a-Computer**, Calle 11 Y Av Guerrero, above Café Nacional, T441-7632, US$2.50/hr, net phones US$0.61/min to England. **Post office** in Cristóbal Administration Building, on corner of Av Bolívar and Calle 9. **Telephone** Cable & Wireless in Cristóbal.

Isla Grande *p1156*

Telephone There are 2 pay phones on the island, 150 m to the left of the landing jetty, on a small plaza, and to the right beside the basketball court.

San Blas Islands

→ *Colour map 8, B2. Population: 40,092.*

The Archipiélago de San Blas (or Las Mulatas) is a broad string of 365 islands ranging in size from deserted islets with just a few coconut palms to inhabited islands, about 50 in total and home to hundreds of Kuna people. Lying off the Caribbean coast east of Colón, the archipelago stretches along the coast for over 200 km from the Gulf of San Blas to the Colombian border. The islands' distance from the mainland ranges from 100 m to several kilometres. ▸▸ *For Sleeping, Eating and all other listings, see pages 1162-1163.*

Ins and outs

There are about 20 airstrips in the San Blas Islands and province, but most are 'larger' than the islands or places on which they are built. They include: El Porvenir, Cartí, Río Sidra, Río Azúcar, Narganá, Corazón, Río Tigre, Playón Chico, Tupile, Tikankiki, Ailigandi, Achutupu (also known as Uaguitupu), Mamitupu, Ogobsucum, Ustupu, Mansucum, Mulatupu, Tubuala, Calidonia and Puerto Obaldía. You can be dropped off at any island or village and picked up later, subject to negotiations with the pilot, but though this may sound appealing, it is probably not wise since there is no drinking water or food. One of the best islands to visit from the Porvenir area is **Dog Island** with a superb beach and great snorkelling on a wreck just 20 m off shore. Hotel prices usually include a trip here. There is a 'local' tax of US$1 per island.

Any travel agent in Panama can book a San Blas tour.

An alternative route to San Blas is to walk over the continental divide from Cañita to Sarti. Take a bus from Panama City towards Darién and get off at Cañita, then walk two to three hours to the **EcoLodge** at Burbayar (there is also a lodge at Nusagrande). The following day camp on the coastal side of the Serranía de San Blas and on the third day make sure that you reach **Cartí** before 1600 when the last boat leaves for the islands – US$20-30 to El Porvenir, or US$10 (20 minutes) to Isla Naranjos. At Cartí there is a museum of Kuna culture.

The most common point of entry into the San Blas, **El Porvenir** is taken up with an airstrip, customs and immigration offices. On a sailing journey this is the place to obtain your final exit stamp from Panama, or to check in if coming from Colombia. El Porvenir has a rustic hotel and is not unattractive, with a nice palm fringed beach at the northern end. Reef systems around the island invite snorkelling but intensive fishing means large marine life is scarce.

Background

The Kuna (Cuna or Tule) are the most sophisticated and politically organized of the country's seven indigenous groups (Kuna, Embera, Waounan, Ngobe, Bugle, Nassau and Terribe). They run the San Blas Territory virtually on their own terms after a rebellion in 1925, with internal autonomy and, uniquely among Panama's indigenous groups, they send their representative to the National Assembly. Each community is presided over by a *sáhila* (chief). Land is communally owned but coconut trees may belong to individuals. The Kuna have their own language although Spanish is widely spoken. The women wear gold nose- and earrings, costumes with unique designs and *molas*, see box, page 1165, based on local themes, geometric patterns, stylized fauna and flora and pictorial representations of current events or political propaganda. They are outside the Panamanian tax zone and have negotiated a treaty perpetuating their long-standing trade with small craft from Colombia.

Photographers need plenty of cash, as the set price for a Kuna to pose is US$1 per photo.

Sailing to Colombia via the San Blas Islands

With the price of a plane ticket to Cartagena costing around US$170, an alternative, more adventurous route to Colombia could be spending several days travelling by boat. It's adventurous, a true travel experience and a chance to see part of the world normally reserved for those with very big budgets.

Two types of boat can take you to Colombia. The first are local trading vessels, which occasionally head to Colombia stopping at many of the more inhabited Kuna islands and settlements along the coast. These usually cost around US$200 per person, if heading all the way to Cartagena, Barranquilla or Santa Marta. You may be able to track one down at the port in Colón (see crossing the Darién by sea section, page 1202, for further details of ports along the route).

A second option is recreational yachts, often foreign-owned and destined for Cartagena. Some boats are on round the world trips, but a small number make it their business to ferry adventurous travellers to and from Colombia. Price is between US$250-200, including basic food. These boats usually leave from Portobelo or Isla Grande. Ask in Hostel Voyager in Panama City, contact Sr Burgos at Hotel San Blas or Casa Viena, www.casaviena.com, in Cartagena if coming from Colombia.

Sailing vessels usually head along the coast using the most northerly islands of the San Blas, such as Cayos Holandés as overnight stops before the two- to three-day sail across the open sea to Colombia. Prevailing winds and currents make it a rougher ride from Panama to Colombia.

Choosing a boat and captain is important. Sailing is not a risk-free business as demonstrated by the multitude of wrecks in the San Blas area. Talk to your captain about previous experience and look at the boat. If in doubt, listen to your instincts. And as ever, when leaving a country, paperwork is important. Make sure you've completed exit formalities as directed by your captain.

Wichub-Huala and Nalunega

Just south of Porvenir, Wichub-Huala and Nalunega are heavily inhabited labyrinths of huts and alleys and are culturally fascinating. Both have communal halls where the political decisions of the villages are made, and both have simple accommodation and general stores. The shop on the south side of Wichub-Huala (the island closer to Porvenir) seems to be better stocked; it's a good place for last minute supplies.

Cayos Chichime

Not more than a couple of hours sail to the east lie the idyllic islands of the Cayos Chichime, also known as Wichudup or Wichitupo in the Kuna language. The deep-water channel entering the harbour is only 30 m wide with reefs on both sides, and requires care even from experienced captains. Both islands are beautiful and inhabited by only a handful of Kuna who survive through a combination of fishing, harvesting coconuts and selling *molas* to passing boats. The Kuna are friendly, easy-going people and interesting to talk to. Many of the Kuna who live on the islands only do so for four to five months per year before returning to the more inhabited islands or moving on to another island. One of the islands' more permanent residents seems to be Umburto who, if he has space, will let you stay in a hut for US$5 per night – he might even throw in some food. And for a small fee the family will also cook locally caught seafood (through don't accept lobster or crab due to over-fishing, and certainly not the meat or eggs of sea turtles which are sometimes caught). Umburto has a boat with a motor and will take you to Porvenir for a negotiated price.

The Kuna will try and sell you *molas*, one of their few methods of obtaining cash income – if you're not interested, it will be sufficient to decline politely.

Cayos Holandés

To the east of Chichime lies a long chain of sparsely inhabited islands known as Cayos Holandés or Dutch Keys. Some of the islands have no permanent residents, but most have at least one family of Kuna harvesting coconuts. These *cayos* are the furthest from the mainland in Kuna Yala and have a rugged, remote feel. Washed by strong Caribbean swells the Cayos Holandés harbor abundant marine life along the barrier reef and in the deepwater channels at either end of the group – in these areas Caribbean reef sharks, tarpon and rays are often seen. Even on the sheltered southern side there exist some pristine patch reefs only metres from islands themselves. Toward the eastern end of the chain is an excellent protected anchorage know to local yacht types as 'the swimming pool', due to its clear, calm water and location surrounded on all sides by islands. As with Chichime, caution and good navigational charts are required when entering this area.

Sleeping

San Blas Islands *p1160*

Camping is generally discouraged on the islands but if you want to, make sure that you speak to the *sáhila* first.

It may be possible to book direct with a hotel; bear in mind that when coming to these islands, you will always need to book somewhere for the first night.

LL Dolphin Lodge, Narganá, about halfway along the coast between El Porvenir and the Colombian border, T225-8435. Owned by a Kuna family on Uaguitupu, US$139 including air fare, meals and overnight stay.

LL Iskardup Ecoresort, on Isla Tigre, a short canoe trip east from Narganá, T269-6047. With cabins, bar, restaurant, solar power, package tours include trips to the mainland.

L Kwadule, near Corazón de Jesús and Narganá. Very nice restaurant/bar over the reef, some cabins over the water, with bath.

A Kuanidup, Achutupo Island, T227-6026. 7 huts, good food, lovely beaches, no electricity, bathrooms in centre of island.

B Hotel El Porvenir, El Porvenir, T221-1397, simple option close to airstrip, good for boat trips.

D Narganá Lodge Hotel, Narganá, the best option, with a basic hotel (**F**) and restaurant, **El Caprichito**, serving good crab dishes.

D Sugtupu Hotel, Cartí-Sugtupu, south of El Porvenir, reached by boat from El Porvenir or the coastal town of Soledad. Simple option.

Wichub-Huala and Nalunega, *p1161*

A Hotel Anai, Wichub-Huala, T239-3025. Price includes food. Ask for Israel Fernández on arrival at El Porvenir.

B Hotel San Blas, Nalunega Island, 10 mins by boat from the El Porvenir airstrip. T262-5410. Traditional cane and thatch, shared showers, price includes breakfast, lunch, lobster dinner and 2 excursions, owner Sr Burgos meets incoming flights every morning and boats to Cartagena pick up passengers from here.

C Cabañas Ukuptupu, Wichub-Huala, T220-4781 or T299-9011. Run by the family Juan García, canoes for hire. Recommended.

Festivals and events

San Blas Islands *p1160*

All the following fiestas involve dances, games, meals and speeches and are traditional, except those on Narganá, which have a stronger Western element (but also typical dancing and food).

Feb Anniversary of the Tule Revolution, at Playón Chico, Tupile, Ailigandi and Ustupu.

19 Mar Fiesta patronal on Narganá.

8 Jul Anniversary of Inakiña on Mulatupo.

29-31 Jul Fiesta patronal on Fulipe.

20 Aug Charles Robinson anniversary on Narganá.
3 Sep Anniversary of Nele-Kantule on Ustupo.
11 Sep Anniversary of Yabilikiña on Tuwala.

Shopping

San Blas Islands *p1160*
Molas (see box, page 1165) cost upwards of US$10 each. You can also try the San Blas perfume *Kantule*. Both *molas* and *Kantule* are also obtainable in many Panama City and Colón shops).

Transport

San Blas Islands *p1160*
Air
Several companies fly from **Panama City** (Albrook) including Aeroperlas (T315-7500), Ansa (T315-0300), Transpasa (T236-0842) and Aerotaxi (T264-8644) .

The most popular destination is **El Porvenir**, on the north side of the Golfo de San Blas, where tourists are picked up by boat to go to a neighbouring island, about 20 mins. One-way fares to the islands are US$32 to **El Porvenir** and US$52 to **Puerto Obaldía**. All other air fares are scaled in between (price includes a 5% sales tax). You must take your passport because every once in a blue moon a hijack attempt to Colombia is made. All flights leave between 0600 and 0630, Mon-Sat, returning 0800-0830. Evening and Sun flights must be booked privately. Baggage over 15 kg is charged at US$0.50 per kg, so wear your heavy stuff.

Sea
There are occasional boats to the San Blas Islands from **Colón**, but there is no scheduled service and the trip can be rough. One ship that goes from time to time is the *Almirante*; try to find the captain, Figueres Cooper, who charges US$30 for the trip. The port captain's office at Coco Solo may have information on boat departures, T441-5231 or 445-1055, although most boats are not keen to take gringos. Alternatively, go to Portobelo and try for a boat from there, 9 hrs to **El Porvenir**, every other day, US$17.

The Interior

→ *Colour map 8, B1.*

Cross the Puente de las Américas from Panama City and you enter the most densely populated rural quarter of the country, a Panama that is in great contrast to the cosmopolitan capital and the Canal: colonial towns, varied agriculture, traditional crafts and music, Pacific beaches and beautiful mountain landscapes with good walking options. The Pan-American Highway crosses the region known as 'El Interior' (though the term can refer to any area outside the capital), en route to Costa Rica.

» For Sleeping, Eating and other listings, see page 1166.

Panama City to Costa Rica

The Pan-American Highway, also known as the *Interamericana*, heads westwards along a well graded and completely paved road from Panama City through Concepción to the Costa Rican border for 489 km. Leaving Panama City, the Pan-American Highway crosses the **Puente de las Américas** over the Canal at the Pacific entrance (if on a bus, sit on the right-hand side – north – for the best views). The bridge was built between 1958 and 1962 by the USA to replace the ferry crossing. It is 1653 m long and, with a road surface to seaway distance of 117 m, there is ample room for all ships to pass below. The bridge, which has three lanes, is the only vehicular crossing on the Pacific side of the canal. There is also a pedestrian walkway for the length of the bridge, but muggings have occurred on the bridge even in broad daylight so take care. Buses run to a *mirador* on the far side of the bridge from the city.

La Chorrera → *Colour map 8, B1. Population: 37,000.*

The first place you reach, 13 km from Panama City, is the small town of **Arraiján**. Another 21 km by four-lane highway (toll US$0.50) takes you to La Chorrera with an interesting store, **Artes de las Américas,** filled with wooden carvings. A branch road (right) leads 1.5 km to **El Chorro,** the waterfall from which the town takes its name. At Km 20, among hills, is the old town of **Capira** (good food is on offer next to the Shell station, run by Chinese). Just west of Capira is a sign indicating the turn-off to **Lídice,** 4 km north of the highway. At the foot of Cerro Trinidad, which local tradition calls 'the end of the Andes'. The town was the home of Czech immigrants who in 1945 succeeded in having the name changed from Potero to commemorate Lídice in their homeland, which suffered heavily in the Second World War.

The highway passes through the orange groves of Campana, where a 4-km road climbs to **Parque Nacional Altos de Campana**. Created in 1966, the 4816-ha park – the first in Panama – protects humid tropical forest growing on mountainous volcanic rock that forms picturesque cliffs ideal for walking and hiking.

San Carlos and beaches → *Colour map 8, B1.*

At Bejuco, 5 km east of Chame, the road stretches down a 28-km peninsula to **Punta Chame,** with a white-sand beach, a few houses, and just one hotel/restaurant. At low tide the sand is alive with legions of small pink crabs. There is a splendid view northeast to Taboga Island and the entrance to the Canal in the distance. Food is prepared by the beach, there are several bars and a pick-up running between the highway and the beach costing US$1 is your link to the outside world.

Beyond Chame are two beaches: **Nueva Gorgona**, 3 to 4 km long, waves increasing in size from west to east, and a well-stocked grocery store. A little further along the Pan-American is **Playa Coronado,** the most popular beach in Panama, but rarely crowded. Homeowners from Playa Coronado have installed a checkpoint at the turning, unaffiliated with the police station opposite. Be polite, but do not be deterred from using the public beach.

Opposite the turning to Playa Coronado is a road inland to Las Lajas and beyond to the hills and **Lagunas del Valle,** about one hour from the highway. Ten kilometres beyond Playa Coronado is the town of **San Carlos,** wjere there's good river and sea bathing (beware of jelly fish and do not bathe in the estuarine lake). There are not many restaurants in San Carlos, but there are plenty of food shops.

El Valle

Five kilometres on, a road to the right leads, after a few kilometres, to a climb through fine scenery to the summit of **Los Llanitos** (792 m) (direct bus from Panama City US$3.50, or US$1 from San Carlos), and then down 200 m to a mountain-rimmed plateau (7 by 5.5 km) on which is the comparatively cool, summer resort of El Valle. Four kilometres before El Valle is a parking spot with fine views of the village and a waterfall nearby. Soapstone carvings of animals, straw birds, painted gourds (*totumas*), carved wood tableware, pottery and *molas* are sold in the famous Sunday market, which is very popular with Panamanians and tourists. There is also a colourful flower market. The orchid nursery has a small zoo and Panama's best-known **petroglyphs** can be seen near the town. This is one of many good walks in the vicinity (ask directions); another is to the cross in the hills to the west of town.

Beyond El Valle is the **Canopy Adventure** ⓘ *T983-6547 (in El Valle, Spanish only), T264-5720 (in Panama City), daily, 0600-1700, US$40*, with a series of cables and wires whizzing you through the forest; the last stage swoops across the face of a waterfall. It's good for all ages and the whole experience takes about 1½ hours and includes a short hike through the forest. To get there from El Valle take a bus to El Chorro Macho or taxi to La Mesa.

La mola

You might not know what it is until you see one, but the mola – literal translation a 'blouse' – is the most colourful artistic expression of Kuna Yala – the San Blas archipelago. A mola is a reverse appliqué, or 'cut-out', decorative textile made by Kuna women. First created in the mid-19th century it is still worn daily on the front and back of a blouse.

Usually measuring 40 by 33 cm, molas are made out of up to seven (but on average three to four) superimposed, differently coloured materials. Each layer is cut to make up a design element constituted by the unveiled layer beneath it. The ragged hem is folded over and sewn down with concealed stitching. This careful craftwork and step-by-step process slowly reveals a design of a bird, aquatic creature, monster, a generic scene such as fishing or even perhaps a protecting spirit or a wild dance of colours, but always something personal to the creator's imagination.

The traditional mola, the 'serkan' design, with its small range of totemic objects, has been added to by the Kuna encounter with modern Panama and you are as likely to see a mola depicting an aeroplane, map, flag, political leanings, or an American invasion, which can be just as interesting. Another development is machine-made molas with simplistic motifs and gaudy colours.

As gifts and souvenirs, molas make great miniature wall-hangings and have the advantage of being light and small, so they don't take up too much precious space in the backpack. It's worth seeking out a good quality one. Don't worry about exact symmetry, but do look for fine and even outlines, the narrower, the better. The larger pattern should come out of the top layer, often black or maroon, and the detail mainly from lower layers. Some molas have appliqué – sewed on, as opposed to cut away, motifs – and they can create additional depth and enliven the surface, but try to avoid those with fill-in – dots and triangles and small circles roughly applied to fill up space. Stitching should be even and usually hidden, never substituted with tape, and where there is decorative surface stitching it shouldn't compete with the more graphic cut-away. Check the quality of the material in the lower layers and run your hand across the surface of the mola to make sure the layers are not scrunching up.

Santa Clara and Antón

Santa Clara, with its famous beach, 115 km from Panama City, is the usual target for motorists. The beach is about 20 minutes from the Pan-American Highway, with fishing, launches for hire and riding. About 13 km beyond is Antón, which has a special local *manjar blanco* (a gooey fudge) and a crucifix reputed to be miraculous.

Penonomé → *Colour map 8, B1. Population: 10,715.*

A further 20 km is the capital of Coclé province, Penonomé, an old town even when the Spaniards arrived. An advanced culture which once thrived here was overwhelmed by volcanic eruption. Objects revealed by archaeologists are now in Panama City, in the American Museum of Natural History in New York, and in the local **Museo Conte de Penonomé** ⓘ *Tue-Sat 0900-1230, 1330-1600, Sun 0830-1300*. The local university and the **Mercado de Artesanato** on the highway are worth a visit. There is a delightful central plaza with the air of a tiny provincial capital of times past. The town is often a lunch stop for motorists making the trip from Panama City to the western border.

Balneario Las Mendozas and Churuquita Grande

Just under 1 km northwest of Penonomé is Balneario Las Mendozas, on a street of the same name, an excellent river pool for bathing in deep water. Further down the Río Zaratí, also known as the Santa María, is **La Angostura** where the river dives down a canyon. The dirt access road is usually suitable for ordinary cars. There are copper- and gold-mining activities in this area and further north, beyond La Pintada, where a new 35-km road has been built to Coclecito on the Caribbean side of the Continental Divide. The operating mining company is also involved in conservation work including reforestation near La Angostura. Northeast of Penonomé is Churuquita Grande (camping is possible near the river with a waterfall and swimming hole). There's a **Feria de la Naranja** (orange festival) held on the last weekend of January: the inauguration and dancing is on Saturday; the big day, Sunday, includes a colourful parade and huge displays of fruit. From Penonomé you can visit **La Pintada** (buses every 30 minutes), a mountain village that makes a quiet stopping-off point for hiking and horse riding.

El Caño, El Copé and Natá

El Caño is 24 km west of Penonomé, and 3.5 km from the main road is the **Parque Arqueológico del Caño** ⓘ *Tue-Fri 0900-1600, Sat-Sun 1030-1300, US$1*, which has a small museum, some excavations (several human skeletons have been found in the burial site) and standing stones.

From El Caño (the ruins) you can take a *chiva* up into the mountains, changing to another at Río Grande, to the village of **El Copé** (direct buses from Panama City), which gives access to the **Parque Nacional Omar Torrijos** a protected forest of rubber trees with some good trails.

A further 7 km along the Pan-American Highway is **Natá,** one of the oldest towns in Panama and the Americas (1520). The early colonists fought constant attacks led by Urracá. The Iglesia de Santiago Apóstol (1522) is impressive, with interesting wood carvings. It is sady run-down now; donations gratefully received for restoration work.

Aguadulce → *Colour map 8, B1. Population: 14,800.*

Some 10 km beyond is Aguadulce, a prosperous supply centre (bus from Panama, US$6), with local pottery for sale and *salinas* (saltworks) nearby.

Another 17 km further on, just after the large Santa Rosa sugar plantation, a road leads off right to the mountain spa of **Calobre** (31 km). The hot springs are, however, a good hour's drive away, on a very rough road, through great mountain scenery.

Sleeping

La Chorrera *p1164*

D Hospedaje Lamas, on side street just right of Tropical. A/c or fan, clean, big rooms, TV. Recommended.

D Tropical, pink and green building on Pan-American. With fan and private bath. Recommended.

San Carlos and beaches *p1164*

A Río Mar, beyond San Carlos on the Río Mar beach, T223-0192. Has a good seafood restaurant.

B Cabañas de Playa Gorgona, San Carlos, T269-2433. Cheaper, with kitchenettes, BBQ, pool, shade, hammocks, on the ocean.

B Gorgona Hayes, San Carlos, T223-7775. With pleasant pool, fountain, tennis court, restaurant, good.

B Hostal Chiquito, Lagunas del Valle information T236-4632 (Panama City). A 160-ha farm with 8 guest rooms, 2 double rooms in separate units, meals included, riding, hiking, lake swimming, electricity evenings only, transport provided from Panama City.

Camping

Camping is possible on Palmar Beach.

El Valle *p1164*

The town has no real centre; everyone cycles. Accommodation is hard to find at weekends.

B Cabañas Las Mozas, T983-6071. Restaurant serves Arabic food.
B Hotel Campestre, at the foot of Cara Coral Hill, T983-6146, www.hotel campestre.com. 40 tidy rooms and restaurant serving Swiss-style lunch dishes from US$6.
D El Greco Motel, Calle Central, T983-6149. With a restaurant.
E-F Pensión Niña Dalia. No towels or soap, will look after bags. Private houses nearby rent cheaper rooms.

Santa Clara and Antón *p1165*
L-AL Cabañas Las Sirenas, Santa Clara, T993-3235, www.panamainfo.com/lassirenas. *Cabañas* to rent for 5 or 8 people in an attractive landscaped environment.
D Hotel Rivera, Antón, Km 131, T987-2245. With bath and a/c or fan, cheaper without bath, clean.
E Pensión Panamá, Antón, across the Pan-American Highway. Friendly, clean, safe, a/c.

Penonomé *p1165*
C-D Dos Continentes, Av Juan D Arosemena, T997-9325. With shower, a/c, pool, restaurant.
D-E Pensión Los Pinos, on left of highway to Panama City. With bath and a/c (cheaper with fan).
E Pensión Dos Reales, Calle Juan Vásquez. Basic, mosquitoes, noisy.
E Residencial El País, Calle Juan Arosemena near church and Parque, no sign but look for black lanterns on wall. With bath, good value.

Balneario Las Mendozas and Churuquita Grande *p1166*
AL Posada del Cerro La Vieja, Chiguirí Arriba, Coclé (Apdo 543 Estafeta 9A Carrasquilla, Panama City), T223-4553, posada97@ hotmail.com. An excellent purpose-built lodge for walkers and ecotourists. It offers guided treks on foot or mule, including through the mountains to El Valle, or across the isthmus to the Atlantic coast with the final stage by dugout.
E No Name, La Pintada, in front of the church. Juan Cedeno has a house with a couple of large, clean rooms, a/c. hot water.

Aguadulce *p1166*
C El Interamericano, on Pan-American Highway, T997-4148. With bath, a/c, TV, balcony, clean rooms and a swimming pool.
D Pensión Sarita, T997-4437, and others. It may be possible to sleep by the fire station.

Transport

San Carlos and beaches *p1164*
Bus Panama City-San Carlos, frequent from 0615, US$3.50, San Carlos-**David**, US$10.

The Azuero Peninsula → *Colour map 8, C1.*

The small town of Divisa, 61 km beyond Penonomé, is the crossroads for a major paved road that branches south into the Azuero Peninsula, one of the earliest parts of Panama to be settled. Despite recent road paving in the south and east, many of the peninsula's small towns are still remote and preserve much of their 400-year-old colonial traditions, costumes and a number of white churches. In addition to its tranquillity, the region's cleanliness and prosperity are a welcome change from Panama City. Most towns of any size on the peninsula have annual carnivals (the four days before Ash Wednesday) but the one in Las Tablas is especially picturesque and popular with visitors. Accommodation is in short supply at this time throughout the region. ▸▸ *For Sleeping, Eating and other queries, see pages 1173-1177.*

Chitré and around ▸▸ *pp1173-1177. Colour map 8, C1.*

→ *Population: 40,000.*

Passing through **Parita,** with a church dating from 1556, the road reaches the cattle centre of Chitré (37 km), capital of Herrera Province and the best base for exploration.

The cathedral (1578) is imposing and beautifully preserved. The small **Museo de Herrera** ⓘ *C Manuel Correa, Tue-Sat 0900-1230, 1330-1500, Sun 0900-1200, US$1,* has historical exhibits, a few archaeological artefacts, and some local ethnographic displays. The town is known primarily for its red clay pottery, especially its roofing and floor tiles, which are exported, and for its woven mats and carpets.

There are some nice beaches close to Chitré served by local buses, for example **Playa Monagre** and **El Rompio** ⓘ *Take the Santa Ana bus from Chitré terminal, frequent services during the day, 30 mins, US$1 to Monagre,* busy at weekends and holidays. It is a 30-minute walk south along the beach from Monagre to El Rompío, where you can catch a bus back to Chitré or head further south at low tide for mangroves and solitude. There are a few restaurants at Monagre but no accommodation.

At **Puerto Agallito**, 15 minutes by bus from Chitré, many migratory birds congregate and are studied at the Humboldt Ecological Station. Along the swampy coast just to the north is the 8000-ha **Parque Nacional Sarigua**, established in 1984 to preserve the distinctive tropical desert and mangrove margins of the Bahía de Parita. Ancient artefacts have been unearthed within the park's boundaries. The pre-Columbian site of **Monegrillo** is considered very significant but there is little for the non-specialist to appreciate.

La Arena, the centre for Panamanian pottery, is 2 km west of Chitré. The Christmas festivities here, 22-25 December, are worth seeing, with music, dancing, bull running in the Plaza de Toros and cock fights (popular all over Panama). To get there, take a bus from Chitré (US$0.30; taxi US$1.50). Alternatively, tour operators in Panama City can arrange shopping tours here.

Los Santos, only 4 km across the Río La Villa from Chitré in Los Santos province, is a charming old town with a fine 18th-century church (San Anastasio) containing many images. The first call for Independence came from here, recognized in the interesting **Museo de la Nacionalidad** ⓘ *Plaza Bolívar, Tue-Sat 0900-1600, Sun 0900-1200, US$1,* set in a lovely house where the Declaration was signed on 10 November 1821. **Azuero regional IPAT office** ⓘ *T966-8072, Mon-Fri 0830-1630,* is next door.

The main road continues 22 km southeast through agricultural country to the tiny town of **Guararé**, notable only for its folkloric museum, the **Museo Manuel** Zárate ⓘ *2 blocks behind the church, T996-2535,* where examples of Azuero's many traditional costumes, masks and crafts are exhibited in a turn-of-the-20th-century house. There is also a wealth of traditional dance, music and singing contests during the annual National Festival of **La Mejorana** (24 September).

Las Tablas and around → *Colour map 8, C1. Population: 22,140..*

Las Tablas (6 km further) is capital of Los Santos province and the peninsula's second-largest city, 67 km from the Divisa turn-off. The central **Iglesia de Santa Librada** with its gold-leaf altar and majestic carvings is one of the finest churches in this part of Panama and is now a National Historic Monument. **El Pausilipo,** former home of thrice-President Porras – known to Panamanians as 'the great man' – is in the process of being turned into a museum. Las Tablas is widely known for its **Fiesta de Santa Librada** (19-23 July, see Festivals and events).

The lovely and unspoilt beach of **El Uverito** is located about 10 km to the east of town but has no public transport (taxi US$4.50). A paved road runs to **Mensabé.**

Smaller paved roads fan out from Las Tablas to the beaches along the south coast and the small villages in the hills of the peninsula. A circular tour around the eastern mountain range can be done by continuing south to **Pocrí** and **Pedasí** (42 km), then west to **Tonosí,** all with their ancient churches and lack of spectacular sights, but typical of the Azuero Peninsula. Another 57 km of paved road runs directly over the hills from Tonosí to Las Tablas.

Pedasí → *Colour map 8, C1.*

Pedasí is a peaceful little town and the municipal library near the church has many old volumes. The local festival, on 29 June is **Patronales de San Pablo**. President Mireya Moscoso was born in Pedasí and the family figures prominently in the town's history. Beautiful empty beaches (**Playa del Toro**, **Playa La Garita** and **Playa Arena**) and crystal-clear seas are 3 km away, but beware of dangerous cross-currents when swimming. There is no public transport to the beaches but it is a pleasant walk early in the morning. You can also walk along the seashore from one beach to another, best at low tide. The local fishing craft are based at **Playa Arena** (also the safest for swimming) and boats can be hired for sport fishing, whale watching and visits to to **Isla Iguana**, a wildlife sanctuary 8 km offshore, protecting the island's birdlife, reptiles (including turtles) and forest. Locally hired boats cost about US$40 for half a day. The **IPAT** office in Los Santos arranges tours with knowledgeable naturalist René Chan who lives locally.

Playa Venado and Tonosí

About 31 km from Pedasí, and 12 km before Cañas, a small sign points to the black-sand beach of **Playa Venado**, a surfers' paradise. There are five *cabañas* for rent here. The road onwards goes to **Cañas** (no hotel), running near the Pacific coast for a short distance, with a string of lovely coves and sandy beaches accessible by rough tracks.

From Tonosí a branch road goes a few kilometres further south to **Cambutal**, west of which begins **Parque Nacional Cerro Hoya**, where sea turtles come ashore to lay their eggs from July to November. There is also a 20-km long beach at Guánico Abajo, 20 minutes' drive from Tonosí, but no public transport.

An alternative to the main road returning to Las Tablas takes the inland road north following the Río Tonosí. Crossing a saddle between the two mountain ranges that occupy the centre of the Peninsula (picturesque views of forested Cerro Quema, 950 m), the road arrives at **Macaracas**, another attractive but unremarkable colonial town, from where two paved roads return to Los Santos and Chitré (35 km).

Ocú → *Population: 2750.*

About 45 km west of Chitré is Ocú, an old colonial town, whose inhabitants celebrate a few notable fiestas during the year with traditional dress, music, masks and dancing. Ocú is also known for its woven hats, which are cheaper than elsewhere in Panama.

The central mountains effectively cut off the western side of the pensinsula from the more developed eastern half. There is only one road down from the highway, a gruelling gravel/dirt ribbon which staggers from near Santiago down the western coastline of the Peninsula as far south as the village of Arenas (80 km) before giving up in the face of the surrounding scrubby mountain slopes. Eastward from here the Peninsula reaches its highest point at Cerro Hoya (1559 m). No roads penetrate either to the coast or into the mountains, ensuring solitude for the **Parque Nacional Cerro Hoya**, which protects most of the southwest tip. The 32,557-ha park protects four life zones in a region that has been devastated by agriculture, over-grazing, season burning and human population pressure. More than 30 species of endemic plants have been recorded in the park and it is one of the last known sites to see the red macaw. One research trip in 1987 even found an endemic species of howler monkey. Turtles also use the coastal beaches for nesting from July to November. There are no refuges.

Santiago and around » pp1173-1177. *Colour map 7, C6.*

→ *Population: 69,117.*

Back on the Pan-American Highway, from the junction at Divisa the roads enters the Province of Veraguas – the only one with seaboards on both oceans – and arrives

The harpy's call

The wildest and most remote forests of Panama still play host to one of Latin America's most magnificent predator, the harpy eagle (*harpia harpyja*). Standing 1 m tall and with 5-cm talons that rival the claws of a grizzly bear, the harpy is the world's most powerful bird of prey. In comparison to its huge body size, the eagle's wingspan (around 2.1 m) is not large, an adaptation that allows it to glide between the trees with exceptional stealth and agility, searching for its favoured prey of monkeys and sloths.

Harpy eagles need huge territories with good wildlife populations in order to survive. Massive deforestation in Panama and elsewhere in Latin America has resulted in its disappearance from vast swathes of its former habitat. Due to its rarity, and the fact that the harpy does not often soar, this bird is tough to track down. But Panama is perhaps the harpy's greatest stronghold in Central America, and several nest sites have been identified in the Darién and Canal areas. Agencies in Panama City can arrange trips to these nest sites.

after 37 km in Santiago. Capital of the province, Santiago is one of the oldest towns in the country, in a grain-growing region that is very dry in summer. Very good and cheap *chácaras* – macramé bags used by male *campesinos* as a convenient hold all for lunch and other necessities in the fields – are sold in the market here. Heading north for 18 km is **San Francisco**; which has a wonderful old church with wooden images, altar pieces and pulpit. The swimming pool is adjacent to the church.

East of Santiago is the turn-off to **La Atalaya**, site of a major pilgrimage and festival in honour of a miraculous statue of Christ, and home of the **Instituto Jesús Nazareno** ⓘ *open to visitors on Sun*, an important agricultural school for rural boys. West of Santiago is **La Mesa** (turn-off at Km 27), with a beautiful, white colonial church. The old rough road heads south through **Soná** and rejoins the Pan-American at **Guabalá**. The paved highway from Santiago to Guabalá saves a couple of hours.

Las Lajas ⓘ *20 km west of Guabalá*, has good beaches. Facilities are limited: there is a small restaurant, **La Estrella del Pacífico**, about 1 km to the east, but apart from that remember to bring your own food and drink from town. Watch out for strong waves and sharks. To get there, take the turn-off at San Félix or take a bus from David to Las Lajas at 1145 and 1245, US$4. From there it's a short taxi trip to the beach (taxis US$3), or you can walk the 3 km from San Félix. A turning left, 38 km west of Las Lajas, leads to Horconcitos and 13 km beyond on a dirt road, is the tiny fishing village of Boca Chica. From there you can cross in a few minutes to the island of **Boca Brava** ⓘ *US$1 per person* in the **Parque Nacional Marítimo Golfo de Chiriquí**.

Isla de Coiba

Some 80 km to the southeast is Isla de Coiba, which, at 503 sq km, is the largest island within Panamanian territory. A former penal colony, the limited interaction has ensured the protection of the plant, animal and marine life in the area which has been protected since 1992 as **Parque Nacional Coiba**. The park itself covers over 2700 sq km and includes areas of rich open ocean, Coiba and outlying islands and the second largest coral reef in the Eastern Pacific. On land the mostly untouched rainforest supports Panama's largest surviving colony of scarlet macaws, along with 146 other avian species. The marine environment, which in terms of pelagic life can only be rivalled by islands such as Cocos and the Galapagos, boasts 23 recorded species of whales and dolphins, including humpback, sperm and killer whales, some of which can spotted on dive trips to the island. Marine life of the fishy kind includes whitetip, bull, hammerhead and whale sharks in addition to manta and eagle rays. **Santa Catalina**, accessible from Santiago and then the small town of Sona, a route served by a few local buses per day, is a relaxed but fast-developing coastal village. Santa Catalina's main claim to fame has been as the location of some of Central America's best surfing breaks. **ScubaCoiba** ⓘ *on the main street, T/F263-4366, www.scubacoiba.com*, provides access to Coiba's unique submarine world. Numerous hotels in Santa Catalina cater to a wide range of budgets. There's also a surf school. It may be possible to arrange an independent trip to Coiba for US$50-60 by chartering a local boat.

David

» *pp1173-1177. Colour map 7, C5.*

➔ *Population: 124,500.*

David, capital of Chiriquí Province and a hot and humid city, rich in timber, coffee, cacao, sugar, rice, bananas and cattle, is the second city of the republic. Founded in colonial times as San José de David, it has managed to keep its traditions intact while modernizing itself. The attractive city is safe and friendly and a gateway to the Chiriquí Highlands and the Caribbean province of Bocas del Toro. With a wide selection of hotels and restaurants, it is a good place to break the trip from Costa Rica to become acquainted with Panama and its people.

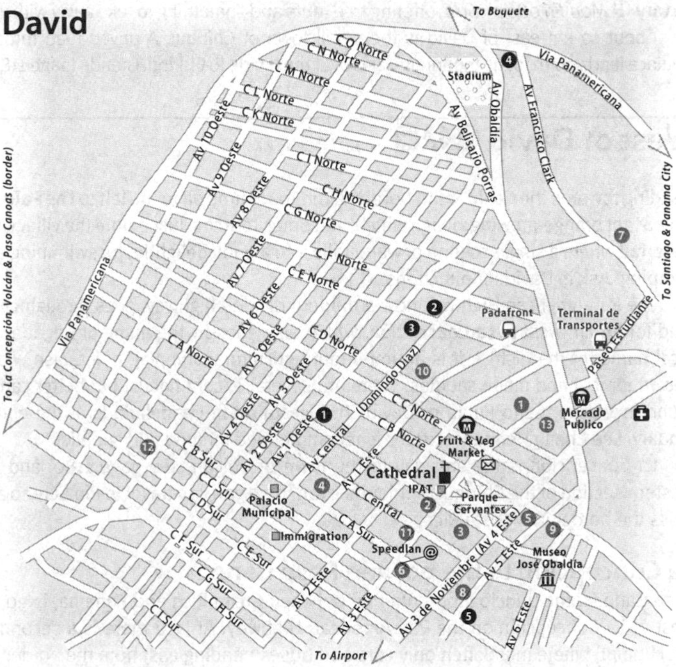

Sleeping
Alcalá 1
Castilla 2
Iris 3
Nacional 4
Occidental & Multi-Café 5
Panamá Rey 6
Pensión Clark 7
Pensión Costa Rica 8
Pensión Fanita 9
Pensíon Saval 10
Puerto del Sol 11
Purple House 12
Residencial La Avenida 13

Eating
El Fogón 1
El Palacio Oriental 2
Helados Jackelita 3
La Cacerola 4
Panadería Pinzón 5

N
Not to scale

Ins and outs

Getting around David presents a significant navigational challenge to the visitor. It is perfectly flat with no prominent landmarks, the central plaza is not central, there are no street signs, some streets have two names and the locals use neither, preferring nostalgic points of reference (eg: across the street from where the old oak used to be) to genuinely useful guidance. City bus routes are circuitous and generate additional confusion. When you get hopelessly lost take a taxi – for US$0.65 it's not such a bad idea. The **IPAT tourist office** ⓘ *Av 3 Este y Calle A Norte on Parque Cervantes, T775-4120, Mon-Fri, 0830-1630,* is friendly and helpful.

Sights

The city of Davis focuses on the fine central plaza, **Parque Cervantes**, which teems with birds in the early morning, providing good birdwatching from the balconies of the Hotel Occidental or Iris. The colonial-style **Iglesia de San José** is on the west side of the park. The bell tower in Barrio Bolívar was built separately as a defence against tribal attacks. The Palacio Municipal is opposite Hotel Nacional on Avenida and Calle Central. The **Museo José de Obaldía** ⓘ *Av 8 Este 5067 y Calle A, Norte, 4 blocks from Plaza, Mon-Sat 0830-1630, US$0.25,* is a museum of history and art in the house of the founder of Chiriquí Province.

A few kilometres north of David on the Boquete road is **Balneario Majagua**, where you can swim in a river under a waterfall (cold drinks for sale). There is another bathing place on the right 10 km further on. Take a Dolega or Boquete bus and ask the driver to drop you off. About 2 km along the main road to the border is the **Carta Vieja rum factory** ⓘ *Mon-Fri 0800-1600,* offering free tours and something to take away with you.

About 10 km east of David is the small town of **Chiriquí**. A paved road through Gualaca leads north to the mountains and over the divide to Chiriquí Grande (page 1187).

West of David » *pp1173-1177.*

Heading towards the Costa Rican border, a dirt road turns off to the left to **Las Palmas**, a pleasant orange-growing village which welcomes tourists. Just before the village is a **waterfall** where a single column of water falls into a pool, delightful for swimming and camping. Ask in David for directions.

The Pan-American Highway, now a modern divided highway, goes through cattle land for 26 km west to **La Concepción**, which also goes by the name of Bugaba, the local name for the district. It is an important agricultural shipping point, also widely known for its hand-made saddles. There are several decent hotels, but better can be found in Volcán, Cerro Punta or David. The **Fiesta de la Candelaria** is at the end of January. **Lee Chang Hermanos** stores is recommended for food and supplies.

La Concepción is the gateway to the town of Volcán, see page 1180, and the western section of the Chiriqui Highlands. From here you can travel to Río Sereno and cross the border into Costa Rica.

La Concepción to the border, Paso Canoas

Paso Canoas, the principal port of entry between Costa Rica and Panama, is 30 km west of La Concepción on the Pan-American Highway. At Jacú there is a secondary checkpoint, where most often only cars and buses heading east from the border are checked. Have passport, tourist card, vehicle permit and driver's licence handy in case they are asked for (usually hassle free).

Paso Canoas is a busy border town. There are also many good eating places, especially open-front restaurants opposite Costa Rican Customs. Informally crossing back and forth between shops and business areas is easy, but travellers intending to leave one country for the other must submit to formalities before proceeding.

Border Essentials: Panama-Costa Rica

Pasa Canoas

Currency exchange Money changers will change colones into dollars at a good rate; the Banco Nacional de Panama cashes TCs and also has Visa ATM.

Panamanian immigration Panamanian customs are open 24 hrs; the Costa Rican side is open 0500-2100 Panama time. After checking in at Entrada, buy a tourist card from the IPAT tourist office around the corner of the building to the left. Return to Entrada for an entry stamp. All relatively quick and painless, unless an international bus has arrived just before you. Free maps of Panama available at IPAT.

Sleeping E Palace, clean bathroom, basic. There is a reasonable restaurant at the border. Greater choice, although not necessarily better, on the Costa Rican side.

Time Panama is 1 hour ahead

Transport Buses to Panama City via La Concepción and David with Padafront, T775-8913, 11 daily every 1½-2 hrs, from terminal on northeast corner of main intersection. Fare to Panama City, US$12; express 2300, 2400, US$17. Regular buses run to David for US$1.50, 1½ hrs.

Sleeping

Chitré and around *p1167*

B **Hong Kong**, Av Carmelo Espadafora, Chitré, T996-4483. A/c, pool, restaurant.

B **Versalles**, Paseo Enrique Grensier, near entry to Chitré, T996-4422. A/c, pool, restaurant.

C **El Prado**, Av Herrera and Calle Correa, Chitré, T996-4620. Clean, quiet, well run, a/c, cheaper with fan, restaurant. Recommended.

C **La Villa de Los Santos**, Calle Alzamora Julio, Los Santos, T/F996-8201. A/c caravans, with swimming pool and good restaurant.

C **Residencial Mejorana**, Guararé, T994-5794. A/c, TV, restaurant.

C **Rex**, Calle Maliton Matín by main plaza, Chitré, T/F996-4310. A/c, restaurant downstairs.

D **Cabañas Bayano Mar**, near El Rompío. Pleasant cabins with private bath and fan, nice setting, restaurant and bar.

D **Pensión Central**, Av Herrera next to El Prado, Chitré, T996-0059. With bath, a/c, cheaper with fan, noisy in front rooms.

D **Pensión Colombia**, Calle Manuel Correa near museum (3 blocks from plaza), Chitré, T996-1856. Fan, private bath, basic.

D **Santa Rita**, Calle Manuel Correa y Av Herrera, Chitré, T996-4610. Friendly, clean, restaurant, good value. Recommended.

E **Pensión Deportiva**, Los Santos. No single rooms, private showers.

E **Pensión Herrerana**, Av Herrera 4072, Chitré, T996-4356. Small rooms with fan, private bath, very hot, clean, parking, basic.

Las Tablas and around *p1168*

D **Zafiro**, Av Belisario Porras, across from main plaza, T/F994-8200. Modern, a/c, TV.

E **Pensión Mariela**, Av Belisario Porras, opposite Zafiro. Basic and run-down.

Pedasí *p1168*

C **Hotel Residencial Pedasí**, at the entrance to town, T995-2322. A/c, spacious grounds.

D **Dim's**, Av Principal, T995-2303. A/c, lovely garden with hammocks.

D-E **Residencial Moscoso**, T995-2203. With shower, TV, a/c, cheaper with fan, clean, good, friendly, meals arranged by owner at nearby bar.

Playa Venado and Tonosí *p1169*

D **Pensión Boamy**, Playa Tonosí, T995-8142. With a/c, cheaper with fan, friendly.

D **Playa Venado**. There are 5 *cabañas* for rent here (no electricity, very basic, overpriced), and plenty of idyllic **camping** spots (camping free, showers cost US$0.25), as well as a combined open-air restaurant.

D-E **Pensión Roslyn**, Playa Tonosí. A/c, cheaper with fan, basic.

E Playa Tonosí. There are *cabañas* for rent (price per person), plenty of idyllic **camping** spots and a small restaurant.

Ocú *p1169*

E Posada San Sebastián, on the plaza. Fans, clean bathrooms, patio, charming.

Santiago and around *p1169*

C Roselas Apartotel, Vía San Francisco, T998-7269. Apartments with kitchen, a/c, hot water, clean, friendly, safe parking for motorcycles.
C-E Gran David, on Pan-American Highway, T998-4510. A/c, TV, cheaper with fan, private bath, clean, pool, good restaurant. Recommended.
D Piramidal, on Pan-Am Highway nearing stopping point for David-Panama buses, T998-3123. A/c, TV, shower, clean, quiet, good pool. Recommended.
D Santiago, Calle 2 near the cathedral, T998-4824. Clean, with a/c, TV and shower, cheaper with shared bath. Noisy and run-down.
D-F Restaurante Boca Brava, Boca Brava, T8731-774-3117. With cabins, cane huts and camping. Lots of wildlife and interesting flora, snorkelling on the nearby rocks, German owners.
E Cabañas La Lajas, Las Lajas. Sleeps 2-4 people with views out to sea, cold showers, kitchen and friendly people.
E Central, next to Jigoneva, T998-6116. Basic, all rooms with shower, Chinese owner.
E Jigoneva, Av Central 2038. Basic, friendly.

Camping

Campana Esperanza, some 28 km west of Santiago, off the road to Canazas. A beautiful setting on a lake with a few cabins.

David *p1171, map p1171*

Most cheap hotels are on Av 5 Este.
A Nacional, Av and Calle Central, T775-2222, www.panamainfo.com/granhotelnacional. Clean rooms, good restaurant, gaming room.
B Castilla, Calle A Norte between Av 2 and 3 Este, T774-5260. Modern and comfortable, centrally located.
B Fiesta, on Pan-American Highway, T775-5454. Restaurant, good pool (US$2 for non-residents).
B Puerto del Sol, Av 3 Este y Calle Central, T774-8422. New, clean, well furnished, TV, a/c, internet US$1/hr.
C Alcalá, Av 3 Este between Calle D and E Norte, T774-9018. With parking, comfortable, pleasant.
C Panamá Rey, Av 3 Este y Calle A Sur, T775-0253. Modern high-rise building, with restaurant.
C-D Iris, Calle A Norte, on Parque Cervantes T775-2251. With bath and a/c, cheaper with fan. Friendly and clean.
D Occidental, Av 4 Este on Parque Cervantes, T775-4695. With bath and a/c, cheaper with fan, nice balcony overlooking park, good value. Recommended.
D Pensión Costa Rica, Av 5 Este, Calle A Sur, T775-1241. Variety of rooms, with shower and/or a/c, basic, clean, safe, friendly and good value, but a bit run-down and noisy.
D Residencial La Avenida, Av 3 Este between Calle D and E Norte, T774-0451. With bath and a/c, cheaper with fan, parking, good value.
D-E Pensión Saval, Calle D Norte between Cincuentenario and Av 1 Este, across Plaza Oteima, T775-3543. With bath and a/c, cheaper with fan, basic, run-down but friendly.
D-E The Purple House, Calle C Sur and Av 6 Oeste, Barrio San Mateo, T774-4059, www.purplehousehostel.com. Hostel close to the centre of town with private and dormitory rooms. Also use of kitchen, free internet access and good information on travel throughout the country and Central America. Good reports but cold showers. Taxi from bus terminal is US$1.
E Pensión Clark, Av Francisco Clark, north of bus terminal, T774-3452. With bath.
E-F Pensión Fanita, Calle 5 between 5 Este and 6 Este, T775-3718. Family-run in an old wooden house.

West of David *p1172*

C Koco's Place, Puerto Armuelles, T770-7049. A/c, TV and small restaurant.

Eating

Chitré and around *p1167*

Many restaurants serving economical *comida corriente*, plus a few Chinese.
TT El Mesón in the Hotel Rex. Upmarket, national and international dishes.
T El Chitreano, Calle Antonio Burgos. Good food and large portions.

Pedasí *p1168*

¶¶¶ **Turístico JR's**, T995-2176. Owner was formerly head chef at **El Panamá**, (see page 1134). Swiss/French dishes, good quality and variety, expensive. Recommended.

¶ **Angela**, Pedasí. Local fare, good.

David *p1171, map p1171*

¶¶¶ **Mar del Sur**, Av Central y Calle H Norte. International menu.

¶¶ **Café Don Dicky**, Calle C Norte near Av Domingo Díaz (Central). Better than it looks.

¶¶ **El Steak House**, Pan-American Highway west of Av Obaldía. Good Chinese and moderate prices.

¶¶ **Mariscos Daiquirí**, Av Central, Calle Sur. Fish and seafood, not cheap, but good.

¶¶ **Parrillada El Portal**, Calle A Sur, Av 5 Este. Good.

¶ **El Fogón**, Av 1 Este y Calle B Norte. Good, reasonable prices.

¶ **El Palacio Oriental**, Av Domingo Díaz (Central) y Calle E Norte. Chinese.

¶ **Ely's**, Av 3 E y Calle A Norte, also at Plaza OTEIMA. Good bread and pastries.

¶ **Helados Jackelita**, Calle E Norte y Av Domingo Díaz. Very good fresh fruit ice cream.

¶ **La Cacerola**, Av Obaldía behind **Super Barú**, just off Pan-American Highway. Self-service, clean, fresh Panamanian dishes all day, a/c, good value. Highly recommended.

¶ **Multi-Café**, in **Hotel Occidental**, Av 4 Este on Parque Cervantes. Popular with locals, good quality, variety and value.

¶ **Nueva China**, Av Obaldía. Chinese.

¶ **Panadería Pinzón**, Av 5 Este, Calle A Sur, opposite **Pensión Costa Rica**. Excellent shop/café with sandwiches, cakes.

¶ **Pizzería Mio Bello**, Calle A Sur y Av 5 Este. Good Italian.

West of David *p1172*

Puerto Armuelles has plenty of cheap eating places.

¶ **Club Social**, Puerto Armuelles, on water (ask any taxi). Chicken and rice dishes.

Festivals and events

Chitré and around *p1167*

May/Jun Feast of Corpus Christi (40 days after Easter) is a 4-day feast celebrated in Los Santos with one of the country's most famous and popular festivals, a glorious distillation of the Peninsula's strong Spanish roots and well worth attending.

End Apr The Feria de Azuero. 'Little devil' (*diablito*) and other masks featuring in the *fiestas* are the local handicraft speciality and may be purchased from stalls or workshops around town and in Parita.

24 Jun **Fiesta de San Juan Bautista**, and the preceding week.

19 Oct **The district's founding** (1848) is celebrated with colourful parades and historical events.

Las Tablas *p1168*

19-23 Jul **Fiesta de Santa Librada** and incorporated **Fiesta de la Pollera**. Las Tablas is widely known for this festival. The *pollera* is a ruffled, intricately embroidered in a single colour, off-the-shoulder dress based on colonial fashions and is now the national costume of Panama; *polleras* are made in villages near Las Tablas, the most beautiful coming from Santo Domingo (5 km east).

Ocú *p1169*

19-24 Jan **San Sebastián**, the district's patron saint, is celebrated with costumed folklore groups.

Aug **El Matrimonio Campesino**, **El Penitente de la Otra Vida** and **El Duelo del Tamarindo**, are straight from medieval Spain and well-worth witnessing.

15 Aug **The Festival del Manito** at the Assumption.

David *p1171, map p1171*

Mid-Mar Major week-long international fair and fiesta.

Activities and tours

David *p1171, map p1171*

Servicios Turísticos, Calle Central, T775-4644. Regional tours.

Travesías, Calle B Norte between Av 5 and 6 Este, T/F774-5352, travesias@mixmail.com. Regional tours.

Transport

Chitré and around *p1167*

Bus Chitré is the transport hub of the peninsula, there is a bus terminal just outside town, take city bus **Las Arenas**.

To **Panama City** (250 km), regular buses by several companies 4 hrs, US$6. To **Santiago**, frequent service, 1 hr, US$2. There is no direct service to **David**, change at Santiago. To **Divisa**, 30 mins, US$1.30; same fare and time to **Las Tablas** (buses leave when full). To **Tonosí**, 3 hrs, US$4.15; to **Santiago**, 1½ hrs, US$2.50.

Las Tablas and around *p1168*
Bus To **Panama City**, several buses daily, 4½ hrs, US$7; to **Santo Domingo**, 10 mins, US$0.40; to **Tonosí**, 2½ hrs, US$4.25. Last bus from Los Santos to **Las Tablas** at 1800.

From Las Tablas buses to **Pedasí** leave when full, 1 hr, US$2, bumpy trip.

Playa Venado and Tonosí *p1169*
Bus 1 a day to Playa Venado from **Las Tablas** at 1300, about 2 hrs, US$3.20, return at 0700. No direct bus Pedasí-Tonosí.

Pedasí-Cañas around 0700 and 1500, US$2; **Cañas**-Tonosí 1 a day. Tonosí-**Las Tablas**, 4 a day between 0700 and 1300, US$3, 1 hrs, leave when full.

A milk truck leaves Tonosí at 0700 for **Chitré**, via Cañas, Playa Venado, Pedasí and Las Tablas, takes passengers, returns 1230.

Bus Tonosí-**Chitré** via Macaracas, 4 a day before 1100, 3 hrs, US$4, mostly paved road.

Hitching is difficult as there is little traffic.

Ocú *p1169*
Bus Several buses a day from Chitré, 1 hr, US$1.75, and buses on to **Panama City**, US$7. Those with limited time can get a glimpse of the Peninsula and villages by taking a bus from Chitré to **Pesé**, **Los Pozos** or **Las Minas**, all in the foothills of the western range, and then another to Ocú; staying the night and taking another bus on to Santiago to return to the Panama City-David highway.

Santiago and around *p1169*
Bus From **Penonomé**, US$4; from **Aguadulce**, US$2.50. Panama City-David buses stop outside **Hotel Piramidal**. Bus to **David** from here costs US$7. To **Panama City** US$7.

David *p1171, map p1171*
Air
Aeroperlas, Calle A Norte y Av 3 Este next to Hotel Castilla, T721-1195. Several flights a day from **Panama City**, US$59 one-way. Also to **Bocas del Toro** and **Changuinola**, both US$32 one-way (occasional seasonal offers, eg US$20). Daily service to **San José**, Costa Rica, US$83, one way.

Mapiex Aero, Plaza OTEIMA, CDN between Av 1 and 2 Este, T775-0812, also flies to **Panama City** (3 daily), **Changuinola** and **Bocas del Toro.**

Bus
Local US$0.20; taxis US$0.65 in city.
Long distance The main bus terminal is at Av 2 Este, 1 block north of Av Obaldía. Taxi to centre US$1. All companies use this except Padafront, whose terminal is nearby at Av 2 Este y Av Obaldía, T775-8913.

To **Panama City** regular buses US$10.60, express US$15, 3 hrs, 10 daily with Padafront, good service.

To **Paso Canoas** (border with Costa Rica), US$1.50, 1½ hrs, every 15 mins 0500-1830. Direct to **San José** with **Tracopa**, 0830 daily, US$12, 8 hrs, with stop in San Isidro.

Regular buses go to **Boquete** every 25 mins, 0600-2145, 1 hr, US$1.20; **Volcán**, every 15 mins, 0700-1800, 1½ hrs, US$2.30; **Chiriquí Grande**, every 90 mins, 0630-1600, 3 hrs, US$7; buses to **Almirante** every 40 mins, 0500-1900, 4 hrs, US$8; **Cerro Punto**, 2¼ hrs, US$3.

Car
Budget, T775-5597; **Hertz**, T775-6828; Mike's, T775-4963. Rent a 4WD vehicle in David if going to Volcán Barú.

Car Ocú can be reached directly from the Pan-American Highway (19 km) by a paved turn-off south just past the Río Conaca bridge (11 km west of Divisa); *colectivos* run from here for US$0.80. Alternatively, a mostly gravel road runs west from Parita along the Río Parita valley, giving good views of the fertile landscapes of the northern Peninsula.

West of David *p1172*
Bus From David via **Concepción** and **Paso Canoas** buses run every 15 mins, 0500-2000, 2½ hr, US$3.

Train Chiriquí Railway: passenger service Puerto Armuelles-**Progreso** (half way to Paso Canoas), twice a day each way, 2 hr,

US$1. There is also a 'Finca Train',4 decrepit, converted banana trucks, leaving at 1500 for the banana *fincas*, returning, by a different route, at 1800. No charge for passengers. Minibuses also leave all day for the *fincas*.

Directory

Chitré and around *p1167*
Internet at **Econoútiles** stationary store, Av Herrera 1 block from cathedral, US$3 per hr. Also at **Abacus**, Belarmino Urriola, US$2.50 per hr.

David *p1171, map p1171*
Banks **Banistmo**, Av 2 Este y Calle A Norte, also on Av Obaldía, for Visa cash advances, changes AMEX TCs without commission. **Banco Nacional de Panamá**, 0800-1330 (generally very convenient, but guards have been known to turn away travellers wearing shorts), changes Amex TCs, 1% commission plus US$0.10 tax per cheque. **Banco General**, Av 3 Este y Calle C Norte, changes TCs, 1% commission, Visa ATM. **Caja de Ahorro** (Caja Pronto), Av 2 Este y Calle Central, for MasterCard and Amex TCs. **Embassies and consulates** Costa Rica, Urbanización El Bosque, 2 blocks west of clinic, best take a taxi, T774-1923. **Immigration** Immigration office Calle C Sur between Av Central and 1 Este, T775-4515, Mon-Fri 0800-1500. **Ministerio de Hacienda y Tesoro** Calle C Norte, 1 block from Parque Cervantes, near the post office. **Internet** **Sinfonet**, Calle E Norte y Av Domingo Díaz, daily 0800-0000, US$1 per hr; **Speedlan**, Av 3 este y Calle A Sur, beside Panamá Rey hotel, T777-2438, US$1/hr. **Instituto OTEIMA**, C D N between Av 1 and 2 Este, daily 0800-1200, 1330-2000, US$1 per hr; **Electrónica Nacional**, Av Obaldía, opposite Domino's Pizza, US$1.50 per hr. **Laundry** **Lavandería One**, Av Centenario Central y 1A Sur; **Lavafast**, 1 Av Obaldia. **Post office** Calle C Norte y Av 3 Este.

Chiriquí Highlands

The Tierras Altas de Chiriquí include the highland areas around Boquete, Volcán Barú and Cerro Punta. The mingling of Atlantic and Pacific winds creates a year-round spring-like climate. The so-called bajareque *(literally 'falling down') shrouds the area in a fine mist-creating cloud forests at higher altitudes. Closer to the ground, the black volcanic soil creates highly fertile conditions. Coffee* fincas *and intensive farming that produces most of the country's vegetables are interspersed with tourist resorts, popular with Panameños seeking to escape the tropical heat during vacations (December to March). It's an ideal place to spend some time hiking, horse riding, fishing, rafting and birdwatching.*

Daytime temperatures are cool; evenings and nights chilly. Some days can be rather windy in the dry season. Mornings are especially clear and beautiful all year round. Travellers entering Panama from the north should consider a visit before pushing on to Panama City. ▸▸ *For Sleeping, Eating and other listings, see pages 1183-1187.*

Boquete and the Eastern Highlands

▸▸ *pp1183-1187. Colour map 7, B5.*

Heading north towards Boquete in the heart of the cool Eastern Highlands, a well-paved road climbs gently from David, passing (after 10 km) a waterfall with a swimming hole, open-air restaurant/bar and space for wild camping. It passes through **Dolega** (swimming pool, one *pensión*, notable for its carnival four days before Ash Wednesday) before reaching (after 40 km) the popular mountain resort of Boquete, at 1060 m in the valley of the Río Caldera, with the slopes of Volcán Barú to the west. It is a beautiful panorama of coffee plantations and orange groves, strawberry fields and gardens.

Good lodging and facilities make Boquete an excellent base for fishing, riding, river rafting and hiking in the area, see Activities and tours, below. It is a slow-paced, predominantly wood-built town with several attractive landscaped parks, including the main plaza and the nearby Parque de las Madres. The fairground east of the river is the site for the annual **Feria de las Flores y del Café**, usually held mid-January. In April, a **Feria de las Orquídeas** is held with many varieties of local and exotic orchids, as well as other flowers. The **cemetery** ⓘ *Mon-Sat 0930-1300, 1400-1800*, is worth a visit, there is a small museum of *huacas* (funerary sculptures) in the centre and a fine panoramic view from the 'Bienvenidos a Boquete' arch at the entrance to the town.

Boquete has gained international recognition as a producer of fine coffees and freelance tour guides *Terry van Niekerk* and *Hans van der Vooren* provide tours of fine local coffee operations. Very comprehensive, informative 2½- to three-hour tours that cover everything from plant to production, harvesting to roasting to a tasting of the final product. Tours visiting **Café Ruiz** ⓘ *T720-1392, www.caferuiz.com, US$17.50 per person,* are available in English, Spanish and Dutch, minimum two people. There's also **Café Kotowa** ⓘ *T720-1430, www.myroaster.com*, and a **tourist office** (CEFATI) at the entrance to town.

Volcán Barú

The highest point in the country, Volcán Barú rises to an altitude of 3475 m and is reached easily from Boquete, 21 km to the east, and not so easily from Volcán to the west. The summit lies within the boundaries of **Parque Nacional Volcán Barú** which covers some 14,000 ha and borders the vast La Amistad International Park, to the north, which itself spans the Panamanian-Costa Rican border covering much of the Cordillera Talamanca. Rainfall in the park ranges between 3000 and 4000 mm a year, and temperatures range from a subtropical 17°C to a distinctly chilly 7°C. Rich cloud forest makes ideal conditions for reptiles, amphibians and birds, with around 40 species endemic to the park.

From Boquete it is 21 km to the summit. The first 7 km is paved, sometimes lined with aromatic pines, goes through coffee groves, most numerous in the area during the year-end harvest season, mainly tended by Ngöbe-Buglé (Guaymí) people. The paved road ends at a small, usually unmanned, ANAM office, from where the track winds up from the office through tall, impressive cloud forest, thick with hanging creepers, lichen and bromeliads. The steep cuttings are carpeted with a glorious array of ferns and colourful flowers; many birds can be seen, including bee hummingbirds, as well as wild turkeys and squirrels. The perfume from the flowers, especially in the wet season when there are many more blooms, is magnificent.

As the road rises, increasingly steeply, there are wonderful views of the Boquete valley, the Río Caldera running through a steep gorge, and the misty plain beyond stretching to the Pacific. Some 9 km from the park entrance is a sign on the right, 'La Nevera' (the ice-box). A small side-trail here leads to a cool mossy gully where there is a stream for water, but no flat ground to camp. This is the only reliable water source during the dry season, so take plenty with you.

At the summit the cloud forest is replaced by a forest of TV and radio aerials in fenced-off enclosures. A short path leads to a small cross and a trigonometric point, from where the best views of dusty craters and the valleys of Volcán, Bambito and Cerro Punta stretch out below. The high-altitude brush contrasts spectacularly with the dark green forest, wisps of mist and cloud clinging to the treetops. Occasionally horizontal rainbows can be seen in the haze, formed in the *bajareque* drizzle. There are many craters around the main summit, with dwarf vegetation, lichens and orchids. Even in the dry season, you will be lucky to have a clear view of both oceans.

In a suitable vehicle it takes about two hours to the top (depending on the weather); or it's a 4½- to six-hour hike up, three hours down, from the park office. Zona Urbana minibuses (US$1) go to El Salto, 4 km from Boquete and 3 km from the end of the asphalt. Vehicles which service the antenna installations often go up to the summit. Officially they are not allowed to take passengers, but drivers may give you a lift. They are also very friendly and like a chat. A taxi to the end of the paved road costs US$4 (recommended during the wet season as there is little chance of hitching and because the mountain summit usually clouds over in the afternoon making an early start your best option). Hiking from the summit all the way back to Boquete takes at least six hours. For those wishing to continue over Barú to Volcán on the mountain's west side, a trail begins 50 m before the cross, descending steeply over loose sand and scree before entering the forest. It's eight to 12 hours to Volcán, and there's no water until you are halfway down; a challenging and rewarding hike (see page 1180).

The managers of the **Hotel Panamonte** in Boquete own **Finca Lérida**, on the slopes of Volcán Barú, tours can be arranged. Ask at the hotel's front desk.

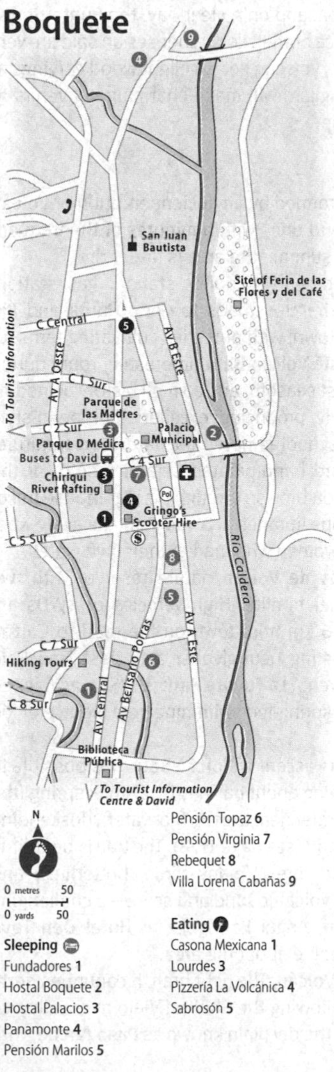

Other hikes and excursions

Twenty-seven kilometres north of the Pan-American Highway (13 km south of Boquete) is a turn-off east to Caldera (14 km), from where a 25- to 30-minute walk leads to **Los Pozos de Caldera** ⓘ *no facilities, options for camping, entry US$1*, a well-known series of hot springs said to be good for rheumatism sufferers. River-rafting trips on the Chiriquí start from Caldera (see Activities and tours). There are six buses a day from David to Caldera, four a day from Boquete to Caldera, and pick-ups from the main road to the village.

Across the suspension bridge, **Conservas de Antaño** ⓘ *T720-1539*, is a very friendly family-owned business that makes old-fashioned fruit preserves. **Café Ruiz** ⓘ *2 km north of Boquete, T720-1392*, is a small factory known for its premium-grade roasted coffees. They welcome visitors for a guided tour (Don José Ruiz speaks English, starting 0900, three hours, US$14), explaining the whole process from harvesting to hand selecting only the best beans and vacuum packing the product. Next door is **Villa Marta**, a private mansion with a huge landscaped garden open to the public, and a sign: *'Mi jardín es su jardín'*. **Los Ladrillos**, a few kilometres further up the Caldera Valley, is a small area of basalt cliffs with octagonal fingers of rock in clusters. Beyond is **Horqueta**, a picturesque hillside area of coffee groves, with a roadside waterfall and banks of pink impatiens; beautiful views to the south.

Volcán and the Western Highlands

➡ pp1183-1187.

The western section of the Tierras Altas (highlands) de Chiriquí is bounded on the north by the Cordillera and on the west by the Costa Rican border, a prosperous and dynamic agricultural region renowned for vegetables, flowers, superb coffees, and the brown Swiss and Holstein dairy herds that thrive in the cool highland pastures. The area is a birdwatchers' mecca and is also popular with residents of Panama City wishing to cool off for a few days.

Heading away from La Concepción there is a very good paved road north, rising 1200 m in 32 km to Volcán. From Cuesta de Piedra, a turning to the right will take you to the canyons of the **Macho de Monte**, a rather small river which has worn deep and narrow gorges. Further on, to the left, is the **Mirador Alan Her** ① *US$0.10*, with good views from the purpose-built tower to the sea, and on a clear day, the Punto Burica peninsula which marks the Panama-Costa Rica border. Local cheeses on sale are very good, especially the mozzarella. Near Volcán, you can get excellent wood carvings at **Artes Cruz** where Don Cruz, who speaks English, will make charming souvenirs to order and have them ready on your return trip.

Volcán and around ➔ *Colour map 7, B5.*

Volcán sits on a broad 1450-m high plateau formed by an ancient eruption of Volcán Barú. The pumice soil is extremely porous and dries within minutes of the frequent torrential downpours in the rainy season; in summer the area is tinder dry.

The town is very spread out. The centre (with police station, gas station, supermarket and bakery) clusters around the crossroads to Cerro Punta and Río Sereno. Volcán is a rapidly growing farming town, with nurseries cultivating ferns for export, the **Beneficio Café Volcán Barú** (interesting tours during October-February harvest season), and a small factory owned by the Swiss Bérard family producing excellent European-style sausages. San Benito school is noted for hardwood furniture, woodcarvings using *cocobolo* hardwood and hand-painted ceramics sold for the benefit of the school. Brother Alfred will let you browse through his warehouse full of English books from the now-closed Canal Zone libraries and you can take away what you will. **Cerámica Beija-Flor** is run by local women who market their own wares.

> *Guides can be arranged in Volcán; climbers sometimes get lost.*

Southwest of town is the **Las Lagunas de Volcán** nature reserve, with two beautiful lakes, abundant aquatic and other birdlife. High vehicles or 4WDs are required in the wet season. **Sitio Barriles**, 6 km from town on the road to Caizán (several buses daily, US$0.50), has interesting petroglyphs; also past Fina Palo Santo, 5 km from town on the road to Río Sereno. **La Fuente Park** ① *US$0.25* (signed from the main road) has playing fields and a spring-fed swimming hole (source of Río Gariché) that's excellent for children.

Volcán is a good jumping-off place for the ascent of **Volcán Barú**. It is possible to climb the west side in one or two days, camping about halfway by a small spring (the only reliable water in the dry season) or in a crater near the top (no water), descending the following day to Boquete on the vehicle road (see page 1178). The trail is beautiful, climbing gently at first through lush cloud forest (many birds, butterflies, and orchids), then scrambling steeply over loose volcanic sand and scree – a challenging but rewarding hike. For **tourist information**, Angel Rodríguez at **Hotel Don Tavo** speaks fluent English and is very knowledgeable about the area.

The road divides at the police station in Volcán. The right branch continues north to tiny **Bambito** and **Cerro Punta** (22 km), following the Chiriquí Viejo river valley up the northwest foothills of Volcán Barú. Cross the dry plain known as **Paso Ancho**, with coffee farms in the hill to the west.

Cerro Punta » pp1183-1187. Colour map 7, B5.

→ *Altitude: 2130 m.*

Heading north from Volcán, at the end of the road is Cerro Punta (buses from David via La Concepción and Volcán, two hours, US$2.65). Set in a beautiful valley, it is at the heart of a vegetable- and flower-growing zone, and a region of dairy farms and racehorse stables. It is sometimes called 'Little Switzerland' because of its Alpine-style houses and the influence of Swiss and former-Yugoslav settlers (there is a settlement called **Nueva Suiza** just south of town). The countryside, full of orchids, is beautiful, though economic pressures push the potato fields ever higher up the hillsides, to the cost of the wooded areas, and sadly encourage the extensive use of agro-chemicals. There are many fine walks in the crisp mountain air. Continue through Cerro Punta to follow the main street as it curves to the left. **Haras Cerro Punta** (topiary initials clipped in the hedge) and **Haras Carinthia** (name visible on stable roof) are well-known thoroughbred farms who will usually receive visitors and show them round. Further on is the small bridge at Bajo Grande. The right fork leads to **Respingo**, where there is a small forest ranger station.

Hikes and nature trails

Camino Los Quetzales Continuing along the main road in Cerro Punta through town is the starting point of the easy six-hour hike, mostly downhill after an initial climb, to Boquete. The track is clear in places and there are a few signs showing the direction and time to Boquete, with the last section following the Río Caldera canyon. It is easier in the dry season (December-April), but can be enjoyed throughout the year. Take food, insect repellent and rain gear. This hike is also recommended for

Around Boquete

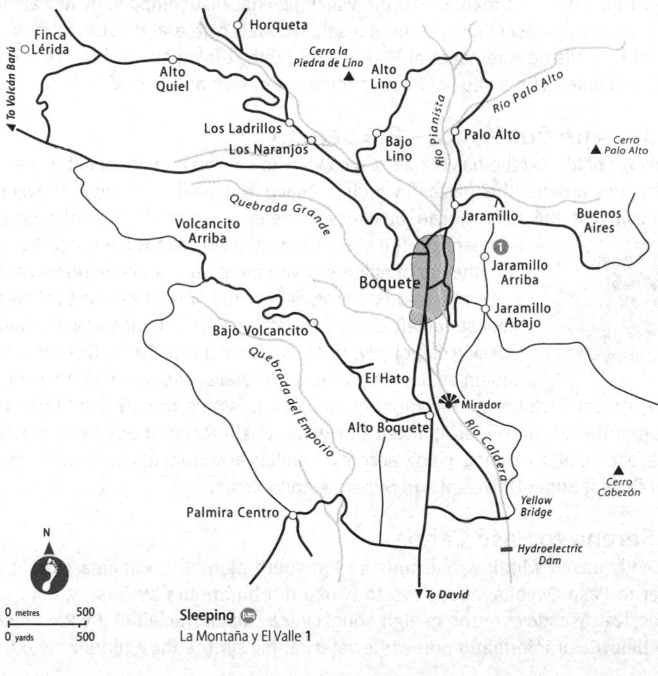

 birdwatching; quetzales and many other species may be seen. Take a taxi (4WD) from Cerro Punta to the Respingo ranger station, US$10. You can stay overnight here in the rangers' quarters (F per person), clean, shared bath and kitchen. The Camino Los Quetzales leads to **Bajo Mono**, from which there are irregular local buses to Boquete (20 minutes, US$1). The walk can also be done in the opposite direction (uphill). It is possible to set out from and return to Boquete in one (very long) day.

Parque la Amistad ⓘ *7 km from the centre of Cerro Punta (signposted at road junction, entrance fee US$1, payable at Las Nubes)*, has been open since 1991, with two trails, good for birdwatching, including quetzales. Nature buffs should also visit Los Quetzales reserve inside Parque La Amistad. See Sleeping.

Volcán to the border

» pp1183-1187. Colour map 7, B5.

From the fork at the police station in Volcán, the left branch loops 48 very scenic kilometres west, climbing over the Cerro Pando, and passing through beautiful cattle country and coffee plantations on a well-paved, little-travelled, winding road to the Costa Rican border. **Los Pozos**, an area of small thermal pools beside a rushing river, is a good campsite, but only accessible by 4WD vehicles and hard to find as the turn-off from Volcán-Río Sereno road is unmarked. Enquire at **Panadería Mollek** (good espresso and pastries), opposite the police station in Volcán. Sr Juan Mollek has a farm at Los Pozos and can provide information. At **Río Colorado**, 15 km from Volcán, **Beneficio Café Durán**, a coffee processing plant whose delicious aroma of fermenting pulp and drying beans will announce its proximity from kilometres away, is hospitable to visitors. At **Santa Clara**, 25 km from Volcán, is the **Finca Hartmann**, 1300-1800 m, where the US **Smithsonian Tropical Research Institute** maintains a biological research station devoted to ecological studies. Enter the unmarked drive 50 m west of petrol station, next to a green house with 'Ab Santa Clara No 2' sign and proceed 1 km on a dirt road. Latest birdwatching checklist compiled by researchers lists 277 species observable on the densely wooded coffee and cattle farm which borders La Amistad International Park to the north. Biologists and the Hartmann family welcome visitors and have information in Spanish and English.

Border with Costa Rica – Río Sereno

The village of Río Sereno has the air of a cowboy town. The Panamanian businesses are centred around the plaza (including **Banco Nacional** – changes traveller's cheques), and the Costa Rican businesses along a street right on the border. Approaching the village from Volcán, abandoned installations from the era of military government are visible on the right. The bus station is just to the right of the *alto* (stop) sign. Follow the main street left along the plaza to where it ends at a steep road crossing diagonally. This is the border with Costa Rica, otherwise unmarked. Numerous vendors' stalls, especially Sunday during coffee harvest (October to December or January). It is safe to park (and lock) your vehicle in the open area of **Almacén Universal**. Costa Rican shops selling leather goods, a few crafts, clothing, gladly accept US dollars at current rates. Do not miss the upper floor of **Super Universal** and **Supermercado Xenia**.

> *If entering Panama, sell colones here; it will be much more difficult at Volcán or David and rates are worse in Panama City.*

Río Sereno to Paso Canoas

A recently paved winding road runs 50 km south along the Panama side of the border to Paso Canoas, about two to two and a half hours by bus. At Km 41 an impressive cascade over 100 m high pours over a cliff on the left of the Río Chiriquí Viejo below. For information on whitewater rafting on the Río Chiriquí Viejo from

Border Essentials: Panama-Costa Rica

Río Sereno

Crossing to Costa Rica This is a minor international crossing post, recommended because the area is prettier and cooler than Paso Canoas (see page 1172), but only for those using public transport. Private vehicles cannot complete formalities here, and Panamanian tourist cards are not available.

Panamanian immigration Immigration and customs are in the wooden police station visible on the hill north of the main Panamanian street. Departing travellers who have been in Panama for over 30 days should see Essentials for details on exit permits. Those entering Panama with a visa, or from countries which require neither visa nor tourist card, will be admitted; those requiring a tourist card or a visa will be directed to Paso Canoas.

Costa Rican immigration The office is in a new white building at Río Sereno, open 0800-1600 Costa Rican time, Sunday till 1400. Departing travellers who have overstayed their 90-day permit will be directed to Paso Canoas for the required tax payments and fines.

Transport There is a frequent bus service dawn to dusk from David to Río Sereno, 3 hours, US$4, via La Concepción, Volcán, Santa Clara; several minibuses daily Río Sereno-Paso Canoas, 2½ hours, US$2.50. On the Costa Rican side bus from San Vito via Sabalito (see page 1073) to the border.

Breñón during the dry season, see Boquete, Acitivities and tours. There is a good view of the river valley at Km 47, with Volcán Barú visible to the northeast.

Sleeping

Boquete and the Eastern Highlands
p1177, map p1179

Accommodation is difficult to find during the feria.

AL **La Montaña y el Valle – The Coffee Estate Inn**, Jaramillo Arriba, T/F720-2211, www.coffeeestateinn.com. 2.5 km from San Juan Bautista church in Boquete (pass church, turn right at fork, cross river, turn left at intersection, then follow signs), Canadian run, 3 deluxe cottages in 2.5 ha (with kitchen, hot water, spacious), fine views, breakfast and dinner available. DirecTV and freshly roasted coffee from their farm is available to guests. Also **camping** (dry season only) US$10 for 2.

AL **Panamonte**, Av Central, north of town, T720-1327, www.hotelpanamonte.com. With bath, some with kitchen, dinner (US$13.50) is highly recommended, popular, garden has over 200 varieties of orchid, very attractive surroundings, built in 1919 and well maintained, charming, run by the Collins family (Swedish/American), day spa introduced (massages, facials and aromatherapy). Tours available, see below.

A **Tinamou Cottage**, 10 mins from town, T720-3852, habbusdekwie@cwpanama.net. 1 cottage for up to 3 people (1 double, 1 single) set on a private coffee farm. Cost includes breakfast. Perfect for nature lovers. Can arrange pick up in town.

A-C **Cabañas Isla Verde**, convenient location on main street, follow signs posted just before the **Casona Mexicana** restaurant. T/F720-2533, www.escapetoboquete.com/islaverde.htm. 6, 2-storey *cabañas*, 2 'suites' overlooking a small stream and a cheaper room with outside bathroom. Good value with lots of space and in a very relaxing environment. German owner Eva Kipp is friendly and knowledgeable. Discounts available in the low season.

B **Villa Lorena Cabañas**, by bridge near **Panamonte**, T/F720-1848. Comfortable cottages for 4-6 persons, overlooking the Río Caldera.

C Fundadores, Av Central at south end of town, T720-1298, hotfundland@cwp.net.pa. Restaurant, beautiful grounds with stream.

C Hostal Mozart, on the Volcancito road, 5 mins' drive from central Boquete, T720-3764. Charming brightly decorated house with outside patio offering nice views. Friendly owner Lorenza speaks German, English and Spanish. Breakfast and dinners are delicious! **Camping** also available.

C Rebequet, Av A Este y Calle 6 Sur, T/F720-1365.Excellent spacious rooms and cabins around a garden, with bath, TV and fridge, kitchen and eating area for guests' use, popular, friendly and helpful. Recommended.

D Hostal Boquete, just off Calle 4 Sur to left of bridge, T720-2573. clean, TV, terrace and garden overlooking river. Recommended.

D-E Hostal Palacios, Av Central on main plaza, T720-1653. With bath and hot water, cheaper without, basic, use of kitchen. Friendly with good information on hiking. Recommended.

D-E Pensión Topaz, behind Texaco station at south end of town, T/F720-1005. With bath, cheaper without, garden with view of Volcán Barú, small pool, good breakfasts, run by Schöb family (artist/anthropologist), tours arranged, beer garden at the family *finca* during the dry season.

E Pensión Marilós, Av A Este y Calle 6 Sur, opposite **Rebequet**, T720-1380, with bath, hot water, English spoken, very clean and well run, motorcycle parking. Often full but permits sharing, tours organized, stores bags. Recommended.

E Pensión Virginia, main plaza, T692-7171, www.geocities.com/pensionvirginiaboquete. The food and lodging isn't remarkable, but the owners are extremely helpful and speak several languages, internet and laundry service available.

Volcán and around *p1180*

Hotels are often fully booked during holidays. Price categories shown for cottages are for 1 or 2 persons, but most for larger groups for the same price or slightly more.

L Bambito Camping Resort, Bambito, T265-5103. Luxury cottages, also camping in tents (**A**) provided by the resort.

AL Hostal Cielito Sur B&B, 9 km from Volcán, past **Hotel Bambito** but before town of Cerro Punta, T/F771-2038, www.cielitosur.com. A lovely place to stay, personal attention, each room is decorated with artwork from Panama's indigenous groups, delicious country-style breakfast is included. Good information about the area from owners Janet and Glenn Lee.

A Cabañas Dr Esquivel, on the road behind **Supermercado Bérard**, Volcán, T771-4770. Several large houses in a compound, friendly.

A Las Huacas, main street at west end of Volcán,T771-4363. Nice cottages, hot water, clubhouse, elaborate gardens, interesting aviaries, English spoken.

C Cabañas Las Reinas, Volcán, signed from main road, T771-4338. Self-contained units with a kitchen in lawn setting.

C Don Tavo, main street, Volcán, T/F771-5144. Comfortable, garden, private baths, hot water, restaurant, clean, friendly. Recommended.

C Dos Ríos, Volcán, T771-4271. Older wooden building (upper-floor rooms quieter), restaurant, bar, garden with stream, private baths, hot water unreliable.

D Cabañas Señorial, main street at entrance to town, Volcán, T771-4239. Basic, for short-stay couples.

D El Oasis, behind restaurant Calle La Fuente, El Valle, Volcán, T771-4644. Bar can be noisy, owner also rents rooms in her home by **La Fuente** pool.

D La Nona, Calle La Fuente, El Valle, T771-4284. Cabins for up to 5, friendly, good value.

D Motel California, on main street, Volcán, T771-4272. Friendly Croatian owner (Sr Zizic Jr) speaks English, clean private baths, hot water, parking, larger units for up to 7, restaurant, bar, quiet, good but check beds, some are very old and soft.

Cerro Punta *p1181*

AL Cabañas Los Quetzales, T771-2182, www.losquetzales.com, at Guadalupe. A true forest hideaway, 5 self-contained cabins, baths, hot water, no electricity, on a cloud forest reserve at 2020 m, inside Volcán Barú National Park, nearly 100 bird species, including quetzales, visible from porches, streams, trout hatchery, primeval forest, 4WD vehicles only, bit of a hike from parking area, but worth it. Owner Carlos Alfaro, fluent English, can arrange transport or daily cook.

B Hotel Cerro Punta, T720-2020. With 9 simple rooms and a quite good restaurant, just before the turning to La Amistad.
D Pensión Eterna Primavera, in Cerro Punta town. Basic.

Volcán to the border *p1182*
AL The Hartmanns, 1 km beyond the end of the dirt road, Santa Clara, T/F775-5223, www.fincahartmann.com. Have a comfortable wooden cabin available in the woods, no electricity but with bath and hot water. They're also excellent auto mechanics.

Border with Costa Rica *p1182*
D Hotel Los Andes, Río Sereno. Good.

Eating

Boquete and the Eastern Highlands *p1177, map p1179*
₸₸ El Explorador, a 45-min walk from Boquete (past Hotel Panamonte) across from La Montaña and El Valle. Beautiful location, picnic area, children's playground, hammocks, etc, entrance to area, US$1, but free to restaurant (excellent local food, breakfast and dinner), open weekends and holidays only.
₸₸ Palo Alto, past the Hotel Panamonte, cross bridge, take left and 400 m after that on the left. Beautiful country-style decor set beside the gurgling Río Caldera. Lunch and dinner. International fare and good coffee.
₸₸-₸ Restaurante Hotel Panamonte, Av Central, north end of town. Open for breakfast, lunch and dinner. Fantastic meals, pricey but well worth the treat. Quaint and charming, succulent trout, fresh juices and delicious desserts.
₸₸ Sabrosón, on Av Central near church. Good quality and value.
₸₸ Salvatore, Av Central at south end of town. Good Italian and pizza.
₸ Bistrot Boquete, on main street past the Mandarin supermarket. A Boquete hang-out, great atmosphere, menu includes chicken curry salad and *filet mignon*. Excellent brownies. Open Thu-Mon 1100-2200.
₸ Casona Mexicana, Av Central, near Lourdes. Good Mexican food.
₸ La Huaca, near Hotel Panamonte. Serves pizza, US owned.
₸ Los Arcos, Calle 1 Sur ½ block from Av Central. Good seafood, open 1600-0000, popular disco at night.
₸ Los Puentes, just past Da Sandwich Shop, main street diagonal to the Texaco gas station. Great value and excellent typical Panamanian food. Breakfast is good and cheap, best corn tortillas in town!
₸ Lourdes, Av Central. Good spot with an outside terrace, but mixed reports on the food.
₸ Pizzería La Volcánica, Av Central, ½ block from main plaza. Good pizzas and pasta at reasonable prices, popular.
₸ Punto de Encuentro, Av A Este, near Pensión Marilo's. Breakfast only, pancakes, fruit salad and juices.
₸ Santa Fe, east of river, near the *feria* ground. A nice place to watch sporting events on cable. US-owned serving US-style food, nachos, burgers, sandwiches and bar in a nice spot.

Bakeries
Da' Sandwich Shop, main street diagonal to the Texaco gas station. US-style deli sandwiches, large portions, fresh juices and fruit salads. Cheap.
King's, Av B Este near Parque a las Madres, is a particularly good bakery.
Pastelería Alemana, south of the arch at the entrance to town. Delicious coffee and pastries.

Volcán and around *p1180*
₸₸ La Hacienda Restaurant, Bambito, T771-4152. Fresh trout, barbecued chicken. Recommended.
₸ Hotel Don Tavo, Volcán. Restaurant in hotel, serving pizza and local dishes.
₸ La Luna, 4 km on the road to Cerro Punta in Paso Ancho. Good Chinese food.
₸ Lizzy's, near post office, Volcán. Fast food, English spoken.
₸ Lorena, on road to Río Sereno. Tables on porch. Good fish brought from coast daily.
₸ Marisquería El Pacífico, main road east of main intersection, Volcán. Recommended.

Border with Costa Rica *p1182*
₸₸ Bar Universal, Río Sereno. Recommended for fried chicken with plantain chips (family atmosphere during the day, more raucous Sat pm and on pay day during the coffee harvest).
₸₸ Sr Eli, top end of the Costa Rican street. Unnamed restaurant, serving good food, friendly and helpful.

Entertainment

Volcán and around *p1180*

Weekend discos at **Eruption** and **Kalahari**, rustic, good places to meet young locals.

Festivals and events

Boquete and the Eastern Highlands *p1177, map p1179*

Jan Feria de las Flores y del Café is a 2-week-long festival (starts 2nd week of Jan) highlighting Boquete's abundance of exotic and colorful flowers. This time of year coffee harvesting season is in full swing and the fair exhibits coffee and coffee-based products. Vendors come from all over Central America to sell their wares. Lodgings fill up, so make reservations in advance.

28 Nov Independence from Spain. Boquete erupts in a day-long parade hosting marching bands of schools from all over Panama.

Volcán and around *p1180*

Dec Feria de las Tierras Altas is held during the 2nd week of Dec in La Fuente Park, with rodeo, dancing, crafts fair and many other attractions.

Activities and tours

Boquete and the Eastern Highlands *p1177, map p1179*

River rafting

Chiriqui River Rafting, Av Central, next to Lourdes, T720-1505, www.panama-rafting.com. Open 0830-1730. Bilingual father-and-son team Héctor and Ian Sánchez, offer 4-hr Class III and IV trips with modern equipment on Río Chiriquí, US$75-90 per person. They can arrange lodging and transport to starting-point or vehicle delivery to landing point. During dry season, Dec-Apr, they arrange trips on Río Chiriquí Viejo (Class III/IV Technical, US$90-100). Recommended.

Panama Rafters, just below the square on Av Central, T/F720-2712, www.panama rafters.com. Good, solid rafting operation with quality gear, guides and a strong emphasis on safety. Kayak and multi-day trips are available, but most trips are run on the excellent Río Chiriquí Viejo. Half day on the Class III Harpia section US$75, full day on the Class IV Jaguar section US$90.

Tour operators

Feliciano Tours, T624-9940, provides tours and transport of the area US$20-US$60. Good for those needing guidance on trails of the area, some English spoken.

Hiking/Birdwatching Tours, T720-3852. Run by Terry Van Niekerk, who speaks English, Spanish and Dutch, and provides hiking and birdwatching tours of the area surrounding Boquete. Highly recommended for the **Los Quetzales** hike (5 hrs) which also includes transport back from Cerro Punta to Boquete (2 hrs). Tours include fresh coffee and snacks and some include a light breakfast. Prices from US$20-US$60 per person depending on tour.

Hiking Tours, Av A Ote on road to cemetery, T/F720-2726. Friendly and helpful owner Sr Bouttet arranges guided tours in the area including Volcán Barú, Cerro Punta (around US$50 per day for a group of up to 3) and can give advice on where to stay overnight.

Hotel Panamonte, Av Central, north end of town, organizes day trips to Volcán Barú, birdwatching and coffee plantations, US$150 for a group of up to 4.

Sr Frank Glavas at Pensión Marilo's, Av A Este y Calle 6 Sur, organizes guides and trips throughout the area.

Transport

Boquete and the Eastern Highlands *p1177, map p1179*

Bike and scooter Estate Office-Gringo's Scooter Hire, Av Central near park. Infomation on hiking, bike hire (US$2.50/hr, US$10/day 8 hrs), scooter hire (US$6.50/hr, US$20/day), pay deposit.

Bus Local buses depart from the main plaza, called El Parque, old fashioned and pretty, every 20 mins to **Volcán** (US$1.65), **David** (US$0.50), and **Paso Canoas** (US$0.75).

10 buses daily to **Panama City** via David with **Padafront**, US$11, 7 hr; terminal beside Delta petrol station next to El Sótano restaurant, east of Volcán intersection on Pan-American Highway, T770-4485.

◐ Directory

Boquete and the Eastern Highlands *p1177, map p1179*
Banks Global Bank, Mon-Fri, 0800-1500, Sat 0800-1500 changes TCs with a commission of US$1 per cheque. Same hours at **Banco Nacional** and **Banolar**, on the main street, who will both cash TCs. **Internet** Oasis Internet, near Pastelería Alemán; **Kelnix**, beside Chiriquí River Rafting, T720-2803, daily 0800-2000, US$1.80/hr. **Laundry** Lavomático Las Burbujas, just south of church, very friendly, US$1 to wash. **Post office** In the Palacio Municipal.

Volcán and around *p1180*
Banks Banco Nacional and Banco de Istmo, Mon-Fri 0800-1500, Sat 0800-1200, both change dollar TCs. **Internet** Sinfonet, in Hotel Don Tavo, US$1 per hr, friendly and helpful. Hardware store **Ferremax**, main road opposite police station, T771-4461, sends and receives international faxes, 0700-1200, 1400-1800, US$1.50 per page plus telephone charge, English spoken. **Laundry** Lava mático Volcán, main road opposite Jardín Alegría dancehall. Service only US$2.50, wash, dry and fold, reliable, Doña Miriam will have washing ready when promised.

Northwest coast

Panama's Caribbean banana-growing region has historical links with Columbus' fourth voyage and with the black slaves imported to work the plantations. Ports of varying age and activity lie on the Laguna de Chiriquí, providing an alternative land route to Costa Rica. This region is subject to heavy rainfall which may be daily afternoon downpours or violent tropical storms. Only from January to March is there much respite from the regular soakings. ➤➤ *For Sleeping, Eating and other listings, see pages 1191-1197.*

Towards Laguna de Chiriquí

From Chiriquí on the Pan-American Highway, 14 km east of David, there is a road north over the mountains to Chiriquí Grande (98 km). Beyond Gualaca the road passes the Fortuna hydroelectric plant, the Cricamola Indigenous Reservation and descends through virgin rainforest to the Caribbean. On the way up the hill, just north of Valle de la Mina is **Mary's**, a simple restaurant. If travelling under your own steam you can stop to admire the views across Lago Fortuna resevoir, from where the road is a tough, steep and twisting climb to the the continental divide, 62 km from the Pan-American Highway, and marked by nothing more than an altitude marker sign.

There is a 10-m waterfall 2.5 km north of the divide. Going north from the continental divide to Chiriquí Grande is a cyclist's delight – good road, spectacular views, little traffic and downhill all the way, but nowhere to eat until Punta Pena, just outside Chiriquí Grande. The road reaches the sea at **Chiriquí Grande**, once the embarkation point for travellers catching the ferry to Almirante and beyond, but now, with the new road heading north, rarely visited.

Banana coast

Fifty kilometres north of Chiriquí Grande one of Central America's most important banana-growing regions extends from **Almirante** northwest across the border to Costa Rica. Today Almirante is a small commercial port, usually just a transit point for tourists heading to or from the Bocas archipelago. The banana railway starts/ends here. In the 1940s and 50s, disease virtually wiped out the business and plantations were converted to *abacá* and cacao. With the development of disease resistant strains of banana, the *abacá* and cacao have been all but replaced, and banana plantations once again thrive. The main players in the industry are large multinational companies. **Cobanat**, who export through **Chiquirí Land Company** (a subsidiary of **Chiquita Brands**) and **Dole** (a subsidiary of **Standard Brands**), who export bananas to

Europe and the US from Almirante. In April 1991 a devastating earthquake struck northwest Panama and southeast Costa Rica. An island in the bay which sank during the earthquake now shows as nothing more than a patch of shallow turquoise water.

Isla Colón and Bocas del Toro

▸▸ pp1191-1197. Colour map 7, B5.

Across the bay are the rainforest, reefs and beaches of the **Bocas Islands**, the most important of which is **Isla Colón**. The protected bay offers all forms of watersport and diving, beautiful sunrises and sunsets. All the islands harbour plenteous

Bocas del Toro

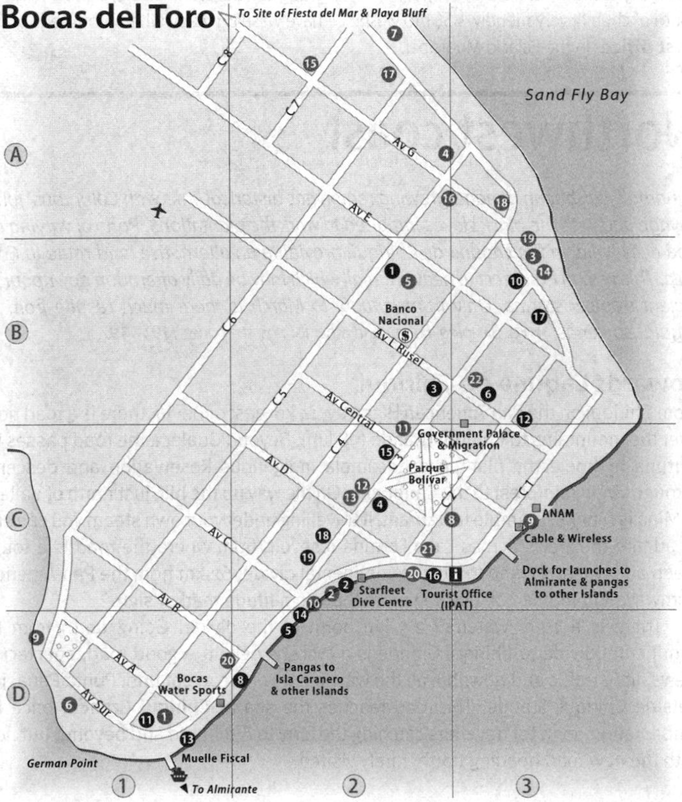

N

0 metres 100
0 yards 100

Sleeping
Bahía 1 *D1*
Bocas del Toro 2 *C2*
Bocas Inn Lodge 3 *B3*
Casa Amarilla 4 *A2*
Cala Luna 5 *B2*
Cayos Zapatillas 12 *C2*
Cocomo-on-the-Sea 7 *A2*
Del Parque 8 *C2*
Dos Palmas 9 *D1*
El Limbo 10 *C2*
Heike 11 *C2*
Hospedaje E & L 20 *D1*
Hotelito del Mar 21 *C2*
La Casbah 19 *B3*
Laguna 13 *C2*
Las Brisas 14 *B3*
La Veranda 15 *A2*
Los Delfines 16 *A2*
Lula's B&B 17 *A2*
Mondo Taitu 18 *A3*
Olas de la Madrugada 6 *D1*
Swan's Cay 22 *B3*

Eating
Alberto's 1 *B2*
Big Bamboo Bar & Grill 11 *D1*
Buena Vista Bar & Grill 2 *C2*
Café Olga 17 *B3*
Chitre 18 *C2*
Cocina del Mar 2 *C2*
El Lorito Don Chicho 3 *B2*
El Pecado 4 *C2*
El Pirate 5 *D2*
Helados Bocatoreños 19 C2
Kun Jah 14 D2
La Ballena 6 *B3*
Lily's Café 16 *C2*
Mc Douglas Golden Grill 15 *C2*
Om Café 12 *B3*
Pargo Rojo 10 *B3*
Reef 13 *D1*
Starfish Coffee 8 *D2*

Bars & clubs
Barco Hundido 9 *C3*
Iguana 20 *C2*

wildlife but especially those east of Colón where tropical birds, butterflies, red, yellow and orange frogs and a great variety of other wildlife abounds. For some, this is being called the new Galápagos, but, as in that fragile paradise, attraction and concern walk hand in hand. Formerly a major banana producer, the industry failed to revive alongside the mainland plantations and the main sources of income are now fishing and tourism. Bocas del Toro town, where most visitors stay, is on the southeast tip of the island. Most activity takes place around the broad main street – Calle 3 – and the leafy square. The **Feria del Mar** is at the end of September/early October, but for most of the rest of the year it is peaceful and quiet, although more hotels are appearing each year. English is spoken by most of the black population. At the **tourist office** ⓘ *on the seafront, T757-9642, www.bocas.com, daily 0830-1630*, there is an informative permanent exhibit, with English translations, about Columbus' landfall, indigenous peoples in the province, the fire at Bocas in 1904 and the United Fruit Company years.

Bocas del Toro and Bastimentos are two of the most rapidly developing places in Cental America.

Islands and island trips

Trips can be made to the islands of the archipelago (Bastimentos – see below, **Caranero** and **Solarte** – also known as Nancy); to the bird sanctuary of **Swan Cay (Isla del Cisne)**; and to the beautiful **Islas Zapatillas**, for beaches and fishing.

On Isla Colón there are some attractive beaches: **Playa Bluff**, 8-9 km northwest of Bocas, is one hour by bike; take the paved road out of town past the cemetery until it runs out and then carry straight on following the shoreline; **Playa Boca del Drago**, on the northwest point, is reached by a newly improved road across the island. Regular buses head over to **Boca del Drago** daily, leaving from the main square in town. This is a little-visited part of the island. Behind the beach there's a good restaurant and a cheap hostel. A local conservation project has an office here and it might be possible to hire dive and snorkel gear.

Do not go to deserted stretches of beach alone; if you do go, be wary of strong ocean currents.

Opposite Bocas, 200 m across the channel, is the small island of **Caranero**, reached by *panga* either flagged down from a waterfront restaurant/bar, or boarded at the small quay just beyond **Le Pirate** or **Taxi 25's** quay next to the tourist office.

A 15-minute boat ride from Bocas town, the quiet island of **Solarte** is a very quiet retreat and good for day trips. For those into frogs, **Hospital Point** (good snorkelling) is the orange frog hangout.

The **National Marine Park** ⓘ *tours US$15-20 per person, US$75 per boat, 0900-1600, entry to the Cayos Zapatillas section of the park is US$10 extra, see Tour operators, page 1196*, on **Isla Bastimentos** encompasses virtually the whole island, bar the small town of Bastimentos on the western tip. Both this island and Isla Colón are turtle-nesting grounds and their protection is being improved with the help of organiatzions like **Caribaro**, on Calle 3, who set up beach patrols. There is snorkelling and a lunch stop at Cayo Crawl. Many tour boats also visit **Laguna Bocatorito** (no snorkelling), part of Isla Cristóbal, to view dolphins before going on to the Zapatillas Cays in the park. Colón also has **La Gruta del Drago**, a cave occupied by long-beaked white bats, which fly out at dusk (tour US$10 plus US$5 for lunch on beach). You can walk to the cave, a pleasant day, but ask locals for directions and advice on safety.

On **Bastimentos** it's a 30-minute walk to northern beaches with soft off-white sand and strong undertow; ask directions, take food and drink, or ask if anywhere is open selling meals. **Red Frog Beach** is the best known; it has a strong rip tide (there

Many of the names relate to Columbus' landfall here on his fourth voyage in October 1502 (Carenero was where he careened his ships, Bastimentos where he took on supplies). The islands also have a rich buccaneering history.

have been three drownings in recent years), but **Polo's Beach** (with red-and-black frog accompaniment) is also recommended – look out for sloths and monkeys. **Playa Larga**, halfway along the north shore, is best reached by boat, as is nearby Polo's Beach. The Ngobe indigenous community of Bahiá Honda on the South Side of Bastimentos have recently opened a restaurant and small ecotourism project the **'Trail of the Sloth'**, which involves a dugout canoe trip and hike through the rainforest to a cave that plays host to an important bat colony. The restaurant offers traditional food in addition to the more common Panamanian dishes. For more information call T603-1857 (mob), or check the website bocas.com/indians/bahiahonda.htm.

Bastimentos village is a stilted, ramshackle, wooden affair clinging to a steep slope on the leeward side of the island. Tourism once skirted round it, helping the place hold on to its old-style Caribbean charm; now a few smart places are opening up, but it is still very quiet.

Cayos Zapatillas Norte is the quieter of the two Zapatillas because the tour boats do not generally stop here.

Isla Popa and **Cayo Agua**, the other main islands in the area, are sparsely settled, heavily forested and have no beaches.

Diving

Several places throughout the archipelago are popular for diving. The joy of diving in Bocas lies in the details, with some wonderful intact coral gardens (74 out of 79 Caribbean coral species exist here) that seem to play host to a multitude of little gems. Brittle stars, spotted morays, arrow crabs, toadfish and squid are just some of the inhabitants you can expect to see, along with most of the common Caribbean reef fish. Occasionally larger grouper, rays and nurse sharks also put in an appearance.

Good dive sites include: **Tiger Rock** with stronger currents, deeper dives, larger fish and sometimes nurse and whitetip reef sharks; dolphin and wash rocks with rock pinnacles, overhangs and caverns and **La Gruta Polo** with good coral, canyons and caverns. **Hospital Point** is popular for both day and night dives. Several good locations near the resort for scuba diving and for snorkelling in the clear waters around **Mangrove Point**.

Cavern diving at **Polo's Beach**, only in calm sea, **Punta Vieja** on the northeast shore of Bastimentos and boat dives at **Cayos Zapatillas**.

The best **snorkelling** sites are **Hospital Point** on Cayo Nancy, **Punta Vieja**, **Islas Zapatillas**, but only outside the reef – tour boats will just drop you off at North Cay for snorkelling off the beach (points en route on tours are also disappointing – **Cayo Crawl** has two great sites with very colourful coral, known as Cayo Crawl Inside and Outside, referring to reefs several hundred meters offshore to the east and west – the area directly around the island is seagrass only; hire a boat and guide from one of the dive shops to see the best of the reef. Some areas, such as the islands around the entrance to **Laguna Bocatorito**, harbour habitats were large coral and sponge colonies run right up to the edges of the mangroves creating the unique and fascinating ecosystem. These areas are as a beautiful as they are fragile and require great caution to avoid damaging the reef and its inhabitants, so if not experienced and confident with your snorkelling ability it's best to leave these areas alone and stick to corals in deeper water.

Surfing

The break on the point of Bastimentos where the island curves away from Carenero to meet First Beach (or Playa Wizard) is the renowned and occasionally terrifying (reaching up to 25 ft) **Silver Back**, which attracts surfers from around the globe (peaks December to February).

Playa Bluff is a good beach break, **Playa Paunch** is mostly reef, both are excellent breaks on Colón, and the northeast point of **Caranero**, a full reef, and the most popular of the island breaks. ▸▸ *For board rental, see page 1196.*

Towards Costa Rica » pp1191-1197.

Changuinola

Between Almirante and the Costa Rica border is sprawling Changuinola, the main commercial centre in the region which, although architecturally not attractive, has an airport and lively nightlife with local bars. Changuinola is good for shopping (the food markets are great) if you are planning on staying on the islands for some time, there are also several banks where you can change traveller's cheques and use ATMs. Visitors should take care going out at night here; women should be particularly careful (women alone will almost certainly be approached if they enter bars, and maybe on the street). Excursions can be made to Naso/Teribe indigenous villages. **Wekso Ecolodge** is reached by taxi to El Silencio (US$5), then launch on Río Teribe (US$30 per boat, or US$5 on local boat). Organize in advance through **ODESEN** (National Organization for Sustainable Ecotourism Development) ⓘ *T620-0192, www.ecotour.org/destinations/wekso.htm.*

Sleeping

Towards Laguna de Chiriquí *p1187*

B **Finca La Suiza**, on the southern side of the Fortuna Reserve, Quadrifoglio, T6615-3774 (in David) www.panama.net.tc. Owned by a Swiss couple, Herbert Brüllmann and Monika Kohler, excellent for birdwatching on 20 km of forest trails, very good food, comfortable accommodation with bath and hot water, breakfast US$3.50, dinner US$8.50. To get there from Gualaca: pass the sign to Los Planes (16.4 km) and the turning to Chiriquicito; 300 m after this junction is the sign for the Fortuna Reserve, 1 km beyond the sign is the gate to the Finca on the right.

D **Pensión Emperador**, Chiriquí Grande, T757-9656. With balconies overlooking the wharf. Clean and friendly.

E **Buena Vista**, Chiriquí Grande, T756-9726. Friendly, breakfast available, shared baths

Bocas del Toro Archipelago

Banana coast *p1187*

D-E San Francisco, Almirante. A/c or fan, small dark rooms, overpriced.

E Albergue Bahía, Almirante, T778-9211. Clean, friendly owner, will store belongings.

Isla Colón and Bocas del Toro *p1188*

AL Bocas del Toro, Calle 2 y Av C, T/F757-9018, www.hotelbocasdeltoro.com. On the seafront, large clean rooms, some with excellent sea views.

AL Cocomo-on-the-Sea, Av Norte y Calle 6, Bocas del Toro, T/F757-9259, www.panamainfo.com/cocomo. 4 rooms on the seafront with a/c, private bathroom, huge breakast included, simple and clean, home-cooked meals, book swap. US owner Douglas is very helpful. Sundeck and free use of 2 kayaks. Good.

AL El Limbo, on the front street next to Bocas del Toro, T757-9062, www.ellimbo.com. Great location overlooking the channel between Isla Colón and Carenero. Good but pricey restaurant, businesslike rooms with a/c, TV, fridge. Rooms with balconies are better.

AL La Estrella de Bocas, Calle 1, T757-9011, www.bocas.com/estrella.htm. Attractive and immaculate hotel. Accommodation ranges from apartments with fully equipped kitchen and rooms with a/c, cable TV and private bath.

AL Swan's Cay, opposite the municipal building on main street, Bocas del Toro, T757-9090, www.swanscayhotel.com. Pricey and upkarket, 2 restaurants, internet, laundry, swimming pool in 2nd building on the seafront.

AL-D Las Brisas, Bocas, on the sea at north end of the main street (formerly **Botel Thomas**), T/F757-9549, hotel_lasbrisas@yahoo.com. Wooden building on stilts with nice veranda over the sea. Cheaper rooms upstairs have private bath and fan, good but the occasional cockroach and thin walls. Downstairs rooms are more expensive rooms have a/c, cable TV and some have fridge. They have fully equipped rooms with kitchenettes.

AL-E Hotel La Rumba, 1.5 km out of town at Big Creek, T757-9961. Rooms of varying sizes and facilities in a round, thatched hotel, with restaurant and bar overlooking the sea. Games, happy hours and satellite showing sport.

A Hotelito del Mar, Calle 1, T757-9861, www.hotelitodelmar.com. A recent edition to Isla Colón, very friendly owner, sparkling clean rooms, all very conventional with private bath, hot water and a/c. Good central location. Tours arranged.

A-B Bahía, south end of main street, Bocas, T757-9626. Building formerly the HQ of the **United Fruit Company** built in 1905, remodelled rooms with balcony are more expensive, all rooms with hot water, TV and a/c, laundry service available and restaurant in front.

A-B Bocas Inn Lodge, north end of Main St, Bocas, T757-9600, bocasinn@anconexpeditions.com. Run by tour operator Ancon Expeditions (see page 1142), comfortable and simple with pleasant, spacious bar and terrace and communal veranda upstairs, good platform for swimming. Water heated with solar panels, Crab and lobster off the menu due to overfishing concerns.

A-B Laguna, on main street with Av D, T757-9091, www.hotellaguna.net. Breakfast terrace and bar.

A-B Los Delfines, Av G y Calle 5, Bocas, T/F757-9963, www.posadalosdelfines.com. Clean, reasonable-sized rooms with cable TV and a/c. Restaurant.

A-B Punta Manglar (formerly **Mangrove Point**), T/F757-9541, www.puntamanglar.com. Cabins sleeping 2-8 set amongst the mangroves and accessible by boat – the hotel offers dive courses up to dive master and fun dives.

B Cala Luna, behind **Alberto's Restaurant**, Calle 5 and Av E, Bocas, T757-9066, calaluna@cwp.net.pa. A hidden gem in the backstreets. Rooms are spacious with a very appealing, sparse, almost Japanese style. Same owners as **Alberto's**.

B Lula's B&B, Av Norte, across street from Cocomo on the Sea, T757-9057, www.lulabb.com. Old style and homely with huge kitchen and living area downstairs, continental breakfast included. All rooms with a/c and private bath, family-run. Recommended.

B-C Casa Amarilla, Calle 5 y Av G, Bocas, behind Mondo Taitu, T757-9938, dennis@cwp.net. 4 Large airy rooms with good beds, a/c, fridge, digital safe and large cable TV. Owner lives upstairs and is very helpful. Free coffee and fruits in the morning – good value. Recommended.

B-C Hotel La Veranda, Calle 7, Av G, 1 block after **Supermarket Ahorros**, T757-9211, laverandapanama.tripod.com. Beautiful wooden, original Bocas-style house, rooms come with private or shared bath and hot water – feels like home. Large veranda on 1st floor has a communal kitchen and a spacious area to eat or relax.

C Del Parque, seaward side of square, Bocas, T757-9008. Well-kept old town house with light rooms and good beds, hot water, free coffee and fruit. Discounts in low season.

C Dos Palmas, Av Sur y Calle 6, Bocas, T757-9906. Quaint with lots of local charm, built over water, a/c, cheaper with fan, clean, swim off platform at back, free coffee before midday.

C Hotel Olas de la Madrugada, Av Sur, T757-9930, www.hotelolas.com. New and already popular hotel built over the water. Clean and bright rooms, all with a/c, cable TV and private hot water shower, good for the price. Friendly owners are opening a bar and restaurant, they also have jet-ski and wake-board rental.

D Hotel Cayos Zapatillas, on the High St, odd-looking building overlooking the park. Good rooms, very reasonably priced for location and with private hot water shower and cable TV. Laundry service.

D Sagitarius, 1 block from main street on Av D, Bocas, T757-9578. With hot water, bath, a/c, cheaper with fan, TV. Clean and good.

D-E Hospedaje E & L, Main St, T757-9206. Friendly, budget accommodation, conveniently located, cold water, shared kitchen available.

D-E Heike, on main square, Bocas, T757-9708. 9 rooms, shared bathrooms, kitchen for lodgers and a communal veranda. Inexpensive, friendly and highly recommended.

E La Casbah, Bocas. Not too clean but cheap, very local, and overlooking the water.

E Mondo Taitu, Bocas, T757-9425. Cheap surfers' hostel at far end of island near **Hotel Las Brisas**. Good place to meet other travellers. Good kitchen, dorms and some private rooms, shared hot water bath, apartment with private bath for couples and a cool little bar tucked in at the back.

Islands and island trips *p1189*

L-AL Al Natural, Old Point, Bastimentos, T/F757-9004, alnaturalbocas@cwpanama.net. Belgian-owned eco-lodge bungalows using traditional techniques and native fallen trees – electricity provided by solar power. Bungalows consist of 3 walls, leaving 1 side open and exposed to a spectacular view of the ocean and Zapatillas Keys in the distance – a truly natural experience. Price includes transport from Isla Colón, 3 meals with wine, use of kayaks and snorkelling gear. Highly recommended.

L-AL Careening Cay Resort, Isla Carenero – facing Isla Colón, T757-9157, www.careeningcay.com. Cottages in a tranquil, well-manicured location, some equipped with gas stove, microwave and fridge, others without, all with a/c and sleep 1-6. Their **Sunset Grill** restaurant serves dinner Tue-Sun.

AL Coral Cay, east of Bastimentos island, T626-1919, www.bocas.com/coralcay.htm. Rustic cabins built over the water. Beautiful surroundings and outstanding seafood. Price includes 2 meals per day, snorkelling equipment and the use of a traditional dugout canoe. Watch out for the sandflies.

AL Solarte del Caribe, Isla Solarte (Cayo Nancy), T6593-2245, www.solarteinn.com, B&B on the southern side. Comfortable beds, colorful, tropical surroundings and good food. Breakfast and roundtrip transport included.

AL-A Buccaneer Resort, on the east side of Isla Caranero, T/F757-9042, www.buccaneer-resort.com. High-end suites and cabinas, all with a/c on the beach. Breakfast included.

A Acuario, Isla Caranero, T757-9565. Nicely situated on a pontoon, rooms come with direct TV, a/c and balconies over the water, there is a kitchen and bar, American owned.

A-B Hotel Tierra Verde, Isla Carenero. T757-9903, www.hoteltierraverde.com. Well-maintained hotel situated among the palms a stone's throw from the shore. Rooms have private showers and hot water, internet use available.

B Caribbean View Hotel, Bastimentos Town, T757-9442, www.bocas.com/caribbean-view.htm. Wooden, traditional-style hotel, with lovely local owners, upmarket for the rustic Bastimentos Town. Rooms available with a/c or fan, all have private shower and hot water and TV. There is a communal deck over the water.

C-D Hotel Bastimentos, Bastimentos Town. An elevated position overlooking the town, islands and surrounding waters. Attractive budget accommodation, with shared dorms and private rooms with showers. Communal kitchen and TV, friendly owners.

D-E Pensión Tío Tom, Bastimentos Town, T757-9831, www.tio-tom.com. Rustic, budget accommodation on the water, rooms with mosquito nets and private bath. Chilled vibe, friendly and helpful owners who also run the internet café a couple of doors down. Recommended.

Changuinola *p1191*
C Alhambra, on the main street (Calle 17 de Abril), T758-9819. Large rooms, hot water TV, a/c, telephone.
C Semiramis, diagonally opposite the Alhambra, T758-6006. Dark rooms with outstandingly kitsch pictures, a/c, TV, restaurant serving Chinese plus standard Panamanian food.
D Taliali, 150 m from bus station, set back from Calle 17 de Abril. A/c, TV, hot water.
D-E Carol, T758-8731, 200 m from bus station. With bath, hot water, a/c (cheaper rooms without), TV, small dark rooms, restaurant next door same ownership.

Eating

Towards Laguna de Chiriquí *p1187*
¥ **Café**, Chiriquí Grande. Good.
¥ **Dallys**, Chiriquí Grande, to right of wharf. Popular.

Isla Colón and Bocas del Toro *p1188*
¥¥¥ **Cocina del Mar**, next to Buena Vista. Very pricey, but top-end seafood cuisine, with views of the bay.
¥¥¥ **La Ballena**, next to Swan Cay Hotel, Bocas. Bit pricey but delicious Italian seafood pastas and cappuccinos, good for breakfast and tables outside.
¥¥¥-¥¥ **Bongos**, main street. Slightly overpriced American-style food.
¥¥¥-¥¥ **El Pecado**, on southwest corner of parque, Bocas. Panamanian and intenational food including Lebanese, one of the best restaurants in town, not too expensive. Great drinks and good wines worth splashing out on, also try their early evening hummous with warm Johnny Cakes (coconut bread).
¥¥ **Alberto's Restaurant**, Calle 5, Bocas. Great pizza, pasta and lasagne, reasonable prices.
¥¥ **Bar y Restaurante Le Pirate**, Calle 3, next to El Limbo Hotel, Bocas. Outstanding lobster for very reasonable prices. Built over the water, full bar, mixed drinks and happy hour.
¥¥ **Big Bamboo Bar and Grill**, next to Super Gourmet opposite ferry pier. A diverse mix of Caribbean cuisine, grills, burgers, hummous, fish and chips, some excellent dishes, others a little too heavy on the oil. Show movies and sports on a big screen, and host live music.
¥¥ **Boca Bills**, main street. Caribbean and local food, they also rent DVDs.
¥¥ **Pargo Rojo**, new location opposite Hotel Las Brisas. Long-standing Iranian chef Bernard has finally moved his restaurant from Carenero to Bocas, bringing his excellent culinary delights to town. The new premises, in a recently renovated building overlooking the street, are very attractive and the restaurant has already had great reviews. Recommended.
¥¥ **Restaurant Claudios at Hotel Laguna**, opposite the park in main street. Reasonably priced, good Italian food, pizzas and pastas are home- made. Big breakfast menu.
¥¥ **Shelly's BBQ Mexican Food**, located behind Claudios, T757-9779. First Mexican eatery in Bocas, enchiladas, mole, guacamole and barbecued meats. They also do home delivery (plus taxi cost) and sell a range of frozen specials in Bocas's Super Gourmet store.
¥¥ **Starfish Coffee**, new coffee shop on Calle 3, just before Bocas Water Sports, Bocas. Cappuccino, pastries, croissants and brownies. Excellent breakfast deals at reasonable prices. Owner offers yoga classes in the morning for US$5 and tours of their environmentally friendly coffee plantation on the mainland on request.
¥¥ **The Reef**, end of main street, opposite Super Gourmet. Local food with seafood specials, cocktail bar with terrace over the water.
¥¥-¥ **Helados Bocatoreños**, main street. Ice cream delights till 2200, also breakfasts, toasts, eggs and fruit salads and juices.
¥¥-¥ **Kalamazu**, located at La Feria, Saigon. Soulful restaurant serves home-made Caribbean fish and vegetarian cuisine, and fantastic home-made desserts – this is food cooked with love and care.
¥ **American And Caribbean Food To Go**, main street, opposite Taxi Marítimo. Sandwiches, subs, chose your own fillings, great for days out and beach tour picnics.
¥ **Buena Vista Bar and Grill**, Bocas. Long-standing American-style sports bar, shows games on direct TV, run by very friendly

Panamanian and his American girlfriend. Good menu for both bar snacks and main meals, grills, tacos, fish and vege options. Nice spot over the water to relax and chat with a beer or cocktail.

Café Olga, opposite Hotel Las Brisas. Good budget local food, rice and beans and the daily special.

El Lorito Don Chicho, main street, Bocas. Most popular – and oldest – local café in town, cheap, good dishes and cakes. Ask for the delicious pudding – unique to Bocas – and their malted milkshakes.

Kun Jah, close to Hotel Limbo. Very reasonable Chinese food, huge plates – fried rice, noodles, sweet 'n' sour, etc, good food, great for those on a budget. Terrace over the water.

Lily's Café, next to Tropical Suites Hotel. Caribbean food with a health food twist, pastas, soups, salads and sandwiches, open for breakfast and lunch only.

Mc Douglas Golden Grill, opposite park, main street. The fast-food emporium of Bocas – burgers, chips and hotdogs, cheap. Also pizzas with loads of cheese, and breakfast eggs and pancakes – good for those on a budget, but not on a diet.

Om Café, now located over Flow Surf Shop, close to La Ballena. Excellent, home-made Indian food served in very relaxing and ambient surroundings. Tables are available on the balcony or private rooms for larger parties. Om also serves good breakfasts with home-made granola and yoghurt, lassis, fruit salads and bagels. Recommended. Closed Wed.

Restaurant Chitre, main street. Best *fonda* in town, good, local food, nice owners, and good spot for watching street traffic.

Islands and island trips *p1189*

Pickled Parrot, Carenero. Bar and restaurant. Draft beers and American BBQs, happy hr 1500-1700 every day. Lovely spot at sunset, facing Bastimentos Island.

Blue Marble, next to Roots, on the water in Bastimentos. Breakfasts, sandwiches, salads, cakes and pastries and an endless list of teas. Friendly people, great spot to chill in the afternoon with a cup of tea and slice of cake. Owners also run island biological tours, including night tours.

Restaurant Doña Mara, Carenero. Excellent seafood and typical Panamanian food.

Roots, Bastimentos village, just east of the centre. Bar and restaurant with a nice terrace, run by Oscar who will also guide tourists to visit the lake in the middle of the island.

Entertainment

Isla Colón and Bocas del Toro *p1188*

Bars and clubs

Barco Hundido, Calle 1, next to Cable & Wireless office, Bocas. Thatched-roof watering hole, affectionately known as the Wreck Deck (its original name) built over the water and above a wrecked, sunken boat. Lights illuminate the boat at night making it a perfect spot to watch the local marine life *and* the local nightlife! *The* place to hang out, dancing, Caribbean scene, mixed drinks, good music and on occasion – at the owners whim – 'pizza and movie night.'

The Blue Nasty Mermaid (at Piña Colada), Main St. Big deck over the water, happy hours and sushi.

Bocas Beach Club, on the waterfront near the firestation. New, very large and looks completely out of place in the town. Despite the fact it has a wooden 'effect', the huge neon guitar that adorns its frontage is not at all Bocas style. Inside, upstairs is a vast nightclub and bar, downstairs a shopping mall, and high-class bar and restaurant.

El Encanto, Main St. The only truly local spot, they play salsa at volume and have a pool hall.

Iguana Bar, Bocas. New smart establishment, surf videos and gringos, good music, another pre-Barco spot.

Mondo Taitu, Bocas, T757-9425. Relaxed, good for cocktails and for warming up for the Barco Hundido or Blue Monday (see Islands and island trips, below).

Islands and island trips *p1189*

Every Mon anyone who wants to party heads over to Isla Bastimentos to Blue Mondays, a largely local event with live Calypso music and the full Caribbean vibe. Hugely popular.

Activities and tours

Isla Colón and Bocas del Toro *p1188*

Diving and snorkelling

Starfleet, near tourist office, T/F757-9630, www.starfleetscuba.com, have years of experience in the Bocas waters, German and

Dutch spoken, PADI course US$200, discounts for cash and groups, US50.00 for 2 dives for qualified divers, snorkel trips, US$15. Good instructors, equipment and safety.

Bocas Watersports, T757-9541, www.bocaswatersports.com, on Calle 3. Dive courses, water skiing and kayak rental. Night dives run at US$50, with longer 2 tank trips to Tiger Rock and the Zapatilla Cayes running at around US$75. Snorkelling gear can be hired from several places, US$5 a day. Affiliated to the Punta Manglar resort.

Surfing

You can rent boards from a small shop next to **The Yellow House** or in **Mondo Taitu**. There are 2 surf shops in town, **Tropix**, on main street (T757-9415) who make custom boards and **Flow**, located under **Om Café**.

Tour operators

There are now numerous tour operators, so many that you should be able to plan your own day if you have a big enough group and know where you want to go – most operators have maps and pictures of the surrounding islands. Usual tours visit either Dolphin Bay, Hospital Point, Cayo Coral, and Red Frog Beach (Bastimentos), or Boca del Drago and Swans Cay (Bird Island). For a little extra you can add Cayos Zapatilla to the first tour.

Blue Marble Tours, located on Bastimentos, T6632-6269. Very enthusiastic guide, a knowledgeable biologist, offers day- and, unusually, night-time wildlife tours in their jungle grounds on Isla Solarte. Recommended.

Cap'n Don's, T6487-8460, www.capndons.com. Private boat rental, windsurfing equipment, kayaks, hobie cats, pedal boats and snorkeling.

Catamaran Sailing Adventures, main street beyond the **Le Pirate**, T757-9710, movida@cwp.net.pa. Owner Marcel offers popular day sailing tours on his 12-m catamaran around the Bocas Islands. For US$25 he includes lunch and snorkelling gear, and he's very knowledgeable when it comes to finding the best reef areas – you can also hire the whole boat for US$250 and do a customized trip. Marcel has plans to move his office to Isla Carenero in the near future.

J&J and **Transparente Tours**, main street beside **Le Pirate**, T757-9915, transparentetours@hotmail.com, US$20 to Laguna Bocatorito, Cayo Crawl, Zapatillas or Red Frog Beach, and sometimes snorkelling at Hospital Point.

Mouth of the Bull Adventures, T6561-0460, mouthofthebulladventures@yahoo.com, organized or customized adventure tours, snorkelling and jungle tours.

Transport

Towards Laguna de Chiriquí *p1187*

Boat Water taxi from Almirante to **Bocas** US$3. To get to the muelle from bus station, cross over railway line, bear left following far side of fence across scrub land to road, head left along road 2 blocks to the quay.

Bus From Almirante to **David**, every 40 mins, 4 hrs, US$7; **Changuinola**, 30 mins, US$1.

Car The road between Chiriquí Grande and Almirante is in excellent condition for the 74 km length of the new road.

Train See under Changuinola.

Isla Colón and Bocas del Toro *p1188*

Air

Bocas del Toro can be reached by **Aeroperlas** (T757-9341) from Albrook Airport, Panama City (US$58 one-way). To **David** US$32. **Panama Air** (www.turismoaereo.com) and **Nature Air** (Costa Rica, www.natureair.com) now both operate international flights between Bocas del Toro and San José, Costa Rica. US$110 one-way. Call **Bocas International Airport** for more details T757-9841.

Boat

Water taxis to and from **Almirante** daily from 0530-1830, 30 mins minimum, US$3.

Taxi 25 and **Taxi Marítimo**, T757-9033, on Calle 3 next to Le Pirate, offer routes to include Bocas-**Changuinola** (US$7 round trip) via the historic Snyder Canal, a 15 km canal built in the late 1800s to transport bananas from Changuinola to awaiting ships in the open sea. Travellers going to Costa Rica can now avoid going through Almirante in order to catch a bus from Changuinola. The water taxi will drop you off at Finca 63 where you can catch a taxi for a short ride to the bus terminal in Changuinola (US$2) or take a local mini bus that runs approximately every 20 mins (US$0.50) or take a taxi direct to the border (US$5 per person).

Cycle hire
Plenty of bike rentals, and some scooter rentals. US$1.50/hr, US$7.50/day.

Boat
Palanga, the car ferry, runs between **Almirante** and Bocas every day, leaving at 0900 and returning from Bocas at 1200. US$15 per car (more for large vehicles), US$1 foot passengers.

Hire boats or **water taxis** in Bocas del Toro to Bastimentos and the other islands. Boat to **Bastimentos** US$2 per person one-way, ask around Le Pirate Bar or Taxi 25 dock next to IPAT, elsewhere along waterfront. Inter-island boats also go from the water-taxi *muelle*, near the tourist office. From Carenero or Bastimentos town it is easy to flag down a passing boat taxi, however, from more out of the way locations, like beaches on Bastimentos or other islands. Don't forget to arrange a time to be picked up. If hiring a boat, try to arrange it the day before, usually at least US$60 per day, depending on the boatman, 4 hrs minimum, can take 9 people or more, depending on boat size. If going on to Costa Rica from Bocas, get the first water taxi for connections at Sixaola. It is better to travel early if you are headed to Costa Rica; a bus leaves Changuinola direct for San José at 10.00. However, if you are simply going to **Puerto Viejo** or **Cahuita**, you can leave anytime before lunch. The border closes at 1700 and Costa Rica is 1 hr behind Panama.

Costa Rica immigration at the Sixaola border crossing requires you to have proof of a return flight out of the country or back to Panama and will ask to see it. Currently you can buy bus tickets at the border that are sufficient, however Costa Rica are cracking down on their '72 hour' law (you can re-enter the country after leaving for 72 hours) and are toughening up on those foreigners who appear to be 'living' permanently in Costa Rica without official residence.

Towards Costa Rica *p1191*
Changuinola
Air To **David**, daily Mon-Fri, US$32 with Aeroperlas, T758-7521.

Bus
There is a road from Changuinola to **Almirante** (buses every 30 mins till 2000, 30 mins, US$1.25). Bus to **San José** leaves Changuinola 1000 daily (no office – pay on bus) US$8, 6-7 hrs, 1 stop for refreshments in Limón, but many police checks (this bus may not always run). Bus to **David**, 4 hrs, US$7.

Trains
The banana railways provide links between **Guabito** on the Costa Rican border, Changuinola and **Almirante**. No passenger trains, and banana trains are incredibly slow, although passage can be negotiated with officials. Schedules and fares should be checked with the **Chiriquí Land Company**, Almirante T758-3215, should leave for border every day.

Directory

Isla Colón and Bocas del Toro *p1188*
Banks Banco Nacional de Panamá, Calle 4 and Av E, T757-5948, Mon-Fri 0800-1500, Sat 0900-1200, 24-hour ATM machine. At Changuinola: **Banistmo**, same hrs, changes AMEX TCs and cash advances on Visa and MasterCard. **Immigration** Migración office, at the back of the Palacio, is for visitors arriving by air or boat. Official waits at the airport to stamp passports of those arriving nationals covered by the '*convenio*' and to provide tourist cards for others (eg US citizens arriving from Costa Rica; see Visas and immigration page 1114). Those requiring visas must go to the Banco Nacional to purchase the relevant documentation (US$10) and then go to the office in the Palacio. This office does not renew tourist cards or visas (done in Changuinola). **Internet** Don Chicho's Internet, next to El Lorito restaurant, US$2/hr, and **Bocas Internet Café**, next to the M/S Isla Colón Supermarket on the main street, also US$2/hr. **Bravo Centre** is fast and has an international call centre US$2/hr. **Laundry** **Lavamático**, on the right, just beyond Hostal Ancón at north end of town, US$3 per load, wash and dry, pick up following day.

Changuinola *p1191*
Bank Bancistmo. **Immigation** Oficina de Migración for renewal of visas and tourist cards.

Darién

→ Colour map 8, B3.

As one of the great impenetrable wildernesses of the world, crossing the Darién Gap is the dream of many, but not a trip to be undertaken lightly. By all accounts good Spanish, good guides, serious planning and lots of money are essential. If you're looking for an exciting route to Colombia, the river crossings and jungle treks of the Darién are one option; alternatively, you can use use launches and canoes to skip along the Pacific or Caribbean coastline. But neither option is cheap.

East of Chepo the Darién stretches out over a third of the area of Panama and is almost undeveloped. Most villages are accessible only by air, river or on foot. The Pan-American Highway ends at Yaviza; from there, if you want to cross by land to South America, it's on foot through the jungles of Darién.

At the end of 1992, Panama and Colombia revealed a plan to build a road through the Darién Gap, which includes environmental protection. Construction of a previous project had been halted in the 1970s by a lawsuit filed by US environmental groups who feared deforestation, soil erosion, endangerment of indigenous groups and the threat of foot-and-mouth disease reaching the USA. Even if the plan is completed, the Darién Gap road linking Panama with Colombia will not be open for many years, so the usual way of getting to Colombia is by sea or air. It is possible to go overland, but the journey is in fact more expensive than by air – and considerably more dangerous. ▸▸ *For Sleeping, Eating and other listings, see page 1204.*

Towards Colombia

The Pan-American Highway runs east 60 km from Panama City to the sizeable town of **Chepo**. There are no hotels or *pensiones* in Chepo, but if you are stuck there, ask at the fire station, they will be able to find a place for you. There is a document check in Chepo and at one or two other places. From Chepo the highway has been completed as far as **Yaviza** (225 km). It is gravel from Chepo until the last 30 km which are of earth (often impassable in the rainy season).

From **El Llano**, 18 km east of Chepo, a road goes north to the Caribbean coast. After 27 km it passes the **Nusagandi Nature Lodge** in the Pemansky Nature Park. The lodge is in Kuna (Cuna) territory, in an area of mostly primary forest. The coast is reached at Cartí, 20 km from Nusagandi. From here there is access to the Archipiélago de San Blas (see page 1160).

Thirty-five kilometres east of Chepo the Pan-American crosses the Lago Bayano dam by bridge (the land to the north of the highway as far as Cañazas is the **Reserva Indígena del Bayano**). Lago Bayano dam supplies a significant amount of Panama's electricity, and has been a source of friction with the Kuna people who occupy the land around the lake and especially above in the catchment area.

The main villages (Yaviza, Púcuro, Paya and Cristales) have electricity, radios and cassette decks; canned food (but no gasoline) is available in Yaviza, Pinogana, Unión de Chocó, Púcuro and Paya, only the Emberá-Wunan (also spelt Wunaan) of the Chocó and Kuna women retain traditional dress. Organized **jungle tours** to Kuna and Emberá-Wunan villages and the Río Bayano costing from US$65 to over US$300 can be purchased through **Extreme Tours** in Panama City. Two of the easiest villages to visit on your own are Mogue, 45 minutes upriver from La Palma (at high tide), US$10 (possible to see harpy eagles in this area) and at Puerto Lara – an hour's walk from turning off the main road just south of Santa Fe (four-person huts, US$20 per person, including meals).

The private **Punta Patiño Nature Reserve** owned by the Panamanian NGO **ANCON** is 25 km southwest of La Palma. Covering some 260 sq km, the reserve protects diverse habitats ranging from rare Pacific Dry forest through to mangroves. Punta Patiño is a good place to get a feel for the Darién and offers rewarding wildlife viewing, including

130 species of birds including the possibility of seeing a harpy eagle, and marmosets, kinkajous, tamanduas and at times the big cats. Heading back from Punta Patiño you pass the small fishing village of **Punta Alegre**, known for frequent fiestas, with a population of Colombian immigrants and Emberá tribesmen. Access within the region is by collective boat (US$3.50 to Mogué, similar to Punto Alegre). Organized trips can be arranged through **Ancon Expeditions** – see Panama City page 1142.

The bus service from Panama City (see below) has its problems; the road is bad and may be washed out after rains. Find out before you leave how far you can get. Alternatively there is an irregular boat to Yaviza, going about once a week, US$12 including meals, leaving from the harbour by the market in the old city, information from Muelle Fiscal, Calle 13 next to the Mercado Público. The only sleeping accommodation is the deck (take a hammock) and there is one primitive toilet for about 120 people. The advertised travel time is 16 hours, but it can take as long as two days.

Yaviza/El Real

Another possibility is to fly to La Palma and take the shorter boat trip to Yaviza, or direct to El Real (three a week, US$68 return), which is about 10 km from Yaviza. There is only one hotel at **Yaviza** ; there is also a TB clinic and a hospital. Crossing the river in Yaviza costs US$0.25. From Yaviza it is an easy two-hours' walk to **Pinogana** (small and primitive), where you have to cross the Río Tuira by dugout, US$1 per person. From Pinogana you can walk on, keeping the river to your left, to Vista Alegre (three hours), recross the river and walk 30 minutes to **Unión de Chocó** (some provisions and you can hammock overnight; you can sleep in the village hall but use a net to protect against *vinchucas* – Chagas disease). It's 1 km upriver to Yape, on the tributary of the same name, then three to four hours' walk to Boca de Cupe. Alternatively, you can go by motor dugout from Pinogana to Boca de Cupe (about US$65 per boat). Or take a boat from Yaviza to **El Real** (US$10), where there is a basic place to stay (E **El Nazareno**, T228-3673). Opposite there is a lady who will prepare meals if given notice. From there, take a motor dugout to Boca de Cupe, about US$15-20 per person, five hours (if possible, take a banana dugout, otherwise bargain hard on boats). A boat to Paya costs about US$35 per person for groups of four or five. Boats from El Real are infrequent and may only go to Unión de Chocó or Pinogana. A jeep track runs from El Real to Pinogana.

There are various other combinations of going on foot or by boat, prices for boat trips vary widely, so negotiate. They tend to be lower going downstream than up. It is wise to make payment always on arrival.

Boca de Cupe → *Colour map 8, B3.*

You can stay overnight at Boca de Cupe with a family. Food and cold beer is on sale here (last chance if you are going through to Colombia), and **Restaurant Nena** (blue building near landing dock) serves meals for US$2 and is a good source of information. Lodging (D) in Boca de Cupe with Antonio (son of María who helped many hikers crossing Darién, but who died in 1989). Don Ramón will prepare meals for US$2 and let you sleep on his floor. You can go with Emberá-Wunan people to Unión de Chocó, stay one or two days with them and share some food (they won't charge for lodging). The Emberá-Wunan are very friendly and shy, and it's best not to take pictures. In Boca de Cupe get your exit stamp (though you may be told to get it at Púcuro) and keep an eye on your luggage. From Boca de Cupe to Púcuro by dugout, US$20-50, to Paya (if river level is high enough), US$80. The section Boca de Cupe-Púcuro is possible on foot.

Púcuro

Púcuro is a Kuna village and it is customary to ask the chief's permission to stay (he will ask to see your passport). Immigration here, if arriving from Colombia, can be very officious. The women wear colourful ornamented *molas* and gold rings through their noses. There is a small shop selling basic provisions, such as tinned meats and salted biscuits. Visitors usually stay in the assembly house. People show little interest in travellers. From Púcuro you can walk through lush jungle to Paya, six hours (guide costs US$20, not really necessary, do not pay in advance), which was the capital of the Kuna Empire. From Púcuro to Paya there are four river crossings. The path is clear after the first kilometre.

Paya

In Paya you may be able to stay in the assembly house at the village, but it is usual to stay 2 km away eastwards in the barracks; US$2.50 per person, recommended. There's a passport check, baggage search and, on entry into Panama at least, all gear is treated with a chemical which eats plastic and ruins leather – wash it off as soon as possible. For US$2-2.50 you will get meals. The Kuna people in Paya are more friendly than in Púcuro. From Paya there are two routes.

Paya to Turbo

Route one From Paya, the next step is four to six hours' walk to **Palo de las Letras**, the frontier stone, where you enter Los Katíos, one of Colombia's national parks (see below). The path is not difficult, but is frequently blocked up to the border. From there you go down until you reach the left bank of the Río Tulé (three hours, no water between these points), you follow it downstream, which involves seven crossings (at the third crossing the trail almost disappears, so walk along the river bed – if possible – to the next crossing). If any of these watercourses are dry, watch out for snakes. About 30 minutes after leaving this river you cross a small creek; 45 minutes further

on is the abandoned camp of the Montadero, near where the Tulé and Pailón rivers meet to form the Río Cacarica. Cross the Cacarica and follow the trail to the MA (**Ministerio del Medio Ambiente** – Colombian National Parks) abandoned rangers' hut at **Cristales** (seven hours from Palo de las Letras). Guides from Paya to Cristales (they work in a rota and always go in pairs), charge US$55-200. They each carry a gun and a small bag of provisions and travel very fast.

If you insist on walking beyond Montadero, a machete, compass and fishing gear (or extra food) are essential. The path is so overgrown that it is easier, when the river is low, to walk and swim down it (Cristales is on the left bank, so perhaps it would be better to stick to this side). Occasional dugout will take you to **Bijao** (or Viajado), two hours, for around US$120 per boat. There is no village nearby, so arrive prepared. It is possible to walk to Bijao down the right (west) bank of the Río Cacarica (heavy going). From the bend to the east of the river the path improves and it is one hour to Bijao. At Bijao ask for the ANAM station, where you can eat and sleep (floor space, or camp). At the end of 1998 guerrillas seized Bijao, killing several people and driving out others, so it is unclear what facilities are available now.

From Bijao a motor dugout used to run to **Travesía** (also called Puerto América) for US$40 per person (two to five hours), from where motorboats go to Turbo for US$10 (in scheduled boat – if it stops; if not it'll cost you about US$250 to hire a boat). Travesía has some accommodation and provisions but has been reported as expensive and anti-gringo. Once again, there is a walking route south to Limón (two hours) and east to La Tapa (30 minutes). A cargo boat may be caught from here to Turbo. There is one *residencial* and a shop in Travesía. The last section from Travesía down the Atrato goes through an area full of birdlife including hummingbirds, kingfishers, herons, and 'screamers', which are about the size of turkeys and are believed to be endemic to the Atrato valley. The river enters the Great Atrato swamp and from there to the Bahía de Colombia. Turbo is on the opposite coast.

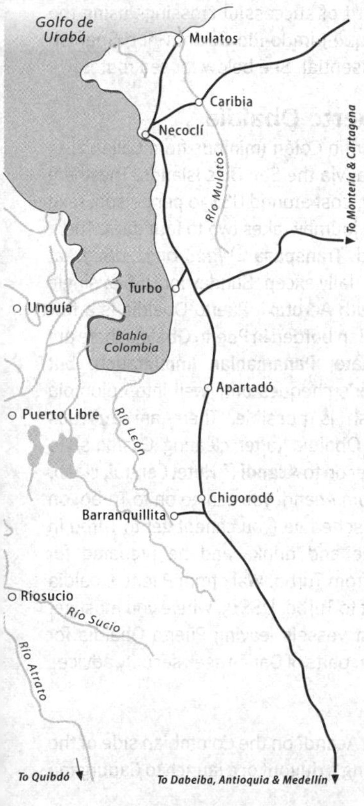

On arrival in Turbo, you must go to the **DAS office** (**Security Police**) ⓘ *Postadero Naval, north along Carrera 13 near airport, open 0800-1630*, to get your entrance stamp. If you fail to do this, you will have to wait until Cartagena, or elsewhere, and then explain yourself in great detail to DAS and quite likely you will be fined. If you arrive at the weekend and the DAS is closed, make sure you obtain a letter or document from the police in Turbo that states when you arrived in Colombia. The problems with this route are mostly on the Colombian side, where route finding is difficult, the undergrowth very hard to get through, and the terrain steep. Any rain adds to the difficulties though equally, when the water is low, boats need more pole assistance and the cost increases.

If you are coming into Panama from Colombia by these routes, and you have difficulty in obtaining entry stamps at Púcuro or Boca de Cupe, obtain a document from an official en route stating when you arrived in Panama. This may be equally hard to get. When you arrive in Panama City, go to the **Oficina Nacional de Migración** (who may send you to the port immigration) and explain the problem. One traveller reports hearing of several arrests of travellers caught without their entry stamp. Many of these 'illegals' stay arrested for weeks. It may help to be able to prove that you have sufficient money to cover your stay in Panama.

The **Parque Nacional Katios**, extending in Colombia to the Panamanian border, can be visited with mules from the MA headquarters in Sautatá. Look out for the Tilupo waterfall, 125 m high, where the water cascades down a series of rock staircases, surrounded by orchids and other fantastic plants. The Alto de la Guillermina is also in the park, a mountain behind which is a strange forest of palms called 'mil pesos', and the Ciénagas de Tumaradó, with red monkeys, waterfowl and alligators.

Entry by motorized vehicle is prohibited.

Route two The second route is a strenuous hike up the Río Paya valley through dense jungle (machete country) for about 16 hours to the last point on the Paya (fill up with water), then a further three hours to the continental divide where you cross into Colombia. Down through easier country (three to four hours) brings you to **Unguía** where motor boats are available to take you down the Río Tarena, out into the Gulf of Urabá, across to Turbo. This trip should not be taken without a guide, though you may be lucky and find some local people making the journey and willing to take you along. They will appreciate a gift when you arrive in Unguía. Hazards include blood-sucking ticks, the inevitable mosquitoes and, if that weren't enough, thirst.

There are many other possible routes from Panama crossing the land border used by locals. Most involve river systems and are affected by water levels. There are few tracks and no reliable maps. We have heard of successful crossings using the Salaqui and Balsas rivers, and a land route Jaqué-Jurado-Río Sucio. Good Spanish and guides, serious planning and money are essential. See below for sea routes.

By sea: the Caribbean route via Puerto Obaldía

Boats leave, irregularly, from the Coco Solo wharf in Colón (minibus from Calle 12, 15 minutes, US$0.80, taxi US$4) for Puerto Obaldía, via the San Blas Islands. These are small boats and give a rough ride in bad weather, cost around US$30 per person, take your own food, water and shade; with stops, the journey takes two to four days. There are flights with **Ansa** ⓘ *T226-7891/6881*, and **Transpasa** ⓘ *T226-0932/0843*, at 0600-0630 from Panama City to Puerto Obaldía, daily except Sunday for US$44 single (book well in advance). There are also flights with **Aerotaxi**. Puerto Obaldía is a few kilometres from the Colombian border. In Puerto Obaldía there are shops, **Colombian Consulate, Panamanian Immigration,** but nowhere to change traveller's cheques until well into Colombia (not Turbo); changing cash is possible. There are *expresos* (speedboats) from Puerto Obaldía (after clearing Customs) to Capurganá, and then another on to **Acandí** (F **Hotel Central,** clean, safe; F **Hotel Pilar**, safe). From Acandí you can go on to Turbo, on the Gulf of Urabá, no fixed schedule (you cannot get to Turbo in the same day; take shade and drinks and be prepared for seasickness). Medellín can be reached by road from Turbo. Walk from Puerto Obaldía to Zapzurro, just beyond the border, for a dugout to Turbo, US$15, where you must get your Colombia entry stamp. It seems that most vessels leaving Puerto Obaldía for Colombian ports are contraband boats. As in other parts of Darién seek security advice.

Arriving in Puerto Obaldía you have to pass through the military control for baggage search, immigration (proof of funds and onward ticket asked for) and malaria control.

Capurganá (Colombia)

Alternatively you can get from Puerto Obaldía to Acandí on the Colombian side of the border, either by walking for nine hours or by hiring a dugout or a launch to Capurganá

Cautions and notes on crossing the Darién Gap

When planning your trip by land or along the coast to Colombia, remember there are strict rules on entry into Colombia and you must aim for either Turbo or Buenaventura to obtain your entry stamp. Failure to do this will almost certainly involve you in significant fines, accusations of illegal entry, or worse in Colombia. Do not enter Darién without full details of which areas to avoid because of the activities of drug traffickers, bandits and guerrilla groups, mostly from Colombia, but operating on both sides of the border.

The best time to go is in the dry months (January to mid-April); the trip would be considerably harder in the wet season (May to December). Even when totally covered in mosquito repellent you will get bitten and run the risk of contracting dengue fever. Travel with a reliable companion or two. Talk to knowledgeable locals for the best advice. Hire at least one indigenous guide, but do it through the village *corregidor*, whose involvement may add to the reliability of the selected guides. (Budget up to US$8 per day for the guide and his food. Negotiate with the chief, but do not begrudge the cost.) Travel light and move fast. The journey described here takes about seven days to Turbo.

Maps of the Darién area can be purchased from the Ministerio de Obras Públicas, Instituto Geográfico Nacional Tommy Guardia, in Panama City (US$4, reported to contain serious mistakes). Information is also available from Asociación Nacional para la Conservación de la Naturaleza, Calle Amela Dennis de Icaza, Ancón Hill, T314-0060, www.ancon.org.

(US$8), and then another launch at 0715, which takes one hour and costs US$3. The snorkelling is good in Capurganá. There is a Panamanian consul (Roberto) who issues visas for Panama. There are **Twin Otter** flights to Medellín. To walk to Capurganá takes four hours, guide recommended (they charge US$10); first go to **La Miel** (two hours), then to **Zapzurro** (20 minutes), where there are shops and cabins for rent, then an hour to 90 minutes to Capurganá. Most of the time the path follows the coast, but there are some hills to cross (it's hot, take drinking water). From Acandí a daily boat is scheduled to go at 0800 to Turbo (US$15, three hours). Take pesos, if possible, to these Colombian places, the rate of exchange for dollars is poor.

The Pacific route

Although not quick, the Pacific coastline provides another relatively straightforward route across the Darién (Spanish is essential). Take a bus from Panama City (Plaza 5 de Mayo) to **Metetí** (D-E **Hospedaje Feliz,** basic 'box' rooms), 50 km from Yaviza , the junction for transport to **Puerto Quimba**, where boats can be taken to La Palma. Alternatively, take a bus to **Santa Fe**, which is 75 km short of Yaviza and off to the south, a rough but scenic six to eight hours (US$8, three a day, check times). In Santa Fe it is possible to camp near the police post. Then hitch a ride on a truck (scarce), or walk two hours to the Río Sabanas at Puerto Larda (11 km) where you must take a dugout or launch to La Palma, or hire one (US$5, two hours). **La Palma** is also reached by boat from Yaviza (US$3, eight hours). It is the capital of Darién – you can change cash and traveller's cheques – has one *pensión* (F, friendly, English-speaking owners, with cooking and laundry facilities), or see if you can stay with the *guardia*). **Jaqué** is on the Pacific coast, near Puerto Piña, 50 km north of the Colombian border (one hotel). **Bahía Piña** has a runway, used mainly by the expensive fishing resort. If you want to stay in the area, there is a range of options provided as part of the **Darién**

 Paradise Trail ⓘ *T226-7000, darientrail.tripod.com*, a community-based ecotourism circuit with accommodation in Santa Fe, Boca Lara, La Palma, Sambu, Meteti-Canglón and Ipeti Embera. Hotels tend to be in the E category.

These isolated settlements on the Pacific coast are close to the **Parque Nacional Darién**, Panama's largest and wildest protected area. Cana and Cerro Pirre are at its heart but at present it is not advisable to visit because of the various armed bands that use the jungle as cover. From Jaqué you can catch a launch to Jurado in Colombia (US$25, four 'murderous' hours, take something to sit on). The launch continues to Bahía Solano or there are weekly cargo boats to Buenaventura (**M/N Fronteras** US$45 including food, 36 hours, bunks but OK), where there is a DAS office where you can sort out your paperwork.

Alternatively, at the Muelle Fiscal in Panama City (by the main waterfront market, near Calle 13), ask for a passenger boat going to Jaqué. The journey takes 18 hours, is cramped and passengers cook food themselves, but costs only US$12. Jaqué is only reached by sea or air (the airstrip is used mostly by wealthy visitors going sports fishing); there are small stores, a good *comedor*, and one *hospedaje*.

The guard post is open every day and gives exit stamps. Canoes from Jaqué go to Juradó (US$20, 4½ hours) or Bahía Solano (US$45, 160 km, with two overnight stops) in Chocó. The first night is in Jurado. There are flights from Jurado to Turbo, but you can get 'stuck' in Jurado for several days. Bahía Solano is a deep-sea fishing resort with an airport and *residencias*. Flights from Bahía Solano go to Quibdó, connecting to Cali, or Medellín (book flights in advance; the town is popular with Colombian tourists). On this journey, you sail past the lush, mountainous Pacific coast of Darién and Chocó, with its beautiful coves and beaches, and you will see a variety of marine life.

Sleeping

Yavisa/El Real *p1199*

E **Tres Américas**, pay in Casa Indira shop next door. Take mosquito coils – there isn't anywhere to hang a net – basic, but friendly.

Paya to Turbo *p1200*

F **Doña Julia**, Unguia. With bath.
F **Residencias Viajero**, Unguia. With bath.

Puerto Obaldía *p1202*

E **Residencia Cande**. A good *pensión*, nice and clean, which also serves very good meals for US$1.50, order meals in advance.

Capurganá (Columbia) *p1202*

Several hotels including B **Calypso**, D **Náutico**, E **Uvita** and E **Al Mar**. There are also *pensiones* and you can camp by the beach.

The Pacific route *p1203*

A **Cana Field Station**, Cana, T269-9415 (Panama City), www.anconexpeditions.com. Mainly used by groups and ornithologists.
E **Guacamaya**, Santa Fe, T299-6727.
F **Chavela**, Jaqué, clean, basic, friendly.

It is easy to find accommodation with local families), and camping is possible on the beach.

Transport

Towards Columbia *p1198*

Bus From bus terminal in Panama City, buses leave every 2 hrs 0630-1430 for **Pacora**, US$0.80, **Chepo**, US$1.60, **Cañitas**, 4 hrs, US$3.10, **Arretí**, 6 hrs, US$9, **Metetí** and **Canglón**, 8 hrs, US$11.20. Beyond, to **Yaviza**, in the dry season only (Jan-Apr), US$15, 10 hrs minimum. Plenty of pick-ups run on the last stretch to Yaviza, eg about 3 hrs from Metetí to Yaviza.

The Pacific route *p1203*

Air and boat There are 2 daily Aeroperlas flights from Panama City to **La Palma**, US$40, and 1 a day to **Jaqué** on the Pacific shore, US$49; also to **Yaviza** 3 days a week, but check with the airline **Parsa**, T226-3883. They have an office at the domestic airport in Panama City.
If you cannot get a plane from **La Palma** to **Jaqué**, there are boats, US$15. En route there is an Ancón lodge at Punta Patino. Details from **Ancón Expediciones** in Panama City, page 1142.

Background

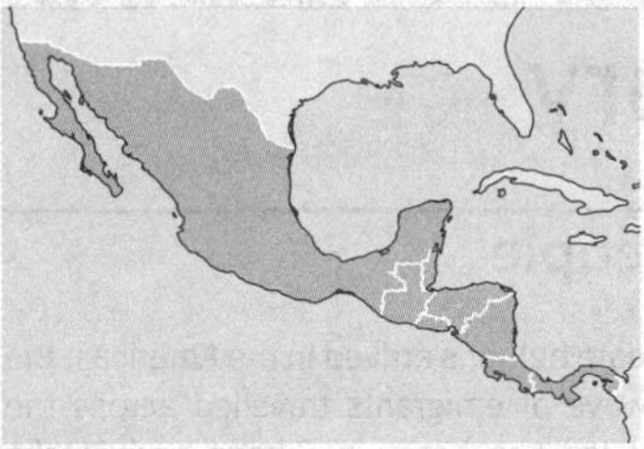

Footprint features

Regional history

Arrival of the American people

While controversy exists around the precise date humans arrived in the Americas, the current prevailing view suggests the first wave of emigrants travelled across the Bering Strait ice bridge created in the last Ice Age between Siberia and Alaska approximately 15,000 years ago. Small groups of peoples quickly moved through the region as the migratory lifestyle of the hunter-gather explored the Americas. In fertile lands the development of farming and the reduced reliance on hunting and migrating encouraged groups to settle. By 1500 BC villages were developing and growing in many parts of the Americas including Mesoamerica.

Pre-Columbian civilizations

The **Aztec** Empire which Spanish conqueror Hernán Cortés encountered in 1519 and subsequently destroyed was the third major power to have dominated what is now known as Mexico. Before it, the empires of **Teotihuacán** and **Tula** each unified what had essentially been an area of separate indigenous groups. All three, together with their neighbours such as the Maya (dealt with below) and their predecessors, belong to a more or less common culture called **Mesoamerica**. Despite the wide variety of climates and terrains that fall within Mesoamerica's boundaries, from northern Mexico to El Salvador and Honduras, the civilizations that developed were interdependent, sharing the same agriculture (based on maize, beans and squash) and many sociological features. They also shared an enormous pantheon, with the god of rain and the feathered serpent-hero predominant; the offering of blood to the gods, from oneself and from sacrificial victims usually taken in war; pyramid-building; a game played with a rubber ball; trade in feathers, jade and other valuable objects, possibly from as far away as the Andean region of South America; hieroglyphic writing; astronomy; and an elaborate calendar.

The **Mesoamerican calendar** was a combination of a 260-day almanac year and the 365-day solar year. A given day in one of the years would only coincide with that in the other every 52 years, a cycle called the **Calendar Round**. In order to give the Calendar Round a context within a larger timescale, a starting date for both years was devised; the date chosen by the Classic Maya was equivalent to 3113 BC in Christian time. Dates measured from this point are called Long Count dates. Historians divide Mesoamerican civilizations into three periods, the **pre-Classic**, which lasted until about AD 300, the **Classic**, until AD 900, and the **post-Classic**, from 900 until the Spanish conquest. An alternative delineation is: Olmec, Teotihuacán and Aztec, named after the dominant civilizations within each of those periods.

Olmecs

Who precisely the Olmecs were, where they came from and why they disappeared, is a matter of debate. It is known that they flourished from about **1400-400 BC**, that they lived in the **Mexican Gulf coast** region between Veracruz and Tabasco, and that all later civilizations have their roots ultimately in Olmec culture. They carved **colossal heads**, stelae (tall, flat monuments), jade figures and altars; they gave great importance to the jaguar and the serpent in their imagery; they built large ceremonial centres such as **San Lorenzo** and **La Venta**. Possibly derived from the Olmecs and gaining importance in the first millennium BC was the centre in the Valley of Oaxaca at

Monte Albán. This was a major city, with certain changes of influence, right through until the end of the Classic period. Also derived from the Olmecs was the **Izapa** civilization, on the Pacific border of present-day Mexico and Guatemala. The progression from the Olmec to the Maya civilization seems to have taken place here with obvious connections in artistic style, calendar use, ceremonial architecture and the transformation of the Izapa long-lipped god into the Maya long-nosed god.

Teotihuacán

Almost as much mystery surrounds the origins of Teotihuacán as those of the Olmecs. Teotihuacán, **'the place where men become gods'**, was a great urban state, holding in its power most of the **Central Highlands** of Mexico. Its influence can be detected in the Maya area, Oaxaca and the civilizations on the Gulf coast which succeeded the Olmecs. The monuments in the city itself, which still stands beyond the outskirts of Mexico City, are enormous, the planning precise; it is estimated that by the seveth century AD some 125,000 people were living in its immediate vicinity. Early evidence did not suggest Teotihuacán's power was gained by force, but research indicates both **human sacrifice** and **sacred warfare** took place. For reasons unknown, Teotihuacán's influence over its neighbours ended around 600 AD. Its glory coincided with that of the Classic Maya, but the latter's decline occurred some 300 years later, at which time a major change affected all Mesoamerica.

Toltecs

The start of the post-Classic period, between the Teotihuacán and Aztec horizons, was marked by an upsurge in **militarism.** In the semi-deserts to the north of the settled societies of central Mexico and Veracruz lived groups of nomadic hunters. These people, who were given the general name of **Chichimecs,** began to invade the central region and were quick to adopt the urban characteristics of the groups they overthrew. The **Toltecs** of **Tula** were one such invading force, rapidly building up an empire stretching from the Gulf of Mexico to the Pacific in central Mexico. Infighting by factions within the Toltecs split the rulers and probably hastened the empire's demise sometime after 1150. The exiled leader **Topíltzin Quetzalcóatl** (Feathered Serpent) is possibly the founder of the Maya-Toltec rule in the Yucatán (the Maya spoke of a Mexican invader named Kukulcán – Feathered Serpent). He is certainly the mythical figure the Aztec ruler, Moctezuma II, took Cortés to be, returning by sea from the east.

Zapotecs and Mixtecs

Another important culture to develop in the first millennium AD was the Mixtec, in western Oaxaca. The Mixtecs infiltrated all the territory held by the Zapotecs, who had ruled Monte Albán during the Classic period and had built many other sites in the Valley of Oaxaca, including Mitla. The Mixtecs, in alliance with the Zapotecs, successfully withstood invasion by the Aztecs.

Aztecs

The process of transition from semi-nomadic hunter-gathering to city and empire-building continued with the **Aztecs,** who bludgeoned their way into the midst of rival city states in the vacuum left by the destruction of Tula around 1150. They rose from practically nothing to a power almost as great as Teotihuacán in about 200 years. From their base at **Tenochtitlán in Lake Texcoco** in the Valley of Mexico they aggressively extended their sphere of influence from the Tarascan Kingdom in the north to the Maya lands in the south. Not only did the conquered pay heavy tribute to their Aztec overlords, but they also supplied the constant flow of **sacrificial victims** needed to satisfy the deities, at whose head was **Huitzilopochtli,** the warrior god of the Sun. The speed with which the Aztecs adapted to a settled existence and

Mexico Central America in figures

	Population (million)	Area (sq km)	People (per sq km)
Mexico	100.9	1,908,700	50.5
Guatemala	12	108,900	110.2
Belize	0.253	22,960	11
El Salvador	6.4	21,040	304
Honduras	6.8	112,100	60.6
Nicaragua	5.3	130,000	40.7
Costa Rica	3.9	51,100	76.3
Panama	2.9	75,520	38.1

Source: World Development Indicators 2004

fashioned a highly effective political state is remarkable. Their ability in sculpting stone, in pottery, in writing books, and in architecture (what we can gather from what the Spaniards did not destroy) was great. Surrounding all this activity was a strictly ritual existence, with ceremonies and feasts dictated by the two enmeshing calendars. It is impossible to say whether the Aztec Empire would have gone the way of its predecessors had the Spaniards not arrived to precipitate its collapse. Undoubtedly, the Europeans received much assistance from people who had been oppressed by the Aztecs and who wished to be rid of them. Within two years Cortés, with his horses, an array of military equipment and relatively few soldiers, brought to an end an extraordinary culture.

Maya

The best known of the pre-Conquest indigenous civilizations of the present Central American area was the Maya, thought to have evolved in a formative period in the **Pacific highlands** of Guatemala and El Salvador between **1500 BC** and about **100 AD**. After 200 years of growth it entered what is known today as its Classic period when the civilization flourished in Guatemala, El Salvador, Belize, Honduras and Mexico (Chiapas, Campeche and Yucatán). The Maya civilization was based on independent and antagonistic city states, including Tikal, Uaxactún, Kaminaljuyú, Iximché, Zaculeu and Quiriguá in Guatemala; Copán in Honduras; Altún Ha, Caracol, Lamanai in Belize; Tazumal and San Andrés in El Salvador; and Palenque, Bonampak (both in Chiapas), Uxmal, Mayapán, Tulum, Cobá and the Puuc hill cities of Sayil, Labná and Kabah (all on the Yucatán Peninsula) in Mexico. Recent research has revealed that these cities, far from being the peaceful ceremonial centres once imagined, were **warring adversaries**, striving to capture victims for sacrifice. Furthermore, much of the cultural activity, controlled by a theocratic minority of priests and nobles, involved blood- letting, by even the highest members of society. Royal blood was the most precious offering that could be made to the gods. This change in perception of the Maya was the result of the discovery of defended cities and of a greater understanding of the **Maya's hieroglyphic writing**. Although John Lloyd Stephens' prophecy that "a key surer than that of the Rosetta stone will be discovered" has not yet been fulfilled, the painstaking decipherment of the glyphs has uncovered many secrets of Maya society (see *Breaking the Maya Code* by Michael D Coe, Thames and Hudson).

Alongside the preoccupation with blood was an artistic tradition rich in **ceremony, folklore and dance**. They achieved paper codices and glyphic writing, which also appears on stone monuments and their fine ceramics; they were skilful

Population Growth (%)	Life expectancy (years)	GNI (US$ per capita)	GDP (US$billion)
1.5	73.6	5910	637.2
2.6	65.5	1760	23.3
2.4	74.1	2970	0.84
1.7	70.1	2110	14.3
2.5	66.1	930	6.6
2.6	68.7	710	4
1.8	77.6	4070	16.8
1.5	74.9	4020	12.3

weavers and traded over wide areas, though they did not use the wheel and had no beasts of burden. The cities were all meticulously dated. Maya art is a mathematical art: each column, figure, face, animal, frieze, stairway and temple expresses a date or a time relationship. When, for example, an ornament on the ramp of the Hieroglyphic Stairway at Copán was repeated some 15 times, it was to express that number of elapsed 'leap' years. The 75 steps stand for the number of elapsed intercalary days. The Maya calendar was a nearer approximation to sidereal time than either the Julian or the Gregorian calendars of Europe; it was only .000069 of a day out of true in a year. They used the zero centuries in advance of the Old World, plotted the movements of the sun, moon, Venus and other planets, and conceived a cycle of more than 1800 million days.

Their tools and weapons were flint and hard stone, obsidian and fire-hardened wood, and yet with these they hewed out and transported great monoliths over miles of difficult country, and carved them over with intricate glyphs and figures which would be difficult enough with modern chisels. Also with those tools they grew lavish crops. To support urban populations now believed to number tens of thousands, and a population density of 150 per sq km (compared with less than 1 per sq km today), an agricultural system was developed of raised fields, fertilized by fish and vegetable matter from surrounding canals.

The height of the Classic period lasted until AD 900-1000, after which the Maya concentrated into Yucatán after a successful invasion of their other lands by non-Maya people (this is only one theory; another is that they were forced to flee due to drought and a peasant rebellion). They then came under the influence of the Toltecs who invaded Yucatán (Chichén Itzá is seen as an example of a Maya city which displays many Toltec features). From then on their culture declined. The Toltecs gradually spread their empire as far as the southern borders of Guatemala. They in turn were conquered by the Aztecs, who did not penetrate Central America.

Conquest

It was only during his fourth voyage, in 1502, that **Columbus** reached the mainland of Central America; he landed in **Costa Rica** and Panama, which he called **Veragua**, and founded the town of Santa María de Belén. In 1508 Alonso de Ojeda received a grant of land on the Pearl coast east of Panama, and in 1509 he founded the town of San Sebastián, later moved to a new site called Santa María la Antigua del Darién (now in Colombia). In 1513 the governor of the colony at Darién was **Vasco Núñez de Balboa**.

 Taking 190 men he crossed the isthmus in 18 days and caught the first glimpse of the Pacific; he claimed it and all neighbouring lands in the name of the King of Spain. But from the following year, when Pedrarias de Avila replaced him as Governor, Balboa fell on evil days, and he was executed by Pedrarias in 1519. That same year Pedrarias crossed the isthmus and founded the town of Panamá on the Pacific side. It was in April 1519, too, that **Cortés** began his conquest of Mexico. Central America was explored from these two nodal points of Panama and Mexico. By 1525 Cortés' lieutenant, **Pedro de Alvarado,** had conquered as far south as San Salvador. Meanwhile Pedrarias was sending forces into Panama and Costa Rica (the latter was abandoned due to the hostile natives, but was finally colonized from Mexico City when the rest of Central America had been taken). In 1522-1524 Andrés Niño and Gil González Dávila invaded **Nicaragua** and **Honduras**. Many towns were founded by these forces from Panama. Spanish forces from the north and south sometimes met and fought bitterly. At this time the gentle **Bartolomé de las Casas**, the 'apostle of the Indies', was active as a Dominican missionary in Central America in the 1530s.

Settlement

The groups of Spanish settlers were few and widely scattered, a fundamental point in explaining the **political fragmentation** of Central America today. Panama was ruled from Bogotá, but the rest of Central America was subordinate to the Viceroyalty at Mexico City, with Antigua, Guatemala, as an Audiencia for the area until 1773, and thereafter Guatemala City. Panama was of paramount importance for colonial Spanish America for its strategic position, and for the trade passing across the isthmus to and from the southern colonies. The other provinces were of comparatively little value.

The small number of **Spaniards intermarried** freely with the locals, accounting for the predominance of mestizos in present-day Central America. But the picture has regional variations. In Guatemala, where there was the highest native population density, intermarriage affected fewer of the natives, and over half the population today is still purely *indígena* (**indigenous**). On the Meseta Central of Costa Rica, the natives were all but wiped out by disease and as a consequence of this great disaster, there is a community of over two million whites, with little *indígena* admixture, in the highlands. **Blacks** predominate along the Caribbean coast of Central America. Most were brought in as cheap labour to work as railway builders and banana planters in the 19th century and canal cutters in the 20th. The **Garífuna** people, living from southern Belize to Nicaragua, arrived in the area as free people after African slaves and indigenous Caribbean people intermingled following a shipwreck off St Vincent.

Independence and after

On 5 November 1811, **José Matías Delgado,** a priest and jurist born in San Salvador, organized a revolt with another priest, Manuel José Arce. They proclaimed the independence of El Salvador, but the Audiencia at Guatemala City suppressed the revolt and took Delgado prisoner.

It was the revolution of 1820 in Spain itself that precipitated the independence of Central America. When on 24 February 1821, the Mexican **General Agustín de Iturbide** announced his *Plan de Iguala* for an independent Mexico, the Central American *criollos* decided to follow his example, and a **declaration of independence**, drafted by José Cecilio del Valle, was announced in Guatemala City on 15 September 1821. Iturbide invited the provinces of Central America to join with him and, on 5 January 1822, Central America was declared annexed to Mexico. Delgado refused to accept this decree and Iturbide, who had now assumed the title of **Emperor Agustín I,** sent an army south under Vicente Filísola to enforce it in the regions under Delgado's influence. Filísola had completed his task when he heard of Iturbide's abdication, and at once convened a general congress of the Central American provinces. It met on 24 June 1823, and established the **Provincias Unidas del Centro de América**. The Mexican Republic acknowledged their independence on 1 August 1824, and Filísola's soldiers were withdrawn.

The congress, presided over by Delgado, appointed a provisional governing *junta* which promulgated a constitution modelled on that of the United States in November 1824. The Province of Chiapas was not included in the Federation, as it had already adhered to Mexico in 1821. Guatemala City, by force of tradition, soon became the seat of government.

The first President under the new constitution was **Manuel José Arce**, a liberal. One of his first acts was to **abolish slavery**. El Salvador, protesting that he had exceeded his powers, rose in December 1826. Honduras, Nicaragua and Costa Rica joined the revolt, and in 1828 **General Francisco Morazán,** in charge of the army of Honduras, defeated the federal forces, entered San Salvador and marched against Guatemala City. He captured the city on 13 April 1829, and established that contradiction in terms: a liberal dictatorship. Many conservative leaders were expelled and church and monastic properties confiscated. Morazán himself became President of the Federation in 1830. He was a man of considerable ability; he ruled with a strong hand, encouraged education, fostered trade and industry, opened the country to immigrants, and reorganized the administration. In 1835 the capital was moved to San Salvador.

These reforms antagonized the conservatives and there were several uprisings. The most serious revolt was among the *indígenas* of Guatemala, led by Rafael Carrera, an illiterate mestizo conservative and a born leader. Years of continuous warfare followed, during the course of which the Federation withered away. As a result, the federal congress passed an act which allowed each province to assume the government it chose, but the idea of a federation was not quite dead. Morazán became President of El Salvador. Carrera, who was by then in control of Guatemala, defeated Morazán in battle and forced him to leave the country. But in 1842, Morazán overthrew Braulio Carrillo, then dictator of Costa Rica, and became president himself. At once he set about rebuilding the Federation, but was defeated by the united forces of the other states and was shot on 15 September 1842. With him perished any practical hope of Central American political union.

The separate states

The history of **Guatemala, El Salvador, Honduras** and **Nicaragua** since the breakdown of federation has been tempestuous in the extreme (**Costa Rica,** with its mainly white population and limited economic value at the time, is a country apart, and **Panama** was Colombian territory until 1903). In each the ruling class was divided into pro-clerical conservatives and anti-clerical liberals, with constant changes of power. Each was weak, and tried repeatedly to buttress its weakness by alliances with others, which invariably broke up because one of the allies sought a position of mastery. The wars were mainly ideological wars between conservatives and liberals, or wars motivated by inflamed nationalism. Nicaragua was riven internally by the mutual hatreds of the Conservatives of Granada and the Liberals of León, and there were repeated conflicts between the Caribbean and interior parts of Honduras.

Of the four republics, **Guatemala** was the strongest and in some ways the most stable. While the other states were skittling their presidents like ninepins, Guatemala had a succession of strong dictators: Rafael Carrera (1844-1865), Justo Rufino Barrios (1873-1885), Manuel Cabrera (1898-1920), and Jorge Ubico (1931-1944). These were separated by intervals of constitutional government, anarchy, or attempts at dictatorship which failed. (Few presidents handed over power voluntarily, most were forcibly removed or assassinated.)

 Despite the permutations and combinations of external and civil war there has been a recurrent desire to re-establish some form of *La Gran Patria Centroamericana*. Throughout the 19th century, and far into the 20th, there have been ambitious projects for political federation, usually involving El Salvador, Honduras and Nicaragua; none of them lasted more than a few years.

Regional integration

Poverty, the fate of the great majority, has brought about closer economic cooperation between the five republics, and in 1960 they established the **Central American Common Market** (CACM). Surprisingly, the Common Market appeared to be a great success until 1968, when integration fostered national antagonisms, and there was a growing conviction in Honduras and Nicaragua, which were doing least well out of integration, that they were being exploited by the others. In 1969 the 'Football War' broke out between El Salvador and Honduras, basically because of a dispute about illicit emigration by Salvadoreans into Honduras, and relations between the two were not normalized until 1980. Hopes for improvement were revived in 1987 when the Central American Peace Plan, drawn up by President Oscar Arias Sánchez of Costa Rica, was signed by the Presidents of Guatemala, El Salvador, Honduras, Nicaragua and Costa Rica. The plan proposed formulae to end the civil strife in individual countries, achieving this aim first in Nicaragua (1989), then in El Salvador (1991). In Guatemala, a ceasefire after 36 years of war led to the signing of a peace accord at the end of 1996. With the signing of peace accords, emphasis has shifted to regional, economic and environmental integration.

In October 1993, the presidents of Guatemala, El Salvador, Honduras, Nicaragua and Costa Rica signed a new **Central American Integration Treaty Protocol**, to replace that of 1960 and set up new mechanisms for regional integration. The Treaty was the culmination of a series of annual presidential summits held since 1986 which, besides aiming for peace and economic integration, established a Central American Parliament and a Central American Court of Justice.

Attempts at further economic and regional integration continue. Plans to create the a **Free Trade Area of the Americas** (FTAA) by 2005 (agreed in Monterrey, in January 2004), have stalled. The **Central American Free Trade Agreement** (CAFTA) was signed by El Salvador, Guatemala, Honduras and Nicaragua in 2003 and shortly after by Costa Rica. The Trade Agreement went into effect on March 1, 2006 for El Salvador following completion of all necessary steps, including delivery of signed Treaty copies to the OAS, which was the final step. Honduras and Nicaragua followed suit on April 1, 2006, with Guatemala expected to complete sometime in 2006, followed by Costa Rica. This regional integration supports the **Plan Puebla Panama**, the development of an economic corridor stretching from Puebla, west of Mexico City, as far as Panama. Strongly promoted by Mexico's President Fox, supporters of the plan see it as a means for economic development. Critics, of which there are many in each Central American nation, as well as Mexico and the United States, see it as a way of draining cheap labour resources with little concern for environmental concerns and long-term progress.

While the Plan Puebla may continue to simmer on the back burner, the desire for Central American nations to strengthen ties is regularly voiced. Regional meetings occur periodically to promote and encourage trust and co-operation, and while the final destination of such co-operation is far from clear, the Central America of today is far more productive and safer than it was in the 1980s and early 1990s.

Mexico

History

Pre-conquest history

Of the many indigenous nations in the vast territory of Mexico, the two most important before the Conquest were the Aztecs of Tenochtitlán (now Mexico City) and the Maya of the Yucatán. The Aztecs, a militarist, theocratic culture, had obtained absolute control over the whole Valley of México and a loose control of some other regions. The Maya were already in decline by the time the Spaniards arrived. A brief history of these and other pre-Conquest, Mexican people is given above.

For more on the region's early history, see page 1206.

Spanish rule

The remarkable conquest of Mexico began when 34-year-old **Hernán Cortés** disembarked near the present Veracruz with about 500 men, some horses and cannon, on 21 April 1519. They marched into the interior, arrived at Tenochtitlán in November and were admitted into the city as guests of the reigning monarch, Moctezuma. There they remained until June of the next year, when Pedro de Alvarado, in the absence of Cortés, murdered hundreds of natives to quell his own fear of a rising. At this treacherous act they did in fact rise, and it was only by good luck that the Spanish troops, with heavy losses, were able to fight their way out of the city on the Noche Triste (the Night of Sorrows) of 30 June. Next year Cortés came back with reinforcements and besieged the city. It fell on 30 August 1521, and was utterly razed. Cortés then turned to the conquest of the rest of the country. One of the main factors in his success was his alliance with the Tlaxcalans, old rivals of the Aztecs. The fight was ruthless, the Aztecs were soon overcome and 300 years of Spanish rule followed.

In the early years all the main sources of gold and silver were discovered. Spanish grandees stepped into the shoes of dead Aztec lords and inherited their great estates and their wealth of savable souls with little disturbance as Aztec and Spanish ways of holding land had broad similarities. The *ejido* (or agrarian community holding lands in common), the *rancho*, or small private property worked by the owner; and that usually huge area that paid tribute to its master, the Spanish *encomienda*, soon to be converted into the hacienda, with its absolute title to the land and its almost feudal way of life. Within the first 50 years all the *indígenas* in the populous southern valleys of the plateau had been Christianized and harnessed to Spanish wealth-getting from mine and soil. The more scattered and less profitable natives of the north and south had to await the coming of the missionizing Jesuits in 1571, a year behind the Inquisition. Too often, alas, the crowded Jesuit missions proved as fruitful a source of smallpox or measles as of salvation, with the result that large numbers of *indígenas* died, their deserted communal lands promptly taken by some neighbouring *encomendero* (a thieving of public lands by private interests, which continued for 400 years).

By the end of the 16th century the Spaniards had founded most of the towns that are still important, tapped great wealth in mining, stock raising and sugar-growing, and firmly imposed their way of life and beliefs. Government was by a Spanish-born upper class, based on the subordination of the *indígena* and mestizo populations and there was a strict dependence on Spain for all things. As with the rest of Hispanic America, Spain built up resistance to itself by excluding from government both Spaniards born in Mexico and the small body of educated mestizos.

Revolution and civil war

The standard of revolt was raised in 1810 by the curate of Dolores, **Miguel Hidalgo**. The Grito de Dolores (*Mueran los gachupines* – Perish the Spaniards), collected 80,000 armed supporters, and had it not been for Hidalgo's loss of nerve and failure to engage the Spaniards, the capital might have been captured in the first month and a government created not differing much from the royal Spanish government. But 11 years of fighting created bitter differences.

A loyalist general, **Agustín de Iturbide**, joined the rebels and proclaimed an independent Mexico in 1821. His *Plan of Iguala* proposed an independent monarchy with a ruler from the Spanish royal family, but on second thoughts Iturbide proclaimed himself Emperor in 1822: a fantasy that lasted a year. A federal republic was created on 4 October 1824, with General Guadalupe Victoria as President. Conservatives stood for a highly centralized government; Liberals favoured federated sovereign states. The tussle of interests resulted in endemic civil war. In 1836, Texas, whose cotton-growers and cattle-ranchers had been infuriated by the abolition of slavery in 1829, rebelled against the dictator, Santa Ana, and declared its independence. It was annexed by the United States in 1845. War broke out and US troops occupied Mexico City in 1847. Next year, under the terms of the treaty of Guadalupe Hidalgo, the US acquired half Mexico's territory: all the land from Texas to California and from the Río Grande to Oregon.

Benito Juárez

A period of reform dominated by independent Mexico's great hero, the Zapoteco, **Benito Juárez**, began in 1857. The church, in alliance with the conservatives, hotly contested by civil war his liberal programme of popular education, freedom of the press and of speech, civil marriage and the separation of church and state. Juárez won, but the constant civil strife wrecked the economy, and Juárez was forced to suspend payment on the national debt. Spain, France and Britain promptly landed a joint force at Veracruz to protect their financial rights. The British and the Spanish soon withdrew, but the French force pushed inland and occupied Mexico City in 1863. Juárez took to guerrilla warfare against the invaders.

The **Archduke Maximilian of Austria** became Emperor of Mexico with Napoleon III's help, but US insistence and the gathering strength of Prussia led to the withdrawal of the French troops in 1867. Maximilian, betrayed and deserted, was captured by the *Juaristas* at Querétaro, tried, and shot on 19 June. Juárez resumed control and died in July 1872. He was the first Mexican leader of any note who had died naturally since 1810.

General Porfirio Díaz

Sebastián Lerdo de Tejada, the distinguished scholar who followed Juárez, was soon tricked out of office by General Porfirio Díaz, who ruled Mexico from 1876 to 1910. Díaz's paternal, though often ruthless, central authority introduced a period of 35 years of peace. A superficial prosperity followed; a civil service was created, finances put on a sound basis, banditry put down, industries started, railways built, international relations improved, and foreign capital protected. But the main mass of peasants had never been so wretched; their lands were stolen, their personal liberties curtailed, and many were sold into forced labour on tobacco and *henequen* plantations from which death was the only release. It was this open contradiction between dazzling prosperity and hideous distress that led to the upheaval of November 1910 and to Porfirio Díaz's self-exile in Paris.

Mexican revolution

A new leader, **Francisco Madero**, who came from a landowning family in Coahuila, championed a programme of political and social reform, which included the restoration of stolen lands. Madero was initially supported by revolutionary leaders such as **Emiliano Zapata** in Morelos, **Pascual Orozco** in Chihuahua and **Pancho Villa** in the north. During his presidency (1911-1913), Madero neither satisfied his revolutionary supporters, nor pacified his reactionary enemies. After a coup in February 1913, led by Gen Victoriano Huerta, Madero was brutally murdered, but the great cry, '*Tierra y Libertad*' (Land and Liberty) was not to be quieted until the revolution was made safe by the election of Alvaro Obregón to the Presidency in 1920. Before then, Mexico was in a state of civil war, leading first to the exile of Huerta in 1914, then the dominance of Venustiano Carranza's revolutionary faction over that of Zapata (assassinated in 1919) and Villa. Later, President **Lázaro Cárdenas** fulfilled some of the more important economic objectives of the revolution; it was his regime (1934-1940) that brought about the division of the great estates into *ejidos* (or communal lands), irrigation, the raising of wages, the spread of education, the beginnings of industrialization, the nationalization of the oil wells and the railways. Later presidents nationalized electric power, the main airlines and parts of industry, but at the same time encouraged both Mexican and foreign (mainly US) entrepreneurs to develop the private sector. All presidents have pursued an independent and non-aligned foreign policy.

Recent politics

In 1946, the official party assumed the name **Partido Revolucionario Institucional (PRI)**, and held a virtual monopoly over all political activity. Having comfortably won all elections against small opposition parties, in the 1980s electoral majorities were cut as opposition to dictatorship by the party grew. Corruption and fraud were claimed to be keeping the PRI in power. The PRI candidate in 1988, Carlos Salinas de Gortari, saw his majority dramatically reduced when **Cuauhtémoc Cárdenas** (son of the former president), at the head of a breakaway PRI faction, stood in opposition to him. The disaffected PRI members and others subsequently formed the **Partido de la Revolución Democrática (PRD)**, which rapidly gained support as liberalization of many of the PRI's long-held political and economic traditions became inevitable. In 1989, for the first time, a state governorship was conceded by the PRI, to the right wing party, **Partido de Acción Nacional (PAN)**. On New Year's Day of the election year, 1994, at the moment when the North American Free Trade Agreement (NAFTA – Mexico, the US and Canada) came into force, a guerrilla group briefly took control of several towns in Chiapas. The **Ejército Zapatista de Liberación Nacional** (EZLN) demanded social justice, indigenous people's rights, democracy at all levels of Mexican politics, an end to government corruption, and land reform for the peasantry. Peace talks were overshadowed by the assassination in Tijuana on 23 March of the PRI's appointed presidential candidate, Luis Donaldo Colosio, the murder of the Tijuana police chief and the kidnapping of several prominent businessmen in subsequent months. To replace Colosio, President Salinas nominated **Ernesto Zedillo Ponce de León,** a US-trained economist and former education minister. Despite continued unrest in Chiapas, Zedillo won a comfortable majority in the August elections, as did the PRI in Congress. Zedillo's opponents, Cuauhtémoc Cárdenas of PRD and Diego Fernández Cevallos of PAN claimed fraud, to no effect.

The 1994 devaluation

On 20 December, just after his inauguration, Zedillo devalued the peso, claiming that political unrest was causing capital outflows and putting pressure on the currency. On 22 December a precipitate decision to allow the peso to float against the dollar caused an immediate crisis of confidence and investors in Mexico lost billions of dollars as the peso's value plummeted. Economic problems grew in the first half of 1995 and Mexicans were hard hit by the recession. The ruling position of the PRI was damaged once more. The party was heavily defeated by the PAN in state elections in Jalisco

 (February) and in Guanajuato (May). In the same month, a narrow PRI victory in Yucatán was hotly disputed. In August the PAN retained the state governorship of Baja California Norte. In Chiapas, Zedillo suspended the controversial PRI governor, but the tension between EZLN and the army continued as a 72-hour campaign to apprehend the EZLN leader, Subcomandante Marcos, failed. Talks recommenced in April, with the EZLN calling a ceasefire but the first peace accord was not signed until February 1996.

Intrigue, corruption and political reform

Investigation into Colosio's murder uncovered PRI involvement and the attorney-general Antonio Lozano of PAN ordered the arrest of Raúl Salinas, brother of ex-president Carlos Salinas, for masterminding the murder of PRI general secretary José Ruiz Massieu in 1994. This broke the convention granting former presidents and their families immunity from criticism or prosecution. Carlos Salinas left Mexico under a cloud and scandals within the PRI continued to further alienate the ruling party.

Political reform

Political reform advanced in 1996 with the introduction of direct elections for the mayoralty of Mexico City, the abolishing of government control of the Federal Electoral Institute, the introduction of constitutional reforms to allow referendums and guarantee fairer access to the media for party broadcasts during elections. The President's campaign to clean up government was strengthened when he sacked the governor of Guerrero for his alleged involvement in a peasant massacre. But mid-term congressional elections held in July 1997 for six state governorships, showed the PRI's grip on power was beginning to fade. The PRI suffered a huge blow at the polls, and for the first time ever it lost control of Congress, winning only 239 seats. The PRD surged to become the second largest party in the lower house, with 125 deputies, while the PAN won 122.

The Chiapas massacre

In 1997 the EZLN renewed its protests at the slow pace of change after a year of no negotiations, accusing the government of trying to change the terms of the agreed legal framework for indigenous rights. The low-intensity war continued in Chiapas, where 60,000 troops heavily outnumbered the EZLN fighters hiding in the Lacandón forest. In December 1997, 45 people – mostly women and children – were massacred in Acteal, Chenalhó, near San Cristóbal de las Casas, by paramilitaries linked to the PRI. Human rights groups and church leaders blamed the government for failing to disarm paramilitary groups and not negotiating a solution to the conflict. The local mayor was implicated and arrested with 39 others, charged with taking part in the massacre. Calls for more senior government officials to be removed saw the resignation of the Interior Minister and State Governor in early in 1998. The army increased its pressure on the EZLN and its civilian supporters and foreign observers were deported for violating tourist visas and engaging in 'political activity' in Chiapas.

Presidential elections in the new millennium

During 1999 the political parties manoeuvred and schemed prior to choosing their presidential candidates. President Zedillo relinquished his traditional role in nominating his successor and the PRI had a US-style primary election to select a candidate. **PAN**, meanwhile, chose former Coca-Cola executive **Vicente Fox** to lead their campaign. On 2 July 1999, Mexicans give power to Fox, former governor of Guanajuato, and the PAN, prising it from the PRI for the first time in 71 years.

Fox promoted himself as a down-to-earth man of the people and he spent much time in the lead-up to elections, touring the country on horseback. An admirer of 'third way' politics and of ex-US President Bill Clinton and UK Prime Minister Tony Blair, Fox, who took office on 1 December 2000, announced czar-led initiatives that would tackle government corruption, drug-trafficking, crime and poverty, and the economic conditions that drive migration to the US. One critic dismissively said Fox was "90% image and 10% ideas".

Mid-term elections saw the pendulum swing against Fox with the old-guard PRI winning a majority of seats in the Chamber of Deputies and with it the possibility to thwart any reforms introduced by Fox. Parliamentary and regional elections continue to undermine Fox's authority and with it the hope of the wide-sweeping change he promised to introduce.

Elections in July 2006 will see a new president leading Mexico. A close electoral result appeared to have given Felipe Calderón, the candidate of the ruling conservative National Action Party (PAN) a narrow win over Andrés Manuel López Obrador of the centre-left Party of the Democratic Revolution (PRD), pushing Roberto Madrazo of the Institutional Revolutionary Party (PRI) into third place. However, the outcome is being strongly contested, and it remains to be seen who will take office in December 2006.

Economy

Mexico has been an **oil** producer since the 1880s and was the world's leading producer in 1921. By 1971 the country had become a net importer, a position reversed in 1972 with the discovery of major new reserves. Today Mexico benefits greatly from the reserves and is the world's sixth largest producer with 65% of production coming from offshore wells in the Gulf of Campeche. Roughly one third of government revenues come from oil. Attempts by Fox at reducing reliance on revenues through tax reform were largely unsuccessful. Mexico's **mineral resources** are legendary and it is the world's leading producer of silver, fluorite and arsenic, and a major producer of many other minerals. Agriculture has been losing importance since the beginning of the 1970s and now contributes only 4.1% of GDP (2004).

Manufacturing contributes 17.6% of GDP. While the capital used to be a focal point for manufacturing the government now offers incentives to companies relocating away from major industrial centres. The boom has been with the creation of 3600 *maquiladoras* along the US border which employ some 1.3 million people, earning US$1.5 bn for the economy. **Tourism** is a large source of foreign exchange and the largest employer (about a third of the total workforce). About 22 million international visitors travelled to Mexico in 2005, with about 75% coming from the US.

Recent trends

In 1982 Mexico, like many countries, was unable to service its debts forcing the economy to restructure under the guidance of the International Monetary Fund. Improving economic conditions stimulated negotiations with the US and Canada on the creation of the North America Free Trade Agreement (NAFTA) to open markets, encourage investment and prepare for migration of many state-owned industries. Growth in the early 1990s wobbled with domestic political unrest, which saw the peso devalued and allowed to float freely against the dollar. The loss of US$4 bn in just two days created the 'Tequila effect' which rippled through Latin markets. Economic figures began to recover but the pain of austerity measures laid the foundations of dissent in middle and lower classes. Towards the end of the 1990s devaluation in Brazil caused the stock market to tumble, weakening the peso just months before presidential elections. The increasingly international nature of business in Mexico was reinforced with the purchase of *Banamex* by *Citigroup* in 2001. HSBC continued the trend acquiring Grupo Financiero Bital for US$1.14 bn in 2002.

 The 2000 Census confirmed the importance of the *maquila* industry to the Mexican economy, as well as over US$9 bn sent home from family living abroad, expected to rise to over US$10 bn in 2003. While Mexico's performance in the first three years of the Fox presidency were seen as broadly acceptable, attempts to raise income from non-oil sources failed, in part due to the opposition led Congress that took power in 2003.

Government

Under the 1917 Constitution Mexico is a federal republic of 31 states and a Federal District containing the capital, Mexico City. The President, who appoints the Ministers, is elected for six years and can never be re-elected. The next elections are scheduled for 2006. Congress consists of the 128-seat Senate, half elected every three years on a rotational basis, and the 500-seat Chamber of Deputies, elected every three years. There is universal suffrage.

The states enjoy local autonomy and can levy their own taxes, and each state has its Governor, legislature and judicature. The President has traditionally appointed the Chief of the Federal District but direct elections were held in 1997 for the first time.

Culture

People

The Census of 2000 gave Mexico a total population of 97.4 million people. The 2006 estimate is 107.5 mn. About 9% are considered white, about 30% *indígena* (indigenous); with about 60% mestizos, a mixture in varying proportions of Spanish and *indígena*. Mexico also has infusions of Europeans, Arabs and Chinese. There is a national cultural prejudice in favour of the indigenous rather than the Spanish element, though this does not prevent *indígena* from being looked down on by the more Hispanic elements. There is hardly a single statue of Cortés in the whole of Mexico, although he does figure, pejoratively, in the frescoes of Diego Rivera and his contemporaries. On the other hand the two last Aztec emperors, Moctezuma and Cuauhtémoc, are national heroes.

Indigenous peoples

Among the estimated 24 million *indígenas* there are 54 groups or sub-divisions, each with its own language. Generally, indigenous people are far from evenly distributed; 36% live on the Central Plateau (mostly Hidalgo, and México); 35% are along the southern Pacific coast (Oaxaca, Chiapas, Guerrero), and 23% along the Gulf coast (mostly Yucatán and Veracruz): 94% of them, that is, live in these three regions. There are also sizeable concentrations in Nayarit and Durango, Michoacán, and Chihuahua, Sinoloa and Sonora. The main groups are: **Pápago** (Sonora); **Yaqui** (Sonora); **Mayo** (Sonora and Sinaloa); **Tarahumara** (Chihuahua); **Huastec** and **Otomí** in San Luis Potosí; **Cora** and **Huichol** (Nayarit); **Purépecha/Tarasco** (Michoacán); scattered groups of **Nahua** in Michoacán, Guerrero, Jalisco, Veracruz and other central states; **Totonac** (Veracruz); **Tiapaneco** (Guerrero); in Oaxaca state, **Mixtec**, **Mixe** and **Zapotec**; in Chiapas, **Lacandón, Tzoltzil, Tzeltal, Chol** and others; **Maya** in Campeche, Yucatán and Quintano Roo.

Land ownership

The issue of access to the land has always been the country's fundamental problem, and it was a despairing landless peasantry that rose in the Revolution of 1910 and swept away Porfirio Díaz and the old system of huge estates. The accomplishments of successive PRI governments have been mixed. Life for the peasant is still hard. The minimum wage barely allows a simple diet of beans, rice and *tortillas*. The home is still, possibly, a shack with no windows, no water, no sanitation, and the peasant may still not be able to read or write, but something was done to redistribute the land in the so-called *ejido* system, which gave either communal or personal control of the land. The peasant was freed from the landowner, and his family received some basic health and educational facilities from the state. In 1992 new legislation radically overhauled the outdated agricultural sector with far-reaching political and economic consequences. Farmers now have the right to become private property owners, if two-thirds of the *ejido* votes in favour; to form joint ventures with private businessmen; and to use their land as collateral for loans. Private property owners may form joint stock companies, thereby avoiding the constitutional limits on the size of farms and helping them raise capital. The failure of any agricultural reforms to benefit the peasants of Chiapas was one of the roots of the EZLN uprising in early 1994.

Music and dance

Mexican music is particularly attractive and vibrant and a vigorous radio, film and recording industry has helped make it highly popular throughout Latin America. There can be no more representative an image of Mexico than the *mariachi* musician and his *charro* costume. The Spanish conquistadores and the churchmen that followed them imposed European musical culture on the defeated natives with a heavy hand and this influence remains predominant. Nobody knows what pre-Columbian music sounded like and even the music played today in the *indígena* communities is basically Spanish in origin although African slaves introduced a third ingredient. The music brought from Europe has over the centuries acquired a highly distinctive sound and style of which every Mexican is justly proud, even if many of the young now prefer to listen to Anglo-American rock and pop.

There is a basic distinction between *indígena* and mestizo music. The former is largely limited to festive rituals and dances, religious in nature and solemn in expression. The commonest instruments are flute and drum, with harp and violin also widely used. Some of the most spectacular dances are those of the Concheros (mainly urban), the Quetzales (from the Sierra de Puebla), the Voladores (flying pole – also Sierra de Puebla and Veracruz), the Tarascan dances from around Lake Pátzcuaro and the Yaqui deer dance (Sonora).

Mestizo music clearly has more mass appeal in what is an overwhelmingly mixed population. The basic form is the *son* (also called *huapango* in eastern areas), featuring a driving rhythm overlaid with dazzling instrumentals. Each region has its own style of *son*, such as the *son huasteco* (Northeast), *son calentano* (Michoacán/ Guerrero), *chilena* (Guerrero coast), *son mariachi* (Jalisco), *jarana* (Yucatán) and *son jarocho* (Veracruz). One *son jarocho* that has achieved world status is *La Bamba*. Instrumental backing is provided in almost all these areas by a combination of large and small guitars, with the violin as virtuoso lead in the *huasteca* and the harp in Veracruz. The *chilena* of Guerrero was inspired by Chilean sailors performing their national dance, the *cueca*, during a naval visit to Acapulco in 1822, while Yucatán features a version of the Colombian *bambuco*. The *son* is a dance form for flirtation between couples and often involves spectacular heel-and-toe stamping by the man. Another widespread dance rhythm is the *jarabe*, including the patriotic 'Jarabe Tapatío', better known to the English-speaking world as the 'Mexican Hat Dance'. Certain regions are known for more sedate rhythms and a quite different choice of instruments. In the north, the Conjunto Norteño leads with an accordion and favours the polka as a rhythm. In Yucatán they prefer wind and brass instruments, while the Isthmus of Tehuantepec is the home of the *marimba* (xylophone), which it shares with neighbouring Guatemala.

For singing, as opposed to dancing, there are three extremely popular genres. First is the *corrido*, a narrative form derived from old Spanish ballads, which swept across the country with the armies of the Revolution and has remained a potent vehicle for popular expression. A second is the *canción* (literally 'song'), which gives full rein to the romantic, sentimental aspect of the Mexican character, and is naturally slow and languid. *Las Mañanitas* is a celebrated song for serenading people on their birthdays. The third form is the *ranchera*, a sort of Mexican Country and Western, associated originally with the cattle-men of the Bajío region. Featured in a whole series of Mexican films of the 1930s and 1940s, *rancheras* became known all over the Spanish-speaking world as the typical Mexican music. The film and recording industry turned a number of Mexican artists into household names throughout Latin America. The 'immortals' are Pedro Infante, Jorge Negrete, Pedro Vargas, Miguel Aceves Mejía and the Trio Los Panchos, with Agustín Lara as an equally celebrated and prolific songwriter and composer, particularly of romantic *boleros*. To all outsiders and many Mexicans, however, there is nothing more musically Mexican than *mariachi*, a word said to be derived from the French *mariage*, introduced at the time of Maximilian and Carlota.

Originating in the State of Jalisco, *mariachi* bands arrived in Mexico City in the 1920s and have never looked back. Trumpets now take the lead, backed by violins and guitars and the players all wear *charro* (cowboy) costume, including the characteristic wide-brimmed hat. They play all the major musical forms and can be found almost every evening in Mexico City's Plaza Garibaldi, where they congregate to be seen, heard and hired. This is the very soul of Mexico.

Finally, there are a number of distinguished 20th-century composers who have produced symphonies and other orchestral works based on indigenous and folk themes. Carlos Chávez is the giant and his *Sinfonía India* a particularly fine example. Other notable names are Silvestre Revueltas (*Sensemayá*), Pablo Moncayo (*Huapango*), Blas Galindo (*Sones de Mariachi*) and Luis Sandi (*Yaqui Music*).

Religion

Roman Catholicism is the principal religion, but the state is determinedly secular. Because of its identification firstly with Spain, then with the Emperor Maximilian and finally with Porfirio Díaz, the Church has been severely persecuted in the past by reform-minded administrations, and priests are still not supposed to wear ecclesiastical dress (see *The Lawless Roads* and *The Power and the Glory* by Graham Greene). Rapprochement between State and Church was sought in the early 1990s.

Land and environment

Geography

Mexico is roughly a quarter of the US in size, with which it has a frontier of 2400 km. The southern frontier of 885 km is with Guatemala and Belize. There is 2780 km of coast on the Gulf of Mexico and the Caribbean, and 7360 km on the Pacific.

The structure of the land mass is extremely complicated, but may be simplified (with large reservations) as a plateau flanked by ranges of mountains roughly paralleling the coasts. The northern part of the plateau is low, arid and thinly populated; it takes up 40% of the total area of Mexico but holds only 19% of its people. From the Bolsón de Mayrán as far south as the Balsas valley, the level rises considerably; this southern section of the central plateau is crossed by a volcanic range of mountains in which the intermont basins are high and separated. The basin of Guadalajara is at 1500 m, the basin of México at 2300 m, and the basin of Toluca, west of Mexico City, is at 2600 m. Above the lakes and valley bottoms of this contorted middle-land rise the volcano cones of Orizaba (5700 m), Popocatépetl

(5452 m), Iztaccíhuatl (5286 m), Nevado de Toluca (4583 m), Matlalcueyetl or La Malinche (4461 m), and Cofre de Perote (4282 m). This mountainous southern end of the plateau, the heart of Mexico, has ample rainfall. Only 14% of the area of Mexico, it holds nearly half of the country's people. Its centre, in a small high intermont basin measuring only 50 sq km, is Mexico City, with 20 or so million inhabitants.

The two high ranges of mountains which rise east and west of the plateau, between it and the sea, are great barriers against communications: there are far easier routes north along the floor of the plateau to the US than there are to either the east coast or the west. In the west there are transport links across the Sierra Madre Occidental from Guadalajara to the Pacific at the port of Mazatlán, continuing northward through a coastal desert to Nogales. The Sierra Madre Oriental is more kindly; in its mountain ramparts a pass inland from Tampico gives access to Monterrey, a great industrial centre, and the highland basins; and another from Veracruz leads by a fair gradient to the Valley of México.

South of the seven intermont basins in the south-central region the mountainland is still rugged but a little lower (between 1800 and 2400 m), with much less rainfall. After some 560 km it falls away into the low-lying Isthmus of Tehuantepec. Population is sparse in these southern mountains and is settled on the few flat places where commercial crops can be grown. Subsistence crops are sown on incredibly steep slopes. The Pacific coast here is forbidding and its few ports of little use, though there is massive development of tourism in such places as Acapulco, Zihuatanejo, Puerto Escondido and Huatulco. Very different are the Gulf coast and Yucatán; half this area is classed as flat, and much of it gets enough rain the year round, leading to its having become one of the most important agricultural and cattle raising areas in the country. The Gulf coast also provides most of Mexico's oil and sulphur. Geographically, North America may be said to come to an end in the Isthmus of Tehuantepec. South of the Isthmus the land rises again into the thinly populated highlands of Chiapas.

The complex land mass that is Mexico is the result of millions of years of geological moulding, a process that still continues today. The country was ignited literally by the spectacular eruptions of Popocatépetl, 60 km to the east of the capital, in 2001, which has been slowly wakening from a 65-year slumber for several years. Likewise to the west of the capital, Colima Volcano is closed to climbers, as activity that has been growing steadily in the last few years looks certain to result in an eruption.

Climate

Climate and vegetation depend upon altitude. The *tierra caliente* takes in the coastlands and plateau lands below 750 m. The *tierra templada*, or temperate zone, is at 750 to 2000 m. The *tierra fría*, or cold zone, is from 2000 m upwards. Above the tree line at 4000 m are high moorlands (*páramos*). The climate of the inland highlands is mostly mild, but with sharp changes of temperature between day and night, sunshine and shade. Generally, winter is the dry season and summer the wet season. There are only two areas where rain falls the year round: south of Tampico along the lower slopes of the Sierra Madre Oriental and across the Isthmus of Tehuantepec into Tabasco state; and along the Pacific coast of the State of Chiapas. Both areas together cover only 12% of Mexico. These wetter parts get most of their rain between June and September, when the skies are so full of clouds that the temperature is lowered: May is a hotter month than July. Apart from these regions, the rest of the country suffers when the rainy season hardly lives up to its name and the dry season almost always does. Extremes of weather do happen, however. In October 2005, the Yucatán Peninsula was savaged by Hurricane Wilma which stayed in the area for close to three days. Damage caused by Wilma is believed to have reduced income to the area by as much as US$800 million. Wilma hit the area shortly after Tropical Storm Stan which caused landslides and early Hurricane Emily.

Books and films

Books

Archaeological sites

Do not expect to find leaflets or books at the sites, so stock up before you visit.

Bloomgarden, Richard *Panorama Guides* and *Easy Guides*. Reliable, widely available and with plans and good illustrations. (Also available are *Miniguides* to archaeological and historical sites, published in various languages by INAH, US$0.75 each.)

Coe, MD *The Maya*, (Pelican Books, or large format edition, Thames and Hudson). Essential recommended reading for the Maya archaeological area.

Birdwatching

Edwards, Ernest P *Finding Birds in Mexico*, Box AQ, Sweet Briar, Virginia 24595, US. Detailed and thorough.

Peterson and Chalif *A Field Guide to Mexican Birds*, Houghton Mifflin, 1973.

Mexican history

Prescott, William *History of the Conquest of Mexico* (1849) Reliable, dated, old favourite.

Thomas, Hugh *Conquest: Cortes, Montezuma, and the fall of the Old Mexico* (1995). A more up-to-date overview.

Travel

Franz, Carl *The People's Guide to Mexico* (John Muir Publications, Santa Fe, NM, 1998). Highly recommended, practical, entertaining and now in its 11th edition. there is also a *People's Guide Travel Letter*.

Burlison, Bob and Riskind, David H *Back Country Mexico, A Traveller's Guide and Phrase Book*, (University of Texas Press, Box 7819, Austin, Texas, 78713-7819).

Robins, Rudi *One-day Car Trips from Mexico City*, and *Weekend Trips to Cities near Mexico City*.

Tree, Isabella *Sliced Iguana – Travels in Mexico* (Penguin Books, 2002). Gets the real flavour of Mexico and is a great travel companion.

Films

On the international big screen Mexico has probably suffered more than most from stereotypical images painting the whole nation as a bunch of lazy, good-for-nothing scoundrels, crooks and corrupt officials. The Western genre relied heavily on the scenic locations around Durango producing classics from the 1950s through the works of Sam Peckinpah up to the more recent all-star *Mask of Zorro*. Many other US productions have used Mexico's tropical locations for films such as *Night of the Iguana*, *Romancing the Stone* and *Medicine Man*, and the blockbuster *Titanic*, which was shot at Rosarito, Baja California, close to Tijuana. But the national film industry has grown in prominence in recent years with international successes including *Como agua para chocolate* (*Like Water for Chocolate)*, *Danzón*, *Amores Perros* (nominated for an Oscar and winner of the 2002 Bafta for best foreign film), and *Y tu mamá también*, a road movie about love, sex, friendship, politics and the blind haste to grow up. Another hit, *Frida*, celebrates the life of the painter Frida Kahlo and her relationship with Diego Rivera, how the couple took the art world by storm and her controversial affair with Leon Trotsky.

Guatemala

History

On the eve of the Spanish conquest of Guatemala there were a number of dominant Maya groups, but dissent within some of these groups was exploited by the invading Spanish, who conquered the country bit by bit from 1524 through to 1697. Under Pedro de Alvarado the *encomienda* system was introduced whereby the Maya were forced to work land that was previously theirs and pay tribute to the colonialists in the form of crops. In return they received Christian instruction. They were treated like slaves and gradually died in their thousands from western diseases. At the end of the 18th century, Spanish power began to wane and Central American Independence was signed in 1821, followed by the creation of the Central American Federation. Full independence came in 1839. Liberals and Conservatives see-sawed in and out of power until 1944. Between 1839 and 1842 the Conservatives restored Spanish institutions. This hark back to the colonial era was continued by the fiercely pro-church Rafael Carrera who became president in 1844. He set about restoring church power and reinviting the Jesuits back into the country (they had been expelled in 1767). He went into exile in 1848 before returning to power in 1851 where he remained until 1865.

For more on the region's early history, see page 1206.

The 1871 Liberal Revolution

On Carrera's death, General Vicente Cerna ruled Guatemala, where he repeatedly suffered Liberal opposition, continuing the Conservative bent until 1871. In 1867, a Liberal revolt was launched in Guatemala, headed by Mariscal Cruz, an ally of the Liberal general Justo Rufino Barrios. Then, a small group of men, led by Barrios' troops invaded from Mexico. Initially they were forced back, but eventually Barrios' troops overthrew the Cerna regime, introducing a wave of Liberal leadership. During his short term, Barrios supporter Miguel García Granados (1871-1873) expelled leading clerics and overturned Carrera's invitation to the Jesuits.

Justo Rufino Barrios (1873-1885) was elected president. He too was vehemently anti-clerical and church power was reined in. He expropriated church property, using the proceeds to found a national bank, secularized education and marriage, and aimed to restore the federation. This idea floundered and he resorted to dictatorial methods. When El Salvador refused to accept the notion of the federation he invaded and died in a battle at Chalachuapa. His term of office was characterized by huge infrastructure projects, including the construction of ports and railways. Coffee production was reformed, which transformed Guatemala into a major producer, but had detrimental effects on the lives of the *indígenas*, who saw their plots of lands seized for coffee plantations, and who were forced to work the plantations. Until 1857, cochineal and indigo were the great exports, but both were wiped out by competition from synthetic dyes. The export vacuum left by indigo and cochineal was filled by *cacao*, followed by coffee and bananas, and essential oils.

Manuel Lisandra Barillas (1885-1892) followed in the presidency and again tried to re-establish Central American union. He was in the same mould as Barrios and continued supporting the expanison of the coffee economy. In his Liberal footsteps followed General José María Reina Barrios (1892-1898) who confiscated his enemies' property and spent much time quashing internal rebellion. During his term the price of coffee crashed on the world market, but public works using public money continued to be built, causing widespread outrage and revolts. He was assassinated.

Dictatorship and the rise of the United Fruit Company

In his place Manuel Estrada Cabrera (1898-1920) came to power. His was the longest one-man rule in Central American history. Cabrera encouraged foreign investment, expansion of the railways and encouraged the United Fruit Company's foray into Guatemala with the planting of bananas. The company acquired privileges, a monopoly on transport and free rein on their affairs without too much state intervention. The United Fruit Company's first plantations were at the mouth of the Río Motagua, near Puerto Barrios, then little more than a village. The company managed the electricity plant, ran supply shops, and was handed the contract to finish the railway line to the Atlantic and granted a 99-year right to use the existing railway line and the port. Land rights saw the company granted some 800,000 ha. Exports soared and American interests in Guatemala grew to the point where 40% of all exports were US controlled. The nail in the coffin of the Cabrera government was its response to the 1917 earthquake and Cabrera was eventually toppled.

Carlos Herrera followed as president and started on a fairly liberal path, but the old style military did not like his approach, and he was overthrown in a bloodless military coup, bringing José María Orellana to power. During Herrera's short presidency (1920-1921) there were strikes against the United Fruit Company and the International Railways of Central America, which the fruit company also ran. Out of this anti-American sentiment again rose the idea of Central American unity, but Orellana knocked this idea on the head and negotiated more concessions for United Fruit and the railway company. However, workers' demands for rights were not to be suffocated, organized protest grew and periodically met with government crackdowns. Orellana, unlike some of his predecessors, died a natural death in 1926.

Social reform

Jorge Ubico was an efficient but brutal dictator who came to power in 1931. He tightened political control, introduced a secret police, clamped down on workers' discontent and Communist movements, persecuted writers and intellectuals, and restricted books coming into the country because of his fear of Communism. He promoted forced labour, fixed low wage rates, and introduced an anti-vagrancy law, whereby the Maya had to work for free on a landlords's farm for 150 days a year. Ubico supported the US government during the Second World War, and during this period sent Germans living in Guatemala back to their homeland, or to camps in the US. He followed this up with expropriating German-owned land. He also extended privileges to the United Fruit Company. These, and other issues, and the fact that he sought constant re-election, provoked demonstrations and a demand for his resignation. The demonstrations led to the suspension of constitutional rights. After a teacher was shot dead during a demonstration demanding university autonomy, the demonstrators called for Ubico's resignation. He resigned in June 1944 and a triumvirate of generals assumed power.

October Revolution

On 20 October 1944 there was an armed uprising of La Guardia de Honor, backed by popular support. The military leaders drew up a democratic constitution, abolished forced labour, and upheld the autonomy of the university. Teacher **Juan José Arévalo** of the **Frente Popular Libertador** party was then elected president and drew up a plan of social reform. He separated the powers of state, introduced *comedores* for children of poor workers, set up the Department for Social Security, and accepted the existence of the Communist Party. He survived more than 20 military coups and finished his term of five years (1945-1950).

1954 US-backed military coup

Jacobo Arbenz Guzmán, a member of the 1944 military triumvirate, became the elected president in 1950. His biggest reforms focused on land reform and the breaking up of American business monopolies in Guatemala. This set him on a collision course with the United Fruit Company. His 1952 Agrarian Reform Law saw the expropriation of large, under-utilized estates without adequate compensation awarded to their owners. The land was then distributed among the numerous landless peasantry, which aroused huge opposition from landowners. The value of the land was based on its declared taxable worth. Altogether, about 1.5 million acres of land was redistributed to around 100,000 families, at a cost of nearly US$8.5 million in government bonds. The biggest voice of discontent came from United Fruit, which for years had been under-declaring the value of its land for tax reasons. According to the company, of its 550,000 acres around the Caribbean, 85% of it was not farmed. It was offered a measly US$2.99 an acre for land (440,000 acres) which it said was worth US$75 – the seeds of the coup had been sown.

Arbenz also attempted to dismantle the monopolies created by the likes of United Fruit. He made moves to build a government-funded port on the Caribbean coast, and started the construction of the Atlantic Highway to transport goods to compete with the fruit company-run railway line. In addition, he also ordered the construction of a hydroelectricity plant to compete with the existing plant run by an American company.

At the same time reports suggested there was increased Communist infiltration of the government. The reforms threatened American commercial interests in Guatemala, especially that of the United Fruit Company. The company's connections with the high-powered within the US Government and the CIA, and its constant complaint that Communism was percolating through the Guatemalan corridors of power, eventually persuaded the US to sponsor an overthrow of the Arbenz government.

According to the excellent investigative report *Bitter Fruit: The Story of the American Coup in Guatemala,* the US waited for tangible proof of the Guatemalan government's 'communist identity' before sponsoring the overthrow of the Arbenz regime. When a boat stockpiled with Czech weapons docked at Puerto Barrios there was no longer any need to delay action. According to the book's authors Stephen Schlesinger and Stephen Kinzer, President Eisenhower said weapons were one step away from establishing a Communist dictatorship.

A well-orchestrated propaganda war was also put in motion by United Fruit to persuade international opinion of the Communist threat. Military strikes were launched on the country in June 1954. At the end of the month Arbenz, under pressure from Guatemalan military and the US ambassador John Peurifoy, resigned. Arbenz went into exile. According to *Bitter Fruit*, the Eisenhower administration tried to distance itself from growing international criticism and it launched an anti-trust suit against United Fruit after investigating its land holdings in Guatemala. This, the book alleges, it did in an attempt to distance itself from the debacle and the opinion that it was defending United Fruit.

Military rule

In June 1954, **Colonel Carlos Castillo Armas**, took over the presidency. He persecuted and outlawed Communists. He was assassinated in 1957, which provoked a wave of violence and instability in Guatemala and for the next three decades the army and its right-wing supporters suppressed left-wing efforts, both constitutional and violent, to restore the gains made under Arévalo and Arbenz; many thousands of people, mostly leftists but also many Maya without political orientation, were killed during this period.

The rise of the guerrilla movement

On 13 November 1960, a military group, inspired by revolution in Cuba, carried out an uprising against the government. It was suppressed but spawned the

 Movimiento 13 de Noviembre, which then joined forces with the **Guatemalan Worker's Party.** In 1962, student demonstrations ended in bloodshed, which resulted in the creation of the **Movimiento 12 de Abril.** These movements then merged to form **Fuerzas Armadas Rebeldes (FAR)** in 1962.

During this period, Arévalo made a move to re-enter the political fold. A coup d'état followed. Guerrilla and right-wing violence began to increase in the late 1960s. In the early 1970s the guerrillas re-focused. The FAR divided into FAR and the EGP (**Ejército Guerrillero de los Pobres,** Guerrilla Army of the Poor) which operated in the north of the country. In 1972 the **Organización Revolucionaria del Pueblo en Armas** (ORPA) was formed. The EGP was led by Rolando Morán, a supporter of the Cuban Revolution. The group's first action took place in the Ixil Triangle in 1975. The ORPA was led by Commandante Gaspar Ilom, also known as Rodrigo Asturias, son of Nobel Prize for Literature winner Miguel Angel Asturias.

The worst of the conflict

Throughout the 1970s and early 1980s the worst atrocities of the war were committed. General Kjell Eugenio Laugerud García's presidency was characterized by escalating violence, which led the US to withdraw its support for the Guatemalan government in 1974 and demand that human rights be respected.

A devastating earthquake struck Guatemala in 1976 killing 23,000 people. This prompted widespread social movements in the country to improve the lives of the poor. At the same time guerrilla activity surged. In 1978-1982, during the term of General Romeo Lucas García and the presidency of **Efraín Ríos Montt**, the violence reached its peak.

The US, believing the human rights situation had improved, resumed military sales to Guatemala. But in 1981 the military unleashed a huge offensive against the guerrillas who united to confront it with the formation of the **Unidad Revolucionaria Nacional Guatemalteca** (URNG) in 1982. The government also set up the civil defence patrols, which were like neighbourhood watch movements, but with a sinister edge. They would set brother against brother and father against son, and were aimed at assisting the army in stopping the infiltration of guerrilla forces into Guatemalan society. Ríos Montt came to power in 1982 following a coup d'état. He and his predecessor presided over the worst period of violence in the civil war with the introduction of the scorched-earth policy, which saw massacres of whole villages in an attempt to root out bands of guerrillas in a massive counter-insurgency campaign. Ríos Montt was ousted by his defence minister, General Oscar Mejías Victores, in a coup in August 1983.

Return of democracy

Mejía Victores permitted a Constituent Assembly to be elected in 1984, which drew up a new constitution and worked out a timetable for a return to democracy. He also created numerous 'model villages' to rehouse the displaced and persecuted Maya, who had fled in their thousands to the forests, the capital, Mexico and the US. Presidential elections in December 1985, were won by civilian Vinicio Cerezo Arévalo of the Christian Democrat party (DC), who took office in January 1986. He was the first democratically elected President of Guatemala since 1966. He opened the door to the first political dialogue between the government and the URNG in 1987. This was preceded by the establishment of the Commission for National Reconciliation formed in attempt to resolve the violent conflicts that had enveloped the entire region. In the 1990 elections the DC fared badly, their candidate failing to qualify for run-off elections between the eventual winner, **Jorge Serrano Elías** of the Solidarity Action Movement and **Jorge Carpio** of the National Centrist Union. Serrano Elías made Guatemalan history by being the first civilian to succeed a previous civilian president in a change of government.

Civil unrest

By 1993, however, the country was in disarray. Political, social and economic policies pursued by the government had alienated nearly everybody and violence erupted on the streets led by a wave of student riots. Amid growing civil unrest, President Serrano suspended the constitution, dissolved Congress and the Supreme Court, and imposed press censorship, with what appeared to be military support for his auto-coup. International and domestic condemnation of his actions was immediate and most foreign aid was frozen. After only a few days, Serrano was ousted by a combination of military, business and opposition leaders and a return to constitutional rule was promised. Congress approved a successor to Serrano, electing Ramiro de León Carpio, previously the human rights ombudsman. This spectacular choice led to much optimism, which proved short-lived. Although progress was made in talks between the government and the URNG, human rights violations continued. Some communities, displaying no faith in the security and justice systems, took the law into their own hands in dealing with criminals. Land invasions also continued and strikes in the public and private sectors continued in 1994 and early 1995. In this climate, the public's distaste of corrupt congressional deputies and ineffectual government was not diminished. The president seemed powerless to restore any confidence because Congress deliberately failed to approve bills on constitutional, police or tax reform, and other laws. The reform of election procedures and political parties had been called for by a referendum in 1994, which obliged Congressional elections to be called. The result gave a majority of seats to the Guatemalan Republican Front (FRG), led by ex-president Ríos Montt. Despite an alliance of four parties against the FRG's control of Congress, Ríos Montt was elected to the presidency of Congress for 1994-1996. Ríos Montt's candidate in the 1995 presidential election, Alfonso Portillo, lost by a slim margin to Alvaro Arzú of the National Advancement Party. Arzú proposed to increase social spending, curtail tax evasion, combat crime and bring a speedy conclusion to peace negotiations with the URNG guerrillas.

Towards peace

One of the earliest moves made by President Serrano was to speed up the process of talks between the government and the URNG, which began in March 1990. The sides met in Mexico City in April 1991 to discuss such topics as democratization and human rights, a reduced role for the military, the rights of indigenous people, the resettlement of refugees and agrarian reform. Progress, however, was slow. In August 1995 an accord was drawn up with the aid of the UN's Guatemala mission (MINUGUA) and the Norwegian government. The timetable proved over-ambitious, but, on taking office in January 1996, President Arzú committed himself to signing a peace accord. In February 1996 he met the URNG leadership, who called a ceasefire in March. On 29 December 1996 a peace treaty was signed ending 36 years of armed conflict. An amnesty was agreed which would limit the scope of the Commission for Historical Clarification and prevent it naming names in its investigations of human rights abuses. Although a demobilization of the guerrilla was completed successfully, difficulties remained over human rights in the peace process.

Peacetime elections and the Portillo Government

The 1999 elections went to a second round with self-confessed killer Alfonso Portillo of the FRG winning 62% of the vote against his rival Oscar Berger, the candidate of President Arzú's ruling PAN. Portillo, while on the campaign trail, used to say that as someone that had defended his own life he could defend his countrymen's. (After he had gunned down two Mexican students in 1982.) On coming to office in January 2000, Portillo committed his government to uphold the Peace Accord of 1996 adding that "all the political, economic and social changes this country needs are mandated under the peace accord". Portillo subsequently promised to reform the armed forces, solve the killing of Bishop Gerardi and disband the élite presidential guard, so implicated in the human rights abuses. Common crime, as well as more sinister crimes such as lynchings, plagued Portillo's term and seemed to increase. Since the signing of the Peace Accords MINUGUA has verified 347 lynchings throughout the country.

In 2002, human rights activists and forensic teams excavating burial sites of civil war victims continued to be threatened. Ex-paramilitaries blockaded Tikal, trapping tourists in the grounds of the ruins, after they demanded compensation for their roles in the civil war. The government said it would try and levy a tax to pay them compensation. In June, ex-president Jorge Serrano was ordered to be arrested on charges which included embezzlement of state funds. He remains exiled in Panama. The former interior minister Byron Barrientos resigned in December 2001 and faced accusations of misappropriating US$6 million in state funds. He has now voluntarily brought himself before the courts. In October 2002, a former colonel in the Guatemalan army, Colonel Juan Valencia Osorio, was found guilty of ordering the murder of anthropologist Myrna Mack and sentenced to 30 years imprisonment. Myrna's sister Helen had been campaigning for 12 years for the conviction of such a senior military man. However, the appeal court overturned his conviction in 2003. Also in October 2002, the four men imprisoned for their role in the 1998 murder of Guatemalan Bishop Gerardi had their convictions overturned. A retrial was ordered. In 2003 Ríos Montt mounted a legal challenge to a rule which prohibits former coup leaders running for president. The constitutional court ruled he could stand in the autumn parliamentary elections. The UN High Commission for Human Rights announced it would open an office in Guatemala City. More details can be found at www.ghrc-usa.org.

2004 elections

A new era in Guatemalan politics began with the election of **Oscar Berger** as president in December. After coming second to Portillo in the 1999 elections as candidate for PAN, Berger led the newly formed **Gran Alianza Nacional** (GANA) to electoral victory with 54% of the vote over his centre-left rival Alvaro Colom. Internal disputes over leadership of PAN had forced the former Guatemala City mayor to leave the party. While the long-term political future of GANA is uncertain, Berger assumed the presidency promising to improve access to clean water, education and health care for all citizens. He also persuaded indigenous leader and Nobel Prize winner Rigoberta Menchú to join his government to work towards a more just country. As only the second presidential elections since the end of civil war in 1996, many observers feared intimidation. Particular as former military ruler, Rios Montt was defeated in the first round of the election. Montt lost his immunity from prosecution in January 2004 when he gave up his seat in the Guatemalan Congress. Montt was placed under house arrest in March 2004 after appearing in court to testify in connection with the death of a journalist in protests in 2003.

Economy

Tourism is the biggest earner for the country. The agricultural sector accounts for one-quarter of GDP, two-thirds of exports, and half of the labour force. Coffee, sugar, and bananas are the main produce, followed by vegetables, sesame and cardamom. There has been an attempt to diversify agricultural exports with tobacco, fruit and ornamental plants. Beef exports are increasing. The equitable distribution of occupied land is still a pressing problem. US Aid statistics show 68% of cultivable land is in the hands of just 2% of landowners, while medium and small landowners account for 20% and 10% of cultivable land, respectively. The industrial sector, apart from food and drink production, includes rubber manufacture, textiles, paper and pharmaceuticals. Chemicals, furniture, petroleum products, electrical components and building materials are also produced. The encouragement of *maquila* industries in the mid-1980s attracted foreign investment, much of it from the Far East, and created low-paid jobs for about 80,000 Guatemalans, mostly in garment manufacturing. Real GDP growth recovered to 2.7% in 2004 and 3.2%in 2005, despite high international oil prices and the damage from tropical storm Stan. The economy is projected to grow by around 4.5% per year in 2006 and 2007, reflecting improvements in the domestic business climate, higher global economic growth, low interest rates and a rebound in coffee prices.

Government

Guatemala is a Republic with a single legislative house of 80 seats. The Head of State and of government is the President. The country is administratively divided into 22 Departments. The Governor of each is appointed by the President, whose term is for five years. The latest constitution was dated May 1985. The next elections will be in 2009.

Culture

People

The word *ladino* applies to any person with a 'Latin' culture, speaking Spanish and wearing Western clothes, though they may be pure Amerindian by descent. The opposite of *ladino* is *indígena*; the definition is cultural, not racial. Guatemala's population in 2006 is estimated to be 3 million. The indigenous people of Guatemala are mainly of Maya descent. The largest of the 22 indigenous Maya groups are K'iche', Q'eqchi' and Mam. When the Spaniards arrived from Mexico in 1524 those who stayed settled in the southern highlands around Antigua and Guatemala City and intermarried with the groups of native subsistence farmers living there. This was the basis of the present mestizo population living in the cities and towns as well as in all parts of the southern highlands and in the flatlands along the Pacific coast; the indigenous population is still at its most dense in the western highlands and Alta Verapaz. They form two distinct cultures: the almost self-supporting indigenous system in the highlands, and the *ladino* commercial economy in the lowlands. Mestizo are mixed Amerindian-Spanish or assimilated Amerindian – more commonly known as *ladino*. About half the total population are classed as Amerindian (Maya) – estimates vary from 40-65%. The remaining populaton comprises: *ladinos*, over 40%; whites, 5%; black, 2%; and other mixed race or Chinese, 3.9%. A 2001 study revealed that there are 5,944,222 Maya; 3,800,405 *ladinos*; 6539 Garífuna; and 297 Xinca who are physically similar to the *ladinos*.

Costume and dress

Indigenous dress is particularly attractive, little changed from the time the Spaniards arrived: the colourful head-dresses, *huípiles* (tunics) and skirts of the women, the often richly patterned sashes and kerchiefs, the hatbands and tassels of the men vary greatly, often from village to village. Unfortunately a new outfit is costly, the indigenous people are poor, and denims are cheap. While men are adopting Western dress in many villages, women have been slower to change.

Religion

There is no official religion but about 70% consider themselves Roman Catholic. The other 30% are Protestant, mostly affiliated to evangelical churches, which have been very active in the country over the past 25 years.

Land and environment

A lowland ribbon, nowhere more than 50 km wide, runs the whole length of the Pacific shore. Cotton, sugar, bananas and maize are the chief crops of this strip. There is some stock raising as well. Summer rain is heavy and the lowland carries scrub forest. From this plain the highlands rise sharply to heights of between 2500 and 4000 m and stretch some 240 km to the north before sinking into the northern lowlands. A string of volcanoes juts boldly above the southern highlands along the Pacific. There are intermont basins at from 1500 to 2500 m in this volcanic area. Most of the people of Guatemala live in these basins, which are drained by short rivers into the Pacific and by longer ones into the Atlantic. One basin west of the capital, ringed by volcanoes and with no apparent outlet, is Lago de Atitlán. The southern highlands are covered with lush vegetation over a volcanic subsoil. This clears away in the central highlands, exposing the crystalline rock of the east-west running ranges. This area is lower but more rugged, with sharp-faced ridges and deep ravines modifying into gentle slopes and occasional valley lowlands as it loses height and approaches the Caribbean coastal levels and the flatlands of El Petén. The lower slopes of these highlands, from about 600 to 1500 m, are planted with coffee. Above 1500 m is given over to wheat and the main subsistence crops of maize and beans. Deforestation is becoming a serious problem. Where rainfall is low there are savannas; water for irrigation is now drawn from wells and these areas are being reclaimed for pasture and fruit growing. Two large rivers flow down to the Caribbean Gulf of Honduras from the highlands: one is the Río Motagua, 400 km long, rising among the southern volcanoes; the other, further north, is the Río Polochic, 298 km long, which drains into Lago de Izabal and the Bahía de Amatique. There are large areas of lowland in the lower reaches of both rivers, which are navigable for considerable distances; this was the great banana zone. To the northwest, bordering on Belize and Mexico's Yucatán Peninsula, lies the low, undulating tableland of El Petén almost one-third of the nation's territory. In some parts there is natural grassland, with woods and streams, suitable for cattle, but large areas are covered with dense hardwood forest. Since the 1970s large-scale tree-felling has reduced this tropical rainforest by some 40%, especially in the south and east. However, in the north, which now forms Guatemala's share of the Maya Biosphere Reserve, the forest is protected, but illegal logging still takes place.

Guatemala's suffered badly from Hurricane Mitch in 1998, and again in 2005 with the passing of Hurricane Stan which caused landslides in many highland villages, killing at least 1500 people.

Books and films

Books

Balchin de Koose, Barbara Guatemala for You (Piedra Santa, Guatemala City).
Menchú, Rigoberta I, Rigoberta Menchú.
Daniels, Anthony Sweet Waist of America: Journeys around Guatemala (Hutchinson).
Asturias, Miguel Angel Hombres de maíz, Mulata de tal and El señor presidente.
Payeras, Mario Los días de la selva. A first-hand account of the guerrilla movement in the 1970s.

Films

Nava, Gregory El Norte (1983). Follows the plight of a Guatemalan brother and sister who seek a new life after experiencing the trials of their village massacre.
Yates and Sigel When the Mountains Tremble (1983). A hard-hitting film demonstrating the desperation of national governments and guerrillas.

Belize

History

Throughout the country, especially in the forests of the centre and south, there are many ruins of the Classic Maya period, which flourished here and in neighbouring Guatemala from the fourth to the ninth century and then, mysteriously (most probably because of drought), emigrated to Yucatán. It is estimated that the population was then 10 times what it is now.

The first settlers were English, with their black slaves from Jamaica, who came in about 1640 to cut logwood, then the source of textile dyes. The British Government made no claim to the territory but tried to secure the protection of the wood-cutters by treaties with Spain. Even after 1798, when a strong Spanish force was decisively beaten off at St George's Caye, the British Government still failed to claim the territory, though the settlers maintained that it had now become British by conquest.

When they achieved independence from Spain in 1821, both Guatemala and Mexico laid claim to sovereignty over Belize, but these claims were rejected by Britain. Long before 1821, in defiance of Spain, the British settlers had established themselves as far south as the River Sarstoon, the present southern boundary. Independent Guatemala claimed that these settlers were trespassing and that Belize was a province of the new republic. By the middle of the 19th century Guatemalan fears of an attack by the United States led to a rapprochement with Britain. In 1859, a Convention was signed by which Guatemala recognized the boundaries of Belize while, by Article 7, the United Kingdom undertook to contribute to the cost of a road from Guatemala City to the sea 'near the settlement of Belize'; an undertaking which was never carried out.

For more on the region's early history, see page 1206.

Heartened by what it considered a final solution of the dispute, in 1862 Great Britain declared Belize, still officially a settlement, a Colony, and a Crown Colony nine years later. Mexico, by treaty, renounced any claims it had on Belize in 1893, but Guatemala, which never ratified the 1859 agreement, renewed its claims periodically.

Independence and after

Belize became independent on 21 September 1981, following a United Nations declaration to that effect. Guatemala refused to recognize the independent state, but in 1986 President Cerezo of Guatemala announced an intention to drop his country's claim to Belize. A British military force was maintained in Belize from independence until 1993, when the British government announced that the defence of Belize would be handed over to the government on 1 January 1994, and that it would reduce the 1200-strong garrison to about 100 soldiers who would organize jungle warfare training facilities. The last British troops were withdrawn in 1994 and finance was sought for the expansion of the Belize Defence Force. Belize was admitted into the OAS in 1991 following negotiations with Guatemala and Britain. As part of Guatemala's recognition of Belize as an independent nation (ratified by Congress in 1992), Britain will recompense Guatemala by providing financial and technical assistance to construct road, pipeline and port facilities that will guarantee Guatemala access to the Atlantic.

Border friction is an ongoing issue between Belize and Guatemala, and in early 2000 tensions overflowed when Guatemalans took some members of the Belizean Defence Force hostage for several days, eventually resulting in some Guatemalans being shot. Tensions were stretched to the limit, and periodically continue to rise and fall but now seem to have cooled and Guatemala has agreed to pursue its claim to half of Belizean territory through the international courts. Low-key negotiations continue between the two countries and in 2003 both countries agreed a **draft settlement** at Organization of American States (OAS) brokered talks. Progress is painfully slow, with Belize and Guatemala signing up to a negotiation framework at the end of 2005.

Economy

Belize's central economic challenge is how to become self-sufficient in food: imports of food are still some 20% of the total requirement. Conversely food exports – sugar, citrus fruits and bananas – are the most important sector of the Belizean economy, directly or indirectly employing more than half the population and bringing in 65% of the country's total foreign exchange earnings. With government encouragement to develop tourism and related services, the sector is now the largest foreign revenue earner. The surge in growth recent years, particularly with cruise ships, how contributes around US$200 million to the economy, providing employment for around one third of the workforce. Traditional exports include timber and marine products (for example shrimp and conch) both of which have been hit by conservation based protests and over extraction in some areas. Light industry and manufacturing (dominated by sugar refining and citrus processing), contribute about 14% of GDP. The value of clothing exports has risen to 10% of domestic exports.

Economic pressures led to the introduction of new taxes in January 2005 as part of the annual budget, Widespread protests culminated in a two-day national strike. The mood continued with further protests in April.

Government

Belize is a constitutional monarchy. The British monarch is the chief of state, represented by a Governor-General, who is a Belizean. The head of government is the Prime Minister. There is a National Assembly, with a House of Representatives of 29 members (not including the Speaker) elected by universal adult suffrage, and a Senate of eight: five appointed by the advice of the Prime Minister, two on the advice of the Leader of the Opposition and one by the Governor-General after consultation. General elections are held at intervals of no more than five years.

Mr George Price, of the People's United Party (PUP), who had been re-elected continuously as Prime Minister since internal self-government was instituted in 1964, was defeated by Mr Manuel Esquivel, of the United Democratic Party (UDP), in general elections held in December 1984 (the first since independence), but was returned as Prime Minister in 1989. The National Alliance for Belizean Rights (NABR) was created in 1992 by a defector from the UDP. General elections were held early in 1993 and, contrary to forecasts, the PUP was defeated. The UDP, in alliance with the NABR, won 16 of the 29 seats, many by a very narrow margin, and Mr Esquivel took office as Prime Minister with the additional portfolios of Finance and Defence. In the months following the elections, a corruption scandal rocked Belizean politics. Several PUP members, including the former Foreign Minister, were arrested on charges of offering bribes to two UDP members of the House of Representatives to persuade them to cross the floor. They were later acquitted. Mr Price retired from the PUP party leadership in 1996, aged 77, after 40 years in the post. He was succeeded by Mr Said Musa, a lawyer. In 1997 the PUP had a spectacular success in the municipal elections, winning all seven Town Boards for the first time ever, reversing the 1994 position when the UDP had won them all. It continued its electoral success in 1998 in the August general election, when it won an unprecedented 26 of the 29 seats in the House of Representatives.

Elections in March 2003 returned Said Musa to the presidency as head of the PUP with 21 of the 29 assembly seats.

Culture

The 2000 National Census put the population of Belize at 240,204, given an annual population growth of 2.7% from the 1991 census figure of 189,392. The urban/rural distribution continues to be roughly 50:50 as it was In 1991. The fastest growing district over the 10-year period is Cayo which has gained at the expense of Orange Walk District and, to a far lesser extent, Belize District. The town of Orange Walk is now only a couple of hundred people more than San Ignacio/Santa Elena which has grown significantly – by Belizean standards – in the last 10 years.

People

About 30% of the population are predominantly black and of mixed ancestry, the so-called Creoles, a term widely used in the Caribbean. They predominate in Belize City, along the coast and on the navigable rivers. About 44% of the population are mestizo; 11% are Maya, who predominate in the north between the Hondo and New rivers and in the extreme south and west. About 7% of the population are Garífuna (black Caribs), descendants of those deported from St Vincent in 1797; they have a distinct language, and can be found in the villages and towns along the southern coast. They are good linguists, many speaking Mayan languages as well as Spanish and 'Creole' English. They also brought their culture and customs from the West Indies, including religious practices and ceremonies, for example Yankanu (John Canoe) dancing at Christmas time. The remainder are of unmixed European ancestry (the majority Mennonites, who speak a German dialect, and are friendly and helpful) and a rapidly growing group of North Americans. The Mennonites fall into two groups, generally speaking: the most rigorous, in the Shipyard area on The New River, and the more 'integrated' in the west, Cayo district, who produce much of Belize's poultry, dairy goods and corn. The newest Mennonite settlements are east of Progresso Lagoon in the northeast. There are also East Indian and Chinese immigrants and their descendants.

Language and education

English is the official language, although for some 180,000 the lingua franca is 'Creole' English. Spanish is the lingua franca for about 130,000 people and is widely spoken in the northern and western areas. In addition, it is estimated that 22,000 people speak Mayan languages, 15,000 Garífuna and 3000 German. Free elementary education is available to everyone, and all the towns have secondary schools.

Land and environment

The coastlands are low and swampy with much mangrove, many salt and fresh water lagoons and some sandy beaches. In the north the land is low and flat, while in the southwest there is a heavily forested mountain massif with a general elevation of between 2000 and 3000 ft. In the east are the Maya Mountains, not yet wholly explored, and the Cockscomb Range which rises to a height of 3675 ft at Victoria Peak. Further west are some 250 square miles of the Mountain Pine Ridge, with large open spaces and some of the best scenery in the country.

From 10 to 40 miles off the coast an almost continuous, 184-mile line of reefs and cayes (or cays) provides shelter from the Caribbean, and forms the longest coral reef in the Western Hemisphere (the fifth-longest barrier reef in the world). Most of the cayes are quite tiny, but some have been developed into tourist resorts. Many have beautiful sandy beaches with clear, clean water, where swimming and diving are excellent. However, on the windward side of inhabited islands, domestic sewage is washed back on to the beaches, some of which are also affected by tar.

 The most fertile areas of the country are in the foothills of the northern section of the Maya Mountains: citrus fruit is grown in the Stann Creek valley, while in the valley of the Mopan, or upper Belize River, cattle raising and mixed farming are successful. The northern area of the country has long proved suitable for sugar cane production. In the south bananas and mangoes are cultivated. The lower valley of the Belize River is a rice-growing area as well as being used for mixed farming and citrus cultivation.

Ongoing conflict between environmental protection and economic growth over the proposed Chalillo Dam in Mountain Pine Ridge reached new levels. The high level campaign took their appeals to the UK Privy Court, the highest court in the Commonwealth, who dismissed the appeal to overturn the Belizean government's approval. Campaigners say the dam on the Macal River threatens rare species and communities downstream.

Books and films

King, Emory *Hey Dad, this is Belize.* A collection of anecdotes by a local celebrity who found himself in Belize after surviving a shipwreck out on the cayes. He had a cameo role in *The Mosquito Coast* a film starring Harrison Ford.

Warlords and Maize Men (Association for Belize Archaeology), is a guide to Mayan sites.

El Salvador

History

When Spanish expeditions arrived in El Salvador from Guatemala and Nicaragua, they found it quite densely populated by several indigenous groups, of whom the most populous were the **Pipiles**. By 1550, the Spaniards had occupied the country, many living in existing indigenous villages and towns. The settlers cultivated cocoa in the volcanic highlands and balsam along the coast, and introduced cattle to roam the grasslands freely. Towards the end of the 16th century, indigo became the big export crop: production was controlled by the Spaniards, and the indigenous population provided the workforce, many suffering illness as a result. A period of regional turmoil accompanied El Salvador's declaration of independence from the newly autonomous political body of Central America in 1839: indigenous attempts to regain their traditional land rights were put down by force.

For more on the region's early history, see page 1206.

Coffee emerged as an important cash crop in the second half of the 19th century, bringing with it improvements in transport facilities and the final abolition of indigenous communal lands.

The land question was a fundamental cause of the peasant uprising of 1932, which was brutally crushed by the dictator **General Maximiliano Hernández Martínez**. Following his overthrow in 1944, the military did not relinquish power: a series of military coups kept them in control, while they protected the interests of the landowning oligarchy.

1980s Civil War

The most recent military coup, in October 1979, led to the formation of a civilian-military junta which promised far-reaching reforms. When these were not carried out, the opposition unified forming a broad coalition, the Frente Democrático

Revolucionario, which adopted a military wing, the **Farabundo Martí National Liberation Front (FMLN)** in 1980. Later the same year, the Christian Democrat Ingeniero **José Napoleón Duarte** was named as President of the Junta. At about the same time, political tension reached the proportions of civil war.

Duarte was elected to the post of President in 1984, following a short administration headed by Dr Alvaro Magaña. Duarte's periods of power were characterized by a partly successful attempt at land reform, the nationalization of foreign trade and the banking system, and violence. In addition to deaths in combat, 40,000 civilians were killed between 1979 and 1984, mostly by right-wing death squads. Among the casualties was Archbishop **Oscar Romero**, who was shot while saying mass in March 1980. Nothing came of meetings between Duarte's government and the FMLN, which were aimed at seeking a peace agreement. The war continued in stalemate until 1989, by which time an estimated 70,000 had been killed. The Christian Democrats' inability to end the war, reverse the economic decline or rebuild after the 1986 earthquake, combined with their reputation for corruption, brought about a resurgence of support for the right-wing National Republican Alliance (ARENA). An FMLN offer to participate in presidential elections, dependent on certain conditions, was not accepted and the ARENA candidate, Licenciado **Alfredo Cristiani**, won the presidency comfortably in March 1989, taking office in June. Peace talks again failed to produce results and, in November 1989, the FMLN guerrillas staged their most ambitious offensive ever, which paralysed the capital and caused a violent backlash from government forces. FMLN-government negotiations resumed with UN mediation following the offensive, but the two sides could not reach agreement about the purging of the armed forces, which had become the most wealthy institution in the country following 10 years of US support.

Peace negotiations

Although El Salvador's most left-wing political party, the Unión Democrática Nacionalista, agreed to participate in municipal elections in 1991, the FMLN remained outside the electoral process, and the civil war continued unresolved. Talks were held in Venezuela and Mexico after initial agreement was reached in April on reforms to the electoral and judicial systems, but further progress was stalled over the restructuring of the armed forces and disarming the guerrillas. There were hopes that human rights would improve after the establishment in June 1991 of a UN Security Council human rights observer commission (ONUSAL), which was charged with verifying compliance with the human rights agreement signed by the Government and the FMLN in Geneva in April 1990. Finally, after considerable UN assistance, the FMLN and the Government signed a peace accord in New York in January 1992 and a formal ceasefire began the following month. A detailed schedule throughout 1992 was established to demobilize the FMLN, dismantle five armed forces elite battalions and to initiate land requests by ex-combatants from both sides. The demobilization process was reported as completed in December 1992, formally concluding the civil war. The US agreed at this point to 'forgive' a substantial portion of the US$2bn international debt of El Salvador. In March 1993, the United Nations Truth Commission published its investigation of human rights abuses during the civil war. Five days later, the legislature approved a general amnesty for all those involved in criminal activities in the war. This included those named in the Truth Commission report. The Cristiani government was slow to implement not only the constitutional reforms proposed by the Truth Commission, but also the process of land reform and the establishment of the National Civilian Police (PNC). By 1995, when Cristiani's successor had taken office, the old national police force was demobilized, but the PNC suffered from a lack of resources for its proper establishment. In fact, the budget for the implementation of the final peace accords was inadequate and El Salvador had to ask the UN for financial assistance.

1994 elections and after

Presidential and congressional elections in 1994 failed to give an outright majority to any presidential candidate and **Calderón Sol** of ARENA won the run-off election. Besides his government's difficulties with the final stages of the peace accord, his first months in office were marked by rises in the cost of living, increases in crime, strikes and protests, and occupations of the Legislature by ex-combatants. Frustration at the slow rate of reform came in the form of criticism from the United Nations and in March 1997 through the ballot box. Only 41% of the electorate bothered to vote. In the National Assembly, Arena won 29 seats, narrowly beating the FMLN which increased its tally to 28 seats. The National Conciliation Party (PCN) won 11, the Christian Democrats (PDC) nine and minority parties seven seats. FMLN managed to run neck-and-neck with Arena until within a year of the March 1999 presidential elections. The party's inability to select a presidential candidate, however, caused it to lose ground rapidly. Arena's candidate, **Fransisco Flores**, won the election but still with a poor turn-out of less than 40% of the electorate. In the face of such a huge rejection of the political system Flores could not claim a clear mandate. Most interpreted the abstention as a lack of faith in any party's ability to solve the twin problems of poverty and crime. Elections in March 2004 won a five-year term for **Tony Saca**, the fourth successive victory for the right-wing Arena party. The former radio and TV presenter promised to crack down on criminal gangs and promote ties with the US.

Into the 21st century

If the devastating earthquakes of early 2001 were not enough for the country to deal with, droughts through the summer months led to a food crisis that required United Nations intervention. Old rivalries flared briefly as Honduras expelled two Salvadorian diplomats on spying charges, displaying the fragility of the cordial relations with the northern neighbour. El Salvador also hosted the meeting of Mexican and Central America presidents to develop the controversial **Plan Puebla Panama** regional integration project which would link the Mexican city of Puebla with Panama City along an economic investment corridor designed to create jobs. Promising signs of progress, and support for the future led President Bush to drop in on the country in his whirlwind trip to Latin America in early 2002, calling El Salvador one of the "really bright lights" in the region.

The country's lively landscape continued to shape events with the eruption of Ilamatepec volcano, also known as Santa Ana, in October 2005, quickly followed by the destructive floods and mudslides of Hurricane Stan which killed over 70 people, and forced over 36,000 to seek refuge in emergency shelters. In 2006 El Salvador continued to lead the way for regional integration as the first country to fully implement the Central American Free Trade Agreement with the US. The regional confidence was demonstrated with the inauguration of a newly defined border with neighbouring Honduras, which should bring to an end the dispute that led to the outbreak of war between the two nations in 1969.

Economy

Economic growth picked up to 2.8% in 2005, despite high oil prices and damage from Hurricane Stan, after sluggish growth averaging under 2 percent during 2000-2004. Agriculture is the dominant sector of the economy, accounting for three quarters of export earnings. Coffee and sugar are the most important crops, but attempts have been made at diversification and now soya, shrimp, sesame, vegetables, tropical flowers and ornamental plants are promoted as important foreign exchange earners. The sector has been badly affected in recent years by drought, the El Niño phenomenon and Hurricane Mitch.

The most important industries are food processing and petroleum products: others include textiles, pharmaceuticals, shoes, furniture, chemicals and fertilizers, cosmetics, construction materials, drink processing and rubber goods. *Maquila* factories have grown rapidly in recent years, providing an estimated 87,000 jobs. Exports of manufactured goods, mostly to other Central American countries, account for some 27% of foreign exchange earnings. Geothermal power makes an important contribution to energy production with installed capacity of around 160MW. Hydraulic resources are also being exploited as a means of generating power and saving oil import costs.

Government

Legislative power is vested in a unicameral Legislative Assembly, which has 84 seats and is elected for a three-year term. The head of state and government is the president, who holds office for five years. The country is divided into 14 departments.

Culture

People

The population is far more homogeneous than that of Guatemala. The reason for this is that El Salvador lay comparatively isolated from the main stream of conquest, and had no precious metals to act as magnets for the Spaniards. The small number of Spanish settlers intermarried with those indigenous locals who survived the plagues brought from Europe to form a group of mestizos. There were only about half a million people as late as 1879. With the introduction of coffee, the population grew quickly and the new prosperity fertilized the whole economy, but the internal pressure of population has led to the occupation of all the available land. Several hundred thousand Salvadoreans have emigrated to neighbouring republics because of the shortage of land and the concentration of land ownership, and, more recently, because of the civil war.

Of the total population, some 10% are regarded as ethnic indigenous, although the traditional indigenous culture has almost completely vanished. Other estimates put the percentage of the pure indigenous population as low as 5%. The **Lenca** and the **Pipil**, the two surviving indigenous groups, are predominantly peasant farmers. Only 1% are of unmixed white ancestry, the rest are mestizos.

With a population of 304 to the sq km, El Salvador is the most densely populated country on the American mainland. Health and sanitation outside the capital and some of the main towns leave much to be desired, and progress in this area was very limited in the 1980s and early 1990s because of the violence.

Music and dance

The Mexican music industry seems to exert an overwhelming cultural influence, while the virtual absence of an indigenous population may also be partly responsible, since it is so often they who maintain traditions and connections with the past. Whatever the reason, the visitor who is seeking specifically Salvadorean native music will find little to satisfy him or her. El Salvador is an extension of 'marimba country', but songs and dances are often accompanied by the guitar and seem to lack a rhythm or style that can be pinpointed as specifically local. An exception is the music played on the *pito de caña* and *tambor* which accompanies the traditional dances called *Danza de los Historiantes*, *La Historia* or *Los Moros y Cristianos*. Over 30 types of dance have been identified, mostly in the west and centre of the country, although there are a few in the east. The main theme is the conflict between christianized and 'heretic' *indígenas* and the dances are performed as a ritual on the local saint's day.

Education and religion

Education is free if given by the government, and nominally obligatory. There are 43 universities, three national and the others private or church-affiliated. There is also a National School of Agriculture. The most famous are the government-financed Universidad Nacional and the Jesuit-run Universidad Centroamericana. Roman Catholicism is the prevailing religion.

Land and environment

El Salvador is the smallest, most densely populated and most integrated of the Central American republics. Its intermont basins are a good deal lower than those of Guatemala, rising to little more than 600 m at the capital, San Salvador. Across this upland and surmounting it run two more or less parallel rows of volcanoes, 14% of which are over 900 m high. The highest are Santa Ana (2365 m), San Vicente (2182 m), San Miguel (2130 m), and San Salvador (1893 m). One important result of this volcanic activity is that the highlands are covered with a deep layer of ash and lava which forms a porous soil ideal for coffee planting.

The total area of El Salvador is 21,041 sq km. Guatemala is to the west, Honduras to the north and east, and the Pacific coastline to the south is approximately 321 km long. Lowlands lie to the north and south of the high backbone. In the south, on the Pacific coast, the lowlands of Guatemala are confined to just east of Acajutla; beyond are lava promontories before another 30-km belt of lowlands where the 325-km long Río Lempa flows into the sea. The northern lowlands are in the wide depression along the course of the Río Lempa, buttressed to the south by the highlands of El Salvador and to the north by the basalt cliffs edging the highlands of Honduras. The highest point in El Salvador, Cerro El Pital (2730 m) is part of the mountain range bordering on Honduras. After 160 km the Lempa cuts through the southern uplands to reach the Pacific; the depression is prolonged southeast till it reaches the Gulf of Fonseca.

El Salvador is located on the southwest coast of the Central American Isthmus on the Pacific Ocean. As the only country in the region lacking access to the Caribbean Sea, it does not posses the flora associated with that particular coastal zone. El Salvador nevertheless has a wide variety of colourful, tropical vegetation; for example over 200 species of orchid grow all over the country. As a result of excessive forest cutting, and hence the destruction of their habitats, many of the animals (such as jaguars and crested eagles) once found in the highlands of the country, have diminished at an alarming rate. In response to this problem several nature reserves have been set up in areas where flora and fauna can be found in their most unspoilt state. Among these nature reserves are the Cerro Verde, Deininger Park, El Imposible Woods, El Jocatal Lagoon and the Montecristo Cloud Forest.

Books and films

Manlio Argueta, *One day of Life* (1980) and *Cuzcatlán* (1986), look at peasant rebellion during El Salvador's 20th-century history.

Rincón Mágico de El Salvador and *El Salvador Prehistórico*, both available at **Banco Agrícola Comercial**, Paseo Escalón 3635, San Salvador (US$72).

Walter Raudales, *Amor de Jade*, to be published in English too, is a novel based on the life of El Salvador's Mata Hari (now ex-comandante Joaquín Villalobos' wife).

On the big screen **Raúl Julia** takes the lead in *Romero* (1989), which covers the story surrounding the archbishop's assassination.

Oliver Stone's *Salvador* takes the journalist's view of events in the country's civil war circa 1980.

Honduras

History

Honduras was largely neglected by Spain and its colonists, who concentrated on their trading partners further north or south. The resulting disparity in levels of development between Honduras and its regional neighbours caused problems after Independence in 1821. Harsh partisan battles among provincial leaders resulted in the collapse of the Central American Federation in 1838. The national hero, General Francisco Morazán was a leader in unsuccessful attempts to maintain the Federation and the restoration of Central American unity was the main aim of foreign policy until 1922.

For more on the region's early history, see page 1206.

Banana Republic

Honduras has had a succession of military and civilian rulers and there have been 300 internal rebellions, civil wars and changes of government since Independence, most of them in the 20th century. Political instability in the past led to a lack of investment in economic infrastructure and socio-political integration, making Honduras one of the poorest countries in the Western Hemisphere. It earned its nickname of the 'Banana Republic' in the first part of the 20th century following the founding of a company in 1899, by the Vaccaro brothers of New Orleans, which eventually became the Standard Fruit Company and which was to make bananas the major export crop of Honduras. The United Fruit Company of Boston was also founded in 1899 and, 30 years later, was merged with the Cuyamel Fruit Company of Samuel Zemurray, who controlled the largest fruit interests in Honduras. United Fruit (UFCo), known as El Pulpo (the octopus), emerged as a major political influence in the region with strong links with several dictatorships.

The Great Depression

The 1929 Great Depression caused great hardship in the export-oriented economies of the region, and in Honduras it brought the rise of another authoritarian régime. Tiburcio Cariás Andino was elected in 1932 and, through his ties with foreign companies and other neighbouring dictators, he was able to hold on to power until renewed turbulence began in 1948, and he voluntarily withdrew from power a year later. The two political parties, the Liberals and the Nationals, came under the control of provincial military leaders and, after two more authoritarian Nationalist governments and a general strike in 1954 by radical labour unions on the north coast, young military reformists staged a palace coup in 1955. They installed a provisional junta and allowed elections for a constituent assembly in 1957. The assembly was led by the Liberal Party, which appointed Dr Ramón Villeda Morales as President, and transformed itself into a national legislature for six years. A newly created military academy graduated its first class in 1960, and the armed forces began to professionalize their leadership in conjunction with the civilian economic establishment. Conservative officers, nervous of a Cuban-style revolution, pre-empted elections in 1963 in a bloody coup which deposed Dr Villeda, exiled Liberal Party members and took control of the national police, which they organized into special security forces.

Football War

In 1969, Honduras and El Salvador were drawn into a bizarre episode known as the 'Football War', which took its name from its origin in a disputed decision in the third qualifying round of the World Cup. Its root cause, however, was the social tension aroused by migrating workers from overcrowded El Salvador to Honduras. In 13 days, 2000 people were killed before a ceasefire was arranged by the Organization of American States. A peace treaty was not signed until 1980, and the dispute provoked Honduras to withdraw from the Central American Common Market (CACM), which helped to hasten its demise.

Tensions between the two countries can still easily rise. Disputes over the border and fishing rights in the Gulf of Fonseca are a cause of friction, and in August 2001, Honduras expelled two Salvadoreans on spying charges. Honduras also has disputed land claims with Nicaragua to the east. However, regional cooperation is sufficiently well developed for regional conferences to tackle the problems with commitments to non-aggressive solutions.

Transition to democracy

The armed forces, led chiefly by General López Arellano and his protégés in the National Party, dominated government until 1982. López initiated land reform but, despite liberal policies, his régime was brought down in the mid-1970s by corruption scandals involving misuse of hurricane aid funds and bribes from the United Brands Company. His successors increased the size and power of the security forces and created the largest air force in Central America, while slowly preparing for a return to civilian rule. A constituent assembly was elected in 1980 and general elections held in 1981. A constitution was promulgated in 1982 and President Roberto Suazo Córdoba of the Liberal Party assumed power. During this period, Honduras cooperated closely with the USA on political and military issues, particularly in covert moves to destabilize Nicaragua's Sandanista government, and became host to some 12,000 right-wing Nicaraguan contra rebels. It was less willing to take a similar stand against the FMLN left wing guerrillas in El Salvador for fear of renewing border tensions. In 1986 the first peaceful transfer of power between civilian presidents for 30 years took place when José Azcona del Hoyo (Liberal) won the elections. Close relations with the USA were maintained in the 1980s, Honduras had the largest Peace Corps Mission in the world, non-governmental and international voluntary agencies proliferated as the government became increasingly dependent upon US aid to finance its budget.

In 1989, the general elections were won by the right wing Rafael Leonardo Callejas Romero of the National Party, which won a 14-seat majority in the National Assembly. Under the terms of the Central American Peace Plan, the contra forces were demobilized and disarmed by June 1990. The Honduran armed forces have come under greater pressure for reform as a result of US and domestic criticism of human rights abuses. A report published in April 1993 recommended a series of institutional reforms in the judiciary and security services, including the resolution by the Supreme Court of all cases of jurisdictional conflict between civilian and military courts. This and other measures led to some, but by no means all, improvements in respect of human rights.

Liberal government since 1993

In the campaign leading up to the 1993 general elections, the Liberal candidate, Carlos Roberto Reina Idiáquez, pledged to provide every citizen 'techo, trabajo, tierra y tortilla' (roof, work, land and food), arguing for a more socially conscious face to the economic adjustment programme inaugurated by President Callejas. Although many of his economic policies were unpopular, and he was unable to alleviate widespread poverty in the short term, President Reina received approval for his handling of the military and investigations of human rights' abuses.

The 1997 presidential elections were again won by the Liberal candidate, Carlos Flores Facusse. He had the support of the business community, who believed he would control public spending and reduce the government deficit in line with IMF targets, but he also campaigned against economic austerity and in favour of bridging the gap between rich and poor. The passage of Hurricane Mitch over Honduras in October 1998 forced the Flores administration to refocus all its attention on rebuilding the country at all levels, social, economic and infrastructural.

Ricardo Maduro of the National Party was sworn in as president in January 2002. Elections in November 2005 were won by the Liberal Party's Manuel Zelaya, with a majority of just 75,000 votes. Zelaya served in the government of Carlos Flores. On taking office he vowed to continue the fight against gang violence along with tackling corruption in government, creation of hundreds of thousands of badly needed jobs and support for CAFTA free trade agreement with the US.

Economy

Honduras is the second poorest economy in Central America with one of the lowest income rates per head in all Latin America. The distribution of land continues to be a pressing problem, with an estimated 170,000 farming families lacking sufficient land for subsistence agriculture. Unemployment (and under-employment) is about 40% of the working population with estimates that 80% of the population live in poverty and the minimum wage has not kept pace with inflation.

Over half of the population lives by the land: coffee, bananas and shrimp are traditionally the main export crops. Tobacco, maize, beans, rice and sugar are grown mostly for domestic use, but small quantities are sometimes exported. Cigars have a good international reputation. Cattle raising is important and exports of both meat and livestock are growing, as are exports of timber. Honduras has considerable reserves of silver, gold, lead, zinc, tin, iron, copper, coal and antimony, but only lead, zinc and small quantities of gold and silver are mined and exported. Considerable offshore exploration for petroleum is in progress. There is oil storage at Puerto Cortés and a refinery at San Lorenzo on the Pacific. The US$600 mn hydroelectric scheme at El Cajón was constructed to reduce the country's oil bill.

Local industries are small, turning out a wide range of consumer goods. *Maquila* industries, accounting for 20% of total exports, in the northern cities of San Pedro Sula, Choloma, Naco and elsewhere grew rapidly in the 1980s but stagnated in the mid-1990s.

Recent trends

Honduras' total external debt amounted to some US$4. 7 bn in 2004 – roughly one third of foreign exchange receipts are spent on debt servicing. The entire economic framework was shattered by Hurricane Mitch. According to estimates 70% of economic output was lost, with the main export crops (bananas, shrimps) largely destroyed or prevented from reaching ports by road damage. Joblessness, especially in the agricultural sector, increased greatly. By mid-2000 the estimated economic damage caused by Mitch was put at US$3-4 bn. As one of the world's most indebted countries, the 2005 G8 summit in Scotland agreed to cancel the debt of Honduras, The process was well-underway by July 2006 and foreign currency formerly used to pay debt obligations should start going into urgently required programmes on health, education and water access.

President Zelaya's time in office is too short to judge its progress, but his predecessors pro-business and honest style of politics was popular. Attempts to tackle crims, improve the economy will continue. Growth in *maquila* industries is expected to continue. Tourism investment has been a recent years, whith Maduro put as a top national priority. The investment has proved worthwhile with an annual increase of 20% for the last two or three years. Tourist visitors in 2005 was nearly 1.2 million, providing US$400 mn in tourism revenue. But in real terms, the greatest single source of foreign income is from *remesas* money being sent to Honduras from abroad, a fact acknowledged by the United States's decision to extends Temporary Protection Status for 100,000 Honduran immigrants who currently send US$1.1 bn back home every year.

Regionally, Honduras agreed to significant developments, signing up to the Central American Free Trade Agreement with effect from April 2006. Shortly after regional confidence was demonstrated with the inauguration of a newly defined border with neighbouring El Salvador, which should bring to an end small-scale disputes that have persisted since the outbreak of war between the two nations in 1969.

Government

Honduras is a multi-party republic. The Legislature consists of a single 128-seat Chamber. Deputies are elected by a proportional vote. Executive authority rests with a President, directly elected for four years. No President may serve two terms in succession. The National Assembly elects members of the Supreme Court which, together with the Court of Appeal, Justices of the Peace and lesser tribunals, constitutes the judiciary. The Constitution was revised by a Constituent Assembly elected in April 1980. The country is divided into 18 departments, each with its own administrative centre, and further subdivided into 297 municipalities.

Culture

People

The pure indigenous population is only an estimated 7% of the total population, and the percentage of pure Spanish or other European ancestry is even smaller. The two largest indigenous groups are the Chortis from Santa Rosa de Copán westwards to the border with Guatemala, and the Lencas in the departments of Lempira, Intibucá and, above all, in the highlands of La Paz. There are also about 45,000 Miskito people who live on the Caribbean coast, alongside several communities of Garífunas (black Caribs). The population is 90% mestizo. Some 53% are peasant farmers or agricultural labourers, with a low standard of living.

Religion and education

Education is compulsory, but not all the rural children go to school – 33% of the population over the age of 10 have had no formal schooling. According to UNESCO 27.1% of people over 15% are illiterate. The National University is based in Tegucigalpa though it also has departments in Comayagua, San Pedro Sula and La Ceiba. Also in Tegucigalpa are the Universidad José Cecilio del Valle, the Universidad Católica (with campuses in San Pedro Sula and Choluteca), the Universidad Tecnológica Centro Americana and the Universidad Pedagógica Nacional; there is also the Universidad de San Pedro Sula, the Universidad Pedagógica Francisco Morazán and the Universidad Tecnológica Centroamericana. The majority of the population is Catholic, but there is complete freedom of religion.

Music

The visitor seeking specifically Honduran native music will find little to satisfy him or her. Honduras shares with Belize and Guatemala the presence of Garífuna or black Caribs on the Caribbean coast. These descendants of indigenous Caribs and escaped black slaves were deported to the area from St Vincent in the late 18th century and continue to maintain a very separate identity, including their own religious observances, music and dances, profoundly African in spirit and style.

Land and environment

With a territory of 112,492 sq km, Honduras is larger than all the other Central American republics except Nicaragua. Bordered by Nicaragua, Guatemala and El Salvador, it has a narrow Pacific coastal strip, 124 km long on the Gulf of Fonseca, and a northern coast on the Caribbean of 640 km.

Inland, much of the country is mountainous: a rough plateau covered with volcanic ash and lava in the south, rising to peaks such as Cerro de las Minas in the Celaque range (2849 m), but with some intermont basins at between 900 and 1800 m. The volcanic detritus disappears to the north, revealing saw-toothed ranges which approach the coast at an angle; the one in the extreme northwest, along the border with Guatemala, disappears under the sea and shows itself again in the Bay Islands. At most places in the north there is only a narrow shelf of lowland between the sea and the sharp upthrust of the mountains, but along two rivers (the Aguán in the northeast, and the Ulúa in the northwest) long fingers of marshy lowland stretch inland between the ranges. The Ulúa lowland is particularly important; it is about 40 km wide and stretches southwards for 100 km where the city of San Pedro Sula is located. From its southern limit a deep gash continues across the highland to the Gulf of Fonseca on the Pacific. The distance between the Caribbean and the Pacific along this trough is 280 km; the altitude at the divide between the Río Comayagua, running into the Ulúa and the Caribbean, and the streams flowing into the Pacific, is only 950 m. In this trough lies Comayagua, the old colonial capital. The lowlands along the Gulf of Fonseca are narrower than they are along the Caribbean; there is no major thrust inland as there is along the Ulúa.

The prevailing winds are from the east, consequently the Caribbean coast has a high rainfall and is covered with deep tropical forest. The intermont basins, the valleys and the slopes sheltered from the prevailing winds bear oak and pine down to as low as 600 m. Timber is almost the only fuel available. In the drier areas, north and south of Tegucigalpa, there are extensive treeless savannas.

Today, land under some form of cultivation is only 18% of the total, while meadows and pastures make up 14% of total land use. Rugged terrain makes large areas unsuitable for any kind of agriculture. Nevertheless, there is undeveloped agricultural potential in the flat and almost unpopulated lands of the coastal plain east of Tela to Trujillo and Puerto Castilla, in the Aguán valley southward and in the region northeast of Juticalpa. The area to the northeast, known as the Mosquitia plain, is largely unexploited and little is known of its potential.

Climate

Rain is frequent on the Caribbean coast year-round; the heaviest occurs from September to February inclusive. In Tegucigalpa the dry season is normally from November to April inclusive. The coolest months are December and January, but this is when heavy rains fall on the north coast, which could impede travel. The driest months for this area are April and May, though they are very hot. However, weather predictions in this area have become more difficult in recent years, whether because of the *El Niño* phenomenon or for other reasons. Rain, when it comes, is usually heavy, but of short duration.

Books and films

Paul Theroux *The Mosquito Coast* (Penguin, 1996) which was also turned into a film starring Harrison Ford.

Norman Lewis *The Volcanoes Above* (1954).

Haskell Wexler *Latino* (1985), which follows the twists, turns, loves and contradictions of a Latino US soldier drafted to Honduras to provide military training in the mid-1980s.

Nicaragua

History

Nicaragua was at the crossroads of northern and southern prehispanic cultures. In Managua, near the crater lake of Acahualinca, there are some well-preserved human and animal footprints of what appears to be a mass flight from a volcanic eruption 6000 years ago. The best understood cultures are the Chorotegas, who came from Mexico around AD 800, and the Nicaraguas, from the same region who partially displaced the Chorotegas in the Pacific basin around AD 1200. The Nicaraguas set up a very successful society which traded with people from Mexico to Peru. The more primitive Chorotegas (Mangue speakers) remained in the areas not occupied by the Nicaraguas (Nahuat speakers), though some were pushed down into Guanacaste and the complete relationship between the two has yet to be fully explained. The most interesting pre-Columbian remains are the many petroglyphs left by unnamed pre-Chorotega cultures, and the Chorotegas' own large basalt figures found in and around Lake Nicaragua, in particular on the islands of Zapatera and Ometepe. Nicaragua is rich in ceramic history, with traces of 3000 years of continuous occupation being found in some areas. The Ramas and Sumos, of South American lowland origin, populated the eastern seaboard regions, but are almost extinct today. Other pre-Columbian cultures of note were the mountain Matagalpa people, thought to be related to the Lenca, the strangely primitive, understudied Chontales, who inhabited the eastern side of the two lakes and, in the area that is now León, the Subtiava people who are perhaps from Baja California in Mexico.

For more on the region's early history, see page 1206.

Christopher Columbus arrived on the Caribbean shores of Nicaragua in 1502 on his fourth and final voyage. The Spanish explorer Gil González Dávila arrived in 1522 overland from Panama and, searching for the wealthiest chief of all, arrived on the western shores of Lake Nicaragua to meet the famous Nicaraguas chief, Niqueragua. The 16th-century Spanish chroniclers described the Nicaraguas' land as the most fertile and productive they had ever seen in the Americas. The chief Nicaragua and Dávila engaged in long philosophical conversations conducted through a translator and eventually the great chief agreed to accept Christianity. After the conversion to Christianity of more than 900 people, Dávila was chased out of Nicaragua by the fierce Chorotega chieftain Diriangen, whose troops decimated Dávila's small force. In 1524 a stronger army was sent and the populace was overcome by Francisco Hernández de Córdoba. Granada and León were founded on the shores of Lake Nicaragua and Lake Managua respectively. In 1570 both colonies were placed under the jurisdiction of Guatemala.

The local administrative centre was not rich Granada, with its profitable crops of sugar, cocoa, and indigo, but impoverished León, then barely able to subsist on its crops of maize, beans and rice. This reversal of the Spanish policy of choosing the most successful settlement as capital was due to the ease with which León could be reached from the Pacific. In 1852 Managua was chosen as a new capital as a compromise, following violent rivalry between Granada and León.

Nicaragua became an independent state in 1838.

Walker's expedition

The infamous filibustering expedition of William Walker is an important event in Nicaraguan and Costa Rican history. William Walker (1824-1860) was born in Nashville, Tennessee, graduated at the University, and studied medicine at Edinburgh and

Heidelberg, being granted his MD in 1843. He then studied law and was called to the bar. On 5 October 1853, he sailed with a filibustering force to conquer Mexican territory, declared Lower California and Sonora an independent republic and was then driven out. In May 1855, with 56 followers armed with a new type of rifle, he sailed for Nicaragua, where Liberal Party leaders had invited him to help them in their struggle against the Conservatives. In October he seized a steamer on Lake Nicaragua belonging to the Accessory Transit Company, an American corporation controlled by Cornelius Vanderbilt. He was then able to surprise and capture Granada and make himself master of Nicaragua as Commander of the Forces. Two officials decided to use him to get control of the Transit Company; it was seized and handed over to his friends. A new government was formed, and in June 1856 Walker was elected President. On 22 September, to gain support from the southern states in America, he suspended the Nicaraguan laws against slavery. His Government was formally recognized by the USA that year. Walker attempted to take control of La Casona in the Guanacaste province of Costa Rica, only to be repelled by the southern nations forces. A coalition of Central American states, backed by Cornelius Vanderbilt, fought against him until he surrendered to the US Navy to avoid capture in May 1857. In November 1857, he sailed from Mobile with another expedition, but soon after landing near Greytown, Nicaragua, he was arrested and returned to the USA. In 1860 he sailed again from Mobile and landed in Honduras in his last attempt to conquer Central America. There he was taken prisoner by Captain Salmon, of the British Navy, and handed over to the Honduran authorities who tried and executed him on 12 September 1860. Walker's own book, *The War in Nicaragua*, is a fascinating document.

US involvement

US involvement in Nicaraguan affairs stretches back a long way. In 1909, US Marines assisted Nicaraguan Conservative leaders in an uprising to overthrow the Liberal president, José Santos Zelaya. In 1911 the USA pledged help in securing a loan to be guaranteed through the control of Nicaraguan customs by an American board. In 1912 the United States sent marines into Nicaragua to enforce control. Apart from short intervals, they stayed there until 1933. During the last five years of occupation, nationalists under General **Augusto César Sandino** waged a relentless guerrilla war against the US Marines. American forces were finally withdrawn in 1933, when President Franklin Roosevelt announced the 'Good Neighbour' policy, pledging non-intervention. An American-trained force, the Nicaraguan National Guard, was left behind, commanded by **Anastasio Somoza García**. Somoza's men assassinated General Sandino in February 1934 and Somoza himself took over the presidency in 1936. From 1932, with brief intervals, Nicaraguan affairs were dominated by this tyrant until he was assassinated in 1956. His two sons both served a presidential term and the younger, General **Anastasio Somoza Debayle,** dominated the country from 1963 until his deposition in 1979; he was later assassinated in Paraguay.

1978-1979 Revolution

The 1978-79 Revolution against the Somoza Government by the Sandinista guerrilla organization (loosely allied to a broad opposition movement) resulted in extensive damage and many casualties (estimated at over 30,000) in certain parts of the country, especially in Managua, Estelí, León, Masaya, Chinandega and Corinto. After heavy fighting General Somoza resigned on 17 July 1979, and the Government was taken over by a Junta representing the Sandinista guerrillas and their civilian allies. Real power was exercised by nine Sandinista *comandantes* whose chief short-term aim was reconstruction. A 47-member Council of State formally came into being in May 1980; supporters of the Frente Sandinista de Liberación Nacional had a majority. Elections were held on 4 November 1984 for an augmented National Constituent Assembly with 96 seats; the Sandinista Liberation Front won 61 seats, and **Daniel Ortega Saavedra,** who had headed the Junta, was elected president. The Democratic Conservatives won 14 seats, the Independent Liberals nine seats and the Popular Social Christians six (the Socialists, Communists and Marxists/Leninists won two seats each). The failure of the Sandinista Government to meet the demands of a right-wing group, the Democratic Co-ordinating Board (CDN), led to this coalition boycotting the elections and to the US administration failing to recognize the democratically elected government.

The Sandinistas

Despite substantial official and private US support, anti-Sandinista guerrillas (the Contras) could boast no significant success in their war against the Government. In 1988, the Sandinistas and the contras met for the first time to discuss the implementation of the Central American Peace Plan, drawn up by President Oscar Arias Sánchez of Costa Rica and signed in August 1987. To comply with the Plan, the Nicaraguan Government made a number of political concessions. By 1989 the contras, lacking funds and with diminished numbers, following a stream of desertions, appeared to be a spent force. The Sandinista Government brought major improvements in health and education, but the demands of the war against the contras and a complete US trade embargo did great damage to the economy as a whole. The electorate's desire for a higher standard of living was reflected in the outcome of the elections, when the US-supported candidate of the free market National Opposition Union (UNO), Señora **Violeta Chamorro,** won 55.2% of the vote, compared with 40.8% for President Ortega. The 14-party alliance, UNO, won 52 seats in the National Assembly, the FSLN 38 and the Social Christian Party one seat. Sra Chamorro, widow of the proprietor of *La Prensa*, who was murdered by General Somoza's forces in 1978, took office on 25 April 1990. The USA was under considerable pressure to provide substantial aid for the alliance it created and promoted, but of the US$300 mn promised for 1990 by the US Congress, only half had been distributed by May 1991. President Chamorro's refusal to dismiss the Sandinista General Humberto Ortega from his post as head of the armed forces (EPS), and to drop the Nicaraguan case against the USA at the International Court of Justice, were said to be hindrances to more rapid disbursement. In 1986 the Court in The Hague found the USA guilty of crimes against Nicaragua for mining its harbours.

The lack of foreign financial assistance prevented any quick rebuilding of the economy. The Government's scant resources did not permit it to give the disarmed contra forces the land and services that had been promised to them. Demilitarized Sandinistas and landless peasants also pressed for land in 1991, with a consequent rise in tension. Factions of the two groups rearmed, to be known as recontras and recompas; there were many bloody conflicts. Divisions within the UNO coalition, particularly between supporters of President Chamorro and those of vice-president Virgilio Godoy, added to the country's difficulties. Austerity measures introduced in early 1991, including a devaluation of the new córdoba, strained the relationship between the administration, Sandinista politicians and the National Workers' Front (FNT), the so-called 'concertación', a pact which the private sector refused to sign. Pacts signed in January 1992 between Government, recontras and recompas failed to stop occasional heavy fighting over the next two years. In 1994, however, a series of bilateral meetings between previously entrenched parties and ceasefires announced by the EPS and the main recontra group, FN 3-80 (Northern Front 3-80) contributed to a disarmament accord, proposed by archbishop Miguel Obando y Bravo, between the Government and FN 3-80.

Movement towards a real and lasting peace

The achievement of a more peaceful state of affairs, if not reconciliation, did not remove other political tensions. After the UNO coalition realigned itself into new political groupings and returned to the National Assembly following a boycott in 1993, the FSLN began to fall apart in 1994. By early 1995, the Sandinistas had become irrevocably split between the orthodox wing, led by Daniel Ortega, and the Sandinista Renewal Movement (MRS), under Sergio Ramírez. The MRS accused the orthodox wing of betraying Sandinista principles by forming pacts with the technocrats and neo-liberals of the Government. The MRS was itself accused of opportunism. Linked to this was considerable manoeuvring over UNO-inspired constitutional reform. The National Assembly approved 67 amendments of the constitution, among which were the strengthening of the legislative branch of government at the expense of the executive, and the prohibition of relatives of the president from seeking that office. President Chamorro denied the validity of the reforms, but the National Assembly unilaterally adopted them in February 1995.

The 1996 elections

In 1995 the National Assembly approved legislation governing the 20 October 1996 presidential elections. The frontrunner was **Arnoldo Alemán**, former mayor of Managua, of the Liberal alliance. His main opponent was Daniel Ortega of the FSLN, who regarded Alemán's policies as a return to Somoza-style government. After reviewing the vote count because of allegations of fraud, the Supreme Electoral Council (CSE) Arnoldo Alemán had won 51% compared with 37.7% for Daniel Ortega. The FSLN called for new elections in Managua and Matagalpa as the OAS declared the elections fair but flawed. Ortega announced he would respect the legality but not the legitimacy of the Government of Alemán.

The Sandinistas have maintained pressure on the Alemán government, with strikes, protests and intermittent negotiations. A deal was reached in 1997 on compensation for properties expropriated under the Sandinista government, involving 1293 claims by foreigners. The agreement avoided a suspension of US aid and the USA gave Nicaragua a year to sort out property rights involving US citizens.

Nature plays her hand

In 1998 two meteorological events caused even greater hardship for parts of the country: the drought (and related fires) from the El Niño phenomenon and, much more costly in terms of lives lost and property destroyed, the floods and storm damage from Hurricane Mitch. In July of 2000 an earthquake measuring almost six points on the Richter scale hit western Nicaragua killing four people and causing damage near the epicentre at Laguna de Apoyo, near Masaya.

A new opportunity

In November of 2001, Daniel Ortega of the FSLN lost to Enrique Bolaños of the ruling Liberal Party (PLC). Voters chose Enrique Bolaños by more than 15-points in what many believed to be a vote against Ortega rather than approval of the Liberal Party. In Enrique Bolaños' first 3 months of office in 2002 he shocked many by taking a very aggressive stance against corruption and his administration has exposed several cases of embezzlement under the Alemán adminstration. The desire to cleanse the past and clear the way for the future was apparent when in December 2003 former president **Arnoldo Alemán** was sentenced to 25 years in prison, later transferred to house arrest, for corruption including money laundering and embezzlement to a value of nearly US$100m.

President Bolaños' agreement to allow his predecessor to be investigated has led to his alienation by some in the Liberal Party. The delicate balance of power in Congress has restricted the president's powers, and further changes to weaken the powers of the president were only avoided at the last minute when President Bolaños made a pact with Sandinista leader Ortega.

Early positioning for elections in November 2005 are beginning, but it the outcome is uncertain. But in April 2006, the US urged Nicaragua to shun Ortega's left-wing Sandinista party. A move that may backfire and boost support for Ortega.

Economy

The **World Bank** classes Nicaragua among the world's poorest countries and its per capita income is the lowest in Latin America. The economy is based on agriculture, which contributes almost 20% of GDP. The principal export items are coffee, seafood, cotton, tobacco, beef, sugar and bananas. Main industries are food processing (sugar, meat, shrimps), textiles, wood, chemical and mineral products. Mineral resources are scarce but there are gold, copper and silver deposits.

Since the late 1970s GDP has fallen, starting with a decline of 29% in 1979. In 1981-90 it fell by an annual average of 2.4%, with only one year of positive growth. In the same period per capita income fell by an average of 5.6% a year, a collapse caused by guerrilla insurgency, the US trade embargo, fluctuations in Central American Common Market trade, floods, drought and changing commodity prices.

In 1990 the US-supported Government of President Violeta Chamorro took office amid great optimism that the economy could be revived on the back of renewed trade with the USA. Trade sanctions were lifted and the US Congress was asked to provide US$300 mn in aid immediately, to be followed by a further US$200 mn.

President Alemán promised to continue the structural adjustment programme of the Chamorro government but Nicaragua's entire economic outlook was radically altered by Hurricane Mitch in 1998 which killed over 3000 and caused damage of over US$500 m. The extent of economic problems in Nicaragua was reinforced when in January 2004 the World Bank cleared 80% of Nicaragua's debt to the institution. Nicaragua also benefitted from the 2005 G8 summit which cleared 100% of international debt to Nicaragua. In 2006, Nicaragua joined El Salvador and Honduras as fully signed up members of the Central America Free Trade Agreement with the US.

Government

A new Constitution was approved by the 92-member National Constituent Assembly in 1986 and signed into effect on 9 January 1987. Legislative power is vested in a unicameral, directly elected National Assembly of 92 representatives, each with an alternate representative, with a six-year term. In addition, unelected presidential and vice presidential candidates become representatives and alternates respectively if they receive a certain percentage of the votes. Executive power is vested in the President, assisted by a Vice President and an appointed Cabinet. The Presidential term is five years. The next elections are scheduled for November 2006.

Culture

People

Population density is low: 40.7 persons to the sq km, compared with El Salvador's 304. Nine out of 10 Nicaraguans live and work in the lowlands between the Pacific and the western shores of Lake Nicaragua, the southwestern shore of Lake Managua, and the southwestern sides of the row of volcanoes. It is only in latter years that settlers have taken to coffee-growing and cattle-rearing in the highlands at Matagalpa and Jinotega. Elsewhere, the highlands, save for an occasional mining camp, are very thinly settled.

The densely forested eastern lowlands fronting the Caribbean were neglected, because of the heavy rainfall and their consequent unhealthiness, until the British settled several colonies of Jamaicans in the 18th century at Bluefields and San Juan del Norte. But early this century the United Fruit Company of America (now United Brands) opened banana plantations inland from Puerto Cabezas, worked by blacks from Jamaica. Other companies followed suit along the coast, but the bananas were later attacked by Panama disease and exports today are small. Along the Mosquito coast there are still English-speaking communities of African, or mixed African and indigenous, descent. Besides the mestizo intermixtures of Spanish and indigenous (69%), there are pure blacks (9%), pure indigenous (5%) and mixtures of the two (mostly along the Atlantic coast). A small proportion is of unmixed Spanish and European descent. For a brief survey of the people of eastern Nicaragua, see the introductory paragraphs of Caribbean coast.

Music and dance

Nicaragua is 'marimba country' and the basic musical genre is the *son*, this time called the *Son Nica*. There are a number of popular dances for couples with the names of animals, like *La Vaca* (cow), *La Yeguita* (mare) and *El Toro* (bull). The folklore capital of Nicaragua is the city of Masaya and the musical heart of Masaya is the indigenous quarter of Monimbó. Here the marimba is king, but on increasingly rare occasions may be supported by the *chirimía* (oboe), *quijada de asno* (donkey's jaw) and *quijongo*, a single-string bow with gourd resonator. Some of the most traditional *sones* are *El Zañate*, *Los Novios* and *La Perra Renca*, while the more popular dances still to be found are *Las Inditas*, *Las Negras*, *Los Diablitos* and *El Torovenado*, all involving masked characters. Diriamba is another centre of tradition, notable for the folk play known as *El Güeguense*, accompanied by violin, flute and drum and the dance called *Toro Guaco*. The Caribbean coast is a totally different cultural region, home to the Miskito people and English-speaking black people of Jamaican origin concentrated around Bluefields. The latter have a maypole dance and their music is typically Afro-Caribbean, with banjos, accordions, guitars and of course drums as the preferred instruments.

Religion and education

Roman Catholicism is the prevailing religion, but there are Episcopal, Baptist, Methodist and other Protestant churches. Illiteracy was reduced by a determined campaign by the Sandinista government in the 1980s. Higher education at the Universidad Nacional Autónoma de Nicaragua at León, with three faculties at Managua, and the private Jesuit Universidad Centroamericana (UCA) at Managua is good. There are two separate Universidades Nacionales Autónomas de Nicaragua (UNAN).

Land and environment

There are three well-marked regions: (1) A large triangular-shaped central mountain land beginning almost on the southern border with Costa Rica and broadening northwards; the prevailing moisture-laden northeast winds drench its eastern slopes, which are deeply forested with oak and pine on the drier, cooler heights. (2) A belt of lowland plains which run from the Gulf of Fonseca, on the Pacific, to the Costa Rican border south of Lake Nicaragua. Out of it, to the east, rise the lava cliffs of the mountains to a height of 1500-2100 m. Peninsulas of high land jut out here and there into the lowland, which is generally from 65 to 80 km wide along the Pacific, but is at its narrowest 20 km between La Virgen on Lake Nicaragua and San Juan del Sur. (3) A wide belt of eastern lowland through which a number of rivers flow from the mountains into the Atlantic. In the plains are the two largest sheets of water in Central America and 10 crater lakes. The capital, Managua, is on the shores of Lake Managua (Xolotlán), 52 km long, 15-25 km wide, and 39 m above sea-level. Its maximum depth is only 30 m. The Río Tipitapa drains it into Lake Nicaragua, 148 km long, about 55 km at its widest, and 32 m above the sea; Granada is on its shores. The 190-km Río San Juan drains both lakes into the Caribbean and is one of 96 principal rivers in the country. The longest at 680 km is the Río Coco, on the border with Honduras.

Volcanoes

Lying at the intersection of three continental plates, Nicaragua has a very unstable, changing landscape. Through the Pacific basin runs a row of 28 major volcanoes, six of which have been active within the 20th century. The northernmost is Cosigüina, overlooking the Gulf of Fonseca, at 800 m with a lake in its crater. Its final eruption was in 1835. Northeast of Chinandega begins the Maribios volcanic chain, with Chonco (1105 m) and the country's highest, the cone of San Cristóbal (1745 m), which recommenced erupting in 1971 after a long period of inactivity. This volcano's lava discharge was used as a lighthouse by Pacific pirates in a very destructive raid on the colonial capital of León in 1685. Just south rises Volcán Casita which is notable for its pine forest, the southernmost of its kind in the American continent's northern hemisphere. A side of Casita collapsed during the torrential rains of Hurricane Mitch (1998), burying numerous villages in Posoltega and killing hundreds of people. Further south, just before León, is the very active Telica (1061m) with eruptions occurring every five years, and the extinct cones of little Santa Clara and Orata (836 m), which is believed to be the oldest in the chain. Just south of León is one of the youngest volcanoes on the planet, Cerro Negro, which was born in 1850 and has risen from sea level to 450 m in this short period. Its most recent eruptions occurred in 1992 and 1995 and it frequently coats León in a thick black soup. Volcán Pilas is formed of various craters, the highest of which rises to 1001 m and contains one active crater known as El Hoyo, which last erupted in 1954. Other extinct cones lie between Pilas and the majestic Momotombo (1300 m), which overlooks the shores of Lake Managua and last erupted in 1905, though a geothermal plant utilizes its energy daily. The chain ends with little Momotombito, which forms an island in Lake Managua. Managua's volcanoes are all extinct and six contain crater lakes. The Dirianes volcanic chain begins just north of Masaya with the complex of the same name, including the smoking, lava-filled Santiago crater and four extinct craters and a lagoon. Masaya is the only volcano on the American continent with a consistent lava pool. The last eruptions occurred in 1965 and 1979 and, after a nine year period of calm, it began to smoke heavily again in 1995 with an eruption expected soon. South between Masaya and Granada is the extinct Apoyo, which died very violently 2000 years ago, leaving the deep blue Laguna de Apoyo, 6 km in diameter. Along the shores of Lake Nicaragua, and shadowing Granada, is Volcán Mombacho (1345 m), wrapped in cloud forest. Mobacho had a major structural collapse in 1570 and the resultant explosion not only wiped out an indigenous village at its base, but also fathered hundreds of Las Isletas in nearby Lake Nicaragua. The volcanoes of Lake Nicaragua include the Isla de Zapatera (600 m), a national park and pre-Columbian site, and the final two in the Nicaraguan chain which make up the stunning Isla de Ometepe: the symmetrical and active cone of Concepción (1610 m), which last erupted in 1956, and the cloud forest covered Maderas (1394 m), which holds a lake at its summit.

Climate

The wet, warm winds of the Caribbean pour heavy rain on the Atlantic coastal zone, especially in the southern basin of the Río San Juan, with more than 6 m annually. While the dry season on the Atlantic coast is only short and not wholly dry, the Pacific dry season, or summer (November to April), becomes very dusty, especially when the winds begin to blow in February. There is a wide range of climates. According to altitude, average annual temperatures vary between 15° and 35°C. Midday temperatures at Managua range from 30° to 36°C, but readings of 38° are not uncommon between March and May, or of 40° in January and February in the west. It can get quite cold, especially after rain, in the Caribbean lowlands. Maximum daily humidity ranges from 90% to 100%.

Books and films

Rubén Darío *Cuentos Completos*, the collected stories of this great Nicaraguan poet, the quintessential Latin American author.
Omar Cabezas *Fire from the Mountain: The Making of a Sandinista.* Descriptions of León's fight against the Somoza régime.
Salman Rushdie *The Jaguar Smile*, which romanticizes the Revolution, but maybe that's only with the benefit of hindsight.
Edward Marriott *Savage Shore: Life and Death with Nicaragua's Last Shark Hunters*, looks at the life of the shark hunters of Lake Nicaragua.
Ken Loach *Carla's Song*, set during the Revolution and starring Nick Nolte and Gene Hackman, is an insightful, if feverishly pro-Sandinista portrayal of Nicaragua post-Revolution.
Under Fire is a film which mixes a lot of fact with some fiction. While the setting may be Nicaragua, it was filmed in Mexico.

Costa Rica

History

Spanish settlement

During his last voyage in September 1502, Columbus landed on the shores of what is now Costa Rica. Rumours of vast gold treasures (which never materialized) led to the name of Costa Rica (Rich Coast). The Spaniards settled in the Meseta Central, where the numbers of several thousand sedentary indigenous farmers were soon greatly diminished by the diseases brought by the settlers. Cártago was founded in 1563 by Juan Vásquez de Coronado, but there was almost no expansion for 145 years, when a small number left Cártago for the valleys of Aserrí and Escazú. They founded Heredia in 1717, and San José in 1737. Alajuela, not far from San José, was founded in 1782. The settlers were growing in numbers but were still poor and raising only subsistence crops.

For more on the region's early history, see page 1206.

Independence and coffee

Independence from Spain was declared in 1821 whereupon Costa Rica, with the rest of Central America, immediately became part of Mexico. This led to a civil war during which, two years later, the capital was moved from Cártago to San José. After independence, the government sought anxiously for some product which could be exported and taxed for revenue. Coffee was successfully introduced from Cuba in 1808, making Costa Rica the first of the Central American countries to grow what was to become known as the golden bean. The Government offered free land to coffee growers, thus building up a peasant landowning class. In 1825 there was a trickle of exports, carried by mule to the ports. By 1846 there were ox-cart roads to Puntarenas. By 1850 there was a large flow of coffee to overseas markets which was greatly increased by the opening of a railway in 1890 from San José and Cártago to Puerto Limón along the valley of the Reventazón. From 1850, coffee prosperity began to affect the country profoundly: the birth rate grew, land for coffee was free, and the peasant settlements started spreading, first down the Río Reventazón as far as Turrialba, then up the slopes of the volcanoes, then down the new railway from San José to the old Pacific port of Puntarenas.

The national adjective, 'costarricense', is rather a mouthful: the universal short form is 'tica'.

Banana industry

Bananas were first introduced in 1878; Costa Rica was also the first Central American republic to grow them and is now the second largest exporter in the world. Labour was brought in from Jamaica to clear the forest and work the plantations. The industry grew and in 1913, the peak year, the Caribbean coastlands provided 11 mn bunches for export. Since then the spread of disease has lowered exports and encouraged crop diversification. The United Fruit Company then turned its attentions to the Pacific littoral, especially in the south around the port of Golfito. Although some of the Caribbean plantations were turned over to cacao, abacá (Manilla hemp) and African palm, the region has regained its ascendancy over the Pacific littoral as a banana producer. By the end of the century over 50,000 ha were planted to bananas, mostly in the Atlantic lowlands.

In the 1990s Chiquita, Dole and Del Monte, the multinational fruit producers, came under international pressure over labour rights on their plantations. Two European campaign groups targeted working conditions in Costa Rica where, despite constitutional guarantees of union freedom, there was a poor record of labour rights abuse. Only 10% of Costa Rica's 50,000 banana workers were represented by unions. The rest preferred to join the less political solidarista associations, which provide cheap loans and promote savings, and thus avoid being blacklisted or harassed. Del Monte agreed in 1998 to talk to the unions after a decade of silence, while Chiquita declared its workers were free to choose trade union representation.

Democratic government

Costa Rica's long tradition of democracy began in 1889 and has continued to the present day, with only a few lapses. In 1917 the elected president Alfredo González was ousted by Federico Tinoco, who held power until 1919, when a counter-revolution and subsequent elections brought Julio Acosta to the presidency. Democratic and orderly government followed until the campaign of 1948 when violent protests and a general strike surrounded disputed results. A month of fighting broke out after the Legislative Assembly annulled the elections, leading to the abolition of the constitution and a junta being installed, led by José Figueres Ferrer. In 1949 a constituent assembly drew up a new constitution and abolished the army. The junta stepped down and Otilio Ulate Blanco, one of the candidates of the previous year, was inaugurated. In 1952, Figueres, a socialist, founded the Partido de Liberación Nacional, and was elected President in 1953. He dominated politics for the next two decades, serving as President in 1953-1958 and 1970-1974. The PLN introduced social welfare programmes and nationalization policies, while intervening conservative governments encouraged private enterprise. The PLN was again in power 1974-1978 (Daniel Oduber Quirós), 1982-1986 (Luis Alberto Monge), 19861-1990 (Oscar Arias Sánchez) and 1994-1998 (José María Figueres).

President Arias drew up proposals for a peace pact in Central America and concentrated greatly on foreign policy initiatives. Efforts were made to expel Nicaraguan contras resident in Costa Rica and the country's official proclamation of neutrality, made in 1983, was reinforced. The Central American Peace Plan, signed by the five Central American presidents in Guatemala in 1987, earned Arias the Nobel Peace Prize, although progress in implementing its recommendations was slow. In the 1990 general elections, Rafael Angel Calderón Fournier, a conservative lawyer and candidate for the Social Christian Unity Party (PUSC), won a narrow victory, with 51% of the vote, over the candidate of the PLN. Calderón, the son of a former president who had been one of the candidates in the 1948 disputed elections, had previously stood for election in 1982 and 1986. The President's popularity slumped as the effects of his economic policies were felt on people's living standards, while his Government was brought into disrepute by allegations of corruption and links with 'narco' traffickers.

PLN government, 1994-1998

In the February 1994 elections another former president's son was elected by a narrow margin. José María Figueres of the PLN won 49.6% of the vote, 2.2% points ahead of his PUSC rival. In the Legislature, the PLN won 29 seats and the PUSC 25, while smaller parties won those that remained. The election was won on economic policies. Figueres argued against neo-liberal policies, claiming he would renegotiate agreements with the IMF and the World Bank, but in his first year of office a third Structural Adjustment Programme (backed by the international agencies and drawn up by the previous administration) was approved. A subsequent National Development Plan and a Plan to Fight Poverty contained a wide range of measures designed to promote economic stability and to improve the quality of life for many sectors of society. While the plans were partly responding to the protests that followed the approval of the Adjustment Programme, many of their proposals were at variance with the programme's policies.

1998 and 2002 elections

Elections were held in February 1998 and were won by the PUSC candidate, Miguel Angel Rodríguez, with 46.6% of the vote, 2% ahead of the PLN candidate. Thirty percent of voters abstained. The new president took office in May 1998, promising to make women, the young and the poor a priority for his government. Typically for Costa Rica, the elections of early 2002 ran on a frenzy of neutrality. President Pacheco, 68 years old, stimulated just enough support to win after the election went to a run-off when none of the three candidates won outright victory in the first round. The challenges to the candidates were to restimulate the economy, hit by the global downturn and the low coffee prices, and both claimed to be opposed to privatization of state-run industries.

Arias returns

Having successfully convinced Costa Rica's Congress to change the constitution and allow re-election, Oscar Arias was elected president in 2006, 16 years after serving his first term. The election was extremely close, and only decided after several recounts. President Arias, a strong supporter of the Central America Free Trade Agreement, has promised to stabilise the economy and to make Costa Rica one of the Latin America's most developed countries.

Economy

The country's agricultural economy is based on the export of coffee, bananas, meat, sugar and cocoa. The Meseta Central with its volcanic soil is the coffee-growing area: here too are grown the staple crops: beans, maize, potatoes and sugar cane, and dairy farming is efficient and lucrative. More recently diversification of exports has been successful, with non-traditional crops now accounting for about 60% of revenues. Costa Rica remains the second largest banana exporter in the world, with production dominated by US multinational companies. The country's timber industry is very small although deforestation has occurred at an alarming rate.

High growth in the industrial sector has led to considerable economic diversification, and manufacturing accounts for about 21% of GDP, compared with 8.7% in the case of agriculture. The port of Caldera, near Puntarenas on the Pacific coast, has been improved and manufacturing for export is being encouraged. High education levels have successfully attracted a growing technology sector including the US microprocessor Intel whose assembly plant near San José is expected to earn more than bananas and coffee in exports.

Tourism is a major industry and one of the main sources of foreign exchange revenue, with over 1.4 mn visitors in 2004. The construction of hotels and land prices have soared, driven up by foreign (mainly US) purchasers. Conservation groups have criticized larger developments due to environmental impact, the proximity of national parks and reserves and the destruction of ecosystems.

Recent trends

The Costa Rican economy suffers from large public-sector deficits, partly because of a high level of government spending on social welfare. The country amassed a large foreign debt which, including accumulated arrears, amounted in 1989 to US$5 bn and was one of the highest per capita in the developing world. In the late 1980s, Costa Rica turned to the IMF and the World Bank for help in adjusting its economy, and was one of the first countries to take advantage of a US-sponsored debt reduction proposal.

In 1995 legislation was approved to liberalize the banking system, support privatization and end state monopolies. Labour unions opposed many of the economic measures including the laying off of 8000 public sector workers. There were many strikes, including an extended protest by teachers. Implementation was delayed until 1999, allowing another round of elections in the interim. Despite record growth of 8.3% in 1999, budgetary pressures led the government to announce a privatization programme that has met with more public demonstrations and roadblocks. Resistance to reforming ICE, the state-owned electricity and telecommunications monopoly, which resulted in strikes in May 2003, has hindered the economic restructuring that is considered essential for continued investment in the high-tech industry. The move away from a reliance on coffee and banana exports is gaining pace as historically low coffee prices and reduction in banana production continue to take their toll. While the economic downturn affected the economy overall, the shift towards technology based on high levels of education continue to reap rewards. In 2000 electrical manufacturing generated over US$2 bn for the economy – more than tourism at the time – however, this level of contribution has tailed off in recent years.

Government

Costa Rica is a unitary multiparty republic with one legislative house, the Legislative Assembly of 57 deputies, elected by proportional representation for four years. Executive authority is in the hands of the President, elected for the same term by popular vote. Men and women over 18 have the right to vote. Voting is secret, direct and free. Judicial power is exercised by the Supreme Court of Justice.

Culture

People

In all provinces over 98% of the population are whites and mestizos except in Limón where 33.2% are blacks and 3.1% indigenous, of whom only 5000 survive in the whole country. There are three groups: the Bribri (3500), Boruca (1000) and Guatuso. Although officially protected, the living conditions of the indigenous population are very poor. In 1992 Costa Rica became the first Central American country to ratify the International Labour Organization treaty on indigenous populations and tribes. However, even in Limón, the percentage of blacks is falling: it was 57.1% in 1927. Many of them speak Jamaican English as their native tongue. Much of the Caribbean coastland, especially in the north, remains unoccupied. On the Pacific coastlands a white minority owns the land on the hacienda system which has been rejected in the uplands. About 46% of the people are mestizos. The population has risen sharply in the mountainous Peninsula of Nicoya, which is an important source of maize, rice and beans.

Music and dance

This is the southernmost in our string of 'marimba culture' countries. The guitar is also a popular instrument for accompanying folk dances, while the chirimía and quijongo, already encountered further north, have not yet totally died out in the Chorotega region of Guanacaste Province. This province is indeed the heartland of Costa Rican folklore and the Punto Guanacasteco, a heel-and-toe dance for couples, has been officially decreed to be the 'typical national dance', although it is not in fact traditional, but was composed at the turn of the last century by Leandro Cabalceta Brau during a brief sojourn in jail. There are other dances too, such as the Botijuela Tamborito and Cambute, but it must honestly be said that they will not be found in the countryside as a tradition, but are performed on stage when outsiders need to be shown some native culture. Among the country's most popular native performers are the duet **Los Talolingas**, authors of *La Guaria Morada*, regarded as the 'second national anthem' and **Lorenzo 'Lencho' Salazar**, whose humorous songs in the vernacular style are considered quintessentially Tico.

Some of the Republic's rapidly deculturizing indigenous groups have dances of their own, like the *Danza de los Diablitos* of the Borucas, the *Danza del Sol* and *Danza de la Luna* of the Chorotegas and the *Danza de los Huesos* of the Talamancas. A curious ocarina made of beeswax, the *dru mugata* is still played by the Guaymí people and is said to be the only truly pre-Columbian instrument still to be found. The drum and flute are traditional among various groups, but the guitar and accordion are moving in to replace them. As in the case of Nicaragua, the Caribbean coast of Costa Rica, centred on Puerto Limón, is inhabited by black people who came originally from the English-speaking islands and whose music reflects this origin. The sinkit seems to be a strictly local rhythm, but the calypso is popular and the cuadrille, square dance and maypole dance are also found. There is too a kind of popular hymn called the saki. Brass, percussion and string instruments are played, as well as the accordion.

Land and environment

Costa Rica lies between Nicaragua and Panama, with coastlines on the Caribbean (212 km) and the Pacific (1016 km). The distance between sea and sea ranges from 119-282 km. A low, thin line of hills between Lake Nicaragua and the Pacific is prolonged into northern Costa Rica with several volcanoes (including the active Volcán Arenal), broadening and rising into high and rugged mountains and volcanoes in the centre and south. The highest peak, Chirripó Grande, southeast of the capital, reaches 3820 m. Within these highlands are certain structural depressions; one of them, the Meseta Central, is of paramount importance. To the southwest this basin is rimmed by the comb of the Cordillera; at the foot of its slopes, inside the basin, are the present capital San José, and the old capital, Cártago. Northeast of these cities, about 30 km away, four volcano cones rise from a massive common pedestal. From northwest to southeast these are Poás (2704 m), Barva (2906 m), Irazú (3432 m) and Turrialba (3339 m). Irazú and Poás are intermittently active. Between the Cordillera and the volcanoes is the Meseta Central: an area of 5200 sq km at an altitude of between 900 and 1800 m, where two-thirds of the population live. The northeastern part of the basin is drained by the Reventazón through turbulent gorges into the Caribbean; the Río Grande de Tárcoles drains the western part of it into the Pacific.

There are lowlands on both coasts. On the Caribbean coast, the Nicaraguan lowland along the Río San Juan continues into Costa Rica, wide and sparsely inhabited as far as Puerto Limón. A great deal of this land, particularly near the coast, is swampy; southeast of Puerto Limón the swamps continue as far as Panama in a narrow belt of lowland between sea and mountain.

The Gulf of Nicoya, on the Pacific side, thrusts some 65 km inland; its waters separate the mountains of the mainland from the 900-m-high mountains of the narrow Nicoya Peninsula. From a little to the south of the mouth of the Río Grande de Tercels, a lowland savannah stretches northwest past the port of Puntarenas and along the whole northeastern shore of the Gulf towards Nicaragua. Below the Río Grande de Tercels the savanna is pinched out by mountains, but there are other banana-growing lowlands to the south. Small quantities of African palm and cacao are now being grown in these lowlands. In the far south there are swampy lowlands again at the base of the Península de Osa and between the Golfo Dulce and the borders of Panama. Here there are 12,000 ha planted to bananas. The Río General, which flows into the Río Grande de Térraba, runs through a southern structural depression almost as large as the Meseta Central.

Books

Costa Rica: A Guide to the People, Politics and Culture (1998), In Focus series, Latin America Bureau. A distilled analysis of the country.
Gary Stiles and Alexander Skutch, *Guide to the Birds of Costa Rica*, Cornell University Press (1989). The definitive field guide for birdwatchers.
Les Beletsky, *Costa Rica: The Ecotravellers' Wildlife Guide* (1998). Great nature book.
Mario A Boza *The National Parks of Costa Rica*, (1986), an illustrated book which gives a good impression of the different parks.
Asociación Ecologista de Vida Silvestre *Areas de conservación y sus parques nacionales* (1998), T/F223-0851.
Nature guides can be found at **7th Avenue Books** in San José.

Panama

History

The history of Panama is the history of its pass-route; its fate was determined on 15 September 1513 when Vasco Núñez de Balboa first glimpsed the Pacific (see page 1209). Panama City was of paramount importance to the Spaniards: it was the focus of conquering expeditions both northwards and southwards along the Pacific coasts. All trade to and from these Pacific countries – including the fantastic gold of the Incas – passed across or around the isthmus. As part of Colombia and its predecessors, Panama was traditionally considered part of South America, until recent years, when it has more and more been classed as a Central American republic. The distinction has political significance as international economic integration increases in importance.

For more on the region's early history, see page 1206.

The Camino Real

Panama City was founded in 1519 after a trail had been discovered and opened up between what is now the Bay of Panama on the Pacific and the Caribbean. The Royal Road, or the *Camino Real*, ran from Panama City to Nombre de Dios until it was re-routed to Portobelo. An alternative route was used later for bulkier, less-valuable merchandise; it ran from Panama City to Las Cruces, on the Chagres River but has now been swallowed up in the Gatún Lake. It ran near to Gamboa on the Gaillard / Culebra Cut and was navigable to the Caribbean, particularly during the rainy season. Vestiges of these trails are still in existence, although much of both routes was flooded by the artificial Gatún and Madden/Alajuela lakes created to feed the Canal. It was in these early years that crossing between the Atlantic and Pacific became part of a Panamanian tradition that ultimately led to the construction of the Canal.

Intruders were quickly attracted by the wealth passing over the Camino Real. **Sir Francis Drake** attacked Nombre de Dios, and in 1573 his men penetrated inland to Vera Cruz, further up the Chagres River on the Camino Real, plundering the town. Spain countered later attacks by building strongholds and forts to protect the route: among them San Felipe at the entrances to Portobelo and San Lorenzo at the mouth of the Chagres. Spanish galleons, loaded with treasure and escorted against attack, left Portobelo once a year. They returned with European goods sold at great fairs held at Portobelo, Cartagena and Vera Cruz. Feverish activity either side of the loading and unloading of the galleons made it a favourite time for attack, especially for those with political as well as pecuniary motives. Perhaps the most famous was the attack by **Henry Morgan** in 1671. After capturing the fort of San Lorenzo, he pushed up the Chagres River to Las Cruces. From there he descended to Panama City, which he looted and burnt. A month later Morgan returned to the Caribbean with 195 mules loaded with booty. Panama City was rebuilt on a new site, at the base of Ancón Hill, and fortified. With Britain and Spain at war, attacks reached their climax with Admiral Vernon's capture of Portobelo in 1739 and the fort of San Lorenzo the following year. Spain abandoned the route in 1746 and began trading round Cape Horn. San Lorenzo was rebuilt: it is still there, and has been tidied up and landscaped.

In 1821, Gran Colombia won Independence from Spain. Panama, in an event celebrated annually on 28 November, declared its own Independence and promptly joined Bolívar's Gran Colombia federation. Though known as the 'Sovereign State' of Panama it remained, even after the federation disintegrated, a province of Colombia.

The Panama Railroad

Some 30 years after Independence, streams of men were once more moving up the Chagres and down to Panama City: the forty-niners on their way to the newly discovered gold fields of California. Many perished on this 'road to hell', as it was called, and the gold rush brought into being a railway across the isthmus. The Panama Railroad from Colón (then only two streets) to Panama City took four years to build, with great loss of life. The first train ran on 26 November 1853. The railway was an enormous financial success until the re-routing of the Pacific Steam Navigation Company's ships round Cape Horn in 1867 and the opening of the first US transcontinental railroad in 1869 reduced its traffic. Having been out of operation for several years, a concession to operate the line was awarded to a Kansas rail company in 1998 and service is being restored; initially for freight, perhaps later for passengers.

Building of the Canal

Ferdinand de Lesseps, builder of the Suez Canal, arrived in Panama in 1881 to a hero's welcome, having decided to build a sea-level canal along the Chagres River and the Río Grande. Work started in 1882. One of the diggers in 1886 and 1887 was the painter Gauguin, aged 39. About 30 km had been dug before the Company crashed in 1893, defeated by extravagance, corruption, tropical diseases (22,000 people died, mostly of yellow fever and malaria) and by engineering difficulties inherent in the construction of a canal without lift-locks. Eventually the Colombian government authorized the Company to sell all its rights and properties to the United States, but the Colombian Senate rejected the treaty, and the inhabitants of Panama, encouraged by the United States, declared their dence on 3 November 1903. The United States intervened and, in spite of protests by Colombia, recognized the new republic. Colombia did not accept the severance until 1921.

Within two weeks of its independence, Panama, represented in Washington by the controversial Frenchman **Philippe Bunau-Varilla**, signed a treaty granting to the USA 'in perpetuity' a 16-km wide corridor across the isthmus over which the USA would exercise authority 'as if it were sovereign'. Bunau-Varilla, an official of the bankrupt French canal company, presented the revolutionary junta with the *fait accompli* of a signed treaty. The history of Panama then became that of two nations, with the Canal Zone governor, also a retired US general, responsible only to the President of the USA.

Before beginning the task of building the Canal, the United States performed one of the greatest sanitary operations in history: the clearance from the area of the more malignant tropical diseases. The name of the physician William Crawford Gorgas will always be associated with this, as will that of the engineer George Washington Goethals with the actual building of the Canal. On 15 August 1914, the first official passage was made, by the ship *Ancón*. During this period, and until the military seized power in 1968, a small commercially orientated oligarchy dominated Panamanian politics, although presidential successions were not always smooth.

1939 Treaty with USA

As a result of bitter resentment, the USA ended Panama's protectorate status in 1939 with a treaty which limited US rights of intervention. However, the disparity in living standards continued to provoke anti-US feeling, culminating in riots that began on 9 January 1964, resulting in the death of 23 Panamanians (the day is commemorated annually as Martyrs' Day), four US marines and the suspension of diplomatic relations for some months.

In 1968 **Arnulfo Arias Madrid** was elected president for the third time, having been ousted twice previously. After only 10 days in office he was forcibly removed by the National Guard which installed a provisional junta. Brigadier General Omar Torrijos Herrera ultimately became Commander of the National Guard and principal power in the junta, dominating Panamanian politics for the next 13 years. Gradually, the theoretically civilian National Guard was converted into a full-scale army and renamed the Panama Defence Forces. Constitutional government was restored in 1972 after elections for a 505-member National Assembly of Community Representatives, which revised the 1946 constitution, elected Demetrio Basilio Lakas Bahas as president, and vested temporary extraordinary executive powers in General Torrijos for six years. Torrijos' rule was characterized by his pragmatic nationalism; he carried out limited agrarian reform and nationalized major industries, yet satisfied business interests; he had close links with left wing movements in Cuba, El Salvador and Nicaragua, yet reached agreement with the USA to restore sovereignty over the canal zone to Panama and to close the US military bases by the year 2000. In 1978 elections for a new National Assembly were held and the new representatives elected Arístedes Royo Sánchez president of the country. General Torrijos resigned as Chief of Government but retained the powerful post of Commander of the National Guard until his death in a small plane air-crash in 1981. There followed several years of rapid governmental changes as tension rose between presidents and National Guard leaders.

General Noriega's Administration

Following an election in May 1984, Nicolás Ardito Barletta was inaugurated in October for a six-year term, though the fairness of the elections was widely questioned. He was removed from office by military pressure in September 1985 as he attempted to assert some civilian control and was replaced by Eric Arturo Delvalle. His attempts to reduce military influence in government, by then concentrated principally in the hands of **General Manuel Antonio Noriega** Moreno, led to his own removal by General Noriega in February 1988. Manuel Solís Palma was named President in his place.

With the economy reeling and banks closed as a result of US economic sanctions, the campaign leading up to the election of May 1989 saw the growing influence of a movement called the *Civilista* Crusade, led by upper and middle-class figures. When their coalition candidate, Guillermo Endara Galimany, triumphed over Noriega's candidate, Carlos Duque Jaén, the election was annulled by the military. General Noriega appointed Francisco Rodríguez as provisional President in September, but by December, General Noriega had formally assumed power as Head of State. These events provoked the US military invasion **Operation 'Just Cause'** on 20 December to overthrow him. He finally surrendered in mid-January, having first taken refuge in the Papal Nunciature on Christmas Eve. He was taken to the USA for trial on charges of drugs trafficking and other offences, and sentenced to 30 years in prison. **Guillermo Endara** was installed as President. The Panamanian Defence Forces were immediately remodelled into a new Public Force whose largest component is the civilian National Police, with a compulsory retirement after 25 years' service. More than 150 senior officers were dismissed and many were arrested. Panama has not had a regular army since.

After 'Just Cause'

After the overthrow of General Noriega's administration, the US Senate approved a US$1 bn aid package including US$480 mn in direct assistance to provide liquidity and get the economy moving again. A further US$540 mn aid package was requested from the USA, Japan, Taiwan and the EEC to enable Panama to help clear its US$610 mn arrears with multilateral creditors and support the Panamanian banking system, but inevitably there were delays and little progress was made until 1991. The USA put Panama under considerable pressure to sign a Treaty of Mutual Legal Assistance, which would limit bank secrecy and enable investigation into suspected drug traffickers' bank accounts. Higher levels of crime and drugs trafficking led to the Government passing a law to create the Technical Judicial Police (PTJ) to pursue criminals. While structural, economic and legal changes impacted Panama in the early 1990s, Panama was still not without problems. Charges of corruption at the highest level were made by Panamanians and US officials. President Endara himself was weakened by allegations that his law firm had been involved with companies owned by drugs traffickers. Though the economy grew under Endara, street crime increased, social problems continued, there were isolated bombings and pro-military elements failed in a coup attempt.

1994 elections and after

The 1994 elections took place with 2000 local and international observers, and polling was largely incident-free and open. **Ernesto Pérez Balladares** of the Partido Revolucionario Democrático (PRD), won with less than a third of the popular vote, with a campaign harked back to the record of the party's founder, Omar Torrijos, successfully avoiding any links with its more recent leader Noriega. The PRD also won a narrow majority in the Legislative Assembly. Pérez Balladares, who appointed a cabinet containing members of opposition parties as well as from the PRD, gave priority in his campaign to tackling the problems of social inequality, unemployment, deteriorating education standards and rising crime which had all characterized the end of Endara's term.

In May 1999, Mireya Moscoso emerged victorious in presidential elections which saw a 78% voter turnout. Moscoso obtained 45% of the popular vote, ahead of her closest rival Martín Torrijos (son of General Omar Torrijos) with 38%. Moscoso took office on September 1, becoming the first female president of Panama, enjoying the honour of receiving control of the Panama Canal from the US on 31 December 1999, and the prospect of presiding over the nation's centennial celebrations in 2003.

Elections in May 2004 saw **Martin Torrijos**, son of former dictator Omar Torrijos, win the presidential elections. Commentators believe he gained support from his father's reputation, widely regarded as a hero for negotiating the handover of the Panama Canal. Torrijos Jnr has pledged to improve public finances, judicial reform and the predictable chant of any incoming Latin president, take a firm stance against crime and corruption.

Tax fraud and displaced dictators

Criticisms from the international community in early 2000 suggested that Panama was 'inward looking' and that the country was suffering accordingly. Strong economic growth in 2000 was accompanied by decisions to analyze the past with an announcement by President Moscoso to investigate crimes committed while military goverments were in power between 1968 and 1989.

Two incidents in late 2000 also showed the country's willingness to play a more internationally responsible role. Discussions between Moscoso and the Colombian president Andrés Pastrana produced agreement to strengthen security on their shared border in the Darién region, in an attempt to reduce violence by Colombian rebels and paramilitary groups and to tackle arms and drugs smuggling in region.

The political crisis in Peru in September bought to the fore the country's reputation as the number one destination for politicians seeking exile. Peru's former intelligence chief Vladimiro Montesinos fled to Panama under cover of darkness and, while the Panamanian government was keen to reject his request for political asylum, pressure from Latin American leaders, the US and the Organization of American States led to his temporary political asylum in the interests of stability in Peru. While Panama racks up political points with her neighbours, the country is keen to move away from the image of being a dumping ground for political criminals. This unenviable reputation has seen the Shah of Iran, former Guatemalan President Jorge Serrano Elías, the Haitian military leader Raoul Cedras and the former Ecuadorean President Abdala Bucaram all seek asylum within the country.

Canal area

The former Canal Zone was a ribbon of territory under US control extending 8 km on either side of the Canal, including the cities of Cristóbal and Balboa. The price paid by the United States Government to Panama for construction rights was US$10 mn. The French company received US$40 mn for its rights and properties after the first attempt at constructing a canal finally ground to a halt in 1893 and US$25 mn was given to Colombia in compensation. The total cost at completion was US$387 mn. Panama long ago rejected the perpetuity clause of the original Canal Treaty, but in April 1978 a new treaty was ratified and on 1 October 1979 the Canal Zone, now known officially as the Canal Area, including the ports of Cristóbal and Balboa, the Canal dry docks and the trans-isthmus railway, was formally restored to Panamanian sovereignty. The US Southern Command moved to Miami in 1997, and by the end of 1999 the few remaining bases had closed.

Though polls indicated that many Panamanians supported retention of US military bases, largely because of their employment of civilians and direct governmental expenditures in Panama (about US$350 mn a year in the last years of US operation), vocal minorities demanded their departure. In the run-up to the final hand-over however, there prevailed a curious mixture of national euphoria and apprehension over the country's ability to successfully manage so vital an international resource. US phasing out of the bases was achieved ahead of schedule, though the two countries agreed in 1997 to create a Multilateral Anti-drug Centre which would occupy one of the former US bases and would have some military components. While the doubters are still waiting for problems with the new Canal Administration, the Panamanian Canal authorities are confident they can deliver a world class service. In the first 100 days 3700 vessels transported 61.5 mn tons of cargo through the canal, providing US$143 mn in tolls.

According to figures for 2002, 13,185 ships passed through the Panama Canal, providing US$152 mn for the Panamanian government (out of total Canal revenues of US$588 mn). In 2003 the luxury passenger vessel *Coral Princess* established a new toll record paying US$226,194.25 to transit the canal. In 2004, the Panama Canal posted record revenues of US$1 billion for the financial year. The canal currently operates at

93% of capacity, and at current growth rates will have reached its limit by 2014. A US$5.2 billion investment programme is currently under review to increase capacity.

Economy

Panama's economy has traditionally been founded on income derived from services for visitors, taking advantage of its geographical position, its banking centre, Canal employees and US military personnel spending money in the Republic. However, this contribution is lessening with the departure of the US military and Canal workers, so the country is developing new sources of income including tourism, agricultural exports and industry.

Apart from the Canal the other traditional mainstay of the economy is agriculture, which contributes about 10% of GDP. The leading agricultural export crop is bananas, a large proportion of which are marketed by subsidiaries of the US multinationals Chiquita and Dole. Shrimp is another major export, having grown to about 12% of total earnings. Raw sugar is also an important export item, while smaller quantities of pineapples, coffee and hides and skins are sold abroad. The main industry is food processing but there are also textile and clothing concerns, cement, chemicals, plastics and other light industries. Petroleum products, made from imported crude, are the only industrial export. The lowering of import tariffs in 1993, as a part of trade liberalization measures, contributed to a decline in manufacturing output.

Vast deposits of copper have been found. The mine at Cerro Colorado, if fully developed, could be one of the largest in the world with reserves said to exceed 1 bn tonnes. A 25-year concession granted to a Canadian company is being vigorously opposed by the Ngöbe-Buglé indigenous group. Large coal, gold and silver deposits have been found. So far no oil has been discovered, but exploration is taking place. One of the most dynamic sectors of the economy is banking. There are currently over 100 banks from 32 countries in Panama.

Recent trends

The adoption of neo-liberal economic policies in the 1990s brought rising discontent as spending cuts caused job losses. Strikes and demonstrations became commonplace and poverty increased. The economic plan announced at the outset of Pérez Balladares' term gave priority to reducing poverty by 50%, though it achieved little. Steady inflation, the stable political situation and a growth in tourism are expected to stimulate the economy in the coming years. Panama also hopes to benefit from e-commerce setting up a world-class communications system making the country an important hub in the e-commerce world. While prospects appear to be promising, growing social unrest became apparent in 2001 when general strikes over bus prices (and in 2003 over management of social security funds) paralysed public services and revealed a greater disillusionment amongst those suffering from recession and increased unemployment.

Government

Constitutional reforms were adopted by referendum in April 1983. Legislative power is vested in a unicameral, 72-member Legislative Assembly which is elected by universal adult suffrage for a term of five years (and whose elections are hotly contested, in part because a five-year term yields members total compensation of US$600,000 each). Executive power is held by the President, assisted by two Vice Presidents and an appointed Cabinet. Panama is divided into nine provinces and two semi-autonomous indigenous reservations.

Culture

People

The population is mostly of mixed descent but there are indigenous and black communities and a small Asian population. Most of the rural population live in the six provinces on the Pacific side, west of the Canal. There is only one rural population centre of any importance on the Caribbean: in Bocas del Toro, in the extreme northwest. Of the 60 indigenous tribes who inhabited the isthmus at the time of the Spanish conquest, only three have survived in any number: the Kunas (also spelt Cunas, particularly in Colombia) of the San Blas Islands (50,000), the Guaymíes, who prefer to be called Ngöbe-Buglé, of the western provinces (80,000), and the Emberá-Wunan, formerly known as Chocóes of Darién (10,000). These, and a few others, such as the Teribes, account for 6% of the total population. Indigenous opposition to the opening of copper mines at Cerro Colorado and demonstrations supporting greater autonomy for indigenous people in the area characterized 1996, but were inconclusive. However, an administrative enclave, the Comarca, providing for some Ngöbe-Buglé home rule, has been created. Numbers of African slaves escaped from their Spanish owners during the 16th century. They set up free communities in the Darién jungles and their Spanish-speaking descendants, known as *cimarrones*, still live there and in the Pearl Islands. The majority of Panama's blacks, often bilingual, are descended from English-speaking West Indians, brought in for the building of the railway in 1850, and later of the Canal. There are also a number of East Indians and Chinese, a few of whom, especially in the older generations, tend to cling to their own languages and customs.

Music and dance

Being at the crossroads of the Americas, where Central America meets South America and the Caribbean backs on to the Pacific, and being one of the smallest Latin American republics, Panama possesses an outstandingly rich and attractive musical culture. Albeit related to that of the Caribbean coast of Colombia and Venezuela, it is very different. The classic Panamanian folk dances are the *tambor* or *tamborito*, *cumbia*, *punto* and *mejorana*, largely centred on the central provinces of Coclé, and Veraguas and those of Herrera and Los Santos on the Península Azuero. Towns that are particularly noted for their musical traditions are Los Santos, Ocú, Las Tablas, Tonosí and Chorrera. The dances are for couples and groups of couples and the rhythms are lively and graceful, the man often dancing close to his partner without touching her, moving his hat in rhythmic imitation of fanning. The woman's *pollera* costume is arguably the most beautiful in Latin America and her handling of the voluminous skirt is an important element of the dance. The *tamborito* is considered to be Panama's national dance and is accompanied by three tall drums. The *cumbia*, which has a common origin with the better-known Colombian dance of the same name, has a fast variant called the *atravesado*, while the *punto* is slower and more stately. The name *mejorana* is shared by a small native guitar, a dance, a song form and a specific tune. The commonest instruments to be found today are the tall drums that provide the basic beat, the violin, the guitar and the accordion, with the last-named rapidly becoming predominant. The *tuna* is a highly rhythmic musical procession with women's chorus and massed hand-clapping.

Turning to song, there are two traditional forms, both of Spanish origin: the *copla*, sung by women and accompanying the *tamborito*, and the *mejorana*, which is a male solo preserve, with the lyrics in the form of *décimas*, a verse form used by the great Spanish poets of the Golden Age. It is accompanied by the ukulele-like guitar of the same name. Quite unique to Panama are the *salomas* and *gritos*, the latter between two or more men. The yodelling and falsetto of the *salomas* are in fact carried over into the singing style and it is this element, more than any other, that gives Panamanian folk song its unique and instantly recognizable sound. There are other traditional masked street dances of a carnavalesque nature, such as the very African *Congos*, the *Diablicos Sucios* (dirty little devils) and the *Grandiablos* (big devils). In the area of the Canal there is a significant English-speaking black population, similar to those in Nicaragua and Costa Rica, who also sing calypso, while the Guaymí people (Ngöbe-Buglé) in the west and the Kuna and Chocó (Emberá-Wunan) of the San Blas islands and Darién isthmus possess their own song, rituals and very attractive flute music. When travelling in rural areas during working hours, listen for the distinctive yodelling call of Panamanian farm workers, who greet each other in the fields over long distances with the *saloma*, a cry that slides from a rumble in the throat to a falsetto and back into a rumble, usually rendered in Spanish as *¡Ajuuúa!* Folk tradition says it was adopted from an indigenous custom, and certainly some of its most expert and frequent practitioners are indigenous. Psychologists say letting fly with such a yelp releases the fatigue and heat-induced tension built up by long hours swinging a machete to eliminate weeds from pastures, or to prepare fields for planting. Complex *saloma*-based calls have heavily influenced Panamanian traditional song and the chanting that accompanies much dance. The *¡Ajuuúa!* can also be heard as an expression of approval at baseball games, football matches, and anywhere high spirits provide the occasion for whoops of delight.

The rise in popularity of Latin music has been evident in Panama, in particular as a result of the multi-talented **Rubén Blades**, (currently Minister for Tourism) whose album *Tiempos*, supported by the Costa Rican trio **Editus**, won a Grammy in 2000.

Education

Education is compulsory from the age of six to 15. Ninety-two percent of children attend elementary school. English is the compulsory second language in secondary schools, and many Panamanians speak a little English. There are several universities, including the massive **Nacional**, with 55,000 students, the **Tecnológica**, with 13,000, the important Catholic **Santa María La Antigua** (5000 students), and eight small private ones.

Religion

Panama's Constitution makes Roman Catholicism the official religion of the country, but guarantees freedom of practice to all others. As with neighbouring countries, evangelical churches have been active in recent years. Mosques have been built in Panama City and David, the third city of the Republic.

Land and environment

Panama is most easily visualized as a slightly stretched, horizontal 'S', with the 767 km Caribbean coastline on the north and the 1234 km Pacific coast on the south and lying between 7° and 10° north of the Equator. The Canal, which runs southeast-northwest, bisects the country; the mountains running along the isthmus divide the country from north to south. About one-third of the population lives in Panama City on the east side of the Canal at its southern terminus. Most of the rural population live in the quarter of the country south of the mountains and west of the Canal. At the border with Costa Rica there are several inactive volcanic cones, the boldest of which is the Volcán Barú, 3475 m high and the highest point in the country. The sharp-sided Cordillera de Talamanca continues southeast at a general altitude of about 900 m, but subsides suddenly southwest of Panama City. The next range, the San Blas, rises east of Colón (the city at the north end of the Canal) running parallel to the Caribbean coastline, into Colombia. Its highest peak Tacarcuna, at 1875 m, is in the heart of the Darién. A third range rises from the Pacific littoral in the southeast, running along the Pacific coast of Colombia as the Serranía de Baudó. Nature decreed a gap between the Talamanca and San Blas ranges in which the divide is no more than 87 m high. The ranges are so placed that the gap, through which the Canal runs, follows a line from northwest to southeast. To reach the Pacific from the Atlantic you must travel eastwards so when travelling through the canal, as in much of the country, the sun rises over the Pacific and sets over the Atlantic. The rate of deforestation in Panama has accelerated in the 1980s and early 1990s. Although more of the country is forested than any other Central American republic except Belize, the loss of forest in 1990 was estimated at 220,000 acres, against felling of up to 154,000 acres per year between 1985 and 1989. The government reported a slowing of deforestation during 1993-1995, but in early 1996 estimated it was continuing at 2200 acres (100 ha) a year.

Books and films

For the history of the Canal, see David McCullough's *The Path Between the Seas*. For the era of military rule, John Dinges, *Our Man in Panama*.Graham Greene's *Getting to Know the General* (Torrijos) is subjective and, as such, is not historically reliable, but is worth reading. John Le Carré's recent *Tailor of Panama* is a cynical but entertaining view of Panama City society, recently put on the big screen. Manuel Noriega has written *America's Prisoner* (Random House). Cinema has failed to be inspired by Panama so far. In addition to Le Carré's *Tailor of Panama*, which refreshingly takes Pierce Brosnan out of the Bonded facial expression role, the *Canal Zone*, directed by Frederick Wiseman (1977), is a triology documentary series looking at life in the Canal Zone. For ornithologists, Robert S Ridgely's and John Gwynn's richly illustrated *Guide to the Birds of Panama*, Princeton University Press, describes 929 species and is the definitive guide.

Wildlife

Mexico alone has over 430 mammal species, more than 960 different birds, around 720 reptiles and almost 300 amphibians and as for insects, definitely more than you want to know about, from beautiful butterflies to biting bugs. Even the smallest country in the area, El Salvador, which has little natural habitat remaining, can boast a total of 680 species of vertebrates, the UK has just 280 or so. This diversity is due to the fact that the area is the meeting place of two of the world's major biological regions – the Nearctic to the north and the Neotropical to the south. It has a remarkable geological and climatic complexity and consequently an enormous range of habitats, from desert in the north of Mexico to rainforests, dry forests, cloud forests, mangroves and stretches of wetlands further south in the tropical areas of the region.

When to go?

In terms of wildlife, the best time to visit depends, obviously, on where you are and what you want to see. For instance, if its whale watching you want off Baja California, then go between mid December and mid-March, but if it's the sight of hundreds of thousands of migrating raptors passing over Central America then it will have to be between August and December, or the spectacular mass of Monarch butterflies in the Reserva Ecológica El Campanario, just west of Mexico City, are best visited in January or February. Likewise, the sight of nesting turtles from Mexico to Panama requires planning to get the timing right.

Spotting wildlife

Use local, **experienced guides** as these people will know what species are around and where to look for them and will often recognise bird calls and use these as an aid to spotting them. You should take **binoculars**; get a pair with a reasonable magnification and good light-gathering configurations (ie 10x40 or 8x40) for use in the dim light of the rainforests. They will also need to be reasonably waterproof. Another enormous aid to wildlife watching is a strong torch or, better still, a powerful **headlamp**. The latter not only leaves your hands free but it also helps when trying to spot eye shine of nocturnal mammals, the light reflected back from their eyes direct to yours. Some places, such as Monteverde Cloud Forest Reserve in Costa Rica and the Community Baboon Sanctuary in Belize, offer excellent night walks with guides, but with care you can equally well arrange your own. Another strategy to use is to select a likely looking spot – such as a fruiting fig or a watering hole (in dry country) – and wait for the animals to come to you.

Mammals

In Central America and Mexico mammals tend to be secretive, indeed the majority are nocturnal; hence the need for night walks if you are serious about finding them, though, even then, good views are comparatively rare. That said, you will certainly see some delightful creatures, with views of primates being more or less guaranteed. The rainforests throughout the region contain **spider monkeys, howler monkeys** and/or **capuchin monkeys.** The howlers are probably the most noticeable because, as their name suggests, they are inclined to make a huge row at times, especially early in the mornings and in the late afternoons. The **Community Baboon Sanctuary** in **Belize** was set up especially for the conservation of the black howler monkey and you've a good chance of seeing them in **Tikal, Guatemala,** in **Parque Nacional Pico Bonito** in **Honduras,** on the **Omotepe Islands** in **Nicaragua** and the rainforests of **Costa Rica**. The **spider monkey** is a much more agile, slender primate, swinging around high in the canopy, using its prehensile tail as a fifth limb and again found throughout the region. The smaller, white-throated **capuchins** are also commonly seen, moving around quite noisily in groups, searching for fruit and insects in the trees and even coming down to the ground to find food. Smaller again, and restricted to **Panama** and **Costa Rica**, is the red-backed squirrel monkey. The most likely places to see them are **Parques Nacionales Corcovado** and **Manuel Antonio** in **Costa Rica**. Finally, for the daytime species, you may see a **tamarin**, both Geoffroy's and the cotton-top tamarin are present, but only in **Panama** (try Darién or Natural Metropolitano NPs). The New World, unlike Africa and Asia, has only one group (10 species) of nocturnal primates and this, appropriately enough, is the **night monkey**. Panama is the only country in the region to contain night monkeys. Another mammal you are very likely to see in the southern countries of the region are sloths, good places to look are **Reserva Monteverde** and the forests of **Tortuguero** and **Manuel Antonio** in **Costa Rica**. As they tend to stay in one area for days at a time, local guides are excellent at pointing them out. The most easily seen of the carnivores is not, sadly, the longed for **jaguar**, but the ubiquitous **white-nosed coati**, a member of the racoon family. The females and their offspring go around in groups and are unmistakable with their long, ringed tails, frequently held in the air, and their long snouts sniffing around for insects and fruit in trees and on the ground. At many tourist sites, they hang around waiting to be fed by the visitors, in particular around **Tikal** and in the popular lowland National Parks of **Costa Rica**. Members of the cat family are rarely seen, those in the area include the **bobcat** (in Mexico only), **jaguar**, **puma**, **ocelot** and **margay**. All are more likely to be seen at night, or, possibly, at dawn and dusk. In **Belize**, **Cockscomb Basin Wildlife Sanctuary** is also known as the **Jaguar Reserve**, so this area is as good a place as any to try your luck. **Río Bravo** and **Chan Chich Lodge** in **Belize**, **Corcovado** and **Tortuguero** NPs in **Costa Rica** and **Reserva Biológica Indio Maíz** in **Nicaragua** are also possibilities for the jaguar and the other small cats. The largest land mammal in Central America is **Baird's tapir**, weighing up to 300 kg. It is a forest species and very secretive, particularly so in areas where it is hunted. **Corcovado** and **Santa Rosa** NPs in Costa Rica are all places it might be seen, at least there is a reasonable chance of seeing its hoof prints. They might be seen at waterholes or be spotted swimming in rivers. More likely to be seen are **peccaries**, especially the collared peccary, medium sized pig-like animals that are active both day and night. The **collared peccary** can be found in both dry and rain forests throughout the region, while the **white-lipped peccary** is more common in wetter, evergreen forests. Both live in herds, of up to 100 individuals in the case of the white-lipped species. Found throughout the area, in drier, woodland patches, the **white-tailed deer** can easily be spotted, especially at dawn or dusk, or their bright eyeshine can be seen at night if you are out in a car or on foot with a torch. Also found from Mexico down into South America is the smaller **red brocket**, this, though, is a rainforest species and is more elusive. Rodent species you might see include the **agouti**, which looks rather like a long-legged guinea pig, it can be seen moving around on the forest floor. Considerably larger and stockier is the nocturnal **paca** (**gibnut** in Belize), another forest species found throughout the region, often near water where they hide when chased by predators. The world's largest rodent, the **capybara**, is also found near water, but in this region can be seen only in **Panama**, in Darién, for instance. **Bats** will usually be a quick fly past at night, impossible to identify but for the jagged flight path which is clearly not that of a bird. Perhaps one of the strangest is the **Mexican long-nosed bat**, which forages in groups of 25, feeding on nectar from agaves, in particular, in the desert regions of the country. The nightly exodus of **bats** from caves near to **El Zotz**, in Petén, **Guatemala** is a spectacular sight. Others feed on fish, frogs, fruit and insects; probably the most notorious is the blood-sucking vampire bat, though it rarely attacks humans, instead feeding almost exclusively on domestic stock, such as cattle and goats.

Finally, marine mammals in the area include **whales, dolphins** and **manatees.** The last of these can be seen in Belize's **Southern Lagoon, Lago Izabal** in Guatemala or **Cuero Y Salado Wildlife Reserve in Honduras.** Whales and dolphins occur along both the Pacific and Atlantic coasts and can be watched at a number of sites from **El Vizcaíno Biosphere Reserve** in **Baja California** down the Pacific coast to Puero Vallarta, Escondido and other places along the coast as far south as **Isla Iguana Wildlife Reserve** in **Panama.**

Birds

It is true, the early bird gets the worm and the earlier you get up, the more species you'll see! All countries have very high numbers of birds on their lists but Panama is the haven for birdwatchers in this area; though relatively tiny, it boasts almost as many (922) bird species as Mexico. One of the best places to go in Panama is the **Pipeline Road** (Sendero Oleoducto) in **Parque Nacional Soberanía.** In this lowland rainforest area, brilliantly coloured species such as the violaceous and slaty-tailed **trogans** or the blue-crowned **motmot** can be seen, along with **parrots, tanagers, hummingbirds, antbirds** and many others during the day. It is also a good place to see the spectacular keel-billed **toucan.** At night, eight species of owl, including the crested, can be found, along with potoos and a variety of nightjars. Also, for serious birders, not to be missed in Panama is **Parque Nacional Darién** with mangroves, lowland and montane rainforest where numerous raptors can be seen, including king and black **vultures,** crested **eagles** and, if you're really lucky, the huge, monkey-eating **harpy eagle** with its 2-m wing span. **Macaws, parrots** and **parakeets** are common, along with toucans, hummingbirds, aracaris and tanagers, to mention just a few. At higher altitudes in this park (Cerro Pirre), the golden-headed quetzal can be seen at higher altitudes in Parque Nacional Darién (around Pirre Camp) and nowhere else in Central America.

Many of these birds can be seen outside Panama. Toucans and the smaller toucanets are widespread throughout the tropical areas of the region with the ruins of **Tikal** offering good siting opportunities. Another popular sighting is the scarlet macaw easily spotted near **Puerto Juárez, Costa Rica,** and the region of El Perú and the **Río San Juan** in **Guatemala.** Hummingbirds too are a common sighting throughout the region, frequently drawn to sugar-feeders. The harpy eagle is extremely rare with sightings on the **Osa Peninsula, Costa Rica** a possibility and the in rainforest region of northern Guatemala, Belize and southern Mexico.

To find the **resplendent quetzal,** a brilliant emerald green bird, with males having a bright scarlet breast and belly and ostentatious long green streamers extending as much as 50 cms beyond the end of its tail, **Monteverde Cloud Forest Reserve** or the less atmospheric **Eddie Serrano Mirador** in **Costa Rica** are a couple of the best places to go. You'll also have a good chance of spotting the quetzal in the **Quetzal Biosphere Reserve** in the Sierra de las Minas, **Guatemala,** where the bird is on name of the currency and national symbol.

In addition to the quetzal, Costa Rica, containing around 850 bird species, follows close on the heels of Panama as being a good country to visit for bird watchers and **Monteverde** is one of the hotspots. Species seen there include black **guans, emerald toucanets, violet sabrewings, long-tailed manakins, three wattled bellbirds** and the threatened **bare-necked umbrellabird.** Mixed flocks of small birds such as **warblers, tanagers, woodcreepers** and **wood-wrens** can also be seen in the area. **La Selva Biological Station,** an area of lowland rainforest in Costa Rica, is another area rich in rainforest species such as the **chestnut-billed toucan, mealy parrot** and **squirrel cuckoo.** A very different habitat, with, consequently, different birds, is found in the large wetland area of **Parque Nacional Palo Verde** in Costa Rica. Here one can see **jabirus, black-necked stilts, spotted rails, bare-throated tiger heron, purple gallinule** and many other water birds. In the dry season, **ducks,** including the **black-bellied whistling duck, blue-billed teal, ring-necked duck** and **northern pintail,** congregate in this area in their thousands. More rarely seen here is the **white-faced whistling duck.** Many of these waterbirds can also be seen in **Crooked Tree Wildlife Sanctuary in Belize.**

Of course, all along the coasts are masses of different seabirds, including **pelicans, boobies** and the **magnificent frigate bird.** And in Mexico coastal wetlands near Celestún and in Río Lagarto on the Yucután Peninsula, provide good sightings of **pink flamingoes.**

Maybe you are looking for real rarities, then try spotting the threatened **horned guam,** a highly distinctive and striking bird, that can be found only in high cloud forests of **Mexico** and **Guatemala,** for example, in **El Triunfo Biosphere Reserve** in Mexico. Another species you might consider searching for is the maroon-fronted parrot, endemic to the pine forests of the **Sierra Madre Occidental** in Mexico. This species, strangely for a parrot, nests exclusively in holes in limestone cliffs. The **El Tary Sanctuary,** between the cities of Monterrey and Saltillo, has been created to protect the largest known nesting cliff of this bird, where 100 pairs, a quarter of the breeding population, are found.

Reptiles

This group covers **snakes, lizards, crocodilians** and **turtles.** Mexico has more of these animals than any other country in the world. Throughout the whole region, though, you are not particularly likely to see snakes in the wild, for those wishing to do so, a snake farm or zoo is the best place to go. You might, though, be lucky on one of your walks and see a **boa constrictor** curled up digesting its latest meal, or, again, a guide might know where one is resting. In contrast, **lizards** are everywhere, from small geckos walking up walls in your hotel room, catching insects attracted to the lights, to the large **iguanas** sunbathing in the tree tops. The **American crocodile** and **spectacled caiman** are both found throughout the area, with the latter being seen quite frequently. **Morlet's crocodile,** on the other hand, is found only in Mexico, Belize and Guatemala. Several species of both freshwater and sea **turtles** are present in the region. **Parque Nacional Tortuguero** in **Costa Rica** is a good place to see freshwater and four species of marine turtles, while at **Ostional Beach** in Santa Rosa National Park you can watch masses of olive Ridley turtles coming in to lay their eggs, particularly in September and October. You'll also be able to see nesting turtles along the Pacific coastal beaches of Nicaragua, in La Mosquitia, Honduras,.Monterrico, Guatemala and Mexico, in particular along the southern Pacific around Mazunte and near Bahías de Huatulco.

Amphibians

You'll certainly hear frogs and toads, even if you do not see them. However, the brightly coloured **poison-dart frogs** and some of the tree frogs are well worth searching out. Look for them in damp places, under logs and moist leaf litter, in rock crevices and by ponds and streams, many will be more active at night. **Monteverde** and **La Selva Reserves** are both rich in amphibians, and a visit to **Bocas del Toro** will also reveal colourful amphibians on appropriately named Red Frog Beach.

Invertebrates

There are uncounted different species of invertebrates in the area. Probably, most desirable for ecotourists are the **butterflies,** though some of the **beetles,** such as the jewel **scarabs,** are also pretty spectacular. If you are fascinated by spiders, you can always go hunting for nocturnal **tarantulas; Lamanai** in **Belize** harbours four different species. The gathering of **Monarch butterflies** near Angangueo in Central Mexico is certainly worth a special visit. There are also **butterfly farms** in some of the countries, including in Nicaragua (Los Guatusos Wildlife Reserve) and Costa Rica (eg el Jardín de

Mariposas in Monteverde) that will give you a close up view of many different species. Watching **leaf-cutter ants** marching in long columns from a bush they are systematically destroying and taking the pieces of leaf to their nest, huge mounds on the forest floor, can be a absorbing sight, while marching columns of army ants, catching and killing all small beasts in their path, are best avoided.

Marine wildlife

Predicting the movement and location of marine animals is difficult, and often sightings of sharks and rays is chance. However, the **whale shark** makes a seasonal migration through the coastal waters of Belize and Honduras between March and May. Less natural shark encounters can be had off **Caye Caulker,** Belize, and **Isla Mujeres,** on the Yutatán, Mexico, where hand-feeding brings in **sting rays** and **nurse sharks** for close but safe encounters.

Books

Literature

Books covering the region look like a Who's Who of literature with classic contributions:
Jack Kerouac *On the Road.*
DH Lawrence *The Plumed Serpent.*
Graham Greene *The Lawless Road, The Power and the Glory, The Captain and the Enemy* and *Getting to Know the General.*
Paul Theroux *The Old Patagonian Express* and *The Mosquito Coast.*
Iain Banks *Canal Dreams.*
Norman Lewis *The Volcanoes Above Us.*
Malcolm Lowry Under the Volcano.
Aldous Huxley Eyeless in Gaza and *Beyond the Mexique Bay.*

And that, without touching on the home-grown talents of **Carlos Fuentes, Miguel Angel Asturias, Juan Rulfo, Rubén Darío, Ernesto Cardenal** and the rest. Any of these books would make an excellent choice to accompany the start of your travels.

Jason Wilson, *Traveller's Literary Companion, South and Central America* (Brighton, UK: In Print, 1993), a general guide to the literature of the region with extracts from works by Latin American writers and by non-Latin Americans about the various countries; it also has very useful bibliographies.

History

Michael D Coe *The Maya* (Thames and Hudson), an excellent overview of the Maya.
Michael D Coe *Breaking the Maya Code*, an in-depth account of how the hieroglyphics of the Maya were eventually read.
James Dunkerley *Power in the Isthmus: A Political History of Modern Central America* (1989), a good history of the smaller republics.

Wildlife

If wildlife spotting is the primary reason for your trip, then plan carefully. Specialist advice on where and when to visit should be researched, using advice from detailed sources such as websites or tour companies mentioned throughout this book.

Useful guide books, covering all vertebrate groups, include:
Les Beletsky *Ecotravellers' Wildlife Guides* (one for Costa Rica, one for Tropical Mexico and one for Belize and Northern Guatemala).
F Reid *Field Guide to the Mammals of Central America and Southeast Mexico,* is worth finding.
Louise Emmon *Neotropical Rainforest Mammals: A Field Guide*, will help with identifying wildlife.

For birds:
Steve Howell and Sophie Webb *A Guide to the Birds of Mexico and Northern Central America.*
G Stiles, A Skutch and D Gardner *A Field Guide to the Birds of Costa Rica.*
Steven Howell *A Guide to the Birds of Mexico and Northern Central America.*

R Peterson *Field Guide to Mexican Birds.*
R Ridgeley and J Gwynne *Field Guide to the Birds of Panama.*
www.lab.org.uk (Latin American Bureau) An excellent specialist online guide and bookstore, with country specific titles and international delivery.

Recommended books for countries in Central America and Mexico are listed under the relevant Books sections of each country Background section.

Footnotes

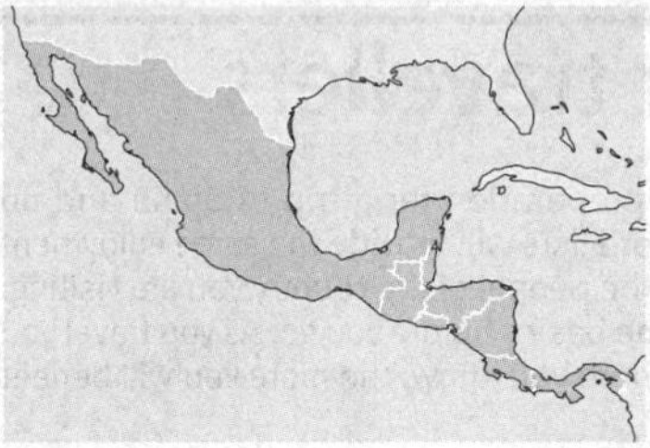

Basic Spanish for travellers

Learning Spanish is a useful part of the preparation for a trip to Spain and no volumes of dictionaries, phrase books or word lists will provide the same enjoyment as being able to communicate directly with the people of the country you are visiting. It is a good idea to make an effort to grasp the basics before you go. As you travel you will pick up more of the language and the more you know, the more you will benefit from your stay.

General pronunciation

For travelling purposes, everyone in Andalucía speaks Spanish, known either as *castellano* or *español*, and it's a huge help to know some. The local accent, *andaluz*, is characterized by dropping consonants left, right and centre, thus *dos tapas* tends to be pronounced *dotapa*. Unlike in the rest of Spain, the letters 'C' and 'Z' in words such as *cerveza* aren't pronounced /th/ (although in Cádiz province, perversely, they tend to pronounce 'S' with that sound).

Vowels

a	as in English *cat*
e	as in English *best*
i	as the *ee* in English *feet*
o	as in English *shop*
u	as the *oo* in English *food*
ai	as the *i* in English *ride*
ei	as *ey* in English *they*
oi	as *oy* in English *toy*

Consonants

Most consonants can be pronounced more or less as they are in English. The exceptions are:

	before *e* or *i* is the same as *j*
h	is always silent (except in *ch* as in *chair*)
j	as the *ch* in Scottish *loch*
ll	as the *y* in *yellow*
ñ	as the *ni* in English *onion*
rr	trilled much more than in English
x	depending on its location, pronounced *x, s, sh* or *j*

Spanish words and phrases

Greetings, courtesies

hello	*hola*
good morning	*buenos días*
good afternoon/evening/night	*buenas tardes/noches*
goodbye	*adiós/chao*
pleased to meet you	*mucho gusto*
see you later	*hasta luego*
how are you?	*¿cómo está?¿cómo estás?*
I'm fine, thanks	*estoy muy bien, gracias*
I'm called...	*me llamo...*
what is your name?	*¿cómo se llama? ¿cómo te llamas?*
yes/no	*sí/no*
please	*por favor*
thank you (very much)	*(muchas) gracias*
I speak Spanish	*hablo español*
I don't speak Spanish	*no hablo español*
do you speak English?	*¿habla inglés?*
I don't understand	*no entiendo/no comprendo*
please speak slowly	*hable despacio por favor*
I am very sorry	*lo siento mucho/disculpe*
what do you want?	*¿qué quiere? ¿qué quieres?*
I want	*quiero*
I don't want it	*no lo quiero*
leave me alone	*déjeme en paz/no me moleste*
good/bad	*bueno/malo*

Basic questions and requests

have you got a room for two people?	*¿tiene una habitación para dos personas?*
how do I get to_?	*¿cómo llego a_?*
how much does it cost?	*¿cuánto cuesta? ¿cuánto es?*
I'd like to make a long-distance phone call	*quisiera hacer una llamada de larga distancia*
is service included?	*¿está incluido el servicio?*
is tax included?	*¿están incluidos los impuestos?*
when does the bus leave (arrive)?	*¿a qué hora sale (llega) el autobús?*
when?	*¿cuándo?*
where is_?	*¿dónde está_?*
where can I buy tickets?	*¿dónde puedo comprar boletos?*
where is the nearest petrol station?	*¿dónde está la gasolinera más cercana?*
why?	*¿por qué?*

Basic words and phrases

bank	*el banco*
bathroom/toilet	*el baño*
to be	*ser, estar*
bill	*la factura/la cuenta*
cash	*el efectivo*
cheap	*barato/a*
credit card	*la tarjeta de crédito*
exchange house	*la casa de cambio*
exchange rate	*el tipo de cambio*
expensive	*caro/a*
to go	*ir*
to have	*tener, haber*
market	*el mercado*
note/coin	*el billete/la moneda*
police (policeman)	*la policía (el policía)*
post office	*el correo*
public telephone	*el teléfono público*
shop	*la tienda*
supermarket	*el supermercado*
there is/are	*hay*
there isn't/aren't	*no hay*
ticket office	*la taquilla*
travellers' cheques	*los cheques de viajero/los travelers*

Getting around

aeroplane	*el avión*
airport	*el aeropuerto*
arrival/departure	*la llegada/salida*
avenue	*la avenida*
block	*la cuadra*
border	*la frontera*
bus station	*la terminal de autobuses/camiones*
bus	*el bus/el autobús/el camión*
collective/fixed-route taxi	*el colectivo*
corner	*la esquina*
customs	*la aduana*
first/second class	*la primera/segunda clase*
left/right	*izquierda/derecha*
ticket	*el boleto*
empty/full	*vacío/lleno*
highway, main road	*la carretera*
immigration	*la inmigración*
insurance	*el seguro*
insured person	*el asegurado/la asegurada*

to insure yourself against	*asegurarse contra*
luggage	*el equipaje*
motorway, freeway	*el autopista/la carretera*
north, south, west, east	*el norte, el sur, el oeste (occidente), el este (oriente)*
oil	*el aceite*
to park	*estacionarse*
passport	*el pasaporte*
petrol/gasoline	*la gasolina*
puncture	*el pinchazo/la ponchadura*
street	*la calle*
that way	*por allí/por allá*
this way	*por aquí/por acá*
tourist card/visa	*la tarjeta de turista/visa*
tyre	*la llanta*
unleaded	*sin plomo*
waiting room	*la sala de espera*
to walk	*caminar/andar*

Accommodation

air conditioning	*el aire acondicionado*
all-inclusive	*todo incluido*
bathroom, private	*el baño privado*
bed, double/single	*la cama matrimonial/sencilla*
blankets	*las cobijas/mantas*
to clean	*limpiar*
dining room	*el comedor*
guesthouse	*la casa de huéspedes*
hotel	*el hotel*
noisy	*ruidoso*
pillows	*las almohadas*
power cut	*el apagón/corte*
restaurant	*el restaurante*
room/bedroom	*el cuarto/la habitación*
sheets	*las sábanas*
shower	*la ducha/regadera*
soap	*el jabón*
toilet	*el sanitario/excusado*
toilet paper	*el papel higiénico*
towels, clean/dirty	*las toallas limpias/sucias*
water, hot/cold	*el agua caliente/fría*

Health

aspirin	*la aspirina*
blood	*la sangre*
chemist	*la farmacia*
condoms	*los preservativos, los condones*
contact lenses	*los lentes de contacto*
contraceptives	*los anticonceptivos*
contraceptive pill	*la píldora anticonceptiva*
diarrhoea	*la diarrea*
doctor	*el médico*
fever/sweat	*la fiebre/el sudor*
pain	*el dolor*
head	*la cabeza*
period/sanitary towels	*la regla/las toallas femeninas*
stomach	*el estómago*
altitude sickness	*el soroche*

Family

family	*la familia*
brother/sister	*el hermano/la hermana*
daughter/son	*la hija/el hijo*
father/mother	*el padre/la madre*
husband/wife	*el esposo (marido)/la esposa*
boyfriend/girlfriend	*el novio/la novia*
friend	*el amigo/la amiga*
married	*casado/a*
single/unmarried	*soltero/a*

Months, days and time

January	*enero*
February	*febrero*
March	*marzo*
April	*abril*
May	*mayo*
June	*junio*
July	*julio*
August	*agosto*
September	*septiembre*
October	*octubre*
November	*noviembre*
December	*diciembre*
Monday	*lunes*
Tuesday	*martes*
Wednesday	*miércoles*
Thursday	*jueves*
Friday	*viernes*
Saturday	*sábado*
Sunday	*domingo*
at one o'clock	*a la una*
at half past two	*a las dos y media*
at a quarter to three	*a cuarto para las tres/a las tres menos quince*
it's one o'clock	*es la una*
it's seven o'clock	*son las siete*
it's six twenty	*son las seis y veinte*
it's five to nine	*son cinco para las nueve/las nueve menos cinco*
in ten minutes	*en diez minutos*
five hours	*cinco horas*
does it take long?	*¿tarda mucho?*

Numbers

one	*uno/una*
two	*dos*
three	*tres*
four	*cuatro*
five	*cinco*
six	*seis*
seven	*siete*
eight	*ocho*
nine	*nueve*
ten	*diez*
eleven	*once*
twelve	*doce*
thirteen	*trece*
fourteen	*catorce*

fifteen	*quince*
sixteen	*dieciséis*
seventeen	*diecisiete*
eighteen	*dieciocho*
nineteen	*diecinueve*
twenty	*veinte*
twenty-one	*veintiuno*
thirty	*treinta*
forty	*cuarenta*
fifty	*cincuenta*
sixty	*sesenta*
seventy	*setenta*
eighty	*ochenta*
ninety	*noventa*
hundred	*cien/ciento*
thousand	*mil*

Food

avocado	*el aguacate*
baked	*al horno*
bakery	*la panadería*
banana	*el plátano*
beans	*los frijoles/las habichuelas*
beef	*la carne de res*
beef steak or pork fillet	*el bistec*
boiled rice	*el arroz blanco*
bread	*el pan*
breakfast	*el desayuno*
butter	*la mantequilla*
cake	*el pastel*
chewing gum	*el chicle*
chicken	*el pollo*
chilli pepper or green pepper	*el ají/el chile/el pimiento*
clear soup, stock	*el caldo*
cooked	*cocido*
dining room	*el comedor*
egg	*el huevo*
fish	*el pescado*
fork	*el tenedor*
fried	*frito*
garlic	*el ajo*
goat	*el chivo*
grapefruit	*la toronja/el pomelo*
grill	*la parrilla*
guava	*la guayaba*
ham	*el jamón*
hamburger	*la hamburguesa*
hot, spicy	*picante*
ice cream	*el helado*
jam	*la mermelada*
knife	*el cuchillo*
lime	*el limón*
lobster	*la langosta*
lunch	*el almuerzo/la comida*
meal	*la comida*
meat	*la carne*
minced meat	*el picadillo*
onion	*la cebolla*
orange	*la naranja*

pepper	*el pimiento*
pasty, turnover	*la empanada/el pastelito*
pork	*el cerdo*
potato	*la papa*
prawns	*los camarones*
raw	*crudo*
restaurant	*el restaurante*
salad	*la ensalada*
salt	*la sal*
sandwich	*el bocadillo*
sauce	*la salsa*
sausage	*la longaniza/el chorizo*
scrambled eggs	*los huevos revueltos*
seafood	*los mariscos*
soup	*la sopa*
spoon	*la cuchara*
squash	*la calabaza*
squid	*los calamares*
supper	*la cena*
sweet	*dulce*
to eat	*comer*
toasted	*tostado*
turkey	*el pavo*
vegetables	*los legumbres/vegetales*
without meat	*sin carne*
yam	*el camote*

Drink

beer	*la cerveza*
boiled	*hervido/a*
bottled	*en botella*
camomile tea	*té de manzanilla*
canned	*en lata*
coffee	*el café*
coffee, white	*el café con leche*
cold	*frío*
cup	*la taza*
drink	*la bebida*
drunk	*borracho/a*
firewater	*el aguardiente*
fruit milkshake	*el batido/licuado*
glass	*el vaso*
hot	*caliente*
ice/without ice	*el hielo/sin hielo*
juice	*el jugo*
lemonade	*la limonada*
milk	*la leche*
mint	*la menta/la hierbabuena*
rum	*el ron*
soft drink	*el refresco*
sugar	*el azúcar*
tea	*el té*
to drink	*beber/tomar*
water	*el agua*
water, carbonated	*el agua mineral con gas*
water, still mineral	*el agua mineral sin gas*
wine, red	*el vino tinto*
wine, white	*el vino blanco*

Index

C

D

E

H

I

J

K

L

M

Footnotes Index

Q

R

S

Map index

Advertisers' index

Map symbols

Administration

- Capital city
- Other city/town
- International border
- Regional border
- Disputed border

Roads and travel

- National Highway
- Paved road
- Unpaved all-weather road
- Seasonal unpaved road/track
- Footpath
- Railway with station
- Airport
- Bus station
- Metro station
- Cable car
- Funicular
- Ferry

Water features

- River, canal
- Lake, ocean
- Seasonal marshland
- Beach, sandbank
- Waterfall
- Reef

Topographical features

- Contours (approx)
- Mountain, volcano
- Mountain pass
- Escarpment
- Gorge
- Glacier
- Salt flat
- Rocks

Cities and towns

- Main through route
- Main street
- Minor street
- Pedestrianized street
- Tunnel
- One way-street
- Steps
- Bridge
- Fortified wall
- Park, garden, stadium
- Sleeping
- Eating
- Bars & clubs
- Building
- Sight
- Cathedral, church
- Chinese temple
- Hindu temple
- Meru
- Mosque
- Stupa
- Synagogue
- Tourist office
- Museum
- Post office
- Police
- Bank
- Internet
- Telephone
- Market
- Medical services
- Parking
- Petrol
- Golf
- Detail map
- Related map

Other symbols

- Archaeological site
- National park, wildlife reserve
- Viewing point
- Campsite
- Refuge, lodge
- Castle
- Diving
- Deciduous/coniferous/palm trees
- Hide
- Vineyard
- Distillery
- Shipwreck
- Historic battlefield

Complete title listing

Footprint publishes travel guides to over 150 destinations worldwide. Each guide is packed with practical, concise and colourful information for everybody from first-time travellers to travel aficionados. The list is growing fast and current titles are noted below. Available from all good bookshops and online at www.footprintbooks.com

(P) denotes pocket guide

Latin America and Caribbean
Argentina
Barbados (P)
Belize, Guatemala & Southern Mexico
Bolivia
Brazil
Caribbean Islands
Central America & Mexico
Chile
Colombia
Costa Rica
Cuba
Cuzco & the Inca heartland
Dominican Republic
Ecuador & Galápagos
Havana (P)
Mexico
Nicaragua
Patagonia
Peru
Peru, Bolivia & Ecuador
Rio de Janeiro (P)
South American Handbook
St Lucia (P)
Venezuela

North America
Vancouver (P)
New York (P)
Western Canada

Africa
Cape Town (P)
Egypt
Kenya
Libya
Marrakech (P)
Morocco
Namibia
South Africa
Tanzania
Tunisia
Uganda

Middle East
Dubai (P)
Israel
Jordan
Syria & Lebanon

Australasia
Australia
East Coast Australia
New Zealand Sydney (P)
West Coast Australia

Asia
Bali
Bhutan
Borneo
Cambodia
Goa
Hong Kong (P)
India
Indian Himalaya
Indonesia
Laos
Malaysia & Singapore
Nepal
Northern Pakistan
Pakistan
Rajasthan
South India
Sri Lanka
Sumatra
Thailand
Tibet
Vietnam
Vietnam, Cambodia & Laos

Europe
Andalucía
Barcelona (P)
Belfast (P)
Berlin (P)
Bilbao (P)
Bologna (P)
Britain
Cardiff (P)
Copenhagen (P)
Croatia
Dublin
Dublin (P)
Edinburgh (P)
England
Glasgow (P)
Ireland
Lisbon (P)
London
London (P)
Madrid (P)
Naples (P)
Northern Spain
Paris (P)
Reykjavík (P)
Scotland
Scotland Highlands & Islands
Seville (P)
Siena (P)
Spain
Tallinn (P)
Turin (P)
Turkey
Valencia (P)
Verona (P)
Wales

Lifestyle guides
Diving the world
European City Breaks
Surfing the World
Surfing Britain
Surfing Europe

Also available:
Traveller's Handbook (WEXAS)
Traveller's Healthbook (WEXAS)
Traveller's Internet Guide (WEXAS)

Credits

Footprint credits

Editor: Felicity Laughton
Assistant editor: Angus Dawson
Map editor: Sarah Sorensen
Picture editor: Kevin Feeney
Proofreader: Claire Boobbyer

Publisher: Patrick Dawson
Editorial: Alan Murphy, Sophie Blacksell, Nicola Jones
Cartography: Robert Lunn, Kevin Feeney
Series development: Rachel Fielding
Design: Mytton Williams and Rosemary Dawson (brand)
Sales and marketing: Andy Riddle, Daniella Cambouroglou
Advertising: Debbie Wylde
Finance and administration: Elizabeth Taylor

Photography credits

Front cover: Superstock (Cactus)
Inside: Alamy, Beth Tierney, Claire Boobbyer, Photolibrary, Superstock, Travel Ink, Willy Urbide
Back cover: Superstock (Local band, Zunil, Guatemala)

Print

Manufactured in Italy by LegoPrint
Pulp from sustainable forests

Footprint feedback

We try as hard as we can to make each Footprint guide as up to date as possible but, of course, things always change. If you want to let us know about your experiences – good, bad or ugly – then don't delay, go to **www.footprintbooks.com** and send in your comments.

Publishing information

Footprint Mexico and Central America
16th edition

August 2006
ISBN 1 904777 65 1

CIP DATA: A catalogue record for this book is available from the British Library

Published by Footprint

6 Riverside Court
Lower Bristol Road
Bath BA2 3DZ, UK
T +44 (0)1225 469141
F +44 (0)1225 469461
discover@footprintbooks.com
www.footprintbooks.com

Distributed in the USA by

Publishers Group West

Acknowledgements

A great deal of work goes into the creation of *Footprint Mexico and Central America*. It's an almost non-stop process which, in some respects, is made easier by the internet but still involves a lot of hard work to get the latest and most up-to-date information possible. A large team of people contribute to this guide, not all of whom are mentioned below: in-country correspondents – both old and new – provide the inside track on developments in each country in a way that only residence allows; readers' letters (credited on the following page) provide personal experiences and stories, while trips by experienced researchers capture the spirit of the very latest happenings in the region.

As editor of the book I have the pleasure of meeting and working with a wide range of people from all kinds of backgrounds and being able to see, first hand, the changing face of the region. I also get the pleasure of working with a varied bunch of people, who are passionate about the region, or their particular patch. And this year, the team somehow managed to have three babies in the six months leading up to publication. Now that's multi-tasking. Hope everyone's getting more sleep.

Specific people should quite rightly be thanked for their contribution particular to *Footprint Mexico and Central America*, 16th edition.

Vast **Mexico** was, as ever, the work of several people. Peter Hutchison covered much of southern Mexico, spending a short time in Mexico City. Claire Boobbyer also visited parts of southern Mexico and worked on the northern and central Mexico sections. It really is a huge, fast-changing country. We tried to get a few fresh faces for this edition and we'll continue to look for more for the next edition.

Claire also provided the attention to detail, thoroughness and dedication to her trips through **Guatemala** and **Belize**.

El Salvador was updated by the on the ground knowledge of Lena Johannessen.

Honduras got the light touch of Howard Rosenzweig who reliably provides information from his base in Copán Ruinas, and from John Dupis in La Ceiba.

Nicaragua was updated by Miguel Castrillo Cheng, who enjoyed travelling through his own country looking with the attentive eye that a guidebook updater has to have.

Costa Rica was updated by Heloise Crowther, with very useful input from Jane Koutnik at times. Heloise also helped out with **Panama**, putting to good use her detailed knowledge of the country.

For specialist contributions from this or previous years, we would like to thank: Caroline Harcourt for wildlife; Nigel Gallop for music and dance; John Alton for details on cargo ship cruises; Binka and Robin le Breton for motoring; Ashley Rawlings for motorcycling; Hallam Murray for cycling; Hilary Bradt for hiking and trekking; David Fishlow for language and Mark Eckstein for responsible tourism.

The health section was written by Professor Larry Goodyer, Head of the Leicester School of Pharmacy and director of Nomad Medical. Additional research was carried out by Joe Copestake.

Claire Boobbyer who updated the Guatemala and Belize chapter would like to thank Patrick Vercoutere at Adrenalina Tours, Thierry Roquet at Mayaexplor, Francisco Sandoval at Uxlabil, Chiminos, Café Rocio in Antigua, Discovery Expeditions in Belize City, Explore in Santa Elena and the INGUAT staff Jorge Lucas Cuxil and Gustavo Rosales and especially Olivier Ordoñez. A particular thanks is due to Neil Rogers for his many many contacts and arrangements in Belize and to Pascale from Sin Fronteras in Antigua who made my trip possible.

Travellers' letters

Travelling through Mexico and Central America you're bombarded with experiences – good and bad. While it's up to you to decide where you go, how you travel and what you do, we try our best to provide up-to-date information to help you on your way. Many travellers assist us in this task by writing to us with information about new hotels that have opened, established hotels that have gone downhill or been refurbished, restaurants that provide a welcome change from the norm, changes in transport prices, routes and options and so on.

Many thanks to the following readers who have taken the time to write notes as they travel and to share their experiences with us by post or, increasingly, by email. It's great to receive letters, from short pithy corrections to colourful, sometimes humorous descriptions of personal journeys.

Carlos Agudelo, Costa Rica (Cos); Alex Ahlberg, Finland ; Allan Ament, (Cos); Ana Elisa Ana, (Mex); Markus Angst, Switzerland (Mex); Krieg Hillebrand & Julia Armin, Austria (Mex, Bel, Gua, El Sal, Hon); Maria-Sol Bachand, (Mex); Adam Beals, US (Cos); Johannes Beck, (Mex, Bel); Ofir Berger, Israel (Mex, Gua); Arlene Black, US (Nic); Clint & Carly Blackbourn, (Hon, Nic, Cos); Julie Blyth, (Gua); Steffan Boerner, Germany (Bel); Elinor Breman, (Nic); Ali Briggs, Australia (Gua); Rosemarie Briggs, Canada (Gua); Howard Buck, US (Mex, Gua, El Sal, Hon, Nic, Cos, Pan); Tony Burton, (Mex); Christophe Caron, (Gua); Carina Cisnero, (Hon); John Clark, Guatemala (Gua); Shlomit Cohen Yashar, Israel (Gua); Jo Collins, Belize (Bel); Clark Conn, (El Sal, Pan); Rebecca Craske, UK (Mex, Gua, Hon, Nic, Cos); Karen Schulpzand & Rudy Cruysbergs, Belgium (Cos); Amy Davis, US (Gua); Sofie De Bauw, Belgium (Gua); Yohai Devir, Israel (Mex, Gua); Thomas Dewijn, Netherlands (Gua); Inge Dix, Netherlands (Mex); Leibbrandt Dominique, Switzerland (Mex); Olivia Duke, UK (Gua); Nalina Dunstan, Australia (Gua, Hon, Nic); Sebastian Erb, (Nic); Lilach Eyal, Israel (Mex); Carolyn Freiwald, US (Mex); Jakob Frost, Germany ; Walter Fuchs, Austria (Gua); Jordan Gabay, Israel (Mex); Karla Galeazzi, (Hon); Pedro Garcia, Panama (Pan); Kent Gardner, Belize (Bel); Magdalena Geigenberger, Germany (Gua); Dagmar Gendera, Guatemala (Gua); Vivian Georgy, UK (Gua); Klaus Giger, Germany (Mex); Pat Horan & Celia Gleeson, UK (Mex); Jane Glover, UK (Pan); Fred Gries, (Mex); Megan Gross, US (Cos); Viviana Gutierrez, Costa Rica (Cos); Mike Haaijer, (Hon); Terry Halpin, US (Nic); Paul Hammer, Austria (Nic); Natalie Harvey, UK (Hon); Nigel Hashim, (Gua); Andreas Henrichs, (Mex); William Hodges, US (Gua, Bel, Hon); Leon Hüppauff, Germany (Mex); Jamie Hustwayte, UK (Gua); Wilma Frankema & Jan Idsardi, Netherlands (Hon); Robert Ingham, UK (Mex, Gua, Nic); Lachance Isabelle, Canada (Cos); David Jackson, Australia (Cos); Tim Jellings, UK (Mex); Schaefer John, US (Pan); Marwin en Jose, Netherlands (Gua); Sann K, Finland (Mex); Timo Kiesel, Germany ; Jon Knight, Australia (Mex); Sebastian Koetter, Germany (Mex); Marceal Kohman, UK ; Marijke Lamers, Netherlands (Gua, Hon, Nic, Cos); Gerhard Landscuetzer, Austria (Nic); Geoff Ledgerwood, US (Cos); Jean-Sebastien Leduc, Canada (Cos); Ina Lockau-Vogel, Germany (Cos); Catherine MacNicol, UK (Nic); Ciara Maguire, Ireland (Mex, Gua, Bel, El Sal, Hon, Nic, Cos, Pan); Tarne Malor, Australia (Mex); Fiechter Manouk, Switzerland (Gua); Jean Pierre Martin, Canada (Cos); Scott & Narelle Mayer, Australia (Gua); Neil McCann, Australia (Hon); Fergus McGaugh, (Mex, Gua); Leslie McGinnis, US (Cos); Donough McGuinnes, Ireland (Bel); Sarah Miles, UK (Nic); Thomas Ming, Switzerland (Nic); Jacques Modiano, Costa Rica (Cos); Edd Morris, UK (Gua); Wolfgang Mühlbauer, Germany (Nic); Meera Nair, UK (Bel); Jen Noone, US (Gua); Claudia Oliveira, Belize (Bel); Lisa Orrenius, Guatemala (Gua); Karol Pastorek, Slovakia (Mex, Gua, El Sal, Hon, Nic, Cos); Nicholas Pelafas, US (Mex); Judith Pisarek,

(Hon); Heloise Plumley, UK (Gua, Hon, Cos); Erin Pugh, Belize (Bel); Alex Putt, Costa Rica (Cos); Nora Pyne, Canada (Mex); Andrew Raffo, Costa Rica (Cos); Sheila Ramclam, Belize (Bel); Ian Rayner, Australia (Nic); George Rentz, US (Gua); Silvia Rey, Switzerland (Nic); Andrew Rhee, US (Cos); Orlando Rivera, US (Cos); Justin Rose, UK (Gua); Gil Rosenstock, Israel (Gua); Nynke van der Schaaf, Netherlands (Gua); Adrian Schaer, Switzerland (Mex, Nic); Karen Scheuerer, (Nic); Volkmar Schuster, Germany (Gua, Bel, El Sal, Nic, Cos); Diane Scully, UK (Nic); Anja Seidel, Costa Rica (Cos); Silvia Senger, Switzerland (Cos); Julien Simard, Canada (Pan); Alejandro Solano, Costa Rica (Cos); Camilla Spears, UK (Mex, Gua); Cheryl Steinmeyer, US (Bel); Claudia Stracke, Germany (Mex); Hisako Tajima, US (Nic); Katharina Vater & Gabriel Tecklenburg, Germany (Cos); Debra Thesken, US (Hon); Daniel Toporoski, US (Mex); Terhi Tuominen, (Mex); Michal Vaadia, Israel (Mex); JRJ van Asperen de Boer, Netherlands (Mex); Dana Verstappen, Costa Rica (Cos); Judith Verwij, Netherlands (Gua); Gordan & Sue Vint, UK (Cos); Otto de Voogd, Netherlands ; Hans Wagenhaus, Belize (Bel); Hans Wagner, Switzerland (Mex); Hans Wagner, Switzerland ; Kristen Walbran, UK (Mex); Tom Walton, UK (Mex); Willi Waschull, Germany (Cos); William Welbourn, Honduras (Hon); Karyn Wesselingh, UK (Mex, Gua, Hon, Cos, Pan); Gerrit Wilmink, Netherlands (Cos); Brian Wilson, US (Gua); Steffan Wofford, Costa Rica (Cos); Nadja Wuest, Switzerland (Cos).

Also many thanks to the many hoteliers, restaurateurs, tour operators and others mentioned in *Footprint Mexico and Central America* who have kindly taken the time to inform us when their contact details have changed. While we are unlikely to include the details of a new establishment without specific recommendations or, ideally, a visit, it is very useful to receive details about changes in telephone numbers, email and postal addresses, services provided, prices and so on. Thanks.

If you have any comments, please send them to: Footprint Handbooks, 6 Riverside Court, Lower Bristol Road, BA2 3DZ, UK or by email to discover@footprintbooks.com.

About the author

Peter Hutchison first travelled through Central and South America between 1993 and 1995 after gaining a degree in Development Studies, specializing in Latin American Studies, from Reading University. During his travels he used both versions of 'The Bible' – Central and South – to guide his path, taking time to stop for almost two years to work on the *Bolivian Times* in La Paz. Since then regular trips to Latin America, travelling popular routes and journeying roads less travelled, have kept the passion alive.

In February and March 2002 a team of five, led by Peter, made the first recorded descent of the River Parapeti (www.coursingtheparapeti.com) with the support of the Royal Geographic Society and funding from a Travelling Fellowship provided by the Winston Churchill Memorial Trust. River travel by canoe continued in Belize 2003 when Peter entered the Macal River Race in Belize with Marc Gussen and Max. Paddling the Devizes Westminster Canoe Marathon down the River Thames in 2004 kept the long distance race going and Peter is currently looking for a new river to explore, preferably in Latin America.

Peter now lives in Hanwell, West London, using this base to work as a freelance journalist and travel writer. Having trained on the kayaking course used in the Mexican Olympics in 1968, he is very excited about watching the developments in London in the build up to 2012.

Notes

Mango Inn
Utila
BAY ISLANDS HONDURAS
Utila Dive Centre
Great Diving
Great Accommodations
Complete Training Facility
Great Value
CDC
Career Development Center
PADI
UTILA
Dive Centre
WWW.UTILADIVECENTRE.COM
WWW.MANGO-INN.COM
EMAIL: INFO@UTILADIVECENTRE.COM

Footprint
Diving the World
Live.
Dive.
Travel.
Only £19.99
Available online and from all
good bookshops Spring 2006
This guide is as vital as a mask and fins.
David Espinosa, Asian Diver magazine
www.footprintbooks.com
Footprint
Travel guides

Mexico & Central America

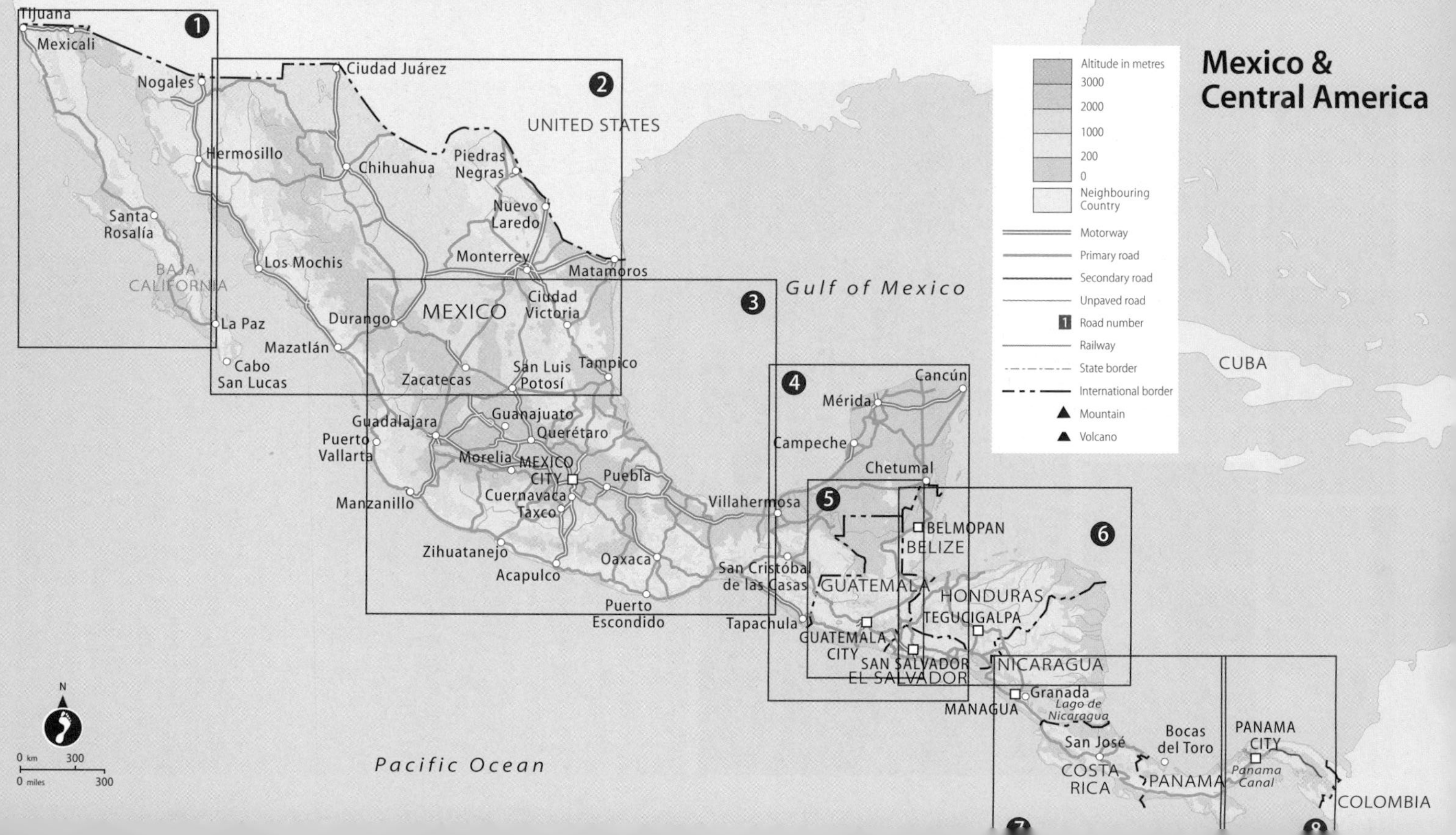

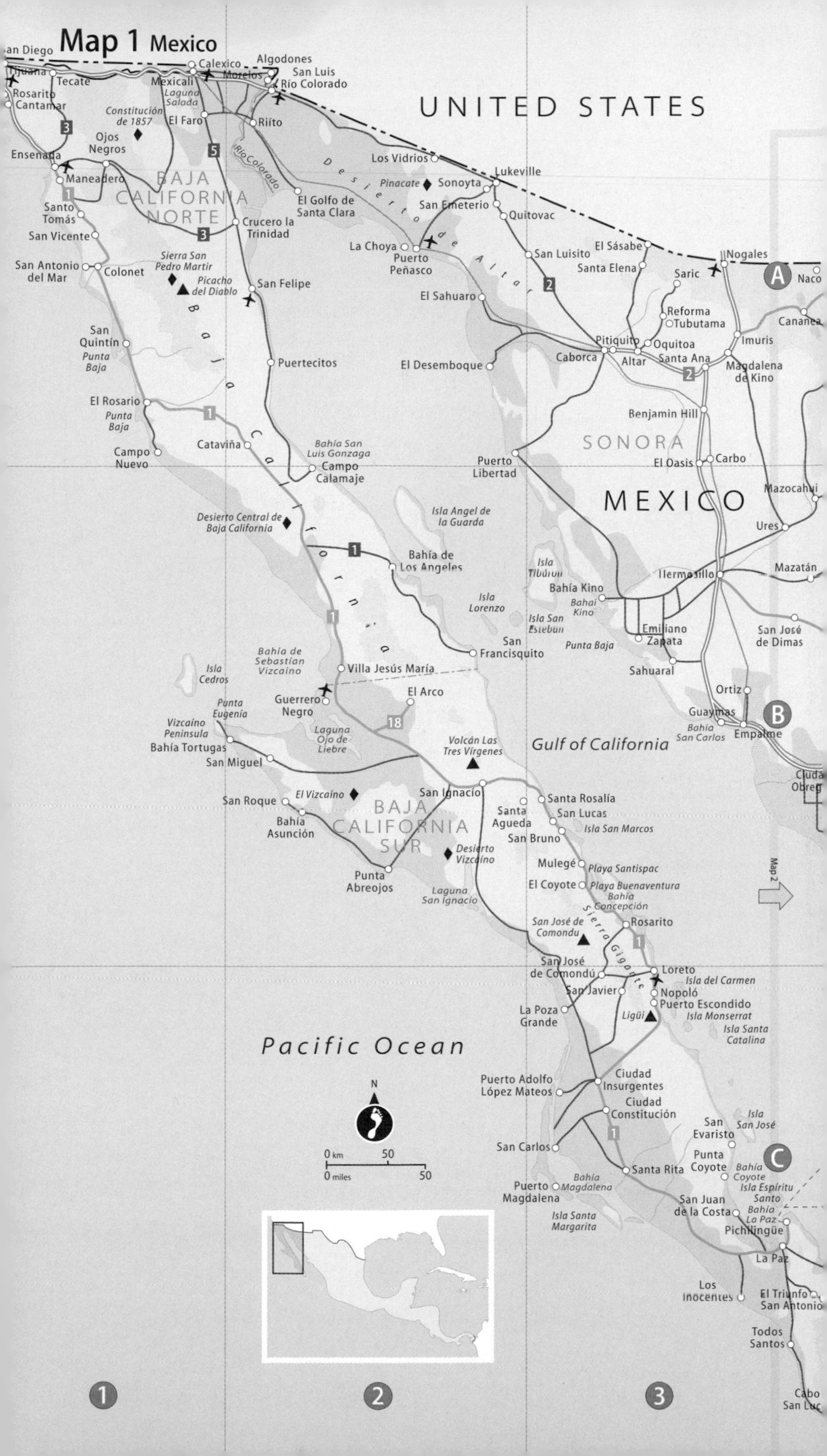

Map 1 Mexico
UNITED STATES
MEXICO
BAJA CALIFORNIA NORTE
BAJA CALIFORNIA SUR
SONORA
Baja California
Desierto de Altar
Gulf of California
Pacific Ocean
San Diego
Tijuana
Tecate
Calexico
Mexicali
Algodones
Morelos
San Luis Río Colorado
Rosarito
Cantamar
Laguna Salada
Constitución de 1857
El Faro
Riíto
Ojos Negros
Río Colorado
Ensenada
Maneadero
Los Vidrios
Lukeville
Pinacate
Sonoyta
San Emeterio
Quitovac
El Golfo de Santa Clara
Santo Tomás
San Vicente
Crucero la Trinidad
La Choya
Puerto Peñasco
San Luisito
El Sásabe
Santa Elena
Nogales
Saric
Naco
San Antonio del Mar
Colonet
Sierra San Pedro Martir
Picacho del Diablo
San Felipe
El Sahuaro
Reforma
Tubutama
Cananea
San Quintín
Punta Baja
Puertecitos
El Desemboque
Pitiquito
Caborca
Oquitoa
Altar
Santa Ana
Imuris
Magdalena de Kino
El Rosario
Benjamin Hill
Cataviña
Campo Nuevo
Bahía San Luis Gonzaga
Campo Calamaje
Puerto Libertad
El Oasis
Carbo
Mazocahui
Desierto Central de Baja California
Isla Angel de la Guarda
Ures
Bahía de Los Angeles
Isla Tiburón
Hermosillo
Mazatán
Bahía Kino
Bahai Kino
Isla Lorenzo
Isla San Esteban
Emiliano Zapata
San José de Dimas
San Francisquito
Punta Baja
Bahía de Sebastían Vizcaino
Isla Cedros
Villa Jesús María
Sahuaral
Ortiz
Guerrero Negro
El Arco
Punta Eugenia
Vizcaíno Peninsula
Guaymas
Bahía San Carlos
Empalme
Bahía Tortugas
Laguna Ojo de Liebre
Volcán Las Tres Vírgenes
San Miguel
Ciudad Obregón
El Vizcaíno
San Ignacio
Santa Rosalía
San Roque
Santa Agueda
San Lucas
Bahía Asunción
Isla San Marcos
San Bruno
Desierto Vizcaíno
Mulegé
Playa Santispac
Punta Abreojos
El Coyote
Playa Buenaventura
Laguna San Ignacio
Bahía Concepción
Map 2
San José de Comondu
Sierra Gigante
Rosarito
San José de Comondú
Loreto
Isla del Carmen
San Javier
Nopoló
Puerto Escondido
La Poza Grande
Ligüi
Isla Monserrat
Isla Santa Catalina
Puerto Adolfo López Mateos
Ciudad Insurgentes
Ciudad Constitución
Isla San José
San Evaristo
San Carlos
Punta Coyote
Bahía Coyote
Santa Rita
Puerto Magdalena
Bahía Magdalena
Isla Espíritu Santo
San Juan de la Costa
Bahía La Paz
Isla Santa Margarita
Pichilingüe
La Paz
Los Inocentes
El Triunfo
San Antonio
Todos Santos
Cabo San Lucas
N
0 km 50
0 miles 50
A
B
C
1
2
3

Map 2 Mexico

Colombus
Palomas
El Paso
Cuidad Juárez
2
Douglas
Naco
Agua Prieta
2
Fronteras
Cananea
San Miguelito
Ascensión
Janos
El Barreal
Imuris
A
Kino
Bacerac
Villa Ahumada
Villa Hidalgo
Casas Grandes
Nuevo Casas Grandes
10
45
Moctezuma
Buenaventura
El Sueco
SONORA
Ricardo Flores Magón
Presidio
Río Grande
Río Bravo
Ojinaga
Zaragoza
Coyame
Mazocahui
Las Varas
Gómez Farías
16
Ures
Nueva Madera
Namiquipa
Madera
San José de Bavicora
Oscar Soto Maynes
Usulután
Mazatán
Sahuaripa
Cumbres de Majalca
Tres Ojitos
Bachiniva
Aldama
San José de Dimas
Alvaro Obregón
Chihuahua
Tonichi
Ciudad Guerrero
La Junta
45
San Nicolas
Yepachic
16
Cuauhtémoc
Yécora
Ciudad Delicias
Ortíz
Map 1
Basaseachi
Basaseachi Falls
Satevó
Empalme
San Juanito
Creel
CHIHUAHUA
Ciudad Camargo
15
Río Conchos
El Divisadero
Cusárare
Valle Zaragoza
Ciudad Obregón
San Rafael
Bahuichivo
Basíhuare
Témoris
Copper Canyon
Cerocahuí
Ciudad Jiménez
B
Río Urique
Urique
Samachique
La Bufa
Hidalgo del Parral
Alamos
Batópilas
Buenavista
Valle de Allende
Navojoa
Río Batopolis
Nachacachi
Satevo
San Francis del Oro
49
Huatabampo
Sinforosa Canyon
Guachochi
Santa Bárbara
Ceballos
15
MEXICO
Río Fuerte
Choix
El Fuerte
Revolución
Guanacevi
Mapimí
El Anuajito
San Blas
Santa María del Oro
Sinaloa de Leyva
Los Mochis
SINALOA
Santiago de los Caballeros
Topolobampo
El Casco
Guasave
Guamuchil
DURANGO
Nazas
Tepehuanes
Las Herreras
Rodeo
Buenavista
Santiago Papasquiaro
San Juan del Río
Nuevo Ideal
15
Culiacán
Guatimape
Donato Guerrero
Altata
Guadalupe Victoria
Canatlán
C
Comedero
Francisco Madero
Pichilingüe
El Dorado
La Paz
Durango
Ensenado de los Muertos
San Ignacio
45
El Salto
40
La Cruz
Coyotitán
La Ciudad
Vicente Guerrero
El Triunfo
15
Los Barriles
Mezquital
La Nona
Todos Santos
Santiago
El Pescadero
Cabo Pulmo
Concordia
Mazatlán
Villa Unión
Colonia Plutarco Elías Calles
San José del Cabo
Pacific Ocean
El Rosario
Escuinapa de Hidalgo
Cabo San Lucas
Teacapan
Acaponeta
Tecuala
El Novillero
Rosamorada
NAYARIT
1
2
3
Chilapa
Tuxpan
Santiago Ixcuintla

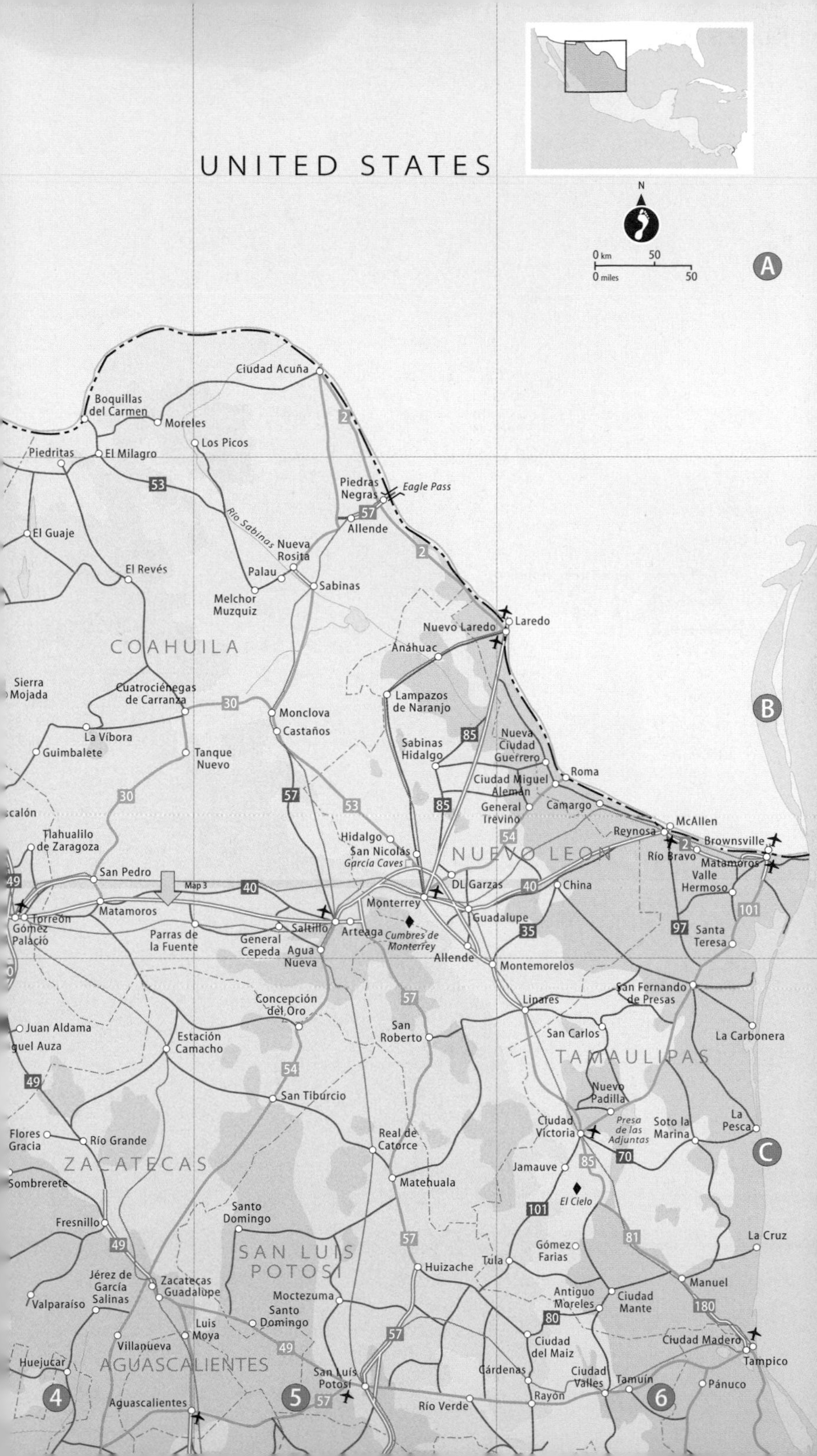

UNITED STATES
N
0 km 50
0 miles 50
A
B
C
4
5
6
Ciudad Acuña
Boquillas del Carmen
Moreles
Los Picos
Piedritas
El Milagro
53
Piedras Negras
Eagle Pass
57
Allende
2
El Guaje
Río Sabinas
Nueva Rosita
Palau
El Revés
Sabinas
Melchor Muzquiz
Laredo
Nuevo Laredo
Anáhuac
COAHUILA
Sierra Mojada
Cuatrociénegas de Carranza
30
Monclova
Castaños
Lampazos de Naranjo
La Víbora
Guimbalete
Tanque Nuevo
Sabinas Hidalgo
85
Nueva Ciudad Guerrero
Roma
Ciudad Miguel Alemán
General Treviño
Camargo
McAllen
Reynosa
Brownsville
Río Bravo
Matamoros
Valle Hermoso
Tlahualilo de Zaragoza
Hidalgo
San Nicolás
García Caves
NUEVO LEON
54
San Pedro
Map 3
40
DL Garzas
China
49
Torreón
Gómez Palacio
Matamoros
Parras de la Fuente
General Cepeda
Saltillo
Arteaga
Monterrey
Cumbres de Monterrey
Guadalupe
35
97
Santa Teresa
101
Agua Nueva
Allende
Montemorelos
San Fernando de Presas
Concepción del Oro
Linares
Juan Aldama
Miguel Auza
Estación Camacho
San Roberto
San Carlos
La Carbonera
TAMAULIPAS
San Tiburcio
Nuevo Padilla
Ciudad Victoria
Presa de las Adjuntas
Soto la Marina
La Pesca
Flores Gracia
Río Grande
Real de Catorce
70
ZACATECAS
Sombrerete
Matehuala
Jamauve
El Cielo
Fresnillo
Santo Domingo
101
81
SAN LUIS POTOSI
Gómez Farias
La Cruz
Huizache
Tula
Jérez de García Salinas
Zacatecas Guadalupe
Valparaíso
Moctezuma
Santo Domingo
Antiguo Moreles
Ciudad Mante
Manuel
180
Luis Moya
80
Villanueva
Ciudad del Maiz
Ciudad Madero
Tampico
Huejucar
AGUASCALIENTES
San Luis Potosí
Cárdenas
Ciudad Valles
Tamuín
Pánuco
Aguascalientes
Río Verde
Rayón

Map 3 Mexico

DURANGO
COAHUILA
NUEVO LEON
ZACATECAS
SAN LUIS POTOSI
MEXICO
NAYARIT
AGUASCALIENTES
GUANAJUATO
JALISCO
MICHOACAN
COLIMA
GUERRERO
Pacific Ocean
A
B
C
1
2
3
del Oro
San Pedro
Gómez Palacio
Torreón
Matamaros
Parras de la Fuente
General Cepeda
Saltillo
Monterrey
Guadalupe
Allende
Montemorelos
Linares
Agua Nueva
San Roberto
Tepehuanes
Las Herreras
Rodeo
Nazas
Santiago Papasquiara
Nuevo Ideal
San Juan del Río
Peñón Blanco
Guatimape
Donato Guerrero
Canatlán
Francisco I Madero
Juan Aldama
Miguel Auza
Guadalupe Victoria
Estación Camacho
Concepción del Oro
San Tiburcio
Durango
El Salto
La Ciudad
Flores Gracia
Río Grande
Vicente Guerrero
Sombrerete
Mezquital
Real de Catorce
Matehuala
Fresnillo
Santa Domingo
Concordia
Villa Unión
El Rosario
Escuinapa de Hidalgo
Valparaíso
Jérez de García Salinas
Chicomostoc
Zacatecas
Guadalupe
Moctezuma
Santo Domingo
Tula
Acaponeta
Tecuala
El Novillero
Rosamorada
Villanueva
Luis Moya
Ciudad del Maí
Huejúcar
San Luís Potosí
Cárdena
Chilapa
Tuxpán
Santispac
Map 2
Huaynamota
Colotlán
Aguascalientes
Río Verde
Rayó
Santiago Ixcuintla
Tlaltenango
Santa María del Río
Jalpa
Encarnación
San Blas
Tepic
Volcán Sangangüey (2286m)
Teocaltiche
Santa Cruz
Compostela
Lagos de Moreno
San Felipe
San Luís de la Paz
Conca
Zacualapan
Las Varas
Dolores Hidalgo
Pozos
Ixtlán del Río
Los Ayala
Rincón de Guayabitos
León
San José Iturbide
Jalostotitlán
Guanajuato
San Miguel de Allende
San Joaquí
Sayulita
Magdalena
Amatlán de Cañas
Etzatlán
Tequila
Punta de Mita
Bucerías
Guadalajara
Cadereyta
Puerto Vallarta
Tonalá
Tepatitlán
Irapuato
Juventino Rosas
Ezequiel Montes
Mascota
Ahualulco de Mercata
Tlaquepaque
Colón
Querétaro
Chimo
Mismaloya
Yelapa
Ameca
Salamanca
Celaya
Tequisquiapán
Villa Corona
Chapala
Ocotlán
La Piedad de Cabadas
Aquiles Serdán
Jocotepec
Ajijic
Lago de Chapala
Valle de Santiago
San Juan del Río
Tecolotlán
Yuriria
Ipala
Ayutla
Juchitán
Sahuayo
Tomatlán
Unión de Tula
Tapalpa
Mazimatla
Zamora
Maravatio
Autlán de Navarro
Ciudad Guzmán
Zacapú
Querendaro
Ixtlahuaca
Campo Acosta
Quiroga
Tamazula
Charapán
Paracho
Morelia
Angangueo
Casimiro Castillo
Nevado de Colima (3,842m)
Los Reyes
Lago Pátzcuaro
Tzintzuntzan
Ciudad Hidalgo
Villa de Allende
Angahuan
Volcán Paricutín
Uruapan
Chamela
La Huerta
Pátzcuaro
Zitácuaro
San Patricio-Melaque
Comala
Allende National Park
Toluc
Cihuatlán
Colima
Benito Juárez
Valle de Bravo
Barra de Navidad
Santiago
Manzanillo
Nevada de Toluca (4583m
Tecomán
Apatzingan
Ixtapa de la Sa
San Juan de Lima
Cutzamala de Pinzón
Ciudad Altamirano
Maruata
Caleta de Campos
Playa Azul
Lázaro Cárdenas
Ixtapa
Zihuatanejo
Petatlan
Estado de Guerrero
Atoyac de Alvárez
Tecpán de Galeana
Coyuca
Taxc
Acapulc
15
35
40
41
45
49
51
54
55
57
70
80
110
134
200

Gulf of Mexico
TAMAULIPAS
VERACRUZ
HIDALGO
QUERETERO
TLAXCALA
PUEBLA
MORELOS
GUERRERO
OAXACA
MEXICO CITY
China
Valle Hermoso
Mezquital
San Fernando de Presas
San Carlos
La Carbonera
Nuevo Padilla
Presa de las Adjuntas
Soto la Marina
La Pesca
Ciudad Victoria
La Cruz
Manuel
Ciudad Mante
Ciudad Madero
Tampico
Pánuco
Tamuín
Ciudad Valles
Santa Catarina
Tempoal de Sánchez
Tancoyol
Xilitla
Jalpan
Tamazunchale
Jacala
Tuxpan
Castillo de Teayo
Barra de Cazones
Zimapán
Zacualtipán
Molango
Poza Rica
Meztitlán
Ixmiquilpan
Papantla
Tecolutla
Xicotepec de Juárez
El Tajín
Gutiérrez Zamora
Actopan
Atotonilco el Grande
Huachinango
Nautla
Cuetzalán
Martínez de la Torre
Pachuca
Tulancingo
Tlapacoyan
Tula
Epazoyucan
Tetela de Ocampo
Teziutlán
Zacatlán
Tepotzotlán
Zaragoza
Chignahuapan
Perote
Naolinco
Tlalnepantla
Xalapa
Teotihuacán
Cofre de Perote (4274m)
Xico
Cempoala
Chachalacas
Oriental
Cardel
Texcoco
Cacaxtla
Apizaco
Veracruz
Totutla
Zacatepec
Boca del Río
Xochimilco
Tlaxcala
Huamantla
Huatusco
Antón Lizardo
Iztaccíhuatl
Pico de Orizaba (5746m)
Amecameca
Puebla
Amozoc
Fortín de las Flores
Los Robles
La Laguna
PN Desierto del Carmen
Atlixco
Acatzingo
Punto Roca Partida
Tepeaca
Córdoba
Alvarado
Tepoztlán
Popocatépetl
Tecamachalco
Orizaba
La Tinaja
Santiago Tuxtla
Cuernavaca
Zongolica
Yanga
Sontecomepan
Paraíso
Xochicalco
Cuautla
Tlacotalpan
Sánchez Magallanes
Catemaco
Amacuzac
Izúcar de Matamoros
San Juan Ixcaquixtla
Tehuacán
Tierra Blanca
San Andrés Tuxtla
Laguna Catemaco
Comalcalco
Taxco
Cosamaloapan
Coatzacoalcos
La Venta
Ajalpan
Temascal
Juan Díaz Covarrubias
Villahermosa
Iguala
Tamazulapan
Presa Miguel Alemán
Papaloapan
Agua Dulce
Acatlán
Huautla
Tuxtepec
Villa Isla
Minatitlán
Huimanguillo
Teotitlán
Loma Bonita
Acayucan
Jalapa
Rodríguez Clara
Sayula
Chiltepec
Chontalpa
La Laguna
Olinalá
Playa Vicente
Valle Nacional
Huajapán de León
Zumpango del Río
Chilapa
Tlapa
Jesús Carranza
Chilpancingo
San Francisco Telixtlahuaca
Istmo de Tehuantepec
Raudales
Petaquillas
Ixtlán de Juárez
Palomares
Mazatlán
Etlá
Tierra Colorado
Tlaxiaco
Guelatao
Oaxaca
El Terrero
Monte Albán
Tlacolula
Matías Romero
Ocozocautla
Tianguis
Ayutla de Los Libres
Mitla
Cintlapa
Zaachila
San Marcos
San Pablo Huixtepec
San Pedro Totolapan
La Ventosa
Ixtepec
Ocotlán
Zanatepec
Cruz Grande
Laguna Tres Palos
Laguna Tecomate
Juchitán
Villa Flores
Tapanatepec
Cuajinicuilapa
Santiago Jamiltepec
Juchatengo
Miahuatlán
Tehuantepec
Arriaga
Tonalá
Pinotepa Nacional
Parque Nacional Lagunillas de Chacahua
Salina Cruz
Parédon
Puerto Arista
Gulf of Tehuantepec
Pochutla
Huatulco
Puerto Escondido
Puerto Angel
N
0 km
50
0 miles
50
A
B
C
4
5
6
Map 4

Map 4 Mexico

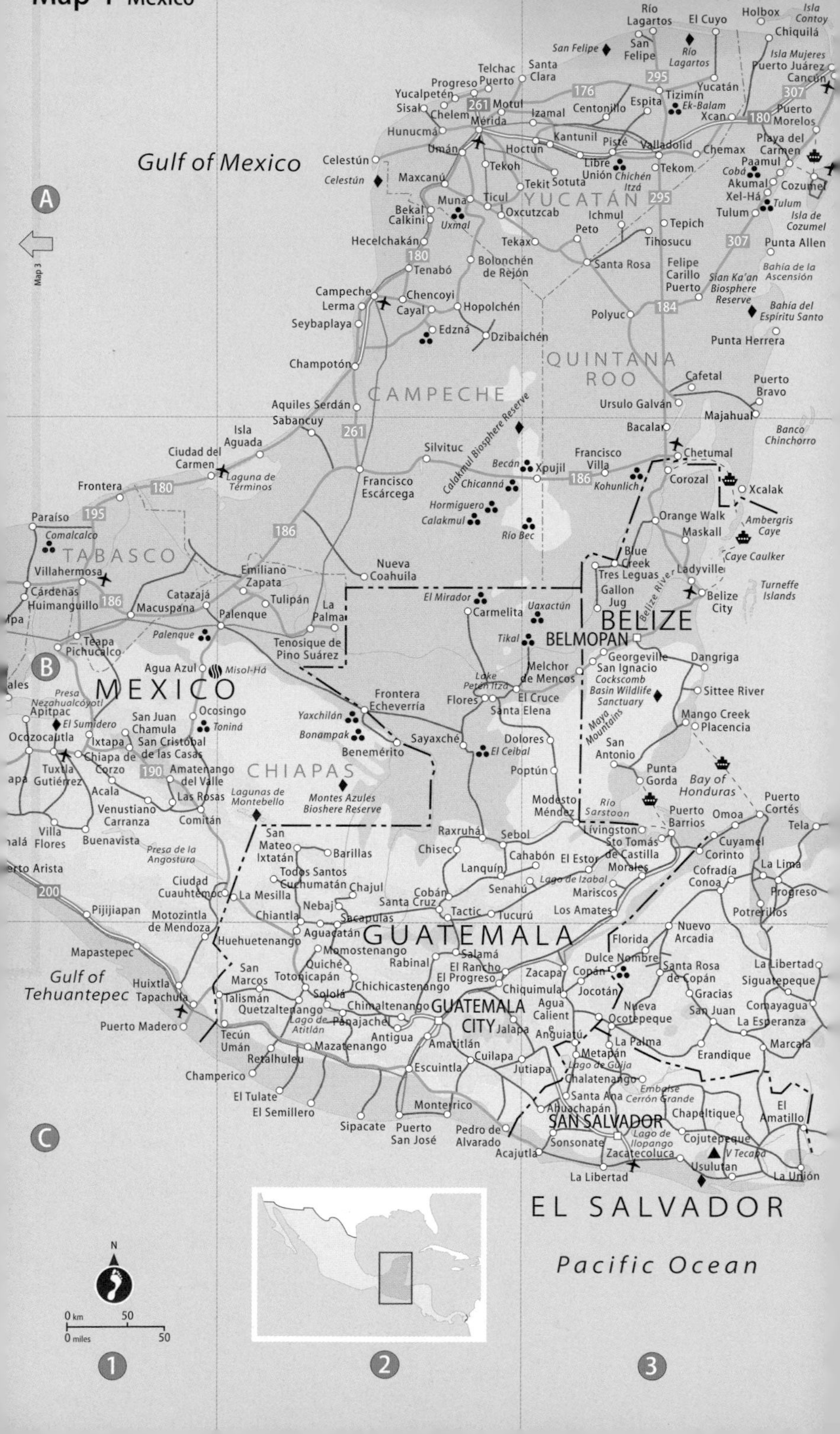
Gulf of Mexico
Río Lagartos
El Cuyo
Holbox
Isla Contoy
San Felipe
Río Lagartos
Chiquilá
Isla Mujeres
Puerto Juárez
Cancún
Telchac Puerto
Santa Clara
Progreso
Yucalpetén
Sisal
Chelem
Mérida
Motul
Izamal
Centonillo
Espita
Tizimín
Ek-Balam
Yucatán
Xcan
Puerto Morelos
Playa del Carmen
Hunucmá
Umán
Hoctun
Kantunil
Pisté
Valladolid
Chemax
Celestún
Maxcanú
Tekoh
Tekit
Sotuta
Libre Unión
Chichén Itzá
Tekom
Cobá
Paamul
Akumal
Cozumel
Xel-Há
Tulum
Isla de Cozumel
Muna
Ticul
Oxcutzcab
YUCATÁN
Bekal
Calkini
Uxmal
Ichmul
Peto
Tepich
Tihosucu
Hecelchakán
Tekax
Punta Allen
Tenabó
Bolonchén de Rejón
Santa Rosa
Felipe Carillo Puerto
Sian Ka'an Biosphere Reserve
Bahía de la Ascensión
Campeche
Lerma
Chencoyi
Cayal
Hopolchén
Polyuc
Bahía del Espíritu Santo
Seybaplaya
Edzná
Dzibalchén
Punta Herrera
Champotón
QUINTANA ROO
CAMPECHE
Cafetal
Puerto Bravo
Aquiles Serdán
Ursulo Galván
Majahual
Sabancuy
Isla Aguada
Calakmul Biosphere Reserve
Bacalar
Banco Chinchorro
Ciudad del Carmen
Laguna de Términos
Silvituc
Francisco Villa
Chetumal
Frontera
Francisco Escárcega
Becán
Xpujil
Chicanná
Kohunlich
Corozal
Xcalak
Paraíso
Comalcalco
Hormiguero
Calakmul
Río Bec
Orange Walk
Maskall
Ambergris Caye
TABASCO
Caye Caulker
Villahermosa
Cárdenas
Huimanguillo
Emiliano Zapata
Nueva Coahuila
Blue Creek
Tres Leguas
Gallon Jug
Ladyville
Belize River
Belize City
Turneffe Islands
Macuspana
Catazajá
Tulipán
La Palma
El Mirador
Carmelita
Uaxactún
BELIZE
Palenque
Tenosique de Pino Suárez
Tikal
BELMOPAN
Teapa
Pichucalco
Georgeville
San Ignacio
Dangriga
Agua Azul
Misol-Há
Melchor de Mencos
Cockscomb Basin Wildlife Sanctuary
MEXICO
Lake Petén Itzá
Flores
El Cruce
Santa Elena
Sittee River
Presa Nezahualcóyotl
Apitpac
El Sumidero
San Juan Chamula
Ocosingo
Toniná
Frontera Echeverría
Yaxchilán
Bonampak
Maya Mountains
Mango Creek
Placencia
Ocozocautla
Ixtapa
San Cristóbal de las Casas
Chiapa de Corzo
Benemérito
Sayaxché
Dolores
El Ceibal
San Antonio
Tuxtla Gutiérrez
Amatenango del Valle
CHIAPAS
Poptún
Punta Gorda
Bay of Honduras
Acala
Las Rosas
Lagunas de Montebello
Montes Azules Bioshere Reserve
Venustiano Carranza
Comitán
Modesto Méndez
Río Sarstoon
Puerto Barrios
Omoa
Puerto Cortés
Villa Flores
Buenavista
San Mateo Ixtatán
Raxruhá
Sebol
Livingston
Sto Tomás de Castilla
Tela
Presa de la Angostura
Barillas
Chisec
Cahabón
El Estor
Cuyamel
Corinto
Todos Santos Cuchumatán
Chajul
Lanquín
Lago de Izabal
Morales
La Lima
Cofradía
Conoa
Ciudad Cuauhtémoc
La Mesilla
Senahú
Mariscos
Progreso
Cobán
Santa Cruz
Pijijiapan
Motozintla de Mendoza
Chiantla
Nebaj
Sacapulas
Tactic
Tucurú
Los Amates
Potrerillos
Aguacatán
GUATEMALA
Huehuetenango
Momostenango
Nuevo Arcadia
Florida
Mapastepec
Quiché
Rabinal
Salamá
Dulce Nombre
Santa Rosa de Copán
La Libertad
Siguatepeque
Gulf of Tehuantepec
Huixtla
Tapachula
San Marcos
Totonicapán
El Rancho
El Progreso
Zacapa
Copán
Chichicastenango
Chiquimula
Jocotán
Gracias
Talismán
Quetzaltenango
Sololá
Chimaltenango
GUATEMALA CITY
Agua Caliente
Nueva Ocotepeque
San Juan
Comayagua
La Esperanza
Puerto Madero
Lago de Atitlán
Panajachel
Jalapa
Anguiatú
Tecún Umán
Antigua
Amatitlán
La Palma
Marcala
Retalhuleu
Mazatenango
Cuilapa
Metapán
Erandique
Lago de Güija
Champerico
Escuintla
Jutiapa
Chalatenango
El Tulate
Santa Ana
Embalse Cerrón Grande
El Semillero
Monterrico
Ahuachapán
Chapeltique
El Amatillo
Sipacate
Puerto San José
Pedro de Alvarado
SAN SALVADOR
Lago de Ilopango
Cojutepeque
Sonsonate
V Tecapa
Acajutla
Zacatecoluca
Usulután
La Unión
La Libertad
EL SALVADOR
Pacific Ocean
N
0 km 50
0 miles 50
261
176
295
180
307
184
186
195
190
200
Map 3
A
B
C
1
2
3

Map 5 Central America

Map 6 Central America

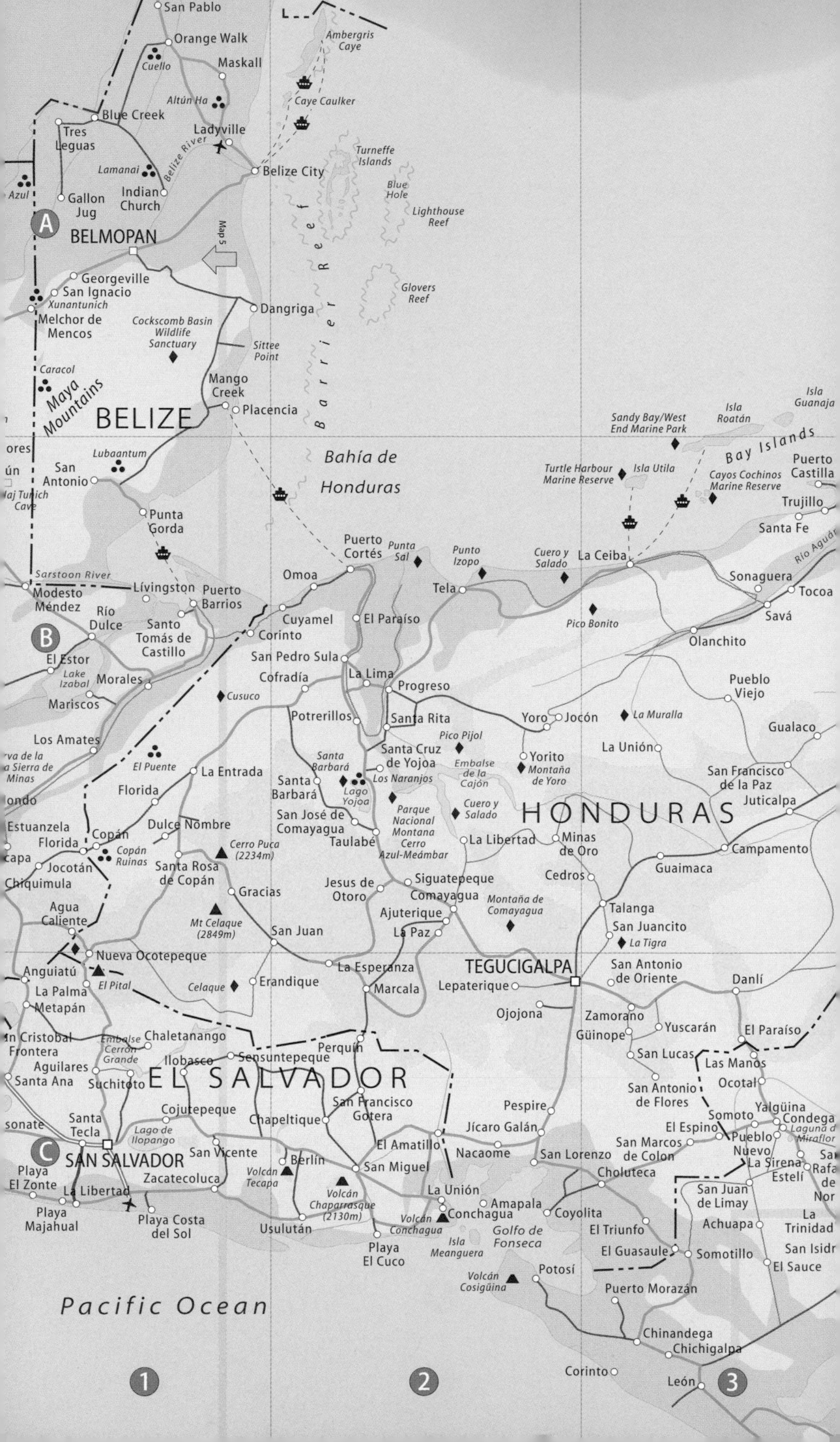

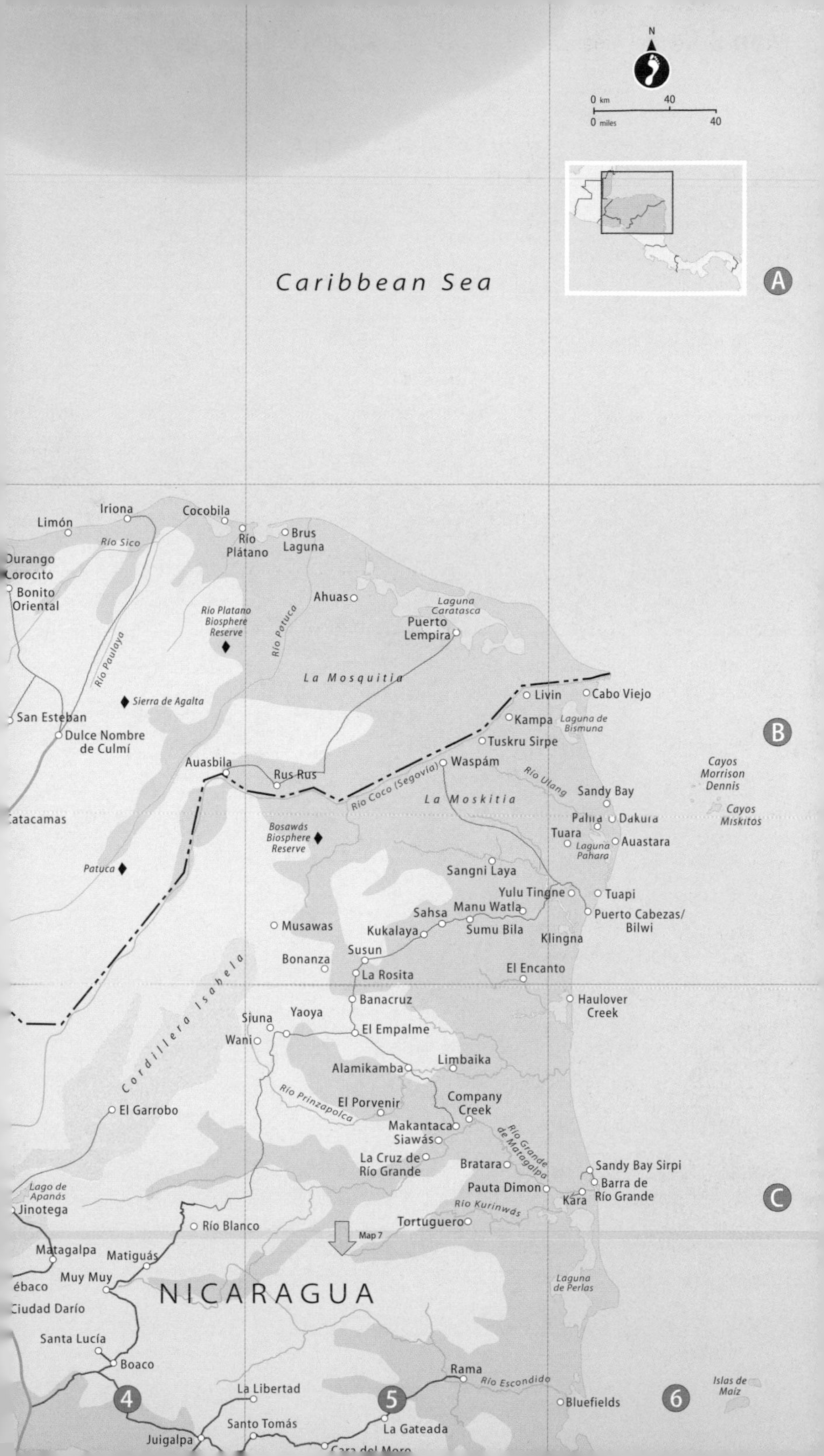
N
0 km 40
0 miles 40
Caribbean Sea
A
B
C
Iriona
Limón
Cocobila
Río Sico
Río Plátano
Brus Laguna
Durango
Corocito
Bonito Oriental
Ahuas
Laguna Caratasca
Río Platano Biosphere Reserve
Puerto Lempira
Río Patuca
Río Paulaya
La Mosquitia
Sierra de Agalta
Livin
Cabo Viejo
Kampa
Laguna de Bismuna
San Esteban
Dulce Nombre de Culmí
Tuskru Sirpe
Auasbila
Rus Rus
Waspám
Río Coco (Segovia)
Río Ulang
Cayos Morrison Dennis
Sandy Bay
La Moskitia
Catacamas
Palma
Dakura
Cayos Miskitos
Bosawás Biosphere Reserve
Tuara
Auastara
Laguna Pahara
Patuca
Sangni Laya
Yulu Tingne
Tuapi
Sahsa
Manu Watla
Puerto Cabezas/ Bilwi
Musawas
Kukalaya
Sumu Bila
Klingna
Susun
Bonanza
La Rosita
El Encanto
Cordillera Isabela
Banacruz
Haulover Creek
Siuna
Yaoya
Wani
El Empalme
Limbaika
Alamikamba
Company Creek
Río Prinzapolca
El Porvenir
El Garrobo
Makantaca
Siawás
Río Grande de Matagalpa
La Cruz de Río Grande
Bratara
Sandy Bay Sirpi
Barra de Río Grande
Lago de Apanás
Pauta Dimon
Kara
Jinotega
Río Kurinwás
Río Blanco
Tortuguero
Map 7
Matagalpa
Matiguás
Laguna de Perlas
Muy Muy
NICARAGUA
Ciudad Darío
Santa Lucía
Boaco
Rama
Río Escondido
Islas de Maíz
La Libertad
4
5
6
Bluefields
Santo Tomás
La Gateada
Juigalpa

Map 7 Central America

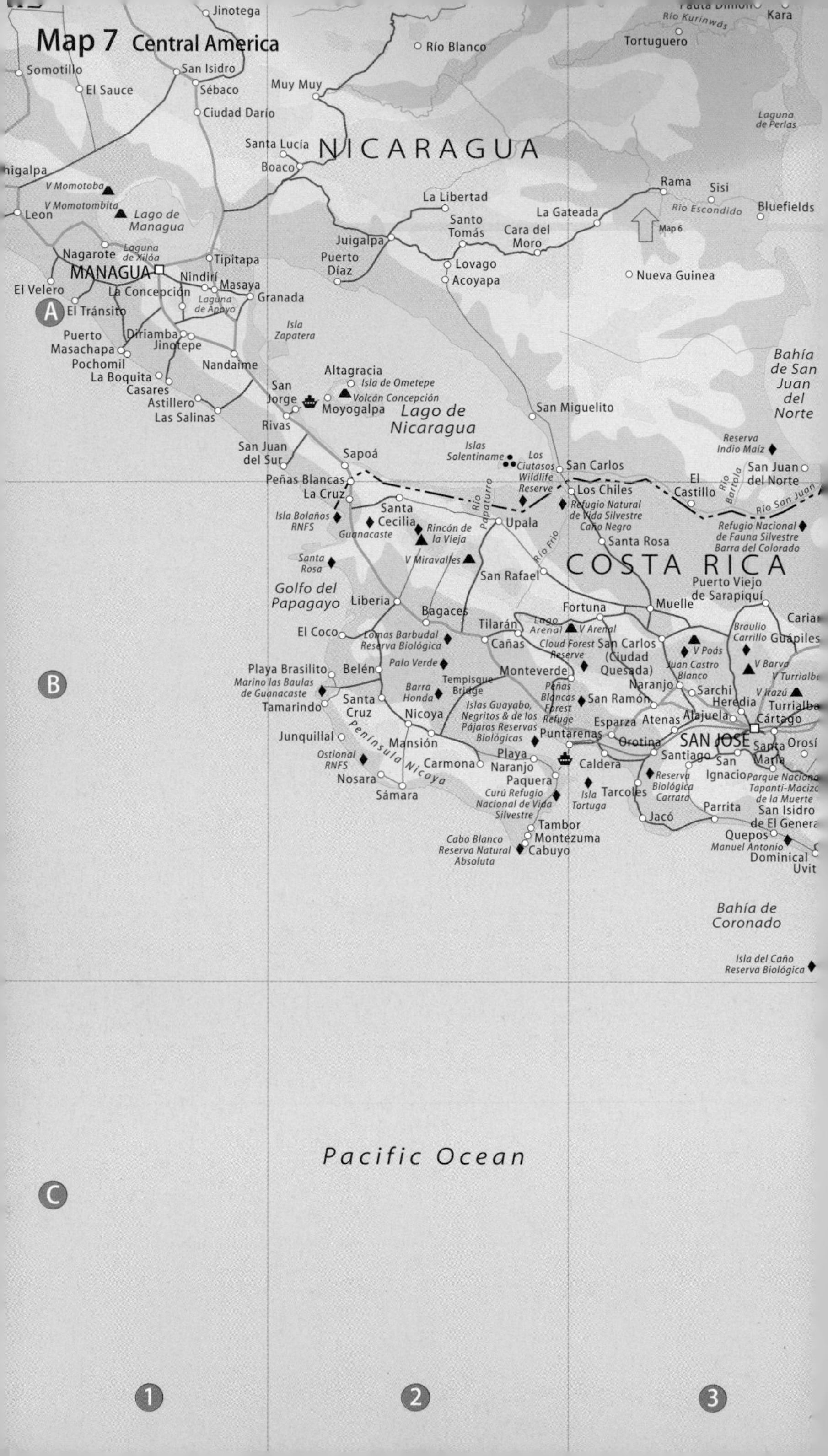

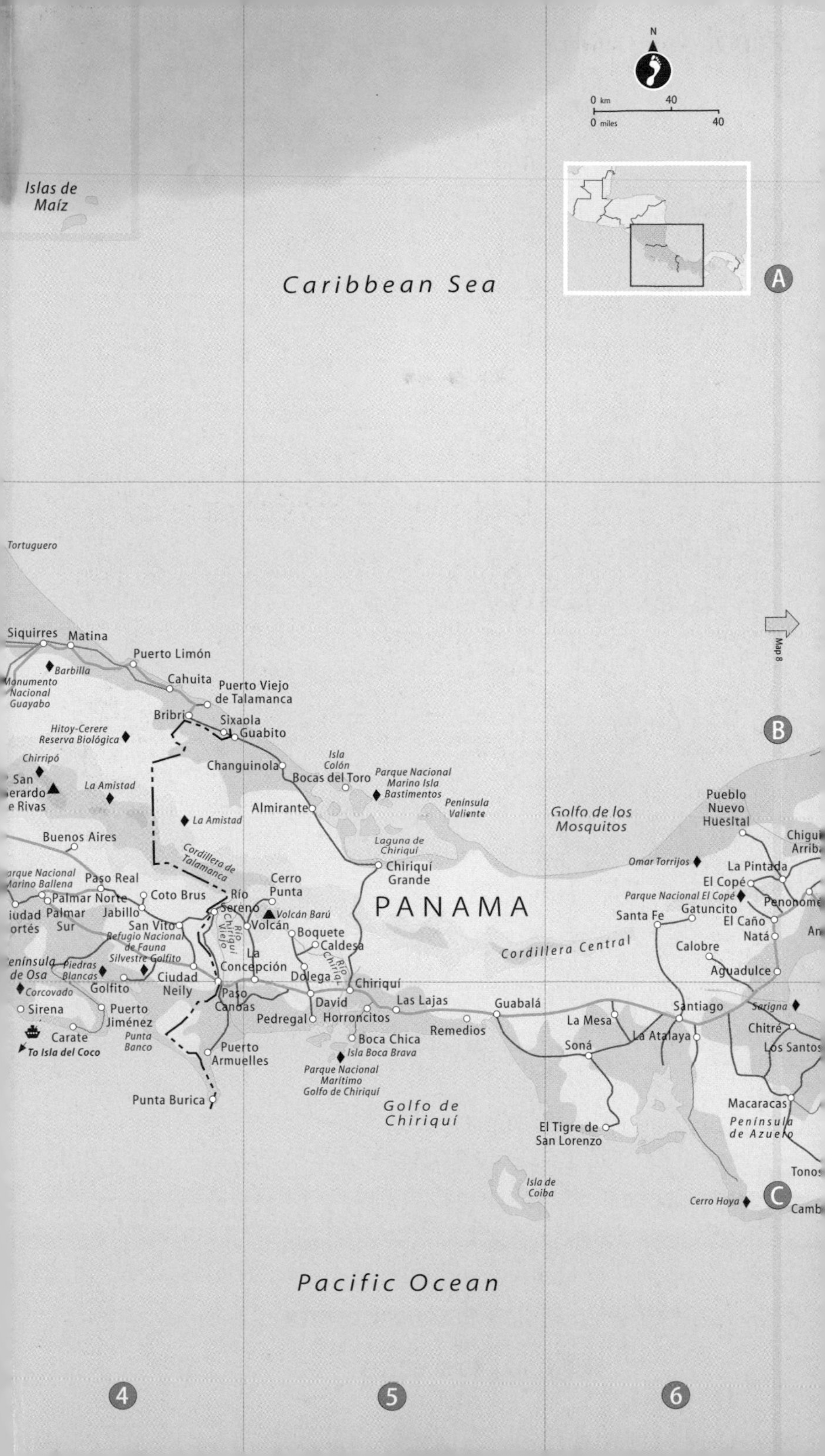

N
0 km 40
0 miles 40
Islas de Maíz
Caribbean Sea
A
Tortuguero
Siquirres
Matina
Puerto Limón
Barbilla
Monumento Nacional Guayabo
Cahuita
Puerto Viejo de Talamanca
Bribri
Sixaola
Guabito
Hitoy-Cerere Reserva Biológica
Chirripó
San Gerardo de Rivas
La Amistad
La Amistad
Changuinola
Isla Colón
Bocas del Toro
Parque Nacional Marino Isla Bastimentos
Península Valiente
Almirante
Golfo de los Mosquitos
Pueblo Nuevo Hueslstal
Chigui Arriba
Map 8
B
Buenos Aires
Laguna de Chiriquí
Cordillera de Talamanca
Chiriquí Grande
Omar Torrijos
La Pintada
Parque Nacional Marino Ballena
Paso Real
Cerro Punta
El Copé
Parque Nacional El Copé
Penonomé
Palmar Norte
Coto Brus
Río Sereno
PANAMA
Gatuncito
Ciudad Cortés
Palmar Sur
Jabillo
Volcán Barú
Santa Fe
El Caño
San Vito
Río Chiriquí Viejo
Volcán
Boquete
Natá
Refugio Nacional de Fauna Silvestre Golfito
Caldera
Cordillera Central
Calobre
Península de Osa
Piedras Blancas
La Concepción
Río Chiriquí
Aguadulce
Golfito
Ciudad Neily
Dolega
Chiriquí
Corcovado
Paso Canoas
David
Las Lajas
Guabalá
Santiago
Sarigna
Sirena
Puerto Jiménez
Pedregal
Horconcitos
Remedios
La Mesa
Chitré
Carate
Punta Banco
Boca Chica
La Atalaya
Los Santos
To Isla del Coco
Puerto Armuelles
Isla Boca Brava
Soná
Parque Nacional Marítimo Golfo de Chiriquí
Punta Burica
Golfo de Chiriquí
Macaracas
Península de Azuero
El Tigre de San Lorenzo
Tonosí
Isla de Coiba
Cerro Hoya
C
Camb
Pacific Ocean
4
5
6

Map 8 Central America

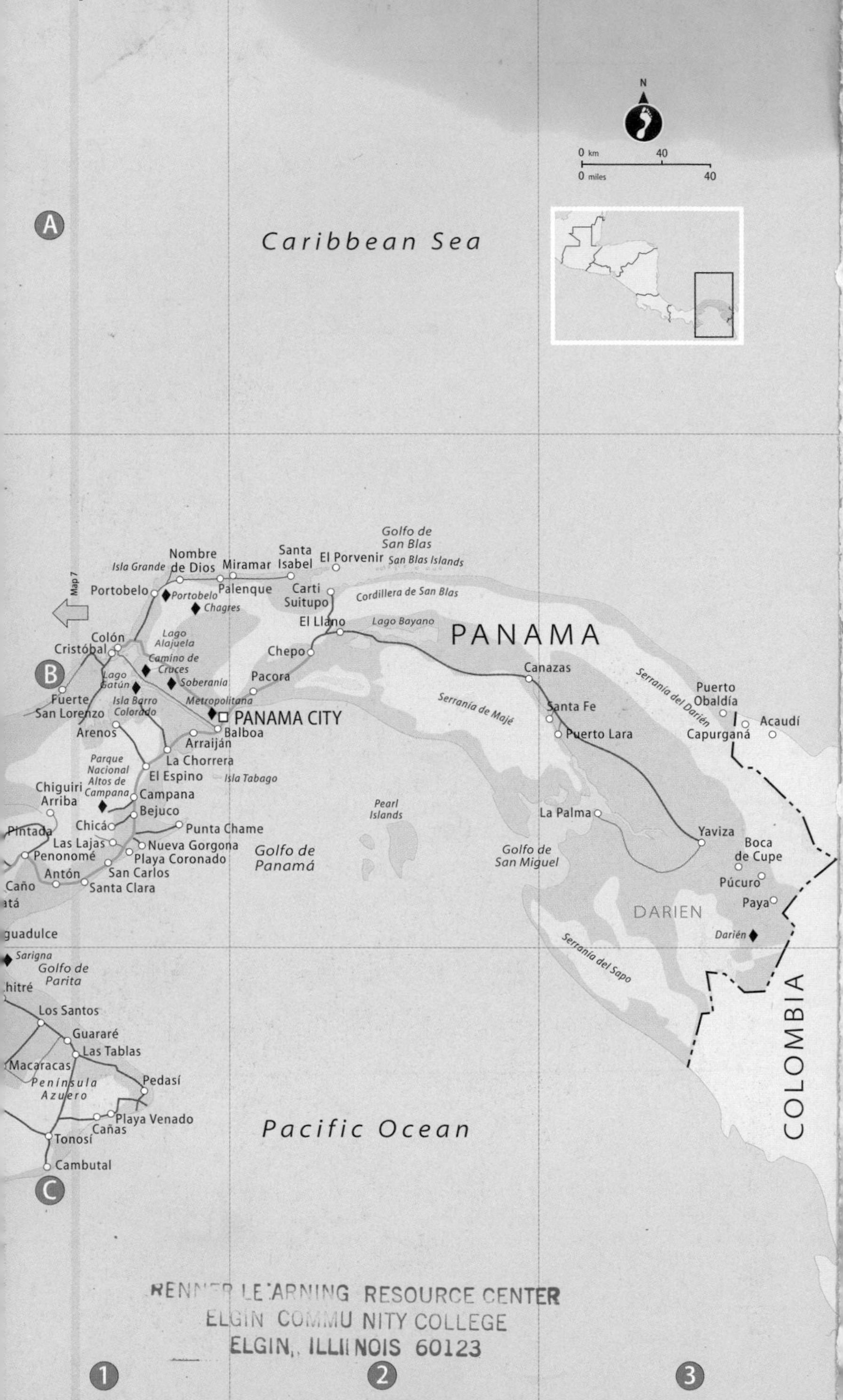